BELLAMY & CHILD
EUROPEAN COMMUNITY
LAW OF COMPETITION

BELLAMY & CHILD

EUROPEAN COMMUNITY LAW OF COMPETITION

SIXTH EDITION

Edited by

PETER ROTH QC

Barrister, Visiting Professor of Law, King's College, London

VIVIEN ROSE

Barrister, Chairman of the Competition Appeal Tribunal

OXFORD

UNIVERSITY PRESS

OXFORD
UNIVERSITY PRESS

Great Clarendon Street, Oxford OX2 6DP

Oxford University Press is a department of the University of Oxford.
It furthers the University's objective of excellence in research, scholarship,
and education by publishing worldwide in

Oxford New York

Auckland Cape Town Dar es Salaam Hong Kong Karachi
Kuala Lumpur Madrid Melbourne Mexico City Nairobi
New Delhi Shanghai Taipei Toronto

With offices in

Argentina Austria Brazil Chile Czech Republic France Greece
Guatemala Hungary Italy Japan Poland Portugal Singapore
South Korea Switzerland Thailand Turkey Ukraine Vietnam

Oxford is a registered trade mark of Oxford University Press
in the UK and in certain other countries

Published in the United States
by Oxford University Press Inc., New York

British Library Cataloguing in Publication Data
Data available

Library of Congress Cataloging in Publication Data
Data available

Typeset by Cepha Imaging Private Ltd, Bangalore, India
· Printed in Italy
on acid-free paper by
L.E.G.O. S.p.A.

ISBN 978–0–19–957222–9 (Set)
978–0–19–928651–5 (Book)

3 5 7 9 10 8 6 4 2

EDITORS

Peter Roth QC
Barrister

Vivien Rose
Barrister

CONTRIBUTORS

Frances Barr
Solicitor

George Peretz
Barrister

Alan Bates
Barrister

Ben Rayment
Barrister

John Boyce
Solicitor

Ashley Roughton
Barrister

Christopher Bright
Barrister

Nicholas Scola
Solicitor

Christopher Brown
Solicitor

John Schmidt
Solicitor

Manish Das
Solicitor

Kassie Smith
Barrister

Josh Holmes
Barrister

Christopher Thomas
Solicitor

Anneli Howard
Barrister

Rhodri Thompson QC
Barrister

Ronit Kreisberger
Barrister

Anny Tubbs
Solicitor

Alistair Lindsay
Solicitor

Christopher Vajda QC
Barrister

Dimitrios Loukas
Solicitor

Tim Ward
Barrister

John O'Flaherty
Barrister

EDITOR OF VOLUME II: APPENDIX MATERIALS

Andrew Macnab
Barrister

CORRESPONDENT EDITORS

Franz Nestl
Austria

Filip Tuytschaever
Belgium

Andreas Christensen
Denmark

Nathalie Lobel-Lastmann
France

Thomas Lübbig
Germany

Gabor Fejes
Hungary

Michael Collins SC
Ireland

Francesca Ammassari
Italy

Weijer VerLoren van Themaat
Netherlands

Robert Gago
Poland

Sofia Belard
Portugal

Iñigo Igartua Arregui
Spain

Elisabeth Legnerfält
Sweden

FOREWORD

We are fortunate indeed that Peter Roth QC, the editor of the fifth edition, and Vivien Rose, the editor of the fourth edition, should have agreed to combine forces to produce this sixth edition of *Bellamy & Child*. This has the happy consequence, among others, that this work has now had only four general editors in the past 35 years, surely something of a record for continuity.

The development of competition law since the publication of the first edition in 1973 has been remarkable, but the pace of change seems to have accelerated markedly since the publication of the fifth edition in 2001. Major developments in this latter period include, in particular, the continued development of an economically based approach to competition law; an increasingly severe approach to hard-core cartels, re-enforced by sophisticated leniency programmes; a revised regime for merger control ; and, perhaps most significantly of all, the famous Modernisation Regulation no.1/2003, which came into force on 1 May 2004. The latter, of course, established that Article 81(1) and Article 81(3) are to be treated as a unitary whole, abolished the system of notification, and devolved enforcement to national authorities who, together with national courts, now share with the Commission the front-line responsibility for enforcing the competition rules of the EC Treaty. In addition to these changes, the accession since 2004 of 12 new Member States, to reach 27 Member States in total, brings its own challenges.

To those developments must be added the increasing globalisation of competition law. Over 100 countries round the world have adopted enforcement regimes, mostly based, in one way or another, on Articles 81 and 82. Global mergers, and global cartels, pose complex problems, with the need for increasing liaison between different competition authorities. In addition, close attention is being paid to the development of private enforcement. And, in some jurisdictions, criminal sanctions are being introduced to supplement systems of administrative penalties.

To these multiple challenges, the General Editors and contributors to this new edition have risen magnificently. The general structure of previous editions has been retained, but each chapter has been thoroughly revised, with some significant new additions – the chapters on market definition and on civil proceedings in the Member States are particularly welcome. As the European Community passes its 50th anniversary, Graham Child and I would like to congratulate most warmly all those who have played a part in producing this sixth edition, particularly the stalwart General Editors, as well as the new publishers, Oxford University Press.

Sir Christopher Bellamy
London
November 2007

PREFACE TO THE SIXTH EDITION

In the six years since publication of the last edition of *Bellamy & Child*, the regime of European competition law has experienced a minor revolution. The so-called 'Modernisation' introduced by Council Regulation 1/2003 brought to an end not just the Commission's exclusive competence to grant exemptions under Article 81(3) but the whole system of notification of agreements to an administrative authority for exemption or clearance. Article 81 became a unitary provision, applied as a whole, and the task of assessing agreements against the complex conditions of Article 81(3) in many cases now rests with the parties themselves, with their national courts being the arbiter of any dispute. Moreover, all the Member States have adopted national competition regimes that largely follow the reformed EC model. Whenever national competition authorities apply their domestic competition law to an agreement or conduct that also falls within Article 81 or 82, they are now required to apply the EC competition rules as well. Compared to the situation that prevailed in the past, EC competition law has been decentralised: although the Commission still plays a pre-eminent role, and the Community Courts are the ultimate forum for determining questions of interpretation of the law, an increasing number of decisions are being taken by national courts in the Member States, often in appeals from decisions of the national competition authority. For their part, the national competition authorities confer and cooperate, pursuant to Regulation 1/2003, through the European Competition Network.

It is no coincidence that the Modernisation regime took effect on 1 May 2004, the same day as the greatest enlargement that the European Union has experienced since its inception with the admission of 10 new Member States. With the recent accession of two further members, the European Union now comprises 27 States and a population of some 490 million. At the same time, greater awareness of competition law among the commercial community (and legal advisers) and among organisations representing consumers—who are intended to be the ultimate beneficiaries of competition law—has fostered increasing reliance on arguments based on Articles 81 and 82, whether by way of complaint to national competition authorities or litigation before national courts. Indeed, in 2008 the Commission is expected to publish a White Paper containing legislative proposals to facilitate more effective private enforcement of competition law.

Alongside the procedural transformation, development of the substantive law of Articles 81 and 82 has continued, both through judgments of the European Court of Justice and the Court of First Instance and by legislation at Community level. New block exemptions have been adopted covering technology transfer and motor vehicle distribution. In the field of mergers, the adoption of a new EC Merger Regulation, Regulation 139/2004, with the attendant implementing regulation, and the issue of a comprehensive Jurisdictional Notice in 2007 (just in time for it to be taken into account in the text of this book), have brought significant changes. In State aids, a process of modernisation is also well under way, in implementation of the Commission's State Aid Action Plan adopted in 2005, leading to new block exemptions and guidelines. Moreover, the fundamental building blocks of the Treaty rules, such as the nature of undertakings and agreements, the responsibilities of dominant firms and what is meant by a restriction of competition, have continued to generate substantial case law exploring the boundaries of the competition law regime.

Such changes present the editors of a treatise on EC competition law that seeks to be comprehensive with a significant challenge. The old chapter on notification of agreements has obviously gone as redundant. There is a completely new chapter on market definition, a topic that is important not only for merger and Article 82 cases but for Article 81 as well, since many of the block exemptions incorporate a market share threshold (or more accurately, ceiling) and consideration of the relevant market is often important more widely under Article 81. Sectoral regulation has become increasingly technical with the liberalising measures for energy markets and a complex regulatory regime for electronic communications. To have maintained the previous format of a chapter on each special sector would have expanded this work beyond manageable proportions. Accordingly, the special sectors are now discussed in a single chapter, providing an overview of the relevant legislation in the various sectors including (unlike previous editions) insurance and postal services.

Altogether the work has undergone substantial re-writing, such that the large team of contributors have in effect produced a new book. Indeed, the number of contributors is testimony to the enormity of the task, to which each of them has contributed much time and effort. Since Vivien Rose is a member of the Government Legal Service and a chairman of the UK Competition Appeal Tribunal, Frances Barr is a member of the Government Legal Service and is employed by the Office of Fair Trading, and Dimitrios Loukas is employed by the European Commission, it should be made clear that any views expressed in the chapters for which they are responsible are not to be attributed to the institutions for which they work, nor should any statement in the book be taken to indicate how the Competition Appeal Tribunal may decide any issue that falls for determination in the future.

Perhaps the most significant innovation in the present edition is the reflection of the decentralised application of competition law by extensive reference to decisions of national courts and tribunals. National judgments are significant not only when applying EC competition law but also when applying the competition provisions of national law, since the same substantive issue may arise under both. *Bellamy & Child* has always incorporated extensive reference to English judgments. The new edition provides a more truly European analysis through the involvement of Correspondent Editors who have supplied us with notes and explanations of significant decisions from their home State. The inclusion of this case law casts valuable light on how different jurisdictions are responding to the issues on which lawyers across the Community are asked to advise. It is notable how many questions that remain to be explored in our own jurisdiction have been the subject of a considered judgment elsewhere. The comparative Table of national legislation that appears at the end of Chapter 14 covers all 27 Member States and also Norway from the EEA. For those countries where we do not have the benefit of a Correspondent Editor, information was supplied by the national competition authorities, whose assistance we appreciate but who are of course not responsible for any errors that may remain.

The Appendices containing legislative materials, Commission guidelines, notices, and so forth, are once again set out in a separate volume for easy use in parallel with the main text. The Appendices volume has been diligently edited by Andrew Macnab and we are very grateful to him for undertaking the complex task of producing consolidated texts of many amended instruments. It is intended that this volume will be regularly updated. It also incorporates cross-references to the relevant paragraphs in the main text.

In addition to the Correspondent Editors, a number of other people have given us the benefit of their expertise in particular areas. Tibor Gold MBE contributed helpful observations on a draft of chapter 9; Wouter Wils gave many detailed and insightful comments on drafts of chapters 13 and (in part) 14; and Michael Bowsher QC helped with the section on arbitration at the end of chapter 14. To all of them we are most grateful, as we are to Sir Jeremy Lever QC who, as for previous editions, shared his wisdom on a number of difficult issues. We also acknowledge with appreciation the assistance that we received from Patricia Boeynaems, James Flynn QC, Max Klasse, Petra Krenz, Justin Menezes, Rita Nina, Irina von Wiese and Julia Xoudis. Production of this work was enormously assisted by our excellent research assistants, whom we are pleased to thank: successively, Kathy Lee, Sarah Darmon, Rebecca Dalzell and, most extensively, Marton Horanyi.

The formidable task of typing up the amendments, re-amendments and updates of the different chapters was undertaken with unfailing cheerfulness, and even enthusiasm, by Linda Antonioni. The copy editing for this edition, like the last, was carried out with efficient skill by Melanie Pepper. And we are grateful to Chris Rycroft and his team at Oxford University Press for their diligence, and patience, in seeing this work through to publication.

We have attempted to ensure that the book is up-to-date to 1 July 2007 and it has proved possible to take account of a few developments since that date. Although the landmark judgment of the Court of First Instance in *Microsoft* came too late to be incorporated into the discussion of Article 82 in the main text, there is included a Postscript which considers the main implications of the judgment and appears at the end of the book before the Index.

Peter Roth QC and Vivien Rose

October 2007

NOTE ON CITATION

The Treaty of Amsterdam, which came into force on 1 May 1999, introduced a renumbering of the articles of the EC Treaty to take account of deletions and additions. In this work, the post-Amsterdam numbering is used throughout, irrespective of the date of the case or decision that is being discussed. However, when the text includes a direct quotation from a judgment that antedates the renumbering, the new Treaty number is given in parenthesis, thus: 'Articles [81] and [82] are complementary inasmuch as they pursue a common general objective set out in Article 3[1][g] of the Treaty . . . .' A Table of Equivalences showing the old and new numbering is at Appendix 1 in Volume II.

For all judgments of the Community Courts, the case number is cited, and reference is given to the official European Court Reports (ECR) and also to the Common Market Law Reports (CMLR) and the All England Reports: European Cases (All ER (EC)) when the case is reported there as well. For all CMLR citations, the reference is to the page number in the report (and not to the unique and confusing CMLR case number adopted since 2001). For those judgments not yet reported at the time of writing, the date of the judgment is stated.

For decisions of the European Commission, reference is given to the Official Journal (OJ) when the decision is published there in full, and to the CMLR if the decision is reported there. The CMLR provides the benefit of a headnote that is particularly useful for longer cartel decisions. However, in recent years the Commission has adopted the practice of publishing only a summary of the longer Article 81 and 82 decisions in the OJ and the full text on the DG Competition website under 'Antitrust—Cases'. For such cases, where the decision is reported in the CMLR that reference is given; otherwise the decision is cited by the Commission case number and the date of the decision (and the OJ short form summary is not cited). The same approach is adopted for Merger decisions, to be found on the DG Competition website under 'Mergers – Cases'.

ACKNOWLEDGMENT

CONTENTS—SUMMARY

VOLUME I

VOLUME II

Appendix Materials
Edited by Andrew Macnab

CONTENTS

VOLUME I

VOLUME II

APPENDIX MATERIALS

TABLES

1. ALPHABETICAL TABLE OF COMMUNITY CASES AND DECISIONS

2. NUMERICAL TABLE OF EUROPEAN COURT OF JUSTICE CASES

3. NUMERICAL TABLE OF
COURT OF FIRST INSTANCE CASES

4. NUMERICAL TABLES OF COMMISSION MERGER AND JOINT VENTURE DECISIONS

MERGER DECISIONS

JOINT VENTURE DECISIONS

5. TABLES OF EUROPEAN COURT OF HUMAN RIGHTS, EFTA COURT AND NATIONAL CASES

EUROPEAN COURT OF HUMAN RIGHTS

EFTA COURT

NATIONAL CASES

Austria

Belgium

Denmark

France

Netherlands

New Zealand

Poland

Spain

Sweden

6. TABLE OF EU/EC TREATIES

7. TABLE OF EC REGULATIONS

8. TABLE OF EC DIRECTIVES

9. TABLE OF EC AND EEA DECISIONS

EEA Joint Committee Decisions

10. TABLES OF EC AND EEA NOTICES, GUIDELINES AND OTHER INFORMAL TEXTS

11. TABLES OF NATIONAL LEGISLATION

12. TABLE OF INTERNATIONAL
TREATIES, CONVENTIONS AND AGREEMENTS

1

THE TREATY AND ITS TERRITORIAL REACH

1

1. Introduction

1.001 **The origins of the Community.**   The origins of the European Community lay in the desire, in the aftermath of the Second World War, to render impossible any further armed conflict between the States of Western Europe, while at the same time laying a firm foundation for European recovery. In memorable language, the preamble to the Treaty establishing the European Coal and Steel Community ('the ECSC Treaty'), signed in 1951, recorded the resolve of the signatories:

> '. . . to substitute for age-old rivalries the merging of their essential interests; to create, by establishing an economic community, the basis for a broader and deeper community among peoples long divided by bloody conflicts; and to lay the foundations for institutions which will give direction to a destiny hence-forward shared.'

That aspiration remains relevant today, as the Community has expanded to embrace the former communist States of Central and Eastern Europe, separated from the West by the 'iron curtain' for most of the second half of the twentieth century.

1.002 **Plan of this Chapter.**   The rules of EC competition law are in part contained in the EC Treaty itself and in part in legislation adopted pursuant to various articles of the Treaty. This Chapter explains the background and context of the EC Treaty, describes its most relevant provisions and discusses some preliminary concepts which are important in applying the competition rules. Section 2 describes the evolution of the Treaty, since it was first signed in 1957, and the various associated Treaties. Section 3 examines the general structure of the Treaty, the competition provisions in particular and other articles which have an important role to play in the application of competition law. These include the rules on free movement of goods, the duties of sincere cooperation between the Community and the Member States and the concept of subsidiarity. Section 4 describes the institutions of the Community focusing on the Directorate-General for Competition and its role in enforcing the competition rules, describing the modernisation of the procedure for enforcement which took place in May 2004. Section 5 discusses the aims of the competition provisions of the Treaty, setting them in the context of the Lisbon Agenda. Section 6 describes the gradual enlargement of the Community from the original six to the current 27 Member States and explains the geographic coverage of the competition rules in relation to the overseas territories of the Member States. It also describes the operation of the EEA Agreement and the Community's bilateral arrangements with third countries for cooperation on competition matters. Section 7 considers issues concerning territorial jurisdiction of the Commission's competence in enforcing the competition rules, as regards activity outside the area of the Community and as against undertakings outside the Member States. Finally, Section 8 considers the requirement in both Articles 81 and 82 that the conduct which affects competition also affects trade between Member States.

2. The Community Treaties

The EC Treaty. This work is principally concerned with the Treaty establishing   **1.003**
the European Community ('the EC Treaty').[1] Building upon the experience of the
ECSC Treaty,[2] and 'determined to lay the foundations of an ever closer union
among the peoples of Europe',[3] the original Member States, France, Germany,
Italy, Belgium, the Netherlands and Luxembourg, signed a Treaty at Rome on
25 March 1957 to establish what was then called the European Economic
Community. Subject to transitional arrangements,[4] that Treaty came into force
on 1 January 1958. It has since been substantially amended, in particular by the
Treaty on European Union signed at Maastricht, which replaced the term 'European
Economic Community' with 'European Community' ('the Community'); and by
the Treaty of Amsterdam, which renumbered the Articles of the amended EC
Treaty.[5] The Treaty of Rome sought to create a common market based on an economic union between the Member States, an objective which received a major
boost from the creation of the single market with effect from 1 January 1993.[6]
The Treaty on European Union marked a further substantial stage in the integration of the Member States by establishing a European Union that embraces a wide
range of additional areas of cooperation alongside the Community itself.[7]

The ECSC Treaty. The Treaty establishing the European Coal and Steel   **1.004**
Community came into force on 23 July 1952 and expired 50 years later on 22 July
2002. It created a competition regime for certain steel and coal products which
operated separately from the regime established under Articles 81 *et seq* of the EC
Treaty.[8] The consequences of expiry were covered in a Protocol to the Nice Treaty
signed in February 2001. The European Commission issued a Communication[9]

---

[1] For an annotated text of the EC Treaty, as amended, see Hunnings (ed), *Encyclopedia of
European Union Law (Constitutional Texts)*, Vol 1, paras 12.0033 *et seq*. For general works on the
EC Treaty see, eg Vaughan and Robertson (eds), *The Law of the European Union* (2003 and supp);
Hartley, *The Foundations of European Community Law* (5th edn, 2003); Craig and de Burca, *EU
Law: Text, Cases and Materials* (3rd edn, 2002); Weatherill, *Cases and Materials on EU Law* (7th edn,
2005); Mathijsen, *A Guide to European Union Law* (8th edn, 2004); Lasok, *Law and Institutions of
the European Union* (7th edn, 2001).

[2] See para 1.004, below.

[3] EC Treaty, first preamble.

[4] Pursuant to Art 8 of the original Treaty of Rome, the transitional period expired on 31 December
1969. The rules on competition came fully into effect with the adoption of Reg 17, the first main
implementing Regulation, on 13 March 1962, see para 1.057, below.

[5] See Table of Equivalences: Vol II, App A.1.

[6] Introduced by the internal market programme following the amendments to the EC Treaty
made by the Single European Act 1986.

[7] The Treaty on European Union came into force on 1 November 1993. See para 1.006, below.

[8] For a brief description of this regime see Chapter 17 of the 5th edition of this work (2001).

[9] ECSC Communication, OJ 2002 C152/5.

clarifying how competition cases would be treated following the expiry. The Communication notes that the expiry of the Treaty means in principle that the sectors previously covered by the ECSC Treaty regime will be subject to the rules of the EC Treaty as well as to the procedural rules and other secondary legislation derived from the EC Treaty. The Communication summarises the most important changes in the applicable substantive and procedural law arising from this transition and explains how the Commission intends to deal with the specific issues raised in the areas of antitrust, merger control and State aid control. If the Commission identifies an infringement in a field covered by the ECSC Treaty, the substantive law applicable will be the law in force at the time when the facts constituting the infringement occurred, even if the investigation takes place after the Treaty expired. As regards procedure, however, the law applicable after the expiry of the ECSC Treaty will be the rules of EC law.[10]

1.005 **The Euratom Treaty.** At the same time as they signed the Treaty of Rome, the original Member States signed the Treaty establishing the European Atomic Energy Community ('the Euratom Treaty'),[11] to coordinate the development of the nuclear industries of the Member States. Unlike the ECSC Treaty, the Euratom Treaty is of indefinite duration.

1.006 **The Treaty on European Union.** The Treaty on European Union ('the TEU') was signed at Maastricht in February 1992 and is often referred to as the 'Maastricht Treaty'.[12] The Treaty came into force on 1 November 1993, when ratifications by the then 12 Member States of the Community took effect. This followed constitutional challenges under national law before the courts in several States.[13]

---

[10] For an illustration of this, see COMP/37.956 *Concrete reinforcing bars*, decn of 17 December 2002 (on appeal, Cases T-27/03 *SP v Commission*, T-98/03 *Alfa Acciai v Commission*, T-77/03 *Feralpi Siderurgica v Commission*, T-94/03 *Ferriere Nord v Commission*, T-97/03 *Ferriera Valsabbia and Valsabbia Investimenti v Commission*, T-79/03 *IRO v Commission*, T-46/03 *Leali v Commission*, T-80/03 *Lucchini v Commission*, T-45/03 *Riva Acciaio v Commission*, not yet decided. The parties challenge, *inter alia*, the power of the Commission to adopt a decn under the ECSC Treaty after its expiry). Similarly, COMP/38.907 *Steel Beams*, decn of 8 November 2006; on appeal Case T-405/06 *Arcelor v Commission*, not yet decided.

[11] Cmnd 7462. For an annotated text, as amended by the Treaty of Amsterdam, see *Encyclopedia of European Union Law (Constitutional Texts)*, Vol 1, paras 11.0001 *et seq*. For a discussion of the scope of the EURATOM Treaty, see Case C-61/03 *Commission v United Kingdom* [2005] ECR I-2477, [2005] 2 CMLR 1209, where the ECJ declined to follow the Opinion of AG Geelhoed and held that the Treaty did not extend to the military nuclear installations.

[12] Cmnd 1934. For the text as amended by the Treaty of Amsterdam, see *Encyclopedia of European Union Law (Constitutional Texts)*, Vol 1, paras 13.0001 *et seq*. and Vol 5, paras 97.001 *et seq*.

[13] England: *R v Secretary of State for Foreign and Commonwealth Affairs, ex p Rees-Mogg* [1994] QB 552, [1994] 1 All ER 457, [1993] 3 CMLR 101 (DC); France: Case 92–308 of 9 April 1992, [1993] 3 CMLR 345 and, following a constitutional amendment, Case 92–312 of 2 September 1992, (1992) JORF 12095 (Conseil Constitutionnel); Germany: *Brunner*, 12 October 1993, 89 BVerf GE 155, [1994] 1 CMLR 57 (Fed Const Ct); and Spain: Case 1236/1992, [1994] 3 CMLR 101 (Const Ct).

The most striking change introduced by the TEU was the establishment of the European Union which, despite popular misconceptions, has not replaced the European Community. The Community continues in its pre-Maastricht structure although the EC Treaty was subject to numerous detailed amendments made by the TEU (including the deletion of 'Economic' from the title of the European Community to reflect its broadened range of application to beyond the purely economic sphere). The European Union is a broader, albeit loose, entity that embraces the European Community as the first of what, under the original TEU, were called its 'Three Pillars'. The Second Pillar (now Title V of the renumbered TEU) is the Common Foreign and Security Policy; and the Third Pillar (now Title VI of the TEU) comprises what was first called Co-operation in the Fields of Justice and Home Affairs but under the Treaty of Amsterdam has been renamed Police and Judicial Cooperation in Criminal Matters. Under the original TEU, the European Court of Justice had no jurisdiction as regards the Second and Third Pillars but, following the Treaty of Amsterdam, it has been given limited jurisdiction as regards Police and Judicial Cooperation. However, in political and administrative respects, a single set of institutions operates in respect of all aspects of the European Union: in particular, the European Parliament, the Council of Ministers and the European Commission: see Section 4, below. The TEU also increased the role of the Parliament by amending the decision-making process under the EC Treaty and gave further recognition to the role of the European Council (not to be confused with the Council of Ministers), a summit of the Heads of Government of the Member States (accompanied by their Foreign Ministers) and the President of the Commission.

The single currency. The Maastricht Treaty added as one of the Community's **1.007** objectives the establishment of 'economic and monetary union'.[14] What is now Article 4 of the TEU committed the Member States to the fixing of exchange rates leading to the introduction of a single currency and the pursuit of a single monetary and exchange rate policy. The common currency, called the euro (and designated by €) was introduced on 1 January 1999 by 11 Member States, namely Austria, Belgium, Finland, France, Germany, Ireland, Italy, Luxembourg, the Netherlands, Portugal, and Spain. Greece joined the 'Euro Zone' on 1 January 2001 and Slovenia on 1 January 2007. Cyprus and Malta are to adopt the Euro on 1 January 2008.[15] During a transitional period, the Member States' existing currencies operated as denominations of the euro but on 1 January 2002, euro notes and coins entered into circulation and by the end of February 2002 the old

---

[14] Art 2 of the EC Treaty as amended by the TEU.
[15] Monaco adopted the euro (OJ 2002 L142/59), as did San Marino (OJ 2001 C209/1) and Vatican City (OJ 2001 C299/1).

notes and coins were withdrawn from circulation.[16] The United Kingdom and Denmark preserved their right to remain outside the third stage of EMU by Protocols added to the EC Treaty by the TEU.[17] Discussion of EMU is beyond the scope of this work.[18] Since 1 January 1999, the turnover figures that apply under EC competition law (for example, jurisdictional thresholds under the Merger Regulation and the turnover of companies that determine a ceiling for fines) are calculated in euros and all fines are imposed in euros. Previously, the Community institutions used European Currency Units ('ECU'), which was the currency in which the EC budget was drawn up and which was calculated daily from a basket of currencies and published regularly in the C-series of the *Official Journal*. Where reference is found to ECUs in legal instruments, it is to be replaced with effect from 1 January 1999 by a reference to euros.[19]

1.008 **The Treaty of Amsterdam.**   The Treaty of Amsterdam, which came into force on 1 May 1999, was essentially an amending Treaty making numerous changes to the TEU and the EC Treaty.[20] Those two Treaties and the Euratom Treaty, as amended, therefore constitute the European Union. The substantive changes made by the Treaty of Amsterdam included: extension to the subjects in respect of which the Council may take decisions by qualified majority voting (as opposed to unanimity); further enhancement of the role of the Parliament; the addition in the TEU of a new Title on 'Closer Co-operation' that in effect allows some Member States to proceed with closer integration while others opt out;[21] the incorporation into the EC Treaty (but subject to opt-outs on the part of the United Kingdom, Ireland and Denmark) of provisions on visas, asylum and immigration that had previously formed part of the Third Pillar;[22] and the incorporation into the EC Treaty of the Social Chapter, which had been confined to a Protocol by the Maastricht Treaty because of the previous opt-out by the United Kingdom.[23] Whereas the political pressures and compromises at Maastricht gave the original TEU an inelegant and cumbersome structure, the Treaty of Amsterdam sought to

---

[16] For a summary description of the process see *Bank charges for exchanging euro-zone currencies*, OJ 2003 L15/1, although the result was annulled on appeal: Cases T-44/02, etc, *Dresdner Bank v Commission* [2006] ECR II-3567, [2007] 4 CMLR 467.

[17] Protocol 25 (United Kingdom); Protocol 26 (Denmark).

[18] For a helpful introduction in a general work, see Lasok (n 1, above) Chap 24. See also Beaumont and Walker (eds), *The Legal Framework of the Single European Currency* (1999).

[19] ie at a conversion of one-to-one: Art 2(1) of Reg 1103/97, OJ 1997 L162/1.

[20] Cm 3780, OJ 1997 C340. See *Encyclopedia of European Union Law (Constitutional Texts)*, Vol 5, paras 97A.0001 *et seq.*

[21] Title VII. This is sometimes referred to as 'variable geometry'.

[22] Title IV (Arts 61–69) EC. The UK and Irish opt-outs are in Protocol 4; the Danish opt-out is in Protocol 5.

[23] Following Maastricht, Protocol 14 to the EC Treaty, agreed to by 11 Member States; now at Arts 137–140 EC. The UK opt-out was ended by the Labour government that came to power in 1997.

produce a more cohesive document, whereby the Second and Third Pillars became Titles V and VI, respectively, of a renumbered TEU and the previously lettered articles of the TEU were given numbers.

The Treaty of Nice. The Treaty of Nice entered into force on 1 February 2003 **1.009** following ratification by all the Member States.[24] It made various amendments to the EU Treaties, in particular, to the provisions in the TEU concerning a common foreign and security policy and to the provisions covering so-called 'enhanced cooperation' in various areas covered by the TEU between a smaller group of Member States (which can now be undertaken between a minimum of eight Member States). The amendments made by the Treaty of Nice to the EC Treaty (and to the Euratom Treaty) are in general not substantial except that majority voting replaces the requirement of unanimity for Council decisions in certain areas and some important changes are made as regards the jurisdiction and structure of the Community Courts[25] and a revised Statute of the Court of Justice was adopted.[26] No amendments were made to the competition provisions of the earlier Treaties.

Charter of Fundamental Rights. In December 2000, at the time of the inter- **1.010** governmental conference that led to the Treaty of Nice, the European Parliament, the Council and the Commission 'solemnly proclaim[ed]' a Charter of Fundamental Rights of the European Union.[27] It incorporates many of the principles found in the European Convention on Human Rights but also enunciates further rights, for example in the field of employment and social benefits. The Charter was not adopted under any of the EU Treaties and is expressly stated not to modify powers and tasks defined by the Treaties.[28] At present, its formal, legal status is unclear, but it is likely to be influential on the actions of the Community institutions.[29] Moreover, if the proposed Reform Treaty agreed between the Heads of Government in June 2007 is adopted, Article 6 of the TEU will be amended to refer to the Charter and make it legally binding.[30] However, on matters of privacy, a fair trial

---

[24] Treaty of Nice, OJ 2001 C80/1. See *Encyclopedia of European Union Law (Constitutional Texts)*, Vol 6, paras 104.0385 *et seq.*

[25] See paras 1.045 *et seq*, below and Vol II, App A.6 which includes the provisions as amended.

[26] Art 7 of the Treaty of Nice and the Protocol annexed.

[27] Charter of Fundamental Rights, OJ 2000 C364/1. See *Encyclopedia of European Union Law (Constitutional Texts)*, Vol 6, paras 104.0100 *et seq.*

[28] Art 51(2). If the Constitutional Treaty had been adopted (see para 1.012, below), the Charter would have been incorporated into the Treaty although it is not clear to what precise effect.

[29] Note also the reference to the Charter in Recital (37) of Reg 1/2003, stating that the Regulation should be interpreted and applied with regard to those principles: Vol II, App B.3.

[30] This will be subject to a 'UK opt-out' in the form of a Protocol annexed to the TEU providing that the Charter does not 'extend the ability' of the courts to find the laws or administrative practices or action of the United Kingdom are inconsistent with the rights and principles in the Charter. See Presidency Conclusions —Brussels, 21/22 June 2007 (Doc 1117/07), Ann 1, available at: http://www.consilium.europa.eu/ueDocs/cms_Data/docs/pressData/en/ec/94932.pdf.

and the rights of defence, which are the provisions that are likely to be of greatest relevance in the field of competition law, the Charter does not appear to go further than the analogous provisions of the European Convention, as interpreted by the European Court of Human Rights.[31]

1.011 **The Laeken Declaration and the Constitution.** Meeting in Belgium in December 2001, the European Council (comprising the Heads of Government and President of the Commission) considered the challenges facing the Union and adopted the Laeken Declaration.[32] The Declaration recognised that 'Europe is on its way to becoming one big family, without bloodshed, a real transformation clearly calling for a different approach from fifty years ago, when six countries first took the lead'. The Declaration highlighted three basic challenges; how to bring citizens closer to the European design and the European institutions; how to organise politics and the European political area in an enlarged Union; and how to develop the Union into a stabilising factor and a model in the new, multi-polar world. To address these issues, the Council convened a Convention under the Presidency of Valery Giscard D'Estaing to prepare a response to be presented at an Intergovernmental Conference. The Convention's members came from 28 countries: the 15 then Member States, the 10 countries due to accede to the Union in May 2004, and the three then candidate countries, Romania, Bulgaria and Turkey. The Convention's recommendations took the form of a draft Constitutional Treaty which was considered and adopted at an Inter-Governmental Conference in 2004.[33] However, for the Treaty to come into force, it had to be ratified by all the (by then) 25 Member States. Although the Treaty was ratified by Austria, Germany, Greece, Hungary, Italy, Latvia, Lithuania, Slovakia, Slovenia and Spain,

---

[31] Note also Art 41, the right to good administration, which provides that 'every person has the right to have his or her affairs handled impartially, fairly and within a reasonable time' by the EU institutions. See paras 13.026, *et seq*, below, for the application of these principles in the enforcement of the competition rules. In Case T-112/98 *Mannesmannröhren-Werke v Commission* [2001] ECR II-729, [2001] 5 CMLR 54, para 76, the CFI rejected an application to re-open the hearing to receive submissions concerning the Charter, on the grounds that it could be of no relevance to the contested decision since that was taken before the date of the Charter. In Case T-210/01 *General Electric v Commission* [2005] ECR II-5575, [2006] 4 CMLR 686, para 725, the CFI noted that the Charter rights being invoked were already protected as fundamental principles of EC law. But see Case C-540/03 *European Parliament v EU Council* [2006] ECR I-5769, [2006] 3 CMLR 779, [2007] All ER (EC) 193, paras 38 and 59, for reliance by the ECJ on the Charter along with other human rights instruments. See generally Craig, *EU Administrative Law* (2006), Chap 14; and for analysis of various provisions of the Charter, see Peers and Ward (eds), *The European Union Charter of Fundamental Rights* (2004). For discussion of its legal effect, see the article by the former UK Attorney General, Lord Goldsmith, 'The Charter of Rights: a brake not an accelerator' [2004] EHRLR 473, and the response by Roy Davis, 'A Brake? The Union's New 'Bill of Rights'' [2005] EHRLR 449.

[32] (2001) 12 EU Bull, point I.1.

[33] *Encyclopedia of European Union Law (Constitutional Texts)*, Vol 6, paras 104.1700, *et seq*.

the French and Dutch electorate voted against the Treaty in referenda and thereafter the ratification process was effectively suspended.

The Reform Treaty.   Following the abortive Constitutional Treaty, the Heads of **1.012**
Government meeting in Brussels on 21–22 June 2007 under the German presidency agreed on a Reform Treaty that will preserve some of the elements of the Constitution by way of amendment to the TEU and the EC Treaty.[34] The latter is to be renamed the Treaty on the Functioning of the Union, the two treaties will formally be given equal legal status, and the term 'Union' will replace 'Community' throughout. The size of the European Commission is to be reduced, the six-month rotating Presidency is to be replaced with a full-time President, and, most contentiously, the voting system is to be significantly changed to reflect the larger size of the Union. As mentioned above, the TEU will formally incorporate by reference the Charter of Fundamental Rights.[35] Although the statement of the objectives of the Union taken over from the Constitution into a new Article 3 of the TEU will not mention free and undistorted competition (as had the equivalent provision of the Constitution), a change for which the French President was responsible and which provoked much outrage from competition specialists,[36] it is to be noted that this is not among the enumerated objectives of the Union in the present Article 2 of the TEU (which the new Article 3 will replace) or in Article 2 of the EC Treaty.[37] Moreover, no amendment is proposed to Article 3(1) of the EC Treaty which includes in the list of activities of the Community 'a system ensuring that competition in the internal market is not distorted'.[38] It is the intention to have the Reform Treaty drafted by the end of 2007, but it will then require ratification by all Member States and is unlikely to come into effect before 2009 at the earliest. It remains to be seen whether the Reform Treaty will fare better than the Constitutional Treaty during the ratification process.

3. The EC Treaty

(a) Generally

The aims of the EC Treaty.   Since the Community was established, its aims have **1.013**
been considerably broadened. Today they are, in essence: the creation of a single, internal market in which goods, services, persons and capital move at least as freely

---

[34] See Presidency Conclusions —Brussels, 21/22 June 2007 (n 30, above).
[35] See para 1.010, above.
[36] See, eg 'Removal of competition clause causes dismay', *Financial Times*, 23/24 June 2007, p 6.
[37] As the ultimate political compromise, there is also to be a Protocol annexed to the Treaties stating that the Member States consider that the internal market as set out in Art 3 TEU 'includes a system ensuring that competition is not distorted'.
[38] Art 3(1)(g) EC.

throughout the Community as they do within the national territory of each Member State; the promotion of a high level of employment, social protection and equality between men and women; and the progressive coordination of the economies of the Member States so as to create an economic and monetary union. Those aims are set out in the amended Article 2 of the Treaty, which provides:

> 'The Community shall have as its task, by establishing a common market and an economic and monetary union and by implementing common policies or activities referred to in Articles 3 and 4, to promote throughout the Community a harmonious, balanced and sustainable development of economic activities, a high level of employment and of social protection, equality between men and women, sustainable and non-inflationary growth, a high degree of competitiveness and convergence of economic performance, a high level of protection and improvement of the quality of the environment, the raising of the standard of living and quality of life, and economic and social cohesion and solidarity among Member States.'

1.014 **The structure of the EC Treaty.** Articles 1–16 provide the basic framework of the Treaty. Article 1 establishes the Community. Articles 7–9 provide for the main institutions: under Article 7, a European Parliament, a Council, a Commission, a Court of Justice and a Court of Auditors; under Article 8, a European Central Bank and a European System of Central Banks; and under Article 9, a European Investment Bank. Other pertinent articles are Article 2 (aims of the Community), Article 3 (activities of the Community), Article 5 (subsidiarity), Article 6 (environmental protection), Article 10 (duties of Member States) and Article 12 (prohibition of discrimination on grounds of nationality).[39] Part Two of the Treaty, 'Citizenship of the Union', added by the TEU, comprises Articles 17–22 and concerns the rights which result from the citizenship of the European Union that is bestowed on the citizens of each Member State, for example the right to vote and stand as a candidate in municipal (but not national) elections. Part Three of the Treaty contains its most fundamental provisions, including the four 'freedoms', namely the free movement of goods (Articles 23–31), persons (Articles 39–48), services (Articles 49–55) and capital (Articles 56–60). Part Three also contains provisions relating to the common agricultural policy (Articles 32–38) and the common transport policy (Articles 70–80). The Treaty provisions relating to agriculture and transport are discussed briefly in Chapter 12, below.

1.015 **Interpretation of the Treaty.** The competition rules in Articles 81 to 89 must always be considered in their context in the Treaty as a whole. In dealing with any given problem, therefore, other provisions may be relevant. This is particularly so in respect of the general principles set out in Articles 2, 3, 5, and 10 and the Treaty

---

[39] See Vol II, App A.3.

provisions relating to the freedom of movement for goods, discussed below.[40] In addition, the provisions of the Treaty must be applied in accordance with certain general principles common to the Member States.[41] In the present context, the relevant general principles include proportionality (that is the principle which requires that measures implemented through Community provisions must be appropriate for attaining the objective pursued and not go beyond what is necessary to achieve it),[42] equality and non-discrimination,[43] legitimate expectation (that is that the Community will not act contrary to expectations legitimately held by those affected by the proposed action),[44] legal certainty[45] and the right to a fair hearing.[46]

---

[40] Paras 1.032 *et seq*, below. For a description of the correct approach to the interpretation of Treaty provisions, see Cases T-22 & 23/02 *Sumitomo v Commission* [2005] ECR II-4065, [2006] 4 CMLR 42, paras 42 *et seq*. That case also confirms that the same principles apply to interpreting Community secondary legislation: para 77. For a similar exercise in interpreting the corresponding provisions of the EEA Agreement, see Case E-8/00 *LO and NKF v KS* [2002] Rep EFTA Ct 114, [2002] 5 CMLR 160.

[41] See generally Craig, *EU Administrative Law* (2006); Hartley, *The Foundations of European Community Law* (5th edn, 2003), Chap 5; Tridimas, *The General Principles of EU Law* (2nd edn, 2006); Schermers and Waelbroeck, *Judicial Protection in the European Community* (6th edn, 2001), paras 53 *et seq*; Vaughan and Robertson (n 1, above), sect 3 (by Lasok).

[42] See, eg Case C-491/01 *British American Tobacco (Investments) and Imperial Tobacco* [2002] ECR I-11453, [2003] 1 CMLR 395, [2003] All ER (EC) 604, para 122; Case C-479/04 *Laserdisken v Kulturministeriet* [2006] ECR I-8089, [2007] 1 CMLR 187, para 53; and in the context of judicial control of a competition investigation by the Commission, Case C-94/00 *Roquette Frères* [2002] ECR I-9011, [2003] 4 CMLR 46, [2003] All ER (EC) 920, paras 71–80. The principle of proportionality is now prescribed by the third para of Art 5 of the EC Treaty, introduced by the TEU: see Vol II, App A.3.

[43] See, eg Cases 117/76 & 16/77 *Ruckdeschel v Hauptzollamt Hamburg-St. Annen* [1977] ECR 1753, [1979] 2 CMLR 445; Cases 103 & 145/77 *Royal Scholten-Honig v Intervention Board* [1978] ECR 2037, [1979] 1 CMLR 675, paras 26–27. See also the argument put forward (unsuccessfully) by ICI regarding the level of its fine compared with the fines imposed on other members of the polypropylene cartel: Case T-13/89 *ICI v Commission* [1992] ECR II-1021, paras 380–388; Case T-352/94 *Mo och Domsjö v Commission* [1998] ECR II-1989, paras 378 *et seq*; and Cases T-305/94, etc, *Limburgse Vinyl Maatschappij v Commission ('PVC II')* [1999] ECR II-931, [1999] 5 CMLR 303, paras 1211 *et seq*.

[44] See, eg Case C-506/03 *Germany v Commission*, judgment of 24 November 2005 (unpubd), para 58; Cases C-182 & 217/03 *Belgium and Forum 187 v Commission* [2006] ECR I-5479, para 147.

[45] See, eg Case 85/76 *Hoffmann-La Roche v Commission* [1979] ECR 461, [1979] 3 CMLR 211, paras 4–6; Cases 209/84, etc, *Ministère Public v Asjes* [1986] ECR 1425, [1986] 3 CMLR 173; Case T-51/89 *Tetra Pak Rausing v Commission* [1990] ECR II-309, [1991] 4 CMLR 334; Cases T-79/89, etc, *BASF v Commission ('PVC I')* [1992] ECR II-315, [1992] 4 CMLR 357, paras 71–77, appeal dismissed Case C-137/92P [1994] ECR I-2555 (infringement of Commission's rules of procedure violates legal certainty); Case T-229/94 *Deutsche Bahn v Commission* [1997] ECR II-1689, [1998] 4 CMLR 220 (answer to Parliamentary Question cannot affect the legal situation); Case C-286/95P *Commission v ICI* [2000] ECR I-2341, [2000] 5 CMLR 413; and Cases C-287 & 288/95P *Commission v Solvay* [2000] ECR I-2391, [2000] 5 CMLR 454; *Sumitomo* (n 40, above) para 80: 'The principle of legal certainty aims to ensure that situations and legal relationships governed by Community law remain foreseeable'; Case C-3/06 P *Groupe Danone v Commission* [2007] 4 CMLR 701 (no breach of the principle of legal certainty for the Commission to increase fine because of prior infringements occurring beyond the limitation period).

[46] Referred to as the rights of the defence. See paras 13.028 *et seq*, below.

1.016 **Fundamental human rights.** The original Community Treaties made no reference to human rights. However, the Court of Justice held that fundamental rights,
as derived from the constitutional traditions of the Member States and as set out
in the European Convention for the Protection of Human Rights and Fundamental
Freedoms, constitute general principles of Community law.[47] This is now expressly
stated in Article 6(2) of the TEU.[48] The jurisdiction of the Community Courts in
respect of the acts of the institutions embraces this provision, in contrast to many
other parts of the TEU outside the three Community Treaties.[49]

1.017 **A presumption of compliance: *Bosphorus Airways.*** In the important case of
Bosphorus Airways v Ireland,[50] the European Court of Human Rights considered
the relationship between a Member State's obligations to apply EC law and its
obligations under the European Convention on Human Rights. The case arose
from the impounding of an aircraft by the Irish authorities in compliance with EC
Regulation 990/93 imposing sanctions against the former Federal Republic of
Yugoslavia. Could an act which the Member State was bound by Community law
to perform nonetheless amount to an infringement of the applicant's property
rights under the Human Rights Convention? The Court held that a Contracting
Party to the Convention cannot avoid responsibility for its conduct simply because
it is bound, by the rules of an international organisation of which it is a member,
to carry out that act. However, State action taken in compliance with such legal
obligations is justified as long as the organisation from which they derive protects
fundamental rights in a manner which is at least equivalent to that for which the
Convention provides. If such equivalent protection is provided by the organisation, the presumption will be that a State is complying with the Convention when
it does no more than implement legal obligations flowing from its membership of

---

[47] See Case 36/75 *Rutili v Minister for the Interior* [1975] ECR 1219, [1976] 1 CMLR 140,
paras 31–32; Case C-260/89 *ERT* [1991] ECR I-2925, [1994] 4 CMLR 540, paras 41 *et seq*
(national courts applying provisions of the Treaty must have regard to all the rules of Community
law including the fundamental right to freedom of speech as enshrined in Art 10 ECHR); Case
C-404/92P *X v Commission* [1994] ECR I-4737 (right to respect for private life under Art 8
ECHR and Aids testing of Community employee); Case C-112/00 *Schmidberger* [2003] ECR
I-5659, [2003] 2 CMLR 1043, para 71 and case law cited (failure to ban political demonstration
which resulted in 30 hour closure of main trunk route through Austria restricted free movement
of goods but was justified by protection of freedom of expression and the right to demonstrate);
Laserdisken (n 42, above) paras 60 *et seq* (exercise of copyright does not breach right to freedom of
expression under Art 10 ECHR). For application of the ECHR in the field of competition law, see
Mannesmannröhren-Werke v Commission (n 31, above) and paras 13.026 *et seq*, below.

[48] Under the proposed Reform Treaty, Art 6 will be amended to provide for the EU to accede to the
ECHR; and see further para 1.012, above, as regards incorporation of the Charter of Fundamental
Rights.

[49] Art 46(d) TEU.

[50] Application No. 45036/98 *Bosphorus Hava Yollari Turizm ve Ticaret Anonim Sirketi (Bosphorus
Airways) v Ireland,* judgment of 30 June 2005, (2006) 42 EHRR 1. The case was heard by the Grand
Chamber with the European Commission, amongst others, participating in the oral hearing.

the organisation. However, any such presumption can be rebutted if, in the circumstances of a particular case, it is considered that the protection of Convention rights by the body imposing the obligations was manifestly deficient. The Court considered carefully the development of EC jurisprudence on the role of fundamental rights in the system of Community law. It found that the protection of fundamental rights by EC law can be considered to be 'equivalent' to that of the Convention system. Consequently, there was a presumption that Ireland did not depart from the requirements of the Convention when it implemented legal obligations flowing from its membership of the Community. Further, the protection of the applicant's Convention rights was not manifestly deficient so as to rebut the presumption of Convention compliance. The Court unanimously found that there had been no violation of the applicant's rights.

(b) The main competition provisions

Generally. Against the above background, Articles 81–89 of the Treaty provide **1.018**
rules governing competition within the Community. Those provisions, which implement Article 3(1)(g), constitute Chapter 1 of Title VI of the Treaty and comprise two main sections, namely 'rules applying to undertakings' (Articles 81–86) and 'aids granted by States' (Articles 87–89). The full text is at Appendix A.2.

Article 81. The first paragraph of Article 81 prohibits all agreements between **1.019**
undertakings, decisions by associations of undertakings and concerted practices which may affect trade between Member States and which have as their object or effect the prevention, restriction or distortion of competition within the common market. The essential feature of Article 81(1) is that its application in any given case depends upon the economic aims or effects of transactions entered into between undertakings. Article 81(2) provides that any agreements or decisions prohibited under Article 81(1) shall be automatically void. This has been interpreted by the Court of Justice to mean that only those provisions of the agreement which restrict competition contrary to Article 81(1) are void.[51] The doctrine of direct effect has the consequence that provisions of an agreement which are void by reason of Article 81(2) are unenforceable in the national courts of the Member States.[52] Article 81(3) provides that the prohibition may be declared to be inapplicable to agreements, decisions or concerted practices, or categories thereof, which contribute to improving the production or distribution of goods, or to promoting technical or economic progress, provided that they also allow consumers a fair share of the resulting benefit, only impose restrictions indispensable to achieving

---

[51] Case 56/65 *Société Technique Minière v Maschinenbau Ulm* [1966] ECR 235, 250, [1966] CMLR 357, 376; Case 319/82 *Soc de Vente de Ciments et Bétons v Kerpen & Kerpen* [1983] ECR 4173, 4184–4185, [1985] 1 CMLR 511, 526–527.
[52] See Chap 14, below.

those objectives and do not permit the elimination of competition. Under the first procedural regime for enforcement of Article 81,[53] the European Commission had exclusive competence to apply Article 81(3) either by individual decision on particular agreements or by adopting regulations which applied Article 81(3) to categories of agreements fulfilling certain criteria. Individual applications of Article 81(3) by the Commission under that regime are commonly referred to as 'exemptions', although this word does not appear in the Treaty itself; and the regulations exempting categories of agreements are known as 'block exemptions'. However, since Regulation 1/2003[54] came into force on 1 May 2004, the national competition authorities and national courts can apply all aspects of Article 81. The term 'individual exemption' is therefore no longer apposite for such application of Article 81(3) under the new regime.

1.020 **Article 82.** Article 82 provides that an abuse by one or more undertakings of a dominant position within the common market or in a substantial part of it shall be prohibited insofar as it may affect trade between Member States.[55] Whereas Article 81 strikes at various forms of cooperation between undertakings, Article 82 strikes at unilateral conduct by an undertaking (or occasionally several undertakings) with market power. Both Articles 81 and 82 seek to achieve the same paramount aim, the maintenance of effective competition within the common market.[56] There is no equivalent to Article 81(3) providing for exemption under Article 82.[57]

1.021 **Article 83.** Article 83 imposes upon the Council, acting on a proposal from the Commission and after consulting the European Parliament, the duty to adopt appropriate regulations or directives[58] to give effect to the principles set out in Articles 81 and 82. Such regulations and directives may be designed in particular: (i) to ensure compliance with the prohibitions of Article 81(1) and Article 82 by making provision for fines and other penalty payments; (ii) to lay down detailed rules for the application of Article 81(3); (iii) to define the scope of Articles 81 and 82 'in various branches of the economy'; (iv) to define the respective functions of

---

[53] Under Reg 17/62, see Vol II, App B.1.

[54] Reg 1/2003, OJ 2003 L1/1: Vol II, App B.3. See paras 1.058 *et seq* and Chap 13, below.

[55] See generally Chap 10, below.

[56] Case 6/72 *Europemballage and Continental Can v Commission* [1973] ECR 215, [1973] CMLR 199, para 25; Case 66/86 *Ahmed Saeed Flugreisen v Zentrale zur Bekämpfung Unlauteren Wettbewerbs* [1989] ECR 803, [1990] 4 CMLR 102; *Tetra Pak Rausing* (n 45, above).

[57] For the relationship between Arts 81(3) and 82, see *Tetra Pak Rausing* (n 45, above) and para 3.012, below.

[58] Regulations made by the Council or the Commission have general application. According to Art 249 of the EC Treaty, they are binding in their entirety and directly applicable in all Member States. By contrast, directives are binding upon Member States as to the result to be achieved, but leave to the national authorities the choice of form and methods of achieving that objective.

the Commission and the Court of Justice; and (v) to determine the relationship between national laws and Community laws.[59]

Regulations and directives under Article 83.   The Council has exercised its **1.022**
power under Article 83 to make the five principal regulations establishing the current competition regime: Regulation 1/2003[60] sets out the general implementing provisions; Regulations 19/65, 2821/71 and 1534/91 enable the Commission to adopt block exemption regulations covering various fields;[61] and Regulation 139/2004 sets out the regime for merger control.[62] These Regulations in turn empower the Commission to make subordinate regulations. No directives have yet been adopted under Article 83. Article 89 similarly empowers the Council to make regulations for the application of the State aid provisions in Articles 87 and 88. Under this provision, the Council adopted Regulation 994/98 which enables the Commission to adopt block exemption regulations, and Regulation 659/1999 which sets out general procedural rules for State aid notifications.[63]

Articles 84 and 85.   Article 84 provides transitional provisions relating to the **1.023**
enforcement of Articles 81 and 82 pending the entry into force of measures taken under Article 83. Since all areas of the economy are now covered by the procedural rules laid down in Regulation 1/2003, Article 84 has become otiose.[64] Article 85 provides that the Commission 'shall ensure the application of the principles laid down in Articles 81 and 82'. It also set up some machinery for the Commission to

---

[59] A national court is under a duty to construe its national law, so far as possible, to achieve the result pursued by the directive: Case C-106/89 *Marleasing v La Comercial* [1990] ECR I-4135, [1992] 1 CMLR 305; Cases C-397/01, etc, *Pfeiffer Deutsches Rotes Kreuz* [2004] ECR I-8835, [2005] 1 CMLR 1123. For a comprehensive analysis by the English Court of Appeal of European and UK authorities on the correct approach to construing EC legislation, see *HM Revenue and Customs v IDT Card Services Ireland Ltd* [2006] EWCA Civ 29, [2006] STC 1252. Under the doctrine of 'vertical direct effect', certain directives can become binding on bodies that constitute 'emanations of the State' and thereby confer rights on private individuals and other non-State undertakings, but they cannot impose obligations on private undertakings until incorporated into national law: see Case 152/84 *Marshall* [1986] ECR 723, [1986] 1 CMLR 688; Cases C-6 & 9/90 *Francovich v Italian Republic* [1991] ECR I-5357, [1993] 2 CMLR 66; and in England, *R v Durham County Council, ex p Huddelston* [2000] 1 WLR 1484 (CA). See further Prechal, *Directives in European Community Law* (2nd edn, 2005), and the works cited at n 1 to para 14.001, below.
[60] Replacing Reg 17/62. See paras 1.058 *et seq*, below.
[61] Para 1.065 and Chap 3, below.
[62] Reg 139/2004, OJ 2004 L24/1: Vol II, App D.1, replacing Reg 4064/89. For merger control generally see Chap 8, below.
[63] Reg 994/98, OJ 1998 L142/1: Vol II, App G.9; Reg 659/1999, OJ 1999 L83/1, as amended by Act of accession of Czech Republic, Estonia, Cyprus, Latvia, Lithuania, Hungary, Malta, Poland, Slovenia and Slovakia, OJ 2003 L236/345: Vol II, App G.1, both discussed in Chap 15, below.
[64] Air transport between Community and third country airports was brought within the general regime by an amendment to Reg 1/2003 in Reg 411/2004, OJ 2004 L68/1; international tramp vessels and intra-Member State maritime transport were brought within Reg 1/2003 by Reg 1419/2006, OJ 2006 L269/1.

investigate infringements in the absence of implementing legislation that empowers the Commission directly to enforce the competition rules.

1.024 **Article 86.** The purpose of Article 86 is to ensure that Member States do not adopt legislation which favours undertakings in the public sector of the economy or on whom the State has conferred special rights. It differs from Articles 81 and 82 in being directed at Member States rather than at undertakings, although a breach of a Treaty provision by an undertaking is an essential component in any breach of Article 86. Article 86(2) provides that undertakings entrusted with the operation of services 'of general economic interest' or 'having the character of a revenue-producing monopoly' are subject to the competition rules only insofar as the application of those rules 'does not obstruct the performance in law or fact of the particular tasks assigned to them'. The application of Article 86 has assumed ever-increasing significance in recent years and is discussed in Chapter 11, below.

1.025 **Articles 87–89.** Since 'State aid generally means a conflict of interests between the recipient economic agents and their competitors in other Member States',[65] Article 87(1) declares incompatible with the common market, insofar as it affects trade between Member States, 'any aid granted by a Member State which distorts or threatens to distort competition by favouring certain undertakings or the production of certain goods'. Article 87, and the ancillary provisions in Articles 88 and 89, are considered in Chapter 15, below.

(c) **Other provisions of the Treaty**

1.026 **Article 3: the activities of the Community.** Article 3(1) provides that the activities of the Community shall include the prohibition, as between Member States, of customs duties and quantitative restrictions on the import and export of goods, and of all other measures having equivalent effect;[66] the abolition of obstacles to freedom of movement of goods,[67] persons,[68] services[69] and capital;[70] the adoption

---

[65] *1st Report on Competition Policy* (1971), point 133.

[66] See in particular Arts 23 and 25 (prohibition of customs duties on imports and exports between Member States and of all charges having equivalent effect); Arts 28–29 (prohibition of quantitative restrictions on imports and exports between Member States and all measures having equivalent effect); and Art 30 (certain exceptions to Arts 28–29).

[67] ibid.

[68] See Arts 39–42 (workers), Arts 43–48 (right of establishment), Arts 136–145 (social provisions). Note also Arts 61–69, added by the Treaty of Amsterdam (visa, asylum and immigration policies) from which the United Kingdom and Ireland have an opt-out: n 22, above.

[69] See Arts 49–50. By Art 51(1) transport services are governed by Arts 70–80.

[70] See Arts 56–60 (as replaced by the TEU).

of a common policy in the spheres of agriculture and fisheries[71] and of transport;[72] and encouragement for the establishment of trans-European networks.[73]

Article 3(1)(g).   The list of activities of the Community in Article 3 includes, **1.027** as Article 3(1)(g), 'a system ensuring that competition in the internal market is not distorted'. This has been described by the Court of Justice as a 'requirement so essential that without it numerous provisions of the Treaty would be pointless'.[74] Article 3(1)(g) is implemented by the rules on competition set out in Articles 81–89.

Article 5: subsidiarity.   The Maastricht amendments enshrined in the EC Treaty **1.028** the principle of subsidiarity by introducing into the Treaty what is now Article 5:

'The Community shall act within the limits of the powers conferred upon it by this Treaty and of the objectives assigned to it therein.

In areas which do not fall within its exclusive competence, the Community shall take action, in accordance with the principle of subsidiarity, only if and in so far as the objectives of the proposed action cannot be sufficiently achieved by the Member States and can, therefore, by reason of the scale or effects of the proposed action, be better achieved by the Community.'

The principles in the two paragraphs of Article 5 are distinct. The first paragraph limits the scope of Community law. This provision was relied on by the Court of Justice in holding that the Community did not have competence to accede to the European Convention on Human Rights.[75] Formally, the principle of subsidiarity, set out in the second paragraph of Article 5, is a principle of allocation of jurisdiction to apply the Community objectives set out in the Treaty.[76] When legislation is contemplated to cover a particular area, the principle of subsidiarity requires that this should not be undertaken at Community level if it could be adequately done by the individual Member States. The principle of subsidiarity has been amplified by the Protocol on Subsidiarity and Proportionality, added to the EC Treaty by the Treaty of Amsterdam. This Protocol makes clear that for Community

---

[71] Arts 32–38. The common agricultural policy is implemented by a series of regulations establishing a common organisation of the market for each product sector; see generally Chap 12, below.

[72] Arts 70–80; see Chap 12, below.

[73] Arts 154–156, added by the TEU.

[74] *Europemballage and Continental Can v Commission* (n 56, above) para 24. On Art 3(1)(g), see also Cases 6 & 7/73 *Commercial Solvents v Commission* [1974] ECR 223, [1974] 1 CMLR 309, para 32; Case 26/76 *Metro v Commission (No. 1)* [1977] ECR 1875, [1978] 2 CMLR 1, para 20. Note that the proposed Reform Treaty, para 1.012, above, does not amend this provision.

[75] Opinion 2/94 *Accession to the European Convention for the Protection of Human Rights and Fundamental Freedoms* [1996] ECR I-1759, [1996] 2 CMLR 265.

[76] See the annotation to Art 5 in *Encyclopaedia of European Law (Constitutional Texts)*, Vol I, paras 12.0120A *et seq*. See also Craig, *EU Administrative Law* (2006), 419–428. For application of the principle, see, eg *British American Tobacco (Investments) and Imperial Tobacco* (n 42, above) paras 177–185; Case T-253/02 *Ayadi v Council* [2006] ECR II-2139, on appeal, Case C-403/06, not yet decided, paras 105 *et seq*.

action to be justified, both the negative and the positive aspects of the principle of subsidiarity must be met.[77]

1.029 **Subsidiarity and decentralisation of competition law.** As the Community competition rules concern a matter within the Community's exclusive competence, it is arguable that subsidiarity in the strict sense has no application to EC competition law at all. However, subsidiarity has come to embrace a broader concept, indicated in the preamble to the TEU, that expresses the resolution of the Member States that 'decisions [should be] taken as closely as possible to the citizen in accordance with the principle of subsidiarity'. This wider principle of subsidiarity, which has never been precisely defined, therefore links with the objective of decentralisation.[78] The Protocol on Subsidiarity indicates that action to prevent distortion of competition comes within the scope of the principle.[79] In *GlaxoSmithKline Services*[80] the Court of First Instance stated that in the context of Article 81(1), the principle of subsidiarity 'is given concrete form' by the limitation of the prohibition to conduct which may affect trade between Member States. If this condition is satisfied then it is appropriate for the Community to take action and where that action takes the form of a Commission decision, the Commission complies with the principle of subsidiarity if it establishes to the requisite legal standard that trade between Member States is capable of being affected by the conduct it is examining. Paragraph 34 of the Preamble to Regulation 1/2003 now refers to Article 5 in describing the enhanced role of national competition authorities in the enforcement of EC competition law.

1.030 **Article 10: duties of Member States.** The signatories to the Treaty are of course the Member States and they have each taken appropriate steps to incorporate the

---

[77] Protocol 30 EC; for the text see *Encyclopedia of European Union Law (Constitutional Texts)*, Vol I, para 12.3280.

[78] See *per* AG Jacobs in Case C-91/95P *Tremblay v Commission* [1996] ECR I-5547, Opinion at para 20, distinguishing between subsidiarity and the decentralised application of EC competition law. The ECJ did not address this issue in its judgment.

[79] Protocol on Subsidiarity (n 77, above).

[80] Case T-168/01 *GlaxoSmithKline Services v Commission* [2006] ECR II-2969, [2006] 5 CMLR 1589, paras 201 *et seq* (on appeal, Cases C-501/06P, etc, *GlaxoSmithKline Services v Commission*, not yet decided); Cases T-259/02, etc, *Raiffeisen Zentralbank Österreich v Commission*, judgment of 14 December 2006, para 162 (on appeal, Cases C-125/07, etc, not yet decided). In Case T-65/98 *Van den Bergh Foods v Commission* [2003] ECR II-4653, [2004] 4 CMLR 14, paras 197–198, the ECJ rejected an argument that the Commission's proceedings commenced in parallel with a case pending in the Irish High Court offended against the principle of subsidiarity holding that the direct effect of Arts 81 and 82 'does not mean that the Commission has no right to adopt a position in a case, even though an identical or similar case is pending before one or more national courts, provided in particular that trade between Member States is capable of being affected'. Various aspects of the case indicated, in the Court's view, that the issues dealt with had a wider Community importance (upheld on appeal, Case C-552/03P *Unilever Bestfoods v Commission* [2006] ECR I-9091, [2006] 5 CMLR 1460.

provisions of the Treaty into national law.[81] In addition to the various specific requirements of the Treaty, Article 10 provides:

'Member States shall take all appropriate measures, whether general or particular, to ensure fulfillment of the obligations arising out of this Treaty or resulting from action taken by the institutions of the Community. They shall facilitate the achievement of the Community's tasks.

They shall abstain from any measure which could jeopardise the attainment of the objectives of this Treaty.'[82]

In the present context, Article 10 is relevant, *inter alia*, to the exercise by the Member States of their parallel jurisdiction to enforce competition law under Regulation 1/2003;[83] to whether they may enforce laws which detract from the principles of the free movement of goods or which distort competition within the common market;[84] to the remedies available in national law for breach of Community law;[85] and more generally to the duty of 'sincere cooperation' which the Court of Justice has held exists between the Member States and the Community institutions.[86] Although Article 81 is addressed only to undertakings and not to Member States, the Court of Justice has applied Article 10 in conjunction with Article 81 to place on Member States an obligation not to give legislative effect to anti-competitive agreements concluded by undertakings in breach of that Article.[87] This is considered further in Chapter 11, below.

Article 12: non-discrimination. Article 12 of the Treaty provides: **1.031**

'Within the scope of application of this Treaty, and without prejudice to any special provisions contained therein, any discrimination on grounds of nationality shall be prohibited.'

---

[81] eg for the United Kingdom, see para 14.002, below.

[82] For the significance of Art 10 in competition law, see, eg Case 66/86 *Ahmed Saeed Flugreisen v Zentrale zur Bekämpfing Unlauteren Wettbewerbs* [1989] ECR 803, [1990] 4 CMLR 102; Case C-185/91 *Reiff* [1993] ECR I-5801, [1995] 5 CMLR 145; Case C-153/93 *Delta Schiffarts und Speditionsgesellschaft* [1994] ECR I-2517, [1996] 4 CMLR 21; *Van den Bergh Foods* (n 80, above); Case C-209/00 *Commission v Germany* [2002] ECR I-11695 (recovery of State aid). See also Temple Lang, 'The Core of the Constitutional Law of the Community—Article 5 EC' in Gormley (ed), *Current and Future Perspectives on EC Competition Law* (1997).

[83] See para 14.003, below.

[84] For the enforceability of the laws of Member States see Chap 11, below.

[85] For the duty of national courts to ensure that the rights granted under Community law are fully effective, and the effect of this on civil remedies for breaches of Arts 81 and 82, see Chap 14, below.

[86] See, eg Case 68/88 *Commission v Greece* [1989] ECR 2965, [1991] 1 CMLR 31, paras 22–28; Case 230/81 *Luxembourg v European Parliament* [1983] ECR 255, [1983] 2 CMLR 726, para 37; Case C-2/88 *Zwartveld* [1990] ECR I-3365, [1990] 3 CMLR 457; Case C-234/89 *Stergios Delimitis v Henninger Brau* [1991] ECR I-935, [1992] 5 CMLR 210.

[87] See, eg Case C-198/01 *Consorzio Industrie Fiammiferi and Autorità Garante della Concorrenza e del Mercato* [2003] ECR I-8055, [2003] 5 CMLR 829, [2004] All ER (EC) 380, paras 45 *et seq.*

The general principle of non-discrimination on grounds of nationality does not apply to disparities in treatment which result solely from divergences existing between the laws of Member States.[88] Article 12 does, however, strictly prevent Member States from applying their national laws (for example, national competition laws) differently according to the nationality of the parties concerned.[89]

1.032   **Article 28: the free movement of goods.**   At the heart of the Community is the customs union.[90] Articles 23–27 of the Treaty require the abolition between Member States of all customs duties and charges having equivalent effect and the creation of a common external tariff to be uniformly applied in trade between Member States and third countries.[91] However, the abolition of customs barriers within the Community is not sufficient in itself to create a true common market because Member States could still limit imports or exports by establishing quotas or by adopting a multitude of other measures. Accordingly, Articles 28 and 29 of the Treaty supplement the provisions establishing the customs union by prohibiting, subject to Article 30, all 'quantitative restrictions and measures having equivalent effect' on imports and exports between Member States. There is no need to show an appreciable effect on trade under Article 28,[92] unlike Article 81.[93] Articles 28–30 of the Treaty have 'direct effect' which means that they can be relied on by individuals before national courts to impugn national laws.[94]

1.033   **The *Cassis de Dijon* principle and the *Keck* distinction.**   In the leading case of *Cassis de Dijon*,[95] German legislation prevented the sale in Germany of alcoholic liquor below a specified minimum content. That legislation had the effect of preventing the import into Germany of French cassis which had a low alcohol content. The Court of Justice effectively struck down the German legislation

---

   [88] Case 14/68 *Wilhelm v Bundeskartellamt* [1969] ECR 1, [1969] CMLR 100, para 13. See also *GlaxoSmithKline Services* (n 80, above) para 174 (national disparities in regulation of the pharmaceuticals market meant that sales to distributors in different Member States were not equivalent transactions for the purposes of Art 81(1)(d)).

   [89] *Wilhelm*, above.

   [90] See generally Oliver, *Free Movement of Goods in the European Community* (4th edn, 2003); Baquero Cruz, *Between Competition and Free Movement* (2002). See also Philipson, *Guide to the Concept and Practical Application of Articles 28–30 EC* (DG Internal Market, January 2001) available at
   http://ec.europa.eu//enterprise/regulation/goods/docs/art2830/guideart2830_en.pdf.

   [91] But note also the extension of these provisions under the EEA Agreement to cover the European Economic Area: para 1.086, below.

   [92] Case 16/83 *Prantl* [1984] ECR 1299, [1985] 2 CMLR 238, para 20; Cases 177 & 178/82 *Van de Haar* [1984] ECR 1797, [1985] 2 CMLR 566. See also Case C-67/97 *Bluhme* [1998] ECR I-8033 (restriction covering only a small and remote Danish island fell within Art 28).

   [93] For the *de minimis* rule under Art 81, see paras 2.121 *et seq*, below.

   [94] For 'direct effect' see para 14.004, below. The question whether Arts 28–30 may be invoked against private acts of individuals unconnected with State measures seems to have been answered in the negative in Case 65/86 *Bayer v Sullhofer* [1988] ECR 5249, [1990] 4 CMLR 182; see also Case 311/85 *VVR v Sociale Dienst* [1987] ECR 3801, [1989] 4 CMLR 213, para 30.

   [95] Case 120/78 *Rewe-Zentral v Bundesmonopolverwaltung für Branntwein* [1979] ECR 649, [1979] 3 CMLR 444. See also the Commission's Communication relating to that case, OJ 1980 C256/2.

under Article 28 and thus established the important principle that Article 28 may apply to any national measure which has the effect of preventing the sale in one Member State of any product lawfully produced and marketed in another Member State, even though the national measure applies to domestic and imported products alike. That principle is subject to the exceptions specifically provided by Article 30 and by certain other considerations of public policy (referred to as 'mandatory requirements') such as the effectiveness of fiscal supervision, the protection of public health, the fairness of commercial transactions, the defence of the consumer, and the plurality of the media.[96] The *Cassis de Dijon* principle has been applied in many subsequent cases.[97] However, there was considerable criticism of the potential breadth of this principle, that came to a head when it was relied on in a series of challenges to rules that restricted shop opening hours. In the landmark case of *Keck and Mithouard*,[98] the Court of Justice finally modified the approach to be adopted. The issue there was whether French legislation that prohibited traders from selling goods at a loss infringed Article 28 of the Treaty. The Court distinguished between 'rules that lay down requirements to be met by goods' (such as those relating to designation, size, weight, composition, labelling and packaging) and 'selling arrangements'.[99] The former are to be dealt with on the basis of the previous case law whereas rules under the latter are subject to different principles. The Court held that rules in the second category, like the legislation in *Keck* itself, fall outside the scope of Article 28 altogether provided that they 'apply to all affected traders operating within the national territory and provided that they affect in the same manner, in law and in fact, the marketing of domestic products and of those from other Member States'.[100] Prior decisions

---

[96] eg Case C-368/95 *Familiapress v Bauer Verlag* [1997] ECR I-3689, [1997] 3 CMLR 1329, para 18 (prohibition on promotion of newspapers by prize competitions enacted for the purpose of maintaining press diversity).

[97] For more recent examples, see, eg Case C-434/04 *Ahokainen and Leppik* [2006] ECR I-9171, [2007] 1 CMLR 345 (authorisation requirement for import of denatured alcohol not contrary to Art 28 unless disproportionate to the objective of protecting public health); Case C-366/04 *Schwarz v Burgermeister der Landeshauptstadt Salzburg* [2005] ECR I-10139, [2006] 1 CMLR 895 (Austrian law banning sale of unwrapped chewing gum in vending machines justified on grounds of public health); Case C-166/03 *Commission v France* [2004] ECR I-6535, [2004] 3 CMLR 108 (French law requiring gold items below a certain fineness to be restamped as 'gold alloy' contrary to Art 28); Case C-14/00 *Commission v Italy (re labelling of cocoa products)* [2003] ECR I-513, [2005] 2 CMLR 832 (Italian legislation requiring the re-labelling as 'chocolate substitute' of chocolate products containing vegetable fats other than cocoa butter contrary to Art 28).

[98] Cases C-267 & 268/91 *Keck and Mithouard* [1993] ECR I-6097, [1995] 1 CMLR 101.

[99] ibid, paras 15–16.

[100] For analysis of the judgment and its relevance in the area of free movement of goods in general, see Oliver (n 90, above)pp 122–133; Oliver, 'Some Further Reflections on the Scope of Articles 28–30 (*ex* 30–36)' (1999) CMLRev 783. For some recent applications of the *Keck* distinction see, eg Case C-20/03 *Burmanjer* [2005] ECR I-4133, [2006] 1 CMLR 621 (Belgian restrictions on itinerant sales of subscriptions to periodicals not caught by Art 28); Case C-71/02 *Karner* [2004] ECR I-3025, [2004] 2 CMLR 75 (Austrian law restricting advertisements for sales of goods from insolvent estates not caught by Art 28).

concerning 'selling arrangements' must therefore be read in the light of this judgment.

1.034 **Article 29.** Article 29 of the EC Treaty provides:

'Quantitative restrictions on exports, and all measures having equivalent effect, shall be prohibited between Member States.'

Article 29 applies to:

'. . . national measures which have as their specific object or effect the restriction of patterns of exports and thereby the establishment of a difference in treatment between the domestic trade of a Member State and its export trade in such a way as to provide a particular advantage for national production or for the domestic market for the State in question.'[101]

Article 29 thus applies to a national measure which directly restricts exports, such as a requirement to obtain an export licence,[102] or to sell exclusively to undertakings in the same Member State,[103] or which prohibits exports by producers who are not registered with a specified organisation.[104] But Article 29 does not apply to national measures which are not directed towards the restriction of exports.[105]

1.035 **Article 30.** Articles 28 and 29 are to be read subject to Article 30, which provides:

'The provisions of Articles 28 and 29 shall not preclude prohibitions or restrictions on imports, exports or goods in transit justified on grounds of public morality, public policy or public security; the protection of health and life of humans, animals or

---

[101] See, eg Case 238/82 *Duphar v Netherlands* [1984] ECR 523, [1985] 1 CMLR 256, para 25. For more recent cases on Art 29, see Case C-12/02 *Grilli* [2003] ECR I-11585 (rules banning fixing of temporary number plates to cars bought in Germany); Case C-469/00 *Ravil* [2003] ECR I-5053 (law requiring Grana Padano cheese to be grated in the region of origin caught by Art 29 but justified provided proportionate to aim of protecting industrial and commercial property).

[102] See, eg Case 53/76 *Procureur de la République v Bouhelier* [1977] ECR 197, [1977] 1 CMLR 436; Case 68/76 *Commission v France ('Potatoes')* [1977] ECR 515, [1977] 2 CMLR 161; Case C-47/90 *Delhaize Frères v Promalvin* [1992] ECR I-3669; and Case C-388/95 *Belgium v Spain* [2000] ECR I-3123, [2002] 1 CMLR 395.

[103] See, eg Case 83/78 *Pigs Marketing Board v Redmond* [1978] ECR 2347, [1979] 1 CMLR 177 (pig producers required to sell to a statutory body which therefore becomes the sole exporter); Case 172/82 *Fabricants Raffineurs D'Huile de Graissage v Inter-Huiles* [1983] ECR 555, [1983] 3 CMLR 485; Case 295/82 *Rhône Alpes Huiles v Syndicat National des Fabricants Raffineurs D'Huile de Graissage* [1984] ECR 575 (waste oils could not be disposed of to undertakings in other Member States); cf Case 174/84 *Bulk Oil v Sun International* [1986] ECR 559, [1986] 2 CMLR 732 (restriction on delivery of oil to Israel amounted to a 'measure' but was not contrary to Art 29 as it involved exports to a third country).

[104] Case C-293/02 *Jersey Produce Marketing Organisation* [2005] ECR I-9543, [2006] 1 CMLR 738 (law affecting only exports of new potatoes between Jersey and the UK still caught by Art 29 because potatoes might then be exported from UK to other Member States).

[105] See, eg Case 15/79 *Groenveld* [1979] ECR 3409, [1981] 1 CMLR 207; Case 155/80 *Oebel* [1981] ECR 1993, [1983] 1 CMLR 390; Cases 141/81, etc, *Holdijk* [1982] ECR 1299, [1983] 2 CMLR 635; Case 286/81 *Oosthoek* [1982] ECR 4575, [1983] 3 CMLR 428. But see Case C-350/97 *Monsees* [1999] ECR I-2921, [2001] 1 CMLR 16: restriction on transit times for animals that impeded journeys to the frontier fell within Art 29 as well as Art 28.

plants; the protection of national treasures possessing artistic, historic or archaeological value; or the protection of industrial and commercial property. Such prohibitions or restrictions shall not, however, constitute a means of arbitrary discrimination or a disguised restriction on trade between Member States.'

The effect of Article 30 on the exercise of patent, trade mark and similar rights is discussed in Chapter 9, below. Specialist works should be consulted for an account of the case law under Article 30 and on the exceptions to the *Cassis de Dijon* principle already mentioned.[106]

Article 31: State monopolies.   Article 31 of the Treaty complements Articles 28–30 **1.036** by requiring the adjustment of certain state monopolies of a commercial character so as to eliminate discrimination between nationals of Member States regarding the conditions under which goods are procured and marketed. Article 31 is discussed in Chapter 11, below.

Other relevant Treaty provisions.   Other substantive provisions of the EC **1.037** Treaty which may be relevant to competition within the Community include those establishing the common agricultural policy (Articles 32–38) and the common transport policy (Articles 70–80), discussed briefly in Chapter 12, below, and the provisions concerning the promotion of trans-European networks in the fields of transport, telecommunications and energy, also referred to in Chapter 12, below. Article 151(4) provides that in its action under other provisions of the Treaty, the Community shall take cultural aspects into account, 'in particular in order to respect and to promote the diversity of its cultures'. This might be relevant as regards enforcement of competition rules in the media sector, although it has not so far been referred to in that context.[107] Article 174 sets out the objectives of Community environmental policy which, although that provision does not contain an equivalent exhortation to Article 151(4), are now taken into account in dealing with environmental agreements under the competition rules.[108] Article 296 allows a Member State to derogate from other Treaty provisions on matters affecting its essential interests of national security, including weapons production; that provision is of particular relevance in merger control,[109] but application of the exception is strictly construed and is subject to review by

---

[106] See Oliver (n 90, above) Chap VIII.

[107] In *Laserdisken* (n 42, above), the ECJ held that the Community institutions in the drafting and adoption of Dir 2001/29 took fully into account the cultural aspects specific to the Member States and the right to education, which the Community legislature must take into account in its action, so that the Directive did not infringe Arts 151(1) or 153(1).

[108] Note also Art 6 EC. See *CECED*, OJ 2000 L187/47, [2000] 5 CMLR 635, where an exemption under Art 81(3) was granted largely because of the environmental benefits expected from the agreement; and the section on 'Environmental Agreements' in the Commission's Guidelines on Horizontal Cooperation Agreements, OJ 2001 C3/2: Vol II, App C.12, paras 179 *et seq*.

[109] See para 8.105, below.

the Court of Justice.[110] Also relevant on occasion are the taxation provisions (Articles 90–93) which prohibit discriminatory taxation[111] and provide for the harmonisation of VAT and other taxes. Article 133, which is part of the common commercial policy established under Title IX, provides the legal basis for the control of dumping into the Community, and Article 134 enables Member States to be authorised to take certain protective measures against imports from third countries.[112] Treaties with third countries are made under Articles 133(3) and 300. The social policy of the Community, which may also be relevant in certain competition cases, is governed principally by Articles 136–145 of the Treaty, which should be read in conjunction with the provisions on free movement of workers in Articles 39–42.[113]

4. The Institutional Structure of the Community

(a) The Community institutions

1.038 **The institutions of the Community.** The main institutions which variously impinge upon the development of the Community and the enforcement of the EC Treaty are established under Article 7 of the EC Treaty. This provides that the tasks of the Community shall be carried out by (a) a European Parliament; (b) a Council; (c) a Commission; (d) a Court of Justice; and (e) a Court of Auditors.[114] In addition, the European Council, which is distinct from (b) and comprises the Heads of Government of the Member States and the President of the Commission, meets at least twice a year.[115] Apart from the obvious influence that results from its

---

[110] On reference by the Commission or another Member State under Art 298. Note also Art 297 re serious internal civil disturbance within a Member State.

[111] See, eg Case 170/78 *Commission v United Kingdom* [1980] ECR 417, [1980] 1 CMLR 716 and [1983] ECR 2265, [1983] 3 CMLR 512 (the 'beer and wine' case).

[112] Dumping is outside the scope of this work: see, eg Van Bael and Bellis, *Anti-Dumping and other Trade Protection Laws of the EC* (4th edn, 2004).

[113] The social provisions were relied on by the ECJ to conclude that collective labour agreements concerning conditions of work and employment fall outside the scope of Art 81(1): Case C-67/96 *Albany* [1999] ECR I-5751, [2000] 4 CMLR 446; Cases C-115 to 117/97 *Brentjens* [1999] ECR I-6025, [2000] 4 CMLR 566; Case C-219/97 *Drijvende Bokken* [1999] ECR I-6121, [2000] 4 CMLR 599. Employment consequences are also relevant, eg to the application of Art 81(3): Case 26/76 *Metro v Commission (No. 1)* [1977] ECR 1875, [1978] 2 CMLR 1; Case 42/84 *Remia v Commission* [1985] ECR 2545, [1987] 1 CMLR 1. See, eg *Synthetic Fibres*, OJ 1984 L207/17, [1985] 1 CMLR 787, and *Stichting Baksteen*, OJ 1994 L131/15, [1995] 4 CMLR 646, in both of which the coordination of plant closures was exempted under Art 81(3), *inter alia*, on the ground that the social consequences could be thereby softened.

[114] The TEU also established a European Central Bank and European Investment Bank: Arts 8–9 EC. For further discussion of the institutions, see Lasok (n 1, above); Lenaerts and Van Nuffel, *Constitutional Law of the European Union* (2nd edn, 2005). For a 'who's who' of the Community institutions, see *Vacher's European Companion* (quarterly, Vacher Dod Publishing).

[115] Art 4 of the TEU.

composition, it has a particular role under Title V of the TEU as regards a common foreign and security policy.[116] The activities of the Community are financed from the Community budget which is in turn financed by a variety of sources including a percentage of the VAT collected by Member States. Fines paid for infringements of the competition rules also contribute to the Community budget.

The official languages of the Community.   When the European Community   **1.039** first began operations in 1958, there were four official languages and 15 staff interpreters employed. At the end of 2006, there were 20 official languages and a staff of 500 permanent interpreters and 300–400 freelance interpreters used each day. A meeting conducted in 20 official languages requires 60 interpreters to achieve 'total symmetry', that is translation in to and out of each language. The translation of written material is carried out by a permanent staff of some 1650 linguists based in Brussels and Luxembourg.[117] On 1 January 2007, Bulgarian, Romanian and Irish were added to the 20 existing official languages: Czech, Danish, Dutch, English, Estonian, Finnish, French, German, Greek, Hungarian, Italian, Latvian, Lithuanian, Maltese, Polish, Portuguese, Slovak, Slovenian, Spanish and Swedish.

The European Parliament.   The Members of the European Parliament ('MEPs') are   **1.040** directly elected in elections held throughout the Community every five years.[118] Following the accession of Bulgaria and Romania, there are now 785 MEPs, who sit in party political groups and not as national delegations.[119] The importance of the European Parliament was considerably enhanced by the amendments to the EC Treaty made by the TEU and the Treaty of Amsterdam. In particular, through the so-called 'co-decision' procedure, the Parliament has a substantive role alongside the Council of Ministers in adoption of legislation in certain areas. The relevant provisions of the EC Treaty are complex and beyond the scope of this work, but the areas of co-decision include the internal market and consumer affairs.[120] The European Parliament is also empowered to appoint an Ombudsman;[121] the nomination for appointment as the President of the Commission and of the Commissioners as a body must be approved by vote of the Parliament;[122] and

---

[116] Arts 13 *et seq*, TEU.

[117] For the relevance of the language skills of Commission staff handling a particular case file see Case C-328/05P *SGL Carbon v Commission* [2007] 5 CMLR 16, Opinion of AG Mazák, para 67.

[118] See generally Arts 189–201 EC.

[119] After the 2009 EP elections, the number of MEPs will reduce to 736 and the number of seats for the United Kingdom will decrease from 78 to 72: Act of Accession of Bulgaria and Romania, Arts 9 and 24, OJ 2005 L157/203.

[120] See Arts 251–252 and Hartley, *The Foundations of European Community Law* (5th edn, 2003), 43–47.

[121] Art 195.

[122] Art 214.

Parliament can force the Commissioners as a body to resign by a vote of censure passed by a two-thirds majority.[123] The Council and the Commission have the duty to give oral or written answers to questions put by MEPs.[124] Parliamentary resolutions and debate occur on matters affected by competition policy. Parliamentary Committees (principally the Economic and Monetary Affairs Committee and the Legal Affairs Committee) discuss the Commission's proposals and monitor its activities.

1.041 **The Council.**   The Council of the European Communities ('the Council') consists of one representative from the government of each Member State.[125] The Presidency of the Council can carry considerable political influence and rotates every six months among the Member States in alphabetical order.[126] The Council is variously constituted depending on the business in question and may at any one time consist of, for example, foreign, agricultural or finance ministers.

1.042 **Functions of the Council.**   The Council has a duty to ensure that the objectives of the Treaty are attained and must ensure coordination of the general economic policies of the Member States.[127] Even with the increased role of the Parliament under the 'co-decision' procedure, the Council is the primary legislative body of the Community and takes the major economic and political decisions about Community policy. That policy is normally implemented by regulations and directives proposed by the Commission.[128] The Council acts either unanimously or by a qualified majority, depending on the Treaty provision in question.[129] Under Article 83 of the Treaty,[130] the Council is charged with the duty, acting by a qualified majority on a proposal from the Commission, and after consulting the European Parliament, to adopt appropriate regulations or directives to give effect to the principles set out in the competition rules of the Treaty.

---

[123] Art 201. The threat of such a vote prompted the resignation of the Santer Commission in 1999. For the effect of this mass resignation on the Commission's decision-making power, see Case T-219/99 *British Airways v Commission* [2003] ECR II-5917, [2004] 4 CMLR 1008, [2004] All ER (EC) 1115, para 55 (appeal on other grounds dismissed, *British Airways v Commission* [2007] 4 CMLR 982).

[124] Art 197.

[125] See Arts 202–210. The Council of the European Communities is not to be confused with the Council of Europe, an organisation of European States founded on 5 May 1949 through which was established the European Convention for the Protection of Human Rights and Fundamental Freedoms: para 1.016, above; nor with the European Council, which consists of Heads of Government of the Member States: para 1.038, above.

[126] Art 203.

[127] Art 202.

[128] See para 1.022, above.

[129] Although Art 205 states that the Council shall act by a majority 'save as otherwise provided' by the Treaty, few decisions under the Treaty are not subject to such special provision. For a qualified majority, see Art 205(2).

[130] Para 1.021, above.

The Commission.   The Commission is a separate institution, independent of   **1.043**
the Council. The Commission itself consists of 27 members,[131] nominated by the
governments of the Member States and supported by the services of the
Commission, a permanent staff of about 15,000. Article 211 of the EC Treaty
provides that the Commission is charged with ensuring that the provisions of the
Treaty, and the measures taken pursuant thereto, are applied. The Commission is
the executive of the Community and is responsible for implementing the decisions of the Council and for putting forward opinions or recommendations on
matters dealt with in the Treaty, where the Treaty so provides or where the
Commission considers it necessary. The Commission also has power to take its
own decisions, to participate in the shaping of legislative measures enacted by the
Council, and to exercise powers conferred on it by the Council to implement
the Regulations laid down by the latter.[132] Under many provisions of the Treaty
the Council may legislate only on a proposal from the Commission. The taking of
decisions by the Commission is governed by its own Rules of Procedure.[133] The
Commission is of central importance to the enforcement of Community competition law and the Directorate-General of Competition is discussed further below.

The services of the Commission.   The Commission includes a Secretariat-   **1.044**
General and a Legal Service, which are both responsible directly to the President
of the Commission, currently José Manuel Durão Barroso. The Legal Service
advises the Commission, checks on the legality of its decisions and represents the
Commission in the Court of Justice and the Court of First Instance. The work of
the Commission is carried out by Directorates-General and specialised services,
for each of which a particular Commissioner has responsibility. At the time of
writing, the Commissioner responsible for Competition is Mrs Neelie Kroes.

(b) The Community and EFTA Courts

The Community Courts.   There are two tiers of judicial decision-making in the   **1.045**
Community: the Court of First Instance of the European Communities and the
European Court of Justice, both of which sit in Luxembourg. In addition, by an
amendment to the EC Treaty introduced by the Treaty of Nice with the object of
relieving the burden on the Court of First Instance, judicial panels may be attached
to that Court to exercise its jurisdiction in specific areas.[134] The judgments of the

---

    131 Art 213(1) EC Treaty as amended.
    132 Art 211 EC. See also Art 202. The Commission also enjoys powers to enact directives under
Art 86(3): see paras 11.022 *et seq*, below.
    133 For the current rules, see Commission decn of 15 November 2005, OJ 2005 L347/83.
    134 Arts 220, 225a EC: a judicial panel is established by a unanimous decision of the Council,
and the decision shall specify the extent of the panel's jurisdiction. A Civil Service Tribunal was
established to hear EU civil service cases, and constituted with effect from December 2005: Council
Decn 2004/752, OJ 2004 L333/7.

Courts are binding in matters of law in all the Member States.[135] The procedure of the Courts is governed by the Statute of the Court of Justice annexed as a Protocol to the Treaty[136] and by the Rules of Procedure.[137]

1.046 **The Court of First Instance.** This Court was established by a Council Decision of 24 October 1988, adopted pursuant to Article 225 of the Treaty and is now directly constituted by the amended Article 220. The Court now has 27 judges and has jurisdiction to hear all cases brought under the Treaty by natural or legal persons. It will therefore hear applications by undertakings under Article 230 for the annulment of Commission decisions relating to the implementation of the competition rules of the Treaty.[138] Under Article 229 of the Treaty, the Court of First Instance has unlimited jurisdiction to review the decisions of the Commission imposing penalties in respect of infringements of the rules on competition. The members of the Court are divided into Chambers of three or five judges, the competition cases normally being assigned to Chambers of three judges and State aids and dumping being heard by five judges. Following a Council Decision[139] and consequent amendment to the Rules of Procedure in 1999,[140] certain cases (but not competition cases) may be heard by a single judge. In February 2001, a new expedited procedure was introduced for the review of certain cases, particularly merger cases.[141] In cases of particular legal difficulty or factual complexity or where the Court sits in plenary session, one of the judges may be appointed to sit as Advocate General, but this is rarely done. The Court of First Instance therefore differs from the Court of Justice in that it normally operates without the assistance of an Advocate General. The Court of First Instance does not presently hear references for preliminary rulings but the Treaty of Nice has enabled that development to take place in specific areas by a future amendment of the Statute of the Court of Justice.[142]

1.047 **The Court of Justice.** The Court of Justice of the European Communities consists of one judge from each Member State, assisted by eight Advocates General.[143]

---

[135] For the United Kingdom, see s 3(1) of the European Communities Act 1972, incorporating this obligation into domestic law; see further para 14.002, below.

[136] Protocol on the Statute of the Court of Justice. A consolidated text of the Statute is available on the Court website, and also in *Encyclopedia of European Union Law (Constitutional Texts)*, Vol 4, para 60.0214.

[137] Consolidated texts of the Rules of Procedure of the ECJ and the CFI are available on the Court website, and also in *Encyclopedia of European Union Law (Constitutional Texts)*, Vol 4, paras 60.0580, 61.0254. See also Chap 13, below.

[138] The grounds of annulment are lack of competence, infringement of an essential procedural requirement, infringement of the Treaty or any rule of law relating to its application, or misuse of powers: see paras 13.222 *et seq*, below.

[139] OJ 1999 L114/52.

[140] OJ 1999 L135/92.

[141] OJ 2000 L322/4; see Fountoukakos, 'Judicial Review and Merger Control: the CFI's Expedited Procedure' (2002) 3 Competition Policy Newsletter 7. See also para 8.236, below.

[142] Art 225(3).

[143] Arts 221–222. For general works on the ECJ, see n 1072 to para 13.211, below.

The Court has two main jurisdictions relevant here.[144] First, an appeal lies to the Court of Justice against a decision of the Court of First Instance on the grounds of lack of competence, breach of procedure before the Court of First Instance or infringement of Community law.[145] Secondly, under Article 234 of the Treaty, the Court has jurisdiction to give preliminary rulings, at the request of a court of a Member State, concerning, *inter alia*, the interpretation of the Treaty and of acts of the Council and the Commission.

Judgments of the Community Courts. The decisions of the Court of First **1.048** Instance and of the Court of Justice under Articles 230 and 234 of the Treaty are of fundamental importance in the interpretation of Community competition law. Judgments under Article 230, which relates to appeals from decisions of the Commission, are concerned with whether the Commission has reached its decision in accordance with the proper interpretation of the Treaty and in accordance with due process. On substantive issues, the Court of First Instance will investigate the merits to see whether the decision is adequately reasoned or whether it is vitiated by a manifest error of fact or appreciation.[146]

References under Article 234. By contrast, in references under Article 234 of **1.049** the Treaty, the Court of Justice is not primarily concerned with the facts of the case. Under this jurisdiction, the Court of Justice is responding to a request by a national court to give an interpretative ruling in relation to a matter of Community law that has arisen in the course of domestic litigation within a Member State. Where such a question arises, the national court may, and a national court of final resort normally must, refer that question to the Court of Justice for a ruling.[147] In such cases, the Court seeks to avoid determining questions of fact or questions of national law, which are a matter solely for the national court. Its function is rather to lay down, in the abstract, the principles of Community law to be applied to the case in question. However, the Court can, where appropriate, provide clarification designed to give the national court guidance in its interpretation of the relevant provisions.[148] The Court often adopts a broad teleological approach, interpreting the legislation in the light of the spirit and general objectives of

---

[144] Other jurisdictions of the ECJ in which competition issues may arise include infraction proceedings against Member States under Art 226; actions for failure to act under Art 232; and actions for damages against the Community under Art 288.

[145] Art 225(1) EC; Statute of the Court of Justice (n 136, above) Art 51.

[146] See generally para 13.227, below.

[147] Save that in future some such references may be assigned to the CFI. For Art 234 proceedings, see Chap 14, below.

[148] See, eg Cases C-295/04, etc, *Manfredi* [2006] ECR I-6619, [2006] 5 CMLR 980, [2007] All ER (EC) 27, paras 47 *et seq*; Case C-217/05 *Confederación Española de Empresarios de Estaciones de Servicio v CEPSA* [2006] ECR I-11987, [2007] 4 CMLR 181, para 50; Case C-238/05 *Asnef-Equifax v Ausbanc* [2006] ECR I-11125, [2007] 4 CMLR 224, para 40.

the Treaty.[149] The Court has delivered a number of wide-ranging judgments which have done much to clarify the rules on competition.

1.050 **Opinions of the Advocates General.** The Advocate General summarises the arguments of the parties and makes his or her own submissions to the Court in a role akin to that of an *amicus curiae*. Such submissions often contain useful summaries of the relevant principles and case law. The Advocates General rank equally in precedence with the Judges of the Court. Their opinions are authoritative. If an Advocate General is not followed by the Court, the opinion is probably equivalent to a dissenting judgment.[150] Under the Statute of the Court of Justice adopted by the Treaty of Nice, the Court has the power to determine a case without a submission from the Advocate General if the case involves no new point of law.[151] The Court of First Instance does not have a separate body of Advocates General but may appoint one of its members to act as Advocate General in cases of particular factual complexity or legal difficulty or where the Court sits in plenary session. This power is seldom exercised.

1.051 **The EFTA Court.** The EFTA Surveillance Authority, applying the analogous competition provisions of the EEA regime, takes decisions of an equivalent nature to those of the Commission under the EC Treaty.[152] The EFTA Court, similarly, has a jurisdiction analogous to that of the Community Courts, and determines both references from national courts of the three participating EFTA States[153] and challenges to decisions of the Surveillance Authority.[154] The EEA Agreement and the EFTA Surveillance and Court Agreement state that provisions which correspond to those in the EC Treaties, and the incorporated EC legislation, are to be implemented and applied in accordance with any relevant ruling of the Court of Justice given prior to the date of the EEA Agreement (ie 2 May 1992).[155] Although the EFTA Court is accordingly not bound by decisions of the Court of Justice given after that date, it must 'pay due account' to those judgments and in practice seeks to follow the rulings of the Community courts on identically-worded

---

[149] See Schermers and Waelbroeck, *Judicial Protection in the European Union* (6th edn, 2001), paras 40 *et seq.*

[150] Schermers and Waelbroeck, above, para 1347.

[151] Art 20, 5th paragraph, of the Statute of the Court of Justice.

[152] The EFTA Surveillance Authority and the EFTA Court are established under the Agreement between the EFTA States on the Establishment of a Surveillance Authority and a Court of Justice, OJ 1994 L344/3: see paras 1.087 *et seq*, below. The text of the Agreement and the EFTA Court's Rules of Procedure are available on the EFTA Court's website under 'legal texts' and in *Encyclopedia of European Union Law (Constitutional Texts)*, Vol 2, paras 30.3190 *et seq*, and Vol 3, paras 62.2001 *et seq*. Protocol 5 to the Agreement is the Statute of the EFTA Court, setting out its constitution.

[153] Under Art 34 of the EFTA Surveillance and Court Agreement. Such references are referred to as requests for an Advisory Opinion. See the discussion of the 'homogeneity objective' at para 1.089, below.

[154] Under Arts 35–36 of the EFTA Surveillance and Court Agreement.

[155] Art 6 EEA; Art 3(1) of the EFTA Surveillance and Court Agreement.

provisions of EC law,[156] and the Commission, as well as the Surveillance Authority, has a right to be heard in proceedings. Although the EFTA Court has so far given few judgments as regards competition law, its decisions have strong persuasive authority within the Community.

(c) The Directorate-General for Competition

(i) Structure

The Directorate-General for Competition ('DG Competition').   DG Competi-   **1.052**
tion was reorganised in 2003. Whereas previously it was divided up according to the nature of the investigation being undertaken, the new structure is based on industrial sectors. It is headed by a Director-General[157] and three Deputies (for antitrust, mergers and State aid), and now comprises 10 Directorates and in addition a Chief Competition Economist with his or her Team.[158] The former Merger Taskforce was therefore disbanded and mergers are now dealt with by specialist units within each industry-specific Directorate unit:

— Directorate R: Registry and resources
— Directorate A: Policy and Strategic Support (including the European Competition Network and international relations)
— Directorate B: Energy, Basic Industries, Chemicals and Pharmaceuticals
— Directorate C: Information, Communication and Media
— Directorate D: Services (including financial services and transport)
— Directorate E: Industry, consumer goods and manufacturing
— Directorate F: Cartels[159]
— Directorate G: State Aid I: Cohesion and Competitiveness
— Directorate H: State Aid II: Network industries, liberalised sectors and services
— Directorate I: State aid policy and strategic coordination

The Chief Economist Team.   The Chief Economist Team ('CET') is a separate   **1.053**
unit reporting directly to the Director-General.[160] Its role is to provide guidance on methodological issues of economics and econometrics in the application of EU competition rules and assist in the development of general policy instruments with an economic context. The team also provides general guidance in individual

---

156 Art 3(2) of the EFTA Surveillance and Court Agreement. See Case E-2/94 *Scottish Salmon Growers Association v EFTA Surveillance Authority* [1994–5] Rep EFTA Ct 59, [1995] 1 CMLR 851, paras 11–13. For a survey of the case law, see Baudenbacher (President of the EFTA Court), *EFTA Court: Legal Framework and Case Law* (2nd edn, October 2006), available on the Court website.
157 Currently Mr Philip Lowe.
158 There is an organigramme of DG Competition at the back of each issue of the Commission's Competition Policy Newsletter, giving contact details for staff in the different units within the Directorates.
159 This was formed in 2005.
160 See *Report on Competition Policy 2004*, Vol 1, p 16.

competition cases from their early stages and on occasion more detailed guidance in the most important competition cases involving complex economic issues. In the more complex cases, a member of the CET may be seconded to work on the Commission case team though the CET team member retains his or her independent status and reports directly to the Chief Competition Economist. The Chief Competition Economist is also responsible for maintaining contact with the academic world and organises and chairs meetings of the Economic Advisory Group for Competition Policy.

1.054 **The Economic Advisory Group for Competition Policy ('EAGCP').** The EAGCP is a group of leading academics from different fields of research and academic centres in Europe all of whom specialise in industrial economics. The Group is a forum for the discussion of competition policy matters, its main purpose being to support DG Competition by improving the quality of economic reasoning in competition policy analysis. Within the framework of the EAGCP, three sub-groups have been set up to work on issues related to antitrust, mergers and State aid. On request by the Commissioner for Competition or the Director-General, members may also be asked on an ad hoc basis to provide economic advice on issues of relevance. [161]

1.055 **Consumer Liaison Officer.** The first Consumer Liaison Officer within the DG Competition was appointed in December 2003[162] to ensure a permanent dialogue with European consumers who are intended to be the beneficiaries of the Community's competition policy. The post also provides a focus for contact between DG Competition and other Directorates-General within the Commission, for example that for Health and Consumer Protection. The Consumer Liaison Officer acts as primary contact point for consumer organisations and for individual consumers, and alerts consumer groups to competition cases when their input might be useful, advising them on the way they can provide input and express their views. The Officer also maintains contacts with national competition authorities regarding consumer protection matters.

1.056 **The Hearing Officer.** The post of Hearing Officer was established in 1982 to provide an independent component in the Commission's decision-making process and to ensure that the rights of the defence are protected.[163] The role of the Hearing Officer was strengthened by the adoption of a new mandate in 2001.[164]

---

[161] See, eg the EAGCP report on 'An economic approach to Article 82' (July 2005), available on the DG Comp website.

[162] See *XXIIIrd Report on Competition Policy* (2003), p 16.

[163] See Durande and Williams, 'The practical impact of the exercise of the right to be heard: A special focus on the effect of Oral Hearings and the role of the Hearing Officers' (2005) 2 EC Competition Policy Newsletter 22.

[164] Commission Decn 2001/462, OJ 2001 L162/21. See further para 13.102, below.

The Officer organises and conducts the oral hearings before the Commission; acts as arbitrator between the Commission and the undertaking being investigated if there are disputes about access to the Commission's file and reports directly to the Commissioner for Competition on his conclusions about whether the right to be heard was observed in the particular case. The final report of the Hearing Officer covers not only whether the parties were afforded the right to be heard but also any views he has on the objectivity of the investigation carried out by the Commission. This final report goes to the Commission, the competent authorities of the Member States and the EFTA Surveillance Authority.

(ii) Enforcement through investigation and decision

Regulation 17.   Council Regulation 17[165] was the first regulation implementing   **1.057** the competition rules of the Treaty and came into force in the then Member States on 13 March 1962. Article 1 of that Regulation provided that the prohibitions of Articles 81 and 82 take effect without any prior decision being required. However, the application of Article 81(3) was reserved exclusively for the Commission.[166] The Regulation established a procedure whereby parties could notify an agreement to the Commission with a request for a declaration that it did not fall within the scope of Article 81 (known as a 'negative clearance') or for exemption under Article 81(3). The Regulation also dealt with the making of complaints by aggrieved parties; and with the Commission's powers of enforcement, which include powers to require information, to order the termination of infringements, and to impose fines. The notification procedure gave rise to substantial delays in determining the legality of agreements and led to the creation of the 'comfort letter', an informal indication from the Commission to the parties of its views on the agreement. The legal status of these letters was unclear,[167] and the inability of national courts, before which Article 81 disputes were increasingly litigated, to apply Article 81(3) further stultified the enforcement process.[168]

Modernisation.   In May 2004 a new enforcement regime was established with   **1.058** the coming into force of Regulation 1/2003.[169] The then Commissioner for

---

[165] Reg 17/62, JO 1962 13/204: Vol II, App B.1.

[166] Reg 17/62, Art 4.

[167] See earlier editions of this work; eg 5th edn (2001), para 11–017.

[168] For the problems caused by the exclusive competence of the Commission, see, eg the procedural history of the analysis of ice cream freezer exclusivity clauses described in Case T-65/98 *Van den Bergh Foods Ltd v Commission* [2003] ECR II-4653, [2004] 4 CMLR 14, [2005] All ER (EC) 418, appeal dismissed Case C-552/03P *Unilever Bestfoods v Commission* [2006] ECR I-9091, [2006] 5 CMLR 1460.

[169] Reg 1/2003, OJ 2003 L1/1: Vol II, App B.3. See generally the special edition of the EC Competition Policy Newsletter issued in May 2004; Rocca *et al*, 'Regulation 1/2003: a modernised application of EC competition rules' (2003) 1 EC Competition Policy Newsletter 3; Gauer *et al*, 'Regulation 1/2003 and the Modernisation Package fully applicable since 1 May 2004' (2004) 2 EC Competition Policy Newsletter 1; *XXIVth Competition Policy Report* (2004), p 29. The new enforcement regime is considered in detail in Chap 13, below.

Competition, Mario Monti, described the new regime as 'a mature system in which law-abiding companies that do business in Europe will be freed from decade-old legal straightjackets and will benefit from less bureaucracy and a more level playing field in the European single market'.[170] On the basis that Member States now have their own competition law and enforcement mechanisms and substantial experience in dealing with competition law cases, it was determined that the whole of Article 81, along with Article 82, should be enforceable by domestic competition authorities and national courts. Further, now that companies 'know the Highway Code',[171] it was no longer considered necessary for them to seek a decision of the Commission for innocuous agreements under the notification system. By freeing the resources previously devoted to scrutinising many notified agreements, the Commission has been able to focus on investigating and punishing 'hard-core' cartels and serious abuses by dominant undertakings. However, the Commission remains able to monitor how enforcement is progressing in the Member States through the mechanisms for information exchange and consultation set up under Regulation 1/2003.[172]

1.059 **Regulation 1/2003: the main changes.**   The key change is made in Article 1(2) of Regulation 1/2003 which provides that agreements, decisions and concerted practices caught by Article 81(1) of the Treaty which satisfy the conditions of Article 81(3) of the Treaty shall not be prohibited, no prior decision to that effect being required. The Regulation imposes a *duty* on national competition authorities and national courts, when they are applying their domestic competition law to a matter affecting trade between Member States, also to apply Articles 81 and 82.[173] To ensure the smooth running of these parallel jurisdictions, the Regulation restricts the scope for divergent application of national and EC competition law and gives priority to decisions by the Commission;[174] and it sets up a system under which competition authorities notify the Commission and each other of their respective enforcement activities.[175] Regulation 1/2003 also significantly strengthened the investigation powers of the Commission, introducing a power to enter and search the homes of company directors and other members of

---

170 See the special edition of the EC Competition Policy Newsletter, May 2004.

171 ibid. 'They know', he stated 'that meeting secretly in a hotel to fix prices for the vitamins used in everything from cereals to cosmetics and dog food is illegal'.

172 See paras 14.018 and 14.022, below.

173 Reg 1/2003, Art 3.

174 See, eg Art 3(2) (national authorities and courts cannot prohibit an agreement which would not contravene Art 81) and Art 16 (national courts and competition authorities must not rule in a way which runs counter to an existing Commission decision under Art 81 or 82). But the Commission does not have to follow an earlier decision of a national competition authority: see Case 298/83 *CICCE v Commission* [1985] ECR 1105, [1986] 1 CMLR 486, para 27; Case T-67/01 *JCB Service v Commission* [2004] ECR II-49, [2004] 4 CMLR 1346, para 93, appeal dismissed Case C-167/04P [2006], ECR I-8935, [2006] 5 CMLR 1303.

175 Reg 1/2003 (n 169, above) Arts 11 and 12.

staff, subject to obtaining a court order,[176] and a power to interview any natural or legal person who consents to be interviewed for the purposes of an investigation.[177] The Regulation also established a formal procedure whereby the Commission can close its file on a case by accepting legally binding commitments from undertakings as to their future conduct.[178] All these aspects of Regulation 1/2003 are considered in more detail in Chapter 13, below.

Other elements of the Modernisation package. Article 33 of Regulation 1/2003 empowers the Commission to take appropriate measures to implement the Regulation. The Commission has adopted a number of formal measures and issued substantial informal guidance as part of the overall Modernisation package of measures. Regulation 773/2004[179] sets out further detailed provision of the enforcement procedure to be adopted by the Commission, concerning the handling of complaints, the exercise of the right to be heard and access to the file. The Commission also issued notices concerning cooperation between the Commission and national courts and competition authorities[180] explaining the new competences and describing how the Commission is able to assist them with handling particular cases. Further assistance to national courts and competition authorities comes from the Commission's Notices on substantive issues in competition law issued to coincide with the coming into force of Regulation 1/2003.[181] **1.060**

The European Competition Network. Article 35 of Regulation 1/2003 requires Member States to designate the domestic competition authority or authorities responsible for the application of Articles 81 and 82. These national competition authorities together form the European Competition Network 'dedicated to the effective enforcement of EC competition rules throughout the Community'.[182] The ways in which these authorities are expected to cooperate with the Commission and with each other, and the manner in which cases are allocated among them, are set out in the Commission's Notice on cooperation within the network of competition authorities.[183] Representatives from the Network members meet together **1.061**

---

[176] ibid, Art 21.
[177] ibid, Art 19.
[178] ibid, Art 9.
[179] Reg 773/2004, OJ 2004 L123/18: Vol II, App B.4. The Commission elaborated on certain aspects of the new procedure by issuing Notices on its handling of complaints (OJ 2004 C101/65: Vol II, App B.10) and on the issue of Guidance letters (OJ 2004 C101/78: Vol II, App B.11).
[180] See Notice on cooperation between the Commission and the courts of the EU Member States in the application of Articles 81 and 82 EC, OJ 2004 C101/54: Vol II, App B.9; Notice on cooperation within the network of competition authorities, OJ 2004 C101/43: Vol II, App B.8.
[181] See Guidelines on the effect on trade concept contained in Articles 81 and 82 of the Treaty, OJ 2004 C101/81: Vol II, App C.17; Guidelines on the application of Article 81(3) of the Treaty, OJ 2004 C101/97: Vol II, App C.18.
[182] See the Joint Statement of the Council and the Commission on the Functioning of the Network of Competition Authorities, 10 December 2002, Doc. 15435/02 ADD1: Vol II, App B.7.
[183] Notice on cooperation within the network of competition authorities (n 180, above).

to discuss areas of competition policy to help ensure a consistent approach to difficult issues which arise across all Member States.[184]

1.062 **Direct effect: enforcement at the national level.** The Court of Justice decided early on that Articles 81 and 82 have direct effect, which means that they create rights for individuals which must be enforced by the national courts.[185] The decisions of national courts therefore provide source material for the application of the Treaty rules on competition.[186] As a matter of EC law, a judgment of a national court of one jurisdiction is not binding in another, save where the same parties are seeking to re-litigate a dispute which has been judicially determined elsewhere.[187] In *Consorzio Industrie Fiammiferi*[188] the Court of Justice held that the primacy of Community law requires any provision of national law which contravenes a Community rule to be disapplied, regardless of whether it was adopted before or after that rule. Further, the duty to disapply such national legislation is owed not only by national courts but by all organs of the State, including administrative authorities. Thus the national competition authority is responsible for ensuring, *inter alia*, that Article 81 EC is observed and must not apply national legislation which contravenes the Member State's duty under Article 10 to refrain from introducing measures contrary to the Community competition rules.

1.063 **The outcome of an investigation under Regulation 1/2003.** The culmination of an investigation by the Commission into an alleged infringement of Articles 81 or 82 will be a decision adopted under Chapter III of Regulation 1/2003. A decision of the Commission is binding in its entirety on those to whom it is addressed.[189] The Commission must publish its decisions applying Article 81 or 82, but

---

[184] See, eg note on 'Energy day', the first high level sectoral meeting of the Network held in September 2004 to discuss competition in the electricity and gas markets; (2004) 3 EC Competition Policy Newsletter 33 and the creation of the 'insurance network' which met for the first time in June 2003 to improve information sharing on insurance issues, (2003) 3 EC Competition Policy Newsletter 60.

[185] See para 14.004, below. For the direct effect of the provisions relating to State aids see paras 15.108 *et seq*, below.

[186] A summary of many decisions is included in the Report on the competition rules in the EU, published with the Commission's annual Report on Competition Policy. See also Braakman (ed), *The Application of Articles 85 & 86 of the EC Treaty by National Courts in the Member States* (European Commission, 1997); Report on the application of EC State aid law by the Member State courts (1999), available on the DG Comp website at http://europa.eu.int/comm/competition/state_aid/others. See further Chap 14, below.

[187] In which case the judgment of the court of another Member State on a competition matter receives recognition under Regulation 44/2001 ('the Brussels Regulation').

[188] Case C-198/01 *Consorzio Industrie Fiammiferi and Autorità Garante della Concorrenza e del Mercato* [2003] ECR I-8055, [2003] 5 CMLR 829, [2004] All ER (EC) 380.

[189] Art 249 EC, 4th para. Strictly, the Commission's decisions are 'not law creating', *per* AG Warner, Case 19/77 *Miller v Commission* [1978] ECR 131, 161, [1978] 2 CMLR 334, 346. Nonetheless, the Commission's decisions are legally binding upon those to whom they are addressed: see also the discussion of *Courage v Crehan* in para 14.080, below.

publication of 'the main contents of the decision, including any penalties imposed' is sufficient[190] and increasingly only such a summary of long decisions is published in the *Official Journal*.

Sectoral inquiries.   Under Article 12 of Regulation 1/2003, the Commission   **1.064** may initiate general inquiries into those sectors of the economy where it believes competition might be restricted or distorted. The aim of this provision is to allow the Commission to investigate suspicious pricing structures or other practices indicating a possible anti-competitive situation across a whole industry. It is regarded as particularly suitable for examining established oligopolistic markets where the presence of a small number of important players may encourage concerted practices. It is also an appropriate instrument for inquiring into sectors where business practices are not yet established and where the future competitive environment will be shaped by industry-wide agreements which have been concluded but whose effects are not fully known.[191] Sector inquiries also allow the Commission to analyse allegedly anti-competitive practices in a systematic and transparent manner and give the opportunity to national authorities to launch their own parallel national investigations on the basis of the Commission's findings.

(iii) Enforcement through legislation and guidance

The Commission's legislative powers.   The Commission is empowered to adopt   **1.065** legislation by a number of Council Regulations. Council Regulations 19/65 (as amended by 1215/1999), 2821/71 and 1534/91 empower the Commission to exempt *en bloc* under Article 81(3) certain categories of agreements, such as agreements relating to industrial property rights, 'vertical' agreements between undertakings at different levels of the production or distribution chain, certain categories of standardisation, research and development and specialisation agreements, and certain agreements in the insurance industry. The Commission has over time adopted a series of block exemptions covering various sectors and kinds of agreement. These regulations are discussed in Chapter 3, below.[192]

General notices and guidance.   In addition, the Commission from time to time   **1.066** issues notices and guidelines which provide guidance for undertakings and indicate the Commission's view on various matters relating to the application of the

---

[190] Art 30 of Reg 1/2003. The full text of decisions is published on the Commission's website in the language of the case and the main Community languages, often before any publication in the *Official Journal*.

[191] For a description of the Commission's policy regarding use of this power, see Crawford and Adamopoulos 'Using the instrument of sector-wide inquiries: inquiry into content for 3G services' (2004) 2 EC Competition Policy Newsletter 63.

[192] Council Reg 994/98 empowers the Commission to adopt block exemption regulations in relation to State aids: for the exercise of this power see Chap 15, below.

competition rules. Examples are the *De Minimis* Notice, the Guidelines on Vertical Restraints, the Horizontal Cooperation Guidelines and the Relevant Market Notice. In *Dansk Rørindustri*,[193] the Court of Justice considered whether the application of the Commission's Guidelines on Fines to conduct which had occurred before those Guidelines had been published was contrary to the principle of the non-retrospectivity of punishment. The Court of First Instance had rejected this plea on the ground that the Guidelines do not form part of the legal framework for the imposition of fines. The Court of Justice dismissed the plea but disagreed with that aspect of the Court of First Instance's analysis. The Court of Justice held that internal measures adopted by the administration, although they may not be regarded as rules of law which the administration is always bound to observe, nevertheless form rules of practice from which the administration may not depart in an individual case without giving reasons that are compatible with the principle of equal treatment. The Court stated:

'In adopting such rules of conduct and announcing by publishing them that they will henceforth apply to the cases to which they relate, the institution in question imposes a limit on the exercise of its discretion and cannot depart from those rules under pain of being found, where appropriate, to be in breach of the general principles of law, such as equal treatment or the protection of legitimate expectations. It cannot therefore be excluded that, on certain conditions and depending on their conduct, such rules of conduct, which are of general application, may produce legal effects.'[194]

A Notice may subsequently be withdrawn, although the Commission is probably estopped from imposing a fine in respect of an agreement clearly covered by the relevant Notice.[195] All the Notices are subject to any ruling on the point at issue by the Community Courts which may decide not to follow the Commission's approach.

1.067 **Other pronouncements by the Commission.** Guidance as to the Commission's views on particular matters can be obtained from a number of other official and semi-official pronouncements. Most important are the Reports on Competition Policy, published annually in conjunction with the Commission's General Report on the Activities of the Communities.[196] The Reports on Competition Policy

---

193 Cases C-189/02P, etc, *Dansk Rørindustri v Commission* [2005] ECR I-5425, [2005] 5 CMLR 796.

194 ibid, para 211. The ECJ found that there had been no breach of the principle of non-retroactivity on the facts of the case.

195 Case 19/77 *Miller* (n 189, above) 342–343, per AG Warner. See the *De Minimis* Notice, OJ 2001 C368/13: Vol II, App C.13, para 5.

196 Note Cases C-319/93, etc, *Dijkstra* [1995] ECR I-4471, [1996] 5 CMLR 178, para 32, where the ECJ stated that the practice of the Commission is to be discerned not only from its decisions but also from its Reports on Competition Policy and its communications. Between 1995 and 2003, with this annual Report of the Commission there was published a Report by DG Competition on the application of the competition rules in the EU that included also details of selected cases. The EFTA Surveillance Authority also publishes an annual report that contains a section on competition policy and enforcement.

survey the Commission's activity in this field during the year and give helpful indications as to the Commission's general policy and its approach to various issues. Also of value is the Competition Policy Newsletter, published three times a year by DG Competition, which contains short articles by Commission officials discussing significant developments, including cases settled without a formal decision following the Commission's intervention. The Commission's written answers to questions put to it by Members of the European Parliament give general indications of the Commission's views on particular matters. The Commission also circulates to trade associations and other interested parties discussion papers on legislative proposals or other developments and may also publish these on its website.

The DG Competition website.   The Competition section of the Commission's   **1.068**
website at http://europa.eu.int/comm/competition contains a wide range of useful information enabling the practitioner to keep up-to-date with developments in the competition law field. It includes press releases,[197] gives details of recent decisions and reproduces the text of speeches given by the Commissioner for Competition and other leading officials.[198] It also contains electronic versions of the annual Reports on Competition Policy and the Competition Policy Newsletter.

'Competition Advocacy'.   The Commission sometimes holds meetings with   **1.069**
important 'stakeholders' to consider how competition can be improved in the markets in which they are active.[199] Twice yearly 'Competition Days' are hosted by the Member State holding the Presidency.[200]

The Commission on the international stage.   A further source of law or guid-   **1.070**
ance is provided by certain international conventions to which the Member States and the Community itself are parties. These include the European Patent Convention,[201] and the Community Patent Convention.[202] Where a Member State, but not the Community itself, is party to an agreement with one or more

---

[197] Some of the more important press releases are published in the CMLR and CCH reports and referred to in the Commission's annual Reports on Competition Policy.

[198] The Commission has stressed the importance of the 'transparency' and greater public awareness of its competition policy as an essential prerequisite for decentralisation of the enforcement of competition laws by the national courts of the Member States: *XXIst Report on Competition Policy* (1991), points 66–68.

[199] See, eg the Commission's approach to improving competition in the liberal professions: Amato and others, 'Professional services: more competition, more competitiveness, more consumer orientation' (2004) 2 EC Competition Policy Newsletter 71; and the discussion of the need for greater competition scrutiny of legislation by Emberger, 'How to strengthen competition advocacy through competition screening' (2006) 1 EC Competition Policy Newsletter 28.

[200] Details of the Competition Days are given in the Commission's Competition Policy Newsletters. The Stockholm day in June 2001 was 'dedicated to the citizens of the European Union who are not really aware of the positive impact of competition policy on their day-to-day life'!

[201] eg in the field of intellectual property: see para 9.003, below.

[202] ibid.

third countries concluded prior to the entry into force of the Treaty or that State's accession to the Community, Article 307 provides that the EC Treaty shall not affect that State's obligations under the agreement; but Member States cannot rely on the terms of an international convention to justify restrictions between themselves that are contrary to the EC Treaty.[203] Similarly, Member States cannot set aside the rules of the Treaty by entering into international agreements or conventions which contain terms in conflict with their Community obligations.[204]

5. The Aims of the Community Rules on Competition

1.071 **Purpose of the EC competition rules.** The Court of Justice has stated that the maintenance of effective competition is so essential 'that without it numerous provisions of the Treaty would be pointless'.[205] Although not articulated in the Treaty, Community competition law has two basic and complementary aims: the promotion of a competitive market economy and the prevention of barriers to integration of the single market.

1.072 **A competitive market economy.** Like competition rules elsewhere, the Community rules on competition are founded on the principle that a competitive market, rather than state control or private monopoly, is the best means of securing economic efficiency, as regards both allocation of resources and efficient production. In a society characterised by a market economy, the competitive activities of undertakings, driven by self-interest,[206] will further economic development, and therefore the welfare of consumers[207] and, at least in the long term, higher employment. As the current Commissioner for Competition, Neelie Kroes, stated on taking up her post:

> 'Market based competition rewards strong firms that offer better goods and services at lower prices. And it penalizes those which make less efficient choices about how they organise themselves and what they produce. . . . [C]ompanies which face strong

---

[203] Case 121/85 *Conegate v HM Customs & Excise* [1986] ECR 1007, [1986] 1 CMLR 739; Cases C-241 & 242/91P *RTE and ITP v Commission ('Magill')* [1995] ECR I-743, [1995] 4 CMLR 718, [1995] All ER (EC) 416, paras 72 *et seq.*

[204] *Magill*, ibid.

[205] Case 6/72 *Europemballage and Continental Can v Commission* [1973] ECR 215, [1973] CMLR 199, para 24.

[206] cf Adam Smith: 'Although an individual undertaking striving to maximise profits intends only his own gain. . . he is in this, as in many other cases, led by an invisible hand to promote an end which was no part of his intention . . . By pursuing his own interest he frequently promotes that of society more effectually than when he really intends to promote it'. *The Wealth of Nations* (Cannan ed, University of Chicago, 1977), 477.

[207] The CFI has recently stressed that the function of the competition rules is to increase consumer benefit, see Case T-168/01 *GlaxoSmithKline Services v Commission* [2006] ECR II-2969, [2006] 5 CMLR 1589; on appeal, Cases C-501/06P, etc, *GlaxoSmithKline Services v Commission* not yet decided.

competition in their home markets are more likely to become successful on a global scale.'[208]

A detailed discussion of the economic theories that have been advanced in support of the desirability of competition and the role of the law in maintaining an effective competitive structure lies outside the scope of this work.[209]

The Lisbon Agenda. The European Council held a special meeting in March **1.073** 2000 in Lisbon to consider the strategic direction of the European Union. The Presidency Conclusions of that meeting – often referred to as the Lisbon Agenda or Strategy – state that the goal of the Community over the next decade is 'to become the most competitive and dynamic knowledge-based economy in the world, capable of sustainable economic growth with more and better jobs and greater social cohesion'. In April 2004, a High Level Group was set up, under the chairmanship of Mr Wim Kok, former Prime Minister of the Netherlands, to give renewed stimulus to the attainment of these goals. The Commission has identified three areas where competition policy can make an important contribution to the success of the Lisbon Agenda:

- Promoting the knowledge-based society: strong competitive pressure can provide incentives for companies to engage in innovation and research and development.

- Fostering the internal market: competition enforcement and advocacy can contribute to better functioning of the internal market; the enforcement of competition law helps create sound conditions for growth.

- Promoting a favourable business climate: State aid rules increase the availability of risk capital for start ups and small- and medium-sized enterprises; competition principles can allow screening of new and existing regulatory frameworks in other important policy areas so as to ensure that regulation does not unnecessarily curb competition.[210]

Market integration. The Community competition rules also have the distinct **1.074** objective of preventing barriers to achievement of a single market. As seen above, the EC Treaty is designed to abolish all national barriers to intra-Community trade and to create a single Community market in which the conditions prevailing in a national market are reproduced on a Community scale. A single market presupposes the free flow of goods and services throughout that market. If such a

---

[208] (2004) 1 EC Competition Policy Newsletter 1.

[209] See generally, Ehlerman and Laudati (eds), *European Competition Law Annual 1997: Objectives of Competition Policy* (1998); Bishop and Walker, *The Economics of EC Competition Law* (2nd edn, 2002); Bergh and Camesasca, *European Competition Law and Economics: A Comparative Perspective* (2nd edn, 2006). For a historical perspective, see Gerber, *Law and Competition in Twentieth Century Europe* (2003); and, for a brief introduction, Whish, *Competition Law* (5th edn, 2003), Chap 1.

[210] *XXIVth Report on Competition Policy* (2004), p 6.

market is working effectively, it becomes impossible to maintain artificially different prices in different parts of the market because goods will freely flow from the low-price areas into the high-price areas, undercutting the higher prices. The result should be that prices settle down at broadly the same level so that, subject to transport costs, the price of a given brand of (say) hi-fi equipment eventually becomes the same whether it is purchased in Manchester, Madrid or Munich.[211] The rules on free movement seek to prevent barriers to trade being maintained by Member States. The competition rules may be seen as complementing those provisions in preventing such barriers being re-erected by private agreements, for example by a manufacturer prohibiting its distributors from supplying customers outside a defined territory. The Court of Justice has said:

> '. . . an agreement between a producer and a distributor which might tend to restore the national divisions in trade between Member States might be such as to frustrate the most fundamental object of the Community. The Treaty, whose preamble and content aim at abolishing the barriers between States . . . could not allow undertakings to reconstruct such barriers. Article [81(1)] is designed to pursue this aim, even in the case of agreements between undertakings placed at different levels in the economic process.'[212]

Similarly, achievement of a truly integrated market would be hampered if a Member State were to subsidise its industries, and thereby hinder imports from other Member States or artificially stimulate exports to other Member States. The State aid rules, which are a particular feature of Community competition law, therefore play an essential role in furtherance of this fundamental objective. However, parallel trade is not protected as an end in itself but because it usually optimises consumer welfare by reducing prices and increasing the range of goods on offer.[213]

1.075 **Importance of parallel trading.** The principle that the consumer should be able to buy goods from the cheapest source anywhere in the Community leads in particular to the need to protect trading by intermediaries who buy from the manufacturer to sell on to consumers, thereby competing either directly with the manufacturer's own sales arm or with the manufacturer's approved dealer network. The term 'parallel trading' refers to such trading across frontiers by intermediaries, normally operating outside 'authorised' channels of distribution. Parallel traders typically buy goods in low-priced areas of the Community and export

---

[211] cf Cases 100/80, etc, *Musique Diffusion Française v Commission* ('the *Pioneer* case') [1983] ECR 1825, [1983] 3 CMLR 221. The reality is often rather different: see the Commission's biannual Reports on car price differentials within the EU, available at http://ec.europa.eu/comm/competition/sectors/motor_vehicles/prices/report.html.

[212] Cases 56 & 58/64 *Consten and Grundig v Commission* [1966] ECR 299, 340, [1966] CMLR 418, 471. See also *XXIst Report on Competition Policy* (1991), points 43–44.

[213] *GlaxoSmith Kline Services* (n 207, above).

them cheaply to the higher priced areas, thus making it impossible for the higher prices to be maintained. Many of the cases arising under the rules on competition are concerned with the right of 'parallel imports' to move between Member States[214] and increasingly heavy penalties are imposed on undertakings that attempt to prevent such trade.[215]

Liberalisation of markets. The Commission has stressed the importance of opening up markets which were traditionally heavily regulated or operated by a single, often State-owned undertaking.[216] Telecommunications, the energy industries, air transport and, most recently, postal services are the subject of Community initiatives in this regard.[217] The Commission sees the enforcement of the general competition rules as one weapon in its overall armory in opening up these markets. More recently the Commission's focus has moved to eliminating restrictions which govern the liberal professions.[218] **1.076**

Other objectives. Although these are the primary aims of the competition rules, in certain circumstances other objectives affect the application of those principles or sit alongside them.[219] The special position of agriculture, where the common **1.077**

---

[214] See generally paras 6.053 *et seq*, below. For a case under Art 82 see *Tetra Pak II*, OJ 1992 L72/1, [1992] 4 CMLR 551, 162–164 (note that the remedies ordered by the Commission included an obligation not to refuse orders on the ground that the customer was not an end-user of Tetra Pak's product); appeals dismissed, Case T-83/91 *Tetra Pak v Commission* [1994] ECR II-755, [1997] 4 CMLR 726; Case C-333/94P [1996] ECR I-5951, [1997] 4 CMLR 662. It has been questioned whether the 'free riders' associated with parallel trading really do assist the integration of the common market, eg Korah, 'EEC Competition Policy—Legal Form or Economic Efficiency', *Current Legal Problems* (1986). In Case T-204/03 *Haladjian Frères v Commission* [2006] ECR II-3779, [2007] 4 CMLR 1106, the CFI appears to have accepted that it was legitimate for a manufacturer to try to control imports of cheap spare parts from outside the EEA if they undermined the viability of the investment made by its official distributors.

[215] See, eg Case T-62/98 *Volkswagen v Commission* [2000] ECR II-2707, [2000] 5 CMLR 853: fine of €90 million, as revised by the CFI; upheld on further appeal, Case C-338/00P [2003] ECR I-9189, [2004] 4 CMLR 351.

[216] See *XXth Report on Competition Policy* (1990), point 53, and more recently, *XXXIInd Report on Competition Policy* (2002), points 74 *et seq*; *XXXIIIrd Report on Competition Policy* (2003), points 86 *et seq*; *Report on Competition Policy 2005*, pts 36 *et seq*.

[217] See Chap 12, below. For an example of the interrelation of EC liberalising legislation and the application of the competition rules see *Deutsche Telekom*, OJ 2003 L263/9, [2004] 4 CMLR 790 (on appeal, Case T-271/03, not yet decided).

[218] See 'Report on Competition in Professional Services', February 2004; 'Stocktaking Exercise on Regulation of Professional Services – Overview of Regulation in the New EU Member States', November 2004; the follow-up report, 'Professional Services – Scope for more reform', September 2005: all available with other material in the Professional Services section of DG Competition's website. See also Deisenhofer, 'Towards a proportionality test in the field of the liberal professions?' (2005) 3 EC Competition Policy Newsletter 25.

[219] For a critique of EC competition law as failing to pursue only an antitrust objective, see Amato, *Antitrust and the Bounds of Power* (1997). There was similar controversy in the past regarding the extent to which wider, non-economic considerations should be taken into account under US antitrust law: see, eg Pitofsky, 'The Political Content of Antitrust' (1979) 127 U of Pa. Law Rev 1051, and Comment by Schwartz, ibid, 1076.

agricultural policy is a protected regime in marked contrast to the free market model applied to the rest of the Community economy, leads to a modified application of competition rules in that sector.[220] More generally, protection of the environment and maintenance of cultural diversity are now expressed as distinct objectives under the Treaty and will be taken into account, as appropriate, in particular cases.[221] The Community seeks in certain circumstances to give protection to small- and medium-sized enterprises, although this may not be consistent with a 'pure' economic approach to competition.[222] The conditions imposed for the application of Article 81(3) sometimes seek to impose a standard of fairness in commercial dealing and do not merely have regard to competition concerns.[223]

6. Territorial Ambit of EC Competition Rules

(a) The Member States: enlargement

1.078 **The Member States.** The territory to which the EC Treaty extends is determined by Article 299 which provides that the Treaty applies in its entirety, save for express provisions to the contrary, to the territories of the Member States and the European territories for whose external relations a Member State is responsible.[224] The Member States were originally six, namely Belgium,[225] Germany,[226] France, Italy, Luxembourg and the Netherlands.

---

[220] See Chap 12, below.

[221] See para 1.037, above. See, eg Nehl and Nuijten 'Commission ends competition proceedings regarding German book price fixing agreements following acceptance of an undertaking on cross border sales' describing how the Commission 'showed its readiness to take into account the national interest in maintaining systems that are aimed at preserving cultural and linguistic diversity in Europe' (2002) 2 EC Competition Policy Newsletter 35; Horizontal Cooperation Guidelines, OJ 2001 C3/2: Vol II, App C.12, sect 7 Environmental Agreements

[222] See, eg the Commission's block exemption for State aid to SMEs, Reg 70/2001, OJ 2001 L10/33: Vol II, App G.11.

[223] eg as between supplier and dealer, as shown by the block exemption Reg 1400/2002 (distribution of motor vehicles), OJ 2002 L203/30: Vol II, App C.6.

[224] Art 299(4) and see the Answer of Commission President Delors to a Parliamentary Question, OJ 1992 C102/77.

[225] In Cases 43 & 63/82 *VBVB and VBBB v Commission* [1984] ECR 19, [1982] 1 CMLR 27, paras 47–48, the ECJ rejected an argument that, for the purpose of assessing an effect on trade between Member States, the Flemish-speaking part of Belgium could linguistically be regarded as forming a single entity with the Dutch-speaking Netherlands.

[226] Following the reunification of Germany under Art 23 of the Constitution of the Federal Republic, the territory of the former German Democratic Republic became part of the territory of the Community, but various transitional arrangements were necessary: see *XXth Report on Competition Policy* (1990), points 33–40.

Accessions before 2000.   The expansion of the Community in the second half   **1.079**
of the last century was a gradual process. With effect from 1 January 1973, the
United Kingdom, Denmark and Ireland acceded to the EC Treaty, subject to
certain transitional arrangements.[227] Greece acceded with effect from 1 January
1981;[228] Spain and Portugal acceded with effect from 1 January 1986;[229] and
Austria, Finland and Sweden acceded with effect from 1 January 1995.[230] In each
case, the accession was subject to transitional arrangements.

Enlargement into Eastern Europe.   After the collapse of the Soviet Union, the   **1.080**
EC quickly established diplomatic relations with the countries of Central and
Eastern Europe and, through the PHARE Programme created in 1989, provided
considerable financial support for these countries' efforts to reform and rebuild
their economies. In 1993, at a meeting in Copenhagen, the European Council
agreed that 'the associated countries in Central and Eastern Europe that so desire
shall become members of the European Union'.[231] At the same time it defined the
membership criteria, which are often referred to as the 'Copenhagen criteria'. The
criteria laid down that a candidate country must have achieved (a) stability of
institutions guaranteeing democracy, the rule of law, human rights and respect for
and protection of minorities; (b) the existence of a functioning market economy
as well as the capacity to cope with competitive pressure and market forces within

---

[227] Cmnd 7463. For an annotated text, see *Encyclopedia of European Union Law (Constitutional Texts)*, Vol 1, paras 20.0008 *et seq*. The rules on competition took effect on 1 January 1973, subject to transitional rules for the notification of existing agreements under Art 25 of Reg 17; see the 5th edn of this work (2001), paras 11–030 *et seq*.

[228] The Treaty concerning the Accession of Greece was signed at Athens on 28 May 1979: Cmnd 7650. For an annotated text, see *Encyclopedia of European Union Law (Constitutional Texts)*, Vol 1, paras 21.0046 *et seq*. The rules on competition took effect on 1 January 1981, subject to transitional rules for the notification of existing agreements under Art 25 of Reg 17.

[229] The Treaty concerning the Accession of Spain and Portugal was signed in Madrid and Lisbon on 12 June 1985: Cmnd 9634. For an annotated text, see *Encyclopedia of European Union Law (Constitutional Texts)*, Vol 1, paras 22.0028 *et seq*. The transitional arrangements relating to the accession of Spain and Portugal were complex, but in principle the transitional period continued until 1 January 1993, subject to certain exceptions, including special arrangements regarding pharmaceutical products operating until 7 October 1995: see Case C-191/90 *Generics and Harris Pharmaceuticals* [1992] ECR I-5335, [1993] 1 CMLR 89, arising from the fact that patents were not permitted for such products prior to October 1992. The rules on competition took effect on 1 January 1986, subject to transitional rules for the notification of existing agreements under Art 25 of Reg 17.

[230] The Treaty of Accession was signed at Corfu on 24 June 1994: Cmnd 2887. Norway was also a State party to the Treaty but the subsequent Norwegian referendum voted against accession. The Treaty provided that the annexed Act of Accession could be amended in such circumstances by unanimous decision of the Council of the EU, which duly took place so as to remove those aspects relating to Norway. For the text of the Treaty and Act of Accession as amended, see *Encyclopedia of European Union Law (Constitutional Texts)*, Vol 2, paras 23.0034 *et seq*.

[231] Conclusions of the Presidency of the European Council Meeting in Copenhagen, 21–22 June 1993, doc SN 180/1/93 REV 1, available on the Council's website at http://www.consilium. europa.eu/ueDocs/cms_Data/docs/pressdata/en/ec/72921.pdf.

the Union; and (c) the ability to take on the obligations of membership including adherence to the aims of political, economic and monetary union. The membership criteria also require that the candidate country must have created the conditions for its integration through the adjustment of its administrative structures, as underlined by the Madrid European Council in December 1995.[232] The Madrid meeting concluded that although it is important that EC legislation is transposed into national legislation, it is even more important that the legislation is implemented effectively through appropriate administrative and judicial structures. Following the Luxembourg European Council of December 1997, accession negotiations were opened with Cyprus, the Czech Republic, Estonia, Hungary, Poland and Solvenia ('the Luxembourg group'). Following the Helsinki European Council of December 1999, negotiations were opened with Bulgaria, Latvia, Lithuania, Malta, Romania and Slovakia (the 'Helsinki group'). The negotiations were guided by the principle of differentiation which means that each candidate country was assessed on its own merits.

1.081 **The competition law dimension of accession negotiations.** Accession negotiations are sub-divided into a number of topical chapters, one of which concerns competition policy. Candidate countries are regarded as ready for accession only if their companies and public authorities have become accustomed, well before the date of accession, to a competition discipline similar to that of the EU. In translating these principles into concrete requirements, there are three elements that must be in place in a candidate country before the competition chapter negotiations can be closed. First, the necessary legislative framework with respect to antitrust and State aid must be in place; secondly, the State must demonstrate an adequate administrative capacity, in particular a properly functioning competition authority; and thirdly, it must have a credible enforcement record of the *acquis* in all areas of competition policy. To evaluate whether these conditions are met, DG Competition[233] carries out a detailed assessment, including the examination of cases which the competition authorities of the country have handled.

1.082 **Becoming 27.** A single Treaty of Accession for 10 new Member States was signed in Athens on 16 April 2003 and came into force on 1 May 2004. By this Treaty, the Czech Republic, Estonia, Cyprus, Latvia, Lithuania, Hungary, Malta, Poland, Slovenia and Slovakia became Members of the European Union, bringing the total number of Member States to 25. Annexed to the Treaty and forming

---

232 Conclusions of the Presidency of the Madrid European Council Meeting, 15–16 December 1995, available at: http://www.consilium.europa.eu/ueDocs/cms_Data/docs/pressdata/en/ec/00400-C.EN5.htm.

233 See para 1.052, above.

an integral part of it is an Act setting out the conditions for Accession of each new Member.[234] The Protocols to the Accession Agreement cover a wide range of issues from the restructuring of the Czech and Polish steel industries to the acquisition of secondary residences in Malta.[235] Protocol 10 covers the position of Cyprus in the light of the failure of the unification talks prior to Accession. Bulgaria and Romania signed Accession Treaties in Luxembourg on 25 April 2005 and became Member States on 1 January 2007.[236] The Union now comprises 27 Member States with a total population of almost 500 million people.

Further enlargement. Turkey was accepted as a candidate country in 1999 but negotiations on membership commenced only in October 2005 and, at the time of writing, political opposition from existing Member States makes the prospect of Turkish membership uncertain. In October 2005, negotiations on accession also started with Croatia and, in December 2005, the former Yugoslav Republic of Macedonia was granted the status of Candidate Country but accession negotiations have not yet started. In July 2006, the Council adopted an Instrument for Pre-Accession Assistance which provides targeted assistance to candidate and potential candidate countries.[237]   **1.083**

(b) The Member States: current geographic scope

The current Member States: overseas territories, etc. Several of the Member States have overseas territories for whom special arrangements are in place regarding which aspects of the EC Treaty, if any, apply to them. These arrangements are to be found in Articles 188 and 299 of the EC Treaty and in the Accession Treaties. The scope of the Community customs territory is set out in Regulation 2913/92.[238] Generally, the customs territory of the EC includes the territorial waters, the inland maritime waters and the airspace of those parts of   **1.084**

---

[234] The Treaty, Act of Accession, 18 Annexes and 10 Protocols are printed in OJ 2003 L/236 (with the Appendices to the Annexes printed in OJ 2003 C/227 E). See also *Encyclopedia of European Union Law (Constitutional Texts)*, Vol 1, paras 24.0002 *et seq.*

[235] For the transitional arrangements in place relating to the application of competition law to each of the new Member States, see *XXIIIrd Report on Competition Policy* (2003), point 659. These mostly relate to the phasing out of fiscal aids.

[236] For texts, see *Encyclopedia of European Union Law (Constitutional Texts)*, Vol 2, paras 25.0051 *et seq.* See also article on Romanian preparation for accession and the closure of the competition chapter of the negotiations (2005) 1 EC Competition Policy Newsletter 39.

[237] Reg 1085/2006, OJ 2006 L210/82. See further para 1.098, below.

[238] Reg 2913/92, OJ 1992 L302/1. A consolidated text is available on the website of the Commission's Taxation and Customs Directorate General. The Commission has published a proposal for a new modernised customs code which would replace Reg 2913/92: see COM(2005) 608 final 30 November 2005.

the Member States which are included in the Community. The current position is as follows:

State	Territory	Status
Cyprus	Northern Cyprus	Although Cyprus as a whole is a member of the EU, application of EC law is suspended in those areas in which the government of the Republic of Cyprus is not in control[239]
Denmark	Greenland	EC law not in force and not part of the customs territory but there are special arrangements for association with the EC[240]
	Faroe Islands	EC law not in force[241]
Finland	Åland Islands	EC law in force with some exceptions[242]
France	Guadeloupe French Guiana Martinique Réunion	EC law in force[243]
	French Polynesia French Southern and Antarctic Territories Mayotte New Caledonia and Dependencies Saint-Pierre and Miquelon Wallis and Fortuna Islands	EC law not in force and not part of the customs territory but there are special arrangements for association with the EC[244]
Germany	Büsingen Island of Heligoland	Excluded from the customs union[245]
Italy	Communes of Livigno and Campione d'Italia and the national waters of Lake Lugano	Excluded from the customs union[246]
The Netherlands	Aruba Dutch Antilles	EC law not in force but there are special arrangements for association with the EC[247]

---

[239] Protocol 10 to the Act of Accession (n 234, above) Art 1. And see Reg 886/2004, OJ 2004 L161/128 (corr OJ 2004 L206/51) for a regime under Art 2 of Protocol 10. See, eg *Orams v Apostolides* [2006] EWCH 2226, [2007] 1 WLR 241: English High Court held that Brussels Regulation on recognition of judgments does not apply in respect of land in Northern Cyprus.

[240] Arts 188 and 299(3) and Ann II EC, and Protocol 15 on special arrangements for Greenland. See also Art 3(1) of Reg 2913/92.

[241] Art 299(6)(a) EC

[242] Art 299(5) EC and Protocol 2 to the Treaty of Accession of Austria, Finland and Sweden.

[243] Subject to the Councils right to adopt specific measures in relation to them in the interests of their development: Art 299(2) EC.

[244] Arts 188 and 299(3) and Ann II EC; Art 3(1) Reg 2913/92.

[245] Art 3(1) of Reg 2913/92, OJ 1992 L302/1. These areas are subject to Treaty provisions between Germany and Switzerland.

[246] Art 3 of Reg 2913/92.

[247] Art 3 of Reg 2913/92.

State	Territory	Status
Portugal	Azores Madeira	EC law in force[248]
Spain	Ceuta Melilla Canary Islands	Excluded from the customs union but EC law otherwise applies[249] EC law in force[250]

United Kingdom	Gibraltar
	Channel Islands
	Isle of Man
	UK Sovereign Base
	  Areas of Akrotiri and
	  Dhekelia in Cyprus
	
	Anguilla
	Bermuda
	British Antarctic Territory
	British Indian Ocean
	  Territory
	British Virgin Islands
	Cayman Islands
	Falkland Islands
	Montserrat
	Pitcairn
	Saint Helena and Dependencies
	South Georgia and the
	  South Sandwich Islands
	Turks and Caicos Islands
		EC law in force with some exceptions[251]
		Part of the customs union. EC law
		not in force but some chapters
		apply[252]
		Part of the customs union. EC law
		applies to some extent[253]
		
		EC law not in force but there are
		special arrangements for association
		with the EC[254]

[248] Subject to the Council's right to adopt specific measures in relation to them in the interests of their development: Art 299(2) EC.

[249] See Art 3(1) of Reg 2913/92 and Art 25 of the Act of Accession of Spain and Portugal (n 229, above) subject to the derogations stated therein.

[250] Subject to the Council's right to adopt specific measures in relation to them in the interests of their development: Art 299(2) EC.

[251] Gibraltar is *prima facie* covered by Art 299(4) but is outside the common customs territory under Reg 2913/92 and certain other Treaty rules by virtue of Art 28 of the Act of Accession (n 227, above): see Case C-30/01 *Commission v United Kingdom* [2003] ECR I-9481. However, the competition rules should apply to Gibraltar. See also Case C-145/04 *Spain v United Kingdom* [2006] ECR I-7917, [2007] 1 CMLR 87, [2007] All ER (EC) 486.

[252] The Isle of Man and the Channel Islands are part of the common customs territory under Reg 2913/92 so the rules on free movement of goods apply to them but it seems that the competition rules of the Treaty do not apply: Art 299(6)(c) EC and Protocol 3 to the Treaty of Accession (n 227, above). See Case C-171/96 *Pereira Roque v Lieutenant Governor of Jersey* [1998] ECR I-4607, [1998] 3 CMLR 143, Opinion of AG La Pergola, para 8. See also Case C-293/02 *Jersey Produce Marketing Organisation* [2005] ECR I-9543, [2006] 1 CMLR 738: Jersey and the United Kingdom were to be regarded as the same Member State but a law affecting only exports of new potatoes between Jersey and the United Kingdom was still caught by Art 29 because the potatoes might then be exported from the United Kingdom to other Member States.

[253] See Art 199(6)(b) as amended by Protocol 3 to the Treaty of Accession of April 2003: OJ 2003 L236/940.

[254] Arts 188 and 299(3) and Ann II EC.

State	Territory	Status
Other European states[255]	Monaco	Included in the customs union[256]
	The Vatican	Outside the EU
	San Marino	Subject to a special agreement[257]
	Andorra	Subject to a special agreement[258]

(c) EFTA and the EEA

1.085 **EFTA.** The European Free Trade Association ('EFTA') was established in 1960 under the EFTA Convention signed in Stockholm. That Convention mainly covered trade in industrial goods but was updated by the Vaduz Convention which entered into force in June 2002. The Convention covers many other areas of trade, such as the free movement of goods and persons, and allows undertakings in the EFTA countries to benefit from most of the rights provided for in the EEA Agreement. It now comprises Switzerland, Iceland, Norway and Liechtenstein.

1.086 **The EEA Agreement.** In 1992, the European Communities, the Member States and the EFTA countries signed an Agreement on the European Economic Area ('the EEA Agreement')[259] which came into force on 1 January 1994. The EEA Agreement aims at ensuring free movement of goods, persons, services and capital among the Contracting Parties[260] and at setting up a system of undistorted competition. The Agreement also provides for closer cooperation in other fields such as research and development, the environment, education and social policy. Although Switzerland signed the EEA Agreement, it subsequently withdrew from

---

255 Information about the EU's relations with these and other States is available on the website of the Commission's Directorate-General of External Relations.

256 Art 3(2) of Reg 2913/92 as amended by Reg 82/97, OJ 1997 L17/1. It is unclear whether it should be treated as part of France for the purposes of the competition rules by virtue of Art 299(4) of the EC Treaty. See the Opinion of AG Fennelly in Case C-220/98 *Estée Lauder Cosmetics v Lancaster Group* [2000] ECR I-117, [2000] 1 CMLR 515, [2000] All ER (EC) 122, approving (at para 12) the submissions of France and the Commission that Monaco is a third country for EC law purposes. (This issue is not addressed in the judgment of the ECJ.)

257 Since 1992 San Marino's trade relations with the EC have been governed by a special international agreement: see most recently Council Decn 2002/245/EC, OJ 2002 L84/41. It is uncertain how far it may be treated as part of Italy for the purposes of the competition rules by virtue of Art 299(4) EC.

258 See OJ 1990 L374/16. An additional cooperation agreement with Andorra and an agreement on taxation of savings came into force in July 2005.

259 Cmnd 2073. The Agreement was signed at Oporto on 2 May 1992. See the Opinions of the ECJ: Opinion 1/91 [1991] ECR I-6079, [1992] 1 CMLR 245; Opinion 1/92 [1992] ECR I-2821, [1992] 2 CMLR 217. For the text of the EEA Agreement as amended by the 'Swiss Protocol' (to take account of the absence of Switzerland), see *Encyclopedia of European Union Law (Constitutional Texts)*, Vol 2, paras 30.0042 *et seq*. See also [1993] 1 ECLR Supp for the parts of the Agreement and the Protocols relating to competition.

260 See Information Note *The Four Freedoms and the EEA* prepared by DG External Relations for the European Parliament, 27 October 2004, Doc DEEA20050413_10EN.doc.

the EEA after the Swiss electorate voted against the Agreement in a referendum. The accession of Austria, Finland and Sweden to the European Community on 1 January 1995 reduced the number of non-EC signatory States to two: Iceland and Norway. Liechtenstein, which had withdrawn from the EEA along with Switzerland, joined the EEA after the Agreement had been suitably amended, on 1 May 1995. Accordingly, the non-EC signatory States are now Iceland, Liechtenstein and Norway.

The EFTA institutions.   Article 108 of the EEA Agreement provides for the establishment of an independent EFTA surveillance authority, with an analogous role to that of the European Commission, and an EFTA Court of Justice. This provision was implemented by the Agreement between the EFTA States on the establishment of a Surveillance Authority and a Court of Justice ('the EFTA Surveillance and Court Agreement').[261] Protocol 5 to the Agreement on the EFTA Surveillance and Court Agreement constitutes the Statute of the EFTA Court.[262]   **1.087**

Uniform application of competition policy in the EEA.   Article 1 of the EEA Agreement provides that the aim of the Agreement is to promote a continuous and balanced strengthening of trade and economic relations between the Contracting Parties with equal conditions of competition, and the respect of the same rules, with a view to creating a homogeneous European Economic Area. The Commission and the EFTA Surveillance Authority are charged by Article 55(1) of the EEA Agreement with ensuring the application of the competition rules set out in Articles 53 and 54 of the EEA Agreement.   **1.088**

Homogeneity objective in the application of EC jurisprudence in the EEA.   Article 6 of the EEA Agreement provides that, without prejudice to future developments of case law, the provisions of the Agreement, insofar as they are identical in substance to corresponding rules of the EC Treaty and to acts adopted pursuant to that Treaty, shall be implemented and interpreted in accordance with the case law of the European Court of Justice given prior to the date of the Agreement. Moreover, Article 3(2) of the EFTA Surveillance and Court Agreement provides that the Surveillance Authority and the Court shall take 'due account' of the relevant rulings of the European Court of Justice given after the date of the EEA Agreement. On that basis, the EFTA Court has referred to the 'homogeneity objective' and applies the case law of the two Community Courts when ruling on   **1.089**

---

[261] OJ 1994 L344/3: see paras 1.051 *et seq*, above. The text of the Agreement and the EFTA Court's Rules of Procedure are available on the EFTA Court's website under 'legal texts.' See also *Encyclopedia of European Union Law (Constitutional Texts)*, Vol 2, paras 30.3190 *et seq.*

[262] For a discussion of the role of the ECJ under the EEA Agreement see Opinion 1/92 of the ECJ (n 259, above).

competition law.[263] The EC Commission as well as the EFTA Surveillance Authority has a right to be heard in proceedings.[264]

1.090   **The competition provisions of the EEA Agreement.**   The competition provisions in Articles 53, 54 and 59 of the EEA Agreement mirror Articles 81, 82 and 86 of the EC Treaty, and Article 57 of the EEA Agreement incorporates control of concentrations.[265] The State aids provisions in Article 87 of the EC Treaty are similarly mirrored in Article 61 of the EEA Agreement and provisions for notification of proposed aid analogous to Article 88 of the EC Treaty are found in the EFTA Surveillance and Court Agreement.[266] Relevant EC legislative instruments are incorporated into the EEA Agreement by decision of the EEA Joint Committee.[267] Thus, pursuant to Article 60 and under Annex XIV of the EEA Agreement, most of the various EC Council and Commission Regulations concerning competition law have been adopted, subject to necessary amendments so that they apply to the EFTA States.[268] The EFTA Surveillance Authority also promulgates notices and guidance which mirror those issued by the Commission.[269] By amendment to Protocol 4 to the EFTA Surveillance and Court Agreement, the EFTA States adopted the Modernisation package[270] as regards the application of the EEA competition rules with effect from 20 May 2005.[271] However, since only the contracting EFTA States are parties to that Agreement, the national competition authorities of only

---

263   Case E-1/94 *Restamark* [1994–5] Rep EFTA Ct 15, [1995] 1 CMLR 161, paras 32–35; Case E-2/94 *Scottish Salmon Growers Association v EFTA Surveillance Authority* [1994–5] Rep EFTA Ct 59, [1995] 1 CMLR 851, paras 11–13; Case E-8/00 *LO and NKF v KS* [2002] Rep EFTA Ct 114, [2002] 5 CMLR 160, para 39: 'It is a fundamental objective of the EEA Agreement to achieve and maintain uniform interpretation and application of those provisions of the EEA Agreement that correspond to provisions of the EC Treaty, and to arrive at equal treatment of individuals and economic operators as regards conditions of competition in the whole European Economic Area'.

264   Protocol 5 EEA, Arts 17, 20.

265   See Fenger, Sanchez Rydelski and van Stiphout, *International Encyclopaedia of Laws: Intergovernmental Organisations*, Supplement 24: European Free Trade Association (EFTA) and European Economic Area (EEA) (2005).

266   Protocol 3 to the EFTA Surveillance and Court Agreement (n 261, above). See also Art 62 EEA.

267   These Decns are reported in the *Official Journal* and also, in Norwegian and Icelandic, in the EEA Supplement to the OJ. The EEA Supp also reports other matters of relevance only to the EFTA Contracting States.

268   See eg the block exemptions dicussed at para 3.093, below.

269   The texts of these Notices are published in English and German in the *Official Journal*, eg the Notice on Cooperation between the EFTA Surveillance Authority and the courts of the EFTA States, OJ 2006 C305/19. The Notices are also available on the EFTA Surveillance Authority's website: www.eftasurv.int.

270   See at paras 1.058–1.060, above. For the EEA modernisation, see further the EFTA Surveillance Authority Annual Report 2005, pp 38–39.

271   Agreement between the EFTA States of 24 September 2004, replacing Protocol 4, Part I, Chap II to the EFTA Surveillance and Court Agreement, OJ 2005 C304/24. A consolidated version of Protocol 4 is on the EFTA Surveillance Authority website.

those States[272] are required to enforce the EEA competition rules; the national competition authorities of the EC Member States have not been given such power. This does not affect the jurisdiction of either the EFTA Surveillance Authority or the Commission. Furthermore, the competition rules of the EEA Agreement have direct effect in the Member States of the EU, on the corresponding basis to the competition rules of the EC Treaty,[273] and are therefore enforceable in the national courts of the Member States. By contrast with EC law, there is no general principle of direct effect under the EEA Agreement; however, Norway and Iceland adopted domestic legislation incorporating Articles 53 and 54 EEA into their national legal order, and Liechtenstein follows the monist tradition whereby the State's international obligations are part of its domestic law: accordingly, the courts of the three contracting EFTA States have power to apply the EEA competition rules.[274]

Allocation of jurisdiction under the EEA Agreement. The basis on which cases **1.091** are allocated between the Commission and the EFTA Surveillance Authority is set out in Article 56 of the EEA Agreement. If the conduct under investigation affects only trade between Member States the Commission has competence and applies the EC Treaty.[275] If the conduct affects only trade between EFTA or EEA states, then the EFTA Surveillance Authority alone is competent and applies the EEA competition rules. Where, however, the effect on trade is mixed, the Commission is the competent authority and may apply both the EC Treaty and the EEA Agreement where either (a) the conduct in question has an appreciable effect on trade between Member States and on competition within the Community; or (b) the combined turnover of the undertakings concerned in the territory of the EFTA states is less than 33 per cent of their turnover in the EEA.[276] Cases under Article 54 concerning abuse of a dominant position are allocated to the authority in the territory in which a dominant position is found to exist. If dominance exists

---

[272] However, there is a special reservation for Liechtenstein, which does have a competition authority, absolving it from this requirement: Art 41 of Protocol 4.

[273] See by analogy Case T-115/94 *Opel Austria v Council* [1997] ECR II-39, [1997] 1 CMLR 733, [1997] All ER (EC) 97 (concerning the prohibition of customs duties).

[274] Further, Art 6 of the amended Protocol 4 to the Surveillance and Court Agreement requires the national courts of the EFTA States to have power to apply the competition rules. See *International Encyclopaedia of Laws: Intergovernmental Organisations*, Supplement 24 (n 265, above) paras 211–216.

[275] For examples of the application of these principles see eg COMP/37.857 *Organic Peroxide*, 10 December 2003, [2005] 5 CMLR 579, paras 287–293 and para 368 (on appeal, Cases T-99/04 *AC Treuhand*, not yet decided, and T-120/04 *Peróxidos Orgánicos* [2007] 4 CMLR 153, appeal dismissed); *Video games Nintendo Distribution*, OJ 2003 L255/33, [2004] CMLR 421, para 241 (on appeal, Cases T-18/03 *CD-Contact Data*, T-12/03 *Itochu Corporation*, T-398/02 *Linea Gig (in liquidation)* and T-13/03 *Nintendo Corp and Nintendo of Europe*, not yet decided).

[276] See Case T-67/00 *JFE Engineering v Commission* [2004] ECR II-2501, [2005] 4 CMLR 27, paras 484 *et seq* (point not considered on appeal, Cases C-403 & 405/04P *Sumitomo Metal Industries v Commission* [2007] 4 CMLR 650).

in the territories of both the authorities, the Commission has jurisdiction where the tests in (a) or (b) above are satisfied.

1.092 **Powers of the Commission and the EFTA Surveillance Authority.**   Where cases under the EEA Agreement are allocated to the EC Commission, the same rules as to procedure and as to the Commission's powers of investigation and enforcement apply as for cases under the EC Treaty alone.[277] The EFTA Surveillance Authority has equivalent powers and functions in relation to investigation and enforcement to those granted to the Commission by Regulation 1/2003. These powers are set out in Chapter II of Protocol 4 to the EFTA Surveillance and Court Agreement.[278] Further provisions in Chapters III (as amended) and V set out rules as to the conduct of proceedings and as to limitation periods that are materially identical to the equivalent EC rules. Article 11(1) of Protocol 23 to the EEA Agreement provides that a complainant may address a complaint to either authority. If it is, or becomes, apparent that the complaint was addressed to the wrong authority, the authority that received the complaint must transfer the case to the other.[279]

1.093 **Cooperation in 'mixed' cases.**   Under Article 58 of the EEA Agreement[280] the Commission and the EFTA Surveillance Authority consult each other on general policy issues and on individual cases. The manner in which they cooperate is set out in Protocols 23 and 24 to the Agreement.[281] In 'mixed' cases which affect both EFTA and EC Member States, each authority sends to the other authority copies of notifications and complaints over which it has jurisdiction and informs the other about the opening of any *ex officio* procedures. The authority which is not competent to deal with the case may at any stage of the proceedings make observations to the authority which is dealing with the case. Each authority, and representatives of the States in its jurisdiction, are entitled to attend, but not to vote at, meetings of the Advisory Committee of the other authority, and to see the relevant papers.[282] Each authority must also consult the other when it addresses a statement of objections to undertakings.[283] The other authority, and the authorities of the States in the other authority's territory, are entitled to attend oral hearings concerning mixed cases.[284] The rules relating to professional secrecy or the restricted use of information set out in Article 28 of Regulation 1/2003[285] do not

---

[277] *JFE Engineering*, above.

[278] See n 271, above.

[279] Art 11(2) and (3) of Protocol 23 to the EEA Agreement. Once a case has been transferred under these provisions, it may not be transferred again. Nor may a case be transferred once a complaint has been definitively rejected or after a Statement of Objections has been issued: ibid, Art 10(4).

[280] See also Art 109 which imposes a general duty to cooperate.

[281] Protocol 24 deals specifically with cooperation with regard to control of concentrations.

[282] Protocol 23, Art 6(1).

[283] ibid, Art 3.

[284] ibid, Art 5.

[285] And in Art 28 of Chapter II of Protocol 4 to the EFTA Surveillance and Court Agreement.

apply to the exchange of information between the Commission and the EFTA Surveillance Authority. But each authority is bound by equivalent obligations of confidentiality in respect of information obtained from the other.[286]

Cooperation in investigations.   Where, under Article 18 of Regulation 1/2003   **1.094** (or under Article 18 of Chapter II of Protocol 4 to the EFTA Surveillance and Court Agreement), one authority addresses a request for information to (or takes a decision requiring the provision of information by) an undertaking in the other authority's territory[287] it must send a copy of that request or decision to the other authority.[288] Where an authority wishes an investigation to take place in the other authority's territory under Article 20 of Regulation 1/2003,[289] it must request the other authority to undertake that investigation; the other authority must comply with that request.[290]

Review of competition decisions by the EFTA Court.   The EFTA Court has,   **1.095** under Articles 35–37 of the EFTA Surveillance and Court Agreement, substantially the same powers of judicial review in relation to the conduct of the EFTA Surveillance Authority as does the Court of First Instance in relation to the conduct of the Commission.[291] Its procedures are closely modelled on those of the Court of Justice.[292] The Court is composed of three judges and sits in Luxembourg. The European Commission as well as the EFTA Surveillance Authority has the right to appear in cases before the EFTA Court.[293]

(d) Agreements between the Community and third countries

Switzerland.   In order to minimise the negative consequences of being the only   **1.096** State within EFTA that was not also in the EEA, Switzerland[294] and the Community entered into a series of bilateral agreements covering a range of areas including free movement of persons, public procurement and transport. Seven initial bilateral

---

[286] Arts 9–10 of Protocol 23 to the EEA Agreement, and Art 122 EEA.

[287] That is to say, the EFTA States in the case of the Commission and the EC in the case of the EFTA Surveillance Authority.

[288] Art 8(1) and (2) of Protocol 23 to the EEA Agreement.

[289] Or the corresponding Art 20 of Chapter II of Protocol 4 to the EFTA Surveillance and Court Agreement.

[290] The requesting authority is entitled to be present at, and to play an active part in, the investigation, and to receive the information obtained: Art 8(3) and (4) of Protocol 23 to the EEA Agreement.

[291] For the EFTA Court generally, see Baudenbacher, 'The EFTA Court: An Actor in the European Judicial Dialogue' (2005) 28 Fordham Int Law J353.

[292] See the Statute of the EFTA Court in Protocol 5 to the EFTA Surveillance and Court Agreement.

[293] ibid, Art 17.

[294] The website of the Swiss Integration Office contains useful information about Switzerland's relationship with the EU including the current status of the various bilateral agreements: see www.europa.admin.ch/e/.

agreements came into force in June 2002.[295] The Agreement relating to air transport which sets out the rules for the Contracting Parties in the field of civil aviation contains provisions mirroring Articles 81, 82, 86 and the State aid provisions of the EC Treaty and control of mergers.[296] After several years of subsequent negotiation, a further nine sectoral agreements were signed in June 2005 concerning topics including the taxation of savings; the cooperation in the fight against fraud; the association of Switzerland to the Schengen acquis; and Swiss participation in the Media plus and Media training programmes. In addition, a protocol to the existing agreement on free movement of persons was signed, extending this agreement to the 10 Member States who joined the EU in 2004. These Agreements came into force during the second half of 2005.

1.097 **Turkey.**   Relations between the EU and Turkey are governed by the Association Agreement of 1963 ('the Ankara Agreement').[297] Decision 1/95 of 22 December 1995 of the EC-Turkey Association Council,[298] implementing the final phase of the customs union under the Ankara Agreement, contains detailed competition provisions that mirror Articles 81 and 82 of the EC Treaty.[299] However, as regards those provisions no implementing rules have yet been adopted, although in 2001 the Commission submitted a 'proposal on the position to be adopted by the Community within the EC-Turkey Association Council, concerning a Decision of the Association Council adopting the implementing rules necessary for the application of the provisions on competition policy referred to in Article 37 of Decision No 1/95'.[300] The proposal contains chapters on procedural provisions, substantive provisions and provisions relating to dispute avoidance. The Court of Justice has ruled on the direct effect of various provisions in Decision 1/80 which was adopted by the EC–Turkey Association Council in order to ensure the progressive implementation of the freedom of movement for workers, for example provisions laying down an obligation of equal treatment in access to education

---

[295] OJ 2002 L114/1.

[296] OJ 2002 L114/73. See Arts 8–14. Art 10 provides that anti-competitive agreements and abuses which may only affect trade within Switzerland remain in the exclusive competence of the Swiss authorities.

[297] JO 3687/64 and (English text) OJ 1973 C113/1, supplemented by Additional Protocols. See *Encyclopedia of European Union Law (Constitutional Texts)*, Vol 3, paras 40.1884 *et seq*. For a case on direct application of the Ankara Agreement, see Case C-37/98 *Savas* [2000] ECR I-2927, [2000] 3 CMLR 729, [2000] All ER (EC) 627. By an Additional Protocol of July 2005, the Agreement was extended to the 10 new Member States, including significantly Cyprus. However, Turkey attached a declaration to its signature that qualifies its position as regards relations with Cyprus. See Katselli, 'The Ankara Agreement, Turkey and the EU' (2006) 55 ICLQ 705.

[298] Decn 1/95 of 22 December 1995, OJ 1996 L35/1.

[299] ibid, Arts 32–33. Art 35 provides that any practices contrary to those rules are to be assessed on the basis of the criteria arising from the application of Arts 81 and 82 and the secondary legislation thereunder.

[300] COM(2001) 632.

and vocational training.[301] Such free movement provisions could be relied on by an individual before a national court in order to request it to disapply the discriminatory provisions of the legislation of a Member State, no further implementing measures being required. It is arguable that such considerations do not apply equally to the competition provisions, which cannot be regarded as sufficiently precise and unconditional to be capable of being applied by a national court and, therefore, of governing the legal situation of undertakings. On the other hand, perhaps direct effect should not be rejected as entirely implausible, given the similarity in wording of the provisions in Decision 1/95 to Articles 81 and 82 EC which are directly effective,[302] and given the nature and purpose of the Ankara Agreement. Decision 1/95 constituted the final phase of the customs union rather than a mere transitional stage intended to facilitate accession to the European Communities. Its provisions could therefore hardly be deemed as being 'final' if they are not to be given full effect within the Community. Accession negotiations were opened with Turkey on 3 October 2005, but the proposal for Turkish accession has attracted opposition in several Member States and is compounded by the problem of Turkey's position regarding Cyprus.

Croatia, the FYR of Macedonia, and Albania.   The former Yugoslav Republic **1.098** of Macedonia and Croatia were the first and second countries respectively to sign a Stabilisation and Association Agreement ('SAA') with the EU.[303] The SAA constitutes an essential element of the EU's Stabilisation and Association Process with the Western Balkans.[304] The SAA is similar to the earlier 'Europe Agreements' with previous candidate countries[305] and provides a contractual framework with mutual rights and obligations between the EU and the countries until accession, including provisions on competition. Articles 70(1) and 70(2) of the Agreement

---

[301] Case C-374/03 *Gürol v Bezirksregierung Köln* [2005] ECR I-6199, [2005] 3 CMLR 44; Case C-192/89 *Sevince* [1990] ECR I-3461, [1992] 2 CMLR 57.

[302] But cf *Barkoci and Malik* [2001] ECR I-6557, [2001] 3 CMLR 48: mere similarity in the wording of a provision of one of the Treaties establishing the Communities and of an international agreement between the Community and a non-Member country (in that case the Association Agreement with the Czech Republic) is not sufficient to give the wording of that agreement the same meaning as it has in the Treaties. However, that was stated in relation to the scope of the provision rather than to its direct effect.

[303] The SAA with the former Yugoslav Republic of Macedonia entered into force on 1 May 2004. The text is at OJ 2004 L84/1, also *Encyclopedia of European Union Law (Constitutional Texts)*, Vol 3, paras 40.2646 *et seq*. The SAA with Croatia entered into force on 1 February 2005 and is published at OJ 2005 L26/3. An Enlargement Protocol, necessary to take into account the accession of ten New Member States on 1 May 2004 was signed in December 2004 and is published at OJ 2005 L26/222. See also Council Decn 2006/145 on principles, priorities and conditions on Accession Partnership with Croatia, OJ 2006 L155/30.

[304] Albania, Bosnia and Herzegovina, Croatia, the former Yugoslav Republic of Macedonia, Serbia and Montenegro.

[305] ie with Bulgaria, the Czech Republic, Estonia, Hungary, Latvia, Lithuania, Poland, Romania, the Slovak Republic and Slovenia.

with Croatia, for example, essentially mirrors similar competition provisions in the previous Europe Agreements,[306] and 'appropriate measures' may be taken in respect of practices contrary to Article 70(1) after consultation within the Stabilisation and Association Council or after 30 working days following referral for such consultation.[307] Article 69 provides for the approximation of laws which will extend to all elements of the Community *acquis* within six years after the entry into force of the Agreement.[308] However, none of the specific implementing rules have been adopted at the time of writing. Albania signed an SAA in June 2006 with an interim agreement coming into force in December 2006.

1.099 **International cooperation beyond Europe.** Cooperation between competition law enforcement authorities is an important part of the Commission's enforcement policy. The Commission aims to develop bilateral cooperation with the EC's main trading partners and to participate in various fora where States meet for multilateral cooperation on competition issues. With regard to bilateral arrangements, the EU has concluded dedicated cooperation agreements with the United States, Canada and Japan. The principal elements are the coordination of enforcement investigations and the non-confidential information. The agreements also contain provisions for one party to request the other to take enforcement action (positive comity) and for one party to take into account the important interests of the other party in the course of enforcement activities (traditional comity).

1.100 **Comity agreements with the United States.** The first cooperation agreement on competition matters with the United States was concluded by the Commission in 1991. After litigation challenging the Commission's *vires* to conclude the Agreement,[309] the Council and the Commission adopted a joint decision in April 1995,[310] approving the Agreement and declaring it applicable as from the date it was signed by the Commission. On 4 June 1998, a further agreement was concluded[311] strengthening the provisions of the earlier Agreement, in particular

---

[306] See para 2–162 of the 5th edition of this work. Art 70(2) provides that any practices contrary to those rules are to be assessed on the basis of the criteria arising from the application of Arts 81 and 82 EC and the secondary legislation thereunder.

[307] ibid, Art 70(9).

[308] ibid, Art 5.

[309] See Case C-327/91 *France v Commission* [1994] ECR I-3641, [1994] 5 CMLR 517.

[310] US Comity Agreement, OJ 1995 L95/45, OJ 1995 L131/38, [1991] 4 CMLR 823, [1995] 4 CMLR 677. The Agreement is published at OJ 1995 L95/47 together with the text of an exchange of interpretative letters between the EC and the USA occasioned by the litigation.

[311] OJ 1998 L173/26, [1999] 4 CMLR 502. This Agreement, unlike the 1991 Agreement does not cover mergers. The CFI has held that the purpose of the 1998 Agreement is not to implement a principle of *non bis in idem* but rather to enable the authorities of one of the Contracting Parties to take advantage of the practical effects of a procedure initiated by the authorities of the other: see Cases T-71/03, etc, *Tokai Carbon v Commission (speciality graphite)* [2005] ECR II-10, [2005] 5 CMLR 489, para 116 (appeal dismissed, Case C-328/05P, *SGL Carbon v Commission* [2007] 5 CMLR 16). The Commission is therefore not required to set off a fine imposed by the US authorities against the fine imposed in a decision: Case T-224/00 *Archer Daniels Midland and Archer*

introducing a positive comity clause whereby the competition authorities of one Party may request the other to investigate and, if warranted, remedy anti-competitive practices occurring in its territory. The influence of US antitrust analysis can be felt in the Commission's effort consciously to establish an economically more realistic application of competition law to commercial conduct. For example, the Commission's preparation of the Horizontal Cooperation Guidelines[312] involved discussion with the US antitrust authorities that were at the same time preparing guidelines on the same topic,[313] with a view to achieving a consistent approach.[314] The US Guidelines for the Licensing of Intellectual Property may be of value in considering the equivalent problems within the framework of EC competition law.

Cooperation with the United States under the comity agreement. The EC–USA **1.101** Competition Laws Cooperation Agreement provides for the exchange of information between the EC and US competition authorities, subject to their respective rules on confidentiality and 'important interests'.[315] Under the Agreement, each party will provide the other with 'any significant information' that comes to its attention about anti-competitive activities that may warrant enforcement activity by the other party.[316] Each party may also request the other to initiate enforcement activities in respect of anti-competitive activities occurring substantially in the territory of the requested party that adversely affect the interests of the requesting party.[317] The latter, 'positive comity', provision was strengthened by the 1998 Agreement which defines the circumstances in which the competition authorities of the requesting party will normally suspend or defer their investigations in reliance on enforcement activities of the requested party. In its 2005 Annual Report,[318] the Commission described its cooperation with the US Department of Justice and Federal Trade Commission as 'frequent and intense' in particular in relation to investigations into cartel activity.

Bilateral comity arrangements with other States. In 1999 the EC entered into **1.102** an agreement[319] with the government of Canada to promote cooperation and

---

Daniels Midland Ingredients v Commission [2003] ECR II-2597, [2003] 5 CMLR 583, paras 96 *et seq* (appeal dismissed, Case C-397/03P [2006] ECR I-4429).

[312] Horizontal Cooperation Guidelines, OJ 2001 C3/2: Vol II, App C.12.

[313] The Antitrust Guidelines for Collaborations Among Competitors were issued by the FTC and Dept of Justice in April 2000.

[314] Schaub, 'EC Competition Law—the Millennium Approaches' in Hawk (ed), *1997 Fordham Corp. L. Inst.* (Juris, 1998), 234.

[315] Agreement (n 310, above) Art VIII(1); for the provisions on confidentiality affecting the Commission, see para 13.095, below.

[316] ibid, Art III(3). There were 82 formal notifications by the EU to the US in 2005, and 27 from the US to the EU: *Report on Competition Policy 2005*, para 685.

[317] ibid, Art V.

[318] Paras 678 and 682.

[319] OJ 1999 L175/50. The Commission has stated that its contacts with the Canadian Competition Bureau have been 'frequent and fruitful', taking the form of 'regular telephone

coordination of their competition authorities and to lessen the possibility or impact of differences between the parties in the application of their competition laws. Under the agreement, each Party agrees to notify the other of enforcement activities which may affect 'the important interests' of the other Party, to render each other assistance and to coordinate their enforcement activity where both have an interest in a particular case. In 2003, an agreement in similar terms was concluded with the government of Japan.[320] In May 2004, the Commission signed detailed terms of reference for a dialogue with the government of China on competition matters.[321] The primary aim of this agreement is to establish a permanent forum of consultation and transparency between China and the EU in this area and to enhance the EU's technical and capacity-building assistance to China with regard to competition policy. Cooperation between the Commission and the competition authorities of other OECD member countries is carried out on the basis of a Recommendation adopted by the OECD in 1995.[322] International bodies such as the OECD and UNCTAD also promulgate voluntary codes containing provisions about competition.[323]

1.103 **Other association agreements.** The Community has bilateral agreements establishing an association with a number of other countries. [324] Most of these agreements contain some reference to competition but in many cases the relevant provisions are of a rather general and exhortatory nature. Those which have specific

---

calls, e-mails, and conference calls between case teams'. See *Report on Competition Policy 2005*, paras 686–687. Under the 1999 Agreement, there were eight formal notifications by the Commission in 2005 and one notification by the Canadian authorities; ibid, para 689.

320 Agreement with Japan, OJ 2003 L183/12. The Commission has stated that its contacts with the Japanese competition authority increased considerably in 2005: see *Report on Competition Policy 2005*, para 690.

321 See (2004) 2 EC Competition Policy Newsletter 27.

322 Recommendation of the Council concerning Cooperation between Member Countries on Anti-Competitive Practices Affecting International Trade, 27 July 1995, C(95)130/Final.

323 See, in particular, the OECD Recommendation concerning Cooperation between Member Countries on Anticompetitive Practices Affecting International Trade (1995), C(95)130/Final; and its Recommendation concerning Effective Action Against 'Hard-Core' Cartels (1998), C(98)35/Final. See also Suurnäkki, 'OECD peer review gives positive assessment on competition policy and enforcement in the European Union' (2006) 2 EC Competition Policy Newsletter 7.

324 The Community is also bound by the World Trade Organisation ('WTO') Agreement and the annexed multilateral agreements, including the General Agreement on Tariffs and Trade 1994 (GATT) and the Agreement on Trade-Related Aspects of Intellectual Property Rights (TRIPS): see OJ 1994 L336/3 and Opinion 1/94 (*'the WTO Case'*) [1994] ECR I-5267, [1995] 1 CMLR 205. But these Agreements do not have direct effect or create rights in individuals: Case C-149/96 *Portugal v Council* [1999] ECR I-8395, [2001] 1 CMLR 857; Cases C-300 & 392/98 *Dior v TUK Consultancy* [2000] ECR I-11307; save that exceptionally the legality of a Community measure may be reviewed in the light of the WTO Agreement where it was designed to implement a particular obligation in the context of the WTO: Case T-19/01 *Chiquita Brands v Commission* [2005] ECR II-315, [2006] All ER (EC) 63, para 115. See further Case T-201/04 *Microsoft v Commission*, judgment of 17 September 2007, paras 798–802 (rejecting the argument that Art 82 must be interpreted consistently with the TRIPS Agreement); see Postscript below.

competition provisions include the so-called Euro-Med Agreements forming an association with north African and Middle Eastern countries[325] and in the EC–South Africa Agreement of 1999.[326] DG Competition maintains a list on its website, in the section relating to International: Bilateral Relations which has a link to a table showing the Community's relationships with countries from Albania to Zimbabwe and providing links to the competition provision extracts from the relevant agreements.

The International Competition Network.   The International Competition **1.104** Network ('ICN')[327] was launched in New York in October 2001. Membership is open to national and multinational competition agencies entrusted with the enforcement of antitrust laws and the ICN currently has over 80 members. The ICN operates through working groups devoted to selected topics (for example, mergers, cartels, leniency programmes and unilateral conduct) which aim to produce guidelines as to best practice. The ICN as a whole holds an annual conference, hosted by a different member authority each year. Despite being non-binding (or perhaps as a result), the ICN has proved very successful in fostering cooperation between authorities around the world and in promoting convergence of ideas and practice.[328]

7. The Territorial Jurisdiction of the Community Institutions

In general.   On the face of it, the territorial ambit of EC competition rules is **1.105** very wide since it strikes at any agreement or abusive conduct which has the necessary effect on competition and trade between Member States, whatever the nationality or territorial location of the undertakings concerned. Agreements which are directly or overtly concerned only with exports from or imports to the Community may nevertheless have an effect upon intra-Community trade and so fall within the scope of the competition rules. The following topics are considered here: (i) the application of Article 81(1) to agreements affecting trade into the Community from third countries; (ii) the application of Article 81(1) to agreements affecting trade from the Community to third countries; and (iii) the extent

---

[325] The Euro-Med process, launched in Barcelona in November 1995, is intended to embrace 12 Mediterranean counterparts in a free-trade zone by 2010. See Lenaerts and Van Nuffel, *Consitutional Law of the European Union* (2nd edn, 2005), para 20–020. See, eg the Euro-Med Agreements with Morocco and Algeria in *Encyclopedia of European Union Law (Constitutional Texts)*, Vol 3, paras 46.0071, 46.0301.

[326] Agreement on Trade, Development and Co-operation between the EC, its Member States and the Republic of South Africa, OJ 1999 L311/1.

[327] See generally the ICN website at http://www.internationalcompetitionnetwork.org/.

[328] For discussion of the first two years of the ICN's activities, see (2003) 3 EC Competition Policy Newsletter 37. The activity of the ICN is now summarised in the 'International activities' section of DG Comp's annual Report on Competition Policy.

to which jurisdiction to apply Articles 81 and 82 and the Merger Regulation is asserted over undertakings outside the Community. The scope of the territory of the Community and the effect of the EEA Agreement and other bilateral arrangements between the Community and third countries has already been considered above.[329]

(a) Trade into the Community from third countries

1.106 **Agreements on imports into the Community.** It is well established that a restrictive agreement between undertakings within the Community and their competitors in third countries intended to reduce the supply, within the Community, of products originating in third countries is capable of falling within Article 81(1).[330] Further, an agreement relating to imports into the Community from third countries which has as its object or effect an appreciable restriction of competition within the Community, such as an exclusive distributorship for a territory within the Community, is likely to fall within Article 81(1).[331] The Commission emphasised this principle over 30 years ago in a Notice on Imports of Japanese Products[332] and it has been reiterated in many other decisions.[333] Indeed, any agreement which potentially reduces competition in the Community by undertakings in third states may fall under Article 81(1) and it is irrelevant that one or more parties are situated outside the Community.[334] Once it is established that the agreement in question restricts competition in relation to the import of goods into the Community, it is not thereafter difficult to find that the agreement is liable to interfere with the natural movement of trade within the Community and thus, at least potentially, to affect trade between Member States.[335]

---

[329] Paras 1.084 and 1.086, above.

[330] Case 51/75 *EMI Records v CBS United Kingdom* [1976] ECR 811, [1976] 2 CMLR 235, para 28; *Aluminium Imports from Eastern Europe*, OJ 1985 L92/1, [1987] 3 CMLR 813.

[331] Case 22/71 *Béguelin Import v GL Import Export* [1971] ECR 949, [1972] CMLR 81; Case 71/74 *Frubo v Commission* [1975] ECR 563, [1975] 2 CMLR 123.

[332] Notice in imports of Japanese products, OJ 1972 C111/13.

[333] eg *Franco-Japanese Ballbearings*, OJ 1974 L343/19, [1975] 1 CMLR D8; *Preserved Mushrooms*, OJ 1975 L29/26, [1975] 1 CMLR D83; *Ansac*, OJ 1991 L152/54 (US Webb-Pomerene Act association of soda-ash producers; the Commission rejected the argument that the cartel enabled a strong market entrant from the United States, despite having condemned ICI and Solvay for sharing the EC market).

[334] eg *Reuter/BASF*, OJ 1976 L254/40, [1976] 2 CMLR D44 (restrictive covenant affecting transfer of know-how to undertakings outside the Community that could become suppliers in the Community); *Siemens/Fanuc*, OJ 1985 L376/29, [1988] 4 CMLR 945 (cooperative exclusive dealing agreement between German and Japanese manufacturers); *Quantel International-Continuum/ Quantel SA*, OJ 1992 L235/9, [1993] 5 CMLR 497 (market-sharing on de-merger by French company of its US subsidiary); *Cartonboard*, OJ 1994 L243/1, [1994] 5 CMLR 547, para 139 (cartel of which many of the members had their head offices outside the EC); *GEAE/P&W*, OJ 2000 L58/16, [2000] 5 CMLR 49 (joint venture between two major US manufacturers to develop engine for very large commercial aircraft; now would fall under the amended Merger Reg).

[335] *Frubo v Commission* (n 331, above). But Art 81(1) is not infringed if, on the facts, the relevant trade is plainly confined to trade between one Member State and a non-Member State:

(b) Trade from the Community to third countries

Agreements concerning exports from the Community.   In general, agreements   **1.107**
or clauses in agreements relating exclusively to trade outside the Community do
not fall within Article 81(1).[336] However, it does not necessarily follow that an
agreement falls outside Article 81(1) merely because it relates to trade outside the
Community since the agreement itself may still have a significant effect upon
competition within the Community. Therefore, a cartel of undertakings in the
Community concerning only markets outside the Community will infringe
Article 81(1) if it has the object of diverting surpluses from within the Community,
or of preventing re-export to home markets.[337] A cargo-sharing agreement between
carriers operating on routes from one Member State to third countries distorts
competition with carriers in other Member States and also as between Community
exporters.[338] An export ban on sales to third countries included in a distribution
agreement for territories in the Community, even if it does not have the object of
restricting trade between Member States may nonetheless have that effect, and
accordingly infringe Article 81(1), if in the absence of such a restriction there
would be a realistic possibility of re-import of the products into the Community,
having regard, for example, to the level of customs duties.[339] Similar considerations
apply to a licensing agreement for production in the Community that prohibits

---

Case 28/77 *Tepea v Commission* [1978] ECR 1391, 3 CMLR 392, para 48 (no infringement prior to UK accession to the Community).

[336] Case 174/84 *Bulk Oil v Sun International* [1986] ECR 559, [1986] 2 CMLR 732, para 44. See generally *Rieckermann*, JO 1968 L276/25, [1968] CMLR D78; *DECA*, JO 1964 2761, [1965] CMLR 50; *VVVF*, JO 1969 L168/22, [1970] CMLR Dl. See also *Zinc Producer Group*, OJ 1984 L220/27, [1985] 2 CMLR 108, para 84 (Commission considered Art 81(1) did not apply to those members of an international cartel outside the Community who scarcely participated in the Community market; *sed quaere*).

[337] Cases 40/73, etc, *Suiker Unie v Commission* [1975] ECR 1663, [1976] 1 CMLR 295, paras 558 *et seq*; Cases T-25/95, etc, *Cimenteries v Commission* [2000] ECR II-491, [2000] 5 CMLR 204, paras 3851 *et seq* (esp at paras 3920–3930).

[338] *French-West African Shipowners' Committee*, OJ 1992 LI34/1, [1993] 5 CMLR 446, para 43: the less favourable terms which participants in the agreement can impose on exporters places shipments from that State at a disadvantage, and thereby also distorts competition between Community ports. See also the more recent liner conference cases, para 5.033, below.

[339] *SABA (No. 1)*, OJ 1976 L28/19, [1976] 1 CMLR D61, para 35; *Junghans*, OJ 1977 L30/10, [1977] 1 CMLR D82. However, in both cases, once the free trade area came into effect with the EFTA States on 1 July 1977, a restriction on sale to those States would infringe Art 81(1) as the customs duties that made re-importation uneconomic would cease to apply. And see *Tretorn*, OJ 1994 L378/45, [1997] 4 CMLR 860, paras 65–66: although re-exportation from Switzerland was unlikely, a ban on sales to Swiss dealers was nonetheless held to infringe Art 81(1) since it prevented them from buying in one Member State and reselling in another without physically importing into Switzerland. Note that in its Art 19(3) Notice in *Chanel*, OJ 1994 C334/11, the Commission required deletion from Chanel's agreements with its selected retailers for watches of the ban on export to all countries which had concluded free trade agreements with the Community. See also *The Distillers Company Limited*, OJ 1978 L50/16, [1978] 1 CMLR 400, paras 72–73 (appeal on other issues dismissed, Case 30/78 *Distillers v Commission* [1980] ECR 2229, [1980] 3 CMLR 121).

export to a third country.[340] Moreover, if an agreement relates to exports to an EEA State, the parallel competition provisions of the EEA Agreement will apply.[341] In each case a careful examination of the individual circumstances is required to determine the likely or foreseeable effect of the agreement.[342]

1.108 **Likelihood of re-imports.** When territorial restrictions that prevent sale in the Community are included in an agreement for distribution, or a licence to manufacture, outside the Community, the application of Article 81(1) depends on the legislative and economic context of the agreement. Where the distributor or licensee is situated in a third country, an effect on trade within the Community could arise only by importation. If that is not a realistic commercial prospect, for example because of the nature of the product or because any price differential would be eroded by transport costs or customs duties, the agreement falls outside Article 81(1).[343] Where the distributor is another Community undertaking, a third country 'destination clause' operates also to prevent direct sales between Member States. If competition for such products in the Community is limited, a clause that prevents parallel imports may have an appreciable anti-competitive effect and infringe Article 81(1).[344] In *Javico v YSLP*,[345] the Court of Justice

---

[340] *Kabelmetal/Luchaire*, OJ 1975 L222/34, [1975] 2 CMLR D40 (re-importation unlikely because the products were not suitable for sale through intermediaries); *Campari*, OJ 1978 L70/69, [1978] 2 CMLR 397, para 60 (double excise duties, taxes and trade margins would preclude re-importation). See also *Schlegel/CPIO*, OJ 1983 L351/20, [1984] 2 CMLR 179 (negative clearance granted to manufacturing licence restricted to the Community but sales permitted worldwide: no grounds to suggest that it would affect competition within the Community).

[341] See paras 1.086 *et seq*, above. Decisions pre-1994 must be read subject to that qualification.

[342] See also Art 82 cases, where the ECJ has held that if the abuse of a dominant position adversely affects a competitor within the Community, this has repercussions on the competitive structure within the common market and it is therefore irrelevant that the abusive conduct relates only to activities outside, or exports from, the Community: Cases 6 & 7/73 *Commercial Solvents v Commission* [1974] ECR 223, [1974] 1 CMLR 309, paras 33–34; Case 22/79 *Greenwich Film Production v SACEM* [1979] ECR 3275, [1980] 1 CMLR 629, paras 11–13.

[343] eg *Raymond-Nagoya*, JO 1972 L143/39, [1972] CMLR D45 (licence to Japanese company to manufacture in Japan with exclusive territory in the Far East: technical nature of the products made it necessary to be close to the customers); *Grosfillex-Fillistorf*, JO 1964 915, [1964] CMLR 237 (distributor in Switzerland: no material price difference between Switzerland and the Community, where there was substantial competition for such products). cf *BBC Brown Boveri*, OJ 1988 L301/68, [1989] 4 CMLR 610 (exclusive know-how licence to Japanese company for manufacture and sale of products in the Far East in the context of a joint research and development agreement: because exports of the product to the Community would have been feasible, notwithstanding the large distances involved, the licence came within Art 81(1)). See also the decisions concerning intra-Community agreements in nn 339 and 340, above.

[344] See Cases 29 & 30/83 *CRAM and Rheinzink v Commission* [1984] ECR 1679, [1985] 1 CMLR 688: German producer supplied sheet zinc to a Belgian purchaser on condition that he resold the goods in Egypt; the vendor was the only producer in Germany and the ECJ held that the clause was 'essentially designed to prevent the re-export of goods to the country of production so as to maintain a system of dual prices and restrict competition on the common market' (para 28).

[345] Case C-306/96 *Javico v YSLP* [1998] ECR I-1983, [1998] 5 CMLR 172. Case 14967, NJ 1993/382 *Philips Information Systems BV and Solid International BV*, judgment of Dutch

considered the exclusive agreements entered into by Yves Saint Laurents Parfums (YSLP) with a German company for distribution in Russia/Ukraine and Slovenia,[346] in circumstances where YSLP's selective distribution system for territories within the Community was covered by a decision applying Article 81(3). Noting that the restriction covered not only the Community but all third countries other than the contractual territories, the Court held that the restrictions 'must be construed as not being intended to exclude parallel imports and marketing of the contractual products within the Community but as being designed to enable the producer to penetrate a market outside the Community by supplying a sufficient quantity of contractual products to that market'.[347] Whilst the agreements therefore did not have the object of restricting competition within the Community, it was necessary to consider whether they had such an effect. That would depend on the degree to which the Community market in products of that kind was already competitive and, as regards the potential for re-imports, whether there was a substantial price difference that would not be eroded by the costs involved in re-importation.[348] Although the judgment is somewhat confusing in its lack of distinction between inter-brand and intra-brand competition,[349] the Court's approach is that unless the Community market is oligopolistic, prevention of direct, parallel imports by such a third country destination clause should not be regarded as having an anti-competitive effect, and that the test under Article 81(1) is then the same as if the distributor was itself outside the Community: ie whether there is a realistic likelihood of re-imports from the country of destination.

Imports into the Community: *de minimis.*   In accordance with general principles, an agreement that restricts imports into the Community may fall outside Article 81(1) under the *de minimis* rule if it affects trade between Member States only to an extent which is not appreciable.[350] Moreover, in *Javico v YSLP*, the   **1.109**

Supreme Court, 23 April 1993 concerned a shipment of outdated personal computers, produced in Canada, and sold by Philips to Solid International. Both Philips and Solid International were based in the Netherlands. The purchasing agreement contained an export clause stipulating that the goods be sold outside the Community in Eastern Europe. However, Solid sold the complete shipment within the Netherlands claiming the clause contravened Art 81. Philips argued that the export clause could not affect inter-State trade since the computers were produced outside the Community, were to be transported outside the Community, and were destined to be sold outside the Community. The Dutch Supreme Court decided that the Court of Appeal had not properly considered these facts and annulled the Court's judgment.

346 At that time not a Member State.

347 *Javico v YSLP* (n 345, above) para 19.

348 The judgment refers to customs duties, transport costs and the other costs resulting from export to a third country and re-importation into the community: para 24. The reference to other costs ('*les autres coûts*') is omitted from the English translation.

349 There is also no discussion of the potential exhaustion of YSLP's trade mark rights, perhaps because that was not part of the questions referred.

350 *Tepea* (n 335, above) para 47. See para 1.124, below.

Court of Justice stated: 'In that regard, intra-Community trade cannot be appreciably affected if the products intended for markets outside the Community account for only a very small percentage of the total market for those products in the territory of the Common Market'.[351] This appears to go somewhat further than the usual *de minimis* threshold, especially as the quantity of luxury perfume exported to the Russian/Ukrainian market was evidently not insignificant.[352] On the other hand, even if the conduct of an individual party to an agreement does not itself appreciably affect trade within the Community, the small scale of that party's participation in the agreement will not exculpate it if the effect of the agreement as a whole is appreciable.[353]

(c) Jurisdiction over undertakings outside the Community

1.110 **The issue.** The question of substantive, or subject-matter, jurisdiction under Community competition law arises not only as regards Article 81 but also in connection with Article 82 and the Merger Regulation. When a non-EC undertaking engages in conduct directly within the Community, such conduct is clearly subject to Community law on the basis of territorial jurisdiction. It is the application of Community competition law to activity carried on outside the Community (and now the European Economic Area), especially by non-EC undertakings, that gives rise to a problem. How far a State may properly apply its laws to conduct carried out beyond its territory is a controversial issue under public international law.[354] On the one hand, the application by one State, or group of States, of their law to conduct on the territory of another State can be regarded as an infringement of the latter State's sovereignty. On the other hand, in an increasingly interdependent world, competition law that is based primarily on economic consequences becomes stunted and artificial if it cannot reach any activity conducted beyond the legislating State's territorial boundaries. The extraterritorial reach of US antitrust law in the past provoked strong reaction from other countries, including some of the EC Member States, but the Community has itself had to confront such issues in the exercise of its own jurisdiction.[355]

---

[351] *Javico v YSLP* (n 345, above) para 26.

[352] See the Opinion of AG Tesauro, ibid, paras 14–15, noting that it was undisputed that large volumes of re-importation had in fact occurred and that as it was the policy of large groups to purchase the products throughout the European market, subsequent re-export to another Member State was almost inevitable. However, the ECJ declined to make any determination on the facts.

[353] *Aluminium Imports from Eastern Europe* (n 330, above) para 13; see further para 1.127, below.

[354] See Jennings and Watts (eds), *Oppenheim's International Law* (9th edn, 1992), Vol I, pp 472–478.

[355] See generally Neale and Stephens, *International Business and National Jurisdiction* (1988); Roth, 'Reasonable Extraterritoriality: Correcting the Balance of Interests' (1992) ICLQ 245.

Wood Pulp.   The application of Article 81 to agreements concluded between under-   **1.111**
takings outside the Community was the principal issue arising in *Wood Pulp I*.[356]
The Commission's decision[357] concluded that 41 wood pulp producers, and two
of their trade associations, all having their registered offices outside the Community,
had engaged in concerted practices relating to the prices charged through subsidiaries or agents to paper-makers within the Community. The decision was challenged on a number of grounds and the Court of Justice ordered that the
jurisdictional issues be determined separately from the substantive issues.[358]

Wood Pulp: **the implementation doctrine.**   The Court of Justice rejected the   **1.112**
argument that the Commission had incorrectly assessed the territorial scope of
Article 81. The Court stated that where producers established in third countries
sell directly to purchasers established in the Community and engage in price competition in order to win orders from those customers, that constitutes competition
within the common market. It follows that where those producers concert on the
prices to be charged and put that concertation into effect by selling at prices
which are coordinated, they are taking part in concertation which has the object
and effect of restricting competition within the common market. The Court
continued:

> 'It should be observed that an infringement of Article [81], such as the conclusion of
> an agreement which has had the effect of restricting competition within the common
> market, consists of conduct made up of two elements, the formation of the agree-
> ment, decision or concerted practice and the implementation thereof. If the applica-
> bility of prohibitions laid down under competition law were made to depend on the
> place where the agreement, decision or concerted practice was formed, the result
> would obviously be to give undertakings an easy means of evading those prohibi-
> tions. The decisive factor is therefore the place where it is implemented.

> The producers in this case implemented their pricing agreement within the common
> market. It is immaterial in that respect whether or not they had recourse to subsidiar-
> ies, agents, sub-agents, or branches within the Community in order to make their
> contacts with purchasers within the Community.

---

[356]   Cases 89/85, etc, *Åhlström v Commission ('Wood Pulp I')* [1988] ECR 5193, [1988] 4 CMLR 901.
For a later example of a cartel of undertakings in non-Member States, see *Ansac*, OJ 1991 L152/54.
In Case T-395/94 *Atlantic Container v Commission (TAA Agreement)* [2002] ECR II-875, [2002]
4 CMLR 1008, the CFI, citing *Woodpulp*, stated 'where producers established outside the Community
sell directly to purchasers established in the Community and engage in price competition in order to
win orders from those customers, that constitutes competition within the common market, so that
concertation between those producers on the prices to be charged to their customers in the Community
has the object and effect of restricting competition within the common market' (para 72).

[357]   OJ 1985 L85/1, [1985] 3 CMLR 474.

[358]   Much of the decision was subsequently annulled by the ECJ in its substantive judgment:
Cases C-89/85, etc, *Åhlström Osakeyhtiö v Commission ('Wood Pulp II')* [1993] ECR 1–1307, [1993]
4 CMLR 407. See further para 2.046, below.

Accordingly the Community's jurisdiction to apply its competition rules to such conduct is covered by the territoriality principle as universally recognised in public international law.'[359]

The Court accordingly articulated a principle based on the territorial implementation of a cartel, irrespective of where the cartel agreement was made or the parties were based.[360]

1.113 *Gencor:* **the effects doctrine.** Further consideration was given to the scope of the Community's jurisdiction by the Court of First Instance, in the context of the Merger Regulation, in the *Gencor* case.[361] The Regulation applies to a concentration according to quantitative thresholds based on worldwide and Community-wide turnover.[362] The Commission prohibited a proposed joint venture between a South African and a British company on the grounds that this would bring under common control the platinum metals production carried on by their respective subsidiaries, which were located in South Africa.[363] One of the grounds on which the parties challenged the decision was that it involved an impermissible assertion of extra-territorial jurisdiction. The Court of First Instance upheld the Commission's jurisdiction under the Merger Regulation on the basis that the concentration would be implemented in the Community, since the parties made significant sales to purchasers in Member States. The Court here stated that it was following *Wood Pulp.* However, the focus of merger control is on structural arrangements rather than conduct, and the structural change produced by this concentration would essentially take place outside the Community. Implicitly acknowledging that jurisdictionally sensitive issues could arise, the Court went on to consider expressly the compatibility of the decision with public international law.[364] In an important passage, the Court adopted what might be described as a 'qualified effects test' of the kind urged by AG Darmon in *Wood Pulp I:*[365]

'Application of the Regulation is justified under public international law when it is foreseeable that a proposed concentration will have an immediate and substantial effect in the Community.'[366]

---

[359] *Wood Pulp I* (n 356, above) paras 16–18.

[360] The ECJ declined to follow the Opinion of AG Darmon, ibid, paras 54–58, who urged it to adopt a criterion of 'direct, substantial and foreseeable effect', discussing the US and international law on the subject.

[361] Case T-102/96 *Gencor v Commission* [1999] ECR II-753, [1999] 4 CMLR 971, [1999] All ER (EC) 289. See Broberg, (2000) ICLQ 172.

[362] See Chap 8, below.

[363] Case M.619 *Gencor/Lonrho*, OJ 1997 LI 1/30, [1999] 4 CMLR 1076. The arrangement constituted a full-function, concentrative JV and so came within the then Merger Reg.

[364] Community law must comply with public international law: see Cases 21/72, etc, *International Fruit Co v Produktschap voor Groenten en Fruit* [1972] ECR 1219, [1975] 2 CMLR 1, para 6; Case C-286/90 *Poulsen and Diva Corp* [1992] ECR I-6019, para 9.

[365] *Wood Pulp I* (n 356, above). The CFI substituted 'immediate' for 'direct' but this seems to make no practical difference.

[366] *Gencor v Commission* (n 361, above) para 90.

Noting that the concentration, by creating a dominant duopoly, would give rise to a situation where effective competition would have been significantly impeded on the common market, the Court proceeded to find that the three criteria of 'immediate, substantial and foreseeable effect' were satisfied on the facts of the case. Accordingly, the Court in *Gencor* did not enunciate the qualified effects doctrine in substitution for the implementation doctrine as the basis of Community jurisdiction, but as placing a boundary on the jurisdiction that might otherwise result from application of the implementation doctrine. Formally, therefore, jurisdiction over undertakings outside the Community must satisfy both doctrines; but in practice, at the Community level, this seems unlikely to produce a different result from application of the effects doctrine alone.[367]

International comity.   In *Gencor*, one of the parties was incorporated in a **1.114** Member State, although the concentration was to be put into effect outside the Community. However, the same criteria would apply when a concentration involves no Community undertakings, a matter that caused controversy in the Commission's scrutiny of the high-profile merger between two major US aircraft manufacturers in *Boeing/McDonnell Douglas*, although that was finally cleared subject to undertakings.[368] In the United States, in response to foreign concerns about the application of their antitrust laws, courts and scholars have developed the concept that the exercise of an extraterritorial jurisdiction may be limited to take account of important policy interests of another State where the activities in question take place.[369] In *Eastern Aluminium*,[370] the Commission reflected this approach in indicating that it would be appropriate to show self-restraint in the exercise of jurisdiction when it would require any of the undertakings to act in a way contrary to the requirements of their domestic laws, or when the application of Community law might adversely affect the important interests of a non-Member State. But such an interest 'would have to be so important as to prevail over the fundamental interest of the community that competition within the common market is not distorted'. In *Gencor*, the Court of First Instance referred to the parties' contention that there was such a principle of 'non-interference', but

---

367 A theoretical example of the distinction is a collective boycott of the Community by undertakings situated outside. But given the commercial importance of the EC market, such an absolute restriction seems very unlikely; cf the position for a single Member State.

368 Case M.877 *Boeing/McDonnell Douglas*, OJ 1997 L336/16. See further para 8.060, below.

369 See in particular *Timberlane Lumber Co v Bank of America*, 549 (9th Cir 1976); *Mannington Mills Inc v Congoleum Corp* 595 F. 2d 1287 (3rd Cir 1979); *Restatement (Third) of the Foreign Relations Law of the United States*, para 403. But cf *Hartford Fire Insurance Co v California*, 509 US 764, 113 S Ct 2891 (1993). See also the reliance on comity by the US Supreme Court in interpreting the Foreign Trade Antitrust Improvements Act 1982, which provides a limited exclusion to the application of the Sherman Act to foreign commerce, in *F Hoffmann-La Roche v Empagran*, 542 US 155, 124 S Ct 2359 (2004).

370 *Aluminium Imports from Eastern Europe* (n 330, above) para 14.7. No such interests were found in that case.

found on the facts that there was neither a conflict between what was required by the Community and by the South African government nor any basis for showing that the concentration would affect South Africa's vital economic or commercial interests. Therefore the Court expressly declined to decide whether such a principle of non-interference exists in public international law.[371] As regards enforcement by the Commission, the difficulties can be minimised through international cooperation agreements whereby the Community and the other contracting State agree to consult and have regard to the important interests of each other when deciding on investigations and remedies.[372] However, such international agreements cannot solve the problems that may be caused by private actions in national courts. In such cases, it is not yet clear that Community law requires the controversial 'balancing of interests' that some United States courts have adopted.[373]

8. Effect on Trade between Member States

(a) Generally

1.115 **Rule of jurisdiction.** The expression 'which may affect trade between Member States' is common to both Article 81 and Article 82[374] and defines the boundary between conduct which is subject to Community law and conduct which is governed solely by national law.[375] The concept of 'effect on trade between Member States' is thus best understood as a rule of jurisdiction, enabling Community law to regulate all restrictive agreements and abusive conduct by dominant undertakings having appreciable repercussions at Community level.[376] The limitation

---

[371] *Gencor* (n 361, above) paras 103–105. Although the US *Restatement* (n 369, above) expresses this approach as a rule of international law, it is probably better regarded today as principle of comity that may, in time, develop into a rule of law. For comity, see *Oppenheim's International Law* (n 354, above), 50–51; Brownlie, *Principles of Public International Law* (6th edn, 2003), 28.

[372] For the cooperation agreements entered into by the Community, see paras 1.096 *et seq*, above.

[373] See n 369, above, and Roth (n 355, above). It is unclear whether that approach governs *existence* of jurisdiction, the *exercise* of jurisdiction, or merely the remedies that may be imposed.

[374] See generally Faull & Nickpay, *The EC Law of Competition* (2nd edn, 2007), paras 3.337 *et seq*; O'Donoghue and Padilla, *The Law and Economics of Article 82 EC* (2006), Chap 14.

[375] Cases 56 & 58/64 *Consten and Grundig v Commission* [1966] ECR 299, 341, [1966] CMLR 418, 471; Cases 6 & 7/73 *Commercial Solvents v Commission* [1974] ECR 223, [1974] 1 CMLR 309, paras 30–33; Case T-395/94 *Atlantic Container v Commission (TAA Agreement)* [2002] ECR II-875, [2002] 4 CMLR 1008, [2002] All ER (EC) 684, para 80; Cases C-295/04, etc, *Manfredi* [2006] ECR I-6619, [2006] 5 CMLR 980, [2007] All ER (EC) 27, para 41; Case C-238/05 *Asnef-Equifax v Ausbanc* [2006] ECR I-11125, [2007] 4 CMLR 224, para 33. See also para 12 of the Effect on Trade Notice, OJ 2004 C101/81: Vol II, App C.17.

[376] However, an undertaking is not entitled to refuse to supply the Commission with information on the ground that, in its view, the agreement is not capable of affecting trade: *RAI/UNITEL*, OJ 1978 L157/39, [1978] 3 CMLR 306; *Fire Insurance (D)*, OJ 1982 L80/36, [1982] 2 CMLR 159. See also para 13.034, below.

imposed on the prohibitions in the competition rules by this requirement also means that action taken at a Community level to enforce those rules complies with the principle of subsidiarity.[377] Moreover, the concept has assumed additional importance under the Modernisation regime introduced by Regulation 1/2003:[378] where an agreement or practice has an effect on inter-State trade, a national court or competition authority is obliged to apply EC competition law as well as national competition law, and cannot prohibit under national competition law an agreement which does not infringe Article 81.[379] The same concept also applies as a condition of the exceptional jurisdiction of the Commission under the Merger Regulation to investigate, on request from a Member State, a concentration which does not have a 'Community dimension'.[380] However, as regards the State aids rules, the formulation in Article 87 of the Treaty is subtly different, in that it refers to aid which 'affects trade between Member States'. Although the omission of the word 'may' found in Articles 81 and 82 has been held not to be significant, the effect on trade criterion under Article 87 has nonetheless received a slightly different interpretation and does not incorporate an inherent appreciability threshold.[381] The effect on trade criterion in the context of State aid is accordingly discussed separately in Chapter 15, below.[382]

The Commission's Notice. As part of the Modernisation package,[383] the **1.116** Commission issued in May 2004 a Notice ('the Effect on Trade Notice') setting out guidelines on the effect on trade concept in Articles 81 and 82 of the Treaty.[384] The aim of the Notice is to give guidance to the courts and authorities of the Member States on the methodology for applying this requirement and to describe its application in frequently occurring situations. The Notice also explains the Commission's approach to the requirement that the effect on trade must be appreciable, and sets out for the purpose of Article 81(1) a presumption as to when agreements will not appreciably affect inter-State trade.

---

[377] Case T-168/01 *GlaxoSmithKline Services v Commission* [2006] ECR II-2969, [2006] 5 CMLR 1589, paras 201 *et seq* (on appeal, Cases C-501/06P, etc, *GlaxoSmithKline Services v Commission*, not yet decided); Cases T-259/02, etc, *Raiffeisen Zentralbank Österreich*, judgment of 14 December 2006, para 165 (on appeal, Cases C-125/07, etc, not yet decided); and see paras 1.028 *et seq*, above.

[378] See para 1.058, above.

[379] Art 3 of Reg 1/2003: Vol II, App B.3. This also triggers the rights and obligation of a national competition authority as regards notification of the case to the Commission and the exchange of information: ibid, Arts 11–12. See generally paras 14.018 *et seq*, below.

[380] Art 22 of Reg 139/2004, OJ 2004 L24/1: Vol II, App D.1. See paras 8.097–8.100, below.

[381] Such a qualification, although not for all sectors, was therefore introduced by regulation: see now Reg 1998/2006, OJ 2006 L379/5.

[382] See paras 15.026–15.028, below.

[383] See para 1.058, above.

[384] Effect on Trade Notice, OJ 2004 C101/81: Vol II, App C.17. The Notice does not provide guidance on the effect on trade concept contained in Art 87 on State aid: para 4.

1.117 **Trade.** The concept of 'trade' has been described by the Court of Justice as having 'a wide scope'.[385] It covers all economic activity, including not only the supply of goods but also the supply of services such as banking and money transmission,[386] insurance,[387] loss adjustment,[388] foreign exchange broking,[389] postal services,[390] the management of artistic copyrights,[391] the organisation of trade fairs,[392] employment agency services,[393] television broadcasts,[394] public services such as ambulance services,[395] the services of public utilities, such as gas and electricity,[396] and the economic aspects of sports, including the rules of sporting bodies governing entitlement to compete in sporting events.[397] The performance of individual artistes,[398] the provision of consulting services by an individual[399] and the supply of professional services[400] have all been held to be 'trade' for the purposes of Article 81. 'Trade' covers the establishment of a presence in a Member State[401]

---

[385] Case 172/80 *Züchner v Bayerische Vereinsbank* [1981] ECR 2021, [1982] 1 CMLR 313, para 18. *Quaere* the position of charitable activities: *Re Dutch Banks*, OJ 1989 L253/1, [1990] 4 CMLR 768, para 59.

[386] eg *Züchner v Bayerische Vereinsbank*, above; *Uniform Eurocheques*, OJ 1985 L35/43, [1985] 3 CMLR 434; Cases C-215 & 216/96 *Bagnasco* [1999] ECR I-135, [1999] 4 CMLR 624, [1999] All ER (EC) 678; *Raiffeisen Zentralbank Österreich* (n 377, above).

[387] Case 45/85 *Verband der Sachversicherer v Commission* [1987] ECR 405, [1988] 4 CMLR 264; *Manfredi* (n 375, above).

[388] Case 90/76 *Van Ameyde v UCI* [1977] ECR 1091, [1977] 2 CMLR 478.

[389] *Sarabex* [1979] 1 CMLR 262; *VIIIth Report on Competition Policy* (1978), points 35–37; Cases T-44/02, etc, *Dresdner Bank v Commission* [2006] ECR II-3567, [2007] 4 CMLR 467.

[390] *REIMS II*, OJ 1999 L275/17, [2000] 4 CMLR 704; Cases C-147 & 148/97 *Deutsche Post/ GZS (Remail)* [2000] ECR I-825, [2000] 4 CMLR 838.

[391] See, eg Case 127/73 *BRT v SABAM* [1974] ECR 51 and 313, [1974] 2 CMLR 238, 269 and 282.

[392] See, eg *SMM&T Exhibition Agreement*, OJ 1983 L376/1, [1984] 1 CMLR 611, and paras 5.152 *et seq*, below.

[393] Case C-41/90 *Höfner & Elser v Macrotron* [1991] ECR I-1979, [1993] 4 CMLR 306 (a case under Art 82).

[394] eg Case 155/73 *Sacchi* [1974] ECR 409, [1974] 2 CMLR 177; *Eurovision*, OJ 2000 L151/18, [2000] 5 CMLR 650, on appeal Cases T-185/00, etc, *Métropole Télévision -M6 v Commission* [2002] ECR II-3805, [2003] 4 CMLR 707 (further appeal dismissed, Case C-470/02P *UER v M6*, Order of 27 September 2004).

[395] Case C-475/99 *Ambulanz Glöckner* [2001] ECR I-8089, [2002] 4 CMLR 726, paras 44 *et seq*.

[396] eg Case C-393/92 *Almelo* [1994] ECR I-1477 (electricity); *Transgás/Turbogás*, XXVIth Report on Competition Policy (1996), p 135 (gas).

[397] Case C-519/04P *Meca-Medina v Commission* [2006] ECR I-6991, [2006] 5 CMLR 1023, [2006] All ER (EC) 1057.

[398] *RAI/UNITEL*, OJ 1978 L157/39, [1978] 3 CMLR 306; *XIIth Report on Competition Policy* (1982), point 90 (Opera singers at La Scala).

[399] *Reuter/BASF*, OJ 1976 L254/40, [1976] 2 CMLR D44.

[400] eg Case T-513/93 *CNSD* [2000] ECR II-1807, [2000] 5 CMLR 614 (customs agents in Italy, classified under Italian law as a liberal profession); Cases C-180 to 184/98 *Pavlov* [2000] ECR I-6451, [2001] 4 CMLR 30 (specialist medical services). For legal services, see Case C-309/99 *Wouters* [2002] ECR I-1577, [2002] 4 CMLR 913, [2002] All ER (EC) 193; Cases C-94 & 202/04 *Cipolla* [2006] ECR I-11421, [2007] 4 CMLR 286.

[401] *Wouters*, above, para 95; *Ambulanz Glöckner* (n 395, above) para 49.

and in some circumstances, it seems that the flow of profits from one Member State to another may in itself constitute 'trade' between Member States.[402]

Relevant factors.   The effect on trade may arise from a combination of several **1.118** factors, none of which individually would necessarily be decisive.[403] The nature of the goods or services covered by the agreement or practice is important and it is sufficient that the products concerned are traded, or likely to be traded, between Member States.[404] An effect is more readily established where, by their nature, the products are easily traded across borders or are important for undertakings that want to enter the market in another Member State.[405] The characteristics of the agreement or practice are also important. Thus, an effect on inter-State trade will normally be presumed where an agreement or practice directly relates to international transactions,[406] especially if it restricts imports or exports,[407] or where it applies to more than one Member State[408] or throughout the Community[409] or

---

[402] *Fire Insurance (D)* (n 376, above) paras 29–36; on appeal, *Verband der Sachversicherer v Commission* (n 387, above). Although the insurance contracts in question were written locally in respect of German risks, Community issuers outside Germany earned profits from their branch offices in Germany and bore the risk of losses. For other aspects of effect on trade in the insurance sector, see *Assurpol*, OJ 1992 L37/16, [1993] 4 CMLR 338; *Manfredi* (n 375, above).

[403] Case C-250/92 *Gøttrup-Klim v Dansk Landbrugs Grovvareselskab AmbA* [1994] ECR I-5641, [1996] 4 CMLR 191, para 54.

[404] eg *Rockwell/Iveco*, OJ 1983 L224/19, [1983] 3 CMLR 709; *BPCL/ICI*, OJ 1984 L212/1, [1985] 2 CMLR 330; *Synthetic Fibres*, OJ 1984 L207/17, [1985] 1 CMLR 787; *ENI/Montedison*, OJ 1987 L5/13, [1988] 4 CMLR 444. Trade across at least one frontier is sufficient: see, eg Cases 40/73, etc, *Suiker Unie v Commission* (n 337, above) para 193 (Belgium/Netherlands); *Amersham/Buchler*, OJ 1982 L314/34, [1983] 1 CMLR 619 (UK/Germany); *Langenscheidt/Hachette*, OJ 1982 L39/25, [1982] 1 CMLR 181 (France/UK); *Mitchell Cotts/Sofiltra*, OJ 1987 L41/31, [1988] 4 CMLR 111 (UK/Ireland).

[405] Effect on Trade Notice (n 384, above) para 30.

[406] eg *Züchner v Bayerische Vereinsbank* (n 385, above). In *Greek Ferries*, OJ 1999 L109/24, [1999] 5 CMLR 47, para 143, the Commission stated that any agreement that affects demand for services between two Member States (such as an agreement between major providers of that service) is likely to deflect demand both as between the parties to the agreement and with third parties, and thus alter the pattern of trade in that service between Member States. In one of the appeals from that decn, Case T-61/99 *Adriatica di Navigazione v Commission* [2003] ECR II-5349, [2005] 5 CMLR 1843, the CFI rejected a challenge to the finding of an effect based on the fact that the volume of traffic and the number of operators had increased on the route in question: para 165 (further appeal dismissed, Case C-111/04P, [2006] ECR I-22). In Cases T-24/93, etc, *Compagnie Maritime Belge v Commission* [1996] ECR II-1201, [1997] 4 CMLR 273, paras 202 *et seq*, the CFI rejected the argument that there was no effect on trade between Member States because the shipping services in question were made from Community ports to third countries, noting that the affected market was not that in the export of goods to third countries but the market in liner transport services; competition as between different Community ports would also be indirectly affected by the agreements in question; further appeal dismissed on other grounds, Cases C-395 & 396/96P [2000] ECR I-1365, [2000] 4 CMLR 1076, [2000] All ER (EC) 385.

[407] Para 1.120, below.

[408] Cases 43 & 63/82 *VBVB and VBBB v Commission* [1984] ECR 19, [1985] 1 CMLR 27.

[409] eg *P&I Clubs*, OJ 1985 L376/2, [1989] 4 CMLR 178; *X/Open Group*, OJ 1987 L35/36, [1988] 4 CMLR 542; *Ford/ Volkswagen*, OJ 1993 L20/14, [1993] 5 CMLR 617. See also *Breeders rights: roses*, OJ 1985 L369/9, [1988] 4 CMLR 193 (where the Community-wide effect was established by virtue of a network of similar agreements).

establishes a Community-wide distribution system.[410] It may be sufficient if the agreement applies to a branch,[411] or a subsidiary, of an undertaking based in another Member State.[412] The fact that the participants in a national arrangement include undertakings from other Member States is an important element in the assessment but is not enough by itself to establish the necessary effect.[413] In addition, account must be taken of the legal and factual environment in which the agreement or practice operates. For example, in *Viho/Toshiba*[414] the Commission held that the existence of price differentials led to conditions in which parallel trading would take place so that any restriction on exports affected trade to an appreciable extent.

1.119 **The basic test: alteration of the pattern of trade.**   The Court of Justice has consistently held that in order for an agreement or conduct to affect trade between Member States:

> '. . . it must be possible to foresee with a sufficient degree of probability on the basis of a set of objective factors of law or fact that it may have an influence, direct or indirect, actual or potential, on the pattern of trade between Member States, such as might prejudice the aim of a single market in all the Member States.'[415]

In practice, this requirement is met if the agreement alters the normal flow or pattern of trade, or causes trade to develop differently from the way it would have developed in the absence of the agreement.[416] It is irrelevant that the agreement or

---

[410] *SABA (No. 2)*, OJ 1983 L376/41, [1984] 1 CMLR 676; *Grohe distribution system*, OJ 1985 L19/17, [1988] 4 CMLR 612 on appeal Case 49/85; *Ideal Standard distribution system*, OJ 1985 L20/38, [1988] 4 CMLR 627 on appeal Case 55/85; *Grundig distribution system*, OJ 1985 L233/1, [1988] 4 CMLR 865; *Ivoclar*, OJ 1985 L369/1, [1988] 4 CMLR 781. But cf Case 107/82 *AEG v Commission* [1983] ECR 3151, [1984] 3 CMLR 413, paras 54–60, where the Commission conceded that it was the improper application of the AEG system and not the mere fact that it applied to more than one Member State that brought Art 81(1) into play. See also AG Reischl at 3265 (ECR), 376–77 (CMLR). In *Grohe, Ideal Standard*, above, and *Rodenstock/Metzler, XVth Report on Competition Policy* (1985), point 65, the Commission left open what the position would be if the agreement were confined to one Member State.

[411] *Verband der Sachversicherer v Commission* (n 387, above).

[412] *ABI*, OJ 1987 L43/51, [1989] 4 CMLR 238; *TEKO*, OJ 1990 L13/34, [1990] 4 CMLR 957.

[413] *Manfredi* (n 375, above) para 44; *Asnef-Equifax* (n 375, above) para 36.

[414] *Viho/Toshiba*, OJ 1991 L287/39, [1992] 5 CMLR 180.

[415] Case 42/84 *Remia v Commission* [1985] ECR 2545, [1987] 1 CMLR 1, para 22. The test was first stated in Case 56/65 *Société Technique Minière v Maschinenbau Ulm* [1966] ECR 235, 249 and 251, [1966] CMLR 357, 375 and 377, and has often been repeated; see, eg *Raiffeisen Zentralbank Österreich* (n 377, above) para 163.

[416] See, eg Case 71/74 *Frubo v Commission* [1975] ECR 563, [1975] 2 CMLR 123, para 38 ('liable to interfere with the natural movement of trade'); Case T-61/89 *Dansk Pelsdyravlerforening v Commission* [1992] ECR II-1931, para 143 ('liable to deflect trade flows from their natural course and thereby affect trade between Member States'); Case T-395/94 *Atlantic Container v Commission (TAA Agreement)* (n 375, above) para 81 ('capable of modifying the pattern of trade in goods'); Case T-61/99 *Adriatica di Navigazione* (n 406, above) para 163: the agreement alters the normal pattern of trade flows and thus harms intra-Community trade by causing trade to develop differently than it would in the absence of the agreement.

conduct produces an increase in trade, even a large one,[417] since the aim of the Treaty is not to increase trade as an end in itself but rather to create a system of undistorted competition.[418]

Partitioning the market. The Court of Justice stated in *Société Technique* **1.120** *Minière*[419] that 'special attention' should be given to whether the agreement is capable of partitioning the market in certain products between Member States. The requirement of an effect on inter-State trade is clearly satisfied if the agreement or conduct could result in the compartmentalisation of markets on a national basis, thereby impeding the economic interpenetration and objectives of a single market which the Treaty is designed to bring about.[420] At the manufacturing level, agreements which fix prices, limit production, share markets or sources of supply, control channels of distribution or limit advertising or promotion,[421] hold up the economic interpenetration which the Treaty is designed to achieve and therefore 'affect trade between Member States'. At the distribution level, agreements likely to partition markets include first and foremost restrictions on imports or exports. Such measures 'of their nature' affect trade between Member States,[422] especially if they give rise to 'absolute territorial protection' or otherwise obstruct parallel imports. Indeed, in *Pronuptia* the Court of Justice went so far as to state that:

'. . . distribution franchise agreements which contain clauses effecting a partitioning of markets between franchisor and franchisees or between franchisees are *per se* capable of affecting trade between Member States, even if they are concluded between enterprises established in the same Member State, to the extent that they prevent the franchisees from setting themselves up in another Member State.'[423]

---

[417] *Consten and Grundig v Commission* (n 375, above) (ECR) 341, (CMLR) 429. See, eg *CSV*, OJ 1978 L242/15, [1979] 1 CMLR 11 (Art 81); *Napier Brown-British Sugar*, OJ 1988 L284/41, [1990] 4 CMLR 196 (Art 82).

[418] *Milchförderungsfonds*, OJ 1985 L35/35, [1985] 3 CMLR 101; *Eirpage*, OJ 1991 L306/22, [1993] 4 CMLR 64, para 13; *Raiffeisen Zentralbank Österreich* (n 377, above) para 164.

[419] Case 56/65 *Société Technique Minière v Maschinenbau Ulm* [1966] ECR 235, 251, [1966] CMLR 357, 377.

[420] These phrases are often used: see, eg Case 126/80 *Salonia v Poidomani and Giglio* [1981] ECR 1563, [1982] 1 CMLR 64, paras 12–14; *Remia* (n 415, above); Case C-407/04P *Dalmine v Commission*, judgment of 25 January 2007, paras 89–91. But market partitioning is only one aspect of effect on inter-State trade: see Cases 240/82, etc, *SSI v Commission* [1985] ECR 3831, [1987] 3 CMLR 661.

[421] See, eg Case T-213/00 *CMA CGM v Commission* [2003] ECR II-913, [2003] 5 CMLR 268 (appeal on other grounds dismissed, Case C-236/03P *Commission v CMA CGM*, order of 28 October 2004), para 221 (prior definition of the relevant markets for services was not necessary since the price-fixing agreement was capable *per se* of affecting trade to an appreciable extent, not only in maritime transport services, but also in the other services to which the charges and surcharges in question apply). See also Effect on Trade Notice (n 384, above) paras 61 *et seq*, and paras 4.005 *et seq*, below. The same applies to agreements on trade exhibitions, paras 5.152 *et seq*, below.

[422] Case 19/77 *Miller v Commission* [1978] ECR 131, [1978] 2 CMLR 334, paras 14–15. See also Cases C-89/85, etc, *Åhlström Osakeyhtiö v Commission* ('*Wood Pulp II*') [1993] ECR I-1307, [1993] 4 CMLR 407, para 176 (irrelevant that economic factors make cross-border trade unlikely).

[423] Case 161/84 *Pronuptia* [1986] ECR 353, [1986] 1 CMLR 414, para 26. This case indicates the very wide meaning the ECJ may give to 'effect on trade between Member States'. On the facts, it

Thus, so far as services are concerned, the effect on trade may arise from a partitioning of the market in a way which either prevents operators established in Member States other than the Member State in question from providing the services or hinders an undertaking in another Member State from establishing itself in the Member State in question with a view to providing services there.[424]

1.121   **Altering the structure of competition.**   In addition, trade between Member States may be affected within the meaning of the competition rules if the agreement or conduct alters the competitive structure within the common market to an appreciable extent. In *Commercial Solvents*,[425] the conduct complained of was the elimination of a competitor within the Community, although most of the competitor's production was exported outside the Community. The Court of Justice stated that the requirement that the conduct may affect trade could not be interpreted as limiting the prohibitions contained in Articles 81(1) and 82 to industrial and commercial activities supplying the Member States. The Community authorities must consider the effect of the agreement on the competitive structure of the common market. If the conduct has 'repercussions' for that competitive structure, the requirement of effect on trade is satisfied.[426] This formulation of the test is often used in cases concerning Article 82 [427] but is also relevant to Article 81(1).[428] The question of the impact on competitive structures will also be important in joint venture and similar cases.[429]

---

must surely have been unlikely that a retail franchisee would have wished to open a shop in another Member State: see Venit, (1986) EL Rev 213. But this was an Art 234 reference, so the ECJ's remarks are not determinative of the facts; and cf Cases C-215 & 216/96 *Bagnasco* [1999] ECR I-135, [1999] 4 CMLR 624, [1999] All ER (EC) 678: see para 1.132, below. For franchising agreements, see paras 6.171 *et seq*, below.

[424]   *Ambulanz Glöckner* (n 395, above) para 49.

[425]   Cases 6 & 7/73 *Commercial Solvents v Commission* [1974] ECR 223, [1974] 1 CMLR 309, paras 30–35. Note that in *Soda-ash-Solvay*, OJ 1991 L152/21, [1994] 4 CMLR 645, para 66, the Commission held that the fact that Solvay's conduct was aimed principally at imports from the United States did not preclude the application of Art 82 since such imports were perceived as the main threat to Solvay's domination of Western Europe; the decision was annulled on procedural grounds, Case T-32/91 *Solvay v Commission* [1995] ECR II-1825, [1996] 5 CMLR 91, further appeal dismissed, Cases C-287 & 288/95P, [2000] ECR I-2391, [2000] 5 CMLR 454.

[426]   See also para 20 of the Effect on Trade Notice (n 384, above).

[427]   See, eg Case 27/76 *United Brands v Commission* [1978] ECR 207, [1978] 1 CMLR 429, para 201 (Art 82 applies even if the abuse does not relate to transactions directly concerning inter-State trade); Case 22/79 *Greenwich Film Production v SACEM* [1979] ECR 3275, [1980] 1 CMLR 629, para 11 (where the ECJ held that *Commercial Solvents* applied equally to the provision of services such as management of copyright as to supply of goods).

[428]   Case T-2/89 *Petrofina v Commission* [1991] ECR II-1087, para 222. Note Case T-29/92 *SPO v Commission* [1995] ECR II-295, para 238: rules on the allocation of tendering costs in the Netherlands construction industry gave Dutch undertakings an advantage in tendering for contracts outside Holland and thereby affected trade between Member States; further appeal dismissed, Case C-137/95P [1996] ECR I-1611.

[429]   eg, *BPCL/ICI*, OJ 1984 L212/1, [1985] 2 CMLR 330, para 32 (third party competitors confronted with different trading conditions as a result of rationalisation); *British Interactive*

Potential effect.   It is not necessary to establish that the agreement or conduct **1.122** has in fact affected trade between Member States; it is enough to show that it is capable of having an effect.[430] A sufficient degree of probability must be demonstrated[431] and the Commission must clearly set forth how it is envisaged that trade could be affected.[432] A speculative or contrived possibility is not enough,[433] but a potential effect is sufficient if it is appreciable[434] and this is the case even if the conduct being examined occurred in the past.[435] It is not necessary to calculate the actual volume of trade between Member States affected by the agreement or to estimate what would have been the level of parallel trade in the absence of the agreement, so long as the effect is appreciable.[436] Arguments that inter-State trade is not affected because the parties were not interested in trading

---

Broadcasting/Open ('BiB'), OJ 1999 L312/1, [2000] 4 CMLR 901, paras 153–157 (JV affected the competitive structure in the United Kingdom and thereby made market entry more difficult for potential competitors); *KSB/Goulds/Lowara/ITT*, OJ 1991 L19/25, [1992] 5 CMLR 55 (should consumers ultimately prefer new products being developed by JV, trade in the Community would shift in favour of the JV parents that would become the suppliers); *Asahi/St Gobain*, OJ 1994 L354/87 (similarly); *GEAE/P&W*, OJ 2000 L58/16, [2000] 5 CMLR 49 (potential customers of the JV include airlines based in the EEA and airlines carrying passengers between Member States). See also, under Art 22 of the Merger Reg (see para 1.115, above), Case T-22/97 *Kesko v Commission* [1999] ECR II-3775, [2000] 4 CMLR 335, paras 105–109 (combination of purchasing of the two parties reduces the number of distribution channels for suppliers and therefore limited the possibility of foreign suppliers gaining access to the national market). But in most JV cases falling under Art 81(1), the parents are based in different Member States or the JV itself operates in two or more Member States so that the JV of its nature affects inter-State trade: Effect on Trade Notice (n 384, above) paras 67–68.

[430]   *Miller v Commission* [1975] ECR 1491, [1976] 1 CMLR 589, para 15; Case 322/81 *Michelin v Commission* [1983] ECR 3461, [1985] 1 CMLR 282, para 104; Case C-219/95P *Ferriere Nord v Commission* [1997] ECR I-4411, [1997] 5 CMLR 575, para 19; Case T-86/95 *Compagnie Générale Maritime v Commission* [2002] ECR II-1011, [2002] 4 CMLR 1115, para 145.

[431]   eg in *Cobelpa/VNP*, OJ 1977 L242/10, [1977] 2 CMLR D28, the Commission said it was not possible to work out the figures expressing how trade would have developed in the absence of collusion, but it was clear that normal competitive behaviour would have had a different effect on the flow of trade.

[432]   *Papiers Peints v Commission* [1975] ECR 1491, [1976] 1 CMLR 589 (Commission decision went appreciably further than earlier cases without adequate reasoning). But cf *Michelin v Commission* (n 430, above) where the applicant unsuccessfully accused the Commission of 'a purely abstract and theoretical analysis'.

[433]   Case 22/78 *Hugin v Commission* [1979] ECR 1869, [1979] 3 CMLR 345: para 1.130, below; Effect on Trade Notice (n 384, above) para 43.

[434]   *Miller v Commission* (n 422, above). A striking example is *Vacuum Interrupters (No. 1)*, OJ 1977 L48/32, [1977] 1 CMLR D67. At the time there was not a single manufacturer in the Community making or selling vacuum interrupters. However, the parties to the JV were potential competitors and it was reasonable to assume that manufacturers in other Member States would develop competing products and would be less able to penetrate the UK market if that market was occupied by an economically and technically strong JV. Further, exports from the UK were likely to start earlier and form a different pattern, thus affecting the flow of trade.

[435]   *Raiffeisen Zentralbank Österreich* (n 377, above) para 166.

[436]   Effect on Trade Notice (n 384, above) para 27.

between Member States,[437] or were not in a position to do so,[438] will generally be rejected, not least because the situation may change from year to year. It is necessary to take account of foreseeable development of trade, including possible development of cross-border activities by reason of policy or legislative initiatives to reduce legal or technical barriers.[439] Conversely, evidence showing that the parties were concerned to prevent imports can, of itself, indicate that inter-State trade can be affected.[440]

1.123   **Indirect effects.**   It is sufficient if the agreement or conduct affects a raw material for a product which is traded between Member States, even if the raw material itself is not.[441] Agreements or practices relating to transport of goods can affect both the pattern of the relevant transport market, and, indirectly, both the provision of port and auxiliary services and the pattern of trade in the goods transported.[442] Where a manufacturer limits warranties to products sold by distributors within their allocated territory, exports are indirectly affected.[443] Similarly, with regard to the supply of services, the market which is affected by an unlawful agreement or conduct may not be the same as the market for the individual services which are the subject of the unlawful price-fixing agreement or the abuse. Thus, for example, the fixing of prices for a large range of banking services was capable of having

---

437 *Miller v Commission* (n 422, above) paras 11–12; *Wood Pulp II* (n 422, above) paras 172, 176.

438 *AEG v Commission* (n 410, above) paras 63–66. See also Case 48/69 *ICI v Commission* [1972] ECR 619, [1972] CMLR 557, paras 120–124; Case 7/82 *GVL v Commission* [1983] ECR 483, [1983] 3 CMLR 645. In *Building and construction in the Netherlands*, OJ 1992 L92/1, [1993] 5 CMLR 135, the Commission found that low penetration by foreign undertakings did not demonstrate a *de minimis* effect; 'on the contrary, the restrictive practices. . . are all the more harmful as they occur in a domain where interpenetration of national markets is relatively limited, thus affecting intra-Community trade in all the more appreciable a manner' (para 107). The Commission also found that competition was distorted as the arrangements gave Dutch contractors an artificial advantage over foreign contractors when tendering for contracts outside the Netherlands (para 113); appeals dismissed, *SPO v Commission* (n 428, above). See also the finding of a potential effect on trade because of the proposed development of the interconnector despite limited current trade in electricity: *Scottish Nuclear Energy Agreement*, OJ 1991 L178/31.

439 Case C-238/05 *Asnef-Equifax v Ausbanc* [2006] ECR I-11125 [2007] 4 CMLR 224, para 44. See eg *Ambulanz Glöckner* (n 395, above) (statutory restriction on operation of ambulance services in frontier region).

440 Cases T-202/98, etc, *Tate & Lyle v Commission* [2001] ECR II-2035, [2001] 5 CMLR 859, [2001] All ER (EC) 839, para 81 ('. . .one of the major preoccupations of British Sugar and Tate & Lyle was to limit imports to a level which would not threaten their ability to sell their production in the national market') (appeal dismissed, Case C-359/01P *British Sugar v Commission* [2004] ECR I-4933, [2004] 5 CMLR 329). See also Effect on Trade Notice (n 384, above) para 81, stating that the extent to which cartel members monitor prices and competitors in other Member States indicates how tradeable the goods are.

441 Case 123/83 *BNIC v Clair* [1985] ECR 391, [1985] 2 CMLR 430; *Wood Pulp II* (n 422, above) para 142; Effect on Trade Notice (n 384, above) para 38.

442 Case T-395/94 *Atlantic Container v Commission (TAA Agreement)* (n 375, above) paras 80 *et seq*; Case T-86/95 *Compagnie Générale Maritime v Commission* (n 430, above) para 148.

443 Effect on Trade Notice, para 39.

repercussions on markets other than the markets for those services themselves.[444] But some effects on trade may be too remote from the restriction to establish Community law jurisdiction.[445]

Appreciable effect. The Court of Justice established a *de minimis* principle as **1.124** regards the requirement of an effect on inter-State trade, as it did similarly as regards the requirement of an effect on competition under Article 81.[446] The jurisdictional requirement is not met unless the effect is appreciable. In those Article 81 cases with a clear element of trade between Member States, the appreciability requirement as regards these two aspects generally goes together. But in other cases, the degree of effect on inter-State trade requires separate consideration. Indeed, in some more recent cases, the Court of Justice has added that the influence on trade 'must not be insignificant'.[447] And whereas the issue of appreciability of an effect on competition for the purpose of Article 81(1) is now determined primarily by considering the market shares of the parties,[448] the Effect on Trade Notice applies to the issue of appreciability of an effect on inter-State trade a combination of market share and absolute turnover thresholds.[449] Indeed, the Commission's earlier Notice giving *de minimis* guidelines as regards an effect on competition[450] states that agreements between small- and medium-sized enterprises ('SMEs') are rarely capable of affecting trade between Member States.[451] The Effect on Trade Notice appears to qualify that indication by explaining it on the basis that the activities of SMEs are normally local or regional, adding that where SMEs engage in cross-border activity they may be subject to Community jurisdiction.[452]

---

[444] *Austrian Banks (Lombard Agreement)*, OJ 2004 L56/1, [2004] 5 CMLR 399, paras 456–459; upheld on appeal *Raiffeisen Zentralbank Österreich* (n 377, above) para 174. See also *Virgin/ British Airways*, OJ 2000 L244/56, [2000] 4 CMLR 999, paras 112–113, where the Commission noted that the abuse in the market for the purchase of the services of UK travel agents would also affect airline transport markets which involved cross-border trade, although there was no finding of dominance on those markets (appeals on other grounds dismissed, Case T-219/99 *British Airways v Commission* [2003] ECR II-5917, [2004] 4 CMLR 1008, [2004] All ER (EC) 1115, Case C-95/04P, *British Airways v Commission* [2007] 4 CMLR 982).

[445] See the example given in para 43 of the Effect on Trade Notice.

[446] Case 5/69 *Völk v Vervaeke* [1969] ECR 295, [1969] CMLR 273. See further paras 2.121 *et seq*, below.

[447] See *Manfredi* (n 375, above) para 42, referring to Case C-306/96 *Javico v YSLP* [1998] ECR I-1983, [1998] 5 CMLR 172, para 16.

[448] See paras 2.129, *et seq*, below.

[449] Effect on Trade Notice, OJ 2004 C101/81: Vol II, App C.17.

[450] Notice on agreements of minor importance which do not appreciably restrict competition (*'De Minimis* Notice'), OJ C368/13: Vol II, App C.13.

[451] ibid, para 3. Such 'SMEs' are now defined as enterprises which have fewer than 250 employees and have an annual turnover of no more than €50 million and/or an annual balance sheet total not exceeding €43 million: Recommendation concerning the definition of micro, small and medium-sized enterprises, OJ 2003 L124/36, Annex, Art 1: Vol II, App C.15.

[452] Effect on Trade Notice, para 50.

1.125 **The 'NAAT-rule'.**   In the Effect on Trade Notice, the Commission sets out, as a general principle for Article 81(1) cases, what it calls the 'NAAT-rule' (standing for 'no appreciable affectation of trade'[453]). The Commission considers that inter-State trade is normally not capable of being affected when two cumulative conditions are satisfied:

(a) the aggregate market share[454] of the parties on any relevant market in the Community affected by the agreement does not exceed 5 per cent; and

(b) —in the case of *horizontal agreements*, the aggregate annual Community turnover of the undertakings concerned in the products covered by the agreement does not exceed €40 million;[455] or

— in the case of *vertical agreements*, the aggregate annual Community turnover of the supplier in the products covered by the agreement does not exceed €40 million.[456]

Although described as a 'rule', the principle is expressed as a negative, rebuttable presumption applying to all agreements, including those containing 'hard-core' restrictions.[457] In cases where the thresholds are not exceeded, the Commission will normally not institute proceedings either upon application or on its own initiative. Where the undertakings assume in good faith that the agreement is covered, the Commission will not impose fines. However, where the agreement concerns a market which does not yet exist so that the parties neither generate relevant turnover nor accumulate any relevant market share, the NAAT-rule does not apply and the Commission will assess appreciability on the basis of the position of the parties on a related product market or their strength in technologies relating to the agreement.[458]

1.126 **Presumption of appreciable effect in relation to certain agreements.**   The Effect on Trade Notice states that, in general, agreements which do not fall below the thresholds of the NAAT-rule are not to be regarded automatically as having an

---

[453] ibid. The word 'affectation' in the English version of the Notice appears to be a mistranslation of *'incidence'* in the French text.

[454] This should be calculated, if possible, on sales or purchase value data as appropriate: ibid, para 55. In the case of networks of agreements entered into by the same supplier with different distributors, sales made through the entire network are taken into account: ibid, para 56.

[455] ibid, para 52. Where the agreement concerns the joint buying of products, the relevant turnover is the parties' combined purchases of the products covered by the agreement.

[456] ibid. In the case of a technology licence agreement, the relevant turnover is the aggregate turnover of the licensees in the products incorporating the technology and the licensor's own turnover in such products. Where the agreement is between a buyer and several suppliers, the relevant turnover is the buyer's combined purchases of the products covered by the agreement: ibid.

[457] There is some leeway when the turnover or market share thresholds are marginally exceeded for no more than two successive calendar years: ibid. For 'hard-core' restrictions, see para 2.097, below.

[458] Effect on Trade Notice, para, 52.

appreciable effect.[459] However, where an agreement by its very nature is capable of affecting trade because it concerns imports and exports or covers several Member States, there is a rebuttable positive presumption that there is an appreciable effect if the agreement does not fall below both the market share and turnover thresholds.[460] This presumption does not arise where the agreement covers only part of a Member State. Neither the NAAT-rule nor the positive presumption applies to Article 82 cases.

(b) Particular aspects

Effect of agreement as a whole in Article 81 cases.   The Treaty does not require   **1.127** that each clause which restricts competition in an agreement should individually be capable of affecting intra-Community trade.[461] Similarly, where the infringement arises out of the activities of a series of different committees, it is not necessary to examine whether each committee individually is capable of affecting trade.[462] Indeed, the effect on inter-State trade is normally the result of a combination of factors, which considered separately may not be decisive.[463] If the agreement as a whole satisfies the test, there is jurisdiction to apply Community law to the entire agreement. In cases where the contractual relations between the same parties cover several activities, these activities must be directly linked and form an integral part of the same overall arrangement in order to be considered together.[464] Moreover, it is not necessary to show that the participation of a particular party to the agreement has that effect in order to establish an infringement by that party.[465]

Effect of conduct in Article 82 cases.   Although, for the purposes of Article 81   **1.128** there is no need to show a link between the effect on trade and the restriction of competition, in applying Article 82 the effect on trade must arise from the abuse. However, conduct which forms part of an overall strategy pursued by a dominant undertaking must be assessed in terms of its overall impact.[466] Generally, if an

---

[459] ibid, para 51.

[460] ibid, para 53.

[461] Case 193/83 *Windsurfing International v Commission* [1986] ECR 611, [1986] 3 CMLR 489, para 96; Case T-77/94 *VGB v Commission* [1997] ECR I-759, [1997] 5 CMLR 812, para 126, appeal on other grounds dismissed, Case C-266/97P *VBA v VGB and Commission* [2000] ECR I-2135.

[462] *Raiffeisen Zentralbank Österreich* (n 377, above) para 177.

[463] Cases C-295/04, etc, *Manfredi* [2006] ECR I-6619, [2006] 5 CMLR 980, [2007] All ER (EC) 27, para 43.

[464] *VGB* (n 461, above) paras 126, 142–144; *Raiffeisen Zentralbank Österreich* (n 377, above) para 168. See also Effect on Trade Notice (n 384, above) para 14.

[465] *Petrofina v Commission* (n 428, above) para 227; Case T-141/89 *Tréfileurope Sales v Commission* [1995] ECR II-791, para 122; Case T-17/99 *Ke KELIT v Commission* [2002] ECR II-1647, para 58; *Raiffeisen Zentralbank Österreich* (n 377, above) para 196.

[466] Effect on Trade Notice (n 384, above) para 17.

undertaking is dominant in more than one Member State and engages in abusive conduct in more than one of those States, trade between Member States is likely to be affected. By the very nature of the undertaking's market position, its conduct is likely to affect the competitive structure within those States in the Community, and to do so in a manner which is appreciable. Where the conduct is an exploitative abuse, for example the imposition of excessive or discriminatory pricing, the effect on trade is likely to arise from an alteration of the trading patterns of the dominant firm's downstream trading partners.[467] Exclusionary abuses, such as predatory pricing or fidelity rebates, are likely to divert trade from the course which it would have followed in the absence of the abuse.[468]

1.129 **Barriers to entry.** One of the objective factors to be taken into account in determining whether an agreement or practice may affect trade is the existence of entry barriers, including in particular a network of agreements between, for example, a manufacturer and its distributors.[469] Other relevant barriers might be the degree of saturation of the market, the number and size of the existing suppliers, and customer brand loyalty.[470] In the Effect on Trade Notice, the Commission states that if there are absolute barriers to cross-border trade, then trade is only capable of being affected if those barriers are likely to disappear in the foreseeable future,[471] and in that regard it is necessary to take account of any policy or legislative initiatives designed to reduce such barriers.[472] But in cases where the barriers are not absolute but merely render cross-border activities more difficult, it is of the utmost importance to ensure that an agreement or practice does not further hinder such activities. Generally, arguments that inter-State trade cannot take place because of technical barriers are treated with scepticism.[473]

---

[467] ibid, para 74.

[468] ibid, para 75. See, eg Cases C-241 & 242/91P *RTE and ITP v Commission ('Magill')* [1995] ECR I-743, [1995] 4 CMLR 718, [1995] All ER (EC) 416, para 70: exclusion of competitor from geographical market comprising Ireland and Northern Ireland.

[469] Case C-234/89 *Delimitis* [1991] ECR I-935, [1992] 5 CMLR 210. See also the German ice cream cases: Case T-7/93 *Langnese-Iglo v Commission* [1995] ECR II-1533, [1995] 5 CMLR 602, [1995] All ER (EC) 902, appeal dismissed, Case C-279/95P [1998] ECR I-5609, [1998] 5 CMLR 933; and Case T-9/93 *Schöller v Commission* [1995] ECR II-1611, [1995] 5 CMLR 659.

[470] *Delimitis*, above, para 22.

[471] Effect on Trade Notice (n 384, above) para 32

[472] *Asnef-Equifax* (n 439, above) para 44. See also Effect on Trade Notice, para 41.

[473] eg *AEG v Commission* (n 410, above) paras 62 *et seq*. See also Cases 209/78, etc, *Van Landewyck v Commission ('FEDETAB')* [1980] ECR 3125, [1981] 3 CMLR 134, para 169; and Cases 240/82, etc, *SSI v Commission* (n 420, above) (fact that technical and fiscal barriers exclude the possibility of parallel imports irrelevant if the parties to the agreement themselves sell imported products). Similarly, the fact that there is only a small volume of trade because of 'the business and legal environment' does not necessarily negative a finding of effect on inter-State trade: *Fire Insurance(D)* (n 376, above), on appeal *Verband der Sachversicherer v Commission* (n 411, above); *Assurpol*, OJ 1992 L37/16, [1993] 4 CMLR 338 (although only limited trade in certain liability insurance was possible, 'this situation is likely to change in the future'). But cf the approach where the case concerns re-importation of exports outside the Community: para 1.108, above.

Agreements or practices confined to a single Member State. If the agreement **1.130**
or conduct is capable of appreciably affecting patterns of trade and competition
in the common market, it makes no difference that the parties are situated in one
Member State or that the conduct in question takes place in one Member State.[474]
Hence if the flow of trade or the structure of competition is affected in the manner already indicated,[475] Articles 81(1) or 82 may apply. The Court of Justice
held in *Cementhandelaren*,[476] that an agreement extending over the whole territory of a Member State by its very nature has the effect of reinforcing the compartmentalisation of markets on a national basis and therefore impeding the aims
of the EC Treaty. This principle has since been reaffirmed many times.[477]
However, despite such apparently unequivocal statements, it is necessary to consider (i) the nature of the products or services at issue to ascertain whether they
are in fact tradeable across borders, and if they are, whether it is reasonably likely
that there would be significant cross-border trade in the absence of the restrictive
practice concerned; or alternatively (ii) whether foreign entry onto the national
market is sufficiently impeded by reason of the agreement or practice. For this
purpose, an effect in a frontier region may be sufficient.[478] If on the facts the
agreement directly affects imports or exports[479] or hinders penetration of a

---

[474] eg *Michelin v Commission* (n 430, above) paras 100–105 (Art 82).

[475] Paras 1.119–1.123, above.

[476] Case 8/72 *Cementhandelaren v Commission* [1972] ECR 977, [1973] CMLR 7. eg Case
246/86 *Belasco v Commission* [1989] ECR 2181, [1991] 4 CMLR 96 (roofing felt cartel); Case
T-66/89 *Publishers' Association v Commission* [1992] ECR II-1995, [1992] 5 CMLR 120 (net book
agreement); Case 311/85 *VVR* [1987] ECR 3801, [1989] 4 CMLR 213 (national arrangements
among travel agents and tour operators).

[477] *Remia* (n 415, above) paras 22–23; and see the cases cited at n 476, above. For information
exchange, see *UK Agricultural Tractor Registration Exchange*, OJ 1992 L68/19, [1993] 4 CMLR 358,
paras 57–58 (industry-wide arrangement including all major importers from other Member States);
appeals on other grounds dismissed, Case T-34/92 *Fiatagri and New Holland Ford v Commission*
[1994] ECR II-905. For rules of a professional association, see *Wouters* (n 400, above) para 96 ('That
effect is all the more appreciable. . .because [the agreement] applies equally to visiting lawyers who
are registered members of the Bar of another Member State, because economic and commercial
law more and more frequently regulates transnational transactions and, lastly, because the firms
of accountants looking for lawyers as partners are generally international groups present in several
Member States'); Case C-35/99 *Arduino* [2002] ECR I-1529, [2002] 4 CMLR 866; Cases C-94 &
202/04 *Cipolla* [2006] ECR I-11421, [2007] 4 CMLR 286; *Asnef-Equifax* (n 439, above).

[478] *AEG v Commission* (n 410, above) paras 65–66 (demand in frontier region of France for sets
manufactured to receive German broadcasting systems); Cases T-13/95 & T-18/96 *SCK and FNK v
Commission* [1997] ECR II-1739, [1998] 4 CMLR 259, para 177 (Dutch cranes hired in frontier region of Belgium). In *Film Purchases by German television stations*, OJ 1989 L284/36, [1990]
4 CMLR 841, the necessary effect was found because the agreement included Luxembourg and the
South Tyrol region of Italy.

[479] See, eg *FEDETAB* (n 473, above); Cases 240-242/82, etc, *Stichting Sigarettenindustrie v
Commission* [1985] ECR 3831, [1987] 3 CMLR 661 (irrelevant that imports were by way of supply
from companies in the same corporate group); *Vimpoltu*, OJ 1983 L200/44, [1983] 3 CMLR 619;
Eirpage (n 418, above); *Stichting Baksteen*, OJ 1994 L131/15, [1995] 4 CMLR 646.

national market,[480] even if the market is regulated and transport costs make imports difficult,[481] an effect on inter-State trade is readily established. The contrary position is illustrated by the judgments of the Court of Justice in *Hugin* and *Bagnasco*, concerning Articles 82 and 81 respectively. In *Hugin*,[482] a Swedish manufacturer of cash registers refused to supply Liptons, a UK company, with spare parts to enable Liptons to offer service and repair facilities to customers who had installed Hugin cash registers. The servicing and repair of cash registers were essentially local in character and could not be operated profitably beyond a certain area around the commercial base of an undertaking. The Court of Justice annulled the Commission's decision condemning the refusal as an abuse, holding that the spare parts were 'not such as to constitute a commodity of commercial interest in trade between Member States' especially since Hugin did not apply different prices in different markets. The fact that Liptons had tried to obtain spare parts from other Member States did not alter the position, since that was an exceptional occurrence; in normal circumstances there was no inter-State trade in spare parts. In the more recent judgment in *Bagnasco*,[483] the Court of Justice held that, although the great majority of Italian banks were members of the Association of Italian Banks (ABI), the ABI standard conditions that governed contracts for current accounts, and in particular the provisions that governed the provision of a general guarantee for the opening of a credit facility, did not have an appreciable effect on inter-State trade. The participation of subsidiaries or branches of non-Italian banks in the ABI was limited and, in any event, the recourse to credit facilities and general guarantees by 'the main customers' of foreign banks was not significant.[484] This decision demonstrates that the application of an agreement or concerted practice to the whole of a Member State does not in itself establish an effect on inter-State trade: save in obvious cases, at least some evaluation of the

---

[480] Case 61/80 *Coöperatieve Stremsel-en Kleurselfabriek v Commission* [1981] ECR 851, [1982] 1 CMLR 240 (exclusive purchasing prevented imports); *Stichting Sigarettenindustrie*, above, para 50 (limitation of distributors' margins reduced incentive to promote sales of imported products rather than other products); Case C-393/92 *Almelo* [1994] ECR I-1477. See also paras 5.062 and 6.053 *et seq*, below.

[481] Cases T-202/98, etc, *Tate & Lyle v Commission* [2001] ECR II-2035, [2001] 5 CMLR 859, [2001] All ER (EC) 839, para 80; appeal dismissed Case C-359/01P *British Sugar v Commission* [2004] ECR I-4933, [2004] 5 CMLR 329.

[482] Case 22/78 *Hugin v Commission* [1979] ECR 1869, [1979] 3 CMLR 345. The ECJ expressly stated that the same jurisdictional test as for Art 81 applied.

[483] Cases C-215 & 216/96 *Bagnasco v BPN and Carige* [1999] ECR I-135, [1999] 4 CMLR 624. See also *ABI*, OJ 1987 L43/51, [1989] 4 CMLR 238.

[484] The ECJ accepted the arguments of the Commission and declined to follow the strong Opinion of AG Ruiz-Jarabo Colomer. Note that the point was decided on the basis of an effect on inter-State trade and the ECJ did not consider whether the standard guarantee condition had an effect on competition (cf the contrary approach in the same case to another provision in the standard conditions, the prevention of offering a fixed interest rate, which the ECJ surprisingly held did not appreciably affect competition between the banks).

consequences is required.[485] In the light of *Bagnasco*, the Court of First Instance has referred to a 'strong presumption' that an agreement covering the territory of a Member State may affect trade, that presumption being rebuttable if the analysis of the characteristics of the agreement and the economic context in which it operates prove the contrary.[486] In *Manfredi*,[487] the Court of Justice held that the mere fact that foreign insurance companies doing business in Italy participated in a nationwide arrangement for exchange of information was insufficient in itself to establish an effect on inter-State trade; however, this indicated the potential for foreign companies to enter the Italian market and it was therefore necessary to determine whether the effects of the agreement might deter such entry.

Particular kinds of domestic agreements.   In the light of the somewhat diverse   **1.131**
jurisprudence, the Effect on Trade Notice devotes considerable discussion to the question of when a domestic agreement or practice meets the effect on inter-State trade criterion under Articles 81(1) or 82.[488] In that regard, the Notice distinguishes between different forms of domestic agreements:

(a) *Cartels* which cover the whole of a Member State will in general be capable of affecting inter-State trade, if the product is tradeable.[489]

(b) *Horizontal cooperation agreements* may affect trade by foreclosing markets. Agreements which establish sector-wide standardisation and certification regimes, which either exclude undertakings from other Member States or which are more easily fulfilled by undertakings from the Member State in question because of national rules or traditions, may make it more difficult for undertakings from other Member States to penetrate the market and hence have the necessary effect.

---

[485] See similarly *Re Dutch Banks*, OJ 1989 L253/1, [1990] 4 CMLR 768 (certain interbank services by their very nature only performed locally; safe deposit and safe custody services, hire of safes); *Nederlandse Vereniging van Banken (1991 GSA Agreement)*, OJ 1999 L271/28, [2000] 4 CMLR 137 (Commission applied *Bagnasco* in finding that agreement between all the Dutch banks for standard interbank commissions for the processing of giro payments did not appreciably affect inter-State trade, although the agreement did appreciably affect competition and foreign banks participated). See also the English Court of Appeal in *Higgins v Marchant & Eliot Underwriting Ltd* [1996] 2 Lloyd's Rep 31 (funding arrangements between Name at Lloyd's and the managing agents of the syndicate of which he is a member).

[486] Cases T-259/02, etc, *Raiffeisen Zentralbank Österreich*, judgment of 14 December 2006, paras 180 *et seq*, distinguishing *Bagnasco* and also *Nederlandse Vereniging van Banken (1991 GSA Agreement)*(above) as concerning a particular banking service and not the full range of operations. The CFI upheld the Commission's decision in *Austrian Banks (Lombard Agreement)* (n 444, above) which had rejected the argument that there was a special test for effect on trade in the banking sector (on appeal, Cases C-125/07P, etc, not yet decided).

[487] *Manfredi* (n 463, above) paras 44, 50–51. See also *Asnef-Equifax* (n 439, above) para 37.

[488] Effect on Trade Notice, OJ 2004 C101/81: Vol II, App C.17, paras 77–99.

[489] The dicta in the case law that agreements covering a whole Member State 'by their nature' affect inter-State trade generally concern cartels or agreements adopting national tariffs. The Commission explains this on the basis that to maintain the cartel's effectiveness the participants normally need to take action to exclude competitors from other Member States: Effect on Trade Notice, paras 79–80. See, eg *Belasco* (n 476, above) paras 34–35.

(c) *Joint venture agreements* may affect trade by preventing undertakings from another Member State from benefiting from an important channel of distribution or source of demand.[490]

(d) *Vertical agreements* establishing exclusive distribution may foreclose outlets making it more difficult for undertakings from other Member States to penetrate the market.[491] Resale price maintenance will have a direct effect on trade by increasing imports from and decreasing exports to other Member States.

1.132 **Particular kinds of domestic abuse.**   For the purpose of analysing the position of an undertaking whose dominant position covers only one Member State, the Effect on Trade Notice distinguishes between exclusionary and exploitative abusive practices:[492]

(a) *Exclusionary abuse* that involves binding customers to the dominant undertaking will generally affect inter-State trade since it means it impedes access to those customers by suppliers from other Member States. Therefore, fidelity rebates[493] and exclusive purchasing arrangements[494] will meet the requirement since they foreclose foreign competitors.

(b) *Exclusionary abuse* that seeks to eliminate or weaken a competitor of the dominant undertaking, such as predatory pricing or a refusal to supply, will obviously affect inter-State trade if the target is a foreign competitor; but if the target is a domestic competitor that neither engages in exports or imports nor itself also operates in other Member States, there will not be an effect on inter-State trade.[495] The Notice observes that an indirect effect on inter-State

---

[490] See cases cited at n 429, above.

[491] *Coöperatieve Stremsel-en Kleurselfabriek v Commission* (n 480, above). See also the decns concerning the 'Green Dot' waste packaging recycling scheme: *DSD*, OJ 2001 L319/1, [2002] 4 CMLR 405, para 131 (Germany) (appeal dismissed, Case T-289/01, *Duales System Deutschland v Commission* [2007] 5 CMLR 356); *ARA and ARGEV, ARO*, OJ 2004 L75/59, [2004] 5 CMLR 1101, paras 263–265 (Austria). Foreclosure effects normally apply to foreign suppliers as much as to domestic suppliers, but a reservation in favour of access by suppliers from other Member States will preclude an effect on inter-State trade if its terms provide a real possibility for foreign supply: *Delimitis* (n 469, above) paras 28–33.

[492] Effect on Trade Notice (n 488, above) paras 93–96. For discussion of different kinds of abuse, see paras 10.058 *et seq*, below.

[493] Case 322/81 *Michelin v Commission* [1983] ECR 3461, [1985] 1 CMLR 282, paras 100–105.

[494] For exclusive or tying arrangements, the same considerations apply under Art 82 as under Art 81: see eg *Van den Bergh Foods Ltd*, OJ 1998 L246/1, [1998] 5 CMLR 530, paras 201 and 271 (appeals on other grounds dismissed: Case T-65/98 *Van den Bergh Foods v Commission* [2003] ECR II-4653, [2004] 4 CMLR 14, [2005] All ER (EC) 418; Case C-552/03P *Unilever Bestfoods v Commission* [2006] ECR I-9091, [2006] 5 CMLR 1460).

[495] See, eg *Hugin*, discussed in para 1.130, above. But the exports need not be to another Member State: see Cases 6 & 7/73 *Commercial Solvents v Commission* [1974] ECR 223, [1974] 1 CMLR 309, paras 30–34, where the refusal by a US company, dominant throughout the Community, to supply a raw material to a customer in Italy was held to affect inter-State trade irrespective of the fact that this customer sold 90% of its finished product outside the Community: see para 1.121, above.

trade may also be found if the conduct has a dissuasive effect on potential market entrants from other Member States.[496]

(c) *Exploitative abuse*, such as excessive pricing or price discrimination, is stated by the Notice to present a 'more complex' situation. The Notice states that price discrimination between domestic customers will not normally affect trade between Member States, but that it may do so if the disadvantaged buyers are engaged in export activities.[497] Where the discrimination consists in offering lower prices to those customers most likely to import from another Member State, for example customers in a border region, an effect on trade may be readily established.[498] Presumably, analogous reasoning should apply to excessive pricing, on which the Notice is silent.[499]

As regards the requirement of appreciability, the very presence of an undertaking which is dominant in a national market is likely already to hinder penetration of that market by a competitor, and accordingly any abuse which increases the difficulty of market entry will probably have an appreciable effect on inter-State trade. Therefore even if such abuse covers only part of the national territory or affects only certain buyers, an effect on inter-State trade is likely to be significant.[500] But if the abuse involves only an insignificant share of the dominant undertaking's sales within the State, trade between Member States may not be appreciably affected.

Agreement or dominance in only part of a Member State.   The Effect on Trade **1.133** Notice discusses also the application of the criterion where an agreement or dominant position covers only part of a Member State.[501] For an agreement, the assessment is approached in the same way as when considering an agreement covering the whole of a Member State. But to determine appreciability, where an

---

[496] Effect on Trade Notice, para 94.

[497] ibid, para 95. See, eg *Portuguese airports* [1999] 5 CMLR 103, para 20: Commission found no effect on inter-State trade caused by discriminatory landing fees at four airports in the Azores since the traffic was either entirely domestic or from third countries, by contrast with the position at mainland airports (appeal on other grounds dismissed, Case C-163/99 *Portugal v Commission* [2001] ECR I-2613, [2002] 4 CMLR 1319).

[498] eg Case T-228/97 *Irish Sugar v Commission* [1999] ECR II-2969, [1999] 5 CMLR 1300, [2000] All ER (EC) 198, paras 169, 185; appeal dismissed, Case C-497/99P *Irish Sugar v Commission* [2001] ECR I-5333, [2001] 5 CMLR 29. Such conduct may equally be categorised as an exclusionary abuse.

[499] See, eg *Der Grüne Punkt – Duales System Deutschland*, OJ 2001 L166/1, [2001] 5 CMLR 609, paras 155–158: fees under trade mark agreement for use of 'Green Dot' on packaging regardless of whether the packaging was recycled under the licensor's scheme or that of a competitor; appeal dismissed, Case T151/01 *Duales System Deutschland v Commission*, apppeal dismissed, Case T-151/01 *Duales System Deutschland v Commission* [2007] 5 CMLR 300. cf Case T-229/05 *AEPI v Commission*, appeal dismissed, judgment of 12 July 2007 (challenge to Commission's rejection of complaint concerning high level of music and recording copyright charges levied in Greece as not appreciably affecting inter-State trade).

[500] Effect on Trade Notice, para 96.

[501] ibid, paras 89–92, 97–99.

agreement forecloses access to a regional market, the best indicator is the share of the national market in terms of volume that is being foreclosed. In such a case, the geographic extent of the regional market, or the parties' market shares (of that regional market) are of limited weight. If the proportion of the national market affected is not significant, there is unlikely to be an appreciable effect on inter-State trade.[502] The Effect on Trade Notice suggests that even in an Article 81 case, guidance can be derived from the case law under Article 82 concerning the concept of a 'substantial part of the common market'.[503] And in an Article 82 case, where an undertaking is dominant only in part of a Member State, the effect on trade requirement can be considered together with this other requirement under Article 82 that the dominant position must cover a 'substantial part of the common market'. Therefore, if a port, by reason of its significance, constitutes a substantial part of the common market and the abuse makes it more difficult for competitors from other Member States to gain access to that port, the appreciable effect on trade requirement will be satisfied.[504] However, abuse that is purely local in nature is unlikely to have an effect on inter-State trade.[505] The fact that the affected region is of substantial size does not of itself establish an appreciable affect on inter-State trade. For example, in *Ambulanz Glöckner*, concerning a limitation of the right to operate ambulance services, the Court of Justice noted that the affected *Land* of Rheinland-Pfalz might by its geographic area and population be regarded as constituting a 'substantial part of the common market' for the purpose of Article 82,[506] but the question of an appreciable effect on inter-State trade depended upon whether there was a sufficient degree of probability that operators from neighbouring States might have sought, but for the restriction, to operate ambulance services in Rheinland-Pfalz.[507]

1.134 **Restrictions arising from activities in non-Member States.** An agreement between undertakings all of which are outside the Community may still restrict competition within the Community and affect trade between Member States. The jurisdiction to apply the competition rules in such circumstances is considered in Section 7, above.[508] In the case of agreements which do not have the object

---

[502] ibid, para 90. See eg *Industrieverband Solnhofener Natursteinplatten*, OJ 1980 L318/32, [1981] 2 CMLR 308, paras 40–41 (standardised exchange arrangements between competing local producers of a particular natural stone had no effect on inter-State trade, although the stones were exported).

[503] Effect on Trade Notice, para 92. For discussion of this concept and citation of authorities, see para 10.014, below.

[504] Effect on Trade Notice (n 500, above) paras 97–98. See, eg Case C-179/90 *Merci convenzionale porto di Genova* [1991] ECR I-5889, [1994] 4 CMLR 422, para 15.

[505] Effect on Trade Notice (n 500, above) para 99.

[506] Case C-475/99 *Ambulanz Glöckner* [2001] ECR I-8089, [2002] 4 CMLR 726, para 38.

[507] ibid, paras 48–50, and see Opinion of AG Jacobs at paras 168–173. Since this was a reference for preliminary ruling, it was for the national court to determine these issues on the facts.

[508] See also Effect on Trade Notice (n 500, above) paras 100 *et seq*.

of restricting competition inside the Community, it is still necessary to consider whether patterns of trade are capable of being affected, for example by considering the effect of the agreements on customers and other operators inside the Community that rely on the products or services of the parties to the agreement, or whether the likelihood of goods being re-imported has been altered.[509] The mere fact that conduct produces certain effects, no matter what they may be, on the Community economy does not in itself constitute a sufficiently close link to be able to found Community competence.[510] Thus, where an equipment manufacturer took steps to limit exports of spare parts from the United States to Europe where the parts were more expensive, the Court of First Instance upheld the Commission's finding that there was an insufficient effect on trade.[511] Similarly, where an agreement, albeit between undertakings inside the Community, concerns only exports to a non-Member State, the question whether a restriction on re-export into the Community gives rise to an appreciable effect on inter-State trade is to be determined on the basis of the quantity of products affected in relation to the total market for those products in the Community.[512]

---

[509] See paras 106 *et seq* of the Effect on Trade Notice.

[510] Case T-204/03 *Haladjian Frères v Commission* [2006] ECR II-3779, [2007] 4 CMLR 1106.

[511] ibid. There was evidence that the system established was necessary to support the official spare parts distribution network and still allowed substantial parallel importing to take place. Note that there were no restrictions on parts moving between one EU Member State and another, only between the United States and the EEA.

[512] Case C-306/96 *Javico v YSLP* [1998] ECR I-1983, [1998] 5 CMLR 172, paras 25–26. See further paras 1.108–1.109, above.

2

ARTICLE 81(1)

1. Introduction

Article 81(1).   Article 81(1) provides: **2.001**

'The following shall be prohibited as incompatible with the common market: all agreements between undertakings, decisions by associations of undertakings and concerted practices which may affect trade between Member States and which have as their object or effect the prevention, restriction or distortion of competition within the common market, and in particular those which:
(a) directly or indirectly fix purchase or selling prices or any other trading conditions;
(b) limit or control production, markets, technical development or investment;
(c) share markets or sources of supply;
(d) apply dissimilar conditions to equivalent transactions with other trading parties, thereby placing them at a competitive disadvantage;
(e) make the conclusion of contracts subject to acceptance by the other parties of supplementary obligations which, by their nature or according to commercial usage, have no connection with the subject of such contracts.'

2.002 **The constituent elements.**   In deciding whether any particular transaction falls within Article 81(1) it is necessary to consider:

(a) whether there exists an agreement, decision or concerted practice made between or observed by undertakings;

(b) whether competition within the common market may thereby be prevented, restricted or distorted; and

(c) whether trade between Member States may thereby be affected.

The last requirement of an effect on trade between Member States is considered in Chapter 1, above.[1] The other elements of the Article 81(1) prohibition are examined in this Chapter.

2. Undertakings

(a) Generally

2.003 **Undertakings.**   The word 'undertaking' is not defined in the EC Treaty.[2] In the context of competition law, it appears in Articles 81 and 82 and is of fundamental importance under the Merger Regulation,[3] and it should receive a consistent interpretation. It is a wide term which extends to any entity engaged in an economic activity, regardless of its legal status or the way in which it is financed.[4] The Court of First Instance has stated that Article 81 is addressed to economic entities made up of a collection of physical and human resources being capable of taking part in the commission of an infringement of the kind referred to in that Article.[5] The term thus includes, for example, limited companies,[6] partnerships,[7] agricultural

---

[1] See paras 1.115 *et seq*, above.

[2] But note that the EEA Treaty (see para 1.086, above) defines an undertaking as 'any entity carrying out activities of a commercial or economic nature': Art 1 of Protocol 22.

[3] Reg 139/2004: see Chap 8, below.

[4] Case C-41/90 *Höfner & Elser v Macrotron* [1991] ECR I-1979, [1993] 4 CMLR 306, para 21; Case C-309/99 *Wouters* [2002] ECR I-1577, [2002] 4 CMLR 913, [2002] All ER (EC) 193, and case law cited there; Cases C-189/02P, etc, *Dansk Rørindustri v Commission* [2005] ECR I-5425, [2005] 5 CMLR 796, para 112.

[5] Case T-6/89 *Enichem v Commission* [1991] ECR II-1623, para 235 (on appeal, Case C-49/92P *Commission v Anic Partecipazioni* [1999] ECR I-4125, [2001] 4 CMLR 602); Cases T-71/03, etc, *Tokai Carbon v Commission (Speciality Graphite)* [2005] ECR II-10, [2005] 5 CMLR 489, para 54 (further appeal regarding the level of fine dismissed, Case C-328/05P *SGL Carbon v Commission* [2007] 5 CMLR 16); Case T-352/94 *Mo och Domsjö v Commission* [1998] ECR II-1989; Case T-66/99 *Minoan Lines v Commission* [2003] ECR II-5515, [2005] 5 CMLR 1957, para 122 (appeal dismissed, Case C-121/04P, Order of 17 November 2005).

[6] In all their corporate forms, including, eg a limited partnership, as in Case 258/78 *Nungesser v Commission* [1982] ECR 2015, [1983] 1 CMLR 278; or a trust company, as in *Fides*, OJ 1979 L57/33, [1979] 1 CMLR 650 (Societa fiduciaria under Italian law providing secretarial services to a cartel). For the treatment of a corporate group as a single undertaking see para 2.017, below.

[7] See, eg *Breeders' rights: roses*, OJ 1985 L369/9, [1988] 4 CMLR 193. In *Price Waterhouse/ Coopers & Lybrand*, OJ 1999 L50/27, the Commission concluded that the international networks of

cooperatives,[8] sole traders and self-employed professionals,[9] and State corporations.[10] A trade association can be both an association of undertakings and an undertaking itself by virtue of the economic activity it pursues.[11] Whether the undertaking is profit-making is immaterial, provided that it carries out economic or commercial activities.[12] It is not necessary for the entity to have legal personality under the law of the Member State where it operates in order for it to be an undertaking.[13] Further, a change in the legal form and name of an undertaking does not necessarily have the effect of creating a new undertaking free of liability for the anti-competitive behaviour of its predecessor when, from an economic point of view, the two are identical.[14]

Individuals as undertakings. An individual will be an undertaking for the **2.004** purposes of Article 81(1) if and insofar as he engages in economic or commercial activity in his own right, for example as a sole trader.[15] In *Wouters*[16] the Court of

---

separate and autonomous national firms were sufficiently integrated to be regarded as single undertakings for the purposes of the Merger Reg.

[8] Case 61/80 *Coöperatieve Stremsel-en Kleurselfabriek v Commission* [1981] ECR 851, [1982] 1 CMLR 240; Case T-61/89 *Dansk Pelsdyravlerforening v Commission* [1992] ECR II-1931, para 50 (cooperative is both an undertaking itself and an association of undertakings). See also *Meldoc*, OJ 1986 L348/50, [1989] 4 CMLR 853; *Bloemenveilingen Aalsmeer*, OJ 1988 L26/27, [1989] 4 CMLR 500.

[9] Para 2.004, below.

[10] Paras 2.007 *et seq*, below. For foreign State trading corporations, see para 2.006, below.

[11] Case T-193/02 *Piau v Commission* [2005] ECR II-209, [2005] 5 CMLR 42, para 72 (appeal dismissed Case C-171/05P [2006] ECR I-37). In *UEFA Champions League*, OJ 2003 L291/25, [2004] 4 CMLR 549, the Commission held that UEFA was an association of associations of undertakings, an association of undertakings and also an undertaking itself because it engaged in commercial activity. cf *Wouters* (n 4, above) where the ECJ held that the Dutch Bar Association was an association of undertakings but not an undertaking in its own right. In Case T-253/03 *Akzo Nobel Chemicals and Akcros Chemicals v Commission* [2004] ECR II-1603, the CFI rejected an application to intervene made by the Business Law section of the International Bar Association on the basis that the section was not itself a representative body.

[12] Cases 209/78, etc, *Van Landewyck v Commission* [1980] ECR 3125, [1981] 3 CMLR 134, para 88; *GVL*, OJ 1981 L370/49, [1982] 1 CMLR 221 (this point was not challenged on appeal in Case 7/82 *GVL v Commission* [1983] ECR 483, [1983] 3 CMLR 645); *P & 1 Clubs*, OJ 1985 L376/2, [1989] 4 CMLR 178 (non-profit making mutual insurance associations); *Höfner & Elser* (n 4, above) (State-run employment recruitment agency); *EBU*, OJ 1993 L179/23, [1995] 4 CMLR 56 (public television broadcasting stations acquiring rights to sporting events).

[13] *Dansk Rørindustri* (n 4, above) para 113.

[14] See Cases 29 & 30/83 *CRAM and Rheinzink v Commission* [1984] ECR 1679, [1985] 1 CMLR 688, para 9; Cases C-204/00P, etc, *Aalborg Portland A/S v Commission* [2004] ECR I-123, [2005] 4 CMLR 251, para 59 and paras 354 *et seq*, where the ECJ deals with the question of which undertaking is liable to be fined.

[15] eg Mr Eisele, a plant breeder, in *Nungesser v Commission* (n 6, above); Mr Segers, a supplier of tobacco products, in Case 35/83 *BAT v Commission* [1985] ECR 363, [1985] 2 CMLR 470; Mr Schmidt, a shopkeeper, in Case 210/81 *Demo-Studio Schmidt v Commission* [1983] ECR 3045, [1984] 1 CMLR 63.

[16] Case C-309/99 *Wouters* [2002] ECR I-1577, [2002] 4 CMLR 913, [2002] All ER (EC) 193. See also Cases C-180/98, etc, *Pavlov* [2000] ECR I-6451, [2001] 4 CMLR 30, para 77 (medical practitioners).

Justice considered whether members of the Dutch Bar are undertakings for the purposes of Article 81. It held that since they offer services for a fee and bear the financial risk attaching to the performance of those services, they should be regarded as carrying on an economic activity. The lawyers are therefore undertakings for the purposes of the competition rules and the 'complexity and technical nature' of their work and the fact that the profession is regulated does not alter that conclusion.[17] Licensors of intellectual property rights,[18] performing artistes[19] and consultants[20] have also been held to be undertakings. An individual cannot be an undertaking solely in his capacity as a member of or shareholder in a company,[21] but may be as the future purchaser of a business.[22]

2.005 **Economic or commercial activity.**   Undertakings engaged in the supply of services are 'undertakings' within the meaning of Article 81(1) as well as undertakings engaged in the supply of goods. But it is essential that the 'undertaking' should carry on some economic or commercial activity; bodies which are not engaged in any such activity are not 'undertakings' within the meaning of Article 81(1). It is activity consisting in offering goods and services on a given market that is the characteristic feature of an economic activity.[23] This delimitation is applied by considering the nature and aim of the activities of the body in question and how it is financed. Therefore, a public placement office, which had an exclusive right under domestic law to act as an employment agency, is an undertaking because employment procurement is to be regarded as an economic activity which is not necessarily carried out by public entities.[24] The fact that an activity may be carried

---

17 *Wouters*, above, para 48. See also *EPI Code of Conduct*, OJ 1999 L106/14, [1999] 5 CMLR 540 upheld on appeal Case T-144/99 *Institute of Professional Representatives v Commission* [2001] ECR II-1087, [2001] 5 CMLR 77; Case C-35/96 *Commission v Italy* [1998] ECR I-3851, [1998] 5 CMLR 889; and *CNSD* (n 23, above) (customs agents in Italy, classified under Italian law as a liberal profession); *Pavlov*, above (medical specialists); *COAPI*, OJ 1995 L122/37, [1995] 5 CMLR 468 (industrial property agents in Spain).

18 eg *AOIP/Beyrard*, OJ 1976 L6/8, [1976] 1 CMLR D14; *Vaessen/Moris*, OJ 1979 L19/32, [1979] 1 CMLR 511; *Theal/Watts*, OJ 1977 L39/19, [1977] 1 CMLR D44, on appeal Case 28/77 *Tepea v Commission* [1978] ECR 1391, [1978] 3 CMLR 392.

19 *RAI/Unitel*, OJ 1978 L157/39, [1978] 3 CMLR 306 (four leading opera singers performing Don Carlos at La Scala, Milan). For subsequent proceedings, see *XIIth Report on Competition Policy* (1982), point 90.

20 *Reuter/BASF*, OJ 1976 L254/40, [1976] 2 CMLR D44 (Dr Reuter acted as commercial adviser to third parties, as well as being economically active as a controlling shareholder and exploiting the results of his own research).

21 *Dansk Rørindustri* (n 4, above) at para 111. cf *Vaessen/Moris* (n 18, above); *Reuter/BASF*, above.

22 *Nutricia*, OJ 1983 L376/22, [1984] 2 CMLR 165; on appeal Case 42/84 *Remia v Commission* [1985] ECR 2545, [1987] 1 CMLR 1.

23 Case C-35/96 *Commission v Italy* [1998] ECR I-3851, [1998] 5 CMLR 889, para 36; Case T-513/93 *CNSD v Commission* [2000] ECR II-1807, [2000] 5 CMLR 614, para 36; Case T-155/04 *SELEX Sistemi Integrati v Commission* [2007] 4 CMLR 372, para 61 (on appeal Case C-113/07p *Selex Sistemi Integrati v Commission*, not yet decided).

24 *Höfner & Elser* (n 4, above); Case C-55/96 *Job Centre (No. 2)* [1997] ECR I-7119, [1998] 4 CMLR 708.

out by a private undertaking indicates that it is a business activity – the fact that the services in question are not at present offered by private undertakings does not prevent them being described as economic activity if it is possible for them to be carried on by private entities.[25] The fact that the service is provided free of charge is also not determinative.[26] However, the purchase of goods or services cannot be dissociated from the activity in which those goods or services will be used and so does not constitute a separate economic activity.[27]

Undertakings outside the common market. An undertaking situated outside **2.006**
the common market is still an undertaking and an agreement made by such an undertaking may fall within Article 81(1) if the agreement has effects ('*produit ses effets*') on the territory of the common market.[28] A foreign state trading corporation is an undertaking even, it seems, if it is the alter ego of a foreign government.[29]

(b) The State as an undertaking

Member States and the essential functions of the State. Member States are not **2.007**
undertakings when they act in the performance of their sovereign or administrative functions.[30] But the question of when the State, or a State–owned body, is engaging in commercial activity so as to place it within the sphere of competition law has generated a substantial jurisprudence. Some activities have been classified as part of the exercise of the sovereign power of the State such that they are not subject to competition law rules. These include the provision of air space management

---

[25] *SELEX Sistemi* (n 23, above) para 89.

[26] *Höfner & Elser* (n 4, above); *SELEX Sistemi* (n 23, above) para 90.

[27] Case T-319/99 *Federación Nacional de Empresas de Instrumentación Científica, Médica, Técnica y Dental (FENIN) v Commission* [2003] ECR II-357, [2003] 5 CMLR 34, [2004] All ER (EC) 300, para 36, upheld on appeal by the ECJ, Case C-205/03P, [2006] ECR I-6295, [2006] 5 CMLR 559, para 26; *SELEX Sistemi* (n 23, above) para 65.

[28] See Cases 89/85, etc, *Åhlström v Commission (Wood Pulp I)* [1988] ECR 5193, [1988] 4 CMLR 901, paras 12–13; Case T-395/94 *Atlantic Container Line AB v Commission* [2002] ECR II-875, [2002] 4 CMLR 1008, [2002] All ER (EC) 684, para 72. As to extraterritorial jurisdiction generally, see paras 1.105 *et seq*, above.

[29] eg *Cafeterios de Colombia*, OJ 1982 L360/31, [1983] 1 CMLR 703 (Colombian coffee marketing authority); *Aluminium imports from Eastern Europe*, OJ 1985 L92/1, [1987] 3 CMLR 813 (Communist state trading organisation); *Cane Sugar*, OJ 1980 L39/64, [1980] 2 CMLR 559 (agreements with sugar trading corporations owned by Commonwealth countries described in the decision as 'agreements with States').

[30] See, eg Case 52/76 *Benedetti v Munari* [1977] ECR 163, 191–192, per AG Reischl (State intervention agency an administrative organ acting in a sovereign capacity); Case 82/77 *Van Tiggele* [1978] ECR 25, 47–49, [1978] 2 CMLR 528, 539–542, per AG Capotorti (Dutch Produktschap performing public function in setting price rules not within Art 81(1)); *AROW/ BNIC*, OJ 1982 L379/1, 10, [1983] 2 CMLR 240, 254–255 (price decision of civil commissioner not within Art 81(1) as such). See also Case C-364/92 *SAT Fluggesellschaft v Eurocontrol* [1994] ECR I-43, [1994] 5 CMLR 208 (international organisation to coordinate air navigation control is exercising State functions). The same presumably applies to foreign States acting in their sovereign capacity.

services,[31] pollution control services in a harbour[32] and the collection of taxes.[33] The fact that a charge is made for a service does not automatically mean that the provision of that service is an economic activity.[34] But the fact that the service is provided free of charge is also not determinative.[35] The dilemma involved in assessing the conduct of State bodies has been summed up as follows:

> 'In seeking to determine whether an activity carried on by the State or a State entity is of an economic nature, the Court is entering dangerous territory, since it must find a balance between the need to protect undistorted competition on the common market and respect for the powers of the Member States. The power of the State which is exercised in the political sphere is subject to democratic control. A different type of control is imposed on economic operators acting on a market: their conduct is governed by competition law. But there is no justification, when the State is acting as an economic operator, for relieving its actions of all control. On the contrary, it must observe the same rules in such cases.'[36]

2.008 **State-owned corporations and statutory bodies.** State-owned corporations are undertakings within the meaning of Article 81(1) insofar as they carry on economic or commercial activities, which include the supply of public services.[37] Agreements between trading interests made within a public law framework may

---

[31] *Eurocontrol* (n 30, above): organisation established by an international Convention, whose activities included the provision of air traffic control services and the collection of route charges, was not an undertaking. The collection of route charges could not be separated from Eurocontrol's other activities and make it an undertaking. More recently, the CFI held that Eurocontrol's activity developing and adopting technical standards was not an economic activity because Eurocontrol in this role was merely a forum for concerted action of the Member States in coordinating their technical standards. However, the provision of advice by Eurocontrol to national authorities for drafting contract documents and carrying out calls for tender is an economic activity within Art 82: *SELEX Sistemi* (n 23, above). See also Case 123/83 *BNIC v Clair* [1985] ECR 391, 395, [1985] 2 CMLR 430, 441, per AG Slynn (a body created by ministerial decree whose sole function was to make rules to regulate others was not an 'undertaking' because it did not carry out an economic activity, although it could be an association of undertakings).

[32] Case C-343/95 *Cali & Figli v SEPG* [1997] ECR I-1547, [1997] 5 CMLR 484.

[33] Case C-207/01 *Altair Chimica v ENEL Distribuzione* [2003] ECR I-8875, [2003] 5 CMLR 867 (where an electricity generating company collected a surcharge imposed by the Italian government to pay for decommissioning nuclear power plants, it was acting as a tax collector rather than performing an economic activity).

[34] *Eurocontrol* (n 30, above).

[35] See para 2.005, above.

[36] Case C-205/03P *FENIN v Commission* (n 27, above), Opinion of AG Maduro, para 26. The Opinion contains a useful account of the jurisprudence on this topic. The ECJ agreed and upheld the judgment of the CFI in Case T-319/99 *FENIN* (n 27, above).

[37] eg Case 155/73 *Sacchi* [1974] ECR 409, 428–432, [1974] 2 CMLR 177, 203–205 (State television company); *British Telecommunications*, OJ 1982 L360/36, [1983] 1 CMLR 457, on appeal Case 41/83 *Italy v Commission* [1985] ECR 873, [1985] 2 CMLR 368 (rule-making activities of public telecommunications undertaking subject to Art 82); *NAVEWA/ANSEAU*, OJ 1982 L167/39, [1982] 2 CMLR 193, on appeal Cases 96/82, etc, *IAZ v Commission* [1983] ECR 3369, [1984] 3 CMLR 276 (water supply companies); Cases C-147 & 148/97 *Deutsche Post* [2000] ECR I-825, [2000] 4 CMLR 838 (postal service).

fall under Article 81(1).[38] Further, the fact that an entity carrying on an economic activity has public service obligations imposed on it by the State may place it at a competitive disadvantage but does not deprive the activity of its economic character.[39] A statutory body performing quasi-governmental functions is an undertaking in respect of its own commercial agreements.[40] If a statutory body is composed essentially of trading interests, it may be regarded as an 'association' of the undertakings whose interests are represented.[41]

Activities of State body to be considered individually. It is clear that each **2.009** activity carried on by the State or other public entity falls to be analysed separately so that it is possible for the body to be an undertaking in respect of some of its activities and not in respect of others.[42] Economic activity is contrasted with what the Court of Justice has described as the performance of 'a task in the public interest which forms part of the essential functions of the State'.[43] This distinction is not always readily apparent.[44] There are three situations in particular where the dividing line between the exercise of State function and the carrying on of economic activity have been considered: (i) where the State grants access to public property to an undertaking to enable that undertaking to carry out an activity, often coupled with the grant of a licence or concession to that undertaking for a fee; (ii) where the State organises social insurance or healthcare provision;

---

[38] Case 123/83 *BNIC v Clair* (n 31, above).

[39] Case C-475/99 *Ambulanz Glöckner* [2001] ECR I-8089, [2002] 4 CMLR 726 (ambulance services and patient transport services considered under Art 86).

[40] eg *Nungesser v Commission* (n 6, above) (INRA, the French national institute for agricultural research, treated as an undertaking despite the doubts of AG Rozés at [1982] ECR 2015, 2105–2106, [1983] 1 CMLR 278, 314–316); Case T-128/98 *Aéroports de Paris* (n 42, below) (airport authority in respect of its contracts for groundhandling services); see also *Höfner & Elser* (n 4, above).

[41] Case C-35/96 *Commission v Italy and CNSD* (n 23, above); *Pabst & Richarz/BNIA*, OJ 1976 L331/24, [1976] 2 CMLR D63; *AROW/BNIC* (n 30, above). See also *BNIC v Clair* (n 31, above).

[42] Case 118/85 *Commission v Italy* [1987] ECR 2599, [1988] 3 CMLR 255, para 7; and Case T-128/98 *Aéroports de Paris v Commission* [2000] ECR II-3929, [2001] 4 CMLR 1376, para 108 (upheld on appeal Case C-82/01P *Aéroports de Paris v Commission* [2002] ECR I-9297, [2003] 4 CMLR 609); *SELEX Sistemi* (n 23, above) para 54.

[43] *Cali & Figli v SEPG* (n 32, above) para 22 (activity of anti-pollution surveillance carried out by a limited company set up by public port authority did not come within Art 82 although financed by dues paid by port users).

[44] The UK Competition Appeal Tribunal in *Bettercare Group v Director General of Fair Trading* [2002] CAT 7, [2002] CompAR 299, distinguished between cases where the competition rules do not apply because the conduct complained of is that of the State 'exercising its sovereign powers in the regulatory and administrative sphere' and other cases where the activity was not 'economic' because it is 'an exclusively social function' and is 'based on the principle of solidarity'. The Tribunal considered that the *Eurocontrol* and *Cali & Figli* cases were examples of the former category and the *Poucet and Pistre* cases (para 2.012, below) of the latter. This judgment was described as 'particularly noteworthy' by AG Maduro in *FENIN*, (n 36, above). See also *Institute of Independent Insurance Brokers v Director General of Fair Trading* [2001] CAT 4, [2001] CompAR 62, paras 252 *et seq*.

(iii) where the State delegates the task of supervising a profession or other activity to a regulatory body.

2.010 **Occupation and use of publicly owned facilities.** These principles were applied by the Court of First Instance and the Court of Justice in *Aéroports de Paris*. ADP was a public corporation governed by French law but financially autonomous. It was responsible under the French Civil Aviation Code for the Paris airports. It granted concessions to two airline catering providers, allowing them to occupy premises on land within the airport perimeter and to use the airport's facilities as necessary to provide their catering service to airlines using the airport. The fee payable by the catering companies was in part a fixed amount for the use of the land and in part a 'commercial fee' calculated as a proportion of the turnover of their business. The Commission found that ADP had abused its dominant position because the fees charged to the different companies amounted to discrimination.[45] One of the issues raised on appeal was whether ADP was an undertaking for the purposes of Article 82. The Court of First Instance reaffirmed[46] that the fact that ADP was a public corporation placed under the authority of the Minister responsible for civil aviation and that it managed facilities in public ownership did not in itself mean that it could not be an undertaking.[47] It was necessary first to determine what the relevant activities are and then to consider whether or not they constitute economic activities. The Court upheld the Commission's conclusion that the variable commercial fee charged by the airport was not simply a fee for the occupation of the land but rather related to the activities which ADP carried on in managing and maintaining the airport infrastructure for the benefit of the caterers as well as for other businesses using those facilities. The Commission had been correct to draw a distinction between the part of the fee payable purely for the private occupation of publicly owned land, and that payable for the provision by ADP of management services and licensing of the catering concession. The activity covered by the commercial fee was therefore an economic activity which fell within Article 82.[48] The Court considered that its conclusion in this regard was supported by the fact that in some Member

---

[45] *Alpha Flight Services/Aéroports de Paris*, OJ 1998 L230/10, [1998] 5 CMLR 611.

[46] Case T-128/98 *Aéroports de Paris v Commission* [2000] ECR II-3929, [2001] 4 CMLR 1376.

[47] The CFI also held that it was irrelevant that that the agreements between ADP and the groundhandlers were concluded under French law applicable to agreements for the occupation of publicly-owned property (para 120).

[48] The CFI referred in its judgment to Case 41/83 *Italy v Commission* [1985] ECR 873, [1985] 2 CMLR 368, where the ECJ held that the activity whereby BT managed public telecommunications equipment and placed such equipment at the disposal of users on payment of a fee amounted to an economic activity, and Case T-229/94 *Deutsche Bahn v Commission* [1997] ECR II-1689, [1998] 4 CMLR 220, where it was held that that the provision of locomotives, traction and access to the railway infrastructure is to be regarded as an economic activity.

States the management of airports was carried out by private undertakings.[49] The Court of Justice upheld this analysis holding that the activity of managing and operating the Paris airports could be separated from ADP's purely administrative and supervisory activities and did fall within Article 82.[50]

Practice in the Member States. In its judgment in *Aéroports de Paris*, the Court **2.011** of First Instance referred to the litigation in the French courts concerning complaints by TAT European Airlines.[51] TAT complained that ADP had grouped Air France's activities at Orly-Ouest airport and required several airlines including TAT to transfer their services to Orly Sud. TAT also complained about the fact that it was forced to use ADP's ground handling services. The Tribunal des Conflits found [52] that the decisions to group Air France's activities at Orly-Ouest air terminal and to refuse TAT's request to open new lines from this air terminal constituted the use of public power prerogatives. The decisions could not be separated from the reorganisation of Orly decided by ADP and approved by the Minister of Equipment and Transportation. However, the requirement imposed on TAT to use ADP's groundhandling services could be separated from their public activities and was therefore subject to competition law. The Brussels Court of Appeal applied *Aéroports de Paris* in holding that although some activities of the Diamond Council were economic activities within Article 82, the functions conferred on it by Royal Decree to control the value, weight, qualification and origin of imported or exported diamonds were part of its public function and not subject to competition rules.[53] In two decisions under the Dutch Competition Act, the terms of leases granted by municipal authorities were held to be part of their public function and not susceptible to challenge on competition grounds.[54]

---

[49] The CFI referred to the Commission's decn in *FAG - Flughafen Frankfurt/Main AG*, OJ 1998 L72/30 where the Commission found that the undertaking which owns and operates Frankfurt airport is a private undertaking approved in accordance with German law.

[50] Case C-82/01P *Aéroports de Paris v Commission* [2002] ECR I-9297, [2003] 4 CMLR 609.

[51] Case T-128/98 *Aéroports de Paris* (n 46, above) para 129.

[52] *Aéroports de Paris et Air France v TAT European Airlines*, judgment of 18 October 1999, AJDA 1999.996. On subsequent referral back, the Paris Court of Appeal upheld the finding of the French competition authority that the requirement to use ADP's groundhandling services breached the French domestic equivalent of Art 82: judgment of 23 September 2003, ref in Report of the Conseil de la Concurrence 2003.

[53] *International Gemmological Institute BVBA v Hoge Raad voor Diamant Antwerpen VZW*, judgment of the Brussels Court of Appeal (2004/MR/1), 31 January 2006.

[54] Case 99/1690 *Van Vollenhoven Olie v Municipality of Venlo and Schreurs Oliemaatschappij BV*, judgment of 1 August 2001 (Rotterdam District Court held that the municipality had not been acting as an undertaking when it granted exclusivity to a supplier of petrol in a newly developed industrial site); Case 101 *Laddrak v Municipality of Amsterdam*, decn of Dutch Competition Authority, 26 November 1998 (restriction in a lease of a stall in a flower market limiting products sold to fresh or dried flowers was part of the public zoning plan for the market).

2.012 **Insurance and social security schemes.** The distinction between economic activity and tasks carried out in the public interest has arisen particularly in the context of independently managed social security schemes. In *Poucet and Pistre*,[55] the Court of Justice held that two autonomous schemes set up under French law, one for sickness and maternity insurance and the other for old age insurance, were not undertakings: they pursued only a social objective and were based on the principle of solidarity in that the benefits were not related to the level of compulsory contribution which was determined by reference to individual income.[56] By contrast, a non-profit organisation that operated an optional pension scheme on the basis of capitalisation, was held to be an undertaking.[57] Moreover, in the *Dutch Sectoral Pension Funds* cases,[58] the Court held that pension funds which were established by collective agreements in particular sectors of industry, and to which affiliation was *prima facie* compulsory under Dutch law, were undertakings: the benefits that they provided depended on the performance of their investments and the funds could grant exemption from affiliation where an employer gave its workers benefits of at least an equivalent level. The fact that the bodies operating those pension schemes and funds were to an extent in competition with private insurance companies pointed to their carrying out an economic activity. The reasoning in these cases has since been applied to organisations managing a national health system which, since they operate according to the principle of solidarity

---

55 Cases C-159 & 160/91 *Poucet and Pistre v AGF and Cancava* [1993] ECR I-637. In Cases C-264/01, etc, *AOK Bundesverband* [2004] ECR I-2493, [2004] 4 CMLR 1261, the fact that the fund was compelled by law to offer identical benefits and had no influence over those benefits pointed to it not being an economic activity. Further, the ancillary function performed by the fund of setting the maximum amount paid to pharmaceutical companies for medicines paid for by the fund was a part of the exclusively social objective of the fund and not a separate economic activity.

56 See also *Pavlov* (n 16, above) (supplementary pension scheme for medical specialists); Case C-218/00 *Cisal* [2002] ECR I-691, [2002] 4 CMLR 833 (body providing compulsory insurance against accidents at work not an undertaking).

57 Case C-244/94 *Fédération Française des Sociétés d'Assurances (FFSA) v Ministère de l'Agriculture et de la Pêche* [1995] ECR I-4013, [1996] 4 CMLR 536 (benefits were based on the financial results of the fund's investments and were proportionate to the contributions paid).

58 Case C-67/96 *Albany* [1999] ECR I-5751, [2000] 4 CMLR 446; Cases C-115–117/97 *Brentjens* [1999] ECR I-6025, [2000] 4 CMLR 566; Case C-219/97 *Drijvende Bokken* [1999] ECR I-6121, [2000] 4 CMLR 599; and subsequently Case C-222/98 *Van der Woude* [2000] ECR I-7111, [2001] 4 CMLR 93; Case E-8/00 *Lo and NKF v KS* [2002] EFTA Ct Rep 114, [2002] 5 CMLR 160. See also *Pavlov* (n 16, above) where, in a complex judgment, the ECJ held that a pension fund, which determines itself the amount of the contributions and benefits and operates on the basis of the principle of capitalisation, which has been made responsible for managing a supplementary pension scheme set up by the medical practitioners' representative body and membership of which has been made compulsory by the public authorities for all members of that profession, is an undertaking. Further, the ECJ held that a decision taken by the members of a liberal profession to set up the fund and to request the public authorities to make membership of that fund compulsory fell within the scope of Art 81 but that the decision had no appreciable effect on competition. It was not contrary to Art 10 in conjunction with Art 81 for the public authorities to make membership of the scheme compulsory.

and provide services free of charge to members on the basis of universal cover, are not to be regarded as carrying on economic activity.[59]

Regulatory bodies.   In *Wouters*,[60] the Court of Justice considered whether the rules promulgated by the Netherlands Bar Association could be regarded as decisions of an association of undertakings even though the power to adopt binding rules was conferred on it by statute. The Court held that the fact that the constitution of the Bar Association was regulated by public law did not take the body outside the ambit of Article 81(1). The Court drew a distinction between two situations. The first is where a Member State grants regulatory powers to a professional association and defines public interest criteria and other principles in accordance with which the body must act. In such a situation, where the Member State also retains its power to adopt decisions in the last resort, the rules adopted by the association remain State measures and are not covered by Article 81. In the second situation where the rules are adopted by the association alone, they are subject to the competition rules. The Court held that the rule in question, prohibiting multi-disciplinary partnerships, was a rule regulating the economic activity carried on by advocates and so fell within the scope of the competition rules. In *Institute of Independent Insurance Brokers*,[61] the United Kingdom Competition Appeal Tribunal, considering the rules of a trade association regulating aspects of the conduct of insurance business, stated that it was doubtful whether, as a matter of Community law, the notion of the exercise of 'official authority' or 'public powers' can extend to cases where the legal basis of the activity in question is not derived from the public law of the Member State but derives entirely from contracts between private parties. The Irish High Court did not regard the regulatory bodies governing the conduct of opticians or dentists as undertakings subject to the competition rules.[62]

2.013

Activities ancillary to exercise of public functions.   An organisation which purchases goods in order to use them for the purposes of an activity which would

2.014

---

[59] Case T-319/99 *FENIN* (n 36, above). The CFI declined to consider the question whether the fact that the hospitals also on occasion provided health services for which they made a charge affected their status as economic entities since this fact had not been brought to the Commission's attention before it rejected the complaint. This jurisprudence was applied by the Brussels Court of Appeal in *Cools v De Christelijke Mutualiteiten Antwerpen* judgment of 25 January 2005 (Case No 2003/MR/14), holding that an Antwerp health insurance fund was not an undertaking for the purposes of the Belgian domestic equivalent of Art 81 since the system of reimbursement was characterised by the principle of solidarity (the benefits were not related to the level of compulsory contribution).

[60] *Wouters* (n 16, above).

[61] *Institute of Independent Insurance Brokers v Director General of Fair Trading* (n 44, above) para 256.

[62] *Easy Readers Limited v Bord na Radharcmhastori* (2003) IEHC 67 (15 October 2003) (opticians); *Kenny trading as Denture Express v Dental Council* (2004) IEHC 29 (27 February 2004) (dentists).

itself not constitute economic activity does not act as an undertaking simply because it is a purchaser in a given market. Although such an entity may wield very considerable economic power, if the activity for which the entity purchases goods is not an economic activity, then it is not acting as an undertaking in making those purchases.[63] Similarly, the acquisition of prototype equipment and the management of intellectual property rights used in the development of technical standards cannot be separated out from the production and adoption of technical standards which was not a commercial activity.[64] The EFTA Court has held[65] that if an association of municipalities engages in collective bargaining in respect of employees who are engaged exclusively in the realm of public administration, neither the organisation nor its members could in that respect be considered an undertaking within the meaning of Article 53 EEA. However, if the collective agreement covers municipal employees of all groups, not only employees engaged in the realm of public administration, then the municipality is protecting its interests as an employer engaged in economic activities and may act as an undertaking within the meaning of Article 53 EEA.

2.015 Article 86. In the case of 'public undertakings and undertakings to which Member States grant special or exclusive rights', Member States are required by Article 86(1) of the Treaty neither to enact nor to maintain in force any measure contrary, *inter alia*, to Articles 81–89. However, by virtue of Article 86(2), '[u]ndertakings entrusted with the operation of services of general economic interest or having the character of a revenue-producing monopoly' have a limited dispensation from the rules on competition. The application of these provisions is discussed in Chapter 11, below.[66]

2.016 Local authorities and municipalities. Whether Member States' regional or local authorities are 'undertakings' in respect of their commercial agreements is an open question. Probably their position is to be assimilated to that of a Member State. In *Bettercare*,[67] the UK Competition Appeal Tribunal held that

---

63 Case T-319/99 *FENIN* (n 36, above) upheld on appeal Case C-205/03P (n 36, above) where the ECJ said at para 26: 'there is no need to dissociate the activity of purchasing goods from the subsequent use to which they are put in order to determine the nature of that purchasing activity, and . . . the nature of the purchasing activity must be determined according to whether or not the subsequent use of the purchased goods amounts to an economic activity'.

64 *SELEX Sistemi* (n 23, above) paras 75 *et seq*.

65 *Lo and NKF v KS* (n 58, above) para 65.

66 See also Art 31 EC: paras 11.036 *et seq*, below.

67 *Bettercare Group v Director General of Fair Trading* (n 43, above); see also the cases concerning Dutch municipal authorities (n 54, above). In *NAVEWA/ANSEAU* (n 37, above) the membership of the ANSEAU association fined for infringement of Art 81(1) appears to have included certain local water authorities. But contracts for concessions concluded between French communes acting in their capacity as public authorities and undertakings entrusted with the operation of a public service do not constitute agreements between undertakings: Case 30/87 *Bodson v Pompes Funèbres* [1988] ECR 2479, [1989] 4 CMLR 984. See also para 2.009, above.

local authorities were undertakings in their acquisition and provision of care home services. The EFTA Court also applied the Court of Justice's jurisprudence in concluding that an association of municipalities was an association of undertakings when it entered into a collective labour agreement which covered both employees who worked in the municipality's economic activities and those who worked exclusively in the municipality's public administration activities.[68]

(c) Treatment of economically linked legal entities

Group of companies as a single undertaking.   The focus of Community law   **2.017**
on the economic rather than legal scope of the entity means that a corporate group made up of a number of individual legal bodies can be treated as a single undertaking for the purposes of competition law.[69] For the purpose of applying the rules on competition, the formal separation between two parties resulting from their separate legal personality is not conclusive; the decisive test is the unity of their conduct on the market.[70] This is relevant to three issues in particular: (i) the application of Article 81(1) to an agreement between companies in the same group; (ii) whether the conduct of a subsidiary company can be imputed to a parent company, usually in the context of imposing a fine; and (iii) which associated undertakings should be taken into account when calculating the turnover of an undertaking for the purpose of applying a turnover threshold, for example, in a block exemption regulation. In the first situation, it is in the interest of the companies concerned to be considered as a single undertaking. By contrast, in the context of the other two cases, they may wish to argue that the subsidiary should be regarded as a distinct undertaking. The first issue is discussed here and the other two issues are considered further in Chapter 13, below. However, the principles established by the case law apply without distinction to all three situations. Thus an agreement between a parent company and a subsidiary or between two companies which are under the common control of a third does not fall within Article 81(1) if the companies form an economic unit within which the subsidiary has no real freedom to determine its course of action on the market.[71] Since entities which form part of the same economic unit cannot be expected to compete with one another, relations

---

68 *Lo and NKF v KS* (n 58, above) paras 60 *et seq.*

69 Case 170/83 *Hydrotherm v Compact* [1984] ECR 2999, [1985] 3 CMLR 224, para 11; Case T-234/95 *DSG v Commission* [2000] ECR II-2603, para 124 (appeal dismissed, Case C-323/00P [2002] ECR I-3919); *Pre-insulated Pipe Cartel*, OJ 1999 L24/1, [1999] 4 CMLR 402, para 154, upheld on appeal in Case T-9/99 *HFB v Commission* [2002] ECR II-1487, paras 54–68; and *Dansk Rørindustri* (n 4, above) paras 103 *et seq* (further appeal dismissed, Cases C-189/02P, etc, [2005] ECR I-5425, [2005] 5 CMLR 796); *Minoan Lines* (n 5, above) para 122.

70 Case C-217/05 *Confederación Española de Empresarios de Estaciones de Servicio v CEPSA* [2006] ECR I-11987, [2007] 4 CMLR 181, para 41.

71 Case T-102/92 *Viho v Commission* [1995] ECR II-17, [1997] 4 CMLR 469, [1995] All ER (EC) 371; upheld on appeal, Case C-73/95P [1996] ECR I-5457, [1997] 4 CMLR 419, paras 16–18. See also *Double Quick Supplyline Ltd v Office of Fair Trading* [2007] CAT 13, paras 69 *et seq.*

between such entities, although they have separate legal personality, cannot give rise to an agreement or concerted practice that restricts competition.[72] For the same reason, for the purpose of a block exemption which applies to an agreement 'to which only two undertakings are party',[73] a parent company and its subsidiary or subsidiaries forming a single economic unit will be counted as a single undertaking.[74]

2.018 **Subsidiary companies and branches.** There is in effect a presumption, at least in the case of a wholly owned subsidiary, that its commercial policy is decisively influenced by its parent so as to constitute a single undertaking.[75] However, on the basis of the governing test, the possibility cannot be altogether excluded of showing that a subsidiary is in fact free independently to determine its conduct on the market.[76] Therefore, in justifying the imputation of the conduct of a subsidiary to its parent for the purpose of the imposition of a fine, the fact of ownership, or common ownership is important but is not conclusive and the Commission takes additional factors into account.[77] However, a subsidiary company may be an undertaking which is liable in its own right for infringement of the competition rules.[78] A branch office

---

[72] Case C-73/95P *Viho* (above) per AG Lenz at para 67; his Opinion reviews the conflicting strands in the previous case law.

[73] eg the block exemption for technology transfer agreements, Reg 772/2004: OJ 2004 L123/11, Vol II, App C.7.

[74] *Hydrotherm v Compact* (n 69, above).

[75] Case T-354/94 *Stora Kopparbergs Bergslags v Commission* [1998] ECR II-2111, para 80, confirmed by the ECJ in Case C-286/98P *Stora Kopparbergs Bergslags v Commission* [2000] ECR I-9925, [2001] 4 CMLR 370, paras 27–29; *Tokai Carbon (Speciality Graphite)* (n 5, above) para 60; Case T-325/01 *DaimlerChrysler v Commission* [2005] ECR II-3319, [2007] 4 CMLR 559, paras 219–220.

[76] In Decn No 03-D-01 of 14 January 2003, BOCCRF 8 October 2003, the French Conseil de la Concurrence fined three companies in the Air Liquide Group for collusive tendering for public contracts. Although the Conseil confirmed that an agreement between companies within the group as to which would submit a bid would not have breached Art 81 if they were not commercially independent, it was a breach to deceive the recipient of the bids into believing that they were genuinely competing with each other by submitting separate bids when in fact they had colluded. See further para 2.047, below.

[77] *Dansk Rørindustri* (n 4, above) para 118; Case C-196/099 *Aristrain v Commission* [2003] ECR I-1105, para 99; COMP 37.533 *Choline Chloride*, 9 December 2004, [2006] 4 CMLR 159, paras 172–175, on appeal Case T-112/05 *Akzo Nobel v Commission*, not yet decided.

[78] See eg Case C-279/98P *Cascades v Commission* [2000] ECR I-9693, where the ECJ held that an undertaking is not responsible for the cartel participation of other entities before they became its subsidiaries. The case was remitted back to the CFI to assess fines on the two subsidiary companies: Case T-308/94 *Cascades SA v Commission* [2002] ECR II-813, [2002] 4 CMLR 1381; similarly Case T-354/94 *Stora Kopparbergs Bergslags* (n 75, above). For cases where a subsidiary has been fined for distinct infringements from those committed by its parent, see, eg *BPB Industries/British Gypsum*, OJ 1989 L10/50 (am OJ 1989 L52/42), [1990] 4 CMLR 464, on appeal Case T-65/89, [1993] ECR II-389, [1993] 5 CMLR 32, on further appeal Case C-310/93P, [1995] ECR I-865, [1997] 4 CMLR 238. In Cases T-71/03, etc, *Tokai Carbon* (n 5, above) the subsidiary had been involved in the cartel meetings and its behaviour was imputed to its parent, making them jointly and severally liable to be fined.

is not an undertaking.[79] Although it remains unclear whether a division within a company could constitute an undertaking,[80] for the purpose of enforcement it is necessary for a decision finding an infringment to be addressed to entities with legal personality.[81]

Partly owned subsidiaries.   A substantial minority shareholding by one com-   **2.019** pany in another will not render the two a single economic unit.[82] Difficulties may arise, however, in the case of partly owned subsidiaries. In *Gosme/Martell–DMP*,[83] the Commission considered an agreement between Martell and DMP, the latter being a joint subsidiary owned 50 per cent by Martell and 50 per cent by Piper-Heidsieck. The Commission found that Martell and DMP were independent undertakings. At the relevant time Martell was not in a position to control the commercial activity of DMP because:

(a) the parent companies each held 50 per cent of the capital and voting rights of DMP;

(b) half the supervisory board members represented Martell shareholders and half Piper-Heidsieck shareholders;

(c) DMP also distributed brands not belonging to its parent companies;

(d) Martell and Piper-Heidsieck products were invoiced to customers on the same document; and

(e) DMP had its own sales force and it alone concluded the conditions of sale with its customers.[84]

In *IJsselcentrale*,[85] the Commission rejected an argument that the four parties (electricity generating companies) and their jointly owned subsidiary (SEP) formed a single economic entity. The four companies did not belong to a single group and were not controlled by a single person; each company determined its own conduct independently and the fact that the generators formed part of a single indivisible system of public supply did not change their position. SEP was

---

[79] *Fire Insurance (D)*, OJ 1982 L80/36, [1982] 2 CMLR 159. For subsequent proceedings see *Fire Insurance (D)*, OJ 1985 L35/20, [1985] 3 CMLR 246; on appeal, Case 45/85 *Verband der Sachversicherer v Commission* [1987] ECR 405, [1988] 4 CMLR 264.

[80] See Wils, 'The Undertaking as subject of EC competition law and the imputation of infringe-ments to natural or legal persons' (2000) 25 ELR 99, arguing that a division cannot constitute an undertaking.

[81] Cases T-305/94, etc, *Limburgse Vinyl Maatschappij v Commission* ('PVC No. 2') [1999] ECR II-931, [1999] 5 CMLR 303, para 978; further appeals only on procedural grounds largely dismissed, Cases C-238/99P, etc, [2002] ECR I-8375, [2003] 4 CMLR 397.

[82] See, eg Case T-145/89 *Baustahlgewebe v Commission* [1995] ECR II-987, para 107 (on appeal on other grounds, Case C-185/95P [1998] ECR I-8417, [1999] 4 CMLR 1203).

[83] *Gosme/Martell-DMP*, OJ 1991 L185/23, [1992] 5 CMLR 586.

[84] ibid, para 30. The Commission also noted that neither DMP nor Martell had contested the view that they were independent; on the contrary, they had written to the Commission to underline this independence.

[85] *IJsselcentrale*, OJ 1991 L28/32, [1992] 5 CMLR 154.

a joint venture controlled by its parents together and so did not form an economic unit with one or more of the parents.[86]

2.020 **Agents.** An independent agent is probably an undertaking, but an agreement between a principal and its agent strictly so-called may fall outside Article 81(1).[87] Where an agent works for his principal, he may be regarded as an auxiliary organ bound to carry out the principal's instructions and thus, like a commercial employee, form part of the same economic unit as the principal.[88] Whether the agent is to be regarded as so integrated with the principal depends on whether the agent takes on an economic risk which is more than negligible and whether he determines his conduct on the market independently.[89] This question must be determined by looking at the clauses of the agreement, implied or express, relating to the assumption of financial and commercial risks, but taking account of the real economic situation rather than the legal classification of the contractual relationship under national law. Hence, in *DaimlerChrysler*,[90] the Court of First Instance carried out a careful analysis of the arrangements between Mercedes Benz and its commercial agents in Germany, annulling the finding of the Commission that the agents carried sufficient commercial risks to bring the agency agreement within the scope of Article 81. Although the agents were able to negotiate discounts with customers that were deducted from their commission, and were required to purchase demonstration vehicles and to set up a workshop to carry out guarantee repair work, the Court found that the Commission had overstated the resulting

---

[86] See also *Optical Fibres*, OJ 1986 L236/30 in which there was a series of interlocking JVs in the UK, France and Germany. Corning's interest in each JV was 50 per cent in the UK and Germany and 40 per cent in France. Each JV was technologically dependent on Corning. Corning had certain veto rights (but not voting control), and actively participated in the management. Without discussion the Commission treated each JV as a separate undertaking and held that the arrangements were likely to restrict competition between them. For the application of Art 81(1) to JVs generally, see Chap 7, below.

[87] See paras 6.028 *et seq*, below.

[88] Case T-56/99 *Marlines v Commission* [2003] ECR II-5225, [2005] 5 CMLR 1761, para 60: Commission was entitled to treat the manager of the vessels as part of the same economic unit as the ship owners. The fact that the ship owners had not given the agent authority to take part in the cartel was not relevant here (appeal dismissed Case C-112/04P *Marlines v Commission*, Order of 15 September 2005 (unpublished)). See also Case T-59/99 *Ventouris Group Enterprises v Commission* [2003] ECR II 5257, [2005] 5 CMLR 1781, paras 147 *et seq*.

[89] Case T-325/01 *DaimlerChrysler v Commission* (n 75, above) paras 87–88. See, eg Case T-66/99 *Minoan Lines v Commission* [2003] ECR II 5515, [2005] 5 CMLR 1957, paras 121 *et seq*: ETA was Minoan's 'right hand man' and the two companies formed a single economic entity for the purposes of competition law (appeal dismissed Case C-121/04P *Minoan Lines v Commission*, Order of 17 November 2005); *CEPSA* (n 70, above) para 61.

[90] Case T-325/01 *DaimlerChrysler v Commission* [2005] ECR II-3319, [2007] 4 CMLR 559. See also *CEPSA* (n 70, above) (the allocation of financial and commercial risks between a petrol service station operator and the supplier of fuel must be analysed on the basis of criteria such as ownership of the goods, the contribution to the costs linked to their distribution, the safe keeping of and liability for any damage caused to the goods or by the goods to third parties and the making of investments specific to the sale of those goods: para 60).

commercial risks (the demonstration vehicles were supplied on preferential terms and could then be resold and the agents received a guaranteed payment in advance from the manufacturer to cover the cost of repair work). Further, there were many substantial differences between the position of these agents and independent Mercedes dealers: in particular, the contractual sales to customers were always made by the agents in the name of Mercedes Benz, who bore the main share of the price risk, and the agents were not required to hold a stock of cars.

Employees and trade unions.   An employee is not an undertaking.[91] A workers' **2.021**
organisation is probably not an undertaking, at least as regards its industrial relations activities where it acts on behalf of its members;[92] and collective labour
agreements concerning conditions of work and employment in any event fall
outside the scope of Article 81(1).[93] But a trade union may be an undertaking
subject to the competition rules insofar as it carries on an economic activity in its
own right, such as the operation of a savings bank or travel agency.[94]

3. Agreements, Decisions and Concerted Practices

Generally.   The concepts of 'agreement', 'decision of an association of under- **2.022**
takings' and 'concerted practice' overlap.[95] The Commission may characterise the
arrangements made by the parties to a complex cartel as constituting an agreement and/or a concerted practice, and this approach has been upheld by the
Community Courts.[96] The Court of Justice has stated:

> 'The list in Article [81(1)] of the Treaty is intended to apply to all collusion between
> undertakings, whatever form it takes. There is continuity between the cases listed.
> The only essential thing is the distinction between independent conduct, which is

---

[91] Cases 40/73, etc, *Suiker Unie v Commission* [1975] ECR 1663, [1976] 1 CMLR 295, para 539. As regards ex-employees, see *Reuter/BASF* (n 20, above).

[92] See *Les Meilleures Éditions v Comité Intersyndical du Livre Parisien*, Paris Court of Appeal, 29 February 2000, BOCCRF 31 March 2000 (agreement between a publisher and the union to acquire all its printing needs from companies where the CILP was in charge of placing workers not covered by French competition rules). But a trade union may have *locus* to make a complaint to the Commission: *BP/TGWU*, XVIth Report on Competition Policy (1986), point 43; for the rights of employee representatives under the Merger Regulation, Reg 139/2004, Art 18(4), see paras 8.131 and 8.241, below.

[93] *Albany* (n 58, above) paras 59–60; *Lo and NKF v KS* (n 58, above). See further para 2.034, below.

[94] *Dutch Sectoral Pension Funds* cases, per AG Jacobs, Opinion at para 226.

[95] Thus an 'agreement' can also be a 'decision': *FEDETAB*, OJ 1978 L224/29, 40, [1978] 3 CMLR 524, 539, on appeal Cases 209/78, etc, *Van Landewyck v Commission* ('*FEDETAB*') [1980] ECR 3125, [1981] 3 CMLR 134, paras 85–89; and an 'informal agreement' may also be a 'concerted practice': paras 2.038 *et seq*, below.

[96] See, eg *Polypropylene*, OJ 1986 L230/1, [1988] 4 CMLR 347, paras 86–87; appeals largely dismissed: *PVC No. 2* (n 81, above) paras 696–698, 72.

allowed, and collusion, which is not, regardless of any distinction between the types of collusion.'[97]

(a) Agreements

2.023 **Agreements may be informal.** The word 'agreements' in Article 81(1) is not confined to legally binding contracts;[98] it is sufficient if the undertakings in question have expressed their joint intention to conduct themselves on the market in a specific way.[99] A 'gentlemen's agreement', as the expression of a morally binding commitment, is therefore an 'agreement' within the meaning of Article 81(1).[100] Such an agreement may be written or oral, it may be inferred from all the circumstances,[101] and can consist in the continuing business relationship between the parties.[102] Summarising the effect of the case law, the Court of First Instance has stated that:

> 'the concept of an agreement within the meaning of Article [81(1)] . . . centres around the existence of a concurrence of wills between at least two parties, the form in which it is manifested being unimportant so long as it constitutes the faithful expression of the parties' intention.'[103]

The concept of agreement can cover the inchoate understandings and partial and conditional agreements in the bargaining process which lead up to a

---

[97] Case C-49/92P *Commission v Anic Partecipazioni* [1999] ECR I-4125, [2001] 4 CMLR 602, para 108 (one of the *Polypropylene* appeals). For a useful exposition of the law see the judgment of the UK Competition Appeal Tribunal in *JJB Sports plc v Office of Fair Trading* [2004] CAT 17, [2005] Comp AR 29, paras 150 *et seq*.

[98] *Van Landewyck* (n 95, above) paras 85–91; *Polypropylene* (n 96, above) para 81.

[99] Case T-7/89 *Hercules v Commission* [1991] ECR II-1711, [1992] 4 CMLR 84, para 256; appeal dismissed, Case C-51/92P [1999] ECR I-4235, [1999] 5 CMLR 976. See also Case 41/69 *ACF Chemiefarma v Commission* [1970] ECR 661, para 112; *Van Landewyck* (n 95, above) para 86. For a case where the CFI found that the Commission had failed to prove that a meeting at which banks discussed prices for currency swaps gave rise to a price-fixing agreement, see Cases T-44/02, etc, *Dresdner Bank v Commission* [2006] ECR II-3567, [2007] 4 CMLR 467.

[100] eg *Interbrew and Alken-Maes ('Belgian beer')*, OJ 2003 L200/1, [2004] 4 CMLR 80, paras 247 and 248 (appeals dismissed: Case T-38/02 *Groupe Danone v Commission* [2005] ECR II-4407, [2006] 4 CMLR 1429 (small reduction in the fine) (further appeal dismissed: C-3/06P [2007] 4 CMLR 701) and Case T-48/02 *Brouwerij Haacht v Commission* [2005] ECR II-5259, [2006] 4 CMLR 621); *Minoan Lines* (n 89, above) para 207; *Ventouris* (n 88, above) para 52; *Vitamins*, OJ 2003 L6/1, [2003] 4 CMLR 22, para 554 (fines reduced on appeal, Cases T-15/02, etc, *BASF v Commission* [2006] ECR II-497, [2006] 5 CMLR 27).

[101] eg Case 28/77 *Tepea v Commission* [1978] ECR 1391, [1978] 3 CMLR 392, paras 17–57 (informal oral agreement inferred from dealings between the parties); Cases 32/78, etc, *BMW v Commission* [1979] ECR 2435, [1980] 1 CMLR 370 (circular signed by dealers); *National Panasonic*, OJ 1982 L354/28, 32, [1983] 1 CMLR 497, 504–505 (terms of unwritten dealer agreements clearly understood by the parties); *Viho/Toshiba*, OJ 1991 L287/39, [1992] 4 CMLR 180 (understanding that export ban would apply).

[102] *Konica*, OJ 1988 L78/34, [1988] 4 CMLR 848, para 40, although this must now be read subject to the *ADALAT* line of decisions discussed in paras 2.025 *et seq*, below.

[103] Case T-41/96 *Bayer v Commission ('ADALAT')* [2000] ECR II-3383, [2001] 4 CMLR 126, [2001] All ER (EC) 1.

definitive agreement.[104] Furthermore, the process of negotiation and preparation culminating effectively in the adoption of an overall plan to regulate the market may well also (depending on the circumstances) be correctly characterised as a concerted practice.[105] If the parties combine informally to restrict competition, but those arrangements are neither legally nor morally binding, they may give rise to a 'concerted practice'.[106] A series of connected agreements that pursue the same overall objective may be read together as one agreement,[107] and the agreement can encompass not only the overall plan and the terms expressly agreed but also the implementation of what has been agreed in pursuance of the same common purpose.[108]

Unilateral action. Action taken by an undertaking without any agreement or concert with another undertaking does not infringe Article 81(1),[109] although an undertaking in a dominant position may by unilateral conduct infringe Article 82.[110] However, care needs to be taken in determining whether particular conduct is truly 'unilateral'. If, for example, a supplier operates a restricted system of distribution, the apparently 'unilateral' exclusion of a particular dealer may infringe Article 81(1) if it results from an understanding, tacit or express, between the supplier and his existing dealers, to exclude certain dealers from the distribution network.[111]   **2.024**

The *ADALAT* case. The distinction between unilateral conduct and conduct which falls within Article 81(1) was considered by the Community Courts in the   **2.025**

---

[104] COMP/37.857 *Organic Peroxides*, 10 December 2003, [2005] 5 CMLR 579, para 297 (appeal on other grounds dismissed, Case T-120/04 *Peróxidos Orgánicos v Commission* [2007] 4 CMLR 153). cf Case E-3/97 *Jaeger v Opel Norge* [1988] Rep EFTA Ct 1, [1999] 4 CMLR 147, where the EFTA Court held (para 38) that if parties are still in negotiations and have not reached a consensus there can be no agreement within Art 53(1) EEA.

[105] *Organic Peroxides*, above, para 301.

[106] Paras 2.038 *et seq*, below.

[107] Cases T-25/95, etc, *Cimenteries CBR v Commission ('Cement')* [2000] ECR II-491, [2000] 5 CMLR 204, paras 4019–4058. See also *BP Kemi/DDSF*, OJ 1979 L286/32, [1979] 3 CMLR 684; *ENI/Montedison*, OJ 1987 L5/13, [1989] 4 CMLR 444.

[108] *Vitamins* (n 100, above) para 558.

[109] Cases 228 & 229/82 *Ford v Commission* [1984] ECR 1129, [1984] 1 CMLR 649, 16. But cf Cases 25 & 26/84 *Ford v Commission (No. 2)* [1985] ECR 2725, [1985] 3 CMLR 528. Conduct which begins unilaterally can thereafter become part of an agreement: *Scottish Salmon Board*, OJ 1992 L246/37, [1993] 5 CMLR 602. See also *Richard Cound Ltd v BMW (GB) Ltd* [1997] EuLR 277 (English Court of Appeal): termination by contractual notice, without any reason, of a distribution agreement was a unilateral act.

[110] See Chap 10, below. Note also that there is some authority for the proposition that an agreement which does not otherwise fall within Art 81(1) may do so if it is operated abusively: Case 262/81 *Coditel v Ciné-Vog Films (No. 2)* [1982] ECR 3381, [1983] 1 CMLR 49, paras 17–20; Case 35/83 *BAT v Commission* [1985] ECR 363, [1985] 2 CMLR 470.

[111] Case 107/82 *AEG v Commission* [1983] ECR 3151, [1984] 3 CMLR 325, paras 31–39; Case 75/84 *Metro v Commission (No. 2)* [1986] ECR 3021, [1987] 1 CMLR 118, para 72; *Jaeger v Opel Norge* (n 104, above) (EFTA Ct), paras 40–42; and see the English High Court in *Holleran v Thwaites* [1989] 2 CMLR 917 (ChD). cf Case 210/81 *Demo-Studio Schmidt v Commission* [1983] ECR 3045, [1984] 1 CMLR 63, paras 17–20. See generally paras 6.055 and 6.090, below. For a supplier acting on complaints from a distributor, see para 2.048, below.

leading case of *ADALAT*.[112] As a result of a substantial price differential between France and Spain on the one hand and the United Kingdom on the other, the French and Spanish wholesalers of Bayer's cardio-vascular medicine started re-exporting ADALAT to the British market, undercutting UK distributors. In response, Bayer introduced a policy of restricting the quantities supplied to its French and Spanish wholesalers according to the level of their previous orders. Although this strategy was consciously designed to maintain national partitioning of the market, the Court of First Instance annulled the Commission's decision[113] that an export ban was thereby tacitly incorporated into the distribution agreements. Conducting a thorough evaluation of the evidence, the Court found, first, that Bayer had not itself sought to monitor the conduct of individual wholesalers or to make supply conditional on the final destination of the products; and secondly, that the wholesalers themselves attempted by various means to obtain additional supplies so that they could continue exporting to customers in the United Kingdom. The Commission's appeal was dismissed by the Court of Justice,[114] which held that in order to find that an agreement has been concluded by tacit acceptance, 'it is necessary that the manifestation of the wish of one of the contracting parties to achieve an anti-competitive goal constitute an invitation to the other party, whether express or implied, to fulfil that goal jointly, and that applies all the more where, as in this case, such an agreement is not at first sight in the interests of the other party, namely the wholesalers'. Further, in considering how the alleged export restriction fitted in with the pre-existing neutral contractual relationship between Bayer and its wholesalers, the Court of Justice held that the mere fact that the anti-competitive measure 'falls within the context of continuous business relations between the manufacturer and its wholesalers' is not sufficient for a finding that an agreement contrary to Article 81(1) exists.

2.026 **Cases applying *ADALAT*.** Following the Court of First Instance's judgment in the *ADALAT* case, a number of undertakings accused of imposing export restrictions on their distributors argued that their conduct was merely unilateral and did not form part of its agreement with its wholesale network.[115] Such arguments

---

112 For a discussion of the impact of the *ADALAT* judgment on the earlier case law on concerted practices, see the judgment of the UK Competition Appeal Tribunal in *Argos Ltd and Littlewoods Ltd v Office of Fair Trading* [2004] CAT 24, [2005] CompAR 588, paras 666 *et seq.*

113 *ADALAT*, OJ 1996 L201/1, [1996] 5 CMLR 416, on appeal Case T-41/96 *Bayer v Commission* [2000] ECR II-3383, [2001] 4 CMLR 126, [2001] All ER (EC) 1. The Commission had imposed a fine of 3 million ECU.

114 Cases C-2 & 3/01P *BAI and Commission v Bayer* [2004] ECR I-23, [2004] 4 CMLR 653, [2004] All ER (EC) 500.

115 For an application of the *Bayer* 'concurrence of wills' test to an alleged horizontal agreement, see Cases T-44/02, etc, *Dresdner Bank v Commission* [2006] ECR II-3567, [2007] 4 CMLR 467 (Commission had failed to prove that meeting of banks resulted in an anti-competitive agreement).

have met with varying degrees of success. In *Opel Nederland*,[116] the Court of First Instance found that Opel had adopted a policy of trying to restrict exports but held that the Commission had failed to prove that this policy had ever been communicated to wholesalers, still less that it had formed part of the contract between them. However, the Court of First Instance upheld the Commission's finding in the same decision[117] that a policy of excluding parallel export sales from the distributors' bonus scheme did constitute an agreement. Applications for bonuses were treated in accordance with the conditions then applicable, which excluded export sales from the scope of the bonus system. The new conditions thus became an integral part of the dealership contracts between Opel Nederland and its dealers and became incorporated into a series of continuous commercial relations governed by a pre-established general agreement. The measure was not therefore a unilateral act but an agreement within the meaning of Article 81(1).[118] In *Volkswagen*,[119] the Court of Justice considered again the question whether or not anti-competitive instructions issuing from a supplier to its distributors should be regarded as part of the apparently benign underlying agreement between them. In that case, the dealership agreement provided that the dealer had to comply with all instructions issued for the purposes of the agreement regarding the distribution of new Volkswagen cars. The contract also referred expressly to Volkswagen issuing non-binding price recommendations concerning retail prices and discounts. Volkswagen subsequently issued to its dealers instructions attempting to increase retail prices. The Commission contended that, in signing a dealership agreement, dealers give their prior consent to all measures adopted by the motor vehicle manufacturer in the context of that contractual relationship, lawful or not.[120] The Court of First Instance annulled the decision on the grounds that a dealer who has signed a dealership agreement which complies with competition law cannot be deemed to have accepted in advance a later variation which would make the agreement unlawful. On further appeal, the Court of Justice held that the lower Court

---

[116] Case T-368/00 *General Motors Nederland and Opel Nederland v Commission* [2003] ECR II-4491, [2004] 4 CMLR 1302, [2004] All ER (EC) 674 (appeal dismissed, Case C-551/03P, [2006] ECR I-3173, [2006] 5 CMLR 9). See also Case T-67/01 *JCB Services v Commission* [2004] ECR II-49, [2004] 4 CMLR 1346 (manufacturer's expression of concern on level of retail prices to association of its network dealers did not establish an agreement to fix prices: para 128).

[117] *Opel*, OJ 2001L59/1, [2001] 4 CMLR 1441.

[118] The CFI also upheld the finding that there was 'a meeting of minds' between Opel and nine of its dealers that they would not export so that there were Art 81(1) agreements between Opel and each of them.

[119] Case C-74/04P *Commission v Volkswagen* [2006] ECR I-6585, [2007] ICR 217 (on appeal from Case T-208/01 *Volkswagen v Commission* [2003] ECR II-5141, [2004] 4 CMLR 727, [2004] All ER (EC) 674. This was the appeal from the Commission's decision (June 2001) concerning alleged price-fixing for the Passat model at OJ 2001 L262/14, [2001] 5 CMLR 1309.

[120] The ECJ noted that the Commission had not put its case on the basis that there was either explicit or tacit acquiesence in the instructions by the dealers but relied solely on the authorisation of the calls by the underlying agreement.

had erred in law in holding that neutral clauses which comply with the competition rules cannot, as a matter of principle, be treated as authorising calls which are contrary to those rules. It was necessary to examine the clauses of the dealership agreement individually, taking account, where applicable, of other factors, such as the aims pursued by that agreement in the light of the economic and legal context in which it was signed to determine whether they authorised the unlawful calls in question. The Court then upheld the Court of First Instance's finding that the contract did not in fact authorise the issue of the binding price instructions and so did not disturb the annulment of the Commission's decision. In contrast, in the earlier *Volkswagen* case,[121] the Court of First Instance found that an export ban had been incorporated into the pre-existing contract between the manufacturer and its dealers and largely upheld the Commission's finding of infringement.

2.027 **Incorporation of terms in an agreement.** The *ADALAT* line of cases tends to blur the distinction between a finding that an agreement exists and a finding that a particular objectionable term is incorporated into an underlying benign agreement. The latter issue was addressed in the case law prior to *ADALAT*. In *Sandoz*,[122] the Court of Justice held that the systematic dispatching by a supplier to his customers of invoices bearing the words 'export prohibited' rendered that restriction part of an agreement when this occurred in the context of the continuous business relations governed by a general agreement drawn up in advance. The tacit acceptance of the term by the customer could be inferred from renewed orders placed without protest on the same conditions. The mere fact that a supplier may not have taken steps to ensure the observance of a clause by his customers is not sufficient to remove that clause from the ambit of Article 81(1).[123] This must now be read subject to the more recent case law. The fact that a written agreement expressly

---

[121] Case T-62/98 *Volkswagen v Commission* [2000] ECR II-2707, [2000] 5 CMLR 853. This is the appeal from the Commission's decision concerning export restrictions on dealers in Italy, OJ 1998 L124/60, [1998] 5 CMLR 33; upheld by the ECJ on further appeal Case C-338/00P *Volkswagen v Commission* [2003] ECR I-9189, [2004] 4 CMLR 351. See also Case T-168/01 *GlaxoSmithKline Services v Commission* [2006] ECR II-2969, [2006] 5 CMLR 1589, paras 75–90 (CFI held there was an agreement where GSK sent the terms and conditions to the wholesalers and asked them to send back a signed sheet saying that they accepted those terms) (on appeal, Cases C-501/06P, etc, *GlaxoSmithKline Services v Commission*, not yet decided).

[122] Case C-277/87 *Sandoz v Commission* [1990] ECR I-45. See also *Bayo-n-ox*, OJ 1990 L21/71, [1990] 4 CMLR 930; *Vichy*, OJ 1991 L75/57, para 17; *Gosme/Martell–DMP*, OJ 1991 L185/23, [1992] 5 CMLR 586; *Tretorn*, OJ 1994 L378/45, [1997] 4 CMLR 860; Case T-43/92 *Dunlop Slazenger v Commission* [1994] ECR II-441. Note also *D'Ieteren Motor Oils*, OJ 1991 L20/42, [1992] 4 CMLR 399: a 'strong recommendation' by a supplier in a circular sent to dealers found by the Commission to create *de facto* an economic obligation on the dealer to conform to that recommendation and therefore tantamount to a condition of the dealer agreement.

[123] *Sandoz*, above.

allows exports will not preclude the existence of an underlying agreement or concerted practice to prohibit them.[124]

Horizontal and vertical agreements. Both 'horizontal' agreements (that is, **2.028** agreements between two or more suppliers or two or more acquirers *inter se*) and 'vertical' agreements (that is, agreements between a supplier and one to whom he supplies, such as a dealer) may fall within Article 81(1).[125]

Government measures. National legislative measures may restrict competition **2.029** but they cannot, as such, constitute an 'agreement' in violation of Article 81(1).[126] In certain circumstances a Member State may be in breach of its obligations under the Treaty by adopting such measures, as explained elsewhere in this work.[127] Where under a national measure rates or specifications are fixed by a public body that includes members appointed by undertakings or trade associations, the decisions of that body will not give rise to an agreement between undertakings if the members act in their personal capacity in the public interest.[128] But the position will be otherwise if they act as representatives of the associations or enterprises which appointed them.[129] The question whether an agreement made pursuant to

---

124 *Video Games, Nintendo distribution*, OJ 2003 L255/33, [2004] CMLR 421, para 111 (on appeal, Cases T-18/03 CD-*Contact Data v Commission*; T-12/03 *Itochu Corporation v Commission*; T-398/02 *Linea Gig v Commission*; T-13/03 *Nintendo Corp and Nintendo of Europe v Commission*, not yet decided).

125 See the early cases of Case 56/65 *Société Technique Minière v Machinenbau Ulm* [1966] ECR 235, [1966] CMLR 357; Cases 56 & 58/64 *Consten and Grundig v Commission* [1966] ECR 299, [1966] CMLR 418; and more recently Case C-217/05 *Confederación Española de Empresarios de Estaciones de Servicio v CEPSA* [2006] ECR I-11987, [2007] 4 CMLR 181, para 37.

126 Case 5/79 *Buys* [1979] ECR 3203, [1980] 2 CMLR 493, paras 29–31 (national legislation imposing price freeze); Case 811/79 *Ariete* [1980] ECR 2545, [1981] 1 CMLR 316 (national taxation); Case 174/84 *Bulk Oil v Sun International* [1986] ECR 559, [1986] 2 CMLR 732 (Member State policy of preventing export of oil to a non-Member country on the basis of Art 10 of Reg 2603/69 not contrary to Art 81); Case 267/86 *Van Eycke v ASPA* [1988] ECR 4769, [1990] 4 CMLR 330 (tax exemption limited in order to reduce bank interest rates); Case T-325/01 *DaimlerChrysler v Commission* [2005] ECR II-3319, [2007] 4 CMLR 559, para 156 (Spanish legislation requiring supplier of a leased car to have identified a lessee at the time the vehicle is acquired). See also *Franco-Japanese ballbearings*, OJ 1974 L343/19, [1975] 1 CMLR D8 (export restriction imposed by Japanese authorities).

127 For the application of the Art 10 duty on Member States in combination with Arts 81 and 82, see paras 11.029 *et seq*, below, and cases there cited. Chap 11 also covers the specific prohibition in Art 86 on Member States as regards public undertakings or undertakings granted special or exclusive rights.

128 Case C-185/91 *Reiff* [1993] ECR I-5801, [1995] 5 CMLR 145 (board fixing long-distance road haulage tariffs in Germany); Case C-153/93 *Delta Schiffarts- und Speditionsgesellschaft* [1994] ECR I-2517, [1996] 4 CMLR 21 (commission fixing inland waterways tariffs in Germany); Case C-35/99 *Arduino* [2002] ECR I-1529, [2002] 4 CMLR 866 (draft tariffs for legal fees fixed by barristers' professional body); Case C-198/01 *CIF* [2003] ECR I-8055, [2003] 5 CMLR 829, [2004] All ER (EC) 380 (obligation of national competition authority to disapply national measures which contravene Art 81(1)).

129 Case 123/83 *BNIC v Clair* [1985] ECR 391, [1985] 2 CMLR 430. See also *Pabst & Richarz/ BNIA*, OJ 1976 L331/24, [1976] 2 CMLR D63 (statutory body limiting exports ostensibly on

legislative measures or under pressure from public authorities comes within Article 81(1) is discussed in Chapter 11, below.

2.030 **Infringement action.**   The mere exercise of a legal right, for example, by bringing an infringement action under a patent or trade mark[130] or registered design[131] does not, as such, fall within Article 81(1); but the position may be different if the action is brought pursuant to a continuing agreement or concerted practice and has the effect of dividing markets[132] or restricting competition in some unreasonable or exploitative manner.[133] The bringing of an infringement action may also, in certain circumstances, infringe Article 82 or the rules on the free movement of goods.[134]

2.031 **Assignments and licences of intellectual property rights.**   An executed assignment or exclusive licence of intellectual property rights may, in some circumstances, fall outside Article 81(1).[135] However, the present position is not wholly clear[136] and in any event other provisions of the assignment or licence may infringe Article 81(1).[137] Where the rights to a particular output, such as the broadcast of a football match, are jointly owned by a number of bodies, the agreement between those bodies as to the grant of licences of the rights is not caught by Article 81(1).[138]

2.032 **Terminated or 'spent' agreements.**   Article 81(1) applies to agreements which are no longer in force if they continue to produce their effects after they have been formally terminated.[139] In practice, it may be difficult to show that an agreement

---

quality grounds caught by Art 81(1) as an association of undertakings). In that regard it is relevant if the industry-appointed members of the body are in a minority: Case C-96/94 *Centro Servizi Spediporto* [1995] ECR I-2883, [1996] 4 CMLR 613 (road haulage tariffs in Italy); Cases C-140/94, etc, *DIP* [1995] ECR I-3257, [1996] 4 CMLR 157 (committees advising local authorities on trading licences).

[130] Case 24/67 *Parke Davis v Centrafarm* [1968] ECR 55, [1968] CMLR 47 (patent); Case 51/75 *EMI v CBS* [1976] ECR 811, [1976] 2 CMLR 235, paras 26–27 (trade mark).

[131] Case 144/81 *Keurkoop v Nancy Kean Gifts* [1982] ECR 2853, [1983] 2 CMLR 47, paras 27–28.

[132] *Consten and Grundig v Commission* (n 125, above); Case 40/70 *Sirena v Eda* [1971] ECR 69, [1971] CMLR 260; Case 15/74 *Centrafarm v Sterling Drug* [1974] ECR 1147, [1974] 2 CMLR 280; *EMI v CBS* (n 130, above) paras 5–39; *Keurkoop v Nancy Kean Gifts*, above, paras 25 *et seq*; Case 170/83 *Hydrotherm v Compact* [1984] ECR 2999, [1985] 3 CMLR 224. See generally paras 9.066 *et seq*, below.

[133] *Coditel v Ciné-Vog Films (No. 2)* (n 110, above). See further para 9.069, below.

[134] For Art 82, see paras 9.072 and 14.136 *et seq*, below. For the rules on free movement in this context, see paras 9.007 *et seq*, below.

[135] Case 258/78 *Nungesser v Commission* [1982] ECR 2015, [1983] 1 CMLR 278, paras 44–67 ('open' patent licence); *Coditel v Ciné-Vog Films (No. 2)* (n 110, above) paras 9 *et seq* (licence to exhibit cinema film).

[136] See generally paras 9.075 *et seq*, below.

[137] See generally paras 9.086 *et seq*, below. Note that the technology transfer block exemption, Reg 772/2004, may apply: see Chap 9, below.

[138] *UEFA Champions League*, OJ 2003 L291/25, [2004] 4 CMLR 549, para 124.

[139] Case 243/83 *Binon* [1985] ECR 2015, [1985] 3 CMLR 800; *Hercules v Commission* (n 99, above); *EMI v CBS* (n 130, above). cf *Sirena v Eda* (n 132, above).

had ceased to have an effect, particularly if the parties' behaviour continues to be convergent. In *Soda-ash–Solvay, ICI*[140] the Commission found that the formal termination of a market-sharing agreement on the accession of the United Kingdom did not result in or reflect any alteration in practice of the strict market separation between the two suppliers: the continuing cooperation between the former parties to the agreement therefore amounted at least to a concerted practice. The fact that an agreement has come to an end does not preclude the Commission from taking proceedings in respect of its period of operation. However, this power is subject to the Commission establishing that it has a legitimate interest in investigating the infringement even though the parties have already brought it to an end.[141]

Judicial settlements. It is as yet undecided whether a judicial settlement reached **2.033** before a national court which constitutes a judicial act can be invalid for breach of Article 81(1). In *Bayer v Süllhöfer*,[142] the Court of Justice considered a no-challenge clause in an agreement which had been entered into to settle a dispute about the validity of certain industrial property rights. The Court rejected the argument, advanced by the Commission, that such a clause should be regarded as compatible with Article 81(1) when it is included in an agreement to settle pending court proceedings provided that the existence of the industrial property right in question was genuinely in doubt. There, the clause was part of an out-of-court settlement and the Court of Justice stated: 'Article [81(1)] makes no distinction between agreements whose purpose is to put an end to litigation and those concluded with other aims in mind'.[143] The wider question of the application of Article 81(1) to judicial settlements was expressly left open.

Collective labour relations agreements. The Court of Justice has recognised **2.034** that certain restrictions of competition are inherent in collective agreements

---

[140] *Soda-ash–Solvay, ICI*, OJ 1991 L152/1. However, that decision was annulled on procedural grounds for breach of the rights of the defence in failing to give full access to the file: Case T-30/91 *Solvay v Commission* [1995] ECR II-1775, [1996] 5 CMLR 57; Case T-36/91 *ICI v Commission* [1995] ECR II-1847; [1995] All ER (EC) 600 (both). A similar point was made by the Commission in *Nintendo* (n 124, above) para 111.

[141] Art 7(1) Reg 1/2003, OJ 2003 L1/1: Vol II, App B.3. See also Case 7/82 *GVL v Commission* [1983] ECR 483, [1983] 3 CMLR 645, paras 24 *et seq*; Cases T-22 & 23/02 *Sumitomo v Commission* [2005] ECR II-4065, [2006] 4 CMLR 42, paras 129–140, which also held that the limitation period applies only to the imposition of penalties for infringements and does not rule out an investigation of infringements. For limitation periods, see Art 25(1) of Reg 1/2003, above, and para 13.208, below.

[142] Case 65/86 *Bayer v Süllhöfer* [1988] ECR 5249, [1990] 4 CMLR 182. AG Darmon thought that 'giving special status to settlements putting an end to litigation might give rise to fictitious disputes whose aim was to achieve an otherwise prohibited agreement': at 5278 (ECR), 188 (CMLR).

[143] ibid, para 15. See also *Nungesser v Commission* (n 135, above) paras 80–90 (obligation arising out of judicial settlement may violate Art 81(1)); *Eleco-MiTek*, OJ 1991 C285/8 (divestment following report by UK Monopolies and Mergers Commission). See also para 2.118, below.

between organisations representing employers and workers.[144] Referring to the objectives set out in Article 2 of the Treaty and to the Agreement on Social Policy then in force[145] the Court has held that those social policy objectives would be seriously undermined if management and labour were subject to Article 81(1) when seeking jointly to adopt measures to improve conditions of work and employment so that 'agreements concluded in the context of collective negotiations between management and labour in pursuit of such objectives must, by virtue of their nature and purpose, be regarded as falling outside the scope of Article [81(1)] of the Treaty'.[146] This approach was refined by the EFTA Court in a case concerning a Norwegian collective agreement relating to a pension scheme.[147] The Court held that an agreement was not taken outside the scope of Article 53 EEA simply because the parties were a labour union and an employer or an association of employers, or because the agreement could generally be characterised as having the nature and purpose of a typical collective agreement. It was also necessary to show that the agreement was 'concluded in pursuit of the objective of improving conditions of work and employment'.[148] Account must also be taken of the form and content of the agreement and of its various provisions, and of the circumstances under which they were negotiated. The subsequent practice of the parties to the agreement may be important, as may the effect, in practice, of its provisions. The Court also stated that the national court must consider the aggregate effect of the provisions. Even if individually, the provisions would not lead to any certain resolution of the status of the collective agreement in relation to the applicability of Article 53 EEA, their aggregate effect may bring the agreement within the scope of that Article. These cases should be seen as establishing a

---

[144] Case C-67/96 *Albany* [1999] ECR I-5751, [2000] 4 CMLR 446, paras 59 and 60; Cases C-115–117/97 *Brentjens* [1999] ECR I-6025, [2000] 4 CMLR 566; Case C-219/97 *Drijvende Bokken* [1999] ECR I-6121, [2000] 4 CMLR 599. Similarly, Case C-222/98 *Van der Woude* [2000] ECR I-7111, [2001] 4 CMLR 93 (compulsory sickness insurance scheme under collective labour agreement for the hospital sector). But note that the decision by a professional organisation to set up a compulsory pension fund did not fall outside Art 81(1) since it was not concluded in the context of a collective labour agreement: Cases C-180/98, etc, *Pavlov* [2000] ECR I-6451, [2001] 4 CMLR 30.

[145] The Agreement on Social Policy, signed in December 1991, was incorporated into the Social Chapter of the EC Treaty by the Treaty of Amsterdam.

[146] *Albany* (n 144, above) para 60.

[147] Case E-8/00 *Lo and NKF v KS* [2002] EFTA Ct Rep 114, [2002] 5 CMLR 160.

[148] The EFTA Ct held that the term 'conditions of work and employment' must be interpreted broadly as including not only wages and working hours but also matters such as safety, the workplace environment, holidays, training and continuing education, and consultation and co-determination between workers and management. Provisions relating to the total remuneration were included, eg the assumption by an employer of an obligation to establish and contribute to an occupational pension scheme. The Court noted: 'At present, there may appear to be a tendency to include in collective agreements elements that reflect changing needs and interests of the parties'. Such novel elements of a collective agreement may require particular scrutiny by the national court to determine whether they aim to improve conditions of work and employment (para 54).

sui generis rule for collective labour agreements and not a more general principle excluding from the scope of Article 81(1) agreements which are consistent with, and intended to facilitate, the achievement of other Community objectives.[149]

Restrictions assessed as part of concentration or State aid.   Council **2.035** Regulation 139/2004 provides a specific regime under which the Commission considers the compatibility of mergers and 'full-function' joint ventures with the common market. Restrictions accepted by the parties to such a concentration and which are directly related and necessary to the concentration are also considered pursuant to the Merger Regulation.[150] This regime is considered in detail in Chapter 8, below. The question as to how far Articles 81 (and 82) can be applied by the national courts to agreements establishing concentrations is also discussed in that Chapter.[151] Similarly, agreements between private undertakings which are indissolubly linked to the grant of a State aid will be evaluated under the State aid regime and not under Article 81(1).[152]

Accession agreements.   Agreements that were in existence at the time when **2.036** a State joined the Community and which fall within Article 81(1) solely as a result of that State's accession are referred to throughout this work as 'Accession agreements'. In general terms, Accession agreements are agreements that fell outside the Treaty prior to the date of a particular Member State's accession in that they affected trade either only between an acceding Member State and an existing Member State or only between acceding Member States, or they restricted competition or affected trade only outside the Community.[153] But Accession agreements do not include agreements which, prior to the relevant date of accession, affected trade between the then Member States and restricted competition within the then common market, notwithstanding that the parties to such agreements were, at that time, situated outside the Community.[154] The application of

---

[149] See also Case 90/76 *Van Ameyde v UCI* [1977] ECR 1091, [1977] 2 CMLR 478 (restrictions inherent in green card vehicle insurance scheme which facilitates free movement of persons and goods do not fall within Art 81(1)).

[150] See Recital (21) to Reg 139/2004, OJ 2004 L24/1: Vol II, App D.1 and see paras 8.170 *et seq*, below.

[151] See paras 8.262 *et seq*, below.

[152] Cases T-197 & 198/97 *Weyl Beef Products v Commission* [2001] ECR II-303, [2001] 2 CMLR 459, para 83.

[153] eg *Vacuum Interrupters (No. 1)*, OJ 1977 L48/32, [1977] 1 CMLR D67 (JV between UK parties); *SMM&T Exhibition Agreement*, OJ 1983 L376/1, [1984] 1 CMLR 611 (agreement affecting UK exhibitors only).

[154] For the potential application of the Europe Agreements, see para 2–162 of the 5th edn of this work. There are many instances of the application of Art 81 for periods prior to Accession: eg *Tepea v Commission* (n 101, above) (arrangement between UK and Dutch suppliers to protect Dutch market from UK imports did not affect trade between Member States prior to UK accession on 1 January 1973); *Vegetable Parchment*, OJ 1978 L70/54, [1978] 1 CMLR 534 (agreement by continental suppliers not to supply UK market contrary to Art 81(1) from 1 January 1973 but not

these principles is illustrated by the Commission's decision in *Organic Peroxides*[155] concerning a cartel which involved producers in many European States over almost 30 years both before and after those States acceded to the EEA or the Community. In applying Article 81 EC and Article 53 EEA, the Commission distinguished between the effects of the cartel on the Community and the effects within the individual States. Thus, the Commission found that Community rules applied to the Spanish producer even before Spain's accession insofar as the cartel affected trade within the Community but that the effects of the arrangement in Spain were not subject to Article 81 prior to Spain's accession. Insofar as the cartel arrangements covered Austria, Finland, Norway and Sweden prior to the EEA Agreement entering into force in 1994, they were not considered to be a violation of Article 81. During 1994 (that is the period when the EEA Agreement was in force but before Austria, Finland and Sweden acceded to the Community) the cartel was a violation of both Article 81 EC and Article 53(1) EEA insofar as it affected trade between the EEA and the Community and was also a violation of Article 53(1) EEA insofar as it affected trade within those States. After the accession of Austria, Finland and Sweden in 1995, Article 81(1) EC became applicable insofar as it affected those markets and the operation of the cartel within Norway remained in violation of Article 53(1) EEA. After the accession of the United Kingdom (1973), Greece (1981) and Spain and Portugal (1986) to the Community, Article 81(1) EC became applicable to the cartel insofar as it affected the markets within those States. Accession agreements fall within Article 81(1) if their effects continue to be felt within the enlarged common market after the date of accession.[156] Their civil validity is not affected in respect of any period prior to accession.[157]

---

apparently before); *Campari*, OJ 1978 L70/69, [1978] 2 CMLR 397 (licence to Danish licensee did not fall within Art 81(1) prior to Danish accession on 1 January 1973 despite export ban because of customs and tax regulations); *Cast iron and steel rolls*, OJ 1983 L317/1, [1984] 1 CMLR 694 (UK undertakings fined in respect of cartel having perceptible effect within the Community prior to 1 January 1973); *Aluminium imports from Eastern Europe*, OJ 1985 L92/1, [1987] 3 CMLR 813 (UK undertakings did not infringe Art 81(1) by protecting UK market against imports of Eastern bloc aluminium prior to 1 January 1973 but did infringe Art 81(1) insofar as intra-Community trade was affected within the then Community). See also Cases 97/87, etc, *Dow Chemical Iberica v Commission* [1989] ECR 3165, [1991] 4 CMLR 410, paras 61 *et seq* (use of Commission's powers under Art 14 of Reg 17 in Spain to obtain information relating to activities prior to Accession). For extra-territoriality generally, see paras 1.105 *et seq*, above.

155 COMP/37.857 *Organic Peroxides*, 10 December 2003, [2005] 5 CMLR 579, paras 296 and 368–372 (appeal on other grounds dismissed, Case T-120/04 *Peróxidos Orgánicos v Commission* [2007] 4 CMLR 153).

156 *Tepea v Commission* (n 101, above) paras 45 *et seq*.

157 ibid; see also Case 13/61 *Bosch v De Geus* [1962] ECR 45, [1962] CMLR 1; *Applications des Gaz v Falks Veritas* [1974] Ch 381 (CA). Before the Modernisation regime was introduced in May 2004, certain agreements duly notified to the Commission or exempt from notification at the date of accession enjoyed 'provisional validity': see paras 11–029 *et seq* of the 5th edn of this work.

Agreements between parent and subsidiary or principal and agent. In prin- **2.037**
ciple, an agreement between a parent company and a subsidiary should fall outside Article 81(1). In its earlier judgments, the Court of Justice seems to have
based this principle on two conditions: first, that the undertakings form a single
economic unit within which the subsidiary has no effective freedom to determine
its course of action on the market; and secondly, that the agreement or concerted
practice in question was concerned merely with the internal allocation of tasks as
between the undertakings.[158] However, in *Viho* the Court of First Instance in
effect abandoned the second condition and its decision was upheld by the Court
of Justice.[159] Similarly, agreements between a principal and agent, properly so
called, do not fall within Article 81(1) because the two entities form a single economic unit.[160]

(b) Concerted practices

In general. The concept of 'concerted practices' in Article 81(1) has been **2.038**
defined by the Court of Justice as covering:

> '. . . a form of co-ordination between undertakings which, without having reached
> the stage where an agreement properly so called has been concluded, knowingly
> substitutes practical co-operation between them for the risks of competition.'[161]

As the Court of Justice subsequently observed, the concepts of 'agreement' and
'concerted practice' used in Article 81(1) are intended:

> 'to catch forms of collusion having the same nature and . . . only distinguishable
> from each other by their intensity and the forms in which they manifest
> themselves.'[162]

---

[158] See Case 22/71 *Béguelin Import v GL Import Export* [1971] ECR 949, [1972] CMLR 81;
Case 15/74 *Centrafarm v Sterling Drug* [1974] ECR 1147, [1974] 2 CMLR 480; and in particular
Case 30/87 *Bodson v Pompes Funèbres* [1988] ECR 2479, [1989] 4 CMLR 984.

[159] Case T-102/92 *Viho v Commission* [1995] ECR II-17, [1997] 4 CMLR 469, [1995] All
ER (EC) 371, para 51; on appeal, Case C-73/95P [1996] ECR I-5457, [1997] 4 CMLR 419,
paras 16–18. This issue is discussed at paras 2.017 *et seq*, above.

[160] See para 2.020, above.

[161] Originally stated in Cases 48/69, etc, *ICI v Commission ('Dyestuffs')* [1972] ECR 619, [1972]
CMLR 557, para 64; and repeated many times since, eg *Vitamins* (n 100, above) para 556. See also
Interbrew and Alken-Maes (n 100, above) para 254 where the Commission stated 'Although it cannot be established with certainty from the available evidence that there was an agreement between
the four brewers, it is at any rate proven that there was a concerted practice'. In *Competition Authority
v Norsk Hydro Olje Aktiebolag* (Case No. MD 2005:7 judgment of 22 February 2005) the Swedish
Market Court found that meetings between petrol companies gave rise to a concerted practice on
rebates but that the existence of an agreement had not been proven. In *Organic Peroxides* (n 155,
above) the Commission found that, during a period of power struggles within the cartel, there was
at least a concerted practice even if not a continuing agreement: para 413.

[162] Case C-49/92P *Commission v Anic Partecipazioni* [1999] ECR I-4125, [2001] 4 CMLR 602,
para 131.

Accordingly, and particularly as the Commission is entitled to characterise collusive arrangements in the case of a complex cartel as constituting either an agreement or a concerted practice,[163] the importance of the concept of a concerted practice is not its distinction from an agreement but from parallel behaviour which does not infringe the competition rules. The concept has been developed and reaffirmed in a number of leading cases concerning cartels discussed in this Section. There are many others.[164] This Section contains a brief account of the relevant aspects of those decisions followed by some general conclusions.

2.039 ***Dyestuffs*: coordinated course of action among competitors.** In *Dyestuffs*, nearly all the undertakings that produced aniline dyestuffs in Italy and Benelux made a series of simultaneous and uniform price increases. In its decision,[165] the Commission held that the parties were guilty of concerted practices and imposed fines. The parties contended that the price increases merely reflected parallel behaviour in an oligopolistic market where each producer followed the price-leader which initiated the increase. This behaviour, it was argued, was quite natural in a closely-knit industry where all producers were equally affected by the continual erosion of margins.

2.040 **The Court of Justice's decision in *Dyestuffs*.** Dismissing the appeal,[166] the Court of Justice, after explaining the concept of concerted practice as set out above,[167] said that although parallel behaviour by itself did not constitute a concerted practice, it may amount to strong evidence of such a practice if it leads to conditions of competition which do not correspond to the normal conditions of the market.[168] In order to decide whether market conditions diverge from the normal, it is necessary to examine the nature of the market for the products in question. The Court found[169] that the market for dyestuffs was fragmented and divided along national lines. The similarity of the rates and timing of the price increases could not be explained away as the result of parallel yet independent behaviour prompted by market forces. In particular, the concerted prior announcement of price changes enabled the undertakings to eliminate in advance all uncertainty between them as to their future conduct on the various markets. The Court said:

> 'Although every producer is free to change his prices, taking into account in so doing the present or foreseeable conduct of his competitors, nevertheless it is contrary to the rules on competition contained in the Treaty for a producer to co-operate with his competitors, in any way whatsoever, in order to determine a co-ordinated course

---

163 See para 2.022, above.
164 See the cases discussed in Chap 5, below.
165 *Dyestuffs*, JO 1969 L195/11, [1969] CMLR D23.
166 Cases 48/69, etc, *ICI v Commission* (n 161, above).
167 Para 2.038, above.
168 *ICI v Commission* (n 161, above) paras 65–68.
169 ibid, paras 69–124.

of action relating to a price increase and to ensure its success by prior elimination of all uncertainty as to each other's conduct regarding the essential elements of that action, such as the amount, subject-matter, date and place of the increases.'[170]

Sugar: disclosure of policy to competitors. The *Sugar* case concerned a vari- **2.041**
ety of anti-competitive activities which were alleged against most of the then Community sugar producers.[171] Two of the alleged parties argued that there was no 'concerted practice' because the evidence had failed to establish any plan and merely indicated that the parties knew of each other's commercial policies and had independently adopted their own policies accordingly. In its judgment,[172] the Court of Justice substantially repeated the general definition of a concerted practice from the *Dyestuffs* judgment[173] and proceeded to a careful factual analysis of the evidence. The Court held that the concept of a concerted practice 'did not require the working out of an actual plan', and:

> '. . . must be understood in the light of the concept inherent in the provisions of the Treaty relating to competition that each economic operator must determine independently the policy which he intends to adopt on the common market including the choice of the persons and undertakings to which he makes offers or sells. Although it is correct to say that this requirement of independence does not deprive economic operators of the right to adapt themselves intelligently to the existing and anticipated conduct of their competitors, it does, however, strictly preclude any direct or indirect contact between such operators, the object or effect whereof is either to influence the conduct on the market of an actual or potential competitor or to disclose to such a competitor the course of conduct which they themselves have decided to adopt or contemplate adopting on the market.'[174]

The Court held that a concerted practice was established by the evidence.[175]

---

[170] ibid, para 118. The removal of uncertainty as to the other undertakings' future action is a key factor in information exchange agreements: see, eg Case C-238/05 *Asnef-Equifax v Ausbanc* [2006] ECR I-11125, [2007] 4 CMLR 224, para 51.

[171] *Sugar*, OJ 1973 L140/17, [1973] CMLR D65, paras 74–226. The infringements alleged included: (1) concerted practice to protect the Italian market: paras 29–73 (the parties succeeded on the ground that Community and national legislation made competition virtually impossible: see para 11.006, below); (2) concerted practice to protect the Southern part of the Federal Republic of Germany: paras 311–364 (the ECJ held that a concerted practice was not proved: there were other plausible explanations for the parties' conduct); (3) undue economic pressure on Belgian exporters contrary to Art 82: paras 365–402; (4) restrictions on resale by agents, and loyalty rebates contrary to Art 82: paras 421–528; (5) agreements with agents contrary to Art 81(1): paras 529–557; (6) concerted practice in relation to export tenders for third countries (the ECJ held that the concerted practice was proved).

[172] Cases 40/73, etc, *Suiker Unie v Commission* [1975] ECR 1663, [1976] 1 CMLR 295.

[173] Para 2.040, above.

[174] *Suiker Unie* (n 172, above) paras 173–174. This formula has also been repeated many times since, eg Case T-325/01 *DaimlerChrysler v Commission* [2005] ECR II-3319, [2007] 4 CMLR 559, para 200.

[175] ibid, paras 167–192. See also the more recent case concerning the sugar industry, Cases T-202/98, etc, *Tate & Lyle v Commission* [2001] ECR II-2035, [2001] 5 CMLR 22, [2001] All ER (EC) 839, discussed at para 2.044, below.

2.042 *Polypropylene*: **presumption as regards effect on participants' conduct.** In its decision condemning the polypropylene cartel,[176] the Commission imposed substantial fines on 14 companies. All of them appealed to the Court of First Instance;[177] and there were eight further appeals to the Court of Justice, although mostly only on procedural grounds.[178] The Court of First Instance upheld the findings of fact by the Commission that the undertakings had attended meetings to fix prices and exchange information. This concerted action was intended to influence their conduct on the market and could not fail to have done so:

> 'Thus not only did the applicant pursue the aim of eliminating in advance uncertainty about the future conduct of its competitors but also, in determining the policy which it intended to follow on the market it could not fail to take account, directly or indirectly, of the information it obtained during the course of those meetings. Similarly, in determining the policy which they intended to follow, its competitors were bound to take into account the information disclosed to them by the applicant about the course of conduct which the applicant itself had decided upon or which it contemplated adopting on the market.'[179]

Responding to the arguments by several appellants that there was insufficient proof that they had participated in the concerted practice, the Court confirmed that in order to establish the existence of a concerted practice it is necessary to show conduct on the market pursuant to those collusive practices, and a relationship of cause and effect between the two.[180] Although taking part in discussions did not necessarily establish that those discussions influenced the participant's conduct, when the participant remained active in the market there was a 'presumption' that it took account of the information exchanged in determining its conduct, particularly when the exchange was sustained on a regular basis over a long period.[181] As the appellants had failed to rebut that presumption, the appeals were dismissed.

2.043 *Cement*: **degree of reciprocity required.** The Commission's decision[182] concerning the cement cartel imposed a total of 248 million ECU in fines on

---

176 *Polypropylene*, OJ 1986 L230/1, [1988] 4 CMLR 347.

177 Each appeal was the subject of a separate judgment although many passages in the judgments are identical. Note that Judge Vesterdorf, acting as AG, gave a comprehensive Opinion covering all the appeals: reported with Case T-1/89 *Rhone-Poulenc v Commission* [1991] ECR II-867.

178 Only three of the appeals to the ECJ raised substantive issues under Art 81(1): *Commission v Anic Partecipazioni* (n 162, above); Case C-199/92P *Hüls v Commission* [1999] ECR I-4287, [1999] 5 CMLR 1016; and Case C-235/92P *Montecatini v Commission* [1999] ECR I-4539, [2001] 4 CMLR 691.

179 This form of words was repeated in a number of the judgments: see, eg Case T-7/89 *Hercules v Commission* [1991] ECR II-1711, [1992] 4 CMLR 84, paras 259–261; Case T-1/89 *Rhône-Poulenc v Commission* (n 177, above).

180 *Commission v Anic Partecipazioni* (n 162, above) para 118. Similarly, *Hüls v Commission* (n 178, above) paras 161–166. For appreciable effect, see paras 2.121 *et seq*, below.

181 *Hüls v Commission* (n 178, above) paras 158–166.

182 *Cement*, OJ 1994 L343/1, [1995] 4 CMLR 327.

42 companies for price-fixing and market-sharing arrangements. The many appeals were resolved in one consolidated judgment of the Court of First Instance that contains a comprehensive analysis of the numerous and varied procedural and substantive points raised by the different defendants.[183] For present purposes, it is sufficient to consider the Court's observations as regards the degree of reciprocity necessary to establish a concerted practice in the context of a challenge to the Commission's finding[184] of two particular concerted practices, based on bilateral contacts between the Italian cement producer, Buzzi, on the one hand, and two French cement producers on the other. The Commission found the first of those concerted practices was established by the note of a meeting in which Buzzi informed a French producer, Lafarge, that it regarded the south of France market as belonging to Lafarge and had no desire to enter that market in competition. Although there was no evidence that Lafarge disclosed its own strategy, it had requested the meeting and did not appear to express any reservations or objections when informed of Buzzi's intentions. On that basis the Court was satisfied that the contacts 'were motivated by the elements of reciprocity essential to a finding of concerted practice'.[185] Moreover, by its statements Buzzi gave Lafarge 'an assurance, with an anti-competitive intent as to the— in this case peaceful—attitude which the latter could count on as regards the market in the south of France'.[186] The second Franco–Italian concerted practice involved the supply to Buzzi by another French producer (Ciments Français) of its current prices with a statement of the increases envisaged in the current year. As these were transmitted in response to Buzzi's request, the Court held that this was sufficient to establish the necessary element of reciprocity.[187] Relying on the *Polypropylene* cases, the Court found that disclosure of such information had the effect on Buzzi of, at the very least, reducing in advance any uncertainty as to Ciments Français' pricing policy in the market concerned.[188] The Court seems to have accepted the Commission's inference that the information was disclosed in order to enable Buzzi to align its prices with those of its French competitor.[189]

---

[183] Cases T-25/95, etc, *Cimenteries CBR v Commission ('Cement')* [2000] ECR II-491, [2000] 5 CMLR 204. The judgment runs to 5134 paragraphs. These aspects of the case were not challenged on appeal to the ECJ: Cases C-204/00P, etc, *Aalborg Portland v Commission* [2004] ECR I-123, [2005] 4 CMLR 251, where the focus was on how far attendance at cartel meetings is sufficient to establish membership of the cartel: see para 2.054, below.

[184] *Cement* (n 182, above) Art 3(1) of the decn.

[185] *Cimenteries CBR* (n 183, above) paras 1849–1850.

[186] ibid, para 1852.

[187] ibid, para 1887.

[188] ibid, para 1896. However, although the CFI upheld the Commission's finding that Buzzi had participated in these two (and a third) bilateral concerted practices, it annulled the Commission's determination that Buzzi was thereby a part of the larger Cembureau cartel: paras 4110–4113. As the Commission had fined Buzzi only on the latter basis, and had not imposed separate fines for the three concerted practices, the fine on Buzzi was annulled: para 4719.

[189] Note also the Commission's statement in *Hasselblad*, OJ 1982 L161/18, [1982] 2 CMLR 233, para 47: 'For a concerted practice to exist it is sufficient for an independent undertaking

2.044   *British Sugar/Tate & Lyle*: **unilateral disclosure of information.**   In *British Sugar*,[190] the Court of First Instance analysed what had taken place at meetings between British Sugar, a competing sugar producer Tate & Lyle, and the sugar merchant Napier Brown, which was both a competitor and customer of British Sugar. It was accepted that at the meetings, British Sugar had notified the others present of its pricing intentions. The Court held that the fact that only one of the participants in the meetings revealed its intentions did not exclude the possibility of an agreement or concerted practice arising. The Court found that the information supplied by British Sugar was not otherwise readily accessible market data and the meetings allowed the participants to become aware of that information 'more simply, rapidly and directly, than they would be able to via the market'.[191] Further, the Court upheld the Commission's finding that 'the systematic participation of the applicant undertakings in the meetings in question allowed them to create a climate of mutual certainty as to their future pricing policies'. Napier Brown argued that as a customer of the sugar producers its participation was devoid of any anti-competitive spirit. The Court rejected this, finding that 'at the very least, it gave the impression that its participation took place in the same spirit as that of its competitors'. Moreover, by merely participating in the meetings, each participant could not fail to take account, directly or indirectly, of the information obtained during those meetings in order to determine the market policy which it intended to pursue.

2.045   **Concerted practices: the requisite elements.**   In the light of the above cases, it appears that a concerted practice will be held to exist where: (i) there is some positive contact between undertakings, that will often consist of meetings, discussions, disclosure of information, or 'soundings out', whether oral or written; (ii) such contact involves cooperation that is contrary to the normal competitive processes, for example by removing, or substantially reducing, uncertainty as to the future competitive conduct of an undertaking; and (iii) that contact has the effect – or can be assumed to have had the effect[192] – of maintaining[193] or altering the commercial conduct of the undertakings concerned.[194]

---

knowingly and of its own accord to adjust its behaviour in line with the wishes of another undertaking'.

   190 Cases T-202/98, etc, *Tate & Lyle v Commission* [2001] ECR II-2035, [2001] 5 CMLR 859, [2001] All ER (EC) 839 (appeal on other grounds dismissed, Case C-359/01P *British Sugar v Commission* [2004] ECR I-4933, [2004] 5 CMLR 329).

   191 ibid, para 60.

   192 See the presumption in *Polypropylene*: para 2.042, above, and para 2.050, below.

   193 In Case 172/80 *Züchner v Bayerische Vereinsbank* [1981] ECR 2021, [1982] 1 CMLR 313, para 20, the ECJ said that a concerted practice existed if it enabled the parties 'to congeal conditions in their present state thus depriving their customers of any genuine opportunity to take advantage of services on more favourable terms which would be offered to them under normal conditions of competition'.

   194 *Commission v Anic Partecipazioni* (n 162, above) para 131 (reversing the CFI on this point). But such conduct may be presumed: para 2.050, below. Note that this is distinct from the requirement that for an infringement of Art 81(1) the concerted practice must have as its object *or effect*

Alternative explanations for parallel behaviour. In practice, if parallel behav- **2.046**
iour in the market is established and contact between the parties is proved, a concerted practice will readily be inferred.[195] The exchange of commercially
confidential information,[196] or other close contact,[197] will usually enable a concerted practice to be proved. The proximity of relevant dates[198] and the absence of
competitive trading[199] will be relevant, as will a previous agreement between the
parties.[200] Where a finding of infringement rests entirely on observed parallel conduct in the absence of any direct documentary evidence,[201] a stringent test of parallelism is applied. In *Wood Pulp II*[202] the Court of Justice confirmed that parallel

---

an *appreciable* effect on competition; ie although the conduct on the market resulting from the
concertation may not in fact have had a significant anti-competitive effect, Art 81(1) will be
infringed if that was the object of the parties' acting in concert: ibid, paras 122–125. For appreciable
effect, see paras 2.121 *et seq*, below.

[195] See generally Cases 29 & 30/83 *CRAM and Rheinzink v Commission* [1984] ECR 1679,
[1985] 1 CMLR 688. In his Opinion (at [1984] ECR 1712–1713, [1985] 1 CMLR 701), AG Rozes
cited the test formulated by AG Mayras in *Dyestuffs* (n 161, above) (at 673 (ECR), 574 (CMLR)):
'I think that it is necessary at the least to show: first, that the conscious parallel behaviour is not
exclusively or even mainly due to economic conditions or to the structure of the market; secondly,
that, where there is no express meeting of minds, sufficiently clear, unequivocal presumptions lead
to the conviction that the parallel conduct was the result of concertation, of a coordinated policy'.
For further discussion on adequacy of proof, see para 13.226, below.

[196] eg *Zúchner v Bayerische Vereinsbank* (n 193, above) para 21 (exchange of information on bank
charges); *BP Kemi/DDSF* (n 107, above) (regular exchange of information on sales); Case 86/82
Hasselblad v Commission [1984] ECR 883, [1984] 1 CMLR 559 (price lists, prices, and serial numbers of equipment sold).

[197] eg meetings, letters, telexes, telephone calls: see generally *Sugar, Hasselblad* and the *Polypropylene*
cases, above. cf. Cases T-68/89, etc, *Società Italiano Vetro v Commission* [1992] ECR II-1403.

[198] eg *Dyestuffs* (n 161, above) (price increases on identical dates); cf *CRAM and Rheinzink*
(n 195, above).

[199] eg *Sugar* (n 171, above); *Vegetable Parchment* (n 154, above).

[200] *BP Kemi/DDSF* (n 107, above); *White lead*, OJ 1979 L21/16, [1979] 1 CMLR 464; Case
243/83 *Binon* (n 139, above); *Nintendo* (n 124, above) (agreements had contained express restrictions on exports and when these clauses were deleted, the practice of restricting exports continued
as before).

[201] The issue of whether there is another plausible explanation for the perceived parallel conduct
of the undertakings on the market is only relevant when there is no documentary or other evidence
of contact between the parties: Cases T-67/00, etc, *JFE Engineering v Commission* [2004] ECR
II-2501, [2005] 4 CMLR 27, para 186; upheld on appeal Cases C-403 & 405/04P *Sumitomo v
Commission* [2007] 4 CMLR 650.

[202] Cases C-89/85, etc, *Åhlström Osakeyhtiö v Commission* ('Wood Pulp II') [1993] ECR I-1307,
[1993] 4 CMLR 407, para 71. See also *Dyestuffs* (n 161, above) paras 65–68; *Zúchner v Bayerische
Vereinsbank* (n 193, above) paras 11–22; *Suiker Unie* (n 172, above) paras 199–210 and paras 403–
420 contrasting especially with paras 282–283; Cases 110/88, etc, *Ministère Public v Tournier* [1989]
ECR 2521, [1991] 4 CMLR 248, para 24; Cases T-68/89, etc, *Società Italiano Vetro v Commission*
[1992] ECR II-1403, paras 174–193 and paras 326 *et seq*. Among Commission decisions, *Zinc
Producer Group*, OJ 1984 L220/27, [1985] 2 CMLR 108, para 75 (barometric price leadership not
proved to be collusive). See also Case No. VIA Ca 1146/04 *Agri – Maszewo (yeast producers) v Polish
Office of Competition and Consumer Protection*, decn of the Court of Appeal in Warsaw 5 October
2005: court upheld the competition authority's decision that parallel price rises by yeast producers
were sufficient evidence of collusive price-fixing. The court found that producers had traditionally
raised their prices at different times and by different amounts. A simultaneous price rise by a similar

conduct cannot be regarded as furnishing proof of concertation unless it is the only plausible explanation. In that case, the Court engaged experts to analyse the characteristics of the market. The experts' report found that the operation of market forces was a more plausible explanation for parallelism in prices and that various features of the market were incompatible with a finding of concertation.[203] The Court therefore annulled most of the Commission's decision.

2.047 **Concerted practices among potential contract tenderers.** In a series of cases the UK Competition Appeal Tribunal has considered the degree of contact that is necessary to establish a concerted practice between potential bidders for contracts to carry out building work. In *Apex*,[204] the Tribunal set out 12 principles derived from the case law of the Community Courts holding that a concerted practice may arise if there are reciprocal contacts between the parties which have the object or effect of removing or reducing uncertainty as to future conduct on the market. Such reciprocal contacts are established where one competitor provides information as to its future intentions or conduct on the market to another when the latter requests it, or at the very least accepts it. Such contacts, together with the presumption that the undertakings which remain active in the market take account of the information exchanged when determining their commercial conduct, are enough to establish an infringement.

2.048 **Concerted practices to prevent parallel imports.** The *Pioneer* case[205] illustrates a concerted practice operating at distributor, rather than producer, level. The parties were the main European subsidiary of Pioneer, a Japanese supplier of hi-fi equipment, and Pioneer's exclusive distributors in France, Germany and the United Kingdom. Pioneer argued that it was not a party to the concerted practices between its distributors. However, the Court of Justice upheld the Commission's findings that Pioneer had participated in the concerted practice by forwarding

---

amount in September 2001 could not be explained by external factors in the industry. The case was upheld on appeal to the Supreme Court, judgment of 9 August 2006.

[203] *Wood Pulp II*, above, paras 73–127. In *Motor-fuels on the motorway ('carburants sur autoroute')* judgment of 9 December 2003, BOCCRF no. 2 of 12 March 2004, the Paris Court of Appeal overturned a finding that French oil companies had colluded on price and infringed the French equivalent of Art 81. Although petrol service stations regularly exchanged information about current prices and transmitted this to their respective head offices where it was used to determine pricing policy, the Court held that the oil companies had set their prices independently and that price convergence arose from the transparency prevailing in an oligopolistic market and not from the exchange of information. See further para 5.089, below.

[204] *Apex Asphalt and Paving Co v Office of Fair Trading* [2005] CAT 4. See also the later case of *Makers UK Ltd v Office of Fair Trading* [2007] CAT 11: concerted practice would be established where one tenderer obtains a quotation for subcontracting the work from another undertaking which it knows is also an existing tenderer or subcontractor and incorporates the prices from that quotation in its own bid. On the facts as found, it was not necessary for the Tribunal to rely on this exposition.

[205] Cases 100/80, etc, *Musique Diffusion Française v Commission* [1983] ECR 1825, [1983] 3 CMLR 221 (on appeal from *Pioneer Hi-Fi Equipment*, OJ 1980 L60/21, [1980] 1 CMLR 457).

MDF's complaints about the presence on its market of parallel imported goods to the other distributors, and by convening and presiding over meetings where parallel imports were discussed. In relation to Pioneer, the Court held that 'on account of its central position, it was obliged to display particular vigilance in order to prevent concerted efforts of that kind from giving rise to practices contrary to the competition rules'.[206] The making of a complaint by one supplier to another may give rise to a concerted practice if it is acted upon,[207] even if that action is taken as a result of economic pressure.[208] Collaboration between a manufacturer and distributor designed to identify the source of parallel imports and to put a stop to them also gives rise to a concerted practice to ban exports and to protect the distributor from price competition.[209] 'Checking up' actions, such as supplying serial numbers or price lists, may constitute a concerted practice.[210]

Disclosure of pricing information from retailers to suppliers. In *Replica* **2.049**
Football Kit,[211] the UK Competition Appeal Tribunal considered when a concerted practice arises where a retailer discloses to his supplier the price at which he intends to resell the goods in the expectation that the supplier will pass this information to another retailer. The Tribunal stated:

> '. . . if one retailer A privately discloses to a supplier B its future pricing intentions in circumstances where it is reasonably foreseeable that B might make use of that information to influence market conditions, and B then passes that pricing information on to a competing retailer C, then in our view A, B and C are all to be regarded on those facts as parties to a concerted practice having as its object or effect the prevention, restriction or distortion of competition. The prohibition on direct *or indirect* contact between competitors on prices has been infringed.'[212]

---

[206] ibid, para 75. See also paras 79 and 132. This reference to 'particular vigilance' was cited by the Commission in *Nintendo* (n 124, above) para 293, where the Commission imposed heavy fines for a two-tiered arrangement whereby Nintendo cooperated with its exclusive distributors, retail and wholesale customers to restrict parallel imports and one of those distributors, John Menzies, entered into similar arrangements with its own retail customers.

[207] *Sugar* (n 171, above) para 283; *Musique Diffusion Française* (n 205, above) paras 72 *et seq*; *Hasselblad v Commission* (n 196, above) paras 24–29; *Gosme/Martell—DMP*, OJ 1991 L185/23.

[208] *Hasselblad* (n 189, above). See, eg the more recent Commission decisions concerning two export ban arrangements: *Nintendo* (n 124, above) and COMP/37.980 *Souris – Topps*, 26 May 2004, [2006] 4 CMLR 1713 (Pokemon collectibles). See also the other cases referred to in paras 6.053 *et seq*, below.

[209] *Newitt/Dunlop Slazenger*, OJ 1992 L131/32, on appeal Case T-43/92 *Dunlop Slazenger v Commission* [1994] ECRII-441; *Nintendo* (n 124, above).

[210] *Hasselblad* (n 189, above); *Ford Agricultural*, OJ 1993 L20/1; *Gosme/Martell—DMP* (n 207, above). However, it may be legitimate to operate a system which seeks to controls imports into the EU/EEA from lower price countries and to monitor sales in that lower price country for that purpose: Case T-204/03 *Haladjian Frères v Commission* [2006] ECR II-3779, [2007] 4 CMLR 1106 (CFI upheld Commission rejection of a complaint by importer).

[211] *JJB Sports plc and Allsports plc v Office of Fair Trading* [2004] CAT 17, [2005] CompAR 29.

[212] ibid, para 659; and see the same formulation in *Argos and Littlewoods v Office of Fair Trading* [2004] CAT 24, [2005] CompAR 588, para 779.

On appeal, the Court of Appeal considered that this statement 'may have gone too far'[213] but it did not have to decide whether such a wide proposition could be supported since the facts as found fell squarely within established case law. The Court stated the position in more restricted terms:

> '. . . if (i) retailer A discloses to supplier B its future pricing intentions in circumstances where A may be taken to intend that B will make use of that information to influence market conditions by passing that information to other retailers (of whom C is or may be one), (ii) B does, in fact, pass that information to C in circumstances where C may be taken to know the circumstances in which the information was disclosed by A to B and (iii) C does, in fact, use the information in determining its own future pricing intentions, then A, B and C are all to be regarded as parties to a concerted practice having as its object the restriction or distortion of competition. The case is all the stronger where there is reciprocity: in the sense that C discloses to supplier B its future pricing intentions in circumstances where C may be taken to intend that B will make use of that information to influence market conditions by passing that information to (amongst others) A, and B does so.'[214]

2.050 Proof of resulting conduct. Although, as explained above, conduct of the undertaking caused by the concertation is a distinct ingredient of a concerted practice,[215] this generally does not present difficulties of proof. When an undertaking remains active on the market it is presumed to take into account the information exchanged with its competitors, subject to its proving the contrary.[216] That will be a high burden to discharge. For example, in *Cement*,[217] Buzzi's participation in the bilateral concerted practice with Ciments Français was not negated by evidence that its prices in fact remained lower than those of the French producer since that did not make it 'inconceivable that the Italian undertaking, despite everything, allowed the information . . . to influence its export prices'. However, the Commission cannot simply infer from the fact that the parties continued to meet frequently over a long period that the cartel must have had some effect on the market.[218]

---

213 *Argos & Littlewoods and JJB Sports v Office of Fair Trading* [2006] EWCA Civ 1318, para 140. The appeal against the *Replica Football Kit* decision was consolidated with the appeal from *Argos and Littlewoods* (above) resulting in a single, combined judgment.

214 ibid, para 141. This tripartite structure was distinguished from a case where one competitor discloses its pricing intentions to another: cf *Makers UK Ltd v Office of Fair Trading* (n 204, above).

215 Para 2.045, above.

216 *Commission v Anic Partecipazioni* (n 162, above) para 121; *Hüls v Commission* (n 178, above) paras 162–167. For a case in which the CFI analysed, in the context of reviewing the level of penalty, whether prices charged by the parties to the cartel reflected market forces or demonstrated the implementation of a price-fixing agreement see Case T-224/00 *Archer Daniels Midland v Commission* [2003] ECR II-2597, [2003] 5 CMLR 583, paras 153 *et seq* (appeal dismissed, Case C-397/03P *Archer Daniels Midland v Commission* [2006] ECR I-4429; [2006] 5 CMLR 230).

217 Cases T-25/95, etc, *Cement* (n 183, above) at para 1912: see para 2.043, above.

218 Case T-224/00 *Archer Daniels Midland* (n 216, above) para 159.

Duration of concerted practice.   It is not always easy to determine the precise   **2.051**
duration of a concerted practice, but the burden of proof rests on the Commission.[219]
Generally, once the undertaking has ceased to take part in collaborative discussions, participation may come to an end with the last overt act that can fairly be
attributed to the concerted practice. In *Dunlop Slazenger*,[220] where the length of
infringement found by the Commission was significantly reduced on appeal, the
Court of First Instance stated that the principle of legal certainty 'requires that, if
there is no evidence directly establishing the duration of an infringement, the
Commission should at least adduce evidence of facts sufficiently proximate in
time for it to be reasonable to accept that the infringement continued uninter-
ruptedly between two specific dates'.

(c) Agreements and concerted practices: other issues

Single overall infringement.   A cartel is usually not based on a single, isolated   **2.052**
act but operates through a complex pattern of conduct involving a series of
agreements and concerted practices entered into over a period of time. Those
agreements and concerted practices may also vary to adapt to new circumstances;
sub-agreements or inner circles of closer cooperation may be established and new
implementing mechanisms developed. Some participants may drop out, others
may join in, and not every company is necessarily involved in every aspect. Where
it is established that a set of individual agreements are interlinked in terms of pursuing the same object or as part of a common plan, they can be characterised as
constituting a single continuous infringement.[221] Similarly, a series of bilateral

---

[219] Cases T-25/95, etc, *Cement* (n 183, above) paras 2800–2803, distinguishing the observations of AG Slynn in *Pioneer* that a concerted practice is presumed to continue until the contrary is
shown: [1983] ECR 1825, 1941–1942, [1983] 3 CMLR 221, paras 299–300. See also Case 41/69
ACF Chemiefarma v Commission [1970] ECR 661 at paras 693–700 (analysis of the evidence as to
termination); *Hasselblad v Commission* (n 196, above) paras 24–29 (and see AG Slynn at [1984]
ECR 883, 928, [1984] 1 CMLR 559, 580); Case 35/83 *BAT v Commission* [1985] ECR 363,
[1985] 2 CMLR 470 (no evidence that party had withdrawn from agreement). Note also *Zinc
Producer Group* (n 202, above) (presumption exercised in firm's favour that infringement ended
when the last recorded instance occurred of the effect of the relevant agreement or practice). In
Case T-44/00 *Mannesmannröhren-Werke v Commission* [2004] ECR II-2223, [2005] 4 CMLR 182
(a seamless steel tubes appeal), the Commission had conceded that the infringement should be
subject to fine only during the period after a voluntary restraint agreement between the EC and
Japan on the import of seamless tubes came to an end. However, since the Commission lost the
documentation showing when this was, the CFI held that it was precluded from denying the applicant's contention on this issue; see para 262 (further appeal dismissed, Case C-411/04P *Salzgitter
Mannesmann v Commission* [2007] 4 CMLR 682).

[220] *Dunlop Slazenger v Commission* (n 209, above) para 79. The fine was accordingly reduced
from 5 million to 3 million ECU. For the relevance of duration to the level of fine, see paras 13.155
et seq, below.

[221] The concept was first applied in *Polypropylene*, OJ 1986 L230/1, [1998] 4 CMLR 347, paras
81–83; of the various appeals, see Case T-15/89 *Chemie Linz v Commission* [1992] ECR II-1275,
para 308; Case C-49/92P *Commission v Anic* [1999] ECR I-4125, [2001] 4 CMLR 602, para 113,

agreements may form part of an overall scheme and therefore be considered as a common enterprise giving rise to one multilateral infringement.[222] Determining that various agreements give rise to a single continuous infringement has significant consequences. If there is only one infringement, it can attract only a single fine, and since each separate fine is subject to a ceiling of 10 per cent of worldwide turnover that can result in a lower, overall penalty.[223] On the other hand, the level of fine reflects the duration of the infringement, so that a finding of a continuous infringement over a sustained period may well increase the penalty.[224] Moreover, the five-year limitation period for imposition of a penalty runs from the end of a period of continuing infringement; finding a single continuous infringement may therefore enable the Commission to penalise conduct that would otherwise have been time barred.[225] The facts taken into account to determine whether there is a single continuous infringment or distinct infringements include: the existence of an overall plan pursuing a common anti-competitive objective, the identity of the participating parties, the time frame of the arrangements, the similarities in the instruments and mechanisms used, the structure of the cartel, the substitutability of the products and the characteristics of the affected geographic areas.[226]

---

and Opinion of AG Cosmas at paras 79–81 on the criminal law origins of the concept. See also Cases T-25/95, etc, *Cement* (n 183, above) paras 4025 *et seq*; and in relation to a two-tiered vertical agreement to restrict exports: *Nintendo* (n 124, above) para 261; COMP/37.980 *Souris/Topps* ('*Pokémon Cards*'), 26 May 2004, [2006] 4 CMLR 1713, paras 122–128. The Commission has also applied the concept of single continuous infringement under Art 82: COMP.37.507 *AstraZeneca*, 19 July 2006, [2006] 5 CMLR 287, paras 774–776 and 861–862 (on appeal, Case T-321/05 *AstraZeneca v Commission*, not yet decided). For further discussion, see Faull & Nikpay, *The EC Law of Competition* (2nd edn, 2007), paras 8.498–8.501.

222 COMP/38.338 *Needles*, 26 October 2004, [2005] 4 CMLR 792, paras 249 *et seq* (on appeal Cases T-30/05 *Prym and Prym Consumer v Commission*; T-36/05 *Coats Holdings and Coats v Commission*, not yet decided).

223 Reg 1/2003, OJ 2003 L1/1: Vol II, App B.3, Art 23(2).

224 See para 13.155, below. Determination that there is a single or several distinct infringements can also be significant in the operation of the leniency discounts for cooperation: see Faull & Nikpay (n 221, above) para 8.498 and n 187.

225 Reg 1/2003 (n 223, above) Art 25(2). See, eg COMP/37.533 *Choline Chloride*, 9 December 2004, [2006] 4 CMLR 159, paras 145–148; on appeal against the finding of a single continuous infringement, Cases T-111/05 *UCB v Commission* and T-101/05 *BASF Ludwigshafen v Commission*, not yet decided (and appeal on other grounds, Case T-112/05 *AKZO Nobel v Commission*, not yet decided).

226 In addition to the cases cited in n 221, above, see Cases T-259/02, etc, *Raiffeisen Zentralbank Österreich v Commission*, judgment of 14 December 2006, paras 111 *et seq* (finding of single continuous infringement upheld) (on appeal, Cases C-125/07P, etc, not yet decided); Case T-43/02 *Jungbunzlauer v Commission* [2006] ECR II-3435, paras 309 *et seq* (finding that two cartels were distinct upheld). See also COMP/38.238 *Spanish Raw Tobacco*, 20 October 2004, [2006] 4 CMLR 866, paras 275–277, 296–297, 326–327 (on appeal, Cases T-24/05 *Standard Commercial*, T-29/05 *Deltafina*, T-33/05 *Cetarsa*, T-37/05 *World Wide Tobacco Espana*, T-38/05 *Agroexpansion*, T-41/05 *Dimon*, not yet decided); COMP/38.354 *Industrial Bags*, Press Release IP/05/1508 (30 November 2005) (on appeal on this ground, Case T-53/06 *UPM-Kymmene v Commission*, not yet decided; on other grounds, Cases T-26/06, etc, *Trioplast Wittenheim v Commission*, not yet decided).

However, separate infringements can still be dealt with by a single set of proceedings, provided that the ultimate decision makes this clear and that no producer is held responsible for collusion in a product in which it was not involved.[227] For example, in two decisions adopted in 2001 and 2002 concerning, respectively, cartels in graphite electrodes and certain speciality graphites (isostatic graphite and extruded graphite), the Commission held that there were three separate infringements and accordingly imposed three sets of fines.[228] In *Tokai Carbon*,[229] the Court of First Instance rejected a challenge to these cumulative penalties on the basis that the arrangements should have been considered as a single continuous infringement. The Court noted that the products involved belonged to three distinct product markets, that the three cartels had very limited overlap in their membership, and that they involved different anti-competitive mechanisms (the graphite electrodes cartel included market-sharing but this was not a feature of the speciality graphite cartel).

Parties to the agreement/concerted practice.   The identity of the parties to a   **2.053**
particular agreement is a question of fact. The conduct of a subsidiary may be imputed to a parent, at least if the parent has controlled or decisively influenced the activities of the subsidiary.[230] The parties may include an undertaking assisting, but not directly participating, in the infringement.[231] It is not necessary for an undertaking to be present at every (or any) meeting of a cartel in order for it to be a party.[232] This raises the question of the extent to which one undertaking can be

---

[227] *Vitamins*, OJ 2003 L6/1, [2003] 4 CMLR 22, para 580 (fines reduced on appeal Cases T-15/02, etc, *BASF v Commission* [2006] ECR II-497, [2006] 5 CMLR 27); *Tokai Carbon* (n 229, below) para 125.

[228] *Graphite Electrodes*, OJ 2002 L100/1, [2002] 5 CMLR 829; COMP 37.667 *Speciality Graphite*, Press Release IP/02/1906 (17 December 2002).

[229] Cases T-71/03, etc, *Tokai Carbon v Commission (Speciality Graphite)* [2005] ECR II-10, [2005] 5 CMLR 489, paras 117–124 (further appeal on other grounds dismissed, Case C-328/05P *SGL Carbon v Commission* [2007] 5 CMCR 16). Similarly *Jungbunzlauer* (n 226, above) as regards the citric acid and sodium gluconate cartels.

[230] Case 107/82 *AEG v Commission* [1983] ECR 3151, [1984] 3 CMLR 325, paras 47–53; Case 48/69 *ICI v Commission ('Dyestuffs')* [1972] ECR 619, [1972] CMLR 557; Case C-286/98P *Stora Kopparbergs v Commission* [2000] ECR I-9925, [2001] 4 CMLR 370, paras 22–30. See further para 13.205, below.

[231] eg by providing secretarial services as in *Italian Cast Glass*, OJ 1980 L383/19, 26, [1982] 2 CMLR 61. See COMP/37.857 *Organic Peroxides*, 10 December 2003, [2005] 5 CMLR 579: fine on a Swiss-based entity which had provided administrative and secretariat services to the cartel. The fine was nominal because of the novelty of penalising a trade association for involvement of that kind (para 454) and the decn is on appeal, Case T-99/04 *AC Treuhand v Commission*, not yet decided. cf *UK Agricultural Tractor Registration Exchange*, OJ 1992 L68/19 (proceedings not pursued against computer bureau which provided members of exchange with confidential information); *Building and construction industry in the Netherlands*, OJ 1992 L92/1 (association not fined as it performed a purely administrative function).

[232] *Vitamins* (n 227, above) para 563; *Tokai Carbon v Commission (Speciality Graphite)* (n 229, above) para 67 (fact that one undertaking did not attend top level meetings did not mean it was not part of the cartel) (appeal on other grounds dismissed, Case C-328/05P *SGL Carbon v Commission*

held to be a participant in the practices proved against other undertakings. Although most of the appeals against the *Polypropylene* decision were dismissed, the Court of First Instance annulled part of that decision insofar as it attributed responsibility to one of the undertakings, Anic, for certain conduct carried out by others.[233] On the Commission's appeal and Anic's cross-appeal, the Court of Justice stated:

> 'When . . . the infringement involves anti-competitive agreements and concerted practices, the Commission must, in particular, show that the undertaking intended to contribute by its own conduct to the common objectives pursued by all the participants and that it was aware of the actual conduct planned or put into effect by other undertakings in pursuit of the same objectives or that it could reasonably have foreseen it and that it was prepared to take the risk.'[234]

On that basis, the Court of Justice allowed the Commission's appeal, holding that Anic was responsible throughout the period of its participation in the concerted practices for the conduct of the other participants in pursuit of the same end.[235] Passive participation is sufficient: once an undertaking is aware of the conduct planned or implemented by the other undertakings, the undertaking's failure publicly to distance itself from the content of the unlawful initiative or report it to the administrative authorities may be found to constitute tacit approval that effectively encourages the continuation of the infringement.[236] However, where a party participates in what it thinks is a national cartel, it is not responsible for the wider European cartel of which the national cartel was a part unless it knew or ought to have known that the wider cartel existed.[237]

[2007] 5 CMLR 16). See the arguments on 'collective responsibility' in, eg *Hercules v Commission* (n 179, above) paras 282 *et seq* (appeal on other grounds dismissed, Case C-51/92P [1999] ECR I-4235, [1999] 5 CMLR 976).

[233] Case T-6/89 *Enichem Anic v Commission* [1991] ECR II-1623.

[234] *Commission v Anic* (n 221, above) paras 87, 203; applied in Case T-28/99 *Sigma Tecnologie v Commission* [2002] ECR II-1845 (a pre-insulated pipes appeal) para 40. See also *Interbrew and Alken-Maes* (*'Belgian Beer'*), OJ 2003 L200/1, [2004] 4 CMLR 80 (appeals dismissed: Case T-38/02 *Groupe Danone v Commission* [2005] ECR II-5407, [2006] 4 CMLR 1429 (small reduction in the fine) (further appeal dismissed, Case C-3/06P [2007] 4 CMLR 701) and Case T-48/02 *Brouwerij Haacht v Commission* [2005] ECR II-5259, [2006] 4 CMLR 621).

[235] ibid, paras 190 *et seq*. The Commission stated (para 175) that it brought the appeal to establish the principle that 'where a group of undertakings agree to maintain the price level of a product, each undertaking is responsible for all the activities aimed at maintaining prices, even those in which it did not actually collaborate'. See also *Video Games, Nintendo distribution*, OJ 2003 L255/33, [2004] CMLR 421, paras 282 *et seq* (distributors in high price countries participate in arrangement to prevent parallel exports occurring from low price countries by reporting incidence of imports into their territory to the manufacturer); *Vitamins* (n 227, above) para 562; Cases T-67/00 *JFE Engineering* (n 201, above) para 370.

[236] Cases C-204/00P *Cement* (n 183, above) paras 83–84. But see also in the CFI, Cases T-25/95, etc, (ibid) at para 4267, annulling part of the decision as regards the duration of infringement by eight participants. Infrequent attendance at meetings, however, may indicate that the undertaking took a passive rather than an active role in the cartel, a factor which may mitigate the fine imposed: see Case T-220/00 *Cheil Jedang v Commission* [2003] ECR II-2473, paras 168 *et seq*.

[237] *Sigma Tecnologie* (n 234, above) paras 40 *et seq*.

Distancing oneself from the cartel: passive attendance at meetings. Once it **2.054** has been established that an undertaking had attended meetings, even without playing an active role, and that those meetings had included discussion of, for example, price initiatives, the undertaking is presumed to have subscribed to the initiative agreed at the meeting.[238] In *Cement*,[239] the Court of Justice reaffirmed earlier case law[240] holding that it is sufficient for the Commission to show that an undertaking participated in meetings at which anti-competitive agreements were concluded, without manifestly opposing them, to prove to the requisite standard that the undertaking participated in the cartel.[241] Such conduct encourages the continuation of the infringement and compromises its discovery. The burden lies on the undertaking concerned to put forward evidence demonstrating that it had indicated to its competitors that it was participating in those meetings in a spirit that was different from theirs.[242] Without such 'public distancing', the fact that an undertaking does not abide by the outcome of meetings which it has attended does not relieve it of full responsibility for its participation in the cartel if those meetings had a manifestly anti-competitive purpose.[243] In *Adriatica di Navigazione*,[244] the Court of First Instance held that to avoid liability an undertaking must not only come to an internal decision not to participate in the cartel but must make this clear to the other participants. The notion of public distancing as a means of excluding liability must be interpreted narrowly so that silence by an operator in a meeting during which the parties colluded unlawfully on a precise question of pricing policy is not tantamount to an expression of firm and unambiguous disapproval.[245]

---

[238] See *Hüls v Commission* (n 178, above) para 174; *Commission v Anic* (n 221, above) para 96.

[239] Cases C-204/00P, etc, *Aalborg Portland v Commission ('Cement')* [2004] ECR I-123, [2005] 4 CMLR 251; see further para 2.043, above. The formula has been repeated many times, eg Cases C-189/02P *Dansk Røindustrie v Commission* [2005] ECR I-5425, [2005] 5 CMLR 796, para 142; Cases C-403 & 405/04P *Sumitomo v Commission* [2007] 4 CMLR 650, para 47.

[240] See, eg Case T-141/89 *Tréfileurope v Commission* [1995] ECR II-791.

[241] *Hüls v Commission* (n 178, above) para 155; *Montecatini v Commission* (n 178, above) para 181.

[242] *Aalborg Portland* (n 239, above) paras 81–82 and the case law cited there; *Adriatica di Navigazione*, discussed below.

[243] *Tréfileurope v Commission* (n 240, above) para 85; *Cimenteries CBR v Commission* (n 183, above) para 1389; Case T-56/99 *Marlines v Commission* [2003] ECR II-5225, [2005] 5 CMLR 1761, para 61 (appeal dismissed Case C-112/04P *Marlines v Commission*, Order of 15 September 2005 (unpublished)); Cases T-71/03, etc, *Tokai Carbon* (n 229, above) para 74 (deceiving other cartel members is no answer).

[244] Case T-61/99 *Adriatica di Navigazione* [2003] ECR II-5349, [2005] 5 CMLR 1843, paras 135 *et seq* (on appeal from *Greek Ferries*) where the CFI said '. . . given that the applicant's desire not to adhere to the cartel was expressed in an internal document, but not externalised, it is legitimate to conclude that that was an attempt to mislead the other members of the cartel, in the hope that it would nevertheless remain in force, which, as the Commission states, confirms the undertaking's (albeit disloyal) participation in the cartel'.

[245] Case T-303/02 *Westfalen Gassen Nederland v Commission* [2007] 4 CMLR 334, paras 76 *et seq*: 'The applicant . . . did not express a view which would have left the other undertakings

2.055 **Proof of participation.** In a number of recent cartel cases,[246] the Court of First Instance has examined the adequacy of the evidence relied on against each party to the cartel and the Court of Justice has broadly upheld the principles applied by the Commission and Court of First Instance. In particular, the Court of Justice has acknowledged that the existence of an anti-competitive agreement must often be inferred from a number of coincidences and indicia which, taken together may, in the absence of another plausible explanation, be enough to establish an infringement.[247] The judgments of the Community Courts in these cases contain helpful guidance on how questions of evidence and proof will be addressed. A document found at the premises of one party to a cartel can be used as evidence against a different undertaking, provided that there is evidence to suggest that the content of the document is an objective reflection of the content of the meetings.[248] Similarly, a statement made by an employee of one member of the cartel can be used to incriminate the other members[249] although it must be corroborated by other evidence.[250] In contrast to circumstantial evidence, when the proof of concerted action is based on documents, the burden is on the defendant undertakings not merely to put forward an alternative explanation for the facts found by

---

in no doubt that it was distancing itself from the idea of such [a price] increase'; Case T-325/01 *DaimlerChrysler v Commission* [2005] ECR II-3319, [2007] 4 CMLR 559, para 206 '[MBBel's] silence on that occasion can be interpreted only as an approval of and participation in the action against "price slashing" which had already been decided upon by the Belgian dealers'.

[246] See, eg Case T-56/99 *Marlines v Commission* (n 243, above) para 41; Cases T-67/00 *JFE Engineering* (n 201, above); *DaimlerChrysler* (above) para 215 (the insertion in a document of an exclamation mark after a figure showing percentage discount was considered incriminating).

[247] Cases C-204/00P, etc, *Aalborg Portland* (n 239, above) para 57, but see the comment of the UK Competition Appeal Tribunal on this passage in the ECJ's judgment: *JJB Sports v Office of Fair Trading* (n 213, above) para 206; Cases T-44/02, etc, *Dresdner Bank v Commission* [2006] ECR II-3567, [2007] 4 CMLR 467, para 64: 'The fragmentary and sporadic items of evidence which may be available to the Commission should, in any event, be capable of being supplemented by inferences which allow the relevant circumstances to be reconstituted'. See also the application of this 'alternative plausible explanation' test in *Makers UK Ltd v Office of Fair Trading* (n 204, above).

[248] Case T-3/89 *Atochem v Commission* [1991] ECR II-1177, paras 31–38; *JFE Engineering* (n 201, above) para 192. See also Case T-11/89 *Shell* [1992] ECR II-757 where, in relation to one item of evidence, the CFI stated 'The note itself is free of ambiguity and the fact that it is badly written, unsigned and undated is quite normal since it is a note taken during a conversation, probably over the telephone, and the anti-competitive object of the note was a reason for its author to leave the least trace possible . . . Furthermore, the fact that the information is reported second hand is immaterial . . . the precise, detailed nature of that information makes it wholly unlikely that it simply reflected market gossip, was completely wrong or invented'. But note that the Commission must be able to specify in relation to each item of evidence the producers against whom the item is probative and the period of infringement established by the item: see the ECJ's curt rejection of the Commission's more generalised approach in *Wood Pulp II* (n 202, above) paras 68–69.

[249] *JFE Engineering* (n 201, above): 'If that were not the case, the burden of proving conduct contrary to [Arts 81 and 82]. . .would be unsustainable and incompatible with the task of supervising the application of those provisions which is entrusted it by the EC Treaty' (para 192).

[250] ibid, paras 219 and 335.

the Commission but to refute the facts established by the documents.[251] If the undertaking wishes to dispute the accuracy of a document, it must put forward evidence in the form of its own notes of the meetings or from the members of its personnel who took part in the meetings. Moreover, the absence of any minutes or notes of meetings between competitors may indicate that the participants were attempting to hide the true nature of the discussion.[252] Where it is clear from the documents that the other parties involved in the cartel believed that a particular undertaking was a willing participant in it, if that undertaking admits having received the documents addressed or copied to it and was thus aware of the cartel's existence, and it took no steps to disabuse them, the Court will conclude that the undertaking was content to allow the authors of the documents to assume that their belief was well founded.[253]

Duration of individual members' participation.   As far as concerns the dura- **2.056** tion of each undertaking's participation in a multilateral concerted practice, it is clear from the *Polypropylene* and *Cement* judgments that although the conduct of the parties can be treated as constituting a single infringement, each undertaking is a party to that infringement only for the period during which it is proved that that undertaking was a party to the agreement.[254] In *Union Pigments*,[255] the evidence showed that the applicant had told the other cartel members that it was withdrawing from the cartel and that it had not participated in cartel meetings over a four-month period. However, the Court of First Instance upheld the Commission's conclusion that the applicant had continued to participate in the cartel without interruption. The applicant had not resumed a 'genuinely autonomous policy' in the market and the benefit it obtained from access to the information from other cartel members before its withdrawal did not cease to exist on the day it withdrew. Moreover, when it rejoined the cartel, it provided members with statistics retroactively covering the whole period of its purported withdrawal.

---

[251] Cases T-305/94, etc, *Limburgse Vinyl Maatschappij v Commission* ('*PVC No. 2*') [1999] ECR II-931, [1999] 5 CMLR 303. In *Dresdner Bank* (n 247, above) the CFI held on a close analysis of the allegedly incriminating documents and the context in which the banks had met (the introduction of the euro) that it was impossible to reject the appellants' alternative explanation of what had taken place at the meeting.

[252] Case T-334/94 *Sarrio v Commission* [1998] ECR II-1439, [1998] 5 CMLR 195, para 227; upheld on appeal, Case C-291/98P [2000] ECR I-9991.

[253] *Marlines v Commission* (n 243, above) para 41.

[254] Among the *Polypropylene* cases, see, eg *Shell* (n 248, above) (duration of infringement found to be less and fine reduced in consequence from 9 to 8.1 million ECU); Cases T-25/95, etc, *Cement* (n 183, above) para 4267, annulling part of the decision as regards the duration of infringement by eight participants. Infrequent attendance at meetings may also indicate that the undertaking took a passive rather than an active role in the cartel, a factor which may mitigate the fine imposed: see Case T-220/00 *Cheil Jedang v Commission* [2003] ECR II-2473, paras 168 *et seq*.

[255] Case T-62/02 *Union Pigments v Commission* [2005] ECR II-5057, [2006] 4 CMLR 1005 (zinc phosphate cartel) paras 37 *et seq*.

The Court also commented that the applicant did not withdraw from the cartel in order to report it to the Commission but rather 'the better to exploit the cartel for its own benefit'.

2.057 **Participation under duress.** An agreement allegedly 'imposed' by a supplier on his customers is still an 'agreement' within the meaning of Article 81(1).[256] Acquiescence under pressure to the wishes of a supplier may also give rise to a 'concerted practice'.[257] The argument raised on appeal by one of the participants in the *Welded Steel Mesh* cartel, that it took part in discussions against its will under pressure from other producers, was robustly dismissed by the Court of First Instance:[258] the company should have complained to the competent national authorities or the Commission instead of taking part.

2.058 **Authority to enter into agreements.** An 'agreement between undertakings' may be made on the undertakings' behalf by employees acting in the ordinary course of their employment despite the ignorance of more senior management.[259] This may be so even if the employees are acting contrary to instructions. Similarly, the fact that a ferry operator chartered its ships and had not been authorised by the owners of the vessels to enter into the cartel agreement did not prevent it from being a member.[260]

(d) Decisions by associations of undertakings

2.059 **Associations of undertakings.** Although trade associations of various kinds are the most common form of 'associations of undertakings', the word 'association' in Article 81(1) is not limited to any particular type of association. It includes

---

[256] *BMW Belgium*, OJ 1978 L46/33, 41 [1978] 2 CMLR 126, 139–140; on appeal Cases 32/78, etc, *BMW v Commission* [1979] ECR 2435, [1980] 1 CMLR 370, paras 35–37.

[257] *Hasselblad* (n 189, above) para 47 (acquiescence by Irish dealer to wishes of Swedish supplier). However, in a situation of unequal bargaining power where the smaller parties had in effect little option but to agree, this factor is very relevant to the determination of the fines: see para 13.172, below.

[258] *Tréfileurope Sales v Commission* (n 240, above) para 58. See also, eg Case T-368/00 *General Motors Nederland and Opel Nederland v Commission* [2003] ECR II-4491, [2004] 4 CMLR 1302, para 147 (appeal dismissed Case C-551/03P, [2006] ECR II-3173, [2006] 5 CMLR 9); Case T-59/99 *Ventouris Group Enterprises v Commission* [2003] ECR II 5257, [2005] 5 CMLR 1781, para 90. In Cases T-71/03, etc, *Tokai Carbon* (n 229, above) para 77, the CFI rejected the argument that the undertaking participated for fear of retaliatory measures, holding that it could have contacted the Commission anonymously or sought confidential treatment of its complaint.

[259] *Musique Diffusion Française* (n 205, above) para 97; *Viho/Parker Pen*, OJ 1992 L233/27, [1993] 5 CMLR 382, para 16: 'the company remains liable whether on the principle of *culpa in eligendo* or of *culpa in vigilando*'; appeals dismissed, Case T-77/92 *Parker Pen v Commission* [1994] ECR II-549, [1995] 5 CMLR 435; Case T-66/92 *Herlitz v Commission* [1994] ECR II-531, [1995] 5 CMLR 458.

[260] Case T-56/99 *Marlines v Commission* (n 243, above) para 60. Further, the CFI held that the Commission had been right to treat the agent and the shipowner as a single undertaking.

agricultural cooperatives,[261] professional regulatory bodies,[262] associations without a legal personality,[263] non-profit making associations,[264] associations of associations[265] and an association outside the Community.[266] A statutory body entrusted with certain public functions and including some members appointed by the government of a Member State may be an 'association of undertakings' if it represents the trading interests of other members and takes decisions or makes agreements in pursuance of those interests.[267]

Decisions. Where the activities of an association of undertakings produce **2.060** the results prohibited under Article 81(1), little will turn on an exact analysis of the measures taken.[268] The concept of 'decision' includes the rules and regulations of the association in question,[269] decisions binding upon the members[270]

---

[261] Case 61/80 *Coöperatieve Stremsel-en Kleurselfabriek v Commission* [1981] ECR 851, [1982] 1 CMLR 240; Case T-61/89 *Dansk Pelsdyravlerforening v Commission* [1992] ECR II-1931; *MELDOC*, OJ 1986 L348/50, [1989] 4 CMLR 853; *Campina, XXIst Report on Competition Policy* (1991), point 83; *Milk Marketing Board, XXIInd Report* (1992), points 161–167.

[262] If they comprise representatives of the independent practitioners: eg *EPI Code of Conduct*, OJ 1999 L106/14, [1999] 5 CMLR 540, upheld on appeal Case T-144/99 *Institute of Professional Representatives v Commission ('EPI')* [2001] ECR II-1087, [2001] 5 CMLR 77; and see the cases cited at n 17 to para 2.004, above.

[263] *Cecimo*, JO 1969 L69/13, [1969] CMLR Dl; exemption under Art 81(3) renewed *sub nom Emo*, OJ 1979 LI 1/16, [1979] 1 CMLR 419. An EIG is an association of undertakings: *Assurpol*, OJ 1992 L37/16.

[264] *FEDETAB*, OJ 1978 L224/29, 40.

[265] *BPICA*, OJ 1977 L299/18, [1977] 2 CMLR 43; *Milchförderungsfonds*, OJ 1985 L35/35, [1985] 3 CMLR 101; Case T-193/02 *Piau v Commission* [2005] ECR II-209, [2005] 5 CMLR 42, para 72 (appeal dismissed Case C-171/05P [2006] ECR I-37); Cases T-217 & 245/03 *FNCBV and FNSEA v Commission ('French Beef')*, judgment of 13 December 2006, paras 48–54 (on appeal Case C-110/07P, not yet decided). In *UEFA Champions League*, OJ 2003 L291/25, [2004] 4 CMLR 549, the Commission held that UEFA was an association of associations of undertakings, an association of undertakings and also an undertaking itself because it engages in commercial activity.

[266] Cases 89/85, etc, *Åhlström v Commission ('Wood Pulp I')* [1988] ECR 5193, [1988] 4 CMLR 901 (US Webb Pomerene Act export association).

[267] *Pabst & Richarz/BNIA*, OJ 1976 L331/24, [1976] 2 CMLR D63; *AROW/BNIC*, OJ 1982 L379/1, [1983] 2 CMLR 240; Case 123/83 *BNIC v Clair* [1985] ECR 391, [1985] 2 CMLR 430; *EPI Code of Conduct* (n 262, above); *COAPI*, OJ 1995 L122/37, [1995] 5 CMLR 468; Case C-35/96 *Commission v Italy* [1998] ECR I-3851, [1998] 5 CMLR 889, para 40.

[268] Case 71/74 *Frubo v Commission* [1975] ECR 563, 583, [1975] 2 CMLR 123, para 30 (agreements between associations infringe Art 81(1)). See also *FEDETAB* (n 264, above) paras 85–89; Cases 96/82, etc, *IAZ v Commission* [1983] ECR 3369, [1984] 3 CMLR 276, paras 19–21.

[269] eg *BPICA* (n 265, above) exemption under Art 81(3) renewed, OJ 1982 L156/16, [1982] 1 CMLR 123; *National Sulphuric Acid Association*, OJ 1980 L260/24, [1980] 3 CMLR 429; *EPI Code of Conduct* (n 262, above) (limited exemption granted); *COAPI* (n 267, above). But 'the rules' can also be an agreement: *London Sugar Futures Market Limited*, OJ 1985 L369/25; and see the cooperative tendering arrangements under the rules of the Dutch construction industry association: Case T-29/92 *SPO v Commission* [1995] ECR II-755, appeal on other grounds dismissed, Case C-137/95P [1996] ECR I-1611.

[270] *FEDETAB* (n 264, above); *Milchförderungsfonds* (n 265, above).

and recommendations,[271] or codes of conduct[272] and in fact anything which accurately reflects the association's desire to coordinate its members' conduct in accordance with its statutes. An act of an association can be regarded as a decision even if it is not binding on the members, at least if the members comply with it.[273] Agreements implemented within the framework of the association concerned may be analysed either as 'decisions' of that association[274] or 'agreements' between the members.[275]

2.061 **Association as party to an agreement.**   Whether an association is a party to an agreement in its own right is a matter of fact. An association may itself enter into an anti-competitive agreement for the benefit of its members.[276] Further, an association and its members may be held to have participated in the same agreement if it is established that the conduct on the part of the association was distinct from that of its members.[277]

4. Restriction of Competition

2.062 **Plan of this topic.**   Article 81(1) does not apply unless the agreement in question has as its 'object or effect the prevention, restriction or distortion of competition within the common market'. In many cases it will be self-evident that the agreement has such an object or effect. In other cases it will be far from obvious, partly because of the conceptual difficulty of defining a 'restriction of competition' and partly because of the diversity and complexity of the case law. This Section (a) draws attention to some of the difficulties of defining a prohibited 'restriction of competition'; (b) traces some of the main decisions of the Community Courts;

---

[271] eg Case T-193/02 *Piau v Commission* (n 265, above) para 75; Case C-309/99 *Wouters* [2002] ECR I-1577, [2002] 4 CMLR 913, [2002] All ER (EC) 193, para 64. The Opinion of AG Leger in *Wouters* was applied by the UK Competition Appeal Tribunal in *Institute of Independent Insurance Brokers v Director General of Fair Trading* [2001] CAT 4, [2001] CompAR 62.

[272] Case T-144/99 *EPI* (n 262, above).

[273] *IAZ v Commission* (n 268, above) para 20; *DaimlerChrysler v Commission* (n 246, above) para 210.

[274] *AROW/BNIC* (n 267, above). In *Piau* (n 265, above) the CFI held that the regulations adopted by the association of national football clubs associations resulted in those national associations holding a collective dominant position.

[275] *BNIC v Clair* (n 267, above). See, eg *Belgische Vereniging der Banken/Association Beige des Banques*, OJ 1987 L7/27, [1989] 4 CMLR 141; Cases T-5 & 6/00 *Nederlandse Federatieve Vereniging voor de Groothandel op Elektrotechnisch Gebied v Commission* [2003] ECR II-5761, [2004] 5 CMLR 969; further appeals dismissed, Cases C-105 & 113/04P, [2006] 5 CMLR 1257.

[276] eg COMP/38.238 *Spanish Raw Tobacco* (n 226, above). See also Cases T-39 & 40/92 *CB and Europay v Commission* [1994] ECR II 49: Groupement des Cartes Bancaires 'CB', an economic grouping of French banks, had infringed Art 81(1) by reason of its agreement with Eurocheque International concerning the basis of acceptance of Eurocheques by its members in France.

[277] Cases T-25/95, etc, *Cement* (n 183, above) paras 1322–1328: Cembureau separately responsible from its members as a participant in the cement cartel arrangements.

and finally (c) attempts a practical summary of the present law. Readers not wishing to be detained by detailed discussion should go straight to sub-section (c).[278]

(a) Some conceptual issues

Generally. In most antitrust systems the definition of a 'restriction' of competition poses conceptual problems.[279] In one sense, almost every commercial contract can be said to 'restrict' competition, since once A has sold goods to B, A cannot sell those goods to anyone else and B is no longer interested in obtaining them elsewhere.[280] Similarly, in many cases one party (for example a patent licensee or a franchisee) would, in the absence of the agreement, have had no ability to trade in the goods at all. Does an agreement that confers a freedom, albeit a qualified freedom, to trade in the goods, where previously there was no freedom at all, 'restrict' competition? More generally, in many cases the overall purpose of the agreement may be to enhance competition. For example, is competition 'restricted' if a combination between two undertakings enables them to enter a new market or develop new technology which neither could achieve alone? This gives rise to the basic question: is such an agreement, which *prima facie* enhances competition, to be treated as prohibited under Article 81(1) but capable of benefiting from the application of Article 81(3)? Or does the overall benefit to competition arising from the agreement mean that Article 81(1) does not apply at all?[281]

2.063

The competition rules and consumer detriment. In *GlaxoSmithKline*, the Court of First Instance emphasised the role of Article 81(1) in protecting

2.064

---

[278] Paras 2.094 *et seq*, below.

[279] For the 'peculiar conceptual difficulty' of defining a covenant in restraint of trade at common law, see *Chitty on Contracts* (29th edn, 2004, and 3rd Supp, 2006), Vol 1, paras 16–077 *et seq*. In US antitrust law, the prohibition in s 1 of the Sherman Act of 'every contract, combination . . . or conspiracy in restraint of trade' was derived from the common law and has of course spawned an immense and sophisticated case law.

[280] See Case T-168/01 *GlaxoSmithKline Services v Commission* [2006] ECR II-2969, [2006] 5 CMLR 1589, para 171: '. . . not every agreement which restricts the freedom of action of the participating undertakings, or of one of them, necessarily falls within the prohibition in Article 81(1) EC. . . . In particular, any contract concluded between economic agents operating at different stages of the production and distribution chain has the consequence of binding them and, consequently, of restricting them, according to the stipulated terms, in their freedom of action. . . . However, as the objective of the Community competition rules is to prevent undertakings, by restricting competition between themselves or with third parties, from reducing the welfare of the final consumer of the products in question . . . it is still necessary to demonstrate that the limitation in question restricts competition, to the detriment of the final consumer' (on appeal, Cases C-501/06P, etc, *GlaxoSmithKline Services v Commission*, not yet decided); Case C-519/04P *Meca-Medina and Majcen* [2006] ECR I-6991, [2006] 5 CMLR 1023, para 42. See also Neale and Goyder, *The Antitrust Laws of the USA* (3rd edn, 1981), 25: 'There is a sense in which any one bargain excludes others; when a bargain is sealed, the competition for that particular portion of trade is at an end. It would be a *reductio ad absurdum* to call trade itself restraint of trade; yet some types of bargain may preclude a great deal of potential competition'.

[281] See discussion in paras 2.088 *et seq*, below. For the present law on joint ventures, see Chap 5, below.

the interests of consumers.[282] According to the Court, the objective assigned to Article 81(1) is to prevent undertakings, by restricting competition between themselves or with third parties, from reducing the welfare of the final consumer of the products in question. Thus the Court held that even where an agreement was intended to limit parallel imports, this was not sufficient to bring the agreement within Article 81(1) if a competitive analysis of the market showed that final consumers of the product were not affected by a restriction on parallel trade. In the particular circumstances of the pharmaceuticals market it could not be presumed that parallel trade had an impact on prices charged to the final consumer for medicines reimbursed by the State health service. The fact that wholesale distributors of the pharmaceutical products were prevented from making profits from exploiting the price differences between Member States did not bring the agreement within Article 81(1).[283] Further, the Court there stated that the form of competition with which the Treaty is concerned is 'effective competition':

> 'that is to say, the degree of competition necessary to ensure the attainment of the objectives of the Treaty. Its intensity may vary to an extent dictated by the nature of the product concerned and the structure of the relevant market. Furthermore, its parameters may assume unequal importance, as price competition does not constitute the only effective form of competition or that to which absolute priority must in all circumstances be given . . .'[284]

2.065 **Horizontal agreements.** In analysing the concept of 'restriction of competition', it is useful to distinguish broadly between 'horizontal' and 'vertical' restrictions.[285] A horizontal agreement is an agreement between undertakings at the same level of supply, usually an agreement between competitors, for example an agreement not to compete on price, or to share out or allocate markets. The Community Courts have described the ambit of the prohibition in Article 81(1) as it applies to horizontal agreements in the following terms:

> '. . . it is inherent in the Treaty provisions on competition that every economic operator must determine autonomously the policy which it intends to pursue on the common market. Thus, according to the case-law, such a requirement of autonomy precludes any direct or indirect contact between economic operators of such a kind as either to influence the conduct on the market of an actual or potential competitor or to reveal to such a competitor the conduct which an operator has decided to follow

---

282 *GlaxoSmithKline Services* (n 280, above) paras 109 *et seq*. See also the Irish Supreme Court in *Competition Authority v O'Regan* [2007] IESC 22, per Fennelly J at para 106: 'The entire aim and object of competition law is consumer welfare' (Fennelly J is a former Advocate General of the ECJ).

283 *GlaxoSmithKline Services* (n 280, above) para 171.

284 ibid, para 109.

285 However, the Commission does not have to specify in the statement of objections whether it regards an alleged agreement as horizontal or vertical: *DaimlerChrysler v Commission* (n 245, above) para 192.

itself or contemplates adopting on the market, where the object or effect of those contacts is to give rise to conditions of competition which do not correspond to the normal conditions of the market in question, taking into account the nature of the products or the services provided, the size and number of the undertakings and also the volume of the market'.[286]

Vertical agreements.   A vertical agreement is an agreement between a supplier and   **2.066**
a customer whom he supplies. 'Vertical' agreements often contain: (a) a restriction accepted by the supplier not to supply goods of that type to anyone except the acquirer, for example a distributor or dealer in a particular area; (b) a restriction accepted by the acquirer not to acquire goods of that type from anyone except the supplier; and (c) restrictions on the acquirer's freedom to determine the resale price of the goods, or where, or to whom, the goods may be resold.

Inter-brand and intra-brand competition.   So far as vertical agreements are   **2.067**
concerned, the competition which is affected by the agreement or practice may be competition between different distributors of the same supplier's products (intra-brand competition) or competition between the products of that supplier and the suppliers of competing products (inter-brand competition). In many cases, a manufacturer will be unable to sell his goods at all unless he persuades a distributor to handle them. But building a market for a particular manufacturer may be both costly and risky for the distributor; hence a distributor may be unwilling to take on the manufacturer's products unless he is protected from competition from the manufacturer or from other distributors. In particular, the distributor will wish to protect himself from 'free riders' who, after the distributor has established the market, come into his territory and undercut him with cheaper goods of the same brand obtained from other sources.[287] In an analogous context, the licensee of intellectual property rights may be unwilling to take a licence, invest in the development of a new product, and pay a royalty, unless he has some protection against competition from the licensor or other licensees. In such cases it may be necessary to accept certain restrictions on intra-brand competition between dealers in the goods from the same manufacturer or 'second line' competition, in order to promote more effective inter-brand or 'first line' competition between dealers of goods from different manufacturers.

---

[286] Case C-49/92P *Commission v Anic* [1999] ECR I-4125, [2001] 4 CMLR 602, paras 116 and 117, cited recently in Case C-238/05 *Asnef-Equifax v Ausbanc* [2006] ECR I-11125, [2007] 4 CMLR 224, para 52.
[287] See, eg the dilemma faced by the Distillers Company in Case 30/78 *Distillers Company v Commission*, as described by AG Warner at [1980] ECR 2229, 2283–2290, [1980] 3 CMLR 121, 146–154. cf the subsequent distribution arrangements: *Distillers Company plc (Red Label)*, OJ 1983 C245/3, [1983] 3 CMLR 173 (never the subject of a final decision). See also *Haladjian Frères* (n 210, above) where the CFI, upholding the Commission's rejection of a complaint, regarded the manufacturer's desire to support its official distributors of spare parts against cheap imports from outside the EEA as legitimate: paras 58–59.

2.068 **Need to prevent absolute territorial protection.** The problem of restrictions on intra-brand competition in distribution and licence agreements gives rise to a dilemma under Community law. On the one hand, the protection sought by the distributor or licensee may be a legitimate means of enhancing competition by enabling undertakings to enter new markets or develop new technology. On the other hand, to give the distributor or licensee a 'protected' territory may artificially partition the common market, contrary to the basic aims of the Treaty. In particular, the distributor or licensee may be able to maintain prices higher than those prevailing for the same goods elsewhere in the common market because he is not exposed to competition from 'parallel imports' of those goods originating from other intermediaries outside the distributor's territory.[288] A distributor who is protected from 'parallel imports' (normally by contractual restraints on the supplier and on other distributors preventing them from selling into his territory) is said to enjoy 'absolute territorial protection'.[289] Here the issue in Community law is how to strike the balance between the legitimate interest of the distributor or licensee in a degree of protection and the Community interest in the free movement of goods: should that balance be struck under Article 81(1) or under Article 81(3), or by a combination of the two?

(b) The main decisions

2.069 **Generally.** The case law of the Community Courts has tended to distinguish between restrictions which constitute clear anti-competitive conduct, such as price-fixing and market-sharing, and other kinds of restrictions. The first category, sometimes referred to as 'hard-core' restrictions, will, subject to the *de minimis* threshold, fall within Article 81(1) if they affect trade between Member States.[290] Many of the cases coming before the Community Courts have involved agreements of the classic 'cartel type' to fix prices or share markets and the Courts have had no hesitation in holding that agreements to fix prices or divide markets 'of their nature' (that is *per se*[291]) restrict competition within the meaning of Article 81(1). Such cases raised few issues regarding the restriction of competition

---

[288] See generally paras 1.074 and 1.075, above. Parallel imports may arise where goods are sold to an intermediary by an official distributor in another territory and then imported by that intermediary into the other Member State or where a customer in one territory buys the goods from a distributor outside his home country.

[289] For the *locus classicus* on absolute territorial protection, see Cases 56 & 58/64 *Consten and Grundig v Commission* [1966] ECR 299, [1966] CMLR 418: paras 2.072 *et seq*, below.

[290] For 'hard-core' restrictions, see further para 2.097, below.

[291] The expression '*per se*' that also derives from US antitrust law, above, must be used with caution in the Art 81(1) context because (i) even an agreement which 'of its nature' infringes Art 81(1) may benefit from the *de minimis* rule (paras 2.121 *et seq*, below); and (ii) there remains the theoretical possibility of satisfying the criteria in Art 81(3). In Case T-17/93 *Matra Hachette v Commission* [1994] ECR II-595, para 85, the CFI stated that in principle the Commission had power to exempt any anti-competitive practice if the conditions of Art 81(3) were fulfilled. See also the CFI's decision

and are not further discussed here.[292] With regard to other kinds of restrictions, the Community Courts have stressed that thorough analysis of the economic context surrounding the agreement and the effect of the agreement in the relevant market is necessary to determine whether the obligations are anti-competitive to any significant extent. The following Section considers first the two seminal cases from which the competition law of the Community has developed: *Société Technique Minière* (1966) and *Consten and Grundig* (1966). There follows discussion of three leading cases concerned with market analysis: *Völk* (1969), *Delimitis* (1991) and *European Night Services* (1998).

(i) The two seminal cases

***Société Technique Minière*: market analysis necessary.** The first case of sig- **2.070**
nificance is *Société Technique Minière*,[293] decided in 1966, in which the Court of
Justice declined to adopt a formalistic interpretation of 'restriction of competition' under Article 81(1). A French company (Technique Minière) was given the
exclusive right to sell in France certain levelling machines manufactured by
a German company (Maschinenbau Ulm) and agreed not to sell competing
machines. The French company sought to renege on payment for the machines
on the grounds that the agreement contravened Article 81(1). However there was
no 'absolute territorial protection' and no impediment to parallel imports.[294] On
a reference from the French court for a preliminary ruling, the Court of Justice
rejected the Commission's argument that the restriction accepted by Maschinenbau
Ulm not to compete with Technique Minière necessarily amounted to a prohibited 'restriction of competition'. The Court of Justice held that agreements merely
granting an exclusive right of sale did not 'of their very nature' restrict competition
within the meaning of Article 81(1).[295] The relevant part of the Court's judgment
is of sufficient importance to set out in full:

> 'Finally, for the agreement at issue to be caught by the prohibition contained in
> Article [81(1)] it must have as its "object or effect the prevention, restriction or dis-
> tortion of competition within the Common Market".

---

in *European Night Services*, Cases T-374/94, etc, *ENS v Commission* [1998] ECR II-3141, [1998] 5 CMLR 718, para 136: discussed at paras 2.084 *et seq*, below.

[292] Some have raised issues about the meaning of 'concerted practice': see paras 2.038 *et seq*, above; and many involve significant procedural issues: see generally Chap 13, below.

[293] Case 56/65 *Société Technique Minière v Maschinenbau Ulm* [1966] ECR 235, [1966] CMLR 357. The ECJ's approach in *Société Technique Minière* has been affirmed many times since.

[294] ie no export bans were imposed on the French distributor nor, apparently, on any other dis-tributor of the products of Maschinenbau Ulm. The agreement in question would now benefit from block exemption under Art 81(3) by virtue of Reg 2790/1999, provided that Maschinenbau Ulm's market share did not exceed 30 per cent. For further discussion of exclusive distribution agreements, see paras 6.039 *et seq*, below.

[295] *Société Technique Minière* (n 293, above) at 251 (ECR), 376 (CMLR).

The fact that these are not cumulative but alternative requirements, indicated by the conjunction "or," leads first to the need to consider the precise purpose of the agreement, in the economic context in which it is to be applied. This interference with competition referred to in Article [81(1)] must result from all or some of the clauses of the agreement itself. Where, however, an analysis of the said clauses does not reveal the effect on competition to be sufficiently deleterious, the consequences of the agreement should then be considered and for it to be caught by the prohibition it is then necessary to find that those factors are present which show that competition had in fact been prevented or restricted or distorted to an appreciable extent.

The competition in question must be understood within the actual context in which it would occur in the absence of the agreement in dispute. In particular it may be doubted whether there is an interference with competition if the said agreement seems really necessary for the penetration of a new area by an undertaking. Therefore, in order to decide whether an agreement containing a clause "granting an exclusive right of sale" is to be considered as prohibited by reason of its object or of its effect, it is appropriate to take into account in particular the nature and quantity, limited or otherwise, of the products covered by the agreement, the position and importance of the grantor and the concessionaire on the market for the products concerned, the isolated nature of the disputed agreement, or, alternatively, its position in a series of agreements, the severity of the clauses intended to protect the exclusive dealership or, alternatively, the opportunities allowed for other commercial competitors in the same products by way of parallel re-exportation and importation.'[296]

2.071 **Result of *Société Technique Minière*.** Because *Société Technique Minière* was a reference for a preliminary ruling, the Court was not able to apply its judgment to the particular facts of the case. Nonetheless, in interpreting Article 81(1) the Court clearly rejected the simple *per se* approach put forward by the Commission in argument[297] and decided in favour of a limited kind of 'rule of reason'.[298] *Société Technique Minière* seems to yield the following propositions, which have been further developed in later cases:

(1) In deciding whether Article 81(1) applies, it is first necessary to consider 'the object' of the agreement.

(2) The grant of an exclusive right of sale does not of its nature have 'the object' of restricting competition, at least where the exclusive right is necessary for the penetration of a new area by an undertaking.

(3) If the 'object' of the agreement does not of its nature restrict competition, it is next necessary to consider the 'effect' of the agreement on competition, taking into account the whole economic context in which the agreement operates.

---

[296] ibid, at 249–250 (ECR), 375–376 (CMLR).

[297] ibid, at 239–241 (ECR), (not in CMLR).

[298] The expression is used in the Opinion of AG Roemer in *Société Technique Minière* (n 293, above). But see para 2.091, below.

(4) In judging the 'effect' of the agreement, regard must be had to the competition that would occur in the absence of the agreement in dispute.

(5) The effect on competition must be shown to be appreciable.

(6) Factors relevant to determining whether the agreement appreciably affects competition include, in particular: (a) the market shares of the parties in the relevant market; (b) whether the agreement stands alone or is part of a network of similar agreements; and (c) whether the agreement precludes the possibility of parallel imports.

These conditions remain a convenient checklist for deciding whether Article 81(1) applies.[299]

***Consten and Grundig*: export bans 'of their nature' restrictive.**   The rejection   **2.072**
of *per se* arguments in *Société Technique Minière* may be contrasted with the contemporaneous result in *Consten and Grundig*,[300] the *fons et origo* of much Community competition law. That case established the basic principle that agreements which prohibit exports within the common market of their nature restrict competition within the meaning of Article 81(1), irrespective of their actual effects. That is so even if the competition which is restricted is not between the parties to the agreement (ie a producer and his distributor) but between one of those parties and third parties (ie between that distributor and other distributors of the same brand).[301]

The facts of *Consten and Grundig*.   In *Consten and Grundig*, Consten was   **2.073**
appointed exclusive distributor in France of Grundig radios and televisions. Consten undertook, *inter alia*, not to deliver any Grundig products directly or indirectly outside France. Grundig undertook not to deliver its products directly or indirectly to anyone in France except Consten. At the same time, Grundig assigned to Consten the trademark 'GINT' which was affixed to all Grundig products in addition to the 'Grundig' mark. This assignment enabled Consten to sue any third party importing Grundig products into France for infringement of the 'GINT' trade mark. Moreover Grundig imposed on all its other distributors and dealers obligations not to deliver directly or indirectly outside their respective territories. The purpose of the Grundig system was to protect Consten, as far as possible, from competition from imports of Grundig products obtained by third parties from outside France (ie 'parallel imports'). By imposing export bans on each dealer, and by assigning to Consten the trademark 'GINT', Grundig sought

---

[299] For a more comprehensive summary, see paras 2.094 *et seq*, below.

[300] Cases 56 & 58/64 *Consten and Grundig v Commission* [1966] ECR 299, [1966] CMLR 418. For other aspects of this case, see para 9.068 (intellectual property rights), below.

[301] *Consten and Grundig*, above, at 339–343 (ECR), 469–474 (CMLR). See also Case 32/65 *Italy v Council and Commission* [1966] ECR 389, 407–408, [1966] CMLR 39, 62–64.

to protect Consten absolutely from such imports ('absolute territorial protection'). As a result, Grundig products obtainable more cheaply elsewhere in the Community could not be sold on the French market.

2.074 **Restriction of competition in *Consten and Grundig*.** The Commission held[302] that the Grundig system restricted competition within the meaning of Article 81(1). On appeal,[303] it was argued that the concept of 'restriction of competition' under Article 81(1) applied mainly to competition *between manufacturers*: the Commission should have considered the whole market for radio and television products in which Grundig faced fierce competition from other brands. Had it done so, it would have found that the overall effect of the Grundig system was to increase competition between Grundig products and competing makes. The Court of Justice, however, rejected those arguments,[304] and held that Article 81(1) extended to agreements which restricted competition *between distributors of the same brand of products* (ie intra-brand or 'second line' competition). The Grundig system of export bans on Grundig dealers prevented any parallel trading in Grundig products between the territories of the Community, thus enabling higher prices for Grundig products to prevail in some territories than in others and preventing the creation of a true common market. The Court said that the Grundig system:

> '. . . results in the isolation of the French market and makes it possible to charge for the products in question prices which are sheltered from all effective competition[305] . . . Since the agreement thus aims at isolating the French market for Grundig products and maintaining artificially, for products of a very well-known brand, separate national markets within the Community, it is therefore such as to distort competition within the Common Market.'[306]

However, the Court confined its reasoning to the export bans imposed on the Grundig dealers and the associated agreement regarding the 'GINT' trade mark.[307] The Court annulled for lack of reasoning the Commission's decision insofar as it also condemned the obligation on Grundig not to make direct deliveries in France except to Consten.[308]

---

302 *Consten and Grundig*, JO 1964 2545/64, [1964] CMLR 489.

303 *Consten and Grundig* (n 300, above).

304 ibid, at 342–343 (ECR), 472–174 (CMLR).

305 It is clear that the ECJ is referring to effective competition between Grundig dealers, which was seen by the ECJ as a means of removing price disparities between Grundig products within the Community.

306 *Consten and Grundig* (n 300, above) at 340 and 343 (ECR), 471 and 474 (CMLR). See also Case 32/65 *Italy v Council and Commission* (n 301, above).

307 *Consten and Grundig*, ibid, at 342–343 and 344–346 (ECR), 472–474 and 474–475 (CMLR).

308 *Consten and Grundig*, ibid, at 344 (ECR), 474–475 (CMLR). The Commission had given no reasons for prohibiting under Art 81(1) Grundig's obligation to deliver only to Consten in France. In annulling this part of the Commission's decision, the ECJ was acting consistently with its judgment in *Société Technique Minière* (n 293, above).

'Object or effect' in *Consten and Grundig*. The Court of Justice also held that **2.075**
once it was shown that the *object* of the agreement was to restrict competition
within the meaning of Article 81(1), it was irrelevant to consider the effects:

> '. . . there is no need to take account of the concrete effects of an agreement once
> it appears that it has as its object the prevention, restriction or distortion of
> competition.'[309]

Moreover, the Court said that once it was established that the agreement restricted
competition between the Grundig distributors by preventing parallel imports it
was irrelevant that the agreement might increase competition between manufacturers of radios and televisions or have other favourable effects.[310] Such effects
were for consideration, if at all, only under Article 81(3).[311]

The two cases contrasted: agreements 'of their nature' restrictive. The con- **2.076**
trast between *Société Technique Minière* and *Consten and Grundig* seems to derive
from the distinction between agreements which 'of their nature' restrict competition (ie restrict competition *per se*[312]), and those which do not necessarily do
so.[313] The export bans considered in *Consten and Grundig* were perceived as contrary to the fundamental objective of market integration under the Treaty. The
Court of Justice was therefore prepared to regard an export ban as a *per se* 'restriction of competition' within the meaning of Article 81(1), regardless of its actual
effects.[314] On the other hand, in *Société Technique Minière* the Court was concerned with a single exclusive dealing agreement of a common commercial kind
between two companies of modest importance. Such an agreement was not in
fundamental conflict with the objectives of the Treaty. The Court therefore felt
able to adopt a different approach to the application of Article 81(1), emphasising
the need for a market analysis and paying particular regard to the competition
likely to occur in the absence of the agreement.

The interpretation of *Consten and Grundig* in *GlaxoSmithKline*. The judg- **2.077**
ment in *Consten and Grundig* has recently been considered by the Court of
First Instance in *GlaxoSmithKline*, a case concerning the restrictions imposed by a
manufacturer on distributors to prevent parallel trade in its pharmaceutical products.

---

309 *Consten and Grundig* (n 300, above) at 342 (ECR), 473 (CMLR).
310 *Consten and Grundig* (n 300, above) at 343 (ECR), 473–474 (CMLR).
311 The ECJ also upheld the Commission's refusal to grant an exemption under Art 81(3) for
a system including absolute territorial protection: ibid, at 347–350 (ECR), 477–80, (CMLR).
312 Subject, however, to the *de minimis* rule (paras 2.121 *et seq,* below) and the exceptional possibility of applying Art 81(3).
313 See the contrast made between the two cases by the CFI in *GlaxoSmithKline Services* (n 280,
above) paras 111 and 112.
314 Similarly, see Case 19/77 *Miller v Commission* [1978] ECR 131, [1978] 2 CMLR 334; Case
28/77 *Tepea v Commission* [1978] ECR 1391, [1978] 3 CMLR 392; and many subsequent cases:
para 6.053, below.

There, the Court of First Instance, rejecting the Commission's argument, expressed a more qualified interpretation of the prohibition on export bans set out in *Consten and Grundig*:

'... the Court of Justice ... did not hold that an agreement intended to limit parallel trade must be considered by its nature, that is to say, independently of any competitive analysis, to have as its object the restriction of competition. On the contrary, the Court of Justice merely held, first, that an agreement between a producer and a distributor which might tend to restore the national divisions in trade between Member States might be of such a kind as to frustrate the most fundamental objectives of the Community . . ., a consideration which led it to reject a plea alleging that Article 81(1) EC was not applicable to vertical agreements . . . . The Court of Justice then carried out a competitive analysis, *abridged but real*, during the course of which it held, in particular, that the agreement in question sought to eliminate any possibility of competition at the wholesale level in order to charge prices which were sheltered from all effective competition, considerations which led it to reject a plea alleging that there was no restriction of competition . . . .

While it has been accepted since then that parallel trade must be given a certain protection, it is therefore not as such but, as the Court of Justice held, in so far as it favours the development of trade, on the one hand, and the strengthening of competition, on the other hand . . ., that is to say, in this second respect, in so far as it gives final consumers the advantages of effective competition in terms of supply or price . . . Consequently, while it is accepted that an agreement intended to limit parallel trade must in principle be considered to have as its object the restriction of competition, that applies in so far as the agreement may be presumed to deprive final consumers of those advantages.'[315] (Emphasis added)

(ii) Market analysis

2.078 ***Völk*: the requirement of appreciable effect.** In 1969, *Völk v Vervaecke*[316] established the principle, already foreshadowed in *Société Technique Minière*,[317] that an agreement falls outside Article 81(1) where it is unlikely either to affect trade between Member States or to restrict competition to any appreciable extent. In that case, a German manufacturer of washing machines, Völk, appointed the Belgian firm, Vervaecke, as exclusive distributor in Belgium and Luxembourg. Völk undertook to ensure that Vervaecke would be absolutely protected against parallel imports and Vervaecke undertook not to sell competing machines. A dispute arose and Vervaecke alleged that the agreement was void under Article 81(1). It transpired that Völk's production of washing machines varied between 0.2 per cent

---

[315] *GlaxoSmithKline Services* (n 280, above) paras 120–121. The judgment is under appeal: Cases C-501 & 513/06P, etc.

[316] Case 5/69 *Völk v Vervaecke* [1969] ECR 295, [1969] CMLR 273. See also Case 1/71 *Cadillon v Höss* [1971] ECR 351, [1971] CMLR 420, para 9; Case 22/71 *Béguelin Import v G.L Import Export* [1971] ECR 949, [1972] CMLR 81, paras 16–18; *Miller v Commission* (n 314, above). See generally paras 2.121 *et seq*, below, and the Commission's *De Minimis* Notice, OJ 2001 C368/13: Vol II, App C.13.

[317] Para 2.070, above.

and 0.5 per cent of production in Germany. The Court of Justice said that the requirements of Article 81(1) must be considered in the actual circumstances of the agreement. Consequently, it held:

> '. . . an agreement falls outside the prohibition in Article [81] when it has only an insignificant effect on the markets, taking into account the weak position which the persons concerned have on the market of the product in question.'[318]

Comment on *Völk*. *Völk* decides that if, having conducted a market analysis in **2.079** accordance with *Société Technique Minière*, the effect on the market is insignificant, Article 81(1) does not apply even where the agreement gives rise to 'absolute territorial protection'.[319] That rule makes it necessary to identify the market in which the agreement is likely to have effect, that is to say 'the relevant market', which is further discussed below.[320] The requirement of appreciable effect, also known as the *de minimis* rule, is of major importance in Community law.[321]

***Delimitis*: wide market analysis required.** In its 1991 judgment in *Delimitis*,[322] **2.080** the Court of Justice gave detailed guidance on the factors to be taken into account in assessing the compatibility of an exclusive purchasing obligation in a vertical agreement, in this case a brewery tie agreement. First, the Court described the advantages which each party derived from the exclusive purchasing obligation. The supplier obtains a guaranteed outlet and ensures that the reseller concentrates his sales efforts on the distribution of the contract goods; the reseller gains access to the beer distribution market under favourable conditions and their shared interest in promoting sales of the contract goods 'secures for the reseller the benefit of the supplier's assistance in guaranteeing product quality and customer service'. The Court appeared to conclude from this that the contract does not therefore have as its *object* the restriction of competition, so that it is necessary to ascertain whether it has the *effect* of preventing restricting or distorting competition.

***Delimitis*: ease of market entry must be analysed.** The Court of Justice indi- **2.081** cated that the key question to be addressed in determining whether an exclusive purchasing obligation restricted competition was the extent of other barriers to

---

318 *Völk v Vervaecke* (n 316, above) para 5/7.

319 In *Miller v Commission* (n 314, above) at 157–158 (ECR), 341–342 (CMLR), AG Warner considered that *Société Technique Minière* and *Völk* yield slightly different principles: in *Société Technique Minière* the submission was that, without the exclusive dealing agreement, the relevant trade could not take place at all whereas in *Völk* the submission was *de minimis non curat lex*.

320 Para 2.101, below.

321 Paras 2.121 *et seq*, below.

322 Case C-234/89 *Delimitis* [1991] ECR I-935, [1992] 5 CMLR 210. This important case is discussed further at para 6.146 *et seq*, below.

entry, or to growth, for participants in the market. Referring to *Brasserie de Haecht*,[323] the Court held that:

'. . . the cumulative effect of several similar agreements *constitutes one factor amongst others* in ascertaining whether, by way of a possible alteration of competition, trade between member-States is capable of being affected.

Consequently, in the present case it is necessary to analyse the effect of a beer supply agreement, taken together with other contracts of the same type, on the opportunities of national competitors or those from other member-States, to gain access to the market for beer consumption or to increase their market share and, accordingly, the effects on the range of products offered to consumers.'[324] (Emphasis added)

2.082 **Contribution to barriers of agreement in question.** Thus the Court of Justice made clear that, in considering this question, the existence of a bundle of similar contracts, even if they had a considerable effect on the opportunities for gaining access to the market, was not sufficient, in itself, to support a finding that the market was inaccessible. Account must be taken of the possibilities for a new competitor to penetrate the market by acquiring a brewery already established on the market or by opening new public houses. Account must also be taken of 'the conditions under which competitive forces operate on the relevant market'; for example, the number and size of producers, the degree of saturation of the market, customer brand loyalty and trends in beer sales.[325] If the market analysis reveals that it is difficult to gain access to the relevant market, the Court held that it is then necessary to assess the extent to which the agreements entered into by the brewery in question contribute to that difficulty. If the contribution of the particular brewery is insignificant, its agreements will not fall within Article 81(1). This will depend on the market position of the contracting parties and the duration of the obligation.[326]

2.083 ***Delimitis*: comment.** The Court of Justice in *Delimitis* propounded a two-stage test.[327] First, is the market in which the agreement operates one which is difficult for new suppliers to enter or in which existing suppliers cannot easily increase their market share? To determine this one must look at all the circumstances, including the existence of other networks of agreements. Secondly, if the market does pose barriers to entry or growth, one must examine whether the agreement in question contributes significantly to those barriers. Subsequent decisions have made it clear that this approach applies generally to consideration of exclusive

---

[323] Case 23/67 *Brasserie De Haecht v Wilkin* [1967] ECR 407, [1968] CMLR 26.
[324] *Delimitis* (n 322, above) paras 14–15.
[325] ibid, para 22.
[326] ibid, paras 24 *et seq*.
[327] See, eg the English court's approach to this two-stage test in *Crehan v Inntrepreneur Pub Company* [2003] EWHC 1510 (Ch), [2003] UKCLR 834, [2003] EuLR 663, ultimately upheld by the House of Lords in *Inntrepreneur Pub Company v Crehan* [2006] UKHL 38, [2006] 3 WLR 148, [2006] 4 All ER 465.

purchasing agreements.[328] The complexity of the analysis involved greatly increases the burden for a national court having to determine the validity of such clauses. However, the practical implications are considerably alleviated by the Commission's block exemption for vertical agreements[329] under which, unless the supplier's share of the relevant market exceeds 30 per cent, the agreement will normally benefit from automatic exemption and the question of whether or not it would fall within Article 81(1) in the first place therefore becomes academic; equally, if that market share exceeds 30 per cent, the agreement will probably fall within Article 81(1) on a *Delimitis* analysis and individual exemption will be required.[330]

European Night Services. The 1998 judgment of the Court of First Instance in **2.084** *European Night Services* [331] highlights the importance of proper market analysis in the context of a horizontal cooperation agreement. European Night Services (ENS) was a joint venture set up by the British, German, Dutch and French national railway operators to provide overnight cross-Channel rail passenger services between the United Kingdom and continental European cities through the Channel Tunnel. The undertakings notified to the Commission both the agreement establishing ENS and the operating agreements whereby each parent undertook to provide various services to ENS, including traction (ie the provision of locomotives, crew and train paths) on each national network, and the British and French operators agreed to provide the specialised traction required for the Channel Tunnel.

---

328 Case C-393/92 *Almelo* [1994] ECR I-1477. In two parallel judgments, the CFI applied such a detailed analysis of the cumulative effect of a network of exclusive purchasing agreements for impulse ice cream in Germany, instead of the simpler approach that had been adopted by the Commission: Case T-7/93 *Langnese-Iglo v Commission* [1995] ECR II-1533, [1995] 5 CMLR 602, [1995] All ER (EC) 902, appeal dismissed, Case C-279/95P [1998] ECR I-5609, [1998] 5 CMLR 933; Case T-9/93 *Schöller v Commission* [1995] ECR II-1611, [1995] 5 CMLR 659. See also Case T-65/98 *Van den Bergh Foods v Commission* [2003] ECR II-4653, [2004] 4 CMLR 14, [2005] All ER (EC) 418 (principles applied to ice cream cabinet exclusivity clauses), appeal dismissed Case C-552/03P *Unilever Bestfoods v Commission* [2006] ECR I-9091, [2006] 5 CMLR 1460. In Case C-214/99 *Neste v Yötuuli Ky* [2000] ECR I-11121, [2001] 4 CMLR 993, [2001] All ER (EC) 76, the ECJ stressed the importance of the duration of the particular restraint (measured by reference to the notice period for terminating the agreement) in assessing the foreclosure effect. See further paras 6.148 *et seq*, below. It seems that, in principle, the same approach should apply to exclusive distribution agreements, which commonly impose a restriction on supplies to other outlets in the reseller's territory.

329 Reg 2790/1999, OJ 1999 L336/21: Vol II, App C.3. See paras 6.010 *et seq*, below, for a discussion of Reg 2790/1999 and paras 6.164 *et seq*, below, for the application of Art 81(3) to single branding agreements.

330 However, if the agreement in question is less restrictive than the type of agreement more widely used by the supplier, that agreement may fall outside Art 81(1) even if his overall market share exceeds 30 per cent: *Neste v Yötulli* (n 328, above).

331 Cases T-374/94, etc, *ENS v Commission* [1998] ECR II-3141, [1998] 5 CMLR 718.

2.085 ***European Night Services*: the Commission's decision.** The Commission held[332] that ENS was a cooperative joint venture (JV) where the individual parents all continued to operate in the upstream market for rail services that they supplied to the JV. Since each parent had the financial and technical resources to set up other groupings that could provide overnight passenger transport services, competition between them was restricted; and since the formation of ENS might impede access by other railway operators to the necessary rail services for use of the Channel Tunnel it also had an anti-competitive effect *vis-à-vis* third parties. The Commission found that those restrictions were enhanced because ENS was only one of a number of JVs concluded by or between the parent undertakings. The Commission therefore held that both the JV agreement itself and the operating agreements came within Article 81(1) but granted an exemption[333] for eight years on condition that the parties supplied the same necessary services, on the same terms, to any other operator wishing to operate night passenger trains through the Channel Tunnel.

2.086 ***European Night Services*: the Court of First Instance judgment.** On a challenge brought by the parties to ENS, the Court of First Instance annulled the decision and held that the Commission had failed to establish that the agreements fell within Article 81(1) at all.[334] In an important passage, the Court stated:

> '. . . it must be borne in mind that in assessing an agreement under Article [81(1)], account should be taken of the relevant conditions in which it functions, in particular the economic context in which undertakings operate, the products or services covered by the agreement and the actual structure of the market concerned . . . unless it is an agreement containing obvious restrictions of competition such as price-fixing, market-sharing or the control of outlets. . . . In the latter case, such restrictions may be weighed against their claimed pro-competitive effects only in the context of Article [81(3)] of the Treaty, with a view to granting an exemption from the prohibition in Article[81(1)].'[335]

Applying that approach, the Court found that none of the three grounds on which the Commission had based its decision that competition was restricted could be upheld. As regards competition between the parties, there was no actual competition between them on their national networks and potential competition between

---

[332] *Night Services*, OJ 1994 L259/20, [1995] 5 CMLR 76.
[333] The exemption was granted under the then implementing regulation for rail transport, Reg 1017/68, not under Art 81(3), but the provision was in similar terms.
[334] Cases T-374/94, etc, *ENS v Commission* (n 331, above). The decision was annulled also on other grounds including a failure to establish an appreciable effect on trade between Member States.
[335] ibid, para 136.

them for international services through the Channel Tunnel was unrealistic as none of them individually could take the financial risk involved in establishing such an operation. The Commission's finding that there was a restriction in the supply of services to third parties was vitiated by the Court's previous judgment which had annulled the Commission's analysis of the Eurotunnel agreements.[336] And as regards the other JVs entered into by the parents, on which the Commission relied, the Commission had failed to explain how participation in those JVs, which concerned the transport of goods,[337] affected competition regarding the creation or operation of ENS, which concerned the transport of passengers and therefore operated in a different market.

***European Night Services*: comment.** The Court's judgment presents one of **2.087** the clearest articulations of the division of restrictive provisions in agreements into two categories. For 'hard-core' restrictions which clearly have the object of restricting competition, there is effectively a presumption that they fall within Article 81(1); the assessment can therefore proceed straight away to ask whether the conditions for exemption might be satisfied. But for any other form of restriction, careful consideration of the effect of the agreement is required. That involves examination of the realistic, as opposed to theoretically possible, commercial options for the parties in the absence of such an agreement, having regard to the market affected.[338] In that determination, the Court leaves scope for the pro-competitive effects of the agreement to be brought into account. Significantly, the Court referred to both *Delimitis*[339] and *Gøttrup-Klim*[340] in its reasoning. This judgment served as a catalyst to the Commission's adoption of an economically more realistic approach to the analysis of the effect on competition, which had previously been employed in some of its joint venture decisions but had not been adopted on a consistent basis.[341] It is now the dominating feature of the new block exemptions and Guidelines adopted in recent years.[342]

---

[336] Cases T-79 & 80/95 *SNCF and British Railways v Commission* [1996] ECR II-1491, [1997] 4 CMLR 334, annulling *Eurotunnel III*, OJ 1994 L354/66, [1995] 4 CMLR 801.

[337] Moreover, those services were not marketed by the parties to ENS.

[338] See also Case T-328/03 *O2 (Germany) v Commission* [2006] ECR II-1231, [2006] 5 CMLR 258, discussed at para 2.093, below, where the CFI also annulled a decision granting exemption under Art 81(3) finding that the agreement did not fall within Art 81(1).

[339] Para 2.080, above.

[340] Case C-250/92 *Gøttrup-Klim v Dansk Landbrugs Grovvareselskab AmbA* [1994] ECR I-5641, [1996] 4 CMLR 191. See para 2.090, below.

[341] eg *ElopakMetal Box-Odin*, OJ 1990 L209/15, [1991] 4 CMLR 832. See para 7.069, below.

[342] See in particular Reg 2790/1999 (n 329, above); Reg 2659/2000, OJ 2000 L304/7: Vol II, App C.5; Reg 772/2004, OJ 2004 L123/11 and the Guidelines published in relation to each Reg.

(iii) Consideration of pro- and anti-competitive effects

2.088 **The ambit of the prohibition under Community law.** Given the structure of Article 81, there are two possible approaches to the definition of a 'restriction of competition' under Article 81(1). The first approach is to interpret the prohibition of Article 81(1) widely, permitting restraints on competition only when applying Article 81(3). Under this wide approach, almost every restriction on conduct accepted as between the parties is regarded as falling under Article 81(1), to be permitted only under Article 81(3). The second approach takes the view that not every restriction on conduct is necessarily a restriction of *competition* within the meaning of Article 81(1). The Community Courts have generally adopted the latter approach: if an agreement can be seen to be pro-competitive overall, any restrictions which are essential to the performance of the agreement fall outside Article 81(1).[343] With the advent of Regulation 1/2003 allowing national courts and competition authorities to apply Article 81(3) as well as Article 81(1),[344] the practical significance of this issue has greatly diminished.[345] But the cases are still important for what they say about the nature of competition, and hence about the nature of restrictions and distortions of competition.

2.089 *Metro*: **objective criteria and 'workable competition'.** In 1977, a different approach to deciding what is a 'restriction of competition' emerged in *Metro (No. 1)*, to be confirmed in 1986 by *Metro (No. 2)*.[346] In the *Metro* cases the Court of Justice decided that certain 'restrictions' do not amount to restrictions on competition within the meaning of Article 81(1) if they are 'objectively justified' by certain policy considerations, such as the need to ensure adequate distribution of high quality or high technology products. Metro was a 'cash and carry' outlet which had been refused supplies of SABA electrical products. SABA operated a system of selective distribution, whereby SABA distributors agreed to supply only to 'appointed' SABA wholesalers or retailers. The technical (or so called 'qualitative') requirements were that the dealer specialise in electrical products, maintain

---

[343] The dichotomy is not strict. Hence in *Gøttrup-Klim* (n 340, above) the ECJ made reference to the economic conditions on the market in which the cooperative purchasing association operated.

[344] See paras 1.058 *et seq*, above and Chap 13, below.

[345] But the burden of proof under Art 81(1) is on the party alleging violation, whereas under Art 81(3) it is on the party seeking to bring the agreement within the exempting provision: Art 2 of Reg 1/2003, OJ 2003 L1/1: Vol II, App B.3.

[346] Case 26/76 *Metro v Commission (No. 1)* [1977] ECR 1875, [1978] 2 CMLR 1; Case 75/84 *Metro v Commission (No. 2)* [1986] ECR 3021, [1987] 1 CMLR 118. Those cases arose out of Metro's challenge to the Commission's decision to grant exemption under Art 81(3) in *SABA (No. 1)*, OJ 1976 L28/19, [1976] 1 CMLR D61, renewed in *SABA (No. 2)*, OJ 1983 L376/41, [1984] 1 CMLR 676. The facts of *Metro (No. 1)* are summarised here but were essentially the same in *Metro (No.2)*: para 12 of that judgment. For further comment and selective distribution generally, see paras 6.086 *et seq*, below.

adequate premises, employ qualified staff and supply aftersales service. The commercial (or 'quantitative') requirements were that the dealer be prepared to enter into six-month forward supply contracts based on targets set by SABA, to achieve an 'adequate' turnover, and to maintain specified stock levels. The Court of Justice upheld the Commission's decision that the qualitative criteria did not fall within Article 81(1) stating:

> 'The requirement contained in Articles 3 and [81] of the [EC] Treaty that competition shall not be distorted implies the existence on the market of workable competition, that is to say the degree of competition necessary to ensure the observance of the basic requirements and the attainment of the objectives of the Treaty, in particular the creation of a single market achieving conditions similar to those of a domestic market. In accordance with this requirement the nature and intensiveness of competition may vary to an extent dictated by the products or services in question and the economic structure of the relevant market sectors.'[347]

In the case of high quality and technically advanced consumer durables, the Court held that the Commission was justified in recognising that selective distribution systems constituted, together with others, an aspect of competition which did not contravene Article 81(1) provided, first, that resellers were chosen on the basis of objective criteria of a qualitative nature and, secondly, that such conditions are laid down uniformly for all potential resellers and are not applied in a discriminatory fashion.[348] However, Article 81(1) was infringed by the requirements imposed on SABA wholesalers which went further than strictly qualitative requirements[349] and which excluded access to SABA products by dealers technically qualified to handle them, thereby limiting outlets.[350] The Court also upheld the Commission's decision under Article 81(3),[351] but said that the Commission should reconsider the matter if the structural rigidity of the SABA system were to become reinforced

---

[347] *Metro (No. 1)* above, para 20. There seems to be no practical difference between the term 'workable competition', as there used by the ECJ, and the term 'effective competition' that is more commonly employed by economists today and has been used in more recent judgments (and see also Art 2 of the Merger Reg, Reg 139/2004: Vol II, App D.1). See *GlaxoSmithKline Services*, para 2.077, above. Both expressions are intended to contrast with the economic model of 'perfect competition' and imply a competitive market which is efficient, responsive to consumer demand and without insuperable barriers to entry; see generally Scherer and Ross, *Industrial Market Structure and Economic Performance* (3rd edn, 1990), Chap 2.

[348] *Metro (No. 1)* (n 346, above). The ECJ confirmed this approach in *Metro (No. 2)* (n 346, above) para 40, subject to the qualification that Art 81(1) might exceptionally apply if the cumulative effect of such 'simple' selective distribution systems was to eliminate other forms of distribution from the relevant market or if there was no effective competition. See further paras 6.086 *et seq*, below.

[349] Such as the obligations on wholesalers to promote SABA products, to achieve sales targets and maintain stocks: *Metro (No. 1)* (n 346, above) paras 39 *et seq*.

[350] *Metro (No. 1)* paras 34–41, esp paras 37, 39, 40.

[351] ibid, paras 40–50.

by an increase in the number of selective distribution systems in the sector in question.[352]

2.090 **Other instances.**   This approach has been confirmed in subsequent cases concerning selective distribution networks.[353] Similar analysis has been applied in other contexts:

- **Franchise network.** In *Pronuptia*,[354] the Court of Justice held that restrictions in an agreement between a franchisor and its franchisee network did not fall within Article 81(1) if they were essential to maintain the inherent characteristics of the franchised business.

- **Grant of intellectual property rights.** In *Nungesser*,[355] the Court of Justice considered whether the grant of exclusive plant breeder rights was *per se* within Article 81 (1).[356] The Court appears to have accepted, on the facts, that protection of plant breeders' rights, and the granting of exclusive licences of such rights, encouraged technical innovation and the development of new markets.[357] A total prohibition of such licences under Article 81(1) would, therefore, be prejudicial to the Community interest. An 'open' exclusive licence which allowed parallel imports and did not purport to confer absolute territorial protection was not contrary to Article 81(1).[358]

---

[352] ibid, paras 21–22, and see *Metro (No. 2)* (n 346, above).

[353] eg Case 107/82 *AEG v Commission* [1983] ECR 3151, [1984] 3 CMLR 325, para 42, where the ECJ said the restriction of price competition inherent in selective distribution systems 'is counterbalanced by competition as regards the quality of services supplied to customers which, would not normally be possible in the absence of an appropriate profit margin making it possible to support the higher expenses connected with those services'. But note *Metro (No. 2)* (n 346, above) paras 40–45: where the number of selective distribution systems was such that there was no room for other forms of distribution or resulted in a rigid price structure that was not counterbalanced by other aspects of intra-brand and inter-brand competition, the ECJ stated that Art 81(1) would apply. This appears to introduce a limited form of economic analysis, subsequently developed in *Delimitis*, para 2.080, above.

[354] Case 161/84 *Pronuptia* [1986] ECR 353, [1986] 1 CMLR 414. See generally Venit, 'Pronuptia: ancillary restraints or unholy alliances' (1986) EL Rev 213.

[355] Case 258/78 *Nungesser v Commission* [1982] ECR 2015, [1983] 1 CMLR 278. See also Case 262/81 *Coditel v Ciné-Vog Films (No. 2)* [1982] ECR 3381, [1983] 1 CMLR 49: an exclusive licence to exhibit a cinema film did not in itself fall within Art 81(1) in the light of the particular characteristics of the cinema industry. On the application of Art 81(1) to various specific provisions in patent licences, see also Case 193/83 *Windsurfing v Commission* [1986] ECR 611, [1986] 3 CMLR 489, and the discussion at paras 9.086 *et seq*, below.

[356] *Nungesser*, above, paras 44–67. See also paras 9.079 *et seq*, below, for discussion of *Nungesser* in the context of intellectual property licensing.

[357] ibid, paras 55–56.

[358] *Nungesser* (n 355, above) para 61. cf Case 27/87 *Erauw-Jacquery v La Hesbignonne* [1988] ECR 1919, [1988] 4 CMLR 576, where the ECJ held that an export ban in a licence to propagate and sell certain varieties of seed protected by plant breeders' rights fell outside Art 81(1) because the licensor must be entitled to restrict propagation to selected licensees. However, a minimum sales price in the same licence did restrict competition since the existence of such a clause in a series of licences had the same effect as a horizontal price-fixing agreement.

- **Vendor non-compete covenant.** In *Remia*,[359] the Court of Justice held that a covenant of reasonable length included in the agreement for the sale of a business did not fall within Article 81(1) although the express object of a vendor/purchaser covenant is to prevent the vendor from competing with the undertakings which had been sold.
- **Agricultural cooperative rules**. In *Gøttrup-Klim*,[360] the Court of Justice considered the rules of a Danish agricultural purchasing cooperative (DLG) which prohibited members from participating in any other association that was in competition with DLG as regards the purchase of fertilisers or plant protection products. The Court found that dual membership would jeopardise both the proper functioning of the cooperative and its contractual power in relation to producers. Prohibition of dual membership did not, therefore, necessarily constitute a restriction of competition within the meaning of Article 81(1) and may even have had beneficial effects on competition provided that they were limited to what was necessary to ensure that the cooperative functioned properly and maintains its contractual power in relation to producers.[361]

'Rule of reason' in Community law?   The approach taken in the cases men- **2.091** tioned in the previous paragraph have some similarity with the 'rule of reason' applied under US antitrust law[362] to the prohibition in section 1 of the Sherman Act. The 'rule of reason' in that context distinguishes between certain kinds of agreement which are illegal *per se* (for example price-fixing) and other restrictive agreements which are illegal only if they are shown to be in 'unreasonable restraint of trade'.[363] Deciding whether an agreement is an unreasonable restraint of trade will often involve balancing the 'pro-competitive' and 'anti-competitive' effects of the agreement. Whether such a 'rule' exists as a matter of Community law has

---

359 Case 42/84 *Remia v Commission* [1985] ECR 2545, [1987] 1 CMLR 1.

360 Case C-250/92 *Gøttrup-Klim v Dansk Landbrugs Grovvareselskab AmbA* [1994] ECR I-5641, [1996] 4 CMLR 191. See also Case C-399/93 *Oude Luttikhuis v Coberco* [1995] ECR I-4515, [1996] 5 CMLR 178.

361 *Gøttrup-Klim*, above, paras 31–35.

362 The 'rule of reason' has been described as 'a shorthand and somewhat dangerous phrase for the various techniques adopted over the years by the courts of the United States to mitigate the absolute prohibition of "every contract, combination (. . .) or conspiracy in restrict of trade" to be found in section 1 of the Sherman Act 1890, which has no provision for exemption equivalent to Article 81(3)': see judgment of the UK Competition Appeal Tribunal in *Institute of Independent Insurance Brokers v Director General of Fair Trading* [2001] CAT 4, [2001] CompAR 62, paras 174 *et seq.*

363 For enunciation of the rationale and basis of the *per se* rule in US antitust, see the majority and dissenting judgments in the US Supreme Court in *Leegin Creative Products Inc v PSKS Inc*, judgment of 28 June 2007. See also Hovenkamp, *Federal Antitust Policy: The Law of Competition and Its Practice* (3rd edn, 2005), para 255-259.

been much debated.[364] In *Métropole Télévision (M6)*[365] the Court of First Instance said that the Community Courts had been 'at pains to indicate that the existence of a rule of reason in Community competition law is doubtful' and took the view that Article 81(3) 'would lose much of its effectiveness' if an examination of the pro- and anti-competitive aspects of a restriction fell to be weighed under Article 81(1). Advocate General Léger in his Opinion in the *Wouters* case sought to reconcile such a rule with the existence of Article 81(3) by limiting 'rule of reason' considerations 'to a purely competitive balance-sheet of the effects of the agreement'.[366] According to that analysis, it is only those aspects of agreement which promote competition which can be weighed against the restrictive effect of an agreement under Article 81(1); wider public interest issues such as were raised in that case to support the professional rule prohibiting multi-disciplinary partnerships only fell to be considered under Article 81(3). But this approach was not adopted by the Court of Justice.

2.092 **Wouters and Meca-Medina.**   Delineation of the scope of analysis embraced by Article 81(1) has become less clear in the light of the landmark judgments of the Court of Justice in these two cases. In *Wouters*,[367] a preliminary ruling decided in 2002, the Court found that the professional rule of the Dutch Bar which imposed an absolute prohibition on lawyers entering into partnership with accountants, appreciably restricted competition. But contrary to the approach of the Advocate General, the Court continued:

> 'However, not every agreement between undertakings or every decision of an association of undertakings which restricts the freedom of action of the parties or of one of them necessarily falls within the prohibition laid down in Article [81(1)] of the Treaty. For the purposes of application of that provision to a particular case, account must first of all be taken of the overall context in which the decision of the association of undertakings was taken or produces its effects. More particularly, account must be

---

364 See Case T-148/89 *Tréfilunion v Commission* [1995] ECR II-1063, para 109; Case C-235/92P *Montecatini v Commission* [1999] ECR I-4539, [2001] 4 CMLR 691, para 133: both judgments stated that if a 'rule of reason' does apply under Art 81(1), it would not apply where the restriction of competition was 'clear cut'. The English authorities have been more willing to apply the concept: *Society of Lloyd's v Clementson* [1996] CLC 1590, [1996] ECC 193 (QBD), holding that the rule of reason applied to the Central Fund arrangements of Lloyd's (citing the 4th edition of this work); *Racecourse Association v Office of Fair Trading* [2005] CAT 29, [2006] CompAR 99 (Competition Appeal Tribunal).

365 Case T-112/99 *Métropole Télévision (M6) v Commission* [2001] ECR II-2459, [2001] 5 CMLR 1236, paras 72–74; see also Case T-65/98 *Van den Bergh Foods Ltd v Commission* (n 328, above) para 106 ('the existence of such a rule in Community competition law is not accepted'). In *Racecourse Association*, above, the CAT noted that this approach could not 'obviously be reconciled' with the approach in *Gøttrup-Klim* and *Wouters* and concluded that the application of Art 81(1) 'is a rather more flexible exercise than the CFI was perhaps willing to appreciate'.

366 *Wouters* (n 367, below) Opinion para 104.

367 Case C-309/99 *Wouters* [2002] ECR I-1577, [2002] 4 CMLR 913, [2002] All ER (EC) 193.

taken of its objectives, . . . It has then to be considered whether the consequential effects restrictive of competition are inherent in the pursuit of those objectives.'[368]

The Court proceeded to hold that the rule had the objectives of ensuring the necessary independence and guarantee of professional secrecy in the interest of consumers of legal services. The restriction could reasonably be considered necessary in order to ensure the proper practice of the legal profession in the Netherlands and the Dutch Bar 'was entitled to consider' that the objectives pursued by the rule could not be achieved by less restrictive means.[369] *Wouters* was followed and applied in 2006 in *Meca-Medina*,[370] where the Court of Justice held that the general objective of the anti-doping rules adopted by the International Olympic Committee was to safeguard equal chances for athletes, athletes' health, the integrity and objectivity of competitive sport and ethical values in sport. Since it was not shown that the substantive content of the rule in question was disproportionate (as regards the level of prohibited substance) the rule did not infringe Article 81(1) because the penalties were necessary to ensure enforcement. These judgments go beyond the earlier case law in accepting necessary and proportionate restraints which are ancillary to an objective which is not related to a pro-competitive purpose, or indeed a specifically commercial purpose at all.[371]

Article 81(1) and Article 81(3) relationship illustrated.   The subtlety of the **2.093** relationship between Article 81(1) and Article 81(3) is illustrated by the different approaches of the Commission and the Court of First Instance in *O₂ (Germany)*.[372] That case concerned an agreement for infrastructure sharing and roaming arrangements between T-Mobile, the incumbent German mobile operator, and O₂,

---

[368] ibid, para 97. The only authority cited for this approach was a decision in the field of free movement (Case C-3/95 *Reisebüro Broede v Sandker* [1996] ECR I-6511, [1997] 1 CMLR 224) and the Court may have been drawing on the concept of 'mandatory requirements' that were established by the case law as an exception from the free movement rules: see para 1.033, above.

[369] ibid, para 108. The articulation of an apparently subjective test is surprising. It seems preferable that the test of proportionality should be applied objectively, as the ECJ did in *Meca-Medina* (below).

[370] Case C-519/04P *Meca-Medina and Majcen v Commission* [2006] ECR I-6991, [2006] 5 CMLR 1023, [2006] All ER (EC) 1057.

[371] In *Wouters* (n 367, above) AG Léger regarded it as clear that the rule of the Dutch Bar prohibiting multi-disciplinary partnerships infringed Art 81(1). See, eg Case T-144/99 *Institute of Professional Representatives v Commission* [2001] ECR II-1087, [2001] 5 CMLR 77: CFI upheld the Commission's decision that a professional rule banning comparative advertising contravened Art 81(1) but could be granted exemption under Art 81(3); Case 243/83 *Binon* [1985] ECR 2015, [1985] 3 CMLR 800: argument that rpm for newspapers was necessary to maintain wide selection of newspapers and periodicals in the public interest held to be relevant only to the application of Art 81(3), not to Art 81(1). But cf Case 90/76 *Van Ameyde v UCI* [1977] ECR 1091, [1977] 2 CMLR 478: certain exclusive rights under the green card insurance system not contrary to Art 81(1) provided third party intermediaries not unreasonably excluded, since otherwise the national legislation controlling insurance would be undermined.

[372] Case T-328/03 *O2 (Germany) v Commission* [2006] ECR II-1231, [2006] 5 CMLR 258.

a potential market entrant. The Commission accepted that this was not an agreement which had an anti-competitive object. Its analysis of the effect of the agreement assumed that, in the absence of the agreement to share T-Mobile's facilities, O_2 would enter the market by rolling out its own rival network. The Commission found, looking at the matter in general, that roaming agreements between rival providers restrict competition because the roaming operator does not roll out its own network and is therefore dependent on the network quality and transmission rates of the host operator. Having found that the agreement therefore fell within Article 81(1), the Commission granted an individual exemption under Article 81(3) finding that the agreement enabled O_2 to enter the market more rapidly than it could have done in the absence of the agreement. The Court of First Instance annulled the decision on the grounds that the Commission had failed to carry out an adequate degree of market analysis. The Commission should have considered whether this particular roaming agreement, not roaming agreements in general, restricted competition by appraising realistically how likely it was that O_2 would be able to enter the market in the absence of the agreement. Carrying out this assessment in the context of Article 81(1) did not amount to applying a rule of reason but was simply an application of the *Société Technique Minière* principles.

(c) The present law

2.094 **In general.** In the light of the foregoing judgments and the many other decisions of the two Community Courts and the Commission, this sub-section attempts to explain the present law on whether an agreement has as its 'object or effect the prevention, restriction or distortion of competition'. The words 'prevention, restriction or distortion' are used collectively as a comprehensive description of the 'anti-competitive' nature of the agreement or concerted practice in question. The expression is to be read with the general objective of the Community set out in Article 3(1)(g) of the Treaty: 'the institution of a system ensuring that competition in the common market is not distorted'. The competition referred to here is taken to mean effective competition, that is to say, the degree of competition necessary to ensure the attainment of the objectives of the Treaty.[373] The intensity of competition may vary to an extent dictated by the nature of the product concerned and the structure of the relevant market. The analysis of the agreement is essential not just for determining whether an agreement falls within Article 81(1) but also for determining the gravity of the infringement for the purpose of assessing the fine to be imposed.[374] Much of

---

[373] Case T-168/01 *GlaxoSmithKline Services v Commission* [2006] ECR II-2969, [2006] 5 CMLR 1589, para 109 (on appeal, Cases C-501/06P, etc, *GlaxoSmithKline Services v Commission*, not yet decided).

[374] See, eg Case T-224/00 *Archer Daniels Midland v Commission* [2003] ECR II-2597, [2003] 5 CMLR 583, where the Commission and the CFI examined whether the cartel had actually raised

the discussion by the Community Courts of anti-competitive effect now takes place in the context of considering the amount of the penalty to be imposed for the infringement.

The main considerations.   In practice, in determining whether competition[375]   **2.095** is 'distorted' three main considerations are important. First, it is necessary to consider the competition that would occur in the absence of the agreement in dispute.[376] If the agreement contributes to an appreciable divergence from 'normal' conditions of competition there is a 'distortion' within the meaning of Article 81(1). Secondly, it is inherent in the concept of undistorted competition that 'each economic operator must determine independently the policy which he intends to adopt on the common market'.[377] Article 81(1) thus requires that every undertaking must act independently, taking its own decisions without cooperation with its competitors. An agreement whereby competitors exchange confidential and commercially sensitive information,[378] or jointly subsidise selling

---

prices not in order to establish the infringement but in order to determine whether the infringement was properly characterised as 'very serious' (further appeal dismissed, Case C-397/03P [2006] ECR I-4429, [2006] 5 CMLR 230).

[375] There is no definition of 'competition' in Community law but it may be broadly described as the process by which commercial operators strive for the patronage of customers; see, eg Scherer and Ross, *Industrial Market Structure and Economic Performance* (3rd edn, 1990). Competition law is essentially concerned with 'effective competition', the expression used in the Merger Regulation, Reg 139/2004, Art 2: Vol II, App D.1. That concept is well-recognised in economic writing and is usually defined as the absence of market power, ie the ability of an enterprise to raise prices above the competitive level. However, developing that definition further raises a host of economic issues, some of which are the subject of lively debate. See also Bishop and Walker, *The Economics of Competition Law* (2nd edn, 2002); Faull and Nikpay, *The EC Law of Competition* (2nd edn, 2007), Chap 1. The meaning of 'workable competition', the expression found in some of the earlier decisions, is in practice the same as 'effective competition'.

[376] See para 2.099, below. This position which would have pertained in the absence of the agreement is often referred to as the 'counterfactual'.

[377] Cases 40/73, etc, *Suiker Unie v Commission* [1975] ECR 1663, [1976] 1 CMLR 295, paras 173–174; Case 172/80 *Züchner v Bayerische Vereinsbank* [1981] ECR 2021, [1982] 1 CMLR 313, paras 13 *et seq;* Cases C-89/85 *Ahlström Osakeyhtiö v Commission ('Wood Pulp II')* [1993] ECR I-1037, [1995] 4 CMLR 407, paras 63–65. See also, eg *French inland waterway charter traffic: EATE levy*, OJ 1985 L219/35, 42, [1988] 4 CMLR 698: '[T]he commercial independence and freedom of choice of economic agents are an essential condition for the existence of effective and adequate competition on the market.'

[378] eg Case T-34/92 *Fiatagri and Ford New Holland v Commission* [1994] ECR II-905; and Case T-35/92 *John Deere v Commission* [1994] ECR II-957, upholding *UK Agricultural Tractor Registration Exchange*, OJ 1992 L68/19, [1993] 4 CMLR 358: system of regular exchange of precise information on recent sales reduced uncertainty and therefore reduced further the already weak competition in a concentrated market; further appeals dismissed, Case C-7/97P [1998] ECR I-3111, [1998] 5 CMLR 311, and Case C-8/95P [1998] ECR I-3111, [1998] 5 CMLR 362. cf Case T-16/98 *Wirtschaftsvereinigung Stahl v Commission* [2001] ECR-II 1217, [2001] 5 CMLR 310 (Commission decision annulled because of factual error about the nature of the information exchanged), see esp para 44. See further paras 5.084 *et seq*, below.

activities,[379] or confer on themselves a competitive advantage denied to others,[380] may therefore 'distort' competition although such an agreement does not involve any restriction. Thirdly, the competition which Article 81(1) seeks to protect is that which would occur in a true common market in which goods and services flow freely throughout the Community.[381] Thus an agreement which hinders the integration of the single market is a particularly important example of a 'distortion' of competition within the meaning of Article 81(1).[382]

2.096 **The object.** In many cases, no clear distinction is made between 'object' and 'effect'. However, unlike the terms 'prevention, restriction or distortion' discussed above, the terms 'object' and 'effect' used in Article 81(1) express true alternatives and require separate consideration.[383] It is therefore appropriate to consider first 'the object' of the agreement before considering its 'effects'.[384] This has been referred to as the 'two-stage examination' required by Article 81(1).[385] The 'object' of the agreement is to be found by an objective assessment of the aims of the agreement in question,[386] and it is unnecessary to investigate the parties' subjective intentions.[387] Generally, if the obvious consequence of the agreement is to

---

[379] eg *Milchsförderungsfonds*, OJ 1985 L35/35, [1985] 3 CMLR 101 (collective agreement by German dairy industry to subsidise branded exports 'distorted' competition; if the advertising had been generic, competition would not have been distorted because all undertakings would have benefited equally). See paras 5.146 *et seq*, below.

[380] eg *French inland waterway charter traffic: EATE levy* (n 377, above) (levy on export traffic distorted competition by giving unfair advantage to certain carriers); *X/Open Group*, OJ 1987 L35/36, [1988] 4 CMLR 542 (undertakings belonging to the X/Open Group creating an open industry standard for computer software had an important competitive advantage in lead time over non-members, as well as the possibility of excluding non-members from membership of the Group). See also para 2.103, below.

[381] Also throughout the European Economic Area, pursuant to the EEA Agreement, paras 1.088 *et seq*, above.

[382] eg Cases 56 & 58/64 *Consten and Grundig v Commission* [1966] ECR 299, [1966] CMLR, esp at 343 (ECR), 474 (CMLR): 'Since the agreement thus aims at isolating the French market for Grundig products and maintaining artificially, for products of a very well known brand, separate national markets within the Community, it is therefore such as to distort competition within the Common Market'.

[383] Although in the Italian text of the Treaty they are expressed as cumulative ('*per oggetto e per effetto*'), that version must yield to all the other language versions in which they are stated as alternatives: Case C-219/95P *Ferrière Nord v Commission* [1997] ECR I-4411, [1997] 5 CMLR 562, paras 14–15. See also *per* Lord Bingham MR in *The Society of Lloyd's v Clementson* [1995] CLC 117, 126 (English Court of Appeal).

[384] Case 56/65 *Société Technique Minière v Maschinenbau Ulm* [1966] ECR 235, 249, [1966] CMLR 357, 375; Case C-234/89 *Delimitis* [1991] ECR I-935, [1992] 5 CMLR 210, both discussed earlier in this Chapter; *GlaxoSmithKline Services* (n 373, above) where the CFI disagreed with the Commission's analysis of the object of the agreement but upheld the decision on the basis of its effects.

[385] *Gøttrup-Klim* (n 360, above) per AG Tesauro at para 16.

[386] Cases 29 & 30/83 *CRAM & Rheinzink v Commission* [1984] ECR 1679, [1985] 1 CMLR 688, paras 24–31.

[387] *Société Technique Minière* (n 384, above); Case 19/77 *Miller v Commission* [1978] ECR 131, [1978] 2 CMLR 334, para 7; Case 123/83 *BNIC v Clair* [1985] ECR 391, 399, [1985] 2 CMLR 430, 445 (AG Slynn).

restrict or distort competition, as a matter of law that is its 'object' for the purposes of Article 81(1), even if the parties claim that such was not their intention, or if the agreement has other objects.[388]

'Hard-core' restrictions: objects restrictive *per se*.   In *Consten and Grundig*,   **2.097** the Court of Justice said:

> '. . . there is no need to take account of the concrete effects of an agreement once it appears that it has as its object the prevention, restriction or distortion of competition.'[389]

In the context of horizontal agreements, the Community Courts have confirmed that agreements which, in themselves, pursue the object of restricting competition and fall within a category of agreements expressly prohibited by Article 81(1) cannot be justified by an analysis of the economic context of the anti-competitive conduct concerned.[390] Thus, if an agreement is indisputably intended to restrict competition, for example by price-fixing or by limiting output or allocating customers, it is unnecessary to show that price competition has in fact been affected, or that exports have in fact been restricted, in order to establish the infringement.[391] It is therefore unnecessary for the Commission to carry out a detailed market analysis or to come to a precise conclusion on the proper definition of the relevant market in such cases.[392] Agreements that have been held by the Court of Justice and

---

[388] eg Cases 96/82, etc, *IAZ v Commission* [1983] ECR 3369, [1984] 3 CMLR 276, paras 22–25; *CRAM & Rheinzink v Commission* (n 386, above); *AROW/BNIC*, OJ 1982 L379/1, [1983] 2 CMLR 240 (object allegedly to guarantee the quality of cognac but also in fact intended to restrict price competition).

[389] *Consten and Grundig* (n 382, above) at 342 (ECR), 473 (CMLR). This statement has been repeated many times, eg recently Case T-395/94 *Atlantic Container Line AB v Commission* [2002] ECR II-875, [2002] 4 CMLR 1008, [2002] All ER (EC) 684, para 76.

[390] Cases T-67/00, etc, *JFE Engineering v Commission* [2004] ECR II-2501, [2005] 4 CMLR 27, paras 181–184; upheld on appeal, Cases C-403 & 405/04P *Sumitomo v Commission* [2007] 4 CMLR 650, para 42.

[391] See, eg *Miller v Commission* (n 387, above); Cases 32/78, etc, *BMW v Commission* [1979] ECR 2435, [1980] 1 CMLR 370; Case 86/82 *Hasselblad v Commission* [1984] ECR 883, [1984] 1 CMLR 559, para 46; Cases T-305/94, etc, *Limburgse Vinyl Maatschappij v Commission* ('*PVC No. 2*') [1999] ECR II-931, [1999] 5 CMLR 303, para 741 (on further appeal, Cases C-238/99P, etc, appeals on procedural grounds only largely dismissed, [2002] ECR I-8375, [2003] 4 CMLR 397); Cases T-25/95, etc, *Cimenteries CBR v Commission* [2000] ECR II-491, [2000] 5 CMLR 204, para 1531; Case T-213/00 *CMA CGM v Commission* [2003] ECR II-913, [2003] 5 CMLR 268 (appeal on other grounds dismissed, Case C-236/03P *Commission v CMA CGM*, order of 28 October 2004); Case T-61/99 *Adriatica di Navigazione v Commission* [2003] ECR II-5349, [2005] 5 CMLR 1843, paras 26 *et seq* (appeal dismissed: Case C-111/04P [2006] ECR I-22); Cases T-202/98, etc, *Tate & Lyle v Commission* [2001] ECR II-2035, [2001] 5 CMLR 859, [2001] All ER (EC) 839, para 72 (appeal dismissed Case C-359/01P *British Sugar v Commission* [2004] ECR I-4933, [2004] 5 CMLR 329).

[392] Case T-213/00 *CMA CGM v Commission* [2003] ECR II-913, [2003] 5 CMLR 268, paras 201–235 (appeal dismissed, Case C-236/03P, [2005] 4 CMLR 557, order of 28 October 2004) discussed at paras 4.005 *et seq*, below. However, the combined market share of the undertakings attending a meeting is relevant to whether they were likely to have concluded a price-fixing

the Court of First Instance to have, by their very nature, the object of restricting competition include 'horizontal' agreements to fix prices,[393] partition markets,[394] or deal exclusively through agreed channels,[395] and 'vertical' agreements imposing export bans,[396] or otherwise restricting the buyer's freedom to deal with the goods.[397] The Commission has followed the same approach.[398] Agreements of this kind are often referred to as *per se* infringements of Article 81(1), subject to the *de minimis* rule and provided that the agreement has the potential to affect inter-State trade.[399] However, in the light of the Court of First Instance's judgment in *GlaxoSmithKline Services*, it may be more appropriate, at least as regards export bans, to refer to a strong presumption that such agreements violate

---

agreement at that meeting since this is less likely if the participants do not control a substantial proportion of the business: Cases T-44/02, etc, *Dresdner Bank v Commission* [2006] ECR II-3567, [2007] 4 CMLR 467, para 85.

[393] Art 81(1)(a). See, eg Case 41/69 *ACF Chemiefarma v Commission* [1970] ECR 661, 696 (manufacturers' price cartel); Cases 43 & 63/82 *VBVB and VBBB v Commission* [1984] ECR 19, [1985] 1 CMLR 27, paras 32–49 (collective resale price maintenance for books); Case 123/83 *BNIC v Clair* (n 387, above) para 22 (minimum price for cognac); and more recently Case T-224/00 *Archer Daniels Midland* (n 374, above) para 120; Case T-213/00 *CMA CGM* (n 391, above) para 175 (agreement prohibited grant of discounts from published prices). See generally paras 5.015 *et seq*, below.

[394] Art 81(1)(b) and (c). See, eg COMP/37.750 *French Beer (Brasseries Kronenbourg, Brasseries Heineken)*, 29 September 2004, [2006] 4 CMLR 577, para 53. See generally paras 5.048, 5.059 *et seq*, below.

[395] eg Case 61/80 *Coöperatieve Stremsel-en Kleurselfabriek v Commission* [1981] ECR 851, [1982] 1 CMLR 240, paras 12–13. See generally paras 5.098 *et seq*, below.

[396] eg *Consten and Grundig v Commission* (n 382, above); *Miller v Commission* (n 387, above) para 7; Cases 32/78, etc, *BMW v Commission* [1979] ECR 2435, [1980] 1 CMLR 370, para 31; Case T-66/92 *Herlitz v Commission* [1994] ECR II-531, [1995] 5 CMLR 458, para 29; and Case T-77/92 *Parker Pen v Commission* [1994] ECR II-549, [1995] 5 CMLR 435, para 37. See generally paras 6.053 *et seq*, below.

[397] eg Case 319/82 *Soc de Vente de Ciments et Bétons v Kerpen & Kerpen* [1983] ECR 4173, [1985] 1 CMLR 511, para 9 (obligations to use goods for own needs, not to resell in specified area, and to consult seller before soliciting business); *Hasselblad v Commission* (n 391, above) para 46 (prohibition on sales between authorised dealers).

[398] In addition to numerous decisions, note the 'prohibited restrictions' under the block exemption for vertical agreements, Reg 2790/1999, OJ 1999 L336/21, Vol II, App C.3; the Commission's Guidelines on Vertical Restraints, OJ 2000 C291/1: Vol II, App C.11 paras 46–56; and the Horizontal Cooperation Guidelines, OJ 2001 C3/2, paras 24–25. See further for horizontal agreements, Chap 5, below; for vertical agreements, Chap 6, below.

[399] See further paras 2.121 *et seq*, below (*de minimis*) and paras 1.115 *et seq*, above (effect on trade). The expression '*per se* infringement' comes from US antitrust law: n 291, above. See also the interesting discussion in the CAT's judgment in *Cityhook Ltd v Office of Fair Trading* [2007] CAT 18, paras 249 considering what is meant by the term 'hard-core' restriction and whether it is synonymous with infringements which have as their 'object' the restriction of competition or is simply a short hand term to refer to really serious infringements. The CAT noted that the term does not appear in the case law of the Community Courts though it is used frequently by the Commission and concluded (para 262) that 'there does not appear to be a universally accepted use of the term "hard-core".... If the relevant competition authority decides that an agreement does not constitute a "hard-core" infringement under the [Competition Act 1998], that agreement may nonetheless have as its object the restriction of competition; such a restriction by object, however, does not fall into the class which is so serious as to be categorised as a "hard-core" infringement.'

Article 81(1), that may be rebutted in exceptional circumstances.[400] For a concerted practice, the position is theoretically more complicated since it is necessary to show that the cooperation between the participants had some actual effect on their conduct. But if the object of the cooperation was a hard-core restriction of this kind, Article 81(1) will apply without it being necessary to establish that the conduct has appreciably effected competition.[401] Even where the agreement obviously restricts competition, some analysis of its actual or potential effects will be necessary to determine (i) whether the agreement satisfies the requirement of appreciable effect; (ii) whether the agreement affects trade between Member States; (iii) in the case of an infringement, the level of fine; and (iv) whether the conditions for the application of Article 81(3) apply. In practice, therefore, considerable analysis of the effects of the agreement is to be found in almost all the decisions of the Commission and the Community Courts, even where reliance is placed primarily on the 'object' of the agreement.[402]

Where objects ambivalent. In cases where it is not plain and obvious that the object of the agreement is to restrict competition, it will be necessary to consider the effects of the agreement in considerable detail.[403] In many cases the agreement, while in one sense restrictive, will also, or even primarily, be intended to achieve some pro-competitive purpose, such as new market entry or the development of a new product,[404] or some other improvement of competition.[405] In such cases, it seems difficult to regard the agreement as having 'the object' of restricting competition. Probably the correct analysis is that an agreement is not to be regarded as having 'the object' of restricting competition within the meaning of Article 81(1) **2.098**

---

[400] *GlaxoSmithKline Services* (n 373, above): see paras 2.077, above and 2.110, below.

[401] Case C-49/92P *Commission v Anic Partecipazioni* [1999] ECR I-4125, [2001] 4 CMLR 602, para 121; Case C-199/92P *Hüls v Commission* [1999] I-4287, [1999] 5 CMLR 1016, paras 163–166. In practice, the threshold of an effect on conduct is readily established: para 2.050, above.

[402] The Commission relies on 'the object' mostly in cases involving price-fixing, market-sharing or exclusive dealing cartels (Chap 5, below) or export bans, (Chap 6, below). But the issue is one of fact and sometimes the Commission will find on specific facts that the agreement had 'the object' of restricting competition, eg *Video cassette recorders*, OJ 1978 L47/42, [1978] 2 CMLR 160 (uniform application of technical standards). Note that the question of 'the object' is of some importance if the agreement is never put into 'effect': para 2.106, below.

[403] See, eg Case C-238/05 *Asnef-Equifax v Ausbanc* [2006] ECR I-11125, [2007] 4 CMLR 224 (credit reference data base had both pro- and anti-competitive effects).

[404] eg *Société Technique Minière* (n 384, above) (exclusive distribution agreement to penetrate new market); *Nungesser* (n 355, above) (exclusive licence to promote dissemination of new technology); *O2 (Germany)* (discussed at para 2.093, above) and see also the agreements on R & D, specialisation and production joint ventures discussed in Chap 7, below.

[405] eg the better distribution of technically complex goods as in *Metro (No. 1)* [1977] ECR 1875, [1978] 2 CMLR 1 and *(No. 2)* [1986] ECR 3021, [1987] 1 CMLR 118, and many other cases discussed at para 2.089, above and paras 6.086 *et seq*, below; or the advantages to retail distribution which stem from franchise agreements of the kind considered in *Pronuptia* (n 354, above) and further discussed at paras 6.171 *et seq*, below; or the benefits of collective purchasing by small enterprises to achieve volume discounts, as in *Gøttrup-Klim* (n 360, above).

unless it is an agreement of a kind which restricts competition 'of its nature'.[406] In practice, the Commission often avoids this analytical problem by failing to distinguish between 'object' and 'effect'. In some cases, notably joint venture agreements, the Commission has relied entirely on the 'effects'.[407]

2.099 **The effects on competition: the whole economic context.** As appears from *Société Technique Minière*, reaffirmed many times since, the effect of the agreement is to be judged by reference to the competition which would occur in the absence of the agreement in question.[408] In determining this, regard must be had to the whole economic context in which competition would occur in the absence of the agreement in dispute. This hypothetical position which would pertain in the absence of the agreement is often referred to as the 'counterfactual' and the correct determination of what this position would be is critical to a proper assessment of the effect of the agreement. The relevant factors include, in particular:

> '. . . the nature and quantity, limited or otherwise, of the products covered by the agreement, the position and importance of the [parties] on the market for the products concerned, the isolated nature of the disputed agreement or, alternatively, its position in a series of agreements.'[409]

The examination of competition in the absence of an agreement is particularly necessary when the relevant market under consideration is undergoing liberalisation or is an emerging market where effective competition may be problematic owing, for example, to the presence of a dominant operator, the concentrated nature of the market structure or the existence of significant barriers to entry.[410] It is necessary to consider not only what the parties have expressly agreed to do, or have done, but also their implied obligations, and the way they are likely to behave, even if they have not agreed to act in any particular way.[411] The potential effects

---

[406] On the present case law, it appears that it is only in plain and obvious cases involving very clear restrictions of the kind discussed in para 2.097, above, that 'the object' as distinct from 'the effect' has been held to be determinative.

[407] See Chap 7, below.

[408] *Société Technique Minière* (n 384, above); Case 31/80 *L'Oréal v De Nieuwe AMCK* [1980] ECR 3775, [1981] 2 CMLR 235, para 19; *Remia v Commission* (n 359, above) para 18; Case 31/85 *ETA v DK Investment* [1985] ECR 3933, [1986] 2 CMLR 674, para 11. But arguments that the parties were only doing under the agreement what they would have done separately anyway were not accepted by the Commission, eg in *BPCL/ICI*, OJ 1984 L212/1, [1985] 2 CMLR 330. In *ENI/Montedison*, OJ 1987 L5/13, [1989] 4 CMLR 444, the Commission held that although some withdrawal from the market was inevitable, the pattern would have been different but for the agreement.

[409] *Société Technique Minière* (n 384, above) at 250 (ECR), 375 (CMLR); *L'Oréal v De Nieuwe AMCK*, above, para 19.

[410] *O2 (Germany)* (n 372, above) para 72 (3G mobile communications market).

[411] eg *Bayer/Gist Brocades*, OJ 1976 L30/13, [1976] 1 CMLR D98 (parties to specialisation agreement likely to obtain all their requirements from each other although not contractually bound to do so); see also *Olivetti/Canon*, OJ 1988 L52/51, [1989] 4 CMLR 940; *Alcatel Espace/ANT*, OJ 1990 L32/19, [1991] 4 CMLR 208.

are relevant as well as the actual effects.[412] For example, the formation by competitors of a joint venture may, in itself, restrict or distort competition even if there are no express provisions to that effect;[413] but it should not do so if individually each lacked the technical or financial capacity to establish or implement the joint venture project.[414] It is also relevant to consider the effects of the agreement on other activities of the parties even if those activities fall outside the scope of the agreement.[415]

Material factors. In *Delimitis*,[416] the Court of Justice held that account must be **2.100** taken of the conditions under which competitive forces operate on the relevant market: it is necessary to know the number and the size of producers present on the market and customer fidelity to existing brands. Other material factors include[417] the existence or exercise of any intellectual property rights,[418] and the

---

[412] Among many examples, see cases concerned with the development of a new product, eg *Ford/Volkswagen*, OJ 1993 L20/14: para 7.108, below; *Konsortium ECR 900*, OJ 1990 L228/31, [1992] 4 CMLR 4; *Asahi/St Gobain*, OJ 1994 L354/87: para 7.075, below; and *X/Open Group* (n 380, above) (possibility of distortion may result 'from future decisions' of Group setting up industry software standard). See also para 2.102, below.

[413] *GEC/Weir*, OJ 1977 L327/26, [1978] 1 CMLR D42; *Ford/Volkswagen*, above (exemption conditional on information barriers being put in place to prevent JV influencing other activities). See generally paras 7.035 *et seq*, below.

[414] eg *Elopak/Metal Box-Odin*, OJ 1990 L209/15, [1991] 4 CMLR 832. See para 7.105, below.

[415] For examples of cases in which there was held to be a restrictive 'spill-over' effect into other areas of the parties' activities, see para 7.046, below.

[416] *Delimitis* (n 384, above) and para 2.080, above. See also Case T-7/93 *Langnese-Iglo v Commission* [1995] ECR II-1533, [1995] 5 CMLR 602, [1995] All ER (EC) 902, appeal and cross-appeal dismissed, Case C-279/95P, [1998] ECR I-5609, [1998] 5 CMLR 933; and Case T-9/93 *Schöller v Commission* [1995] ECR II-1611, [1995] 5 CMLR 659 (effect of the network of agreements with retailers of the two leading suppliers of ice cream on the German market); for further analysis see paras 6.147 *et seq*, below.

[417] On such an assessment that is sensitive to the actual conditions of competition in the market in question, there can be no exhaustive list of relevant considerations. Note the somewhat surprising ruling of the ECJ in Cases C-215 & 216/96 *Bagnasco* [1999] ECR I-135, [1999] 4 CMLR 624, [1999] All ER (EC) 678, that the standard current account conditions of the Italian banking association, that precluded member banks from charging fixed rates of interest on borrowing, did not have an appreciable effect on competition because 'any variation of the interest rate depends on objective factors, such as changes occurring in the money market' (para 35). In reaching this view, the ECJ declined to follow the strong Opinion of AG Ruiz-Jarabo Colomer. More understandably, the ECJ also held that Art 81(1) did not apply for lack of an appreciable effect on inter-State trade: see further para 1.130, above. cf the Commission's decision in *Nederlandse Vereniging van Banken (1991 CSA Agreement)*, OJ 1999 L271/28, [2000] 4 CMLR 137: multilateral fixing of interbank commission limited the freedom of banks to determine their own policy and so had an appreciable effect on competition (but, following *Bagnasco*, did not appreciably affect inter-State trade).

[418] For intellectual property rights generally, see Chap 9, below. In certain circumstances the exercise of intellectual property rights by the bringing of an action for infringement may be contrary to Art 81(1), eg where the object or effect is to obstruct parallel imports: see para 2.030, above and para 9.067, below. But it is only the improper exercise, and not the grant of the right itself, to which Art 81(1) applies: Case 8/74 *Procureur du Roi v Dassonville* [1974] ECR 837, [1979] 2 CMLR 436. See also Case 170/83 *Hydrotherm v Compact* [1984] ECR 2999, [1985] 3 CMLR 224.

effect of national laws or Community measures.[419] In general, however, it is the situation of the parties in the context of the relevant market, discussed in the following paragraph, that is the most important factor in assessing the effect of an agreement.

2.101 **The relevant market.** Save in obvious cases, such as international cartels,[420] the Commission's decisions normally define the relevant market and a decision may be annulled if the analysis is incorrect.[421] Reference should be made to the discussion of market definition in Chapter 4, below.[422] In summary, the relevant product market comprises all products (or services) considered by consumers to be interchangeable or substitutable, having regard to their characteristics, price and intended use.[423] The relevant geographic market is the area in which the parties to the agreement are involved in the supply of products (or services) in which 'the conditions of competition are sufficiently homogeneous and which can be distinguished from neighbouring areas because, in particular, conditions of competition are appreciably different in those areas'.[424] This may be the whole of the Community (or EEA) where the goods are regularly bought and sold in all

---

[419] eg where parallel imports may be obstructed by an agreement in conjunction with the French law of unfair competition: Cases 56 & 58/64 *Consten and Grundig v Commission* (n 382, above); Case 22/71 *Béguelin Import v CL Import Export* [1971] ECR 949, [1972] CMLR 81; or by an agreement in conjunction with national customs legislation (*Procureur du Roi v Dassonville* (n 418, above) paras 11–15). As to measures taken in conjunction with national authorities, or where it is alleged that national laws preclude competition between the parties, see paras 11.004 *et seq*, below; as to the compatibility of national laws themselves with Art 81(1) see paras 11.029 *et seq*, below.

[420] See n 390, above and para 4.006, below.

[421] eg Case 6/72 *Europemballage and Continental Can v Commission* [1973] ECR 215, [1973] CMLR 199; Cases 19 & 20/74 *Kali und Salz und Kali Chemie v Commission* [1975] ECR 499, [1975] 2 CMLR 154; and see the comments of the CFI in Cases T-68/89, etc, *Società Italiano Vetro SpA v Commission* [1992] ECR II-1403, [1992] 5 CMLR 302, para 159. In the German ice cream cases, *Langnese-Iglo v Commission* and *Schöller v Commission* (n 416, above) the CFI held that the relevant product market was broader than that determined by the Commission but did not annul the decision on that ground as the wider market definition did not substantially affect the analysis of the agreements at issue. But the Commission is not obliged to define the market if it is self-evident that the agreement has an appreciable effect on competition and on trade between Member States: Case T-62/98 *Volkswagen v Commission* [2000] ECR II-2707, [2000] 5 CMLR 853, paras 230–231 (appeal and cross appeal on other grounds dismissed, Case C-338/00P, [2003] ECR I-9189, [2004] 4 CMLR 351). Note that where the determination of the case will not be affected if a wider market definition is adopted, the Commission often leaves open the precise market definition.

[422] Market definition is also of central importance under the Merger Reg, although the focus of analysis in that context is slightly different: see paras 8.186 *et seq*, below. For the different role of market definition under Arts 81 and 82, see Case T-29/92 *SPO v Commission* [1995] ECR II-289, para 74 (appeal on other grounds dismissed, Case C-137/95P, [1996] ECR I-1611).

[423] Relevant Market Notice, OJ 1997 C372/5: Vol II, App C.10, para 7. See also the cases under Art 82 discussed at paras 10.015 *et seq*, below. For judgments on relevant market under Art 81(1) see, eg *Hasselblad v Commission* (n 391, above) paras 19–23; *Langnese-Iglo v Commission*, and *Schöller v Commission* (n 416, above).

[424] Case T-310/01 *Schneider Electric v Commission* [2002] ECR II-4071, [2003] 4 CMLR 768, para 153, following para 8 of the Relevant Market Notice. See also *Fiatagri and Ford New Holland v Commission* (n 378, above) para 56.

Member States, or a narrower market, such as a single Member State, or the whole world where competition takes place on a global basis.[425] The nature and characteristics of the goods or service, consumer preferences, high transport costs and other barriers restricting the free movement of the goods will all be relevant considerations. Each case has to be considered on its own facts.[426]

Effect on potential competition.   An important question is whether the   **2.102**
agreement is likely to affect potential competition which might otherwise take place and, in particular, whether the parties are at least potential competitors[427] even if they are not actually in competition at present. If it is established that the parties are not potential competitors then to that extent Article 81(1) is not infringed, although Article 81(1) may still apply for other reasons.[428] In the *European Night Services* judgment, the Court of First Instance emphasised that the assessment of potential competition must be made in an economically realistic fashion.[429]

Effect on third parties.   Article 81(1) may apply if third parties are adversely   **2.103**
affected, for example if the agreement prevents parallel imports by third parties,[430] or restricts third parties' access to supplies,[431] or to technology,[432] or reduces the number

---

[425] See, eg *Nederlandse Vereniging van Banken (1991 GSA Agreement)*, OJ 1999 L271/28, [2000] 4 CMLR 137 (Dutch market); *TPS*, OJ 1999 L90/6, [1999] 5 CMLR 168 (French market or French-speaking European market: upheld on appeal Case T-112/99 *Métropole Télévision(M6) v Commission* [2001] ECR II-2459, [2001] 5 CMLR 33, [2002] All ER (EC) 1); *CECED*, OJ 2000 L187/47, [2000] 5 CMLR 635 (the EEA); *GEAE/P&W*, OJ 2000 L58/16, [2000] 5 CMLR 49 (world market).

[426] eg in *European Night Services*, para 2.084, above, following its general practice in transport cases, the Commission defined two relevant service markets: transport for business passengers and for leisure passengers; and each distinct route was regarded as a separate geographic market. These definitions were not challenged before the CFI.

[427] As to when the parties are to be regarded as potential competitors, see, eg para 7.044, below. See also *Tariff structures in the combined transport of goods*, OJ 1993 L73/38 (agreed tariff structure affected potential competition which would arise following the liberalisation of the rail transport sector).

[428] eg where the parties are not potential competitors Art 81(1) may be infringed as a result of the effect on third parties (para 2.103, below) or for other reasons, eg the coordinative effect of a series of interlocking joint ventures: para 7.050, below.

[429] Cases T-374/94, etc, *ENS v Commission* [1998] ECR II-3141, [1998] 5 CMLR 718, para 137. The CFI quoted para 18 from the Commission's 1993 Joint Venture Notice to that effect, and proceeded to find on the facts that the Commission had failed to apply that approach: para 2.086, above; see further para 7.026, below.

[430] Cases 56 & 58/64 *Consten and Grundig v Commission* (n 382, above) and many other cases: see Chap 6, below.

[431] As, eg in exclusive dealing or market-sharing agreements or agreements under which supplies of goods or services are limited to, or obtainable from, particular persons only, whether in horizontal agreements between competitors or vertical agreements for distribution or supply.

[432] As, eg in certain exclusive licensing agreements, paras 9.075 *et seq*, below, or where the parties agree to licence technology only jointly: eg para 7.073, below.

of independent suppliers,[433] or discriminates against third parties,[434] or makes it more difficult for third parties to compete with the parties to the agreement[435] or deprives third parties of competitive opportunities.[436] But it may be that on the facts third parties are unaffected by the agreement in question.[437]

2.104 **Networks of agreements.** The existence of similar agreements is part of the economic and legal context in which the agreement is to be appraised,[438] but the existence of a network of similar agreements is only one of many factors to be taken into account.[439] In *Van den Bergh Foods*,[440] the Court of First Instance

---

[433] As, eg where the parties agree to sell only jointly, paras 5.106 *et seq*, below; or to enter into production specialisation agreements or production joint ventures, Chap 7, below.

[434] Either overtly, eg *French inland waterway charter traffic: EATE levy* (n 377, above) on appeal Case 272/85 *ANTIB v Commission* [1987] ECR 2201, [1988] 4 CMLR 677 (discriminatory levy on traffic destined for abroad); or by taking exclusionary measures, eg in agreements on technical standards (paras 5.139 *et seq*,below); collective agreements to deal through approved channels or 'members only' arrangements (paras 5.124 *et seq*,below); agreements on access to trade exhibitions (paras 5.152 *et seq*, below); or selective distribution systems limited to 'approved dealers only' (paras 6.086 *et seq*, below). Note also Art 81(1)(d).

[435] eg by acting collectively to the disadvantage of third parties by concerted predatory pricing, as in *Roofing Felt*, OJ 1986 L232/15, [1991] 4 CMLR 130, on appeal Case 246/86 *Belasco v Commission* [1989] ECR 2117, [1991] 4 CMLR 96; by concerted action to prevent imports, as in *MELDOC*, OJ 1986 L348/50, [1989] 4 CMLR 853; by jointly subsidising the promotion of their own branded products as in *Milchförderungsfonds* (n 379, above); or even by taking structural measures such as setting up a joint venture making market penetration by third parties more difficult, as in *Astra*, OJ 1993 L20/23, [1994] 5 CMLR 226.

[436] eg exclusive purchasing agreements foreclose the market to third parties, see paras 6.139 *et seq*, below; agreements restricting participation in trade exhibitions preclude opportunities for organisers, and intermediaries who would wish to attend, see paras 5.152 *et seq*, below; the formation of a joint venture may make the parties more reluctant to deal with outside suppliers, para 7.048, below; and the denial of membership of a distribution system or 'members only' group may be a significant competitive disadvantage: see n 434, above and, eg *X/Open Group* (n 380, above) (non-members unable to participate in setting industry standard at a disadvantage in lead time).

[437] eg *Optical Fibres*, OJ 1986 L236/30, where, after amendments to the agreements, it was held that third parties were not affected. But note the requirement for a careful market analysis: *ENS v Commission* (n 429, above) paras 2.084 *et seq*, above. See also *Mitchell Cotts/Sofiltra*, OJ 1987 L41/31, [1988] 4 CMLR 111 (on the facts, the formation of the JV did not foreclose opportunities to third parties).

[438] See also *Procureur du Roi v Dassonville* (n 418, above) para 13 (relevance of agreements between same producer and concessionaires in other Member States); Case 75/84 *Metro v Commission (No. 2)* [1986] ECR 3021, [1987] CMLR 118, para 40 (existence of selective distribution systems maintained by other suppliers relevant to the application of Art 81(1)); Case 27/87 *Erauw-Jacquery v La Hesbignonne* [1988] ECR 1919, [1988] 4 CMLR 576 (network of licences setting minimum price had same effect as horizontal price agreement). Consideration of the 'network effect' is of particular importance in the distribution sector: see generally Chap 6, below.

[439] *Delimitis* (n 384, above) para 14.

[440] Case T-65/98 *Van den Bergh Foods v Commission* [2003] ECR II-4653, [2004] 4 CMLR 14, [2005] All ER (EC) 418 (appeal dismissed Case C-552/03P *Unilever Bestfoods v Commission* [2006] ECR I-9091, [2006] 5 CMLR 1460) applying the two-fold test laid down in *Delimitis* discussed at para 2.080, above. The contracts were different from those in the earlier ice cream cases (Case T-7/93 *Langnese-Iglo v Commission* and Case T-9/93 *Schöller v Commission* (n 416, above)) because they did not prevent the retailer from selling competing ice cream from the outlet if stocked in his own or a competitor's freezer.

examined whether an agreement between an ice cream manufacturer and the network of retail outlets in Ireland, which prevented the retailer from stocking competing ice cream in the freezer cabinet supplied by the manufacturer, appreciably restricted competition. The Court stated that its task was:

> 'to consider whether all the similar agreements entered into in the relevant market and the other features of the economic and legal context of the agreements at issue, show that those agreements cumulatively have the effect of denying access to that market to new competitors. If, on examination, that is found not to be the case, the individual agreements making up the bundle of agreements cannot impair competition within the meaning of Article [81(1)] of the Treaty. If, on the other hand, such examination reveals that it is difficult to gain access to the market, it is then necessary to assess the extent to which the agreements at issue contribute to the cumulative effect produced, on the basis that only those agreements which make a significant contribution to any partitioning of the market are prohibited.'[441]

Markets where scope for competition is limited. Where there is limited scope **2.105** for competition in the relevant market, any additional restriction or distortion arising from the agreement will be regarded as having a significant impact. In *CMA CGM*,[442] the Court of First Instance considered a price-fixing agreement between the members of a liner conference and independent shipping lines operating the same route. Price competition between the members of the liner conference was already greatly reduced because the block exemption then in force allowed the members to apply common freight rates. The additional restriction on competition arising from the agreement in question was therefore all the more appreciable since it prevented the maintenance of effective competition in particular on the part of the non-conference shipping lines. The existence of such competition was one of the main justifications for the block exemption.

Agreements never put into effect. If an agreement clearly has the object of **2.106** restricting competition and potentially affects inter-State trade, arguments that it was never put into effect are generally irrelevant to the application of Article 81(1),[443] save in mitigation of any fine.[444]

---

[441] *Van den Bergh Foods*, above, para 83.

[442] Case T-213/00 *CMA CGM v Commission* [2003] ECR II-913, [2003] 5 CMLR 268, para 180 (appeal on other grounds dismissed, Case C-236/03P *Commission v CMA CGM*, order of 28 October 2004). See also *GlaxoSmithKline Services*, discussed at para 2.077, above: CFI held that the agreements had an anti-competitive effect so as to come within Art 81(1) since they restricted yet further the limited intra-brand competition in the pricing of pharmaceutical medicines (although Commission's finding of anti-competitive object was annulled).

[443] eg Case 19/77 *Miller v Commission* (n 387, above) paras 7–10, and other cases on export bans; paras 6.053 *et seq*, below. See also, eg COMP/37.750 *French Beer* [2006] 4 CMLR 577 (agreement not implemented but clearly had the object of restricting competition); Case C-277/87 *Sandoz v Commission* [1990] ECR I-45 (clause not enforced nonetheless had object of restricting competition); *WANO Schwarpulver*, OJ 1978 L232/26, [1979] 1 CMLR 403 (restrictive JV abandoned before implementation had object of restricting competition and would, if put into effect, have done so to an appreciable extent).

[444] See paras 13.66 *et seq*, below.

2.107 **Typical restrictions on competition.** Typical examples of 'horizontal' restrictions of competition are discussed in Chapter 5, below, and include agreements which directly or indirectly fix selling prices, or terms of trading, or involve the exchange of competitive information, or which limit production or investment, or technical standards, or whereby the parties agree to limit or control markets (for example, by market-sharing agreements), or agree to deal exclusively with each other, or only through agreed channels of distribution, or unreasonably exclude third parties from trading facilities, or engage in joint purchasing, joint selling, or joint advertising, or agree to restrict advertising, or to limit promotional activities such as trade exhibitions.

2.108 **Restrictions on research, development, etc.** Other horizontal agreements capable of giving rise to restrictions of competition are discussed in Chapter 7, below, and include agreements to cooperate in research and development, or to specialise in the manufacture of particular products, or to establish a joint venture for the production of certain products or the operation of a particular business.

2.109 **Vertical restrictions.** Article 81(1) may also be infringed by 'vertical' restrictions on competition which are discussed more fully in Chapter 6, below. The main kinds of agreement in which vertical restrictions may arise are exclusive supply agreements, distribution and selective distribution agreements, exclusive purchasing agreements, franchise agreements, tying arrangements and certain kinds of subcontracts.

2.110 **Vertical restrictions affecting exports or imports.** An export ban or other similar measure which directly or indirectly restricts exports or imports between Member States generally constitutes a serious contravention of Article 81(1), irrespective of its actual effect. However, in *GlaxoSmithKline Services* the Court of First Instance held that this was in effect a strong presumption, which in exceptional circumstances might be rebutted: hence where regulation controlled the final prices of pharmaceutical drugs and the market was shielded from the free play of supply and demand, parallel trade may not bring the benefits of price competition to final consumers. In such a case, provisions to restrict exports did not necessarily have restriction of competition as their 'object' so that it was necessary to consider whether they had an effect on competition.[445] The judgment is under appeal, and at the time of writing it is uncertain whether the Court of Justice will uphold this approach.[446] However, it is clear that in normal circumstances

---

[445] Case T-168/01 *GlaxoSmithKline Services v Commission* [2006] ECR II-2969, [2006] 5 CMLR 1589, paras 118 *et seq*; see para 2.077, above. The CFI proceeded to hold that there was an anti-competitive effect bringing the agreements within Art 81(1), but annulled the Commission's refusal to grant exemption under Art 81(3).

[446] On appeal, Cases C-513/06P, etc, *GlaxoSmithKline Services v Commission*, not yet decided.

measures restricting parallel imports will attract heavy fines.[447] Article 81(1) applies even if the ban extends only to 'active' as distinct from 'passive' sales.[448]

Restrictions in licences of intellectual property rights.   Complex issues arise   **2.111** as to the circumstances in which an exclusivity provision in a licence of intellectual property rights,[449] or other provisions commonly found in licensing agreements, infringe Article 81(1). The relevant considerations are discussed in Chapter 9, below.

Ancillary restrictions not within Article 81(1).   As seen earlier in this   **2.112** Section,[450] there are now a considerable number of 'restrictions' which have been held not to fall with Article 81(1). The Commission has used the term 'ancillary restrictions' to describe those restraints included in an agreement which is not in itself anti-competitive and that can be regarded as necessary for the agreement to be workable or achieve its purpose. The concept was considered by the Court of First Instance in *Métropole (M6)*.[451] The Court stressed that the requirement for objective necessity did not imply a need to weight the pro- and anti-competitive effects of the agreement:

'. . . examination of the objective necessity of a restriction in relation to the main operation cannot but be relatively abstract. It is not a question of analysing whether, in the light of the competition situation on the relevant market, the restriction is

---

[447] *Miller v Commission* (n 387, above) para 7, following the general principle established in *Consten and Grundig* (n 382, above). See, eg Case T-62/98 *Volkswagen v Commission* (n 421, above): fine of €90 million; *Video Games, Nintendo distribution*, OJ 2003 L255/33, [2004] CMLR 421: fine of €149 million (on appeal Cases T-18/03 *CD-Contact Data v Commission*; T-12/03 *Itochu Corporation v Commission*; T-13/03 *Nintendo Corp and Nintendo of Europe v Commission*, not yet decided).

[448] A 'passive' sale occurs where the supplier has simply responded to an unsolicited request from an individual customer but has not specifically targeted advertising at or established distribution arrangements in the territory: see Guidelines on Vertical Restraints, OJ 2000 C291/1, Vol II, App C.11, para 50. See also para 6.054, below, and, eg *Optical Fibres*, OJ 1986 L236/30; *Mitchell Cotts/Sofiltra* (n 437, above); *Bossies/Interpane*, OJ 1987 L50/30, [1988] 4 CMLR 124; *Novalliance/Systemform*, OJ 1997 L47/11, [1997] 4 CMLR 876, para 60. The distinction between active and passive sales is of considerable relevance to the application of the block exemption for vertical agreements, Reg 2790/1999: see para 6.023, below. A restriction on active sales will have a more appreciable effect if there is no intermediate trade: *Mitchell Cotts/Sofiltra*, above.

[449] *Nungesser v Commission* (n 355, above); Case 262/81 *Coditel v Ciné-Vog Films (No. 2)* [1982] ECR 3381, [1983] 1 CMLR 49; Case T-504/93 *Tiercé Ladbroke v Commission* [1997] ECR II-923, [1997] 5 CMLR 309. See generally paras 9.075 *et seq*, below, and Reg 772/2004, OJ 2004 L123/11, Vol II, App C.7.

[450] See paras 2.088–2.093, above.

[451] Case T-112/99 *Métropole Télévision (M6) v Commission* [2001] ECR II-2459, [2001] 5 CMLR 33, [2002] All ER (EC) 1, on appeal from *TPS*, OJ 1999 L90/6, [1999] 5 CMLR 168. The Commission held that a non-compete clause between the partners was 'logical' in view of the heavy investment needed for the project and hence was ancillary to the setting up of the joint company which was not, in itself, anti-competitive. But the obligations on the parties to channel their programming through the joint vehicle were not ancillary and were granted exemption under Art 81(3). The CFI upheld this analysis.

indispensable to the commercial success of the main operation but of determining whether, in the specific context of the main operation, the restriction is necessary to implement that operation. If, without the restriction, the main operation is difficult or even impossible to implement, the restriction may be regarded as objectively necessary for its implementation.'[452]

The Court gave as an example a non-compete clause in a transfer of undertakings; if the vendor remained free to win back his former customers immediately after the transfer and thereby drive the purchaser out of business, the transaction could not take place. Even if a restriction is objectively necessary to implement the main operation, one must still verify whether its duration and scope are limited to what is necessary. Where it is established that a restriction is ancillary then the compatibility of that restriction with Article 81(1) must be examined with that of the main operation.[453] If the main operation does not fall within the scope of the prohibition, the same holds for the ancillary restrictions. If, on the other hand, the main operation is a restriction within the meaning of Article 81(1) but fulfils the criteria in Article 81(3), the benefit of Article 81(3) also covers those ancillary restrictions.

2.113 **Ancillary restrictions in practice.** Although as a concept this is not always easy to apply,[454] it has been elucidated by a substantial body of decisions in the field of joint ventures[455] and concentrations.[456] As regards the latter specific guidance can be obtained from the Commission's Notice on this subject.[457] It is on the basis of such reasoning that a vendor/purchaser covenant, if reasonable in time and scope,[458] and various restrictions essential to the efficacy of a franchising agreement[459] have been held to fall outside Article 81(1). Similarly, where a supplier contracts out the manufacture of all or part of a product or the carrying out of certain work, and provides the sub-contractor with confidential information or the use of his intellectual property rights for that purpose, restrictions on the sub-contractor supplying the resulting product to third parties generally do not fall

---

[452] ibid, para 109.

[453] Similarly agreements which are 'indissolubly linked' to the purpose of a State aid must be evaluated under the State aid regime and not under Art 81(1): Cases T-197 & 198/97 *Weyl Beef Products v Commission* [2001] ECR II-303, [2001] 2 CMLR 459, para 83.

[454] See Faull & Nikpay, *The EC Law of Competition* (2nd edn, 2007), para 3.213: 'it is clear that the concept still raises more questions than it answers'.

[455] See *Elopak/Metal Box—Odin*, OJ 1990 L209/15, [1991] 4 CMLR 832 and paras 7.104 *et seq*, below. See also the Commission's old Notice on Cooperative Joint Ventures, OJ 1993 C43/2.

[456] See paras 8.263 *et seq*, below.

[457] Ancillary Restraints Notice, OJ 2005 C56/24, Vol II, App D.10. However, a restriction that is ancillary to a concentration may not be ancillary in a non-structural context and care must be taken in applying the reasoning in decisions under the Merger Reg to cases involving Art 81(1).

[458] Case 42/84 *Remia v Commission* [1985] ECR 2545, [1987] 1 CMLR 1. See generally para 8.266, below.

[459] Case 161/84 *Pronuptia* [1986] ECR 353, [1986] 1 CMLR 414. See generally paras 6.171 *et seq*, below.

within Article 81(1).[460] It has been doubted whether Article 81(1) applies to an exclusivity clause in an 'open'[461] distribution agreement if the restriction seems really necessary for the penetration of a new area by an undertaking.[462] An 'open' exclusive licence of intellectual property rights involving the dissemination of new technology has been held not to infringe Article 81(1),[463] as has an exclusive licence to exhibit a cinema film;[464] a restriction on the resale of technically complex goods based on objective qualitative criteria applied without discrimination falls outside Article 81(1),[465] as does a prohibition on a wholesaler supplying consumers,[466] or on a specialist distributor supplying retailers outside his specialised area.[467] Article 81(1) has been held not to apply to an obligation not to disclose secret know-how,[468] nor to a prohibition on export of seeds to Member States that do not grant legal protection to new plant varieties.[469]

Qualitative restrictions based on objective criteria. Technical restrictions **2.114** that are based on objective criteria and are applied in a non-discriminatory manner generally do not fall within Article 81(1). Therefore the Commission has decided that Article 81(1) does not apply to restrictions that are necessary to maintain quality control[470] or to avoid causing damage to the product,[471] or that are designed to safeguard the health of the consumer.[472]

---

[460] Subcontracting Notice, OJ 1979 C1/2: Vol II, App C.8. (The Notice continues to be effective: Horizontal Cooporation Guidelines, OJ 2001 C3/2: Vol II, App C.12, para 81, n 39). See paras 6.189 *et seq*, below.

[461] ie an agreement without absolute territorial protection: see para 2.068, above.

[462] *Société Technique Minière* (n 384, above). But for the general position as to exclusivity in distribution agreements, see paras 6.039 *et seq*, below.

[463] Case 258/78 *Nungesser v Commission* [1982] ECR 2015, [1983] 1 CMLR 278. But for exclusive licences of intellectual property rights see paras 9.095 *et seq*, below.

[464] Case 262/81 *Coditel v Ciné-Vog Films (No. 2)* [1982] ECR 3381, [1983] 1 CMLR 49.

[465] *Metro v Commission (No. 1)* [1977] ECR 1875, [1978] 2 CMLR 1 and *(No. 2)* [1986] ECR 3021, [1987] 1 CMLR 118, para 2.089, above, and many other cases discussed at paras 6.086 *et seq*, below.

[466] *Metro v Commission (No. 1)* above; para 6.101, below.

[467] See the Commission's decisions in *Distillers-Victuallers*, OJ 1980 L233/43, [1980] 3 CMLR 244; *Villeroy & Boch*, OJ 1985 L376/15, [1988] 4 CMLR 461, para 6.066, below.

[468] Among many examples see, eg *Campari*, OJ 1978 L70/69, [1978] 2 CMLR 397; *Boussois/Interpane*, OJ 1987 L50/30, [1988] 4 CMLR 124; *X/Open Group*, OJ 1987 L35/36, [1988] 4 CMLR 542.

[469] *Sicasov*, OJ 1999 L4/27, [1999] 4 CMLR 192.

[470] eg *Campari* (n 468, above) (licensor entitled to veto a change in the place of manufacture adversely affecting quality, and to require licensee to follow licensor's instructions on manufacture and quality control, and to obtain certain raw materials from licensor); *Carlsberg*, OJ 1984 L207/26, [1985] 1 CMLR 735 (licensor obliged by agreement to impose same technical standards on all licensees); *Pronuptia*, OJ 1987 L13/39, [1989] 4 CMLR 355 (provision to maintain quality of goods and reputation of franchisor fell outside Art 81(1), including requirement to obtain products from sources nominated by franchisor). See also Case 193/83 *Windsurfing v Commission* [1986] ECR 611, [1986] 3 CMLR 489, paras 43 *et seq* (licensor's quality control outside Art 81(1) only if relating to specific subject-matter of patent and based on objective criteria agreed in advance).

[471] *D'Ieteren Motor Oils*, OJ 1991 L20/42, [1992] 4 CMLR 399, para 11.

[472] *Kathon Biocide*, OJ 1984 C59/6, [1984] 1 CMLR 476. But the Commission will scrutinise such arguments with care, and they will not be accepted if a less restrictive alternative was

2.115 Positive obligations as restrictions.   The fact that a given clause imposes a positive obligation, as distinct from a restriction, does not necessarily preclude the
application of Article 81(1).[473] For example, a dealer's obligation to maintain
stocks and achieve a certain minimum turnover in the supplier's products may
give rise to a *de facto* 'tie' which, coupled with other restrictive aspects of the agreement, may make Article 81(1) applicable.[474] Altogether, the development of a
more economically-based approach to the assessment of Article 81(1) means that
regard should be had to the actual, commercial effect of a provision in an agreement, considered together with the other obligations and restrictions: hence a contract may fall within, or outside, Article 81(1) depending on its duration.[475] But a
normal commercial contract of sale will not, of itself, infringe Article 81(1).[476]

2.116 Restrictions necessary and proportionate to legitimate objective.   In its
landmark judgments in *Wouters* and *Meca-Medina*, discussed above,[477] the Court of
Justice has developed the concept that although a restriction may have the effect
of appreciably restricting competition, having regard to the overall context in
which the restriction is applied, it will not give rise to an infringement of
Article 81(1) provided that (i) its purpose is to achieve a legitimate objective;
(ii) such a restriction is inherent in the pursuit of that objective; and (iii) the
restriction goes no further than necessary, or in other words, is proportionate.
In *Meca-Medina*,[478] the Court overruled the reasoning of the Court of First
Instance,[479] which had held that purely 'sporting rules' are outside Article 81(1),

---

available: *Bayo-n-ox*, OJ 1990 L21/71, [1990] 4 CMLR 930 (circular prevented authorised as well
as unauthorised trade), appeal held inadmissible; Case T-12/90 *Bayer v Commission* [1991] ECR
II-219, [1993] 4 CMLR 30, further appeal dismissed, Case C-195/91P [1994] ECR I-5619, [1996]
4 CMLR 32; *Tetra Pak II*, OJ 1992 L72/1, [1992] 4 CMLR 551, para 119 (in the context of Art
82), on appeal Case T-83/91 *Tetra Pak International v Commission* [1994] ECR II-755, [1997] 4
CMLR 726, paras 138–139, further appeal dismissed Case C-333/94P, [1996] ECR II-5951. See
also *Distribution of package tours during 1990 World Cup*, OJ 1992 L326/31 (exclusive rights to
sell World Cup tickets not justified by need to keep spectators apart).

[473] For a striking example of a positive obligation constituting a restriction, see *Windsurfing
International v Commission* (n 470, above) where the licensees' obligation to affix the notice 'Licensed
by Windsurfing International' to the sailboards was held to fall under Art 81(1), because the sailboards were not covered by the patent and the licensor thus 'encouraged uncertainty as to whether
or not the board too was covered by the patent and thereby diminished the consumer's confidence
in the licensees so as to gain a competitive advantage for itself' (para 73).

[474] See *Metro (No. 1)* (n 465, above) and *(No. 2)* ibid; paras 6.096 and 6.157, below. cf the position in a franchise agreement, para 6.187, below.

[475] See generally the Guidelines on Vertical Restraints (n 448, above) and paras 6.140 and 6.150,
below.

[476] Note *BPCL/ICI*, OJ 1984 L212/1, [1985] 2 CMLR 330 (as to BPCL's obligation to purchase
ethylene from ICI).

[477] See para 2.092, above.

[478] Case C-519/04P *Meca-Medina and Majcen v Commission* [2006] ECR I-6991, [2006] 5
CMLR 1023, [2006] All ER (EC) 1057.

[479] Case T-313/02 *Meca-Medina and Majcen v Commission* [2004] ECR II-3291, [2004] 3
CMLR 60.

and on the contrary held that the anti-doping rules of the International Olympic Committee fell within the scope of the competition rules since they could lead to the exclusion of an athlete from sporting events. However, applying *Wouters*, the Court of Justice held that the particular rule at issue did not infringe Article 81(1). To combat doping in order that competitive sport could be conducted fairly was clearly a legitimate objective and it had not been shown that the substantive provisions of the rule (as regards the level at which doping was established or the penalties applied) went beyond what was necessary. It is as yet unclear by what criteria the condition of 'legitimate objective' will be determined in borderline cases but it seems unlikely that the concept will be extended to purely commercial considerations.

Restraint on 'competitiveness'.   At one time, the Commission was inclined to **2.117** hold that Article 81(1) could apply to an agreement on the basis that it had the effect of making one of the parties 'less competitive', for example where a licensee was subject to an onerous obligation to pay royalties after the expiry of a patent.[480] But the current approach pays greater respect to a freely negotiated commercial agreement, unless it has an appreciable foreclosure effect on third party suppliers or customers.[481] The purpose of Article 81(1) is not to provide a general escape route for those wishing to avoid complying with contractual obligations which turn out to be more onerous than expected.[482]

Restrictions on remedies.   Article 81(1) extends to restrictions on the exercise **2.118** of legal remedies, for example an agreement not to challenge a patent.[483] Similarly an agreement which purports to oust the jurisdiction of the national courts to apply Article 81(1) may itself infringe Article 81(1).[484] However, a trade mark delimitation agreement which is genuinely intended to define legal rights and to avoid confusion in the least restrictive manner does not fall under Article 81(1).[485] But in principle, the fact that an agreement is made in settlement of litigation does not provide any shield from Article 81(1). For example, cross-licensing arrangements in settlement of a patent dispute may appreciably restrict competition in the same way as if the agreement was entered into without litigation.[486]

---

[480] *AOIP/Beyrard*, OJ 1976 L6/8, [1976] 1 CMLR D14.

[481] *Boussois/Interpane* (n 468, above) (payment of royalties after know-how in public domain); Case 320/87 *Ottung v Klee* [1989] ECR 1177, [1990] 4 CMLR 915; Case 65/86 *Bayer v Süllhöfer* [1988] ECR 5249, [1990] 4 CMLR 182. See generally paras 9.118 *et seq*, below.

[482] See the English Court of Appeal in *Chemidus Wavin v TERI* [1978] 3 CMLR 514, on appeal from [1976] 2 CMLR 387 (ChD).

[483] eg *Windsurfing International v Commission* (n 470, above). See paras 9.115 (patents) and 9.175 (trade mark), below.

[484] *CBR*, OJ 1978 L20/18, [1978] 2 CMLR 194. See also *Nungesser* (n 463, above) paras 80 *et seq* (obligation arising under a judicial settlement).

[485] Case 35/83 *BAT v Commission* [1985] ECR 363, [1985] 2 CMLR 470, para 33. For the cases and the relevant principles as implemented by the Commission, see para 9.177, below.

[486] See para 9.120, below and para 2.033, above.

However, where the opinion of a professional association regarding the level of a fee enables the professional to invoke a summary legal procedure for recovery of the fee, but the client is able to challenge that opinion before the court, this does not give rise to a restriction of competition.[487]

2.119   **'Unfair' competition not deserving protection.**   It is sometimes alleged that an agreement does not fall within Article 81(1) because it is designed to combat 'unfair' competition, such as dumping.[488] However, such arguments will generally fail since the control of unfair commercial practices is the function of the public authorities acting in the public interest and cannot be left to agreements between private parties acting in their own interest.[489] Similarly an agreement not to sell 'defective' products may infringe Article 81(1),[490] as may an export ban contained in an agreement for the sale of 'seconds'[491] or an agreement which is allegedly designed to prevent 'slavish' imitation.[492] The proper way to control such matters is by public law regulation or by recourse to the courts in a private law action for passing-off (in common law countries) or unfair competition (in civil law countries).[493]

2.120   **Restriction of competition outside common market.**   Article 81(1) is confined to agreements which restrict competition within the common market. Therefore, agreements which restrict competition only outside the common market do not infringe Article 81(1). Each case will, however, depend on its own circumstances.[494]

5. Appreciable Effect on Competition

2.121   **In general.**   An agreement falls outside Article 81(1) if it is not capable of having an *appreciable* effect either on competition or on trade between Member States.[495] The *de minimis* principle was established by the Court of Justice in

---

[487] Case C-221/99 *Conte* [2001] ECR I-9359, [2002] 4 CMLR 269: no breach of Art 10 in combination with Art 81.

[488] eg Cases 43 & 63/82 *VBVB and VBBB v Commission* [1984] ECR 19, [1985] 1 CMLR 27, paras 35 *et seq*; see also the following Commission decisions: *IFTRA rules on glass, containers*, OJ 1974 L160/1, [1974] 2 CMLR D50; *Aluminium imports from Eastern Europe*, OJ 1985 L92/1, [1987] 3 CMLR 813; *MELDOC*, OJ 1986 L348/50, [1989] 4 CMLR 853. In any event, parallel importation can never be an 'unfair' commercial practice: Cases 100/80, etc, *Musique Diffusion Française v Commission* [1983] ECR 1825, [1983] 3 CMLR 221, paras 88–90.

[489] eg *VBVB and VBBB v Commission*, above; *Aluminium imports from Eastern Europe*, above.

[490] *IFTRA rules on glass containers* (n 488, above). See also Case T-30/89 *Hilti v Commission* [1991] ECR II-1439, [1992] 4 CMLR 16, paras 115–119 (under Art 82); appeal on other grounds dismissed, Case C53/92P [1994] ECR I-667, [1994] 4 CMLR 614.

[491] Case 58/80 *Dansk Supermarked v Imerco* [1981] ECR 181, [1981] 3 CMLR 590.

[492] *Windsurfing International v Commission* (n 470, above) para 44.

[493] ibid; *VBVB and VBBB v Commission* (n 488, above) para 37.

[494] Paras 1.105 *et seq*, above. See also para 6.064, below.

[495] The principle is stated most succinctly in Case 22/71 *Béguelin Import v GL Import Export* [1971] ECR 949, [1972] CMLR 81, para 16: '. . . in order to come within the prohibition imposed

Völk, which has already been discussed,[496] and applies to 'object' cases as well as to 'effect' cases.[497] The concept has been developed both in the jurisprudence of the Community Courts and by a series of Notices issued by the Commission, indicating that the Commission will not institute proceedings in cases which fall below the thresholds set out. It is the agreement as a whole, rather than the participation of any particular party, which can be *de minimis*.[498] This Section considers the application of the appreciability threshold to the effect on competition of an agreement, concerted practice or decision of an association of undertakings. The issue of *de minimis* in relation to the effect on trade between Member States is considered in Chapter 1, above in the context of the effect on trade requirement.

(a) Jurisprudence of the Community Courts

Market shares and other factors.   In *Völk* the products concerned represented   **2.122** between 0.2 per cent and 0.5 per cent of production in Germany. Subsequently, in *Miller*[499] the defendant undertaking sought to take advantage of the principle in circumstances where Miller had on average about 5 per cent of the total market in sound recordings in Germany, with higher market shares in some sectors and a turnover in 1975 of DM34 million. The Court of Justice held:

> 'It is evident that Miller's sales constitute a not inconsiderable proportion of the market and that it specialises in the production of certain distinct categories for which it occupies a position on the market which, if not strong, is at any rate important . . . it must accordingly be concluded that Miller . . . is an undertaking of sufficient importance for its behaviour to be, in principle, capable of affecting trade.'[500]

The appraisal of the appreciable effect of an agreement will therefore include consideration of 'the position and importance of [the parties] on the market for

---

by Article [81], the agreement must affect trade between Member States and the free play of competition to an appreciable extent'.

[496] Case 5/69 *Völk v Vervaeke* [1969] ECR 295, [1969] CMLR 273; para 2.078, above. The ECJ did not in terms hold that the agreement in question was *de minimis* (as the Commission submitted) since the case was a reference for a preliminary ruling; but the inference is clear. See also Case 56/65 *Société Technique Minière v Maschinenbau Ulm* [1966] ECR 235, 249, [1966] CMLR 357, 375. In Case 126/80 *Salonia v Poidomani and Giglio* [1981] ECR 1563, [1982] 1 CMLR 64, para 17, the ECJ said that in the case of newspapers and periodicals the assessment of appreciable effect is stricter than in the case of other products.

[497] Indeed, *Völk* involved an export ban giving absolute territorial protection, an agreement which has been regarded as having an anti-competitive object: paras 2.078–2.079, above.

[498] Case T-6/89 *Enichem Anic v Commission* [1991] ECR II-1623, para 216 (argument that Enichem's small market share allowed it to benefit from the *de minimis* principle rejected).

[499] Case 19/77 *Miller v Commission* [1978] ECR 131, [1978] 2 CMLR 334.

[500] ibid, para 10.

the products concerned'.[501] The Court's decision in *Miller* was regarded as establishing a presumption that an undertaking with 5 per cent of the market is of sufficient importance for its agreements to fall within the scope of Article 81(1).[502]

2.123 **Exceptions to the market share presumption.** Undertakings with a market share of less than 5 per cent may still be caught by Article 81(1) if, on the facts, a sufficiently appreciable effect can be demonstrated in the light of the competitive structure of the market. Thus in *Pioneer*,[503] two of the applicants contended that their behaviour did not appreciably affect inter-State trade because their market shares were only 3.38 per cent in France, and 3.18 per cent in the United Kingdom. The Court of Justice rejected that argument on the grounds that the total market, although very large, was fragmented; the applicants' market shares by brand were greater than those of most of their competitors, and higher still if regard was had to imported brands only. On those facts, and taking into account the parties absolute turnover (FF77 million and £7 million respectively in 1976) the Court held that an appreciable effect was established.[504] Although the contention there was considered in terms of an effect on trade between Member States, the same considerations apply to an effect on competition. Conversely, the fact that the market share exceeds 5 per cent does not in itself establish that the agreement has an appreciable effect, especially when it is not significantly above that threshold. In *European Night Services*,[505] where the Commission's decision was annulled, *inter alia*, because of insufficient reasoning to support a finding of an appreciable effect on inter-State trade, the Court of First Instance held that 'the mere fact that the [5 per cent] threshold may be reached and even exceeded does not make it possible to conclude with certainty that an agreement is caught by Article [81(1)]'. That was particularly so in that case since the train operators that were parties to the agreements operated on markets largely dominated by air transport and it was expected that the market share of the ENS joint venture would either fall or remain stable in the future.

2.124 **Market structure.** Where the market is concentrated, the effect on competition of restrictive or cooperative provisions involving major competitors is

---

[501] *Société Technique Minière* (n 496, above) paras 2.070–2.071, above. See, eg Case T-77/92 *Parker Pen v Commission* [1994] ECR II-549, [1995] 5 CMLR 435, paras 39 *et seq*.

[502] *Miller v Commission* (n 499, above). See, eg Case 107/82 *AEG v Commission* [1983] ECR 3151, [1984] 3 CMLR 325, para 58. In Case 28/77 *Tepea v Commission* [1978] ECR 1391, [1978] 3 CMLR 392, para 50, the ECJ held that agreements which affected 15 per cent of the product market in the Netherlands thereby had an appreciable effect on inter-State trade.

[503] Cases 100/80, etc, *Musique Diffusion Française* [1983] ECR 1825, [1983] 3 CMLR 221.

[504] *Musique Diffusion Française*, above, paras 81–87. See also Case 30/78 *Distillers Company v Commission* [1980] ECR 2229, [1980] 3 CMLR 121, paras 27–28 (re Pimm's).

[505] Cases T-374/94, etc, *ENS v Commission* [1998] ECR II-3141, [1998] 5 CMLR 718, paras 102–103 and see para 2.084, above. See also the German ice cream cases, n 440, above; Case T-77/94 *VGB v Commission* [1997] ECR II-759, [1997] 5 CMLR 812, paras 131–144.

enhanced; this has been important, and even critical, to a number of decisions.[506] In contrast, in a competitive market the effect of provisions in a particular agreement will be less significant.[507] The Herfindahl-Hirschmann Index ('HHI'), developed in the context of US antitrust law, and the leading firm concentration ratio (the aggregate market share of the three, four or five largest competitors) may be useful means of assessing market concentration.[508] Whether the market is expanding or declining will also be relevant.[509]

Relevance of parallel networks of agreements.   One issue which frequently **2.125** arises in relation to vertical agreements is the extent to which other networks of agreements operated by competing suppliers in the market should be taken into account in determining whether the effect on competition (and on trade between Member States) was appreciable. In *Delimitis*,[510] the Court of Justice held that the existence of networks of agreements was only one among many factors to be taken into account in assessing the scale of barriers to entry into the market, and that it was the ease or difficulty of entry into the market by competitors and the contribution made by the agreement which determined whether the agreement had an

---

[506] eg Case T-34/92 *Fiatagri and Ford New Holland v Commission* [1994] ECR II-905; and Case T-35/92 *John Deere v Commission* [1994] ECR II-957, upholding *UK Agricultural Tractor Registration Exchange*, OJ 1992 L68/19, [1993] 4 CMLR 358: system of regular exchange of information on past sales by location (but not price) had an anti-competitive effect in an oligopolistic market as it reduced uncertainty, although it might benefit competition in a truly competitive market; further appeals dismissed: Case C-7/97P [1998] ECR I-3111, [1998] 5 CMLR 311, and Case C-8/95P [1998] ECR I-3111, [1998] 5 CMLR 362. See also *BP Kemi/DDSF*, OJ 1979 L286/32, [1979] 3 CMLR 684 (weak competitive structure on relevant market); *Floral*, OJ 1980 L39/51, [1980] 2 CMLR 285, paras 49–52 (joint sales organisation had only 2 per cent of German market but the parties were major producers and the market was oligopolistic); *Carlsberg* (n 470, above) (long-term purchasing agreement between brewers assessed in context of already concentrated UK beer market); *Optical Fibres*, OJ 1986 L236/30 (market already highly oligopolistic).

[507] eg *Villeroy & Boch*, OJ 1985 L376/15, [1988] 4 CMLR 461 (highly competitive nature of market for ceramic tableware relevant to decision that Art 81(1) did not apply); *Elopak/Metal Box–Odin*, OJ 1990 L209/15, [1991] 4 CMLR 832, para 27: number of competitors in the fields of both partners to the joint venture meant no foreclosure effect.

[508] The HHI is the sum of the squares of the individual market shares of all competitors. See Guidelines on Vertical Restraints (n 448, above) paras 119(1), 143, 189, and see further para 2.130, below. See also Horizontal Cooperation Guidelines, OJ 2001 C3/2, para 29. For the relative merits of the HHI compared to concentration ratios, see Bishop and Walker, *The Economics of Competition Law* (2nd edn, 2002), 36–38.

[509] eg *Fatty Acids*, OJ 1987 L3/17, [1989] 4 CMLR 445 (economic recession, surplus capacity and falling prices part of economic context in assessing restrictive nature of the agreement). cf *Télécom Développement*, OJ 1999 L218/24, [2000] 4 CMLR 124 (JV to develop telecommunications network on newly liberated French market that many other operators were planning to enter). See also *European Night Services*, para 2.084, above.

[510] Case C-234/89 *Delimitis* [1991] ECR I-935, [1992] 5 CMLR 210. For 'network effect', see para 2.104, above. For further discussion of *Delimitis*, see paras 2.080 *et seq*, above and paras 6.146 *et seq*, below.

appreciable effect.[511] The Court therefore propounded a two-fold test. First, one must examine whether the existence of similar contracts entered into by other suppliers on the relevant market have the cumulative effect of denying access to that market to new national and foreign competitors. If there is no market foreclosure, the agreements of the particular supplier in question cannot be held to restrict competition within the meaning of Article 81(1). However, if it is difficult to gain access to the relevant market, one must go on to assess the extent to which the agreements entered into by the supplier in question contribute to the cumulative effect produced in that respect by the totality of the similar contracts found on that market. If the contribution of the particular network to the cumulative foreclosure effect is insignificant, then the agreements in that network do not fall under the prohibition under Article 81(1).[512]

2.126   **Application of *Delimitis*.**   In two parallel cases concerning the standard-form supply agreements for 'impulse' ice cream concluded by the two leading German producers with retailers, that included exclusive purchasing and non-competition provisions, the Commission[513] held that, as the market share covered by the agreements represented more than 15 per cent in the one case and more than 10 per cent in the other case of the relevant market, it was not necessary to examine the cumulative effect of parallel networks. The Court of First Instance disagreed[514] and, applying *Delimitis*, proceeded to conduct such an analysis. The Court noted, first, the extent of tying-in achieved by the two agreements together; and, secondly, the substantial barriers to entry by other producers arising from supply to retailers of freezer cabinets by the leading producers on terms that the cabinets could be used only for their products, the rebates granted for exclusive supply, the large number of small retailers which made a profitable distribution system expensive to establish, and the fact that the appellants' product brands were well-known. In those circumstances, the Court concluded that the networks of exclusive purchasing agreements of two-and-a-half years duration had the effect of restricting access to the German market for domestic and foreign competitors, thereby appreciably affecting competition and trade between Member States. Consequently,

---

[511] cf *Yves Saint Laurent Parfums*, OJ 1992 L12/24, [1993] 4 CMLR 120, para 42, where the Commission stated that the YSL network formed part of an economic context in which selective distribution systems comprising similar restrictions of competition were the rule and that the appreciable nature of the restrictions may be said to derive from the cumulative effect inherent in such a distribution structure. But in that case, YSL Parfums had a market share well in excess of 5 per cent in several Member States.

[512] *Delimitis* (n 510, above) paras 23–24.

[513] *Langnese-Iglo*, OJ 1993 L183/19, [1994] 4 CMLR 51; *Schöller Lebensmittel*, OJ 1993 L183/1, [1994] 4 CMLR 51.

[514] Case T-7/93 *Langnese-Iglo v Commission* [1995] ECR II-1533, [1995] 5 CMLR 602, [1995] All ER (EC) 902, paras 94–132 (appeal and cross-appeal dismissed, Case C-279/95P [1998] ECR I-5609, [1998] 5 CMLR 933); and Case T-9/93 *Schöller v Commission* [1995] ECR II-1611, [1995] 5 CMLR 659, paras 71–99. cf *VGB v Commission* (n 505, above) paras 140–144.

all the agreements in the network were caught by Article 81(1), even if some of them, on their own, might not have had an appreciable anti-competitive effect. However, when the degree of restraint imposed by agreements in a network differs in a fundamental respect, the cumulative effects of different categories of agreement may have to be considered separately. This was made clear by the Court of Justice in the *Neste* case, a preliminary ruling concerning a petrol service station agreement in Finland that contained an exclusive purchasing obligation.[515] The great majority of service station agreements in Finland included such a tie, and Neste's contracts, taken together, made a significant contribution to closing off the market since it supplied petrol to about a third of the Finnish service stations. But because the effective duration of the particular agreement at issue was only one year, whereas most of Neste's agreements had much longer, fixed terms, and since the length of such a tie is of particular significance in considering its anti-competitive effect, the Court of Justice held, rejecting the argument of the Commission, that it was appropriate to subdivide Neste's network for the purpose of a *Delimitis* analysis. Article 81(1) applied only to agreements of a type which, together, contributed significantly to the cumulative sealing off of the market and not, therefore, to the agreement at issue.

Other reasons for lack of appreciable effect. Apart from the weakness of the **2.127** parties on the market, the agreement may lack appreciable effect for many other reasons. In rare circumstances, national laws may preclude competition.[516] More commonly, a lack of appreciable effect may be the result of the nature of the product,[517] or of the trade restrained.[518] Each case will turn upon its own facts. In *Pavlov*,[519] it was acknowledged that competition between medical specialists as regards purchasing of supplementary pensions was restricted by the decision of their professional organisation that obliged them to contribute to a particular pension fund. However, the Court of Justice held that as that was a relatively insignificant cost factor as regards the services offered by self-employed medical specialists, in comparison to their other costs, the restriction had only a marginal

---

[515] Case C-214/99 *Neste v Yötuuli Ky* [2000] ECR I-11121, [2001] 4 CMLR 993, [2001] All ER (EC) 76. See further para 6.148, below.

[516] Cases 40/73, etc, *Suiker Unie v Commission* [1975] ECR 1663, [1976] 1 CMLR 295, paras 29–73. But this is exceptional: see para 2.029, above and Chap 11, below.

[517] eg *Salonia v Poidomani and Giglio* (n 496, above) paras 15–17 (Italian newspapers: availability of other channels of distribution for publications from other Member States and rigidity of demand relevant to assessing appreciable effect); cf Case 45/85 *Verband der Sachversicherer v Commission* [1987] ECR 405, [1988] 4 CMLR 264 (fact that direct effect was only on local branches of insurers from other Member States, mainly because of restrictions under German law on cross-border supply of insurance services, did not exclude appreciable effect on inter-State trade).

[518] eg *Distillers Victuallers*, OJ 1980 L233/43, [1980] 3 CMLR 244 (restrictions relating to duty-free sales only not likely to have appreciable effect). See also *Villeroy & Boch*, OJ 1985 L376/15, [1988] 4 CMLR 461 (resale to specialised traders).

[519] Cases C-180/98, etc, *Pavlov* [2000] ECR I-6451, [2001] 4 CMLR 30.

influence on the final costs of the doctors' services and therefore was not appreciable.[520] In *UEFA Brodcasting Regulations*,[521] the Commission had objected to earlier versions of the regulations whereby the member national football associations were required to impose terms in the sale of broadcast rights to football matches abroad that largely blocked the broadcasting of those matches at times when local matches were being played. But the Commission held that, after revisions, the form of restriction on broadcast times was sufficiently limited that the remaining effect on competition was no longer appreciable, and accordingly the regulations did not infringe Article 81(1).[522]

(b) Commission guidance

2.128   **In general.**   Since the *de minimis* principle was established in the *Völk* judgment, the Commission has issued a series of Notices giving guidance on the thresholds it will apply in its own consideration of anti-competitive agreements and practices. Early versions of this guidance relied on a combination of market share and turnover thresholds but it has been increasingly recognised that the condition of appreciability depends, at least as regards the anti-competitive effect of an agreement, primarily on the parties' market power.[523] The latest version of the Notice on agreements of minor importance which do not appreciably restrict competition under Article 81(1) of the Treaty ('the *De Minimis* Notice') was published at the end of 2001.[524] It states that it is 'without prejudice to the principles for assessment' expressed in the Horizontal Cooperation Guidelines[525] and the Guidelines on Vertical Restraints.[526] It also does not deal with the issue of whether an agreement is capable of appreciably affecting trade between Member States;

---

[520] Curiously, the ECJ did not consider the effect of the restriction in a related market: that for the provision of pension arrangements to the self-employed. As between competing pension providers, the effect of the decision might be more significant; *quaere* whether the effect on that market should be analysed in the context of similar compulsory pension arrangements pursuant to decisions of other professional bodies in the Netherlands. Note that the judgment distinguished the *Dutch Sectoral Pension Funds* cases, para 2.034, above, holding that the arrangement did not by its nature fall outside the scope of Art 81(1) since it was not concluded pursuant to a collective labour agreement. Nonetheless, there appears to be a strong element of policy in this decision.

[521] *UEFA Broadcasting Regulations*, OJ 2001 L171/12, [2001] 5 CMLR 654.

[522] In summary, the national association could block broadcasting of live matches for a maximum of two-and-a-half hours on either Saturday or Sunday, excluding excerpts during non-sporting programmes. See further para 5.162, below.

[523] see *VGB v Commission* (n 505, above) paras 131–144 (exclusive purchasing agreements by Dutch wholesalers with major growers' cooperative did not appreciably hinder inter-State trade in flowers).

[524] *De Minimis* Notice, OJ 2001 C368/13, Vol II, App C.13. The Notice was first issued on 27 May 1970 and revised on 19 December 1977, again on 3 September 1986 and again on 9 December 1997. The EFTA Surveillance Authority issued an equivalent Notice for the purpose of the EEA Agreement: OJ 2003 C67/20 and EEA Supplement to the OJ 2003, No 15 p 11.

[525] Horizontal Cooperation Guidelines, OJ 2001 C3/2: Vol II, App C.12.

[526] Guidelines on Vertical Restraints, OJ 2000 C291/1: Vol II, App C.11.

that is now covered by the Guidelines on the Effect on Trade Concept.[527] There are now therefore four sources of guidance[528] on the appreciability threshold under Article 81(1).

De Minimis Notice.   Where an agreement is made between undertakings **2.129** which are actual or potential competitors, the Commission holds the view that agreements do not appreciably restrict competition if the aggregate market share held by the parties[529] to the agreement does not exceed 10 per cent on any of the relevant markets.[530] Where the agreement is between non-competitors, the market share threshold is 15 per cent. In a case where it is difficult to classify whether the agreement involves competitors or not, the 10 per cent threshold applies. There is a margin of tolerance in that the Commission does not regard the agreements as restrictive of competition if the market share is exceeded by not more than 2 percentage points in any two successive calendar years.[531] Where the relevant market is characterised by networks of agreements, it will be regarded as significantly foreclosed if 30 per cent or more of the market is covered by parallel networks of agreements.[532] Where that is the case, individual suppliers or distributors with a market share below 5 per cent are not regarded as contributing significantly to the cumulative foreclosure effect.[533] The Notice then lists a number of 'hard-core' restrictions which will deprive the agreement of the benefit of the Notice, including price-fixing, market-sharing, resale price maintenance and export restrictions.[534] Where an agreement falls within the thresholds set by the Notice, the Commission will not institute proceedings either in response to a complaint or on its own initiative. Where undertakings assume in good faith that an agreement is covered by the Notice, the Commission will not impose fines. The Notice is not binding on the courts or competition authorities of the Member States but is intended to give guidance to them in their application of Article 81.

---

[527] Guidelines of the Effect on Trade Concept, OJ 2004 C101/81: Vol II, App C.17. This is discussed at paras 1.115 *et seq*, above.

[528] In addition, the Commission cross-refers to the Relevant Market Notice, OJ 1997 C372/5, Vol II, App C.10, in relation to the calculation of market shares necessary for the application of the guidance on appreciable effect.

[529] Para 12 of the *De Minimis* Notice provides guidance on which entities are considered connected to the party to the agreement such that their market share falls to be included.

[530] For an unsuccessful attempt to rely on the *De Minimis* Notice, see *Quantel International-Continuum/Quantel SA*, OJ 1992 L235/9, para 43.

[531] *De Minimis* Notice, para 9.

[532] ie when considering the first stage of the *Delimitis* test; see paras 2.081 and 2.126, above.

[533] ie when considering the second stage of the *Delimitis* test; ibid.

[534] Nonetheless, it appears that the Commission is unlikely to commence proceedings as regards agreements containing restrictions of that kind that fall below the thresholds in the Notice: Faull and Nikpay (n 375, above) para 3.164. Moreover, the application of Art 81(1) to such agreements is still subject to an appreciability threshold (as acknowledged in the Guidelines on Vertical Restraints (n 526, above) para 10).

2.130 **Vertical restraints: market shares of the parties to the agreement.** The Guidelines on Vertical Restraints[535] provide guidance on the application of the block exemption for vertical agreements contained in Regulation 2790/1999 and also on the treatment of agreements where the relevant party's market share exceeds 30 per cent, taking it outside the ambit of the block exemption.[536] However, as regards parties with a low market share and the issue of appreciability, there is a 'disconnect' between the 1999 Guidelines and the 2001 *De Minimis* Notice. The Guidelines state a general rule[537] that vertical agreements entered into by undertakings whose share on the relevant market does not exceed 10 per cent will generally fall outside Article 81(1). However, this figure reflects the 1997 version of the *De Minimis* Notice that was current at the time the Guidelines were issued; since vertical restraints generally arise in agreements between non-competitors, the current Notice, as stated above, provides for a 15 per cent 'safe harbour'. But the Guidelines state in addition that the Commission considers that, subject to the cumulative effect of networks of agreements and to the existence of hard-core restrictions, agreements between SMEs are rarely capable of appreciably affecting competition.[538] The later paragraphs of the Guidelines describe, in relation to many kinds of vertical agreement, the factors which indicate whether or not they are likely to have an appreciable effect on competition.

2.131 **Vertical restraints: unconcentrated markets.** The Guidelines on Vertical Restraints provide an alternative way of analysing appreciable effect on competition. The Commission's view is that for most vertical restraints, competition concerns only arise if there is insufficient inter-brand competition, that is, if there exists a certain degree of market power at the level of the supplier or the buyer or both. Where there are many firms competing in an unconcentrated market, it can be assumed that non hard-core vertical restraints will not have appreciable negative effects.[539] A market is deemed to be unconcentrated where the HHI index is below 1,000.[540] This rule holds, irrespective of the market share of the company, for two years after the first putting on the market of the product, and it applies to all non hard-core vertical restraints.[541]

---

[535] Guidelines on Vertical Restraints, OJ 2000 C291/1: Vol II, App C.11.

[536] See Chap 6.

[537] Guidelines on Vertical Restraints (n 526, above) para 9. This principle is said to be subject to the conditions set out in the *De Minimis* Notice precluding its application to hard-core restrictions, such as export bans or retail price-fixing.

[538] Guidelines, para 11, SMEs are now defined in Commission Rec 2003/361/EC OJ 2003 L124/36: Vol II, App C.15. cf *De Minimis* Notice, para 3, which refers to SMEs only as regards an appreciable effect on trade between Member States.

[539] ibid, para 119.

[540] ie the sum of the squares of the individual market shares of all companies in the relevant market, see further para 2.124, above.

[541] There are further rules covering agreements establishing new geographic or product markets: see para 119 of the *De Minimis* Notice.

Horizontal cooperation agreements. In the Horizontal Cooperation **2.132** Guidelines, the Commission states that if the parties to a horizontal cooperation agreement [542] together have a low combined market share, a restrictive effect on competition is unlikely. Further, if one of just two parties has an insignificant market share and does not possess important resources, even a high combined market share does not normally indicate a restrictive effect on competition in the market.[543] Given the variety of types of cooperation, the Commission regards it as impossible to give a general market share threshold above which sufficient market power for causing restrictive effects can be assumed. Additional factors to take into account are the degree of market concentration, entry barriers and likelihood of market entry, and the nature of the products .

---

[542] Defined as agreements on R&D, production, purchasing, commercialisation (ie cooperation in selling, distribution or promotion), standardisation and environmental agreements: Horizontal Cooperation Guidelines (n 525, above) para 10. The Guidelines do not apply to other types of agreement, eg for exchange of information.

[543] Horizontal Cooperation Guidelines (n 525, above) para 28.

3

ARTICLE 81(3)

1. Introduction

Article 81(3). The prohibition contained in Article 81(1) is not absolute. **3.001**
Article 81(3) provides[1] that the prohibition can be disapplied in the following
circumstances:

'The provisions of paragraph 1 may, however, be declared inapplicable in the case of:
— any agreement or category of agreements between undertakings;
— any decision or category of decisions by associations of undertakings;
— any concerted practice or category of concerted practices;
which contributes to improving the production or distribution of goods or to
promoting technical or economic progress, while allowing consumers a fair share
of the resulting benefit, and which does not:
(a) impose on the undertakings concerned restrictions which are not indispensable
to the attainment of these objectives;

---

[1] The terms of Art 53(3) of the EEA Agreement are identical to those of Art 81(3) of the EC
Treaty: see Vol II, App A.8. Its application is discussed at paras 3.090 *et seq*, below.

(b) afford such undertakings the possibility of eliminating competition in respect of a substantial part of the products in question.'

3.002 **Single substantive test for all sectors.** As from 1 May 2004, the criteria for disapplying the prohibition in Article 81(1) set out in Article 81(3) apply regardless of the sector of the economy concerned. Previously, agreements in the rail, road and inland waterway sector were assessed by reference to the criteria set out in Article 5 of Regulation 1017/68. That provision was repealed as part of the Modernisation package.[2]

3.003 **Direct application of Article 81(3).** A key change to the regime for enforcing Community competition law brought about by Regulation 1/2003 was that, as from 1 May 2004, any agreements, decisions and concerted practices caught by Article 81(1) which satisfy the conditions of Article 81(3) escape the prohibition in Article 81(1) and are fully valid and enforceable. No prior decision to that effect is required.[3] Article 81(3) can now therefore be applied directly not only by the European Commission but also by the competition authorities of the Member States and by national courts.[4] This directly applicable system created by Regulation 1/2003 replaces the former regime under Regulation 17, in which Article 81(3) could only be applied by the Commission and then, generally, only if the agreement had been notified to the Commission for this purpose.[5] As discussed below, Article 81(3) may also be applied in the form of a regulation exempting certain categories of agreements (a 'block' or 'group' exemption).

3.004 **Commission Guidelines.** To coincide with the coming into force of Regulation 1/2003, the Commission issued Guidelines on the application of Article 81(3) of the Treaty ('the Article 81(3) Guidelines') setting out its own views and discussing typical scenarios.[6] Other notices concerning cooperation between the Commission and the national competition authorities ('NCAs') and between the Commission

---

[2] Reg 1/2003, OJ 2003 L1/1, Vol II, App B.3, Art 36(4). The Commission had in any event considered that Reg 1017/68, Art 5 and Art 81(3) were cumulative so that both had to be satisfied for individual exemption to be granted: *Tariff structures in the combined transport of goods*, OJ 1993 L73/38, para 19; *Far Eastern Freight Conference*, OJ 1994 L378/17, para 96 (appeal largely dismissed, Case T-86/95 *Compagnie Générale Maritime v Commission* [2002] ECR II-1011, [2002] 4 CMLR 1115). Reg 1/2003 was amended by Council Reg 411/2004, OJ 2004 L68/1, which brought all air transport into the new regime. For the background to the Modernisation package, see paras 1.057 *et seq*, above.

[3] Reg 1/2003, Art 1(2).

[4] Reg 1/2003, Arts 4–6. Art 6 thus reverses the finding in Case 31/80 *L'Oréal v De Nieuwe AMCK* [1980] ECR 3775, [1981] 2 CMLR 235, para 13, that national courts could not apply Art 81(3) directly. That ruling was based on the exclusive competence then held by the Commission under Reg 17, Art 9(1).

[5] See Reg 1/2003 (n 2, above) Recitals (1) to (4).

[6] Guidelines on the application of Art 81(3) of the Treaty, OJ 2004 C101/97: Vol II, App C.18. For discussion by a Commission official, see Kjølbye, 'The New Commission Guidelines on the Application of Article 81(3): An Economic Approach to Article 81' (2004) ECLR 566.

and the national courts serve further to explain the new relationship between the enforcement bodies as regards the application of Article 81(3). In addition, the Commission's Guidelines on the applicability of Article 81 to horizontal cooperation agreements ('the Horizontal Cooperation Guidelines')[7] and Guidelines on Vertical Restraints[8] contain discussion of the circumstances in which agreements of those kinds satisfy the conditions of Article 81(3). Both those Guidelines, which were issued in 2000, continue to be valid. They are considered in detail in, respectively, Chapters 5 and 6, below. Many of the agreements covered by the Horizontal Cooperation Guidelines are in the form of joint ventures: see further Chapter 7, below.

Cessation of prospective assessment of agreements. The simplicity of Article 1(2) **3.005** of Regulation 1/2003, which swept away the earlier notification and individual exemption regime, disguises the complex way in which the relationship between Article 81(1) and Article 81(3) has changed. Under the former enforcement regime set out in Regulation 17,[9] the balancing of the restriction of competition caused by an agreement with its objective benefits was carried out by a single administrative decision-maker, acting at Community level. Under the post-Modernisation system, that balance can be carried out by a multitude of different decision-makers, both administrative and judicial, and at both Community and national level. Under the Regulation 17 regime, the assessment was generally conducted prospectively, considering whether the conditions were likely to be satisfied in the future (even though the agreement may already have been brought into effect). The Commission's assessment was also usually carried out at a time when the parties were still able (and willing) to amend the terms of their agreement to allay concerns expressed by the Commission if that was needed to achieve the legal certainty that an exemption decision offered. Under the post-Modernisation system, the question of whether the conditions of Article 81(3) are satisfied will generally arise only when the legality of the operation of the agreement in the past is challenged and at a time when there can be no retrospective adjustment of the terms of the agreement. The effect of these changes on the interpretation and application of Article 81(3) is as yet unknown.

Relevance of pre-Modernisation jurisprudence. The move to the direct appli **3.006** cation of Article 81(3) has clearly made redundant much of the old law, for example, that relating to the notification procedure for applying for a Commission

---

[7] Horizontal Cooperation Guidelines, OJ 2001 C3/2: Vol II, App C.12. The Guidelines accompany the new block exemption regulations for R&D and Specialisation Agreements, Regs 2659/2000 and 2658/2000.

[8] Guidelines on Vertical Restraints, OJ 2000 C291/1: Vol II, App C.11.

[9] Reg 17 of 1962, JO 1962 13/204, OJ 1959–62, 87: Vol II, App B.1. The former regime is briefly described in Chap 13, below.

exemption decision. Although the cases concerning the interpretation of the criteria in Article 81(3) may appear still to be relevant, it must be borne in mind that they were decided in the context of a regime whereby individual exemptions could be of limited duration; could be made subject to conditions and reporting obligations; and could be revoked or reviewed at the Commission's initiative. Whether that context affects the value of those judgments needs to be considered individually in each case.

3.007 **The convergence rule under Regulation 1/2003.** Under the regime established by Regulation 1/2003, most Commission decisions applying Article 81(3) will be infringement decisions, and thus will be decisions finding that the criteria are not satisfied.[10] In some cases, the affected party or parties may offer commitments to change an agreement or arrangement to meet concerns expressed by the Commission in relation to the Article 81(3) criteria, with the consequence that the Commission adopts a decision on that basis making those commitments binding.[11] In exceptional cases where the public interest of the Community so requires, the Commission may adopt a decision finding that Article 81 is not applicable to an agreement, decision or concerted practice, for example because the conditions of Article 81(3) are satisfied.[12] Decisions of this type by the Commission have Community-wide effect, in that when a national court or NCA rules on agreements, decisions or practices under Article 81 which are already the subject of a Commission decision, it cannot take a decision running counter to the Commission's decision.[13]

3.008 **Continued effect of extant Commission exemption decisions.** Individual exemptions granted by the Commission under the former regime of Regulation 17 and its equivalent regulations in the transport sector have not been repealed by Regulation 1/2003. Until the expiry of the time limits set in those decisions, they therefore remain binding on national courts and on the competition authorities of the Member States.[14] In some decisions taken shortly before the repeal of

---

[10] Reg 1/2003 (n 2, above) Art 1(1).

[11] ibid, Art 9.

[12] ibid, Recital (14) and Art 10.

[13] ibid, Arts 16(1) and 16(2). But the binding effect under Art 16 does not apply to the rejection by the Commission of a complaint, although that rejection may be on the basis that the Commission considers that the matter does not come within Art 81(1) or that the conditions of Art 81(3) are fulfilled, nor does it apply to a decision by the Commission accepting commitments under Art 9 of Reg 1/2003: see para 14.092, below. Note also that Reg 1/2003 does not provide that decisions applying Art 81(3) adopted by a NCA are binding on the courts of that or other Member States; this is accordingly a matter of national law. See paras 14.064 *et seq*, below.

[14] In Case 31/80 *L'Oréal v De Nieuwe AMCK* (n 4, above) para 8, the ECJ made clear that an exemption decision granted by the Commission could be relied upon before a national court. Reg 1/2003, Arts 16(1) and 16(2), provides for a similar rule binding on both national courts and the competition authorities of the Member States, which is expressed in terms of agreements, decisions and concerted practices 'which are already the subject of a Commission decision'. This expression

Regulation 17, the Commission expressly hinted that the conditions for the application of Article 81(3) might continue beyond the expiry date of the exemption.[15] The Commission retains the power under Regulation 17, Article 8(3), to revoke or amend exemption decisions, or prohibit specified acts by the parties.[16] Furthermore, if a condition of an exemption decision is no longer satisfied, the exemption will automatically cease to apply, although it is now possible to argue that the criteria of Article 81(3) are satisfied nonetheless.

Lapse of extant notifications for exemption.   As at 1 May 2004, there were very **3.009** many notifications applying for exemption to which the Commission had not yet made any response. Indeed, the burden of dealing with the large number of notifications was part of the rationale for the Modernisation reform.[17] Pursuant to Article 34(1) of Regulation 1/2003, all such notifications automatically lapsed. It would appear that the basis of the post-Modernisation regime is that the Commission can no longer adopt a decision in response to a notification. However, the Court of First Instance has held, when annulling decisions of the Commission granting individual exemption pre-Modernisation,[18] that the Commission could take a new decision on the notified agreement and adjudicate on the application

---

appears wide enough to include surviving exemption decisions adopted under the former Reg 17 and equivalent regulations. Exemption decisions must be interpreted restrictively so as to ensure that their effects are not extended to situations which they are not intended to cover: Case C-306/96 *Javico v YSLP* [1998] ECR I-1983, [1998] 5 CMLR 172, para 32. An individual exemption of a distribution system does not regulate the activities of third parties who may operate on the market outside that network: Case T-87/92 *Kruidvat v Commission* [1996] ECR II-1931, [1997] 4 CMLR 1046, para 71 (appeal dismissed, Case C-70/97P, [1998] ECR I-7183, [1999] 4 CMLR 68).

[15] eg, *O₂ UK Limited/T-Mobile UK Limited- UK network sharing agreement*, OJ 2003 L200/59, [2004] 4 CMLR 1401, para 152; *T-Mobile Deutschland/ O₂ Germany – Network Sharing Rahmenvertrag*, OJ 2004 L75/32, [2004] 5 CMLR 762, para 149 (decn in part annulled on appeal, Case T-328/03 *O₂ (Germany) v Commission* [2006] ECR II-1231, [2006] 5 CMLR 258).

[16] Reg 1/2003 (n 2, above) Art 43(1) repeals Reg 17 except for its Art 8(3), which makes such provision (a) where there has been a change in any of the facts which were basic to the making of the decision; (b) where the parties commit a breach of any obligation attached to the decision; (c) where the decision is based on incorrect information or was induced by deceit; and (d) where the parties abuse the exemption from the provisions of Art 81(1) granted to them by the decision. In cases where (b), (c) or (d) apply, the decision may be revoked with retroactive effect. Note that, while the Commission's power under Reg 17, Art 15(2)(b), to impose fines for breach of an obligation attached to an exemption decision has been repealed without the insertion of an obviously equivalent provision in Reg 1/2003, the Commission might claim the ability to revoke the exemption with retroactive effect and then impose a fine for infringement of Art 81. The equivalent powers have been retained for road, rail and inland waterway transport (Reg 1/2003, Art 36(4) preserves Reg 1017/68, Art 13(3)); maritime transport (Reg 1/2003, Art 38(4) preserved Reg 4056/86, Art 13(3), but now see Reg 1419/2006, OJ 2006 L269/1, repealing the block exemption subject to a two-year transitional period: para 3.083, below); and air transport (Reg 411/2004, Art 1, preserves Reg 3975/87, Art 6(3)).

[17] See para 1.057, above.

[18] *O₂ Germany v Commission* (n 15, above) paras 47–49. See similarly Case T-168/01 *GlaxoSmithKline Services v Commission* [2006] ECR II-2969, [2006] 5 CMLR 1589, paras 318–320, on appeal Cases C-513/06P, etc, *GlaxoSmithKline Services v Commission*, not yet decided.

for negative clearance and exemption by reference to the date of the notification, carrying out its examination under Regulation 17. This approach seems difficult to reconcile with Article 34(1) of Regulation 1/2003 and the abolition of the procedural provisions of Regulation 17, without any saving transitional provisions.[19] At the time of writing, the issue is pending before the Court of Justice.[20]

3.010 **Application of Article 81(3) by national courts.**   Given that the balancing often involves a comparison of very different factors, the challenge for national judges should not be underestimated. The objective benefits and the anti-competitive effects of an agreement may not be experienced to the same extent in all Member States and there may be limited opportunities for national courts, or even NCAs, to balance objective benefits in their own Member State with anti-competitive effects felt in other Member States.[21] It remains to be seen whether such issues will be resolved through the use of Article 234 of the EC Treaty to refer questions on the application of Article 81(3) to the Court of Justice.[22] Under the former regime under Regulation 17, the Community Courts granted a margin of appreciation to the Commission in its 'complex economic assessment' of agreements under Article 81(3). Thus the Court of First Instance has stressed that in the context of an action for annulment pursuant to Article 230 of the Treaty, 'the review undertaken by the Court of the complex economic appraisals made by the Commission when it exercises the discretion conferred on it by Article [81(3)] of the Treaty, with regard to each of the four conditions laid down in that provision, is necessarily limited to verifying whether the rules on procedure and on the giving of reasons have been complied with, whether the facts have been accurately stated and whether there has been any manifest error of assessment or a misuse of powers.'[23] But the Court of Justice may have a growing role in the establishment

---

[19] The Community Courts cannot bind the Commission in an 'annulment' judgment as to the future conduct of the case.

[20] Cases C-501/06P, etc, *GlaxoSmithKline Services v Commission*, not yet decided. In the earlier case, *O2 Germany* (n 15, above), the applicant did not seek a fresh decision from the Commission so the conundrum did not have to be resolved.

[21] As to whether it is appropriate to offset benefits in one market against detriments in another, see paras 3.022 and 3.023, below.

[22] See paras 14.092 *et seq*, below.

[23] Case T-395/94 *Atlantic Container Line v Commission* ('*TAA*') [2002] ECR II-875, [2002] 4 CMLR 1008, para 257, citing Cases 142/84 & 156/84 *BAT and Reynolds v Commission* [1987] ECR 4487, [1988] 4 CMLR 24, para 62; Cases T-39 & 40/92 *CB and Europay v Commission* [1994] ECR II-49, para 109; Case T-17/93 *Matra Hachette v Commission* [1994] ECR II-595, para 104; Case T-29/92 *SPO v Commission* [1995] ECR II-289, para 288; and Cases T-213/95 & T-18/96 *SCK and FNK v Commission* [1997] ECR II-1739, [1998] 4 CMLR 259, para 190. See also Case T-86/95 *Compagnie Générale Maritime v Commission* [2002] ECR II-1011, [2002] 4 CMLR 1115, para 126: 'It is not for the Court of First Instance to substitute its assessment for that of the Commission, or to rule on pleas, complaints or arguments which, even if they were well founded, would not lead to the annulment of the contested decision.' But see *GlaxoSmithKline Services v Commission* (n 18, above), where the CFI annulled the Commission's conclusion that the first condition of Art 81(3) was not

of a single set of legal benchmarks for the balancing required under Article 81(3), and in assisting national courts to apply that provision appropriately where agreements affect various Member States differently. National courts may also seek the opinion of the Commission about the economic legal or factual analysis of an agreement or conduct at issue in the case before them.[24] The Commission will not, however, advise the court on the merits of the case.

Relationship between Article 81(1) and 81(3).   There is continuing discussion **3.011** in the case law of the Community Courts as to the extent to which the weighing of the pro- and anti-competitive effects of an agreement should be considered as part of determining whether it falls within Article 81(1) at all, or only as to whether it benefits from the application of Article 81(3). The question whether Article 81(1) incorporates a 'rule of reason' test whereby pro-competitive agreements escape Article 81(1) altogether is discussed in Chapter 2, above.[25] Although the Court of First Instance has generally held that such a balancing is only relevant to the application of Article 81(3),[26] the Court of Justice determined in a number of cases that agreements which do not contain restrictions going beyond what is necessary to achieve some other benefit fall outside Article 81(1).[27] The significance of this debate has lessened following the direct applicability of Article 81(3) post-Modernisation.

Relationship between Article 81(3) and Article 82.   According to longstanding **3.012** case law of the Court of Justice, the fact that an agreement benefits from the disapplication of Article 81(1) does not mean that it also escapes the application of Article 82.[28] However, the Court of First Instance has held that where the

---

satisfied on the basis that the Commission had failed to take into account and assess all the relevant information.

   [24] See Commission Notice on cooperation with the courts of the Member States ('National Courts Cooperation Notice'), OJ 2004 C101/54, Vol II, App B.9, paras 21–30, and paras 14.064 *et seq*, below.

   [25] See paras 2.088 *et seq*, above.

   [26] Case T-112/99 *M6 v Commission* [2001] ECR II-2459, [2001] 5 CMLR 1236, [2002] All ER (EC) 1, paras 72–74; and also Case T-65/98 *Van den Bergh Foods v Commission* [2003] ECR II-4653, [2004] 4 CMLR 14, [2005] All ER(EC) 418, para 106 ('the existence of such a rule in Community competition law is not accepted') (appeal on other grounds dismissed: Case C-552/03P, [2006] 5 CMLR 1460, [2006] ECR I-9091,). cf Case T-328/03 *O2 (Germany) v Commission* (n 15, above) where the CFI annulled the Commission's decn on a national roaming agreement because factors which the Commission had held allowed the agreement to benefit from Art 81(3) should have been considered to determine whether the agreement came outside the scope of Art 81(1) in the first place.

   [27] See, eg Case C-309/99 *Wouters* [2202] ECR I-1577, [2002] 4 CMLR 913, [2002] All ER (EC) 193; Case C-519/04P *Meca-Medina and Majcen v Commission* [2006] 5 CMLR 1023, [2006] All ER (EC) 1057.

   [28] Case C-310/93 *BPB Industries and British Gypsum v Commission* [1995] ECR I-865, [1997] 4 CMLR 238, para 11, relying upon the opinion of AG Léger at para 67; Cases C-395 & 396/96P *Compagnie Maritime Belge Transports v Commission* [2000] ECR I-1365, [2000] 4 CMLR 1076, [2000] All ER (EC) 385, para 130 (on appeal from Cases T-24/93, etc, [1996] ECR II-1201,

Commission granted an individual exemption pursuant to Article 81(3) in respect of agreements notified by undertakings holding a dominant position it indirectly bars itself, in the absence of a change in the facts or the law, from considering that the same agreement constitutes an abuse contrary to Article 82.[29] Less controversially, the fact that an agreement falls within a block exemption does not give rise to any presumption regarding the applicability of Article 82.[30] Moreover, the fact that an agreement falls within Article 81(3) does not preclude its implementation from giving rise to sufficient links between the undertakings concerned that they may be viewed as collectively dominant and therefore liable to infringe Article 82 by abusive conduct.[31]

2. Application in Individual Cases

(a) Generally

3.013 **Unlimited theoretical application of Article 81(3).** In principle, no anti-competitive practices are excluded from the possible application of Article 81(3) if, having regard to their effects on a given market, they satisfy the conditions laid down in Article 81(3). There are thus no infringements that are inherently incapable of benefiting from the disapplication of the prohibition in Article 81(1).[32] That said, serious restrictions of competition, and in particular restrictions that are prohibited in block exemption regulations or identified as hard-core restrictions in Commission guidelines or notices, are unlikely to fulfil all the conditions of Article 81(3).[33]

3.014 **Substantive conditions are cumulative.** Article 81(3) lays down four substantive conditions for escaping the prohibition in Article 81(1). These conditions are cumulative: if any one is not established, Article 81(3) cannot apply regardless

---

[1997] 4 CMLR 273, para 152); Case T-51/89 *Tetra Pak v Commission* [1990] ECR II-309, [1991] 4 CMLR 334, para 25. In the last mentioned case (to which Reg 17 applied), it was held, at paras 27–28, that any subsequent application of Art 82 to the operation of an agreement must, unless the factual and legal circumstances have altered, take account of the earlier findings made when the Commission granted that agreement exemption under Art 81(3). In particular, the Commission would have found that the agreement did not afford the undertakings concerned the possibility of eliminating competition in respect of a substantial part of the products in question.

29 Cases T-191/98, etc, *Atlantic Container Line v Commission* ('*TACA*') [2003] ECR II-3275, [2005] 4 CMLR 1283, para 1456.

30 *Tetra Pak* (n 28, above) paras 79–81.

31 Cases C-395 & 396/96P *Compagnie Maritime Belge Transports* (n 28, above) para 44.

32 *Matra Hachette v Commission* (n 23, above) para 85; *GlaxoSmithKline Services* para 233.

33 Art 81(3) Guidelines (n 6, above) para 46; Guidelines on Technology Transfer Agreements, OJ 2004 C101/2: Vol II, App C.16, para 37.

of the situation with respect to the others.[34] The agreement must therefore satisfy each of the following conditions:

(1) it contributes to improving the production or distribution of goods or to promoting technical or economic progress;
(2) it allows consumers a fair share of the resulting benefit;
(3) it does not impose on the undertakings concerned restrictions which are not indispensable to the attainment of these objectives; and
(4) it does not afford those undertakings the possibility of eliminating competition in respect of a substantial part of the products in question.

Burden of proof. In any national or Community proceedings, the undertaking **3.015** or association of undertakings claiming the benefit of Article 81(3) bears the burden of proving that the conditions of that paragraph are fulfilled.[35] This approach is similar to that previously applied as regards applications to the Commission for exemption decisions under Regulation 17. In that context, it was held that it was in the first place for the undertakings concerned to present to the Commission the evidence intended to establish the economic justification for the exemption.[36]

Relevant considerations. Under the former regime of Regulation 17, the **3.016** Community Courts provided guidance as to how the Commission should carry out its Article 81(3) assessment. This guidance would appear equally valid under Regulation 1/2003, for the Commission, for national courts and for NCAs. Thus, the decision-maker is under a duty to examine carefully and impartially all the relevant aspects in the individual case.[37] For example, the Commission could not apply Article 81(3) to the rules of an association set up to negotiate certain exclusive rights for its members without examining whether the association's

---

[34] For an early case establishing this, see Cases 56 & 58/64 *Consten and Grundig v Commission* [1966] ECR 299, 350, [1966] CMLR 418, 480. For more recent cases, see, eg Case T-86/95 *Compagnie Générale Maritime v Commission* (n 23, above) para 349; *TAA* (n 23, above) para 264; Cases T-185/00, etc, *Métropole Télévision (M6) v Commission* [2002] ECR II-3805, [2003] 4 CMLR 707, para 86; Case C-167/04P *JCB Service v Commission* [2006] ECR I-8935, [2006] 5 CMLR 1303, para 187.

[35] Reg 1/2003 (n 2, above) Art 2. For the compatibility of such a presumption with Art 6(2) of the European Convention on Human Rights, see *Salabiaku v France* (1991) 13 EHRR 379; and the more recent European and UK authorities discussed by the House of Lords in *Sheldrake v DPP* [2004] UKHL 43, [2005] 1 AC 264. The factual evidence on which a party relies may be of such a kind as to require the other party to provide an explanation or justification, failing which it is permissible to conclude that the burden of proof has not been discharged: Cases C-204/00P, etc, *Aalborg Portland v Commission* [2004] ECR I-123, [2005] 4 CMLR 251, para 79.

[36] See, eg Case C-552/03P *Unilever Bestfoods (Ireland) v Commission*, [2006] ECR I-9091, [2006] 5 CMLR 1460, paras 102–103.

[37] Cases T-528/93, etc, *Métropole Télévision v Commission* [1996] ECR II-649, [1996] 5 CMLR 386, para 93. This principle derives from Case C-269/90 *Technische Universität München* [1991] ECR I-5469, [1994] 2 CMLR 187, para 14, where the ECJ held that when the Community institutions have a power of appraisal, respect for the rights guaranteed by the Community legal order, including the duty of the competent institution to examine carefully and impartially all the relevant aspects of the individual case, is of fundamental importance

membership rules were objective and sufficiently determinate and capable of uniform, non-discriminatory application.[38] More generally, the decision-maker must take account of all the circumstances surrounding the application of the agreement.[39] In examining the economic context of an agreement, it must take account of the effect on the competitive situation of similar agreements.[40] Finally, when exercising its power under Article 81(3), the decision-maker should take account of the particular nature of different branches of the economy and the problems peculiar to them.[41]

3.017 **Effect of changing circumstances.** Under the former regime of Regulation 17, the Court of First Instance emphasised that the duration of an exemption granted by the Commission must be sufficient to enable the beneficiaries to achieve the benefits justifying the exemption. Where those benefits cannot be achieved without considerable investment, the length of time required to ensure a proper return on that investment is necessarily an essential factor to be taken into account. The period of time for which it can reasonably be supposed that market conditions will remain substantially the same cannot be regarded as decisive, on its own, for determining how long Article 81(3) applies, without also taking account of the length of time necessary to enable the parties to achieve a satisfactory return on their investment.[42] In the Article 81(3) Guidelines, the Commission emphasises that Article 81(3) applies as long as the four conditions are fulfilled and ceases to apply when that is no longer the case.[43] Nonetheless, the Commission accepts that it is necessary to take into account the time needed and the restraints required to commit and recoup an efficiency-enhancing investment.

3.018 **Breach of Article 82 and other unilateral conduct may preclude exemption.** The decision-maker is entitled to regard unilateral conduct, such as a refusal to supply, as a circumstance which prevents an agreement benefiting from the application of Article 81(3). This will be the case in particular where a manufacturer refuses to supply dealers within a selective distribution network with goods which would be exported to another Member State.[44] Such a refusal is part of the circumstances

---

[38] *Métropole Télévision v Commission* (n 37, above) paras 93–102.

[39] Cases 25 & 26/84 *Ford v Commission* [1985] ECR 2725, [1985] 3 CMLR 528, para 33.

[40] Case 75/84 *Metro v Commission* ('*Metro No. 2*') [1986] ECR 3021, [1987] 1 CMLR 118, paras 41, 43.

[41] Case 45/85 *Verband der Sachversicherer v Commission* [1987] ECR 405, [1988] 4 CMLR 264, para 15; Case T-29/92 *SPO v Commission* [1995] ECR II-289, para 253 (appeal on other grounds dismissed: Case C-137/95P *SPO v Commission* [1996] ECR II-1611).

[42] Cases T-374/94, etc, *European Night Services v Commission* [1998] ECR II-3141, [1998] 5 CMLR 718, paras 230, 231. The Court thus annulled an exemption granted for only eight years, pointing to the fact that the financing of the project was arranged over 20 years.

[43] Art 81(3) Guidelines (n 6, above) paras 44–45.

[44] Cases 228 & 229/92 *Ford v Commission* [1984] ECR 1129, [1984] 1 CMLR 649, para 22. The English version of this judgment is misleading in that the relevant passage is introduced by the

surrounding the application of the agreement and must therefore be taken into account when balancing the benefits deriving from the agreement with the disadvantages in terms of competition.[45] The Commission has emphasised that price-discrimination by a supplier against tied resellers may preclude the application of Article 81(3) to an exclusive purchase agreement.[46] The Court of First Instance has expressly left open the question whether an established violation of Article 82 should preclude the application of Article 81(3),[47] but there appears to be no reason why Article 82 abuse should be treated differently from other unilateral conduct.[48] However, as the Commission stresses in its Article 81(3) Guidelines, not all restrictive agreements concluded by a dominant undertaking constitute an abuse of a dominant position.[49] The mere hypothetical possibility that an agreement would enable the undertakings concerned to acquire a collective dominant position and that they would then commit an abuse under Article 82 does not preclude the application of Article 81(3).[50] Nonetheless, it should be recalled that Article 81(3) does not apply if the agreement affords the undertakings concerned the possibility of eliminating competition in respect of a substantial part of the products in question.

Effect of other Treaty provisions.   In some circumstances an agreement may **3.019** need to be assessed both under Article 81 and under the Articles of the Treaty relating to free movement of goods or service. Pre-Modernisation, and following the *Bosman* judgment,[51] the Commission stated that in addition to the requirements in Article 81(3), it would not grant exemption to rules of sporting bodies or associations that contravene the Treaty provisions on free movement of persons; and the discontinuance of an investigation under Article 81 of the FIFA rules on player transfers followed amendments to those rules which also took

---

phrase 'on the assumption that'. It is clear from the French original text, which uses the expression '*en admettant que*', and from para 23, which refers to the possibility of withdrawing immunity from fines in these circumstances, that the ECJ intended to make a positive assertion.

[45] Cases 25 & 26/84 *Ford v Commission* (n 39, above) para 33; see also Case T-208/01 *Volkswagen v Commission* [2004] ECR II-5141, [2004] 4 CMLR 727, para 51 (appeal on other grounds dismissed, Case C-74/04P, [2006] ECR I-6585).

[46] *Whitbread*, OJ 1999 L88/26, [1999] 5 CMLR 118, paras 155–170 (appeal on other grounds dismissed, Case T-131/99 *Shaw v Commission* [2002] ECR II-2023, [2002] 5 CMLR 81).

[47] *Matra Hachette v Commission* (n 23, above) paras 124, 154. But see *Atlantic Container Line v Commission* ('*TACA*') (n 29, above) para 1456.

[48] In Case 43/85 *Ancides v Commission* [1987] ECR 3131, [1988] 4 CMLR 821, para 14, the ECJ specifically observed in the context of a challenge to the renewal of an exemption that the applicant had failed to establish that the beneficiary of the exemption had a dominant position or that it had abused such a position.

[49] Article 81(3) Guidelines (n 6, above) para 106.

[50] *Matra Hachette v Commission* (n 23, above) paras 124, 154.

[51] Press Release IP/99/133 (24 February 1999), [1999] 4 CMLR 596; for *Bosman* and the application of the competition rules to sport, see paras 5.156 *et seq.*, below.

account of free movement concerns.[52] However, the approach adopted by the Court of Justice in its recent judgment in *Meca-Medina* to the relationship between the free movement rules and the rules on competition in a sporting context suggests that perhaps the application of the former is of less relevance to the application of the latter.[53] The Commission also considers that cultural benefits are relevant to whether Article 81(1) should be disapplied, having regard to Article 151(4) of the Treaty. That Article provides that the Community, in its action under other provisions of the Treaty, must take cultural aspects into account 'in particular in order to respect and to promote the diversity of its cultures'.[54]

(b) The first condition: economic and other benefits

(i) *Generally*

3.020 **Benefits must be objective.**   The first condition laid down in Article 81(3) is that the agreement must contribute 'to improving the production or distribution of goods or to promoting technical or economic progress'. Improvements falling within the scope of Article 81(3) are not the same thing as the advantages which the parties obtain from their agreement. A relevant 'improvement' must show appreciable objective advantages of such a character as to compensate for the disadvantages caused by the agreement in the field of competition.[55] This fundamental requirement implies that the subjective business reasons for entering into an agreement, however compelling, cannot in themselves fulfil the conditions of Article 81(3). The Commission emphasises this point in its Article 81(3) Guidelines, as it did in the past in individual decisions.[56]

---

[52] Press Release IP/01/314 (6 March 2001).

[53] Case C-519/04P *Meca-Medina and Majien v Commission* (n 27, above): see further para 5.161, below.

[54] The quoted phrase was introduced by the Treaty of Amsterdam. See Parliamentary Answer by Commissioner Monti to Written Question E-1401/99, OJ 2000 C27E/46. As regards the effect of the original Art 128 (introduced by the Maastricht Treaty), see *XXIIIrd Report on Competition Policy* (1993), points 175–177.

[55] *Consten and Grundig v Commission* (n 34, above) at 348 (ECR) and 478 (CMLR); Case T-7/95 *Langnese-Iglo v Commission* [1995] ECR II-1533, [1995] 5 CMLR 602, [1995] All ER (EC) 908, para 180 (appeal dismissed on other grounds Case C-279/95P [1998] ECR I-5609, [1998] 5 CMLR 933); T-9/95 *Schöller v Commission* [1995] ECR II-1611, [1995] 5 CMLR 602, para 142; Case T-65/98 *Van den Bergh Foods v Commission* [2003] ECR II-4653, [2004] 4 CMLR 14, [2005] All ER(EC) 418, para 139 (appeal on other grounds dismissed, Case C-552/03P (n 36, above)).

[56] Art 81(3) Guidelines (n 6, above) para 49; *Quantel International-Continuum/Quantel SA*, OJ 1992 L235/9, [1993] 5 CMLR 497, para 52; *Schöller Lebensmittel*, OJ 1993 L183/1, [1994] 4 CMLR 51, para 117 (appeal dismissed, n 55, above); *Langnese-Iglo*, OJ 1993 L183/19, [1994] 4 CMLR 51, para 118 (appeals dismissed, n 55, above); *Stichting Certificate Kraanverhuurbedrijf and the Federatie van Nederlandse Kraanverhuurbedrijven*, OJ 1995 L312/79, [1996] 4 CMLR 565, para 33; (appeal dismissed, Cases T-213/95 & T-18/96 *SCK and FNK v Commission* [1997] ECR II-1739, [1998] 4 CMLR 259); *Van den Bergh Foods*, OJ 1998 L246/1, [1998] 5 CMLR 530, para 224.

Efficiencies and other benefits.   In its Article 81(3) Guidelines, the Commission   **3.021**
equates 'improving the production or distribution of goods' and 'promoting
technical or economic progress' with 'efficiency gains', and exclusively uses the language of 'efficiencies' when referring to the benefits that might justify the application of Article 81(3).[57] This is a departure from its previous practice. Indeed, the
first exemption decision which clearly applied the language and approach outlined in the Guidelines was the *Telenor/Canal+/Canal Digital* case decided shortly
before the Guidelines were published.[58] As will be seen below, both the Community
Courts and historically the Commission have accepted a more extensive view of
the kind of benefits that are relevant under Article 81(3). The Commission alludes
to this in the Guidelines, indicating that goals pursued by other Treaty provisions
can be taken into account to the extent that they can be subsumed under the four
conditions of Article 81(3), but makes no further reference to such matters.[59]
In *GlaxoSmithKline*, the Court of First Instance referred to efficiency gains in the
context of the first condition of Article 81(3), but described the task of assessment
under Article 81(3) generally as weighing up the advantages expected from implementation of the agreement and the disadvantages which the agreement entails
for the final consumer owing to its impact on competition, 'a balancing exercise
conducted in the light of the general interest appraised at Community level'.[60]

Benefits in various markets.   According to the Court of First Instance,   **3.022**
Article 81(3) envisages that it will apply to agreements which contribute to promoting technical or economic progress but does not require a specific link with
the relevant market in which competition is restricted. When examining the
application of Article 81(3), regard should be had to the advantages arising from
the agreement not only for the relevant market but also, in appropriate cases, for
every other market on which the agreement in question might have beneficial
effects. Indeed, in a more general sense, any potential improvements in the quality
or efficiency of any service that might arise from the existence of that agreement
should be taken into account.[61] In its Article 81(3) Guidelines, the Commission

---

[57] Art 81(3) Guidelines (n 6, above) paras 48 *et seq.*
[58] COMP/38.287 *Telenor/Canal+/Canal Digital*, decn of 29 December 2003, paras 197 *et seq*
and see Note on this decision in (2004) 2 EC Competition Policy Newsletter 56. cf *SAS Maersk
Air*, OJ 2001 L265/15, [2001] 5 CMLR 1119, para 77, where the Commission inserted a reference
to the public interest into a statement adopted from the *Consten and Grundig* judgment: 'in order
for Article 81(1) to be declared inapplicable, the agreements should produce appreciable objective
advantages *in the public interest* of such a character as to compensate for the disadvantages in the field
of competition' [emphasis added].
[59] Art 81(3) Guidelines (n 6, above) para 42.
[60] Case T-168/01 *GlaxoSmithKline Services v Commission* (n 18, above) para 244; and see at
paras 247 *et seq* re efficiency gains.
[61] Case T-86/95 *Compagnie Générale Maritime v Commission* (n 23, above) para 343;
GlaxoSmithKline Services v Commission (n 18, above) para 248. See also Case T-213/00 *CMA
CGM v Commission* [2003] ECR II-2913, [2003] 5 CMLR 268, where the CFI indicated at

takes a contrary position, arguing that in principle the benefits flowing from a restrictive agreement must be assessed within the confines of each relevant market. Further, the efficiencies generated by an agreement in a relevant market must outweigh the anti-competitive effects in that same market.[62]

3.023 **Geographic location of benefits.**   The relevant benefits under Article 81(3) are not limited to those occurring in the Member State or States in which the parties to the agreement are established and may thus include those occurring in other Member States.[63] It is unclear whether a benefit arising exclusively outside the Community could justify the restriction of competition within it.

3.024 **Benefits must result from the agreement.**   The benefits claimed for an agreement must actually result from that agreement.[64] Although this may be clear in some cases, proof of causation may be difficult, for example, where the benefit relates to the overall health of the sector concerned or where it is not based on specific contractual obligations.[65] In its Article 81(3) Guidelines, the Commission argues that the causal link must normally be direct.[66] Moreover, the benefits must be linked to the restrictions in the agreement that attract the prohibition in Article 81(1). Hence in dismissing a challenge to the Commission's refusal of an exemption in *Van den Bergh Foods*,[67] the Court of First Instance noted that the benefits to retailers of having freezer cabinets for the storage of ice cream were the result of HB making those cabinets available free of charge; those benefits accordingly could be achieved without the exclusivity obligation on retailers to use the cabinets to stock only HB ice creams. Further, the Court held that the Commission could validly conclude that it was unlikely, as a matter of

---

paras 225–227 that it is not even necessary to define the relevant market before applying the first three criteria of Art 81(3) (Commission's appeal on other grounds dismissed as inadmissible, Case C-236/03P, order of 28 October 2004).

[62] Art 81(3) Guidelines (n 6, above) para 43. The Commission thus seeks to limit the CFI rulings to situations where markets are related, and involve the same group of consumers. cf Horizontal Cooperation Guidelines (n 7, above) paras 192–198, where the Commission accepts that general environmental benefits can justify the application of Art 81(3).

[63] Case C-360/92P *Publishers Association v Commission* [1995] ECR I-23, [1995] 5 CMLR 33, para 29 (on appeal from Case T-66/89 [1992] ECR II-1995, [1992] 5 CMLR 120).

[64] Case T-19/91 *Vichy v Commission* [1992] ECR II-415, para 93; Case T-29/92 *SPO v Commission* (n 41, above) para 291.

[65] *Vichy v Commission*, above, para 93; Case T-29/92 *SPO v Commission* (n 41, above) para 291. See also *Vichy*, OJ 1991 L75/57, para 25; *Astra*, OJ 1993 L20/23, [1994] 5 CMLR 226, para 19; *Trans-Atlantic Agreement*, OJ 1994 L376/1, paras 475–476; *Far Eastern Freight Conference* (n 2, above) paras 110–111; *Coapi*, OJ 1995 L122/37, [1995] 5 CMLR 468, para 41; *Trans-Atlantic Conference Agreement*, OJ 1999 L95/1, [1999] 4 CMLR 1415, paras 410–413.

[66] Art 81(3) Guidelines (n 6, above) para 54.

[67] Case T-65/98 *Van den Bergh Foods Ltd v Commission* (n 55, above) paras 142–143; upheld by the ECJ, Case C-552/03P *Unilever Bestfoods (Ireland) Ltd v Commission* [2006] ECR I-9091, [2006] 5 CMLR 1460.

commercial reality, that HB would cease to supply cabinets to retailers if it was unable to impose an exclusivity obligation on their use.

Benefits must be sufficient to compensate for the restriction of competition.   There will be no 'improvement' within the meaning of Article 81(3) if the disadvantages of an agreement in terms of competition are greater than its objective benefits.[68] Put another way, the agreement's objective advantages must compensate for the disadvantages caused in the field of competition.[69] Where the anti-competitive effect is the result of the cumulative impact of a network of agreements, it is not necessary to establish whether the claimed benefits compensate for the negative features of each individual agreement considered in isolation: since the adverse impact on competition relates to the situation of the parties to the agreements as a whole, the countervailing benefits should be analysed similarly with regard to the market generally.[70]   **3.025**

Goods and services included.   Although Article 81(3) refers expressly to the production and distribution of goods, without any reference to services, agreements which contribute to improving the provision of services may fulfil the criteria in Article 81(3).[71] The Council and Commission block exemptions in the insurance sector, and for road and inland waterway groupings, liner conferences and liner consortia all assume the inclusion of services within Article 81(3).   **3.026**

Classification of benefits not relevant.   Neither the Commission nor the Community Courts has attached any particular significance to the characterisation of a given benefit as improving the production of goods, improving the distribution of goods, promoting technical progress or promoting economic progress. Indeed, the Court of Justice has referred simply to the 'economic justification for an exemption' and to an agreement benefiting from Article 81(3) because of its 'beneficial economic effects'.[72]   **3.027**

---

[68] *Verband der Sachversicherer v Commission* (n 41, above) para 61.

[69] *Consten and Grundig v Commission* (n 34, above); *Matra Hachette v Commission* (n 23, above) para 135; Case T-7/95 *Langnese-Iglo v Commission* (n 55, above) para 180; T-9/95 *Schöller v Commission* (n 55, above) para 142. See also *Verband der Sachversicherer v Commission* (n 41, above) para 61; and Cases 209/78, etc, *Van Landewyck v Commission* ('*FEDETAB*') [1980] ECR 3125, [1981] 3 CMLR 134, para 185. For a good concise example of this balancing, see *Van den Bergh Foods v Commission* (n 55, above) para 140.

[70] *Shaw v Commission* (n 46, above) para 163 (foreclosure of the market by 'pub tie' agreements) ['the average lessee does enjoy' in the official English translation might better be rendered 'the average of tied lessees enjoy' ('*la moyenne des débitants liés*' in the French original)].

[71] *Verband der Sachversicherer v Commission* (n 41, above) para 58. See also Art 81(3) Guidelines (n 6, above) para 48.

[72] Cases 43 & 63/82 *VBVB and VBBB v Commission* [1984] ECR 19, [1985] 1 CMLR 27, para 52; Case 66/86 *Ahmed Saeed Flugreisen v Zentrale zur Bekämpfung unlauteren Wettbewerbs* [1989] ECR 803, [1990] 4 CMLR 102, para 25.

3.028 **Commission's current approach.** In its Article 81(3) Guidelines, the Commission proposes that the benefits claimed for an agreement (or, in the Commission's terminology, the 'efficiency claims') should be substantiated so that the following can be verified: the nature of the claimed efficiencies; the link between the agreement and the efficiencies; the likelihood and magnitude of each claimed efficiency; and how and when each claimed efficiency would be achieved.[73]

(ii) Cost efficiencies

3.029 **Typical cost efficiencies.** In the Article 81(3) Guidelines, the Commission draws a distinction between cost efficiencies and what it describes as qualitative efficiencies. Its previous practice focused on the latter. The Commission emphasises that the development of new production technologies and methods offer great potential for cost savings. Also, the combination of two existing technologies with complementary strengths may reduce production costs or lead to the production of a higher quality product. Cost efficiencies may result from economies of scale and from economies of scope. Finally, they may derive from better planning of production, reducing the need to hold expensive inventory and allowing for better capacity utilisation.[74]

3.030 **Improvements to the structure of production.** Historically, the Commission extended this analysis to the point at which it accepted a collectively agreed restructuring to eliminate surplus capacity, on the basis that this would enable production to be concentrated on the remaining, more efficient, capacity in the industry.[75] Similarly, an agreement which enabled nuclear power stations to be operated at full capacity and thus permitted the elimination of power stations with higher generation and transmission costs was viewed as objectively beneficial.[76] But a temporary capacity non-utilisation agreement was not viewed as offering such benefits.[77]

3.031 **Stability and flexibility of supply.** The Court of Justice has held that supply contracts for a certain duration may ensure a degree of stability in the supply of the relevant products, allowing the requirements of users to be more fully satisfied,

---

[73] Art 81(3) Guidelines (n 6, above) paras 51–58.
[74] ibid, paras 64–68.
[75] *Stichting Baksteen*, OJ 1994 L131/15, [1995] 4 CMLR 646. See further paras 5.051 *et seq*, below.
[76] *Scottish Nuclear, Nuclear Energy Agreement*, OJ 1991 L178/31 (but exemption limited to 15 years not 30 years requested, as sufficient to give stability to the industry). More recently in *Viking Cable*, OJ 2001 C247/11, the Commission issued a negative clearance-type comfort letter to a JV to build a sub-sea cable for the transmission of high voltage electricity between Norway and Germany thereby removing the need to construct of a new power plant in Germany. See also *Bacton-Zeebrugge Gas Interconnector, XXVth Report on Competition Policy* (1995), p 125, and para 7.113, below.
[77] *Europe Asia Trades Agreement*, OJ 1999 L193/23, [1999] 5 CMLR 1380, para 199.

and may also ensure, where the duration is relatively short, a degree of flexibility enabling production to be adapted to the changing requirements of the market.[78] Accordingly, the enhanced availability of stocks and stability of supply are relevant factors when considering the benefits of distribution arrangements,[79] and many such arrangements have long benefited from a block exemption. Insofar as they came outside the terms of the relevant block exemption, the Commission in its assessment under Regulation 17 sometimes granted individual exemption to exclusive distribution arrangements on this basis, coupled with the increased incentive which they gave to the distributor to devote its efforts to marketing the goods.[80] In emergency situations, such as disruption to the supply of oil, agreements which reduce the inconvenience and share the difficulties are viewed by the Commission as beneficial.[81] Similarly, an agreement which improved electricity generation and coal production was approved as promoting security of energy supply.[82]

Danger of relying on cost efficiencies.   Even before the Article 81(3) Guidelines, **3.032** the Commission had invoked cost savings achieved through economies of scale and scope, and various forms of integration and rationalisation of business activities.[83] However, the Court of Justice has emphasised that consumers will only obtain a fair share of any such benefit, so as to satisfy the second condition under Article 81(3), where the pressure of competition is sufficient to induce the undertakings to pass on some of the cost savings.[84] Care should in any case be taken when equating cost savings with objective benefits where the savings result from conduct which has been found genuinely to restrict competition. Without clear evidence of lower prices being charged, it may well be that in these circumstances any 'efficiencies' represent a subjective gain that is of benefit only to the undertakings concerned. Accordingly, such considerations alone were usually judged

---

[78]   Case 26/76 *Metro v Commission (Metro No. 1)* [1977] ECR 1875, para 43.

[79]   *Vichy v Commission* (n 64, above) para 92.

[80]   *Pasteur Mérieux-Merck*, OJ 1994 L309/1, para 103; *BASF Lacke-Farben and Accinauto*, OJ 1995 L272/16, [1996] 4 CMLR 811, para 96 (appeals on other grounds dismissed, Case T-175/95 [1999] ECR II-1581, [2000] 4 CMLR 33, Case T-176/95, [1999] ECR II-1635, [2000] 4 CMLR 67). See further para 3.036, below; Guidelines on Vertical Restraints (n 8, above) paras 115–166; and para 6.081, below.

[81]   *International Energy Agency*, OJ 1994 L68/35, para 6.

[82]   *Jahrhundertvertrag*, OJ 1993 L50/14, para 31. See also *Scottish Nuclear, Nuclear Energy Agreement* (n 76, above) para 33.

[83]   *Sippa*, OJ 1991 L60/19, [1992] 5 CMLR 528, para 17; *IATA Passenger Agency Programme*, OJ 1991 L258/18, [1992] 5 CMLR 496, para 56; *IATA cargo agency programme*, OJ 1991 L258/29, [1992] 5 CMLR 496, para 50; *Exxon/Shell*, OJ 1994 L144/20, para 69; *BT-MCI*, OJ 1994 L223/36, [1995] 5 CMLR 285, para 53; *LH/SAS*, OJ 1996 L54/28, [1996] 4 CMLR 845, paras 69–72; *Phoenix/Global One*, OJ 1996 L239/57, [1997] 4 CMLR 147, para 57; *Unisource*, OJ 1997 L318/1, [1998] 4 CMLR 105, para 87; *P & O Stena Line*, OJ 1999 L163/61, [1999] 5 CMLR 682, paras 15, 62, 132.

[84]   *Metro No.1* (n 78, above).

insufficient to outweigh the anti-competitive effects of exclusive purchasing or single brandings arrangements made by parties with a market share above the ceiling prescribed by the applicable block exemption, unless very substantial investments were involved.[85] Furthermore, the Commission has indicated that it does not take into account cost savings that arise from output reduction, market-sharing or from the mere exercise of market power.[86]

(iii) Qualitative efficiencies

3.033 **Typical qualitative efficiencies.** In its Article 81(3) Guidelines, the Commission stresses that technical and technological advances form an essential and dynamic part of the economy, generating significant benefits in the form of new or improved goods and services. The combination of production assets may lead to higher quality products or products with novel features; it may enable the more rapid dissemination of technology, or allow new or improved products to be introduced more quickly or at lower cost.[87]

3.034 **New or improved products, and expanded range of products.** The Court of First Instance has recognised that the improvement of products may cause an agreement to come within Article 81(3), even where some of the improvements merely bring together in a single product techniques which already exist, although used in isolation, on different models.[88] The Article 81(3) Guidelines are consistent with numerous decisions by the Commission based on the introduction of new or improved products (whether goods or services),[89] including products with

---

[85] eg *Schöller Lebensmittel* (n 56, above) paras 115–120; *Van den Bergh Foods v Commission* (n 55, above) paras 140–141. See also *Langnese-Iglo* (n 56, above) paras 116–120, where the agreements came within the block exemption but the Commission withdrew that benefit because they did not contribute to improving the distribution of goods. cf *Isab Energy, XXVIth Report on Competition Policy* (1996), p 133 (15-year exemption-type comfort letter for agreements for exclusive supply of electricity from new power station in Sicily in favour of ENEL who would be exclusive purchaser and undertook to buy the entire output). See further paras 6.164 *et seq*, below.

[86] Horizontal Cooperation Guidelines (n 7, above) para 33.

[87] See, generally, Art 81(3) Guidelines (n 6 above) paras 69–72.

[88] *Matra Hachette v Commission* (n 23, above) para 110. See also *Fiat/Hitachi*, OJ 1993 L20/10, [1994] 4 CMLR 571, para 25; *Ford/Volkswagen*, OJ 1993 L20/14, [1993] 5 CMLR 617, paras 24–26.

[89] eg *BT-MCI* (n 83, above); *ACI*, OJ 1994 L224/28, para 48; *Banque Nationale de Paris-Dresdner Bank*, OJ 1996 L188/37, [1996] 5 CMLR 582, para 18; *Atlas*, OJ 1996 L239/23, [1997] 4 CMLR 89, paras 49, 50; *Phoenix/Global One* (n 83, above) para 57; *Unisource* (n 83, above) para 88; *Uniworld*, OJ 1997 L318/24, [1998] 4 CMLR 145, paras 68–72; *TPS*, OJ 1999 L90/6, [1999] 5 CMLR 168, paras 114, 115; *P & O Stena Line* (n 83, above) paras 62, 132; *GEAE/P & W*, OJ 2000 L58/16, [2000] 5 CMLR 49, para 79; *REIMS II*, OJ 1999 L257/17, [2000] 4 CMLR 704, paras 70–76; *British Interactive Broadcasting/Open ('BiB')*, OJ 1999 L312/1, [2000] 4 CMLR 901, para 159; *IFPI 'Simulcasting'*, OJ 2003 L107/58, [2003] 5 CMLR 386, para 87; *UEFA Champions League*, OJ 2003 L291/25, [2004] 4 CMLR 549, paras 144–145; *Reims II renotification*, OJ 2004 L56/76, [2004] 5 CMLR 123 paras 111–117. See also para 7.059, below.

particular advantages in terms of health and safety.[90] It has also recognised that an existing product may depend on continued cooperation.[91] The improvement may take the form of the availability of a wider range of products or, in the case of services, products of a broader scope than previously available.[92] It may also involve the creation of a brand associated with quality and thus attractive to consumers, and the creation of new forms of media rights.[93] The benefit may simply be that the improved product is available more rapidly and efficiently than would otherwise have been possible.[94] It may also imply the making available to consumers in the Community of advanced technology already available elsewhere,[95] or the more rapid dissemination of such technology.[96] A particular example in the services sector is the raising of the professional and ethical standards of football players' agents.[97] In an industry where innovation is an important parameter of competition and where research and development costs are generally funded from income rather than loans, restrictions which optimise income through price discrimination may, exceptionally, benefit from Article 81(3).[98]

New or improved production process. As indicated by the Court of First **3.035**
Instance, the first application of an advanced manufacturing process by a European manufacturer constitutes an optimisation of the manufacturing process within Article 81(3).[99] The Commission's previous decision-making practice recognised the development of new production technologies as a relevant benefit.[100]

---

90 *Pasteur Mérieux-Merck* (n 80, above) para 84 (multivalent vaccines); *Asahi/Saint-Gobain*, OJ 1994 L354/87, para 24 (safer glass in motor cars).

91 *P & I Clubs, IGA*, OJ 1999 L125/12, [1999] 5 CMLR 646, para 106 (pooling agreement to enable provision of higher level of P&I cover).

92 *LH/SAS* (n 83, above) paras 64–68; *Atlas* (n 89, above) para 48; *Phoenix/Global One* (n 83, above) paras 57, 58; *Unisource* (n 83, above) paras 85, 86; *Uniworld* (n 89, above) paras 69, 71; *Telenor/Canal+/Canal Digital* (n 58, above) para 209. See also Case CE/2611/03 *Pool Reinsurance Co Ltd* [2004] UKCLR 893:individual exemption under UK equivalent of Art 81(3) for pool arrangements providing reinsurance for terrorism risk to commercial property in Great Britain, thereby enabling insurance for such risk to become available again (following IRA London bombings).

93 *UEFA Champions League* (n 89, above) paras 154, 160.

94 *Eirpage*, OJ 1991 L306/22, [1993] 4 CMLR 64, para 14; *BT-MCI* (n 83, above) para 53; *Pasteur Mérieux-Merck* (n 80, above) paras 83, 85; *Unisource* (n 83, above) para 85; *Uniworld* (n 89, above) para 69; *UK Network Sharing Agreement* (n 15, above) paras 137–139; *Network Sharing Rahmenvertrag* (n 15, above) para 122, 124, 126, although the CFI annulled part of the decision on the basis that the fact that the service might not be provided at all in the absence of the agreement meant that it fell outside Art 81(1) rather than needing to benefit from Art 81(3): Case T-328/03 *O₂ Germany v Commission* [2006] ECR II-1231, [2006] 5 CMLR 258.

95 *BT-MCI* (n 83, above) para 53. See also *Sicasov*, OJ 1999 L4/27, [1999] 4 CMLR 192, para 74 (dissemination throughout the Community of seeds developed in France).

96 *Olivetti-Digital*, OJ 1994 L309/24, para 30.

97 Case T-193/02 *Piau v Commission* [2005] ECR II-209, [2005] 5 CMLR 42, paras 102–103.

98 *GlaxoSmithKline Services* (n 18, above).

99 *Matra Hachette v Commission* (n 23, above) para 109. See also *Exxon/Shell* (n 83, above).

100 *Pasteur Mérieux-Merck* (n 80, above) para 86.

The Commission has applied Article 81(3) on the basis of the elimination of obsolete production capacity and its replacement with more efficient facilities.[101] It has accepted that the fact that a common tariff structure may remain in force for several years is an incentive for users to invest in up to date, suitable rolling stock.[102]

3.036 **Improved distribution.** The Commission has recognised as an objective benefit the fact that a licensee or distributor concentrates his marketing efforts on a given territory.[103] Similarly, the creation of a network of distributors prepared to make a particular effort to distribute the manufacturer's products may justify requirements relating to minimum stocks and carrying a full range.[104] Exclusivity may lead to intensive marketing of a supplier's services and to the provision of higher quality ancillary services by the distributor.[105] When applying Article 81(3) to exclusive purchase and non-compete restrictions, the Commission has also relied on the incentive for the reseller to devote all his resources to the sale of the supplier's goods, and the consequent durable cooperation between the two.[106] In a duopolistic market, limited term vertical restrictions may promote efforts to enhance distinctive branding and channel penetration.[107] Collective arrangements for the EEA-wide distribution of music rights may significantly reduce transaction costs and facilitate the creation of an EEA market.[108]

3.037 **Creation of infrastructure.** The creation or improvement of the tangible and intangible infrastructure on which the European economy depends is a relevant benefit under Article 81(3). Thus the Commission has previously applied Article 81(3) to the establishment of trade fairs,[109] improvement of

---

[101] *Philips-Osram*, OJ 1994 L378/37, [1996] 4 CMLR 48, para 25.

[102] *Tariff structures in the combined transport of goods*, OJ 1993 L73/38, para 52. But the Commission does not accept that price-fixing can be justified by the encouragement of new investment by the price-fixing undertakings themselves. In its view, elimination of the prospect of gaining market share by charging lower prices reduces the incentive to invest in new equipment and technology: see *Trans-Atlantic Agreement* (n 65, above) paras 475–476, and *Far Eastern Freight Conference* (n 2, above) paras 110–111.

[103] *BT-MCI* (n 83, above) para 53; *Novalliance/Systemform*, OJ 1997 L47/11, [1997] 4 CMLR 876, para 70; *Unisource* (n 83, above) para 89; *Uniworld* (n 89, above) para 75; *Sicasov* (n 95, above) para 74.

[104] *Grundig's EC distribution system*, OJ 1994 L20/15, [1995] 4 CMLR 658, para 36.

[105] *Cégétel* + 4, OJ 1999 L218/14, [2000] 4 CMLR 106, para 58.

[106] *Whitbread* (n 46, above) para 151; *Bass*, OJ 1999 L186/1, [1999] 5 CMLR 831, para 169 (appeal dismissed, Case T-231/99 *Joynson v Commission* [2002] ECR II-2085, [2002] 5 CMLR 123; further appeal dismissed, Case C-204/02P [2003] ECR I-14763); *Scottish & Newcastle*, OJ 1999 L186/28, [1999] 5 CMLR 831, para 138. See para 6.165, below.

[107] *Telenor/Canal+/Canal Digital* (n 58, above) paras 204, 212–213.

[108] *IFPI 'Simulcasting'* (n 89, above) paras 89–92. See para 5.113, below.

[109] *Sippa* (n 83, above) para 18 (the Commission emphasised that the trade fair was aimed at informing consumers about as complete a range as possible of products on the market).

telecommunications,[110] improvements to the generation and distribution of electricity,[111] and the construction and operation of the Channel Tunnel.[112] However, if the parties can establish that the infrastructure would not be built at all in the absence of their cooperation, the agreement may fall outside Article 81(1) entirely.[113]

Satisfaction of subjective consumer desires. The Commission has held that **3.038** Article 81(3) is satisfied by agreements intended to protect the consumer's image of a product in terms of exclusivity and prestige, where this image is valued by the consumer.[114]

(iv) Improvements to market dynamics

Promotion of competition. In the *TPS* decision, the Commission viewed the **3.039** promotion of competition on one market (pay-TV) as justifying the exemption of an agreement that it had held to restrict competition on another market (supply of special interest channels).[115] This approach was upheld by the Court of First Instance in the *Métropole Télévision* judgment, where the Court held that the pro- and anti-competitive effects of an agreement should be balanced within Article 81(3) and not under Article 81(1).[116] The Commission has reflected that statement of principle in *Métropole Télévision* in its Article 81(3) Guidelines but also considers that the benefits produced by an agreement in one market must outweigh the restrictive effects in that same market.[117] It is possible, therefore, in

---

110 *Eirpage* (n 94, above) paras 14 and 15; *Atlas* (n 89, above) para 51. cf *Cégétel+4*, OJ 1999 L218/14 (corr L237/10), [2000] 4 CMLR 106 discussed at paras 7.121 *et seq*, below where the Commission held that the creation of the joint venture did not fall within Art 81(1) though an exclusivity restriction did require the application of Art 81(3).

111 *Scottish Nuclear, Nuclear Energy Agreement* (n 76, above) para 33. See also the more recent cases discussed in paras 7.112 and 7.113, below.

112 *Night Services*, OJ 1994 L259/20, [1995] 5 CMLR 76, para 59; *Eurotunnel*, OJ 1994 L354/66, [1995] 4 CMLR 801, para 97. These decisions were annulled on other grounds in Cases T-374/94, etc, *European Night Services v Commission* (n 42, above); and Cases T-79 & 80/95 *SNCF and British Railways v Commission* [1996] ECR II-1491, [1997] 4 CMLR 334.

113 See *O₂ UK Limited/T-Mobile UK Limited-UK network sharing agreement*, OJ 2003 L200/59, [2004] 4 CMLR 1401, para 152; Case T-328/03 *O₂ (Germany) v Commission* [2006] ECR II-1231, [2006] 5 CMLR 258, paras 47–49 (on appeal from *T-Mobile Deutschland/O₂ Germany – Network Sharing Rahmenvertrag*, OJ 2004 L75/32, [2004] 5 CMLR 762). See further the cases discussed in paras 7.111 *et seq*, below.

114 *Yves Saint Laurent Parfums*, OJ 1992 L12/24, [1993] 4 CMLR 120, paras II.B.2, II.B.3; *Parfums Givenchy system of selective distribution*, OJ 1992 L236/11, [1993] 5 CMLR 579, paras II.B.2, IIB.3. cf *Vichy* (n 64, above) para 27.

115 *TPS* (n 89, above) para 114, where the exclusive rights of a pay-TV joint venture over certain channels produced by its parents, which restricted competition in the market for such channels, were exempted because they facilitated the entry of the JV onto the pay-TV market.

116 Case T-112/99 *M6 v Commission* [2001] ECR II-2459, [2001] 5 CMLR 1236, [2002] All ER (EC) 1, para 74.

117 Article 81(3) Guidelines, OJ 2004 C101/97: Vol II, App C.18, para 43.

the Commission's view for the promotion of competition to be a benefit justifying the application of Article 81(3), even with respect to markets where there is a restriction of competition under Article 81(1).[118]

3.040 **Price transparency.** In the past, the Commission was prepared to accept common tariff structures as justified, *inter alia* because they better enabled users to compare competing products. It invoked this justification even where the agreement included price-fixing on an element that is 'absolutely secondary' to the overall tariff.[119] However, the Court of First Instance has indicated that an increase in market transparency is inherent in any system of recommended rates set and published by an association which represents a significant proportion of undertakings operating in a given market. Demonstrating such an increase is thus not sufficient to qualify for an exemption.[120] The Commission subsequently drew a distinction between transparency as between competitors and transparency as between suppliers and consumers; an increase in price transparency does not benefit consumers when it is accompanied by a lessening of price competition.[121] The Commission also took the view that the enhancement of consumer awareness as to the range of products available on the market was an objective benefit.[122]

3.041 **Price stability.** In the past, the Commission has accepted price stability as a relevant benefit in markets characterised by considerable temporal fluctuations in supply and demand. The main instance where such arguments have been accepted was in relation to the application of Article 81(3) to liner conferences.[123] The preamble to Regulation 4056/86[124] states that liner conferences 'have a stabilizing effect, assuring shippers of reliable services' and that these results cannot be obtained without the cooperation that shipping companies promote within conferences in relation to rates and, where appropriate, availability of capacity or allocation of cargo for shipment, and income. However, stability is a legitimate objective only to the extent that it enables regular and reliable supplies, and

---

[118] *UK Network Sharing Agreement* (n 113, above) paras 122 and 140; *Network Sharing Rahmenvertrag* (n 113, above) paras 110, 112, 127.
[119] *Tariff structures in the combined transport of goods* (n 102, above) paras 50, 53.
[120] *SCK and FNK v Commission* (n 56, above) para 210.
[121] *FETTCSA*, OJ 2000 L268/1, [2000] CMLR 1011, para 169.
[122] *Sippa* (n 83, above) para 18.
[123] A liner conference is a group of shipping companies who agree rates and share capacity on a particular route, see paras 5.033 *et seq*, and Chap 12, below. For the repeal of this block exemption see para 3.083, below. See also *Trans-Atlantic Agreement* (n 65, above) para 467; *Far Eastern Freight Conference*, OJ 1994 L378/17, paras 104, 105 (upheld on appeal Case T-86/95 *Compagnie Générale Maritime v Commission* [2002] ECR II-1011); *Trans-Atlantic Conference Agreement* (n 65, above) para 4.
[124] Reg 4056/86, OJ 1986 L378/4: Vol II, App E.5, repealed by Reg 1419/2006, OJ 2006 L269/1, subject to a two-year transitional period: para 3.083, below).

cannot be invoked as a euphemism for the survival of existing undertakings on the market and the preservation of their profits.[125] This block exemption has recently been repealed since the Commission considers that the conditions in Article 81(3) are no longer met.

Profitability of investments. The Court of First Instance indicated in *Vichy* **3.042** that the profitability of an investment made by a producer in connection with the launch of a product or range of new products may, depending on the specific circumstances of the case in question, be one of the advantages which may be taken into account as regards the contribution made to economic progress.[126] However, the profits made by undertakings belong in principle to their shareholders, and by definition have not been passed on to consumers. Therefore, in principle the profitability of an investment ought to be taken into account only where it serves to incentivise the undertaking concerned to proceed with an investment which gives rise to benefits which themselves are recognised under Article 81(3).[127] Indeed, the Court of First Instance has subsequently rejected an argument that an agreement should be denied exemption because it rendered one of the parties less profitable than its competitors: profitability is relevant only to the extent that it may affect the materialisation of the benefits claimed for the agreement.[128]

(v) General public benefits

Introduction. In the Article 81(3) Guidelines, the Commission accepts that **3.043** goals pursued by other Treaty provisions can be taken into account to the extent that they can be subsumed under the four conditions of Article 81(3).[129] Indeed, the Community Courts and, historically, the Commission have taken a wide variety of public benefits into account when applying Article 81(3).

Environmental protection. In the Horizontal Cooperation Guidelines, the **3.044** Commission indicates that it takes a positive stance on the use of environmental agreements as a policy instrument to achieve the goals enshrined in Article 2 and Article 174 of the EC Treaty as well as in Community environmental action plans.[130] The Guidelines refer to 'net benefits in terms of reduced environmental pressure resulting from the agreement, as compared to the baseline where no action is taken', and give an example of an industry-wide agreement to produce

---

125 *Trans-Atlantic Agreement* (n 65, above) paras 388–392.
126 Case T-19/91 *Vichy v Commission* (n 64, above) para 94.
127 See *UEFA Champions League* (n 89, above) para 150, where the Commission pointed to the fact that the agreement in question reduced financial risk, enabling greater investment and thus a more improved product.
128 *Joynson v Commission* (n 106, above) para 50.
129 Art 81(3) Guidelines (n 117, above) para 42.
130 Horizontal Cooperation Guidelines, OJ 2001 C 3/2: Vol II, App C.12, para 192.

only energy-efficient washing machines, which reduces emissions from electricity generation.[131] The Commission has relied on a reduction in air pollution and energy use, as well as the prospect of the development of lead-free materials.[132] It has also invoked a reduction in the use of raw materials and the volume of waste products, together with the environmental benefits of eliminating the transport of a particular hazardous substance.[133] Similarly, the development of a product with reduced or eliminated environmentally hazardous materials, low emissions and fuel consumption, and increased recyclability was viewed as beneficial.[134] The Commission has approved cooperation in the insurance sector which was expected to lead to the development of industrial production techniques less hazardous to the environment.[135] The Commission applies a similar policy with respect to voluntary agreements between government and industry, and measures of self-regulation.[136]

3.045 **Provision of employment.** According to the Court of Justice, the provision of employment comes within the framework of Article 81(3) in that it improves the general conditions of production, especially when market conditions are unfavourable.[137] The Commission has previously relied on the fact that coordinated closures of production capacity allow the restructuring of an industry to take place in acceptable social conditions, including the redeployment of employees.[138]

3.046 **Sport.** In the *Laurent Piau* case concerning the FIFA rules governing football players' agents, the Commission expressed the view that the protection of players, the promotion of ethical standards in sport, the maintenance of a balance between clubs, the preservation of a certain equality of chance and unpredictability of results, and encouragement of the recruitment and training of young players, may all justify an exemption under Article 81(3).[139] However, the Commission's

---

131 Horizontal Cooperation Guidelines, paras 192–198. The example is based on *CECED*, OJ 2000 L187/47, [2000] 5 CMLR 635. See also *XXVIIIth Report on Competition Policy* (1998), point 129 that 'When the Commission examines individual cases, it weighs up the restrictions of competition arising out of an agreement against the environmental objectives of the agreement.'

132 *Philips-Osram* (n 101, above) paras 25, 27; and see *EACEM, XXVIIIth Report on Competition Policy* (1998), p 152 (comfort letter).

133 *Exxon/Shell* (n 83, above) paras 67, 69.

134 *Ford/Volkswagen* (n 88, above) para 26.

135 *Assurpol*, OJ 1992 L37/16, [1993] 4 CMLR 338, para 38.

136 *XXVth Report on Competition Policy* (1995), points 83–85. See also the cases concerning recycling of packaging where the Commission granted negative clearance rather than exemption to some aspects of the agreements: paras 6.196 *et seq*, below.

137 *Metro No. 1* (n 78, above) para 43; Case 42/84 *Remia v Commission* [1985] ECR 2545, [1987] 1 CMLR 1, para 42.

138 *Stichting Baksteen* (n 75, above) para 27. See also *Ford/Volkswagen* (n 88, above).

139 COMP/37.124 *Laurent Piau v FIFA*, decn of 15 April 2002, para 29; see also the Opinion of AG Lenz in Case C-415/93 *Union Royale des Sociétés de Football Association v Bosman* [1995] ECR I-4921, [1996] 1 CMLR 645, [1996] All ER (EC) 97, para 278.

actual decision granting an exemption to the modified rules was based on the protection of the economic interests of players, and not some special exception based on the specific nature of sport, as the Court of First Instance pointed out when dismissing the appeal.[140] In *UEFA Champions League*, the Commission highlighted the benefits for smaller football clubs of the agreement for collective selling of media rights, but declined formally to express a view on arguments that the agreement would promote financial solidarity between football clubs and thus stimulate the development of the sport; indeed, the original arrangements were regarded by the Commission as too anti-competitive to qualify for exemption.[141] However, more recently in *Meca-Medina*, the Court of Justice held that anti-doping rules would fall outside Article 81(1) altogether provided that they were a proportionate measure containing only such restrictions as are inherent in achieving the legitimate objective of ensuring that competitive sport is conducted fairly, including safeguarding equal chances for athletes, athletes' health, the integrity and objectivity of competitive sport and ethical values in sport.[142] If the rules were not proportionate, whether on account of the standard imposed or the severity of the penalty for infringement, they would come within Article 81(1), and by implication there would be no scope for the application of Article 81(3).

General public interest. In *Métropole Télévision v Commission*, the Court of   **3.047**
First Instance annulled the exemption granted by the Commission to statutes and regulations of the European Broadcasting Union ('EBU'), which provided for considerable coordination between the EBU members, including the acquisition of broadcasting rights to sporting events, and the exchange of broadcasts to sports and cultural events through the Eurovision system. One ground of the Commission's decision was the public mission of the EBU members 'to provide varied programming including cultural, educational, scientific and minority programmes without any commercial appeal and to cover the entire national population irrespective of the costs'.[143] On appeal, the Court held that such factors cannot constitute a criterion for the application of Article 81(3) in the absence of other justification.[144] Although considerations of that kind connected with the pursuit of the public interest are relevant, it was necessary to demonstrate that such considerations required exclusivity of rights to transmit sports events, and that exclusivity was 'indispensable' in economic terms in order for the EBU

---

140 Case T-193/02 *Piau v Commission* [2005] ECR II-209, [2005] 5 CMLR 42, para 105 (further appeal to the ECJ dismissed as manifestly unfounded: Case C-171/05P, [2006] ECR I-37). See further para 5.163, below.

141 *UEFA Champions League* (n 89, above) paras 163–167: see further para 5.117, below.

142 Case C-519/04P *Meca-Medina and Majeen v Commission* [2006] 5 CMLR 1023, [2006] All ER (EC) 1057. See further para 5.161, below.

143 *EBU/Eurovision System*, OJ 1993 L179/23, [1995] 4 CMLR 56, para 5.

144 Cases T-528/93, etc, *Métropole Télévision v Commission* [1996] ECR II-649, [1996] 5 CMLR 386, paras 116–123.

members to obtain a fair return on their investments. Moreover, exemption was inappropriate when the rules were not amenable to uniform, non-discriminatory application. This judgment is consistent with that of the Court of Justice in *Binon v AMP*, where it was held that maintaining the availability to readers of a wide selection of newspapers and periodicals is a factor that may be taken into account under Article 81(3).[145] The Commission has stated that cultural benefits may justify exemption.[146] It has exempted an agreement which would prevent damage to the image of institutions participating in the administration of justice.[147] And the Commission has highlighted the benefits of an agreement for rural areas.[148] The correct approach appears to be that such considerations can come within the first condition of Article 81(3), which is therefore not strictly confined to economic 'efficiencies', but it is necessary to show that the achievement of those benefits is indeed dependent upon the restriction at issue.

3.048 **General Community interest.** In *Ford/Volkswagen*, the Commission indicated that the motor vehicle manufacturing project in that case was the largest ever foreign investment in Portugal and would create many thousands of jobs and attract additional investment. According to the Commission, it therefore contributed to the promotion of the harmonious development of the Community and the reduction of regional disparities, one of the basic aims of the Treaty. It also furthered European market integration by linking Portugal more closely to the Community through one of its important industries. The Commission indicated that this 'would not be enough to make an exemption possible unless the conditions of Article [81(3)] were fulfilled, but it is an element that the Commission has taken into account'.[149] This reliance on social factors has been strongly criticised as diluting antitrust principles;[150] and in its judgment dismissing the appeal against the decision, the Court of First Instance declined to review this part of the Commission's reasoning on the basis that it had not affected the outcome of the case.[151] In the post-Modernisation environment, it is questionable whether the reduction of regional disparities within the Community could legitimately be invoked by a NCA or court of the 'beneficiary' Member State in order to justify the restriction of competition in other Member States.

---

[145] Case 243/83 *Binon v AMP* [1985] ECR 2015, [1985] 3 CMLR 800, para 46. See also *Newspaper distribution contracts in Belgium-AMP, XXIXth Report on Competition Policy* (1999), p 161.

[146] See para 3.019, above.

[147] *EPI code of conduct*, OJ 1999 L106/14, [1999] 5 CMLR 540, para 46.

[148] *UK Network Sharing Agreement* (n 113, above) para 141.

[149] *Ford/Volkswagen*, OJ 1993 L20/14, [1993] 5 CMLR 617, para 36.

[150] Amato, *Antitrust and the Bounds of Power* (1997), pp 59–62.

[151] Case T-17/93 *Matra Hachette v Commission* [1994] ECR II-595, para 139.

(vi) Absence of benefit

No benefit from certain hard-core restrictions. The Court of Justice has **3.049**
ruled that an agreement which has as its sole purpose the prevention of sales of
certain products in a Member State does not fulfil the conditions laid down in
Article 81(3) and in particular does not contribute to improving the production
or distribution of the products in question.[152] In exceptional circumstances, the
Commission has accepted an absolute export ban imposed on the distributor
or licensee, provided that purchasers within the relevant territory are themselves
able to export.[153] Similar positions of principle have been adopted in Commission
decisions, for example in relation to resale price maintenance.[154]

No benefit from duplication of action by public authorities. It is in principle the **3.050**
task of public authorities and not of private bodies to ensure that statutory requirements are complied with. Therefore a scheme set up by private agreement may not
add sufficient value to fulfil the criteria in Article 81(3). An exception to this rule may
be allowed where the public authorities have, of their own will, decided to entrust the
monitoring of compliance with statutory requirements to a private body.[155]

No benefit from counteracting unfavourable market regulation. It is unac- **3.051**
ceptable for suppliers to counteract legislation which they consider excessively
favourable to users by entering into restrictive arrangements intended to offset the
advantages granted to users.[156]

(c) The second condition: fair share of benefits for consumers

Generally. The second condition for the application of Article 81(3) is that the **3.052**
agreement must allow consumers a fair share of the resulting objective benefit
described in the previous Section. The agreement must be appraised as objectively

---

[152] Case 28/77 *Tepea v Commission* [1978] ECR 1391, [1978] 3 CMLR 392, para 57; Case 35/83 *BAT v Commission* [1985] ECR 363, [1985] 2 CMLR 470, paras 39, 41.

[153] *Sicasov* (n 95, above) para 74.

[154] See, *eg Hennessy-Henkell*, OJ 1980 L383/11, [1981] 1 CMLR 601; *Volkswagen*, OJ 2001 L262/14, [2001] 5 CMLR 1309, para 95 (annulled on other grounds, Case T-208/01 *Volkswagen v Commission* [2003] ECR II-5141, [2004] 4 CMLR 727, [2004] All ER (EC) 674) (further appeal on other grounds dismissed, Case C-74/04P *Commission v Volkswagen* [2006] ECR I-6585). See also *French Beef*, OJ 2003 L209/12, [2003] 5 CMLR 891, para 130, concerning an agreement between farmers and slaughterhouses to set minimum prices because of crisis caused by BSE ('mad cow disease'): the Commission noted that even if application had been made for exemption, the first two conditions of Art 81(3) were not satisfied.

[155] Cases T-213/95 & T-18/96 *SCK and FNK v Commission* [1997] ECR II-1739, [1998] 4 CMLR 259, para 194. See also Case T-30/89 *Hilti v Commission* [1991] ECR II-1439, [1992] 4 CMLR 16, para 118, with respect to Art 82 (appeal on other grounds dismissed, Case C-53/92P [1994] ECR I-667).

[156] Case T-29/92 *SPO v Commission* [1995] ECR II-289, para 256 (appeal on other grounds dismissed: Case C-137/95P *SPO v Commission* [1996] ECR II-1611); Cases T-49/02, etc, *Brasserie Nationale v Commission* [2005] ECR II-3033, [2006] 4 CMLR 266, para 81.

as possible, without in any way considering its appropriateness by reference to other technically possible or economically viable choices. The issue of whether the same benefits can be achieved by other means is part of the third condition for exemption, relating to the indispensability of the restrictions.[157]

3.053 **'Consumers' includes all users.**   The term 'consumers' is not limited to private individuals in the sense of consumer protection legislation. It includes all users of the goods or services concerned, whether undertakings or private individuals, and at whatever stage of the production and distribution chain. For example, contract awarders faced with a bid-rigging agreement between tenderers are consumers within the meaning of Article 81(3).[158] This broad view of consumers appears to imply that undertakings do not need to establish that the benefits of their agreement will be passed all the way down to the final consumer, and it is reflected by the Commission in its Article 81(3) Guidelines.[159]

3.054 **Carrying out the assessment.**   In its Article 81(3) Guidelines, the Commission advances a number of propositions about how, in its view, the assessment should be carried out. First, the net effect of the agreement must be neutral from the point of view of those consumers directly or most likely to be affected by the agreement, with this balancing taking place within each relevant market.[160] Here, the Commission appears to go beyond the express wording of Article 81(3), which requires only that the objective benefits of an agreement outweigh the restriction of competition, and that consumers receive a fair share of those benefits. As described above, the Commission also does not explain how its position can be reconciled with the Court of Justice's view that benefits in all affected markets may be taken into account, and that consideration may be given to non-market benefits, such as the environment and culture. Secondly, the Commission asserts that the value of a gain for consumers in the future has less value than a present gain for consumers, and indicates that a discount rate should be applied, reflecting the rate of inflation and lost interest.[161] This approach may have some merit where the claimed benefits for consumers are future price reductions achieved through cost savings, but it is difficult to apply in other contexts. Thirdly, the Commission states that the second condition of Article 81(3) incorporates a sliding scale. If the

---

[157] *Matra Hachette v Commission* (n 151, above) para 122.

[158] Case T-29/92 *SPO v Commission* (n 156, above) para 300.

[159] Art 81(3) Guidelines, OJ 2004 C101/97: Vol II, App C.18, para 84.

[160] ibid, paras 85–86, and fn 81 in particular. The Commission cites Cases 56 & 58/64 *Consten and Grundig v Commission* [1966] ECR 299, [1966] CMLR 418, where the ECJ stated that the improvement within the meaning of the first condition of Art 81(3) must show appreciable objective advantages of such a character to compensate for the disadvantages which they cause in the field of competition. However, the ECJ did not specify that there must be net advantages at the level of consumers, nor that the consumers in each affected market must be assessed in isolation.

[161] Art 81(3) Guidelines, para 88.

restrictive effects of an agreement are relatively limited and the efficiencies are substantial, it is likely that a fair share of the cost savings will be passed on to consumers: a detailed analysis is normally not necessary. If the restrictive effects are substantial and the cost savings are relatively insignificant, it is very unlikely that the second condition of Article 81(3) will be fulfilled. If an agreement has both substantial anti-competitive effects and substantial pro-competitive effects, a careful analysis is required.[162] This third proposition of the Commission appears to be a reasonable approach to the consumer pass-on issue.

Cost efficiencies.   Benefits which are essentially internal to the operations of **3.055** the parties to the agreement, such as rationalisation of production or distribution, or economies of scale, must be passed on to consumers in the form of lower prices. Whether the benefits are passed on will depend on the pressure of competition.[163] In its Article 81(3) Guidelines, the Commission stresses the need to take into account the characteristics and structure of the market, the nature and magnitude of the efficiency gains, the elasticity of demand and the magnitude of the restriction of competition.[164] The Commission offers interesting insights into this assessment. If undertakings compete mainly on price and are not subject to significant capacity constraints, pass-on may occur relatively quickly. If competition is mainly on capacity and capacity adaptations occur with a certain time lag, pass-on will be slower. Pass-on is also likely to be slower when the market structure is conducive to tacit collusion. If competitors are likely to retaliate against an increase in output by one or more parties to the agreement, the incentive to increase output may be tempered, unless the competitive advantage conferred by the efficiencies is such that the undertakings concerned have an incentive to break away from the common policy adopted on the market by the members of the oligopoly. In other words, the efficiencies generated by the agreement may turn the undertakings concerned into so-called 'mavericks'. In previous decisions, the Commission has rejected the possibility that economies of scale would be passed on where the supplier concerned enjoyed a dominant position,[165] or where

---

[162] ibid, paras 90–92. See, eg COMP/38.287 *Telenor/Canal +/Canal Digital*, decn of 29 December 2003, para 231, where the Commission indicated merely that certain cost efficiencies were 'not unlikely' to translate into price advantages for consumers in the face of the tight competition existing in the market (albeit a market characterized by duopoly). See also the Note on that decision in the (2004) 2 EC Competition Policy Newsletter 56. See also COMP/38.479 *British Airways/Iberia/GB Airways*, decn of 10 December 2003, para 47: although there were at the time only a few indications that the various cost and qualitative efficiencies claimed for the agreement had indeed been passed on to consumers, there was no reason to believe that they would not be on those routes where the parties were subject to sufficient competitive constraints from actual and/or potential competitors.

[163] *Metro No. 1* (n 78, above) para 48.

[164] Art 81(3) Guidelines (n 159, above) paras 95–101.

[165] *Van den Bergh Foods*, OJ 1998 L246/1, [1998] 5 CMLR 530, para 240; appeals to CFI and ECJ dismissed, Case T-65/98 *Van den Bergh Foods v Commission* [2003] ECR II-4653, [2004] 4

competition was limited by parallel agreements.[166] Conversely, it has accepted that cost savings would benefit consumers where a detailed analysis led it to conclude that a joint venture would not result in price parallelism in the context of a duopolistic market structure.[167] In its last decision granting individual exemption under Article 81(3) prior to the introduction of the Modernisation regime, concerning the *Air France/Alitalia* strategic alliance,[168] the Commission found that it was uncertain that the cost efficiencies resulting from the alliance would be passed on to consumers in the absence of sufficient competition on the various affected routes, and imposed detailed commitments for release of slots at the relevant airports to facilitate such competition; on that basis, it was assumed that the requisite pass-on would occur.

3.056 Qualitative and other benefits. Some kinds of objective benefits recognised under Article 81(3) are directly beneficial to consumers. In these circumstances, the examination of whether consumers receive a 'fair share' of the benefits will ordinarily duplicate the analysis of whether they constitute an 'improvement' within the meaning of the first condition in Article 81(3) in that they sufficiently compensate for the restriction of competition. The decision-maker must simply evaluate the extent of the benefit and compare it with the importance of the restriction of competition.[169] As the Commission indicates in its Article 81(3) Guidelines, any such assessment necessarily requires value judgement.[170] Examples of benefits where this approach has been followed include new or improved products and expanded ranges of products and services,[171] improved frequency

---

CMLR 14, [2005] All ER(EC) 418; Case C-552/03P *Unilever Bestfoods v Commission* [2006] ECR I-9091, [2006] 5 CMLR 1460.

[166] *Schöller Lebensmittel*, OJ 1993 L183/1, [1994] 4 CMLR 51, para 122 (appeal dismissed T-9/95 *Schöller v Commission* [1995] ECR II-1611, [1995] 5 CMLR 602); *Langnese-Iglo*, OJ 1993 L183/19, [1994] 4 CMLR 51, para 123 (appeals dismissed Case T-7/95 *Langnese-Iglo v Commission* [1995 ECR II-1533, [1995] 5 CMLR 602, [1995] All ER (EC) 908 and Case C-279/95P [1998] ECR I-5609, [1998] 5 CMLR 933).

[167] *P & O Stena Line*, OJ 1999 L163/61, [1999] 5 CMLR 682, paras 63, 69–127.

[168] COMP/38.284 *Air France/Alitalia*, 7 April 2004, [2005] 5 CMLR 1504, paras 137, 160 *et seq*; on appeal Case T-300/04 *EasyJet v Commission*, not yet decided. See further paras 7.134 *et seq*, below.

[169] See Case 26/76 *Metro v Commission* ('*Metro No. 1*') [1977] ECR 1875, [1978] 2 CMLR 1, para 48. In *BT-MCI*, OJ 1994 L223/36, [1995] 5 CMLR 285, para 55, the Commission remarked in particular that the new services to be provided would enable large companies to 'operate more effectively on a global scale and to better compete with their global as well as Community and EEA competitors'. In *Assurpol* (n 135, above) para 39, the Commission emphasised the benefits of the agreement for small and medium-sized enterprises.

[170] Art 81(3) Guidelines (n 159, above) para 103.

[171] *BT-MCI* (n 169, above) para 55; *ACI*, OJ 1994 L224/28, para 52; *Pasteur Mérieux-Merck*, OJ 1994 L309/1, paras 89, 90; *Asahi/Saint-Gobain*, OJ 1994 L354/87, para 26; *LH/SAS*, OJ 1996 L54/28, [1996] 4 CMLR 845, paras 69–72; *Banque Nationale de Paris–Dresdner Bank*, OJ 1996 L188/37, [1996] 5 CMLR 582, para 19; *Atlas*, OJ 1996 L239/23, [1997] 4 CMLR 89, paras 53–54; *Phoenix/Global One*, OJ 1996 L239/57, [1997] 4 CMLR 147, para 60; *Unisource*, OJ 1997 L318/1, [1998] 4 CMLR 105, para 90; *Uniworld*, OJ 1997 L318/24, [1998] 4 CMLR 145,

of services,[172] stability and flexibility of supply,[173] environmental protection,[174] the satisfaction of subjective consumer desires,[175] and the avoidance of confusion in the mind of the public.[176] This would appear to apply also where the benefit identified is the promotion of competition on another market.[177] However, undertakings will always have to show that any alleged benefits for consumers are not outweighed by disadvantages.[178] Where the Commission has exempted an agreement on the basis that it promotes competition in a market where the Commission had earlier – in its Article 81(1) analysis – detected an aspect of competition which was restricted, the Commission has no difficulty in concluding that consumers will benefit appropriately.[179]

Disadvantages for consumers.   Some agreements will have clear disadvantages **3.057** for consumers and these may outweigh any benefits. For example, an agreement may restrict the consumer's choice of products,[180] or prevent efficient undertakings

---

para 76; *Sicasov* (n 95, above) para 75; *TPS*, OJ 1999 L90/6, [1999] 5 CMLR 168, para 118, appeal dismissed, *M6 v Commission* (n 116, above) para 144; *P & I Clubs, IGA*, OJ 1999 L125/12, [1999] 5 CMLR 646, para 107; *P & O Stena Line* (n 167, above) paras 63, 133; *GEAE/P & W*, OJ 2000 L58/16, [2000] 5 CMLR 49; *AuA/LH*, OJ 2002 L242/25, [2003] 4 CMLR 252, para 90. In *P & I Clubs*, the Commission referred not only to the benefits for immediate consumers (shipowners enjoying insurance cover) but also (at para 108) for downstream consumers (the customers of the shipowner that would then be able to obtain compensation when needed). Similarly, in *GEAE/P & W*, the Commission referred to both airframe manufacturers and airlines in the context of a JV to develop a new engine (para 81). See also the Art 81(3) Guidelines, para 104.

172 *P&O Stena Line* (n 167, above) paras 62, 132.

173 *Metro No. 1* (n 169, above) para 48. See also *Sicasov* (n 95, above) para 75; *Whitbread*, OJ 1999 L88/26, [1999] 5 CMLR 118, para 151 (appeal dismissed, Case T-131/99 *Shaw v Commission* [2002] ECR II-2023, [2002] 5 CMLR 81).

174 *CECED* (n 131, above) paras 47–57; *Exxon/Shell*, OJ 1994 L144/20, para 71; *Philips-Osram* (n 101, above) para 27. In *Exxon/Shell*, the Commission felt it necessary to indicate that the environmental advantages in question 'will be perceived as beneficial by many consumers at a time when the limitation of natural resources and threats to the environment are of increasing public concern'. In *CECED*, the Commission considered separately the individual economic benefits for consumers and the collective environmental benefits: it placed specific numerical value on the environmental benefits, and compared this with the aggregate anticipated purchase costs that would result for consumers.

175 *Yves Saint Laurent Parfums* (n 114, above) para II.B.3; *Parfums Givenchy* (n 114, above) para II.B.3.

176 *EPI code of conduct* (n 147, above) para 46.

177 *TPS* (n 171, above) para 119. In this case, the Commission was able to give details of the effect that the entry of a new operator onto the market had on prices over an 18-month period. But the Commission must be entitled to assume that consumers will benefit from increased competition, and this data should therefore be viewed as evidence of the extent of the benefit.

178 Case T-19/91 *Vichy v Commission* [1992] ECR II-415, para 98; Case T-29/92 *SPO v Commission* (n 156, above) paras 295–300.

179 *UK Network Sharing Agreement* (n 113, above) para 142; *Network Sharing Rahmenvertrag* (n 113, above) para 129.

180 *Cewal*, OJ 1993 L34/20, [1995] 5 CMLR 198, para 44; *Schöller Lebensmittel* (n 166, above) para 123; *Langnese-Iglo* (n 166, above) para 124; *Van den Bergh Foods* (n 165, above) para 239 (the CFI did not address this issue on the appeal, ibid).

from passing on cost savings to consumers.[181] Price-fixing by competitors will maintain prices above market rates,[182] as will limits on capacity utilisation.[183] The Commission has historically viewed absolute export bans imposed on distributors or licensees as preventing consumers from taking advantage of differences in price between Member States and restricting 'the right of consumers to buy goods of their choice anywhere they want in the single market', thus precluding exemption.[184] In exceptional circumstances, the Commission has accepted an absolute export ban imposed on the distributor or licensee, provided that its customers within the relevant territory are themselves free to export.[185] However, the fact that there are some consumers who may not derive a benefit from the restrictive agreement, or are indeed disadvantaged as a result, does not preclude the second condition from being fulfilled: it is the beneficial nature of the effect on consumers generally in the relevant markets that has to be considered.[186]

3.058 **Views of consumers.** Historically, the Commission has been willing to take into consideration views expressed directly by consumers or consumer associations.[187] Indeed, the Court of First Instance has even indicated that the Commission was entitled to infer from the large number of complaints from users that a particular

---

[181] *Far Eastern Freight Conference* (n 123, above) para 116.

[182] ibid, para 115; *Coapi*, OJ 1995 L122/37, [1995] 5 CMLR 468, para 43; *SCK and FNK* (n 155, above) para 34; *Trans-Atlantic Conference Agreement*, OJ 1999 L95/1, [1999] 4 CMLR 1415, para 414 (upheld as regards the application of Art 81 on appeal: Cases T-191/98, etc, *Atlantic Container v Commission* [2003] ECR II-3275, [2005] 4 CMLR 1283). In *REIMS II*, OJ 1999 L257/17, [2000] 4 CMLR 704, paras 77–85, the Commission accepted that a price-fixing agreement would raise prices for some consumers but nonetheless considered that, in the circumstances of the case, consumers would receive a 'fair' share of the benefits of an agreement that offered considerable improvements in cross-border mail services.

[183] *Trans-Atlantic Agreement*, OJ 1994 L376/1, para 412 (the CFI did not address this issue in dismissing the appeal, Case T-395/94 *Atlantic Container Line v Commission* ('TAA') [2002] ECR II-875, [2002] 4 CMLR 1008, [2002] All ER (EC) 684); *Europe Asia Trades Agreement*, OJ 1999 L193/23, [1999] 5 CMLR 1380, paras 208–209.

[184] *VW*, OJ 1998 L124/60, [1998] 5 CMLR 33, para 189; appeal dismissed, Case T-62/98 *Volkswagen v Commission* [2000] ECR II-2707, [2000] 5 CMLR 853; appeal and cross appeal on other grounds dismissed, Case C-338/00P, [2003] ECR I-9189, [2004] 4 CMLR 351. See also *BASF Lacke-Farben and Accinauto*, OJ 1995 L272/16, [1996] 4 CMLR 811, para 99 (appeals on other grounds dismissed, Case T-175/95 *BASF v Commission* [1999] ECR II-1581, [2000] 4 CMLR 33, Case T-176/95 *Accinauto v Commission* [1999] ECR II-1635, [2000] 4 CMLR 67); *Opel*, OJ 2001 L59/1, para 160 (appeals on other grounds dismissed, Case T-368/00 *General Motors Nederland and Opel Nederland v Commission* [2003] ECR II-4491, [2004] 4 CMLR 1302, [2004] All ER (EC) 674; Case C-551/03P *General Motors v Commission* [2006] ECR I-3173, [2006] 5 CMLR 9); *Novalliance/Systemform*, OJ 1997 L47/11, [1997] 4 CMLR 876, para 74; COMP/37.975 *Yamaha*, decn of 16 July 2003, para 178; COMP/37.980 *Souris-Topps*, 26 May 2004, [2006] 4 CMLR 1713, para 142.

[185] *Sicasov*, OJ 1999 L4/27, [1999] 4 CMLR 192, para 75.

[186] Case C-238/05 *Asnef-Equifax v Ausbanc* [2006] ECR I-11125, [2007] 4 CMLR 224, paras 66–71.

[187] eg *Trans-Atlantic Agreement* (n 183, above) paras 413, 479, 480; *Far Eastern Freight Conference* (n 123, above) para 117; *Europe Asia Trades Agreement* (n 183, above) paras 143–147, 213; *GEAE/P & W* (n 171, above) para 81.

agreement did not take fair account of their interests.[188] However, it would seem inappropriate to draw conclusions from the mere number of complaints against an agreement without reference to the merits of those complaints.

(d) The third condition: indispensability of restrictions

Generally. The third condition is that the agreement does not impose on the **3.059** undertakings concerned restrictions which are not indispensable to the attainment of the benefits concerned. This requirement goes beyond the establishment of a simple causal link between the restrictive provisions of an agreement and the benefits claimed.[189] The parties to the agreement must show that the benefits claimed for it cannot be attained by other less restrictive means. The mere fact that the advantages in question are 'underwritten' by the agreement is not enough.[190] In its Article 81(3) Guidelines, the Commission stresses that the efficiencies claimed for an agreement must be specific to that agreement in the sense that there are no other economically practicable and less restrictive means of achieving the efficiencies; the Commission will not second guess the business judgement of the parties and will intervene only where it is reasonably clear that there are realistic and attainable alternatives.[191]

Establishing indispensability. Where the 'break-even' point for the investment **3.060** necessary to enter the European market for a particular product, and the anticipated sales, are such that undertakings acting alone would only have been able to penetrate the market at a loss, it is *ipso facto* established that the restriction of competition implicit in a joint venture between those undertakings is indispensable in order to attain the improved production process and improved product that would result from the venture.[192] In contrast, bid-rigging is clearly not

---

188 Case T-86/95 *Compagnie Générale Maritime v Commission* [2002] ECR II-1011, [2002] 4 CMLR 1115, para 371 (on appeal from *Far Eastern Freight Conference* (n 123, above)).

189 In the absence of such a relationship, no 'improvement' would result from the agreement within the meaning of the first condition under Art 81(3): para 3.024, above.

190 Case 71/74 *Frubo v Commission* [1975] ECR 563, [1975] 2 CMLR 123, para 42. See also *Trans-Atlantic Conference Agreement* (n 182, above) para 433; *Visa International - Multilateral Interchange Fee*, OJ 2002 L318/17, [2003] 4 CMLR 283, para 98, where the Commission insisted that the restrictions must be indispensable for the benefits as such, and not merely for the contractual system said to give rise to those benefits.

191 Art 81(3) Guidelines (n 159, above) para 75. The Commission goes on to explain at para 76 that it is particularly relevant to examine whether the parties could have achieved the efficiencies by means of another less restrictive type of agreement and, if so, when they would likely be able to obtain the efficiencies. It may also be necessary to examine whether the parties could have achieved the efficiencies on their own; eg for the claimed efficiencies of a JV in the form of cost reductions resulting from economies of scale or scope, the undertakings must explain and substantiate why these would not be likely to be attained through internal growth and price competition.

192 *Matra Hachette v Commission* (n 151, above) para 138. The CFI was not asked to rule whether in these circumstances the joint venture fell within Art 81(1).

indispensable to ensure the comparability of tenders.[193] With respect to individual restrictions, the Commission indicates in its Article 81(3) Guidelines that a restriction is indispensable if its absence would eliminate or significantly reduce the efficiencies that follow from the agreement or make it significantly less likely that they will materialise; the assessment of alternative solutions must take into account the actual and potential improvement in the field of competition by the elimination of a particular restriction or the application of a less restrictive alternative; and the more restrictive the restraint the stricter the test under the third condition.[194] In particular circumstances, market share may be relevant to the analysis. Thus a cooperative of cheese producers which produced rennet for use in cheese production, and which enjoyed a near monopoly of the rennet market, could not justify the imposition of an obligation on its members to purchase 100 per cent of their rennet requirements by invoking the undoubted benefits generated by the cooperative.[195] The indispensability of a restriction may apply for a limited time period; for example, during a start-up phase or even where an industry needs a transitional period to make changes needed to operate in a more competitive manner.[196]

3.061 **Absolute territorial protection.**   The Court of Justice held in *Nungesser* that absolute territorial protection for seeds for the production of maize, 'an important product for human and animal foodstuffs', manifestly went beyond what was indispensable for the improvement of production or distribution or the promotion

---

[193] Case T-29/92 *SPO v Commission* (n 156, above) para 311.

[194] Art 81(3) Guidelines, para 79. See also *Compagnie Générale Maritime v Commission* (n 188, above) paras 392–395.

[195] Case 61/80 *Coöperatieve Stremselen Kleurselfabriek v Commission* [1981] ECR 851, [1982] 1 CMLR 240, para 18. cf Case CE/2611/03 *Pool Reinsurance Co Ltd* [2004] UKCLR 893: exclusivity obligations on insurers of commercial property using the pooled reinsurance scheme, requiring them to place reinsurance of all terrorism cover for all their commercial property in Great Britain with the pool; individual exemption granted by UK Office of Fair Trading under the UK equivalent of Art 81(3) since the reinsurance was provided on standard terms and the obligations were necessary to prevent adverse selection. See also *Competition Authority v Beef Industry Development Society Ltd* [2006] IEHC 294, paras 133–134, where the Irish High Court held that the indispensability condition was satisfied by a rationalisation scheme to reduce overcapacity in the Irish beef slaughtering and processing industry following reports on the future of the industry: market forces had failed to achieve the necessary reduction and the industry was 'in survival mode'; the judgment is on appeal to the Irish Supreme Court, not yet decided.

[196] See also the Art 81(3) Guidelines (n 159, above) para 81. *IFPI 'Simulcasting'*, OJ 2003 L107/58, paras 106–107. See also *DSD*, OJ 2001 L319/1, [2002] 4 CMLR 405: so as to satisfy Art 81(3), grant of exclusivity to waste packaging collectors reduced from 15 years to 11 years which gave the collectors sufficient time to achieve an economically satisfactory return of their investment (appeal on other grounds dismissed, Case T-289/01 *Der Grüne Punkt — Duales System Deutschland v Commission* [2007] 5 CMLR 356). For recycled waste system cases generally, see paras 6.196 *et seq*, below.

of technical progress.[197] Similarly, the Commission states in its Article 81(3) Guidelines that restrictions which disentitle an agreement to the benefit of a block exemption or which are identified as hard-core restrictions in Commission guidelines and notices are unlikely to be considered indispensable.[198]

(e) The fourth condition: no elimination of competition

Generally. The fourth condition is that the agreement must not afford the **3.062** undertakings concerned the possibility of eliminating competition in respect of a substantial part of the products in question. The prohibition on eliminating competition is a narrower concept than that of the existence or acquisition of a dominant position, so that an agreement could be regarded as not eliminating competition within the meaning of Article 81(3) and therefore escape the prohibition, even if it established a dominant position for the benefit of its parties.[199] The fourth condition in Article 81(3) reflects an endeavour to maintain in the market 'real or potential competition' even in cases in which restraints on competition are permitted.[200] This expression has been equated with 'effective competition' as mentioned in the former block exemption for exclusive purchasing agreements, Regulation 1984/83.[201] It may also be referred to as 'workable competition', the degree of competition necessary to ensure the observance of the basic requirements and the attainment of the objectives of the Treaty, in particular the creation of a single market achieving conditions similar to those of a domestic market.[202] The Commission takes the view that where an undertaking is dominant or becoming dominant as a consequence of an agreement, an agreement that has appreciable anti-competitive effects cannot, in principle, satisfy Article 81(3).[203]

Framework for analysis. The possibility of eliminating competition in respect **3.063** of a substantial part of the products in question must be assessed as a whole, taking

---

[197] Case 258/78 *Nungesser v Commission* [1982] ECR 2015, [1983] 1 CMLR 278, para 77. cf the more empirical examination contemplated by the ECJ in *Consten and Grundig v Commission* (n 160, above) at 347–350 (ECR), 477–480 (CMLR).

[198] Article 81(3) Guidelines, para 79.

[199] *Atlantic Container Line v Commission ('TAA')* (n 183, above) para 330.

[200] Case 6/72 *Europemballage and Continental Can v Commission* [1973] ECR 215, [1973] CMLR 199, para 25; Case T-7/95 *Langnese-Iglo v Commission* (n 166, above) para 148.

[201] Case T-7/95 *Langnese-Iglo v Commission* (n 166, above) para 148. See Reg 1984/83, OJ 1983 L173/5, Art 14(a); Reg 2790/1999, which replaced Reg 1984/83, does not use this formulation. In *Atlantic Container Line v Commision ('TAA')* (n 183, above) para 355, the CFI assessed whether rivals were able to exert 'effective competitive pressure' on the parties to the agreement.

[202] *Metro No. 1* (n 169, above) paras 20–21.

[203] Guidelines on Vertical Restraints, OJ 2000 C291/1: Vol II, App C.11, para 135 (however, the agreement may fall outside Art 81(1) if there is an objective justification for the restraint: eg the protection of relationship-specific investments or the confidentiality of the know-how transferred); Horizontal Cooperation Guidelines, OJ 2001 C3/2: Vol II, App C.12, para 36.

into account in particular the specific characteristics of the relevant market, the restrictions of competition brought about by the agreement, the market shares of the parties to that agreement and the extent and intensity of external competition, both actual and potential. In the context of this comprehensive approach, those different elements are closely interlinked or may balance each other out. Thus, the greater the restrictions of internal competition between the parties, the more necessary it is for external competition to be keen and substantial if the agreement is to escape the prohibition. Similarly, the larger the market shares of the parties to the agreement, the stronger the potential competition must be.[204]

3.064 **Market shares.** Application of the fourth condition will often depend on the market share of the undertakings concerned. For example, an agreement between manufacturers on the profit margins to be allowed to their distributors was not acceptable where those manufacturers together held 95 per cent of the relevant market.[205] Similarly, a cooperative of cheese producers which produced rennet for use in cheese production, and which enjoyed a near monopoly of the rennet market, was not permitted to require its members to purchase from it all of their rennet requirements.[206] Where many other undertakings in the market have similar agreements, these parallel networks may cumulatively eliminate competition.[207] Continuing marginal competition from sources outside the properly defined relevant market will not affect the analysis.[208] Where the economies of scale are such that it would be uneconomic to have more than one firm carrying out a particular activity, regular tendering for the contract to carry out that activity may avoid the elimination of competition.[209]

3.065 **Other key factors.** The decision-maker cannot, in principle, rely merely on the fact that the agreement in question eliminates competition between those parties and that they account for a substantial part of the relevant market. As mentioned above, the prohibition on eliminating competition is a narrower concept than that of the existence or acquisition of a dominant position. It is thus necessary to take into account and analyse external competition, both actual and potential: in particular, potential competition must be taken into consideration before concluding that an agreement eliminates competition for the purposes of Article 81(3).[210]

---

[204] *Atlantic Container Line v Commission ('TAA')* (n 183, above) para 300.

[205] Cases 209/78, etc, *Van Landewyck v Commission ('FEDETAB')* [1980] ECR 3125, [1981] 3 CMLR 134, paras 131, 188–189.

[206] *Coöperatieve Stremselen Kleurselfabriek v Commission* (n 195, above) para 18.

[207] *Metro No. 1* (n 169, above) paras 21, 50. In *Whitbread* (n 173, above) para 177, the Commission accepted exclusive purchase *obligations* imposed by a supplier accounting for 13 per cent of the market, while parallel agreements accounted for at most 58 per cent in total.

[208] *Atlantic Container Line v Commission ('TAA')* (n 183, above) paras 272–273, 282, 287, 294.

[209] *ARA, ARGE and ARO*, OJ 2004 L75/59, [2004] 5 CMLR 1101, paras 278–284.

[210] *Atlantic Container Line v Commission ('TAA')* (n 183, above) paras 330–332. At paras 360–363 in particular, the CFI carried out a detailed examination of potential competition and the barriers

Competition from rivals may be limited by capacity constraints, or the smaller range of services that they offer.[211] The Commission has suggested that if rivals have relatively higher costs of production their competitive response will necessarily be limited.[212] The importance of competition from external rivals may be such that the undertakings concerned must commit to deal with third parties on non-discriminatory terms.[213] Similarly, the Commission has in the past negotiated elaborate schemes designed to remove barriers to entry before accepting that an agreement did not eliminate competition (and thus also fail to pass on cost savings to consumers): in future undertakings in equivalent situations must presumably contemplate the adoption of such measures as a spontaneous initiative to ensure the compatibility of their agreement with Article 81(3).[214] The degree of concentration is a factor to be taken into consideration if it affects the structure of competition on the relevant market.[215] Such an effect will not always occur where the concentration is at the level of production and the agreements to be examined concern the distribution of products. But it may do so, for example, if the trend towards concentration helps to eliminate price competition or oust other channels of distribution.[216] The Commission also points to the fact that the elimination of a maverick or of a particularly close competitor in a differentiated product market may have a disproportionate effect on competition; it calls for claims relating to potential competition to be fully substantiated.[217]

Price competition.   The Court of Justice has stated that price competition is so **3.066** important that it should never be eliminated.[218] Given that the fourth condition

---

to entry and exit, including references to the maintenance of excess capacity which deterred entry, and to the empirical fact that no entry had occurred despite substantial price rises. See also *British Airways/Iberia/GB Airways* (n 162, above) paras 51–70; *Air France/Alitalia*, (n 168, above) paras 142–143.

[211] *Atlantic Container Line v Commission ('TAA')* (n 183, above) paras 339–343 (see also the Art 81(3) Guidelines, OJ 2004 C101/97: Vol II, App C.18, para 109). At paras 337–338, the CFI also pointed to the fact that the parties to the agreement had been able to impose substantial price rises, following which the market shares of rivals rapidly stabilised and even fell.

[212] Art 81(3) Guidelines, para 109. However, it is arguable that the inability of less efficient competitors to constrain the undertakings concerned should not be taken as an indicator of the elimination of competition.

[213] *REIMS II renotification*, OJ 2004 L56/76, [2004] 5 CMLR 123, paras 145–157. In Cases T-185/00, etc, *Métropole Télévision (M6) v Commission* [2002] ECR II-3805, [2003] 4 CMLR 707, the CFI annulled the decision of the Commission, holding that the Commission had committed a manifest error of assessment when it found on the facts that a sub-licensing scheme for television rights operated by EBU guaranteed access for third party competitors of the EBU's members and consequently avoided the elimination of competition in that market.

[214] See, eg *AuA/LH* (n 171, above) paras 93, 97–103 and 105–114.

[215] Case 75/84 *Metro v Commission ('Metro No. 2')* [1986] ECR 3021, [1987] 1 CMLR 118, para 88; Case 43/85 *Ancides v Commission* [1987] ECR 3131, [1988] 4 CMLR 821, para 13.

[216] *Metro No. 2*, above, para 88.

[217] Article 81(3) Guidelines (n 211, above) paras 112–116.

[218] Case 26/76 *Metro v Commission ('Metro No. 1')* [1977] ECR 1875, [1978] 2 CMLR 1, para 21. See also *Metro No. 2* (n 215, above) para 88.

of exemption relates to the elimination of competition in respect of a substantial part of the products in question, this observation must be taken as referring to the elimination of price competition in the relevant market and not to its elimination merely as between the parties to an agreement. A certain degree of price rigidity may be acceptable where the agreement promotes improved competition relating to factors other than price.[219]

3.067 **Channels of distribution.**   In both *Metro* cases, the Court of Justice appears to contemplate that the elimination from the relevant market of a particular channel of distribution, in that case, self-service wholesale traders, could result in the elimination of competition in the sense of Article 81(3).[220] The mere fact that an individual trader cannot obtain supplies of the products of a particular manufacturer is insufficient.[221] Arguably, the elimination of a channel of distribution should preclude exemption under the fourth condition only if the effect is to eliminate price competition in the market. Nonetheless, Article 81(3) refers to the elimination of competition in respect of a 'substantial part' of the products in question. Where a distribution channel potentially accounting for a substantial part of the goods sold in the market is eliminated, this may therefore preclude exemption without further examination of the effect on price competition.[222]

3. Block Exemption

(a) Generally

3.068 **Function of block exemptions.**   When an agreement falls within a block exemption adopted by the Council or the Commission, the prohibition in Article 81(1) is automatically disapplied. Block exemptions do not have the effect of amending the content of an agreement, nor is an agreement rendered void merely because it does not satisfy all the conditions laid down in the regulation.[223]

---

219 *Metro No. 1*, above, para 22.
220 ibid, para 50; *Metro No. 2* (n 215, above) paras 65, 66.
221 *Metro No. 2* (n 215, above) para 64.
222 Note that in *REIMS II* (n 182, above) para 90, the Commission indicated that, while the price-fixing agreement in that case might be expected to reduce to a very large extent arbitrage-based remail, it would be inappropriate to regard this as an elimination of competition because the cost-based remuneration system foreseen in the agreement would only restore normal competitive conditions.
223 Case 10/86 *VAG France v Magne* [1986] ECR 4071, [1998] 4 CMLR 98, para 12; Case C-226/94 *Grand Garage Albigeois v Garage Massol* [1996] ECR I-651, [1996] 4 CMLR 778, para 15; Case C-309/94 *Nissan France v Dupasquier* [1996] ECR I-677, [1996] 4 CMLR 778, para 15; Case C-41/96 *VAG Handlerbeirat v SYD-Consult* [1996] ECR I-3123, [1997] 5 CMLR 537, para 16; Case C-230/96 *Cabour and Nord Distribution Automobile v Arnor* [1998] ECR I-2055, [1998] 5 CMLR 679, para 47; Cases T-185/96, etc, *Riviera Auto Service v Commission* [1999] ECR II-93, [1999] 5 CMLR 31, para 30.

Similarly, parties are not obliged to amend their contracts so as to satisfy the terms of the regulation.[224] Where an agreement does not satisfy all the conditions provided for by an exempting regulation, it will be caught by the prohibition laid down in Article 81(1) only if its object or effect is appreciably to restrict competition within the common market and it is capable of affecting trade between Member States.[225] Thus the mere fact that an agreement is one of a category covered by a block exemption does not imply that it must fall within Article 81(1).[226] The same applies to agreements falling within a category specified by a regulation empowering the Commission to adopt a block exemption.[227]

Agreements outside a block exemption may benefit from Article 81(3). The **3.069** parties to an agreement which does not satisfy all the conditions laid down by a particular block exemption may nonetheless argue that Article 81(3) applies on an individual basis, or may claim that the conditions of another exemption regulation for other categories of agreements are fulfilled.[228] There is no presumption that that the agreement is illegal.[229] Where an agreement does not comply with the terms of a block exemption because of a purely technical matter which does not prevent it from complying with the spirit of the regulation, the decision-maker is right to refer to the framework of analysis provided by the regulation in the context of examining the possibility of the individual application of Article 81(3).[230]

Interpretation of block exemptions. Provisions in a block exemption which **3.070** derogate from the general principle prohibiting anti-competitive agreements laid down in Article 81(1) cannot be interpreted widely and cannot be construed

---

[224] *VAG France v Magne* (n 223, above) para 12; *Grand Garage Albigeois v Garage Massol* (n 223, above) para 15; *Nissan France v Dupasquier* (n 223, above) para 15; *VAG-Händlerbeirat v SYD-Consult* (n 223, above) para 16; *Riviera Auto Service v Commission* (n 223, above) para 30.

[225] *Cabour and Nord Distribution Automobile v Amor* (n 223, above) para 48; *Riviera Auto Service v Commission* (n 223, above) para 31. See also Case C-39/92 *Petrogal* [1993] ECR I-5659, para 68. The Commission has stated in its Guidelines on Vertical Restraints (n 203, above) para 62, that vertical agreements falling outside Reg 2790/1999 will not be presumed to be illegal; the authority or party contending that such an agreement violates Art 81(1) accordingly has the burden of proof to establish this: Reg 1/2003, OJ 2003 L1/1: Vol II, App B.3, Art 2.

[226] Case 32/65 *Italy v Council and Commission* [1966] ECR 389, 405–406 [1969] CMLR 39, 61; T-61/89 *Dansk Pelsdyravlerforening v Commission* [1992] ECR II-1931, para 98.

[227] Case 32/65 *Italy v Council and Commission*, above, at 406 (ECR), 61 (CMLR).

[228] *VAG France v Magne* (n 223, above) para 13; Case C-234/89 *Delimitis* [1991] ECR I-935, [1992] 5 CMLR 210, para 41. However, see Reg 1400/2002, OJ 2002 L203/30: Vol II, App C.6, Recital 2, which states that the sector-specific character of the exemption for motor vehicle distribution precludes application of the more general Reg 2790/1999 on vertical agreements.

[229] Guidelines on Vertical Restraints (n 203, above) para 62; Guidelines on Technology Transfer Agreements, OJ 2004 C101/2: Vol II, App C.16, para 37.

[230] Case T-231/99 *Joynson v Commission* [2002] ECR II-2085, [2002] 5 CMLR 123, paras 58–59; appeal dismissed as manifestly inadmissible or unfounded, Case C-204/02P [2003] ECR I-14763.

in such a way as to extend the effects of the regulation beyond what is necessary to protect the interests which they are intended to safeguard.[231] The Community Courts have spoken of the need to interpret block exemptions 'strictly' or 'narrowly'.[232] There have been judgments of the Court of Justice running contrary to this approach, but they appear to reflect a concern for the enforceability of a particular type of agreements, that would no longer be applicable today.[233]

3.071 Commission's explanatory notices. Several of the block exemptions have been accompanied by explanatory notices or guidelines issued by the Commission. Although such notices may clarify the terms used in a block exemption regulation and indicate the Commission's approach, they cannot alter the scope of the regulation as a matter of law.[234]

3.072 Burden of proof. Under the former regime of Regulation 17, the Court of First Instance rejected a challenge to a Commission infringement decision on the basis that the undertaking concerned had not proved that its agreement could be covered by a block exemption.[235] This mirrored the Court's approach to the burden of proof as regards satisfying the conditions of Article 81(3) so as to obtain an individual exemption.[236] Article 2 of Regulation 1/2003 has codified the rule that the burden of proof rests on the party claiming the benefit of Article 81(3), and although that provision does not expressly refer to a block exemption it should apply equally in that context.

---

[231] Case C-70/93 *BMW v ALD* [1995] ECR I-3439, [1996] 4 CMLR 478, para 28; Case C-266/93 *Bundeskartellamt v Volkswagen and VAG Leasing* [1995] ECR I-3477, [1996] 4 CMLR 505, para 33; *Cabour and Nord Distribution Automobile v Arnor* (n 223, above) para 30; Case T-9/92 *Peugeot v Commission* [1993] ECR II-93, [1995] 5 CMLR 696, para 37.

[232] 'Strictly' in Cases T-24/93, etc, *Compagnie Maritime Belge Transports v Commission* [1996] ECR II-1201, [1997] 4 CMLR 273, para 48; and in Cases T-191/98 *Atlantic Container Line v Commission ('TACA')* [2003] ECR II-3275, [2005] 4 CMLR 1283, para 568; 'narrowly' in Case T-67/01 *JCB Service v Commission* [2004] ECR II-49, [2004] 4 CMLR 1346, para 164 (appeal on other grounds dismissed, Case C-167/04P, [2006] ECR I-8935, [2006] 5 CMLR 1303).

[233] Case 63/75 *Fonderies Roubaix v Fonderies Roux* [1976] ECR 111, [1976] 1 CMLR 538, paras 12–19; Case 47/76 *De None v Brouwerij Concordia* [1977] ECR 65, [1977] 1 CMLR 378, paras 14–21. In these cases, the ECJ applied a very broad interpretation of a block exemption regulation, even contrary to its express wording, in order to exempt purely domestic agreements of the same type as certain multi-national agreements which clearly were exempted and which seemed more likely to prejudice the working of the common market. Current block exemption texts do not make this distinction and, in any event, parties seeking to enforce such agreements are now able to rely on the direct effect of Art 81(3).

[234] *Grand Garage Albigeois v Garage Massol* (n 223, above) para 21; *Nissan France v Dupasquier* (n 223, above) para 22.

[235] *JCB Service v Commission* (n 232, above) para 168.

[236] See para 3.015, above.

Third party activities.   Third parties may be affected where an agreement   **3.073**
benefits from a block exemption, in that they might have wished to rely on the
invalidity of that agreement under Article 81(1). But block exemptions do not
regulate the activities of third parties, who may operate outside the framework of
an exempted agreement. Thus the fact that a manufacturer's distribution network
falls within the motor vehicle block exemption does not affect the rights of an
independent dealer trading in that make of car outside the network.[237]

Council block exemptions.   The Council has adopted block exemptions in   **3.074**
the road and inland waterway sectors, and in the maritime transport sector.[238]
It has also established exceptions to Article 81(1) applicable in the agricultural
sector,[239] and for technical agreements in the road, rail and inland transport
sectors, and the maritime transport sector.[240]

Council enabling regulations.   The Council has adopted various regulations   **3.075**
empowering the Commission to grant block exemptions to certain defined
categories of agreements:

- Regulation 19/65 applies to vertical agreements and those concerning the
  acquisition or use of industrial property rights;[241]

- Regulation 2821/71 applies to agreements on the application of standards
  or types, research and development and specialisation;[242]

- Regulation 3976/87 applies to certain categories of agreements relating to air
  transport;[243]

- Regulation 1534/91 applies to certain categories of agreement relating to
  insurance;[244]

- Regulation 479/92 applies to liner consortia.[245]

---

[237] *Grand Garage Albigeois v Garage Massol* (n 223, above) paras 18–20; *Nissan France v Dupasquier* (n 223, above) paras 18, 20; Case C-128/95 *Fontaine v Aqueducs Automobiles* [1997] ECR I-967, [1997] 5 CMLR 39, paras 15, 17; *VAG-Händlerbeirat v SYD-Consult* (n 223, above) para 17. See further para 6.117, below.

[238] Reg 1017/68, Art 4, see para 3.082, below; Reg 4056/86, Arts 3–6, para 3.083, below. See also Chap 12, below.

[239] Reg 1184/2006, OJ 2006 L 214/7, Vol II, App E.30 and see Chap 12, below.

[240] Reg 1017/68, Art 3. See also Reg 4056/86, Art 2 recently repealed by Reg 1419/2006, OJ 2006 L269/1, para 3.083, below.

[241] Reg 19/65, OJ 1965 L36/533: Vol II, App C.1.

[242] Reg 2821/71, OJ 1971 L285/46: Vol II, App C.2.

[243] Reg 3976/87, OJ 1987 L374/9: Vol II, App E.9.

[244] Reg 1534/91, OJ 1991 L143/1: Vol II, App E.26.

[245] Reg 479/92, OJ 1992 L55/3: Vol II, App E.6.

(b) Current block exemption regulations

3.076 **Specialisation/production agreements.** Subject to various conditions, Regulation 2658/2000,[246] which came into force on 1 January 2001, exempts agreements whereby:

(a) one party agrees not to manufacture certain products and to purchase them from a competitor who agrees to produce and supply those products (unilateral specialisation or outsourcing);

(b) two or more parties agree on a reciprocal basis not to manufacture certain, but different, products and to purchase them from the other parties who agree to supply them (reciprocal specialisation); and

(c) two or more parties agree to produce certain products jointly.[247]

This exemption applies only if the parties' combined share of the relevant market does not exceed 20 per cent.[248] Regulation 2658/2000 will expire on 31 December 2010.[249]

3.077 **Research and development.** Subject to various conditions, Regulation 2659/2000, which came into force on 1 January 2001, exempts agreements entered into between two or more parties under which those parties 'pursue (a) joint research and development of products or processes and joint exploitation of the results of that research and development; (b) joint exploitation of the results of research and development of products or processes jointly carried out pursuant to a prior agreement between the same undertakings; or (c) joint research and development of products or processes excluding joint exploitation of the results', insofar as such agreements fall within the scope of Article 81(1).[250] The duration of the applicable exemption is determined according to whether the parties are competitors and their combined market share.[251] Regulation 2659/2000 will expire on 31 December 2010.[252]

3.078 **Vertical restraints.** The block exemption for vertical restraints, Regulation 2790/1999,[253] came into force on 1 June 2000 and will expire on 1 June 2010.[254] The exemption applies to 'agreements or concerted practices entered into between

---

[246] Reg 2658/2000, OJ 2000 L304/3: Vol II, App C.4. This block exemption is considered in detail at paras 7.097 *et seq*, below.

[247] Reg 2658/2000, Art 1.

[248] ibid, Art 4.

[249] ibid, Art 9.

[250] Reg 2659/2000, OJ 2000 L304/7: Vol II, App C.5, and see paras 7.078 *et seq*, below.

[251] Reg 2659/2000, Art 4.

[252] ibid, Art 9.

[253] Reg 2790/1999, OJ 1999 L336/21: Vol II, App C.3. This block exemption is discussed in detail in Chap 6, below

[254] ibid, Art 13.

two or more undertakings each operating, for the purposes of the agreement, at a different level of the production and distribution chain and relating to the conditions under which the parties may purchase, sell or resell certain goods or services', subject to certain exceptions.[255] The block exemption includes all vertical restraints except those relating to industrial property rights, in all sectors of distribution other than motor vehicles. It is subject to a market share limit of 30 per cent,[256] and excludes hard-core restrictions such as fixed or minimum resale prices and export bans.[257]

Motor vehicle distribution. Subject to various conditions, Regulation 1400/2002 exempts 'vertical agreements under which the parties may purchase, sell or resell new motor vehicles, spare parts for motor vehicles or repair and maintenance services for motor vehicles'.[258] It is subject to varying market share limits, depending on the circumstances: no limits for qualitative selective distribution, supplier maximum 40 per cent share for quantitative selective distribution, buyer maximum 30 per cent share where agreement contains an exclusive supply obligation, and otherwise supplier maximum 30 per cent share.[259] Regulation 1400/2002 expressly states that stricter rules than those of Regulation 2790/1999 are needed in this sector. The Regulation entered into force on 1 October 2002 (although one provision only came into effect on 1 October 2005) and is due to expire on 31 May 2010.[260]   **3.079**

Technology transfer agreements. Subject to various conditions, Regulation 772/2004 exempts patent, know-how and software copyright licensing agreements entered into between two undertakings permitting the production of contract products.[261] Different lists of hard-core restrictions apply to agreements between competitors and those between non-competitors, and the exemption is also subject to combined market share limits of 20 per cent and 30 per cent respectively. [262] Regulation 772/2004 entered into force on 1 May 2004 and is due to expire on 30 April 2014.[263]   **3.080**

Insurance. Subject to various conditions, Regulation 358/2003 exempts agreements entered into between undertakings in the insurance sector with respect to the joint establishment of certain calculations and tables, the carrying out of   **3.081**

---

255 ibid, Art 1.
256 ibid, Art 3.
257 ibid, Art 4.
258 Reg 1400/2002, OJ 2002 L203/30: Vol II, App C.6, Art 2(1). This block exemption is discussed in detail at paras 6.109 *et seq*, below.
259 Reg 1400/2002, Art 3(1) and (2).
260 Reg 1400/2002, Art 12.
261 Reg 772/2004, OJ 2004 L123/11: Vol II, App C.7, Art 1(1)(b) and Art 2. This block exemption is discussed in detail in Chap 9, below.
262 Reg 772/2004, Art 4 and Art 3.
263 ibid, Art 11.

certain studies, the establishment of non-binding standard policy conditions for direct insurance and other matters.[264] Regulation 358/2003 entered into force on 1 April 2003 and is due to expire on 31 March 2010.

3.082 Road and inland waterway groupings. Subject to various conditions, Regulation 1017/68 exempts agreements, decisions and concerted practices between small and medium-sized undertakings where their purpose is the constitution and operation of groupings of road or inland waterway transport undertakings with a view to carrying on transport activities, and for the joint financing or acquisition of transport equipment or supplies to this end.[265] Regulation 1017/68 entered into force on 1 July 1968 for an indefinite period.[266] The provisions in the original Regulation which set up a notification and exemption procedure for those sectors were repealed by Regulation 1/2003.

3.083 Liner conferences. Until recently, Regulation 4056/86 exempted agreements, decisions and concerted practices of all or part of the members of one or more liner conferences which had as their objective the fixing of rates and conditions of carriage, and, as the case may be, certain other objectives including the regulation of carrying capacity offered by each member and the allocation of cargo or revenue among members.[267] This exemption was subject to detailed conditions and obligations. In addition, and also subject to conditions, Regulation 4056/86 exempted agreements, decisions and concerted practices between transport users and conferences concerning rates, conditions and quality of liner services, and agreements between transport users which may be necessary to that end.[268] The Commission carried out an extensive review to determine whether liner conferences still fulfilled the four cumulative conditions of Article 81(3). A White Paper was published in October 2004[269] and the Commission adopted a legislative proposal in December 2005.[270] Regulation 1419/2006[271] has repealed Regulation 4056/86 subject to a transitional period. Article 1 of Regulation 1419/2006 provides that certain provisions of the block exemption continue to apply in respect of line shipping conferences satisfying the requirements of Regulation 4056/86 until

---

[264] Reg 358/2003, OJ 2003 L53/8: Vol II, App E.27, Art 1. This block exemption is considered at paras 12.170 *et seq*, below.

[265] Reg 1017/68, OJ 1968 L175/1: Vol II, App E.1, Art 4. This block exemption is considered at paras 12.010 *et seq*, below.

[266] ibid, Art 30.

[267] Reg 4056/86, OJ 1986 L378/4: Vol II, App E.5. This block exemption is considered at paras 12.021 *et seq*, below.

[268] ibid, Art 6.

[269] See Press Release IP/04/1213 (13 October 2004).

[270] See Press Release IP/05/1586 (14 December 2005) and MEMO/04/480 (14 December 2005).

[271] Reg 1419/2006, OJ 2006 L269/1. See further paras 12.019 *et seq*, below.

18 October 2008.[272] The terms of the block exemption therefore remain relevant for liner shipping conferences before that date.

Liner consortia. Subject to various conditions and obligations, Regulation **3.084** 823/2000 exempts certain agreements relating to the joint operation of liner shipping transport services, when entered into in the context of a consortium between vessel-operating carriers.[273] Regulation 823/2000 entered into force on 26 April 2000 and, after amendment, is due to expire on 25 April 2010.[274]

Slot allocation and passenger tariff consultations. Regulation 1617/93, as **3.085** amended, exempted certain agreements between undertakings in the air transport sector for consultations on passenger tariffs, slot allocation and airport scheduling. Regulation 1617/93 expired on 30 June 2005, but the Commission subsequently adopted a new block exemption providing short-term exemption to slot allocation agreements and passenger tariff consultations. Regulation 1459/2006[275] granted a temporary exemption with retrospective effect to agreements which fulfilled the conditions set out in the Regulation. It applied to two different kinds of agreements: (i) (until 31 December 2006) the holding of consultations on slot allocation and airport scheduling insofar as they concern air services which start or finish at a point within the Community; and (ii) (until 31 October 2007) the holding of consultations on tariffs for carriage of passengers with their baggage on scheduled air services. In respect of both kinds of consultation, the Regulation gives the Commission and Member States the right to send observers to the consultations.[276] The exemption in respect of (i) expired on 31 December 2006 and the expiry of the exemption in respect of (ii) varies according to the geographical scope of the service involved but in any event expires on 31 October 2007.[276A] The Commission gas announced that the block exemption for passenger tariff consoltations will not be renewed.[276B]

(c) Withdrawal and disapplication

Withdrawal from individual agreements. Regulation 1/2003 provides that **3.086** where the Commission, empowered by a Council Regulation, has declared Article 81(1) inapplicable to certain categories of agreements, decisions or

---

272 These are Art 1(3)(b) and (c) which define certain terms, Arts 3–7 which contain the block exemption, Art 8(2) which empowers the Commission to withdraw the benefit of the block exemption from an individual agreement and Art 26 which empowers the Commission to adopt implementing measures.

273 Reg 823/2000, OJ 2000 L100/24, Vol II, App E.7, Art 3. This block exemption is discussed in Chap 12, below.

274 ibid, Art 14.

275 Reg 1459/2006, OJ 2006 L272/3: Vol II, App E.12. The Reg will not be renewed: Press Release IP/07/973 (29 June 2007). This block exemption is discussed at paras 12.043, *et seq* below.

276 ibid, Arts 2(2) and 3(3).

276A See para 12.046 below.

276A Press release IP/07/973 (29 June 2007).

concerted practices, it may, acting on its own initiative or on a complaint, withdraw the benefit of such an exemption regulation when it finds that in any particular case an agreement, decision or concerted practice has certain effects which are incompatible with Article 81(3).[277] The similar provision in Council Regulation 4056/86 has been kept in force over the two-year transitional period before the maritime shipping block exemption expires.[278] Withdrawal of a block exemption has been carried out in at least two cases, and threatened in others.[279] The block exemptions for liner conferences and liner consortia may also be withdrawn where the persons concerned are in breach of certain obligations laid down in the applicable regulation or where the conduct of the conference or consortium concerned has effects incompatible with Article 82.[280] A complainant is entitled to a decision on a request for withdrawal of a block exemption,[281] and it may be inferred that this must be given within a reasonable period.[282]

3.087 **Withdrawal by Member State authorities.**   Where, in any particular case, agreements, decisions or concerted practices to which a Commission block exemption regulation applies have effects which are incompatible with Article 81(3) of the Treaty in the territory of a Member State, or in a part thereof, which has all the characteristics of a distinct geographic market, Regulation 1/2003 empowers the competition authority of that Member State to withdraw the benefit of the regulation in question in respect of that territory.[283] This creates a jurisdiction concurrent with that of the Commission as regards withdrawal, but the Commission may be expected to leave such cases to the authority of the relevant Member State

---

[277] Reg 1/2003, OJ 2003 L1/1, Vol II, App B.3, Art 29(1). Various Commission block exemptions contain similar powers, often specifying the types of effect or conduct that may lead to the withdrawal of the exemption. See Reg 2658/2000, Art 7; Reg 2659/2000, Art 7; Reg 2790/1999, Art 6; Reg 1400/2002, Art 6(1); Reg 772/2004, Art 6(1); Reg 358/2003, Art 10; Reg 823/2000, Art 12(1); Reg 1617/93, Art 10. The Guidelines on Vertical Restraints, OJ 2000 C291/1: Vol II, App C.11, paras 71–79, offer guidance on withdrawal of the Reg 2790/1999 exemption by the Commission or Member States.

[278] Reg 4056/86, Art 7(2) and Reg 1419/2006, Art 8(2). Interestingly, Reg 1017/68 relating to road, rail and inland waterway transport does not contain a withdrawal power. But Art 4(2) empowers the Commission to require undertakings or associations of undertakings to make any effects of their agreements, decisions or concerted practices that are incompatible with the requirements of Art 81(3) cease.

[279] *Eco System/Peugeot*, OJ 1992 L66/1, [1993] 4 CMLR 42, para 33 (withdrawal conditioned on non-compliance with requirement to terminate infringement); *Langnese-Iglo*, OJ 1993 L183/19, [1994] 4 CMLR 51, paras 115–148 (appeals dismissed Case T-7/95 *Langnese-Iglo v Commission* [1995 ECR II-1533, [1995] 5 CMLR 602, [1995] All ER (EC) 908 and Case C-279/95P [1998] ECR I-5609, [1998] 5 CMLR 933).

[280] Reg 4056/86, Arts 7(1) and 8; Reg 823/2000, Art 12.

[281] Case T-24/90 *Automec v Commission* [1992] ECR II-2223, [1992] 5 CMLR 431, para 75.

[282] Cases T-213/95 & T-18/96 *SCK and FNK v Commission* [1997] ECR II-1739, [1998] 4 CMLR 259, para 55. See also Case T-95/96 *Gestevisión Telecinco v Commission* [1998] ECR II-3407, [1998] 3 CMLR 1112, [1998] All ER (EC) 918 (a State aid case) para 73.

[283] Reg 1/2003, Art 29(2). Certain Commission block exemptions contain parallel provisions. See Reg 2790/1999, Art 7; Reg 1400/2002, Art 6(2); Reg 772/2004, Art 6(2); Reg 823/2000, Art 12(2).

save where a particular Community interest is involved.[284] There is no provision for Member States to withdraw exemptions arising under Council Regulations 4056/86 or 1017/68, on maritime, rail, road and inland waterway transport.

No withdrawal for future agreements.   There is no power to withhold the ben-   **3.088**
efit of a block exemption from future agreements that have not been concluded at the time of the withdrawal decision. Moreover, to decide that certain undertakings could not enjoy the benefit of the block exemption as regards their future dealings while their competitors were under no such disability would be contrary to the principle of equal treatment.[285]

Disapplication of block exemption in respect of networks of agreements.   Com-   **3.089**
mission block exemptions adopted under Council Regulation 19/65 may include a power for the Commission to exclude from the application of the exemption certain parallel networks of similar agreements or concerted practices operating on a particular market; that power is to be exercised by regulation, which must specify a period of at least six months before the exclusion takes effect.[286] Such a power is included in Regulation 2790/1999 on vertical agreements (six months), Regulation 1400/2002 on motor vehicle distribution (one year) and in Regulation 772/2004 on technology transfer agreements (six months).[287] But the adoption of a regulation disapplying the block exemption does not imply that any particular agreement infringes Article 81(1), or indeed that it cannot benefit from the individual application of Article 81(3).[288]

4. Article 53(3) of the EEA Agreement

General.   Article 53(3) of the EEA Agreement is expressed in terms identical   **3.090**
to those of Article 81(3) of the EC Treaty. The Modernisation package in Regulation 1/2003 was reflected in corresponding EEA legislation bringing about the direct applicability of Article 53(3) of the EEA Agreement in national courts and the abolition of individual exemptions by the European Commission and the EFTA Surveillance Authority. The EEA provisions came into effect as from 19 May 2005.[289]

---

[284] See the Guidelines on Vertical Restraints (n 277, above) para 77.

[285] Case T-7/95 *Langnese-Iglo v Commission* (n 279, above) paras 208–209, upheld on appeal in Case C-279/95P *Langnese-Iglo v Commission* (n 279, above) para 74; T-9/95 *Schöller v Commission* [1995] ECR II-1611, [1995] 5 CMLR 602, 659, paras 162–163.

[286] Reg 19/65, Art 1(a).

[287] Reg 2790/1999, Art 8; Reg 1400/2002, Art 7; Reg 772/2004, Art 7. The Guidelines on Vertical Restraints (n 277, above) paras 80–87, offer guidance on the disapplication of the Reg 2790/1999 exemption.

[288] See further the Guidelines on Vertical Restraints (n 277, above) para 81.

[289] EEA Joint Committee Decn 130/2004, OJ 2005 L64/57, and the amended Chapter II of Protocol 4 to the Surveillance and Court Agreement entered into force on 19 May 2005. Further

3.091 **EFTA Surveillance Authority guidance and past practice.** The Authority has issued guidelines on the application of Article 53(3) of the EEA Agreement which are modelled very closely on the equivalent guidelines issued by the European Commission.[290] It has also issued guidelines on specific types of cooperation matching those of the Commission. Under the pre-Modernisation regime, the Authority issued two formal decisions rejecting requests for individual exemptions.[291] It has also issued various 'comfort' letters for arrangements which met the conditions of Article 53(3).[292]

3.092 **Block exemption.** Annex XIV to the EEA Agreement[293] contains block exemptions based upon the relevant EC regulations. The EC regulations are adopted by reference and with certain modifications which may be important in particular cases. Under Article 98 of the EEA Agreement, the EEA Joint Committee may by decision amend Annex XIV, and under Article 102 the Joint Committee is required to take such a decision 'as closely as possible' to the adoption by the Community of the corresponding EC legislation. By the Joint Committee taking decisions to update the content of Annex XIV, the EEA Agreement should be kept in step with legislative developments in the EC competition rules. However, that is not always achieved. In particular, when an EC block exemption is extended immediately prior to its expiry, this can cause a temporal gap in the coverage of the equivalent EEA block exemption. That happened with the old motor vehicle block exemption, Regulation 123/85, and for over a year there was no block exemption covering motor vehicle distribution agreements in the EEA States.[294] The EFTA Court held that this gap could not be

---

necessary changes were brought about by EEA Joint Committee Decn 178/2004, OJ 2005 L133/35, and by corresponding changes to the Surveillance and Court Agreement, which entered into force only on 1 July 2005. (The delay was due to the late notification by Iceland.)

[290] Guidelines on the application of Article 53(3) of the EEA Agreement (adopted on 18 May 2005 by College Decision 123/05/COL), not yet published, but available on the website of the EFTA Surveillance Authority.

[291] *NSF*, OJ 1997 L284/68, (refusal of exemption for certain restrictive arrangements on the sellers' side in the Norwegian timber industry); *TFB*, OJ 1997 L 284/91 (refusal of exemption for certain restrictive arrangements on the buyers' side in the Norwegian wood processing industry).

[292] See, eg *Association of Norwegian Insurance Companies, ESA Annual Report '98*, para 5.1.2.2.4 (rules adopted by the Norwegian insurance industry for the approval of security devices and installation undertakings: comfort letter issued after modification of the rules); *Supply of pharmaceuticals and healthcare products in Norway, ESA Annual Report '01*, para 5.3.4 (p 70) (exemption-type comfort letter for agreements imposing purchasing obligations on pharmacies); *Norwegian insurance agreements, ESA Annual report '02*, para 6.2.6 (p 71) (exemption-type comfort letters provided for various agreements on standard policy conditions, methods for valuing building materials, cooperation on medical risk assessment and on the time taken for motor vehicle repairs).

[293] OJ 1994 L1/446. An updated text of Annex XIV is available at the EFTA Secretariat and Surveillance Authority websites.

[294] Reg 123/85 was due to expire on 30 June 1995, but was extended until 30 September 1995 by Reg 1475/95, adopted on 28 June 1995. Art 3 of Decn 46/96 of the EEA Joint Committee, OJ 1996 L291/39, adopted on 19 July 1996, which incorporated reference to Reg 1475/95 into Annex XIV, indicated that the EFTA States might lay down transitional measures for the period between

overcome by interpreting Article 53(1) EEA in the light of Regulation 123/85 for reasons of homogeneity.[295] However, the new block exemption on vertical restraints, Regulation 2790/1999, was adopted by the EEA Joint Committee on 28 January 2000 with retroactive effect as from 1 January 2000.[296]

Current block exemptions.   The block exemptions contained as at 1 May 2007   **3.093** in Annex XIV to the EEA Agreement, subject to the modifications described in that annex, are set out below.

	EC Regulation	*EEA Annex XIV*
Specialisation/production agreements	2658/2000	point 6[297]
Research and development	2659/2000	point 7[298]
Vertical restraints	2790/1999	point 2[299]
Motor vehicle distribution	1400/2002	point 4b[300]
Technology transfer	772/2004	point 5[301]
Insurance	358/2003	point 15b[302]
Road, rail and inland waterway	1017/68	point 10[303]
Liner conferences	4056/86	point 11[304]
Liner consortia	823/2000	point 11c[305]
	1419/2006	point 11d[306]
Air passenger tariff conferences	1459/2006	point 11e[307]

1 July 1995 and 19 July 1996 to the extent necessary for constitutional reasons, but Norway adopted no such measures.

[295] Case E-3/97 *Jaeger v Opel* Norge [1998] Rep EFTA Ct 1, [1999] 4 CMLR 147, paras 27–32.

[296] Decn 18/2000, OJ 2001 L103/36.

[297] Text replaced by Decn 113/2000, OJ 2001 L52/38, am by the EEA Enlargement Agt, OJ 2004 L130/3 and by Decn 130/2004, OJ 2005 L64/57. See also Guidelines on Horizontal Cooperation issued by the EFTA Surveillance Authority, OJ 2002 C266/1, which discuss the block exemption and the application of Art 53 to cooperation agreements more generally.

[298] Text replaced by Decn 113/2000 and am by the same instruments as Reg 2658/2000 above, and see Guidelines on Horizontal Cooperation Agreements, above.

[299] Text replaced by Decn 18/2000, OJ 2001 L 103/36, am by the EEA Enlargement Agt, OJ 2004 L130/3, by Decn 29/2004, OJ 2004 L127/137 and by Decn 130/2004, OJ 2005 L64/57. See also EFTA Surveillance Authority Guidelines on Vertical Restraints, OJ 2002 C122/1.

[300] Point inserted by Decn 136/2002, OJ 2002 L336/38, am by the EEA Enlargement Agt, Decn 29/2004, and Decn 130/2004, above.

[301] Text replaced by Decn 42/2005, OJ 2005 L198/42. See also EFTA Surveillance Authority Guidelines adopted on 21 September 2005 by College Decn 228/05, not yet published but available on EFTA Surveillance Authority website.

[302] Point inserted by Decn 82/2003, OJ 2003 L257/37.

[303] Text replaced by Decn 130/2004, OJ 2005 L64/57.

[304] Text replaced by Decn 130/2004, above.

[305] Text replaced by Decn 49/2000, OJ 2000 L237/60.

[306] Point inserted by Decn 153/2006, OJ 2007 L89/25, with effect from 1 August 2007, following notification by Norway of fulfilment of the constitutional requirements.

[307] Point inserted by Decn 156/2006, OJ 2007 L89/31. Reg 1459/2006 expired 31 October 2007 and will not be renewed: Press Release IP/07/973 (29 June 2007).

4

MARKET DEFINITION

1. Introduction and Overview

In general. An economic market comprises those goods or services which pro- **4.001**
vide a close competitive constraint on one another.[1] Market definition has an
important role in competition law which is concerned with undertakings' ability

---

[1] See generally: Bishop & Walker, *The Economics of EC Competition Law* (2nd edn, 2002); Faull
& Nikpay, *The EC Law of Competition* (2nd edn, 2007), paras 1.130 *et seq*; Motta, *Competition
Policy – Theory and Practice* (2004), sect. 3.2; Geroski and Griffith, 'Identifying Anti-trust Markets'
in Neumann and Weigand (eds), *The International Handbook of Competition* (2004), 290–305. See
also the works on merger control, eg Struys & Robinson (eds), *EC Merger Decisions Digest* (2005);
Levy, *European Merger Control Law: A Guide to the Merger Regulation* (2003); Lindsay, *The EC
Merger Regulation: Substantive Issues* (2nd edn, 2006); and the International Competition Network
('ICN') Project on Merger Guidelines, Chapters 1 and 2:
   (http://www.internationalcompetitionnetwork.org/seoul/analysisofmerger.html).

to distort competition and therefore frequently involves consideration of market power. More particularly, the process of market definition serves as a prerequisite to the calculation of market shares, which are commonly used as a proxy[2] for market power,[3] and provides a conceptual framework within which the evaluation of the competitive effect of the conduct or transaction in question takes place.[4] Hence market definition is a means to an end and not an end in itself. A relevant economic market has two principal dimensions: the goods or services comprising it (the 'product market') and the area within which the undertakings operating in the market are involved in the supply of those goods or services (the 'geographic market'). However, it is sometimes necessary to consider also a third dimension: the times or periods during which supply and demand on that market occur (the 'temporal market').[5]

4.002 **Structure of this Chapter.** This Chapter begins by defining a 'market' for the purposes of EC competition law and then examines the practical significance of market definition in cases under Articles 81 and 82 and the merger regime. It describes the development of the concept with reference, in particular, to the Commission's current approach to defining markets and its Notice on the definition of the relevant market (the 'Relevant Market Notice'). The latter parts of Section 1 of this Chapter examine the methodology for defining markets, including the 'hypothetical monopolist' or 'SSNIP' test and its limitations. Sections 2, 3 and 4 of this Chapter examine in detail the three dimensions of a relevant economic market, namely the product dimension, the geographic dimension and the temporal dimension. Although these dimensions together form a single economic market, it is common to talk of a 'product market', a 'geographic market' and a 'temporal market'. When determining the scope of each dimension, it is necessary to examine two different forms of substitution: demand-side substitution (which examines the scope for purchasers to switch to alternatives in response to a price increase); and supply-side substitution (which examines the

---

[2] Market definition would generally be redundant if market power could be estimated directly (eg by estimating the residual demand curve faced by a supplier or a proposed merged group). However, this is generally not possible and market definition therefore remains a valuable tool in seeking to assess the extent to which a supplier, or a proposed merged group, enjoys, or may enjoy, market power.

[3] See generally Chap 8 in relation to mergers and Chap 10 in relation to abuse of a dominant position.

[4] eg in Case M.3197 *Candover/Cinven/Bertelsmann-Springer* (29 July 2003), para 13, the Commission rejected a possible definition of the market (based on demand-side considerations alone) in part on the grounds that it would not allow proper assessment of the competitive relations between the different suppliers and therefore the effect of the notified merger on competition.

[5] eg, there may be separate markets for on-peak and off-peak travel or for the supply of fruit and vegetables during the domestic season and at other times (when demand is met by imported products). See further paras 4.089–4.090, below.

scope for suppliers to commence supply in response to a price increase).[6] Finally, Section 5 describes the way markets have been defined in several particular fields.

(a) The concept of the relevant market

Specific meaning of a 'relevant market'.   The concept of a 'relevant market' has   **4.003**
a specific meaning in competition law which is narrower than the general use of the word 'market' in a commercial context. For example, suppliers may use the term 'market' in its non-technical sense to refer to the areas in which they sell their products, or to refer broadly to the industry or sector to which they belong.[7] But for the purposes of competition law, a relevant market comprises those goods or services[8] in a specified area and, where appropriate, over an identified time period that provide a close competitive constraint on one another, ie which are economic substitutes.[9] The Relevant Market Notice describes the position as follows:

> 'The objective of defining a market in both its product and geographic dimension is to identify those actual competitors of the undertakings involved that are capable of constraining those undertakings' behaviour and of preventing them from behaving independently of effective competitive pressure.'[10]

This approach to defining the relevant market does not imply that products which fall outside the relevant market do not pose *any* competitive constraint on products within it; rather, it implies that only products which are directly substitutable impose a sufficiently strong constraint to be regarded as part of the relevant market. Potential competition from firms that might enter the market may also constitute an important competitive constraint but it is not relevant to market definition.[11]

Risk of error in defining markets.   The process of defining markets is complex   **4.004**
and there is a material risk of error. If markets are defined too narrowly, suppliers may be subject to competition law restrictions (on their freedom to make agreements, pursue a course of conduct or merge with other undertakings) that are unnecessary since, in the absence of market power, those activities would be unlikely to harm consumers. By contrast, if markets are defined too widely, suppliers which do in fact have significant market power may be subject to a

---

  [6] Case 6/72 *Europemballage and Continental Can v Commission* [1973] ECR 215, [1973] CMLR 199.
    [7] Relevant Market Notice, OJ 1997 C372/5 see Vol II, App C.10, para 3.
    [8] In the remainder of this Chapter, references to 'products' or 'goods' include goods and services, unless the context indicates otherwise.
    [9] The fact that two products are complementary (ie demand for product A increases as the price of product B decreases) does *not* mean that they form part of the same economic market; see, eg Case M.3396 *Group 4 Falck/Securicor* (28 May 2004), para 25.
    [10] Relevant Market Notice, para 2.
    [11] ibid, para 24. See further para 4.020, below.

lower standard of competition law obligations, enabling them profitably to act in ways that harm consumers (by raising prices or reducing quality, innovation or choice). Because of the difficulty of conclusive definition of the relevant market, it is often sufficient to establish a few alternative relevant markets and if none of the possible alternatives means that the operation in question gives rise to competition concerns, the actual market definition can be left open.[12]

(b) Relevance of market definition in EC competition law

4.005 **Article 81 cases.** In *European Night Services*,[13] the Court of First Instance held that the relevant economic market must be defined when this is necessary to determine whether the agreement or concerted practice has as its object or effect the prevention, restriction or distortion of competition within the common market and is liable to affect trade between Member States.[14] For example, in *Roberts*[15] the Court of First Instance stated that 'delimitation of the relevant market is essential in order to analyse the effects on competition of beer supply agreements with an exclusive purchasing obligation, and in particular to analyse the opportunities available to new domestic and foreign competitors to establish themselves in the market of the consumption of beer or to increase their market shares.' However, it follows from the Court's formulation in *European Night Services* that there are cases in which the Commission is entitled to make a finding of infringement of Article 81 without first arriving at a fully specified determination of the relevant economic market.[16] It may be evident (without the need to reach a precise conclusion on the definition of the relevant market) that an agreement or concerted practice is liable to affect trade between Member States and has an anti-competitive object or effect. For example, in *CMA CGM v Commission*,[17] the Court of First

---

[12] See Speech by Commr Monti, 'Market definition as a cornerstone of EU Competition Policy', 5 October 2001 (Speech/01/439). The UK OFT Guidelines on Market Definition (OFT 403, 2004) adopt the same approach: para 2.14. See also the ICN Project on Merger Guidelines (n 1, above) which refers to the identification of the 'spectrum of substitution possibilities that the analytical framework needs to accommodate' (Chap 1, para 17).

[13] Cases T-374/94, etc, *European Night Services v Commission* [1998] ECR II-3141, [1998] 5 CMLR 718, paras 93–95 and 103. See also Case T-62/98 *Volkswagen v Commission* [2000] ECR II-2707, [2000] 5 CMLR 853, para 230 (appeal on other grounds dismissed, Case C-338/00P [2003] ECR I-9189, [2004] 4 CMLR 351).

[14] The Commission may identify the relevant market in its decision for the purposes of finding an infringement of Art 81 without needing to address this issue separately: see Case T-86/95 *Compagnie Générale Maritime v Commission* [2002] ECR II-1011, [2002] 4 CMLR 1115, para 114.

[15] Case T-25/99 *Roberts v Commission* [2001] ECR II-1881, [2001] 5 CMLR 828, para 26.

[16] But cf Cases T-68/89, etc, *Società Italiana Vetro (SIV) v Commission (Italian Flat Glass)* [1992] ECR II-1403, [1992] 5 CMLR 302, in which the CFI stated: 'The Court considers, on the contrary, that the appropriate definition of the market in question is a necessary precondition of any judgment concerning allegedly anti-competitive behaviour' (para 159).

[17] Case T-213/00 *CMA CGM v Commission* [2003] ECR II-913, [2003] 5 CMLR 268, paras 201–235, appeal dismissed, Case C-236/03P *Commission v CMA CGM*, [2005] 4 CMLR 557.

Instance held that, in the case of horizontal price fixing affecting a significant part of the price of transport on a major cargo route, the Commission was entitled to find that the agreement had as its object a restriction of competition and that it was capable *per se* of affecting trade between Member States to an appreciable extent without fully defining the relevant markets.[18] Further, there is no need for the Commission to reach a final conclusion on market definition if its conclusions would be the same on each candidate market definition.[19]

Cartel cases. Although the Community Courts have recognised that it is not **4.006** necessary in all Article 81 cases for the Commission to reach a final determination of the relevant economic market for the purposes of establishing an infringement, they have nevertheless stated that the Commission should clearly define the markets in complex cartel cases since the relevant market is material to other matters in the context of a cartel investigation. In *Adriatica di Navigazione*,[20] the Court of First Instance stated that the determination of the relevant market could affect the scope of the cartel, whether it is specific or general, and the extent of individual participation of each of the undertakings concerned. The Court specifically identified the risk for undertakings of civil proceedings arising from the Commission's findings in such cases and stated: 'where it adopts a decision in which it finds that an undertaking has participated in a complex, collective and continuous infringement (which cartels often are) . . . the Commission ought to examine the relevant market or markets and identify them in a statement of reasons which it gives for any decision sanctioning an infringement of Article [81(1)] of the Treaty, and it should do so with sufficient precision so as to be able to

---

[18] See also Case T-61/99 *Adriatica di Navigazione v Commission* [2003] ECR II-5349, paras 28–29 (appeal dismissed, Case C-111/04P [2006] ECR I-22); Cases T-25/95, etc, *Cimenteries CBR v Commission* [2000] ECR II-491, [2000] 5 CMLR 204, para 1094 (judgment set aside in part on other grounds, Cases C-204/00, etc, *Aalborg Portland v Commission* [2004] ECR I-123, [2005] 4 CMLR 251); Case T-44/00 *Mannesmannröhren-Werke v Commission* [2004] ECR II-2223, at paras 132 *et seq*). In Cases T-5 & 6/00 *Nederlandse Federatieve Vereniging voor de Groothandel op Elektrotechnisch Gebied v Commission* [2003] ECR II-5761, [2004] 5 CMLR 969, appeal largly dismissed, Case C-105/04P [2006] ECR I-8725, [2006] 5 CMLR 1223, the CFI concluded that the Commission had been right for the purposes of establishing an infringement under Art 81 to take the view that the undertaking in question had a strong, or very strong, position on each of the different markets in question, regardless of which market definition was chosen. In *Volkswagen v Commission* (n 13, above), the CFI held that, in the context of Volkswagen's partitioning of the Italian market, there was no need to define the relevant geographic market to find that the infringement was capable of affecting trade between Member States (para 231).

[19] eg Cases T-185/00, etc, *Métropole Television (M6) v Commission* [2002] ECR II-3805, [2003] 4 CMLR 707, para 57: failure to define precisely the relevant product market did not affect the analysis of whether the Eurovision system satisfied the conditions for exemption in Art 81(3), as the Commission had assumed the existence of the narrowest possible market for the purposes of its analysis (although the decision was annulled on other grounds) (appeal dismissed, Case C-470/02P *UER v Commission*, Order of 27 September 2004).

[20] See *Adriatica di Navigazione* (n 18, above).

identify the operating conditions in the market in which competition has been distorted and to satisfy the essential requirements of legal certainty.'[21]

4.007 **Anti-competitive effect under Article 81(1).**   Market definition is important in determining the impact on competition arising from an agreement or concerted practice. In *Völk v Vervaecke* the Court of Justice held that an agreement falls outside the prohibition in Article 81 when it has only an insignificant effect on the market, taking into account the weak position which the persons concerned have on the market of the product in question.[22] The Commission's *De Minimis* Notice uses market share thresholds to identify agreements that are not to be regarded as having an *appreciable* effect on competition.[23] Moreover, for agreements that do not involve hard-core restrictions,[24] the question of whether or not the parties have market power may be critical to the analysis of anti-competitive effect. The Commission's Guidelines on Horizontal Cooperation Agreements use market shares and market concentration as the starting point for analysis of those agreements that may, but will not necessarily, come within Article 81(1).[25] The Guidelines on Vertical Restraints similarly set out, as important factors to be considered, the market shares of the supplier, the buyer and competitors.[26] Therefore, defining the relevant market (or at least the range of candidate markets) will be necessary whenever the competitive effect of an agreement is in issue.

4.008 **Elimination of competition under Article 81(3).**   The criteria in Article 81(3) for the non-application of the prohibition in Article 81(1) include, as the fourth condition, that the agreement or concerted practice does not afford 'the possibility of eliminating competition in respect of a substantial part of the products in question.' This inevitably involves consideration of the market in which those products compete, as discussed further in paragraphs 3.062 *et seq*, above.

4.009 **Thresholds in block exemptions.**   The Commission often uses market share thresholds in block exemptions as a condition for an agreement to be eligible for exemption from the prohibition under Article 81(1). For example, the Vertical Agreements Block Exemption provides for an exemption for undertakings operating at different levels of the production or distribution chain provided

---

[21] ibid, para 32. The CFI held that the effect of an incorrect or confused definition of the relevant market on the validity of such a decision had to be considered on a case-by-case basis but, in the case itself, the Commission's definition of the relevant market and its findings of infringement were not ambiguous (para 36).

[22] Case 5/69 *Völk v Vervaecke* [1969] ECR 295, [1969] CMLR 273. See generally paras 2.121 *et seq*, above on appreciable effect.

[23] The *De Minimis* Notice, OJ 2001 C368/13, see Vol II, App C.13.

[24] For the concept of hard-core restrictions, see the *De Minimis* Notice, ibid, para 11.

[25] Guidelines on Horizontal Cooperation Agreements, OJ 2001 C3/2, see Vol II, App C.12, paras 27 *et seq*.

[26] Guidelines on Vertical Restraints, OJ 2000, C291/1, see Vol II, App C.11, paras 121–125.

that the market share held by the supplier does not exceed 30 per cent of the relevant market on which it sells contract goods or services.[27] The Motor Vehicle Block Exemption similarly applies a 30 per cent threshold.[28] The Technology Transfer Block Exemption provides for an exemption for technology transfer agreements permitting the production of contract products provided that the combined market share of the parties on the affected relevant technology and product market does not exceed 20 per cent (in the case of competing undertakings) or 30 per cent (in the case of non-competing undertakings).[29] The block exemptions for specialisation agreements and for research and development agreements incorporate threshold conditions that the combined market share of the parties does not exceed, respectively, 20 per cent[30] and 25 per cent (in the case of competing undertakings).[31]

Application of guidelines on fines.   The definition of the relevant market is also **4.010** relevant in the application of the Commission's Guidelines on the Method of Setting Fines. The 1998 Guidelines provided that when assessing the gravity of the infringement, the Commission must have regard to the 'actual impact on the market, where this can be measured, and the size of the relevant geographic market'.[32] Although replaced in June 2006, those Guidelines continue to apply in cases where a statement of objections was issued before 1 September 2006. The new Guidelines provide that the basic amount of a fine will be set in relation to a proportion of the value of the undertakings' sales of the goods or services affected; and in determining the appropriate proportion, one factor to be considered is the combined market share of all the undertakings concerned.[33]

Article 82 cases.   Article 82 applies only to undertakings which, individually or **4.011** collectively, hold a dominant position on the relevant market. Since definition of the relevant market is a prerequisite to any finding of dominance, the relevant market (or at least a range of candidate markets) must be identified in all Article 82 cases.[34]

---

[27] Reg 2790/99, OJ 1999 L336/21, see Vol II, App C.3, Arts 2(1) and 3(1). In the event that the agreement contains exclusive supply obligations, the market share condition applies to the buyer: Art 3(2). See further paras 6.018 *et seq*, below.

[28] Reg 1400/2002, OJ 2004 L203/30, see Vol II, App C.6, Arts 2(1) and 3(1).

[29] Reg 772/2004, OJ 2004 L123/11, see Vol II, App C.7, Arts 3(1) and 3(2). See also Glynn and Randall, 'Technology transfer – the draft block exemption – the role of market definition' (2004) Competition Law Insight 13. For technology markets, see para 4.068, below.

[30] Reg 2658/2000, OJ 2000 L304/3, see Vol II, App C.4, Art 4.

[31] Reg 2659/2000, OJ 2004 L304/7, see Vol II, App C.5, Art 4(2)–(3).

[32] Guidelines on Setting Fines, OJ 1998 C9/3, see Vol II, App B.5, sect 1.A.

[33] Guidelines on the method of setting fines imposed pursuant to Article 23(2)(a) of Regulation 1/2003, OJ 2006 C210/2, see Vol II, App B.13, para 22.

[34] See *Società Italiana Vetro (SIV) v Commission* (n 15, above) para 159; and Case T-29/92 *SPO v Commission* [1995] ECR II-289, para 74 (appeal on other grounds dismissed, Case C-137/95P [1996] ECR I-1611). In *Adriatica di Navigazione* (n 17, above) para 27, the CFI stated: 'It is clear . . . that the approach to defining the relevant market differs according to whether Article [81] or

4.012 **Merger cases.** In *France v Commission*, the Court of Justice, when considering an earlier version of the substantive test under the EC Merger Regulation, stated that 'a proper definition of the relevant market is a necessary precondition for any assessment of the effect of a concentration on competition.'[35] Since 1 May 2004, the substantive test under the Merger Regulation has been whether the transaction in question would 'significantly impede effective competition in the common market or in a substantial part of it, in particular as a result of the creation or strengthening of a dominant position.'[36] The key concepts in this test (significant impediment of effective competition and dominance) were also present in the previous formulation of the substantive test[37] and the Court of Justice's conclusion therefore remains good law.[38] Furthermore, referral of a concentration by the Commission to the competent authority of a Member State under Article 9 of the Regulation is dependent upon the concentration affecting competition in 'a distinct market' within that Member State.

4.013 **Sectoral regulation: electronic communications.** In 2002 the European Parliament and Council adopted a new regulatory framework for electronic communications networks and services.[39] This involves *ex ante* regulation to be undertaken by the national regulatory authorities ('NRAs') of the individual Member States. Under Directive 2002/21, the basic framework Directive, NRAs are required to carry out an analysis of each relevant market to determine whether it is effectively competitive and, if not, to identify the undertakings with significant market power (defined as a position equivalent to dominance) upon whom appropriate regulatory obligations must then be imposed.[40] Market definition therefore plays a fundamental role in the operation of this sectoral regime.[41] The new framework requires NRAs to define the relevant markets in accordance with the principles of competition law, while recognising that the markets defined on an *ex post*

Article [82] of the Treaty is to be applied. For the purposes of Article [82], the appropriate definition of the relevant market is a necessary precondition for any judgment concerning allegedly anticompetitive behaviour ... since, before an abuse of a dominant position is ascertained, it is necessary to establish the existence of a dominant position in a given market, which presupposes that such a market has already been defined.' See also *Volkswagen v Commission* (n 13, above) para 230.

[35] Cases C-68/94 & 30/95 *France v Commission* [1998] ECR I-1375, [1998] 4 CMLR 829, para 143. See also Case T-2/93 *Air France v Commission* [1994] ECR II-323, para 80; and Case T-342/99 *Airtours v Commission* [2002] ECR II-2585, [2002] 5 CMLR 317, [2002] All ER (EC) 783, para 19.

[36] Merger Reg 139/2004, OJ 2004 L24/1, see Vol II, App D.1, Art 2(2). See further Chap 8, below.

[37] Reg 4064/89, Art 2(2): App 33 to the 5th edn of this work.

[38] See further Merger Reg 139/2004 (n 36, above) Recital (26), which states that one of the aims, in formulating the revised substantive test, was to preserve the guidance which might be drawn from past judgments of the Community Courts.

[39] See further paras 12.087 *et seq*, below.

[40] Dir 2002/21, OJ 2002 L108/33, Arts 14–16.

[41] For market definition in this sector, see paras 4.093 *et seq*, below.

basis for the purpose of Articles 81 and 82 may sometimes differ from those identified on a forward-looking basis for the purpose of sector-specific regulation.[42]

State aid cases.   The process of market definition may also be important in   **4.014**
certain State aid cases. Article 87(1) prohibits as incompatible with the common
market aid which 'distorts or threatens to distort competition by favouring certain
undertakings or the production of certain goods . . . [and which] affects trade
between Member States.' In determining whether aid does distort or threaten
to distort competition, the Commission may need to determine the relevant
economic market.[43]

(c) Methodology for determining market definition

(i) Jurisprudence and guidelines

Judgments of the Community Courts.   The Community Courts have consist-   **4.015**
ently defined the relevant product market as comprising all those products and/or
services which are regarded as interchangeable or substitutable by the consumer,
by reason of the products' characteristics, their prices and their intended use.
The overall effect of the case-law was summarised in the judgment of the Court of
First Instance concerning Article 82 in *Tiercé Ladbroke*:

> 'the relevant product or service market includes products or services which are sub
> stitutable or sufficiently interchangeable with the product or service in question, not
> only in terms of their objective characteristics, by virtue of which they are particularly
> suitable for satisfying the constant needs of consumers, but also in terms of the
> conditions of competition and/or the structure of supply and demand on the market
> in question'.[44]

---

[42] Dir 2002/21 (n 40, above) Art 15(1); Commission Guidelines on market analysis and the assessment of significant market power under the Community regulatory framework for electronic communications networks and services (the 'SMP Guidelines'), OJ 2002 C165/6, see Vol II, App E.25, paras 25–27. See further para 4.093, below.

[43] In Cases C-329/93, etc, *Germany v Commission* [1996] ECR I-5151, [1998] 1 CMLR 591, the ECJ overturned the Commission's decision that a guarantee infringed the State aid rules, in part because the decision 'contains no information whatever as to the situation on the market in question, KAE's share of that market or the position of competing undertakings' (para 53). Further, market definition may be relevant to questions arising in relation to other parts of the State aid rules: see, eg Case T-155/98 *Société Internationale de Diffusion et d'Édition v Commission* [2002] ECR II-1179, [2002] 1 CMLR 1658, concerning Art 87(3)(d). But a finding of market definition will not be necessary in every State aid case. In Case C-351/98 *Spain v Commission* [2002] ECR I-8031, para 58, the ECJ held that 'in certain cases the very circumstances in which the aid has been granted show that it is liable to affect trade between Member States and to distort or threaten to distort competition.' See further Chap 15, below.

[44] Case T-504/93 *Tiercé Ladbroke v Commission* [1997] ECR II-923, [1997] 5 CMLR 309, para 81 (citing Case 31/80 *L'Oréal* [1980] ECR 3775, [1981] 2 CMLR 235, para 25; Case 322/81 *Michelin v Commission* [1983] ECR 3461, [1985] 1 CMLR 282, para 37; Case C-62/86 *AKZO Chemie v Commission* [1991] ECR I-3359, [1993] 5 CMLR 215, para 51; Case T-30/89 *Hilti v Commission* [1991] ECR II-1439, [1992] 4 CMLR 16, para 64; and Case T-83/91 *Tetra Pak v Commission* ('*Tetra Pak II*') [1994] ECR II-755, [1997] 4 CMLR 726, para 63).

The relevant geographic market is defined as comprising:

> 'the area in which the undertakings concerned are involved in the supply and demand of products or services, in which the conditions of competition are sufficiently homogeneous and which can be distinguished from neighbouring areas because, in particular, the conditions of competition are appreciably different in those areas.'[45]

4.016 **The Relevant Market Notice.**   The publication of the Relevant Market Notice in December 1997[46] was highly significant as it marked the adoption by the Commission of a more systematic and conceptually rigorous approach to market definition.[47] The Notice provides explanations, based on the previous case law, of the relevant product and geographic market definitions and describes the concept of a relevant market within the context of competition policy. It gives more detailed guidance on the assessment of competitive constraints in the context of the product and geographic dimensions of the market before providing examples of the evidence that may be used to establish the relevant market. Finally, the Commission provides details of how market shares are calculated with reference to market definition and concludes by identifying certain 'additional considerations' which are relevant. Moreover, the Notice incorporates the methodology of assessment known as the 'hypothetical monopolist' or 'SSNIP' test. The operation of this test is described in detail in paragraphs 4.024 to 4.028, below. The SSNIP test is viewed as providing the theoretical foundation for the definition of a particular economic market. However, the Notice does not hold out the SSNIP test as the exclusive test for market definition: it is described as 'one way' of determining the relevant market.[48] The Commission seeks to reconcile the described methodology with the earlier judgments of the Community Courts by stating that the Commission interprets the Court of Justice's definitions according to the orientations defined in the Notice.[49]

---

[45] Case T-310/01 *Schneider Electric v Commission* [2002] ECR II-4071, [2003] 4 CMLR 768, para 153, following para 8 of the Relevant Market Notice. See also Merger Reg (n 36, above) Art 9(7); Case 27/76 *United Brands v Commission* [1978] ECR 207, [1978] 1 CMLR 429, paras 11 and 44; *Michelin* (n 44, above), para 26; Case 247/86 *Alsatel v Novasam* [1988] ECR 5987, [1990] 4 CMLR 434, para 15; *Tiercé Ladbroke* (n 44, above), para 102; and *France v Commission* (n 35, above), para 143.

[46] Relevant Market Notice, OJ 1997 C372/5, see Vol II, App C.10. For commentary, see Desai, 'The European Commission's Draft Notice on Market Definition: a Brief Guide to the Economics' (1997) ECLR 473; Baker and Wu, 'Applying the Market Definition Guidelines of the European Commission' (1998) ECLR 273.

[47] In the *XXVIIth Report on Competition Policy* (1997), point 44, the Commission stated (in the context of the publication of the Relevant Market Notice): 'Such clarification is evidence of the Commission's willingness to increase the predictability of its market analyses for practitioners of Community competition law.'

[48] Relevant Market Notice, para 15. Similarly, the subsequent SMP Guidelines (n 42, above), refer to the SSNIP test as 'but one example of methods used for defining the relevant market' (at n 26). See also the UK OFT Guidelines on Market Definition (n 12, above) at para 2.5, stating that the SSNIP test is 'usually' employed.

[49] Relevant Market Notice, para 9. As a Commission Notice, it is binding on the Commission to the extent that it does not depart from the rules of the Treaty as interpreted by the Community Courts: Case T-114/02 *BaByliss v Commission* [2003] ECR II-1279, [2004] 5 CMLR 21, para 143.

Limited application of the SSNIP test. The judgments of the Community **4.017**
Courts since publication of the Relevant Market Notice continue to reflect the
traditional approach to market definition. For example, in *Ambulanz Glöckner*
(an abuse of dominance case), the Court of Justice held that transport services
provided by medical aid organisations fell into two distinct product markets, the
market for emergency transport and the market for patient transport, which were
not substitutable for one another. Emergency transport services require highly
qualified personnel and sophisticated equipment 24 hours a day; and since
emergency transport is particularly costly, it was not a valid substitute for non-
emergency services.[50] Even in the field of merger control, the Commission itself
expressly applies the SSNIP test relatively rarely.[51] In a merger notification, the
Commission seeks specific information from customers and competitors to assist
in defining the relevant product and geographic markets. The merging parties
sometimes submit analyses to show the correlation that exists between prices of
different products or to estimate cross-elasticities of demand.[52] But even then, the
Commission uses these in addition to, not in substitution for, other approaches to
market definition.[53] As regards Article 81, for undertakings seeking to calculate
whether they meet the market share threshold of a block exemption or carrying
out self-assessment pursuant to Regulation 1/2003, information for a SSNIP
analysis is generally not available. In Article 82 cases, there is the additional
problem that the dominant undertaking's prevailing price may well exceed the
competitive price.[54] Proper application of the test therefore involves determination of a hypothetical competitive price, an exercise which is difficult, if not
impossible, to conduct with sufficient accuracy: see further paragraph 4.031,
below. Moreover, in *Roberts*, the Court of First Instance held that when consumer
choice is influenced by considerations other than price, it is inappropriate to
define the market only by the criterion of price.[55] The Court therefore rejected a
challenge, based on failure to apply the SSNIP test, to the Commission's determination that both pubs and clubs selling alcoholic beverages for consumption on
the premises were in the same market.

---

[50] Case C-475/99 [2001] ECR I-8089, [2002] 4 CMLR 726, para 33. See also Case T-65/96
Kish Glass v Commission [2000] ECR II-1885, [2000] 5 CMLR 229, para 62 (appeal dismissed,
Case C-241/00 [2001] ECR I-7759, [2002] 4 CMLR 586).

[51] In a large sample of Phase II merger cases from the period 1990–2001, it was found that the
Commission referred expressly to the use of the SSNIP test in just 4 per cent of geographic market
definitions and 11 per cent of product market definitions: Copenhagen Economics, *The internal
market and the relevant geographical market* (2003), http://europa.eu.int/comm/enterprise/library/
lib-competition/doc/marketdef_final_report.pdf.

[52] For the cross-elasticity of demand, see para 4.043, below.

[53] Monti (n 12, above) who observes: 'As an economist, I know well the limitations of our
discipline!'.

[54] This may result in the so-called 'cellophane fallacy': see para 4.030, below.

[55] *Roberts v Commission* (n 15, above) paras 38, *et seq.*

4.018 **Reconciling the various approaches to market definition.** The adoption of a more developed approach to market definition has helped to focus on the issue of substitutability as a competitive constraint. This highlights the role of the marginal consumers: the critical question is whether a sufficient number of consumers would switch their purchases to product B so as to render unprofitable a small increase in the price of product A. In *Airtours*, a merger case, one issue was whether package holidays to short-haul destinations constituted a different market from package holidays to long-haul destinations. The Court of First Instance upheld the Commission's finding that these were two distinct product markets on the basis of (a) objective characteristics: there was a substantial difference between the average flight times; (b) pricing differences: the average prices of long-haul packages were about double those of short-haul packages; and (c) conditions of competition: Airtours itself published separate brochures for short- and long-haul package holidays. In response to the argument that the use of averages disguised the position at the margins, the Court accepted the significance of the marginal customers but held that the Commission had not erred in concluding that where the differences were so significant it was unlikely that a sufficient number of customers would react to price increases in short-haul package holidays by purchasing long-haul package holidays so that the price of the one constrained the price of the other.[56] Thus the SSNIP test can perhaps best be regarded as a conceptual foundation for market definition. Product characteristics, prices and intended use may serve as a practical proxy in defining the product market, and the divergence in prices, local preferences and the conditions of competition may similarly serve as a proxy in defining the geographic market. More particularly, the SSNIP test is a quantitative test and, if sufficient reliable data[57] is available, then it will generally be applied to determine the relevant market. However when sufficient and reliable data are not available, then a qualitative assessment is carried out, taking into account all relevant available evidence to identify those goods or services that provide a close competitive constraint on one

---

[56] n 34, above. The Commission's decision was annulled on other grounds. cf *United Brands v Commission* (n 45, above), where the ECJ upheld the Commission's finding that there was a market for bananas which was distinct from soft fruit as whole on the basis of the particular physical characteristics of bananas and the existence of certain categories of consumers (such as the very young and the elderly) who were able to eat bananas but not other soft fruit. However the unwillingness of only some customers to switch to other soft fruit by no means establishes whether a small increase in the price of bananas would be profitable. See n 77, below for criticism of the ECJ's approach in *United Brands*.

[57] eg survey evidence may not be reliable as explained in n 150, below. Accordingly, in COMP/38.233 *Wanadoo Interactive*, 16 July 2003, [2005] 5 CMLR 120, the Commission applied a SSNIP test based directly on the results of a customer survey, but also took account of other relevant available evidence to supplement its conclusions, basing its finding that residential high-speed internet access was a distinct market from low-speed access on the differences in use, technical features and performances, and prices (appeal dismissed, Case T-340/03 *France Télécom v Commission* [2007] 4 CMLR 919, on appeal, Case C-202/07P, not yet decided). See also the SMP Guidelines (n 42, above) para 48.

another in order to provide the best possible approximation for the SSNIP test. Altogether, the Relevant Market Notice and the subsequent case law and decisional practice now point to a more multifaceted approach.[58] This approach was expressed by the United Kingdom Competition Appeal Tribunal, applying a domestic statutory prohibition that mirrors Article 82, in *Aberdeen Journals (No. 1)*:

> 'The . . . relevant product market is to be defined by reference to the facts in any given case, taking into account the whole economic context which may include notably (i) the objective characteristics of the products; (ii) the degree of substitutability or interchangeability between the products, having regard to their relative prices and intended use; (ii) the competitive conditions; (iv) the structure of the supply and demand; and (v) the attitudes of consumers and users. . . However, this check list is neither fixed, nor exhaustive, nor is every element mentioned in the case law necessarily mandatory in every case. Each case will depend on its own facts, and it is necessary to examine the particular circumstances in order to answer what, at the end of the day, are relatively straightforward questions: do the products concerned sufficiently compete with each other to be sensibly regarded as being in the same market? Are there other products which should be regarded as competing in the same market? The key idea is that of competitive constraint; do the other products alleged to form part of the same market act as a competitive constraint on the conduct of the allegedly dominant firm?'[59]

(ii) Factors relevant to defining markets

Three types of competitive constraints. In defining relevant markets it is **4.019** important to distinguish between demand-side substitution, supply-side substitution and potential competition as competitive constraints facing suppliers.[60] Of these, only demand- and supply-side substitution may be considered to be sufficiently direct in their competitive impact to be relevant for the purposes of market definition. By way of hierarchy, demand-side substitution is regarded as the more important criterion in assessing the relevant market since it constitutes the most immediate and effective disciplinary force on the suppliers of a given product, in particular in relation to their pricing decisions.[61] Demand-side substitution comprises purchasers' willingness to switch to other products (or to equivalent products from other geographic areas) in response to an increase in price of the product under consideration. Supply-side substitution (ie the possibility that suppliers not currently supplying the product could begin production, or that

---

[58] Note the observation by Geroski and Griffith, n 1 above: 'Identifying market boundaries is as much an art as it is a science, and it sometimes requires fairly finely tuned judgments to do the exercise properly.' (Prof Geroski was Dep Chairman and then Chairman of the UK Competition Commission.)

[59] *Aberdeen Journals Ltd (No 1) v Director General of Fair Trading* [2002] CAT 4, [2002] CompAR 167, paras 96 and 97.

[60] Relevant Market Notice (n 46, above) para 13.

[61] Case T-177/04 *easyJet v Commission* [2006] ECR II-1931, [2006] 5 CMLR 663, at para 99, approving Relevant Market Notice, para 13.

suppliers outside the relevant geographic area could start to supply within it) may also be taken into account where its effects are sufficiently direct and immediate.

4.020 **Potential competition.**   When potential supply-side considerations are not sufficiently direct and immediate to qualify as supply-side substitution, they are regarded as *potential* competition and are therefore taken into account at the stage of substantive assessment of market power and not when defining the relevant market.[62] The significance of potential competition depends on various considerations, in particular the barriers to entry.[63] There may also be relevant competition (from both demand- and supply-side perspectives) from products or services that are outside the relevant market. By definition, such products or services do not provide a close and immediate competitive constraint on products and services within the market. However, this does not mean that they exercise no competitive constraint and such products or services may therefore still be relevant to the overall assessment of competition.[64]

4.021 **Market definitions are contextual.**   Market definitions may differ depending on the context in which they arise because they are simply a means of identifying the close competitive constraints faced by the supplier, or suppliers, of a particular set of products in a particular area and in the particular circumstances under review. Thus, given that behavioural cases are essentially retrospective (assessing, broadly speaking, whether consumers have suffered in the past) whereas merger control and sectoral regulation are essentially prospective (assessing, broadly speaking, whether consumers will suffer in the future), different market definitions may be adopted in different cases in the same industry.[65] On a prospective basis, the proposed liberalisation of a market[66] or the launch of a new technology may mean that a different market definition is appropriate. The activities of the parties to a merger may affect the relevant market definition when examining whether the merged group would be able profitably to harm consumers through price increases, reductions in quality, choice or innovation (rather than whether each of the parties separately could do so). For example, markets for glass packaging

---

[62] See further para 4.054, below.

[63] Relevant Market Notice, para 24.

[64] Vickers 'Competition Economics and Policy', speech of 3 October 2002 (www.oft.gov.uk/News/Speeches+and+articles/2002/index.htm), refers to the 'pitfall [of] the "zero-one" fallacy—the tendency, once "the market" is defined, to think of all products within it as extremely substitutable for the products at the centre of concern, and those products beyond the boundaries as irrelevant. In reality matters are of varying degrees, and the useful tool of market definition must be employed with this in mind'. See also, eg Case M.72 *Sanofi / Sterling Drug* (10 June 1991), in which competition from outside the product market was taken into account in clearing a merger.

[65] Relevant Market Notice, para 12; SMP Guidelines (n 42, above) paras 26–27.

[66] See, eg Case M.3440 *ENI/EDP/GDP* (9 December 2004), para 16 (taking into account proposed liberalisation of energy markets) (appeal on other grounds dismissed, Case T-87/05 *EDP v Commission* [2005] ECR II-3745).

might generally be national, but in the case of a merger between suppliers with plants in southern France and northern Spain, the relevant geographic market might include southern France and northern Spain to reflect the fact that the parties' plants compete with one another.[67] Further, when products are bundled in the market, there may be numerous different markets comprising different groups of bundled and unbundled supply.[68]

'One-way' markets.   Market definitions are not necessarily symmetrical. It does **4.022** not follow from the fact that product X exerts a close competitive constraint on product Y, that product Y exerts a close competitive constraint on product X: whether it does so is an empirical question in each case. For example, in *Group 4 Falck/Securicor*, the Commission found that suppliers of service A could readily commence the supply of service B, whereas the reverse was not true, and stated that, since the merger related exclusively to the supply of service B, the market should include both service A and service B (while noting that a different market definition might be appropriate in a merger affecting the supply of service A).[69]

Market definitions are not static.   Market definitions may change over time, for **4.023** example because of changes in the structure of demand or supply or as a result of technological or legislative changes. It is therefore necessary to consider the market afresh as each case arises.[70] Accordingly, under the regulatory framework for electronic communications introduced in 2002, the Commission is under an obligation regularly to review its recommendation on relevant product and service

---

[67] See, by analogy, Case M.3397 *Owens-Illinois/BSN Glasspack* (9 June 2004), paras 24–26. See also UK OFT Guidelines on Market Definition (n 12, above) n 32 and para 5.10 (since there is no clear cut-off in differentiated products, products which were identified as forming parts of separate markets in one case may be found to form part of a single product market in a second).

[68] See Europe Economics, *Market Definition in the Media Sector – Economic Issues* (Report for the European Commission, 2002) (http://europa.eu.int/comm/competition/publications/studies/european_economics.pdf), paras 2.3.15–2.3.32 and A1.74–A1.82.

[69] Case M.3396 *Group 4 Falck/Securicor* (28 May 2004), para 16 and n 1. In Case COMP/37.792 *Microsoft* [2005] 4 CMLR 965 (on appeal Case T-201/04 *Microsoft v Commission*, judgment of 17 September 2007, see Postscript below), the Commission concluded that customers wanted media players that were able to play *and stream* audio and video files, and stated: 'While a streaming media player is therefore a substitute for media players which deliver less functionality, substitution the other way round is not readily available as less performing media players do not satisfy specific consumer demand' (para 415). In Case T-191/98 *Atlantic Container Line v Commission* [2003] ECR II-3275, [2005] 4 CMLR 1283, which concerned the activities of shippers between ports in Northern Europe and the US, the CFI upheld the Commission's finding that whereas northern European ports were substitutable for Mediterranean ports, the converse was not the case. See also Case M.2547 *Bayer/Aventis Crop Science*, OJ 2004 L107/1; Case M.3431 *Sonoco/Ahlstrom*, OJ 2005 L159/13, paras 26 and 27.

[70] Cases T-125 & 127/97 *Coca-Cola v Commission* [2000] ECR II-1733, [2000] 5 CMLR 467, [2000] All ER (EC) 460, paras 81–82. In *GSM radiotelephony services in Italy*, OJ 1995 L280/49, the Commission identified a distinct market for cellular digital mobile radiotelephony services, whilst recognising that, in time, those services might form part of a single telecommunications systems market.

markets and NRAs are expected periodically to review their decisions as to whether markets are competitive.[71]

(iii) The SSNIP test

4.024 **SSNIP test.** The SSNIP test involves identifying the smallest group of products sold over the smallest area[72] in which a hypothetical monopoly supplier could *profitably* apply a 'Small, but Significant, Non-transitory Increase in Price'.[73] For that reason, it is also known as the 'hypothetical monopolist' test. The SSNIP might be defeated (ie rendered not profitable) by customers switching to alternative products or locations (demand-side substitution) or suppliers of other products, or suppliers present in other locations commencing supply (supply-side substitution). The test therefore focuses on the question of economic substitutability. It is analytically rigorous because the objective of market definition is to identify *close* competitive constraints. The test assumes, in summary, that a market is 'something worth monopolising'.[74] The test is usually applied on the basis of a 5 to 10 per cent increase in the hypothetical monopolist's prices,[75] with the prices of other products remaining constant. The postulated increase in price is considered on a '*non-transitory*' basis, meaning that purchasers would not be able to avoid the hypothetical price increase by merely delaying purchases until the price returns to its previous level.

4.025 **The SSNIP test focuses on *marginal* purchasers and suppliers.** A relevant market will be found when the application of the SSNIP test reveals that the number of purchasers that would switch to alternative products or would cease purchasing (and/or the number of suppliers that would commence supplying) within a relatively short time frame is sufficiently small that the price increase would be profitable. Therefore, looking at the demand side by way of illustration, the SSNIP test does not examine whether *all* customers would switch, or even whether a *majority*

---

[71] Framework Directive (n 40, above) Arts 15(1) and 16(1); SMP Guidelines (n 42, above) para 28 and see paras 4.093 *et seq*, below.

[72] It may also be necessary to identify the time period in question, ie the temporal dimension of the market (see paras 4.089–4.090, below).

[73] See Geroski and Griffith, n 1, above; Niels, 'The SNNIP Test: Some Common Misconceptions' (2004) Comp Law 267; Crocioni, 'The Hypothetical Monopolist Test: What it can and cannot tell you' (2002) ECLR 354; Kokkoris, 'The Concept of Market Definition and the SSNIP Test in the Merger Appraisal' (2005) ECLR 209. The test was first adopted by a competition authority in the US Dept of Justice 1984 Merger Guidelines.

[74] For a theoretical application of the SSNIP test in a very local market, see the judgment of the UK Competition Appeal Tribunal in *JJ Burgess v Office of Fair Trading* [2005] CAT 25, [2005] CompAR 1151 (funeral services in Stevenage and Knebworth) para 216.

[75] See the discussion in the ICN Project on Merger Guidelines, Chap 2, para 1.32 (n 1, above) about the circumstances in which a smaller price increase might be relevant. The UK OFT Guidelines on Market Definition (n 12, above) state that 5 to 10 per cent is merely an 'indicative range'.

of customers would switch.[76] Rather, it asks whether a *sufficient* number of customers would switch to render the price increase unprofitable. Switching to alternative products by a relatively small proportion of customers may be sufficient to render the price increase unprofitable. The existence of a significant proportion of customers that is unwilling or unable to switch to alternative products is therefore irrelevant[77] (unless such customers in themselves constitute a distinct market).[78] The same principles apply in relation to supply-side substitution: the issue is not whether all potential suppliers would commence production, but whether a sufficient number would do so to render the SSNIP unprofitable for the hypothetical monopolist. The logic behind focusing on the actions of marginal purchasers and suppliers is that, in the absence of price discrimination, non-marginal purchasers are protected from anti-competitive price rises by the willingness of the marginal purchasers to switch to alternative products or the willingness of marginal suppliers to commence supply. The time period in which the substitution should occur will depend on the industry in question but it is clear that it must occur within the short-term since the market comprises only direct competitive constraints; a one year period may be taken as a working starting point.[79]

SSNIP test focuses on whether a price increase would be profitable. The **4.026** SSNIP test is applied to determine whether a price increase by a hypothetical monopolist would be profitable, assuming that all other conditions remain the same.[80] The test of 'profitability' is important because suppliers can (leaving legal restrictions on pricing to one side[81]) set their prices at any level they choose, but have an incentive to raise prices only if this increases their profitability. Whether a SSNIP would be profitable will depend on whether the increased revenues from sales at a higher price and the savings in costs derived from reduced output exceed

---

[76] Contrast in this respect Case M.3779 *Pernod Ricard/Allied Domecq* (24 June 2005), para 12.

[77] For this reason, the significance attached by the Commission to the existence of certain very young and old 'captive' consumers of bananas in *United Brands* (n 45, above) has been criticised: eg Bishop & Walker (n 1, above) para 4.24.

[78] See para 4.046, below, regarding the possibility of a group of customers constituting a distinct market.

[79] Relevant Market Notice (n 44, above) paras 16 and 20; SMP Guidelines (n 42, above) n 37. See in this regard Case M.2420 *Mitsui/CVRD/Caemi*, OJ 2004 L92/50, n 29 to para 111; cf Case M.53 *Aérospatiale-Alenia/de Havilland*, OJ 1991 L334/42, [1992] 4 CMLR M2, para 14, ruling out supply-side substitution on the basis that it would take three to four years to adapt). See also the UK OFT's Guidelines on Market Definition (n 12, above) paras 3.6 and 3.15.

[80] In Case M.2947 *Verbund/Energie Allianz*, OJ 2004 L92/91, para 75, the Commission stated: 'Even if a new market entry coincides with a small but permanent price increase (in the range of 5–10%) by the monopolistic undertaking and the undertaking loses market share as a result, this still does not prove that it would not profit from the price increase nevertheless, on account of a marked increase in the profit margin.'

[81] See, in particular, paras 10.104 *et seq*, below, in relation to the pricing constraints imposed on dominant suppliers under Art 82.

the revenues foregone through lost sales.[82] This calculation therefore depends on two factors: first, the extent to which demand for the product forming the subject of the price increase would decrease as a result (referred to as the 'own-price elasticity of demand'); and secondly, the extent to which demand must fall before the price increase ceases to be profitable taking into account any costs saved as a result of the reduction in output (referred to as the 'critical loss'). The use of these concepts is explained further in paragraphs 4.043 and 4.044, below.

4.027   **SSNIP test applied iteratively.**   The SSNIP test is applied by considering as a starting point the products that are actually supplied by the undertaking(s) in question and the area in which the undertaking(s) supply the goods or services, and progressively expanding the products and areas under analysis until a group of products is identified within a particular area for which a SSNIP would be profitable.[83] This means that the relevant market is generally[84] the narrowest product and geographic grouping in which a hypothetical monopoly supplier could profitably impose a SSNIP. Although complex questions could arise about the order in which products or areas are added to the analysis, in practice such questions rarely prove problematic because there is usually a small number of credible 'candidates' for the relevant market definition.[85]

4.028   **Application of the SSNIP test in practice.**   If the SSNIP test were to be applied directly and literally, it would require a great deal of evidence which is not normally available in competition cases. This practical concern is less daunting when it is recalled that the SSNIP test is a 'speculative experiment': it articulates the rationale for the process of market definition (based on the identification of close competitive constraints that would prevent a hypothetical monopolist from exercising market power) and therefore provides a structural discipline for the process of market definition. Against this background, the fact that the relevant market is defined using the best evidence available, even if this evidence does not permit a direct application of the SSNIP test, is not problematic.

---

[82]   There will be relatively few circumstances in which a SSNIP results in an *increase* in the output of a given product, although it is possible to imagine circumstances in which the image of a premium or luxury good could be enhanced by an increase in price (particularly if the existing price led customers to believe that the product was of inferior quality).

[83]   In the case of the temporal dimension of the market, it is necessary to consider the time at which the goods or services are purchased or supplied (eg peak-time travel). Theoretically, the product, geographic and temporal dimensions of a market should be defined simultaneously: eg the same product may form part of different product markets in different areas because of different local preferences.

[84]   For a discussion of 'concentric' markets, see Lindsay (n 1, above) para 3-002(b).

[85]   See Relevant Market Notice (n 47, above) para 26.

(iv) Limitations on the SSNIP test

Circumstances where the SSNIP test cannot be applied.   The SSNIP test **4.029**
focuses on the response of purchasers and suppliers to a SSNIP applied to the prevailing, market price (or, in certain cases, the competitive price).[86] However, in
some instances, there is no meaningful 'market price'. This applies in particular in
the case of products, such as infrastructure projects, which are bespoke and where
competition often takes the form of a bidding market. In such cases, the
Commission is likely to focus to a greater extent on an analysis of the closeness of
competition between various suppliers, for example through a bidding study.
Further, the SSNIP test may not be appropriate when the price is subject to
regulation (rather than being freely determined);[87] or when one of the products is
supplied without any charge at the point of consumption (eg free newspapers or
public broadcasting);[88] or in the case of a new product that has not been supplied
before;[89] or when the conduct being considered is alleged predatory pricing.[90]

The 'cellophane fallacy'.   A supplier with a monopoly in a relevant economic **4.030**
market will, if acting rationally, price at a level (the monopoly price) at which any
further increase in price is inevitably unprofitable. A price increase by a supplier
with significant market power, falling short of monopoly, may also be unprofitable for similar reasons. Applying the SSNIP test to the prevailing price in those
circumstances would therefore result in an erroneously wide market definition.
This is the so-called 'cellophane fallacy', named after a decision of the United
States Supreme Court concerning the dominant supplier of cellophane, Du Pont,
which had raised prices to such a level that consumers were prepared to substitute
other materials. The Court found that cellophane was therefore part of a wider,
flexible packaging market, although it appears that the other materials would not
have been regarded as substitutes had the price of cellophane been competitive.[91]

---

[86] See para 4.031, below.

[87] See the SMP Guidelines (n 42, above) para 42.

[88] But, cf Europe Economics, *Market Definition in the Media Sector – Economic Issues* (n 65,
above) paras 2.4.21 and 3.4.81–3.4.90, raising the possibility of applying the SSNIP test in this
context on the basis of a small reduction in *quality* rather than a small increase in price.

[89] See, eg the decision of the UK Competition Appeal Tribunal, *The Racecourse Association v
Office of Fair Trading* [2005] CAT 29, [2006] CompAR 99 which concerned the collective selling of
broadcasting rights of horseracing for use in interactive betting (paras 139 *et seq*).

[90] eg judgment of the UK Competition Appeal Tribunal in *Aberdeen Journals Ltd (No. 2) v The
Office of Fair Trading* [2003] CAT 11, [2003] CompAR 67 (paras 259 *et seq*).

[91] *United States v Du Pont de Nemours & Co.* 351 US 377, 76 S Ct 994 (1956). In *United States v
Eastman Kodak Co.* 853 F Supp. 1454 (WD NY), the US District Court pithily summarised the
problem as being that 'at a high enough price, even poor substitutes look good to the consumer.'
In that case, the Court of Appeals upheld the conclusion that foreign films were part of the same
market as Kodak's film in the US: *United States v Eastman Kodak Co.* 63 F.3d 95 (2nd Cir, 1995).
The Court distinguished *Du Pont* on the grounds that foreign film and Kodak film were close substitutes (whereas cellophane and wax paper were very different products) and the 'premium' being
charged by Kodak was small and not manifestly above competitive levels.

The existence of the cellophane fallacy means that particular care is needed in defining the market in Article 82 cases.

4.031 **Applicable price for the SSNIP test.** As a result of the cellophane fallacy, it is necessary to consider whether the SSNIP test should be applied to the prevailing (market) price or another price (the 'competitive' price).[92] In merger cases, the price level at which the SSNIP test is applied should, in principle, be the prevailing market price, reflecting the competitive conditions operating within that market. This is because the issue under investigation is the effect of the merger on the market as it currently operates, not on a more or less competitive market.[93] By contrast, in behavioural cases, the SSNIP test should, in principle, be applied to the competitive price. However, the difficulties in identifying the level of a hypothetical, competitive price mean that, in practice, the SSNIP test can rarely be relied upon for an accurate market definition in an Article 82 case. It may still be used on the assumption that the prevailing price is the competitive price, but it will be necessary to use various other criteria to check the robustness of possible market definitions.[94]

4.032 **Varying strength of competition within the market: differentiated products.** Differentiated products exist when consumers perceive differences between them although they are sufficiently close substitutes that they form part of the same product market. For example, in the case of branded goods, customers may perceive differences between two otherwise similar products. When markets include differentiated products, the strength of the competitive constraint exercised by one product on another will vary. This has particular importance in the case of merger control: an assessment of the 'closeness' of competition between the products supplied by the merging parties may be more important than the definition of the market; for example, a merger between suppliers of products which are one another's closest competitors in 'product space' may harm consumers even if the merged group has a relatively low combined market share.[95]

---

[92] There are suggestions that the use of the SSNIP test may lead to an unduly *narrow* market definition if parties in the market are engaging in very low pricing in an attempt to build up customers in a market which is expected to 'tip' (ie a market in which the presence of network effects suggests that a supplier which builds a critical mass is likely to become so attractive to customers that it will evolve into a dominant, or the sole, supplier) or to benefit from economies of scale; see OECD, *Merger Review in Emerging High Innovation Markets*, DAFFE/COMP(2002)20 (http://www.oecd.org/dataoecd/40/0/2492253.pdf), 8.

[93] Relevant Market Notice, para 19. It is arguable that the competitive, rather than the prevailing, price should be used in merger cases when there is some form of coordination in the setting of prices: see the UK Competition Commission's Merger Reference Guidelines (CC2, 2003) para 2.10.

[94] This difficulty is recognised in the DG Competition discussion paper on the application of Art 82 to exclusionary abuses (December 2005), paras 13–16. See also *Attheraces Ltd v British Horseracing Board* [2007] EWCA Civ 38, where in a case alleging excessive pricing the English Court of Appeal held that the competitive price was not necessarily cost plus a reasonable profit margin.

[95] See Baker and Wu (n 46, above), who note that 'classifying firms as either "in" or "out" of the market would misrepresent competition in a differentiated products market, for such an approach

2. Product Market

(a) Demand-side substitution

In general.   Demand-side substitution exists when a sufficient[96] number of   **4.033**
purchasers of product A regard product B as a credible alternative and would
switch from A to B in response to a small change in relative prices. The Relevant
Market Notice states that demand-side substitution is the most important factor
in determining the relevant product market:

> 'From an economic point of view, for the definition of the relevant market, demand
> substitution constitutes the most immediate and effective disciplinary force on the
> suppliers of a given product, in particular in relation to their pricing decisions. A firm
> or a group of firms cannot have a significant impact on the prevailing conditions
> of sale, such as prices, if its customers are in a position to switch easily to available
> substitute products or to suppliers located elsewhere.'[97]

In those cases in which the Commission seeks to reach a conclusion on market
definition, it is willing to consider a broad range of evidence regarding demand-
side substitution and does not follow a rigid hierarchy of different sources or types
of evidence.[98]

Product characteristics and functional interchangeability.   Products that have   **4.034**
materially different characteristics[99] and/or are not functionally interchangeable[100] generally do not form part of the same economic market. In *Hoffmann-La
Roche*, the Court of Justice stated: 'The concept of the relevant market in fact
implies that there can be effective competition between the products which form
part of it and this presupposes that there is a sufficient degree of interchangeability
between all the products forming part of the same market in so far as a specific use

---

fails to recognise that there may be a range of products that compete with varying degrees of
intensity with the products under investigation.' See generally Chap 8, below in relation to merger
control analysis.

[96]   ie focusing on the behaviour of *marginal* purchasers: see para 4.025, above.

[97]   Relevant Market Notice, OJ 1997 C372/5: Vol II, App C.10, para 13. This passage was
approved and adopted by the CFI in Case T-177/04 *easyJet v Commission* [2006] ECR II-1931,
[2006] 5 CMLR 663, para 99.

[98]   ibid, para 25.

[99]   In Case M.3333 *Sony/BMG*, OJ 2005 L62/30, the Commission placed great weight on a
comparison of product characteristics when defining a market for recorded music excluding online
music (paras 22–23); annulled on other grounds, Case T-464/04 *Impala v Commission* [2006] ECR
II-2289, [2006] 5 CMLR 1049, further appeal pending, Case C-413/06P .

[100]   Products with different characteristics may be used for the same purposes (eg cable and
satellite connections to access the internet) and products with the same purpose may form separate
markets (eg paging services and mobile telephony, both of which enable customers to send two-way
short messages): see the SMP Guidelines (n 42, above) para 45.

of such products is concerned.'[101] However, the mere fact that products have similar characteristics or serve the same functions is not sufficient to show that they form part of the same relevant market: the focus of market definition is on economic substitutability and, more particularly, whether purchasers of product A would switch to product B in response to a small relative increase in the price of product A.[102] The Court of Justice has accordingly emphasised that reference to the characteristics of the products in question is, by itself, insufficient for the purposes of market definition.[103] In particular, switching costs, brand preferences or other consumer preferences may prevent two products with similar characteristics from forming part of a single relevant product market.[104] For example, in appraising the *Nestlé/Perrier* merger, the Commission found that products such as bottled waters, tea and milk were not in the same market merely because they served the broad purpose of quenching thirst, as they were not sufficiently close alternatives that a SSNIP in relation to bottled waters would be defeated by purchasers switching to another product.[105] In *Atlantic Container Line*, the applicants challenged the Commission's finding that the relevant market was containerised liner shipping between northern Europe and the US using sea routes between ports in northern Europe and ports in the US and Canada, arguing that there was competition from air transport and conventional (bulk-break) liner transport. The Court of First Instance rejected this argument on the basis that, except in limited cases, other forms of maritime transport and air transport were not substitutes for container shipping.[106]

4.035 **Switching data.** In assessing the likelihood of substitution, and the extent to which two products can genuinely be said to be substitutable in the eyes of consumers,[107] it is important to have regard to previous examples of switching,

---

[101] Case 85/76 *Hoffmann-La Roche v Commission* [1979] ECR 461, [1979] 3 CMLR 211, para 28.

[102] See Relevant Market Notice, para 36. See also Europe Economics, *Market Definition in the Media Sector – Economic Issues* (n 68, above) para 3.4.10.

[103] See *Michelin* (n 44, above) para 37, where the ECJ emphasised that the competitive conditions and the structure of supply and demand on the market must also be taken into consideration.

[104] See the UK OFT Guidelines on Market Definition (n 12, above) para 3.7.

[105] Case M.190 *Nestlé/Perrier*, OJ 1992 L356/1, para 9.

[106] Case T-395/94 *Atlantic Container Line v Commission* [2002] ECR II-875, [2002] 4 CMLR 1008, [2002] All ER (EC) 684, paras 269–290. See also Case 66/86 *Ahmed Saeed Flugreisen v Zentrale zur Bekämpfung unlauteren Wettbewerbs* [1989] ECR 803, [1990] 4 CMLR 102, para 40; *Compagnie Générale Maritime v Commission* (n 14, above) para 48. In *Société Routière de l'Est Parisien* (Cour de Cassation, commercial chamber, 22 May 2001), BOCCRF No. 9, 23 June 2001, the French Supreme Court (applying the domestic equivalent to Art 82), quashed the decision of the Court of Appeal that rejected a single market encompassing both landfill sites and waste recycling: the Court of Appeal had based its decision only on the different technical characteristics and the intrinsic nature of the two services without applying the criterion of demand-side substitution.

[107] Care should, however, be taken in examining switching data where there is evidence that the market is not operating competitively since customers' behaviour may have been artificially influenced by existing distortions in competition: for a recent UK case, see *Aberdeen Journals (No. 2)* (n 90, above) para 262.

provided that such evidence is probative of current market conditions (or of future market conditions in the context of a merger): the fact that switching has taken place historically may not be reliable evidence that this would occur again. Similarly, evidence showing that purchasers had switched from product A to product B does not necessarily establish that purchasers would in the future switch from product B to product A.[108]

Stability of demand.   If demand for a product has been stable over a long period, **4.036** this suggests that the product comprises a distinct product market. In particular, such evidence will be strongest when there have been developments in relation to similar products that have failed to impact to a material extent on demand for the product in question. In *Tetra Pak v Commission*, the Court of Justice upheld the Court of First Instance's assessment that the fact that packaging materials other than carton were able to gain only a marginal share of UHT-milk packaging over a 15-year period was evidence that non-carton packaging was not a viable substitute for carton. The Court of Justice found that 'such stability in demand is a relevant criterion for determining whether carton is interchangeable with other materials.'[109]

Consumer preferences and perceptions.   Consumer preferences may affect the **4.037** question of what products are properly considered to be part of the same market. This may mean that products which are functionally interchangeable nevertheless comprise distinct product markets. For example, luxury and standard versions of a product may form separate product markets because customer preferences for the luxury products depend less on the product's functionality and more on its perceived quality and image.[110] In *Airtours*, one element in the Commission's determination that long-haul and short-haul package holidays were in separate markets was the 'image or idea of the holiday' with long-haul packages seeming more exotic and therefore appealing to single people or couples without children whereas short-haul package holidays, for example to Mediterranean resorts, are of more interest to families.[111] In assessing customer preferences, the Commission

---

108 For the concept of 'one-way' markets, see para 4.022, above.

109 Case C-333/94P *Tetra Pak v Commission* [1996] ECR I-5951, [1997] 4 CMLR 662, [1997] All ER (EC) 4, para 15.

110 In *Yves Saint Laurent Parfums*, OJ 1992 L12/24, [1993] 4 CMLR 120, when considering the perfumes which formed the subject of selective distribution systems, the Commission stated: 'Their nature as luxury products ultimately derives from the aura of exclusivity and prestige that distinguishes them from similar products falling within other segments of the market and meeting other consumer requirements'. The Commission also referred to the maintenance of a prestige brand image on the 'luxury cosmetics products market' (para 5). The CFI noted on appeal (on other grounds) that '[luxury cosmetics, in particular luxury perfumes] enjoy a 'luxury image' which distinguishes them from other products lacking such an image': Case T-19/92 *Leclerc v Commission* [1996] ECR II-1851, [1997] 4 CMLR 995, para 114.

111 *Airtours*, OJ 2000 L93/1, [2000] 5 CMLR 494 (decision quashed on other grounds, n 35, above). See further para 4.018, above.

takes account of the way in which products are branded and marketed. In *Guinness/Grand Metropolitan*, the Commission noted that product development, advertising and promotional expenditure was determined by the particular brand of spirit and brands did not appear to be easily transferable between different spirit types; the Commission therefore concluded that consumer demands in terms of taste, price and image were focused on each individual type of spirit rather than wider categories of drinks.[112]

4.038 **Switching costs and other barriers.** In considering whether a sufficient number of purchasers would switch to alternative products, it is necessary to identify the *costs to customers* of switching[113] and any additional *barriers to switching*. For example, a manufacturer purchasing alternative components for use within a production process may need to adjust or replace machinery, adjust moulds or dies, or re-train staff.[114] In assessing switching costs and other barriers, the extent to which switching has occurred in the past is of obvious importance.

4.039 **Order and bidding data.** Order and bidding data may provide valuable information about the products which consumers regard as economic substitutes at prevailing prices. For example, in *Bertelsmann/Springer/JV*, the Commission examined order patterns which showed that customers requiring the printing of large orders or of publications with more than 64 pages almost invariably used rotogravure printing, rather than offset, indicating that there was a separate market for the supply of rotogravure printing.[115] Similarly, in *Oracle/Peoplesoft*, the Commission carried out a bid study to identify the suppliers which had been invited to tender, with the aim of identifying which suppliers formed part of the relevant economic market.[116]

4.040 **Shock analysis or event evidence.** Shock analysis or event evidence involves examining the effect on the market of changes or shocks which altered its operation. Such evidence may provide powerful, practical information on the likely effect of a SSNIP. If the relative prices of two products change (for example because of a change in raw material prices affecting just one of the two products), then it may be possible to assess the effect on sales of both products to determine whether material switching occurred as a result.[117] Similarly, if a new brand or

---

[112] Case M.938 *Guinness/Grand Metropolitan*, OJ 1998 L288/24, para 14.
[113] eg, if the costs of switching exceed 5 to 10 per cent, then a SSNIP in relation to product A would be unlikely to be defeated by switching to product B (unless the pre-SSNIP price of product A was sufficiently high relative to product B that a SSNIP in relation to product A was sufficient to induce customers to switch to product B in sufficient numbers to render the SSNIP unprofitable).
[114] See further Relevant Market Notice (n 97, above) para 42.
[115] Case M.3178 *Bertelsmann/Springer/JV* (3 May 2005), paras 41 and 44.
[116] Case M.3216 *Oracle/Peoplesoft*, OJ 2005 L218/6, paras 98, 129, 136, 142 and 144.
[117] See further Kokkoris (n 73, above, 213); and Harkrider, 'Operationalizing the Hypothetical Monopolist Test', http://www.usdoj.gov/atr/public/workshops/docs/202598.pdf.

type of product is launched, it may be possible to identify the products from which it won share; if a new product has only a marginal impact on the sales of existing products, it may be possible to conclude that the new product is not regarded by consumers as an effective substitute for the original ones.[118] Finally, if supplies of a product are dramatically reduced (for example, because of the financial difficulties of a supplier or because of an explosion in a plant) it may be possible to identify which products gained sales.[119] Such evidence is objective and, depending on its type and quality, may come close to a 'real life SSNIP experiment', therefore providing very valuable evidence of the relevant market definition.[120]

Demand-side substitution evidence: an example of past event evidence. 4.041 In *Procter & Gamble/Schickendanz*,[121] the question arose whether tampons and sanitary towels formed part of the same relevant product market. Both products broadly served the same basic function, but the issue was whether there was a *sufficient* degree of substitutability that an attempt by a hypothetical monopolist to raise the price of tampons would be rendered unprofitable by a sufficient number of consumers switching to sanitary towels. The Commission was able to examine the effect of the launch of a major new brand of sanitary towels. The evidence showed that the launch of the new brand did not reduce the share of female hygiene supplies accounted for by tampons (suggesting that the new brand won share from other sanitary towel brands and not from tampon brands) and that, following the launch of the brand, the price of tampons rose whereas the price of sanitary towels remained constant (suggesting that, following the launch of the new product, competition was relatively more intense in the supply of sanitary towels than in the supply of tampons). The Commission concluded that there were separate relevant product markets for tampons and sanitary towels.

Different absolute price levels. Products that are priced at materially different 4.042 absolute levels are less likely to form part of the same relevant product market, as the inference from the disparity in prices is that customers place relatively greater

---

[118] See, eg *Tetra Pak v Commission* (n 44, above), where the CFI analysed the effect of the introduction of systems for aseptic packaging in plastic bottles, returnable glass bottles and pouches on demand for aseptic systems using cartons.

[119] See, eg Case M.3570 *Piaggio/Aprilia* (22 November 2004), in which the Commission examined which products customers bought when Aprilia's sales of 50cc scooters were reduced as a result of its financial difficulties.

[120] See Relevant Market Notice (n 97, above) para 38: 'this sort of information will normally be fundamental for market definition. If there have been changes in relative prices in the past (all else being equal), the reactions in terms of quantities demanded will be determinant in establishing substitutability. Launches of new products in the past can also offer useful information, when it is possible to precisely analyse which products lost sales to the new product.'

[121] Case M.430 *Procter & Gamble/Schickendanz*, OJ 1994 L354/32, paras 62–71.

value on the more expensive product.[122] In *Microsoft*,[123] the Commission identified a separate market for workgroup server operating systems (excluding operating systems for other types of server) because there were clearly identifiable bands of prices charged for different types of server operating system. Microsoft had argued that the fact that higher-level versions of its server operating system could also carry out workgroup server tasks pointed towards a single market. However, the Commission rejected this argument on the ground that users of higher-level server operating systems would be unlikely to pay the premium for a higher-level system to perform the (comparatively simple) tasks of a workgroup server.[124] However, there are exceptions to this general approach. In particular, products of different qualities (with different prices) would form part of the same market if consumers reacted to a change in relative prices by switching between them.[125] Further, the products may be functionally interchangeable (a kitchen roll with 80 sheets is the same as two rolls each with 40 sheets and rational customers would pay twice the price for a roll with twice as many sheets) and, separately, there may be a continuous chain of substitution across a range of products with different prices, eg laptop computers ranging from £500 to £1,000.[126] Equally, there may be other considerations relating to the way in which the product or service is provided which mean that it would be inappropriate to draw conclusions on demand-side substitution on the basis of price differentials alone.[127]

4.043 **Price elasticity.** The Commission states that it takes account of quantitative data, when available, on own-price elasticity and cross-price elasticity that is capable of withstanding rigourous scrutiny:[128]

---

[122] The converse clearly does not follow: the fact that two dissimilar products have the same, or similar, prices in no way suggests that they are in the same relevant market.

[123] *Microsoft* (n 69, above) paras 369–382. See also the judgment of Paris Court of Appeal, 1st ch, 24 May 2005, *Digitechnic v Microsoft* (BOCCRF 20 September 2005), where the Court criticised the market analysis of software applications by the Conseil de la Concurrence.

[124] In this context, the Commission also pointed (at para 376) to Microsoft's own marketing material which stated that customers were able to tailor their investment to their needs 'without overbuying for operations that don't require maximum uptime.'

[125] In *Microsoft* (n 69, above) para 372, it was clear that the price differentials were such that a SSNIP of one grade of server operating system would not have made the price in any way comparable to that charged for the next higher grade of server. See the SMP Guidelines (n 41 above) para 46: 'A low quality product or service sold at a low price could well be an effective substitute to a higher quality product sold at higher prices. What matters in this case is the likely response of consumers following a relative price increase.' See also ICN, *Investigative Techniques Handbook for Merger Review* (2005) (http://www.internationalcompetitionnetwork.org/handbook_5-5.pdf) 59–60; UK OFT Guidelines on Market Definition (OFT 403, 2004) para 3.5.

[126] See further para 4.066, below, in relation to continuous chains of substitution.

[127] See *Roberts v Commission*, para 4.017, above. In *Société Routière de l'Est Parisien* (n 106, above) the French Supreme Court held that a significant and sustained difference in price between the two waste disposal services was not enough by itself to support a finding of separate markets.

[128] Relevant Market Notice (n 97, above) para 39.

(i)   Own-price elasticity measures the effect on the demand for a product (or group of products)[129] of an increase (or reduction) in the price of that product (or group of products), assuming that the prices of all other products are held constant. If the own-price elasticity exceeds one,[130] then demand for the product (or group of products) is relatively sensitive to changes in its price: ie demand is 'elastic'. By contrast, if the own-price elasticity is less than one, then price changes do not have such a significant effect on purchasing patterns (ie demand is 'inelastic'), which *suggests* that there are not close economic substitutes and therefore that the product (or group) forms a separate relevant product market.[131] Data on the own-price elasticity of demand can therefore play a key role in determining the relevant market. However, in order to determine whether a SSNIP would be *profitable* (which is the relevant issue for the purposes of market definition), it is necessary also to consider the relevant supplier's (or suppliers') costs structure (effectively to understand how much profit is derived from each sale).

(ii) Cross-price elasticity measures the effect on demand for one product of an increase (or reduction) in the price of another particular product, assuming that the prices of all other products are held constant. Analysis of the cross-price elasticities of different products indicates whether there is a competitive relationship between them and can also show which product provides the closest competitive constraint.[132] The Commission has used cross-price elasticity data on a number of occasions,[133] although such evidence is of

---

[129] There is an important distinction between the own-price elasticity of demand for *a product generally* (which is the relevant analysis for the purposes of applying the SSNIP test, since the issue is whether a hypothetical monopolist of all examples of that product could profitably raise its prices) and own-price elasticity of demand for *a particular supplier's product* (which may be high if there are other suppliers offering similar products).

[130] The elasticity is calculated as the percentage change in the quantity demanded divided by the percentage change in the price. eg, if a price increase from €10 to €10.25 reduces demand from 10,000 to 9,500 units, the own-price elasticity of demand is -2. However, since it is very unusual for demand to rise as price rises (which would produce a positive elasticity), it is common practice to discuss negative own-price elasticities as if they were positive numbers.

[131] See, eg Case M.619 *Gencor/Lonrho*, OJ 1997 L11/30, [1999] 4 CMLR 1076 (upheld on appeal in Case T-102/96 *Gencor v Commission* [1999] ECR II-753, [1999] 4 CMLR 971, [1999] All ER (EC) 289).

[132] This may be relevant if it is necessary to widen the hypothetical product market to encompass additional products when applying the SSNIP test: see para 4.027, above.

[133] In *Hilti*, OJ 1988 L65/19, [1989] 4 CMLR 677 (appeal and further appeal dismissed: Case T-30/89 *Hilti v Commission* (n 44, above); Case C-53/92P [1994] ECR I-667, [1994] 4 CMLR 614), the Commission examined the cross-price elasticity of demand between powder activated fastening systems and other fixing methods. Since changes in the price of one method did not appear to cause an appreciable shift of demand to (or from) the alternative method of fixing, the cross-price elasticities of demand for the different types of fixing method suggested that they did not form part of a single market.

secondary importance when compared with own-price elasticity data (which bears more directly on the likely outcome of a SSNIP).[134]

4.044 **Critical loss analysis.** The critical loss is the smallest percentage of sales which, if lost, would render unprofitable a hypothetical price increase of 5 to 10 per cent in relation to a given product, or group of products. It is calculated mathematically using data on the incremental margin.[135] In general, the higher the profit on marginal sales, the lower the critical loss because the sales that are 'lost' following the increase in price result in a greater loss of profit than in cases of lower margins.[136] Once the critical loss is identified, the next step is to estimate the proportion of sales which would in fact be lost by a hypothetical monopolist seeking to apply a SSNIP (based on the own-price elasticity of demand). If the actual predicted loss that would result from a SSNIP is larger than the critical loss for a given product, then a SSNIP would be unprofitable and it is necessary to re-run the analysis on a wider candidate market. By contrast, if the actual predicted loss is smaller than the critical loss, then the SSNIP would be profitable and a relevant economic market has been identified.

4.045 **Price correlations.** If there is good quality data on the prices of two products over time, then it is possible to calculate the *price correlation*, ie the extent to which the two data series follow one another.[137] Generally, if the two price series track one another closely (ie if the correlation is positive and high) then this suggests that the two products form part of the same market (as the price of one

---

[134] See ICN, *Investigative Techniques Handbook for Merger Review* (n 125, above) 58: 'In fact, cross elasticities are not really the issue at all – it is the own-price elasticity that is of the greatest consequence'. In Case M.1313 *Danish Crown/Vestjyske Slagterier*, OJ 2000 L20/1, the Commission found that price developments of different meats were '*to a certain extent linked*', as evidenced by positive cross-price elasticities between the different types of meat, but relied on the fact that the own-price elasticities for beef, pork and poultry were inelastic as evidence that there were distinct markets for fresh beef, fresh pork and fresh poultry (paras 27–29).

[135] For a full explanation of the use of critical loss analysis as a step in the application of the SSNIP test, see: Epstein and Rubinfeld, Report for European Commission: 'Effects of Mergers Involving Differentiated Products', (http://europa.eu.int/comm/competition/mergers/others/effects_mergers_involving_differentiated_products.pdf), 28–33; Harris and Veljanovski, 'Critical Loss Analysis: Its Growing Use In Competition Law' (2003) ECLR 213. See also the UK OFT Guidelines on Market Definition (n 125, above) para 3.7; and Kokkoris, 'Critical Loss Analysis: Critically Ill?' (2005) ECLR 518.

[136] The UK OFT Guidelines on Market Definition (n 125, above) para 3.7, note that the fact that an undertaking can set a high price might suggest in itself that its current customer base is not particularly price sensitive.

[137] A price correlation of +1 implies that the prices track one another perfectly. A price correlation of -1 implies that the prices move in opposite directions in a perfect pattern. A price correlation of 0 implies that there is no relationship between movements in the prices of the two products. For the use of price correlation analysis see, eg Case M.1939 *Rexam (PLM)/American National Can* (19 July 2000), para 12; Case M.2187 *CVC/Lenzing*, OJ 2004 L82/20; Case M.2972 *DSM/Roche Vitamins*, OJ 2004 L82/73, para 43; and *ENI/EDP/GDP* (n 66, above) para 92 (appeal on other grounds dismissed, *EDP v Commission* (n 66, above)).

appears to be influencing the second).[138] However, in drawing such a conclusion, it is necessary to confirm that there is not a *false correlation* created, for example, by a common inflationary trend, common exchange rate changes or changes in common components or inputs.[139] For example, it may be possible to observe similarities in the price movements of plastics and petrol over time, caused by underlying movements in the price of oil, but that does not mean that consumers regard plastics and petrol as substitutes.

Price discrimination resulting in distinct markets. If price discrimination is **4.046** practicable, there may be a separate market for supply to the category of customers willing to pay higher prices. In order to identify a separate market on this basis, it is necessary to show (a) that suppliers are able to charge different prices to objectively distinct groups of customers; and (b) that there is no possibility of arbitrage.[140] Price discrimination may occur, for example, in relation to the time at which the service is purchased[141] or the identity of the customer (eg discount travel tickets for students or the elderly). Arbitrage occurs when consumers being charged higher prices can instead obtain supplies (whether directly or indirectly) from those charged low prices. For example, price discrimination led the Commission to identify a distinct product market in *Microsoft*. The Commission found that Microsoft was able to price discriminate in the supply of server operating systems depending on the intended use of the product by the purchaser.

---

[138] In merger control cases, the Commission has regarded correlations of more than 0.80 as high and of below 0.65 as low: see *Rexam (PLM)/American National Can* (n 137, above) paras 11–13; *CVC/Lenzing* (n 137, above) paras 21, 73, 74 77 and 108–115.

[139] In order to overcome the false correlation issue, standard price correlation can be supplemented with more sophisticated techniques, such as Granger causality tests and co-integration tests (see Ivaldi et al, 'The Economics of Unilateral Effects', November 2003, Report for the EuropeanCommission,(http://europa.eu.int/comm/competition/mergers/review/the_economics_of_unilateral_effects_en.pdf) 97).

[140] cf Relevant Market Notice (n 97, above) para 43. In Case T-5/02 *Tetra Laval v Commission* [2002] ECR II-4381, [2002] 5 CMLR 1182, [2002] All ER (EC) 762, paras 259–269, the CFI annulled the Commission's definition of distinct sub-markets, in effect because there was insufficient evidence that these conditions were fulfilled: see, on further appeal, Case C-12/03 *Commission v Tetra Laval* [2005] ECR I-987, [2005] 4 CMLR 573, para 103. Note also the Opinion of AG Tizzano (at para 143): 'the fact that a single operator (not followed by its competitors) adopts a pricing policy that discriminates against a particular group of customers does not of itself make it possible to identify a specific market in relation to that group of customers, for the presence of other operators that do not practise the same policy may prevent the establishment of essentially different market conditions for the group of customers in question.' The AG's reasoning reflects the fact that an application of the SSNIP test would have required consideration of whether *all of the suppliers acting together* (ie equivalent to the hypothetical monopolist) could profitably have raised their prices to the distinct group of consumers. For the position when the groupings used for the discrimination overlap and a product which is priced differently between different groups competes with a product for which no price discrimination is attempted, see Europe Economics, *Market Definition in the Media Sector – Economic Issues* (n 68, above) paras 2.2.15 and 2.2.16.

[141] These situations may instead be analysed as part of the temporal market: see paras 4.089–4.090, below.

Substantially higher prices were charged for server operating systems with higher workload levels.[142]

4.047 **Trade relationships.** Identical or similar products may form separate markets if they are produced for, or sold to, different categories of customers, or if they are sold through different distribution channels. In *Endemol Entertainment v Commission*, the Court of First Instance upheld the Commission's determination that, as regards the production of Dutch language television programmes, the market for independent production of programmes was separate from the market for in-house productions of the public broadcasters.[143] In addition to objective differences between the kind of programmes produced, the in-house productions of the public broadcasters were essentially for their own use and any sales to third parties were made on the international market whereas the independent producers sold on the domestic, Dutch market. In *SCA/Metsä Tissue*, the Commission identified separate markets for identical (tissue-paper) products for 'away from home' and domestic use, since they were sold to different customers through different distribution channels.[144] Similarly, the Commission has regularly identified separate markets for the supply of vehicle parts to original equipment manufacturers ('OEM') and, separately, the independent aftermarket ('IAM').[145]

4.048 **Shares of supply.** If the shares of supply accounted for by producers differ materially between product types, this suggests that the product types form parts of separate product markets.[146]

4.049 **Demand-side substitution evidence: views of customers and competitors.** Evidence on the likely response of *customers* to a SSNIP can be obtained by asking them directly.[147] The Relevant Market Notice states that the Commission often contacts the main customers and competitors of the companies involved to

---

[142] In this instance, the price discrimination that indicated distinct product markets was made not on the basis of the identity of the customer, but rather on the intended use of the product by that consumer: *Microsoft* (n 69, above) paras 369–382. See also *Piaggio/Aprilia* (n 119, above): distinct market for motor scooters with engines under 50cc, largely because the most significant source of demand for these scooters derived from a distinct group of customers (people between 14 and 16 years of age) in several Member States who were not permitted by law to drive scooters with larger engines.

[143] Case T-221/95 *Endemol Entertainment v Commission* [1999] ECR II-1299, [1999] 5 CMLR 611, paras 106–112 (dismissing a challenge to the Commission's prohibition of a joint venture under the Merger Regulation).

[144] Case M.2097 *SCA/Metsä Tissue*, OJ 2002 L57/1, para 17; similarly Case M.623 *Kimberly Clark/Scott*, OJ 1996 L183/1, paras 29–33.

[145] See, eg Case M.3436 *Continental/Phoenix* (26 October 2004), paras 14–15. See also Case M.3658 *Orkla/Chips* (3 March 2005), para 9, following a line of cases distinguishing the supply of food products to the retail sector, on the one hand, and the food service sector on the other.

[146] See, eg Case M.3083 *GE/Instrumentarium*, OJ 2004 L109/1, para 29.

[147] See Hildebrand, 'The European School in EC Competition Law' (2002) 25(1) World Competition 3, 11–16.

gather their views on the relevant product market and to inquire about the likely result of a SSNIP analysis.[148] Hence, in *Guinness/Grand Metropolitan*,[149] the Commission considered whether there were separate product markets by spirit type or wider markets (for example, for white or brown spirits). It placed weight on evidence that third parties characterised spirits drinkers as having a degree of loyalty towards one or two brands within a particular category and that they were likely to enjoy occasion-based consumption patterns which were well-entrenched and unlikely to be changed in response to a SSNIP. However, answers to hypothetical questions need to be treated with caution.[150] The views of *competitors* are treated with particular care when they comprise mere assertion because the evidence may be self-serving and/or inaccurate, but are accorded more weight when there is factual evidence in support (for example, referring to past behaviour).

Demand-side substitution evidence: internal company documents. Documents **4.050** created by or for the relevant undertakings relating to the question of consumer demand and competition from other products generally constitute valuable evidence in defining the market, provided that they have not been produced for the purposes of the case in question.[151] Such documents may include analyses produced by the undertaking itself or market surveys or reports drawn up by third parties for the undertaking's commercial purposes. Such pre-existing internal documents often provide evidence on the competitive constraints faced by the undertaking in question that reflect its genuinely-held assessment of market conditions.[152] For example, in *De Post-La Poste* the Commission relied on evidence from internal documents showing that La Poste recognised a distinction on the demand side between general letter post (for correspondence with the general public) and business-to-business mail (for delivery to a closed group

---

148 Relevant Market Notice (n 97, above) para 40.

149 *Guinness/Grand Metropolitan* (n 112, above) para 13.

150 See the UK OFT Guidelines on Market Definition (n 125, above) para 3.7; McFadden, 'Economic Choices' (2001) 91 The American Economic Review 373; Hughes and Beale, 'Customer Surveys in UK Merger Cases' (2005) ECLR 297, 302–303. Concerns about the unreliability of responses to general hypothetical questions can be mitigated by careful structuring of the questions (as explained in the ICN, 'Developing Reliable Evidence in Merger Cases' (http://www.internationalcompetitionnetwork.org/Reliable.pdf) 13) or the use of conjoint analysis (ie surveying customers by asking them to choose between alternative products; the customer preferences can be used to build up a model of market demand: see Dubow, 'Understanding Consumers: The Value of Stated Preferences in Antitrust Proceedings' (2003) ECLR 141).

151 In Case C-62/86 *AKZO Chemie v Commission* [1991] ECR I-3359, [1993] 5 CMLR 215 the ECJ noted (in the context of AKZO's challenge to the finding that there was a single market for organic peroxides) that 'it may be seen from AKZO's internal documents . . . that AKZO itself regarded organic peroxides as a single market, since it calculates its market share in relation to these products as a totality' (para 53).

152 See, eg *ENI/EDP/GDP* (appeal on other grounds dismissed, *EDP v Commission*) (n 66, above) para 267.

of users).[153] However, the Commission treats with caution customer surveys produced by the merging parties themselves for the purposes of the case in question (even when these have been carried out by independent third parties acting on behalf of the relevant parties) because of the risk that the evidence will be skewed or distorted by the commissioning party's objectives in the investigation or dispute.[154]

(b) Supply-side substitution

4.051 **In general.** Supply-side substitution focuses on the extent to which alternative suppliers would switch, or begin, production in response to a hypothetical price increase. The relevance of supply-side substitution in market definition was established relatively early in the history of Community competition law. In *Continental Can*, the Court of Justice ruled that supply-side substitution forms an essential element of market definition.[155] The Court annulled the Commission's finding that there were distinct markets for different types of light metal containers in part because the Commission had failed adequately to evaluate the possibility that suppliers of other types of light metal containers might commence supply. A market for light metal containers for meat and fish could not be established unless it was proved that competitors from other sectors of the market for light metal containers were not in a position to enter that market, by a simple adaptation, with sufficient strength to create a serious counterweight.

4.052 **Use of supply-side substitution in practice.** Supply-side substitution is generally of secondary importance to demand-side substitution in defining relevant product markets because the criteria for its application are difficult to satisfy. In terms of the types of situation in which supply-side substitution arises, the Relevant Market Notice gives the example of paper. From a demand-side perspective, it may not be possible to use a different grade of paper as a substitute. However, from a supply-side perspective, if producers of one grade of paper can readily adjust their output to supply a different quality, then the market comprises papers of all grades.[156] Similarly, in a merger case concerning academic publishing, the Commission found on the demand-side that there was little substitution between (and even within) subjects, but identified a broader market on the basis

---

[153] *De Post-La Poste*, OJ 2002 L61/32, [2002] 4 CMLR 1426. See also *Aberdeen Journals Ltd (No. 1) v Director General of Fair Trading* (n 59, above) (judgment of the UK Competition Appeal Tribunal), para 104.

[154] Relevant Market Notice, OJ 1997 C372/5, see Vol II, App C.10, para 41.

[155] Case 6/72 *Europemballage and Continental Can v Commission* [1973] ECR 215, [1973] CMLR 199.

[156] Relevant Market Notice, para 22. The example is based on Case M.166 *Torras/Sarrio* (24 February 1992), para 18.

of supply-side considerations.[157] In *Kish Glass*, the Court of First Instance dismissed a challenge to a Commission decision which had rejected a complaint under Article 82 on the ground that Pilkington did not hold a dominant position in the market for the sale of float glass to dealers. As regards the argument that the relevant product market should have been defined more narrowly as the market for only 4mm float glass, the Court upheld the Commission's finding that since production of 4mm glass is technically almost identical to that of glass of other thicknesses, glass manufacturers can convert production 'rapidly and without excessive cost'.[158]

Conditions for consideration of supply-side substitution. The Relevant **4.053** Market Notice states that supply-side substitution should be taken into account when defining markets provided that the competitive constraint is sufficiently close and equivalent to demand-side substitution in terms of effectiveness and immediacy.[159] More particularly, the Notice provides that supply-side substitution is taken into account when two conditions are met: first, suppliers must be able to switch to supply the product in the 'short term'; and secondly, suppliers must be able to switch 'without incurring significant additional costs or risks'. The Notice does not identify a specific period within which a supplier must be able to commence supply in order for this to be regarded as 'short term', but refers to 'a period that does not entail a significant adjustment of existing tangible and intangible assets.'[160] In *Michelin*, the Court of Justice upheld the Commission's finding that there was a distinct market for replacement tyres for heavy vehicles (excluding car and van tyres) in part because: 'The fact that time and considerable investment are required in order to modify production plant for the manufacture of light-vehicle tyres instead of heavy-vehicle tyres or vice versa means that there is no discernible relationship between the two categories of tyre enabling production to be adapted to demand on the market'.[161]

Relationship between supply-side substitution and potential competition. If **4.054** potential rival suppliers do not pose a sufficiently close competitive constraint to be treated as part of the relevant market through supply-side substitution, the

---

[157] M.3197 *Candover/Cinven/Bertelsmann-Springer* (29 July 2003) para 14. See also Case M.3805 *Crompton/Great Lakes* (15 June 2005), paras 25–28 (supply-side substitution between different types of antioxidants).

[158] Case T-65/96 *Kish Glass v Commission* [2000] ECR II-1885, [2000] 5 CMLR 229, paras 68–69. The CFI stated that the argument based on lack of cross-price elasticity between supply of 4mm glass and glass of other thicknesses therefore cannot be upheld. Appeal on other grounds dismissed, Case C-241/00p [2001] ECR I-7759, [2002] 4 CMLR 586.

[159] Relevant Market Notice, para 20.

[160] Relevant Market Notice, n 4. See further n 79, above, in relation to the meaning of '*short term*'. See also para 4.056, below, in relation to technological barriers to supply-side substitution.

[161] Case 322/81 *Michelin v Commission* [1983] ECR 3461, [1985] 1 CMLR 282, para 41. See also Relevant Market Notice, para 23: for branded beverages, the lead time involved in advertising, testing and distributing bottled beverages means that alternative producers are not considered as close competitive constraints in terms of supply-side substitution.

scope for them to commence supply may nevertheless form part of the substantive competitive assessment under the potential competition principle (or new entry). The Court of First Instance has stated that although supply-side substitution and potential competition are conceptually different issues, there is 'overlap in part' since the distinction between them lies primarily in whether the competitive constraint is immediate or not.[162] For example, in *Enso/Stora*, the Commission found that although it was technically possible to produce different grades of virgin-based packaging board from the same machine, switching production to a different grade involved significant cost and that a quick supply response was not possible; the Commission therefore considered those factors not in the market definition but under potential competition.[163]

4.055 **Supply-side substitution evidence: switching costs.** In assessing supply-side substitution, it is accordingly necessary to assess the costs which would be incurred by suppliers in switching to supply the product in question. The Commission may therefore contact possible alternative suppliers to obtain evidence of the likely costs involved. These typically include changes to manufacturing equipment, training of staff, marketing costs and any distribution costs[164] associated with the product. In addition, there may be opportunity costs in giving up the profits associated with the supply of other products, depending in particular on whether the supplier has spare capacity. In *Microsoft*, the Commission evaluated potential supply-side substitution in the provision of client personal computer operating systems (having already found that there were no realistic substitutes on the demand side). The Commission highlighted the significant marketing costs that would be required in order to launch a new product in this area, since familiarity

---

[162] *Atlantic Container Line v Commission* (n 69, above) para 834. In that case, at paras 827–836, the CFI rejected the applicants' arguments that the Commission had failed to examine the possibility of supply-side substitution (by converting non-containerised vessels into containerised liners), finding that the Commission's discussion of the absence of potential competition was sufficient also to justify the absence of supply-side substitution. Commission Guidelines on market analysis and the assessment of significant market power under the Community regulatory framework for electronic communications networks and services (the 'SMP Guidelines'), OJ 2002 C165/6, see Vol II, App E.25, note that distinguishing between supply side substitution and potential competition may be particularly difficult in electronic communications markets given their dynamic character. 'What matters, however, is that potential entry from suppliers is taken into consideration . . . either at the initial market definition stage or at the subsequent stage of assessment of significant market power' (at n 24). See also the UK OFT's Market Definition Guidelines (n 125, above) para 3.18.

[163] Case M.1225 *Enso/Stora*, OJ 1999 L254/ 9, [1999] 4 CMLR 372, paras 37–40

[164] In *Irish Sugar*, OJ 1997 L258/1, [1997] 5 CMLR 666, para 90 (appeal dismissed, Case T-228/97 *Irish Sugar v Commission* [1999] ECR II-2969, [1999] 5 CMLR 1300, [2000] All ER (EC) 198; further appeal on other grounds dismissed, Case C-497/99P [2001] ECR I-5333, [2001] 5 CMLR 1082), the Commission identified separate markets for each of retail and industrial uses for sugar because the pack sizes in the different channels were very different, the customers were largely distinct and the distribution channels were different. It would therefore not have been possible for a supplier of one quantity of sugar quickly and easily to have switched to supplying the other quantity, bearing in mind the need to find a route to market.

with the look and feel of a product was considered to be of paramount importance for many customers.[165] This contributed to the Commission's conclusion that there was no supply-side substitution.[166]

Supply-side substitution evidence: other barriers to switching.   There may **4.056** be barriers to switching (other than costs) which prevent alternative suppliers from commencing supply. For example, statutory or other, similar restrictions may prevent alternative suppliers from being considered part of the market.[167] Technological barriers may have a similar effect. For example, in *Microsoft*, the Commission examined whether there was supply-side substitutability in the provision of streaming media players from developers of other software applications. The Commission found that existing suppliers of streaming media players controlled the technology through intellectual property rights, effectively creating a barrier to entry, which meant that supply-side substitution was unlikely to have a disciplinary effect on competitive behaviour.[168]

Supply-side substitution: shock analysis or event evidence.   Evidence regard- **4.057** ing suppliers' responses to actual, past events is of particular value on the question of supply-side substitution. For example, there may be evidence about whether alternative suppliers switched production in response to increases in prices by existing suppliers or changes in the pattern of demand. In *Michelin*, the Court of Justice upheld the Commission's decision to exclude car and van tyres from the

---

165 *Microsoft* (n 69, above) paras 334–341.

166 Together with other factors (ie significant technical barriers which would be expected to take significantly over a year to overcome).

167 In Case T-229/94 *Deutsche Bahn v Commission* [1997] ECR II-1689, [1998] 4 CMLR 220 (appeal on other grounds dismissed, Case C-436/97P *Deutsche Bahn v Commission* [1999] ECR I-2387, [1999] 5 CMLR 776), the CFI upheld the Commission's finding that the provision of rail services constituted the relevant product market, distinct from the wider provision of railway transport services, in part because railway undertakings held a statutory monopoly in the provision of rail services in their respective countries (para 55). The fact that these services were linked to the provision of railway transport services more generally (in which there was competition) did not prevent rail services constituting a separate economic market. See also *DSD*, OJ 2001 L166/1, [2002] 4 CMLR 609 (appeal dismissed, Case T-151/01 *Duales System Deutschland v Commission* [2007] 5 CMLR 300): requirement under German law that a system for recovery of sale packaging should operate in an area covering at least a *Land* meant that substantial initial investment and a long development period would be required prior to commencing supply; it was therefore unlikely that other suppliers in the general waste management sector would enter the market in the short term.

168 *Microsoft* (n 69, above) paras 418–422. The Commission pointed to n 4 of its Relevant Market Notice: see at n 156 above. See also Case T-83/91 *Tetra Pak v Commission* (*'Tetra Pak II'*) [1994] ECR II-755, [1997] 4 CMLR 726 para 69, in which the CFI upheld the Commission's reasoning, concluding that: 'the manufacture of machinery for the aseptic packaging of UHT milk in cartons requires complex technology, which only Tetra Pak and its competitor PKL had succeeded in developing and making operational during the period considered in the Decision. Manufacturers of non-aseptic machinery using cartons, operating on the market closest to the market in the aseptic machinery in question, were therefore not in a position to enter the latter market by modifying their machinery in certain respects for the market in aseptic machinery' (further appeal to the ECJ dismissed: *Tetra Pak v Commission*, n 109, above).

market for replacement tyres for heavy vehicles, in part because when there had been insufficient supply of tyres for heavy vehicles some years previously, Michelin NV had granted an extra bonus rather than using surplus production capacity for car tyres to meet demand (as would have been expected if supply-side substitutability had existed).[169]

4.058 **Application of the SSNIP test.** On the supply side, application of the SSNIP test involves examining whether a price rise of 5 to 10 per cent by a hypothetical monopoly supplier would be rendered unprofitable as a result of suppliers of other products beginning to supply the product in question.[170] The issue is therefore the same as that considered in relation to demand-side substitution, namely whether there are sufficiently close competitive constraints to prevent suppliers in the hypothetical market from harming consumers by raising prices or reducing quality, consumer choice or innovation.

(c) Particular issues in determining the product market

(i) Connected markets

4.059 **Connected markets.** Connected markets[171] arise when products are related by their function or usage[172] (such as printers and printer cartridges or mainframe computers and maintenance and repair services for those computers).[173]

---

[169] *Michelin v Commission* (n 161, above) para 41. This conclusion was reviewed and reaffirmed by the Commission in its more recent decision, *Michelin II*, OJ 2002 L143/1, [2002] 5 CMLR 388, appeal on other grounds dismissed: Case T-203/01 *Michelin v Commission* [2003] ECR II-4071, [2004] 4 CMLR 923.

[170] See Niels (n 73, above) 273–275, for discussion of whether supply-side substitution should also include suppliers which already produce the product in question but would respond to a SSNIP by *increasing* their levels of supply by diverting production capacity away from the production of other similar products.

[171] cf so-called 'two-sided' markets, where a single product market may itself be two-sided, ie where a common platform brings together two distinct sets of customers, with the benefit derived by one set of customers increasing in line with the increased size of the other set: eg heterosexual dating agencies (men and women), telephone directories (advertisers and consumers) and credit card suppliers (retailers and consumers). When applying the SSNIP test to define such two-sided markets, account must be taken of the effect of the SSNIP on both groups of customers. See Evans, 'The Antitrust Economics of Two-Sided Markets' (2002) (http://ssrn.com/abstract=332022); and Oldale and Wang, 'A Little Knowledge Can be a Dangerous Thing: Price Controls in the Yellow Pages Industry' (2004) ECLR 607.

[172] Separately, two or more products may form a 'cluster' or 'bundled' market if a monopoly supplier of the cluster could profitably impose a SSNIP (ie if the SSNIP would not be defeated by customers choosing to purchase from suppliers offering the products separately). 'Cluster' markets typically arise when customers value the convenience of 'one-stop shopping' (eg supermarkets). See the UK OFT Guidelines on Market Definition (n 125, above) para 5.11; Veljanovski, 'Banking Mergers: Transaction Costs and Market Definition' (2000) ECLR 195.

[173] See generally the discussion of connected/secondary markets in NERA, *Switching Costs*, Economic Discussion Paper 5 (http://www.oft.gov.uk/NR/rdonlyres/CFD52220-7862-41A7-8F6F-53F3B4FE78FE/0/oft655.pdf), paras 7.10–7.17; and Europe Economics, *Market Definition in the Media Sector – Economic Issues* (n 68, above) paras 2.3.33–2.3.44.

The question arises whether each product forms part of a separate market or the products together form a single (or 'system') market. For example, there could be a market for printers in which X and Y compete and then two separate downstream markets for cartridges for X's printers and cartridges for Y's printers; or there might be a market for all printers and a separate market for all printer cartridges; or there might be just one market for printer systems of which the printer and the cartridges are integral parts. In the early case of *Hugin*, the Court of Justice held that the relevant market was for spare parts for Hugin cash registers because those parts were not interchangeable with spare parts for cash registers of other makes.[174] In *Hilti* the Commission concluded that there were separate product markets for nail guns, Hilti-compatible cartridge strips and Hilti-compatible nails. This was because the Commission found that nail guns and consumables were not purchased together and cartridge strips and nails were specifically manufactured for use in a single brand of gun.[175] Hilti challenged the Commission's conclusion, arguing that guns, cartridge strips and nails should be regarded as forming a complete 'powder-actuated fastening system.' However, this argument was rejected by the Court of First Instance on the grounds that its acceptance would be 'tantamount to permitting producers of nail guns to exclude the use of consumables other than their own branded products in their tools' whereas, in fact, there was evidence that there were independent manufacturers of gun nails, including manufacturers of gun nails for Hilti guns.[176]

System markets. System markets are more likely when consumers identify the **4.060** total costs of ownership, including secondary products (ie the 'whole-life cost') when acquiring the primary product.[177] It follows that 'whole-life costing' can be excluded when customers cannot form reasonable expectations about the likely costs of secondary product purchases when they acquire the primary product.

---

[174] Case 22/78 *Hugin v Commission* [1979] ECR 1869, [1979] 3 CMLR 345. See also the UK OFT Guidelines on Market Definition (n 125, above) para 6.4.

[175] *Hilti*, OJ 1988 L65/19, [1989] 4 CMLR 677.

[176] Case T-30/89 *Hilti v Commission* [1991] ECR II-1439, [1992] 4 CMLR 16; further appeal to the ECJ dismissed Case C-53/92P [1994] ECR I-667, [1994] 4 CMLR 614. In *Tetra Pak II* (n 168, above) Tetra Pak challenged the Commission's determination of separate markets for aseptic packaging machines and the aseptic cartons themselves, arguing that there was a 'natural and commercial link' between the machines and the cartons and that separating the machines and the packaging potentially created public health risks. The CFI (at paras 79–83) rejected both points: in terms of commercial usage, there were independent producers of the cartons; on public safety, any appropriate concerns were matters for resolution by separate legislation or regulations, and not for resolution by the manufacturers themselves; further appeal on other grounds dismissed (n 109, above).

[177] See Case 238/87 *Volvo v Veng* [1988] ECR 6211, [1989] 4 CMLR 122: on the question whether there was a distinct market for Volvo body panels, AG Mischo noted the possibility that purchasers of a new car might have regard to the price of replacement body panels but pointed out that, for an owner of a vehicle who decides to repair the bodywork, the relevant market is for body panels relating to a particular make of car. This issue was not addressed in the ECJ's judgment.

In *Pelikan/Kyocera*, the Commission concluded that there was a single 'system' market for printers and printer cartridges because 'purchasers were well informed about the price charged for consumables and appeared to take this into account in their decision to buy a printer. "Total cost per page" was one of the criteria most commonly used by customers when choosing a printer. This was due to the fact that life-cycle costs of consumables (mainly toner cartridges) represented a very high proportion of the value of a printer. Therefore, if the prices of consumables of a particular brand were raised, consumers would have a strong incentive to buy another printer brand.'[178] The Commission also takes into account the relative prices of the primary and secondary products, whether there are any undertakings which are active only in the supply of the secondary products[179] and whether the same undertakings are responsible for purchasing the primary and secondary products. When purchasers of the primary product are not also responsible for purchasing the secondary product, it becomes less likely that their purchase of the primary product would be influenced by the price paid (by another entity) in the secondary market.[180] It may also be relevant to consider, in particular, the frequency with which products are purchased in the primary market, the amount of information available to consumers about the cost of the secondary products and the sophistication of the buyers.

4.061 **Market in licences or access to facilities.** Analogous to the spare parts cases is the situation where an undertaking grants licences which are necessary to enable its customers to carry on a particular commercial activity. It is clear that such licences can form a distinct product market. In *General Motors v Commission*, concerning the prices charged by General Motors for issuing certificates of conformity with Belgian law for vehicles imported into Belgium, General Motors

---

[178] *Pelikan/Kyocera, XXVth Report on Competition Policy* (1995), point 87. Similarly, *Info-Lab/Ricoh, XXIXth Report on Competition Policy* (1999), point 169 (toner cartridges and photocopiers). The UK OFT Guidelines on Market Definition (n 125, above) at para 6.7, suggest that a system market may also be appropriate when reputational effects mean that setting a supra-competitive price for the secondary product would significantly harm a supplier's profits on future sales of its primary products.

[179] See, eg Case T-86/95 *Compagnie Générale Maritime v Commission* [2002] ECR II-1011, [2002] 4 CMLR 1115 paras 128–129, upholding the Commission's finding that there were separate markets for inland transport of containers and maritime transport of containers, in part on the basis that there existed independent suppliers for the inland transport service. See also, eg Case M.986 *Agfa-Gevaert/Du Pont*, OJ 1998 L211/22, para 36; Case M.2220 *General Electric/Honeywell*, OJ 2004 L48/1, paras 35 and 96 (appeals on other grounds dismissed: Case T-209/01 *Honeywell International v Commission* and Case T-210/01 *General Electric v Commission* [2005] ECR II-5527, 5575, [2006] 4 CMLR 652, 686).

[180] In *Hugin v Commission* (n 170, above) paras 4–10, the ECJ found that users of Hugin cash registers did not themselves purchase spare parts but instead purchased repair and maintenance services (either from Hugin or an independent supplier); the secondary product market (for the sale of Hugin parts) comprised purchases by independent suppliers of repair and maintenance services. Hugin's argument that the supply of spare parts formed an essential parameter of competition in the (primary) market for cash registers therefore failed.

argued that issuing such certificates was an activity merely ancillary to the market in motor cars, in which it did not hold a dominant position. The Court of Justice rejected that argument, holding that the issue of such certificates constituted a distinct market.[181] In *Aéroports de Paris v Commission*, the Court of Justice upheld the finding that the management of airport facilities was the relevant product market since a licence for access to those facilities was necessary for suppliers of groundhandling services.[182]

Applying the SSNIP test in systems cases. The SSNIP test can be applied to **4.062** connected products in the same way as to stand-alone products. However, when two products are connected, the SSNIP test is applied at the time of the purchase of *each* product to determine the relevant product market. In this situation, if a SSNIP in relation to one (or both) of the products taken individually would not be profitable, then it is necessary to assess whether a SSNIP in the primary *and* secondary products taken together would be profitable. A SSNIP in mechanical equipment may be defeated by customers increasing their spending on maintenance and repair services (to extend the effective life of existing equipment), whereas a SSNIP in maintenance and repair services for the mechanical equipment in question might be profitable (because insufficient consumers would react by seeking to mitigate their costs through purchases of new equipment); if a SSNIP in mechanical equipment *and* maintenance and repair services (taken together) were also profitable, then there would be (i) a market for maintenance and repair services; and (ii) a system market for the mechanical equipment *and* the maintenance and repair services.[183] A hypothetical monopoly supplier of the secondary products who did not also sell primary products would not be concerned about the effect of lost sales of the primary product except insofar as those lost sales translated into reduced sales of the secondary product. More particularly, the fact that the same manufacturers may be active in the primary and secondary markets should not alter the way in which the SSNIP test is applied (ie with reference to effect on profitability of the supply of the products in question).

---

181 Case 26/75 *General Motors Continental v Commission* [1975] ECR 1367, [1976] 1 CMLR 95, paras 7–11; followed in Case 226/84 *British Leyland v Commission* [1986] ECR 3263, [1987] 1 CMLR 185. See also *Volvo Italy, XVIIth Report on Competition Policy* (1987), point 82.

182 Case C-82/01P *Aéroports de Paris v Commission* [2002] ECR I-9297, [2003] 4 CMLR 609, paras 84–96. See also two Swedish cases: *FAC Flygbussarna Airport Coaches AB v Luftfartsverket* (Case No. MD 2005:27, judgment of the Market Court, 30 August 2005): market for supply of infrastructure for passenger traffic to and from the terminal areas at Arlanda Airport; *Luftfartsverket (Swedish Airport and Navigation Services) v Scandinavian Airline Systems (SAS)* (Case No. T 33-00, judgment of the Göta Court of Appeal, 27 April 2001): market for granting of use of Arlanda Airport to airlines.

183 See *Digital Undertaking*, Press Release IP/97/868 (10 October 1997). cf the UK OFT's decision in Case CA/98/6/201 *ICL/Synstar*, finding a single market for mainframe computers and maintenance services.

4.063 **Separate markets for different stages of the production and distribution chain.** There may be separate markets for different stages of the production and distribution chain. In particular, there may be distinct markets for raw materials and for the finished products,[184] and for wholesale and retail distribution.[185]

(ii) Branded goods

4.064 **Separate markets for branded and own label products.** The question may arise as to whether own label goods form part of the same product market as their branded equivalents. This depends, in particular, on consumer preferences for the products in question. When own label products are strong (eg because they are supported by a strong retail brand) or branded products are weak, there is more likely to be a single market. However, if the own label products are weak relative to the branded products, there are likely to be separate markets for branded and own label products. For example, in *SCA/Metsä Tissue*, the Commission identified separate markets for branded and own label tissues for the consumer market because the two markets were served by different competitors and supermarkets purchased branded and own label products in markedly different ways.[186] By contrast, in the 'away from home' market (for supplies to hotels, restaurants and catering firms and other corporate customers), there was a single market comprising both branded and own label tissues, because purchasers tended to focus on the quality of the product, and not on the question of whether it was branded.

(iii) In-house production

4.065 **In-house production.** Whether the market is limited to third party (or 'merchant') supply or also includes in-house (or 'captive') production depends on whether a SSNIP by a hypothetical monopoly supplier to third parties would be defeated by decisions by in-house producers to supply third parties (ie on the basis of a consideration of supply-side substitution[187]). Commonly, in-house producers would not commence supply to third parties in such a situation because they need the capacity to supply their own downstream business, and this has led to a working presumption that in-house supplies are distinct from the third party or merchant market. Prior to the judgment of the Court of First Instance in

---

[184] eg Cases 6 & 7/73 *Commercial Solvents v Commission* [1974] ECR 223, [1974] 1 CMLR 309, para 22. cf the UK OFT Guidelines on Market Definition (n 125, above) para 5.12, postulating that a SSNIP by third party suppliers at a wholesale level may be defeated by the presence on a downstream retail market of a vertically integrated supplier (who does not supply third parties at the wholesale level).

[185] eg Case T-139/98 *AAMS v Commission* [2001] ECR II-3413, [2002] 4 CMLR 302 (cigarettes in Italy); *Repsol CPP SA*, OJ 2004 C258/7 (wholesale and retail distribution of fuel in Spain).

[186] Case M.2097 *SCA/Metsä Tissue*, OJ 2002 L57/1, paras 23–28 and 33.

[187] On the demand side, if purchasers would switch to self-supply in response to a SSNIP, this could render the SSNIP by the hypothetical third party monopolist unprofitable. See n 190, below, in relation to the possibility of customers commencing self-supply.

Schneider Electric v Commission, the Commission's practice in merger cases was accordingly to exclude in-house production from the market (and therefore from the calculation of market shares).[188] However, in *Schneider Electric*, the Court of First Instance found that the Commission's decision to exclude sales by vertically integrated suppliers of electrical panel boards from the market share calculations overstated the economic significance of the non-vertically integrated suppliers and was therefore erroneous.[189] Whilst the Court of First Instance's reasoning did not directly apply a SSNIP test,[190] it is consistent with the basic principle that, in determining whether in-house production should be included in the market, it is necessary to assess whether that production operates as a competitive constraint on third party suppliers.[191] Hence in *Endemol v Commission*, the Court of First Instance upheld the Commission's finding that the in-house production of Dutch public broadcasters did not form part of the same market as that for independent production of Dutch language television programmes: the in-house producers did not offer their programmes for sale to other Dutch broadcasters, whereas the in-house producers were constrained in commissioning programmes from independent producers by the investment they had made in developing their own in-house production capacity.[192]

(iv) Continuous chains of substitution

Continuous chains of substitution. In certain situations, a continuous chain of substitution serves to unite into a single market a series of products which would otherwise comprise separate markets. For example, laptop computers in the price range £500 to £1,000 may form part of the same relevant product market although a SSNIP in relation to £500 to £600 laptops would not lead directly to any material switching to laptops in the £900 to £1,000 bracket; however, if customers would react to such a SSNIP by switching to computers in the £600 to £700 range, and so on, then there may be a 'ripple effect', where changes in competitive

4.066

---

[188] See, eg Case M.2002 *Preussag/Thomson* (26 July 2000), para 11. For a post-*Schneider* decision focusing on the merchant market (but taking account of the fact that 97 per cent of production was used for intra-group supplies), see Case M.3056 *Celanese/Degussa/European Oxo Chemicals* (11 June 2003).

[189] T-310/01 *Schneider Electric v Commission* [2002] ECR II-4071, [2003] 4 CMLR 768, paras 281–283.

[190] For application of the SSNIP test in this context, see eg *Oracle/Peoplesoft* (n 116, above) para 115. cf Case M.3396 *Group 4 Falck/Securicor* (28 May 2004), paras 15 and 31, in which the Commission considered whether an increase in merchant prices would result in customers commencing self-supply (and did not also consider expressly the supply-side question, namely whether such an increase would lead those suppliers who currently self-supplied to offer services to third parties). See also Case M.2978 *Lagardère/Natexis/VUP*, OJ 2004 L125/54, paras 154–156.

[191] For criticism of the Commission as relying on a formalistic separation of captive and in-house suppliers, see Baker, 'The Treatment of Captive Sales in Market Definition: Rules or Reason' (2003) ECLR 161.

[192] *Endemol v Commission* (n 143, above).

conditions in one part of the market affect the remainder of the market. The chain of substitution operates if a SSNIP in relation to any part of the chain would be rendered unprofitable by purchasers switching to products elsewhere in the chain. The Commission's Relevant Market Notice states: 'From a practical perspective, the concept of chains of substitution has to be corroborated by actual evidence, for instance related to price interdependence at the extremes of the chains of substitution, in order to lead to an extension of the relevant market in an individual case.'[193] Chains of substitution have been found by the Commission in markets as diverse as spirits of different quality levels (ie premium and secondary brands),[194] premium and economy cruises,[195] pet foods of different quality[196] and the provision of hospital ventilation equipment.[197]

(v) Procurement markets

4.067 **Supply and procurement markets.** Markets are typically defined in terms of the *supply* of goods or services. However, it may also be appropriate to define markets for the *procurement* of goods and services.[198] In *British Airways v Commission*, British Airways challenged the Commission's finding that it was dominant (as a purchaser) on the UK market for the provision of air travel agency services to airlines, arguing that the nature of competition was properly assessed by reference to British Airways' flight sales to end consumers and not the services provided to a supplier (ie British Airways) by the retailers who were the point of sale (ie the travel agents). The Court of First Instance, however, upheld the Commission's definition of the market, noting that the specific services supplied by travel agents to the airlines (advertising and commercial promotional services) meant that there was a distinct procurement market, separate from the market for the supply of airline tickets. The Court stated:

'Article 82 EC applies both to undertakings whose possible dominant position is established, as in this case, in relation to their suppliers and to those which are capable of being in the same position in relation to their customers . . . The Commission did not therefore make any error of assessment in defining the relevant product market as that for services provided by travel agents in favour of airlines, for the pur-

---

[193] Relevant Market Notice, OJ 1997 C372/5: Vol II, App C.10, para 58. Although the first part of para 58 appears, like para 57, to apply to both geographic and product markets, the Commission's subsequent statement in para 58 that 'Price levels at the extremes of the chains would have to be of the same magnitude as well' should be understood as referring to the application of chains of substitution in the determination of the geographic dimension to the market (as discussed in the preceding para 57); in a product market analysis, a budget product at one end of the spectrum would clearly be expected to be cheaper than a premium product at the other end of the spectrum.

[194] Case M.2268 *Pernod Ricard/Diageo/Seagram Spirits* (8 May 2001) para 16.

[195] Case M.2706 *Carnival Corporation/P&O Princess*, OJ 2003 L248/1, paras 78, 91 and 112.

[196] Case M.2544 *Masterfoods/Royal Canin* (15 February 2002) paras 15–17.

[197] Case M.2861 *Siemens/Drägerwerk/JV*, OJ 2003 L291/1, paras 16–19.

[198] Such markets may be relevant, for example, to assess whether a supermarket chain has market power in the procurement of products for subsequent retail sale.

poses of establishing whether BA holds a dominant position on that market in its capacity as bidder for those services.'[199]

In situations involving a procurement market, the SSNIP test is applied from the standpoint of the monopsony purchaser (rather than the monopoly supplier) to determine whether it would be able profitably to *decrease* by 5 to 10 per cent the prices at which it purchases the products.

(vi) Technology and innovation markets

Technology markets.   There may be separate markets for the licensing of technol-   **4.068**
ogy, particularly if rights to technology, for example through the granting of patent licences, are sold separately from the underlying product. Thus in *Shell/Montecatini*, the Commission concluded that there was a market for the licensing of polypropylene technology, involving the licensing and use of catalysts and technological processes, distinct from the market for the production and sale of polypropylene.[200] This approach to product market definition can be relevant for other technology-driven industries, especially where licensing is an accepted form of exploiting technology. The block exemption for technology transfer agreements, Regulation 772/04, accordingly distinguishes between the 'relevant technology market' and the 'relevant product market'.[201] The relevant technology market will include the technology that is licensed and its close substitutes.[202] The market share of an undertaking on a technology market is calculated on the basis of the total sales of the licensor and all its licensees of products incorporating the licensed technology.[203]

Innovation markets.   Innovation markets involve firms which take preparatory   **4.069**
steps with the objective of selling innovative products in the future.[204] In this

---

[199] Case T-219/99 *British Airways v Commission* [2003] ECR II-5917, [2004] 4 CMLR 1008, [2004] All ER (EC) 1115, paras 101 and 107; on appeal on other grounds, Case C-95/04P, [2007] 4 CMLR 982. See also, eg Case M.3605 *Sovion/HMG* (21 December 2004), paras 12-16 (purchase of live pigs and sows for slaughtering); Case M.3579 *WPP/Grey* (24 January 2005), para 36, (procurement markets for the purchase by media buyers of advertising time and space); Case M.2876 *NewsCorp/Telepiù*, OJ 2004 L110/73, [2004] 5 CMLR 1619, paras 49-77 (markets for the purchasing of broadcasting rights). See further Veljanovski, 'Markets in Professional Sports: Hendry v. WPSBA and the Importance of Functional Markets' (2002) ECLR 273, 277.

[200] Case M.269 *Shell/Montecatini*, OJ 1994 L332/48. And see also, eg Case M.550 *Union Carbide/Enichem* (13 March 1995); Case M.2299 *BP Chemicals/Solvay/HDPE JV* (29 October 2001), para 16; Case M.2396 *Industri Kapital/Perstop (II)* (11 May 2001), paras 33 and 34.

[201] Reg 772/04 on the application of Article 81(3) of the Treaty to categories of technology transfer agreements, OJ 2004 L123/11, see Vol II, App C.7, Art 1(1)(j). See further para 9.088, below.

[202] ibid. See also Commission Notice on Guidelines on the applicability of Article 81 of the EC Treaty to horizontal cooperation agreements, OJ 2001 C3/02, see Vol II, App C.12, paras 47–48.

[203] Reg 772/04, Art 3(3). For the rationale for this approach, see Commission Notice on Guidelines on the application of Article 81 to technology transfer agreements, OJ 2004 C101/2, see Vol II, App C.16, para 23.

[204] See Glader, *Innovation Markets and Competition Analysis* (2006); and the 1995 US Dept of Justice and Federal Trade Commission, *Antitrust Guidelines for the Licensing of Intellectual Property* (http://www.usdoj.gov/atr/public/guidelines/0558.htm).

respect, they are quite unlike orthodox markets which involve existing buyers and sellers. It may be relevant to define an innovation market to assess whether a merger or agreement is likely to reduce the parties' incentives to innovate in the future.[205] In its Guidelines on the Assessment of Horizontal Mergers,[206] the Commission refers to the possibility of effective competition being 'significantly impeded by a merger between two important innovators, for instance between two companies with "pipeline" products related to a specific product market.' Further, in relation to behavioural cases, the Commission states in its Guidelines on the Application of Article 81 to Technology Transfer Agreements:[207] 'In a limited number of cases, . . . it may be useful and necessary to. . . define innovation markets. This is particularly the case where the agreement affects innovation aiming at creating new products and where it is possible at an early stage to identify research and development poles.'

3. Geographic Market

(a) Overview

4.070 **Definition of the relevant geographic market.** The relevant geographic market comprises the area in which the undertakings concerned are involved in the supply and demand of products or services, in which the conditions of competition are sufficiently homogeneous and which can be distinguished from neighbouring areas because the conditions of competition are appreciably different in those areas.[208] It is not necessary for the conditions of competition to be perfectly homogeneous, so long as they are similar or sufficiently homogeneous.[209] In *AAMS (Italian Cigarettes)*[210] the Court of First Instance considered the distribution of cigarettes in Italy. Three relevant product markets were identified: the market for cigarettes, the market for wholesale distribution of cigarettes, and the market for retail distribution of cigarettes. In each case, the Court upheld the Commission's conclusion that the relevant geographic market was Italy. The Court stated that the facts that (a) AAMS supplied cigarette distribution services only in Italy and was not active in any other Member State; and (b) it had enjoyed a *de facto*

---

[205] See, eg Case M.1846 *Glaxo Wellcome/SmithKline Beecham* (8 May 2000), paras 70–72. For a controversial US decision involving a merger to monopoly in an innovation market, see Statement of FTC Chairman Muris in *Genzyme Corporation/Novazyme Pharmaceuticals* (http://www.ftc.gov/os/2004/01/murisgenzymestmt.pdf).

[206] Guidelines on Assessment of Horizontal Mergers, OJ 2004 C31/5, see Vol II, App D.6, at para 38. See further Chap 8, below, in relation to merger control analysis.

[207] Guidelines on Technology Transfer Agreements (n 203 above) para 25. See further Chap 9, below.

[208] See at para 4.015, above.

[209] Case T-229/94 *Deutsche Bahn v Commission* (n 167, above) para 92.

[210] Case T-139/98 *AAMS v Commission* [2001] ECR II-3413, [2002] 4 CMLR 302.

monopoly over the wholesale distribution of cigarettes in Italy for many years; were sufficient on their own to support the Commission's analysis that the geographic market was Italy. The Court, however, went on to list the other facts which supported the definition of the relevant geographic market, namely the existence in Italy of legislation governing all operations concerning cigarettes; considerable differences in retail sale prices between Italy and other Members States; the lack of parallel imports of cigarettes into Italy; the fact that Italian consumers have particular preferences; and the very large market share held by AAMS brands of cigarettes while they were virtually non-existent in the other Member States.

Methodology. The starting point for the analysis is the activities of the party **4.071** (or parties) concerned.[211] From this a working hypothesis can be developed regarding the geographic market, normally based on market shares and prices in different areas, before testing that hypothesis using demand- and supply-side analyses.[212] On the demand side, it is necessary to consider purchasers' willingness to acquire products from other areas. On the supply side, attention focuses on the willingness of suppliers in other areas to commence supply in (or into) the area in question. In principle, supply-side substitution (ie whether suppliers will travel further to deliver their products) is as likely to lead to wider geographic markets as demand-side substitution (ie whether customers will travel further to acquire their products) and there is no reason to treat demand-side substitution as more significant in the context of defining the geographic market.[213] In merger cases, the four most frequent reasons for identifying smaller geographic markets have been: regulatory barriers, transport cost and delivery time, distribution cost and national preferences.[214]

Geographic market definition in the context of the removal of barriers to **4.072** **trade.** In many situations, the geographic market may be affected by national legislation or regulation, customs duties, taxation or other barriers to trade. Such provisions may have an effect on consumers' willingness to purchase products outside a particular territory or on suppliers' abilities and incentives to start

---

[211] In Case M.3397 *Owens-Illinois/BSN Glasspack* (9 June 2004) the Commission identified relevant geographic markets for the supply of glass packaging in Barcelona/south-western France and northern Italy/south-eastern France because the parties had plants which were relatively close to one another in those areas (albeit in different Member States) and the evidence was that the plants competed with one another across national boundaries (paras 24–26).

[212] Relevant Market Notice (n 193, above) paras 28–30. See, eg Case M.3099 *Areva/Urenco/ ETC JV* (6 October 2004), para 75.

[213] cf para 4.019, above: the Commission regards demand-side substitution as the most important criterion in defining the market, apparently as regards the geographic dimension as well as the product dimension.

[214] *The internal market and the relevant geographical market* (n 51, above) 60. Note also the criteria set out in Art 9(7) of the Merger Regulation for assessment of whether there is a distinct geographic market in a Member State for the purposes of a reference back to the national competition authorities of a merger with a Community dimension: Reg 139/2004, OJ 2004 L24/1, see Vol II, App D.1 (for the application of Art 9, see paras 8.091 *et seq*, below).

supplying within it. The internal market programme has sought to remove or reduce some of these barriers and its effects are therefore taken into account, where relevant, when defining the relevant geographic market.[215]

(b) Demand-side substitution

4.073 **Transport costs.** Transport costs are particularly important when analysing the relevant geographic market.[216] If transport costs are high relative to the value of the product, customers are unlikely to be willing to pay the additional costs in sourcing from suppliers located in more distant areas.[217] In *Irish Sugar*, the Commission rejected an argument that the geographic market for the supply of retail and industrial white granulated sugar was wider than Ireland, notwithstanding the existence of substantial sugar surpluses in France, Germany, Denmark, Belgium and the Netherlands, since the cost of freight was a significant barrier to trade.[218]

4.074 **Pricing data.** Products of higher value (with higher prices) are more likely to form parts of wider geographic markets as it becomes worthwhile for customers to travel further in order to find a cheaper supplier.[219] Separately, if prices in two areas are materially different, this suggests, without being decisive, that the two areas comprise parts of two different geographic markets, as such differences would normally be eroded through competition in a single geographic market.[220] For example, in *Michelin II*, the Commission produced detailed pricing tables, for both replacement tyres and re-treaded tyres for heavy vehicles, covering a number of Members States over several years (including both list prices and post-rebate prices). Persistent price differences between Member States over time supported the conclusion that the relevant geographic market was national.[221]

4.075 **Differences in prices: further considerations.** Evidence of differences in prices in different areas is not conclusive that the two areas form separate markets.

---

[215] Relevant Market Notice, para 32. cf *The internal market and the relevant geographical market* (n 49, above) 8, finding no evidence that the size of the geographic market in merger cases had increased over the period 1990 to 2001.

[216] It may also be relevant to consider the mobility of customers: see the UK OFT Guidelines on Market Definition (n 125, above) para 4.3.

[217] See, eg Case M.3625 *Blackstone/Acetex* (13 July 2005) paras 42–45 and 63–67.

[218] *Irish Sugar* (n 164, above) para 95 (appeals on other grounds to the CFI and ECJ dismissed, ibid).

[219] See the UK OFT Guidelines on Market Definition (n 125, above) para 4.3

[220] See, eg *GE/Instrumentarium* (n 146, above) paras 72–74, 82 and 83.

[221] *Michelin II* (n 169, above) paras 134–139 and 158–164 (appeal on other grounds dismissed, ibid). See also *Lagardère/Natexis/VUP* (n 190, above) at paras 353, 374 and 383, where the Commission compared the discounts agreed by suppliers in different Member States: when the level of discount was not related to the location of the dealer, this was relied on to establish that the relevant geographic market was international; when the discount *was* related to the location of the dealer, this pointed to there being a national market.

First, differences in prices may arise because of transport costs. For example, if the price is £100 in area A and £105 in area B, and purchasers from one area incur costs of £7 in purchasing from the other area, then a price rise in area B would lead to customers switching to area A (pointing towards a one-way market including areas A and B, notwithstanding the differences in prices).[222] In *Procter & Gamble/ Wella*, the Commission emphasised the importance of transport costs, stating: 'Persistent price differences that are not due to transport costs are a strong indicator that hair care products in one Member State do not exercise a competitive constraint on hair products in other Member States.'[223] Secondly, it is necessary to determine whether any price differences arise from objective differences in the competitive structure operating in different areas, in which case a narrower market would indeed be justified; or whether they arise artificially from present (and potentially remediable) distortions of competition, in which case a wider geographic market may be appropriate. The distinction between these situations is not always easy to draw. The former case is illustrated by the decisions in *Soda Ash – Solvay* and *Soda Ash – ICI*, in which the Commission found that conditions of competition for the purchase of soda ash were objectively different in the UK compared to the rest of Europe (although the differences had arisen, at least in part, because of existing anti-competitive arrangements involving Solvay and ICI).[224] By contrast, in *Hilti* the Court of First Instance found that large differences in the prices of Hilti products in different Member States, coupled with low transport costs, meant that parallel trading would normally have been expected if the market were operating competitively. As such, the existence of price disparities was explained by artificial barriers erected by market participants, rather than the structure of competition, and the relevant geographic market was therefore the Community as a whole.[225] Finally, as in the case of product market definition, evidence that there is a high correlation between prices in different areas suggests

---

222 The market would be one-way because area A would itself also constitute a separate geographic market: a 5 to 10 per cent increase in the price of the products in area A would not lead to purchasers in area A sourcing from area B. For one-way markets, see para 4.022, above.

223 Case M.3149 *Procter & Gamble/Wella* (30 July 2003) para 27.

224 *Soda Ash – Solvay*, OJ 2003 L10/10 (on appeal, Case T-57/01 *Solvay v Commission*, not yet decided); and *Soda Ash – ICI*, OJ 2003 L10/33 (on appeal, Case T-66/01 *ICI v Commission*, not yet decided). ICI was the sole producer of soda ash in the UK. Solvay and other western European producers did not market their products in ICI's 'home territory'. Since ICI's important customers in the Community were all located in the UK, this effectively separated the UK from the remainder of the Community.

225 *Hilti v Commission* (n 176, above) para 81 (appeal on other grounds to the ECJ dismissed, ibid). See also Case T-83/91 *Tetra Pak v Commission* ('*Tetra Pak II*') [1994] ECR II-755, [1997] 4 CMLR 726, para 96 (appeal on other grounds to the ECJ dismissed, ibid): differences in prices between Member States were evidence of artificial partitioning of the markets, rather than objective differences in conditions of competition.

that the two areas form part of the same geographic market, provided that the correlation is not spurious.[226]

4.076 **National preferences and cultural features.** Other barriers to switching by customers may include linguistic requirements, cultural features, consumer-led standards, requirements specific to a local area, or local or national preferences more generally.[227] The nature of the product itself may point to a national or linguistic boundary to the geographic market. In *Cableuropa v Commission*, the Court of First Instance upheld the Commission's decision that Spain constituted a distinct geographic market for the sale of television broadcasting rights for films, for football matches involving Spanish teams, and for other sporting rights and entertainments (considered to be three distinct products) because of language barriers and cultural factors and the way that broadcasting rights were generally sold on the basis of national exclusivity.[228] Certain products require a local presence, for example for after-sales support or service, meaning that it is not feasible for customers to purchase outside a particular area.[229] Equally, in certain industries, there may be regulatory barriers or safety restrictions which narrow the geographic market.[230] For example, in *United Brands*, the Court of Justice upheld the Commission's finding that the geographic market for the supply of bananas comprised six Member States,[231] but excluded the (then) remaining three (France, Italy and the UK) because the particular purchasing preferences resulting from

---

[226] For price correlation evidence, see para 4.045, above. See, eg *Blackstone/Acetex* (n 217, above) paras 34, 35, 57 and 77. In *The internal market and the relevant geographical market* (n 51, above) 67–88, Copenhagen Economics argue for the use of price correlation or co-integration as the standard tools for evaluating geographic market definition and provide a detailed proposed methodology.

[227] See, eg Case M.2283 *Schneider Electric/Legrand*, OJ 2004 L101/1, paras 193–242 (annulled on other grounds, *Schneider Electric v Commission* n 189, above); Case M.2621 *SEB/Moulinex* (8 January 2002), paras 26–30, a Phase I merger decision concerning at least 13 distinct product markets (mostly for different small electrical kitchen appliances), where the Commission found that in each case there were distinct geographic markets as between the different Member States (application to annul on other grounds dismissed, Case T-119/02 *Royal Philips Electronics v Commission* [2003] ECR II-1433, [2003] 5 CMLR 53).

[228] Cases T-346 & 47/02 *Cableuropa v Commission* [2003] ECR II-4251, [2004] 5 CMLR 1216 (a challenge to the Commission's decision referring a merger back to the Spanish authorities under Art 9 of the Merger Reg).

[229] See, eg *Siemens/Drägerwerk/JV* (n 197, above) para 47; and *GE/Instrumentarium* (n 146, above) paras 75, 84 and 96. For a case where the geographic market was confined to a small area, see the judgment of the UK Competition Appeal Tribunal in *JJ Burgess v Office of Fair Trading* [2005] CAT 25, [2005] CompAR 1151 (funeral services in Stevenage and Knebworth).

[230] See generally the Relevant Market Notice (n 193, above) paras 46 and 50.

[231] Germany, Denmark, Ireland, the Netherlands, Belgium and Luxembourg. This was notwithstanding the fact that applicable tariff provisions and transport costs differed between them: the ECJ emphasised that, in respect of all six, the markets were '*completely free*' and the conditions of competition were the same for all: Case 27/76 *United Brands v Commission* [1978] ECR 207, [1978] 1 CMLR 429, paras 36–57.

the national organisation of supply in those Member States meant that United Brands' bananas did not compete on equal terms.[232]

Geographic purchasing patterns and trade flows. Existing purchasing patterns **4.077** may provide useful evidence in defining the geographic market.[233] For example, in *Michelin v Commission*, the Court of Justice upheld the Commission's finding that the relevant geographic market was the Netherlands because there was evidence that dealers in the Netherlands obtained their tyre supplies only from suppliers operating within the Netherlands.[234] In *Blackstone/Acetex*, the Commission relied on fluctuations in trade flows as evidence of a wider geographic market, since supplies appeared to move easily across regions to satisfy changes in demand, regardless of location.[235] The Relevant Market Notice also refers to the examination of bidding or tender evidence to determine the relevant geographic market.[236] For example, in *Oracle/Peoplesoft*, the Commission carried out a bid study to identify whether customers requested tenders only from suppliers in particular areas and, since they did not, concluded that the market was global.[237] However, the Relevant Market Notice notes that trade flow data is not, taken in isolation, conclusive and that it is necessary to understand the underlying rationale behind the trade flows.[238] Furthermore, it cannot be inferred from the absence of trade

---

[232] In France, two-thirds of the market was reserved for overseas départements (including certain jurisdictions with which France had special relations, which enjoyed duty-free imports of bananas). In the UK, preference was given to the developing countries of the Commonwealth. In Italy, a national system of quota restrictions operated.

[233] Since the SSNIP test focuses on marginal consumers (see para 4.025, above) the fact that a relatively small minority of customers purchases a product from a particular territory at pre-SSNIP prices may be sufficient to indicate that the application of the SSNIP test to a more restricted area would be unprofitable (demonstrating that a wider market is appropriate); the issue is whether a sufficient number of other purchasers would begin to purchase outside the candidate market to defeat the SSNIP.

[234] *Michelin v Commission* (n 161, above) para 26. See further *Michelin II* (n 169, above) (appeal on other grounds dismissed, ibid), where the Commission held that the relevant geographic market was France. Michelin had argued that the supply of replacement tyres had changed since the earlier decision, with international suppliers competing across the EU. The Commission rejected this argument on the basis that dealers in France nevertheless still tended to purchase nationally because: they would not obtain rebates from foreign Michelin subsidiaries; dealers remained in close contact with the manufacturer in France because of the absence of wholesalers; and dealers required regular and secure supply across the range which could not be satisfied by parallel imports. As such, purchases from suppliers outside France were sporadic and small in quantity and those replacement tyres purchased from Asia and Eastern Europe comprised 'third line' tyres which did not compete strongly with Michelin's core business and which had, in any event, achieved relatively weak penetration in France. See also, eg Case M.3314 *Air Liquide/Messer Targets* (15 March 2004), para 37; and Case M.3431 *Sonoco/Ahlstrom*, OJ 2005 L159/13, paras 57–64.

[235] Case M.3625 *Blackstone/Acetex* (13 July 2005) paras 32, 33, 54 and 55. See also para 78, relying on high levels of world trade and high margins as pointers towards a global market.

[236] Relevant Market Notice, OJ 1997 C372/5: Vol II, App C.10 para 48.

[237] Case M.3216 *Oracle/Peoplesoft*, OJ 2005 L218/6.

[238] Relevant Market Notice, para 49. Trade flows are sometimes referred to as 'shipping patterns.' See also the UK OFT Guidelines on Market Definition (OFT 403, 2004) para 4.6: in some

flows that the geographic market is necessarily narrow: it may be that consumers are not purchasing from a particular location at current price levels, but they would do so in the event of a small increase in price (SSNIP); the issue in each case is whether there is some form of barrier (financial or other) that is effectively preventing trade from taking place.[239]

4.078 **Shares of supply.** If the shares of supply accounted for by producers differ materially between areas, this suggests that the areas form parts of separate geographic markets.[240] Further, the fact that suppliers are able to maintain high and stable market shares for a long period in particular areas suggests that they may not face substantial competition from outside the area and that the relevant geographic market may therefore be narrow but the inference may be rebutted if there is an explanation for the differences that is not inconsistent with the existence of a broader geographic market.[241]

4.079 **Shock analysis or event evidence.** Evidence of consumers' responses to a price change in the past, that may resemble, or serve as a useful proxy for, a SSNIP (in particular events which cause relative prices in the two areas to change significantly and suddenly) can be a valuable indicator of the scope of substitution but, as with all evidence of this kind, requires scrutiny for alternative explanations.[242] For example, in *Irish Sugar*, the Commission relied on the fact that, during a price war in the UK, Irish Sugar was able to maintain its price premium in Ireland, which suggested that the relevant market should not extend to the UK.[243] In *Blackstone/Acetex*, the Commission examined the effect of unexpected outages in capacity to produce chemicals; it found that unexpected outages in the EEA caused surges of imports from North America, indicating that the relevant market included at least the EEA and North America.[244]

---

circumstances imports may not be evidence of an international market since they may come only from the international operations of domestic suppliers, importers may need to invest in distribution facilities or marketing and there may be quotas.

[239] Relevant Market Notice, para 50.

[240] See Relevant Market Notice, para 28; and, eg Case M.2947 *Verbund/Energie Allianz*, OJ 2004 L92/91, para 58; *GE/Instrumentarium* (n 146, above) para 80; *Procter & Gamble/Wella* (n 223, above) para 25; and *Continental/Phoenix* (n 145, above) paras 41, 42 and 110–112. In *Lagardère/Natexis/VUP* (n 190, above) the Commission stated, at para 362, that differences in market shares by area were not sufficient in themselves to justify a finding of separate geographic markets.

[241] *Areva/Urenco/ETC JV* (n 212, above) paras 76 and 83.

[242] ibid, para 45, noting also the need to take account of exchange rate movements, taxation and product differentiation when comparing price levels across different Member States.

[243] *Irish Sugar* (n 160, above) para 96 (appeals on other grounds to the CFI and ECJ dismissed, ibid). See also *Areva/Urenco/ETC JV* (n 212, above) para 90.

[244] *Blackstone/Acetex* (n 235, above) para 41 (see also paras 36–37, 39–40 and 59–62); and see Durand and Rabassa, 'The Role of quantitative analysis to delineate antitrust markets' (2005) 3 EC Competition Policy Newsletter 118. In T-395/94 *Atlantic Container Line v Commission* [2002] ECR II-875, [2002] 4 CMLR 1008, [2002] All ER (EC) 684, paras 291–298, the appellants argued that transatlantic trade from Mediterranean ports was substitutable with that from northern European

Demand-side substitution evidence: market structure.   The way in which the   **4.080**
market is structured, and in particular, whether undertakings have been organised
internally in a particular way in order best to meet local patterns of demand, can
be a useful indication of the relevant geographic market. In *Michelin*, the Court of
Justice held that the existence of autonomous commercial policies of subsidiaries
of tyre manufactures in the Netherlands, 'generally adapted to the specific conditions existing on each market', was evidence of a distinct national market.[245]
Similarly, in *Procter & Gamble/Wella*, the Commission relied, as evidence of the
geographic markets being national, on the fact that virtually all manufacturers
had production sites in various locations in the EC and that there were national
sales and marketing teams.[246]

Demand-side substitution evidence: internal company documents.   As in the   **4.081**
case of the relevant product market, internal documents produced by (or for)
the undertakings themselves may provide significant evidence in the form of the
undertakings' own views of the geographic market.[247]

Demand-side substitution evidence: views of customers and competitors.   **4.082**
Views of customers and/or competitors on the question of geographic market
definition may be of particular relevance. For example, customers may express
cultural or 'lifestyle' reasons for purchasing within a specific area (typically a local
region or within their own Member State). The weight to be attached to this evidence will depend on the quality and perceived objectivity of the information

---

ports and relied on evidence of increases in trade through Mediterranean ports following the entry
into force of increased freight rates by Trans-Atlantic Agreement members. However, the CFI noted
that, although trade from Mediterranean ports had increased by 14 per cent following the price
increases, it had also increased by 9 per cent from northern European ports; further, the increase
in Mediterranean trade could be explained on other grounds (eg growth in exports to the US from
southern regions of Europe). The CFI therefore held that the event evidence was insufficient to
warrant overturning the Commission's market definition.

[245] *Michelin v Commission* (n 161, above) para 26. The position was re-examined by the
Commission in *Michelin II* (n 169, above) and the same conclusion was reached in respect of the
French market: Michelin itself confirmed that 'dealers, at least as regards their regular supplies,
generally use the Michelin company established in their country' (paras 125–126) (appeal on other
grounds dismissed, *Michelin v Commission*, ibid).

[246] *Procter & Gamble/Wella* (n 223, above) paras 22–24 and 26. In addition, several manufacturers used different brands in different Member States. See also *Blackstone/Acetex* (n 216, above) paras
48 and 69 (planned capacity developments existed outside the EEA, although there was a deficit
in the EEA and a surplus in the areas where new plants were being installed; this suggested that the
market was wider than the EEA). In Case M.3436 *Continental/Phoenix* (26 October 2004) the
Commission relied, at paras 38–40, on the fact that all foreign manufacturers had set up, or were
setting up, manufacturing capability in Europe as evidence that the relevant geographic market
was European (and not wider). Conversely, the fact that manufacturers operated a small number
of plants in the EEA pointed towards a wider geographic market in *Sonoco/Ahlstrom* (n 234, above)
para 30.

[247] See para 4.050, above, in relation to the use of internal company documents.

available. The Relevant Market Notice points out the need for such views to be backed sufficiently by factual evidence.[248]

4.083 **Application of the SSNIP test.** The issue to be determined is whether a hypothetical monopolist could profitably impose a SSNIP in a particular geographic area. If such an attempt would be defeated by purchasers switching to obtain supplies outside the area in question, then the relevant geographic market is wider. The Relevant Market Notice states[249] that the switch must be made in the 'short term' and at 'negligible cost', reflecting the fact that the hypothetical price increase for the purposes of the SSNIP test is small, albeit significant, ie 5 to 10 per cent. If customers would incur material costs in switching, or would switch only in the longer term, such a constraint is not sufficiently direct to warrant inclusion within the relevant geographic market.[250] In practice, at least in relation to merger decisions, the Commission applies a somewhat cruder approach to geographic market definition, relying most commonly on trade flow data and a comparison of price levels and rarely applying or referring directly to the SSNIP test.[251]

(c) Supply-side substitution

4.084 **Conditions for supply-side substitution.** The Commission takes into account the effect of supply-side substitution when defining the relevant geographic market only when its effects are equivalent to those of demand-side substitution in terms of effectiveness and immediacy.[252] In practical terms, this means that to come within the relevant market a supplier must be able easily and quickly to divert or commence supply. When the goods in question can be transported relatively easily and cheaply, this may simply involve transporting them further.

---

[248] Relevant Market Notice (n 236, above) para 47. See also Case T-504/93 *Tiercé Ladbroke v Commission* [1997] ECR II-923, [1997] 5 CMLR 309 where the Commission and the CFI focused on demand-side considerations at the level of the final consumer in finding that the geographic market for transmission of pictures from French racecourses was limited to Belgium so that there was no breach of Art 82 by the owners of the rights to the pictures.

[249] ibid, para 29.

[250] See *Alpha Flight Services/Aéroports de Paris*, OJ 1998 L230/10, [1998] 5 CMLR 611 (appeals on other grounds to the CFI and ECJ dismissed: Case T-128/98 *Aéroports de Paris v Commission* [2000] ECR II-3929, [2001] 4 CMLR 1376; and Case C-82/01P, n 178, above): for the large majority of passengers, alternative airports were clearly not substitutable for Paris Orly and Paris CDG, with the result that the relevant geographic market was the supply of services to Paris airports (and since Orly and CDG were under common ownership, it was unnecessary to determine the degree of substitution between them). Similarly, *Flughafen Frankfurt/Main AG*, OJ 1998 L72/30, [1998] 4 CMLR 779: Frankfurt airport was the relevant geographic market for the provision of airport facilities for aircraft to land and take off; although Lufthansa could in theory switch its hub for indirect services, it would do so only to a German airport and there was no alternative German airport that could host the Lufthansa hub in the short term.

[251] *The internal market and the relevant geographical market* (n 51, above) 59 and 61.

[252] Relevant Market Notice, para 20. See also paras 4.053–4.054, above, in relation to the necessary conditions for supply-side substitution to be considered for the purposes of market definition.

When the products are costly or awkward to transport, or have specialised transportation requirements, the time and costs involved may enable a hypothetical monopoly supplier profitably to impose a price rise without being constrained by other suppliers. For example, in *GVG/FS*, the Commission considered the appropriate geographic market for the supply of traction services (ie the provision of a rail locomotive and driver ready for use, together with back-up services) to operate from Domodossola (on the Swiss–Italian border) to Milan.[253] The relevant geographic market was found to be confined to the region of Milan because of the need for the traction provider to be able to call upon a pool of locomotives in the event of a technical failure: the pool had to be close to the route in order to ensure that a replacement could be obtained without incurring disproportionate time and costs.

Supply-side substitution evidence: generally.   The approach to evidence of   **4.085**
supply-side substitution when defining geographic markets is similar to that used in relation to product market definition: one must examine whether alternative suppliers could switch to supplying the product in question in the relevant geographic area.[254]

Supply-side substitution evidence: trade flow and pricing data.   Trade flow   **4.086**
data is often important on the supply side. By identifying the distances over which providers currently supply and comparing those distances with any relevant price differences between locations,[255] it may be possible to draw conclusions about the circumstances in which suppliers would be likely to start supplying a particular location.[256]

Supply-side substitution evidence: legislative requirements or other barriers to   **4.087**
switching.   It is important to consider whether there are particular legislative or regulatory barriers which mean that alternative suppliers would be unlikely to commence supply into the area. For example, labelling requirements may render it more difficult for alternative suppliers to commence supply. In *AAMS v Commission*, the reasons for the Court of First Instance upholding the Commission's conclusion that the relevant geographic markets for the wholesale and distribution of cigarettes were limited to Italy included the Italian legal requirements that manufactured tobaccos were kept on separate premises from other goods, so that market entry would involve substantial investment for other

---

[253] *GVG/FS*, OJ 2004 L11/17, para 58.
[254] See paras 4.055–4.058, above.
[255] In comparing prices across borders, it is necessary to take account of exchange rate movements and differences in local taxation treatments: see the Relevant Market Notice, para 45.
[256] See the discussion of one-way markets in para 4.022, above, and the factual illustration in para 4.075, above.

distributors, and that cigarette packages carry a health warning in Italian.[257] In *DSD*, the Commission considered that Germany was the relevant geographic market for the organisation of the take-back and recovery from private final consumers of used sales packaging, despite the increasing internationalisation of the waste management sector generally. This was because laws and regulations regarding the disposal of packaging differed from country to country, meaning that conditions of supply to meet particular national requirements tended to remain organised at a national level.[258] Similarly, in *British Airways*, where the Court of First Instance upheld the finding that British Airways was dominant as a purchaser of travel agent services to airlines, the Court further agreed that the relevant market was a national one because IATA regulations prevented tickets sold outside the United Kingdom being used for departures from United Kingdom airports.[259]

(d) Particular issues in determining the geographic market

4.088 **Continuous chains of substitution.** A continuous chain of substitution may result in a single geographic market in the same way that it can create a single product market.[260] For example, if there are 11 motorway petrol stations each at five-mile intervals, there may be a continuous chain creating a single geographic market although the petrol station at one end of the chain cannot directly be said itself to exercise a close competitive constraint on the petrol station 50 miles away. However, a continuous chain of substitution is unlikely to be found if there is a material difference in prices at opposite ends of the spectrum.[261] The Relevant Market Notice states in this respect that: 'From a practical perspective, the concept of chains of substitution has to be corroborated by actual evidence, for instance related to price interdependence at the extremes of the chains of substitution, in order to lead to an extension of the relevant market in an individual case. Price levels at the extremes of the chains would have to be of the same magnitude as well.'[262] In *Laurus/Groenwoudt*, the Dutch Competition Authority found a national geographic market for the sale of daily consumer goods through supermarkets,

---

[257] *AAMS v Commission* (n 210, above) para 42. The CFI held that the fact that the legislation had been imposed by a Community directive did not preclude it being taken into consideration as a determining factor.

[258] *DSD* (n 167, above) and para 4.070, above, for a discussion of other barriers to switching in relation to supply-side substitutability.

[259] *British Airways* (n 199, above).

[260] See para 4.066, above.

[261] In *Sonoco/Ahlstrom* (n 234, above) at paras 53 and 75, the Commission considered a different issue, namely whether the degree of interpenetration of market shares was extensive; it relied on the limited degree of interpenetration to reject an argument that continuous chains of substitution gave rise to a national market.

[262] Relevant Market Notice (n 238, above) para 58.

in part on the grounds that there was a continuous chain of substitution.[263] By contrast, in *Owens-Illinois/BSN Glasspack*, the Commission rejected an argument based on continuous chains of substitution on the grounds that suppliers could price discriminate according to the location of the customer, meaning that all customers located in the catchment areas of a given set of plants formed a separate relevant geographic market.[264]

4. Temporal Market

Existence of temporal dimension.   Each relevant market has a temporal dimen-   **4.089**
sion as well as product and geographic dimensions.[265] The temporal dimension defines the period of time over which the market operates: it may relate, for example, to the time of day or the season. The temporal dimension is often not expressly addressed in the Commission's decisions, and in many cases when it is defined, it is incorporated within the definition of the relevant product market (for example, the supply of 'peak-time rail travel').[266] But it may be important to consider whether consumers could purchase the product or service at a different time or whether alternative suppliers could commence supply during the period in question.

Definition of temporal market in practice.   It is evident in many cases that there   **4.090**
are no meaningful time constraints on the purchase or supply of a given product. However, in other cases, the temporal dimension to the market requires more careful consideration: it is not self-evident, for example, whether there should be delimited temporal markets for the supply of fresh fruit, cinema tickets, impulse ice-cream, package holidays or ski equipment, all of which experience significant fluctuations in demand and/or supply depending on the time of day or year. In considering demand-side substitution, the issue is whether any attempt by the supplier to raise prices during a particular period would be defeated by customers switching their purchases to other periods. If so, then the relevant temporal market is wider. For example, in the case of peak-time rail travel, there may be

---

[263] *Laurus/Groenwoudt* (Decn of Dutch Competition Authority of 4 July 2000). See Baker, 'Unilateral effects in retail chain mergers: an application to supermarkets' (2002) ECLR 180. See also *Air Liquide/Messer Targets* (n 234, above) para 37 (finding a national market on the basis of a continuous chain of substitution *and* a series of local markets).

[264] Case M.3397 *Owens-Illinois/BSN Glasspack* (9 June 2004), para 25 and n 6. See also *Group 4 Falck/Securicor* (n 190, above) para 34, in which the Commission stated: 'even when two catchment areas overlap, it may be questioned whether there is actually a substitution chain in a similar manner as for retail activities. Contrary to retailers, the . . . suppliers are fully aware of the location of the customers that they serve . . . As a result, there is not necessarily a transmission chain of the competitive environment along the overlapping catchment areas.'

[265] See the UK OFT Guidelines on Market Definition (n 238, above) n 17 and paras 5.1–5.3.

[266] ibid, para 5.1. The Relevant Market Notice appears to take this approach since it does not refer specifically to the existence of a separate temporal dimension to the market.

'captive' consumers who cannot switch outside the market (ie to a non-peak service). If sufficiently few commuters are able to delay their journey until after the start of non-peak travel, the relevant market might properly include a temporal dimension.[267] In relation to supply-side substitution, the analysis would consider whether a supplier who increased the price of goods or services supplied during a particular period would be defeated by other suppliers commencing supply. For example, if the price of a particular fruit were increased during the domestic season, the question would arise whether importers (which generally supply outside the domestic season) could increase their supplies.

5. Market Definitions in Particular Sectors

4.091　**Introduction.**　As noted in paragraphs 4.021 and 4.023, above, market definitions are specific to the context in which they are employed and are dynamic in that they change to reflect developments in market conditions over time. It should not, therefore, be assumed that because a particular market definition was adopted in a particular sector in the past, the same definition will necessarily apply in the future. However, as a practical matter, guidance may be obtained from reviewing the approach that the Commission has taken when defining markets in previous cases, not least because this is likely to indicate the evidence used to reach any conclusions and which it might be appropriate to investigate again. This Section sets out brief, illustrative outlines of the approach to market definition that has been taken by the Commission in a number of key sectors.[268]

4.092　**Pharmaceuticals.**　For merger cases, the Commission has adopted the third level of the Anatomical Therapeutic Classification ('ATC') of medicines which groups medicines according to their therapeutic qualities, that is to say their intended use as an operational market definition.[269] However, the Commission noted that 'it is inevitable that any workable market definition will involve a certain amount of

---

[267] This is distinct from the question as to whether passengers would switch to alternative rail routes or alternative modes of transport, which would be considered as part of the product market definition.

[268] For a detailed account of market definitions reached in previous Commission merger cases, see Struys & Robinson (eds), *EC Merger Decisions Digest* (2005).

[269] Case M.072 *Sanofi/Sterling Drug* (10 June 1991), para 14; See also Case M.2922 *Pfizer/ Pharmacia* (27 February 2003), para 15; and Case M.3544 *Bayer Healthcare/Roche (OTC Business)* (19 November 2004), para 12; Case T-168/01 *GlaxoSmithKline Services v Commission* [2006] ECR II-2969, [2006] 5 CMLR 1589, paras 155 *et seq*. Further appeals pending, Cases C-501/06P, etc, In certain circumstances, several third level categories could be grouped together as one market, or, alternatively, a narrower fourth level classification could be required: see generally Case M.737 *Ciba-Geigy/Sandoz*, OJ 1997 L201/1, paras 15 *et seq*; *Glaxo Wellcome/SmithKline Beecham* (n 205, above); Case M.1878 *Pfizer/Warner-Lambert* (22 May 2000), paras 11 *et seq*; *Bayer Healthcare/Roche (OTC Business)*, above, para 12; *Pfizer/Pharmacia*, above, paras 16–17.

arbitrariness, because, in the final resort, substitutability among medicines may not only depend on the intrinsic characteristics of the drug itself, but also their intended use, taking into account the patient's overall condition.'[270] The Commission also distinguishes between ethical drugs which can only be dispensed against a prescription and over-the-counter ('OTC') medicines which are more widely available.[271] This means that if some products in an ATC3 category are available OTC and others only on prescription, there will generally be separate markets for pharmaceuticals in the different categories. However, the ATC classification does not distinguish between branded and own label products, with the result that the starting point for analysis is that they form part of the same market.[272] The geographic market for the supply of pharmaceuticals is essentially national as the pharmaceutical industry operates within a tight national legal framework.[273] The evaluation of a drug and the final decision on whether to authorise its marketing still resides mainly at the national level; the prices of ethical drugs are directly or indirectly regulated by widely varying national laws and the market for OTC medicines is also primarily national.[274] Wholesale pharmaceutical markets also remain national, or even regional.[275] However, the ongoing harmonisation of authorisation procedures within the Community suggests that this national market definition may change over time. The Commission has also[276] identified separate innovation markets[277] for new products and the geographic markets in such cases are at least Community-wide, and perhaps global.[278] However, the same approach to market definition does not necessarily apply in cases under Articles 81 and 82. Where the conduct being investigated affects pharmaceutical wholesalers engaged in parallel trading the market may be defined as all the medicines reimbursed by the national sickness insurance scheme which are capable of being sold at a profit owing to the price differential between two Member States. In that situation the characteristic of the product which is of most interest to the wholesaler is whether there is a sufficient price differential to render parallel trade lucrative rather than its therapeutic indication

---

[270] *Sanofi/Sterling Drug*, above, para 12.

[271] *Sanofi/Sterling Drug*, above.

[272] However, this presumption may be displaced if it is possible to show that own label products do not provide a close competitive constraint on branded goods: see para 4.064, above.

[273] *GlaxoSmithKline Services* (n 269, above) para 150.

[274] See *Ciba-Geigy/Sandoz* (n 269, above) paras 47–49; and *Bayer Healthcare/Roche (OTC Business)* (n 269, above) paras 31–32.

[275] Case M.718 *Phoenix/Comifar* (20 March 1996); Case M.572 *Gehe/AAH* (3 April 1995); and *Angelini/Phoenix/JV*, OJ 2001 C281/9, para 13.

[276] Sales by wholesalers and sales directly from the laboratory have been held to constitute two separate markets: *Gehe/AAH*, above; and *Angelini/Phoenix/JV*, above, para 9.

[277] See para 4.069, above; and *Glaxo Wellcome/SmithKline Beecham* (n 205, above) paras 70–72.

[278] *Glaxo/Wellcome*, above; *Gehe/AAH* (n 275, above); Case M.631 *Upjohn/Pharmacia* (28 September 1995); and *Ciba-Geigy/Sandoz* (n 269, above) para 51.

or pharmacological properties.[279] Everything will depend on the context of the arrangement under consideration.[280]

4.093 **Telecommunications.**[281]   The telecommunications sector is one area in which the Commission has taken an active and interventionist role in respect of how markets are defined by national authorities. First, the Commission has provided detailed guidance as to how demand- and supply-side substitutability should be assessed, and as to how the SSNIP test should be applied, in the context of electronic communications. In its SMP Guidelines,[282] the Commission provides specific examples of the evidence to be used by national authorities in determining the relevant market in this area, as well as giving an overview of the Commission's own decisional practice. Although the Commission highlights the difficulty of relying on precedents in 'a sector characterised by constant innovation and rapid technological development [where a recent precedent] runs the risk of becoming inaccurate or irrelevant in the near future',[283] it nevertheless points to certain aspects of its practice in this area by way of guidance. As an illustration, the Commission first distinguishes between two main types of markets: those involving the provision of a service to end users (services markets) and those involving provision to other operators of access to the facilities required to provide such services (access markets). Secondly, the Commission indicates that it will normally differentiate between services markets and the provision of the underlying network infrastructure, which itself may be differentiated on the basis of type of network infrastructure and by the class of users (business and residential customers) to whom the infrastructure is provided. Thirdly, the Commission will differentiate retail markets based on the identity of the consumer as between residential and business customers. Fourthly, the Commission will differentiate on the basis of demand-side considerations between mobile and fixed telephony services.

4.094 **Telecommunications: the Commission's Recommendation on Relevant Markets.** In line with its responsibilities under the Directive for the Common Framework for electronic communication networks and services,[284] the Commission published

---

[279] *GlaxoSmithKline Services* (n 269, above) paras 156 *et seq*.

[280] See, eg the UK Competition Appeal Tribunal in *Genzyme Ltd v Office of Fair Trading* [2004] CAT 4, [2004] CompAR 358, paras 197–221 (under the UK equivalent of Art 82).

[281] See further Nihoul and Rodford, *EU Electronic Communications Law* (2004), paras 3.213–3.266; and for an economic perspective, Gual, 'Market definition in the telecoms industry' in Buigues and Rey (eds), *The Economics of Antitrust and Regulation in Telecommunications* (2004), Chap 4.

[282] The Commission Guidelines on market analysis and the assessment of significant market power under the Community regulatory framework for electronic communications networks and services (the 'SMP Guidelines'), OJ 2002 C165/6, see Vol II, App E.25. These Guidelines are discussed further in Chap 12.

[283] ibid, para 63.

[284] Dir 2002/21 of the European Parliament and of the Council on a common regulatory framework for electronic communication networks and services ('Framework Directive'), OJ 2002 L108/33, see Vol II, App E.17.

in 2003 a Recommendation on relevant markets within the electronic communications sector outlining those markets that it regards as potentially susceptible to *ex ante* regulation.[285] The Recommendation provides a list of identified telecommunications markets as an annex, differentiating between services provided at retail and wholesale level. The Recommendation notes, however, that it is for national regulatory authorities to define relevant geographic markets within their territory.[286] Although the Commission has itself acknowledged the possibility that markets defined for the purposes of determining the scope of appropriate prospective regulation may differ from those adopted for the purposes of applying the competition rules to a situation occurring in the past, it has nevertheless urged national competition authorities to seek methodological consistency between the approach adopted in each case.[287]

Telecommunications: Commission's veto under Framework Directive. The **4.095** Commission has, on several occasions, employed its veto powers under Article 7 of the Framework Directive[288] in respect of measures proposed by national authorities. In the case of a draft measure of the Austrian Telecommunications Regulatory Authority,[289] the Commission vetoed the national measure on the basis of the approach taken to market definition. The case concerned the fixed telephony network, and in particular the provision of ancillary services, such as transit services, which enable calls to be carried between different local or regional telephone exchanges. The Commission clarified that, in analysing the scope of the relevant markets, it is necessary to take account of demand- and supply-side substitutability only when the constraint is real (as opposed to merely hypothetical) and would occur in the short term.[290] The Commission's intervention serves to show that it

---

[285] Commission Recommendation on relevant product and service markets within the electronic communications sector susceptible to ex ante regulation in accordance with Dir 2002/21/EC of the European Parliament and of the Council on a common regulatory framework for electronic communication networks and services, OJ 2003 L114/45. In June 2006, the Commission issued for consultation a draft revised Recommendation, which reduces the list of 18 specified markets to 12; the Commission expects to adopt a new Recommendation in 2007: Press Release IP/06/874 (29 June 2006). See further para 12.101, below.

[286] Commission Recommendation, para 2.

[287] SMP Guidelines (n 282, above) para 37. The Commission notes, however, that 'markets defined under sector-specific regulation are defined without prejudice to markets that may be defined in specific cases under competition law.'

[288] Framework Directive (n 284, above) Art 7.

[289] Draft measure of Austrian Telecommunications Regulatory Authority (AT/2004/0090).

[290] The draft Austrian measure had included within the market for transit services, operators that had established direct connections between networks, which the Commission found was based on insufficient evidence. See generally (2005) 1 EC Competition Policy Newsletter 49 and, for a discussion of the Commission's veto decision of 20 February 2004 related to the draft regulatory measures of the Finnish Communications Regulatory Authority, (2004) 2 EC Competition Policy Newsletter, 52. See further Chap 12 below.

will use its powers under the Framework Directive to uphold the standard of market definition analysis expected and required of national authorities.

4.096 **Broadcasting and television.**   As a result of the progressive liberalisation of the telecommunications sector in Europe, and the continuous development of new technologies and services, a large and increasing number of distinct product markets have emerged in the broadcasting and television industry. These can broadly be divided into three categories: programme procurement, broadcasting and infrastructure. Several subdivisions can be made in relation to content, for example news, film, sports[291] and children's programming;[292] delivery means, such as cable, satellite and terrestrial frequencies;[293] and technical and administrative matters. In *Endemol Entertainment v Commission*, the Court of First Instance upheld the Commission's decision that, as regards the production of Dutch language television programmes, the market for independent production of programmes was separate from the market for in-house productions of the public broadcasters.[294] The distinction derives from the fact that those in-house programmes were essentially for own use and not sold to third parties on the Dutch market.[295] Television broadcasting can be divided between free access and pay-TV on the basis that revenue for each activity is derived from different sources and that subscribers are willing to pay significant sums for pay-TV.[296] However, in the case of mixed financing by advertising revenue and subscriber fees, this

---

[291] In *Joint Selling of the Commercial Rights of the UEFA Champions League*, OJ 2003 L291/25, [2004] 4 CMLR 549, paras 63 *et seq*, the Commission considered that the relevant product market was the acquisition of TV broadcasting rights of football events played regularly throughout the year: football events created a particular brand image for a TV channel and allowed the broadcaster to reach a particular audience at a retail level that could not be achieved by other programmes. This meant that even other sporting events or feature films did not provide a competitive constraint on the holder of the TV rights to such events (para 77).

[292] See, eg Case M.566 *CLT/Disney/Super RTL* (17 May 1995), para 14; Case M.779 *Bertelsmann/CLT* (7 November 1996), para 18; Case JV.46 *Blackstone/CDPQ/Kabel Nordrhein-Westfalen* (19 June 2000).

[293] The Commission has stated (in *Joint Selling of the Commercial Rights of the UEFA Champions League* (n 291, above)) that, in relation to new media, such as wireless and Internet content rights, 'it is likely that each different form of exploitation will provide a specific service to specific consumers. On demand services delivered via wireless mobile devices or via the Internet will not compete with live TV broadcasting. Likewise mobile clip services will not compete with television highlights packages' (para 84). Therefore, the Commission expected that new media markets would emerge to parallel those previously existing in the pay-TV sector.

[294] Case T-221/95 *Endemol Entertainment v Commission* [1999] ECR II-1299, [1999] 5 CMLR 611, paras 106–112: in addition to objective differences between the kind of programmes produced, the in-house productions of the public broadcasters were essentially for their own use and any sales to third parties were made on the international market whereas the independent producers sold on the domestic, Dutch market.

[295] See further Case M.1943 *Telefónica/Endemol* (11 June 2000), para 8.

[296] See, eg Case M. 2483 *Group Canal+/RTL/GJCD/JV* (13 November 2001); Case M.584 *Kirch/Richemont/Multichoice/Telepiu* (5 May 1995), para 15; *Bertelsmann/CLT* (n 292, above).

distinction can become blurred.[297] Separate markets have also been identified for television and radio advertising.[298] As regards infrastructure, the Commission has adopted a market definition for administrative and technical services for suppliers of pay-TV,[299] which includes, *inter alia*, the making available of decoders and the settlement of accounts with programme suppliers. The question has arisen[300] whether the operation of a network constitutes a separate market from the provision of services on that network, and the Commission may in future adopt such distinct market definitions. It should be noted that, due to the growing convergence of the media, telecommunication and computer sectors, media markets are currently in a transitional phase and product market definitions adopted by the Commission in this sector can quickly become outdated. As regards geographic market definition, broadcasting is generally still to be regarded as a national operation. Television and radio stations in Europe are mostly national in coverage and in their audiences, mainly for linguistic reasons but also as a result of consumer preferences,[301] regulatory constraints,[302] different conditions of competition and other technical factors.[303] However, some TV and radio channels serve audiences in a broader linguistic region, which might therefore be the relevant geographic market.[304]

Transport routes. As regards the provision of transport services, to assess **4.097** whether different modes of transport (road, rail, air and sea) are substitutable for each other, it is necessary to consider the precise route involved.[305] In general,

---

[297] See Case M.469 *MSG Media Service*, OJ 1994 L364/1, para 32; Case M.993 *Bertelsmann/Kirch/Premiere*, OJ 1999 L53/1, [1999] 4 CMLR 700, para 18, where the Commission noted that with the spread of digitalisation there may be a convergence of pay- and free access TV in the future. However in Case JV.48 *Vodafone/Vivendi/Canal Plus* (20 July 2000), the Commission rejected the parties' argument that digitalisation meant there was a convergence between pay- and free access TV on the basis that there would remain a separate market for pay-TV while 'there nonetheless remains a sufficiently large body of consumers whose demand for particular television channels is sufficiently strong for those consumers to fund a pay television service through a subscription fee' (para 63).

[298] See, eg *Bertelsmann/CLT* (n 292, above) para 15; Case M.553 *RTL/Veronica/Endemol*, OJ 1996 L134/32, para 23 (appeal on other grounds dismissed, *Endemol Entertainment v Commission*, n 289, above).

[299] *MSG Media Service* (n 297, above) para 20; Case M.1022 *Cable I Televisio de Catalunya (CTC)* (28 January 1998), para 29; *Bertelsmann/Kirch/Premiere* (n 292, above) paras 19–21.

[300] eg Case M.887 *Castle Tower/TDF/Candover/Berkshire-HSCo* (27 February 1997), para 6.

[301] See, eg *MSG Media Service* (n 297, above).

[302] See, eg *RTL/Veronica/Endemol* (n 298, above).

[303] See, eg Case M.490 *Nordic Satellite Distribution*, OJ 1996 L53/20, para 73. And see generally Cases T-346 & 47/02 *Cabeleuropa v Commission* [2003] ECR II-4251, [2004] 5 CMLR 1216 (Spanish market for pay-TV, for film broadcasting rights and for broadcasting rights for sports events).

[304] *Bertelsmann/Kirch/Premiere* (n 296, above) para 25 (the whole German-speaking area was the relevant market for technical services for pay-TV); cf Case M.1027 *Deutsche Telekom/BetaResearch*, OJ 1999 L53/1, [1999] 4 CMLR 700, 748, para 24 (relevant market for cable networks confined to Germany).

[305] See generally Case 66/86 *Ahmed Saeed Flugreisen v Zentrale zur Bekämpfung unlauteren Wettbewerbs* [1989] ECR 803, [1990] 4 CMLR 102, paras 30–40; Faull & Nikpay (eds), *The EC Law of Competition* (1999), paras 12.30–12.37.

assessed on the basis of demand-side substitutability, alternative forms of transport constitute separate markets. However, in some cases, the possible transport alternatives are actual substitutes and form part of the same market.[306] Particular attention has focused on the appropriate market definition in air transport passenger cases. In *Air France v Commission*,[307] the Court of First Instance upheld the decision of the Commission that the London–Paris and London–Lyons routes were distinct markets and rejected the contention that air transport between Member States anywhere in the Community should be regarded as the relevant market. In *KLM/Alitalia*,[308] the Commission considered that each point-of-origin/point-of-destination ('O&D') pair constitutes a separate market, but that for passengers travelling between those locations, the market embraced not only direct flights between the two airports involved but also flights between other airports within the respective catchment areas of the airports concerned as well as, potentially, other forms of transport. Hence in *Air France/KLM*,[309] the two Paris airports (CDG and Orly) were considered substitutable as regards routes from Paris. In *Air France/Sabena*[310] it was held that market analysis of longer routes[311] through different gateway airports could be by means of individual routes or be bundles of substitutable routes, depending on the circumstances. And in *United Airlines/US Airways*[312] it was held that for long-haul routes, indirect services

---

[306] See *P & O Stena Line*, OJ 1999 L163/61, [1999] 5 CMLR 682, a decision under Art 81 relating to a JV that would now fall within the Merger Regulation; Case M.806 *British Airways/TAT (II)* (26 August 1996). See also the Commission's approach in its decisions concerning the Channel Tunnel: eg *Night Services*, OJ 1994 L259/20, [1995] 5 CMLR 76, paras 17–27 (annulled on other grounds: Cases T-374/94, etc, *European Night Services v Commission* [1998] ECR II-3141, [1998] 5 CMLR 718).

[307] Case T-2/93 *Air France v Commission* [1994] ECR II-323. The Commission did, however, assess the transaction also at the wider level of international operations from France.

[308] Case JV.19 *KLM/Alitalia* (11 August 1999), paras 21–25; see also Case M.2008 *AOM/Air Liberté/Air Littoral* (27 July 2000), in which the position regarding catering services and groundhandling services was also considered.

[309] Case M.3280 *Air France/KLM* (11 February 2004); appeal dismissed Case T-177/04 *easyJet v Commission* [2006] ECR II-1931, [2006] 5 CMLR 663 . It was there held also that Milan-Linate and Milan-Malpensa, and New York JFK and Newark were substitutable. cf Case M.278 *British Airways/Dan Air* (17 February 1993), [1993] 5 CMLR M61 (whether Heathrow and Gatwick constituted separate markets for the purpose of the London-Brussels service was left open); Case M.967 *KLM/Air UK* (22 September 1997), para 24 (low degree of substitutability between Amsterdam Schipol and the nearest Dutch, Belgian and German airports for services to London).

[310] Case M.157 *Air France/Sabena* (5 October 1992), [1994] 5 CLMR M2. See also Case M.616 *Swissair/Sabena* (20 July 1995).

[311] *Lufthansa/AuA*, OJ 2002 L242/25, [2003] 4 CMLR 252, confirmed that indirect flights do not pose a sufficiently strong competitive constraint on non-stop flights in relation to short-haul flights. In Case M.2672 *SAS/Spanair* (5 March 2002), para 14, the Commission considered that 'on medium-haul flights such as Spain-Scandinavia, indirect flights are at a lower disadvantage than on short-haul service, because, on the one hand, intermediate stops have a lower relative impact on total elapsed time as the total trip duration increases and, on the other hand, the number of daily direct frequencies in the city-pairs considered is very reduced (3 or less).'

[312] Case M.2041 *United Airlines/US Airways* (12 January 2001), para 17.

should fall within the same market as direct flights where they are marketed as connecting flights on the O&D pair in question and involve only a limited extension of the trip duration. The Commission has subsequently confirmed that such a time extension should not exceed 150 minutes.[313] Accordingly, in considering the various forms of transport for an O&D route, the Commission has stated that 'whether those alternatives are substitutable amongst themselves depends on a multiplicity of factors, such as the travel time, number of frequencies, service features and the price of the different alternatives.'[314] The Commission considered in *Air France/KLM*[315] whether this O&D approach should be replaced by consideration of network competition reflecting the existence of airline alliances but concluded that demand-side substitution justified the retention of the O&D approach when defining the market, whilst recognising that network effects should be taken into account in the overall substantive analysis.

Air transport: business and leisure passengers; cargo. Business travel ('time-sensitive' passengers) and leisure travel ('price-sensitive' passengers) may constitute separate markets, particularly in relation to intra-European flights, reflecting their different willingness to pay for schedule flexibility.[316] Airports may also be substitutable for leisure travellers but not for business passengers by reason of the number of connections which they offer.[317] For cargo transport, different considerations obviously apply: indirect routes with multiple stopovers are likely to be acceptable substitutes, so the market definition is likely to be wider. **4.098**

Defence markets. In defence markets, a distinction is drawn between cases in which the relevant ministry of defence seeks to award contracts to domestic suppliers for policy reasons and is able to do so, in which case the relevant geographic market is national, and cases in which there is no national supplier and competition therefore necessarily occurs on an international basis.[318] **4.099**

---

[313] *Air France/KLM* (n 304, above) para 22.

[314] COMP/38.284 *Air France/Alitalia*, 7 April 2004, [2005] 5 CMLR 1504, para 40; on appeal, Case T-300/04 *easyJet v Commission*, not yet decided. See Gremminger, 'The Commission's approach towards global airline alliances - some evolving principles' (2003) 1 EC Competition Policy Newsletter 75.

[315] n 309 above, paras 10–18.

[316] See *P&O Stena Line* (n 306, above) (different markets for cross-Channel services); *KLM/Alitalia* (n 308, above) (generally different for air transport services); and *Air France/KLM* (n 309, above) para 19; but cf *Air France/Sabena*, n 309, above (same market in air travel from Brussels). The issue was expressly left open in *KLM/Air UK* (n 310, above).

[317] *Air France/KLM* (n 309, above) para 28. However, this did not affect the overall conclusion that Paris Orly and Paris CDG were substitutable on the demand side.

[318] See, eg Case M.1745 *EADS* (11 May 2000); Case M.2938 *SNPE/MBDA/JV* (30 October 2002); Case M.3680 *Alcatel/Finmeccanica/Alcatel Alenia Space & Telespazio* (28 April 2005), para 54. See also Burnside and Brooks, 'EU market definition in the defence sector' (2003) 6(3)Global Competition Review 16.

5

COMMON HORIZONTAL AGREEMENTS

1. Introduction

Scope of this Chapter. This Chapter considers various common types of agree- **5.001** ment in the light of the general principles discussed in Chapters 2 and 3, above. Each type of agreement is considered under Article 81(1) and, more briefly, under Article 81(3). The types of agreement discussed are very varied but all are 'horizontal' agreements between undertakings at the same level of supply. Horizontal agreements relating to joint ventures, or similar collaborative arrangements concerning research and development or production, are considered separately in

303

Chapter 7; and agreements which give rise to a 'concentration' within the scope of the Merger Regulation are considered in Chapter 8, below. 'Vertical' agreements – arrangements between a supplier and an acquirer at a different level of the production or distribution chain – are discussed in Chapter 6.

5.002   **Structure of this Chapter.** Sections 2 to 5 of this Chapter concentrate on restrictions on price and output, followed by arrangements to share customers or markets. Most of these are 'hard-core' restrictions and, in that regard, the application of Article 81(1) is relatively uncontroversial: there is only limited scope for the application of Article 81(3) and substantial fines are likely to be imposed for infringement. However, agreements on non-price trading conditions may involve different considerations, and those are considered in Section 3. Sections 6 to 8 deal with a number of other areas where undertakings enter into cooperative arrangements that are less easy to classify under Article 81 and where the Community Courts and the Commission have taken a more cautious approach, particularly in relation to the activities of trade associations and cooperative organisations. The activities of sporting bodies bear some similarities to those of trade associations, but give rise to specific problems as regards both membership rules and the regulation of sporting competitions because of the particular characteristics of sport. These are therefore separately considered in Section 9.

5.003   **Refinement of classical analysis.** In common with US antitrust policy, Community analysis of horizontal arrangements emerged from an analytical model of price competition based on the operation of durable commodity markets. On various assumptions as to the operation of such markets, in particular that the goods are readily tradeable and that consumers are well informed,[1] price and output are bound by a rigid inverse correlation. Although this model offers 'useful benchmarks for predicting whether competition is likely to be healthy in a given real world market',[2] difficulties inevitably arise in markets for more sophisticated products or where the market structure is very different from that assumed by the classical model. However, the central tenets of Community competition law derive largely from early (and continuing) experience in dismantling cartels in commodity markets.[3] The more refined administrative and theoretical principles needed to address other more complicated products, services and market structures have developed more recently.[4]

---

   [1] For an overview, see Wood, 'The role of economics and economists in competition cases' (1999) 1 OECD Journal of Competition Policy 82. See also Alfter and Young, 'Economic Analysis of Cartels - Theory and Practice' (2005) 10 ECLR 26 546–557.

   [2] Wood, above, p 84.

   [3] Sections 3 and 4 of this Chapter set out the application of the classical model to restrictions on price and output, largely, although not exclusively derived from international goods cartels.

   [4] See in particular the issues raised by the approach to service industries discussed in Section 2 of this Chapter and collective arrangements discussed in Sections 7 and 8 of this Chapter.

Other horizontal agreements: Commission Notice.   At the same time, the   **5.004**
Commission has taken steps to clarify and accelerate its procedures for types of
horizontal arrangements other than cartels. In December 2000, the Commission
adopted Guidelines on the applicability of Article 81 to horizontal cooperation
agreements ('the Horizontal Cooperation Guidelines') that seek to promote a
more economically based approach to the assessment of those forms of cooperation that may have efficiency benefits, such as agreements on research and development, purchasing and standardisation.[5]

2. Cartels and Other Covert Conduct

(a) The Commission's approach to cartel activity

The harm caused by cartels.   The Commission has described the effect of cartels   **5.005**
on the European economy in the following terms:

> 'Secret cartels are among the most serious restrictions of competition. They lead to
> higher prices and less choice for consumers. And they have a negative impact on the
> whole of European industry by increasing the cost of services, goods and raw materi-
> als for European enterprises obtaining their supplies from cartel members. In the
> longer term, they reduce European industry's overall competitiveness.'[6]

This approach was affirmed by the Court of Justice in the *Cement* case:

> 'Participation by an undertaking in anti-competitive practices and agreements con-
> stitutes an economic infringement designed to maximise its profits, generally by an
> intentional limitation of supply, an artificial division of the market and an artificial
> increase in prices. The effect of such agreements or of such practices is to restrict free
> competition and to prevent the attainment of the common market, in particular by
> hindering intra-Community trade. Such harmful effects are passed directly on to
> consumers in terms of increased prices and reduced diversity of supply. Where an
> anti-competitive practice or agreement is adopted in the cement sector, the entire
> construction and housing sector, and the real-estate market, suffer such effects.'[7]

Increasing focus of law enforcement.   The Commission has increasingly   **5.006**
focused its resources on tackling cartels. Regulation 1/2003 which abolished the

---

   [5] Horizontal Cooperation Guidelines, OJ 2001 C3/2: Vol II, App C.12. The Guidelines accompany the new block exemption regulations for R & D and Specialisation Agreements, Regs 2659/2000
and 2658/2000. Many of the agreements covered by the Guidelines will be in the form of joint
ventures: see generally Chap 7, below. Moreover, 'full-function' JVs with a Community dimension
have since 1 March 1998 been subject to control under the Merger Regulation: Chap 8, below.
   [6] *XXXIst Report on Competition Policy* (2001), point 32.
   [7] Cases C-204/00P, etc, *Aalborg Portland v Commission* [2004] ECR I-123, [2005] 4 CMLR
251, para 53. See also Harding and Gibbs 'Why go to Court in Europe? An analysis of cartel appeals
1995–2004' (2005) 30 EL Rev 349–369. There is wider global action against cartels: see, eg *Hard
Core Cartels:Recent Progress and Challenges Ahead* (OECD, 2003) and discussion in Azevedo, 'Crime
and Punishment in the fight against cartels: the gathering storm' (2003) 24 ECLR 400–407.

procedure for notification of agreements to the Commission and strengthened the Commission's powers of investigation has enhanced its ability to tackle multi-national, covert activity.[8] A new Directorate with three units devoted exclusively to cartel enforcement was set up in the Directorate-General of Competition in 2005.[9] Increasingly, the illegality of cartel activity has been accepted by those involved and the focus in appeals against Commission decisions has been on the nature of the evidence, the administrative procedure and the level of fines imposed.[10] The Commission publishes the statistics charting its activity in this area in its annual Reports on Competition Policy:[11] in 2001 it took 10 decisions and imposed total fines of €1800 million; in 2002 nine decision and total fines of about €1 billion; in 2003 five decisions and total fines of €405 million; in 2004 six decisions and total fines of €390 million and in 2005 five decisions and total fines of €683 million. In 2006 the Commission took six decisions and imposed fines totalling €1,843 million. Commenting on the fines of over €344.5 million imposed on four producers in May 2006 for participation in a cartel for acrylic glass, Commissioner Kroes stated: 'These fines will serve as a cold shower for the management and shareholders of all these companies, who have to realise that cartels cannot and will not be tolerated.'[12]

5.007 **Application of Commission guidance to cartels.** The serious adverse effect of cartels is reflected in the Commission Guidelines on setting fines. The new Guidelines adopted in 2006 increased the likely penalties.[13] The Commission states that the basic amount of the fine is set at a proportion of up to 30 per cent of the value of sales, depending on the gravity of the infringement. For horizontal price-fixing, market-sharing and output limitation agreements, since they are by their very nature 'among the most harmful restrictions of competition' the proportion of the value of sales taken into account will generally be at the higher end of the scale.[14] Furthermore, the Commission will include an additional

---

   [8] See, eg *XXXIst Report on Competition Policy* (2001), point 32. The Commission does not limit its investigations to products with high volumes of sales: the market considered in *Methylglucamine*, OJ 2004 L38/18, [2004] 4 CMLR 1591 had a total annual value of €3 million and was the smallest product market for which the Commission has adopted a cartel decision.
   [9] Directorate F with a staff around 60: See *Commission action against cartels–Questions and Answers* MEMO/05/454, 30 November 2005. This followed a period in 2003–2004 when cartel activity was undertaken by all antitrust units of DG Competition.
   [10] See Harding and Gibbs (n 7, above).
   [11] The decisions are often noted in the Commission's EC Competition Policy Newsletter published three times a year.
   [12] Press Release IP/06/698 (31 May 2006). The fines incorporated discounts of 40 per cent and 30 per cent for two of the participants for their disclosure of information to the Commission. A fifth participant received full immunity from fines.
   [13] Guidelines on the method of setting fines, OJ 2006 C210/2: Vol II, App B.13.
   [14] ibid, paras 21–23. The 2006 Guidelines apply in cases commenced by a statement of objec-tions served after 1 September 2006. For all earlier cases, the previous Guidelines on setting fines

sum above the basic amount of between 15 and 25 per cent of the value of sales in order to deter undertakings from entering into such arrangements.[15] Further, the thresholds set out in the Commission's *De Minimis* Notice[16] for determining whether an agreement has an appreciable effect on competition do not apply to agreements containing 'hard-core' restrictions such as price-fixing, limitation of output and allocation of markets or customers.

(b) Anatomy of a classic cartel

How and why cartels form: *Choline Chloride*. Before considering particular **5.008** kinds of horizontal restrictions, it is helpful to understand how and why cartels are formed. There is now an extensive body of economic literature devoted to this subject, partly theoretical and partly based on empirical study.[17] There seems little doubt that growth in demand or excess capacity and stocks, whether triggered by abrupt changes or prolonged adverse conditions, are factors that encourage collusion, and that cartels are facilitated in a concentrated market where few players together hold a large market share. By contrast, persistent demand instability and ease of entry into the market make cartel activity harder to sustain. A description of the Commission's cartel infringement decision in Choline Chloride[18] provides a convenient illustration. Choline chloride is an additive used in the animal feed industry. It is a typical cartel product because it is a low price and low margin product so that transport and storage costs tend to make selling in distant areas unprofitable. Nevertheless, there is always a risk with such products in a mature market that producers will offload any surplus production[19] in the

---

continue to apply: OJ 1998 C9/3: Vol II, App B.5. Under those Guidelines, there is a category of 'very serious infringements', encompassing such horizontal arrangements as price cartels and market-sharing quotas, to which the highest level of the basic amount is applied: sect 1.A. See also Chap 13, below on the enforcement of the antitrust rules.

[15] 2006 Guidelines (n 13, above) para 25.

[16] Notice on agreements of minor importance, OJ 2001 C368/13: Vol II, App C.13, para 11 (see para 2.129, above). This was applied in *Luxembourg Breweries*, OJ 2002 L253/21, [2002] 5 CMLR 1279, para 83 (appeals dismissed Cases T-49/02, etc, *Brasserie Nationale v Commission* [2005] ECR II-3033, [2006] 4 CMLR 266).

[17] See, eg Grout and Sonderegger, *Predicting Cartels* (OFT Economic discussion paper, March 2005); Harrington, 'Behavioural Screening and the Detection of Cartels' in Ehlermann and Atanasiu (eds), *European Competiton Law Annual 2006: Enforcement of Prohibition of Cartels* (forthcoming). For a survey of the earlier literature, see Motta, *Competition Policy – Theory and Practice* (2004, sect 4.2). Empirical studies are subject to possible sampling error in that of their nature they can analyse only cartels that have been discovered.

[18] Case COMP/37.533 *Choline Chloride*, 9 December 2004, [2006] 4 CMLR 159. The three European producers have lodged appeals but do not challenge the existence of the cartel: Cases T-101/05 *BASF v Commission* (appeal on fine only); T-111/05 *UCB v Commission*; T-112/05 *Akzo Nobel v Commission*, not yet decided.

[19] When rejecting an argument that the fines should be reduced because the choline chloride market was 'in crisis', the Commission said 'As a general rule, cartels risk coming into play not

form of occasional spot exports, to help cover their fixed production costs. Even in small quantities, such exports can spoil the price climate in the import market, since customers use their potential occurrence to negotiate price reductions from the home producer. The initial cartel contacts in this market were triggered by a sudden and dramatic rise in exports by the US producers into the European market between 1989 and early 1992 followed by a 'retaliatory' export into the US market by one of the European producers' Mexican subsidiaries.

5.009 *Choline Chloride:* **the global aspect of the cartel.** The cartel involved three European producers and three US producers, who between them accounted for over 80 per cent of the world market. Their resulting arrangements operated at two levels: the global level where the European and North American producers met regularly to fix prices and share markets; and subsequently at the EEA level where the European producers met amongst themselves to fix prices and allocate customers. At both levels there was extensive exchange of commercially sensitive information to enable the parties to monitor the operation of the agreement. The cartel was found to have operated at the global level between October 1992 and April 1994. At the initial 1992 meeting the producers drew up the framework for their regulation of the international market. They then met at regular intervals around the world to monitor compliance with the initial agreements and to update prices and market share allocations.[20] The key element was an agreement for the European producers not to export to the North American market and vice versa. Through this market allocation, the remaining market players could stabilise their home market and improve profitability in their area. In those areas of the world where there was no domestic production and where all or most participants would continue to supply, profitability would be increased and stability created by agreeing on the volumes to be marketed and by avoiding price competition. An agreement was made to increase prices worldwide to identical levels, something which would not only increase profitability but also help to avoid destabilising exports between regions. Finally, steps were taken to ensure that distributors of the product did not disrupt the agreement by undercutting the fixed prices.

---

when undertakings make large profits but precisely when a sector encounters problems' (para 216). See further para 5.028, below, on the relevance of decline in the relevant industry.

   [20] Complex cartels often involve parallel meetings between representatives at different levels of seniority with the senior executives agreeing the principles of the cartel and the more junior managers meeting to monitor compliance and discuss implementation: see, eg 'Masters' and 'Sherpas' meetings in *Citric Acid*, OJ 2002 L239/18, [2002] 5 CMLR 24 (appeals largely dismissed, Cases T-59/02 *Archer Daniels Midland* [2006] ECR II-3627, [2006] CMLR 1494 (further appeal pending, Case C-511/06P) and T-43/02 *Jungbunzlauer* [2006] ECR II-3435 and the 'Top Guy' and 'working level' meetings in *Graphite Electrodes*, OJ 2002 L100/1, [2002] 5 CMLR 829 (some fines reduced on appeal, Cases T-236/01, etc, *Tokai Carbon v Commission* [2004] ECR II-1181, [2004] 5 CMLR 1465; Commission's further appeal allowed, Case C-301/04P *Commission v SGL Carbon* [2006] ECR I-5915, [2006] 5 CMLR 877; other appeals dismissed, Cases C-289/04P *Showa Denko v Commission* and C-308/04P *SGL Carbon v Commission* [2006] ECR I-5859, 5977, [2006] 5 CMLR 840, 922).

Choline Chloride: **the European aspect of the cartel.**   At the European level the   **5.010**
cartel was found to have operated between March 1994 and October 1998. The
European producers met to allocate market shares, to fix prices and in some cases
to allocate specific customers. At a typical cartel meeting the companies exchanged
detailed information regarding their sales volumes and prices to named clients in
Germany, the Netherlands and Belgium. They also agreed the allocation of lists
of named clients in each of these three Member States, agreeing the price which
the chosen producer would offer to that customer so that the other producers
could ensure that they quoted a higher price.

Choline Chloride: **the Commission's findings.**   The Commission concluded   **5.011**
that the object of the cartel was to restrict competition so that there was
no need, in order to establish a breach of Article 81, to show that the cartel had an
effect on the market. The Commission held that the involvement of the European
producers in the global and European levels of the agreement was a single and
continuous infringement between 1992 and 1998.[21] This was important because
the Commission investigation had started more than five years after the last of the
global level meetings. No fines could therefore be imposed on the US producers
because of the limitation period set by Article 25 of Regulation 1/2003,[22] but fines
were imposed on the European producers for the full duration of the cartel. In setting the fines for the European producers, the Commission regarded the cartel as
a very serious infringement covering the whole of the EEA. It had been implemented and thus had an impact on the market, although the precise significance
of that impact could not be measured. All three European producers received a
reduction in the amount of the fine because of their cooperation with the
Commission's investigation. The level of fines was relatively low, partly because
the total value of the European market in the product was small.[23]

(c) Ancillary restrictions supporting cartel activity

Restrictions ancillary to the main anti-competitive restrictions.   Complex   **5.012**
international cartels involving many participants tend to exhibit certain features
designed to support the primary anti-competitive agreements on price-fixing or
market allocation. Large scale exchange of information on prices charged, volumes
of sales and customer base is often needed to monitor compliance with the overall
goals.[24] Cartels may be either 'gentlemen's agreements' relying for enforcement

---

[21] It is this aspect of the decision which is challenged by UCB on appeal: n 18, above.
[22] See para 13.208, below.
[23] After reductions of 20–30 per cent for cooperation, the fines were: BASF: €34.97 million;
Akzo Nobel: €20.99 million; and UCB: €10.38 million. The EEA market value of choline chloride
in the last full year of the infringement was €52.6 million.
[24] eg in *Methionine*, OJ 2003 L255/1, [2004] 4 CMLR 1062 (reduction in fine on appeal Case
T-279/02 *Degussa v Commission* [2006] ECR II-897, further appeal pending, Case C-266/06P);

solely on peer pressure brought to bear at cartel meetings[25] or they may set up a more formal system of sanctions for breach. Thus, some cartels establish 'compensation' mechanisms whereby a cartel member who exceeds his allotted market share must pay financial compensation or purchase products from a member who has underperformed.[26] Other restrictions that may play a part in a formalised cartel include:

(a) an agreement not to transfer technology outside the group;[27]

(b) an agreement to respect a 'cease fire' period following a price increase during which they would not approach each other's customers;[28]

(c) an agreement to buy up the relevant business of undertakings that did not take part in the cartel.[29]

All these aspects of the agreement are likely to be condemned as anti-competitive under Article 81(1).

5.013 **Restrictions on advertising.** Some recent cartels have included restrictions on the parties advertising in certain ways. In *Fine Art Auction Houses*,[30] the parties, Christie's and Sotheby's, agreed to limit their marketing effort by avoiding statements

---

Interbrew and Alken-Maes ('Belgian Beer'), OJ 2003 L200/1, [2004] 4 CMLR 80 (appeals dismissed: Case T-38/02 *Groupe Danone v Commission* [2005] ECR II-4407, [2006] 4 CMLR 1429 (small reduction in the fine) and Case C-3/06P [2007] 4 CMLR 701; and Case T-48/02 *Brouwerij Haacht v Commission* [2005] ECR II-5259, [2006] 4 CMLR 621).

[25] eg *Zinc Phosphate*, OJ 2003 L153/1, [2003] 5 CMLR 731, para 72 (appeals dismissed, Cases T-33/02 *Britannia Alloys and Chemicals v Commission*, T-52/02 *Société Nouvelle des Couleurs Zinciques v Commission*, T-62/02 *Union Pigments v Commission*, T-64/02 *Dr Hans Heubach v Commission* [2006] 4 CMLR 1046, 1069, 1105, 1157; further appeal dismissed, Case C-76/06P *Britannia Alloys and Chemicals v Commission* [2007] 5 CMLR 251).

[26] eg *Citric Acid* (n 20, above) para 88; *Vitamins*, OJ 2003 L6/1, [2003] 4 CMLR 1030 (on appeal, Cases T-15/02 *BASF* [2006] ECR II-497, [2006] 5 CMLR 27 (fines reduced); T-22 & 23/02 *Sumitomo Chemicals* [2005] ECR II-4065, [2006] 4 CMLR 42 (decn annulled on procedural grounds); T-26/02 *Daiichi Pharmaceuticals* [2006] ECR II-713, [2006] 5 CMLR 169 (fine reduced)).

[27] *Graphite Electrodes* (n 20, above); Case COMP/37.370 *Sorbates*, 2 October 2003, [2005] 5 CMLR 2054, para 280: 'While, as a general rule, no undertaking can be obliged to provide technology to actual or potential competitors, agreements between undertakings not to supply such technology to other undertakings go beyond acceptable business practice and constitute an infringement of competition rules' (on appeal, Case T-410/03 *Hoechst v Commission*, not yet decided).

[28] *Industrial and medical gases*, OJ 2003 L84/1, [2004] 5 CMLR 144, para 158 (appeals dismissed, Case T-304/02 *Hoek Loos v Commission* [2006] ECR II-1887, [2006] 5 CMLR 590; Case T-303/02 *Westfalen Gassen Nederland v Commission* [2007] 4 CMLR 334).

[29] Case COMP/37.857 *Organic Peroxide*, 10 December 2003, [2005] 5 CMLR 579, para 271 (appeal dismissed, Case T-120/04 *Peróxidos Orgánicos v Commission* [2007] 4 CMLR 153).

[30] COMP/37.784 *Fine Art Auction Houses*, 22 December 2004, [2006] 4 CMLR 90. See also *Austrian Banks (Lombard Agreement)* OJ 2004 L56/1, [2004] 5 CMLR 399, para 79 (renunciation of advertising of lending and deposit rates agreed by the banks aimed at avoiding competition 'at this information level') (fines reduced on appeal: Cases T-259/02, etc, *Raiffeisen Zentralbank Osterreich v Commission*, judgment of 14 December 2006, further appeal pending: Cases C-125/07P, etc); *Belgian Beer* (n 25, above) para 47 (agreed levels of advertising spend); Case COMP/38.359 *Electrical and mechanical carbon and graphite products*, 3 December 2003, [2005] 5 CMLR 1062, para 240 (agreement not to advertise or participate in sales exhibitions) (on appeal, Cases T-68/04, etc, *SGL Carbon v Commission*, not yet decided).

regarding market share or claims to be the market leader in any segment of the art market. Sotheby's argued that this would not constitute an infringement of Article 81(1) since it aimed to create transparency in the market about correct market shares and to avoid the making of false claims. The Commission, however, considered that since clients were often attracted on the basis of image and reputation and market share was often used to impress clients, advertising was a relevant tool in the competition that did exist between Christie's and Sotheby's, especially since they were charging the same or very similar commission rates.

Cartel 'consultancy'.   Usually the parties to a cartel are the producers or suppli-   **5.014**
ers of the product in question. But cartels can also involve the industry trade association, which may be used as a venue for the cartel meetings or as a cover for covert meetings which take place at the fringes of legitimate industry business.[31] In *Organic peroxide*[32] a fine was imposed on AC Treuhand, a Swiss consultancy firm, for its role in the organisation and operation of the cartel. It was not involved in the market covered by the cartel but the Commission noted that it played a key role in organising meetings, mediating conflicts, proposing market shares (producing 'pink' and 'red' papers with the agreed market shares which could not be taken outside its premises) and hiding incriminating evidence (reimbursing travel expenses to avoid any trace of meetings). The Commission held that it acted as an association of undertakings and/or as an undertaking. It received a fine of only €1000 because of the relative novelty of the circumstances; but the Commission has made clear that larger fines may be imposed on organisers or facilitators of cartels in future cases.[33] At the time of writing, an appeal against the decision by AG Treuhand is pending.[34]

3. Agreements on Prices and Trading Conditions

(a) Price-fixing

(i) *Generally*

Price-fixing prohibited.   Since price is the main instrument of competition in   **5.015**
most markets, Article 81(1)(a) expressly mentions as restrictive of competition agreements which 'directly or indirectly fix purchase or selling prices or any other trading conditions'. An agreement to fix prices[35] by its very nature constitutes a

---

[31] eg *Carbonless Paper*, OJ 2004 L115/1, [2004] 5 CMLR 1303, para 123: the room booking at the Sheraton Hotel covered both the legitimate trade association meeting and the subsequent cartel meeting.

[32] Case COMP/37.857 *Organic Peroxide*, n 29, above.

[33] See Press Release IP/03/1700 (10 December 2003).

[34] Case T-99/04 *AC Treuhand v Commission*, not yet decided.

[35] For agreements on purchase prices, see para 5.027, below and Section 7(e), below.

restriction on competition within the meaning of Article 81(1).[36] The fixing of target prices constitutes the direct or indirect fixing of prices within Article 81(1)(a) even if there is no evidence that the target price had any influence on the actual selling price[37] because it enables all the participants in a cartel to predict with a reasonable degree of certainty what the pricing policy pursued by their competitors will be. As the Court of First Instance has stated: 'By expressing a common intention to apply a given price level for their products, the producers concerned cease independently determining their policy in the market and thus undermine the concept inherent in the provisions of the Treaty relating to competition.'[38] Article 81(1) is infringed by an explicit agreement between suppliers to fix prices, and also by a concerted practice to restrict price competition, for example informal concertation on the dates and amounts of price increases.[39] In many of its cartel decisions, the Commission adopts similar wording to address price-fixing:

> 'Price being the main instrument of competition, the various collusive arrangements and mechanisms . . . were all ultimately aimed at an inflation of the price to their benefit and above the level which would be determined by conditions of free competition'.[40]

5.016 **What constitutes price-fixing.** There are many ways in which prices can be fixed in addition to setting the price itself, such as determining components of the price, setting a minimum price or establishing a percentage for increase or a range.

---

[36] See, eg Case 123/83 *BNIC v Clair* [1985] ECR 391, [1985] 2 CMLR 430; Case 243/83 *Binon v AMP* [1985] ECR 2015, [1985] 3 CMLR 800; Case 246/86 *Belasco v Commission* [1989] ECR 2181, [1991] 4 CMLR 96; Case 27/87 *Erauw-Jaquery v La Hesbignonne* [1988] ECR 1919, [1988] 4 CMLR 576 (minimum price set by plant breeder for a number of growers equivalent to a horizontal price-fixing agreement).

[37] Case T-13/89 *ICI v Commission* [1992] ECR II-1021. See also *Methionine* (n 25, above); *Vitamins* (n 27, above) (setting of target and minimum prices for various vitamins); *Sorbates* (n 28, above); and *Industrial copper tubes*, OJ 2004 L125/50, [2005] 5 CMLR 1186, para 214 where target prices were agreed (on appeal Cases T-127/04 *KM Europa Metal v Commission*, T-122/04 *Outokumpu v Commission*, T-116/04 *Wieland Werke v Commission*, not yet decided).

[38] Case T-224/00 *Archer Daniels Midland and Archer Daniel Midlands Ingredients v Commission* [2003] ECR II-2597, [2003] 5 CMLR 583 (appeal from *Amino Acids*), para 120; further appeal against level of fines dismissed, Case C-397/03P, [2006] ECR I-4429, [2006] 5 CMLR 230.

[39] See, eg Cases 48/69, etc, *ICI v Commission* ('*Dyestuffs*') [1972] ECR 619, [1972] CMLR 557. See also COMP/37.667 *Speciality graphite*, decn of 17 December 2002: parties discussed who would announce what price on which date (on appeal, fines were reduced Cases T-71/03, etc, *Tokai Carbon v Commission* [2005] ECR II-10, [2005] 5 CMLR 489, further appeal dismissed, Case C-328/05P *SGL Carbon v Commission* [2007] 5 CMLR 16); *Vitamins* (n 27, above): parties agreed on and implemented price increases.

[40] eg, *Methionine* (n 24, above) para 215. See also the Commission's description of the effect of price-fixing and cartels in its Competition Policy Reports, eg 'Cartel participants conspire to maintain an illusion of competition while in reality customers have no effective choice and pay higher prices . . . . Moreover since cartel prices are commonly fixed in line with the costs of the least competitive producer, they create disincentives for more efficient companies to improve quality, technology and generally rationalise production and sales methods': *XXXth Report on Competition Policy* (2000), points 68–69.

A price-fixing agreement may have only an indirect effect on prices to be charged. The prohibition of Article 81(1) covers not only the direct fixing of sales prices in the narrow sense but any agreement relating to elements of the price. In *Electrical and mechanical carbon and graphite products*,[41] the parties encountered resistance from customers in Germany to price increases at a time of low inflation. The price increases were therefore 'camouflaged' as charges for particular services performed or additional costs incurred by the cartel members. Other elements of price-fixing which fall within Article 81(1) include agreements as to:

(a) discounts;[42]

(b) surcharges[43] and charges for ancillary services;[44]

(c) margins;[45]

(d) commission rates;[46]

---

[41] Case COMP/38.359 *Electrical and mechanical carbon and graphite products*, 3 December 2003, [2005] 5 CMLR 1062, para 111 (on appeal, Cases T-68/04, etc, *SGL Carbon v Commission*, not yet decided).

[42] See, eg Case 246/86 *Belasco v Commission* [1989] ECR 2181, [1991] 4 CMLR 96 (agreed discounts for supply of roofing felt); Case 311/85 *VVR v Sociale Dienst* [1987] ECR 3801, [1989] 4 CMLR 213 (prohibition of non-standard discounts by travel agents); *Vimpoltu*, OJ 1983 L200/44, [1983] 3 CMLR 619 (agreement by Dutch importers of tractors to observe maximum discounts and standard delivery and payment terms for imported products); *Citric Acid* (n 20, above) (parties agreed that all customers would be expected to pay the list price except for the five major customers who could be offered a discount of up to 3 per cent off the list price); *Electrical and mechanical carbon and graphite products* (n 41, above) (discounts for alternative delivery options and for early payment). See also the English Court of Appeal, *JJB Sports v Office of Fair Trading (Replica football kit)* [2006] EWCA Civ 1318, judgment of 19 October 2006 (agreements/concerted practices fixing the retail selling price of England and Manchester United shirts for certain key selling periods by agreement not to discount on the understanding that other retailers also would not discount).

[43] *Ferry Operators–Currency surcharges*, OJ 1997 L26/23, [1997] 4 CMLR 798 (coordinated introduction of a freight surcharge designed to compensate cross-Channel ferry companies for the devaluation of the pound in September 1992). See also *Alloy surcharge*, OJ 1998 L100/55, [1998] 4 CMLR 973; on appeal, Cases T-45/98, etc, *Krupp Thyssen Stainless and Acciai Speciali Terni v Commission* [2001] ECR II-3757, [2002] 4 CMLR 521: CFI upheld the finding of infringement in respect of fixing a component of the final price through the use by producers of the same reference values for calculating alloy surcharge (paras 156–157) (further appeals dismissed, Cases C-65 & 73/02P [2005] ECR I-6773, [2005] 5 CMLR 773); *Electrical and mechanical carbon and graphite products* (n 41, above) (surcharges for recycling of used products, packaging and carriage and costly raw material).

[44] eg *Industrial and medical gases* (n 28, above) paras 241 *et seq* (parties agreed transport charges for gases supplied in cylinders; minimum levels for cylinder rent; the introduction of a drop charge for bulk delivery of gases; the introduction of environmental and safety charges for gases in cylinders and charges for renting bulk tanks).

[45] Cases 209/78, etc, *Van Landewyck v Commission* ('*FEDETAB*') [1980] ECR 3125, [1981] 3 CMLR 134, paras 94–112 (manufacturers and importers of tobacco in Belgium fixed trade and retail margins); *VVR* (n 42, above) (contractual and statutory ban on the passing on of commission from travel agents to customers in Belgium).

[46] See *Fine Art Auction Houses* (n 30, above): Christie's and Sotheby's agreed on an increase of the so-called 'vendor's commission'. See also *Eurocheque: Helsinki Agreement*, OJ 1992 L95/50, [1993] 5 CMLR 323. Although the Commission has insisted on the abandonment of fixed commission rates on the London commodity markets, it permitted a rule to the effect that a commission should be charged in transactions off the floor of the market: *The London Sugar Futures Market Limited*,

(e) rebates[47] (or an agreement not to give other than cost related rebates);[48]

(f) interest rates and other credit terms;[49]

(g) a common tariff structure;[50]

(h) 'standard' exchange rates;[51]

(i) not to submit quotations without prior consultation;[52]

(j) not to deviate from published prices,[53] or not to make public any deviations from published prices;[54]

(k) not to quote other than delivered prices;[55]

OJ 1985 L369/25, [1988] 4 CMLR 138 (see ibid, for cocoa L369/28, coffee L369/31 and rubber L369/34; [1988] 4 CMLR 143, 155 and 149 respectively). The Commission adopted similar decisions on *The Petroleum Exchange of London*, OJ 1987 L3/27, [1989] 4 CMLR 280; and on the futures markets for meat, potatoes, grain and soya beans: OJ 1987 L19/18, etc.

[47] *FEDETAB* (n 45, above) paras 142–146; Cases 240/82, etc, *SSI v Commission* [1985] ECR 3831, [1987] 3 CMLR 661 (Dutch importers and manufacturers of cigarettes agreed 'specialist retailers bonus'). For aggregated rebates cartels, see para 5.101, below.

[48] *IFTRA Aluminium*, OJ 1975 L228/3, [1975] 2 CMLR D20.

[49] eg *Austrian Banks ('Lombard Agreement')* (n 30, above) (agreement covered all banking products and services including interest rates for loans and savings for commercial customers, fees for certain services, money transfer and export financing); *Vimpoltu* (n 42, above). *Fine Art Auction Houses* (n 31, above) (agreement on minimum interest rates for loans and to refrain from giving advances to vendors on single auction lots). The giving of extended credit may be a form of price reduction if interest is not charged at a commercial rate. cf Cases C-215 & 216/96 *Bagnasco* [1999] ECR I-135, [1999] 4 CMLR 624, [1999] All ER (EC) 678 (standard banking terms requiring banks to lend only at variable rates alterable without notice held to fall outside Art 81).

[50] *Tariff structures in the combined transport of goods*, OJ 1993 L73/38, L145/31; *GEN (Global European Network), XXVIIth Report on Competition Policy* (1997), p 104, [1997] 5 CMLR 824 (comfort letter on condition that price-fixing eliminated from access arrangements to high quality digital telecommunications network). But cf *REIMS II*, OJ 1999 L275/17, [2000] 4 CMLR 704 (negative clearance, subject to conditions, for agreed 'terminal dues' for international mail, ie agreed payments to the national postal service responsible for delivery: see further para 12.189, below). In the context of a joint venture, a common charging structure between the partners may be ancillary and therefore outside Art 81: eg *Iridium*, OJ 1997 L16/87, [1997] 4 CMLR 1065 (guidelines for distribution of charges between partners in different territories to global digital telecommunications satellite): see further Chap 7, below.

[51] eg *Speciality graphite* (n 39, above) para 100.

[52] *Cast Iron and Steel Rolls*, OJ 1983 L317/1, [1984] 1 CMLR 694; cf *Building and construction industry in the Netherlands*, OJ 1992 L92/1, [1993] 5 CMLR 135, upheld on appeal in Case T-29/92 *SPO v Commission* [1995] ECR II-289, and Case C-137/95P, [1996] ECR I-1611 (price-fixing meetings in relation to bids for contracts put out to tender); *Astra*, OJ 1993 L20/23, [1994] 5 CMLR 226.

[53] *IFTRA Glass Containers*, OJ 1974 L160/1, [1974] 2 CMLR D50 (so-called 'fair trading rules' promulgated by trade association of glass container manufacturers and administered from Vaduz); *IFTRA Aluminium* (n 48, above) ('fair trading rules' promulgated by trade association of primary aluminium manufacturers, similarly administered from Vaduz); cf *VVR* (n 42, above).

[54] Case 73/74 *Papiers Peints v Commission* [1975] ECR 1491, [1976] 1 CMLR 589, paras 8–10. See also in *UK Replica football kit* (n 42, above): 'price pegging' agreement that Sportsetail's retail prices for England replica kit would be aligned with JJB's retail prices for the same products to avoid Sportsetail undercutting JJB (although the Competition Appeal Tribunal found that there was insufficient evidence to demonstrate that JJB was a party to this agreement once it became illegal following the coming into force of the Competition Act 1998).

[55] *IFTRA Glass Containers* (n 53, above); *Vimpoltu* (n 42, above).

(l)   not to sell 'below cost';[56]
(m) to grant parties 'most favoured nation' status.[57]

An agreement on list prices or a prohibition on advertising specially reduced prices restricts competition even if the parties are free to grant discounts or to sell at lower prices.[58] The agreement of 'basic rates' from which individual prices are calculated will also constitute an infringement.[59] Agreement on guaranteed purchases between competing suppliers in return for price stability may also constitute price-fixing.[60] A national initiative to impose maximum prices may involve companies affected by the initiative on infringements of Article 81(1).[61]

Price recommendations.   Article 81(1) may also be infringed by price 'recommendations' relating, for example, to the 'target' prices to be achieved,[62] the 'basic'   **5.017**

---

[56] *IFTRA Glass Containers* (n 53, above); *IFTRA Aluminium* (n 48, above); Case 8/72 *Cementhandelaren v Commission* [1972] ECR 977, [1973] CMLR 7 (obligation imposed on cement merchants to make 'a demonstrable profit'); *Belasco* (n 42, above).

[57] The Commission closed the investigation into the 'most favoured nation' clauses in the 'output deal' contracts of certain Hollywood film studios with pay television companies following certain studios' waiver of the clause in existing agreements: Press Release IP/04/2004 (26 October 2004). Studios agreed to sell broadcasters their entire film production for a set period with the right to enjoy the most favourable terms agreed between a pay-TV company and any one of them. The Commission's initial assessment was that the cumulative effect of such clauses was an alignment of prices paid to the studios because any increase paid by one studio led to a parallel price increase for other studios.

[58] *Franco-Japanese Ball Bearings*, OJ 1974 L343/19, [1975] 1 CMLR D8; *FEG–Dutch association of electrotechnical equipment wholesalers*, OJ 2000 L39/1, [2000] 4 CMLR 1208, para 114 (upheld on appeal, Cases T-5 & 6/00 *Nederlandse Federative Vereniging voor de Groothandel op Elektrotechnisch Gebiedand and Technische Unie v Commission* [2003] ECR II-5761, [2004] 5 CMLR 969; further appeals dismissed, Cases C-105 & 113/04P, [2006] ECR I-8725, 8831, [2006] 5 CMLR 1223); *Methylglucamine*, OJ 2004 L38/18, [2004] 4 CMLR 1591 and *XXXIInd Report on Competition Policy* (2002), points 48–49.

[59] *Nuovo CEGAM*, OJ 1984 L99/29, [1984] 2 CMLR 484 (Italian insurers' agreement on basic premiums); cf *Industrieverband Solnhofener Natursteinplatten*, OJ 1980 L318/32, [1981] 2 CMLR 308 (a rare example of price arrangements for cross deliveries between small producers benefiting from the *de minimis* rule).

[60] *Soda-ash–Solvay CFK*, OJ 1991 L152/16, annulled on appeal on procedural grounds in Cases T-31 & 32/91 *Solvay v Commission* [1995] ECR II-1821, 1825, [1996] 5 CMLR 91; further appeals dismissed, Cases C-287 & 288/95P, [2000] ECR I-2391, [2000] 5 CMLR 454; see also para 5.075, below.

[61] Cases T-113/89, etc, *Nefarma v Commission* [1990] ECR II-797 (Dutch system for the control of pharmaceutical prices: provisional view expressed by the Commission); *Danish Ministry of Health and Life*, Press Release IP/99/633 (17 August 1999) (agreement with Danish Association of Pharmaceutical Producers to allocate quota of overall public expenditure on pharmaceuticals based on previous year's market share; arrangement amended after intervention by the Commission who stated that a price freeze designed to limit public expenditure can in itself be compatible with Art 81).

[62] *Cementhandelaren* (n 56, above); Case T-13/89 *ICI v Commission* [1992] ECR II-1021; *Welded Steel Mesh*, OJ 1989 L260/1, [1991] 4 CMLR 13 (appeals dismissed save for reduction in some of the fines: Cases T-141/89, etc, *Tréfileurope Sales v Commission* [1995] ECR II-791; on further appeal: Cases C-185/95P *Baustahlgewebe v Commission* [1998] ECR I-8417, [1999] 4 CMLR 1203, C-219/95P *Ferrière Nord v Commission* [1997] ECR I-4411, [1997] 5 CMLR 575).

prices to be applied,[63] or the price increases to be sought.[64] A horizontal agreement to publish recommended prices is capable of restricting competition[65] even though the prices themselves are fixed independently.[66]

5.018 **Price transparency.** The Commission's approach to exchanges of price information among competitors is considered in Section 6, below. Price transparency may be an issue in considering whether an industry practice whereby each manufacturer announces publicly the prices it intends to charge for some future period can amount to a concerted practice within Article 81. In *Wood Pulp II*,[67] the Court of Justice considered an alleged cartel among United States, Canadian and Scandinavian producers of bleached sulphate pulp used for the manufacture of paper. The market for the supply of wood pulp was characterised by long-term relations between the producers and their customers and by a system of 'quarterly announcements' whereby the producer would inform his customers of the maximum price which would prevail during the following quarter and would guarantee a quantity of pulp reserved for that customer. The customer was free to purchase a greater or smaller quantity and could negotiate discounts and rebates from the 'announced price'. The price at which the pulp was actually sold, referred to in the judgment as the 'transaction price', was thus either the same as or lower than the announced price. The Commission's decision had condemned the producers for concerting on both the announced prices and the transaction prices. The Court of Justice annulled most of the Commission's decision on a variety of grounds.

---

[63] Cases 209/78, etc, *FEDETAB* (n 45, above) paras 102 *et seq* (recommendation on trade margins, etc). See also *SCK and FNK*, OJ 1995 L312/79, [1996] 4 CMLR 565: publication by the Dutch crane hire association of cost calculations and recommended rates based upon them, together with an obligation on the members to charge 'reasonable rates' (fine of 11.5 million ECU imposed on FNK); upheld on appeal, Cases T-213/95 & 18/96 [1997] ECR II-1739, [1998] 4 CMLR 259: see also para 5.142, below. In *Fenex*, OJ 1996 L181/28, [1996] 5 CMLR 332, the practice of a Dutch association of freight forwarders in circulating recommended tariff increases to its members was similarly held to violate Art 81(1), but only a very small fine was imposed in the particular circumstances of the case.

[64] Case 45/85 *VdS v Commission* [1987] ECR 405, [1988] 4 CMLR 264 (recommendation by German fire insurers' association to increase prices); cf *TEKO*, OJ 1990 L13/34, [1990] 4 CMLR 957 (group reinsurance company's compulsory premium recommendations on basis of optional risk assessment); and *Concordato Incendio*, OJ 1990 L15/25, [1991] 4 CMLR 199 (association of fire insurance companies setting common insurance tariff): both exempted under Art 81(3). For the insurance sector, see now Reg 358/2003, OJ 2003 L53/8: paras 3.081, above and 12.189 *et seq*, below.

[65] In *Belgian Architects*, OJ 2005 L4/10, [2005] 4 CMLR 677 the Commission noted the negative impact of recommended prices. They can facilitate coordination of prices between service providers and can mislead consumers as to the price levels that might be reasonable. There are alternative methods for providing consumers with average costs of services, eg the publication of historical or survey based price information. See De Waele, 'Liberal professions and recommended prices: the Belgian architects case' (2004) 3 EC Competition Policy Newsletter 44.

[66] *Vimpoltu* (n 42, above) paras 38–41; cf Case 161/84 *Pronuptia* [1986] ECR 353, [1986] 1 CMLR 414 (recommended prices acceptable in a vertical franchise agreement provided franchisee is free to disregard them).

[67] Cases C-89/85, etc, *Ahlström v Commission* [1993] ECR I-1307, [1993] 4 CMLR 407, on appeal from Commission decision in *Wood Pulp*, OJ 1985 L85/1, [1985] 3 CMLR 374.

As far as the concertation on announced prices was concerned, the Court held that, as a matter of law, a system of quarterly price announcements did not, of itself, infringe Article 81(1).[68] The Court rejected the Commission's arguments that such a system led to artificial price transparency and held that the system did not 'lessen each undertaking's uncertainty as to the future attitude of its competitors'. The Court also rejected on the facts the allegations that the system of announced prices was evidence of concertation on prices by the producers.

Price agreements among distributors.   It is also an infringement of Article 81(1)   **5.019**
for distributors to agree prices among themselves, or for a manufacturer to seek to restrict price competition at the level of distribution.[69]

(ii) Imports and exports

Price agreements on imports into the Community.   Horizontal agreements   **5.020**
which restrict price competition in respect of goods imported into the Community from third countries may well infringe Article 81(1).[70] The most striking example to date is *Wood Pulp II,*[71] where the parties were situated outside the Community but supplied virtually all the bleached sulphate pulp for paper manufacture within the Community, and they were alleged to have followed a concerted pricing policy over many years. Although the Court of Justice annulled most of the decision's findings on concertation, it upheld the finding that the US producers who were

---

[68] *Ahlström*, above, paras 55–65.

[69] *Hasselblad*, OJ 1982 L161/18, [1982] 2 CMLR 233, on appeal Case 86/82 *Hasselblad v Commission* [1984] ECR 883, [1984] 1 CMLR 559. See also Cases 100/80, etc, *Musique Diffusion Française v Commission ('Pioneer')* [1983] ECR 1825, [1983] 3 CMLR 221; para 2.048, below; *Fisher Price/Quaker Oats Ltd–Toyco*, OJ 1988 L49/19, [1989] 4 CMLR 553 (Irish retailers prevented from purchasing at lower prices enjoyed by Northern Irish purchasing group); cf *D'Ieteren Motor Oils*, OJ 1991 L20/42, [1992] 4 CMLR 399 (a recommendation to a motor dealer not to charge for an approved oil the same resale price as for another oil of higher quality prevents misinformation and is not the subject of the competition rules). In *French Beef*, OJ 2003 L209/12, [2003] 5 CMLR 891, the agreement was made between four organisations representing cattle farmers and two organisations representing slaughterers. The Commission noted in determining the level of fines that this was the first case concerning an agreement entirely between federations, related to a basic agricultural product and involving two links in the production chain (on appeal, Cases T-217 & 245/03 *FNCBV and FNSEA v Commission*, judgment of 13 December 2006, paras 356–361, the CFI reduced the fines because of the exceptional circumstances in the industry resulting from 'mad cow' disease, further appeals pending, Cases C-101 & 110/07P). In *Vitamins* (n 26, above), the Commission noted the role of the major producers, particularly BASF and Roche, as producers of pre-mixes themselves as well as suppliers of vitamins to other pre-mixers and therefore in a position to squeeze margins and damage the business of customers by increasing the price of vitamins to them. For discussion of market-sharing, see paras 5.059 *et seq*, below. See also the judgment of the English Court of Appeal concerning (a) an agreement between manufacturer (Umbro) and distributors, and (b) a concerted practice between manufacturer of toys (Hasbro) and distributors (Argos and Littlewoods): *Argos and Littlewoods v Office of Fair Trading ('Toys'), JJB Sport v Office of Fair Trading* (n 42, above).

[70] See *Aluminium Imports from Eastern Europe*, OJ 1985 L92/1, [1987] 3 CMLR 813: para 5.070, below.

[71] *Ahlström* (n 67, above); and see para 5.018, above. For the jurisdiction of EC law as regards conduct outside the Community, see para 1.105, above.

members of KEA, an association set up under the Webb Pomerene Act, had infringed Article 81(1). Similarly, the Commission has struck down agreements between Community undertakings and foreign undertakings fixing prices for goods imported into the Community.[72] Even if the agreement is limited to an undertaking in a single Member State and an undertaking in a non-Member State, trade between Member States may be affected if the agreement is likely to have repercussions outside the single Member State in question.[73]

5.021 **Price agreements on exports out of the Community.**   In its early decisions, the Commission held that an agreement which fixes prices solely in respect of exports out of the Community does not fall within Article 81(1),[74] although subsequently in *Centraal Stikstof Verkoopkantoor*[75] the Commission left the point open. In a case concerning a vertical agreement, *Javico v Yves Saint Laurent*,[76] the Court of Justice considered an agreement under which Javico undertook to distribute YSL products in Russia and the Ukraine. The Court held, on a reference under Article 234, that an obligation to sell only in the contract territories and not to re-import the goods into the Community did not have as its object the suppression of parallel imports and that it was for the national court to assess, looking at the characteristics of the market, whether it had that effect.

5.022 **Domestic price agreements extending to imports or exports.**   Agreements between undertakings situated in the same Member State fall within Article 81(1) where the parties fix prices in respect of products imported from,[77] or exported

---

[72] eg *French and Taiwanese Mushroom Packers*, OJ 1975 L29/26, [1975] 1 CMLR D83 (agreement between French and Taiwanese producers to undertake concerted action on the German market); *Sorbates* (n 27, above).

[73] See generally para 1.106, above.

[74] *DECA*, JO 1964 2761, [1965] CMLR 50; *VVVF*, JO 1969 L168/22, [1970] CMLR D1.

[75] *Centraal Stikstof Verkoopkantoor*, OJ 1978 L242/15, [1979] 1 CMLR 11. In the view of the Commission, since the agreement in question also covered domestic sales, there was no need to decide whether cooperation which consisted 'simply and solely of making specified quantities of products available to a distribution agency for sales in non-member countries' had an appreciable effect on competition and trade between Member States.

[76] Case C-306/96 *Javico v YSLP* [1998] ECR I-1983, [1998] 5 CMLR 172: see further paras 1.108 *et seq*, above and 6.059, below.

[77] See, eg *FEDETAB* (n 45, above) (Belgian manufacturers' and importers' agreement on trade margins, end of year rebates, and terms of payment for tobacco products likely to distort trade patterns in manufactured tobacco and reduce competition between imported products); *SSI v Commission* (n 48, above) (Dutch manufacturers and importers agreements and concerted practices on prices and rebates for tobacco products); *Vimpoltu* (n 42, above) (agreement on maximum discounts by Dutch importers of tractors). But cf *Papiers Peints* (n 54, above): ECJ quashed the fines imposed by a Commission decision condemning an 'aggregated rebates' cartel which affected 10 per cent of Belgian imports and five per cent of the total Belgian market, and to which no foreign manufacturer was a party. The ECJ held (at paras 29–33) that the Commission had not sufficiently explained why the agreement was liable to affect trade between Member States. The same principles apply to suspension of imports. See *French Beef* (n 69, above): parties agreed to suspend imports of beef into France. The CFI noted that this suspension was properly regarded as linked to the agreement on minimum prices to be paid by abbatoirs, since the suspension was designed to prevent

to,[78] other Member States. The same applies if prices are fixed for a raw material used in the production of finished products likely to be exported, even if the raw material itself is not normally traded between Member States.[79] Similarly Article 81(1) may be infringed by a price agreement relating to services, if the services extend to property situated in other Member States[80] or, conversely, are supplied in one Member State by undertakings situated in other Member States.[81]

Domestic price agreements not extending to imports or exports.   Price-fixing   **5.023**
agreements between undertakings in the same Member State may fall within Article 81(1) even if they do not expressly extend to imports or exports between Member States.[82] Whether such an agreement has the potential appreciably to affect inter-State trade is a question of fact in each case, taking into account, *inter alia*, the relative importance of the agreement on the market concerned and the economic context in which it exists.[83] Hence in *British Sugar*, the Court of Justice dismissed a challenge to the finding of infringement by an arrangement between British producers that covered marketing of sugar only in Great Britain, since that market is susceptible to imports and defence against imports was one of the major

---

importation at lower prices and thus to support the efficacy of the agreed price scale: *FNCBV and FNSEA v Commission* (n 69, above) paras 81–82.

[78]   See, eg *VVVF* (n 74, above) (prices for exports of paints to other Member States fixed by Dutch trade association); *Cimbel*, JO 1972 L303/24, [1973] CMLR D167 (equalisation scheme between home and export prices inevitably influenced export prices and distorted pattern of exports from Belgium to other Member States); *Industrieverband Solnhofener Natursteinplatten* (n 59, above) (fixing of export prices and aggregated rebates by small and medium sized suppliers of German Solnhofen natural stone); *AROW/BNIC*, OJ 1982 L379/1, [1983] 2 CMLR 240 (minimum prices for cognac sold in France and for export to other Member States); see also *BNIC v Clair* (n 36, above).

[79]   *BNIC v Clair* (n 36, above); cf *Industrieverband Solnhofener Natursteinplatten* (n 59, above) (fixing of 'base prices' for deliveries of stone between producers: held, on the facts, not to be an appreciable restriction of competition). See also *Spanish Raw Tobacco* (n 96, below) where the Commission concluded that the agreement extended over the whole of Spain since the undertakings concerned were the only processors recognised in Spain and bought most of the raw tobacco produced in Spain each year which once processed was sold primarily for export. The agreement therefore had an effect on trade between Member States. In addition, although the three agricultural producers' representatives argued that their conduct could not have an effect on trade because tobacco can only be exported upon processing, the Commission found that there can be an effect on patterns of trade where the agreement relates to an intermediate product and the final product is itself traded.

[80]   *Nuovo CEGAM* (n 59, above); *Assurpol*, OJ 1992 L37/16, [1993] 4 CMLR 338.

[81]   *Fire Insurance* (D), OJ 1985 L35/20, [1985] 3 CMLR 246, on appeal Case 45/85 *VdS v Commission* (n 64, above); *Assurpol* (n 80, above). For two national price-fixing regimes for services, see *CNSD*, OJ 1993 L203/27, [1995] 5 CMLR 495; appeal dismissed Case T-513/93 *CNSD v Commission* [2000] ECR II-1807, [2000] 5 CMLR 614 (scheme relating to goods imported into or exported from Italy); *COAPI*, OJ 1995 L122/37, [1995] 5 CMLR 468 (minimum scale of charges affected non-Spanish residents seeking to register intellectual property rights in Spain and Spanish residents seeking to register such rights abroad).

[82]   *Cementhandelaren v Commission* (n 56, above); *Belasco v Commission* (n 43, above); *Dutch Banks*, OJ 1989 L253/1, [1990] 4 CMLR 768, appeal dismissed Case T-138/89 *Nederlandse Bankiervereniging v Commission* [1992] ECR II-2181, [1993] 5 CMLR 436; *Building and construction industry in the Netherlands* (n 52, above).

[83]   For appreciable effect, see generally paras 2.121 *et seq*, above.

concerns of the cartel participants.[84] Similarly, an agreement can fall within Article 81 because it affects the parties' position in export markets, or alters the pattern of exports that might otherwise occur.[85]

(iii) Resale and purchase prices

5.024 **Collective resale price maintenance.** A horizontal agreement whereby suppliers collectively agree to operate a system of resale price maintenance infringes Article 81(1) if the agreement extends to imported goods, even if the parties are each free to set their own minimum resale prices.[86] A collective agreement to operate resale price maintenance in respect of domestically produced goods sold in the home market can also infringe Article 81(1), but only if the requisite effect is shown on trade between Member States.[87]

5.025 **Resale price maintenance for books.** In many Member States the last overt example of collective resale price maintenance was in relation to books. The position in the United Kingdom was the subject of a Commission decision, *Publishers' Association–Net Book Agreements*,[88] which held that the practice was contrary to Article 81(1) and refused to grant exemption under Article 81(3). The decision was upheld by the Court of First Instance[89] but the Court of Justice allowed the further appeal,[90] finding that the Commission had incorrectly evaluated the conditions for exemption.[91] The Commission has noted that it does not object to

---

[84] Case C-359/01P *British Sugar v Commission* [2004] ECR I-4933, [2004] 5 CMLR 329, paras 28–30 (upholding the judgment of the CFI in Cases T-202/98, etc, *Tate & Lyle v Commission* [2001] ECR II-2035, [2001] 5 CMLR 859, [2001] All ER (EC) 839). For effect on imports, see also *Cementehandelaren v Commission* (n 56, above) para 30; *MELDOC*, OJ 1986 L348/50, [1989] 4 CMLR 853; *Building and construction industry in the Netherlands* (n 52, above).

[85] eg *Centraal Stikstof Verkoopkantoor* (n 75, above); *Italian Cast Glass*, OJ 1980 L383/19, [1982] 2 CMLR 61.

[86] Cases 43 & 63/82 *VBVB and VBBB v Commission* [1984] ECR 19, [1985] 1 CMLR 27; see, eg *ASPA*, JO 1970 L148/9, [1970] CMLR D25; *CBR*, OJ 1978 L20/18, [1978] 2 CMLR 194; *Dutch Pharmaceuticals Agreement*, VIIIth Report on Competition Policy (1978), point 81; *Binon v AMP* (n 36, above) paras 39–47 (newspaper distribution: special characteristics of market might justify application of Art 81(3)).

[87] *GERO-fabriek*, OJ 1977 L16/8, [1977] 1 CMLR D35 (domestic rpm tends to deflect trade flows from natural channels).

[88] *Publishers' Association – Net Book Agreements*, OJ 1989 L22/12, [1989] 4 CMLR 825.

[89] Case T-66/89 *Publishers Association v Commission* [1992] ECR II-1995, [1992] 5 CMLR 120.

[90] Case C-360/92P *Publishers Association v Commission* [1995] ECR I-23, [1995] 5 CMLR 33, [1996] ICR 121. In *VBVB and VBBB* (n 86, above) paras 30–31 and Case 229/83 *Leclerc v Au Ble Vert* [1985] ECR 1, [1985] 2 CMLR 286, the ECJ had left open how far a domestic rpm agreement on books infringed Art 81(1). See also AG Verloren van Themaat in *VBVB and VBBB*, above, at para II(3).

[91] The UK agreement was also subject to scrutiny by the national competition authorities in both Ireland and the UK in 1994 and has now been abandoned (as a matter of law, the Restrictive Practices Court finally ruled the agreement contrary to the public interest under the Restrictive Trade Practices Act 1976, on the basis of fundamental changes of circumstances since its original exemption in 1962: *Re Net Book Agreement (No. 4)* [1998] ICR 753).

'truly national resale price maintenance agreements' for printed products provided that they do not appreciably affect trade between Member States. It has closed and settled the major cases on that basis. The *Sammelrevers*[92] case concerning prices in Germany and Austria was closed by negative clearance comfort letter based on the lack of an appreciable effect on trade between Member States, after a commitment was given which would guarantee the freedom of direct cross-border selling by foreign traders of German language books to final consumers in Germany, in particular via the internet. The Commission has noted that it will keep under review any unjustified cross-border price differentials which trigger complaints, following the enhanced transparency in the print sector as a result of the introduction of the euro.[93]

Individual resale price maintenance.   An agreement between a supplier and a customer whereby the former agrees or imposes a minimum resale price will often also infringe Article 81(1).[94] Vertical provisions on resale prices are discussed in Chapter 6, below.[95]   **5.026**

Fixing of purchase prices.   An agreement on purchase prices restricts the ability of the parties to purchase individually at different prices and normally thus restricts competition within the meaning of Article 81(1). For example, in *Spanish Raw Tobacco*[96] and *Italian Raw Tobacco*[97] the Commission fined the members of a cartel of tobacco processors who agreed on the maximum prices they would pay   **5.027**

---

92 *Sammelrevers, Internetbuchhandel, Proxis/KNO et al*, Press Release IP/02/461 (22 March 2002), *XXXIInd Report on Competition Policy* (2002), page 203. See also the Note on these proceedings and text of the commitment in (2002) 2 EC Competition Policy Newsletter 35. As regards book prices, Art 151(4) EC may be relevant to the application of Art 81(3): see Council Resolution on fixed book prices in homogeneous cross-border linguistic areas, OJ 1999 C42/3.

93 *XXXIInd Report on Competition Policy* (2002), points 152–153.

94 See, eg *GERO-fabriek* (n 87, above); *Hennessy/Henkell*, OJ 1980 L383/11, [1981] 1 CMLR 601. See also comments of the UK Competition Appeal Tribunal in the *Toys* case (n 70, above) in its separate judgment on penalty. In relation to the trilateral concerted practice in which one major retailer communicated with the supplier to ascertain that another major retailer would not sell below recommended resale prices, the Tribunal stated: 'We do not, moreover, share the appellants' view that this case was necessarily less serious than a "classic" price fixing agreement . . . . In our view this case involved subtle and largely oral agreements or concerted practices in which Argos and Littlewoods contrived, with Hasbro acting as middleman and go-between, to raise retail prices to RRPs on the basis of assurances from Hasbro that they would not be undercut by the other party if they did so . . . . In our view, agreements or concerted practices of this kind are no less serious than more formal price-fixing agreements.' [2005] CAT 13, [2005] CompAR 834, para 217. The Tribunal's judgment was upheld by the Court of Appeal, *Argos Ltd and Littlewoods Ltd v Office of Fair Trading* (n 43, above).

95 See paras 6.050 *et seq*, below.

96 COMP/38.238 *Spanish Raw Tobacco*, 20 October 2004, [2006] 4 CMLR 866 (on appeal Cases T-24/05 *Standard Commercial*; T-29/05 *Deltafina*; T-33/05 *Cetarsa*; T-37/05 *World Wide Tobacco Espana*; T-38/05 *Agroexpansion*; T-41/05 *Dimon*, not yet decided).

97 COMP/38.281 *Italian Raw Tobacco*, 20 October 2005, [2006] 4 CMLR 1766 (on appeal Cases T-11/06; T-12/06; T-19/06 and T-25/06, not yet decided) (the parties were largely the same undertakings in both decisions).

producers for each kind and quality of tobacco. The Commission stated that purchase price is a fundamental aspect of the competitive conduct of any undertaking operating in a processing business and is also, by definition, capable of affecting the behaviour of the same companies in any other market in which they compete, including downstream markets. This was particularly so since the raw tobacco is a substantial input of the activities carried on by the participants. In *French Beef* [98] there was a commitment to apply 'the slaughterhouse entry purchase price scale to culled cows' with a list of prices for certain categories.[99] Different considerations apply in the context of the collective buying arrangements considered in Section 7, below.

(iv) Application of Article 81(3)

5.028 **Relevance of state of the industry.** In special circumstances, the Commission has granted exemption (under the former regime of Regulation 17) to horizontal agreements fixing standard tariffs or common prices, as discussed below.[100] In cases of chronic overcapacity in an industry, a 'restructuring agreement' involving a specified programme to reduce capacity, for instance by plant closures, has also been given exemption.[101] But restructuring agreements do not involve coordination of prices, and the fact that an industry is in decline, or even in crisis, does not generally enable price-fixing arrangements to meet the conditions for the application of Article 81(3).[102] In *French Beef,* concerning an agreement between French farmers' and slaughterhouses' representatives to set minimum prices for culled cows in France because of the serious crisis in the industry caused by BSE ('mad cow disease'), the Commission noted that even if exemption had been applied for, the agreement could not satisfy the first two conditions of Article 81(3): the agreement did not improve the production or distribution of goods or promote technical or economic progress, nor did it allow consumers a fair share of the resulting benefit.[103] On appeal, although the Court of First Instance did not specifically address Article 81(3) it emphasised that the supposed inadequacy of governmental measures to deal with the crisis in the agricultural sector cannot justify private undertakings engaging in measures contrary to the competition rules or arrogating to themselves the role of public authorities.[104] The agreement at issue in

---

[98] *French Beef,* OJ 2003 L209/12, [2003] 5 CMLR 891; appeals dismissed save for reduction in the fines, Cases T-217 & 245/03 *FNCBV and FNSEA v Commission,* judgment of 13 December 2006, further appeals pending, Cases C-101 & 110/07P.

[99] See also *Spanish Raw Tobacco* and *Italian Raw Tobacco* (nn 96 and 97, above) where processors agreed on purchase prices to be paid to growers for raw tobacco.

[100] See paras 5.032–5.034, below.

[101] See paras 5.051–5.054, below.

[102] *Cast Iron and Steel Rolls,* OJ 1983 L317/1, [1984] 1 CMLR 694.

[103] *French Beef* (n 98, above) para 130.

[104] *FNCBV and FNSEA v Commission* (n 98, above) para 91. cf Cases C-238/99P, etc, *LVM v Commission* ("*PVC II*") [2002] ECR I-8375, where the ECJ (at para 487) approved the dictum of

French Beef was publicly announced;[105] it seems inconceivable that a covert price-fixing agreement would fulfil the requirements of Article 81(3), whatever the situation in the industry. At most, these are factors that might be relevant to the level of penalty to be imposed.[106] In *Steel Beams*,[107] the fact that there had been delivery and production quotas and minimum prices imposed by the Commission between October 1980 and June 1988 was not accepted as any justification for the price-fixing and production limitations agreed by the producers themselves (although no fine was imposed in relation to that period). Similarly, it is no justification that the object of a cartel is to counter trading by others in an anti-competitive or unfair manner. In *Citric Acid*,[108] the parties argued that the pressure that they were alleged to have brought to bear on Chinese producers to increase their prices was legitimate because the Chinese were dumping citric acid on the European market. The Commission made clear that although an industry may lawfully discuss whether an anti-dumping complaint should be filed with the Commission, it is not for the main producers in a given market segment to take concerted action themselves to evict third parties from the market. The Commission characterised the behaviour of the cartel members towards the Chinese producers as 'a strategy aimed at protecting the cartel from an unexpected competitive threat, irrespective of the question of the lawfulness, under EC anti-dumping law, of the prices charged by the Chinese producers'.[109]

---

the CFI that the existence of a crisis in the market might in an appropriate case be relied on with a view to obtaining an exemption; however, the observation was *obiter* as the agreement had not been notified and no analysis of how Art 81(3) might apply was carried out.

[105] In the Finnish roundwood sector, where an extremely diverse sellers' market, comprising hundreds of thousands of smallholdings, is confronted with a heavily concentrated buyers' market, the Commission, developing the EFTA Surveillance Authority's approach prior to 1 January 1995, has allowed the sellers to be represented by committees mandated to agree on 'the market situation and the price expectations' with the major buyers, while limiting the degree of information exchange and avoiding central decisions on prices or target prices: *Finnish timber, XXVIth Report on Competition Policy* (1996), para 126–127 (misdescribed as a decision granting five-year exemption but in fact only a comfort letter).

[106] As was the case in *French Beef*. For determination of fines, see paras 13.135 *et seq*, below.

[107] *Steel Beams*, OJ 1994 L116/1, [1994] 5 CMLR 353. The Commission's decisions were substantially upheld by the CFI: see eg, Case T-141/94 *Thyssen Stahl v Commission* [1999] ECR II-347, [1999] 4 CMLR 810; Case T-134/94 *NMH Stahlwerke v Commission* [1999] ECR II-239, etc. On appeal to the ECJ, six of the eight appeals were dismissed: eg, Cases C-179/99P *Eurofer v Commission*; C-194/99P *Thyssen Stahl v Commission* [2003] ECR I-10725, 10821, etc. In Case C-176/99P *ARBED v Commission* [2003] ECR I-10687, [2005] 4 CMLR 530, the decision as regards one defendant was annulled on procedural grounds and the Commission re-adopted the decision against that corporate group in 2006: Press Release IP/06/1527 (8 November 2006); on appeal, Case T-405/06 *Arcelor v Commission*, not yet decided.

[108] *Citric Acid*, OJ 2002 L239/18, [2002] 5 CMLR 1070 (appeals on other grounds largely dismissed, Cases T-59/02 *Archer Daniels Midland* and T-43/02 *Jungbunzlauer* (n 20, above).

[109] ibid, para 165. See also *Interbrew and Alken-Maes ('Belgian Beer')*, OJ 2003 L200/1, [2004] 4 CMLR 80, para 254 (argument that pricing collusion aimed at preventing abusive predatory pricing by Interbrew to Alken-Maes' tied estate rejected); appeals dismissed: Case T-38/02 *Groupe*

5.029 **Relevance of legislative price controls.** Generally it is no defence that national authorities connived at the infringement.[110] In *Belgian Beer*,[111] the Commission noted that state price controls could not justify restrictions on price competition. The Belgian system obliged the parties to request approval for a price increase either individually or collectively through their trade association but not to conclude agreements or consult about prices. Equally, price control could not be a justification for the exchange of information. Although detailed information had to be submitted together with a request for a price increase, this information was to be submitted to the Confederation of Belgian Brewers and not exchanged among the brewers. This information had also been submitted every month by Interbrew and Alken-Maes although the obligation was only to do so each time a request for a price increase was submitted. On appeal, the Court of First Instance rejected the applicants' argument that the Commission erred in failing to take account of the influence of the price control regime.[112]

5.030 **Price agreements in privatised industries: *Scottish Nuclear.*** In *Scottish Nuclear*,[113] the Commission held that Article 81(3) would be satisfied for a period of 15 years by an agreement fixing prices and quotas for purchases by the newly privatised Scottish electricity companies from the Scottish nuclear power generating company, Scottish Nuclear. Under the agreement, the two new companies,

---

Danone v Commission [2005] ECR II-4407, [2006] 4 CMLR 1429 (small reduction in the fine), Case C-3/06P [2007] 4 CMLR 701 and Case T-48/02 *Brouwerij Haacht v Commission* [2005] ECR II-5259, [2006] 4 CMLR 621.

[110] See, eg *Zinc Producer Group*, OJ 1984 L220/27, [1985] 2 CMLR 108; *Building and construction industry in the Netherlands* (n 52, above). See also the arguments rejected by the Commission in *Re Sugar Beet*, OJ 1990 L31/35, [1991] 4 CMLR 629, regarding the effect of the EC sugar quota system. In the appeals against the Commission decision in *Greek Ferries*, OJ 1999 L109/24, [1999] 5 CMLR 47, the CFI rejected the argument that national legislation aimed at preventing a price war robbed the undertakings of their autonomy in fixing prices:

Case T-65/99 *Strintzis Lines Shipping v Commission* [2003] ECR II-5433, [2005] 5 CMLR 1901, Case T-66/99 *Minoan Lines v Commission* [2003] ECR II-5515, [2005] 5 CMLR 1957 (further appeals dismissed: Cases C-110/04P *Strintzis Lines* [2006] ECR I-44, order of 30 March 2006; C-121/04P *Minonan Lines*, order of 17 November 2005) and Case T-59/99 *Ventouris Group v Commission* [2003] ECR II-5257, [2005] 5 CMLR 1781.

[111] *Belgian Beer* (n 109, above) paras 247 and 248.

[112] *Group Danone* (n 109, above) at para 409. See also *French Beef* (n 98, above) (Commission acknowledged the involvement of the French state in encouraging the agreement but noted that it had not forced the agreement which remained one between private parties); *Spanish Raw Tobacco* (n 97, above) (the Commission noted that the agreements in place were not necessary for agricultural purposes and that price competition was essential to meet objectives of agricultural reform. The Commission also found that neither national law nor Ministerial practice required the processors to agree on the prices or share quantities. But the involvement of the Ministry in approving certain standard contracts and schedules was relevant to the level of fine imposed); *Italian Raw Tobacco* (n 98, above) (Commission noted Italian law providing for collective negotiation of minimum prices in the agricultural sector 'had a clear effect on the conduct' of the two associations).

[113] *Scottish Nuclear*, OJ 1991 L178/31. cf *Verbändevereinbarung*, *XXVIIIth Report on Competition Policy* (1998) pp 156–159 (provisional approval for joint tariff structure for German electricity in context of transition to open access to German market).

Scottish Power and Hydro-Electric, were required to purchase the entire production of Scottish Nuclear in a fixed ratio and at an identical price. The Commission considered that it was necessary to introduce competition gradually into the market and to reduce overcapacity. The exemption granted was limited to 15 years, rather than the 30 years requested, since the shorter period was sufficient to give stability to the industry.

Royalty rates charged by collecting societies. Recent decisions on collective **5.031** buying and selling of intellectual property rights are considered in Section 7, below. As regards price-fixing, in *IFPI 'Simulcasting'*[114] the Commission considered an agreement whereby any collecting society in the EEA was empowered to grant a licence for the total repertoire of the other record companies' collecting societies provided it charged the same fee for that repertoire as the society which owned the repertoire would charge. Thus the global simulcasting tariff to be charged to a user for a multi-repertoire/multi-territory licence was the aggregation of all the copyright royalties determined at national level and so remained pre-determined and unchangeable by the society that granted the simulcasting licence. The Commission considered an alternative model, whereby the granting society was free to set the royalty for the other collecting societies' repertoire included in the licence as well as for its own. The Commission concluded that the resulting loss of control would be a serious deterrent to societies from participating in the agreement. A society which contributed its members' repertoire to the 'one-stop' package of repertoires would incur the risk that another participating society, in order to attract users, lowered the global royalty fee below the level considered to be acceptable by the former society and/or its members. In this situation, such society (and its members) would lose revenues when compared with the scenario where it did not participate in the arrangement. Therefore, the absence of a certain degree of control over the licensing terms as regards the royalty level would cause the economic incentive to participate in the reciprocal agreement to disappear and the term was thus entitled to exemption under Article 81(3).

Price agreements in service industries. Article 81 applies to services,[115] but **5.032** some service industries, such as postal services, banking and insurance and professional services, exhibit special characteristics which are recognised in the way that Article is applied. Where there is specific legislation which affects the application

---

114 *IFPI 'Simulcasting'*, OJ 2003 L107/58, [2003] 5 CMLR 386. 'Simulcasting' is the simultaneous transmission by radio and TV stations via the internet of sound recordings included in their broadcasts of radio and/or TV signals. Other aspects of the case are considered in para 5.113, below. See also the Note on this decision in (2003) 1 EC Competition Policy Newsletter 44.

115 See para 2.005, above. See also *VVR v Sociale Dienst* (n 42, above) (price-fixing by tour operators and travel agents); *Fine Art Auction Houses* (n 30, above) (price-fixing by Christie's and Sotheby's), on which Commr Monti commented: 'This case again shows that illegal cartels can appear in any sector, from basic industries to high profile service markets': Press Release IP/02/1585 (30 October 2002).

of competition law to the sector, this is considered in Chapter 12, below. Banking and financial services, and the professions, are not covered by a special regime but the decisions regarding those sectors often cover agreement also on terms other than price and are discussed in sub-sections 3(c) and (d) below.[116]

5.033 **Liner conferences.** Exceptionally, price-fixing agreements in the context of a shipping liner conference have benefited from a block exemption, Council Regulation 4056/86.[117] A liner conference is defined by the Regulation as '. . . a group of two or more vessel-operating carriers which provides international liner services for the carriage of cargo on a particular route or routes within specified geographical limits and which has an agreement or arrangement, whatever its nature, within the framework of which they operate under uniform or common freight rates and any other agreed conditions with respect to the provision of liner services.' The application of that block exemption is considered in Chapter 12, below, and it has been repealed with effect from October 2008.[118] In the meantime, the Commission has taken a series of decisions in recent years concerning price-fixing in maritime freight tariffs, some of which were concluded between members of a liner conference, reflecting the Commission's view that the exemption should be limited to its strict wording. The more general price-fixing aspects of those cases are discussed here. The Court of First Instance has generally upheld the Commission's restrictive interpretation of the exemption. In particular, in *Far Eastern Freight Conference (FEFC)*[119] the Court held that the exemption does not apply to price-fixing for the non-maritime segments of multi-modal carriage but only to the maritime component of the journey. Further, the fixing of prices for the inland carriage element of the journey was not entitled to exemption under Article 81(3).[120] In *Far East Trade Tariff Charges and Surcharges Agreement (FETTCSA)*[121] the Court of First Instance upheld the Commission's finding that

---

[116] Paras 5.037 *et seq*, below.
[117] Reg 4056/86, OJ 1986 L378/4: Vol II, App E.5.
[118] Press Release IP/06/1249 (25 September 2006): see further para 12.021, below.
[119] Case T-86/95 *Compagnie Générale Maritime and others v Commission* [2002] ECR II-1011, [2002] 4 CMLR 1115, paras 241 *et seq* (association of liner conferences operating between northern Europe and South-East), dismissing the appeals from *Far Eastern Freight Conference (FEFC)*, OJ 1994 L378/17, save only that the nominal fines imposed were set aside: this was an open tariff agreement not a secret cartel and the scope of Reg 4056/86 had been uncertain.
[120] This was the case whether or not that aspect of the agreement was covered by Reg 1017/68, the regulation applying the competition rules to inland transport.
[121] Case T-213/00 *CMA CGM v Commission* [2003] ECR II-913, [2003] 5 CMLR 268, on appeal from *Far East Trade Tariff Charges and Surcharges Agreement (FETTCSA)*, OJ 2000 L268/1. The CFI stated (para 180): 'the additional restriction on competition arising from the agreement in question is all the more appreciable since it prevents the maintenance of effective competition in particular on the part of the non-conference shipping lines'. However, the fines imposed by the Commission were annulled because the five-year limitation period had expired; appeal by the Commission against the annulment of the fines dismissed by the ECJ, Case C-236/03P *Commission v CMA CGM*, Order of 28 October 2004.

the agreement, entered into between carriers who belonged to the Far East liner conference and some carriers who did not, was not a liner conference agreement and so could not benefit from the block exemption. Furthermore, the carriers had not agreed to charge a uniform tariff but that they would not grant discounts or rebates from their individual published tariffs. The Court held that this agreement was not entitled to exemption.

Uniformity of prices within the liner conference. It is of the essence of a liner **5.034** conference that the conference puts itself forward as an entity on the market in the sense that the same price will be charged for the carriage of the same cargo from point A to point B, regardless of which shipowning member of the conference is responsible for carriage.[122] Thus in *Transatlantic Agreement (TAA)*,[123] the Commission held that the agreement did not benefit from the block exemption because (i) the agreement between carriers provided for a scheme of tariffs which varied according to the members rather than a uniform tariff; (ii) it included a capacity management programme which went beyond what was permitted under the Regulation; and (iii) it extended the price-fixing to the inland transport part of the multi-modal freight rate. The Court of First Instance only found it necessary to determine that the first of these elements precluded the application of the block exemption. But it upheld the Commission's decision that none of the elements of the agreement qualified for exemption under Article 81(3). Similarly, in *Transatlantic Conference Agreement (TACA)*[124] the Court of First Instance agreed with the Commission that the fixing of commissions paid to freight forwarders and the designation of cargo brokers[125] by the shipping companies was not covered by the block exemption.

---

122 Cases C-395 & 396/96P *Compagnie Maritime Belge de Transports and others v Commission* [2000] ECR I-1365, para 48.

123 *Transatlantic Agreement (TAA)*, OJ 1994 L376/1 (agreement on the scheduled transport of containers across the Atlantic between northern Europe and the United States of America and on the inland carriage of containers); on appeal Case T-395/94 *Atlantic Container Line AB v Commission* [2002] ECR II-875, [2002] 4 CMLR 1008, [2002] All ER (EC) 684. (There was a hiatus in the progress of the appeal because a preliminary ruling raising similar issues was requested from the ECJ under Art 234 by the English High Court in Case C-339/95 *Compagnia di Navigazione Marittima and others*. However, when the underlying litigation settled, that request for a ruling was withdrawn and the proceedings in Case T-395/94 resumed.)

124 *Transatlantic Conference Agreement (TACA)*, OJ 1999 L95/1, [1999] 4 CMLR 1415. The agreement replaced the TAA and contained provisions identical to those of the TAA on the fixing of prices for inland transport services provided within the Community, and also a number of rules concerning other aspects of transport, in particular as regards the conclusion of service contracts and the remuneration of freight forwarders. On appeal, Cases T-191/98, etc, *Atlantic Container Line v Commission* [2003] ECR II-3275, [2005] 4 CMLR 1283: the decision in relation to Art 81(1) were largely upheld but the Commission's findings that the agreement also constituted an abuse of a collective dominant position were annulled in part, as were the fines imposed. See Jaspers, (2004) 1 EC Competition Policy Newsletter 34.

125 See Cases T-191/98, etc, *Atlantic Container Line v Commission* [2003] ECR II-3275, [2005] 4 CMLR 1283, paras 560 *et seq.*

(b) Agreements on other trading conditions

5.035 **Collective fixing of terms and conditions.** Collective horizontal agreements often regulate not only the prices but also the conditions upon which goods or services may be supplied. Since Article 81(1)(a) mentions as restrictive of competition agreements which 'fix . . . any other trading conditions', such collective horizontal agreements are likely to infringe Article 81(1), particularly if they purport to restrict the terms upon which,[126] or the persons to whom, goods or services may be supplied.[127] Vertical agreements on conditions of resale made bilaterally between a supplier and a customer are discussed in Chapter 6, below.[128]

5.036 **Classification of such restrictions.** As with other horizontal arrangements, such as market-sharing or information exchange, agreement on particular terms and conditions of trade can act as a powerful means of reinforcing agreements to fix prices and restrict output. However, agreements on terms and conditions include a wide range of possibilities and may be entered into for a number of reasons, some of which are entirely legitimate. Such arrangements can be broadly classified into four categories:

(1) measures designed to reinforce price-fixing or the restrictions on output discussed in Section 4, below;[129]

(2) measures complementary to or equivalent to the collective trading arrangements discussed in Section 7, below: collective exclusive dealing, collective selling or collective buying;

(3) measures adopted under the aegis of a trade association, in particular the use of standard forms or common trading standards, discussed in Section 8, below; and

(4) measures adopted by a professional body or association in exercise of its regulatory function.

---

[126] See, eg *Vimpoltu*, OJ 1983 L200/44, [1983] 3 CMLR 619 (standard terms of business); *Pabst & Richarz/BNIA*, OJ 1976 L331/24, [1976] 2 CMLR D63 (prohibition of bulk deliveries); *Industrial and medical gases*, OJ 2003 L84/1, L123/49, [2004] 5 CMLR 144 (parties agreed to trading conditions when offering gases to new customers including rent for cylinders, a safety and environment charge for supplies in cylinders, transportation costs charges and a delivery charge for liquid gases), appeals dismissed, Case T-304/02 *Hoek Loos v Commission* [2006] ECR II-1887, [2006] 5 CMLR 590 and Case T-303/02 *Westfalen Gassen Nederland v Commission* [2007] 4 CMLR 334; *Fine Art Auction Houses* (n 30, above) (agreement included cessation of the giving of guarantees to sellers for auction results). See also the Commission decisions granting exemption under Art 81(3) to various uniform arrangements made by national banking associations, discussed in para 5.043, below.

[127] See Section 7, below for a discussion of these issues, particularly Section 7(a) in respect of collective exclusive dealing. See also Section 8(b), below, in relation to common standards.

[128] See paras 6.062 *et seq*, below.

[129] eg *TACA* (n 124, above) (price-fixing combined with restrictions on the terms on which services could be supplied to shippers); upheld in relation to Art 81 on appeal Cases T-191/98P, etc, *Atlantic Container Line* [2003] ECR II-3275. cf *Europe Asia Trades Agreement ('EATA')*, OJ 1999 L192/23, [1999] 5 CMLR 1380 (capacity management programme intended to reverse decline in freight rates).

Category (1) arrangements stand to be condemned alongside the 'hard-core' infringements of which they form part. Category (2) and category (3) agreements require more detailed analysis and are discussed in Sections 7 and 8, below. Category (4) arrangements are discussed in the next sub-section, followed by consideration of uniform arrangements adopted in the banking and financial payments sector.

(c) Professional services

Professional services.   The Commission has recognised the role to be played by **5.037** professional services in improving the competitiveness of the European economy as part of the Lisbon Agenda[130] and there has been an increased focus on this area.[131] Professional services are usually characterised by a high level of regulation, either by the state or professional bodies. These regulations are potentially restrictive and so may fall within Article 81(1). The five main categories identified by the Commission are (i) price-fixing, (ii) recommended prices, (iii) advertising regulations, (iv) entry requirements and reserved rights and (v) regulations governing business structure and multi-disciplinary practices. The Commission acknowledged that some regulation may be justified, for example in order to reduce the asymmetry of information between customers and service providers, but also noted that in some cases different mechanisms could be used. It has stated that in all scrutiny of professional regulation, a proportionality test should be applied and that rules must be objectively necessary to attain a clearly articulated and legitimate public interest objective. They must also be the mechanism least restrictive of competition to achieve that objective. This follows the approach adopted by the Court of Justice in the landmark case of *Wouters*,[132] considered below.

Professional services: fee scales.   In *CNSD*,[133] the Commission condemned a **5.038** compulsory tariff established by a trade association representing customs agents

---

130 See para 1.073, above.

131 *XXXIVth Report on Competition Policy* (2004), point 324. There has been considerable discussion of these policy issues: see Commission Communication 'Professional Services - Scope for more reform' (overview of changes to regulatory restrictions for lawyers, notaries, engineers, architects, pharmacists and accountants (including tax advisers)): MEMO/05/299, Press Release IP/05/1089 (5 September 2005); Commission Report on Competition in Professional Services, COM (2004) 83 final, 9 February 2004; Paterson, Fink and Ogus, 'Economic Impact of regulation in the field of liberal professions in different EU Member States', Institute for Advanced Studies, Vienna, January 2003; 'Better Regulation of Professional Services', speech by Commr Kroes, 21 November 2005; 'Competition in professional services: new light and new challenges', speech by Commr Monti, 21 March 2003; *XXXIIIrd Report on Competition Policy* (2003), point 187.

132 Case C-309/99 *Wouters v Algemene Raad van de Nederlandse Orde Van Advocaten* [2002] ECR I-1577, [2002] 4 CMLR 913, [2002] All ER (EC) 193: see para 5.039, below.

133 *CNSD*, OJ 1993 L203/27, [1995] 5 CMLR 495; appeal dismissed Case T-513/93 *CNSD v Commission* [2000] ECR II-1807, [2000] 5 CMLR 614.

in Italy, and the decision was upheld by the Court of First Instance. In *COAPI*,[134] the target of the Commission's decision was minimum rates for services established by the Spanish professional association of agents of industrial property. Both cases are significant in that the services in question were classified as 'professions' under national law and the price-fixing arrangements were expressly provided for (although not specifically required) by national legislation governing those services.[135] More recently, in *Belgian Architects' Association*[136] the Commission categorised as a restriction by object the minimum fee scale adopted by the National Council of the Belgian Architects' Association for services performed by architects in independent practice in Belgium. Although described as a 'guideline', the fee scale was rule-making in tone and the Association had used a standard contract for 18 years in which the only option for determining fees was a reference to the scale and there was evidence that the scale was applied. The Commission held that the fee scale was not necessary in order to ensure the proper practice of the architects' profession and therefore did not fall outside Article 81(1) on the basis of the principle established in *Wouters*. Similar decisions have been taken by a number of national competition authorities.[137] However, where a scale proposed by a professional body is adopted by the State so as to achieve the character of legislation, it constitutes a State measure and the decision of the body and its professional members falls outside the scope of Article 81, although in some circumstances, adoption of such a rule may place the State in breach of Article 10 of the Treaty in combination with Article 81.[138]

---

[134] *COAPI*, OJ 1995 L122/37, [1995] 5 CMLR 468.

[135] The Commission also successfully challenged the compatibility of the Italian legislation at issue in *CNSD* with Arts 3(l)(g) and 10, read in conjunction with Art 81: Case C-35/96 *Commission v Italy* [1998] ECR I-351, [1998] 5 CMLR 889. The appeal to the CFI by CNSD (Case T-513/93) was stayed pending the outcome of the ECJ proceedings. For State authorisation, see Chap 11, below.

[136] *Belgian Architects' Association*, OJ 2005 L4/10, [2005] 4 CMLR 677. In *Eddy Lodiso v La SPRLU MONDE* (2002/MR/6), judgment of 28 September 2004, the Brussels Court of Appeal, referring to this decision and applying the convergence rule in Art 16(1) of Reg 1/2003, ruled that the practice of the Belgian Architects' Association was invalid and could not be enforced against third parties.

[137] eg the UK Office of Fair Trading concluded in 2001 that the indicative fee guidance issued by the Royal Institute of British Architects could facilitate collusion but in 2003 accepted new fee guidance based on historical information and the collation of price trends that did not reveal the current year's prices (OFT Weekly Gazette, Competition Act: competition case closure summaries, 1–31 March 2003). The Law Society of Northern Ireland has changed its practice regulations following an OFT investigation: prohibitions on fee advertising, comparative fee advertising or charging uneconomic fees have been revoked and soliciting including all direct and unsolicited approaches to existing or potential clients is now permitted: OFT Press Release 218/05, 25 November 2005. The Portuguese Competition Authority imposed fines on the professional bodies of the veterinary surgeons and dentists for the operation of codes that effectively imposed minimum or fixed scale fees: Communications nos 7 & 8/2005, respectively. See also Commission Communication (n 132, above).

[138] C-35/99 *Arduino* [2002] ECR I-1529, [2002] 4 CMLR 866; followed and applied by the Italian Court of Cassation, judgments no. 5252 of 4 April 2003 (lawyers) and no. 12825 of 12 July 2004 (engineers and architects); cf Case C-250/03 *Mauri* [2005] ECR I-1267, [2005] 4 CMLR 723. See further paras 11.029 *et seq*, below.

Professional services: other restrictions.   In *Wouters*[139] the Court of Justice held   **5.039**
that regulations which are objectively necessary to guarantee the proper practice
of the profession, as organised in the Member State concerned, fall outside the
prohibition in Article 81(1). The rule of the Dutch Bar Council which prohibited
lawyers from entering into partnership with non-lawyers was challenged by
Mr Wouters and Mr Savelbergh who wished to practise as lawyers in a firm of
accountants. A number of questions were referred to the Court of Justice. The
Court found that a prohibition on multi-disciplinary partnerships 'is liable to limit
production and technical development within the meaning of Article 81(1)(b)' and
that it had an effect on trade. However, the Court then stated that it was necessary
to have regard to the overall context of the rule:

> 'More particularly, account must be taken of its objectives, which are here concerned
> with the need to make rules relating to organisation, qualifications, professional
> ethics, supervision and liability in order to ensure that the ultimate consumers of
> legal services and the sound administration of justice are provided with the necessary
> guarantees in relation to integrity and experience.'[140]

The Court proceeded to hold that Article 81(1) would not be infringed where the
rule could 'reasonably be considered to be necessary in order to ensure the proper
practice of the legal profession, as it is organised in the Netherlands'.[141]

Professional services: current practice.   Any examination of purely 'deontologi-   **5.040**
cal' (professional ethics) rules in competition terms must apply the Court of Justice's
ruling that they are not called into question so long as they are reasonably necessary
to guarantee the proper exercise of the profession; and to this extent they are not
caught by Article 81(1). Any rules not reasonably necessary need to be assessed under
Article 81(3). The Commission has also noted that this will affect its approach to
other types of restrictive rules and practices, including restrictions on advertising,[142]

---

139 *Wouters* (n 132, above).
140 ibid, para 97.
141 ibid, para 107.
142 See *EPI code of conduct*, OJ 1999 L106/14, [1999] 4 CMLR 513, largely upheld on appeal
Case T-144/99 *Institute of Professional Representatives v Commission* [2001] ECR II-1087, [2001]
5 CMLR 77 (restrictive rules on advertising by patent agents; the Commission required substantial
relaxation of rules but accepted a prohibition on comparative advertising for a short transitional
period ending on 23 April 2000). In Case Vj-180/2004, decn of 14 June 2006, the Hungarian
Competition Authority (GVH) held that the general prohibition of advertising in the rules of
the Hungarian Bar Association infringed Art 81 and the equivalent provision of Hungarian competition law. Applying *Wouters* and having regard to the similar rules and codes in other major EU
jurisdictions, the GVH found that the extent of the prohibition was disproportionate and could
not be justified by the ethical values of the profession. The decn is on appeal to the Budapest
Metropolitan District Court (case no. 7.K.33.763/2006), which granted an interim suspension
of the decn pending the appeal. See also case involving Law Society of Northern Ireland (n 137,
above).

soliciting clients and access to the profession.[143] The full implications and limits of the ruling in *Wouters* have still to be worked out.[144]

(d) Banking and payment services

5.041 **Banking.** Article 81(1) applies to agreements between banks as it applies in any other sector.[145] However, the question whether any concerted action by banks affects competition or trade between Member States *appreciably* must be examined carefully in each case. In its preliminary ruling in *Bagnasco*,[146] the Court of Justice found that standard terms agreed between Italian banks requiring current account lending to be conducted only at rates variable by the bank (and not at fixed rates) did not have an appreciable effect on competition because the opening of such a facility was a banking transaction which 'by its very nature, is linked with the right of the bank to change the agreed rate of interest by reference to factors such as, in particular, the conditions for the refinancing of the loan by the banks'. In *Identrus*,[147] the Commission gave negative clearance for agreements between a number of banks creating a global network for the authentication of electronic signatures and other aspects of e-commerce transactions: there was no risk of foreclosure and there were competing systems which provided a competitive check.[148]

---

[143] *XXXIInd Report on Competition Policy* (2002), point 203.

[144] See further para 2.116, above.

[145] For a discussion of the policy issues raised by agreements between suppliers of financial services, see Faull & Nikpay (eds), *The EC Law of Competition* (2nd edn, 2007), pp 1308–1330. The ECJ ruled in Case 172/80 *Züchner v Bayerische Vereinsbank* [1981] ECR 2021, [1982] 1 CMLR 313, that coordination of bank charges fell in principle within the scope of Art 81(1). However, as described below, the relevant principles have been significantly developed in recent years. The Committee of Wise Men on the Regulation of European Securities Markets published its final report on 15 February 2001 suggesting the Commission examine the market in clearing and settlement in order to ensure that Community competition policy is being properly implemented in the sector: *XXXIst Report on Competition Policy* (2001), points 191–195. The Commission has published a study: 'An overview of current arrangements in securities trading, clearing and settlement in EU 25' (*2004 Report on Competition Policy*, point 311).

[146] Cases C-215 & 216/96 *Bagnasco* [1999] ECR I-135, [1999] 4 CMLR 624, [1999] All ER (EC) 678, para 35. See also *Irish Banks Standing Committee*, OJ 1986 L295/28, [1987] 2 CMLR 601 (agreement on bank opening hours). But cf *Belgische Vereniging der Banken/Association Belge des Banques* ('*Belgian Banks*'), OJ 1987 L7/27, [1989] 4 CMLR 141; *ABI*, OJ 1987 L43/51, [1989] 4 CMLR 238 (inter-bank commissions, etc); *Nederlandse Bankiersverniging* ('*Dutch Banks*'), OJ 1989 L253/1, [1990] 4 CMLR 768 (simplified clearance procedures for cheques denominated in guilders and foreign currency infringed Art 81(1), but granted exemption under Art 81(3)); appeal dismissed as inadmissible, Case T-138/89 *Nederlandse Bankiervereniging v Commission* [1992] ECR II-2181, [1993] 5 CMLR 436.

[147] *Identrus*, OJ 2001 L249/12, [2001] 5 CMLR 1294.

[148] The decision also shows the importance the Commission attaches to the development of competitive e-commerce related markets: *XXXIst Report on Competition Policy* (2001), point 132. See also *Eurex*, *XXXIst Report on Competition Policy* (2001), point 196: negative clearance comfort letter issued to a joint venture between Deutsche Borse and SWX Swiss Exchange establishing a cross-border exchange for electronic trading in financial derivatives. Similarly, *Centradia*, *XXXIInd Report on Competition Policy* (2002), p 188, a business-to-business online trading platform, established by

However, in *Austrian Banks (Lombard Agreement)*[149] eight Austrian banks were fined a total of €124.26 million for their participation in a wide-ranging cartel. A highly institutionalised price-fixing scheme covered the whole of Austria and all banking products and services including interest rates for loans and savings for private/household and for commercial customers, the fees customers had to pay for certain services, money transfers and export financing as well as advertising.[150] The Commission rejected the assertion by the parties that their actions should not be assessed in terms of normal market economy criteria because of the special role banks play in the economy and the particular risks attendant on a failure in the banking system. Referring back to earlier case law,[151] the Commission stated that the parties could have been in no doubt that the prohibition on price-fixing agreements applied to credit institutions.[152]

Banking and effect on trade between Member States. The *Bagnasco* ruling also **5.042** involved standard terms for bank guarantees. The Court of Justice held that there was no effect on inter-State trade[153] and this was followed by the Commission in granting negative clearance to an agreement among Dutch banks relating to the terms of acceptance giros.[154] In *Austrian Banks (Lombard Agreement)*,[155] however, the Commission held that whereas the banking services involved did not by their

---

four European banks to offer a range of foreign exchange products to commercial clients: the Commission considered that it did not raise competition problems in light of the constant movement in the prices of the current range of foreign exchange products on the interbanking market and that collusion on prices was unlikely.

[149] *Austrian Banks (Lombard Agreement)*, OJ 2004 L56/1, [2004] 5 CMLR 399, para 79 (fines reduced on appeal: Cases T-259/02, etc, *Raiffeisen Zentralbank Österreich v Commission*, judgment of 14 December 2006, on appeal on other grounds, Cases C-125/07P, etc, not yet decided).

[150] *XXXIInd Report on Competition Policy* (2002) p 175.

[151] In particular *Züchner* (n 146, above); and *Eurocheque: Helsinki Agreement*, OJ 1992 L95/50, [1993] 5 CMLR 323 (appeals largely dismissed, save that decision in respect of Eurocheque annulled on procedural grounds: Cases T-39 & 40/92 *CB and Europay v Commission* [1994] ECR II-49).

[152] The Commission had launched an investigation against a large number of banks and bureaux de change in Austria, Belgium, Finland, Germany, Ireland, the Netherlands and Portugal following complaints about high exchange rate commissions after the introduction of the euro in January 1999. The proceedings were ended against most of the banks concerned after they presented proposals for significantly reducing their exchange charges for in-currency bank notes and abolishing all such charges by October 2001 at the latest for buying transactions by account holders. The Commission took into account the exceptional circumstances of the disappearance of the market concerned and the immediate benefit to consumers: *XXXIst Report on Competition Policy* (2001) p 205, Press Release IP/01/1159 (31 July 2001).

[153] *Bagnasco* (n 146, above) para 53.

[154] *Nederlandse Vereniging van Banken (1991) GSA Agreement*, OJ 1999 L271/28, [2000] 4 CMLR 137: agreement for standard form credit transfers between Dutch banks appreciably restricted competition but received negative clearance on the basis that it had no effect on inter-State trade. Similarly, in *Dutch Banks* (n 146, above), the agreement concerning uniform conditions for the hire of safes was found not appreciably to restrict inter-State trade since little use of such safes was made by consumers from other Member States and branches of overseas banks seldom offered safes for hire.

[155] *Austrian Banks (Lombard Agreement)* (n 149, above).

nature have any cross-border dimension and hence were too minor to be able to affect trade between Member States, the agreement on interest rates and other loan terms did have the necessary effect. The Commission found that some banking services inherently affect cross-border trade.[156] These include agreements relating to cross-border payment transactions, documentary business and the buying and selling of securities (since foreign nationals purchase large volumes of Austrian securities and Austrians purchase large volumes of foreign securities). Other aspects of the agreements did not have any 'natural connection' with cross-border transactions but exercise an indirect influence: for example, lending rates necessarily affect the investment and production decisions both of subsidiaries of foreign firms and of Austrian firms in Austria. The network of agreements also affected 'supply-side' decisions by foreign banks whether to enter the Austrian market.[157]

5.043   **Banking agreements and Article 81(3).**   Standard multilateral bank arrangements which do not involve fixing of prices or commission rates may satisfy the conditions of Article 81(3). Hence in *Dutch Banks*,[158] after the Commission made clear that the regulations fixing minimum commissions for services, rates and margins for dealings in foreign currency could not receive exemption, those provisions of the Dutch banking organisations were withdrawn; the Commission then granted exemption to the uniform procedures for clearance for cheques denominated both in guilders and foreign currencies since they resulted in simplified clearance and therefore faster crediting of customers' accounts. Similarly, in *Belgian Banks*,[159] the provisions fixing common charges for various inter-bank services were found to restrict competition but received exemption since they improved the functioning and reduced the costs and inconvenience to customers of the various transactions involved.

5.044   **Cross-border credit transfers.**   In its Notice on the application of the EC competition rules to cross-border credit transfers,[160] the Commission indicates that

---

[156] See also *Bank charges for exchanging euro-zone currencies - Germany*, OJ 2003 L15/1, [2003] 4 CMLR 842, where the Commission found that the service of buying and selling euro-zone banknotes was cross-border in nature. The decision was annulled on appeal because the Commission had not proved the existence of an agreement and there were other possible explanations for the allegedly parallel conduct: Cases T-44/02, etc, *Dresdner Bank v Commission* [2006] ECR II-3567, [2007] 4 CMLR 467; T-56/02 *Bayerische Hypo- und Vereinsbank v Commission* [2004] ECR II-3495, [2004] 5 CMLR 1592, etc. See also *Belgian Banks* (n 146, above) where it was noted that if many foreign banks operating an agreement do so through branches not subsidiaries, the agreement will intrinsically have a cross-border element.

[157] *Austrian Banks (Lombard Agreement)* (n 149, above) paras 438 *et seq.*

[158] *Dutch Banks* (n 146, above).

[159] *Belgian Banks* (n 146, above). See also the decision regarding the Italian banking association, *ABI*: ibid.

[160] Notice on cross-border credit transfers, OJ 1995 C251/3, [1995] 5 CMLR 551. Note the closure by comfort letters of the following cases concerning cross-border payment systems: *IBOS*

multinational pricing agreements between banks who participate in such transfers may fall within Article 81(1); in order to benefit from Article 81(3), such arrangements must not only be necessary to achieve some identifiable benefit, for example to avoid double charging, but must also (i) relate to average additional costs and (ii) be subject to alternative bilateral arrangements between participants.

Credit cards and payment systems.   Collective exclusive dealing between the   **5.045**
member banks of a credit card network may also attract the application of Article 81 since such arrangements may have a distorting effect on competition in the supply of credit card services.[161] In *Visa International: Rules*,[162] the Commission found that certain provisions of the Visa International payment card scheme fell outside the scope of Article 81. The decision covered five particular provisions:

(i)   the 'no discrimination' rule which prohibits merchants from charging cardholders extra for using their Visa card. The Commission considered that this rule limits the freedom of merchants to set their own prices but does not have an appreciable restrictive effect on competition. The Commission noted that studies in countries where the rule had been abolished showed that this did not have a significant effect on merchants' fees;

(ii)   the modified rules on cross-border card issuing and merchant acquiring which allow Visa members to issue cards to consumers and to contract with all types of merchants in other Member States without first establishing a branch/subsidiary in the Member State concerned;

(iii)   the principle of territorial licensing according to which banks normally need a licence to issue and acquire for each Member State. The Commission considered that this did not constitute an appreciable restriction of competition

---

(international data transfer system with a membership from several Member States); *Eurogiro* (system of bulk transfers between post/girobanks); and *Finansrådet (Danish Bankers' Association)* (agreement within Denmark for handling charge by correspondent bank to beneficiary bank on cross-border transfers, but considered *de minimis* as less than 5 per cent of relevant Danish business): *XXVIth Report on Competition Policy* (1996), pp 128–130.

161   For economic analysis and reference to the US cases, see 'Symposium – Antitrust Issues in Payment Card Systems' (2006) 73 Antitrust LJ 571.

162   *Visa International: Rules*, OJ 2001 L293/24, [2002] 4 CMLR 168. In the earlier case *Amex and Dean Witter/Visa, XXVIth Report on Competition Policy* (1996), p 140, the Commission made clear that it would not accept the adoption of a rule prohibiting member banks which were able to issue Mastercards and Diners cards from also being able to issue the competing American Express cards. See also the decns of the Netherlands Competition Authority ('NMa') in *Interpay*, Case 29100–700, 28 April 2004, revised on administrative appeal in Case 2910–864, 21 December 2005, fining eight Dutch banks for infringement of the national equivalent of Art 81. Interpay was a JV owned by the banks and the NMa did not object to its acquiring and issuing operations or its processing of electronic funds transfers, but to the extension of its activities to the joint sale of network services for PIN (direct debit) transactions, which precluded the banks from providing such services in competition with each other. See discussion of this case by Bos, 'International Scrutiny of Payment Card Systems' in the Symposium (above) at 756–761.

because banks can obtain additional trade mark licences for all Member States in which they are authorised to carry on banking activities;

(iv) the 'no acquiring without issuing' rule which requires banks to issue a reasonable number of cards to cardholders before starting merchant acquiring activities. The Commission considered that this rule promoted the development of the system by ensuring a large card base which made the system more attractive for merchants; and

(v) the 'honour all cards' rule which requires merchants to accept all valid cards with either the Visa or Electron brand irrespective of the identity of the issuer, the nature of the transaction or the type of card (credit or deferred debit) being issued. This rule was held to promote the development of the Visa payment scheme because it ensures the universal acceptance of Visa cards, the development of a payment system depending on issuers being able to rely on the acceptance of their cards by merchants contracted to other acquirers.

5.046 **Multilateral interchange fee.** In a subsequent decision, the Commission granted a conditional exemption to the Visa multilateral interchange fee (MIF) for cross-border payment transactions using Visa consumer cards within the EEA.[163] An MIF is an inter-bank payment made for each transaction carried out with a payment card. In the Visa system, it is paid to the cardholder's bank by the retailer's bank. The cost is usually passed on to retailers as part of the fee they pay to their bank for each Visa card payment. The default level of the Visa MIF, which applies unless two banks agree otherwise, is set by the Visa Board and laid down in the Visa International payment card rules. The exemption was granted subject to conditions aimed at reducing the overall level of fees, relating them more closely to costs and increasing the transparency of this element of the overall charge.[164]

5.047 **Sectoral inquiry and payment cards.** In January 2007, the Commission published the final report of its sectoral inquiry into retail banking,[165] conducted

---

[163] *Visa International – Multilateral Interchange Fee*, OJ 2002 L318/17, [2003] 4 CMLR 283. See also *Visa International: Rules* (n 162, above).

[164] A statement of objections was sent to MasterCard concerning its MIF for cross-border transactions with payment cards in the EU and EEA: *XXXIIIrd Report on Competition Policy* (2003), points 182–184. The Commission noted that the MIF was not in line with the basic principles set out in the *Visa* decision; merchants have no choice but to accept MasterCard cards; the MIF should be transparent and cost based in order to prevent MasterCard setting its MIF at a revenue maximising level irrespective of the benefits to merchants and customers. The Commission's preliminary conclusions were that the MIF restricts competition and does not meet the conditions of Art 81(3). Subsequently the Commission welcomed announcements by Visa and MasterCard to publish their MIF rates for European cross-border payments: *Europay (Eurocard – Mastercard)*, Press Release IP/04/616 (7 May 2004). However, the Commission's main concern about the composition of MasterCard's MIF remained: *Report on Competition Policy* (2005), point 118.

[165] Final Report: Sector Inquiry under Art 17 of Reg 1/2003 on retail banking COM(2007) 33 final, 31 January 2007, available at http://ec.europa.eu/comm/competition/antitrust/others/sector_inquiries/financial_services/com_2007_033_en.pdf.

pursuant to Article 17 of Regulation 1/2003. The report sets out a number of competition concerns regarding the markets for payment cards, payment systems, and retail banking products. The inquiry found highly concentrated markets, high entry barriers, and sustained high profitability indicating significant market power in all of these markets. Furthermore, divergent technical standards, regulatory obstacles and other factors lead to the partitioning of the markets along national boundaries. In the market for payment cards, this results in large variations in merchant fees and interchange fees across the Community. Competition at the retailer level is also weakened by the behaviour of the issuing banks. The inquiry also found structural and behavioral concerns in the retail banking products market. Credit registers used to set loan rates and some other aspects of cooperation among banks can reduce competition and raise entry barriers. Competition in retail banking products is also weakened by product tying and a generally low level of customer mobility. Based on the findings of the inquiry, the Commission intends to use its powers under the competition rules in individual cases to tackle any serious abuses on these markets.[166]

4. Output Restrictions

Limitation of output. Agreements to maintain prices by restricting output constitute classic restrictions on competition. Such agreements are commonly found as part of wider cartel agreements to fix prices[167] or share markets. Article 81(1)(b) mentions as restrictive of competition agreements which 'limit or control production . . . or investment', and which 'limit or control . . . markets'. Similarly, Article 81(1)(c) mentions agreements which 'share markets or sources of supply'. **5.048**

Limitation of production. According to classic cartel theory, an agreement between participants in a cartel to limit production is the natural and inevitable complement to an attempt to maintain or inflate price levels. In the absence of such restrictions on output, market forces would undermine the price-fixing arrangements by driving down prices to their competitive levels. However, not all markets conform to the standard model and agreements to limit production have **5.049**

---

[166] See Press Release IP/07/114 (31 January 2007).

[167] See, eg *Graphite Electrodes*, OJ 2002 L100/1, [2002] 5 CMLR 829 (no expansion of capacity, Japanese producers agreed to reduce capacity, no transfer of technology outside the group) (appeals dismissed save for variation of the fines, Cases T-236/01, etc, *Tokai Carbon v Commission* [2004] ECR II-1181, [2004] 5 CMLR 28; Commission's further appeal allowed, Case C-301/04P *Commission v SGL Carbon* [2006] ECR I-5915, [2006] 5 CMLR 877; other appeals dismissed, Cases C-289/04P *Showa Denko v Commission* and C-308/04P *SGL Carbon v Commission* [2006] ECR I-5859, 5977, [2006] 5 CMLR 840, 922). The major cartels in *Steel beams*, OJ 1994 LI 16/1, [1994] 5 CMLR 353, and *Cartonboard*, OJ 1994 L243/1, [1994] 5 CMLR 547, are also good examples of production limitations combined with wider cartel agreements to fix prices or share markets.

also occurred in the context of attempts to deal with structural overcapacity in various European industries. Although such 'restructuring' agreements may have anti-competitive effects, and cannot be entered into by undertakings without careful scrutiny by the competition authorities, in certain circumstances the conditions of Article 81(3) may be fulfilled. Production restrictions also arise, at least as a matter of theory, in other contexts, in particular production and specialisation joint ventures and arrangements for collective sale, where more complex analytical issues again arise.

5.050 **Cartel agreements to limit production.**   An agreement among competing undertakings to adopt production quotas or otherwise limit output is contrary to Article 81(1).[168] A typical example occurred in *Zinc Producer Group*,[169] where the participants agreed to keep within collectively agreed production quotas and also not to build any new zinc production capacity without obtaining approval from ZPG. The Commission held that Article 81(1) was infringed. Any problem of overcapacity in the industry should have been resolved by seeking exemption under Article 81(3) for a restructuring agreement.[170] The same reasoning applies to restrictions on utilisation of capacity. Such capacity management programmes agreed between shipping lines have been held to violate Article 81(1); and since they do not lead to a permanent reduction in capacity, and have generally been introduced for trades where rates were fixed by a liner conference,[171] the Commission has refused to grant exemption under Article 81(3).[172]

5.051 **Restructuring agreements.**   Certain Community industries are affected by chronic overcapacity as a result of changes in market demand. One of the Commission's general objectives is to enable structural overcapacity to be eliminated so that the industries concerned can recover profitability.[173] The Commission has pursued this policy by controlling State aids and by granting exemption under Article 81(3) to certain so-called 'restructuring agreements'. Three pertinent decisions are *Synthetic Fibres, BPCL/ICI* and *Stichting Baksteen ('Dutch Bricks')*.

---

[168] Early cases include Case 41/69 *ACF Chemiefarma v Commission* [1970] ECR 661, 699 (agreement not to manufacture synthetic quinidine); *Lightweight Paper,* JO 1972 L182/24, [1972] CMLR D94 (production quotas); Case 246/86 *Belasco v Commission* [1989] ECR 2181, [1991] 4 CMLR 96; see also *Flat Glass* (n 252, below). Agreements establishing sales quotas also tend to limit production. Exceptionally, the Commission decided not to proceed as regards a quota scheme for the sale of prescription drugs to the Danish Ministry of Health, designed to control public expenditure, after the arrangement had been modified: Press Release IP/99/633 (17 August 1999).

[169] *Zinc Producer Group*, OJ 1984 L220/27, [1985] 2 CMLR 108.

[170] A proposed restructuring agreement for zinc (OJ 1983 C164/3) was later abandoned when market conditions improved: Press Release IP/84/8 (9 January 1984), [1984] 1 CMLR 263.

[171] As permitted under the block exemption, Reg 4056/86: see para 5.033, above and para 12.021, below.

[172] *Transatlantic Agreement (TAA)* (n 123, above); *EATA* (n 129, above).

[173] See *XXIst Report on Competition Policy* (1991), points 207 *et seq.*

Restructuring agreements: *Synthetic Fibres*. In *Synthetic Fibres*,[174] the **5.052**
Commission granted exemption under Article 81(3) to what is known as a 'crisis
cartel'. The synthetic fibre industry of the Community suffered from chronic
overcapacity. About 70 per cent of production capacity was being used, whereas
the minimum economic level was about 85 per cent. Under the agreement all
the major Community producers agreed to make specific production cutbacks
in order to bring capacity into line with demand. The Commission held that
Article 81(1) was infringed but that exemption could be granted. Although in
principle it was for each undertaking to determine its level of capacity, the agreement was necessary to re-establish the viability of the industry and eliminate
losses. Market forces were working too slowly to achieve the desired results.
Since effective competition would remain after the restructuring programme was
complete, exemption was justified.

Bilateral restructuring: *BPCL/ICI*. A restructuring agreement may also be **5.053**
bilateral, as in *BPCL/ICI*.[175] In that case BPCL and ICI both produced polyvinyl
chloride (PVC) and low density polyethylene (LdPE), both petrochemical-based
plastics. There was serious European overcapacity in petrochemicals; ICI saw its
future primarily as a manufacturer of PVC, while BPCL thought it had advantages in the supply of LdPE. Accordingly, BPCL sold its main PVC plant to ICI,
together with the goodwill of its PVC business, and withdrew from the supply of
PVC. At the same time ICI sold to BPCL its main LdPE plant, together with its
associated goodwill, with the result that ICI withdrew from the supply of LdPE
in the United Kingdom. The Commission held that Article 81(1) was infringed.
The Commission was, however, prepared to grant an exemption under Article 81(3)
on the grounds that the agreement enabled the parties to eliminate under-utilised
capacity, improve unit costs and eliminate losses, results which market forces
were too slow to bring about. Although short-term price rises were inevitable, that
was the result of the industry returning to normal levels of profitability. Consumers'
long-term interests were best served by healthy industries rather than loss-making
ones. In the United Kingdom effective competition was provided by imports of
PVC and LdPE from elsewhere in the Community.[176]

---

174 *Synthetic Fibres*, OJ 1984 L207/17, [1985] 1 CMLR 787.
175 *BPCL/ICI*, OJ 1984 L212/1, [1985] 2 CMLR 330. See also the abandoned restructuring
agreement for the zinc industry (n 170, above); *Rovin*, OJ 1983 C295/7, [1984] 1 CMLR 87; *ENI/
Montedison*, OJ 1987 L5/13, [1988] 4 CMLR 444; *Montedison/Hercules (Himont), XVIIth Report on
Competition Policy* (1987), point 69; *Enichem/ICI*, OJ 1988 L50/18, [1989] 4 CMLR 54; *PRB/Shell*,
XVIIth Report on Competition Policy (1987), point 74 (project ultimately abandoned, in part
because of conditions imposed by Commission); *Bayer/BP Chemicals*, OJ 1988 L150/35, [1989]
4 CMLR 24; also OJ 1994 L174/34; and cf *Exxon/Shell*, OJ 1994 L144/20 (production joint venture
for linear polyethylene). See more generally the position regarding joint ventures: Chap 7, below.
176 The decns in *PVC*, OJ 1989 L74/1, [1990] 4 CMLR 345, and *LdPE*, OJ 1989 L74/21,
[1990] 4 CMLR 382, demonstrate that exemption of specific restructuring agreements within an

5.054 **Domestic restructuring of a national industry: *Dutch Bricks*.** This case[177] illustrates the Commission's approach to such an agreement limited to a single national market. In order to resolve the crisis of overcapacity in the Dutch brick industry, the major producers concluded an agreement providing for a collective reduction in production, with coordination and compensation for the cost of closures placed in the hands of a foundation financed by the 16 participating manufacturers. The Commission found that the agreement fell within Article 81(1) but after the agreement was amended to remove the provision for production quotas, the Commission granted an exemption for five years on condition that the parties to the agreement did not divulge to one another any data in respect of individual outputs and deliveries.

5.055 **Production limitation combined with supply arrangements.** A particular kind of agreement limiting production is where two or more parties agree to cease or limit production and obtain their requirements of the products concerned from the other parties, often exclusively. Since the parties are by implication at least potential competitors, such reciprocal specialisation agreements are likely to infringe Article 81(1).[178] Thus in *Rolled Zinc*,[179] one party (PYA) agreed to cease production of rolled zinc and to acquire supplies of rolled zinc exclusively from the other party (CRAM). In return CRAM agreed to limit its production of zinc alloys, and to obtain supplies of zinc alloys from PYA to enable the latter to increase its production. The agreement was for 15 years. Various further arrangements between the parties indicated that they intended to coordinate their sales policies

---

industry subject to serious overcapacity does not give general protection to the industry to indulge in anti-competitive practices. Those decisions relate to the same period as the exemptions discussed in this Section. See also *Polypropylene*, OJ 1986 L230/1, [1988] 4 CMLR 347 and, on appeal, the comments of Judge Vesterdorf (acting as AG) that it was 'hardly surprising' that the undertakings should 'consider steps to avoid devastating price competition . . . by reaching a mutual arrangement in order to survive for the time being pending the advent of better times': Case T-1/89 *Rhône-Poulenc v Commission* [1991] ECR II-867, 877, [1992] 4 CMLR 84, 92.

[177] *Stichting Baksteen*, OJ 1994 L131/15, [1995] 4 CMLR 646. See also *Competition Authority v Beef Industry Development Society Ltd* [2006] IEHC 294, where the Irish High Court held that a rationalisation scheme to reduce serious overcapacity in the Irish beef slaughtering and processing industry did not infringe Art 81(1) since it had not been shown that it was likely to lead to price increases, given the fragmented nature of the market and low barriers to entry. On appeal, the Irish Supreme Court referred to the ECJ the question whether such a scheme falls within Art 81(1) on the basis of its object as opposed to its effect: Case C-209/07 *Beef Industry Development and Barry Brothers*, not yet decided.

[178] *Rolled Zinc Products and Zinc Alloys*, OJ 1982 L362/40, [1983] 2 CMLR 285, on appeal on other aspects Cases 29 & 30/83 *CRAM and Rheinzink v Commission* [1984] ECR 1679, [1985] 1 CMLR 688. See also *Billiton/M & T*, VIIth *Report on Competition Policy* (1977), point 131 (agreement not to manufacture tin tetrachloride but instead obtain supplies from the other party); *BP Kemi/DDSF* (n 268, below); *BPCL/ICI* (n 175, above) in which a five-year supply arrangement was exempted under Art 81(3).

[179] *Rolled Zinc*, above.

and to refrain from competitive conduct. The Commission found that Article 81(1) was infringed. Although it might have been prepared in principle to consider an exemption to permit the 'rationalisation' of production, the agreement did not satisfy Article 81(3) on the facts. More recently, a German Court[180] condemned an agreement under which two producers of construction vehicles agreed to limit their product range to complementary products which would be distributed under the same trade mark. The contract eliminated competition between the parties and was therefore harmful to competition by its very nature. Further, the Court found that the provisions regarding the use of the trade mark also had to be considered to be void, since their sole purpose was to distribute the complementary products under the same brand. The parties' single-brand strategy only made sense as long as competition was eliminated between them. The whole agreement was therefore unenforceable.

Specialisation block exemption. However, if the parties' combined market **5.056** share does not exceed 20 per cent of the relevant market, a specialisation agreement of the kind described in the preceding paragraph may fall within the block exemption for specialisation agreements, Regulation 2658/2000.[181] The application of this block exemption is discussed in Chapter 7, below.[182]

Joint production. An agreement which may limit the parties' individual free- **5.057** dom to control production also occurs if the parties establish joint arrangements for production, usually through the medium of a joint venture. Such collaborative arrangements, which may also benefit from Regulation 2658/2000, are similarly discussed in Chapter 7, below.[183]

Production limitation under Article 81(3). Agreements to limit production **5.058** are unlikely to satisfy the conditions of Article 81(3) except in the context of genuine restructuring, specialisation, or joint production arrangements. In such cases, if an agreement does not come within the block exemption because the market share condition is exceeded, it will require very careful consideration to determine whether the criteria of Article 81(3) can be satisfied.[184]

---

[180] Case 13 U 227/02, judgment of the Oberlandesgericht Celle of 6 June 2003 (published at: www.judicialis.de). The case was decided under Art 81.

[181] Reg 2658/2000, OJ 2000 L304/3: Vol II, App C.4 which replaced Reg 417/85, OJ 1985 L53/1 (as am by Reg 151/93, OJ 1993 L21/8 and Reg 2236/97, OJ 1997 L306/12) subject to transitional provisions.

[182] See paras 7.097 *et seq*, below.

[183] See paras 7.089 *et seq*, below, and *Ford/Volkswagen*, discussed at paras 7.108 *et seq*, below.

[184] Horizontal Cooperation Guidelines, OJ 2001 C3/2: Vol II, App C.12, para 101.

5. Market-sharing and Customer Allocation

(a) Generally

5.059 **Market-sharing.** Horizontal agreements between competitors to refrain from supplying into each other's markets within the Community directly frustrate the aims of the EC Treaty and constitute very serious infringements of Article 81(1)(b) and (c). Such agreements often include arrangements to fix prices and limit production.[185] In the context of Community competition law, where many of the most significant distortions of competition result from the insulation of national markets from foreign competition, market-sharing on geographical, and in particular national, lines has been a central concern of the Commission and Community Courts. The Court of First Instance has recently confirmed the seriousness of market-sharing in its judgment in the appeal against the fines imposed by the Commission in relation to the *SAS/Maersk* cooperation agreement.[186] The Court rejected the parties' arguments that the infringement should have been classified as 'serious' rather than 'very serious' for the purpose of determining the level of fine, noting that market-sharing is expressly declared incompatible with the common market in Article 81(1)(c): 'Apart from the serious distortion of competition which they entail, such agreements, by obliging the parties to respect distinct markets, often delimited by national frontiers, cause the isolation of those markets, thereby counteracting the EC Treaty's main objective of integrating the Community market'.[187]

5.060 **Market-sharing between producers.** Article 81(1) is infringed if two or more producers agree to a territorial division of markets within the Community, for example by agreeing to keep out of each other's territories ('*chacun chez soi*'), as in *Sugar*,[188] or by establishing quotas. Numerous decisions have condemned such agreements.[189] A recent example of a classic market-sharing cartel is the

---

[185] See, eg *Soda-ash—Solvay, CFK*, OJ 2003 L10/01, on appeal Case T-58/01 *Solvay v Commission*, not yet decided: purchases of guaranteed quantities by competing supplier in return for price stability in German market. This decn was the re-taking of a 1991 Commission decn to the same effect that had been annulled by the CFI for procedural irregularity: Case T-31/91 *Solvay v Commission* [1995] ECR II-1821; appeal by the Commission dismissed, Cases C-287 & 288/95P [2000] ECR 1–2391, [2000] 5 CMLR 454.

[186] Case T-241/01 *Scandinavian Airline Systems v Commission* [2005] ECR II-2917, [2005] 5 CMLR 922.

[187] ibid, para 85.

[188] Cases 40/73, etc, *Suiker Unie v Commission* [1975] ECR 1663, [1976] 1 CMLR 295.

[189] See, eg *Benelux Flat Glass*, OJ 1984 L212/13, [1985] 2 CMLR 350: price-fixing agreement among Benelux producers included an agreement to share the market in a 60:40 ratio which reflected the parties' capacity; *PVC* (n 176, above); *LdPE* (n 176, above); *Welded Steel Mesh*, OJ 1989 L260/1, [1991] 4 CMLR 13 (appeals dismissed save for reduction in some of the fines: Cases T-141/89, etc, *Tréfileurope Sales v Commission* [1995] ECR II-791; on further appeal: Cases C-185/95P *Baustahlgewebe v Commission* [1998] ECR I-8417, [1999] 4 CMLR 1203, C-219/95P *Ferrière Nord v Commission* [1997] ECR I-4411, [1997] 5 CMLR 575); *Pre-insulated Pipes cartel*, OJ 1999 L24/48, [1999] 4 CMLR 402; *Seamless Steel Tubes*, OJ 2003 L140/1, [2003] 5 CMLR 683 (appeals dismissed

Zinc Phosphate decision and the *Needles* case illustrates a market-sharing arrangement of a different kind.

Market-sharing in a cartel: *Zinc Phosphate*. The *Zinc Phosphate*[190] decision **5.061** illustrates how a market-sharing cartel operates. Zinc phosphate is used by paint manufacturers as an anti-corrosion pigment in industrial paints for cars, aircraft and ships. Virtually the whole of the world market was supplied by five producers located in western Europe. The Commission found that the allocation of sales quotas was 'the cornerstone of the cartel'. Respective market shares were initially calculated in 1994 on the basis of the undertakings' sales for the years 1991 to 1993 and each cartel member was expected to adhere to its allocated market share. During the meetings, information about specific customers was exchanged and on some occasions this resulted in customer allocation. To monitor compliance, each producer sent its sales volumes data on a monthly basis to a trade association of which they were all members. The association compiled the figures and sent them to all the five producers concerned. Being in possession of the exact size of the market, the producers could then meet and provide each other with their individual sales volumes, thereby verifying via this exchange of information their mutual adherence to the agreed market shares. The Commission held that this represented a very serious infringement of Article 81(1) and imposed substantial fines.

Market-sharing in product and geographic markets. Market-sharing may be **5.062** organised on the basis that parties agree which products each of them will supply or on the basis of which territories they will supply. In *Needles*,[191] the Commission

---

save for reductions in the fines due to shorter duration of the cartel: Cases T-44/00 *Mannesmannröhren-Werke v Commission*, T-48/00 *Corus UK v Commission*, T-50/00 *Dalmine v Commission* T-67/00, etc, *JFE Engineering v Commission* [2004] ECR II-2223, 2325, 2395, 2501, [2005] 4 CMLR 182; further appeals dismissed, Case C-411/04P *Mannesmannröhren-Werke v Commission*, [2007] 4 CMLR 682, Case C-407/04P *Dalmine v Commission*, judgment of 25 January 2007, Cases C-403 & 405/04P *Sumitomo Metal Industries v Commission* [2007] 4 CMLR 650): domestic markets of different producers respected by other producers not supplying those markets; *Interbrew and Alken-Maes ('Belgian beer')*, OJ 2003 L200/1, [2004] 4 CMLR 80, paras 247 and 248 (appeals dismissed: Case T-38/02 *Groupe Danone v Commission* [2005] ECR II-4407, [2006] 4 CMLR 1429 (small reduction in the fine), Case C-3/06P [2007] 4 CMLR 701 and Case T-48/02 *Brouwerij Haacht v Commission* [2005] ECR II-5259, [2006] 4 CMLR 621): 'non aggression pact' including the allocation of customers in the 'on trade' sector (hotels, cafes and restaurants) as well as the limitation of investments and advertising; *Vitamins*, OJ 2003 L6/1, [2003] 4 CMLR 1030 (on appeal, Cases T-15/02 *BASF* [2006] ECR II-497, [2006] 5 CMLR 27 (fine reduced), T-22 & 23/02 *Sumitomo Chemicals* [2005] ECR II-4065, [2006] 4 CMLR 42 (decn annulled on procedural grounds); T-26/02 *Daiichi Pharmaceuticals* [2006] ECR II-713, [2006] 5 CMLR 169 (fine reduced)).

[190] *Zinc Phosphate*, OJ 2003 L153/1, [2003] 5 CMLR 731 (appeals against fines dismissed Case T-33/02 *Britannia Alloys & Chemicals* [2005] ECR II-4973, [2006] 4 CMLR 1046, further appeal dismissed Case C-76/06P, [2007] 5 CMLR 251, Case T-52/02 *SNCZ* [2005] ECR II-5005, [2006] 4 CMLR 1069; Case T-64/02 *Heubach* [2005] ECR II-5057, [2006] CMLR 1157; Case T-62/02 *Union Pigments* [2005] ECR II-5137, [2006] 4 CMLR 1105 (appeal against duration of infringement and fine dismissed).

[191] COMP/38.338 *Needles*, 26 October 2004, [2005] 4 CMLR 792 (on appeal Cases T-30/05 *Prym and Prym Consumer v Commission*; T-36/05 *Coats Holdings and Coats v Commission*, not yet decided). See the note on this case in (2005) 1 EC Competition Policy Newsletter 59.

analysed a complex series of bilateral agreements between undertakings involved in the needles[192] and other hard haberdashery items product markets. The main manufacturers in the European needles market were Prym, Entaco and Coats, and Coats was also the main distributor of haberdashery products. Prym and Entaco agreed that Entaco would restrict its manufacturing and distribution activities in the haberdashery sector to hand sewing needles and special needles only and also that Entaco would not supply continental European markets for needles (with some exceptions), thereby reserving those markets for Prym. This agreement was conditional on the signing of an agreement between Entaco and Coats and on the sale of the remainder of Coats' needle manufacturing business to Entaco. Coats also entered into an exclusive supply relationship with Entaco whereby it undertook to buy all its requirements in the United Kingdom and (partially) Italy for the Milward brand of needles from Entaco provided that Entaco abided by the market-sharing agreement which it had entered into with Prym. The Commission found that the bilateral agreements together formed a tripartite market-sharing agreement between the parties, allocating markets in terms of products and in terms of territory.

5.063 **Market-sharing between purchasers.**   A less frequent occurrence is collusion among undertakings in the acquisition of their raw materials. In *Raw Tobacco (Spain)*[193] and *Raw Tobacco (Italy)*[194] the processors of tobacco fixed their shares of the available supply of raw tobacco and allocated suppliers amongst themselves. By doing so, the Commission held, they restricted competition for market share downstream and also prevented each allocated supplier from being able to play buyers off one against the other as happens in a normal competitive market. The purchasing cartel had the potential to affect the producers' willingness to generate output, and thus to reduce global tobacco production to the ultimate detriment of consumers.

5.064 **Domestic market-sharing agreements.**   A market-sharing agreement confined to the territory of one Member State may still infringe Article 81(1), since it is liable to affect the patterns of imports or exports that might otherwise take place.[195]

---

[192] Needles here included crochet hooks and knitting needles. The case concerned only needles for home use, not for industrial sewing.

[193] Case COMP/38.238 *Spanish Raw Tobacco*, 20 October 2004, [2006] 4 CMLR 866 (on appeal, Cases T-24/05 *Standard Commercial*; T-29/05 *Deltafina*; T-33/05 *Cetarsa*; T-37/05 *World Wide Tobacco Espana*; T-38/05 *Agroexpansion*; T-41/05 *Dimon*, not yet decided).

[194] COMP/38.281 *Italian Raw Tobacco*, 20 October 2005, [2006] 4 CMLR 1766 (on appeal, Cases T-11/06; T-12/06; T-619/06; T-25/06, not yet decided). The parties were largely the same undertakings in both decisions.

[195] See, eg *Italian Cast Glass*, OJ 1980 L383/19, [1982] 2 CMLR 61 (quotas for cast glass established on the Italian market restricted competition and also affected ability to export elsewhere in the EC); *Italian Flat Glass*, OJ 1981 326/32, [1982] 3 CMLR 366 (quotas for flat glass agreed between the main Italian producers and Italian wholesalers, who also agreed to deal exclusively with the Italian producers and not purchase from foreign producers, in return for a special rebate); *Belasco* (n 168, above); *MELDOC*, OJ 1986 L348/50, [1989] 4 CMLR 345 (concerted action to prevent

If the agreement covers the whole territory of a Member State, Article 81(1) will almost certainly be infringed.[196] Whether a domestic agreement to share local or regional markets within a Member State falls within Article 81(1) will be a matter of fact and degree depending on all the circumstances.[197]

Control over imports and exports. A particularly clear case of a domestic agree- **5.065** ment affecting inter-State trade is *IJsselcentrale*,[198] where the Dutch electricity generating companies operated a joint distribution system which gave them exclusive control over all imports and exports of electricity to and from the Netherlands by the imposition of restrictive terms in all electricity distribution contracts. In *Luxembourg breweries*,[199] three Luxembourg breweries agreed to consult each other if a foreign brewer attempted to negotiate a supply contract with one of their tied outlets and then to give priority to one of the other parties in negotiating with the tied outlet for a change of supplier. Compensation had to be provided if the 'Luxembourg colleague' was successful in winning the business. Further, any party which cooperated with a foreign brewer or distributed its beer was excluded from the cartel. The Commission condemned the agreement as aimed at preventing foreign brewers from concluding exclusive contracts with Luxembourg outlet operators and the Court of First Instance upheld the decision.

Market-sharing and trade with third countries. As has been seen, a market- **5.066** sharing agreement between undertakings within the Community and undertakings in third countries which restricts competition from, or reduces the supply of, imports into the Community may infringe Article 81(1).[200] A market-sharing agreement in respect of exports from the Community may also fall within Article 81(1) if it impinges on competition within the Community.[201]

---

dairy imports to Holland from Belgium); cf *Building and construction industry in the Netherlands*, OJ 1992 L92/1, [1993] 5 CMLR 135 (appointment of 'entitled undertaking' on the basis of comparison of proposed bids at price-fixing meeting; appeals dismissed in Case T-29/92 *SPO v Commission* [1995] ECR II-289 and Case C-137/95P [1996] ECR I-1611). See also *Luxembourg breweries* (n 199, below).

[196] eg *TFB*, OJ 1997 L284/91 and see para 1.130, above.

[197] The principal issue will be whether there is a potential effect on inter-State trade. See, eg the decisions at n 195, above, and *IJsselcentrale*, para 5.065, below.

[198] *IJsselcentrale*, OJ 1991 L28/32, [1992] 5 CMLR 154.

[199] *Luxembourg breweries*, OJ 2002 L253/21, [2002] 5 CMLR 1279, para 83 (appeals dismissed, Cases T-49/02, etc, *Brasserie Nationale v Commission* [2005] ECR II-3033, [2006] 4 CMLR 266).

[200] Para 1.106, above. See also *White Lead*, OJ 1979 L21/16, [1979] 1 CMLR 464 (a quota system purportedly applied only to third countries found to affect intra-EC deliveries). In *Seamless steel tubes* (n 189, above), the agreement to respect domestic markets included Japanese producers.

[201] Paras 1.107 *et seq*, above and cf para 5.021, above. See also *French-West African Shipowners' Committees*, OJ 1992 L134/1, [1993] 5 CMLR 446, where the Commission condemned an agreement among French shipowners who operated a quota system for cargoes bound for certain African ports, and the other liner conference cases discussed at paras 5.033 and 5.034, above.

5.067 **Market-sharing under Article 81(3).** An agreement to divide the common market will not fulfil the conditions for the application of Article 81(3). But limited territorial restrictions may be permissible in the context of certain agreements on research and development, specialisation or joint production, distribution agreements, and licences of intellectual property rights, and a relevant block exemption may apply: those topics are discussed elsewhere in this work.[202]

(b) Buying and selling among competitors

5.068 **Collective dealing between manufacturers.** Multipartite horizontal exclusive dealing agreements, considered in more detail later in this Chapter,[203] represent a further means by which manufacturers may share markets. In *Sugar*,[204] the producers in Belgium and the Netherlands agreed to channel all cross-border deliveries solely through each other on a 'producer-to-producer' basis; and in *Soda-ash—Solvay, ICI*,[205] the producers in the continental Member States agreed to supply the British market solely via ICI, the British manufacturer. In those cases the Commission held that Article 81(1) was infringed. It is only in exceptional circumstances that such an exclusive dealing agreement between competitors will fall outside Article 81(1).

5.069 **Exclusive supply from one producer to another.** Even if there is no reciprocal agreement to supply between competitors, a one way supply arrangement can infringe Article 81(1). In *Seamless Steel Tubes*,[206] the Commission examined the 'Europe-Japan Club' established by producers of seamless steel pipes and tubes, including oil country tubular goods (OCTG). The fundamental principle of the Club was that producers would not sell into each other's domestic market. The United Kingdom at this stage was a 'semi-protected market' which meant that a competitor had to contact the local producer of oil pipes and tubes before bidding for business. In 1990, the domestic producer in the United Kingdom, British Steel, ceased making the relevant product when it closed its plant in Clydesdale. However it still required a supply of plain end tubes to supply its heat treating and tube threading plant. This created the risk that Japanese producers would start to supply British Steel's requirements. The European producers agreed

---

[202] Research and development agreements, paras 7.067 *et seq*, below; specialisation agreements, paras 7.087 *et seq*, below; distribution agreements, paras 6.039 *et seq*, below; licences of intellectual property rights paras 9.075 *et seq*, below.

[203] Paras 5.098 *et seq*, below.

[204] Cases 40/73, etc, *Suiker Unie v Commission* [1975] ECR 1663, [1976] 1 CMLR 295.

[205] *Soda-ash—Solvay, ICI*, OJ 1991 L152/1, [1994] 4 CMLR 454. The decision was annulled for breaches of the rights of defence: Case T-30/91 *Solvay v Commission* [1995] ECR II-1775, [1996] 5 CMLR 57; and Case T-36/91 *ICI v Commission* [1995] ECR II-1847, [1995] All ER (EC) 600: see para 5.075, below.

[206] *Seamless Steel Tubes* (n 189, above). See also *Soda-ash—Solvay, ICI*, above.

that they would share British Steel's requirements for seamless steel tubes among themselves and the three producers accordingly entered into long-term supply contracts with British Steel. The Commission concluded without difficulty that the fundamental arrangement of the Europe-Japan Club infringed Article 81(1); but in addition it found that three aspects of the arrangements made by a number of producers with British Steel also constituted an infringement.[207] First, the quantities of tubes to be supplied by the three producers were set not in absolute terms but as percentages of British Steel's requirement. The suppliers were therefore unable to take advantage of any increase in demand for threaded pipes, since British Steel's right to ask them for unlimited additional quantities of plain ends enabled it to satisfy any increase in demand itself. Further, the pricing formula in the supply contracts made the price of plain ends dependent on the prices of British Steel's threaded pipes. This meant that the European suppliers had no interest in initiating competition on the prices of threaded pipes in the United Kingdom because a reduction in the prices of threaded pipes would have led to a reduction in the prices of the plain ends they sold to British Steel. This, the Commission found, ensured that prices in the United Kingdom remained high. Thirdly, the information which British Steel was obliged by the contracts to supply to the other parties (concerning prices and quantities) was information normally covered by business secrecy. Communication of this information preserved control over the conditions on the British market.

Collective purchasing to prevent imports. An example of limiting or controlling markets based on exclusive dealing between producers occurred in the earlier case of *Aluminium imports from Eastern Europe*.[208] Fearing that low-priced imports of aluminium from State trading companies would disrupt western European markets, all the primary aluminium producers of the Community agreed to purchase at a common price the entire supplies of aluminium offered by the State trading agencies of Eastern bloc countries, while those agencies (principally Raznoimport of the USSR) agreed to sell exclusively to the EC producers. The purpose of the arrangement was to ensure that Eastern aluminium was not sold at unfairly low prices. The Commission held that there was an infringement of Article 81(1). It was no defence that the undertakings had acted so as to prevent 'Eastern bloc dumping', since appropriate measures to counter such alleged dumping could lawfully be adopted only by public authorities.[209] **5.070**

Emergency allocation of supplies. The Commission considers that even in an emergency an agreement allocating supplies of essential products may give rise to **5.071**

---

[207] *Seamless Steel Tubes*, para 153.
[208] *Aluminium Imports from Eastern Europe*, OJ 1985 L92/1, [1987] 3 CMLR 813.
[209] ibid, para 12.2.

a breach of Article 81(1). In the unusual case of *International Energy Agency*,[210] such an agreement relating to oil supplies was made between 21 members of the OECD, including every Member State except France. The Commission took the view that the exchanges of information associated with the agreement might restrict competition and give rise to market-sharing between the oil companies, who necessarily participated in the arrangements. However, the Commission granted an exemption under Article 81(3).

5.072 **Reciprocal assistance agreements.** Other agreements between competitors to make supplies available to each other may evidence an intention to share markets. In *CRAM*,[211] three competing manufacturers agreed to make reciprocal supplies available 'in the event of serious technical or other disruption resulting in significant loss of production.' The agreement was vague, was not limited to *force majeure*, and appeared to envisage considerable tonnages. The Commission held that the contract gave rise to a system of 'mutual aid' which prevented the parties from taking advantage of any reductions in output sustained by others. The Commission's finding that Article 81(1) was infringed was upheld by the Court of Justice.

5.073 **Inter-producer deliveries.** Subject to the foregoing, inter-producer deliveries are not as such caught by Article 81(1), although they may evidence some underlying concertation to share markets.[212] In *CRAM*,[213] the Commission stated that it did not object to 'occasional and irregular deliveries between competitors' and would be prepared to consider exemption under Article 81(3) in respect of non-exclusive agreements limited in time and made for the purpose of guaranteeing supplies.

(c) Bilateral market-sharing

5.074 **Generally.** Market-sharing agreements between manufacturers are not confined to multipartite cartels, but also occur bilaterally. Such agreements take many forms, including a simple agreement between manufacturers to keep out of each other's markets,[214] distribution arrangements between competitors,[215] and collaboration in manufacture[216] or in research and development.[217] Some agreements

---

[210] *International Energy Agency*, OJ 1983 L376/30, [1984] 2 CMLR 186; and OJ 1994 L68/35 (exemption renewed for a further period of 10 years).

[211] *CRAM*, OJ 1982 L362/40, [1983] 2 CMLR 285, on appeal Cases 29 & 30/83 *CRAM & Rheinzink v Commission* [1984] ECR 1679, [1985] 1 CMLR 688. Note that in Cases T-68/89, etc, *Società Italiano Vetro (SIV) v Commission* [1992] ECR II-1403, [1992] 5 CMLR 302, the CFI annulled the Commission's finding (*Flat Glass*, OJ 1989 L33/44, [1990] 4 CMLR 535, paras 53–58) that the producers had set up an institutionalised system for exchanges of glass with the intention of sharing markets.

[212] eg *Suiker Unie* (n 204, above) para 182.

[213] *CRAM* (n 212, above); and see *SIV v Commission* (n 211, above).

[214] *Van Katwijk*, OJ 1970 L242/18, [1970] CMLR D43; *Soda-ash—Solvay, ICI*, para 5.075, below.

[215] See para 5.076, below.

[216] See paras 7.087 *et seq*, below.

[217] See paras 7.067 *et seq*, below.

may benefit from the application of Article 81(3);[218] but the difficulties are illustrated by the three cases discussed in the following paragraphs: *Soda-ash—Solvay, ICI* (involving a mutual obligation to keep out of their principal competitor's markets); *Siemens/Fanuc* (grant of exclusive selling rights to competitor); and *French Beer.*[219]

Bilateral market-sharing: *Soda-ash.* In *Soda-ash—Solvay, ICI,*[220] Solvay and   **5.075**
ICI were fined by the Commission for a market-sharing agreement between the two companies in relation to the supply of synthetic soda-ash to the Community. Solvay and ICI were the two largest suppliers of soda-ash to the Community but for many years ICI had sold exclusively into the Irish and United Kingdom markets whereas Solvay sold exclusively into continental Europe. The infringement was exacerbated by purchases by ICI from Solvay for resale by ICI in its 'home' market, which the Commission held were intended to prevent any competition between the companies. However, on appeal the decisions were annulled by the Court of First Instance for breach of the rights of defence by failing to give proper access to the file.[221]

Exclusive territorial rights granted to competitor. A further kind of agreement   **5.076**
giving rise to a form of market-sharing likely to infringe Article 81(1) occurs where one manufacturer grants exclusive selling rights to a competitor in respect of a particular territory.[222] Thus in *Siemens/Fanuc,*[223] the Japanese firm Fanuc

---

[218] Note the block exemptions for specialisation agreements (Reg 2658/2000) and for research and development agreements Reg 2659/2000: see paras 7.097, 7.078 *et seq*, below. See also *Sole Distribution Agreements for Whisky and Gin*, OJ 1985 L369/19, [1986] 2 CMLR 664. For market-sharing arrangements in airline alliance agreements see, eg COMP/38.477 *BA/SN Brussels Airlines*, decn of 10 March 2003, relating to pricing, scheduling and capacity: *XXXIIIrd Report on Competition Policy* (2003), points 50–53, and other cases discussed at paras 7.133 *et seq*, below.

[219] For market-sharing by allocation of customers, see para 5.083, below.

[220] *Soda-ash— Solvay, ICI*, OJ 1991 L152/1, [1994] 4 CMLR 454.

[221] Cases T-30/91 *Solvay v Commission* [1995] ECR II-1775, [1996] 5 CMLR 57, and T-36/91 *ICI v Commission* [1995] ECR II-1847. See also *Soda-ash—Solvay, CFK* (n 185 above). Unlike the latter decision and two other decisions of the same date against Solvay and ICI under Art 82, all of which were annulled for procedural irregularity, the Commission did not 're-take' the decision discussed in the text following its annulment; ICI and Solvay had contended that their previous market-sharing arrangement had ended on the UK's accession to the Community.

[222] See, eg *Pripps/Tuborg, XXVIIIth Report on Competition Policy* (1998) p 148 (licence from Carlsberg group to the leading Swedish brewer to manufacture, sell and distribute Tuborg beer in Sweden received an exemption-type comfort letter only after it was amended to become non-exclusive and a second licensee was appointed); *Carlsberg/Interbrew, XXIVth Report on Competition Policy* (1994), p 351 (Commission required significant amendments to an agreement between the leading suppliers of beer in Denmark and Belgium/Luxembourg giving exclusive rights for the Belgium/Luxembourg market). See also the Commission's intervention in relation to an agreement under which the cigarette manufacturer Philip Morris granted an exclusive licence to the Spanish cigarette manufacturer Tabacalera to produce Philip Morris' branded cigarettes for the Spanish market. The Commission considered there was no reason for Philip Morris not to make and import cigarettes into Spain itself: and the agreement was modified accordingly: Note by Rayners Fontana, (2001) 2 EC Competition Policy Newsletter 40.

[223] *Siemens/Fanuc*, OJ 1985 L376/29, [1988] 4 CMLR 945.

granted Siemens, a competitor, exclusive selling rights for the whole of Europe in respect of Fanuc numerical controls ('NCs'– special purpose computers used in the machine tool industry). The Commission held that the agreement infringed Article 81(1): Fanuc was an important, and generally cheaper, alternative source of supply for NCs and the agreement prevented Fanuc from selling NCs itself, or supplying third parties, in the Community. However, the non-reciprocal appointment of a competing manufacturer as a distributor may benefit from block exemption under Regulation 2790/1999 if the agreement otherwise complies with that Regulation and the distributor has a turnover not exceeding €100 million;[224] and in certain circumstances Article 81(3) might apply to an individual agreement.[225]

5.077　**Agreements on vertical integration.**　In *French Beer*,[226] the Commission considered an agreement between the two main breweries in France concerning the acquisition of wholesaling businesses. Prior to the agreement, the volume of each brewer's beer distributed by wholesalers linked with the competing brewer was the same. But an acquisition by one brewer of a wholesaler which distributed a significant volume of the other's beer led to a 'retaliatory' acquisition and then a bidding war which pushed up the price of wholesaling businesses. The brewers agreed an 'armistice' whereby they would stop buying up wholesalers and re-establish an equilibrium so that neither became dominant in the distribution of beer. The Commission stated[227] that an agreement designed to bring wholesaler acquisition costs under control in the short term by putting an end to an acquisition war cannot be regarded as a clear infringement on a par with price-fixing but it was an agreement designed to limit or control investment. The agreement to establish longer-term equilibrium between the two distribution networks was 'akin to a market-sharing agreement'. This was not market-sharing in a conventional sense since it was mainly intended to prevent one group from dominating the market rather than to eliminate all competition between the groups or impede third parties.

(d) Sharing access to infrastructure or facilities

5.078　**The *Channel Tunnel* cases.**　The opening of the Channel Tunnel provided the occasion for the Commission to adopt a series of decisions relating to agreements

---

[224] Art 2(4) of Reg 2790/1999, OJ 1999 L336/21: Vol II, App C.3, discussed paras 6.010 *et seq*, below.

[225] Application of Art 81(3) is unlikely if the parties' market share is significant: see para 6.085, below. See also *Sole Distribution Agreements for Whisky and Gin* (n 218, above).

[226] COMP/37.750 *French Beer (Brasseries Kronenbourg, Brasseries Heineken)*, 29 September 2004, [2006] 4 CMLR 577.

[227] ibid, para 83.

to share access to an 'essential facility'.[228] In *ACI*,[229] British Railways ('BR'), SNCF and Intercontainer (a combined transport operator owned by 24 railway undertakings) agreed to the joint marketing of combined road and rail services between the United Kingdom and continental Europe via the Channel Tunnel. The Commission considered that the three parent companies were potential competitors on the relevant market and that there was a risk that access to BR and SNCF networks and services would be limited. However, a five-year exemption was granted subject to conditions, the most significant being an obligation on BR and SNCF to supply services to competitors of ACI on a non-discriminatory basis. *Eurotunnel III*[230] concerned the agreement by Eurotunnel, the company responsible for the Channel Tunnel, to grant BR and SNCF exclusive rights to 50 per cent of the capacity of the Channel Tunnel (the remainder being reserved to Eurotunnel itself). This arrangement was interpreted by the Commission as foreclosing access to the Tunnel to competitors of BR and SNCF in the supply of international train services and to fall within Article 81. The decision was found on appeal to have been based on an error of fact, in that Eurotunnel was free to grant access to third parties up to its total limit of 50 per cent of capacity and its own shuttle services did not exhaust that capacity. The decision was therefore annulled.[231] The Commission subsequently conducted a fresh analysis and, having regard also to changed circumstances, concluded that Article 81(1) did not apply to the agreement: usage of the Tunnel was not saturated, and since the agreement was not exclusive it had neither the purpose nor the effect of restricting competition in the market for access to the Tunnel, nor was it a market-sharing agreement.[232]

Mobile telephony site sharing.   Another market in which sharing of infrastructure has been considered beneficial is where mobile telephony operators cooperate by sharing sites and allowing reciprocal use of their networks to ensure that new products are rolled out to less populated areas of the country. In *O2 UK Limited / T-Mobile UK Limited ('UK Network Sharing Agreement')*[233] the parties had agreed   **5.079**

---

[228] For the concept of 'essential facilities', see para 10.135, below.

[229] *ACI*, OJ 1994 L224/28. See also *Night Services*, OJ 1994 L259/20, [1995] 5 CMLR 76, on appeal Cases T-374/94, etc, *ENS v Commission ('European Night Services')* [1998] ECR II-3141, [1998] 5 CMLR 718 (joint venture to operate night passenger services between the United Kingdom and continental Europe on four specific routes. The CFI held that there was no basis for a finding that Art 81 was infringed.)

[230] *Eurotunnel III*, OJ 1994 L354/66, [1995] 4 CMLR 801.

[231] Cases T-79 & 80/95 *SNCF and British Railways v Commission* [1996] ECR II-1491, [1997] 4 CMLR 334.

[232] *Eurotunnel*, XXIXth Report on Competition Policy (1999), p 163.

[233] *O2 UK Limited / T-Mobile UK Limited ('UK Network Sharing Agreement')*, OJ 2003 L200/59, [2004] 4 CMLR 1401. See note in (2003) 3 EC Competition Policy Newsletter 43 and the similar decn in *T-Mobile Deutschland/O2 Germany – Network Sharing Rahmenvertrag*, OJ 2004 L75/32, [2004] 5 CMLR 762 (on appeal, Case T-328/03 *O2 (Germany) GmbH & Co v Commission* [2006] ECR II-1231, [2006] 5 CMLR 258, the CFI annulled the different finding that cooperation on

to cooperate in the planning, acquiring, building and deploying and sharing of sites for the roll-out of their 3G mobile networks. The sites involved shared structures including mast, materials and equipment such as power supply, racking and cooling. The Commission considered that such far-reaching cooperation between two key players in a market with only a limited number of competitors and high, if not absolute, barriers to entry raised competition concerns. Site sharing could have an adverse impact on competition, in particular by reducing network competition, denying competitors access to necessary sites and site infrastructure, thus foreclosing competitors and, possibly in some cases, facilitating collusive behaviour. However, the need for up to a twofold increase in the number of sites for 3G network heightens environmental and health concerns. Site sharing is therefore increasingly favoured for policy considerations and is expressly encouraged by Community rules. After a detailed review of the market conditions the Commission concluded that the provisions of the agreement relating to site sharing did not fall within Article 81(1).

(e) Other market-sharing

5.080 Market division between or involving distributors.   An agreement to divide markets also infringes Article 81(1) if it is made at the level of distribution, either between the manufacturer and his distributors or between the distributors themselves.[234]

5.081 Market division by intellectual property rights.   Undertakings may seek to achieve a *de facto* division of the common market by licences of intellectual

---

national roaming fell within Art 81(1): see paras 7.127 and 12.139, below. See also Chap 12, below in relation to sharing of gas pipelines and other energy transmission infrastructure.

234 Many such cases combine 'vertical' and 'horizontal' elements. See, eg Cases 100/80, etc, *Musique Diffusion Française v Commission* ('*Pioneer*') [1983] ECR 1825, [1983] 3 CMLR 221 (agreement to divide markets involving Pioneer and its British, French and German distributors); *Video games Nintendo Distribution*, OJ 2003 L255/33, [2004] CMLR 421, on appeal Cases T-12/03 *Itochu Corporation v Commission*, T-13/03 *Nintendo v Commission*, T-18/03 *CD Contact Data v Commission*, not yet decided ('shared understanding' among Nintendo and its exclusive distributors that they had to prevent parallel exports from their territory); *Luxembourg breweries* (n 200, above); *Needles* (n 191, above); *Ducros/DHL*, *XXIVth Report on Competition Policy* (1994), point 192 and Annex II, p 370 (cooperation agreement between express delivery services: a French company, Ducros, pooled its services in France with services provided by DHL and its German subsidiary, Elan, in other Member States, operating under a common name and granting reciprocal exclusive rights in their respective territories; the Commission treated the agreement as a transport agreement and granted a three-year exemption under the opposition procedure pursuant to Regulation 1017/68); *Eudim*, OJ 1996 C111/8, [1996] 4 CMLR 871 (association of national distributors of plumbing, heating and sanitary products limited membership to one per country and provided for extensive exchange of information: agreement cleared after parties adopted a formal declaration that they were 'free to sell their products and to establish their businesses wherever they feel is appropriate'). See the EFTA Surveillance Authority decision in *TFB*, OJ 1999 L284/91 for an agreement between purchasers. For the application of Art 81 to distribution agreements generally, see Chap 6, below.

property rights. It is well established that the exercise of rights under a trade mark licence to achieve a partitioning of the common market is contrary to Article 81(1).[235] Similar principles apply to patent licences[236] although certain patent licences may benefit from block exemption under Regulation 772/2004. An agreement between the holders of intellectual property rights not to grant licences to exploit those rights to third parties may have an anti-competitive effect and so violate Article 81(1).[237] The exercise of intellectual property rights generally is further affected by the rules on the free movement of goods.[238] The whole topic of the exercise of, and licences for, such rights is discussed in Chapter 9, below.

Trade mark delimitation agreements.   Although a bona fide agreement not to use a trade mark confusingly similar to that of another undertaking does not in itself infringe Article 81(1), an agreement not to use a trade mark may in certain circumstances be regarded as a market-sharing agreement.[239]   **5.082**

(f) Customer allocation

Customer allocation.   Another method of market-sharing is where the parties to the agreement determine who will supply each customer. The cartel members then ensure that the price quoted to the customer by those who are not intended to be the supplier is higher than the price quoted by the chosen supplier. In *Choline Chloride*[240] the European producers' meetings included the allocation of individual clients among themselves. Some clients were allocated to a single producer but with the larger consumers, the parties agreed the share of that customer's demand that each would supply. In *Luxembourg breweries*,[241] three Luxembourg breweries agreed to respect each other's tied house arrangements with drinks outlets. The Commission held that this was clearly a restriction within Article 81(1) in cases where there was no formal contractual tie but where one of the brewers had financed the fitting out of the outlet and in cases where there was a contractual   **5.083**

---

[235] cf Cases 56 and 58/64 *Consten and Grundig* [1966] ECR 299, [1966] CMLR 418; Case 40/70 *Sirena v Eda* [1971] ECR 69, [1971] CMLR 260; Case 16/74 *Centrafarm v Winthrop* [1974] ECR 1183, [1974] 2 CMLR 480. See further paras 9.032 *et seq*, below.

[236] Case 15/74 *Centrafarm v Sterling Drug* [1974] ECR 1147, [1974] 2 CMLR 480.

[237] Case T-504/93 *Tiercé Ladbroke v Commission* [1997] ECR II-923, [1997] 5 CMLR 309, paras 156–160.

[238] Paras 9.007 *et seq*, below.

[239] Case 35/83 *BAT v Commission* [1985] ECR 363, [1985] 2 CMLR 470. See also *Hershey/Herschi*, XXth *Report on Competition Policy* (1990), point 111, and the German case referred to in para 5.055, above (at n 180).

[240] Case COMP/37.533 *Choline Chloride*, 9 December 2004, [2006] 4 CMLR 159. The three European producers have lodged appeals but do not challenge the existence of the cartel: (T-101/05 *BASF* (appeal on fine only); T-111/05 *UCB*; T-112/05 *Akzo Nobel*, not yet decided). See also *Zinc phosphate* (n 190, above) where information was exchanged about customers which were then allocated: the Finnish customer, Teknos Witner, was allocated successively to the members of the cartel.

[241] *Luxembourg breweries* (n 199, above) para 83.

tie but it was invalid under national law. Even where there was a valid tie in place, the Commission held that the agreement was contrary to Article 81(1) because the restraint imposed on competitors covered a wider range of products than could lawfully be tied. The agreement also precluded a tied house operator from breaching his tie contract in circumstances where it would be commercially beneficial for him to do so. By rendering this type of 'arbitrage' impossible, the agreement 'serves to maintain inefficient brewer-operator relationships'.[242]

6. Information Exchange

5.084 **Information agreements.** A cartel usually requires the exchange of information on prices and markets if the intended coordination of its participants' commercial strategies is to be achieved. Agreements or practices of that kind are likely to constitute or form part of serious infringements of Article 81(1). At the other end of the spectrum, dissemination by a trade association of anonymised, historical statistical data may be unobjectionable. Between these two extremes, difficult issues arise. In general, whether the exchange of information between competitors infringes Article 81(1) depends on whether or not that information would normally be regarded as a business secret.[243]

5.085 **Information exchange ancillary to a cartel.** The role of information exchanges in the context of a complex price-fixing and market-sharing cartel[244] was

---

[242] See in particular the domestic market-sharing arrangements referred to in para 5.064, above; and also Case 41/69 *ACF Chemiefarm v Commission* [1970] ECR 661 (agreement not to manufacture synthetic quinidine); *BP Kemi/DDSF*, OJ 1979 L286/32, [1979] 3 CMLR 684 (sectoral division of Danish market for synthetic ethanol between BP Kemi: larger customers; and DDSF: smaller customers); *Methylglucamine*, OJ 2004 L38/18, [2004] 4 CMLR 1591 and *XXXIInd Report on Competition Policy* (2002) points 48–49, p 179 (parties ensured no major customer changed supplier); Case COMP/37.370 *Sorbates*, 2 October 2003, [2005] 5 CMLR 2054, on appeal, Case T-410/03 *Hoechst v Commission*, not yet decided (allocation of market shares). See also *Industrial and medical gases*, OJ 2003 L84/1, [2004] 5 CMLR 144, appeals dismissed, Case T-304/02 *Hoek Loos v Commission* [2006] ECR II-1887, [2006] 5 CMLR 590 and Case T-303/02 *Westfalen Gassen Nederland v Commission* [2007] 4 CMLR 334: parties agreed not to deal with each other's customers for a period of two to five months each year in order to implement agreed price increases; *Belgian beer* (n 189, above): Interbrew and Alken-Maes in Belgium agreed with the French company Danone as to customer sharing in the 'on-trade'. In *French Beer* (n 226, above), Groupe Danone/Brasserie Kronembourg and Heineken NV/Heineken France agreed to a temporary freeze on acquisitions of wholesalers outside an agreed list as well as the establishment of an equilibrium between the two groups distribution networks. The Commission noted, however, in considering the level of fine that in determining the gravity of infringement this was not on a par with a price-fixing agreement since it was not 'market sharing in the "conventional" sense, since the agreement was intended mainly to prevent one group from dominating the market rather than to eliminate all competition between the groups or impede third parties' (para 83).

[243] See paras 5.090 *et seq*, below for the kinds of information which undertakings would be expected to regard as confidential.

[244] Information exchange in various forms has been the subject of many recent Commission decisions, eg *Plasterboard*, OJ 2005 L166/8, paras 444 *et seq*: 'The fact that the data exchanged were

considered by the Court of the Justice in the *Cement* appeals.[245] In relation to the exchange of price information, the parties argued that the exchange of information was lawful because the information exchanged was in the public domain or related to historical or purely statistical prices. The Court upheld the Court of First Instance's rejection of this argument, holding that there was an infringement of Article 81(1) where information exchange underpins another anti-competitive arrangement. The circulation of price information limited to the members of an anti-competitive cartel has the effect of increasing transparency on a market where competition is already much reduced and of facilitating control of compliance with the cartel by its members.[246] The information served as a basis for discussion and therefore the fact that it was provided before the meeting was irrelevant; the Court noted that the precise chronology and the lack of a temporal link between the exchanges and meetings was not important where exchanges formed part of an overall plan.[247] The Court also rejected the argument that the circulation of the information by a trade association such as Cembureau was lawful.[248] It upheld the Court of First Instance's finding that the exchanges were intended to curb intra-Community imports of cement.[249]

Price information agreements outside a cartel. Price competition will be **5.086** restricted if competing manufacturers exchange information about their prices when such exchanges are made in advance and are not shared with customers. Such contact between competitors infringes Article 81(1), in particular by eliminating uncertainty and replacing 'the risks of competition and the hazards of competitors' spontaneous reactions by co-operation.'[250] The Commission has stated expressly:

'It is contrary to the provisions of Article [81(1)]. . . for a producer to communicate to his competitors the essential elements of his price policy, such as price lists, the

---

"historical" does not suffice to exclude the possibility that this data exchange system may have permitted the existence of mutual monitoring by the parties to the exchange' (para 446); *Methionine*, OJ 2003 L255/1, [2004] 4 CMLR 1062 (on appeal, fine reduced: Case T-279/02 *Degussa* [2006] ECR II-897, further appeal pending, Case C-266/06P) (data on sales volumes exchanged which was then used in the discussion to determine target prices); Case COMP/37.370 *Sorbates* (n 242, above) (on appeal, Case T-410/03 *Hoechst v Commission*, not yet decided) (information exchanged on sales volumes and market shares); *Industrial copper tubes*, OJ 2004 L125/50, [2005] 5 CMLR 1186 para 214 (on appeal, Cases T-127/04 *KM Europa Metal v Commission*, T-122/04 *Outokumpu v Commission*, T-116/04 *Wieland Werke v Commission*, not yet decided) (information exchanged on sales volumes and prices charged).

[245] Cases C-204/00P, etc, *Aalborg Portland v Commission* [2004] ECR I-123, [2005] 4 CMLR 251.

[246] ibid, para 281.

[247] ibid, paras 282, 290.

[248] ibid, para 282.

[249] ibid, para 288.

[250] Cases 48/69, etc, *ICI v Commission* [1972] ECR 619, [1972] CMLR 557, para 119. See also Cases 40/73, etc, *Suiker Unie v Commission* [1975] ECR 1663, [1976] 1 CMLR 295.

discounts and terms of trade he applies, the rates and date of any change to them and the special exceptions he grants to specific customers.'[251]

5.087 *The United Kingdom Agricultural Tractor Registration Exchange.*   The Court of First Instance and Court of Justice considered the operation of such agreements in determining the appeals against the Commission's decision in *United Kingdom Agricultural Tractor Registration Exchange*.[252] The case concerned the detailed exchange of information in relation to retail sales and market shares between the leading eight suppliers of agricultural tractors to the UK market (whose combined market share was found to be 87–88 per cent). Although the exchange of information between the main suppliers did not directly concern prices or 'underpin any other anti-competitive arrangement', the Courts accepted the Commission's argument that the regular and frequent sharing of information regarding registered vehicles and their place of registration served to reduce uncertainty and impair competition on such a highly concentrated market. An important further objection to the arrangement was that participation in the exchange of information was in practice limited to the major suppliers.

5.088 *Wirtschaftsvereinigung Stahl.*   In *Wirtschaftsvereinigung Stahl*,[253] concerning detailed exchanges of data between members of the German steel industry trade association, the Commission drew a distinction between exchanges of sensitive, recent and individualised information on a concentrated market in homogeneous products, and exchanges of such information on less concentrated or more diverse markets. The Commission's reasoning is based on the idea that excessive market transparency on an oligopolistic market for homogeneous products acts as a significant deterrent to competitive conduct on that market, because of rapid detection of such conduct by competitors.[254] However, the Commission's decision

---

[251] *IFTRA Glass Containers*, OJ 1974 L160/1, [1974] 2 CMLR D50, para 43. See also *Vimpoltu*, OJ 1983 L200/44, [1983] 3 CMLR 619 (exchange of price lists to police price agreement between Dutch tractor importers); *Fatty Acids*, OJ 1987 L3/17, [1989] 4 CMLR 445; *Flat Glass*, OJ 1989 L33/44, [1990] 4 CMLR 535, on appeal Cases T-68/89, etc, *Società Italiano Vetro (SIV) v Commission* [1992] ECR II-1403, [1992] 5 CMLR 302 (in large part annulling the decn on evidential grounds); *Building and construction industry in the Netherlands*, OJ 1992 L92/1, [1993] 5 CMLR 135, appeals dismissed, Case T-29/92 *SPO v Commission* [1995] ECR II-289, Case C-137/95P, [1996] ECR I-1611. cf Frignani and Rossi, 'Exchanges of Information among Competitors: a comparative survey' [2003] 1 BLI 54 (International Bar Association), considering whether an effect of exchange of price sensitive information should be required, at least in a non-oligopolistic market, and criticising the Italian car insurance decision, n 261, below.
[252] *UK Agricultural Tractor Registration Exchange*, OJ 1992 L68/19, [1993] 4 CMLR 358; on appeal, Case T-34/92 *Fiatagri and New Holland Ford v Commission* [1994] ECR II-905 and Case T-35/92 *John Deere v Commission* [1994] ECR II-957 (CFI); on further appeal, Case C-7/95P *Deere v Commission* [1998] ECR I-3111, [1998] 5 CMLR 311, and Case C-8/95P *New Holland Ford v Commission* [1998] ECR I-3175, [1998] 5 CMLR 362.
[253] *Wirtschaftsvereinigung Stahl*, OJ 1998 L1/10, [1998] 4 CMLR 450. Because the case fell under Art 65 ECSC, there was no jurisdiction to grant exemption.
[254] ibid, para 39.

condemning the arrangements was annulled by the Court of First Instance,[255] which emphasised that on the facts the data exchanged did not enable the participants to do more than estimate the participants' relative market shares. The Court stated: 'information agreements are not generally prohibited automatically but only if they have certain characteristics relating, in particular, to the sensitive and accurate nature of recent data exchanged at short intervals.'[256] The Court distinguished the *United Kingdom Tractor Registration Exchange* case, on which the Commission had relied, on the basis that there the information which was exchanged was extremely precise and permitted the identification of each individual sale which had been made.

Artificial market transparency. Where pricing information is made available by   **5.089** the market leader to its competitors unilaterally rather than exchanged, this may still amount to an unlawful restriction on competition.[257] Further, Article 81(1) is infringed even if the information could have been obtained from other, less convenient, sources.[258] The question is whether the exchange creates an artificial transparency of information limited to the participants, which would not be available in the absence of these arrangements and is therefore liable to affect their competitive conduct. The exchange of information is especially liable to distort competition in an oligopolistic market.[259] But where there is already a high degree of price transparency in the market, price information arrangements even in an oligipolistic market may not have any distorting effect. This distinction is illustrated by two contrasting judgments of the Paris Court of Appeal, the one overturning and the other upholding the condemnation of a price exchange agreement by the French Conseil de la Concurrence. In *Motor-fuels on the motorway*

---

[255] Case T-16/98 *Wirtschaftsvereinigung Stahl v Commission* [2001] ECR-II 1217, [2001] 5 CMLR 310.

[256] ibid, para 44. See also Case C-238/05 *Asnef-Equifax v Ausbanc* [2006] ECR I-11125 where the ECJ stated (para 54) that the compatibility of information exchange agreements with Art 81(1) 'depends on the economic conditions on the relevant markets and on the specific characteristics of the system concerned, such as, in particular, its purpose and the conditions of access to it and participation in it, as well as the type of information exchanged – be that, for example, public or confidential, aggregated or detailed, historical or current – the periodicity of such information and its importance for the fixing of prices, volumes or conditions of service'.

[257] Cases T-202/98, etc, *Tate & Lyle, Napier Brown and British Sugar* [2001] ECR II-2035, [2001] 5 CMLR 859 (appeal on other grounds dismissed, Case C-359/01P *British Sugar* [2004] ECR I-4933, [2004] 5 CMLR 329). The CFI rejected British Sugar's argument that earlier accusations of predatory pricing justified its disclosure to competitors and held that 'the systematic participation of the applicant undertakings in the meetings in question allowed them to create a climate of mutual certainty as to their future pricing policies': para 60.

[258] *Cobelpa/VNP*, OJ 1977 L242/10, [1977] 2 CMLR D28; *Vegetable Parchment*, OJ 1978 L70/54, [1978] 1 CMLR 534; *Hasselblad* OJ 1982 L161/18, [1982] 2 CMLR 233, on appeal Case 86/82 *Hasselblad v Commission* [1984] ECR 883, [1984] 1 CMLR 559; *Asnef-Equifax v Ausbanc* (n 256, above) para 58.

[259] *Plasterboard* (n 244, above) para 165.

(*'carburants sur autoroute'*),[260] the Court held that the regular exchange of price information between motorway service stations did not affect the individual pricing decisions of each company: fuel prices were openly displayed and although the information exchanged was communicated to the fuel companies' head offices, the convergence in prices was the result of the transparency that otherwise existed in this oligopolistic market. On the other hand, in *Palaces parisiens*,[261] the Court upheld the Conseil's imposition of penalties on six luxury hotels in Paris for the regular exchange of information, including their occupancy rates, average room prices and marketing strategies, and even the number of Japanese-speaking staff they employed (which was relevant in attracting Japanese guests). This sharing of confidential and strategic information in an oligopolistic market created an artificial 'collusive equilibrium'.

5.090   **Information on output and sales.**   There is no objection to the collection by a trade association of statistical information giving an aggregate picture of the output and sales of the relevant industry without identifying individual undertakings.[262] In *CEPI-Cartonboard*,[263] the Commission issued a negative clearance comfort letter for a statistical exchange system for the cartonboard industry to replace the arrangements condemned in 1994 in its *Cartonboard* decision. The new system was based on aggregated information and was approved on the basis that it would not be discussed between competitors, would not be accompanied by comments, analyses, observations or recommendations, and would not cover prices,

---

260 *Esso, Total, BP and Shell v Minister of the Economy, Finance and Industry*, judgment of 9 December 2003, BOCCRF no. 2 of 12 March 2004, [2005] ECC 51, further appeal to the Cour de Cassation dismissed as inadmissible: judgment of 25 January 2005.

261 *Hotel Le Bristol v Minister of the Economy, Finance and Industry*, judgment of 26 September 2006 (the case was decided under the French equivalent of Art 81). In *Axa Assicurazioni et a v Autorità Garante della Concorrenza e del Mercato*, Administrative Tribunal of Lazio, no. 6139/2001, 5 July 2001, the Court upheld the Italian competition authority's decision that arrangements for detailed exchange of information between 38 car insurance companies (constituting about 85 per cent of the market) about premiums, policy terms, compensation paid, etc, violated the Italian equivalent of Art 81; a further appeal to the Consiglio di Stato was dismissed, save for reduction in some of the fines: Decn no. 129/2002 of 27 February 2002. For exchange of pricing information in the context of a bid tendering process, see *Apex Asphalt and Paving Co Ltd v Office of Fair Trading* [2005] CAT 4, [2005] CompAR 507 (UK Competition Appeal Tribunal).

262 For a discussion of these issues, see *UK Agricultural Tractor Registration Exchange*, para 5.087, above; and the judgment of the CFI in *Wirtschaftsvereinigung Stahl*, para 5.088, above: information as to deliveries and market shares. See also *Cobelpa/VNP* and *Vegetable Parchment* (n 258, above).

263 *CEPI-Cartonboard*, XXVIth *Report on Competition Policy* (1996), p 127; see also OJ 1996 C310/3, [1996] 5 CMLR 725 (Art 19(3) Notice under Reg 17). In *Operational riskdata eXchange (ORX)*, XXXIInd *Report on Competition Policy* (2002), p 188, the provision of operational risk related loss information in a standardised and anonymous form by the creation of an electronic data pool received a negative clearance comfort letter. ORX was established by global banks to help improve the measurement of risks with a view to lowering the minimum capital requirements in relation to a new capital adequacy framework for the banking industry.

production forecasts or forecasts of capacity utilisation rates.[264] Similarly there is no objection under Article 81(1) if information as to the production or sales of particular undertakings is made publicly available under the auspices of a trade association provided the information is sufficiently historical that it no longer has any real impact on future behaviour.[265] However, the private exchange between competitors of information normally kept confidential, for example a breakdown of deliveries by product[266] or customer,[267] or the disclosure of invoices[268] or of capacity utilisation,[269] will often infringe Article 81(1). Any 'market transparency' attained is offset by the fact that the information remains private to the undertakings concerned.[270]

Other exchanges of information.   In its Notice on Cooperation Agreements,   **5.091** issued in 1968, the Commission indicated that the 'exchange of opinion or experience' and the joint compilation of market research, general industry studies, or statistics, did not infringe Article 81(1).[271] The Horizontal Cooperation Guidelines adopted in 2000 to replace the 1968 Notice do not expressly cover agreements on

---

[264] The Commission has also obtained agreement from tractor suppliers throughout the Community to abide by two principles in the exchange of information: only to exchange individual figures after a period of 12 months; and only to exchange more recent historical data where at least three industrial or financial groupings or more than 10 entities are involved. The Commission stated that these principles should serve as guidelines for any similar exchanges of information in other highly concentrated sectors although the application of the '10 units rule' is stated to be specific to tractors and agricultural machinery: *Exchange of information between tractor and agricultural machinery manufacturers, XXIXth Report on Competition Policy* (1999), p 156.

[265] *UK Agricultural Tractor Registration Exchange* (n 252, above).

[266] *Cobelpa/VNP* (n 258, above); *Fatty Acids* (n 251, above); *UK Agricultural Tractor Registration Exchange* (n 263, above). In the context of restructuring agreements, see also *Stichting Baksteen*, OJ 1994 L131/15, [1995] 4 CMLR 646, where the Commission imposed conditions on the exchange of information in relation to individual output and deliveries as part of a decision under Art 81(3).

[267] *Vegetable Parchment* (n 258, above); *White Lead*, OJ 1979 L21/16, [1979] 1 CMLR 464; *BP Kemi/DDSF*, OJ 1979 L286/32, [1979] 3 CMLR 684; *UK Agricultural Tractor Registration Exchange* (n 252, above).

[268] *Vegetable Parchment* (n 258, above).

[269] *Europe Asia Trades Agreement ('EATA')*, OJ 1999 L192/23, [1999] 5 CMLR 1380. cf *Bouygues Télécom, Orange France, SFR*, judgment No 1020 of 29 June 2007, where the French Cour de Cassation held that the regular exchange of unpublished information between competitors, even in an oligopolistic market, does not *per se* restrict competition; to uphold the Conseil de la Concurrence's finding of infringement, it was necessary to show that the information (as to the gross and net numbers of new subscribers and terminating subscribers) actually reduced the uncertainty of the operators as to the performance of each of their competitors. See also *Palaces parisiens* (n 261, above and discussed at para 5.089, above).

[270] *Cobelpa/VNP, Vegetable Parchment Parchment* (n 258, above); *UK Agricultural Tractor Registration Exchange* (n 252, above). In *EATA* (n 269, above) the Commission noted that the defendant undertakings claimed confidentiality vis-à-vis complainants in the procedure for the capacity information exchanged under the agreement, thereby confirming the commercially sensitive nature of that information (para 156).

[271] Notice on Cooperation Agreements, OJ 1968 C75/3, para II(1): see *Department Stores, IXth Report on Competition Policy* (1979), point 89. See also *Zinc Producer Group*, OJ 1984 L220/27, [1985] 2 CMLR 108; *European Wastepaper Information Service, XVIIIth Report on Competition Policy* (1988), point 63.

the exchange of information,[272] but this statement probably still holds true: there is no objection to the compilation of general information, whether by a trade association or otherwise. However, it is essential that the information exchanged does not extend to truly confidential competitive information relating to individual undertakings.

5.092 **Exchange of information between distributors.** The same principles apply to the exchange of price information between distributors.[273] But a supplier may lawfully ask a distributor for price information provided he does not pass that information on to other distributors.[274]

5.093 **Information on costs and investment.** The exchange of information on costs is likely to infringe Article 81(1), especially if there is reason to infer that the underlying purpose of the exchange is to diminish price competition.[275] Exchange of detailed information on proposed investment may well infringe Article 81(1).[276]

5.094 **Information on debtor credit worthiness.** In *Asnef-Equifax*[277] the Court of Justice was asked by a Spanish court whether a system for the exchange between financial institutions of credit information concerning the identity and economic activity of debtors was compatible with Article 81. The Court acknowledged that by reducing the risk of defaults, the register could bring down the overall cost of borrowing. Further, by reducing the significance of the information held by financial institutions regarding their own customers, such registers were, in principle, capable of increasing the mobility of consumers of credit making it easier for new competitors to enter the market. Provided that the relevant market or markets are not highly concentrated, that the system does not permit lenders to be identified either directly or indirectly and that the conditions of access and use

---

[272] Horizontal Cooperation Guildelines, OJ 2001 C3/2: Vol II, App C.12, paras 8, 10.

[273] *Hasselblad* (n 258, above): exchange of information on prices and discounts between distributors at a time when parallel imports were occurring. Where a market is not oligopolistic, the Commission has been prepared to accept even the exchange of individual and confidential information concerning costs, sales volumes and market shares, so long as it did not include prices or individual customer-related information: *Eudim*, OJ 1996 C111/8, [1996] 4 CMLR 871 (Art 19(3) Notice under Reg 17).

[274] *Hasselblad* (n 258, above). See also *SABA (No. 1)*, OJ 1976 L28/19, [1976] 1 CMLR D61.

[275] *IFTRA Glass Containers* (n 252, above); *IFTRA Aluminium*, OJ 1975 L228/3, [1975] 2 CMLR D20. See also *Stack, XXVIIIth Report on Competition Policy* (1998), p 153: company set up by major IT component purchasers whose activities included central monitoring of prices paid and the reporting of benchmark prices to members; comfort letter issued after the Commission was satisfied that no commercially sensitive price information was exchanged.

[276] *Zinc Producer Group* (n 271, above).

[277] Case C-238/05 *Asnef-Equifax v Ausbanc* [2006] ECR I-11125. See also *EFTA Surveillance Authority Annual Report 2002*, para 6.2.6 (p 72): exchange of information between Norwegian motor insurance companies as to the risks of policyholders did not come within Art 53(1) EEA.

by financial institutions are not discriminatory, the Court held that such a register is not, in principle, liable to have the effect of restricting competition. The Court observed that each lending institution could still be expected to act autonomously in its lending decisions, and that although such a system reduced uncertainty as to the risk of borrower default, it did not reduce uncertainty as to the risks of competition.

Disclosure of technology.   The disclosure of know-how and similar informa-   **5.095**
tion is discussed elsewhere in this work.[278]

Information agreements under Article 81(3).   Generally, there appears to be   **5.096**
little scope for the application of Article 81(3) to the kind of agreements here discussed: either they fall outside Article 81(1) altogether, or they are clearly anti-competitive.[279] In the insurance sector, however, special considerations have been found to apply: as with price-fixing arrangements, Regulation 358/2003[280] grants exemption to certain specific information agreements in relation to the supply of insurance services. In *TEKO*,[281] the Commission found that the exchange of information for the purposes of coordinated risk assessment and the setting of common premiums by a number of insurance companies, although falling within the scope of Article 81(1), qualified for exemption.

7. Collective Trading Arrangements

Traditional cartel analysis and collective selling and purchasing arrangements.   **5.097**
Collective selling and purchasing arrangements could be characterised as involving a form of price-fixing and output restriction: the participants in such arrangements necessarily agree to buy or sell only at the centrally agreed price and not to buy or sell the product to which the agreement relates otherwise than through the central body. However, the Community Courts and Commission have regularly accepted that in certain markets (notably those involving intellectual property rights and perishable goods such as agricultural products) and certain market structures (in particular those involving substantial countervailing market power)

---

[278] See Chap 9, below.
[279] But see *Irish Club Rules*, OJ 1991 C166/6, [1991] 4 CMLR 704 (possibility of exemption of information exchange agreement between cargo shipping lines in the exceptional competitive situation of sea trade between Ireland and continental Europe). The Commission closed its file and sent a comfort letter to the parties with respect to the amended *Irish Club Rules*, OJ 1993 C263/6 (Notice under Reg 4956/86), *XXIIIrd Report on Competition Policy* (1993), point 233.
[280] Reg 358/2003, OJ 2003 L53/8: Vol II, App E.27, discussed at paras 12.169 *et seq*, below.
[281] *TEKO*, OJ 1990 L13/34, [1990] 4 CMLR 957 (individual exemption for 10 years where parties' combined market share no more than 20 per cent). But cf the Italian car insurance case, n 261, above. And note the Commission's sector inquiry into business insurance, which may lead it to modify its approach: see para 5.143, below.

analysis in terms of price-fixing, or restriction of supply or demand, may be inappropriate and a more subtle analysis is called for. Collective trading arrangements are often organised under the auspices of a trade association or other industry-wide body. Cases relating more specifically to the rules of such organisations are considered in Section 8 of this Chapter.

(a) Boycotts and collective exclusive dealing

5.098 **Collective exclusive dealing.** The term 'collective exclusive dealing agreement' is used here to describe an agreement whereby groups of suppliers agree to deal exclusively through certain distribution channels (typically 'approved dealers' only) or reciprocal exclusive arrangements are entered into between groups of suppliers and groups of dealers (typically the 'approved dealers' in question) to deal only with one another.[282] Alternatively, such arrangements may be couched in negative terms as agreements to refuse to deal with particular individuals or categories of purchaser, competitor or supplier.

5.099 **Collective exclusive dealing agreements.** Collective exclusive dealing agreements for ordinary manufacturing products have been consistently condemned under Article 81(1).[283] Such agreements tend, by their nature, to perpetuate the division of the common market along national lines. In *FEG and TU*[284] the Court of First Instance considered an appeal by a Dutch association of wholesalers of electrotechnical fittings and one of its members against a Commission decision,[285] condemning an exclusive dealing arrangement between FEG and NAVEG, the

---

[282] Particular kinds of multipartite exclusive dealing require specific analysis, eg between manufacturers *inter se* at paras 5.068 *et seq*, above; and on purchases of raw material at paras 5.125 *et seq*, below. For exclusive dealing in vertical distribution and supply agreements see Chap 6, below.

[283] See, eg Case 8/72 *Cementhandelaren* [1972] ECR 977, [1973] CMLR 7 (Dutch cement dealers recommended prices and sold only to approved resellers); Cases 209/78, etc, *Van Landewyck* ('*FEDETAB*') [1980] ECR 3125, [1981] 3 CMLR 134 (agreement between Belgian tobacco manufacturers and importers and Belgian wholesalers provided for sales to 'approved wholesalers' and 'approved retailers' only, in support of an agreement maintaining fixed trade margins in the supply of tobacco products in Belgium); Cases 43 & 63/82 *VBVB and VBBB* [1984] ECR 19, [1985] 1 CMLR 27 (Dutch and Belgian publishers of Flemish books agreed to deal only with 'recognised' booksellers and wholesalers who observed publishers' resale prices); Case 243/83 *Binon v AMP* [1985] ECR 2015, [1985] 3 CMLR 800 (selective distribution by Belgian press agency acting on behalf of Belgian and foreign newspapers publishers); and see also *AMP*, OJ 1987 C164/2, [1987] 3 CMLR 445; Case 246/86 *Belasco* [1989] ECR 2117, [1991] 4 CMLR 96 (agreement on concerted action by Belgian roofing felt manufacturers against competitors not members of the Belasco cartel); *Auditel I*, OJ 1993 L306/50, [1995] 5 CMLR 719 (agreement by Auditel shareholders, comprising in practice television broadcasters and advertising associations, to use exclusively the Italian audience ratings provided by Auditel); *SCK and FNK*, OJ 1995 L317/79, [1996] 4 CMLR 565, upheld on appeal Cases T-213/95 and T-18/96 [1997] ECR II-1739, [1998] 4 CMLR 259 (Dutch crane-hirers affiliated to the domestic certification institution prevented from engaging non-affiliated crane hirers as subcontractors).

[284] Cases T-5 & 6/00 *Nederlandse Federative Vereniging voor de Groothandel op Elektrotechnisch Gebied and Technische Unie v Commission* [2003] ECR II-5761, [2004] 5 CMLR 969.

[285] *FEG and TU*, OJ 2000 L39/1, [2000] 4 CMLR 1208.

latter being an association of importers and agents representing foreign manufacturers of electrotechnical fittings. Under the arrangement, NAVEG members agreed to supply only members of FEG. However, the arrangement was not reciprocal and FEG members were free to purchase their supplies from non-members of NAVEG. The Commission held that the gentlemen's agreement between NAVEG and FEG on not supplying non-members of FEG constituted an agreement within the meaning of Article 81(1). The agreements between individual suppliers of electrotechnical fittings and the FEG and its individual members on not supplying non-members of the FEG should be regarded as concerted practices within the meaning of Article 81(1). The arrangements restricted the freedom of suppliers to determine for themselves through whom to distribute their goods so that both suppliers and non-member wholesalers were placed at a disadvantage. The FEG's strict admissions policy made it difficult for new wholesalers from outside the Netherlands to join. On appeal, FEG denied the existence of the arrangements, arguing that a non-reciprocal exclusive dealing agreement did not make economic sense; members of NAVEG would have no incentive to bind themselves to FEG if FEG members were free to make purchases outside NAVEG. The Court of First Instance upheld the Commission's finding because the members of FEG together held such a strong market position that NAVEG could not afford to refuse to enter into the arrangements, and the further appeals to the Court of Justice were dismissed.[286] The Commission has always refused exemption under Article 81(3) for a collective exclusive dealing agreement affecting the supply of goods. However, the Court of Justice's recent case law (considered below[287]) in respect of collective buying and selling of agricultural products suggests that a more complex analysis may be required in at least some markets.

Collective refusal to deal. The ordinary means of enforcing a collective exclu- **5.100**
sive dealing agreement is by a collective boycott or concerted refusal to deal. A boycott in support of an infringing agreement itself infringes Article 81(1)[288] as

---

[286] Case C-105/04P *FEG v Commission*, Case C-113/04P *TU v Commission* [2006] ECR I-8725, 8831, [2006] 5 CMLR 1223.

[287] See the discussion of collective selling and purchasing arrangements in paras 5.106 *et seq*, below. Some Commission initiatives appear to reflect a similar approach: eg in *IFCO*, OJ 1997 C48/4, [1997] 5 CMLR 943, the Commission issued a Notice under Reg 17 stating its intention to approve a system for the transport of fruit and vegetables developed by a 'pool' of German food trading companies and based on the use of standardised, collapsible and reusable plastic crates manufactured by a particular group of manufacturers of plastic products and containers. However, the Commission's approval was conditional on substantial amendments to the arrangements preventing (i) the participants entering into joint marketing of the IFCO system; (ii) IFCO promoting the system as a horizontal exclusive agreement; (iii) agreed rebates to participants in the recycling system; and (iv) information exchange as to the commercial strategy of members' suppliers. The Commission was then satisfied that IFCO could be regarded as a 'market product based on standard general terms' rather than an exclusive dealing arrangement.

[288] Cases involving alleged boycotts or concerted refusals to deal include Case 73/74 *Papiers Peints v Commission* [1975] ECR 1491, [1976] 1 CMLR 589 (boycott of Mr Pex, a price cutter);

does a collective refusal to supply a customer who is not a domestic national.[289] Refusal to supply by a dominant undertaking (including collectively dominant undertakings) is discussed in Chapter 10, below in the context of Article 82.[290]

5.101 **Aggregated rebates cartels.** An effect similar to a collective exclusive dealing agreement is achieved where a group of suppliers agree to grant rebates, discounts or bonuses based on the total purchases of the customer from all the suppliers, thus tending to tie the customer to the group as a whole. Such agreements infringe Article 81(1) and do not benefit from Article 81(3).[291]

5.102 **Appreciable effect.** In exceptional cases a collective exclusive dealing agreement may fall outside Article 81(1) for lack of appreciable effect.[292] Thus in *Salonia*,[293] an agreement existed between the Italian Federation of Newspaper Publishers and the Italian Federation of Newsagents whereby Italian newspapers and periodicals would be delivered to approved newsagents only. The agreement did not cover newspapers and periodicals of other Member States. While indicating that such a 'closed circuit' distribution system might have 'repercussions' on the distribution of imported newspapers and periodicals, the Court of Justice, on a reference under Article 234, left open the possibility that the agreement might lack any appreciable effect on trade between Member States.[294]

Case 90/76 *Van Ameyde v UCI* [1977] ECR 1091, [1977] 2 CMLR 478 (possible exclusion of loss adjuster from insurance business); *Cauliflowers*, OJ 1978 L21/23, [1978] 1 CMLR D66 (exclusion of non-members from auctions not based on objective criteria); *RAI/Unitel*, OJ 1978 L157/39, [1978] 3 CMLR 306, *XIIth Report on Competition Policy* (1982), point 90, (boycott of TV broadcast of 'Don Carlos'); *SMM & T Exhibition Agreement*, OJ 1983 L376/1, [1984] 1 CMLR 611 (boycott of Earls Court 'Motorfair'); *Binon v AMP* (n 283, above) (collective refusal to supply newspapers to non-selected newsagent).

[289] *Re Sugar Beet*, OJ 1990 L31/32, [1991] 4 CMLR 629.

[290] Paras 10.125 *et seq*, below.

[291] See, eg *German Ceramic Tiles Discount Agreement*, JO 1971 L10/15, [1971] CMLR D6 (aggregated rebate scheme among German ceramic tile suppliers); *Industrieverband Sohnhofener Natursteinplatten*, OJ 1980 L318/32, [1981] 2 CMLR 308 (aggregated sales bonus for Belgian and French customers for German natural stone); Cases 240/82, etc, *SSI v Commission* [1985] ECR 3831, [1987] 3 CMLR 661 (aggregated rebate to specialist tobacco retailers, as defined, based on collective purchases from members of SSI). In *Société des Caves et des Producteurs réunis de Roquefort* Decn No. 04-D-13 of 8 April 2004, BOCCRF 31 March 2005, the Conseil de la Concurrence condemned the *Société* under Art 82 for operating a rebate system which aggregated sales of all its members.

[292] For appreciable effect generally see paras 2.121 *et seq*, above.

[293] Case 126/80 *Salonia v Poidomani and Giglio* [1981] ECR 1563, [1982] 1 CMLR 64. The case was only sketchily argued: the plaintiff in the main action failed to file any written observations in due time and the defendant filed no written observations at all; another person, who was not a party to the action, sought to file observations, which were rejected as inadmissible; cf generally *Binon v AMP* (n 283, above) where a similar agreement extended to foreign publications and apparently had an appreciable effect on the facts.

[294] *Salonia*, above, paras 15–18. Under Art 234 the ECJ had no jurisdiction to decide the facts, but nonetheless drew attention to (i) the possible use of other channels of distribution and (ii) the apparent lack of effect of the agreement on demand for foreign newspapers and periodicals: note that in oral argument (at 1573 (ECR)) the Commission expressed the view that the agreement had had no restrictive effect on the import of foreign newspapers in Italy.

Qualitative criteria.   Also in *Salonia*, the Court of Justice indicated that a collec- **5.103** tive exclusive dealing agreement might fall outside Article 81(1) if it was based purely on objective qualitative criteria, such as the technical qualifications of the reseller and the suitability of his premises and staff.[295] However, instances of collective exclusive dealing agreements based on genuine qualitative criteria are likely to be rare.[296]

Collective exclusive dealing in financial services.   The Commission seems to **5.104** take a more favourable attitude to collective exclusive dealing agreements affecting financial services such as insurance[297] and commodity trading.[298]

Collective exclusive dealing in the airline industry.   In two decisions, *IATA* **5.105** *Passenger Agency Programme,*[299] and *IATA Cargo Agency Programme,*[300] the Commission applied Article 81(3) to collective distribution arrangements operated by all the members of the International Air Transport Association (IATA). Membership of IATA is open to all air transport enterprises operating an air service between two or more countries and the rules in question governed the sale of passenger and cargo services of IATA members through common standards for appointment as IATA agents. After considerable amendments to the rules designed

---

[295] ibid, paras 23–27. For a further discussion of 'qualitative' as distinct from 'quantitative' criteria, see paras 6.094 *et seq*, below.

[296] In most cases it will be impossible to justify a collective agreement based on quantitative criteria (although the Commission has in some cases been prepared to allow a network of national operators in the financial services and telecommunications fields: see n 126, above and para 5.035, above); so-called 'qualitative' criteria are capable of being invoked for ulterior purposes, as shown by the cases at n 283, above; but see *AMP* (n 283, above).

[297] See, eg *Nuovo CEGAM*, OJ 1984 L99/29, [1984] 2 CMLR 484 (Italian insurers agreed to place all their re-insurance with specified re-insurers: Art 81(3) exemption granted); cf *Dutch Transport Insurers, VIth Report on Competition Policy* (1976), point 120. See also *Van Ameyde v UCI* (n 288, above) (certain business reserved to national insurers' bureaux in implementation of the 'green card' scheme not incompatible with Art 81). See also *Visa International rules* discussed at para 5.045, above, and *XVIIIth Report on Competition Policy* (1998), points 111–119 (Commission policy in relation to aviation and maritime insurance of major risks) and Chap 12, below.

[298] *The London Sugar Futures Market Limited* (also cocoa, coffee, and rubber terminal markets), OJ 1985 L369/25, etc, [1988] 4 CMLR 138 (negative clearance for rules of London commodity markets). See also *The Petroleum Exchange of London*, OJ 1987 L3/27, [1989] 4 CMLR 280, and similar decisions on the London futures markets for soya bean, grain, potatoes and meat: OJ 1987 L19/18, [1989] 4 CMLR 287; *Baltic International Foreign Futures Exchange*, OJ 1987 L222/24, [1989] 4 CMLR 314. See also *Sarabex, VIIIth Report on Competition Policy* (1978), points 35–37, [1979] 1 CMLR 262 (rules for foreign exchange transactions in the London market); para 5.138, below.

[299] *IATA Passenger Agency Programme*, OJ 1991 L258/18, [1992] 5 CMLR 496. For air transport generally, see Chap 12, below.

[300] *IATA Cargo Agency Programme*, OJ 1991 L258/29, [1992] 5 CMLR 496. In *IATA-Currency Rules*, rules that prevented purchases by consumers from outside the country of travel origin were modified after intervention by the Commission so as not to apply to travel within the EC and Norway: *XXIIIrd Report on Competition Policy* (1993), point 237. See also *Sabre/Air France and Iberia* (refusal by Air France and Iberia to participate in a competing computerised reservation system): *XXIIIrd Report on Competition Policy* (1993), point 239; and see para 12.048, below.

to facilitate access into the agency market, the Commission was prepared to grant a 10-year exemption in each case.

(b) Collective selling of goods

5.106 **In general.** In certain circumstances undertakings may seek to cooperate in the joint selling of their products, for example through a joint subsidiary formed for the purpose, or a joint sales agency. However, Article 81(1) proceeds on the basis that every undertaking must compete independently and not coordinate its activities with any other undertaking unless the agreement fulfils the criteria in Article 81(3). Thus joint selling arrangements between competitors in the supply of goods or services will normally infringe Article 81(1) if the requisite effect on trade between Member States is shown, since they eliminate price competition and may also restrict the volume of products delivered by the individual participants through the operation of a system for allocating orders.[301] Similar principles apply to joint advertising and promotion.[302]

5.107 **Joint selling by agricultural cooperatives:** *Oude Luttikhuis*.[303] In line with its approach in relation to collective purchasing by agricultural cooperatives,[304] the

---

[301] Horizontal Cooperation Guidelines, OJ 2001 C3/2: Vol II, App C.12, paras 143–145. See, eg *Floral*, OJ 1980 L39/51, [1980] 2 CMLR 285; *Centraal Stikstof Verkoopkantoor*, OJ 1978 L242/15, [1979] 1 CMLR 11; *Bayer/BP Chemicals*, OJ 1988 L150/35, [1989] 4 CMLR 24 (12-year exemption for joint selling by two competitors in the polyethylene sector in the context of a restructuring agreement: see also OJ 1992 C44/11); *Hudson's Bay/Dansk Pelsdyravlerforening*, OJ 1988 L316/43, [1989] 4 CMLR 340, on appeal Case T-61/89 *Dansk Pelsdyravlerforening v Commission* [1992] ECR II-1931; *UIP*, OJ 1989 L226/25, [1990] 4 CMLR 749 (joint distribution and licensing joint venture between US film makers exempted by the Commission after amendment); also *XXIXth Report on Competition Policy* (1999), p 148 (exemption renewed by comfort letter for amended agreement subject to undertakings designed to enhance parties' individual autonomy and ensure fair treatment for cinemas); *Finnpap*, OJ 1989 C45/4, [1989] 4 CMLR 413, *XIXth Report on Competition Policy* (1989), point 44 (joint selling of Finnish newsprint; case closed after amendment of rules – no appreciable effect on inter-State trade); *Ecomet*, *XXIXth Report on Competition Policy* (1999), p 153 (grouping set up by national meteorological institutes for joint sale of their data but prices determined by each individual institute for its own data: comfort letter issued). Both *ACI* and *Night Services*, para 5.078, above, contained aspects of joint selling. See also *Norwegian Filmdistributors Association/Films & Kino*, *EFTA Surveillance Authority Annual Report 2003*, p 51 and Press Release PR(03)33 (12 November 2003): ESA accepted commitments to bring to an end a long-standing agreement between the associations comprising, respectively, film distributors and cinemas and which had covered all commercial distribution of films to cinemas in Norway: the distributors undertook not to engage in joint negotiations for film distribution in the future.

[302] See paras 5.146 *et seq*, below. See especially *Milchförderungsfonds*, OJ 1985 L35/35, [1985] 3 CMLR 101. As discussed below, the analysis in respect of the parties to the joint arrangements will differ from that in respect of customers and competing undertakings. Problems arise in practice where the parties to the joint arrangements collectively are in a position to exercise significant market power at the expense of their customers and/or their competitors: in those circumstances, Art 82 may also apply.

[303] Case C-399/93 *Oude Luttikhuis v Coberco* [1995] ECR I-4515, [1996] 5 CMLR 178.

[304] See Case C-250/92 *Gøttrup-Klim v Dansk Landbrugs Grovvare AmbA* [1994] ECR I-5641, [1996] 4 CMLR 191, discussed at para 5.126, below.

Court of Justice accepts that the creation of such cooperatives as a means of encouraging modernisation and rationalisation in the agricultural sector does not in itself constitute anti-competitive conduct and therefore does not generally have an anti-competitive *object* for the purposes of Article 81(1). However, the Court of Justice equally does not accept that such arrangements automatically fall outside the scope of Article 81(1), on the basis of their *effect*. A full economic assessment of the market in which they operate must be undertaken to assess whether the restrictions imposed by the cooperative are 'limited to what is necessary to ensure that the cooperative functions properly and in particular to ensure that it has a sufficiently wide commercial base and a certain stability in its membership.'[305]

Joint selling within the Community. Subject to these qualifications in particular economic contexts, Article 81(1) is normally infringed if undertakings jointly sell to purchasers in other Member States.[306] Thus in *Floral*,[307] the three largest French producers of compound fertilisers set up a jointly owned company for the promotion of their exports to Germany. Although the undertakings did not explicitly agree to sell all their exports to Germany through the joint company, they in fact did so for several years. The Commission held that Article 81(1) was infringed. It was irrelevant that, on one view, the agreement led to an overall increase in trade; the effect of the agreement was that the parties did not offer compound fertilisers for sale in Germany in competition with each other. German customers were confronted with uniform terms of supply. The Commission refused an exemption under Article 81(3) and imposed fines. There were no countervailing benefits to outweigh the restrictions of competition arising between the parties each of whom, so the Commission found, would have been capable of setting up an independent sales organisation. Article 81(1) may also be infringed by a joint selling agreement between undertakings in the same Member State, although ostensibly confined to the national territory.[308] In certain circumstances, the Commission has recognised the necessity for collective arrangements to protect the interests of small producers, while increasingly seeking to facilitate

5.108

---

[305] *Oude Luttikhuis* (n 303, above) para 14. See also COMP/38.238 *Spanish Raw Tobacco*, 20 October 2004, [2006] 4 CMLR 866; and COMP/38.281 *Italian Raw Tobacco*, 20 October 2005, [2006] 4 CMLR 1766 which included agreements between processors' and growers' trade unions and agricultural cooperatives.

[306] In some very early cases the Commission held that in ordinary circumstances, joint selling solely to countries outside the Community did not fall within Art 81(1): *DECA*, JO 1964 2761, [1965] CMLR 50; *VVVF*, JO 1969 L168/22, [1970] CMLR Dl; *Supexie*, JO 1971 L10/12, [1971] CMLR Dl; but in *Centraal Stikstof Verkoopkantoor* (n 301, above) the Commission left open whether Art 81(1) could apply to arrangements to make available specified quantities of products to a joint distribution agency for resale to third countries.

[307] *Floral*, OJ 1980 L39/51, [1980] 2 CMLR 285.

[308] *Centraal Stikstof Verkoopkantoor* (n 301, above).

individual sales by larger producers capable of operating competitively outside the collective scheme.[309]

5.109 **Joint selling from third countries:** *Ansac.* In the course of its investigation of the Community soda-ash industry, the Commission considered a notification from the American Natural Soda Ash Corporation ('Ansac')[310] seeking negative clearance or exemption in respect of arrangements entered into by the six United States producers of natural soda-ash for joint export sales exclusively through Ansac. The Commission had concluded, in the course of its investigation of the market, that the United States suppliers of natural soda-ash were the 'major competitive threat' to the European manufacturers and that natural soda-ash enjoyed a significant cost advantage over the synthetic soda-ash produced in Europe which enabled it to be sold at prices which undercut European prices without dumping. The Commission found that the arrangement infringed Article 81(1) and it was not prepared to grant an exemption despite the participants' argument that Ansac would serve to offer new competition to the 'present rigidly oligopolistic structure' of the Community market. The Commission's view was that the individual undertakings were capable of entering the Community market independently, although it was prepared to give favourable consideration to arrangements limited to joint storage and transport facilities.

5.110 **Joint ventures and specialisation agreements.** A 'joint venture' limited to selling activities only will ordinarily infringe Article 81(1), as shown by *Floral*.[311] Distribution arrangements arising in connection with research and development, specialisation of manufacture or joint production are discussed in Chapter 7, below. There is no objection to undertakings collaborating in a consortium to tender for a specific project, if none can complete the project by itself.[312]

---

[309] eg Cases T-70 & 71/92 *Florimex and VGB v Commission* [1997] ECR II-693, [1997] 5 CMLR 769, [1997] All ER (EC) 788 (auction sales of flowers); appeals dismissed, Case C-265/97P *VBA v Florimex* [2000] ECR I-2061, [2001] 5 CMLR 1343 and Case C-266/97P *VBA v VGB and Florimex* [2000] ECR I-2135. See para 5.107, above, in relation to collective sale of agricultural products and para 5.111, below, in relation to collective selling of rights. In each case, the specific justification for collective selling derives from the existence of large numbers of small producers of products that are inherently exposed to market failure.

[310] *Ansac*, OJ 1991 L152/54; see also para 5.075, above.

[311] *Floral* (n 307, above and discussed at para 5.108, above).

[312] Horizontal Cooperation Guidelines (n 301, above) para 143. See *Eurotunnel*, OJ 1988 L311/36, [1989] 4 CMLR 419 (negative clearance of the construction contracts between 10 major British and French construction and engineering companies); *Eurotunnel II, XIXth Report on Competition Policy* (1989), point 57; see also OJ 1988 C292/2, [1989] 4 CMLR 210 (three-year exemption of cooperation agreement between British Rail and SNCF; in *Eurotunnel III*, the exemption was renewed for 30 years, on stipulated conditions, in view of the exceptional nature of the tunnel and the need to create a successful environment for its successful use: see para 5.078, above). For the application of Art 81 to research, development and production joint ventures generally, see Chap 7, below.

The block exemption for vertical agreements, Regulation 2790/1999, does not cover reciprocal distribution arrangements between competitors.[313] The primary concern in such cases is that the arrangement may lead to market partitioning: the Commission has stated that the key question for assessment is whether the agreement is objectively necessary for the parties to enter each other's market.[314] The risk of market partitioning is less where competitors enter into a non-reciprocal distribution agreement and in certain conditions Regulation 2790/1999 may provide such an agreement with exemption; but if the block exemption does not apply, the agreement will generally fall within Article 81(1) if there might be a mutual understanding between the competitors not to enter each other's market. However, the Horizontal Cooperation Guidelines state that Article 81(1) will generally not apply to an agreement which does not involve price-fixing unless the parties have 'some degree of market power'; and that this is unlikely if the parties' combined market share is below 15 per cent.[315]

(c) Collective selling of intellectual property and media rights

Joint selling of rights.   Particular difficulties arise in relation to the collective   **5.111**
sale of intellectual property rights. The application of Article 81 to the creation and operation of patent pools where several licensors pool their rights and provide a one-stop shop for licensees is discussed in Chapter 9, below. The joint selling of rights in music or film recordings or the broadcasting rights to sporting events gives rise to issues which, the Community authorities have recognised, derive from three main sources. First, there is a risk of administrative chaos or market failure if there is no central point from which users can purchase a licence for the rights to many hundreds of individual copyright items. Secondly, however, there may be concentration in the buying market for such rights. More recently, the Commission has had to grapple with the complex question of market definition in cases concerning rights to broadcast a sporting competition which is centrally organised but involves a group of economically independent undertakings (whether the participating clubs or teams or the national organisers of an international series of events) and where there is potential for the rights to be exploited in a multitude of different media. The Commission is concerned that existing methods of licensing and royalty collection should not impede the development

---

[313] Reg 2790/999, OJ 1999 L336/21: Vol II, App C.3, Art 2(4). For Reg 2790/1999, see generally Chap 6, below.

[314] Horizontal Cooperation Guidelines (n 301, above) para 147; but any vertical restrictions in the agreement will have to be assessed according to the principles which govern vertical restraints: Chap 7, below.

[315] ibid, paras 148–149; if that share is exceeded, the structure of the affected market may determine whether agreement falls within Art 81(1) or qualifies for exemption under Art 81(3): para 150 and example at para 158.

of new media and that, where feasible, competition between national licensing bodies for internet rights (which are necessarily pan-European rights) should be encouraged.[316] Arrangements for reciprocal licensing of rights, in particular to television programming, are considered later in this Section.[317]

5.112 **Collective selling of rights: music and films.** The Commission has until recently taken a relatively benign approach to collective arrangements for licensing rights in music and film. It has accepted that such arrangements reflect ordinary commercial practice and that the activities of such bodies should be addressed under Article 82 rather than Article 81.[318] In particular cases, for example where national collecting societies cooperate to segment the national markets, Article 81 may apply. The Court of Justice and the Commission have been slow to infer such cooperation without specific evidence.[319] However, there are indications that this approach may be changing. For example, the Commission adopted the stance that the major record companies should negotiate prices independently of a collective sale of musical video rights, while accepting that the collective administrative arrangements fell outside Article 81(1).[320] Likewise, the Court of First Instance has indicated that an agreement between the operators of French racecourses not to enter the Belgian market for the sale of 'sound and pictures' of French horse races could fall within the scope of Article 81.[321]

5.113 **Licensing use of rights on the internet.** In two recent cases, the Commission has considered collective management and copyright licensing for the purpose of exploitation of musical works on the internet. In both cases, it has insisted that the licensee must be free to obtain its 'one-stop' licence for European repertoire from any of the collecting societies operating in Europe and that each such society must

---

[316] See eg *BUMA + SACEM + 9 (Santiago Agreement)*, OJ 2005 C200/11.

[317] See the discussion *Eurovision* in paras 5.130 *et seq*, below.

[318] See paras 10.134, *et seq*, below.

[319] eg Case T-224/95 *Tremblay v Commission* [1997] ECR II-2215, [1998] 4 CMLR 427, para 60, citing Case C-395/87 *Ministère Public v Tournier* [1989] ECR 2521, [1991] 4 CMLR 248; Cases C-110 & 241–2/88 *Lucazeau v SACEM* [1989] ECR 2811, [1991] 4 CMLR 248.

[320] This case was the subject of parallel proceedings under Arts 81 and 82 before the Commission and in the English courts (the English litigation was ultimately settled): the case is described in *MTV Europe v BMG Records (UK) Ltd* [1995] 1 CMLR 437 (Ch); [1997] 1 CMLR 867, [1997] EuLR 100 (CA). See also *Universal International Music BV/MCPS (The Cannes Extension Agreement)*, OJ 2006 C122/02: Commission sought views on proposed commitments to abandon clauses whereby mechanical copyright collecting societies undertook to the music publishers (i) that no society would grant a rebate to the licensed record companies without seeking the consent of all the society's members; and (ii) that no society would engage in the business of music publishing or record producing. The Commission subsequently accepted the commitments and closed its case: Press Release IP/06/1311 (4 October 2006).

[321] However, the CFI also found that a collective and exclusive sale of such rights for Germany with a prohibition on sub-licensing outside the territory did not fall within Art 81, although that had the consequence that the German rights holder was unable to sub-license those rights to Belgium: Case T-504/93 *Tiercé Ladbroke v Commission* [1997] ECR II-923, [1997] 5 CMLR 309.

be able to grant a pan-European licence regardless of where the licensee carries on its business. In *IFPI 'Simulcasting'*[322] the agreement as originally drafted provided that a collecting society could only grant an international simulcasting licence to broadcasting stations whose signals originated in its territory. This meant that broadcasters were required to approach the producers' collecting society in their own Member State in order to be granted a multi-territory simulcasting licence. At the request of the Commission, the agreement was modified to allow TV and radio broadcasters to obtain a 'one-stop shop' licence from any of the collecting societies located in the EEA.[323] In *BUMA and SABAM (Santiago Agreement)*,[324] commitments were offered to address similar competition concerns. The 'Santiago Agreement' is a standard agreement entered into between national collecting societies allowing each to grant a multi-territorial, multi-repertoire licence of the public performance rights of the repertoire in an online environment.[325] The structure of the cross-licensing arrangements in the original agreement effectively transposed onto the internet the national monopolies that the collecting societies have traditionally held in the offline world. BUMA and SABAM offered commitments that they would not enter into agreements which contained an 'economic residency' clause limiting themselves to licensing only those content providers who had their actual and economic location in that society's territory.

Licensing of music rights: further steps. The Commission has issued a **5.114**
Communication[326] setting out principles for the sector, including the need to avoid territorial restrictions, the proper mix between individual rights management and collective management of music rights and favourable treatment of one-stop shop arrangements and related reciprocal agreements between collective rights management systems.

Collective selling of rights: sporting events. Since the ruling of the Court of **5.115**
Justice in *Bosman*, the arrangements made by major national and international

---

[322] *IFPI 'Simulcasting'*, OJ 2003 L107/58, [2003] 5 CMLR 386. 'Simulcasting' is the simultaneous transmission by radio and TV stations via the internet of sound recordings included in their broadcasts of radio and/or TV signals. The Commission also found that the fact that the fee charged for the licence did not distinguish between the royalty for record producers' rights and the collecting society's fee unnecessarily restricted competition between the societies and did not qualify for exemption. On the parties' undertaking to provide greater transparency as to their costs, exemption was granted. The price-fixing aspect of this case is considered in para 5.031, above. See the Note on this decision in (2003) 1 EC Competition Policy Newsletter 44.

[323] See also *XXXIInd Report on Competition Policy* (2002), point 150.

[324] *BUMA + SACEM + 9 (Santiago Agreement)*, OJ 2005 C200/11.

[325] See Press Release IP/04/586 (3 May 2004).

[326] Communication from the Commission to the Council, the European Parliament and the European Economic and Social Committee – The Management of Copyright and Related Rights in the Internal Market, COM/2004/261, 16 April 2004. See also the Commission's recommendation 2005/737/EC (OJ 2005 L276/54) concerning the ability of the rights holder to use any collecting society in the EEA regardless of his nationality.

sporting associations have increasingly become the subject of scrutiny by the Commission (and by national competition authorities).[327] In May 1998 the Commission issued an 'orientation document' intended 'to lay down some broad lines identified to date for the application of competition law in a sector in which the structure and economics are very complex and which is the subject of continuous and very rapid developments.'[328] More recently, the Commission has noted the characteristics of the media market that may lead to competition concerns:

> 'Firstly, only a few powerful players are active on the different levels of the value chain for valuable audiovisual sport content, which want to protect their return on investment. Secondly, the rapid technological developments in the media sector and the limited market experience with new media content leads to insecurity, rightly or not, about the future consumption patterns . . . In order to maximise consumer choice, encourage innovation and foster competition, the European Commission advocates a competition policy that assures that access to sports rights for distribution over mobile platforms is not unduly restricted through anti-competitive practices resulting in output limitations'.[329]

5.116 **Commission policy: sports content rights and broadcasting.** The Commission has noted that competition problems in the markets for sports content rights are often caused by joint selling arrangements and exclusive rights contracts that have a wide scope and/or long duration. Such arrangements can lead to foreclosure of other operators in the downstream market; and to output restrictions when the collective rights holders withhold certain parts of the rights from the market so as to attract a higher price for the rights sold, with the result that the development of new internet and mobile media markets is impeded. Promoting efficient competition for sports TV rights is likely to improve competition on TV broadcasting markets and give viewers access to quality TV services, which are reasonably priced, innovative and varied. Commission policy[330] is therefore to ensure that

---

[327] See speech by Toft, 'EC Competition Law aspects: Sports Rights in a converging media technology market' (30 March 2006), available at: http://ec.europa.eu/comm/competition/speeches/text/sp2006_002_en.pdf

[328] *Broadcasting of sports events and competition law* (1998) 2 EC Competition Policy Newsletter 18 (prepared in consultation with Member State authorities). The Commission notes that '[b]efore considering the applicability of Community competition law, the ownership of rights needs to be taken into account as there is a danger that commercial agreements may collapse in a dispute about ownership, as has been witnessed in the Netherlands': para IV(2).

[329] Commission and EFTA Surveillance Authority Report on the sector inquiry into the provision of sports content over third generation mobile networks, 21 September 2005, paras 56–57: available at http://ec.europa.eu/comm/competition/antitrust/others/sector_inquiries/new_media/3g/final_report.pdf. See further para 5.119, below.

[330] See speech by Toft (n 327, above). The right of sports associations to sell their broadcasting rights is also affected by the national measures adopted to implement Dir 89/552 as amended by Dir 97/36, OJ 1997 L202/60, as to which see Fleming, 'Television without frontiers: The Broadcasting of Sports Events in Europe' (1997) Ent LR 281. In the UK, the concept of 'listed events' requires that certain major sporting events of general interest will be made available on a non-exclusive basis on both subscription and free-to-air television: Broadcasting Act 1996, ss 97–105 (as amended by

TV rights are regularly offered to the market in a manner which allows potential bidders a genuine chance of winning them and does not weight the process towards the incumbent national broadcaster. Not only the duration but also the scope of the packages of rights may need to be limited, so as to permit several buyers to acquire different rights; and provision should be made that rights not sold by the joint selling entity should revert to the individual clubs (the so-called 'fall-back option') to reduce the risk that those rights are not used. Subject to such qualifications, the efficiencies that result from joint selling may satisfy the requirements of Article 81(3).[331] Cases on selling of media rights by sports leagues have generally focused on the horizontal agreement pooling the rights. However, many of the same principles should apply as regards the terms of a vertical agreement under which a single sporting body that holds all the rights sells them to broadcasters.[332]

UEFA Champions League.   The Commission's approach to joint selling of sports   **5.117**
rights is illustrated by its decision granting exemption under Article 81(3), subject to the imposition of conditions, to UEFA's modified selling arrangements for the media rights to the Champions League.[333] Initially the arrangements provided for UEFA to sell all TV rights in one package to a single broadcaster on an exclusive basis for four years in each Member State. Many rights remained unused because only one or two matches were broadcast live out of a maximum of 16. No new media rights were exploited and football clubs could not exploit any media rights individually themselves. Following negotiations with the Commission, which

---

the Communications Act 2003). See the challenge to the inclusion of FIFA World Cup matches in the UK's list in Case T-33/01 *Infront WM v Commission* [2005] ECR II-5897, on appeal, Case C-125/06P *Commission v Infront WM*, not yet decided.

[331] In some cases, the bodies engaged in joint selling may also hold a collectively dominant position on a relevant market so as to engage Art 82, but an arrangement which satisfies the conditions of Art 81(3) is unlikely to constitute an abuse

[332] Although objections to such an arrangement could be framed in terms of Art 82 where the sporting body holds a dominant position, competition authorities may prefer to approach this under Art 81 since the broadcast channel is often just as, if not more, responsible for any restrictive provisions. See *Polish Football Association and Canal+ v Office for Competition and Consumer Protection*, judgment of the Polish Court for Competition and Consumer Protection, Case XVIAmA 98/06, 14 February 2007, upholding the decision that an 'English clause' in the four-year agreement for exclusive sale of rights to Canal+ violated the Polish equivalent of Art 81 since it placed Canal+ in a favoured position on the retendering of the rights at the end of the four-year period.

[333] *UEFA Champions League*, OJ 2003 L291/25, [2004] 4 CMLR 549. See Toft, 'Football: joint selling of media rights' (2003) 3 EC Competition Policy Newsletter 47. The Commission stated that it will apply the same principles to scrutinise similar national and Europe-wide agreements: *XXIInd Report on Competition Policy* (2002), point 139. Note also the outcome of the Commission's investigation of the arrangements governing Formula One and other international motorracing competitions, which included issues of assignment and collective sale of broadcasting rights: the commercial arrangements were changed so as to reduce the length of contracts to five years for some hosting broadcasters and three years for other broadcasters: IP/01/1523 (30 October 2001).

made clear that the existing rules distorted competition and did not qualify for exemption, the arrangements were changed to ensure that:

(i) all media rights would be sold using a tender procedure in various separate packages with a maximum duration of three years;

(ii) UEFA no longer had an exclusive right to sell any TV rights that it had not managed to sell by a given date;

(iii) UEFA and the individual clubs could exploit in parallel certain live TV rights, deferred TV rights, archive rights and new media rights;

(iv) in addition to UEFA producing a wide selection of League products, football clubs were allowed to produce new club-branded products emphasising individual clubs' action in the UEFA Champions League on their websites, mobile services and DVD.

5.118 **National leagues.** The Commission has also adopted a commitments decision[334] in relation to the joint selling of *Bundesliga* media rights.[335] The Commission identified joint selling as hindering competition between the clubs in terms of prices, innovation and fan services and products. It also led to the league selling the rights in a single bundle or very few packages on an exclusive basis, typically to incumbent broadcasters. The clubs were prevented from dealing independently with television and radio operators and/or sports rights agencies. The Commission also noted the adverse effect on the downstream markets in television and new media since the possibility of supplying football content plays an important role in competition between programme suppliers for advertising revenues and subscribers or pay-per-view customers. The commitments resulted in the rights being offered in several packages in a transparent, non-discriminatory procedure subject to a maximum duration. Clubs would be able to sell home games and exploit unused rights.[336]

5.119 **Licensing rights to mobile telephone networks.** This approach has been applied also in the new media sector, in relation to the provision of sports content

---

[334] ie a decision under Art 9 of Reg 1/2003.

[335] *Joint selling of the media rights to the German Bundesliga*, OJ 2005 L134/46, [2005] 5 CMLR 1715. Note the Commission's approach in Case M.2876 *NewsCorp/Telepiu*, OJ 2004 L110/73, [2004] 5 CMLR 1619 (a condition for clearance of the merger that contracts with football clubs would not exceed two years and that their exclusivity would be limited to direct-to-home transmission).

[336] See also COMP/38.173 *Joint selling of the media rights to the FA Premier League*, decn of 22 March 2006, [2006] 5 CMLR 1396: Commission accepted binding commitments that TV rights would be sold by an open bidding process in six packages; no single broadcaster would be allowed to buy all the packages and the sale would be monitored by a trustee appointed by the Commission. cf Cases no. 2005/MR/2 & 5 *Telenet and BeTV v Belgacom Skynet and Professional Football League*, judgment of 28 June 2006, where the Brussels Court of Appeal upheld the decision of the Belgian Competition Council rejecting a complaint about the sale of all six packages of broadcasting rights to Belgium's main football competition to Belgacom Skynet. The packages had been sold in an open and non-discriminatory manner and were limited to three years' duration; the Court considered the *UEFA* and *Bundesliga* decisions and held that in the circumstances the conditions of Art 81(3) were fulfilled.

over third generation mobile networks ('3G rights').[337] In their report, the Commission and EFTA Surveillance Authority advocate:

> 'a policy that guarantees that 3G rights are exploited to the maximum. The efficiency argument in favour of joint selling of 3G rights cannot be accepted where the selling body fails to find demand in the market for the 3G rights. When collective selling of 3G rights is unsuccessful, the rights should fall back to the individual rights owners to be exploited individually'.[338]

The report also notes the need to address cases where rights to premium sports remain under-exploited through the bundled sales of rights and where there are timing embargoes.[339]

(d) Joint tendering

Generally.   The Community law obligation placed on Member States to seek   **5.120** tenders for all significant public procurement contracts[340] has given rise to a number of cases in the national competition authorities and courts concerning collusive bidding by tenderers. In some cases, the anti-competitive nature of the conduct has been clear. Other cases have considered the advantages and disadvantages of allowing potential competitors to submit joint bids.

Submission of joint bids.   Provided that the cooperation is carried out openly   **5.121** and made known to the tenderee, joint bids by competing companies may not infringe competition law. The position is illustrated by two contrasting French cases. The Minister of Economy, Finance and Industry referred 15 tender bids for road developments to the Conseil de la Concurrence.[341] The Conseil noted that the constitution of interest groups in a tender bid process is not in itself anti-competitive. Such groups can benefit competition if they allow participation

---

[337] Report on the sector inquiry into the provision of sports content over third generation mobile networks (n 329, above).

[338] ibid, para 50.

[339] ibid, paras 38–39, 45–46.

[340] ie under Dir 2004/18/EC, OJ 2004 L134/114.

[341] Decn no. 05-D-24 of 21 May 2005. See also *ÁB-Aegon/Allianz Hungária/Generali-Providencia/OTP Garancia/Uniqua* (Case Vj-149/2003) where the Hungarian Competition Office ('GVH') granted an individual exemption to a consortium agreement among Hungarian insurers bidding to provide State-wide insurance for children and young people. The GVH took the view that it was a restriction of competition if undertakings, which would otherwise be able to participate on their own in a public procurement tender, instead established a consortium. Such a consortium would escape the cartel prohibition only if there are objective economic reasons underlying its creation and there were no such grounds in this case. However, the GVH went on to hold that the consortium satisfied the conditions for exemption under the domestic regime: in particular, it created a significantly larger number of contact points for potential claimants, making it easier and cheaper for young people to use the scheme; and it enabled the parties to allocate their risks more efficiently and thereby provide a very favourable and much lower price compared with general insurance prices.

by companies which would not have been able to make a stand-alone bid or if they enable companies to submit more competitive bids. On the other hand, common bids are anti-competitive when they artificially lower the number of candidates and disguise an agreement on prices or market-sharing.[342] The Conseil accepted the groups' arguments that their formation was justified by the fact that a great number of tender bids were launched at the same time and that starting dates for the works were unknown at the time the bids had to be submitted. These factors made it very difficult for the bidders to anticipate their organisational needs in terms of materials and work force. Interest groups in these circumstances legitimately wanted to share out the workload between the partners. The Conseil also emphasised that members of a group can complement each other if they cover different specialties, have access to different technology and can facilitate access to raw materials or the necessary workforce. Common bids can also spread costs for equipment rental. By contrast, in *Air Liquide Group*[343] the Conseil condemned an agreement between two bidders who presented themselves to the public authority as submitting two independent bids relating to hospital medical gas supply when in fact they had colluded over the contents of their bids.

5.122 **'Cover' bidding.** In *Apex Asphalt and Paving Co Ltd v Office of Fair Trading*,[344] the UK Competition Appeal Tribunal considered a tendering process involving cover bidding, that is where one bidder submits a bid which it knows is higher than the bid submitted by another bidder.[345] The Tribunal considered that the absence of any contact between bidders was fundamental to the tendering process and this was all the more so in a selective tendering process where the number of bidders was limited. Any interference with the independence of the bids could result in significant distortions of competition. The Tribunal held that where a bidder submits a cover bid rather than simply declining to submit a bid at all, this deprives the tenderee of the opportunity of seeking a replacement competitive bid and prevents other contractors wishing to place competitive bids in that particular tender from doing so. It gives the tenderee a false impression of the nature of competition.[346] The Tribunal accepted that there was a presumption that the exchange of information about the level of proposed bids influenced the conduct of the other bidder. The elements of a concerted practice were therefore made out although the proposed cover bidder did not, in the event, submit a tender.

---

[342] cf *Floral*, para 5.108, above.
[343] Decision no. 03-D-01 of 14 January 2003.
[344] *Apex Asphalt* [2005] CAT 4, [2005] CompAR 507; see in particular paras 208 *et seq*, on the nature of the tendering process. See also para 2.047 above.
[345] The motive for cover bidding may be that undertakings invited to tender perceive an advantage in taking part in the competition even if they do not, in fact, want to win that particular contract, in order to ensure that they will be asked by the tenderee to participate in subsequent competitions when they may want the work: see *Apex Asphalt*, above, para 249.
[346] ibid, paras 208–253.

Bidders' reciprocal sub-contracting arrangements. In *Baucont/ÉPKER/* **5.123**
KÉSZ,[347] the Hungarian Competition Office examined an agreement between
two construction companies tendering for a public procurement contract. Under
this agreement each agreed that, if successful, they would involve the other in the
execution of the contract as a sub-contractor. The Office held that such an agreement was liable substantially to reduce the risks inherent in taking part in an open
competition. It was those risks which were intended to prompt each party to
enhance efficiency to the maximum extent possible and to submit the most competitive bids. Although it was not alleged that the parties influenced each other's
bids, or that they had jointly decided who should be the winner, the Office found
that the syndicate agreement seriously reduced the risk of the bidding procedures
and therefore was liable to increase the bidding prices.

(e) Collective buying of goods

In general. Joint purchasing agreements require consideration under Article 81(1) **5.124**
where groups of purchasers (i) agree the prices which they are prepared to pay,
or (ii) agree to purchase wholly or mainly through agreed arrangements. Such
agreements may involve both a horizontal element (that is, the agreement between
the purchasers to buy jointly) and a vertical element (for example, the arrangements made with third party suppliers). The Horizontal Cooperation Guidelines
indicate that the horizontal aspect of such arrangements should be considered
first: if that produces a favourable assessment, it is then necessary to consider the
vertical aspect in accordance with the principles governing vertical agreements
and the possible application of the block exemption for vertical agreements,
Regulation 2790/1999.[348] This Section considers the horizontal aspects of collective buying arrangements. The vertical aspects, along with bilateral vertical agreements between individual suppliers and acquirers, are discussed in Chapter 6,
below.

Collective purchasing of raw materials: the early cases. In the past the **5.125**
Commission tended to regard a collective agreement to purchase raw materials
exclusively through agreed arrangements as falling squarely within the scope of
Article 81(1). The Commission was, however, prepared to grant exemption under
Article 81(3) in certain circumstances, for example where there was a modified
obligation to purchase only a proportion of requirements or where the arrangements led to a more flexible and secure system of supply.[349]

---

[347] *Baucont/ÉPKER/KÉSZ* Case Vj-28/2003; on appeal to the Metropolitan Court of Budapest
(case no. FB. 19.K.764/2005, not yet decided).
[348] Horizontal Cooperation Guidelines (n 301, above) paras 117–118.
[349] *National Sulphuric Acid Association*, OJ 1980 L260/24, [1980] 3 CMLR 429 (obligation to buy
100 per cent of sulphur requirements through the pool reduced to 25 per cent at Commission's behest).

5.126 **Collective purchasing of raw materials: *Gøttrup-Klim.*** In this important case, the Court of Justice held[350] that a provision in the rules of a cooperative purchasing organisation which forbade its members from participating in other forms of organised cooperation in direct competition with it, was not caught by Article 81(1). This was the case so long as the provision was restricted to what was necessary to ensure that the cooperative functions properly and maintains its contractual power in relation to producers. The Court considered that the rules in question were necessary in that case to enable individual farmers to combine their limited individual purchasing power in the face of very powerful world suppliers of fertilisers and plant protection products. Advocate General Tesauro in his fully-reasoned Opinion stated that the earlier cases were best interpreted by reference to the economic circumstances prevailing on the markets in issue in those cases.[351] In *Gøttrup-Klim* the cooperative in question enjoyed a much less powerful market position, both in respect of competing purchasers and in respect of its suppliers. A more qualified application of Article 81(1) was therefore appropriate.[352]

5.127 **Collective priority to domestic sources of supply.** In *Re Sugar Beet*,[353] the Commission condemned an agreement among Belgian sugar refiners which provided for them to give priority to beet growers established in Belgium. The agreement had serious adverse effects on growers on the Belgo-French border who had traditionally supplied their harvest to Belgian refineries. The Commission rejected the argument that the agreement followed the 'logic' of the Community rules which allocated sugar production quotas to each Member State, stating that this was not intended to impede the sales of beet across frontiers.

5.128 **Collective purchasing: economics-based approach.** The Commission's Horizontal Cooperation Guidelines, adopted in December 2000,[354] reflect the development of a more economics-based approach to collective purchasing agreements.[355] The Commission states that such an agreement does not of its

---

See also the 'bark pool' in *Quinine*, JO 1969 L192/5, [1969] CMLR D41 and Case 61/80 *Coöperatieve Stremsel-en Kleursfabriek* [1981] ECR 851, [1982] 1 CMLR 24 (obligation to buy all rennet from the cooperative infringed Art 81(1) and not exempt under Art 81(3)).

[350] Case C-250/92 *Gøttrup-Klim v Dansk Landbrugs Grovvare selskat AmbA* [1994] ECR I-5641, [1996] 4 CMLR 191.

[351] *Gøttrup-Klim*, above, Opinion of AG Tesauro at para 24.

[352] Note also *LIS*, OJ 1999 C330/8 (EFTA Surveillance Authority notice concerning the statutes of an organisation, LIS, comprising 18 Norwegian counties, for the joint purchasing and delivery of medicines for use in county hospitals. The Authority indicated its intention to take a favourable view of the rules after they had been amended so as to permit members to participate in other forms of joint purchasing of medicines. The LIS held about 11 per cent of the market for purchasing pharmaceuticals in Norway but about 66 per cent of the market for pharmaceuticals only used in hospitals).

[353] *Sugar Beet*, OJ 1990 L31/35, [1991] 4 CMLR 629.

[354] Horizontal Cooperation Guidelines, OJ 2001 C3/2: Vol II, App C.12.

[355] See, eg AG Tesauro's Opinion in *Gøttrup-Klim*, discussed at para 5.126, above.

nature fall within Article 81(1) unless it is operated with the object of creating a disguised cartel.[356] Two distinct markets have to be considered: (i) the relevant purchasing market, and (ii) the downstream selling market (or markets) where the participants in the agreement are active as sellers (ie as re-sellers if the goods concerned are finished products).[357] If the parties to the joint purchasing agreement are not competitors in the downstream market, Article 81(1) is unlikely to apply to the agreement unless they have a very strong position on the purchasing market.[358] On the other hand, if they have market power in the downstream market, it is less likely that the cost savings achieved by the joint purchasing will be passed on to consumers; and the higher the level of that market power, the greater will be their incentive to coordinate their behaviour as sellers. The Notice sets out market share thresholds below which the agreement is unlikely to cause concern. Other factors such as the market structure (for example, the number and size of other competitors) and any countervailing power of suppliers on the purchasing market must also be considered.[359] In particular, a joint purchasing agreement between small- and medium-sized enterprises to achieve volume discounts or economies of scale obtained by their larger competitors may be pro-competitive; and if it falls within Article 81(1) at all, it should benefit from the application of Article 81(3).[360]

(f) Collective buying of intellectual property and media rights

Collective purchasing in the audiovisual media. The Commission has developed its policy in this area over a number of years through a number of 'flagship' **5.129**

---

[356] Horizontal Cooperation Guidelines, para 124.

[357] ibid, paras 119–122.

[358] Note that as regards cross-border groups, if the relevant downstream market is national, the members are not competitors on those markets and the agreement is therefore unlikely to restrict competition. See generally Lücking, 'Retailer Power in EC Competition Law' in Hawk (ed), *2000 Fordham Corp. L. Inst.* (2001).

[359] ibid, paras 128–131.

[360] ibid, para 116 and examples at paras 136, 138. The only EC decisions concerning retail groups are relatively old: *Intergroup Trading (Spar)*, OJ 1975 L212/23, [1975] 2 CMLR D14; see also *Socemas*, JO 1968 L201/4, [1968] CMLR D28. But see *Legemiddel Innkjøp Samarbeid ('LIS')*, *EFTA Surveillance Authority Annual Reports 1999*, point 5.1.3.3 and *2001*, point 5.3.4: negative clearance-type comfort letter under Art 53 EEA for joint purchasing of medicines for use in 17 Norwegian county hospitals, accounting for 66 per cent of all Norwegian hospital purchasing and involving common invitations to tender, after LIS statutes amended to allow member hospitals the option to make their own purchasing arrangements; *Films & Kino*, *EFTA Surveillance Authority Annual Report 2003*, p 51 and Press Release PR(03)33 (12 November 2003): negative clearance-type comfort letter for joint purchasing from film distributors by smaller Norwegian cinemas (this replaced a previous agreement which had involved joint selling as well as joint buying covering all commercial distribution of films to cinemas in Norway and which was found to infringe Art 53 EEA: n 301, above).

cases relating to the joint purchasing of rights to show films and sports on television.[361] As a matter of policy, the Commission has stated that:

> 'the joint acquisition or distribution of television rights, which in principle are covered by Article [81(1)] of the [EC] Treaty, could be exempted if they allow rationalisation, provided that they do not prevent market access for competitors.'[362]

The Commission's approach to collective purchasing of rights to sporting events now reflects the increasing price that such rights can command.[363]

5.130 **The Eurovision System.** The European Broadcasting Union ('EBU') is an association of national broadcasters who act collectively in the acquisition of rights to televise international sports events together. The EBU also operates a scheme ('the Eurovision System') for the exchange of programmes between its members. The case raised far-reaching questions concerning the future of television in the context of the rapidly developing market for commercial television making use of satellite and cable transmission. The combined purchasing power of the national broadcasters was considered by the Commission to restrict competition: (i) between EBU members insofar as they transmitted to the same national audiences (as is the case in Belgium, France, Denmark, Germany and the United Kingdom); and (ii) in relation to non-EBU members. However, the Commission recognised considerable public interest benefits in the Eurovision System that provided free exchange and access (and particularly benefited the smaller public service broadcasters). Following an extensive investigation and negotiations with the parties, the Commission therefore decided[364] to grant a five-year exemption. This was made subject to a detailed access scheme whereby individual EBU members were required to give third parties access to the acquired rights under specified minimum conditions (eg relating to live access, specified periods of delay and news access). The Commission also noted developments in the cooperation between *commercial* broadcasters but indicated that it was not yet able to evaluate how those would be assessed under the competition rules. However, the decision was annulled by the Court of First Instance[365] on two fundamental grounds: that the

---

361 *Film purchases by German television stations*, OJ 1989 L284/36, [1990] 4 CMLR 841; *Screensport/EBU Members*, OJ 1991 L63/32, [1992] 5 CMLR 273 (see *Eurosport Mark III*, OJ 1993 C76/8); *Astra*, OJ 1993 L20/23, [1994] 5 CMLR 226.

362 *XXth Report on Competition Policy* (1990), point 82. See more recently *XXXIst Report on Competition Policy* (2001), points 165–169; *XXXIInd Report on Competition Policy* (2002), points 134–153 and the discussion of the Commission's policy in relation to collective selling of such rights: paras 5.111 *et seq*, above.

363 See the Commission's 'orientation document' *Broadcasting of sports events and competition law* (n 328, above) para VI(l)–(2). The Commission notes that the removal of joint selling arrangements will minimise the need for collective purchasing.

364 *EBU/Eurovision System*, OJ 1993 L179/23, [1995] 4 CMLR 56.

365 Cases T-528/93, etc, *Métropole Télévision v Commission* [1996] ECR II-649, [1996] 5 CMLR 386, paras 102 and 123. Appeal lodged (Case C-320/96 P) on 30 September 1996 but removed

criteria for membership of the EBU were too vague and imprecise to enable the Commission to assess whether those criteria were indispensable within the meaning of Article 81(3); and that it was a misinterpretation of Article 81(3) to treat fulfilment of a particular public mission as a criterion for granting exemption.[366]

Eurovision: **subsequent proceedings.**   The Commission subsequently took a **5.131** further decision granting exemption to the Eurovision system in the light of the changed circumstances in the broadcasting sector.[367] This exemption was annulled by the Court of First Instance and the appeal by the EBU against that annulment was dismissed by the Court of Justice.[368] The case concerned the rules within the European Broadcasting Union governing the joint acquisition of sport television rights, the sharing of jointly acquired sport television rights, the exchange of the signal for sporting events and the sub-licensing scheme for contractual access to Eurovision sports rights for third parties. The Court of First Instance found that the Eurovision system led to two types of restriction:

(i) joint acquisition and sharing of television rights to sporting events and the exchange of the signal restricts or eliminates competition among EBU members which are competitors on both the upstream and downstream markets. The restriction arose because of the structure of the market, the market position of the EBU and the degree of vertical integration of the EBU and its members.[369]

---

from register by Order on 14 November 2000 (OJ 2001 C118/27). *BSB/Football Association* concerned the joint acquisition of exclusive rights to English Football Association matches for four years by BSkyB (formerly BSB) and the BBC; after the removal of a similar exclusivity for foreign football matches, the Commission stated that exemption was justified to facilitate BSkyB's entry into the market: *XXIIIrd Report on Competition Policy* (1993), p 459.

366 Following the annullment of the exemption, Métropole Télévision reapplied to join Eurovision and was rejected. It then complained to the Commission which rejected the complaint. The CFI then annulled the rejection of the complaint on the grounds of inadequate reasoning and a failure to deal properly with the complaint: Case T-206/99 *Métropole Télévision v Commission* [2001] ECR II-1057.

367 *Eurovision*, OJ 2000 L151/18, [2000] 5 CMLR 650.

368 Cases T-185/00, etc, *Métropole Télévision (M6) v Commission* [2002] ECR II–3805, [2003] 4 CMLR 707 (appeal dismissed, Case C-470/02P, *Union européene de radio-télévision (UER) v Commission,*Order of 27 September 2004, OJ 2004 C314/2).

369 *Métropole Télévision (M6) v Commission*, above, para 68. See also *GIE Sport Libre*, Paris Court of Appeal (1st ch), 4 June 2002, BOCCRF no. 12, 22 August 2002, upholding the decision of the Conseil de la Concurrence imposing interim measures on the main French radio stations which had combined in an economic interest group called 'Sport libre' to which they granted exclusive rights to negotiate the purchase of sporting rights, in particular in relation to the football World Cup. The Court held that the strict terms of this collective purchasing arrangement, whereby any member wishing to acquire rights individually had to withdraw from the group, with two months' prior notice and the loss of all rights negotiated collectively, were likely to dissuade a member to leave the GIE and thus threatened the commercial autonomy of the members. (The radio stations then reached a commercial settlement with the complainant and the Conseil did not pursue the case further.)

(ii) the system led to a foreclosure effect with respect to third parties since the sports rights are generally sold on an exclusive basis and non-EBU members are refused access. This foreclosure effect could not be remedied by the sub-licensing scheme.

The Court held that the Commission had committed a manifest error of assessment in concluding that the sub-licensing scheme meant that competition was not eliminated in respect of a substantial part of the product market and therefore annulled the decision granting exemption.

5.132 **Exclusivity clauses in rights exploitation agreements.** In *TPS*[370] the Commission considered a partnership set up by television production companies to enter the market for pay-TV in France. TPS was a new entrant into a market traditionally dominated by the established operator Canal+. The agreement included a non-compete clause whereby the six partners promised not to acquire interests in other companies active in the market. There was also a special interest channels clause according to which they promised to give TPS first refusal for any special interest channel content they produced and an exclusivity clause whereby they promised to broadcast all their general interest material for pay-TV through TPS. The Commission granted negative clearance to the non-compete clause and granted a three-year exemption under Article 81(3) for the special interest and exclusivity clauses. The Court of First Instance[371] upheld the finding that the exclusivity clause restricted competition, holding that the effect of the clause was that competitors to TPS did not have access to attractive programming produced by the six partners in TPS. It also upheld the Commission's conclusion that the special interest channels clause and the exclusivity clauses were not ancillary restrictions essential to the operation of the partnership and that they should be exempted only for three years.

8. Trade Associations, Cooperatives and Exhibitions

5.133 **Introduction.** Several issues considered in this Section have close affinities to the issues considered in the context of collective exclusive dealing in Section 7, above.[372] Although trade associations and cooperative bodies are commonplace in many industries and can often be regarded as beneficial complements to a competitive market, there are obvious risks to the competitive process where

---

[370] *TPS*, OJ 1999 L90/6, [1999] 5 CMLR 168.

[371] Case T-112/99 *Métropole Télévision (M6) v Commission* [2001] ECR II-2459, [2001] 5 CMLR 1236.

[372] See generally Temple Lang, 'Trade Associations and Self Regulation', in Hawk (ed), *1984 Fordham Corp. L. Inst.*, 613; Watson and Williams, 'The Application of the EEC Competition Rules to Trade Associations' (1988) 8 YEL 121.

membership rules act as a significant barrier to entry to new competitors or where membership provides a vehicle for collusive conduct. Clear examples of these risks have already been described earlier in this Chapter.[373] This Section concentrates on a number of features of trade associations and cooperatives and their treatment under Article 81: membership rules; common standards; joint marketing; and trade exhibitions and auctions.

(a) Membership rules

Membership of trade associations and cooperative organisations.   Membership   **5.134** of such organisations can be an essential pre-condition for competition in a particular market. For example, access to the auctions selling 90 per cent of Brittany cauliflowers, artichokes and early potatoes was restricted to those dealers who: (i) established a local packing centre (even though most of the vegetables were auctioned pre-packed), and (ii) were members of the local dealer association, admission to which could be easily blocked by the existing members.[374] Similarly in *Dansk Pelsdyravlerforening*,[375] the applicant was an association of Danish fur breeders which organised auctions through which the majority of mink and fox skins in Denmark were sold. The Court of First Instance held that in the light of the width of the loyalty obligation imposed, and the strong position of the applicant on the market, the effect of the obligation was to render it extremely difficult for third parties to enter the market. The loyalty obligation therefore fell within Article 81(1).

The Commission's attitude to membership rules.   Generally, the Commission   **5.135** requires the rules of admission to membership to be based on objective criteria, with a proper appeal procedure in the event of refusal.[376] The Court of First

---

[373] See, eg the position of Cembureau in Cases C-204/00P, etc, *Aalborg Portland v Commission* [2004] ECR I-123, [2005] 4 CMLR 251, para 282, discussed at para 5.085, above; *Coöperatieve Stremsel-en Kleursfabriek* (n 350, above), para 102; *Gøttrup Klim* (n 350, above) discussed at para 5.126, above; *EBU/Eurovision System*, para 5.130, above (collective purchasing).

[374] *Cauliflowers* (n 288, above), D66; cf *SWIFT, XXVIIth Report on Competition Policy* (1997), p 120 (worldwide cooperative between banks for the supply of data communication and processing; the Commission suspended its investigation under Arts 81 and 82 on the basis that access to SWIFT's services would be granted to 'any institution in the European Union which provides cross-border payment services to the public and fulfils the criteria laid down by the European Monetary Institute (or any successor organisation) for admission to domestic payment systems').

[375] Case T-61/89 *Dansk Pelsdyravlerforening v Commission* [1992] ECR II-1931 (on appeal from *Hudson's Bay/Dansk Pelsdyravlerforening*, OJ 1988 L316/43, [1989] 4 CMLR 340). This case has obvious affinities to the collective buying and selling cases discussed in Section 7, above. In his Opinion in *Gøttrup-Klim* (n 350, above), AG Tesauro suggested (at n 26 to his Opinion) that some of the CFI's statements of law were excessively wide.

[376] See *Sarabex, VIIIth Report on Competition Policy* (1978), points 35–37, [1979] 1 CMLR 262, discussed at para 5.138, below; *The London Sugar Futures Market Limited* and similar cases, OJ 1985 L369/25, etc, [1988] 4 CMLR 138; *Retel 1988*, OJ 1991 C121/2, [1991] 4 CMLR 487 (negative clearance of rules for recognition of private telecommunications and data-processing equipment

Instance has now made clear that in order for the Commission to be able to assess whether membership rules were indispensable within the meaning of Article 81(3), it is necessary for the rules to be objective and sufficiently determinate, and capable of non-discriminatory application.[377]

5.136 **Unreasonable refusal of membership.** Analogous to a boycott is a refusal to admit a new member to the agreement or association in question. Where the agreement or association controls access to some important economic activity, unreasonable refusal to admit to membership may, in itself, infringe Article 81(1).[378] Thus, for example, in *Cauliflowers*[379] the Commission held that Article 81(1) was infringed. The agreement did not qualify for exemption since the conditions of admission were neither reasonable nor objective.

5.137 **Restrictions on ceasing membership.** The Commission has also expressed concern where members are prevented from leaving an association.[380] The effect of such restrictions in some circumstances may be to prevent members of cooperative organisations developing legitimate competitive opportunities where such conduct would not undermine the benefits derived from the cooperative's activities on behalf of its members. In the context of agricultural cooperatives, where a large number of small undertakings act collectively to sell their produce or acquire their supplies, the Community Courts recognise that it may be essential to the cohesion and effectiveness of the cooperative arrangement that members should be required to deal only through the collective body. Complex issues arise in balancing the interests of the smaller members (who derive legitimate benefits from the collective sale or purchase) and of the larger members (who may wish to trade independently and thereby to create a more competitive buying or selling process). In *Oude Luttikhuis*[381] the Court of Justice indicated that rules requiring payment of 'excessive fees' on withdrawal from a cooperative could fall within the

---

installers). cf the *IATA* cases (nns 299 and 300, above); and the Commission's insistence on an appeal procedure on exclusion from a trade exhibition, para 5.154, below, and on an admissions procedure in cases of selective distribution, para 6.098, below. The Commission's Notice on the application of the EC competition rules to cross-border credit transfers, OJ 1995 C251/3, [1995] 5 CMLR 551, requires cross-border credit transfer systems to be open to further members and to have objectively justified membership rules where they represent an 'essential facility' for a bank to compete on the relevant market.

[377] Cases T-528/93, etc, *Métropole Télévision* (n 365, above) para 102, annulling the Commission's decision in *EBU/Eurovision System*: see further para 5.130, above.

[378] cf the Commission's analogous policy regarding agreements on technical standards, para 5.139, below; patent pools, para 9.128, below; trade exhibitions, paras 5.152 *et seq*, below; and in selective distribution systems paras 6.086 *et seq*, below. See also *Sarabex*, para 5.138, below; and cf the amendments required by the Commission in the *IATA* cases, para 5.105, above.

[379] *Cauliflowers*, OJ 1978 L21/23, [1978] 1 CMLR D66. See also *Dansk Pelsdyravlerforening* (n 375, above).

[380] For shipping liner conferences see para 5.033, above.

[381] Case C-399/93 *Oude Luttikhuis v Coberco* [1995] ECR I-4515, [1996] 5 CMLR 178, para 15.

scope of Article 81(1). In *Florimex*[382] the Court of First Instance found that fees levied by a powerful cooperative on direct supplies by non-members to wholesalers established on its premises, that were not made through its auction facilities, could operate anti-competitively by restricting the freedom of members to leave the cooperative and that they were not justified by the interests of the cooperative in maintaining its cohesion.

Membership of regulated bodies.   In *Sarabex*,[383] refusal to admit to member-   **5.138**
ship occurred in a sphere subject to regulation, namely foreign exchange dealing in the City of London. Sarabex complained to the Commission that it was unable to trade in scheduled currencies, which were reserved to members of the FECDBA, a dealing association recognised by the Bank of England. Following the Commission's intervention, the rules for the recognition of foreign exchange brokers in London were revised under the aegis of the Bank of England, recognition being based on objective criteria with provision for appeal to the Panel on Takeovers and Mergers.

(b) Common standards

Agreements on technical standards.   A particular type of horizontal agreement   **5.139**
which may limit production or divide markets is an agreement on technical standards. Such an agreement is likely to infringe Article 81(1) if it prevents the parties from selling differentiated products, or limits technical development or is used to obstruct imports. However, in certain circumstances the adoption of common standards may be desirable; many agreements on technical standards do not infringe Article 81(1) and of those that do fall within Article 81(1), many fulfil the criteria for the application of Article 81(3).

Agreements on standards outside Article 81(1).   Article 81(1) is not normally   **5.140**
infringed where participation in the setting of standards is unrestricted and transparent, and the parties are free to diverge from the agreed standards, or to make or market other products which do not conform to the standards.[384] Similarly, Article 81(1) is not normally infringed by an agreement whereby the use of a

---

[382] Cases T-70 & 71/92 *Florimex and VGB v Commission* [1997] ECR II-693, [1997] 5 CMLR 769, [1997] All ER (EC) 788; appeals dismissed, Cases C-265/97P *VBA v Florimex* [2000] ECR I-2061, [2001] 5 CMLR 1343, and Case C-266/97P *VBA v VGB and Florimex* [2000] ECR I-2135.

[383] *VIIIth Report on Competition Policy* (1978), points 35–37, [1979] 1 CMLR 262 (an inquiry under both Arts 81 and 82). See also the decisions on commodity markets (n 298, above).

[384] Horizontal Cooperation Guidelines (n 354, above), para 163. See, eg Stack, *XXVIIIth Report on Competition Policy* (1998), p 153 (company set up by major IT companies within and outside the EC with the task of defining specifications and standard for components and then certifying compliance; but no obligation on members to buy certified components and membership open to any interested company); COMP/38.401 *EMC/European Cement Producers*, decn of 28 September 2005 (complaint about cement standard rejected because producers were not obliged to comply with it).

particular quality mark is restricted to products which meet certain agreed technical standards, provided that the mark is freely available, that the parties are free to manufacture products with different characteristics, and that the agreement does not otherwise restrict competition.[385] Article 81(1) is not infringed if the standards are objectively justified, for example, for consumer protection, or do not significantly affect competition.[386] In industries characterised by competition over networks operated independently of or jointly by the competitors, such as the telecommunications and energy markets, the Commission is prepared to accept that common standards are inevitable and operate in the interests of consumers, provided that the competitive process is safeguarded.[387] Standards adopted by recognised standards bodies which are based on non-discriminatory, open and transparent procedures generally do not fall within Article 81(1).[388] A horizontal agreement which limits differentiation or technical development by the restrictive use of technical standards may fall within Article 81(1).[389] But where the agreement

---

[385] *VVVF*, JO 1969 L168/22, [1970] CMLR Dl. See also *TÜV/Cenelec*, XXVIIIth Report on Competition Policy (1998), p 159 (commonly agreed 'Keymark' of conformity with technical standards for household electrical appliances).

[386] See, eg *Industrieverband Solnhofener Natursteinplatten*, OJ 1980 L318/32, [1981] 2 CMLR 308. The Commission did not object to rules directed towards 'quality control and observance of building regulations and standards'. See also the Art 19(3) Notices under Reg 17 in *Pasta Manufacturers*, OJ 1986 C266/5, [1986] 3 CMLR 639 (agreement on standard ingredients) and *Retel 1988*, OJ 1991 C121/2, [1991] 4 CMLR 487 (recognition rules for installers of telecommunications and data-processing equipment based on objective criteria). Note also Cases C-215 & 216/96 *Bagnasco v Banco Popolare di Novara* [1999] ECR I-135, [1999] 4 CMLR 624, and the decisions on various standard arrangements in the banking sector (para 5.041, above). In *Video Cassette Recorders*, OJ 1978 L47/42, [1978] 2 CMLR 160 the Commission refused to exempt an agreement which locked VCR manufacturers into Philips' technical standards to the exclusion of competing systems. See also *IGR Stereo Television*, XIth Report on Competition Policy (1981), point 94; *IGR*, XIVth Report on Competition Policy (1984), point 92; *EACEM*, XXVIIIth Report on Competition Policy (1998), p 152: agreement between 16 major manufacturers of TV sets and video recorders to introduce only products that consume reduced level of power; Commission found that the energy-saving and environmental benefits justified exemption.

[387] See, eg *The GSM MoU standard international roaming agreement*, XXVIIth Report on Competition Policy (1997), p 115 (standard agreement to enable mobile phone users in different countries to use the networks in other countries; the Commission approved the system on condition that consumers were free to take out subscriptions cross-border and that information exchange between operators did not go beyond what was necessary for the 'roaming agreements').

[388] eg bodies recognised under Dir 98/34, OJ 1998 L204/37. See Horizontal Cooperation Guidelines (n 354, above) para 163 and example at para 176.

[389] Horizontal Cooperation Guidelines (n 354, above) paras 166–167. See, eg *Transocean Marine Paint Association* JO 1967 163/10, [1967] CMLR D9, (exemption under Art 81(3) renewed subject to conditions: OJ 1974 L19/18, [1974] 1 CMLR Dll; one of the conditions annulled in Case 17/74 *Transocean Marine Paint v Commission* [1974] ECR 1063, [1974] 2 CMLR 459); further renewed, OJ 1980 L39/73, [1980] 1 CMLR 694; and OJ 1988 L351/40, [1989] 4 CMLR 621). See also Case 246/86 *Belasco v Commission* [1989] ECR 2181, [1991] 4 CMLR 96; *Uniform Eurocheques*, OJ 1989 L36/16, [1989] 4 CMLR 907 (guidelines for standard production and finishing of cheques and cheque cards); *Dutch banks*, OJ 1989 L253/1, [1990] 4 CMLR 768; *P & I Clubs*, OJ 1999 L125/12, [1999] 5 CMLR 646, and see para 12.174, below for insurance pools generally.

on standards affects only a minor part of the relevant market, it will have no appreciable effect on competition and accordingly fall outside Article 81(1).[390]

Use of technical standards to hinder imports. Article 81(1) is infringed if **5.141** technical standards are used to obstruct imports. Thus, in *IAZ*[391] the Belgian Association Nationale des Services d'Eau (Anseau) agreed with Belgian manufacturers and sole importers of washing machines and dishwashers to ensure that all appliances sold in Belgium bore a conformity label signifying that they complied with certain technical requirements laid down by Belgian law. However, the conformity labels were made available only to Belgian manufacturers or sole importers, thereby making parallel imports into Belgium virtually impossible. The Court of Justice upheld the fines imposed by the Commission. Similarly, if imports are obstructed by standards laid down by national law or by public bodies, such standards may be open to attack under the rules on free movement of goods in Article 28 of the Treaty. If undertakings have participated in the setting of the standards, it is possible that Article 81 may also be infringed. The maintenance of national quality standards cannot be invoked to justify restrictions on exports[392] or prices.[393]

Common standards additional to a national statutory scheme: *SCK and* 5.142 *FNK.* The issue of common standards was considered in detail by the Commission and the Court of First Instance in *SCK and FNK*.[394] This case concerned the rules of two trade associations in the Dutch mobile crane market, whose members accounted for between 37 and 40 per cent of the Dutch market. In relation to SCK, its members were required to hire only cranes certified by SCK.[395] Although the associations vigorously defended the rules as necessary to maintain industry standards, both the Commission and the Court of First Instance found that they fell within the scope of Article 81(1) and could not be justified for the purposes of Article 81(3). The rules, which applied throughout the Netherlands, were found to have a materially restrictive effect on competing crane operators, including those from Belgium. Neither the Commission nor the Court

---

390 Horizontal Cooperation Guidelines (n 354, above) para 164.

391 Cases 96/82, etc, *IAZ v Commission* [1983] ECR 3369, [1984] 3 CMLR 276. See also *Belgian Central Heating*, JO 1972 L264/22, [1972] CMLR D130 (Belgian manufacturers and installers agreed *inter alia* to deal solely in equipment approved by the trade association).

392 *Pabst & Richarz/BNIA*, OJ 1976 L231/24, [1976] 2 CMLR D63.

393 *AROW/BNIC*, OJ 1982 L379/1, [1983] 2 CMLR 240; Case 123/83 *BNIC v Clair* [1985] ECR 391, [1985] 2 CMLR 430.

394 *Stichting Certificatie Kraanverhuurbedrijf and Federatie van Nederlandse Kraanverhuurbedrijven*, OJ 1995 L312/79, [1995] 4 CMLR 565; on appeal Cases T-213/95 & T-18/96 *SCK and FNK v Commission* [1998] ECR II-1739, [1997] 4 CMLR 259.

395 The case in relation to FNK concerned the setting of recommended rates for its members and was condemned as a price-fixing arrangement for which a fine of 11.5 million ECU was imposed: see n 63, above.

of First Instance was satisfied that the private certification system had been shown to be necessary having regard to the public monitoring system operated by the Dutch authorities in accordance with Dutch law. This Dutch law itself in part implemented a Community directive on the approximation of the laws of the Member States relating to machinery.[396] The mere fact that the private scheme laid down additional requirements and was more frequently monitored by SCK did not demonstrate that the statutory scheme was inadequate.

5.143 **Use of standard forms, etc.** A trade association may make available to its members a standard form of contract for the members to use or not as they see fit. There should be no anti-competitive effect merely from the use of standardised printed forms unless their use is combined with an understanding or tacit agreement on uniform prices, rebates or conditions of sale. A trade association's standard terms relating, *inter alia*, to price changes, ownership and risk, terms of payment, warranty, liability, advertising, after-sales service and settlement of disputes, have been held 'to regulate important secondary aspects of competition' and to 'reinforce' the restrictive effects of a price-fixing agreement among the members of the association.[397] As in other areas, the Commission has traditionally taken a more lenient approach to pooling arrangements in the financial services sector, in particular in relation to settlement arrangements in the banking and insurance sector.[398] However, there are signs that this is changing. In 2005, the Commission accepted undertakings from the International Underwriting Association of London and the Lloyd's Market Association providing for changes in the way standard clauses are drawn up for aviation insurance policies. This followed an investigation into the degree of coordination on the London market, introducing greater transparency and involvement of customers.[399] At the time of writing, the Commission is conducting a sector inquiry under Article 17 of Regulation 1/2003 into business insurance, looking at the extent of cooperation among insurers and insurance associations on matters such as setting standard conditions.[400]

5.144 **Agreements on standards under Article 81(3).** If a bona fide agreement on technical standards falls within Article 81(1), it may benefit from the application of Article 81(3) if sufficient countervailing benefits can be demonstrated.[401]

---

[396] Dir 89/392, OJ 1989 L183/9.

[397] *Vimpoltu*, OJ 1983 L200/44, [1983] 3 CMLR 619.

[398] See paras 5.041 *et seq*, above, with regard to banking and para 12.173, below, with regard to insurance. See also the insurance cases summarised at *XXVIth Report on Competition Policy* (1996), pp 131–132.

[399] Press Release IP/05/361 (23 March 2005).

[400] Commission Decn of 13 June 2005; see at http://ec.europa.eu/comm/competition/antitrust/others/sector_inquiries/financial_services/decision_insurance_en.pdf.

[401] eg *Transocean Marine Paint Association* (n 389, above); *X/Open Group*, OJ 1987 L35/36, [1988] 4 CMLR 542 (five-year exemption granted for agreement among computer systems manufacturers to develop 'open' industry standard for software). For technical requirements imposed on

The Horizontal Cooperation Guidelines state that the Commission generally takes a positive approach to 'agreements that promote economic interpenetration of the common market or encourage the development of new markets and improved supply conditions.' However, for Article 81(3) to apply, the relevant standard must be set in a transparent manner involving an appreciable proportion of the industry; it should not limit innovation, and the necessary information to apply the standard must be available to anyone wishing to enter the market.[402] Under the enabling Regulation 2821/71,[403] the Commission has power to grant block exemption to agreements which have as their object 'the application of standards or types', but that power has not been exercised. However, the block exemption in the insurance sector, Regulation 358/2003, exempts agreements on technical specifications for security devices and for rules to approve firms that carry out their installation and maintenance.[404]

Agreements protecting the environment. The Horizontal Cooperation **5.145** Guidelines[405] include as a separate category agreements whereby the parties undertake to achieve the reduction of pollution or other environmental objectives (in particular as set out in Article 174 of the Treaty) and indicates when the Commission is likely to regard such agreements as falling within Article 81(1). The Commission generally takes a favourable approach to such an agreement, having regard to the objectives in Article 174 of the Treaty.[406] But the benefits of

---

licensees of industrial property rights, see paras 9.101 *et seq*, below. The position has been complicated in recent years by the widespread use by the Community itself of common technical standards as a central element in the programme of harmonisation aimed at creating the Single Market (see, eg the Commission Communication, Standardisation in the European Economy, OJ 1992 C96/2 at 5: 'European standardisation. . . is recognised as a fundamental instrument for achieving the full economic benefit of a single market'). See also the Notice on the application of the EC competition rules to cross-border credit transfers, OJ 1995 C251/3, [1995] 5 CMLR 551, paras 30–34, for the Commission's views on the applicability of Art 81(1) and Art 81(3) to agreements between participants in cross-border credit transfer systems on common operational standards: see also *XXVth Report on Competition Policy* (1995), points 47–48; *Canon/Kodak*, OJ 1997 C330/1O, [1999] 4 CMLR 318 (Art 19(3) Notice under Reg 17 in respect of agreements, after they had been amended, for development and licensing of new advanced photographic system (APS) between major film and camera producers); and the cases concerning common standards adopted in the rules of the Association of Norwegian Insurance Companies as regards security devices and the approval procedure for installers; as regards determination of the value of building materials; and for repairs for motor vehicle damage; in each case the EFTA Surveillance Authority issued exemption-type comfort letters after the agreements were amended to make the standards non-binding and applicable on a non-discriminatory basis: *EFTA Surveillance Authority Annual Reports 1998*, para 5.1.2.2.4; *2002*, para 6.2.6.

[402] Horizontal Cooperation Guidelines (n 354, above) paras 169 *et seq*; and see example at para 178.

[403] Reg 2821/71, OJ 1971 L285/46: Vol II, App C.2, Art 1(l)(a).

[404] For discussion of Reg 358/2003 exempting agreements relating to the introduction, installation and maintenance of security devices in the insurance sector, see para 12.178, below.

[405] Section 7: paras 179, *et seq*.

[406] Apart from the general objective of 'preserving, protecting and improving the quality of the environment', the most relevant objective here appears to be the 'prudent and rational utilisation of natural resources.'

the agreement must outweigh the costs in terms of lessened competition and any compliance costs.[407] In *CECED*,[408] the Commission granted an exemption to an agreement between major domestic appliance manufacturers, together holding 90 per cent of the EEA market, to phase out production of washing machines that do not meet energy efficiency criteria, thereby reducing CO_2 emissions. The Commission considered that the environmental benefits for society met the criteria for exemption even if there were no benefits for individual purchasers.[409]

(c) Joint marketing

5.146 **In general.** The main kinds of horizontal agreement relating to advertising and promotion requiring consideration under Article 81(1) are those which (i) restrict undertakings' freedom to advertise; or (ii) enable undertakings to engage in joint advertising or promotion. Agreements or concerted practices which restrict the ability of undertakings to advertise represent an important restriction on competitive freedom and may therefore infringe Article 81(1).[410] The use of advertising

---

[407] Horizontal Cooperation Guidelines, OJ 2001 C3/2: Vol II, App C.12, paras 193–194.

[408] *CECED*, OJ 2000 L187/47, [2000] 5 CMLR 635.

[409] See also *CECED: dishwashers and water heaters*, Press release IP/01/1659 (26 November 2001) (issue of an exemption-type comfort letter for horizontal agreements relating to the energy efficiency of household dishwashers and water heaters); and see the note on this case by Martinez-Lopez, (2002) 1 EC Competition Policy Newsletter 50; *EACEM* (n 386, above) (agreement between leading suppliers of televisions and video recorders to reduce energy consumption in standby mode; the Commission considered that the restrictive effects of the scheme were essential to achieving the environmental and energy-saving benefits; environmental benefits for society met the criteria for exemption even if there were no benefits for individual purchasers); cf *CEMEP*, Press Release IP/00/508 (23 May 2000) (negative clearance-type comfort letter issued for agreement between 80 per cent, of manufacturers of standardised low voltage motors, which introduced efficiency classifications and joint targets but did not impose individual obligations). See also *ZVEI/Arge Bat*, OJ 1998 C171/13, [1999] 4 CMLR 526 (German trade association agreements for cooperation in the disposal of pollutants contained in used batteries). The Commission has exempted arrangements between mobile operators to cooperate by site sharing. Where the parties retain independent control of their core networks site sharing was found not to restrict competition and considered to be beneficial for environmental and health reasons: *O2 UK Limited/T-Mobile UK Limited - UK network sharing agreement*, OJ 2003 L200/59, [2004] 4 CMLR 1401; *T-Mobile Deutschland/O2 Germany - Network-sharing Rahmenvertrag*, OJ 2004 L75/32 (on appeal, Case T-328/03 *O2 (Germany) GmbH & Co v Commission* [2006] ECR II-1231, [2006] 5 CMLR 258, CFI annulled distinct part of the decn that cooperation on national roaming fell within Art 81(1): see para 7.127, below).

[410] See, eg *Groupements des Fabricants de Papiers Peints de Belgique*, OJ 1974 L237/3, [1974] 2 CMLR D102 (agreement prevented members of association from seeking competitive advantage through own advertising: abandoned on appeal in Case 73/74 *Papiers Peints v Commission* [1975] ECR 1491, [1976] 1 CMLR 589); *Boat Equipment, Xth Report on Competition Policy* (1980), point 119 (Belgian manufacturers persuaded Belgian magazine not to carry advertisements for British boat equipment); *FEG and TU*, OJ 2000 L39/1, [2000] 4 CMLR 1208 (decision by Dutch association of electrotechnical equipment wholesalers prohibiting members from advertising specially-reduced or loss leader prices: upheld on appeal Cases T-5 & 6/00 *Nederlandse Federative Vereniging voor de Groothandel op Elektrotechnisch Gebied and Technische Unie v Commission* [2003] ECR II-5761, [2004] 5 CMLR 969; further appeals dismissed, Case C-105/04P *FEG v Commission*, Case

to obstruct imports may also infringe Article 81 (1).[411] Agreements not to use particular trade marks may infringe Article 81(1), at least if they go beyond the minimum necessary to protect the mark and avoid confusion to the public.[412]

Joint advertising.   In the Horizontal Cooperation Guidelines, joint advertising   **5.147** is treated along with agreements on joint selling or joint distribution as part of a broad category of 'commercialisation agreements'.[413] The Commission's main concerns as regards an agreement jointly to advertise appear to be whether operation of the agreement may lead to a coordination of pricing strategy, or whether the sharing of advertising costs means that a significant input into the parties' final product cost becomes common, thereby limiting the scope for price competition.[414] If the agreement does not involve price-fixing, the Commission states that it will only be subject to Article 81(1) if the parties have 'some degree of market power'.[415]

Milchförderungsfonds.   This decision[416] concerned a 'Milk Promotion Fund'   **5.148** set up by the German dairy industry and financed by a voluntary levy on each litre of milk delivered to dairies. The resulting funds were used *inter alia* to promote the export of milk and other dairy products both to other Member States and non-Member countries. The methods of promotion involved both subsidised sales and brand advertising campaigns. The Commission held that both aspects of the arrangements distorted competition contrary to Article 81(1) by artificially strengthening the position of German exporters in their Community markets as against their competitors. However, as regards advertising the Commission distinguished between brand advertising and generic advertising:

> 'The situation would be different were the export support to be used for advertising and sales promotion of a general nature that is not brand orientated. In such a case

---

C-113/04P *TU v Commission* [2006] ECR I-8725, 8831, [2006] 5 CMLR 1223. See also para 5.013, above and the cases cited there.

[411] *Ford Garantie Deutschland, XIIIth Report on Competition Policy* (1983), points 104–106 (German dealers placed advertisements stating that they need not carry out warranty work on Ford cars purchased elsewhere in the Community); *Euglucon 5*, ibid, points 107–109 (circular announcing new version of drug in Germany (Euglucon N) omitted to mention that the old version (Euglucon 5) was still on sale more cheaply in other Member States).

[412] See generally para 9.177, below.

[413] Horizontal Cooperation Guidelines (n 407, above) section 5.

[414] ibid, paras 144–146. Indeed, restrictions on advertising are sometimes imposed as part of a price-fixing and market-sharing cartel: See, eg *Belasco* (n 389, above) (joint advertising contrary to Art 81(1) where it serves to intensify the restrictive effects of a cartel) and cases cited at para 5.013, n 31, above.

[415] Horizontal Cooperation Guidelines (n 407, above), paras 148–150. If the parties' combined market share is below 15 per cent, this is unlikely to be the case. Above that level of market share, the impact of the agreement on the market must be assessed to establish whether it falls within Art 81(1) and, if so, whether it can benefit from Art 81(3).

[416] *Milchförderungsfonds*, OJ 1985 L35/35, [1985] 3 CMLR 101.

the promotion would benefit all competitors and there would not be an appreciable distortion of competition. However, the promotion would not have to seek to discourage the foreign consumer from buying dairy products not from Germany or to disparage such products in the eyes of the foreign consumer. Nor must it commend German dairy products to the foreign consumer simply on the basis of their national origin.

Likewise, there would not be an appreciable restriction of competition if the advertising stressed the special features of the dairy products in question or used the special characteristics of particular kinds of dairy product as a selling point, even if those kinds were typically German, since such advertising is too indefinite to have a practical effect on competition.'[417]

It seems to follow from *Milchförderungsfonds* that purely generic advertising, which does not disparage foreign (or otherwise competing) products or aim to discourage their purchase, is accepted by the Commission as unobjectionable under Article 81(1). Similarly, advertising referring only to the special characteristics of the product in question is unobjectionable.[418]

5.149 **Joint brand advertising.** Although the Commission's principal objection in *Milchförderungsfonds* was to the export subsidy, the Commission also objected to 'brand-orientated' advertising beneficial to German suppliers. It is not clear whether that case concerned marks of individual producers, which were advertised collectively, or whether a jointly owned mark was involved. The case seems best understood as a further example of the application of Article 81 to practices which are harmless or beneficial in the case of small- or medium-sized enterprises, enabling them to compete effectively with their larger rivals, but which threaten to restrict or distort competition where larger-scale cooperation is involved.[419]

5.150 **Joint promotion.** It is clear from *Milchförderungsfonds* that an agreement between undertakings for the joint funding of price reductions, discounts and other promotional allowances for branded products sold in other Member States will be contrary to Article 81(1), subject to the usual requirements of appreciability.[420]

5.151 **Common quality marks.** It is not an infringement of Article 81(1) to use a common quality mark or label which is used to designate goods or services meeting particular specifications or having particular characteristics, provided that the mark is available to all products meeting the stipulated requirements, regardless of

---

[417] ibid, paras 38–39. The Commission's approach was apparently inspired, *inter alia*, by Case 222/82 *Apple & Pear Development Council v Lewis* [1983] ECR 4083, [1984] 3 CMLR 733, para 33.

[418] See also *Apple & Pear Development Council*, above.

[419] cf paras 5.124 *et seq*, above, in respect of 'joint purchasing'. See further Vollebrecht, 'Joint brand advertising: is it allowed?' (1997) 4 ECLR 242.

[420] See also *VVVF* (n 385, above).

the Member State from which they come.[421] Similarly it is not contrary to Article 81(1) to reserve the mark solely for use in connection with products meeting the standards in question so long as participating enterprises are not obliged to manufacture or supply only products conforming to those standards.[422]

(d) Trade exhibitions and auctions

Trade exhibitions. In certain circumstances agreements relating to trade exhibitions may fall within Article 81(1). The Commission has considered a number of cases in which a trade association has imposed a prohibition against exhibiting at exhibitions other than those organised by the association itself. In most cases the sanction for breach of the agreement is exclusion from the fair in a subsequent year or the imposition of fines or less favourable terms of re-entry. In *VIFKA*,[423] exhibitors at an office equipment trade fair agreed not to participate in any other office equipment fair or exhibition not organised or approved by VIFKA in the same calendar year; and in *Internationale Dentalshau*[424] exhibitors at a fair for manufacturers of dentistry articles agreed not to take part in any other exhibition for a period of three months before and two months after the IDS fair. At a national level, in *British Dental Trade Association*[425] the Commission considered both the subsisting and the previous rules governing the prestigious triennial BDTA dental equipment exhibitions. The previous rules had limited participation at the exhibition to members of the Association (in effect, therefore, to United Kingdom undertakings) or had imposed less favourable terms on non-UK exhibitors and

5.152

---

[421] See, eg *Association pour la promotion du Tube d'Acier soudé électriquement*, JO 1970 L153/14, [1970] CMLR D31; *Milchförderungsfonds* (n 416, above); *Retel 1988* (n 386, above) (Art 19(3) Notice under Reg 17). Access must be on equitable terms: *Poroton, Xth Report on Competition Policy* (1980), points 130–132; *TÜV/Cenelec, XXVIIIth Report on Competition Policy* (1998), p 159.

[422] eg *Association Pharmaceutique Belge*, OJ 1990 L18/35, [1990] 4 CMLR 619 (quality stamp introduced by APB for parapharmaceutical products to be distributed exclusively through Belgian pharmacies).

[423] *VIFKA*, OJ 1986 L291/46. See also *SMM & T Exhibition Agreement*, OJ 1983 L376/1, [1984] 1 CMLR 611. For earlier cases see, eg *Cematex*, JO 1971 L227/26, [1973] CMLR D135, exemption under Art 81(3) (renewed OJ 1983 L140/27, [1984] 3 CMLR 69); *CECIMO*, OJ 1969 L69/13, [1969] CMLR Dl (exemption renewed OJ 1979 L11/16, [1979] 1 CMLR 419 and OJ 1989 L37/11, [1990] 4 CMLR 231); *BPICA*, OJ 1977 L299/18, [1977] 2 CMLR D43 (exemption renewed OJ 1982 L156/16, [1983] 2 CMLR 40); *UNIDI*, OJ 1975 L228/14, [1975] 2 CMLR D51 (renewed OJ 1984 L322/10, [1985] 2 CMLR 38, on appeal Case 43/85 *Ancides v Commission* [1987] ECR 3131, [1988] 4 CMLR 821).

[424] *Internationale Dentalshau*, OJ 1987 L293/58. The exemption which was originally granted expired in December 2000 and the Commission issued a comfort letter in respect of the new rules that reduce the periods of restraint to eight weeks before, and four weeks after, the exhibition: *XXIXth Report on Competition Policy* (1999), p 160.

[425] *British Dental Trade Association*, OJ 1988 L233/15, [1989] 4 CMLR 1021. The exemption expired in December 1996 and the Commission issued a exemption-type comfort letter: *XXVIIth Report on Competition Policy* (1997), p 134. See also *Sippa*, OJ 1991 L60/19, [1992] 5 CMLR 528 (French paper industry exhibition).

for this infringement of Article 81(1) a fine was imposed. The Commission stated that the rules unnecessarily restricted competition in the sales of imported goods; but it granted exemption to the amended rules which included a 'closed period' during which the participants could not exhibit elsewhere but from which all forms of discrimination between BDTA members and non-members had been eliminated.

5.153 **Application of Article 81(1).** In each of the above cases the Commission held that the arrangements fell within Article 81(1). Competition was restricted (i) between organisers of exhibitions, since only in certain years could such organisers hope to compete with the approved exhibition; (ii) between manufacturers of the products concerned, who were deprived of freedom to promote their products at other fairs; and (iii) between distributors and intermediaries who were also deprived of the freedom to participate in other exhibitions or to make contacts with new customers. Trade between Member States was affected because organisers of other exhibitions could not hold exhibitions exhibiting products from other Member States, and manufacturers and distributors could not exhibit at exhibitions elsewhere in the Community. The same effects were present at national level in the *UNIDI* and *SMM & T Exhibition Agreement* cases: importers from other Member States were denied access to any other exhibition in the country concerned, and national exhibition organisers could not organise a rival exhibition for imported goods.[426]

5.154 **Trade exhibitions: Article 81(3).** However, in each of the above cases where the arrangements were notified, the Commission was prepared to grant exemption under Article 81(3), although it required several of the agreements to be amended.[427] In general, there are benefits from the rationalisation of such

---

[426] n 423, above. cf *Vidal v Fédération française des sociétés d'assurances*, Cour de Cassation (ch. Com) 22 October 2002, BOCCRF no. 17, 25 November 2002 (FFSA asked its members to postpone their registration at Vidal's fair and subsequently told its members that Vidal had agreed to open the fair to a larger number of participants in the commercial industry and that its members should decide whether or not to participate in light of this. As a consequence, the 1992 Assure Expo was less successful than previously. The Court noted that 'a boycott constitutes a deliberate action aimed at evicting an operator from the market' and that in this case the actions did not constitute a boycott since the FFSA's desire to evict VIDAL had not been established and there was no significant effect on the market. In *WEX v FEBIAC* (2004/MR/8), judgment of 10 November 2005, the Brussels Court of Appeal considered a regulation of the FEBIAC union of Belgian importers of motor vehicles which prohibited members from taking part in a rival trade exhibition within six months prior to the annual FEBIAC trade fair. Although it held that the restriction had not been established to have an appreciable effect on competition for the purposes of Art 81(1), the Court went on to decide that the restriction was an abuse by FEBIAC of its dominant position on the market of services for organising exhibitions of utility vehicles in Belgium because the absolute ban did not allow any derogation for participation in a competitor's exhibition which did not seriously threaten to reduce the impact of the FEBIAC trade fair.

[427] In the case of *VIFKA* (n 423, above) the amendments were substantial. In *Sippa* (n 425, above), the version of the regulations 'endorsed' by comfort letter in 1986 was redrafted in negotiation with the Commission after withdrawal of the comfort letter.

exhibitions, but the Commission is concerned to ensure that the restrictions are no more than reasonably necessary, particularly as regards the period of protection and the extent of the restraint.[428] The Commission is also concerned to secure that the rules should be based on objective criteria,[429] and be non-discriminatory.[430] The Commission usually requires to be informed of refusals of admission and in certain cases has insisted on an appeals procedure from such a refusal.[431]

Auctions. In two decisions relating to fruit and vegetable auctions[432] it has been **5.155** held that Article 81(1) may be infringed by provisions which (i) require certain undertakings to deal exclusively through the auction in question; or (ii) impose unreasonable restrictions on access to the auction. In both cases exemption was refused. The same approach applies to auctions of other kinds, at least where the products concerned are traded appreciably between Member States. For example, a cooperative society organising a major Dutch flower auction[433] was found to be

---

[428] In *Sippa* (n 426, above) the Commission referred to *VIFKA, Internationale Dentalschau and British Dental Trade Association*, para 5.152, above, and summarised its policy in relation to exhibitions and trade fairs as being 'to allow agreements or arrangements which result in rationalisation or cost savings and which at the same time contain advantages for consumers, the benefits of which outweigh the restrictive elements'.

[429] See, eg *BPICA* (n 425, above) where the Commission insisted on an objective definition of the exhibitions to which the rules applied, to prevent arbitrary decisions by the trade association.

[430] See *British Dental Trade Association* (n 425, above). But it is not discriminatory to charge a higher entrance fee to non-members if justified on cost grounds: *UNIDI* (n 423, above); and a discount to signatories of the agreement is permissible: *SMM & T Exhibition Agreement* (n 423, above).

[431] See, eg renewal of the exemptions under Art 81(3) in *Cematex, CECIMO* and *UNIDI* (n 423, above).

[432] *Frubo*, OJ 1974 L237/16, [1974] 2 CMLR D89, on appeal Case 71/74 *Frubo v Commission* [1975] ECR 563, [1975] 2 CMLR 123 (Dutch wholesalers agreed in effect to buy fruit imported from third countries exclusively through the Rotterdam auctions, *inter alia* preventing importers established elsewhere in the Community supplying the Dutch market without going through the auctions); *Cauliflowers* (n 380, above) (agreement by dealers to deal through specified auctions in Brittany only). See also Note regarding *Dutch Fishermen* (2001) 2 EC Competition Policy Newsletter 43 (rules which obliged members of private trade associations to land their catches of fish in the Netherlands and to have those catches auctioned through auctions that were recognized by the association unacceptable). See also paras 5.134 *et seq*, above.

[433] *Verenigde Bloemenveilingen Aalsmeer*, OJ 1988 L262/27, [1989] 4 CMLR 500 (for subsequent proceedings see Case C-265/97P *VBA v Florimex and VGB* [2000] ECR I-2061 and Case C-266/97P *VBA v VGB Florimex* [2000] ECR I-2135). In *CVBA Belgische Fruitveiling and CVBA Veiling Borgloon v VZW Nationale Unie van Belgische Exporteurs van Land- en Tuinbouwproducten* (2002/MR/10–2002/MR/11), judgment of 29 September 2004, the Brussels Court of Appeal upheld the Competition Council's decision that the rules rules of certain firms organising auctions for fruit growers infringed the Belgian counterpart of Art 81(1). The grounds for exclusion of buyers must be objective and are so only if they are clearly described and if the sanction of exclusion from the auction is proportionate so that it cannot be used as an arbitrary means to put pressure on a given buyer. See also Case 2269, *Dutch Shrimp producers and wholesalers agreement*, decn of Dutch Competition Authority, 24 December 2004 (agreement entered into by associations of Dutch, German and Danish shrimp producers with an association of Dutch shrimp wholesalers limited catches, set minimum prices and hindered new entrants trying to acquire shrimp by auction in the Netherlands, in breach of Dutch competition law and Art 81(1) EC).

in contravention of Article 81(1) by requiring its wholesalers to sell only products purchased at its auction; and an association constituting Europe's leading fur auctioneer[434] was fined for requiring its members to sell only through its own subsidiary.

9. Sporting Bodies and Competitions

5.156 Introduction. Sporting activity is not in itself subject to the competition rules of the EC Treaty.[435] The practice of sport is subject to Community law only insofar as it constitutes an economic activity.[436] In recent years, the continuing development in economic activities connected with sport, in particular the escalating value of rights to broadcast major sporting events,[437] largely as a result of the technological revolution in broadcasting, and the transformation in the conduct of the major sporting clubs and federations, has led to increasing application of competition law to the rules and arrangements made by sporting bodies. However, in applying competition law in this field, regard must be had to the social and cultural role played by sport. The Commission recognises the public interest in the solidarity between professional and amateur clubs and in permitting wealthier clubs in some sports to subsidise or promote the weaker clubs for the advancement of the sport generally. This reflects the Declaration on Sport made by the EU Intergovernmental Conference and annexed to the Treaty of Amsterdam, which states:

> 'The Conference emphasises the social significance of sport, in particular its role in forging identity and bringing people together. The Conference therefore calls on the bodies of the European Union to listen to sports associations when important questions affecting sport are at issue. In this connection, special consideration should be given to the particular characteristics of amateur sport.'[438]

---

[434] *Hudson's Bay/Dansk Pelsdyravlerforening*, OJ 1988 L316/43, [1989] 4 CMLR 340; this point upheld on appeal, Case T-61/89 *Dansk Pelsdyravlerforening v Commission* [1992] ECR II-1931.

[435] See generally Lewis and Taylor, *Sport: Law and Practice* (2003), Chap B2.

[436] Case 36/74 *Walrave v Union Cycliste Internationale* [1974] ECR 1405, [1975] 1 CMLR 320, para 4; Case 13/76 *Donà v Mantero* [1976] ECR 1333, [1976] 2 CMLR 578, para 4; Cases C-51/96 & C-191/97 *Deliège v Ligue Francophone de Judo* [2000] ECR I-2549, [2002] 2 CMLR 1574, para 51.

[437] The value of broadcast rights for the Olympic Games increased from $287 million for Los Angeles in 1984 to $1.5 billion for Athens in 2004: IOC Fact Sheet: Revenue Generation and Distribution, December 2005. The experience for soccer has been similar and FIFA earned an estimated $1.3 billion from sale of the broadcast rights for the 2006 World Cup (WIPO Magazine, August 2006).

[438] OJ 1997 C340/136. The Declaration was referred to by the ECJ in Case C-176/96 *Lehtonen and Castors Braine* [2000] ECR I-2681, [2000] 3 CMLR 409, [2001] All ER (EC) 97, para 33. See also the Commission Statement: 'The application of the EU's Competition rules to sports', MEMO/02/127 (5 June 2002).

In addition, as regards sporting competitions and tournaments, particular restrictions may be required to reflect the characteristics of the sport or competition in question (for example, the representative character of international sporting competitions such as the Olympic Games) and, especially in a league context, to protect a degree of uncertainty of the result. The question of the collective selling and buying of broadcasting rights to sporting events and tournaments is discussed above.[439] This Section considers other aspects of the application of Article 81 to sporting bodies and competitions. Where such bodies occupy a powerful position in a particular market, their conduct may at the same time constitute an abuse of a dominant position within Article 82.[440]

Bosman: **international rules governing the terms on engagement of players.**   **5.157**
The landmark judgment of the Court of Justice in *Bosman*[441] highlighted the impact of the EC Treaty on arrangements made by sporting bodies. The issues in the case related to national and international rules restricting (i) the circumstances in which professional football players could be registered to play in national leagues of other Member States without the payment of an agreed 'transfer fee' to their previous club; and (ii) the numbers of 'foreign' players who could take part in competitions organised by UEFA. Although the Court of Justice decided the case only under the rules on free movement in Article 39 and did not address the issues under competition law,[442] the case was argued also under Articles 81 and 82. Advocate General Lenz considered the analysis under Article 81 in some detail, finding that there was an agreement between the member clubs of UEFA and FIFA, or alternatively there were decisions of associations of undertakings, to which Article 81(1) applied. The rules had not been notified to the Commission for exemption under Article 81(3) but Advocate General Lenz considered that such an exemption should have been refused in any event because the rules violated Article 39.[443] Both the Court of Justice and the Advocate General were of the view that the ultimate interests of UEFA in the preservation of competitive balance and the health of the smaller clubs could be achieved

---

439 See paras 5.115–5.119 and 5.129–5.131, above.

440 In Case T-193/02 *Piau v Commission* [2005] ECR II-209, [2005] 5 CMLR 42, paras 113–116, the CFI held that the national football associations, and therefore FIFA which was to be regard as their emanation, occupied a collective dominant position on the market in question; appeal on other grounds dismissed, Case C-171/05P [2006] ECR I-37, order of 23 February 2006. For dominance, see further paras 10.015 *et seq*, below. In this respect, the sale of sports rights has many of the same characteristics as the sale of music or film rights, where the Commission and ECJ have traditionally placed the primary emphasis on Art 82: see also para 5.112, above.

441 Case C-415/93 *Union Royale des Sociétés de Football Association v Bosman* [1995] ECR I-4921, [1996] 1 CMLR 645, [1996] All ER (EC) 97.

442 Case C-264/98 *Balog v Royal Charleroi Sporting Club*, in which the issue was raised directly on a reference to the ECJ, was withdrawn the day before the AG was due to deliver his opinion.

443 *Bosman* (n 441, above) Opinion at paras 277–278.

without the rules at issue in *Bosman*, in particular by redistribution of receipts from sales of television rights.[444]

5.158 *Bosman*: **analysis.** The classification of the *Bosman* case under Article 81 is rather difficult. But it seems best to regard it as an unusual example of restrictions on the terms on which the clubs agreed to carry on their business as participants in professional football competitions, the effect of the restrictions being to suppress demand for players and thus artificially to restrict output on the player market. This is apparently confirmed by the effect of the abandonment of the rules, under pressure from the Commission, in the national as well as international market, which led to a rapid and significant increase in player wages and club wage costs, particularly for players attractive on the international market.[445]

5.159 **Scope of Article 81(1) in relation to sporting events.** Article 81(1) could apply only where there is an appreciable effect on competition between undertakings engaged in sport as an economic activity and where a sufficient effect on inter-State trade is found. However, there are so many economic activities related to sports, in particular broadcasting on television and radio, advertising and sponsorship, that Article 81(1) is likely to apply to a number of national as well as international contests. It cannot be assumed that 'amateur' or individual sports, such as judo, will be held to fall outside the competition rules.[446] Moreover, not only national but also regional events are often conducted under the rules of the relevant international sporting body, and that body may well constitute an association of undertakings even if it is not an undertaking in its own right,[447] whose rules can attract the application of Article 81. In addition, broadcasting contracts between sporting associations and television companies will fall within the scope of Article 81 even if the participants in the sport are not regarded as themselves falling within the meaning of 'undertaking'.

---

[444] For AG Lenz's analysis, see ibid, paras 254 *et seq.*

[445] cf para 262 of AG Lenz's Opinion (ibid), where he refers to the rules on foreign players and on transfers as sharing 'sources of supply' within Art 81(l)(c) and replacing 'the normal system of supply and demand by a uniform machinery . . .'. Player wage inflation was the subject of detailed evidence before the UK Restrictive Practices Court in the *Premier League* case, concerning collective selling of broadcasting rights, *In re the Supply of Services facilitating the broadcasting on television of Premier League football matches* [1999] UKCLR 258.

[446] See *Deliège* (n 436, above) para 46. *Deliège* concerned rules limiting the number of individual participants from one country in international judo competitions; see also *Lehtonen* (n 438, above): rules limiting the period during which transfers of basketball players could take place. In both these cases, the ECJ held that the national court making the reference had insufficiently explained the factual background for it to deal with the questions referred under the competition rules and therefore confined its decision to the free movement rules. For the general principles governing the meaning of 'undertaking' and appreciability, see Chap 2, above.

[447] See eg *Piau v Commission* (n 440, above) paras 69–72: both the national football associations and FIFA are associations of undertakings.

Meca-Medina **and 'sporting rules'.** The Commission had adopted the prelimi- **5.160**
nary view that Article 81(1) did not apply to rules that 'are inherent to sport and/
or necessary for its organisation'.[448] Hence the Commission rejected a complaint
regarding the UEFA Cup 'at home and away from home' rule, that required each
club to play its home match on its own ground, on the basis that this was adopted
by UEFA as part of its legitimate self-regulation as a sports organisation in order
to secure equality between clubs.[449] Similarly, the Commission rejected a complaint by Mr Meca-Medina and another professional swimmer who had been
banned from competitions following a positive test for prohibited anabolic substances after finishing first and second in the Long-distance Swimming World
Cup.[450] Their appeal to the Court of Arbitration for Sport had been dismissed
(although the length of the ban was subsequently reduced). The two swimmers
argued that the rules adopted by the IOC and by FINA (the Fédération
Internationale de Natation Amateur) regarding the definition of doping, the
threshold for defining the presence of a banned substance in the body as doping
and recourse to the Court of Arbitration had restricted competition within the
meaning of Article 81 and unjustifiably restricted the freedom of swimmers to
provide services under Article 49. The Court of First Instance upheld the
Commission's decision, stating that the competition provisions of the Treaty, like
the provisions concerning free movement, do not affect 'purely sporting rules,
that is to say rules concerning questions of purely sporting interest and, as such,
having nothing to do with economic activity'.[451]

Meca-Medina: **the Court of Justice's analysis.** However, on the further appeal **5.161**
in *Meca-Medina and Majcen v Commission*, the Court of Justice expressly overruled this approach. In a passage that is not altogether easy to understand, the
Court of Justice held that the fact that a rule falls outside the free movement provisions because it concerns questions of purely sporting interest and thus has nothing to do with economic activity, does not preclude the application of the
competition rules.[452] However, the Court proceeded to apply a proportionality
test to the application of Article 81 to the FINA and IOC rule. Drawing on the

---

[448] See Press Release IP/99/133 (24 February 1999), [1999] 4 CMLR 596, 'Commission debates application of its competition rules to sports'.
[449] *Lille/UEFA ('the Mouscron case'), XXIXth Report on Competition Policy* (1999) p 166. The complaint was made by the Communauté Urbaine de Lille which was unable, as a consequence of the rule, to hire out its stadium for a UEFA Cup game between Excelsior Mouscron and FC Metz. The rule allowed for exceptions but the Commission also found that there were insufficient grounds to investigate whether the conditions imposed for such exceptions by UEFA might infringe Art 82.
[450] *Meca Medina and Majcen/IOC, XXXIInd Report on Competition Policy* (2002), p 200.
[451] Case T-313/02 *Meca-Medina and Majcen v Commission* [2004] ECR II-3291, [2004] 3 CMLR 60, paras 41–42.
[452] Case C-519/04P *Meca-Medina and Majcen v Commission* [2006] 5 CMLR 1023, [2006] All ER (EC) 1057, paras 24–34.

approach enunciated in *Wouters*,[453] the Court held that the questions to be addressed are whether the rule or decision pursued a legitimate objective, whether the restrictions of competition were inherent in the pursuit of that objective and whether the restrictions were limited to what was necessary for that purpose.[454] The combat of doping in sport was clearly a legitimate objective, inherent in the organisation and proper conduct of sport. Nonetheless, the penalties applied under the anti-doping rules could produce anti-competitive effects if the penalty was unjustified, since in that case an athlete would be prevented from engaging in sporting events. As to the third element of proportionality, the Court significantly stated:

> 'Rules of that kind could indeed prove excessive by virtue of, first, the conditions laid down for establishing the dividing line between circumstances which amount to doping in respect of which penalties may be imposed and those which do not, and second, the severity of those penalties.'[454]

The appeal was dismissed since the evidence had not established that the threshold had been set too low, and the appellants had not alleged that the penalties in themselves were too severe.

5.162 **Proportionality under Article 81 in the sporting context.** The full implications of the *Meca-Medina* judgment have still to be worked out. Many rules governing sporting competitions can have significant economic implications and thus affect competition: for example, the specified size of a football pitch will determine which grounds are eligible to host matches, and the tie-break rule in tennis may affect the outcome of a tournament and hence the earnings of the players. But it is difficult to see how the reasonableness of those rules can be assessed in terms of their effect on competition. If the objective of the rule is legitimate, and provided that the rule operates in a non-discriminatory way,[455] any resulting restriction of competition should not readily be found to be excessive, particularly where the rule is adopted by a sporting body which generally has the proper conduct of the sport as its aim. However, the further the subject of the rule is from the inherent conduct of the sport, the more intensive may be the scrutiny to which it is subject on proportionality grounds under Article 81. This approach derives

---

[453] See para 5.039, above.

[454] This approach was foreshadowed in the Opinion of AG Lenz in *Bosman* (n 441, above) at paras 268–270. In this respect, AG Lenz was consciously applying the more flexible approach to Art 81 exemplified by the ECJ's decision in Case C-250/92 *Gøttrup-Klim v Dansk Landbrugs Grovvareselskab AmhA* [1994] ECR I-5461, [1996] 4 CMLR 191.

[455] A discriminatory rule, in either its form or its application, could not satisfy the proportionality test: CFI judgment in *Meca-Medina* (n 452, above) para 49. And see the judgment of the English High Court, *adidas-Salomon v Draper* [2006] EWHC 1318 (Ch), [2006] EuLR 1057: interim injunction concerning application of the jointly agreed dress rules of the four Grand Slam tennis tournaments and the International Tennis Federation to the '3-Stripes' design of adidas, on the grounds of discriminatory treatment in contravention of Art 81. (The case subsequently settled.)

support from the decisional practice of the Commission already prior to the *Meca-Medina* judgment. Hence the Commission rejected a complaint about the UEFA rule preventing any company or individual being directly or indirectly in control of more than one club participating in a UEFA competition.[456] The multi-ownership rule was justified by the need to preserve the integrity of the competition and therefore fell outside Article 81.[457] In *UEFA broadcasting regulations*,[458] the Commission granted negative clearance to the revised regulations that allowed national football associations to prevent the broadcasting of football within their territory for two and a half hours at the weekend at a time that corresponds to their main match fixtures. The Commission had issued a statement of objections regarding the original regulations notified to it, which were much more extensive in scope and also very complicated, providing for a time window covering the whole week and different authorisation requirements. As revised, the rules were found to be reasonable to meet the objective of allowing national football associations to schedule fixtures at times when they were not liable to be disturbed by simultaneous broadcasts of football, to the detriment of stadium attendance and amateur participation in the sport.[459]

Application of Article 81(3). In rejecting a complaint against the FIFA rules **5.163** governing the activity of players' agents, the Commission stated that the requirement for agents to be licensed met the conditions for exemption under Article 81(3).[460] The Commission had objected to the original rules, in particular because they had prevented access by those with the requisite skills and qualifications by the requirement of payment of a substantial deposit. The new rules replaced the deposit obligation with the option of taking out professional liability insurance. The Commission considered that this removed the main objection on competition grounds. The rules met the aims of extending good practice, raising professional standards and protecting players and clubs from unqualified and

---

456 COMP/37.806 *ENIC/UEFA*, decn of 25 June 2002, and see Press Release IP/02/942 (27 June 2002). Note also the rejection by the Court of Arbitration for Sport of the contention that the rule distorted competition (dismissing a related challenge by two of the ENIC-owned clubs): *AEK PAE and SK Slavia Praha v UEFA*, CAS 98/2000, award of 20 August 1999, *Digest of CAS Awards II 1998–2000* (2002), p 36.

457 See also Decn no. 2004-E/A-25 *URBSFA*, CONC-E/A-01/0039, 4 March 2004, in which the Belgian Competition Council held that the rules of the Belgian football association concerning the technical and financial qualifications for a club to be licensed to play in the national leagues, and the conditions for relegation of a club due to financial difficulties were both non-discriminatory and proportionate to the objective of maintaining a fair, healthy and balanced sporting event and so, although restricting competition, fell outside the Belgian equivalent of Art 81.

458 *UEFA broadcasting regulations*, OJ 2001 L171/12, [2001] 5 CMLR 654.

459 Commissioner Monti referred at the time of the decision to the Commission's attempt 'to play the role of impartial referee between the different interests of broadcasters and football clubs': Press Release IP/01/583 (20 April 2001).

460 Commission decn of 15 April 2002, *XXXIInd Report on Competition Policy* (2002), p 197.

unscrupulous agents. In *Piau v Commission*, the Court of First Instance upheld the Commission's decision that in the circumstances there was no further Community interest in pursuing the complaint.[461] The Court agreed that the requirement of a licence as a condition for acting as a players' agent necessarily affected competition since it constituted a barrier to access to an economic activity. It could therefore only be accepted if the conditions of Article 81(3) were met. The Court took account of FIFA's explanation that this rule was pursuing a 'dual objective of raising professional and ethical standards for the occupation of players' agent in order to protect players, who have a short career' noting also that there were virtually no national rules and no collective organisation for players' agents. The Court found that the licence system 'appears to result in a qualitative selection, appropriate for the attainment of the objective or raising professional standards for the occupation of players' agent, rather than a quantitative restriction on access to that occupation.' Accordingly, the conditions of Article 81(3) appeared to be satisfied.[462]

5.164 *FIFA/UEFA*: **international football transfers.** After the *Bosman* judgment, the Commission took up the matter of the regulations governing transfers with UEFA and FIFA, respectively the European and world bodies for the regulation of football. Following the issue of a statement of objections to FIFA and extensive negotiations, agreement was reached in 2001 as to the principles according to which the transfer regulations would comply with EC law, and UEFA and FIFA agreed to amend their regulations accordingly.[463] The Commission finally closed its investigation in May 2002 after rejecting the two remaining complaints and the withdrawal of others.[464] The new rules strike a balance between players' right to free movement and stability of contract and the legitimate objective of integrity of sport and the stability of championships. In case of any dispute, the new rules make clear that players may have recourse to voluntary arbitration or to the national courts. The Commission noted that the discussions with the football authorities and the rejection of the two complaints have helped to confirm that EC and national law apply to football and that EC law is able to take into account the specificity of sport and in particular to recognise that sport performs an important social, integrating and cultural function.

---

[461] Case T-193/02 *Piau v Commission* (n 440, above). For the same reason, the CFI held that there was no violation of Art 82. The appeal to the ECJ was dismissed as manifestly unfounded: Case C-171/05P, order of 23 February 2006.

[462] ibid, paras 102–104. Applying the pre-*Meca-Medina* approach, the CFI also held that these regulations could not be regarded as pure 'sporting rules' since they concerned an economic activity peripheral to the sporting activity in question: para 76.

[463] Press Release IP/01/314 (6 March 2001). For the earlier stages, see *XXVIth Report on Competition Policy* (1996), points 104–107.

[464] *SECTA+FGTB/FIFA* and *Sport et libertés/FIFA, XXXIInd Report on Competition Policy* (2002) p 197.

Formula One. The prolonged investigation of various arrangements governing   **5.165** motorsport illustrates the Commission's concerns and approach. Notifications of the agreements relating to the FIA Formula One Championship were made in 1994 and 1997, and the Commission then received several complaints. The cases concerned the organisation and promotion of cross-border motorsport series; the certification/licensing of motorsport events' organisation and participants; and the broadcasting rights of the FIA Formula One Championship. The Commission objected to several aspects of the agreements, and extensive modifications were then offered by the Fédération Internationale de l'Automobile (FIA) and the Formula One Adminstration (FOA) to address the competition concerns identified.[465] Those changes included a complete separation between the commercial and regulatory functions in relation to the FIA Formula One World Championship and the FIA World Rally Championship; improved transparency of decision-making and appeals procedures to create greater accountability; guaranteed access to motorsport to any person meeting the relevant safety and fairness criteria; FIA's approval to all events meeting certain safety and sporting criteria without any restrictions placed on access to external independent appeals; and modification of the duration of free-to-air broadcasting contracts in relation to the FIA Formula One World Championship. As a result, the Commission issued both negative clearance-type and exemption-type comfort letters in 2001, but continued to monitor compliance with the undertakings it had received from the FIA and FOA. After two years, the Commission was satisfied that the terms of the settlement had been complied with and that the new model of organisation and commercial exploitation had introduced an environment which took into account the character of the sport while guaranteeing 'a reasonable degree of competition at the same time'.[466] The monitoring was therefore brought to an end.

---

[465] *Fédération Internationale de l'Automobile — FIA* and *FIA Formula One World Championship, XXXIst Report on Competition Policy* (2001), p 203; see also Press Release IP/01/1523 (30 October 2001).
[466] Press Release IP/03/1491 (31 October 2003).

6

VERTICAL AGREEMENTS AFFECTING DISTRIBUTION OR SUPPLY

1. Introduction

Preliminary. There are many means by which producers can sell and distribute **6.001**
their products. An undertaking may carry out a large part of the distributive function itself, using its own employees or its own branches, or through wholly owned
subsidiaries. In some cases (for example, petrol companies) the undertaking will
own some of the retail outlets for its goods. In many cases, however, undertakings
rely substantially upon intermediaries. The agreements with which this Chapter

is mainly concerned are vertical agreements[1] between a supplier and the purchasers of its goods or services at a different level of the production or distribution chain. Such a purchaser may be an intermediary in the distribution sector, buying the products for resale under a contract in which one or both parties accept restrictions on their trading activities; or it may be an end-user, buying raw materials or components for use in manufacturing another product. This Chapter also deals with subcontracts whereby an undertaking arranges to have produced by a third party all or part of the goods or services that it has agreed to supply to its customers. In certain circumstances, the agreements considered here may also infringe Article 82, which is discussed in Chapter 10, below.

6.002 **Vertical restraints under Article 81.** Any of the agreements discussed in this Chapter may involve (a) exclusive dealing obligations and (b) restrictions relating to resale or supply of the products in question. Exclusivity provisions in vertical agreements may bring economic benefits by improving efficiency, reducing transaction costs and enabling suppliers to penetrate new markets. The need for efficient distribution arrangements has increased with the application of information technology and 'just-in-time' methods of supply. Without the protection of a restriction on the supplier or purchaser, there may be a disincentive for the other party to an agreement to incur investments for fear of 'free-riding' or so-called 'hold-ups'.[2] Some vertical restraints may therefore be necessary to promote inter-brand competition. However, vertical restrictions can have anti-competitive effects in foreclosing access to markets and preventing intra-brand competition. Moreover, territorial exclusivity or customer allocation can operate to partition markets in a manner that undermines the integration of a single Community market that is one of the fundamental objectives of the Treaty. The extent to which many of the vertical restraints of the kind discussed here come within Article 81(1), and therefore must fulfil the criteria of Article 81(3) to be valid, or fall outside Article 81(1) altogether, has not been clearly resolved and may be impossible to determine in the abstract. Although the Commission in the past often adopted a 'maximalist' approach, contending that most restraints that have an appreciable effect should be regarded as falling within Article 81(1), the Court of Justice has

---

[1] For 'vertical' and 'horizontal' agreements, see para 2.028, above. See generally, Wijckmans, Tuytschaever and Vanderelst, *Vertical Agreements in EC Competition* Law (2006); Goyder, *EU Distribution Law* (4th edn, 2005); Christou, *International Agency, Distribution and Licensing Agreements* (4th edn, 2003); Korah and O'Sullivan, *Distribution Agreements under the EC Competition Rules* (2002).

[2] 'Free-riding' occurs when the competitors of the person incurring the investment are able to appropriate the resulting benefit ('the beneficial externality'): eg when expenditure by one distributor on the promotion of a brand thereby attracts customers for other distributors. 'Hold-ups' refer to the situation where significant sunk costs would not be incurred by one party without the security of supply by or to the other trading partner on terms that would cover those costs: eg investment in equipment or training that is related to a specific product.

been more sensitive to the economic circumstances of the particular case. For agreements that do not involve undertakings holding a significant market share, the new regime for vertical restraints introduced in 2000 may render this issue largely irrelevant in practice.

Appreciable effect: the Commission's presumptions.   The Notice on agree-   **6.003** ments of minor importance issued by the Commission in 1997[3] already adopted the approach that more vertical agreements than horizontal agreements could be regarded as not having an appreciable effect and therefore not coming within Article 81(1).[4] The 1997 Notice was replaced in 2001, but the principles underlying the Commission's approach to vertical agreements remained similar. The 2001 Notice ('the *De Minimis* Notice')[5] states that the Commission considers that agreements between non-competing undertakings (that is, undertakings which are neither actual nor potential competitors on the markets concerned) do not appreciably restrict competition where the market share of each of the parties to the agreement does not exceed 15 per cent[6] on any of the relevant markets affected by the agreement.

Situations where the presumption in the Notice does not apply.   The   **6.004** Commission's view in this regard does not apply to agreements which contain hard-core restrictions, that is restrictions which have as their object the fixing of resale prices or conferring territorial protection. A clause which fixes a maximum sales price or which recommends a sales price is not treated for this purpose as having the object of fixing prices, unless the existence of pressure from, or incentives offered by, any of the parties means that in effect it operates as fixing a minimum price.[7] The market share thresholds also do not apply where the agreement restricts the territory into which, or the customers to which, the buyer may resell the contract goods or services if those restrictions go beyond the kinds of restrictions which are generally regarded as acceptable in vertical agreements of different sorts.[8]

Cumulative effect of parallel agreements under the Notice.   The 1997 Notice   **6.005** simply provided that it did not apply in circumstances where competition was

---

    3 1997 *De Minimis* Notice, OJ 1997 C372/13.

    4 The Guidelines on Vertical Restraints (discussed at para 6.008, below) state (para 8) that they are 'without prejudice to the application of the present or any future "*de minimis*" notice'.

    5 Notice on agreements of minor importance which do not appreciably restrict competition under Art 81(1) ('*De Minimis* Notice'), OJ 2001 C368/13: Vol II, App C.13, and see para 2.129, above.

    6 This compares with an *aggregate* market share of 10 per cent for the parties to a horizontal agreement. In cases where it is difficult to classify the agreement as either horizontal or vertical, the 10 per cent threshold applies: *De Minimis* Notice, para 7.

    7 These types of price related clauses are discussed at paras 6.051 *et seq*, below.

    8 Para 11(2)(b) of the Notice. See generally paras 6.053 *et seq*, below.

restricted by parallel networks of similar agreements.[9] The 2001 *De Minimis* Notice deals expressly with this situation, in effect setting market share thresholds for the two stage test propounded in the *Delimitis* decision.[10] Where competition is restricted by the cumulative effect of parallel agreements, the Commission will not regard the effect of a particular agreement as being appreciable if less than 30 per cent of the relevant market is covered by parallel networks of similar agreements and if the particular supplier's and the particular distributor's share of their respective markets is less than 5 per cent.

6.006 **Legislative approach to vertical restraints.** The legislative approach to vertical restraints was transformed by the block exemption for vertical agreements, Regulation 2790/99,[11] which took effect on 1 June 2000. Until the introduction of this regime, the Commission had dealt with vertical restrictions by a series of block exemptions, which addressed different categories of vertical agreements of a narrowly defined kind.[12] By Regulation 1215/1999, the Council amended the enabling Regulation 19/65 so as to permit the Commission to adopt a 'simpler, more flexible and better targeted' block exemption covering all types of vertical agreements.[13] Pursuant to this provision, the Commission adopted Regulation 2790/99 granting exemption to a wide range of vertical agreements, subject to a 30 per cent market share ceiling. This was followed by the Guidelines on Vertical Restraints,[14] published in October 2000, setting out the Commission's approach both to the application of the block exemption and to individual agreements. However, one category of vertical agreements, contracts for motor vehicle distribution and servicing, was expressly excluded from the scope of the Commission's review and these agreements are covered by a separate block exemption, Regulation 1400/2002, discussed in Section 5(d) of this Chapter.

6.007 **Economic analysis and market power.** The new regime reflects the modern economic thinking that vertical restraints are not *per se* anti-competitive. Instead, the impact on competition and efficiency of vertical arrangements and distribution systems depends to a great extent on the market context and barriers to entry.[15]

---

[9] 1997 Notice, n 3 above, para 18. But in 1992, following the *Delimitis* judgment, a *de minimus* provision specifically concerning beer supply agreements concluded by a brewery was introduced by amendment into the Notice on Regulations 1983/83 and 1984/83 [the then block exemptions]: OJ 1992 C121/2.

[10] Para 8 of the *De Minimis* Notice. For *Delimitis* see para 6.146, below.

[11] Reg 2790/99, OJ 1999 L336/21: Vol II, App C.3 and see paras 6.010 *et seq*, below.

[12] For discussion of the terms of the former block exemptions, see Chap 7 of the 4th edition of this work (1993 and Supp, 1996).

[13] Recital (9) to Reg 1215/1999, OJ 1999 L148/1. For Reg 19/65 as amended, see Vol II, App C.1.

[14] Guidelines on Vertical Restraints, OJ 2000 C291/1: Vol II, App C.11 and see para 6.008, below.

[15] See Hildebrand, *Economic Analyses of Vertical Agreements - A Self-Assessment* (2005). For a sophisticated analysis of the problem generally, see Lever and Neubauer, 'Vertical Restraints, Their Motivation and Justification' (2000) ECLR 7, who observe (at para 2.4) that '[t]he ambivalence

In the Guidelines, the Commission states that:

> 'For most vertical restraints, competition concerns can only arise if there is insuffi-
> cient inter-brand competition, ie if there is some degree of market power at the level
> of the supplier or the buyer or at both levels. If there is insufficient inter-brand com-
> petition, the protection of inter- and intra-brand competition becomes important.'[16]

'Market power' for this purpose is defined in classic economic terms to mean the
ability to raise prices above the competitive level (that is, the level that would
prevail in a competitive market) and, at least in the short term, to obtain supra-
normal profits.[17] The Commission further states:

> 'Where there are many firms competing in an unconcentrated market, it can be
> assumed that non-hardcore vertical restraints will not have appreciable negative
> effects.'[18]

To measure market concentration, the Commission principally uses the
Herfindahl-Hirschmann Index ('HHI'),[19] following the practice of the US anti-
trust enforcement agencies, or alternatively the five-firm concentration ratio
('CR5'), that is, the aggregate market share held by the five largest suppliers.[20]

The Guidelines.   The Commission's Guidelines on Vertical Restraints[21] provide   **6.008**
a commentary on Regulation 2790/99 and set out the Commission's approach
and methodology as regards the various types of vertical restraints, albeit with little reference to decided cases. The Guidelines outline a framework of four categories that describe the basic components of vertical restraints: single branding;
limited distribution; resale price maintenance; and market partitioning.[22] But as

---

of economic theory and the complexity of possible motives and of possible effects render the
rational application of competition policy to vertical restraints extremely difficult.' For discussion
of the Commission's approach, see Biro and Fletcher, 'The EC Green Paper on Vertical Restraints:
an Economic Comment' (1998) ECLR 129. For a sustained argument that vertical restraints in
distribution arrangements where neither party has market power on balance promote economic
efficiency, see Xoudis, *Les accords de distribution au regard du droit de la concurrence* (2002).

   [16] Guidelines on Vertical Restraints (n 14, above) para 6.
   [17] The increase in price will involve a restriction of output. It follows from this definition that a
firm can have market power below the level of dominance for the purpose of Art 82.
   [18] Guidelines on Vertical Restraints (n 14, above) para 119(1). For hard-core restraints, see para
6.023, below.
   [19] The HHI is the sum of the squares of the individual market shares of all companies in the
relevant market. The Commission states that a market is deemed unconcentrated when the HHI
is below 1000: ibid; and moderately concentrated when the HHI is between 1000 and 1800: *Bass*,
OJ 1999 L186/1, [1999] 5 CMLR 782, para 22. See also the Horizontal Cooperation Guidelines,
OJ 2001 C3/2: Vol II, App C.12, para 29.
   [20] See, eg Guidelines on Vertical Restraints (n 14, above) paras 143, 189. For the methodology of
HHI and its relative merits compared to concentration ratios, see Bishop and Walker, *The Economics
of Competition Law* (2nd ed, 2002), 56–59.
   [21] Guidelines on Vertical Restraints, OJ 2000 C291/1: Vol II, App C.11. The EFTA Surveillance
Authority issued an equivalent version of the Guidelines for application as regards the EEA
Agreement: OJ 2002 C122/1.
   [22] Guidelines on Vertical Restraints, above, paras 104–114.

some of those categories are very broad and since in practice many agreements combine restraints falling within different categories, the Guidelines also provide separate analysis of eight common forms of vertical restraints: single branding; exclusive distribution; exclusive customer allocation; selective distribution; franchising; exclusive supply; tying; and recommended and maximum resale prices.[23] Although comprehensive, this structure makes the Guidelines complex to use since, save for the separate section concerning the block exemption, they need to be read as a whole. The Guidelines suggest that once the relevant party is below the 30 per cent market share ceiling for the block exemption to apply, the agreement does not require individual consideration unless it contains hard-core restraints.[24] But the detailed discussion of particular forms of restraint shows that certain situations falling below that ceiling may be viewed with concern by the Commission and thus lead to withdrawal of the benefit of the block exemption from individual agreements or groups of agreements. Altogether, the Guidelines adopt a sophisticated approach that is sensitive to the economic and commercial aspects of particular kinds of agreement. They are not to be applied mechanically but in a reasonable and flexible manner.[25]

6.009 **Structure of this Chapter.** The next Section of this Chapter describes in detail the exemption conferred by Regulation 2790/99. The subsequent Sections consider various kinds of agreements and vertical restraints under the following classifications:

(i) *Agency agreements:* the relationship between the parties is one of principal and agent, strictly so called.[26] The principal is typically restricted as to the other agents through whom it may supply while the agent may be restricted from acting for another principal. Such agreements are discussed in Section 3;

(ii) *Exclusive distribution and supply agreements:* the supplier appoints a distributor for a territory or for a particular class of customer; that distributor buys the goods from the supplier on its own account and resells them, normally to retailers or direct to consumers or users. The supplier is typically restricted from supplying customers itself directly[27] or from appointing another distributor in the territory or for those customers. This category also includes

---

[23] ibid, paras 137–228.

[24] ibid, para 120(2).

[25] ibid, para 1(3).

[26] The expression 'agent' is sometimes loosely used to describe a distributor who buys for his own account. In this chapter 'agent' refers only to an agent strictly so called, ie one who merely passes orders to his principal or makes contracts on his principal's behalf.

[27] If the restriction on the supplier does not prevent the supplier himself making direct supplies then the agreement is, strictly speaking, 'sole' rather than 'exclusive'; but these expressions tend to be used interchangeably in the context of distribution agreements.

exclusive supply agreements, whereby the supplier agrees to sell in the Community to only one purchaser,[28] who may be an end-user that incorporates the products in his industrial process. This category is discussed in Section 4;

(iii) *Selective distribution agreements:* the supplier operates a restricted system of distribution in which it appoints only a limited number of wholesale or retail dealers who agree not to supply unauthorised dealers outside the network. Such agreements are discussed in Section 5. Motor vehicle dealerships typically constitute such a system, and this Section considers the block exemption for such agreements, Regulation 1400/2002;

(iv) *Exclusive purchasing, single branding and tying agreements:* Section 6 considers these different, but related, forms of restraint that are often found in combination in the same agreement. In exclusive purchasing, the person to be supplied undertakes to obtain all his requirements of specified goods from a particular supplier. In single branding (or a non-compete obligation), the purchaser agrees not to obtain goods of the type being supplied which are not of the specified brand. Exclusive purchasing and single branding obligations are found in 'tied house' agreements for beer and 'solus' agreements for petrol. This Section also considers minimum purchasing obligations that may have an equivalent effect. In a tying arrangement, the purchaser is obliged when purchasing one kind of product to purchase also a second (tied) product;

(v) *Franchise agreements:* the franchisor licenses a retail dealer to sell goods under the franchisor's trade mark, usually in retail premises 'got up' in accordance with the franchisor's specifications. The franchisor normally requires the franchisee to sell only at the approved location and to obtain goods from the franchisor or sources specified by him. Franchise agreements are discussed in Section 7;

(vi) *Subcontracting agreements:* a supplier contracts for the manufacture of the products which it supplies, or of certain components which it incorporates in those products, to be carried out to its instructions and specifications by an independent subcontractor. Subcontracting agreements are discussed in Section 8;

(vii) *Packaging waste recovery systems:* an undertaking contracts with producers and distributors of packaged goods to arrange the collection and recycling of the waste packaging from consumers and then contracts also with local authorities, waste collectors and waste recyclers to ensure the proper disposal of the packaging. These systems are discussed in Section 9.

---

[28] Or a single purchaser for a particular application.

2. Regulation 2790/99

6.010 **In general.** Regulation 2790/99[29] was adopted by the Commission on 22 December 1999. It came into force on 1 June 2000 and applies until 1 June 2010.[30] The background to the new regime created by this block exemption is discussed above. Altogether, the block exemption adopts a broad approach to exemption of vertical restraints based not so much on the terms of the agreement but on the market power of the parties. Interpretation of Regulation 2790/99 is assisted by the Commission's Guidelines.[31]

(a) Scope

6.011 **'Vertical agreement'.** For the purpose of Regulation 2790/99, the term 'vertical agreement' is defined in Article 2 as an agreement or concerted practice entered into between two or more undertakings that meets two conditions:

(a) each undertaking operates at a different level of the production or distribution chain for the purposes of the agreement; and

(b) the agreement relates to the conditions under which the parties may purchase, sell or resell certain goods or services.

Accordingly, Regulation 2790/99 applies to agreements concerning services as well as agreements concerning goods. Unlike the three former block exemptions which it replaces, it is not limited to agreements between only two undertakings. An agreement between a manufacturer, a wholesaler and a retailer may accordingly fall within the exemption. There is no requirement that the goods be purchased for resale: they may be bought for use, either in themselves or to be incorporated in a manufactured product,[32] or for renting to third parties. But a rental or lease agreement in itself is not covered by the block exemption. The requirement that the parties should be operating at different levels of 'the production or distribution chain' would appear to exclude from the scope of the block exemption an arrangement whereby a retailer grants franchises to independent third parties to carry on an equivalent retail operation in other territories.

---

[29] Reg 2790/99, OJ 1999 L336/21: Vol II, App C.3. Subject to necessary modifications, Reg 2790/99 has been adopted under the EEA Agreement by EEA Joint Committee Decn 18/2000 of 28 January 2000, with retroactive effective from 1 January 2000: OJ 2001 L103/36.

[30] Reg 2790/99, above, Art 13 (except for the extension of the validity of Regs 1983/83, 1984/83 and 4087/88, which applied as from 1 January 2000: ibid)

[31] Guidelines on Vertical Restraints, OJ 2000 C291/1: Vol II, App C.11, see para 6.008, above.

[32] Although both seller and purchaser may be manufacturers, *for the purposes of the agreement* they would be operating at different levels of the production chain.

Competing undertakings. The block exemption will not in general apply to **6.012** agreements between competing undertakings,[33] which are defined for this purpose as actual or potential suppliers in the same product market, irrespective of their geographic market.[34] For example, if a manufacturer supplies raw materials used in its products to another manufacturer of the same or competing products, the agreement between them will not be covered. However, this exclusion is subject to three exceptions for non-reciprocal agreements[35] which may therefore be covered by the exemption:

(a) if the buyer's annual turnover[36] does not exceed €100 million; or
(b) if the supplier is a manufacturer and a distributor of goods whereas the buyer is a distributor but not also a manufacturer of competing goods; or
(c) if the supplier is a provider of services at several levels of trade whereas the buyer does not provide competing services at the level at which he purchases services from the supplier.

By virtue of the second exception, a distribution agreement made by a producer which also distributes its own products alongside its appointed distributors (that is, dual distribution) may benefit from the block exemption. The third exception achieves the same result as regards the supply of services.

Retailers' associations. The block exemption will apply to vertical agreements **6.013** made by an association of distributors selling goods to final consumers and either its members, or its suppliers, on condition that no individual member (and its connected undertakings) has a total annual turnover[37] exceeding €50 million. An agreement whereby an individual member of a retailers' joint buying association purchases supplies from the association would therefore be covered, subject to the turnover condition. However, a purely horizontal agreement, for example that the members should sell only certain categories of goods, would not be covered.[38] Therefore a decision by the association that the members should buy specified goods only from the association would first have to be assessed as a horizontal agreement before consideration of the application of the block exemption to the vertical agreements for purchase by the members from the association.[39]

---

[33] Reg 2790/99 (n 29, above) Art 2(4).
[34] ibid, Art 1(a).
[35] eg where one manufacturer becomes the distributor of the products of a second manufacturer but the second manufacturer does not become the distributor of the products of the first manufacturer.
[36] See para 6.014, below.
[37] For annual turnover and 'connected undertaking', see para 6.014, below.
[38] Reg 2790/99 (n 29, above) Art 2(2).
[39] Guidelines on Vertical Restraints (n 31, above) para 29. For the horizontal aspects, see Chap 5, above.

6.014 **Turnover calculations.** For the purpose of calculating the annual turnover under the Regulation, the turnover in the previous financial year of the undertaking in question and all connected undertakings, in respect of all goods and services, is to be used.[40] However, the exemption still applies if the threshold is exceeded by no more than 10 per cent in any two consecutive financial years.[41] 'Connected undertakings' is given an extended definition based on control.[42]

6.015 **Other block exemptions.** Regulation 2790/99 does not apply to agreements the subject-matter of which falls within another subsisting block exemption.[43] Accordingly, it does not currently apply to:

(a) agreements covered by the motor vehicle dealing block exemption, Regulation 1400/2002;[44]

(b) agreements covered by the technology transfer block exemption, Regulation 772/2004;[45]

(c) vertical restraints in connection with agreements concerning specialisation or research and development covered by Regulations 2658/2000 or 2659/2000, respectively.[46]

Therefore if, for example, an agreement within the scope of the motor vehicle dealing block exemption, Regulation 1400/2002, does not because of its terms satisfy the conditions of exemption under that Regulation, it cannot be 'saved' by Regulation 2790/99.

6.016 **Intellectual property rights.** In many cases, restrictions concerning intellectual property rights (IPR) may not come within Article 81(1) at all.[47] However, insofar as they may do so, Article 2(3) of Regulation 2790/99 provides that the block exemption applies to a vertical agreement concerning the assignment to, or use by, the buyer of IPR on condition that (i) those provisions are not the primary object of the agreement; (ii) they are directly related to the use, sale or resale by the buyer or his customers of the goods or services in question; and (iii) in relation to the contract goods or services those provisions do not contain restrictions that have the same object or effect as vertical restraints that are not exempted under the block exemption. Those requirements are designed to ensure that the block exemption will only apply to agreements containing provisions on IPR when the

---

[40] Reg 2790/99 (n 29, above) Art 10(1).

[41] ibid, Art 10(2).

[42] ibid, Art 11(2).

[43] ibid, Art 2(5).

[44] Reg 1400/2002, OJ 2002 L203/30: Vol II, App C.6. This Reg is discussed at paras 6.109 *et seq*, below.

[45] Reg 772/2004, OJ 2004 L123/11: Vol II, App C.7. See paras 9.129 *et seq*, below.

[46] Reg 2658/2000, OJ 2000 L304/3: Vol II, App C.4 and Reg 2659/2000, OJ 2000 L304/7: Vol II, App C.5, and see paras 7.097 and 7.078 *et seq*, below.

[47] See generally Chap 9, below.

main object of the agreement is the purchase or distribution of goods.[48] It will not apply, for example, to a pure licensing agreement, or to the assignment or licensing of IPR for the purpose of manufacture. Therefore subcontracting agreements, where the supplier transfers know-how to a subcontractor, will not be covered. But provisions on know-how and trade marks in franchise agreements normally concern the marketing of the goods or services by the franchisee-purchaser and accordingly such an agreement should satisfy the requirements of Article 2(3).[49]

(b) Market share

Threshold. According to Article 3 of Regulation 2790/99, the block exemption **6.017** will apply only if the market share held by the relevant party does not exceed 30 per cent. This reflects the fact that it is generally only where at least one party has market power that a vertical agreement may produce significant anti-competitive effects or effects that are not necessarily counterbalanced by benefits.[50] Although market share is not the same as market power, this condition is intended to provide a 'safe harbour' for agreements on the basis that if the relevant party does not have a high market share it is very unlikely to have market power. Although the 30 per cent condition is referred to as a 'threshold', it should be remembered that Regulation 2790/99 serves to apply Article 81(3) to many agreements that fall within Article 81(1), and includes the power to withdraw or disapply the block exemption in appropriate cases.[51] As regards vertical agreements that fall outside the block exemption because the threshold is exceeded, the Commission has made clear that they are not to be presumed to be illegal but may benefit from the individual application of Article 81(3).[52]

Relevant party. In most cases, the threshold of 30 per cent applies to the share **6.018** held by the supplier (and its connected undertakings) of the market in which it sells the contract goods or services.[53] But where the agreement contains an 'exclusive *supply* obligation', the threshold applies instead to the buyer (and its connected undertakings).[54] That approach reflects the fact that where a single buyer has the exclusive right to purchase particular goods or services, the relevant effect on competition arises from the enhancement of that buyer's market power,

---

[48] See the Guidelines on Vertical Restraints (n 31, above) paras 30 *et seq.*

[49] ibid, paras 42–44; see further paras 6.171 and 6.183, below.

[50] ibid, Recitals (8)–(9): the impact of vertical restraints is approached in the framework of Art 81(3); Recital (4) states that it is not necessary to determine for this purpose whether agreements in fact come within Art 81(1).

[51] It is therefore more accurate to describe the 30 per cent condition as a ceiling for the application of Reg 2790/99. For withdrawal and disapplication, see paras 6.025 *et seq*, below.

[52] Guidelines on Vertical Restraints (n 31, above) para 63.

[53] Reg 2790/99 (n 29, above) Arts 3(1), 11(1).

[54] ibid, Arts 3(2), 11(1).

even if the supplier's market share is relatively small. However, 'exclusive supply obligation' is narrowly defined as:

'any direct or indirect obligation causing the supplier to sell the goods or services specified in the agreement *only to one buyer inside the Community* for the purposes of a specific use or for resale.'[55] [emphasis added]

The fact that when the exclusivity relates, for example, only to a single Member State, the applicable threshold under the regulation is the supplier's market share and not the buyer's market share, although that Member State may be the relevant market, appears anomalous. The rationale seems to be that parallel trading by buyers in other areas of the Community should counter any anti-competitive effects.[56]

6.019 **Calculation of market share.** Although determining the market share is very important for the application of the block exemption, the provisions in Article 9 dealing with how this is done are relatively sparse. Where the market share of the *supplier* has to be determined, the primary test is share by value, calculated on the basis of sales of the contract goods or services and other substitutable goods or services made by the supplier and its connected undertakings.[57] If value data are not available, 'estimates based on other reliable market information, including market sales volumes' can be used. However, where the market share in purchases by the *buyer* is the determining factor,[58] only data or estimates by value, not by volume, must be used. Article 9(1) refers to goods regarded as substitutable or interchangeable by consumers on the basis of the products' characteristics, prices and intended use. Determination of the relevant product and geographic market for the purpose of assessment of market share should be undertaken on the basis of the Commission's Notice on the definition of relevant market ('the Relevant Market Notice'),[59] discussed in detail in Chapter 4, above. But for the purpose of the block exemption, the market in question is that on which the supplier, or buyer, itself sells the contract goods to, or buys them from, its trading partners: the share held of a downstream market is not taken into account;[60] nor is in-house

---

[55] ibid, Art 1(c).

[56] This would depend, however, on whether such parallel trading was practicable. Note that if a supply contract restricts the supplier from selling to anyone else in a Member State, although the threshold under Reg 2790/99 is based on the *supplier's* market share, if the State is regarded as a distinct market and the *buyer's* share of that market renders the contract anti-competitive, the State's competent authority may withdraw the benefit of the block exemption from that contract for its territory: para 6.026, below.

[57] Where the supplier shares control of a 'connected' undertaking with a third party (eg a joint venture), the market share of that undertaking is to be apportioned: Reg 2790/99 (n 29, above) Art 11(3).

[58] See para 6.018, above.

[59] Guidelines on Vertical Restraints (n 31, above) para 94; the Relevant Market Notice is at Vol II, App C.10.

[60] Guidelines on Vertical Restraints (n 31, above) paras 91–92. The Commission considers that in view of the 30 per cent threshold, the effect on a downstream market is likely to be limited: ibid,

production of an intermediate product for own use.[61] However, if the wholesale market is the relevant market, supplies to integrated distributors for sale are to be included in calculation of the supplier's market share.[62] The Commission's Guidelines state that in cases involving three parties operating at different levels of trade (for example, producer, wholesaler and distributor), the market share at both levels of supply must fall below the threshold for the block exemption to apply.[63] As regards repair or replacement parts, the original equipment manufacturer is often the sole or major source of supply. The Guidelines state that the relevant market for the application of Regulation 2790/99 in such a case may be either the original equipment market including the spare parts or a distinct after-market, depending on the circumstances, including the lifetime of the equipment and the importance of the repair or replacement costs.[64]

Relevant period. Article 9(2) provides that the relevant market share should be **6.020** calculated on the basis of data relating to the preceding calendar year. Although the threshold is 30 per cent, the block exemption incorporates limited extensions that allow for expansion in market share. If the share rises to between 30 and 35 per cent, the block exemption continues to apply for the next two consecutive calendar years. If it rises above 35 per cent, the block exemption continues to apply for the next calendar year. But the benefit of these two provisions cannot be combined to obtain an overall extension in excess of two years. The wording of these provisions makes clear that the application of the block exemption to an agreement is not determined on a once-and-for-all basis at the time the agreement is entered into but that, subject to these limited extensions, it depends on continuing satisfaction of the market share threshold. For example, if a five-year exclusive distribution agreement is entered into in March 2006 and the supplier's market share was below 30 per cent in the calendar year 2005 but rises to 34 per cent in 2007, the agreement will cease to come within the block exemption at the end of 2009. If instead it rises in 2007 to 38 per cent, it will cease to come within the block exemption at the end of 2008.

---

para 22. But note that where a franchisor supplies not goods but a bundle of services and IPR that form the business method being franchised, the Guidelines state that the franchisor's market share as the provider of a business method is based on the market where the method is exploited, ie by the franchisees. Its market share should therefore be calculated on the basis of the franchisees' share of that market, which will include suppliers of substitutable goods and services that are not franchised: ibid, para 95. This approach is hard to reconcile with Art 3(1) of Reg 2790/99 (n 29, above). Where the franchisor also supplies goods, a separate market share calculation for the supply of goods to retailers needs to be made.

[61] Guidelines on Vertical Restraints (n 31, above) para 98.
[62] Reg 2790/99 (n 29, above) Art 9(2)(b).
[63] Guidelines on Vertical Restraints, OJ 2000 C291/1: Vol II, App C.11, para 93.
[64] ibid, para 94; and see the discussion in paras 4.060, above.

6.021 **Vertical agreement covering several products.** A supplier may distribute a range of different products under the same vertical agreement. It may satisfy the market share threshold as regards some of those products but not for the others. In those circumstances, the block exemption will apparently apply to the agreement in respect of the former goods. The Guidelines state that in such a case, if the conditions for the application of Article 81(3) are not fulfilled in respect of the latter goods, consideration should be given as to whether 'appropriate remedies' can be found to solve the competition problem within the existing distribution system.[65]

(c) Terms and conditions

6.022 **Scheme of the block exemption.** Regulation 2790/99 distinguishes between two kinds of prohibited restrictions. Article 4 lists a number of 'hard-core' restraints. If the agreement, whether on its own or in combination with other factors under the control of the parties, has the object of imposing any of these hard-core restraints, the whole agreement will fall outside the block exemption and all restrictions coming within Article 81(1) will be void. By contrast, Article 5 sets out a list of non-exempted restrictions. Although none of those terms in an agreement receives the benefit of block exemption, that does not affect the application of the block exemption to other restrictions in the agreement. Whether such severance for the purposes of Article 81(2) renders the agreement, shorn of these restrictions, enforceable is a question of domestic law.[66]

6.023 **Hard-core restrictions.** The block exemption will not apply to an agreement that directly or indirectly has the object of imposing any of the following restraints:

(a) Imposition of a fixed or minimum resale price. The agreement may set a recommended or maximum resale price provided this does not in practice amount to a fixed or minimum price.[67]

(b) In the case of a selective distribution system,[68] any restriction of (i) resales by a retail distributor to end-users, whether active or passive, save that the distributor may be prohibited from operating out of an unauthorised place of business;[69]

---

[65] Guidelines on Vertical Restraints (n 63, above) para 69.

[66] See paras 14.101 *et seq*, below.

[67] Reg 2790/99 (n 29, above) Art 4(a). The Guidelines on Vertical Restraints (n 63, above) para 47, list a range of measures that may indirectly impose RPM, eg granting rebates or reimbursement of promotional costs subject to observance of a recommended price.

[68] For definition, see Reg 2790/99 (n 29, above) Art 1(d); and see further paras 6.086 *et seq*, below.

[69] Reg 2790/99 (n 29, above) Art 4(c). The distributors may therefore effectively be restricted in their location, including a defined territory for a mobile distributor: Guidelines on Vertical Restraints (n 63, above) para 54. But they cannot be prevented from advertising or selling over the internet: ibid, para 53. See, eg *Selective distribution system for Yves Saint Laurent perfume*, Press Release IP/01/713 (17 May 2001): system satisfied Reg 2790/99 since authorised retailers operating a physical sales point were allowed to sell also via the internet.

or (ii) cross-supplies by any distributor to other distributors within the system.[70] The agreement may restrict resales to unauthorised distributors.[71] Therefore a supplier cannot combine selective distribution with exclusive purchasing obligations.

(c) In all other cases, any restriction[72] concerning the territory into which or the customers to whom resales can be made, except:[73]

  (i) a buyer may be restricted from making active resales in the exclusive territory or to the exclusive customer group given to another buyer or reserved by the supplier[74] but no obligation may be placed on a buyer to limit resales by its customers;[75]

  (ii) a wholesaler may be restricted from selling to end-users;[76]

  (iii) in the case of components[77] supplied for the purposes of incorporation into another product, the buyer may be restricted in selling them to customers who would use them to manufacture 'the same type of goods' as those sold by the supplier.[78] Therefore independent repairers who purchase spare parts for the purposes of their repair service cannot otherwise be restricted in reselling those spare parts (unless the repairers form part of a selective distribution system).

---

[70] Reg 2790/99 (n 29, above) Art 4(d).

[71] ibid, Art 4(b), 3rd indent.

[72] See eg *Nathan-Bricolux*, OJ 2001 L54/1, [2001] CMLR 1122, where the absolute territorial protection precluded the application of the block exemption. The Guidelines on Vertical Restraints (n 63, above) emphasise, at para 49, that indirect restrictions may have that effect, eg when a supplier offering a guarantee does not reimburse distributors for this service in relation to products sold by other distributors into their territory. If the supplier operates a system that seeks to monitor the destination of its goods, that may reinforce the possibility of a practice being found to constitute an indirect restriction.

[73] The Guidelines on Vertical Restraints (n 63, above) state, at para 49, that a prohibition on sales to certain end-users will also not be regarded as hard-core if it is objectively justified by reference to the product, eg a general ban on selling dangerous substances to certain customers for health and safety reasons. This is obviously sensible (eg a restriction on sale to children) although it requires a generous interpretation of the language of Art 4. An obligation on the reseller regarding display of the supplier's brand name is not a hard-core restriction: ibid.

[74] For the Commission's interpretation of 'active' and 'passive' sales, see Guidelines on Vertical Restraints (n 63, above) para 50. Note that use of the internet for promotion and sale is not regarded as active selling; cf sending unsolicited emails to potential customers: ibid, para 51. The scope of this exemption is more limited than the analogous provision of the former block exemption for exclusive distribution agreements, which permitted a general restriction on active sales outside the distributor's territory, irrespective of whether the area so prohibited had been reserved for anyone else: Art 2(2)(c) of Reg 1983/83, OJ 1983 L173/1.

[75] Reg 2790/99 (n 29, above) Art 4(b), 1st indent.

[76] ibid, Art 4(b), 2nd indent.

[77] 'Components' includes any intermediate goods: Guidelines on Vertical Restraints (n 63 above) para 52.

[78] Reg 2790/99 (n 29, above) Art 4(b), 4th indent.

(d) In the case of agreements between a supplier of components and buyers who incorporate those components, any restriction on the supplier also selling the products as spare parts (i) to end-users; or (ii) to independent repairers or service providers who have not been entrusted by the buyer with the repair or servicing of the final product.[79] This means that the supplier can be prevented from supplying spare parts to those repairers and service providers who form part of the buyer's own network, thereby enabling the buyer to require his authorised repairers and service providers to obtain their spare parts from him.

6.024 **Non-exempted restrictions.** The specified conditions listed in Article 5 that do not receive exemption are:

(a) A direct or indirect non-compete obligation for a period in excess of five years or an indefinite period.[80] It should be noted that this limit is not related to the duration of the agreement itself. Furthermore, 'non-compete obligation' is given an extended definition to cover also an obligation to purchase more than 80 per cent of the buyer's requirements of such goods or services from the supplier or from a third party designated by the supplier.[81] But there is an exception where the goods or services are supplied by the buyer from premises owned or leased[82] by the supplier, for example a 'tied' pub or petrol service station: in such a case the non-compete obligation may extend for the period of occupancy.

(b) A direct or indirect obligation or restriction on the buyer as regards manufacture, purchase, distribution or sale that applies after termination of the agreement, except for a post-termination non-compete obligation as regards competing goods or services which is not more than one year's duration, provided that (i) it is indispensible to protect know-how[83] transferred to the buyer by the supplier; and (ii) it is 'limited to the premises and land from which the buyer has operated during the contract period.' This condition does not affect a prohibition on use or disclosure of know-how that is not in

---

[79] ibid, Art 4(e).

[80] A non-compete obligation which is automatically renewed beyond five years unless terminated is deemed to be of indefinite duration. Note that the Commission takes a strong line as to what constitutes pressure to extend a non-compete obligation thereby indirectly prolonging its duration and taking the obligation outside the exemption. The Guidelines on Vertical Restraints (n 63, above) state that when the supplier provides equipment which is not 'relationship-specific', the buyer should have the opportunity to take over that equipment at its market value at the end of the non-compete obligation: para 58.

[81] Reg 2790/99 (n 29, above) Art 1(b).

[82] Provided that the landlord is an independent third party and not connected to the buyer. This is an anti-avoidance provision.

[83] For definition of 'know-how', see Reg 2790/99 (n 29, above) Art 1(f).

the public domain. Nonetheless, the condition as regards location is much narrower than is commonly found in many post-termination restrictions.

(c) Any direct or indirect obligation on members of a selective distribution system not to sell specified brands of *particular* competing suppliers. Although the supplier can impose on its selective distributors a general non-compete obligation for up to five years, if it does not do so, it cannot impose a restriction that is targeted at specific competing brands. Although that may appear to be a narrower restriction, the Commission explains this provision as designed to avoid a situation where a number of suppliers use the same selective distribution outlets and require those outlets not to carry the goods of particular competitors. This could significantly foreclose access to the market for those targeted suppliers.[84]

(d) Withdrawal and disapplication

Withdrawal by the Commission. Regulation 2790/99[85] provides, by Article 6, **6.025** that where the Commission finds that in a particular case, agreements otherwise within the block exemption have effects that are incompatible with the criteria of Article 81(3), it may withdraw the benefit of the block exemption from those agreements. In view of the market share threshold that usually applies to the supplier, the Regulation indicates that grounds for withdrawal may arise when the buyer has significant market power in the relevant downstream market where it resells the goods; or when the cumulative effect of similar vertical restraints in parallel networks of agreements implemented by competing suppliers or buyers restricts competition or access to the market.[86] That may be the case, for example, with a selective distribution system that includes non-compete obligations. The Guidelines also envisage that vertical restraints may have a stronger adverse impact, that may justify withdrawal of the benefit of the Regulation, when they apply to the distribution of goods to final consumers.[87] Withdrawal cannot be retrospective. A decision to withdraw under Article 6 implies that the Commission

---

[84] Guidelines on Vertical Restraints (n 63, above) paras 61 and 192. See also Recital (11) to Reg 2790/99 (n 29, above). If this amounted to a collective boycott by the suppliers, it would also infringe Art 81(1) as a horizontal agreement.

[85] Reg 2790/99, OJ 1999 L336/21: Vol II, App C.3.

[86] Reg 2790/99, above, Art 6 and Recital (13). See also Guidelines on Vertical Restraints (n 63, above) para 204. Note that in *Langnese-Iglo*, OJ 1993 L183/19, [1994] 4 CMLR 83, the Commission acted under the analogous provision of Reg 1984/83 to withdraw the benefit of that block exemption from a network of exclusive purchasing agreements for ice cream when it found a cumulative foreclosure effect on the German market; the decision was upheld on appeal: Case T-7/93 *Langnese-Iglo v Commission* [1995] ECR II-1533, [1995] 5 CMLR 602, [1995] All ER (EC) 902, paras 145–154: see further para 6.147, below.

[87] Guidelines on Vertical Restraints (n 63, above) para 71.

has concluded that the agreements in question infringe Article 81(1) and do not merit exemption.[88]

6.026 **Withdrawal by a national authority.** Article 7 of Regulation 2790/99 gives a similar power of withdrawal to the competent national authority where a vertical agreement, or network of agreements, has effects incompatible with Article 81(3) in the whole or part of the territory of a Member State that has all the characteristics of a distinct geographic market.[89] In such a case, therefore, the Commission and national authority have concurrent jurisdiction to withdraw the benefit of the block exemption. However, withdrawal by a national authority has effect only as regards its own national territory. A competent national authority may be expected to consult with the Commission before taking a decision of withdrawal under Article 7.[90]

6.027 **Disapplication by regulation.** Although the relevant parties to individual agreements may each have well below a 30 per cent market share, a market may be characterised by networks of parallel agreements containing similar restrictions[91] which, taken together, have a significant anti-competitive effect. Where such networks cover more than 50 per cent of a relevant market, Article 8 of Regulation 2790/99 gives the Commission power to disapply the block exemption altogether to vertical agreements relating to that market that contain specific restrictions.[92] This power is to be exercised by the making of a regulation, which must identify the type of vertical restraint and the market in respect of which the block exemption will no longer apply. Such a regulation may not take effect earlier than six months after its adoption,[93] and the Commission should set this transitional period to allow the parties time to adapt their agreements.[94] Moreover, as such disapplication applies generally in the market, the possibility remains that particular agreements may fulfil the criteria of Article 81(3).[95] Accordingly, before exercising the general power under Article 8 to disapply the block exemption, the Commission will consider whether individual withdrawal under Article 6 would be a more appropriate remedy. That is likely to depend on the number of

---

[88] ibid, para 81.

[89] cf Art 9 of the Merger Regulation (Reg 139/2004) and in particular Art 9(2) and (7): see para 8.094, below.

[90] Guidelines on Vertical Restraints (n 63, above) paras 77–78.

[91] The Commission states that it will normally regard restrictions as similar if they come within the same category in its classification of four types of restraints: Guidelines on Vertical Restraints (n 63, above) para 82, and see para 6.008, above. However, some of those categories (eg single branding) comprise very different kinds of restrictions and the Commission also notes that the disapplication may be limited only to specific kinds of restriction within a category.

[92] Reg 2790/99, OJ 1999 L336/21: Vol II, App C.3, Art 8(1).

[93] Reg 2790/99, above, Art 8(2).

[94] Guidelines on Vertical Restraints (n 63, above) para 86. It will not affect the validity of agreements prior to its entry into force: ibid, para 87.

[95] ibid, para 81.

undertakings that contribute to the cumulative effect or the number of affected geographic markets within the Community.[96]

3. Agency Agreements

Introduction.   The term 'agent' is sometimes used loosely to describe a distributor who may act exclusively as the intermediary promoting the products of a particular supplier but in fact buys and resells those products for his own account. In the case of genuine agency agreements, the obligations imposed on the agent as to the contracts that he negotiates or concludes on behalf of his principal do not fall within the scope of application of Article 81(1). This is usually explained on the basis that a genuine agent is to be regarded as merely an auxiliary organ forming an integral part of the principal's business; therefore obligations imposed on the agent that relate only to activity which he undertakes on his principal's behalf cannot be regarded as, in themselves, restrictive of competition.[97] By contrast, 'non-genuine' agency agreements may fall within Article 81(1) and be treated in the same way as ordinary distribution agreements. It is therefore critical to establish whether or not an agency agreement is to be regarded as 'genuine'.[98]   **6.028**

Commission Guidelines.   The Commission's Guidelines on Vertical Restraints[99] define an agency agreement as covering: **6.029**

> 'the situation in which a legal or physical person (the agent) is vested with the power to negotiate and/or conclude contracts on behalf of another person (the principal), either in the agent's own name or in the name of the principal, for the:
> — purchase of goods or services by the principal, or
> — the sale of goods or services supplied by the principal'.[100]

---

[96]   ibid, para 84.

[97]   In a different context, namely the attribution of cartel participation of an agent to its principal, the CFI has stated that 'where an agent works for his principal, he can in principle be regarded as an auxiliary organ forming an integral part of the latter's undertaking, bound to carry out the principal's instructions and thus, like a commercial employee, forms an economic unit with this undertaking': see Case T-56/99 *Marlines v Commission* [2003] ECR II-5225, [2005] 5 CMLR 1761, para 60 (appeal dismissed, Case C-112/04P, order of 15 September 2005); and Case T-66/99 *Minoan Lines v Commission* [2003] ECR II-5515, [2005] 5 CMLR 1957, paras 121 *et seq* (appeal dismissed, Case C-121/04P, order of 17 November 2005).

[98]   In Case VI-U(Kart)43/02, judgment of the Oberlandesgericht Düsseldorf of 24 March 2004 (published at: www.justiz.nrw.de/RB/nrwe/index.html), the owner of a petrol station alleged that his supply agreement contravened Art 81(1) because it required him to pay two days in advance for expected sales of petrol. The Court held, having analysed the allocation of risks under the contract, that the agreement was a genuine agency agreement that fell outside Art 81(1).

[99]   Guidelines on Vertical Restraints, OJ 2000 C291/1: Vol II, App C.11.

[100]   ibid, para 12. The section on agency agreements in the Guidelines (paras 12–20) replaces the Commission's Notice on Exclusive Dealing Contracts with Commercial Agents of 24 December 1962, JO 1962 139/2921 (sometimes called 'the Christmas message'): see App 21 to the 4th ed of this work.

6.030 **Financial or commercial risk.** In *Sugar*,[101] the Court of Justice held that agents who by agreement carry out 'duties which from an economic point of view are approximately the same as those carried out by an independent dealer' cannot be regarded as auxiliary organs forming an integral part of the principal's undertaking 'because . . . the said agents [accept] the financial risks of the sales or of the performance of contracts entered into with third parties'.[102] This reasoning was applied in *Bundeskartellamt v Volkswagen and VAG Leasing*,[103] where the Court took the view that the question whether or not the 'agent' assumes financial risk was the essential factor in determining whether there was a true agency agreement. The Court stated that 'representatives can lose their character as independent traders only if they do not bear any of the risks resulting from the contracts negotiated on behalf of the principal and they operate as auxiliary organs forming an integral part of the principal's undertaking'.[104] However, the reference to 'any of the risks' is not to be taken literally: in *CEPSA*,[105] the Court made clear that the test is whether or not the operator assumes one or more of the financial and commercial risks 'to a non-negligible extent'.

6.031 **The analysis of the Court of First Instance in *DaimlerChrysler*.** In its decision in *Mercedes-Benz*[106] the Commission held that the agreements which DaimlerChrysler entered into with its German agents for the distribution of Mercedes-Benz cars should be treated in the same way as its dealership arrangements with distributors in other Member States. The Commission held that the agent bore a considerable share of the price risk because any price concessions, volume or user discounts offered by the agent were deducted in whole or in part from the agent's commission. According to the contract terms, the agent also bore the cost of transporting a new vehicle to a customer who did not wish to collect at the factory; he had to acquire demonstration vehicles for his own account and set up a workshop for his own account to offer customer and guarantee services.

---

[101] Cases 40/73, etc, *Suiker Unie v Commission* [1975] ECR 1663, [1976] 1 CMLR 295, paras 530–557 (see also paras 458–498).

[102] *Suiker Unie*, above, at paras 541–542; similarly at paras 482–483. See also *ARG/Unipart*, OJ 1988 L45/34, [1988] 4 CMLR 513 (genuine agency); *Fisher-Price/Quaker Oats—Toyco*, OJ 1988 L49/19, [1989] 4 CMLR 553; *Distribution of package tours during 1990 World Cup*, OJ 1992 L326/31, [1994] 5 CMLR 253 (role of 90 Tour Italia went well beyond that of a mere agent).

[103] Case C-266/93 *Bundeskartellamt v Volkswagen AG and VAG Leasing* [1995] ECR I-3477, [1996] 4 CMLR 478, paras 4 and 19.

[104] ibid, para 19. The ECJ noted that the dealers assumed, at least in part, the financial risks linked to the transactions concluded on behalf of VAG Leasing insofar as they repurchased the vehicles from it upon expiry of the leasing contracts. This approach is reflected in the Guidelines, which state that the determining factor in assessing whether an agency agreement falls within the scope of Art 81(1) is the financial or commercial risk borne by the agent in relation to the activities for which he has been appointed as an agent by the principal: para 13.

[105] Case C-217/05 *Confederación Española de Empresarios de Estaciones de Servicio ("CEPSA")*, [2006] ECRI-11987, [2007] 4 CMLR 181.

[106] *Mercedes-Benz*, OJ 2002 L257/1, [2003] 4 CMLR 95.

Having examined in detail the nature of the relationship, and having noted that the agency agreements placed requirements on agents which were identical to those placed on Mercedes-Benz dealers outside Germany, the Commission concluded that Article 81(1) was applicable to the agreements in the same way as to the agreements with dealers. The Commission went on to find that instructions by DaimlerChrysler to its agents not to sell vehicles outside their contract territory were attempts to partition markets and contravened Article 81(1). The Court of First Instance annulled the findings in the decision regarding agency.[107] The Court found that it was Mercedes-Benz, not its German agents who determined the conditions of each sale for a particular vehicle, including the sale price, and who bore the main risks relating a sale. The agent was prohibited by the agency contract from buying and maintaining stocks of vehicles for sale. The Court concluded that they sold the vehicles 'essentially under the direction of' Mercedes-Benz and 'must thus be assimilated to employees and considered as integrated in this undertaking, and being part of the same economic entity'.[108] It was also Mercedes-Benz which assumed the risks of the transaction, including the failure to deliver, delivery of a faulty vehicle or non-payment of the price. The Court criticised the Commission for exaggerating the impact of the risks assumed by the agent, saying that the Commission had simply listed the obligations imposed under the contract without demonstrating the extent to which these obligations in practice created a commercial risk for the agent. The agents' provision of repairs and after-sales service were not associated with a commercial risk which would require them to be classified as independent operators.

Types of risk.   The Guidelines on Vertical Restraints must, on this point, now   **6.032** be read in the light of the *DaimlerChrysler* judgment. They distinguish two types of financial or commercial risk that are relevant to the assessment of the genuine nature of an agency agreement for the purpose of Article 81(1): (i) risks that are directly related to the contracts concluded and/or negotiated by the agent on behalf of the principal; and (ii) risks related to market-specific investments.[109] The first category includes such matters as the financing of stock. The second category comprises investments that are specifically required for the type of activity for which the agent has been appointed by the principal, ie which are required to enable the agent to conclude and/or negotiate such contracts. If upon leaving that particular field of activity, the agent cannot use the investment for other activities or sell them other than at a significant loss, they represent sunk costs. On the other hand, risks that are related to the activity of providing agency services in general, such as the dependence of the agent's income upon his success as an agent or

---

[107] Case T-325/01 *DaimlerChrysler v Commission* [2005] ECR II-3319, [2007] 4 CMLR 559.
[108] ibid, para 102 [editors' translation].
[109] Guidelines on Vertical Restraints (n 99, above) para 14.

general investments in premises or personnel, are not relevant to this assessment. Although the list set out in the Guidelines is helpful, it is expressly stated not to be exhaustive in establishing that an agency agreement falls outside Article 81(1). In giving a preliminary ruling in *CEPSA*, the Court of Justice indicated the relevant risks to be considered in determining whether a service station operator is to be regarded as the agent of the fuel supplier, including the ownership of the goods, the contribution to the costs of their distribution, their safe-keeping, liability for damage caused to the goods or by the goods to third parties, and the making of investments specific to the sale of the goods.[110]

6.033 **Agent acting for more than one principal.**   The mere fact that an agent acts for more than one principal does not make Article 81(1) applicable.[111] However, different considerations may arise where two or more parties in competition with each other agree to appoint the same agent to transact business on their behalf. In the *Flemish Travel Agents* case,[112] the Court of Justice held that where travel agents sold travel on behalf of a large number of tour operators and tour operators marketed travel through a large number of agents, the travel agents had to be regarded as providing services on 'an entirely independent basis', notwithstanding that they contracted with their clients in the name of and on behalf of the tour operators.

6.034 **Cartels facilitated by agents.**   An arrangement between competitors to appoint the same agent may well be a concerted practice to which Article 81(1) may therefore apply irrespective of the nature of the agency. That would be the case if this is used as a means of collusion, for example by collectively excluding others from those agents or for coordination of marketing strategy or the exchange of information.[113] Similarly, if an independent trader freely participates in a cartel which infringes Article 81(1), it is clearly no defence that he carried out the wishes of the cartel 'as an agent'.[114] Moreover, the Commission is concerned about the attenuation of competition that would result if an undertaking appointed a direct competitor to act also as its agent.[115]

---

[110] *CEPSA* (n 105, above) para 60.

[111] Guidelines, para 13. See also per AG Slynn in Case 243/83 *Binon v AMP* [1985] ECR 2015, [1985] 3 CMLR 800 at 2025–2026 (ECR), 812–813 (CMLR); the ECJ did not address this point.

[112] Case 311/85 *VVR v Sociale Dienst* [1987] ECR 3801, [1989] 4 CMLR 213, paras 19–20. See also *Distribution of railway tickets by travel agents*, OJ 1992 L366/47; annulled on other grounds, Case T-14/93 *Union Internationale des Chemins de Fer v Commission* [1995] ECR II-1503, [1996] 5 CMLR 40; appeal dismissed, Case C-264/95P *Commission v UIC* [1997] ECR I-1287, [1997] 5 CMLR 49.

[113] Guidelines on Vertical Restraints (n 99, above) para 20. And see, eg *SCPA/Kali und Salz*, OJ 1973 L217/3, [1973] CMLR D219; *CSV*, OJ 1978 L242/15, [1979] 1 CMLR 11.

[114] *Aluminium Imports from Eastern Europe*, OJ 1985 L92/1, [1987] 3 CMLR 813.

[115] See *Eirpage*, OJ 1991 L306/22, [1993] 4 CMLR 64: before granting exemption under Art 81(3), the Commission required that provisions preventing direct competitors from acting as

Agent also acting on own account.   Article 81(1) may apply where the agent,   **6.035**
although acting as agent vis-à-vis his principal, also carries on a separate business
of his own. In *Pittsburgh Corning Europe*,[116] the Commission held that an apparent agent could not be regarded as a true auxiliary, integrated fully into the distribution system of its principal, when it made the main part of its turnover as an
independent manufacturer of its own products unconnected with the agency.
This approach derives support from the Court of Justice's subsequent decision in
Sugar, where certain large business houses acted as agents in respect of sales of
sugar for consumption in specified territories within the Community but also
acted as independent dealers on their own account in respect of sugar exports to
non-Member countries and sugar supplies for denaturing. The Court held that
the 'ambivalent relationship' under which the same undertaking was both an
agent and an independent trader in relation to the same commodity, depending
on how it best suited the supplier, could not escape Article 81(1).[117]

Terms and conditions falling outside Article 81(1).   If an agency agreement is   **6.036**
a genuine agency agreement and does not fall within the scope of the application
of Article 81(1), all obligations imposed on the agent are also outside Article 81(1)
as long as they relate to the contracts to be negotiated by the agent on behalf of the
principal.[118] The Guidelines state that the following obligations on the agent's
part will generally be considered to fall outside the scope of Article 81(1):

(a) limitations on the territory in respect of which the agent may act and may sell
     the goods or services;
(b) limitations on the clients to whom the agent may sell the goods or services;
     and

---

agents be added to the standard agency agreement for the marketing of a new nationwide paging
system in Ireland.

[116] *Pittsburg Corning Europe*, JO 1972 L272/35, [1973] CMLR D2. In that case, however the
'agency' agreement relied on what appears to have been a temporary expedient adopted for tax reasons. See also *ARG/Unipart* (n 102, above), where the agreement was held to fall within Art 81(1)
because it covered also the distributor's business in non-ARG parts.

[117] *Suiker Unie* (n 101, above) paras 544–547. In effect, this system enabled the 'agents' to operate independently in areas where their independent activities could do little harm while preventing
competition in the supplier's principal home market. However, because the supplier might have been
misled by the Commission's Notice on Commercial Agents (n 100, above) the resulting infringement was to be disregarded for the purposes of the fines: paras 555–557. See also *Bundeskartellamt v
Volkswagen AG and VAG Leasing* (n 103, above) para 19: dealers' main business was not leasing but
sales and after-sales service.

[118] In COMP/37.980 *Souris – Topps*, 26 May 2004, [2006] 4 CMLR 1713 (concerning the
distribution of Pokemon collectibles), the Commission (at para 103) rejected arguments that two
of the dealers were 'genuine' agents and held that in any event the restrictions imposed on parallel
imports did not correspond to any of the obligations which relate to the ability of the principal to
fix the scope of activity of the agent in relation to the contract goods and which are, therefore, mentioned in para 18 of the Guidelines, nor did they concern exclusive agency provisions within para
19 of the Guidelines.

(c) the prices and conditions at which the agent must sell or purchase the goods or services.[119]

Such restrictions are regarded as an inherent part of an agency agreement since they relate to the ability of the principal to fix the scope of activity of the agent in relation to the contract goods or services. This is essential if the principal is to undertake all the risks and therefore be in a position to determine commercial strategy.

6.037 **Other terms and conditions.** However, provisions in the agency agreement that concern the relationship between the agent and the principal are subject to different considerations. Provisions that prevent the principal from appointing other agents in respect of certain types of transaction, client or territory, affect only intra-brand competition and therefore will generally not be regarded as producing anti-competitive effects. By contrast, provisions that prevent the agent from acting as an agent or distributor of undertakings which compete with the principal, affect inter-brand competition and may infringe Article 81(1) if they lead to foreclosure on the relevant market.[120] In *Bundeskartellamt v Volkswagen and VAG Leasing*,[121] the Court of Justice considered the form of exclusive agency agreements between Volkswagen and Audi dealers and Volkswagen's subsidiary, VAG Leasing, as regards the leasing of vehicles. The dealers were obliged to procure leasing contracts solely for VAG Leasing and were prevented from selling new motor vehicles to an independent leasing company except when that company had introduced a customer directly or a customer had spontaneously asked for a particular company to be involved. Accordingly, there was an absolute ban on supplying independent leasing companies where the aim of the purchase was to build stocks. The exclusivity clause in the agency agreements was held to restrict competition and hence to fall within Article 81(1) in two respects: first, it limited access for leasing companies to Volkswagen and Audi vehicles since they could not use the dealer network; and, secondly, it prevented dealers from developing a leasing business in their own name and for their own account.[122]

6.038 **Application of Regulation 2790/99.** Where an agency agreement comes within the scope of Article 81(1), all the ordinary rules regarding vertical agreements will apply. The fact that the agent is not trading on his own account does not preclude

---

[119] Guidelines on Vertical Restraints, OJ 2000 C291/1: Vol II, App C.11, para 18. And see *ARG/Unipart* (n 102, above) paras 7(c), 26.

[120] Guidelines, above, para 19. For post-termination non-compete provisions, see Art 5(a) of Reg 2790/99 (n 92, above).

[121] *Bundeskartellamt v Volkswagen AG and VAG Leasing* (n 103, above).

[122] The ECJ also held that the agreements did not come within the then motor vehicle block exemption, Reg 123/85: for discussion of the current motor vehicle block exemption, see paras 6.109 *et seq*, below.

application of the block exemption regulation to the agreement between principal and agent: 'buyer' under Regulation 2790/99 expressly includes an undertaking selling goods or services on behalf of another undertaking.[123] But a restriction that prevents the agent from 'sharing' his commission with his customer (that is, without affecting the income of the principal) will be regarded as a 'hard-core' resale price-fixing restraint that precludes application of the block exemption.[124]

4. Exclusive Distribution and Supply Agreements

(a) Generally

Definitions. An exclusive distribution agreement, in the broad sense, is one **6.039** where a supplier appoints one distributor to be the exclusive outlet for his products, either for a defined territory or for a particular class of customers. The supplier thereby agrees that his other distributors will be restricted as regards sales in that territory or to those customers (and usually he is subject to equivalent restrictions as regards his own sales).[125] The Commission uses the term 'exclusive distribution agreement' to refer only to those agreements by which the distributor is allocated a territory; if the distributor is allocated a group of customers, the agreement is called an 'exclusive customer allocation agreement'.[126] These two forms may be combined, where different distributors are appointed for different classes of customer within a particular territory. The term 'exclusive supply' is used by the Commission for the situation where a supplier agrees to sell to only one purchaser inside the Community, either for the purpose of a specific use (industrial supply) or as an extreme form of exclusive distribution (that is, where the appointed territory is the whole of the Community).[127] Agreements that involve quantity forcing on the supplier, by incentives that make him concentrate his sales to a particular buyer, indirectly have a similar effect.[128] 'Selective distribution' refers to the situation where the criteria used by the supplier for selection of distributors have the effect of limiting their numbers but the distributors are not allocated either a protected territory or a customer group. In its Guidelines, the Commission uses the term 'limited distribution' to cover all the above arrangements since they all have the effect of limiting the sales possibilities used by the

---

[123] Reg 2790/99 (n 92, above) Art 1(g). For Reg 2790/99 generally, see paras 6.010 *et seq*, above.

[124] Reg 2790/99 (n 92, above) Art 4(a) and see Guidelines on Vertical Restraints (n 119, above) para 48.

[125] If he does not, the agreement is sometimes described as a 'sole' distributorship.

[126] Guidelines on Vertical Restraints (n 119, above) paras 161, 178.

[127] ibid, para 202; and see Art 1(c) of Reg 2790/99 (n 92, above). See, eg *ARG/Unipart* (n 102, above) where a motor manufacturer agreed to carry out all its distribution of spare parts through a single distributor.

[128] Guidelines on Vertical Restraints (n 119, above) para 214.

supplier.[129] However, this Section considers only exclusive distribution (and customer allocation) and supply agreements. Selective distribution agreements, which raise distinct considerations, are discussed separately in Section 5, below.

6.040 **Economic effects of exclusive distribution/supply agreements.** Exclusive distribution and supply agreements give rise to certain problems for competition policy.[130] They particularly affect *intra-brand* competition as they prevent the supplier from appointing another distributor in the territory or, normally, selling directly in the territory itself. This may have the effect of partitioning the market, thereby enabling the implementation of different prices in different territories. Secondly, other buyers will no longer be able to buy from the supplier in question, which may lead to foreclosure on the purchase market. Moreover, such agreements may also affect *inter-brand* competition. When exclusive distribution at the retail level is used in such a way that few outlets can carry the goods in question, that leads to less in-store competition between brands. If inter-brand competition is already weak, reduction of intra-brand competition has a general effect in lowering pressure on prices. And if most competing suppliers implement exclusive distribution arrangements, that may facilitate collusion at either supplier or distributor level, particularly if the same distributor acts exclusively for several brands. On the other hand, three considerations militate against the potential anti-competitive effects of limited distribution agreements. First, in many cases, the supplier will lack its own distributive organisation and the appointment of an exclusive distributor may be its most effective means of penetrating the market since the distributor is thereby given an enhanced interest in promotion of the supplier's products. Indeed, exclusive distribution and similar restrictions may be necessary to protect distributors from free-riding.[131] It is questionable whether competition is 'restricted' if the supplier would not have been able to penetrate the market successfully in the absence of such an agreement.[132] Secondly, by appointing an exclusive distributor, the supplier avoids numerous dealings with a large number of traders; it is able to intensify its sales effort and rationalise its distribution, particularly where international trade is concerned.[133] Thirdly, since inter-brand competition will normally be decisive in maintaining a competitive market, it is argued that where inter-brand competition is strong there is little need to regulate the vertical relationship between supplier

---

[129] ibid, para 109.

[130] ibid, paras 110, 161, 204. See also Green Paper on Vertical Restraints in EC Competition Policy, COM(96) 721 final, [1997] 4 CMLR 519, Chap II; see also Biro and Fletcher, 'The EC Green Paper on Vertical Restraints; An Economic Comment' (1998) ECLR 129 at 131–132.

[131] Guidelines on Vertical Restraints (n 119, above) para 116(1). For free-riding, see n 2 to para 6.002, above.

[132] Case 56/65 *Société Technique Minière v Maschinenbau Ulm* [1966] ECR 235, [1966] CMLR 357. See also Case 258/78 *Nungesser v Commission* [1982] ECR 2015, [1983] 1 CMLR 278.

[133] Guidelines on Vertical Restraints (n 119, above) para 116(6).

and distributor which primarily affects only intra-brand competition.[134] This economics-based approach has considerably influenced the Commission in its formulation of the Guidelines.

Economic effects of exclusive customer allocation. Exclusive customer alloca- **6.041** tion usually applies either to intermediate products or, in the case of final products, at the wholesale level or for sales to sophisticated purchasers. It gives rise to some of the same objections as exclusive distribution by territory. But in addition, the Commission points out that allocation of customers makes arbitrage by customers, and also by non-appointed distributors, more difficult and therefore leads to the almost total elimination of intra-brand competition.[135] However, customer allocation can lead to efficiencies, particularly when the distributors of intermediate products are obliged to incur investments to adapt to the distinct needs of their particular class of customers.[136]

Combination with other vertical restraints. Exclusive distribution raises **6.042** particular problems when it is combined with single branding (for example, non-compete) or exclusive purchasing obligations on the distributor. This may lead to significant foreclosure both at the resale (downstream) level and at the supplier (upstream) level, making arbitrage by final customers or distributors more difficult and thereby hindering market integration.[137] On the other hand, if it does not lead to foreclosure, this combination may be pro-competitive by increasing the incentive for the distributor to concentrate his efforts on the particular brands covered by the agreement.[138] A combination of exclusive customer allocation and selective distribution is regarded by the Commission as a hard-core restriction as it restricts active selling by the appointed distributors to end-users.[139]

Structure of this Section. Under Regulation 2790/99, many exclusive distribu- **6.043** tion and supply agreements will be automatically exempted if the relevant market share ceiling of 30 per cent is not exceeded. However, it remains relevant to consider the position of agreements even below that market share figure. First, inclusion of certain hard-core restrictions will take the agreement outside Regulation 2790/99. Secondly, the Commission may withdraw the benefit of the block exemption from an agreement when the effects on competition are particularly strong and are not counterbalanced by benefits that would otherwise fulfil

---

[134] ibid, paras 6 and 119(1). See also the Communication on the Application of the Community Competition Rules to Vertical Restraints, OJ 1998 C365/5, [1999] 4 CMLR 281, sect III. Some of the considerations are set out by AG Verloren van Themaat in Case 161/84 *Pronuptia* [1986] ECR 353, [1986] 1 CMLR 414.

[135] Guidelines on Vertical Restraints (n 119, above) para 180.

[136] ibid, para 182.

[137] ibid, para 172.

[138] ibid, para 171.

[139] ibid, para 179; and see Reg 2790/99 (n 92, above) Art 4(c).

the criteria of Article 81(3). Accordingly, it is necessary in such cases to consider the question of the individual application of Article 81(3). This Section accordingly considers, first, the general analysis of exclusive distribution and supply agreements under Article 81(1), including the approach to particular terms and conditions; and secondly, the application of Article 81(3). For discussion of Regulation 2790/99, see Section 2, above.

(b) Application of Article 81(1)

6.044 **In general.** Community competition law is not ill-disposed towards exclusive distribution agreements, provided that they do not contain 'hard-core' restrictions. In *Technique Minière*[140] the Court of Justice held that an agreement which merely granted exclusive distribution rights, but conferred no absolute territorial protection and contained no export bans, did not necessarily fall within the prohibition of Article 81(1), especially if the exclusivity was really necessary for the penetration of a new market. Similarly, in *Consten and Grundig*,[141] although the Court upheld the condemnation of those terms in Grundig's distribution agreements that secured absolute territorial protection of the French market, the decision was annulled (for lack of reasoning) insofar as it had also held that the restriction on Grundig not to make direct deliveries to France except to Consten infringed Article 81(1). This approach has been followed many times since.[142] Accordingly, in determining whether a limited distribution agreement appreciably affects competition, it is necessary to have regard to all the surrounding circumstances and to consider the competition that would have occurred in the absence of the agreement. In the *L'Oréal* case[143] concerning a selective distribution agreement, but in a passage that is of general application and has often been repeated, the Court of Justice stated:

> 'it is appropriate to take into account in particular the nature and quantity, limited or otherwise, of the products covered by the agreement, the position and importance of the parties on the market for the products concerned, and the isolated nature of the disputed agreement or, alternatively, its position in a series of agreements.'

The Guidelines set out the approach that the Commission now takes in assessing agreements in their economic context.[144]

---

140 *Technique Minière* (n 132, above). See also paras 2.070 *et seq*, above.
141 Cases 56 & 58/64 *Consten and Grundig v Commission* [1966] ECR 299, [1966] CMLR 418.
142 See, eg *Nungesser* (n 132, above) para 58: an 'open' exclusive licence which did not affect the position of third parties such as parallel importers and licensees for other territories was not in itself contrary to Art 81(1); Case T-61/89 *Dansk Pelsdyravlerforening v Commission* [1992] ECR II-1931, para 99: concerning the obligations of the members of an agricultural cooperative outside the scope of Reg 26 to deal exclusively with that cooperative in certain circumstances.
143 Case 31/80 *L'Oréal v De Nieuwe AMCK* [1980] ECR 3775, [1981] 2 CMLR 235, para 19.
144 Guidelines on Vertical Restraints, OJ 2000 C291/1: Vol II, App C.11, see para 6.008, above, and paras 102, 121–133 of the Guidelines.

Inter-brand competition and market power.   A critical factor in the assessment   **6.045**
of the effect of a limited distribution agreement is the degree of inter-brand competition. As the Guidelines state: 'the loss of intra-brand competition can only be
problematic if inter-brand competition is limited.'[145] The primary indicator of
the degree to which inter-brand competition is affected is the market power of the
supplier. If the supplier's market share is above the 30 per cent ceiling for the
purpose of Regulation 2790/99, the Commission has generally presumed that it
has market power and individual consideration of Article 81(3) will therefore be
required. However, the significance of the supplier's market share will vary according to the nature of the market. In a dynamic market, with growing demand and
developing technologies, the loss of intra-brand competition is less significant
than in a mature market where market shares are relatively stable.[146] Where
the supplier is selling a new product, or an existing product in a new geographic
market, where exclusivity is intended to secure effective market entry, a high
market share[147] does not in itself mean that exclusive protection will distort
competition. For example, the Commission states that Article 81(1) should not
apply to any non-hard-core vertical restraints for two years after the product is first
introduced on the relevant market.[148] In the case of an exclusive supply agreement, it is the market power not of the supplier but of the buyer that is the most
important criterion, as the buyer provides the sole outlet in the Community for
the supplier's products. But it is important to note that the Commission takes a
broader approach to market power in the assessment of individual agreements
than is the case under Regulation 2790/99.[149] All affected markets are to be considered, including downstream markets in which the goods are resold.[150] Further,
the Commission looks at the market shares not only of the parties to the agreement but also of their competitors, to determine whether or not the market is
concentrated: in an unconcentrated market, non-hard-core restraints are assumed
not to have appreciable anti-competitive effects.[151]

Foreclosure issues.   Foreclosure can operate as regards other suppliers or as   **6.046**
regards other distributors. Foreclosure of other suppliers is a potential problem
only if an exclusive distribution agreement includes also non-compete obligations

---

[145] Guidelines, above, para 163. See also para 119(1).

[146] ibid, para 168.

[147] The distinctive nature of the product may lead to a narrow product market definition, resulting in a high share of a narrow market.

[148] Guidelines on Vertical Restraints (n 144, above) para 119(10).

[149] Under Reg 2790/99 (n 92, above), only the market as between seller and buyer are considered: see para 6.018, above.

[150] Guidelines on Vertical Restraints (n 144, above) para 96.

[151] ibid, para 119(1). The Guidelines refer to the Herfindahl-Hirschmann Index and state that
when the HHI index is below 1000, the market is deemed to be unconcentrated. See para 6.007,
above.

restricting the distributor from selling competing goods. In that case, it is necessary to consider what entry barriers there are to other suppliers trying to arrange for distribution of their products.[152] Foreclosure of other distributors may be a problem if the appointed distributors are given very large, exclusive territories, particularly when they have market power in their downstream market. That is especially the case if the distributor is reselling to final consumers. The Guidelines give the example of a supermarket chain that becomes the only distributor of a leading brand on a national food retail market.[153] The Commission is also likely to be concerned by limited distribution agreements when, in addition to a reduction in intra-brand competition, more efficient distributors or distributors having a different distribution format are foreclosed.[154] As regards an exclusive supply agreement, whilst the market power of the buyer on the upstream market is important for assessing whether there is any real foreclosure of other buyers, it is his market power on the downstream market that is the more significant when considering the effect of any such foreclosure on consumers.[155]

6.047 **Cumulative effect.** Even if the individual agreement does not fall within the scope of Article 81(1), the cumulative effect of several similar agreements may appreciably restrict competition. That may be the case if an individual agreement forms part of a network, of which the overall effect must be considered, especially if other suppliers operate similar networks.[156] In those circumstances, the combination of exclusive distribution with non-compete provisions may have a significant foreclosure effect on suppliers.[157] But a cumulative effect may also be relevant to multiple exclusive dealerships, that is if the same distributor is appointed by several competing suppliers to be their exclusive distributor in the same territory. When the distributor is in consequence exclusively setting the resale price for several competing brands, a reduction in inter-brand price competition is likely. Therefore, even if the individual suppliers' market shares are below 30 per cent, if

---

[152] Guidelines on Vertical Restraints (n 144, above) para 165 and see also para 171. Reg 2790/99 (n 92, above) grants exemption provided that the non-compete restriction does not exceed five years. For individual application of Art 81(3), see paras 6.079 *et seq*, below. But note that if entry barriers in the particular market are already high for structural reasons, it is possible that exclusivity provisions in an agreement have no independent foreclosure effect: *Europay+ETCI+Thomas Cook, XXVIth Report on Competition Policy* (1996), p 135 (distribution arrangements for travellers cheques).

[153] Guidelines on Vertical Restraints (n 144, above) para 166.

[154] ibid, para 119(3).

[155] ibid, paras 96(i) and 204–210. Market power here embraces not just market share but also the relative strength of other buyers, entry barriers and the countervailing power of suppliers.

[156] ibid, para 133. For assessment of the cumulative effect of networks, see paras 6.100 and 6.145 *et seq*, below.

[157] Guidelines on Vertical Restraints (n 144, above) para 171.

the cumulative share is significantly higher, that may be a ground for the Commission to withdraw the benefit of Regulation 2790/99.[158]

Individual clauses. A considerable body of case law has developed on the appli- **6.048** cation of Article 81(1) to particular restrictions. Although the general approach to vertical restraints changed considerably with the introduction of Regulation 2790/99, the prior case law complements the Guidelines, which in any event do not bind the courts, when considering a limited distribution agreement to which the block exemption does not apply. The application of Article 81(1) to such individual restraints is, of course, subject to establishment of an appreciable effect on trade between Member States, and to possible exclusion as *de minimis.*[159]

(i) The hard-core restrictions

Limited distribution agreements containing hard-core restrictions. Limited **6.049** distribution agreements which contain hard-core restrictions fall outside the block exemption and may infringe Article 81(1) even below the 15 per cent threshold in the *De Minimis* Notice.[160] Two hard-core restrictions are particularly relevant to limited distribution agreements: resale price maintenance and territorial restrictions on resale or other measures obstructing parallel imports.

Resale price maintenance. Resale price maintenance ('RPM') has the direct **6.050** effect of reducing, or even eliminating, intra-brand competition. It can also facilitate horizontal price-fixing cartels since the increased transparency of prices makes price cuts at the retail level easier to detect. The reduction in intra-brand competition may, as it leads to less downward pressure on the price for particular goods, also have as an indirect effect a reduced level of inter-brand competition.[161] However, it is necessary to distinguish between strict RPM, that sets a fixed or minimum resale price, and recommended or maximum resale prices. RPM that establishes a fixed or minimum resale price completely eliminates intra-brand price competition. It is only RPM of this type, and arrangements that indirectly achieve the same object, that are treated as a hard-core restriction under Regulation 2790/99.[162] Such agreements are regarded as the vertical version of price-fixing,

---

[158] ibid, para 164.

[159] See paras 2.129 *et seq*, above.

[160] ibid.

[161] Guidelines on Vertical Restraints (n 144, above) para 112.

[162] Reg 2790/99, OJ 1999 L336/21: Vol II, App C.3, Art 4(a) and see para 6.023, above. For similar arrangements, see Case 86/82 *Hasselblad v Commission* [1984] ECR 883, [1984] 1 CMLR 559, para 49 (clause controlling advertisements used to prevent price-cutting); *Rover Group, XXIIIrd Report on Competition Policy* (1993), point 228 (limitation on the maximum amount of discount); *Novalliance v Systemform*, OJ 1997 L47/11, [1997] 4 CMLR 876 (joint setting of prices). In the Communication on Vertical Restraints (n 134, above) sect III.4, the Commission stated: 'RPM is usually considered to be more restrictive than the other vertical restraints. In case of efficiencies it can often be replaced by other less competition distorting restraints with similar positive effects.

expressly prohibited by Article 81(1)(a).[163] A ban on making special offers, rebates or clearance sales 'liable to damage' the brand name of the products has been condemned by the Commission even where there was no explicit or objective definition of the level at which such damage might arise.[164] The Commission regards such RPM obligations as a restriction of competition by object, thus obviating the need to show any actual or potential anti-competitive effect.[165] However, although strict RPM is similarly treated as a hard-core restriction under the *De Minimis* Notice,[166] thereby depriving an agreement of the benefit of that Notice, where the supplier's market share is very small any potential effect on competition may not be appreciable and thus the agreement could fall outside Article 81(1).[167]

6.051 **Recommended resale prices.** Provided that recommended or maximum resale prices are truly only recommended or maximum, they are not regarded as inherently restrictive of competition.[168] In *JCB Service*[169] the Court of First Instance

---

This is reflected by the current policy in most countries which tends to be very strict on RPM while allowing exclusive distribution in certain market conditions'.

[163] See, eg Case 243/83 *Binon v AMP* [1985] ECR 2015, [1985] 3 CMLR 800 (RPM for newspapers infringed Art 81(1) but might qualify for exemption under Art 81(3); see further para 6.084, below). See also *GERO-fabriek*, OJ 1977 L16/8, [1977] 1 CMLR D35; *Hennessy-Henkell*, OJ 1980 L383/11, [1981] 1 CMLR 601 (RPM clause in exclusive distribution agreement precluded exemption under Art 81(3)). The various national agreements fixing prices for the resale of books have involved collective RPM by the publishers and are therefore discussed in the context of horizontal agreements: para 5.025, above.

[164] *Nathan-Bricolux* (n 72, above) para 86.

[165] See, eg Case COMP/37.975 *Yamaha*, decn of 16 July 2003, paras 127, 137, 144, 155–156 (RPM in the supply of musical instruments in the Netherlands, Italy and Austria).

[166] OJ 2001 C368/13: Vol II, App C.13, point 11(2)(a).

[167] See Guidelines on Vertical Restraints (n 144, above) para 10 (referring to the 10 per cent threshold under the then applicable Notice; now 15 per cent: para 6.003, above). Although the reasoning in *Yamaha* (n 165, above), suggests there is no need to consider appreciability in this regard, the Commission nonetheless noted Yamaha's important position on the affected markets and the application of the restrictions to 'an important number' of dealers on such markets: para 154. And see Cases 04/237 and 04/249, LJN AU8309 *Secon Group and G-Star International v NMa*, 7 December 2005, where the Dutch Trade and Industry Appeals Tribunal quashed the decision of the Netherlands Competition Authority (the 'NMa') condemning, under the Dutch equivalent of Art 81, a clause in a standard form distribution agreement for jeans and other clothing, setting a retail price and prohibiting sale to other than end-users. The Court held that the NMa should not have rejected an argument of *de minimis* without considering the actual situation in which the agreement took effect, in particular with regard to the size of the undertakings involved, their position on the relevant markets, the structure of those markets and the other circumstances in which this agreement had been enforced.

[168] Communication on Vertical Restraints (n 134, above) sect III.4; Guidelines on Vertical Restraints (n 142, above) para 47. And see *Pronuptia* (n 134, above) para 27(4) (in the context of franchising agreements).

[169] Case T-67/01 *JCB Service v Commission* [2004] ECR II-49, [2004] 4 CMLR 1346 (on appeal from *JCB*, OJ 2002 L69/1, [2002] 4 CMLR 1458); further appeal on other grounds dismissed, Case C-167/04P [2006] ECR I-8935, [2006] 5 CMLR 1303). See also *D'Ieteren motor oils*, OJ 1991 L20/42, [1992] 4 CMLR 399, para 11 (a recommendation to a motor dealer not to charge for an oil approved by the supplier the same retail price as was charged for another oil of higher quality served to prevent 'misinformation' to the consumer and did not affect competition).

disagreed with the Commission's inference that JCB had operated a system of retail price-fixing by means of recommending prices and then expressing its own price to its dealers as an amount discounted from the recommended price. The Court confirmed that there is a difference between the establishment of recommended prices and the fixing of retail prices. It accepted that the documents showed that JCB was concerned about the level of retail prices which it felt were too low and that studies and discussions were conducted on that subject within the JCB Dealers Association at JCB's request. But the Court did not agree that this warranted the Commission's conclusion that there was a horizontal price-fixing agreement among the dealers. The documents showed that, in France, 'it was not rare' for dealers to sell below the recommended price and to ask JCB to invoice them at a lower price in order to preserve their own profit margin. JCB was not, however, obliged to grant that request. The Court of First Instance concluded:

> 'In short . . . JCB's actions amounted to the fixing of its own prices ex-works, details of which were negotiable, and the drawing up of suggested scales for retail prices. The influence of JCB on retail sale prices was therefore significant, but essentially that of a manufacturer who draws up suggested lists of retail sale prices and fixes invoicing prices internal to its network according to the retail sale prices desired. Moreover, the retail sale price scales, although strongly indicative, were none the less not binding. There is nothing to indicate that JCB's efforts to influence dealers and discourage them from agreeing to sale prices considered to be too low involved coercion.'[170]

Maximum retail prices. The setting of maximum prices may not only have no **6.052** adverse effect on competition but may actually limit the potentially negative effect of an exclusive distribution agreement, by controlling the price increases which the distributor might otherwise be able to impose under the protection of his exclusivity.[171] The Commission has therefore stated that it no longer believes that an obligation not to exceed a maximum resale price in itself necessarily restricts competition.[172] Such an obligation may have positive effects on economic efficiency in allowing distributors and manufacturers to set a price likely to maximise their joint profits (thus avoiding 'double marginalisation'). However, the Commission is concerned that the setting of a maximum resale price may become a focal point for all distributors. This risk should only be serious if the supplier has a strong market position, but in such circumstances if the result is a uniform price level the Commission has stated that it may regard the practice as an infringement

---

[170] *JCB Service*, above, para 130.
[171] See Guidelines on Vertical Restraints (n 144, above) para 119(6).
[172] *Nathan-Bricolux* (n 72, above) para 87, referring to the Communication on Vertical Restraints (n 134, above). The Commission held in that case that by setting a maximum price and prohibiting sepcial offers and discounts, the supplier 'is endeavouring artificially to harmonise prices and discounts'.

of Article 81(1).[173] Furthermore, in a narrow oligopolistic market the consequent price transparency may lead to tacit collusion on price as between suppliers, in which case the Commission also considers that the practice may contravene Article 81(1).[174]

6.053 **Measures obstructing parallel imports.** It is a basic principle of Community law that an agreement falls within the prohibition of Article 81(1) when it establishes absolute territorial protection for exclusive distributors, by preventing, in law or in fact, either re-export of the contract products by the distributor to other Member States or import of such products by third parties from other Member States.[175] That is so whether the prevention of imports or exports results from export bans, discriminatory pricing policies or other measures. An export ban imposed on the distributor is prohibited and void, whether it takes the form of a simple instruction to dealers to cease exporting[176] or is imposed by conduct.[177] The prohibition applies irrespective of whether the supplier takes active steps to enforce it,[178] and even if the agreement contains a clause stating that the ban is

---

[173] Guidelines on Vertical Restraints (n 144, above) para 227. In its Notice under Art 27(4) of Reg 1/2003 in *Repsol*, OJ 2004 C258/7, [2004] 5 CMLR 1708, paras 18–20, the Commission noted that it had not find indications that the setting of maximum prices had created significant alignment effects that might affect intra-brand competition. (Appeal on other grounds, Case T-274/06, not yet decided.)

[174] Guidelines on Vertical Restraints, para 228. Presumably, in the absence of active collusion, the relevant agreement for the purpose of Art 81(1) is that between supplier and distributor.

[175] For important early judgments, see Case 22/71 *Béguelin Import v G.L. Import Export* [1971] ECR 949, [1972] CMLR 81, para 12; *Consten and Grundig* (n 141, above). For more recent cases, see n 180, below. Note that the CFI held that although in principle agreements which aim to impede parallel trade must be regarded as having as their *object* the restriction of competition, in the particular circumstances of the pharmaceutical markets where the pricing of drugs is highly regulated it cannot be taken for granted at the outset that parallel trade tends to reduce those prices. The Court explained that the objective of Art 81(1) is not to bring about the single market but to prevent undertakings, by restricting competition between themselves or with third parties, from reducing the welfare of the final consumer of the products in question. If parallel imports had no effect on the pricing of the products then a more detailed analysis was needed to determine whether the *effect*, rather than the object, of the restriction fell within Art 81(1): Case T-168/01 *GlaxoSmithKline Services v Commission* [2006] ECR II-2969, [2006] 5 CMLR 1589 (on appeal from *Glaxo Wellcome*, OJ 2001 L302/1, [2002] 4 CMLR 335) (on appeal, Cases C-501/06P, etc, *GlaxoSmithKline Services v Commission*, not yet decided).

[176] eg Case T-368/00 *General Motors Nederland and Opel Nederland v Commission* [2003] ECR II-4491, [2004] 4 CMLR 1302, [2004] All ER (EC) 674, regarding nine dealers (paras 146 *et seq*). Dismissing the appeal, the ECJ stated that a distribution agreement 'clearly demonstrating the will to treat export sales less favourably than national sales' has a restrictive object for the purpose of Art 81: Case 551/03P *General Motors v Commission* [2006] ECR I-3173, [2006] 5 CMLR 9.

[177] eg *Video Games, Nintendo distribution*, OJ 2003 L255/33, [2004] CMLR 421 (written agreements from which express export ban had been removed thereafter proceeded on the 'shared understanding' that dealers would not export); on appeal, Cases T-18/03 *CD-Contact Data v Commission*; T-12/03 *Itochu Corporation v Commission*; T-398/02 *Linea Gig (in liquidation) v Commission*; T-13/03 *Nintendo Corp and Nintendo of Europe v Commission*, not yet decided.

[178] *Sandoz*, OJ 1987 L222/28, [1989] 4 CMLR 628, appeal dismissed, Case C-277/87 *Sandoz v Commission* [1990] ECR I-45; Case 19/77 *Miller v Commission* [1978] ECR 131, [1978] 2 CMLR 334, para 7; Case T-175/95 *BASF v Commission* [1999] ECR II-1581, [2000] 4 CMLR 33,

---

inapplicable if prohibited by law.[179] Such a ban is regarded as a serious violation and will attract heavy fines in appropriate cases.[180]

'Active' and 'passive' sales and absolute territorial protection.   However, for   **6.054** this purpose, Community competition law draws a distinction between 'active' and 'passive' sales, which is reflected in the block exemption.[181] Active sales are where the distributor seeks customers, establishes a branch or maintains a distribution depot outside the territory. Passive sales are where the distributor merely responds to unsolicited orders from outside its territory or customer group. Only a restraint on passive sales is a hard-core restriction since this confers what is known as 'absolute territorial protection' on the dealer by preventing other dealers from making sales to customers within its territory. Where distributorships are allocated on a territorial basis, the supplier may impose obligations on distributors restricting active sales to their exclusively allocated territories or customer groups. However, the distributor must always remain free to accept unsolicited orders from outside its territory or customer group.[182] Thus an obligation on a dealer to refer orders from customers in other territories to other distributors or to obtain prior approval before accepting such orders[183] amounts to an unlawful restriction. Even if the wording of the dealership contract is limited to banning passive sales, extraneous documents may demonstrate that the actual restriction accepted by the dealers goes further.[184] Where a distributor receives an order from another company in the same ownership outside its contract territory, this is to be regarded as active sales promotion outside the territory by the distributor which

---

para 156; Case T-176/95 *Accinauto v Commission* [1999] ECR II-1635, [2000] 4 CMLR 67, para 123. See also *Novalliance v Systemform* (n 162, above) para 60.

[179] *Novalliance v Systemform* (n 162, above) para 57. See also *Kodak*, JO 1970 L147/24, [1970] CMLR D19, D22; *John Deere*, OJ 1985 L35/58, [1985] 2 CMLR 554, paras 24–29.

[180] Various recent examples are referred to in other footnotes, eg (the first two in the context of selective distribution agreements) see *VW*, OJ 1998 L124/60, [1998] 5 CMLR 33: fine of €102 million, reduced on appeal to €90 million: Case T-62/98 *Volkswagen v Commission* [2000] ECR II-2707, [2000] 5 CMLR 853; further appeal dismissed, Case C-338/00P [2003] ECR I-9189, [2004] 4 CMLR 351); *Opel*, OJ 2001 L59/1, [2001] 4 CMLR 1441: fine of €43 million (appeals dismissed, n 176 above); *JCB* (n 169, above): fine of €39.6 million; *Mercedes Benz*, OJ 2002 L257/1, [2003] 4 CMLR 95: fine of €72 million; reduced on appeal to €9.8 million, Case T-325/01 *DaimlerChrysler v Commission* [2005] ECR II-3319, [2007] 4 CMLR 559; *Video games, Nintendo distribution* (n 177, above): fines totalling €167.8 million; *Souris – Topps* (n 118, above): fine of €1.59 million. Although fines may be imposed on the distributors/purchasers as well as on the supplier, the fine on the supplier is usually significantly greater: see generally para 13.172, below.

[181] Reg 2790/99 (n 162, above) Art 4(c). See also Guidelines on Vertical Restraints (n 144, above) para 50, and para 6.023(c), above.

[182] This principle was recently reaffirmed in *Video Games, Nintendo distribution* (n 177, above) para 331.

[183] eg *Windsurfing*, OJ 1983 L229/1, [1984] 1 CMLR 1, paras 111–112.

[184] Case T-67/01 *JCB Service v Commission* (n 169, above) para 88 (appeal dismissed, ibid); *Nathan-Bricolux*, OJ 2001 L54/1, [2001] CMLR 1122.

the supplier is justified in trying to stop.[185] The Commission has indicated that sales on the internet should, in general, be considered to be passive sales, insofar as a website is not clearly designed to reach primarily customers inside the territory of, or a customer group exclusively allocated to, another distributor. But the sending of unsolicited email to such customers would constitute active selling.[186]

6.055 **Unilateral conduct or unlawful agreement.** Following the important judgment of the Court of First Instance (upheld by the Court of Justice) in the *ADALAT* case,[187] a number of cases have re-examined the earlier case law concerning when restrictions which a manufacturer wanted to impose on its dealers have become incorporated into the dealership agreement so as to constitute an arrangement falling within Article 81(1) rather than simply unilateral conduct escaping censure. The point can be illustrated by comparing two cases in the Community Courts involving the distribution of Volkswagen cars. The earlier of the two *Volkswagen*[188] cases concerned distribution of VW and Audi cars made in Germany and imported into Italy by VW's subsidiary Autogerma. Autogerma was the exclusive importer into Italy and distributed the cars through a selective distribution network of dealers. Devaluation of the Italian lire made it very attractive for German and Austrian customers to buy cars in Italy for immediate export. Autogerma took steps to restrict supply to its Italian dealers in order to limit such exports. The Court of Justice noted that the dealership contract provided for the possibility of limiting supplies to Italian dealers and that the Court of First Instance had found that the limitation was imposed with the express aim of blocking re-exportation from Italy of the vehicles delivered to those dealers. The Court of Justice held that by accepting the dealership contract, the Italian dealers consented to a measure which was subsequently used for the purpose of blocking re-exports from Italy and thus of restricting competition within the Community. In the later *Volkswagen*[189] case, the Commission argued that in the context of a selective and exclusive distribution

---

[185] *Novalliance v Systemform* (n 162, above) paras 4, 50 and 62.

[186] Guidelines on Vertical Restraints (n 144, above) para 51.

[187] Case T-41/96 *Bayer v Commission* [2001] 4 CMLR 126, [2001] All ER (EC) 1; on appeal, Cases C-2 & 3/01P *Commission v Bayer* [2004] ECR I-23, [2004] 4 CMLR 13, [2004] All ER (EC) 500: see further paras 2.025 *et seq*, above.

[188] Case C-338/00P *Volkswagen v Commission* [2003] ECR I-9189, [2004] 4 CMLR 351, paras 63–65, dismissing the appeal from Case T-62/98 *Volkswagen v Commission* [2000] ECR II-2707, [2000] 5 CMLR 853.

[189] Case C-74/04P *Commission v Volkswagen* [2006] ECR I-6585, affirming on other grounds Case T-208/01 *Volkswagen v Commission* [2003] ECR II-5141, [2004] 4 CMLR 727, [2004] All ER (EC) 674. The earlier cases analysed by the Commission and the Courts were: Case 107/82 *AEG v Commission* [1983] ECR 3151, [1984] 3 CMLR 325; Case T-43/92 *Dunlop Slazenger v Commission* [1994] ECR II-441; Cases 25 & 26/84 *Ford v Commission (No. 2)* [1985] ECR 2725, [1985] 3 CMLR 528; and the earlier *Volkswagen* case (n 188, above). See also *General Motors Nederland and Opel Nederland v Commission* (n 176, above), where the CFI held that although a minute of a senior management meeting did evince an intention to try to prevent passive sales, it had not been shown that this had been communicated to the dealers 'still less that that measure entered into the field of the contractual relations between Opel Nederland and its dealers' (para 88).

network, it was not necessary to look for acquiescence on the part of the dealer to the manufacturer's instruction not to sell below recommended selling prices following the receipt of that instruction. According to the Commission, such acquiescence must be regarded as established as a matter of principle by the mere fact that the dealer had entered the manufacturer's distribution network and is therefore deemed to have been given in advance. The Commission asserted that it was of little importance whether the contract contained an express reservation which allowed such instructions. Such an instruction could still become an integral part of the contract, or form part of the contract; the decisive point is the purpose of that call, which is to influence dealers in the performance of that contract. The Courts rejected this analysis. The Court of Justice accepted that a contractual variation could be regarded as having been accepted in advance by a seemingly neutral clause in the dealership agreement, even where it is a variation which is contrary to the competition rules. However, the clauses in the agreements did not authorise VW to issue binding price recommendations; and in the absence of such prior agreement, the instructions to dealers did not in themselves constitute an 'agreement' for the purpose of Article 81.

Financial disincentives for dealers who export.   Indirect measures aimed at induc-   **6.056**
ing the distributor not to resell to customers in other territories will also bring the agreement within the scope of Article 81(1): for example, a refusal or reduction of bonuses or discounts.[190] In *Opel Nederland*[191] the Court of First Instance upheld the finding that during several sales promotion campaigns, Opel had excluded sales outside the contract territory from the calculations on which the sales bonuses awarded to dealers were based. The Court held that this was contrary to Article 81, stating:

> 'As bonuses were no longer granted for export sales, the margin of economic manoeu-
> vre which dealers have to carry out such sales was reduced in comparison with that
> which they have to carry out domestic sales. Dealers are thereby obliged either to
> apply less favourable conditions to foreign customers than domestic customers, or to
> be content with a smaller margin on export sales. By withdrawing bonuses for export
> sales, the latter became less attractive to foreign customers or to dealers. The measure
> was therefore, by its very nature, likely to inhibit export sales, even without any
> restriction on supply.'[192]

Further the CFI refused to infer from the existence of export bans imposed on nine dealers that there was a wider arrangement covering all 20 dealers.

[190] *Sperry New Holland*, OJ 1985 L376/21, [1988] 4 CMLR 306 (bonuses withdrawn for exported product); *Ford Agricultural*, OJ 1993 L20/1, [1995] 5 CMLR 89 (higher prices or reclaimed discounts for exported product); *Organon*, XXVth Report on Competition Policy (1995), points 37–38 (only contraceptive pills to be sold in the United Kingdom, not those intended for export, qualified for discount); *JCB Service v Commission* (n 169, above) (bonuses and fee system that disadvantaged out of territory sales).

[191] Case T-368/00 *General Motors Nederland and Opel Nederland v Commission* (n 176 above); appeal to the ECJ, dismissed (ibid, and following AG Tizzano's Opinion of 25 October 2005 (not in CMLR)).

[192] para 100.

Similarly, in *Volkswagen*[193] the Court of Justice upheld earlier findings that a '15% rule', according to which the dealer's sales bonus took into account his sales outside the contract territory only up to a limit of 15 per cent of total sales, was contrary to Article 81. The Court held that imposing a limit on the volume of export sales on which the dealer could earn a bonus was liable to induce dealers to sell at least 85 per cent of their sales in their contract territory and therefore made it more difficult for German and Austrian consumers to find an Italian dealer prepared to sell to them. However, a manufacturer who granted a price discount to a dealer when the dealer had itself to grant its customer a volume rebate on selling multiple machinery to that customer, was entitled to limit the grant of such a discount to cases where the customer was an end-user rather than another dealer.[194] The result would have been different if the manufacturer had stipulated that the end-user had to be inside the dealer's contract territory.

6.057 **Support to dealers disadvantaged by parallel imports into their territory.** In some dealership arrangements, there is provision for a payment to a dealer, particularly one located close to a national border, when a customer in his territory is supplied by a dealer in another territory. This payment may be made by the manufacturer as a form of dealer support or by the dealer who makes the sale, in order to compensate the recipient dealer for having to service the vehicle in future without having had the benefit of selling it. In *JCB Service*[195] the Court of First Instance noted that the Commission conceded that the latter arrangement of dealer to dealer payments was not open to criticism as a matter of principle. The Court held that it was important to know whether the amount of the fee imposed on the exporting dealer was a realistic assessment of the cost of after-sales service which the recipient dealer would have to provide or whether it was set at an excessive level in order to deter exports. Since JCB put forward a cost justification for the flat rate fee and the Commission did nothing to counter this, the Court annulled the Commission's finding that the fee prevented sales outside territory. Further, the Court held that the existence of clear guidelines as to the fee payment may, by preventing unstructured negotiations between the two dealers concerned, make out-of-territory sales easier. Similarly, the Paris Court of Appeal has held that subsidies granted by Peugeot to dealers based close to frontiers and facing competition from cross-border agents and independent resellers ('budget frontiers') were not anti-competitive.[196]

---

193 Case C-338/00P *Volkswagen v Commission* (n 188, above).
194 Case T-67/01 *JCB Service v Commission* (n 169, above) paras 149 *et seq*.
195 ibid, paras 137 *et seq*.
196 *SPEA v GCAP and Peugeot*, 21 September 2004, BOCCRF, 8 November 2004. As regards the 'budget frontiers', the Court observed that the granting of commercial specific subsidies by a manufacturer to its dealers in order to support its network, to develop its sales or to avoid its collapse, is not in itself anti-competitive as long as the conditions of the granting are not anti-competitive.

Other indirect measures preventing parallel imports.   Other indirect measures to   **6.058**
prevent parallel imports which have been held to infringe Article 81(1) include: the
exercise of trade mark rights;[197] the reservation of recommendation labels to products
sold through exclusive distributors;[198] the buying back of parallel imports;[199] the use
of national laws to obstruct parallel imports;[200] contractual provisions that require
the purchaser to use the goods himself,[201] or not to make cross-supplies to other
dealers,[202] or to supply to end-users only,[203] or to provide information for the purpose
of monitoring the destination of products;[204] or a warning that resale abroad may
infringe unspecified regulations or third party rights;[205] the denial of a standard

---

The Court emphasised that the dealers based in other countries were not prevented from selling cars
to French citizens, and that Peugeot's subsidies represented a small percentage of the car price, far
from covering the substantial price gap between different countries. (The case was decided under
both Art 81 and the French domestic law equivalent.)

[197] *Consten and Grundig* (n 141, above); Case 28/77 *Tepea v Commission* [1978] ECR 1391,
[1978] 3 CMLR 392; cf Case 170/83 *Hydrotherm v Compact* [1984] ECR 2999, [1985] 3 CMLR
224. Arts 28 and 30 EC on the free movement of goods may also be relevant. On trade marks and
the exercise of intellectual property rights generally, see Chap 9, below.

[198] *Newitt/Dunlop Slazenger International*, OJ 1992 L131/32, [1993] 5 CMLR 352, para 60
(appeal dismissed, *Dunlop Slazenger v Commission* (n 189, above)).

[199] ibid, para 58.

[200] *Consten and Grundig* (n 141, above) (French law of unfair competition); Case 22/71 *Béguelin
Import v G.L. Import Export* (n 175, above) (French law of unfair competition); Case 8/74 *Procureur
du Roi v Dassonville* [1974] ECR 837, [1974] 2 CMLR 436 (Belgian law of unfair competition
in combination with certificate of origin requirements); *Ford Agricultural* (n 190, above) (refusal
to supply English manual to parallel importers faced with safety regulations requiring supply of
manual with each tractor). As with trade mark rights (n 197, above), the Treaty provisions on free
movement of goods may also be relevant.

[201] *Cafeteros de Colombia*, OJ 1982 L360/31, [1983] 1 CMLR 703; Case 319/82 *Société de
Vente de Ciments et Betons v Kerpen & Kerpen* [1983] ECR 4173, [1985] 1 CMLR 511; *Bayo-n-ox*,
OJ 1990 L21/71, [1990] 4 CMLR 930 (appeal dismissed as out of time, Case C-195/91P *Bayer v
Commission* [1994] ECR I-5619, [1996] 4 CMLR 32).

[202] See para 6.065, below. See also *IJsselcentrale*, OJ 1991 L28/32, [1992] 5 CMLR 154, where
the Commission found that a series of exclusive purchasing obligations imposed at different levels
of the distribution chain operated to render imports impossible; on appeal Case T-16/91 *Rendo v
Commission* [1992] II-ECR 2417, Case C-19/93P *Rendo v Commission* [1995] ECR I-3319, [1997]
4 CMLR 392 and Case T-16/91 *RV Rendo v Commission* [1997] ECR II-1827, [1997] 4 CMLR
453. See also the reference to the ECJ from parallel proceedings in the Dutch courts, Case C-393/92
Almelo [1994] ECR I-1477.

[203] See para 6.065, below.

[204] See *Hasselblad*, OJ 1982 L161/18, [1982] 2 CMLR 233, paras 23–25 and 48 (provision of
serial numbers); *Gosme/Martell—DMP*, OJ 1991 L185/23, [1992] 5 CMLR 586 (encoding of Cognac
bottles); *Newitt/Dunlop Slazenger International* (n 198, above) (marking of tennis balls); *Ford Agricultural*
(n 190, above) para 15 (die stamping tractors and using vehicle registration documents to identify
exports); *Tretorn*, OJ 1994 L378/45, [1997] 4 CMLR 860, paras 59–61 (marking of tennis balls) (appeal
dismissed, Case T-49/95 *Van Megen Sports v Commission* [1996] ECR II-1799, [1997] 4 CMLR 843).
cf Case T-204/03 *Haladjian Frères v Commission*, [2006] ECR II-3779, [2007] 4 CMLR 1106
(monitoring of sales legitimate to control imports from low price countries outside the EU).

[205] *Bayer Dental*, OJ 1990 L351/46, [1992] 4 CMLR 61: distributors were also prohibited from
repackaging the goods to avoid this risk. See also *Ford Agricultural* (n 190, above).

manufacturer's guarantee to parallel imports;[206] the charging of different prices according to the territory into which the goods are to be delivered;[207] or refusal to supply.[208] Product differentiation can also be used to give territorial protection contrary to Article 81(1). The Commission held that where the formulation of a herbicide requires approval under the law of one Member State in order to be sold, offering slightly different formulations in other Member States has the effect of a ban on parallel imports.[209] Similarly, a commitment by a distributor to his retail customers that he will himself buy up any contract goods that are imported from another Member State infringes Article 81(1).[210] So also does a requirement that the distributors should include in their resale contracts territorial restrictions on where their customers may in turn resell the goods.[211]

6.059 **Obligation to export only outside the Community.** An obligation on the distributor to export the goods only outside the Community will normally infringe Article 81(1) when it has the object of preventing parallel trading[212] but the position may be otherwise if the agreement complements an intra-Community exclusive distribution network which has exemption under Article 81(3) and is designed to assist in penetration of a particular external market.[213]

---

[206] Case 31/85 *ETA v DK Investment* [1985] ECR 3933, [1986] 2 CMLR 674.

[207] See *Newitt/Dunlop Slazenger International* (n 198, above); *The Distillers Company Limited*, OJ 1978 L50/16, [1978] 1 CMLR 400, (appeal dismissed Case 30/78 *Distillers Company v Commission* [1980] ECR 2229, [1980] 3 CMLR 121). See also *Kodak* (n 179, above) (orders from outside the territory to be met at the price ruling in the territory where the order originated, not where the order was received); *Pittsburg Corning Europe*, OJ 1972 L272/35, [1973] CMLR D2 (differential prices according to territory to prevent parallel imports); *Hennessy-Henkell* (n 163, above) (distributor guaranteed a price and margin sufficient to protect him from 'infiltration'); *Moet et Chandon (London) Ltd*, OJ 1982 L94/7, [1982] 2 CMLR 166 (clause in terms of sale that prices apply only to goods intended for consumption in the territory, orders for export to be referred to overseas parent of supplier); *Polistil/Arbois*, OJ 1984 L136/9, [1984] 2 CMLR 594 (a similar price clause inserted to combat possible competition from parallel importers); *Bayo-n-ox* (n 201, above). But see *GlaxoSmithKline Services* (n 175, above) paras 155 *et seq*: Glaxo Wellcome's dual pricing system in Spain, under which it charged higher prices to Spanish wholesalers for pharmaceuticals intended for export where the domestic prices in Spain were set by the Spanish authorities held to have an anti-competitive effect but not an anti-competitive object.

[208] See *Dunlop Slazenger* (n 189, above); *Tretorn* (n 204, above). See also *Euglucon 5, XIIIth Report on Competition Policy* (1983), point 108 (withdrawal of product with intent to affect parallel imports).

[209] *Zera/Montedison*, OJ 1993 L272/28, [1995] 5 CMLR 320; and see *XXIIIrd Report on Competition Policy* (1993), point 212.

[210] *Konica*, OJ 1988 L78/34, [1988] 4 CMLR 848. For horizontal arrangements between distributors to prevent parallel imports, see para 5.080, above.

[211] See Reg 2790/99, OJ 1999 L336/21: Vol II, App C.3, Art 4(b), 1st indent. See also *Video Games, Nintendo Distribution* (n 177, above) para 265 (agreement between Nintendo and its exclusive UK distributor, John Menzies, restricted John Menzies to selling only to retailers who sold the products to final consumers).

[212] Cases 29 & 30/83 *CRAM and Rheinzink v Commission* [1984] ECR 1679, [1985] 1 CMLR 688. See also para 6.064, below.

[213] Case C-306/96 *Javico v YSLP* [1998] ECR I-1983, [1998] 5 CMLR 172: see further para 1.108, above. See also Case 14967 *Philips Information Systems and Solid International*,

Export bans at dealer level.   Where a distributor includes an export ban in its   **6.060**
onward sales, those agreements will infringe Article 81(1),[214] as will an undertaking by the supplier to the distributor to procure that no third party exports into
the contract area.[215] Thus in *Gaz de France*,[216] the Commission examined a contract between Gaz de France DF (GDF) and ENI, whereby GDF transported
natural gas acquired by ENI in northern Europe over French territory to the Swiss
border. The Commission held that a clause requiring ENI to market the gas exclusively 'downstream of the redelivery point' (that is, after leaving France), restricted
the territory in which the parties could use the gas and was designed to partition
national markets. It were therefore in breach of Article 81(1).

Measures aimed at monitoring and identifying the source of parallel imports.   **6.061**
In cases involving long-standing restrictions on exports operated by a supplier
and its distributors, there are often measures put in place to alert the supplier to
instances of parallel imports and to identify the origin of such imports. In *Video
Games, Nintendo Distribution*,[217] the Commission imposed heavy fines both on the
Nintendo group of companies and on various of its distributors. The Commission
found that various methods had been used over a long period to enforce the
restriction on parallel imports. Statistical methods, such as close monitoring of
the ratio of orders of consoles and cartridges by dealers could be used to discern
patterns of trade indicating sales to non-end-users. Nintendo also sent out questionnaires to its dealers asking for information about any imports they encountered in their territories. It instructed its local subsidiaries to make test purchases

---

Dutch Supreme Court, 23 April 1993, NJ 1993/382. Philips sold a shipment of outdated personal
computers, produced in Canada, to Solid International. Both Philips and Solid International were
based in Eindhoven, the Netherlands. The purchasing agreement contained an export clause stipulating that the goods must be sold outside the Community in Eastern Europe. However, Solid sold
the complete shipment to a company seated in Eindhoven, and in injunction proceedings the Court
of Appeal held that the clause contravened Art 81. Philips argued that the export clause could not be
held to affect inter-State trade since the computers were produced outside the Community, were to
be transported outside the Community, and were destined to be sold outside the Community. The
Dutch Supreme Court held that the Court of Appeal had not properly considered these facts and
annulled the Court's judgment.

[214] *Sandoz* (n 178, above), where 'export prohibited' was printed on the supplier's invoices.
Although this was held to be a term of the agreement with the wholesalers and pharmacies to whom
sales were made, the Commission decided that the supplier alone was responsible for the infringement. See also *Gosme/Martell—DMP* (n 204, above).

[215] See, eg Case 25/75 *Van Vliet Kwastenfabriek v Dalle Crode* [1975] ECR 1103, [1975] 2
CMLR 549.

[216] COMP/38.662 *Gaz de France*, decn of 26 October 2004. Taking account of the specific
nature of the gas market and the circumstances of the case, however, the Commission decided not to
impose fines. The Commission reached a similar conclusion regarding a clause in a contract between
GDF and ENEL which contained a clause requiring ENEL to use the gas in Italy.

[217] *Video Games, Nintendo distribution*, OJ 2003 L255/33, [2004] 4 CMLR 421; on appeal,
Cases T-18/03 *CD-Contact Data v Commission*, T-12/03 *Itochu Corporation v Commission*,
T-398/02 *Linea Gig (in liquidation) v Commission*, T-13/03 *Nintendo Corp and Nintendo of Europe
v Commission*, not yet decided.

from other dealers and introduced a tagging system to help identify parallel exporters. The Commission held that even those distributors in the high price countries from which exports were unlikely to originate participated in the agreement by informing Nintendo when imports were found in their territory in the expectation that Nintendo would put pressure on dealers in the low price countries to prevent exports.[218] The implementation of a system (for example, differentiated labels or serial numbers) aimed at verifying the effective destination of the supplied goods that is used by the supplier to monitor the activity of individual distributors may indicate the implementation of a ban.[219]

(ii) Particular clauses

6.062 **Distributor's obligation not to sell competing products.** When an exclusive distribution or supply agreement contains an obligation on the distributor not to manufacture or sell competing products (now referred to by the Commission as 'single branding'), the Commission takes the view that this is in principle an infringement unless it benefits from Article 81(3).[220] That is generally so where the market share condition of the block exemption is exceeded, or the agreement is part of a network which forecloses a substantial part of the market.[221] Moreover, even for an isolated agreement where the supplier's market share is below 30 per cent, a non-compete obligation which lasts for more than five years will not benefit from exemption under Regulation 2790/99.[222]

6.063 **Distributor's exclusive purchasing obligation.** An obligation on the distributor to obtain all his supplies of the contract goods from the supplier may infringe Article 81(1).[223] Such an obligation may well be coupled with the more extensive obligation not to deal in competing goods, discussed above.[224]

---

[218] ibid, para 282.

[219] See, eg *Gosme/Martell—DMP* (n 204, above).

[220] ibid, para 171. See also, eg *Goodyear Italiana*, OJ 1975 L38/10, [1975] 1 CMLR D31; *Hennessy-Henkell* (n 163, above); *Sole distribution agreements for whisky and gin*, OJ 1985 L369/19, [1986] 2 CMLR 664; *Moosehead/Whitbread*, OJ 1990 L100/32, [1991] 4 CMLR 391. Different principles apply to franchising agreements: paras 6.173 *et seq*, below.

[221] Cases 40/73, etc, *Suiker Unie v Commission* [1975] ECR 1663, [1976] 1 CMLR 295, paras 549–552. See further the cases on selective distribution agreements and on the cumulative effect of networks: paras 6.100 and 6.145 *et seq*, below. For application of Art 81(3) to individual agreements, see para 6.079, below.

[222] Art 5(a) of Reg 2790/99 (n 211, above): an obligation that is tacitly renewable beyond a period of five years is similarly not exempt. See para 6.024(a), above.

[223] Guidelines on Vertical Restraints (n 144, above) para 172. And see *Hennessy-Henkell* (n 163, above); *Sole distribution agreements for whisky and gin* (n 220, above). Again different principles apply to franchising agreements, paras 6.171–6.176, below. *Quaere* whether those principles are relevant to distribution agreements.

[224] See, eg *Hennessy-Henkell*, above, where the modified agreement contained differing obligations on the distributor in respect of the purchase of Hennessy cognac, cognac generally and other wine-based spirits.

Restrictions on export to or import from third countries. A clause restricting **6.064** exports outside the Community may well fall outside Article 81(1) but the question is one of fact in each case. Ordinarily, the accumulation of consecutive profit margins, transport costs and customs duties will mean that if the goods were exported from the Community, there is little likelihood that they would be re-imported into the Community and then further traded between Member States.[225] Similar considerations arise as regards 'destination clauses' in a distribution agreement covering a third country, which restrict re-export into the Community.[226] However, a restriction affecting trade with the EEA States would infringe the competition provisions of the EEA Agreement[227] and may also infringe Article 81(1).[228] A distribution or supply agreement under which a supplier outside the Community appoints a distributor for a territory in the Community is governed by the same rules as apply where both parties are situated in the Community.[229]

Restrictions as to persons to whom goods may be resold. Provisions restricting **6.065** the persons to whom goods may be resold require close scrutiny under Article 81(1). Ordinarily, it is contrary to Article 81(1) to prohibit a reseller from

---

[225] *Omega*, OJ 1970 L242/22, [1970] CMLR D49, para 5; *Goodyear Italiana* (n 220, above); *Campari*, OJ 1978 L70/69, [1978] 2 CMLR 397, para 60; *Distillers Company Limited*, OJ 1978 L50/16, [1978] 1 CMLR 400 (appeal on other issues dismissed, Case 30/78 *Distillers v Commission* [1980] ECR 2229, [1980] 3 CMLR 121). cf *Kabelmetal-Luchaire*, OJ 1975 L222/34, [1975] 2 CMLR D40. In *Tretorn* (n 204, above), the Commission held that a ban on parallel exports from the EC into Switzerland had a potential effect on trade between Member States although prices were higher in Switzerland, as Swiss dealers 'would, in the absence of the restrictive practices, buy tennis balls at the lowest Community prices and resell them, even without physically shipping them to Switzerland, in Member States where prices are higher' (para 65).

[226] See Case C-306/96 *Javico v YSLP* (n 213, above). See also *Tretorn* (n 204, above) para 66: the prevention of parallel exports from the USA into Switzerland was also held to affect trade between Member States since the price differentials made re-exportation into the Community 'highly probable'; Cases 29 & 30/83 *CRAM and Rheinzink v Commission* [1984] ECR 1679, [1985] 1 CMLR 688 (German producer supplied sheet zinc to a Belgian purchaser on condition that he resold the goods in Egypt; the vendor was the only producer in Germany and the ECJ held that the clause was 'essentially designed to prevent the re-export of goods to the country of production so as to maintain a system of dual prices and restrict competition on the common market') (para 28).

[227] Art 53(1) EEA: see paras 1.085 *et seq*, above. See the treatment of Bergsala, Nintendo's exclusive distributor in Norway and Iceland in *Video Games, Nintendo distribution* (n 217, above) paras 239 *et seq.*

[228] *SABA (No. 1)*, OJ 1976 L28/19, [1976] 1 CMLR D61, para 35 (upheld on appeal: Case 26/76 *Metro v Commission (No. 1)* [1977] ECR 1875, [1978] 2 CMLR 1); see also *Junghans*, OJ 1977 L30/10, [1977] 1 CMLR D82. In *Campari* (n 225, above) such a restriction was held not to fall within Art 81(1), since trade in alcoholic beverages with EFTA countries remained subject to customs duties. The same principles apply to other third countries that have concluded free trade agreements with the EC: see the Art 19(3) Notice under Reg 17/62 in *Chanel*, 1994 OJ C334/11.

[229] *Béguelin Import v G.L. Import Export* (n 175, above). See also *Siemens/Fanuc*, OJ 1985 L376/29, [1988] 4 CMLR 945, where agreements between a Japanese and a German company granting reciprocal exclusive distribution rights infringed Art 81(1) insofar as they provided for exclusive distribution in the EC but the Commission did not condemn Siemens' exclusive distribution rights in Asia.

supplying the products in question to resellers in other Member States[230] since 'such bans on horizontal supplies can have the same effect on cross-frontier trade as export bans.'[231] An exclusive customer allocation agreement, where the distributor is restricted as regards active sales to customers reserved to another distributor or to the supplier, is covered by Regulation 2790/99[232] but almost certainly falls within Article 81(1) if the market share threshold of 30 per cent under the block exemption is exceeded.[233] Similarly, provisions in a distribution agreement, whether or not the distributor is given an exclusive territory, that prohibit him from supplying certain kinds of customer,[234] or require him to supply only to end-users,[235] will generally infringe Article 81(1). The exclusive distributor must therefore be free to sell the goods to other, non-appointed dealers, save that if the exclusive distributor himself has to satisfy certain objective criteria (for example, as regards premises or staff), it seems that he can be prohibited from making sales to other dealers at the same level of the distribution chain who do not also satisfy those criteria. If a producer of intermediate goods acts as his own distributor, selling the product direct to end-users, a requirement that the purchasers must use the product only for their own requirements (thus preventing resale) infringes Article 81(1).[236] However, particular considerations apply (i) when the distributor is a wholesaler; and (ii) in the context of a selective distribution system.

6.066 **Restrictions on resale by wholesalers.** In *Metro (No. 1)*, the Court of Justice held that a ban on direct supplies by a wholesaler to private consumers did not distort competition since it merely corresponds to the separation of functions

---

[230] When the restriction concerns only supply in the same Member State, the position will depend on whether there is an appreciable effect on inter-State trade. cf *Hasselblad*, OJ 1982 L161/18, [1982] 2 CMLR 233, affirmed on appeal, Case 86/82 *Hasselblad v Commission* [1984] ECR 883, [1984] 1 CMLR 559, para 48: selective distribution agreement in which the ban on resale infringed Art 81(1) including as regards resale within the United Kingdom.

[231] *Deutsche Philips*, OJ 1973 L293/40, [1973] CMLR D241, para II.2(d). See further the position in selective distribution agreements, para 6.101, below.

[232] Art 4(b), 1st indent, of Reg 2790/99 (n 211, above). A prohibition that extends to passive sales deprives the agreement of exemption and is regarded as a hard-core restriction: see para 6.023, above.

[233] See Guidelines on Vertical Restraints, OJ 2000 C291/1: Vol II, App C.11, paras 179–180. For possible application of Art 81(3), see para 6.079, below.

[234] *Ivoclar*, OJ 1985 L369/1, [1988] 4 CMLR 781 para 15(b) (exclusive distribution agreement: exemption granted); *Cafeteros de Colombia*, OJ 1982 L360/31, [1983] 1 CMLR 703 (non-exclusive distribution agreements by major coffee supplier: exemption refused).

[235] eg *Windsurfing*, OJ 1983 L229/1, para B.I.2(b), [1984] 1 CMLR 1, paras 114–116. See also *Menrad/Silhouette* and *Rodenstock/Metzler*, *XVth Report on Competition Policy* (1985), points 64 and 65; also *Interlübke*, ibid, point 61, where both a positive obligation to sell only to end-users and a prohibition on cross-supplies to other dealers were held to fall within Art 81(1). cf *Mitsui/Bridgestone*, ibid, point 60 (restriction on selling to non-authorised dealers treated as *de minimis*). For the position in franchise agreements, see para 6.181, below.

[236] *Bayo-n-ox* (n 201, above).

between wholesaler and retailer.[237] This approach is adopted in Regulation 2790/99[238] and reflected in the Guidelines.[239] In *Distillers-Victuallers*,[240] a similar logic was applied to specialist wholesalers: a condition was imposed by a whisky distiller on victuallers who supplied duty-free goods to ships, airports and the like, requiring them to resell only for duty-free consumption and to ensure that their purchasers entered into a similar obligation. The Commission held that in practice this did not restrict competition because the victuallers' business was orientated towards duty-free sales. Moreover, there was little possibility of the duty-free goods being supplied otherwise than for duty-free consumption because of national and international legislation governing duty-free concessions.

Selective distribution systems.   A particular example of a supplier wishing to restrict the persons to whom his goods may be resold occurs where the supplier seeks to limit his goods to outlets that fulfil certain criteria, for example dealers who fulfil certain technical requirements or who achieve a certain minimum turnover. Broadly speaking, such 'selective distribution systems' do not fall within Article 81(1) if supplies are limited on purely qualitative grounds, such as to dealers employing qualified staff or maintaining suitable premises. But Article 81(1) may apply if additional quantitative criteria are used, such as the attainment of an agreed level of ordering or the limitation of the number of dealers per territory. Selective distribution agreements are dealt with separately below, taking into account all aspects of Article 81.[241]   **6.067**

Other restrictions on resale.   It will not ordinarily be permissible under Article 81(1) to impose on the distributor restrictions as to the end use or purpose for which the goods may be resold, for example in the case of a drug, only for medical and not for veterinary purposes.[242] On the other hand, end use   **6.068**

---

237 Case 26/76 *Metro v Commission (No. 1)* [1977] ECR 1875, [1978] 2 CMLR 1, paras 28–29. The permissible ban was confined to private as opposed to trade consumers: paras 31–32. For a subsequent Commission decision, see *Grundig's EEC distribution system*, OJ 1985 L233/1, [1988] 4 CMLR 865.

238 Reg 2790/99 (n 211, above) Art 4(b), 2nd indent.

239 Guidelines on Vertical Restraints (n 233, above) para 170, stating that as long as the manufacturer is not dominant, if he appoints an exclusive wholesaler there should not be any anti-competitive effects arising from its appointment of an exclusive wholesaler provided that the wholesaler is free to resell to downstream retailers without restriction; implicitly, the wholesaler may be precluded from selling to end-users.

240 *The Distillers Co. Ltd—Victuallers*, OJ 1980 L233/43, [1980] 3 CMLR 244; cf the requirement to sell only Italian produced Campari to victuallers in *Campari* (n 225, above). See also *Villeroy & Boch*, OJ 1985 L376/15, [1988] 4 CMLR 461 (resale restrictions affecting specialised suppliers to hotels and restaurants and distributors of advertising gifts).

241 See paras 6.086 *et seq*, below.

242 *Beecham Pharma-Hoechst, VIth Report on Competition Policy* (1976), points 129 *et seq*.

restrictions justifiable on grounds of health protection do not fall within Article 81(1).[243]

6.069 **Provision of information by distributor.** An obligation on the distributor to provide the supplier with information as to his trading position, sales trends, market situation, stocks, expected demand, gross income, discounts granted, or other information will not ordinarily infringe Article 81(1), even though the supplier thereby learns of the ways in which his dealers compete *inter se*, provided that the supplier does not use the information for an improper purpose, for example to influence the distributor as to the area in which, or the prices at which, he should sell the products[244] or to identify parallel importers and cut off supplies to them.[245] However, it is contrary to Article 81(1) for a manufacturer to supply competitive information gathered from some of his dealers to other dealers.[246]

6.070 **Restrictions on advertising.** An obligation to follow the supplier's instructions with regard to advertising does not infringe Article 81(1), provided that those instructions do not seek to regulate the advertising of prices or conditions of sale.[247] It is not settled how far the supplier may prohibit the distributor from exhibiting in trade fairs and exhibitions.[248]

6.071 **Obligation to advertise and promote.** An obligation to advertise the contract products and to promote them does not infringe Article 81(1).[249]

---

[243] *Kathon Biocide*, OJ 1984 C59/6, [1984] 1 CMLR 476. See also Guidelines on Vertical Restraints (n 233, above) para 49. However, the Commission will be concerned to establish whether less restrictive provisions may provide sufficient protection: *Bayo-n-ox* (n 201, above), dismissing Bayer's argument that the own-use restriction was designed to prevent unauthorised trade.

[244] *BMW*, OJ 1975 L29/1, [1975] 1 CMLR D44; *SABA (No. 1)* (n 228, above); *Junghans*, ibid.

[245] *Tretorn* (n 204, above) paras 57–58; *Video Games, Nintendo Distribution* (n 217, above). However, it may be legitimate to operate a system which seeks to controls imports into the EU/EEA from lower price countries and to monitor sales in that lower price country for that purpose: *Haladjian Frères v Commission* (n 204, above) (CFI upheld Commission rejection of a complaint by importer).

[246] *Hasselblad* (n 230, above); and see also *BP Kemi/DDSF*, OJ 1979 L286/32, [1979] 3 CMLR 684, where the Commission condemned an information exchange agreement between a supplier and his distributor where the supplier himself competed in the distributor's territory. See also *Argos & Littlewoods and JJB Sports v Office of Fair Trading* [2006] EWCA Civ 1318, para 140 (concerted practice arising where a retailer discloses to his supplier the price at which he intends to resell the goods in the expectation that the supplier will pass this information to another retailer).

[247] *BMW* (n 244, above); *Murat*, OJ 1983 L348/20, [1984] 1 CMLR 219, para 15 (requirement to use supplier's promotional aids did not infringe Art 81(1)); Case 161/84 *Pronuptia* [1986] ECR 353, [1986] 1 CMLR 414, para 22. cf *Spices*, OJ 1978 L53/20, [1978] 2 CMLR 116, where the supplier reserved the power to decide on the manner of display of the products, and imposed resale prices: Art 81(1) was held to be infringed. For cases of infringement by a supplier seeking to control price advertisements in the context of selective distribution agreements, see, eg *Hasselblad v Commission* (n 230, above) paras 47–49; *AEG v Commission* (n 189, above) paras 130, 135(a).

[248] *BMW*, (n 244, above) para 20. See generally paras 5.152 *et seq*, above.

[249] See, eg *SABA (No. 1)* (n 228, above); *Krups*, OJ 1980 L120/26, [1980] 3 CMLR 274. In *Campari* (n 225, above), an obligation to spend a standard minimum sum on advertising fell outside Art 81(1). For promotional obligations in selective distribution systems, see para 6.096, below.

Trade marks.   An obligation to sell under the supplier's trade marks,[250] or to use   **6.072**
the supplier's trade marks without alteration or addition and only in a proper
manner in connection with the business,[251] do not in themselves fall within Article
81(1). But, as has been seen, the exercise of a trade mark right to prevent parallel
imports bearing the same mark will ordinarily be prohibited.[252] An obligation on
the distributor not to challenge the validity of the supplier's trade mark may
infringe Article 81(1), but only if the mark is sufficiently well established for the
limitation on its use to have an appreciable effect on competition.[253]

Packaging and presentation.   Article 81(1) is not ordinarily infringed by an   **6.073**
obligation to resell in the manufacturer's original packaging, unless this will
impede exports by making it difficult to comply with foreign legal requirements.[254]
But where products are delivered in bulk, it may be contrary to Article 81(1) to
provide that they may be resold only in packaged form.[255]

Complete range and minimum quantities.   It is ordinarily permissible to   **6.074**
require the distributor to purchase a complete range or minimum quantities
without infringing Article 81(1).[256] However, if a minimum quantities requirement operates in effect as a non-compete obligation, it will be assessed
accordingly; under Regulation 2790/99, a requirement for the buyer to purchase
more than 80 per cent of his total requirements on the relevant market from a
designated supplier is treated as a non-compete obligation.[257] Moreover, such
obligations in a long-term supply contract, where the parties have a significant
market share, may infringe Article 81(1).[258]

Maintenance of stocks and sales network.   It will ordinarily be permissible to   **6.075**
require a distributor to maintain a sales network and adequate stocks.[259] Different
considerations may arise if it is sought to restrict the distributor's freedom to resell

---

[250] *Omega* (n 225, above).

[251] *BMW* (n 244, above) para 21.

[252] See n 197 to para 6.058, above.

[253] *Moosehead/Whitbread* (n 220, above). See also para 9.175, below.

[254] *Dupont de Nemours*, OJ 1973 L194/27, [1973] CMLR D226, para II; cf *Bayer Dental*,
OJ 1990 L351/46, [1992] 4 CMLR 61, where the prohibition referred also to the supplier's
registered trade mark and was intended to discourage exports by creating the prospect of trade
mark infringement.

[255] *Pabst & Richarz/BNIA*, OJ 1976 L331/24, [1976] 2 CMLR D63; *Beecham Pharma-Hoechst*
(n 242, above).

[256] *Omega* (n 225, above); *BMW* (n 244, above).

[257] Reg 2790/99 (n 211, above) Art 1(b). See also Green Paper on Vertical Restraints in EC
Competition Policy, COM(96) 721 final, [1997] 4 CMLR 519, para 147.

[258] *Carlsberg*, OJ 1984 L207/26, [1985] 1 CMLR 735 (exemption granted). Note also that in
the context of selective distribution systems, such obligations may go beyond so-called qualitative
criteria and thus will need to fulfil the criteria of Art 81(3) to be valid: para 6.096, below.

[259] See, eg *Omega* (n 225, above); *Krups* (n 249, above).

only to persons who accept obligations of this kind, since in that case the principles governing selective distribution systems apply.[260]

6.076 **Provision of supporting services.** Obligations on an exclusive distributor to provide after-sales service, to sell products with a warranty and to employ properly qualified staff will fall outside Article 81(1).[261]

6.077 **Customer and guarantee service.** It is contrary to Article 81(1) for a manufacturer to refuse to honour his guarantee in respect of parallel imported products.[262] Similarly, it is contrary to Article 81(1) for a manufacturer or distributor to stipulate that a guarantee applies only to products acquired in the territory from an authorised distributor.[263] The general principle is that a manufacturer's guarantee or warranty service must be made available on the products he distributes throughout the Community irrespective of their original place of purchase.[264] Similarly, it is contrary to Article 81(1) to discriminate against parallel imports in the speed of repair service provided under the manufacturer's guarantee.[265] The same principle applies to the provision to dealers of after-sales services and other essential services, including the provision of technical information.[266] But it is not contrary to Article 81(1) for a distributor to provide an additional guarantee, going beyond the manufacturer's guarantee, which is not available to parallel imported products.[267]

---

[260] See paras 6.086 *et seq*, below.

[261] See, eg *Omega* (n 225, above); *IBM Personal Computer*, OJ 1984 L118/24, [1984] 2 CMLR 342. The imposition of such obligations may also be necessary to avoid 'free-riding' and thereby secure one of the major benefits to economic efficiency of permitting distributors to have exclusive territories: para 6.040, above. For the position of such obligations in selective distribution systems, see paras 6.094–6.096, below.

[262] Case 31/85 *ETA v DK Investment* [1985] ECR 3933, [1986] 2 CMLR 674.

[263] *Zanussi*, OJ 1978 L322/36, [1979] 1 CMLR 81; *Ford Agricultural* (n 190, above). See also *Ideal-Standard's distribution system*, OJ 1985 L20/38, [1988] 4 CMLR 627 (where such a clause was included to reinforce a customer class restriction placed on the distributor); *Sony*, *XVIIth Report on Competition Policy* (1987), point 67.

[264] *Fiat*, *XIVth Report on Competition Policy* (1984), points 70–71; *Alfa Romeo*, ibid, point 72. See generally, *Consumer guarantees*, *XVIth Report on Competition Policy* (1986), point 56; Fine, 'EEC Consumer Warranties: A new Antitrust Hurdle Facing Exporters' (1989) ECLR 233. In its decision renewing individual exemption for Grundig's selective distribution network, the Commission records that, pending Grundig's introduction of a Europe-wide contractual warranty, the company had undertaken that its distributors would allow consumers to claim in their country of residence the benefit of statutory warranty rights under the law of the country of purchase: *Grundig (No. 2)*, OJ 1994 120/15, [1995] 4 CMLR 658, para 19 (renewing exemption granted in *Grundig's EEC distribution system*, OJ 1985 L233/1, [1988] 4 CMLR 865).

[265] *Hasselblad* (n 230, above); on appeal, reversed on this point on the facts: *Hasselblad v Commission* (n 230, above) paras 32–34. See also, per AG Slynn at 929–931 (ECR), 582–583 (CMLR).

[266] *AKZO Coatings*, *XIXth Report on Competition Policy* (1989), point 45.

[267] *Hasselblad*, and *Hasselblad v Commission* (n 230, above).

Termination for breach. The usual right of the supplier to terminate for breach **6.078** cannot be regarded as anti-competitive unless there is evidence to suggest that the power might be used as an economic sanction to impose conditions more restrictive than those appearing on the face of the agreement.[268] Even then, the infringement of Article 81(1) arises from the incorporation into the agreement of a restriction that is implied by reason of the threat of termination when the distributor acts to the contrary.

(c) Application of Article 81(3) to individual agreements

In general. If an agreement falls within Article 81(1) but outside Regulation **6.079** 2790/99, it may still fulfil the criteria of Article 81(3). Because of the very different approach of the previous block exemptions covering exclusive distribution agreements, which did not include a market share limitation, there are few decisions concerning the application of Article 81(3), outside the field of selective distribution agreements, that are relevant to the application of the Article 81(3) criteria to those agreements that do not fall within Regulation 2790/99.[269] For case law on Article 81(3), reference should therefore be made to Section 5, below. The following observations are based largely on the approach set out in the Commission's Guidelines.

The conditions of Article 81(3). The general principles governing the applica- **6.080** tion of Article 81(3) are discussed in Chapter 3, above. Because one of the conditions that must be fulfilled is that the agreement does not afford the undertakings the possibility of eliminating competition in respect of a substantial part of the products in question,[270] it is unlikely that Article 81(3) will apply to a vertical restraint that benefits a party that is dominant, or would become dominant as a result of the restraint in question.[271] When Regulation 2790/99 does not apply because the relevant party exceeds the market share limit of 30 per cent, that may appear to leave a relatively narrow area for the application of Article 81(3) in individual circumstances. But it should be remembered that dominance does

---

[268] *BMW* (n 244, above) para 22; *Hasselblad* and *Hasselblad v Commission*, above.

[269] But see the application of Art 81(3) in *ARG/Unipart*, OJ 1988 L45/34, [1988] 4 CMLR 513 (exclusive supply agreement which contained some customer restrictions on the distributor); *Delta Chemie/DDD*, OJ 1988 L309/34, [1989] 4 CMLR 535 (temporary exclusive distribution linked to transfer of know-how for manufacture). Note also *Bayer/BP Chemicals*, OJ 1988 L150/35, [1989] 4 CMLR 24, where a competitor was appointed as distributor in return for the licensing of technology as part of a restructuring arrangement: individual exemption granted; *Bayer/BP Chemicals (No. 2)*, OJ 1994 L174/34 (amending the conditions for plant closure included in the previous decision); *Sony España*, OJ 1993 C275/3, [1994] 4 CMLR 581 (Art 19(3) Notice under Reg 17/62 expressing the intention to grant exemption to the closed distribution network being established by Sony's Spanish subsidiary for professional electronic equipment that combined exclusive distribution of some products and selective distribution of other products).

[270] See paras 3.062 *et seq*, above.

[271] Guidelines on Vertical Restraints (n 233, above) para 135.

not simply depend on market share but also on the nature of the market and product in question: the degree of market concentration, barriers to entry and extent of product innovation will all be relevant to a determination of dominance.[272] In general, parties arguing that an agreement satisfied the Article 81(3) criteria will need to substantiate the consumer benefits claimed to result from the restraint, for example, economies of scale resulting from concentration of distribution in a limited number of distributors.[273] It will also be necessary to consider whether a less restrictive obligation might be sufficient for the purpose relied on.[274]

6.081 **Application of Article 81(3) to exclusive distribution agreements.** The Commission has stated that in order for Article 81(3) to apply, the risk of a significant reduction of intra-brand competition which arises when the supplier's market share exceeds 30 per cent needs to be balanced by real efficiencies.[275] Those may comprise savings due to economies of scale in distribution; or the need to protect investment costs by distributors related to the brand.[276] The latter will be easier to establish for new or complex products or for products of which the qualities are difficult to judge before, or even after, consumption. In considering the combination of exclusive distribution with other restraints, the Commission distinguishes between (i) a non-compete obligation ('single branding'), where the distributor is prevented from selling products that compete with the contract products; and (ii) an exclusive purchasing obligation, where the distributor is prevented from obtaining the contract products other than from the supplier:

(a) If exclusive distribution is combined with a non-compete obligation, that may lead to significant foreclosure of the market to other suppliers; but if there is no such foreclosure, the combination may be pro-competitive by increasing the incentive on the exclusive distributor to focus his efforts on the particular brand. Accordingly, such a combination, particularly at the wholesale level,[277] may fulfil the Article 81(3) criteria for the whole duration of the agreement.

(b) If exclusive distribution is combined with exclusive purchasing, the possible competition risks of reduced intra-brand competition and market partitioning will be increased since the authorised distributors are prevented from making cross-supplies to each other. Unless there are very clear and

---

[272] See paras 10.015 *et seq*, below.

[273] Guidelines on Vertical Restraints (n 233, above) paras 136, 116(6).

[274] ibid, para 118.

[275] ibid, para 163.

[276] ibid, para 174. See also *Pasteur Mérieux-Merck*, OJ 1994 L309/1, para 103 (sole distribution agreement for Hepatitis B vaccine).

[277] ibid, para 171. cf Reg 2790/99 (n 211, above) Art 5(a), whereby a non-compete obligation is not exempted if it exceeds five years.

substantial efficiencies leading to lower prices to all final consumers, it is unlikely that the agreement will benefit from Article 81(3).[278]

Application of Article 81(3) to exclusive customer allocation agreements.   An **6.082** agreement containing exclusive customer allocation provisions where the parties' market shares exceed the thresholds of Regulation 2790/99 will not fulfil the criteria in Article 81(3) except in cases of clear and substantial efficiency benefits.[279] Such benefits are most likely where distributors are required to make investments in specific equipment, skills or know-how and where the products in question are new or complex or for products requiring adaptation to the needs of the particular customer or class of customers. The depreciation period of those investments indicates the justified duration of the exclusivity. Allocation of final, non-professional customers is unlikely to qualify.[280] As regards the combination of customer allocation with non-compete or exclusive purchasing obligations, the same considerations apply as to exclusive distribution agreements.[281]

Application of Article 81(3) to exclusive supply agreements.   The application **6.083** of Article 81(3) to an exclusive supply agreement is complicated by the fact that for such an agreement the market share threshold under Regulation 2790/99 applies to the buyer's share of the upstream market on which he purchases the goods whereas the anti-competitive effects of such an agreement will depend not only on the degree of foreclosure on the upstream market but also on the buyer's share of the downstream market.[282] The question of dominance on the latter market therefore needs to be considered. The principal efficiency that can constitute justification is a hold-up problem, where exclusivity is needed to protect substantial and contract-specific investments made by the buyer.[283] The duration of the agreement and the nature of the goods supplied will be of particular significance. As a working rule, the Commission considers that most types of investments cannot provide justification for exclusivity of supply for longer than five years[284] and that such justification is more likely when the supply is of intermediate and not final products.[285] When the supply is of homogeneous intermediate products, Article 81(3) is likely to apply below the level of dominance.[286] Moreover, some very substantial investments may exceptionally justify longer terms of

---

[278] Guidelines on Vertical Restraints (n 233, above) para 172 and the example at para 177.

[279] ibid, para 180.

[280] ibid, para 182 and example at para 183.

[281] ibid, para 179: see para 6.081, above.

[282] See para 6.018, above. The distinction is of particular importance as exclusive supply agreements often concern intermediate goods that are used to manufacture a different product.

[283] Guidelines on Vertical Restraints (n 233, above) para 211. For hold-ups, see n 2 to para 6.002, above.

[284] ibid, para 205.

[285] ibid, para 211. See also example at para 213.

[286] ibid, para 210.

exclusivity, even where the purchaser is dominant. The Commission has been prepared to regard the conditions in Article 81(3) as satisfied for a period of 15 years in respect of exclusive supply agreements linked to major power plant projects undertaken by the supplier, where the purchaser undertakes a corresponding obligation to purchase the entire output of the new power station and thereby provides the necessary security for the capital costs incurred.[287] However, in any case of exclusive supply, it is also important to consider less restrictive alternatives, such as quantity forcing on the supplier.[288]

6.084 **Application of Article 81(3) to hard-core restrictions.** If a vertical agreement contains a hard-core restriction and violates Article 81(1), it is highly unlikely that Article 81(3) will be fulfilled,[289] unless the essential character of the trade or industry requires such a restriction.[290]

6.085 **Agreements between competing undertakings.** Regulation 2790/99 does not apply to agreements between undertakings that supply competing products, even if they operate in different geographical markets, unless the agreement is non-reciprocal and either (i) the buyer's turnover does not exceed €100 million; or (ii) the supplier is a manufacturer and distributor and the buyer is only a distributor but not a manufacturer of competing goods; or (iii) the supplier provides services at several levels of trade while the buyer does not provide services at the level at which it purchases the contract services.[291] Therefore an agreement by a manufacturer in one Member State granting exclusive distribution rights of its products to a manufacturer in another Member State will not come within the block exemption. Where the parties' market shares are significant, such an exclusive cooperation agreement is unlikely to satisfy Article 81(3) because of its foreclosure effect.

---

[287] *Isab Energy, XXVIth Report on Competition Policy* (1996), p 133 (20-year agreements for exclusive supply of electricity from new power stations in Italy in favour of ENEL who undertook to purchase the entire output. Exemption-type comfort letters issued for 15 years only); *REN/ Turbogás*, ibid, p 134 (25-year agreement for supply of electricity by Turbogás from new power station, which would be the largest in Portugal, to the operator of the Portuguese electricity grid; comfort letter given after the agreement was amended to enable Turbogás to sell electricity to third parties after the first 15 years).

[288] Guidelines on Vertical Restraints (n 233, above) para 212.

[289] ibid, para 46. See *Distillers Company (Red Label)*, where the Commission published an Art 19(3) Notice under Reg 17/62 stating that it was minded to grant exemption for differential price terms for a limited period to facilitate the reintroduction of Johnnie Walker Red Label whisky into the UK market: OJ 1983 C245/3, [1983] 3 CMLR 173; but then concluded that exemption would not be justified: *XVIIth Report on Competition Policy* (1987), point 65. The terms were then withdrawn.

[290] eg *Newspaper distribution contracts in Belgium—AMP, XXIXth Report on Competition Policy* (1999), p 161: exemption-type comfort letter for newspaper and magazine distribution contracts in Belgium that included a fixed resale price obligation, in circumstances where the product had a very short life-span and effective distribution was dependent on sale-or-return terms. For RPM in books see para 5.025, above.

[291] Arts 1(a) and 2(4) of Reg 2790/99 (n 211, above): see further para 6.012, above.

A less restrictive form of restraint, such as non-exclusive distribution combined with minimum purchasing obligations, may be acceptable.[292]

5. Selective Distribution Systems

(a) Generally

Preliminary. Some suppliers, especially those supplying sophisticated consumer **6.086** products, wish to limit the resale of their goods to 'approved dealers only'. In adopting such a policy, a supplier may be concerned that its products are sold only through outlets that possess at least a minimum of technical expertise or that are consistent with the products' 'luxury' image. Additionally, or alternatively, it may wish to supply only dealers prepared to undertake specific obligations such as sales promotion or regular ordering, or it may wish to limit the number of dealers handling its product in a particular area. Whatever selection criteria a supplier may use, it will normally wish to prevent its approved dealers selling to any non-approved dealer since, without such a restriction, his policy of limiting resale to 'approved dealers only' might be frustrated. By contrast with an exclusive distribution system, in a selective distribution system the distributor is normally not allocated a territory and the restriction on its resales is therefore not prescribed on a territorial basis. In this Section, the term 'selective distribution system' has the same meaning as that adopted by Regulation 2790/1999, namely a system of distribution whereby the supplier limits, on the basis of specified criteria, the distributors it is prepared to supply and the appointed distributors are forbidden to resell to anyone other than end-users or other appointed distributors.[293] The goods subject to selective distribution are almost always branded, final products.

---

[292] See *Seamless Steel Tubes*, OJ 2003 L140/1, [2003] 5 CMLR 683 (appeals dismissed save for reductions in the fines: Cases T-44/00 *Mannesmannröhren-Werke v Commission*, T-48/01 *Corus UK v Commission*, T-50/01 *Dalmine v Commission*, T-67/01, etc, *JFE Engineering v Commission* [2004] ECR II-2223, 2325, 2395, 2501, [2005] 4 CMLR 182; further appeal dismissed, Case C-411/04P *Mannesmannröhren-Werke v Commission* [2007] 4 CMLR 682), where an agreement under which British Steel bought its requirements for tubes from its European competitors in the context of a cartel to exclude Japanese suppliers was condemned. Note also the Commission's intervention in relation to an agreement under which the cigarette manufacturer Philip Morris granted an exclusive licence to the Spanish cigarette manufacturer Tabacalera to produce Philip Morris' branded cigarettes for the Spanish market. The Commission considered there was no reason for Philip Morris not to make and import cigarettes into Spain itself: (2002) 2 EC Competition Policy Newsletter 40. cf *Pripps/Tuborg, XXVIIIth Report on Competition Policy* (1998), p 148: licence from Carlsberg group to the leading Swedish brewer to manufacture, sell and distribute Tuborg beer in Sweden received an exemption-type comfort letter after it was amended to become non-exclusive and a second licensee was appointed; although that was as much a horizontal as a vertical agreement, a similar approach should apply to a simpler distribution arrangement.

[293] Reg 2790/99 (n 211, above) Art 1(d). In some more restrictive selective distribution systems, appointed distributors are further prohibited from supplying other appointed distributors,

6.087 **Effect on competition.** Selective distribution systems are extremely common but because they limit the outlets through which goods are supplied, such arrangements pose certain problems for competition law.[294] On the one hand, selective distribution systems can be pro-competitive: they provide protection from free-riding[295] to those outlets that are prepared to invest in staff training or technical facilities to promote the manufacturer's particular range of products, and they may help to create a brand image for luxury goods, thereby furthering inter-brand competition. On the other hand, the limitation of outlets may be used by the manufacturer and appointed distributors to exclude price discounters and thereby maintain higher prices. As with other types of limited distribution arrangements, the principal effects of a selective distribution system are therefore a reduction in intra-brand competition and the foreclosure of distributors.[296] But these adverse effects are unlikely to be appreciable when inter-brand competition is strong, and any negative effects may be countered by the pro-competitive effect of the restrictions in avoiding free-riding or promoting a brand image. However, the foreclosure of other distributors assumes greater significance when the number of authorised distributors is very small, or when most major suppliers use selective distribution. Moreover, in that situation a further problem may be the increased risk of collusion between, respectively, distributors or suppliers.[297] Foreclosure of suppliers is not usually a consequence of selective distribution, so long as the authorised distributors may deal in competing brands (that is, provided that selective distribution is not combined with non-compete obligations) and are not curtailed in their freedom to do so by quantitative obligations in their distribution agreements.[298]

6.088 **Approach of this Section.** Prior to Regulation 2790/99, selective distribution in general was not covered by the previous block exemptions and therefore

---

eg *Hasselblad* (n 230, above). Such provisions normally infringe Art 81(1): see para 6.101, below. cf *Konica* (n 210, above), where the distributors were not prohibited from selling outside the network. See also the Commission's decision to continue to exempt Grundig's selective distribution agreement which contained bans on supplies to non-approved dealers, and on wholesalers supplying to final consumers, as well as a clause requiring approved dealers to give details of any supplies to other approved dealers: *Grundig (No. 2)* (n 264, above).

[294] It should be noted that the manufacturer's policy of it supplying only selected outlets does not infringe Art 81(1) since unless it is dominant it is entitled to refuse to supply anyone without reason; the competition rules apply only as a result of the restriction imposed on the selected dealers that prohibits them from reselling to non-authorised dealers.

[295] For free-riding, see para 6.002, above.

[296] See para 6.002, above. But note that the Commission considers that these effects may be more pronounced with a selective distribution system than with exclusive distribution because in the former, non-authorised dealers who may be more efficient are precluded from obtaining supplies from the authorised distributors: Guidelines on Vertical Restraints (n 233, above) para 188.

[297] ibid.

[298] ibid, para 193.

generated a considerable body of case law. The new block exemption applies to selective distribution agreements provided that the market share held by the supplier does not exceed 30 per cent of the relevant market on which he sells the goods.[299] For those selective distribution agreements which exceed that threshold, guidance as to the basis on Article 81(3) will be applied is set out in the Commission's Guidelines.[300] The Guidelines also indicate the circumstances in which the Commission might withdraw the benefit of the block exemption from a selective distribution agreement that satisfies the market share condition. This Section accordingly first considers the application of Article 81(1) to selective distribution systems in more detail and assesses the effect of Regulation 2790/99. Next, the question of the application of Article 81(3) to individual agreements is discussed. The final part of this Section considers separately motor vehicle distribution and servicing agreements, which are subject to a distinct regime under a separate block exemption, Regulation 1400/2002. Sometimes selective distribution systems are also part of a system of exclusive distribution, or involve exclusive purchasing or non-compete obligations, in which case reference should also be made to the matters discussed in the other relevant Sections of this Chapter.

(b) Article 81(1)

The leading cases. The principles for assessing selective distribution systems under Article 81(1) were laid down by the Court of Justice in the leading decisions of *Metro (No. 1)*, *Metro (No. 2)*, *AEG* and *Ford (No. 2)*. The *Metro* cases[301] concerned a selective distribution system in Germany and other Member States for television, radio and tape recording equipment operated by a German company, SABA. In *Metro (No. 1)*, the Court of Justice upheld the Commission's view that selective distribution systems based on objective qualitative criteria are compatible with Article 81(1). The Court said:

6.089

> '. . . selective distribution systems constitute [. . .], together with others, an aspect of competition which accords with Article 81(1), provided that resellers are chosen on the basis of objective criteria of a qualitative nature relating to the technical qualifications of the reseller and his staff and the suitability of his trading premises and that such conditions are laid down uniformly for all potential resellers and are not applied in a discriminatory fashion.'[302]

---

[299] Reg 2790/99 (n 211, above) Art 3(1). Additional restrictions in the agreements may preclude application of the block exemption. See paras 6.022 *et seq*, above.

[300] Guidelines on Vertical Restraints (n 233, above).

[301] Case 26/76 *Metro v Commission (No. 1)* [1977] ECR 1875, [1978] 2 CMLR 1 (on appeal from *SABA (No. 1)*, OJ 1976 L28/19, [1976] 1 CMLR D61); Case 75/84 *Metro v Commission (No. 2)* [1986] ECR 3021, [1987] 1 CMLR 118 (on appeal from *SABA (No. 2)*, OJ 1983 L376/41, [1984] 1 CMLR 676, in which the Commission renewed the exemption it had granted in *Saba (No. 1)*).

[302] *Metro (No. 1)*, above, para 20.

The Court acknowledged that in such systems 'price competition is not generally emphasized' but held that 'price competition . . . does not constitute the only effective form of competition' and that:

> 'For specialist wholesalers and retailers the desire to maintain a certain price level, which corresponds to the desire to preserve, in the interests of consumers, the possibility of the continued existence of this channel of distribution in conjunction with new methods of distribution based on a different type of competition policy, forms one of the objectives which may be pursued without necessarily falling under the prohibition contained in Article 81(1), and, if it does fall thereunder, either wholly or in part, coming within the framework of Article 81(3).'[303]

Metro (No. 1) thus establishes that, in principle, Article 81(1) does not apply to a 'simple' selective distribution system based solely on objective, qualitative criteria that are appropriate for the products in question. However, in *Metro (No. 2)* the Court added the qualification that:

> '. . . there may nevertheless be a restriction or elimination of competition where the existence of a certain number of such [simple] systems does not leave any room for other forms of distribution based on a different type of competition policy or results in a rigidity in price structure which is not counterbalanced by other aspects of competition between products of the same brand and by the existence of effective competition between different brands.'[304]

Therefore, if 'simple' selective distribution systems become the norm in a given industry, resulting in a serious lack of effective competition, Article 81(1) might, exceptionally, apply.[305] *Metro (No. 1)* also establishes that Article 81(1) applies to additional requirements which exceed strictly 'qualitative' criteria relating to the technical qualifications of the reseller and the suitability of its premises.[306]

6.090 **Unilateral conduct or agreement within Article 81(1).** *AEG-Telefunken* was the first case where the Commission fined a company for operating a selective distribution system that was contrary to Article 81(1).[307] In dismissing AEG's appeal from the Commission decision, the Court of Justice[308] rejected AEG's submission that its failure to admit certain traders as dealers even though they met

---

[303] ibid, para 21. See generally paras 2.088 *et seq* above, for whether such considerations fall to be judged under Art 81(1) or Art 81(3). For comment on *Metro (No. 1)*, see also para 2.089, above.

[304] *Metro (No. 2)* (n 301, above) at para 40. See also the opinion of AG Verloren van Themaat.

[305] See further para 6.100, below.

[306] See further paras 6.096 *et seq*, below.

[307] *AEG Telefunken*, OJ 1982 L117/15, [1982] 2 CMLR 386.

[308] Case 107/82 *AEG v Commission* [1983] ECR 3151, [1984] 3 CMLR 325, paras 37–38.

the qualitative criteria for membership was a unilateral act which fell outside Article 81(1).[309] The Court held that:

'. . . where the manufacturer, with a view to maintaining a high level of prices or to excluding certain modern channels of distribution, refuses to approve distributors who satisfy the qualitative criteria of the system . . .'

the manufacturer's conduct is not truly unilateral but:

'. . . forms part of the contractual relations between the undertaking and resellers. Indeed, in the case of the admission of a distributor, approval is based on the acceptance, tacit or express, by the contracting parties of the policy pursued by AEG which requires *inter alia* the exclusion from the network of all distributors who are qualified for admission but are not prepared to adhere to that policy.'[310]

Thus systems of selective distribution which exclude certain qualified dealers infringe Article 81(1); and an infringement is established if there are a sufficient number of such refusals to prove systematic conduct.[311] Moreover, the Court rejected AEG's argument that specialist dealers fulfilling the necessary qualitative criteria were entitled to a guaranteed profit margin.[312]

Basic principles. The principles derived from the decisions of the Court of **6.091** Justice can be summarised as follows. In general, Article 81(1) does not apply to a selective distribution system if four conditions are satisfied:[313] (i) the nature of the goods in question means that such a system is a legitimate requirement;[314] (ii) the distributors are selected solely on the basis of non-discriminatory, qualitative criteria relating to their technical ability to handle the goods and the suitability of

---

[309] On the distinction between unilateral conduct and an agreement within Art 81(1), see now the *ADALAT* case: Case T-41/96 *Bayer v Commission* [2001] 4 CMLR 126, [2001] All ER (EC) 1; on appeal Cases C-2 & 3/01P *Commission v Bayer* [2004] ECR I-23, [2004] 4 CMLR 13, [2004] All ER (EC) 500; see para 2.025, above. See also para 6.055, above and Cases 25 & 26/84 *Ford v Commission (No. 2)* [1985] ECR 2725, [1985] 3 CMLR 528 where an ostensibly 'unilateral' decision taken by a supplier with a selective distribution system to cease supplying a product (right-hand drive cars) may infringe Art 81(1) if the purpose of the decision is to obstruct parallel imports, although it is still necessary to show that a restraint on such importing was by implication accepted by the dealers.

[310] *AEG v Commission* (n 308, above) paras 37–38.

[311] *AEG v Commission*, above, paras 36–39. The ECJ held that the refusals were systematic although the Commission relied on only 18 cases (some involving the same retailers) over a six-year period when AEG had 12,000 distributors in the Community. cf the opinion of AG Reischl who found insufficient grounds on the facts to support the Commission's conclusion. And see also *Metro (No. 2)* (n 301, above) para 73.

[312] ibid, paras 40–43.

[313] Case T-19/92 *Leclerc v Commission* ('*YSL*') [1996] ECR II-1851, [1997] 4 CMLR 995, para 112; Case T-88/92 *Leclerc v Commission* ('*Givenchy*') [1996] ECR II-1961, para 106. See also the Guidelines on Vertical Restraints, OJ 2000 C291/1: Vol II, App C.11, para 185.

[314] See paras 6.092 and 6.093, below.

their premises;[315] (iii) those criteria do not go beyond what is necessary;[316] and (iv) the system seeks to achieve a result which enhances competition and therefore counterbalances the reduction in competition, particularly as regards price, inherent in such systems.[317] Conversely, and subject to the *de minimis* rule,[318] Article 81(1) will usually apply where the supplier selects dealers also on the basis of 'quantitative' criteria: for example, by reference to minimum sales requirements or a limitation on the number of appointed dealers in a given area.[319] Similarly, Article 81(1) will apply if the supplier prevents cross-supplies between authorised dealers or takes measures to limit parallel imports.[320] In assessing whether Article 81(1) applies in any given case, it is relevant to take into account the features of the relevant market and, in particular, the character of competition in that market.[321]

6.092 **The nature of the products: objective technical requirements.** Even if the supplier operates a simple selective distribution system based on 'objective technical requirements', such a system will fall outside Article 81(1) only if those requirements are reasonably necessary for the proper sale of the particular product. As expressed by the Court of Justice, this involves consideration whether 'the characteristics of the product in question necessitate a selective distribution system in order to preserve its quality and ensure its proper use'.[322] The Commission has held that a system limiting supplies to resellers having suitable premises, trained staff and adequate servicing arrangements is acceptable in respect of cameras,[323] televisions, hi-fi and similar products,[324] high quality watches

---

[315] *Metro (No. 1)*, para 20, quoted in para 6.089, above. This statement has often been repeated: eg *AEG* (n 308, above) para 35.

[316] Case 31/80 *L'Oréal v De Nieuwe AMCK* [1980] ECR 3775, [1981] 2 CMLR 235, para 16; Case T-19/91 *Vichy v Commission* [1992] ECR II-415, paras 69–71 (on appeal from *Vichy*, OJ 1991 L75/57).

[317] See *AEG* (n 308, above) paras 34, 37: refusal to approve distributors in order to maintain price levels.

[318] Note the Commission's position in the Perfumes cases: Cases 253/78, etc, *Procureur de la République v Giry and Guerlain* [1980] ECR 2327, [1981] 2 CMLR 99; Case 37/79 *Marty v Lauder* [1980] ECR 2481, [1981] 2 CMLR 143; Case 99/79 *Lancôme v Etos* [1980] ECR 2511, [1981] 2 CMLR 164.

[319] *Metro (No. 1)* (n 301, above); *Vichy* (n 316, above). See further para 6.096, below.

[320] *Ford (No. 2)* (n 309, above); *Hasselblad*, OJ 1982 L161/18, [1982] 2 CMLR 233. See further para 6.101, below.

[321] A relevant feature is how far other suppliers use selective distribution systems: *Metro (No. 2)* (n 301, above). See further para 6.100, below.

[322] *L'Oréal* (n 316, above) para 16; *AEG* (n 308, above) para 33.

[323] *Kodak*, JO 1970 L147/24, [1970] CMLR D19, D22.

[324] *SABA (No. 1)* (n 301, above) and *SABA (No. 2)* (n 301, above), upheld by the ECJ in *Metro (No. 1)* and *(No. 2)* (n 301, above): see in particular *Metro (No. 2)* at paras 54–56; *Grundig distribution system* and *Grundig (No. 2)* (n 264, above) (renewal of exemption); and the dismissal of a complaint, upheld in Case 210/81 *Demo-Studio Schmidt v Commission* [1983] ECR 3045, [1984] 1 CMLR 63. See also *Kenwood Electronics Deutschland*, OJ 1993 C67/9, [1993] 4 CMLR 389 (car audio equipment); *Sony España*, OJ 1993 C275/3, [1994] 4 CMLR 581 (professional electronic equipment); *Sony Pan-European Dealer Agreement*, XXVth *Report on Competition Policy* (1995), p 135 (comfort letter).

and clocks,[325] jewellery,[326] glass crystal,[327] computers,[328] ceramic tableware[329] and newspapers[330] but not for tobacco products[331] or mass produced watches.[332] The position is doubtful in respect of plumbing equipment.[333] Selective distribution is not justifiable if the quality of the product is already adequately regulated by public law[334] for example, with regard to cosmetics or body-care products which are not at the luxury end of the market, the existence of national and Community rules which ensure that such products do not pose a danger to health limits the need for qualitative control of outlets.[335] Despite the many examples in previous decisions, precisely which products justify a selective distribution system may not be easy to determine in a particular case.[336]

Luxury and prestige products.   In the two *Leclerc* cases,[337] the Court of First   **6.093**
Instance considered the distribution systems for Yves Saint Laurent and Givenchy

---

[325] *Junghans*, OJ 1977 L30/10, [1977] 1 CMLR D82. And see Case C-376/92 *Metro SB-Grossmärkte v Cartier* [1994] ECR I-15, [1994] 5 CMLR 331; but cf Case 31/85 *ETA v DK Investment* [1985] ECR 3933, [1986] 2 CMLR 674, where the ECJ refused to accept that a selective distribution system was justified for mass produced 'Swatch' watches. See also *Chanel, XXVth Report on Competition Policy* (1995), p 136, where the Commission granted clearance (by comfort letter) to a selective distribution system for luxury watches after amendment to incorporate objective qualitative criteria for selection of dealers.

[326] *Murat*, OJ 1983 L348/20, [1984] 1 CMLR 219.

[327] *Compagnie des Cristalleries Baccarat, XXIst Report on Competition Policy* (1991), point 98; *Schott-Zwiesel-Glaswerke*, OJ 1993 C111/4, [1993] 5 CMLR 85.

[328] *IBM Personal Computer*, OJ 1984 L118/24, [1984] 2 CMLR 342. cf *Computerland*, OJ 1987 L222/12, [1989] 4 CMLR 259.

[329] *Villeroy & Boch*, OJ 1985 L376/15, [1988] 4 CMLR 461.

[330] This point was left open in Case 126/80 *Salonia v Poidomani and Giglio* [1981] ECR 1563, [1982] 1 CMLR 64, but was accepted in Case 243/83 *Binon v AMP* [1985] ECR 2015, [1985] 3 CMLR 800, 32. See also *AMP*, OJ 1987 C164/2.

[331] Cases 209/78, etc, *Van Landewyck v Commission* ('*FEDETAB*') [1980] ECR 3125, [1981] 3 CMLR 134, paras 138–140.

[332] *ETA v DK Investment* (n 325, above).

[333] *Grohe's distribution system*, OJ 1985 L19/17, [1988] 4 CMLR 612; *Ideal-Standard distribution system*, OJ 1985 L20/38, [1988] 4 CMLR 627.

[334] *L'Oréal v De Nieuwe AMCK* (n 316, above) para 16.

[335] *Vichy*, OJ 1991 L75/57, para 18(2)(c), appeal dismissed, *Vichy v Commission* (n 316, above); and see *APB*, OJ 1990 L18/35, [1990] 4 CMLR 619, where the Commission objected to a collective agreement limiting the distribution of parapharmaceutical products to pharmacies. cf *LCJ Diffusion v La Roche Posay*, Paris Court of Appeal, RG no. 2003/11305, 8 June 2005, which concerned proceedings brought by La Roche Posay against LCJ Diffusion under the French law on unfair competition as a result of LCJ having distributed La Roche Posay's dermo-cosmetic products in a store outside the scope of its selective distribution network. LCJ was enjoined to stop selling La Roche Posay products and, on appeal, the Court of Appeal confirmed this decision. The Court rejected the argument that the restrictions imposed by the La Roche Posay network were contrary to Art 81, holding that they were justified by the high technicality and quality of the products. The distribution of the La Roche Posay products required an organised space in which some advice could be given (by a dermatologist or a pharmacist), although these products were not medicines. The Court also found that the agreements came within Reg 2790/99.

[336] See also Faull & Nikpay (eds), *The EC Law of Competition* (2nd edn, 2007), para 9.332.

[337] *Leclerc* (*YSL*) and *Leclerc* (*Givenchy*) (n 313, above).

beauty products, including both perfumes and high quality cosmetics and body-care products. Leclerc, the French supermarket chain, applied for annulment of the Commission decisions which had granted individual exemption (under the pre-Modernisation regime) in respect of those systems after finding that many of the provisions in the agreements did not fall within Article 81(1).[338] The Court held that these products, in particular perfume, were high quality products with a luxury image which was of great importance to consumers. The nature of the products in question therefore encompassed not just their material quality but also their 'aura of luxury'. Since it was in the interests of consumers to buy luxury products in appropriate surroundings which maintained that image of exclusivity, the restriction on competition that is inherent in selective distribution systems was justified.[339] Yves Saint Laurent and Givenchy were therefore justified in specifying detailed criteria for the location, aesthetic and functional qualities of the outlets admitted to the network, in line with the luxurious and exclusive nature of the product. However, in order to counterbalance the restriction on competition inherent in selective distribution, the systems had to be open to all retailers who could present the products in their appropriate setting and thereby preserve their luxury image.[340]

6.094 **Qualitative criteria.** Assuming that selective distribution is appropriate to the products in question, criteria such as technically qualified staff, suitable premises,[341]

---

[338] *Yves Saint Laurent Parfums*, OJ 1992 L12/24, [1993] 4 CMLR 120; *Parfums Givenchy*, OJ 1992 L236/11, [1993] 5 CMLR 579. See also the Report by the UK Monopolies and Mergers Commission ('MMC'), *Fine Fragrances* (1993, Cm. 2380), which concluded that the selective distribution systems for these products did not operate against the public interest in the United Kingdom.

[339] *Leclerc (YSL)* (n 313, above) paras 114–123; *Leclerc (Givenchy)*, ibid, paras 108–117. This conclusion was not invalidated by the fact that in certain Member States, including the UK, a proportion of sales took place outside the selective distribution network: the CFI held that those sales resulted in part from the luxury image that had been preserved, at least partly, by the selective distribution system. See Art and Van Liedekerke, 'Developments in EC Competition Law in 1996 – An Overview' (1997) 34 CMLRev 895 at 911, criticising this approach on the grounds that appraising the interests of consumers is a highly subjective exercise: whilst some consumers of luxury cosmetics may give priority to their sale in luxurious surroundings, others may consider that the sale of the same products at the lowest possible price takes precedence. cf *Vichy v Commission* (n 316, above) where the CFI held that general cosmetics (ie face-care and body-care products, but not perfumes) did not justify a distribution system that allowed only retail pharmacies to be distributors. See also, the decision of the Paris Court of Appeal in *LCJ Diffusion v La Roche Posay* (n 335, above). For the Commission's treatment of other luxury products, see *Baccarat* (glass crystal) (n 327, above); *Chanel* (luxury watches) (n 325, above).

[340] *Leclerc (YSL)* (n 313, above) para 122; *Leclerc (Givenchy)*, ibid, para 116.

[341] In *Leclerc (YSL)* (n 313, above) paras 139–147, similarly *Leclerc (Givenchy)*, paras 132–140, the CFI held that this could include obligations as to the external appearance of the retail outlet. Restrictions as to the shop's name were also, in principle, legitimate as a shop name could be 'down market' in consumers' eyes and so detract from the luxury image of the products. However, national authorities had a particular responsibility to ensure that such requirements were not applied in a discriminatory, unjustifiable or disproportionate manner and the contention that a particular shop

the maintenance of a specialist department, a ban on sale of 'downmarket' goods in proximity to the contract goods[342] and the ability to display the products and provide after-sales service are accepted as qualitative criteria falling outside Article 81(1).[343] In *Grundig*, the Commission held that a requirement not to advertise at 'cash and carry, self-service or take away' prices could be subsumed under qualitative selective criteria, since the dealer was impliedly waiving after-sales services, and that a ban on mail order supplies could be subsumed under the dealer's qualitative obligations to give advice and to display the products.[344] An obligation to hold stocks has on occasion been assimilated to a qualitative obligation,[345] but in other cases such an obligation is treated as quantitative.[346] Exceptionally, however, Article 81(1) might apply even to a system based on qualitative criteria if the cumulative effect of such systems precluded other methods of distribution from competing in the relevant market.[347]

Restriction on sales over the internet.   If it is legitimate for the supplier to   **6.095** require distributors to maintain a luxury setting for the goods, can the supplier also exclude internet online resellers from the network? In *Depotkosmetik im Internet*,[348] the German Federal Supreme Court held that the producer of luxury

---

name was perceived as 'down market' had to be established objectively, eg by reference to consumer surveys and market studies: *Leclerc* (*YSL*), paras 158–161; *Leclerc* (*Givenchy*), paras 150–153. But a retailer's policy on prices could not be regarded as making a shop 'down market': shops could offer products at reduced prices in product-enhancing conditions.

342 However, in *Leclerc* (*Givenchy*), above, paras 141–144, it was held that an obligation to ensure that the sale of the luxury cosmetic products accounted for at least 50 per cent of the total activities in the retail outlet was disproportionate and had no inherent connection with the legitimate aim of preserving the products' luxury image; it was discriminatory and anti-competitive and fell within Art 81(1). Similarly, *Leclerc* (*YSL*) (above), paras 151–153 (analogous 60 per cent requirement).

343 *Leclerc* (*YSL*) and *Leclerc* (*Givenchy*) (above). See also the Commission decisions in *Murat* (n 326, above); *IBM Personal Computer* (n 328, above). In *Villeroy & Boch* (n 329, above), the company dropped a requirement that the premises should be in a central location. In *Baccarat* (n 327, above), the Commission approved a minimum business turnover requirement (not limited to sales of the contract goods) provided that it was kept at a reasonable level.

344 *Grundig distribution system* and *Grundig (No. 2)* (n 264, above). cf the restrictions on price advertising condemned in Case 86/82 *Hasselblad v Commission* [1984] ECR 883, [1984] 1 CMLR 559, paras 47–49. See also the CFI's attitude to price discounters in the *Leclerc* judgments (n 313, above).

345 See, eg *Murat* (n 326, above) (retailers' obligation to order three months' stock not restrictive of competition since the quantities were less than those customary in the trade); *Villeroy & Boch* (n 329, above) (promotional obligations and stockholding did not restrict competition on the facts where the supplier had a small market share). See also *Krups* (n 249, above) (obligation on 'appointed' dealers to maintain stocks, etc outside Art 81(1) where supplier in fact supplied other dealers outside the system and the dealers' obligations were held on the facts not to restrict competition appreciably).

346 See para 6.096, below.

347 See para 6.100, below.

348 *Depotkosmetik im Internet*, judgment of 4 November 2003, WuW/E DE-R 1203. See also the decision of the Belgian Supreme Court in *MAKRO v Beauté Prestige International*, 10 October 2002, where it was held in the context of a selective distribution network of perfumes, that the need to give personal advice could serve as an objective justification for prohibiting Internet sales and

perfume operating a selective distribution network of authorised retail stores was not required to admit a purely online distributor to its network. This was the case even where its authorised retailers were allowed to achieve up to 50 per cent of their individual turnover by way of online distribution via the internet. The Court analysed the distinction between traditional, stationary, cosmetic retail and online trade and concluded that the Commission's practice drew a clear distinction between selective distribution in traditional retail outlets and online trade. Regulation 2790/99 allows suppliers to restrict distribution to outlets which satisfy certain minimum quality requirements. Online distribution via the internet clearly does not meet these requirements and, therefore, does not communicate the aura of luxury which is a key feature of selective distribution. The Court referred to Article 4(c) of Regulation 2790/99[349] and to the Guidelines on Vertical Restraints[350] which stipulated that even in a selective distribution system, the manufacturer is not allowed to prevent its distributors from all use of online trade as a means of distribution. However, the Court held that this rule did not require the manufacturer to waive the requirement of a stationary retail outlet as a prerequisite for distributors to be admitted to the selective system.[351]

6.096 **Quantitative restrictions.** Article 81(1) may apply if the system involves additional, 'quantitative' requirements. These may include obligations to purchase a minimum quantity of goods;[352] to achieve a particular turnover in the supplier's products; to enter into formal contracting commitments; to maintain stocks; or to promote the products of the supplier in question.[353] However, such obligations do not invariably infringe Article 81(1)[354] and the distinction between purely qualitative criteria and those requirements that are regarded as additional, and therefore quantitative, can be somewhat elusive.[355] It seems that the matter will be

---

promotion. The Court considered that the restriction fell within Art 4(b) of Reg 2790/99 but referred to para 51 of the Guidelines on Vertical Restraints in holding that a total ban on internet sales could be objectively justified.

[349] Reg 2790/99, OJ 1999 L336/21: Vol II, App C.3.

[350] Guidelines on Vertical Restraints (n 313, above).

[351] Note also the Commission approval of the selective distribution system of Yves Saint Laurent Parfums for the period following the expiry of the earlier exemption: Press Release IP/01/713 (17 May 2001). Approved retailers operating a physical premises were permitted to sell via the internet, and the Commission stated that this met the conditions of Reg 2790/99.

[352] *Yves Saint Laurent Parfums* (n 338, above) (exemption granted subject to a reporting condition which would enable the Commission to monitor the economic effect of the minimum purchase levels set by YSL).

[353] *Metro (No. 1)* (n 301, above) upholding *SABA (No. 1)*; *BMW*, OJ 1975 L29/1, [1975] 1 CMLR D44; *SABA (No. 2)* (n 301, above); *Grundig* (n 293, above).

[354] See, eg *Krups*, OJ 1980 L120/26, [1980] 3 CMLR 274; *Murat* (n 326, above); *Villeroy & Boch* (n 329, above).

[355] Note also the different approach taken in relation to franchise agreements where similar obligations have been held to fall outside Art 81(1): *Pronuptia*, OJ 1987 L13/39, [1986] 1 CMLR 414, para 27. For franchising, see generally paras 6.171 *et seq*, below.

one of fact and degree in the circumstances of each case. Article 81(1) is more likely to apply if dealers are required to achieve a specified turnover, or a sales target. In *Grundig (No. 2)*,[356] the Commission held that requirements as to the range of products carried and levels of stock went beyond what was necessary for an 'appropriate' distribution of the products and meant that the dealers 'must take sales promoting measures that restrict their commercial independence'.[357] These obligations therefore came within Article 81(1) but the exemption previously granted to the network agreement was renewed for 10 years. A more restrictive form of quantitative criterion seeks directly to limit the number of authorised dealers, for example by reference to the purchasing power or population of the region, or the distance from the nearest existing authorised dealer. However, these are not restrictions or obligations in the agreements themselves but are more appropriately regarded as a form of discrimination in operation of the other criteria for selection; in any event, a selective system operated on that basis will come within Article 81(1).[358]

Open admission to the network for qualifying resellers. In order to fall outside **6.097** Article 81(1), the qualitative requirements must be objectively applied without discrimination to all resellers seeking admission to the system,[359] ie the system must be an 'open' system. Conversely, Article 81(1) applies if the system restricts the admission of dealers who satisfy the qualitative criteria, ie if the system is a 'closed' system of selective distribution which limits, for example, the number of resellers appointed in a particular territory.[360] In some cases, the Commission

---

[356] *Grundig (No. 2)*, OJ 1994 L20/15, [1995] 4 CMLR 658, renewing exemption granted in *Grundig's EEC distribution system*, OJ 1985 L233/1, [1988] 4 CMLR 865. See also *Grohe distribution system* (n 333, above), and *Ideal-Standard distribution system*, ibid, where it was doubted that the obligation to stock a whole range fell outside Art 81(1).

[357] *Grundig (No. 2)* above, para 35.

[358] See Green Paper on Vertical Restraints in EC Competition Policy, COM (96) 721 final, [1997] 4 CMLR 519, para 127.

[359] See especially *Metro (No. 1)* (n 301, above) discussed at para 6.089, above, and the definition of 'qualitative selective distribution system' in the context of motor vehicle dealerships, in Reg 1400/2002, OJ 2002 L203/30: Vol II, App C.6, Art 1(1)(h). Note also that in *Vichy* (n 335, above), the Commission appeared to regard the coexistence of two different distribution systems in the common market as requiring justification; see similarly *Konica*, OJ 1988 L78/34, [1988] 4 CMLR 848. In *Magneti Marelli*, Press Release IP/92/262 (6 April 1992), the Commission intervened when a supplier's differential pricing for spare parts discriminated against members of its distribution system as compared to its direct sales to car manufacturers.

[360] See, eg *Omega*, OJ 1970 L242/22, [1970] CMLR D49 (retailer appointments limited by purchasing power of local clientele); *BMW* (n 353, above) (BMW entitled to exclude undertakings meeting the objective criteria): *Hasselblad* (n 320, above), and *Hasselblad v Commission* (n 344, above) (only 100 out of 2000 possible dealers appointed on the ground that otherwise dealers could not obtain sufficient turnover to justify holding stock); *AEG-Telefunken*, OJ 1982 L117/15, [1982] 2 CMLR 386, on appeal *AEG v Commission* (n 308, above) (low price dealers excluded); *Ivoclar*, OJ 1985 L369/1, [1988] 4 CMLR 781 (some dental depots meeting qualitative criteria excluded); see also *Ivoclar (No. 2)*, OJ 1993 C251/3, [1994] 4 CMLR 578 (proposal to extend exemption).

sought to ensure that the admission criteria are applied in a non-discriminatory way by persuading the supplier to allow wholesalers also to appoint dealers, and to give objectively verifiable reasons before a dealership is withdrawn.[361] In the *Leclerc* judgments, the Court of First Instance made it clear that the application of the qualitative requirements was to be reviewed by the national courts and that any applicant refused admission to a selective distribution network who considered that the criteria at issue had been applied to him in a manner inconsistent with Article 81(1), and, in particular, in a discriminatory or disproportionate fashion, may bring a case before the national courts or authorities responsible for the application of Community competition law.[362]

6.098 **Procedure for admission to the network.** The Commission has intervened to speed up the procedures adopted by the manufacturer for assessing whether an outlet is entitled to join the network. In *Yves Saint Laurent Parfums*[363] the Commission required amendments to the system to ensure that admission was not unduly delayed and in particular that the procedure did not enable YSL to postpone admission until such time as it judged that a new account in a particular region was justified by the strength of local demand. The terms were amended to specify: (i) strict time limits for the inspection of the applicant's outlet and for a decision on admission; and (ii) the provision of a written and reasoned response to the application, identifying if possible the works needed to be done at the outlet to bring it up to the standard required and giving the applicant an opportunity to carry out such works.

---

[361] *SABA (No. 2)* (n 301, above); *Grundig* (n 356, above).

[362] Case T-19/92 *Leclerc v Commission ('YSL')* [1996] ECR II-1851, [1997] 4 CMLR 995, paras 124–130; Case T-88/92 *Leclerc v Commission ('Givenchy')* [1996] ECR II-19614, paras 118–124. However, the CFI also held, referring to *AEG*, that an applicant refused admission to the network could, subject to the principles laid down in Case T-24/90 *Automec v Commission ('Automec II')* [1992] ECR II-2223, [1992] 5 CMLR 431, submit a complaint to the Commission, in particular if the conditions for admission are systematically used in a manner incompatible with EC law.

[363] *Yves Saint Laurent Parfums*, OJ 1992 L12/24, [1993] 4 CMLR 120. See also *Parfums Givenchy* (n 338, above) (exemption granted to standard terms similar to those in YSL). These terms were not challenged before the CFI. See also the Commission's approach to the notifications by Sony of its selective distribution networks for electronic equipment. In *Sony España* (n 324, above), the Commission obtained Sony's agreement that a distributor would automatically be admitted to the network in Spain if their application had not been rejected, with written reasons, six months after application. In *Sony Pan-European Dealer Agreement*, ibid, the Commission approved Sony's pan-European dealer agreement after it was changed to provide that Sony may not refuse to supply a product to an authorised distributor without written justification, and for an independent arbitration procedure to which a dealer refused authorisation may appeal. In *Grundig (No. 2)* (n 356, above) para 33, the Commission held that Grundig's procedure for the admission of wholesalers and retailers was unobjectionable from a competition policy point of view since applications for admission were decided within an appropriate period of four weeks. In *Fine Fragrances* (n 338, above), the UK MMC recommended that fragrance houses should set up an arbitration scheme for cases where a retailer considers that authorised status has been refused contrary to the criteria for selection (at para 8.188).

Application of Regulation 2790/99.   If the supplier's share of the market on   **6.099**
which he sells the contract goods does not exceed 30 per cent, a selective distribution agreement may fall within the block exemption for vertical agreements.[364]
Regulation 2790/99 applies to such agreements irrespective of the nature of the
products or the criteria by which distributors are selected.[365] However, in the light
of the case law discussed above, the Commission has indicated two circumstances
in which it is likely to consider withdrawal of the block exemption: (i) if the nature
of the product does not require selective distribution *and* the system in place has
appreciable anti-competitive effects;[366] or (ii) in the case of significant cumulative
effects.[367] It appears that so long as the nature of the product justifies a selective
distribution system, agreements containing quantitative restrictions should,
without more, continue to enjoy the benefit of the block exemption.[368] However,
as it is the character of the product that leads to a selective distribution arrangement, and since the block exemption would only apply in the first place where the
supplier's market share is no more than 30 per cent, the application of selective
distribution by several other suppliers is not unlikely and the cumulative effect
then has to be considered.

Cumulative effect.   In *Metro (No. 2)*, the Court of Justice indicated that   **6.100**
the cumulative effect of several selective distribution systems, even when only
objective, qualitative criteria are employed, could lead to the application of
Article 81(1).[369] However, in the *Leclerc* judgments, the Court of First Instance
emphasised that even where most manufacturers of a product use selective distribution systems based only on qualitative criteria, that does not lead automatically
to the application of Article 81(1). The Court held that the systems will only be
caught by the competition rules if:

> 'it is established either that there are barriers preventing access to the market by new
> competitors capable of selling the products in question, so that the selective distribu-
> tion systems at issue have the effect of constraining distribution to the advantage of
> certain existing channels . . ., or that there is no workable competition, in particular
> as regards price, taking account of the nature of the products at issue.'[370]

---

[364] See paras 6.010 *et seq*, above.
[365] Reg 2790/99 (n 349, above). See the definition of 'selective distribution system' in Art 1(d).
[366] Guidelines on Vertical Restraints (n 313, above) para 186.
[367] ibid, para 189.
[368] ibid, para 187.
[369] See para 6.089, above.
[370] *Leclerc (YSL)* (n 362, above) para 182; *Leclerc (Givenchy)*, ibid, para 174. The CFI held that
the applicant had not discharged this evidential burden. Note that in the decisions challenged the
Commission regarded it as important that customers for whom price rather than prestige was a
priority could choose from a range of competing goods sold in the adjacent non-luxury market
through an unrestricted range of outlets, thereby 'penalising' the choice of distribution method
adopted by the luxury suppliers.

Therefore if sufficient strong competitors do not apply selective distribution, there is unlikely to be any anti-competitive effect. In its Guidelines, the Commission states its view that a problem of cumulative effect is unlikely to arise when: (i) the share of the market covered by selective distribution is below 50 per cent; and (ii) the aggregate market share of the five largest suppliers is below 50 per cent. However, if all five largest suppliers apply selective distribution, competition concerns will in particular arise regarding agreements that apply quantitative selection criteria which directly limit the number of dealers.[371] Whether the application of more indirect quantitative criteria (for example, minimum purchasing requirements or the obligation to reserve a minimum shelf-space for the supplier's products) produces net negative effects will depend on the particular facts.[372] The Commission can therefore be expected to adopt this approach as regards both withdrawal of the block exemption from an individual selective distribution system and the exercise of its power to issue a regulation disapplying the exemption to all agreements containing specific restraints in a particular market.[373] In any event, when an individual supplier has a low market share, its agreements will not be regarded as contributing significantly to a cumulative effect.[374]

6.101 **Territorial and other restrictions on resale.** It is inherent in a selective distribution system that the supplier seeks to limit distribution of its products to authorised distributors. Accordingly a restriction on the authorised distributors in such a system selling to unauthorised distributors does not infringe Article 81(1).[375] Restrictions that are ancillary to this objective should therefore also fall outside Article 81(1): for example, in the *Cartier* case,[376] the Court of Justice held that a manufacturer's restriction of his guarantee to goods sold only by authorised dealers is to be regarded as a means of preventing persons outside the network from marketing the goods and so does not infringe the competition rules. Article 81(1)

---

[371] Guidelines on Vertical Restraints (n 313, above) para 189 and example at para 198.

[372] The Commission states that they are 'less likely' to produce net negative effects if they do not relate to a 'significant' proportion of the dealer's total turnover in the products in question nor go beyond what is 'necessary' for the supplier to recover any investment related to that relationship and/or realise economies of scale in distribution: ibid, para 189; see also para 193. This guidance begs as many questions as it answers.

[373] Reg 2790/99 (n 349, above) Art 8 permits such general withdrawal where parallel networks of similar restraints cover more than 50 per cent of a relevant market: see paras 6.025 *et seq*, above.

[374] Guidelines on Vertical Restraints (n 311, above) para 189: the Commission considers 5 per cent to be the threshold for this purpose. See also Case C-214/99 *Neste Markkinointi Oy v Yötuuli Ky* [2000] ECR I-11121, [2001] 4 CMLR 993 (in the context of an exclusive purchasing agreement).

[375] If the agreement otherwise comes within Art 81(1), such a restriction is exempt under Art 4(b), 3rd indent, of Reg 2790/99 (n 349, above). The enforceability of this restriction as a matter of EC law is not dependent upon the supplier imposing such an obligation on all its authorised distributors in the Community, or taking steps to prevent supplies to unauthorised dealers: ie the principle of *Lückenlosigkeit* ('imperviousness') that applies under German unfair competition law is not relevant for EC law: *Metro SB-Grossmärkte v Cartier* (n 325, above).

[376] *Metro SB-Grossmärkte v Cartier* (n 325, above); see further para 6.077, above.

will apply if the system includes territorial restrictions on the resale of the products,[377] or is operated in such a way as to obstruct parallel imports.[378] In particular, and by contrast with an exclusive distribution system, active as well as passive sales must be permitted without territorial limitation. Therefore Article 81(1) will apply to bans on cross-supplies to other appointed resellers,[379] and to bans on supplying particular kinds of customer. Hence, a requirement that authorised retailers sell only to end-users, or obtain supplies only from the national distributor, infringes Article 81(1) and the Commission now regards such provisions as 'hard-core' restrictions.[380] However, wholesalers may be required to sell only to retailers and not direct to end-users since this corresponds to their separate functions in the distribution chain,[381] and certain specialised traders may be prohibited from reselling to the general trade.[382] A restriction on retailers engaging in active sales of a new addition to the product range which has not yet been launched in his territory falls within Article 81(1) but can be justified if it is imposed only for a reasonable time so as not to interfere with the manufacturer's launch publicity campaign.[383]

---

[377] See, eg *Kodak* (n 323, above) (export restrictions and price terms designed to prevent inter-State exports); *Omega* (n 360, above); *SABA (No. 1)* (n 301, above); *Ford Agricultural*, OJ 1993 L20/1, [1995] 5 CMLR 89.

[378] *Ford (No. 2)* (n 309, above). Similarly, *Peugeot*, OJ 1986 L295/19, [1989] 4 CMLR 371; *Lee Cooper*, *XXIXth Report on Competition Policy* (1999), p 138; and note Case 226/84 *British Leyland v Commission* [1986] ECR 3263, [1987] 1 CMLR 185 (refusal to issue certificates of conformity in order to obstruct parallel imports infringed Art 82). See also Art 4(d) of Reg 2790/99 (n 349, above): restriction of cross-supplies precludes application of the block exemption. In *Yves Saint Laurent Parfums* (n 363, above), before granting exemption the Commission required deletion of a clause providing that purchases by a retailer did not count towards his minimum purchase obligation if they were resold to other dealers in the network.

[379] See, eg *Kodak* (n 323, above); *Hasselblad* (n 320, above); *Grohe's distribution system* (n 333, above) and *Ideal-Standard's distribution system*, ibid (resale permitted only to plumbing contractors and not to other retailers, held to infringe Art 81(1)). The Commission considered whether that restriction was objectively justified under Art 81(3) but rejected the arguments put forward. The Commission left open what the position would be if the restriction had applied only within one Member State); *Ivoclar* (n 360, above) (resale limitation to dentists, dental technicians, laboratories, hospitals, etc infringed Art 81(1) but exemption granted); *Ivoclar (No. 2)*, ibid. See also *Pronuptia* (n 355, above) para 24; *Interlübke, Menrad-Silhoutte*, and *Rodenstock/Metzler*, *XVth Report on Competition Policy* (1985), points 61, 64–65 (in *Rodenstock/Metzler*, the Commission left open the question whether Art 81(1) applied to a ban confined to resellers in the same Member State). A requirement to sell to end-users only has the same effect as a ban on cross-supplies: see para 6.065, above.

[380] Case COMP/37.975 *Yamaha*, decn of 16 July 2003. See further para 6.106, below.

[381] *Metro (No. 1)* (n 301, above) paras 28–29. The ECJ accepted that without this restriction, wholesalers would enjoy an unjustified competitive advantage over retailers. See also *Grundig* (n 356, above); *Villeroy & Boch* (n 329, above); and note Art 4(c) of Reg 2790/99 (n 365, above).

[382] *Villeroy & Boch* (n 329, above). See also *Distillers-Victuallers*, OJ 1980 L233/43, [1980] 3 CMLR 244.

[383] *Yves Saint Laurent Parfums*, OJ 1992 L12/24, [1993] 4 CMLR 120. This aspect of the case was not considered by the CFI.

6.102 **Resale price maintenance.** If the agreements contain provisions that directly or indirectly limit the freedom of the distributor as regards pricing, other than the fixing of a maximum resale price, Article 81(1) will apply[384] and the agreements will not be covered by the block exemption.[385] The fixing of maximum resale prices does not preclude application of the block exemption and the Commission has stated that such a restriction in a selective distribution agreement (as in an exclusive distribution agreement) may have the effect of limiting the price increases that the distributor would otherwise seek to introduce.[386]

6.103 **Effect of refusal of admission.** If a dealer fulfilling objective, qualitative require-ments is refused admission to a selective distribution system that does not come within the block exemption and infringes Article 81(1), then unless the system fulfils the criteria of Article 81(3), the system may be legally unenforceable, the Commission may take a decision of prohibition and the parties may be liable to fines. Nonetheless, in *Automec II,* the Court of First Instance held that the Commission does not have, in the context of its powers to put an end to infringe-ments, the power to order a party to enter into a contractual relationship in circumstances where several means exist for ending the infringement. The parties must be free to exercise their own choice among the different potential courses of action which would bring their behaviour into compliance with the Treaty.[387]

(c) Application of Article 81(3)

6.104 **Generally.** If a selective distribution system falls outside Regulation 2790/99 because the supplier's market share exceeds the 30 per cent threshold, the agree-ments may nonetheless benefit from the application of Article 81(3). The Com-mission's Guidelines, following the previous case law, indicate the circumstances in which the criteria under Article 81(3) will be met.[388]

6.105 **Criteria under Article 81(3).** Since the loss of intra-brand competition result-ing from the selective distribution system is primarily of concern only if there is insufficient inter-brand competition, the principal considerations governing the application of Article 81(3) are the market position of the supplier and his com-petitors and the existence of parallel networks of selective distribution. Therefore the relative market shares of the supplier's main competitors, the distribution methods that they use and the entry barriers for non-authorised dealers have to be

---

[384] See *Yamaha* (n 380, above), and the discussion of RPM in the context of exclusive distribu-tion agreements, paras 6.050 *et seq,* above.

[385] Art 4(a) of Reg 2790/99 (n 349, above).

[386] Communication on the Application of the Community Competition Rules to Vertical Restraints, OJ 1998 C365/5, [1999] 4 CMLR 281, para III.2.2.

[387] Cases T-24 & 28/90 *Automec v Commission ('Automec II')* [1992] ECR II-2223, [1992] 5 CMLR 431.

[388] Guidelines on Vertical Restraints, OJ 2000 C291/1: Vol II, App C.11, paras 186 to 198.

assessed. For a supplier who is not dominant,[389] if the nature of the goods justifies a selective distribution system and Article 81(1) applies only because of the inclusion of quantitative criteria that are necessary to ensure efficient distribution of those goods, the agreement may escape the prohibition in the absence of cumulative effect.[390] That is particularly the case where those criteria are obligations of a promotional nature, such as stockholding or minimum sales targets.[391] But if the system is one of a number of parallel networks, the considerations set out in the discussion of Article 81(1), above, will apply.[392] A particular concern is to ensure that more efficient or price discounting distributors are not foreclosed from competing in the relevant market.[393] In *Metro (No. 1)*,[394] the Court of Justice held that although the SABA system restricted access to supplies of SABA products, those restrictions could have been complied with by Metro and similar self-service wholesalers; but the Court stated that the outcome might be different if such wholesalers were in fact eliminated as distributors in the consumer electronics market or if the rigidity of prices was unduly reinforced.[395] When the application of Article 81(3) to the SABA system was challenged in *Metro (No. 2)*,[396] the Court concluded, after detailed examination, that these consequences had not in fact occurred.[397] Even a dominant supplier's selective distribution arrangements which specifically seek to limit the number of distributors may, exceptionally, satisfy the conditions under Article 81(3), provided that the selection criteria used are non-discriminatory and transparent, for example where supply is limited and safety considerations require monitoring of the distributors' sales.[398]

Hard-core restrictions. A restriction, whether direct or indirect, on cross-supplies between authorised distributors leads to partitioning of the market and **6.106**

---

389 In *Hilti*, OJ 1988 L65/19, [1989] 4 CMLR 677, para 89(2), the Commission stated, *obiter*, that a dominant firm could not impose quantitative restrictions in a selective distribution system (appeal on other grounds dismissed, Case T-30/89 [1991] ECR II-1439, [1992] 4 CMLR 16).

390 Guidelines on Vertical Restraints (n 388, above) para 187 and example at para 197.

391 *Metro (No. 1)* (n 394, below) paras 43–50: the establishment of supply forecasts and six-month supply contracts was held to further stability of production and distribution, since close cooperation between wholesalers and manufacturers was essential to ensure efficient planning, manufacture and marketing of goods. See also *Grundig distribution system*, OJ 1985 L233/1, [1988] 4 CMLR 865; *Grundig (No. 2)*, OJ 1994 L20/15, [1995] 4 CMLR 685; and the Commission's Green Paper (n 358, above) para 128.

392 Para 6.100, above.

393 Guidelines on Vertical Restraints (n 388, above) paras 188–189.

394 Case 26/76 *Metro v Commission (No. 1)* [1977] ECR 1875, [1978] 2 CMLR 1.

395 *Metro (No. 1)*, above, paras 50 and 22.

396 Case 75/84 *Metro v Commission (No. 2)* [1986] ECR 3021, [1987] 1 CMLR 118, paras 34 *et seq*.

397 Upholding the Commission and declining to follow the opinion of AG van Themaat.

398 See *1998 Football World Cup*, XXVIIth *Report on Competition Policy* (1997), p 122 (only five tour operators selected to act as distributors of tickets; exemption-type comfort letter issued). cf the subsequent, and distinct, Commission decision finding a violation of Art 82 in the sale of tickets that favoured French purchasers: OJ 2000 L5/55, [2000] 4 CMLR 963.

will almost certainly not benefit from Article 81(3).[399] Similarly, a direct or indirect territorial restriction as regards the end-users to whom retail distributors may sell,[400] or any combination of selective distribution and exclusive customer allocation,[401] is generally viewed as a hard-core restriction as it restricts parallel imports. Restrictions regarding sales to end-users in general will not benefit from Article 81(3), unless justified by objective considerations.[402] An agreement that directly or indirectly operates to impose fixed or minimum resale prices will not benefit from exemption,[403] save in exceptional circumstances where the nature of the product or trade is dependent on such a restriction.[404]

6.107 **Combination with other restraints.**   Where selective distribution is combined with other non-hard-core restraints, the Commission indicates that the following factors will be relevant to the application of Article 81(3):

(i) If selective distribution is combined with exclusive distribution, that is generally regarded as leading to a division of the markets out of proportion to the benefits derived from those forms of distribution when considered separately.[405] Only exceptionally would such a combination fulfil the conditions of Article 81(3), if it were truly indispensable to protect substantial investments made by the authorised dealers that are specifically related to their distributorship, and thereby avoid a 'hold-up' problem.[406] But the Commission has stated that it accepts in principle the idea of territorial responsibility on the part of distributors. Therefore, provided that each authorised retailer is under no territorial restrictions as regards his resales, whether active or passive, his agreement may include a limitation on the freedom of the supplier to appoint other distributors in his 'territory'. As regards wholesalers, it seems that a greater degree of protection may be

---

[399] See *Yamaha* (n 380 above) paras 175–178.

[400] eg *Ford (No. 2)* (n 309, above) (exemption precluded by refusal to supply RHD cars in Germany in order to obstruct parallel trade to UK); *Peugeot*, OJ 1986 L295/19, [1994] 4 CMLR 371 (exemption precluded by dissuasive measures taken to prevent parallel exports to UK); *Ford Agricultural* (n 377, above) (territorial restrictions external to the written agreement not exempted). Significant price disparities between Member States often indicate an impediment to parallel trade.

[401] Guidelines on Vertical Restraints (n 388, above) para 179. See *Grohe's distribution system* (n 333, above) and *Ideal-Standard distribution system*, ibid. cf *Ivoclar*, OJ 1985 L369/1, [1988] 4 CMLR 781, where limitations on resale to authorised dealers, dentists, hospitals, etc were justified by the specific needs of the distribution of dental supplies and granted exemption; *Ivoclar (No. 2)*, OJ 1993 C251/3, [1994] 4 CMLR 578 (intention to extend exemption).

[402] See para 6.101, above.

[403] *AEG v Commission* (n 308, above); *Hasselblad v Commission* (n 344, above).

[404] See para 6.102, above.

[405] eg *Motor cycle distribution*, XXVIth Report on Competition Policy (1996), p 132.

[406] Guidelines on Vertical Restraints (n 388, above) para 195; and see *Omega* (n 360, above); *BMW*, OJ 1975 L29/1, [1975] 1 CMLR, D44; *Ivoclar* (n 401, above). For hold-ups, see n 2 to para 6.002, above.

permitted, so that a restriction of active distribution outside the allocated territory may be acceptable.[407]

(ii) If selective distribution is combined with a non-compete obligation, fulfilment of the criteria in Article 81(3) depends upon whether there is an appreciable risk of foreclosure of other suppliers on the market. That in turn is dependent on the supplier's market share, whether the supplier has a dense network of authorised distributors and the question of cumulative effect with other suppliers' systems.[408] It should be noted that under Regulation 2790/99, exemption is not granted to a non-compete obligation that exceeds five years (save where the supplier owns or rents the premises from which the distributor operates),[409] and for this purpose an obligation to buy more than 80 per cent of total purchases of the contract goods from the supplier is deemed to be a non-compete obligation.[410] The Commission is also concerned about 'targeted' non-compete obligations that prevent the distributor from stocking the brands only of specified competitors and such a provision in an agreement is excluded from the block exemption.[411] If several leading suppliers adopted this practice and used the same outlets, this could have the effect of foreclosing a particular competitor. In *Parfums Givenchy*,[412] the standard agreement required distributors to carry a minimum of four competing brands from a list drawn up by Givenchy, in order to create the specialised environment that supported the luxury brand image. Before granting individual exemption under the pre-Modernisation procedure, the Commission required that the agreement be amended to leave distributors free to make their own choice of the competing luxury brands.

(d) Motor vehicle distribution and servicing

In general.   The application of Article 81 to agreements between motor vehicle **6.108** manufacturers and dealers results from their use in common form in the manufacturers' distribution networks, generally with one or more standard forms used in each Member State and sometimes in several States together.[413] In 1985,

---

[407] See, eg *Schott-Zwiesel Glaswerken*, OJ 1993 C111/4, [1993] 5 CMLR 85 (Art 19(3) Notice under Reg 17/62), but the market share in that case was almost certainly below 30 per cent so Reg 2790/99 (n 349, above) would now apply.

[408] Guidelines on Vertical Restraints (n 388, above) para 193; and see further para 6.100, above.

[409] Reg 2790/99, OJ 1999 L336/21: Vol II, App C.3, Art 5(a): including an obligation which is tacitly renewable beyond five years.

[410] ibid, Art 1(b).

[411] ibid, Art 5(c).

[412] *Parfums Givenchy*, OJ 1992 L236/11, [1993] 5 CMLR 579, para B(4). See also Guidelines on Vertical Restraints (n 388, above) para 61.

[413] See Swaak, *European Community Law and the Automobile Industry* (1999), Chap 7. The DG Competition website has a special site devoted to the car sector with links to key documents at http://ec.europa.eu/comm/competition/sectors/motor_vehicles/overview_en.html.

following its experience since its decision in *BMW*,[414] the Commission concluded that the agreements used for distribution and servicing systems for motor vehicles could be exempted *en bloc* provided that certain conditions as regards, in particular, the availability and price of motor vehicles and spare parts were fulfilled. The Commission stated:

> 'The exclusive and selective distribution clauses can be regarded as indispensable measures of rationalisation in the motor vehicle industry because motor vehicles are consumer durables which at both regular and irregular intervals require expert maintenance and repair, not always in the same place. Motor vehicle manufacturers co-operate with selected dealers and repairers in order to provide specialised servicing for the product. On grounds of capacity and efficiency alone, such a form of co-operation cannot be extended to an unlimited number of dealers and repairers'.[415]

Accordingly, motor vehicle distribution systems are not selective distribution systems of the 'classic' type considered in the *Metro* cases and *AEG*.[416] The necessary cooperation between manufacturers and dealers could not be extended to an unlimited number of dealers who might satisfy objective quality criteria. The requirement developed in the case law regarding selective distribution systems that all suitably qualified resellers should be admitted to the network[417] therefore cannot be met in this sector. The form of agreement discussed in this Section may be characterised as falling somewhere between selective distribution and exclusive distribution, but rather close to the latter.[418]

6.109 **Regulation 1400/2002.** The Commission's first block exemption for selective distribution systems for motor vehicles was Regulation 123/85[419] which was replaced with effect from 1 October 1995 by Regulation 1475/95.[420] In November 2000, the Commission published an extensive evaluation of Regulation 1475/95, concluding that the regime had not achieved part of its aims.[421] In particular, consumers suffered from the maintenance of high price differentials between Member States and dealers remained heavily dependent upon manufacturers. The report found that there was no longer a natural link between the

---

[414] *BMW*, OJ 1975 L29/1, [1975] 1 CMLR D44.
[415] Recital (4) to Reg 123/85, OJ 1985 L15/16.
[416] See paras 6.089 *et seq*, above.
[417] See also the definition of 'selective distribution system' in Art 1(d) of Reg 2790/99 (n 407, above) and para 6.086, above.
[418] Case E-3/97 *Jaeger v Opel Norge* [1998] Rep EFTA Ct 1, [1999] 4 CMLR 147, paras 61, 67.
[419] Reg 123/85, OJ 1985 L15/16.
[420] Reg 1475/95, OJ 1995 L145/25. Reg 123/85 would have expired on 30 June 1995 but continued to apply until 30 September 1995 by reason of Art 13 of Reg 1475/95. Reg 1475/95 was adopted with necessary qualifications for the purposes of the EEA Agreement by EEA Joint Committee Decision 46/96 of 19 July 1996, OJ 1996 L291/39: EEA Agreement, Annex XIV, point 4a.
[421] COM (2000) 743 final. See also the speech by Commissioner Monti, 'Who will be in the driver's seat?' (2000) 2 EC Competition Policy Newsletter 1.

sale of new cars and after-sales servicing.[422] The new Regulation 1400/2002[423] was designed to resolve these problems, while recognising the special features of the motor vehicle sector. The new Regulation, which entered into force on 1 October 2002, introduced a number of substantial changes as regards the exemption of distribution agreements for new motor vehicles and spare parts. It also made major changes as regards the exemption of agreements for the provision of repair and maintenance services by authorised and independent repairers and other independent operators, such as on-road assistance operators, distributors of spare parts and providers of training for repairers. The Commission issued an Explanatory Brochure which provides detailed guidance to the application of the new Regulation, including illustrative examples.[424] It is described by the Commission as a 'legally non-binding guide' but has been referred to by the Community Courts.[425] The new Regulation only became fully applicable after the end of the transitional periods.[426]

Aims of Regulation 1400/2002. The Commission's evaluation report[427] had **6.110** concluded that Regulation 1475/95 did not achieve some of its principal aims. The Commission considered that applying the general vertical restraints block exemption Regulation (Regulation 2790/1999) would also not solve all the problems identified in the evaluation report. Regulation 1400/2002 reflects the more economics-based approach taken to the assessment of vertical restraints in Regulation 2790/1999 by, in particular, its use of market share thresholds. Consequently, the new Regulation is less prescriptive than Regulation 1475/95, with a view to avoiding the 'straitjacket' effect observed in the case of Regulation 1475/95 whereby, by exempting only one model for distribution, the previous block exemption had encouraged suppliers to use near identical distribution systems, leading to rigidity. It was hoped that the new approach would allow the development of innovative distribution formats. However, in some respects the

---

[422] Press Releases IP/00/1306 (15 November 2000) and IP/01/204 (14 February 2001).

[423] Reg 1400/2002, OJ 2002 L203/30: Vol II, App C.6. See Commissioner Monti, 'The new legal framework for car distribution', Speech/03/59, Brussels, 6 February 2003; Tsoraklidis, 'Towards a new Motor Vehicle Block Exemption' (2002) 2 EC Competition Policy Newsletter 31; and Clark, 'New rules for Motor Vehicle Distribution and Servicing' (2002) 3 EC Competition Policy Newsletter 3; Automotive Groups of Houthoff Buruma and Liederkerke Wolters Waelbroek Kirkpatrick, 'Flawed Reform of the Competition Rules for the European Motor Vehicle Distribution Sector' (2003) ECLR 254; Wijckmans, Tuytschaever and Vanderelst, *Vertical Agreements in Competition Law* (2006), Chap 11.

[424] *Distribution and Servicing of Motor Vehicles in the European Union* ('Explanatory Brochure'): Vol II, App C.14 (published only on the DG Comp website).

[425] Case C-125/05 *Vulcan Silkeborg* [2006] ECR I-7637; Cases C-376 & 377/05 *A Brünsteiner v Bayerische Motorenwerke* [2006] ECR I-11383, [2007] 4 CMLR 259, paras 13–14.

[426] See para 6.138, below and Reg 1400/2002 (n 423, above) Arts 10 and 12.

[427] See the Commission's report of 15 November 2000 (n 421, above).

new Regulation is stricter than Regulation 1475/95 and it also addresses competition issues relating to the repair and maintenance markets.

6.111 **Regulation 1400/2002: summary.** In addition to setting market share thresholds, the Regulation only covers agreements when certain general conditions are fulfilled,[428] for example, in relation to dispute resolution by an arbitrator. The Regulation sets out a list of very serious restrictions (commonly called 'hard-core restrictions') clarifying what is not normally permitted.[429] Where these restrictions are present, not only will the agreement no longer benefit from the block exemption, but the criteria in Article 81(3) are unlikely to apply. In addition to the hard-core restrictions list, the Regulation imposes specific conditions on certain vertical restraints, particularly non-compete obligations and location clauses.[430] When these specific conditions are not fulfilled, the vertical restraints are excluded from the block exemption. However, the Regulation will continue to apply to the rest of a vertical agreement, if the remainder of the agreement can operate independently from the non-exempted vertical restraint. The non-exempted vertical restraint will need an individual assessment under Article 81(3).[431]

6.112 **Selective and exclusive distribution.** As regards the distribution of new motor vehicles, the Regulation is built around the following principles.[432] First, the Regulation distinguishes between exclusive distribution systems and selective distribution systems. An exclusive distribution system is defined as one where the suppliers sells the contract goods or services only to one buyer inside the common market. A selective distribution system is defined as a system whereby the supplier undertakes to sell the contract goods or services only to distributors or repairers selected on the basis of specified criteria and where those distributors and repairers undertake not to sell on to distributors or repairers outside the network. Selective distribution systems are further divided into 'quantitative selective distribution systems' where the criteria for selection limit the number of appointed distributors or repairers and 'qualitative selective distribution systems' where admission to the network is open to anyone who fulfils the qualitative criteria without any direct or indirect limit on the numbers admitted.

6.113 **Principles underlying Regulation 1400/2002.** One key underlying principle of Regulation 1400/2002 is the importance of reinforcing competition between dealers in different Member States (intra-brand competition) and improving market integration. This is achieved in particular by not exempting distribution agreements which restrict passive sales; by not exempting distribution agreements

---

[428] See paras 6.123 *et seq*, below and Reg 1400/2002 (n 423, above) Art 3.
[429] See paras 6.124 *et seq*, below and Art 4.
[430] See paras 6.132 *et seq*, below and Art 5.
[431] See paras 6.104 *et seq*, above.
[432] Section 3.2 of the Explanatory Brochure (n 424, above).

in selective distribution systems which restrict active sales; and by not exempting clauses (commonly referred to as 'location clauses') prohibiting dealers in selective distribution systems from establishing additional outlets elsewhere in the common market.[433] The Regulation also prohibits a requirement that the same firm carries out both sales and servicing (commonly referred to as the 'sales-service link') by not exempting agreements that do not allow dealers to subcontract servicing and repair to authorised repairers who belong to the authorised repair network of the brand in question and who therefore fulfil the manufacturer's quality standards.[434] The Regulation also aims to facilitate multi-branding by not exempting 'non-compete obligations' which restrict the sale of motor vehicles of different brands by one dealer.[435] Suppliers may however impose an obligation for motor vehicles of different brands to be exhibited in different areas of the same showroom. The Regulation maintains the 'availability clause' by not exempting agreements that limit a dealer's ability to sell cars with different specifications from the equivalent models within the dealer's contract range. This should make it possible for a consumer to obtain vehicles from a dealer in another Member State with the specifications current in the consumer's home Member State, for example allowing UK and Irish consumers to buy new right-hand drive cars in mainland Europe.[436] The Regulation supports the use of intermediaries or purchasing agents by consumers[437] and strengthens dealers' independence from manufacturers, both by stimulating multi-brand sales and by strengthening minimum standards of contractual protection (including retaining the minimum notice periods provided for in Regulation 1475/95) and by allowing dealers to realise the value that they have built up by giving them the freedom to sell their businesses to other dealers authorised to sell the same brand.[438]

Underlying principles regarding exemption of repair and maintenance arrangements. As regards repair and maintenance of motor vehicles, Regulation 1400/2002 is based on the same stricter approach, while retaining certain elements of the previous Regulation 1475/95. The Regulation has the following aims:[439] **6.114**

— to allow manufacturers to set selection criteria for authorised repairers, provided that these do not prevent the exercise of any of the rights enshrined in the Regulation;

---

[433] Art 5(2)(b) of Reg 1400/2002 (n 423, above) which came into effect on 1 October 2005: Art 12(2). With a location clause, a manufacturer obliges a dealer only to operate from a certain place of establishment, which may be an address, a town or a territory.

[434] Reg 1400/2002 (n 423, above) Art 4(1)(g).

[435] ibid, Arts 5(1)(a) and (c).

[436] ibid, Art 4(1)(f).

[437] ibid, Recital (14).

[438] ibid, Arts 3(3) and 3(5).

[439] See Sect 3.2 of the Explanatory Brochure (n 424, above).

— to ensure that if a supplier of new motor vehicles sets qualitative criteria for the authorised repairers belonging to its network, all operators who fulfil those criteria can join the network;

— to improve authorised repairers' access to spare parts which compete with parts sold by the vehicle manufacturer;

— to preserve and reinforce the competitive position of independent repairers, that is repairers who do not operate within the distribution system of a vehicle manufacturer.[440] Independent repairers outnumber authorised repairers in all European markets, although their turnover has not grown as fast as that of authorised repairers.[441] The Regulation improves their position by reinforcing their ability to gain access to spare parts and technical information in line with technical advances, especially in the field of electronic devices and diagnostic equipment. The access right is also extended to training and to all types of tools, since access to all four of these elements is necessary if an operator is to be able to provide after sales services.

6.115 **Relationship with Regulation 2790/99 and Article 81(3).** Article 2(5) of Regulation 2790/99[442] which confers block exemption on certain vertical agreements declares that it does not apply to vertical agreements whose subject matter falls within the scope of any other block exemption regulation. It follows that Regulation 2790/99 does not apply to vertical agreements that concern new motor vehicles, repair and maintenance services for motor vehicles and spare parts for motor vehicles, as defined in Regulation 1400/2002. An agreement whose subject-matter falls within the scope of application of the Regulation[443] but which fails to meet its requirements does not fall within the scope of application of Regulation 2790/99. In *Citroën*,[444] the German Federal Supreme Court considered a claim by Citroën car dealers that certain clauses in Citroën's dealership agreement should be omitted in future. The proceedings were commenced before Regulation 1/2003 came into effect, but the Court decided that in claims relating to future conduct it had to take the change of law into consideration even at the appeal stage and to apply the new regime. The Court adopted a threefold approach: for the time before the implementation of Regulation 1400/2002 it considered the clauses under the earlier motor vehicle block exemption, Regulation 1475/95; for the period between the coming into force of Regulation 1400/2002 and 1 May 2004, it considered the clauses under Regulation 1400/2002; and for the time

---

[440] Reg 1400/2002 (n 423, above) Art 1(1)(m).

[441] See Part II of *Study in car retailing and after-sales markets under Regulation no 1400/2002*, Report by London Economics for DG Comp (June 2006), available at http://ec.europa.eu/comm/competition/sectors/motor_vehicles/documents/retailing.html.

[442] Reg 2790/99, OJ 1999 L336/21: Vol II, App C.3.

[443] Reg 1400/2002 (n 423, above) Art 2.

[444] *Citroën*, judgment of the Bundesgerichtshof of 13 July 2004, WuW/E DE-R 1335.

after 1 May 2004, it considered the clauses under both Regulation 1400/2002 and Article 81(3). The Court found that the agreement did not fall within either block exemption and referred the case back to the Court of Appeal for further consideration of the application of Article 81(3).

Scope of application of Regulation 1400/2002.   Article 2(1) of Regulation **6.116** 1400/2002 provides that the provisions of Article 81(1) will not apply to vertical agreements where they relate to the conditions under which the parties may purchase, sell or resell new motor vehicles, spare parts for motor vehicles or repair and maintenance services for motor vehicles. The Regulation does not apply, *inter alia*, to vehicles which are not motor vehicles;[445] to motor vehicles which are not new; to loans by banks which finance the purchase of a vehicle by an end-user or to goods which are not spare parts as defined in the Regulation.[446]

Third parties.   Regulation 1400/2002 does not lay down mandatory provisions **6.117** but prescribes conditions under which agreements between suppliers and approved distributors are removed from the scope of the prohibition in Article 81(1).[447] Therefore, although the Regulation states what the supplier and dealer may or may not do in their relations with third parties, it does not regulate the activities of third parties themselves, who may operate outside the framework of the Regulation. The block exemption is therefore irrelevant as regards the operation of an independent dealer who does not belong to the manufacturer's distribution network and who may be a parallel importer of motor vehicles.[448] Similarly, the Regulation does not give any third party an enforceable right to a distribution agreement, even if the third party meets the specified qualitative criteria for the manufacturer's selective distribution system. The consequence of the manufacturer's failure to apply those conditions in a non-discriminatory manner may simply be to remove the benefit of the block exemption from its agreements.[449]

---

[445] The definition of motor vehicles is found in Art 1(1)(n) and is the same as under Reg 1475/95 (n 420, above). In Case T-67/01 *JCB Service v Commission* [2004] ECR II-49, [2004] 4 CMLR 1346, paras 126–133 (further appeal on other grounds dismissed: Case C-167/04P, [2006] ECR I-8935, [2006] 5 CMLR 1303), the CFI held that construction site machinery intended for earth moving and construction fell outside Reg 1475/95 although it may be used on public roads.

[446] As defined in Art 1(1)(s) of Reg 1400/2002 (n 423, above). Items may not be 'spare parts' because they are not necessary for the use of a motor vehicle, although they may be fitted in it, eg a tape or CD player, or other accessories according to trade usage.

[447] Case 10/86 *VAG France v Magne* [1986] ECR 4071, [1988] 4 CMLR 98; Case C-230/96 *Cabour and Nord Distribution Automobiles v Arnor* [1998] ECR I-2055, [1998] 5 CMLR 679, para 47.

[448] See Case C-226/94 *Grand Garage Albigeois v Garage Massol* [1996] ECR I-651, [1996] 4 CMLR 778; Case C-309/94 *Nissan France v Dupasquier* [1994] ECR I-677, [1996] 4 CMLR 778; Case C-128/95 *Fontaine v Aqueducs Automobiles* [1997] ECR I-967, [1997] 5 CMLR 39; Case C-41/96 *VAG-Händlerbeirut v SYD—Consult* [1997] ECR I-3123, [1997] 5 CMLR 537 (all re Reg 123/85 but equally applicable to Reg 1400/2002).

[449] *Qualitative Selektion*, judgment of the German Federal Supreme Court of 28 June 2005, case KZR 26/04, WuW/E DE-R 1621. But cf *Garage Gremeau v Daimler Chrysler France*, Cass. Com.,

6.118 **Types of vertical agreements covered by Regulation 1400/2002.** The Regulation applies to vertical agreements[450] in the motor vehicle sector at all levels of trade from the stage of first supply of a new motor vehicle by its manufacturer to the final resale to end consumers. It also applies from the first supply of spare parts by their manufacturer to the provision of repair and maintenance services to end consumers. The scope of application of the Regulation is broader than Regulation 1475/95 as it includes agreements, for instance, with importers or wholesalers of motor vehicles which do not provide after-sales services, with repairers who do not sell cars and with suppliers who provide spare parts to repairers.

6.119 **Agreements between competing undertakings.** Generally, Regulation 1400/2002 does not apply to vertical agreements entered into between competing undertakings.[451] However, Article 2(3) of the Regulation provides that it applies to non-reciprocal vertical agreements which a motor vehicle manufacturer that sells directly to end-users may conclude with an individual member of its network of authorised dealers (where the dealer has a total annual turnover not exceeding €100 million). The exemption also applies to a vertical agreement between a manufacturer of motor vehicles or spare parts and an association of authorised or independent dealers or repairers who jointly buy motor vehicles or spare parts, provided that none of the individual members of the association has a total annual turnover exceeding €50 million.[452] Article 2(3) also provides that the exemption will apply to the vertical agreements between such an association and its individual members, but this is without prejudice to the application of Article 81(1) to the horizontal agreements entered into between the members of the association.

6.120 **Agency agreements.** Agency agreements are common in the motor vehicle industry. Genuine agency agreements, that is, those where the agent bears insignificant or no financial and commercial risk in respect of the contract concluded or negotiated on behalf of its principal and in respect of market-specific investments for that field of activity, are not prohibited under Article 81(1)[453] and do

---

case no. 982, 28 June 2005 (am by case no. 1319, 12 July 2005), where the French Supreme Court annulled the lower court's dismissal of a claim by dealer who had been refused a new distribution contract, holding that the court should have examined whether the manufacturer's criteria for selecting its dealers were objective and applied in a non-discriminatory manner. The reasoning in the judgment is sparse and the Court's application of Reg 1400/2004 is difficult to follow. Note that on reference back to the Paris Court of Appeal, the Commission for the first time exercised its power under Art 15(3) of Reg 1/2003 to intervene in national court proceedings: see para 14.070, below. However, the Court of Appeal postponed ruling until after judgment in a fresh action brought by DaimlerChrysler alleging fraud on the part of Garage Gremeau: judgment No 188/07 of 7 June 2007.

[450] As defined in Art 1(1)(c) of Reg 1400/2002 (n 423, above).

[451] ibid, Art 2(3).

[452] Reg 1400/2002 (n 423, above) Art 2(2)(a). Art 9 prescribes how turnover is to be calculated and provides some leeway where the threshold is slightly exceeded.

[453] See paras 6.028 *et seq*, above, and Guidelines on Vertical Restraints, OJ 2000 C291/1: Vol II, App C.11, Sect II.2 Agency Agreements, paras 12–20.

not fall within the scope of Regulation 1400/2002. Non-genuine agency agreements, on the other hand, do fall within the scope of the Regulation.[454]

Exclusive or selective distribution. To benefit from the new Regulation **6.121**
1400/2002, when appointing their distributors, manufacturers have to choose
between creating an exclusive distribution system, where dealers are allocated a
given territory, or a selective distribution system. In a major change from
Regulation 1475/95, a system combining these features is not covered by the
block exemption, although a manufacturer could adopt a selective distribution
system in one area (for example, one Member State) and an exclusive distribution
system in a distinct area. If a selective distribution system is chosen, the manufacturer may apply a combination of qualitative and quantitative criteria or it may
select its dealers according to purely qualitative criteria. If the manufacturer
chooses the latter option, it will not be able to place a ceiling on the number of
dealers and any dealer who meets the criteria may join the network.[455] If the
manufacturer chooses a quantitative system, although Regulation 1400/2002
does not appear to require that the selection of dealers must be conducted in a
non-discriminatory manner or according to objective criteria, the French Supreme
Court has held that there is in effect such an obligation.[456] In all selective systems,
be they qualitative and/or quantitative, the manufacturer may require that sales
are made only to final consumers and other members of the authorised network.[457]
However, if an exclusive distribution system is adopted, the manufacturer cannot
prohibit its distributors making passive sales to dealers outside the network.[458]

---

[454] As they did under Reg 1475/95 (n 420, above). See *Mercedes-Benz*, OJ 2002 L257/1, [2003]
4 CMLR 95, and, on appeal, Case T-325/01 *DaimlerChrysler v Commission* [2005] ECR II-3319,
[2007] 4 CMLR 559, discussed at paras 6.031 *et seq*, above.

[455] Reg 1400/2002 (n 423, above) Art 1(1)(h).

[456] *Garage Gremeau v Daimler Chrysler France* (n 449, above). The definition of 'quantitative
selective distribution system' in Art 1(1)(g) of Reg 1400/2002, to which the Court exclusively
referred, does not include the reference to non-discrimination found in Art 1(1)(h) defining a
'qualitative selective distribution system'. See comment by Chagny, JCP E no. 47, 24 November
2005, p 1701.

[457] See, generally, COMP/38.554 *PO/Audi-Werkstattverträge*, Press Release IP/03/80
(20 January 2003) (Audi system of qualitative selective distribution for the provision of after-sales
services established to benefit from the new block exemption). See also the closure of investigation
into BMW's and General Motor's distribution and servicing agreements following amendments:
IP/06/302 and IP/06/303 (13 March 2006), and in MEMO(06)120, 13 March 2006 discussed at
para 6.133, below.

[458] Reg 1400/2002 (n 423, above) Art 4(1)(b)(i). Similarly, if a selective distribution system is adopted for only one region, the dealers in that system cannot be prevented from making
passive sales to independent dealers outside the region covered by the system: Recital (13) to
Reg 1400/2002. See also Automotive Groups of Houthoff Buruma and Liederkerke Wolters
Waelbroek Kirkpatrick, article cited n 423, above.

Almost all manufacturers have chosen selective distribution throughout the single market (apart from Suzuki which operates an exclusive distribution system).[459]

6.122 **Market share thresholds.** Article 3 of Regulation 1400/2002 sets out five general conditions which agreements must fulfil for the block exemption to apply. The first of these imposes market share thresholds for all agreements covered by the exemption except a purely qualitative selective distribution system.[460] Generally, the exemption applies only on condition that the supplier's market share on the relevant market on which it sells the new motor vehicles, spare parts or repair and maintenance services does not exceed 30 per cent. In the case of a quantitative selective distribution system for the sale of new motor vehicles, the market share of the supplier must not exceed 40 per cent. In the case of an exclusive supply obligation, the relevant market share is that of the buyer rather than the supplier and must not exceed 30 per cent of the relevant market in which it purchases the contract goods or services.[461] Article 8 of the Regulation provides further detail about the calculation of market shares for this purpose.[462] For new motor vehicles shares are to be calculated by volume, if possible, whereas the more usual criterion of value is to be preferred for spare parts and repair and maintenance services.[463]

6.123 **Other conditions for the application of the exemption.** Article 3 of Regulation 1400/2002 imposes four further general conditions. First, the agreement must oblige the supplier to agree to the transfer of the dealership or authorised repair business together with all related rights and obligations to another member within the brand network.[464] The second condition limits the manner in which the supplier can terminate the agreement.[465] The agreement must provide that the supplier is required to give notice to terminate in writing and include 'detailed, objective and transparent reasons' for the termination. This is to prevent the supplier from attempting to terminate the agreement as a means of enforcing a restriction which is not permitted under the Regulation, for example on sales to foreign consumers. Thirdly, minimum contract duration terms are fixed; a fixed term contract must be for at least five years and require six months' notice of

---

[459] Press Release IP/03/1318 (13 September 2003) (new rules for car sales and servicing); and IP/04/585 (3 May 2004) (Porsche distribution and after-sales service arrangements).

[460] Reg 1400/2002 (n 423, above) Art 3(1).

[461] ibid, Art 3(2). 'Exclusive supply obligation means that the supplier must sell the contract goods or services to only one buyer inside the common market': ibid, Art 1(1)(e).

[462] See also Art 3(7) regarding apportionment of market share in the case of joint ventures.

[463] See generally Sect 6 of the Explanatory Brochure (n 424, above).

[464] ibid, Art 3(3).

[465] ibid, Art 3(4). But the Reg does not preclude an express termination clause permitting the supplier to terminate without a period of notice in the event of breach: Case C-421/05 *City Motors Groep v Citroën Belux* [2007] 4 CMLR 455.

intention not to renew.[466] An indefinite contract must provide for two years' notice of termination, reduced to one year where the supplier will pay compensation on termination or where termination is 'necessary' to reorganise the network.[467] Finally, the agreement must confer on each of the parties a right to refer disputes concerning the fulfilment of the contractual obligations to an independent expert or arbitrator.[468] That includes a dispute as to whether termination of the agreement was justified by the reasons given in the notice, as to which the expert or arbitrator must be in a position to carry out an effective review.[469] The conditions on contractual protection[470] apply to restrictive agreements to which distributors or repairers are a party. The condition regarding the minimum duration of contracts and periods of notice only applies to agreements between suppliers of new motor vehicles and their distributors or authorised repairers.

Hard-core restrictions.   Article 4 of Regulation 1400/2002 contains a list of 13   **6.124** hard-core restrictions. The Regulation defines hard-core restraints as provisions which, directly or indirectly, in isolation or in combination with other factors under the control of the parties, have the object of restricting certain conduct,[471] or a certain type of sale.[472] This broad definition means that each of the hard-core restrictions can be brought about through one or more indirect means and that in practice this may result in an anti-competitive outcome similar to that resulting from the express inclusion of the restriction in question in the written contract. Hard-core restrictions may of course take the form of outright prohibitions, but may also consist of limitations, financial disincentives, pressures or obstacles to certain activities or transactions.[473] The presence of one or more of these restrictions in an agreement automatically leads to the agreement in its entirety losing

---

[466] Reg 1400/2002 (n 423, above) Art 3(5)(a).

[467] ibid, Art 3(5)(b). If reorganisation of the network is relied on as grounds for the shorter period of notice, the test of necessity is objective: it must be justifiable on grounds of economic effectiveness by comparison with termination by the primary, two-year notice period: *Vulcan Silkeborg* (n 425, above) (re the equivalent provision of Reg 1475/95). The need to comply with a new block exemption may permit the reduction to one year's notice, depending on the particular nature of the distribution network: *A Brünsteiner v Bayerische Motorenwerke* (n 425, above); similarly Case C‑273/06 *Auto Peter Petschenig v Toyota Frey Austria* [2007] 4 CMLR 913. For an application of these principles, see the judgments of the French Cour de Cassation in *Garage de Bretagne v Daimler Chrysler France* and *Ferry Automobiles v Peugeot*, 6 March 2007.

[468] Reg 1400/2002 (n 423, above) Art 3(6). However, this right must not preclude each party's right to make an application in the national court: ibid.

[469] Reg 1400/2002 (n 423, above) Art 3(6)(g); *City Motors Groep v Citroën Belux* (n 465, above) para 30. But whether such review must include the power to grant interim relief is determined according to whether there is such power as regards similar provisions of domestic law, according to the principle of equivalence: ibid, paras 34–37.

[470] Set out in Reg 1400/2002 (n 423, above) Art 3(3), (4) and (6).

[471] ibid, Arts 4(1)(a), (f), (g), (h), (j), (k) and (l).

[472] ibid, Arts 4(1)(b), (c), (d), (e), and (i).

[473] ibid, Recitals (12)–(26) set out some of many possible examples of agreements or practices which may indirectly constitute hard-core restrictions for the purposes of the Regulation.

the benefit of the block exemption. However, in *Wegfall der Freistellung*,[474] the German Federal Supreme Court dismissed an independent distributor's claim for compensation for a refusal to supply by members of a car manufacturer's selective distribution system because the claimant could not, as required under the German law of torts, prove that the manufacturer's alleged restrictive practices caused the refusal to supply. The Court found that the manufacturer acted contrary to the terms of Regulation 1475/95 (the motor vehicle block exemption then in force) when it asked its German distributors for pricing discipline: this was a prohibited practice under the Regulation. However, the Court concluded that this did not disapply the block exemption to the selective distribution system as a whole, but only to the geographic area in which the practice distorted competition, and only for the duration of the unlawful practice. As the request for pricing discipline covered only Germany, the obligation on the network members not to sell new cars to unauthorised distributors still benefited from the exemption in the Netherlands and in Denmark. And since the claimant had not solicited orders in Germany, where the manufacturer was found to have been in breach of Article 81(1), the claim was unfounded.

6.125 **Hard-core restrictions: price-fixing.** The first set of five hard-core restrictions applies to all arrangements covered by the Regulation, that is both arrangements concerning the sale of new motor vehicles and those covering repair and maintenance services or the supply of spare parts. The first hard-core restriction is any obligation which has as its object the restriction of the distributor's or repairer's ability to determine its sale price. This is, however, without prejudice to the supplier's ability to impose a maximum sale price or to recommend a sale price, provided that this does not amount to a fixed or minimum sale price as a result of pressure from, or incentives offered by, any of the parties.[475] In *JCB Service*[476] the Court of First Instance, considering an agreement which fell outside the motor vehicle block exemption, held that where the manufacturer expresses his prices to the dealers as a discount from a recommended retail price, this did not amount to price-fixing although there was evidence that the manufacturer had been concerned that retail prices were too low.[477]

---

[474] *Wegfall der Freistellung*, judgment of the Bundesgerichtshof, 30 March 2004, WuW/E DE-R 1263.

[475] Reg 1400/2002 (n 423, above) Art 4(1)(a). For recommended prices generally see para 6.051, above.

[476] Case T-67/01 *JCB Service v Commission* [2004] ECR II-49, [2004] 4 CMLR 1346, paras 126–133, allowing on this point JCB's appeal (further appeal by JCB on other grounds dismissed, Case C-167/04P, [2006] ECR I-8935, [2006] 5 CMLR 1303.

[477] There was evidence of negotiations on price between JCB and its dealers and that 'it was not rare' for dealers to sell below the suggested price: ibid, para 129.

Hard-core restrictions: territorial ban on sales. The second hard-core restric- **6.126**
tion of general application is any obligation in the agreement which has the object
of restricting the territory into which, or the customers to whom, the distributor
or repairer may sell the contract goods or services. This covers direct or indirect
limitation of sales.[478] However, the exemption does still apply to:

(i) the restriction of active sales into the exclusive territory or to an exclusive
customer group reserved to the supplier or allocated by the supplier to
another distributor or repairer, where such a restriction does not limit sales
by the customers of the distributor or repair;

(ii) the restriction of sales to end-users by a distributor operating at the wholesale level of trade;

(iii) the restriction of sales of new motor vehicles and spare parts to unauthorised
distributors by the members of a selective distribution system in markets
where selective distribution is applied, subject to the provisions of point (i);

(iv) the restriction of the buyer's ability to sell components, supplied for the purposes of incorporation, to customers who would use them to manufacture
the same type of goods as those produced by the supplier.[479]

Accordingly, any limitation of the freedom of a retail dealer to sell to end-users,
except only for a restriction on active sales into the territory or to customers
covered by an exclusive distribution system, constitutes a hard-core restriction
and takes the agreement outside the block exemption.

Other hard-core restrictions of general application. Regulation 1400/2002 **6.127**
also prohibits any provision which has as its object:

(i) the restriction of cross-supplies between distributors or repairers within a
selective distribution system, including between distributors or repairers
operating at different levels of trade;[480]

(ii) the restriction of active or passive sales of new passenger cars or light commercial vehicles, spare parts for any motor vehicle or repair and maintenance
services for any motor vehicle to end-users by members of a selective distribution system operating at the retail level of trade in markets where selective
distribution is used. The exemption applies to agreements containing a
prohibition on a member of a selective distribution system from operating
out of an unauthorised place of establishment[481] but must not limit the

---

[478] See examples in Recital (16) of Reg 1400/2002 (n 423, above). Motor distribution cases in
which restrictions are imposed outside the formal terms of the dealership agreement are discussed in
the context of the prohibition on export bans more generally: see paras 6.053 *et seq*, above.
[479] ibid, Art 4(1)(b).
[480] ibid, Art 4(1)(c).
[481] ibid, Art 4(1)(d).

distributor's ability to establish additional outlets at other locations in the territory where selective distribution is applied;[482]

(iii) the restriction of active or passive sales of new motor vehicles (other than passenger cars or light commercial vehicles) to end-users by members of a selective distribution system operating at the retail level of trade in markets where selective distribution is used, although the supplier may prohibit a member of that system from operating out of an unauthorised place of establishment.[483]

6.128 **Active and passive sales.** The Commission has indicated[484] that, for the purposes of Regulation 1400/2002, 'active sales' involve actively approaching individual customers by, for example, direct mail or visits, advertisement in media, or other promotions not normally available or in circulation at the authorised place of establishment of a dealer or repairer.[485] Active sales are also those achieved by establishing a warehouse or sales or delivery outlet at another place of establishment to facilitate dealings with customers or their intermediaries. 'Passive sales' involve responding to unsolicited requests from customers or their duly authorised intermediaries, including delivery of motor vehicles or spare parts to such customers or intermediaries. General advertising or promotions in media which are normally available or in circulation at the authorised place of establishment of the dealer or repairer or on the internet are passive sales methods.[486]

6.129 **Hard-core restrictions concerning only the sale of new motor vehicles.** The second set of hard-core restrictions applies only to arrangements concerning the sale of new motor vehicles. These are restrictions which have as their object:

(i) the restriction of the distributor's ability to sell any new motor vehicle which corresponds to a model within its contract range;[487]

(ii) the restriction of the distributor's ability to subcontract the provision of repair and maintenance services to authorised repairers.[488] However, it is not regarded as a restriction on this ability if the contract requires the distributor to give end-users the name and address of the authorised repairer or repairers in question before the conclusion of a sales contract and, if any of these authorised repairers is not in the vicinity of the sales outlet, also to tell

---

[482] ibid, Art 5(2)(b) and para 6.134, below.

[483] ibid, Art 4(1)(e).

[484] See Sect 4.4 of the Commission's Explanatory Brochure (n 424, above).

[485] In a distribution system based on territorial exclusivity the place of establishment is deemed to be his exclusive territory.

[486] As regards internet sales, see Recital (15) of Reg 1400/2002 (n 423, above).

[487] ibid, Art 4(1)(f).

[488] See, eg *Porsche, XXXIVth Annual Report on Competition Policy* (2004), p 51 (restriction on Porsche dealers subcontracting provision of after-sales service to authorised Porsche service centre lifted to ensure compliance with Reg 1400/2002).

end-users how far the repair shop or shops in question are from the sales outlet. However, such obligations may only be imposed provided that similar obligations are imposed on distributors whose repair shop is not on the same premises as their sales outlet.[489]

Hard-core restrictions concerning only the supply of repair and maintenance services and sale of spare parts. The third set of hard-core restrictions applies only to arrangements concerning the supply of repair and maintenance services and the sale of spare parts. These are restrictions which have as their object: **6.130**

— the restriction of the authorised repairer's ability to limit its activities to the provision of repair and maintenance services and the distribution of spare parts;[490]
— the restriction of sales of spare parts by members of a selective distribution system to independent repairers which use these parts for the repair and maintenance of a motor vehicle;[491]
— the restriction agreed between a supplier of original spare parts or spare parts of matching quality, repair tools or diagnostic or other equipment and a manufacturer of motor vehicles, which limits the supplier's ability to sell these goods or services to authorised or independent distributors or to authorised or independent repairers or end-users;[492]
— the restriction of a distributor's or authorised repairer's ability to obtain original spare parts, or spare parts of matching quality, from a third undertaking of its choice and to use them for the repair or maintenance of motor vehicles. However, a supplier of new motor vehicles may require the use of original spare parts supplied by it for repairs carried out under warranty, free servicing and vehicle recall work;[493]
— the restriction agreed between a manufacturer of motor vehicles which uses components for the initial assembly of motor vehicles and the supplier of such components which limits the component supplier's ability to place its trade mark or logo effectively and in an easily visible manner on the components supplied or on spare parts.[494]

Hard-core restrictions concerning access to information. Finally, Article 4(2) of Regulation 1400/2002 provides that the block exemption does not apply where **6.131**

---

[489] Reg 1400/2002 (n 423, above) Art 4(1)(g).
[490] ibid, Art 4(1)(h). See, eg *Porsche* (n 488, above) (requirement on Porsche service centres to sell new cars lifted to ensure compliance with Reg 1400/2002).
[491] Reg 1400/2002 (n 423, above) Art 4(1)(i).
[492] ibid, Art 4(1)(j).
[493] ibid, Art 4(1)(k).
[494] ibid, Art 4(1)(l).

the supplier of motor vehicles refuses to give independent operators[495] access to any technical information, diagnostic and other equipment, tools including any relevant software, or training required for the repair and maintenance of these motor vehicles or for the implementation of environmental protection measures. Such access must include in particular the unrestricted use of the electronic control and diagnostic systems of a motor vehicle, the programming of these systems in accordance with the supplier's standard procedures, the repair and training instructions and the information required for the use of diagnostic and servicing tools and equipment. Access must be given to independent operators in a non-discriminatory, prompt and proportionate way and the information must be provided in a usable form. If the relevant item is covered by an intellectual property right or constitutes know-how, access shall not be withheld in any abusive manner.

6.132 **Specific conditions: non-compete clauses.** Article 5 sets out specific obligations which do not benefit from exemption under Regulation 1400/2002. However, these are not regarded as hard-core restrictions and there remains the possibility in a particular case that such an obligation may satisfy the criteria of Article 81(3). If it does not satisfy Article 81(3), then if it can be severed from the rest of the agreement, the remaining part of the agreement continues to benefit from the block exemption. The specific conditions exclude both direct and indirect means of attaining the anti-competitive outcome of such obligations. In accordance with one of the objectives of the block exemption of facilitating 'multi-branding', most of the specific conditions seek to ensure access to markets and to give distributors and repairers opportunities to sell and repair vehicles from different suppliers. Article 5 excludes obligations contrary to this aim from the block exemption. Specifically, as regards the sale of vehicles, repair and maintenance services or spare parts, the block exemption does not cover:

—any non-compete obligation;[496]

---

[495] ibid, Art 4(2) defines 'independent operator' as meaning 'undertakings which are directly or indirectly involved in the repair and maintenance of motor vehicles, in particular independent repairers, manufacturers of repair equipment or tools, independent distributors of spare parts, publishers of technical information, automobile clubs, roadside assistance operators, operators offering inspection and testing services and operators offering training for repairers.'

[496] Reg 1400/2002 (n 423, above) Art 5(1)(a). 'Non-compete obligation' is defined in Art 1(1)(b) as direct or indirect obligation on distributors or repairers to buy more than 30 per cent of their purchases of vehicles or spare parts pertaining to the same relevant market from a single supplier is treated as a non-compete obligation. However, an obligation that the distributor may sell other car makes only in separate areas of the show room in order to avoid confusion is not a non-compete obligation. An obligation to have brand specific sales personnel for different car makes does constitute a non-compete obligation unless this is the result of the distributor's choice and the supplier meets all additional costs involved. The Reg also covers an obligation to display the full range of motor vehicles in the showroom provided that such an obligation does not prevent the display or sale of motor vehicles from other suppliers or render the display or sale of such vehicles unreasonably difficult: see Recital (27) and also *BMW* (n 500, below) (whether obligation to display minimum number of vehicles in the showroom was an indirect non-compete obligation).

—any obligation limiting the ability of an authorised repairer to provide repair and maintenance services for vehicles from competing suppliers;[497]

—any restriction on members of a distribution system preventing them from selling motor vehicles or spare parts of particular competing suppliers or providing repair and maintenance services for motor vehicles of particular competing suppliers;[498]

—any obligation requiring the distributor or authorised repairer, after termination of the agreement, not to manufacture, purchase, sell or resell motor vehicles or not to provide repair or maintenance services.[499]

Obstacles to multi-brand distribution and servicing. On 13 March 2006, **6.133** the Commission closed its investigations into the distribution and servicing agreements of *BMW* and *General Motors*, following changes to bring them into line with Regulation 1400/2002.[500] The Commission indicated that the solutions found in these cases would serve as guidance on the application of the Regulation for the vehicle distribution sector in general.[501] Both car makers clarified a number of ambiguities in their existing contracts so that dealers knew their contractual rights and obligations should they opt for a multi-brand retailing format. In particular, BMW and GM clearly communicated to their respective networks that they accepted the joint and non-exclusive use of all facilities other than the part of a showroom which was dedicated to the sale of their brands. In addition, both car makers explicitly recognised the principle of co-existence of competing brands, allowing their respective trade marks, distinctive signs or other corporate identity elements to be displayed in and outside the dealership premises. In addition, they accepted that their dealers could use generic (multi-brand) informatics infrastructure and management systems, including accounting methodology and accounting frames, provided that such systems have equivalent functionality and quality as the solutions recommended by BMW and GM. As regards in particular GM, its contracts were adjusted to ensure that 'sales targets' and 'performance targets' did not operate as an indirect restriction on the capacity of dealers to sell competing brands. GM also clarified that its dealers could set up multi-brand internet sites and that GM trained sales personnel could also be used for selling cars of other brands whereas GM-specific training would

---

[497] Reg 1400/2002 (n 423, above) Art 5(1)(b).

[498] ibid, Art 5(1)(c).

[499] ibid, Art 5(1)(d).

[500] *BMW*, Press Release IP/06/302 (13 March 2006); and *General Motors*, IP/06/303 (13 March 2006). See Becker and Hamilton, 'Multi-brand distribution and access to repairer networks under Motor Vehicle Block Exemption Regulation 1400/2002: the experience of the BMW and General Motors cases' (2006) 2 EC Competition Policy Newsletter 33.

[501] See MEMO(06)120, 13 March 2006.

no longer be required in respect of staff entrusted with the sale of competing brands.

6.134 **Specific conditions: leasing services and 'location clauses.'** The second specific condition set out in Article 5 of Regulation 1400/2002 provides that, as regards the sale of new motor vehicles, the block exemption does not cover any obligation causing the retailer not to sell leasing services relating to contract goods or corresponding goods.[502] As regards repair and maintenance services or the supply of spare parts, the exemption does not cover any restriction on the location of the authorised repairer's workshop where selective distribution, whether quantitative or qualitative is applied.[503] Moreover, as of 1 October 2005, the block exemption no longer covers any restriction on any authorised distributor of passenger cars or light commercial vehicles[504] freely establishing additional sales or delivery outlets at other locations in the Community where selective distribution (whether quantitative or qualitative) is applied.[505] The use of 'location clauses' in agreements for the distribution of such vehicles will thus be incompatible with the Regulation. The intention is that dealers should be able to expand their business by establishing additional outlets, for example in other Member States or areas where consumers previously had little choice of dealer. The potential remains for individual assessment of such location clauses, but the Commission doubts that prohibition of the establishment of an additional *sales* outlet could satisfy the conditions of Article 81(3). However, if the clause restricts only the establishment of an additional place for *delivery*, the Commission considers that it might come within Article 81(3) when such an outlet brought a real risk of free-riding on the investment, promotional efforts and goodwill of a dealer in the second location.[506] As regards the sale of other motor vehicles, such as trucks and buses, location clauses in the context of a selective distribution network are allowed.[507] Since such vehicles are generally bought by commercial purchasers, the Commission assumes that those buyers are in a better position than private consumers to purchase from a dealer located in another area and that they will have access to better sales terms.[508]

6.135 **Withdrawal of the benefit of the block exemption.** The Commission may withdraw the benefit of Regulation 1400/2002 in respect of specific agreements if

---

[502] Reg 1400/2002 (n 423, above) Art 5(2)(a).

[503] ibid, Art 5(3). See also definitions of 'selective distribution' in Arts 1(1)(f), (g) and (h).

[504] 'Light commercial vehicle' means a motor vehicle intended to carry goods or passengers with a maximum mass of no more than 3.5 tonnes. However, if such a light commercial vehicle is also sold in a version with a maximum mass exceeding 3.5 tonnes, all versions of that vehicle are considered light commercial vehicles: ibid, Art 1(1)(p).

[505] ibid, Arts 4(1)(d), 5(2)(b) and 12(2).

[506] *Report on Competition Policy 2005*, points 17–19.

[507] Reg 1400/2002 (n 423, above) Art 4(1)(e).

[508] Commission's Explanatory Brochure (n 424, above) Sect 5.3.3.

it finds that due to specific circumstances the conditions for exemption set out in Article 81(3) are not met. Article 6 contains a non-exhaustive list of circumstances in which the Commission may decide to use this power, including where one supplier is not exposed to effective competition from other suppliers or where prices or conditions of supply for the goods differ substantially between geographic markets. The competition authority of a Member State, where that State or a part of it constitutes a distinct geographic market, has the equivalent power to withdraw the benefit of application of Regulation 1400/2002 in respect of that territory.[509]

Disapplication to parallel networks in a relevant market. Where parallel **6.136** networks of similar vertical restraints cover more than 50 per cent of a relevant market, the Commission may provide that the block exemption should no longer apply to vertical agreements containing specific restraints relating to that market.[510] The Commission may disapply the Regulation in respect of entire vertical agreements or in respect of specific restrictions or stipulations. It does this by promulgating a specific regulation disapplying the block exemption from the vertical restraints in question. The Commission's Guidelines on Vertical Restraints provide indications of procedure and substance about the disapplication.[511] However, any such specific regulation disapplying the block exemption cannot become applicable earlier than one year following its adoption.[512]

Enforcement and severance. Once an agreement is outside the terms of **6.137** Regulation 1400/2002, it falls to be assessed under Article 81 in the ordinary way. If it (either alone or considered in the context of a network of agreements) has an appreciable effect on competition that may affect trade between Member States, all the provisions of the agreement restrictive of competition are void under Article 81(2), subject only to the possibility of the agreement satisfying the conditions of Article 81(3), which in those circumstances is unlikely.[513] The result may be to deprive the dealer of many of the commercial safeguards in the agreement, since some of the restrictive provisions would have operated for his benefit. Severance of the restrictions from the agreement is a matter for national law, but in many

---

[509] Reg 1400/2002 (n 423, above) Art 6(2). The Guidelines on Vertical Restraints, OJ 2000 C291/1: Vol II, App C.11, Sect IV, paras 71–79, provide indications of procedure and substance about withdrawal by the Commission and the Member States. This power is different from the power of a national court to hold that restrictions in an agreement deprive it of the benefit of the block exemption: see Case T-115/99 *Système Européen Promotion (SEP) SARL v Commission* [2001] ECR II-691, [2001] 5 CMLR 579, para 47.

[510] Reg 1400/2002 (n 423, above) Art 7.

[511] Guidelines on Vertical Restraints (n 509, above) Sect IV, paras 80–89.

[512] Reg 1400/2002 (n 423, above) Art 7(2).

[513] Explanatory Brochure (n 424, above) Sect 3.1, p 12; cf answer to Q.8, p 25. (The language there used requires adaptation as it is no longer possible to apply for individual exemption since the coming into force of Reg 1/2003.)

cases so many provisions fundamental to the character of the agreement are affected that severance is likely to be impossible, leaving the dealer with no agreement at all.[514] That may be the result, for example, if the agreement contains less than the prescribed period of notice or the safeguard against termination under Article 3(4) and (5).[515] The dealer can complain to the Commission or to its national competition authority and request it to take action in respect of infringements. In many cases, the Commission is likely to decide that the matter is not of sufficient Community interest to justify intervention on its part,[516] and it is a matter of national law as to whether a national authority enjoys a similar discretion as to priorities. Although action by the national authority may lead the supplier to amend its agreements so as to make them comply with the block exemption, the dealer does not have the right under EC law to require such an amendment and it seems unlikely that this could be ordered if the dealer brought a private action before the national court.[517]

6.138 **Entry into force and transitional provisions.** The Regulation entered into force on 1 October 2002 and will expire on 31 May 2010.[518] However, Article 5(2)(b) applied only from 1 October 2005.[519] New agreements entering into force after 1 October 2002 have to be compatible with the Regulation for the benefit of the block exemption to apply. However, transitional provisions were included to allow operators time to adapt existing vertical agreements which were compatible with Regulation 1475/95 and which were still in force when that Regulation expired on 30 September 2002. Such agreements benefited from a transitional period until 30 September 2003, during which time the new Regulation exempted

---

[514] See per AG Tesauro in Case C-230/96 *Cabour and Nord Distribution Automobiles v Arnon* [1998] ECR I-2055, [1998] 5 CMLR 679, paras 39–42. Under English law, see the judgment of the Court of Appeal in *Richard Cound Ltd v BMW (GB) Ltd* [1997] EuLR 277.

[515] If such an agreement from which the benefit of the block exemption was removed were susceptible to severance, it is unclear whether the notice term itself would be void as contrary to Art 81(1). In *First County Garages v Fiat (Auto) UK* [1997] EuLR 712 (ChD), which otherwise followed *Cound* (above), the English High Court held (as an alternative ground of judgment) that such a term was not anti-competitive. In that case the difference was trivial (365 days instead of the one year prescribed by the then block exemption, Reg 123/85); but a significantly shorter period would increase the dealer's economic dependence on the supplier and therefore has an anti-competitive effect: see Recital (9) to Reg 1400/2002. If the notice term is void, there is presumably implied a reasonable period of notice, which might be that prescribed under the block exemption.

[516] See the applications for judicial review in Case T-186/94 *Guérin Automobiles v Commission* [1995] ECR II-1753, [1996] 4 CMLR 685, on appeal Case C-282/95P [1997] ECR I-1503, [1997] 5 CMLR 447; and Case T-38/96 *Guérin Automobiles v Commission* [1997] ECR II-1223, [1997] 5 CMLR 352 (actions dismissed because the Commission finally adopted a decision but it was ordered to contribute to the costs on account of its delays.)

[517] The dealer would presumably also be able to rely on national competition law. See *Qualitative Selektion* (n 449, above), where the German Federal Supreme Court held that Reg 1400/2002 does not, directly or indirectly, create obligations enforceable before the civil courts.

[518] Reg 1400/2002 (n 423, above) Art 12(1) and (3).

[519] See para 6.134, above.

them from the prohibition laid down in Article 81(1).[520] All agreements and all their relevant provisions had to conform to the requirements of Regulation 1400/2002 as of 1 October 2003 if they were to benefit from the block exemption. The Munich Court of Appeal[521] held that a car manufacturer was entitled to give notice under the contractual termination clause on the grounds that the restrictive clauses in its distribution contracts would have become void on the coming into effect of Regulation 1400/2002. In answer to questions referred to it by the German Federal Supreme Court, the Court of Justice held that Regulation 1400/2002 did not, of itself, require the reorganisation of the distribution network of a supplier within the meaning of the first indent of Article 5(3) of Regulation 1475/95. However, in the light of the particular nature of the distribution network of each supplier, the new block exemption may have required changes that were so significant that they amount to a true reorganisation within the meaning of that provision. It is for the national courts to determine, the Court said, in the light of all the evidence in the case before them, whether that is the position.[522]

6. Exclusive Purchasing, Single Branding and Tying

(a) Generally

Definitions. Exclusive purchasing is the mirror image of exclusive supply and **6.139** distribution. Under an exclusive purchasing contract, the purchaser must buy the contract goods or services exclusively from one supplier. However, the supplier is under no restriction as to his sales to other purchasers. Furthermore, if the purchaser is a distributor, he is not restricted as to the area in which he can seek to resell the goods. A minimum purchasing obligation, depending on the quantities involved, is a weaker form of exclusive purchasing. 'Single branding' is the term now used by the Commission to cover non-compete obligations and quantity forcing arrangements that have a similar effect.[523] A non-compete obligation requires the purchaser not to use or resell products of a particular type on a particular market that are not produced by one supplier. By contrast with an exclusive

---

[520] Reg 1400/2002 (n 423, above) Art 10.

[521] Case U (K) 5664 03, judgment of the OLG Munich of 26 February 2004, Betriebsberater (BB) 15/2004, p 79.

[522] *A Brünsteiner v Bayerische Motorenwerke* (n 467, above). The ECJ also held that, once the transitional period provided for by Art 10 had expired, a contract which had satisfied the conditions for block exemption under Reg 1475/95 but which had as its object at least one of the hard-core restrictions listed in Art 4 of the new Reg did not benefit at all from the new block exemption. The result was that all restrictions in such contracts were liable to be caught by Art 81(1), if Art 81(3) did not apply. See also Case C-125/05 *VW-Audi Forhandlerforeningen v Skandinavisk Motor Co* [2006] ECR I-7637, [2007] 4 CMLR 1071, paras 58–65.

[523] Guidelines on Vertical Restraints, OJ 2000 C291/1: Vol II, App C.11, para 138.

purchasing obligation, the purchaser is not restricted as to the source from which he obtains those goods (that is, he does not have to obtain them directly from the supplier). However, an exclusive purchasing agreement also frequently contains non-compete obligations. Quantity forcing is a weaker form of obligation, where incentives or requirements make the purchaser concentrate his purchases to a large extent with one supplier, whether by minimum purchasing requirements or by non-linear pricing, such as a quantity rebate scheme or loyalty discounts.[524] Tying, in the strict sense, refers to the situation where a supplier makes the purchase of one product ('the tying product') conditional upon the purchase of another distinct product ('the tied product') from the supplier or someone designated by him.[525]

6.140 **Economic effects of exclusive purchasing/single branding.**   Unlike standard contracts for the sale and purchase even of large quantities of goods or services,[526] long-term exclusive purchasing reduces intra-brand competition by preventing alternative sourcing of the contract goods. It may thereby enable the supplier to engage in differential pricing and partition the market.[527] Single branding, whether or not combined with exclusive purchasing, deprives the purchaser of the freedom to obtain substitute products made by competing manufacturers. By limiting the distributor or user to one manufacturer, it thereby denies other manufacturers an outlet for their products. If the manufacturer has significant market power or several manufacturers operate the same practice, this may lead to foreclosure of the market and, in the case of distribution of final products, reduce in-store competition between competing brands. Single branding therefore affects inter-brand competition. Where large purchasers or very many smaller purchasers in a particular market enter into exclusive purchasing and single branding agreements, that may not only form a substantial barrier to entry by other suppliers into the market but also make existing market shares more rigid, which can facilitate collusion as between suppliers. However, such arrangements may bring significant benefits. As stated by the Commission in its Green Paper:

> 'they can improve the production and distribution of goods because they enable the parties to plan production and sale with greater precision and for a longer period, to limit the risk to them of variation in market conditions, and to lower the costs of

---

[524] ibid, para 152. Non-linear pricing means that the average price per unit varies according to the quantity purchased, either of that product or of another product.

[525] ibid, para 215. Note that the expressions 'tying' and 'tied outlet' are also used more generally to describe exclusivity obligations imposed on a purchaser towards his supplier, ie non-compete or exclusive purchasing restrictions.

[526] For the Commission's explanation of the distinction between an exclusive purchasing obligation and the apparent 'anti-competitive' effect of any contract to purchase a large quantity of goods, see *BP Kemi/DDSF*, OJ 1979 L286/32, [1979] 3 CMLR 684, para 60. See also *Cane Sugar*, OJ 1980 L39/64, [1980] 2 CMLR 559 (long-term bulk purchasing contracts outside Art 81(1)).

[527] Guidelines on Vertical Restraints (n 523, above) para 114.

production, stocks and marketing. For small and medium sized enterprises such agreements are often the only way of entering the market and thus stimulating competition. They facilitate sales promotion and intensive marketing, because the supplier will generally help to improve the distribution network. Consumers benefit, because they can obtain the goods more regularly and more easily.'[528]

Moreover, the security of such restraints may be necessary in order to overcome a 'hold-up' problem as regards the supplier, for example where a manufacturer has to build new machines or tooling to produce goods to the specification of a particular client[529] or as a guarantee for investment made in the purchaser by the supplier, whether through the provision of equipment or by way of a loan on more favourable terms than could be obtained in the financial markets.[530] Altogether, in addition to the market position of the supplier, the specific terms and duration of the restraint will often be critical in assessing the net effect of the arrangement on competition.

Economic effects of tying.   Tying involves a form of quantity forcing on the   **6.141** purchaser in respect of the tied product. The main anti-competitive effect of tying is possible foreclosure on the market of the tied product. Where the purchaser also accepts a non-compete obligation in respect of the tied product, the possible foreclosure effect is increased. There may also be a problem with the supplier charging higher prices for the tied product: normally that arises only if the supplier is dominant, as otherwise purchasers would obtain the tying product from a competitor. But the Commission points out that it can arise on sales to end-users when the tying enables the supplier to charge different prices according to the use which the customer makes of the tying product; and in long-term contracts or when replacement of components is long postponed, where it becomes difficult for customers to calculate the consequences of the tying condition.[531]

Structure of this Section.   As with other vertical restraints, following the entry   **6.142** into force of Regulation 2790/99 many exclusive purchasing, single branding and tying agreements will be automatically exempted if the relevant market share ceiling of 30 per cent is not exceeded. However, if an agreement does not fall within the terms of the block exemption, that does not mean that it is automatically caught by Article 81(1) or, for example where it comes within Article 81(1) but the market share condition of Regulation 2790/99 is exceeded, that it cannot nonetheless fulfil the criteria of Article 81(3). This Section accordingly considers,

---

[528] Green Paper on Vertical Restraints in EC Competition Policy, COM (96) 721 final, [1997] 4 CMLR 519, para 125. See also Guidelines on Vertical Restraints (n 523, above) para 116.

[529] For hold-ups, see n 2 to para 6.002, above.

[530] Guidelines on Vertical Restraints (n 523, above) para 116(4) and (7). Such facilities are commonly the case in connection with petrol service station agreements and 'tied' public house leases.

[531] ibid, paras 107, 217. The Commission states that tying may also lead to higher entry barriers both on the market of the tying product and on the market of the tied product.

first, the general analysis of exclusive distribution and supply agreements under Article 81(1), including the approach to particular terms and conditions; and secondly, individual application of Article 81(3). For discussion of Regulation 2790/99, see Section 2, above.

(b) Application of Article 81(1)

6.143 **In general.** In 1967, the Court of Justice held in *Brasserie de Haecht*,[532] a case concerning a tie between a brewery and a café, that exclusive purchasing agreements do not by their nature necessarily have the object or effect of restricting competition. Whether such an agreement contravenes Article 81(1) has to be determined in the light of the economic and legal context in which it is made. In the *Delimitis* case,[533] the Court developed this approach, stating that such an agreement will infringe Article 81(1) only if two cumulative conditions are met: (i) there are significant barriers to competitors entering the relevant market or increasing their market share; and (ii) the agreement in question makes a significant contribution to those barriers. As regards the first condition, the existence of a number of exclusive purchasing agreements that have the cumulative effect of foreclosing access to the market is only one factor among others to be considered in assessing whether access to the market is indeed difficult.

6.144 **Exclusive purchasing and single branding agreements: similar approach.** Whereas the Commission's Guidelines on Vertical Restraints analyse exclusive purchasing agreements as coming within a different category[534] of restraint from single branding, only single branding agreements receive extended discussion.[535] However, since it is common for exclusive purchasing agreements to contain non-compete restrictions, it seems that some of the guidance given as to the Commission's approach to single branding agreements applies also to exclusive purchasing agreements. Nonetheless, as noted, above, a 'simple' exclusive purchasing agreement (ie that does not, directly or indirectly, include a non-compete obligation) primarily affects only intra-brand competition whereas single branding inevitably affects inter-brand competition which is generally regarded as more serious in its impact on consumers.[536] Accordingly, a simple exclusive purchasing

---

[532] Case 23/67 *Brasserie de Haecht v Wilkin (No. 1)* [1967] ECR 407, [1968] CMLR 26.

[533] Case C-234/89 *Delimitis v Henninger Brau* [1991] ECR 935, [1992] 5 CMLR 210, para 27. Although stated in the context of a beer supply agreement, the principles set out in this judgment are of general application: see, eg Case T-61/89 *Dansk Pelsdyravlerforening v Commission* [1992] ECR II-1931, paras 98–99 (Danish fur breeders cooperative); Case C-393/92 *Almelo* [1994] ECR I-1477 (exclusive purchasing agreements in the Dutch electricity market).

[534] They are classified as within the 'market partitioning' category: Guidelines on Vertical Restraints (n 523, above) para 113.

[535] ibid, paras 138 *et seq.*

[536] Foreclosure of the market to other brands may prevent those goods reaching the consumer: ibid, para 119(2).

obligation, viewed in isolation, is unlikely to infringe Article 81(1) if it contains no hard-core restrictions and neither party is dominant.[537] The relevant hard-core restrictions are resale price maintenance and measures obstructing parallel imports, which are dealt with in more detail elsewhere in this Chapter.[538] Whether a single branding agreement, viewed in isolation, that contains no hard-core restrictions, falls within Article 81(1) depends on the market position of the supplier and the duration of the non-compete obligation. These aspects are discussed further below. If the supplier is dominant, any exclusive purchasing or single branding agreement is likely to come within Article 81(1).

Cumulative effect.   Neither exclusive purchasing nor single branding agree-   **6.145**
ments commonly exist in isolation: they generally fall to be assessed in terms of the effect of a number of such agreements in the relevant market, often agreements between large suppliers and relatively small purchasers. Following the seminal judgment in *Delimitis*, the treatment of cumulative effect has been developed further by the Community Courts in the *Langnese-Iglo/Schöller Lebensmittel* cases and the judgment in *Neste v Yötuuli* which are discussed in the following paragraphs.

Delimitis v Henninger Brau.   This case[539] concerned a domestic 'tied house'   **6.146**
agreement between a single café in Frankfurt and a local brewery. The operator of the café was obliged to obtain all his supplies of beer and soft drinks from the brewery or its associated companies, was prohibited from obtaining such drinks from any other supplier in Germany but could do so from undertakings in other Member States. In assessing whether the agreement was caught by Article 81(1), the Court of Justice held that the fact that the agreement was part of a network of similar agreements was only one of several factors to be assessed in determining, on consideration of the agreement in its legal and economic context, whether the agreement contributed significantly to foreclosure of the market:

(a)   The relevant market had to be defined, both as a product market and as a geo-
      graphical market.[540] To assess the degree of foreclosure of that market, the

---

[537] cf *Nutrasweet, XVIIIth Report on Competition Policy* (1988), point 53 (contracts whereby Coca-Cola Co. and Pepsico Inc., the two largest purchasers in the EC of the sweetener, Aspartame, agreed to purchase all their requirements for two years from Nutrasweet, the world's largest producer, amended after the Commission's intervention to substitute minimum fixed quantities, thereby enabling new competitors to enter the market to supply the balance). See also *Industrial Gases, XIXth Report on Competition Policy* (1989), point 62 (exclusive purchasing obligations imposed on customers contrary to Art 82 and replaced with fixed maximum or minimum/maximum quantities).

[538] See paras 6.049 *et seq*, above. See also the Commission's Communication on Vertical Restraints (n 134, above) Sect V.3; and Case 319/82 *Soc. de Vente de Ciments et Bétons v Kerpen & Kerpen* [1983] ECR 4173, [1985] 1 CMLR 511.

[539] Case C-234/89 *Delimitis v Henninger Brau* [1991] ECR 935, [1992] 5 CMLR 210.

[540] *Delimitis*, above, paras 16–18.

nature and importance of the totality of tying contracts had to be considered.[541] That depended in particular on the proportion of total outlets subject to a tie, the duration of the ties and the quantity of the products supplied by tied outlets as compared to the total sold. Also relevant was the scope for new entry into the market by acquisition of an existing outlet or opening of a new one, having regard to the necessary economies of scale and any applicable domestic controls.

(b) It was also necessary to assess the competitive conditions on the market and, in particular, whether there were real and specific possibilities for competitors to penetrate the market despite the existence of a network of exclusive purchasing agreements. The number and size of producers, the existence of independent wholesalers, the degree of market saturation and the level of brand loyalty were all relevant, as were restrictions imposed by the supplier on use of equipment lent to the reseller and the grant of rebates to resellers for compliance with exclusive agreements.[542] If the above analysis showed that entry to the market was difficult for foreign or domestic producers, it was necessary to assess the extent to which the contested agreements contributed to the cumulative effect produced. Only agreements which made a significant contribution to any foreclosure of the market would be prohibited. This involved consideration not only of the market position of the contracting parties but also of the number of the supplier's tied outlets relative to the market as a whole and the duration of the exclusive agreements.[543]

6.147 *Langnese-Iglo/Schöller.* The application of *Delimitis* was clarified by the judgments of the Court of First Instance on the appeals from the Commission's final decisions in *Schöller Lebensmittel* and *Langnese-Iglo*.[544] The parallel cases

---

[541] *Delimitis*, above, para 19. The judgment indicates that only contracts with domestic producers are to be considered for this part of the analysis, but there seems to be no logic in leaving out of account ties of domestic outlets to foreign producers. See Lasok, 'Assessing the Economic Consequences of Restrictive Agreements: A Comment on the Delimitis Case' (1991) 5 ECLR 194, 197–98. See also the CFI's judgments in *Langnese-Iglo* (n 544, below) para 101; and *Schöller*, ibid, para 78.

[542] *Delimitis* (n 539, above) para 22. The ECJ observed that the barriers to entry are generally higher in a market with a small number of large producers commanding major brand loyalty. See also *Langnese-Iglo*, paras 106–110; *Schöller*, paras 82–85, discussed in para 6.147, below.

[543] *Delimitis* (n 539, above) paras 24–26. See also *Langnese-Iglo* (n 544, below) paras 103–105; *Schöller*, ibid, paras 80–81.

[544] *Schöller Lebensmittel*, OJ 1993 L183/1, [1994] 4 CMLR 51, on appeal Case T-9/93 *Schöller v Commission* [1995] ECR II-611, [1995] 5 CMLR 659; *Langnese-Iglo*, OJ 1993 L183/19, [1994] 4 CMLR 83, on appeal Case T-7/93 *Langnese-Iglo v Commission* [1995] ECR II-1533, [1995] 5 CMLR 602, [1995] All ER (EC) 902. In its decision in *Langnese-Iglo*, the Commission disapplied the then block exemption, Reg 1984/83, from that network of agreements and held in *Schöller Lebensmittel* that the duration of the agreements took them outside the block exemption. See also the order in Cases T-7 & 9/93R *Langnese-Iglo and Schöller v Commission* [1993] ECR II-131 (dismissal in large part of the applications to suspend enforcement of the Commission's decisions pending appeal); and Korah, 'Exclusive Purchasing Obligations: Mars v. Langnese and Schöller' (1994)

concerned the networks of agreements entered into with retailers by, respectively, the two leading suppliers of ice cream on the German market, that included both exclusive purchasing and non-compete obligations. Upon complaints brought by Mars, the Commission decided that the relevant agreements contravened Article 81(1) because the parties' market shares[545] far exceeded the limit set out in the then *De Minimis* Notice.[546] Therefore, the Commission held that it was unnecessary to examine the cumulative effect of parallel networks of agreements of other ice cream manufacturers on the German market, distinguishing *Delimitis* as applying only where an undertaking's network of agreements did not, in itself, have an appreciable effect on competition. That approach was overruled on appeal.[547] The Court of First Instance held that the *De Minimis* Notice indicated only those agreements that did *not* appreciably affect competition; it could not be assumed, conversely, that if the market share condition of the Notice was exceeded an agreement did appreciably affect competition.[548] The Court proceeded to apply *Delimitis* and carried out an elaborate market share analysis, considering first the cumulative effect of parallel networks of agreements on the market and then whether the parties' networks contributed significantly to the cumulative position. The Court also considered the various other barriers to entry for new competitors, including the system of suppliers lending freezer cabinets to retailers on condition that the cabinets were used exclusively for the suppliers' products; and the fragmentation of demand resulting from the small size of most retailers and the absence of wholesalers. On that basis, the Court upheld the Commission's conclusion in each case that the network of agreements had an appreciable effect on competition and that consequently all the agreements in the network were caught by Article 81(1). The Court also held that it was not possible to argue that a supplier's network of agreements did not have an appreciable effect because one of its rival's networks had been prohibited by the Commission.[549] A further appeal by *Langnese-Iglo* to the Court of Justice was dismissed.[550]

---

3 ECLR 171. A similar approach was taken by the Commission in *Amex and Dean Witter/Visa*, *XXVIth Report on Competition Policy* (1996), p 140 (proposed Visa rule banning its member banks from issuing a competing card would have significant foreclosure effect).

[545] On the market definition in this case see *Langnese-Iglo v Commission* and *Schöller v Commission* (n 544, above) paras 60–72 and paras 39–51, respectively.

[546] The 1986 Notice then applicable specified a market share threshold of five per cent for all agreements: OJ 1986 C231/2. For the position under the current 2001 version of the Notice (Vol II, App C.13), see para 6.003, above.

[547] *Langnese-Iglo v Commission* (n 544, above); *Schöller v Commission*, ibid.

[548] *Langnese-Iglo v Commission*, above, para 98; *Schöller v Commission*, above, para 75.

[549] *Schöller v Commission* (n 544, above) para 96.

[550] Case C-279/95P *Langnese-Iglo v EC Commission* [1998] ECR I-5609, [1998] 5 CMLR 933, [1999] All ER (EC) 616. The ECJ held (paras 32–41) that Langnese could not contest the CFI's decision that Langnese's network of agreements involved an appreciable restriction on competition as that decision was based on the CFI's assessment of the facts; this ground of appeal was thus inadmissible.

6.148 **Individual agreement in a network: *Neste v Yötuuli*.** In the German ice cream cases, Langnese and Schöller had argued that, since a supplier whose network of agreements below the ceiling would escape the prohibition in Article 81(1), the Commission was under an obligation to consider their individual agreements separately and decide which of them were valid. The Court of First Instance rejected this argument, holding that a bundle of similar agreements must be considered as a whole and that the Commission was therefore correct in refusing to examine separately each agreement within the network.[551] The position of an individual agreement in a network was considered further by the Court of Justice in *Neste v Yötuuli*,[552] a reference from a Finnish court concerning a petrol service station agreement. Neste was engaged in marketing petrol products and had a network comprising about a third of the service stations in Finland. The overwhelming majority of service station agreements in Finland included a tie to one supplier for up to 10 years and the national court found that Neste's network as a whole made a significant contribution to the closing off of the market. However, the agreement between Neste and Yötuuli included the right for the retailer to give one year's notice of termination and only five per cent of Neste's contracts contained such a provision. On the question of whether that agreement violated Article 81(1), the Court of Justice noted that an exclusive purchasing obligation in a petrol service station agreement effectively involves single branding since only one brand of motor fuel is sold in practice. Rejecting the approach advocated by the Commission, the Court of Justice ruled that, in view of the fundamental importance of the duration of such a restraint in assessing foreclosure, contracts which may be terminated on one year's notice,[553] and which represent only a small proportion of that supplier's exclusive purchasing agreements, must be regarded as making no significant contribution to the cumulative effect and therefore fall outside Article 81(1). Such a subdivision of the supplier's network was appropriate when a supplier entered into different categories of contract which had different foreclosing effects.

6.149 **Application of the two stage *Delimitis* test in Member States.** National courts are often called upon to consider the legality of networks of exclusive purchasing agreements. For example, in *Masterfoods*,[554] the Paris Court of Appeal applied the two stage test in *Delimitis* to find that a network of exclusive freezer cabinet

---

[551] *Langnese-Iglo v Commission* (n 544, above) para 129; *Schöller v Commission*, ibid, para 95. A similar argument as regards application of Art 81(3) also failed.

[552] Case C-214/99 *Neste v Yötuuli Ky* [2000] ECR I-11121, [2001] 4 CMLR 993, [2001] All ER (EC) 76.

[553] Although the judgment refers to the contract being terminable 'upon one year's notice at any time', in fact it was for a 10-year minimum duration and only so terminable thereafter: para 4. The contrast appears to have been with agreements that were for renewable 10-year terms without such a break clause, and therefore came within the former block exemption, Reg 1984/83.

[554] *Masterfoods*, Paris Court of Appeal, 7 May 2002, BOCCRF no. 10, 24 June 2002.

agreements did not fall within Article 81(1). Having found that the market share of all the suppliers who operated similar networks was over 60 per cent, the Court considered the other criteria relevant to establishing cumulative effect. The Court found that new companies had entered the market; the contracts could be cancelled with a short notice period of 15 days; 20 per cent of freezers were returned each year, indicating that the market was relatively fluid; 27 per cent of distributors owned their freezers; 52 per cent of distributors had the option of installing several freezers on their premises; the market did not appear to be saturated; and finally, the co-existence of companies of varying sizes meant that a high degree of competition could be maintained. The Court of Appeal concluded that there was no firm evidence that the cumulative effect of parallel contracts to loan freezers, accompanied by brand exclusivity clauses, would have anti-competitive effects over the period in question. Similarly, in *Crehan Inntrepreneur*[555] the English High Court, considering a claim by a public house tenant for damages for breach of Article 81(1), held that the first stage of the *Delimitis* test was not satisfied because access to the British licensed on-trade was not foreclosed. The judgment was reversed on appeal but then reinstated by the House of Lords.[556]

Duration of restraint. As the *Neste* case[557] emphasises, in considering an exclusivity restriction on a purchaser, the anti-competitive effect results from the duration of the obligation rather than the fact of the exclusivity itself. In *Delimitis*, the Court of Justice observed that a supplier with a relatively small market share which ties its outlets for many years may make as significant a contribution to the foreclosure of the market as a supplier in a strong market position which regularly releases its purchasers from exclusive obligations at shorter intervals.[558] Under Regulation 2790/99, save for special provisions that apply when the purchaser operates from premises belonging to the supplier,[559] a non-compete obligation on the purchaser will not receive block exemption if it lasts longer than five years or if it is indefinite; and an obligation which is tacitly renewable beyond a period of five years is deemed to be of indefinite duration.[560] In its Guidelines, the Commission sets out its approach to the duration of a non-compete obligation entered into by non-dominant companies.[561] Such an obligation for less than one

6.150

[555] *Crehan v Inntrepeneur Pub Co* [2003] EWHC 1510 (Ch), [2003] EuLR 663.

[556] *Inntrepreneur Pub Company v Crehan* [2006] UKHL 38, [2006] 4 All ER 465. This case is discussed at paras 14.080 and 14.114, below.

[557] *Neste v Yötuuli Ky* (n 552, above).

[558] *Delimitis* (n 539, above) para 26. In Case T-25/99 *Roberts and Roberts v Commission* [2001] ECR II-1181, para 77, the CFI held nine years was not excessive having regard to average durations apparent from Commission's consideration of the pub lease agreements of three major brewers in the UK (*Whitbread, Bass* and *Scottish & Newcastle* (nn 570–572 below)).

[559] See para 6.152, below.

[560] Art 5(a) of Reg 2790/99, OJ 1999 L336/21: Vol II, App C.3.

[561] Guidelines on Vertical Restraints, OJ 2000 C291/1: Vol II, App C.11, para 141.

year is in general not considered to give rise to appreciable anti-competitive effects or net negative effects. An obligation of between one and five years requires a balancing of pro- and anti-competitive effects. And an obligation for more than five years is in general not considered necessary to achieve the claimed efficiencies or those efficiencies are not regarded as sufficient to outweigh the foreclosure effect. Therefore, it appears that if an agreement is not *de minimis*[562] and includes a non-compete obligation that lasts for more than five years, it is likely to fall within Article 81(1) and the application of Article 81(3) will need to be considered. However, in certain circumstances, an exclusivity obligation imposed even by a dominant supplier may fall outside Article 81(1). In *Heineken Nederland BV*,[563] Heineken applied to the Netherlands Competition Authority for an exemption under the national equivalent of Article 81(3) for its standard beer contracts. These contracts provided for financial support by Heineken for cafés that sold draught beer exclusively from Heineken. The Authority held that, despite Heineken's market share of between 50 to 60 per cent on the relevant market for the sale of draught beer for consumption at cafés and other premises, these contracts did not contravene the Dutch equivalent of Article 81(1) and thus did not need exemption. The decision was based on three grounds: all other brewers in the Dutch market took advantage of Regulation 2790/1999 to impose beer ties of five years; Heineken's outlets were permitted to terminate the beer tie at any time; and the fact that the exclusivity applied only to draught beer and not to bottled beer meant that intra-brand competition was still possible. Finally, the Authority required Heineken to remind its buyers each year that they could terminate their contract at any moment and that they were permitted to switch to Heineken's competitors. Heineken, on the other hand, was not allowed to terminate any of the contracts unless the café was in breach of its obligations.

6.151 **Longer duration may be justified.** Where an agreement would involve the transfer of substantial know-how to the purchaser which is not otherwise readily available, without a non-compete obligation for longer than five years, the supplier may be reluctant to enter into the agreement at all, since that would enable the know-how to be used to benefit the sale of his competitors' products. This is a form of specific 'hold-up' and, provided that the know-how is truly indispensable to the operation of the agreement, in those circumstances a non-compete obligation of longer duration may fall outside Article 81(1).[564]

---

[562] See para 6.003, above.

[563] Case 2036 *Heineken Nederland BV*, decn of Netherlands Competition Authority, 28 May 2002.

[564] Guidelines on Vertical Restraints (n 561, above) para 118(5); but cf para 157 and see para 6.167, below. For 'hold-ups', see n 2 to para 6.002, above.

Resale from supplier's premises.   In certain sectors, it is a frequent arrangement   **6.152**
for the buyer to operate from premises owned or leased by the supplier. This is
particularly a feature of supply agreements concerning petrol service stations and
bars and public houses ('tied pubs'). The former block exemption for exclusive
purchasing agreements, Regulation 1984/83, contained detailed special provisions governing agreements in those sectors.[565] By contrast, Regulation 2790/99
has a simple provision stating that in those circumstances a non-compete
obligation need not be limited to five years but may extend for the period of
occupancy of the premises and land by the buyer.[566] The Commission can be
expected to follow the same approach as regards agreements that fall outside
Regulation 2790/99 because the market share condition is exceeded. The Guidelines
state that the possibility of imposing effective remedies for a possible foreclosure
effect are limited in such a case, so that intervention by the Commission below
the level of dominance is unlikely.[567] In *Repsol*,[568] the Commission accepted
commitments from the Spanish petrol supplier to phase out its long-term exclusive purchasing contracts with the owners of petrol stations. Under Repsol's
contracts, land owners granted a 'right in rem' for a long period (from 25 to 40
years) to Repsol on their land and Repsol would then finance the construction or
refurbishment of the station, rent the station back to the owner and, for the
duration of the 'right in rem', be the exclusive supplier of motor fuel to the station.
The Commission found that the market for retail supply of motor fuel in Spain was
highly concentrated with Repsol holding a market share of 40 per cent. It was also
characterised by a high degree of vertical integration foreclosing new entry. Repsol
undertook to allow all service stations to terminate their contracts subject to compensating Repsol for the loss of its right in rem and further undertook not to enter
into any new exclusive supply contracts with longer than five years duration.

Market share and the *Delimitis* criteria.   The need to consider the cumulative   **6.153**
effect on the market means that it is obviously important to consider the market
position not only of the supplier in question but also of his competitors. The
Commission's approach in practice to this assessment, following the German ice

---

[565] See 5th edn of this work, paras 7-162 and 7-163.
[566] Reg 2790/1999, OJ 1999 L336/21: Vol II, App C.3, Art 5(a), 3rd sentence. This applies
where the premises and land are owned by the supplier or leased by the supplier 'from third parties
not connected with the buyer'; that qualification is an anti-avoidance provision: Guidelines on
Vertical Restraints (n 561, above) para 59.
[567] Guidelines on Vertical Restraints (n 561, above) para 150.
[568] COMP/38.348 *Repsol CPP*, decn of 12 April 2006, Press Release IP/06/495. Repsol also
undertook to abstain from purchasing stations that it did not currently supply and to ensure complete freedom to all service stations in its network to offer discounts on the retail price. The decn was
adopted under Art 9(1) of Reg 1/2003. See Note on the case in (2006) 2 EC Competition Policy
Newsletter 25. The decn is under appeal: Case T-274/06 *Estaser El Mareny v Commission*, not yet
decided.

cream cases,[569] can be seen from its recent decisions concerning various standard form agreements for tied 'pubs' in the United Kingdom. Considering the pub lease agreements of three major brewers, *Whitbread,*[570] *Bass*[571] and *Scottish & Newcastle,*[572] the Commission concluded that the British on-trade beer market was foreclosed. At least 50 per cent by volume of the on-trade was covered by property-tied, loan-tied and managed outlets of brewers operating in the United Kingdom. In assessing the tied market share, it was relevant to include a brewer's managed outlets (that is, the vertically integrated part of their on-sales to consumers) although such arrangements did not come within Article 81(1), because they contributed to the foreclosing effect.[573] On that basis, the Commission held that the tied networks of the three major brewers contributed significantly to the foreclosure and accordingly came within Article 81(1).[574] Turning to Article 81(3), the Commission found that the conditions for the application of Article 81(3) were fulfilled and exemptions (under the pre-Modernisation procedure) were accordingly granted.[575]

6.154 **Inclusion of wholesaling business in brewer's network.** In *Roberts and Roberts v Commission,*[576] the Court of First Instance considered the situation where agreements entered into by Greene King (a regional brewery) did not contribute significantly to foreclosure of the market. However, the appellants argued that, in assessing cumulative effect, the Court should also take into account the wholesale agreements that Greene King had with various other national breweries. It was argued that the 'upstream' agreements and the 'downstream' agreements together contributed significantly to foreclosure of the market. The Court held[577] that before it was appropriate to take the 'upstream' agreements into account, two conditions must be satisfied. First, the beer supply agreements concluded between the wholesaling brewery, in this case Greene King, and the supplying national

---

569 See para 6.147, above.

570 *Whitbread*, OJ 1999 L88/26, [1999] 5 CMLR 118 (appeal dismissed, Case T-131/99 *Shaw v Commission* [2002] ECR II-2023, [2002] 5 CMLR 81, [2002] All ER (EC) 501).

571 *Bass*, OJ 1999 L186/1, [1999] 5 CMLR 782 (appeal dismissed, Case T-231/99 *Joynson v Commission* [2002] ECR II-2085, [2002] 5 CMLR 123; further appeal dismissed, Case C-204/02P [2003] ECR I-14763).

572 *Scottish & Newcastle*, OJ 1999 L186/28, [1999] 5 CMLR 831.

573 *Whitbread* (n 570, above) para 134; *Bass* (n 571, above) para 151; *Scottish & Newcastle* (n 572, above) para 121. See also Art 9(2)(b) of Reg 2790/99.

574 *Bass* at paras 145–155; *Whitbread* at paras 128–138; *Scottish & Newcastle* at paras 115–125. But cf *Crehan v Inntrepeneur Pub Co* [2003] EWHC 1510 (Ch), [2003] EuLR 663, where the English High Court held, after a thorough examination of the evidence at trial, that access to the British on-trade was not foreclosed (on appeal, the House of Lords held that the judge was not bound by the Commission decns involving other parties and had correctly made his own assessment: see para 14.080, below).

575 See para 6.165, below.

576 *Roberts & Roberts* (n 558, above).

577 ibid, paras 104–107.

breweries, may be regarded as forming part of the supplying breweries' networks of agreements if they contained terms which may be analysed as a purchasing obligation (commitments to purchase minimum quantities, stocking obligations or non-competition obligations). It follows that a supply contract which does not contain a purchasing obligation, in whatever form, does not form part of the network of agreements of a supplying brewery, even if it relates to a substantial proportion of the beer sold by the establishments tied to the wholesaling brewery. Secondly, in order for both the 'upstream' agreements and the 'downstream' agreements between the wholesaling brewery and its tied outlets to be attributed to the supplying breweries' networks of agreements, it is also necessary for the agreements between the supplying breweries and the wholesaling brewery to be so restrictive that access to the wholesaling brewery's network of downstream agreements is no longer possible, or at least very difficult, for other breweries in the United Kingdom or elsewhere. If the restrictive effect of the upstream agreements is limited, other breweries are also able to conclude agreements with the wholesaling brewery and so enter the latter's network of downstream agreements. They are thus in a position to have access to all the establishments in that network without it being necessary to conclude separate agreements with each outlet. The existence of a network of downstream agreements therefore constitutes a factor which can promote penetration of the market by other breweries.

Tied estate owned by non-brewer. In *Inntrepreneur-Spring*,[578] the Commission considered standard form tenancy agreements entered into by a free-standing pub company (which did not brew its own beer) with several thousand tied pubs and held that it fell outside the scope of Article 81(1). Although the tenancy agreements contained exclusive purchasing and non-compete obligations, they did not contribute to, but rather mitigated, foreclosure on the market. This was because the pub company in turn obtained its supplies from a number of different brewers and subjected its two- to five-year contracts with those supplying brewers to a process of periodic tendering, thereby allowing other brewers access to its network of tied houses.[579] Those decisions were taken in respect of a period prior to the application of Regulation 2790/99. However, since Regulation 2790/99 came

6.155

---

[578] *Inntrepreneur-Spring*, OJ 2000 L195/49, [2000] 5 CMLR 948. The decision concerned only the period after the tied estate had been acquired by a subsidiary of Nomura and so was no longer owned by brewers. See also *Allied Domecq*, OJ 1999 C82/5, [1999] 4 CMLR 1568: intention to grant negative clearance to Allied's tenancy agreements for the period after it ceased brewing itself and entered into a series of beer supply agreements with UK national and regional brewers, none of which contained a minimum purchase obligation.

[579] The Commission (at para 57) differentiated the 'upstream' beer supply contract from the 'downstream' tie agreement in the pub leases. But where the upstream supply agreement contained exclusive purchasing and non-compete obligations, it was to be considered part of the brewer's tied network. Those agreements therefore might fall within Art 81(1) but were not at issue in the decision.

into force, if there is a cumulative effect but each supplier individually satisfies the 30 per cent market share condition, the Commission may withdraw the benefit of the block exemption if the criteria in Article 81(3) are not satisfied.[580] In its Guidelines on Vertical Restraints, the Commission states that if the market share of the largest supplier is below 30 per cent and the aggregate shares of the five largest suppliers ('CR5') is below 50 per cent, there is unlikely to be a single or cumulative anti-competitive effect.[581] If the block exemption is withdrawn, such withdrawal should not apply to suppliers whose agreements do not contribute to the cumulative effect. A tied market share of less than 5 per cent is not considered, in general, to contribute significantly to a cumulative foreclosure effect.[582]

6.156 **Other factors.** There can be no exhaustive list of the factors that may be relevant in assessing the anti-competitive effect of a particular agreement or network of agreements. However, in addition to the matters discussed above, the Commission notes that the following may be significant: entry barriers; the countervailing power of buyers (although agreements concluded with major buyers may have a strong foreclosure effect); and the level of trade and nature of the product to which the restriction applies.[583] As regards the latter criteria, distinction may be drawn (i) between intermediate and final products, and (ii) between the wholesale and retail stages of supply. For *intermediate products*, appreciable foreclosure is unlikely in the case of a single supplier below the level of dominance, in the absence of a cumulative effect. The Commission considers that a serious cumulative effect is unlikely unless at least 50 per cent of the market is tied.[584] For *final products*, the foreclosure effect depends not only on the tied market share but on the possibility of manufacturers establishing their own operation at the next level of trade. At the wholesale level, the entry barriers for manufacturers will depend in part on the nature of the product, whereas at the retail level entry barriers for manufacturers

---

[580] See Recital (13) and Art 6 of Reg 2790/99 (n 566, above); also the power by regulation adopted under Art 8 to disapply the block exemption generally for a market where parallel networks cover more than 50 per cent. In *Langnese-Iglo* (n 544, above), the Commission withdrew the benefit of the then block exemption, Reg 1984/83, from a major supplier's the network of agreements because of cumulative effect. Note also that a 'tie' lasting for more than five years where the purchaser does not operate from premises belonging to or leased by the supplier will not come within Reg 2790/99 at all: see para 6.150, above.

[581] Guidelines on Vertical Restraints, OJ 2000 C291/1: Vol II, App C.11, para 143. Although the Guidelines here refer simply to 'market share', it is the *tied* market share that is relevant. cf paras 146, 149. In the UK brewery cases, the Commission did not use the CR5 ratio but applied the HHI to find that the UK market in brewing was 'moderately concentrated': *Whitbread* (n 570, above) para 19; similarly *Bass* (n 571, above) para 22; *Scottish & Newcastle* (n 572, above) para 20. For CR5 and HHI, see para 6.007, above.

[582] Guidelines on Vertical Restraints (n 581, above) para 142. See, eg *Greene King/Roberts*, *XXVIIIth Report on Competition Policy* (1998), p 167 (small brewers do not contribute significantly to foreclosure of UK on-trade beer market), on appeal *Roberts and Roberts* (n 558, above).

[583] Guidelines on Vertical Restraints (n 581, above) paras 144–146; see also paras 121–133.

[584] ibid, para 146.

are likely to be significant.[585] For final products at the retail level, the Commission considers that there is likely to be appreciable foreclosure if the supplier ties 30 per cent or more of the relevant market. As regards cumulative effect, the Commission states that this is unlikely if either all companies have market shares below 30 per cent and the total tied market share is less than 40 per cent; or if some companies have shares above 30 per cent but none is dominant and the total tied market share is less than 30 per cent.[586]

Quantity forcing. A purchasing agreement may have a significant restrictive **6.157** effect even if it does not impose total exclusivity when it obliges the purchaser to buy a considerable proportion of his requirements from the supplier or gives him significant incentives for doing so. A minimum quantity may be specified either by reference to a share of the purchaser's total requirements or in numerical terms. Regulation 2790/99 defines a 'non-compete obligation' as covering not only a prohibition on dealing in competing products but also:

> 'any direct or indirect obligation on the buyer to purchase from the supplier or another undertaking designated by the supplier more than 80 per cent of the buyer's total purchases of the contracts goods or services and their substitutes on the relevant market.'[587]

When the proportion of requirements involved is considerably lower, it is a question of fact and degree whether such an obligation over a period of years can fall within Article 81(1). For example, in *Carlsberg*[588] the Commission decided that a brewer's obligation to buy a specified quantity of lager for a period of 11 years, when that quantity represented over half of its annual requirements, restricted competition because it prevented the purchaser from producing that volume itself

---

[585] ibid, para 147.

[586] ibid, paras 148–149.

[587] Reg 2790/99 (n 566, above) Art 1(b).

[588] *Carlsberg*, OJ 1984 L207/26, [1985] 1 CMLR 735. Note that the Commission also held that Carlsberg's obligation to supply GM's requirements fell within Art 81(1), as did GM's obligation to supply Carlsberg with rolling sales forecasts; Art 81(3) was applied. See also: *BP Kemi/DDSF* (n 526, above) (exclusive purchasing obligation for six years was of excessive duration; customers' interests could have been met by concluding purchasing agreements stipulating fixed quantities which could be regularly renegotiated in the light of market circumstances); *Olivetti/Digital*, OJ 1994 L309/24 (four year commitment by Olivetti to purchase at least half its requirements of the relevant products came within Art 81(1) but also Art 81(3) as forming part of a strategic alliance which overall had a positive impact on the developing market for RISC computers); *Re Tabaqueira*, Press Release IP/88/656 (28 October 1988), [1989] 4 CMLR 208 (minimum purchasing requirements imposed on tobacco wholesalers by state monopoly producer; the Commission closed its investigation when the supplier greatly reduced the level of purchases required so as to leave ample scope for competing suppliers); *MD Foods/FDB*, *XXVth Report on Competition Policy* (1995), p 136 (five-year minimum purchasing obligation in favour of the largest Danish dairy producer agreed for about 90 per cent of the purchaser's requirements: amended on the Commission's instigation to 70 per cent of requirements reducing to 30 per cent during the term of the agreement; negative-clearance type comfort letter then issued).

or purchasing it from other producers, and because it prevented the seller from selling a considerable proportion of its output to other breweries.

6.158 **Exclusive use of equipment.** The Court of First Instance in *Van den Bergh Foods*[589] considered an appeal from a finding by the Commission that Article 81(1) was infringed where an ice cream producer provided freezer cabinets to retailers without extra charge on condition that the cabinets were used exclusively to store that producer's ice cream. The Court noted that the exclusivity clause did not require retailers to sell only HB products in their sales outlets and so was not, in formal terms, an exclusive purchasing obligation whose object is to restrict competition on the relevant market. The Court therefore had to examine whether the Commission had adequately proved, in the specific circumstances of the relevant market, that the exclusivity clause relating to freezer cabinets in reality imposed exclusivity on some sales outlets and whether the Commission had correctly quantified the degree of that foreclosure. The Court agreed with the Commission that the provision of a freezer without charge, the evident popularity of HB's ice cream, the breadth of its range of products and the benefits associated with the sale of them, are very important considerations in the eyes of retailers when they consider whether to install an additional freezer cabinet in order to sell a second, possibly reduced, range of ice cream or, a *fortiori*, to terminate their distribution agreement with HB in order to replace HB's freezer cabinet either by their own cabinet or by one belonging to another supplier, which would, in all probability, be subject to a condition of exclusivity. Moreover, 83 per cent of all retail outlets in Ireland selling ice cream for immediate consumption had freezer cabinets subject to such an exclusivity obligation, and HB had held a dominant position on that market for several years.[590] The Court of First Instance also upheld the Commission's rejection of the argument that that the exclusivity condition contained in its freezer cabinet agreements fell outside Article 81(1) as a restraint

---

[589] Case T-65/98 *Van den Bergh Foods v Commission* [2003] ECR II-4653, [2004] 4 CMLR 14, on appeal from *Van den Bergh Foods Ltd*, OJ 1998 L246/1, [1998] 5 CMLR 530. The case had a tortuous procedural history: the Commission's decision, which differed from its earlier view of these arrangements (*Unilever/Mars*, XXVth *Report on Competition Policy* (1995), p 137) was contrary to the finding of the Irish High Court after full trial in proceedings between Van den Bergh (then called HB Ice Cream) and its main competitor, Masterfoods, a subsidiary of Mars: *Masterfoods Ltd v H.B. Ice Cream Ltd* [1992] 3 CMLR 830, [1993] ILRM 145. However, on a reference from the Irish Supreme Court, the ECJ held that the decision of the Commission must prevail, Case C-344/98 *Masterfoods* and *HB* [2000] ECR I-11369, [2001] 4 CMLR 449, [2001] All ER (EC) 130. See further, para 14.078, below. For comment, see Robertson and Williams, 'An Ice Cream War: The Law and Economics of Freezer Exclusivity' (1995) 1 ECLR 7; Rowe 'Ice Cream: The Saga Continues' (1998) ECLR 479.

[590] cf *Masterfoods* (n 554, above), where the Paris Court of Appeal held, on a detailed analysis of the characteristics of the French market, that although the market share of all the suppliers who operated similar exclusive freezer cabinet agreement networks was over 60 per cent, other factors indicated that the market was fluid and the cumulative effect of parallel contracts to loan freezers, accompanied by brand exclusivity clauses, did not have anti-competitive effects.

ancillary to the legitimate object of those agreements, the provision of equipment to resellers to enable them to stock ice cream for resale. The exclusivity condition could not be considered ancillary as there was no objectively indispensable link between the supply of freezer cabinets to retailers and that condition.[591] On further appeal, the judgment of the Court of First Instance was upheld by the Court of Justice.[592]

'English clause'. A so-called 'English clause' to some extent mitigates the effect **6.159** of an exclusivity obligation by permitting the purchaser to obtain products from other sources offering lower prices than the supplier if, after being informed of those prices, the supplier declines to match them. However, in practice such a provision may lead to the same foreclosure of other suppliers as an unqualified exclusivity obligation. Moroever, if in order to benefit from this clause the customer has to inform the supplier of the identity of the person making the better offer, that gives the supplier competitive information which he would not normally have and, by increasing the transparency of the market, may also facilitate collusion among suppliers. The Commission has therefore regarded such provisions as contrary to Article 81(1)[593] and states in the Guidelines that it views such a clause as having the same effect as a non-compete obligation.[594] Where an exclusive agreement is for a fixed term but includes an 'English clause' governing the entry into a subsequent agreement, it means that other potential suppliers (or distributors, if it is a distribution agreement) are not on an equal footing in negotiating for an agreement upon expiry of that fixed term, and therefore extends the period for which competition is affected.[595]

Tying obligations. In general, tying obligations are imposed by the supplier. **6.160** If the buyers have sufficient countervailing power, tying is therefore usually not

---

[591] The CFI also dismissed the argument that application of Art 81(1) to the exclusivity provision would be tantamount to interference with its property rights, contrary to Art 295 EC, in that it would permit other suppliers' products to be stored in its freezer cabinets: the right to property could be restricted in the public interest and Art 81(1) was a public interest provision; moreover, the application of Art 81(1) did not concern Van den Bergh's use of its own property but the restrictions which it imposed on others to whom it had granted the use of its property: ibid, para 170.

[592] Case C-552/03P *Unilever Bestfoods (Ireland) v Commission* [2006] ECR I-9091, [2006] 5 CMLR 1460.

[593] *BP Kemi/DDSF*, OJ 1979 L286/32, [1979] 3 CMLR 684. When used by a dominant supplier such a clause may infringe Art 82: see, eg *Industrial Gases* (n 537, above) (exclusive purchasing obligations imposed on customers contrary to Art 82 as well as Art 81 and replaced with fixed maximum or minimum/maximum quantities). See para 10.099, below.

[594] Guidelines on Vertical Restraints (n 581, above) para 152.

[595] See *Polish Football Association and Canal+ v Office for Competition and Consumer Protection*, judgment of the Polish Court for Competition and Consumer Protection, Case XVIAmA 98/06, 14 February 2007, upholding the decision that an 'English clause' in the four-year agreement with Canal+ for exclusive sale of rights to broadcast football matches, giving Canal+ the right to match any offer for the rights for subsequent seasons, violated the Polish equivalent of Art 81 since it placed Canal+ in a favoured position on the retendering of the rights at the end of the four-year period.

anti-competitive as they would not accept such obligations without a share in any resulting efficiencies.[596] In the absence of significant buyer power and where the supplier's market share is above the 30 per cent condition of Regulation 2790/99, the anti-competitive effect of a tying obligation will depend on the market position of the supplier as regards the tying product. If the supplier's competitors are sufficiently numerous and strong, the Commission states that in the absence of a cumulative effect the tying arrangement should not appreciably distort competition.[597]

6.161 **Hard-core restrictions.**   As with other types of vertical agreements, an exclusive purchasing or single branding agreement that contains minimum or fixed resale price maintenance or territorial restrictions as to where the purchaser may resell will come within Article 81(1).[598] If an agreement contains a hard-core restriction, it will not be covered by Regulation 2790/99.[599]

6.162 **Effect on trade between Member States.**   In *IJsselcentrale*,[600] the Commission found that a series of exclusive purchasing obligations imposed at various levels of the distribution chain operated to exclude any possibility of imports by anyone other than the producer at the head of the chain. Where the exclusivity imposed by an agreement is qualified in that the purchaser is permitted to obtain supplies from other Member States, the restriction will not affect trade between Member States within the terms of Article 81(1) provided that there is a real opportunity for the purchaser to obtain such foreign supplies.[601] For example, if the purchaser is permitted to purchase only directly from foreign suppliers and not from other importers on the domestic market, the qualification may be insufficient to take the agreement outside Article 81(1). Moreover, if the agreement also includes a

---

[596] ibid, para 221.

[597] ibid, para 220. Note also Art 81(1)(e) EC.

[598] See paras 6.049 *et seq*, above.

[599] Reg 2790/1999 (n 566, above) Art 4(a)–(b).

[600] *IJsselcentrale*, OJ 1991 L28/32, [1992] 5 CMLR 154. The case concerned the distribution of electricity by the Dutch generating companies. The complainants' appeal was dismissed, Case T-16/91 *Rendo v Commission* [1992] ECR II-2417, but in Case C-19/93P *Rendo v Commission* [1995] ECR I-3319, [1997] 4 CMLR 392, the ECJ set aside the judgment of the CFI insofar as it had held that the Commission decision had had no legal effect in respect of the application of Art 81 to the import restrictions applicable in the period before the 1989 Dutch Electricity Law came into effect, dismissed the remainder of the appeal and referred the case back to the CFI. The CFI then annulled that part of the Commission's decision: Case T-16/91RV *Rendo v Commission* [1997] ECR II-1827, [1997] 4 CMLR 453. See also the reference to the ECJ from parallel proceedings in the Dutch courts, Case C-393/92 *Almelo* [1994] ECR I-1477, where the ECJ held that Art 81(1) prevented a regional electricity distributor from using an exclusive purchasing clause so as to prohibit a local distributor from importing electricity for public supply, but that those restrictions might be justifiable under Art 86(2). For further cases concerning exclusive purchasing in the energy industry, see Chap 12, below.

[601] *Delimitis* (n 539, above) paras 28–33. Such a provision is referred to in French as a *'clause d'ouverture'*.

substantial minimum purchasing requirement, the practical effect of a clause expressly allowing foreign supplies may be questionable.

Article 82.   In some circumstances Article 82 may also apply in that the exclusiv-   **6.163**
ity obligation in a single branding or exclusive purchasing agreement may constitute an abuse by the supplier of its dominant position.[602]

(c) Application of Article 81(3)

In general.   If an agreement falls within Article 81(1) but outside Regulation   **6.164**
2790/99, it may still be valid if it meets the criteria set out in Article 81(3).
The general principles governing the application of Article 81(3) are discussed in
Chapter 3, above.

Article 81(3) and exclusive purchasing/single branding agreements.   If the   **6.165**
supplier is not dominant, an exclusive purchasing/single branding agreement may
fulfil the criteria of Article 81(3), if the supplier can establish that the arrangement
provides efficiencies which justify the restrictions.[603] In *Whitbread*,[604] *Bass*[605]
and *Scottish & Newcastle*,[606] the Commission applied Article 81(3) to give retroactive validity to the standard leases of three major United Kingdom brewers
because of the improvements to distribution which agreements for the lease
of pubs combined with exclusive purchase/non-compete obligations offered.
The Commission indicated that such improvements could be outweighed where
a brewer used the tie to extract higher prices from its tied customers than those
charged to non-tied customers, even when adjusted for the increased benefits
which tied customers obtained from a brewery. However, the countervailing benefits offered by the brewers accounted for the difference between the prices at

---

[602] In *Van den Bergh Foods Ltd* (n 589, above), the Commission held that the freezer cabinet exclusivity infringed Art 82 as well as Art 81(1). See also *Industrial Gases* (n 537, above) (exclusivity clauses contrary to Art 82 and replaced with fixed maximum or minimum/maximum quantities); *UBC-Almirall, XXIVth Report on Competition Policy* (1994), p 362 (exemption-type comfort letter for a supply agreement between the dominant manufacturer of an active pharmaceutical ingredient (Piracetam) and the most important European purchaser of Piracetam, after the agreement had been amended, *inter alia*, by reducing the proportion of the purchaser's requirements that it had to buy from this supplier and the duration of the obligation from five to three years, thereby removing provisions which the Commission considered an abuse of the manufacturer's dominant position). The Guidelines on Vertical Restraints (n 581, above) para 1, state that they are expressly without prejudice to the possible parallel application of Art 82. For application of Art 82 to exclusivity, see paras 10.098 *et seq*, below.

[603] For cases where the criteria in Art 81(3) were held not to have been met, see eg *Spices*, OJ 1978 L53/20, [1978] 2 CMLR 116; *Schöller Lebensmittel* (n 544, above) paras 114–147, upheld on appeal *Schöller v Commission* (n 544, above) paras 125–149; and *Van den Bergh Foods Ltd* (n 589, above) paras 221–247. See also see the Investigation by the EFTA Surveillance Authority regarding *Service station agreements in Austria*, ESA Annual Report '94, para 4.9.2.

[604] *Whitbread* (n 570, above).

[605] *Bass* (n 571, above).

[606] *Scottish & Newcastle* (n 572, above).

which they supplied loan-tied and non-loan-tied customers.[607] By contrast, if the supplier has a significant share of the market, simply the benefit of being able better to plan production and avoid shortages or excessive storage costs is unlikely to bring an exclusive purchasing obligation of even five years within Article 81(3), since there may be less restrictive means of achieving predictability of demand.[608]

6.166 **Particular efficiencies achieved.** The Guidelines indicate some of the factors which might justify restraints of this kind: (i) the need to avoid free-riding by other suppliers; (ii) the existence of capital market imperfections; and (iii) the prevention of hold-up problems. As regards the first two benefits, the Commission states that quantity forcing may be a less restrictive alternative that should be considered.[609] Capital market imperfection refers to the situation where it may be more efficient for the supplier to provide the purchaser with a loan or capital equipment than for the purchaser to obtain funding from a bank, either because the supplier has better information on the purchaser's financial position or is better able to take security. But the Commission states that this situation will not normally save a non-compete obligation that has a foreclosure effect on the market unless the purchaser is able to repay the loan, and thereby terminate the non-compete obligation, without penalty at any time; and if the supplier provides equipment, the purchaser should be able to take over the equipment at its market value.[610] As regards a claimed hold-up problem,[611] the investment that is sought to be protected must be specific to the particular contractual relationship at issue. Investment by the supplier to increase capacity for a market is not normally regarded as relationship-specific so as to justify a non-compete obligation, by contrast with investment that caters for the requirements only of a particular buyer. In the latter case, non-compete or quantity forcing arrangements for the period of depreciation of the investment will generally justify the application of Article 81(3).[612] Where the agreement involves the transfer to the purchaser of substantial know-how that could be used to benefit the supplier's competitors, if a non-compete obligation on the purchaser comes within Article 81(1) at all it should fall within Article 81(3) for the duration of the agreement.[613] In other

---

[607] See also *Allied Domecq*, OJ 1999 C82/5, [1999] 4 CMLR 1568 (Art 19(3) Notice under Reg 17/62; exemption-type comfort letter subsequently issued).

[608] See Guidelines on the application of Art 81(3) of the Treaty, OJ 2004 C101/97: Vol II, App C.18, para 82, 2nd example.

[609] Guidelines on Vertical Restraints, OJ 2000 C291/1: Vol II, App C.11, paras 153–154. Note the exemption for a long-term minimum purchasing obligation in *Carlsberg*, para 6.157, above, where that furthered Carlsberg's expansion in the UK market.

[610] Guidelines on Vertical Restraints, above, paras 116(7), 156; and see para 58. Repayment instalments should therefore not increase over time. See also the example of a quantity forcing obligation that would qualify for exemption, ibid, para 160.

[611] For hold-ups, see n 2 to para 6.002, above.

[612] Guidelines on Vertical Restraints (n 609, above) paras 116(4), 155.

[613] ibid, para 157; see also para 116(5).

cases, a non-compete restriction lasting for longer than the five years permitted under Regulation 2790/99 may prove difficult to justify.

Article 81(3) and tying agreements.   Tying agreements may qualify for the   **6.167** application of Article 81(3), provided that the supplier is not dominant. For tying to satisfy the necessary criteria, it must be shown that at least part of the cost reductions gained from any efficiencies created from joint production or joint distribution, or from economies of scale in purchasing by the supplier, are passed on to the consumer. Accordingly, tying is not normally justified when the retailer is able to obtain, on a regular basis, supplies of the same or equivalent products on the same or better conditions than those offered by the supplier. Article 81(3) is also unlikely to apply when a tying obligation is combined with a non-compete obligation, either in respect of the tied or the tying product.[614]

Combination with other vertical restraints.   Either non-compete or exclusive   **6.168** purchasing obligations may be included in exclusive or selective distribution agreements. Exclusive purchasing may be particularly objectionable when combined with exclusive distribution or selective distribution; the effect being market foreclosure both at the supplier (upstream) level and at the resale (downstream) level, making arbitrage by final customers or distributors more difficult, facilitating price discrimination and thereby hindering market integration. If the 30 per cent ceiling of Regulation 2790/99 is exceeded, that combination is unlikely to be justified 'unless there are very clear and substantial efficiencies leading to lower prices to all final consumers.'[615] The Commission further states that the lack of compensating efficiencies may lead to withdrawal of the block exemption where the supplier's market share is below 30 per cent.[616] However, the net effect of the combination of a non-compete obligation with exclusive distribution is not necessarily anti-competitive. Whilst it can create foreclosure both for suppliers and distributors, if it does not lead to significant foreclosure then it may promote competition by encouraging the exclusive distributor to concentrate his efforts on the particular brand. The Commission states that in those circumstances, below the level of dominance, this combination may satisfy Article 81(3) for the whole length of the agreement.[617]

---

[614] ibid, paras 222–223. See *Vaessen/Moris*, OJ 1979 L19/32, [1979] 1 CMLR 511 (exemption refused for tying clause in patent licence from supplier of specialised product; however the decision contains little economic analysis and the case might be approached differently today).

[615] Guidelines on Vertical Restraints (n 609, above) para 172. See also Communication on the Application of the Community Competition Rules to Vertical Restraints, OJ 1998 C365/5, [1999] 4 CMLR 281, Sect III(2.2).

[616] Guidelines on Vertical Restraints (n 609, above) para 172.

[617] ibid, paras 158 and 171.

6.169 **Long-term industrial supply agreements.** Minimum purchasing agreements between major industrial companies are more likely to qualify for exemption over a longer period if that can be justified either by the purchaser's need for security and continuity of supply (for which the supplier requires the minimum purchasing commitment)[618] or by the equivalent need on the part of the supplier, for example if such a forward contract enables it to incur substantial investment in the construction of new plant. In those circumstances, exclusive supply and exclusive purchasing obligations are often combined.[619] However, the Commission is concerned that the foreclosing effect of such arrangements should be limited, particularly where it could hold back the liberalisation of previous monopoly industries; this may be achieved by limiting the period of exclusivity or using minimum instead of exclusive purchasing obligations, with the specified quantities or proportions fixed to decline over the period of the contract.[620] Considering the long-term contracts for gas supply which E.ON Ruhrgas had concluded with local distributors, covering either all or 80 per cent of the distributor's requirements for a period of 10–15 years (and in some cases even longer), the Düsseldorf Court of Appeal rejected the argument that this was necessary to match the long-term contracts with 'take or pay' obligations which E.ON held with gas producers.[621] The Court held that obligations upstream had nothing to do with the downstream market and that the risk to E.ON (which had a market share of up to 75 per cent) of not being able to sell enough gas downstream reflected the risk facing any supplier. The Court therefore refused to suspend the decision of the German competition authority (the *Bundeskartelamt*) that the contracts infringed both EC and German national competition law. The Court noted that the decision did not create any threat to continuity of supply.

6.170 **Hard-core restrictions.** If a vertical agreement contains a hard-core restriction and it violates Article 81(1), it is highly unlikely that it will satisfy the criteria in Article 81(3).[622]

---

[618] eg *Shotton/Maybank, Shotton-Davidsons*, OJ 1990 C106/3, [1990] 4 CMLR 596 (Art 19(3) Notice under Reg 17/62).

[619] For exclusive supply, see paras 6.039 *et seq*, above.

[620] See, eg *Isab Energy, XXVIth Report on Competition Policy* (1996), p 133 (20 years' agreement but exemption-type comfort letter only for 15 years); *Electrabel/Mixed intercommunal electricity distribution companies in Belgium, XXVIIth Report on Competition Policy* (1997), p 127.

[621] Case No. VI-2 Kart 1/06 (V), OLG Düsseldorf, 20 June 2006, 2006 WuW/E DE-R 1757-E.ON Ruhrgas. The Bundeskartelamt also prohibited E.ON from entering into any new supply contracts with a distributor for more than 50 per cent of its total demand with a duration in excess of four years; or for more than 80 per cent of its total demand with a duration in excess of two years.

[622] Guidelines on Vertical Restraints, OJ 2000 C291/1: Vol II, App C.11, para 46.

7. Franchising Agreements

(a) Generally

Franchising.   The term franchising, in its modern sense and as used in this 6.171
work,[623] usually means an arrangement whereby the proprietor of a trade mark,
trade name or other distinctive marketing presentation (the franchisor) grants one
or more parties (the franchisees) a licence to use that trade mark, trade name, or
presentation in the supply of goods or services and to arrange their premises in
accordance with the distinctive layout or format associated with the franchisor.
Each franchisee remains an independent trader bearing his own financial risk, but
pays a fee or royalties to the franchisor. The franchisor's aim is to create a chain of
franchisees using a uniform presentation and selling products or services of uniform quality; to the outside observer the outlets look like subsidiaries or branches
of the franchisor. To achieve that uniformity, the franchisor normally requires the
franchisee to obtain his stock from the franchisor or from sources nominated by
him or to produce it in accordance with the franchisor's specifications. He usually
retains the right to supervise the location, layout and decor of the franchisee's
premises. In addition to the know-how and a marketing image, which usually has
proven market appeal, the franchisor generally provides the franchisee with
commercial and technical assistance for the duration of the agreement. In general
terms, the franchising relationship involves a greater degree of cooperation and a
greater involvement of the supplier in the licensed enterprise than is found in
other kinds of vertical agreement.

Varieties of franchise.   There has been a marked expansion of franchising within 6.172
the Community.[624] Four kinds of franchise can be distinguished: a production or
industrial franchise, under which the franchisee manufactures products according
to the franchisor's specifications and sells them under his trade mark; a distribution franchise, under which the franchisee sells certain products from a retail outlet that bears the franchisor's business name; a service franchise, under which the
franchisee offers a service under the business name and in accordance with the
style of the franchisor; and a wholesale franchise, under which the franchisees
similarly distribute certain products but supply only retailers and not end-users.
Following an important decision of the Court of Justice in 1986 concerning a
distribution franchise, there were a number of Commission decisions on the
application of Article 81(3) to franchise agreements and in 1988 the Commission

---

[623] See also the Guidelines on Vertical Restraints, above, para 42.
[624] See the Commission's Green Paper on Vertical Restraints in EC Competition Policy, COM
(96) 721 final, [1997] 4 CMLR 519, paras 36 and 266. See also OECD report, *Competition Policy
and Vertical Restraints: Franchising Agreements* (1994).

issued Regulation 4087/88,[625] which granted block exemption to distribution and service franchises satisfying certain requirements. Regulation 4087/88 has been replaced by Regulation 2790/99, which covers all types of franchising agreements that comply with the conditions of the block exemption. This Section examines, first, the approach to franchise agreements under Article 81 and, secondly, the application of Regulation 2790/99 to franchise agreements.

(b) Application of Article 81(1)

6.173 **The Court of Justice's attitude to franchise agreements.** The position of franchise agreements under Article 81(1) was partly elucidated by the Court of Justice in the *Pronuptia* case.[626] This was a reference from a German court before which a franchisee sought to avoid an obligation to pay royalties by contending that the franchise agreement was contrary to Article 81(1) and void. The Court of Justice held that franchise agreements were not as such restrictive of competition. The Court recognised that the use of franchise agreements to establish a distribution network brings benefits to both parties. It often enables the franchisor to exploit the expertise he has acquired through success in other markets, without having to invest substantial capital in setting up a retail network. It also gives an inexperienced retailer access to trading methods which have already been tested whilst enabling him to retain his independence. The Court held that the obligations in the agreement which were necessary to support the essential ingredients of the franchising relationship do not fall within Article 81(1),[627] but that certain other clauses may do so. It is accordingly necessary to analyse the various clauses in a franchise agreement, and this is assisted by the Commission's five subsequent decisions under Article 81(3)[628] and the discussion of franchising in the Guidelines on Vertical Restraints.[629]

(i) Clauses falling outside Article 81(1)

6.174 **The essential ingredients.** The Court held in *Pronuptia* that in order for a franchise system to work, there are two essential ingredients. The first ingredient is

---

[625] Reg 4087/88, OJ 1988 L359/46.

[626] Case 161/84 *Pronuptia* [1986] ECR 353, [1986] 1 CMLR 414. The judgment is not easy to follow but is analysed by Venit, 'Pronuptia–ancillary restraints or unholy alliances' (1986) EL Rev 213.

[627] *Pronuptia* (n 626, above) para 27(2)–(3).

[628] *Yves Rocher*, OJ 1987 L8/49, [1988] 4 CMLR 592; *Pronuptia*, OJ 1987 L13/39, [1989] 4 CMLR 355; *Computerland*, OJ 1987 L222/12, [1989] 4 CMLR 259; *ServiceMaster*, OJ 1988 L332/38, [1989] 4 CMLR 581 (which concerned a service franchise); *Charles Jourdan*, OJ 1989 L35/31, [1989] 4 CMLR 591 (which concerned not only franchised shops but franchised 'corners' within shops). See also *Texaco Ltd*, *XXIIIrd Report on Competition Policy* (1993), point 225, in which the Commission considered the compatibility with Reg 4087/88 of various requirements in franchise agreements for the operation of Texaco service stations and integrated on-site shops.

[629] Guidelines on Vertical Restraints, OJ 2000 C291/1: Vol II, App C.11, see para 6.008, above.

that the franchisor must be able to give the franchisee the benefit of his know-how and business expertise without fearing that the information will reach the hands of a competitor, even indirectly. The second ingredient is that the franchisor has sufficient control over the operation of the retail outlet to enable him to protect the reputation of his trade name and business image. Clauses designed to achieve these objects fall outside Article 81(1).

Protection of know-how and expertise.   The Court of Justice examined which   **6.175** of the clauses in Pronuptia's agreement may be justified as ensuring legitimate protection of the franchisor's know-how and expertise. On that ground, the Court held that Article 81(1) is not infringed if the franchisee is prohibited from opening a shop of the same or similar nature in an area where he may compete with a member of the network during the currency of the agreement.[630] The Court also said that such a restriction may extend for a reasonable period after the expiry of the franchise.[631] The period will be such as is necessary for a new franchisee to be established and start acquiring goodwill.[632] The franchisee can also be prevented from transferring his shop to another party without the prior approval of the franchisor.[633] On the same basis, restrictions and other obligations in relation to the use of the franchisor's trade mark and logo have subsequently been held by the Commission to fall outside the scope of Article 81(1) in individual cases.[634]

---

[630] *Pronuptia* (n 626, above) para 16. This can be framed as a general non-compete obligation, subject to appropriate territorial limitation: see *Computerland* (n 628, above) para 22(ii); see also the Guidelines (n 629, above) para 200(2). But in *Computerland*, ibid, a prohibition on the franchisee having an interest in a competing business was modified at the Commission's request to permit the holding of a financial interest short of control; cf *ServiceMaster* (n 628, above) para 10, where in the context of a service franchise a stricter limitation of interest in a competing company was accepted: the franchisee could acquire only a financial interest not exceeding 5 per cent in a publicly quoted company.

[631] *Pronuptia* (n 626, above) para 16.

[632] In general, a period of one year from termination is considered reasonable. But cf *Charles Jourdan* (n 628, above) para 27, where the Commission stated that, in the circumstances of the case, any post-termination non-competition clause would not have been justified: the relevant know-how included a large element of general commercial techniques and the type of franchise under consideration was primarily granted to retailers who were already experienced in the field. It is not clear whether, in any circumstances, a restraint period longer than one year could be regarded as reasonable. See, eg *Computerland* (n 628, above) para 22(ii), where the post-termination restraint was reduced, following comments by the Commission, from three years to one and its geographical extent was also limited to a 10km radius of the franchisee's previous outlet. And see also the approach of national courts: eg in England: *Budget Rent A Car International v Mamos Slough Ltd.* (1977) 121 SJ 374 (CA); *Prontaprint plc v London Litho Ltd* [1987] FSR 315 (ChD); *Kall-Kwik Printing (UK) Ltd v Bell* [1994] FSR 674 (ChD): *Kall-Kwik Printing (UK) Ltd v Rush* [1996] FSR 114 (ChD); *Dyno Rod Plc v Reeve* [1999] FSR 148 (ChD); *Convenience Co Ltd v Roberts* [2001] FSR 625 (ChD) (nationwide restraint unreasonable); in France: *vêtements 'Z'*, BOCCRF no.7 of 22 April 1997, p 267 (Paris CA), noted at (1997) 4 ECLR R-80 (two-year post termination restraint excessive to safeguard the identity of a network of children's clothing shops).

[633] *Pronuptia* (n 626, above) para 16.

[634] See Commission Decisions in *Pronuptia* (n 628, above) para 26; *Computerland* (n 628, above) para 23(ii).

In particular, an obligation to sell only products bearing the franchisor's trade mark was upheld as 'inherent in the very nature of the [chosen] distribution formula'.[635] In the context of a service franchise, where it was stated that the protection of the franchisor's know-how and reputation can be 'even more essential',[636] the Commission held that an obligation for one year after termination not to solicit customers of the franchised business in the previous two years fell outside Article 81(1).[637] An obligation to preserve the secrecy of all confidential information and know-how, both before and after termination of the agreement, and to impose a similar obligation on employees, as well as the obligation to cease using the know-how upon termination unless it has come into the public domain, are not caught by Article 81(1).[638]

6.176 **Protection of network reputation.** Obligations on the franchisee to apply the franchisor's business methods and know-how and to set up and decorate his premises in accordance with the franchisor's specifications are justified by the need to protect the reputation and identity of the network and therefore fall outside Article 81(1),[639] as does an obligation to stop using the franchisor's system immediately upon leaving the network.[640] Similarly, a requirement that the franchisee confines his activities at the premises to the franchised business is necessary to maintain the uniform character of the network.[641] A prohibition on the assignment by the franchisee of his rights and obligations under the contract without the franchisor's approval protects the latter's right to ensure that his franchisees have the qualifications which will maintain the reputation of the network.[642] In this context, the Commission has also upheld restrictions and prohibitions on the sale of goods to resellers outside the franchise network, since to allow distribution by non-franchised dealers would render meaningless many of the other obligations under the contract.[643] The franchisor will also be concerned that the goods supplied by his franchisees are of a uniform quality. In circumstances where it is impractical to lay down objective quality specifications, a requirement that the franchisee sell only products supplied by the franchisor or by

---

[635] *Yves Rocher* (n 628, above) para 45.

[636] *ServiceMaster* (n 628, above) para 6: on the basis that carrying out a service, often at the customer's premises, involves closer personal contact than arises in the mere sale of goods.

[637] ibid, para 11.

[638] eg *ServiceMaster* (n 628, above) paras 7–9; *Computerland* (n 628, above) para 22(i).

[639] *Pronuptia* (n 626, above) para 19.

[640] *Computerland* (n 628, above) para 23(ii): note that the Commission required that franchisees be expressly entitled to continue using any innovations and improvements they had developed which were demonstrably separable from the Computerland system.

[641] *Computerland* (n 628, above) para 22(vi).

[642] *Pronuptia* (n 626, above) para 20.

[643] *Yves Rocher* (n 628, above) para 46; *Charles Jourdan*, ibid, para 28. But cf *Computerland*, para 6.181, below.

suppliers selected by him does not infringe Article 81(1).[644] The franchisee may also be required to submit advertising material to the franchisor for approval.[645] The franchisee can be required to communicate any improvements which he makes in the operation of the business, as this encourages the free interchange of improvements between all franchisees.[646]

Other clauses held to fall outside Article 81(1). The Commission in *Pronuptia* **6.177** also held that a number of clauses, which would be regarded as restricting competition in a selective distribution system, did not fall within the ambit of Article 81(1) in the context of the particular franchise agreement under consideration. These included an obligation to pay a minimum amount of royalty each year, an obligation to order in advance according to a fixed timetable at least 50 per cent of the estimated sale requirements and an obligation to hold stock.[647] In its other decisions, the Commission held that clauses allowing the franchisor to inspect stock levels, accounts and balance sheets were essential to enable the franchisor to verify that the franchisees are discharging their obligations.[648] An obligation on the franchisee to form a corporation is also justified in terms of business efficiency.[649]

(ii) Clauses falling within Article 81(1)

Exclusivity for franchisees. The Court of Justice stated in *Pronuptia* that clauses **6.178** which did not relate to the two essential ingredients of franchising might fall within Article 81(1), particularly provisions which might lead to market-sharing between the franchisor and franchisees or between franchisees. Most franchise agreements include the grant of some exclusivity by the franchisor, who normally agrees neither to operate in the area in question himself nor to license any other franchisee to do so. In addition, franchisees are often required to sell only at a specified location, which means in practice that one franchisee cannot set up in another franchisee's area. That was the situation in *Pronuptia* in which the franchisees were, therefore, absolutely protected from competition from the

---

[644] Guidelines on Vertical Restraints (n 629, above) para 200(2); *Pronuptia* (n 626, above) para 21. The Commission has often insisted that franchisees should be allowed to purchase goods from any other franchisee or other retailer within the network, see Commission Decision in *Pronuptia* (n 628, above) para 25(ii); and *Charles Jourdan*, ibid, para 28. In *Computerland* (n 628, above) para 34, a relaxation of an otherwise restrictive clause, so as to allow franchisees to sell to other franchisees within the network was an important consideration in the application of Art 81(3).

[645] *Pronuptia* (n 626, above) para 22.

[646] *ServiceMaster* (n 628, above) para 14.

[647] *Pronuptia* (n 628, above) para 27. See also Commission Green Paper (n 624, above) para 156.

[648] *Yves Rocher* (n 628, above) para 50; *Computerland* (n 628, above) para 23(vii); *ServiceMaster* (n 628, above) para 19.

[649] *Computerland* (n 628, above) para 24(ii).

franchisor or other franchisees. The Court, citing *Consten and Grundig*,[650] held that such a system gave rise to market partitioning which was contrary to Article 81(1) since it 'concerns a business name or symbol which is already well known'.[651] According to the Court, although a franchisee might reasonably require some protection from competition from the franchisor and other franchisees before taking on the franchise, that issue was relevant only to the application of Article 81(3) and not to the application of Article 81(1). Moreover, the Court held that a provision which prevents a franchisee from opening a shop in another Member State affected trade between Member States within the meaning of Article 81(1) even if the agreement was entered into by undertakings in the same Member State.[652] The Commission's decisions following *Pronuptia* regarded almost any form of exclusivity clauses, even those that were very limited in scope, as falling within the ambit of Article 81(1),[653] although exemptions were granted in each case.

6.179 **Comment on the treatment of exclusivity in *Pronuptia*.** The Court of Justice's treatment of the exclusivity issue in *Pronuptia* is not, at first sight, entirely consistent with its judgments in *Technique Minière*[654] and *Nungesser*,[655] in which the Court said that an exclusivity provision does not fall within Article 81(1) at all if it is really necessary to persuade a distributor or licensee to undertake the risk involved in entering into the agreement.[656] However, those dicta of the Court were made in relation to 'open' exclusive licences where the supplier undertakes not to supply other dealers within the contract territory and not to deal there himself, but does not undertake to prevent supplies being brought into the contract territory by others. The Court made it clear in *Nungesser* that arguments based on risk could not prevent Article 81(1) applying to a grant of absolute territorial protection. In *Pronuptia*, the Court held that the combination of clauses whereby the franchisee was obliged to sell goods only from the premises

---

[650] Cases 56 & 58/64 *Consten and Grundig v Commission* [1966] ECR 299, [1966] CMLR 418, para 6.044, above.

[651] *Pronuptia* (n 626, above) para 24. It is still not clear whether similar principles would apply if the mark were not well known.

[652] ibid, para 26.

[653] See, eg *Computerland* (n 628, above) para 25, where the 'protected area', within which no other outlet was allowed, was limited to 1km from the original outlet and franchisees were permitted to effect sales outside their allocated territory; *ServiceMaster*, ibid, para 22, where franchisees were only prevented from actively seeking customers outside their territory. The Commission, nevertheless, took the view that this provided a certain degree of market-sharing and therefore fell within Art 81(1). See also *Charles Jourdan*, ibid, para 32; Commission Green Paper (n 624, above) para 142.

[654] Case 56/65 *Société Technique Minière v Maschinenbau Ulm* [1966] ECR 235, [1966] CMLR 357: see paras 2.070 *et seq*, above.

[655] Case 258/78 *Nungesser v Commission* [1982] ECR 2015, [1983] 1 CMLR 278; see also Case 27/87 *Erauw-Jacquery v La Hesbignonne* [1988] ECR 1919, [1988] 4 CMLR 576.

[656] See generally paras 2.070 *et seq*, above.

specified in the agreement, and the franchisor granted him an exclusive right to use the name in the contract territory, amounted to a grant of absolute territorial protection: the franchisee could not open a second shop in another franchisee's territory and the franchisor undertook in effect to prevent other network members opening shops in the franchisee's area. For those reasons, it seems, the Court considered such a system as more analogous to *Consten and Grundig* than to the 'open licences' in *Technique Minière* and *Nungesser*. The arrangement was regarded as leading to market-sharing between franchisees, and therefore was treated by the Court as in effect a ban on direct competition between them.

Pricing by franchisees.   The Court of Justice stated in *Pronuptia* that provisions **6.180** which prevent franchisees from engaging in price competition with each other are restrictions on competition within Article 81(1). However, where the franchisor communicates only recommended resale prices to the franchisee, there is no violation of Article 81(1) so long as there is no concerted practice between franchisor and franchisee or between franchisees to apply those prices.[657] A stipulation of maximum prices should not infringe Article 81(1) unless this has the effect of leading to fixed prices.[658]

Other clauses held to fall within Article 81(1).   In *Computerland*, the Commis- **6.181** sion held that an obligation to sell only to end-users and other franchisees was a restriction of competition in circumstances where the product sold was of a more generic nature and did not itself bear the franchisor's name or trade mark, so that the obligation could not be said to relate to the protection of that trade mark and the associated know-how.[659]

(c) Regulation 2790/99 and franchise agreements

General approach.   In accordance with its approach of providing a single block **6.182** exemption for vertical restraints, Regulation 2790/99 does not contain any specific provisions concerning franchise agreements or, indeed, a definition of franchising. The Commission stated that franchising will not be given any preferential treatment under the block exemption. Instead, a franchise agreement is to

---

[657] *Pronuptia* (n 626, above) para 25. In *Bestseller v Danish Competition Council*, case VL B-2807–04, judgment of 27 November 2006, the Danish High Court upheld a decision that the provisions of a franchise agreement for 'concept' clothing stores that required the stores to report their sales prices and profit margins to the franchisor through a joint IT system had a similar effect to an obligation to follow recommended prices (which had been deleted from the agreement) and infringed the Danish domestic equivalent of Art 81; Bestseller was ordered to change its IT system accordingly.

[658] See para 6.052, above. See also the Commission in *Pronuptia* (n 628, above) para 26; *Yves Rocher* (n 628, above) para 26.

[659] *Computerland* (n 628, above) para 26. In this case the trade mark covered the business format as such, but not the products sold, which bore the name and trade mark of each individual manufacturer.

be treated as a combination of selective distribution and non-compete obligations in relation to goods that are the subject-matter of the franchise, sometimes including other elements such as a location clause or exclusive territory, each of which are to be examined according to the general criteria set out in the block exemption.[660] The problem with this approach is that franchising not only combines a number of restraints but does so in the context of a distinct marketing concept, which can make it difficult to fit a franchise network within the broader definitions in Regulation 2790/99. For general discussion of Regulation 2790/99, reference should be made to Section 2 of this Chapter. Only those provisions of the block exemption that particularly concern franchising agreements are considered further here.

6.183 **Intellectual property rights.** Franchising agreements almost invariably provide for the licensing of trade mark rights to the franchisee for use in the distribution of goods or the supply of a service, along with the provision of know-how; and sometimes other intellectual property rights ('IPRs') are licensed as well, such as patents for use in production of the goods. Article 2(3) of Regulation 2790/99 sets out the conditions on which the block exemption will apply to an agreement that contains provisions relating to the assignment to or use by the buyer of IPRs. Such an agreement will be covered by Regulation 2790/99 only if (i) those provisions are not the 'primary object' of the agreement; (ii) those provisions relate to the use, sale or resale of goods or services by the buyer or its customers; and (iii) the agreement does not contain restrictions of competition having the same effect as vertical restraints which are not exempted by the Regulation. Subject to point (iii), which is discussed further below, a franchising agreement generally complies with these conditions. The IPRs help the franchisee either to resell products supplied by the franchisor (or his nominated suppliers) or to use those products in the sale of related goods or services. However, where the franchise only or primarily concerns licensing of IPRs and know-how, it will not fulfil the conditions of Article 2(3) and accordingly falls outside the block exemption.[661]

6.184 **Market share.** A franchise agreement will only come within Regulation 2790/99 if the franchisor's share of the relevant markets does not exceed 30 per cent.[662] In a goods franchise, the franchisor himself frequently supplies goods to his franchisees for resale, in which case his share of the market in which he sells those goods must not exceed 30 per cent. If he does not himself supply the goods but a business method combined with IPRs, with a requirement that the franchisee

---

[660] Communication on the Application of the Competition Rules to Vertical Restraints (n 615, above) Sect V.3.

[661] See Guidelines on Vertical Restraints (n 629, above) para 43; for the application of Art 81(3) in such a case, see para 6.188, below.

[662] Art 3(1) of Reg 2790/99, OJ 1999 L336/21: Vol II, App C.3.

obtains specified goods or equipment elsewhere, the relevant market for application of the block exemption is that of the exploitation of the business method.
The Commission explains that this is to be calculated by reference to the value of
goods or services supplied by franchisees as a share of the market for substitutable
goods or services (whether or not by way of franchised operations). If the
franchisor supplies primarily a business method but also some input products
used in the franchise operation, he will have to satisfy the market share condition
in both respects.[663]

Location and sales restrictions.   It is normal practice for a franchise agreement   **6.185**
to incorporate a 'location clause' requiring the franchisee to operate only from
premises approved by the franchisor and the agreement may also include provision for territorial exclusivity. As has already been discussed,[664] the former but not
the latter is regarded as falling outside Article 81(1). However, Article 4 of
Regulation 2790/99 sets out a list of prohibited restrictions none of which may be
included in an agreement for the block exemption to apply.[665] For a franchise
agreement to benefit from the block exemption, it is therefore necessary to ensure
that it does not include such a prohibited provision. However, it is not altogether
clear whether inclusion of any of the provisions specified in Article 4 precludes
application of Regulation 2790/99 only if that provision is a restriction of competition (that is, if it comes within Article 81(1)) or in any event. The former seems
to be the more appropriate interpretation: if an agreement otherwise fulfils the
criteria in Article 81(3), there would be no purposes in denying the disapplication
of the Article 81(1) prohibition only because it includes a provision which does
not, in that context, appreciably affect competition.[666] The distinction may be
important because of the particular requirements set out in Article 4 as regards
agreements which are, and which are not, part of a selective distribution system.
Although the Commission appears to take the contrary view,[667] in many cases a
franchise will not satisfy the definition of 'selective distribution system' in
Regulation 2790/99.[668] If the particular franchising arrangement is not formally

---

663   Guidelines on Vertical Restraints (n 629, above) para 95.

664   See paras 6.173 *et seq*, above.

665   See generally para 6.023, above.

666   See also Reg 2790/99 (n 662, above) Recital (10) which refers to 'severely anti-competitive
restraints'.

667   See the Guidelines on Vertical Restraints (n 629, above) para 201; the Communication on the
Application of the Competition Rules to Vertical Restraints (n 615, above) Sect V.3, 13th indent.

668   See Art 1(d) of Reg 2790/99 (n 662, above). Three elements of that definition cause potential
difficulties in a franchising context: (i) the system must involve the sale of contract goods or services
by the supplier; (ii) the supplier must undertake to sell them only to the selected distributors; and
(iii) the distributors must be selected on the basis of 'specified criteria'. However, in franchising:
(i) the franchisor may not necessarily be the supplier but may specify that supplies be obtained
from third parties; (ii) the franchisor may himself operate outlets in the network, or (if he is a supplier of goods) wish to supply them to some non-franchised distributors away from the franchised

a selective distribution system, as defined, then to comply with Regulation 2790/99 the franchisee may be restricted as regards active sales only into the territory of other franchisees but he cannot be restricted as regards customers within his territory.[669] The problems raised by that analysis are that: (i) once a franchise is not a selective distribution system, there is no requirement under the block exemption that the franchisees should be free to make cross-supplies to each other,[670] whereas the Commission in its decisions has regarded that as an essential requirement for the application of Article 81(3);[671] (ii) the requirement that a franchisee may operate only out of premises approved by the franchisor might be regarded as a form of territorial restriction, which is not permitted unless the franchise is a selective distribution system;[672] and (iii) unless a franchise is a selective distribution system, a franchisee cannot be prevented from reselling the franchised goods to other, non-franchised, distributors.[673] The first problem should probably be dealt with in practice by including such a right in the franchise agreements.[674] The second problem does not arise if the basic interpretation of Article 4 set out above is correct since, following *Pronuptia*, a location clause of that kind does not fall within Article 81(1). The third problem can be overcome only by omitting any such restriction from the agreements, unless the franchised network clearly is a selective distribution system. On the other hand, if the franchise is a selective distribution system, a prohibition on active sales outside the franchised territory is not permitted under Regulation 2790/99.[675] In reality, a franchise network is a particular kind of hybrid between selective distribution and exclusive distribution. The practical result may be that many franchises cannot readily fit within

territories; and (iii) franchisees are frequently selected on the basis only of financial standing and a subjective assessment by the franchisor of their entrepreneurial aptitude: cf *Yves Rocher* (n 628, above). Note also Mendelsohn and Rose, 'The New Block Exemption Regulation Has Arrived' (1999) Int. J. of Franchising and Distribution Law 291 at 293, stating that 'it would be most unusual' for a franchisor to undertake to sell the franchised merchandise only to franchisees.

[669] Reg 2790/99 (n 662, above) Art 4(b), 1st indent.

[670] cf ibid, Art 4(d).

[671] See para 6.188, below. cf Reg 2790/99 (n 662, above) Art 4(d). For the provisions concerning selective distribution agreements generally, see paras 6.086 *et seq*, above. The right to obtain the merchandise from other franchisees was also a condition for application of the old block exemption: Art 4(a) of Reg 4087/88, OJ 1988 L359/46.

[672] Reg 2790/99 (n 662, above) Art 4(c).

[673] cf ibid, Art 4(b), 1st and 3rd indents.

[674] It should be remembered that even if Reg 2790/99 is to be interpreted as not importing such a requirement, Art 6 entitles the Commission to withdraw the benefit of the block exemption in a particular case where it finds that the agreements are incompatible with Art 81(3): see para 6.025, above.

[675] ie the franchisee must be free to target customers in the territory of another franchisee although he cannot open a branch there: Art 4(c) of Reg 2790/99 (n 662, above). cf Art 2(d) of Reg 4087/88, OJ 1988 L359/46 which permitted a restriction on active sales outside the contract territory. Note that in *ServiceMaster* (n 628, above) which benefited from the application of Art 81(3) prior to the adoption of Reg 4087/88, the agreement contained such a restriction.

these requirements of Regulation 2790/99 but should nonetheless benefit from the individual application of Article 81(3).

Non-compete obligations.   Two kinds of non-compete obligation need to be   **6.186** considered: (i) a restriction during the term of the franchise; and (ii) a restriction for a period after termination of the franchise. As regards an obligation not to deal in competing goods or services during the currency of the franchise, such a restriction does not fall within Article 81(1) when it is necessary to maintain the common identity and reputation of the franchised network. Accordingly, inclusion of such a provision generally does not affect the application of the block exemption.[676] Post-termination, an obligation for a 'reasonable period' not to open an outlet of the same or similar nature in an area where it may compete with a shop in the franchised network similarly falls outside Article 81(1);[677] but a wider non-compete obligation does come within Article 81(1).[678] Article 5(b) of Regulation 2790/99 gives exemption to a post-termination non-compete obligation only if it is limited to one year and if three conditions are met:

(i) it relates to goods or services which compete with the goods or services that were the subject of the franchise;

(ii) it is limited to the premises and land from which the franchisee had to operate during the franchise; and

(iii) it is indispensable to protect know-how transferred by the franchisor to the franchisee.[679]

However, a post-termination restriction on a franchisee using or disclosing know-how which has not entered the public domain may be unlimited in time.

---

[676] Guidelines on Vertical Restraints (n 629, above) para 200(2). In that case, the non-exemption under Art 5(a) of Reg 2790/99 of such an obligation lasting in excess of five years is irrelevant. But if such a restriction may be wider than necessary, it will fall within Art 81(1) and, if the agreement lasts for more than five years, this restriction will not be exempted under Reg 2790/99 and application of Art 81(3) will be required: see para 6.188, below.

[677] *Pronuptia* (n 626, above) para 16. See para 6.175, above.

[678] See Guidelines on Vertical Restraints (n 629, above) para 200(2).

[679] Note the definition of 'know-how' in Art 1(f) of Reg 2790/99 (n 662, above). The requirement that the know-how should be 'identified' does not mean that it has to be set out in the agreement: cf the know-how licensing agreement considered in *Rich Products/Jus-rol*, OJ 1988 L69/21, [1998] 4 CMLR 527 (notes of oral discussions). The requirement that the know-how should be 'substantial' is further defined as meaning that it 'includes information which is *indispensable* to the buyer for the use, sale or resale of the contract goods or services' [emphasis added]. This is the same definition as in the block exemption for research and development agreements, Reg 2659/2000, OJ 2000 L304/7: Vol II, App C.5, Art 2(10); cf the more recent block exemption for technology transfer agreements, Reg 772/2004, OJ 2004 L123/11: Vol II, App C.7, Art 1(1)(i), stating that know-how is 'substantial' means '*significant and useful* for the production of the contract products' [emphasis added]. Although the criterion of indispensability in the definition of 'know-how' may be difficult to satisfy, in practice Art 5(b) is of relevance to franchise agreements only as regards the use or disclosure of know-how outside the public domain, since a one-year post-termination restriction that fulfils the three conditions of Art 5(b) is likely to fall outside Art 81(1) in any event.

6.187 **Other restrictions.** The general approach of Regulation 2790/99 is that restrictions in an agreement that comes within its scope are permitted unless they are specifically prohibited. Accordingly, the exemption will cover obligations on the franchisee (if they fall within Article 81(1) at all) (i) to communicate to the franchisor any experience gained in exploiting the franchise and to grant it and other franchisees a non-exclusive licence for the know-how resulting from that experience; and (ii) to inform the franchisor of infringements of licensed intellectual property rights and either to take legal action himself against infringers or to assist the franchisor in any such action.[680] Furthermore, an obligation on the franchisor not to approve other franchised premises within the territory granted to a franchisee, and not himself to operate within that territory, does not affect the application of the block exemption.[681] However, hard-core pricing restrictions which require the franchisee to charge a fixed or minimum price, will take an agreement outside Regulation 2790/99.[682]

(d) Application of Article 81(3)

6.188 **Application of Article 81(3).** When a franchising agreement that contains provisions falling within Article 81(1) is not covered by the block exemption under Regulation 2790/99, the agreement may nonetheless escape the prohibition if the criteria in Article 81(3) are met. If a franchise agreement falls outside Regulation 2790/99 because the agreement primarily concerns IPRs,[683] the Commission has stated that it will approach the application of Article 81(3) according to the principles set out in the block exemption.[684] If a restriction regarding the input products which the franchisee can use to produce the goods being sold may be wider than is necessary to protect the franchise reputation, with the risk that this restriction will therefore attract the operation of Article 81(1),[685] and the restriction is not covered by Regulation 2790/99 because the agreement lasts for more than five years, the Commission has indicated that Article 81(3) should apply.[686] However, if the reason why Regulation 2790/99 does not apply is that the franchisor's market share is above 30 per cent, there is at present little

---

[680] Guidelines on Vertical Restraints (n 629, above) para 44. The other obligations there listed are discussed above. See similarly Recital (11) and Art 3(2) of Reg 4087/88, OJ 1988 L359/46.

[681] See Guidelines on Vertical Restraints (n 629, above) para 53. This result corresponds to Art 2(a) of Reg 4087/88, OJ 1988 L359/46.

[682] Art 4(a) of Reg 2790/99 (n 662, above).

[683] See para 6.183, above.

[684] Guidelines on Vertical Restraints (n 629, above) para 43. For an apparent example (only summary facts are set out), see *BWI, XXVIIth Report on Competition Policy* (1997), p 125 (master franchise for Best Western hotels).

[685] cf para 6.176, above.

[686] This appears to be the explanation of the example in the Guidelines on Vertical Restraints (n 629, above) para 201.

guidance as to how Article 81(3) will apply.[687] An agreement which includes fixed or minimum resale price obligations or a prohibition on cross-supplies between franchisees[688] is very unlikely to escape the prohibition in Article 81(1).

8. Subcontracting

Generally. An undertaking may choose to have its products made wholly or in part by some independent third party. The arrangement whereby a third party carries out part or all of a manufacturing function is often known as a subcontracting agreement, although the expressions 'contract manufacturing', 'contracting out' or 'tolling' may also be appropriate. Subcontracting may also involve an agreement whereby one party entrusts another with the carrying out of certain services under his direction. In discussing subcontracting agreements, the undertaking which entrusts to another the manufacture or provision of services is referred to as 'the contractor' and the undertaking which carries out the manufacture or provides the services is referred to as 'the subcontractor'. However, as legal and economic concepts, the categories of subcontracting agreements and of long-term supply agreements for input products (for example, components) have considerable overlap. When the purchaser (contractor) makes available to the supplier (subcontractor), for example, equipment or technology, intellectual property rights ('IPRs') or know-how, to manufacture an input product for his benefit, that can be regarded as a particular form of agreement. Guidance as to whether such a subcontracting agreement falls within Article 81(1) is found in the Commission's Subcontracting Notice. But it should be noted that the Commission now refers also to a wider category of 'subcontracting agreements' as extending to any agreement whereby one competitor 'entrusts' another with the production of a product.[689] If a subcontracting agreement does fall within Article 81(1), it may benefit from block exemption under Regulation 2790/99, although the extent to which the Regulation applies to subcontracting agreements is not altogether clear; and otherwise it may benefit from the application of Article 81(3). These issues are considered in turn in this Section.

6.189

---

[687] Save that the Guidelines state that the more important the transfer of know-how, the more easily the vertical restraints fulfil the conditions for exemption: para 200(1).

[688] See *Yves Rocher* (n 628, above), where the agreements were altered to allow cross-supplies before exemption was granted.

[689] Horizontal Cooperation Guidelines, 2001 OJ C3/2: Vol II, App C.12, paras 79–81: those Guidelines are stated to apply when the parties are competitors, and the Guidelines on Vertical Restraints, OJ 2000 C291/1: Vol II, App C.11, when the parties are not competitors. This serves to indicate some of the dangers of over-categorisation.

6.190 **The Subcontracting Notice.** The Commission's Notice on subcontracting agreements, issued in 1978 ('the Subcontracting Notice'),[690] covers agreements whereby the subcontractor agrees to carry out work in accordance with the contractor's instructions and for that purpose has to make use of particular technology or equipment provided by the contractor. In the Commission's view,[691] Article 81(1) does not apply to clauses in such an agreement whereby: (i) technology or equipment provided by the contractor may not be used except for the purposes of the subcontracting agreement; or (ii) technology or equipment provided by the contractor may not be made available to third parties; or (iii) the goods, services or work resulting from the use of such technology or equipment may be supplied only to the contractor or performed on his behalf. But the Commission considers that such clauses fall outside Article 81(1) only if and insofar as the technology or equipment is necessary to enable the subcontractor under reasonable conditions to manufacture the goods, to supply the services or to carry out the work in accordance with the contractor's instructions. This will be so, for example, where performance of the subcontracting agreement makes necessary the use by the subcontractor of IPRs or know-how belonging to the contractor. The same is true where the subcontractor needs to use studies, plans or documents prepared by or for the contractor, or dies, patterns, tools or accessory equipment that are distinctively the contractor's and that permit the manufacture of goods which differ in form, function or composition from other goods manufactured or supplied on the market. Situations of this type are to be distinguished, however, from those where the subcontractor has at his disposal, or could under reasonable conditions obtain access to, the technology and equipment needed to produce the goods, provide the services or carry out the work. When the contractor provides no more than general information describing the work to be done, the criteria set out in the Subcontracting Notice are accordingly not fulfilled. If the input product could not be manufactured by the subcontractor using his own technology, then by definition the parties are not competitors in relation to the supply of an input product of that specific description; it appears to be on this basis that the Commission states in its recent Horizontal Cooperation Guidelines that the Notice will not apply to agreements between competitors.[692] However, the agreement may benefit from exemption under Regulation 2790/99.[693]

---

[690] Subcontracting Notice, OJ 1979 C1/2: Vol II, App C.8. The Notice continues to be effective: Horizontal Cooperation Guidelines (n 689, above) para 81, n 39. The EFTA Surveillance Authority has issued an equivalent Notice on subcontracting agreements: OJ 1994 L153/1, 30, [1994] 4 CMLR 353.

[691] Subcontracting Notice, above, para 2.

[692] Horizontal Cooperation Guidelines (n 689, above) paras 80–81. If the subcontractor can produce the subcontracted product without technology (including know-how or IPRs) or equipment from the contractor, it would appear that he should be regarded as at least a potential competitor in respect of that product.

[693] Para 6.193, below.

Additional provisions which may fall outside Article 81(1).   If an agreement   **6.191**
falls outside Article 81(1) on the basis of the criteria set out in the Subcontracting
Notice, it may further include any of the following provisions without attracting
the operation of Article 81(1):

  (i) an undertaking by each party to preserve the secrecy of the other's secret
processes or know-how not in the public domain;[694]

 (ii) an undertaking by the subcontractor not to make use, after expiry of the
agreement, of secret manufacturing processes or know-how received by him
during the currency of the agreement;[695]

(iii) an undertaking by the subcontractor to pass on to the contractor on a
non-exclusive basis any technical improvements which he makes during the
currency of the agreement or, where a patentable invention has been discovered by the subcontractor, to grant to the contractor, for the term of the
patent, non-exclusive licences in respect of patented inventions relating to
improvements and new applications of the original invention.[696] Such
licences may, however, be exclusive insofar as the relevant improvement or
invention made by the subcontractor during the currency of the agreement
is incapable of being used independently of the contractor's secret know-
how or patent rights.[697]

Unacceptable restrictions.   If limitations are placed on the subcontractor re-   **6.192**
garding disposal of the results of his own research and development work where
such results are capable of being used independently, the subcontracting agreement will not benefit from the Notice.[698] Although such a restriction does not
preclude an agreement from benefiting from Regulation 2790/99, if the agreement is otherwise outside the scope of the block exemption, the general competition rules on know-how and IPRs will apply as regards such restrictions.[699]

Application of Regulation 2790/99.   It is not altogether clear to what extent   **6.193**
the block exemption for vertical agreements, Regulation 2790/99,[700] applies to

---

  694 Subcontracting Notice (n 690, above) para 3, 1st indent. For the position as regards know-
how agreements generally, see Chap 9, below.

  695 Subcontracting Notice (n 690, above) para 3, 2nd indent. For the position under a full know-
how licence, see para 9.118, below.

  696 ibid, para 3, 3rd indent.

  697 ibid, para 3, 2nd para.

  698 ibid, para 3, 3rd para. But the Notice also states that the subcontractor may be restricted in
the use he makes of the contractor's trade mark: ibid, para 4. This would normally be the case under
the general law in any event.

  699 See Chap 9, below.

  700 Reg 2790/99, OJ 1999 L336/21: Vol II, App C.3. For Reg 2790/99 generally, see
paras 6.010 *et seq*, above. The Guidelines on Vertical Restraints (n 689, above) contain no separate
discussion of subcontracting, but see para 213. See also Horizontal Cooperation Guidelines (n 689,
above) paras 100 and 114 for subcontracting between competitors.

subcontracting agreements. Although both parties may be manufacturers, a subcontracting agreement is a vertical agreement for the purpose of the Regulation since they operate, for the purpose of the agreement, at a different level of the production chain.[701] However, as noted above, such agreements frequently involve the use by the subcontractor of IPRs or know-how made available by the contractor. Article 2(3) of Regulation 2790/99 makes provision for application of the block exemption to vertical agreements which contain provisions for assignment of IPRs to, or their use by, *the buyer*. The Commission interprets Regulation 2790/99 in the light of this provision as by implication excluding from the scope of the block exemption all other vertical agreements containing provisions concerning IPRs.[702] If the Commission is correct in so interpreting the Regulation, then since the IPRs in a subcontracting arrangement are made available for use by *the seller*, subcontracting which involves the transfer of IPRs to the subcontractor is not covered by Regulation 2790/99. Moreover, in its Guidelines on Vertical Restraints the Commission goes further and states that subcontracting which involves the transfer of *know-how* to the subcontractor also does not benefit from Regulation 2790/99.[703] Since know-how is defined in Regulation 2790/99 in a manner that appears to exclude IPRs, the Commission's view in this regard appears unwarranted.[704] In any event, if the contractor provides to the subcontractor only specifications (without IPRs) for the goods or services to be supplied, the agreement is within the scope of Regulation 2790/99 and will benefit from the block exemption if the other conditions of the Regulation are satisfied.[705] In that regard, it should be noted that, if the subcontractor is supplying components for incorporation into the contractor's products, Article 4(e) of Regulation 2790/99 proscribes, as a hard-core restriction, a prohibition on the subcontractor also selling those components to end-users or repairers, save that if the supplier has his own network of authorised repairers or service providers the subcontractor may be prevented from selling the components to them so that the authorised repairers and service providers have to obtain their supplies from the contractor.[706] If the parties are competitors, the agreement constitutes a non-reciprocal vertical agreement and application of Regulation 2790/99 is subject to the further conditions that the contractor's turnover does not exceed €100 million or that the contractor does not manufacture the subcontracted product.[707]

---

[701] Art 2(1) of Reg 2790/99 (n 700, above); see also Guidelines on Vertical Restraints (n 689, above) para 27. But if the parties are potential suppliers of substitutable products, note the conditions of Art 2(4) read with Art 1(a).

[702] Guidelines on Vertical Restraints (n 689, above) para 30.

[703] Guidelines on Vertical Restraints, OJ 2000 C291/1: Vol II, App C.11, para 33.

[704] cf Art 1(e) and (f) of Reg 2790/99 (n 700, above).

[705] Guidelines on Vertical Restraints (n 703, above) para 33.

[706] See the explanation of this provision, ibid, para 56.

[707] Art 2(4) of Reg 2790/99 (n 700, above).

Application of Article 81(3).   If the Subcontracting Notice does not apply to an **6.194**
agreement, so that the agreement falls within Article 81(1), and the conditions of
Regulation 2790/99 are not fulfilled, the agreement may still be lawful if it
satisfies the criteria in Article 81(3). In that event, the exclusivity obligations
should be assessed according to the general criteria discussed earlier in this Chapter
(if those obligations do not concern IPRs or know-how) or in Chapter 9, below
(if those obligations do concern IPRs or know-how). In *ICL/Fujitsu*,[708] the Commission considered a number of agreements in connection with the production
and sale by ICL of its own-brand computers. Under one of those agreements,
Fujitsu undertook to manufacture and supply large mainframe computers to ICL
on an original equipment manufacturer (OEM) basis, on terms that ICL could
resell them only in specified territories and Fujitsu would supply those computers
in England exclusively to ICL. That agreement was cancelled after the Commission
made clear that such territorial restrictions were unlikely to qualify for exemption
under the pre-Modernisation procedure. However, an exemption-type comfort
letter was issued for the other agreements that covered the production and supply
of components by Fujitsu to ICL for 10 years: under those agreements Fujitsu
undertook to supply exclusively to ICL components made to ICL's designs; ICL
undertook to purchase exclusively from Fujitsu components embodying Fujitsu
know-how; and ICL undertook to give Fujitsu first priority in the supply of other
components and equipment.

Approval of subcontractors.   It is commonplace in the building industry for **6.195**
the contract between the employer and main contractor to include requirements
that the contractor use only specified subcontractors. In *Eurotunnel*,[709] the agreements between a consortium of major building and civil engineering contractors with Eurotunnel for the construction of the Channel Tunnel contained such
provisions whereby certain subcontracting activities were subject to the prior
approval of Eurotunnel. The Commission decided that this condition did not
fall within Article 81(1), noting that the approval or supervision of Eurotunnel
was required only to the extent that it had a legitimate financial or technical interest. The position should clearly be the same for projects of a lesser scale.[710]

---

[708] *ICL/Fujitsu, XVIth Report on Competition Policy* (1986), point 72. See also the Notice
(under Art 19(3) of the old Reg 17) at OJ 1986 C210/3, [1986] 3 CMLR 154. cf *Bramley/Gilbert,
Xth Report on Competition Policy* (1980), point 128 (exclusive supply and purchase obligations
disapproved where parties where joint inventors of a patented invention).

[709] *Eurotunnel*, OJ 1988 L311/36, [1989] 4 CMLR 419. See also *FIEC/CEETB*, OJ 1988
C52/2, [1988] 4 CMLR 508 (standardisation of tender procedures: Commission notified its
intention to take no action).

[710] And see *Uniform Eurocheques*, OJ 1989 L36/16, [1989] 4 CMLR 907 (printing of cheques
and cheque cards for banks belonging to international payment system restricted to authorised firms
for security reasons: not within Art 81(1)).

9. Waste Packaging Recycling Arrangements

6.196 **Generally.** Directive 94/62 on packaging and packaging waste placed various obligations on Member States designed to reduce the amount of packaging used in the distribution of products and to increase the volume of reused and recycled waste.[711] In several Member States, the implementation of these obligations gave rise to new businesses which took over from manufacturers and distributors their responsibilities for collecting and recycling the packaging that they use for their products. Indeed, many of the companies operating such a system have been established on a collective basis by the producers of packaging and packaged products themselves. The operator of such a system generally does not itself either collect or recycle waste but makes arrangements with other companies for the supply of such services, often with different companies for different categories of waste (paper, glass, aluminium, plastic, etc). Further agreements may be made, either directly by the system operator or by the sectoral recycling companies, with local firms or local authorities to provide the actual waste collection and sorting services. The result of such arrangements is a complex structure of interrelated agreements. The Commission has taken a number of decisions concerning these arrangements and, drawing on this experience, the Commission's Competition Directorate-General published in 2005 a discussion paper on competition issues arising in the field of waste management in relation to packaging waste, end of life vehicles and waste electrical and electronic equipment. In addition to the avoidance of obvious hard-core restrictions such as price-fixing and market-sharing, the paper expresses the Commission's concerns (a) to ensure a legal environment that will allow the existence of several competing operators; and (b) that exclusive arrangements of all kinds should be avoided without solid and convincing economic justification.[712]

6.197 **The use of the 'Green Dot'.** All the Commission decisions to date in this area have concerned a form of 'Green Dot' scheme. The Green Dot (*Grüne Punkt*) is a symbol widely used to mark consumer packaging produced by a company that has participated in the financing of a collection and recovery system. Producers of products who want to use the Green Dot mark on their packaging must obtain a licence to do so. The mark is administered by a company called Pro Europe set up by the main recycling system operators in the Community to licence its use

---

[711] Directive 94/62, 1994 OJ L 365/10.
[712] Report of 22 September 2005, para 13, published at http://ec.europa.eu/comm/competition/antitrust/others/waste.pdf. See also *Report on Competition Policy 2005*, point 145.

outside Germany,[713] whereas within Germany the licensing is carried out directly by the mark owner, Duales System Deutschland ('DSD'). The licensees of the mark in each territory grant sub-licences to producers and distributors of goods who participate in their recycling system. The Commission regards it as important to ensure that control by the leading domestic recycling operator of the licensing of the Green Dot mark does not enable that operator to restrict the development of competing recycling systems. In *Eco-Emballages*,[714] concerning the Green Dot arrangements in France, the Commission approved the principal exclusive licence between Pro Europe and Eco-Emballages on the grounds that the licence required Eco-Emballages to sub-licence competing system operators. In considering the other issues that have arisen, it is convenient to distinguish between (a) the arrangements between the systems operator in a Member State and the producers and distributors of packaged goods; and (b) the arrangements made with the undertakings that actually carry out the collection and sorting of waste.

Relationship between the system operator and the producers and distributors   **6.198**
of packaged goods.   In *Eco-Emballages*,[715] the form of agreement between Eco-Emballages and producers was amended after the Commission indicated that the original agreement infringed Article 81(1) and did not satisfy the conditions of Article 81(3). The amended agreements provided that if the packaging covered by the system accounted for most of the producer's packaging, the producer was allowed to affix the Green Dot mark to all its packaging including that covered by its own system. The producer in this position could be required, if requested by Eco-Emballages, to provide an auditor's statement attesting to the quantity of packaging to which it attached the mark. On the other hand, if the packaging covered by the producer's own recycling system accounted for most of its requirements, the producer could be required to fix the mark only to the quantity covered by Eco-Emballages system 'except where it does not consider this to be adequate and rational'. In that situation, it is entitled to fix the mark to all its packaging provided that it can show that its individual system meets an appropriate standard. Further, the agreements enabled the producer to leave the system after a year and at the end of every subsequent year. On this basis, the Commission issued a negative clearance decision. In *ARA and ARGEV, ARO*,[716] concerning

---

713 See COMP/38.051 *Pro Europe*, 2001 OJ C153/4 (Carlsberg notice relating to the Articles of Association and the principal licence agreements).

714 *Eco-Emballages*, OJ 2001 OJ L233/37, [2001] 5 CMLR 1096.

715 *Eco-Emballages* (above) paras 61(j) and (k) which also deal with the fixing of the mark on packages bound for export. For discussion of this case and the Art 81 decn in *DSD* (below), see Gremminger, Laurila and Miersch 'The Commission defines principles of competition for the packaging waste recovery markets' (2001) 3 EC Competition Policy Newsletter 29.

716 *ARA and ARGEV, ARO*, OJ 2004 L75/59, [2004] 5 CMLR 1101.

the arrangements in Austria, ARO, which held the licence to the Green Dot mark, undertook, as a condition for the agreements with producers being found to fall outside Article 81(1), that it would not invoke its licence rights to collect a fee from manufacturers and distributors of packed goods for use of the mark unless they actually used the ARA recycling arrangements. In *DSD*,[717] concerning the arrangements in Germany, the producers who collectively owned DSD were free to enter into contracts with competing organisations (albeit that at the time none existed), and the agreements constituting DSD therefore contained no restriction of competition. However, in a separate decision under Article 82, the Commission held that DSD's trade mark agreement for the Green Dot mark constituted an abuse of its dominant position, and this decision was upheld by the Court of First Instance.[718] DSD licensed producers to include the Green Dot mark on their packaging so that consumers would know that they should dispose of that package in the Green Dot bin rather than the public waste disposal bin. DSD charged for the service by setting a licence fee for all use of the mark regardless of whether DSD was responsible for the final collection of the actual package, with the consequence that producers had in effect to pay DSD for all their packaging even if, in a particular area of Germany, they self-collected or appointed a rival operator (should one exist in the future).

6.199 **Arrangements with waste collectors.** So far as concerns the agreements with the undertakings which collect the waste, the Commission's decisions indicate that the following principles apply:

(a) Any territorial exclusivity given by the system operator to a collector must be limited in duration to such period as allows the collector to achieve a satisfactory return on its investment. In *DSD*, the Commission made clear that the agreements with collectors providing for 15-years exclusivity could not satisfy Article 81(3), and granted an exemption (under the pre-Modernisation system) after the agreements had been amended to last for up to 11 years, as an exceptional duration permissible only for the initial period; the Commission stated that thereafter, with the system well established, exclusive agreements could be economically justified for no more than three years.

(b) The collectors must be expressly permitted to make their local collection facilities available to competing operators. Given that duplication of local disposal and collection facilities is often not economically viable, unrestricted

---

[717] *DSD*, OJ 2001 L319/1, [2002] 4 CMLR 405, paras 104–107. However, the standard form of service agreement that DSD entered into with collection undertakings was found to foreclose the market and exemption under Art 81(3) was granted only on the basis of undertakings and subject to obligations: see para 6.199(b) below.

[718] *Der Grüne Punkt – Duales System Deutschland*, OJ 2001 L166/1, [2001] 5 CMLR 609; appeal dismissed, Case T151/01 *Der Grüne Punkt – Duales System Deutschland v Commission*, [2007] 5 CMLR 300. See further para 9.178, below.

access to and the unlimited sharing of the collection facilities is a pre-condition for the development of competition on the downstream market for organising take back and recovery of packaging. In *DSD*,[719] the Commission imposed a condition on its grant of exemption that collectors could make arrangements for joint use of containers or facilities for collection and sorting of waste with organisations competing with DSD, and prohibited DSD from requiring the collecting companies to inform it of the volumes collected that were outside the DSD system. Similarly, as regards the three-tier system considered in *ARA and ARGEV, ARO*,[720] the Commission found considerable economies of scale and scope in the arrangements made by the major sectoral recycling companies (each responsible for a particular category of waste) on the one hand and their local or regional partners on the other hand that actually carried out the collection, sorting and recycling of waste ('disposal firms'). But as a condition of granting exemption under Article 81(3) to the five-year, exclusive arrangements which precluded the sectoral companies using other local disposal firms, the Commission required that there should be no restriction on the disposal firms that prevented shared use of their collection containers for waste to be collected on behalf of a competing system.

(c) Collectors cannot be prohibited from selling the recovered waste on their own account, so as to compete in the secondary market for recycled materials. In *DSD*, the original agreements with collectors contained such a restriction, which was removed following negotiations with the Commission.[721]

---

[719] n 717, above. The appeal against this aspect of the decn was dismissed, the CFI upholding the finding that the DSD system formed a bottleneck to which access was necessary in order for other competing waste collection undertakings to penetrate the German market, and that the obligations were not disproportionate: Case T-289/01 *Der Grüne Punkt – Duales System Deutschland v Commission* [2007] 5 CMLR 356.

[720] n 716, above.

[721] *DSD* (n 717, above) paras 47–48. The restriction continued to apply for plastics, but due to the particular circumstances where such materials had a negative market price the Commission held that this was not caught by Art 81(1): paras 110–116.

7

JOINT VENTURES AND SIMILAR
COLLABORATIVE ARRANGEMENTS

1. Introduction

Plan of this Chapter. This Section explains the various types of joint venture **7.001** and the jurisdictional distinction between joint venture arrangements which are treated as concentrations under the Merger Regulation[1] (and are therefore discussed in Chapter 8) and those which may be treated as restrictive agreements

---

[1] Reg 139/2004, OJ 2004 L24/1, Vol II, App D.1.

under Article 81 (and are therefore discussed in this Chapter). Section 2 provides an outline of the Commission's evolving approach to the treatment of joint ventures under the Community competition rules. Section 3 deals with the general application of Article 81(1) to joint ventures, both as regards their formation and as regards specific restrictions in the joint venture agreement. Section 4 deals with the application of Article 81(3) following the 'modernisation' under Regulation 1/2003 of the procedure for the enforcement of Article 81. Section 5 deals with research and development agreements, which generally do not provide for production, and considers the block exemption for such agreements. Section 6 deals with production and specialisation agreements and considers the block exemption for such agreements. Section 7 contains an account of some joint venture cases both within the traditional manufacturing sphere and in some rapidly evolving technological sectors of industry such as e-commerce and mobile telephony. This Chapter does not deal with the question of effect on trade between Member States,[2] which is discussed in Chapter 1 above.

(a) Definitions

7.002 **'Joint venture'.** The term 'joint venture' ('JV'), as used by industry, resists clear definition.[3] JVs range from arrangements which are akin to mergers through to mere cooperation agreements for research and development, production or distribution (although many JVs do not contain all of these features). Terms such as joint venture, strategic alliance[4] and cooperative arrangement are loosely applied to commercial agreements between two or more parties with a wide variety of objectives and economic effects. However, in the context of the EC competition rules, the Commission has applied the term 'joint venture' only to an undertaking that is (i) a separate business entity,[5] and (ii) jointly controlled by at least two parents.[6] That definition will be used in this Chapter. Nonetheless, it has been observed that 'some of the competition issues concerning jointly *owned* companies

---

[2] But see Temple Lang, 'International Joint Ventures under Community Law' in Hawk (ed), *1999 Fordham Corp. L. Inst.* (2000), 381 at 384: 'Almost every joint venture to which Community anti-trust law applies is an international joint venture in the sense that more than one State is involved'.

[3] Brodley, 'Joint Ventures and Antitrust Policy' (1982) 95 Harvard Law Rev 1523. See also Hawk, 'Joint Ventures under EC Law' in Hawk (ed), *1991 Fordham Corp. L. Inst.* (1992), 557; Ribstein and Kobayashi, 'Joint Ventures' in Newman (ed), *The New Palgrave Dictionary of Economics and the Law* (1998).

[4] See para 7.009, below.

[5] The Commission has described JVs as a 'special, institutionally fixed form of co-operation between undertakings. They are versatile instruments at the disposal of the parents with the help of which different goals can be pursued and attained': see para 1 of the now superseded Notice concerning the assessment of cooperative JVs under Art 81, OJ 1993 C43/2 Vol II, App C.9 ('Cooperative JV Notice').

[6] The term 'joint control' has the same meaning in this context as under the Merger Reg: see paras 8.033 *et seq*, below.

arise whether or not they are jointly *controlled'* so the distinction is primarily for procedural purposes.[7]

Functions of joint ventures. JV agreements are mainly agreements the immedi- **7.003** ate or ultimate aim of which is to establish a new entity. That entity may complement some other form of activity by the parents or integrate some of their existing activities or develop an entirely new area of activity. The now defunct Commission Notice concerning the assessment of cooperative JVs under Article 81 of 1993[8] identified numerous applications to which JVs can be put.[9] That 1993 Notice distinguished between a number of JV categories:[10] pure R&D JVs, sales JVs, purchasing JVs, and production JVs. Production JVs come in many shapes and sizes and may involve upstream operations, such as research and development activities, and downstream operations, such as marketing and sales activities *relating to the JV's own production activities*. A JV may also be concerned with upstream and downstream operations *for its parents*, such as providing them with research and development, or supplying them with primary materials or intermediate components for their final products, or manufacturing the final products which they will market independently. A 'final product' JV is a JV where the product which it manufactures is ready for distribution to customers.[11] A JV which produces goods and services for its parents is known as an 'input' JV if it supplies an upstream market or an 'output' JV if it supplies a downstream market.[12]

Full-function and partial function joint ventures. The significance of the dis- **7.004** tinction between full-function and non-full function JVs is primarily procedural.

---

[7] See Temple Lang (n 2, above) at 383, who nonetheless observes that, from a substantive viewpoint, there is a distinction in that jointly controlled JVs enable each parent to veto the JV's expansion into that parent's market, whereas this is not necessarily possible where an enterprise is simply jointly owned, but not jointly controlled: see at 395. For recent cases where the 'joint venture' was not jointly controlled by its parents but where the Commission nevertheless treated the case substantively as a JV, see, eg *Covisint*, para 7.130, below; *Eutilia*, OJ 2001 C100/14 and Press Release IP/01/1775 (10 December 2001).

[8] n 5, above. Although replaced by the Horizontal Cooperation Guidelines, OJ 2001 C3/2, Vol II, App C.12, the Cooperative JV Notice remains of assistance on certain matters: see paras 7.027, 7.045 (competition between parents) and 7.055 (ancillary restrictions), below. For 'cooperative' JVs, see para 7.006, below.

[9] Cooperative JV Notice (n 5, above) para 2: 'JVs can form the basis and the framework for cooperation in all fields of business activity. Their potential area of application includes, *inter alia*, the procuring and processing of data, the organisation of working systems and procedures, taxation and business consultancy, the planning and financing of investment, the implementation of research and development plans, the acquisition and granting of licences for the use of intellectual property rights, the supply of raw materials or semi-finished products, the manufacture of goods, the provisions of services, advertising, distribution and customer service.'

[10] Cooperative JV Notice (n 5, above) paras 59–62; cf the categories in the Horizontal Cooperation Guidelines (n 8, above): para 7.028, below.

[11] See, eg *Ford/Volkswagen*, para 7.108, below.

[12] See *XXIVth Report on Competition Policy* (1994), points 164–165; and for an input JV see, eg *Asahi/St Gobain*, para 7.075, below.

Since an amendment to the Merger Regulation that took effect on 1 March 1998,[13] all 'full-function' JVs with a 'Community dimension' are notifiable to the Commission under the Merger Regulation. By contrast, JVs which are not 'full-function' (and full-function JVs which lack a 'Community dimension') are assessed under Article 81. Moreover, post-modernisation, the latter are no longer notifiable to the Commission or national competition authorities. Full-function JVs are 'autonomous economic entities'[14] which operate on a 'lasting basis' and which perform 'all the functions' of such entities.[15] This Chapter therefore deals with those JVs which do not fall within the Merger Regulation, that is to say, JVs which:

(a) are full-function JVs without a Community dimension; or

(b) are not full-function JVs because they are not autonomous economic entities; or they do not operate on a lasting basis; or they do not perform all the usual functions of an autonomous economic entity. In this work, JVs that are not full-function JVs are referred to as 'partial function' JVs.

A full-function JV may have contractual relationships mainly or only with third parties whereas the primary purpose of a partial function JV will be to provide input into its parents' activities, as a result of which it may need neither its own resources nor relationships with third parties. The distinction between full-function and partial function JVs was clarified by the Commission's Notice on the concept of full-function JVs under the original Merger Regulation, Regulation 4064/89, recently repalced by the Jurisdictional Notice,[16] and is discussed in Chapter 8 below.[17] The division of jurisdiction in the control of JVs is explained below.[18] However, since some of the leading decisions concern JVs notified prior to the amendment of the Merger Regulation, some of the cases discussed in this Chapter involve full-function JVs that remain relevant as illustrating the appropriate analysis under Article 81.

7.005 **Structural joint ventures.** A further concept employed by the Commission is that of a 'structural' JV, that is a JV which involves an important change in the structure and organisation of the business assets of the parents. Such operations therefore are characterised by significant financial investment and the commitment of significant tangible or non-tangible assets such as know-how or intellectual

---

[13] Reg 1310/97, OJ 1997 L180/1, corr by OJ 1998 L3/16, amending the old Merger Reg, Reg 4064/89, OJ 1990 L257/13.

[14] However, a full-function JV need not be a separate legal entity.

[15] See Art 3(4) of the Merger Reg, Reg 139/2004, OJ 2004 L24/1, Vol II, App D.1.

[16] Full-function JV Notice, OJ 1998 C66/1, replaced by Jurisdictional Notice, published on 10 July 2007, Vol II, App D.13.

[17] See paras 8.052 *et seq*, below.

[18] See paras 7.011 *et seq*, below.

property rights. Structural JVs are generally intended to operate for the medium or long-term. However, although many structural JVs will be full-function, that is not necessarily the case. A structural JV will be partial function when it takes over one or more specific functions either within the parents' existing activities, or develops new functions exclusively on its parents' behalf and without access to the market, for example, research and development and/or production.[19] The distinction between structural and non-structural JVs is largely historical since under the pre-modernisation notification regime structural JVs could benefit from a 'fast track' notification procedure.

Concentrative and cooperative joint ventures. The concept of a 'concentrative' **7.006**
JV (and the distinction between concentrative and cooperative JVs) was developed by the Commission to reflect the jurisdictional boundary under the original Merger Regulation prior to its amendment in 1997. The original Merger Regulation provided that a JV would only constitute a concentration if it did not give rise to coordination of the competitive behaviour of the parties as between themselves, or as between them and the JV.[20] Such a JV was therefore referred to as a 'concentrative' JV, whereas any other JV—which by definition did give rise to such coordination—was referred to as a 'cooperative' JV. This distinction does not correspond to any economic categorisation and the exclusion of all cooperative JVs from the ambit of the Merger Regulation was widely criticised. It was abandoned in the first amendment of the Merger Regulation which brought all full-function JVs within its scope with effect from 1 March 1998.[21]

JVs with coordinative effects. However, a remnant of the concept survives in **7.007**
the assessment of JVs that involve coordinative aspects since these aspects are separately assessed under Article 2(4) of the new Merger Regulation.[22] Such JVs are sometimes referred to as 'cooperative full-function' JVs. In the hope of avoiding confusion, that term will not be used in this work and such a JV will be described as 'a JV with coordinative effects'.

Joint ownership without joint control. As explained above, an entity that is **7.008**
not subject to joint control is not strictly classified as a JV but Article 81 may nevertheless apply. In particular, concerns as regards potential coordination between minority shareholder and the majority shareholder (or as between several major shareholders) can arise. The application of Article 81 to minority share

---

[19] eg *Exxon/Shell*, OJ 1994 L144/20, a production JV the activity of which was limited to supply to its parents.

[20] Art 3(2) of Reg 4064/89. The original Merger Reg was published (as corrected) at OJ 1990 L257/13. Reg 1310/97 which amended that Reg was published at OJ 1997 L180/1, corrected by OJ 1998 L40/17.

[21] See para 7.023, below. The text of the original Art 3(2) was accordingly replaced.

[22] For Art 2(4) of the Merger Reg, see below at paras 7.017 and 8.233 *et seq*.

acquisitions is considered in Chapter 8 below.[23] Although the Court of Justice has confirmed the potential for Article 81 to apply in such circumstances (the so-called *Philip Morris* doctrine),[24] there has to date been little application of this principle by the Commission.[25] By contrast in the field of merger control, existing minority participations by the merging companies (even where they do not confer control) are increasingly taken into account in the substantive assessment of the merger.[26] Where a new enterprise is established by several partners without, however, creating joint control, the assessment of the arrangements by the Commission under Article 81 seems in practice to be the same as in the case of a JV.[27]

7.009 **Strategic alliances.**   The term 'strategic alliance' has no precise meaning but is often used by the parties themselves to cover transactions ranging from partial concentrations or focused JVs to wider-ranging collaboration. The Commission recognises that 'strategic alliances can be co-operative arrangements of varying scope involving the creation of several contractual and structural links, such as the creation of a joint venture, specialisation in certain markets, joint R&D, technology transfer, cross-supply agreements, commitments to co-operate in other fields in the future and the acquisition of cross-shareholdings'.[28] Such arrangements were originally a particular feature of newly liberalised markets, such as telecommunications and air transport, prompted by the international potential, the respective benefit to undertakings well-established in different sectors of the market of linking with each other to offer a global, or at least multi-national, service and the convergence or complementarity of information technologies and networks. In 1995, the Commission described the treatment of these alliances as 'one of the major challenges for EU competition policy in recent years'.[29] Because of the variety and complexity of the arrangements involved, the Horizontal Cooperation Guidelines expressly do not cover strategic alliances.[30]

7.010 **The Commission's approach to strategic alliances.**   A strategic alliance needs to be analysed both as regards its particular elements and in its totality. As alliances are usually concluded between actual or potential competitors, they give rise to

---

   23 See paras 8.273 *et seq*, below.
   24 Named after Cases 142 & 156/84 *BAT and Reynolds v Commission* [1987] ECR 4487, [1988] 4 CMLR 24, concerning the acquisition by Philip Morris of a 30 per cent shareholding, but just under 25 per cent of the voting rights, in its competitor, Rothmans.
   25 See Temple Lang (n 2, above), who suggested that if the Modernisation package was adopted, use of the *Philip Morris* doctrine by the Commission might revive as a means of controlling anti-competitive effects in concentrated industries.
   26 See, eg Case M.2431 *Allianz/Dresdner* (19 July 2001); Case M.3653 *Siemens/VA Tech* (13 July 2005).
   27 See *TPS*, discussed at paras 7.115 *et seq*, below.
   28 *XXIVth Report on Competition Policy* (1994), point 156.
   29 *XXVth Report on Competition Policy* (1995), point 55.
   30 Horizontal Cooperation Guidelines (n 8, above) para 12. However, various aspects of an alliance may be appraised with the help of the corresponding section of the Guidelines: ibid.

particular 'spill-over'[31] concerns because they may create a tendency for the parties to seek more generally to cooperate rather than compete. However, alliances, like JVs, can lead to the creation of new services, reductions in costs, and the establishment of trans-European networks; and they may be essential to enable the participants to remain competitive in a dynamic, global market. The Commission attempts to take all these factors into account. In addition to 'spill-over', the Commission has shown particular concern that the creation of an alliance does not unduly strengthen the position of a well-established home operator (for example, an incumbent telecommunications operator or a flag carrier airline) against existing competitors or potential new entrants. Strategic alliance arrangements are not confined to these specific sectors and the Commission has taken decisions regarding alliances in, for example, banking[32] and computer software.[33]

(b) Article 81 and the Merger Regulation

Division of jurisdiction. All full-function[34] JVs with a Community dimension **7.011** are assessed exclusively by the Commission under the Merger Regulation. This precludes the application of national competition law.[35] By contrast, all partial function JVs and any full-function JV that does not have a Community dimension might fall within the regime of Article 81 if it is more than *de minimis* and has an effect on trade between Member States.[36] It may also be subject to national merger and competition laws.[37]

The tests applied. In the case of a JV which falls outside the Merger Regulation, its **7.012** establishment (with regard to coordination, foreclosure or network effect issues[38])

---

[31] For spill-over, see para 7.046, below.

[32] *Banque Nationale de Paris/Dresdner Bank*, OJ 1996 L188/37, [1996] 5 CMLR 582 (exemption for 10 years for agreement between fourth largest French bank and second largest German bank for cooperation that includes exchange of information and joint EDP developments on their home markets and joint activity in third country markets; a provision giving a right of veto when one party wished to conclude a cooperation agreement with a home competitor of the other party was held to be ancillary).

[33] *Olivetti/Digital*, OJ 1994 L309/24 (strategic alliance involving cooperation to develop and promote operating systems and software given negative clearance; linked requirements purchasing contract exempted for four years; minority stake held by Digital in Olivetti given negative clearance). See also *Fiat/General Motors*, OJ 2000 C170/8, Press Release IP/00/932 (16 August 2000) (strategic alliance concerning production of power trains, the purchasing of car components and parts, and financial services for dealers and consumers: exemption-type comfort letter issued).

[34] See para 7.004, above.

[35] Merger Reg (n 15, above) Art 21(3).

[36] See the Cooperative JV Notice (n 5, above) para 15, confirming that some JVs are outside Art 81. For the application of Art 81 to full-function JVs without a Community dimension, see para 7.017 (C)–(D), below.

[37] See para 8.279, below for a table showing the national merger control in the EC Member States. National competition laws are discussed in Chap 14.

[38] See paras 7.046 *et seq*, below.

and any specific restrictions[39] are considered under EC competition law according to the substantive tests in Article 81(1) and 81(3). Assessment by the Commission, national competition authorities or national courts follows the procedural rules of Regulation 1/2003. In the case of a JV that falls within the Merger Regulation, its establishment (*excluding* any coordinative effects) is considered according to the substantive test provided in the Merger Regulation. Any specific restrictions are currently considered in accordance with the Commission's Notice on restrictions directly related and necessary to concentrations.[40] The coordinative effects of a JV falling within the Merger Regulation remain subject to the substantive test of Article 81(1).[41] However, the entire assessment of such a JV is conducted according to the Merger Regulation procedures and the application of national law is excluded even in respect of the coordinative effects.

7.013 **Different substantive tests.**   Article 81(1) and the Merger Regulation contain different substantive tests for establishing whether agreements are compatible with Community law. The test under Article 81 is stricter in two respects. First, agreements attract the prohibition of Article 81(1) if they may affect trade between Member States and have, as their object or effect, 'the prevention, restriction or distortion of competition', provided only that this will be or is 'appreciable'.[42] This falls short of the 'significant impediment' to effective competition which is required under the Merger Regulation. Secondly, Article 81(3)(b) will not apply to such an agreement if it gives the parties even the *possibility* of eliminating competition.[43] The Merger Regulation, by contrast, as it seeks to deal with arrangements involving a change in market structure, takes a broader view of what needs, or does not need, to be regulated. The Merger Regulation therefore allows intervention against transactions only if competition 'would be', in other words, will in fact be, significantly impeded. The rationale for the more favourable treatment of concentrations, and of affording this 'concentration privilege' to full-function JVs, is that those transactions which involve a sufficient degree of economic integration between undertakings are presumed to give rise to significant efficiency gains that compensate for their potential anti-competitive effects.[44]

7.014 **Advantages and disadvantages of the different procedures.**   From the perspective of a JV parent, once a JV has a Community dimension for the purpose of the thresholds under the Merger Regulation, it is often preferable if the JV meets the

---

[39] See para 7.052 *et seq*, below.
[40] The Ancillary Restraints Notice, OJ 2005 C56/24, Vol II, App D.10 and see paras 7.053 *et seq*, below.
[41] See paras 8.232 *et seq*, below.
[42] See paras 1.115 *et seq*, above (effect on trade) and paras 2.121 *et seq*, above (appreciable effort).
[43] See paras 3.062 *et seq*, above.
[44] See Faull & Nikpay, *The EC Law of Competition* (2nd edn, 2007), 667–668.

criteria of being 'full-function'. The reasons are twofold. First, the JV will be assessed (except for coordination issues) under the less onerous Merger Regulation test rather than being subject to scrutiny in its entirety under Article 81. Secondly, a full-function JV will provide the JV parents with a definitive Commission ruling on the legality of the JV whereas, following modernisation of Article 81 enforcement, a partial function JV will not be able to achieve such a level of certainty.[45] Obtaining such certainty may be particularly important for structural JVs involving significant capital and other resources. In such a case, the potential invalidity of the JV may carry with it an unacceptable level of commercial risk.[46]

Duration and outcome of investigation. The modernisation of Article 81 **7.015** enforcement has significantly exacerbated the procedural differences between the two regimes under which JVs are assessed. First, a JV under the Merger Regulation will be dealt with within a maximum of 25 (or 35) working days plus an extra 90–125 working days if a 'serious doubts' investigation ('Phase II') is initiated.[47] By contrast, procedures under Article 81 no longer allow for the possibility of notification. Thus even parties to structural (but non-full function) JVs cannot achieve certainty on the legality of their venture either at Community or at national level. Secondly, JVs cleared under the Merger Regulation will receive a formal, binding and permanent decision, whereas even if the JV fulfils the criteria of Article 81(3) at the time the agreement is entered into, circumstances may change in the course of the agreement with the result that the conditions of Article 81(3) are no longer fulfilled. This could mean that a previously 'exempt' agreement loses the benefit of Article 81(3) without the parties being able to obtain prospective certainty through a fixed term exemption (or through an extension to an exemption).[48] Thirdly, as a general rule, where the Merger Regulation applies to a transaction, Member States' national merger and competition laws do not apply so that the Merger Regulation ensures a 'one-stop-shop'. By contrast, Article 81 jurisdiction over a JV potentially results in the parallel application of national merger or competition laws in one or more Member States. Fourthly, however, the block exemptions for horizontal agreements concerning R&D and for specialisation/production agreements embrace a wide range of JVs (subject to the market share limits) which therefore receive automatic exemption

---

[45] Unless the JV falls within a block exemption: see para 7.030, below.

[46] Even a reduction of the duration of exclusivity provisions or non-compete obligations may undermine or in any event negatively affect the economics of the transaction: see Case T-112/99 *Métropole Télévision-M6 v Commission* [2001] ECR II-2459, [2001] 5 CMLR 1236, [2002] All ER (EC) 1, para 40.

[47] See paras 8.133 and 8.142, below.

[48] As they did, for example, in *P&O Stena Line 2*, Press Release IP/01/806 (7 June 2001) (exemption extended for six years under the opposition procedure of Reg 4056/86); or *European Rail Shuttle*, IP/02/575 (17 April 2002) (exemption extended for three years under the opposition procedure of Reg 1017/68).

under Article 81(3).[49] Similarly, partial function JVs (even structural JVs) which do not involve a significant amount of capital and other resource commitment from the parents and where the commercial risk of invalidity is consequently low, benefit from the fact that Article 81 no longer requires a notification. By contrast, any concentration with a Community dimension (even if it raises no substantive issues) has to be notified.

(c) Jurisdictional categories

7.016 **Jurisdictional categories.** The Table below lists six categories of JVs with a guide as to which regime is applicable to each. Those categories reflect the fundamental jurisdictional division as between full-function and partial function JVs.

Type of JV	Competition Analysis			
	ECMR	Article 81	National Merger Rules	National Competition Laws
A. **Full-function;** Community dimension; no 'coordinative effects'	✓	✗	✗	✗
B. **Full-function;** Community dimension; with 'coordinative effects'	✓ (single assessment under ECMR)		✗	✗
C. **Full-function;** no Community dimension; no 'coordinative effects'	✗	✗	✓	✓
D. **Full-function;** no Community dimension; with 'coordinative effects'	✗	✓[50]	✓	✓
E. **Partial function; structural;** with or without 'coordinative effects'	✗	✓	✓	✓
F. **Partial function; non-structural;** with 'coordinative effects' (eg a cooperative R&D agreement)	✗	✓	✗	✓

---

[49] Regs 2659/2000 and 2658/2000. See paras 7.078-7.086 and 7.097-7.103, respectively, below, for discussion of the block exemptions.

[50] The Commission will normally leave national authorities to assess such cases, but in *Eurex, XXXIst Report on Competition Policy* (2001), points 196–199 (see also Press Release IP/02/4 (3 January 2001)) it issued a negative clearance-type comfort letter where the subject matter of the JV was inherently cross-border and the transaction did not require notification to any national authority. The purpose of the JV was the creation of a cross-border electronic derivatives exchange.

Full-function JVs. All full-function JVs constitute concentrations under **7.017** Community law.[51] The control of such a concentration under the Merger Regulation is dependent upon whether or not it has a 'Community dimension'.[52] Four categories of such JVs can be distinguished:

A. Full-function; Community dimension; no coordinative effects

Such a JV falls exclusively under the Merger Regulation. It is subject to the same substantive test and procedures as a full merger.

B. Full-function; Community dimension; with coordinative effects

Such a JV is also assessed under the Merger Regulation. However, whilst establishment of the JV and its specific restrictions will be assessed under the substantive test applied to mergers, the coordinative effects on the conduct of the parents will be assessed under the substantive Article 81(1) test in accordance with Article 2(4) of the Merger Regulation. The Article 81(1) assessment will be made only in respect of actual or potential coordination of the parent companies' behaviour which is the consequence of the creation of the JV. In other words, there must be a direct causal link between the creation of the JV and the coordination of the parents' activities. If the agreement creating the JV contains provisions giving rise to coordination that are not to be regarded as the result of the JV, those restrictions fall outside of the Merger Regulation and thus are subject to self-assessment under Regulation 1/2003.

C. Full-function; no Community dimension; no coordinative effects

Because of the lack of a Community dimension, such a JV is not subject to the automatic jurisdiction of the Merger Regulation. It is still a concentration, and the implementing regulations for Article 81 do not apply to it.[53] The Commission therefore does not have power to apply Article 81 to its formation; the question whether the transitional rules in Articles 84 and 85 of the Treaty would apply, such that national authorities might apply Article 81, has not been clearly resolved.[54] However, the formation of such a JV can be referred to the Commission for review under the Merger Regulation at the request of the parties pursuant to Article 4(5) of the Merger Regulation or at the request of a Member State pursuant to Article 22 of the Merger Regulation.[55] In that event, the assessment is whether the JV would significantly impede effective competition within that Member State.

---

[51] Art 3(4) of the Merger Reg (n 15, above).
[52] See paras 8.060 *et seq*, below.
[53] Art 21(1) of the Merger Reg (n 15, above).
[54] See the discussion in para 8.261, below.
[55] Art 22(1) of the Merger Reg (n 15, above); see generally paras 8.081 *et seq*, below.

National merger control laws may otherwise apply to such full-function JVs, as the equivalent turnover (and other) thresholds for the applicability of national merger laws are generally lower than the Community thresholds and many JVs without a Community dimension will thus have a 'national dimension'. National competition laws may also be applicable.

D. Full-function; no Community dimension; with coordinative effects

As with Category C, the Merger Regulation will not apply unless it is invoked by a Member State by a referral under Article 22 (or by the parties under Article 4(5)). Again, national merger control laws or competition laws may be applicable. However, in this case the implementing regulations for Article 81 do apply, so the Commission, national competition authorities and national courts each have jurisdiction to examine such a JV under Article 81. Since modernisation, no notification procedure exists under Community or national rules that would allow the parties to force a decision by the relevant authorities prior to or at the time of engaging in the venture.[56] The Commission is therefore unlikely ever to become involved in the assessment of such a JV, unless it involved a novel question of law[57] or unless any proposed action by a national competition authority were to threaten the uniform application of EC competition law.[58]

7.018 **Partial function JVs.** A JV that is not full-function is not a 'concentration' and there is no scope for the Merger Regulation to apply in such a case. Article 81 may apply in full but the block exemptions for R&D agreements or production/specialisation agreements and the Commission's Horizontal Cooperation Guidelines may be relevant: these are discussed in Sections 5 and 6 of this Chapter.

E. Partial function; structural; with or without coordinative effects

The application of Article 81 to this category of JV has significantly changed following adoption of Regulation 1/2003. Previously, parties were able to take advantage of the 'fast-track' procedure to obtain a relatively speedy response from the Commission. This process has disappeared so that parties must now rely on their internal legal assessment. In respect of JVs involving the pooling of assets (especially in the production field and in connection with the manufacture and marketing of goods purchased by the JV) this can cause significant problems.

---

[56] ibid, Art 21(1).

[57] See Commission Notice on informal guidance relating to novel questions concerning Arts 81 and 82 of the EC Treaty that arise in individual cases ('the Informal Guidance Notice') OJ 2004 C101/78, Vol II, App B.11.

[58] See Arts 11(6) and 16(2) of Reg 1/2003 and Commission Notice on cooperation within the Network of Competition Authorities ('the Network Notice') OJ 2004 C101/43, Vol II, App B.8, paras 43 *et seq.*

Some production JVs can benefit from full exemption under the specialisation block exemption[59] and some R&D JVs will fall within the R&D block exemption.[60] For all other partial function JVs, the question of obtaining certainty is more problematic. National merger or competition laws may also be applicable to cases in this category and the national merger rules may give the parties a route to obtaining a positive decision that could mitigate the remaining Article 81 risk.

F. Partial function; non-structural; entirely coordinative

Non-structural JVs that result in coordination of the competitive behaviour of the parties who are, at least, potential competitors and that affect trade between Member States will fall under Article 81(1). National competition laws may also be applicable to such arrangements. Notification of such a JV for exemption under Article 81(3) is no longer available but if an agreement comes within either of the block exemptions it will of course still benefit from the application of Article 81(3) and will then similarly be protected under national competition law.[61]

2. Developing Treatment of JVs under EC Competition Law

Benefits of JVs. In contrast to many of the horizontal agreements considered in **7.019** Chapter 5 above, competition analysis perceives many JVs as likely in general terms to increase, rather than reduce, competition. Joint research and development may lead to new and better products being developed more quickly and efficiently; joint production may enhance efficiency and reduce costs.[62] The cost of developing or improving a product may otherwise be too great for either parent to proceed alone and/or the venture may require particular skills or abilities which

---

[59] Reg 2658/2000: see paras 7.097 *et seq*, below.

[60] Reg 2659/2000: see paras 7.078 *et seq*, below.

[61] By reason of Art 3 of Reg 1/2003.

[62] See *XVth Report on Competition Policy* (1985), point 26, as follows: '[J]oint ventures can contribute to a number of general economic objectives: (i)integration of the internal market, especially by means of cross-border co-operation; (ii) facilitation of risky investments; (iii) promotion of innovation and transfer of technology; (iv) development of new markets; (v) improvement of the competitiveness of Community industry; (vi) strengthening the competitive position of small and medium sized firms; (vii) elimination of structural overcapacity.' See also the Preamble to the *Antitrust Guidelines for Collaborations Among Competitors* (2000) issued by the US Dept of Justice and the Federal Trade Commission and available on *http://www.ftc.gov/opp/jointvent* ('*US Competitor Collaboration Guidelines*'): 'Competitive forces are driving firms toward complex collaborations to achieve goals such as expanding into foreign markets, funding expensive innovation efforts, and lowering production and other costs. Such collaborations often are not only benign but procompetitive.' For illustrative cases, see Section 7, below. For reference to the economic litereature on JVs, see Ribstein and Kobayashi (n 3, above).

neither parent could supply by itself. A JV may thus create a new competitive force in the market place or it may enable the parents to improve on products in a sector in which they were already active. More generally, JVs may enable smaller undertakings to compete more effectively with larger undertakings.

7.020 **Possible anti-competitive effects of JVs.** The establishment of the JV itself may have anti-competitive effects when the combination in a single enterprise of activities previously carried out by independent undertakings means that the creation of the new enterprise itself leads to a significant impediment to competition, for example if the JV has, or is likely to achieve, a dominant position in the market. This aspect is often referred to as the structural effect of the JV. However, for both full- and partial function JVs, the cooperation between the parents may bring about a reduction of competition such as, most obviously, the competition which would (or might) otherwise have existed between them in the market of the JV, or may stifle further innovation by removing a likely innovator from the competitive process.[63] The parents may either entirely cease their independent activities in that sector with regard to a particular product or territory (or both) or partially withdraw from that sector. This diminution of actual or potential competition will be even greater if the JV agreement carries the risk of 'spill-over', ie of coordination in markets outside the JV's market.[64] The JV may also have foreclosure effects where its activity has a vertical relationship to the activities of the parents: it may, for example, reduce the opportunities for third parties to act as suppliers to, or customers of, the JV's parents, which is a particular concern where the industry concerned is already concentrated.[65] The Commission has also expressed concerns about 'network effects', ie the anti-competitive potential associated with the creation of a series of parallel, commonly-controlled JVs.[66]

7.021 **Initial application of Article 81 to all JVs.** Prior to the adoption of the original Merger Regulation in 1989, the Commission could rely only on Article 81 as an instrument for controlling JVs. This encouraged the Commission to adopt an expansive approach to the application of Article 81(1) to JVs, thereby obtaining jurisdiction to examine a broad range of JV agreements. The Commission commonly considered the JV parents to be at least potential competitors and also readily found that there was a likelihood of an appreciable effect on competition for the purposes of Article 81(1).[67] Although block exemptions were issued for

---

[63] JVs can 'lead to market sharing, raising of barriers to entry, and the intensification of market power' (*XVth Report on Competition Policy* (1985), point 26 and for actual/potential competition, see Section 3, below. See also *GEC/Weir*, OJ 1977 L327/26, [1978] 1 CMLR D42, and the discussion of that decision in Faull & Nikpay (n 44, above) 668.

[64] See paras 7.046 *et seq*, below. Note that the Commission uses the term 'spill-over' in a broader sense to cover any effect on the behaviour of the parents, whether in the market of the JV or in other markets.

[65] See paras 7.048 *et seq*, below.

[66] See paras 7.050 *et seq*, below.

[67] See paras 2.121 *et seq*, above.

specialisation agreements and R&D agreements,[68] the latter in particular was of limited application and JV agreements that fell outside those categories were subject to the uncertain and protracted application of the Article 81(3) conditions under the then applicable Regulation 17 procedures.

The introduction of the Merger Regulation.   By 1990 there were signs that the **7.022** Commission's traditional approach to the application of Article 81(1) would on occasion give way to a more detailed, economically-based analysis of the impact of the JV on competition.[69] Although it is impossible to trace a consistent line of development, the decision in *Elopak/Metal Box-Odin*,[70] discussed in detail below, provides a clear exposition of the more sensitive and flexible analytical framework for the assessment of JVs under Article 81(1). When the Community introduced a regime for merger control in 1989, the original Merger Regulation applied also to JVs that did not give rise to the 'coordination' of the competitive behaviour of the parties.[71] A concentrative JV that met the threshold of the Merger Regulation was thereafter appraised under faster procedures and according to a single test of whether it created or strengthened a dominant position as a result of which effective competition would be impeded in the common market. Unless that was held to be the result, the JV was declared compatible with the common market and thereby received permanent approval.

Amendment of the Merger Regulation.   The first amendment of the Merger **7.023** Regulation in 1997 removed the difficult and awkward distinction between concentrative and cooperative JVs.[72] All full-function JVs became concentrations, even if they had coordinative effects. Any such coordinative effects were still assessed under Article 81(1) but within the Merger Regulation procedure.[73] Partial function JVs or full-function JVs without a Community dimension remained outside the Merger Regulation and were exclusively regulated by Article 81. Substantively, the Commission sought to bring some consistency of approach to an area where this had often been distinctly lacking.[74] In the context of some

---

[68] Reg 417/85 (specialisation) and Reg 418/85 (R&D). For the current block exemptions, see paras 7.097–7.103 and 7.078–7.086 *et seq*, below.

[69] Already in its *XIIIth Report on Competition Policy* (1983), points 53–55, the Commission committed itself to 'make its assessment of potential competition in the most realistic way possible.' See also Faull, 'JVs under the EEC Competition Rules' (1984) ECLR 358.

[70] *Elopak/Metal Box-Odin*, OJ 1990 L209/15, [1991] 4 CMLR 832. See para 7.105, below.

[71] Reg 4064/89, Art 3(2), prior to 1997 amendment.

[72] By Reg 1310/97, OJ 1997 L180/1 (corrected OJ 1998 L3/16, L40/17), which deleted the relevant passages from Art 3(2) of Reg 4064/89 (the original version of which was published (as corrected) at OJ 1990 L257/13).

[73] Art 2(4) of Reg 4064/89, as amended.

[74] See Temple Lang (n 2, above): 'In future, the apparent differences in style and approach in the past between the Commission's handling of JVs under Reg 17 and under the EC Merger Reg will disappear, and a single intermediate economics-based approach will emerge more clearly'. See also Faull & Nikpay (n 44, above) 678–679.

significant cases, many of which are concerned with the telecommunications market,[75] the Commission seemed prepared to conduct a more realistic economic assessment of the likelihood of the parents being potential competitors and the extent of the effect of any restrictions when considering whether the JV will have an 'appreciable' effect on the market concerned.

7.024 **Modernisation of Article 81 enforcement.**   In May 2004 there was a sea change in the procedures for enforcing Article 81 with the introduction of Regulation 1/2003 as a new implementing regulation.[76] The 'prior authorisation' system, whereby application of Article 81(3) could be achieved only as a block exemption or as an individual exemption following advance notification, was replaced by a 'directly applicable exception' system, whereby Article 81(3) became directly applicable alongside Article 81(1) without the need (or ability) to pre-notify the agreement. The reform also removed the Commission's monopoly on granting individual exemptions under Article 81(3) and allows national courts or competition authorities to apply Article 81(3) in cases which come before them.[77]

7.025 **No prior clearance for JVs.**   The fact that particularly structural JVs can no longer be notified for prior exemption under Article 81(3) attracted considerable criticism as providing insufficient legal certainty for some major investments.[78] Such uncertainty is not limited to the substantive issue of whether or not an agreement is void but also to the procedural uncertainty that the JV could be examined or attacked by a number of national competition authorities and/or national courts.[79] The Commission still retains the right to take a decision 'on its own initiative' that Article 81 is inapplicable to an agreement either because the agreement falls outside Article 81(1) or because the conditions of Article 81(3) are satisfied.[80] However, such decisions are reserved for exceptional cases of Community public interest, for example where this involves a new type of agreement or one not covered by pre-existing Commission practice. Although parties may seek informal 'guidance' from the Commission on novel questions of Article 81,[81] such guidance letters (and even more so formal decisions) are reserved

---

[75] See, eg *Cégétel + 4*, para 7.121, below, (a full-function JV notified in 1997 under the then Reg 17 regime but which now would be considered under the amended Merger Reg).

[76] Reg 1/2003 OJ 2003 L1/1, Vol II, App B.3. See generally para 1.058, above for modernisation and Chap 13, below for procedure under the new Reg.

[77] Reg 1/2003, Arts 1(3), 5 and 6.

[78] See, eg 'Reforming EC Competition Procedures' HL Select Committee on the European Union, Session 1999–2000, 4th Report (HL Paper 33).

[79] For a detailed discussion on case allocation within the ECN see Chap 13, below and Brammer, 'Concurrent Jurisdiction under Reg 1/2003 and the Issue of Case Allocation' (2005) 42 CML Rev 1383.

[80] Reg 1/2003 (n 76, above) Art 10 and Recital (14).

[81] ibid, Recital (38). See Commission Notice on informal guidance relating to novel questions concerning Articles 81 and 82 of the EC Treaty that arise in individual cases ('Informal Guidance Notice'), OJ 2004 C101/78: Vol II, App B.11.

for exceptional cases of Community public interest, for example where this involves a new type of agreement or one not covered by pre-existing Commission practice. The fact that a particular transaction involves significant investments (but is insufficiently structural to qualify for assessment under the Merger Regulation) will not in itself justify a decision or guidance letter.[82]

Judicial review of Commission decisions. Under the previous *ex ante* **7.026** notification system, the Commission tended to grant individual exemption to notified JVs (or to give a negative clearance 'comfort letter'), albeit sometimes after requiring amendment to the transaction. The parties therefore generally had no incentive to seek judicial review of the Commission's decision (if there was a formal decision at all).[83] None of the cases where a JV was actually prohibited by the Commission has been the subject of a judicial decision.[84] However, in *European Night Services*,[85] decided in 1998, the Court of First Instance quashed the Commission's decision that the JV established by four railway companies for the operation of night passenger transport services through the Channel Tunnel came within Article 81(1). The Court held that the Commission's finding that the JV was likely to restrict competition was vitiated by an inadequate analysis of the actual market conditions. The judgment emphasises the need for an economically realistic approach to the application of Article 81(1) to JVs:

'. . . it must be borne in mind that in assessing an agreement under Article [81(1)], account should be taken of the relevant conditions in which it functions, in particular the economic context in which undertakings operate, the products or

---

[82] Informal Guidance Notice, para 8(b) mentions this as only one among a number of considerations that need to be satisfied.

[83] In Case T-17/93 *Matra Hachette v Commission* [1994] ECR II–595, a third party competitor unsuccessfully challenged the grant of individual exemption to a JV, but in that case the application of Art 81(1) was not in doubt. Note that even when the Commission considered that a JV merited exemption, it often closed the case by a comfort letter. See also Case T-300/04 *easyjet v Commission*, not yet decided: challenge by a competitor to the Commission's decision of 7 April 2004 granting exemption, subject to commitments, to the *Air France/KLM* strategic alliance.

[84] Proceedings were started before the CFI to challenge the prohibition decision in *Screen Sport/ EBU*, OJ 1991 L63/32, [1992] 5 CMLR 273, but the case was discontinued.

[85] Cases T-374/94, etc, *ENS v Commission* [1998] ECR II–3141, [1998] 5 CMLR 718. This was an appeal against an exemption granted only on conditions and for eight years, claiming that the JV should have been granted negative clearance: see para 2.085, above. See also Case T-328/03 *O2 (Germany) GmbH v Commission* [2006] ECR II-1231, [2006] 5 CMLR 258: successful appeal against decision finding that a mobile telecommunications roaming agreement came within Art 81(1) although it had been granted exemption for a limited period under Art 81(3); see further para 7.127, below. And note the proceedings brought by the parties to the arrangement in *TPS*, paras 7.115 *et seq*, below, challenging the finding that certain restrictions in an agreement otherwise given negative clearance were not ancillary and should receive exemption for only a short period: Case T-112/99 *Métropole Télévision-M6 v Commission* (n 46, above).

services covered by the agreement and the actual structure of the market concerned'.[86]

Only if an agreement contained 'obvious restrictions of competition', such as price fixing, market sharing or control of outlets, could the Commission readily conclude that Article 81(1) applied and proceed to consider the claimed pro-competitive effects in the context of an exemption under Article 81(3).

7.027 **Horizontal Cooperation Guidelines.** The *European Night Services* judgment reinforced the need for the Commission to abandon its broad view of the application of Article 81(1) to JVs in favour of a more economically realistic assessment of a JV's potential effect on competition.[87] Following its similar approach as regards vertical agreements,[88] in November 2000, the Commission issued Guidelines on the applicability of Article 81 to horizontal cooperation agreements ('the Horizontal Cooperation Guidelines').[89] The Guidelines set out an analytical framework for the analysis of the common forms of potentially beneficial horizontal cooperation. They therefore include, but are not restricted to, JVs but they expressly do not cover agreements on the exchange of information or minority shareholdings or strategic alliances.[90] The Guidelines also do not apply to sectors that are covered by specific rules, ie the various transport sectors and insurance.[91] Concentrations falling within the Merger Regulation are not covered by the Guidelines. The Guidelines enunciate and clarify the more economically-based approach to assessment of horizontal agreements that has been developed by the Commission in recent years. The key elements for analysis are the market power of the parties and the structure of the market in which the cooperation takes place. The Horizontal Cooperation Guidelines are stated to replace not only the Commission's Notice on Cooperation Agreements (1968)[92] but also the 1993 Cooperative JV Notice.[93] However, the new Guidelines make scant reference to the case law whereas the Cooperative JV Notice refers to many of the Commission's decisions and still appears helpful in its conceptual approach to various forms of JV. Accordingly, in this work reference continues to be made to the Cooperative

---

[86] *ENS v Commission*, ibid, para 136. The CFI also cites (at para 137) with approval the Cooperative JV Notice (n 5, above) para 18, to that effect, proceeding to find that the Commission had failed to adopt such an approach in this case.

[87] See further para 7.044, below.

[88] See paras 6.006 *et seq*, above.

[89] Horizontal Cooperation Guidelines, OJ 2001 C3/2, Vol II, App C.12.

[90] The Guidelines state that exchange of information and shareholding agreements will be 'addressed separately' (para 10). Strategic alliances are considered too complex an amalgam of arrangements to be the subject of general guidelines (para 12).

[91] ibid, para 13. For insurance, see Chap 12, below.

[92] Notice on Cooperation Agreements, OJ 1968 C75/3: see the 4th edn of this work.

[93] Cooperative JV Notice (n 5, above).

JV Notice but that should now be read in the context of the Horizontal Cooperation Guidelines.

Categories under the Guidelines.   Reference to the general approach of the   **7.028**
Horizontal Cooperation Guidelines is made throughout this Chapter. However, as well as a general section, the Guidelines consider cooperation arrangements more specifically in six categories:

(i)   R&D agreements;
(ii)   Production agreements, including agreements on specialisation;
(iii) Joint purchasing agreements;
(iv)   'Commercialisation' agreements: this embraces collaboration in marketing and selling, distribution and promotion such as advertising;
(v)   Standardisation agreements: that is agreements that cover technical or quality standards;
(vi)   Environmental agreements: that is agreements intended to achieve environmental objectives, including the abatement of pollution.

'Centre of gravity' test.   The first two categories, which are particularly impor-   **7.029**
tant in the context of JVs, are given further consideration in Sections 5 and 6 of this Chapter. The other forms of agreement are discussed in Chapter 5, above. However, many agreements combine different forms of collaboration. The Commission has therefore adopted the concept of the 'centre of gravity' of the cooperation, to be determined on the basis of the starting point of the collaboration, and the degree of integration of the different functions being combined.[94] The relevant section of the Guidelines will be that which corresponds to the centre of gravity of the arrangements. For example, a JV that involves R&D leading, if successful, to joint production, is classified as an R&D agreement given that R&D is the starting point of the cooperation. On the other hand, if there is only partial cooperation on R&D but full integration of production facilities is envisaged, this would be examined as a production agreement. While some cases will be obvious, this approach illustrates the impossibility of strict categorisation and the need to scrutinise each JV on the facts.

Block exemptions.   Together with the Horizontal Cooperation Guidelines, the   **7.030**
Commission issued revised block exemptions to replace Regulations 417/85 and 418/85, the block exemptions for specialisation agreements and for R&D agreements, which expired on 31 December 2000. Regulations 2658/2000 and 2659/2000 are described in Sections 5 and 6 below. They reflect the more economically-based approach set out in the Guidelines. The revised block exemptions recognise that most agreements of this kind should satisfy the

---

[94] Horizontal Cooperation Guidelines (n 89, above) para 12.

conditions of Article 81(3), provided that the parties' market share is limited[95] and that the agreement does not include certain 'hard-core' restrictions.

3. The Application of Article 81(1) to Joint Ventures

(a) Generally

7.031 **The Commission's approach.** In its pre-modernisation decisions, the Commission developed a two-stage analysis of JVs under Article 81(1). They are examined first to establish whether their very formation is anti-competitive; and secondly, to ascertain if the JV agreement contains specific anti-competitive restrictions. For the first stage, the primary issue is whether the mere existence of the JV and its interrelationship with the parents or other parties may have a restrictive effect on competition. For the second stage, each specific restriction is analysed to establish whether it is directly related to and necessary for the JV (and therefore 'ancillary') or an additional restriction that requires independent assessment. The same approach applies in the self-assessment of post-modernisation JVs.

7.032 **Form of the JV.** The legal form of a JV is not material to the applicability of Article 81. The relevant factor is the economic reality of the situation. The Commission has in the past reviewed under Article 81 the establishment of unlimited partnerships,[96] entities established by contract alone[97] and business associations without legal personality.[98]

7.033 **Effect on competition: markets which can be affected.** It must be established whether competition may be affected in either the JV's market or other markets. A JV that sells products manufactured by its parents is likely to eliminate competition between them in respect of the sales of those products (ie on the JV market) and will generally be treated as a joint selling agreement.[99] Other affected markets may be related to the JV market in that they are immediately upstream of, or downstream to that market; or may be unrelated ('adjacent') markets. The effect of restrictions on competition affecting such related and unrelated markets are generally referred to as 'spill-over effects' of the formation of the JV.[100]

---

[95] Subject to a safety margin, the limits are 25 per cent for R&D agreements and 20 per cent for production/specialisation agreements.

[96] eg *Optical Fibres*, OJ 1986 L236/30.

[97] eg *GEC/Weir* (n 63, above).

[98] eg *De Laval/Stork*, OJ 1977 L215/11, [1977] 2 CMLR D69.

[99] eg *Floral*, OJ 1980 L39/51, [1980] 2 CMLR 285. See paras 5.106 *et seq*, above.

[100] Note that the Commission (and writings by Commission officials) use the term 'spill-over' in a broader sense to mean all the economic effects on the behaviour of the JV parents or third parties, including those in the JV market (eg Faull & Nikpay (n 44, above) 672–676).

Effect on competition: persons who may be affected. It must be established **7.034**
whether the JV itself will have a dominant position on a particular market,[101] and
whether either the JV itself or any specific provisions in the agreements:

— are likely to restrict or distort competition between the parents themselves or
   between the JV and one or more of its parents; or
— have a restrictive effect on competition with third parties.

The Commission stated in the now superseded Cooperative JV Notice that the
effect on competition as between the JV and its parents requires assessment only
in the case of a full-function JV.[102] However, Article 2(4) of the Merger Regulation
appears to provide that the Article 81 appraisal of a full-function JV falling under
the merger regime is directed only at potential coordination between the parents.
That is a more restricted scrutiny than had previously been applied by the
Commission under Article 81 to such cases outside the merger regime (ie before
the Merger Regulation was amended in 1997). Where a full-function JV does not
have a Community dimension, and therefore does not fall under the Merger
Regulation, it appears that an appreciable restriction of competition as between
the JV and one or more parents that was not directly related to and necessary for
the JV, could still infringe Article 81.[103]

(b) Formation of the JV

Key indicators of applicability of Article 81(1). When the Commission **7.035**
considers the effect of the formation of a JV, it reviews several areas of possible
concern. There are four principal indicators of a restriction on competition;
removal of actual or potential competitors; spill-over effect; foreclosure effect; and
network effect.

Removal of actual or potential competitors. Where the parents are *actual* com- **7.036**
petitors, the Commission has in the past generally assumed that the establishment
of the JV will reduce at least the intensity of competition between the parents.
It is also likely to lead to an exchange of information and therefore a coordination
of policy, unless cooperation through the JV is the only way for the parents to
remain in that market. However, the Commission now recognises that there
may well not be an anti-competitive effect from a production JV established by

---

[101] Art 81 is generally the relevant provision for dominance issues as regards the establishment
of a JV. But where either one parent individually or both parents jointly already hold a dominant
position on the market, it could be an abuse under Art 82 for them to set up a JV that eliminated
further what little competition existed between them: see Temple Lang (n 2, above) 435–436. Art 82
could of course also apply in the usual way to subsequent conduct by the JV.

[102] Cooperative JV Notice, OJ 1993 C43/2, Vol II, App C.9, para 17.

[103] See González-Díaz, 'Joint Ventures under EC Competition Law: the New Boundaries', in
Mélanges M. Waelbrock (1999), Vol II, 1019 at 1027, 1046.

competitors that results in only a low commonality of total costs.[104] If the parents are *potential* competitors who could have entered the JV's market independently, in whatever is considered a reasonable period in the circumstances, there could be an anti-competitive effect, as the JV probably reduces the likelihood of separate entry into the market by one or both parents or limits the possibility of a company associated with one parent from competing with a company in the group of the other parent. If the parents are not potential or actual competitors, a JV could only exceptionally come within Article 81(1) where it involves one or more dominant firms and is likely to lead to problems of foreclosure as regards third parties.[105]

7.037 'Spill-over' effects.   Whether the parents are competitors in any related or even unrelated markets or whether the JV (if full-function) may become a competitor of a parent in such other markets, the Commission considers whether the JV is likely to have a spill-over effect.[106] Spill-over effects may result from express contractual provisions, or simply be a foreseeable consequence of the effect of the JV on its parents' activities or of the effect of the parents' direct relationship with the JV. Even where there is no active coordination in such other markets, there may be a lessening of the competitive tension between the parents in those fields.[107]

7.038 'Foreclosure' effects.   A JV may have foreclosure effect if it reduces any commercial opportunities for others.[108] The issue is whether the JV results in the foreclosure of competitive opportunity for a third party or for one of the parents in a market where the other parent is active. If the JV supplies its parents with goods or services, this may effectively prevent competing third parties from being their suppliers. Similarly, if the parents constitute the major customer(s) for the JV's products, then other potential customers may be unable to acquire products required for their businesses. Alternatively, the JV may result in vertical integration between the JV and its parents, thereby increasing the likelihood of exclusive dealing by the parents with the JV. Specific restrictions, such as exclusive supply or licensing arrangements, can also create a foreclosure effect.

7.039 'Network' effects.   Where the JV is part of a network of two or more competing JVs, there is a possibility of coordination of behaviour by several JVs, such as geographic market sharing.[109] It is therefore important to establish whether the JV is part of a series of JVs between the same two (or more) parents or belongs to a network of JVs connecting different parent companies.

---

104 See the Horizontal Cooperation Guidelines (n 89, above) para 88 and para 7.044, below.
105 Para 7.049, below; and see Horizontal Cooperation Guidelines (n 89, above) para 24.
106 Note that in this work 'spill-over' refers to the effect on a market other than that of the JV.
107 See *GEC/Weir* (n 63, above).
108 See paras 7.048 *et seq*, below.
109 See paras 7.050 *et seq*, below.

Article 81(1): practical approach for the parties.   If it appears that the forma-   **7.040**
tion of the JV may have an anti-competitive effect because certain of these key
indicators are present, the extent of that effect has to be assessed. If it is likely to be
appreciable, the parties should consider whether the agreement falls within the
production/specialisation or R&D block exemptions[110] or whether it is possible
to structure the JV in such a way that it becomes full-function so that it can be
notified under the Merger Regulation. If, however, none of the indicators listed
above is present, Article 81(1) should not apply to the formation of the JV as such.
In those circumstances it is nonetheless necessary to proceed to the second stage
of analysis and consider whether Article 81(1) applies to any of the specific restrictions contained in the JV agreement.[111]

Effect on competition: 'appreciability'.   The Horizontal Cooperation Guide-   **7.041**
lines emphasise that Article 81(1) will not necessarily apply even if the agreement
limits competition between the parties. The agreement must also reduce competition in the market to such an extent that negative market effects as to prices, output, innovation or the variety or quality of goods and services can be expected.[112]
In assessing such effects, it is important to 'distinguish between effects which are
certain to occur (but which may not be very important) and effects (such as lessening the chances of independent entry by the parent companies) which are not
certain (since they might not have entered separately) but which would be important if they did occur'.[113] Where the object of a JV is to restrict competition by
means of 'hard-core' restrictions, such as price-fixing, limitation of output or
market sharing (whether for suppliers, areas or customers), the agreement will
usually be presumed to have the effect of appreciably distorting competition. Save
in those cases, the relevant considerations will be the areas and extent of cooperation, and how close these are to the marketing level. Therefore cooperation only
on R&D will in general be less likely to have an appreciable effect on competition
than cooperation on production.[114]

Appreciability and market share.   If the parties (and their connected undertak-   **7.042**
ings) have only a low market share, it is unlikely that the agreement has an appreciable effect on competition in the market.[115] Even if the combined market share is
high, it is necessary to consider the individual shares of the parties. If one party
has only an insignificant share, its combination in a JV with a party that already
has a high share is unlikely to cause any appreciable further restrictive effect

---

[110] See paras 7.097-7.103 and 7.078-7.086, below.
[111] See paras 7.052 *et seq*, below.
[112] Horizontal Cooperation Guidelines, OJ 2001 C3/2, Vol II, App C.12, para 19.
[113] Temple Lang (n 2, above), at 390.
[114] See, respectively, paras 7.071 and 7.090 *et seq*, below.
[115] The Horizontal Cooperation Guidelines state (para 28) that in those circumstances no further analysis is required. For a discussion of market definition see Chap 4, above.

on competition. If the addition of market shares is significant, the following are the most important criteria for assessment of the situation: whether the relevant product and geographic market is competitive or concentrated; the market shares of the competitors; the economic and financial strengths of the parents and any technological or commercial advantages which they have; and the extent to which there are barriers to entry by third parties.[116] Whether the parents are vertically integrated may be significant in this context. Other issues which may be important are the presence of price transparency, stable prices, stable market shares, market size, stable technology, competitors' spare capacity or lack of it, the likelihood or otherwise of new market entrants and the size and negotiating strength of buyers.

7.043 **Effect on competition: causation.** Article 81(1) should similarly apply only if the creation of the JV (rather than any other factor such as previous links between the parent companies) is the real cause of the probable coordination of the competitive behaviour of the parents. Whilst there has hitherto been no specific reference to this aspect in the case law or associated Notices concerning JVs under Article 81(1), the Commission's decisions under the amended Merger Regulation applying the Article 81(1) test to the coordinative aspects of JVs have considered causation as a distinct aspect. In several cases the Commission has concluded that, while there were potential markets for coordination, in the particular circumstances either this was unlikely to happen[117] or, if it did happen, it would not be as a result of the JV.[118] This aspect overlaps with the question of appreciable effect discussed above. As regards both issues, it is to be expected that the Commission's approach to the analysis of JVs in cases coming under the Merger Regulation will be adopted in cases falling outside that Regulation.[119]

(c) Actual or potential competitors

7.044 **The emergence of a realistic economic analysis.** As stated above, if the parents are actual competitors in the product and geographical markets of the JV and have reasonably large market shares, the Commission used to assume that there would be a restriction on competition. However, the Horizontal Cooperation Guidelines

---

[116] See Horizontal Cooperation Guidelines (n 112, above) paras 29–30. Barriers to the entry of third parties may include the existence of patents, exclusive distribution arrangements, long-term supply contracts with large buyers and the high cost of changing suppliers.

[117] eg Case JV.1 *Telia/Telenor/Schibsted* [1999] 4 CMLR 216 (coordination unlikely on the dial-up internet access market despite the parents' high market shares because the market is characterised by high growth and relatively low barriers to entry).

[118] eg Case JV.2 *ENEL/FT/DT*, Decn of 22 June 1998, paras 37–39 (coordination the result not of the Wind JV but of the parents' previous association through Atlas/GlobalOne approved by the Commission in 1996). See Faull & Nikpay (n 44, above) p 684 n 91.

[119] See paras 7.023, *et seq*, above. As most non-Merger Reg JV cases did not result in a formal, published decision, even pre-modernisation, this trend is not immediately apparent.

recognise that, for production JVs, it is necessary to consider also the proportion of the parties' total costs that become common costs.[120] For example, where the JV concerns manufacture of an intermediate product and the costs of such manufacture represent only a small part of the total costs of production of the final product into which the JV product will be incorporated, an effect on the parties' competitive behaviour is unlikely. Traditionally, if the parents were not actual competitors the Commission was quick to find that they were potential competitors.[121] Its decisions in this regard were based on 'presumptions related to the previous activities and expertise of the parent companies, their theoretical access to the necessary technology and their financial resources'.[122] Subsequently, however, as with actual competitors, the Commission sought to take a more realistic approach, considering whether the parents are indeed potential competitors given the nature of the product or activity and the market concerned, so that individual entry into the market of the JV needs to be more than just a theoretical possibility. Several decisions taken in the 1990s display a much more sensitive and thorough assessment.[123] The strictures of the Court of First Instance when it annulled the Commission's 1994 decision in *European Night Services*[124] reinforces this approach. In reaching a view, therefore, one needs to ascertain the *real concrete possibilities* which exist for competition by the parents or other parties. The time frame within which the parents would be able to enter the market independently must also be realistic.[125] Accordingly, although the parents may be competitors in a market

---

[120] Horizontal Cooperation Guidelines (n 112, above) para 88.

[121] eg *KEWA*, OJ 1976 L51/15, [1976] 2 CMLR D15 (JV to erect plant for nuclear fuel reprocessing); *Vacuum Interrupters (No. 1)*, OJ 1977 L48/32, [1977] 1 CMLR D67 (JV to develop produce and sell vacuum interrupters).

[122] Faull & Nikpay (n 44, above) p 670.

[123] See, eg *Elopak/Metal Box-Odin* (n 70, above) (negative clearance for JV to research, develop and produce a new form of paperboard-based carton with laminated metal lid; parents not actual or potential competitors outside JV but new JV vehicle might become competitor of one of them); *Konsortium ECR 900*, OJ 1990 L228/31, [1992] 4 CMLR 54 (negative clearance for JV to develop a new digital cellular mobile telephone system, which parties could not do individually because of high costs involved); cf *Philips-Osram*, OJ 1994 L378/37, where the Commission found that Osram had the financial, technical and research capabilities to set up a new facility to manufacture independently the JV product (lead glass); *KSB/Goulds/Lowara/ITT*, OJ 1991 L19/25, [1992] 5 CMLR 55 (JV for R&D of advanced pump components for water pumps where the Commission found that the parties were potential competitors as each would have been able to acquire the basic technology necessary, eg by licensing; the fact that individual development would not have been cost-effective because of the lower volume of production was dismissed on the basis that development costs could be recouped in other ways). In both the latter cases, Reg 418/85 was inapplicable because the particular market shares exceeded the threshold set by the block exemption, and individual exemptions were granted. See also the careful evaluation of the prospects for competition as regards the different vaccines to be developed by the JV in *Pasteur Mérieux-Merck*, OJ 1994 L309/1, paras 59–69.

[124] Case T-374/94, etc, *ENS v Commission* [1998] ECR II–3141, [1998] 5 CMLR 718, paras 137 *et seq*.

[125] See, eg *Konsortium ECR 900* (n 123, above) para 25 (parties could not individually meet the tight deadlines imposed by national network operators for development and supply of GSM system).

closely related to that of the JV, they may not be potential competitors in the JV market itself.[126] Many of the more recent Commission decisions which evidence such an approach are in the telecommunications industry.[127] That market is characterised by very fast change, necessitating a pragmatic assessment of the potential current and future coordinative effects of JVs.[128] In such cases, one may conclude that the parents are not potential competitors if the JV's product uses advanced technology in which at least one parent has no or little experience. Further, the greater the funding required and the risks undertaken in such projects, the more likely is it to conclude that the parents are not potential competitors.[129]

7.045 **Assessment of a party's capability to achieve task alone.** The now superseded Cooperative JV Notice published in 1993[130] set out certain questions which aim to clarify whether any party alone is in a position to fulfil the tasks assigned to the JV and, if so, whether it ceases to be likely to do so as a result of the creation of the JV. Although framed in terms of a production JV, the questions are relevant also to other types of JV. If the parents 'could reasonably be expected to act autonomously' in the light of the factors identified in those questions, then the parents are potential competitors. However, these factors may be given different weight in varying circumstances. The criteria should now be applied in the light of the Commission's more realistic appraisal of the commercial circumstances discussed above. The questions relate to the research and development, production, marketing and sales stages of a JV's operations and are as follows:

(i) *Contribution to the JV*—Does each parent company have sufficient financial resources to carry out the planned investment? Does each parent company have sufficient managerial qualifications to run the JV? Does each parent company have access to the necessary input products?

---

126 Horizontal Cooperation Guidelines (n 112, above) para 82. As is often the case, market definition can be critical to the analysis.

127 But see also for an airline strategic alliance, the Commission's assessment that Alitalia was not a potential competitor to Air France on the Paris–Turin route: *Air France/Alitalia*, 7 April 2004, [2005] 5 CMLR 1504, paras 111-126.

128 Temple Lang, 'Telecommunications JVs and the revised European Community Merger Regulation' (1999) BLI 1 at 4. For telecoms generally see Chap 12, below. See, eg *Cégétel + 4*, para 7.121, below (four-party JV to provide full telecommunications service in France in competition with France Télécom). But where the parents include incumbent telecommunications operators, an effect on actual or potential competition is generally found: see the decisions on major JVs in *Atlas*, OJ 1996 L239/23, [1997] 4 CMLR 89; *Phoenix/GlobalOne*, OJ 1996 L239/57, [1997] 4 CMLR 147; *Unisource*, OJ 1997 L381/1, [1998] 4 CMLR 105; *Uniworld*, OJ 1997 L381/24, [1998] 4 CMLR 145; and *British Interactive Broadcasting Open ('BiB')*, OJ 1999 L312/1, [2000] 4 CMLR 901.

129 eg *International Private Satellite Partners*, OJ 1994 L354/75 (JV to provide international business telecommunications services using its own satellite system); *Iridium*, OJ 1997 L26/87, [1997] 4 CMLR 1065 (JV to provide global satellite wireless communications services via mobile telephones).

130 Cooperative JV Notice, OJ 1993 C43/2, Vol II, App C.9, para 19.

(ii) *Production by the JV*—Does each parent know the production technique? Does each parent make the upstream or downstream products itself and does it have access to the necessary production facilities?

(iii) *Sales by the JV*—Is actual or potential demand such as to enable each parent company to manufacture the product on its own? Does each parent company have access to the distribution channels needed to sell the product manufactured by the JV?

(iv) *Risk factors*—Can each parent company on its own bear the technical and financial risks associated with the production operations of the JV?

(v) *Access to the relevant market*—What is the relevant geographic and product market? What are the barriers to entry into that market? Is each parent company capable of entering that market on its own? Can each parent overcome existing barriers within a reasonable time and without undue effort or cost?

Furthermore, when multi-party cooperation is an essential element for the service that the JV provides, it may not be anti-competitive but in fact produce efficiencies even where it involves most competitors in the market, provided that it is conducted in a transparent fashion and with appropriate safeguards. This is particularly evident in arrangements to establish Business-to-Business (B2B) internet market places or jointly operated electronic platforms selling to consumers.[131]

(d) 'Spill-over'

'Spill-over' effects generally in related and unrelated markets. Spill-over effects   **7.046** (sometimes also referred to as 'group' effects) may result from express contractual clauses or simply be a foreseeable consequence of the effect of the JV on its parents' activities or of the parents' direct relationship with the JV. The Commission has set out its approach to spill-over effects on related markets as follows:[132]

> 'In cases involving input JVs[133] . . . the spill-over effects on the final product market depends principally on two factors: the importance of the jointly produced input in the cost of the final product (ratio of common cost/total final cost) and the market position of the parents. The higher the common cost and the combined market share of the parents in the final product market, the greater the risk of spill-over effects is likely to be. In the case of final product JVs, the commonality of costs and the proximity of the parents' co-operation to the final product market are such that

---

[131] See eg *Covisint*, Press Release IP/01/1155 (31 July 2001) and *XXXIst Report on Competition Policy* (2001), p 58 (Box 4): B2B e-marketplace created by most of the world's car manufacturers primarily to serve their procurement needs. See further paras 7.128–7.132, below.

[132] *XXIVth Report on Competition Policy* (1994), point 65. For an application of this approach, see *Exxon/Shell*, OJ 1994 L144/20 (a final product JV) para 63.

[133] See para 7.003, above.

appreciable spill-over effects are very likely to occur (for instance by alignment of sales prices), in particular where the parties have important market shares or operate in an oligopolistic market'.[134]

The Commission is also concerned about coordinative spill-over on adjacent or unrelated markets.[135] As with the question of whether the parents are potential competitors, the Commission is appraising the issue of the likelihood of appreciable coordination between the parents on the basis of more realistic economic analysis. In addition to the matters discussed above, such factors as the ownership and control structure of the JV, the size of the JV in comparison to that of the parents' separate operations and the duration of the agreement will, in general, be relevant to that assessment.[136]

7.047 **'Spill-over' effects in the case of a full-function JV.** An effect on competition as between the JV and one or more of its parents is generally relevant only in the case of a full-function JV.[137] Brodley[138] identifies several areas which can suffer from such spill-over effects. These are horizontal JVs (where the JV enters the market of one of the parents); market extensions (where the JV enters a different geographic market but the same product market as the parents); and product extensions

---

134 See, eg *Philips-Osram* (n 123, above) (JV to produce lead glass for lamps but despite parents' very high market share, the Commission found spill-over effect on lamp market to be insignificant as lead glass accounted for only c. 2–3 per cent of the final product cost. JV nonetheless held to be within Art 81(1) because of anti-competitive effect on market for lead glass; exemption granted). cf *Asahi/St Gobain*, OJ 1994 L 354/87 where a JV for R&D and licensing of bi-layer glass technology for windscreens, allowing parent companies to compete in finished products was granted exemption for 10 years although the parents together held over 50 per cent of European market: this case is discussed at paras 7.075 *et seq*, below; *Fujitsu/AMD Semi-conductor*, OJ 1994 L341/66 (JV to design, construct, and operate a plant to produce semi-conductor wafers of certain types of non-volatile memory (NVM); held to restrict competition between parents in NVM market but exemption granted). See also the final product JV, *Olivetti/Canon*, OJ 1988 L52/51, [1989] 4 CMLR 940 (JV to develop, design and produce copying, laser printer and facsimile products, which were then sold independently by the parents using their own distribution networks and brand names; held that each party had less autonomy in sales pricing than if production costs were different but exemption granted).

135 eg *Ford/Volkswagen*, OJ 1993 L20/14, [1993] 5 CMLR 617, para 21: the Commission noted that the cooperation to make 'people carriers' would lead to extensive sharing of technical know-how 'which could affect the competitive behaviour of the two partners in neighbouring market segments like those of estate cars or light vans'; *GEAE/P&W*, OJ 2000 L58/16, [2000] 5 CMLR 49: full-function JV between two of the only three potential aircraft engine manufacturers to develop, manufacture and supply engines for future, very large commercial aircraft (Airbus A3XX and possible Stretch versions of Boeing B747–400), where the Commission was concerned also about potential coordination on the neighbouring market for engines for existing commercial wide-body aircraft on which the parents compete. See also *Atlas* (n 128, above), in which there was concern that neither parent would enter the other's domestic market after full telecommunications liberalisation.

136 For discussion of the economic literature on the coordinative effects of JVs, see González-Díaz (n 103, above) at 1035–1043.

137 See para 7.004, above.

138 Brodley, 'Joint Ventures and Antitrust Policy' (1982) 95 Harvard Law Rev. 1523.

(where the JV enters a product market different from, but related to, that of the parents). Even if the parents themselves do not compete in related or unrelated product markets, the product developed by the JV may sometimes be expected to compete to some extent with the existing products of one of the parents in a related market. In such circumstances there is a risk of the coordination of commercial behaviour between the JV and the parent in a related area. This might result in at least a softening of the competition that would otherwise have prevailed and, at worst, in market-sharing or price collusion. If one parent is an actual competitor of the JV in respect of such a related market and the other a potential competitor, this may result in collusion between the JV and the actual competitor or the loss of eventual competition by the potential competitor. The situation in respect of parties in a different product market but the same geographic market is particularly an issue in high technology industries, where the boundaries between product markets fluctuate.[139]

(e) Foreclosure

Foreclosure effects generally. Article 81(1) will apply to the establishment of a **7.048** JV if its creation alters the structure of the market in such a way as to make it appreciably more difficult for third parties to compete. This tends to arise when there is an element of exclusive dealing between the parents and the JV, either where the parents will be obliged, or are in fact likely, to purchase all their requirements of particular goods (or services) from the JV (thereby preventing competing suppliers from selling to the parents) or, conversely, where the JV will be obliged, or is likely, to supply goods (or services) only to its parents (thereby preventing its parents' competitors from obtaining their requirements).[140] The Commission's analysis in respect of foreclosure to a great extent depends upon the market power of the parents and the level of competition likely to prevail in the market after the establishment of the JV. Article 81(1) is more likely to apply where the market is concentrated.[141] Foreclosure can involve impeding the

---

[139] See, eg *BT/MCI(I)*, OJ 1994 L223/36, [1995] 5 CMLR 285 (JV to develop and market internationally value-added telecommunications services for large multinational companies and a reciprocal territorial non-compete obligation on the parents; exemption granted for seven years in respect of the JV itself and five years in respect of the territorial non-compete clause). Under the amended Merger Reg, the JV would constitute a concentration. Note that in *Unisource* (n 128, above) whereas the full-function JV between major telecommunications operators was at the outset held to fall clearly within Art 81(1) and exempted subject to detailed conditions, when the JV's activity was subsequently much reduced and the original exclusivity provisions ceased to apply, the JV was given negative clearance: OJ 2001 L52/30.

[140] See, eg *GEC/Weir* (n 63, above) where customers were faced with only one source of supply of the product concerned rather than two, and other third parties were restricted in their opportunities to participate with either the parents or the JV in development or manufacturing work.

[141] eg *Eirpage*, OJ 1991 L306/22, [1993] 4 CMLR 64; *Astra*, OJ 1993 L20/23, [1994] 5 CMLR 226.

growth of existing competitors of the parents and creating or increasing entry barriers for new entrants.[142] The Commission will consider the possibility of market entry by companies outside the JV's market and the parents' geographic market, and whether they would be independent entrants or possible partners of existing competitors. Foreclosure can also restrict the opportunities for former suppliers or customers.[143] For example, a JV is likely to reduce the willingness of its parents to cooperate with third parties in the same field. The combination of the JV's parents may also effectively deny third parties the possibility of operating in the JV's field if, for example, the combination gives the JV an entrenched advantage of some kind that others cannot match.[144] In addition, the JV agreements may contain specific arrangements which will have a similar foreclosing effect on third parties: for example, the grant to the JV of licences of key intellectual property rights or technology.[145]

7.049 **Foreclosure effects where a parent is in special or dominant position.** The process of liberalisation of the various telecommunications markets in the Community gave rise to foreclosure concerns. For example, the Commission reviewed several JVs which involved the incumbent monopolist telecommunications operator (TO) linking up with a partner in order to enter particular submarkets or adjacent markets. In such cases 'the Commission must examine whether the still existing special and/or exclusive rights of the TO in question cause its participation in the JV company to place the latter in an unjustifiably favourable position *vis-à-vis* competitors'.[146] Similarly, where a JV parent is the operator of a network infrastructure to which competitors may require access, there will be a risk of foreclosure by discrimination.[147]

---

[142] See, eg *Eurosport*, OJ 1991 L63/32, [1991] 4 CMLR 228, in which the Commission held that the formation of the JV gave rise to a foreclosure effect in the markets for (i) the broadcasting of sports programming; (ii) the acquisition of sports programming rights; and (iii) the marketing of cable distribution rights. See also *Elopak/Metal Box—Odin* (n 70, above) para 27: foreclosure effect was precluded by the fact that there were several other large competitors with at least equivalent know-how and access to the same or additional technology.

[143] See, eg *Optical Fibres* (n 96, above), where the agreements (as amended) provided *inter alia* that the JVs would sell to third parties on non-discriminatory terms and could obtain supplies from third parties. The JV may also impact adversely on the number and identity of suppliers and purchasers: see *Olivetti/Canon* (n 134, above), where the JV limited opportunities for manufacturers to supply the parents on an OEM basis, for distributors to purchase the JV's products from a parent for resale and for third parties to obtain manufacturing licences from either parent.

[144] See, eg the complaints in *KSB/Goulds/Lowara/ITT* (n 123, above) that the combination of JV partners would result in denying third parties the possibility of operating in the JV field since others alone or in combination could not achieve the requisite scale for entry. These complaints were rejected by the Commission on the facts. It seems that a JV with powerful parents may even be regarded as a 'psychological' deterrent to third party entry: *Eirpage* (n 141, above) para 12.

[145] See para 7.054(iv), below.

[146] *XXIIIrd Report on Competition Policy* (1993), point 218. See also paras 12.144 *et seq*, below.

[147] See, eg *Screensport/EBU members*, OJ 1991 L63/32, [1992] 5 CMLR 273.

(f) Network effect

Parallel JVs with the same parents. A situation of particular concern arises **7.050**
where a series of JVs is established, each with a common parent or parents. The
Commission has remarked that such networks of JVs can have a restrictive effect
on competition by intensifying 'the effects of individual JVs on the policy of the
parent undertakings and the market position of third parties'.[148] The Commission
considers that competition between the parents is reduced as a result of increasingly closer ties between them formed by each new JV.[149] Moreover, the existence
of two or more such JVs may evidence an agreement between the parents not to
enter certain markets separately, thereby foreclosing potential competition.

Parallel JVs connecting different parents. A network concern can also arise **7.051**
where competing parents set up several JVs for production and distribution, or in
respect of networks between non-competing parents where one parent is common to all the JVs. The concern may arise regardless of the fact that each JV, if
subjected to an individual analysis under Article 81(1), would not be considered
restrictive of competition. However, where the various JVs are not active in the
same market, it is necessary to show how the fact that there is a common parent or
parents has an actual anti-competitive effect.[150] Aside from this, a network of
interlocking JVs could create or contribute to collective dominance. They may
also provide the opportunity for a collusive exchange of information, especially if
all the members of an oligopoly are involved.

(g) Specific restrictions

Nature of restrictions. Once the JV itself has been examined, it is necessary to **7.052**
consider specific restrictions in the JV agreement. The restrictions may be express
or implicit. The Commission distinguishes between, on the one hand, restrictions
which are necessary and directly relevant to the JV and on the other hand

---

[148] *XXIVth Report on Competition Policy* (1994), point 187.
[149] See *Optical Fibres* (n 96, above) which established the Commission's view of network effect.
Corning established three JVs with makers of optical cables in France, Germany and the United
Kingdom. The Commission found no relevant restriction of competition as between the JV parents
in each country but held that because the arrangements created 'a network of interrelated JVs with
a common technology provider in an oligopolistic market' (para 48), competition between the JVs
themselves would be restricted within the meaning of Art 81(1). An exemption was granted after
various amendments were made to the agreements. For criticism of the Commission's analysis on the
facts, see Pathak, 'The EC Commission's Approach to Joint Ventures: A Policy of Contradictions'
(1991) ECLR 171, 178–179.
[150] On this basis the CFI annulled the Commission's finding of an anti-competitive network
effect arising from the JVs entered into by five public railway undertakings for the operation of
goods and passenger services for night passenger trains between the UK and continental Europe
using the Channel Tunnel, where each parent was involved in other JVs to transport goods through
the Tunnel: *ENS v Commission* (n 124, above) paras 155–160.

restrictions that are not intrinsic to the JV. The former are regarded as 'ancillary' to the JV while the latter are 'additional' restrictions. Since the Commission established this approach only in 1988–1990,[151] the analysis in earlier decisions should be approached with caution.

7.053 **Ancillary restrictions.** The Commission has described[152] ancillary restrictions as 'restrictions only imposed on the parties or the JV (not on third parties) which are objectively necessary for the successful functioning of the JV and thus by their very nature inherent in the operation concerned . . . '. Ancillary restrictions must be subordinate in importance to the main object of the JV. A restriction will therefore only be regarded as ancillary if it is no more than is *objectively* necessary to ensure the start-up and proper functioning of the JV. In that regard, the assessment is relatively abstract, based upon the nature of the JV rather than the competitive situation in the market. In *Métropole Télévision-M6*,[153] the Court of First Instance held that it is not a question of whether the restriction is indispensable to the *commercial* success of a JV but whether the JV would be difficult, if not impossible, to implement without it. Moreover, the Court stressed that necessity involves consideration not only of the nature of the restriction but whether it is proportionate: the duration and geographical scope of the restriction need to be evaluated. Any restriction which is not objectively necessary in that sense but which in a particular case may be commercially indispensable does not qualify as ancillary and therefore has to be assessed separately under Article 81(3). The Court rejected the parties' argument that such clauses should be subjected to a 'rule of reason', balancing the positive and negative effects of the restriction, under Article 81(1).[154] The ancillary restrictions concept is also used in the assessment of concentrations under the Merger Regulation. Merger decisions and the Commission's Ancillary Restraints Notice[155] therefore provide helpful guidance on this point for JVs under Article 81.[156]

---

[151] See in particular *Mitchell Cotts/Sofiltra*, OJ 1987 L41/31, [1988] 4 CMLR 111; *Elopak/Metal Box-Odin* (n 70, above).

[152] *XXIVth Report on Competition Policy* (1994), point 166.

[153] Case T-112/99 *Métropole Télévision-M6 v Commission* [2001] ECR II-2459, [2001] 5 CMLR 1236, [2002] All ER (EC) 1, paras 104–117. This gives a good judicial summary of the concept of ancillary restrictions and the consequences of being classified as such.

[154] paras 68–80 and, in particular, para 78. This aspect of the judgment is further considered at para 2.091, above.

[155] See the Notice on restrictions directly related and necessary to concentrations ('The Ancillary Restraints Notice') OJ 2005 C56/24, Vol II, App D.10, especially paras 36–44 and paras 8.263 *et seq*, below.

[156] The Commission's practice has evolved over time so that earlier merger decisions arrive at results that may differ from the Commission's more recent approach or that adopted in the Ancillary Restraints Notice.

Application of Article 81 to specific restrictions. Ancillary restrictions will not **7.054** be assessed separately from the JV itself. Therefore, if the JV itself does not fall within Article 81(1), nor do the ancillary restrictions. Conversely, if the JV itself falls within Article 81(1) and also fulfils the criteria of Article 81(3), the ancillary restrictions will also be covered without an independent evaluation. By contrast, restrictions that are not ancillary may fall within Article 81(1) where the JV does not. And even if the conditions of Article 81(3) are satisfied, the additional restrictions require separate evaluation.

Examples of ancillary restrictions. The new Horizontal Cooperation Guide- **7.055** lines do not explicitly address the question of specific restrictions.[157] However, the 1993 Cooperative JV Notice gave guidance as to what restrictions may be imposed on both the JV and on the parents as ancillary restrictions[158] and further illustrations are found in the Commission's decisions. The provisions below have been found to constitute ancillary restrictions:

(i) Restrictions on the parents competing with the JV, or with each other, as regards the specific activity of the JV. The Commission has moved away from its previous position whereby it generally accepted non-compete restrictions for the lifetime of the JV.[159] In *TPS*, the Commission limited the negative clearance which it granted to the partnership for the establishment and operation of a digital platform for satellite pay-TV services to three years on the ground that the non-competition clause could be classified as ancillary only during the launch period.[160] And in a number of relatively recent decisions under the Merger Regulation, the Commission was prepared to accept only a finite period of five years rather than the usual lifetime of a JV.[161] The new Ancillary Restraints Notice reverts back to the lifetime of the JV, however, but only in respect of controlling parents.[162] If a non-compete obligation extends beyond the JV's geographic field of operation or product

---

[157] Horizontal Cooperation Guidelines (n 112, above).

[158] OJ 1993 C43/2, Vol II, App C.9, paras 70–76 (now superseded by the Horizontal Cooperation Guidelines).

[159] *XXIVth Report on Competition Policy* (1994), point 166; and see, eg for input JVs: *Asahi/St Gobain* (n 133, above) para 29; *Philips/Osram* (n 123, above) paras 19–20.

[160] OJ 1999 L60/6. See further paras 7.115–7.117, below. On appeal, the CFI held that this did not infringe the principle of legal certainty since the Commission's statement in its *XXIVth Report on Competition Policy*, n 159, above, was only an indication not a strict rule: *Métropole Télévision-M6* (n 153, above) paras 168–172.

[161] See, eg Case JV.51 *Bertelsmann/Mondadori/BOL Italia* (1 September 2000) para 31; and Case M.1807 *FNAC/COIN/JV* (14 January 2000) para 20; Case M.2243 *Stora Enso/AssiDomän* (22 December 2000) para 49.

[162] See paras 36 and 41. Although the Ancillary Restrictions Notice strictly only covers full-function JVs, there is no reason why the approach should be different in respect of partial function JVs. See also *Pfizer/Aventis* (*XXXIst Report on Competition Policy* (2001), points 241–243) for a 20-year non-compete (reduced from 30 years) that was treated as ancillary.

scope, it is unlikely to be ancillary.[163] In *BT/MCI (1)*,[164] the arrangements included financial disincentives (by loss of rights) to either parent competing in basic public telephony in the other parent's 'home' market (ie for MCI the Americas and for BT the rest of the world). As that field was not a JV activity, the provision could not be regarded as an ancillary restriction (although it was granted individual exemption for five years).[165]

(ii) Non-compete restrictions that apply for a limited period after the sale of a parent's shareholding in a JV.[166] However, such covenants are not always regarded as ancillary and in the past did generally not receive exemption,[167] although conceptually they do not differ from a standard vendors' non-compete designed to ensure the (re-)transfer of the goodwill to the JV partner who acquires the business.

(iii) Obligations on the JV (or the parents) to purchase exclusively from, or to supply exclusively to, its parents (or their JV). Such restrictions may be ancillary (at least for a start-up period) or alternatively fall within Article 81(3).[168] Where the JV supplies its parents, it may also be required to give them preference when there are capacity shortages, on the basis that the parents may have established the JV principally to supply their own needs.[169] A 'most favoured nation' obligation imposed on the JV for the parents' benefit may also be ancillary.[170] However, for a final product JV, an agreement that the

---

163 See paras 37–39 of the Ancillary Restraints Notice (n 155, above).

164 *BT/MCI (1)*, OJ 1994 L223/36, [1995] 5 CMLR 285, para 48.

165 See also para 39 of the Ancillary Restraints Notice (n 155, above) on this point.

166 eg *Fujitsu/AMD Semiconductor* (n 134, above) para 35 (two-year non-compete obligation after sale of shares within first 10 years); *BiB* (n 128, above) paras 148 (restriction for 12 months as regards any party losing control within three years of the decision: justified to prevent parent withdrawing and taking unfair advantage of know-how). Note that in *Pasteur Mérieux-Merck* (n 123, above), Merck accepted a post-termination restriction on supplying or licensing to a third party a JV product or a competing product for five years (para 41); this was not addressed in the legal analysis under Art 81 in the decision.

167 See *Eirpage* (n 141, above) para 7(5) (three years post-termination obligation deleted at Commission's request); *Alenia-Honeywell*, *XXIIIrd Report on Competition Policy* (1993), point 216 ('very stringent' post-termination non-competition obligations were considered by the Commission to be non-ancillary and had to be deleted before full-function JV could receive negative clearance). By contrast in *Pfizer/Aventis* (n 162, above) for a three-year post termination non-compete (reduced from five years at the Commission's instigation) was regarded as ancillary.

168 *Philips/Osram* (n 123, above) paras 19–20; *Atlas* (n 128, above) para 42; *Phoenix/GlobalOne* (n 128, above) para 52–53. See also *Olivetti-Canon* (n 134, above) (minimum purchasing obligation on parents held to be ancillary); but cf *Olivetti-Digital*, OJ 1994 L309/24 (a strategic alliance in which the obligation on one party to purchase 50 per cent of requirements from the other was held to be an additional (not an ancillary) restriction that received exemption under Art 81(3) whereas the alliance itself fell outside Art 81(1)). Similarly, in *TPS*, OJ 1999 L60/6 a provision for the exclusive supply by the (non-controlling) parents of a JV was not regarded as ancillary but received a clearance for three years under Art 81(3). See also para 44 of the Ancillary Restraints Notice (n 155, above).

169 *Philips/Osram* (n 123, above).

170 *International Private Satellite Partners* (n 129, above) para 61(b).

---

parents shall be exclusive distributors of the output of the JV will not normally be an ancillary restriction since the JV's purpose would also be served by having them as non-exclusive distributors, thereby avoiding partitioning of the market.[171]

(iv) Exclusive technology licences: an exclusive licence by the parents of their technology or intellectual property rights to the JV that is limited to the field of activity of the JV may be ancillary.[172] In the case of a full-function JV that potentially competes with one of its parents, such an exclusive restriction that extends beyond a start-up period may not be ancillary, particularly if it is coupled with territorial sales provisions.[173] However, the Ancillary Restraints Notice allows for these irrespective of duration.[174]

(v) Post-termination restrictions on use of technology: an obligation on a parent for a limited period after dissolution of, or the parent's departure from, the JV whereby the parent is restricted from giving to a third party the benefit of technology or rights developed by the JV may be ancillary.[175]

4. Application of Article 81(3)

(a) Introduction

Block exemptions.   Certain JVs may benefit from the block exemptions granted   **7.056** for R&D and production/specialisation agreements. Those two categories, along with the respective block exemption Regulations, are discussed in Sections 5 and 6 below. However, there are no other block exemptions for horizontal cooperation agreements, and there is now no possibility of obtaining an individual decision on

---

[171] See the Commission's decisions on major telecommunications JVs in each of which this term was nonetheless found to be 'indispensable' and so met the criteria for exemption, which was granted for the same period as the JV; it was noted that exclusive distributorship also better protected the intellectual property rights of the parents: *Atlas* (n 128, above) paras 43, 57; *Phoenix/GlobalOne* (n 128, above) paras 54, 62–64; *Unisource* (n 128, above) paras 83, 93; *Uniworld* (n 128, above) paras 66, 81. *BT/MCI (I)* (n 139, above) paras 47, 59–60. But cf *Iridium* (n 129, above) paras 42–46, where exclusive territorial rights to parties to provide 'gateway' (ie interface switching) services and to designate service providers for satellite digital communications system were held to be ancillary restrictions: the number of gateways was limited and exclusivity was necessary to attract operators to assume the high risk investments involved. For a Merger Reg case in which an exclusive supply of one product to one of the parents was refused ancillary treatment see Case M.835 *Recticel/Greiner* (19 March 1997) para 28.

[172] *Asahi/St Gobain* (n 134, above) paras 19, 29; *Elopak/Metal Box-Odin*, OJ 1990 L209/15, [1991] 4 CMLR 832, paras 30–31.

[173] See *Mitchell Cotts/Sofiltra* (n 151, above) (JV received negative clearance but specific restrictions granted exemption for c.10 years).

[174] Ancillary Restraints Notice (n 155, above) para 42.

[175] eg by licensing the rights: *Konsortium ECR 900* (n 123, above); or using them with a competitor of the other parent: *Elopak/Metal Box-Odin* (n 172, above). The ban was five years in each case.

the application of Article 81(3) for any JV that falls within Article 81(1) but outside the relatively strict parameters of those Regulations. In such cases the parties themselves will have to decide whether the criteria of Article 81(3) are fulfilled (so-called 'self-assessment'). Although this introduces flexibility, the absence of formal decisions may become problematic where a JV involves companies with significant market shares making a substantial financial commitment. Similarly, even if the parties do not exceed the market share thresholds under the relevant block exemption at the inception of the JV, the agreement may lose the protection of the block exemption if the JV is successful.

7.057　**Application of Article 81(3): the conditions.**　In order for Article 81(3) to apply, an agreement must meet two positive and two negative conditions. These are designed to establish whether the beneficial effects of an agreement outweigh its anti-competitive consequences and are discussed in general in Chapter 3, above. In *Matra Hachette*[176] (concerning the *Ford/Volkswagen* JV[177]), the Court of First Instance stated that the Commission must establish that any adverse effects on competition resulting from the project are 'proportionate' to the contribution that it makes to technical or economic progress. The Commission's Cooperative JV Notice (now superseded by the Horizontal Cooperation Guidelines) stated that the 'pros and cons of a JV will be weighed against each other on an overall economic balance, by means of which the type and the extent of the respective advantages and risks can be assessed'.[178] There is no equivalent general statement in the Horizontal Cooperation Guidelines, but they reflect this approach in the guidance that they give as to how the Article 81(3) conditions are to be applied for the particular categories of agreements discussed.[179] The Commission's pre-modernisation administrative practice as well as the approach adopted by the Community Courts remain valid under the new regime of Regulation 1/2003, subject to the caveat that the enforcing authority is now more likely be one or more national competition authorities or courts.

(b) Application of the Article 81(3) conditions

7.058　**The first Article 81(3) condition: efficiencies or economic benefits.**　Common benefits resulting from JVs are the development of new and often advanced technology products (or services) and production methods;[180] and the creation of new

---

[176] Case T-17/93 *Matra Hachette v Commission* [1994] ECR II–595, para 135.
[177] See paras 7.108 *et seq*, below.
[178] OJ 1993 C43/2, Vol II, App C.9, para 57.
[179] Horizontal Cooperation Guidelines, OJ 2001 C3/2, Vol II, App C.12, eg paras 68–71, 102 *et seq*.
[180] In *Ford/Volkswagen* (n 135, above), the Commission found that the use of a pioneering components delivery system in the manufacturing process satisfied the first condition of Art 81(3): see para 7.110, below. This conclusion was upheld by the CFI: *Matra Hachette* (n 176, above) para 109.

industry capacity.[181] Other benefits which JVs can typically provide are an ability to undertake speculative or long-term R&D by sharing risks and costs;[182] the hastening of the entry of a new competitor,[183] particularly when facing existing larger suppliers;[184] and improved distribution arrangements (including after-sales service).[185] Such new entry or improved market penetration may be in relation to either a product or a geographic market. However, no account is to be taken of cost savings that arise from output reductions, market sharing or 'the mere exercise of market power'.[186]

Promotion of new technology. The Commission has stated[187] that it: **7.059**

'. . . is generally favourable to R&D and production JVs which promote the development and production of *new* products or services which did not exist before or which improve the quality of existing products and thus increase the output on the market and the choices available to consumers. Such JVs create new competition which normally outweighs possible disadvantages for competition overall, provided there remains effective competition from other competitors on the market, even if the market is characterised by an oligopolistic structure'.

The Commission has on this basis granted exemption to JVs between major competitors where it was satisfied that the JV enables the parties to overcome technical difficulties and major financial risks associated with the development of advanced technology products.[188] Consequently, the following aspects will be favourable to the assessment of the JV: the fact that the JV brings together complementary skills

---

[181] eg *Exxon/Shell* (n 132, above); see also *Philips/Osram* (n 123, above) para 25.

[182] eg *Beecham-Parke Davis*, OJ 1979 L70/11, [1979] 2 CMLR 157 (R&D programme which had especially long duration). Several nuclear industry JVs ameliorated risk: eg *GEC/Weir*, OJ 1977 L327/26, [1978] 1 CMLR D42; *KEWA* (n 121, above) (joint building and operating of reprocessing plant); *United Reprocessors*, OJ 1976 L51/7, [1976] 2 CMLR D1 (agreement to reprocess oxide fuels).

[183] eg *Amersham-Buchler*, OJ 1982 L314/34, [1983] 1 CMLR 619 (quicker entry of parent into the German market); *Rockwell/Iveco*, OJ 1983 L224/19, [1983] three CMLR 709 (emergence of new competitor through JV); *Eirpage* (n 141, above) (parents could not independently have achieved JV objective on the same 'rapid timescale').

[184] *VW/Man*, OJ 1983 L376/11, [1984] 1 CMLR 621 (VW network alone was not equipped for truck servicing); *Sopelem/Vickers*, OJ 1983 L70/4, (JV for technical cooperation in field of microscopy and for future distribution system); *Ford/Volkswagen* (n 135, above).

[185] *Langenscheidt Hachette*, OJ 1982 L39/25, [1982] 1 CMLR 181 (publication and sale of foreign language learning materials); *Amersham Buchler* (n 183, above) (JV to distribute Amersham's radioactive products in Germany); *VW/Man*, above; *IVECO-Ford*, OJ 1988 L230/39 (increasing car distribution network and ranges); *UIP*, OJ 1989 L226/25, [1990] 4 CMLR 749 (pooling of film distribution for the Community), exemption renewed by comfort letter, *XXIXth Report on Competition Policy* (1999), p 148.

[186] Horizontal Cooperation Guidelines (n 179, above) para 33.

[187] *XXIVth Report on Competition Policy* (1994), point 155.

[188] This aspect therefore overlaps with the 'indispensability' requirement in the third Art 81(3) condition. See, eg *KSB/Goulds/Lowara/ITT* (n 123, above); *Asahi/St Gobain* (n 134, above) and para 7.075, below; *GEAE/P&W* (n 135, above); and the decisions in the telecommunications field discussed at paras 12.144 *et seq*, below.

and expertise, enabling development problems to be solved more 'effectively, economically and quickly' than if the parties had proceeded independently;[189] that the product to be developed is of major economic importance[190] or represents a breakthrough;[191] or that a successful solution is particularly sought by customers. In *Pasteur Mérieux-Merck*,[192] the Commission noted that the JV would be the first entity with access to the full range of antigens necessary to develop new generation multivalent vaccines, thereby accelerating the availability of such vaccines in Europe. The Commission has in the past also taken account of the fact that the JV will strengthen the competitiveness of the Community industry by transferring important technology from outside the Community to an EC producer.[193]

7.060 **The second Article 81(3) condition: allowing consumers a fair share of the benefit.** This condition is closely related to the first condition. Provided that effective competition continues on the market (ie that the fourth condition is fulfilled), it can be assumed that the competitive process ensures that the benefits of the JV encompassed in the first condition will be passed on to the consumer.[194]

7.061 **The third Article 81(3) condition: indispensability.** The parties to an agreement generally take the view that they would not have undertaken the operation that is the subject of the JV separately. But the examining authority or court will need to be satisfied that the parties *could* not do so, or that, if they could do so, they had substantial reasons for not doing so. As indicated above, where the JV involves considerable financial investment or commercial risk, or will result in the earlier introduction of a new product than would be likely if the parents were to develop it independently, the Commission has in the past generally found that this condition was satisfied.[195] In *Ford/Volkswagen*,[196] the condition was met because individual penetration of the market by either of the parents could have been

---

[189] See, eg *GEC/Weir* (n 182, above); *Vacuum Interrupters (No. 1)* (n 121, above); and *Vacuum Interrupters (No. 2)*, OJ 1980 L383/1, [1981] 2 CMLR 217; *Beecham-Parke Davies* (n 182, above); *GEAE/P&W* (n 135, above).

[190] *Optical Fibres* (n 96, above).

[191] See, eg *Beecham/Parke Davis* (n 182, above); and *VIIIth Report on Competition Policy* (1978), point 93, where the fact that the product would be pharmacologically and therapeutically different from all known medicines was described as the 'conclusive element' in granting exemption.

[192] *Pasteur Mérieux-Merck*, OJ 1994 L309/1. See also *Bayer/Hoechst*, *XXth Report on Competition Policy* (1990), point 99 (R&D and marketing of AIDS drug).

[193] *Olivetti/Canon* (n 134, above). See also *Philips-Thomson-Sagem*, *XXIIIrd Report on Competition Policy* (1993), point 215 (full-function JV for active matrix liquid crystal displays that was means for development and mass production in Europe for a market with strong competition from Japanese producers: exemption-type comfort letter issued).

[194] Horizontal Cooperation Guidelines (n 179, above) para 35. See, eg *Philips-Osram* (n 123, above) para 27; *Ford/Volkswagen* (n 135, above) para 27; *P&O Stena Line*, OJ 1999 L163/61, [1999] 5 CMLR 682, para 63.

[195] See, eg *Asahi/St Gobain* (n 134, above) paras 27–28: *GEAE/P&W* (n 135, above) paras 83–84.

[196] See para 7.108, below.

achieved only at a loss. However, an important question may be whether a less restrictive form of collaboration would have been sufficient to achieve the benefits of the JV.[197] In *GEC/Weir*,[198] the Commission accepted that any less close form of technical cooperation, for instance a licensing and information-exchange agreement or a specialisation arrangement, would not achieve the desired objectives as quickly or efficiently. In *P&O Stena Line*,[199] concerning a full-function JV for the integration of the parties' cross-Channel ferry operations, the Commission found that lesser forms of cooperation (such as interlining or joint scheduling) would not achieve the same cost savings. Similarly the Commission has considered whether the full extent of the JV is necessary. In *Pasteur Mérieux-Merck*,[200] distribution by the JV of the products which resulted from its collaborative R&D work was held to be justified because Merck did not have its own Europe-wide distribution network. But in *Astra*,[201] a JV to provide capacity on one of the parent's satellites for the transmission of television channels, the Commission found that collaboration with British Telecommunications (the other party) was not indispensable to ensure successful entry into the United Kingdom market, and exemption was refused. The third condition of Article 81(3) is of particular significance in the consideration of specific restrictions in the JV agreements.[202] Shifting the examination of exemptability from *ex ante* to *ex post* removes clearly some of the more speculative aspects of reaching a decision. However, it gives rise to

---

[197] This consideration of alternatives is not relevant to assessment under the second Art 81(3) condition: *Matra Hachette* (n 176, above) para 122.

[198] *GEC/Weir*, OJ 1977 L327/26, [1978] 1 CMLR D42; similarly *Olivetti/Canon*, OJ 1988 L52/51, [1989] 4 CMLR 940 (licensing arrangement would not achieve the same effect because major involvement of the parties in a manufacturing JV permits 'a permanent and intense flow of technology.') See also the Commission's Guidelines on the Application of Art 81(3), OJ 2004 C101/97, Vol II, App C.18, paras 76–77.

[199] *P&O Stena Line*, OJ 1999 L163/61, [1999] 5 CMLR 682, para 65. See further para 7.063, below. The exemption was extended until March 2007: see Press Release IP/01/806 (7 June 2001).

[200] *Pasteur Mérieux-Merck* (n 192, above) paras 91–94; see also *Alcatel Espace/ANT*, OJ 1990 L32/19, [1991] 4 CMLR 208, para 20 (option of separate marketing after joint R&D and manufacturing was not practicable as customers for satellite communications expect all members of the consortia to be involved in the technical discussions).

[201] *Astra*, OJ 1993 L20/23, [1994] 5 CMLR 226. See also *Eurosport*, OJ 1991 L63/32, [1992] 5 CMLR 273: exemption refused to JV between Sky Television and the Eurosport consortium to operate a sports-dedicated TV channel transmitted either by cable or from the Astra satellite; the alliance of the consortium members (backed by the EBU) with the most likely competitor was 'excessive' and could not be regarded as indispensable to the establishment of such a channel (para 74). (In *Eurosport Mark III*, OJ 1993 C67/8, the Commission indicated its intention to take a favourable view of revised arrangements.) In *Bayer/Gist-Brocades*, OJ 1976 L30/13, [1976] 1 CMLR D98, arrangements for joint control of production and investment were held not be indispensable to achieve benefits of specialisation; the agreement was exempted after amendment to remove those elements. In *Scandairy*, XXVIIth *Report on Competition Policy* (1997), p 107, a JV between the dominant Danish and Swedish dairy cooperatives was restricted to new, 'functional' (ie having a physiological as well as a nutritional value) products and amended to exclude cooperation as regards conventional dairy products in order to obtain an exemption-type comfort letter.

[202] See paras 7.052 *et seq*, above.

another problem: although with hindsight it may become clear that a less restrictive form of collaboration would have sufficed (and hence the protection of Article 81(3) may not be available), this may not have been clear to the parties (or any of their competitors) at the time of forming the JV. In other words, if the uncertainty, risks and doubts of the parties are not fully documented at the time of the inception of the JV, they will open themselves up to a subsequent argument that the success of the JV demonstrates that each of the parties could have undertaken the project on its own.

7.062 **The fourth Article 81(3) condition: no elimination of competition.** Article 81(3)(b) provides that the Commission may not exempt an arrangement that would give the parties 'the possibility of eliminating competition' in respect of a 'substantial' part of the market concerned. In practice, this refers to the elimination of actual rather than potential competition. The analysis of the market is essentially the same as is conducted to assess the application of Article 81(1). But a degree of increase in market power, and consequent adverse effect on competition, may be permitted. There is, however, no clear rule to determine when the reduction in competition involved is sufficiently material to preclude the application of Article 81(3). Each case turns on the structure of the particular market involved and the attainable benefits concerned.[203] The more significant the efficiencies or technical benefits for which the JV has been found to be indispensable, the greater degree of reduction in competition that may be permitted.[204]

7.063 **Relationship between elimination of effective competition and dominant position.** No benefits can outweigh the elimination of 'effective competition'. The Commission takes the view that this will occur if the parties will, or are likely to become, dominant, so that a JV which creates a dominant position may never be permitted under Article 81(3)(b).[205] However, the relationship between the test under Article 81(3)(b) and the test of dominance, as applied for the purposes of Article 82, remains uncertain in the absence of a determination by the Community Courts.[206] In *P&O Stena Line*[207] the Commission considered a

---

[203] cf Faull & Nikpay (eds), *The EC Law of Competition* (2nd edn, 2007), 311. This condition 'requires a careful analysis of the various sources of competitive constraint'.

[204] See, eg paras 7.058 *et seq*, above.

[205] Horizontal Cooperation Guidelines (n 179, above) para 36. But note that in *Matra Hachette* (n 176, above) the CFI held that the risk that the partners may in time become collectively dominant could not justify withholding of an exemption where that risk would not materialise within the period of validity of the decision (at para 153).

[206] See Temple Lang, 'International JVs Under Community Law' in Hawk (ed), *1999 Fordham Corp. L. Inst.* (2000), who considers that the test is stricter than that of dominance; cf Waelbroeck and Frignani (eds), *Commentaire J. Megret: Vol 4, Concurrence* (2nd edn, 1997), 222–23, arguing that creation of a dominant position does not in itself preclude exemption.

[207] *P&O Stena Line*, OJ 1999 L163/61, [1999] 5 CMLR 682. The JV was notified also to the UK and French competition authorities. In the United Kingdom, it was classified as a merger and

full-function JV that consolidated the 'Short Sea' cross-Channel ferry services of
P&O and Stena. The purpose of the JV was to achieve cost savings and economies
of scale and thereby enable the combined business to compete more effectively
with Eurotunnel which had acquired (since its inception in 1995) approximately 37 per cent of the tourist market. Most of the Commission's analysis concentrated on whether the JV would give the parties the opportunity to eliminate
competition in respect of a substantial part of the Short Sea tourist market.[208]
P&O had 27 per cent, Stena 18 per cent and Eurotunnel 37 per cent of this
market, with the remainder of the market split between three operators. In those
circumstances, there was a risk of duopolistic behaviour developing between
Eurotunnel and the JV. However, the parties successfully argued that there existed
significant over-capacity in the market, leading both Eurotunnel and the JV to
keep down prices in order to increase use of capacity. The Commission accepted
that, as a result, Eurotunnel and the JV would almost certainly continue to compete with each other and the other three operators also offered competition.[209]
What is clear is that where a JV involves major competitors in the market, this
condition will receive careful consideration, focusing on the strength and number
of the other competitors and any countervailing power exercised by customers.
For example, in *Exxon/Shell*,[210] which concerned an oligopolistic market (for low-
density polyethylene) of which the parents jointly held 22 per cent, the Commission
concluded that the size of the remaining competitors 'guarantees that workable
competition is not eliminated'. Even when an undertaking with a high market
share concludes a production JV with a competitor, the presence of a potentially

---

referred to the Monopolies and Mergers Commission which recommended that the JV should
be permitted only on the basis of very stringent conditions: *The Peninsular and Oriental Steam
Navigation Co and Stena Line AB* (November 1997, Cm. 3664); however, after discussion with the
European Commission, the Secretary of State cleared the JV subject only to a conditional imposition of a cap on fares should a duopoly develop in the passenger services market after the abolition of duty-free: DTI Press Notice P/97/757 (19 November 1997). In France, the Conseil de la
Concurrence advised that the JV did not constitute a concentration under French competition law
(Advice no. 97 of 1 April 1997) but the Finance Minister warned the parties that he would carefully
monitor the conduct of the JV under the French domestic equivalent of Arts 81 and 82.

[208] There was not the same concern as regards the Anglo-Continental freight market, which was
characterised by strong price competition, low barriers to entry and powerful customers.

[209] Following expiry of the original exemption, the parties re-notified the JV to the Commission
and received a further six-year exemption under the then opposition procedure of Reg 4056/89:
P&O Stena Line 2, Press Release IP/01/806 (7 June 2001).

[210] *Exxon/Shell*, OJ 1994 L144/20, para 81. See also *Philips-Thomson-Sagem*, *XXIIIrd Report
on Competition Policy* (1993); *P&O Stena Line* (n 207, above) where this issue received extensive consideration. But cf *GEAE/P&W* (n 135, above) para 88, where in granting exemption to a collaboration between two of the three manufacturers capable of developing
and producing a new jet engine for very large commercial aircraft, the Commission simply
found that this condition was satisfied because Rolls Royce remained as a significant competitor.
(However, safeguards were imposed to prevent spill-over restricting competition as regards other
types of engines.)

effective new entrant may be sufficient to satisfy this condition.[211] But in some cases, this condition has been met by the imposition on the parties of strict conditions as regards access or even divestiture.[212]

(c) Duration of Article 81(3) protection

7.064 **Relevance of past decisions.** Under the new regime of Regulation 1/2003, neither the Commission nor national authorities or courts can limit the application of Article 81(3) to a particular prospective period. They will only decide whether the conditions of Article 81(1) and 81(3) are met at the time of taking the decision. Nevertheless, the previous administrative practice in relation to duration remains to some extent relevant in deciding at what point a JV may no longer benefit from Article 81(3).

7.065 **Pre-existing Commission practice.** The Commission's past approach to duration of an exemption depended to a large extent on the nature of the agreement and of the industry concerned. A JV involving significant expense and technical risks in a highly specialised industry was capable of receiving a far longer exemption than, for example, a JV in a simpler market that involves neither. In its judgment in *European Night Services*,[213] the Court of First Instance found that the time needed to get a return on investment was an 'essential factor to be taken into account' and held that the period for which market conditions were likely to remain the same could not itself be decisive.[214] In *Olivetti/Canon*,[215] the Commission stated that in a case of production JVs 'requiring substantial long term investments and concerning a new product not yet fully established on the market, a period of 12 years appears indispensable to enable the parties to rely on the enforceability of the agreements and to obtain a satisfactory return on their capital.' For R&D JVs, the maximum duration of an individual exemption was unlikely to be longer than that provided under the block exemption.[216]

7.066 **Limitations of past cases.** The temporal limitation of past exemption decisions did not mean that after such period the conditions of Article 81(3) were no longer met. It simply meant that they had to be re-examined and often a further

---

[211] Guidelines on the Application of Art 81(3) (n 198, above) paras 115–116 (3rd example).

[212] eg *Atlas* (n 128, above); *British Interactive Broadcasting/Open ('BiB')* (n 128, above).

[213] Cases T-374/94, etc, *ENS v Commission* [1998] ECR II–3141, [1998] 5 CMLR 718, paras 230–231.

[214] But cf *P&O Stena Line* (n 207, above) where exemption for only three years was granted because of the uncertainty as to how market conditions might change with the ending of the duty-free concessions. The exemption was subsequently extended for a further six years: n 209, above.

[215] *Olivetti/Canon*, OJ 1988 L52/51, [1989] 4 CMLR 940. See also *GEAE/P&W* (n 135, above) 15-years exemption to reflect the long development period for aircraft engines in which investments are typically not recovered.

[216] See para 7.084, below.

exemption was issued.[217] This is important to bear in mind when relying on past cases in the context of self-assessment (or *ex post* assessment) under the new regime of Regulation 1/2003.[218]

5. R&D Agreements

(a) Generally

Introduction. The general principles discussed above apply directly or by anal-   **7.067**
ogy to R&D agreements. Horizontal arrangements for collaboration on R&D may be in the form of a simple agreement between undertakings or in the more elaborate form of a JV.[219] This Section supplements the foregoing analysis by concentrating on matters of special relevance to R&D agreements, including the block exemption regulation, Regulation 2659/2000.

R&D cooperation. As underlined in the EC Treaty,[220] cooperation between   **7.068**
undertakings in research and technological development represents an essential tool in making Community industry internationally competitive. Collaboration in R&D may bring significant advantages, including a more efficient allocation of tasks and resources and the likelihood of earlier breakthroughs. However, an agreement which restricts the parties' freedom in R&D or which prevents one party obtaining a competitive advantage in R&D over the other is likely to restrict competition within the meaning of Article 81(1), particularly in research-based or technologically dynamic industries. In 1985, the Commission summarised the factors weighing on each side as follows:

'R&D collaboration has various economic advantages:

(i) Investment in R&D can be kept to a minimum. Economies of scale can be achieved.

---

[217] See, eg *Bayer/Gist-Brocades* (n 201, above), point 101 (comfort letter that exemption conditions 'remain fulfilled'); *United International Picture (UIP)*, *XXIXth Report on Competition Policy* (1999), p 148 (comfort letter renewing exemption after agreement had been amended and subject to undertakings); *P&O Stena Line 2* (n 209, above) (no objection raised under the then opposition procedure of Reg 4056/89 since there were no 'material changes in the market that would justify denying a further clearance'); *European Rail Shuttle*, OJ 2002 C13/5/2, Press Release IP/02/575 (17 April 2002) (non-opposition given the continued countervailing benefits).

[218] Horizontal Cooperation Guidelines (n 179, above) para 74.

[219] Note also that a JV responsible for R&D, licensing, production and distribution of the products, may be a full-function JV falling under the EC Merger Reg: see paras 8.052 *et seq*, below.

[220] Art 163(2) states: '... the Community shall, throughout the Community, encourage undertakings, including small and medium-sized undertakings, research centres and universities in their research and technological development activities of high quality; it shall support their efforts to co-operate with one another, aiming, notably, at enabling undertakings to exploit the internal market potential to the full, in particular through the opening up of national public contracts, the definition of common standards and the removal of legal and fiscal obstacles to the co-operation'.

(ii) Research budgets can be made to go further and risks spread by sharing the costs and benefits of a project between several firms or spreading a given sum over a series of relatively independent projects.

(iii) Cross-frontier R&D collaboration within the Community can help to open up national markets . . . . International R&D collaboration can enlarge markets and supply for the products (high technology or otherwise) incorporating the results of the joint research to a Community or even world scale.

But the economic effects of R&D are not always wholly beneficial:

(iv) Powerful firms may enter into R&D agreements with potentially very innovative rivals in order to be able to control technological progress. In other cases, R&D collaboration may raise entry barriers to non-participating competitors.

(v) R&D collaboration can also facilitate coordination of pricing and production and enable abnormal profits to be made from innovations. Such dangers are greatest where, as is frequently the case in the Community, there are non-tariff barriers between national markets. In such cases, cross-frontier collaboration at the R&D stage may give way to geographical division of the market on national lines for the product resulting from the R&D.'[221]

7.069 **The Commission's approach.** In the past, in order to establish jurisdiction to control R&D agreements, the Commission often took a wide view as to the circumstances in which Article 81(1) applied[222] and expressed its detailed stance in relation to exemption (with any necessary modifications of the arrangement) under Article 81(3). However, as discussed above, during the 1990s the Commission developed a more realistic economic approach to the analysis of JVs.[223] *Elopak/Metal Box-Odin,*[224] a landmark decision in this process, concerned a JV with a major R&D element which had originally been notified under the 'opposition procedure' of the then block exemption Regulation 418/85.[225] Most of the Commission's decisions on R&D agreements have concerned JVs, but an R&D agreement which does not constitute a JV (for example, because it does not involve joint control) should benefit from the same approach.[226] In practice, the most clear-cut result can be achieved, if possible, by drafting R&D agreements so as to fall within the block exemption.[227] Where this is not possible either for

---

[221] *XVth Report on Competition Policy* (1985), point 282.

[222] eg *BBC Brown Boveri,* OJ 1988 L301/68, [1989] 4 CMLR 610 (JV between electrical engineering company and technical ceramic manufacturer to develop sodium-sulphur high performance battery).

[223] See paras 7.022 *et seq,* above.

[224] *Elopak/Metal Box-Odin,* OJ 1990 L209/15, [1991] 4 CMLR 832; paras 7.105 *et seq,* below.

[225] Reg 418/85, OJ 1985 L53/5 amended by Reg 151/93 OJ 1993 L21/8. Its application was extended by Reg 2236/97, OJ 1997 L306/12.

[226] See, eg *Canon/Kodak, XXVIIIth Report on Competition Policy* (1998), p 147 (agreements between major film and camera producers re development and licensing of new advanced photographic system (APS)).

[227] Reg 2659/2000, OJ 2000 L304/7, Vol II, App C.5. This applies (as did Reg 418/85) to R&D agreements whether or not they are in the form of a JV: see paras 7.079 *et seq,* below.

commercial reasons or, for example, because the parties' combined share of the relevant market exceeds the limit permitted under the Regulation, the agreement may still fall within the criteria of Article 81(3). Thus in *Asahi/St Gobain*,[228] the JV was exempted for a certain period because of the large R&D element.

(b) Application of Article 81 to R&D agreements

Application of Article 81(1).   Many agreements on R&D do not appreciably **7.070** restrict competition. In general, Article 81(1) should not apply to agreements relating solely to a stage prior to commercial exploitation and having as their sole object the cooperation on pure R&D projects; or to the placing of R&D contracts, typically with specialised companies or research institutes, which are not active in the exploitation of the results.[229] Moreover, an R&D agreement is unlikely to constitute a restriction of competition if it is not made between actual or potential competitors in an affected field. That may involve consideration of the competitive position both as regards existing products and as regards new products with which the product being developed will compete over time.[230] If the product is a key input into another, final product and the parties are competitors in the supply of those final products, the effect on the final product market will also have to be considered. An R&D agreement may restrict competition, and therefore come within Article 81(1), if it contains particular restrictions relating to independent R&D activity, access to the results, or exploitation of the results of joint research. Although in most cases competition could only be restricted if the parties are actual or potential competitors, a restriction of exploitation of the results of joint research may also bring an agreement within Article 81(1). This may be the case even when the parties are not actual or potential competitors if one of them is dominant in respect of key technology. These aspects are described in the following paragraphs.

Independent research precluded.   In principle, Article 81(1) is applicable if poten- **7.071** tial competitors with a significant share of the market agree not to carry out independent R&D.[231] Even if the parties do not formally agree to forgo independent

---

[228] *Asahi/St Gobain*, OJ 1994 L 354/87 discussed at paras 7.075 *et seq*, below. See also *Continental/Michelin*, OJ 1988 L305/33, [1989] 4 CMLR 920 (exemption granted to collaboration on R&D and initial commercial development of new 'drive flat' tyre between the two largest tyre manufacturers in the Community whose combined market share was almost 50 per cent). Conversely, in *Co-operation agreements between Peugeot and Fiat involving the Sevel JV*, XXIIIrd *Report on Competition Policy* (1993), point 227; and *Exxon/Hoechst*, XXVth *Report on Competition Policy* (1995), p 125, agreements that were notified for an individual exemption were found by the Commission to come within Reg 418/85.

[229] Horizontal Cooperation Guidelines (n 179, above) paras 55 *et seq*.

[230] ibid, para 43.

[231] See, eg *Alcatel Espace/ANT* (n 200, above) (allocation of R&D projects exclusively to one or other party restricted competition in R&D despite the fact that results were to be cross-licensed on royalty-free basis).

research, Article 81(1) will apply if the effect of the agreement is that *de facto* the parties will no longer conduct research independently of one another or, to put it another way, if they preclude themselves from gaining a competitive advantage over each other in R&D.[232] Therefore, if the parties were realistically capable of performing the R&D alone, Article 81(1) may apply to their arrangements to cooperate on R&D or exchange research results, in pursuit of a joint project.[233] Even more general sharing of information on research between potential competitors may lead to coordination of their activity. In particular, this may lead to a diminution in individual initiative with a potential effect in underlying markets.[234]

7.072 **Access to the results.** Payments of royalties by the parties to each other may infringe Article 81(1) unless justifiable by unequal contributions to the joint R&D or to inequalities in the exploitation of the results.[235] In *EUCAR*,[236] the

---

[232] *Henkel/Colgate*, JO 1972 L14/14 and *VIIth Report on Competition* (1978), points 89–90; *Vacuum Interrupters (No. 1)*, OJ 1977 L48/32, [1977] 1 CMLR D67; *GEC/Weir* (n 198, above). In *Continental/Michelin* (n 228, above), despite the freedom of the parties as a matter of formal contract to pursue independent R&D in competition with the JV, the Commission inferred that in practice they did not do so and that this was indeed part of the understanding between them; see also *Olivetti/Canon* (n 215, above) (because of joint development via JV the parties were taken to have no interest in investing resources in independent development).

[233] eg *Asahi/St Gobain* (n 228, above); *Beecham/Parke-Davis* (n 182, above); *Pfizer/EISAI*, *XXXIst Report on Competition Policy* (2001), points 239-40, where one of the parties gave up its pipeline product so that both companies' efforts were concentrated on one product. Conversely, the Commission found Art 81(1) inapplicable in respect of an R&D project to develop inhalable insulin where one party was not active in the insulin market at all and the other was only the third largest player: see *Pfizer/Aventis* (n 162, above).

[234] In *Bayer/BP Chemicals*, OJ 1988 L150/35, [1989] 4 CMLR 24, the Commission stated simply 'Continual co-operation between competitors at the R&D level is bound to have a direct impact on competition between them.' See *Pasteur Mérieux-Merck* (n 192, above), where the Commission carefully assessed the effect on potential competition as regards the various groups of vaccine products on which the parties were cooperating. As regards future monovalent products, the Commission found (para 63) that because new discoveries will be discussed between the parents, there was an appreciable risk of coordination of basic R&D which, in view of the parties' important position on the vaccine markets, constituted a restriction of potential competition. Nevertheless exemption was granted. In *Canon/Kodak* (n 226, above), the Commission issued an exemption-type comfort letter in respect of far-reaching cooperation agreements between five major producers for R&D and cross-licensing of technology for APS film and cameras, was granted. But it only did so after the agreements had been amended to allow for competition from third party licensees.

[235] In *Beecham/Parke Davis* (n 182, above), the parties had made equal contributions to the work but had agreed on cross-royalty provisions on sales made by each other, apparently at different rates for packaged and bulk sales. The Commission condemned these arrangements as 'likely to create a considerable disincentive for the parties to compete with one another, particularly where marketing raises difficulties, since substantial returns through royalties would have been obtained without production or marketing expenditure' (para 43(c)). The Commission, however, recognised that the position would be different if the parties had made unequal contributions. *A fortiori*, cross-royalty provisions will also be condemned if they are related to marketing territories allocated to the participants: *Re Research and Development* [1971] CMLR D31.

[236] *XXVIIIth Report on Competition Policy* (1998), point 132. The agreement doubtless fell outside Reg 418/85 because the market share criterion was exceeded. See also the Art 19(3) Notices

Commission issued a comfort letter in respect of an agreement between the major European motor manufacturers for the establishment of cooperative research projects concerning experimental products. These products were being developed with a view to achieving higher environmental standards and had no direct commercial application. The Commission regarded this R&D as being at the 'precompetitive stage', the results from which were to be made available to all participants for independent commercial development. The Commission noted that if in any case partners in a project wished to proceed with joint exploitation of the results and this involved appreciable restrictions of competition, any such further agreement would need to be considered separately under Article 81. However, the conditions of Article 81(3) may not be fulfilled if the parties do not all have access to the results of the joint work.[237]

Restriction on exploitation of results. Article 81(1) applies if the parties accept, **7.073** expressly or by implication, restrictions on their ability independently to exploit the results of the joint research. For example, they may commit themselves to joint production or joint marketing of the products in question[238] or accept other restrictions on production or marketing,[239] particularly restrictions which might impede the free flow of the products of the joint research throughout the Community.[240] If the parties individually or together have a large share of the

---

under Reg 17/62 in *Re the Application of the Twinning Programme Engineering Group*, OJ 1992 C148/8, [1992] 5 CMLR 93; *Re the European Fuel Cycle Consortium*, OJ 1993 C351/6, [1994] 4 CMLR 589.

[237] See Art 3(2) of Reg 2659/2000 (n 227, above) which makes an exception for research institutes or academic bodies that may confine their use of results for the purpose only of further research. See also the Horizontal Cooperation Guidelines (n 179, above) para 67: 'agreements which restrict access of a party to the results of the work . . . do not, as a general rule, promote technical and economic progress by increasing the dissemination of technical knowledge between the parties.' But if there are compelling economic reasons for exclusive access in view of the risks and scale of investment, Art 81(3) may be satisfied: ibid.

[238] See Art 3(3) and (4) of Reg 2659/2000 and, eg *Vacuum Interrupters (No. 1)* (n 232, above) and *(No. 2)*, OJ 1980 L383/1, [1981] 2 CMLR 217; *GEC/Weir* (n 198, above); *Pasteur Mérieux-Merck* (n 192, above) (joint distribution by the JV of products manufactured by the parents on the basis of R&D by the JV). See also *Alcatel Espace/ANT* (n 200, above) (despite provision for independent marketing, the nature of the communications satellites meant that joint marketing was likely wherever possible; but as this was to meet the wishes of customers who insisted on a high degree of cooperation with all parties involved in development, exemption was granted). cf *Asahi/St Gobain* (n 228, above) where the two parties would compete with each other as regards manufacture and sale.

[239] See, eg *Siemens/Fanuc*, OJ 1985 L376/29, [1988] 4 CMLR 945 (joint determination of how the products developed were to be manufactured and how intellectual property rights were to be exploited); *VW/MAN* (n 184, above) (common distribution arrangements).

[240] See, eg *Siemens/Fanuc*, above (cross-exclusive licensing, to Siemens for Europe and to Fanuc for Asia); *Rank/Sopelem*, OJ 1975 L29/20, [1975] 1 CMLR D72 (export restrictions on products concerned); *Beecham/Parke-Davis* (n 182, above) (exclusion of France meant that free movement throughout the common market of the goods derived from the joint research was unjustifiably impeded; the Commission stated that exemption would be granted only 'if the results of such joint research can

market, restrictions on the grant of licences to third parties may have a foreclosure effect.[241] Restrictions on exploitation which apply after the termination of the agreement may also infringe Article 81(1). In principle, the parties should be able to use the results of the joint work after termination on the basis of equal access to research results.[242] An obligation to preserve the confidentiality of know-how after the expiry of the agreement does not infringe Article 81(1).

7.074 **Duration.** Past Commission practice granted exemptions covering (i) the period of the R&D phase and (ii) where the JV provides for subsequent exploitation of the product, the relevant start-up period. A 'first mover advantage' provides the incentive for the risk and investment involved in undertaking the R&D and will not usually be regarded as anti-competitive.[243] In *Continental/Michelin*,[244] the exemption for a JV to develop a new type of 'drive-flat' tyre extended to five years following the first marketing of the product by one of the partners, but following discussion with the Commission, the period of commercial cooperation (ie as regards marketing and not merely further product development) was restricted to two years. In exceptional cases, the Commission took the view that individual

---

be used by both parties freely and independently without any territorial or other restrictions on production or marketing within the common market', para 42). Note also *Quantel International Continuum/Quantel SA*, OJ 1992 L235/9, [1993] 5 CMLR 497 (Commission condemned so-called R&D agreements ancillary to a business transfer because, *inter alia*, the agreements prevented one party from having access to the Community market for an indefinite period). In *Pfizer/EISAI* (n 232, above) the Commission did not object to a co-promotion arrangement for pharmaceutical products (ie where the jointly developed product was sold under a single trade mark by the JV parents) in its exemption-type comfort letter. Moreover in *Pfizer/Aventis* (n 162, above) the Commission granted a negative clearance-type comfort letter despite the co-promotion arrangement.

[241] In *Continental/Michelin* (n 228, above), notwithstanding that there was provision for the JV on request of one of the parties and after consulting the other to license to third parties, the Commission concluded that in practice this entailed both parties' agreement. However, the parties' statement that 'they will offer licences on reasonable terms to all interested competitors,' was a material factor in the decision to grant exemption. In *Pasteur Mérieux-Merck* (n 192, above), the agreements were amended to provide for the grant of production and distribution licences for HIB vaccines in Germany and France in order to secure exemption (paras 111–113). Similarly in *Asahi/St Gobain* (n 228, above) where there was no restriction on independent exploitation, the fact that the JV agreement provided that third parties would be licensed with the bi-layer technology on a non-discriminatory basis was relevant to the Commission's finding that the JV met the conditions for exemption. See also *Beecham/Parke-Davis* (n 182, above).

[242] *Rank/Sopelem* (n 240, above) (obligations likely to put parties out of business following termination held to infringe Art 81(1)); *Beecham/Parke Davis* (n 182, above) (obligations after termination to pay 75 per cent of other parties' costs if exploiting products emanating from that party based on joint work held to infringe Art 81(1) but exempted under Art 81(3)); *Carbon Gas Technologie*, OJ 1983 L376/17, [1984] 2 CMLR 275 (obligation on withdrawing shareholder not to use joint know-how for five years infringed Art 81(1) but exempted under Art 81(3)). cf *Elopak/Metal Box-Odin* (n 224, above) para 7.105, below: five-year ban post dissolution of or departure from a full-function JV on use of other party's or JV-developed know-how with a competitor held to be an ancillary restriction and so outside Art 81(1).

[243] Horizontal Cooperation Guidelines, OJ 2001 C3/2, Vol II, App C.12, para 73.

[244] *Continental/Michelin*, OJ 1988 L305/33, [1989] 4 CMLR 920.

exemption may be possible for a longer period than would have applied had the agreement fallen within the block exemption if it can be shown that such a period is needed to guarantee a sufficient return on the investment involved.[245] As already noted above,[246] the periods for which an exemption was previously available are relevant but not determinative for a (prospective or *ex post*) self-assessment under Regulation 1/2003. If an R&D JV is examined after the period set out by the Commission, Article 81(3) may still apply if the criteria continue to be met.[247]

R&D joint venture (extending to production): *Asahi/Saint Gobain.* The **7.075** Commission's approach to R&D agreements is illustrated by the decision in *Asahi/Saint Gobain*.[248] Saint Gobain and Asahi set up a JV for the joint research, development and production of new products called 'bi-layer' products intended for use in the manufacture of safety glass for automotive vehicles. The new glass was expected to offer important advantages over conventional laminated glass with which the bi-layer glass was nonetheless expected to compete. The parties agreed to coordinate their respective R&D activities on bi-layer technology through the JV. The cooperation was divided into two stages: the first stage consisted in a joint R&D programme and the establishment of a pilot plant (for R&D and pre-marketing purposes); the second stage commenced when a second pilot plant for the commercial production of bi-layer film in the European market became operational. The parties agreed that nothing would prevent them from competing with each other in the manufacture, the marketing or the sale of bi-layer products. However, the JV agreement restricted each party from constructing another plant for the production of bi-layer film prior to the construction of the two pilot plants and from expanding existing capacity without the prior consent of the other party.

Asahi/Saint Gobain: **Article 81(1).** The JV parents were strongly positioned **7.076** in the glass industry in general and in the automotive safety glass market in particular so that they were major competitors in the market at which the R&D was primarily aimed. The Commission considered that the parties could have carried out the R&D projects individually and that either party could have developed its own new product. The cooperation extended to the joint exploitation of the intellectual property rights to development of bi-layer technology, as the JV would be exclusive licensor of the technology both to the parents and to interested third parties, not only during the R&D period but also during the production stage covered by the JV agreement. Although the end product (bi-layer safety

---

[245] Horizontal Cooperation Guidelines (n 243, above) para 73.
[246] See para 7.066, above.
[247] Horizontal Cooperation Guidelines (n 243, above) para 74.
[248] *Asahi/Saint Gobain,* OJ 1994 L354/87.

glass) was to be competitively manufactured and marketed, the Commission therefore concluded that there was a restriction of competition.

7.077 *Asahi/Saint Gobain:* **Article 81(3).**   The Commission readily found the requisite contribution to the improvement of production, technical and economic progress and consumer benefit. On indispensability, the Commission concluded that the parties had reached a comparable level of knowledge and that in the field of bi-layer technology this knowledge was largely complementary. The Commission accepted that the commercial viability of the new product was still uncertain and that the efforts and risks involved, if undertaken independently by each party, would most certainly not lead to results as rapid, efficient and economic as those envisaged. The agreement originally provided for cooperation between the parties for a 30-year period and that the JV would be the exclusive licensor of bi-layer technology for the duration of the patents. However, the Commission made clear that although it was favourably disposed to R&D joint ventures, it was not prepared to permit such a long period of cooperation where the parties held such a strong position on the market.[249] Although Regulation 418/85 did not apply because of the parties' combined market share, the Commission saw no reason to depart from the period of five years set out in the block exemption. The parties amended the agreement so that the JV company would be dissolved at the end of a five-year period beginning with the date on which the second pilot plant began commercial production and on this basis the Commission granted individual exemption to expire at the end of that period.

(c) Regulation 2659/2000: the R&D block exemption

7.078 **In general.**   Regulation 2659/2000 replaced the old block exemption, Regulation 418/85.[250] It came into force on 1 January 2001[251] and will expire on 31 December 2010.

7.079 **The agreements covered.**   Regulation 2659/2000 applies to agreements[252] entered into between any number of undertakings for the purposes of:

(a) joint research and development of products or processes and joint exploitation of the results of that research and development;

---

[249] The parties together held more than 50 per cent of the European market: *XXIVth Report on Competition Policy* (1994), point 177.

[250] See n 225, above.

[251] Reg 2659/2000, OJ 2000 L304/7, Vol II, App C.5. Reg 2659/2000 has been adopted, with appropriate amendments, for the purpose of the EEA Agreement: Decn 113/2000 of the EEA Joint Committee, OJ 2001 L52/38. The transitional provisions which covered agreements already in force on 31 December 2000 expired on 30 June 2002 and are therefore no longer relevant (Reg 2659/2000, Art 8).

[252] Reg 2659/2000 applies to decisions of associations of undertakings or concerted practices as well as agreements: Art 2(1).

(b) joint exploitation of the results of research and development of products or processes jointly carried out pursuant to a prior agreement between the same undertakings; or

(c) joint research and development of products or processes excluding joint exploitation of the results;

insofar as such agreements fall within the scope of Article 81(1).[253]

Definition of terms. 'Research and development' is defined as 'the acquisition of know-how[254] relating to products or processes and the carrying out of theoretical analysis, systematic study or experimentation, including experimental production, technical testing of products or processes, the establishment of the necessary facilities and the obtaining of intellectual property rights for the results.'[255] 'Exploitation of the results'[256] means 'the production or distribution of the contract products[257] or the application of the contract processes[258] or the assignment or licensing of intellectual property rights or the communication of know-how required for such manufacture or application.' The block exemption therefore covers: (i) R&D agreements up to the stage of industrial application; (ii) R&D agreements extending to joint manufacture or collaboration in licensing; and (iii) R&D agreements extending through to joint selling in certain circumstances.   **7.080**

Meaning of 'joint' exploitation. 'Joint' exploitation occurs: (i) where the exploitation is carried on by a joint team or is jointly entrusted to a third party or is allocated between the parties by way of specialisation in research, development or production; or (ii) the parties collaborate in any way in the assignment or licensing of intellectual property rights or the communication of know-how resulting from the joint R&D.[259]   **7.081**

Conditions for exemption. The block exemption applies only if all parties have access to the results (save that research institutes or academic bodies may agree to   **7.082**

---

[253] Reg 2659/2000, Art 1(1). Recital (3) of Reg 2659/2000 states: 'Agreements on the joint execution of research work or the joint development of the results of research, up to but not including the stage of industrial application, generally do not fall within the scope of Art 81(1) of the Treaty', unless the parties are restricted in carrying out independent R&D.

[254] 'Know-how' in turn is given a full definition: Reg 2659/2000, Art 2(10).

[255] Reg 2659/2000, Art 2(8).

[256] ibid, Art 2(8).

[257] 'Contract product' means a product 'arising out of the joint research and development or manufactured or provided [sic] applying the contract processes': Reg 2659/2000, Art 2(7).

[258] 'Contract process' means a technology or process 'arising out of the joint research and development': Reg 2659/2000, Art 2(6). In *Continental/Michelin* (n 244, above), the Commission held that insofar as technical knowledge owned by the parties individually prior to the collaboration had become a component in the joint development and was necessary for its exploitation, that technical knowledge was part of the contract products and processes as defined in Reg 418/85 and accordingly could itself be jointly exploited (if decisive in the production or processing) within the terms of the block exemption.

[259] Reg 2659/2000, Arts 2(8) and 11.

confine their use of the results for further research[260]). Further, in the case of an R&D agreement up to the stage of industrial application, each party must be free independently to exploit the results and any pre-existing know-how necessary for such exploitation.[261] However, non-competitors may agree to limit their right to exploitation to particular technical fields, in order to facilitate cooperation between parties with complementary skills.[262] In the case of an R&D agreement which extends to joint exploitation, the requirement of independent exploitation *ex hypothesi* does not apply. However, the joint exploitation must relate only to intellectual property or know-how which makes a substantial contribution to technical or economic progress and the result of the joint research must be 'decisive' for the manufacture of the contract products or the application of the contract processes.[263] This provision ensures that the 'joint exploitation' is confined to cases where the joint results are really significant, ie that the agreement is not a device to cloak other arrangements of which R&D is only an ancillary aspect.[264] Undertakings which, pursuant to the agreement, are to specialise in the manufacture of products must meet orders from all the parties to the agreement except where the agreement also provides for joint distribution.[265]

7.083 **Broad approach to exemption.** The block exemption abandoned the 'clause-based' approach of the previous block exemption. Rather than setting out a list of restrictions that may be included and an opposition procedure for certain other restrictions, Regulation 2659/2000 adopts a more economics-based approach that reflects the impact of an agreement on the relevant market.[266] For that reason, the market share limits and the list of prohibited restrictions are considered adequate to avoid exempting agreements that are likely to have an anti-competitive effect. Subject to those limitations, any agreement within the scope of the R&D block exemption is exempted under Article 81(3) and there is accordingly no longer a need for a list of permitted restrictions. The fact that an agreement does not fall within the block exemption does not mean that it cannot or does not fulfil the criteria of Article 81(3). It only means that the agreement does not fall 'within a category of agreements for which it can be *assumed with sufficient certainty* that they satisfy the conditions of Article 81(3)' (emphasis added).[267]

---

[260] ibid, Art 3(2).

[261] ibid, Art 3(3).

[262] ibid, Recital (14).

[263] Reg 2659/2000, Art 3(4). cf the less exacting Art 81(3) criterion of a mere 'contribution to the promotion of technical or economic progress' (*KSB/Goulds/Lowara/ITT*, OJ 1991 L19/25, [1992] 5 CMLR 55, para 26).

[264] Reg 2659/2000, Recital (14).

[265] ibid, Art 3(5).

[266] ibid, Recital (7).

[267] ibid, Recital (9).

Market share limits and duration.   Regulation 2659/2000 does not apply at all   **7.084**
to agreements between parties who are actual or potential[268] manufacturers of
existing products capable of being improved or replaced by the contract products
where those manufacturers' combined[269] production of such existing products
exceeds 25 per cent of the relevant market at the time the agreement is entered
into.[270] Where the parties (or their related undertakings) are either not competing
manufacturers (actual or potential)[271] or their market share falls below this limit,
the exemption will apply for the duration of the R&D. Where the project involves
joint exploitation of the results, the exemption will continue to apply for seven
years after contract products are first put on the market in the Community.[272] The
exemption will continue to apply thereafter for so long as the parties' combined
market share does not exceed 25 per cent of the total market for the contract
products.[273] For these purposes, market share is to be calculated on the basis of
preceding year data. There is a safety margin extending the exemption when the
market share subsequently rises to between 25 and 30 per cent (two year extension) or above 30 per cent (one year extension).[274]

Provisions which must not be included.   Exemption under Regulation 2659/   **7.085**
2000 is precluded[275] if the parties are: (a) restricted from carrying out independent R&D in an unconnected field,[276] or in the field of the joint programme after
its termination; (b) restricted after completion of the R&D from challenging
intellectual property rights relevant to the R&D or to its results; (c) restricted as
to output or sales;[277] (d) restricted in the determination of prices, save that they
may agree the prices charged to immediate customers where they undertake joint
distribution;[278] (e) restricted in respect of the customers whom they may serve
after the end of seven years from the time when the products were first marketed
in the Community; (f) prohibited from making passive sales for the contract

---

[268] ibid, Art 2(12).

[269] Production by related undertakings is also to be taken into account in this assessment: ibid,
Art 2(2) and (3).

[270] ibid, Art 4(2).

[271] This covers the situation when the objective of the R&D is the development of a new product
which will create a completely new demand: Horizontal Cooperation Guidelines (n 243, above)
para 54.

[272] ibid, Art 4(1) and (2).

[273] ibid, Art 4(3).

[274] ibid, Art 6.

[275] ibid, Art 5(1).

[276] See also Art 1(2).

[277] But the setting of production or sales targets is permitted where that is necessary for the integration of production or sales functions: ibid, Art 5(2).

[278] ibid. Reg 418/85 did not contain this proviso. cf *Alcatel Espace/ANT* (n 200, above) where
the parents engaged in joint bidding for satellite projects and therefore were restricted in their independent determination of prices. The JV therefore did not come within Reg 418/85 but individual
exemption for 10 years was granted.

products in territories reserved for other parties; (g) restricted from putting the contract products on the market, or pursuing an active sales policy in territories reserved to other parties after the end of seven years from the time when the products were first marketed in the Community; (h) required not to grant third party licences in respect of the products or processes arising from the joint R&D where the exploitation by the parties themselves of the results is either not provided for or does not take place; (i) required to refuse to meet demand from users or dealers in their respective territories who would market the products elsewhere in the common market; or (j) required to take other measures to hinder parallel imports.

7.086 **Withdrawal of block exemption.** As with other block exemption regulations, Regulation 2659/2000 provides[279] that the Commission may withdraw its benefit from a particular agreement which has effects that are incompatible with Article 81(3). The specified circumstances that may trigger such a withdrawal are designed to cover the risk of foreclosure either as regards research opportunities (because of the limited research capacity elsewhere) or as regards access to contract products (because of the structure of supply on the market); the situation where the parties do not exploit the results of their joint R&D; and the case where the contract products are not subject to effective competition.

6. Specialisation/Production Agreements

(a) Generally

7.087 **Introduction.** Many JVs involve production. Where the JV extends also to distribution of the products manufactured, it will often be a 'full-function' JV that will be appraised under the Merger Regulation if it meets the thresholds of that Regulation.[280] Where cooperation on production is by way of specialisation and not joint production, it will more usually be achieved through contractual arrangements that may technically not amount to a JV. This Section, which is to be read with Sections 1 to 4 above, considers some specific aspects of joint production and specialisation agreements, (whether or not in the form of a JV) and the block exemption regulation for such agreements, Regulation 2658/2000. Following the approach of the Horizontal Cooperation Guidelines, an arrangement will be considered a production/specialisation agreement when its 'centre of gravity' concerns joint or specialised production.[281]

---

[279] Art 7.
[280] See para 7.004, above. Where a full-function JV does not have a 'Community dimension' in this sense, it may nonetheless fall to be assessed under Art 81: para 7.017 (C) and (D), above.
[281] See para 7.029, above.

Specialisation agreements. The term 'specialisation agreement' refers to **7.088**
agreements which bring about specialisation at the production level between
competing or potentially competing manufacturers. Such agreements may be for
reciprocal or unilateral specialisation. Reciprocal specialisation involves an
agreement by each party to specialise in the production of certain products to the
exclusion of other products which are to be produced by the other party. As a
corollary, each party agrees to obtain exclusively from the other its requirements
of those products which it has itself agreed not to manufacture and to supply to
the other party the products in the manufacture of which it has itself specialised.
The products may be final products ready for distribution and sale;[282] or intermediate products that each party will use in its independent manufacture of the finished goods.[283] Unilateral specialisation involves an agreement whereby only one
party ceases to manufacture certain products, agreeing to take its requirements
exclusively from the other. It is often referred to as 'out-sourcing' and has become
increasingly important in many industries.

Joint production agreements. The Commission originally adopted a block **7.089**
exemption for specialisation agreements in 1972.[284] In 1985, Regulation 417/85
already extended the scope of the exemption, notably by allowing the parties to
agree to manufacture '*only* jointly'. The most recent block exemption, Regulation
2658/2000,[285] came into force on 1 January 2001. It no longer includes the qualification of 'only' and covers all agreements for joint manufacture, thereby further
enlarging the scope of agreements that benefit. The Horizontal Cooperation
Guidelines similarly treat specialisation and joint production agreements as one
category. In this Section, the term 'production agreements' is used to cover both
specialisation and joint production agreements.

The Commission's approach. The principal substantive concern to which pro- **7.090**
duction agreements may give rise is the possibility of restraint on the parties' competitive efforts as suppliers. However, most types of production agreement can be
assumed to bring some economic benefits by way of economies of scale or scope
or the introduction of new technologies, unless they are a disguised means of price
fixing or output limitation, or market or customer sharing. Regulation 2658/2000
accordingly abandons the clause-based approach of its predecessor,[286] in favour of
a broad exemption of all production agreements that do not contain specified
'hard-core' restrictions and where the parties' combined market share does not

---

[282] eg *Sopelem/Langen*, JO 1972 L13/47, [1972] CMLR D77.
[283] eg *VW/MAN* (n 184, above).
[284] Reg 2779/72, JO 1972 L292/23; replaced successively by Reg 3604/82, OJ 1982 L376/33,
by Reg 417/85, OJ 1985 L53/1 and most recently by Reg 2658/2000, OJ 2000 L304/3.
[285] Reg 2658/2000, OJ 2000 L304/3, Vol II, App C.4; see further paras 7.097 *et seq*, below.
[286] Which exempted agreements that contain specific restrictions and obligations.

exceed 20 per cent.[287] This means that most production agreements should be covered by the block exemption and thus are unlikely to require a full self-assessment under Article 81. However, where the market share limit is exceeded, the parties and their advisors need to balance carefully potential anti-competitive effects of the agreement against its benefits to ascertain whether Article 81(3) can apply.

(b) Assessment under Article 81

7.091 **Actual or potential competitors.** Where the parties are not actual or potential competitors in either of the products or markets covered by the agreement, Article 81(1) should not apply save in two very limited situations. These are where there are spill-over effects into other markets, or where there is a risk of foreclosure. The Horizontal Cooperation Guidelines state that even where parties are competitors, a production agreement will not necessarily lead to the coordination of competitive behaviour. If collaboration between firms provides the only commercially justifiable way of entering a new market, or of carrying out a specific project, such collaboration should not fall within Article 81(1).[288] However, in such instances the parties ought not to be regarded as potential competitors in respect of the subject-matter of the collaboration. When the parties are competitors, a distinction has to be made between a production agreement concerning a final product and one concerning an intermediate product.

7.092 **Production of final product.** An agreement relating to the production of a final product in which the parties are actual or potential competitors will ordinarily fall within Article 81(1). Such collaboration may have an anti-competitive effect as regards output, innovation or prices. The test is whether, on the facts, the parties have expressly or by implication[289] renounced the possibility of engaging in the (otherwise quite feasible) separate development and manufacture of products.[290] Reduction of capacity or investments in itself may have an impact on competition.[291] Where the scope of the cooperation extends to joint development

---

[287] cf the similar approach of Reg 2659/2000 (R&D): para 7.083, above.

[288] Horizontal Cooperation Guidelines, OJ 2001 C3/2, Vol II, App C.12, para 87. This suggests that whereas previously such commercial justification was assessed with regard to 'indispensability' as a condition for exemption under Art 81(3), the current view is that it may preclude Art 81(1) from applying in the first place.

[289] eg *Bayer/Gist-Brocades* (n 201, above) para 51: '. . . it would serve neither the spirit nor the purpose of the agreement if, during its course, one party were able to become an independent competitor in the manufacturing preserve of the other.'

[290] eg by agreeing not to extend their range and to purchase from each other, as in *Sopelem/ Langen*, JO 1972 L13/47, [1972] CMLR D77; or to develop a new joint range as in *VW/MAN*, OJ 1983 L376/11, [1984] 1 CMLR 621; or by accepting an express restriction as in *JAZ/Peter (No. 1)*, JO 1969 L195/1, [1970] CMLR 129.

[291] *Bayer/BP Chemicals* (n 234, above) para 21.

or cross-licensing of technology, competitive initiative regarding development of new products will also be affected.[292] Even if the agreement covers only production and the parties engage in separate distribution, their identical production costs will usually have an impact on their sales prices.[293]

Production of intermediate product.   For an intermediate product or compo-   **7.093**
nent, it is necessary to consider the effects not only on the market for the intermediate product itself but also on the downstream, final product market.[294] Moreover, the higher the parties' market share, the greater the potential for foreclosure of supplies to or purchases from third parties. In *Philips/Osram*,[295] where 80 per cent of the JV's production of lead glass was to supply the requirements of the parents for use in their manufacture of incandescent and fluorescent lamps, the jointly produced lead glass accounted for only two to three per cent of the costs of a lamp. The Commission therefore found that there was no appreciable anti-competitive effect on the lamp market. However, the JV was held to come within Article 81(1) because of the removal of Osram as a potentially competitive supplier of lead glass to third party lamp manufacturers. By contrast, where the input product accounts for a significant proportion of the production costs of the final product, an appreciable anti-competitive effect as regards the final product is likely.[296]

Degree of commonality of costs.   The Horizontal Cooperation Guidelines   **7.094**
note that an effect on the parties as suppliers of the final product is unlikely if the area covered by the collaboration concerns only a small proportion of their total costs.[297] Therefore, when an agreement covers only a small proportion of the parents' total output, for example a JV to establish a particular new plant, the formation of the JV may in itself have little impact on prices and so fall outside Article 81(1).[298] The Guidelines further indicate that for heterogeneous products, where substantial marketing costs are also involved, the impact of joint

---

[292] eg *Olivetti-Canon* (n 215, above); *Bayer/Gist-Brocades* (n 201, above); *Ford/Volkswagen*, OJ 1993 L20/14, [1993] 5 CMLR 617; and see paras 7.108 *et seq*, below.

[293] See *Olivetti-Canon* (n 215, above) (JV to develop, design and manufacture copying and fax machines, as to which parents were actual or potential competitors; also laser printers, in which market only Canon had been involved); *Exxon/Shell*, OJ 1994 L144/20 (JV plant to produce linear low-density polyethylene: a homogeneous product so that competition was based on investment and production strategy, that is coordinated by the JV).

[294] For this aspect of spill-over, see also para 7.046, above.

[295] *Philips/Osram*, OJ 1994 L378/37.

[296] eg *Fujitsu/AMD Semiconductor*, OJ 1994 L341/66 (JV to manufacture semi-conductor wafers that account for more than half of the price of non-volatile memory devices).

[297] Horizontal Cooperation Guidelines (n 288, above) para 88.

[298] See *Solvay-Sisecam*, OJ 1999 C272/14, [1999] 5 CMLR 1444 (Art 19(3) Notice indicating negative clearance for JV to operate soda production plant in Bulgaria).

production on final prices will be much less and Article 81(1) might not apply.[299] Similarly, such 'low degree of commonality of total costs' may arise when the specialisation or joint production covers an intermediate product that accounts for a small proportion of the cost of manufacture of the final product.

7.095 **'Hard-core' restrictions.**   Restrictions regarding pricing or limiting output and arrangements for sharing markets or customers are regarded as intrinsically anti-competitive and will almost always come within Article 81(1). In *Solvay-Sisecam*,[300] the original agreement for a production JV established the transfer price for sales by the JV of soda (the JV product) to its parents by reference to their selling prices to third parties. Following the Commission's concern that this might lessen price competition between the parties in distribution, the transfer price mechanism was changed to reflect independently established international prices. Further, to take the agreement outside the scope of Article 81(1), a clause prohibiting one party from actively marketing soda produced by the JV in Italy (where it had an independent soda facility) was deleted after discussion with the Commission. In *Fujitsu AMD Semiconductor*,[301] non-exclusive licences to the one parent to sell in the UK and Ireland and to the other to sell in the rest of Europe were held to fall within Article 81(1); but because the restriction covered only active not passive sales, it did not preclude the application of Article 81(3) to the agreement.

7.096 **Individual application of Article 81(3).**   Where the market share threshold of the block exemption is exceeded, the application of Article 81(3) will depend on overall analysis of the market structure. The individual and combined shares of the parties, the market concentration and barriers to entry and the extent of any over-capacity in the industry are all relevant factors in this assessment. The Horizontal Cooperation Guidelines give examples of production JVs where the structure of the market makes the application of Article 81(3) unlikely.[302] However, even when the parties are competitors with a high market share, the conditions of Article 81(3) may be met. In *Philips/Osram*,[303] the two parents accounted for

---

[299] Horizontal Cooperation Guidelines (n 288, above) para 88. No doubt this is a matter of degree: see *Electrolux/AEG*, OJ 1993 C269/4, [1994] 4 CMLR 112 where the agreement was considered to fall within Art 81(1); but the Commission's approach may have developed since then.

[300] *Solvay-Sisecam* (n 298, above).

[301] *Fujitsu/AMD Semiconductor* (n 296, above). See also *Bayer/BP Chemicals* (n 234, above) where a specialisation agreement covering distribution and production was granted exemption as it formed part of rationalisation of the EC polyethylene business that was in need of serious restructuring in the face of imports from outside the EC; conditions of exemption modified, OJ 1994 L174/34.

[302] At paras 106 *et seq*.

[303] *Philips/Osram*, OJ 1994 L378/37, [1996] 4 CMLR 48. See also *BPCL/ICI*, OJ 1984 L212/1, [1985] 2 CMLR 330 (reciprocal specialisation agreement between two major UK groups designed to rationalise their production of petrochemical plastics; 15-year exemption granted (subject to reporting conditions), despite their high shares of the UK market and the avowed purpose of the agreement to reduce capacity, because of the extent of competition on the broader EC market and the industry-wide structural over-capacity for the products in question); *GEAE/P&W*, OJ 2000 L58/16, [2000]

66 per cent of European production of lead glass but the JV was found to satisfy the conditions for exemption because of the number of major alternative sources of supply outside the Community and the substantial spare production capacity amongst suppliers generally.

(c) Regulation 2658/2000: the specialisation block exemption

In general. The current block exemption for specialisation agreements, **7.097** Regulation 2658/2000, is a reincarnation of a long line of previous block exemptions, albeit modified and extended.[304] It came into force on 1 January 2001 and will expire on 31 December 2010.[305]

Scope. Regulation 2658/2000 covers agreements, decisions of associations of **7.098** undertakings or concerted practices whereby, as regards goods or services:

(a) one party agrees to cease production of certain products or to refrain from producing those products and to purchase them from the other party that agrees to supply them, where those parties are actual or potential competitors (unilateral specialisation); or

(b) two or more parties agree on a reciprocal basis to cease or refrain from producing certain but different products and to obtain them from the other parties, who agree to supply them (reciprocal specialisation); or

(c) two or more parties agree to produce certain products jointly (joint production);

to the extent that those agreements fall within Article 81(1).

This represents a significant extension of the scope of the previous block exemption which did not cover unilateral specialisation (or outsourcing) at all.[306] Furthermore, joint production agreements are included irrespective of whether

---

5 CMLR 49 (full-function JV for production of new aircraft engine for envisaged very large aircraft, where the two parties accounted for 63 per cent of the adjacent market for engines for existing wide-body commercial aircraft and Rolls Royce was the only independent competitor; 15-years exemption granted but, because of concern about spill-over to that adjacent market, subject to conditions confining the scope of the JV to the particular new engine). (The JV was notified prior to the amendment to the Merger Reg and so was assessed under Reg 17 as a 'cooperative JV'.) See also the example in Commission Guidelines in the Application of Art 81(3), OJ 2004 C101/97, Vol II, C.18, para 116.

[304] Reg 417/85, OJ 1985 L53/1, replaced the previous Reg 3604/82, OJ 1982 L376/33, the scope of which was expanded by Reg 153/93. The duration of the block exemption was further extended by Reg 2236/97, OJ 1997 L306/12 until 31 December 2000.

[305] Reg 2658/2000, OJ 2000 L304/3, Vol II, App C.4. The Reg contains transitional provisions for agreements already in force on 31 December 2000 but since these provisions expired on 30 June 2002, they are not further discussed.

[306] In many cases outsourcing agreements constitute a concentration to be assessed under the EC Merger Reg either because they involve the transfer of previously internal operations and thus an acquisition of sole or joint control or because they involve the creation of a full-function joint venture. See, eg Case M.791 *British Gas Trading / Group 4 Utility Services* [1996] 5 CMLR 526; Case M.2122 *BAT / CAP Gemini / Iberian* (11 September 2000).

the parties retain independent production facilities or not.[307] However, Regulation 2658/2000 only covers a reciprocal specialisation agreement where parties agree on cross-supplies. That condition prevents an agreement to partition the market passing under the block exemption under the guise of a reciprocal specialisation agreement.[308]

7.099 Ancillary restrictions. Regulation 2658/2000 also expressly covers provisions that are directly related to and necessary for the operation of the agreement.[309] This should include provisions that concern the assignment or use of intellectual property rights; the capacity or production volume of a JV or the quantity of products to be supplied under a specialisation agreement; and the fixing of prices towards third parties of a production JV where its functions extend to distribution.[310]

7.100 Purchasing and marketing arrangements. The exemption in Regulation 2658/2000 extends to arrangements whereby:

(a) the parties accept exclusive purchase and/or exclusive supply obligations; or
(b) the parties to a joint production agreement agree on joint distribution or distribution by a third party, on an exclusive or non-exclusive basis, provided that the third party is not a competitor.[311]

However, such exclusivity arrangements which are not agreed in the context of specialisation or joint production will not be exempt under this provision and will require separate assessment under Article 81.[312]

7.101 Other obligations. The restrictions expressly set out in Regulation 2658/2000 do not purport to be exhaustive. The block exemption covers all specialisation or production agreements, as defined, subject to a market share limit, provided that they do not contain 'hard-core' restrictions to fix prices,[313] limit output[314] or sales or allocate markets or customers.[315]

---

[307] cf Reg 417/85 (n 304, above) Art 1(b): 'to manufacture certain products or have them manufactured only jointly'.

[308] cf *SPELL*, OJ 1978 L191/41, [1978] 2 CMLR 758.

[309] Reg 2658/2000 (n 305, above) Art 1(2).

[310] The first category is expressly mentioned in Art 1(2). Note that the last category is in any event likely to be a full-function JV.

[311] Art 3.

[312] See, eg *Hydro Texaco Holdings–Preem*, XXVIIth *Report on Competition Policy* (1997), pp 107–108: production JV to manufacture lubricants for the parents, combined with a trade mark licence and distribution agreement granting one party an exclusive licence to distribute lubricants under the other's trade mark in Sweden. The Commission considered that the second agreement was not ancillary to the first and examined it separately (and two separate comfort letters were issued).

[313] Save in the case of a production and distribution JV, which inherently involves joint determination of prices: Art 5(2)(b) of Reg 2658/2000.

[314] Save in the case of a unilateral or reciprocal specialisation agreement or a production JV: ibid, Art 5(2)(a).

[315] Art 5(1).

Market share and turnover limits.   The exemption under Regulation 2658/   **7.102**
2000 will apply provided that the combined share of the relevant market[316] held
by the participating undertakings (and their related undertakings) is no more
than 20 per cent.[317] The market share is to be calculated on the basis of preceding
calendar year data and there is a safety margin that continues the benefits of
exemption when the market share subsequently rises to between 20 and 25 per cent
(two year extension) or above 25 per cent (one year extension).[318]

Withdrawal of block exemption.   Regulation 2658/2000 includes provision   **7.103**
for the Commission to withdraw its application to a particular agreement where
the benefits envisaged by the block exemption, and therefore the justification
for the application of Article 81(3), are not being realised.[319] This includes cases
where the agreement does not yield significant results in terms of rationalisation
or where the products that are the subject of the agreement are not subject to
effective competition from identical or equivalent products.

7. Joint Ventures in Practice

Introduction.   This Section contains some illustrations of how JV practice has   **7.104**
developed in particular sectors of the economy. It begins with a description of two
production joint ventures in traditional industries *Elopak/Metal Box-Odin* and
Ford/Volkswagen. The first of these marked a step change in the Commission's
approach to the application of Article 81(1). The Section then focuses on how
joint ventures are developing in sectors of the economy characterised by the
requirement for major capital investment. These include major infrastructure
projects for exploiting natural resources and the expanding markets for TV and
media broadcasting, mobile telephony and e-commerce.

(a) Production joint ventures

An R&D, production and sales JV: *Elopak/Metal Box-Odin.*   A 50/50 owned   **7.105**
JV company, Odin, was established by Elopak and Metal Box to carry out R&D
concerning a new type of paperboard carton container with a separate metal lid to
hold UHT-treated, non-liquid foods and to develop the machinery and technology required to fill such containers. If the R&D phase was successful, Odin would
produce and distribute both containers and filling machines. The JV was of

---

[316] Defined as the relevant product and geographic market(s) to which the products that are the
subject-matter of the agreement belong: Art 5.
[317] Arts 2(2) and 4.
[318] Art 6.
[319] Art 7.

indefinite duration. It was likely that, once developed, the new container would compete with metal cans, glass jars and 'brick' cartons but not with cartons for fresh liquids packaging; it might however come to constitute a distinct market.[320] The Commission decided[321] that Article 81(1) did not apply to the formation of the JV itself. Although Odin was a full-function JV, the Commission's analysis remains of general relevance for its assessment of various possible effects on competition.

7.106 *Elopak/Metal Box-Odin*: **application of Article 81(1).** The Commission first considered whether the parents were actual or potential competitors. The Commission took account of the particular structural and dynamic market characteristics which, given the costs involved, 'would realistically preclude' each party from entering the field independently. These included the parents' existing technical capabilities, the commercial risks inherent in over-coming consumer resistance to innovation and the need to provide extensive customer support on launch. The conclusion was that neither party could in the short term enter the market alone since expertise in the other's technology could not be developed without significant and time-consuming investment. Further, the whole project involved considerable commercial risks as it would be necessary not only successfully to develop the product but also to gain consumer acceptance and persuade food processors and packers to invest in the expensive new packaging and equipment. Because the two parents therefore were not potential competitors in the JV field, the creation of the JV involved no restriction as between them.

—Potential competitors: JV and a parent.

As the JV was full-function, the Commission also considered the risk of coordination between Metal Box and Odin. Although it was possible that the new container would compete with Metal Box products, the Commission did not consider that this situation brought the JV within Article 81(1). The extensive post-termination cross-licensing provisions, which could be triggered by Elopak unilaterally dissolving the JV, would tend to deter any anti-competitive coordination of the commercial behaviour of Odin and Metal Box.

---

[320] cf the market definition in *Tetra Pak II*, OJ 1992 L72/1, [1992] 4 CMLR 551 (carton packaging treated as distinct from other forms of packaging and aseptic cartons for liquids held to be a separate market); upheld on appeal; Case T-83/91 *Tetra Pak v Commission* [1994] ECR II–755, [1997] 4 CMLR 726; further appeal dismissed; Case C-333/94P [1996] ECR I-5951, [1997] 4 CMLR 662.

[321] *Elopak/Metal Box-Odin*, OJ 1990 L209/15, [1991] 4 CMLR 832.

—'Spill-over' effects.

The Commission concluded that Elopak and Metal Box were neither actual nor potential competitors outside the JV field since the former was a manufacturer of cartons for fresh or pasteurised liquids, a market in which the latter was not involved.[322]

—Foreclosure.

Despite the concentrated character of the various packaging markets (cans, jars and brick cartons), there were other large metal can makers with technical know-how equivalent to that of Metal Box. Similarly, the aseptic technology used by Elopak was used also by other companies. The collaboration of Metal Box and Elopak in the JV on an exclusive basis therefore would not foreclose the possibility of development of potential competition to the Odin product.

Elopak/Metal Box-Odin: **specific restrictions.** The Commission also examined **7.107** the specific restrictions in the agreements and concluded that all were properly to be regarded as necessary to ensure the creation and proper operation of a non-infringing JV. Accordingly, they did not come within Article 81(1). In particular, the following provisions were regarded as ancillary:

— the exclusive licences from the parents to Odin to exploit their know-how relevant to the field of the JV[323] (ie field-of-use exclusivity);
— the provision for non-exclusive licence-back by Odin to both parents of improvements which it did not wish to exploit or of which the likely use would not conflict with Odin (ie licence for use outside the JV field);
— the provision that whereas each parent was free to compete in the JV field at R&D, production and marketing levels, it could not use the other parent's know-how or Odin improvements to do so;
— in the event of dissolution of the JV or sale by one party of its interests, non-exclusive cross-licensing arrangements ensuring equal access to the extant Odin technology (including that originally contributed by both parents), subject only to (i) a field-of-use restriction on each parent as regards the technology originally contributed by the other parent (ie use for Odin container only) and (ii) a five year ban on use by either parent of the other's know-how (or of Odin improvements thereto) with a competitor of the other parent;
— the prohibition on either party disposing of its interests in Odin without the consent of the other and, should one parent buy out the other, a provision that

---

[322] The Commission noted in passing that the JV entailed no network effect (para 28).

[323] The Commission noted that the scope of the JV's activity was 'very narrowly defined to include only the highly specific product in question' (para 30).

the 'inheritor' may not sell its shares in Odin for five years to any third party without first offering them on equal terms to the former parent.

7.108 **JV for development and production (but not marketing):** *Ford/Volkswagen*. This decision[324] concerned the formation of a 50/50 JV company by Ford and VW to develop, engineer and manufacture, at a new, purpose-built plant in Portugal, a new MPV car ('multi-purpose vehicle' or 'people-carrier'). The expected life cycle of this MPV, and so of the JV, was 10 years and the total investment required was approximately US$3 billion. VW would take the lead on product development, Ford on manufacturing and plant engineering. The JV would make differentiated vehicles for both parents under their respective trade marks; the parents would buy at 'cost plus' and all distribution, marketing and sales would be carried out by the parents independently. The parents would supply engines and transmissions to the JV but other components would be externally sourced. The vehicles made for Ford would be differentiated from those made for VW in terms of exterior design, optional extras, product range and engines (all VWs having VW engines and all standard Fords having Ford engines; top-of-the-range and diesel Fords would use VW engines). The parents each accepted a fixed quantity minimum purchasing obligation covering both MPVs and parts and equating in each case to half of the JV's likely output.

7.109 *Ford/Volkswagen*: **Article 81(1).**   The Commission held that the agreement came within Article 81(1). MPVs were held to constitute a distinct market dominated by the Renault Espace which had over 50 per cent of the Community market, with the next largest player having a market share of only 16 per cent. The market was small and, although relatively fast-growing, was unlikely to reach any very large volume overall. Entry was difficult inasmuch as the development and production costs were considerable, the minimum efficient scale of production being around 110,000 units p.a.

—Actual or potential competitors.

Although neither Ford nor VW had produced MPVs, the agreement was between two of the Community's major car manufacturers, each of whom was capable of producing an MPV independently. Since new vehicle development was a key element of competition between car manufacturers, the agreement to cooperate on an MPV rather than compete was seen as inherently a serious restriction of competition.

---

[324] *Ford/Volkswagen*, OJ 1993 L20/14, [1993] 5 CMLR 617. See also *PSA/Fiat (Sevel) agreement*, *XXVth Report on Competition Policy* (1995), p 127 (exemption-type comfort letter).

—'Spill-over' effects.

In addition, there was a risk, arising particularly from the extensive sharing of technical knowledge that would be involved in the JV, that cooperation could spill over into adjacent markets such as light vans and estate cars.

Ford/Volkswagen: **Article 81(3).** The Commission granted an exemption, finding that the conditions of Article 81(3) were fulfilled because of the exceptional circumstances of the market and subject to conditions. This assessment was upheld by the Court of First Instance against a challenge by the manufacturer of the Renault Espace.[325] Exemption was granted for 13 years to allow the high investment of the parties to become profitable. The exemption was subject to a number of conditions and obligations which had three principal objectives: first, to contain the collaboration to the JV purpose and prevent spill-over;[326] secondly, to enable the parents to compete against one another as vigorously as possible at the distribution and sales level;[327] and, thirdly, to deter market sharing in the Community.[328] Finally, the Commission required the parents to provide for effective separation should the exemption not be renewed and imposed certain reporting obligations to enable it to monitor the development of competition in the MPV market.

7.110

(b) Infrastructure and natural resources projects

Natural resources projects: general. Large natural resources projects such as the exploration and development of oil or gas fields or other mines often involve significant project risks. In order to minimise such risks, these projects tend to be undertaken as JVs between a number of competitors covering one or more of the necessary elements such as exploration/research, extraction of the materials and selling the extracted materials as final products. Where these JVs are self-standing, full-function operations they will be assessed under the Merger Regulation.[329]

7.111

---

[325] Case T-17/93 *Matra Hachette v Commission* [1994] ECR II–595. (Matra was independent of Renault, which marketed and distributed the Espace). It has been suggested that the fact that the complainant was the parties' dominant competitor may have influenced the decision, which has been strongly criticised as displaying a weakening of antitrust principles on industrial policy grounds since the general concepts of productive improvement and technical progress referred to in the decision could apply to many new plants: see Amato, *Antitrust and the Bounds of Power* (1997), 59–62. Note also *BPCL/ICI* (n 303, above), where the Community-wide over-capacity in the relevant industry was expressly a ground for exemption of a reciprocal specialisation agreement designed to rationalise production between two major UK producers.

[326] The parents were to establish certain procedures and safeguards regarding the types of information that could be exchanged and the persons to whom and the basis on which it could be disclosed.

[327] Ford was not to use VW engines in more than 25 per cent of its MPVs over any three-year period.

[328] The MPVs must be offered throughout the EC and an EC type-approval sought.

[329] See paras 7.011 and 7.017, above.

Where the JV is not full-function, the entire operation requires an examination under Article 81 on the principles set out in the earlier parts of this Chapter.[330] Given that such markets tend to involve only relatively few players, a careful analysis of potential 'spill-over' and 'network effects' is required.[331]

7.112 **Natural resource projects: joint selling.**   One specific area of concern can arise if the parties intend to extend the JV's activities to joint selling. This will benefit from the application of Article 81(3) only within the very narrow parameters of the Horizontal Cooperation Guidelines. In *Corrib*,[332] the owners of Ireland's only and newly discovered gas field sought to justify joint marketing on the basis that the purchasers were duopsonists (Ireland's state-owned gas company, BGE and its state-owned electricity company, ESB). The Commission rejected the argument that joint selling was needed as a counterweight to the purchasing power of BGE and ESB. This led the parties to abandon the joint marketing aspects of the JV. In *GFU*[333] the Commission initiated proceedings against some 30 Norwegian gas producers for participating in the Norwegian Gas Negotiation Committee, GFU. The purpose of GFU was to negotiate sales contracts on behalf of all Norwegian gas producers. Following the Commission's investigation, the parties agreed to market their gas individually and to discontinue all joint marketing activities. A similar marketing structure existed in Denmark which was similarly abandoned following the Commission's investigation (in liaison with the Danish competition authority) in *Dong/DUC*.[334]

7.113 **Infrastructure JVs: cross-border power interconnectors.**   Issues similar to those set out above are likely to arise in other infrastructure projects, such as power stations, pipelines or interconnectors. The deal economics of large infrastructure projects also closely mirror those of natural resource projects.[335] *Viking Cable*[336]

---

[330] See para 7.018, above. Note also that some national merger regimes (notably that of Germany) may also still apply.

[331] For spill-over, see para 7.046, above; and for network effects, see para 7.050, above.

[332] See *Corrib*, Press Release IP/01/578 (20 April 2001). See also *Britannia Gas Condensate Field, XXVIIth Report on Competition policy* (1997), p 115 where the Commission cleared an oral joint marketing arrangement on the basis of absence of effect on trade between Member States. However, given that the Bacton-Zeebrugge Interconnector was commissioned since then, that facts have significantly moved on.

[333] See also *GFU*, Press Release IP/02/1084 (17 July 2002). The Commission and not the EFTA Surveillance Authority was the competent authority for the purpose of this case because the arrangement had an appreciable effect on trade between EC Member States: see para 1.091, below.

[334] See See *XXXIIIrd Report on Competition Policy* (2003), points 95–99. See also Press Release IP/03/566 (24 April 2003); and MEMO/03/89, 16 April 2003.

[335] Again, where such infrastructure projects are themselves designed to operate as full-function market participants, they are most likely to fall within the ambit of the EC or national merger regimes.

[336] *Viking Cable*, OJ 2001 C247/11 (Notice under Art 19(3) of Reg 17). The project was subsequently discontinued but the Commission has been concerned to ensure effective third party access

concerned a JV between E.ON, Statkraft and Statnet to build a sub-sea cable for the transmission of high voltage electricity between Norway and Germany. The main purpose was to export electricity from Norway (which has a hydro-power electricity system) to Germany, which has a predominantly thermal-based electricity system, thereby avoiding the construction of a new power plant in Germany. Part of the arrangement was a provision granting Statkraft and E.ON exclusive rights for the use of the interconnector for a period of 25 years. Given the significant level of financial investment and the fact that the project added a further connection to transmission links between Norway and Germany, the Commission considered that it would be justified in granting negative clearance in respect of both Articles 81 and 82. In the earlier case of *Bacton-Zeebrugge Gas Interconnector*,[337] the Commission exempted, rather than cleared, a JV between nine companies to build a gas interconnector between the UK and Belgium. The arrangement divided the entire capacity between the JV shareholders for a period of 20 years.It appears that the key factor leading the Commission to consider that the arrangement fell within Article 81(1) was that the agreements provided for a limited amount of joint selling. The Commission granted an exemption-type comfort letter since the joint selling would only occur in very limited circumstances.[338]

Infrastructure: plant construction. A long term supply contract with the JV **7.114** parents in an infrastructure project was also an issue in *Synergen*.[339] The project involved the construction of a gas-fired power plant as a JV between Norwegian gas company Statoil and Ireland's dominant electricity supplier ESB. A 30-year long exclusive gas supply agreement was regarded as reasonable, given the dominance of the incumbent gas supplier BGE, the fact that Statoil was a new entrant with a share just above *de minimis* level and the fact that the price formula took account of the long term nature. Similarly, a three-year supply contract for the JV's output was cleared on the basis that it would provide the JV operators with certainty for medium term planning.[340] The above cases, contrasted with the Commission's approach to incumbent (usually ex-monopolist) suppliers'

---

to congested interconnectors between different States: *XXXIst Report on Competition Policy* (2001), point 97. See also Press Release IP/01/30 (11 January 2001).

[337] *XXVth Report on Competition Policy* (1995), p 125.

[338] It is important to remember that there was a factually very specific pro-competitive element of the JV that is unlikely to arise in most other JVs: linkage of the UK gas market to the continent at a time when energy liberalisation and market integration was a key Commission objective: see, in particular, ibid, point 82.

[339] *Synergen*, Press Release IP/02/792 (31 May 2002).

[340] In order to clear the JV the Commission also negotiated a commitments which would allow Statoil to enter the market in competition with the JV and which forced ESB and the JV to make some of the output openly available on the market.

infrastructure[341] suggests that the pro-competitive effects of new infrastructure justifies exclusivity for significant periods of time to allow the JV partners the benefit of their investment. In *EHP*,[342] the Commission also cleared a JV which combined the respective hydropower businesses of Germany's E.ON and the Austrian electricity producer Verbund. As the purpose of the JV was to supply only the parents, the JV was only partial function. The Commission based its clearance-type comfort letter on the fact that the parents' market position in the Austrian and German electricity markets would not appreciably change as a result of the JV. While this case involved the combination of pre-existing power stations, the reasoning should equally apply by analogy to new ventures,[343] subject to possible network and spill-over issues.

(c) TV and other media

7.115 **Partnership for launch and management of digital platform for distribution of satellite pay-TV services: *TPS*.** The Commission has stated[344] 'Digital TV is to TV what CD is to sound' in that it provides a superior picture and sound quality and is also used for interactive services such as pay-per-view TV. Like telephony, it is a sector in which the Commission is keen to encourage new entrants to challenge the ability of an incumbent which, with the advantage of many years of national monopoly in the old technology, is likely to become dominant in the new technology. The *TPS*[345] decision was one of the few where an appeal against the grant of an exemption was considered by the Court of First Instance.[346] Because the participating partners did not exercise joint control, Télévision par satellite ('TPS') was not strictly a JV,[347] but it was analysed by the Commission in a similar manner. The shares in TPS were held by four parties each having an equal stake: TF1, France Télévision Enterprises (jointly owned, in turn, by France Télécom and France Télévision), M6 Numérique and Lyonnaise Satellite. TPS operates on the pay-TV market, which the Commission distinguished from the market for free-access television. The Commission identified a separate product market for technical services for pay-TV. In addition, the Commission considered relevant the markets for the acquisition of broadcasting rights and for the distribution and

---

341 As, for example, in the press releases in *Marathon – Thyssengas*, IP/01/1641 (23 November 2001); *Marathon – Gasunie*, IP/03/547 (16 April 2003); *Marathon – BEB*, IP/03/1129 (29 July 2003); and *Marathon – EdF and Ruhrgas*, IP/04/573 (30 April 2004). See also *XXXIst Report on Competition Policy* (2001), point 97.
342 *EHP*, OJ 2001 C316/15 and Press Release IP/02/62 (15 January 2002).
343 See, eg *Pilkington/Saint-Gobain*, OJ 2001 C132/4.
344 *NSAB/Modern Times Group*, Press Release IP/01/1845 (20 December 2001).
345 *TPS*, OJ 1999 L90/6, [1999] 5 CMLR 168.
346 Case T-112/99 *Métropole Télévision-M6 v Commission* [2001] ECR II-2459, [2001] 5 CMLR 33, [2002] All ER (EC) 1. The judgment of the CFI contains important comments on the nature of ancillary restrictions in JVs: see para 7.053, above.
347 For joint control, see para 7.002, above.

operation of special interest channels. On all those markets Canal+, the established incumbent, had a strong position, with 4.3 million subscribers, a strong brand image in France and considerable acquired know-how in the management of pay-TV services; the Commission estimated Canal+ to have approximately a 70 per cent share of the French pay-TV market.

TPS: **formation of the enterprise.** The Commission held that the creation of **7.116** TPS did not infringe Article 81(1).[348]

—Competitors.

The Commission concluded that there was no risk of coordination between the partners. None of the members of TPS was already a competitor on the pay-TV market. TF1, France Télévision and M6 (the parent of M6 Numérique) were all present on the unencrypted television market, where they had continued to compete fiercely; whereas the cable operator members (France Télécom and Lyonnaise) did not compete with each other as they operated in different geographic areas. Only France Télécom was active in the market for technical services for pay-TV. On the market for the acquisition of broadcasting rights, particularly for films and sporting events, the Commission held that there was little risk of coordination between the broadcaster members, provided that their main activity continued to be unencrypted TV broadcasting and that the resulting competition between them on that market was maintained.

—'Spill-over' effects.

All the TPS members had stakes of varying sizes in special-interest channels but the Commission held that the risk of coordination of competitive behaviour on the market for the distribution of special-interests channels was not realistic. As far as concerned satellite transmission, a clause in the agreement between the parties gave TPS a priority right to the special-interest channels of the TPS members; and, as far as concerned the distribution of special-interest channels via cable, the differences between the commercial value of the different channels involved led the Commission to conclude that coordination between the parties, particularly as regards price, was 'hardly conceivable'.

—Foreclosure.

The notified agreements included a clause whereby the two shareholding cable operators agreed to give priority on their networks to programmes supplied by TPS. As they together held more than half of the cable market, that provision

---

[348] As the ultimate aim of TPS was to serve French-speaking Belgium and Luxembourg, the agreements had an effect on inter-State trade.

would have had a significant effect in restricting access by independent channels to the cable network. The clause was deleted at the Commission's request, removing the risk of foreclosure.

7.117 *TPS: specific restrictions.* The Commission considered whether three clauses in the agreement fell within Article 81(1):

(i) The parties undertook not to become involved in any way in companies engaged in the distribution and marketing of television programmes and services for payment which are broadcast in digital mode by satellite to French-speaking homes in Europe. In view of the fact that TPS was a high-risk venture, this non-compete obligation was held by the Commission to be ancillary but only for the launch phase, which the Commission estimated to cover the initial three years.

(ii) The parties agreed, for a 10-year period, to give TPS first refusal in respect of the special-interest channels and services operated, controlled or produced by any of the parties. The Commission concluded that although this provision might be regarded as ancillary to the launch of the new service, it resulted in a limitation of the supply of special-interest channels and television services and its imposition for such a long period came within Article 81(1). The Commission granted this provision an exemption for three years. This aspect of the decision was challenged on appeal (the parties had sought a 10-year exemption). The Court of First Instance upheld the findings both that the clause fell within Article 81(1) and that there was no manifest error in limiting the exemption to three years.[349]

(iii) Similarly, the parties agreed to grant TPS the exclusive right to broadcast the general-interest terrestrial channels of TF1, France Télévision and M6 in encrypted form and digital mode by satellite. The Commission regarded this exclusivity as a restriction on competition coming within Article 81(1), as competitors of TPS were thereby denied access to 'attractive programmes'. However, TPS faced a considerable handicap in having to compete with Canal+, which held much more extensive sporting and film broadcasting rights. In order to formulate an attractive choice for subscribers in the face of such competition, TPS relied on the exclusive presence of the general-interest channels. Accordingly, the restriction qualified for exemption but the Commission regarded the 10 years exclusivity provided by the clause as excessive. On the basis that TPS had to establish its subscriber base as quickly as possible, the Commission granted exemption for three years as 'the minimum period' during which it considered that the exclusive right

---

[349] *Métropole Télévision-M6 v Commission* (n 346, above).

was essential.[350] Again, both aspects of the Commission's decision on this clause were upheld by the Court of First Instance.

Exclusivity following demerger. In *Telenor/Canal+/Canal Digital*[351] the **7.118** Commission issued a complex and lengthy decision which considered the relationship between direct-to-home and cable network delivery of satellite channels and the different characteristics of pay-TV, pay-per-view and near-video-on-demand retail products. Telenor is a Nordic media and telecom operator in Norway under the sole control of the Norwegian State. Canal+ produces, acquires and distributes feature films, audio-visual works and acquires and exploits film licences and sports broadcasting rights for the purpose of pay-TV distribution. It also produces pay-TV channels and markets bouquets of such channels via cable and satellite. In 1997 Canal+ and Telenor established a joint venture, Canal Digital but in 2001, Canal+ sold its 50 per cent share in Canal Digital to Telenor. The agreements notified to the Commission were intended to ensure a continuation of the exclusive satellite distribution of Canal+ Nordic's premium pay-TV channels through the direct-to-home satellite TV platform Canal Digital. The Commission decided that Article 81 was applicable to 'demerger' agreements entered into between economically distinct undertakings as part of an overall divestment transaction and the separation of previously vertically integrated companies.

Telenor: **specific restrictions.** The Commission considered various bundles of **7.119** provisions which gave rise to competition concerns. First, the arrangements gave Canal Digital the exclusive right to direct-to-home (as opposed to cable network) satellite distribution of Canal+ Nordic's pay-TV channels for a period of 10 years. The parties agreed to shorten this to a maximum period of four years. The parties also entered into various non-compete obligations which shielded DTH satellite distribution of Canal+ Nordic's pay-TV channels by Canal Digital from competition emanating from both third party pay-TV channel suppliers and from the Telenor group itself. Again the Commission found that these had a substantial foreclosure effect. The Commission analysed the restrictions in part as horizontal and in part as vertical[352] and found that these clauses had a considerable foreclosure effect in a market where barriers to entry were already high. It granted a five-year exemption to the arrangement, and found that the arrangements relating to pay-per-view did not fall within Article 81(1).

---

[350] *TPS* (n 345, above) para 134.

[351] *Telenor/Canal+/Canal Digital*, Decn of 29 December 2003, Press Release IP/04/2 (5 January 2004).

[352] In commenting on this case, the Commission stated that this was the first time that it had, in this sector, explicitly drawn on the principles laid down in the Guidelines on Vertical Restraints issued in October 2000: see *XXXIIIrd Report on Competition Policy* (2003), point 185.

7.120 **Use of satellite transponders.** The sale agreement in the *Telenor/Canal+* case obliged Canal+ Nordic to continue to retransmit its premium content channels for DTH reception exclusively via satellites owned and operated by Telenor during the five year period rather than via competing satellite service providers. Telenor continued to be free to offer spare satellite transponder capacity to third party TV channel providers and Canal+ Nordic remained free to use third parties' satellite capacity retransmission of its premium content channels to cable network operators' head-ends. The Commission concluded that the satellite transponder non-compete obligation formed an integral part of the vertical relationship created between Canal+ Nordic and Telenor/Canal Digital for the purpose of the exclusive distribution of Canal+ Nordic's pay-TV premium content channels via direct-to-home and could not be separated from the latter without undermining its efficiencies. The restriction therefore received exemption alongside the overall arrangement. In this, the Commission was following its earlier response to an arrangement between the other major player in the Nordic pay-TV market. In *Nordic Satellite AB/Modern Times Group*[353] the Commission had issued a comfort letter in respect of an agreement between NSAB and MTG setting the conditions for the migration of MTG's analogue satellite broadcasting operations in the Nordic region to digital satellite broadcasting operations from NSAB's satellites. According to the agreement, NSAB would be the exclusive provider of satellite transponder capacity to MTG for digital transmission of television signals for a five-year period. This was provided that NSAB's rates were competitive and further that NSAB accepted certain restrictions regarding the lease of transponder capacity for digital transmission of advertising funded, general entertainment, non-encrypted television channels. The Commission's view was that although the agreement, at first sight, presented certain restrictions of competition, it was in fact pro-competitive since it facilitated the upgrading from analogue to digital transmission of television programmes to viewers receiving satellite television direct-to-home. It also permitted a more efficient use of NSAB's satellite transponders, which could lead to more competition in this market in Scandinavia.

(d) Fixed and mobile telecommunications

7.121 **JV to operate as full service telecommunications provider: *Cégétel+4*.** The notified agreements in the *Cégétel+4* decision[354] concerned the restructuring of

---

353 *NSAB/MTG*, Press Release IP/01/1845 (20 December 2001).

354 *Cégétel+4*, OJ 1999 L218/14 (correcting L237/10), [2000] 4 CMLR 106. For other telecommunications alliances, see *Atlas*, OJ 1996 L239/23, [1997] 4 CMLR 89; and *Phoenix/GlobalOne*, OJ 1996 L239/57, [1997] 4 CMLR 147 (which concerned linked JVs and related distribution and agency arrangements involving France Télécom, Deutsche Telekom and Sprint Corporation; after the agreements were modified exemptions were granted for, respectively, five and seven years subject to a series of conditions, including non-discriminatory access, restrictions on cross-subsidies

Cégétel as a JV between its original French parent, CGE (re-named Vivendi), and British Telecommunications (BT), Mannesmann and the American telecommunications operator, SBC International. The transaction was intended to enable Cégétel to expand its operations into all segments of the French telecommunications markets, in particular fixed voice-telephony, as a 'full service' provider that would be the major competitor to France Télécom. This was a full-function JV, established for an indefinite duration and involving a very large financial commitment by all the participants. Before the notification, Cégétel's only operations in France had been in the mobile telephony sector, of which it had had a market share of 38 per cent of all French subscribers. BT had its own subsidiary in France that was engaged in the provision of corporate telecommunications services, but with a very low market share. As part of the agreements, that business was to be transferred to Cégétel. Just prior to notification, Mannesmann had become (through another JV) a new entrant on the fixed telecommunications market in Germany, but it had no operations in France. SBC was a regional telecommunications provider in the US, but was not involved in the French market.

Cégétel: **application of Article 81(1).** The Commission found that the restructuring of Cégétel did not appreciably restrict actual or potential competition and so fell outside Article 81(1). However, the reasoning was strongly influenced by the fact that the JV would introduce significant competition on the newly liberalised market to the incumbent operator, France Télécom. None of the parents competed to any significant extent on the French telecommunications market, except in mobile telephony. The activity of BT and Cégétel in corporate communications services was dismissed as unimportant, in view of their low market shares and the dominance of this segment by France Télécom. As regards mobile telephony, the Commission found that competition between the parents was not affected as the agreements concerned only the French market.[355] The decision significantly contains no reference in that regard to 'spill-over' or network effects. The Commission noted that 'formally' all the parent companies had the technical and

7.122

---

and the divestiture by France Télécom of its corporate service provider in Germany; moreover the commencement of the period of exemption was contingent upon the further liberalisation of the telecommunications markets which the French and German governments had undertaken to carry out). cf *GEN (Global European Network), XXVIIth Report on Competition Policy* (1997), p 104 (international agreement to create a multilateral, high capacity, fibre optic telecommunications network; the provisions for collective price-fixing and restrictions on access had to be deleted before the Commission granted negative clearance by comfort letter); *BT/MCI,* OJ 1994 L223/36, [1995] 5 CMLR 285 (JV to develop and market international value-added telecommunications services for large multi-national companies, and agreement by the parents to a reciprocal, territorial non-competition clause, was granted an exemption for seven years in respect of the JV itself and five years in respect of the non-competition clause).

355 This aspect is only briefly dealt with in the decision in a passage (at para 39) that is hard to follow, not least because it states that there is no effect on 'potential competition'.

financial resources to enter the French market separately. However, experience in other European markets showed that even well-established international telecommunications operators would not attempt entry into a recently liberalised national market without a financial or strategic partner.

7.123 *Cégétel:* **ancillary restrictions.** The restriction preventing competition between the participants within the French market (subject to any rules relating to passive sales) was considered to be ancillary to the creation of a new 'full service' telecommunications operator in the French market and therefore fell outside Article 81(1). So too did a 'preferred supplier' clause in favour of all parent company dealings with Cégétel, and a 'preferred supplier' and 'preferred customer' clause in relation to the provision of international traffic services between BT and Cégétel. However, the 'preferred supplier' clauses did not entitle any party to review the terms of any third party offer (Cégétel remained free to deal with a third party that offered better terms), and did not result in price transparency which might prejudice third parties. Their purpose was to enable Cégétel to develop its business in the most competitive way possible.

7.124 *Cégétel:* **exemption for specific restrictions.** Under the agreements, Cégétel became the exclusive distributor for BT's 'Concert' services, its enhanced international telecommunications product for corporate customers. Cégétel was prevented from supplying any similar product unless that was expressly requested by a customer. Because of its tendency to isolate the French market against supply of such services from other Member States, this restriction was held to fall within Article 81(1) and it was not ancillary to the JV. However, this provision was given a 10-year exemption under Article 81(3) because of the potential benefit to customers of having Cégétel market and develop the 'Concert' product. The Commission noted that, in global telecommunications JVs, exclusive distribution protects the intellectual property rights of the parents better than other arrangements.[356] Moreover, the exclusivity was not absolute as regards either Cégétel or BT in a market that was highly competitive.

7.125 **Mobile telecommunications: the development of 3G technology.** In Europe, the first generation ('1G') of mobile communication systems was based on analogue technology. This was followed at the beginning of the 1990s by the second generation ('2G') systems which introduced digital technology but which required a physical terrestrial path between the two connected points to be set up for each call for the duration of the connection. Enhanced '2.5G' mobile technologies used more efficient packet-switched communications to send data in packets to their destinations, via different routes, without requiring the reservation of a

---

[356] At para 65; cf *Atlas* (n 354, above) para 58; *Unisource*, OJ 1997 L381/1, [1998] 4 CMLR 105, para 93.

dedicated transmission channel. This provided a greater range of services including mobile e-mail, visual communications, multimedia messaging and location-
based services. The third generation ('3G') of mobile technology builds on 2.5G
technology but has much faster data transmission speeds capable of supporting
multimedia services such as GSM and also of combining the use of terrestrial and
satellite components to transmit the data. Establishing a national 3G network
therefore requires the construction of sites containing satellite transmission masts
and other costly physical infrastructure. [357]

Mobile telecommunications: 3G network sharing. 3G network sharing **7.126**
between operators can take place at a number of different levels and involve varying degrees of cooperation. The degree of independence retained by an operator
depends on which network elements are being shared and its remaining ability to
install separate elements (planning freedom). Site sharing between competitors
has been commonplace in 2G but principally on an ad hoc basis. The need for
a substantial increase in the number of sites to support a national 3G network
heightens environmental and health concerns so that site sharing is expressly
encouraged by Community rules. However, site sharing may have an adverse
impact on competition, in particular by reducing network competition, denying
competitors access to necessary sites and site infrastructure, thus foreclosing
competitors and possibly, in some cases, facilitating spill-over and collusive
behaviour. In *O₂ UK Limited/T-Mobile UK Limited ('UK Network Sharing
Agreement')*[358] the parties were direct competitors in 2G and 3G wholesale and
retail markets and had well-established positions in 2G mobile telephony. Their
cooperation in a market with only a limited number of competitors and high, if
not absolute, barriers to entry raised competition concerns. However, having
examined the plans in detail, the Commission concluded that they retained
independent control of their networks, including the critical core network.
They would be able to differentiate their services downstream since the level of
common costs brought about by site sharing was not significant. The provisions
whereby they granted each other a degree of exclusivity over shared sites did not

---

[357] See also *Patent Platform Partnership ('3G3P')*, Press Release IP/02/1651 (12 November
2002): negative clearance-type comfort letter for a set of agreements dealing with patents which are
essential for 3G equipment manufacturers who need to comply with the IMT-2000 3G standard.
The Commission insisted that each licence agreement was limited to essential patents only; that the
agreements do not foreclose competition in related or downstream markets; that licensing should be
on non-discriminatory terms and that sensitive commercial information is not exchanged. Further,
3G manufacturers should not be forced to pay for patents that they do not need and the licensing
arrangements should not discourage further R&D and innovation in the mobile communications
sector.

[358] *O₂ UK Limited/T-Mobile UK Limited ('UK Network Sharing Agreement')*, OJ 2003
L200/59, [2004] 4 CMLR 1401. See also *T-Mobile Deutschland/ O₂ Germany: Network
Sharing Rahmenvertrag*, OJ 2004 L75/32 (a different part of the decision annulled by the CFI: see
para 7.127, below).

lead to widespread foreclosure for third party operators since there was no short-age of sites available in the United Kingdom. In any event, if there were specific problem sites, the recently introduced regulatory framework operating in the United Kingdom allowed the National Regulatory Authorities to impose site sharing. The agreement initially provided for third parties to pay a licence fee for use of the site equal to or higher than that of the parties. The parties modified the clauses to remove the concern over possible price fixing and also to ensure that they could not raise the entry costs for third party operators by requiring them to pay a higher licence fee. The Commission therefore concluded that the network sharing aspect of the agreement did not fall within Article 81(1).[359]

7.127 **Mobile telecommunications: reciprocal national roaming arrangements.** Mobile roaming occurs when customers use their mobile telephone on a different mobile network (host or visited network) from that to which they subscribe and which issued their SIM card (home network). Roaming can be either national or international. In both cases it is based on agreements between the home net-work operator and the visited network operator for the provision of wholesale roaming access to the visited network which is then passed on as a retail service by the home network to its subscribers. Cooperation between operators is aimed at providing 'seamless national roaming', which will allow calls to be handed over when the caller moves across the networks without the call being dropped or any loss of service functions. Unless parties to a roaming agreement would be unable to roll out their networks individually, such an agreement may raise significant competition concerns. But close examination of what is likely to happen in the absence of the agreement is vital to an assessment of the competitive effect of the agreement. In *T-Mobile Deutschland (Network Sharing Germany)*[360] the Commission concluded that the reciprocal roaming arrangement between two major players in the market had an appreciable effect on competition since it lim-its the parties' ability to compete at the network level on coverage, quality and transmission rates. It also had effects downstream since the parties were depend-ent on the coverage, quality and transmission rates of each others' networks to provide services. On appeal,[361] the Court of First Instance annulled this part of the

---

[359] The Commission also cleared the information exchange aspect of the agreement. Although the information to be exchanged included business secrets, it was primarily of a technical nature and did not allow one party to understand the overall competitive strategy of the other party. The parties introduced safeguards to limit the risk that the cooperation could spill over into anticompetitive activity in downstream markets. The agreement prohibited the exchange of information on the pricing of products and services, product development and launch plans, and the parties undertook to ensure that employees engaged in the project were provided with appropriate guidance as to competition law, confidentiality and regulatory obligations.

[360] n 358, above.

[361] Case T-328/03 *O2 (Germany) GmbH v Commission* [2006] ECR II-1231, [2006] 5 CMLR 258.

decision on the basis that the Commission had failed to carry out a full analysis of whether the operators would be able to penetrate this new market without entering into the agreement. The examination of competition in the absence of an agreement was especially necessary as regards markets undergoing liberalisation or emerging markets, as in the case of the 3G mobile communications market, where effective competition may be problematic owing, for example, to the presence of a dominant operator, the concentrated nature of the market structure or the existence of significant barriers to entry. The Court held that the factors which the Commission had considered relevant only to the application of Article 81(3) could well take the agreement outside Article 81(1) altogether. The Court concluded that:

> '. . . it cannot therefore be ruled out that a roaming agreement of the type concluded between T-Mobile and O2, instead of restricting competition between network operators, is, on the contrary, capable of enabling, in certain circumstances, the smallest operator to compete with the major players . . . on the retail market, or even dominant operators . . . on the wholesale market.'[362]

(e) E-commerce platforms

E-commerce platforms: general.   The expanding success of the internet has **7.128** given rise to a number of ventures in which companies use the internet to create electronic market places to buy and sell goods. Some of these have been examined under the Merger Regulation,[363] but where the structure does not constitute a 'concentration' within the terms of the merger regime, for example when the parties owning the company do not exercise joint control, the assessment has been conducted under Article 81.[364] Trading platforms operate like an exchange in which buyers and sellers are brought together through an electronic platform (rather than in a physical building such as a market hall or stock exchange). Consequently, the legal analysis of such cases does not differ from the analysis of physical market places. However, by their very nature, such platforms tend to give rise to similar issues which are highlighted here. The Commission regards trading platforms as generally benign, given that they increase transparency in a market and thus lead to a reduction in search and switching costs. However, anti-competitive

---

[362] ibid, para 109.

[363] eg, Case M.1969 *UTC/Honeywell/i2/MyAircraft.com* (4 August 2000); Case M.2027 *Deutsche Bank/SAP/JV* (13 July 2000); Case M.2374 *Telenor/Ergogroup/DNB/Accenture/JV* (2 May 2001); Case M.2747 *Onedeo – Thames Water/ Water Portal* (28 May 2002); Case M.2830 *Lufthansa Cargo/ Air France Finance/British Airways/Global Freight Exchange/JV* (25 October 2002); Case M.3334 *Arcelor/ThyssenKrupp/Steel 24-7* (16 February 2004).

[364] See paras 7.002 and 7.004, above. And see, eg *Eurex*, Press Release IP/02/4 (3 January 2002): full-function JV that fell below the EC Merger Reg thresholds notified to the Commission for a ruling on any Art 81 issues; the Commission found no risk of coordination since the parents were active in different product markets and issued a negative clearance-type comfort letter.

effects are likely to outweigh those benefits if the JV involves joint purchasing/selling, exchange of commercially sensitive information, discrimination or foreclosure.[365]

7.129 **E-commerce platforms: basic analysis.** As with other JV cases, the analysis falls into two parts: first, whether the creation of the JV itself is anti-competitive and, secondly, whether any particular clauses have anti-competitive effects. The first part has not so far given rise to significant issues, given the amount of other sources of competition (in particular from other platforms) and the fact that a new platform tends to create an additional source of procurement or supply.[366] As for the second part of the analysis, the vast majority of cases have hitherto been structured (or restructured) in such a way that they fall outwith Article 81(1), since in this context forms of cooperation that fall within Article 81(1) (such as joint selling or purchasing) are unlikely to meet the criteria of Article 81(3).

7.130 **E-commerce platforms: Article 81(1).** *Covisint*[367] involved a joint venture between the car manufacturers DaimlerChrysler, Ford, GM, Nissan, Renault and Peugeot Citroën to provide the automotive industry with procurement, collaborative product development and supply chain management tools. The Commission identified a number of situations in which electronic trading platforms could fall within the scope of Article 81(1). This will be the case where the platform (i) leads to discrimination between classes of users or, *a fortiori*, if the platform is discriminatory in terms of access to the platform; (ii) where market sensitive data is exchanged through the platform; or (iii) where the platform is essentially a tool for joint purchasing (or selling). In that case, the Commission granted a negative clearance comfort letter on the basis that the platform was open to all firms in the industry on the basis of open standards; there was no discrimination between shareholders and other users; joint purchasing was precluded; and appropriate firewalls and other security measures were put in place to prevent the exchange of sensitive information.[368]

---

[365] See Lücking, 'B2B e-marketplaces and EC Competition Law – where do we stand?' (2001) three EC Competition Policy Newsletter 14. See also OFT Economic Discussion Paper No. 1, *E-commerce and its implications for competition policy* (OFT 308, August 2000).

[366] One open question that may come to fore in future is whether bricks and mortar outlets form part of the same market as electronic trading platforms.

[367] *Covisint+5*, Press Release IP/01/1155 (31 July 2001); and *XXXIst Report on Competition Policy* (2001), p 42, Box 4.

[368] The FTC also closed its investigation into Covisint without taking action under US antitrust law as regards the formation of the JV but reserved its position for the future: Press Release of 11 September 2000 (available at www.ftc.gov/opa/2000/09/covisint.htm); in Germany, the Bundeskartellamt approved the JV based on the fact that Covisint would face competition from a variety of sources: Decn B5-40/00, 30 September 2000.

E-commerce platforms: subsequent practice. In a number of subsequent **7.131** cases[369] the Commission also granted negative clearance-type comfort letters provided the JV remained within the parameters of *Covisint*. The same principles were also applied to trading platforms that did not amount to a formal JV.[370] In *Opodo*[371] the JV parents were nine of the largest European airlines. They created the JV (Opodo) as a pan-European electronic travel agent providing a sales outlet direct to consumers for airline tickets, hotel bookings, car hire and insurance. The Commission sought commitments to prevent spill-over effects to the parents' activities and to stop the parents from favouring the e-platform outlet. These resulted in a negative clearance-type comfort letter under both Article 81 and Article 82. The clearance gave rise to a complaint from a leading German travel agent on the basis that the platform amounted to nothing less than joint selling. The Commission rejected the complaint[372] on the basis that Opodo operates as an independent travel agency and on an arms-length basis from its shareholders. Moreover, the airlines would continue to distribute the majority of their tickets indirectly through other travel agents. In *Volbroker*[373] the Commission issued an exemption-type comfort letter, rather than a negative clearance. However, the issues which arose in *Volbroker* that led to the exemption do not seem to be any different from the cases discussed above which were granted negative clearance-type comfort letters. In particular, non-discriminatory access to the platform and ring-fencing of commercially sensitive information had to be safeguarded before the Commission would issue the comfort letter. Moreover, subsequently the Commission granted a negative clearance-type comfort letter to a similar platform[374] in the same market as *Volbroker*, which suggests an evolution in the Commission's approach. In this context, the criteria of Article 81(3) seem

---

[369] *Eutilia* and *Endorsia*, Press Release IP/01/1775 (10 December 2001): Eutilia was set up by major European electricity utilities including Scottish Power, RWE and Iberdrola, to provide electronic auctions and purchasing, buy/sell enquiries and database services. Endorsia was set up by component manufacturer to support the buying and selling requirements of manufacturers, distributors and end-users of branded industrial goods. In its Press Release the Commission stated: 'the two Internet portals will be open to all potential users on a non-discriminatory basis and all exchange members will be free to do business through other on- and offline methods. Furthermore, the ventures will not act as a buying club, but rather operate as an intermediary. They will also provide appropriate protection of confidential information: firewalls and other safeguards will ensure that no commercially sensitive data is disclosed between competitors'. See also COMP/38.380 *Whirlpool+3*, OJ 2002 C139/5 (new business 2 business portal and possibly an e-market place in the household appliances industry).

[370] *Inreon*, *XXXIInd Report on Competition Policy* (2002) p 188.

[371] *Opodo*, *XXXIInd Report on Competition Policy* (2002) p 190. See also Tomboy, 'Commission clears online travel agency Opodo' (2003) 1 EC Competition Policy Newsletter 54.

[372] The decision rejecting the complaint (published on the DG Comp website) provides a detailed examination of the relevant markets and the assessment of the JV.

[373] *Volbroker*, Press Release IP/00/896 (31 July 2000); and *XXXth Report on Competition Policy* (2000) p 66.

[374] *Centradia*, *XXXIInd Report on Competition Policy* (2002) p 188.

limited to those outlined in the Commission's Horizontal Cooperation Guidelines, for example, joint purchasing by small- and medium-sized enterprises.[375]

7.132 **E-commerce: secure electronic payment system.** In *Identrus*,[376] the Commission granted negative clearance to a multi-lateral agreement enabling the participants to issue digital certificates certifying the identity of their clients engaging in electronic transactions. Each participant in the system operates as an individual and competing certification authority and posts a deposit with a bank for the benefit of third parties who rely on the certificates. The Commission noted that due to the developing nature of the markets in question it did not have a 'comprehensive overview' of the competitive situations or of the parties' future competitors. But it predicted that because of the rapidly increasing demand for authentication services, Identrus would soon be confronted by numerous potential competitors. The Commission found that under the agreements, access was open to all, subject to objective criteria. Identrus had no incentive to exclude participants as it is inherent in the system to attract as many participants as possible to increase its revenues. Further, Identrus participants were free to take part in any other competing scheme if they chose to do so. The Commission concluded that the system did not create any foreclosure risk and there was no adverse effects on input markets. There was nothing to bring the agreement within Article 81(1).

(f) Airline alliances

7.133 **Collaborative arrangements.** The Commission has monitored the increasing trend towards establishing alliances in the air transport sector.[377] Such alliances can benefit consumers by providing a larger product offering or more competitive prices. On the other hand, competition issues may arise if the airlines are particularly strong on certain routes and/or where they hold a large number of slots on capacity constrained airports (such as London Heathrow). Airlines often use strategic alliances because national laws prevent a full merger or takeover. The structure can vary from something that falls within the Merger Regulation[378] to a 'partial function' JV or even a much looser collaboration through agreements

---

[375] See paras 115 *et seq* and also, eg *XVth Report on Competition Policy* (1985), point 26.

[376] *Identrus*, OJ 2001 L249/12, [2001] 5 CMLR 1294.

[377] See Gremminger, 'The Commission's approach towards global airline alliances – some evolving assessment principles' (2003) 1 EC Competition Policy Newsletter 75. For a comparison of the US and EC approaches, see Cheng-Jui Lu, *International Airline Alliances: EC Competition Law, US Antitrust Law and International Air Transport* (2003).

[378] eg Case JV.19 *Alitalia/KLM* (11 August 1999); Case M.2672 *SAS/Spanair* (5 March 2002); Case M.3280 *Air France/KLM* (11 February 2004), appeal dismissed, Case T-177/04 *easyJet v Commission* [2006] ECR II-1931, [2006] 5 CMLR 663.

creating a 'strategic alliance'.[379] All have been approved,[380] but in many cases subject to conditions designed to facilitate new entry into the routes affected, in particular by the requirement that the partners surrender a significant number of slots at the relevant capacity constrained airports.

Air France/Alitalia.   The Commission's approach to airline alliances is illus-   **7.134** trated by the *Air France/Alitalia* decision.[381] Through their cooperation, the two airlines sought to establish a far-reaching strategic bilateral alliance, the main elements of which were (a) the creation of a European multi-hub system based on Air France's hub at Paris Charles de Gaulle and Alitalia's hubs at Rome Fiumicino and Milan Malpensa, in order to interconnect their worldwide networks; (b) coordination of the parties' passenger service operations, including extensive use of code-sharing, coordination of their scheduled passenger network, sales, revenue management, mutual recognition of their respective frequent flyer programmes, marketing coordination and share of lounge usage; and (c) cooperation in other areas, such as cargo operations, passenger handling, maintenance, purchasing, catering, information technology, fleet development and purchase, crew training and revenue accounting.

The France–Italy 'bundle' of routes.   The Commission considered first the   **7.135** parties' planned cooperation on the various routes between France and Italy. On these routes, the parties agreed to coordinate prices and to share their earnings; further, they would coordinate frequencies and schedules, share capacity, and exchange sensitive information as regards their respective sales and yield management systems. The Commission held that the agreements had the object of

---

[379] For other airline alliance decisions, see *LH/SAS*, OJ 1996 L54/28, [1996] 4 CMLR 845; *bmi/ LH/SAS*, Press Release IP/01/831 (13 June 2001); and *XXXIst Report on Competition Policy* (2001), points 136-139; *AuA/LH*, OJ 2002 L242/25, [2003] 4 CMLR 252; COMP/38.477 *BA/SN Brussels Airlines*, Press Release IP/03/350 (10 March 2003); COMP/38.479 *British Airways/Iberia/GB Airways*, Press Release IP/03/350 (10 December 2003). See also *Austrian Airlines/SAS*, OJ 2005 C233/18, where the Commission's intervention lead to the abandonment of the JV and its replacement with a lesser form of cooperation.

[380] Before 1 May 2004 (when Reg 1/2003 as amended by Reg 411/2004 came into effect), agreements relating to air transport services between Community airports could be notified under Art 5 of Reg 3975/87. Unless the Commission raised 'serious doubts' about the arrangement within 90 days of publication of the details in the OJ, the arrangement was treated as exempt for six years. But cf *SAS Maersk Air*, OJ 2001 L265/15, [2001] 5 CMLR 1119, where the investigation of a collaboration agreement relating to code sharing and frequent flyer programmes uncovered a hard-core market sharing agreement; see also *XXXIst Report on Competition Policy* (2001), p 21 (appeal against the level of the fine dismissed, Case T-241/01 *Scandinavian Airlines System v Commission* [2005] ECR II-2917). In *SkyTeam*, the Commission continued an investigation of an arrangement originally notified in 2002 (OJ 2002 C76/12) and issued a statement of objections in mid-2006 (see MEMO/06/243 of 19 June 2006): although the Commission does not object to the alliance as a whole it has concerns about a number of overlap routes where the alliance partners previously competed but no longer face competition from outside the alliance.

[381] Case COMP/38.284 *Air France/Alitalia* (7 April 2004), [2005] 5 CMLR 1504; on appeal, Case T-300/04 *easyJet v Commission*, not yet decided.

reducing competition and that, as a matter of both fact and of law, all competition among the parties would be eliminated. The Commission analysed each route segment as a separate relevant market and calculated the parties' market share on that route. In relation to some routes, the market was further divided between time-sensitive and flexibility-focused passengers on the one hand and price-sensitive passengers, who might regard a rail journey as an acceptable alternative, on the other. On the overlap routes,[382] where the parties were currently both operating services, the Commission had no difficulty in concluding that competition would be appreciably affected. However, in relation to non-overlap routes where, at the time of the agreement, only one party was operating, the Commission considered whether the non-operating party was a potential entrant onto that segment and concluded that it was not.[383]

7.136 **Other intra-European routes.** For routes outside the France-Italy 'bundle', the cooperation between the parties was looser. The parties agreed to make extensive use of code-sharing on a 'free-flow' basis (ie there was no restriction on the number of seats each could sell on the shared flight). They agreed to implement price coordination where possible and to use reasonable efforts to coordinate their flight schedules. The Commission held that these parameters are key elements on which airlines normally compete with each other. Moreover, the parties would share sensitive information as regards their respective sales and yield management systems and in order to cooperate on their frequent flyer programmes. The Commission held that this aspect of the agreement also fell within Article 81(1).

7.137 **Application of Article 81(3).** The Commission accepted that the cooperation agreement was likely to generate benefits in terms of creating a more extensive network which would offer customers better services in terms of an increased number of direct and indirect flights: 'While an increase in the airlines' size does not necessarily lead to a cost reduction because of constant economies of scale, savings may be realised due to an increase in traffic throughout the network, better planning of frequencies, a higher load factor, and so forth.'[384] The parties intended to add additional frequencies on the France–Italy routes offering customers more convenient scheduling and a better spread of flights during the day. Although the parties argued that the alliance would lead to cost savings and efficiencies, the Commission was concerned that, on the routes where the parties

---

[382] Paris-Milan, Paris-Rome, Paris-Venice, Paris-Florence, Paris-Bologna, Paris-Naples and Milan-Lyon.

[383] An airline would, in principle, be considered a potential entrant on a specific non-overlapping route only if that route was either directly linked to one of its hubs or was sufficiently large and frequented by local traffic to allow market entry on a point-to-point basis, while taking into account the operational requirements and benchmarks of the respective business strategy (para 111).

[384] Para 132.

would stop competing with each other, there may not be enough competitive pressure to ensure that the savings would be passed on to consumers. In order to create the potential for future market entry, and thereby ensure that competition was not eliminated in the relevant markets, the Commission required the parties to release slots at congested airports to carriers proposing to start operating on the key routes.[385] This helped reduce one of the main barriers to entry. The parties made other commitments aimed at facilitating new entry: in particular, they agreed to allow new entrants to participate in their frequent flyer programmes; to permit interlining so that passengers can fly out with the parties and return with a competitor or vice versa on a given journey, using a single ticket; and to refrain from increasing their schedule of flights ('frequency freeze') during a start-up period to ensure that a new entrant was not squeezed out of the market shortly after entry. The Commission was satisfied that, on the basis of these commitments, there were several competitors seriously interested in entering the routes at issue. The alliance agreements were therefore granted an exemption for six years under Article 81(3).

Transatlantic alliances. As regards the air transport sector, the adoption of procedural rules implementing Article 81 in respect of all international air travel has been a gradual process. For a long time the Commission had full enforcement powers only in respect of transport between Community airports, but since 1 May 2004 the procedural regime of Regulation 1/2003 applies to all air transport, irrespective of the routes involved.[386] In 2002, under its previous, more limited jurisdiction, the Commission adopted a formal position as regards two transatlantic alliances, *KLM/NorthWest* and *Lufthansa/SAS/United Airlines (STAR alliance)*.[387] In the former, although competition was appreciably restricted on two routes, since there was no capacity constraint at the affected airports the Commission concluded that the parties' behaviour was sufficiently constrained by existing or potential competitors. By contrast, in the *STAR alliance* decision the Commission found that there were substantial entry barriers of both a structural and a regulatory nature. The parties agreed to adopt a number of

7.138

---

[385] See similarly *bmi/LH/SAS* (n 379, above): parties required to release slots at Frankfurt airport allowing for four daily frequencies to address competition concerns. In *AuA/LH*, ibid, given the serious effects of the alliance, the Commission imposed a price reduction mechanism and an obligation to enter into special prorate agreements and inter-modal agreements. Where new players enter the markets, this may reduce the number of slots required to be divested. Conversely, if competitors leave the routes in question additional slots may have to be made available (eg *AirFrance/Alitalia*, OJ 2003 C297/10 at paras 20–22).

[386] This results from the amendment to Reg 1/2003 made by Reg 411/2004, OJ 2004 L68/1, deleting the exclusion of air transport between Community airports and third countries.

[387] *LH/SAS/United Airlines* and *KLM/NorthWest* (both decns of 28 October 2002), Press Release IP/02/1568 (29 October 2002); and see Negenman, 'Commission closes investigation into Lufthansa/SAS/United Airlines and KLM/NorthWest alliances' (2003) 1 EC Competition Policy Newsletter 70.

remedies proposed by the Commission, including the surrender of slots at capacity constrained airports[388] and the offer to new entrants operating a non-stop service of interlining facilities and participation in their frequent flyer programme. In both these cases involving long-haul services, indirect services were regarded as providing actual or potential competition, in contrast to the position taken by the Commission when considering short-haul routes.

---

[388] To allow competition on the routes between Frankfurt and Chicago, Los Angeles, San Francisco and Washington DC.

8

MERGER CONTROL

1. Introduction

(a) Summary

The Merger Regulation.[1]   After many years of deliberation and negotiation the   **8.001**
Community introduced a specific regime for merger control in December 1989
with the adoption of Council Regulation 4064/89 ('the original Merger
Regulation') which came into force on 21 September 1990.[2] Following a wide-
ranging consultation exercise intiated by a Commission Green Paper in 2001,[3]
the original Merger Regulation was replaced by Council Regulation 139/2004[4]
which was adopted in January 2004 and came into force on 1 May 2004.
Regulation 139/2004 (referred to in this Chapter as 'the Merger Regulation') is
the main instrument for the control of mergers, acquisitions and other concentrations under EC competition law. It applies throughout the EEA.[5]

Jurisdictional scope.   The jurisdictional position is considered in more detail in   **8.002**
Section 2 of this Chapter and can be summarised as follows:

(a) *Overview.* Where a 'concentration' has a 'Community dimension', it is sub-
    ject to review by the Commission on a 'one-stop shop' basis for the EEA. This
    allocation of exclusive jurisdiction is subject to certain exceptions.

---

¹ See generally: Struys & Robinson (eds), *EC Merger Decisions Digest* (2005); Levy, *European Merger Control Law: A Guide to the Merger Regulation* (2006); Cook & Kerse, *EC Merger Control* (4th edn, 2005); Navarro, Font, Folguera & Briones, *Merger Control in the European Union* (2nd edn, 2005); Lindsay, *The EC Merger Regulation: Substantive Issues* (2nd edn, 2006); Drauz & Jones (eds), *EU Competition Law, Vol II: Mergers and Acquisitions* (2006).

² Reg 4064/89, OJ 1989 L395/1, corr by OJ 1990 L257/13. It was subject to a series of amendments that took effect on 1 March 1998, by Reg 1310/97, OJ 1997 L180/1, corr by OJ 1998 L3/16, L40/17. For a consolidated text, see App 33 to the 5th ed of this book. For background to the introduction of the Merger Reg, see Brittan, *Competition Policy and Merger Control in the Single European Market* (1991), 25–32. See also paras 8.257 *et seq*, below regarding the position prior to the Merger Regulation.

³ Commission Green Paper COM (2001) 745 of 11 December 2001.

⁴ Merger Reg, Reg 139/2004, OJ 2004 L24/1: Vol II, App D.1. The jurisdictional scope of the original Merger Reg was varied by allowing for the possibility of pre-notification reallocation of jurisdiction between the Member States and the Commission: see para 8.100 and also paras 8.081 *et seq*, below, for the current position. Some procedural changes were introduced, includ-ing extending the timing of most Phase I and Phase II investigations: see paras 8.133 and 8.142, below. The key substantive change was the introduction of the so-called 'SIEC' test (ie whether the merger would significantly impeded effective competition) to replace the earlier 'dominance' test for assessing the compatibility of mergers with the common market: see paras 8.192–8.197, below. For a further explanation of the principal changes introduced, see Commission MEMO/04/9 of 20 January 2004, 'New Merger Regulation frequently asked questions.'

⁵ The Merger Reg has been incorporated by reference into the EEA Agreement by EEA Joint Committee Decn 78/2004 and Joint Committee Decn 79/2004 (the latter dealing specifically with Arts 13 and 22 of the Merger Reg), which came into force on 9 June and 1 July 2005 respectively: see OJ 2004 L219/13 and OJ 2004 L219/24, corr at OJ 2004 L349/70. For the application of the EEA Agreement to mergers, see paras 8.280 *et seq*, below.

(b) *Concentrations.* The Merger Regulation only applies if a transaction gives rise to a 'concentration' involving a change in the control of the undertakings concerned: see paragraphs 8.015 *et seq*, below.

(c) *Full-function joint venture undertakings.* The creation of a full-function joint venture undertaking (and other transactions resulting in an undertaking jointly controlled by two or more other undertakings) will give rise to a concentration: see paragraphs 8.052 *et seq*, below.

(d) *Community dimension.* The levels of the parties' turnovers (worldwide and within the EC) determine whether a concentration has a 'Community dimension': see paragraphs 8.060 *et seq*, below.

(e) *Pre-notification reallocation of jurisdiction.* Generally, concentrations with a Community dimension fall to be investigated by the Commission, whereas those without a Community dimension fall to be investigated by the national competition authorities ('NCAs') in accordance with their domestic merger control rules.[6] As an exception to this general rule, parties can engage in pre-notification contacts with the authorities with a view to reallocating jurisdiction between the Commission and NCAs, either from the Commission to the NCAs or from the NCAs to the Commission: see paragraphs 8.081 *et seq*, below.

(f) *Post-notification reallocation of jurisdiction.* There are also procedures for the reallocation of jurisdiction after a case has been notified to a competent authority. Where a concentration with a Community dimension has been notified to the Commission, in certain circumstances a Member State may request that it be referred (in whole or part) for review under national merger control rules. Conversely, where a concentration without a Community dimension has been notified to one or more of the NCAs, in certain circumstances they may transfer jurisdiction to the Commission. See paragraphs 0 *et seq*, below.

(g) *National investigations on grounds other than competition.* In certain strictly circumscribed situations relating to legitimate issues other than competition, Member States may investigate and even impose conditions on some concentrations with a Community dimension: see paragraphs 8.101 *et seq*, below.

8.003 **Procedure.** A number of procedural consequences flow from the fact that a transaction gives rise to a concentration with a Community dimension. They are considered in more detail in Section 3 of this Chapter and may be summarised

---

[6] Summaries of the national merger control rules in the EU Member States and three EFTA States that are party to the EEA Agreement are provided in the tables at para 8.279, below.

as follows:

(a) *Mandatory notification and waiting period.* Concentrations with a Community dimension must be formally notified to the Commission. Generally, they cannot be put into effect until the Commission has taken a formal clearance decision: see paragraphs 8.111 *et seq*, below.

(b) *Commission investigations.* Formal procedures apply to cases investigated under the Merger Regulation. Most investigations are completed within a period of about five weeks following the formal notification ('Phase I' investigations: see paragraphs 8.133 *et seq*, below). Some cases, however, are subjected to more detailed proceedings which typically last a further four or five months ('Phase II' investigations: see paragraphs 8.141 *et seq*, below). Parties may offer formal commitments to the Commission in order to enable clearance at Phase I or Phase II (see paragraphs 8.162 *et seq*, below). The Commission has wide powers of investigation (see paragraphs 8.172 *et seq*, below); it also has powers to impose fines and other sanctions for infringement of the Merger Regulation (see paragraphs 8.178 *et seq*, below).

Substantive appraisal of concentrations. Various factors must be taken into **8.004** account under the Merger Regulation when assessing whether a notified concentration is compatible with the common market and more specifically whether it would significantly impede effective competition, as considered in Section 4 of this Chapter. Where the notified concentration involves the establishment of a full-function joint venture undertaking which may lead to the coordination of the competitive behaviour of undertakings which remain independent, the Commission can also use its Merger Regulation powers to appraise whether those coordinative aspects are caught by the Article 81(1) prohibition and, if so, whether they may satisfy the criteria for the disapplication of that prohibition in Article 81(3).

Judicial review. Decisions and other acts of the Commission under the Merger **8.005** Regulation are subject to judicial review by the Community Courts, as considered in Section 5 of this Chapter.

Application of Articles 81 and 82 in the field of mergers and acquisitions. **8.006** Although the Merger Regulation is the main instrument for the control of mergers, Articles 81 and 82 of the EC Treaty remain relevant for certain purposes.[7] This is considered in Section 6 of this Chapter. Where parties agree 'ancillary restrictions' which are directly related to, and necessary for, the implementation of a concentration, whether with or without a Community dimension, these will

---

[7] The equivalent provisions under the EEA Agreement are Arts 53 and 54.

fall outside the scope of Article 81(1). However, where restrictions of competition are neither an integral part of the concentration itself (for example, for the establishment of a full-function joint venture undertaking), nor ancillary to the concentration, they may be subject to investigation by the Commission or NCAs under Articles 81 and 82 in accordance with the regime established under Regulation 1/2003. Furthermore, the national courts of the Member States may rule on such aspects and indeed may still have direct jurisdiction under Article 82 in respect of some 'concentrations', whether or not they have a Community dimension.

8.007 **National merger control and international cooperation.** Particularly in the case of high profile cross-border mergers, there may be close cooperation and sometimes tensions between the Commission and other competition authorities considering the case, both within the EEA and globally. This is considered further in Section 7 of this Chapter. For concentrations that do not have a Community dimension, in principle jurisdiction within the EEA falls to the NCAs. For certain concentrations affecting the contracting EFTA States (whether with or without a Community dimension), the EFTA Surveillance Authority plays a significant role under the EEA Agreement. Furthermore, when investigating some international mergers the Commission will generally maintain contacts with other competition authorities outside the EEA under bilateral agreements, for example with the authorities in the United States. The Commission also participates in various multilateral initiatives at a broader policy level.

(b) Commission guidance

8.008 **Implementing Regulation and Notices.** The principal Commission measures applicable to concentrations are set out below. Although the Commission's notices and guidelines are not legislative instruments, they are binding on the Commission in its application of the merger control regime, unless they are inconsistent with the Treaty or the Merger Regulation.[8]

(a) *Implementing Regulation* (2004). The current Commission Implementing Regulation is Regulation 802/2004, which entered into force on 1 May 2004.[9] This addresses various procedural matters, including the calculation

---

[8] Case T-114/02 *BaByliss v Commission* [2003] ECR II-1279, [2004] 5 CMLR 21, para 143.

[9] Implementing Reg, Reg 802/2004, OJ 2004 L133/1: Vol II, App D.2. Until the adoption of an equivalent Implementing Reg at the EEA level, Art 5 of Council Reg 2894/1994, OJ 1994 L305/6, enables the Commission to apply the same rules as it does in respect of the implementation of the Merger Reg. eg, DG Comp has published on its website an unofficial version of Form RS which gives guidance on the extension of the Art 4 pre-notification referral procedures to the three contracting EFTA States.

of time limits and the conduct of hearings. Annexed to it are the various questionnaire forms (notably Form CO) which must be answered by parties when notifying transactions under the Merger Regulation.

(b) *Jurisdictional Notice* (2007). The Commission adopted a new Notice on jurisdictional issues in July 2007.[10] The new Notice consolidates, updates and simplifies four Notices which had been adopted in 1998 in respect of the original Merger Regulation: the Concentration Notice,[11] the Full-function Joint Venture Notice,[12] the Undertakings Concerned Notice[13] and the Turnover Notice.[14] The new Notice takes account of changes introduced in 2004 by the new Merger Regulation. It also reflects recent judgments of the Community Courts. After a short introduction (Part A) the Notice is structured in two parts:

  (i) Part B addresses the concept of 'concentration' under Article 3 of the Merger Regulation, including the notions of 'sole control', 'joint control' and changes in the 'quality of control'. It also specifically deals with joint ventures and the concept of 'full-functionality';

  (ii) Part C deals with the concept of 'Community dimension' which depends on the turnovers of the undertakings concerned. It clarifies the interpretation of the concept of 'undertakings concerned' under Articles 1 and 5 of the Merger Regulation and provides guidance on practical issues associated with the calculation of turnover for Merger Regulation purposes.

(c) *Case Referral Notice* (2004). This provides guidance on the general principles applied by the Commission and NCAs when considering requests for pre-notification reallocation of jurisdiction and also when considering post-notification referrals.[15]

(d) *Best Practice Guidelines* (2004). These provide guidance on the conduct of merger control proceedings, including contact with the Commission prior to and during the notification process.[16]

---

[10] Consolidated Jurisdictional Notice published on 10 July 2007, Vol II, App D.13.

[11] Commission Notice on the concept of concentration, OJ 1998 C66/5.

[12] Commission Notice on the concept of full-function joint ventures, OJ 1998 C66/1.

[13] Commission Notice on the concept of undertakings concerned, OJ 1998 C66/14.

[14] Commission Notice on calculation of turnover, OJ 1998 C66/25.

[15] Commission Notice on case referral in respect of concentrations, OJ 2005 C56/2: Vol II, App D.9.

[16] DG Comp Best Practices on the conduct of EC merger proceedings, available at DG Comp's website (http://ec.europa.eu/comm/competition/mergers/legislation/regulation): see Vol II, App D.7. See paras 8.109 *et seq*, below. The Commission has also published Best Practices for merger investigations which are subject to transatlantic cooperation between the Commission and the US antitrust agencies: Vol II, App D.18. See para 8.284, below.

(e) *Simplified Procedure Notice* (2004). This provides guidance on which cases are eligible for a simplified procedure. For these cases, the notifying parties can use a Short Form notification, rather than the Full Form CO questionnaire, and the Commission issues only a short-form decision at the end of the Phase I procedure.[17]

(f) *Remedies Notice* (2001). This provides guidance on the types of commitments which may be acceptable to the Commission to address competition concerns which it has identified.[18] At the time of writing, the Commission has published for consultation a draft revised version of this Notice to reflect the adoption of Regulation 139/2004 and the developments in the Commission's practice since 2001. Some of the proposed amendments, such as a new information form, Form RM, to be submitted by the parties to describe their remedies proposals, will also require an amendment of the Implementing Regulation, Regulation 802/2004. The draft revised Notice sets out what the Commission already requires of the parties in practice and the Commission encourages parties to use the new form in anticipation of its adoption of the revised Remedies Notice later in 2007.

(g) *Horizontal Merger Guidelines* (2004) and *Non-horizontal Merger Guidelines* (2007). The Horizontal Merger Guidelines provide guidance on how the Commission assesses concentrations where the undertakings concerned are actual or potential competitors on the same relevant market. The Commission is also proposing to adopt complementary Non-horizontal Merger Guidelines (ie addressing vertical and conglomerate effects). These substantive issues are addressed in detail in Section 4 of this Chapter.[19]

(h) *Ancillary Restraints Notice* (2004). This provides guidance on restrictions which are considered to be ancillary to concentrations, meaning that they are not caught by the Article 81(1) prohibition.[20]

---

[17] Commission Notice on a simplified procedure for treatment of certain concentrations, OJ 2005 C56/32: Vol II, App D.11. See paras 8.122 *et seq*, below.

[18] Commission Notice on remedies, OJ 2001 C68/3: Vol II, App D.4. The Commission has also published Best Practice Guidelines on divestiture commitments as well as Model Texts for such commitments and for the trustee mandate. These are available on DG Comp's website. For the draft revised Remedies Notice see Press Release IP/07/544 (27 April 2007) and Vol II, App D.15. The Press Release also contains a link to the text of the proposed revisions to the Implementing Reg introducing Form RM: see also Vol II, App D.3. See generally paras 8.162 *et seq*, below.

[19] Guidelines on the assessment of horizontal mergers, OJ 2004 C31/5: Vol II, App D.6; draft Guidelines on the assessment of non-horizontal mergers: Vol II, App D.14, see Press Release IP/07/178 (13 February 2007).

[20] Commission Notice on restrictions directly related and necessary to concentrations, OJ 2005 C56/24: Vol II, App D.10. These issues are addressed at paras 8.263 *et seq*, below.

Other Commission guidance. Other Commission Notices which are relevant **8.009**
to the Merger Regulation include:

(a) *Relevant Market Notice* (1997). This provides guidance on how the
Commission applies the concepts of relevant product markets and geographic
markets in its enforcement of the competition rules including under the
Merger Regulation.[21] For detailed discussion, see Chapter 4, above.

(b) *Access to File Notice* (2005). This explains the Commission's approach to
granting parties subject to investigation under the Merger Regulation or
Articles 81 or 82 access to documents on the Commission's case file.[22] This
right is only available insofar as those documents do not contain third party
business secrets, other confidential information or internal Commission
communications. The Notice also sets out procedures for claiming confidentiality for documents supplied to the Commission.[23]

(c) Case law and statistics

Case law. Further guidance can be obtained from the case law of the Community **8.010**
Courts and from past decisional practice of the Commission under the
Merger Regulation.[24] All significant Merger Regulation decisions are published
subject to the redaction of business secrets, providing useful insights into how
the Commission has defined markets in previous cases.[25] Summaries of the prin-
cipal cases and developments under the Merger Regulation are included in the
Commission's Annual Reports on Competition Policy, as well as in DG
Competition's Competition Policy Newsletters.[26]

Statistics. Since the implementation of the original Merger Regulation in **8.011**
September 1990, the Commission has received formal notifications of well over
3,000 transactions. In recent years it has received some 250 to 350 or so formal

---

[21] Commission Notice on the definition of the relevant market for the purposes of Community
competition law, OJ 1997 C372/5: Vol II, App C.10. Market definition issues with respect to
concentrations are considered further at paras 8.186 *et seq,* below.

[22] Commission Notice on the rules for access to the Commission's file, OJ 2005 C325/7: Vol II,
App B.12. Access to file issues with respect to concentrations are considered further at para 8.146,
below.

[23] Confidentiality issues are considered further at paras 8.176–8.177, below.

[24] For the role played by the Community Courts, see paras 8.235 *et seq,* below.

[25] The DG Comp website contains an exhaustive list of the Commission's decisions under the
Merger Reg, sorted according to a number of criteria (case number, company name, date, decision
type, NACE Code product classification): http://ec.europa.eu/comm/competition/mergers/cases/.
In most cases, a non-confidential version of the decision can be accessed this way, together with any
other published information (eg press releases).

[26] The Commission's *Annual Reports on Competition Policy* and DG Comp's Competition Policy
Newsletters are available on DG Comp's website (http://ec.europa.eu/comm/competition/
publications).

notifications a year (with a new peak of 356 in 2006). The following tables provide statistics on cases handled under the Merger Regulation:

(a) Total number of notifications and referrals by year[27]

Year	Notifications to Commission	Referrals from Member States to Commission		Referrals from Commission to Member States	
		Pre-notification (Art 4(5))	post-notification (Art 22)	pre-notification (Art 4(4))	post-notification (Art 9)
1990	11	-	-	-	-
1991	64	-	-	-	-
1992	59	-	-	-	1
1993	59	-	1	-	1
1994	95	-	-	-	1
1995	110	-	1	-	-
1996	131	-	1	-	3
1997	168	-	1	-	7
1998	224	-	-	-	4
1999	276	-	-	-	5
2000	330	-	-	-	5
2001	335	-	-	-	7
2002	277	-	2	-	11
2003	211	-	1	-	9
2004	247	16	1	2	3
2005	313	24	3	11	6
2006	356	39	3	13	2
Total	3,266	79	14	26	65

(b) Different Phase I outcomes by year

Year	Clearance decisions				No jurisdiction		Referred to Phase II decisions		Notifications withdrawn during Phase I	
	Unconditional		Conditional							
1990	5	(71%)	-		2	(29%)	-		-	
1991	47	(77%)	3	(5%)	5	(8%)	6	(10%)	-	
1992	43	(68%)	4	(6%)	9	(14%)	4	(6%)	3	(5%)
1993	49	(84%)	-		4	(7%)	4	(7%)	1	(2%)
1994	78	(80%)	2	(3%)	5	(5%)	6	(6%)	6	(6%)
1995	90	(80%)	3	(3%)	9	(8%)	7	(6%)	4	(4%)

---

[27] The introduction of the Art 4(4) and (5) pre-notification referral procedures in 2004 has increased the overall number of formal notifications to the Commission (as well as involving the Commission and NCAs in the Form RS process for each pre-notification request). eg in 2006 39 pre-notification referrals were made to the Commission with a view to subsequent formal notifications under the Merger Reg, whereas only 13 pre-notification referrals were made to the NCAs (which would otherwise have involved formal notifications to the Commission, possibly followed by post-notification Art 9 referrals). This equates to a net increase of 26 notifications (ie 7 per cent of the total number of notifications to the Commission in the same period).

Year	Clearance decisions				No jurisdiction		Referred to Phase II decisions		Notifications withdrawn during Phase I	
	Unconditional		Conditional							
1996	109	(87%)	-		6	(5%)	6	(5%)	5	(4%)
1997	118	(82%)	2	(1%)	4	(3%)	11	(8%)	9	(6%)
1998	196	(86%)	12	(5%)	4	(2%)	11	(5%)	5	(2%)
1999	225	(84%)	16	(6%)	1	(0%)	20	(7%)	7	(3%)
2000	278	(84%)	26	(8%)	1	(0%)	18	(5%)	8	(2%)
2001	299	(88%)	10	(4%)	1	(0%)	21	(6%)	8	(2%)
2002	238	(92%)	11	(3%)	1	(0%)	7	(3%)	3	(1%)
2003	203	(91%)	11	(5%)	-	-	9	(4%)	-	-
2004	220	(91%)	12	(5%)	-	-	8	(3%)	3	(1%)
2005	276	(90%)	15	(5%)	-	-	10	(3%)	6	(2%)
2006	323	(91%)	13	(4%)	-	-	13	(4%)	7	(2%)
Total	2,797	(87%)	140	(4%)	52	(2%)	161	(5%)	75	(2%)

(c) Different Phase II outcomes by year

Year	Clearance decisions				Prohibition decisions[28]		Notifications withdrawn during Phase II	
	Unconditional		Conditional					
1991	1	(20%)	3	(60%)	1[a]	(20%)	-	-
1992	1	(25%)	3	(75%)	-	-	-	-
1993	1	(25%)	2	(50%)	-	-	1	(25%)
1994	2	(40%)	2	(40%)	1[b]	(20%)	-	-
1995	2	(29%)	3	(42%)	2[c]	(29%)	-	-
1996	1	(12%)	3	(38%)	3[d]	(38%)	1	(12%)
1997	1	(11%)	7	(78%)	1[e]	(11%)	-	-

[a] Case M.053 *Aerospatiale/Alenia/De Havilland*, OJ 1991 L334/42, [1992] 4 CMLR M2.

[b] Case M.469 *MSG Media Service*, OJ 1994 L364/1.

[c] Case M.490 *Nordic Satellite Distribution*, OJ 1996 L53/32; Case M.553 *RTL/Veronica/Endemol*, OJ 1996 L134/32 (completed merger; also an Art 8(4) decision requiring divestments), appeal dismissed, Case T-221/95 *Endemol Entertainment v Commission* [1999] ECR II-1299, [1999] 5 CMLR 611.

[d] Case M.619 *Gencor/Lonrho*, OJ 1997 L11/42, [1999] 4 CMLR 1076, appeal dismissed, Case T-102/96 *Gencor v Commission* [1999] ECR II-879, [1999] 4 CMLR 971; Case M.784 *Kesko/Tuko*, OJ 1997 L110/53 (completed merger; also an Art 8(4) decision imposing divestments), appeal dismissed, Case T-22/97 *Kesko v Commission* [1999] ECR II-3775, [2000] 4 CMLR 335; Case M.774 *Saint Gobain/Wacker Chemie/NOM*, OJ 1997 L247/1.

[e] Case M.890 *Blokker/Toys "R" Us*, OJ 1998 L316/1 (completed merger; also an Art 8(4) decision requiring divestments).

---

[28] For ease of reference, the 19 Art 8(3) prohibitions for each year in the period to end 2006 are separately listed in the notes beneath the table. The Commission adopted its 20th prohibition decision in Case M.4439 *Ryanair/Aer Lingus* (27 June 2007), Press Release IP/07/893.

Year	Clearance decisions				Prohibition decisions		Notifications withdrawn during Phase II	
	Unconditional		Conditional					
1998	3	(25%)	4	(30%)	2[f]	(15%)	4	(30%)
1999	--		7	(54%)	1[g]	(8%)	5	(38%)
2000	3	(14%)	12	(55%)	2[h]	(9%)	5	(23%)
2001	5	(22%)	9	(39%)	5[i]	(22%)	4	(17%)
2002	2	(25%)	5	(62%)	-	-	1	(13%)
2003	2	(25%)	6	(75%)	-	-	-	-
2004	2	(22%)	4	(44%)	1[j]	(11%)	2	(22%)
2005	2	(25%)	3	(38%)	-	-	3	(38%)
2006	4	(33%)	6	(50%)	-	-	2	(17%)
Total	32	(20%)	79	(50%)	19	(12%)	28	(18%)

[f] Case M.993 *Bertelsmann/Kirch/Premiere*, OJ 1999 L53/1, [1999] 4 CMLR 700; Case M.1027 *Deutsche Telekom/BetaResearch*, OJ 1999 L53/31, [1999] 4 CMLR 700.

[g] Case M.1524 *Airtours/First Choice*, OJ 2000 L93/1, [2000] 5 CMLR 494, annulled on appeal, Case T-342/99 *Airtours v Commission* [2002] ECR II-2585, [2002] 5 CMLR 317, [2002] All ER (EC) 783 (but merger abandoned). See also Case T-212/03 *MyTravel v Commission*, not yet decided (damages claim against the Commission).

[h] Case M.1672 *Volvo/Scania*, OJ 2001 L143/74; Case M.1741 *MCI Worldcom/Sprint*, OJ 2003 L300/1, annulled on appeal, Case T-310/00, *MCI v Commission* [2004] ECR II-3253, [2004] 5 CMLR 1274 (but merger abandoned).

[i] Case M.2097 *SCA/Metsä Tissue*, OJ 2002 L57/1; Case M.2220 *General Electric/Honeywell*, OJ 2004 L48/1, appeals dismissed, Cases T-209/01 *Honeywell v Commission* and T-210/01 *General Electric v Commission* [2005] ECR II-5527, 5575, [2006] 4 CMLR 652, 686 (but merger abandoned); Case M.2283 *Schneider/Legrand*, OJ 2004 L101/1 and L101/134 (completed merger; also an Art 8(4) decision requiring divestments), annulled on appeal, Case T-310/01 *Schneider Electric v Commission* [2002] ECR II-4071, [2003] 4 CMLR 768, [2004] All ER (EC) 314, but renewed Phase II proceedings subsequently opened and merger abandoned by way of divestment. See also Case T-351/03 *Schneider Electric v Commission*, judgment of 11 July 2007 (damages claim against the Commission). Case M.2187 *CVC/Lenzing*, OJ 2004 L82/20; Case M.2416 *Tetra Laval/Sidel*, OJ 2004 L38/1(divestiture decision) and L43/13 (prohibition decision), both decisions annulled on appeal: the prohibition decision in Case T-5/02 *Tetra Laval v Commission* [2002] ECR II-4381, [2002] 5 CMLR 1182 further appeal dismissed, Case C-12/03P [2005] ECR I-987, [2005] 4 CMLR 573 and the divestiture decision Case T-80/02 *Tetra Laval v Commission* [2002] ECR II-4519, [2002] 5 CMLR 1271, no ruling on further appeal Case C-13/03P [2005] ECR I-1113, [2005] 4 CMLR 667, merger subsequently approved subject to conditions in renewed Phase I proceedings (13 January 2003).

[j] Case M.3440 *ENI/EDP/GDP* (9 December 2004); appeal dismissed, Case T-87/05 *EDP-Energias de Portugal v Commission* [2005] ECR II-3745 [2005] 5 CMLR 1436.

2. Jurisdictional Scope of the Merger Regulation

(a) Overview of 'one-stop shop' principle

8.012 In general. The Merger Regulation applies to any 'concentration' which has, or is deemed to have, a 'Community dimension'. For these purposes:

(a) *Concentration*: the concept of 'concentration' is widely defined to cover mergers, acquisitions of control and the creation of full-function joint venture undertakings;[29]

---

[29] See paras 8.015 *et seq*, below.

(b) *Community dimension*: a concentration has a 'Community dimension' where certain turnover thresholds are met.[30]

Where a transaction gives rise to a concentration with a Community dimension, in principle it must be notified to the Commission which has exclusive jurisdiction to investigate without the NCAs being able to apply their national merger control rules. This 'one-stop shop' principle is set out at Article 21(2) and (3) (and Recitals (8) and (11)) of the Merger Regulation.[31] Conversely, concentrations which do not have a Community dimension are subject to the jurisdictions of the NCAs under their national merger control rules, without the Commission having any jurisdiction to investigate.[32]

Exceptions to general rule on case allocation. This simple allocation of juris- **8.013**
diction is, however, subject to a number of exceptions. For these purposes, it is convenient to distinguish:

(a) *Pre-notification reallocation of jurisdiction*: the Merger Regulation includes procedures which allow for the possibility of proposed concentrations to be reallocated at the initiative of the parties, although only at the pre-notification stage. These Article 4(4) and (5) referral procedures (which were introduced on 1 May 2004) are considered at paragraphs 8.081 *et seq*, below;

(b) *Post-notification reallocation of jurisdiction*: the Merger Regulation also maintains and extends procedures (which already existed under the original Merger Regulation) under which notified concentrations can be referred from the Commission to the NCAs or vice versa at the request of Member States. These referral procedures under, respectively, Articles 9 and 22, are considered at paragraphs 8.091 *et seq*, below.

Otherwise, there are only limited circumstances in which a Member State may intervene to impose measures in respect of a concentration which is subject to review by the Commission.[33]

Guiding principles for reallocation of cases. The steps involved in the pre- **8.014**
notification or post-notification referral of cases are illustrated in the chart

---

[30] See paras 8.060 *et seq*, below.

[31] For the Commission's exclusive competence as regards the EFTA States in respect of concentrations with a Community dimension, see Art 57 of the EEA Agreement and paras 8.280 *et seq*, below.

[32] Where a case does not have a Community dimension but has an 'EFTA dimension' in accordance with the provisions of the EEA Agreement, the EFTA Surveillance Authority is competent to review the case as regards its effects on the EFTA pillar (currently Iceland, Liechtenstein and Norway) but not as regards its effects in the EC where the NCAs will remain competent. However, no such case has arisen to date.

[33] For these circumstances, as covered in particular by Art 21(4), see paras 8.101 *et seq*, below.

on page 687.[34] Decisions taken with regard to the referral of cases should take due account of the principle of subsidiarity, in particular which is the 'more appropriate authority' for carrying out the investigation, the benefits inherent in a 'one-stop shop' system, and the importance of legal certainty with regard to jurisdiction.[35] Above all, in considering whether or not to exercise their discretion to make or accede to a referral, the Commission and Member States should bear in mind the need to ensure effective protection of competition in all markets affected by the transaction.[36]

(b) Concentrations

(i) In general

8.015 **Change of control on a lasting basis.** The Merger Regulation applies to 'concentrations'. The concept is widely defined to cover various operations which bring about a 'change in the control on a lasting basis' of the undertakings concerned and therefore in the structure of the market.[37] The definition of a concentration is broad, so many different types of transaction can fall within the Merger Regulation. These range from public takeover bids and private share purchase or business sale agreements, to the creation and break-up of joint ventures, management buy-outs and private equity deals. In accordance with Article 3(1) of the Merger Regulation, these various types of concentration can each be classified under the general headings of 'mergers' and/or 'acquisitions of control':[38]

(a) *Mergers:* ie where two or more previously independent undertakings merge;[39] and

(b) *Acquisitions of control:* ie where one or more undertakings (or one or more persons already controlling at least one undertaking) acquire, whether by purchase of securities or assets, by contract or by any other means, direct or indirect control of the whole or parts of one or more other undertakings.[40]

---

[34] Further illustrations are included as flowcharts annexed to the Case Referral Notice, OJ 2005 C56/2: Vol II, App D.9.

[35] Case Referral Notice, above, paras 8–14.

[36] ibid.

[37] Merger Reg, Reg 139/2004, OJ 2004 L24/1: Vol II, App D.1, Art 3(1) and Recital (20); Jurisdictional Notice (n 10, above) para 28. A change of control on a lasting basis may occur even if the agreements are limited to a definite period of time, provided the agreements are renewable. A concentration may arise even if the agreements have a definite end date, provided the period is sufficiently long to lead to a lasting change in control of the undertaking concerned. For concentrations involving different steps or closely linked transactions, see paras 8.044 *et seq*, below. For specific operations which are deemed not to be sufficiently lasting to give rise to a concentration, see paras 8.049 *et seq*, below.

[38] Jurisdictional Notice (published on 10 July 2007, Vol II, App D.13) para 8 (previously Concentration Notice, OJ 1998 C66/5, para 5).

[39] See paras 8.021–8.022, below.

[40] See paras 8.023–8.043, below.

This distinction between 'mergers' and 'acquisitions of control' is not material as regards substantive assessment. However, it can have a bearing on identifying the undertakings concerned for jurisdictional purposes, as well as which parties should notify the concentration under Article 4(2) of the Merger Regulation.[41]

The concept of control.   The qualitative concept of 'control' and how it is capable of being exercised is central to identifying the existence of concentrations.[42] This is as true for 'mergers' where the control of formerly independent undertakings comes together as it is for 'acquisitions of control' where the control of one undertaking becomes vested in one or more other undertakings. The concept of control is discussed in more detail in the following paragraphs. The concept of an 'undertaking' has the same meaning as in the case law under Articles 81 and 82 of the EC Treaty.[43]   **8.016**

Internal corporate restructurings.   Since a concentration covered by the Merger Regulation must involve a merger between, or change in control of, independent undertakings, a mere internal restructuring within a group of companies cannot constitute a concentration.[44]   **8.017**

State-controlled undertakings.   In cases where both the acquiring and acquired undertaking are public bodies owned by the same State (or the same public body or municipality), the question arises as to whether or not the transaction amounts to a mere internal restructuring. The analysis in such cases depends upon whether or not both undertakings were part of the same economic unit prior to the transaction.[45] Where the State-controlled undertakings were part of different economic units which had independent power of decision, the transaction will be regarded as a concentration rather than an internal restructuring.[46] If the undertakings concerned are grouped under the same holding company such independent power of decision will not normally exist.[47] The rights and prerogatives which a State may exercise as a public authority or in a regulatory capacity, focused on protecting the public interest, do not constitute control for   **8.018**

---

[41] For the concept of 'undertakings concerned' see para 8.070, below. For details as to who is obliged to notify, see para 8.112, below.

[42] Jurisdictional Notice, para 7 (previously Concentration Notice, para 4).

[43] See paras 2.003 *et seq*, above.

[44] Jurisdictional Notice (n 38, above) para 51 (previously Concentration Notice, para 8).

[45] Merger Reg (n 37, above) Recital (22); and Jurisdictional Notice (n 38, above) para 52 (previously Concentration Notice (n 38, above) para 8).

[46] Case M.097 *Péchiney/Usinor-Sacilor* (24 June 1991); Case M.216 *CEA Industrie/France Telecom/Finmeccanica/SGS-Thomson* (22 February 1993); Case M.931 *Neste/IVO* (2 June 1998).

[47] Jurisdictional Notice (n 38, above) para 52 (previously Concentration Notice (n 38, above) para 8) and paras 153 and 192–194 (previously Undertakings Concerned Notice, OJ 1998 C66/14, paras 55–56). See also para 8.075, below.

Merger Regulation purposes, to the extent that they have neither the object nor the effect of enabling the State to exercise decisive influence over the activities of the undertaking.[48]

8.019 **Management buyouts.** The Jurisdictional Notice confirms that an acquisition of control of an undertaking by its management is an acquisition by individuals.[49] The management team may pool their interests through a 'vehicle company' (that in some cases may be treated as a separate 'undertaking concerned', depending on the facts) to ensure that they act with a single voice and to facilitate coherence in decision-making. The management may also seek investors in order to finance the acquisition, for example through venture capital or private equity investment funds which may acquire certain rights resulting in control within the meaning of Article 3 of the Merger Regulation being conferred upon them, as considered in the following paragraph.

8.020 **Venture capital and private equity investment funds.** Investment funds invest in and acquire businesses in transactions which may or may not include participation by the target's management. The Commission analyses structures involving investment funds on a case-by-case basis. Often the investment company exercises control over the fund by means of its organisational structure, eg by directly or indirectly controlling the general partner where the funds are organised as limited partnerships or by other contractual arrangements. Where an investment company establishes separate investment funds, these may be treated as economically linked and subject to common control by virtue of their relationships with the investment company. For example they may be operated under a common brand, a common organisational structure, or common management arrangements resulting from advisory agreements.[50]

(ii) Mergers

8.021 **Legal mergers.** A concentration within the meaning of Article 3(1)(a) of the Merger Regulation occurs when at least two previously independent undertakings amalgamate into a new undertaking, so that they cease to exist as separate legal

---

[48] Jurisdictional Notice, para 53 (previously Concentration Notice, para 19); see, eg Case M.493 *Tractebel/Distrigaz II* (1 September 1994).

[49] Jurisdictional Notice (n 38, above) para 152 (previously Undertakings Concerned Notice (n 47, above) para 53). See also para 8.023, below.

[50] ibid, paras 14–15 and 189–191 (expanding on the Undertaking Concerned Notice, para 54). There have been numerous such deals notified under the Merger Reg. They are generally assessed under the simplified procedure (see paras 8.122 *et seq*, below) provided that the investors do not have controlling interests in any competing undertakings. For a private equity deal which did raise substantive issues leading to a Phase II prohibition decision, see Case M.2187 *CVC/Lenzing*, OJ 2004 L82/20. See also para 8.074, below on the calculation of turnover for such structures.

entities creating, instead, a new undertaking.[51] Such a concentration may also be found to occur where one previously independent undertaking is absorbed into another, so that only the latter retains its legal identity.[52] Such legal mergers involve the restructuring of shareholdings, with either both sets of shareholders accepting shares in an entirely new legal entity or one set of shareholders accepting shares in the other legal entity into which their company is being absorbed. For the purposes of Article 3(1)(a) a merger is not deemed to arise if a target is merged with the subsidiary of the acquiring company such that the parent company acquires control of the target under Article 3(1)(b).[53]

Mergers by contract or other arrangements.   For the purposes of Article 3(1)(a)   **8.022**
of the Merger Regulation, a merger can also be effected by contract if it results in the *de facto* creation of a single economic unit (subject to a permanent single economic management), notwithstanding the absence of a legal merger.[54] For example, in *RTZ/CRA* the merger was effected by a contract which led *inter alia* to an identity of economic interest for all shareholders by equalising dividend and capital entitlements.[55] This left the shareholders of each company in the same position as if they held shares in a single group which owned all the assets of both companies.

---

[51] Jurisdictional Notice, para 9. Relatively few cases are expressly identified by the Commission as constituting 'mergers' within the meaning of Art 3(1)(a) of the Merger Reg: eg Case M.596 *Mitsubishi Bank/Bank of Tokyo* (17 July 1995); Case M.759 *Sun Alliance/Royal Insurance* (18 June 1996); Case M.768 *Lucas/Varity* (11 July 1996); Case M.1184 *Travelers/Citicorp* (23 June 1998); and Case M.2681 *Conoco/Phillips Petroleum* (6 March 2002). See also Case M.938 *Guinness/Grand Metropolitan*, OJ 1998 L288/24; Case M.1380 *Siebe/BTR* (13 January 1999); and Case M.1972 *Granada/Compass* (29 June 2000) concerning mergers within Art 3(1)(a) that were effected by means of inter-conditional schemes of arrangement under the UK Companies Act 1985, a procedure which can result in a similar outcome to legal fusion. The merger in Case M.1595 *British Steel/Hoogovens* (15 July 1999) was implemented by the acquisition of British Steel by a vehicle company, pursuant to a scheme of arrangement (under which British Steel's shares were cancelled and reissued), and by a public offer by that vehicle company for the Hoogovens shares.

[52] See, eg Case M.69 *Kyowa/Saitama* [1992] 4 CMLR M105, where the notified operation (in the form of absorption) was found to constitute a merger in accordance with the statutory provisions of the Japanese Commercial Code; Case M.642 *Chase Manhattan/Chemical Banking Corporation* (26 October 1995); Case M.1383 *Exxon/Mobil*, OJ 2004 L103/1; Case M.1878 *Pfizer/Warner-Lambert* (22 May 2000). Case M.1673 *Veba/VIAG*, OJ 2001 L188/1; Case M.1806 *AstraZeneca/Novartis*, OJ 2004 L110/1; Case M.2208 *Chevron/Texaco* (26 February 2001).

[53] Jurisdictional Notice (n 38, above) para 9. See, eg Case M.2510 *Cendant/Galileo* (24 September 2001); Case M.3732 *Procter & Gamble/Gillette* (15 July 2005).

[54] Jurisdictional Notice, para 10 (expanding on Concentration Notice (n 38, above) para 7) which refers to examples such as the establishment of a *Gleichordnungskonzern* under German law, certain *Groupements d'Intérêt Economique* under French law, the amalgamation of partnerships as in Case M.1016 *Price Waterhouse/Coopers & Lybrand* (20 May 1998); or other contractual arrangements as in Case M.2824 *Ernst & Young/Andersen Germany* (27 August 2002).

[55] Case M.660 *RTZ/CRA* (7 December 1995). See also Case M.2413 *BHP/Billiton* (14 June 2001); Case M.3071 *Carnival Corporation/P&O Princess II* (10 February 2003).

(iii) Acquisitions

8.023 **Acquisition of control.** Article 3(1)(b) of the Merger Regulation provides that a concentration also occurs in the case of an acquisition of control. The concept of control is applied broadly. Thus, the existence of a concentration under the Merger Regulation is to a great extent determined by qualitative rather than quantitative criteria, focusing on the concept of control.[56] These criteria include considerations of both law and fact. Control may be acquired by an undertaking acting alone (sole control) or by a number of undertakings acting jointly (joint control). It may also be acquired by a person who already controls (solely or jointly) at least one other undertaking.[57] Equally, a combination of undertakings and/or persons (controlling another undertaking) can acquire joint control of another undertaking. 'Person' in this context can extend to public bodies (including the State itself), private entities and individuals.[58]

8.024 **Definition of control.** Article 3(2) of the Merger Regulation provides that:

> 'control shall be constituted by rights, contracts or any other means which, either separately or in combination and having regard to the considerations of fact or law involved, confer the possibility of exercising decisive influence on an undertaking, in particular by:
>
> (a) ownership or the right to use all or part of the assets of an undertaking;
> (b) rights or contracts which confer decisive influence on the composition, voting or decisions of the organs of an undertaking.'

In essence, 'control' relates to the possibility of exercising decisive influence over an undertaking on the basis of rights, contracts or other means.[59] Control may thus be acquired by the purchase of shares or assets, or on a contractual basis if the contract confers rights over the management and the resources of the other undertaking, similar to those that would be acquired by purchasing the shares or assets of the undertaking.[60] Article 3(2)(a) of the Merger Regulation specifies that

---

[56] Jurisdictional Notice (n 38, above) para 7 (previously Concentration Notice (n 38, above) para 4).

[57] See Case M.3762 *Apax/Travelex* (16 June 2005) where a private individual acquiring joint control was not considered to be an undertaking concerned.

[58] Jurisdictional Notice, para 12 (previously Concentration Notice, para 8).

[59] The same concept of control is equally relevant for the purposes of Art 81 EC: see paras 2.017 *et seq*, above; and in particular Case T-102/92 *Viho v Commission* [1995] ECR II-17, [1997] 4 CMLR 469, [1995] All ER (EC) 371; appeal dismissed: Case C-73/95P [1996] ECR I-5457, [1997] 4 CMLR 419.

[60] Jurisdictional Notice, para 18 specifies that such contracts must be of long duration and without the possibility of early termination by the party granting the contractual rights. In Case M.2632 *Deutsche Bahn/ECT International/United Depots/JV* (11 February 2002) the contract had a duration of eight years. In Case M.3858 *Lehman Brothers/SCG/Starwood/Le Meridien* (20 July 2005) the management contracts had a duration of 10–15 years.

control may be conferred by a right to use all or part of the assets of the business.[61] Depending on the facts, such contracts may lead to situations of sole control or joint control. It is the *possibility* of exercising decisive influence, rather than the actual exercise of such influence, that determines whether control has been acquired.[62] In practice, whether a transaction gives rise to an acquisition of control depends on a number of legal and/or factual elements. Decisive influence may include both positive rights to manage and determine the commercial policy of another undertaking, as well as the ability to veto decisions relating to the strategic commercial behaviour of another undertaking such as, typically, the budget and the business plan in the context of a JV undertaking.

Direct or indirect control. Normally control is acquired by the persons or **8.025** undertakings which hold, or are entitled to, the rights conferring control over the undertaking.[63] The obvious example is direct ownership of shares giving the right to cast sufficient votes to exercise decisive influence over the undertaking concerned. Less commonly, the formal holder of the rights conferring control differs from the person or undertaking which can actually exercise the rights. For example, undertakings may use another person or undertaking as a vehicle for the acquisition of the shares necessary for a controlling interest, and may also exercise the rights through that person or undertaking. In such circumstances control is acquired by the person or undertaking which, in reality, has the power to control the target undertaking and not the formal holder.[64] In *Cementbouw*[65] the Court of First Instance concluded that where rights conferring control are held by a commercial company these can be attributed to its sole or majority

---

[61] See, eg Case M.2060 *Bosch/Rexroth*, OJ 2004 L43/1 involving a control contract (*Beherrschungsvertrag*) under German law in combination with a business lease; *Deutsche Bahn/ECT International/United Depots/JV*, above involving a business lease; Case M.3136 *GE/Agfa NDT* (5 December 2003) involving a contract to transfer control over business resources, management and risk. The Jurisdictional Notice, n 20 to para 18 refers to examples of specific contracts under national law such as the *Beherrschungsvertrag* under German law and *Contrato de subordinação* under Portuguese law.

[62] Jurisdictional Notice (n 38, above) para 16 (previously Concentration Notice (n 38, above) para 9). In Case T-282/02 *Cementbouw v Commission* [2006] ECR II-319, [2006] 4 CMLR 1561, para 58 the CFI observed that the possibility of exercising such influence must be effective; on the facts of that case the three shareholders had notified to the Dutch NCA a proposed pooling agreement but the CFI found that the mere fact of notification did not prove that there was effective joint control (on appeal, Case C-202/06P *Cementbouw v Commission*, not yet decided).

[63] Merger Reg (n 37, above) Art 3(3)(a); Jurisdictional Notice (n 38, above) para 13 (previously Concentration Notice, para 10).

[64] ibid, Art 3(3)(b). See, eg Case M.683 *GTS-Hermes Inc./Hit Rail BV* (5 March 1996) where 10 European National railway undertakings controlled the joint venture Hermes jointly with GTS, but where the 10 undertakings acted together through a Dutch company, HIT Rail. This structure was devised to ensure that the 10 companies spoke and acted as one and avoided a situation whereby GTS could exercise sole control because of the inability of the 10 companies to reach a unified position on any decision.

[65] Case T-282/02 *Cementbouw v Commission* (n 62, above), paras 71–74.

shareholder or to those jointly controlling the company since the company will comply in any event with the decisions of its shareholder(s). Where a number of different entities in the same group each hold shares which when combined give rise to a controlling shareholding, the combined interests will normally be attributed to the parent company. In other cases, indirect control may be established by other evidence, including factors such as shareholdings, contractual relations, sources of financing or family links.[66]

8.026 **Object of control.** The object of control can be undertakings which constitute legal entities or the assets of such entities or only some of the assets.[67] As defined in Article 3(1)(b) of the Merger Regulation, a concentration can occur where control of the whole or part of one or more undertakings is acquired. Thus, a concentration may arise where only some of the assets of an entity such as intellectual property rights (trade marks, patents or copyrights) are acquired or licensed on an exclusive basis, provided that those assets constitute a business which has a market presence and to which a market turnover can be 'clearly attributed'.[68]

8.027 **Outsourcing arrangements.** Specific issues arise where an undertaking 'outsources' to a third party service provider activities which were previously sourced 'in-house' (eg outsourcing of IT services to a specialised IT company). Depending on the surrounding circumstances, such arrangements may give rise to a concentration.[69] A simple outsourcing contract, without transfer of assets or employees, will not give rise to a concentration (even if the service supplier is given a right to use or direct assets and employees of the customer exclusively to service the customer). By contrast, if assets and/or personnel are transferred, these may constitute a business with access to the market – provided the service supplier is able to use them to provide services also to third parties, either immediately or within a short period after the transfer.

---

[66] See, eg Case M.754 *Anglo American/Lonrho*, OJ 1998 L149/21.

[67] Jurisdictional Notice (n 38, above) para 24 (previously Concentration Notice (n 38, above) para 11).

[68] There have been many such cases under the Merger Reg. The Jurisdictional Notice, para 24 (previously Concentration Notice, para 11) refers only to Case M.3867 *Vattenfall/Elsam and E2 Assets* (22 December 2005) and Case M.2857 *ECS/IEH* (23 December 2002) which involved the transfer of the customer base of a business.

[69] Jurisdictional Notice, paras 25–27: see eg Case M.1841 *Celestica/IBM* (25 February 2000); Case M.1849 *Solectron/Ericsson Switches* (29 February 2000); Case M.2479 *Flextronics/Alcatel* (29 June 2001); Case M.2629 *Flextronics/Xerox* (12 November 2001); Case M.3583 *Flextronics/Nortel* (28 October 2004). For further observations on calculation of turnover in respect of outsourcing arrangements, see para 8.062, below.

(iv) Sole control

Acquisition of sole control. Sole control is usually acquired by an undertaking **8.028**
acquiring the majority of the voting rights in a company (ie *de jure* control).[70]
A classic acquisition of control is where 100 per cent of the share capital is acquired,
for example through a public takeover bid or a private share acquisition. However,
the level of shareholding is not determinative in itself. Even if an undertaking
acquires more than 50 per cent of the share capital, this will normally not confer
control unless it involves the acquisition of the majority of the voting rights.[71]
Indeed, where the company's statutes or a shareholders agreement requires a
supermajority for strategic decisions, even a simple majority will normally not be
sufficient to confer sole control.[72] There can be other exceptional circumstances
where a shareholder does not enjoy sole control (but rather only joint control)
despite having a casting vote, eg if another (minority) shareholder enjoys extensive rights such that the casting vote can only be exercised after a series of stages of
arbitration and attempts at reconciliation, or if exercise of the casting vote would
trigger a put option implying a serious financial burden, or if the mutual interdependence of the parent companies makes exercise of the casting vote unlikely.[73]
Furthermore, sole control will not be conferred if any other shareholder enjoys
similar rights, although this may give rise to a situation of joint control.[74]

Sole control through minority shareholding. Sole control may also occur **8.029**
where specific rights attach to a minority shareholding whether under the terms
of a shareholders agreement, in accordance with rights attaching to certain preferential shares or otherwise such that the minority shareholder has a majority of the
voting rights or is able to appoint a majority of the directors on the board and thus
determine the strategic commercial behaviour of the company.[75] A substantial

---

[70] Jurisdictional Notice (n 38, above) paras 55–58 (previously Concentration Notice, para 13).
[71] ibid, para 56.
[72] ibid, para 56. eg in Case M.293 *Philips/Thomson/Sagem* (18 January 1993), Philips held 80 per
cent of the voting rights in the policy committee of the JV, but did not acquire 'sole control' because
major strategic decisions concerning the JV required a voting majority of more than 80 per cent. See
also Case M.904 *RSB/Tenex/Fuel Logistic* (2 April 1997).
[73] Jurisdictional Notice, para 82 (previously Concentration Notice, para 37) and, eg Case M.258
CCIE/GTE (25 September 1992).
[74] The concept of control under EC law differs from the concept of control for UK merger
control purposes under the Enterprise Act 2002. Thus, a minority shareholder may have sufficient
rights to be able individually to exercise 'material influence' and therefore control for UK purposes,
even where the company is already subject to the legal or *de facto* control of another undertaking
(eg another shareholder holding the majority, or near-majority, of the share capital). For Merger Reg
purposes, however, such a minority shareholder would not be able to exercise 'sole' control, although
its rights could mean that it enjoys 'joint' control (with the majority or near-majority shareholder).
[75] Jurisdictional Notice (n 38, above) para 57 (previously Concentration Notice (n 38, above)
para 14). cf Case M.3411 *UGC/NOOS* (17 May 2004): minority board representation and limited
veto rights (typically intended to protect minority shareholders) were deemed insufficient for the
purposes of conferring control.

minority shareholder may be regarded as having *de facto* control if, for example, it is highly likely that it will achieve a majority of the votes cast at shareholders meetings. This will typically arise where ownership of the remaining shares is widely dispersed. If it is unlikely that all the small shareholders will be present or represented by proxy at the shareholders' meeting, the substantial minority shareholder will effectively be able to exercise sole control. To determine whether or not sole control exists in a particular case, the Commission considers evidence of attendance at shareholders' meetings in previous years.[76] For example, in *Société Générale de Belgique/Générale de Banque*[77] an increase in shareholding from 20.94 per cent to 25.96 per cent was held to be sufficient to move from a position of absence of control to a position of sole control, taking account of the level of votes cast at the previous three annual general meetings. A controlling interest (based on the likelihood that the minority shareholder will achieve a majority at the shareholders meeting) may also be acquired passively, following a change in another shareholder's ownership interest.[78]

8.030 **Negative control.** In some situations a minority shareholder may be able to veto strategic decisions in an undertaking, even though it does not have the positive ability to impose such decisions on its own. Since such a shareholder is able to produce a deadlock situation, it is able to exercise 'negative control' sufficient to confer decisive influence and therefore sole control for the purposes of the Merger Regulation.[79] Where a shareholder acquires the ability to exercise

---

[76] Jurisdictional Notice, para 59 (previously Concentration Notice, para 14). The Commission should carry out a prospective analysis, taking account of foreseeable changes in shareholder presence which might arise following the operation. This may involve a case-by-case analysis of the positions of other shareholders and whether they are likely to support or destabilise the position of the large minority shareholder: see, eg Case M.025 *Arjomari/Wiggins Teape* (10 December 1990); *Anglo American/Lonrho* (n 66, above).

[77] Case M.343 *Société Générale de Belgique/Générale de Banque* (3 August 1993). See also Case M.613 *Jefferson Smurfit Group/Munksjö AB* (31 July 1995), where the acquisition of a 29.04 per cent interest was held to give Jefferson Smurfit sole control over Munksjö AB: the remaining shares were widely dispersed, with the next largest shareholder having only a 5.9 per cent interest; and the voting patterns at the two previous annual general meetings showed that the seller of the shareholding accounted for a majority of the votes cast and there seemed no reason why that position should change. See also Case M.3502 *Accor/Club Méditerranée* (19 October 2004): holding of 28.9 per cent of the shares sufficient to confer sole control; Case M.2117 *Aker Maritime/Kværner* (11 December 2000): Phase II proceedings terminated after Aker reduced the level of the stake it would acquire from 26.7 per cent to 17.8 per cent and withdrew its notification under the Merger Reg; and Case M.4336 *MAN/Scania* (20 December 2006): VW's 21.6 per cent stake considered insufficient to obtain a majority at MAN shareholders' meeting. In Case M.3445 *Microsoft/Time Warner/ContentGuard JV* (withdrawn on 9 March 2005): parties restructured the deal (following the launch of a Phase II investigation by the Commission) so that the transaction was no longer subject to review under the Merger Reg.

[78] See, eg Case M.3330 *RTL/M6* (12 March 2004): RTL acquired sole control of M6 only by reason of the divestiture by Suez of its 37.6 per cent stake in M6, as a result of which RTL's retained 48.4 per cent stake meant that it moved from joint to sole control.

[79] Jurisdictional Notice (n 38, above) para 60 (previously Concentration Notice (n 38, above) para 39). See Case M.258 *CCIE/GTE* (25 September 1992): CCIE, with a shareholding of only

'negative control' it is the only undertaking acquiring decisive influence, so is the only undertaking required to submit a notification under the Merger Regulation (if the transaction has a 'Community dimension'). In contrast to the situation in a jointly controlled company, there are no other shareholders able to exercise such influence and the shareholder enjoying negative sole control does not have to cooperate with specific other shareholders in excercising its veto rights. For the assessment of moves from negative to positive (full) sole control, see paragraph 8.042, below.

Option rights.   An option to purchase a controlling shareholding cannot in   **8.031** itself confer sole control, given the uncertainty over whether it will be exercised. Exceptionally, however, the grant of an option may be found to confer control if it is clear that the option will be exercised in the near future in accordance with legally binding agreements which cannot be unilaterally rescinded.[80] Generally, the Commission considers that it is the exercise of the option rather than its grant which may give rise to a notifiable concentration. However, the likely exercise of such an option can be taken into account as an additional element which, together with other factors, may lead to the conclusion that there is in fact sole control.[81]

Other factors leading to *de facto* control.   Sole control can also be exercised by   **8.032** a minority shareholder if it has the right to manage the activities of the company and determine its strategic business policy.[82] In exceptional circumstances, purely

---

19 per cent, was able to veto strategic decisions through its appointee on the GTE board. See also Case M.2777 *Cinven Limited/Angel Street Holdings* (8 May 2002) para 8 referring to Cinven's veto rights which enabled it to 'create a deadlock structure by blocking key decisions' and so 'exert decisive influence over the target and therefore sole control'; Case M.3198 *VW-Audi/VW-Audi Vertriebszentren* (29 July 2003) para 8; related Cases M.3537 *BBVA/BNL* (20 August 2004); and M.3768 *BBVA/BNL* (27 April 2005) para 3 referring to how the second operation would enable BNL to 'acquire full sole control' as distinct from the negative control it had acquired under the first operation; Case M.3876 *Diester Industrie/Bunge/JV* (30 September 2005) where the D2I JV would hold 50 per cent of NEW (the remaining shares being held 25 per cent by a third party and 25 per cent by another) resulting, according to the Jurisdictional Notice (at para 58, n 38, above), in D2I acquiring 'negative sole control' of NEW.

⁸⁰ Jurisdictional Notice, para 60 (previously Concentration Notice, para 15). See, eg Case M.259 *British Airways/TAT* (27 November 1992); appeal dismissed, Case T-2/93 *Air France v Commission (TAT)* [1994] ECR II-323. The subsequent exercise of the option giving BA sole control was cleared: Case M.806 *British Airways/TAT (II)* (26 August 1996). See also Case M.3068 *Ascott Group/Goldman Sachs/Oriville* (13 February 2003).

⁸¹ Jurisdictional Notice (n 38, above) para 60 (previously Concentration Notice (n 38, above) para 15). See, eg Case M.625 *Nordic Capital/Transpool* (23 August 1995); Case M.1037 *Nomura/ Blueslate* (17 November 1997). Even though an option does not normally in itself give rise to a concentration, it can be taken into account for the substantive assessment of a related concentration: see Case M.3696 *E.ON/MOL*, OJ 2006 L253/20 at paras 12–14, 480, 762 *et seq.*

⁸² Jurisdictional Notice, paras 20 and 61 (previously Concentration Notice, para 14). See, eg *CCIE/GTE* (n 79, above): CCIE with a shareholding of 19 per cent was found to exercise sole control because the 81 per cent shareholder had delegated its management powers and ceded its veto rights. Effectively, CCIE had the right to manage the affairs of the company through which the acquisition was carried out.

economic relationships, usually reflecting some form of economic dependence, may also lead to *de facto* sole control. For example, significant long-term supply agreements or credits provided by suppliers or customers coupled with structural links may confer decisive influence and be sufficient to lead to a change of control on a lasting basis.[83] Control can also be acquired for Merger Regulation purposes even in circumstances when it is not the intention of the parties to acquire control or where control is not deemed to exist for the purpose of other legislation such as taxation, prudential rules, media or air transport ownership rules.[84]

(v) Joint control

8.033 **Concept of joint control.**   Joint control exists where two or more undertakings or persons have the ability to exercise decisive influence over another undertaking. The acquisition of joint control can occur on a *de jure* or *de facto* basis. Unlike sole control, where a specific shareholder has the power to determine the strategic decisions of an undertaking, joint control normally means that there is the possibility of deadlock because two or more shareholders (or the parent companies of a joint venture undertaking) each have the power to reject strategic proposals. The element of 'joint control' arises, therefore, because these share-holders must reach a common agreement or understanding on major decisions concerning the undertaking in question such that they are required to cooperate on a lasting basis.[85]

8.034 **Equality in voting rights and appointments.**   Joint control clearly exists where there are only two parents which share equally voting rights or the rights to appoint the decision-making bodies of the joint venture (JV), such that neither of the parents can determine alone the business policy of the JV. In such a situation, there is no need for a formal agreement. However, if there is such a shareholders agreement, joint control will exist if it treats each parent equally, eg with each having the same number of representatives in management bodies and none having a casting vote.[86]

---

[83] Jurisdictional Notice, paras 20 and 61. See, eg Case M.625 *Nordic Capital/Transport* (23 August 1995); Case M.697 *Lockheed Martin Corporation/Loral Corporation* (27 March 1996); Case M.794 *Coca-Cola/Amalgamated Beverages GB*, OJ 1997 L218/15; See, eg Case M.2060 *Bosch/Rexroth*, OJ 2004 L43/1; cf *CCIE/GTE* (n 79, above) where various supply, licensing and other supporting agreements were found not to be sufficiently long-lasting to confer decisive influence on Siemens.

[84] Jurisdictional Notice, para 23 (previously Concentration Notice, para 9). See, eg Case M.157 *Air France/Sabena* (5 October 1992).

[85] Jurisdictional Notice (n 38, above) paras 62–63 (previously Concentration Notice, paras 18–19). Art 3(4) of the Merger Reg (n 37, above) provides that 'full-function' JVs constitute concentrations subject to the Merger Reg. The meaning of 'full-function' JVs is explained at paras 8.052 *et seq*, below.

[86] ibid, para 64 (previously Concentration Notice, para 20). See, eg Case M.272 *Matra/CAP Gemini Sogeti* (17 March 1993); Case M.724 *GEC/Thomson-CSF (II)* (15 May 1996); Case M.744 *Thomson/Daimler-Benz* (21 May 1996); Case M.2645 *Saab/WM-Data AB/Saab Caran JV* (6 December 2001); Case M.3097 *Mærsk Data/Eurogate IT/Global Transport Solutions JV* (12 March 2003).

Veto rights for minority shareholders. Joint control can also exist where there **8.035** is no equality in votes or representation on decision-making bodies, or where there are more than two parent companies, provided that the minority shareholders in question have the power to veto strategic commercial decisions.[87] These veto rights may be set out in the articles of association of the JV company or form part of a JV agreement between the parents. They may also arise, for example, because of procedural requirements, such as where the minority shareholders form part of the quorum needed for the decision.

Focus on strategic business policy. In order to confer control for these pur- **8.036** poses, the veto rights must relate to the strategic business policy of the JV and not merely to changes to the constitutive documents, capital increases or decreases, or liquidation.[88] Where the veto rights protect only the usual rights of minority shareholders, they will not be regarded as indicating joint control. The acquisition of joint control does not necessarily mean that the acquirer has decisive influence over the JV's day-to-day operations; veto rights giving parents decisive influence over strategic business decisions are sufficient. Furthermore, the right to exercise such influence is sufficient to establish the existence of joint control; it is not necessary to establish that the acquirer will exercise that influence.[89] As explained below, a minority shareholder is likely to be found to enjoy joint control if it has the right to veto senior management appointments, budget matters, the business plan and major investments. However, joint control can be acquired without the minority shareholder having veto rights in respect of all these matters. Whether any particular veto, or use of veto rights, can constitute joint control depends

---

[87]   ibid, para 65 (previously Concentration Notice, paras 21–29). See, eg Case T-2/93 *Air France v Commission* (n 80, above); Case M.522 *Scandinavian Project* (28 November 1994): certain major decisions required unanimous consent of the board so the seven notifying parties were found to exercise joint control; Case M.526 *Sappi/DLJMB/UBS/Warren* (28 November 1994): key decisions, eg the annual business plan, the budget, and appointment of the Chief Executive Director and Chief Financial Officer, needed the approval of at least one director of each of the parents; Case M.2766 *Vivendi Universal/Lagardère/Multithématiques* (3 May 2002): Lagardère deemed to have retained joint control through such veto rights, notwithstanding its minority shareholding.

[88]   A veto right preventing sale or winding-up of the JV does not confer joint control on the minority shareholder: Jurisdictional Notice, para 66 (previously Concentration Notice, para 22). See, eg Case M.062 *Eridania/ISI* (30 July 1991). cf Case M.710 *BHF-Bank/Crédit Commercial de France* (2 May 1996): both parents had a 30 per cent shareholding and could veto strategic decisions; although the parents could not impose a decision, this ability to create deadlock was found to confer joint control. See also Case T-282/02 *Cementbouw v Commission* (n 62, above), paras 71–75: joint control of a JV although the parents had only minority representation on the company's supervisory board and none on the managing board, since they appointed the members of those boards.

[89]   Jurisdictional Notice (n 38, above) paras 16 and 67 (previously Concentration Notice (n 38, above) paras 9 and 23). Even if one parent plays a modest or non-existent role in the day-to-day management of the JV (being motivated more by longer-term financial or other considerations) it may nevertheless retain the real possibility of contesting strategic decisions, sufficient to confer joint control: see Jurisdictional Notice, para 81 (previously Concentration Notice, para 36).

upon the exact nature of the veto and its importance in the context of the business of the undertaking.[90]

8.037 **Examples of strategic veto rights.** The Jurisdictional Notice gives examples of strategic veto rights that the Commission will generally regard as establishing joint control.[91] The two most important veto rights usually relate to decisions on senior management appointments and the budget. The power to block decisions on these issues enables the minority shareholder to exercise decisive influence over the commercial policy of the undertaking, giving that shareholder joint control. Similarly, where the minority shareholder has a veto right over the type of business plan which determines objectives and the specific measures to be undertaken in order to achieve them, this may be sufficient to confer joint control. However, a veto right over a business plan which merely declares general business aims will not of itself be sufficient to confer joint control, although it will be a factor to be taken into account in an overall assessment of whether the shareholder enjoys joint control. A veto right over investment decisions is also a factor which could significantly affect the commercial policy of the undertaking and so confer joint control. Whether the veto is of sufficient commercial significance depends on two criteria: first, the level of investments subject to the veto; and secondly, the extent to which investments are an essential feature of the undertaking's market.[92] Finally, the Commission refers to veto rights relating to specific decisions which in particular markets are key to the commercial policy of the undertaking, for example which technology to use or which product lines to develop, and thus may confer joint control on the holder of the right.[93]

8.038 *De facto* **joint control.** Two or more minority shareholders may acquire joint control if (i) together they will hold a majority of voting rights; and (ii) they will act together in the exercise of them. Such a situation may result from an agreement to transfer their rights to a holding company or some form of pooling

---

[90] ibid, para 68 (previously Concentration Notice, para 24). In assessing the relative importance of veto rights, where there are a number of them, they should be evaluated not in isolation but as a whole: Jurisdictional Notice, para 73 (previously Concentration Notice, para 29).

[91] ibid, paras 69–73 (previously Concentration Notice, paras 23–27).

[92] With regard to the first criterion, para 71 of the Jurisdictional Notice (previously para 27 of the Concentration Notice) specifies that where a parent company has veto rights only over high levels of investment, it may amount to rights akin more to standard minority protection than conferring power of co-decision over the undertaking's commercial policy. As to the second criterion, normally the investment policy of an undertaking is essential to its commercial policy. There may be markets, however, where investments do not play a significant role in an undertaking's market behaviour such that a veto right carries less weight in the assessment of joint control. See Case M.295 *SITA-RPC/SCORI* (19 March 1993): three minority shareholders had a veto over certain aspects of the growth policy of the undertaking but not over its commercial policy or competitive strategy; they were held not to enjoy control.

[93] For further guidance, see Jurisdictional Notice (n 38, above) para 72 (previously Concentration Notice (n 38, above) para 28).

agreement whereby the undertakings agree to act together.[94] Exceptionally, a *de facto* pooling of voting rights may exist without the need for a formal agreement if there are such strong common interests between the minority shareholders that none would act against the other in relation to the undertaking.[95] Existing prior links may indicate such a common interest, as may the establishment of a JV where each parent contributes a different element to its business (such as technology, local know-how or supply agreements). In such circumstances the parents may need to cooperate fully on a lasting basis despite the absence of any legal requirement to do so, even if one parent company alone technically has a casting vote (usually considered as precluding joint control).[96] Similarly, *de facto* joint control may be found to exist if there is a high degree of dependency of a majority shareholder on a minority shareholder.[97] The likelihood of such *de facto* joint control decreases as the number of minority shareholders concerned increases above two. Indeed, in any case where parties seek to notify deals on the basis of *de facto* joint control, the Commission will require the parties to put forward convincing

---

[94] Jurisdictional Notice, paras 74–75 (previously Concentration Notice, paras 30–31). See, eg Case M.331 *Fletcher Challenge/Methanex* (31 March 1993); Case M.382 *Philips/Grundig* (3 December 1993); Case M.1745 *EADS* (11 May 2000); and Case M.1853 *EDF/EnBW*, OJ 2002 L59/1.

[95] Jurisdictional Notice, paras 76–77 (previously Concentration Notice, paras 32-34). See *Cementbouw* (n 62, above) paras 42, 52, 67. See also Case JV.55 *Hutchison/RCPM/ECT* (3 July 2001), where the Commission found joint control on the basis of strong interests and mutual dependency between Hutchison and RCPM ('strategic investors' each holding a 35 per cent interest with the remaining shares held by a bank and an employees' trust), including investment guarantees, such that the parties, when voting, would not act against each other. Case M.2066 *Dana/GETRAG* (7 November 2000) where the Commission found that the various commercial links between the minority shareholder and the majority shareholder meant that it was 'inconceivable under the given circumstances that one party might act independently from the other even if it might have contractually the power to do so.' These criteria apply to the formation of a new JV as well as to acquisitions of minority shareholdings resulting in joint control. Where two (or more) parties act in concert to acquire shareholdings, there is a higher probability of a commonality of interest: Jurisdictional Notice, para 79 (previously Concentration Notice, para 34).

[96] See the CFI's judgment in Case T-221/95 *Endemol Entertainment v Commission* [1999] ECR II–1299, [1999] 5 CMLR 611, [1999] All ER (EC) 385, paras 161–164; dismissing the appeal against the Commission's prohibition decn in Case M.553 *RTL/Veronica/Endemol*, OJ 1996 L294/14. The Commission had found that although one parent company held a casting vote over certain issues, if reconciliation was not possible, this did not preclude joint control: the use of the contested casting vote by RTL would, in practice, only be used in exceptional circumstances. Furthermore, certain other aspects of the JV's strategy remained subject to unanimous agreement by RTL and VMG. See also Case M.3556 *Fortis/BCP* (19 January 2005) where the Commission found that BCP's 49 per cent minority interest conferred joint control over NHC despite the fact that Fortis's 51 per cent majority holding gave it the right to determine the business plan and the budget; in reaching the conclusion that there was *de facto* joint control, the Commission took account of all the surrounding circumstances including the fact that BCP exercised certain veto rights over NHC's product range and over its distribution channels.

[97] See, eg Case M.967 *KLM/Air UK* (22 September 1997); Case M.4085 *Arcelor/Oyak/ Erdemir* (13 February 2006).

evidence of strong common interests.[98] In the absence of such evidence, joint control cannot be assumed: see observations on shifting alliances in the following paragraph.

8.039 **Shifting alliances.** Without strong common interests as referred to above, the possibility of changing coalitions between minority shareholders usually excludes joint control. If the majority in the decision-making procedure can be achieved by different combinations of shareholders, joint control cannot be assumed. It is not sufficient for two or more minority shareholders to agree identical rights and powers in relation to the undertaking in question. The Jurisdictional Notice gives examples of circumstances in which joint control on a lasting basis would not be established, eg where the shares in the company are held equally by three shareholders in circumstances where decisions are taken on a simple majority basis.[99]

(vi) Changes in quality of control

8.040 **In general.** Particular issues arise in relation to transfers of shareholdings between existing shareholders and other shifts in control structures. These issues are dealt with in the Jurisdictional Notice (at paragraphs 83 to 90), discussed here in the following paragraphs.

8.041 **Changes from joint to sole control.** Typically, a move from joint to sole control will arise where one shareholder acquires the shareholding held by one or more other shareholders. In the case of a 50/50 JV, the acquirer moves from joint to sole control of the entire undertaking which, as a result, ceases to be a JV. A change from joint control to sole control constitutes a concentration within the meaning of the Merger Regulation, as it substantially alters the nature of control over the

---

[98] The number of formal decisions finding no jurisdiction under Art 6(1)(a) has declined significantly in recent years, with no such decisions at all in the 2003 to 2006 period: see statistics at para 8.011, above. See, eg Case M.1095 *NEC/Bull/PBN* (6 February 1998) where the Commission concluded that the assertion that NEC (with 49 per cent of the shares) and Bull (with 12.6 per cent) 'both have long term common interests as external investors in PBN [and] should be treated for the purposes of this notification as voting in concert' was 'a pure assumption by the notifying parties which is not sufficient, in the absence of stronger legal or factual elements, to prove the existence of a situation of joint control within PBN'. Subsequently, in Case M.1276 *NEC/PBN* (3 September 1998), NEC increased its interest from 49 per cent to 52.8 per cent and this was found to confer sole control.

[99] Jurisdictional Notice, (published on 10 July 2007, Vol II, App D.13) para 80 (previously Concentration Notice, OJ 1998 C66/5, para 35); see, eg Case JV.12 *Ericsson/Nokia/Psion/Motorola* (22 December 1998) where the Commission found no evidence that the four shareholders would always vote together on strategic matters. In M.2425 *Coop Norden* (26 July 2001) the Commission likewise concluded that the three retail cooperative societies did not have joint control of the JV: 'Even though the parents will transfer their core businesses to the joint venture, i.e. their entire retailing, wholesaling and procurement business of daily consumer goods, it is unclear why this fact should make the parents co-ordinate their voting behaviour. Therefore, it cannot be ruled out that the parent would vote disparately. Consequently, no joint control can safely be established.'

undertaking on a lasting basis.[100] In the course of its substantive assessment, the Commission will consider whether the move from joint to sole control is likely to change materially the commercial policy of the undertaking concerned to the detriment of competition.[101]

Changes from negative to full sole control. The Jurisdictional Notice expressly **8.042** provides that a concentration does not arise when a shareholder which is already able to exercise negative control acquires additional rights enabling it positively or unilaterally to impose strategic decisions and to determine strategic decisions on its own.[102] Accordingly, where an operation leads to a change from negative to full sole control, the Commission should not regard this as a change in the quality of control giving rise to a concentration.[103]

Other changes in shareholdings of existing undertakings. In considering **8.043** whether a change in shareholdings in an existing undertaking gives rise to a concentration, the critical question is whether it may lead to a change in the quality of control, for example from sole to joint control or from joint to sole control. Each transaction has to be analysed on its particular facts, with different possible jurisdictional assessments.[104] The Jurisdictional Notice draws a distinction between transactions involving the entry of new controlling shareholders and those involving a reduction in the number of shareholders:[105]

(a) *Entry of controlling shareholders:* Changes in shareholdings only give rise to a concentration if the company is subject to *de jure* or *de facto* control after

---

[100] Jurisdictional Notice, para 89 (previously Concentration Notice para 16); Undertakings Concerned Notice, OJ 1998 C66/14, paras 30–32. Examples of moves from joint to sole control include Case M.023 *ICI/Tioxide* (28 November 1990); Case M.400 *Allied Lyons/HWE-Pedro Domecq* (28 April 1994); and Case M.563 *British Steel/UES* (17 March 1995).

[101] See, eg Case M.2838 *P&O/P&O Stena Line* (7 August 2002); Case M.2761 *BP/Veba Oel* (1 July 2002); and Case M.3561 *Deutsche Telekom/EuroTel* (15 December 2004). Since such changes from joint to sole control generally do not raise significant competition issues, they are usually assessed under the simplified procedure: paras 8.122 *et seq*, below.

[102] Jurisdictional Notice (n 99, above) para 83.

[103] Prior to the adoption of the Jurisdictional Notice, in exceptional circumstances, the Commission had considered that a move from negative to full (positive) control might have resulted in a sufficient change in the quality of control to give rise to a concentration. See eg *BBVA/BNL* and *VW-Audi/VW Audi Vertriebszentren* (both n 79, above). The concept of negative control is considered at para 8.030, above.

[104] Where a transaction concerns the acquisition of (sole) control of the parent company of a group, the latter may in turn have pre-existing joint control of a JV undertaking with a third party. As an indirect consequence of the transaction, the JV will ultimately become jointly controlled by the acquirer (indirectly) and the third party. In such a situation, the Commission's practice is to regard the transaction as giving rise to just one concentration within the meaning of the ECMR: see Jurisdictional Notice, para 41 (and also Green Paper on the Review of Council Reg 4064/89, COM(2001) 745/6 final, 11 December 2001, paras 131–132).

[105] Jurisdictional Notice (n 99, above) paras 85–90 (replacing Undertakings Concerned Notice (n 100, above) paras 33–45).

the transaction.[106] If a shareholder moves from sole control (whether positive or negative) to joint control with one or more other shareholders, this will give rise to a change in the quality of control. The Jurisdictional Notice proceeds on the basis that there is also a change in the quality of control (giving rise to a concentration) if a new controlling shareholder enters a pre-existing JV undertaking – either in addition to the existing controlling shareholders or by replacing one of them – even though the undertaking remains subject to 'joint control' both before and after the transaction.[107] In such circumstances, where each shareholder alone has a blocking right concerning strategic decisions, the jointly controlling shareholders have to take account of each other's interests and cooperate on a lasting basis in determining the JV's strategic behaviour.[108] Accordingly, where a new controlling shareholder enters (eg if a competitor acquires a direct controlling interest in the JV which had previously been held by a financial investor) the control structure and incentives of the JV may change significantly, not only due to the entry of the new controlling shareholder but also due to the change in the behaviour of the other controlling shareholder(s).

(b) *Reduction in the number of shareholders*: Where the exit of one or more shareholders results in another shareholder moving to a position of 'sole control', this clear change in the quality of control gives rise to a concentration.[109] By contrast, if the exit and reduction in numbers still leaves the JV subject to the joint control of two or more remaining shareholders, this will normally not be treated as a change in the quality of control. Prior to the adoption of the Jurisdictional Notice, in exceptional circumstances, the Commission had considered that where a change in structure left the JV subject to the joint control of only two shareholders, and the operation gave those remaining two shareholders additional veto rights or considerably more weight in the decision-making process (rather than simply a numerical increase in their voting rights), this might have changed the incentives and nature of the JV's control structure sufficiently to give rise to a change in the quality of control.[110]

(vii) Interrelated transactions

8.044 **Transactions involving different steps.** Commercial transactions raising Merger Regulation issues are often implemented in two or more identifiable stages

---

[106] ibid, para 88: see para 8.039, above on shifting alliances which do not give rise to a change in control on a lasting basis.

[107] ibid, para 87. See, eg Case M.3440 *ENI/EDP/GdP* (9 December 2004) (appeal dismissed, Case T-87/05 *EDP v Commission* [2005] ECR II-3745, [2005] 5 CMLR 1436).

[108] *Cementbouw* (n 62, above) para 67.

[109] See para 8.041, above.

[110] Jurisdictional Notice (n 99, above) para 90. See eg Case M.993 *Bertelsmann/Kirch/ Premiere*, OJ 1999 L53/1 focusing on the transfer of additional assets; Case M.1889 *CLT-UFA/Canal+/VOX* (21 March 2000); Case M.1863 *Vodafone/BT/Airtel* (18 December 2000).

or are closely connected with other related transactions. In looking at any complex operation implemented in separate steps or involving more than one acquisition, it is necessary to consider whether the operation gives rise to one or more distinct 'concentrations'.[111] The Commission will generally treat interrelated transactions as distinct concentrations if there are differences in the resulting quality of control or in the identity of the undertaking exercising control on a lasting basis over distinct sets of assets (such that there is an absence of economic unity between the transactions).[112] Where, however, the transactions at issue are inter-conditional and indicate an economic unity between the transactions, with the resulting quality of control, and the identity of the undertakings involved in the transfer of control, being the same, these interrelated transactions may be considered to give rise to one single concentration. In *Cementbouw Handel v Commission*, the Court of First Instance stated that to determine the unitary nature of the transactions in question, 'it is necessary, in each individual case, to ascertain whether those transactions are interdependent, in such a way that one transaction would not have been carried out without the other.'[113] Recital (20) of the Merger Regulation also provides the following general guidance: 'It is moreover appropriate to treat as a single concentration transactions that are closely connected in that they are linked by condition or take the form of a series of transactions in securities taking place within a reasonably short period of time'.[114] Where an undertaking acquires joint control of one business and sole control of another, the two transactions may be treated as one concentration if they are closely linked.[115]

---

[111] In the case of a sale of parts of an undertaking in two or more transactions, the anti-avoidance provision in Art 5(2) of the Merger Reg deems the transactions to be legally and economically linked if they take place within a two-year period: see para 8.065, below.

[112] See Jurisdictional Notice, paras 41 and 44–47 (replacing Concentration Notice, OJ 1998 C66/5, para 16). This provides (at para 41) that several transactions, linked by condition upon each other, can only be treated as a single concentration if control is ultimately acquired by the same undertaking(s); see eg Case M.4521 *LGI/Telenet* (26 February 2007).

[113] *Cementbouw* (n 62, above) paras 105–109. See also, eg Case M.861 *Textron/Kautex* (18 December 1996); Case M.2737 *Royal Bank Private Equity/Cinven/ Chelwood* (13 March 2002); Case M.2724 *Royal Bank Private Equity/Cinven/Ambion* (13 March 2002); and Case M.2926 *EQT/ H&R/Dragoco* (16 September 2002). In Case M.3571 *IBM/Mærsk Data/DMdata* (18 November 2004), IBM's consecutive acquisitions of Mærsk Data and DMdata were treated as a single concentration since the different parts of the transaction were linked by legal conditionality, the signing of the different agreements occurred on the same day and the closing of the transfer of the remaining shares in DMdata was to occur immediately following the closing of IBM's purchase of Mærsk Data.

[114] As part of the review of Reg 4064/1989 (the original Merger Reg), the Commission had proposed extending the application of the Merger Reg to interrelated transactions, with the insertion of new provisions in the main body and recitals: see the Green Paper (n 3, above) paras 128–136. However, the European Parliament and Council did not adopt the Commission's proposals and retained only the wording of Recital (20).

[115] Jurisdictional Notice, para 42, reasoning by analogy with the situation where a specific corporate entity is acquired in circumstances where it has sole control of one undertaking and joint control of another (which will invariably be treated as one concentration). This represents a shift in Commission policy (relying on the interpretation foreseen in Recital (20) of the new Merger Reg)

8.045 **Asset swaps.** Where two or more undertakings exchange assets, regardless of whether these constitute legal entities or not, each acquisition of control constitutes an independent concentration.[116] Although the relevant operations can be considered by the parties to be interdependent, the legal link and interconditionality between them is not sufficient for them to qualify as a single concentration, given that each undertaking is to acquire control over distinct assets.

8.046 **Break-up bids and other operations with on-sale arrangements.** Two or more undertakings may come together to acquire another undertaking, for example, by setting up a JV or other special purpose vehicle company in which each party has a shareholding or by entering into back-to-back agreements where one party agrees to on-sell certain assets to the other. Where the parties use a jointly owned bidding vehicle to acquire the target's shares, but have agreed to divide up the target's assets immediately or shortly after the acquisition in accordance with a pre-existing plan, there will be no acquisition of joint control on a lasting basis over the target as a whole. Instead, the Commission analyses such operations as giving rise to two or more distinct concentrations whereby each of the acquiring undertakings is deemed to acquire sole control on a lasting basis only over the part of the target company that it will ultimately hold.[117] The same analysis applies

---

compared with its interpretation of the original Merger Reg, eg in Case M.2046 *Valeo/Robert Bosch/ JV* (28 July 2000) where Valeo's acquisition of sole control of certain Bosch group activities had been regarded as a separate and distinct concentration from the establishment of joint control by Valeo and Bosch over certain activities; see also Case M.1587 *Dana/GKN* (4 November 1999) where the Commission had considered two transactions forming part of a larger Umbrella Agreement (with Dana acquiring sole control of GKN's medium and heavy propeller shaft businesses and joint control of GKN's light propeller shaft business) but where the Commission had nevertheless considered that these should in principle be regarded as two separate concentrations under the original Merger Reg and that no specific circumstances justified a deviation from that principle.

[116] Jurisdictional Notice, para 41 (replacing Undertakings Concerned Notice (n 100, above) para 49). This is consistent with the principles considered at para 8.044, above. See Case M.042 *Alcatel/Telettra* (12 April 1991); and Case M.043 *CEAC/Magneti Marelli* (29 May 1991): framework agreement between Fiat and Alcatel Alsthom provided for (i) an acquisition by Alcatel (an Alcatel Alsthom subsidiary) of Telettra (a Fiat subsidiary) and (ii) an acquisition by Magneti Marelli (a Fiat subsidiary) of CEAC (an Alcatel Alsthom subsidiary); the two acquisitions were viewed as distinct concentrations, each with a 'Community dimension', and were notified separately to the Commission. Similarly, Case M.251 *Allianz/DKV* (10 September 1992), para 3, considered only Allianz's acquisition of sole control of DKV, although this was part of an extensive exchange of shares between Allianz and Munich-Re affecting a total of seven German insurance companies. See also, eg Case M.1056 *Stinnes/BTL* (4 February 1998).

[117] Jurisdictional Notice, paras 30–33 (replacing Undertakings Concerned Notice, paras 24–25). See, eg Case M.1630 *Air Liquide/BOC*, OJ 2004 L92/1; see also *ENI/EDP/GDP* (n 107, above): transaction structured in two phases: (i) the acquisition by ENI, EDP and REN of joint control over the whole of GDP's share capital and (ii) the subsequent spin-off from GDP and transfer to REN of the gas pipeline network; considering the purely transitional nature of the first phase of the transaction, its relatively short time frame and the clear break-up situation which would result after the second phase, the Commission found that the operation resulted in two distinct concentrations: the first concentration (ie acquisition by ENI and EDP of joint control over GDP) had a Community dimension whereas the second concentration (ie acquisition by REN of sole control

where as a first step one or more of the bidders acquires the target with a view to the agreed subsequent break-up or on-sale; that first step will not be sufficiently long lasting to give rise to a separate concentration but may instead be treated as an integral part of the overall break-up operation, such that it should not be put into effect until merger control clearances have been obtained for all the concentrations resulting from the break-up.[118] For example, in *UPM-Kymmene/Haindl*[119] and *Norske Skog/Parenco/Walsum*[120] the Commission opened two parallel Phase II investigations into a transaction under which UPM-Kymmene acquired Haindl (including six paper mills) and sold two paper mills on to Norske Skog; the way in which the transaction was structured meant that the first deal could proceed on its own but the second deal was dependent on the first one, so there were two distinct concentrations which had to be separately notified.[121] Similarly, in *Allied Domecq*[122] the parties structured their operation in two steps: first, Pernod Ricard was to acquire the whole of Allied, then within six months it was to divest certain brands/assets to Fortune Brands. The Commission examined the operations as giving rise to two distinct concentrations and conducted its review of Pernod Ricard's acquisition on a 'look through' basis, disregarding those brands which would subsequently be divested to Fortune Brands.[123] If a break-up operation is structured in a way which leaves uncertainty over whether the second step will proceed within a short time of the first acquisition, the first step may instead be treated as a separate concentration involving the acquisition of control of the entire target undertaking on a lasting basis.[124]

Demergers and the break-up of JV undertakings. Where a company demerges or a JV is broken up, the division of assets and activities between the demerging parties   **8.047**

---

over the gas pipeline network) did not, and accordingly had been notified to the Portuguese NCA. sf Case M.2384 *Ratos/3i Group/Atle* (2 April 2001).

[118] Jurisdictional Notice, paras 31–32. This is in line with the stand-still period under Merger Reg Art 7(1): see para 8.126, below.

[119] Case M.2498 *UPM-Kymmene/Haindl* (21 November 2001), paras 7–8.

[120] Case M.2499 *Norske Skog/Parenco/Walsum* (21 November 2001), paras 7–8.

[121] Jurisdictional Notice (n 99, above) paras 33 and 38–40. See also parallel cases in Cases M.3293 *Shell/BEB* and M.3294 *Exxon Mobil/BEB* (both 20 November 2003).

[122] Parallel investigations in Cases M.3779 *Pernod Ricard/Allied Domecq* (24 June 2005) and M.3813 *Fortune Brands/Allied Domecq* (10 June 2005).

[123] See also Cases M.4685 *Enel/Acciona/Endesa* (5 July 2007) and M.4672 *E.ON/Endesa Europa/Viesgo* (6 August 2007). In other break-up operations, the first step may involve an acquisition by a jointly-owned bidding vehicle: see, eg *Air Liquide/BOC* (n 117, above); Case M.1922 *Siemens/Bosch/Atecs* (11 August 2000); Case M.2059 *Siemens/Dematic/VDO Sachs* (29 August 2000).

[124] Jurisdictional Notice (n 99, above) para 33. This is the case if the first transaction may also proceed independently of the second transaction: see parallel investigations in *UPM-Kymmene/Haindl* (n 119, above) and *Norske Skog/Parenco/Walsum* (n 120, above). It is likewise the case if a longer transitory period is needed for the break-up: see Case M.3372 *Carlsberg/Holsten* (16 March 2004).

will usually result in two or more concentrations.[125] This will notably be the case where the demerger or break-up gives rise to a different asset configuration or where the operation results in a durable change in the quality of decisive influence from joint to sole control.[126] The undertakings concerned for each concentration will be the undertaking acquiring control and the part of the assets or JV it is acquiring.

8.048 **'Warehousing' arrangements.** Where a party seeking to purchase an undertaking does so through arrangements involving a third party which will hold them on a temporary 'warehousing' basis, such interrelated arrangements may be viewed as giving rise to one single concentration. The step under which the assets would be 'parked' or 'warehoused' may not be viewed as sufficiently long lasting to give rise to a separate concentration, but may instead be treated as an integral part of the single concentration comprising the lasting acquisition of control by the ultimate buyer, such that it should not be put into effect until merger control clearance has been obtained for that concentration, resulting from the operation, unless the Commission grants a derogation from the standstill period under Article 7 of the Merger Regulation.[127]

(viii) Specific operations that are not concentrations

8.049 **Temporary holdings by financial institutions.** Acquisitions of securities on a temporary basis with a view to resale will not give rise to a concentration if made by insurance companies, credit institutions or other financial institutions[128] whose

---

[125] Jurisdictional Notice, para 41 (replacing Undertakings Concerned Notice (n 100, above) paras 46–48). See, eg Case M.197 *Solvay-Laporte/Interox* (30 April 1992): the two parents had notified their intention to break up the Interox JV as one concentration, arguing that the operation was governed by one master agreement, related to the division of a single undertaking and involved closely related products and activities. The Commission, however, held that two concentrations arose because two independent undertakings were moving from a position of joint to sole control in relation to two different sets of specific assets and products. Similarly, whereas the establishment of the DuPont Dow Elastomers JV had been notified as one concentration: Case M.663 *Dow/DuPont* (21 February 1996); its subsequent break-up gave rise to two concentrations: Case M.3743 *DuPont/DDE* (12 April 2005) and Case M.3733 *Dow/DDE* (26 April 2005). See also parallel proceedings in Cases M.3293 *Shell/BEB* and M.3294 *Exxon Mobil/BEB* (n 121, above).

[126] The Commission has held that there could be exceptional circumstances in which the division of an undertaking between its owners could be treated as one concentration: Case M.138 *Campsa* (19 December 1991), which involved the division of the retailing activities of the Spanish petroleum monopoly. *Campsa* was distinguished in *Solvay-Laporte/Interox*, above, on the basis that where 'exogenous constraints falling outside the scope of the control of the owners (ie the political imperative that the petrol monopoly be broken up in accordance with the Act of Accession of Spain to the EC) are imposed on the parties or products concerned', they 'necessarily confer a unity of character on the division'.

[127] Jurisdictional Notice, para 35; see also general observations on interrelated transactions at para 8.044, above and on operations involving on-sales at para 8.046, above. See also Art 3(5)(a) of the Merger Reg: para 8.049, below. For the effect of the standstill period and the possibility of derogations, see paras 8.126–8.130, below.

[128] For the meaning of these terms, see Jurisdictional Notice (n 99, above) para 207 (previously Turnover Notice, OJ 1998 C66/25, paras 51–52), adopting the definitions in the First and Second

normal activities include transactions and dealing in securities for their own account or for the account of others.[129] For this exception under Article 3(5)(a) of the Merger Regulation to apply, the institution must not exercise any voting rights with a view to determining the strategic commercial behaviour of the undertaking in which those securities have been acquired. However, it may exercise such voting rights with a view to preparing the disposal of the undertaking, its assets or securities, provided that the disposal takes place within one year of the acquisition. The Commission may extend that period where the acquiring institution can show that the disposal was not reasonably possible within that time, for example because of the market price for the securities.[130] In practice, the provisions of Article 3(5)(a) are of little relevance to merger transactions, particularly given that the concept of concentration only applies to operations involving a change of control on a lasting basis.[131] Indeed, if a financial institution were to agree to 'warehouse' certain assets or securities for a short period with a view to subsequent resale to another party, the two steps may be treated as economically linked such that they are treated as parts of one and the same concentration (see para 8.048, above).[132]

Liquidation and insolvency.   The acquisition of control by a liquidator or similar office-holder in accordance with a Member State's laws on insolvency, winding-up or analogous proceedings, will not constitute a change of control on   **8.050**

Banking Dirs: hence 'credit institution' is defined to mean 'an undertaking whose business is to receive deposits or other repayable funds from the public and to grant credits of its own account'; 'financial institution' is defined to mean an undertaking other than a credit institution the principal activity of which is to acquire holdings or carry on certain of the activities listed in the Annex to the Second Banking Dir (including financial leasing, trading in financial instruments, money broking, portfolio management and safe custody services).

129   Merger Reg, Reg 139/2004, OJ 2004 L24/1: Vol II, App D.1, Art 3(5)(a); see also Jurisdictional Notice (n 99, above) para 111 (previously Concentration Notice (n 112, above) para 42).

130   In Case M.116 *Kelt/American Express* (20 August 1991), Art 3(5)(a) was held to be inapplicable, because there was no indication that the banks would dispose of the Kelt securities within a year; but given the need to effect the restructuring operation quickly, the Commission granted a derogation from the applicable suspensory period. The Art 3(5)(a) exception will generally not apply to 'rescue operations', involving the conversion of existing debt into a new company, through which a syndicate of banks may acquire joint control of the company concerned. Although the primary intention of the banks is to restructure the financing of the undertaking concerned for subsequent resale, the Commission normally takes the view that this constitutes a concentration involving joint control since a restructuring programme will normally take longer than a year and will require the controlling banks to determine the strategic commercial behaviour of the rescued undertaking: see Jurisdictional Notice, para 116 (previously Concentration Notice, para 45).

131   See para 8.015, above.

132   The scope of Art 3(5)(a) is the subject of proceedings in Case T-279/04 *Editions Odile Jacob v Commission*, not yet decided regarding certain 'warehousing' or 'parking' arrangements whereunder Natexis acquired Vivendi Universal Publishing subject to a commitment to sell it on to Largardère in circumstances where the subsequent sale was investigated and approved by the Commission in Case M.2978 *Lagardère/Natexis/VUP*, OJ 2004 L125/54.

a lasting basis. It will not therefore give rise to a concentration.[133] However, the sale of an undertaking by such an office-holder to a third party will generally give rise to a concentration.[134]

8.051 **Acquisitions by financial holding companies.** The acquisition of control of an undertaking by certain 'financial holding companies'[135] for the purpose of managing their investment without being involved in the day-to-day management of the undertaking will not give rise to a concentration.[136] For this exception to apply, the holding company may exercise voting rights, in particular in relation to the appointment of members of the management and supervisory bodies of the undertaking in which they have holdings, only in order to maintain the full value of the investment but 'not to determine, directly or indirectly, the competitive conduct' of the undertaking.[137]

(c) Full-function joint venture undertakings

(i) In general

8.052 **Background.** The meaning of joint control is discussed above: see paragraphs 8.033 *et seq*. As a result of an amendment to the original Merger Regulation that took effect in March 1998, there is no longer a jurisdictional distinction to be drawn between 'concentrative' JVs (which fall outside the scope of Article 81(1) but have been subject to review since the original Merger Regulation came into force) and so-called 'cooperative' JVs (which had previously not been caught by the Merger Regulation but were instead subject to review and appraisal under Article 81).[138] Article 3(4) of the Merger Regulation now provides that: 'The creation of a joint venture performing on a lasting basis all the functions

---

[133] Merger Reg (n 129, above) Art 3(5)(b); see also Jurisdictional Notice, para 112 (previously Concentration Notice, para 43). The position is less clear where control results from insolvency in accordance with the law of a non-Member State, although in practice the Commission has not required the notification of any acquisitions of control by liquidators operating in accordance with third country rules.

[134] See, eg Case M.497 *Matra Marconi Space/Satcomms* (14 October 1994); Case M.573 *ING/Barings* (11 April 1995).

[135] As defined at Art 5(3) of the Fourth Company Law Dir (Council Dir 78/660, OJ 1978 L222/11) on the annual accounts of certain types of companies, as amended by the Seventh Company Law Dir (Council Dir 83/349, OJ 1983 L193/1).

[136] Merger Reg (n 129, above) Art 3(5)(c); see also Jurisdictional Notice, para 113 (previously Concentration Notice (n 112, above) para 44).

[137] See Case M.669 *Charterhouse/Porterbrook* (11 December 1995), where the exception was held to be inapplicable.

[138] The concept of 'cooperative' JVs had been necessary prior to 1998 as Art 3(2) of the original Merger Reg had provided that: 'An operation including the creation of a joint venture, which has as its object or effect the coordination of the competitive behaviour of undertakings which remain independent shall not constitute a concentration.'

of an autonomous economic entity shall constitute a concentration'.[139] Thus since 1998, all 'full-function' JVs constitute concentrations with the meaning of the Merger Regulation, regardless of whether there may be coordination of the competitive behaviour of the parents.[140] Accordingly, it is necessary to identify, on a case-by-case basis, whether the transaction gives rise to a JV which will perform on a lasting basis all the functions of an autonomous economic entity.

Commission guidance.   Guidance on whether a JV has the characteristics nec-   **8.053** essary to be 'full-function' can be found in the Jurisdictional Notice.[141] The Notice clarifies the distinction between (i) JVs 'performing on a lasting basis all the functions of an autonomous economic entity' under Article 3(4) of the Merger Regulation; and (ii) 'partial function' JVs and other forms of horizontal cooperation (which do not come within the scope of the Merger Regulation but may instead be subject to Article 81 of the Treaty, as discussed in Chapter 7, above). The Notice also considers that a concentration may arise where two or more parties acquire joint control of a pre-existing undertaking (with a market presence) even if it will not subsequently operate as a full-function undertaking, given that it nevertheless leads to a structural change in the market as set out in Recital (20) of the Merger Regulation.[142]

(ii) Full functionality

Key principles of full functionality.   To be 'full-function' (or autonomous), a JV   **8.054** must perform the usual functions of an undertaking operating on the same market. The JV must have management for its day-to-day operations and access to sufficient resources, including finance, personnel and assets (tangible and intangible), to be able to conduct its business activities within the area provided

---

[139] During the period 1998–2002, a total of 51 such 'cooperative JVs' were examined not by the former specialist mergers Directorate within DG Comp (the 'Merger Task Force': see n 299, below) but by the relevant sectoral Directorates; these were distinguished by having a 'JV' case number rather than a 'M' case number.

[140] See also Recital (20) to the Merger Reg, Reg 139/2004, OJ 2004 L24/1: Vol II, App D,1. But to the extent that the concentration has as its object or effect the coordination of the competitive behaviour of its parents, such coordination is to be appraised in accordance with the criteria of Art 81(1) and (3) EC: Merger Reg, Art 2(4) and (5). See further paras 8.232 *et seq*, below.

[141] Jurisdictional Notice, paras 91–109 (previously Full-function JV Notice, OJ 1998 C66/1).

[142] Jurisdictional Notice, para 91. Such a situation might arise where an undertaking producing certain industrial inputs is jointly acquired by two of its customers which would subsequently use the JV's production solely for their own requirements and cease selling to third parties (such that the JV would not be regarded as full-function). The Notice proceeds on the basis that such an acquisition of joint control will of itself lead to a change in control on a lasting basis within the meaning of Art 3(1) of the Merger Reg, regardless of whether the resulting joint venture is full-function or has effects which may be subject to review under Art 81 EC.

for in the JV agreement on a lasting basis.[143] Personnel do not necessarily need to be employed by the JV, particularly if it is standard practice in the industry for third parties to supply staff under an operational agreement or from a temporary employment agency. The secondment of personnel by the parent companies may also be sufficient if done either only for a start-up period or if the JV deals with the parent companies in the same way as with third parties (on arm's length commercial terms).[144]

8.055 **JV scope and degree of dependence.** A JV cannot be regarded as full-function if it is only assigned one specific function within its parents' commercial activities without having access to the marketplace; for example, pure research and development or production joint ventures will not be regarded as full-function.[145] The same is true for those JVs which, by being limited to distribution or sales of parents' products, are essentially confined to a sales agent role.[146] However, use of its parent companies' distribution networks will not disqualify a JV from being full-function, so long as they are acting mainly as sales agents of the JV.[147] If the parent companies remain strongly active in upstream or downstream markets so

---

[143] Jurisdictional Notice, para 94 (previously Full-function JV Notice, para 12). Many full-function JVs have been notified under the Merger Reg. See, eg Case M.523 *Akzo Nobel/Monsanto* (19 January 1995); Case M.966 *Philips/Lucent Technologies* (20 August 1997); Case JV.51 *Bertelsmann/Mondadori/BOL Italia* (1 September 2000); Case JV.54 *Smith & Nephew/Beiersdorf/ JV* (30 January 2001); Case M.3134 *Arcelor/Umicore/Duology JV* (4 July 2003). In Case JV.19 *KLM/Alitalia* (11 August 1999), although the two airlines would continue to operate as air carriers, contractual arrangements between them progressively to integrate their scheduled passenger and cargo services in JVs that would be jointly run and marketed (sharing costs and revenues and with unconditional access to the parents' aircraft) were held to constitute a full-function JV undertaking.

[144] Jurisdictional Notice, para 94.

[145] Jurisdictional Notice, paras 95–96 (previously Full-function JV Notice, para 13). See, eg Case M.904 *RSB/Tenex/Fuel Logistic* (2 April 1997): the 'forwarding functions' of the JV were essentially limited to auxiliary functions for the forwarding activities of its parent. For such partial function JVs, see Chap 7, above. The Jurisdictional Notice (at para 92) refers to the common example of JVs established to hold real estate property (often for tax or other financial reasons) which cannot be considered as full-function as they lack an autonomous long-term business activity on the market. Such JVs can be contrasted with full-function real estate property management JVs which act on their own behalf on the market: eg Case M.929 *DIA/Veba Immobilien/Deutschbau* (23 June 1997); Case M.3325 *Morgan Stanley/Glick/Canary Wharf* (20 February 2004).

[146] See Case M.551 *ATR/BAe* (25 July 1995): re existing aircraft, the JV would be acting as sales agent for its parents, at least initially, given the extent of market risk and responsibility that the parent companies would retain. Moreover, the parties' commitment to the JV was not irreversible until the successful completion and implementation of feasibility studies for new aircraft and the progress of the parties' existing activities at least to the stage of limited financial integration. Employees were, at least initially, to be seconded by the parent companies. The Commission thus found that the activities and nature of the JV were not sufficient to give it a full-function character. cf Case M.788 *AgrEvo/Marubeni* (3 September 1996): JV sold only a limited proportion of its parents' products; it was therefore not just a sales agency and was full-function.

[147] Jurisdictional Notice, para 95 (previously Full-function JV Notice (n 141, above) para 13). See, eg Case M.102 *TNT/Canada Post* (2 December 1991); Case M.3556 *Fortis/BCP* (19 January 2005).

that substantial provision of services, sales or purchases between parents and the JV take place for more than an initial start-up period, the JV is unlikely to be regarded as full-function.[148] For these purposes, the Commission considers that the start-up period should not usually exceed a period of three years, although its actual length will depend on conditions in the market in question. The degree and significance of the JV's dependence on its parents is assessed on a case-by-case basis, having regard to the prevailing conditions in each market.[149]

Sales to parents. Where the JV will make sales to its parents on a lasting **8.056** basis beyond an initial start-up period, the essential question is whether the JV will nonetheless be able to play an active role in the market. An important factor is whether the proportion of sales to the parents compared with the JV's total production allows the JV to be a credible supplier to the market. Another significant factor is whether the sales to the parents are made on arm's length commercial terms. If the answer to both these questions is positive, the JV will most likely be considered to be full-function even if it makes substantial sales (for example 50 to 80 per cent of its output) to its parents.[150]

Purchases from parents. Where the JV will make substantial purchases from its **8.057** parents beyond an initial start-up period, the characterisation of the JV as full-function or not hinges upon the focus of its activities. If the JV adds little value to the products or services in question, it may be treated as closer to a joint sales agency. However, if its role is to be active at an intermediate wholesaling or trading

---

[148] Jurisdictional Notice, para 97 (previously Full-function JV Notice, para 14). For cases where the JV was regarded as full-function notwithstanding its dependence on its parents for the provision of certain services or purchases/sales or access to facilities for an initial period, see, eg Case M.468 *Siemens/Italtel* (17 February 1995): sales by JV to its parents caused by a legal monopoly downstream of the JV; Case M.550 *Union Carbide/Enichem* (13 March 1995): sales by JV to its parent consisted of by-products of minor importance to the JV; Case M.560 *EDS/Lufthansa* (11 May 1995); Case M.686 *Nokia/Autoliv* (5 February 1996); Case M.1020 *GE Capital/Sea Containers* (28 April 1998); Case M.2299 *BP Chemicals/Solvay/HDPE JV* (29 October 2001); Case M.3056 *Celanese/Degussa/JV* (11 June 2003). cf Case M.904 *RSB/Tenex/Fuel Logistic* (2 April 1997); Case M.979 *Preussag/Voest Alpine* (1 October 1997): the JV was essentially unable to determine its own commercial policy and was dependent on its parents for the supply of raw materials necessary to perform its functions. See also Case M.3003 *Electrabel/Energia Italiana/Interpower* (23 December 2002): JV not full-function since the greatest part of its turnover depended upon sales to its parents and it had no independent commercial strategy.

[149] See Case T-87/96 *Assicurazioni Generali and Unicredito v Commission* [1999] ECR II -203, [2000] 4 CMLR 312, paras 71–79: in life assurance market, although it is common practice for life assurance company to have recourse to outside companies for distribution and assistance in actuarial matters, internal auditors, choice of doctors and IT procedures, when JV is dependant on its parents for provision of all these services beyond initial start-up period it was not operationally autonomous.

[150] Jurisdictional Notice, paras 98–100 (previously Full-function JV Notice, para 14). See, eg Case M.556 *Zeneca/Vanderhave* (9 April 1996); Case M.751 *Bayer/Hüls-Newco* (3 July 1996); Case M.2645 *Saab/WM-Data AB/Saab Caran JV* (6 December 2001); Case M.3178 *Bertelsmann/ Springer* (3 May 2005).

level, it may be viewed not as performing an auxiliary sales function but as a full-function JV performing all the functions of a trading company on the trade market in question.[151] To fulfil such a role the JV must have the necessary facilities and resources and be likely to obtain substantial supplies not only from its parents but also from their competitors. [152]

(iii) Lasting basis

8.058 **Durability.** The other element of the definition in Article 3(4) of the Merger Regulation is whether the JV can be regarded as performing its functions 'on a lasting basis'. This durability can usually be demonstrated if the parent companies commit the necessary financial and other resources to the JV. If an operation leads to joint control for only a limited start-up period (generally up to one year) but under legally binding arrangements where it will then convert to sole control by one of the parents, the whole operation will normally be considered to be an acquisition of sole control.[153] If a JV is established only for a short, finite duration or for a specific project (for example, a construction project), it will not be regarded as operating on a lasting basis.[154] Even if the JV has a specified duration, provided that the period is sufficiently long to result in a lasting change in the undertakings concerned, or provision is made for the JV to continue beyond the specified period in certain circumstances, it can still be considered as full-function.[155] The fact

---

[151] Jurisdictional Notice, para 101 (previously Full-function JV Notice, para 14).

[152] See, eg Case M.788 *AgrEvo/Marubeni* (3 September 1996); Case M.2048 *Alcatel/Thomson Multimedia/JV* (26 October 2000); Case M.2403 *Schneider/Thomson Multimedia/JV* (13 June 2001).

[153] Jurisdictional Notice, para 34. The Commission had in the past accepted that a longer start-up period could be acceptable: see Case M.425 *British Telecom/Banco Santander* (28 March 1994); and also the 1998 Concentration Notice, para 38 (which had provided that such a start-up period could last for as long as three years). However, in its restated policy under the Jurisdictional Notice it concludes that the period should, in general, not exceed one year and there should be clear indications that the joint control is only transitory in nature: see Case M.2389 *Shell/DEA*, OJ 2003 L15/35 where the ultimate acquirer of sole control had a strong influence in the operational management during the joint control period; and Case M.2854 *RAG/Degussa* (18 November 2002) where the transitional period was designed to facilitate internal post-merger restructuring.

[154] Jurisdictional Notice, paras 103–104 (previously Full-function JV Notice (n 141, above) para 15). A JV exceeding 10 years in duration can generally be expected to fulfil the 'lasting basis' requirement of the Merger Reg: see, eg Case M.2903 *DaimlerChrysler/Deutsche Telekom/JV*, OJ 2003 L300/62, [2004] 5 CMLR 169. Short-term jointly owned vehicle companies, established for the purpose of making a joint bid for a company, will not be regarded as operating on a lasting basis: see para 8.046, above.

[155] Jurisdictional Notice, para 103 (previously Full-function JV Notice, para 15). In particular, this may be the case depending on the specific market conditions and the specific termination/renewal rights attached to the JV agreement: see, eg Case M.259 *British Airways/TAT* (27 November 1992); Case M.791 *British Gas Trading/Group 4 Utility Services* (7 October 1996). cf Case M.722 *Teneo/Merrill Lynch/Bankers Trust* (15 April 1996): although a share purchase agreement establishing the JV referred to a five-year strategic business plan, the intention of the parties was to set up a vehicle for the temporary holding of shares with a view to selling the underlying assets within three years; held not to constitute a concentration.

that the parents make provision for the dissolution of the JV in prescribed circumstances or for the withdrawal of one or more parents in cases of fundamental disagreement will not prevent the JV from being regarded as operating on a lasting basis.[156] A JV will not be regarded as full-function if the commencement of its activities remains subject to essential decisions on the part of third parties, for example if it depends upon the award of a contract by public tender, a licence as in the telecoms sector, or access rights to property such as exploration rights for oil or gas.[157]

Changes in joint venture's activities.   If the parents of a full-function JV subse-   **8.059**
quently decide to enlarge its field of activities, eg by transferring additional assets to it (or through the acquisition of the whole or part of another undertaking), this will generally give rise to a new concentration. However, if the scope of a JV is enlarged without additional assets, contracts, know-how or rights being transferred, no concentration will arise.[158] Thus, where a full-function JV expands its activities through organic growth, this will not be regarded as a new concentration unless there is evidence that the parent companies are in fact the real players behind this operation. For this purpose, the criteria to be applied are the same as for evaluating acquisitions made by a full-function JV (including the extent of the parents' involvement in the initiation, organisation and financing of the operation).[159]

(d) Community dimension

(i) Turnover thresholds

Worldwide and Community-wide turnover.   The Merger Regulation gives the   **8.060**
Commission jurisdiction over concentrations which have a 'Community dimension', a concept which depends on the respective turnovers of the undertakings concerned.[160] The jurisdictional tests relate only to the economic size of the parties and do not depend on the market shares of the parties or substantive impact of the transaction, nor on whether the concentration will have any effects within the Community.[161] This means that the Merger Regulation can apply to concentrations which take place outside the Community and regardless of the

---

[156] Jurisdictional Notice, para 103 (previously Full-function JV Notice (n 141, above) para 15). See, eg Case M.891 *Deutsche Bank/Commerzbank/J.M. Voith* (23 April 1997).

[157] Jurisdictional Notice, para 105.

[158] Jurisdictional Notice, paras 106–108. See also Case M.3039 *Soprol/Cérérol/Lesieur* (30 January 2003).

[159] See para 8.070(e), below.

[160] For 'undertakings concerned', see paras 8.070 *et seq*, below.

[161] For notifications of full-function JVs with no effects within the EC (but between parent companies which satisfy the turnover tests), see, eg Case M.2278 *Lafarge/Blue Circle JV* (29 January 2001); Case M.2871 *Air Liquide/BOC/Japan Air Gases* (10 October 2002). Such cases are generally handled under the simplied procedure (see paras 8.122 *et seq*, below).

nationalities of the parties.[162] There are two sets of turnover tests, as illustrated by the diagram [opposite]):[163]

(a) The 'original' tests (unchanged since their introduction in 1990) involve three cumulative criteria:
  (i) *Worldwide threshold*: the combined aggregate worldwide turnover of all the undertakings concerned exceeds €5,000 million; and
  (ii) *Community-wide threshold*: the aggregate Community-wide turnover of each of at least two of the undertakings concerned exceeds €250 million; and
  (iii) *Two-thirds rule*: a concentration does not have a 'Community dimension' if each of the undertakings concerned achieves more than two-thirds of its aggregate Community-wide turnover within one and the same Member State.

(b) If these original tests are not satisfied, there will still be a Community dimension if the 'alternative' tests (introduced in 1998) are satisfied:
  (i) *Lower worldwide threshold*: the aggregate worldwide turnover of all the undertaking concerned exceeds—€2,500 million; and
  (ii) *Lower Community-wide threshold*: the aggregate Community-wide turnover of each of at least two of the undertakings concerned exceeds €100 million; and
  (iii) *Additional three Member States threshold*: in each of at least three Member States:
    — the combined aggregate turnover of all the undertakings concerned is more than €100 million; and
    — each of at least two of the undertakings concerned achieves a turnover of more than €25 million (in each of the same three Member States identified); and
  (iv) *Two-thirds rule*: a concentration does not have a 'Community dimension' if each of the undertakings concerned achieves more than two-thirds of its aggregate Community-wide turnover within one and the same Member State.

---

[162] High profile Phase II cases between non-European companies include Case M.619 *Gencor/Lonrho*, OJ 1997 L11/30; Case M.877 *Boeing/McDonnell Douglas*, OJ 1997 L336/16; Case M.1069 *Worldcom/MCI II*, OJ 1999 L116/1; Case M.2220 *General Electric/Honeywell*, OJ 2004 L48/1; Case M.3216 *Oracle/PeopleSoft*, OJ 2005 L218/6.

[163] Merger Reg (n 140, above) Art 1(1)–(3). In its Green Paper review of the Merger Reg, the Commission had originally proposed automatic Community competence over cases subject to filing requirements in three or more Member States (n 3, above) at paras 21 *et seq*. Because of the legal uncertainty that was likely to arise from the divergence of national merger control rules, this was abandoned in favour of a streamlined system of pre-notification referrals: see paras 8.081 *et seq*, below. Art 1(4)–(5) of the Merger Reg envisages that the Commission will report to the Council on the operation of the thresholds and criteria by 1 July 2009.

The two-thirds rule. The two-thirds rule accordingly applies to both the origi- **8.061** nal and alternative tests, on the basis that a Member State should retain jurisdiction over concentrations that are expected to have effects primarily within its territory, in line with the principles of subsidiarity and efficient allocation of jurisdiction.[164] Nonetheless, it means that the test for Community dimension will be satisfied provided at least one of the undertakings concerned has less than

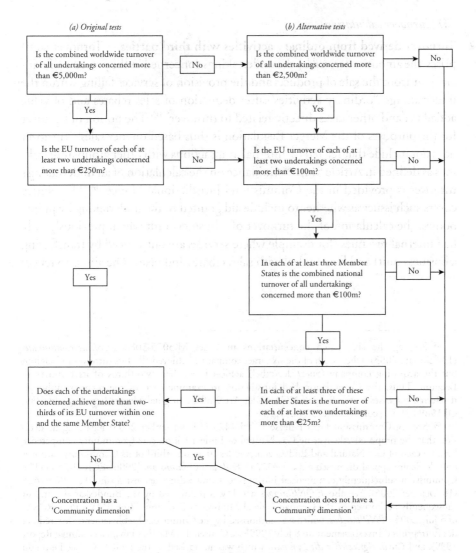

---

[164] In applying the two-thirds rule, no account is to be taken of turnover in jurisdictions outside the EC. Accordingly, mergers involving undertakings active in the EFTA States will remain subject to review by the Commission under Art 57 of the EEA Agreement where a 'Community dimension' exists, even if most of their turnover is achieved in an EFTA State (eg Norway). For the EEA Agreement, see paras 8.280 *et seq*, below.

two-thirds of its turnover in the same Member State as the others.[165] The application of the two-thirds rule has raised some controversy with regard to transactions consolidating the presence of strong national players, particularly in the energy and financial services sectors where the Commission has voiced concerns regarding the creation of 'national champions' which could impede internal market integration objectives.[166]

(ii) Turnover calculation

8.062 **Turnover derived from ordinary activities with third parties.** Turnover comprises 'the amounts derived by the undertakings concerned in the preceding financial year from the sale of products and the provision of services falling within the undertakings' "ordinary activities" after deduction of sales rebates and of value added tax and other taxes directly related to turnover'.[167] The notion of turnover for the purposes of the Merger Regulation is thus based on 'net sales'. Turnover does not include that related to 'internal' transactions with other group undertakings as defined in Article 5(4).[168] Guidance on the calculation of an undertaking's turnover is provided in the Commission's Jurisdictional Notice.[169] The Notice covers such issues as whether to include aid granted to the undertaking by public bodies, the calculation of the turnover of a business unit which previously only had internal revenues (for example where services are outsourced by transferring a business unit) and how to deal with sales rebates and taxes. The aim is to reflect

---

[165] See, eg the six related concentrations in Cases M.3075-3080 *ECS/Intercommunales* (13 February 2003), where each of the six target companies achieved all of its turnover in Belgium but the acquiring company (Suez/Electrabel) achieved less than two-thirds of its turnover in Belgium. Thus, the Commission had jurisdiction to examine each of the mergers, although it referred the cases to the Belgian NCA under Art 9 of the original Merger Reg, Reg 4064/89, OJ 1989 L395/1, corr by OJ 1990 L257/13.

[166] See, eg Commission Press Release IP/05/1425 (15 November 2005) regarding its decision that the proposed takeover by Gas Natural of Endesa fell outside Community competence because each of Gas Natural and Endesa achieved less than one-third of its Community turnover outside Spain; appeal dismissed Case T-417/05 *Endesa v Commission*, [2006] ECR II-2533. The Commission subsequently commenced infringement proceedings against Spain: see IP/06/1426 (18 October 2006). See also *E.ON/Ruhrgas* which was prohibited by the Bundeskartellamt, but subsequently authorised by the German Federal Minister of Economics (see BMWi Press Release of 5 July 2002); *BNP/Paribas*, which was authorised by the Comité des Etablissements de Crédit et des Entreprises d'Investissement on 8 July 1999 (see Conseil des Marchés Financiers Annual Report 1999); and *Crédit Agricole/Crédit Lyonnais*, which was authorised by the DGCCRF (see Lettre du Ministre de l'Economie, des Finances et de l'Industrie, NOR: ECOC0400146Y, 28 January 2003).

[167] Merger Reg (n 140, above) Art 5(1). For 'undertakings concerned', see paras 8.070 *et seq*, below.

[168] Jurisdictional Notice, para 167. See also paras 8.076 *et seq*, below.

[169] Jurisdictional Notice, paras 157 *et seq* (replacing Turnover Notice, OJ 1998 C66/25). Calculation of turnover in services generally uses the same method as for goods, unless the specific conditions of the service provided warrant adjustments (see paras 131–133). For further observations on outsourcing arrangements see para 8.027, above.

only transactions with third parties.[170] When a merger is notified, turnover figures are to be submitted in euros. Where the company's accounts are not expressed in euros, the conversion calculations should be made using the average exchange rate for the 12-month period in question using the official exchange rates as published by the European Central Bank for the same period.[171]

Audited accounts for relevant financial year and adjustments. The Merger **8.063** Regulation refers to turnover in the undertaking's preceding financial year and, in practice, the Commission generally looks at the most recent audited accounts. Only in cases where there are major differences between the Community's accounting standards and those of a third country may the Commission look behind the audited figures.[172] However, when calculating turnover, it will generally make adjustments to take into account subsequent acquisitions, divestments[173] or entry into new JVs.[174]

Acquisition of parts of a company. Special rules apply for the calculation of **8.064** turnover when part of an undertaking is sold. Under Article 5(2) of the Merger Regulation, whether or not the part sold constitutes a separate legal entity, 'only the turnover relating to the parts which are the subject of the transaction shall be taken into account with regard to the seller or sellers'.

Acquisitions within two-year period. Article 5(2) also provides that where two **8.065** or more transactions consisting of the acquisition of a part of an undertaking take place within a period of two years between the same parties, they shall be treated as one and the same concentration occurring on the date of the last transaction.[175] The provision was included as an anti-avoidance measure to ensure that parties could not avoid the obligation to notify a concentration with a Community

---

[170] Merger Reg (n 140, above) Art 5(1); Jurisdictional Notice, para 167 (previously Turnover Notice, paras 22–23).

[171] Averages are available from the ECB Monthly Bulletin (www.ecb.int/pub/mb/html). See also Jurisdictional Notice, paras 204–205 (previously Turnover Notice (n 169, above) paras 49–50).

[172] Jurisdictional Notice, paras 169–174 (previously Turnover Notice, paras 24–28). The Commission seeks to base itself upon the most accurate and reliable figures available, and thus generally refers to audited and other definite accounts. In exceptional circumstances, however, it may also rely on management or other forms of provisional accounts. See the CFI's judgment in *Endesa* (n 166, above), dismissing the appeal against the Commission's rejection of Endesa's complaint that various adjustments should be made to its 2004 audited accounts for the purposes of calculating its turnover.

[173] In order for turnover to be excluded from the calculation, the divestiture should be effected either between the closing of the relevant accounts and the time of signature of the merger agreement or as part of the notified concentration by means of an irrevocable condition precedent: Case M.1741 *MCI WorldCom/Sprint*, OJ 2003 L300/1, paras 6 *et seq;* annulled on other grounds, Case T-310/00 *MCI v Commission* [2004] ECR II-3253, [2004] 5 CMLR 1274. See also Jurisdictional Notice, paras 172–173.

[174] See, eg Case M.936 *Siebe/APV* (16 June 1997).

[175] Jurisdictional Notice, paras 48–50 (previously Turnover Notice (n 169, above) paras 32–35). See also para 8.044, above, on interrelated transactions.

dimension by implementing it over a period of time in staged transfers each falling below the relevant turnover thresholds. However, the provision applies to any transactions which the parties may have entered into at different times within a two-year period.[176] This applies even if the first transaction had already been notified under the Merger Regulation and the second one is relatively small.[177]

8.066 **Geographic allocation of turnover.** Article 5(1) provides that: 'Turnover, in the Community or in a Member State, shall comprise products sold and services provided to undertakings or consumers, in the Community or in that Member State as the case may be'.[178] The allocation of turnover thus generally depends on the location of the customer or the place of the performance of the contract. However, it will not always be clear in which Member State supply takes place, for example in the case of services provided over the Internet or services involving on element of cross-border travel. The Commission may therefore consider alternative methods for allocating turnover, with a view to ensuring that the resulting figures represent economic reality, particularly with regard to the place where competition is actually taking place.[179] Where the audited accounts are not prepared in a manner which provides the required geographic breakdown, the Commission will use the best figures available.[180]

8.067 **Banks and other credit and financial institutions.** In accordance with Article 5(3)(a) of the Merger Regulation, turnover calculations for credit and financial institutions[181] are based on a definition which corresponds to the format of banks' profit and loss accounts, as required under the Directive on Annual

---

[176] See, eg Case M.522 *Scandinavian Project* (28 November 1994); Case M.1630 *Air Liquide/BOC* (18 January 2000); Case M.2639 *Compass/Réstorama/Rail Gourmet/Gourmet Nova* (26 February 2002).

[177] See, eg Case M.224 *Volvo/Lex* (21 May 1992) and Case M.261 *Volvo/Lex (II)* (3 September 1992); Case M.769 *Norsk Hydro/Annya (Enichem Agricoltura)* (29 July 1996) and Case M.832 *Norsk Hydro/Enichem Agricoltura – Terni (II)* (25 October 1996); Case M.3725 *Cargill/Pagnan* (22 March 2005) and Case M.4082 *Cargill/Pagnan II* (6 February 2006); Case M.4005 *Ineos/Innovene* (9 December 2005) and Case M.4094 *Ineos/BP Dormagen* (10 August 2006). Case M.4540 *Nestlé/Novartis* (29 June 2007) and Case M.4688 *Nestlé/Gerber* (27 July 2007).

[178] See also Jurisdictional Notice, paras 195–202 (previously Turnover Notice (n 169, above) paras 45–48).

[179] Jurisdictional Notice, paras 197–202, provides some guidance on relevant factors for the cross-border supply of goods and provision of services (including travel, transport and telecoms services).

[180] Jurisdictional Notice, para 195 (previously Turnover Notice (n 169, above) para 29). Turnover in a relatively new Member State will be relevant provided that it is a Member State at the time of the concentration, even if, during some or all of the periods in question, it was not part of the EU: see Case M.122 *Paribas/MTH/MBH* (17 October 1991).

[181] For these terms, see n 128, above. A financial leasing company is treated as a financial institution within the meaning of Art 5(3)(a) of the Merger Reg: see Jurisdictional Notice, paras 211–213 (previously Turnover Notice, para 55).

Accounts of Banks and other Credit Institutions.[182] Turnover is defined as the sum of:[183]

(a) interest income and similar income;
(b) income from securities (ie from shares and other variable yield securities, from participating interests and from shares in affiliated undertakings);
(c) commissions receivable;
(d) net profit on financial operations; and
(e) other operating income.

Interest payable and similar charges, commissions payable and net losses of financial operations are not deducted; extraordinary income and extraordinary profits are not included in the calculation. As regards geographic allocation of turnover, Article 5(3) also provides that: 'the turnover of a credit or financial institution in the Community or in a Member State shall comprise the income items . . . which are received by the branch or division of that institution established in the Community or in the Member State in question, as the case may be'.

Insurance companies. In accordance with Article 5(3)(b) of the Merger **8.068** Regulation, turnover calculations for insurance companies are based on the values of gross premiums written worldwide and with Community residents are used in place of worldwide and Community-wide turnover respectively.[184] The two-thirds rule is similarly adapted. Gross premiums written comprise all insurance and reinsurance amounts received and receivable in respect of insurance contracts issued by or on behalf of the insurance companies concerned, after deduction of taxes and any parafiscal contributions or levies charged by reference to the amount of individual premiums or the total volume of premiums. Reinsurance premiums paid out by the undertaking concerned to obtain reinsurance cover are not to be deducted from the gross premiums written.

Mixed groups. Where a group's activities include businesses of a mixed nature **8.069** (eg where a group with banking or insurance activities also has activities in other areas), the Commission's approach is to apply the appropriate tests to the different parts of the group and then to aggregate the resulting sub-totals.[185]

---

[182] Council Dir 86/635, OJ 1986 L372/1.

[183] Merger Reg (n 140, above) Art 5(3)(a); Jurisdictional Notice, para 210 (previously Turnover Notice (n 169, above) paras 51–55).

[184] Merger Reg, Art 5(3)(b); Jurisdictional Notice, paras 214–216 (previously Turnover Notice, paras 56–58).

[185] Jurisdictional Notice, paras 217–220 (previously Turnover Notice paras 59–61). This is consistent with Art 5 (4) of the Merger Reg, which provides that the aggregate turnover of an undertaking is to be calculated by adding together the respective turnovers of the undertaking itself and the other companies belonging to the same group; see paras 8.076 *et seq*, below.

(iii) Undertakings concerned

8.070 **Key principles.** The 'undertakings concerned' for the purposes of the Merger Regulation are the direct participants in a merger or acquisition of control, ie the undertakings that are merging or the undertaking (or undertakings) acquiring sole (or joint) control and the undertaking over which control is being acquired. The Jurisdictional Notice provides detailed guidance.[186] The Commission bases itself upon the configuration of the undertakings concerned at the relevant date for establishing the Commission's jurisdiction.[187] By way of overview:

(a) *Mergers*: in the case of a merger, the undertakings concerned are each of the merging entities;[188]

(b) *Acquisitions of sole control*: in the case of an acquisition of sole control over the whole of a company, the undertakings concerned are the acquiring company and the acquired or target company. Where sole control is acquired over parts of a company, the undertakings concerned will be the acquirer and the acquired parts of the target company, and the seller is to be ignored for the purposes of identifying the undertakings concerned;[189]

(c) *Moves from joint to sole control*: where one party to a joint venture acquires its JV partner's stake, so moving from joint to sole control, the undertakings concerned are the acquiring company and the JV undertaking. The exiting shareholder is to be ignored for the purposes of identifying the undertakings concerned;[190]

(d) *Acquisitions of joint control*: in the case of an acquisition of joint control over a newly-created JV company, the undertakings concerned are each of the companies acquiring control of the newly set-up company (which, as such, has no turnover of its own). Where joint control is acquired over a pre-existing company or business, the undertakings concerned are each of the companies acquiring joint control and the acquired pre-existing entity or business;[191]

---

[186] Jurisdictional Notice, paras 129–153 (replacing the Undertakings Concerned Notice, OJ 1998 C66/14, paras 5 *et seq*). The concept of 'undertaking concerned' should not be confused with the wider concept of identifying all the legal entities in a corporate group which constitutes a single undertaking and therefore whose turnovers need to be aggregated in order to arrive at the turnover of the undertaking concerned, for the purposes of determining jurisdiction: see paras 8.076 *et seq*, below.

[187] See para 8.111, below.

[188] Jurisdictional Notice, para 132 (previously Undertakings Concerned Notice, paras 6 and 12).

[189] ibid, paras 133-137 (previously Undertakings Concerned Notice, paras 13–20). See also para 8.064, above. A part may be, eg a legally independent subsidiary, an internal subdivision within the seller (eg a division or unit), or specific assets (such as a brand or licence) to which a market turnover can be clearly attributed; see para 8.026, above).

[190] ibid, para 138.

[191] ibid, paras 133 and 139–141 (previously Undertakings Concerned Notice (n 186, above) paras 21–25). Where the pre-existing company was previously under the sole control of one of the

(e) *Acquisitions by a joint venture:* where a full-function JV undertaking acquires control of another undertaking,[192] the former will normally be the undertaking concerned rather than its parents,[193] although its parents' turnovers will be aggregated with that of the JV under Article 5(4) of the Merger Regulation because they are part of the same 'undertaking' under ordinary Community law principles. However, if the JV is essentially a shell or vehicle company set up for the purposes of the acquisition, or an existing JV which is being used by the parents as a legal vehicle for their joint transaction, the parents and not their JV will be regarded as constituting the undertakings concerned.[194] This distinction may be significant in terms of the Community-wide turnover test that must be satisfied by at least two of the 'undertakings concerned'.[195]

Changes in shareholdings.   Changes in shareholdings can take various forms.   **8.071**
If existing shareholders leave so as to give a remaining shareholder sole control, then the undertakings concerned are the shareholder acquiring sole control and the former jointly controlled company. If a change in shareholdings results in a new shareholder enjoying joint control of a pre-existing undertaking, the undertakings concerned are the two or more shareholders which subsequently exercise joint control and the pre-existing jointly controlled company.[196]

Closely linked transactions.   Where a number of interrelated transactions are to   **8.072**
be treated as two or more distinct concentrations, the undertakings concerned will be, for each property transfer, the acquiring company and the company or assets it acquires.[197] These considerations are relevant for transactions such as asset swaps, joint bids, demergers and the break-up of JV companies and on-sale agreements discussed in paragraphs 8.044 *et seq*, above.

Acquisitions by individuals.   An acquisition by an individual will only give rise   **8.073**
to a concentration within the meaning of the Merger Regulation where the acquiring individual already has sole or joint control of another undertaking.[198] In such circumstances, he or she will be treated as an undertaking concerned and the

---

companies acquiring joint control, the target company is not an undertaking concerned and its turnover is attributed to its parent; ibid, para 199.

[192] ibid, paras 145–147 (previously Undertakings Concerned Notice, paras 26–29).

[193] This is the case where the acquisition is carried out by a full-function JV undertaking: ibid, para 146 (previously Undertakings Concerned Notice, para 27).

[194] ibid, para 147.

[195] See, eg Case M.102 *TNT/Canada Post* (2 December 2001); Case M.402 *PowerGen/NRG Energy/Morrison Knudsen/Mibrag* (27 June 1994); Case M.689 *ADSB/Belgacom* (29 February 1996); see also the hypothetical example at foonote to para 145 of the Jurisdictional Notice.

[196] See para 8.043, above on the circumstances in which a change in shareholdings in an existing undertaking gives rise to a concentration.

[197] Jurisdictional Notice, paras 141 and 148–150 (previously Undertakings Concerned Notice (n 186, above) paras 46–50).

[198] Merger Reg (n 140, above) Art 3(1)(b).

turnover calculation will be made in the usual way, with the turnover of the undertaking(s) controlled by the individual being included in the calculation of the individual's turnover.[199]

8.074 **Management buy-outs, venture capital and private equity deals.** The same principle applies to management buy-outs which are acquisitions by individuals.[200] If the persons concerned form a jointly controlled vehicle company to carry out the acquisition, the rules governing acquisitions by a JV will apply.[201] If outside investors are brought in, the principles are the same: it is necessary to identify who acquires control within the meaning of Article 3 of the Merger Regulation.[202]

8.075 **Acquisitions by State-controlled companies.** The basic principle is that there should be no discrimination as between the private and public sectors.[203] Therefore, the rules set out above should apply in the case of an acquisition by a State-owned company. However, where one State-owned company acquires another, it is necessary to determine whether it should be treated as a concentration (in which case the acquiring and acquired entities are each undertakings concerned) or as an internal restructuring (within a single group of companies).[204] The Commission proceeds on the basis that, when calculating turnover of undertakings in the public sector, 'account is only to be taken of those undertakings which belong to the same economic unit, having an independent power of decision'.[205]

(iv) Identification of corporate group

8.076 **Group turnover for the purposes of Article 5(4).** In order to arrive at the aggregate turnover figures for each of the various 'undertakings concerned', it is necessary to aggregate the turnovers of each of the legal entities which are sufficiently linked to the undertaking concerned to be treated as part of the relevant 'group' for the purposes of calculating whether the turnover thresholds in the Merger Regulation are satisfied.[206] The aim is to capture the total volume of the economic resources that are being combined through the operation.[207] Articles 5(4) and (5) of the Merger Regulation list the various direct or indirect links that determine

---

[199] Jurisdictional Notice, para 151 (previously Undertakings Concerned Notice (n 186, above) paras 51–52).

[200] ibid, para 152 (previously Undertakings Concerned Notice, paras 53–54). See also para 8.019, above.

[201] See para 8.070, above, in particular sub-para (e).

[202] See para 8.020, above.

[203] Recital (22) of the Merger Reg; Jurisdictional Notice, para 192.

[204] See para 8.018, above.

[205] Jurisdictional Notice, paras 153 and 192–194 (previously Undertakings Concerned Notice (n 186, above) para 56); See also Case M.216 *CEA Industrie/France Télécom/Finmeccania/SGS-Thomson* (22 February 1993).

[206] ibid, paras 130–131.

[207] Jurisdictional Notice, para 175 (previously Turnover Notice, OJ 1998 C66/25, para 36).

which other undertakings are to be regarded as part of this group.[208] In applying these rules, the Commission does not limit itself to theoretical control, but will look at what has tended to happen in practice.[209]

Parent companies, subsidiaries and sister companies.   Parent companies of the   **8.077** undertakings concerned are regarded as part of the group. This rule applies even where the undertaking concerned is a JV such that it will have two or more parent companies.[210] Subsidiaries are included to the extent that the undertaking concerned exercises a controlling influence over them, whether as a result of owning more than half the capital or business assets, controlling more than half the voting rights, the composition of certain of the subsidiary's bodies or having the right to manage the subsidiary's affairs.[211] Subsidiaries of a parent company (sister companies) are also included to the extent that the common parent exercises decisive influence over both the undertaking concerned and the sister company in question.

Joint ventures between the undertakings concerned.   Article 5(5) of the Merger   **8.078** Regulation deals with the situation in which two or more of the undertakings concerned have joint control of a third undertaking.[212] It provides that no account is to be taken of the turnover resulting from the sale of products or the provision of services between the JV and each of the undertakings concerned or any other undertaking connected with any one of them as set out in Article 5(4). The purpose of such a rule is to avoid double counting. As far as transactions with third parties

---

[208] For detailed guidance and a graphic illustration, see Jurisdictional Notice, paras 176–184 (previously Turnover Notice paras 36–42). Art 5(4)(b)(i)–(iii) of the Merger Reg list quantitative criteria according to which a company shall be considered as part of a group if (i) more than half of its capital or assets are owned by the group; (ii) more than half of its voting rights can be exercised by the group; or (iii) the group can appoint more than half of its Board. Art 5(4)(b)(iv) states that a company shall be included in the group if the group has the right to manage its affairs. This 'right to manage' is of a more qualitative nature and is similar to the qualitative test of 'control' in the sense of decisive influence within the meaning of Art 3(3) of the Merger Reg (see paras 8.024–8.025, above).

[209] See, eg Case M.025 *Arjomari/Wiggins Teape Appleton* (10 December 1990): Groupe Saint Louis' 45.12 per cent stake in Arjomari was held not to confer the necessary level of control taking account of voting patterns at the previous annual general meeting. In Case M.187 *Ifint/Exor* (2 March 1992), the Commission, in calculating Exor's turnover, included the turnover of a company in which Exor held a 28.69 per cent interest (conferring 33.29 per cent of the votes) since at a previous annual general meeting of the company, Exor had held 52.1 per cent of the votes actually present or represented. See also Case M.062 *Eridania/ISI* (30 July 1991) and Case M.147 *Eurocom/RSCG* (18 December 1991): minority shareholders were held to have the required powers of decisive influence. But cf Case M.940 *UBS/Mister Minit* (9 July 1997): ownership by a franchisor of over half the franchisees' business assets was not sufficient to bring the franchisees' turnover into the calculation of aggregate turnover, since the franchisees paid rent for use of those assets and the franchise relationship was one of economic independence.

[210] Merger Reg, Reg 139/2004, OJ 2004 L24/1: Vol II, App D.1, Art 5(4); Jurisdictional Notice, para 182 (previously Turnover Notice (n 207, above) para 38 and remark 3 to the chart).

[211] Merger Reg, Art 5(4); Jurisdictional Notice, para 179 (previously Turnover Notice, para 38); see also para 8.024, above.

[212] See Jurisdictional Notice, paras 168 and 186 (previously Turnover Notice (n 207, above) para 38 and Undertakings Concerned Notice (n 186, above) paras 26–29).

are concerned, turnover is to be apportioned equally between the undertakings concerned, to reflect the joint control.

8.079 **Joint ventures between an undertaking concerned and a third party.** Where an undertaking concerned has a JV with one or more third parties, the Commission's practice is to allocate that JV's turnover equally between each of that JV's parents.[213]

8.080 **State-controlled companies.** The fact that two companies are both State-owned does not make them part of the same group for these purposes. Rather, the question is whether each company constitutes an independent economic unit.[214]

(e) Pre-notification reallocation of jurisdiction

(i) Article 4(4) referrals from Commission to NCAs

8.081 **Suitable cases for Article 4(4) referral.** There may be some circumstances in which parties to a proposed concentration with a Community dimension conclude that it would be simpler or more advantageous if their transaction could be reviewed either in whole or part at the Member State level, rather than by the Commission under the Merger Regulation.[215] This might be the case, for example, if the only competition issues of any significance are limited to one Member State, particularly if they are issues over which the relevant NCA would be likely to seek to assert jurisdiction in a post-notification referral under Article 9.[216]

8.082 **Voluntary procedure.** For such cases, with effect from 1 May 2004 the Merger Regulation introduced a voluntary procedure under which the parties may opt to apply to have the case referred, in whole or part, to the NCA in question instead of notifying it for formal review by the Commission. The procedures may only be used if the parties have not already formally notified the transaction to one (or more) of the NCAs under the national merger control rules.[217] The parties must prepare and submit a reasoned submission using Form RS[218] to the Commission

---

[213] Jurisdictional Notice, paras 168 and 187 (previously Turnover Notice, para 40).

[214] Jurisdictional Notice, paras 192–194. See para 8.018, above.

[215] Merger Reg (n 210, above) Art 4(4). For guiding principles for the reallocation of cases, see para 8.014, above.

[216] The same option is available as regards the review of a case by the NCA of an EFTA State: see Art 6(4) and Art 13 of Protocol 24 to the EEA Agreement. See the Commission's Note of 14 October 2004 on 'Case Referral under the EEA Agreement' at Vol II, App D.19. For the EEA Agreement, see further paras 8.280 *et seq*, below.

[217] Before formally using the procedure, the parties will generally have engaged in pre-notification contacts with the Commission and relevant NCA(s); see paras 8.109 *et seq*, below.

[218] Merger Reg (n 210, above) Art 4(4). Form RS is annexed to the Implementing Reg, Reg 802/2004, OJ 2004 L133/1: Vol II, App D.2. See also the informal version of the Form RS covering EEA aspects, as published on DG Comp's website.

which will then forward copies to all the NCAs.[219] The identified NCA then has 15 working days in which to agree or object to the proposed referral, with absence of a decision being deemed as agreement.[220] If the NCA agrees, the Commission must then decide within a maximum of 25 working days from the submission of the Form RS whether or not to make the requested referral. These procedures are illustrated by the diagram on page 687.

Legal requirements under Article 4(4). In order for a referral to be made by the   **8.083**
Commission to one or more Member States pursuant to Article 4(4), two formal legal requirements must be fulfilled:

(a) there must be indications that the concentration may significantly affect competition in a market or markets; and
(b) the market(s) in question must be within a Member State and present all the characteristics of a distinct market.

As regards the first criterion, while the requesting parties are not required to demonstrate that the effect on competition is likely to be an adverse one, they should point to indicators which are generally suggestive of the existence of some competitive effects stemming from the transaction.[221] As regards the second criterion, the requesting parties are required to show that a geographic market in which competition is affected by the transaction is national, or narrower than national.[222] If a case may give rise to competition concerns in a number of Member States, and require coordinated investigative and remedial action, this would generally make it more likely that the Commission would retain jurisdiction over the entirety of the case.[223] Consideration should also be given to whether the NCA(s) to which referral of the case is contemplated may possess specific

---

[219] For further guidance, see Ryan, 'The revised system of case referral under the Merger Regulation – experiences to date' (2005) 3 EC Competition Policy Newsletter 38. The Commission has developed the practice of accompanying the Form RS which it transmits to Member States with a short memorandum indicating whether, on a preliminary examination, it considers that the case is appropriate for referral.

[220] Merger Reg (n 210, above) Art 22(3) expressly provides that notwithstanding the exclusivity of jurisdiction enjoyed by the Commission for concentrations with a Community dimension, Member States may carry out investigations necessary for the application of Art 4(4).

[221] See Case Referral Notice, OJ 2005 C56/2: Vol II, App D.9, para 17. The existence of 'affected markets' within the meaning of Form RS would generally be considered sufficient to meet the requirements of Art 4(4). cf the standard for post-notification referrals under Art 9(2)(a) of the Merger Reg, which refers to 'a real risk that the transaction may have a significant adverse impact on competition'. The parties can also point to any factors which may be relevant to the competitive analysis (market overlap, vertical integration, etc).

[222] Case Referral Notice, above, para 18; similarly, see para 36 re post-notification referral requests pursuant to Art 9 of the Merger Reg. For market definition, see generally Chap 4 above, and the Relevant Market Notice: OJ 1997 C372/5: Vol II, App C.10. See Merger Reg, Art 9(7) (which applies by reason of Art 4(4), last sentence) re the criteria to be applied in determining the geographic reference market.

[223] Case Referral Notice (n 221, above) para 22.

expertise concerning local markets, or be examining or about to examine another transaction in the sector concerned.[224]

8.084 Consequences of Article 4(4) referral. If the Commission agrees to refer the case in whole, it will then only be necessary for the parties to notify the case to the NCA in question. That NCA will then review the case under its applicable national merger control rules, save that it must inform the parties of the result of its preliminary assessment within 45 working days.[225] If the Commission agrees to a partial referral request, the aspects concerned will be reviewed by the NCA in question but the parties will also need to make a notification to the Commission under the Merger Regulation in respect of the remaining aspects of the concentration. In either case, the concentration continues to have a 'Community dimension' such that the other NCAs will not be able to apply their national merger control rules unless, in the event of a partial referral, the Commission were to agree to a subsequent Article 9 request to another NCA in respect of the aspects notified to the Commission.

(ii) Article 4(5) referrals to Commission

8.085 Suitable cases for Article 4(5) referral. Many cross-border mergers which fall below the Merger Regulation's thresholds are subject to notification and review by a number of NCAs within the EEA. Recognising that there could be advantages to business if some of these transactions could also benefit from the one-stop shop principle, with effect from 1 May 2004 the Merger Regulation introduced a voluntary procedure under which parties may seek to have cases handled by the Commission if they would otherwise have been subject to investigation by the NCAs in at least three Member States.[226]

8.086 Voluntary procedure. To take advantage of these pre-notification procedures, before notifying the concentration to any of the NCAs the parties must prepare and submit a reasoned submission to the Commission (using Form RS) which

---

[224] ibid, para 23.

[225] The period starts on the working day following that of receipt of the notification: Merger Reg, Art 9(6) (n 210, above) applied by reason of Art 4(4), last sentence. UK procedures for Art 4(4) referrals are laid down in the Enterprise Act 2002, ss 34A–34B.

[226] Merger Reg (n 210, above) Art 4(5). For guiding principles for the reallocation of cases, see para 8.014, above. The EEA Agreement also provides for pre-notification referrals from the EFTA States, by allowing the parties to a concentration to request that the Commission examine a concentration which is 'capable of being reviewed under the national competition laws of at least three EC Member States and at least one EFTA State' (Art 6(5) of Protocol 24 to the EEA Agreement): see generally paras 8.280 *et seq*, below. This constitutes an optional 'add-on' for the parties: see the Commission's Note, 'Case Referral under the EEA Agreement' (n 216, above); eg see Case M.3692 *Reuters/Telerate* (23 May 2005) where the transaction would otherwise have been subject to review by 12 Member States.

will then be forwarded to all the NCAs.[227] Each of those NCAs, which would in principle have jurisdiction to investigate under its national merger control rules, then has 15 working days from receipt of the Form RS in which to object. If no NCA objects, the transaction is deemed to have a Community dimension and must be notified to the Commission. However, if any of the Member States which would have been competent to examine the concentration under its merger control rules formally objects (even if only one of them) then jurisdiction is not transferred and the deal remains subject to notification and review at the Member State level.[228] These procedures are illustrated in the diagram on page 687.

Legal requirements under Article 4(5).   In order for a referral to be made by the **8.087** Commission to one or more Member States pursuant to Article 4(5), two formal legal requirements must be fulfilled:

(a) the transaction must be a 'concentration' within the meaning of Article 3 of the Merger Regulation; and

(b) the concentration must be capable of being reviewed under the national competition laws on the control of mergers in at least three Member States.

In considering whether a case is a suitable candidate for Article 4(5) treatment, the Commission and NCAs will have regard to whether it is genuinely cross-border in nature, where any significant effects on competition are likely to arise, and what investigative and enforcement powers are likely to be required to address any such effects.[229]

Consequences of Article 4(5) referral.   If no NCA objects, the transaction is **8.088** deemed to have a Community dimension and must be notified to the Commission in accordance with the same procedures as any other concentration with a Community dimension.[230] No NCAs will be able to apply their national merger control rules unless the Commission were to agree to a subsequent Article 9 request.

---

[227] The Commission encourages the notifying parties to conduct a thorough research with respect to the Member States identified as competent to review the case, making direct contact with the relevant NCAs as appropriate prior to submitting their Art 4(5) reasoned submission. For pre-notification contacts, see paras 8.109 *et seq*, below.

[228] For further guidance, see Ryan (n 219, above). Significantly more requests have been made under Art 4(5) than under Art 4(4): see statistics in table (a) at para 8.011, above. In the UK, where parties make use of this Form RS procedure the Office of Fair Trading will refrain from investigating the case under the national merger control rules: Enterprise Act 2002, s 22(3)(f) and 22(3A).

[229] Case Referral Notice (n 221, above) paras 26–27. See also European Competition Authorities network, 'Principles on the application, by National Competition Authorities within ECA, of Articles 4(5) and 22 of the EC Merger Regulation' (www.oft.gov.uk/ECA/Working+groups.htm); and 'Case referral under the EEA Agreement' (n 216, above).

[230] See paras 8.111 *et seq*, below. Such a notification should be made using Form CO (see para 8.117, below) or the Short Form (see paras 8.124 *et seq*), as applicable.

(iii) Formalities and review

8.089 **Form RS.** Form RS, which is annexed to the Implementing Regulation, specifies the information to be provided by parties when they submit a reasoned submission requesting a case referral pursuant to Article 4(4) or (5) of the Merger Regulation.[231] It requests a considerable amount of information which can require substantial work by the requesting parties.[232] Form RS includes an introductory section explaining (a) the purpose of the Form; (b) the need for a correct and complete reasoned submission; (c) who is entitled to submit a reasoned submission; (d) how to make such a submission; (e) confidentiality issues; and (f) definitions and instructions for the purposes of the Form. The Form RS questionnaire itself contains seven sections:

— *Section 1*: various background information on the parties including names, addresses and contact details;
— *Section 2*: background and details of the concentration (structure, economic sectors involved, parties' turnovers, etc);
— *Section 3*: details of undertakings owned or controlled by the parties to the concentration;
— *Section 4*: description of markets affected by the concentration and other markets on which the operation will have an impact;
— *Section 5*: certain information on the affected markets including market size, market shares, market entry, vertical integration issues);
— *Section 6*: details of the referral request and reasons why the case should be referred pursuant to Article 4(4) or (5) of the Merger Regulation;
— *Section 7*: each submission must conclude with a declaration to the effect that, to the best of the knowledge and belief of the signatory, the information supplied is true and complete.

---

[231] Implementing Reg, Reg 802/2004, OJ 2004 L133/1: Vol II, App D.2 Art 6 and Annex III. See also the additional informal Form RS that has been supplemented to take account of the provisions of the EEA Agreement (available on DG Comp's website). According to para 66 of the Case Referral Notice, pre-filing referrals must concern concentrations the plans for which are sufficiently concrete; ie there must at least exist a good faith intention to merge on the part of the undertakings concerned, or, in the case of a public bid, at least a public announcement of an intention to make such a bid (see also para 8.111, below). Essentially, the same procedural rules apply as for formal notifications using Form CO or the Short Form.

[232] Before submitting the final Form RS, the parties will normally engage in pre-notification discussions with the Commission: see paras 8.109 and 8.110, below. The formal signed copy of the Form RS (including a set of all supporting documents and other annexes) must be submitted to the Commission on paper. This must be accompanied by five paper copies, together with one copy in CD- or DVD-ROM format. The requirement of a copy in CD- or DVD-ROM format was introduced in November 2006: see para 8.118, below. In the case of Form RS, the electronic files comprising the relevant submission should generally not exceed 1 MB each; if they cannot be kept below that size, or if the total size of all the files exceeds 5 MB, then the parties must submit 32 copies in CD- or DVD-ROM format (rather than just one).

Review of pre-notification referral procedures.   Article 4(6) of the Merger   **8.090**
Regulation envisages that the Commission will report to the Council on the
operation of the pre-notification referral regime by 1 July 2009. If the Commission
proposes changes to the regime, the Council could revise the regime by
adopting a Regulation by a qualified majority.

(f) Post-notification reallocation of jurisdiction

(i) *Article 9 referrals from Commission to NCAs*

Legal requirements under Article 9.   At the request of a Member State acting on   **8.091**
its own initiative or at the invitation of the Commission, the Commission may
refer a notified concentration with a Community dimension, or a part thereof, to
the competent authority of that Member State for assessment under its national
merger control rules.[233] This might be appropriate, for example, if the only competition issues of any significance are limited to one Member State, particularly if
the markets affected by the concentration are geographically restricted to local
areas which are not a substantial part of the Community since then it will not be
possible for the Commission to prohibit the concentration under the Merger
Regulation.[234] In particular, a case can be referred by the Commission to a Member
State's NCA under Article 9 of the Merger Regulation,[235] if the concentration
either:

(a)   threatens to affect significantly competition in a market within that Member
     State, which presents all the characteristics of a distinct market;[236] or

---

[233] Merger Reg (n 210, above) Art 9(1). For guiding principles for the reallocation of cases, see
para 8.014, above. The Art 9 post-notification referral procedure existed under the original Merger
Reg. Similarly, the Commission may refer a notified concentration to an EFTA State: see Art 6(1)
of Protocol 24 to the EEA Agreement. Where issues of allocation of jurisdiction may arise, parties
may engage in informal pre-notification discussions with the Commission and the relevant NCA(s),
in some cases with a view to making a pre-notification referral request pursuant to Art 4(4) of the
Merger Reg: see paras 8.081 *et seq,* above.

[234] See para 8.184, below. In Case M.3669 *Blackstone (TBG CareCo)/NHP* (1 February 2005),
where the parties had notified the concentration to the Commission without making use of the
Art 4(4) pre-notification referral procedures, the Commission's announcement that the whole case
had been referred to the UK under Art 9 noted that it would have been an appropriate candidate for
a pre-notification referral request: Press Release IP/05/125 (2 February 2005).

[235] Referral decisions taken by the Commission in respect of an EFTA State are addressed to the
EFTA Surveillance Authority. In addition, under Art 9 of Part III, Chapter XIII of Protocol 4 to the
Agreement between the EFTA States on the establishment of a Surveillance Authority and a Court
of Justice, the EFTA Surveillance Authority may refer cases notified to it to the competent NCAs of
the EFTA States; this provision mirrors Art 9 of the Merger Reg.

[236] Merger Reg (n 210, above) Art 9(2)(a). See, eg Case M.3823 *MAG/Ferrovial Aeropuertos/
Exeter Airport* (8 August 2005): referral of the joint acquisition of Exeter Airport by the Macquarie
Airport Group and Ferrovial Aeropuertos to the OFT for review under Art 9(2)(a), as the concentration threatened to significantly affect competition between airports (in the provision of services to
airlines) in South-West England.

(b) affects competition in a market within that Member State, which presents all the characteristics of a distinct market and which does not constitute a substantial part of the common market.[237]

As regards the first situation, a requesting State is essentially required to demonstrate that there is a real risk that the transaction may have a significant adverse effect on competition (based on preliminary indications) and that the geographic markets in which competition is affected are national or narrower than national in scope.[238] As regards the second situation, a requesting State is required to show that the concentration is liable to affect competition in a market (based on preliminary indications) and that the geographic market in which competition is affected (i) is generally narrower than national in scope and (ii) does not constitute a substantial part of the common market.[239]

8.092 **Degree of Commission's discretion.** If the Commission considers that such a distinct market or threat does not exist, it shall reject the Member State's referral request.[240] Where the Commission considers that there is a distinct market which is a substantial part of the common market and that the concentration threatens to affect competition significantly (situation (a) at paragraph 8.091, above), it has broad discretion to take one of the following three courses of action:[241]

---

237 Merger Reg (n 210, above) Art 9(2)(b).

238 Case Referral Notice (n 221, above) paras 35–36; as for pre-notification referral requests, various other factors may also be pertinent. For further guidance on the concept of 'distinct market', see para 8.094, below.

239 Case Referral Notice (n 221, above) paras 39–40. Cases referred under Art 9(2)(b) have essentially related to local markets, ie markets that were narrower than national in scope: see, eg Case M.3669 *Blackstone (TGB CareCo)/NHP* (1 February 2005) concerning the supply of care home services in a number of local markets in the UK. For the concept of 'substantial part of the common market', see para 8.095, below. For guiding principles for the reallocation of cases, see further para 8.014, above.

240 Merger Reg, Art 9(3), second para. See, eg Case M.165 *Alcatel/AEG Kabel* (18 December 1991): although a distinct market did exist, the concentration did not threaten to create or strengthen dominance within it (in accordance with the substantive the test under the original Merger Reg); Case M.1346 *EDF/London Electricity* (27 January 1999): UK request rejected by the Commission as it found that the concentration was unlikely to lead to an adverse effect on competition (see *XXIXth Report on Competition Policy* (1999), point 193); Case M.2978 *Lagardère/Natexis/VUP*, OJ 2004 L125/54 (rejection of request 23 July 2003): referral request with regard to most markets forming part of the 'book chain' rejected, since they had a supranational geographical dimension, covering the whole of the French-speaking area in Europe; Case M.3130 *Arla Foods/Express Dairies* (10 June 2003): referral request rejected re the market for the procurement of raw milk in the UK, since the transaction did not threaten to create or strengthen a dominant position.

241 Merger Reg (n 210, above) Art 9(3), first para. See Case T-119/02 *Royal Philips Electronics v Commission* [2003] ECR II-1433, [2003] 5 CMLR 53, para 344: judicial review, in the light of Art 9(3) and (8) of the Merger Reg, is restricted to establishing whether the Commission was entitled, without committing a manifest error of assessment, to consider that the referral would enable the NCA to safeguard or restore effective competition on the relevant market, so that it was unnecessary for the Commission to deal with the case itself.

(a) deal with the case itself in order to maintain or restore effective competition on the market concerned;[242]

(b) refer part of the case to the competent authority of the Member State concerned for the application of national competition law;[243] or

(c) refer the whole case to the competent authority of the Member State concerned for the application of national competition law.[244]

However, the Commission has no discretion and must refer all or any relevant part of the transaction to the relevant NCA for review if the concentration affects competition in a distinct market which is not a substantial part of the common market (situation (b) at paragraph 8.091, above).[245] In such cases involving local

---

[242] See, eg Case M.1920 *Nabisco/United Biscuits* (5 May 2000): UK's referral request declined, following the Commission's initial investigation and the receipt of satisfactory Phase I commitments from the parties which resolved all competition concerns, although the conditions for referral under Art 9 were met. See also *Lagardère/Natexis/VUP* (n 240, above): although the market for the sale of school books constituted a separate national market, the Commission declined to refer the case, given the substantial overlap between that market and other markets of supranational geographic dimension that formed part of the book chain. In the Interpretative Notes annexed to the original Merger Reg (available on DG Comp's website at http://ec.europa.eu/comm/competition/mergers/legislation/regulation/notes.html), it was stated that the Council and Commission consider that where the distinct market represents a substantial part of the common market, the referral procedure should be applied only in exceptional cases where the competition interests of the Member State concerned cannot be adequately protected in any other way. However, the Commission has increasingly been prepared to grant referral requests where the markets have been defined as national in scope: see para 8.096, below.

[243] The Commission has made several partial referrals under Art 9(3)(b) of the Merger Reg, generally because an Art 9 request was made in respect of only part of the affected markets. See, eg Case M.3905 *Tesco/Carrefour (Czech Republic and Slovakia)* (22 December 2005): referral of part of Tesco's proposed acquisition of Carrefour's Czech and Slovak retailing business to the Slovak Antimonopoly Office, on the basis that the transaction affected competition in three distinct local markets within the Slovak Republic that did not form a substantial part of the Common Market; but the Commission approved the deal with regard to the Czech Republic as it would not significantly impede effective competition in the Czech retailing sector. See also *Arla Foods/Express Dairies* (n 240, above) re the market for the supply of fresh processed milk in the UK and the market for the supply of fresh potted cream (non-bulk cream) in the UK; Case M.2639 *Compass/Restorama/Rail Gourmet/Gourmet Nova* (26 February 2002) re the UK on-train catering services market; Case M.2662 *Danish Crown/Steff-Houlberg* (14 February 2002) re the Danish markets for (i) the purchase of live pigs, (ii) the sale of fresh pork for direct human consumption, (iii) the supply of fresh pork for further processing, (iv) the supply of processed pork products, and (v) the collection of abattoir by-products; Case M.2502 *Cargill/Cerestar* (18 January 2002) re the supply of glucose syrups and blends in the UK.

[244] See, eg Cases M.3075-3080 *ECS/Intercommunales* (13 February 2003): referral to the Belgian NCA of the acquisition by Electrabel of six local authority energy suppliers in Flanders, following a referral request under Art 9(2)(a) of the Merger Reg to ensure consistency with the Belgian NCA's previous decisions; *MAG/Ferrovial Aeropuertos/Exeter Airport* (n 236, above).

[245] Merger Reg, Art 9(3), third para. See, eg *Blackstone (TBG CareCo)/NHP* (n 234, above). See also Case M.3754 *Strabag/Dywidag* (23 June 2005): Commission approved the acquisition by Strabag of parts of the bankrupt German construction company Walter Bau, but referred the assessment of the Hamburg regional asphalt market to Germany's Federal Cartel Office following a request pursuant to Art 9(2)(b) of the Merger Reg; similarly, Case M.3373 *Accor/Colony/Desseigne-Barriere/JV* (4 June 2004): partial referral following a request by the French authorities; *Arla Foods/Express Dairies* (n 240, above) partial referral re the supply of bottled milk by doorstep deliveries in the UK.

markets, the Commission would not have had jurisdiction to prohibit the concentration under the Merger Regulation.[246]

8.093 **Procedure.** The procedure under Article 9 can be invoked only by a Member State acting on its own initiative or at the invitation of the Commission. The Member State has 15 working days, following receipt of a copy of the notification from the Commission, to lodge a referral request. If such a request is made, the Phase I timetable is extended by 10 working days (from 25 to 35 working days).[247] The Commission must inform the undertakings concerned if such a request is made.[248] It is then required to determine whether or not to refer the case to the Member State within 25 working days from the effective date of the notification[249] or, where the Commission launches Phase II proceedings under Article 6(1)(c) of the Merger Regulation, within 65 working days from the effective date of the notification.[250] The Member State concerned is able to make its views known up to the adoption of the Commission's decision and, to this end, it is given access to the file.[251] If the Commission accepts the request and the case is referred to the Member State, the relevant NCA has no fixed time frame within which to reach its final decision; it must, however, inform the parties of its preliminary assessment and proposed future actions within 45 working days and must reach a final decision without undue delay.[252] If the Commission rejects the referral request, it is then open to the Member State to appeal the Commission's decision to the Court of Justice and apply for interim measures, with a view to applying its national competition law.[253] Third parties may also appeal referral decisions.[254]

8.094 **Concept of distinct market.** Article 9(7) of the Merger Regulation sets out the criteria to be applied in determining the geographic reference market for the purpose of establishing whether a distinct market exists. The relevant geographic

---

[246] Since the concentration would not significantly impede effective competition 'in the common market or in a substantial part of it': see para 8.184, below.

[247] Merger Reg, Reg 139/2004, OJ 2004 L24/1: Vol II, App D.1, Art 10(1), second para.

[248] ibid, Art 9(2).

[249] ibid, Art 9(4)(a). Any public offer subject to the (UK) City Code on Takeovers and Mergers must include a term that it will lapse in the event that an Art 9 reference to a competent authority is made before the first closing date or the date when the offer becomes unconditional as to acceptances, whichever is later (Rule 12). In addition, except in the case of a Rule 9 mandatory offer, the bidder can make the offer conditional on there not being a reference.

[250] ibid, Art 9(4)(b) and (5).

[251] ibid, Art 19(2). It may also appeal to the ECJ (and apply for interim measures) in the event that the Commission does not accede to an Art 9 request: ibid, Art 9(9).

[252] ibid, Art 9(6). If an Art 9 request is granted, the Member State may take only the measures strictly necessary to safeguard or restore effective competition on the market concerned: Art 9(8). UK procedures for Art 9 referrals are laid down in the Enterprise Act 2002, ss 34A and 34B.

[253] ibid, Art 9(9).

[254] *Royal Philips Electronics v Commission* (n 241, above) paras 267–300.

market must be an area: (i) where the undertakings are involved in a market in which there is supply and demand for their products or services; (ii) where competitive conditions are sufficiently homogenous; and (iii) where the market can be distinguished from neighbouring geographic areas because, in particular, conditions of competition are appreciably different in those areas.[255] The requesting Member State is in essence required to show that a geographic market in which competition is affected by the transaction is national, or narrower than national in scope.[256]

Concept of a substantial part of the common market.   There is no precise   **8.095** definition of the concept of a substantial part of the common market in the Merger Regulation and accompanying Commission Notices. Based on past practice and case law, the Commission tends to regard the concept of a distinct market that does not constitute a substantial part of the common market as generally limited to markets with a narrow geographic scope, within a Member State.[257] Indeed, the Commission has been prepared to apply a broad notion of what may constitute a substantial part of the common market with a view to retaining jurisdiction.[258]

Commission practice.   In general, an Article 9 request is more likely to succeed   **8.096** where the relevant geographic market is smaller than the territory of the Member State concerned and the issues are genuinely local or regional, or where there are special circumstances (such as concurrent analysis of a related transaction by national authorities).[259] However, the Commission has also accepted Article 9

---

[255] The assessment of the geographic reference market must also take account of the nature and characteristics of the products or services involved, the existence of barriers to entry, consumer preferences, and the presence of any appreciable differences of prices and the parties' market shares in those areas.

[256] See para 8.096, below; Case Referral Notice (n 221, above) para 36. cf para 18 of the Case Referral Notice concerning pre-notification referral requests pursuant to Art 4(4) of the Merger Reg.

[257] Case Referral Notice (n 221, above) para 40 (including n 34).

[258] See, eg *EDF/London Electricity* (n 240, above) where the Commission noted that the London Electricity authorised area could likely be regarded a substantial part of the common market in view of the number of LE's customers and sales as compared to other EC regions, electricity being an essential input of business and industry, and the importance of London, although the proportion of electricity concerned represented only about 2 per cent of total EC consumption. Similarly, see Case M.2822 *ENBW/ENI/GVS* (17 December 2002): State of Baden-Württemberg constituted a substantial part of the common market, as the quantities of gas supplied roughly corresponded to those supplied, eg in Austria or Denmark.

[259] See, eg *MAG/Ferrovial Aeropuertos/Exeter Airport* (n 236, above); *Blackstone (TBG CareCo)/ NHP* (n 239, above); Case M.3373 *Accor/Colony/Barrière* (4 June 2004); Case M.3754 *Strabag/ Dywidag* (23 June 2005); Case M.3318 *ECS/Sibelga* (19 December 2003); Case M.2760 *Nehlsen/ Rethmann/SWB/Bremerhavener Entsorgungswirtschaft* (30 May 2002); and Case M.2446 *Govia/ Connex South Central* (20 July 2001).

requests where the geographic reference area is an entire Member State.[260] On the other hand, where the reference area is wider than national in scope, an Article 9 request is typically unlikely to succeed.[261]

(ii) Article 22 referrals to Commission

8.097 **Legal requirements under Article 22.** Article 22 of the Merger Regulation permits Member States, either individually or jointly, to request the Commission to investigate a concentration under the Merger Regulation where the parties do not meet the turnover criteria for it to constitute a concentration with a 'Community dimension'.[262] This option is available only if both of two conditions are fulfilled:

(a) *The concentration has an effect on trade between Member States.* The requesting State is required to demonstrate that the concentration is liable to have some discernible influence on the pattern of trade between Member States. This is assessed on the same basis as for Articles 81 and 82 of the Treaty; a potential effect is therefore sufficient.[263]

(b) *The concentration threatens significantly to affect competition within the territory of the Member State (or States) making the request.* The requesting State is essentially required to show that there is a real risk (based on preliminary indications) that the transaction may significantly impede effective competition, thereby deserving closer scrutiny. As post-notification referrals may entail additional costs and delay, the Commission takes the view that they should be limited to those cases presenting a real risk of negative effects on competition and trade between Member States, and where it appears that these would be best addressed at the Community level.[264]

---

[260] See, eg Case M.1555 *Heineken/Cruzcampo* (17 August 1999); Case M.2621 *SEB/Moulinex* (8 January 2002); appeals dismissed, *Royal Philips Electronics v Commission* (n 241, above) and Case T-114/02 *BaByliss v Commission* [2003] ECR II-1279, [2004] 5 CMLR 21; Case M.2845 *Sogecable/Canalsatéllite Digital/Vía Digital* (14 August 2002); appeal dismissed, Case T-346/02 *Cableuropa v Commission* [2003] ECR II-4251, [2004] 5 CMLR 1216; Case M.3248 *BAT/Ente Tabacchi Italiani* (23 October 2003); Case M.3275 *Shell España/CEPSA/SIS JV* (23 November 2004).

[261] See, eg *Lagardère/Natexis/VUP* (n 240, above).

[262] Merger Reg (n 247, above) Art 22(1). For guiding principles for the reallocation of cases, see para 8.014, above.

[263] Case T-22/97 *Kesko v Commission* [1999] ECR II-3775, [2000] 4 CMLR 335, paras 106–107.

[264] Case Referral Notice (n 221, above) paras 42–45. See also 'Principles on the application, by National Competition Authorities within ECA, of Articles 4(5) and 22 of the EC Merger Regulation' (n 229, above); and 'Case referral under the EEA Agreement' (n 216, above). Post-notification referrals from an EFTA State to the Commission are limited to situations where an EFTA State joins a request for referral put forward by one or more Member States (Art 6(3) of Protocol 24 to the EEA Agreement). This request can be made where a concentration may affect trade between one or more Member States and one or more EFTA States, and it threatens significantly to affect competition in one or more EFTA States. This is without prejudice to the EFTA States' right to request that the EFTA Surveillance Authority review a case under Art 22 of Part III, Chapter XIII of Protocol 4 to the Surveillance and Court Agreement (where such a case affects trade between EFTA States and threatens significantly to affect competition within the territory of the EFTA State or States making the request).

Procedure.   The request must be made by a Member State within 15 working **8.098** days from the date of national notification or, where no notification is required, the date when the concentration was made known to the Member State concerned.[265] The Commission shall inform all Member States (and the undertakings concerned) of the request without delay; any other Member State can decide to join the initial request within a period of 15 working days of being informed by the Commission of the initial request.[266] The Commission may also, at its own initiative, inform one or several Member State(s) that the criteria for an Article 22 referral are fulfilled and invite them to refer the transaction at issue to the Commission.[267] At the latest 10 working days following the expiry of the 15 working day period, the Commission must decide whether to accept the case from the requesting Member State(s).[268] If the Commission accepts jurisdiction, it informs all Member States and the undertakings concerned of its decision; national proceedings in the referring Member State(s) are terminated and the Commission examines the case on behalf of the requesting State(s).[269] However, non-requesting States can continue to apply their national merger control rules.[270]

Commission's powers upon referral.   Once a referral has been made, the **8.099** Commission follows the procedural rules set out in the Merger Regulation as if the concentration had a Community dimension.[271] It may require the undertakings concerned to submit a Form CO notification.[272] It will conduct a formal Phase I investigation; in appropriate cases, it may then open a Phase II investigation. The Commission will not examine the effects of the concentration in the territory of Member States which have not made or joined the request, unless such an examination is necessary for the assessment of the effects of the concentration

---

[265] Merger Reg (n 247, above) Art 22(1). The reference to the date when a concentration is 'made known' is particularly relevant to the UK where the merger control system does not involved a mandatory notification requirement. According to the Commission, the notion of 'made known' implies the provision of sufficient information for the national competition authority (eg the OFT in the UK) to make a preliminary assessment as to the existence of the criteria for the making of such a referral request: Case Referral Notice (n 221, above) para 50. On timing under the EEA Agreement, see Art 13 of Protocol 4.

[266] Merger Reg, Art 22(2). All national time limits relating to the concentration are suspended until it has been decided, in accordance with the procedure set out in Art 22, where the concentration shall be examined. As soon as a Member State has informed the Commission and the undertakings concerned that it does not wish to join the request, the suspension of its national time limits ceases.

[267] ibid, Art 22(5).

[268] ibid, Art 22(3); Case Referral Notice, para 50. If the Commission does not take a decision within the specified period, it shall be deemed to have accepted the request.

[269] Merger Reg, Art 22(4).

[270] Case Referral Notice (n 221, above) para 50.

[271] Merger Reg (n 247, above) Art 22(4).

[272] ibid, Art 22(3); if the Commission does not require a Form CO notification, the Phase I timetable shall commence on the working day following that on which the Commission informs the undertakings concerned that it has decided to accept the request.

within the territory of the requesting Member States.[273] Article 22 confers no power on Member States to control the scope of conduct of the Commission's investigation.[274] Upon referral, the concentration is suspended to the extent that it has not been implemented on the date on which the Commission informs the undertakings concerned that a request has been made.[275]

8.100 **Practice.** Referrals to the Commission pursuant to Article 22 of the Merger Regulation have been rare.[276] In the early years of the Merger Regulation, some Member States did not have their own merger control rules and Article 22(3) enabled them to seek the intervention of the Commission in regulating concentrations which did not have a Community dimension.[277] Although all Member States other than Luxembourg now have merger control, and despite the introduction of the possibility of pre-notification referrals to the Commission pursuant to Article 4(5) of the Merger Regulation, Article 22 has continued to be used. For example, Article 22 may be used by Member States where a transaction is subject to multiple national merger filings but the remedies available to the individual NCAs may be ineffective, particularly in view of the supranational scope of the transaction. Although it is not entirely beyond doubt, the Merger Regulation appears to permit a Member State to make use of Article 22 even in cases where the concentration falls below the thresholds under its domestic merger control regime.[278]

(g) National investigations on grounds other than competition

(i) Legitimate interests under Article 21(4)

8.101 **In general.** Article 21(3) of the Merger Regulation provides that no Member State may apply its domestic competition legislation to any concentration with a Community dimension. However, under Article 21(4), Member States are

---

[273] Case Referral Notice (n 221, above) n 45.

[274] Case T-221/95 *Endemol Entertainment v Commission* [1999] ECR II–1299, [1999] 5 CMLR 611, [1999] All ER (EC) 385, para 40.

[275] Merger Reg, Art 22(4); cf Case M.890 *Blokker/Toys R Us*, OJ 1998 L316/1, where the merger was put into effect and the Commission subsequently made a divestiture order pursuant to Art 8 (4) when it found that the merger would strengthen a dominant position in the Netherlands.

[276] See statistics in table (a) at para 8.011, above. On 27 October 2005, the Commission rejected the Portuguese and Italian Art 22 requests to consider the effects of the proposed *Gas Natural/Endesa* merger on their markets: Press Release IP/05/1356 (27 October 2005).

[277] Case M.278 *British Airways/Dan Air* (17 February 1993) from Belgium; Case M.553 *RTL/Veronica/Endemol*, OJ 1996 L294/14 from the Netherlands; Case M.784 *Kesko/Tuko*, OJ 1997 L110/53 from Finland; *Blokker/Toys R Us* (n 275, above) from the Netherlands.

[278] This has already happened in practice as regards Member States joining requests made by another Member State: see, eg the requests made by France and Sweden in Case M.3796 *Omya/JM Huber* (19 July 2006). To date, all *initial* requests under Art 22 have been made either by Member States which did not have domestic merger control rules at the time or in respect of concentrations which met the relevant domestic merger control thresholds.

Pre-notification and post-notification referral procedures

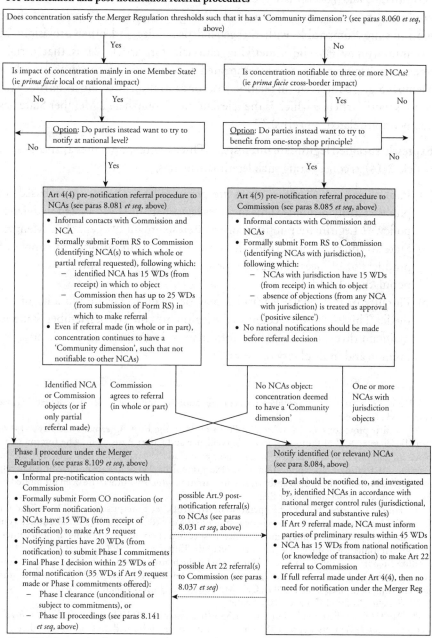

Does concentration satisfy the Merger Regulation thresholds such that it has a 'Community dimension'? (see paras 8.060 *et seq*, above)

Yes — Is impact of concentration mainly in one Member State? (ie *prima facie* local or national impact)

No — Is concentration notifiable to three or more NCAs? (ie *prima facie* cross-border impact)

No / Yes — Option: Do parties instead want to try to notify at national level?

Yes / No — Option: Do parties instead want to try to benefit from one-stop shop principle?

Art 4(4) pre-notification referral procedure to NCAs (see paras 8.081 *et seq*, above)
- Informal contacts with Commission and NCA
- Formally submit Form RS to Commission (identifying NCA(s) to which whole or partial referral requested), following which:
  – identified NCA has 15 WDs (from receipt) in which to object
  – Commission then has up to 25 WDs (from submission of Form RS) in which to make referral
- Even if referral made (in whole or in part), concentration continues to have a 'Community dimension', such that not notifiable to other NCAs

Art 4(5) pre-notification referral procedure to Commission (see paras 8.085 *et seq*, above)
- Informal contacts with Commission and NCAs
- Formally submit Form RS to Commission (identifying NCAs with jurisdiction), following which:
  – NCAs with jurisdiction have 15 WDs (from receipt) in which to object
  – absence of objections (from any NCA with jurisdiction) is treated as approval ('positive silence')
- No national notifications should be made before referral decision

Identified NCA or Commission objects (or if only partial referral made)

Commission agrees to referral (in whole or part)

No NCAs object: concentration deemed to have a 'Community dimension'

One or more NCAs with jurisdiction objects

Phase I procedure under the Merger Regulation (see paras 8.109 *et seq*, above)
- Informal pre-notification contacts with Commission
- Formally submit Form CO notification (or Short Form notification)
- NCAs have 15 WDs (from receipt of notification) to make Art 9 request
- Notifying parties have 20 WDs (from notification) to submit Phase I commitments
- Final Phase I decision within 25 WDs of formal notification (35 WDs if Art 9 request made or Phase I commitments offered):
  – Phase I clearance (unconditional or subject to commitments), or
  – Phase II proceedings (see paras 8.141 *et seq*, above)

possible Art.9 post-notification referral(s) to NCAs (see paras 8.031 *et seq*, above)

possible Art 22 referral(s) to Commission (see paras 8.037 *et seq*)

Notify identified (or relevant) NCAs (see para 8.084, above)
- Deal should be notified to, and investigated by, identified NCAs in accordance with national merger control rules (jurisdictional, procedural and substantive rules)
- If Art 9 referral made, NCA must inform parties of preliminary results within 45 WDs
- NCA has 15 WDs from national notification (or knowledge of transaction) to make Art 22 referral to Commission
- If full referral made under Art 4(4), then no need for notification under the Merger Reg

Note: WD indicates working days.

permitted to take appropriate measures to protect legitimate interests which are not taken into consideration under the Merger Regulation,[279] provided those measures are 'compatible with the general principles and other provisions of Community law'.[280] The underlying rationale for Article 21 is that certain important 'legitimate' interests, unrelated to competition concerns, entitle a Member State to intervene in relation to a concentration affecting its territory (in contrast with Article 9 which is the relevant provision where a Member State has competition-related concerns).[281]

8.102   **Expressly specified legitimate interests.**   Three matters are expressly specified in Article 21(4) as constituting such legitimate interests:

(a) Public security: Member States are permitted to take measures based on public security grounds. This includes legitimate interests related to defence policy.[282] Legitimate public security interests might also enable a Member State to intervene in relation to a merger to ensure security of supply of products or services considered vital or essential for the protection of the population's health.[283]

(b) Plurality of the media: Measures may be taken to ensure plurality of the media. This exception recognises the legitimate concern of Member States to maintain diversified sources of information in order to ensure diversity of opinion and multiplicity of views.[284]

---

[279] For the matters which are taken into consideration for appraisal under the Merger Reg, see para 8.183 *et seq*, below.

[280] Similar provisions apply at Art 7 of Protocol 24 to the EEA Agreement and Art 21(4) of Part III, Chapter XIII of Protocol 4 to the Surveillance and Court Agreement. The Interpretative Notes to the original Merger Reg (n 247, above) include general guidelines provided by the Commission relating to the application of this exception. Member States are not permitted to rely on legitimate interest grounds to authorise a concentration which has otherwise been prohibited by the Commission under the Merger Reg.

[281] For the UK procedures re the operation of Art 21(4), see Enterprise Act 2002, s 67 and the Enterprise Act 2002 (Protection of Legitimate Interests) Order 2003, SI 2003/1592. The Secretary of State may serve a 'European intervention notice' in specified circumstances relating to 'public interest considerations' (as defined in ss 42(3) and 58 of the Enterprise Act 2002). The OFT must then produce a report, and the Secretary of State may refer the matter to the Competition Commission. See, eg Case M.3418 *General Dynamics/Alvis* (26 May 2004); Case M.3559 *Finmeccanica/Agusta-Westland* (20 September 2004); Case M.3720 *BAES/AMS* (14 March 2005).

[282] See also Art 296 EC: para 8.105, below.

[283] Art 21(4) was first invoked in Case M.336 *IBM France/CGI* (19 May 1993), *XXIIIrd Report on Competition Policy* (1993), point 321: the French authorities informed the Commission that they were taking measures to protect French legitimate interests linked to public security. See also Case M.1858 *Thomson-CSF/Racal (II)* (15 June 2000), Press Release IP/00/628 (16 June 2000): transaction cleared by the Commission but the UK authorities announced their intention to consider the public security aspects of the transaction.

[284] See, eg Case M.423 *Newspaper Publishing* (14 March 1994): Commission had cleared the acquisition of Newspaper Publishing (which produced *The Independent* and *The Independent on Sunday*) by a consortium headed by Mirror Group Newspapers, but accepted that the UK authorities could take measures in accordance with Art 21(4) as 'the transaction involves issues such as the

(c) *Prudential rules*: Rules to protect 'prudential interests' are of particular relevance in the area of financial services. Most Member States have supervisory regimes in place for banks, investment firms and insurance companies. This exception makes it possible for Member States to apply such national rules to concentrations in those sectors.[285] For example, a national authority could prevent a bank within the Member State from being acquired by a business which does not meet acceptable capital adequacy requirements or supervisory standards.[286]

Scope of the exceptions. If there is doubt as to whether one of the express grounds in Article 21(4) applies, the Member State wishing to intervene against a concentration should notify the Commission. In *BSCH/A. Champalimaud*[287] the Portuguese authorities took measures to block a financial restructuring that would give the Spanish banking group, Banco Santander, joint control over a Portuguese insurance company. When the Portuguese government sought to justify its action on the basis of prudential rules, the Commission expressed the strong suspicion that the real motive had been to curb foreign ownership in the financial sector and found that there was no basis for concluding that the transaction would be detrimental to the prudent management of the insurance company involved. Portugal was ordered to suspend the measures.[288] For this purpose the Commission assumed that it had such power although not expressed in the Merger Regulation. **8.103**

Other legitimate public interest grounds. Article 21(4) provides a non-exhaustive list of legitimate interests, so enabling the Commission to permit national **8.104**

---

accurate presentation of the news and the free expression of opinion' and the UK Secretary of State had powers to address these under applicable legislation on newspaper ownership. However, any such measures must be appropriate for their objective, go no further than necessary for the protection of the legitimate interest in question, and objectively be the least restrictive available. The UK authorities were required to keep the Commission informed of any conditions they attached to the transaction.

[285] See Interpretative Notes to the original Merger Reg (n 242, above).

[286] See, eg Case M.759 *Sun Alliance/Royal Insurance* (18 June 1996): the Commission decided not to oppose the merger of the two insurance companies, but granted jurisdiction for the UK Department of Trade and Industry (DTI) to carry out its regulatory functions under the Insurance Companies Act 1982 (ie to consider whether the prospective new controller is a fit and proper person and whether criteria of sound and prudent management are met). Nevertheless, the Commission required the DTI to liaise with it in so doing. See also Case M.1616 *Antonio de Sommer Champalimaud/Banco Santander Central HispanoAmericano* (3 August 1999) for further guidance on the concept of 'prudential rules' under Community law.

[287] *BSCH/A. Champalimaud* (n 286, above). A new concentration was subsequently notified in place of the previous one and authorised by the Commission: Case M.1799 *BSCH/Banco Totta Y CPP/A. Champalimaud* (11 January 2000).

[288] The Commission first made such an order by interim decision on 20 July 1999, which it made final on 20 October 1999: *XXIXth Report on Competition Policy* (1999), points 194–195. The infringement proceedings which the Commission opened against Portugal for not complying with the suspension order were subsequently closed: Press Release IP/00/296 (27 March 2000).

intervention on other legitimate interest grounds, if appropriate. In the event that a Member State wishes to take measures based on other public interest grounds, it must first inform the Commission which will then examine the compatibility of those grounds with Community law. The Member State must be informed of the Commission's decision within 25 working days of that communication. In the event that a Member State intervenes to block or impose measures on a concentration with a Community dimension without having informed the Commission of any legitimate interest grounds, the Commission is entitled to decide whether the Member State's interests are legitimate and compatible with Community law, seeking information from the Member State for this purpose and otherwise relying on the information which it has at its disposal.[289] Article 21(4) has to date been invoked only very rarely in relation to interests other than those expressly specified.[290] Following the Commission's clearance decision in *Unicredito/HVB*,[291] the Polish Treasury instructed UniCredito to sell its shares in BPH (a Polish subsidiary of HVB). It cited a breach of UniCredito's obligations under a non-compete clause of a 1999 privatisation agreement (under which Unicredito acquired Polish bank Polska Kasa Opieki) and threatened to revoke the agreement in question failing such a sale. Poland also brought an action against the Commission's clearance decision before the Court of First Instance.[292] The Commission launched infringement proceedings against Poland under Article 21 of the Merger Regulation on

---

[289] Case C-42/01 *Portugal v Commission* [2004] ECR I-6079, [2004] 5 CMLR 363. The Portuguese Government issued two decisions refusing to authorise the proposed takeover of the largely privatised Portuguese cement manufacturer under national law which restricted the acquisition of stakes representing more than 10 per cent of a privatised company, although the transaction had been notified to the Commission under the Merger Reg (Case M.2054 *Secil/Holderbank/Cimpor*). The Portuguese Government had not notified the Commission of these rules in accordance with Art 21(4) but the Commission examined them of its own initiative, held that they were not compatible with Community law (the objective of the Portuguese legislation being essentially protectionist) and ordered their withdrawal The ECJ upheld the Commission's right to intervene, noting that otherwise the controls in Art 21(4) would be largely ineffective. See Mäkelä, 'The Court of Justice rules for the first time on Article 21(3)', (2005) 1 EC Competition Policy Newsletter 19.

[290] But see Case M.567 *Lyonnaise des Eaux/Northumbrian Water*: the UK regulatory framework for the water industry provides that there should be a sufficient number of independent water enterprises to allow the Director General of Water Services to make comparisons of efficiencies; the Commission accepted this as a legitimate interest, but specified that the UK authorities should concern themselves solely with the issues set out in that legislation (Decn of 29 March 1995). The UK authorities recognised that in evaluating the proposed merger it could not take account of the potential implications of the merger for competition, employment or regional policy: Report of the Monopolies and Mergers Commission, Cm 2936 (July 1995), para 1.9; but nevertheless concluded that the merger could be expected to operate against the public interest. The merger was subsequently approved by the Commission under the Merger Reg (21 December 1995), but blocked by the UK authorities on other grounds. cf Case M.1346 *EDF/London Electricity* (27 January 1999): request under Art 21(4) refused because the UK public interest issues could legitimately be protected under its electricity regulatory system and were not directed at the concentration itself. The Commission also refused the related UK request for referral of the whole case under Art 9.

[291] Case M.3894 *Unicredito/HVB* (18 October 2005).

[292] Case T-41/06 *Republic of Poland v Commission*, not yet decided.

the basis that the measures did not fall within the expressly available exceptions and were not otherwise justifiable.[293]

(ii) Defence sector

Defence interests under Article 296 EC. The legitimate interests which Member States may invoke under Article 21(4), in particular under the expressly recognised 'public security' heading, are without prejudice to the general derogation under Article 296(1)(b) of the EC Treaty which provides:

> '[A]ny Member State may take such measures as it considers necessary for the protection of the essential interests of its security which are connected with the production of or trade in arms, munitions and war material; such measures shall not adversely affect the conditions of competition in the common market regarding products which are not intended for specifically military purposes.'

For a concentration with a Community dimension concerning an undertaking active in specifically military products, this derogation would permit a Member State to impose conditions or alternatively to allow it to proceed without any investigation or review of competitive overlaps. However, this provision is strictly construed.[294] To the extent that military products have dual application (ie if they can also be used for civil purposes), the Commission remains fully competent under the Merger Regulation. Some Member States have actively sought to preclude the Commission from exercising jurisdiction in the defence sector (including by directly instructing parties to a concentration with a Community dimension only to provide the Commission with information relating to civil or dual use products).[295]

8.105

---

[293] Case M.4125 *Unicredito/HVB* (8 March 2006): see Commission Press Release IP/06/277 (8 March 2006). See also Art 21 decisions addressed to Spain in Case M.4197 *E.ON/Endesa* (26 September 2006 and 20 December 2006) concerning various national measures taken in respect of a proposed merger which the Commission had approved under the Merger Reg in Case M.4110 *E.ON/Endesa* (25 April 2006). In 2006 the Commission also commenced infringement proceedings against Italy, following intervention by the Italian government in the proposed acquisition of control (by a consortium including a Spanish company) of formerly state-owned Autostrade, approved under the Merger Reg in Case M.4249 *Abertis/Autostrade* (22 September 2006): see Press Release IP/06/1418 (18 October 2006) and MEMO/06/414 (7 November 2006).

[294] For Art 296, see also paras 11.057 *et seq*, below. For the Commission's views on the limited scope of Art 296, see the reply to a question in the European Parliament in May 1990, OJ 1991 C130/2. See also the Commission's Green Paper on Defence Procurement, September 2004 (COM(2004) 608).

[295] See, eg Case M.529 *GEC/VSEL* (7 December 1994); Case M.724 *GEC/Thomson-CSF (II)* (15 May 1996); Case M.820 *British Aerospace/Lagardère* (23 September 1996), Press Release IP/96/851 (25 September 1996); Case M.1258 *GEC Marconi/Alenia* (28 August 1998), IP/98/82 (31 August 1998); Case M.1438 *British Aerospace/GEC Marconi* (25 June 1999), IP/99/426 (28 June 1999); Case M.1858 *Thomson-CSF/Racal (II)* (15 June 2000). However, aspects of other transactions pertaining to the defence sector have also been reviewed by the Commission: eg Case M.1745 *EADS* (11 May 2000) re the markets for military satellites, guided weapons, unmanned air vehicles (drones) and defence electronics; Case M.3985 *EADS/BAES/FNM/NLFK* (7 February 2006) re guided weapons and weapons systems.

In such circumstances, the Commission has requested that Member States provide it with sufficient information to assess the applicability of Article 296. Article 298 of the EC Treaty expressly gives the Commission or any Member State the right to bring the matter directly before the Court of Justice if it considers that another Member State is making improper use of the defence derogation:

> 'If measures taken in the circumstances referred to in Articles 296 and 297 have the effect of distorting the conditions of competition in the common market, the Commission shall, together with the State concerned, examine how these measures can be adjusted to the rules laid down in the Treaty . . . the Commission or any Member State may bring the matter directly before the Court of Justice if it considers that another Member State is making improper use of the powers provided for in Articles 296 and 297.'

3. Procedure

(a) In general

(i) *Commission hierarchy for merger control proceedings*

8.106 **The Commission.** The Competition Commissioner is empowered by the College of Commissioners to adopt most decisions and measures under the Merger Regulation, with management and administrative measures generally delegated to the Director-General of DG Competition and other senior officials within DG Competition.[296] Thus, Phase I clearance decisions can be adopted by the Competition Commissioner acting alone, subject to (i) prior approval of the Commission Legal Service; and (ii) consultation by DG Competition with the other Directorates-General primarily responsible for the products, services or policy areas in question (whose approval is required if the market share of the undertakings concerned exceeds 25 per cent). Decisions to open Phase II proceedings or to issue a statement of objections are subject to prior approval of the Legal Service and the President of the Commission.[297] However, the power to adopt Phase II decisions and various other decisions which are viewed as going beyond measures of administration or management, such as the imposition of fines, the revocation of a clearance decision, or the refusal to refer a case to a Member State following an Article 9 request, has not been delegated; these decisions have to be adopted by the full College of Commissioners. Furthermore, if

---

[296] Commission Decn of 28 April 2004, SEC(2004)518, PV(2004)1655; and Arts 12–14 of the Commission's Rules of Procedure, OJ 2000 L308/26. If the Competition Commissioner may have a conflict of interest, procedures exist for the reallocation of cases by the President either to himself or to another Commissioner, generally the Internal Market Commissioner: see, eg Case M.3576 *ECT/PONL/Euromax* (22 December 2004). The Code of Conduct for Commissioners is available on the Commission's website.

[297] For the role of the Legal Service, see para 8.153, below.

the Legal Service did not approve a draft decision to be adopted by the Competition Commissioner under the empowerment procedure, this would negate the empowerment and require the decision to be adopted by the full College of Commissioners.

DG Competition.   The investigation of merger cases is undertaken by DG   **8.107**
Competition. Within DG Competition, the current hierarchy for merger policy and investigations includes the position of a Deputy Director-General with special responsibility for mergers who reports to the Director-General. The Director-General is supported by a Unit whose resposibilities include formulation and coordination of merger policy and enforcement, as well as the allocation of new cases to case teams in the Mergers Units within the operational Directorates and ensuring that they are adequately resourced. New cases are generally allocated to case teams at DG Competition's merger management meetings, which usually take place on Monday afternoons.[298] These officials with general responsibilities for mergers liaise closely with the case-handling officials within the Mergers Units as part of a group within DG Competition known as the 'Merger Network' aimed at maintaining consistency of standards in merger control cases handled by DG Competition.[299]

Case teams.   Within DG Competition, each operational Directorate has at   **8.108**
least one Mergers Unit. These officials comprise the case team staff with day-to-day responsibility for handling Merger Regulation cases allocated to them; they include a number of officials seconded from the NCAs known as 'national experts'.

(ii) Pre-notification contacts

Initial contact.   The possibility of pre-notification discussions between the   **8.109**
notifying parties and the Commission is specifically referred to at Recital (11) of the Implementing Regulation. The Commission actively encourages parties and their advisers to have pre-notification contacts with the Commission, even in seemingly non-problematic cases.[300] These discussions are confidential and sometimes commence before the transaction is announced; in general, initial contacts

---

[298] In order that new cases may be allocated in an efficient manner at DG Comp's weekly management meetings, parties are encouraged to provide details to the Merger Registry by 12 noon on the previous Friday.

[299] As part of an internal reorganisation of DG Comp in 2004, the former specialised Directorate for Mergers (the so-called 'Merger Task Force' or MTF) was dissolved. The MTF's role had been to examine all notifications and prepare decisions under the Merger Reg, regardless of their subject-matter. In some respects the MTF's role within DG Comp has now been assumed by the broader 'Merger Network'.

[300] See the introduction to the Form CO. For further guidance, see paras 5–15 of the Best Practices Guidelines; DG Comp Best Practices on the conduct of EC merger proceedings, available at DG Comp's website and see Vol II, App D.7. For cases with a strong transatlantic element,

tend to be made at least two weeks prior to formal notification and in some cases even months in advance.[301] As part of this process the Commission will allocate the case team, to whom the parties will usually submit a briefing paper or a draft notification in advance of any meeting to discuss specific aspects of the case. Irrespective of whether pre-notification meetings take place or not, notifying parties are encouraged to provide a substantially complete draft of the notification at least five working days before the formal filing; this should provide the case team with sufficient time to review the draft and comment on its adequacy.[302]

8.110 **Usefulness of pre-notification contacts.** Pre-notification discussions with the case team can be helpful to the parties for a number of reasons, including the following:

(a) they enable the parties to obtain informal advice on jurisdictional issues such as the calculation of turnover or whether a JV undertaking is 'full-function';[303]

(b) in some cases they can be used to discuss whether it may be appropriate to take advantage of the voluntary pre-notification referral procedures of Article 4(4) or (5) (see paragraphs 8.081 *et seq*, above);

(c) in some cases they can be used to discuss whether the simplified procedure may be available, such that the parties need only submit a Short Form notification (see paragraphs 8.120 *et seq*, below);[304]

(d) they allow the parties to discuss waivers from the strict requirements of the Form CO questionnaire, thereby minimising the risk of a formal notification being subsequently declared incomplete;[305]

(e) they assist in identifying any special concerns the case team may have, thereby enabling the parties to address these in the notification (and, if appropriate, to consider changes to the transaction); and

---

see also the EU-US Best Practices on cooperation in merger investigations (Vol II, App D.18) and para 8.284, below.

[301] See the Best Practices Guidelines, above, para 10.

[302] ibid, para 15.

[303] Following pre-notification discussions, if the Commission is satisfied that it does not have jurisdiction, it may issue an informal letter to this effect. The legal effect of such a letter is unclear, although it may give rise to certain legitimate expectations on the part of the recipients as it effectively absolves them from the obligation to notify under Art 4(1) of the Merger Reg. But cf the Commission's Best Practice Guidelines (n 300, above) at n 9: 'Such informal guidance cannot be regarded as creating legitimate expectations regarding the proper interpretation of applicable jurisdictional or other rules'.

[304] See Simplified Procedure Notice, OJ 2005 C56/32: Vol II, App D.11, para 15.

[305] See para 8.114, below.

(f) where the parties consent, and the existence of the proposed concentration is already in the public domain, they may even enable the Commission to start the process of third party consultation before formal notification.[306]

(iii) Obligation to notify

Timing of formal notification. Article 4(1) of the Merger Regulation provides **8.111** that concentrations with a Community dimension must be formally notified to the Commission prior to their implementation unless they have been the subject of a pre-notification referral in whole to a NCA pursuant to the Article 4(4) procedures. The relevant date for establishing the Commission's jurisdiction is the earlier of (a) the date of the conclusion of the binding agreement, the announcement of the public bid, or the acquisition of a controlling interest; or (b) the date of the first notification (to the Commission or a Member State's national competition authority) of a good faith intention to conclude such an agreement or make such a bid.[307] Thus the notification can be made at an earlier stage than a binding agreement if:[308]

(a) the undertakings concerned demonstrate to the Commission a good faith intention to conclude an agreement;[309] or
(b) in the case of a public bid, the acquirer has publicly announced an intention to make such a bid.[310]

Who must notify? The persons by whom notifications must be submitted are **8.112** specified at Article 4(2) of the Merger Regulation.[311] Where a concentration consists

---

[306] Best Practice Guidelines (n 300, above) para 26.

[307] Jurisdictional Notice, paras 154–156.

[308] Merger Reg (n 247, above) Art 4(1) and Recital (34). This possibility of earlier notification (prior to conclusion of a binding agreement) was introduced on 1 May 2004 to provide greater flexibility in the notification process and allow better coordination with merger investigations in jurisdictions outside the EEA: see Green Paper (n 3, above) paras 180–186.

[309] Merger Reg, Recital (34): in particular, they must demonstrate to the satisfaction of the Commission that their plan for the proposed concentration is sufficiently concrete, eg on the basis of an agreement in principle, a memorandum of understanding or letter of intent.

[310] Hence notification of a public bid can be made where there is no agreement or recommendation by the target's board, eg in a hostile bid situation. Similarly, a potential bidder can notify at the stage that it announces a 'pre-conditional' bid (ie that it will launch a bid provided it first obtains Merger Reg and other regulatory approvals); see, eg Case M.1630 *Air Liquide/BOC* (18 January 2000); and Case M.2706 *Carnival Corporation/P&O Princess*, OJ 2003 L248/1. Likewise, in the context of a bid to be implemented by way of a court-approved scheme of arrangement of a UK target company (under s 425 of the Companies Act 1985), the acquirer can notify at the stage of the announcement of the proposed scheme (including in circumstances where it is pre-conditional upon first obtaining Merger Reg and other regulatory approvals): see, eg Case M/3209 *WPP/Cordiant* (25 July 2003); Case M.3304 *GE/Amersham* (21 January 2004); Case M.3572 *Cemex/RMC* (8 December 2004); Case M.3783 *TPG/British Vita* (6 July 2005); Case M.4141 *Linde/BOC* (6 June 2006).

[311] See also Implementing Reg, Reg 802/2004, OJ 2004 L133/1: Vol II, App D.2, Art 2(1) and Part 1.2 of the Introduction to Form CO. Joint notifications should be submitted by a joint

---

of a merger (within the meaning of Article 3(1)(a)) or in the acquisition of joint control, it must be notified jointly by the parties to the merger or by those acquiring joint control as the case may be. In all other situations, only the undertaking or undertakings acquiring control, and not the target or vendor, are required to notify. However, 'other involved parties', that is the parties to the proposed concentration other than the notifying parties (the seller or the target) have certain rights to be heard which are greater than those of third parties.[312] In most cases, other involved parties will be supportive of the notifying parties, with submissions often being made on a 'joint' basis;[313] however, in the case of 'hostile' takeovers, sometimes the target may take a stance against the merger.[314] The act of notification does not constitute voluntary submission to the jurisdiction of the Commission.[315]

8.113 **Effective date of notification.** A notification becomes effective on the date it is received by the Commission unless it is incomplete in a material respect.[316] The Commission has expressed concerns about the number of notifications that it has had to declare incomplete.[317] If the Commission requires additional information before it will consider the notification to be materially complete, it must inform the parties in writing without delay and fix an appropriate time limit for the supply of the information. In such cases, the notification will become effective on the date on which that information is received by the Commission.[318]

---

representative who is authorised to transmit and receive documents on behalf of all notifying parties.

[312] See Implementing Reg (n 311, above) Arts 11 and 14(2). For the rights of third parties, see para 8.131, below.

[313] In the event of a 'contested' bid situation involving competing bids from two or more bidders, the target may need to adopt a more neutral stance. See, eg the UK City Code on Takeovers and Mergers, Rule 20.2 which requires that any information given to one actual or potential bidder must, on request, be given equally and promptly to any other bidder or bona fide potential bidder, even if that other bidder is less welcome.

[314] See, eg Case M.3216 *Oracle/PeopleSoft*, OJ 2005 L218/6. The board of a target subject to a hostile takeover will, however, need to take account of fiduciary duties owed to shareholders and other stakeholders; eg for bids governed by the UK City Code on Takeovers and Mergers, General Principle 7 and Rule 21.1 restrict the board from taking frustrating action without stakeholder approval.

[315] Case T-102/96 *Gencor v Commission* [1999] ECR II-753, [1999] 4 CMLR 971, [1999] All ER (EC) 289, para 76.

[316] Implementing Reg (n 311, above) Art 5(1) and (2). The fact that the notification has been made is publicised by the Commission.

[317] See, eg *XXVIIIth Report on Competition Policy* (1999), points 172–173. A declaration of incompleteness may delay the commencement and consequently the expiry of Phase I for several weeks.

[318] In some cases, the parties may use these procedures in order to give the Commission more time to investigate a notified transaction with a view to avoiding the launch of Phase II proceedings which might have been inevitable on the original Phase I timetable: eg in Case M.1795 *Vodafone Airtouch/Mannesmann* (12 April 2000), the notification was received by the Commission on 14 January 2000 and declared incomplete on 22 February 2000; see also Case M.1745 *EADS* (11 May 2000); Case M.2345 *Deutsche BP/Erdölchemie* (26 April 2001), initially examined by the

Where there are material changes in the facts contained in a notification which the notifying parties know or ought to have known, these changes must be communicated to the Commission without delay.[319] If the material changes could have a significant effect on the appraisal of the concentration, the notification will not become effective until the date on which the information on the material change is received by the Commission.[320] The Commission may declare a notification incomplete at any time throughout Phase I.

Waivers regarding provision of information.   The Commission may excuse the   **8.114** parties from the obligation to provide particular information in the notification where it considers the information is not necessary for the examination of the case.[321] In practice, DG Competition case teams have been willing to use the waiver provisions, particularly where a concentration does not raise major competition issues.

Supply of incorrect or misleading information.   The negligent or intentional   **8.115** supply of incorrect or misleading information in the notification, or in response to subsequent information requests addressed to the notifying parties by the Commission, may expose the parties to the possibility of fines.[322]

Failure to notify.   The consequences of putting a concentration with a Community dimension into effect without first having notified to the Commission are   **8.116** considered at paragraph 8.130, below.

(iv) Formalities

Form CO.   Form CO is annexed to the Implementing Regulation and specifies   **8.117** the information to be provided by parties when notifying a concentration with a Community dimension.[323] It requests a large amount of information; the preparation of a notification in accordance with Form CO can therefore require considerable work on the part of the notifying parties, particularly in cases which raise significant competition issues. Form CO includes an introductory section explaining matters such as the possibility of notification in short-form, and how

---

Commission as Case M.2624; Case M.3561 *Deutsche Telekom/Eurotel* (15 December 2004); Case M.3664 *Repsol Butano/Shell Gas (LPG)* (2 March 2005).

[319] Implementing Reg (n 311, above) Art 5(3).

[320] See, eg Case M.1377 *Bertelsmann/Wissenschaftsverlag Springer* (15 February 1999): material changes in the circumstances of the transaction, as communicated by the parties post-notification, were deemed to have potentially significant effects on the Commission's appraisal so as to warrant a belated effective date of the notification.

[321] Implementing Reg (n 311, above) Art 4(2) and Introductions to Annexes I, II and III. See also Best Practice Guidelines (n 300, above) para 19.

[322] Merger Reg, Art 14(1). See para 8.180, below.

[323] Implementing Reg (n 311, above) Art 3(1) and Annex I.

confidentiality issues are handled. The Form CO questionnaire itself contains 11 sections:

— *Section 1*: description of the concentration, including an executive summary specifying the nature and parties to the concentration, the main 'affected markets',[324] the economic rationale for the transaction, etc;

— *Section 2*: information about the parties, their addresses, contact details, legal representatives, etc;

— *Section 3*: details of the concentration, the structure and economic sectors involved, the parties' turnovers, the economic rationale for the transaction, etc;[325]

— *Section 4*: information on undertakings owned or controlled by the parties to the concentration and information on personal and financial links with other undertakings active on affected markets;

— *Section 5*: supporting documentation;

— *Section 6*: a description of markets affected by the concentration and other markets on which the operation will have an impact;

— *Section 7*: detailed information on all 'affected markets', including market size, market shares, import data, barriers to entry, vertical integration issues, etc;

— *Section 8*: information on general conditions in the 'affected markets', including contact details for the parties' five largest independent suppliers and customers,[326] information on distribution systems, capacity levels, record of market entry, R&D levels, cooperative agreements, trade associations, etc;

— *Section 9*: other general market information, including on the worldwide context of the operation and on possible efficiency gains;

— *Section 10*: information on the cooperative effects if the case concerns a full-function JV, in particular regarding the parents' activities in the JV's market or in upstream, downstream or neighbouring markets. To the extent that the operation may have Article 81(1) cooperative effects, Form CO requests

---

324 The term 'affected markets' is defined in Section 6.III of Form CO. See para 8.186, below.

325 This includes information on the parties' turnovers in Iceland, Liechtenstein and Norway, for the purpose of determining whether the case qualifies as a 'mixed case' in accordance with Art 2 of Protocol 24 to the EEA Agreement and is subject to cooperation between the Commission and the EFTA Surveillance Authority (Form CO, para 3.5 and n 1): see further paras 8.280–8.281, below.

326 In cases raising significant competition issues, the Commission often asks the parties to provide contact details for substantially more customers (and competitors if appropriate), so broadening the scope of the Commission's market investigations. The Best Practice Guidelines (n 300, above) para 21, request that these details be provided electronically (in accordance with a standard Excel spreadsheet, a copy of which can be obtained from the Commission case team).

the parties to give reasons why the exemption criteria of Article 81(3) may be met;[327]

—*Section 11*: each notification must end with a declaration to the effect that, to the best of the knowledge and belief of the notifying parties, the information supplied is true and complete.

Submission of notification and supporting documentation. The original and several copies of each notification must be supplied to the Commission.[328] The original Form CO notification must include the original proof of authority to act as given to the representative(s) who signed the notification.[329] There are no filing fees payable for notifications under the Merger Regulation. The original signed copy of the notification (including a set of all supporting documents and other annexes) must be submitted to the Commission on paper. This must be accompanied by five paper copies, together with 32 copies in CD- or DVD-ROM format.[330] The required supporting documents are listed at section 5 of Form CO:[331]

8.118

(a) copies of the final or more recent versions of all documents bringing about the concentration;

(b) in a public bid, a copy of the offer document which, if unavailable on notification, should be submitted as soon as possible and not later than when posted to shareholders;

(c) copies of the parties' most recent annual reports and accounts; and

(d) copies of all analyses, reports, studies, surveys, and any comparable documents prepared by or for any member(s) of the Board of directors, or the supervisory Board, or the other person(s) exercising similar functions, or the

---

[327] For cooperative effects, see paras 8.232 *et seq,* below (re substantive assessment).

[328] Implementing Reg (n 311, above) Arts 3(2) and 23. Technically this only required 35 copies without specifying the format; however, in practice this has been superseded by a move to copies on CD- or DVD-ROM and by the subsequent accession of Bulgaria and Romania to the Community. Additional security procedures for the delivery of notifications and merger related documents are set out on DG Comp's website at http://ec.europa.eu/comm./competition/mergers/others.

[329] Implementing Reg, Art 2(2).

[330] These electronic files should be in PDF format and should generally not exceed 5 MB each; where documents were originally produced in other formats (Word, Excel, PowerPoint) they should also be saved in PDF format on the CD- or DVD-ROM. Each file should bear the relevant Commission case number and name (and be named in a way which allows easy identification of the section in the notification to which it relates), and there should be a separate file on the CD- or DVD-ROM containing a list of all the different files it contains. The requirement of copies in CD- or DVD-ROM format was introduced in November 2006 in accordance with a Commission Communication, OJ 2006 C251/2: Vol II, App D.12 issued pursuant to Art 3(2) of the Implementing Reg (n 311, above), with the number of CD- or DVD-ROMs increased from 30 to 32 following the accession of Bulgaria and Romania to the Community. The same procedures apply for Short Form notifications (see para 8.124, below) and, by virtue of Implementing Reg Art 6(2), for reasoned submissions under Form RS (see para 8.089, above).

[331] Implementing Reg (n 311, above) Art 3(2) and (3); for notification made using the Short Form (see para 8.124, below) only the documents listed at (a) and (c) need be supplied (Section 5 of the Short Form).

shareholders meeting, for the purpose of assessing or analysing the concentration with respect to market shares, competitive conditions, competitors (actual and potential), the rationale of the concentration, potential for sales growth or expansion into other markets, and/or general market conditions.[332] Legal professional privilege should protect certain communications with external lawyers from disclosure to the Commission.

8.119 **Language.** The notification must be made in one of the official languages of the Community which becomes the language of the proceedings for all notifying parties.[333] Other parties, including the company being acquired, as well as third parties involved in the proceedings, may use another official language if they wish. Supporting documents should be provided in their original language and translated into the language of the proceedings if their original language is not an official language of the Community.

8.120 **Business secrets.** Although there is a relatively high degree of transparency in respect of the Commission's assessment of concentrations, including through the publication of Commission decisions, both Article 287 of the EC Treaty and Article 17(2) of the Merger Regulation require the Commission to protect business secrets.[334] Parties can identify which aspects of the deal and which materials in their notification or other communications constitute business secrets by expressly alerting the Commission and, if necessary, marking the appropriate pages, usually with the words 'Business Secrets'.[335] Where it is necessary not to disclose material in a notification to another notifying party, the material is placed in a separate, clearly marked annex. In all cases where confidentiality is required, reasons should be given as to why the material should not be divulged or published.[336]

---

[332] The scope of the supporting documentation required by Form CO was broadened under the Implementing Reg adopted in 2004 (n 311, above), although a proposal also to cover similar documentation prepared by investment banks or management consultancy agencies was not ultimately included. Where a transaction raising significant competition issues also requires a filing to the US authorities, it is common practice to supply the Commission with copies of the documents submitted in the US under Item 4(c) of the HSR notification form, together with any other documents that may be relevant in a European context. The Commission tolerates the practice of parties supplying these documents to it on a standalone basis, subject to certain key background materials being included in the Form CO notification.

[333] Implementing Reg, Art 3(4) and (5). For the official languages, see para 1.039, above. Where notifications are made pursuant to Art 57 of the EEA Agreement (see para 8.280, below), they may be submitted in one of the official languages of the EFTA States (so technically adding the possibility of notifying in Norwegian or Icelandic) but must be accompanied by a translation into a Community language.

[334] See also paras 8.176–8.177, below.

[335] Implementing Reg (n 311, above) Art 18(2).

[336] ibid, Art 18(2).

Need for full and accurate disclosure. The notifying parties should provide all **8.121** the information requested by Form CO or the Short Form[337] unless either the Commission has waived the obligation to provide it,[338] or the parties have good reasons why they are unable to provide it.[339] Any material changes in the facts specified in the notification which the parties know or ought to know must be communicated to the Commission without delay.[340]

(v) Simplified procedure

In general. In 2000 the Commission introduced a simplified procedure **8.122** applicable to notifications of concentrations which do not raise competition concerns.[341] Following receipt of such a notification, for which the parties may use the Short Form, introduced in 2004, the Commission publishes a notice in the *Official Journal* providing information about the notified concentration including a statement that the concentration may qualify for treatment under the simplified procedure. If the Commission is satisfied that the concentration fulfils the criteria for the simplified procedure, it will normally adopt a short-form clearance decision at the end of the Phase I investigation period.[342] This procedure has significantly eased the administrative burden on DG Competition by enabling its staff to focus their resources on cases that may raise competition concerns. Approximately half of all notifications are handled under this simplified procedure.

Eligible cases. The simplified procedure is available for the following three **8.123** categories of cases:[343]

(a) The establishment of any full-function JV undertaking which has no, or negligible, actual or foreseen activities within the EEA. That is stated to be the case where:

    (i) the EEA turnover of the JV and/or of the activities contributed to the JV is less than €100 million; and

---

[337] ibid, Arts 3(1) and 4(1).

[338] See para 8.112, above.

[339] See para 1.3(f) and (g) of the Introduction to Form CO and para 1.5(f) and (g) of the Introduction to the Short Form.

[340] Implementing Reg (n 311, above) Art 5(3).

[341] For further guidance, see Simplified Procedure Notice, OJ 2005 C56/32: Vol II, App D.11.

[342] Simplified Procedure Notice, above, paras 17–18. Unlike the formal reasoned decisions issued at the end of standard investigations under the Merger Reg, a short-form clearance decision only contains the information about the concentration published in the OJ at the time of notification (names of the parties, their country of origin, nature of the concentration and economic sectors concerned) and a statement that the cleared concentration falls within an identified category or categories of qualifying cases under the Simplified Procedure Notice.

[343] ibid, para 5.

    (ii) the total value of assets transferred to the JV is less than €100 million in the EEA.

(b) Any concentration where there are no 'affected markets',[344] either because:

    (i) the parties do not engage in business activities in the same product or geographic market ('horizontal relationships') or in a product market that is upstream or downstream of a market in which another party is engaged ('vertical relationships'); or

    (ii) in the event of such horizontal relationships, the parties' combined market share does not exceed 15 per cent; or

    (iii) in the event of such vertical relationships, the parties' individual or combined market shares do not exceed 25 per cent.

(c) Transactions where one party is to acquire sole control of an undertaking over which it already has joint control.[345]

8.124 **Short Form.** The Short Form is set out at Annex II to the Implementing Regulation and can be used (instead of Form CO) for any concentration which would qualify for treatment under the simplified procedure.[346] The original signed copy of the Short Form (including a set of all supporting documents and other annexes) must be submitted to the Commission on paper. This must be accompanied by five paper copies, together with 32 copies in CD- or DVD-ROM format.[347]

8.125 **Exceptions.** The Commission may require a full Form CO notification where it appears either that the conditions for using the Short Form are not met or, exceptionally, where the Commission determines that a more detailed Form CO notification is warranted to ensure an adequate investigation. This will generally be discussed during pre-notification contacts or the Commission may declare the notification incomplete or request additional information.[348] The Commission's Notice also states that it will not apply the simplified procedure if a Member State or a third party has expressed substantiated concerns about the concentration.[349]

---

344 For the concept of 'affected markets', see para 8.186, below.

345 For moves from joint to sole control, see para 8.041, above. In Case M.3768 *BBVA/BNL* (27 April 2005) the Commission concluded that the simplified procedure was also available for a move from negative to full sole control: see para 8.042, above.

346 Implementing Reg (n 311, above) Art 3(1) and Annex II to the Implementing Reg. It is considerably shorter than Form CO and contains nine Sections.

347 The requirement of CD- or DVD-ROM format was introduced in November 2006: see para 8.118, above.

348 Simplified Procedure Notice (n 341, above) paras 6–11.

349 ibid, paras 12–13.

(vi) Suspension of concentrations

Standstill period. A concentration with a Community dimension cannot be **8.126** put into effect or completed unless and until it has been declared compatible with the common market pursuant to a Phase I or Phase II clearance decision or is deemed to have been so declared pursuant to Article 10(6).[350] This general rule is subject to exceptions only in the case of public bids or if an express derogation has been granted.

'Gun-jumping' issues. Questions sometimes arise as to whether parties to a **8.127** proposed concentration can engage in cooperation before expiry of this waiting period.[351] The appraisal of such pre-closing cooperation can involve different considerations. In some cases, extensive cooperation could be viewed as partial implementation of the concentration in breach of Article 7(1) of the Merger Regulation, thereby exposing the parties to the risk of infringement proceedings and fines under Article 14(2)(b) of the Merger Regulation.[352] In other cases, such cooperation may be benign or there may even be scope for treating it as an integral part of the concentration itself or as directly related and necessary for the implementation of the concentration. More generally, there may sometimes be wider concerns under Article 81 (or occasionally Article 82) of the EC Treaty if the pre-closing cooperation could have the object or effect of appreciably restricting competition between undertakings which remain independent during the period prior to closing. In practice, these various considerations generally arise in the following contexts:

(a) *Due diligence and transition planning*: due diligence and transition planning conducted by the parties in the period prior to closing will not of itself raise competition concerns. Such preparatory work can, however, involve the sharing of sensitive information. Accordingly, when the parties are competitors, pre-closing information exchange will raise Article 81 issues if it could affect the parties' independent competitive activities in the market place in the period prior to closing.[353]

---

[350] Merger Reg, Art 7(1). In practice, the Commission has accepted that this does not prevent the purchaser from paying the purchase price to the vendor in advance of clearance and completion of the transaction: see facts of Case M.4404 *Universal Music Group/BMG Music Publishing* (22 May 2007).

[351] See Modrall and Ciullo, 'Gun-Jumping and EU Merger Control' (2003) ECLR 424.

[352] See para 8.181, below. The Commission considered bringing such proceedings during the administrative procedure in Case M.993 *Bertelsmann/Kirch/Premiere*, OJ 1999 L53/1: see Press Release IP/97/1119 (1 December 1997), which refers to the formal undertaking given by the parties to suspend Premiere's use and marketing of Kirch's d-box decoder as it amounted to partial implementation of the proposed merger of the parties' digital pay-TV interests. (The proposed merger was subsequently prohibited.)

[353] Parties negotiating a proposed merger will generally put in place a confidentiality agreement early in the process. Other safeguards can also be put in place to minimise the competition law risks

(b) *Anticipating post-closing expenditure:* the purchaser may seek to impose restrictions in the transaction agreements giving it some level of veto or consultation right over significant expenditure in the period prior to closing, particularly if it involves large sums or activities outside the normal course of the target's business, which will have an effect on the value of the business post-closing. The Commission's Ancillary Restraints Notice recognises that it is legitimate to impose some limitations on the target business prior to closing.[354] However, if those restrictions have the effect of preventing a party from implementing its competitive strategy, in some cases they could be unenforceable under Article 81 and may expose the parties to the risk of infringement proceedings.

(c) *Joint activity:* in some cases, merging parties may wish to approach customers following the announcement and prior to closing to explain the benefits of the merger. Such joint or coordinated courtesy calls, effectively marketing the transaction itself, ought to be possible without having broader spill-over effects on competition between the parties; however, more market-focused joint activity could raise Article 81 concerns if it were to affect the intensity of pre-closing competition between the parties. In some cases, pre-merger cooperation may be compatible with Article 81, for example if the parties' market positions are such that the cooperation is covered by one of the Commission's vertical or horizontal block exemptions or is otherwise compatible with the criteria of Article 81(3); however, this will generally not extend to any discussion or coordination of prices or allocation of customers or markets in the period prior to closing. Furthermore, and regardless of the Article 81 assessment, particular care needs to be taken to ensure that any pre-merger cooperation does not amount to early implementation during the period prior to the Commission's clearance decision.[355]

8.128 **Public bids.** Public bids duly notified to the Commission may be implemented before the Commission's decision. However the acquirer must not exercise the voting rights attached to the securities in question or may do so only to maintain the full value of those investments and on the basis of a derogation granted by the

---

and ensure that the scope of such information exchange is reasonable: eg while the purchaser may need information on the business it is proposing to acquire, it is generally not necessary for the vendor to receive information on the purchaser's business (although two-way exchanges may be necessary for the establishment of a full-function JV). It may be appropriate to put in place limited teams of personnel, as distinct from sales and marketing personnel, who will have access to competitively sensitive information (eg detailed pricing and customer information, future plans) or to outsource some aspects of integration and planning activities to external consultants.

[354] Ancillary Restraints Notice, OJ 2005 C56/24: Vol II, App D.10, para 14, referring to such restrictions in the context of a joint bid: see para 8.264(b), below.

[355] See *Bertelsmann/Kirch/Premiere* (n 352, above).

Commission in accordance with the procedures considered in the following paragraph.[356]

Derogations. The Commission, acting on a reasoned request, may grant a dero- **8.129** gation from the suspension period, either unconditionally or subject to conditions to ensure effective competition.[357] In deciding on the request, the Commission shall take into account *inter alia* the effects of the suspension on one or more undertakings concerned by a concentration or on a third party and the threat to competition posed by the concentration. Derogations can be applied for and granted before or after notification. Where the Commission proposes to refuse such a request, or proposes to grant it but subject to conditions, it must first inform the parties, fixing a time limit within which they may make their views known.[358]

Completion in breach. Where a concentration with a Community dimension **8.130** is put into effect without first being notified or before expiry of the suspension period, its validity is dependent on a notification subsequently being made and on the Commission deciding on its compatibility with the common market.[359] Also, the parties are liable for a fine of up to 10 per cent of aggregate turnover.[360] However, transactions in securities on recognised stock exchanges may nevertheless be

---

356 Merger Reg, Reg 139/2004, OJ 2004 L24/1: Vol II, App D.1 Art 7(2). For high profile cases involving public bids, see Case M.2283 *Schneider/Legrand*, OJ 2004 L101/1 and L101/34; and Case M.2416 *Tetra Laval/Sidel*, OJ 2004 L38/1 (divestiture decision) and L43/13 (prohibition decision). In both cases the bids were implemented during the course of the Commission's administrative proceedings, which concluded with prohibition decisions and orders for divestment.

357 Merger Reg, Art 7(3). Statistics on DG Competition's website confirm that such derogations are unusual (10 in 2004, six in 2005, two in 2006). See, eg Case M.116 *Kelt/American Express* (20 August 1991): to allow a financial rescue package to proceed swiftly; Case M.4 *Renault/Volvo* [1991] 4 CMLR 297: to avoid adverse Swedish tax implications; Case M.538 *Omnitel* (27 March 1995): to enable the newly-created JV to meet the deadlines imposed in its GSM licence and to start competing against Telecom Italia; Case M.573 *ING/Barings* (11 April 1995): to prevent substantial damage to Barings and third parties as the Barings holding company was in administration; Case M.1822 *Mobil/JV Dissolution* (2 February 2000), presumably in the absence of competition concerns; and Case M.2777 *Cinven Limited/Angel Street Holdings* (8 May 2002): to facilitate a bid for the purchase of assets, since without a derogation the parties would have effectively been excluded from the auction.

358 Implementing Reg (n 311, above) Art 12(1). Pursuant to Art 12(2) and (3), the Commission may, on the basis of the reasoned request, issue a provisional decision on whether to grant the requested derogation, without having given the notifying parties and other involved parties the opportunity to comment. Once such parties make their views known, the Commission takes a final decision annulling, amending or confirming its provisional decision.

359 Merger Reg (n 356, above) Art 7(4).

360 ibid, Art 14(2)(b). See Case M.920 *Samsung/AST*, OJ 1999 L225/12, notified in April 1997 although Samsung (of Korea) had acquired control of AST (of the USA) in January 1996; fine of only €33,000 because no damage had been caused, the parties did finally notify the agreement, the infringement appeared not to be intentional, and Samsung cooperated with the Commission in its investigations. cf Case M.969 *AP Møller*, OJ 1999 L183/29: total fines of €219,000 for failing to notify and putting into effect three concentrations. See also Case M.166 *Torras/Sarrio* (24 February 1992): agreement notified almost one year late and some time after it had been put into effect, but ('exceptionally') no fine imposed in view of problems relating to the correct method of calculating turnover; Case M.157 *Air France/Sabena* (5 October 1992): no fine imposed because the transaction

deemed valid, unless the buyer and seller knew or ought to have known that the transaction was carried out in breach.[361] The Commission may also take interim measures appropriate to restore or maintain effective competition.[362]

(vii) Role of third parties

8.131   **Formal rights of third parties.**   Article 18(4) of the Merger Regulation obliges the Commission to hear any third party who applies and shows a 'sufficient interest';[363] it refers expressly to members of the administrative or management bodies of the undertakings concerned and to recognised representatives of their employees, although in practice competitors and customers tend to be the categories of third parties who are most likely to express interest in Commission investigations.[364] If third parties so apply in writing to be heard, the Commission must inform them of the nature and subject-matter of the procedure and shall fix a time limit within which they may make known their views.[365] Those third parties may submit written observations within the time limit set by the Commission (and may request the opportunity to participate in the oral hearing).[366] The Commission may also invite other third parties to submit written or oral observations, or to participate in the oral hearing.[367] Where third parties do not make an application to be heard, the Commission is under no obligation to keep them informed.[368] The formal procedural rights of third parties are effectively confined to those set out in Article 18(4).[369] Accordingly, if an interested third party so requests, the Commission must adjudicate formally on the question whether or not a

---

was complex and the agreement had already been notified in good faith under Reg 17 for the purposes of Art 81.

[361]   Merger Reg, Art 7(4).

[362]   This power under Merger Reg Art 8(5)(a) was introduced in 2004.

[363]   See also Merger Reg, Recital (37).

[364]   In Cases C-68/94 & C-30/95 *France v Commission (Kali+Salz)* [1998] ECR I-1375, [1998] 4 CMLR 829, the ECJ indicated that third parties, whom the Commission considers may share a position of collective dominance with the parties as a result of the concentration, are entitled to be heard (paras 55–58).

[365]   Implementing Reg (n 311, above) Art 16(1). In practice, this tends to be done in Phase II proceedings by providing them with a non-confidential version of the statement of objections (and sometimes even of the Art 6(1)(c) decision to open the Phase II investigations). The Best Practice Guidelines (n 300, above) para 36, provide that these documents will be provided only under strict confidentiality obligations and restrictions on use.

[366]   Implementing Reg (n 311, above) Art 16(2).

[367]   ibid, Art 16(3).

[368]   Case T-96/92 *CCE de la Société Générale des Grandes Sources v Commission* [1995] ECR II–1213. The Commission is also under no obligation to inform the employees' representatives of the existence of a notified concentration: Case T-12/93 *CCE de Vittel v Commission* [1995] ECR II–1247, para 62. Both these cases concerned challenges by workers' councils to the Commission decision in Case M.190 *Nestlé/Perrier*, OJ 1992 L356/1, [1993] 4 CMLR M17.

[369]   See *CCE de la Société Générale des Grandes Sources v Commission*, above, para 56; Case T-290/94 *Kaysersberg v Commission* [1997] ECR II-237, [1998] 4 CMLR 336, at para 105.

concentration which has not been notified falls within the scope of the Merger Regulation.[370]

Significance in practice. In practice, third parties which may be affected by **8.132** the concentration (in particular customers, competitors, suppliers, and bodies or associations representing any of these groups) can play a significant role in merger control investigations from an early stage in the proceedings. The Commission generally places significant reliance on their views in the course of its investigation.[371] In this regard:

(a) *Complaints about unnotified concentrations:* in some cases third parties may raise concerns about a transaction before it has been notified to the Commission.[372] This may prompt the Commission to make contact with the parties to the concentration if they are not already engaged in pre-notification discussions;

(b) *Responses to invitations to comment:* the Commission has adopted the practice of requesting third parties to comment by its Article 4(3) publication in the *Official Journal.* They are generally invited to comment within a short period, usually 10 days from the date of publication;[373]

(c) *Market testing:* the Commission often uses its powers to request third parties, notably customers, competitors and suppliers,[374] to reply to specific questions pursuant to Article 11 of the Merger Regulation. It also conducts interviews and holds discussions with third parties. The Commission uses this 'market testing' to verify the arguments developed by the parties in their notification and subsequently on market definition and the substantive appraisal of the concentration. Where parties offer commitments with a view to obtaining Commission clearance (whether at Phase I or Phase II), the

---

[370] Case C-170/02P *Schlüsselverlag J. S. Moser v Commission* [2003] ECR I-9889, [2004] 4 CMLR 27, paras 27–29 (see also n 372, below).

[371] See Best Practices Guidelines (n 300, above) paras 34–37. These also refer to the fact that the Commission welcomes the views of consumer organisations; it has therefore established a Consumer Liaison Officer (within Directorate A of DG Comp) responsible for contacts with consumer organisations.

[372] See *Schlüsselverlag J. S. Moser GmbH v Commission* (n 370, above) para 27.

[373] This reflects the tight 25 working day timetable imposed on the Commission in Phase I proceedings under the Merger Reg. In *Kaysersberg v Commission* (n 369, above) para 113, where the third party competitor was given only two working days in which to submit its comments on proposed amendments to the concentration, the CFI held that the Commission had not failed to have regard to that third party's right to be heard: the legitimate interest of third parties must be adapted to the need for speed which characterises the general scheme of the Merger Reg and which requires the Commission to comply with strict time limits for the adoption of the final decision.

[374] Form CO requires the notifying parties to provide contact details of a potentially large number of third parties (competitors, suppliers and customers) whom the Commission may consult early in the Phase I process.

Commission will also 'market test' these by seeking the views of interested third parties;[375]

(d) *Access to file*: although third parties have no right to access the Commission's file during Phase II proceedings, in some cases the Commission may grant them limited access to non-confidential copies of specific documents (see paragraph 8.146, below);

(e) *Oral hearing*: The Commission may also, where appropriate, afford third parties who have so requested in their written comments the opportunity to participate in a formal hearing during Phase II or to express their views orally (see paragraph 8.148, below).

(b) Initial Phase I investigation

(i) Phase I process

8.133 **Duration of Phase I investigation.** Once it receives a formal notification, the Commission publishes a notice in the *Official Journal*, setting out the date of the notification, the names of the parties, their countries of origin, the nature of the concentration and the economic sectors involved.[376] The information is also publicised on the website of DG Competition, indicating the provisional date for the expiry of Phase I.[377] The Commission must conclude its preliminary examination within 25 working days from the first working day following the date of receipt of the notification or, if the information supplied with the notification is incomplete, from the working date following that of the receipt of the complete information.[378] This period is extended by an additional 10 working days to a total of 35 working days if either (a) the Commission receives a request for referral from a Member State in accordance with Article 9(2);[379] or (b) the notified undertakings submit commitments pursuant to Article 6(2) with a view to rendering the concentration compatible with the common market.[380] In all cases it is

---

[375] For commitments to enable clearance, see paras 8.162 *et seq*, below.

[376] Merger Reg (n 356, above) Art 4(3); Implementing Reg (n 311, above) Art 5(5). The same information is also published in the EEA Supplement to the OJ.

[377] In 2005 DG Comp introduced the practice of publishing on its website a non-confidential executive summary of each case in the form supplied by the notifying parties (pursuant to Section 1.2 of Form CO).

[378] Merger Reg, Art 10(1); Implementing Reg (n 311, above) Art 7.

[379] Merger Reg, Art 10(1). See further paras 8.091 *et seq*, above.

[380] ibid, Art 10(1); Remedies Notice, OJ 2001 C68/3: Vol II, App D.4, para 33 (a revised and updated version of this Notice is under preparation). See further paras 8.162 *et seq*, below. If formal commitments are submitted, the Phase I period is automatically extended even if the proposed commitments are subsequently deemed unsatisfactory or are not acceptable to the Commission. In a few cases, commitments are principally designed to give the Commission the extra 10 working days added to Phase I since this may enable the Commission to investigate further and conclude that there are not sufficient grounds to open Phase II proceedings or to impose conditions at Phase I; in those cases, the Commission may decide that it is not necessary to market test the commitments with third parties.

extended to take account of Commission holidays falling within the review period.[381] A time period calculated in working days expires at the end of the last working day, while a time period set by the Commission in terms of a calendar date expires at the end of that date.[382]

Suspension of Phase I time period.   The Phase I investigation period can be   **8.134** suspended if the Commission adopts a decision formally requesting the parties to provide further information pursuant to Article 11 of the Merger Regulation (if they have failed to provide such information pursuant to an earlier written request) or if a third party fails to provide information requested of it owing to circumstances for which one of the parties is responsible.[383] It could also be suspended if the Commission were to adopt a formal decision ordering an investigation pursuant to Article 13 of the Merger Regulation, following the refusal of the parties to submit to or cooperate in such an investigation.[384] The period is suspended if the parties fail to inform the Commission of material changes in the facts specified in the notification or of any new information.[385] The suspension of the time limit starts on the day following the event causing the suspension and ends with the expiry of the day when the reason for suspension is removed or of the next working day should that day not be a working day.[386]

Scope for modifications or commitments.   Recital (11) to the Implementing   **8.135** Regulation provides that after notification the Commission will maintain close contact with the parties concerned to the extent necessary to discuss any practical or legal problems that may arise and, if possible, to address such problems by mutual agreement. Such contacts may allow the parties to modify the terms of the transaction or make other changes which may serve to remove 'serious doubts'

---

[381] Implementing Reg (n 311, above) Arts 22 and 24. These dates are published in the OJ before the beginning of each year. Apps D.16–17 in Vol II provide a list of Commission holidays planned for 2008 and 2009.

[382] ibid, Art 8.

[383] Merger Reg (n 356, above) Art 10(4); Implementing Reg (n 311, above) Art 9(1)(a) and (b); see also the analogous Phase II suspension: para 8.143, below. There are very few instances of the Commission 'stopping the clock' in this way at Phase I; see, eg Case M.2257 *France Télécom/Equant* (21 March 2001), paras 11–13 and Case M.4533 *SCA/P&G* (5 September 2007). Where the Commission requires information to complete its Phase I investigation in circumstances where that information ought to have been included as part of the Form CO notification, it is open to the Commission to reject the notification as incomplete until such time as the parties supply the complete information (see para 8.121, above). With regard to information to be supplied by third parties, the Commission could, eg suspend the period if a fax requesting information of a third party was sent to the wrong fax number or the wrong individual within a company (such that the reply was delayed) because of incorrect contact details supplied by the parties; alternatively, the Commission could reject the original notification as incomplete pending receipt of the correct contact details.

[384] Implementing Reg (n 311, above) Art 9(1)(c). See also para 8.174, below.

[385] ibid, Art 9(1)(d).

[386] ibid, Art 9(4).

which the Commission might otherwise have had about the concentration's compatibility with the common market. Prior to 1998, the Merger Regulation did not expressly allow for formal commitments to be incorporated in Phase I decisions, so that modification of the terms of the transaction occurred more frequently. Under the current Merger Regulation, substantial amendments of this kind are normally expressed as conditions of the Commission's decision.[387] In the event that a case looks likely to raise 'serious doubts', the Commission's Best Practice Guidelines foresee the possibility of a 'state of play' meeting during the course of Phase I in advance of the 20 working day deadline for the parties to offer such commitments.[388]

(ii) Possible outcomes at Phase I

8.136 **Decisions following the Phase I investigation period.** Following the initial investigation period, the Commission issues one of the following decisions:

(a) *No jurisdiction decision:* the Commission will issue a decision pursuant to Article 6(1)(a) if it finds that it does not have jurisdiction under the Merger Regulation, either because the operation is not a 'concentration' or because the concentration does not have a 'Community dimension';[389] or

(b) *Clearance decision:* the Commission will issue a clearance decision pursuant to Article 6(1)(b) if it finds that the concentration does not give rise to serious doubts about its compatibility with the common market. If it reaches this conclusion as a result of commitments offered by the parties pursuant to Article 6(2) the decision may include conditions and obligations intended to ensure that the parties comply with their commitments;[390] or

(c) *Launch of an in-depth Phase II investigation:* if the Commission finds that the concentration gives rise to serious doubts as to its compatibility with the common market, it takes a decision pursuant to Article 6(1)(c) by which it initiates further investigative proceedings (a Phase II investigation), the progress of which is discussed below.[391]

Also, if the Commission finds that the notified transaction involves a concentration which fulfils the referral criteria under Article 9(3) of the Merger Regulation,

---

[387] See paras 8.162 and 8.163, below.

[388] Best Practice Guidelines; DG Comp Best Practices on the conduct of EC merger proceedings, available at DG Comp's website (www.europa.eu/comm/competition/mergers/ legislation/ regulation): (Vol II, App D.7) para 33. For 'state of play' generally, see para 8.149, below.

[389] Although there were several such decisions in the early years of the Merger Reg (when greater uncertainties prevailed as to its jurisdictional scope), they are now rare: see statistics in table (b) at para 8.011, above.

[390] Approximately 90 per cent of cases dealt with at Phase I are unconditional clearances, while approximately five per cent are clearance decisions attaching conditions/obligations (pursuant to Art 6(2)): see the statistics in table (b) at para 8.011, above.

[391] See paras 8.141 *et seq*, below.

it may decide to refer the whole or part of the case to the relevant NCA(s) for examination in accordance with national merger control rules.[392]

Deemed decisions.   According to Article 10(6) of the Merger Regulation, where **8.137** the Commission has not taken a decision within the strict Phase I time frame, the duly notified concentration shall be deemed to have been declared compatible with the common market.[393]

Communication and publication of Phase I decisions.   The Commission must **8.138** notify its Phase I decision without delay to the notifying parties and NCAs in the Member States.[394] The decision takes the form of a reasoned letter addressed to the notifying parties or their representatives.[395] The Commission is not required to publish its Phase I decisions, although it has adopted the practice of issuing a press release and publishing a short notice in the *Official Journal*. The confidential version of the decision requests that the parties inform the Commission of provisions which they regard as constituting business secrets.[396] Non-confidential versions of Article 6(1)(a) and (b) decisions including commitments where relevant are then made available on the DG Competition website, generally only in the original language of the proceedings in question.

Changes to transaction after Phase I clearance.   In some cases parties may **8.139** subsequently decide not to implement the concentration in the form that had been foreseen in their notification. In such situations, the parties need to establish whether the Commission's clearance decision still covers the revised deal structure. If the revised deal structure is fundamentally different, then it will be regarded as a different concentration and a new notification will be required.[397] However, less significant modifications to the transaction, (eg minor changes in

---

[392] See paras 8.091 *et seq,* above. See statistics in table (a) at para 8.011, above for details of the number of Art 9 (and other) referrals each year.

[393] This is without prejudice to the operation of Art 9 of the Merger Reg; see paras 8.091 *et seq,* above. In Case M.330 *McCormick/CPC/Rabobank/Ostmann* (29 October 1993), the Commission had intended to deal with the case itself, but this option was foreclosed as a result of an error in the calculation of the legal deadlines; however, as the possibility of referral under Art 9 remained open, the Commission referred the case to the German Bundeskartellamt.

[394] Merger Reg (n 356, above) Art 6(5).

[395] Decisions are generally transmitted by fax, the original being sent by ordinary post: see Implementing Reg (n 311, above) Art 21.

[396] See also Implementing Reg (n 311, above) Art 18(3). For further discussion of confidentiality, see paras 8.176–8.177, below.

[397] Jurisdictional Notice, paras 122–123. In Case M.2706 *Carnival Corporation/P&O Princess*, OJ 2003 L248/1 Carnival secured a Phase II clearance of its proposed bid for P&O Princess, being an 'acquisition of control' within the meaning of Merger Reg, Art 3(1)(b). However, it subsequently agreed with the envisaged target company to implement the transaction by way of a dual listed company structure, giving rise to a 'merger' within the meaning of Merger Reg, Art 3(1)(a): see para 8.021, above. The parties therefore had to renotify the revised transaction as a new concentration in Case M.3071 *Carnival Corporation/P&O Princess II* (10 February 2003).

the shareholding percentages which do not involve a change in the quality of control, or a change in the offer price in the case of a public bid) should generally not be treated as a new concentration.

8.140 **Revocation of Phase I decisions.** The Commission is entitled to revoke a decision that a concentration does not fall within the scope of the Merger Regulation or is compatible with the common market where the decision was based on incorrect information for which one of the undertakings was responsible or where it was obtained by deceit,[398] or where the undertakings concerned committed a breach of an obligation attached to the decision.[399] In the event of such a revocation decision, the Commission would then re-examine the concentration in a renewed Phase I proceeding.[400]

(c) In-depth Phase II investigation

(i) Phase II process

8.141 **Formal steps in the investigation.** Phase II proceedings impose significant burdens not only on the parties but also on the Commission and any interested third parties who may be involved in the process. In addition to ongoing information gathering, including site visits in many cases, Phase II proceedings generally involve a number of formal steps to guarantee due process, in particular:

(a) the issue of a written statement of objections by the Commission;
(b) formal access to the Commission's file;
(c) the parties' response to the statement of objections;
(d) the possibility of a formal oral hearing; and
(e) the possibility of 'state of play' meetings at certain points in the process.

8.142 **Duration of Phase II investigation.** After the initial Phase I period the Commission may decide that it has serious doubts about the compatibility of the notified concentration with the common market.[401] In such a case the Commission

---

[398] Merger Reg (n 356, above) Art 6(3)(a). In such a case the Commission is also likely to impose a fine: see further para 8.180, below. See Case M.1397 *Sanofi/Synthélabo*, where the Commission revoked its original unconditional clearance decision (15 March 1999) because of the parties' failure to disclose an area in which their respective subsidiaries were both involved; on re-notification with full disclosure, the Commission cleared the concentration with an undertaking to divest the relevant activities of Synthélabo (17 May 1999). The Commission also proceeded to impose the then maximum fine of €50,000 on both parties: Case M.1543, OJ 2000 L95/34.

[399] Merger Reg, Art 6(3)(b). Before taking such a revocation decision, the Commission must first give the undertakings concerned the opportunity to submit their observations in writing and at a hearing: Merger Reg, Art 18(1); Implementing Reg (n 311, above) Art 14(1).

[400] Merger Reg, Art 10(5), final sub-para: see para 8.256, below, for consequences.

[401] Such a decision under Art 6(1)(c) is the equivalent of an 'initiation of a procedure' under Arts 81 or 82 (see para 13.082, below). Under the UK City Code on Takeovers and Mergers, any

will launch a further in-depth investigation which must generally be completed within 90 working days following the date on which proceedings are initiated.[402] If the parties offer commitments aimed at addressing the Commission's concerns, this Phase II time period is automatically extended to 105 working days unless the parties have offered commitments within 55 working days from the start of Phase II. The Phase II timetable may also be extended by up to 20 working days in complex cases at the request of the parties if requested within 15 working days of the start of Phase II or, at any time, by the Commission with the consent of the parties; these formal 'stop the clock' provisions, which did not exist under the original Merger Regulation, are distinct from the Commission's powers to suspend the timetable using its powers under Article 11 of the Merger Regulation.[403] The Commission must adopt a decision as soon as it appears that the serious doubts referred to in its Article 6(1)(c) initiating Phase II proceedings have been removed.[404] However, even in cases where the parties may be able to address the Commission's concerns relatively quickly following the launch of Phase II proceedings, for example by offering commitments, the formalities which need to be conducted are such that they generally take at least three to four months.[405]

Suspension of Phase II time period. As with Phase I, the Phase II investigation period can be suspended if the Commission adopts a decision formally requesting that the parties provide further information pursuant to Article 11 of the Merger Regulation if they have failed to provide such information pursuant to an earlier request or if a third party fails to provide information requested of   **8.143**

---

public offer which is subject to the Code must include a term that it will lapse in the event that an Art 6(1)(c) decision is made before the first closing date or the date when the offer becomes or is declared unconditional as to acceptances, whichever is later (Rule 12). In addition (except in the case of a Rule 9 mandatory offer), the bidder can make the offer conditional on there not being an Art 6(1)(c) decision.

[402] Merger Reg, Art 10(3). The Phase II period is extended to take account of Commission holidays falling within the review period (as considered at para 8.133, above, in the case of Phase I). For further guidance on the calculation of time-limits, see Implementing Reg (n 311, above) Arts 7–10.

[403] See para 8.175, below.

[404] Merger Reg (n 356, above) Art 10(2).

[405] See, eg Case M.2972 *DSM/Roche Vitamins*, OJ 2004 L82/73, where the Phase II proceedings lasted less than 10 weeks, the parties having offered appropriate commitments addressing the Commission's concerns early in the process; Case M.3975 *Cargill/Degussa Food Ingredients* (29 March 2006) where the proceedings lasted only 15 weeks, as the Commission concluded that its serious doubts were unfounded without the need to issue a statement of objections. cf Case M.3216 *Oracle/PeopleSoft*, OJ 2005 L218/6, where the Phase II proceedings which took 11 months (the longest lasting Phase II procedure to date); and Case M.3796 *Omya/JM Huber* (19 July 2006) where the Phase II proceedings took more than nine months.

it owing to circumstances for which one of the parties is responsible.[406] It could also be suspended if the Commission were to adopt a formal decision ordering an investigation pursuant to Article 13 of the Merger Regulation, following the refusal of the parties to submit to or cooperate in such an investigation. [407] The period can be suspended if the parties fail to inform the Commission of material changes to the facts specified in the notification.[408] Any such suspension of time should continue until such time as complete and correct information is supplied.[409]

8.144 **Rights of defence generally.** Before it takes any final adverse Phase II decision under Article 8 of the Merger Regulation, other than a clearance decision with no conditions or obligations attached, the Commission must give the parties concerned the opportunity to make known their views on the Commission's objections to the transaction.[410] Article 18(3) of the Merger Regulation expressly stipulates that the Commission must fully respect the rights of the defence. The decision may only be based on objections that were submitted to the parties for their observations, and there shall be access to the file at least to the parties directly involved.[411]

8.145 **Statement of objections.** A statement of objections sets out in detail the reasons why the Commission has serious doubts as to the compatibility of the notified transaction with the common market. The Commission must inform the notifying parties of its objections in writing and specify a time limit within which the parties concerned may reply.[412] Typically, a statement of objections is issued about eight to ten weeks after the start of the Phase II investigation. This normally builds

---

[406] Merger Reg (n 356, above) Art 10(4); Implementing Reg (n 311, above) Art 9(1)(a) and (b). There have been several instances of the Commission 'stopping the clock' in this way at Phase II; for an extreme example, see *Oracle/PeopleSoft*, above, where the clock was stopped twice (first for five weeks and then for 24 weeks). In accordance with Art 9(2) of the Implementing Reg, the Commission could issue such a decision without first issuing a simple request for information owing to circumstances for which one of the undertakings involved is responsible.

[407] Implementing Reg, Reg 802/2004, OJ 2004 L133/1: Vol II, App D.2, Art 9(1)(c). See also para 8.175, below.

[408] ibid, Art 9(1)(d).

[409] ibid, Art 9(3)–(4).

[410] Merger Reg (n 356, above) Art 18(1). A decision to grant a derogation from suspension under Art 7(4) (see para 8.129, above) may be taken without the parties having a prior opportunity to comment, provided that they are given such an opportunity as soon as possible afterwards: Art 18(2).

[411] Recital (36) to the Merger Reg provides that it should be interpreted and applied with respect to the fundamental rights and principles recognised in particular by the EU Charter of Fundamental Rights, Art 41 of which states that every citizen has the 'right to have his or her affairs handled impartially, fairly and within a reasonable time by the institutions and bodies of the Union', including 'the right of every person to be heard, before any individual measure which would affect him or her adversely is taken'. For the Charter, see para 1.010 above.

[412] Implementing Reg (n 407, above) Art 13(2). The Commission must also inform in writing other involved parties of these objections and set a time limit within which they may reply.

upon the line of reasoning set out in the Article 6(1)(c) decision, following the Commission's further investigation of all elements pertaining to the case.[413] However, this time frame depends on the scope and depth of the Commission's investigation in each case.

Access to file. There is no formal right of access to the Commission's file unless **8.146** and until the Commission issues a statement of objections.[414] The Commission nevertheless generally aims to give the notifying parties access to non-confidential versions of 'key documents' on its file, notably market studies and third party substantiated submissions running counter to the parties' own contentions, at an earlier stage in the Phase II proceedings.[415] Once they have received the statement of objections, the notifying parties have a formal right of access to the Commission's file for the purpose of preparing their reply as part of their rights of defence.[416] The notifying parties will also be given the opportunity to have access to documents received after the issuing of the statement of objections up until the consultation of the Advisory Committee.[417] The Commission's file will consist of documents including electronic data obtained, produced or assembled by DG Competition during its investigation.[418] However, the right of access to the file does not extend to: (i) documents which contain business secrets of other involved parties (such as the vendor or the target company) or of third parties; (ii) other confidential information the disclosure of which would have a significant adverse effect on the supplier of such information; or (iii) internal documents of the Commission or other authorities, including comments received by the Commission from NCAs.[419] The Commission may therefore need to reconcile opposing interests by preparing non-confidential versions of documents containing business

---

[413] In a significant minority of cases the Commission will decide not to issue a statement of objections. These include cases where the parties have accepted the competition concerns identified by the Commission and offered sufficient remedies early in the Phase II process, as well as cases where upon further investigation the Commission has concluded that the concentration can be approved without conditions.

[414] Access to File Notice, OJ 2005 C325/7: Vol II, App B.12, para 26.

[415] Best Practice Guidelines (n 388, above) paras 45–46; Access to File Notice, above, para 28.

[416] Merger Reg, Art 18(3) and Implementing Reg (n 407, above) Art 17(1); Access to File Notice (n 414, above) para 27. See Case T-221/95 *Endemol Entertainment v Commission* [1999] ECR II–1299, [1999] 5 CMLR 611, [1999] All ER (EC) 385, para 65.

[417] See Access to File Notice, para 28 and Best Practice Guidelines (n 388, above) para 43. Access should be given to all evidence favourable to the notifying parties, which could be used is the defence; however, adverse evidence is relevant only insofar as the Commission itself relies on it, in which case it must be made available, but if the evidence is not so relied on, the fact that it is not made available has no effect on the lawfulness of the procedure: Case T-210/01 *General Electric v Commission* [2005] ECR II-5575, [2006] 4 CMLR 686, para 649.

[418] Access to File Notice (n 414, above) para 8.

[419] Implementing Reg (n 407, above) Recital (16) and Art 17(3); Access to File Notice (n 414, above) para 10. See also, *General Electric v Commission* (n 417, above) para 630.

secrets or other sensitive information.[420] Article 18(3) of the Merger Regulation provides for access to the file to be granted at least to the parties directly involved. Other involved parties, such as the vendor or a target company, have a right of access to the file insofar as this is necessary for the purposes of preparing their observations.[421] Member States are also given access to the Commission file.[422] There is no express provision for third parties to be given access to the file.[423] The procedures for dealing with requests for access to the file are addressed in the Access to File Notice which states that the Commission will provide the notifying parties with an enumerative list of documents setting out the content of the Commission file.[424] In practice, this list identifies each document on the file as accessible, partially accessible or non-accessible. In cases involving complex economic issues and empirical analyses, the Commission has also been prepared to allow the notifying parties' economic advisors to review third party pricing and other data on the Commission's premises, subject to strict confidentiality assurances and undertakings.[425] Documents obtained through access to the file may only be used for the purpose of the relevant Merger Regulation proceeding.[426]

8.147 **Reply to statement of objections.** The notifying parties must make known their views on the statement of objections in writing within the time fixed by the Commission.[427] This response is a critical step in the administrative procedure, as

---

[420] See *Endemol Entertainment v Commission* (n 416, above); and *General Electric v Commission*, above, paras 631 and 653 *et seq.* For the requirement to protect business secrets, see also the Best Practice Guidelines (n 388, above) para 47; Case 53/85 *Akzo Chemie v Commission* [1986] ECR 1965, [1987] 1 CMLR 231, para 28; Case T-353/94 *Postbank v Commission*, [1996] ECR II-921, [1997] 4 CMLR 33, [1996] All ER (EC) 817, para 87.

[421] Implementing Reg (n 407, above) Art 17(2); Access to File Notice (n 414, above) para 33. Art 11 of the Implementing Reg draws a basic distinction between 'other involved parties' and 'third persons' (eg customers, suppliers, competitors and recognised representatives of employees).

[422] Merger Reg (n 356, above) Art 19(2).

[423] See *CCE de la Société Générale des Grandes Sources v Commission* (n 368, above) para 64; the CFI expressly did not consider it necessary to rule on whether, and under what conditions, third parties showing a sufficient interest to be heard may have the right of access to the file, since the applicants had not, even implicitly, requested such access at the time. The Commission may, in the interest of the investigation in appropriate cases, also provide third parties showing a sufficient interest with a redacted version of the statement of objections, in order to allow them to make their views known on the Commission's preliminary assessment: see paras 8.131–8.132, above and Best Practice Guidelines (n 388, above) para 36.

[424] Access to File Notice (n 414, above) paras 44 *et seq.*

[425] See eg Case M.3083 *GE/Instrumentarium*, OJ 2004 L109/1. See also Loriot, Rouxel and Durand, 'GE/Instrumentarium: a practical example of the use of quantitative analyses in merger control' (2004) 1 EC Competition Policy Newsletter 61.

[426] Implementing Reg (n 407, above) Art 17(4).

[427] ibid, Art 13(2) and (3). The parties' response should comprise one original and at least 10 copies and an electronic copy should also be submitted in a format specified by the Commission. The Commission must forward copies of the response without delay to the NCAs. Where particular NCAs are showing a close interest in their case, the parties may already be in contact with them and may brief them and directly supply them with a copy of the response so they are familiar with its contents ahead of the oral hearing.

it enables the parties to rebut the competition concerns raised by the Commission, by setting out in detail all matters relevant to the case and by attaching any relevant supporting documents.[428] The parties may also propose that the Commission hear persons who may corroborate the facts set out in their written replies. The parties will usually be given only a short period in which to submit their formal reply.[429] When assessing alleged infringements of the rights of defence because of the time limits set for the response to the statement of objections, the Community Courts have consistently held that it is necessary to take account of the need for speed which characterises the general scheme of the Merger Regulation.[430] The Commission is not obliged to take into account comments received after the expiry of the time limit set for the reply.[431] The Commission may issue a supplemental statement of objections, although this is rare in Merger Regulation cases.[432]

Oral hearing. The notifying parties may request in their written reply an opportunity to put their views to the Commission at a hearing.[433] Other involved parties such as the vendor or target, who apply in writing to the Commission, have a right **8.148**

---

[428] On the basis of the parties' replies, the Commission has in the past been prepared to abandon the objections in the statement of objections: see, eg Final Report of the Hearing Officer in Case M.3333 *Sony/BMG* OJ 2005 L62/30 (decn annulled on appeal Case T-464/04 *Impala v Commission* [2006] ECR II-2289, [2006] 5 CMLR 1049, on further appeal to the ECJ: Case C-413/06 *Bertelsmann and Sony Corp/Impala,* not yet decided). The CFI's judgment in *Impala* indicates that in cases where the Commission issues a statement of objections but subsequently adopts an unconditional clearance decision, such a 'fundamental U-turn' (para 283) may require the Commission to put forward new evidence that is 'particularly reliable, objective, relevant and cogent' (para 414) and to seek the views of third parties late in the Phase II process. The judgment suggests that failure to conduct such an additional investigation would amount to delegating 'without supervision, responsibility for conducting certain parts of the investigation to the parties to the concentration' (para 415). For an example of a case where the Commission did undertake such a subsequent verification with third parties, see Case M.4094 *Ineos/BP Dormagen* (10 August 2006) para 4.

[429] In fixing the date for the reply, the Commission must have regard to the time required for preparing statements and to the urgency of the case; it should also take account of public holidays in the country of receipt: Implementing Reg (n 407, above) Art 22. The parties concerned may be given more time to reply to the statement of objections, particularly where information pertaining to the target is not readily accessible in the context of a hostile bid: see Case M.2706 *Carnival Corporation/ P&O Princess,* OJ 2003 L248/1, Final Report of the Hearing Officer, OJ 2003 L248/1.

[430] *General Electric v Commission* (n 417, above) para 701; *Endemol Entertainment v Commission* (n 416, above) para 68; *Kaysersberg v Commission* (n 369, above) para 84.

[431] Implementing Reg (n 407, above) Art 13(2).

[432] But see, eg *Tetra Laval/Sidel* (n 356, above) Final Report of the Hearing Officer: supplemental statement of objections issued after the oral hearing; Case M.2547 *Bayer/Aventis Crop Science,* OJ 2004 L107/1, Final Report of the Hearing Officer: short supplemental statement of objections issued, although no oral hearing held; Case M.2876 *NewsCorp/Telepiu,* OJ 2004 L110/73, [2004] 5 CMLR 1619, Final Report of the Hearing Officer: statement of objections was issued in two documents (the second one week after the first) with one deadline (of two weeks after the supplemental documents) to reply to both.

[433] Merger Reg, Art 18(1); Implementing Reg, Art 14(1). It is not uncommon for the parties to waive this right, particularly if they decide to resolve the Commission's concerns by offering commitments (see paras 8.162 *et seq,* below).

to be heard if they demonstrate a sufficient interest.[434] Representatives of the NCAs are also invited to attend.[435] Where appropriate, the Commission may also afford third parties who have formally applied in writing to be heard, and have so requested in their written comments, the opportunity to participate at a hearing.[436] Thus several undertakings may be represented at the same hearing, in which event the Commission will have regard to the parties' business secrets and the Hearing Officer who conducts the hearing may exclude persons from parts of the hearing.[437] The Hearing Officer may also hold a preparatory meeting with the parties and the Commission's services, so as to facilitate the efficient organisation of the hearing.[438] The oral hearing normally takes place within two weeks of the date fixed for the parties' written response to the statement of objections and generally lasts one or two days. The Hearing Officer may allow all parties, the Commission services[439] and the competent authorities of the Member States to ask questions during the oral hearing.[440] The oral hearing is not public.[441]

8.149 **State of play meetings and triangular meetings.** There is also the possibility of voluntary 'state of play' meetings in addition to less formal contacts between the parties and Commission staff at certain points in the process. The Commission's Best Practice Guidelines provide for such meetings at the following stages:[442]

(a) within a couple of weeks of the opening of Phase II proceedings (to facilitate the parties' understanding of the Commission's concerns and the Commission's

---

[434] Implementing Reg (n 407, above) Arts 14(2); see also paras 8.112 and 8.131, above.

[435] ibid, Art 15(3). See also para 8.154, below.

[436] Merger Reg, Art 18(4); Implementing Reg (n 407, above) Art 16(2). The Commission may also hear other persons should it consider this necessary: Implementing Reg, Art 16(3). Based on current practice, third parties are not entitled to an oral hearing in their own right where the notifying parties do not exercise their right to be heard orally: see, eg Case M.2706 *Carnival Corporation/ P&O Princess*, OJ 2003 L248/1, Final Report of the Hearing Officer.

[437] Merger Reg, Reg 139/2004, OJ 2004 L24/1: Vol II, App D.1 Art 18; Implementing Reg (n 407, above) Art 15(6). For the role of the Hearing Officer, see further para 8.150, below; for business secrets, see para 8.176, below.

[438] Implementing Reg (n 407, above) Art 15(7).

[439] In addition to DG Comp, the Commission's Legal Service and other interested Directorates General typically also attend the oral hearing.

[440] Implementing Reg (n 407, above) Art 15(7). The EFTA Surveillance Authority and the competent authorities of the EFTA States may also attend where the case qualifies as a 'mixed' case under Art 2 of Protocol 24 to the EEA Agreement: see para 8.281, below.

[441] Implementing Reg (n 407, above) Art 15(6). Furthermore, it is not necessary for the Commission to draw up minutes of the hearing: *Endemol Entertainment v Commission* (n 416, above) para 94. However, the hearing is recorded and, upon request, the recording is made available to the participants, subject to confidentiality arrangements: Implementing Reg, Art 15(8).

[442] Best Practice Guidelines DG Comp Best Practices on the conduct of EC merger proceedings, available at DG Comp's website and see Vol II, App D.7, para 33. The notifying parties also have the opportunity of such a state of play meeting during the course of Phase I if the case looks likely to raise 'serious doubts' (so that the parties have the opportunity to table Phase I commitments before the expiry of the 20 working days deadline). State of play meetings are generally chaired by the Director of the relevant Directorate within DG Competition or by the Deputy Director with responsibility for mergers.

understanding of the parties' reactions, as well as to discuss the likely time frame for the Phase II proceedings);

(b) shortly in advance of the statement of objections (to help clarify certain issues and facts);

(c) following the reply to the statement of objections and the hearing (to serve as a basis for discussing the scope and timing of any remedial commitments); and

(d) in advance of the Advisory Committee meeting (to discuss the market-testing of any Phase II commitments tabled by the parties and possible final improvements).

In addition to these bilateral meetings between the parties and the DG Competition staff, the Best Practice Guidelines also envisage the possibility of 'triangular meetings' where the views of the notifying parties and opposing third parties can be heard in a single forum, generally in advance of any statement of objections.[443]

(ii) Additional Commission checks and balances

Hearing Officer. The role of the Hearing Officer is to ensure that the proce- **8.150** dural rights of the parties are respected in competition law proceedings.[444] A Hearing Officer will be allocated to a merger case before the statement of objections is sent to the parties and in some cases much earlier in the administrative proceeding should procedural issues arise. In order to emphasise the Hearing Officers' independence from the rest of DG Competition, for administrative purposes they are directly attached to the Competition Commissioner.[445] The Hearing Officers' role extends beyond organising and chairing oral hearings. They ensure that the rights of defence are respected, ruling on whether documents contain business secrets or other confidential information and on procedural issues such as access to material on the Commission's file, time limits for replying to the statement of objections, and the objectivity of any investigations assessing the impact of proposed commitments.[446] Where third parties have stated in writing that they wish to be heard or have access to documents on the Commission file, the Hearing Officer rules on the question and informs them of any reasons for

---

[443] ibid, paras 38–39.

[444] There is a dedicated section on the DG Comp website dealing with the mission and role of the Hearing Officers.

[445] Currently, there are two Hearing Officers each of whom performs these functions for Merger Reg cases (as well as for Arts 81 and 82 proceedings).

[446] See Hearing Officers' Terms of Reference, OJ 2001 L162/21: Vol II, App B.2, Arts 1, 3, 4, 5, 11 and 12; Best Practice Guidelines (n 442, above) para 49; also Access to File Notice, (n 414, above) in particular para 42 (on disagreements on confidentiality claims) and para 47 (on disagreements on the classification of documents on the Commission's file as 'non-accessible'). See also Durande and Williams, 'The practical impact of the exercise of the right to be heard: a special focus on the effect of Oral Hearings and the role of Hearing Officer' (2005) 2 EC Competition Policy Newsletter 22.

finding that an applicant has an insufficient interest.[447] The Hearing Officer also prepares a final written report on the proceedings, which is attached to the draft decision submitted to the Advisory Committee and then to the College of Commissioners and also to the final decision addressed to the notifying parties.[448]

8.151 **Peer review panel.** In most Phase II cases, under a procedure introduced in 2004, DG Competition establishes a peer review panel comprising three or so Commission officials. These officials are given access to the file and scrutinise the draft statement of objections prepared by their colleagues, acting as a 'fresh pair of eyes', with a view to improving the quality of the statement of objections and the prospect of the final Phase II decision withstanding challenge before the Community Courts. These are internal checks within the Commission, intended to improve the quality of the Commission's investigation and decision-making process; accordingly, the parties are not entitled to any formal meetings, consultation or other access rights to the peer review panel.

8.152 **Chief Economist.** The Chief Economist's team within DG Competition is consulted on economic related matters and provides input on selected Merger Regulation cases.[449] Typically, this involves the analysis of complex economic data, as well as the methodology and economic theory underpinning the Commission's assessment.

8.153 **Commission's Legal Service and other Directorates General.** The Commission Legal Service and officials from other interested Directorates General are given the opportunity to review and provide comments on drafts of the statement of objections and the final decision.[450] DG Competition is therefore expected to send a draft to the Legal Service and other interested DGs in good time before sending it to the Commissioner for formal adoption; as a general rule, and if there are no exceptional circumstances necessitating a shorter period, two to three

---

[447] Hearing Officers' Terms of Reference, above, Arts 6–8.

[448] ibid, Art 16. Arts 13–16 further stipulate that the observations in the report shall specifically concern procedural issues, including disclosure of documents and access to the file, time limits for replying to the statement of objections, the proper conduct of the oral hearing, the objectivity of any inquiry into commitments and whether the draft decision only deals with objections in respect of which the parties have been afforded the opportunity to respond. The report is published in the OJ together with the final Phase II decision.

[449] See para 1.053, above. The Chief Economist's team is involved in a number individual merger cases and makes significant contributions to guidelines and policy issues.

[450] Inter-service consultation operates in accordance with the Commission's empowerment procedures and Rules of Procedure, OJ 2000 L308/26. In particular DG Enterprise and Industry and DG Financial Affairs tend to follow Phase II cases. Given the central overseeing role of the Commission's Legal Service on legal matters, its views can play a significant role in the overall shaping and direction of the final decision. According to the Commission's empowerment procedures and Rules of Procedure (Art 21), the Legal Service must be consulted on the text of all documents which may have legal implications and its prior approval is required for all draft decisions.

working days is considered sufficient.[451] These are again internal checks within the Commission, so the parties do not have any formal access or consultation rights.

(iii) Role of Member States

Liaison with the NCAs. The Members States are given the opportunity to make   **8.154** their views known at every stage of the proceedings. The Commission sends the NCAs copies of all notifications and of the most important documents lodged with or issued by the Commission, including any commitments offered by the notifying parties with a view to obtaining clearance.[452] The NCAs are given access to the Commission file for the purpose of exercising their right to request a referral pursuant to Article 9 of the Merger Regulation,[453] and are also invited to attend the formal oral hearing.[454]

Advisory Committee. Before the Commission adopts a final Phase II decision,   **8.155** it must consult the Advisory Committee on concentrations[455] which consists of representatives of the NCAs of the Member States.[456] The Committee's recommendations are not binding, but the Commission must take the utmost account of its opinion.[457] The consultation takes place at a joint meeting at the invitation of and chaired by the Commission. The invitation (accompanied by a summary of the case, an indication of the most important documents and a preliminary draft of the decision) should in principle be sent to the NCAs at least 10 working days before the meeting.[458] The opinion of the Advisory Committee (which may be delivered even if some members are absent and unrepresented) is made known to the notifying parties only with the final decision.

(iv) Possible outcomes at Phase II

Decisions following a Phase II investigation. Following Phase II proceedings,   **8.156** the Commission will generally issue a fully reasoned decision. If the Commission were to fail to issue a final decision within the period prescribed for the Phase II

---

[451] See Memorandum accompanying Commission Decn of 28 April 2004, SEC(2004)518, PV(2004)1655, paras 63–72.

[452] Merger Reg (n 437, above) Art 19(1).

[453] Merger Reg, Art 19(2).

[454] Implementing Reg (n 407, above) Art 15(3).

[455] Merger Reg, Art 19(3). In 'mixed' cases under Art 2 of Protocol 24 to the EEA Agreement, the EFTA Surveillance Authority and the EFTA States are entitled to be present at such Advisory Committee meetings and to express their views: see Art 5(3) of Protocol 24.

[456] Merger Reg (n 437, above) Art 19(4).

[457] ibid, Art 19(6).

[458] ibid, Art 19(5). Exceptionally, the notice period may be shortened in order to avoid serious harm to one or more of the undertakings concerned.

investigation, the concentration would be deemed to have been cleared.[459] The decision is adopted by the full College of Commissioners and will be one of the following:

(a) *Unconditional clearance decision:* a clearance decision pursuant to Article 8(1) of the Merger Regulation declares the concentration compatible with the common market;

(b) *Conditional clearance decision:* where a clearance decision is issued pursuant to Article 8(2), it may attach conditions and obligations intended to ensure that the undertakings concerned comply with the commitments they have entered into vis-à-vis the Commission. Conditions or obligations may require structural changes such as divestment of businesses where there is competitive overlap, or impose behavioural obligations on the parties' future business conduct or relations with competitors or customers;[460] or

(c) *Prohibition decision:* a prohibition decision pursuant to Article 8(3) declares the concentration incompatible with the common market.[461] The Commission may also adopt a decision pursuant to Article 8(4) requiring divestments or other remedies if the parties have already implemented a concentration that is prohibited.[462]

8.157 **Abandonment at Phase II.** If it becomes clear to the parties that the Commission is unlikely to grant approval on acceptable terms, the parties may abandon the transaction during the course of the Phase II proceedings, thereby avoiding a final Phase II decision.[463] The Commission will nonetheless conclude its Phase II proceedings and issue a formal decision, unless the undertakings concerned have demonstrated to the satisfaction of the Commission that they have abandoned the concentration, usually by formally terminating the notified concentration agreement.[464]

---

[459] ibid, Art 10(6). In practice this deemed clearance procedure has not been triggered, see also para 8.137, above.

[460] See paras 8.162 *et seq*, below. When a concentration is cleared subject to divestment or other conditions, the Commission publishes a non-confidential version of the parties' commitments (or at least their salient facts) with its decision.

[461] In the period to end 2006, only 19 prohibition decisions had been adopted: see table (c) at para 8.011, above.

[462] See para 8.160, below. Where such implementation was not permitted, the Commission may also impose fines: Merger Reg (n 437, above) Art 14(2)(c).

[463] For statistics on cases where the transaction has been abandoned at Phase II and the notification withdrawn, see table (c) at para 8.011, above.

[464] Merger Reg, Art 6(1)(c). See also Jurisdictional Notice, paras 117–121 (replacing DG Comp Information Note on abandonment of concentrations issued in 2005). The wording in the last sentence of Art 6(1)(c) was introduced in 2004 because of concerns that the original Merger Reg did not permit the Commission to adopt a Phase II decision if the parties had withdrawn their notification during the course of the Phase II proceedings even if it was not certain whether the transaction had been abandoned: see Case T-310/00 *MCI v Commission* [2004] ECR II-3253, [2004]

Communication and publication of Phase II decisions. The Commission **8.158** must notify its Phase II decision without delay to the undertakings concerned and the NCAs of the Member States.[465] The decision is addressed to the undertakings concerned or their representatives.[466] In practice, the Commission also issues a press release. Final decisions under Article 8(2) to (5) are published in the *Official Journal*, having regard to the legitimate interest of undertakings in the protection of their business secrets.[467] The confidential version of the decision requests the parties to inform the Commission of provisions which the parties regard as constituting business secrets.[468]

Changes to transaction after Phase II clearance. As with a Phase I clearance **8.159** decision, the parties would not be able to rely on a Phase II clearance if they were subsequently to decide to implement the concentration in a fundamentally different form.[469]

Dissolution of prohibited concentrations and other restorative measures. **8.160** Article 8(4) of the Merger Regulation provides that where a concentration has already been implemented and has been declared incompatible with the common market or has been implemented in contravention of an attached condition, the Commission may take any appropriate restorative measures, including dissolution of the merger or the disposal of all shares acquired.[470] The Court of First Instance has observed that the separation of the undertakings involved is the logical consequence of the decision declaring the concentration incompatible

---

5 CMLR 1274. In Case M.3445 *Microsoft/Time Warner/Contentguard* (withdrawn on 9 March 2005) the Commission terminated its Phase II investigation following the restructuring of the deal, after being satisfied that Microsoft would no longer be able to determine Contentguard's licensing policy.

[465] Merger Reg, Art 8(8).

[466] As permitted by Art 21 of the Implementing Reg (n 407, above) decisions are generally transmitted by fax, the original being sent by ordinary post.

[467] Merger Reg, Art 20(1). Nowadays, the Commission only publishes a summary of the decision in the OJ, although a non-confidential version of the full decision is made available on DG Comp's website.

[468] For confidentiality, see paras 8.176–8.177, below. Negotiations with the parties as to what constitutes a business secret sometimes give rise to considerable delay in the publication of the non-confidential version of decisions.

[469] See observations at para 8.139, above.

[470] At the time of writing, the following Art 8(4) decisions had been issued: Case M.784 *Kesko/Tuko*, OJ 1997 L110/53; Case M.890 *Blokker/Toys R Us (II)*, OJ 1998 L316/1; Case M.2416 *Tetra Laval/Sidel*, OJ 2004 L38/1, annulled on appeal, Case T-80/02 *Tetra Laval v Commission (II)* [2002] ECR II-4519, [2002] 5 CMLR 1271 (no ruling on further appeal Case C-13/03P [2005] ECR I-1113); Case M.2283 *Schneider/Legrand* (30 January 2002), annulled on appeal Case T-77/02 *Schneider Electric v Commission (II)* [2002] ECR II-4201. The Commission may also take interim measures to restore or maintain conditions of effective competition pursuant to Art 8(5)(c) of the Merger Reg. See further Fountoukakos, 'Unscrambling the eggs: dissolution orders under Article 8(4) of the Merger Regulation' (2004) 1 EC Competition Policy Newsletter 63.

with the common market.[471] If the the parties do not comply with the Commission's decision under Article 8(4), they are subject to fines.[472]

8.161 **Revocation of Phase II clearance decision.** As with a Phase I clearance decision,[473] the Commission may revoke an Article 8(2) clearance decision if it is based on incorrect information for which one of the undertakings is responsible or where the clearance has been obtained by deceit or where the undertakings concerned commit a breach of an obligation attached to the clearance decision.[474] Where a clearance decision is revoked, the Commission may take a decision prohibiting the concentration without being bound by the usual time limits of Article 10(3).[475] Accordingly, the Commission could re-examine the concentration in renewed Phase II proceedings.[476]

(d) Commitments to enable clearance

(i) Commitments at Phase I or Phase II

8.162 **In general.** Where a proposed concentration gives rise to serious competition concerns, the parties may be able to avoid an adverse decision by offering the Commission remedies that would remove those concerns. In most cases it is not feasible for those remedies to be implemented prior to the Commission's decision, so procedures exist under which the Commission will accept the parties' commitments to implement the remedies; those commitments are then attached to the Commission's Phase I or Phase II clearance decision as conditions or obligations.[477] In such cases, a non-confidential version of the commitments is published together with the decision. Commitments have become increasingly important as the basis on which a large number of concentrations are approved by the Commission.[478] Responsibility for formulating and offering proposed

---

[471] *Tetra Laval v Commission,* above, para 36.
[472] Merger Reg (n 437, above) Art 14(2)(c). cf para 8.130, above.
[473] See para 8.140, above.
[474] Merger Reg, Art 8(6)(a). Before taking such a revocation decision, the Commission must give the undertakings concerned the opportunity to submit their observations in writing and at a hearing and must consult the Advisory Committee: ibid, Arts 18(1) and 19(3); Implementing Reg (n 407, above) Art 14(1).
[475] Merger Reg (n 437, above) Art 8(7).
[476] ibid, Art 10(5), final sub-para; for consequences, see para 8.256, below.
[477] See Remedies Notice, OJ 2001 C68/3: Vol II, App D.4, para 12. The term 'conditions' refers to commitments to achieve measures that result in a change of the market, thereby addressing competition concerns raised by the Commission in the course of its investigation, eg the divestiture of a business. The term 'obligations' comprises the implementing steps which are necessary to achieve such conditions, eg the appointment of a trustee with an irrevocable mandate to sell the business to be divested. The distinction is further explained in the 2007 draft Remedies Notice, discussed below, paras 19–20.
[478] For statistics, see tables at para 8.011, above: some 5 per cent of notifications are concluded with Phase I commitments, and most Phase II proceedings conclude with Phase II commitments.

commitments is exclusively a matter for the parties. In December 2000, the Commission adopted a Notice on remedies acceptable under the Merger Regulation (the 'Remedies Notice'). The Commission has published a revised draft Remedies Notice to reflect the adoption of Regulation 139/2004 and the developments in the Commission's practice since 2001. The draft revised Notice sets out what the Commission already requires of the parties in practice so that reference should be made to both the 2001 Notice and the proposed revised Notice.[479] The Commission has also published standard model texts for divestiture commitments and trustee mandates, designed to serve as best practice guidelines for notifying parties submitting commitments under the Merger Regulation.[480]

Phase I commitments. Where the Commission finds that, following modifica- **8.163** tion by the undertakings concerned, a notified concentration no longer raises serious doubts about its compatibility with the common market, it may attach to its clearance decision conditions and obligations intended to ensure that the undertakings concerned comply with the commitments they have entered into vis-à-vis the Commission.[481] The proposed remedies at Phase I must be sufficiently clear to rule out serious doubts about the concentration.[482] Phase I

---

[479] Remedies Notice (n 477, above) and see speech by Commissioner Monti, 'The Commission notice on merger remedies – one year after', 18 January 2002 (on the DG Comp website). The Commission has also published a study on the design and effective implementation of commitments, on the basis of a representative number of remedies accepted by the Commission in the five-year period 1996–2000: European Commission 'Merger Remedies Study', 21 October 2005 (available on DG Comp's website). For the draft revised Remedies Notice see Press Release IP/07/544 (27 April 2007) and Vol II, App D.15. Some of the proposed amendments, such as a new information form, Form RM, to be submitted by the parties to describe their remedies proposals, will also require an amendment of the Implementing Reg 802/2004. The Commission encourages parties to use the new form in anticipation of its adoption of the revised Remedies Notice later in 2007. For the proposed revisions to the Implementing Regulation including the new Form RM see Vol II, App D.3.

[480] The Best Practice Guidelines on divestiture commitments, including the standard model texts for divestiture commitments and trustee mandates are at Vol II, App D.5 and are also available on DG Comp's website. The model texts are based on the experience the Commission has gained in fashioning remedies and are drafted in line with the policy guidelines set out in the Commission's Remedies Notice. The Best Practice Guidelines on divestiture commitments specify (at para 3) that provisions contained in the standard texts can be used in cases involving commitments other than divestiture commitments.

[481] Merger Reg (n 437, above) Art 6(2).

[482] ibid, Recital (30); and see Remedies Notice (n 477, above) para 11 and at n 11: 'the competition problem needs to be so straightforward and remedies so clear cut that it is not necessary to enter into an in-depth investigation'. Phase I commitments tend to provide for divestment of overlapping businesses, for the removal of structural links between the parties or with third parties or of vertical links likely to obstruct entry or expansion into the market. But even complex remedies may be accepted during Phase I: see Case T-114/02 *BaByliss v Commission* [2003] ECR II-1279, [2004] 5 CMLR 21, paras 176–178; the CFI dismissed a challenge to the Commission's acceptance of commitments (including grant of a trade mark licence), holding that the the proposed remedy had been market tested to a sufficient degree. See also Case M.3680 *Alcatel/Finmeccanica/Alcatel Alenia Space & Telespazio* (28 April 2005). See also the draft revised Remedies Notice (n 479, above) paras 18 and 76–84.

commitments must be submitted by the parties within 20 working days from the date of notification.[483] Where the parties submit formal commitments, the time limit for the Phase I investigation is extended from 25 working days to 35 working days.[484] This gives the Commission time to consult the NCAs on the proposed commitments and, where appropriate, to 'market test' them with interested third parties.[485]

8.164 **Phase II commitments.** Article 8(2) of the Merger Regulation provides for clearance of a concentration at Phase II subject to conditions or obligations. The Commission must adopt a decision as soon as it appears that the serious doubts referred to in its decision to initiate Phase II proceedings have been removed.[486] Commitments must be submitted within not more than 65 working days from the day on which the Phase II proceedings were initiated.[487] If the parties offer commitments, the time limit for the Phase II investigation is automatically

---

[483] Implementing Reg (n 407, above) Art 19(1). Para 37 of the Remedies Notice (n 477, above) further specifies that where the commitments offered are not deemed sufficient to remove competition concerns, only limited modifications can be accepted after the deadline. In practice, however, the Commission has some flexibility in accepting clarifications, refinements and other improvements: see, eg Case M.2050 *Vivendi/Canal+/Seagram* (13 October 2000) where structural undertakings were finally offered in lieu of the original (essentially) behavioural undertakings. In *Babyliss v Commission*, above, the CFI held that although the parties to a concentration cannot oblige the Commission to take account of commitments and modifications to them after the prescribed time limit, the Commission may nevertheless (where it considers that it has the time necessary to examine them) authorise the concentration in light of those commitments. In accordance with the Remedies Notice, such modifications should be limited, and aimed at improving or refining the initial version of the commitments. Similarly, see Case T-119/02 *Royal Philips Electronics v Commission* [2003] ECR II-1433, [2003] 5 CMLR 53, paras 226–250.

[484] Merger Reg, Art 10(1): see para 8.133, above. One original and 10 copies (together with an electronic copy) of the proposed commitments should be submitted: Implementing Reg (n 407, above) Art 20(1). At the time of writing, proposed revisions to the Implementing Reg (n 407, above) providing for the submission of information in accordance with the new Form RM (n 479, above) have yet to be adopted.

[485] Remedies Notice (n 477, above) paras 34–35 and n 40. Depending on the scope of the proposed remedies, consultation may extend to the competent authorities of the EEA and even non-EEA competition authorities (in the framework of the Community's bilateral cooperation agreements with other countries). In theory, where proposed undertakings are not acceptable the parties may avoid a Phase II investigation by withdrawing their notification and re-notifying the transaction with modified commitments; however, in accordance with Art 6(1)(c) of the Merger Reg, the notifying parties would need to demonstrate that they have abandoned the original concentration.

[486] Merger Reg (n 437, above) Art 10(2). See, eg *DSM/Roche Vitamins* (n 405, above). Before the College of Commissioners can adopt the final decision, however, certain formalities need to be followed, including obtaining the opinion of the Advisory Committee (see para 8.155, above).

[487] Implementing Reg (n 407, above) Art 19(2). If the Phase II period has been extended on the basis of an Art 10(3) request, the deadline for submitting Phase II commitments is similarly extended by the same number of working days: Merger Reg, Art 10(3). One original and 10 copies (together with an electronic copy) should be submitted: Implementing Reg, Art 20(1). At the time of writing, the revisions to the Implementing Reg providing for the submission of information responsive to Form RM (n 479, above) have yet to be adopted.

extended from 90 working days to 105 working days, unless the notifying parties have already tabled commitments less than 55 working days from the start of Phase II, in which case the standard time limit of 90 working days applies.[488] Parties are encouraged to discuss suitable commitments prior to the 65 working days deadline and to submit draft proposals dealing with both the substantive and procedural aspects which are necessary to ensure that the commitments are fully workable.[489] The Commission may only in exceptional circumstances grant an extension or accept commitments offered after expiry of the time limit set for their submission.[490] In the course of its assessment of the proposed commitments, the Commission consults the authorities of the Member States and, where considered appropriate, interested third parties including competitors in the form of a market test.[491]

Common principles. The commitments proposed by the notifying parties **8.165** must be proportionate to, and entirely eliminate, the competition problem identified during the course of the administrative procedure.[492] It is the responsibility of the notifying parties to show that the proposed commitments, once implemented, will eliminate such competition problems.[493] In assessing whether or not

---

[488] Merger Reg, Art 10(3).

[489] Remedies Notice (n 477, above) para 40. See also the draft revised Remedies Notice (n 479, above) para 88.

[490] See Remedies Notice, para 39 and draft revised Remedies Notice, para 88. See, eg Case M.1439 *Telia/Telenor*, OJ 2001 L40/1, [2001] 4 CMLR 1226, paras 379–380: exceptional circumstances in that the parties were subject to the additional constraints of having to consult the Swedish and Norwegian Parliaments prior to the submission of the proposed remedies; the Commission also took account of the clear-cut nature of the commitments proposed, which were accepted one week after the expiry of the deadline; cf Case M.1524 *Airtours/First Choice*, OJ 1999 L93/1, [2000] 5 CMLR 494, para 193: no exceptional circumstances to consider modified undertakings submitted over a week after the deadline (annulled on other grounds, Case T-342/99 *Airtours v Commission* [2002] ECR II-2585, [2002] 5 CMLR 317, [2002] All ER (EC) 783). See also Case T-87/05 *EDP v Commission* [2005] ECR II-3745, para 161, confirming that the Commission is not obliged to accept commitments which are submitted after the legal deadline.

[491] Remedies Notice (n 477, above) paras 41–42 and n 40; at the same time as submitting the commitments, the parties should supply a non-confidential version for market testing purposes. NCAs are sent a copy of proposed commitments on receipt by the Commission and, in practice, are consulted when the Advisory Committee meets in Phase II proceedings: Merger Reg, Arts 19(1) and (3). The Commission is not required to obtain views from third parties about the final terms of commitments offered before they are accepted: see Case T-290/94 *Kaysersberg v Commission* [1997] ECR II-237, [1998] 4 CMLR 336, para 120. See also the draft revised Remedies Notice (n 479, above) paras 79 and 90–92.

[492] Merger Reg (n 437, above) Recital (30). For Phase II, this means that commitments must address all problems raised by the Art 6(1)(c) decision or statement of objections that have not been abandoned by the Commission. See also Case T-282/02 *Cementbouw Handel & Industrie v Commission* [2006] ECR II-319, [2006] 4 CMLR 1561, para 307 (on appeal, Case C-202/06P *Cementbouw v Commission*, not yet decided).

[493] Remedies Notice (n 477, above) para 6; the remedy should further be capable of restoring conditions of effective competition on a permanent basis. At time of writing the Commission has proposed amendments to the Implementing Reg, requiring parties to provide certain standard

a remedy will restore effective competition the Commission will consider all relevant factors, including (i) the structure and particular characteristics of the market; (ii) the type, scale and scope of the remedy proposed; and (iii) the likelihood of its successful, full and timely implementation by the parties.[494] Commitments must be capable of being implemented effectively and within a short period of time.[495] Whereas divestiture remedies, once implemented, do not require any further monitoring measures, other types of commitments require monitoring mechanisms to ensure that their effect is not eliminated or diminished by the parties.[496] Before approving the commitments tabled by the notifying parties, the Commission must be satisfied that they are compatible with the competition rules.[497]

(ii) Scope of commitments

8.166 **Structural and behavioural commitments.** Since the Merger Regulation is in principle directed at the maintenance of a competitive market structure, as a rule structural commitments are considered preferable. However, commitments can be behavioural, or a mixture of both structural and behavioural remedies, provided

---

information as specified by a new form, Form RM, which will be added as a new Annex IV to the Implementing Reg, Reg 802/2004. This includes detailed information on the proposed commitments and the conditions for their implementation; an explanation of the suitability of the commitments to remove the competition concerns; and details of any deviations from the Commission's model commitments: see Press Release IP/07/544 (27 April 2007) which contains a link to the draft amendment.

[494] Remedies Notice, para 7 and draft revised Notice paras 11–12. To remove any uncertainties which might cause the Commission to reject the remedy proposed, notifying parties are often prepared to extend their proposals: see, eg Case M.3732 *Procter & Gamble/Gillette* (15 July 2005), para 156: geographic scope of the proposed co-brand licence was extended beyond the affected markets to cover the whole territory of the EEA, to ensure the viability of the divested business; Case M.2621 *SEB/Moulinex* (8 January 2002), paras 141 *et seq*: scope of the licence for the Moulinex trade mark was extended to all categories of small electric appliances although serious doubts were raised with respect to only one category of product (appeals dismissed, *Babyliss v Commission* (n 482, above); and *Royal Philips Electronics v Commission* (n 483, above); Case M.1990 *Unilever/Bestfoods* (28 September 2000), paras 177 *et seq*: scope of the remedy was extended to cover the entire product portfolio associated with specific brands although competition concerns had not been identified in respect of all such products.

[495] Remedies Notice (n 477, above) para 10. In Case M.2220 *General Electric/Honeywell*, OJ 2004 L48/1, the Commission had found that the proposed divestment commitments relating to one of the relevant markets were insufficient as they depended on the resolution of a number of practical issues which had not been addressed by GE (including the necessity for approval by US export control authorities for a divestiture); on appeal, the CFI held that since the commitment offered was 'hypothetical', its realisation being wholly dependent on a decision of the authorities of a non-Member State', the Commission was entitled to reject it: *General Electric v Commission* (n 417, above) para 617.

[496] See draft revised Remedies Notice (n 479, above) para 13 and see Case T-177/04 *easyJet v Commission* [2006] ECR II-1931, [2006] 5 CMLR 663 (paras 186–188).

[497] See *BaByliss v Commission* (n 482, above) para 421.

that they have the effect of removing competition concerns.[498] Although it is not always easy to characterise commitments as either structural or behavioural:

(a) structural remedies accepted by the Commission have related to: the divestiture of specific assets;[499] the licensing of specific assets, preferably exclusive, or re-branding commitments;[500] the termination of an exclusive vertical arrangement with significant foreclosure effects;[501] the reduction in the scope and/or duration of rights of exclusive access;[502] and withdrawal from a particular activity;[503] and a non-competition provision;

---

[498] Remedies Notice (n 477, above) para 9 and draft revised Remedies Notice paras 15–17. See Case T-158/00 *ARD v Commission* [2003] ECR II-3825, [2004] 5 CMLR 681, para 193; and Case T-102/96 *Gencor v Commission* [1999] ECR II-753, [1999] 4 CMLR 971, [1999] All ER (EC) 289, para 319, confirming that structural commitments are generally preferable to behavioural commitments, while the precise categorisation of remedies as structural or behavioural is not material. For the requirement to take into account commitments of a behavioural nature, see also Case T-5/02 *Tetra Laval v Commission* [2002] ECR II-4381, [2002] 5 CMLR 1182, paras 161 and 217–224 (on appeal from Case M.2416 *Tetra Laval/Sidel*, OJ 2004 L43/13); and further appeal dismissed, Case C-12/03P *Commission v Tetra Laval* [2005] ECR I-987, [2005] 4 CMLR 573, paras 71–89. For remedy proposals combining both structural and behavioural elements, see eg *Telia/Telenor* (n 490, above); and Case M.2803 *Telia/Sonera* (10 July 2002) (divestitures combined with network access rights).

[499] See, eg Case M.3225 *Alcan/Pechiney (II)* (29 September 2003); Case M.3314 *Air Liquide/ Messer Targets* (15 March 2004); Case M.3396 *Group 4 Falck/Securicor* (28 May 2004); Case M.3420 *GIMD/Socpresse* (16 June 2004); Case M.3686 *Honeywell/Novar* (31 March 2005); Case M.3436 *Continental/Phoenix* (26 October 2004); Case M.3751 *Novartis/Hexal* (27 May 2005); Case M.3732 *Procter & Gamble/Gillette* (15 July 2005); Case M.3829 *Mærsk/PONL* (29 July 2005); Case M.3687 *Johnson & Johnson/Guidant* (25 August 2005); Case M.4151 *Orica/Dyno Nobel* (23 May 2006); Case M.4137 *Mittal/Arcelor* (2 June 2006); Case M.4141 *Linde/BOC* (6 June 2006). In the aviation sector, competition concerns usually arise from barriers to entry in the form of access to airport slots, so merging parties often agree to put slots at the disposal of competitors to enable them to operate flights on routes where the Commission identified competition concerns: see, eg Case M.3940 *Lufthansa/Eurowings* (22 December 2005); Case M.3770 *Lufthansa/Swiss* (4 July 2005); Case M.3280 *Air France/KLM* (11 February 2002), upheld on appeal in Case T-177/04 *easyJet v Commission* (n 496, above). See also observations on divestiture of assets in the draft revised Remedies Notice (n 479, above) para 37.

[500] See, eg Case M.3692 *Reuters/Telerate* (23 May 2005); *Procter & Gamble/Gillette*, above, where the business divestiture was combined with co-brand licensing; Case M.2544 *Masterfoods/Royal Canin* (15 February 2002); Case M.3149 *Procter & Gamble/Wella* (30 July 2003). In the pharmaceutical sector, licensing has become a relatively standard remedy: see, eg Case M.1846 *Glaxo Wellcome/Smithkline Beecham* (8 May 2000); Case M.3354 *Sanofi-Synthélabo/Aventis* (26 April 2004). See also observations on IP licences and on re-branding commitments in the draft revised Remedies Notice (n 479, above) paras 38–42.

[501] See, eg Case M.291 *KNP/Bührmann-Tetterode/VRG* (4 May 1993); Case M.477 *Mercedes-Benz/Kässbohrer* (14 February 1995).

[502] See, eg Case M.214 *DuPont/ICI* (30 September 1992); Case M.623 *Kimberly-Clark/Scott Paper* (16 January 1996); Case M.737 *Ciba-Geigy/Sandoz*, OJ 1997 L 201/1; Case M.856 *BT/MCI (II)*, OJ 1997 L336/1; Case M.877 *Boeing/McDonnell Douglas*, OJ 1997 L336/16; Case M.950 *Hoffmann-LaRoche/Boehringer Mannheim* (4 February 1998); Case M.986 *Agfa-Gevaert/DuPont* (11 February 1998).

[503] See, eg Case M.269 *Shell/Montecatini*, OJ 1994 L332/48; Case M.553 *RTL/Veronica/Endemol*, OJ 1996 L294/14; *Boeing/McDonnell Douglas*, above; Case M.938 *Guinness/Grand Metropolitan*, OJ 1998 L288/24; Case M.1845 *AOL/Time Warner*, OJ 2001 L268/28, [2002] 4 CMLR 454; and Case M.3863 *TUI/CP Ships* (12 October 2005).

(b) behavioural commitments that have been accepted include:[504] remedies directed at ensuring access to essential inputs, or precluding discrimination in the grant of such access;[505] generally facilitating market entry;[506] supplying products or services to the benefit of third parties;[507] managing assets separately;[508] ensuring interoperability;[509] preventing the flow of commercially sensitive information;[510] publicising information that might otherwise induce anti-competitive parallel behaviour;[511] and providing additional information to an independent regulatory agency so that it can fulfil an increased monitoring role.[512]

8.167 **Divestiture.** A divestment commitment typically relates to tangible and intangible assets, which could take the form of a pre-existing company or group of companies, or of a business activity which was not previously incorporated in its own right.[513] The divested activities must comprise a viable business which, if operated by a suitable purchaser, can compete effectively with the merged entity on a lasting basis.[514] The intended subject of the divestment must be precisely and exhaustively defined and the description should contain all elements of the business that are necessary for it to act as a viable competitor in the market: tangible assets such as production, distribution, sales, R&D and marketing activities, intangible assets such as intellectual property rights, goodwill, personnel, supply and sales contracts with appropriate guarantees about their transferability,

---

[504] For specific observations on behavioural commitments, see the draft revised Remedies Notice (n 479, above) paras 61–69 and 126–127.

[505] See, eg Case M.190 *Nestlé/Perrier*, OJ 1992 L356/1, [1993] 4 CMLR M17; Case M.1717 *Siemens/Italtel* (15 December 1999); *Boeing/McDonnell Douglas* (n 502, above); *Guinness/Grand Metropolitan* (n 503, above); *Hoffmann-LaRoche/Boehringer Mannheim*, ibid; *Telia/Telenor* (n 490, above); Case M.1795 *Vodafone Airtouch/Mannesmann* (12 April 2000); Case M.2389 *Shell/DEA*, OJ 2003 L15/35; *Telia/Sonera* (n 498, above); Case M.2876 *Newscorp/Telepiù*, OJ 2004 L110/73, [2004] 5 CMLR 1619,

[506] See, eg Case M.3280 *Air France/KLM* (11 February 2002).

[507] See, eg Case M.1309 *Matra/Aérospatiale* (28 April 1999); Case M.2050 *Vivendi/Canal+/Seagram* (13 October 2000); *Newscorp/Telepiù*, n 505 above; Case M.3570 *Piaggio/Aprilia* (22 November 2004).

[508] See, eg *Boeing/McDonnell Douglas* (n 502, above); and Case M.3653 *Siemens/VA Tech* (13 July 2005).

[509] See, eg *GE/Instrumentarium* (n 425, above): proposed divestiture coupled with undertakings to ensure interoperability of medical devices.

[510] See, eg Case M.3099 *Areva/Urenco/ETC JV* (6 October 2004).

[511] See, eg *Nestlé/Perrier* (n 505, above).

[512] See, eg *Areva/Urenco/ETC JV* (n 510, above); the relevant authority was the Euratom Supply Agency (ESA).

[513] Usually, a divestment remedy involves an overlapping business, the purpose being to remove horizontal-type concerns. The Merger Remedies Study (n 479, above) confirmed the Commission's preference for divesting stand-alone businesses, while recognising that carve-out divestiture alternatives may be acceptable; in the latter case, appropriate oversight mechanisms must be introduced to ensure an adequate competition outcome of the carve-out process.

[514] See Remedies Notice paras 14 and 46 and the draft revised Remedies Notice paras 22–24.

customer lists, third party service agreements, technical assistance, etc.[515] Divestiture is generally required to be made within a fixed period to a purchaser approved by the Commission. The period set is not disclosed to third parties but usually amounts to several months. The sale must be expressed to be subject to the Commission's prior approval.[516] The purchaser must therefore meet the Commission's criteria of being a viable existing or potential competitor, independent of and unconnected to the parties, possessing the financial resources, proven expertise and having the incentive to maintain and develop the divested business as an active competitive force in competition with the parties.[517]

Upfront buyer, alternative and 'crown-jewel' divestiture remedies. Where the **8.168** viability of the divestiture package depends, in view of the assets being divested, to a large extent on the identity of the purchaser, the Commission may request, as a condition to clearance, that the parties undertake not to implement the notified transaction before having entered into a binding agreement with a purchaser for the divested business (upfront buyer requirement).[518] In cases of uncertainty as to the implementation of the proposed divestiture option, the Commission may also require an alternative commitment which would be triggered if the primary

---

[515] The Merger Remedies Study (n 479, above) identified inadequacies in the scope of some divested businesses, mainly the omission of key assets necessary for its viability and competitiveness. It suggested that the Commission consider more fully the following aspects in order to determine the scope of the divestiture package in each case: (i) the degree of upstream and/or vertical dependence between the divested business and parts of the parties' retained business; (ii) the geographic scope of a viable and competitive business as compared to the geographic scope of the relevant market; (iii) the critical size or mass necessary to ensure the viability of the divested business; (iv) potential product cycle effects, eg the divestiture of mature products to compete against the parties' retained innovative new generation products; and (v) intellectual property rights issues. The Study suggests that the straightforward approach of divesting solely the overlapping business has at times been inadequate.

[516] Remedies Notice (n 477, above) paras 48, 49 and 58 and draft revised Remedies Notice paras 47–52.

[517] See Case T-342/00 *Petrolessence and SG2R v Commission* [2003] ECR II-1161, [2003] 5 CMLR 498, dismissing a challenge to the Commission's rejection of a potential purchaser as unsuitable for maintaining or developing competition; the CFI noted the discretionary margin afforded to the Commission in such an assessment.

[518] Remedies Notice (n 477, above) para 20, draft revised Remedies Notice paras 53–55. An 'upfront buyer' solution was required for the first time in Case M.2060 *Bosch/Rexroth*, OJ 2004 L43/1. See also Case M.2544 *Masterfoods/Royal Canin* (15 February 2002), para 102; and *XXXIst Report on Competition Policy* (2001), points 298–299, re the upfront buyer requirement requested in Cases M.2337 *Nestlé/Ralston Purina* (27 July 2001) and M.1915 *Post Office/TPG/SPPL* (13 March 2001), OJ 2004 L82/1; Case M.2947 *Verbund/Energie Allianz* (11 June 2003); Case M.2972 *DSM/Roche Vitamins* (23 July 2003); Case M.3796 *Omya/JM Huber* (19 July 2006). The Merger Remedies Study (n 479, above) noted the infrequent use of alternative divestiture commitments and considered that recourse to an upfront buyer solution could help to ensure that merging parties make all necessary efforts to implement the remedy effectively and quickly. See also observations on 'fix-it-first' remedies in the draft revised Remedies Notice (n 479, above) paras 56–57 where parties already during the Commission procedure enter into a legally binding agreement with a buyer.

commitment is not implemented by an initial deadline;[519] such an alternative commitment may be broader in scope and easier to implement, although less attractive to the merging parties ('crown-jewel' commitment).[520]

(iii) Implementation of commitments

8.169 **Timing of divestments.** The standard model text for divestiture commitments and the accompanying Best Practice Guidelines provide detailed guidance with regard to the timing of implementation.[521] During a first phase (the so-called 'first divestiture period'), the parties have the sole responsibility for finding a suitable purchaser for the divestment business.[522] If they do not succeed in divesting the business on their own in that period, then a divestiture trustee is appointed with an exclusive mandate to dispose of the business at no minimum price, within a second stage (the so-called 'extended divestiture period'). The Commission will normally consider a period of around six months for the first divestiture period and an additional period of three to six months for the extended divestiture period as appropriate. However, these periods may be modified according to the particular requirements of each case.[523]

8.170 **Role of trustees.** Pending divestiture, the parties are required to offer commitments to maintain the competitiveness of the business to be divested and to continue it as a distinct and saleable business with its own, independent management.[524] In this regard, the Commission will approve the appointment of a third party to oversee the parties' compliance with such preservation measures and their efforts to find a potential purchaser and to transfer the business, referred to by the Commission as a 'monitoring trustee'.[525] In case the parties do not find a suitable purchaser within the first divestiture period, the commitments should grant an

---

[519] Remedies Notice (n 477, above) paras 22–23 and draft revised Remedies Notice paras 44–46. See, eg Case M.3225 *Alcan/Pechiney (II)* (29 September 2003), paras 155 *et seq*.

[520] See, eg Case M.2337 *Nestlé/Ralston Purina* (27 July 2001), para 69; Case M.1813 *Industri Kapital (Nordkem)/Dyno*, OJ 2001 L188/1, paras 132 *et seq*; and *XXXIst Report on Competition Policy* (2001), points 298–299.

[521] Best Practices Guidelines, DG Comp Best Practices on the conduct of EC merger proceedings, available at DG Comp's website (www.europa.eu/comm/competition/mergers/ legislation/ regulation): (Vol II, App D.7) para 15. See also draft revised Remedies Notice (n 479, above) paras 95–98.

[522] Without questioning the Commission's practice of leaving the parties to manage the divestiture process (at least during the first divestiture period), the Merger Remedies Study (n 479, above) suggested that a minimum standard of what constitutes a proper divestiture procedure be established, including the obligation on the seller(s) to provide potential purchasers with full, frank and timely information regarding the scope of the divested business.

[523] The Merger Remedies Study noted that extensions of the divestiture deadlines were granted in about 30 per cent of the cases examined.

[524] Remedies Notice, OJ 2001 C68/3: Vol II, App D.4, paras 50–51 and see draft revised Remedies Notice, Vol II, App D.15, paras 105–109.

[525] ibid, para 52 and paras 110 and 115–117 of the draft revised Remedies Notice.

irrevocable and exclusive mandate to an independent third party, referred to as the 'divestiture trustee', to dispose of the business. These trustees are generally required to supervise and report to the Commission on implementation of the commitments.[526] Depending on the facts of the case, the divesture trustee may be the same as the monitoring trustee. Each trustee's terms of appointment are subject to Commission review and approval and their services are paid for by the parties.[527]

Failure to fulfil commitments. In the case of both Phase I and Phase II commit- **8.171** ments, if the parties fail to comply with an *obligation* attached to the Commission's decision, the Commission may, at its discretion, revoke the clearance of the concentration.[528] On the other hand, when a *condition* is not fulfilled, the Phase I or Phase II clearance decision no longer stands.[529] The Commission may proceed with renewed Phase I or Phase II proceedings (as applicable) without being bound by the time limits that would otherwise apply.[530] In such circumstances, the Commission may order any interim measures appropriate to restore or maintain conditions of effective competition.[531] In addition, the parties may be subject to fines.[532] Since the formal acceptance of commitments by the Commission produces legal effects, a decision to clear a merger on the basis of such commitments is susceptible to appeal by the parties.[533] Where the parties consider that the circumstances which gave rise to the conditions have changed, the Commission may on reasoned application vary its decision by releasing them from the commitments; the Commission's model text commitments include a standard review clause enabling the Commission, if requested by parties showing good cause, to revise deadlines or to waive, modify or substitute, in exceptional circumstances, the commitments.[534]

---

[526] They should have the right to propose, and if deemed necessary impose, all measures necessary to ensure compliance with any of the commitments. However, the Commission must also be satisfied that the proposed purchaser meets the requirements of the commitments. Accordingly, divestiture is ultimately subject to Commission approval; the acquisition by a third party may itself require clearance as a distinct concentration under the Merger Reg or national merger contol rules.

[527] Remedies Notice (n 524, above) para 55 and draft revised Remedies Notice, paras 120–124.

[528] Merger Reg, Reg 139/2004, OJ 2004 L24/1: Vol II, App D.1, Art 6(3)(b) for Phase I (see para 8.137, above); Art 8(6)(b) for Phase II (see para 8.158, above). The parties may also be subject to fines and periodic penalty payments pursuant to Arts 14(2)(d) and 15(1)(c) of the Merger Reg.

[529] Remedies Notice (n 524, above) para 12 and draft revised Remedies Notice, paras 19–20.

[530] Merger Reg, Art 6(4); Art 8(7); also Recital (31).

[531] ibid, Art 8(5)(b). The Commission is not required to consult the parties or the Advisory Committee before taking such interim measures: Arts 18(2) and 19(3).

[532] ibid, Art 14(2)(d). See para 8.181, below.

[533] cf Cases T-125 & 127/97 *The Coca-Cola Co. v Commission* [2000] ECR II–1733, [2000] 5 CMLR 467, where the action was dismissed as inadmissible because the undertakings given were not formally part of the decision.

[534] See draft revised Remedies Notice (n 524, above) paras 70–75 and n 480, above. See eg Case M.269 *Shell/Montecatini* (Decns of 8 June 1994 and 24 April 1996), varying one of the commitments set out in the original 1994 clearance decision upon the parties' reasoned request. In the absence of an explicit 'review clause', it is not entirely clear whether the Commission can modify

(e) Commission's powers of investigation

(i) *Means of obtaining information*

8.172 **Information requests.** Both during the initial Phase I investigation and in any subsequent Phase II investigation, the Commission has powers, under Article 11 of the Merger Regulation, to request information from undertakings which are party to the concentration, including information from individuals acquiring control within the meaning of Article 3(1)(b); and from third parties, in particular customers, suppliers and competitors.[535] Such information requests, which are usually made in the form of a simple request pursuant to Article 11(2), state the legal basis and the purpose of the request, specify what information is required, fix the time limit for a response and indicate the penalties for supplying incorrect or misleading information. The Commission has powers to issue a decision compelling the recipient to supply the information pursuant to Article 11(3) of the Merger Regulation;[536] it may use these powers if, for example, the recipient of a simple Article 11(2) request has failed to provide the information within the period requested or has provided incomplete information. In practice, where a recipient has difficulty in supplying the information requested, it can discuss the scope of the request with the case team and, subject to the constraints under which the Commission operates, request extensions of time. In responding to information requests and generally providing additional information in support of their arrangements, the undertakings concerned can also volunteer additional data and evidence.[537] When the Commission sends an Article 11(3) decision, it must send a copy to the NCA of the Member State in which the recipient of the request

---

previously accepted commitments, in a way that avoids declaring that the original decision is invalid for breach of condition and avoids re-notification. But see Case M.1378 *Hoechst/Rhône-Poulenc* (9 August 1999 and 30 January 2004): Commission accepted Aventis's amendment request, notwithstanding the limited scope of the review clause included in the original 1999 commitments. See also *Siemens/VA Tech* (n 508, above) in which the Commission took a separate decision to release Bombardier from its obligation under Case M.2139 *Bombardier/Adtranz*, OJ 2002 L69/50 to purchase certain traction systems for trams from VA Tech, in order to bring to an end a structural link between competitors Bombardier and Siemens in the market for trams.

[535] Merger Reg (n 528, above) Arts 11(1).

[536] Such a decision shall similarly state the legal basis and the purpose of the request, specify what information is required, fix the time limit for a response and indicate the penalties for failure to comply (as specified in Arts 14 and 15 of the Merger Reg: see paras 8.180–8.182, below). The Commission has no jurisdiction to enforce decisions under Art 11(3) where the recipient of the request has no affiliates or assets within the EU: see Case M.1693 *Alcoa/Reynolds*, OJ 2002 L58/25, para 104, n 23. For the implications of Art 11 on Phase I and II timetables, see para 8.175, below.

[537] Where potentially important information is not clearly ascertainable from pre-existing documentation, the Commission may take account of statutory declarations or affidavits that the parties may submit; see eg Case M.3149 *Procter & Gamble/Wella* (30 July 2003), para 44: affidavit from a Vice-Chairman declaring that Procter & Gamble had never considered independent entry to the market in question, in support of its argument that it was not to be considered a realistic potential entrant.

is situated.[538] In addition, the Commision may request information from Member States.[539]

Interviews. The Commission also has powers to interview any natural or legal person who consents to be interviewed for the purpose of collecting information relating to the subject-matter of the investigation.[540]   **8.173**

Inspections. The Commission has powers, under Article 13 of the Merger Regulation, to carry out investigations at undertakings' premises, including not only those of the parties to the proposed concentration but also those of third parties. These powers extend to entering premises, examining books and other business records, taking copies, sealing business premises, books or records, and asking for explanations on facts or documents and recording the answers.[541] The Commission may exercise these powers by way of a mandate or it may first issue a formal decision. Any such investigation will usually be undertaken with the assistance of the NCA of the relevant Member State.[542]   **8.174**

(ii) Suspension of Phase I and Phase II timetables

Article 11 decisions. The time periods for Phase I and Phase II investigations are suspended where the Commission has had to issue a decision requesting information pursuant to Article 11(3), or ordering an inspection pursuant to Article 13(4) until full compliance.[543] The Commission may also suspend the Phase I and Phase II time periods (or 'stop the clock') by a decision pursuant to Article 11(3), without proceeding first by way of a simple information request, owing to circumstances for which one of the undertakings involved in the concentration is responsible.[544] These Commission powers to suspend the Merger   **8.175**

---

[538] Merger Reg (n 528, above) Art 11(5). See also Art 8(1) of Protocol 24 to the EEA Agreement in respect of requests sent to addressees in the EFTA States.

[539] ibid, Art 11(6): the provision expressly refers to information from 'governments and competent authorities'. Similarly, the Commission can obtain information and assistance from the EFTA Surveillance Authority and the contracting EFTA States: Art 8 of Protocol 24 to the EEA Agreement.

[540] ibid, Art 11(7), which provides further guidance on the procedure to be followed. See also Art 8(2) of Protocol 24 to the EEA Agreement.

[541] See, eg Case M.1157 *Skanska/Scancem* (11 November 1998), point 11: Commission carried out an inspection visit in order to clarify the arrangements relating to the establishment of Scancem and its notifiability under the Merger Regulation; cf Art 20 of Reg 1/2003: see para 13.048, below.

[542] Merger Reg (n 528, above) Art 13(3)–(5); see also Art 12. Similarly, Art 8(4) of Protocol 24 to the EEA Agreement.

[543] Implementing Reg, Reg 802/2004, OJ 2004 L133/1: Vol II, App D.2, Art 9(1). See also paras 8.134 and 8.143, above.

[544] ibid, Art 9(2). See, eg Case M.3796 *Omya/JM Huber* (19 July 2006): Phase II proceedings were suspended on seven separate occasions. Omya has challenged the validity of one of these Art 11 decisions in Case T-145/06 *Omya v Commission,* not yet decided, seeking the annulment of the information request and a declaration that the merger should have been deemed authorised in March 2006, due to the Commission's failure to reach a decision by that deadline. See also

Regulation timetable are distinct from the agreed 'stop the clock' procedures available at Phase II.[545]

(iii) Confidentiality and business secrets

8.176 **Obligation of professional secrecy.** During the course of the investigation of a concentration under the Merger Regulation the Commission will acquire a wealth of information about the parties and relevant markets. Information collected as a result of the application of the Merger Regulation powers may only be used for the purposes of the relevant request, investigation or hearing.[546] In addition, information acquired by the Commission and NCAs through the application of the Merger Regulation may not be disclosed if it is 'of the kind covered by the obligation of professional secrecy'.[547] The obligation of professional secrecy is expressed to be without prejudice to the provisions of Article 18 which relates to the hearing of parties concerned and third parties, and without prejudice to the provisions of Articles 4(3) and 20 which provide for publication by the Commission of the fact that a notification has been received and of decisions following a Phase II investigation.[548] These provisions implement and extend the application of the general rule of Article 287 of the EC Treaty which prohibits the disclosure by Commission officials of 'information of the kind covered by the obligation of professional secrecy, in particular information about undertakings, their business relations or their cost components'.[549]

8.177 **Business secrets and other confidential information.** Where information, including documents, contains business secrets or other confidential information, the Commission will not disclose it or make it accessible, unless it considers it necessary for the purpose of the procedure.[550] Any person submitting information

---

Case M.3083 *GE/Instrumentarium*, OJ 2004 L109/1 (timetable suspended for a month); Case M.3216 *Oracle/PeopleSoft*, OJ 2005 L218/6 (timetable suspended twice, first for one month then for five months); Case M.3333 *Sony/BMG*, OJ 2005 L62/30 (timetable suspended for a month: see Final Report of the Hearing Officer (13 July 2004)); see also Case T-310/01 *Schneider Electric v Commission* [2002] ECR II-4071, [2003] 4 CMLR 768, [2004] All ER (EC) 314, paras 94–113.

545 See para 8.142, above.
546 Merger Reg (n 528, above) Art 17(1).
547 ibid, Art 17(2).
548 ibid, Art 17(2). However, Arts 4(3) and 20(2) of the Merger Reg provide that, when publishing such details of notifications and decisions, the Commission is required to take account of the legitimate interests of undertakings in the protection of their business secrets. This equally applies to other publications, including the making available to interested third parties of non-confidential versions of Phase I and Phase II decisions, or press releases, and the publication in the OJ of the Advisory Committee's opinion on draft Commission decisions in Phase II investigations.
549 See also Art 9 of Protocol 24 to the EEA Agreement. Furthermore, Art 17 of the Commission's Staff Regulations (Council Reg 723/2004, OJ 2004 L124/1) prohibits unauthorised disclosure of information by Commission staff.
550 Implementing Reg (n 543, above) Art 18(1). Where it is necessary to disclose or grant access to such documents, the Commission will generally rely on non-confidential versions of the documents or may prepare a summary of the relevant information: see Access to File Notice, OJ 2005 C325/7: Vol II, App B.12, para 17.

to the Commission must clearly identify any material it considers to be confidential, giving reasons, and providing a separate non-confidential version within time limits set by the Commission.[551] The Commission may also require persons and undertakings to identify any part of the statement of objections, case summary or formal decision which contains business secrets.[552] Any disputes with the Commission on these issues may be referred to the Hearing Officer for a ruling.[553] For these purposes, the Commission provides guidance on these two categories of sensitive information:

(a) *Business secrets:* business secrets comprise information about an undertaking's business activities, disclosure of which could result in serious harm to that undertaking.[554] Examples may include: technical and/or financial information relating to an undertaking's know-how, methods of assessing costs, production secrets and processes, supply sources, quantities produced and sold, market shares, customer and distributor lists, marketing plans, cost and price structure and sales strategy;[555]

(b) *Other confidential information:* in addition to business secrets, other information may be considered confidential if its disclosure would significantly harm a person or undertaking, for example if its disclosure would risk exposing the person or undertaking to the risk of retaliatory measures.[556] Accordingly, the concept of 'other confidential information' may extend to information that would enable the parties to identify complainants or other third parties who have a justified wish to remain anonymous. Other confidential information would also include military secrets.[557]

(f) Commission's powers of sanction

(i) In general

Measures following a prohibition decision. Where the Commission issues a decision prohibiting a concentration which has already been implemented,　**8.178**

---

[551] Implementing Reg (n 543, above) Art 18(2). See also Access to File Notice, above, paras 21–25.

[552] Implementing Reg, Art 18(3).

[553] See Access to File Notice (n 550, above) para 42. For the Hearing Officer, see para 8.150, above.

[554] Access to File Notice (n 550, above) para 18; Case T-353/94 *Postbank v Commission* [1996] ECR II-921, [1997] 4 CMLR 33, [1996] All ER (EC) 817, para 87.

[555] Information which is already known outside the undertaking will not normally be considered confidential; historic information will generally be regarded as no longer being of commercial importance (eg turnover, sales and market shares data which is more than five years old: see Access to File Notice, para 23).

[556] Access to File Notice (n 550, above) paras 19 and 43. See, eg Case T-221/95 *Endemol Entertainment v Commission* [1999] ECR II–1299, [1999] 5 CMLR 611, [1999] All ER (EC) 385, para 60; *Tetra Laval v Commission* (n 498, above) paras 98 *et seq.*

[557] Access to File Notice (n 550, above) para 20. See also para 8.105, above, on defence interests under Art 296 of the EC Treaty.

the Commission may require the undertakings to take steps to restore conditions for effective competition. Such steps may include divestiture.[558]

8.179 The power to fine. The Commission may impose fines or periodic penalty payments on persons or undertakings committing procedural or substantive infringements.[559] Before taking any decision imposing fines or periodic payments the Commission must first give the undertakings concerned the opportunity to submit their observations in writing and at a hearing and must consult the Advisory Committee.[560] In setting the amount of the fine, the Commission must have regard to the nature, gravity and duration of the infringement.[561] Decisions imposing fines are expressed to be not of a criminal nature.[562]

(ii) Fines and penalty payments

8.180 Fines for procedural infringements. Under Article 14(1) of the Merger Regulation, the Commission may impose fines not exceeding one per cent of the aggregate turnover, calculated in accordance with Article 5, on any undertaking or association of undertakings, or on an individual acquiring control within the meaning of Article 3(1)(b), which intentionally or negligently:

(a) supplies incorrect or misleading information in a submission, certification, notification or supplement thereto (made pursuant to Articles 4, 10(5) or 22(3));[563]

---

[558] Merger Reg (n 528, above) Art 8(4); see para 8.160, above.

[559] ibid, Arts 14 and 15. Note that this constitutes a distinct decision from the decision on the concentration and is given a different case number.

[560] ibid, Arts 18(1) and 19(3); Implementing Reg (n 543, above) Art 14(3).

[561] Merger Reg, Art 14(3).

[562] ibid, Art 14(4).

[563] See Case M.3255 *Tetra Laval/Sidel* (7 July 2004): fine of €90,000 on Tetra Laval for providing incorrect or misleading information relating to the existence of its Tetra Fast technology; Case M.2624 *Deutsche BP/Erdölchemie* (19 June 2002): BP fined €35,000 for supplying incorrect (or at least misleading) information on its activities; Case M.1610 *Deutsche Post/trans-o-flex* (14 December 1999); *XXIXth Report on Competition Policy* (1999), p 73: two fines of €50,000 each imposed for the deliberate supply of incorrect and misleading information in connection with Deutsche Post's 1999 notification of its intention to acquire sole control of the German high-speed delivery service trans-o-flex GmbH; it emerged that Deutsche Post might already have acquired indirect control over trans-o-flex in 1997, and the failure to disclose the true position both in the notification and in response to information requests by the Commission was regarded as a serious violation. In Case M.1397 *Sanofi/Synthélabo* (21 April 1999), the parties' failure to disclose that they both had subsidiaries active in the area of morphine and morphine derivatives was brought to the Commission's attention by third parties after the concentration had been cleared; the Commission revoked its clearance decision (see para 8.137, above) and imposed the then maximum fine of €50,000 on each of the parties. See also Case M.1608 *KLM/Martinair* (14 December 1999), *XXIXth Report on Competition Policy* (1999), p 73: fine of €40,000 was imposed for the 'grossly negligent' supply of incorrect information regarding both the destinations served by Transavia and the nature of its operations in the original notification of its proposal to acquire Martinair (the proposed acquisition was subsequently abandoned).

(b) supplies incorrect or misleading information in response to an Article 11 request for information or fails to supply information within the period fixed by a decision taken pursuant to Article 11;[564]

(c) produces incomplete books or records during an inspection or refuses to submit to an inspection;

(d) in response to an oral question, gives an incorrect or misleading answer, fails to rectify within the time limit set by the Commission such an answer or fails or refuses to provide a complete answer on facts relating to the subject-matter and purpose of an inspection; or

(e) breaks seals affixed by the Commission or other authorised persons in the course of inspections.

Fines for substantive infringement. Under Article 14(2) of the Merger **8.181** Regulation, the Commission may impose fines of up to 10 per cent of aggregate turnover (calculated in accordance with Article 5) on any undertaking concerned, or an individual acquiring control within the meaning of Article 3(1)(b) which intentionally or negligently:

(a) fails to notify a concentration prior to its implementation, unless expressly authorised to do so by the Commission;[565]

(b) puts a concentration into effect before it has been the subject of a Commission clearance decision;[566]

(c) puts a concentration into effect in breach of an Article 8(3) prohibition decision or, where the concentration has already been implemented, fails to comply with measures ordered by the Commission under Article 8(4) or (5);

(d) fails to comply with a condition or an obligation attached either to a clearance decision under Articles 6(1)(b) or 8(2) or to a decision granting a derogation from the suspension period under Article 7(3).

Periodic penalty payments. Under Article 15 of the Merger Regulation, the **8.182** Commission may impose periodic penalty payments on any undertaking or

---

[564] See *Tetra Laval/Sidel* and *Deutsche Post*, above. See also Case M.1634 *Mitsubishi Heavy Industries* (14 July 2000): Mitsubishi fined €50,000 and a periodic penalty payment imposed for repeated failure to supply information requested by the Commission for the purposes of its investigation in Case M.1431 *Ahlström/Kværner*. This was the first time that the Commission fined a company other than a notifying party in merger proceedings.

[565] See n 360 to para 8.130, above: in Case M.969 *AP Møller*, OJ 1999 L183/29, a fine of €45,000 was imposed under this head, in respect of three concentrations.

[566] ibid. In *AP Møller*, above, a fine of €6,000 per month was imposed under this head, covering a total period of 29 months in respect of three concentrations.

associations of undertakings, or on an individual acquiring control within the meaning of Article 3(1)(b), in order to compel them to: [567]

(a) supply complete and correct information requested by a Commission decision;[568]

(b) submit to an inspection pursuant to a Commission decision;

(c) comply with an obligation attached to a clearance decision under Articles 6(1)(b) or 8(2) or to a decision granting a derogation from the suspension period under Article 7(3);

(d) where the concentration has already been implemented, comply with any measures ordered by the Commission under Articles 8(4) or (5).

Where the undertaking has subsequently satisfied the obligation which the periodic penalty payment intended to enforce, the Commission may fix the definite amount of the periodic penalty payments at a figure lower than that which would arise under the original decision.[569]

4. Substantive Appraisal of Concentrations

(a) In general

8.183   **Compatibility with the common market.**   Article 2(1) of the Merger Regulation provides that concentrations must be appraised with a view to establishing whether or not they are 'compatible with the common market'. Recital (23) to the Merger Regulation provides that the Commission must place its appraisal within the general framework of the achievement of the fundamental objectives referred to in Article 2 of the EC Treaty[570] and Article 2 of the Treaty on European Union.[571] Article 2(1) of the Merger Regulation contains a non-exhaustive list of considerations which the Commission must take into account when making its appraisal, namely:

(a) the need to maintain and develop effective competition within the common market in view of, among other things:
   — the structure of all the markets concerned; and
   — the actual or potential competition from undertakings located either within or outwith the Community;

---

[567] These powers are similar in object and effect to those under Arts 23–24 of Reg 1/2003: see paras 13.035 and 13.050, below.

[568] See *Mitsubishi Heavy Industries* (n 564, above).

[569] Merger Reg (n 528, above) Art 15(2).

[570] Art 2 EC refers to the task of promoting throughout the EU 'a harmonious, balanced and sustainable development of economic activities' and various other objectives.

[571] Art 2 EU refers to various objectives, including 'to promote economic and social progress and a high level of employment and to achieve balanced and sustainable development.'

(b) the following specific factors:
— the market position of the undertakings concerned and their economic
and financial power;
— the alternatives available to suppliers and users;
— their access to supplies or markets;
— any legal or other barriers to entry;
— supply and demand trends for the relevant goods and services;
— the interests of intermediate and ultimate consumers; and
— the development of technical and economic progress provided that it is
to consumers' advantage and does not form an obstacle to competition.

SIEC test. In appraising the compatibility of a concentration with the common **8.184**
market under the Merger Regulation, the Commission must make a prospective
determination of whether the concentration would 'significantly impede effective
competition in the common market or in a substantial part of it, in particular as a
result of the creation or strengthening of a dominant position' (Article 2(2)
and (3)).[572] This substantive test is known as the 'SIEC' test, to distinguish it from
the 'dominance' test that existed under the original Merger Regulation.[573] The
SIEC test is generally viewed as substantively similar to the substantial lessening
of competition ('SLC') test applied in a number of other jurisdictions, including
the United Kingdom and the United States. The scope and operation of the SIEC
test is considered in more detail at paragraphs 8.192 to 8.231, below.[574]

Spill-over effects of certain joint ventures. In addition, a different substantive **8.185**
assessment must be undertaken if the concentration involves the establishment of
a full-function JV undertaking with potential spill-over effects on competition

---

[572] As part of its assessment, the Commission should identify the markets on which the concentration may have effects (if any): see further paras 8.186–8.191, below and Chap 4, above. Where the affected markets are geographically restricted to local areas which are not a substantial part of the Community, the Commission does not have jurisdictions to prohibit the concentration under the Merger Reg and is likely to agree to a request for a pre-notification referral under Art 4(4) (see paras 8.081 *et seq*, above) or a post-notification referral under Art 9 (see paras 8.091 *et seq*, above).

[573] In the original Merger Reg, Art 2(2) and (3) expressed the substantive test as a determination whether the concentration would 'create or strengthen a dominant position as a result of which effective competition would be significantly impeded in the common market or in a substantial part of it'. That 'dominance' test was held to comprise two cumulative criteria: (i) the creation or strengthening of a dominant position; and (ii) the fact that effective competition would be significantly impeded: Case T-2/93 *Air France v Commission (TAT)* [1994] ECR II-323, para 79; Case T-290/94 *Kaysersberg v Commission* [1997] ECR II-237, [1998] 4 CMLR 336, para 156; Case T-5/02 *Tetra Laval v Commission* [2002] ECR II-4381, [2002] 5 CMLR 1182, para 120; Case T-87/05 *EDP v Commission* [2005] ECR II-3745, [2005] 5 CMLR 1436, para 45; Case T-210/01 *General Electric v Commission* [2005] ECR II-5515, [2006] 4 CMLR 686, para 84.

[574] Art 57 of the EEA Agreement has not yet been amended to adopt the SIEC test as the basis for assessing the compatibility of mergers with the EEA Agreement. However, changes to Annex XIV of the EEA Agreement are intended to incorporate the substantive provisions of the new Merger Reg, including the SIEC test, into the EEA Agreement by reference.

between undertakings that remain independent. According to Article 2(4) and (5) of the Merger Regulation, those coordinative aspects must be appraised not under the SIEC test but in accordance with the criteria of Article 81 of the EC Treaty. These provisions are considered in more detail at paragraphs 8.232 to 8.234, below.

(b) Market definition

(i) *Affected markets for Form CO purposes*

8.186 **Market definition and relevant markets.** The market shares of the parties and their competitors in the relevant market or markets are an important factor in the evaluation of any concentration. Thus, the Commission recognises that the main purpose of market definition is to identify in a systematic way the immediate competitive constraints facing the merged entity.[575] This process of market definition requires the identification of both the relevant product market and the relevant geographic market: for full discussion of the issues involved, see Chapter 4, above.[576] To assist the Commission in making its assessment at Phase I, Form CO requires notifying parties to provide information on so-called 'affected markets', that is those where the parties' activities are *prima facie* sufficient to justify some substantive review. For this purpose, markets are treated as 'affected markets' where the parties' activities overlap (horizontal relationships) or form part of a vertical supply chain (vertical relationships) and specific market share thresholds are met:[577]

(a) *Horizontally affected markets:* there is a horizontally affected market where two or more of the parties to the concentration are engaged in business activities in the same product market and where the concentration will lead to a combined market share of 15 per cent or more; and

(b) *Vertically affected markets:* there is a vertically affected market where one or more of the parties to the concentration are engaged in business activities in a product market which is upstream or downstream of a product market in which any of other party to the concentration is engaged, and any of their individual or combined market shares at either level is 25 per cent or more, regardless of whether or not there is any existing supplier/customer relationship between the parties to the concentration.

---

[575] Horizontal Merger Guidelines, OJ 2004 C31/5: Vol II, App D.6, para 10.

[576] In some cases it may also be appropriate to identify a temporal market, ie the period of time over which the market operates: paras 4.089 *et seq*, above.

[577] See Section 6 (III) Form CO. The Commission's determination of what constitute relevant markets in its substantive assessment is not constrained by the data on affected markets as presented in the notification; it may explore a number of possible alternatives and review the impact of a transaction by reference to various possible market definitions, taking account *inter alia* of views of third parties.

(ii) Product market

Relevant product market. The Commission describes the relevant product   **8.187**
market as comprising 'all those products and/or services which are regarded as
interchangeable or substitutable by the consumer, by reason of the products' characteristics, their prices and their intended use.'[578] In defining relevant product
markets and appraising the parties' market positions, the Commission takes
account of numerous factors as supported by empirical evidence, notably the
competitive constraints placed on the parties by demand-side substitution,
supply-side substitution and potential competition. It is generally not necessary
for the Commission to reach a definitive conclusion on the precise market.
As indicated in its 1997 Notice on definition of the relevant market, if under
the conceivable alternative market definitions the operation in question does not
raise competition concerns, the question of market definition will be left open,
reducing thereby the burden on companies to supply information.[579]

Effect of previous cases. Although previous market definitions determined by   **8.188**
the Commission either in merger cases or under Articles 81 and/or 82 are not
binding on the Commission, the Commission's extensive body of decisions, particularly in merger cases, provides useful guidance on its approach to this task.[580]
Commission decisions on market definition are often cited in later Commission
cases concerning the same sector. Indeed, precedents from previous cases may
have a strong persuasive effect. Although the Commission's views on market definition are not legally binding on national authorities or national courts, they
can also influence subsequent national proceedings.[581] However, since market
definition under the Merger Regulation will necessarily be prospective in nature,
changes in market conditions that have taken place or can be expected to take
place in the near future may require the parties and/or the Commission to distinguish between past and present cases.[582]

Other features specifically relevant to merger control. The Commission's   **8.189**
investigation of transactions under the Merger Regulation generally involves

---

[578] Section 6 Form CO and Relevant Market Notice, OJ 1997 C372/5: Vol II, App C.10, para 7.
[579] Relevant Market Notice, above, para 27.
[580] The DG Comp website contains an exhaustive list of the Commission's decisions
under the Merger Reg, sorted according to a number of criteria http://ec.europa.eu/comm/
competition/mergers/cases/.
[581] eg in its guidance on the substantive assessment of mergers (OFT 516, May 2003 as amended
in October 2004), the UK Office of Fair Trading states that it will have regard *inter alia* to previous
Commission decisions concerning the same industry sectors, 'but does not consider itself bound by
those precedents in particular because markets may change over time' (para. 3.16).
[582] See, eg Case M.2337 *Nestlé/Ralston Purina* (27 July 2001), para 21: Commission concluded,
based on a closer examination of market conditions, that the relevant pet food markets were national
in scope, notwithstanding its findings in previous cases that the relevant geographic market for pet
food was EEA-wide.

consultations with interested third parties. Customers, competitors and suppliers are often requested to respond to detailed questionnaires sent to them by the case team.[583] In this context, the Commission tends to place greater emphasis on customer reactions to a proposed concentration than on the views of competitors. This is also reflected in the weight placed by the Commission on demand-side substitutability as opposed to supply-side factors for the purpose of market definition in its review of mergers. In consumer product markets (where the Commission may be considering a merger at the manufacturing/wholesaling level), this can involve placing significant emphasis on downstream consumer preferences and behaviour (at the retail level), which may in turn be affected by a number of considerations in addition to product prices (such as various cultural factors).

(iii) Geographic market

8.190 **Relevant geographic market.** The Commission refers to the relevant geographic market as: 'the area in which the undertakings concerned are involved in the supply of products or services, in which the conditions of competition are sufficiently homogenous and which can be distinguished from neighbouring geographic areas because, in particular, conditions of competition are appreciably different in those areas'.[584] Where products are traded on a worldwide level and there is significant actual or realistic potential competition from imports from outside Europe, the Commission may recognise the existence of a worldwide market as it did, for example, in *Blackstone/Acetex*.[585] In general, however, for jurisdictional reasons the Commission tends to focus on market shares at the Community/EEA level or national level, while sometimes taking account of the worldwide context. At the other extreme, there will be cases where the geographic reference market is local.[586]

---

[583] See paras 8.131-8.132, above on the role of third parties. Third party views are generally not sought in cases handled under the simplified procedure.

[584] Section 6 of Form CO and para 7 of Relevant Market Notice (n 578, above) para 7. This text follows Art 9(7) of the Merger Reg which lays down the criteria for determining the geographical reference market for Art 9 cases (see para 8.094, above).

[585] Case M.3625 *Blackstone/Acetex* (13 July 2005) (acetic acid, acetic anhydride, VAM and PVOH). See also eg Case M.619 *Gencor/Lonrho*, OJ 1997 L11/30, [1999] 4 CMLR 1076 (platinum); Case M.877 *Boeing/McDonnell Douglas*, OJ 1997 L336/16 (large commercial jet aircrafts); Case M.1671 *Dow Chemical/Union Carbide*, OJ 2001 L245/1 (the market for licensing of PE technology); Case M.2208 *Chevron/Texaco* (28 February 2001) (crude oil); Case M.2413 *BHP/Billiton* (14 June 2001) (copper concentrate).

[586] See, eg Case M.3754 *Strabag/Dywidag* (29 April 2005) which was the subject of a partial referral to the Bundeskartellamt under Art 9(3)(b) of the Merger Reg because of competition concerns in the local asphalt market in Hamburg; Case M.1346 *EDF/London Electricity* (27 January 1999) (supply and distribution of electricity); Case M.2446 *Govia/Connex South Central* (20 July 2001) (passenger rail services and railway routes); Case M.2825 *Fortis AG SA/Bernheim-Comofi SA* (9 July 2002) (car parking and real estate); Case M.3415 *CRH/SEMAPA/Secil JV* (28 May 2004) (certain building materials).

In cases of concentrations relating to the retail sector the Commission has taken account of the choice of alternative points of sale available to shoppers in the local areas covered by the concentration.[587]

A dynamic approach to geographic markets. It may be appropriate to focus on **8.191** a broader geographic market, even where national characteristics are still evident, provided that there are clear trends and a realistic expectation of increased inter-State trade and homogenous conditions of competition across national frontiers.[588] Thus a merger between undertakings from different EEA States may be viewed as part of a trend towards increased cross-border trade in the affected product market. However, a merger resulting in a 'national champion' in an EEA State may actually impede internal market developments and point towards the relevant geographic market being national.[589]

(c) SIEC test

(i) Background

Debate on dominance versus SLC. The question of the most appropriate **8.192** substantive test for European merger control was extensively debated in the consultation process initiated by the Commission at the end of 2001 with its Green Paper on the review of the original Merger Regulation.[590] In its Green Paper, the Commission considered the possibility of replacing the original Merger Regulation's 'dominance' test and aligning with the SLC test as applied in other major jurisdictions, including the United States and the United Kingdom, in light of the increasingly international scope of merger activity. The Commission pointed to similarities, from a substantive standpoint, between the dominance test and the SLC test, given the evolution in the application of the dominance test

---

[587] See, eg Case M.3905 *Tesco/Carrefour* (22 December 2005) which was the subject of a partial referral to the Slovak competition authority under Art 9(3)(b) of the Merger Reg because of competition concerns in three local markets in the cities of Bratislava, Košice and Žilina; Case M.784 *Kesko/Tuko*, OJ 1997 L110/53; Case M.2951 *A.S. Watson/Kruidvat* (27 September 2002). See also Horizontal Merger Guidelines (n 575, above) n 32, which refers to product differentiation based on location as being a meaningful consideration for retail distribution, banks, travel agencies or petrol stations.

[588] See eg Case M.1882 *Pirelli/BICC*, OJ 2003 L70/35, paras 35–55, concerning power cables: the gradual liberalisation of electricity markets, the progressive harmonisation of technical standards and the increasing intra-Community trade flows have led the markets for production and sale of power cables to evolve as Community-wide, even if this was not at the time reflected in market shares. cf the Commission's approach regarding pharmaceutical products, where markets have been consistently defined as national in scope, despite increasing harmonisation at European level: see para 4.092, above.

[589] See eg Case M.3440 *ENI/EDP/GDP* (9 December 2004) (appeal dismissed Case T-87/05 *EDP v Commission* [2005] ECR II-3745, [2005] 5 CMLR 1436).

[590] Commission Green Paper COM (2001) 745 of 11 December 2001.

since its inception.[591] It also acknowledged 'more specific hypothetical questions that have occasionally been raised about the reach of the dominance test,' such as (i) whether it allows for the effective control of mergers where a merged firm could unilaterally exercise market power without achieving levels of 'single-firm dominance' and without the conditions for 'collective dominance' being satisfied (so-called 'gap' cases); as well as (ii) the uncertainties surrounding the scope for giving proper consideration to efficiencies that may result from mergers. Much of this reflection was prompted by the Court of First Instance's judgments in 2002 which annulled three Phase II prohibition decisions on the basis that the Commission had failed to prove that the transactions raised valid concerns under the dominance test.[592]

8.193 **Adoption of the SIEC test.**   In its summary of the comments received on the Green Paper,[593] the Commission set out the arguments received for and against a change in the substantive merger control test from dominance to SLC. Those most favourable to SLC saw the test as more 'intellectually honest' and less constricting than the dominance test, whereas those against it argued that the change would unacceptably increase the scope for Commission intervention and reduce legal certainty. Many saw a possible change to SLC as a matter of semantics and argued that the key consideration was how any substantive assessment is carried out in practice: the Commission was encouraged to formulate its intended approach in guidelines based on sound economic principles. The final substantive test of SIEC, as determined by the Council, reflected consensus for an intermediate position that would clarify the scope for Commission intervention while preserving the value of the bulk of the existing body of precedent and case law on merger control.

8.194 **Implications of the SIEC test.**   The SIEC test is generally considered to have expanded the potential scope of the Merger Regulation to a limited extent, as regards unilateral effects cases which do not result in 'single-firm dominance'. Thus, Recital (25) to the Merger Regulation explains the rationale behind the introduction of the SIEC test in terms of a desire to ensure that the non-coordinated effects of mergers in oligopolistic markets can be reviewed. It states that the notion of a significant impediment to effective competition should be

---

591 The Commission referred to the evolution of the Community Courts' interpretation of the Merger Reg's dominance test, eg in respect of collective dominance in the *Kali+Salz* case Cases C-68/94 & C-30/95 *France v Commission (Kali+Salz)* [1998] ECR I-1375, [1998] 4 CMLR 829; and Case T-102/96 *Gencor v Commission* [1999] ECR II-753, [1999] 4 CMLR 971, [1999] All ER (EC) 289.

592 *Airtours v Commission* (n 781, below) annulling *Airtours/First Choice*; *Schneider Electric v Commission* (n 544, above), annulling *Schneider/Legrand*; Case T-5/02 *Tetra Laval v Commission* (n 781, below) annulling the prohibition decision in *Tetra Laval/Sidel*.

593 See http://ec.europa.eu/comm/competition/mergers/review/comments.html.

extended beyond the existing concept of dominance 'only to the anti-competitive effects of a concentration resulting from the non-coordinated behaviour of undertakings which would not have a dominant position on the markets concerned'. That was the so-called 'gap', referred to above, since the test under the original Merger Regulation was dependent on a finding of dominance.[594]

(ii) Relationship with concept of dominance

Dominance as a concept linked with SIEC.   The substantive test under the **8.195** original Merger Regulation included the creation or strengthening of 'dominance' as a necessary pre-requisite; however, the old test comprised two limbs, the second being that effective competition would be significantly impeded, which is in effect the criterion of the SIEC test under the current Merger Regulation.[595] The Community Courts had nonetheless recognised that 'the strengthening of a dominant position may in itself significantly impede competition and do so to such an extent that it amounts, on its own, to an abuse of that position'.[596] Accordingly, the Court of First Instance concluded: 'a fortiori, that the strengthening or creation of a dominant position . . . may amount, in particular cases, to proof of a significant impediment to effective competition'.[597] However, market power may not be determinative if it is likely to be temporary in nature. Thus in *Aérospatiale-Alenia/de Havilland*,[598] after concluding that a dominant position would be created, the Commission stated: 'in general terms, a concentration which leads to the creation of a dominant position may however be compatible with the common market . . . if there exists strong evidence that this position is only temporary and would be quickly eroded because of high probability of strong market entry. With such market entry the dominant position is not likely to significantly impede effective competition'.

---

594 For further observations, see para 8.206, below.

595 See para 8.184, above, in particular n 573.

596 *General Electric v Commission* (n 798, below) para 86, in line with the ECJ's judgment in Case 6/72 *Europemballage and Continental Can v Commission* [1973] ECR 215, [1973] CMLR 199, para 26. For further observations on the Art 82 dominance test in the context of mergers, see para 8.259, below.

597 *General Electric v Commission* (n 798, below) para 87. Accordingly, under the original Merger Reg the facts of a particular case may make it apparent from a single factual analysis of a given market that both limbs of the old 'dominance' substantive test were met. See also *EDP v Commission* (n 736, below) para 49, where the CFI held that: 'proof of the creation or strengthening of a dominant position . . . may in certain cases constitute proof of a significant impediment to effective competition. That observation does not in any way mean that the second criterion is the same in law as the first, but only that it may follow from one and the same factual analysis of a specific market that both criteria are satisfied'.

598 Case M.53 *Aérospatiale-Alenia/de Havilland*, OJ 1991 L334/42, [1992] 4 CMLR M2, para 53; See also Case M.4 *Renault/Volvo* [1991] 4 CMLR 297, para 53; Case M.222 *Mannesmann/ Hoesch*, OJ 1992 L114/334, paras 90–115.

8.196 **Dominance remains a relevant consideration.** The Commission's Horizontal Merger Guidelines continue to identify 'the creation or strengthening of a dominant position' as 'a primary form of competitive harm' in respect of concentrations.[599] They indicate the Commission's expectation that most cases of incompatibility of a concentration with the common market under the current Merger Regulation will continue to be based upon a finding of 'dominance', such that the concept continues to provide 'an important indication as to the standard of competitive harm that is applicable when determining whether a concentration is likely to impede effective competition to a significant degree' and therefore as to the likelihood of intervention by the Commission.[600] In this respect, the Community Courts have developed a classic definition of dominance as:

> 'A situation where one or more undertakings wield economic power which would enable them to prevent effective competition from being maintained in the relevant market by giving them the opportunity to act to a considerable extent independently of their competitors, their customers, and, ultimately, of consumers.'[601]

The Community Courts have interpreted the concept of 'dominance' to include not only 'single-firm dominance' but also 'collective dominance', so covering mergers in oligopolistic markets that give rise to 'coordinated effects' or 'tacit collusion'.[602]

8.197 **Dominance is no longer a pre-requisite.** The substantive SIEC test under the current Merger Regulation no longer requires a formal finding of 'dominance'.[603] Although the Commission has indicated that past decisional practice and case law on dominance remains relevant,[604] its assessment of the impact of a merger, and in particular of whether a merged entity will be able to increase prices post-merger, can be based on a broad review of underlying market dynamics rather than on static monopoly-based competitive harm theories. The Commission has

---

[599] Horizontal Merger Guidelines (n 575, above) para 2.

[600] ibid, para 4. See also Recitals (25) and (26) to the Merger Reg.

[601] *Gencor v Commission* (n 591, above) para 200, following the much cited formulation in Case 85/76 *Hoffmann-La Roche v Commission* [1979] ECR 461, [1979] 3 CMLR 211, para 38. See also Horizontal Merger Guidelines (n 575, above) para 2. In applying this test, a crucial factor is the price elasticity of demand, to establish whether the concentration will enable the undertaking to increase prices without losing customers.

[602] *Gencor v Commission* (n 591, above) para 277; and *Airtours v Commission* (n 781, below) para 61; see paras 8.210 *et seq*, below and Chap 10 on Art 82. See also n 2 to the Horizontal Merger Guidelines (n 575, above).

[603] Prior to the entry into force of the SIEC test, the Commission had already investigated competition concerns in a number of horizontal mergers where the parties' pro forma market shares were below traditional levels of single-firm dominance and the criteria for collective dominance (tacit collusion) did not appear to be satisfied: see Case M.2861 *Siemens/Drägerwerk*, OJ 2003 L291/1, [2004] 5 CMLR 814; Case M.3216 *Oracle/PeopleSoft*, OJ 2005 L218/6, where the Commission conducted a lengthy Phase II investigation.

[604] Horizontal Merger Guidelines (n 575, above) para 4.

indicated that this new approach is particularly relevant to markets that are highly concentrated or 'oligopolistic'.[605] While recognising that many oligopolistic markets exhibit a healthy degree of competition, the Commission's Horizontal Guidelines observe that by reason of non-coordinated effects, concentrations in such markets may result in a significant impediment to effective competition. This may be so if the concentration involves the elimination of important competitive constraints that the merging parties exerted upon each other, as well as a reduction of competitive pressure on the remaining competitors, regardless of whether (i) the merged group may enjoy 'single-firm dominance' or (ii) there may be the likelihood of coordination between the members of the oligopoly.[606]

(iii) Checks and balances

Prospect of judicial review. The potential for its decisions to be challenged by **8.198** the parties or interested third parties acts as a constraint on the Commission in the interpretation and application of the law to a certain extent.[607] The Court of First Instance has also shown itself ready to undertake detailed scrutiny of the accuracy of primary facts relied on by the Commission.[608] It may also undertake a more restrained review of economic assessments made by the Commission when applying the SIEC test.[609] However, the vast majority of Phase I decisions are not appealed.[610] The great majority of Phase II proceedings have tended to involve investigations of horizontal mergers between competitors, most of which have ultimately been cleared by the Commission with or without conditions and have not been the subject of appeals.[611] The cases in which the Commission's

---

[605] ibid, para 25. And see Röller and de la Mano, 'The Impact of the New Substantive Test in European Merger Control' (2006) 2 European Competition Journal 9, noting that the SIEC test enables the Commission to focus on the market-wide equilibrium effects instead of concentrating exclusively on whether the merger increases the market power of the merged entity to the point of dominance.

[606] See further paras 8.209 *et seq*, below.

[607] For judicial review of Merger Reg decisions see paras 8.235 *et seq*, below. Typically, parties to proposed concentrations expressly provide that closing of the deal is conditional *inter alia* upon approval by the Commission (in some cases at Phase I or in other cases allowing for the possibility of a Phase II investigation) or other applicable merger control authorities, with a deadline or 'drop-dead date' by which the deal will lapse if the conditions have not been satisfied. Accordingly, in many cases a Phase II prohibition (or even the mere opening of Phase II proceedings, eg where a takeover bid is subject to the UK City Code) will cause the deal to lapse or be abandoned. Nevertheless, the parties may still proceed with Phase II proceedings and even appeal a Phase II prohibition decision. In two cases (where the prohibition decision was subsequently annulled by the CFI) the parties have brought claims for damages against the Commission: Case T-212/03 *MyTravel v Commission*, not yet decided; and Case T-351/03 *Schneider Electric v Commission*, judgment of 11 July 2007 (damages awarded against the Commission).

[608] See para 8.249, below.

[609] See paras 8.250–8.252, below.

[610] The small number of challenges to Phase I decisions have tended to relate to jurisdictional or procedural issues. See eg Case T-282/06 *Sun Chemical Group v Commission*, judgement of 9 July 2007.

[611] See the statistics in table (c) at para 8.011, above.

substantive appraisal has been most controversial, and has come under greatest scrutiny from the Community Courts, have tended to involve (i) horizontal effects in situations not giving rise to 'single-firm dominance' (for example coordinated effects cases),[612] (ii) vertical effects,[613] and (iii) conglomerate effects.[614]

8.199 **Commission internal procedural checks.** The Commission has taken various steps to allay concerns as to its approach to the substantive assessment of mergers. In 2004, it published Horizontal Merger Guidelines that aim to set out a sound economic framework for the application of its merger control policy.[615] It has also introduced a number of internal procedural checks and balances to its administrative review process.[616] This has involved the establishment of the Merger Network within DG Competition to ensure a degree of consistency between its investigations of different cases.[617] The thoroughness of the Commission's substantive assessment in Phase II investigations was further improved by the creation in July 2003 of the position of the Chief Competition Economist, whose staff of economists can be called upon to assist the case team, and by the introduction of so-called peer review panels to scrutinise more challenging cases.[618] The role of the Hearing Officer has also been strengthened.[619]

(iv) General content of assessment

8.200 **Impact on consumer welfare and the counterfactual.** The Horizontal Merger Guidelines recognise that effective competition brings benefits to consumers, such as low prices, high quality products, a wide selection of goods and services, and innovation. Accordingly, the focus of the application of the SIEC test is the prevention of mergers that would be likely to deprive customers of these benefits by significantly increasing the market power of firms.[620] For these purposes,

---

612 To date the Community Courts have not ruled on the application of the SIEC test to non-coordinated, unilateral effects in situations not giving rise to single-firm dominance. For horizontal mergers involving single-firm dominance, see para 8.207, below. For cases involving coordinated effects, see paras 8.209–8.214, below.

613 For cases involving vertical effects, see para 8.218, below.

614 For cases involving conglomerate effects, see paras 8.219 *et seq*, below.

615 Horizontal Merger Guidelines, OJ 2004 C31/5: Vol II, App D.6.

616 These specific checks for Merger Reg cases should also be viewed in the context of wider Commission initiatives, eg the adoption of a Code of good administrative behaviour for staff of the European Commission in their relations with the public (annexed to the Commission's Rules of Procedure, OJ 2000 L308/32); this emphasises *inter alia* that the Commission acts in accordance with the law and that staff must act objectively and impartially.

617 See para 8.107, above.

618 See paras 8.151–8.152, above.

619 See para 8.150, above.

620 Horizontal Merger Guidelines (n 615, above) para 8. This observes that 'market power' usually refers to a supplier's market power, as opposed to 'buyer power'. It also notes that references to price increases also relate to situations where 'prices are decreased less, or are less likely to decrease, than they otherwise would have without the merger'.

increased market power means the ability of one or more firms profitably to increase prices, reduce output, choice or quality of goods and services, diminish innovation, or otherwise influence the parameters of competition. This substantive appraisal should compare the competitive conditions that would result from the notified merger with the conditions that would have prevailed without the merger.[621] Thus, it is necessary to compare the likely post-merger market structure not with the pre-merger situation (or *status quo ante*) but rather with the 'counterfactual', that is the market structure which would be likely to develop if the merger did not proceed. In order to assess the foreseeable impact of a merger on the relevant markets, the Commission analyses its possible anti-competitive effects and the relevant countervailing factors such as buyer power, the extent of entry barriers and possible efficiencies put forward by the parties.[622]

Priority principle for contemporaneous transactions. Where two mergers **8.201** affecting the same markets are agreed within a short space of time, such that the applicable investigation periods may overlap, the issue arises whether the Commission should take account of the one when assessing the other. As a general proposition, the Commission is required to carry out a prospective analysis that takes account of future events and market developments. However, the Commission applies a 'priority principle' in cases where the administrative authorisation of both transactions is subject to its own control under the Merger Regulation, assessing each transaction in light of the competitive situation that prevailed at the time of the respective notification.[623] This approach is consistent with the fact that it is inherent in the merger control system established by the

---

[621] The Commission may in some circumstances take into account future changes to the market that can reasonably be predicted: see Case M.950 *Hoffmann-La Roche/Boehringer Mannheim*, OJ 1998 L234/14, [2000] 4 CMLR 735, para 13; Case M.1846 *Glaxo Wellcome/SmithKline Beecham* (8 May 2000) paras 70–72; Case M.2547 *Bayer/Aventis Crop Science* (OJ 2004 L107/1), paras 324 *et seq*. This may extend to the likely entry or exit of firms absent the merger; *Gencor v Commission* (n 591, above) paras 247–263.

[622] Horizontal Merger Guidelines (n 615, above) para 12. See paras 8.225–8.229, below.

[623] See Case M.4601 *KarstadtQuelle/MyTravel* (4 May 2007) paras 48–50; and Case M.4600 *TUI/First Choice* (4 June 2007) paras 66–68: the first transaction was agreed and announced on 12 February 2007 and notified on 26 March 2007, whereas the second was agreed and announced on 19 March 2007 and notified on 4 April 2007. See also Case M.1016 *PriceWaterhouse/Coopers & Lybrand* (OJ 1999 L50/27, [1999] 4 CMLR 665), paras 108–111; Case M.2389 *Shell/DEA*, OJ 2003 L15/35; and Case M.2533 *BP/E.ON* (decision of 20 December 2001), paras 21 and 18 respectively. For further analysis, see Schmidt 'Spotting the Elephant in Parallel Mergers: First Past the Post, or Combined Assessment' (2003) 24 ECLR 183; Stadler 'Conflicting Mergers: Combined Assessment or Priority Rule?' (2003) 24 ECLR 321. See also Case M.4141 *Linde/BOC* (6 June 2006) where the Commission's assessment of certain markets for special gases did not take account of a parallel acquisition being made by Linde, as subsequently notified in Case M.4091 *Linde/Spectra* (20 September 2006); the Commission gave priority to the first transaction to be notified, notwithstanding the fact that the other transaction had already been announced and approved by the US authorities and had been the subject of a Form RS submission to the Commission (on 1 February 2006).

Merger Regulation that any party notifying a concentration that, assessed on its own merits, would not significantly impede effective competition, is entitled to have its operation declared compatible with the common market within the applicable time limits.

8.202 **Horizontal and non-horizontal mergers and their economic effects.** Mergers can be categorised as either horizontal, that is between undertakings operating at the same level in the supply chain, supplying competing or substitute products, or non-horizontal. Within the category of non-horizontal mergers, a further distinction can be drawn between vertical mergers, between undertakings operating at different levels in the supply chain, and conglomerate mergers between undertakings operating in different markets which are not horizontally or vertically related.[624] To the extent that a merger removes the competitive constraints imposed by competing or substitute products, this may increase the market power of the merged entity, or of other competitors, with potential harmful effects for consumers giving rise to a SIEC.[625] For these purposes, the Horizontal Merger Guidelines draw a clear distinction between unilateral effects and coordinated effects:[626]

(a) *Unilateral effects:* in the case of so-called 'unilateral' effects (sometimes called 'non-coordinated' effects), it is necessary to consider whether the merger eliminates important competitive constraints on one or more of the merging parties or even on a third party. If so, that party could consequently enjoy increased market power whether or not single-firm dominance could be established that would have harmful effects on competition;

(b) *Coordinated effects:* in the case of coordinated effects, it is necessary to consider whether the pre- and/or post-merger structure is oligopolistic and whether the merger will facilitate existing or new tacit collusion between the members of that oligopoly, with the consequence of prices being raised, output being reduced or other harmful effects on competition. In making this

---

[624] If an undertaking is active in a number of different product markets or at more than one level in the supply chain, a merger with another undertaking may fall into more than one category and involve a combination of horizontal, vertical and/or conglomerate issues.

[625] Non-horizontal mergers are considered further at paras 8.216–8.224, below. Vertical or conglomerate effects arising in respect of a non-horizontal merger which may result in an increase in market power can, as with horizontal mergers, be classified as either 'unilateral effects' or 'coordinated effects' (concepts considered at paras 8.203–8.215, below).

[626] Horizontal Merger Guidelines (n 615, above) para 22; the same distinction is drawn in the Commission's draft Non-horizontal Merger Guidelines, Vol II, App D.14. A merger, whether horizontal or non-horizontal, may give rise to both unilateral and/or coordinated effects in the same or in different relevant markets. See eg Case M.3465 *Syngenta CP/Advanta* (17 August 2004) in which the Commission considered that the parties' combined sales of sugarbeet, maize, sunflower and spring barley seeds led to the creation of single-firm dominance in each of these respective markets in several Member States, while the merger was also likely to result in the creation of non-coordinated effects in an oligopolistic market for sugarbeet seeds in Belgium and France.

assessment, the Commission will examine the structure of the market and past behaviour of firms on the market.

(d) Unilateral effects

(i) In general

Introduction.   The prospect that a concentration may result in a SIEC because **8.203** of unilateral effects generally arises if it results in (i) a merged entity which will have an appreciably larger market share than its remaining competitors; or (ii) the elimination of important competitive constraints previously exerted by one or other of the merging parties on the market as a whole in oligopolistic markets.[627] The Commission's investigation of such issues will take account of market share and concentration levels as 'useful first indications of the market structure and of the competitive importance of both the merging parties and their competitors'.[628] A number of other factors are also potentially relevant to this appraisal of the likelihood of a SIEC involving unilateral effects.

Relevance of market shares and concentration levels.   In making its substantive **8.204** assessment of potential unilateral effects, the Commission places considerable reliance on the parties' market shares. For the purpose of this evaluation, it is necessary to aggregate the market shares of all undertakings which will, post-merger, be under the same 'control' within the meaning of Article 3(2).[629] The Commission's approach is to treat the *pro forma* sum of the parties' pre-merger market shares as indicative of their post-merger combined market share, with some adjustments where these reflect reasonably certain future changes, for instance in light of entry, exit or expansion.[630] Recital (32) to the Merger Regulation states that a concentration involving limited market shares which do not exceed 25 per cent in the common market or a substantial part of it, may be presumed not to be liable to impede effective competition.[631] The Commission will also consider the concentration levels relevant to any given case, often by reference to the Herfindahl-Hirschman

---

[627] Horizontal Merger Guidelines (n 615, above) paras 24–38.

[628] ibid, para 14.

[629] See eg Case M.3576 *ECT/PONL/Euromax* (22 December 2004), concerning the establishment of a JV for the operation for a container port between PONL (a 100 per cent subsidiary of Royal Nedlloyd) and ECT. P&O, a competing operator of container terminals, held a 25 per cent interest in Royal Nedlloyd which the Commission had previously decided, in Case M.3379 *P&O/Royal Nedlloyd/P&O Nedlloyd* (29 March 2004), did not confer control. In the absence of new elements to change this analysis, the Commission decided that P&O's container terminal activities were not to be added to the parties' activities when examining their market power: decn, para 5 and n 3. Similarly, in Case M.50 *AT&T/NCR* (18 January 1991), in calculating AT&T's market share, the Commission did not aggregate that of Olivetti (in which AT&T held a 20 per cent stake) given that AT&T did not exercise sole or joint control of Olivetti: decn, para 7.

[630] Horizontal Merger Guidelines (n 615, above) para 15.

[631] ibid, para 18, n 24, where the Commission asserts that this indication does not apply to cases where the merger creates or strengthens a collective dominant position.

Index (HHI).[632] Conversely, although high market shares and concentration levels have been significant in causing the launch of Phase II proceedings, the various criteria of Article 2(1)[633] and other relevant factors[634] may lead to the conclusion that a concentration is compatible with the common market.

8.205 **Single-firm dominance.** Dominance equates to a position of market power which allows a party to behave to a considerable extent independently of its competitors, customers and ultimately consumers.[635] In the context of a concentration, the critical factor tends to be the extent to which the merged entity may, as a result of the merger, raise prices (or reduce choice or levels of service or innovation) without losing customers. Traditionally, market share figures of more than 40 per cent have been regarded as indicative of single-firm dominance.[636] There is a tendency for the Commission to define product markets narrowly for these purposes.

8.206 **Non-coordinated effects.** Unilateral effects may also arise outside the realm of traditional single-firm dominance cases, if the market structure is oligopolistic and the merger results in the elimination of important competitive constraints previously exerted by one or other of the merging parties on the market as a whole, thereby changing the competitive balance on that market although the merged firm has not itself become dominant. This is the so-called 'gap' case scenario for which the Commission had been intent on securing clearer powers of review.[637]

---

[632] The HHI is calculated by adding the squares of the individual market shares of all firms in the market, both pre- and post-merger, and using the absolute HHI levels and the 'delta' (being the change in absolute HHI brought about by the merger that can also be measured by doubling the product of the market shares of the merging firms) to measure the competitive pressure in the market and the change directly brought about by the concentration. The HHI theoretically ranges from close to zero (in an 'atomistic market') to 10,000 (in the case of a pure monopoly). The Commission has indicated that, save for special circumstances, it is unlikely to identify horizontal competition concerns in a market with a post-merger HHI below 1,000; with a post-merger HHI between 1,000 and 2,000 and a delta below 250; or with a post-merger HHI above 2,000 and a delta below 150 (paras 19 and 20 of the Horizontal Merger Guidelines (n 615, above)). On the HHI and concentration ratios generally, see Bishop & Walker, *The Economics of EC Competition Law* (2nd edn, 2002), paras 3.25 *et seq*, noting that highly concentrated markets might nevertheless be characterised by fierce competition, for instance when barriers to entry and exit are very low.

[633] See para 8.183, above.

[634] See in particular considerations addressed at para 8.200, above, as well as factors addressed at paras 8.206–8.208, below.

[635] Para 8.196, above. See further Chap 10, below.

[636] Horizontal Merger Guidelines (n 615, above) para 17. For a case where single-firm dominance was found at relatively low levels, see Case M.2337 *Nestlé/Ralston Purina* (27 July 2001), paras 44–50.

[637] See paras 8.192–8.194, above. Case M.3696 *E.ON/MOL*, OJ 2006 L253/20, relating to the acquisition by E.ON (a large integrated German energy supplier) of two subsidiaries of MOL (the incumbent oil and gas company in Hungary), has been identified as an instance of a 'gap' case that could better be assessed under the SIEC test, given that the merged entity did not acquire a dominant position in any of the relevant markets identified by the Commission. The Commission stated, in relation to the perceived incentive for E.ON to foreclose access to downstream gas and electricity

For these purposes, an oligopolistic market is defined by the Commission as 'a market structure with a limited number of sizeable firms. Because the behaviour of one firm has an appreciable impact on the overall market conditions, and thus indirectly on the situation of each of the other firms, oligopolistic firms are interdependent'.[638]

(ii) Relevant considerations

Potentially relevant factors.   The Horizontal Merger Guidelines list the fol-   **8.207** lowing factors as potentially relevant, in addition to the market shares of the merging firms, in determining the likelihood of a SIEC involving unilateral (non-coordinated) effects:

(a) *Whether the merging firms are close competitors:* if the parties' products are particularly close substitutes compared with those of other competitors, this will generally increase the risk of significant price rises following the merger as rivals' products are less likely to act as a constraint on pricing.[639] Some products may be closer substitutes than others in a differentiated market, such that customers may in some instances regard the merging firms' products as their first and second choices. Competition concerns are less likely to arise if other competitors are also offering products with a high degree of substitutability, based for example on brand image, technical specifications, quality or level of service, location or the absence of switching costs for customers, or where suppliers can easily reposition their products or extend their product portfolio without incurring substantial risk and large sunk costs.[640] The Commission has thus dismissed concerns of possible non-coordinated

---

markets in Hungary, that 'a monopoly that integrates downstream may have the ability and incentive to raise its downstream rivals' costs. This can lead to significant price increases downstream even if the merged entity falls short of acquiring downstream dominance in the short term' (see Bartok and colleagues, 'A combination of gas release programmes and ownership unbundling as remedy to a problematic energy merger: E.ON/MOL', (2006) 1 EC Competition Policy Newsletter 73). See also Case M.3916 *T-Mobile Austria/tele.ring* (26 April 2006) where the merged group would have had only about one third of the Austrian mobile telephony market behind the largest operator (Mobilkom) but the Commission nevertheless had concerns about 'non-coordinated effects' in the form of price increases which could follow the removal of tele.ring from the market; this was because tele.ring was viewed as a 'price maverick' providing a greater competitive constraint on T-Mobile than the competition from Mobilkom.

[638] Horizontal Merger Guidelines (n 615, above) para 25 and n 29. Such unilateral effects may arise independently of other coordinated effects which may follow from the reactions of the merged entity's competitors: see paras 8.209 *et seq*, below for the assessment of coordinated effects.

[639] High pre-merger margins may be another factor in appraising whether significant price increases are likely post- merger: Horizontal Merger Guidelines (n 615, above) para 28.

[640] ibid, paras 28–30. On high levels of substitutability between merging firms' products see in particular Case M.2817 *Barilla/BPL/Kamps* (25 June 2002), para 34; Case M.430 *Procter & Gamble/VP Schickedanz (II)*, OJ 1994 L354/32; Case M.2097 *SCA/Metsä Tissue*, OJ 2002 L57/1, [2002] 4 CMLR 1541; and Case T-310/01 *Schneider v Commission* (n 544, above) para 418.

effects despite high combined market shares suggestive of dominance where the parties were not the closest competitors in differentiated product markets.[641] The Commission may seek to rely on customer feedback to determine how closely the parties follow one another in terms of 'essential competition parameters' or 'success factors'.[642] In some cases it may be possible to evaluate data on the extent of substitutability, for example by analysing purchasing patterns, cross-price elasticities for the products involved, diversion ratios and, where relevant, historic bidding data. Where a potential competitor has historically exerted significant competitive constraints on the behaviour of firms active in another market or where there was a significant likelihood that it would grow into an effective competitive force, a merger between an undertaking already active on a relevant market and that potential competitor may also give rise to an SIEC. The Commission has indicated that it is more likely to take this view in respect of a potential competitor that could easily enter the market because there are few sunk costs or because it could incur these in a relatively short time period, and in the absence of other potential competitors that could maintain sufficient competitive pressure after the merger.[643]

(b) *Whether customers can still switch to alternative suppliers:* customers with limited buyer power and which have few alternative suppliers or face substantial switching costs, may be particularly vulnerable to price increases. Some such customers may previously have engaged in dual sourcing from the merging parties to obtain competitive prices.[644]

(c) *Entry and expansion conditions:* if barriers to market entry or expansion by other players are high, in particular due to capacity constraints or high expansion costs, a substantial increase in market share and concentration is more likely to raise competition concerns, since it may facilitate a reduction of output or increase in prices by the merged entity. According to the Horizontal Merger Guidelines,[645] a merger is unlikely to pose significant

---

[641] See, eg Case M.3544 *Bayer Healthcare/Roche* (19 November 2004); Case M.3653 *Siemens/VA Tech* (13 July 2005); Case M.3765 *Amer/Salomon* (12 October 2005).

[642] See, eg Case M.3436 *Continental/Phoenix* (26 October 2004), paras 121–123: customer ranking of the parties and other competitors by reference to a number of categories (technical competence/innovation, quality/reliability, customer service/support, past experience, price and spare capacity). The Commission often asks customers to provide such rankings as part of its Phase I and II investigations.

[643] See Horizontal Merger Guidelines (n 615, above) paras 58–60. See also Case M.1439 *Telia/Telenor*, OJ 2001 L40/1, [2001] 4 CMLR 1226, paras 330–331; Case M.1681 *Akzo Nobel/ Hoechst Roussel Vet* (22 November 1999), para 64; Case M.1630 *Air Liquide/BOC*, OJ 2004 L92/1, para 219; Case M.1853 *EDF/EnBW*, OJ 2002 L59/1, paras 54–64; Case M.3687 *Johnson & Johnson/Guidant* (25 August 2005), para 165.

[644] Horizontal Merger Guidelines (n 615, above) para 31. See *Boeing/McDonnell Douglas* (n 585, above) para 70; Case M.986 *Agfa-Gevaert/DuPont* (11 February 1998), paras 63–71.

[645] Horizontal Merger Guidelines (n 615, above) paras 32–36 and 68–75.

anti-competitive risks where new entry offers a likely, timely and sufficient deterrent to any potential impediments to competition. Entry or expansion is likely to represent a meaningful constraint only where it would be economically viable, taking into account the scale of entry required, the price effects of additional output and the potential response of the incumbents. Entry will be more difficult if incumbents can protect their market shares through long-term agreements or selective rebates to key customers. High risk and high cost may also make entry less attractive, as may regulatory restrictions;[646] the need for access to technical facilities,[647] distribution and sales networks,[648] or experience and an established reputation;[649] consumer brand loyalty;[650] close relationships between customers and suppliers and high switching costs to be incurred by customers. Any predicted changes to market conditions should be taken into account when considering such barriers.[651]

(d) *Actual or potential competition:* the ability of the merged group to raise prices may be constrained by actual or potential competition from other undertakings (within or outside the EU), including their ability to increase output (for example, if they have spare capacity) and increase sales if the merged group were to seek to increase prices. The extent to which the merged entity has the ability to hinder such expansion of competition will involve the review of factors such as its control or influence over raw materials, distribution possibilities, intellectual property rights and, in some cases, interoperability between infrastructures. The financial strength of the merged entity relative to its rivals may also be taken into account.[652]

(e) *Whether the merger eliminates an important competitive force:* Some merging firms may have more of an influence on the competitive process than their market shares may suggest, for example, a recent new entrant which may have

---

[646] Case M.1430 *Vodafone/Airtouch* (21 May 1999), para 27; Case M.2016 *France Télécom/Orange* (11 August 2000), para 33; Case M.1693 *Alcoa/Reynolds* OJ 2002 L58/25, [2002] 5 CMLR 475, para 87.

[647] Case M.269 *Shell/Montecatini*, OJ 1994 L332/48, para 32; Case M.774 *Saint-Gobain/Wacker Chemie/NOM*, OJ 1997 L247/1, paras 184–187; Case M.754 *Anglo American Corp/Lonrho*, OJ 1998 L149/21, paras 118–119.

[648] Case M.833 *The Coca-Cola Company/Carlsberg A/S* (11 September 1997), para 74.

[649] *SCA/Metsä Tissue* (n 640, above) paras 83–84.

[650] *The Coca-Cola Company/Carlsberg A/S* (n 648, above) paras 72–73.

[651] Horizontal Merger Guidelines (n 615, above) paras 32–35. See Case M.2187 *CVC/Lenzing*, OJ 2004 L82/20, paras 162–173; Case M.3178 *Bertelsmann/Springer* (3 May 2005); *Johnson & Johnson/Guidant* (n 643, above).

[652] Horizontal Merger Guidelines (n 615, above) para 36. See also Case T-221/95 *Endemol Entertainment v Commission* [1999] ECR II–1299, [1999] 5 CMLR 611, [1999] All ER (EC) 385, para 167; Case T-22/97 *Kesko v Commission* [1999] ECR II-3775, [2000] 4 CMLR 335, paras 141 *et seq*; Case M.623 *Kimberly-Clark/Scott Paper* (16 January 1996); Case T-114/02 *BaByliss v Commission* [2003] ECR II-1279, [2004] 5 CMLR 2, paras 343 *et seq*.

innovative new products or be expected to play the role of a 'maverick' in a concentrated market.[653]

8.208 Application of unilateral effects analysis in practice. The Commission generally seeks to establish in its investigations (i) whether the parties' *pro forma* combined market share *per se* gives rise to *prima facie* competition concerns; and (ii) to what extent there exist sufficient actual or potential competitors with an appreciable presence on the market, or customers with countervailing power, that will be able to constrain the behaviour of the merging parties. In effect, the dominance and unilateral effects assessments are applied in parallel.[654] This increases the scope for intervention by the Commission under unilateral effects theories in cases where the parties' *pro forma* combined market share falls short of single-firm dominance but is above the 25 per cent 'safe harbour' provided by the Merger Regulation and the Horizontal Merger Guidelines.[655]

(e) Coordinated effects

(i) In general

8.209 Oligopolistic markets. An oligopolistic market is one which is dominated by a relatively small number of major players, even if none enjoys a position of single-firm dominance.[656] The term 'duopoly' may be used to describe a two-firm oligopoly; 'oligopolies' may be found to exist where three or even more substantial players are active in the relevant market. The Court of First Instance has upheld the view of the Commission that a position of collective dominance can occur 'where a mere adaptation by members of the oligopoly to market conditions causes anti-competitive parallel behaviour whereby the oligopoly becomes dominant. Active collusion would therefore not be required for members of the oligopoly to become dominant and to behave to an appreciable extent independently of their remaining competitors, their customers and, ultimately, the consumers.'[657]

8.210 Opportunities for tacit collusion. An oligopolistic market may provide opportunities for tacit collusion by the members of the oligopoly where 'cheating' (that is deviations from the tacitly coordinated pricing or output levels) can be

---

[653] Horizontal Merger Guidelines, paras 37–38.

[654] See observations at paras 8.194–8.196, above.

[655] See eg Case M.3751 *Novartis/Hexal* (27 May 2005): merger between close substitutes; Case M.3916 *T-Mobile Austria/tele.ring* (26 April 2006): elimination of maverick; *Johnson & Johnson/Guidant* (n 643, above): Johnson & Johnson was the second largest player on the market for coronary drug-eluting stents (a kind of cardiology device) and Guidant a potential new entrant; after in-depth investigation the Commission concluded that effective competition would not be significantly impeded.

[656] For further observations on 'oligopolies', see para 8.206, above.

[657] Case M.619 *Gencor/Lonrho*, OJ 1997 L11/30, para 140; upheld by *Gencor v Commission* (n 591, above) paras 276–277. See also Case T-342/99 *Airtours v Commission* [2002] ECR II-2585, [2002] 5 CMLR 317, [2002] All ER (EC) 783, para 61; Horizontal Merger Guidelines (n 615, above) para 39.

monitored because of market transparency and 'punished' through some form of deterrent mechanism or retaliation measures. Tacit collusion has been considered by the Commission in many merger cases involving a reduction of players from three to two; only one such case (*Gencor/Lonrho*) has been prohibited by the Commission.[658] In a number of cases, a reduction of players from four to three has also led to an investigation into tacit collusion. Although the only relevant prohibition decision (*Airtours/FirstChoice*) was annulled by the Court of First Instance,[659] the Court did not suggest that collective dominance could not occur in markets with three or more major firms. Indeed, the Commission has also investigated whether tacit collusion existed amongst four or more players in several cases.[660] The prospect that a concentration may result in a SIEC because of coordinated effects generally arises if it would result in or reinforce a market structure where it would be economically rational for members of the oligopoly, in adapting themselves to market conditions, to act in ways which will substantially reduce competition between them, whether or not they had done so previously. Such tacit collusion or coordination may relate to pricing, so keeping prices above the competitive level. Alternatively, it can relate to limiting supplies, whether by limiting production or new capacity or to some form of market sharing according to different territories or customers.[661]

(ii) Relevant considerations

Characterising a market as oligopolistic.   In assessing the likelihood of a SIEC   **8.211**
involving coordinated effects, the Commission will consider all available relevant information on the characteristics of the markets concerned, including structural features and the past behaviour of firms. Evidence of past coordination in the market may be important; evidence of coordination in similar markets may also be considered relevant.[662] While cautioning against adopting a mechanical 'checklist' approach, the Commission typically expects to find some of the following characteristics in an oligopolistic market:[663]

(a) product homogeneity (typically commodities) with limited differentiation in the nature and pricing of the products. Oligopoly concerns are less likely to

---

[658] *Gencor/Lonrho*, above.

[659] *Airtours/First Choice*, annulled in Case T-342/99 *Airtours v Commission* [2002] ECR II-2585, [2002] 5 CMLR 317, [2002] All ER (EC) 783.

[660] See, eg Case M.1225 *Enso/Stora*, OJ 1999 L254/9, [2000] 4 CMLR 372; Case M.202 *Thorn EMI/Virgin* (27 April 1992); and Case M.3333 *Sony/BMG*, discussed at paras 8.212–8.214, below. The Commission has even found tacit collusion amongst as many as seven firms in one market for motor fuel retailing: Case M.1383 *Exxon/Mobil*, OJ 2004 L103/1 (cleared subject to conditions).

[661] Horizontal Merger Guidelines (n 615, above) para 40.

[662] ibid, para 43. Evidence of past coordination will be given added weight where relevant market characteristics have not changed appreciably or are unlikely to do so.

[663] ibid, paras 44 *et seq.*

arise where suppliers offer differentiated product ranges and/or different distribution methods and associated services with different customers having different requirements in terms of product quality, reliability of supply, contract terms;

(b) high market transparency regarding key competitive parameters such as production capacities, output or prices;

(c) stagnant and inelastic demand and supply conditions, given that volatile demand will generally make coordination less likely;

(d) low levels of technological change, recognising that in markets where innovation is important it will be possible for one firm to gain a major advantage over its rivals, so it will not be attractive to seek a tacitly coordinated outcome;

(e) substantial entry barriers;

(f) interdependence and extensive commercial links, giving rise to multi-market contacts between the major suppliers;

(g) symmetries or similarities between the major suppliers' business activities in terms of cost structures, market shares, capacity levels and levels of vertical integration; and

(h) insignificant buyer power.

8.212 Reaching terms of coordination.   Coordination can only emerge if competitors share a common perception of what the coordination will involve, whether it is on price or market division by allocating customers by geography, customer type or based on their historic purchasing patterns. In the Horizontal Merger Guidelines, the Commission suggests that the establishment of 'simple pricing rules' can help oligopolists to overcome complex economic environments, for instance using a small number of pricing points or a fixed relationship between a base or list price and other prices after discounts or rebates. The Guidelines note that: 'The more complex the market situation is, the more transparency or communication is likely to be needed to reach a common understanding on the terms of coordination'.[664] During the original administrative procedure in *Sony/BMG*[665] the Commission had sought to establish past price coordination by looking at the possible use of record companies' trade list prices (so called 'published prices to dealers' or 'PPDs') as focal points that might facilitate parallelism in the price developments of the recorded music 'majors' which would reduce from five to four as a result of the merger. The Commission also examined the developments of the majors' discounts, but ultimately concluded that certain discounts were not

---

[664] Horizontal Merger Guidelines (n 615, above) para 47. See also *Gencor v Commission* (n 591, above) para 222. The Commission may seek to review efficiency gains in assessing whether a merger may increase the symmetry of the various firms present on the market.

[665] Case M.3333 *Sony/BMG*, OJ 2005 L62/30 annulled by the CFI in Case T-464/04 *Impala v Commission* [2006] ECR II-2289, [2006] 5 CMLR 1049, on further appeal to the ECJ: Case C-413/06 *Bertelsmann and Sony Corp / Impala*, not yet decided.

transparent and so were difficult to monitor. The largely differentiated nature of music content further contributed to its finding, at the end of an in-depth Phase II investigation, that despite a certain homogeneity in the format, pricing and marketing of music CDs, the evidence did not establish an existing collective dominant position of the five majors in the market for recorded music.[666] However, the Court of First Instance annulled the approval decision on the grounds that the two main reasons why the Commission concluded that there was not a collective dominant position on the markets for recorded music, namely lack of transparency and inability to adopt retaliatory measures, were not adequately supported by the statement of reasons or by the Commission's examination of the evidence.

Enforcing coordination.   According to the Horizontal Merger Guidelines, and **8.213** consistent with the judgment of the Court of First Instance in the *Airtours* case,[667] there are three cumulative elements which are necessary for coordination to be sustainable, namely (i) the ability of oligopolistic market players to monitor any deviations from the terms of tacit coordination; (ii) a credible deterrent mechanism; and (iii) the inability of outsiders (competitors or customers) to jeopardise the outcome expected from coordination:[668]

(a) *Monitoring:* the successful monitoring of deviations will depend on market transparency. This will most likely be sufficient where market players can draw inferences[669] from one another's behaviour,[670] based for instance on a small number of players, publicity surrounding transactions[671] as opposed to confidential bilateral transactions between a supplier and its customers[672] and stable market conditions in terms of output, demand and prices. The Commission has also recognised that less visible factors can be enough to facilitate the monitoring of deviations, for example contractual clauses linking prices to prevailing market conditions, the publication of information or announcements, the exchange of information through trade associations and any structural links between companies.

---

[666] The Commission also concluded, as regards the possible *creation* of a collective dominant position in the markets for recorded music, that there was insufficient evidence to prove that the reduction from five to four major players would in itself alter the market structure sufficiently to give rise to prospective coordinated effects.

[667] *Airtours v Commission* (n 659, above).

[668] Horizontal Merger Guidelines (n 615, above) paras 49–57. See also Case M.4601 *KarstadtQuelle/MyTravel* (4 May 2007) paras 87–116.

[669] See Case M.1939 *Rexam(PLM)/American National Can* (19 July 2000), para 24.

[670] See *Shell/DEA* (n 623, above) paras 112 *et seq*; *BP/E.ON*, ibid, paras 102 *et seq*.

[671] See Case M.1313 *Danish Crown/Vestjyske Slagterier*, OJ 2000 L20/1, [2000] 5 CMLR 296, paras 176–178.

[672] See Case M.2640 *Nestlé/Schöller* (25 February 2002), para 37; *Enso/Stora* (n 660, above) paras 67–68.

(b) *Deterrent mechanisms:* the Horizontal Merger Guidelines state that the threat of future retaliation is only credible if there is sufficient certainty that if deviation by one of the market players is detected, a deterrent mechanism will be activated and that this will offset the benefits of deviation.[673] Successful and speedy retaliation will depend on transparency and on there being an incentive for other coordinating firms to retaliate against the deviator. So, for example, temporarily engaging in a short-term price war targeted at the deviator may ultimately assist the resumption of a coordinated regime that provides greater longer-term benefits. Retaliation can also take place in other markets where the coordinating firms interact.[674]

(c) *Reactions of outsiders:* successful coordination is also dependent upon the inability of, or lack of incentive for, non-coordinating firms to react to the behaviour of the coordinating firms. The effects of market entry and countervailing buyer power are given special consideration by the Commission in this respect.[675]

8.214 **Prospective analysis: *Impala*.** In *Impala v Commission*, the Court of First Instance confirmed that the Commission is required to conduct a prospective analysis of whether a concentration may create or strengthen a dominant position, involving close examination of, in particular, the circumstances which, in each individual case, are relevant for assessing the effects of the concentration on competition in the relevant market; the Commission must provide solid evidence to support its findings.[676] The Court of First Instance further noted that, in evaluating the possible *existence* of a collective dominant position (which might be *strengthened* by a concentration) – as opposed to whether a concentration may *create* a collective dominant position – the necessary conditions identified in *Airtours v Commission* 'may, however, in the appropriate circumstances, be established indirectly on the basis of what may be a very mixed series of indicia and items of evidence relating to the signs, manifestations and phenomena inherent in the presence of a collective dominant position'.[677] It suggests that close alignment of prices over a long period of time (especially above a competitive level) might, in the absence of an alternative reasonable explanation, suffice to demonstrate the existence of a collective dominant position, even in the absence of firm direct evidence of strong market transparency.[678]

---

673 Horizontal Merger Guidelines, OJ 2004 C31/5: Vol II, App D.6, paras 52–54.

674 ibid, para 55. See *Gencor v Commission* (n 591, above) para 281.

675 See also observations on countervailing buyer power at paras 8.225–8.227, below.

676 Case T-464/04 *Impala v Commission* (n 665, above), para 248 on further appeal to the ECJ: Case C-413/06 *Bertelsmann and Sony Corp / Impala*, not yet decided.

677 ibid, para 251.

678 *Impala v Commission*, ibid, paras 252 and 254: this formulation, noted as *obiter dictum* in the CFI's judgment, may amount to a qualification of (or departure from) the three *Airtours* conditions in the context of the *existence* of a collective dominance position (as opposed to the *creation* of a

Application of coordinated effects analysis in practice. The Commission **8.215**
investigates whether the concentration will result in or reinforce a market structure which would provide opportunities for the remaining major players on the
relevant markets to constrain capacity, discourage market entry or otherwise
distort competition – to the detriment of customers or of smaller competitors or
'mavericks' outside the oligopoly. For these purposes, historical analyses of the
past level of competition in the relevant market, including variations in market
shares and prices, may assist.

(f) Vertical and conglomerate effects

(i) Vertical effects

Potential foreclosure effects. The concept of 'vertical effects' is used to describe **8.216**
issues which may arise in a merger between undertakings operating at different
levels in the chain of production and/or distribution. Vertical mergers may
give rise to competition concerns, in particular if they could have the effect
of foreclosing market access by, for example, limiting competitor access to
upstream raw materials or components or to downstream distribution channels
or by making such access more expensive, thereby increasing rivals' costs. A vertically integrated supplier may in some situations have the ability and the incentive
to foreclose rivals from an upstream market for the supply of inputs (input
foreclosure) or from a downstream market for distribution or sales (customer
foreclosure). When appraising possible non-coordinated effects, it is necessary
to consider whether competitors will have, post-transaction, sufficient access to
alternative supplies or outlets and whether the notified concentration is likely
to change the incentives of the parties to continue to deal with third parties.
In particular circumstances, the Commission may also examine possible
coordinated effects where vertical integration might facilitate collusion among
competitors, for example by increasing transparency at the upstream market
level or by removing incentives for effective competition at the downstream
market level.[679]

---

collective dominance position); in its judgment, however, the CFI confined its review to considering
whether the *Airtours* conditions had been properly applied, as the applicant had based its appeal on
the incorrect application by the Commission of the *Airtours* conditions (in particular the transparency of the market).

[679] Thus, depending on the circumstances, vertical effects may be categorised either as unilateral
or coordinated: see para 8.202, above. For a detailed analysis of issues raised by non-horizontal
mergers, see Church, 'The Impact of Vertical and Conglomerate Mergers on Competition', commissioned by DG Comp (September 2004), available at http://ec.europa.eu/comm./competition/
mergers/others along with a number of other reports commissioned by DG Comp in connection
with its preparation of guidelines for the assessment of mergers under the SIEC test.

8.217 **Degree of market power.** Serious competition concerns should only arise, however, if the parties to the concentration have a substantial degree of market power in one or more relevant markets in the supply chain, in circumstances where customers may be adversely affected by the concentration.[680] Under the Merger Regulation, there is in effect a presumption that vertical or conglomerate issues should not arise if parties' market shares are below 25 per cent in any relevant market.[681] By reference to any markets above this threshold, the Commission will appraise whether the vertical integration resulting from the concentration and/or greater access to economic, and conceivably financial, power and resources arising from the concentration risks significantly impeding effective competition on any of those markets.[682]

8.218 **In practice.** Some guidance on the Commission's approach to mergers with vertical aspects can be obtained from past practice.[683] The Commission has also issued draft guidelines dealing *inter alia* with its appraisal of vertical effects.[684]

---

[680] To assist the Commission in making these assessments, Form CO requires notifying parties to provide information on 'vertically affected markets', defined to include markets where one or more of the parties to the concentration are engaged in business activities in a product market, which is upstream or downstream of a product market in which any other party to the concentration is engaged, and any of their individual or combined market shares at either level is 25 per cent or more, regardless of whether there is any existing supplier/customer relationship between the parties to the concentration (Form CO, question 6.1(b): see para 8.117, above). It also clarifies that if one party exceeds this 25 per cent threshold in a market upstream or downstream of a market in which the other party is active, then both the upstream and downstream markets are to be treated as 'affected markets', whether or not one or more of the parties is already vertically integrated into both markets.

[681] See para 8.204, above. Accordingly, for the purpose of assessing potential vertical and conglomerate effects Form CO requests data only for markets where any party enjoys a market share of 25 per cent or more. The Commission's draft Non-horizontal Merger Guidelines, Vol II, App D.14, further indicate that the Commission is unlikely to have concerns where the post-merger market share is below 30 per cent with an HHI below 2,000.

[682] See, eg Case M.3943 *Saint-Gobain/BPB* (9 November 2005) where the merged group had strong positions in the upstream markets for plasterboards and insulation products and in the downstream market for the distribution of building products (through builders merchants and retail claims). In concluding that the merger would not result in a SIEC, the Commission took account *inter alia* of the facts that (i) the merged group's positions in the upstream markets (which were in the region of 40–50 per cent) did not give rise to 'dominance'; and (ii) a foreclosure strategy would be unlikely to succeed since BPB's pre-merger sales of plasterboard substantially exceeded Saint-Gobain's pre-merger purchases (see paras 55–56).

[683] See eg Case M.1157 *Skanska/Scancem* (11 November 1998); Case M.1845 *AOL/Time Warner*, OJ 2001 L268/28, [2002] 4 CMLR 454; Case M.2050 *Vivendi/Canal+/Seagram* (13 October 2000); Case M.2803 *Telia/Sonera* (10 July 2002); *Siemens/Drägerwerk* (n 603, above); Case M.2903 *DaimlerChrysler/Deutsche Telekom/JV*, OJ 2003 L300/62, [2004] 5 CMLR 169; Case M.3083 *GE/Instrumentarium*, OJ 2004 L109/1; Case M.4300 *Philips/Intermagnetics* (7 November 2006); Case M.4242 *Thermo Electron/Fisher Scientific* (9 November 2006); Case M.4561 *GE/Smiths Aerospace* (23 April 2007).

[684] The Commission is aiming to adopt these Guidelines before the end of 2007. For the draft Non-horizontal Mergers Guidelines see Vol II, App D. 14.

In applying these guidelines, the Commission must have regard to the relevant case law of the Community Courts.[685] In particular:

(a) In *Tetra Laval*[686] the Court of First Instance reviewed the Commission's theory of competitive harm arising from vertical effects applied in its prohibition of the acquisition by Tetra Laval of Sidel. The Commission had held that the vertically integrated merged entity could use its strong market position as a supplier of stretch blow moulding machines to foreclose independent converters of PET plastic bottles by raising converters' costs and marginalising their market position as suppliers of preforms and turnkey installations.[687] First, the Court found that the Phase II commitment offered by Tetra Laval to divest its interests in PET preforms should have entirely eliminated the Commission's concerns about vertical foreclosure. Turning to the Commission's concern that converters would nevertheless purchase more readily from Sidel once Tetra Laval had divested itself of its interests in preforms, thereby strengthening the position of the merged entity, the Court concluded that no cogent evidence to that effect had been put forward by the Commission in the contested decision, other than the reference to the responses to the market investigation. Consequently, the Commission had not shown that the modified merger would result in sizeable or, at the very least, significant vertical effects on the relevant market for PET packaging equipment.[688]

(b) In *GE/Honeywell*[689] the Court of First Instance reviewed the Commission's finding of competitive harm resulting from the vertical relationship between GE's engine-manufacturing business and Honeywell's manufacture of starters for those engines. The Commission had concluded that the vertical integration between the manufacture of an essential component (engine starters) and the manufacture of the finished product sold in a downstream market would strengthen GE's dominant position in that downstream market for large commercial aircraft jet engines. This was based on the finding that the merged entity would have the incentive to disrupt or delay supplies of engine starters to GE's competitors with the intention to foreclose. However,

---

685 The limited CFI case law on vertical mergers (handled under the 'dominance' test of the original Merger Reg) emphasises the high standard of proof incumbent on the Commission in cases where the theories of competitive harm are based on non-horizontal effects: see paras 8.253–8.255, below.

686 Case T-5/02 *Tetra Laval v Commission* [2002] ECR II-4381, [2002] 5 CMLR 1182 (on appeal from Case M.2416 *Tetra Laval/Sidel*, OJ 2004 L43/13 (prohibition decision)); further appeal dismissed, Case C-12/03P *Commission v Tetra Laval* [2005] ECR I-987, [2005] 4 CMLR 573. The Commission's divestiture decision (*Tetra Laval/Sidel*, OJ 2004 L38/1) was also annulled: Case T-80/02 [2002] ECR II-4519, [2002] 5 CMLR 1271.

687 *Tetra Laval/Sidel* (prohibition decision, above).

688 Case T-5/02 *Tetra Laval v Commission*, above, paras 135–140.

689 Case T-210/01 *General Electric v Commission* [2005] ECR II-5575, [2006] 4 CMLR 686, paras 281–314.

although the Court accepted that such conduct would be in the merged entity's commercial interests, the Court held that the Commission's failure to take into account the deterrent effect of Article 82 had resulted in a distorted analysis. In the course of its investigation, the Commission 'necessarily had available all the evidence required in this case to assess, without the need to carry out a detailed investigation in that regard, to what extent the conduct which it itself anticipated on the engine starter market would constitute infringements of Article 82 and be sanctioned as such'.[690] Accordingly, the Court of First Instance concluded that the finding that GE's dominant position would be strengthened by reason of this vertical relationship was vitiated by a manifest error of assessment.[691]

(ii) Conglomerate effects

8.219 Conglomerate effects. The concept of 'conglomerate effects' is used to describe issues which may arise in a merger between undertakings operating in different product markets which are not horizontally or vertically related. In general, pure conglomerate mergers, involving suppliers of completely unrelated products, should not raise competition concerns.[692] Concerns may nonetheless arise in mergers involving partially substitutable products or complementary products in closely related or neighbouring markets. The Commission will occasionally investigate potential conglomerate effects if a party to the concentration has a substantial level of market power in one or more of these closely related or neighbouring markets.[693] In practice, it tends to do so in cases where the products of the business

---

[690] ibid, para 311. The reference to 'a detailed investigation' seems intended to contrast with the position in Case C-12/03P *Commission v Tetra Laval*, where the ECJ overruled the CFI's holding that the Commission's reasoning was vitiated by failure to have regard to the deterrent effect of Art 82 since there such consideration was too speculative: n 686, above.

[691] However, the appeal was dismissed since the conclusion that the merger would strengthen a dominant position was sufficiently substantiated on other grounds.

[692] As the CFI noted in Case T-5/02 *Tetra Laval v Commission* (n 686, above) para 150: 'in principle, a merger between undertakings which are active on distinct markets is not usually of such a nature as immediately to create or strengthen a dominant position due to the combination of the market shares held by the parties to the merger. The factors which are of significance for the relative positions of competitors within a given market are generally to be found within the market itself, namely in particular the market shares held by the competitors and the conditions of competition on the market. It does not follow, however, that the conditions of competition on a market can never be affected by factors external to that market'.

[693] Form CO accordingly requires information on any product market on which any party is present which is a neighbouring market closely related to a product market in which any other party to the concentration is engaged, and the individual or combined market share is 25 per cent or more (Form CO, question 6.3: see para 8.117, above). Markets are described as closely related neighbouring markets when the products are complementary to each other or when they belong to a range of products that is generally purchased by the same set of customers for the same end use. By way of a hypothetical example of products belonging to a range (but clearly borrowed from the facts of Case M.938 *Guinness/Grand Metropolitan*, OJ 1998 L288/24; and *Tetra Laval/Sidel* (n 686,

being acquired, being partially substitutable or complementary to the acquirer's own products, give rise to concerns relating to so-called 'portfolio power' or 'range effects'.[694] According to these theories of competitive harm, the power deriving from a portfolio of products or brands may exceed the sum of its parts; thus a merger combining products in related markets may confer on the merged entity the ability and incentive to leverage a strong market position from one market to another by means of tying, bundling or other exclusionary practices.[695]

Portfolios of consumer goods.   Some guidance on the Commission's approach **8.220** to assessing such issues can be obtained from past practice in mergers between suppliers of consumer goods sold to retailers for subsequent resale to consumers. In *Gillette/Duracell*,[696] an early case to consider these issues, the Commission investigated whether the combination of these two leading manufacturers of branded fast-moving consumer goods might unfairly reduce third parties' legitimate opportunities of access to markets and supplies. It concluded that there was insufficient evidence that Gillette would be able to exercise influence on distribution in a way that would have a significant adverse foreclosure effect on competition, pointing *inter alia* to the fact that the link between the different products (razor blades and batteries) was 'extremely tenuous'. When called upon to consider similar issues on a greater scale some years later in *Procter & Gamble/Gillette*,[697] the Commission assessed the risks of foreclosure through 'bundling' and 'category management'. It indicated that the potential for pure bundling (that is obliging retailers to buy both 'must stock' and 'weak' products) was only likely to be an issue if the parties' products were highly complementary from a demand perspective. However, mixed bundling (that is offering combined products at a lower price than the combined price for the products if bought individually) was seen as achievable through offering rebates across a range of products or cross-promotions. On the facts, the Commission found that third party concerns were not substantiated, taking note in particular of existing competition between suppliers with similarly broad product ranges, buyer power and the efficiencies generated for retailers and customers from the merged entity's enlarged product portfolio.[698]

---

above)), Form CO refers to 'whisky and gin sold to bars and restaurants' and to 'different materials for packaging a certain category of goods sold to producers of such goods'.

[694] See Detmers, Dodoo and Morfey, 'Conglomerate mergers under EC merger control: an overview' (2005) 1 European Competition Journal 265.

[695] See observations at paras 8.216–8.217, above regarding the similar focus on pre-existing market power in the assessment of vertical effects. The issues relevant to such an assessment are considered further in the Commission's draft Non-horizontal Merger Guidelines, Vol II, App D.14.

[696] Case M.836 *Gillette/Duracell* (8 November 1996), paras 8–12.

[697] Case M.3732 *Procter & Gamble/Gillette* (15 July 2005), paras 110–151.

[698] This express reference to 'portfolio efficiencies' as an objective rationale for 'mixed bundling' indicates that the Commission did not equate 'range effect' concerns to an 'efficiency offence'. See further observations on efficiencies at paras 8.228–8.229, below.

8.221 **Other conglomerate cases.** The Commission's decision in *GE/Amersham*[699] indicated that a necessary pre-condition for mixed bundling to result in fore-closure of competition was that the merged entity would be able to leverage its pre-merger dominance in one product market to another complementary product market.[700] As neither GE nor Amersham had strong enough market posi-tions in the EEA to be qualified as dominant before the merger, the Commission approved the transaction at Phase I.[701] The Commission provides some guidance on the assessment of conglomerate mergers in its draft Non-horizontal Merger Guidelines which reflect Commission case law.[702] These Guidelines also take account of the recent case law of the Community Courts.[703]

8.222 **Difficulty of establishing conglomerate effects.** In its judgment in *Tetra Laval* dismissing the Commission's appeal from the annulment by the Court of First Instance of the prohibition decision in *Tetra Laval/Sidel*, the Court of Justice emphasised the standard of evidence required to find that a merger is anti-competitive by reason of conglomerate effects:

> 'The analysis of a "conglomerate-type" concentration is a prospective analysis in which, first, the consideration of a lengthy period of time in the future and, secondly,

---

[699] Case M.3304 *GE/Amersham* (21 January 2004) (decided under the 'dominance' test of the original Merger Reg): although the concentration did not involve any horizontal or vertical relation-ships, the parties' products were 'complements' since customers (hospitals) needed to procure both of them in order to provide a medical imaging service to patients. The Commission investigated whether the merged entity would be able to foreclose competition through 'commercial bundling' (ie mixed bundling), 'forced bundling' (ie pure tying) or 'technical tying'.

[700] ibid, para 37. Furthermore, the Commission observed that for such a strategy to be plausi-ble there must also be a reasonable expectation that rivals will not be able to make a competitive response, that they will be forced to exit the market and that the merged firm will then be able to sustain increases in price without being threatened by new entry (or re-entry).

[701] But note that this case was handled under the original Merger Reg, prior to the implementa-tion of the SIEC test. In *Procter & Gamble/Gillette* (n 697, above) handled under the new Merger Reg, the Commission expressly referred (at paras 110 and 117) to *Guinness/Grand Metropolitan* (n 693, above) and Case M.2220 *General Electric/Honeywell*, OJ 2004 L48/1 as relevant precedents dealing with conglomerate effects, but not to *GE/Amersham*. It conducted a detailed examination of potential conglomerate effects arising out of the parties' combined ownership of 21 'must stock' consumer brands, each with worldwide turnover of more than $1,000 million, but made no refer-ence to whether pre-existing 'dominance' is necessary in order to base a theory of competitive harm on conglomerate effects resulting from a merger. For an example of a case where conglomerate issues (as well as vertical issues) were considered under the SIEC test, see *GE/Smiths Aerospace* (n 683, above) paras 116–126.

[702] For the draft Guidelines see Vol II, App D.14. In addition to the cases in nn 696–701, above, see Case M.794 *Coca-Cola/Amalgamated Beverages GB*, OJ 1997 L218/15; Case M.833 *Coca-Cola/Carlsberg* (11 September 1997); and *Guinness/Grand Metropolitan* (n 693, above) where the Commission eventually concluded that 'portfolio power' issues were not a cause for concern, albeit only after a Phase II investigation. See also horizontal mergers in which portfolio power is identified as a factor in the Commission's decision: eg Case M.1845 *AOL/Time Warner*, OJ 2001 L268/28; Case M.3440 *ENI/EDP/GDP* (9 December 2004), appeal dismissed, Case T-87/05 *EDP v Commission* [2005] ECR II-3745, [2005] 5 CMLR 1436.

[703] However, at the time of writing, the limited case law on conglomerate mergers (see paras 8.222–8.224, below) involves decisions made under the 'dominance' test of the original Merger Reg.

the leveraging necessary to give rise to significant impediment to effective competition mean that the chains of cause and effect are dimly discernible, uncertain and difficult to establish. That being so, the quality of the evidence produced by the Commission in order to establish that it is necessary to adopt a decision declaring the concentration incompatible with the Common Market is particularly important, since that evidence must support the Commission's conclusion that, if such a decision were not adopted, the economic developments envisaged by it would be plausible.'[704]

Conglomerate effects: *Tetra Laval.* The application of this approach is evident **8.223** from the annulment of the Commission's findings of conglomerate effects in two recent cases. In *Tetra Laval* itself, the Court of First Instance had reviewed the Commission's theories of competitive harm concerning leveraging and mixed bundling, according to which Tetra Laval would be able to leverage its existing dominant position in the market for carton packing and equipment (which was scarcely altered by the merger) in order to achieve dominance in the separate market for PET plastic bottling machines. The Commission's conglomeracy concerns related to a mixed bundling strategy which the merged entity could implement to offer customers a combined package of complementary products at a price below the aggregate price for the same products when purchased individually, to the detriment of competing suppliers of PET bottling machines, thereby turning Sidel's position on that distinct market into a dominant position, with the possible consequence of higher prices for customers. The Court of First Instance did not find the Commission's evidence of market developments convincing[705] and held that the Commission had failed to prove its arguments to the requisite legal standard. As noted above, the Commission's appeal to the Court of Justice was dismissed.

Conglomerate effects: *GE/Honeywell.* In *GE/Honeywell*[706] the Court of **8.224** First Instance reviewed the Commission's finding of competitive harm by way of conglomerate effects arising from (i) the financial and commercial strength of GE and (ii) the bundling of GE's engine products with Honeywell's avionics products. With regard to the first limb, the Court held that the Commission would have had to have established three factors to prove its theory: first, that the merged entity would have had the ability to transfer this strength in the market for large commercial jet engines to the avionics and non-avionics markets after the merger; secondly, that it was likely that it would in fact have engaged in such behaviour; and thirdly, that a dominant position in the market would have been created

---

[704] Case T-5/02 *Tetra Laval v Commission* (n 686, above) para 44, on appeal from Case T-5/02 *Tetra Laval v Commission* (n 686, above). See also *General Electrics v Commission* (n 689, above) paras 65–66.

[705] *inter alia*, the Commission's findings as to the likely growth in the use of PET products were found to be unsubstantiated. As regards the relevance of the potential disincentive to future behaviour by the merged entity resulting from Arts 81 and 82, see para 8.218(b) and n 690, above.

[706] *General Electric v Commission* (n 689, above) paras 315–473.

as a result, in the relatively near future. However, the Court found that only the first of these factors was established. With regard to the second limb, the Court first noted that there were practical barriers to bundling, since the end buyers of the two products were frequently different and, furthermore, purchased the products at different stages in the manufacturing process. The merged entity would therefore have had to make an additional commercial effort to sell products in such a way. The Court then examined in detail three categories of potential bundling: 'pure bundling' (where a company which is dominant in one market ties purchase of products in a second market for purely commercial reasons); 'technical bundling' (where a company which is dominant in one market ties purchase of products in a second market by technically combining the products); and 'mixed bundling' (offering combined products at a lower price than the price of the separate elements). In all three categories, the Court found that the Commission had failed properly to examine the likelihood of such behaviour; had placed too great an emphasis on past behaviour in other markets; and had, moreover, failed to establish sufficient intention or incentive for the behaviour.[707]

(g) Other considerations relevant to substantive appraisal

(i) Buyer power

8.225 **Consideration of buyer power.** Both suppliers and buyers can have market power. Looking at the impact of a concentration from the perspective of demand rather than supply in a relevant market, a substantive appraisal can focus on the creation or strengthening of the buyer power of the merged entity on upstream markets.[708] Conversely, a substantive appraisal may determine that the merged entity will face competitive pressure from customers with countervailing buyer power on the market into which the merged entity is selling.[709]

8.226 **Increased buyer power for the merged entity.** A merged entity with increased buyer power may significantly impede effective competition by reducing its purchases of inputs, thereby causing prices to fall on the upstream market and then lowering its level of output in the final product market to the detriment of consumer welfare.[710] This may occur particularly where upstream sellers are fragmented. Alternatively, the merged entity could use its increased buyer power to foreclose its competitors from certain suppliers.[711] However, the Commission

---

[707] Nonetheless, the Commission's Phase II prohibition decision was upheld because of the horizontal effects arising from the merger.

[708] Horizontal Merger Guidelines (n 673, above) paras 61–63.

[709] ibid, paras 64–67.

[710] See, eg Case M.1221 *Rewe/Meinl*, OJ 1999 L274/1, [2000] 5 CMLR 256, paras 71–74.

[711] See, eg *Kesko v Commission* (n 652, above) para 57; Case M.877 *Boeing/McDonnell Douglas*, OJ 1997 L336/16, paras 105–108.

acknowledges that increased buyer power can also be beneficial for competition where it leads to lower input costs that are likely to be passed on to consumers in the form of lower prices. The likely effects of increased buyer power must therefore be examined individually in each case. The Commission will typically conduct its assessment of buyer market power by examining the competitive structure on both the upstream (procurement) markets and the downstream (selling) markets.[712]

Customers' countervailing buyer power. A merged entity with a high market **8.227** share may not be in a position significantly to impede effective competition where its customers possess sufficient countervailing buyer power, having regard to their size, commercial significance and ability to switch to other suppliers.[713] In certain circumstances the merged entity will not be able to act to an appreciable extent independently of its customers,[714] as these will be able to react to increasing prices[715] or deteriorating quality or conditions of delivery by resorting to alternative sources of supply within a reasonable time frame, including other existing or new suppliers[716] or through vertical integration in the upstream market. However, countervailing buyer power will not sufficiently offset the adverse effects of a merger if it only protects certain customers in the market[717] or if the concentration in fact reduces buyer power by removing a credible alternative supplier. Finally, in some cases the incentives for customers to exercise buyer power may be constrained by their unwillingness to take action, such as sponsoring new entry, that might also benefit their competitors.[718]

(ii) Efficiencies

Efficiency benefits. In appraising concentrations under the Merger Regulation, **8.228** the Commission will also consider any efficiencies that the parties expect to flow from the merger.[719] Efficiencies can counter potential price increases for

---

[712] See, eg *Rewe/Meinl* (n 710, above); Case M.1684 *Carrefour/Promodes* (25 January 2000).

[713] See, eg Case M.1882 *Pirelli/BICC*, OJ 2003 L70/35, paras 73–80.

[714] See *Procter & Gamble/Gillette* (n 697, above) where the Commission pointed to the fact that retailers perform an important 'gatekeeper' function for suppliers, with the parties' overall sales representing on average no more than 2 per cent of the retailers' sales, while certain retailers represented 10 per cent or more of the parties' sales in a given EEA State (para 125). See also Kloc-Evison, Larsson Haug and Siebert, 'Procter & Gamble/Gillette: the role of economic analysis in Phase I case' (2005) 3 EC Competition Policy Newsletter 43.

[715] See, eg Case M.1245 *Valeo/ITT Industries* (30 July 1998), para 26.

[716] See, eg Case M.2187 *CVC/Lenzing*, OJ 2004 L82/20, para 223; *Enso/Stora* (n 660, above) paras 89–91.

[717] See, eg *SCA/Metsä Tissue* (n 640, above) para 88; *Enso/Stora*, above, paras 84–97.

[718] See, eg Case M.2544 *Masterfoods/Royal Canin* (15 February 2002), paras 53–54; *General Electric/Honeywell* (n 701, above) sections 1.B.4–1.B. 5 (paras 224–229); and *CVC/Lenzing* (n 716, above) para 233.

[719] See, Recital (29) to the Merger Reg and Horizontal Merger Guidelines (n 673, above) paras 76–88; cf section 9.3 of the Form CO, providing notifying parties with the option to set out the

consumers insofar as the parties are able, as a result of the merger, to realise benefits which will be passed on to consumers. Such benefits might include economies of scale or scope, benefits from rationalised production, from distribution or marketing activities, or from other synergies in the field of research and development expenditure. Although there is scope for horizontal mergers to bring about efficiencies in terms of marginal cost savings, it is generally recognised that there is greater potential for non-horizontal mergers to offer efficiencies in the form of synergies arising from the combination of complementary assets.[720]

8.229 Proving efficiency benefits. Submitting information on efficiencies is voluntary and the parties are not required to offer any objective justification (or obtain a waiver) for not providing such information with their notification if they do not consider that efficiency arguments are required in support of their case. However, if the parties can quantify and put forward substantiated and verifiable evidence of cost-savings or other merger-specific efficiencies, the Commission may rely on these to find that the merged entity will be better placed to act pro-competitively for the benefit of consumers. This might counteract any adverse effects on competition which the merger might otherwise have.[721] With regard to the merger-specific aspect, it is necessary to demonstrate that there are no less anti-competitive, realistic and attainable alternatives to the notified concentration which could achieve the same efficiencies, whether of a concentrative nature (for example, a differently structured merger) or of a non-concentrative nature such as a licensing agreement, horizontal cooperation agreement or partial function joint venture.

(iii) Failing firm defence

8.230 Failing firms. In very exceptional circumstances, an otherwise problematic merger may nevertheless be compatible with the common market if one of the merging parties is a failing firm.[722]

8.231 Burden of proof. The Commission considers that, given the exceptional nature of the failing firm defence, the burden of proof to show a lack of causality between the concentration on the one hand and the adverse effect on competition arising

---

efficiency gains generated by the concentration which are likely to enhance the ability and incentive of the new entity to act pro-competitively for the benefit of consumers.

[720] See, RBB Economics 'The Efficiency-Enhancing Effect of Non-Horizontal Mergers' (2005), commissioned by DG Enterprise and Industry, available at http://ec.europa.eu.int/comm/enterprise/library/lib-competition/doc/non_horizontal _mergers.pdf.

[721] See eg *Procter & Gamble/Gillette* (n 697, above) paras 131 *et seq*. cf Case M.4000 *Inco/Falconbridge* (4 July 2006) paras 529 *et seq* and earlier cases, notably *Danish Crown/Vestjyske Slagterier* (n 671, above) where the Commission has been reluctant to take into account efficiency arguments put forward by the parties.

[722] See Horizontal Merger Guidelines (n 673, above) paras 89–91. See also Case M4 381 *JCI/FIAMM* (10 May 2007) (Commission took account of target's financial difficulties).

from the exit of one party from the market on the other lies with the notifying parties.[723] This involves demonstrating three elements:

(a) the failing firm would in the near future be forced out of the relevant market because of financial difficulties if not taken over by another undertaking;

(b) there is no less anti-competitive alternative transaction, as may be demonstrated by the fact that various other scenarios have been explored without success; and

(c) in the absence of the merger, the assets of the failing firm would inevitably exit the market. This may, in the case of a merger between the only two players in a market, justify such a merger-to-monopoly on the basis that the market share of the failing firm would in any event have accrued to the other merging party.[724]

(h) Coordinative aspects of certain full-function joint ventures

(i) In general

Spill-over effects. Although all 'full-function' joint ventures give rise to con- **8.232** centrations within the meaning of the Merger Regulation, some of them may nevertheless have as their object or effect the coordination of the competitive behaviour of the parent undertakings that remain independent. In appraising whether a particular JV may have such 'spill-over effects', it is necessary to consider whether two or more of the JV's parents have a presence to a material extent:

(a) in the same markets as the JV;

(b) in markets downstream or upstream from the JV's market; or

(c) in neighbouring markets closely related to the JV's market.

The concern is whether the creation of the JV undertaking may lead to coordination between two or more of its parent companies in relation to prices, markets, output or innovation. Coordination between the parents and the JV undertaking is relevant only insofar as it is an instrument for producing or reinforcing coordination between the parents. This involves an assessment of whether the parents are in fact actual or realistic potential competitors of one another in any product and geographic markets affected by the joint venture. There is normally a higher probability of coordination where two or more parent companies retain significant activities in the same market as the JV undertaking.[725]

---

[723] Case M.308 *Kali+Salz/MdK/Treuhand*, OJ 1994 L186/38, para 72.

[724] See *Kali+Salz/MdK/Treuhand*, above, para 71.

[725] See, eg Case M.578 *Hoogovens/Klöckner* (11 April 1995): both parent companies were active in the same product and geographic market as the JV itself (steel stockholding in an area encompassing the Netherlands, Belgium and north-west Germany) which gave rise to 'a high probability of coordination of competitive behaviour' (para 21); similarly, Case M.538 *Omnitel* (27 March 1995): JV offering GSM mobile phone services in Italy where some of its parents were already active, and

(ii) Concentrations with a Community dimension

8.233 **Article 2(4) of the Merger Regulation.** Where a joint venture has such spill-over effects, those aspects may be caught by the Article 81(1) prohibition. Where these coordinative aspects concern a concentration subject to investigation by the Commission under the Merger Regulation, the Commission must also appraise (in accordance with Article 2(4) of the Merger Regulation) whether they satisfy the exemption criteria of Article 81(3) of the EC Treaty (see Chapter 7, above). As further specified in Article 2(5) of the Merger Regulation, the Commission must take into account:

(a) whether two or more parent companies retain, to a significant extent, activities in the same market as the JV or in a market which is downstream or upstream from that of the JV or in a neighbouring market closely related to this market;

(b) whether the coordination which is the direct consequence of the creation of the JV affords the undertakings concerned the possibility of eliminating competition in respect of a substantial part of the products or services in question.

In effect, the Commission conducts an economic balance sheet analysis. It appraises whether any potential for elimination of competition in respect of a substantial part of the products or services in question, through coordination between the parents, rather than between the parents and the JV, is outweighed by likely benefits which may result from the JV through improvements in production, technology or distribution. A fair share of those benefits should flow to consumers. The Commission also seeks to establish whether there is a causal link between the formation of the JV and any likely and appreciable spill-over effects between the parents.[726] Where a JV raises significant spill-over effects, there is likely to be a Phase II investigation to consider these Article 81 issues. It may therefore prove necessary for the parties to offer commitments in order to ensure

---

others were likely to be active in the near future, in GSM service provision. (Since in both these cases the JV was found to be 'cooperative' and not 'concentrative', the JV did not constitute a concentration under the distinction which applied under the original Merger Reg until its amendment with effect from 1 March 1998; they would both constitute concentrations today.) cf Case M.478 *Voith/ Sulzer II* (29 July 1994): a worldwide paper machinery JV where both parents retained certain paper machinery businesses outside the JV but, on the facts, the Commission concluded that there was no scope for coordination between those retained businesses; Case M.640 *KNP BT/Société Générale* (3 October 1995): both parents kept their Belgian computer activities outside the JV but those activities were marginal both in actual terms and in relative terms (and had been kept outside the JV for purely practical reasons); Case T-464/04 *Impala v Commission* (n 665, above) annulling Commission's decision in *Sony/BMG* (n 665, above) regarding likelihood of coordination between Sony's and Bertelsmann's music publishing businesses that were retained outside the JV.

[726] See, eg *Sony/BMG* (n 665, above) para 176; Case M.2211 *Universal Studio Networks/De Facto 829 (NTL)/Studio Channel Limited* (20 December 2000), para 36.

either that the risk of spill-over effects is removed or that the Article 81(3) criteria are satisfied.[727]

(iii) Concentrations without a Community dimension

Regulation 1/2003.   Although the concentrative aspects of full-function JVs   **8.234** below the Merger Regulation thresholds fall within the competence of the Member States, Regulation 1/2003 remains applicable to any spill-over effects, such that these issues may be investigated either by the Commission or by the NCAs at national level.[728] In practice, however, the Commission would be unlikely to apply Regulation 1/2003 to the coordinative aspects of such JV undertakings but would leave the assessment of those elements to the relevant Member States with jurisdiction to review the transaction.[729]

5. Judicial Review by the Community Courts

(a) Procedures

Action for annulment.   The Community Courts have full and unlimited   **8.235** jurisdiction to re-examine Commission decisions fixing fines or periodic penalty payments, so may cancel, reduce or increase the amounts imposed.[730] They also have jurisdiction under Article 230 of the Treaty to review the legality of decisions taken by the Commission under the Merger Regulation.[731] Actions for annulment brought by natural or legal persons fall within the jurisdiction of the Court of First Instance.[732] The European Court of Justice hears actions for annulment brought by Member States.

Expedited procedure.   Challenges of Merger Regulation decisions may be able   **8.236** to take advantage of the expedited (or 'fast-track') procedure introduced in 2001

---

[727] See, eg Case M.3817 *Wegener/PCM/JV* (7 July 2005); Case JV.15 *BT/AT&T* (30 March 1999); and Case M.1327 *NC/Canal+/CDPQ/Bank America* (3 December 1998).

[728] Merger Reg, OJ 2004 L24/1: Vol II, App D.1, Art 21(1).

[729] In principle, such Art 81 issues may also be assessed by the national courts in the event of private actions.

[730] Merger Reg, Art 16 and Recital (43).

[731] For the general procedural provisions governing such actions, see paras 13.211 *et seq*, below. Given the nature of proceedings under the Merger Reg, and in particular the provision for deemed decisions under Art 10(6) of the Merger Reg, proceedings under Art 232 EC for failure to act are unlikely; however, the Commission's refusal to define its position on the question of its competence to review a concentration under the Merger Reg could amount to such a failure to act: see Case C-170/02P *Schlüsselverlag J. S. Moser v Commission* [2003] ECR I-9889, [2004] 4 CMLR 27, paras 25–30.

[732] For appeals from the CFI to the ECJ, see paras 13.252 *et seq*, below.

for urgent cases before the Court of First Instance.[733] Examples of proceedings brought under the expedited procedure include the appeals brought by the notifying parties against the Commission's Phase II prohibition decisions in *Schneider/Legrand*,[734] *Tetra Laval/Sidel*[735] and *ENI/EDP/GDP*.[736] In the last mentioned case, the Court of First Instance procedure from the lodging of the appeal through to the judgment took just under seven months. These cases can be contrasted with Merger Regulation appeals handled under the normal Court of First Instance procedure where the process from appeal through to judgment can take in the region of three years.[737] The expedited procedure has also been used by other involved parties[738] and by third parties.[739]

8.237 **Interim measures.** An action for annulment under Article 230 of the Treaty does not automatically have suspensive effects. Under Articles 242 and 243 of the Treaty, the Court may order that a contested act be suspended, or prescribe interim measures. However, in merger cases it has proved very difficult to obtain interim measures. The applicant was successful in the *Kali & Salz* case (which predated the introduction of the expedited procedure). The Commission's original

---

[733] See para 13.233, below. The expedited procedure can be of particular importance given the difficulties in obtaining interim measures in such cases: see para 8.237, below.

[734] Case T-310/01 *Schneider Electric v Commission* [2002] ECR II-4071, [2003] 4 CMLR 768, [2004] All ER (EC) 314. As well as requesting the expedited procedure, Schneider applied for interim relief to suspend the Commission divestiture order under Art 8(4) of the Merger Reg: Case T-77/02R *Schneider Electric v Commission*. The Commission was persuaded to grant an extension of the period within which the divestiture was to take place and the application for interim measures was withdrawn.

[735] *Tetra Laval v Commission* (n 686, above). Like Schneider, as well as requesting the expedited procedure, Tetra Laval applied for interim relief to suspend the Commission divestiture order under Art 8(4) of the Merger Reg: Case T-80/02R *Tetra Laval v Commission*. As part of an agreement reached between the parties at the hearing of that case, concerning the postponement of the time limit fixed for Tetra Laval's divestiture of its shares in Sidel pending completion of the main proceedings, Tetra Laval withdrew its application for interim measures.

[736] Case T-87/05 *EDP v Commission* [2005] ECR II-3745, [2005] 5 CMLR 1436.

[737] Indeed, the procedure before the CFI in Case T-210/01 *General Electric v Commission* [2005] ECR II-5575, [2006] ECR II-2533 [2006] 4 CMLR 686 took over four years.

[738] See, eg Case T-417/05 *Endesa v Commission* [2006] ECR II-2533: procedure used by the target of a hostile takeover bid to challenge the decision in Case M.3986 *Gas Natural/Endesa* (15 November 2005) declaring that the concentration lacked a 'Community dimension' (appeal dismissed).

[739] See, eg two appeals brought by third parties in respect of the Art 9 referral granted in Case M.2621 *SEB/Moulinex* (8 January 2002), namely Case T-114/02 *BaByliss v Commission* [2003] ECR II-1279, [2004] 5 CMLR 21 and Case T-119/02 *Royal Philips Electronics v Commission* [2003] ECR II-1433, [2003] 5 CMLR 53. See also Case T-464/04 *Impala v Commission* (n 665, above) a third party appeal against the Commission's Phase II unconditional clearance of *Sony/BMG* (n 665, above), on further appeal to the ECJ: Case C-413/06 *Bertelsmann and Sony Corp/Impala*, not yet decided. In *Impala* the proceedings took longer than 19 months; the CFI found that the applicant should bear a quarter of its own costs as, despite the complexity of the case, it had insisted on use of the expedited procedure and had then acted in a way that slowed down the process and was contrary to the letter or the spirit of the expedited procedure.

decision authorised a joint venture combining the potash and rock salt activities of Kali & Salz and the former East German state enterprise (Mitteldeutsche Kali) subject to various conditions designed to avoid the creation of a collective dominant position.[740] One of those conditions was the withdrawal by Kali & Salz and the JV from Kali-Export, an Austrian company that operated as an export cartel coordinating the non-EU sales of its members. The largest remaining EU producer, SCPA, which held 25 per cent of the shares in Kali Export, sought interim measures to suspend this condition on the basis that it would lead to the automatic dissolution of Kali-Export before SCPA's substantive challenge to the Commission's decision could be determined. On that basis, and as a temporary suspension was unlikely to have an adverse effect on the public interest, an order was granted suspending that condition.[741] However, the cases suggest that a suspension order will be granted only if it appears that, without such relief, the applicants would be in a situation liable to jeopardise their very existence or irreparably modify their market position.[742] The Court will not order the suspension of a Commission investigation of a concentration where the Commission has not yet taken a formal decision, save perhaps in wholly exceptional circumstances.[743]

(b) Acts of the Commission which may be appealed

Legal effects. The scope for judicial review *ratione materiae* (in the sense of which acts of the Commission may be challenged) has been largely clarified by the judgments of the Community Courts. Thus, a challenge can be brought under Article 230 of the Treaty against any measure the legal effects of which are binding on, and capable of affecting the interests of, the applicant by bringing about a distinct change in its legal position.[744] Final Phase I or Phase II conditional or   **8.238**

---

[740] Case M.308 *Kali & Salz/MdK/Treuhand*, OJ 1994 L186/38.

[741] Case T-88/94R *Société Commerciale des Potasses et de l'Azote and Entreprise Minière et Chimique v Commission* [1994] ECR II-401 (see also at [1994] ECR II-263). The decision was subsequently annulled by the ECJ on the substantive appeal in which the French Republic joined as applicant: Cases C-68/94 & C-30/95 *France v Commission (Kali & Salz)* [1998] ECR I-1375, [1998] 4 CMLR 829.

[742] See Case T-417/05R *Endesa v Commission* [2006] ECR II-18, rejecting application for interim measures since the applicant had failed to show that it (as distinct from its shareholders) would suffer serious and irreparable harm in the absence of interim measures. See also the refusal to grant in interim measures in Case T-96/92R *CCE Grandes Source v Commission* [1992] ECR II-2579; and Case T-12/93R *CCE Vittel and CE Pierval v Commission* [1993] ECR II-785 (both concerning the Commission's decn in Case M.190 *Nestlé/Perrier*, OJ 1992 L356/1, [1993] 4 CMLR M17); Case T-322/94R *Union Carbide v Commission* [1994] ECR II–1159 (application by a competitor concerning the conditional clearance in Case M.269 *Shell/Montecatini*, OJ 1994 L332/48); Case T-342/00R *Petrolessence and SG2R v Commission* [2001] ECR II-67, [2003] 5 CMLR 485 (application by potential transferee disapproved by the Commission under divestiture commitments).

[743] Case T-52/96R *Sogecable v Commission* [1996] ECR II–797, [1996] 5 CMLR 570.

[744] See generally paras 13.218 *et seq*, below. See also Cases T-125 & 127/97 *The Coca-Cola Co. v Commission* [2000] ECR II-1733, [2000] 5 CMLR 467, para 77 (and previous case law

unconditional clearance decisions, Phase II prohibition decisions and Article 9 referral decisions under the Merger Regulation can clearly fall within this category.[745] By contrast, preparatory measures do not have such effects, for example an Article 6(1)(c) decision initiating Phase II proceedings, the statement of objections in Phase II proceedings, or a Commission letter inviting parties to notify a concentration considered to have a Community dimension.[746] In *Air France (Dan Air)*, the Court of First Instance held that a statement by a spokesperson for the Competition Commissioner, to the effect that the proposed *British Airways/Dan Air* merger did not have a Community dimension, could be challenged since it was capable of producing a series of legal effects, both with regard to the Member States and with regard to the parties to the concentration.[747] With regard to the parties to the concentration, the statement had the effect of absolving them from their obligation to notify under Article 4(1) of the Merger Regulation, and enabled them to put their plans into effect.[748] Similarly, in *Assicurazioni Generali and Unicredito*, the Court held that a decision under Article 6(1)(a) that a JV does not constitute a concentration and therefore falls to be assessed under Article 81, is susceptible to challenge since it deprives the parties of the opportunity of a decision under the accelerated procedure of the Merger Regulation.[749] The Court has also held that a decision by the Commission to reject a potential purchaser as unsuitable, in the course of the implementation of

---

referred to therein): the action dismissed as inadmissible because the Phase II clearance in Case M.794 *Coca-Cola/Amalgamated Beverages GB*, OJ 1997 L218/15 was not conditional upon the informal assurances given by the parties, so the operative part of the decision (which did not refer to the findings on market definition and dominance of concern to the applicants) did not adversely affect the applicants.

[745] This is so, even if the transaction that was the subject of the challenged decision had been terminated before judgment is given: Case T-102/96 *Gencor v Commission* [1999] ECR II-753, [1999] 4 CMLR 971, [1999] All ER (EC) 289, paras 38–46; Case T-22/97 *Kesko v Commission* [1999] ECR II-3775 [2000] 4 CMLR 335, paras 55–65; Case T-310/00 *MCI v Commission* [2004] ECR II-3253, [2004] 5 CMLR 1274, paras 48–56.

[746] See Case 60/81 *IBM v Commission* [1981] ECR 2639, [1981] 3 CMLR 635; and *Sogecable v Commission* (n 743, above) respectively. See also Case T-48/03 *Schneider Electric v Commission* [2006] ECR II-111, in which the CFI held that an Art 6(1)(c) decision to initiate a Phase II investigation is not appealable under Art 230 EC: it constitutes a simple procedural measure marking the commencement of an in-depth investigation and does not affect the legal position of the undertakings concerned (appeal dismissed, Case C-188/06P, order of 9 March 2007).

[747] Case T-3/93 *Air France v Commission* [1994] ECR II–121.

[748] The CFI rejected, on the basis of procedural economy and the effective exercise of judicial review, the Commission's argument that the applicant could have given it formal notice to invite BA to notify the transaction and thereafter have brought proceedings for failure to act pursuant to Article 232 EC: such a course was incompatible with the urgency which characterises the general scheme of the Merger Reg.

[749] Case T-87/96 *Assicurazioni Generali and Unicredito v Commission* [1999] ECR II-203, [2000] 4 CMLR 312 (the substantive challenge was rejected). This may be of still greater importance since the ending of individual exemption decisions under Art 81(3).

divestiture commitments, can be challenged by that potential purchaser.[750] However, a refusal by the Commission to reopen an investigation that had resulted in a previous decision, at least if that refusal is not based upon any new facts, is merely confirmation of the earlier decision and cannot itself be challenged.[751]

(c) Persons entitled to appeal

(i) In general

Direct and individual concern. The scope for judicial review *rationae personae* **8.239** (in the sense of who can challenge acts of the Commission) has likewise been largely clarified by general case law.[752] Parties to a merger are clearly entitled to bring an action since the Commission's decision is addressed to them. This remains the case even if they have abandoned the transaction, whether after the Commission's adverse decision or before a decision is taken.[753] Under Article 230 of the Treaty, third parties may also bring proceedings in respect of a decision which is 'of direct and individual concern' to them. These criteria are distinct and both must be fulfilled. The Court of First Instance has ruled on the admissibility of actions, relating to Merger Regulation proceedings, brought by a number of different classes of third party: competitors and customers, trade associations and other representative bodies, employee representatives and shareholders.

(ii) Third parties

Competitors and customers. Competing undertakings and customers which **8.240** have participated in the administrative process are generally able to show that they have *locus standi*.[754] In challenges brought against British Airways' acquisitions of Dan Air and TAT, Air France successfully argued that it was directly and individually concerned. In *Air France (Dan Air)*,[755] Air France was held to be directly concerned on the basis that the Commission's announcement would quickly lead to a change in the market, substantially reinforcing BA's position on routes where Air France was particularly active. In *Air France (TAT)*,[756] the Court of First Instance gave three reasons for considering that Air France was individually concerned: first,

---

[750] Case T-342/00 *Petrolessence and SG2R v Commission* [2003] ECR II-1161, [2003] 5 CMLR 498.

[751] Case C-480/93P *Zunis Holding v Commission* [1996] ECR I-1, [1996] 5 CMLR 219.

[752] See para 13.221, below.

[753] *Gencor v Commission; Kesko v Commission; MCI v Commission*: passages cited in n 745, above.

[754] See, eg Case T-177/04 *easyJet v Commission* [2006] ECR II-1931, [2006] 5 CMLR 663, para 35: 'whether a third party is individually concerned . . . depends, on the one hand, on that third party's participation in the administrative procedure and, on the other, on the effect on its market position'. See also Case T-282/06 *Sun Chemical Group v Commission*, judgment of 9 July 2007, paras 49–53.

[755] *Air France v Commission (Dan Air)* (n 747, above).

[756] Case T-2/93 *Air France v Commission (TAT)* [1994] ECR II-323, paras 40–47. It was conceded that Air France was directly concerned.

Air France had made observations during the Commission's investigation; secondly, in the actual wording of the contested decision it was apparent that the Commission had mainly taken into account the position of Air France; thirdly, Air France had been obliged (pursuant to an earlier agreement between Air France, the French Government and the Commission) to give up its previous interest in TAT four months prior to BA's acquisition of its holding in TAT. In *easyJet*[757] the Commission questioned whether the action was admissible, given the applicant's lack of interest in the routes affected by the Air France/KLM merger. But the Court of First Instance found that the applicant was in fact one of the merging parties' main competitors on various routes. In several appeals brought by competitors, the Commission has not sought to contest the admissibility of a competitor's *locus standi* to challenge clearance decisions under the Merger Regulation, and the Court has not considered it necessary to consider the admissibility of the action of its own motion.[758] Potential competitors have also been found to have standing to bring an action for annulment, where they have participated actively in the administrative procedure.[759] Indeed, an action for annulment brought by a third party active only on neighbouring, upstream or downstream markets may, in certain circumstances, be admissible.[760]

8.241 **Trade associations and other representative bodies.** In *Wirtschaftskammer Kärnten*[761] the Court of First Instance considered an appeal brought by two bodies representing the interests of their members against the Commission's Phase II conditional clearance of a merger between the principal electricity generator in Austria and five regional electricity suppliers.[762] It noted settled case law that an action brought by an association of undertakings that is not the addressee of the decision is admissible in two situations. In some cases, the association may have

---

[757] *easyJet* (n 754, above) paras 29 and 37.

[758] See, eg Case T-290/94 *Kaysersberg v Commission* [1997] ECR II-237, [1998] 4 CMLR 336 (a challenge to the Phase II conditional clearance decision in Case M.430 *Procter & Gamble/VP Schickedanz*, OJ 1994 L354/32). cf Case T-156/98 *RJB Mining v Commission* [2001] ECR II-337, [2001] 3 CMLR 308: challenge to admissibility failed (under the less strict regime of the ECSC Treaty).

[759] *BaByliss v Commission* (n 739, above).

[760] Case T-158/00 *ARD v Commission* [2003] ECR II-3825, [2004] 5 CMLR 681.

[761] Case T-350/03 *Wirtschaftskammer Kärnten and best connect Ampere Strompool GmbH v Commission* [2006] ECR II-68: the CFI held that the appeal by the Chamber of Commerce for the Austrian region of Carinthia was inadmissible as it had not participated in any way in the administrative procedure and, furthermore, its members were affected by the merger merely in their general capacity as electricity consumers, a capacity which did not of itself give rise to a direct and individual concern. As regards the appeal by best connect Ampere Strompool, a body which negotiated electricity tariffs on behalf of small consumers (rather than being itself a distributor, purchaser or seller of electricity), the CFI held that it too was only generally affected by the decision; moreover, it had not actively participated in the administrative proceedings, as it had merely responded to a Commission questionnaire and had not participated in the oral hearing.

[762] Case M.2947 *Verbund/EnergieAllianz* (11 June 2003).

a particular interest in bringing the action in its own right, especially if its negotiating position is affected by the contested decision. Alternatively, it may act on behalf of one or more of its members whom it represents, provided those members would themselves have been in a position to bring an admissible action. In *Impala*, an action was brought by an association representing a large number of independent record labels (and which had played an active role during the Commission's administrative procedure).[763]

Employee representatives. In the two *Perrier* cases,[764] the Court of First Ins- **8.242** tance had to consider whether workers' councils had standing to challenge the Commission's Phase II conditional clearance decision in *Nestlé/Perrier*.[765] In both cases, the actions were held to be admissible in principle because, under Article 18(4) of the Merger Regulation, a right to be heard is specifically given to 'recognised representatives' of the employees of the merging parties. However, the Court found that in substance the decision was not of direct concern to the applicants. The applicants failed to prove that harm resulted directly from the Commission's decision. Job losses and reduced social protection were not an inevitable consequence of the merger and the Acquired Rights' Directive,[766] and the French Labour Code protected workers being laid off solely for reasons connected with a concentration. The workers' councils were held to be directly concerned, and therefore entitled to challenge the Commission's decisions, only for the specific purpose of examining whether the procedural guarantees to which they were entitled under Article 18 had been infringed.[767]

Shareholders. Actions brought by minority shareholders have not yet been **8.243** found admissible by Community Courts. In *Zunis*, an action was brought by a group of minority investors in Generali challenging the Commission's refusal to revisit its decision in *Mediobanca/Generali* that the transaction did not fall within the scope of the Merger Regulation.[768] The Court of First Instance held that the action was inadmissible on the basis that the investors were not directly and individually concerned by the decision.[769] On the question of direct concern, the Court held that an Article 6(1)(a) decision 'is not of such a nature as by itself to affect the substance or extent of the rights of shareholders of the notifying parties,

---

[763] *Impala v Commission* (n 739, above).

[764] Case T-96/92 *CCE de la Société Générale des Grandes Sources v Commission* [1995] ECR II–1213; and Case T-12/93 *CCE de Vittel v Commission* [1995] ECR II–1247, both on appeal from Case M.190 *Nestlé/Perrier*, OJ 1992 L356/1, [1993] 4 CMLR M17.

[765] ibid.

[766] Dir 77/187 on the approximation of the laws of the Member States relating to the safeguarding of employees' rights in the event of transfers of undertakings, businesses or parts of businesses, OJ 1977 L61/26.

[767] No such infringement was found.

[768] Case M.159 *Mediobanca/Generali* (19 December 1991).

[769] Case T-83/92 *Zunis Holding v Commission* [1993] ECR II-1169, [1994] 5 CMLR 154.

either as regards their proprietary rights or the ability to participate in the company management conferred on them by such rights'.[770] On the question of individual concern, the Court held that the Commission's decision did not affect the applicants individually. Even if the Commission decided that Mediobanca had acquired control of Generali, such a decision would affect the applicants' interests in the same way as those of all the other shareholders. This was particularly the case here, where the applicants' respective shareholdings at the material time each represented less than 0.5 per cent of the share capital of Generali. On appeal, the decision was upheld by the Court of Justice on other grounds, but Advocate General Lenz agreed with the Court of First Instance that the applicants were not individually concerned and considered that, in general, shareholders of an undertaking involved in merger control proceedings should have no right to challenge Commission decisions.[771]

(d) Scope of judicial review

8.244 Grounds of appeal. The Community Courts have jurisdiction under Article 230 of the Treaty to review the legality of acts on grounds of 'lack of competence, infringement of an essential procedural requirement, infringement of [the] Treaty or any rule of law relating to its application, or misuse of powers'. The degree of the Courts' control of Merger Regulation decisions varies, depending on whether they are reviewing the correctness of the Commission's application of the law, or appreciation of the facts, or the correctness of the Commission's appreciation of complex economic matters.[772]

(i) Application of the law

8.245 Questions of law. In reviewing Commission decisions under the Merger Regulation, the Community Courts have full jurisdiction to interpret the law and to verify that the Commission has applied the correct legal principles. This applies equally to jurisdictional, procedural and substantive considerations.

8.246 Jurisdictional issues. The Courts have ruled on a number of jurisdictional issues (addressed principally in Section 2 of this Chapter), such as the concept

---

[770] at para 35.

[771] Opinion of AG Lenz in *Zunis Holding v Commission* (n 751, above) paras 31–40.

[772] See Vesterdorf, 'Standard of Proof in Merger Cases' and Nicholson, Cardell and McKenna, 'The Scope of Review of Merger Decisions under Community Law', both in (2005) 1 European Competition Journal No 1, 1 and 123 respectively; Reeves and Dodoo, 'Standards of Proof and Standards of Judicial Review in EC Merger Law'in Hawk (ed), *2005 Fordham Corp. L. Inst.*(Transnational Juris/Kluwer 2006); Vesterdorf, 'Certain reflections on recent judgments reviewing Commission merger control decisions' in Hoskins and Robinson (eds), *A True European, Essays for Judge David Edward* (2003), p 117.

of control and the application of the Merger Regulation to interrelated transactions,[773] whether control has been acquired solely or jointly[774] and the correct calculation of turnover.[775]

Procedural issues. The Courts have also ruled on various procedural issues **8.247** under the Merger Regulation (as addressed in Section 3 of this Chapter). These have included whether the Advisory Committee had been duly consulted,[776] whether third parties had been duly consulted on commitments,[777] whether the rights of defence had been respected,[778] and whether the decision is adequately reasoned.[779] A Commission decision will be annulled in whole or part if it infringes an essential procedural requirement.[780]

Substantive issues. In reviewing the scope and application of the substantive **8.248** test under the Merger Regulation (as addressed in Section 4 of this Chapter), the Courts have established criteria which guide the Commission in its enforcement of the merger control rules and assist the legal and business communities in the risk assessment of potential mergers and acquisitions. The Court of First Instance has shown itself ready to assume this role in a number of high profile cases which have raised relatively novel issues regarding the application of the substantive test under the Merger Regulation.[781] Thus, it will annul a Commission decision (in whole or part) if an error in the Commission's substantive assessment goes to the heart of the case. However, the Commission's decision will not be annulled if it is supported by other grounds which are not vitiated by illegality and which provide a sufficient legal basis for the operative

---

[773] See eg Case T-282/02 *Cementbouw Handel & Industrie v Commission* [2006] ECR II-319, [2006] 4 CMLR 1561 (on appeal, Case C-202/06P *Cementbouw v Commission*, not yet decided).

[774] See, eg *Air France v Commission (TAT)* (n 756, above) paras 54–66.

[775] See, eg *Air France v Commission (Dan Air)* (n 747, above) paras 87–108.

[776] See, eg *Kaysersberg v Commission* (n 758, above) paras 86–97.

[777] ibid, paras 105–123.

[778] See, eg Case T-221/95 *Endemol Entertainment v Commission* [1999] ECR II–1299, [1999] 5 CMLR 611, [1999] All ER (EC) 385; *Schneider Electric v Commission* (n 734, above).

[779] See eg *Air France v Commission (TAT)* (n 756, above) paras 89–95; *France v Commission* (n 742, above) paras 179–250; *Kaysersberg* (n 758, above) paras 150–161.

[780] Eg *Schneider Electric v Commission* (n 734, above): decision annulled because a key objection in the Phase II prohibition decision had not been addressed with sufficient clarity in the statement of objections, so depriving Schneider of the opportunity to defend itself or to offer proposals for divestiture. See further paras 13.223 *et seq*, below.

[781] See eg Case T-342/99 *Airtours v Commission* [2002] ECR II-2585, [2002] 5 CMLR 317, [2002] All ER (EC) 783): criteria for the application of the Merger Reg to the creation of collective dominance; Case T-5/02 *Tetra Laval v Commission* [2002] ECR II-4381, [2002] 5 CMLR 1182: assessment of leveraging issues in the context of conglomerate mergers. See Judge Vesterdorf, "Standard of Proof in Merger Cases: Reflections in the Light of Recent Case Law of the Community Courts", in Marsden and Hutchings (eds), *Current Competition Law*, Vol IV (2005), 227.

part of the contested decision.[782] As the Court of First Instance noted in its *Honeywell* judgment:

'. . . where the operative part of a Commission decision is based on several pillars of reasoning, each of which would in itself be sufficient to justify that operative part, that decision should, in principle, be annulled only if each of those pillars is vitiated by an illegality. In such a case, an error or other illegality which affects only one of the pillars of reasoning cannot be sufficient to justify annulment of the decision at issue because it could not have had a decisive effect on the operative part adopted by the Commission.'[783]

(ii) Appreciation of facts

8.249 **Questions of fact.** In a number of landmark cases, the Court of First Instance has closely scrutinised the factual elements underpinning the Commission's decisions under the Merger Regulation in order to assess whether the Commission had correctly established the material facts.[784] The intensity of this control by the Court of First Instance was recognised by Advocate General Tizzano in his Opinion on the Commission's appeal against that Court's judgment the *Tetra Laval* proceedings:

'With regard to the findings of fact, the review is clearly more intense, in that the issue is to verify objectively and materially the accuracy of certain facts and the correctness of the conclusions drawn in order to establish whether certain known facts make it possible to prove the existence of other facts to be ascertained'.[785]

This reflects the role of the Court of First Instance in checking meticulously the accuracy, reliability and consistency of the evidence taken into account by the

---

[782] See *EDP v Commission* (n 736, above): Commission's Phase II prohibition decision vitiated by an error of law insofar as it concluded that there would be a strengthening of GDP's preexisting dominant positions on the gas market (para 133), but the applicant had not demonstrated a manifest error with regard to the Commission's assessment of the impact of the concentration on the electricity market and that was sufficient to uphold the decision declaring the concentration incompatible with the common market (paras 144–146, 238–240). See also *Schneider Electric v Commission* (n 734, above) paras 411–413: inadequacy of analysis in the decision re various other national sectoral markets was not sufficient to call in question the objections to the merger re the French sectoral markets (but the CFI nevertheless annulled the decision for infringement of essential procedural requirements); Case T-5/02 *Tetra Laval v Commission* (n 781, above) para 141 (errors in the analysis of vertical and horizontal effects would not have led to annulment of decision if the analysis of conglomerate effects supported the prohibition of the merger).

[783] Case T-209/01 *Honeywell v Commission* [2005] ECR II-5527, [2006] 4 CMLR 652, para 49. Similarly, *General Electric v Commission* (n 737, above) para 734.

[784] See eg *Airtours v Commission* (n 781, above); *Schneider Electric v Commission* (n 734, above); *Tetra Laval v Commission* (n 781, above); and *BaByliss v Commission* (n 739, above).

[785] Case C-12/03P *Commission v Tetra Laval* [2005] ECR I-987, [2005] 4 CMLR 573, AG Tizzano Opinion, para 86 (appeal from Case T-5/02 *Tetra Laval v Commission* [2002] ECR II-4381, [2002] 5 CMLR 1182 which was in turn an appeal from Case M.2416 *Tetra Laval/Sidel,* OJ 2004 L43/13). The divestiture decision taken by the Commission (OJ 2004 L38/1) was also annulled: Case T-80/02 [2002] ECR II-4519, [2002] 5 CMLR 1271 and no ruling was necessary on the further appeal C-13/03P [2005] ECR I-1113.

Commission in its decisions, so as to ensure that the evidence provides a sound factual basis for the adoption of the contested decision. However, there is not always a clear dividing line between the pulling together of the facts which should provide an objective basis for the Commission's assessment of the concentration and the subsequent appreciation of those facts. The latter is a more subjective concept which may necessitate complex assessments such that there is scope for different persons to disagree on what conclusions to draw from the same facts.

(iii) Economic issues

Appreciation of complex economic assessments. The Commission's review of 8.250 concentrations under the Merger Regulation can involve complex economic assessments where the conclusions ultimately drawn by the Commission from the facts may differ from those advocated by the notifying parties or by third parties opposing the concentration. Although the Court of First Instance has shown itself ready to undertake thorough review of whether the Commission correctly applied the law and accurately established the facts, it has been more restrained in reviewing the complex economic assessments undertaken by the Commission in investigations under the Merger Regulation.

Manifest error. The standard to be applied by the Community Courts for the 8.251 purpose of reviewing the Commission's assessment of complex economic issues (the so-called 'manifest error standard') was reaffirmed by the Court of Justice in 2005 in its judgment in *Tetra Laval*, upholding the test which had been applied by the Court of First Instance in its annulment of the Commission's Phase II prohibition decision:

> '[T]he Court of First Instance correctly sets out the tests to be applied when carrying out judicial review of a Commission decision on a concentration as laid down in the judgment in *Kali & Salz*. In paragraphs 223 and 224 of that judgment, the Court stated that the basic provisions of the [Merger] Regulation, in particular Article 2, confer on the Commission a certain discretion, especially with respect to assessment of an economic nature, and that, consequently, review by the Community Courts of the exercise of that discretion, which is essential for defining the rules on concentrations, must take account of the margin of discretion implicit in the provisions of an economic nature which form part of the rules on concentrations.'[786]

---

[786] *Commission v Tetra Laval*, ibid, para 38. (The *Kali & Salz* case referred to is Cases C-68/94 & C-30/95 *France v Commission* (n 741, above)). See also Opinion of AG Tizzano at para 89: 'The rules on the division of powers between the Commission and the Community judicature, which are fundamental to the Community institutional system, do not . . . allow the judicature to go further, and . . . to enter into the merits of the Commission's complex economic assessments or to substitute its own point of view for that the institution'.

8.252 **Effective but restrained review.** The Court of Justice went on in *Tetra Laval* to confirm that the Community Courts nevertheless have a significant role to play in exercising effective but restrained review of the Commission's interpretation of the facts:

> 'Whilst the Court recognises that the Commission has a margin of discretion with regard to economic matters, that does not mean that the Community Courts must refrain from reviewing the Commission's interpretation of information of an economic nature. Not only must the Community Courts, *inter alia*, establish whether the evidence relied on is factually accurate, reliable and consistent but also whether that evidence contains all the information which must be taken into account in order to assess a complex situation and whether it is capable of substantiating the conclusions drawn from it.'[787]

This suggests that the Court of First Instance, in exercising such effective review, should assess not only whether the evidence relied on by the Commission for its assessment of the economic issues was factually accurate, reliable and consistent but also whether there was any other relevant information which should have formed part of that assessment and, further, whether the evidence as a whole supports the conclusions drawn from it by the Commission in the contested decision. If errors in the Commission's assessment of the evidence amount to a manifest error of appreciation, this would be sufficient to vitiate the conclusions drawn from that evidence in the contested decision.

(e) Standard of proof incumbent on Commission

8.253 **Distinction between the scope of judicial review and the standard of proof.** The scope of judicial review (as considered at paragraphs 8.244 to 8.252, above) relates to the standard to be applied by the Community Courts when reviewing the legality of decisions adopted by the Commission under the Merger Regulation. The standard of proof incumbent on the Commission, when adopting a decision to prohibit or clear a notified concentration, is a closely linked, but theoretically distinct, concept. This distinction was addressed to some extent by Advocate General Tizzano in his opinion in *Tetra Laval* when he referred to the need to assess whether the Court of First Instance 'committed an error of law in applying too rigorous a judicial review or in claiming a standard of proof too high for decisions prohibiting mergers'.[788] Although there is no clear rule on precisely how

---

[787] ibid, para 39, and Opinion of AG Tizzano, para 87. See also *Impala v Commission* (n 739, above) para 328; *General Electric v Commission* (n 737, above) paras 63–64: prospective analysis of how a merger might alter the factors determining competition in a given market makes it necessary to envisage various chains of cause and effect with a view to ascertaining which of them are the most likely.

[788] Opinion of AG Tizzano in Case C-12/03P *Commission v Tetra Laval* (n 785, above) at paras 71–89. See also Vesterdorf (n 781, above).

much evidence the Commission should have before it may adopt a formal decision prohibiting, or indeed approving, a concentration, the Community Courts require the Commission to produce enough evidence to meet the 'requisite legal standard'.[789]

Need for convincing evidence. In *Kali & Salz*[790] the Court of Justice referred to **8.254** the need for the Commission's decision to be 'supported by a sufficiently cogent and consistent body of evidence'. It also held that the concentration's effects on competition on the relevant market must be assessed with a 'sufficient degree of probability' and that the Commission must rely on 'a rigorous analysis'.[791] Similarly, in *Airtours*[792] the Court of First Instance held that it was incumbent on the Commission to produce 'convincing' and 'cogent' evidence. In *Tetra Laval*, the Court of First Instance criticised the Commission's analysis as 'not really very convincing' since its conclusions were not based on a 'prudent analysis of the independent studies or on a solid, coherent body of evidence obtained by it through its market investigation'.[793] If a third party challenges a Commission decision and alleges that the Commission made manifest errors of assessment of economic issues, there is a comparable burden on the applicant to adduce 'serious evidence of the genuine existence of a competition problem which, by reason of that effect, should have been examined by the Commission'.[794]

Borderline cases. In its appeal to the Court of Justice in *Tetra Laval*, the **8.255** Commission argued that the Merger Regulation (at Article 2(2) and (3)) imposes a symmetrical standard for clearance and prohibition decisions, essentially advocating a 'balance of probabilities' standard of the type used in some legal systems for civil disputes, since it must prove the merits of its assessment equally in either case. It argued that the standard of 'convincing evidence' applied by the Court of First Instance differed substantially in degree and nature both from the obligation to produce 'cogent and consistent' evidence established in *Kali & Salz* and from the principle that the Commission's assessment of economic matters must be accepted unless it is shown to be manifestly wrong. The Court of Justice rejected

---

[789] Similarly, for a third party to succeed in challenging a Commission decision to approve a merger, it must produce evidence to the requisite legal standard: see CFI judgment in *easyJet v Commission* (n 754, above).

[790] *Kali & Salz* (n 741, above) para 228.

[791] ibid, para 246.

[792] *Airtours v Commission* (n 784, above) paras 63 and 294.

[793] Case T-5/02 *Tetra Laval v Commission* (n 785, above) para 212. In that case the analysis was required to be be particularly plausible as the prohibition decision was based on 'conglomeracy' concerns: see para 8.222, above.

[794] *easyJet v Commission* (n 754, above) paras 65–74: in the absence of convincing evidence that the merger gave rise to a competition problem of the type alleged by the applicant, the CFI concluded that the applicant had not shown to the requisite legal standard that the Commission had committed a manifest error of assessment in clearing the concentration at Phase I.

the Commission's arguments. It held that the Court of First Instance had correctly applied the test in *Kali & Salz* and had 'by no means added a condition relating to the requisite standard of proof but merely drew attention to the essential function of evidence, which is to establish convincingly the merits of an argument or, as in the present case, of a decision on a merger'.[795] The prospective analysis required in a merger case means that particular care is needed in making a prediction of events which are likely to occur in the future according to whether or not the merger takes place (or proceeds subject to conditions). The judgment of the Court of Justice does not make any further observations on what constitutes the requisite standard of proof. However, Advocate General Tizzano expressly considered in his Opinion the scenario of a borderline case where it would not be possible to adduce convincing evidence either for a clearance or for a prohibition, advocating that in such a situation the Commission should authorise the concentration. In support of this proposition, he pointed out that:[796]

(a) Article 10(6) of the Merger Regulation stipulates that where the Commission fails to take a decision within the Phase I or Phase II time limit the concentration is deemed to have been authorised, thereby indicating a presumption for authorisation; and

(b) It would be preferable to have a presumption of authorisation rather than of prohibition, since even if an anti-competitive concentration were allowed to proceed it would still be possible to correct distortions of competition through *ex post* application of Article 82 of the Treaty.[797]

However, in *General Electric v Commission* the Court of First Instance observed that the Merger Regulation 'does not establish a presumption as to the compatibility or incompatibility with the common market of a transaction which has been notified. It is not the case that the Commission must find in favour of a concentration falling within its jurisdiction in a case in which it might entertain doubts but rather that it must always make an actual decision one way or the other'.[798] Where a case is finely balanced but the Commission is faced with having to decide one way or the other, it would seem that the benefit of doubt should lean towards the notifing parties.[799]

---

[795] Case C-12/03P *Commission v Tetra Laval* (n 785, above); see also para 8.249, above.

[796] Opinion of AG Tizzano in *Tetra Laval v Commission*, ibid, paras 79–81.

[797] Furthermore, Recitals (3) and (4) to the Merger Reg could be viewed as broadly supportive of concentrations.

[798] Case T-210/01 *General Electric v Commission* [2005] ECR II-5575, [2006] 4 CMLR 686.

[799] See Vesterdorf, 'Standard of Proof in Merger Cases: Reflections in the Light of Recent Case Law of the Community Courts' (n 772, above) which observes (at 31) that 'overall a slight inclination towards authorising mergers in cases of significant doubts, uncertainty or inaction is in-built in the EC system of merger control. The balance has to tip one way or the other at the end of the Commission's review, when the College of Commissioners sits round a table in the Berlaymont and decides what to do with a given merger case. In cases that are "too close to call" the benefit of

(f) Consequences of annulment

Reopening of Phase I proceedings.   Article 10(5) of the Merger Regulation pro-   **8.256**
vides that: 'Where the Court of Justice gives a judgment which annuls the whole
or part of a Commission decision which is subject to a time limit set by this
Article, the concentration shall be re-examined by the Commission with a view to
adopting a decision pursuant to Article 6(1).' Thus, the Commission is required
to reactivate its investigation of the case in a new Phase I proceeding, unless the
concentration has been aborted in the meantime.[800] Article 10(5) also expressly
provides that this re-examination is to be undertaken 'in light of current market
conditions', ie not solely by reference to those which prevailed at the time of the
original notification. It also provides that where the original Form CO notification is no longer complete, by reason of intervening changes in market conditions
or in the information provided, the notifying parties should submit a new notification, or supplement the original notification, without delay. If there are no such
changes, they should certify this without delay.[801]

---

the doubt should lean towards authorisation of the merger in question, especially where the alleged
anti-competitive effects are too remote or of a nature that allows effective *ex post* correction using
Article 82 EC'. The article goes on to conclude: 'Prohibiting a transaction between two companies
is a far-reaching measure which requires the Commission to be certain at a relatively high standard
(more than just 51%) that the merger in question is likely to result in significant anticompetitive
effects'.

[800] Such second decisions on a merger after renewed administrative proceedings include:
Case M.308 *Kali & Salz/Mdk/Treuhand* (n 740, above) (Phase II conditional clearance decn of
14 December 1993 annulled, Phase I clearance decn on 9 July 1998); Case M.2621 *SEB/Moulinex*
(Phase I unconditional clearance of 8 January 2002 annulled; Phase II conditional clearance decn
on 11 November 2003, OJ 2005 L138/18); Case M.2416 *Tetra Laval/Sidel*, OJ 2004 L38/1 (divestiture decision) and L43/13 (Phase II prohibition decision); Phase I conditional clearance decn
adopted 13 January 2003; Case M.2283 *Schneider/Legrand* Phase II prohibition decn of 30 January
2002 annulled on appeal Case T-77/02 *Schneider Electric v Commission (II)* [2002] ECR II-4201;
following the CFI annulment of the original Phase II prohibition decision, the Commission initiated new Phase II proceedings, but the file was subsequently closed as the parties abandoned the
deal. In Case M.3333 *Sony/BMG*, OJ 2005 L62/30 following the annulment of the original Phase
II unconditional clearance decision by the CFI in Case T-464/04 *Impala v Commission*, judgment
of 13 July 2006 (n 739, above) the Commission reopened the administrative procedure and, after
new Phase II proceedings, adopted a second unconditional clearance decision on 3 October 2007.

[801] The original Merger Reg had not included such provisions, but merely stated that the periods
laid down in the Merger Reg started again from the date of the judgment. However, in the *Kali &
Salz* case, ibid, the Commission took the view that the determination of whether the timetable
re-started completely depended on whether the original notification could still be regarded as complete at the time of the judgment. If that were the position, the Commission should be able to
proceed with its appraisal of the concentration. There, the Commission concluded that it was not
necessary to re-examine the jurisdictional question of the applicability of the Merger Reg (a part
of the original decision which had not been contested), but that it was necessary to conduct a fresh
substantive appraisal of the concentration in the light of current market conditions: *XXVIIIth Report
on Competition Policy* (1998), paras 175–178.

6. Application of Articles 81 and 82 in Field of
Mergers and Acquisitions

(a) Background

8.257 **Position prior to Merger Regulation.**   Prior to the implementation of the original Merger Regulation in 1990, several mergers and acquisitions had been investigated by the Commission under Articles 81 and 82. Uncertainty as to the applicability of these Treaty provisions to mergers and acquisitions and the fact that neither provision was suited to merger control acted as a spur to the adoption of the Merger Regulation.[802] However, despite the implementation of the Merger Regulation, Articles 81 and 82 continue to play a residual role in specific circumstances.

8.258 **Article 81 and concentrations.**   As long ago as 1966 the Commission drew a distinction between structural concentrations where two or more undertakings are brought together under a single economic management in circumstances where they give up their economic independence and behavioural arrangements between independent undertakings, including cartels.[803] It identified a number of reasons why Article 81 could not in principle be applied to concentrations while stating that Article 81 was applicable 'if the agreement does not lead to a permanent change in ownership but only to a coordination of the market behaviour of undertakings that remain economically independent'. The principle that Article 81 does not apply to concentrations was followed by the decisions and practice of the Commission.[804] However, even prior to the implementation of the Merger Regulation, it was still possible for the Commission to intervene under Article 81 in respect of (i) minority shareholdings and other structural links that did not give rise to concentrations; and (ii) other forms of competition between independent undertakings falling short of a concentration such as partial function JVs.[805] Article 81 also remains applicable in the context of some concentrations, in particular (i) in situations where the creation of a full-function JV has its object or effect the coordination of the competitive behaviour of the parent companies;

---

[802] Recital (7) to the Merger Reg recognises that Arts 81 and 82 were insufficient for the control of concentrations; accordingly the legal basis for the Merger Reg is principally Art 308 of the EC Treaty (not only Art 83).

[803] 'Le problème de la concentration dans le marché commun' Collection Etudes, Série Concurrence no. 3, Brussels 1966, Part III, pp 21 *et seq*.

[804] See, eg *IVth Report on Competition Policy* (1974), points 39 to 42; *VIth Report on Competition Policy* (1976), points 53 to 59; *XIIIth Report on Competition Policy* (1983), points 53 to 55; *XVth Report on Competition Policy* (1985), point 26.

[805] See paras 8.273 *et seq*, below for minority shareholdings and Chap 7, above for partial function JVs.

or (ii) for the assessment of restrictive arrangements which may have been entered into at the time of a concentration but which do not qualify as 'ancillary' to that concentration.

Article 82 and concentrations.   Article 82 is designed to control market behav-   **8.259** iour; it does not prohibit an undertaking from holding a dominant position but prohibits certain anti-competitive conduct by dominant undertakings considered largely on an *ex post* basis.[806] In 1973, the Court of Justice held in *Continental Can*[807] that the acquisition of a competitor by a dominant company may constitute an abuse within the meaning of Article 82 since this may reinforce the acquiror's dominant position. The Court stated (at points 26 and 27) that:

'Abuse may . . . occur if an undertaking in a dominant position strengthens such position in such a way that the degree of dominance reached substantially fetters competition, ie that only undertakings remain in the market whose behaviour depends on the dominant one.

Such being the meaning and the scope of Article [82] . . . the strengthening of the position of an undertaking may be an abuse and prohibited under Article [82] of the Treaty, regardless of the means and procedure by which it is achieved, if it has the effects mentioned above'.

Prior to the adoption of the Merger Regulation, the Commission used its Article 82 powers in investigations of a number of mergers.[808] However, merger control under Article 82 could only apply to an acquisition involving an already dominant undertaking and not to the creation of a dominant position which might result from a merger. Subsequent to the adoption of the Merger Regulation, the Community Courts have reaffirmed that it may be an illegal abuse for a dominant company to acquire a competitor.[809] Likewise, it may be an illegal abuse to acquire a minority shareholding or other structural links with a competitor.[810]

---

[806] See generally Chap 10, below.

[807] Case 6/72 *Europemballage and Continental Can v Commission* [1973] ECR 215, [1973] CMLR 199. However, on the facts the ECJ held that the Commission had failed properly to identify the relevant market and so annulled the Commission's decision that there had been an abuse of a dominant position.

[808] The Commission's *Annual Reports on Competition Policy* refer to a number of cases prior to the implementation of the Merger Reg where the Commission raised objections under Art 82. These include *Pilkington/BSN-Gervais-Danône, Xth Report on Competition Policy* (1980), points 152 to 155; *Michelin/Kléber-Colombes, Xth Report on Competition Policy* (1980), points 156; *Baxter/ SmithKline RIT, Xth Report on Competition Policy* (1980), points 157; *Amicon/Fortia/Wright, XIth Report on Competition Policy* (1981), point 112; *Irish Distillers, XVIIIth Report on Competition Policy* (1988), point 80. The Commission allowed some other concentrations to proceed subject to certain conditions, including *British Airways/British Caledonian, XVIIIth Report* (1988), point 81; *Consolidated Gold Fields/Minorco, XIXth Report on Competition Policy* (1989), point 68; *Stena/ Houlder Offshore, XIXth Report on Competition Policy* (1989), point 70.

[809] See, eg *EDP v Commission* (n 736, above) para 47; Case T-210/01 *General Electric v Commission* [2005] ECR II-5575, [2006] 4 CMLR 686, para 86.

[810] See paras 8.273–8.276, below.

8.260 **Disapplication of other regulations for concentrations.** Article 21(1) and (2) of the Merger Regulation provides that the Regulation alone will apply to 'concentrations' and that the implementing regulations for Articles 81 and 82[811] will not apply to them 'except in relation to joint ventures that do not have a Community dimension and which have as their object or effect the coordination of the competitive behaviour of undertakings that remain independent'.[812] To the extent that Article 83 of the EC Treaty provides a legal basis for the Merger Regulation, and since the definition in Article 3 of the Merger Regulation does not distinguish between concentrations with or without a Community dimension, Regulation 1/2003 and the other implementing regulations are disapplied for all concentrations whether or not they have a Community dimension, with the exception of the coordinative aspects of JVs without a Community dimension.[813]

8.261 **Articles 84 and 85.** To the extent that the Merger Regulation operates as an implementing regulation for Articles 81 and 82 (insofar as they are applicable to certain concentrations), there appears to be no scope for action by the Commission or Member States in respect of concentrations under Articles 84 or 85, the so-called transitional competition rules of the Treaty.[814] This is the case whether or not the concentration has a Community dimension.[815]

---

[811] Council Reg 1/2003, OJ 2003 L1/1: Vol II, App B.3 now implements Arts 81 and 82 for all sectors.

[812] For the assessment of the coordinative aspects of such JVs, see paras 8.232–8.234, above.

[813] Recital (6) to the Merger Reg refers to the need for a specific legal instrument 'to permit effective control of all concentrations in terms of their effect on the structure of competition in the Community and to be the only instrument applicable to such concentrations'. Recital (7) refers to the Merger Reg as being based 'not only on Article 83 but, principally, on Article 308 of the Treaty'.

[814] In *R v Secretary of State for Trade and Industry, ex p Airlines of Britain* [1993] BCC 89, the English Court of Appeal considered that the Merger Reg creates 'a seamless system for dealing with concentrations within the Community'. See also para 14.043, below. Concentrations with a Community dimension are to be dealt with by the Commission under the Merger Reg (unless referred to a Member State under Art 4(4) or Art 9), and concentrations without a Community dimension are to be dealt with by the Member States applying their national merger control rules (unless referred to the Commission under Art 4(5) or Art 22). The Court thus held that the application of Art 84 was precluded in respect of a concentration without a Community dimension, so the UK authorities were right not to take Arts 81 and 82 into account when assessing a concentration.

[815] This issue is not entirely beyond doubt; at the time of the adoption of the Merger Reg, the Commission expressly purported to reserve the right to take action under Art 84 in respect of concentrations without a Community dimension. In the Interpretative Notes annexed to the original Merger Reg (available on DG Comp's website at http://ec.europa.eu/comm/competition/mergers/legislation/regulation/notes.html), the Commission stated that it did not intend to take action in this way unless the parties had a combined worldwide turnover of more than €2,000 million, at least two of the parties had a Community-wide turnover of more than €100 million and the two-thirds test was satisfied – on the grounds that concentrations below these levels (which predated the alternative thresholds introduced in 1998) would not normally have a significant effect on trade between Member States. In practice, if the Commission were to have such concerns with respect to a concentration without a Community dimension, it would be more likely to encourage intervention by the NCAs in accordance with the Case Referral Notice (see para 8.014, above).

Private actions in national courts. There is no scope for private action under **8.262** Article 81 in respect of concentrations, whether with or without a Community dimension.[816] However, as regards Article 82, in principle, a private litigant may be able to bring an action in the national courts, claiming damages or injunctive relief, in respect of any concentration or other transaction involving an abuse of dominance within the meaning of Article 82, whether or not the concentration has a Community dimension.[817] In practice, third parties concerned about a particular merger will in most cases bring their complaints to the Commission or NCAs who will usually be best placed to take those concerns into account as part of the administrative procedure. There could, however, be circumstances in which action before the national courts alleging an abuse of dominance under Article 82 might be appropriate, for example in respect of a completed transaction which is subsequently prohibited by the authorities in circumstances where a third party considers that it has suffered damage as a result of the implementation of the merger.

(b) Ancillary restraints

(i) In general

Restrictions directly related and necessary to the implementation of **8.263** **concentrations.** When parties agree a concentration, they generally enter into contractual arrangements to implement the transaction. In addition to agreements that bring about the concentration itself, such as the transfer of shares, the parties sometimes enter into restrictive arrangements that, while not an integral part of the concentration itself, may be viewed as directly related and necessary to the implementation of the concentration. The term 'ancillary restraints' or 'ancillary restrictions' is used in Community law to describe such restrictions. Provided such restrictions are genuinely directly related and necessary to the implementation of the concentration, they (like the concentration itself) will not be caught by the Article 81(1) prohibition.[818] Consistent with the modernised regime under Regulation 1/2003, parties are generally expected to self-assess whether the contractual restrictions to which they agree come within the definition of ancillary

---

[816] See para 8.258, above.

[817] See *Continental Can* (n 807, above) para 8.259, above. In practice, national courts are likely to be influenced by any pending or completed administrative proceedings under the Merger Reg or applicable national merger control rules; see, Commission Notice on cooperation between the Commission and national courts, OJ 2004 C101/54: Vol II, App B.9 paras 8 and 11–14.

[818] Thus the Merger Reg (n 728, above) at Art 6(1)(b), second sub-para; Art 8(1), second sub-para; Art 8(2), third sub-para provides that a Phase I or Phase II clearance decision 'shall be deemed to cover restrictions directly related and necessary to the implementation of the concentration.' See also Recital (21).

restraints or are otherwise compatible with Articles 81 and 82.[819] To assist parties in undertaking their self-assessments, the Commission has issued a Notice on restrictions directly related and necessary to concentrations (the 'Ancillary Restraints Notice').[820] This provides guidance on contractual restrictions which are commonly encountered in the context of concentrations. Only in cases involving exceptional circumstances presenting 'a novel or unresolved question giving rise to genuine uncertainty' will the Commission respond to the parties' requests that it expressly assess whether a restriction is directly related to, and necessary for, the implementation of the concentration.[821]

8.264 **General principles.** The Ancillary Restraints Notice begins with a reminder of the nature of agreements bringing about a concentration such as those relating to the sale of shares or assets of an undertaking.[822] It then highlights the objective nature of the criteria of direct relation and necessity when identifying which restrictions, although not an integral part of the concentration, are economically related to the main transaction and intended to allow a smooth transition to the changed company structure after the concentration. For these purposes:

(a) The necessity for such restrictions must be borne out by the fact that in their absence the implementation of the concentration would be impossible or more difficult, costly or slower. The restrictions must be objectively the least restrictive of competition while at the same time facilitating the concentration, typically by protecting the value transferred, maintaining continuity of supply or enabling the start-up of a new entity to the extent required in terms of duration, subject-matter and scope.[823]

(b) Although restrictions relating to stages preceding the establishment of control are not covered, parties to an acquisition of joint control can legitimately

---

[819] To the extent that restrictions are not 'ancillary', so that Art 81(1) and even Art 82 may be applicable, undertakings can nevertheless self-assess whether they are covered by any of the Commission's block exemptions or otherwise satisfy the criteria of Art 81(3). Ultimately, disputes on such issues may be resolved before the national courts: see generally paras 3.003 *et seq*, above; for potential 'gun jumping' issues, see para 8.127, above.

[820] Ancillary Restraints Notice, OJ 2005 C56/24: Vol II, App D.10. The current version of this Notice substantially revised and simplified a previous Notice which reflected Commission practice under the original Merger Reg.

[821] Merger Reg, Recital (21); Ancillary Restraints Notice, above, paras 2 and 5. n 3 of the Ancillary Restraints Notice refers to a number of cases under the original Merger Reg which have already addressed specific exceptional circumstances (such that the questions are no longer 'novel or unresolved'), namely: (a) where there is a high degree of customer loyalty – M.1980 *Volvo/Renault* (1 September 2000), para 56; (b) where there is a long product life cycle – Case M.1298 *Kodak/Imation* (23 October 1998), para 73; (c) where there is a limited number of alternative producers – Case M.550 *Union Carbide/Enichem* (13 March 1995), para 99; and (d) where longer protection of know-how is required – Case M.197 *Solvay/Laporte* (30 April 1992), para 50.

[822] Ancillary Restraints Notice (n 820, above) para 10.

[823] ibid, para 13. For these purposes it is necessary to consider not only the nature of the restriction but also its subject-matter, duration and geographic scope.

impose an obligation on the vendor to abstain from material changes in the target's business in the period prior to closing of the transaction. Similarly, joint bidders can agree to refrain from making separate competing offers for the same undertaking or otherwise acquiring control.[824]

(c) Where the arrangements involve the break-up of a pre-existing economic entity, the parties can legitimately enter into agreements on how they will divide up the assets.[825]

(ii) Commonly encountered restrictions in business acquisitions

Restrictions in business acquisitions. As a rule, restrictions imposed by the purchaser on the vendor with the objective of protecting the full value of the acquired business (both physical and intangible assets), are more likely to be legitimately justified than any restrictions that the vendor may seek to impose on the purchaser. The Ancillary Restraints Notice considers three categories of restrictions commonly imposed on the vendor of a business. These are vendor non-compete obligations, licence agreements, and purchase and supply obligations.   **8.265**

Vendor non-compete obligations. Vendor non-compete obligations are generally justified and treated as directly related to the concentration where their duration, geographic scope, subject-matter and those bound by them do not exceed what is reasonably necessary to achieve the legitimate objective of implementing the concentration. In general terms, the Notice states that non-compete obligations are justifiable for up to three years in the case of a transfer of goodwill and know-how, and two years if only goodwill is transferred.[826] Only the vendor and its affiliates (including commercial agents but not third party distributors) can validly be bound, subject always to the geographic scope and subject-matter of the restriction reflecting the actual or clearly and imminently anticipated activities of the business over which control is being transferred.[827] It is also legitimate to oblige the vendor not to acquire an active stake in entities that compete with the business transferred, and not to solicit customers or make use of confidential information for so long as the non-compete restriction validly applies.[828]   **8.266**

---

[824] ibid, para 14.

[825] ibid, paras 15–16.

[826] ibid, paras 20–21: non-compete clauses are not considered necessary for bare acquisitions of physical assets or transfers of exclusive industrial or commercial property rights which can be enforced in any event.

[827] eg in Case M.301 *Tesco/Catteau* (4 February 1993) the geographic scope of the non-compete clause was limited to the French départements and Belgian provinces in which Catteau carried on business.

[828] However, special factors may enable non-compete provisions of potentially long duration to be acceptable. In Case M.57 *Digital/Kienzle* [1992] 4 CMLR M99, the vendor retained a stake in the business being sold; the Commission cleared as ancillary a restriction on the vendor not to compete with the business for so long as it held the stake and for two years thereafter (see further *XXIst Report on Competition Policy* (1991), Annex III, p 370). Similarly, in Case M.105 *ICL/Nokia*

8.267 Licence agreements. The transfer of intellectual property rights to the purchaser as part of the concentration may take the form of licences rather than an outright assignment where the vendor wishes to retain ownership of these rights for exploitation or use in other applications. Such licences may relate to patents, know-how, trade marks, copyrights, business names, design rights or similar rights and may be exclusive or non-exclusive, and of any duration. They will be treated as an integral part of the concentration so long as any express field of use corresponds to the activities of the business transferred.[829] Territorial limitations can legitimately be imposed on the licensor under the same conditions as are laid down for non-compete clauses. In contrast, provisions that bind the licensee and protect the licensor are unlikely to be viewed as necessary to the implementation of the concentration.[830]

8.268 Purchase and supply obligations. The smooth implementation of a business transfer can be supported by the maintenance, for a reasonable transitional period, of the lines of purchase and supply that were present when the business transferred formed part of the vendor's economic group. The Notice specifically treats as legitimate restrictions for periods of up to five years where they ensure the continuity of supply required for the parties to carry on their activities, provided they do not provide for unlimited quantities, or confer exclusivity or preferred party status.[831]

(iii) Commonly encountered restrictions in joint ventures

8.269 Restrictions in joint ventures. As a rule, restrictions which protect the full value of the JV undertaking's business (both physical and intangible assets) are afforded greater protection under the Merger Regulation than provisions which benefit the parent companies. The Ancillary Restraints Notice considers the following

---

Data (17 July 1991) the vendor, which was entitled to one seat on the purchaser's board, accepted a non-compete covenant for three years or, if later, until the vendor ceased to have a director on the purchaser's board, to ensure that the vendor did not use confidential board information in a competing business. The restriction was held to be ancillary since the vendor could free itself of the restriction should it wish to compete with the purchaser at any time after expiry of the three year period, by removing its representative from the board. See, more recently, Case M.1298 *Kodak/Imation* (23 October 1998) and *Volvo/Renault* (n 821, above), where five-year non-compete obligations have been accepted.

[829] Ancillary Restraints Notice (n 820, above) paras 27 *et seq.*
[830] ibid, para 30.
[831] ibid, paras 32 *et seq.* See eg Case M.2355 *Dow/Enichem Polyurethane* (6 April 2001), para 31; *Volvo/Renault* (n 821, above) para 55 (supply arrangements of unlimited duration were not considered ancillary to the concentration). Agreements may provide for shared ancillary services, eg power, sewerage, emergency care: see, eg Case M.113 *Courtaulds/SNIA* (19 December 1991), paras 8 and 33; Case M.1469 *Solvay/BASF* (2 June 1999), para 27. Such arrangements will generally not restrict competition and will be seen as reflecting the establishment of economic unity within the concentrated undertaking.

restrictions commonly imposed on parties in the context of the creation of a full-function JV undertaking: shareholder non-compete obligations, licence agreements, and purchase and supply obligations.

Non-compete obligations. Such obligations, when placed on the JV parents, **8.270** are justified and treated as directly related to the concentration where they relate to the products, services and territories covered by the JV agreement or its by-laws. It is acceptable for the parents to agree not to compete with the JV undertaking for the entire duration of the JV undertaking.[832] Such restrictions express the reality of the lasting withdrawal of the parents from the market assigned to the JV undertaking and are therefore recognised as an integral part of the concentration. The Commission has also treated as ancillary non-compete covenants which apply for a limited period after the parent ceases to hold an interest in the JV undertaking.[833] However, non-compete clauses must be limited to products and services constituting the economic activity of the JV. The presumption that one parent's investment in the JV needs to be protected against competition from the other parent does not extend beyond markets in which the JV undertaking will be active from the outset. Products must be at an advanced stage of development, or fully developed but not yet marketed, in order to be validly covered by the non-compete clause.

Licence agreements. The transfer of intellectual property rights from the par- **8.271** ent undertakings to the JV undertaking will often take the form of licences that are restricted to a particular field of use, corresponding with the intended activities of the JV. Such licences may relate to patents, know-how, trade marks, copyrights, business names, design rights or similar rights and can be exclusive or non-exclusive, and of any duration. They will be treated as an integral part of the concentration. Licences by the JV to one of its parents and cross-licences are also regarded as directly related and necessary to the concentration under the same conditions as for business acquisitions.[834]

Purchase and supply obligations. A JV undertaking may be supported by the **8.272** maintenance of purchase and supply lines between itself and its parents. Such arrangements can generally be justified as ancillary for a transitional period of up to five years, insofar as they are required to allow the parties to carry on their

---

[832] Ancillary Restraints Notice (n 820, above) para 36.

[833] See, eg Case M.86 *Thomson/Pilkington* (23 October 1991), para 10; Case M.113 *Courtaulds/ SNIA* (19 December 1991), para 30; Case M.121 *Ingersoll-Rand/Dresser* (18 December 1991), paras 10 and 18; Case M.180 *Steetley/Tarmac* (12 February 1992), paras 15; Case M.926 *Messer Griesheim/Hydrogas* (23 October 1997), paras 18–19. However, in Case M.852 *BASF/Shell*, para 49, the Commission concluded that a two-year post-termination non-compete clause was not sufficiently justified by the parties.

[834] See para 8.267, above and Ancillary Restraints Notice (n 820, above) paras 42 and 43.

activities and do not provide for unlimited quantities, or confer exclusivity or pre-ferred party status.[835] To the extent that supply obligations extend for longer than five years, they will generally not be regarded as ancillary. Accordingly, their enforceability may be subject to challenge under Article 81.[836]

(c) Minority shareholdings and other structural links

8.273 Links not conferring control. Depending on the facts of each case, the acquisi-tion of a minority shareholding in an undertaking may confer joint or even sole control within the meaning of Article 3(3) of the Merger Regulation. If so, the acquisition will give rise to a concentration.[837] However, if a transaction involves a minority investment or other links between independent undertakings which are insufficient to establish sole or joint control then there is no concentration. Depending on the facts, Articles 81 and 82 may be applicable to any such links or arrangements.

8.274 Article 81. In *BAT and Reynolds* ('the *Philip Morris* case'),[838] which pre-dated the adoption of the Merger Regulation, the Court of Justice considered the rela-tively narrow issue of whether and in what circumstances the acquisition of a minority shareholding in a competing company may constitute an infringement of Articles 81 and 82 of the Treaty. The particular share acquisition was the subject-matter of agreements entered into between companies which remained independent after those agreements entered into force. In that context, the Court made a broad statement on the circumstances in which such share acquisitions could fall within Article 81:

> 'Although the acquisition by one company of an equity interest in a competitor does not in itself constitute conduct restricting competition, such an acquisition may nevertheless serve as an instrument for influencing the commercial conduct of the companies in question so as to restrict or distort competition on the market on which they carry on business.

---

[835] Ancillary Restraints Notice, para 44.
[836] See, eg Case M.3178 *Bertelsmann/Springer/JV* (3 May 2003), para 13.
[837] See paras 8.029, 8.030 and 8.035, above.
[838] Cases 142 & 156/84 *BAT and Reynolds v Commission* [1987] ECR 4487, [1988] 4 CMLR 24. See also *Tetra Pak I (BTG Licence)*, OJ 1988 L272/27, [1990] 4 CMLR 47, where the Commission attacked the transfer to a dominant firm of an exclusive licence held by a company it had acquired, although the Commission stopped short of condemning the acquisition itself. Subsequently, in *Tetra Pak II*, OJ 1992 L72/1, [1992] 4 CMLR 551, 616, the Commission condemned Tetra Pak's acquisition of small competitors which it held was part of an overall strategy to eliminate com-petitors which were developing rival technology (on appeal Cases T-83/91 *Tetra Pak v Commission* [1994] ECR II–755, [1997] 4 CMLR 726; Case C-333/94 *Tetra Pak v Commission* [1996] ECR I–5951, [1997] 4 CMLR 662).

That will be true in particular where . . . the agreement provides for commercial cooperation between the companies or creates such a structure likely to be used for such cooperation.

That may also be the case where the agreement gives the investing company the possibility of reinforcing its position at a later stage and taking effective control of the other company. Account must be taken not only of the immediate effects of the agreement but also of its potential effects and of the possibility that the agreement may be part of a long-term plan.

Finally, every agreement must be assessed in its economic context and in particular in the light of the situation on the relevant market. Moreover, where the companies concerned are multinational corporations which carry on business on a worldwide scale, their relationships outside the Community cannot be ignored. It is necessary in particular to consider the possibility that the agreement in question may be part of a policy of global cooperation between the companies which are party to it'.[839]

Applying these considerations to the facts, the Court of Justice held that the Commission had been entitled to conclude that the agreements were not caught by Article 81.[840]

Article 82. In the *Philip Morris* case, the Court of Justice also held that the acquisition of a minority interest in a competing company can give rise to an abuse of a dominant position under Article 82 'where the shareholding in question results in effective control of the other company or at least in some influence on its commercial policy.'[841] In *Gillette*,[842] the Commission considered that, although Gillette had not acquired control over Eemland (which owned the Wilkinson Sword brand), the relationship did enable Gillette to exercise 'some influence' over Eemland's commercial conduct. The Commission concluded that, notwithstanding the care with which the agreements were drafted, the overall arrangements and Gillette's participation would have an adverse effect on competition in the Community wet-shaving market and that therefore Gillette's acquisition of the interests in Eemland constituted an abuse of its dominant position under Article 82.[843]

8.275

---

[839] ibid, paras 37–40. For further analysis of the *Philip Morris* case and subsequent case law and Commission policy, see Caronna, 'Article 81 as a tool for controlling minority cross-shareholdings between competitors' (2004) 29 ELRev 485.

[840] cf the Commission's position regarding the original arrangements, varied by the parties after the Commission initiated proceedings: *Philip Morris/Rembrandt/Rothmans, XIXth Report on Competition Policy* (1984), points 98–100.

[841] See n 838, above, para 65. The ECJ upheld the Commission's finding that this had not been established on the facts.

[842] *Warner-Lambert/Gillette*, OJ 1993 L116/21, [1993] 5 CMLR 599. For the facts, see n 845, below.

[843] ibid, para 31. The Commission referred to the special responsibility that dominant undertakings bear not to allow their conduct to impair genuine undistorted competition in the common market (see para 10.061, below) and held that 'by participating in the buy-out of the Wilkinson Sword business, Gillette had failed to discharge that special responsibility and has abused its dominant position' (para 23).

8.276 **Commission practice.** The focus of the Commission's inquiry is essentially on whether the acquisition of a minority shareholding in a competitor could affect the parties' incentives to compete or could raise any other competition concerns. Particular concerns may arise where joint cooperation projects are envisaged and where the minority shareholding and ensuing rights may be capable of conferring some influence over a competitor's commercial conduct.[844] For example, in *Gillette*[845] the Commission considered that the arrangements between Gillette and Eemland would lead to continued cooperation between Gillette and Eemland's Wilkinson Sword business and would restrict competition between them in the wet-shaving market in the Community. The Commission examined similar issues in *CCIE/GTE*[846] and *BT/MCI*.[847] Although it can be burdensome for

---

[844] The Commission undertakes a similar analysis generally with regard to structural links between rival competitors in the context of its substantive appraisal of concentrations; see, eg Case M.1383 *Exxon/Mobil*, OJ 2004 L103/1, where the Commission stated, that according to mainstream antitrust economics, the existence of links between two competing undertakings in the form of a significant investment stake of one in the other may change their incentives to compete; see also Case M.2876 *Newscorp/Telepiù*, OJ 2004 L110/73, [2004] 5 CMLR 1619, paras 269–281, where the Commission reiterated its jurisdiction to assess fully the effects of Telecom Italia having a 19 per cent non-controlling shareholding in the merged pay-TV platform (ie whether that minority participation would contribute to strengthening the dominant position of the combined platform on the Italian pay-TV market, essentially by sterilising the potential competitive threat of entry stemming from Telecom Italia). The Commission's approach has been confirmed by the CFI in Case T-22/97 *Kesko v Commission* [1999] ECR II-3775, [2000] 4 CMLR 335.

[845] n 842, above. The case concerned a leveraged buy-out of the Wilkinson Sword wet-shaving business through an investment vehicle company, Eemland. Gillette took a 22 per cent equity stake in Eemland (with no voting rights or board representation attached) and made an unsecured loan to Eemland representing about 12 per cent of Eemland's initial loan capital. As part of the transaction, Eemland sold to Gillette the Wilkinson Sword trade marks in countries outside the EC and the USA. The Commission considered that the geographic separation of ownership of the Wilkinson Sword trade marks between the EC and neighbouring European countries was artificial. In finding that these arrangements infringed Art 81(1) and did not satisfy the exemption criteria of Art 81(3), the Commission concluded that they would lead to continued cooperation between Gillette and Eemland's Wilkinson Sword business and would restrict competition between them in the EU wet-shaving market.

[846] Case M.258 *CCIE/GTE* (25 September 1992) where the Commission considered various financial and commercial agreements between Siemens and EDIL including loans, technology licences and supply agreements made in the context of the acquisition by EDIL of GTE's international (including European) lamps business as notified under the Merger Reg. At the same time as the EDIL acquisition, Siemens acquired GTE's North American lamps business. The Commission held that although the agreements did not give Siemens control (ie decisive influence) over EDIL 'these agreements may afford Siemens some limited influence over EDIL' (para 12). The Commission expressly stated that its conclusions were based on the terms of the financial and commercial arrangement between Siemens and EDIL as submitted in the notification under the Merger Reg and that 'any change in these terms, in particular any prolongation of the agreements, would affect the conclusion' (para 35). The market position of EDIL and Siemens/Osram appears not to have raised issues under Art 82.

[847] *BT/MCI*, OJ 1994 L223/36, [1995] 5 CMLR 285, a complex alliance between two leading telecommunications operators, originally notified under the Merger Reg but converted into a notification under Reg 17 when the Commission concluded that it did not constitute a concentration. The arrangement included the acquisition by BT of a 20 per cent shareholding in MCI with

the Commission to prove on the basis of cogent evidence that the existence of such structural links are capable of producing anti-competitive effects, in practice the Commission is sometimes able to exert significant pressure on the parties to end such links in the context of merger proceedings to avoid Phase II proceedings.[848]

7. National Merger Control and International Cooperation

(a) National merger control regimes within EEA

(i) In general

National merger control requirements. For transactions where the Commission **8.277** does not have jurisdiction under the Merger Regulation because the relevant Community dimension thresholds are not fulfilled or because the transaction does not constitute a concentration, the parties may instead need to obtain approvals under one or more national merger control regimes within the EEA.[849] Detailed discussion of the national merger control rules is beyond the scope of this work. However, the tables at the end of this Chapter provide brief summaries of the jurisdictional criteria and notification requirements in each of the EEA countries. Only Luxembourg and Liechtenstein do not have a domestic merger control

---

corresponding board representation. The agreement, however, also included a 'standstill' provision whereby BT undertook for 10 years not to acquire any further ownership interest or to seek to control or influence MCI. For this reason, and bearing in mind the provisions of US antitrust law that prevented misuse by BT of MCI's confidential information, the Commission concluded that the investment did not come within the scope of Art 81. See also *Phoenix/GlobalOne*, OJ 1996 L239/59, [1997] 4 CMLR 147, para 51.

[848] See, eg Case M.113 *Courtaulds/SNIA* (19 December 1991), where Courtaulds agreed to dispose of its 12 per cent minority interest in rival INACSA in order to secure a Phase I clearance. More recently, in Case M.3547 *Banco Santander/Abbey National* (15 September 2004), there were concerns about the strategic cooperation agreement between Banco Santander and Royal Bank of Scotland, a rival of Abbey National in the UK. Prior to notification, Banco Santander and Royal Bank of Scotland modified their cooperation arrangement, by terminating the representation in each other's Board of Directors, their commercial cooperation, as well as any cooperation in JV operations in Europe. Banco Santander also reduced its shareholding in Royal Bank of Scotland to only 2.54 per cent. In consequence, the Commission concluded that cross-shareholdings would not entitle either of the banks to exercise any substantial influence over the other's commercial activities. See also Case M.1980 *Volvo/Renault* (1 September 2000) where the Commission raised concerns *inter alia* that Renault would in future be able to influence the competitive behaviour of two bus companies in which it held an interest, it being the largest shareholder in Volvo (15 per cent of shares and board representation) and also the controlling shareholder in Irisbus (a competing bus JV with Iveco). In order to secure a Phase I clearance, Renault agreed to rescind the Irisbus JV and also divest a bus business equivalent in size to Volvo's French bus activities.

[849] There is also scope for concentrations with a Community dimension to be referred to Member States for review under national merger control rules pursuant to Art 4(4) (see paras 8.081 *et seq*, above) and Art 9 (see paras 8.091 *et seq*, above).

regime. Although national rules are slowly converging, substantial differences remain, particularly regarding jurisdictional thresholds[850] and with regard to procedures.[851] The substantive legal tests also vary between the Member States.[852]

8.278 **Multiple merger filings.** Regardless of whether or not a concentration has a Community dimension enabling the parties to benefit from the 'one-stop shop' within the EEA, notifications may still be required in jurisdictions outside the EEA. Despite a limited amount of alignment of national laws and the increased role of supra-national bodies, multiple merger filings are often required for multi-jurisdictional transactions which can face significant procedural hurdles in terms of cost and timing. From the practitioner's perspective, the analysis of where filings are required or advisable (as well as coordinating those filings) has become increasingly important.[853]

---

[850] In some Member States (eg Austria, Germany and the United Kingdom), the acquisition of minority shareholdings at levels such as 25 per cent (or lower if it confers material influence) can be subject to review even in circumstances where it would not confer sole or joint control for Merger Reg purposes. In most other Member States, the acquisition of control along similar lines to the Merger Reg is required. The financial thresholds vary considerably. Turnover is most generally used, although both the amount and the basis of calculation differ. In some Member States, domestic turnover is relevant, whereas in others combinations of domestic and worldwide turnover are used. In some Member States, turnover tests are coupled with or are alternatives to market share tests.

[851] Most Member States operate systems of mandatory prior notification, although the UK continues to operate a voluntary notification system but with the possibility of the Office of Fair Trading initiating investigations into proposed or completed mergers which have not been notified. The authorities charged with supervising the merger control process may be a single-tier authority (eg the Bundeskartellamt in Germany) or there may be a two-tier system (eg the Office of Fair Trading and the Competition Commission in the UK and the DGCCRF and the Conseil de la Concurrence in France). The ultimate decision may be taken by a government minister (eg in France), or there may be only limited or no scope for ministerial intervention (eg in Germany and the UK). Generally, the investigation is divided into two distinct phases: the initial investigation to examine whether the case requires a more detailed second phase investigation typically takes one or two months. The second phase proceedings can last anything between two and nine months. The extent of judicial review also varies between the Member States.

[852] The relatively new SIEC standard under the Merger Reg (see Section 4, above) can be viewed as a hybrid between (a) the 'substantial lessening of competition' (SLC) standard applied under the US merger control rules and used in a number of other jurisdictions globally; and (b) the traditional 'dominance' standard applied under the original Merger Reg and also used in a number of other jurisdictions globally. Some Member States already operated comparable hybrid systems (eg France). Others already operated and have maintained an SLC-type standard (eg UK, Ireland). Following the adoption of Reg 139/2004, a number of Member State have adopted essentially the same SIEC test as applies under the Merger Reg (eg Belgium, Poland, Spain). Others continue to use a traditional dominance standard (eg Germany, Italy).

[853] A basic understanding of the different jurisdictional tests under the national merger control rules within the EU is also necessary in order to appraise whether the Art 4(5) pre-notification referral procedures (see paras 8.085 *et seq*, above) may enable the parties to benefit from the 'one-stop shop' even for concentrations which do not meet the Merger Reg thresholds.

(ii) Summary of national regimes

Outline of national merger control rules in the EEA.[854]   The tables below pro-   **8.279**
vide brief summaries of the jurisdictional criteria and notification requirements in
(a) the 27 EU Member States and (b) the three contracting EFTA States (Norway,
Iceland and Liechtenstein). The position under the national merger control rules
is stated as at 1 September 2007.

(A) EU Member States

Jurisdiction	Jurisdictional criteria	Notification requirements
Austria	(a) combined worldwide turnover of €300m; and (b) combined turnover in Austria of €30m; and (c) at least two parties each have worldwide turnover of €5m Exceptionally, no jurisdiction if:(i) only one party has turnover in Austria of more than €5 million; and (ii) combined worldwide turnover of all the other parties is less than €30 million	Mandatory prior notification to Bundeswettbewerbsbehörde (Federal Competition Authority)
Belgium	(a) combined turnover in Belgium of €100m; and (b) at least two parties each have turnover in Belgium of €40m	Mandatory prior notification to Conseil de la Concurrence/ Raad voor de Mededinging (Competition Council)
Bulgaria	Combined turnover in Bulgaria of BGN 15m (c. €8m)	Mandatory prior notification to Commission for Protection of Competition
Cyprus	(a) at least two parties each have turnover in Cyprus of CYP 2m (c. €3.5m); and (b) at least one party carries on business in Cyprus; and (c) combined turnover in Cyprus of CYP 2m (c. €3.5m)	Mandatory prior notification to Commission for the Protection of Competition
Czech Republic	(a) combined turnover in Czech Republic of CZK 1,500m (c. €50m); and (b) each of at least two parties has turnover in Czech Republic of CZK 250m (c. €9m); *or* (a) at least one party (which must be the target in the case of a share or asset acquisition) has turnover in Czech Republic of CZK 1,500m (c. €50m); and (b) at least one other party has worldwide turnover of CZK 1,500m (c. €50m)	Mandatory prior notification to Úřvad pro Ochranu Hospodářské Soutěže (Office for the Protection of Economic Competition)

---

[854] See further Rowley & Baker, *International Mergers – The Antitrust Process* (2000 and Supp);
Dabbah and Lasok *Merger Control Worldwide* (2005 and Supp).

Jurisdiction	Jurisdictional criteria	Notification requirements
Denmark	(a) combined turnover in Denmark of DKK 3,800m (c. €510m); and (b) at least two parties each have turnover in Denmark of DKK 300m (c. €40m); *or* (a) at least one party has turnover in Denmark of DKK 3,800m (c. €510m); and (b) at least one other party has worldwide turnover of DKK 3,800m (c. €510m)	Mandatory prior notification to Koncurrencestyrelsen (Competition Authority)
Estonia	(a) combined turnover in Estonia of EEK 100m (c. €6.5 million); and (b) turnover in Estonia of each of at least two parties of EEK 30m (c. €2m)	Mandatory prior notification to Konkurentsiamet (Competition Board)
Finland	(a) combined worldwide turnover of €350m; and (b) at least two parties each have turnover in Finland of €20m	Mandatory prior notification to Kilpailuvirasto (Competition Authority)
France	(a) combined worldwide turnover of €150m; and (b) at least two parties each have turnover in France of €50m	Mandatory prior notification to DGCCRF (Direction Générale de la Concurrence de la Consommation et de la Répression des Fraudes) at Ministry of Economy, Finance and Industry (MINEFI)

Germany	(a) combined worldwide turnover of €500m; and
	(b) at least one party has turnover of €25m in Germany Exceptionally, no jurisdiction if:
	  (i) there is an independent (non-affiliated) undertaking, merging with another undertaking, which has worldwide turnover of less than €10m; or
	  (ii) the only relevant market is a minor market where goods/services have been offered for at least five years with total annual sales of less than €15m
		Mandatory prior notification to Bundeskartellamt (Federal Cartel Office)

Greece	Pre-merger notification if: (a) combined turnover of €150m; and (b) each of at least two parties has turnover in Greece of €15m Post-merger notification if: (a) combined market share of at least 10 per cent; or (b) at least two undertakings have turnover in Greece of €15m	Mandatory prior or post merger notification to Hellenic Competition Commission (depending on jurisdictional criteria)

Jurisdiction	Jurisdictional criteria	Notification requirements
Hungary	(a) combined turnover in Hungary of HUF 15,000m (c. €60m); and (b) at least two parties each have turnover of HUF 500m (c. €2m)	Mandatory prior notification to Gazdasági Versenyhivatal (Office of Economic Competition)
Ireland	(a) at least two parties each have worldwide turnover of €40m; and (b) at least two parties carry on business in any part of the island of Ireland (ie including Northern Ireland); and (c) at least one party has turnover in the Irish Republic of €40m	Mandatory prior notification to Competition Authority
Italy	(a) combined turnover in Italy of €440m; or (b) target has turnover in Italy of €44m *(Thresholds are revised annually to take account of inflation; above figures were revised in May 2007)*	Mandatory prior notification to the Autorità Garante della Concorrenza e del Mercato (Competition Authority)
Latvia	(a) combined turnover of LVL 25m (c. €37m); and (b) combined market share of 40 per cent	Mandatory prior notification to Konkurences Padome (Competition Council)
Lithuania	(a) combined turnover in Lithuania exceeds LTL 30m (c. €9m); and (b) at least two parties each have turnover in Lithuania of LTL 5m (c. €1.5m)	Mandatory notification to Konkurencijos Taryba (Competition Council)
Luxembourg	no specific merger control regime	Not applicable
Malta	combined turnover in Malta of MTL 750,000 (c. €1.8m)	Mandatory prior notification to Office for Fair Competition
Netherlands	(a) combined worldwide turnover of €113.45m; and (b) at least two parties each have turnover in the Netherlands of €30m	Mandatory prior notification to Nederlandse Mededingingsautoriteit (Dutch Competition Authority)
Poland	(a) combined worldwide turnover of €1,000m or combined turnover in Poland of €50m; and (b) turnover of target in Poland of €10m in either of previous two years	Mandatory prior notification to Urzçąd Ochrony Konkurenciji i Konsumentów (Office for Competition and Consumer Protection)
Portugal	(a) combined turnover in Portugal of €150m; and (b) each of at least two parties has turnover in Portugal of €2m; *or* combined market share in Portugal of 30 per cent	Mandatory prior notification to Autoridade de Concorrência (Competition Authority)
Romania	(a) combined worldwide turnover of €10m; and (b) at least two parties each have turnover in Romania of €4m	Mandatory prior notification to Consiliul Concurentei (Competition Council)

Jurisdiction	Jurisdictional criteria	Notification requirements
Slovak Republic	(a) combined worldwide turnover of SKK 1,200m (c. €30m); and (b) each of at least two parties has turnover in the Slovak Republic of SKK 360m (c. €10m); *or* (a) at least one party has turnover in Slovak Republic of SKK 500m (c. €13m); and (b) at least one party has worldwide turnover of SKK 1,200m (c. €30m)	Mandatory notification to Protimonopolný Úrad (Antimonopoly Office)
Slovenia	(a) combined turnover in Slovenia exceeds €33.38m in each of last two years; *or* (b) combined market share in Slovenia of 40 per cent	Mandatory prior notification to Urad RS za Varstvo Konkurence (Competition Protection Office)
Spain	(a) combined turnover in Spain of €240m; and (b) each of at least two parties has turnover in Spain of €60m; *or* combined market share in Spain of 30 per cent	Mandatory prior notification to Servicio de Comisión Nacional de Competencia
Sweden	(a) combined worldwide turnover in preceding financial year of SEK 4,000m (c. €430m); and (b) each of at least two parties has turnover in Sweden of SEK 100m (c. €11m)	Mandatory prior notification to Konkurrensverket (Competition Authority) Voluntary notification possible (and authority could require notification) if first threshold met but second threshold not met
United Kingdom	(a) target has turnover in the UK of £70m (c. €100m); *or* (b) transaction results in or increases share of supply of goods or services of any description of 25 per cent or more in UK (or a substantial part of the UK)	Voluntary notification to Office of Fair Trading

(B) Contracting EFTA States

Jurisdiction	Jurisdictional criteria	Notification requirements
Iceland	(a) combined turnover of ISK 1,000 million (c. €13m); and (b) at least two parties each have turnover of ISK 50m (c. €0.6m)	Mandatory prior notification to Samkeppnisstofnun (Competition Authority)
Liechtenstein	No specific merger control regime	Not applicable
Norway	(a) combined turnover in Norway of NOK 50m (c. €6m); and (b) each of at least two parties has turnover in Norway of NOK 20m (c. €2.5m)	Mandatory prior notification to Konkurransetilsynet (Competition Authority)

(b) Cooperation under EEA Agreement

(i) Framework for cooperation

EEA Agreement.   Since the entry into force of the EEA Agreement on 1 January   **8.280**
1994, the Commission's exclusive competence to review concentrations extends
to the territory covered by the EEA Agreement.[855] The Commission's competence
thus also extends to the three EFTA States which have ratified the EEA Agreement
(Iceland, Liechtenstein and Norway) in addition to the EU Member States,
thereby creating a 'one-stop shop' for merger review across all 30 EEA States.
Article 57(2)(a) of the EEA Agreement confers exclusive EEA-wide jurisdiction
on the Commission for all cases that have a Community dimension under the
Merger Regulation.[856] Article 57(2)(b) gives the EFTA Surveillance Authority[857]
residual jurisdiction over concentrations which do not have a Community
dimension but which satisfy turnover thresholds in respect of the EFTA pillar that
mirror those used to establish a Community dimension.[858]

Mixed cases under EEA Agreement.   Where the Commission is competent to   **8.281**
handle a case by virtue of Article 57(2)(a), it has an obligation under the EEA
Agreement to cooperate closely with the EFTA Surveillance Authority in the
review of cases that affect both EU and EFTA States. Such cases are generally
known as 'mixed' cases. Protocol 24 to the EEA Agreement contains detailed provisions on the scope of that cooperation. It also specifies the following alternative
criteria for the identification of mixed cases:[859]

(a)   The combined turnover of the undertakings concerned in the three EFTA
      States equals 25 per cent or more of their total EEA turnover;[860]

---

[855] See Broberg, *The European Commission's Jurisdiction to Scrutinise Mergers* (3rd edn, 2006),
Chap VII; Dabbah and Lasok, above, Chap 18 (European Economic Area).

[856] The Commission's review of merger cases is generally carried out by reference to the EEA
Agreement as well as to the Merger Reg, so extending the geographic scope of the operative part of
its decisions. See also details of the extension of the pre- and post-notification referral mechanisms
under the EEA Agreement for suitable cases (at paras 8.081–8.091, above respectively).

[857] See para 1.093, above.

[858] See Annex XIV to the EEA Agreement on the criteria for a concentration to have an 'EFTA
dimension'. In essence, the three 'original' criteria (mirroring the 'original' criteria under the Merger
Reg: see sub-para (a) at para 8.060, above) are: (a) the parties have combined worldwide turnover
of €5,000m; (b) the parties have combined turnover across the three contracting EFTA States of
€250m; and (c) the parties do not each achieve more than two-thirds of its EFTA-related turnover
in one and the same signatory EFTA State (eg in Norway); 'alternative' criteria were also introduced
in 1998 (mirroring the 'alternative' criteria under the Merger Reg: see sub-para (b) at para 8.060,
above). The EFTA Surveillance Authority's competence would exclude jurisdiction of the national
authorities of the contracting EFTA States, but not that of the national authorities of the EU States.
There have been no such 'EFTA dimension' cases to date. The prospect of such a case ever arising is
remote, given the small number of remaining EFTA States and the predominance of Norway.

[859] Art 2 of Protocol 24 to the EEA Agreement. The EFTA Surveillance Authority has, since 2001,
published lists of 'mixed' merger cases in respect of which Protocol 24 applied in its annual reports.

[860] See eg Case M.1439 *Telia/Telenor*, OJ 2001 L40/1, [2001] 4 CMLR 1226; Case M.2491
Sampo/Storebrand (27 July 2001); Case M.3395 *Sampo/IF Skadeförsäkring* (28 April 2004).

(b) Each of at least two of the undertakings concerned has turnover exceeding €250 million in the EFTA States;[861]

(c) The concentration is liable significantly to impede effective competition in the territories of the EFTA States, in particular as a result of the creation or strengthening of a dominant position;[862]

(d) The concentration fulfils the criteria for a referral of the case from the Commission to an EFTA State pursuant to Article 6 of Protocol 24;[863] or

(e) An EFTA State wishes to adopt measures to protect legitimate interests not expressly covered by the Merger Regulation.[864]

(ii)   Cooperation between Commission and EFTA Surveillance Authority

8.282   **Close and constant liaison.**   Once a mixed case has been identified, the Commission must implement Article 57 in 'close and constant liaison' with the Authority.[865] In accordance with Protocol 24, the Commission forwards copies of the notification and any other key documents to the Authority. The Authority reviews the information received independently and informs the Commission of its views, generally following receipt of a copy of the notification and, if the case goes into Phase II, following receipt of the statement of objections and in the context of the Advisory Committee meeting.[866] The Authority's stated aim is to focus

---

861   See eg Case M.2367 *Siemens/E.On/Shell/SSG* (27 March 2001).

862   See eg Case M.2097 *SCA/Metsä Tissue*, OJ 2002 L57/1, [2002] 4 CMLR 1541; Case M.2268 *Pernod Ricard/Diageo/Seagram Spirits* (8 May 2001); Case M.2187 *CVC/Lenzing*, OJ 2004 L82/20; Case M.3149 *Procter & Gamble/Wella* (30 July 2003); Case M.3225 *Alcan/Pechiney (II)* (29 September 2003).

863   Art 6 of Protocol 24 enables such concentrations to be referred to the competition authority of a signatory EFTA State in a similar way to the procedures of Art 9 of the Merger Reg: see para 8.091, above. The first Art 6 reference was made in Case M.2683 *Aker Maritime/Kværner (II)* (23 January 2002), in which the Commission made a partial referral to Norway in respect of certain issues relating to offshore oil rigs, but itself cleared the part of the effects of the concentration relating to the parties' shipbuilding activities.

864   Art 7 of Protocol 24 permits the contracting EFTA States to protect such legitimate interests in a similar way to Art 21(3) and (4) of the Merger Reg: see paras 8.101 *et seq*, above.

865   Section 3 of the Form CO and the Short Form include questions designed to establish whether either of the criteria listed at sub-paras (a) and (b) of para 8.281, above are met. The criteria at sub-paras (c) and (d) apply in cases where the criteria at (a) or (b) are not met but the Commission identifies 'serious doubts' in markets where the geographic scope is considered by the Commission to be EEA-wide or otherwise relate to the contracting EFTA States; in such cases the EEA cooperation mechanisms tend to be triggered at the latest when the Commission adopts an Art 6(1)(c) decision to initiate a Phase II investigation under the Merger Reg. It follows that a relatively high proportion of EEA 'mixed' cases involve a Phase II investigation.

866   See Arts 3, 4, and 5 of Protocol 24 to the EEA Agreement. Art 5(3) provides that the EFTA Surveillance Authority and the EFTA States are entitled to be present and express their views at the Advisory Committee on Concentrations, but that they do not have the right to vote. In practice the Authority prepares and gives the Commission a separate document that mirrors the formal Opinion of the Advisory Committee in question, reflecting the views of the EFTA States on the questions put to the members of the Advisory Committee by the Rapporteur.

on problematic cases where it seeks 'to assist the Commission, in every way possible, in gathering information to secure a comprehensive appraisal of the impact of the concentration on the EFTA pillar.'[867] The Authority also forwards copies of relevant documents to the competition authorities of the EFTA States and sends on any comments received in response, including on the possible referral of a concentration, to the Commission. In general the EEA cooperation mechanism in merger cases is intended to ensure that the Commission's decision including any conditions and obligations imposed on the parties takes full account of competitive conditions in the EFTA States.

(c) Cooperation with countries outside EEA

Bilateral cooperation agreements.   Cooperation with competition authorities   **8.283**
outside the EU is also increasing on the basis of bilateral cooperation agreements.[868] The key elements of these agreements tend to involve the mutual provision of information on, and coordination of, enforcement activities and the exchange of information with regard to particular merger investigations.[869] The European Commission has concluded detailed cooperation agreements with a number of major trading partners.[870]

United States of America.   Cooperation between the European Commission   **8.284**
and US antitrust agencies has been particularly intense. It is based on the EC–USA Competition Laws Cooperation Agreement, originally adopted in 1991, which includes cooperation with regard to the application of the Parties' respective merger control rules.[871] In particular, the Agreement provides for each Party

---

[867] See 'EEA cooperation cases under the merger control regime' available on the EFTA Surveillance Authority website. See also, eg *Telia/Telenor* (n 860, above) which involved the imposition by the Commission of far-reaching commitments to open up access to the local access networks for telephony as well as to divest Telia and Telenor's respective cable-TV businesses and other overlapping businesses; *Procter & Gamble/Wella* (n 862, above) (in which divestments were required to rule out serious doubts in the hair care markets in Norway as well as Ireland and Sweden); and *Pernod Ricard/Diageo/Seagram Spirits* (n 862, above) (where the Commission's concerns about the impact of the concentration on the supply of rum in Iceland were addressed by commitments to maintain separate distribution arrangements).

[868] The Commission's *Annual Reports on Competition Policy* provide useful information on the status of contacts and other cooperation initiatives between the Commission and competition authorities outside the EU. Additional information can be found on DG Comp's website: http://ec.europa.eu/comm/competition/international/overview.

[869] In cases with a significant transatlantic element, the parties often agree to give waivers to the Commission and US antitrust agencies to facilitate the exchange of confidential information between the authorities. Such waivers are also sometimes given to other authorities. DG Comp has published a model waiver letter (as well as a link to ICN materials on confidentiality waivers) on its website at http://europa.eu/ec./competition/mergers/others.

[870] The Commission has also continued its dialogue with other competition authorities worldwide: see, eg *XXXIVth Report on Competition Policy* (2004), paras 657 *et seq*.

[871] US Cooperation Agreement, OJ 1995 L95/45. See para 1.100, above.

to notify the other when its enforcement activities may affect 'important interests' of the other Party.[872] In the case of concentrations, the Commission should give such notification to the US antitrust agencies[873] once notice of the Phase I investigation is published in the *Official Journal* and if it decides to initiate Phase II proceedings. This should enable the views of the US agencies to be taken into account before a decision is adopted.[874] Conversely, the US agencies should notify the Commission if a 'second request' is issued under the Hart-Scott-Rodino Antitrust Improvements Act and if they decide to file a complaint challenging the transaction. This should enable the views of the Commission to be taken into account before the entry of a consent decree.[875] The Agreement also provides for cooperation and coordination of enforcement activities, to the extent permitted by their respective laws, and for the respective authorities to seek to avoid conflicts by accommodating any competing interests.[876] In practice, cooperation on specific merger cases tends to be pragmatic and flexible, adapted to take due account of the particular facts and issues arising in each case.[877] In addition to case-specific cooperation on mergers, there is an ongoing dialogue regarding merger control policy issues.[878]

8.285 **Canada and Japan.** There are similar cooperation arrangements with the Canadian and Japanese national competition authorities pursuant to intergovernmental agreements concluded with Canada and Japan: see further paragraph 1.002, above.[879]

8.286 **Multilateral international cooperation.** The Merger Regulation does not contain any formal provisions regarding relations with third countries.[880] Merger control is, however, an area where there is also increasing cooperation at a broader

---

872 The US agencies should generally be notified of any Commission investigation of a concentration where one or more of the parties to the transaction (or a company controlling one or more such parties) is incorporated under the laws of a State of the USA. Generally, the Commission should be notified if the US agencies are investigating a merger concerning a company incorporated under the laws of an EU Member State: Arts I(2)(C), II(2)(c).

873 The Antitrust Division of the US Department of Justice and the Federal Trade Commission.

874 EC–USA Competition Laws Cooperation Agreement (n 871, above) Art II(3)(b).

875 ibid, Art II(3)(a).

876 ibid, Arts IV–VI.

877 The 2002 EU–US best practices on cooperation in reviewing mergers (see Vol II, App D.18) provide a useful framework for cooperation, in particular by indicating critical points in the procedure where contacts between the respective authorities could be productive.

878 Such dialogue takes place in the context of the so-called EU–US Working Group on Mergers, a standing forum for inter-agency policy discussion, but also on the basis of regular informal contacts.

879 OJ 1999 L175/49 (Canada); OJ 2003 L183/12 (Japan).

880 Art 24 of the Merger Reg does provide for the Commission to draw up periodic reports examining the treatment accorded to EU-based undertakings when entering into mergers outside the EU; see also Recital (44).

policy level on a multilateral basis. These discussions are facilitated by a number of international organisations, in particular the International Competition Network (ICN);[881] and the Organisation for Economic Cooperation and Development (OECD): see further paragraphs 1.102 to 1.104, above.

---

[881] In the field of merger control, examples include the ICN Merger Investigative Techniques Workshop, the ICN Notifications and Procedures Sub-group, the ICN Analytical Framework Sub-group and the ICN Workshop on Capacity Building: see *XXXIVth Report on Competition Policy* (2004), paras 666 *et seq.*

9

INTELLECTUAL PROPERTY RIGHTS

1. Introduction

9.001 **In general.** In this Chapter, the phrase 'intellectual property rights'[1] is used to describe the rights arising under national or Community law for the protection of patents, trade marks, copyright, designs and similar rights of various kinds. Intellectual property rights raise difficult problems under competition law. There is an obvious tension between, on the one hand, systems which confer legal monopolies and, on the other hand, systems which are intended to ensure free competition. For example, the owner of a patent (called the 'proprietor' of that patent) has for a period of years the right to exclude others from making use of his invention or marketing the products manufactured using it. He also has the power to dispose of his right to others by assigning it outright to third parties, or to allow others to exploit his invention by granting an exclusive or non-exclusive licence to them to make, use, dispose of or import his product. Such a licence will usually involve the payment of royalties and observance of other conditions. The proprietor of a patent may, for example, license one person to make, use, dispose of or import only in a defined territory or for a particular product market or end use, while licensing others for other territories, product markets or uses. Similar rights are enjoyed by the owners of trade marks, copyrights, designs and so on. Clearly, the existence of such rights, and the terms upon which such licences are granted, may restrict competition. However, it is generally thought desirable to protect intellectual property rights, primarily as a means of rewarding invention and creativity, and in the case of patents to disseminate, rather than keep secret, technical information. The development and the exploitation of new ideas may require substantial investment, particularly when research and other costs are high. Protecting the resulting intellectual property rights tends to encourage such investment and rewards risk-taking, thereby promoting the development of new or better products and services, to the ultimate benefit of consumers and society as a whole. In these circumstances, the protection of intellectual property rights must be reconciled with the need to avoid unjustified restrictions on competition.[2]

---

[1] Art 30 of the Treaty refers to 'industrial and commercial property' but the phrase 'intellectual property' is now widely used. See, eg the Vertical Restraints block exemption, Reg 2790/1999, OJ 1999 L336/21, Vol II, App C.3, Art 1(e); and see also the Commission's Statement concerning Art 2 of Dir 2004/48, which harmonises enforcement of intellectual property rights, OJ 2005 L94/37. For a general survey, see Cornish and Llewellyn, *Intellectual Property: Patents, Copyright, Trade Marks and Allied Rights* (5th edn, 2003); Tritton, *Intellectual Property in Europe* (2nd edn, 2001).

[2] See generally: Anderman and Kallaugher, *Technology Transfer and the New EU Competition Rules* (2006); Fine, *The EC Competition Law of Technology Licensing* (2006); Korah, *Intellectual Property Rights and the EC Competition Rules* (2006); Keeling, *Intellectual Property Rights in EU Law*, Vol I: Free Movement and Competition Law (2003); Anderman, EC *Competition Law and Intellectual Property Rights* (2nd edn, 2002); Govaere, *The Use and Abuse of Intellectual Property Rights in EC Law* (1996). For the position under US law, see Hovenkamp, Janis and Lemley, *IP and Antitrust: An Analysis of Antitrust Principles Applied to Intellectual Property Law* (2004).

Intellectual property rights and the single market. In the context of the **9.002** Community, these difficulties are compounded by the fact that the Treaty aims to establish a single market, the purpose of which is to reproduce the conditions of one national market on a Community-wide scale.[3] However, despite some progress towards the grant of intellectual property rights at Community level, intellectual property rights are still substantially governed by the laws of each Member State,[4] although significant harmonisation has taken place.[5] Therefore, as a matter of national law, the owner of an intellectual property right in one Member State may, in certain circumstances, prevent the importation of products lawfully marketed in another Member State by suing for infringement of his right under national law. A further, although slowly diminishing, problem is that there may be differences between the extent or content of the rights granted under different national laws, so that what constitutes the lawful protection of a right in one Member State may be unlawful in another.[6]

Community-wide rights. Some progress has been made in establishing Com- **9.003** munity-wide intellectual property rights. The most significant achievements to date are the establishment of the Community Trade Mark ('CTM') system under Regulation 40/94,[7] which creates the right to a Community-wide trade mark, and the establishment of the Community Registered Design system under Regulation 6/2002,[8] which creates the right to a Community-wide registered and unregistered

---

[3] See para 1.074, above. As a result of the EEA Agreement a number of the provisions considered in this Chap extend to the EEA countries that are not members of the Community, ie Norway, Iceland and Liechtenstein: see para 1.086, above. References to 'the Community' or 'Member States' should be taken as also referring to Contracting Parties to the EEA Agreement.

[4] See cases cited at n 40, below.

[5] eg on trade marks: Dir 89/104, OJ 1989 L40/1; on computer programs: Dir 91/250, OJ 1991 L122/42, am by OJ 1993 L11/22 and OJ 1993 L290/9; on the right to authorise and prohibit the rental and lending of copyright works: Dir 92/100, OJ 1992 L346/61; on databases: Dir 96/9, OJ 1996 L77/20; on the protection of designs: Dir 98/71, OJ 1998 L289/28: see further, Cornish and Llewellyn and Tritton (n 1, above). Harmonisation of enforcement so as to create a level playing field for rights holders is being introduced in implementation of Dir 2004/48, OJ 2004 L157/45. Note also that many intellectual property rights, especially patents, trade marks and copyright, are also subject to international Conventions which may be relevant to the interpretation of EC law in any given case: see, eg Case C-9/93 *IHT Internationale Heiztechnik v Ideal Standard* [1994] ECR I-2789, [1994] 3 CMLR 857, paras 25–32. Among relevant international agreements to which the Community is a party, note the Agreement on Trade-Related Aspects of Intellectual Property Rights (TRIPS), OJ 1994 2336/214. Provisions of TRIPS have also been cited in decisions of the ECJ: eg Case C-316/95 *Generics v Smith, Kline & French* ('*Generics No. 2*') [1997] ECR I-3929, [1998] 1 CMLR 1; Case C-53/96 *Hermès International v FHT Marketing Choice* [1998] ECR I-3603; Case 200/96 *Metronome Musik* [1998] ECR I-1953, [1998] 3 CMLR 919.

[6] See, eg Cases C-241 & 242/91P *RTE and ITP v Commission* ('*Magill*') [1995] I-ECR 743, [1995] 4 CMLR 718, [1995] All ER (EC) 416 (UK and Irish copyright legislation gave a copyright to television listings which did not exist elsewhere); and Case 144/81 *Keurkoop v Nancy Kean Gifts* [1982] ECR 2853, [1983] 2 CMLR 47; Case C-38/98 *Renault v Maxicar* [2000] ECR I-2973; Case C-23/99 *Commission v France* [2000] ECR I-7653 (all concerning design rights).

[7] Reg 40/94 on the Community Trade Mark, OJ 1994 L11/1.

[8] Reg 6/2002 on Community designs, OJ 2002 L3/1.

design right. Both rights are obtained by filing an application with the Office for Harmonisation of the Internal Market ('OHIM') in Alicante. Over 500,000 Community trade mark and 227,000 Community registered design applications had been made as at the end of 2006.[9] A similar system exists for Community plant variety rights under Regulation 2100/94.[10] Attempts to create a Community-wide patent have met with less success with two Conventions signed but not ratified.[11] There has been harmonisation of Supplementary Protection Certificates for pharmaceutical and plant protection products.[12] These certificates in effect extend the term of the right in situations where a marketing authorisation is delayed until the final part of the term of the underlying patents. The Biotechnology Directive covers biotechnical inventions.[13] Proposals for closer harmonisation, including the establishment of a Community patent and an Intellectual Property Court in patent actions have also progressed slowly.[14] The Community Patent Convention is different from the Convention on the Grant of European Patents, known as the European Patent Convention,[15] which is not a Community treaty and to which the Contracting Parties include several non-EU States such as Switzerland and Liechtenstein. Under the European Patent Convention it has been possible, since 1 June 1978, to secure a patent for the United Kingdom and for other European countries, under the national law of each country concerned, by applying to the European Patent Office in Munich.

9.004 **The Community approach to competition issues.** In resolving the issues which intellectual property rights pose for competition and the creation of the single market, the Community approach has four main elements. First, in seeking to reconcile the requirements of the free movement of goods and the right to intellectual property, the Court of Justice has developed an extensive case law under Articles 28 and 30 of the Treaty[16] to determine the circumstances in which the exercise of intellectual property rights is justified under Community law.[17]

---

[9] Statistics published on OHIM website. Appeals from decisions of OHIM lie to a board of appeal, thence to the CFI and finally, on a point of law, to the ECJ.

[10] Reg 2100/94 on Community plant variety rights, OJ 1994 L227/1.

[11] The first Community Patent Convention was signed on 15 December 1975 and an agreement for the second Community Patent Convention was signed on 15 December 1989, OJ 1989 L401/1. The 1989 Convention, although not yet ratified, has been cited in the ECJ's judgments: eg Case C-316/95 *Generics v Smith, Kline & French* (*'Generics No. 2'*) [1997] ECR I-3929, [1998] 1 CMLR 1. It is not now expected that the first Convention will ever come into force.

[12] See Reg 1768/92, OJ 1992 L182/1 and Reg 1610/96, OJ 1996 L198/30.

[13] Dir 98/44, OJ 1998 L213/13.

[14] See the Commission's Proposal for a Regulation on the Community Patent, COM (2000) 412 final, OJ 2000 C337 E/278. Detailed discussion of these Conventions and the Commission's harmonisation proposals is outside the scope of this work.

[15] European Patent Convention of 5 October 1973. A consolidated version is available on the website of the European Patent Office.

[16] Vol II, App A.4.

[17] Paras 9.007 *et seq*, below.

Secondly, the Commission and the Court have considered the circumstances in which the exercise of intellectual property rights may be affected by Articles 81 and 82 of the Treaty.[18] Thirdly, the Commission has developed, in its decisions and in a series of block exemptions, notably Regulation 772/2004, the principles upon which intellectual property rights, particularly patents and know-how, may be assigned or licensed without infringing Article 81 of the Treaty.[19] Lastly, but so far to a limited extent, the Community has sought where possible to harmonise national laws on intellectual property rights, notably in the field of trade marks and registered designs, as well as creating Community-based systems for the grant of such rights discussed above.

The move to a more economics-based analysis.   In recent years, the Commission's **9.005** policy has become less formalistic and more attuned to the economic reality of the market, recognising the need to encourage innovation and the transfer of technology.[20] The Commission has described this new policy as intended to 'embody a shift from the formal regulatory approach to a more economic approach in the assessment of horizontal co-operation agreements. . . . to allow competitor collaboration where it contributes to economic welfare without creating a risk for competition'.[21] It is therefore necessary to treat with caution some of the earlier decisions of the Commission in relation to intellectual property rights, particularly as regards the interpretation of Article 81(1). Similarly, the case law of the Community Courts has evolved significantly in certain areas, in a direction generally more favourable to the protection of national intellectual property rights, without however compromising the basic principles of the free movement of goods.[22]

---

[18] Paras 9.066 *et seq*, below.

[19] Paras 9.075 *et seq*, below.

[20] For Reg 772/2004, see paras 9.133 *et seq*, below. See also *De Minimis* Notice, OJ 2001 C368/13, Vol II, App C.13 and paras 2.121 *et seq,* above; the Guidelines on Vertical Restraints, OJ 2000 C291/1, Vol II, App C.11; the block exemption for vertical restraints, Reg 2790/1999, OJ 1999 L336/21, Vol II, App C.3, and see paras 6.006 *et seq*, above; and the Horizontal Cooperation Guidelines, OJ 2001 C3/2, Vol II, App C.12, and see paras 7.027 *et seq*, above.

[21] Press Release IP/00/1376 (29 November 2000).

[22] eg the abandonment of the elusive distinction between the 'existence' and the 'exercise' of the right used in the early case law, para 9.009, below. Also contrast, eg the different attitudes of the ECJ to the now defunct doctrine of common origin in Case 192/73 *Van Zuylen v Hag ('Hag I')* [1974] ECR 731, [1974] 2 CMLR 127; and Case C-10/89 *Hag GF ('Hag II')* [1990] ECR I-3711, [1990] 3 CMLR 571: para 9.034, below and the different attitudes to trade mark assignments in *IHT Internationale Heiztechnik v Ideal Standard* (n 5, above) as compared with Case 40/70 *Sirena v Eda* [1971] ECR 69, [1971] CMLR 260: para 9.068, below. A decision such as *Generics (No. 2)* (n 11, above) shows that the ECJ will not aid infringing third party manufacturers: para 9.020, below. It is however a different matter once products are lawfully in circulation within the single market: see, eg Cases C-267 & 268/95 *Merck v Primecrown* [1996] ECR I-6285, [1997] 1 CMLR 83: para 9.021, below.

9.006 **Plan of this Chapter.** This Chapter deals not only with 'property' rights strictly so-called (patents, trade marks, copyright and designs) but also with similar or cognate rights such as plant breeders' rights, public performance rights, protection from passing off or unfair competition, and the protection of secret know-how. The next Section of this Chapter considers in outline the Treaty rules on the free movement of goods as they affect actions for infringement of intellectual property rights. Section 3 considers the effect of Article 81 and Article 82 on the exercise of intellectual property rights. Section 4 considers the licensing of intellectual property rights under Article 81. Section 5 discusses specifically the application of the block exemption for technology transfer agreements, Regulation 772/2004. Finally, Section 6 considers the licensing of other rights not covered by the block exemption: trade marks, copyright and plant variety rights.

2. Infringement Actions and the Free Movement Rules

(a) Generally

9.007 **Plan of this Section.** The necessary reconciliation between the creation of the single market, on the one hand, and the protection of nationally-based intellectual property rights, on the other hand, has been effected largely by the case law of the Court of Justice under the Treaty rules on the free movement of goods.[23] This Section discusses the Treaty rules on the free movement of goods and services as they affect actions for infringement (a) in general terms, and then, more specifically, in respect of (b) patents (c) trade marks and passing off and (d) copyright and similar rights. In certain circumstances, actions for infringement may be affected by Articles 81 and 82, which are considered in the following Section. When considering any given case, reference should be made to both Sections.

9.008 **The relevant Treaty provisions.** Article 28, which has direct effect,[24] provides:

'Quantitative restrictions on imports and all measures having equivalent effect shall be prohibited between Member States.'

---

[23] Arts 28–30, Vol II, App A.4. Art 30 represents the principal means of reconciling these two imperatives: see, eg *Keurkoop v Nancy Kean* (n 6, above) paras 22–24. The same is true of legislative measures such as Art 7 of Dir 89/104, OJ 1989 L40/1, based on the case law under Art 30: Cases C-427/93, etc, *Bristol-Myers Squibb v Paranova* [1996] ECR I-3457, [1997] 1 CMLR 1151, para 40. See generally, Oliver, *Free Movement of Goods in the European Community* (4th edn, 2002); Toth (ed), *Oxford Encyclopaedia of European Law*, Vol II, The Law of the Internal Market (2005). See also Philipson, *Guide to the Concept and Practical Application of Articles 28-30 EC* (DG Internal Market, January 2001) available at http://ec.europa.eu//enterprise/regulation/goods/docs/art2830/guideart2830_en.pdf. For the interaction of the free movement rules and intellectual property law, see Stothers, *Parallel Trade in Europe* (2007).

[24] This means that it can be enforced in legal proceedings before the national courts of the Member States: see paras 14.001 *et seq*, below.

Article 29 contains similar provision in relation to exports. Both Articles are, however, subject to the derogation in Article 30:

> 'The provisions of Articles 28 and 29 shall not preclude prohibitions or restrictions on imports, exports or goods in transit justified on grounds of . . . the protection of industrial and commercial property. Such prohibitions or restrictions shall not, however, constitute a means of arbitrary discrimination or a disguised restriction on trade between Member States.'

The concept of the 'specific subject-matter' of a right. National legislation **9.009** which entitles the owner of the right to bring an action for infringement against an importer *prima facie* constitutes a measure having equivalent effect within the meaning of Article 28. Such legislation must therefore be justified under Article 30. In determining the extent of the protection offered by Article 30, the jurisprudence of the Court of Justice initially drew a distinction between the 'existence' and the 'exercise' of intellectual property rights, holding that only the 'existence' of the right is safeguarded by Article 30, whereas the 'exercise' of the right is subject to limitations arising from the rules of the Treaty.[25] This theory was partly influenced by the perceived effect of Article 295, which was erroneously thought to limit the application of the Treaty as regards intellectual property rights.[26] However, that approach has now been discarded[27] in favour of the concept of the 'specific subject-matter' of the right in question, according to which the exercise of intellectual property rights is 'justified' under Article 30 if such exercise is for the purpose of safeguarding the rights which constitute 'the specific subject-matter' of the intellectual property right concerned. What constitutes the 'core rights'[28] which comprise the 'specific subject-matter' (in French *objet spécifique*, in German *der spezifische Gegenstand*) varies according to the right in question[29] and

---

[25] The distinction was first developed in cases under Art 81(1), eg Cases 56 & 58/64 *Consten and Grundig v Commission* [1966] ECR 299, 345, [1966] CMLR 418, 474, and *Sirena v Eda* (n 22, above), para 5. Later the principle was reaffirmed in cases dealing directly with Arts 28 and 30: see, eg Case 78/70 *Deutsche Grammophon v Metro* [1971] ECR 487, [1971] CMLR 631, paras 6–12.

[26] Art 295 provides: 'This Treaty shall in no way prejudice the rules in Member States governing the system of property ownership'. The distinction between the 'existence' and the 'exercise' of the right in question was a way of reconciling Art 295 with the requirements of Arts 28 and 30. It has since, however, been recognised that Art 295, which was primarily directed towards matters such as State ownership, does not affect the Treaty rules on the free movement of goods: see Case 30/90 *UK v Commission* [1992] ECR 299, [1992] 2 CMLR 709, para 7; Cases C-92 & 326/92 *Phil Collins v Imrat* [1993] ECR I-5144, [1993] 3 CMLR 773, paras 17–28; Case C-350/92 *Spain v Council* [1995] ECR I-1985, [1996] 1 CMLR 415.

[27] See the Opinion of AG Fennelly in *Merck v Primecrown* (n 22, above) para 93. Mr Fennelly also referred with approval to the Opinion of AG Gulmann in *Magill* (n 6, above) who concluded (at para 31) that 'the distinction between the existence and the exercise of rights has no independent significance for resolving specific questions of delimitation'.

[28] The phrase is used by Oliver (n 23, above) at para 8.120.

[29] For patents, see paras 9.017 *et seq*; for trade marks, para 9.033; for copyright, para 9.052, below.

depends on the 'essential function' of the right.[30] However, as will be seen, the concept of 'the specific subject-matter' invariably includes the right (a) to put the product into circulation on the market in the Community for the first time, either directly or through licensees,[31] and (b) to prevent infringements of the right by third parties unconnected with the proprietor of the right in question. The distinction between specific subject-matter on the one hand and essential function on the other is that the former is used in Community law to define (in summary) what are the 'core rights' enjoyed by the owner of the intellectual property right in question whereas the latter defines the purpose for which the right is conferred in the first place.[32]

9.010 **Exhaustion of rights within the Community.** The right to put the product into circulation in the Community for the first time, which is an essential element of the specific subject-matter, is the positive expression of the principle known as 'the exhaustion of rights'.[33] According to that principle, Articles 28 and 30 of the Treaty provide a complete defence to an infringement action if it is shown that the item in question[34] has been previously marketed in another Member State by the proprietor of the right or with his consent. In other words, the previous marketing 'exhausts' the ability of the owner of the right to prevent the subsequent free circulation of that particular item throughout the Community.[35] The corrollary of this is that rights are not exhausted when the item has been put on the market outside the Community.[36]

9.011 **Exhaustion of rights within the EEA.** The question arises whether goods which are placed on the market with the right owner's consent in a non-EU EEA Member

---

[30] See, eg *Hag II* (n 22, above) para 14.

[31] Note that where a trader introduces the goods into the Community or stores them there in accordance with the customs warehousing procedure of the Community customs code for the purpose of transit to a third country, this does not amount to 'importing' them and therefore is not an interference with the specific subject-matter of the right: Case C-405/03 *Class International* [2005] ECR I-8735, [2006] Ch 154, [2006] 1 CMLR 323; Case C-281/05 *Montex Holdings v Diesel* [2006] ECR I-10881.

[32] See *per* AG Gulmann in *Magill* (n 6, above) at paras 36–37.

[33] This principle was first developed in *Deutsche Grammophon v Metro* (n 25, above) in relation to copyright in sound recordings, and subsequently held to apply to patents and trade marks (*Centrafarm v Sterling Drug*, and *Centrafarm v Winthrop*, discussed at paras 9.018 and 9.032, below respectively) and to design rights in *Keurkoop v Nancy Kean Gifts* (n 6, above). It has been consistently confirmed, but the phrase 'exhaustion of rights' seems to have been used explicitly in the judgment of the ECJ for the first time in *IHT Internationale Heiztechnik v Ideal Standard* (n 5, above) para 34. For a recent restatement of the principle see Cases C-414 & 416/99 *Zino Davidoff and Levi Strauss* [2001] ECR I-8691, [2002] Ch 109, [2002] 1 CMLR 1, [2002] All ER (EC) 55.

[34] The right of first marketing attaches to each individual protected item or copy.

[35] Since the 'specific subject-matter' is limited to the right to put the products on the market in the Community *for the first time*, the right to prevent the subsequent importation of products *previously marketed* by the proprietor or with his consent does not form part of the specific subject-matter: see generally the discussion concerning patents and trade marks, paras 9.011 *et seq*, below.

[36] See, eg paras 9.026 (patents), 9.043 *et seq* (trade marks) and 9.059 (copyright), below.

State should be treated as being in free circulation throughout the EEA in exactly the same way as goods placed on the market in an EU Member State. Articles 11, 12 and 13 of the EEA Agreement reproduce respectively Articles 28, 29 and 30 EC as regards the Contracting Parties. Article 65(2) of the EEA Agreement refers to Protocol 28 and Annex XVII as containing specific provisions and arrangements concerning intellectual, industrial and commercial property. The Protocol and Annex are stated to apply, unless otherwise specified, to all products and services.[37] Article 2(1) of Protocol 28 to the Agreement provides:

> 'To the extent that exhaustion is dealt with in Community measures or jurisprudence, the Contracting Parties shall provide for such exhaustion of intellectual property rights as laid down in Community law. Without prejudice to future developments of case-law, this provision shall be interpreted in accordance with the meaning established in the relevant rulings of the Court of Justice of the European Communities given prior to the signature of the Agreement.'

Annex XVII sets out the Community instruments which have been incorporated into the EEA Agreement with whatever adaptations were necessary. With regard to trade mark rights, EC Directive 89/104 has been incorporated into the EEA Agreement and Article 7 of the Directive refers to the placing of goods on the market in an EEA State rather than to the goods originating in that State. The effect of these provisions is, therefore, that the placing of an item on the market in an EEA State exhausts the owner's rights with regard to the further movement of that item within the EEA.

The meaning of 'put on the market'. In *Peak Holding v Axolin-Elinor*[38] the **9.012** Court of Justice was asked to interpret the words 'put on the market' in Article 7(1) of Directive 89/104 as defining the point at which the trade mark owner's rights in the goods are exhausted. In that case, the trade mark owner had imported the goods into Sweden and had offered them for sale to the public. Some items, however, remained unsold and were returned by the owner to his warehouse. The garments which had not been sold were then sold by the trade mark owner as a consignment to a French wholesaler subject to a contractual stipulation that the majority of them should not be resold within the EEA. The Court held that

---

[37] This would appear to override the more general limitation in Art 8(2) EEA which excludes certain categories of goods from the application of the free movement articles and also provides that the free movement provisions apply only to goods *originating* in an EEA State, not to goods which are placed on the market in such a state but have been imported there from a third party state. In Case E-2/97 *Mag Instrument v California Trading Company Norway, Ulsteen* [1997] Rep EFTA Ct 127, [1998] 1 CMLR 331, the EFTA Court noted that the limitation in Art 8 reflected the fact that the EEA is a free trade area and not a customs union like the Community. The result of that case has probably been overruled by *Silhouette* (see para 9.044, below), interpreting the provision relating to exhaustion specific to trade marks in Art 7 of Dir 89/104.

[38] Case C-16/03 *Peak Holding v Axolin-Elinor* [2004] ECR I-11313, [2005] Ch 261, [2005] 1 CMLR 45, [2005] All ER (EC) 723. See also para 9.025, below.

the act of offering the goods for sale did not amount to a placing of the goods on the market if the goods in fact remained unsold. Such acts do not transfer to third parties the right to dispose of the goods bearing the trade mark since they do not allow the proprietor to realise the economic value of the trade mark. Even after such acts, the Court held, the proprietor retains his interest in maintaining complete control over the goods bearing his trade mark, in order in particular to ensure their quality. However, the sale of the consignment to the French wholesaler did amount to a placing of the goods on the market so that the trade mark owner's rights were exhausted at that point.

9.013 **Arbitrary discrimination or disguised restriction on trade.** Even if the doctrine of exhaustion of rights does not apply, there may be other circumstances in which the exercise of the right may not be 'justified' within the meaning of Article 30 or may amount to 'arbitrary discrimination or a disguised restriction on trade' within the meaning of the second sentence of that Article.[39] In that connection, it is for national law to define the right in question, so that if the discrimination or restriction relied on results simply from a disparity between national laws without more, for example because of a difference in the right granted as between one national law and another, the second sentence of Article 30 will not apply.[40] However, if the national law in question in fact leads to arbitrary discrimination between national and imported products, Article 30, second sentence, may be infringed.[41] Moreover, there are certain circumstances in which the national law may be held to infringe Article 12 of the Treaty, which prohibits discrimination on the grounds of nationality.[42]

9.014 **Articles 81 and 82.** In addition, an action for infringement may in certain circumstances be contrary to Article 81(1) of the Treaty if it is 'the object, the means or the consequence' of a restrictive agreement,[43] and may in some circumstances be contrary to Article 82.[44]

(b) Patents

9.015 **Infringements by importation under UK law.** Under UK domestic law, importing patented goods into the United Kingdom for trade purposes is one of the activities capable of being an infringement of a UK patent even if the goods have

---

[39] See paras 9.027 (patents), 9.049 (trade marks) and 9.056 (copyright), below.

[40] See, eg *Keurkoop v Nancy Kean* (n 6, above) para 18; Case 341/87 *EMI Electrola v Patricia* [1989] ECR 79, [1989] 2 CMLR 413, paras 11–12; *Phil Collins v Imrat* (n 26, above) para 19; Case C-317/91 *Deutsche Renault v Audi* [1993] ECR I-6227, [1995] 1 CMLR 461, paras 28, 31; *IHT Internationale Heiztechnik v Ideal Standard* (n 5, above) paras 21–32.

[41] See paras cited in n 39, above.

[42] *Phil Collins v Imrat* (n 26, above).

[43] Paras 9.067 *et seq*, below.

[44] Paras 9.072 and 10.103, below.

been lawfully manufactured abroad, for example in a country where patent protection had never existed or had expired.[45] However, where the proprietor of the patent has himself marketed the goods abroad, by himself or his agent, he cannot sue for infringement of his UK patent to restrain importation into the United Kingdom unless he can prove that the defendant had notice, at the time of purchase, that the goods were sold subject to a condition limiting the defendant's right to import the goods into the United Kingdom.[46] This proposition probably still holds good because, unlike the position regarding trade marks or registered designs, there is no Community-wide and (importantly) Community-led set of rules relating to infringement. If, on the other hand, the goods sought to be imported into the United Kingdom have been manufactured abroad by a licensee or assignee under a foreign patent, who has been given no licence under the equivalent UK patent, the absence of any licence under the UK patent is taken to imply that no licence authorising importation into the United Kingdom has been given.[47] Thus, where a proprietor of a patent holding parallel patents in the United Kingdom and other countries grants licences under the foreign patents, the proprietor of the patent could, under domestic law, prevent importation into the United Kingdom of goods originating from his foreign licensees by suing for infringement of his UK patent.

Community rules on free movement affecting patents. The effect of the **9.016** Community rules on free movement of goods on actions for patent infringement may be summarised as follows:

(a) Articles 28 and 30 preclude the proprietor of a patent protected by the law of one Member State from suing for infringement to prevent the importation of a product that has been lawfully marketed in another Member State by the proprietor of the patent or with his consent.[48] This is the 'exhaustion of rights' principle and applies even if the product is not patentable in the latter Member State, provided that the marketing in that State was voluntary.[49]

---

[45] Patents Act 1977, s 60. See also *Pfizer v Minister of Health* [1965] AC 512 at 571–573 (HL).

[46] *Betts v Willmott* (1870) LR 6 Ch App 239; *National Phonograph v Menck* (1911) 28 RPC 229.

[47] *Manufactures de Glaces SA v Tilghman's Patent Sand Blast Co* (1884) 25 ChD 1; *Beecham Group Ltd v International Products Ltd* [1968] RPC 129 (Kenya); *Beecham Group Ltd v Shewan Tomes (Traders) Ltd* [1968] RPC 268 (Hong Kong); *Minnesota Mining and Manufacturing Co v Geerpres Europe* [1973] FSR 133. For the contrary case of a limitation on the right to export, which would now infringe the EC Treaty, see *Sterling Drug Co v Beck* [1972] FSR 529.

[48] Case 15/74 *Centrafarm v Sterling Drug* [1974] ECR 1147, [1974] 2 CMLR 480; Case 187/80 *Merck v Stephar* [1981] ECR 2063, [1981] 3 CMLR 463; Case 19/84 *Pharmon v Hoechst* [1985] ECR 2281, [1985] 3 CMLR 775; *Merck v Primecrown* (n 22, above).

[49] *Merck v Stephar, Merck v Primecrown*, above.

(b) Articles 28 and 30 do not preclude the exercise of patent rights to prevent the importation into the Community of goods originating in third countries.[50]

(c) Articles 28 and 30 do not otherwise affect actions for infringement,[51] unless it is shown that for some other reason the infringement action is not 'justified for the protection of industrial or commercial property rights', or amounts to 'arbitrary discrimination' or a 'disguised restriction on trade between Member States' within the meaning of the second sentence of Article 30.[52]

9.017 **Exhaustion of rights and specific subject-matter: patents.** The first case to apply the 'exhaustion of rights' principle to patents was *Centrafarm v Sterling Drug*.[53] In that case Sterling Drug Inc, the proprietor of the patent, held patents in the United Kingdom and the Netherlands relating to a drug sold under the trade name 'Negram'. Its subsidiary companies, Sterling-Winthrop Group Ltd in England and Winthrop BV in the Netherlands, were both licensed under the patent (and associated subsidiary and related patents). Each subsidiary was also the local owner of the trade mark 'Negram'. Centrafarm purchased 'Negram' products in England and imported them into the Netherlands, thereby benefiting from the fact that the price in England was some 50 per cent below that in the Netherlands. Sterling Drug Inc brought an action in the Netherlands for infringement of its Dutch patent and Winthrop BV brought an action for infringement of the trade mark 'Negram'.[54] The Dutch Supreme Court (the Hoge Raad) referred to the Court of Justice various questions covering the compatibility of these actions with the Treaty rules on free movement of goods and with Article 81.

9.018 **The Court of Justice's judgment in *Centrafarm v Sterling Drug*.** In *Centrafarm v Sterling Drug*, the Court of Justice held, in effect, that the exercise of patent rights to prohibit the sale in the Netherlands of goods which had been marketed in another Member State by the proprietor of the patent or with his consent was incompatible with the rules on free movement of goods. The Court said:

> 'Inasmuch as it provides an exception to one of the fundamental principles of the Common Market, Article [30] in fact only admits of derogations from the free movement of goods where such derogations are justified for the purpose of safeguarding

---

[50] That is, countries outside the EEA, by analogy from Case 51/75 *EMI v CBS* [1976] ECR 811, [1976] 2 CMLR 235; Case 270/80 *Polydor v Harlequin Record Shops* [1982] ECR 329, [1982] 1 CMLR 677; Case C-355/96 *Silhouette* [1998] ECR I-4799, [1998] 2 CMLR 953; Case 173/98 *Sebago* [1999] ECR I-4105, [1999] 2 CMLR 1317. See further paras 9.043 *et seq*, below.

[51] *Pharmon v Hoechst* (n 48, above); *Centrafarm v Sterling Drug* (n 48, above).

[52] eg Case 35/87 *Thetford Corporation v Fiamma* [1988] ECR 3585, [1988] 3 CMLR 549; Case 434/85 *Allen & Hanburys v Generics (UK) Limited* [1988] ECR 1245, [1988] 1 CMLR 701; Cases C-235/89 and C-30/90 *Commission v Italy, Commission v United Kingdom* [1992] ECR I-777, 829, [1992] 2 CMLR 709, 759; Case C-191/90 *Generics v Smith Kline & French* [1992] ECR I-5335, [1993] 1 CMLR 89; para 9.027, below.

[53] Case 15/74 *Centrafarm v Sterling Drug* [1974] ECR 1147, [1974] 2 CMLR 480.

[54] The trade mark action is considered at para 9.032, below.

rights which constitute the specific subject matter of this property. In relation to patents, the specific subject matter of the industrial property is the guarantee that the proprietor of the patent, to reward the creative effort of the inventor, has the exclusive rights to use an invention with a view to manufacturing industrial products and putting them into circulation for the first time, either directly or by the grant of licences to third parties, as well as the right to oppose infringements.

An obstacle to the free movement of goods may arise out of the existence, within a national legislation concerning industrial and commercial property, of provisions laying down that a proprietor of the patent's right is not exhausted when the product protected by the patent is marketed in another Member State, with the result that the proprietor of the patent can prevent importation of the product into his own Member State when it has been marketed in another State.

Whereas an obstacle to the free movement of goods of this kind may be justified on the ground of protection of industrial property where such protection is invoked against a product coming from a Member State where it is not patentable and has been manufactured by third parties without the consent of the proprietor of the patent and in cases where there exist patents, the original proprietors of which are legally and economically independent, a derogation from the principle of the free movement of goods is not, however, justified where the product has been put on to the market in a legal manner, by the proprietor of the patent himself or with his consent, in the Member State from which it has been imported, in particular in the case of a proprietor of parallel patents.

In fact, if a proprietor of the patent could prevent the import of protected products marketed by him or with his consent in another Member State, he would be able to partition off national markets and thereby restrict trade between Member States, in a situation where no such restriction was necessary to guarantee the essence of the exclusive rights flowing from the parallel patents'.[55]

The reasoning in *Centrafarm v Sterling Drug*. The underlying basis of the **9.019** judgment in *Centrafarm v Sterling Drug* is seemingly as follows. Article 28 of the Treaty prohibits *inter alia* all 'measures having equivalent effect to a quantitative restriction on imports'. The national law upon which the action for infringement was founded constituted such a 'measure'.[56] That 'measure' could be brought into play only if the circumstances fell within the exception provided by Article 30 of the Treaty, that is, that the measure was (a) 'justified on grounds of the protection of industrial and commercial property' and (b) did not 'constitute a means of arbitrary discrimination or a disguised restriction on trade between Member States'. According to the Court of Justice, the exception in Article 30 can be brought into play only if the infringement action is necessary to protect 'the specific subject-matter' of the patent, which the Court defined as 'the guarantee that the proprietor of the patent, to reward the creative effort of the inventor, has the exclusive

---

[55] *Centrafarm v Sterling Drug* (n 53, above) paras 8–12.
[56] For Art 28, see para 9.008, above. An injunction is, in itself, 'a measure' within Art 28: Case 6/81 *Industrie Diensten Groep v Beele* [1982] ECR 707, [1982] 3 CMLR 102.

right to use an invention with a view to manufacturing industrial products and putting them into circulation for the first time, either directly or through licensees, and to oppose infringements'.[57] The Court thus held, in effect, that a proprietor of a patent or his licensees have the exclusive right to make the product and to put it on the market for the first time; but once this has been done anywhere in the EEA, the right is 'exhausted' and no action can be brought under the patent or any parallel patent[58] to impede the subsequent free circulation of the goods throughout the EEA.[59]

9.020 **Protection of the specific subject-matter:** *Generics (No. 2).* Community law will not, however, undermine the 'core rights' of the proprietor of a patent, as illustrated in *Generics (No. 2)*.[60] In that case, the patent for 'Tagamet' had expired elsewhere in the Community, but not in the Netherlands. While the Dutch patent was still in force, Generics submitted samples of the product to the relevant Dutch authorities in order to obtain a marketing authorisation to sell the product in the Netherlands as soon as the Dutch patent expired. Under Dutch law as it then was, the use of the samples in this way was an infringing act, but it had enabled Generics to obtain a marketing authorisation 14 months earlier than if it had had to wait for the patent to expire before applying. The Dutch court held that the Dutch patent had been infringed and granted an injunction preventing Generics from selling the product in the Netherlands until 14 months after the patent had expired, thus depriving Generics of the 'lead time' gained by the infringement. That ruling was upheld by the Court of Justice on the grounds that the use of the samples in question, which had been manufactured by the patented process, infringed the 'specific subject-matter' of the patent which was 'a monopoly of the first exploitation' of the patented product; the 14-month injunction was a legitimate response to the advantage which Generics had wrongfully gained by its infringement.[61] The law relating to the infringement of patents by acts done for

---

[57] *Centrafarm v Sterling Drug* (n 53, above) para 9. This formulation has been confirmed in subsequent cases, eg *Allen & Hanburys v Generics* (n 52, above); Cases C-235/89 and C-30/90 *Commission v Italy, Commission v United Kingdom*, ibid; Case 191/90 *Generics v Smith Kline & French*, ibid para 23. Following *Merck v Stephar* (n 48, above) para 9, the ECJ said in *Merck v Primecrown* (n 22, above) para 31, that: '... it followed from the definition of the specific purpose of a patent that the substance of a patent right lies essentially in according the inventor an exclusive right to put the product on the market for the first time, thereby allowing him a monopoly in exploiting his product and enabling him to obtain the reward for his creative effort without, however, guaranteeing such reward in all circumstances'. See also *Generics (No. 2)* (n 11, above) para 19.

[58] Whether the patent is a 'parallel' patent is a question of fact: *Centrafarm v Sterling Drug* (n 53, above) para 14. This used to cause problems under the differing patent legislation of Member States, particularly as regards pharmaceutical patents, where the patent in one Member State was for a product but the patent in another Member State was for a process.

[59] *Centrafarm v Sterling Drug* (n 53, above) paras 19–20.

[60] Case C-316/95 *Generics v Smith, Kline & French* ('*Generics (No. 2)*') [1997] ECR I-3929, [1998] 1 CMLR 1.

[61] See paras 20 and 29 of the judgment.

experimental purposes is now governed by European Directives[62] so that the result in the *Generics (No. 2)* case would be different if similar facts arose again.

Exhaustion of rights where product not patentable in State of origin.   In two **9.021** cases, *Merck v Stephar*[63] and *Merck v Primecrown*,[64] the proprietor's rights were held to have been exhausted even where the product concerned was imported from a Member State where patent protection was unavailable, provided that it had been marketed in that State by the proprietor of the patent or with his consent.[65] There are now no differences within the Community as to the scope of the subject-matter of patents. However, temporary provisions are sometimes included in accession agreements, for example in the Treaty of Accession for eight of the ten new Member States which joined the Community on 1 May 2004.[66]

Irrelevant defences.   It has further been held that the doctrine of exhaustion of **9.022** rights applies notwithstanding differences in prices resulting from Government price controls,[67] minor disparities in national laws provided that the identity of the protected invention is the same,[68] or differences in the amount of royalties receivable in the different territories.[69] Considerations of public health are also normally irrelevant to patent infringement suits.[70]

Lack of consent: *Pharmon.*   The doctrine of exhaustion of rights does not, how- **9.023** ever, apply if the goods were originally marketed without the consent of the proprietor of the patent, for example if they were manufactured by third parties, without assistance from the proprietor of the patent, in a Member State where there was no patent protection.[71] Moreover 'consent' must be voluntary,

---

[62] See Dir 2004/27/EC, OJ 2004 L136/34 (medicinal products); Dir 2004/28/EC, OJ 2004 L136/58 (veterinary products).

[63] Case 187/80 *Merck v Stephar* [1981] ECR 2063, [1981] 3 CMLR 463. See also Case 24/67 *Parke, Davis v Probel* [1968] ECR 55, [1968] CMLR 47, where the fact that the infringing product had been manufactured in Italy under licence from the proprietor of the patent emerged at a late stage of the procedure and was not taken into account by the ECJ, which was primarily considering arguments under Arts 81 and 82 rather than Arts 28–30. It is doubtful whether this case would be decided in the same way now on the facts.

[64] Cases C-267 & 268/95 *Merck v Primecrown* [1996] ECR I-6285, [1997] 1 CMLR 83.

[65] Note that in his Opinion, AG Fennelly argued powerfully for the opposite result.

[66] Accession Treaty signed in Athens, 16 April 2003, Part 3, Title II, Annex IV, Section 2: provides a mechanism whereby parallel imports from the Czech Republic, Estonia, Latvia, Lithuania, Hungary, Poland, Slovenia and Slovakia are prevented until the patent or supplementary protection of the medicinal product concerned expires in these Member States.

[67] *Centrafarm v Sterling Drug* (n 53, above) paras 14 *et seq; Merck v Primecrown* (n 64, above) para 47.

[68] *Centrafarm v Sterling Drug* (n 53, above) para 14.

[69] Cases 55 & 57/80 *Musik-Vertrieb Membran v GEMA* [1981] ECR 147, [1981] 2 CMLR 44; Case 402/85 *Basset v SACEM* [1987] ECR 1747, [1987] 2 CMLR 173: see para 9.056, below.

[70] *Centrafarm v Sterling Drug* (n 53, above). See also Case 104/75 *De Peijper* [1976] ECR 613, [1976] 2 CMLR 271.

[71] *Centrafarm v Sterling Drug* (n 53, above) para 11.

as decided in *Pharmon v Hoechst*.[72] In that case, Hoechst owned parallel patents in the United Kingdom and the Netherlands. A British company, DDSA, obtained a compulsory licence under United Kingdom domestic law. DDSA circumvented a prohibition on exports contained in the compulsory licence and the goods were imported into the Netherlands by Pharmon. Hoechst sued for infringement. In a reference to the Court of Justice, the main issue was whether the marketing of the goods by DDSA under the compulsory licence had been 'with the consent' of Hoechst. Pharmon argued that Hoechst had chosen to take out a patent in the United Kingdom and as a result had accepted all the consequences, including the possibility that a compulsory licence might be issued. The Court held, however, that when a compulsory licence is granted the patent owner cannot be deemed to have consented to the grant so that Hoechst was free to sue for infringement under Dutch law.

9.024 **What constitutes consent.** The necessary consent arises when the owner himself markets the goods or does so through a subsidiary undertaking.[73] It is sufficient if the owner and the undertaking which did the first marketing are under common control[74] or linked economically.[75] It seems that the voluntary grant of a licence will be sufficient consent,[76] but an assignment by way of sale, for example on the transfer of a business, will not constitute consent to the subsequent production of items by the assignee when there are no ongoing connections between the parties.[77] The marketing of goods in another Member State where there is a risk that a compulsory licence may be granted,[78] or a risk that the relevant protection may expire before expiry elsewhere in the Community,[79] does not constitute consent.

9.025 **'Previously marketed'.** The exhaustion principle permits a third party purchaser to buy goods in one Member State and import them into another Member State without the risk of an action for patent infringement, provided the goods are placed in circulation in the first Member State by the proprietor of the patent

---

72 Case 19/84 *Pharmon v Hoechst* [1985] ECR 2281, [1985] 3 CMLR 775.

73 For an English case considering this, see *EMI v CD Specialists* [1992] FSR 70 (ChD) which held on a striking out application that the fact that a bootleg recording was on sale in another Member State did not give rise to an inference that the copyright owner had or should be deemed to have consented. For a recent analysis of the concept of consent in the context of trade marks, see *Zino Davidoff and Levi Strauss*, para 9.045, below.

74 *Centrafarm v Sterling Drug* (n 53, above).

75 *IHT Internationale Heiztechnik v Ideal Standard* (n 5, above) paras 30, 40–43.

76 *Centrafarm v Sterling Drug* (n 53, above); *Pharmon v Hoechst* (n 72, above) para 2.

77 *IHT Internationale Heiztechnik v Ideal Standard* (n 5, above) discussed at para 9.045, below.

78 *Pharmon v Hoechst* (n 72, above).

79 See *EMI Electrola v Patricia* (n 40, above) where the manufacturer and copyright holder of sound recordings in Germany was permitted by the ECJ to resist imports into Germany of the recordings manufactured and marketed lawfully, but without its consent, in Denmark where the right had expired.

or with his consent. Whether goods have been 'previously marketed' is a question of fact.[80] It is not finally settled whether patent licensee A in one Member State may successfully bring an infringement action against the licensor or licensee B in another Member State in circumstances where the licensor or licensee B has sold directly into licensee A's territory without the goods having been 'previously marketed' at all. The Commission has expressed the view that a licence of a patent in one Member State is to be deemed to carry with it the right to sell throughout the Community, irrespective of the existence of parallel patents held by other licensees in other territories,[81] but is doubtful whether this is correct where parallel patents exist.[82]

Imports from third countries.   Articles 28 and 30 and the corresponding   **9.026** provisions in the EEA Agreement apply only to the free movement of goods between Member States or between Member States and EFTA States that are signatories to the EEA Agreement.[83] It appears that, in the case of patents,[84] as with trade marks,[85] and copyright,[86] the principle of exhaustion of rights does not apply to products originating in third countries which have not been previously marketed in the EEA.[87]

Unjustified, discriminatory or disguised restrictions.   An action for infringe-   **9.027** ment will normally be 'justified' on grounds of the protection of intellectual property within the meaning of Article 30 if the suit seeks to protect the specific

---

[80] Transit across a Member State does not constitute putting on the market: *Commission v France* (n 6, above). Similarly external transit or storage in a customs warehouse does not constitute importation of the goods and so cannot be opposed by the right owner: see *Class International* and *Montex Holdings v Diesel* (both n 31, above). See also *Peak Holding* (n 38, above).

[81] See the Commission's submissions in *Pharmon v Hoechst* (n 72, above) and the Opinion of AG Mancini at 2285–2286 (ECR), 780–781 (CMLR). See also *Fourth Report on Competition Policy* (1974), points 22–27; *Fifth Report* (1975), point 11.

[82] The Commission's view would mean that a licence for one part of the Community conferred a direct sales licence for the whole of the Community even in territories where parallel patents existed. It this were true, territorial restrictions could only apply if imposed in a licence benefiting from Art 81(3). Where there are parallel patents, the Commission's theory would weaken the 'specific subject-matter' of those patents, whether they were retained by the licensor or licensed to other licensees. Moreover, it may be difficult to say that a licensee, or for that matter the licensor, has 'consented' to sales by other licensees in territories that were not licensed but where there were still parallel patents. If no such consent is to be implied, the licensees of the parallel patents could prevent the importation of goods that had not been previously marketed in the Community by suing for infringement, ie they could prevent *direct* sales if not *parallel* trade. For the effect of Art 81(1) and Reg 776/2003, see paras 9.099 *et seq*, below.

[83] Iceland, Liechtenstein and Norway: see para 1.086, above.

[84] Case 191/90 *Generics v Smith, Kline & French* (n 52, above) para 17; but see para 9.027, below.

[85] Paras 9.043 *et seq*, below.

[86] Para 9.059, below.

[87] For free movement within the EEA see para 9.011, above.

subject-matter of the patent.[88] But in some circumstances it can be shown on some other ground either (i) that the protection is not 'justified on grounds of protection of industrial and commercial property' within the meaning of the first sentence of Article 30; or (ii) that the protection amounts to 'arbitrary discrimination' or 'a disguised restriction' on trade between Member States within the meaning of the second sentence of Article 30. The fact that the discrimination complained of results merely from a difference in national laws, for example because a particular national law confers a wider substantive protection than is available elsewhere in the Community, is not sufficient in itself to constitute arbitrary discrimination or a disguised restriction on trade.[89] Thus the Court of Justice has ruled that the former English law doctrine of 'relative novelty', which enabled a new patent to be granted for an invention which replicated a patent specification filed more than 50 years previously, did not constitute such 'discrimination' or such a 'restriction', where the doctrine applied equally to United Kingdom and other Community nationals.[90] On the other hand, it has been held that section 46(3)(c) of the Patents Act 1977, which had the effect that an undertaking which imported the product into the United Kingdom could not be certain of being granted a licence under a patent endorsed 'licence of right', whereas an undertaking which made the product in the United Kingdom would be sure of obtaining a licence, was contrary to Article 28 of the Treaty and constituted 'arbitrary discrimination or a disguised restriction on trade' within the meaning of Article 30, second sentence.[91] Similarly, section 48 of the Patents Act 1977, which provided that compulsory licences of a patent will not be granted where the patent holder exploits the patent by manufacturing the product in the United Kingdom, but can be granted where the patent holder satisfies domestic demand by importing the product from other Member States, has been held to infringe Article 28 since it is designed to encourage domestic production.[92] The practice of the national authority charged with settling the terms of licences of right whereby the licensee was refused the right to import from third countries in cases where the patent holder manufactured the patented product in the United Kingdom, but was authorised to import from third countries in cases where the patent holder did not make the product in the United Kingdom but imported the product from other

---

[88] Paras 9.017–9.020, above.

[89] *Keurkoop v Nancy Kean Gifts* (n 6, above), and other cases cited at n 40, above.

[90] *Thetford Corporation v Fiamma* (n 52, above).

[91] *Allen & Hanburys v Generics* (n 52, above); Case C-191/90 *Generics v Smith, Kline & French,* ibid. In *Hagen v Fratelli* [1980] 3 CMLR 253, the English Court of Appeal held that it was arguable that it is not 'justified' to confine the defence of 'prior use' on a pre-1977 patent to use in the UK, as distinct from elsewhere in the Community, especially when prior use elsewhere in the Community would be a defence in respect of a post-1977 patent under the Patents Act 1977.

[92] Case C-30/90 *Commission v United Kingdom* (n 52, above).

Member States, was also contrary to Article 28.[93] The 1977 Act was subsequently amended to bring it into compliance.

Pharmaceutical marketing authorisations.   The requirement that pharmaceu-   **9.028**
tical products must be licensed before being supplied within a Member State can result in the national pharmaceutical licensing authority creating barriers to imports independent of the intellectual property rights of the patent holder.[94] According to Directive 2001/83,[95] no medicinal product may be placed on the market of a Member State unless a marketing authorisation has been issued by the competent authorities of that State in accordance with that Directive or a Community authorisation has been granted in accordance with Regulation 2309/93.[96] Article 8 of the Directive details the information which must be submitted to the competent authority with the application for authorisation. According to the jurisprudence of the Court of Justice, these rules are subject to exceptions resulting from the application of the principle of free movement and national authorities must not obstruct parallel imports by requiring parallel importers to satisfy the same requirements as those which apply to undertakings seeking a first time authorisation for the product.[97] In particular, where information necessary for the purpose of protecting public health is readily available to the competent authority of the Member State because the product is already sold in its territory, the parallel-imported product is entitled to follow a proportionately simplified procedure in order to obtain authorisation.[98] The simplified procedure is applicable provided that, first, the imported product has already been granted market authorisation in the Member State from which it is being exported; and, secondly, the imported product is sufficiently similar to a reference product which is already authorised in the importing Member State, even if there are differences between the two.[99] Further the Court has ruled that even if the authorisation of the reference product in the importing State has been revoked,

---

[93] Case C-191/90 *Generics v Smith, Kline & French* (n 52, above). For arbitrary discrimination and disguised restrictions in the context of trade marks, see paras 9.049 *et seq*, below.

[94] See Commission Communication on parallel imports of proprietary medicinal products for which marketing authorisiations have already been granted: COM/2003/0839 final, 30 December 2003 (replacing the 1982 Communication, OJ 1982 C115/5).

[95] Dir 2001/83, OJ 2001 L311/67 (am by Dir 2002/98, OJ 2003 L33/30 and Dir 2003/63, OJ 2003 L159/46). Dir 2001/82, OJ 2001 L311/1, makes similar provision for veterinary medicines.

[96] Reg 2309/93, OJ 1993 L214/1. See Commission Communication on the Community Marketing Authorisation Procedures for Medicinal Products, OJ 1998 C229/4, and Case T-123/00 *Thomae v Commission* [2002] ECR II-5193.

[97] Case 104/75 *De Peijper* [1976] ECR 613, [1976] 2 CMLR 271; Case C-201/94 *Smith & Nephew and Primecrown* [1996] ECR I-5819; C-172/00 *Ferring* [2002] ECR I-6891.

[98] *De Peijper*, above.

[99] In *Smith & Nephew and Primecrown*, above, the ECJ held that two products do not have to be identical in all respects provided that they have been manufactured according to the same formulation, use the same active ingredient and have the same therapeutic effect.

parallel imports are still possible provided that the revocation was not on public health grounds.[100]

(c) Trade marks

9.029 Community trade marks. National rules on trade marks must comply with Directive 89/104.[101] An alternative to registration of a mark in each individual Member State is the acquisition of a Community trade mark under Regulation 40/94.[102] A Community trade mark gives its owner exclusive rights throughout the Community. As regards infringement actions, Community trade marks are governed by the same principles of Community law as national trade marks.[103]

9.030 Summary of the rules on free movement affecting trade marks. Community law on the free movement of goods as it affects suits for trade mark infringement may be summarised as follows:

(1) The principle of exhaustion of rights applies to trade marks.[104]
(2) A parallel importer may 'repack' a product without infringing the trade mark only in accordance with criteria laid down by the Court of Justice.[105]
(3) The principle of exhaustion of rights does not preclude the exercise of trade mark rights to prevent the importation into the Community of goods originating in third countries.[106]
(4) The rules on the free movement of goods do not otherwise affect trade mark rights where, according to national law, a third party has unlawfully used the mark or one confusingly similar, unless an action for infringement is not

---

[100] *Ferring* (n 97, above). In COMP/37.507 *AstraZeneca*, 19 July 2006, [2006] 5 CMLR 287, the Commission condemned the conduct of the patent holder in seeking to withdraw one version of the drug from the market and replace it with another version in order to frustrate the ability of generic manufacturers to supply products which competed with the first version (on appeal Case T-321/05 *AstraZeneca*, not yet decided): see further para 10.154, below.

[101] Dir 89/104, OJ 1989 L40/1.

[102] Reg 40/94 on the Community Trade Mark, OJ 1994 L11/1.

[103] Art 13 of Reg 40/94, above. Since a Community trade mark applies to the whole of the Community and cannot be split, assignments for part only of the Community are not possible (see Art 17 of Reg 40/94). However, the rights may be licensed for the whole or part of the Communtiy (Art 22, ibid).

[104] *Centrafarm v Winthrop* (n 109, below): see para 9.032, below. This principle is now given statutory affect in Art 7(1) of Dir 89/104 (n 101, above) and, in the United Kingdom, by s 12 of the Trade Marks Act 1994.

[105] Paras 9.037 *et seq*, below.

[106] Paras 9.043 *et seq*, below. However, if there has been an unequivocal renunciation by the trade mark proprietor of the right to object to parallel importation either expressly or impliedly (but always clearly), the right to object is exhausted in relation to that set or consignment of goods (but not others): Cases C-414 & 416/99 *Zino Davidoff and Levi Strauss Ltd* [2001] ECR I-8691, [2002] Ch 109, [2002] 1 CMLR 1, [2002] All ER (EC) 55.

'justified' on some other ground or there is some arbitrary discrimination or disguised restriction on trade between Member States.[107]

(5) The doctrine of 'common origin', which used to complicate the legal situation in relation to trade marks, has been abolished by the Court of Justice's ruling in '*Hag II*'.[108] This was replaced by a doctrine of common consent or common exhaustion.

Articles 5 and 7 of Directive 89/104. The exhaustion of rights principle **9.031** was established by the case law of the Court of Justice but in relation to trade mark rights it has now been codified in Directive 89/104 which harmonises the rights that the Member States must confer on the trade mark owner. Article 5 of the Directive provides that the registered trade mark must confer on the proprietor the right to stop all third parties using the mark within his consent, including, amongst other things, the right to prohibit import and export of goods bearing the sign. Article 7(1) of the Directive sets out the principle of the exhaustion of rights and provides:

'(1) The trade mark shall not entitle the proprietor to prohibit its use in relation to goods which have been put on the market in the Community under that trade mark by the proprietor or with his consent.

(2) Paragraph 1 shall not apply where there exist legitimate reasons for the proprietor to oppose further commercialisation of the goods, especially where the condition of the goods is changed or impaired after they have been put on the market.'

Exhaustion of rights and specific subject-matter: trade marks. The application **9.032** of the principle of exhaustion of rights to trade marks was established in *Centrafarm v Winthrop*,[109] the sister case to *Centrafarm v Sterling Drug*.[110] In *Centrafarm v Winthrop*, the Court of Justice held that it was incompatible with the rules on the free movement of goods to exercise trade mark rights to prevent the sale in one Member State of a product that had been previously marketed under the trade mark in another Member State by the trade mark owner or with his consent. As in *Centrafarm v Sterling Drug*, the Court of Justice held that Article 30 admits of derogations from the free movement of goods provisions only when they are justified for safeguarding rights which constitute 'the specific subject-matter of the property'. However the Court held that an action for infringement was not justified:

'when the product has been put on the market in a legal manner in the Member State from which it has been imported, by the trade mark owner himself or with his consent, so that there can be no question of abuse or infringement of the trade mark.'[111]

---

[107] Paras 9.049 *et seq*, below.
[108] Paras 9.034 *et seq*, below.
[109] Case 16/74 *Centrafarm v Winthrop* [1974] ECR 1183, [1974] 2 CMLR 480.
[110] See para 9.019, above.
[111] *Centrafarm v Winthrop* (n 109, above) para 10.

Therefore, Winthrop BV could not use its Dutch trade mark rights to prevent the importation of products lawfully bearing the 'Negram' mark which had been previously marketed in the United Kingdom by its sister company.

9.033 **Specific subject-matter of the trade mark.** The formulation of the specific subject-matter of the trade mark has been refined since the Court's judgment in *Centrafarm v Winthrop*. In *Hag II*[112] the Court of Justice approached the issue in the following terms:

> 'Trade mark rights are, it should be noted, an essential element in the system of undistorted competition which the Treaty seeks to establish and maintain. Under such a system, an undertaking must be in a position to keep its customers by virtue of the quality of its products and services, something which is possible only if there are distinctive marks which enable customers to identify those products and services. For the trade mark to be able to fulfil this role, it must offer a guarantee that all goods bearing it have been produced under the control of a single undertaking which is accountable for their quality.
>
> Consequently, as the Court has ruled on numerous occasions, the specific subject matter of trade marks is in particular to guarantee to the proprietor of the trade mark that he has the right to use that trade mark for the purposes of putting a product into circulation for the first time and therefore to protect him against competitors wishing to take advantage of the status and reputation of the trade mark by selling products illegally[113] bearing that mark. In order to determine the exact scope of this right exclusively conferred on the owner of the trade mark, regard must be had to the essential function of the trade mark, which is to guarantee the identity of the origin of the marked product to the consumer or ultimate user by enabling him without any possibility of confusion to distinguish that product from products which have another origin.'[114]

Thus, provided that the use of the mark by a subsequent purchaser of goods placed on the market in the Community does not interfere with the 'specific subject-matter' of the mark as so defined, no action for infringement will lie.[115]

---

[112] Case C-10/89 *CNL-SUCAL v Hag GF AG ('Hag II')* [1990] ECR I-3711, [1990] 3 CMLR 571.

[113] This use of the word 'illegally' is somewhat circular, since on the facts of the case the mark had been lawfully affixed in the Member State of origin.

[114] *Hag II* (n 112, above) para 14. The cases cited by the ECJ in support of this formulation were: Case 102/77 *Hoffmann-La Roche v Centrafarm* [1978] ECR 1139, [1978] 3 CMLR 217, para 7; and Case 3/78 *Centrafarm v American Home Products Corporation* [1978] ECR 1823, [1979] 1 CMLR 326, paras 11–12. For later cases on the 'specific subject-matter' of a trade mark, see notably Case C-9/93 *IHT Internationale Heiztechnik v Ideal Standard* [1994] ECR I-2789, [1994] 3 CMLR 857, paras 16 and 33 (see para 9.047, below); *Deutsche Renault* (n 40, above) paras 30 and 32; and the repackaging cases cited at paras 9.038 *et seq*, below.

[115] For the use of the mark by unconnected undertakings who sell second hand marked goods or provide repair and maintenance services for the marked goods see Case C-63/97 *BMW v Deenik* [1999] ECR I-905, [1999] 1 CMLR 1099.

The defunct doctrine of 'common origin': *Hag I* **and** *Hag II***.**   Prior to the Court   **9.034**
of Justice's ruling in *Hag II*, it had not always been necessary to rely on the doctrine
of exhaustion of rights as a means of resisting actions for trade mark infringement
because of the principle of 'common origin' established in *Van Zuylen v Hag* (*'Hag
I'*).[116] However following a further reference from the national court, in its decision in *Hag II* in 1990, the Court of Justice overruled its previous decision in *Hag
I*, following Advocate General Jacobs' detailed demonstration that 'the doctrine of
common origin is not a legitimate creature of Community law'.[117]

The reasoning of the Court in *Hag II***.**   In *Hag II*,[118] the Court of Justice   **9.035**
stated that it was necessary to reconsider *Hag I* in the light of the established case
law concerning the relationship between intellectual property and the general rules
of the Treaty, particularly with regard to the free movement of goods.[119] The Court
restated the settled case law in relation to Article 30, in particular the principles
of specific subject-matter and exhaustion of rights.[120] In relation to the facts of
Hag II, the Court then stated:

> 'For the purpose of evaluating a situation such as that described by the national court
> in the light of the foregoing considerations, the determinant factor is the absence of
> any consent on the part of the proprietor of the trade mark protected by national leg-
> islation to the putting into circulation in another Member State of similar products
> bearing an identical trade mark or one liable to lead to confusion, which are manu-
> factured and marketed by an undertaking which is economically and legally inde-
> pendent of the aforesaid trade mark proprietor.'[121]

The Court concluded that Hag AG was able to prevent the importation into
Germany of products bearing the 'Hag' trade mark and originating from Sucal in
Belgium because Hag AG had never consented to the goods being marketed else-
where in the Community.

The transit of marked goods through Community territory.   In two cases   **9.036**
decided in 2005 and 2006,[122] the Court of Justice considered whether the introduction of marked goods into the Community territory[123] amounts to 'importing'

---

[116] Case 192/73 *Van Zuylen v Hag* (*'Hag I'*) [1974] ECR 731, [1974] 2 CMLR 127. See also
Advocaat Zwarte Kip, OJ 1974 L237/12, [1974] 2 CMLR D79; *Velcro/Aplix*, OJ 1985 L233/22,
[1989] 4 CMLR 157.
[117] *Hag II* (n 112, above) Opinion of AG Jacobs at part VIII.
[118] ibid. The Opinion of AG Jacobs sets out in considerable detail the logical basis for the ECJ's
action in expressly reversing its own judgment. He also considers the ECJ's powers and duties to
reverse its judgments: Opinion, part XVI.
[119] *Hag II* (n 112, above) para 10.
[120] ibid, paras 11–14.
[121] ibid, para 15.
[122] Case C-405/03 *Class International* [2005] ECR I-8735, [2006] Ch 154, [2006] 1 CMLR
323; and Case C-281/05 *Montex Holdings v Diesel*, [2006] ECR I-10881.
[123] The same may not apply to the territory of non-EU States within the EEA since the customs
code arrangements only apply to the Community: see *Class International*, above, paras 23–27.

the goods and is thus exclusively reserved to the trade mark owner. Under the Community customs code, goods may transit the Community under the external transit procedure and may be stored in customs warehouses without being subject to Community customs duties. The Court held that this does not constitute importing the goods into the Community and does not infringe the exclusive rights which Directive 89/104 requires to be conferred on trade mark owners.

9.037 **The problem of repackaging.** A particular problem concerning trade marks arises if a parallel importer lawfully buys trade marked goods in one Member State and then re-imports them into another Member State having relabelled or repackaged them.[124] In some circumstances, such repackaging may constitute the only means whereby parallel imports may take place, for example where the trade mark owner seeks to sell the same product under different names or in different packs in different Member States. On the other hand, the guarantee of origin, which is the specific subject-matter of the trade mark, may be impaired if a third party can resell the goods after interfering with their original condition. The legality of repackaging has been considered under Community law in a number of cases in which the Court has developed detailed criteria for determining when an importer may 'repack'. This needs to be considered in the light of both Article 7(2) of Directive 89/104,[125] which provides that exhaustion of rights does not apply 'where there exist legitimate reasons for the proprietor to oppose further dealings in the goods, in particular where the condition of the goods has been changed or impaired', and of Article 30 of the Treaty.

9.038 **Repackaging: different packs or wrapping.** In *Hoffmann-La Roche v Centrafarm*,[126] Centrafarm purchased valium tablets in packs from the United Kingdom, imported them into the Netherlands and then repacked the tablets into different packs. Centrafarm affixed to the new packs the trade marks 'Valium' and 'Roche' which were owned by Hoffmann-La Roche. On a reference from the German court, the Court of Justice held that the essential function of a trade mark is to enable the consumer without any possibility of confusion to distinguish the marked product from products which have a different origin.[127] The Court also held that the 'guarantee of origin' afforded by the trade mark included the guarantee to the consumer that the products had not been interfered with by third parties in a way capable of adversely affecting the condition of the product. In the circumstances, the Court held that a trade mark proprietor would be justified under Article 30 in suing for infringement where his mark had been affixed without

---

[124] For discussion, see the Commission Communication (n 94, above) section 5.
[125] Dir 89/104, OJ 1989 L40/1 and see OJ 1992 L6/35 (bringing it into force at the same time as Reg 40/94 on the adoption of a Community trade mark, OJ 1994 L11/1).
[126] Case 102/77 *Hoffmann-La Roche v Centrafarm* [1978] ECR 1139, [1978] 3 CMLR 217.
[127] ibid, para 7.

his consent by a third party. But the Court also ruled that the trade mark owner could not object if: (i) he had adopted a marketing system tending artificially to partition the common market; (ii) repackaging did not adversely affect the product; (iii) the trade mark owner had prior notice of the repackaging; and (iv) the new packaging stated by whom the product had been repackaged. If these conditions were satisfied, an infringement action would be 'a disguised restriction on trade between Member States' and thus contrary to the second sentence of Article 30.[128] The third of these conditions was clarified in *Boehringer*,[129] where the Court of Justice held that the parallel importer has an obligation to notify the mark holder himself rather than to rely on the licensing authority to do so. He must also provide the mark holder with a sample of the repacked product, if so requested. As to how much notice he must give of his intention to import repacked goods, the Court held that it was for the national court to determine whether the mark holder had been given adequate time to react to the proposed imports, though 15 working days was likely to constitute a reasonable time when notification was accompanied by a sample of the product.

Repackaging: recent case law.   The Court of Justice has subsequently elaborated   **9.039**
this approach in the light of Article 7 of Directive 89/104,[130] which now comprehensively regulates the question of exhaustion of trade mark rights within the Community, and has developed detailed rules as to the circumstances in which 'repackaging' is permitted.[131] In *Boehringer*,[132] the Court of Justice considered a number of questions referred by the English court. The Court of Justice held that repackaging the product is, of itself, an interference with the specific subject-matter of the trade mark and the trade mark holder does not have to show that the repacking has any effect either on the goods or on its reputation. The trade mark owner can exercise its right to stop repackaging unless it is 'objectively necessary' to enable the parallel imported product to be marketed effectively in the importing territory. Repackaging will be objectively necessary in this regard where, for example, national rules or practices relating to packaging prevent the

---

[128]   ibid, paras 10–14. See also *Bayer Dental*, OJ 1990 L351/46, [1992] 4 CMLR 61, where a contractual prohibition on the opening of packages of the seller that bore a registered trade mark, for the purposes of resale to third parties, was found to infringe Art 81(1). The Commission considered that such a provision ran counter to the ruling in *Hoffmann-La Roche v Centrafarm*.

[129]   Case C-143/00 *Boehringer Ingelheim* [2002] ECR I-3759, [2003] Ch 27, [2002] 2 CMLR 623, [2002] All ER (EC) 581.

[130]   See para 9.031, above.

[131]   See Case 1/81 *Pfizer v Eurim-Pharm* [1981] ECR 2913, [1982] 1 CMLR 406; Cases C-427/93, etc, *Bristol-Myers Squibb v Paranova* [1996] ECR I-3457, [1997] 1 CMLR 1151; Cases C-71/94, etc, *Eurim-Pharm v Beiersdorf* [1996] ECR I-3603, [1997] 1 CMLR 1222; Case C-232/94 *Pharma v Rhône-Poulenc* [1996] ECR I-3671; Case C-349/95 *Fritz Loendersloot v George Ballantine* [1997] ECR I-6227, [1998] 1 CMLR 1015; Case C-352/95 *Phytheron International v Bourdon* [1997] ECR I-1729, [1997] 3 CMLR 199.

[132]   Case C-143/00 *Boehringer Ingelheim* (n 129, above).

products being placed on the market in the State of importation in their original packaging, or where sickness insurance rules make reimbursement of medical expenses depend on a certain packaging, or where well-established medical pre-scription practices are based on standard sizes recommended by professional groups and sickness insurance institutions. It is not enough merely that the repack-aging gives the importer a commercial advantage and it is not necessary to show a deliberate intention by the trade mark owner to partition markets.[133] The English High Court has referred further questions to the Court of Justice seeking to clarify aspects of the guidance handed down by the Court in its first judgment.[134]

9.040   **Repackaging: consumer preferences.**   Sometimes the parallel importer's wish to repack the product arises not from national rules or practices but from consumer preferences. In *Merck, Sharp & Dohme*,[135] the parallel importer claimed that it was necessary to repack the product, rather than simply put stickers on the existing packaging, 'because relabelled foreign packs engender reactions of mistrust and rejection from both pharmacists and consumers'. The Court held that the trade mark holder's attempt to prohibit the repackaging amounted to a disguised restriction on trade only if the suspicion of over-stickered product was so strong as effectively to preclude the parallel importer's ability to market the goods. Considerable suspicion was not enough: replacement packaging of pharmaceutical products is objectively necessary within the meaning of the Court's case law only if, without it, 'effective access to the market concerned, or to a substantial part of that market, must be considered to be hindered as the result of strong resistance from a significant proportion of consumers to relabelled phar-maceutical products'.[136] It was for the national court to decide whether this was the case in relation to this particular product.

9.041   **Repackaging: different trade marks.**   In *Centrafarm v American Home Products*,[137] the trade mark owner sold the same tablets under the names 'Serenid D' in the United Kingdom and 'Seresta' in the Netherlands. The composition of the tablets was the same but the taste was different. Centrafarm purchased 'Serenid D' tablets

---

[133] See, eg *Bristol- Myers Squibb v Paranova*, above, paras 52–57; and Case C-379/97 *Pharmacia & Upjohn v Paranova* [1999] ECR I-6927, [2000] 1 CMLR 51.

[134] Case C-348/04 *Boehringer Ingelheim II* [2007] 2 CMLR 1445. Note the robust view exp-ressed by AG Sharpston: 'It seems to me that after 30 years of case-law on the repackaging of phar-maceutical products it should be possible to distil sufficient principles to enable national courts to apply the law to the constantly replayed litigation between manufacturers and parallel importers. . . . . Every judge knows that ingenious lawyers can always find a reason why a given proposition does or does not apply to their client's situation. It should not however in my view be for the Court of Justice to adjudicate on such detail for evermore' Opinion of 6 April 2006, para 3.

[135] Case C-443/99 *Merck, Sharp & Dohme v Paranova* [2002] ECR I-3703, [2003] Ch 27, [2002] All ER (EC) 581, 627. See also *Boehringer Ingelheim* (n 129, above).

[136] *Merck, Sharp & Dohme v Paranova*, above, para 33.

[137] Case 3/78 *Centrafarm v American Home Products* [1978] ECR 1823, [1979] 1 CMLR 326.

in the United Kingdom and repacked them and sold them as 'Seresta' tablets in the Netherlands. The Court of Justice held that Article 30 did not preclude the trade mark owner from suing for infringement of the 'Seresta' mark, which had been affixed in the Netherlands without his consent. The Court, however, indicated that if there was evidence that the trade mark owner was using two different marks for the purpose of artificially partitioning the common market, the enforcement of his trade mark rights would amount to a 'disguised restriction on trade between Member States' within the meaning of the second sentence of Article 30. In the later case of *Pharmacia & Upjohn v Paranova*,[138] where Upjohn marketed tablets under the name 'Dalacin' in Denmark, 'Dalacine' in France and 'Dalacin-C' in Greece, a parallel importer obtained the products in France and Greece and resold them in Denmark repackaged as 'Dalacin'. The Court of Justice held that this was permissible (i) if there was in fact an artificial partitioning of the market, the subjective intention of the proprietor of the mark being an irrelevant consideration; (ii) the repackaging was 'objectively necessary' for the products to be sold in the Member State of importation (thus, if the importer was merely gaining a commercial advantage that would be insufficient); and (iii) the repackaging did not impair or change the quality of the product.

Marketing in a manner that may affect reputation. Apart from the repackaging cases, there may be other circumstances in which a proprietor may oppose the further sale of goods already marketed, in reliance on Article 7(2) of Directive 89/104, for example if the goods are advertised in a manner which could damage the reputation of the trade mark. The scope of this exception seems to be relatively narrow.[139] The Court of Justice has stated that an undertaking which uses the mark either to advertise the sale of second hand marked goods or to advertise that it specialises in repairing and maintaining the marked goods must act fairly in relation to the legitimate interests of the trade mark owner and avoid adversely affecting the value of the trade mark by taking unfair advantage of the distinctive character or repute of the goods.[140] In its Communication on parallel imports of medicinal products,[141] the Commission notes that the public is particularly demanding as to the quality and integrity of pharmaceutical products and defective, poor quality or untidy packaging could damage the trade mark's reputation, particularly where the product is sold directly to patients rather than to hospitals.

9.042

---

[138] Case C-379/97 *Pharmacia & Upjohn v Paranova* (n 133, above). Note also *CHEETAH Trade Mark* [1993] FSR 263 (English High Court, ChD).

[139] See Case C-337/95 *Parfums Christian Dior v Evora* [1997] ECR I-6013, [1998] 1 CMLR 737 (marketing of luxury goods in advertisements by cut-price retailer). Case 58/80 *Dansk Supermarked v Imerco* [1981] ECR 181, [1981] 3 CMLR 590 (re-importation into Denmark of reject products) would presumably now be decided under Art 7(2) of the Directive.

[140] Case C-63/97 *BMW v Deenik* [1999] ECR I-905, [1999] 1 CMLR 1099.

[141] See n 94, above.

9.043 **Trade marked goods from third countries.** In *EMI v CBS*,[142] the Court of Justice held that Articles 28 and 30 did not preclude a trade mark infringement action against goods imported into the Community from third countries. In that case the 'Columbia' trade mark for gramophone records had, prior to 1917, belonged in both the United States and Europe to the same undertaking. By a series of transactions, the mark had become vested in CBS as regards the United States and EMI as regards all of the Member States of the Community. By the time of the action, there was no relevant connection between CBS and EMI. CBS sought to import records into the Community bearing the Columbia mark and EMI began proceedings for trade mark infringement in the United Kingdom, Denmark and Germany. Upon references from courts in each of those countries, the Court of Justice held that:

> '. . . the exercise of a trade mark right in order to prevent the marketing of products coming from a third country under an identical mark, even if this constitutes a mea-sure having an effect equivalent to a quantitative restriction, does not affect the free movement of goods between Member States and thus does not come under the prohibitions set out in Article [28] *et seq* of the Treaty.'[143]

The Court also held that nothing in the Treaty prevents the proprietor of a mark in all the Member States exercising his rights to stop the owner of the mark outside the Community manufacturing the products within the Community and then marketing the products under that mark.[144] However, if goods originating from outside the Community have been placed on the market under a trade mark in one Member State, the doctrine of exhaustion of rights prevents the owner of the mark, or an undertaking economically linked to the owner, from exercising his trade mark right to prevent importation into another Member State.[145]

9.044 **No international exhaustion: *Silhouette*.** In *Silhouette*,[146] the Austrian manu-facturer of top quality fashion spectacles sued for trade mark infringement to pre-vent the re-importation into Austria by a low price retailer of some out-of-fashion 'Silhouette' frames that Silhouette had sold cheaply in Bulgaria. On a reference for a preliminary ruling, the Court of Justice upheld Silhouette's arguments that it had not exhausted its right to sue for infringement since the frames in question had not been previously marketed within the Community, and that Article 7 of

---

[142] Case 51/75 *EMI v CBS* [1976] ECR 811, [1976] 2 CMLR 235.
[143] ibid, para 10.
[144] ibid, para 22.
[145] *Phytheron International v Bourdon* (n 131, above).
[146] C-355/96 *Silhouette International v Hartlauer* [1998] ECR I-4799, [1998] 2 CMLR 953. But cf the decision of the EFTA Court in Case E-2/97 *Mag Instrument v California Trading Company* [1997] Rep EFTA Ct 127, [1998] 1 CMLR 331. English law prior to the introduction of Dir 89/104 (n 101, above) permitted international exhaustion: *Revlon Inc v Cripps & Lee Ltd* [1980] FSR 85 (CA), but cf *Colgate-Palmolive Ltd. v Markwell Finance Ltd* [1989] RPC 497 (CA).

Directive 89/104 provided for exhaustion only in relation to goods put on the market in the Community under that trade mark by the proprietor or with his consent. The Court essentially confirmed this conclusion in *Sebago*,[147] which concerned the importation into Belgium by a low-price retailer of 'Sebago' shoes obtained in El Salvador, the mark 'Sebago' being protected by Benelux trade marks. The Court of Justice again held that the Directive does not permit the doctrine of exhaustion of rights to apply in respect of imports from non-member countries to which the proprietor of the trade mark has not consented.[148] Moreover, it is only if that consent is forthcoming in relation to the specific batch of products which have been put on the market in the territory concerned that the doctrine of exhaustion of rights could apply.

Consent: express or implied.   Article 7(1) provides that the trade mark proprie-   **9.045**
tor's rights are exhausted where the goods have been placed on the market in the Community either by him or with his consent. In *Zino Davidoff and Levi Strauss*, the Court of Justice considered a series of questions referred by the English court arising out of two sets of proceedings.[149] The first set of proceedings concerned the import by parallel traders into the United Kingdom of Davidoff products which had been produced by Davidoff in the EEA but then exported to Singapore pursuant to a contract which forbade their export into the EEA. The second set of proceedings concerned the import into the United Kingdom of Levi jeans which had been manufactured by Levi's licensees outside the EEA. The Court of Justice clarified the circumstances in which the mark owner is to be treated as having consented to the products being placed on the market in the EEA. First the Court held that the concept of consent used in Article 7 of the Directive was a Community law concept rather than a matter of national law.[150] Secondly the Court set a high threshold for the obtaining of consent:

> 'In view of its serious effect in extinguishing the exclusive rights of the proprietors of the trade marks in issue in the main proceedings (rights which enable them to control the initial marketing in the EEA), consent must be so expressed that an intention to renounce those rights is unequivocally demonstrated.
>
> Such intention will normally be gathered from an express statement of consent. Nevertheless, it is conceivable that consent may, in some cases, be inferred from facts and circumstances prior to, simultaneous with or subsequent to the placing of the

---

[147] Case C-173/98 *Sebago* [1999] ECR I-4103, [1999] 2 CMLR 1317; *Zino Davidoff and Levi Strauss*, discussed below.

[148] For a similar ruling in relation to the equivalent provision for copyright items see Case C-479/04 *Laserdisken v Kulturministeriet* [2006] ECR I-8089, [2007] 1 CMLR 187, [2007] All ER (EC) 549.

[149] Cases C-414/99, etc, *Zino Davidoff and Levi Strauss* [2001] ECR I-8691, [2002] Ch 109, [2002] 1 CMLR 1, [2002] All ER (EC) 55.

[150] *Zino Davidoff*, above, paras 37–43.

goods on the market outside the EEA which, in the view of the national court, unequivocally demonstrate that the proprietor has renounced his rights.'[151]

The Court further held that it is irrelevant that the importers of the goods were
not aware that the proprietor objected to their being placed on the market in the
EEA and were not subject, in the contract under which they bought the goods
outside the EEA, to any contractual reservations regarding onward sale.

9.046 **Exhaustion of rights: the burden of proof.** In *Zino Davidoff*, the Court of
Justice went on to consider how consent could be established and which party
bears the burden of proof. The Court held that: (i) it is for the trader alleging
consent to prove it and not for the trade mark proprietor to demonstrate its
absence; (ii) consent cannot be inferred from the 'mere silence' of the proprietor
or from the fact that the goods do not carry a warning that it is prohibited to
place them on the market in the EEA; and (iii) consent cannot be inferred from
the fact that the proprietor sold the goods without imposing a contractual reservation withholding the right to market the goods in the EEA. However, the Court
has subsequently qualified what was said in *Zino Davidoff* about the burden of
proof. In *Van Doren + Q v Lifestyle Sports*[152] the issue between the mark owner
and the importer was not whether the mark owner had consented to the placing
of the goods on the market in the EEA but whether the goods had in fact been
placed on the market inside or only outside the EEA. The Court confirmed that
a national rule of evidence whereby the conditions for exhaustion of the right
must be proved by the third party who relies on it as a defence to an action for
infringement is consistent with Community law. But such a rule must be qualified in a situation where it risks enabling the trade mark owner to partition
national markets. This might arise where the trade mark owner distributes his
goods in the EEA through a network of exclusive distributors and where the
dealer seeking to rely on the defence would find it difficult to compel his own
suppliers to disclose to him how they came by the goods without jeopardising
the continuation of supplies.

---

[151] ibid, paras 45 and 46. For the subsequent English proceedings, see *Levi Strauss & Co v
Tesco Stores Ltd* [2002] ECHC 1625 (Ch), [2002] 3 CMLR 281, [2002] EuLR 610. For analysis
of the *Zino Davidoff* decision by the English Court of Appeal in a case finding implied consent on
the facts, see *Mastercigars Direct Ltd v Hunters & Frankau Ltd* [2007] EWCA Civ 176, [2007] RPC
24; cf *Roche Products Ltd v Kent Pharmaceuticals Ltd* [2006] EWCA Civ 1775, [2007] 93 BMLR 123
(the presence of a CE mark on the packaging of a product that was being marketed in the EEA did
not amount to an unequivocal demonstration of consent by a trade mark proprietor to that product being so marketed). See also *Kabushiki Kaisha Sony Computer Entertainment Inc v Nuplayer
Ltd* [2005] EWHC 1522 (Ch), [2006] FSR 9 (the fact that the goods were sold over the internet,
such that the marks were not visible at the point of sale, did not mean that the marks were not
affixed to the goods).
[152] Case C-244/00 *Van Doren + Q* [2003] ECR I-3051, [2003] 2 CMLR 203, [2004] All ER
(EC) 912.

Consent: assignment on the sale of a business.   Another way in which a propri-   **9.047**
etor might give his consent to the marketing of the goods in the Community
is by licensing or assigning the right to do so. In the *Ideal Standard* case, the Court
of Justice held that the necessary 'consent' is not established by the voluntary
assignment of a trade mark.[153] That case concerned the trade mark 'Ideal Standard'
as applied to heating equipment. The mark was originally held in Germany
and France by the respective subsidiaries of the American Standard group. In
1984, the French subsidiary sold its heating equipment business together with
the trade mark for that sector to an unrelated company which later assigned it
to the parent of IHT. When IHT started marketing in Germany heating equipment bearing the 'Ideal Standard' mark, the German subsidiary, which still held
the mark and applied it to sanitary equipment in Germany, sued IHT for infringement of its German mark. On a reference for a preliminary ruling, the Court of
Justice emphasised that national trade marks were not only territorial in nature,
but independent of each other, with the consequence that it must be possible to
assign the mark for one territory without at the same time assigning it for other
territories. The Court thus distinguished between the case where the imported
goods were produced by an assignee which has no economic link with the owner
of the mark in the importing State and the case where the goods were marketed
by a licensee, distributor or other affiliate of the owner.[154] A contract of assignment by itself, in the absence of any continuing economic link, does not give
the assignor any means of controlling the quality of the products marketed by
the assignee.[155] The consent inherent in the assignment is not the consent required
for the application of the doctrine of exhaustion of rights.[156] For the latter, the
owner of the right in the importing State must, directly or indirectly, be able to
determine the products to which the trade mark is affixed in the exporting State
and to control their quality. According to the Court, the considerations set out

---

[153] Case C-9/93 *IHT Internationale Heiztechnik v Ideal Standard* [1994] ECR I-2789, [1994]
3 CMLR 857.

[154] ibid, paras 40 *et seq.*

[155] ibid, paras 38, 41. See also *Doncaster Pharmaceuticals Group v Bolton Pharmaceutical Co*
[2006] EWCA Civ 661, [2007] FSR 3, where the original owner of a trade mark for pharmaceutical
products had assigned its Spanish trade mark 'KALTEN' to a separate Spanish company, which took
over manufacture of the product in Spain. D imported the product from Spain and repackaged and
relabelled it for sale in the United Kingdom under the KALTEN mark. The original owner then
assigned its UK trade mark KALTEN to B, which began to manufacture and sell the product in the
United Kingdom and sued D for trade mark infringement. The English Court of Appeal, setting
aside summary judgment in favour of B, held that since before the assignments the parallel imports
could not have been prevented because the Spanish rights owner would have exhausted his rights
and the assignment had the potential effect of putting B in a stronger position than the original
owner in relation to the enforcement of the UK trade mark against D, a proper investigation was
required as to whether there were economic links between the varous national proprietors in different Member States to whom the original owner had chosen to divest himself of the trade mark.

[156] ibid, para 43.

in *Hag II* were equally relevant to the case of a voluntary assignment.[157] Accordingly, Ideal Standard Germany succeeded in its infringement action against IHT.

9.048 **Enforcement of trade mark where there is no exhaustion.**   If there is no question of the relevant trade mark rights being exhausted, they may be enforced under national law in the ordinary way. For example, in *Terrapin v Terranova*[158] the registered owners in Germany of the 'Terranova' mark sought to prevent the importation into the Federal Republic from the United Kingdom of certain goods sold under the 'Terrapin' mark. The latter was a lawful mark in the United Kingdom under which the goods could lawfully have been sold. However, the German Federal Supreme Court considered that there was risk of confusion and that sale of the 'Terrapin' marked goods would constitute infringement under German law. No connection existed between the Terrapin and Terranova companies and the marks had been acquired separately and independently. In these circumstances, on a reference from the German court, the Court of Justice held that the rules on the free movement of goods did not preclude Terranova from exercising its rights under national law to prohibit importation of the Terrapin marked goods, otherwise 'the specific objective of industrial and commercial property rights would be undermined'.[159] The Court declined the Commission's request to lay down common rules for deciding what amounted to 'confusion' under the national laws on trade marks and trade names.[160] Similarly, in *Deutsche Renault*,[161] the Court of Justice held that the German trade mark law which allowed Audi to register the word 'Quattro' as a trade mark, and to oppose the use by Renault in Germany of the word 'Quadra', was compatible with Article 28. The question whether any confusion exists is a matter of national law and not Community law.[162] It follows from these decisions that where a confusingly similar mark is owned independently in different Member States, without any connection between the owners, each owner can exercise his right in accordance with the principles of national law to prohibit importation of the goods of the other under the marks.

9.049 **Discriminatory or disguised restriction.**   However, even if there is no question of marketing with the owner's consent, the Court of Justice also stated in *Terrapin v Terranova* that the national judge should:

> '. . . enquire further in the context of [the second sentence of Article 30 of the Treaty] whether the exercise in a particular case of industrial and commercial property rights

---

[157] ibid, paras 42–48.
[158] Case 119/75 *Terrapin v Terranova* [1976] ECR 1039, [1976] 2 CMLR 482.
[159] ibid, para 7. See also *EMI v CBS* (n 142, above) para 23.
[160] *Terrapin v Terranova* (n 158, above) at p 1057 and para 4. See also *per* AG Jacobs in *Hag II* (n 112, above) Opinion parts X–XIII, where he discusses and dismisses the possibility that *Terrapin v Terranova*, rather than *Hag I*, was wrongly decided.
[161] C-317/91 *Deutsche Renault v Audi* [1993] ECR I-6227, [1995] 1 CMLR 461.
[162] ibid, paras 31–32.

may or may not constitute a means of arbitrary discrimination or a disguised restriction on trade between Member States. It is for the national judge in this respect to ascertain in particular whether the rights in question are in fact exercised by the proprietor with the same strictness whatever the national origin of any possible infringer.'[163]

Other possible examples of arbitrary discrimination or disguised restriction have been identified in the repackaging cases already discussed.[164]

Passing-off and unfair competition.　Although rights arising under the laws **9.050** of 'passing-off' and similar concepts are probably not, strictly speaking, 'industrial or commercial property rights' within the meaning of Article 30, the rules on the free movement of goods do not preclude an action for passing-off brought with a view to preventing the importation of imitation goods placed on the market by third parties having no connection with the claimants.[165] Thus in *Industrie Diensten Groep v Beele*,[166] IDG imported into the Netherlands and sold cable ducts originating in Germany which were imitations of the cable ducts which Beele sold in the Netherlands and which were likely to cause confusion to consumers. The Court of Justice held that national laws prohibiting the imitation of another trader's product fell within the concept of 'mandatory requirements for the protection of consumers and the fairness of commercial transactions' and were therefore permitted.

(d) Copyright and similar rights

The Community's approach to copyright.　The case law of the Court of Justice **9.051** has emphasised the common characteristics that copyright and similar rights share with other forms of intellectual property. However, copyright differs from other rights in that the exploitation of copyright or kindred rights may take various forms, for example the sale of the copyright work as goods, or the earning of royalties on the performance of the work, or the renting out of the work in the form of a video or compact disc. In general terms, Community law recognises all these forms of protection. In addition, some harmonisation has taken place in respect of national laws on copyright, notably in respect of the term of copyright, rental and lending rights, rights to satellite broadcasting and cable retransmission,

---

[163]　*Terrapin v Terranova* (n 158, above) para 4.

[164]　See paras 9.037 *et seq*, above.

[165]　For the English law of passing off and the effect of the EC free movement rules, see generally Wadlow, *The Law of Passing Off* (3rd edn, 2004), esp paras 9-33–9-35. In general 'exhaustion of rights' does not arise in respect of the simple resale in one territory of goods previously sold in another territory under a trade name that is not a registered trade mark, in the absence of any deception as to the origin of the goods or change in the packaging, etc.

[166]　Case 6/81 *Industrie Diensten Groep v Beele* [1982] ECR 707, [1982] 3 CMLR 102.

and the protection of computer software, semiconductor topographies and databases.[167]

9.052 **The specific subject-matter of the copyright.**   In the *Phil Collins* case,[168] the Court of Justice stated that the specific subject-matter of copyright was to ensure the protection of the moral and economic rights of the holders. As far as moral rights are concerned, the right is 'to object to any distortion, mutilation or other modification of a work which would be prejudicial to their honour or reputation'. As far as economic rights are concerned, the right is 'to exploit commercially the marketing of the protected work, particularly in the form of licences granted for the payment of royalties'. The content of many aspects of copyright has now been harmonised in Directive 2001/29[169] and the Court of Justice has held that the right of the copyright holder to the first placing of the goods on the market in the EEA cannot be removed by national legislation.[170]

9.053 **Copyright and free movement.**   Copyright applies to a diverse range of rights relating to a number of economic sectors. It is therefore convenient to consider sound recordings separately from films and DVDs and then designs. There are no Court of Justice decisions dealing directly with the rules on free movement in relation to books. It seems likely that the rules on free movement under Articles 28–30 developed in relation to sound recordings apply equally to literary, dramatic, musical and artistic works when supplied in the form of goods.[171] Copyright licensing is discussed in the final Section of this Chapter.

9.054 **Summary of rules on free movement of copyright items.**   The position regarding to the application of the rules of free movement to copyright can be summarised as follows:

(1) Subject to (2) below, the principles of 'specific subject-matter' and 'exhaustion of rights' apply to goods covered by copyright as they do to patent and trade mark rights.[172]

(2) Public performance rights in copyright works are not generally affected by the rules on the free movement of goods.[173]

---

[167] See n 5, above.

[168] Cases C-92 & 326/92 *Phil Collins v Imrat* [1993] ECR I-1985, [1993] 3 CMLR 773, para 20.

[169] Dir 2001/29, OJ 2001 L167/10.

[170] Case C-479/04 *Laserdisken v Kulturministeriet* [2006] ECR I-8089, [2007] 1 CMLR 187, [2007] All ER (EC) 549.

[171] The Commission expressed that view in relation to books in *Ernest Benn, Ninth Report on Competition Policy* (1979), point 119, and it is doubtful whether the issues are affected by the question of resale price maintenance on books, now abandoned in the United Kingdom. As regards artistic works, note the Directive introducing the author's right to a royalty ('*droit de suite*') on the occasion of the resale of an original work of art: Dir 2001/84, OJ 2001 L272/32.

[172] Paras 9.055 *et seq*, below.

[173] Paras 9.060 *et seq*, below.

(3) Rental rights in Member State A are not affected by the fact that copies of the work in question have been imported into Member State A from Member State B where they are available for sale or rental.[174]

(4) The operation of copyright under national law must not constitute a means of arbitrary discrimination or a disguised measure for restricting trade between the Member States.[175]

(5) The rules on free movement of goods do not apply to the importation of copyright goods into the Community from third countries.[176]

(6) Subject to the foregoing and in the absence of harmonising measures at the Community level, it remains for national legislatures to specify the conditions and rules for protection of copyright.[177]

(i) Sound recordings

Exhaustion of rights: *Deutsche Grammophon*. *Deutsche Grammophon*,[178] **9.055** the first case to elucidate the principle of exhaustion of rights, applied that principle to sound recordings. Deutsche Grammophon ('DG') manufactured and sold records in Germany under the Polydor label. Metro, a supplier specialising in selling records at low prices, acquired Polydor records that had originally been sold in France by DG's French subsidiary, Polydor SA. When Metro sought to resell those records in Germany at a price well below that of other DG retailers, DG sought an injunction against Metro to prevent the records being sold in breach of the statutory protection accorded to the manufacture of sound recordings. On a reference from the German court, the Court of Justice stressed that Article 30 only permits derogations from the principle of free movement to the extent that such derogations are needed to safeguard the specific subject-matter of the copyright. The Court went on to hold:

> 'If a right related to copyright is relied upon to prevent the marketing in a Member State of products distributed by the holder of the right or with his consent on the territory of another Member State on the sole ground that such distribution did not take place on the national territory, such a prohibition, which would legitimise the isolation of national markets, would be repugnant to the essential purpose of the Treaty, which is to unite national markets into a single market.'[179]

---

174 Para 9.063, below.
175 See by analogy para 9.049, above. For the position in English law, see ss 22 and 27 of the Copyright, Designs and Patents Act 1988, especially s 27(5) which states that the right to prohibit the import of 'infringing copies' does not apply to any article which may be lawfully imported into the United Kingdom by virtue of any enforceable Community right.
176 Para 9.059, below.
177 Para 9.065, below.
178 Case 78/70 *Deutsche Grammophon v Metro* [1971] ECR 487, [1971] CMLR 631.
179 ibid, para 12.

It follows that a manufacturer of sound recordings cannot exercise his exclusive right to distribute the protected products in such a way as to prohibit the sale in one Member State of products which had been placed on the market by him or with his consent in another Member State.

9.056 **National disparities: additional royalties and other related rights.**   In *Musik-Vertrieb Membran v GEMA*,[180] the Court of Justice held that the rules on free movement of goods prevented GEMA, a copyright management society established in Germany, from levying royalties on records and cassettes imported into Germany which had previously been marketed in the United Kingdom by the copyright owner or with his consent. In that case, a statutorily fixed royalty of 6.25 per cent had already been paid in the United Kingdom.[181] The relevant German provisions required an 8 per cent royalty. GEMA sought to levy the difference, but it was held that such an additional levy could not be justified under Article 30. The Court held that national legislation could not permit a copyright collecting society to charge a levy on products imported from another Member State where those products had been put into circulation by or with the consent of the copyright owner.[182]

9.057 **Performing rights.**   The *GEMA* case contrasts with the Court of Justice's rulings in cases relating to performing rights in sound recordings,[183] where the copyright owner was held to be entitled to rely on his rights under national law, which were different and at least arguably more extensive than his rights under the national law of the country of origin of the imported goods in question. Thus in *Basset v SACEM*,[184] the proprietor of a French discotheque challenged the right of SACEM, the French collecting society, to levy a 'supplementary mechanical reproduction fee' in addition to the ordinary performance fees charged in France as in other Member States. The levy in France was based on the distinction between private and public use of copyright material: only materials used in public were liable for the additional 'mechanical reproduction fee'. The Court of

---

[180] Cases 55 & 57/80 *Musik-Vertrieb Membran v GEMA* [1981] ECR 147, [1981] 2 CMLR 44.

[181] GEMA subsequently abandoned the practice, Press Release IP/85/24 (6 February 1985), [1985] 2 CMLR 1. The statutory UK rate was abolished by the Copyright, Designs and Patents Act 1988 and the rate was subsequently fixed by the Copyright Tribunal which rejected the publishers' argument that the UK rate should be increased to the rate said to be prevailing in the rest of Europe: CT7/90 Decn of 12 March 1992.

[182] *Musik-Vertrieb Membran v GEMA* (n 180, above) para 18.

[183] Case 402/85 *Basset v SACEM* [1987] ECR 1747, [1987] 3 CMLR 173; Case 395/87 *Ministère Public v Tournier* [1989] ECR 2521, [1991] 4 CMLR 248; and Cases 110 & 241–242/88 *Lucazeau v SACEM* [1989] ECR 2811, [1991] 4 CMLR 248, where the ECJ applied the same reasoning in relation to the rules on free movement of both goods and of services, expressly distinguishing between cases where distribution of a copyright article was effected by distribution of a physical object and where it was effected by 'performance' as with film exhibition and the public playing of sound recordings: para 12 of the judgment in *Tournier*.

[184] Case 402/85 *Basset v SACEM* [1987] ECR 1747, [1987] 3 CMLR 173.

Justice considered that the French system did not differ in substance from that prevailing in other Member States where only a performing rights fee was charged, and analysed the fee as being 'part of the payment for the author's rights over the public performance of a recorded musical work'.[185] Despite the different mechanism applied in France, the Court held that this represented 'a normal exploitation of copyright' which did not fall within the scope of Article 28, even if it were to be capable of having a restrictive effect on imports.[186]

Rental rights. In 1992 the Council adopted Directive 92/100 which required **9.058** Member States to establish a right to authorise and prohibit the rental and lending of copyright works.[187] The Court of Justice has upheld the exclusive rental right of the producer of compact discs established under Directive 92/100 to obtain a royalty on the rental of the goods in a particular Member State irrespective of whether the discs originate in another Member State.[188]

Goods imported from third countries. *Polydor v Harlequin Record Shops*[189] **9.059** establishes that the rules on the free movement of goods do not apply to the importation of copyright goods into the Community. In that case, a third party sought to re-import from Portugal (then outside the Community) sound recordings made by the Portuguese licensee of the UK copyright owner. The defendant relied on various provisions of the EFTA Treaty between the Community and Portugal which were similar in wording to Articles 28 and 30, but the Court of Justice held that those provisions did not give rise to a defence where there was no artificial partitioning of markets within the Community.

(ii) Films and DVDs

The public showing of films in cinemas. The position of cinema films differs **9.060** from that of sound recordings or literary and similar works, since in the ordinary way (aside from video cassette, DVD and digital download) such films are not in free circulation but are shown to audiences in cinemas. The distributor of the film usually has an exclusive licence for the territory in question and he sub-licences the right to exhibit the film in the particular cinema where it is showing.

---

185 *Basset v SACEM,* above, para 15.

186 ibid, para 16. AG Lenz compared the situation to that prevailing in the *Coditel (No. 1)* case in relation to film distribution as against the situation in the *GEMA* case: Opinion at 1758–1759 (ECR) 179–180 (CMLR); see para 9.061, below for discussion of *Coditel (No. 1)*.

187 Dir 92/100, OJ 1992 L346/61.

188 Case C-200/96 *Metronome Musik* [1998] ECR I-1953, [1998] 3 CMLR 919; Case C-61/97 *FDV Laserdisken* [1998] ECR I-5171, [1999] 1 CMLR 1297. See also para 9.063, below, as regards video rentals.

189 Case 270/80 *Polydor v Harlequin Record Shops* [1982] ECR 329, [1982] 1 CMLR 677. See also para 9.044, above, and *Laserdisken v Kulturministeriet* (n 170, above).

The more appropriate analysis is thus the supply of services, which are governed by Articles 49 *et seq* of the Treaty, rather than the supply of goods.

9.061 **The right to exhibit protected: *Coditel (No. 1)*.** In *Coditel (No. 1)*[190] the right to exhibit the film 'Le Boucher' in cinemas in Belgium had been licensed to the plaintiffs. In Germany the rights were assigned to a television company for showing on German television. The film was shown by German television, picked up by three Belgian rediffusion companies and distributed by cable to their subscribers in Belgium. The plaintiffs sought to restrain distribution of the film by cable in Belgium. The Court of Justice was asked to rule whether the Treaty, notably Article 49, prevented the plaintiffs from asserting their rights so as to prevent redistribution by cable in Belgium of the film already broadcast in Germany. The Court observed that a film is something which may be infinitely repeated and in this respect the problems were different from those involving literary or artistic works in free circulation. The owner of the copyright in a film and his assignees therefore have a legitimate interest in calculating the fees due in respect of the authorisation to exhibit the film on the basis of the actual or probable number of performances and in authorising a television broadcast of the film only after a limited period of time. The Court held that the right to require a fee for any showing of the film derived from the 'essential function' of the copyright in the film. Moreover, that right could not be properly protected unless the copyright owner could regulate the showing of the film on television. In the circumstances, the Court held that Article 49 of the Treaty did not prevent the plaintiffs from invoking their rights under national law against the cable television companies.[191]

9.062 **Sales of videocassettes and DVDs.** Videocassettes and DVDs raise different considerations from cinema films, since videocassettes and DVDs, like sound recordings, are goods whose free movement within the Community is guaranteed by Articles 28 and 30.[192] Directive 2001/29 harmonising certain aspects of copyright requires Member States to confer on the owner the exclusive right to place copyright items on the market within the EEA for the first time. The Directive does not leave it open to Member States to adopt a wider rule of exhaustion of rights.[193] In addition, the free movement of videocassettes and DVDs is complicated by the development of a significant market in the rental of such cassettes and discs.

---

[190] Case 62/79 *Coditel v Ciné-Vog Films (No. 1)* [1980] ECR 881, [1981] 2 CMLR 362.

[191] ibid, paras 9–19. See also Case 262/81 *Coditel v Ciné-Vog Films (No. 2)* [1982] ECR 3381, [1983] 1 CMLR 49, where the ECJ held that an exclusive licence to exhibit a cinema film did not necessarily infringe Art 81(1) either: para 9.181, below.

[192] See Cases 60 & 61/84 *Cinéthèque v Fédération Nationale des Cinémas Français* [1985] ECR 2605, [1986] 1 CMLR 365, paras 10–11.

[193] *Laserdisken v Kulturministeriet* (n 170, above).

Video rentals: *Warner.* The issues raised by video rentals (which would now **9.063** include DVD rentals) were considered in *Warner Bros v Christiansen*.[194] Warner were the owners of the copyright in the James Bond film 'Never Say Never Again', and had granted another company, Metronome, the video lending rights in Denmark. Mr Christiansen, the owner of a video rental business in Denmark, bought a cassette of the film in London, where the video had been marketed with the consent of Warner, with a view to renting it out in Denmark. Warner and Metronome sought an injunction in Denmark to restrain him from doing so. Video lending rights enjoyed protection in Denmark but not, at that time, in the United Kingdom,[195] and the Court of Justice was asked to rule on the legality of an injunction under Community law. The Court held that Warner and Metronome could enforce their Danish law rights. The case was distinguishable from the *GEMA* case[196] on the grounds that the rental right did not enable the author to collect an additional fee on the actual importation of the goods, nor did it create any further obstacle to the import or resale of the video. On the other hand, because there was a potential indirect effect on imports, the Danish legislation fell within the scope of Article 28. In applying Article 30, the Court stressed that the Danish law did not discriminate against non-nationals and that the Community recognised two essential rights of the author, namely the exclusive right of performance and the exclusive right of reproduction.[197] There was a distinct market for the hiring-out of video recordings, which warranted protection by the Community to guarantee to makers of films a remuneration which reflects the number of occasions on which the videocassettes are actually hired out and which secures for them a satisfactory share of the rental market. The Court rejected the argument of the defendants that Warner had consented to the marketing of the cassettes on the UK market where rental rights were not recognised, and had thereby exhausted its rights:

> 'That objection cannot be upheld. It follows from the foregoing considerations that, where national legislation confers on authors a specific right to hire out video-cassettes, that right would be rendered worthless if its owner were not in a position to authorize the operations for doing so. It cannot therefore be accepted that the marketing by a film-maker of a video-cassette containing one of his works, in a Member State which does not provide specific protection for the right to hire it out, should have repercussions for the right conferred on that same film-maker by the legislation of another Member State to restrain, in that State, the hiring-out of that video-cassette.'[198]

---

[194] Case 158/86 *Warner Bros v Christiansen* [1988] ECR 2625, [1990] 3 CMLR 684.

[195] Although they do now: see s 18A(6) of the Copyright, Designs and Patents Act 1988 and Dir 92/100 (n 187, above).

[196] See para 9.056, above.

[197] *Warner Bros v Christiansen* (n 194, above) paras 12–13.

[198] ibid, para 18. See also *Metronome Musik* (n 188, above); *Laserdisken v Kulturministeriet*, ibid.

9.064 **Television broadcasts.** Television broadcasts are not in 'free circulation' in the same way as goods; they are affected, if at all, by the Treaty rules on services and by Directive 89/552 on 'Television without frontiers'.[199] It has been held that it is not contrary to the Treaty for a Member State to grant an exclusive right to transmit television signals, including advertisements.[200] Nor is it contrary to the Treaty to prohibit or regulate advertisements on television, even if that has the effect of preventing the retransmission in one Member State of advertisements originally transmitted on television in another Member State.[201] Further, *Coditel (No. 1)* itself shows that the retransmission by cable in one Member State of material televised in another Member State may be restrained by an action for the infringement of a copyright held in the State where retransmission takes place.[202]

(iii) Designs

9.065 **Designs.** In *Keurkoop v Nancy Kean Gifts,*[203] the Court of Justice held that the principle of exhaustion of rights applies to products protected by design rights. However, it was clear from *Keurkoop* that in the absence of any previous marketing in the Community by the owner or with his consent, and in the absence of any concertation to divide markets contrary to Article 81(1), the owner of a registered design may sue in the ordinary way to prevent the import of infringing products. Since that case there has been substantial Community harmonisation of national design laws with the adoption of Directive 98/71[204] and the creation of Community registered and unregistered designs.[205]

---

[199] Case 155/73 *Sacchi* [1974] ECR 409, [1974] 2 CMLR 177. Dir 89/552, OJ 1989 L298/23, entered into force on 3 October 1991. For the effect of Art 81 on arrangements for television broadcasts relating, eg to sporting events, see paras 9.183 *et seq,* below. For joint ventures in the audiovisual and media fields, see Chap 7, above.

[200] *Sacchi,* above; Case C-260/89 *ERT* [1991] ECR I-2925, [1994] 4 CMLR 540.

[201] Case 52/79 *Procureur du Roi v Debauve* [1980] ECR 833, [1981] 2 CMLR 362. See also Case C-412/93 *LeClerc-Siplec* [1995] ECR I-174, [1995] 3 CMLR 422; Case C-34/95 *Konsumentombudsmannen v De Agostini* [1997] ECR I-3843; Case C-6/98 *ARD v PRO Sieben Media* [1999] ECR I-7599, [1999] 3 CMLR 769.

[202] See para 9.061, above.

[203] Case 144/81 *Keurkoop v Nancy Kean Gifts* [1982] ECR 2853, [1983] 2 CMLR 47; Case 53/87 *CICRA v Renault* [1988] ECR 6039, [1990] 4 CMLR 265. In the United Kingdom, designs may be registered pursuant to the Registered Designs Act 1949, as amended, and may also be protected by copyright or design right under the Copyright, Designs and Patents Act 1988.

[204] Dir 98/71 on the legal protection of designs, OJ 1998 L289/28.

[205] Reg 6/2002 on Community Designs, OJ 2002 L3/1.

3. Articles 81 and 82 and the Exercise of Intellectual Property Rights

Plan of this Section. This Section deals briefly with the effect of Articles 81 and **9.066** 82 on infringement suits and closely related issues such as the refusal to grant a licence. The licensing of intellectual property rights is dealt with in Section 4, below.

Infringement suits under Article 81(1). Although intellectual property rights **9.067** do not as such fall within Article 81(1), the bringing of an infringement action may contravene Article 81(1) where the proceedings are brought as 'the object, the means or the consequence' of an agreement, notably if the action tends to the partitioning of the common market.[206] The principles were first laid down in *Consten and Grundig*, but for Article 81(1) to apply there must be some continuing connection between the parties[207] and some nexus between the agreement relied on and the infringement.[208] The circumstances in which Article 81(1) may be a defence to an infringement action before courts in the United Kingdom is considered more fully in Chapter 14, below.[209]

Consten and Grundig and later cases. In *Consten and Grundig*,[210] the facts of **9.068** which have already been set out, the absolute territorial protection enjoyed by Consten was reinforced by the assignment to Consten of the 'GINT' trade mark. When a third party obtained and imported Grundig products into France, Consten sued the third party for infringement in reliance on the French registration of the GINT trade mark. The Court of Justice held that the Commission had rightly ordered Consten to refrain from using the GINT trade mark to hinder parallel imports. The Court said:

'The injunction . . . to refrain from using rights under national trade mark law in order to set an obstacle in the way of parallel imports does not affect the grant of

---

[206] See, eg on patents: Case 24/67 *Parke, Davis v Probel* [1968] ECR 55, [1968] CMLR 47; Case 15/74 *Centrafarm v Sterling Drug* [1974] ECR 1147, [1974] 2 CMLR 480, paras 38–40; on trade marks: Case 51/75 *EMI v CBS* [1976] ECR 811, [1976] 2 CMLR 235, para 26; Case C-9/93 *IHT Internationale Heiztechnik v Ideal Standard* [1994] ECR I-2789, [1994] CMLR 857; on designs: *Keurkoop v Nancy Kean Gifts* (n 203, above) paras 24–28.

[207] *EMI v CBS* and *IHT Internationale Heiztechnik*, above.

[208] For cases in UK courts, see, eg *ICI v Berk Pharmaceuticals* [1981] 2 CMLR 91 (ChD); *British Leyland v Armstrong* [1984] 3 CMLR 102 (CA) and the later cases cited at paras 14.138 and 14.139, below. Art 81(1) does not prevent an exclusive licensee from enforcing his rights against an ordinary infringer selling spurious products, *Kalwar/Plast Control v Kabelmetal*, *XIIth Report on Competition Policy* (1982), point 87.

[209] Paras 14.136 *et seq*, below. For a review by the English Court of Appeal of the EC and English authorities, see *Sportswear v Stonestyle Ltd* [2006] EWCA Civ 380, [2006] UKCLR 893, [2006] EuLR 1014, [2006] FSR 11.

[210] Cases 56 & 58/64 *Consten and Grundig v Commission* [1966] ECR 299, [1966] CMLR 418: see at para 2.073, above. For a similar example, see Case 28/77 *Tepea v Commission* [1978] ECR 1391, [1978] 3 CMLR 392.

those rights but only limits their exercise to the extent necessary to give effect to the prohibition under Article 81(1).'[211]

Similarly in *Sirena*,[212] where the same trade mark had come into different hands in different Member States as a result of assignments many years before, the Court of Justice said that the exercise of trade mark rights comes within the Treaty where such exercise is 'the subject, the means or the result, of a restrictive practice.'[213] The exercise of patent rights[214] or rights in registered designs[215] to prevent parallel imports may also infringe Article 81(1). The same applies where several persons act in concert to obtain intellectual property rights in different Member States with the intention of partitioning the market.[216] Thus the exercise of such rights by, for example, a licensee to prevent parallel imports of goods already marketed in the Community would probably infringe Article 81(1) as well as Articles 28–30. However, it is now clear that the exercise of trade mark rights, and presumably other intellectual property rights, deriving from an assignment does not as such contravene Article 81(1) unless there is evidence of continuing concert between the parties to divide markets.[217]

9.069 Article 81 and licences of intellectual property rights: unreasonable exploitation. The application of Article 81 to licences of intellectual property rights, particularly exclusive licences, is considered in detail in the next Section. However, even if, in a given case, Article 81(1) does not apply to the licence in question, there may be exceptional circumstances where the exercise of the licensed rights could bring Article 81(1) into play. Thus in *Coditel (No. 2)*,[218] which was concerned with whether an exclusive licence to exhibit a cinematograph film fell within Article 81(1), the Court of Justice held that:

> 'Although copyright in a film and the right deriving from it, namely that of exhibiting the film, are not, therefore, as such subject to the prohibitions contained in Article [81], the exercise of those rights may, nonetheless, come the exercise of those rights may, nonetheless, come within the said prohibitions where there are economic or legal circumstances the effect of which is to restrict film distribution to

---

[211] above, at 345 (ECR), 476 (CMLR, but slightly different translation).

[212] Case 40/70 *Sirena v Eda* [1971] ECR 69, [1971] CMLR 260. See also *Advocaat Zwarte Kip*, OJ 1974 L237/12, [1974] 2 CMLR D79; *Sirdar/Phildar*, OJ 1975 L125/27, [1975] 1 CMLR D93. On the application of Art 81(1) to assignments, the *Sirena* case is effectively overruled by *EMI v CBS* (n 206, above) and *IHT Internationale Heiztechnik v Ideal Standard* (n 206, above).

[213] ibid, para 9. Today this case would probably be decided under Arts 28 and 30 rather than Art 81.

[214] *Centrafarm v Sterling Drug* (n 206, above). The same applies to plant breeders' rights: Case 258/78 *Nungesser v Commission* [1982] ECR 2015, [1983] 1 CMLR 278, paras 28–43.

[215] *Keurkoop v Nancy Kean Gifts* (n 203, above).

[216] ibid.

[217] *EMI v CBS* (n 206, above); *IHT Internationale Heiztechnik v Ideal Standard* (n 206, above).

[218] Case 262/81 *Coditel v Ciné-Vog Films (No. 2)* [1982] ECR 3381, [1983] 1 CMLR 49.

an appreciable degree or to distort competition on the cinematographic market, regard being had to the specific characteristics of that market. . .

It must therefore be stated that it is for national courts, where appropriate, to make such inquiries and in particular to establish whether or not the exercise of the exclusive right to exhibit a cinematographic film creates barriers which are artificial and unjustifiable in terms of the needs of the cinematographic industry, or the possibility of charging fees which exceed a fair return on investment, or an exclusivity the duration of which is disproportionate to those requirements, and whether or not, from a general point of view, such exercise within a given geographic area is such as to prevent, restrict or distort competition within the common market.'[219]

Article 81(1) and refusal to license.   A unilateral refusal to license can hardly **9.070** infringe Article 81(1), since by definition there is no agreement. Moreover, the refusal to grant a licence by a sub-licensee who is himself prohibited from sub-licensing does not of itself infringe Article 81(1) because the prohibition against sub-licensing forms part of the normal exercise of the intellectual property right vested in the licensor.[220] However, if it is a question of a *collective* refusal to licence, whereby a number of undertakings act jointly in refusing to grant licences to a third party, Article 81(1) may apply.[221]

Infringement suits aimed at forcing acceptance of unlawful licence.   In some **9.071** circumstances, the rights holder brings infringement proceedings at the same time as offering the defendant a licence on terms which the defendant contends would be contrary to Articles 81 or 82 if accepted. In such a case, the infringement action may itself be a violation of the competition rules.[222]

Article 82 and infringement suits.   For Article 82 to apply to the exercise **9.072** of an intellectual property right, it is necessary to establish (i) a dominant position in a relevant product and geographic market in a substantial part of the

---

[219]   ibid, paras 17, 19. For the application of this principle, see Case T-504/93 *Tiercé Ladbroke v Commission* [1997] ECR II-923, [1997] 5 CMLR 304, paras 146–153. See also *UIP*, OJ 1989 L226/1, *XXIXth Report on Competition Policy* (1999), pp 148–150.

[220]   *Tiercé Ladbroke*, above.

[221]   ibid, paras 154–162. Note also the lengthy litigation concerning alleged concertation between various national copyright collecting societies refusing foreign users direct access to their repertoires: *Ministère Public v Tournier* (n 183, above); *Lucazeau v SACEM* (n 183, above); Case T-114/92 *BEMIM v Commission* [1995] ECR II-147, [1996] 4 CMLR 305; and Case T-5/93 *Tremblay v Commission* [1995] ECR II-185, [1996] 4 CMLR 305, 336; Case T-224/95 *Tremblay v Commission* ('*Tremblay II*') [1997] ECR II-2215, [1998] 4 CMLR 427. For collective arrangements in relation to television broadcasts, see paras 9.184 *et seq,* below.

[222]   See the decision of the English Court of Appeal, *Intel v VIA Technologies* [2002] EWCA (Civ) 1905, [2003] EuLR 85, *per* Sir Andrew Morritt VC at [87]: 'If the willingness to grant licences but only on terms which involve breaches of Article 81 is part of the abusive conduct of which complaint is made then I see no reason why those facts may not be relied on both for the purposes of the defence under Article 82 and as a free-standing defence under Article 81'. See also *Philips Electronics NV v Ingman* [1998] 2 CMLR 839; *Holleran v Daniel Thwaites plc* [1989] 2 CMLR 917; and *British Leyland Motor Corporation Ltd v TI Silencers Ltd* [1981] 2 CMLR 75.

common market; and (ii) an abuse of that position in a manner likely to affect trade between Member States.[223] The right to enforce an intellectual property right such as a patent or trade mark does not necessarily give rise to a dominant position,[224] and the exercise of an intellectual property right by suing for infringement is not by itself sufficient to establish an abuse.[225] There are, however, some cases where, if a dominant position is established, an infringement suit can be an abuse, at least if there is a sufficient 'nexus' between the right sought to be enforced and the abuse alleged. In *AstraZeneca*[226] the Commission considered whether it could ever be an abuse of a dominant position for a patent holder to defend an action brought against it for a declaration of the invalidity of the patent. The Commission stated that the conduct of a defence cannot be equated with the institution of legal proceedings but left open the question whether, in exceptional circumstances, it can be an abuse, holding that, the conduct of the defence in that case should be regarded as a continuation of the misrepresentations which had led to the extention of the patent right.[227] This is dealt with more fully in Chapters 10 and 14, below.[228]

9.073 **Article 82 and refusal to licence.** There have been four cases to date decided by the Community Courts on the question whether a refusal by a dominant undertaking to license an intellectual property right could be an abuse in violation of Article 82: *Volvo v Veng,*[229] *Magill,*[230] *Tiercé Ladbroke*[231] and *IMS.*[232] The question

---

[223] See generally Chap 10, below, esp paras 10.129 *et seq.* Note also *Santa Cruz Operation Inc/Microsoft, XXVIIth Report on Competition Policy* (1997), point 79 (contract requiring use of out-of-date technology by competitor found to be abusive).

[224] *Parke, Davis v Probel* (n 206, above); *Sirena v Eda* (n 212, above); *Deutsche Grammophon v Metro* (n 178, above); *EMI v CBS* (n 206, above); Case 102/77 *Hoffmann-La Roche v Centrafarm* [1978] ECR 1139, [1978] 3 CMLR 217.

[225] *Hoffmann-La Roche v Centrafarm,* above, para 16; Case T-198/98 *Micro Leader v Commission* [1999] ECR II-3989, [2000] 4 CMLR 886, [2000] All ER (EC) 361, para 57.

[226] COMP/37.507 *AstraZeneca,* 19 July 2006, [2006] 5 CMLR 287 (on appeal Case T-321/05 *AstraZeneca,* not yet decided).

[227] ibid, paras 736 *et seq.*

[228] See generally, paras 10.129 *et seq,* and paras 14.136 *et seq,* below.

[229] Case 238/87 *Volvo v Veng* [1988] ECR 6211, [1989] 4 CMLR 122; see also Case 53/87 *CICRA v Renault* [1988] ECR 6034, [1990] 4 CMLR 265.

[230] Cases C-241 & 242/91/P *RTE and ITP v Commission* [1995] ECR I-743, [1995] 4 CMLR 718, [1995] All ER (EC) 416, upholding the three decisions of the CFI in Cases T-69/89, etc, [1991] ECR II-485, 535, 575, [1991] 4 CMLR 586, 669, 745 (all on appeal from the Commission's decn in *Magill TV Guide,* OJ 1989 L78/43, [1989] 4 CMLR 749). See also *Ford (Body Panels) XVth Report on Competition Policy* (1985), point 49.

[231] *Tiercé Ladbroke* (n 219, above). Note also *IBM settlement, XIVth Report on Competition Policy* (1984), points 94–95, [1984] 3 CMLR 147 (dominant company gave undertaking to supply 'interface' information enabling other manufacturers to supply products that were 'plug compatible' with the dominant company's mainframe computers). In Case C-41/90 *Höfner & Elser v Macrotron* [1991] ECR I-1979, [1993] 4 CMLR 306, AG Jacobs expressed the view that the failure to exploit an intellectual property right could constitute an abuse: para 46 of his Opinion.

[232] Case C-418/01 *IMS Health* [2004] ECR I-5039, [2004] 4 CMLR 1543, [2004] All ER (EC) 813.

is also a central issue in the *Microsoft* case,[233] where the Commission took a decision imposing a requirement to supply software specifications that, at the time of writing, is on appeal to the Court of First Instance.[234] These cases are discussed in Chapter 10, below.[235]

Acquisition of technology by dominant undertakings. In *Tetra Pak (BTG* **9.074** *Licence),*[236] the Commission held that the acquisition by a dominant undertaking of an exclusive patent licence amounted to an abuse of a dominant position. Tetra Pak was dominant in the production and supply of packaging machines capable of packing milk in sterile surroundings, producing a long life product. It bought an American company, Liquipak, which had the benefit of an exclusive licence for a patented process which had the potential to rival the process used by Tetra Pak. The exclusive element of the licence was held to be abusive because it not only strengthened Tetra Pak's dominance but also prevented or delayed the entry into the market of a competing technology. In the circumstances, the Commission concluded that the exclusivity of the licence was not justified on grounds of providing Tetra Pak with the protection needed to justify investment and risk in developing the patented technology. The Commission also held that had Tetra Pak not agreed to renounce the exclusivity of the licence following the intervention of the Commission, the Commission would have withdrawn the benefit of the then block exemption under Regulation 2349/84.[237] If a patent holder acquires an extention of the protection of its rights by making misleading submissions to the national authorising body this may constitute an abuse, at least if it is part of an overall strategy to take steps to keep competitors out of the market.[238]

---

[233] COMP/37.792 *Microsoft*, 24 March 2004, [2005] 4 CMLR 965.

[234] Case T-201/04 *Microsoft v Commission*, judgment of 17 September 2007; see Postscript below.

[235] Paras 10.130 *et seq*, below. For two English decisions, see *HMSO v Automobile Association* [2000] EuLR 80 (Art 82 rejected as a defence to an infringement action in respect of unauthorised use of Ordnance Survey maps); *Claritas v Post Office* [2001] UKCLR 2 (ChD) (use of Royal Mail logo for mailing in competition with claimant's mailings not an abuse of dominance contrary to s 8 of the Competition Act 1998).

[236] *Tetra Pak (BTG Licence)*, OJ 1988 L272/27, [1990] 4 CMLR 47.

[237] The decision was taken on appeal on the narrow legal issue of whether an agreement which falls within a block exemption can, at the same time, constitute an infringement of Art 82. The CFI held that it could: Case T-51/89 *Tetra Pak Rausing v Commission* [1990] ECR II-309, [1991] 4 CMLR 334.

[238] *AstraZeneca* (n 226, above) paras 626 *et seq*. This case is discussed more fully at paras 10.153 *et seq*, below. The Commission found that AstraZeneca had made 'abusively misleading representations . . . in the context of applications for intellectual property rights, in the absence of which the right or rights in question would not normally have been granted' (para 741).

4. Licensing of Intellectual Property Rights

(a) Introduction

9.075 **Generally.** This Section deals with the application of Article 81 to licensing of intellectual property rights. In considering such agreements it is necessary to take account of the principles discussed in the previous Sections, namely the possible effect of Articles 28–30 and Articles 81(1) and 82 of the Treaty on the exercise of the rights in question.[239] Additionally, however, it is necessary to investigate whether individual clauses of licences or similar agreements contravene Article 81(1). In principle, the test for the application of Article 81(1) is the same as it is with other agreements, namely whether the licence or any of its provisions may affect trade between Member States and prevent, restrict or distort competition within the common market to an appreciable extent.[240] If Article 81(1) applies to the licence in question, there remains the possibility of exemption under Article 81(3). Regulation 772/2004[241] provides block exemption for certain types of technology transfer agreements. If that Regulation does not apply, the agreeement may still fulfil the criteria for the application of Article 81(3).

9.076 **Theoretical approachs to reconciling intellectual property with competition law.** Patent licences, and licences of similar rights, raise a number of issues for Community competition law. In addition to the threshold question as to whether a licence, or certain specific provisions of a licence, restrict competition and affect trade between Member States to an appreciable extent having regard to the whole economic context,[242] there are two theoretical problems which arise specifically in relation to intellectual property rights: (a) the 'limited licence' theory; and (b) the need to encourage the licensing of new technology.

9.077 **Limited licences: 'Opening the door'.** A patent or similar right confers a monopoly on the holder of the right. Without a licence a third party cannot exploit the right at all. Thus the licence, when granted, 'opens a door' that would otherwise be closed. On that basis, it may be argued that any limitations in the licence, for example a limitation on the quantity of licensed products to be manufactured by the licensee, or the end use for which the licensed product may be supplied, are

---

[239] Paras 9.007 *et seq* and 9.066 *et seq,* above.

[240] In Case 193/83 *Windsurfing International v Commission* [1986] ECR 611, [1986] 3 CMLR 489, the ECJ held that the effect on trade between Member States had to be judged in relation to the agreement as a whole rather than individual clauses. An agreement relating to rights protected in several Member States affects trade between Member States even if the parties are in the same Member State: Case 65/86 *Bayer v Süllhöfer* [1988] ECR 5249, [1990] 4 CMLR 182, para 20.

[241] Reg 772/2004, OJ 2004 L123/11, Vol II, App C.7. See paras 9.129 *et seq,* below.

[242] See, eg Case 320/87 *Ottung v Klee* [1989] ECR 1177, [1990] 4 CMLR 915, paras 13, 20; *Bayer v Süllhöfer* (n 240, above) paras 16–19.

not 'restrictions' under Article 81(1) but merely define the ambit of the licence, without which the licensed products would not be produced or sold at all. This approach was largely adopted in the Commission's 1962 Patent Notice, which was not formally withdrawn until 1984.[243] While important elements of this approach still survive, the Commission's position seems to involve a partial rejection of the 'limited licence' concept.[244] On the other hand, it is clear that some provisions in licences will not infringe Article 81(1) if they form part of, or are necessary to protect, the 'specific subject-matter' of the right.[245]

'Restrictions' and the encouragement of licensing.   A further problem in assess-   **9.078**
ing licence agreements under Article 81(1) is that one party, whether licensor or licensee, may regard some restriction on the freedom of the other party as essential if a licence is to be entered into at all. Thus a licensee may regard it as essential to be granted exclusivity and might never have taken a licence on any other basis, particularly where the licensee must incur heavy costs and risks in transforming the technology transferred into a marketable product. Equally, a licensor might be unwilling to grant a licence unless the licensee is prepared to accept various restrictions, for example on supplying territories reserved to the licensor. There is thus a

---

[243] See para I of the Patent Notice of 24 December 1962, JO 1962 C139/2922; withdrawn by OJ 1984 C220/14, in anticipation of the first patent licensing block exemption.

[244] In *Windsurfing v Commission* (n 240, above) para 42, the Commission submitted that 'the fact that an undertaking which has granted licences to other undertakings is the proprietor of an industrial property right does not entitle it to control the market for the products under licence'. Accordingly, the Commission considers that, eg a restriction on the right to export throughout the Community, and a limitation on the quantity of products that the licensee may manufacture, fall within Art 81(1). On the other hand, many of the obligations listed in Art 4 of Reg 772/2004, eg a limitation on the licensee to sell only for a particular end use or in a particular product market, seem to be regarded as not falling within Art 81(1) on the basis of the limited licence theory.

[245] In *Ottung v Klee* (n 242, above) the ECJ held (at para 10) that restrictions imposed by a proprietor of the patent on the reproduction, use or exploitation, without a licence, of a patented invention which result from the application of national intellectual property legislation cannot as such be considered to distort competition within the meaning of Art 81(1). Cases in which 'restrictions' in licence agreements have been regarded as falling outside Art 81(1) because they were essential to protect 'the specific subject-matter' of the right in question include: Case 261/82 *Coditel (No. 2)* [1982] ECR 3381, [1983] 1 CMLR 49 (exclusive licence in respect of the showing of a film necessary to allow licensor to exercise his copyright); Case 27/87 *Erauw-Jacquery v La Hesbignonne* [1988] ECR 1919, [1988] 4 CMLR 576 (restriction on sale or export of basic seed from which other seed is propagated necessary to enable breeder to prevent improper handling of seed and to select licensees; but restrictions relating to the sale of later generation seed produced from the basic seed can fall within Art 81(1)); *Tiercé Ladbroke v Commission* (n 219, above) (restriction on sub-licensing necessary to protect the specific subject-matter of the licensor's copyright). In *Windsurfing v Commission* (n 240, above) the test of whether particular provisions fell within the 'specific subject-matter' of the patent was used by the ECJ to determine the compatibility with Art 81(1) of obligations on the licensee (i) to mount the patented rig only on certain types of (unpatented) sailboard specified by the licensor; (ii) to sell the rigs only in conjunction with (unpatented) sailboards approved by the licensor; (iii) to affix a notice stating that the product was made under licence; (iv) not to challenge the validity of certain patents and trade marks; and (v) to manufacture only at a specific plant: see generally paras 37–94 of the judgment.

conflict: a licence may appear to be 'restrictive', but the acceptance of the restrictions may well lead to the successful conclusion of the licence, with the prospect of the dissemination of new technology, increased innovation, and better exploitation of the patented invention.[246] These benefits are well recognised in the *Antitrust Guidelines for the Licensing of Intellectual Property* issued by the US Department of Justice and Federal Trade Commission,[247] and in recent years, the Commission has taken a more positive attitude to the benefits of technology licensing.[248] It may very well be that, for this reason, certain provisions in patent and know-how licences formerly considered to be restrictive would not now be so regarded.

9.079 **Exclusive licences:** *Nungesser.*   Discussion of how far the terms of a licensing agreement do or do not fall within Article 81(1) begins with the landmark decision in *Nungesser*, also known as *'Maize Seed'*.[249] The French national agricultural research institute, INRA, had developed certain varieties of maize seed, for which INRA held plant breeders' rights. INRA granted the exclusive right to produce and sell INRA varieties in the Federal Republic of Germany to Mr Eisele. Under the arrangements, INRA undertook to ensure that INRA seeds would not be exported to Germany other than via Mr Eisele. Although INRA did not itself produce seeds in France, it had licensees who did. In its decision, the Commission held that the following fell within Article 81(1):

(i)   the obligation on INRA (and those deriving rights through INRA) neither to licence other undertakings to produce, use or sell the relevant seeds in Germany nor to produce, use or sell such varieties in Germany themselves;

(ii)   the obligation on INRA (or those deriving rights through INRA) to prevent third parties from exporting the relevant seeds to Germany without the licencee's authorisation for use or sale there;

---

[246] The ECJ judgment in Case 258/78 *Nungesser v Commission* [1982] ECR 2015, [1983] 1 CMLR 278, paras 9.079 *et seq*, below, effectively accepts this point of view. See also *Moosehead/ Whitbread*, OJ 1990 L100/32, [1991] 4 CMLR 391 as an example of a trade mark licence agreement which enabled a Canadian producer with no facilities in, or knowledge of, the relevant market in the Community to enter that market by granting an exclusive licence to an incumbent producer.

[247] Issued 6 April 1995 and available at http://www.ftc.gov/bc/0558.pdf and in [1995] 7 EIPR Supplement. See also the Federal Trade Commission report. *To Promote Innovation: The Proper Balance of Competition Policy and Patent Law and Policy* (October 2003), available at http://www. ftc.gov/os/2003/10/innovationrpt.pdf.

[248] See, eg the recitals to Reg 772/2004 (n 241, above). In the *XXVIth Report on Competition Policy* (1996), point 27, the Commission acknowledged that 'the recognition that technology transfers are a driving force in the economic development of the European Union, prompted the Commission to carry out a substantial simplification of the rules which have hitherto governed technology transfer agreements'.

[249] *Breeders' rights: maize seed*, OJ 1978 L286/23, [1978] 3 CMLR 434; on appeal, Case 258/78 *Nungesser v Commission* [1982] ECR 2015, [1983] 1 CMLR 278.

(iii) the use by Mr Eisele of his plant breeders' rights to prevent parallel imports by third parties into Germany.

The Commission's decision as regards the prevention of all parallel imports and the grant of absolute territorial protection was in accordance with established case law.[250] On point (i) above, the Commission reasoned, in accordance with its own previous decisions, that by licensing a single undertaking to exploit patent rights in a given territory the licensor deprives himself of the ability to license other undertakings in the same territory; and that by agreeing not to produce or market the product himself the licensor eliminates himself as a supplier in that territory. Until *Nungesser*, this reasoning had not been tested before the Court of Justice.

Nungesser: **the licensee's case.** Before the Court of Justice, Mr Eisele argued that **9.080** an exclusive licence for plant breeders' rights could not be treated as falling under Article 81(1) by its very nature, since such a licence constituted the sole means whereby seeds recently developed in one Member State could penetrate the market of another Member State. He pointed out that no grower or trader would have taken the risk of launching the new product on a new market if he had not been protected against direct competition from the holder of the breeders' rights and from other licensees. It was further argued by various interveners,[251] including the German and British governments, that the Commission's reasoning conflicted with a sensible competition policy and was based on the ill-conceived premise that every exclusive licence, whatever its nature, must be regarded as an agreement falling under Article 81(1) and therefore permissible, if at all, only by exemption under Article 81(3).

Nungesser: **the Court's judgment.** In its judgment, the Court of Justice drew **9.081** a distinction between the various obligations on INRA which had been identified by the Commission. On the one hand, there were the obligations on INRA to refrain from producing or selling the relevant seeds in Germany, either themselves or through other German licensees. On the other hand, there was the obligation to prevent third parties from exporting the relevant seeds to Germany. The Court said:

> 'It should be observed that those two sets of considerations relate to two legal situations which are not necessarily identical. The first case concerns a so-called open exclusive licence or assignment and the exclusivity of the licence relates solely to

---

[250] Cases 56 & 58/64 *Consten and Grundig v Commission* [1966] ECR 299, [1966] CMLR 418: see paras 2.072 *et seq*, above. In *Nungesser*, Mr Eisele had also obtained from a parallel trader, in settlement of infringement proceedings, a formal undertaking not to import INRA seeds from France; this agreement was held by the Commission to constitute a distinct infringement of Art 81(1) and the appeal against that aspect of the decision was dismissed.

[251] *Nungesser v Commission* (n 249, above) p 2041 *et seq* (ECR).

the contractual relationship between the owner of the right and the licensee, whereby the owner merely undertakes not to grant other licences in respect of the same territory and not to compete himself with the licensee on that territory. On the other hand, the second case involves an exclusive licence or assignment with absolute territorial protection, under which the parties to the contract propose, as regards the products and the territory in question, to eliminate all competition from third parties, such as parallel importers or licensees for other territories.'[252]

The Court accepted the argument that the grant of exclusive rights for a limited period is capable of providing an incentive to innovative efforts. The Court stated:

'In fact, in the case of a licence of breeders' rights over hybrid maize seeds newly developed in one Member State, an undertaking established in another Member State which was not certain that it would not encounter competition from other licensees for the territory granted to it, or from the owner of the right himself, might be deterred from accepting the risk of cultivating and marketing that product; such a result would be damaging to the dissemination of a new technology and would prejudice competition in the Community between the new product and similar existing products.

Having regard to the specific nature of the products in question, the Court concludes that, in a case such as the present, the grant of an open exclusive licence, that is to say a licence which does not affect the position of third parties such as parallel importers and licensees for other territories, is not in itself incompatible with Article [81(1)] of the Treaty.'[253]

On the other hand, the Court found that a licence which is not 'open' but which eliminates competition from third parties, in particular parallel importers, will normally fall within Article 81(1):

'As regard to the position of third parties, the Commission in essence criticises the parties to the contract for having extended the definition of exclusivity to importers who are not bound to the contract, in particular parallel importers. Parallel importers or exporters . . . had found themselves subjected to pressure and legal proceedings by INRA . . . and the applicants, the purpose of which was to maintain the exclusive position of the applicants on the German market.

The Court has consistently held . . . that absolute territorial protection granted to a licensee in order to enable parallel imports to be controlled and prevented results in the artificial maintenance of separate national markets, contrary to the Treaty.'[254]

The Court also upheld the Commission's refusal to grant an exemption under Article 81(3) in respect of the absolute territorial protection conferred by the licence.

9.082 **The result of *Nungesser*.** The result of *Nungesser* is to establish that an exclusive production and sales licence of plant breeders' rights over seeds newly developed

---

[252] ibid, judgment at para 53.
[253] ibid, paras 57–58.
[254] ibid, para 60.

in one Member State will not fall within Article 81(1) when granted to an undertaking established in another Member State which might otherwise be deterred from accepting the risks, provided that the licence is 'open', meaning that it does not purport to affect the position of third parties. By 'third parties' the Court referred to parallel importers[255] and also to licensees for other territories.[256] The period for which such rights are granted can be long: *Nungesser* concerned a decision in 1978 relating to rights obtained under arrangements made in the early 1960s. It seems that the reasoning in *Nungesser* is fully applicable to other intellectual property rights, particularly patents and to the licensing of know-how. However, the Commission seems to consider that that exclusive patent or know-how licences fall outside Article 81(1) only:

> 'where they are concerned with the introduction and protection of a new technology in the licensed territory, by reason of the scale of the research which has been undertaken, of the increase in the level of competition, in particular inter-brand competition, and of the competitiveness of the undertakings concerned resulting from the dissemination of innovation within the Community.'[257]

If the facts of a particular case do not fit these circumstances, certain exclusivity provisions may fall under Article 81(1).[258] However, the conditions in Article 81(3) may be fulfilled so that the agreement is valid and enforceable, either on the basis of Regulation 772/2004 or by way of individual assessment.

The Commission's Guidelines.   In 2004, the Commission issued a Notice setting   **9.083** out guidance on the application of Article 81 to technology transfer agreements (the 'Guidelines on Technology Transfer').[259] The Guidelines make clear that the Commission regards intellectual property licensing as mainly pro-competitive.

---

[255] See para 9.100, below.

[256] The Commission has expressed the view that a licence is not 'open' if it prevents another licensee from freely selling in the territory in question: *Boussois/Interpane*, OJ 1987 L50/30, [1988] 4 CMLR 124.

[257] ibid. For past decisions by the Commission applying this approach, see *Velcro/Aplix*, OJ 1985 L233/22, [1989] 4 CMLR 157 (Art 81(1) applied to exclusive grant for improvement patents after expiry of basic patents; the position as to the basic patents prior to expiry being left open); *Knoll/Hille Form*, *XIIIth Report on Competition Policy* (1983), points 142 *et seq* (neither 'newness' nor amount of investment justified exclusivity); *Boussois/Interpane* (n 256, above) (exclusive licence that was not 'open' fell within Art 81(1)). cf *Spitzer/Van Hool*, *XIIth Report on Competition Policy* (1982), point 86 ('Since the licensor was a medium sized enterprise there was no reason to oppose the clauses giving exclusivity to a given territory and providing for slightly higher royalties on sales outside the said territory').

[258] The Commission so found, eg in *Velcro/Aplix*, above; *Boussois/Interpane* (n 256, above); *Rich Products/Jus-rol*, OJ 1988 L69/21, [1988] 4 CMLR 527; *Delta Chemie/DDD*, OJ 1988 L309/34, [1989] 4 CMLR 535. But it is not clear whether the Commission would now analyse the application of Art 81(1) in the same way.

[259] Guidelines on Technology Transfer, OJ 2004 C101/2: Vol II, App C.16. The EFTA Surveillance Authority adopted equivalent Guidelines on 21 September 2005 as regards the EEA Agreement by College Decn 228/05 (available on the EFTA Surveillance Authority website).

In most circumstances, therefore, there will be no concerns raised by the application of Article 81(1) of the Treaty.[260] As well as providing a detailed commentary on the provisions of the block exemption in Regulation 772/2004, the Guidelines aim 'to promote predictability beyond the application of the [block exemption] and to confine detailed analysis to cases that are likely to present real competition concerns'.[261] The Guidelines set out the factors which the Commission considers are relevant in assessing how competition operates on the market in question and hence how the licence under consideration affects that competition.[262] The factors which are particularly relevant are the nature of the agreement, for example whether there are implicit restraints going beyond the express terms of the agreement; the market position of the parties, their competitors and the buyers of the licensed products; the existence of barriers to entry such as 'first mover advantage' or brand loyalty created by strong brand advertising; and the maturity of the technology in the market. Other factors which need to be taken into account are the possible cumulative effect of networks of agreements and whether market behaviour indicates or facilitates price leadership or rigidity.[263] The Guidelines relate only to the application of Article 81 to technology transfer agreements and not to the application of Article 82, a fact which dominant companies need to bear in mind.[264]

9.084 **Safe harbour: four competing technologies.** The Commission states in the Guidelines on Technology Transfer that where the licence does not contain hard-core restrictions,[265] Article 81 is unlikely to be infringed where there are four or more independently controlled technologies which compete with the technologies controlled by the parties to the licence.[266] Whether the independently controlled technologies do compete with the licensed technology depends on whether, for example, consumers have a strong preference for products incorporating the licensed technology so that others available impose only a limited competitive constraint. The Commission has stressed that the fact that a licence falls outside this safe harbour, or outside the block exemption, does not create a presumption either that it falls within Article 81(1) or that it is not entitled to the benefit of Article 81(3).

9.085 **The positive and negative effects of licences on competition.** The Guidelines set out the Commission's approach to the balancing of the positive and negative

---

[260] ibid, paras 8, 9 and 36.
[261] ibid, para 131.
[262] ibid, paras 132 *et seq.*
[263] ibid, para 140.
[264] For Art 82, see generally Chap 10, below; and specifically for intellectual property licences, para 10.150, below.
[265] See paras 9.145 *et seq*, below for what amount to hard-core restrictions in licences.
[266] Guidelines on Technology Transfer (n 259, above) para 131.

potential impact of technology licences on the competitive environment.[267] The negative effects may arise in three ways. First, competition between different technologies may be reduced, particularly where the agreement includes the cross-licensing of rights by competing undertakings in a manner which prevents either competitor gaining a technological lead over the other. Licensing between competitors may also facilitate collusion by increasing transparency in the market and by raising barriers to entry. Secondly, even non-reciprocal licences which preclude or discourage the licensee from licensing competing technology can foreclose opportunities for third parties to expand their market share. Thirdly, licences which impose restraints on the licensee selling his products into the markets of other licensees restrict intra-technology competition. The Commission recognises, however, that even restrictive licence agreements produce pro-competitive effects which need to be assessed within the framework of Article 81(3). Licences have the potential to bring together complementary technologies and other assets allowing new or improved products to be produced at lower costs. Licence agreements may also increase efficiency in the distribution of the goods.

(b) Typical clauses in patent and know-how licences

(i) Introduction

Generally. This Section covers the licensing of intellectual property in the context of agreements for the transfer of technology relating to the manufacture of goods or the provision of services by the licensee himself or for his account. It does not cover licences granted purely for the purposes of sale of the protected product, such as distribution or franchising arrangements. It is convenient to discuss together in this Section patent licences, know-how licences, and mixed patent and know-how licences. Licences very often include both patent and know-how rights and such licences are treated together in Regulation 772/2004.[268] Although 'know-how'[269] is not, strictly speaking, a property right 'good against all the world' in the same way as a patent, national laws generally prohibit the unauthorised disclosure of secret know-how and prevent the use of know-how for purposes other than those for which it was made available. The licensing of patents and

9.086

---

[267] ibid, paras 141 *et seq.*

[268] Reg 772/2004, OJ 2004 L123/11, Vol II, App C.7. See further, paras 9.129 *et seq,* below.

[269] For the purposes of Reg 772/2004, 'know-how' is defined as 'a package of non-patented practical information, resulting from experience and testing which is (i) secret . . . (ii) substantial . . . and (iii) identified': Art 1(i). The meanings of 'secret', 'substantial' and 'identified' are defined in Art 10(i). The requirement that the know-how, including any subsequent improvements, should be identified is important. Some know-how may be protected by intellectual property rights, eg copyright in plans or drawings.

know-how is treated by the Commission according to the same principles.[270] Although some reference is made in this Section to early decisions, the Commission now takes a less restrictive approach to technology transfer agreements under Article 81(1) than was formerly the case.

9.087 **Intra-technology and inter-technology competition.** In describing the general framework for the application of Article 81, the Commission acknowledges that the compatibility of the licence must be assessed within the actual context in which competition would occur in the absence of the agreement and of the contractual restraints within the agreement.[271] Two aspects of competition must be considered; the likely impact of the agreement on inter-technology competition, that is competition between undertakings using different and competing technology, and intra-technology competition, that is competition between undertakings using the same technology; typically the other licensees of the rights.[272] Technology transfer agreements may reduce inter-technology competition where, for example, competitors transfer competing technologies to each other and impose a reciprocal obligation to provide each other with future improvements of their respective technologies. Such an obligation may prevent either competitor from gaining a technological lead over the other and thereby restrict competition in innovation between the parties.[273] The contractual terms of a licence agreement may also reduce intra-technology competition, for example where territorial restraints are imposed on licensees preventing them from selling into each other's territory, or if the agreement facilitates collusion between licensees.[274]

9.088 **Competing and non-competing undertakings.** The Commission's analysis of individual clauses either in the context of the provisions of Regulation 772/2004 or more generally in considering the application of Article 81 refers to undertakings which are competing or which are non-competing. For example, the market share thresholds for the application of the block exemption are different for competing and non-competing undertakings and the analysis of exclusivity provisions differs depending on whether or not the parties to the licence are competitors.

---

[270] The principal early decisions of the Commission on patent and know-how licences are referred to in the 4th edn of this work, para 8-076, n 33. The principal decisions of the ECJ on clauses in patent licences or similar agreements are: *Nungesser v Commission* (n 249, above); *Windsurfing v Commission* (n 240, above); *Erauw-Jacquery v La Hesbignonne* (n 245, above); *Bayer v Süllhöfer* (n 240, above); *Ottung v Klee* (n 242, above). Decisions of the Commission prior to *Nungesser* are of doubtful standing as far as exclusivity is concerned. More generally, the currently favourable approach to technology transfer may result in more agreements falling outside Art 81(1), eg for lack of appreciable effect on competition, or on the basis that the licence was necessary to encourage pro-competitive technology transfer.

[271] Guidelines on Technology Transfer (n 259, above) para 11.

[272] ibid, paras 11, 12.

[273] ibid, paras 12 and 142 *et seq*.

[274] ibid, paras 12 and 145.

There are two types of competing undertaking: those which compete or potentially compete because their products compete; and those which compete because their production methods or technology compete.[275] Undertakings will be regarded as being actual competitors on the relevant product market if, in the absence of the licence, they are both active on the same relevant product and geographic markets and if they are so active without infringing any intellectual property rights of the other party to the licence in question. They will be treated as potential competitors on the same product market if they are likely to enter that market in response to a small but permanent increase in prices and would be able to enter that market without infringing the other's rights.[276] Undertakings are regarded as actually competing on the same relevant technology market if they license out competing technologies without infringing the other's rights. Technologies are considered to be competing if they are regarded as interchangeable with or substitutable for the licensed technology by reason of its characteristics, royalties or intended use.[277] Although potential competitors as regards products are regarded as competing undertakings, undertakings which are only potential, not actual, competitors as regards their technology are not regarded as competing undertakings for the purpose of assessing the licence terms.[278]

Development of competition after conclusion of the agreement. In some **9.089** cases, the parties may become competitors after the conclusion of the agreement, for example where the licensee develops and starts exploiting a competing technology or where the licensor enters the product market either on the basis of the licensed or a different technology. The Commission has stated that it will, in these circumstances, generally not treat the parties as competitors.[279] Conversely, parties who appear to be competitors at the time the licence is granted may in fact not be competitors if the licensor's technology renders the licensee's technology obsolete or uncompetitive. Even if this is not apparent at the time the licence is concluded, the parties may later be treated as non-competitors if it becomes apparent that the licensee's technology has effectively been replaced.[280]

Blocking positions. Sometimes one party owns rights to a technology which **9.090** cannot be used without a licence of the rights to the other party's technology. Such a position is referred to as a one-way blocking position and may arise, for example, where one patent covers an improvement of a technology covered by another patent such that the improvement patent cannot be exploited without a licence of the

---

[275] Reg 772/2004 (n 268, above) Art 1(1)(j).
[276] ibid and Guidelines on Technology Transfer (n 259, above) para 29.
[277] Reg 772/2004, Art 1(1)(j)(i) and see Guidelines on Technology Transfer, para 22.
[278] Guidelines on Technology Transfer, paras 30 and 66.
[279] ibid, para 31. See also Reg 772/2004, Art 4(3) which stipulates this in relation to the application of the prohibitions on hard-core restrictions.
[280] ibid, para 33. The Commission gives the example of CD and vinyl recording technologies.

underlying patent. A two-way blocking position exists where neither party can exploit its own rights without a licence or waiver by the other of his rights. Where parties are in either a one-way or two-way blocking position they are not regarded as competitors, although the Commission will require convincing evidence that this is in fact the case.[281]

9.091 **Reciprocal and non-reciprocal licences.** Another factor relevant when assessing the likely effect of a licence on competition is whether the licence between the parties is reciprocal or non-reciprocal. The terms 'reciprocal agreement' and 'non-reciprocal agreement' are defined in Article 1(1)(c) and (d) of Regulation 772/2004 and are relevant not only for the application of certain provisions of the block exemption but also when considering the application of Article 81 more generally. Technology transfer agreements are reciprocal where each party licenses the other in relation to competing products[282] or competing product methods so that the transfer of technology flows both ways in relation to competing goods or processes. A non-reciprocal licence is where there is a transfer of technology in only one direction or where there is cross-licensing but the licences do not concern competing technologies and cannot be used for the production of competing goods.[283] If the licence is non-reciprocal, the fact that there may be cross-licensing of complementary or non-substitutable product is, in economic terms and for the purposes of Regulation 772/2004, irrelevant to the question relating to the effect of the other cross-licence and whether it may qualify for exemption. This concept does not depend upon whether the parties to the licence or arrangement are competitors. The important factor is whether the licensed processes, or the products obtained by the licensed processes, compete.[284]

(ii) Clauses concerning royalties

9.092 **Royalties generally.** Provisions in a licence concerning the payment of royalties will not normally fall within Article 81(1). However, in a limited number of circumstances where cross-licences are entered into between competitors, the licence may be a disguised means of fixing prices, for example where the royalties are clearly disproportionate to the market value of the licence and have a significant impact on market prices.[285] Article 81(1) may also apply where royalties in reciprocal licences increase as output increases since, if the parties have market

---

[281] ibid, para 32.

[282] The term 'product' includes both intermediary and final goods and services: Art 1(1)(e) of Reg 772/2004.

[283] Reg 772/2004 (n 267, above) Art 1(1)(d).

[284] Guidelines on Technology Transfer (n 259, above) para 78.

[285] In effect the royalty becomes the minimum price for the onward sale of the product: see Guidelines on Technology Transfer, paras 157 *et seq.*

power, such a royalty may act as a limitation on output.[286] Article 81(1) will apply if royalties extend to products produced solely with the licensee's own technology.[287] Where the royalty is calculated on the basis of products using both the licensed technology and products using a third party's technology, the foreclosure effects of the resulting increase in the costs of using the third party's technology will need to be assessed to see if Article 81(1) applies.[288] An obligation to pay a minimum royalty will not in itself amount to price-fixing but an arrangement which creates a disincentive for the licensee to sell below a certain price will do so.[289]

Royalties on partly patented products.   Sometimes royalties may be calculated   **9.093**
not solely on the patented items but by reference to the selling price of another product, for example a product at a more advanced stage of the manufacturing process into which the patented item is incorporated. It appears that Article 81(1) does not apply if this basis of calculation is used because the number or value of patented items manufactured or consumed is difficult to establish separately due to the complexity of the production process, or if there is no separate demand for the patented item on its own. Further, such a clause will not have an anticompetitive effect on the sale of the patented component provided that the amount of royalty payable on the whole product is in fact no higher than would be justified for the component alone.[290] However, Article 81(1) may apply if a royalty is charged on a sale price which includes unpatented items if the effect of the royalty is to discourage the licensee from meeting any separate demand for the unpatented items in question.[291]

Royalties on products not using the patent.   The Commission has held that   **9.094**
a clause which requires the licensee to pay royalties when it manufactures products which are the subject-matter of the agreement without making any use of the licensor's patents falls within Article 81(1).[292] Such a provision may strengthen the effect of a non-competition clause and 'has the effect of burdening manufacturing costs without any economic justification, thereby weakening the

---

[286] Guidelines on Technology Transfer (n 259, above) para 158.

[287] ibid, para 157.

[288] ibid, para 160.

[289] ibid, para 79.

[290] *Windsurfing International v Commission* (n 240, above). The Commission's view of royalties based on sales of the product incorporating the licensed technology appears to be more relaxed: Guidelines on Technology Transfer, para 156.

[291] ibid. But see Stone, 'Some thoughts on the Windsurfing Judgment' (1986) 8 EIPR 242.

[292] *AOIP/Beyrard* (n 308, below) para II (4)(f); *Preflex/Lipski* (n 361, below) (patents); *Spitzer/van Hool* (n 331, below) (know-how); *Neilson-Hordell/Richmark, Twelfth Report on Competition Policy* (1982), points 88 *et seq* (copyright); *UARCO, Fourteenth Report* (1984), point 93 (patents and know-how).

competitive position of the licensee'.[293] It is doubtful how far those considerations are correct.[294] Clauses of this nature are not referred to in Regulation 772/2004.[295]

(iii) Clauses concerning the grant of exclusive territories

9.095 **Exclusive grant by licensor.** According to the Commission's Guidelines, the application of the prohibition in Article 81(1) to an obligation on the licensor not to exploit the licensed technology himself within the licensed territory and not to license any other person to do so, depends on whether the licensor and the licensee are competitors and whether they enter into exclusive cross-licences – or in the terminology used in the Guidelines, whether the licences are reciprocal or non-reciprocal.[296] Where the licensor and the licensee are competitors and they enter into reciprocal licences under which each grants an exclusive licence to the other to use the licensed technology, the licence has the same effect as a market-sharing agreement. It will therefore fall within Article 81(1) and will not benefit from Article 81(3).[297] Where the parties to the licence are competing undertakings but the licence operates in one direction only, Article 81(1) is likely to apply only if the licensor has a significant market position and would have the capacity itself to exploit the technology in the licensed territory. Where the licensor is not involved in production at all, for example where it is a research institute, the licence will not fall within Article 81(1) even if the licensor competes with the licensee on the market for the technology concerned.[298] If the parties are non-competing undertakings, the grant of exclusivity is unlikely to fall within Article 81(1) particularly if (i) the licensee, without such protection, might be deterred from accepting the risk of manufacturing and marketing a newly developed product; and (ii) other provisions of the licence do not purport to restrict the

---

[293] *AOIP/Beyrard* (n 308, below). See also *Windsurfing International*,OJ 1983 L229/1, [1984] 1 CMLR 1; and *Windsurfing International v Commission* (n 240, above) paras 60–67: calculation of the royalty based on the price of the complete sailboard rather than just the rig which was covered by the patent restricted competition.

[294] In *Microsoft's Undertaking, XXIVth Report on Competition Policy* (1994), p 364, the Commission expressed concern about the foreclosure of effect of royalties payable whether or not Microsoft software was used; see also *Microsoft Internet Explorer, XXIXth Report on Competition Policy* (1999), point 56. For minimum royalty provisions, see para 9.092, above.

[295] Reg 772/2004 (n 268, above).

[296] Guidelines on Technology Transfer, OJ 2004 L123/11: Vol II, App C.16, paras 162–167. The Commission distinguishes between an exclusive grant, where the licensor agrees both not to exploit himself and not to licence others, and a sole grant, where the licensor agrees only not to licence others. See para 9.091, above for the distinction between reciprocal and non-reciprocal licences.

[297] ibid, para 163. Such an arrangement involves hard-core restrictions which preclude the application of Reg 772/2004: see Art 4(1)(c). See paras 9.088 and 9.091, above, for when undertakings are regarded as 'competing' and when licences are 'reciprocal'.

[298] ibid, para 164.

freedom of parallel importers and other licensees to sell in the licensed territory.[299] Even if it is doubtful whether these criteria are met, such obligations on the licensor still qualify for exemption under Regulation 772/2004.[300] The only situation in which the Commission envisages that intervention might be necessary is if a dominant undertaking obtains an exclusive licence to one or more competing technologies.[301]

Sales restrictions on the licensor. The Commission regards sales restrictions on the licensor as benign: even if they fall within Article 81(1) they are usually indispensable to induce the licensee to invest in the production, marketing and sale of the products incorporating the licensed technology. The Guidelines acknowledge that '[i]t is likely that the licensee's incentive to invest would be significantly reduced if he would face direct competition from the licensor whose production costs are not burdened by royalty payments, possibly leading to sub-optimal levels of investment'.[302]   **9.096**

Exploitation by licensee in territory of licensor. The question whether Article 81(1) applies if the licence restricts exploitation, including direct sales, by the licensee into the territory of the licensor where the licensor has patent protection did not arise in *Nungesser*, but on the basis of the reasoning in that case, Article 81(1) would not necessarily apply. Where the parties to the licence are competitors and they licence each other with their respective technologies, then restrictions on active and passive sales by one or both of the parties are akin to market-sharing and will be prohibited by Article 81.[303] Where competitors enter into a non-reciprocal licence, restrictions on sales by the licensee in the licensor's territory will fall within Article 81(1) where one or both of the parties has a significant degree of market power. Such a restriction can benefit from the block exemption in Regulation 772/2004 and may fulfil the conditions of Article 81(3) where the Regulation does not apply if the licensor is unlikely to want to licence an undertaking which would then compete with it in its own territory.[304] Where the licence is between non-competing parties, a restriction on the licensee from selling into the licensor's territory will fall outside Article 81(1) if the licensor would not be prepared to licence in the absence of such a restriction.   **9.097**

---

[299] *Nungesser v Commission* (n 249, above); *Velcro/Aplix* (n 257, above); and see Guidelines on Technology Transfer (n 296, above) para 165.

[300] Reg 772/2004 (n 268, above).

[301] Guidelines on Technology Transfer, para 166.

[302] ibid, para 173.

[303] ibid, para 169.

[304] ibid, para 170. Such a restriction is not regarded as a hard-core restriction and will be exempt under Reg 772/2004 if the parties fall within the market share threshold: Art 4(1)(c)(iv).

As the Commission has stated: 'A technology owner cannot normally be expected to create direct competition with himself on the basis of his own technology'.[305]

9.098 **Manufacture or use by licensee outside the licensed territory.** If a patent or know-how licensee is authorised to manufacture or use the patented product in one place, or even in one Member State, Article 81(1) has been held to apply if the clause expressly or impliedly prevents manufacture or use in a territory where there is no patent protection.[306] However, it would seem arguable that Article 81(1) does not apply to the extent that the licensor and those deriving title from the licensor have patent protection in other territories in the Community. In such circumstances, the clause would not restrict any act that could lawfully take place.[307] Moreover, the free movement provisions in Articles 28–30 do not appear to be relevant to a restriction on manufacture and use as distinct from sale.

9.099 **Restrictions on direct sale by licensee into territory of another licensee.** *Prima facie*, an export restriction imposed on a licensee infringes Article 81(1).[308] Any contractual restriction which restricts exports by licensees, whether directly or indirectly, actively or passively, will infringe Article 81(1) if there is no patent protection in the other territories.[309] What is the position if the licence restricts direct sales by one licensee into the territory of another licensee where parallel patents are still in force? On this point, *Nungesser* is somewhat ambiguous: the Court of Justice's principal finding was that Article 81(1) did not apply to a restriction on INRA and those deriving rights through INRA on producing or selling the relevant seeds in Germany themselves.[310] But the Court defined an open exclusive licence as a licence 'which does not affect the position of third parties

---

305 Guidelines on Technology Transfer, para 172. A restriction on sales by the licensee into the licensor's territory will be caught if the licensor has significant market power or networks of similar licences create significant foreclosure of the market.

306 *Windsurfing International v Commission* (n 240, above) paras 82 *et seq*. See also *Velcro/Aplix* (n 257, above) (use of equipment outside licensed territory).

307 But note that in its decision in *Windsurfing International* (n 293, above), the Commission left open whether a licence limited to a part of a Member State infringed Art 81(1); and in *Boussois/Interpane* (n 256, above), the Commission apparently considered that a licence to manufacture limited to one Member State infringed Art 81(1). See also *Rich Products/Jus-rol* (n 258, above).

308 See *AOIP/Beyrard*, OJ 1976 L6/8, [1976] 1 CMLR D14; *Breeders' rights: maize seed* (n 249, above); *Velcro/Aplix* (n 257, above). There may be exceptional circumstances where an export ban is necessary to protect the 'specific subject-matter' of the right in question, as with basic seeds: see *Erauw-Jacquery* (n 245, above).

309 The Commission has taken this position even where direct sales by one licensee into the territory of another would *prima facie* infringe the latter's patent rights since the Commission takes the view that Arts 28–30 EC preclude the exercise of patent rights to prevent direct sales between licensees: submissions in Case 19/84 *Pharmon v Hoechst* [1985] ECR 2281, [1985] 3 CMLR 775. This position was supported *obiter* by AG Mancini in *Pharmon v Hoechst*; but see para 9.023, above.

310 Case 258/78 *Nungesser v Commission* [1982] ECR 2015, [1983] 1 CMLR 278, para 67.

such as parallel importers and licensees for other territories'.[311] The Commission's view is that a restriction on active sales by one licensee into the territory of another licensee ('the protected licensee') is likely to be caught by Article 81(1) where the parties have significant market power. But it is also likely to fulfil the criteria in Article 81(3) if it is imposed for a limited period to allow the protected licensee to become established on the market.[312] Where the licence is between non-competing undertakings, a restriction on the licensee's ability to make active sales into the territory of another licensee will benefit from Article 81(3) where it is necessary to induce the licensee to make the investment necessary for the efficient exploitation of the licensed technology in his own territory.[313] Restrictions on passive sales by the licensee into the territory of another licensee will always be caught by Article 81(1) and will rarely benefit from Article 81(3).[314]

Parallel traders.   As explained in Section 2, above, it is contrary to Articles 28 **9.100** and 30 of the Treaty to bring an infringement action to prevent the import of goods first put on the market in another Member State by the owner of the right or with his consent.[315] The Court of Justice in *Nungesser* was clearly concerned that parties should not seek to retrieve by contract what would be prohibited under the rules on free movement of goods.[316] It is clear that any provision in a licence which prevents parallel trade will normally fall within Article 81(1) and will not fulfil the criteria set out in Article 81(3).[317] Thus a restriction on a licensee or licensor which prevents him from meeting in his own territory orders for goods which might then be exported by third parties will infringe Article 81(1) and not qualify for exemption under Regulation 772/2004.[318]

(iv) Restrictions concerning the licensee's production of goods

Limitation on quantities produced or sold.   It might be argued that a limitation **9.101** of the quantity of products to be manufactured or sold under the licence would

---

[311] ibid, paras 58 *et seq*. It is not easy to reconcile these statements, and *Nungesser* thus seems to leave open the question whether Art 81(1) applies to a provision which prevents direct sales by one licensee into the territory of another where both enjoy patent protection, assuming that parallel imports by third parties are unaffected.

[312] Guidelines on Technology Transfer (n 296, above) para 171.

[313] ibid, para 174.

[314] ibid. Reg 772/2004 (n 268, above) exempts such a restriction only between non-competing undertakings and only for the first two years of the protected licensee's sales into its allocated territory: Art 4(2)(b)(ii).

[315] See paras 9.010 *et seq*, above.

[316] *Nungesser* (n 310, above).

[317] Such a provision 'affects the position of third parties, such as parallel traders' within the meaning of *Nungesser*.

[318] Reg 772/2004 (n 268, above).

fall outside Article 81(1) as an example of a limited licence.[319] However, the Commission has expressed the view that Article 81(1) applies to such a restriction because it prevents the party accepting it from increasing his output and may, when combined with exclusive territories or exclusive customer groups, have an effect similar to an export ban.[320] Reciprocal output restrictions between competing undertakings are treated as a hard-core restriction and will be invalid under Article 81. Where the parties are competitors but the licence is not reciprocal, a limitation on output may benefit from Article 81(3) where the licensor's technology is substantially better than the licensee's and the output limit allows substantial expansion of the licensee's existing business.[321] Where the licence is between non-competitors, it is only likely to contain an output restriction where the licensor would not be prepared to grant the licence without such a restriction. It is therefore likely to fall outside Article 81(1).[322]

9.102 **Captive use restrictions.** One particular form of output restriction is where the licensee is required to use products incorporating the licensed technology only as an input for incorporation into his own production. Where the licensee was not, at the time of the conclusion of the licence, actually supplying competing components to third parties, and was not likely to start such supply, the term will not fall within Article 81(1) provided that the licensee remains free to sell the licensed product as replacement parts for his own products.[323] If, on the other hand, the licensee is an actual or potential supplier of competing components to third parties, the term will fall within Article 81(1) if the result of the agreement is that he ceases to be a component supplier.[324] Where the licensor is not himself a supplier of components there is usually no economic justification for a captive use restriction since a restriction on the licensee not to sell into certain customer groups reserved for the licensor is likely to be a less restrictive alternative.[325]

9.103 **Minimum quality.** An obligation on the licensee to observe specifications concerning the minimum quality of the licensed product will not normally fall within Article 81(1), provided that such specifications are necessary for a technically

---

[319] This view was expressed in the 1962 Patent Notice, JO 1962 C139/2922, para IA3. For 'limited licences' see para 9.077, above.

[320] Guidelines on Technology Transfer (n 296, above) para 177. See also *Breeders' rights—maize seed* (n 249, above) (obligation on licensee to produce only part of requirement and buy in the rest held to fall under Art 81(1)).

[321] Guidelines on Technology Transfer (n 296, above) para 175.

[322] ibid, paras 176–178.

[323] ibid, paras 186 *et seq.*

[324] ibid, para 187.

[325] ibid, para 190.

satisfactory exploitation of the licensed invention,[326] or to ensure that the licensee's products conform to the minimum quality standards applicable to the licensor and other licensees.[327] Where there is an obvious link between the product incorporating the licensed technology and the licensor, he has a legitimate interest to ensure that the quality of the products do not undermine the value of the technology or his reputation. Indeed, a licensee may be unwilling to take a licence unless he is assured that all other licensees will be required to exploit the technology in a satisfactory way. Similarly, an obligation to allow the licensor to carry out checks related to the meeting of such minimum quality requirements does not normally fall under Article 81(1).[328]

Minimum quantities.   An obligation on the licensee to produce a minimum quantity of the licensed products, or to carry out a minimum number of operations exploiting the licensed invention, does not generally fall under Article 81(1),[329] since the purpose of such a provision is usually to ensure the adequate exploitation of the patent.[330] For the same reason, an obligation on the licensee to pay a minimum royalty does not generally fall under Article 81(1).[331] Such a provision ensures adequate exploitation of the patent. Where, exceptionally, Article 81(1) applies, exemption may be available under Regulation 772/2004.[332]   **9.104**

Field of use or product market restrictions.   An obligation on the licensee to restrict his exploitation of the licensed invention to one or more technical fields of application covered by the licensed patent will generally not fall under   **9.105**

---

[326] In *Windsurfing International v Commission* (n 240, above), the ECJ upheld the Commission's contention that standards of quality must be agreed in advance on the basis of objectively verifiable criteria (para 46) and that the holder of the patent for the sail board rig was not entitled to retain a right of approval over the boards to which the rig was attached by the licensee. See also Guidelines on Technology Transfer (n 296, above) para 194, and the application of this aspect of the *Windsurfing* judgment by the Engish Court of Appeal in *Intel Corp v VIA Technologies* [2002] EWCA (Civ) 1905, [2003] EuLR 85.

[327] See Art 2(1)(5) of the old block exemption, Reg 240/96, OJ 1996 L31/2 (App 24 to the 5th edn of this work), which included such an obligation in the 'white list' of clauses 'generally not restrictive of competition'. See also *Delta Chemie/DDD*, OJ 1988 L309/34, [1989] 4 CMLR 535, para 30 (a trade mark licence, where such conformity is of particular significance).

[328] *Raymond/Nagoya*, JO 1972 L143/39, [1972] CMLR D45; and see Reg 240/96 (above), Art 2(1)(5).

[329] See *Becton Dickinson/Cyclopore*, XXIIIrd *Report on Competition Policy* (1993), point 241 and Guidelines on Technology Transfer, para 155(e).

[330] *First Report on Competition Policy* (1971), point 75.

[331] Guidelines on Technology Transfer (n 296, above) para 155(e). cf *Microsoft's undertaking*, XXIVth *Report on Competition Policy* (1994), p 364, where the Commission considers that such a requirement could lead to the foreclosure of competitor licensees, and *Microsoft Internet Explorer*, XXIXth *Report on Competition Policy* (1999), point 56: see para 9.147, below. It may be appropriate for any necessary inspection of the licensee's books to be undertaken by an independent third party: *Spitzer/Van Hool, Twelfth Report on Competition Policy* (1982), point 86.

[332] Reg 772/2004 (n 268, above), Art 4(2)(a).

Article 81(1) where the parties do not compete with each other.[333] However, Article 81(1) is likely to apply if the parties were already competing manufacturers before the grant of the licence and they enter into reciprocal exclusive field of use licensing.[334] Where the parties are competitors but there is no reciprocity, a field of use restriction may result in a diminution of competition by the licensee but is not regarded as a hard-core restriction for the purposes of the block exemption.[335] If the conclusion of the agreement is likely to cause the licensee to cease production that he formerly undertook outside the field of use, the clause will fall within Article 81(1).[336] Conversely where the parties are licensed to use each other's technology in the same field of use the restriction is unlikely to be caught.[337] Field of use restrictions in licences between non-competing undertakings are likely to be pro-competitive and not to fall within Article 81(1).[338]

9.106 Competing products. Obligations which restrict the licensee from competing with the other party, connected undertakings, or third parties, in respect of research and development, production, use or distribution of competing products will fall within Article 81(1) where they result in the significant foreclosure of opportunities for competing technologies to gain access to the market.[339] The Guidelines on Technology Transfer describe the factors which need to be taken into account in considering whether any particular agreement has such an effect, including the presence of networks of similar licences, whether the customers of the licensee are also subject to non-compete clauses and the presence of other barriers to entry.[340] Exemption under Regulation 772/2004 is available in specified circumstances.[341]

---

[333] In *Windsurfing International v Commission* (n 240, above) the Commission contended that restrictions on the field of use are acceptable only if they relate to different products belonging to different markets: para 42 of the ECJ's judgment. It is important to distinguish between a genuine field of use restriction and the allocation of a customer group: see Guidelines on Technology Transfer (n 296, above) para 180.

[334] Guidelines on Technology Transfer (n 296, above) para 181. See also *French State/Suralmo, Ninth Report on Competition Policy* (1979), point 114.

[335] See Reg 772/2004 (n 268, above) Art 4(1)(c)(ii).

[336] Guidelines on Technology Transfer, para 183.

[337] ibid.

[338] ibid, para 184. In agreements between non-competitors, the licensor is normally entitled also to grant sole or exclusive licences in one or more fields of use: para 185.

[339] Guidelines on Technology Transfer, paras 196–203, and see, eg *Breeders' Rights—maize seed* (n 249, above) (prohibition on dealing in competing products); *Velcro/Aplix* (n 257, above). See also *Windsurfing International v Commission* (n 240, above) (prohibition on selling certain non-patented items except in conjunction with patented items). But see *Delta Chemie/DDD* (n 258, above) where in the case of an exclusive know-how and trade mark licence, the Commission held that an obligation on the licensee not to manufacture or distribute similar products without the licensor's consent (which would not be withheld if sufficient certainty existed that the licensee would respect his contractual obligations) was not within Art 81(1).

[340] ibid.

[341] Reg 772/2004 (n 268, above) Art 4(1).

Customer restrictions.   The allocation of exclusive customer groups to licensees **9.107** and restrictions imposed on the parties with regard to their sales to the customer groups allocated to others are generally treated in the same way as the grant of exclusive territory.[342]

Prices.   An obligation on the licensee (or the licensor) relating to the prices upon **9.108** which that party may sell the patented products to third parties will, if it concerns fixed or minimum prices, ordinarily infringe Article 81(1)[343] and will not benefit from Regulation 772/2004.[344] The Commission has stated that an obligation regarding only maximum prices is not necessarily regarded as a restriction of competition in the context of vertical agreements where products are resold: whether a maximum price obligation falls within Article 81(1) depends on the economic context of the agreement and on whether this obligation has the effect of indirectly establishing fixed prices.[345] The same approach applies to price provisions in licences between non-competing undertakings. But a stricter approach appears to be adopted in relation to licences between competitors.[346]

Obligation on licensee to use licensor's get-up.   An obligation to use only the **9.109** licensor's trade mark or get-up may fall within Article 81(1) but is not mentioned in Regulation 772/2004. However, an obligation to mark the licensed product with an indication of the patent proprietor's name, or the patent concerned, or the relevant licence, generally falls outside Article 81(1),[347] provided the obligation does not extend to marking products not covered by the patent protection.[348]

(v) Other restrictions on the licensee

Licensee improvements.   An obligation on the licensee to pass to the licensor **9.110** the benefit of any experience gained in working the invention and to grant the licensor an exclusive licence in respect of any inventions relating to improvements

---

[342] See Guidelines on Technology Transfer (n 296, above) paras 162–174, and paras 9.095 *et seq*, above. See also *Breeders' Rights—maize seed* (n 249, above) (sales to certain dealers only). But for field of use clauses which do not infringe Art 81(1), see paras 9.105, above and 9.151, below.

[343] In *Erauw-Jacquery* (n 245, above) the ECJ held that a clause in a plant breeder's rights licence agreement requiring the licensee to respect the minimum prices fixed by the licensor fell within the prohibition of Art 81(1) where there is an appreciable effect on trade between Member States. See also *Plastic Omnium/GKM* [1988] Press release 6 EC Bull 50 (case closed after minimum price provision dropped); and *Zip Fasteners* (patents), Press Release IP/78/111 (9 June 1978), [1978] 3 CMLR 44.

[344] Reg 772/2004 (n 268, above) Arts 4(1)(a) and 4(2)(a).

[345] See Commission's Guidelines on Vertical Restraints, OJ 2000 C291/1, Vol II, App C.11, paras 225–228 and para 6.052, above.

[346] cf Reg 772/2004 (n 268, above) Arts 4(1)(a) and 4(2)(a); Guidelines on Technology Transfer (n 296, above) paras 79 and 97.

[347] Case 193/83 *Windsurfing International v Commission* [1986] ECR 611, [1986] 3 CMLR 489, para 72 and Guidelines on Technology Transfer, para 155(f).

[348] *Windsurfing International v Commission,* above.

and new applications normally falls within Article 81(1). So will an obligation on the licensee to assign the ownership of such inventions to the licensor.[349] Such a clause also prevents Regulation 772/2004 from applying.[350] However, a grant-back clause normally falls outside Article 81(1) if the licensee is obliged to do no more than grant back a licence to the licensor on a non-exclusive basis and if that obligation is balanced by a reciprocal obligation on the licensor.[351] In *Intel v VIA Technologies*[352] the English Court of Appeal held that the defendant had a real prospect of success in establishing that a reciprocal non-exclusive cross licence of improvements between two manufacturers of computer components arguably fell within Article 81(1) because it was asymmetrical. The licensee, VIA Technologies, was obliged to grant a royalty-free licence in respect of all improvements made to any of its patents whereas Intel was obliged only to grant a royalty-bearing licence to improvements to the technology licensed under the agreement.

9.111 **Tying and bundling obligations.** Article 81(1) does not apply where the licensor reasonably insists that the licensee procures certain products or takes a licence for another technology from the licensor or an undertaking designated by him, if such arrangements are indispensable for the technically proper exploitation of the licensed technology, or for ensuring that production under the licence confirms to quality standards respected by the licensor and other licensees.[353] But where the licensor has significant market power in the tying product and the tie covers a significant proportion of the market for the tied product, the licence may have anti-competitive effects such as foreclosing competing suppliers of the tied product.[354]

9.112 **Restriction on assignment and sub-licensing.** Limitations on the licensee's right to assign or sub-license normally fall outside Article 81(1).[355]

---

[349] *Raymond/Nagoya* (n 328, above); *Velcro/Aplix* (n 257, above); *Breeders' rights: roses*, OJ 1985 L369/9, [1988] 4 CMLR 193. The same applies to an obligation to grant joint ownership: *Nodet-Gougis/Lamazou, Tenth Report on Competition Policy* (1980), point 127.

[350] Reg 772/2004 (n 268, above) Art 5(1).

[351] See, eg *Rich Products/Jus-rol* (n 258, above); *Delta Chemie/DDD,* ibid. For a discussion of circumstances in which nonetheless Art 81(1) might apply, see *Kabelmetal/Luchaire*, OJ 1975 L222/34, [1975] 2 CMLR D40, D46–47 (licensee deprived of competitive advantage because improvements granted back to licensor were made available to all the licensor's other licensees).

[352] *Intel Corp v VIA Technologies* (n 326, above). This was one ground on which the Court discharged an order of summary judgment in favour of Intel.

[353] Guidelines on Technology Transfer (n 296, above) para 194. See also para 9.103, above, on minimum quality obligations. Tying clauses are not treated as hard-core restrictions under Reg 772/2004 and hence can be exempt if the parties' market share falls below the relevant threshold, see paras 9.144 *et seq*, below.

[354] ibid, para 193. Where the licensor has significant market power on the market for the tied rather than the tying product, the licence may operate as a non-compete of quantity forcing clause: ibid.

[355] See, eg *Delta Chemie/DDD* (n 258, above); Case T-504/93 *Tiercé Ladbroke v Commission* [1997] ECR II-923, [1997] 5 CMLR 304; and Guidelines on Technology Transfer, para 155.

Dealing with infringers.   An obligation to assist the other party in dealing with   **9.113**
infringements of the patents or misappropriation of the know-how will not normally come within Article 81(1).[356]

'Most favoured licensee' clause.   An obligation on the licensor to grant the   **9.114**
licensee any more favourable terms that the licensor may grant to another undertaking after the agreement is entered into may fall within Article 81(1) if it leads
to uniformity of pricing.[357]

'No-challenge' clause.   An obligation on the licensee not to challenge the valid-   **9.115**
ity of the patents or the secret and substantial nature of the know-how covered
by the licence may, depending on the legal and economic context, fall within
Article 81(1).[358] Such an obligation prevents the licensee from obtaining release
from the burdens of the licence. However, it has no restrictive effect where the
licence has been granted for no consideration and the licensee accordingly does
not have to suffer the competitive disadvantage of having to pay fees, or where
the licence has been granted for consideration but relates to a technically outdated
procedure not used by the licensee.[359] It further appears that Article 81(1) does
not apply to a provision which permits the licensor to terminate an agreement in
the event of a challenge by the licensee to the validity of the patent or to the secret
and substantial nature of the know-how, and such a provision does not preclude
exemption under Regulation 772/2004.[360] Similarly, a right to terminate the licence
if the licensee claims that the patent is unnecessary falls outside Article 81(1).

(vi) Obligations extending after expiry of the licence or of the rights

Undue prolongation of licence.   It has been held that a patent licence may fall   **9.116**
under Article 81(1) if its duration is automatically prolonged beyond the expiry

---

[356] Guidelines on Technology Transfer, para 155(d).

[357] However, see the Commission's investigation into the 'most favoured nation' clauses in the
'output deal' contracts of certain Hollywood film studios with pay television companies: Press
Release IP/04/2004 (26 October 2004). Studios agreed to sell broadcasters their entire film production for a set period with the right to enjoy the most favourable terms agreed between a pay-TV
company and any one of them. The Commission's initial assessment was that the cumulative effect
of such clauses was an alignment of prices paid to the studios because any increase paid by one
studio led to a parallel price increase for other studios. Similarly, a clause requiring the licensee to
offer the most favourable terms to all its customers may operate as a disincentive to price cutting: see
Guidelines on Technology Transfer, para 97.

[358] *Windsurfing International v Commission* (n 347, above) paras 89–94, upholding many previous decisions of the Commission to that effect; but cf *Raymond/Nagoya*, OJ 1972 L143/39, [1972]
CMLR D45 (restriction on Japanese licensee challenging validity of patents in EC or Far East not
on the facts restrictive of competition within the Community). See also Case 65/86 *Bayer v Süllhöfer*
[1988] ECR 5249, [1990] 4 CMLR 182. For the position on trade marks, see para 9.175, below.

[359] *Bayer v Süllhöfer* (n 358, above).

[360] Reg 772/2004 (n 268, above) Art 5(1)(c). But if the licensor is dominant, such a provision
might infringe Art 82: *AllVoice/IBM, XXXIInd Report on Competition Policy* (2002), p 205.

of the licensed patents existing at the conclusion of the agreement by the inclusion in the licence of any new patent obtained by the licensor, since in such a case the licensor may unilaterally and indefinitely extend the duration of the agreement.[361] However, Regulation 772/2004 is silent about agreements where the initial duration is extended indefinitely by the communication of improvements.

9.117 **Confidentiality of know-how.** An obligation to keep know-how confidential, even after the expiry of the agreement, does not fall under Article 81(1).[362]

9.118 **Non-exploitation after termination.** An obligation on the licensee not to exploit the patent or know-how after termination of the agreement if the patent is still in force or the know-how is not yet in the public domain will not fall under Article 81(1).[363] The Court of Justice has held that such a post-termination restraint which is not so limited constitutes a restriction on competition since the licensee will be at a disadvantage compared to his competitors who can freely manufacture the licensed products after the patent expires (or by analogy, when the know-how becomes public).[364]

9.119 **Duration of royalty obligations.** An obligation to pay royalties after the expiry of a patent may fall within Article 81(1) if the licensing agreement does not entitle the licensee to terminate the agreement within a reasonable period or attempts to restrain his freedom of action after termination.[365] The Guidelines on Technology Transfer states that the parties can normally agree to extend royalty obligations beyond the period of validity of the licensed rights without falling foul of Article 81(1) since the competition provided by non-licensees now able to use the technology should ensure that the royalty obligation does not have appreciable anti-competitive effects.[366] However, it may be that the position is otherwise as regards an obligation to continue to pay royalties in a know-how licence: this may fall within Article 81(1) if it continues after the subject-matter of the licence falls into the public domain through no fault of the licensee, or at least by the action of the licensor.[367]

---

361 *AOIP/Beyrard* (n 308, above) para II(4)(d); *Velcro/Aplix*, OJ 1985 L233/22, [1989] 4 CMLR 157; see also *Preflex/Lipski, Tenth Report on Competition Policy* (1980), point 126.

362 See, eg *Rich Products/Jus-rol*, OJ 1988 L69/21, [1988] 4 CMLR 527; *Delta Chemie/DDD*, OJ 1988 L309/34, [1989] 4 CMLR 535; *Moosehead/Whitbread*, OJ 1990 L100/32, [1991] 4 CMLR 391; Guidelines on Technology Transfer, para 155.

363 Guidelines on Technology Transfer (n 296, above) para 155. In early decisions the Commission took the contrary view: *Cartoux/Terrapin, Tenth Report on Competition Policy* (1980), point 129, but accepted such a provision in cases such as *Rich Products/Jus-rol* (n 362, above); Delta *Chemie/DDD*, ibid; *Moosehead/Whitbread*, ibid. In the *Fourth Report on Competition Policy* (1974), point 29, the Commission refers to the possibility of Art 82 applying if the licence was 'abusively short'.

364 Case 320/87 *Ottung v Klee* [1989] ECR 1177, [1990] 4 CMLR 915, paras 17–18.

365 *Ottung v Klee* (n 364, above) para 13.

366 Guidelines on Technology Transfer, para 159.

367 By analogy with Reg 772/2004, Art 2, and Guidelines on Technology Transfer, para 54. See Anderman and Kallaugher (n 2, above) para 7.69.

Settlement of disputes. The principles discussed in this Section apply equally **9.120**
to licences entered into in settlement of a dispute. Such licences should not contain restrictions on competition which are contrary to Article 81(1).[368]

Jointly held patents or know-how. The joint ownership of patents or know- **9.121**
how deriving legitimately from joint work does not in itself infringe Article 81(1),
but an agreement for joint research and development, or the setting up of a joint
venture or of a patent or know-how pool[369] may do so. Where patents or know-how
are jointly owned the granting of licences should not lead to a covert market-sharing
agreement, for example by a restriction on granting licences except by consent;[370]
and the parties should not restrict their freedom to use rival technologies,[371]
or unreasonably exclude third parties,[372] or charge unduly high royalties.[373]

Cross-licences and assignments. Cross-licensing occurs where holders of dif- **9.122**
ferent patents or know-how license each other. Where a market-sharing agreement
results, Article 81(1) will normally be applicable. Even where no market-sharing
is involved, licensing obligations between competitors or potential competitors
may be caught by Article 81(1).[374] An assignment of a patent or know-how where
the risk associated with exploitation remains with the assignor, for example where
the consideration is related to the use made of the technology, or where it is based
on the turnover or volume of products made with the technology, will usually be
treated as a licence.[375]

---

[368] See *Bayer v Süllhöfer* (n 358, above) concerning no-challenge obligations accepted pursuant
to a patent dispute settlement agreement. See also Case 258/78 *Nungesser v Commission* [1982] ECR
2015, [1983] 1 CMLR 278, paras 78–91; Guidelines on Technology Transfer (n 296, above) para
204. Under US antitrust law, see *US v Singer Manufacturing Co*, 374 US 174 (1963) (cross-licensing
of patents in settlement agreement between competitors, creating a patent pool).

[369] See *Dutch standard agreement on designs and models, Fifth Report on Competition Policy*
(1975), point 69; *Concast-Mannesmann, Eleventh Report* (1981), point 93; *IGR Stereo Television*,
ibid point 94 and *XIVth Report* (1984), point 92; *Philips/Matsushita DCC*, OJ 1992 C333/8, [1995]
4 CMLR 286, *XXIIIrd Report* (1993), p 460 (exemption-type comfort letter). And see Press Release
IP/02/1651 (12 November 2002) (clearance granted to jointly organised set of agreements for
licensing of competing technologies for 3G mobile services after modification of the arrangements
to ensure that competing technologies were not bundled together).

[370] *Bronbemaling v Heidemaatschappij*, OJ 1975 L249/27, [1975] 2 CMLR D67. See also *Bramley/
Gilbert, Tenth Report on Competition Policy* (1980), point 128 (restriction of competition between
joint inventors).

[371] *Video Cassette Recorders*, OJ 1978 L47/42, [1978] 2 CMLR 160.

[372] *IGR Stereo Television, Eleventh Report on Competition Policy* (1981), point 94.

[373] See *Ingman Disc VDC v Philips and Sony, etc, XXXIIIrd Report on Competition Policy* (2003),
p 197 (patent pool of Philips and Sony for compact disc technology infringed Arts 81 and 82
because of inclusion of non-essential and expired patents). See also Peña Castellot, (2003) 3 EC
Competition Policy Newsletter 56; *IGR, Fourteenth Report on Competition Policy* (1984), point 92.

[374] See *Philips/Matsushita DCC* (n 369, above). For licensing in the context of R&D, specialisation and joint venture agreements, see Chap 7, above.

[375] See *Preflex/Lipski* (n 361, above) (assignment coupled with payment in form of a percentage
of turnover with reservations concerning the definitive transfer of ownership of the assigned patents,
treated as a licence).

9.123   **Patent or know-how licences for non-Member States.**   In *Raymond/Nagoya*,[376] the Commission granted negative clearance to a licence granted by a German proprietor of the patent, Raymond, to a Japanese company, Nagoya. Raymond had licensed Nagoya to manufacture in Japan patented plastic attachment components used in the construction of cars. The Commission considered that an export limitation on bringing goods into the Community would not, on the facts, appreciably influence competition within the common market. It was extremely unlikely that the Japanese licensee would, in the absence of the limitation, have exported the goods to the Community. However, in *BBC Brown Boveri*,[377] an exclusive know-how licence for Japan and the Far East in the context of a joint research and development agreement was held to fall within Article 81(1) on the grounds that exports to the Community would have been feasible, notwithstanding the long distances involved.

(c) Technology pools

9.124   **Generally.**   A technology pool arises where two or more parties assemble a package of technology which is licensed to third parties. Such an arrangement may be pro-competitive where it provides a 'one-stop shop' for licensees who need to obtain a number of licences from different licensors in order to produce a particular product. But it can also have anti-competitive effects if it forecloses opportunities for new, or rival, technologies. The Commission's approach to the application of Article 81 to such arrangements is set out in Section 4 of the Guidelines on Technology Transfer.[378] The Commission's analysis depends on whether the technologies within the pool are complementary or substitutes for each other, and whether non-essential technologies are bundled with essential technologies. The Commission also examines particular restraints commonly found in such arrangements. The individual licences granted by the pool to third party licensees are treated like any other licence agreements and may benefit from the application of the block exemption in Regulation 772/2004, discussed in Section 5, below.

---

[376] *Raymond/Nagoya*, JO 1972 L143/39, [1972] CMLR D45.

[377] *BBC Brown Boveri*, OJ 1988 L301/68, [1989] 4 CMLR 610, para II(bb). For the issue of when an agreement concerning third countries may affect trade between Member States, see generally para 1.134, above.

[378] Guidelines on Technology Transfer, OJ 2004 C101/2: Vol II, App C.16. See also the Commission's settlement of complaints under Art 82 against the Sony/Philips patent pool for compact disc technology: *Ingman Disc VDC v Philips and Sony* (n 373, above). For a US perspective, see Skitol and Wu, 'A Transatlantic Swim Through Patent Pools: Keeping Antitrust Sharks at Bay' in Lugard and Hancher (eds), *On the Merits: Current Issues in Competition Law and Policy (Liber Amicorum Peter Plompen)*, Chap 7 (2005).

The nature of the pooled technologies.   Two technologies complement each   **9.125**
other where they are both required to make the product to which the technology
relates. Conversely, two technologies are substitutes where either one allows the
holder to make the product. This distinction may not be clear-cut in practice but
is key to the Commission's analysis. A technology is 'essential' where there are no
substitutes for it inside or outside the pool and it is a necessary part of the package
of rights needed to make the product. Technologies which are essential will, by
necessity, also be complementary.

Application of Article 81 to the creation of the pool.   Where a technology pool   **9.126**
is composed only of technologies which are essential and complementary, the creation of the pool will generally fall outside Article 81(1), irrespective of
the market position of the parties.[379] Where non-essential but complementary
technologies are included, there is a risk of foreclosure of a competing third
party technology because the licensee of the pool's package will have little incentive to pay an additional royalty for a substitute for rights he has already been
licensed to use. A pool which includes non-essential technologies is therefore
likely to be caught by Article 81(1) where the pool has a significant share of the
relevant market.[380] The application of Article 81 to such a pool therefore depends
upon whether there are pro-competitive reasons for including non-essential technologies in the pool; whether the licensors are free to license their technology
independently of the pool; and whether the pool offers differently configured
packages of rights so that the licensee does not have to acquire a package containing the non-essential rights, particularly where the pooled technologies can be
used for a number of different applications. Where the pool contains substitute
rather than complementary technologies, the Commission is likely to regard this
as a restriction on inter-technology competition leading to price-fixing between
competitors.[381] It is not sufficient that the parties remain free to license independently because they will have little incentive to do so since this would undermine
the pool.

Assessment of individual restraints in patent pools.   With regard to the condi-   **9.127**
tions imposed for entry to or licensing by the pool, the Commission's view is that
pools which hold a strong position on the market should be open and non-discriminatory and that pools should also not unduly foreclose third party technologies or limit the creation of alternative pools. Licensees must remain free to
determine the price of products produced under the licence and where the pool
has a dominant position on the market, royalties and other licensing terms must

---

[379] Guidelines on Technology Transfer, above, para 220.
[380] ibid, paras 221 and 222, where the Commission suggests that when a technology becomes
non-essential after the creation of the pool, the parties should consider excluding it from the pool.
[381] ibid, para 219.

be fair and non-discriminatory and licences should be non-exclusive. The treatment of licensees should not depend upon whether they are also licensors. Licensors and licensees must be free to develop competing products and standards and must also be free to grant and obtain licences outside the pool. The obligation on the licensee to grant the licensor rights to any important improvements to the technology must be non-exclusive. In order to limit the risk that a no-challenge clause will shield the inclusion of invalid patents in the pool, such a clause must be limited to the technologies owned by the licensor who is the addressee of the challenge and must not extend to other licensed technologies.

9.128 **The institutional framework of the patent pools.** In considering whether the pool is likely to operate in an open and non-discriminatory manner and reflect the value of the licensed technology, there are various factors which the Commission will take into account. The first is whether the membership of the pool represent different interests rather than just a limited group of technology owners. The second is the extent to which independent experts are involved in the creation and operation of the pool. Thirdly, the Commission will examine whether the pool involves the parties exchanging sensitive commercial information. Finally, the existence of a dispute resolution procedure is important: the more dispute resolution is entrusted to bodies or persons that are independent of the pool and its members, the more likely it is that the mechanism will operate in a neutral way.

5. The Block Exemption for Technology Transfer Agreements

(a) Introduction

9.129 **The move to an economics-based test.** The original block exemption for technology transfer agreements, Regulation 240/96,[382] was replaced as from 1 May 2004 by Regulation 772/2004.[383] Regulation 772/2004 is significantly different from its predecessor. Whereas Regulation 240/96 set out lists of restrictions which were either acceptable, neutral or prohibited, the new block exemption adopts a more economics-based approach, although retaining a list of hard-core, prohibited restrictions.[384] The underlying scheme of Regulation 772/2004 is to prescribe

---

[382] Reg 240/96, OJ 1996 L31/2.

[383] Reg 772/2004 on the application of Art 81(3) of the Treaty to categories of technology transfer agreements, OJ 2004 L123/11, Vol II, App C.7. Subject to necessary modifications, Reg 772/2004 has been adopted under Annex XIV of the EEA Agreement by EEA Joint Committee Decn 42/2005, OJ 2005 L198/42.

[384] See Recital (4) of Reg 772/2004.

a market share threshold above which the exemption does not apply and then to confer the benefit of the block exemption on any technology transfer agreement below that threshold, subject to a list of prohibited clauses. There is also a list of excluded restrictions in Article 5. If a licence contains one of the hard-core restrictions then no part of the agreement can benefit from the block exemption. However, if a licence contains an excluded clause, the disapplication of the exemption relates only to that obligation and the rest of the agreement can benefit from the exemption.

Transitional provisions.   Article 10 of Regulation 772/2004 provides that agree-   **9.130** ments which satisfied the conditions set out in Regulation 240/96 continued to benefit from block exemption until 31 March 2006. Thereafter, however, those agreements must satisfy the requirements of the new Regulation if exemption is to continue.

Interpretation: the Commission's Guidelines.   At the same time as Regulation   **9.131** 772/2004 was published, the Commission issued accompanying Guidelines on the application of Article 81 of the Treaty to technology transfer agreements.[385] The Guidelines provide important insights into the Commission's view as to the operation of Regulation 772/2004, as well as providing guidance on the application of Article 81 to agreements which fall outside the Regulation. Even if the agreement does not fall within the terms of the block exemption in Regulation 772/2004, the agreement may still benefit from the individual application of Article 81(3).[386]

Some basic concepts.   A number of provisions of Regulation 772/2004 refer   **9.132** to undertakings which are competing or which are not competing. The definitions of these terms have been discussed in the previous Section.[387] Similarly, the concept of reciprocal and non-reciprocal agreements between competitors is important in the application of the block exemption as well as in the more general assessment of individual clauses in licences between competing undertakings.[388]

(b) The scope of Regulation 772/2004

Agreements falling within the scope of Regulation 772/2004.   To identify the   **9.133** kinds of agreement which may benefit from the block exemption conferred by Regulation 772/2004, Article 2 of the Regulation has to be read in conjunction

---

[385] Guidelines on Technology Transfer, OJ 2004 C101/2: Vol II, App C.16. The EFTA Surveillance Authority adopted equivalent Guidelines on 21 September 2005 as regards the EEA Agreement by College Decn 228/05 (available on the EFTA Surveillance Authority website). See further para 9.083, above.

[386] ibid, para 65 and Recital (12) of Reg 772/2004.

[387] See paras 9.088 *et seq*, above.

[388] See para 9.091, above.

with the definitions of certain key terms set out in Article 1. Thus, according to the first paragraph of Article 2, the agreement (i) must be a technology transfer agreement; (ii) must be entered into between two undertakings; and (iii) must permit the production of contract products.

9.134 **Technology transfer agreements.** The term 'technology transfer agreement' is defined in Article 1(1)(b) of Regulation 772/2004.[389] Primarily it covers a number of distinct types of intellectual property licence, namely patent licensing agreements, know-how licensing agreements, software copyright licensing agreements and mixed patent, know-how or software copyright licensing agreements. The term 'agreement' is defined to include decisions of associations of undertakings and concerted practices;[390] the term 'patents' is defined to include utility models, designs, topographies of semiconductor products and plant breeder's certificates;[391] and 'know-how' is defined as a package of non-patented practical information resulting from experience and testing which is secret, substantial and identified.[392] The concept of 'transfer' means that technology 'must flow from one undertaking to another'.[393] Such transfers normally take the form of a licence of the right to use the technology in return for payment of royalties. It also includes sub-licences of technology.[394]

9.135 **Supplementary sale and purchase of goods.** A licence of patent, know-how or software copyright rights which also contains provisions relating to the sale and purchase of products may also fall within the definition of technology transfer agreements.[395] This will be the case only if those supplementary provisions (i) do not constitute the primary object of the agreement; and (ii) relate directly to the production of 'contract products', that is of products produced using the licensed technology.[396] This is likely to be the case where the product sold under the licence is something which has been specifically tailored for use with the licensed technology.[397]

9.136 **Supplementary licence of other intellectual property rights.** The definition of technology transfer agreements also covers agreements which license other rights, such as trade mark rights and non-software copyrights, alongside the

---

[389] See also Guidelines on Technology Transfer, paras 46 *et seq.*

[390] Reg 772/2004 (n 383, above) Art 1(1)(a).

[391] ibid, Art 1(1)(h). It also includes applications for protection for the kinds of rights which are covered (ibid).

[392] ibid, Art 1(1)(i) and see Guidelines on Technology Transfer (n 385, above) para 47.

[393] Guidelines on Technology Transfer, para 48.

[394] ibid.

[395] Reg 772/2004, Art 1(1)(b) and see Guidelines on Technology Transfer, para 49.

[396] ibid, Art 1(1)(f). Products includes a good or a service and includes both intermediary and final goods and services: Art 1(1)(e).

[397] Guidelines on Technology Transfer, para 49.

primary technology.[398] Again, this is subject to the requirement that the licence of these other rights is not the primary object of the agreement and that the other rights are directly related to the production of the products in that they serve to enable the licensee better to exploit the licensed technology. For example, the licensor may authorise the licensee to use his trade mark on the products incorporating the licensed technology, thereby allowing consumers to make an immediate link between the product and the licensor.[399] However, pure trade mark licences are not governed by Regulation 772/2004 and should not be assessed in accordance with the principles set out in the Regulation or the Guidelines since the Commission regards them as more akin to a distribuition agreement than to a technology licence.[400]

Assignments. Assignments (even bare assignments) of the patent, know-how or software copyright rights are also treated as technology transfer agreements in certain circumstances. This is the case where the assignor retains part of the risk associated with the exploitation of the technology in question, for example where the payments to the assignor depend on the turnover achieved by the assignee or are linked to the number of products produced using the technology.[401] **9.137**

Agreement between two undertakings. Technology transfer agreements between more than two undertakings are not covered by Regulation 772/2004.[402] However, the term 'undertaking' includes connected undertakings and these are defined in Article 1(2) of the Regulation. Agreements concluded by two undertakings fall within the scope of the Regulation even if the agreement stipulates conditions for more than one level of trade, for example, both the production and distribution stage. Further, the Commission has stated that where a multi-party agreement is of the same nature as a bilateral one, it will apply the principles set out in the Regulation.[403] **9.138**

Production of the contract products. In order for an agreement to benefit from the block exemption in Regulation 772/2004, the licensee must be entitled to make products using the licensed rights; indeed the production and supply of products must be the primary function of the agreement.[404] This means that an agreement which has the grant of sub-licences as its primary object will not be **9.139**

---

[398] Reg 772/2004, Art 1(1)(b).

[399] Guidelines on Technology Transfer, para 50.

[400] ibid, para 53. A licence of copyright for the purpose of reproduction and distribution of the protected work is considered as being similar to a technology transfer licence but a copyright licence for the performance of the work is not: Guidelines, paras 51 and 52.

[401] Reg 772/2004, Art 1(1)(b).

[402] ibid, Art 2.

[403] Guidelines on Technology Transfer (n 385, above) paras 49 and 40.

[404] See Recital (7) of Reg 772/2004 (n 383, above) and paras 41–46 and 49 of the Guidelines on Technology Transfer (n 385, above).

covered although the Commission will apply the principles in the Regulation to such 'master licensing' agreements.[405] The Regulation covers subcontracting whereby the licensee undertakes to produce products using the licensed technology exclusively for the licensor.[406]

9.140 **Duration of protection.** Article 2 of Regulation 772/2004 provides that the exemption conferred applies for as long as the intellectual property right in the licensed technology has not expired, lapsed or been declared invalid. In the case of know-how the exemption lasts for as long as it remains secret. Where the know-how has become publicly known as a result of the actions of the licensee, the exemption applies for the duration of the agreement. Where the licence covers more than one right, the block exemption ceases to apply on the date of expiry, invalidity or coming into the public domain of the last intellectual property right covered.[407]

(c) Market share thresholds

9.141 **Likelihood of economic damage.** The broad exemption set out in Article 2 of Regulation 772/2004 is deceptively simple since it is the exceptions and market threshold requirements which define the true ambit of the exemption. The application of market share thresholds reflects the Commission's assessment of which agreements are likely to cause economic damage and hence need to be prohibited. However, there is no presumption that an agreement between parties with higher market shares falls within Article 81(1) or does not fulfil the conditions of Article 81(3).[408]

9.142 **Market definition.** The application of the market share thresholds requires the definition of the relevant product and geographic markets.[409] The definition of relevant markets is considered in Chapter 4, above.

9.143 **Shares of technology and product markets.** The market threshold tests apply to the parties' shares of both the technology and the product markets. When assessing an undertaking's share of the technology market, any sales by the undertaking of products made using that technology must be aggregated with any sales made by its licensees of products using that technology. Thus if company A licenses both B and C to produce a particular pharmaceutical product but does not

---

405 Guidelines on Technology Transfer, para 42.
406 ibid, para 44, which refers to the Commission's Subcontracting Notice, OJ 1979 C1/2: Vol II, App C.8.
407 Guidelines on Technology Transfer, para 55.
408 See Reg 772/2004 Recital (12) and Guidelines on Technology Transfer, para 65.
409 See the Commission notice on the definition of the relevant market for the purposes of Community competition law, 1997 OJ C372/5: Vol II, App C.10, and the Guidelines on Technology Transfer, paras 19–25.

produce the product itself, A's share of the technology market is arrived at by aggregating the sales of B and C using that technology and determining what share that constitutes of the total value of the market for that product. The total value of the market for that product will include sales of all competing, substitutable products using other technologies as well as the sales of products incorporating A's technology. When assessing an undertaking's share of the product market, all the sales by the particular undertaking of products which compete in the product market are included, regardless of the technology which they use.[410] Thus if, in the above example, B was also licensed with a competing technology from D, B's sales of products incorporating D's technology would be included in assessing B's share of the product market but would not form part of A's share of the technology market.

Market share thresholds for competing and non-competing undertakings. **9.144** Where the parties to the technology transfer agreement are competing undertakings,[411] the exemption conferred by Article 2 of Regulation 772/2004 only applies if the combined market share of both parties is less than 20 per cent in both the affected technology market and the product market.[412] In the case of non-competing undertakings, the market shares of each of the parties must not exceed 30 per cent in order for the exemption to apply.[413] Market shares should be calculated on the basis of sales value data or, if such data are not available, other reliable market information including sales volumes may be used.[414] Market share is calculated on the basis of data realting to the preceding calendar year.[415] Article 8 of Regulation 772/2004 provides for the apportionment of market share between joint controllers of a party to the agreement and for the continued application of the exemption for two years where market shares rise above the relevant threshold.

(d) Hard-core restrictions

Hard-core restrictions: competing and non-competing undertakings.[416] **9.145** Article 4 of Regulation 772/2004 sets out the hard-core restrictions the inclusion of which in any technology transfer agreement will result in the disapplication of the exemption to the whole agreement. Where the parties to the agreement are competing, the hard-core restrictions are those set out in Article 4(1). Where the parties are not competing, the relevant restrictions are those set out in Article 4(2).

---

[410] See the examples given in Guidelines on Technology Transfer (n 385, above) para 73.
[411] Defined in Art 1(1)(j): see paras 9.088 *et seq*, above.
[412] Reg 772/2004 (n 383, above) Art 3(1).
[413] ibid, Art 3(2).
[414] ibid, Art 8(1), 2nd para.
[415] ibid; and see the examples in the Guidelines on Technology Transfer, para 73.
[416] See generally section 4.1 of the Guidelines on Technology Transfer.

Where the parties to the agreement are not competing undertakings at the time of the conclusion of the agreement but become competing thereafter, it is the restrictions in Article 4(2) and not Article 4(1) that apply for the full life of the agreement unless the agreement is subsequently amended in any material respect.[417]

9.146 **Hard-core restrictions and competing undertakings.** The hard-core restrictions relating to competing undertakings[418] are:

— restrictions on the price set for the sale of products to third parties;
— output limitations;
— allocation of markets or customers; and
— limiting own technology exploitation (own use restrictions).

Each of these types of restriction is considered further below. In relation to each restriction, the prohibition will apply wherever the agreement directly or indirectly has as its object the imposition of one of the hard-core restrictions and whether it does so in isolation or in combination with other factors under the control of the parties.

9.147 **Restrictions on price setting between competing undertakings.** The first hard-core restriction is 'the restriction of a party's ability to determine its prices when selling products to third parties'.[419] Any such restriction will exclude exemption whether it concerns fixed, maximum, minimum or recommended prices.[420] An obligation to pay a minimum royalty will not in itself amount to price-fixing but an arrangement which creates a disincentive for the licensee to sell below a certain price will do so.[421] In most circumstances, an arrangement whereby the licensee has to pay the royalty on all products sold by him whether or not they incorporate the licensed technology will constitute a hard-core restriction falling within Article 4(1)(a).[422]

9.148 **Price-fixing in cross-licences.** The Guidelines on Technology Transfer refers to a situation where competitors use cross-licensing combined with royalties calculated on the basis of individual product sales as a means of coordinating prices in downstream product markets. The Commission is therefore alert to the possibility that such arrangements are a sham with no pro-competitive purpose.[423]

---

[417] Reg 772/2004, Art 4(3).
[418] See generally section 4.2 of the Guidelines on Technology Transfer.
[419] Reg 772/2004 (n 383, above) Art 4(1)(a).
[420] Guidelines on Technology Transfer (n 385, above) para 79. cf the more favourable position regarding maximum and recommended prices in other vertical agreements, paras 6.051 and 6.052, above.
[421] ibid.
[422] ibid, para 81. This may not be the case where, eg the licensor's technology leaves no visible trace on the final product and there is no other way of determining how much of the licensee's output should be subject to the royalty.
[423] Guidelines on Technology Transfer, para 80.

Output limitations: reciprocal and non-reciproal agreements between **9.149**
competing undertakings.   The second hard-core restriction is 'the limitation of
output, except limitations on the output of contract products imposed on the
licensee in a non-reciprocal agreement or imposed on only one of the licensees in
a reciprocal agreement'.[424] A restriction on output between competing undertakings is only considered a hard-core restriction if it is (i) imposed on both parties to
a reciprocal agreement; or (ii) if it is imposed on one of the parties to a reciprocal
agreement in respect of products he produces using his own technology rather
than using the technology he is licensed to use under the agreement; or (iii) it is
imposed on the licensor in a non-reciprocal agreement. Output limitations on the
licensee in a non-reciprocal agreement, or on only one party to a reciprocal licence
(provided that the limitation relates to his production of products using the technology being licensed to him) are not hard-core restrictions.[425]

Market allocation and competing undertakings.   The third hard-core restric-   **9.150**
tion is the allocation of markets or customers by the parties.[426] This is, however,
subject to a number of important exceptions which enable the parties to incorporate limited market allocation into their arrangements without losing the benefit
of the exemption. The exceptions fall into three categories: field of use restrictions,
territorial restrictions and customer group restrictions. In relation to some of the
exceptions, the distinction between reciprocal and non-reciprocal agreements,
discussed in paragraph 9.091, above, is relevant. The policy behind the exceptions
appears to be aimed at enabling the licensor to allocate markets but only to the
extent of making any licence attractive to potential licensees.

Field of use restrictions between competing undertakings.   A field of use   **9.151**
restriction in a licence limits the ability of the licensee to use the licensed technology for some of the uses to which it could be put, or to produce some products
which could incorporate the technology.[427] An obligation on a licensee to produce
with the licensed technology only within one or more technical fields of use, or
one or more product markets is permitted.[428] This is the case even in a reciprocal
agreement where the obligation is placed on both parties in relation to the technology licensed to them. In order to distinguish between a field of use restriction
and a customer allocation restriction, the field of use 'must be defined objectively
by reference to identified and meaningful technical characteristics of the licensed
product'.[429] Further, the restriction must not go beyond the scope of the licensed

---

[424] Reg 772/2004, Art 4(1)(b).
[425] See Guidelines on Technology Transfer (n 385, above) paras 82–83 for the economic justification of this difference in treatment.
[426] Reg 772/2004 (n 383, above) Art 4(1)(c).
[427] See the examples given in Guidelines on Technology Transfer, paras 179–183.
[428] Reg 772/2004, Art 4(1)(c)(i).
[429] Guidelines on Technology Transfer, para 180.

technologies and no restriction must be imposed on the licensee in relation to the use of his own technology.[430] In a non-reciprocal agreement, the licensor may also be restricted from producing with the licensed technology within a field of use or product market which is reserved for the licensee.[431] Such a restriction may be necessary to give the licensee an incentive to invest in and develop the licensed technology.[432] It may also be combined with a field of use restriction imposed on the licensee.

9.152 **Territorial restrictions between competing undertakings.** The following territorial restrictions are permitted as exceptions to the prohibition on market allocation:

(a) the licensor in a non-reciprocal agreement may be restricted from producing with the licensed technology in the territory which is exclusively reserved to the licensee, even if this territory encompasses the whole world;[433]

(b) the licensor may be restricted from licensing the technology to another licensee in a particular territory, whether the agreement is reciprocal or non-reciprocal;[434]

(c) both the licensor and the licensee in a non-reciprocal agreement may be restrained from making passive or active sales into the exclusive territory of the other party;[435]

(d) the licensee in a non-reciprocal agreement may be restrained from making active sales into the territory allocated exclusively to another licensee provided that this protected licensee was not a competitor of the licensor at the time of the conclusion of the licence between him and the licensor.[436]

9.153 **Customer group restrictions between competing undertakings.** The following restrictions are permitted as exceptions to the prohibition of customer allocation restrictions:

(a) both the licensor and the licensee in a non-reciprocal agreement may be restrained from making passive or active sales to a customer group exclusively reserved to the other party;[437]

---

430 ibid, para 90.
431 Reg 772/2004, Art 4(1)(c)(ii).
432 Guidelines on Technology Transfer, para 86.
433 Reg 772/2004, Art 4(1)(c)(ii) and see Guidelines on Technology Transfer, para 86.
434 Art 4(1)(c)(iii) and Guidelines, para 88.
435 ibid, Art 4(1)(c)(iv). For the distinction between active and passive sales, see para 6.054, above, and the Commission's Guidelines on Vertical Restraints, OJ 2000 C291/1: Vol II, App C.11, para 50.
436 Reg 772/2004 (n 383, above) Art 4(1)(c)(v). See also Guidelines on Technology Transfer (n 385, above) para 89, where the Commission notes that an agreement amongst the licensees not to sell into each other's territories is a cartel not covered by the block exemption.
437 Art 4(1)(c)(iv).

(b) the licensee in a non-reciprocal agreement may be restrained from making active sales to the exclusive customer group allocated to another licensee provided that this protected licensee was not a competitor of the licensor at the time of the conclusion of the licence between him and the licensor;[438]

(c) the licensee may be required to produce the contract products only for his own use.[439] Where the contract product is a component, the licensee can thus be obliged to produce that component only for incorporation into his own products and can be obliged not to sell the components to other producers. The licensee must be free, however, to sell the components as spare parts for his own products and must thus be able to supply third parties that perform after sale services on these products. Such a restriction, commonly called a 'captive use' restriction,[440] may be necessary to encourage the dissemination of technology, particularly between competitors;

(d) the licensee in a non-reciprocal agreement may be required to produce contract products only for a particular customer where the licence was granted in order to create an alternative souce of supply for that customer.[441]

Restrictions on use and development of technology between competing undertakings. Article 4(1)(d) of Regulation 772/2004 categorises as hard-core restrictions any limit on the licensee's ability to exploit his own technology (including on his ability to sub-license his own technology[442]) and any restriction on either party to the licence to carry out research and development. The latter kind of restriction may be permissible if that is the only way to ensure that licensed know-how is not disclosed to third parties.[443] The mere fact that the parties agree to provide each other with future improvements of their respective technologies does not amount to a restriction on independent research and development.[444] **9.154**

Hard-core restrictions and non-competing undertakings. Article 4(2) of Regulation 772/2004 sets out a different set of hard-core restrictions when the licence is between parties who are not competing. The distinction between competing and non-competing undertakings has been discussed at paragraph 9.088, above. The benefit of the exemption will be lost for the whole agreement if the object of the agreement, either directly or indirectly, in isolation or in combination with other factors within the control of the parties, is to impose one of the prohibited restrictions. As one would expect, a narrower range of restrictions is prohibited as between non-competing undertakings than as between **9.155**

---

[438] Art 4(1)(c)(v). See also Guidelines on Technology Transfer, para 89.
[439] Art 4(1)(c)(vi) and see Guidelines on Technology Transfer, paras 92 and 186–190.
[440] See para 9.102, above.
[441] Art 4(1)(c)(vii).
[442] Guidelines on Technology Transfer (n 385, above) para 95.
[443] ibid, para 94.
[444] ibid.

competing undertakings. This narrower range of prohibited restrictions applies to the agreement throughout its life, even if the parties become competitors during the course of the agreement, unless the agreement is subsequently amended in any material respect.[445]

9.156 **Price restrictions between non-competing undertakings.** Unlike the position in relation to competing undertakings where any price restraint is banned, non-competing undertakings may accept restrictions in the form of a maximum or recommended sale price without losing the benefit of the block exemption. This is subject to the proviso that there is no price-fixing or minimum price-fixing arising as a result of pressure from, or an incentive offered by, either party.[446] The Commission's Guidelines on Technology Transfer give examples of indirect means of price-fixing, such as margin and discount fixing and other price maintenance incentives.[447]

9.157 **Restrictions on sales by licensor in agreement between non-competing parties.** Restrictions on either active or passive sales by the licensor are not regarded as hard-core restrictions.[448]

9.158 **Restriction on active sales by non-competing licensee.** Generally, only restrictions on the licensee making passive sales outside its territory or allocated customer group are prohibited where the parties to the licence are non-competing. Thus, the licensee may be restrained from making active sales into the territory or to a customer group which is supplied by the licensor or another licensee.[449] The only circumstances in which a ban on active sales is regarded as a hard-core restriction is where the licensee is part of a selective distribution system operating at the retail level and the licensee is restricted from making active sales to end-users.[450] A restriction on the licensee's ability to operate out of an unauthorised place of business will not be regarded as a restriction on making active sales to end-users.[451] The ban on active sales is allowed even where the protected territory is not allocated to another supplier on an exclusive basis, for example, where more than one licensee has been appointed for a particular territory or customer group.[452]

---

[445] Reg 772/2004, Art 4(3).
[446] ibid, Art 4(2)(a).
[447] Guidelines on Technology Transfer, para 97.
[448] ibid, para 99.
[449] Reg 772/2004, Art 4(2)(b)(i) and (ii). For the distinction between active and passive sales see para 6.054, above and the Commission's Guidelines on Vertical Restraints, OJ 2000 C291/1: Vol II, App C.11, para 50.
[450] ibid, Art 4(2)(c).
[451] ibid.
[452] Guidelines on Technology Transfer (n 385, above) para 99.

Restriction on passive sales by non-competing licensee.   A restriction on the **9.159** making of passive sales by the licensee will be regarded as a hard-core restriction and forfeit the benefit of the block exemption unless it falls within one of the exceptions listed in Article 4(2)(b). Passive sales may be restricted by direct or indirect means. Limits on the quantity of the contract products which the licensee is allowed to sell will not be assumed to be an indirect means of preventing passive sales unless there are indications that the limits are being imposed to implement an underlying market partitioning agreement, for example the adjustment of the quantity over time to match the demand in the licensee's territory.[453] The licensee may be restricted from making passive sales to the territory or customer group exclusively reserved for the licensor or for another licensee. For a territory or customer group to be regarded as reserved to the licensor it is not necessary that the licensor is actually producing with the licensed technology for those markets – it can be reserved for the licensor for later exploitation.[454] Where the restriction relates to a territory allocated to another licensee, the ban on passive sales is only permissible during the first two years of the protected licensee's sales in that territory or to that group.[455]

Captive use restrictions between non-competing undertakings.   The licensee **9.160** may be required to produce the contract products only for his own use.[456] Where the contract product is a component, the licensee can thus be obliged to produce that component only for incorporation into his own products and can be obliged not to sell the components to other producers. The licensee must be free, however, to sell the components as spare parts for his own products and must thus be able to supply third parties that perform after sale services on these products. Such a 'captive use' restriction may be necessary to encourage the dissemination of technology, particularly between competitors. The licensee may also be required to produce contract products only for a particular customer where the licence was granted in order to create an alternative souce of supply for that customer.[457]

Restrictions on sales to end-users between non-competing parties.   Where the **9.161** licensee operates 'at the wholesale level of trade', it may be prohibited from making sales to end-users, in other words it may be required to sell only to retailers.

---

[453] Other examples are given in Guidelines on Technology Transfer, para 98.

[454] Guidelines on Technology Transfer, para 100.

[455] ibid, para 101.

[456] Reg 772/2004 (n 383, above) Art 4(2)(b)(iii) and see Guidelines on Technology Transfer (n 385, above) paras 102 and 186–190.

[457] Art 4(2)(b)(iv). The Commission does not regard such restrictions as likely to fall within Art 81(1): Guidelines on Technology Transfer, para 103.

This allows the licensor to allocate the wholesale distribution function to the licensee and such a restriction will not normally be caught by Article 81(1).[458]

9.162 **Restrictions in a selective distribution network.** In the context of a selective distribution system, the licensee may be prohibited from supplying to unauthorised distributors.[459] However, a ban on either passive or active sales to end-users by a licensee who operates at the retail level is a hard-core restriction.[460]

(e) Excluded restrictions

9.163 **Excluded restrictions.** Article 5 of Regulation 772/2004 sets out four types of restrictions which do not benefit from the block exemption. The inclusion of such a clause in the licence does not take the whole agreement outside the block exemption. The remainder of the agreement may be covered by the exemption but these clauses must be assessed separately to determine whether they fall within Article 81(1) and, if so, whether the conditions for the application of Article 81(3) are fulfilled.

9.164 **Assignment or licensing of severable improvements.** The first two excluded restrictions concern the situation where the licensee develops improvements to the licensed technology or discovers new applications of that technology. The block exemption does not apply to an obligation on the licensee to grant an exclusive licence of its rights in such improvements or new applications to the licensor[461] or to assign those rights to the licensor.[462] The Article refers to rights in 'severable' improvements, namely an improvement that can be exploited without infringing the licensed technology.[463] Exclusive grant backs and assignments of non-severable improvements do not fall within Article 81(1) since they cannot, in any case, be exploited by the licensee without the licensor's permission.[464] An obligation to grant a non-exclusive right is not excluded and so can benefit from the block exemption, even where the licensor is under no corresponding obligation to pass on improvements to the licensee or where the licensor is entitled under the agreement to 'feed-on' the licensee's improvement by licensing it to other licensees.[465] The exclusion of such 'licence back' clauses from the benefit of

---

[458] Art 4(2)(b)(v) and Guidelines on Technology Transfer, para 104.

[459] Art 4(2)(b)(vi).

[460] Art 4(2)(c). Since a ban on sales to end-users only applies if the licensee operates at the retail level, it is still possible for the licensor to take advantage of the exception in Art 4(2)(b)(v) and restrict the wholesaling licensee from making retail sales: Guidelines on Technology Transfer, para 106.

[461] Art 5(1)(a).

[462] Art 5(1)(b). An obligation to licence or assign to a third party designated by the licensor is also excluded from the block exemption.

[463] Art 1(1)(n).

[464] Guidelines on Technology Transfer (n 385, above) para 109.

[465] ibid.

the block exemption does not depend on whether the licensor is required to pay royalties or other consideration to the licensee, although this will be relevant to the individual assessment of the clause.[466]

'No challenge' clauses. A term which prevents the licensee from challenging the validity of the rights which the licensor holds in the common market does not benefit from the block exemption.[467] However, it is permissible for the licensor to provide that the licence agreement may be terminated if the licensee challenges the validity of one or more of the rights in question.[468]   **9.165**

Exploitation of licensee's own technology. Where the licensee and licensor are non-competing undertakings,[469] any obligation which amounts to a restraint on the licensee's conduct of independent research and technology will be excluded from the benefit of the block exemption.[470] Such a restriction is permitted, however, if it is the only way to ensure that licensed know-how is not disclosed to third parties.[471]   **9.166**

(f) Withdrawal of the block exemption

Withdrawal in individual cases. Situations may arise where the Commission comes to the view that although a licence falls within Regulation 772/2004, it has effects which are incompatible with Article 81(3).[472] This may be because barriers to entry arise from the cumulative effect of networks of licences which prohibit the use of third-party technology by licensees[473] or which prohibit licensors from licencing other licensees,[474] or where the parties do not exploit the licensed technology.[475] Article 6 of the Regulation therefore provides that the Commission may withdraw the benefit of the block exemption in such circumstances. Where a licence has such effects in the territory of a Member State, or a region within a Member State, which constitutes a distinct geographic market, the competition   **9.167**

---

466 ibid, para 110.

467 Reg 772/2004, Art 5(1)(c); and see the comments in Guidelines on Technology Transfer, para 112, concerning the Commission's approach to the individual assessment of such clauses.

468 ibid. The provision therefore ensures that the licensee is in the same position as a third party challenger in that it continues its use of the licensed technology at its own risk.

469 See para 9.088, above.

470 Reg 772/2004, Art 5(2). Where the parties are competitors, such a clause is a hard-core restriction which deprives the whole agreement of the benefit of the block exemption: see Art 4(1)(d).

471 Art 5(2), and see Guidelines on Technology Transfer, paras 114–116.

472 The Commission has stated that since withdrawal implies that the agreement falls within Art 81(1) and does not fulfil the criteria of Art 81(3) it must necessarily by accompanied by a negative decision under Reg 1/2003: Guidelines on Technology Transfer (n 385, above) para 119.

473 Reg 772/2004, Art 6(1)(a).

474 ibid, Art 6(1)(b).

475 ibid, Art 6(1)(c), and see Guidelines on Technology Transfer, para 122.

authority of that Member State also has power to withdraw the benefit of the block exemption as regards that territory.[476]

9.168 **Disapplication to classes of licences.** Where parallel networks of similar technology transfer agreements cover more than 50 per cent of a relevant market, the Commission may make a regulation providing that such agreements do not benefit from Regulation 772/2004 if they contain certain types of specified restraints.[477] The regulation must allow a transitional period of at least six months to enable undertakings to bring their agreements into compliance with Article 81.[478] Agreements from which the benefit of the block exemption is withdrawn by Commission regulation will thereafter need to be individually assessed under Article 81(1) and (3) to determine, for example, whether they have an appreciable effect on competition.[479]

(g) Relationship between Regulation 772/2004 and other block exemptions

9.169 **Generally.** The terms of a licence will need to be assessed not only under Regulation 772/2004 but in the context of other block exemptions, in particular Regulation 2658/2000 regarding specialisation agreements,[480] Regulation 2659/2000 regarding research and development agreements[481] and Regulation 2790/1999 regarding vertical agreements.[482] The interface between these Regulations and Regulation 772/2004 is considered by the Commission in the Guidelines on Technology Transfer.[483]

9.170 **Specialisation and research and development agreements.** An agreement under which two or more undertakings agree to produce certain products jointly will be covered by Regulation 2658/2000[484] and provisions in such an agreement regarding the assignment or use of intellectual property rights needed for the implementation of the agreement should be assessed under that Regulation where they are secondary to the main purpose of the agreement.[485] Similarly, where a production joint venture is established and the joint venture vehicle is licensed with the parents' technology, that licence will also fall to be considered under

---

476 ibid, Art 6(2).
477 Reg 772/2004, Art 7(1). The class of agreements covered by the withdrawal may, therefore, be narrower than the class of agreements which cover 50 per cent of the market: see Guidelines on Technology Transfer, para 127.
478 Reg 772/2004, Art 7(2).
479 Guidelines on Technology Transfer, paras 126–127.
480 Reg 2658/2000, OJ 2000 L304/3: Vol II, App C.4, discussed in Chap 7, above.
481 Reg 2659/2000, OJ 2000 L304/7: Vol II, App C.5, discussed in Chap 7, above.
482 Reg 2790/1999, OJ 1999 L336/21: Vol II, App C.3, discussed in Chap 6, above.
483 Guidelines on Technology Transfer, paras 56 *et seq*.
484 Reg 2658/2000, Art 1(1)(c).
485 Guidelines on Technology Transfer, para 58.

Regulation 2658/2000.[486] Regulation 2659/2000 covers licensing between undertakings which agree jointly to carry out research and development and to exploit the results of that work jointly. Licences between the parties to such an agreement, and between each parent and a joint entity created by them, will be covered by Regulation 2659/2000. However, agreements with third parties licensing the fruits of the research will need to comply with Regulation 772/2004.[487]

Vertical agreements.   Regulation 772/2004 includes within its scope agreements between the licensor and the licensee where the licensee is subject to obligations as to the way in which he sells products incorporating the licensed technology. The subsequent agreements between the licensee and its customers (either retailers or end-users) fall within the remit of Regulation 2790/1999 and must comply with that Regulation in order to benefit from block exemption. Where the different licensees of the licensor sell their products incorporating a brand identity which belongs to the licensor, the Commission may be prepared to treat the distribution networks established by the individual licensees as if they were one large network established by the licensor.[488] Furthermore, where the licence of intellectual proprty rights is ancillary to the sale or resale of goods or services, which constitutes the main object of the agreement, for example where the rights are assigned or licensed to the buyer so that he can use or resell the goods or services more effectively, the agreement may receive exemption under Regulation 2790/1999.[489] Licences which serve the implementation of a vertical agreement in that way generally concern trade marks, copyright or know-how.[490]

9.171

6. Licences of other Intellectual Property Rights

(a) Trade marks

Trade mark licences generally.   Trade mark licences occur in the context of distribution or franchise agreements, as well as in connection with patent and know-how licences, sales of a business, joint ventures, and other similar agreements discussed elsewhere in this work. Reference is made here only to certain points relating specifically to trade mark licences under Articles 81 and 82, and to agreements not to use trade marks, including agreements settling disputes.

9.172

---

[486] ibid.

[487] ibid, para 60.

[488] ibid, para 64.

[489] Reg 2790/1999 (n 482, above) Art 2(3). See para 6.016, above, and for franchising agreements, para 6.183, above.

[490] See Guidelines on Vertical Restraints, OJ 2000 C291/1: Vol II, App C.11, paras 30–43.

9.173 **Exclusive trade mark licences.** Aside from the principle of exhaustion of rights,[491] the exercise of licensed trade mark rights to prevent the import of goods lawfully placed on the market in another Member State may be contrary to Article 81(1),[492] and Article 81(1) may apply if the grant of an exclusive trade mark licence gives rise to a system of absolute territorial protection.[493] Further, in *Campari*[494] the Commission held that Article 81(1) applied to an exclusive trade mark licence where Campari had agreed not to license the mark to anyone else in various Member States nor itself to manufacture products bearing the mark in the territories concerned. In that case, the Commission held that the criteria in Article 81(3) were met. While a trade mark licence that is ancillary to a patent and know-how licence may benefit from exemption under Regulation 772/2004,[495] an agreement which is predominantly a trade mark agreement is not covered by that Regulation.[496]

9.174 **Quality control.** Provisions intended to provide the owner of the trade mark with the means to ensure that the quality associated with the mark is maintained will not usually fall under Article 81(1).[497] Thus in *Campari*, requirements to follow the licensor's instructions, to obtain certain secret ingredients[498] only

---

[491] Para 9.032, above.

[492] Paras 9.066 *et seq*, above.

[493] See, eg Cases 56 & 58/64 *Consten and Grundig v Commission* [1966] ECR 299, [1966] CMLR 418; Case 28/77 *Tepea v Commission* [1978] ECR 1391, [1978] 3 CMLR 392. Assignment of a trade mark does not infringe Art 81(1) in the absence of continuing concertation between the parties: *IHT Internationale Heiztechnik v Ideal Standard*, para 9.047, above.

[494] *Campari*, OJ 1978 L70/69, [1978] 2 CMLR 397. That decision was prior to *Nungesser v Commission*, paras 9.079 *et seq*, above; *quaere* whether the Commission's decision that the grant of an exclusive territory *ipso facto* brings the agreement within Art 81(1) is still correct, (cf also Art 4(1)(c)(ii) of Reg 772/2004, para 9.152, above). But see also *Campari, XVIIIth Report on Competition Policy* (1988), point 69 (informal comfort letter following an application to renew the exemption granted in 1977); and *Moosehead/Whitbread*, OJ 1990 L100/32, [1991] 4 CMLR 391, where the Commission held that an exclusive trade mark licence to produce and market beer in the UK under a particular mark fell within the prohibition of Art 81(1).

[495] Para 9.136, above.

[496] See *Moosehead/Whitbread* (n 494, above) (Reg 556/89 did not apply because trade mark licence was the principal element and the grant of know-how was ancillary). See also Guidelines on Technology Transfer, OJ 2004 C101/2: Vol II, App C.16, para 53.

[497] *Campari* (n 494, above). See also, eg Guidelines on Technology Transfer, para 94.

[498] The requirement to buy from the licensor did not extend to ingredients such as bitters and orange essence; such a requirement could not have been justified under Art 81(1), although the licensor was entitled to exercise quality control. See also *Moosehead/Whitbread* (n 494, above): an exclusive purchasing obligation on the licensee in respect of the yeast to be used in producing the beer did not fall within Art 81(1) as it was necessary to ensure technically satisfactory exploitation of the licensed technology. Similarly, obligations on the licensee with regard to the quality of raw materials and finished product and to the protection of the know-how disclosed under the agreement did not fall within Art 81(1).

from the licensor, and to manufacture only in plants capable of guaranteeing the quality of the product were held to fall outside Article 81(1).[499]

No-challenge clause. In *Moosehead/Whitbread*,[500] the Commission gave detailed **9.175** consideration to a no-challenge clause in an exclusive trade mark licence and held that an obligation on the licensee not to challenge the ownership of the trade mark did not restrict competition within the meaning of Article 81(1). An obligation not to challenge the validity of the trade mark could fall under Article 81(1) because it might contribute to the maintenance of an invalid trade mark that would therefore present an unjustified barrier to entry. However, the restriction on competition would only be appreciable where the use of a well-known trade mark would be an important advantage to a company entering or competing in a given market. In *Moosehead/Whitbread* there was no appreciable restriction of competition because the relevant trade mark was new to the market and the fact that other competitors were not able to use it did not constitute an appreciable barrier to entry.[501]

Restrictions in trade mark licences. The application of Article 81 to other **9.176** restrictions that may be found in trade mark licences, for example relating to sales territories, the supply of competing products and so on, will be governed by the general principles discussed elsewhere in this work.[502]

Agreement not to use trade marks. An agreement not to use a trade mark may, **9.177** in principle, fall within Article 81(1).[503] Such agreements may, however, arise in

---

[499] But cf Case 193/83 *Windsurfing International v Commission* [1986] ECR 611, [1986] 3 CMLR 489, paras 82 *et seq.*

[500] *Moosehead/Whitbread*, OJ 1990 L100/32, [1991] 4 CMLR 391.

[501] But cf *Windsurfing*, OJ 1983 L229/1, [1984] 1 CMLR 1, upheld on this point in *Windsurfing International v Commission* (n 499, above): the Commission held that the acknowledgment by patent licensees that the licensor had valid trade marks (which were not licensed to the licensees) fell within Art 81(1), but left open whether a no-challenge clause falls within Art 81(1) when it is part of the agreement licensing the mark in question. See also *Goodyear Italiana*, OJ 1975 L38/10, [1975] 1 CMLR D31 (no-challenge clause removed at request of Commission); *Glass Containers*, OJ 1974 L160/1, [1974] 2 CMLR D50 (Commission did not object to an agreement not to copy the trade mark of another party). For such clauses in agreements settling disputes between trade mark owners, see para 9.177, below.

[502] See in particular, Chap 6 (distribution and franchise agreements, etc). And see generally *Campari* (n 494, above); *Moosehead/Whitbread* (n 494, above).

[503] *Toltecs/Dorcet*, OJ 1982 L379/19, [1983] 1 CMLR 412, on appeal Case 35/83 *BAT v Commission* [1985] ECR 363, [1985] 2 CMLR 470 (BAT held 'Dorcet' mark in Germany. Agreement by owner of 'Toltecs' mark not to market in Germany infringed Art 81(1). The ECJ found that BAT had no legitimate interest in opposing the 'Toltecs' mark since its own mark Dorcet was dormant and the true purpose of the agreement was market-sharing to which Art 81(1) applied). See also, eg *Syntex/Synthelabo*, Press Release IP/89/108 (28 February 1989), [1990] 4 CMLR 343 (agreement by one party which made the use of its mark more difficult in the UK was considered not necessary to avoid risk of confusion and dropped after Commission intervention); *Sirdar/Phildar*, OJ 1975 L125/27, [1975] 1 CMLR D93 (agreement between owners of Sirdar and Phildar marks not to sell in France and UK respectively: Art 81(1) applied); *Persil,*

the context of a genuine dispute about trade marks. In such circumstances the parties should strive to reach the least restrictive solution, in the first instance agreeing so far as possible to use distinguishing marks, shapes or colours to differentiate their products.[504] A bare agreement not to market goods under a trade mark may infringe Article 81(1), particularly if the underlying purpose is to secure market protection.[505] If the agreement not to use a mark is made to settle a genuine dispute, and does not require the party restrained to re-establish its goodwill under another name, Article 81(1) may not apply. Thus in *Penney's*[506] the Commission granted negative clearance under Article 81(1) for a settlement agreement which involved one party agreeing not to use the mark in question, and not to challenge the other party's rights for five years, in circumstances where the party restrained was already successfully carrying on business under other marks and, in the circumstances, the agreement represented the least restrictive solution to a genuine dispute.

9.178   **Royalties for use of the mark.**   In a series of cases the Commission has considered the licensing of the mark known as '*Der grüne punkt*' or 'the Green Dot'

Seventh Report on Competition Policy (1977), point 138 (owners of Persil trade mark in UK and Germany respectively attempted to stop imports of products bearing the mark originating from each other; the Commission held Art 81(1) applied, and the parties agreed to desist and to differentiate their products); *Winninger Domgarten*, Tenth Report (1980), points 133–134 (British firms holding the trade marks Domgarten and Domgarden threatened proceedings against imports of German wine under the name Winninger Domgarten. Matter settled on basis that use of the British trade mark would infringe Reg 355/79 on general rules for description of wine: Art 81(1) proceedings dropped); *Hershey-Herschi*, Press Release IP/90/87 (2 February 1990), *XXth Report on Competition Policy* (1990*)*, point 111 (litigation concerning the right to use a trade mark settled on the basis that one party assigned the mark to the other and took a limited licence back for certain products, whilst agreeing not to introduce new products under the trade mark. The Commission took the view that the settlement solved the problem of confusion in a manner which did not impede competition. No partitioning of the Community on territorial lines was involved). But the assignment of a trade mark arising on the sale of a business does not infringe Art 81(1): Case C-9/93 *IHT Internationale Heiztechnik v Ideal Standard* [1994] ECR I-2789, [1994] 3 CMLR 857, discussed at para 9.047, above.

[504]   *Penneys*, OJ 1978 L60/19, [1978] 2 CMLR 100. In *BAT v Commission,* above, the ECJ stated (at para 33) that so called 'delimitation agreements' are lawful and useful if they serve to delimit, in the mutual interest of the parties, the spheres within which their respective trade marks may be used and are intended to avoid confusion or conflict between them. That is not to say, however, that such agreements are excluded from the application of Art 81 if they also have the aim of dividing up the market or restricting competition in other ways. See also, eg *Bayer/Tanabe, Eighth Report on Competition Policy* (1978), points 125–127 (trade mark litigation concerning the Bayer 'cross' settled on Tanabe agreeing to use a distinguishing mark: Art 81(1) not applicable to the settlement); *Osram/Airam, Eleventh Report* (1981), point 97 (settlement of proceedings between 'Osram' and 'Airam' not within Art 81(1); note that the complainant, Airam, had alleged that the other party, Osram, had infringed Art 82 by abusively registering the Airam mark in Germany).

[505]   *BAT v Commission* (n 503, above).

[506]   n 504, above. See also *Hershey-Herschi* (n 503, above).

which is affixed to packaging to indicate that it can be recycled. In *DSD*[507] the Commission considered the arrangements set up by the only undertaking that operated a comprehensive packaging take-back system in Germany. DSD licensed manufacturers to include the Green Dot logo on their packaging material so that consumers would know that they should dispose of that package in the Green Dot bin rather than the public waste disposal bin. DSD charged for the service by setting a licence fee for all packaging to which the Green Dot mark was affixed regardless of whether that actual package was finally collected by it. This meant that manufacturers had in effect to pay DSD a royalty for all the packaging they produced even if, in a particular area of Germany, they self-collected or appointed a rival operator (should one exist in the future) to collect their packaging. The Commission found that this was an abuse of DSD's dominant position because it linked the fees for the service DSD provided not to the extent of use of DSD's service but to the extent of use of the logo which might not be the same. DSD appealed against the decision and sought interim measures asking for suspension of the order that it change the way it sets its fees. The President of the Court of First Instance found that DSD had not established that it was likely to suffer irreparable damage and further that the balance of public interest lay in refusing interim measures.[508]

(b) Copyright

Copyright licences generally. As already discussed, copyright or similar protection may exist in many different creations, including sound recordings, literary and artistic works, cinema films, television broadcasts, computer programs, and designs.[509] The licensing arrangements for these different kinds of copyright will vary widely, but the general principle is that restrictions necessary to protect the 'core rights' or the 'specific subject-matter' of the copyright will not fall within Article 81(1).[510] Subject to that proviso, the principles of Article 81(1) apply to copyright licences in the same way as they apply to other licence agreements. Therefore, although the principles of *Nungesser*[511] may apply to certain copyright licences, exclusive provisions in relation to copyright licences may infringe **9.179**

---

[507] *DSD*, OJ 2001 L166/1, [2001] 5 CMLR 609. See also article in (2001) 2 EC Competition Policy Newsletter 27. See paras 6.197 *et seq*, above, for other cases regarding the 'Green Dot' mark.

[508] Case T-151/01R *Der Grüne Punkt - Duales System Deutschland v Commission* [2001] ECR II-3295; substantive appeal dismissed [2007] 5 CMLR 300, on appeal, Case C-385/07P *DSD v Commission*, not yet decided.

[509] For Arts 28 and 30 in this connection, see paras 9.051 *et seq*, above.

[510] See, eg Case 262/81 *Coditel v Ciné-Vog Films (No. 2)* [1982] ECR 3381, [1983] 1 CMLR 49 (exclusive licence to exhibit film in cinemas necessary to protect rights of copyright owner): para 9.181, below; Case T-504/93 *Tiercé Ladbroke v Commission* [1997] ECR II-927, [1997] 5 CMLR 304 (prohibition on sub-licensing necessary to enable copyright owner legitimately to exploit copyright); for software licences, see para 9.186, below.

[511] See paras 9.079 *et seq*, above.

Article 81(1), depending on the circumstances.[512] Export bans on copyright works will usually fall under Article 81(1)[513] as may no-challenge clauses, non-competition clauses, provisions requiring payment of royalties on unprotected products, and clauses requiring the transfer by the licensee to the licensor of title to improvements.[514] Cases concerning copyright licences under Article 82 are discussed in Chapter 10, below.[515]

9.180 **Copyright collecting societies.** An exclusive licence granted by a composer or author to a copyright collecting society does not of itself infringe Article 81(1) but may infringe Article 81(1) or Article 82 if it is too widely expressed.[516] Territorial or market-sharing agreements between different national collecting societies may infringe Article 81(1) if concertation is established.[517] Royalty arrangements based on average selling prices rather than the actual selling prices of sound recordings may also infringe Article 81(1).[518] The application of Article 82 to copyright collecting societies is discussed elsewhere in this work.[519]

9.181 **Exclusive licence to exhibit films in cinemas.** In *Coditel (No. 2)*, the Court of Justice held that an exclusive licence to exhibit a film did not in itself infringe Article 81(1).[520] Having considered the nature of the right in question, and particularly the fact that a film is something that may be infinitely repeated, the Court said:

> '. . . the mere fact that the owner of the copyright in a film has granted to a sole licensee the exclusive right to exhibit that film in the territory of a Member State and, consequently, to prohibit, during a specified period its showing by others, is not sufficient to justify the finding that such a contract must be regarded as the purpose, the means or the result of an agreement decision or concerted practice prohibited by

---

[512] See, eg *Knoll/Hille Form, XIIIth Report on Competition Policy* (1983), points 142–146 (where the requirements of *Nungesser* were not satisfied on the facts); *RAI/Unitel, XIIth Report* (1982), point 90 (proceedings regarding exclusive contracts for artists: exclusive agreements for one operatic work only and one form of exploitation not caught by Art 81(1); *quaere* what period may be imposed). See also *Film Purchases by German Television Stations,* para 9.182, below. For exclusivity in respect of televising sporting events, see para 9.184, below.

[513] eg *Ernest Benn, Ninth Report on Competition Policy* (1979), point 118 (books); *STEMRA, XIth Report* (1981), point 98 (film and video music).

[514] See generally *Neilson-Hordell/Richmark, XIIth Report on Competition Policy* (1982), point 88.

[515] Paras 10.130 *et seq,* below.

[516] *GEMA,* JO 1971 L134/15, [1971] CMLR 035 (exclusive licence by author of all works, present and future, to collecting society too widely expressed).

[517] See cases cited at n 221, above.

[518] *BIEM/IFPI, XIIIth Report on Competition Policy* (1983), points 147–150 (royalty based on average prices reduced incentive for manufacturers to sell at lower prices).

[519] See para 10.134, below.

[520] Case 262/81 *Coditel v Ciné-Vog Films (No. 2)* [1982] ECR 3381, [1983] 1 CMLR 49. Similarly, the owner of copyright in a film has a legitimate interest in calculating fees on the basis of number of performances and that interest is part of the essential function of copyright.

the Treaty. The characteristics of the cinematographic industry and of its markets in the Community, especially those relating to dubbing and subtitling for the benefit of different language groups, to the possibilities of television broadcasts, and to the system of financing cinematographic production in Europe serve to show that an exclusive exhibition licence is not, in itself, such as to prevent, restrict or distort competition.'[521]

However, the Court left open the possibility that Article 81(1) might apply if the exercise of the exclusive right distorted competition in the cinema market by, for example, creating barriers which were artificial and unjustifiable.[522]

Exclusive licence to exhibit films on television. In *Film Purchases by German Television Stations*,[523] the Commission held that agreements relating to the purchase of exclusive television rights in films from the MGM/UA films library (including 14 James Bond films) throughout most of German-speaking Europe could fall within Article 81(1) insofar as the exercise of those rights created artificial and unjustified barriers to other undertakings, thereby restricting competition. Individual exemption was granted after the agreements were amended to give third parties some access to the films through the grant of licences to other television stations during specified 'windows' of time varying from two to six years.[524]   **9.182**

Television: licences to cable operators, etc. In *BBC Enterprises*,[525] the Commission examined a standard copyright licensing agreement designed to facilitate the retransmission of UK television programmes to subscribers in Ireland of cable TV and local distribution system networks. The licensors under the agreement were the UK terrestrial broadcasters and organisations representing the owners of copyright and related rights in TV programme services broadcast in the United Kingdom. The Commission required the parties to modify their agreements to ensure adequate access by broadcasters not originally party to the arrangements. However, the Commission accepted that collective licensing was the most effective means by which a cable TV operator (or other local service provider)   **9.183**

---

[521] ibid, paras 15–16.

[522] See, eg *UIP*, OJ 1989 L226/25, [1990] 4 CMLR 749; renewed subject to further undertakings, *XXIXth Report on Competition Policy* (1999), pp 148–150.

[523] Film Purchases by German Television Stations, OJ 1989 L284/36, [1990] 4 CMLR 841.

[524] The appeal against that decision, Cases T-157 & 168/89 *Nefico* and *MGM v Commission*, was settled the day before the CFI was due to give judgment, so no ruling on the legality of the decision was ever given. Note that with increasing convergence between telecommunications and television, and the development of satellite, cable, and digital television in competition with terrestrial broadcasts, significant competition issues arise in the television and wider communications sectors generally. For cases under Art 82 in those sectors, see Chap 10, below; for joint venture cases, see Chap 7, above; for mergers, see Chap 8, above; and for telecommunications generally, see Chap 12, below.

[525] *BBC Enterprises*, OJ 1993 C105/6, [1993] 5 CMLR 300, and *XXIIIrd Report on Competition Policy* (1993) p 459.

could be sure of not infringing the intellectual property rights held in the programmes retransmitted to its subscribers.

9.184 **Television: transmission of major sporting events.** Arrangements for the exploitation of rights to transmit sporting events have caused difficulty under competition law.[526] The Commission sought to give guidance in its 1998 orientation document, prepared in consultation with Member State authorities, *Broadcasting of sports events and competition law.*[527] This stressed that competition law is neutral as between different types of broadcasting (free-access, pay-TV, pay-per-view, etc) and accepts the principle of joint selling, and joint acquisition, of sports rights. The Commission noted that exclusivity for limited periods should not give rise to competition concerns; but that if the duration of exclusive rights is excessive it may give rise to foreclosure and so fall within Article 81(1). The Commission's policy in this area has focused on (i) unbundling packages of rights so as to ensure that rights to matches are not left unused; (ii) ensuring that the process for awarding rights does not unduly favour the incumbent national broadcaster; and (iii) ensuring that rights to broadcast over new media (such as mobile phones) are properly exploited. The leading decisions in the area of joint selling of sports rights are discussed in Chapter 5, above.[528] So far as collective purchasing of rights is concerned, in *Eurovision*[529] the Commission exempted under Article 81(3) the rules of the European Broadcasting Union ('EBU'), which consists mainly of public service broadcasters, providing for the joint acquisition of sport television rights, the sharing of the jointly acquired sport television rights, the exchange of the signal for sporting events, an access scheme for non-EBU members to Eurovision sports rights, and sub-licensing rules relating to exploitation of Eurovision rights on pay-TV channels. However, the Court of First Instance annulled the decision finding that the system eliminated competition among EBU members who were competitors on both upstream and downstream markets.

---

[526] See, eg Commission and EFTA Surveillance Authority report on the sector inquiry into the provision of sports content over third generation mobile networks, 21 September 2005, paras 56–57, available at http://ec.europa.eu/comm/competition/antitrust/others/sector_inquiries/new_media/3g/final_report.pdf. See further paras 5.115 *et seq*, above.

[527] (1998) 2 EC Competition Policy Newsletter 18. See also *XXVIth Report on Competition Policy* (1996), point 83; *XXIXth Report* (1999), point 141. Market definition in the exploitation of sports rights raises particular problems as between, eg different types of television programmes, and between different kinds of broadcasting (free-to-air, pay-TV) or different modes of transmission: terrestrial, cable, satellite, digital: see the orientation doc, above, at sect II.

[528] *UEFA Champions League*, OJ 2003 L291/25, [2004] 4 CMLR 549; *Joint selling of the media rights to the German Bundesliga*, OJ 2005 L134/46, [2005] 5 CMLR 1715. See paras 5.115 *et seq*, above.

[529] *Eurovision*, OJ 2000 L151/18, [2000] 5 CMLR 650. The Commission's earlier decision, OJ 1993 L179/23, [1995] 4 CMLR 56, was annulled by the CFI in Cases T-528/93, etc, *Métropole Télévision v Commission* [1996] ECR II-649, [1996] 5 CMLR 386, on the grounds that the criteria on access for non-members were inadequate.

The foreclosure effect created by the exclusive grant of the rights to EBU members was not remedied by the sub-licensing scheme incorporated into the system.[530]

Television: retransmission of sound and pictures to specific outlets.   In *PMI-DSV*,[531] which concerned a licence agreement whereby an association of French racing organisations granted DSV, a bookmaking organisation, an exclusive licence to exploit the rights to film and commentary of French horse races in Germany, the Commission held that a clause preventing the licensee from broadcasting the licensed material outside his contract area does not fall within Article 81(1), since it is an inherent part of the copyright. The substance of the Commission's approach was effectively confirmed by the Court of First Instance in *Tiercé Ladbroke v Commission*.[532] In *The Racecourse Association v Office of Fair Trading*,[533] the UK Competition Appeal Tribunal held that an arrangement between a consortium of racecourse owners and a joint venture company formed by broadcasting companies for the licensing of certain media rights in race meetings fell outside Article 81(1) because the collective sale of the rights by the racecourses jointly (rather than the acquisition of rights from individual racecourses) was essential to make the provision of a new service viable. The media rights involved allowed interactive betting via television or the internet and the Tribunal found that the broadcasters needed a 'critical mass' of rights before they could launch an untried and innovative product.[534]   **9.185**

Software licences.   The Software Directive on the legal protection of computer programs sets out the rights enjoyed by the owners of copyright in software, provides for the application of the principle of exhaustion of rights regarding the sale of computer programs in hard copy, and provides that licensees of software have certain rights of decompilation to obtain interface information.[535] The Commission has stated that arrangements or measures going beyond the exercise of the permitted copyright, for example contractual arrangements which extend the permitted copyright, or prohibit acts outside the scope of the copyright, may   **9.186**

---

[530] Cases T-185/00, etc, *Métropole Télévision v Commission (M6) v Commission* [2002] ECR II-3805, [2003] 4 CMLR 707; further appeal to the ECJ dismissed; Case C-470/02P *Union européenne de radio-télévision (UER) v Commission*, Order of 27 September 2004, OJ 2004 C314/2. See also paras 5.129 *et seq*, above.

[531] *PMI/DSV*, OJ 1995 L221/34, [1996] 5 CMLR 320.

[532] Case T-504/93 *Tiercé Ladbroke v Commission* [1997] ECR II-923, [1997] 5 CMLR 309.

[533] *The Racecourse Association and the British Horseracing Board v Office of Fair Trading* [2005] CAT 29, [2006] CompAR 99.

[534] ibid, paras 169 *et seq*.

[535] See Arts 4–6 of Dir 91/250, OJ 1991 L122/42, am by OJ 1993 L11/22 and OJ 1993 L290/9. For discussion, see Forrester, 'Software Licensing in the Light of Current EC Competition Law Considerations' (1992) 1 ECLR 5.

be caught by Article 81(1).[536] In *Microsoft's Undertaking*[537] the Commission expressed concern about the use by Microsoft of 'per processor' or 'per system' licences, namely clauses in software licences to PC manufacturers requiring payment of a royalty, regardless of whether any particular computer was shipped with pre-installed Microsoft software; provisions requiring licensees to pay a minimum royalty to Microsoft regardless of actual use of Microsoft products; and the duration of Microsoft licence agreements. Microsoft gave an understanding, for a period of six-and-a-half years, to modify its licensing practices. It would cease to include 'per processor' clauses in its licences, abandon minimum commitment clauses, and not enter into licences with a duration of more than one year. 'Per system' licences would be granted only if licensees are given flexibility to purchase non-Microsoft products and to avoid the payment of royalties in such cases. In *Microsoft Internet Explorer*[538] the Commission intervened again to ensure that agreements between Microsoft and Internet Service Providers, which required minimum distribution volumes to be attained and restricted the promotion of competing browser software, were modified to eliminate the risk of foreclosure of Microsoft's competitors.

(c) Plant variety rights

9.187 **Licences of plant variety rights.** Licences of plant variety rights do not fall under Article 81(1) to the extent necessary to protect the plant breeder's rights in respect of the basic seed used for propagating other seed. However, Article 81(1) will apply in the normal way to provisions restricting the sale or marketing of second generation or later seed used in crop production.[539]

---

[536] See the Commission's 'conclusions' adopted on the occasion of the issue of the proposal for the Software Directive, OJ 1989 C91/16.

[537] *XXIVth Report on Competition Policy* (1994), p 364; see EU Bull 7/8 1994, p 130, for the text of the undertaking. Note also *IBM settlement, Fourteenth Report on Competition Policy* (1984), points 94–95, [1984] 3 CMLR 147, above, which provided for the supply of interface information as between different items of hardware.

[538] *XXIXth Report on Competition Policy* (1999), points 55–56 and p 162. Note also *Digital, XXVIIth Report on Competition Policy* (1997), p 153 (discriminatory pricing and tying of hardware and software services dropped after Commission's intervention); *Sega and Nintendo, XXVIIth Report on Competition Policy* (1997), point 80 (provisions giving manufacturers of video game consoles the right to vet games independently developed by licensees dropped after Commission's intervention).

[539] See Case 27/87 *Erauw-Jacquery v La Hesbignonne* [1988] ECR 1919, [1988] 4 CMLR 576; *Standard Seed Production and Sales Agreements in France*, OJ 1990 C6/3; *Sicasov*, OJ 1999 L4/27, [1999] 4 CMLR 192.

10

ARTICLE 82

1. Introduction

(a) Generally

Article 82. Article 82 of the EC Treaty provides: **10.001**

'Any abuse by one or more undertakings of a dominant position within the common market or in a substantial part of it shall be prohibited as incompatible with the common market insofar as it may affect trade between Member States. Such abuse may, in particular, consist in:

(a) directly or indirectly imposing unfair purchase or selling prices or other unfair trading conditions;

(b) limiting production, markets or technical development to the prejudice of consumers;

(c) applying dissimilar conditions to equivalent transactions with other trading parties, thereby placing them at a competitive disadvantage;

(d) making the conclusion of contracts subject to acceptance by the other parties of supplementary obligations which, by their nature or according to commercial usage, have no connection with the subject of such contracts.'

10.002 **Article 82 generally.** Article 82 is aimed at controlling the abusive exercise of market power.[1] It is an application of the general objective of Article 3(1)(g) of the Treaty[2] that the activities of the Community shall include the institution of 'a system ensuring that competition in the internal market is not distorted'.[3] Article 82 thus forms one element in the broader objectives of EC competition law policy to promote a competitive market economy as an integral part of the internal market. A dominant undertaking has a 'special responsibility' not to impede such competition as takes place on the market but it remains free to engage in vigorous competition on the merits on the relevant market in relation to pricing, contractual conditions, output, innovation, cost reduction, efficiency and so on.

10.003 **The need to demonstrate both dominance and abuse.** Article 82 does not prohibit dominance as such, only the abuse of dominance. As the Court of Justice held in *Michelin*:

'A finding that an undertaking has a dominant position is not in itself a recrimination but simply means that, irrespective of the reasons for which it has such a dominant position, the undertaking concerned has a special responsibility not to allow its conduct to impair genuine undistorted competition on the common market.'[4]

---

[1] See O'Donoghue and Padilla, *The Law and Economics of Article 82* (2006); Whish, *Competition Law* (5th edn, 2003), Chaps 2 and 5; Faull and Nikpay, *The EC Law of Competition* (2nd edn, 2007), Chap 4; Ritter and Braun, *European Competition Law: A Practitioner's Guide* (3rd edn, 2005), Chap V; Ehlermann and Atanasiu (eds), *European Competition Law Annual 2003: What Is an Abuse of a Dominant Position* (with full bibliog) (2006). For economic background, see Bishop and Walker, *The Economics of EC Competition Law* (2nd edn, 2002); Motta, *Competition Policy Theory and Practice* (2004). For a description of the relevant US law, see Hovenkamp, *Federal Antitrust Policy: The Law of Competition and its Practice* (3rd edn, 2005), Chaps 6–8; control of dominance is achieved through s 2 of the Sherman Act, 15 USC para 2: 'Every person who shall monopolize, or attempt to monopolize, or combine or conspire with any other person or persons, to monopolize any part of the trade or commerce among the several States, or with foreign nations, shall be deemed guilty of a felony . . .'; and, more generally, through s 5 of the Federal Trade Commission Act, 15 USC para 45, which outlaws 'unfair methods of competition'.

[2] See Vol II, App A.3.

[3] Case 85/76 *Hoffmann-La Roche v Commission* [1979] ECR 461, [1979] 3 CMLR 211, para 38.

[4] Case 322/81 *Michelin v Commission* [1983] ECR 3461, [1985] 1 CMLR 282, para 57. See also Case C-250/92 *Gøttrup-Klim v Dansk Landbrugs* [1994] ECR I-5641, [1996] 4 CMLR 191, para 49: 'neither the creation or the strengthening of a dominant position is in itself contrary to Art [82] of

Similarly, in *Matra Hachette v Commission*[5] where the applicant was challenging an exemption granted under Article 81(3) to a joint venture between car manufacturers, the Court of First Instance rejected *inter alia* the applicant's argument that the agreement would have the effect of putting the parties into a collective dominant position. The Court held that since the achievement or strengthening of a dominant position, whether individual or collective, was not itself prohibited by Articles 81 and 82, and since the applicant had failed to establish that the risk of abuse was likely to eventuate during the period of the exemption, the alleged risk of a dominant position resulting from the agreement could not justify withholding exemption.[6] The corollary of there being no infringement by virtue solely of being dominant is that there is no infringement by virtue solely of being abusive: conduct which would be abusive on the part of a dominant undertaking does not infringe Article 82 in the absence of dominance. Thus in *Alsatel*, which concerned certain onerous contractual provisions, the Court of Justice held that 'contractual practices, even if abusive ones, on the part of an undertaking . . . do not fall within the prohibition in Article [82] of the EC Treaty where that undertaking does not occupy a dominant position on the relevant market'.[7]

Link between dominant position and abuse.   Although it is necessary to **10.004** demonstrate dominance on a relevant market in addition to abusive conduct, it is not necessary to show that the abuse complained of took place as a result of the existence and exercise of the economic power enjoyed by the dominant firm.[8] Indeed, certain types of contractual terms may be abusive even if they are included at the request of the customer.[9] In addition, in exceptional circumstances involving related markets, the abusive conduct may take place on another market from that on which the dominant position is enjoyed. For example, in *Tetra Pak II*,[10]

---

the Treaty'. However, the creation or strengthening of a dominant position is a highly material factor in relation to merger control, even after the amendments to the Merger Reg that came into force on 1 May 2004: see paras 8.192 *et seq*, above, and also the early ruling in respect of 'strengthening' of a dominant position in Case 6/72 *Europemballage and Continental Can v Commission* [1973] ECR 215, [1973] CMLR 199, para 27.

5 Case T-17/93 *Matra Hachette v Commission* [1994] ECR II-595, paras 123–124.
6 The CFI added that the likelihood of the risk materialising during the period of validity of the exemption had not been made out, leaving it unclear as to whether the CFI's view would have been different had an imminent risk been established (para 153).
7 Case 247/86 *Alsatel v Novasam* [1988] ECR 5987, [1990] 4 CMLR 434, para 23.
8 *Continental Can* (n 4, above) para 27 ('strengthening of the position of an undertaking may be an abuse . . . regardless of the means and procedure by which it is achieved').
9 eg fidelity rebates; see paras 10.091 *et seq*, below. See also *Van den Bergh Foods Ltd*, OJ 1998 L246/1, [1998] 5 CMLR 530, para 160 (appeals dismissed: Case T-65/98 *Van den Bergh Foods v Commission* [2003] ECR II-4653, [2004] 4 CMLR 14, [2005] All ER (EC) 418; Case C-552/03P *Unilever Bestfoods v Commission* [2006] ECR I-9091, [2006] 5 CMLR 1460).
10 *Tetra Pak II*, OJ 1992 L72/1, [1992] 4 CMLR 551; upheld on appeal, Case T-83/91 *Tetra Pak v Commission* [1994] ECR II-755, [1997] 4 CMLR 726, paras 113 *et seq*, and on further appeal, Case C-333/94P *Tetra Pak v Commission* [1996] ECR I-5951, [1997] 4 CMLR 662. Note that in Case T-65/89 *BPB Industries and British Gypsum v Commission* [1993] ECR II-389, [1993]

the Commission, upheld by the Court of First Instance and the Court of Justice, held that abusive conduct infringing Article 82 could take place on a market on which Tetra Pak was not dominant because that market was a 'neighbouring' market to the market on which Tetra Pak held a very powerful dominant position. The Court of Justice was prepared to endorse the analysis of the Commission and the Court of First Instance on the exceptional basis that 'the quasi-monopoly enjoyed by Tetra Pak on the aseptic markets and its leading position on the distinct, though closely associated, non-aseptic markets placed it in a situation comparable to that of holding a dominant position on the markets in question as a whole'.[11] In a situation of collective dominance, the abuse need not be engaged in by all the parties that are jointly dominant.[12]

10.005 **DG Comp Discussion Paper.** As had been the case with regard to Article 81, at least until 2000 when the Commission adopted its guidelines on vertical restraints and horizontal cooperation agreements, there is a marked tendency among many commentators to criticise existing case law under Article 82 as excessively formalistic and insufficiently sensitive to the underlying economic justifications for regulatory intervention against the exercise of market power on a unilateral basis.[13] At the end of 2005, the Commission's Directorate General for Competition ('DG Comp') launched a consultation exercise with the publication of a detailed discussion paper on the application of Article 82 to exclusionary abuses ('the Discussion Paper').[14] In response, a number of influential studies have been undertaken suggesting possible ways of developing the law on abuse of dominance.[15] Following comments received in the public consultation on the

---

5 CMLR 32, paras 92–96, the CFI upheld a finding that the practice of giving priority supplies of plaster (a product in which BPB was not dominant) could constitute an abuse of its dominant position in plasterboard (upheld on appeal, Case C-310/93P [1995] ECR I-865, [1995] 5 CMLR 14). See also AG Van Gerven in Cases C-48 & 66/90 *Netherlands and PTT v Commission* [1992] ECR I-565, [1993] 5 CMLR 316, Opinion, para 45 (since the Commission had not shown that the post office was dominant in the market for messenger services, it could not be accused of unfair pricing in that market).

[11] Case C-333/94P *Tetra Pak v Commission* (n 10, above) para 31.

[12] Case T-228/97 *Irish Sugar v Commission* [1999] ECR II-2969, [1999] 5 CMLR 1300, [2000] All ER (EC) 198, paras 63–66; appeal dismissed, Case C-497/99P *Irish Sugar v Commission* [2001] ECR I-5333, [2001] 5 CMLR 1082.

[13] See, eg Report by the Economics Advisory Group on Competition Policy ('EAGCP'), '*An economic approach to Article 82*' (July 2005); Vickers, 'Abuse of Market Power' (2005) 115 Economic J F244; Ridyard, 'Exclusionary Pricing and Price Discrimination Abuses under Article 82 — An Economic Analysis' (2002) ECLR 286.

[14] DG Competition discussion paper on the application of Article 82 of the Treaty to exclusionary abuses, 19 December 2005, available on the DG Comp website at http://ec.europa.eu/comm/competition/antitrust/art82/index.html. See also Commr Kroes, 'Tackling Exclusionary Practices to Avoid Exploitation of Market Power' in Hawk (ed), *2005 Fordham Corp Law Inst* (2006), 381.

[15] See, eg research papers on Art 82 produced by the Global Competition Law Centre at the College of Europe (July 2005), published in the research projects section of the Centre's website at www.coleurop.be/content/gclc/documents.

Discussion Paper, at the time of writing the Commission is considering how best to take the matter forward and, in particular, whether to issue guidelines. The outcome of such an exercise is uncertain as the Commission seeks to modernise its approach within the constraints of the established case law of the Community Courts, which bind not only the Commission but also the Member States' national competition authorities and courts in their application of Article 82.

(b) Relationship between Article 82 and other competition rules

(i) Article 81

Generally. In *Tetra Pak I* the Court of First Instance observed that: **10.006**

> 'Articles [81] and [82] are complementary inasmuch as they pursue a common general objective, set out in Article 3[1][g] of the Treaty, which provides that the activities of the Community are to include "the institution of a system ensuring that competition in the common market is not distorted". But they none the less constitute, in the scheme of the Treaty, two independent legal instruments addressing different situations.'[16]

It is clear that the applicability of Article 81 to an agreement does not preclude the application of Article 82 and that in such a case the Commission may apply either of the two provisions to the act in question. In *Ahmed Saeed*[17] the Court of Justice considered whether a tariff-fixing agreement in the air transport sector can in principle constitute an abuse of a dominant position where it is the result of parties engaging in concerted action which, itself, is capable of falling within the prohibition set out in Article 81(1). The Court first reiterated that Article 81(1) does not apply where the concerted practice is carried out by undertakings belonging to a single economic group as parent and subsidiary undertakings; conduct of such a unit on the market is liable to come within the ambit of Article 82. The Court continued:

> 'In contrast, the typical example of an agreement, decision or concerted practice falling within Article [81] is where two undertakings which are economically

---

[16] Case T-51/89 *Tetra Pak v Commission* [1990] ECR II-309, [1991] 4 CMLR 334, para 22; on appeal from *Tetra Pak I (BTG Licence)*, OJ 1988 L272/27, [1990] 4 CMLR 47. The CFI cited *Continental Can* (n 4, above) para 25, where the ECJ stated that Arts 81 and 82 'seek to achieve the same aim on different levels *viz.* the maintenance of effective competition within the Common Market'.

[17] Case 66/86 *Ahmed Saeed Flugreisen v Zentrale zur Bekämpfung unlauteren Wettbewerbs* [1989] ECR 803, [1990] 4 CMLR 102. See also *Hoffmann-La Roche* (n 3, above). In *WEX v FEBIAC* (2004/MR/8), judgment of 10 November 2005, [2006] ECC 343, the Brussels Court of Appeal held that a rule of FEBIAC, the union of Belgian importers of motor vehicles, which prohibited members from taking part in a rival trade exhibition within six months prior to the annual FEBIAC trade fair infringed Art 82 as an abuse of its dominant position on the market of services for organising exhibitions of utility vehicles in Belgium, although the rule did not violate Art 81 since the extent of the ban meant that it did not have an appreciable effect on competition. The Court held that when the extent of competition on a market is very weak, any act by the dominant business having the effect of restricting that market, even slightly, is prohibited.

independent of each other engage, by concerted action, in price fixing or other restrictions of competition on the relevant market.

Those considerations do not exclude the case where an agreement between two or more undertakings which simply constitutes the formal measure setting the seal on an economic reality characterised by the fact that an undertaking in a dominant position has succeeded in having the tariffs in question applied by other undertakings. In such a case, the possibility that Articles [81] and [82] may both be applicable cannot be ruled out.'[18]

10.007 Circumstances where both Articles may apply.   That statement by the Court of Justice suggested that, for Article 82 to apply as well as Article 81, something more than just the making of the agreement is needed: in the example given, the pressure brought to bear by the dominant undertaking on its competitors. In *Tetra Pak I*,[19] the Court of First Instance rejected the argument that for Article 82 to apply as well as Article 81, there must be a supplementary element *external to the agreement*. Although recognising that in *Ahmed Saeed* the Court of Justice had referred to the existence of a supplementary element, the Court of First Instance found that the additional element in the case before it lay in the very context of the case: 'in the fact that Tetra Pak's acquisition of the exclusive licence had the practical effect of precluding all competition in the relevant market'. An agreement between parties may also be relevant under Article 82 in a quite different way, as a circumstance where the market shares of the parties should be aggregated so as to give rise to a collective dominant position. That distinct aspect is discussed in paragraph 10.051, below.

10.008 Article 82 and the effect of an exemption under Article 81(3).   In its decision in *Tetra Pak I*,[20] the Commission had condemned as abusive the exclusivity under a patent licence acquired by Tetra Pak, which was dominant in the market for equipment for the aseptic packaging of UHT-treated milk, to which the patented technology related. The patent licence fell within the terms of Regulation 2349/84, the then patent licence block exemption. In upholding the Commission's decision, the Court of First Instance[21] drew a distinction between the grant of an individual exemption and the application of a block exemption. In a case where an individual exemption has been granted, the Commission must take account, unless the factual and legal circumstances have altered, of the earlier findings

---

[18] *Ahmed Saeed*, above, paras 36–37; In Case T-65/98 *Van den Bergh Foods v Commission* (n 9, above), the CFI confirmed that both Arts 81 and 82 may apply to the same contractual arrangements in appropriate circumstances.

[19] Case T-51/89 *Tetra Pak v Commission* (n 16, above) para 24.

[20] *Tetra Pak I (BTG Licence)*, OJ 1988 L272/27, [1990] 4 CMLR 47. See also Case C-310/93P *BPB Industries and British Gypsum v Commission* (n 10, above) per AG Léger at paras 63–69. His conclusions on this point were adopted by the ECJ.

[21] Case T-51/89 *Tetra Pak v Commission* (n 16, above).

made when exemption was granted. That is because the characteristics of the agreement which would be relevant in applying Article 82 may be taken to have been established by the decision applying Article 81(3).[22] But where an agreement satisfies the requirements of a block exemption without having been subject to any positive assessment under Article 81(3), the block exemption does not amount to a negative clearance of the agreement under Article 82.[23] In *Compagnie Maritime Belge*,[24] the Court of Justice dismissed the argument that, because a practice was exempted for the purpose of Article 81(3) by Regulation 4056/86 laying down rules for the application of Articles 81 and 82 to international maritime transport, it could not amount to an infringement of Article 82 until after the benefit of that block exemption had been withdrawn. The Court stated:

> '. . . the fact that operators subject to effective competition have a practice which is authorised does not mean that adoption of the same practice by an undertaking in a dominant position can never constitute an abuse of that position.'[25]

(ii) Article 86

Public undertakings and undertakings granted special or exclusive rights.   **10.009**
A dominant position may be conferred by statute upon a public body or upon undertakings to which Member States grant special or exclusive rights. But a Member State cannot grant any of its undertakings immunity from the prohibition of Article 82. Article 86(1) of the Treaty imposes a duty on Member States not to adopt or maintain in force any measure which could deprive the competition rules, including Article 82, of their effectiveness. Article 86(2) provides that an undertaking entrusted by the State with the operation of services of general economic interest is still subject to Article 82, which prohibits its abusive conduct so long as it is not shown that the prohibition is incompatible with the performance of its tasks. These provisions must be read with Article 16 which requires Member States to ensure that services of general economic interest (for example, a universal postal service) 'operate on the basis of principles and

---

[22] This aspect is less important under the Reg 1/2003 regime since it is likely that in the future the application of Arts 81(3) and 82 to the agreement will be considered at the same time. But it remains relevant for those agreements which continue to benefit from an extant individual exemption.

[23] ibid, paras 28–29.

[24] Cases C-395 & 396/96P *Compagnie Maritime Belge Transports v Commission* [2000] ECR I-1365, [2000] 4 CMLR 1076, [2000] All ER (EC) 385. See also Cases T-191/98, etc, *Atlantic Container Line v Commission* [2003] ECR II-3275, [2005] 4 CMLR 1283, where the CFI rejected arguments that certain contractual provisions set by the liner conference were justified in order to support the stability of the rate agreement which benefited from the block exemption in Reg 4056/86 (paras 1117 *et seq*). The CFI also compared the arguments on which parties can rely in relation to Art 81(3) with the narrower range of arguments available to provide objective justification under Art 82: see para 10.063, below.

[25] ibid, para 131.

conditions which enable them to fulfil their missions'.[26] Although a State may create a dominant position, it cannot do so in such a way that the undertaking in question inevitably commits abuses.[27] Indeed, Article 82 prohibits an abuse 'even if such abuse is encouraged by a national legislative provision'.[28] Article 86 is discussed in Chapter 11, below.

(iii) The Merger Regulation

10.010 **Generally.** Before the entry into force of the new Merger Regulation on 1 May 2004,[29] there was a clear overlap between the issues of dominance that arise under Article 82 and the substantive criterion for merger control. Article 2(3) of the original Merger Regulation[30] provided that a concentration which created or strengthened a dominant position, as a result of which competition would be significantly impeded in the common market or in a substantial part of it, should be declared incompatible with the common market. Given the large volume of cases in which the Commission has been required to conduct at least preliminary market analyses for the purposes of merger control, there is a substantial body of decisional practice, particularly in the area of market definition, which is of potential value in interpreting and developing the much more limited number of Commission decisions under Article 82. However, even in relation to market definition and dominance, there was no direct read across between findings of dominance under the original Merger Regulation and such findings under Article 82.[31] The prospective analysis required for the purposes of merger control and the historical analysis appropriate to an Article 82 investigation mean that only limited guidance can be derived from merger control cases. This is all the more true since 1 May 2004, as the issue of dominance is no longer the central concept in substantive merger appraisal.[32]

---

[26] The Commission describes the combined effect of Art 16 (inserted by the Treaty of Amsterdam) and Art 86 as reinforcing 'the principle whereby a balance must be struck between the competition rules and the fulfilment of public services' missions': *XXVIIth Report on Competition Policy* (1997), point 97; see also points 96–104. The relative predominance of Art 86 cases in the recent Art 82 case law may form part of the trend of exposing the regulated sector to competition: see Gardner, 'The Velvet Revolution: Art 90 and the Triumph of the Free Market in Europe's Regulated Sectors' (1995) ECLR 78.

[27] Case C-41/90 *Höfner and Elser* [1991] ECR I-1979, [1993] 4 CMLR 306, para 27.

[28] Case 13/77 *INNO v ATAB* [1977] ECR 2115, [1978] 1 CMLR 283, para 34.

[29] Reg 139/2004 on the control of concentrations between undertakings (the EC Merger Regulation), OJ 2004 L24/1: Vol II, App D.1.

[30] Reg 4064/89, OJ 1989 L395/1, as amended by Reg 1310/97, OJ 1997 L180/1.

[31] Cases T-125 & 127/97 *Coca-Cola v Commission* [2000] ECR II-1733, [2000] 5 CMLR 467, [2000] All ER (EC) 460, paras 81–83 (re a finding in the context of a decision under the Merger Reg).

[32] See 'Goodbye to "the dominance test"? Substantive appraisal under the new UK and EC merger regimes' (2003–4) Comp Law 332, for a discussion of this issue and residual role of 'dominance' under the amended Merger Reg. Market definition is discussed in Chap 4, above and the Merger Reg is discussed in Chap 8, above.

(iv) Relationship to other provisions of EC law

Non-discrimination and the maintenance of the internal market.   The Court   **10.011**
of Justice has consistently stated that Article 82 is to be construed as an integral
part of Community law, having regard in particular to the objectives of the EC
Treaty set out in Article 3.[33] Of these wider objectives, the most important are the
prohibition of discrimination on grounds of nationality and the creation of the
internal market. Article 12 of the Treaty prohibits discrimination on grounds of
nationality in wide terms. In the context of Article 82, there have been a number
of cases where a dominant undertaking has discriminated between its customers
or competitors on grounds of nationality.[34] The condemnation of such conduct as
abusive reflects the role of the Court of Justice as the guardian
of the Treaty and the central place that the concept of non-discrimination on
grounds of nationality plays within Community law as a whole.[35]

2. Structure of Article 82

The constituent elements.   There are several constituent elements that need to   **10.012**
be present for a breach of Article 82 to be established:

(1) a dominant position must be held by one or more undertakings;
(2) this position must be held in the common market or a substantial part
     thereof;
(3) there must be an abuse of that dominant position;
(4) there must be an actual or potential effect on trade between Member States.

The principal issues under Article 82 are 'dominance' and 'abuse': these are discussed, respectively, in Sections 3 and 4, below. The concept of 'effect on trade
between Member States' is considered in Chapter 1, above. Civil remedies under
Article 82 before national courts are considered in Chapter 14, below.

---

[33] See *Continental Can* (n 4, above); Case 27/76 *United Brands v Commission* [1978] ECR 207,
[1978] 1 CMLR 429; *Hoffmann-La Roche* (n 3, above); *Michelin* (n 4, above); Case 30/87 *Bodson v
Pompes funèbres des regions libérées* [1988] ECR 2479, [1989] 4 CMLR 984.

[34] See para 10.097 for discrimination on grounds of nationality and para 10.086 for price discrimination on nationality grounds, below.

[35] See, eg Arts 12, 39, 43 and 49–50 EC. See Gerard 'Price Discrimination under Article 82(c)
EC: Clearing up the Ambiguities', Research Paper published by the Global Competition Law Centre
of the College of Europe (n 15, above), arguing that 'protectionist abuses' should be dealt with under
the free movement provisions of the Treaty rather than under Art 82 since they do not display elements of a distortion of competition. For a general discussion of non-discrimination in Community
law, see Craig and de Búrca, *EU Law: Text, Cases and Materials* (3rd edn, 2002), 387–391; Tridimas,
The General Principles of EC Law (2nd edn, 2006).

10.013 Undertakings: imputation of subsidiary's conduct to parent. The meaning of the word 'undertaking' under EC competition law has been considered in Chapter 2, above. In relation to Article 82, the question of whether the conduct of a subsidiary is to be imputed to the parent is a question of fact in each case.[36] In *General Motors*,[37] the Commission proceeded against the Belgian subsidiary, since the decision to engage in the abusive conduct was plainly taken locally, affecting only applicants for the relevant Belgian certificate. In *BPB Industries*[38] the Commission imposed a fine on a wholly-owned subsidiary company, British Gypsum, in respect of its activities on the British market but imposed a fine on the parent, BPB, in respect of British Gypsum's activities on the Northern Irish market where British Gypsum sold product supplied by the Irish subsidiary of BPB. The Court of First Instance held that although the Commission could have fined BPB for all British Gypsum's activities, it was quite proper for the Commission instead to attribute only some of the abuses to the parent. Many of the principal cases under Article 82 have involved the parent company in addition to the subsidiary, since the policies or conduct in dispute were plainly attributable to the parent company. Thus, the Commission issued the relevant decision against the parent company in *Continental Can* (US parent),[39] *Commercial Solvents* (US parent),[40] *United Brands* (US parent),[41] *Hoffmann-La Roche* (Swiss parent),[42] *Hugin* (Swedish parent)[43] and *Hilti* (Liechtenstein parent).[44]

10.014 A substantial part of the common market. Even if an undertaking is dominant, there is a further factual criterion that must be satisfied if the Article 82 prohibition is to apply, namely that the dominant position should be held 'within the common market or in a substantial part of it'.[45] In *Suiker Unie*, the Court of Justice stated:

> 'For the purpose of determining whether a specific territory is large enough to amount to "a substantial part of the common market" within the meaning of Article [82] of

---

36 See also para 13.205, below.

37 Case 26/75 *General Motors Continental v Commission* [1975] ECR 1367, [1976] 1 CMLR 95. See also Case 322/81 *Michelin v Commission* (n 4, above).

38 Case T-65/89 *BPB Industries and British Gypsum v Commission* [1993] ECR II-389, [1993] 5 CMLR 32; appeal dismissed, Case 310/93P [1995] ECR I-865, [1995] 5 CMLR 14.

39 Case 6/72 *Europemballage and Continental Can v Commission* [1973] ECR 215, [1973] CMLR 199.

40 Cases 6 & 7/73 *Commercial Solvents v Commission* [1974] ECR 223, [1974] 1 CMLR 309.

41 Case 27/76 *United Brands v Commission* [1978] ECR 207, [1978] 1 CMLR 429 (on appeal from *Chiquita*, OJ 1976 L95/1, [1976] 1 CMLR D28).

42 Case 85/76 *Hoffmann-La Roche v Commission* [1979] ECR 461, [1979] 3 CMLR 211.

43 Case 22/78 *Hugin v Commission* [1979] ECR 1869, [1979] 3 CMLR 345 (on appeal from *Liptons Cash Registers/Hugin*, OJ 1978 L22/23, [1978] 1 CMLR D19).

44 Case T-30/89 *Hilti v Commission* [1991] ECR II-1439, [1992] 4 CMLR 16 (on appeal from *Hilti*, OJ 1988 L65/19, [1989] 4 CMLR 677).

45 For the distinct but related issue of geographical market definition, see Chap 4, above.

the Treaty the pattern and volume of the production and consumption of the said product as well as the habits and economic opportunities of vendors and purchasers must be considered.'[46]

Thus, in order to determine whether the dominant position is held in a 'substantial' part of the common market, it is necessary to take into account the geographic area in which the dominant position is alleged to exist and the product market in that area. Member States will usually be 'substantial' parts of the common market.[47] In *Suiker Unie*, the Court of Justice held that the Belgium–Luxembourg sugar market was a substantial part of the common market in sugar: Belgian production was between eight per cent and nine and a half per cent of total Community production and Belgian consumption was about five per cent of Community consumption.[48] The Court of Justice also held in *Suiker Unie* that the 'southern part of Germany' (primarily comprising for this purpose Bavaria, Baden-Wurttemberg and part of Land Hessen) was a substantial part of the common market.[49] What is 'substantial' will be a question of fact in each case. For example, the Court of Justice has held that the port of Genoa is a substantial part of the common market, having regard to the volume of traffic and its importance in international trade.[50]

---

[46] Cases 40/73, etc, *Suiker Unie v Commission* [1975] ECR 1663, [1976] 1 CMLR 295, paras 371. In Case 127/73 *BRT v SABAM* [1974] ECR 313, 324, [1974] 2 CMLR 238, 277, AG Mayras stated 'What is essential is the quantitative assessment of the common market in relation to the whole of the market, that is to say its relative economic importance. For this purpose one must consider above all the density of the population, the level of its resources and the extent of its purchasing power'. cf *R. v Monopolies and Mergers Commission, ex p South Yorkshire Transport* [1993] 1 WLR 23, concerning the meaning of 'a substantial part of the United Kingdom' under s 64(3) of the Fair Trading Act 1973 (now repealed), where the House of Lords held that the test was qualitative as well as quantitative and meant 'of such size, character and importance as to make it worth consideration for the purposes of the Act.'

[47] Case 26/75 *General Motors Continental v Commission* [1975] ECR 1367, [1976] 1 CMLR 95; Case 7/82 *GVL v Commission* [1983] ECR 483, [1983] 3 CMLR 645; *British Telecommunications*, OJ 1982 L360/36, [1983] 1 CMLR 457; *Liptons Cash Registers/Hugin*, OJ 1978 L22/23, [1978] 1 CMLR 19; Case 322/81 *Michelin* (n 4, above); Case C-260/89 *Eliiniki Radiofonia Tileorasi v Kouvelas* [1991] ECR I-2925, [1994] 4 CMLR 540; Case T-69/89 *Radio Telefís Éireann v Commission* [1991] ECR II-481, [1991] 4 CMLR 582; Case T-70/89 *British Broadcasting Corpn and BBC Enterprises Ltd v Commission* [1991] ECR II-535, [1991] 4 CMLR 669; Case T-76/89 *Independent Television Publications Ltd v Commission* [1991] ECR II-575, [1991] 4 CMLR 745.

[48] *Suiker Unie* (n 46, above) paras 370–375. In Case 77/77 *BP v Commission* [1978] ECR II-1513, 1537, [1978] 3 CMLR 174, 184, AG Warner stated that there was a danger in focusing attention exclusively on percentages; in his view the fact that Luxembourg had a population equal to only 0.23 per cent of the Community would not preclude it being 'a substantial part'.

[49] *Suiker Unie* (n 46, above) paras 445–448.

[50] Case C-179/90 *Merci convenzionale porto di Genova* [1991] ECR I-5889, [1994] 4 CMLR 422, para 15; see also Case C-18/93 *Corsica Ferries* [1994] ECR I-1783; Case C-163/96 *Raso* [1998] ECR I-533, [1998] 4 CMLR 737, para 26; *Port of Rødby*, OJ 1994 L55/52, [1994] 5 CMLR 457; *B&I Line/Sealink* [1992] 5 CMLR 255 (interim measures: Holyhead harbour a substantial part). However, the English Court held that the north of England is not a 'substantial part' of the common market: *Cutsforth v Mansfield Inns* [1986] 1 WLR 558 (QBD); similarly the Irish High Court in

3. Dominant Position

(a) Generally

10.015 **Definition of dominance.** The Court of Justice has defined a dominant position[51] under Article 82 as:

> '. . . a position of economic strength enjoyed by an undertaking which enables it to hinder the maintenance of effective competition on the relevant market by allowing it to behave to an appreciable extent independently of its competitors and customers and ultimately of consumers.'[52]

10.016 **Analysis of dominance.** Determining whether an undertaking holds a dominant position essentially involves two stages:

(i) *market definition*: defining the relevant market (which must comprise at least a substantial part of the common market) in which the market power of the allegedly dominant undertaking is to be assessed;

(ii) *market power*: assessing the degree of commercial power enjoyed by the undertaking on the market so defined.

The second stage in turn involves consideration of various factors, such as market share, barriers to entry, and competitive constraints.

10.017 **Definition of the relevant market.** Dominance cannot be assessed in a vacuum: it requires an assessment of the undertaking's power on a properly

---

Cadbury Ltd v Kerry Co-op [1982] ILRM 77 (North Kerry not a 'substantial part'). For air transport, see *Ahmed Saeed Flugreisen* (n 17, above) (a route taken by scheduled flights may constitute a substantial part of the common market); *British Midland v Aer Lingus*, OJ 1992 L96/34, [1993] 4 CMLR 596, para 17 (the London—Dublin route significant in both the UK and Ireland and therefore a substantial part of the common market); *Brussels Airport*, OJ 1995 L216/8, [1996] 4 CMLR 232 (the eleventh busiest airport in the Community a substantial part of the common market); *Alpha Flight Services/Aéroports de Paris*, OJ 1998 L230/10, [1998] 5 CMLR 611, upheld on appeal by the CFI in Case T-128/98 *Aéroports de Paris v Commission* [2000] ECR II-3929, [2001] 4 CMLR 1376 and by the ECJ in Case C-82/01 *Aéroports de Paris* [2002] ECR I-9297, [2003] 4 CMLR 609; *FAG — Flughafen Frankfurt/Main*, OJ 1998 L72/30, [1998] 4 CMLR 779.

[51] The task of identifying monopoly power or 'dominance' has exercised economists and lawyers in the US and Europe and is the subject of continuing debate: see, eg O'Donoghue and Padilla (n 1, above) Chap 3; Bishop and Walker (n 1, above) Chap 3. Sharpe proposed a definition based on the ability to influence the market behaviour of others: see 'Predation' (1987) ECLR 53, referred to by the Commission in *Hilti* (n 44, above) paras 71–73.

[52] *Michelin v Commission* (n 4, above) para 30; Case 311/84 *CBEM v CLT and IPB* [1985] ECR 3261, [1986] 2 CMLR 558, para 16. See also *United Brands* (n 41, above) para 65; *Hoffmann-La Roche* (n 42, above) para 38. Depending on the context, the 'customers' may be competitor-customers, distributors, processors, commercial users or direct consumers. The fact that in relation to some customers an undertaking may be subject to effective competition from other undertakings does not rule out the possibility that the same undertaking may be held to be dominant in relation to other customers at different stages of supply: see further para 10.044, below.

defined relevant product and geographic market. Market definition is addressed in Chapter 4, above. This Section is concerned with the issue of market power. It deals first with the the relatively simple case of a single relevant market on which a single undertaking is considered possibly to enjoy market power. This is followed by a discussion of the more complex legal and factual issues that frequently arise where more than one related market is under consideration or where more than one undertaking is alleged to enjoy a position of collective dominance.

The temporal scope of a finding of dominance.   Because a finding of dominance involves assessment of these elements in the circumstances prevailing at the time, it is not binding for the future. Therefore a determination by the Commission of dominance, without a finding of abuse, cannot in itself be the subject of an appeal since it does not produce legal effects,[53] although it will probably have a practical effect on the commercial conduct of the undertaking concerned, given the 'special responsibility' imposed on dominant firms by EC competition law.[54] Should a subsequent allegation of abuse be made, an analysis to determine dominance would have to be conducted afresh.   **10.018**

Degrees of dominance.   The Article 82 prohibition is unitary in form but comprises an inherently flexible test that needs to be applied on the basis of a realistic assessment of market power. The logical implication is that, although all undertakings found to be dominant on a relevant market are subject to the special obligations imposed by Article 82, the precise scope and extent of such obligations should depend on the particular circumstances of the market on which that finding is made. In particular, there is authority for the proposition that there may be cases of 'super-dominance' where conduct will be subject to particularly rigorous scrutiny to protect residual competition on a market where one undertaking enjoys an exceptional degree of market power.[55] In *Compagnie Maritime Belge* Advocate General Fennelly suggested that, for undertakings that are near-monopolists, conduct which is demonstrably intended to prevent the emergence of any competition may be assessed according to a higher standard. The Court of Justice   **10.019**

---

[53] Cases T-125 & 127/97 *Coca-Cola v Commission* [2000] ECR II-1733, [2000] 5 CMLR 467, [2000] All ER (EC) 460, paras 81–83 (re a finding in the context of a decision under the Merger Reg). This was followed by the Brussels Court of Appeal in *Beroepsinstituut van Vastgoedmakelaars* Case 2002/MR/2, judgment of 7 June 2004: BIV, a professional body for real estate agents, was not entitled to appeal against the finding by the Belgian Competition Council that it occupied a dominant position since the Council had held that it had not abused that position (by requiring all real estate agents to be members of the BIV in order to exercise their profession) and therefore the Council's decision did not affect BIV's interests by bringing about a distinct change in its legal position.

[54] For the special responsibility, see para 10.061, below.

[55] See, eg *1998 Football World Cup*, OJ 2000 L5/55, [2000] 4 CMLR 963, para 86; *NDC Health/ IMS Health: Interim Measures*, OJ 2002 L59/18, [2002] 4 CMLR 111, para 58; *Deutsche Post AG – Interception of cross-border mail*, OJ 2001 L331/40, [2002] 4 CMLR 598, paras 103 and 124.

appeared to endorse this approach, holding that the 'actual scope of the special responsibility' depends on the specific circumstances of each case.[56] Hence the use of 'fighting ships', charging lower rates, specifically targeted at a new entrant by the members of a collectively dominant liner conference that held over 90 per cent of the market constituted an abuse.[57] The notion that the 'special responsibility' referred to above may vary according to the degree of dominance seems logical from an economic perspective: it serves to emphasise that the analyses of dominance and abuse are interlinked and therefore confirms the need for an overall appraisal of economic effects. The disadvantage of such a further refinement of Article 82 is that it makes it more difficult to lay down specific criteria as to the scope of the prohibition of abusive conduct.[58]

10.020 **Indicators of dominance.** Analytically, there are three factors to be taken into account in assessing the degree of market power of a single undertaking on a relevant market:

(i) *The market position of the undertaking itself.* The most obvious quantitative indicator of the market position of the undertaking viewed in isolation is its percentage share of the relevant market. Where a business has enjoyed a very high market share, or even a monopoly, for a significant period of time, that may be sufficient in itself to establish dominance for the purposes of Article 82.[59] In addition to its market share, there may be other circumstances concerning the undertaking which contribute to its market power. However, in general it will also be necessary to look at two other factors: the nature of the market and the characteristics of the other participants on that market.

(ii) *Barriers to entry or expansion.* If the market is easily contestable by new entrants or smaller competitors, that will tend to undermine an allegation

---

[56] Cases C-395 & 396/96P *Compagnie Maritime Belge Transports v Commission* (n 24, above) Opinion at para 132; judgment at para 114. See also *Tetra Pak II*, discussed in para 10.004, above, where the exceptional circumstances relied on to establish abuse in a related market appear to be an application of this approach. See further para 10.082, below.

[57] Cases C-395 & 396/96P *Compagnie Maritime Belge Transports v Commission* (n 24, above) paras 118–120. See also *Deutsche Post - Interception of cross-border mail* (n 55, above) para 103: '[the] actual scope of the dominant firm's special responsibility must be considered in relation to the degree of dominance held by that firm and to the special characteristics of the market which may affect the competitive situation'. The concept of 'super-dominance' was applied as regards exclusionary pricing strategies by the UK Competition Appeal Tribunal in *NAPP v Director General of Fair Trading* [2002] CAT 1, [2002] CompAR 13, para 219; and similarly, by the Swedish Market Court in Case A3/98 *Posten Sverige v Swedish Competition Authority*, judgment of 11 November 1998. See also the DG Comp Discussion Paper (para 10.005, above) para 59.

[58] For criticism of 'super-dominance', see O'Donoghue and Padilla (n 1, above), 167–168.

[59] *Hoffmann-La Roche* (n 42, above) para 41; Case C-62/86 *AKZO v Commission* [1991] ECR I-3359, [1993] 5 CMLR 215, para 61, where the ECJ found that a market share of 50 per cent would lead to a presumption of dominance.

of dominance. Conversely, high barriers to entry or expansion will tend to support a finding of market power.

(iii) *Countervailing market power.* If actual or potential competitors of the undertaking enjoy substantial competitive advantages, that will lessen the likelihood that the undertaking holds significant market power. The same may be the case where powerful suppliers or customers are able to exert a strong discipline over any exercise of market power by a company.

There are often strong correlations between these three factors. For example, a very high market share held over a period of years will tend to suggest that there are substantial barriers to entry and may also indicate that there are few actual or potential competitors on that market. However, for the purposes of analysis it is appropriate to consider each in turn.

(b) The market position of the undertaking itself

Market share as an indicator of dominance. Where there is a legal monopoly **10.021** over supply on a relevant market, especially a monopoly conferred by statute, there is by definition no competition and therefore, save in exceptional circumstances, dominance.[60] But a dominant position is not confined to such a case. Indeed a dominant position may exist where there is 'lively competition'.[61] In determining whether a firm is dominant, the obvious starting point is to identify the current market share of the undertaking in question. The Court of Justice has said:

> 'The existence of a dominant position may derive from several factors which, taken separately, are not necessarily determinative but among these factors a highly important one is the existence of very large market shares.'[62]

The reason is that:

> 'An undertaking which has a very large market share and holds it for some time by means of the volume of production and the scale of the supply which it stands for – without those having much smaller market shares being able to meet rapidly the

---

[60] See, eg *General Motors* (n 37, above); Case 226/84 *British Leyland v Commission* [1986] ECR 3263, [1987] 1 CMLR 185; *Höfner and Elser* (n 27, above) para 28; *Merci convenzionale porto di Genova* (n 50, above) para 14; Case C-320/91 *Corbeau* [1993] ECR I-2533, [1995] 4 CMLR 621; Case T-229/94 *Deutsche Bahn v Commission* [1997] ECR II-1689, [1998] 4 CMLR 220, para 57 (appeal on other grounds dismissed, Case C-436/97P, [1999] ECR I-2387, [1999] 5 CMLR 776); *Brussels Airport*, OJ 1995 L216/8, [1996] 4 CMLR 232; Case T-139/98 *Amministrazione Autonoma dei Monopoli di Stato v Commission* ('*AAMS*') [2001] ECR II-3413, [2002] 4 CMLR 302 (on appeal from *Amministrazione Autonoma dei Monopoli di Stato*, OJ 1998 L252/47, [1998] 5 CMLR 786). For the position of, eg patent holders, see paras 10.036 *et seq*, below. The only circumstance where 100 per cent market share may possibly not give rise to dominance is where there is extremely strong countervailing buyer power: see further n 127, below.
[61] *Hoffmann-La Roche* (n 42, above); Case T-210/01 *General Electric v Commission* [2006] ECR II-5575, [2006] 4 CMLR 686, para 117.
[62] *Hoffmann-La Roche* (n 42, above) para 39.

demand from those who would like to break away from the undertaking which has the largest market share – is by virtue of that share in a position of strength which makes it an unavoidable trading partner and which, because of this secures for it, at the very least during relatively long periods, that freedom of action which is the special feature of a dominant position.'[63]

10.022 **General caution about market shares.**   However, except in the most obvious of cases, such as in *Suiker Unie*,[64] where one of the suppliers had a massive share of a commodity product, the proof of a significant market share is seldom a substitute for a full economic analysis of the issue of dominance. First, even if the market share figures are reliable, maintenance of a significant market share provides little information about the competitive process without an understanding of the reasons for, and the pressures determining, the output and price decisions made by the firms in the market. Secondly, even if the market has been defined correctly, market share figures do not show relative efficiencies and do not necessarily show that similar market shares can be sustained in the future. Thirdly, the decisions that any firm makes may be influenced by potential competitors who have not yet entered the market but who would do so if a profitable opportunity were to arise. By their nature, market share figures cannot measure this potential competition, although the threat that it presents may be a powerful influence restraining the independence of an allegedly dominant firm. Fourthly, market power on the part of the customers of the undertaking may limit its ability to act independently of their wishes.[65] Fifthly, market shares as at a given date are less significant for the analysis of a market characterised by the award of a limited number of high-value contracts. On such a 'bidding market', the fact that a particular company has had a number of recent 'wins' does not necessarily mean that one of its competitors will not be successful in the next competition and increase its market share considerably at one go.[66]

10.023 **Measurement of market shares.**   Market shares are generally measured by value and volume; where the relevant products are heterogeneous with varying levels of prices, shares by value may be the more reliable indicator of market strength.[67] The analysis of market shares involves examination of absolute and

---

[63] ibid, para 41; and *AAMS* (n 60, above) para 51.

[64] Cases 40/73, etc, *Suiker Unie v Commission* [1975] ECR 1663, [1976] 1 CMLR 295, paras 452–457. See also *Hoffmann-La Roche* (n 42, above) paras 56 and 60; *Tetra Pak II* (n 10, above) para 100 of the Commission's decision; Cases T-24/93, etc, *Compagnie Maritime Belge Transports v Commission* [1996] ECR II-1201, [1997] 4 CMLR 273, para 76.

[65] eg Case M.1882 *Pirelli/BICC*, OJ 2003 L70/35. See also para 8.226, above.

[66] *General Electric* (n 61, above) paras 148 *et seq* (the CFI nevertheless upheld the Commission's finding that GE was dominant in the market for jet engines for large commercial aircraft: 'Even on a bidding market, the fact of a manufacturer maintaining, or even increasing, its market share over a number of years in succession is an indication of market strength').

[67] See, eg *Warner-Lambert/Gillette*, OJ 1993 L116/21, [1993] 5 CMLR 559, para 22.

relative levels and also of changes, if any, over time. Moreover, the concept of the 'unavoidable trading partner'[68] invites an examination of the stability, or instability, of trading relations between suppliers and their customers. In a market in which demand increases slowly and no substitute products are developed, and in which one firm has far outdistanced its rivals and maintained a high market share, the dominant firm may well have become an 'unavoidable trading partner', reasonably secure in the knowledge that existing competitors cannot, and potential competitors would not, seek to mount an attack on that established position. On the other hand, the opposite may be the case on an emerging market, where even a very high initial market share may be vulnerable to challenge from competing suppliers.

Market share levels: *Hoffmann-La Roche.* In the early and leading case of **10.024** *Hoffmann-La Roche*,[69] the Court of Justice considered the issue of market shares in respect of a series of different markets and gave the following indications:

(i) Market shares over a three-year period ranging between 75 per cent and 87 per cent were held to be 'so large that they are in themselves evidence of a dominant position'[70] and market shares ranging between 84 per cent and 90 per cent over a similar period 'so large that they prove the existence of a dominant position'.[71]

(ii) Market shares ranging between 63 per cent and 66 per cent over a three-year period were held to be 'evidence of the existence of a dominant position' and 'the gap between Roche's shares (64.8 per cent) and those of its next largest competitors (14.8 per cent and 6.3 per cent) was such as to confirm the conclusion which the Commission reached'.[72]

(iii) The Court of Justice said that a market share of 47 per cent in a 'narrow oligopolistic market', in which the shares of the other producers were 27 per cent, 18 per cent, seven per cent and one per cent, 'proves that [Roche] is entirely free to decide what attitude to adopt when confronted by competition'.[73]

(iv) In relation to vitamin B3, the Court of Justice declared that there was 'insufficient evidence of the existence of a dominant position',[74] despite market shares in 1974 of 51 per cent by both volume and value, Roche's shares had been significantly lower over the previous two years (in 1972

---

68 As referred to by the ECJ in *Hoffmann-La Roche* (n 42, above) para 41.
69 Case 85/76 *Hoffmann-La Roche v Commission* [1979] ECR 461, [1979] 3 CMLR 211.
70 ibid, para 56.
71 ibid, para 60.
72 ibid, para 63.
73 ibid, para 51.
74 ibid, para 58.

28.9 per cent by value and only 18.9 per cent by volume). The Court of Justice held that:

'Market shares of this size either in value or in quantity, complemented by the statement in the document jointly prepared by the parties that the figures for 1971 were 6 per cent lower still than those for 1972 do not in themselves constitute a factor sufficient to establish the existence of a dominant position for most of the period considered by the Commission.'[75]

10.025 **Market shares in other cases.** Indications given by the Court of Justice in relation to levels of market share in other cases include the following:

(i) In *Suiker Unie*, a market share of 90 per cent in the southern German market and 85 per cent in the Belgian market for sugar were held to be dominant positions.[76]

(ii) In *Michelin*, the Court of Justice held that a market share of 57 per cent to 65 per cent on the market in new replacement tyres for heavy vehicles (compared with the market shares of Michelin NV's main competitors of between four per cent and eight per cent) 'constitutes a valid indication of Michelin NV's preponderant strength in relation to its competitors . . .'.[77]

(iii) In *AKZO*, a stable market share of 50 per cent over at least three years was held to be proof of a dominant position.[78]

(iv) In *United Brands*, the Court of Justice held that a market share of between 40 per cent and nearly 45 per cent 'does not permit the conclusion that UBC automatically controls the market. It [ie the dominance] must be determined having regard to the strength and number of the competitors.'[79] However, the Court went on to find that that percentage represented a share several times greater than that of its competitors, the rest of whom were far behind. This, together with other factors, afforded 'evidence of UBC's preponderant strength'.[80]

(v) In *Gøttrup-Klim*, in relation to market shares of 36 per cent in fertilizers and 32 per cent in plant protection products, the Court of Justice said:

'While an undertaking which holds market shares of that size may, depending on the strength and number of its competitors, be considered to be in a dominant

---

[75] ibid, para 58.

[76] *Suiker Unie* (n 64, above) paras 452–457.

[77] Case 322/81 *Michelin v Commission* (n 4, above) para 52. cf *Meridian Communication Limited and Cellular Three Limited v Eircell* [2002] 1 IR 17, where the Irish High Court found that on the facts of that case Eircell was not dominant in the market for mobile telephony services despite a market share of approximately 60 per cent. This was based on the facts that Eircell's market share was declining in favour of the competing mobile operator, at the time of the case a third operator had just entered the market, and that the significance of high barriers to entry in the market was vastly reduced by the fact that barriers to expansion were so low.

[78] *AKZO v Commission* (n 59, above) para 61.

[79] *United Brands* (n 41, above) paras 108–110.

[80] ibid, para 112.

position, those market shares cannot on their own constitute conclusive evidence of a dominant position.'[81]

(vi) In *Metro*, a 5 to 10 per cent market share of a market for highly technical products which appear to the majority of consumers to be readily interchangeable normally rules out the existence of a dominant position.[82]

Market shares: Commission electronic communications guidelines. In its **10.026** Guidelines on market analysis and the assessment of significant market power under the Community's regulatory framework for electronic communications networks and services (the 'SMP Guidelines'),[83] the Commission discusses the concept of dominance under Article 82 (as the Framework Directive aligns the definition of significant market power with the Court's definition of dominance) and says:

'Although a high market share alone is not sufficient to establish the possession of significant market power (dominance), it is unlikely that a firm without a significant share of the relevant market would be in dominant position. Thus, undertakings with market shares of no more than 25 per cent are not likely to enjoy a (single) dominant position on the market concerned . . . In the Commission's decision-making practice, single dominance concerns normally arise in the case of undertakings with market shares of over 40 per cent, although the Commission may in some cases have concerns about dominance even with lower market shares . . . as dominance may occur without the existence of a large market share.'[84]

Relative market shares. As illustrated by the above references to *Hoffmann-La* **10.027** *Roche, United Brands, Michelin* and *Gøttrup-Klim*, in determining whether any particular level of market share confers dominance, the relationship between that share and the shares of others in the market will be an important consideration. The implications of a market share of, say, 40 per cent are likely to be very different in circumstances where there are two competitors each with 30 per cent as compared with circumstances where no other competitor has more than 10 per cent. This is a clear example of the overlap between issues relating to the strength of the

---

[81] Case C-250/92 *Gøttrup Klim v Dansk Landbrugs* [1994] ECR I-5641, [1996] 4 CMLR 191, para 48. See also rejection of complaints against *Elmo-Tech Ltd*: 30 per cent share of market for equipment for electronic monitoring of paroled offenders 'not normally indicative of dominance' particularly where there was a wide diversity and abundance of firms active in the market: (2003) 3 EC Competition Policy Newsletter 53.

[82] Case 26/76 *Metro v Commission ('Metro No. 1')* [1977] ECR 1875, [1978] 2 CMLR 1, para 17. See also Case 75/84 *Metro v Commission ('Metro No. 2')* [1986] ECR 3021, [1987] 1 CMLR 118, para 85 (share of less than 10 per cent too small to be evidence of dominance).

[83] SMP Guidelines, OJ 2002 C165/03: Vol II, App E.25. The concept of significant market power in this context is considered at paras 12.097 *et seq*, below.

[84] The Commission indicated at para 75 that market shares greater than 50 per cent would give rise to a presumption of dominance and also indicated the potential importance of a high market share over time.

undertaking itself and the countervailing power of its competitors, customers and suppliers, considered below. In *Van den Bergh Foods*, the Court of First Instance referred to the 'considerable gap between its market share and those of its immediate competitors' as being a relevant factor when considering dominance.[85] And in *British Airways*, the Court of First Instance upheld the Commission's finding that British Airways (BA) was a dominant purchaser in the United Kingdom market for the supply of travel agency services to airlines although its market share was only 39.7 per cent. The Court noted that BA still had a 'preponderant' share of the market compared both to its closest rival and to the cumulative shares of its five major competitors.[86]

10.028   **Stability of market shares.**   As *Hoffmann-La Roche* illustrates, the persistence of a given market share over time will also be important in determining whether that share implies dominance.[87] No minimum period has been stipulated over which a high and stable market share is indicative of dominance, but a period of five years would probably afford sufficient evidence while any period of less than three years, especially in a dynamic market, might be considered too short for a high market share to be an indicator of dominance. The fact that market shares may be declining over time will also be relevant, although, as the Court of First Instance has held, 'a decline in market shares which are still very large [over 90 per cent in the case in question] cannot in itself constitute proof of the absence of a dominant position'.[88]

---

[85] Case T-65/98 *Van den Bergh Foods v Commission* [2003] ECR II-4653, [2004] 4 CMLR 14, [2005] All ER (EC) 418, para 155 (appeal on other grounds dismissed, Case C-552/03P *Unilever Bestfoods (Ireland) Ltd v Commission* [2006] ECRI-9091, [2006] 5 CMLR 1460).

[86] Case T-219/99 *British Airways v Commission* [2003] ECR II-5917, [2004] 4 CMLR 1008, [2004] All ER (EC) 1115, dismissing the appeal against *Virgin/British Airways*, OJ 2000 L244/56, [2000] 4 CMLR 999. This was the first time that a share of less than 40 per cent of the relevant market was held to confer a dominant position. (Dominance not challenged on appeal: Case C-95/04P, [2007] 4 CMLR 982.)

[87] Case 85/76 *Hoffmann-La Roche v Commission* [1979] ECR 461, [1979] 3 CMLR 211, para 41. See also Case 77/77 *BP v Commission* [1978] ECR 1513, [1978] 3 CMLR 174, where AG Warner rejected (at 1537) the proposition that Art 82 is applicable to a situation where 'owing to an emergency causing a temporary scarcity of supplies of a particular commodity, the customers or the "normal" customers of each supplier may become dependent upon him.'; *Der Grüne Punkt - Duales System Deutschland*, OJ 2001 L166/1, [2001] 5 CMLR 609: stability of a high (82 per cent) market share over time supported finding of dominance (appeal on other grounds dismissed, Case T-151/01 *Der Grüne Punkt – Duales System Deutschland v Commission* [2007] 5 CMLR 300, on appeal Case C-385/07P, not yet decided). See also SMP Guidelines in the context of electronic communications networks and services (n 83, above) paras 72 *et seq*.

[88] Cases T-24/93, etc, *Compagnie Maritime Belge Transports v Commission* [1996] ECR II-1201, [1997] 4 CMLR 273, para 77; appeal dismissed, Cases C-395 & 396/96P, [2000] ECR I-1365, [2000] 4 CMLR 1076, [2000] All ER (EC) 385. See also *British Airways* (n 86, above): decline of BA's share from 47.7 per cent in 1990 to 39.7 per cent in 1998 did not rebut dominance.

Market shares indicating dominance.   In the light of the foregoing, the follow-   **10.029**
ing broad comments may be helpful:[89]

(i) Percentages significantly and consistently above 50 per cent are likely to be
   strong indicators of dominance save in exceptional market conditions.
(ii) Percentages above 40 per cent would be regarded as relevant and significant
   in an assessment of dominance, depending upon: (i) changes in the absolute
   level over time; (ii) the level relative to that of the nearest competitors; and
   (iii) the presence of other factors tending to entrench the leading position or,
   conversely, to threaten it.[90] For example, in *AKZO*,[91] emphasis was placed on
   AKZO's belief in its position as a world leader in the peroxide market, on its
   highly developed marketing organisation, and on its superior technological
   knowledge.
(iii) Percentages varying between 30 per cent and 40 per cent fall below the level
   at which dominance can be assumed and evidence would be required of substantial disparities in market share, significant impediments to entry, and so
   on, before dominance could be established.
(iv) It appears that a market share of below 30 per cent in a correctly defined market would not be evidence of a dominant position save in wholly exceptional
   circumstances.[92]

Overall size and strength.   It may be relevant also to consider the overall eco-   **10.030**
nomic and commercial strengths of the undertaking alleged to be dominant and
those of its competitors. Thus in *Michelin*, the Court of Justice took into account
'the advantages which [Michelin and its competitors] may derive from belonging
to groups of undertakings operating throughout Europe or even the world'.[93]
In *Van den Bergh Foods*, the Court of First Instance held that the Commission had
correctly treated as relevant to its finding of dominance that HB had the most
extensive and popular range of products on the relevant market, was the sole supplier of impulse ice creams in some 40 per cent of outlets, was part of a multinational group that had been marketing ice creams for many years, and that it was a

---

[89] For a systematic but somewhat light-hearted description of the significance of specific market
share levels for competition law analysis generally, see Whish (n 1, above), 46–48.
[90] *United Brands* (n 41, above); *Hoffmann-La Roche* (n 87, above). This is also the view of the
Commission, *Tenth Report on Competition Policy* (1980), point 150. See also *Napier Brown/British
Sugar*, OJ 1988 L284/41, [1990] 4 CMLR 196 (57 per cent suffices for dominance where the other
major competitor with 43 per cent is weak); *British Airways* (n 86, above).
[91] *AKZO v Commission* (n 59, above).
[92] In *Metro No. 2* (n 82, above) para 85, the ECJ confirmed that a market share of 10 per cent was
too small to establish a dominant position, at least in the absence of exceptional circumstances. The
Commission's SMP Guidelines leave open the possibility of market shares of between 25 per cent
and 40 per cent establishing dominance: para 10.026, above; see also *Tenth Report on Competition
Policy* (1980), point 150, referring also to *Ninth Report* (1979), point 22.
[93] Case 322/81 *Michelin v Commission* (n 4, above) para 55.

very well-known brand, altogether making it an unavoidable partner for many retailers.[94] By contrast, in *Hoffmann-La Roche*, where the Commission had held that a relevant factor in support of a finding of dominance in the various markets for vitamins was that Roche was the world's largest manufacturer of vitamins and pharmaceuticals, the Court of Justice rejected this ground for the decision.[95] Adding in resources that were not employed in the production or supply of goods within the relevant market was not, on the facts of that case, material. In some cases it may be seriously misleading to add together resources used for different purposes and different markets and seek to infer dominance from the aggregate size of the undertaking in question.[96] It will be a question of fact in each case whether undertakings in the same group are to be treated as one unit for the purposes of Article 82.

10.031 **Anti-competitive conduct as evidence of dominance.**   There are occasions on which behaviour may be taken into account in assessing the market power of the undertaking alleged to be dominant. Although generally the issue of dominance is analysed prior to consideration of abuse, the Court of Justice has held that the acts alleged to constitute abuses may be taken into account in determining whether dominance exists:[97] the very fact that the firm can engage in the conduct in question may suggest that it is able to act independently of its competitors and customers.[98] Such behaviour may consist of a policy of granting rebates,[99] a refusal

---

[94] Case T-65/98 *Van den Bergh Foods v Commission* (n 85, above) para 156. The ECJ did not address this issue.

[95] *Hoffmann-La Roche* (n 87, above) para 47.

[96] *Metro No. 2* (n 82, above) paras 79 *et seq*, in which the ECJ refused to take into account the activities of other undertakings in the Thomson-Brandt group in the absence of evidence that the undertakings in the group followed a coordinated marketing strategy. See also *Suiker Unie* (n 64, above) paras 376–382 and 451–452; *Ahmed Saeed* (n 17, above) para 35. In Case T-340/03 *France Télécom v Commission* [2007] 4 CMLR 919, paras 112–120, the CFI held that the Commission had rightly regarded Wanadoo's strength on the market for high-speed internet access as reinforced by the logistical advantages which it enjoyed from its link-up to France Télécom's distribution network, but that the revenue earned by the Wanadoo group from its directory publishing business could not confirm dominance since that related to a different market. On appeal, Case C-202/07P, not yet decided.

[97] *United Brands* (n 41, above) para 68. See also *Hilti* (n 44, above) para 93: 'it is highly improbable in practice that a non-dominant supplier will act as Hilti did, since effective competition will normally ensure that the adverse consequences of such behaviour outweigh any benefits'; *Tetra Pak II*, OJ 1992 L72/1, [1992] 4 CMLR 551, para 146(1): 'It is barely conceivable that undertakings whose conduct is dictated by the laws of the market would be able to impose contractual clauses on their clients as restrictive as those outlined above. This confirms, if there is still a need to do so, the quasi-monopolistic power which Tetra Pak wields on the aseptic markets'. See also *Genzyme Ltd v Office of Fair Trading* [2004] CAT 4, [2004] CompAR 358, para 255: the ability of Genzyme to resist the wishes of its consumers and users was described by the UK Competition Appeal Tribunal as 'the hallmark of dominance'.

[98] The Report by the EAGCP (n 13 above) p 4, suggested that as a matter of economic theory that there may be no justification for a two-stage analysis and that it would be more appropriate to consider the whole issue of unilateral anti-competitive conduct as a single issue.

[99] *Michelin II*, OJ 2002 L143/1, [2002] 5 CMLR 388, paras 197–199 (appeal dismissed, Case T-203/01 *Michelin v Commission ('Michelin II')* [2003] ECR II-4071, [2004] 4 CMLR 923).

to negotiate any amendments to the onerous terms of the contracts which it offers its customers,[100] the treatment by the firm of its competitors,[101] and the firm's own attitude to its market position.[102] However, the fact that a firm is not charging particularly high prices, or is even making losses, is not incompatible with dominance.[103]

(c) Barriers to entry and expansion

Barriers to entry: generally. Where the undertaking under consideration has a **10.032** high market share, it is important to consider how quickly this share could be eroded by existing competitors increasing their output or by new competitors entering the market in the event that the dominant company started to behave abusively. The expression 'barriers to entry' describes the various difficulties which new undertakings may face in entering a market.[104] These difficulties do not have to be absolute but must materially impede an actual competitor in seeking to compete with the market leader and/or deter any actual or potential competitor from seeking to enter or expand its competing business to provide effective competition. Such difficulties may result from technical resources, economies of scale, intellectual property rights or other attributes of the putatively dominant undertaking.

Barriers to entry and definition of the relevant market. Consideration of barriers to entry may arise at various stages of the analysis under Article 82, including **10.033** at the stage of defining the relevant market as well as in the assessment of market power. As discussed in Chapter 4, above, supply substitutability – the possibility that alternative suppliers can switch their production to make products which compete with those of the putative dominant company – is an essential factor in the definition of the relevant market. But where such switching is not so straightforward as to justify the inclusion of the alternative supplier in the relevant product market, the potential for market entry may still exercise a constraint on the behaviour of the dominant firm. The Commission's Relevant Market Notice suggests that entry barriers will generally not be considered in the context of market definition but rather at the later stage of the analysis of dominance, but adds

---

[100] Case T-139/98 *Amministrazione Autonoma dei Monopoli di Stato v Commission ('AAMS')* [2001] ECR II-3413, [2002] 4 CMLR 302, para 52.

[101] *Hilti* (n 44, above).

[102] *BBI/Boosey & Hawkes*, OJ 1987 L286/36, [1988] 4 CMLR 67.

[103] *Michelin* (n 4, above) para 59; Case T-228/97 *Irish Sugar v Commission* [1999] ECR II-2969, [1999] 5 CMLR 1300, [2000] All ER (EC) 198, paras 102–103; appeal dismissed, Case C-497/99P *Irish Sugar v Commission* [2001] ECR I-5333, [2001] 5 CMLR 1082.

[104] Economists generally take a more limited view of what constitutes a barrier to entry than the Commission or the Community Courts: eg mere cost of entry is not generally regarded as a barrier; see Harbord, 'The Analysis of Barriers to Entry and Exit in UK Competition Policy' (1995) ECLR 319; Turnbull, 'Barriers to Entry, Art 86 EC and the Abuse of a Dominant Position: An Economic Critique of European Competition Law' (1996) ECLR 96. See further O'Donoghue and Padilla (n 1, above), 117–119.

that the Commission may also treat barriers to entry as relevant to the geographic market assessment.[105] Some of the commonly identified barriers are discussed below.

10.034 **Scale economies.** In *United Brands*,[106] the Court of Justice considered a number of factors arising out of the scale of United Brands' activities as a producer and supplier of bananas. It noted the exceptionally large capital investments required for the creation and running of banana plantations; the need to increase sources of supply in order to meet unforeseen crop failure; and the economies of scale in distribution possessed by United Brands that were not available to newcomers.[107] However, in every case it will be important to analyse whether the scale of activities truly precludes entry or expansion by new competitors. If the relevant activities can be effectively conducted by competitors operating efficiently but on a smaller scale, dominance may not be established. It has been alleged that a situation of 'massive excess production capacity', combined with increasing concentration in the motor industry, introduced barriers to entry and the likely elimination of competition (the issue was decided on other grounds by the Commission and the Court of First Instance).[108]

10.035 **Technical barriers.** In *Tetra Pak II*, the Court of First Instance found that Tetra Pak had 'artificially limited competition to the [sale of machines] in which it has the greatest technological lead and where entry barriers are therefore at their highest'.[109] In *Hoffmann-La Roche*,[110] both the Commission and the Court of Justice held that Roche's possession of technological advantages was a relevant consideration in the assessment of dominance. Clearly, an undertaking which possesses the resources, financial or technological, to lead in product development

---

[105] Commission Notice on the definition of the relevant market for the purposes of Community competition law, OJ 1997 C372/5: Vol II, App C.10, paras 24, 28–31.

[106] Case 27/76 *United Brands v Commission* [1978] ECR 207, [1978] 1 CMLR 429.

[107] ibid, para 122. The possession of an established sales network may be important: *Hoffmann-La Roche* (n 87, above) para 48; Case 322/81 *Michelin v Commission* [1983] ECR 3461, [1985] 1 CMLR 282, para 58; Cases T-24/93, etc, *Compagnie Maritime Belge Transports* (n 88, above) para 78. See also *Warner Lambert/Gillette* (n 67, above) para 9 (minimum economically viable size for new razor blade factory); *P&I Clubs, IGA*, OJ 1999 L125/12, [1999] 5 CMLR 646 (economies of scale in insurance and long time lag in achieving them by any potential new entrant).

[108] Case T-17/93 *Matra Hachette v Commission* [1994] ECR II-I-595, paras 141–154.

[109] Case T-83/91 *Tetra Pak v Commission ('Tetra Pak II')* [1994] ECR II-755, [1997] 4 CMLR 726, paras 133 and also 110. (The point was not considered by the ECJ on the further appeal, Case C-333/94P *Tetra Pak v Commission* [1996] ECR I-5951, [1997] 4 CMLR 662.)

[110] Case 102/77 *Hoffmann-La Roche v Centrafarm* [1978] ECR 1139, [1978] 3 CMLR 217. See also Case T-51/89 *Tetra Pak v Commission* [1990] ECR II-309, [1991] 4 CMLR 334, para 23 (obtaining exclusive licence for sterilising technology by purchase of another undertaking reinforces technical advantage and strengthens dominance). But the fact that a particular product is always stocked by a distributor because of its high quality does not establish dominance but is a legitimate form of competition: Case 26/76 *Metro v Commission ('Metro No. 1')* [1977] ECR 1875, [1978] 2 CMLR 1, para 17.

or technical services has a relevant advantage over its competitors. On the other hand, if there exist wide opportunities for technological advance, open to many competitors and not just to one firm, there is a very powerful competitive threat to any incumbent firm irrespective of its position in relation to current products. Similarly, technical resources are likely to be less material in low technology or mature markets where there is little apparent scope for further technological advance. Barriers to entry in the telecommunications and energy sectors are being overcome by various directives and Commission communications requiring access to be given by existing infrastructure owners to new entrants.[111]

Ownership of intellectual property. The legal 'monopoly' conferred by national law through patent, trade mark or copyright protection is to be distinguished from the economic concept of 'dominance' for the purposes of Article 82.[112] The ownership of an intellectual property right may be an important contributory factor in establishing dominance but does not, of itself, do so.[113] Thus in *Deutsche Grammophon v Metro*, the Court of Justice suggested that if recording artists were tied to the manufacturer of sound recording by exclusive contracts, a dominant position might arise, depending on the popularity of the artists, the duration of the contracts and the ability of competitors to obtain the services of comparable performers.[114] The issue is whether the ownership of intellectual property rights is such as to enable the owner to impede effective competition on a relevant product market.[115] In relation to patents, it is clearly possible to envisage a patent, or a series of patents, making a substantial contribution to dominance.[116] In relation to trade marks, the statutory protection from infringement is unlikely to be a serious impediment to competition, although a strong brand image could be a contributory factor to dominance. As to copyright, the Commission and the Court of Justice have in several cases[117] found copyright

10.036

---

[111] See Chap 12, below.

[112] See Chap 9, above, and paras 10.129 *et seq*, below.

[113] In Case 238/87 *Volvo v Veng* [1988] ECR 6211, [1989] 4 CMLR 122, one of the questions referred to the ECJ was whether the owner of the rights in an industrial design for a car body panel necessarily had a dominant position in the supply of that body panel. The ECJ did not answer the question but AG Mischo said that this would depend on whether there were substitutes for that body panel available, ie whether it was possible to make an adequate copy of the part without infringing the industrial design rights.

[114] Case 78/70 *Deutsche Grammophon v Metro* [1971] ECR 487, [1971] CMLR 631, para 18.

[115] See Cases C-241 & C-242/91P *RTE and ITP v Commission ('Magill')* [1995] ECR I-I-743, [1995] 4 CMLR 718, paras 46–47.

[116] See, eg *Hilti* (n 44, above) para 93.

[117] See, in particular, Case 127/73 *BRT v SABAM* [1974] ECR 51, [1974] 2 CMLR 238; Case 22/79 *Greenwich Film Production v SACEM* [1979] ECR 3275, [1980] 1 CMLR 629; Case 7/82 *GVL v Commission* [1983] ECR 483, [1983] 3 CMLR 645; Case 125/78 *GEMA v Commission* [1979] ECR 3173, [1980] 2 CMLR 177; the various GEMA decisions: OJ 1971 L134/15, [1971] CMLR D35; OJ 1972 L166/22, [1972] CMLR D115; OJ 1982 L94/12, [1982] 2 CMLR 482; the *SACEM* decisions: Case 402/85 *Basset v SACEM* [1987] ECR 1747, [1987] 3 CMLR 173;

collecting societies to hold a dominant position where the national systems estab-lished for the protection of individuals created organisations of monopolistic power for the exploitation of the copyrights. In the *Magill* case,[118] whereas the Court of First Instance had explicitly related the dominant positions of RTE and ITP to their copyright in programme listings, the Court of Justice approached the matter on the basis that the television stations (or their agents) were the only source of the basic information about the timing and other details of their own programmes. This meant that, 'by force of circumstance', they held a *de facto* monopoly over the information used to compile listings and were thereby able to prevent effective competition on the market in weekly television magazines, and were thus dominant.[119]

10.037 **Rights over land and ownership of property.** In a narrowly defined market, rights over land may be found to confer dominance by affording the ability to pre-clude entry by potential competitors. In cases where the complainant is an under-taking attempting to provide services from premises or facilities owned by one of its competitors, it is important to distinguish between the market for access to those premises or facilities and the market for the services themselves. Thus in *Aéroports de Paris*,[120] the Court of Justice upheld the finding that ADP, as manager of the Paris airports, was the dominant supplier of airport management services to groundhandlers who need the licence issued by ADP as well as access to its airport facilities in order to offer groundhandling services. Similarly, in *Flughafen Frankfurt/Main AG*[121] the Commission held that Flughafen Frankfurt/Main ('FAG'), which was the owner and operator of Frankfurt airport and the sole supplier of ramp-handling services at the airport, was dominant in the supply of those services since alternative suppliers were not in a position to assail FAG's monopoly so long as FAG denied them access to the ramp where the services had to be provided.

10.038 **Advertising.** High levels of advertising spend may constitute a barrier to entry. For example, in relation to cigarettes, the Commission took the view – which was not materially disputed by the parties – that in a stagnant and oligopolistic market,

---

Case 395/87 *Ministère Public v Tournier* [1989] ECR 2521, [1991] 4 CMLR 248; Cases 110/88, etc, *Lucazeau v SACEM* [1989] ECR 2811, [1991] 4 CMLR 248. See also para 10.134, below.

[118] Cases C-241 & 242/91/P *RTE and ITP v Commission* ('*Magill*') [1995] ECR I-743, [1995] 4 CMLR 718, upholding Case T-69/89 *RTE v Commission* [1991] ECR II-485, [1991] 4 CMLR 586, Case T-70/89 *BBC v Commission* [1991] ECR II-535, [1991] 4 CMLR 669 and Case T-76/89 *ITC v Commission* [1991] ECR II-575 [1991] 4 CMLR 745.

[119] *Magill*, above, para 47.

[120] Case C-82/01P *Aéroports de Paris v Commission* [2002] ECR I-9297, [2003] 4 CMLR 609.

[121] *FAG—Flughafen Frankfurt/Main AG*, OJ 1998 L72/30, [1998] 4 CMLR 779, para 69. See also Case T-9/93 *Schöller v Commission* [1995] ECR II-I-1611, [1995] 5 CMLR 659, paras 83–84: a case under Art 81 where the CFI held that a system of lending freezer cabinets to retailers for the exclusive use of the lender's products constituted a barrier to entry into the ice cream market.

advertising and corporate acquisition were the principal means of increasing market share. Since the market was dominated by large companies with considerable resources and advertising was of great importance, there were very high barriers to entry.[122]

Exchange of information.   In *UK Agricultural Tractor Registration Exchange*,   **10.039** in a decision upheld by the Court of First Instance and Court of Justice, the Commission found that an information exchange agreement made between members of a trade association increased transparency on a highly concentrated market and raised barriers to entry for non-members of the association.[123]

(d) Countervailing market power

Relative market power of competing firms.   The need to take account of the   **10.040** relative market power of competing firms has been considered above in respect of market shares. That is one aspect of the wider issue of whether there are significant actual or potential competitors who may be able, in the particular circumstances of the market in question, to provide effective competition to the leading firm and thereby enable it to rebut any presumption of dominance that might arise on the basis of a narrow consideration of market shares. Examples include the *EMI* cases [124] and *United Brands*.[125]

Countervailing power of buyers.   The presence of powerful purchasers with the   **10.041** strength to stand up to a supplier with a large market share may negate the existence of dominance in a particular market. Assessment of customer power is a frequent feature of merger cases, as discussed in Chapter 6, above.[126] Those decisions are of course of equal relevance to Article 82 and the importance of the countervailing power of customers has been recognised in the latter context by the Community Courts. In the *Italian Flat Glass* case,[127] among the criticisms made

---

[122] Cases 142 & 156/84 *BAT & RJ Reynolds v Commission* [1987] ECR 4487, [1988] 4 CMLR 24, paras 43–44.

[123] *UK Agricultural Tractor Exchange*, OJ 1992 L68/19, [1993] 4 CMLR 358; on appeal, Case T-35/92 *Deere v Commission* [1994] ECR II-957 and Case T-34/92 *Fiatagri and New Holland Ford v Commission* [1994] ECR II-905; on further appeal, Case C-7/95P *Deere v Commission* [1998] ECR I-3111, [1998] 5 CMLR 311 and Case C-8/95P *New Holland Ford v Commission* [1998] ECR I-3175, [1998] 5 CMLR 311, 362.

[124] See, eg Case 51/75 *EMI Records v CBS United Kingdom* [1976] ECR 811, [1976] 2 CMLR 235, para 36. See also Case 86/75 *EMI Records v CBS Grammofon* [1976] ECR 871, [1976] 2 CMLR 235, para 33; Case 96/75 *EMI Records v CBS Schallplatten* [1976] ECR 913, [1976] 2 CMLR 235, para 19.

[125] *United Brands* (n 106, above).

[126] See paras 8.225 *et seq*, above.

[127] Cases T-68/89, etc, *SIV v Commission* ('*Italian Flat Glass*') [1992] ECR II-1403, [1992] 5 CMLR 302, para 366. See also *Hutchison 3G (UK) Ltd v Office of Communications* [2005] CAT 39: UK Competition Appeal Tribunal set aside the finding that a mobile operator had significant

of the Commission's decision by the Court of First Instance was that the Commission 'has not even attempted to gather the information necessary to weigh up the economic power of the three producers [alleged to be collectively dominant] against that of Fiat, which could cancel each other out'.[128] The fact that the main purchasers of a product are public authorities who are bound by EC public procurement rules to put contracts out to tender also indicates lack of market power, particularly where the evidence shows that there are several companies bidding for the contracts.[129]

10.042 **Market power of upstream suppliers.** The contractual power of large producers can clearly constrain the market freedom of their customers and has been recognised by the Court of Justice as a factor in assessing the effect on competition. Thus, in *Gøttrup-Klim*, in the context of a challenge made to the position of a buyers' cooperative, the Court of Justice stated:

> 'In a market where product prices vary according to the volume of orders, the activities of cooperative purchasing associations may, depending on the size of their membership, constitute a significant counterweight to the contractual power of large producers and make way for more effective competition.'[130]

---

market power (corresponding to dominance) in the market for call termination on its network, notwithstanding its 100 per cent market share, on the basis that there had been inadequate assessment of the countervailing buyer power of British Telecom; similarly in Ireland, *Hutchison 3G Ireland Ltd v Commission for Communications*, 26 September 2005, Decn 02/05 of the Electronic Communications Appeals Panel; in the Netherlands, *Kroniklijke KPN NV v Independent Post and Telecommunications Authority*, 29 August 2006, Cases AWB 05/903, etc, judgment of the Trade and Industry Appeals Tribunal.

[128] Although such cases are relatively rare in practice, in principle buying power may itself be such as to constitute dominance. In *British Airways* (n 86, above), BA's dominant position was as a purchaser from travel agents of the services of marketing and distribution of airline tickets. See also report by the UK Competition Commission, *Supermarkets* (Cm 4842, 2000), finding that some of the purchasing practices of the major UK supermarkets operated against the public interest. For the EC Commission's observations on retailing, see *XXVIth Report on Competition Policy* (1996), points 142–144 and 147. See also 'The Welfare Consequences of the Exercise of Buyer Power', OFT Research Paper 16 (1998); Vogel 'Competition Law and Buying Power: the case for a new approach in Europe' (1998) ECLR 4; Bloom, 'Retailer Buyer Power' in Hawk (ed), *2000 Fordham Corp. L. Inst.* (2001). For assessment of buyer power in the context of merger analysis, see the Commission's Guidelines on the assessment of horizontal mergers, OJ 2005 C56/24, Vol II, App D.6, and paras 8.225 *et seq*, above. See also the UK Competition Commission's *Market Investigation References: Competition Commission Guidelines* (CC 3, June 2003) paras 3.37–3.39.

[129] See rejection of complaints against *Elmo-Tech Ltd*, (2003) 3 EC Competition Policy Newsletter 53, citing evidence (i) that contracts for equipment for electronic monitoring of paroled offenders were put out to tender and many companies submitted bids; and (ii) of many 'concrete instances' where penetentiary authorities exercised their countervailing bargaining power: 'In bidding markets, a high market share normally is an *ex post* indicator of low prices, not an *ex ante* indicator of high prices. What really matters in such a market is the existence of a significant number of likely bidders willing to apply for tenders'.

[130] Case C-250/92 *Gøttrup-Klim v Dansk Landbrugs Grovvaresklab AmbA* [1994] ECR I-5641, [1996] 4 CMLR 191, para 32.

(e) Appraisal of market power in more complex cases

Related markets: general.   Market definition for related or connected markets is   **10.043**
discussed at paragraph 4.059, above. This is of considerable importance in the
application of Article 82, because there is an established and developing jurisprudence applying the prohibition of abuse of dominance to a range of situations
where an undertaking enjoys market power on one market but exercises that
power in a way that influences conditions of competition on a related market.
This issue is considered below in relation to abuse but this Section illustrates some
aspects which can arise at the earlier stage of determining market power.

Separate markets for raw materials.   A firm alleged to have abused a domi-   **10.044**
nant position in refusing to supply a raw material to a long-standing customer
who is also, or is about to become, a competitor cannot rely on the existence of
conditions of effective competition in the market for the supply of products processed from that raw material. In such a case, the relevant market is the market for
the raw material, although the adverse impact on competition on the downstream
market may form the basis for a finding of abuse on the upstream market.[131]

Control over other essential inputs and facilities.   The issue of control over a   **10.045**
related market is not limited to monopoly supply of a raw material but extends to
a wide range of goods and services that are in practice necessary inputs for the purposes of competing on another market. Examples are industries that function on
the basis of 'networks' or common industry standards, where the controller of the
network or the holder of proprietary rights over the industry standard may in
practice be able to control competition on the principal market. The privatisation
of the utility markets has led to an Article 82-type system of regulation of the relevant networks to ensure fair access to the network for competing suppliers;[132] and
similar issues have arisen on computer markets where one firm has a commanding
position in relation to the industry standard.[133] There have also been a number of
cases in the transport sector where the operator of a transport hub, for example a
port or airport, has in practice been able to control the conditions of competition
facing actual or potential competitors on the relevant transport market.[134] These
issues are considered in more detail below, in the context of abuse.

---

[131] Cases 6 & 7/73 *Commercial Solvents v Commission* [1974] ECR 223, [1974] 1 CMLR 309,
paras 21–22. Commercial Solvents argued that there was effective competition from other anti-
tuberculosis drugs in the market for the finished product, ethambutol. The ECJ rejected this argument as irrelevant when the complaint was the refusal to supply aminobutanol, the raw material.

[132] See paras 10.142 and 10.143, below.

[133] See, eg Case COMP/37.792 *Microsoft*, 24 March 2004, [2005] 4 CMLR 965 (on appeal, Case
T-201/04 *Microsoft v Commission*, judgment of 17 September 2007; see Postscript below); *France
Télécom v Commission* (n 96, above) paras 112–118 (Wanadoo benefited from technical support and pre-
ferential treatment from the France Télécom group of which it was part); see also para 10.131, below.

[134] See, eg *Port of Rødby*, OJ 1994 L55/52, [1994] 5 CMLR 457; *Sealink/B&I Line* [1992]
5 CMLR 255; *Sea Containers/Stena Sealink*, OJ 1994 L15/8, [1995] 4 CMLR 84; *Brussels Airport*,
OJ 1995 L216/8, [1996] 4 CMLR 232.

10.046 **Separate market for ancillary services.** In *General Motors*,[135] it was alleged that General Motors was charging excessive prices for the issue of certificates of conformity, which were required under Belgian law by importers of motor cars into Belgium and were available only from General Motors in respect of General Motors' cars. General Motors argued that issuing such certificates was an activity merely ancillary to the market in motor cars, in which it did not hold a dominant position. The Court of Justice rejected that argument, treating the issue of certificates of conformity for General Motors cars as a distinct market in which General Motors was dominant by virtue of the legal monopoly delegated to it by the State.[136]

10.047 **The relevant market and the market in which the abuse took place.** Usually the relevant market is the market in which the alleged abuse takes place. However, that is not necessarily the case. In *Tetra Pak II*, the Court of First Instance found that Tetra Pak had committed abuses on the non-aseptic packaging markets without finding the company dominant on those markets in addition to its dominant position on the aseptic markets.[137] Upholding the judgment of the Court of First Instance, the Court of Justice said:

> 'It is true that application of Article [82] presupposes a link between the dominant position and the alleged abusive conduct, which is normally not present where

---

135 Case 26/75 *General Motors v Commission* [1975] ECR 1367, [1976] 1 CMLR 95; followed in Case 226/84 *British Leyland* (n 60, above). The ECJ held that where the alleged abuse relates to the supply of certificates of conformity for imported motor vehicles under the type approval system the relevant market for assessing a dominant position is that of the service of supplying such certificates, which is separate from that of the sale of the vehicles themselves; applied in *Carrozeria Grazia v Volvo Italia*, XVIIth Report on Competition Policy (1987), point 82. See also *XXth Report on Competition Policy* (1990), point 61; Case C-18/88 *RTT v GB-INNO-BM* [1991] ECR I-5941, [1992] 4 CMLR 78; *Netherlands Express Delivery Services*, OJ 1990 L10/47, [1990] 4 CMLR 947 (annulled on other grounds, Cases C-48 & 66/90 *Netherlands v Commission* [1992] ECR I-565, [1993] 5 CMLR 316); *Spanish International Express Courier Services*, OJ 1990 L233/19, [1991] 3 CMLR 560.

136 But cf *Sockell v Body Shop International* [2000] FSR 33, [2000] EuLR 85 (English High Court): a franchisor does not hold a dominant position in relation to its franchisees simply because they depend on the franchisor for supplies of the franchised products.

137 Case T-83/91 *Tetra Pak* (n 109, above) para 122. See also *AENA*, OJ 2000 L208/36, [2000] 5 CMLR 967 (the effect of an abuse in the market for take-off and landing services may be felt in the neighbouring market for passenger and freight transport on short and medium haul flights); COMP/37.507 *AstraZeneca*, 15 June 2005, [2006] 5 CMLR 287, para 775: 'There is no legal requirement that the abusive behaviour is implemented in the relevant geographic market where dominance exists. Indeed, what is relevant is that the behaviour, even if implemented in another relevant geographic market, has the purpose of excluding competitors in a relevant market where the undertaking is dominant' (on appeal, Case T-321/05 *AstraZeneca v Commission*, not yet decided). See also *Telekom Austria*, Case 16 Ok 11/03, 17 November 2003, [2005] ECC 541: Austrian Supreme Court upheld the order of the Austrian competition authority finding abuse by the former incumbent telephone network operator through its sales offer of cordless telephones at half price on condition that the purchaser agreed to exclude call-by-call carrier pre-selection (ie the facility to select which network would carry the call); Telekom Austria was dominant in the market for fixed line call origination but not in the market for the sale of telephones. Note that in *Claritas v The Post Office* [2001] UKCLR 2 (ChD), concerning the Chapter II prohibition under the UK Competition Act, the English court found on the facts that there were no special circumstances in terms of the *Tetra Pak* judgment for finding that conduct on the dominated market (mail deliveries) adversely affected a different market (consumer preference data).

conduct on a market distinct from the dominant market produces effects on that distinct market. In the case of distinct, but associated markets . . . application of Article [82] can only be justified by special circumstances.'[138]

(f) Collective or joint dominance

(i) Generally

Abuse by one or more undertakings.   Article 82 refers to any 'abuse by one or   **10.048**
more undertakings of a dominant position' and thereby envisages that two or more undertakings may jointly hold a dominant position. Although it is well established that Article 82 is capable of applying to situations in which several undertakings together hold a dominant position[139] (without each being dominant individually),[140] the circumstances in which a collective or joint dominant position exists, and in which it is abused, have not yet been fully clarified. It is clear that as regards joint dominance, the words of Article 82 must describe something different from the prohibition of anti-competitive agreements or concerted practices under Article 81. The question whether the market position of the group should be assessed collectively is a separate question from whether the group's position on the market is a dominant one.[141] It is also clear that, for undertakings to be treated collectively, they must adopt in some respects common conduct on the market.[142] What is less clear is the manner in which and the degree to which the policy of those undertakings must be coordinated if they are to be found to be jointly dominant.

Links establishing a common policy on the market.   Whether any, and if   **10.049**
so what, form of connection between the undertakings concerned is a prerequisite to a finding of joint dominance has been the subject of considerable debate.

---

[138] Case C-333/94P *Tetra Pak v Commission* [1996] ECR I-5951, [1997] 4 CMLR 662, para 27. The facts of that case were highly unusual in that Tetra Pak had a quasi-monopoly on the market for aseptic liquid packaging and a 78 per cent market share in the 'related' non-aseptic market in that case, so that, although the Commission had not made a finding of dominance on the non-aseptic market, 'the quasi-monopoly enjoyed by Tetra Pak on the aseptic markets and its leading position on the distinct, though closely associated, non-aseptic markets placed it in a situation comparable to that of holding a dominant position on the markets in question as a whole' (para 31).

[139] Case C-393/92 *Almelo* [1994] ECR I-1477, paras 41–42; Case C-96/94 *Centro Servizi Spediporto v Spedizioni Marittima del Golfo* [1995] ECR I-2883, [1996] 4 CMLR 613, paras 32–33; Cases C-140/94, etc, *DIP v Comune di Bassano del Grappa and Comune di Chiogga* [1995] ECR I-3257, [1996] 4 CMLR 157, paras 25–26; *Italian Flat Glass* (n 127, above) paras 357–359, where the CFI found support for its interpretation in Reg 4056/86, applying the competition rules to maritime transport, which expressly contemplates that the conduct of a shipping conference (necessarily involving an agreement between independent undertakings capable of falling within Art 81(1)) may have effects incompatible with Art 82. See generally Whish, 'Collective Dominance' in O'Keefe (ed), *Judicial Review in the European Union (Liber Amicorum for Lord Slynn)* (2000), 581.

[140] Cases T-24/93, etc, *Compagnie Maritime Belge Transports v Commission* (n 88, above) para 60.

[141] Cases C-395 & 396/96P *Compagnie Maritime Belge* (n 88, above) para 39.

[142] *DIP* (n 139, above) para 26.

In *Kali und Salz*, concerning assessment under the Merger Regulation, the Court of Justice held:

> 'In the case of an alleged collective dominant position, the Commission is therefore obliged to assess, using a prospective analysis of the reference market, where the concentration which has been referred to it leads to a situation in which effective competition in the relevant market is significantly impeded by the undertakings involved in the concentration and one or more other undertakings which together, *in particular because of* [*factors giving rise to a connection between them*], are able to adopt a common policy on the market and act to a considerable extent independently of their competitors, their customers, and also of consumers.' (emphasis added)[143]

In the context of Article 82, the Court of Justice has held: 'In order to find that a collective dominant position exists, the undertakings in question must be linked in such a way that they adopt the same conduct on the market'.[144] This definition was developed further in *Compagnie Maritime Belge*, where the Court of Justice stated[145] that two or more companies may together hold a dominant position 'provided that from an economic point of view they present themselves or act together on a particular market as a collective entity . . .'. These formulations leave the nature of any linkage unspecified, indicating that there is no specific requirement as to the manner in which the undertakings come to adopt common conduct; the necessary connecting factors will depend on an economic assessment, reflecting the conditions in the particular market concerned.[146]

(ii) Legal links between jointly dominant undertakings

10.050 **Relationship between collective dominance and anti-competitive agreements.** It is clear that it is not sufficient to 'recycle' the facts constituting an infringement of Article 81 into a finding that the parties to that agreement jointly hold a dominant position of which the making of the agreement constitutes an abuse.[147]

---

[143] Cases C-68/94 & C-30/95 *France v Commission* ('the *Kali und Salz* case') [1998] ECR I-1375, [1998] 4 CMLR 829, para 221. The words in parenthesis are rendered in the official English translation as 'correlative factors which exist between them', but the version given here seems a better reflection of the original French text ('*des facteurs de correlation existent entre elles*') and follows the wording used by the CFI when paraphrasing this passage in a subsequent merger case: Case T-102/96 *Gencor v Commission* [1999] ECR II-879, [1999] 4 CMLR 971, para 163. See also, per AG Fennelly in *Compagnie Maritime Belge* (n 88, above) para 26 (criticising the official English translation).

[144] *DIP* (n 139, above) para 26.

[145] Cases C-395 & 396/96P *Compagnie Maritime Belge Transports v Commission* [2000] ECR I-1365, [2000] 4 CMLR 1076, [2000] All ER (EC) 385, para 36 (dismissing appeal from Cases T-24/93, etc, *Compagnie Maritime Belge Transports v Commission* [1996] ECR II-1201, [1997] 4 CMLR 273). See also at para 44: 'a collective entity *vis-à-vis* their competitors, their trading partners and consumers'.

[146] Note that in *Irish Sugar* (n 103, above) paras 46–49, the absence of practical control by a company with a 51 per cent shareholding of another did not negate joint dominance; such a finding depends on their ability to adopt a common policy on the market.

[147] *Italian Flat Glass* (n 127, above) para 360.

However, provided that it is not on the basis of such 'recycling', both Article 81 and Article 82 may apply in parallel to the same agreement or concerted practice.[148]

Factors establishing a collective entity.   Relevant connecting factors have been   **10.051**
found to arise as a result of agreement between the jointly dominant undertakings, as in the case of the liner conference agreement between the parties in *Compagnie Maritime Belge*.[149] In *Italian Flat Glass*, while finding that the Commission had failed to establish joint dominance on the facts, the Court of First Instance observed that joint dominance could arise where, for example, two or more independent undertakings jointly have, through agreements or licences, a technological lead that enables them to act independently of the market.[150] The question of whether two or more separate entities occupy a collective dominant position is different from the question whether two or more legally separate entities form a single undertaking so that their market shares should be aggregated in order to establish whether that single undertaking is dominant.[151] In *TransAtlantic Conference Agreement*,[152] the Court of First Instance confirmed that the links between the parties did not need to be as strong as the institutional links existing between a parent and its subsidiaries so that the fact that some competition took place between the undertakings did not negate the existence of a collective dominant position. However, the Court held that significant competition within the liner conference may be capable of showing that, in spite of the various links or factors of correlation existing between the members, they are not in a position to adopt the same course of conduct on the market such as to give third parties the impression that they are a single entity and thus justify a collective assessment of

---

[148] *Hoffmann-La Roche v Commission* (n 87, above); Case 66/86 *Ahmed Saeed Flugreisen v Zentrale zur Bekämpfung unlauteren Wettbewerbs* [1989] ECR 803, [1990] 4 CMLR 102, para 37; *Decca*, OJ 1989 L43/27, [1990] 4 CMLR 627; Cases C-395 & 396/96P *Compagnie Maritime Belge* (n 88, above) para 33.

[149] Cases C-395 & 396/96P *Compagnie Maritime Belge* (n 145, above) para 48.

[150] *Italian Flat Glass* (n 127, above) para 358. In Case C-323/93 *Centre d'Insémination de la Crespelle v Coopérative de la Mayenne* [1994] ECR I-5077, the ECJ, in considering the local monopolies granted under French law to bovine insemination centres, appears to have treated the centres as jointly holding a dominant position by virtue of the rights granted to each of them over a contiguous series of areas. See also Peña Castellot, 'Commission settles allegations of abuse and clears patent pools in the CD market' (2003) 3 EC Competition Policy Newsletter 56: joint operation by Philips and Sony of a patent pool created through a series of cross-licences made it possible to conclude that they were jointly dominant in the market for the licensing of CD technology.

[151] See, eg the discussion in Case T-210/01 *General Electric v Commission* ECR II-5575, [2006] 4 CMLR 686 on whether the market shares of various joint venture companies of which GE was a parent should be aggregated with GE's own share in order to establish dominance: paras 127 *et seq.*

[152] *TACA*, OJ 1999 L95/1, [1999] 4 CMLR 1415, paras 527–531; annulled in part on appeal, Cases T-191/98, etc, *Atlantic Container Line v Commission* ('*TACA*') [2003] ECR II-3275, [2005] 4 CMLR 1283.

their position on the market under Article 82 of the Treaty.[153] On the facts, the Court held that the members had failed to establish this and therefore upheld the Commission's finding of collective dominance.[154]

10.052 **Collective dominance of members of an association of undertakings.** Sports clubs that make up a major professional league may well be in a collectively dominant position.[155] In *Piau*[156] the Court of First Instance considered whether the members of the International Football Federation, FIFA, held a collective dominant position by virtue of the fact that they agreed to be bound by the FIFA regulations, in that case in particular the regulations governing the activities of players' agents. The members of FIFA are the national associations of football clubs. The regulations adopted by FIFA could, where implemented, result in the clubs being so linked as to their conduct on the market that they present themselves on that market as a collective entity *vis-à-vis* their competitors, trading partners and consumers. The Court, overturning the Commission's view that FIFA did not hold a dominant position, stated:

> 'Because the regulations are binding for national associations which are members of FIFA and the clubs forming them, these bodies appear to be linked in the long term as to their conduct by rules that they accept and that other actors (players and players' agents) cannot break on pain of sanctions that may lead to their exclusion from the market, in particular in the case of players' agents. Within the meaning of the case law . . . such a situation therefore characterises a collective dominant position for clubs on the market for the provision of players' agents' services, since, through the rules to which they adhere, the clubs lay down the conditions under which the services in question are provided.'

The Court went on to hold that the fact that FIFA itself was not an economic operator that bought players' agents' services on the market and that its involvement in the market stemmed rather from its rule making activity was irrelevant to the application of Article 82. FIFA was the emanation of the national associations and the clubs who were the actual buyers of the services and therefore operated on the market through its members.[157] By contrast, in *Wouters*, although the Dutch Bar was an association of undertakings for the purpose of Article 81, the heterogenous character of its members and the fact that they engaged in a high degree of competition with each other meant that they were not sufficiently

---

153 Cases T-191/98, etc, *TACA* (n 152, above) para 695.

154 However, the CFI annulled the finding that there had been an abuse.

155 See, per AG Lenz in Case C-415/93 *Union Royale Belge des Sociétés de Football Association v Bosman* [1995] ECR I-4921, [1996] 1 CMLR 645, Opinion, para 285 (the ECJ did not address the point).

156 Case T-193/02 *Piau v Commission* [2005] ECR II-209, [2005] 5 CMLR 42, paras 107 *et seq*.

157 However, it went on to hold that no abuse had been established and so upheld the rejection of Mr Piau's complaint.

connected in their conduct on the market so as to hold a collectively dominant position.[158]

(iii) Links arising from market structure

Market structures and coordinated policy. In discussing this issue in its   **10.053**
Telecoms Access Agreements Notice,[159] the Commission treated the question of
links through such agreements as being no more than one possible cause for a lack
of effective competition as between the jointly dominant firms:

> 'The Commission does not . . . consider that either economic theory or Community
> law implies that such links are legally necessary for a joint dominant position to exist.
> It is a sufficient economic link if there is the kind of interdependence which often
> comes about in oligopolistic situations. There does not seem to be any reason in law
> or economic theory to require any other link between those companies.'[160]

This appears to be the view adopted by DG Competition in its Discussion Paper
on Article 82[161] where it states that the existence of an agreement or of other links
in law is not indispensable to a finding of a collective dominant position. Such a
finding may be based on other connecting factors and depends on an economic
assessment, in particular of the structure of the market in question and the way in
which undertakings interact on that market. The simpler and more stable the
economic environment, the easier it is for undertakings to reach a common understanding and to coordinate their behaviour by observing and reacting to each other's behaviour. The Framework Directive on electronic communications annexes
a list of characteristics which make a market conducive to collective dominance,
and although set out in the context of the telecommunications sector they are of
general relevance.[162]

Collective dominance in oligopolistic markets. The fullest consideration to   **10.054**
date by the Community Courts of the requirements for collective dominance
have come in the sphere of merger control, in the judgments in *Gencor*, *Airtours*
and *IMPALA*.[163] However, the same approach should apply in an assessment of

---

[158] Case C-309/99 *Wouters* [2002] ECR I-1577, [2002] 4 CMLR 913, [2002] All ER (EC) 193, paras 64, 113–114.

[159] Commission Notice on the application of the competition rules to access agreements in the telecommunications sector, OJ 1998 C265/2: Vol II, App E.24, para 79.

[160] ibid, para 79. In *P&I Clubs, IGA* (n 107, above) paras 121–122, the Commission decided that sufficient economic links were provided by (a) the sharing of claims between Clubs, (b) common restrictive procedures in offering cover to members of other Clubs, (c) cooperation in a number of commercial areas and (d) the single and identical level of cover provided to members.

[161] DG Competition, Staff Discussion Paper on the application of Article 82 of the Treaty to exclusionary abuses, 19 December 2005, paras 43–50.

[162] Dir 2002/21 on a common regulatory framework for electronic communications networks and services, OJ 2002 L108/33: Vol II, App E.17.

[163] The ECJ in *Compagnie Maritime Belge* (n 145, above) appeared to suggest a greater degree of connection than the CFI judgment in *Gencor* but did not seek to lay down general criteria applicable

dominance under Article 82.[164] In *Gencor*,[165] the Commission's finding of joint dominance was upheld by the Court of First Instance. The merged concern and a third producer would together account for around 70 per cent of the world market for platinum group metal (expected to rise to 80 per cent on the exhaustion of Russian stocks). The Court stated that, particularly in the case of a duopoly, a large market share is, in the absence of contrary evidence, 'a strong indication of the existence of a collective dominant position'.[166] The Court rejected the submission that structural links between the parties were a necessary condition for a determination of collective dominance. The Court held that broader, economic links between the parties may be sufficient:

> 'Furthermore, there is no reason whatsoever in legal or economic terms to exclude from the notion of economic links the relationship of interdependence existing between the parties to a tight oligopoly within which, in a market with the appropriate characteristics, in particular in terms of market concentration, transparency and product homogeneity, those parties are in a position to anticipate one another's behaviour and are therefore strongly encouraged to align their conduct in the market, in particular in such a way as to maximise their joint profits by restricting production with a view to increasing prices.'[167]

10.055 **Three conditions for establishing collective dominance.**   The approach adopted by the Court of First Instance in *Gencor* was relied on by the Commission in subsequent merger decisions, and in particular in its decisions in *Airtours/First Choice* and *Sony/BMG*. However, on appeal, the Court of First Instance annulled both decisions. In *Airtours*,[168] the Court held that the Commission's decision that the merger would give rise to a collective dominant position had comprehensively failed to demonstrate the necessary adverse impact on competition. The Court accepted that a collective dominant position may arise where, from the characteristics of the relevant market and the way that the structure of the market would be altered if the merger took place, it could be concluded that each member of the dominant oligopoly would, on becoming aware of their common interests, consider it possible, economically rational, and hence preferable, to adopt a common

---

in the absence of 'connecting factors'. The Commission had recognised the need to provide further clarification of its approach to oligopolistic dominance in its *XXIXth Annual Report on Competition Policy* (1999), point 151. It is notable that para 62 of the *Airtours* judgment stresses that the three criteria identified in the judgment were accepted by the Commission itself as correct.

[164] See *Piau* (n 156, above) para 111, applying the three *Airtours* conditions. See also the DG Comp Discussion Paper (para 10.005, above) paras 48–50.

[165] Case T-102/96 *Gencor v Commission* [1999] ECR II-879, [1999] 4 CMLR 971: see paras 8.209 *et seq*, above.

[166] ibid, para 206.

[167] ibid, para 276.

[168] Case M.1524 *Airtours/First Choice*, OJ 2000 L93/1, [2000] 5 CMLR 494, annulled on appeal, Case T-342/99 *Airtours v Commission* [2002] ECR II-2585, [2002] 5 CMLR 317, [2002] All ER (EC) 783. See further paras 8.212 *et seq*, above.

policy on the market with the aim of selling at above competitive prices on a lasting basis. This could be achieved without having to enter into an agreement or resort to a concerted practice within the meaning of Article 81, and without any actual or potential competitors, let alone customers or consumers, being able to react effectively. The Court set out the three conditions necessary for a finding of collective dominance:

(i) *Transparency.* Each member of the dominant oligopoly must have the ability to know how the other members are behaving in order to monitor whether or not they are adopting and maintaining the common policy. There must, therefore, be sufficient market transparency for all members of the dominant oligopoly to be aware, sufficiently precisely and quickly, of the way in which the other members' market conduct is evolving.

(ii) *Existence of mechanisms to deter departure from common policy.* The situation of tacit coordination must be sustainable over time, that is to say, there must be an incentive not to depart from the common policy on the market. The notion of retaliation in respect of conduct deviating from the common policy is inherent in this condition: each member of the dominant oligopoly must be aware that competitive action on its part designed to increase its market share would provoke identical action by the others, so that it would derive no benefit from its initiative.

(iii) *Inability of competitors and consumers to erode the advantages of the common policy.* It must be established that the foreseeable reaction of current and future competitors, as well as of consumers, would not jeopardise the results expected from the common policy.[169]

Theoretical and evidential approaches to establishing collective dominance. **10.056**
In *IMPALA*[170] the challenge concerned the Commission's assessment of whether a collective dominant position already existed in the relevant market rather than whether the merger would create such a position. The Commission in its *Sony/BMG* decision had approved the proposed merger of two of the major record companies on the grounds that the element of transparency needed was not established. The Court considered how the three elements set out in *Airtours* could be satisfied when considering whether a position of collective dominance actually

---

[169] Case T-342/99 *Airtours*, above, paras 61–62. As regard the third requirement, see Rabassa, Simon and Kleiner, 'Investigation into possible collective dominance in the publication paper industry' (concerning proposed mergers *UPM-Kymmene/Haindl* and *UPM/Kymmene / Norske Skog*: market conditions not conducive to collective dominance because smaller players would be able to increase their market share if top players colluded to restrict supply and raise prices) (2002) 1 EC Competition Policy Newsletter 77.

[170] Case T-464/04 *Independent Music Publishers and Labels Association (IMPALA) v Commission* [2006] ECR II-2289, [2006] 5 CMLR 1049, annulling the decn in Case M.3333 *Sony/BMG*, OJ 2005 L62/30. On appeal, Case C-413/06P *Bertelsmann and Sony Corp v IMPALA*, not yet decided.

existed rather than whether it would be created by the merger.[171] In addressing the former question, the Court held that the Commission was not limited to a 'delicate prognosis' of what the parties were likely to do if the merger took place but could consider 'what may be a very mixed series of indicia and items of evidence relating to the signs, manifestations and phenomena inherent in the presence of a collective dominant position.' Thus, the Court suggested, the Commission could have looked at pricing behaviour in the past to see whether in fact prices had been aligned over a considerable period; whether prices had been maintained at a stable level; and whether they were set at a level seen as high in spite of a significant fall in demand. Such evidence, together with other factors, might, in the absence of an alternative explanation, establish the existence of a collective dominant position without having to prove that the market was transparent. The Court concluded that the Commission had erred in finding that the market was not sufficiently transparent.

10.057   *IMPALA:* **retaliatory measures.**   A second question raised in *IMPALA* was whether in a case concerning the existence rather than the creation of a dominant position, the second element set out in *Airtours* required the Commission to show that there had in fact been retaliatory measures taken in the past or whether it was sufficient that mechanisms existed which the parties could use to discipline an undertaking which deviated from the common policy. The appellants argued that the major record companies could exercise such discipline by excluding the artists signed to an errant member of the oligopoly from lucrative compilation discs. The Court held that the mere existence of effective deterrent mechanisms is in principle sufficient since 'the most effective deterrent is that which has not been used'.[172] However, in a case where the existence of collective dominance is in issue, evidence that deviations from common policy had occurred in the past and had not in fact triggered a use of the supposed deterrent mechanism would militate against the existence of collective dominance. In this case, the Court held that the Commission had not proven either deviations from common policy or the absence of retaliatory measures and the Court therefore overturned the Commission's conclusion that the second element was not met. However, the judgment of the Court of First Instance is on appeal to the Court of Justice.[173]

---

[171] ibid, paras 251 *et seq*. Since the case had been argued on the basis that the three *Airtours* factors apply to the existence as well as the creation of collective dominance, the CFI could not step outside the framework of the dispute as defined by the parties and so dealt with the case on that basis. Interestingly, the *Airtours* conditions are not referred to in the CFI's decision in Cases T-191/98, etc, *Atlantic Container Line ('TACA')* (n 153, above), which concerned the existence of a collective dominant position.

[172] *IMPALA* (n 170, above) para 466.

[173] Case C-413/06 *Bertelsmann and Sony Corp v IMPALA*, not yet decided.

4. Abuse of a Dominant Position

(a) Introduction

In general.   Article 82 does not provide a comprehensive definition of abuse.   **10.058**
The specific instances set out at Article 82(a)–(d) seek to specify categories of
prohibited conduct, using pejorative wording such as 'unfair' pricing or trading
conditions, output restrictions 'to the prejudice of consumers', discrimination
that places trading partners 'at a competitive disadvantage', and the imposition of
supplementary obligations which 'by their nature or according to commercial
usage, have no connection with the subject matter of such contracts'. However,
concepts such as 'unfair' and 'competitive disadvantage' are inevitably unclear in
their scope and highly dependent on factual appreciation, so that the distinction
between conduct on the part of a dominant firm which is permissible and conduct
which is prohibited as abusive is often a difficult one. For the dominant firm, the
assessment of its actions in any particular case will be a question of fact and degree,
in which the following considerations are relevant when assessing whether a credible case of anti-competitive conduct is made out:

(i) how far competition on the market is already weakened by the economic
strength of the undertaking concerned;

(ii) the nature of the market on which the alleged abuse takes place, and the
extent to which actual or potential competitors are vulnerable to exclusionary conduct on that market;

(iii) the extent to which the conduct in issue can be seen further to weaken competition to the dominant undertaking on the relevant market or to strengthen
the position of that undertaking (or a related undertaking) on a connected
market;

(iv) the effect, direct and indirect, of the conduct on end consumers;

(v) how far the conduct in issue is normal industry practice or, on the contrary,
is exceptional and plainly restrictive of competition;[174]

(vi) how far the conduct reflects a transitory response to a competitive threat as
against a systematic attempt to exclude or to discipline competitors that
threatens to impose a long-term impediment to effective competition;

---

[174] See, eg COMP/37.507 *AstraZeneca*, 15 June 2005, [2006] 5 CMLR 287 (on appeal Case
T-321/05 *AstraZeneca v Commission,* not yet decided), where the Commission stressed that
AstraZeneca's practices regarding its patent rights were not generally adopted by pharmaceutical
companies. cf Cases T-191/98, etc, *Atlantic Container Line ('TACA')* (n 153, above): 'even if the
practices on service contracts in question represent the standard practice of maritime carriers, therefore, Article [82] of the Treaty prevented the TACA parties, given their special responsibility as a
collective dominant unit on the transatlantic trade, from adopting such practices, notwithstanding
the fact that they were adopted by most, if not all, of their competitors.' (para 1125).

(vii) whether the conduct of the dominant firm is motivated by an exclusionary intent or constitutes a legitimate response to competing firms;

(viii) the extent to which a dominant undertaking can be seen to be 'leveraging' its market power in order to place competing undertakings at a significant disadvantage on parts of the market, or related markets, that are in principle contestable; and

(ix) whether the adverse impact of the conduct in issue is 'proportionate' to any legitimate commercial interest or public policy objective which may be identified as an 'objective justification' for such conduct; and

(x) the connection between the conduct and the general principles of the Treaty, especially the elimination of national boundaries and the absence of discrimination between nationals of different Member States.

10.059 **Governing principles.** The illustrations of abusive conduct contained in Article 82 itself have already been set out.[175] In general, the governing principle of Article 82 is that conduct by a dominant firm which seriously and unjustifiably distorts competition within a properly defined relevant market, or leads to a weakening or further weakening of competition in such a market, will be prohibited insofar as it affects trade between Member States.[176] That principle is based upon Article 3(1)(g) of the Treaty [177] and upon the Community's repeatedly stated commitment to competition as 'bringing out the best in Community industry'.[178] In determining whether a dominant undertaking's commercial conduct unjustifiably distorts competition, the principle of proportionality will be important: in striving to improve its market position and pursue its legitimate interests, the dominant firm may employ only such measures as accord with 'commercial usage' in the market in question and are necessary to pursue those interests. It must not act in a way which foreseeably will limit competition more than is necessary.[179]

10.060 **Abuse as an objective concept.** In *Hoffmann-La Roche*, the Court of Justice, in describing the test that it was applying to the conduct in issue in that case, stated:

'The concept of abuse is an objective concept relating to the behaviour of an undertaking in a dominant position which is such as to influence the structure of a market where, as a result of the very presence of the undertaking in question, the degree of competition is weakened and which, through recourse to methods different from

---

[175] Para 10.001, above.

[176] For the effect on inter-State trade, see paras 1.115 *et seq,* above. Note that an effect on the structure of competition within the Community can itself be a relevant effect on inter-State trade: *Commercial Solvents* (n 131, above).

[177] See para 10.002, above

[178] See, eg *XXIst Report on Competition Policy* (1991), point 3.

[179] See the Opinion of Judge Kirschner, acting as AG in the CFI, in Case T-51/89 *Tetra Pak v Commission* (n 110, above) paras 68–74.

those which condition normal competition in products or services on the basis of the transactions of commercial operators, has the effect of hindering the maintenance of the degree of competition still existing in the market or the growth of that competition.'[180]

The 'special responsibility' of dominant firms. Although in the passage just **10.061** cited the Court of Justice refers to 'recourse to methods different from those which condition normal competition', it is clear that this does not mean that an abuse must comprise conduct peculiar to dominant firms or capable of being indulged in only by reason of dominance. Conduct which may be permissible in a normal competitive situation may amount to an abuse if carried out by dominant firms because such firms have a 'special responsibility' on account of the prejudice that their activities may cause to competition in general and to the interests of competitors, suppliers, customers and consumers.[181] It follows from the nature of the obligations imposed by Article 82 that undertakings in a dominant position may be deprived of the right to adopt a course of conduct or take measures which would be unobjectionable if adopted or taken by non-dominant undertakings.[182] Thus the conclusion of a contract or the acquisition of a right may amount to an abuse for the purposes of Article 82 if that contract is concluded or that right is acquired by an undertaking in a dominant position.[183] Equally, whereas a non-dominant firm will be entitled to choose with whom to do business, a dominant firm may be precluded from refusing to deal or required to allow third parties to have access to its facilities.[184]

---

[180] Case 85/76 *Hoffmann-La Roche v Commission* [1979] ECR 461, [1979] 3 CMLR 211, para 91. This interpretation of 'abuse' is now adopted as a standard formula, even where it is not obviously applicable, eg to excessive pricing, where the structure of the market and the degree of competition are not likely to be affected to any material degree. However, the formula importantly emphasises the need for an adverse effect on the structure of competition on a relevant market rather than any potentially more transient behavioural effects.

[181] Case 322/81 *Michelin v Commission* [1983] ECR 3461, [1985] 1 CMLR 282, para 57; see also *Warner-Lambert/Gillette*, OJ 1993 L116/21, [1993] 5 CMLR 559, para 23.

[182] Case T-111/96 *ITT Promedia v Commission* [1998] ECR II-2937, [1998] 5 CMLR 491, para 139, citing *Michelin* (above), para 57; Case T-65/98 *Van den Bergh Foods v Commission* [2003] ECR II-4653, [2004] 4 CMLR 14, [2005] All ER (EC) 418, para 159 (appeal dismissed, Case C-552/03P *Unilever Bestfoods v Commission* [2006] ECR I-9091, [2006] 5 CMLR 1460); Cases T-191/98, etc, *Atlantic Container Line ('TACA')* (n 152, above) paras 1124–1125. (This passage from the 5th edn was cited as authoritative in the majority judgment of the Privy Council on an appeal from New Zealand: *Carter Holt Harvey Building Products Group v Commerce Commission* [2004] UKPC 37, [2006] 1 NZLR 145, para 64.)

[183] *ITT Promedia*, above, para 139, citing Case 51/89 *Tetra Pak v Commission* (n 110, above) para 23; Cases T-191/98, etc, *Atlantic Container Line ('TACA')* (n 152, above) para 1125: contractual terms can be an abuse even if adopted by most, if not all of the dominant undertakings' competitors since the dominant firm's responsibility is not limited solely to conduct likely to reinforce its dominance or reduce the level of competition on the market; Art 82 concerns not only practices which hinder effective competition but also those which cause damage to consumers directly.

[184] See paras 10.125 *et seq*, below.

10.062 **Abusive intent.** Conduct that may otherwise be permissible even on the part of a dominant firm may be rendered abusive if its purpose is anti-competitive. As the Court of Justice has said:

> 'Although it is true . . . that the fact that an undertaking is in a dominant position cannot disentitle it from protecting its own commercial interests if they are attacked, and that such an undertaking must be conceded the right to take such reasonable steps as it deems appropriate to protect its said interests, such behaviour cannot be countenanced if its actual purpose is to strengthen this dominant position and abuse it.'[185]

Equally, conduct may be abusive where it has failed to achieve its intended effect. Thus in *Compagnie Maritime Belge*, the Court of First Instance held that, where dominant undertakings engaged in a practice with the aim of removing a competitor, 'the fact that the result sought is not achieved is not enough to avoid the practice being characterized as an abuse of a dominant position'.[186]

10.063 **Objective justification.** Article 82 contains no exempting provision equivalent to Article 81(3) but it equally does not operate on a wholly rigid or *per se* basis, outlawing specific types of conduct. Advocate General Jacobs described the position as follows:

> '. . . it is clear that the Community case-law provides dominant undertakings with the possibility of demonstrating an objective justification for their conduct, even if it is *prima facie* an abuse, . . . I would add that the two-stage analysis suggested by the distinction between an abuse and its objective justification is to my mind somewhat artificial. Article 82 EC, by contrast with Article 81 EC, does not contain any explicit provision for the exemption of conduct otherwise falling within it. Indeed, the very fact that conduct is characterised as an "abuse" suggests that a negative conclusion has already been reached, by contrast with the more neutral terminology of "prevention, restriction, or distortion of competition" under Article 81 EC. In my view, it is therefore more accurate to say that certain types of conduct on the part of a dominant undertaking do not fall within the category of abuse at all. However, given that the Commission has, in the light of some previous Community case-law, developed its submissions in terms of objective justification, it may be convenient for present purposes to assume that structure.'[187]

---

185 *United Brands* (n 106, above) para 189.

186 Cases T-24/93, etc, *Compagnie Maritime Belge Transports* (n 145, above) para 149. The ECJ did not address this point. In Case C-53/03 *Syfait v GlaxoSmithKline* [2005] ECR I-4609, [2005] 5 CMLR 7, where the question from the referring court assumed that the dominant undertaking's intention in restricting supplies to its distributors was to impede parallel trading, AG Jacobs cautioned (Opinion, para 71): 'The issue of intent should . . . not deflect attention from the essential question whether such a refusal is in all the circumstances justified'. The ECJ held that the reference was inadmissible and so did not address this issue.

187 *Syfait* above, para 72 of the Opinion. See also *Floe Telecom v Office of Communications* [2006] CAT 17, [2006] Comp AR 637, where the UK Competition Appeal Tribunal held that a refusal to supply would be 'objectively justified' if such supply was unlawful. For a discussion of the 'rule of reason' in relation to Art 82, see the EAGCP Report (n 13, above).

Comparison of objective justification with criteria in Article 81(3).   The con-   **10.064**
cept of 'objective justification' therefore plays a central place in many Article 82
investigations. It is in principle open to a dominant firm to argue that apparently
anti-competitive conduct is in fact justified, provided that the grounds relied on
are more than simply the commercial advantage of the undertaking itself.[188] In
Atlantic Container Line (TACA),[189] the Court of First Instance emphasised the
difference between the defence of objective justification under Article 82 and the
application of Article 81(3). Reaffirming that 'there can be no exceptions to the
prohibition of abuse by dominant undertakings',[190] and after reciting the passage
from *United Brands* set out above,[191] the Court went on to state:

> 'However, the justifications permitted by the case-law in respect of Article [82] of the
> Treaty cannot result in creating exemptions from the application of that provision.
> The sole purpose of those grounds of justification is to enable a dominant undertak-
> ing to show not that the practices in question should be permitted because they
> confer certain advantages, but only that the purpose of those practices is reasonably
> to protect its commercial interests in the face of action taken by certain third parties
> and that they do not therefore in fact constitute an abuse.
>
> In the present case the justifications put forward by the applicants seek to demon-
> strate not that the practices in question concerning service contracts do not consti-
> tute an abuse, but only that those practices are necessary in order to achieve certain
> benefits. . . . It follows that, by the present justifications, the applicants thus seek in
> fact to obtain an exemption for the abuse in question on the ground that those prac-
> tices are necessary to achieve certain advantages resulting from the conference
> system. . . . that is sufficient reason to reject all of the justifications alleging that
> the rules in question are necessary.'[192]

In *Microsoft*, the Court of First Instance made clear that the dominant undertaking bore an evidential burden of putting forward a plea of objective justification;
however, it was then for the Commission to prove that the arguments and evidence
relied on did not constitute an objective justification for the impugned conduct.[192a]
Nonetheless, there is no clear enumeration of the grounds that could constitute
objective justification. One of the most difficult issues is whether, and in what

---

[188] See, eg *United Brands* (n 106, above) paras 189–190; *BBI/Boosey & Hawkes*, OJ 1987
L286/36, [1988] 4 CMLR 67; Case C-95/04P *British Airways v Commission* [2007] 4 CMLR 982
(objective justification of discount scheme).

[189] Cases T-191/98, etc, *Atlantic Container Line ('TACA')* (n 152, above).

[190] ibid, para 1109.

[191] See para 10.062, above.

[192] Paras 1114–1117. The Director General of DG Comp has said that the cases broadly suggest
three types of defence: (i) cases where conduct is legitimate business behaviour, including the defence
that the dominant undertaking was only meeting competition; (ii) cases where the dominant undertaking was pursuing a legitimate public interest objective, such as the health of consumers; and (iii) cases
where the conduct of the dominant firm produced efficiency gains: see Lowe, 'DG Competition's
Review of the Policy on Abuse of Dominance' in Hawk (ed), *2003 Fordham Corp. L. Inst.* (2004), 163.

[192a] Case T-201/04 *Microsoft v Commission*, judgment of 17 September 2007, para 688; see
Postscript below.

circumstances, meeting competition from rivals can justify pricing practices (for example, pricing below cost or price discrimination) that would otherwise infringe Article 82. These issues are considered in the discussion of particular abuses, below. Moreover, the principle of proportionality is clearly relevant in this regard. Even when a dominant firm has identified a justification for its conduct, it must not restrict competition more than is necessary and appropriate to achieve that legitimate objective.[193]

10.065 **Exclusionary and exploitative abuses.** Conduct of a kind prohibited by Article 82 can be categorised in various ways, but a traditional and important classification is by reference to its effects. An 'exclusionary abuse' is conduct which has the economic effect of impeding effective competition on the relevant market (by forcing out or marginalising existing competitors and/or raising barriers to entry for potential new competitors). On the other hand, an 'exploitative abuse' is conduct which is unfair or unreasonable towards those persons who depend on the dominant firm for the supply of goods or services on the relevant market. Predatory pricing is a paradigm of an exclusionary abuse and excessive pricing is a paradigm of an exploitative abuse. Of these two categories, the first is the more important in practice and reflects the increasing focus on the wider economic impact of conduct alleged to be abusive. Nonetheless, the protection of end consumers is an important aspect of competition law and it is often highly relevant to consider whether any allegedly exclusionary conduct has in practice caused detriment to end consumers either in terms of an increase in price or a restriction in output or choice. There is, therefore, no absolute distinction in practice between these two classes of case, and some abuses, such as the imposition of tying clauses, may be both exploitative and exclusionary. In addition, although the concept of abuse is an objective one, a realistic characterisation of an exclusionary abuse will be strengthened by an explanation of the motivation of the dominant firm, in terms of a supra-competitive return resulting from the exclusion of its competitors, so that there is often an explanatory link between an exclusionary and an exploitative element in an individual case.[194]

10.066 **Own market and related market abuses.** Another important classification concerns abuses that affect competition on the market where dominance is enjoyed as against those that restrict or distort competition on a related market, in particular where a dominant firm is able to control competition on a downstream market by the exercise of monopoly power. A classic 'own market' exclusionary abuse would

---

[193] *BBI/Boosey & Hawkes* (n 188, above) para 19; Opinion of AG Kirschner in Case T-51/89 *Tetra Pak v Commission* (n 110, above) paras 67–69.

[194] See the discussion of 'recoupment' in the context of predatory pricing at para 10.076, below. The UK Competition Appeal Tribunal has also considered this issue: see *NAPP v Director General of Fair Trading* [2002] CAT 1, [2002] CompAR 13, para 261; *Aberdeen Journals v Office of Fair Trading* [2003] CAT 11, [2003] CompAR 67, para 445.

be predatory pricing or exclusive dealing obligations that make it difficult or impossible for competitors to establish themselves on the market on which an undertaking is dominant. 'Related market' exclusionary abuses include refusal to supply a raw material or to grant a licence of an intellectual property right or access to a network needed for the purposes of competition on a downstream or related market. The DG Comp Discussion Paper adopts this classification, but since it addresses only exclusionary conduct these two categories are there referred to as 'horizontal foreclosure' and 'vertical foreclosure'.[195] Here again, there is a danger in over-rigid categorisation. Tying and bundling seem more logically regarded as a 'related market' abuse, since a company there uses the dependence of its customers on a product in the market on which it is dominant to force them to buy also a distinct product, and it thereby reduces the number of customers available to its competitors in the related market of the second, 'tied' product. But tying can also be viewed as an 'own market' or 'horizontal' abuse if the tied product is important for most buyers of the tying product, since reduction of the number of suppliers of the tied product may raise barriers to entry in the market for the tying product by making it commercially necessary to supply both products in order to compete effectively (in selling the tying product).[196] However, for convenience the classification as between 'own market' and 'related market' abuses is adopted below, with exclusionary abuses taken before exploitative abuses in each case.

Efficiency and abuse. From an economic perspective, one of the principal issues **10.067** is whether the alleged abuse has resulted in consumer detriment or whether it has in fact increased efficiency, and thus can be 'objectively justified'. One test that has some currency in both the economic and legal literature, particularly in the context of related market abuses, is to consider that conduct is an abuse if a dominant undertaking treats its downstream competitors differently from the way in which it treats its own downstream 'purchaser'. In other words, would the terms of supply being offered by the dominant undertaking in fact make it impossible for an equally (or reasonably) efficient competitor to compete with the dominant supplier's own downstream arm?[197]

---

[195] DG Comp Discussion Paper (para 10.005, above) paras 69–73.

[196] The Discussion Paper (above) accordingly places tying and bundling in the category of 'horizontal foreclosure': ibid, paras 73 and 180–181.

[197] For a clear summary of the economic issues, see Vickers (n 13, above); and a speech by Fletcher (Chief Economist, OFT) 'The reform of Article 82: recommendations on key policy objectives', 15 March 2005, available at http://www.oft.gov.uk/NR/rdonlyres/41543043-1363-4CD5-B21E-87A9A3DFD160/0/SPE0305.PDF. For case law and relevant guidance (of particular relevance to the issue of 'price squeezes'), see, eg *Deutsche Telekom*, OJ 2003 L263/9, [2004] 4 CMLR 790, paras 106–108, 126–127, 140–141 (on appeal, Case T-271/03 *Deutsche Telekom v Commission*, not yet decided); Commission Notice on access agreements (n 159, above) paras 117–119, cited by the UK Competition Appeal Tribunal in *Albion Water v Director General of Water Services* [2005] CAT 40, [2006] CompAR 269, at paras 390–392.

10.068 **Abuses considered in this Section.** The rest of this Chapter considers the following forms of abusive behaviour:

(a) Own market abuses: exclusionary pricing practices:
  (i) Predatory pricing;
  (ii) Price discrimination or targeting;
  (iii) Fidelity rebates and similar practices.

(b) Own market abuses: exclusionary non-price conduct:
  (i) Discrimination;
  (ii) Long-term exclusive dealing;
  (iii) Litigation as an exclusionary abuse.

(c) Own market abuses: exploitative pricing:
  (i) Unfairly high prices.

(d) Related market abuses: exclusionary pricing:
  (i) Margin squeezing;
  (ii) Cross-subsidisation.

(e) Related market abuses: exclusionary non-price practices:
  (i) Tying and bundling;
  (ii) Refusal to supply:
    (1) Discontinuing supply to an existing customer;
    (2) Refusal to licence intellectual property rights;
    (3) Refusal of access to 'essential facilities';

(f) Other forms of abuse:
  (i) Unfair trading conditions;
  (ii) Limiting production, markets or technical development;
  (iii) Abusive alteration of the structure of the market;
  (iv) Misconduct in the acquisition of property rights;
  (v) Impeding parallel imports and excluding competing products;
  (vi) Failure to satisfy demand;
  (vii) Inefficiency.

However, it should be emphasised that many cases finding abuse involve conduct of more than one kind, which sometimes makes it difficult to draw firm conclusions about a particular type of potentially abusive practice in isolation on the basis of those decisions. Furthermore, the categories of abuse are not closed and it is impossible to set out a comprehensive enumeration of all forms of conduct that might violate Article 82.[198]

---

[198] The ECJ has stressed that the list of abusive practices in Art 82(a)–(d) is not exhaustive: Case C-333/94P *Tetra Pak v Commission* [1996] ECR I-5951, [1997] 4 CMLR 662, [1997] All ER (EC) 4, para 37. Similarly under US antitrust law, an appellate court has observed: "Anticompetitive

(b) Own market abuses: exclusionary pricing practices

Categories of exclusionary pricing.   There are numerous examples of cases   **10.069**
under Article 82 concerning the exclusionary pricing practices of dominant
undertakings. In broad terms, they comprise one or more of the following:

(i)   Predatory pricing: the setting of prices at an unfairly low level (usually below
      'cost') to induce a rival firm to exit the market or deter its entry or
      expansion;

(ii) Price discrimination or targeting: the targeting of unfairly low prices
      (although above 'cost') at customers of a competing firm; and

(iii) Loyalty rebates and discounts: the granting of financial advantages to cus-
      tomers to promote customer loyalty and thereby to obtain an unfair advan-
      tage over competing firms.

In each case, difficult questions can arise in determining where the line should be
drawn between fair competition on the merits and unfair, exclusionary pricing
practices.

(i) Predatory pricing

Predatory pricing.   Predatory pricing is in essence the setting of prices by a dom-   **10.070**
inant undertaking at a level which has, as its commercial rationale, the elimination or serious weakening of a competitor rather than the generation of profit.[199]
Predatory pricing normally, but not necessarily, involves: (i) a temporary, substantial reduction in price by the dominant firm in response to anticipated or actual
market entry or growth in sales by a smaller competitor; (ii) price levels that are,
in themselves, unprofitable or barely profitable; and (iii) pricing 'aimed at' eliminating or disciplining a specific competitor. However, in certain circumstances
pricing below cost is normal commercial practice and it is not always easy to distinguish predatory pricing from normal price competition. Central to the distinction between predatory pricing and normal price competition is the assumption
that the former strategy will be profitable for the predator if, but only if, it so
weakens or deters effective competition that it can subsequently raise prices or

---

conduct" can come in too many different forms, and is too dependent upon context, for any court or
commentator to have enumerated all the varieties', *Caribbean Broad Sys Ltd v Cable & Wireless PLC*,
148 F 3d 1080, 1087 (DC Cir, 1998).

[199] See DG Comp Discussion Paper, paras 93–96; OFT Research Paper No. 5, *Predatory
Behaviour in UK Competition Policy* (November 1994); Areeda and Turner, 'Predatory pricing and
related practices under Section 2 of the Sherman Act', (1975) 88 Harvard Law Rev. 637; Baumol,
'Predation and the logic of the average variable cost test' (1996) 39 J Law & Econ. 49; Ordover,
'Predatory pricing' (with bibliog) in Newman (ed), *The New Palgrave Dictionary of Economics
and the Law*, Vol 3 (1998); Mastromanolis, 'Predatory Pricing in the European Union: A Case for
Legal Reform'(1998) ECLR 211; and the Commission's Notice on access agreements (n 159, above)
paras 110–116.

otherwise exploit its market power. Since assessment of profitability involves consideration of costs, that raises the question of what measure of cost should be used, and whether any additional features are required to establish the abuse. The distinguishing feature of predatory pricing, although easily expressed in general terms, is difficult to translate into legal tests of general application that are sufficiently certain.

10.071 **The Court of Justice's approach.** The Court of Justice has held that in order to establish predatory pricing it is necessary to show (i) that the alleged predator is selling at below average total costs;[200] and (ii) (whether by direct evidence or by means of a presumption) that it has the intention of eliminating a competitor.[201] Both raise evidential difficulties. However, the Court of Justice has linked the two points by recognising a legal presumption based on costs analysis: if prices are not only below average total costs but also below average *variable* costs, the Court says that it must be presumed that the purpose is predatory. On this basis, the Court of Justice has sanctioned two different methods of analysis for determining whether pricing has been predatory, enunciated in its landmark judgment in *AKZO*, discussed below, and sometimes referred to as the '*AKZO* rule'. The Court has summarised these as follows:

> 'First, prices below average variable costs must always be considered abusive. In such a case, there is no conceivable economic purpose other than the elimination of a competitor, since each item produced and sold entails a loss for the undertaking. Secondly, prices below average total costs but above average variable costs are only to be considered abusive if an intention to eliminate can be shown.'[202]

To the extent that this implies a rule that pricing below average variable costs ('AVC') must be predatory, it seems too rigid. Prices below AVC may be set pro-competitively: for example, in launching a new product, it may be necessary to sell it initially at a loss in order for that product to gain acceptance.[203] In *Tetra Pak II*, the Court of First Instance recognised that it may be acceptable for a dominant company to sell at a loss in some circumstances;[204] and in *Compagnie Maritime Belge*, Advocate General Fennelly referred to the first part of the *AKZO* rule as a presumption which a dominant firm could rebut by showing that such pricing

---

[200] Total costs comprise the sum of fixed and variable costs. Fixed costs are costs which remain constant in spite of changes in output, such as management overheads, depreciation, interest and property taxes. Variable costs are costs which vary with changes in output such as materials and energy. Average costs are total costs divided by output.

[201] Case C-62/86 *AKZO v Commission* [1991] ECR I-3359, [1993] 5 CMLR 215.

[202] Case C-333/94P *Tetra Pak v Commission (Tetra Pak II)* [1996] ECR I-5951, [1997] 4 CMLR 662, para 41, summarising *AKZO v Commission* (n 201, above) paras 70–72.

[203] But cf *Wanadoo Interactive*, para 10.078, below.

[204] Case T-83/91 *Tetra Pak v Commission* [1994] ECR II-755, [1997] 4 CMLR 726, para 147. The CFI did not elaborate on what these circumstances might be and they did not arise on the facts of that case; the ECJ did not address the point in the appeal (n 202, above).

was not part of a plan to eliminate a competitor.[205] Despite the unequivocal wording used by the Court of Justice, it seems appropriate to regard the rule as setting out a strong evidential presumption which, exceptionally, the dominant firm may be able to displace.[206]

AKZO: the facts.   ECS, a small firm, supplied benzoyl peroxide, a product used **10.072** in two different applications: as an additive in flour milling in the United Kingdom and Ireland, and in plastics manufacture. ECS traditionally sold benzoyl peroxide as a flour additive. ECS complained to the Commission that AKZO, the dominant supplier of benzoyl peroxide, had threatened to drive ECS out of the flour additives business unless ECS refrained from starting to sell benzoyl peroxide for plastics applications. ECS also alleged that AKZO had introduced predatory and discriminatory price cutting directed at ECS's customers for benzoyl peroxide as a flour additive, and it had forced ECS to lower its prices to non-economic levels to retain its customers.

AKZO: the judgment.   The Commission[207] found that in fact AKZO were sell- **10.073** ing below AVC; but in any event the Commission rejected the argument that a *per se* test based on marginal or variable costs should be the sole determinant of whether or not Article 82 applied. In the Commission's opinion a test based on the aggressor's costs would not cover all cases of unfair conduct designed to exclude or damage a competitor. Apart from the inherent difficulty of accurately establishing costs, no such tests would give sufficient weight to the strategic aspect of price cutting behaviour.[208] The Court of Justice[209] approached the matter somewhat differently from the Commission. Applying the principle that abuse is an objective concept, the Court adopted a test that is much more closely based on costs, albeit taking account of the strategy of the dominant undertaking. As noted above, the Court held that prices below AVC must be considered abusive, while prices above AVC but below average total cost may be abusive if they constitute part of a plan to eliminate a competitor. However, having formulated a strict *per se* test where prices were below variable costs, the Court of Justice took a narrower view than the Commission of what constituted 'variable costs'. As a result, the

---

[205] Cases C-395 & 306/96P *Compagnie Maritime Belge Transports v Commission* [2000] ECR I-1365, [2000] 4 CMLR 1076, [2000] All ER(EC) 385, Opinion, para 127.
[206] See in that regard the approach of the UK Competition Appeal Tribunal in *Aberdeen Journals Ltd v Office of Fair Trading (No. 2)* [2003] CAT 11, [2003] CompAR 67, paras 357–358. In *First Edinburgh/Lothian*, 29 April 2004, [2004] UKCLR 1554, the Office of Fair Trading held that pricing by a dominant bus operator that was below AVC was not an abuse.
[207] *ECS/AKZO Chemie*, OJ 1985 L374/1, [1986] 3 CMLR 273. See also *British Sugar/Napier Brown*, OJ 1987 L284/41, [1990] 4 CMLR 196; *Macron/Angus XVIIth Report on Competition Policy* (1987), point 81.
[208] *ECS/AKZO Chemie*, above, para 78.
[209] Case C-62/86 *AKZO v Commission* [1991] ECR I-3359, [1993] 5 CMLR 215, paras 69–74.

Court found that AKZO's prices were above AVC but since the prices were still below average total costs and there was evidence of predatory intent over a period of years,[210] the Court upheld the Commission's finding of predation.

10.074 **Assessment of variable costs in predatory pricing.** In defining variable costs in the *AKZO* decision, the Commission treated items such as labour, maintenance, warehousing and dispatching as variable, on the ground that most accounting systems classify them as such. On appeal, the Court upheld AKZO's contention that their labour costs were fixed. The Court said that 'an item of cost is not fixed or variable by nature. It must be determined, therefore, whether, in the present case, labour costs did vary according to the quantities produced'.[211] On the facts, the Court found that there was no direct correlation between the quantities produced by AKZO and its labour costs, and therefore held that labour costs were fixed not variable.[212] In *Statens Järnvägar v Swedish Competition Authority*,[213] the Swedish Market Court considered whether a proposed bid for a contract for the supply of public transport by rail services would be predatory. The Court had to base its analysis on forecasts of future costs for the four-year period over which the services would be provided. The Court found that the dominant bidder had left out a number of costs which should have been included in the tender, which resulted in the variable costs of offering the service being substantially above the tender price. Further, the Court found that the bidder must have been aware that the tendered price was below its variable costs and that the bid was aimed at undermining its competitor.

10.075 **Other measures of cost.** In network industries, such as telecommunications, the Commission considers that simple application of a test based on AVC would not be appropriate: because such industries have large capital costs, some of which are common costs covering a range of services, a price based only on the costs of each additional unit of output may be substantially lower than needed to cover the operator's costs of supplying the service; instead the Commission suggests that long run average incremental costs ('LRAIC') should be the basis for judging whether prices are predatory.[214] Use of LRAIC may involve some allocation of common costs, which is often problematic. However, to the extent that the

---

[210] For the timescale relevant to a finding of predation, see the UK Competition Appeal Tribunal in *Aberdeen Journals No. 2* (n 206, above) paras 353–356 and 382–387. The Tribunal notes that timescale is likely to be relevant not only to issues of intention but also to the assessment of costs: the longer that a low price is maintained, the more likely it is that costs are to be regarded as largely if not entirely variable rather than fixed.

[211] *AKZO v Commission* (n 209, above) para 94.

[212] ibid, para 95.

[213] Case MD 2000:2 *Statens Järnvägar v Swedish Competition Authority*, judgment of 1 February 2000.

[214] See para 12.157, below.

operator's common costs involve the costs of fulfilling a mandatory service obliga-tion, only those costs exclusively related to the provision of the additional service impugned for predatory pricing should be included: in other words, the costs which the firm would not incur if that additional service was not provided. This may include some fixed costs (and therefore will still be a higher measure than AVC) but may be lower than LRAIC. Thus in finding that Deutsche Post ('DP'), which held a legal monopoly in Germany for ordinary letter post, had engaged in predatory pricing of its mail order parcel service which was open to competi-tion, the Commission took into account only DP's incremental costs of providing that service.[215] The Paris Court of Appeal followed the same approach in dismiss-ing the allegation that a ferry operator engaged in predatory pricing contrary to the French counterpart of Article 82: since the dominant operator was obliged to run a passenger service also in the winter months, when it did not face competi-tion, the costs to be taken into account in assessing the prices charged for that operation in the summer, when it did have competitors, were only the additional costs of continuing the service over that extended period.[216]

Potential for recoupment of losses: *Tetra Pak II*. In *Tetra Pak II*[217] the   **10.076**
Commission concluded that Tetra Pak had engaged in predatory pricing of its non-aseptic cartons in Italy. The Commission's conclusion was upheld by the Court of First Instance[218] and by the Court of Justice.[219] Tetra Pak operated in two markets, aseptic and non-aseptic packaging; it was found to be dominant in the former, but to have engaged in predatory pricing in the latter. The Commission found that Tetra Pak's prices over a seven-year period were not only well below their total average cost but also below their AVC and even (save in one year) below their average direct variable cost.[220] The Courts rejected Tetra Pak's argument[221]

---

[215] *Deutsche Post AG — mail order parcel services*, OJ 2001 L125/27, [2001] 5 CMLR 99 paras 35–36: predatory pricing each year for six years. The decn refers to 'incremental cost' but on the facts this correspond to what is often referred to as 'avoidable cost'. See further the discussion of this decn in para 10.117, below.

[216] *Régie départmentale des passages d'eau de la Vendée*, Paris Court of Appeal, 28 June 2005, BOCCRF, 28 October 2005, dismissing the appeal against Decn 04-D-79 of 23 December 2004 of the Conseil de la Concurrence. The costs related to not only the purchase of the passenger boat but also major repairs and insurance were therefore excluded.

[217] *Tetra Pak II*, OJ 1992 L72/1, [1992] 4 CMLR 551, paras 147–159 (on appeal to the CFI, Case T-83/91 *Tetra Pak v Commission* [1994] ECR II-755, [1997] 4 CMLR 726; on further appeal to the ECJ, Case C-333/94P *Tetra Pak v Commission* [1996] ECR I-5951, [1997] 4 CMLR 662, [1997] All ER (EC) 4).

[218] Case T-83/91 *Tetra Pak v Commission*, above, paras 142–152.

[219] Case C-333/94P *Tetra Pak v Commission* (n 217, above) paras 39–45.

[220] *Tetra Pak II* (n 217, above) para 149. According to n 96 in the Decision, direct variable cost was equated to marginal variable cost, apparently meaning the amount by which costs were directly increased by an additional unit of output.

[221] Based on the US Supreme Court judgment in *Brooke Group v Brown & Williamson Tobacco*, 509 US 209, 113 S.Ct. 2578 (1993); rehearing denied, 509 US 940, 114 S.Ct. 13.

that sales at a loss were only predatory when there was a reasonable prospect of subsequently recouping the losses incurred. Tetra Pak claimed this would be impossible because it was not dominant in the market where the pricing in question had occurred. In upholding the Court of First Instance on this point, the Court of Justice stated:

> '. . . it would not be appropriate, in the circumstances of the present case, to require in addition proof that Tetra Pak had a realistic chance of recouping its losses. It must be possible to penalise predatory pricing whenever there is a risk that competitors will be eliminated. . . The aim pursued, which is to maintain undistorted competition, rules out waiting until such a strategy leads to the actual elimination of competitors'.[222]

Although the first sentence appears to leave open the possibility of a requirement of recoupment in different factual circumstances, and despite the economic logic of including such an element in the test for predation, a requirement to demonstrate the probability of future recoupment would often be very difficult to satisfy in practice.[223] It is notable that since the recoupment requirement was established in US antitrust law in 1993, there have been no judgments in the United States federal courts finding predatory conduct.[224] In *France Télécom v Commission*, the Court of First Instance robustly dismissed this ground of challenge to the Commission's decision in *Wanadoo Interactive*,[225] holding that proof of recoupment of losses was not a precondition to a finding of predatory pricing.[226] That was the case although the appellant contended that low barriers to entry on the market for high-speed internet access and the numerous actual and potential competitors meant that recoupment would be unlikely.[227]

10.077 **Predation in emerging markets.** In *Tetra Pak II*,[228] the Court of First Instance recognised that it may be acceptable for a dominant undertaking to sell at a loss in certain cases, although not with the actual purpose of strengthening and abusing

---

[222] Case C-333/94P *Tetra Pak v Commission* (n 217, above) para 44.

[223] Note that AG Ruiz-Jarobo Colomer expressly considered that prospect for recoupment should not be a requirement: *ibid*, Opinion at para 78.

[224] Fletcher (n 197, above) p 12. Note also that in US antitrust law, unlawful predation is not confined to dominant companies, which may justify placing a higher threshold for the claimant to establish.

[225] COMP/38.233 *Wanadoo Interactive*, 16 July 2003, [2005] 5 CMLR 120.

[226] Case T-340/03 *France Télécom v Commission* [2007] 4 CMLR 919, paras 224–228. The UK Competition Appeal Tribunal had previously held that there is no requirement to show recoupment under EC law: *Aberdeen Journals (No. 2)* (n 206, above) paras 437–443.

[227] In its decn, although stating that recoupment was not necessary to establish abuse, the Commission had in fact gone to some lengths to show that, given the structure of the market, recoupment of losses was indeed a likely scenario: *Wanadoo Interactive* (n 225, above) paras 332–368.

[228] Case T-83/91 *Tetra Pak v Commission* (n 217, above) para 147, not considered by the ECJ on appeal: Case C-333/94P (n 217, above).

its dominance. However in the *Wanadoo Interactive* decision,[229] the Commission rejected, as a matter of principle, various justifications put forward by the dominant firm. Wanadoo was a 72 per cent owned subsidiary of France Télécom which at the relevant time had an almost 100 per cent share of the wholesale ADSL services for internet service providers. The Commission found that in one period Wanadoo was charging prices well below AVC and that thereafter they charged at approximately AVC but well below average total cost. Wanadoo argued, first, that it was not appropriate to allege predation in a market which does not possess a sufficient degree of maturity. In the context of introducing a new service, incurring significant losses was inevitable. The Commission held that nothing in Article 82 or the case law on predation provided an exception for emerging markets: 'To subordinate the application of the competition rules to a complete stabilisation of the market would be to deprive the competition authorities of their power to act in time before the abuses established have exerted their full effect and the position unduly acquired has thus been finally consolidated'.[230]

Possible justifications for below-cost pricing. One justification for below-cost **10.078** pricing which had previously been thought legitimate was where the dominant company prices a new product at a level which anticipates economies of scale which will be achieved once production volumes increase. However, in *Wanadoo Interactive*, the Commission rejected this contention and held that a dominant firm is not entitled to reserve for itself the benefits of future economies of scale by absorbing current losses, since this delays the ability of competitors to arrive at the same volume threshold allowing them such economies.[231] The search for economies of scale did not legitimise below-cost pricing since it has the effect of conferring a more favourable cost structure on the dominant undertaking to the detriment of its competitors. The Commission also rejected a defence that Wanadoo was 'meeting not beating' prices offered by its non-dominant competitors.[232] The Commission stated:

> '. . . from a point of view of principle, it is true that new entrants or undertakings which are not in a dominant position are entitled to charge promotional prices for limited periods. Their sole aim is to draw the consumer's attention to the very

---

229 *Wanadoo Interactive* (n 225, above) para 337; appeal dismissed, *France Télécom v Commission* (n 226, above).

230 *Wanadoo Interactive* (n 225, above) para 301. The Commission also considered that the high-speed internet access market had strong links with the market for local access in the telecommunications sector which was a market in the throes of deregulation. This created risks of leverage effect which justified particular vigilance. cf the discussion by the UK Competition Appeal Tribunal in *Freeserve.com v Director General of Telecommunications* [2003] CAT 5, [2003] CompAR 2002, paras 221–224.

231 *Wanadoo Interactive* (n 225, above) para 307. And see the short dismissal of this argument by the CFI on the appeal: *France Télécom v Commission* (n 226, above) para 217.

232 A justification suggested in, eg *AKZO v Commission* (n 209, above) para 135.

existence of the product, more persuasively than by a mere advertisement, and such offers do not have any negative impact on the market. On the other hand, alignment by the dominant operator on the promotional prices of a non-dominant operator is not justified. Whilst it is true that the dominant operator is not strictly speaking prohibited from aligning its prices on those of competitors, this option is not open to it where it would result in its not recovering the costs of the service in question.'[233]

The Court of First Instance fully endorsed this approach in dismissing the appeal.[234]

10.079 **Proof of 'intention'.** Where prices charged are above AVC, evidence of intention to exclude a competitor is required. In *AKZO*, the Court inferred the necessary intention from the fact that there was no objective justification for the low prices charged over a long period in the absence of any competing quotations.[235] In *Tetra Pak II*, the Commission drew a similar conclusion on the basis that loss-making prices were charged only where it was necessary to win prospective customers or win back customers.[236] The Court of First Instance, in agreeing with the Commission, relied in addition on the evidence of board meeting minutes, the duration, continuity and scale of the losses incurred by Tetra Pak, their behaviour in buying stock and selling it below cost in the Italian market (where the alleged predatory behaviour occurred), the lower prices charged in Italy compared with other Member States and the increasing sales of Tetra Pak on the Italian market, and the decline in sales of their competitor, Elopak.[237] As the UK Competition Appeal Tribunal has observed, interpreting the concept of 'intention to eliminate a competitor' is not entirely straightforward.[238] The competitive process, which competition law seeks to encourage, of its nature involves the effort to take business from (and avoid losing business to) a rival, and therefore potentially drive out a less efficient competitor. The Tribunal held that what is meant is 'conduct on the part of a dominant firm which (i) has the reasonably foreseeable result of driving a rival from the market; (ii) goes beyond a normal competitive response and is disproportionate to the threat; and (iii) has the object or effect of preserving or strengthening a dominant position'. In *Wanadoo Interactive*, the Commission decision included detailed consideration of intent based on internal company documents.[239] On appeal, the Court of First Instance held that statements in management-level communications, in particular formal presentations and corporate planning documents that refer to Wanadoo's intention to 'pre-empt' the

---

[233] *Wanadoo Interactive* (n 225, above) para 315.
[234] *France Télécom v Commission* (n 226, above) paras 183–187.
[235] *AKZO v Commission* (n 209, above).
[236] *Tetra Pak II* (n 217, above) para 158.
[237] Case T-83/91 *Tetra Pak v Commission* (n 217, above) para 151, upheld by the ECJ, Case C-333/94P (n 217, above) para 42.
[238] *Claymore Dairies Ltd v Office of Fair Trading* [2005] CAT 30, [2006] CompAR 1, para 270.
[239] *Wanadoo Interactive* (n 225, above) paras 271–299.

ADSL market, could properly be relied on as indicating a 'plan of predation', especially when that was reinforced by evidence that Wanadoo was aware that its strategy of non-profitable pricing combined with high sales volumes was not sustainable for its competitors: the requisite intention for the purpose of the *AKZO* test was therefore satisfied.[240]

(ii) Price discrimination or targeting

Price discrimination or targeting. Price discrimination involves the treat- **10.080** ment of like cases differently or giving the same treatment to cases that are in fact different.[241] However, in the business world, there are many market factors which may lead to different customers paying different prices for the same product. Moreover, in some circumstances there are strong economic justifications for price discrimination as a way of maximising economic efficiency.[242] It is well established that not all price discrimination by a dominant firm constitutes an abuse. But the boundaries of abusive price discrimination remain uncertain. Article 82(c) refers to 'applying dissimilar conditions to equivalent transactions with other trading parties, thereby placing them at a competitive disadvantage'. This therefore refers to an effect on competition in the related market of the customer, and it is clear that price discrimination which lacks justification and places one customer of the dominant firm at a real competitive disadvantage as against another will generally consitute abuse. However, it also apparent that: (i) selective or targeted price discrimination aimed at excluding a competitor of the dominant firm may constitute an abuse; (ii) the element of 'competitive disadvantage' under Article 82(c) is sometimes interpreted broadly, in particular when price discrimination is based, directly or indirectly, on national grounds; and (iii) price discrimination which directly damages ultimate consumers may be an abuse. Price discrimination is accordingly an infringement of Article 82 that covers both same market and related market exclusionary abuses and also exploitative abuse. Since selective price discrimination is essentially a same market abuse, it will be considered first.

---

[240] *France Télécom v Commission* (n 226 above) paras 199–216.

[241] In its 1993 Statement of Objections regarding HB Ice Cream's arrangements for the distribution of impulse ice cream in Ireland, the Commission provisionally concluded that charging retailers a common price for impulse ice cream that took account of the cost of providing a freezer cabinet, irrespective of whether the retailer actually received a cabinet from HB, violated Art 82; HB thereupon discontinued this practice and introduced differential pricing: *Van den Bergh Foods*, OJ 1995 C211/4, [1995] 5 CMLR 734, paras 33, 41–42 (Art 19(3) Notice issued in respect of the revised arrangements; but those were subsequently found to infringe Art 82 on other grounds: see para 10.100, below).

[242] See the discussion of 'Ramsey pricing' in Bishop and Walker (n 1, above), paras 6.31–6.34. 'Ramsey pricing' (named after the English economist and philosopher, Frank Ramsey) involves differential pricing to reflect the different degree of price sensitivity of different classes of customers for products sharing common or fixed costs, with prices set much lower for price sensitive customers: eg private consumers as against business users.

10.081 **Selective price cutting: the problem.** When a dominant firm reduces its prices only to those customers approached by a competitor, the Community Courts have held that this may be an abuse, although the prices remain above cost and therefore are not predatory. The issue was highlighted in the case of *Compagnie Maritime Belge*, where a shipping conference (Cewal), with a monopoly of the Europe to West Africa routes, responded to the entry of a competing line by selectively lowering its freight rates to match those charged by the new entrant, for ships sailing on the same or similar dates.[243] Those rates were still above cost, but the shortfall in revenue earned by these so-called 'fighting ships' was made up by a contribution from all members of Cewal, and it was evident that the practice was introduced with the aim of forcing the new entrant out of the market. However, such conduct did not violate the *AKZO* test, nor did it fall within Article 82(c). In his Opinion, Advocate General Fennelly addressed the problem as follows:

> '. . . normally, non-discriminatory price cuts by a dominant undertaking which do not entail below-cost sales should not be regarded as being anti-competitive. In the first place, even if they are only shortlived, they benefit consumers and, secondly, if the dominant undertaking's competitors are equally or more efficient, they should be able to compete on the same terms. Community competition law should thus not offer less efficient undertakings a safe haven against vigorous competition even from dominant undertakings. Different considerations may, however, apply where an undertaking which enjoys a position of dominance approaching a monopoly, particularly on a market where price cuts can be implemented with relative autonomy from costs, implements a policy of selective price cutting with the demonstrable aim of eliminating all competition. In those circumstances, to accept that all selling above cost was automatically acceptable could enable the undertaking in question to eliminate all competition by pursuing a selective pricing policy which in the long run would permit it to increase prices and deter potential future entrants for fear of receiving the same targeted treatment.'[244]

10.082 **Selective price cutting: the Courts' approach.** The Court of Justice followed the Advocate General in holding that Cewal's conduct constituted an abuse. The Court stated:

> '. . . where a liner conference in a dominant position selectively cuts prices in order deliberately to match those of a competitor, it derives a dual benefit. First, it eliminates the principal, and possibly the only, means of competition open to the competing undertaking. Secondly, it can continue to require its users to pay higher prices for the services which are not threatened by that competition.'[245]

---

[243] Cases C-395 & 396/96P *Compagnie Maritime Belge Transports v Commission* [2000] ECR I-1365, [2000] 4 CMLR 1076, [2000] All ER (EC) 385.

[244] ibid, Opinion, para 132.

[245] ibid, judgment, para 117. However, the ECJ annulled the fines imposed on individual members of Cewal on the grounds that the Commission had not made it clear in the statement of objections that it intended to impose fines on the shipping lines rather than just on the association.

However, the Court expressly did not rule in general terms on when selective price cutting by a liner conference in order to meet competition might be legitimate. And the Court, as had the Advocate General, emphasised that the case concerned a conference with over 90 per cent market share and that the acknowledged aim of the impugned practice was the elimination of its single competitor from the market. Morever, the decision seems influenced by the fact that the liner conference members already enjoyed a privileged position of being allowed to set a collectively agreed tariff by reason of the then block exemption for shipping conferences in Regulation 4056/86.[246] The earlier judgment of the Court of First Instance in *Irish Sugar* provides another instance of selective price discrimination of this kind being condemned.[247] Irish Sugar was found to have abused its dominant position on the market for the supply of retail sugar in Ireland by granting so-called 'border rebates' to retailers in the border area with Northern Ireland in order to meet competition from Northern Irish suppliers. The Court noted that Irish Sugar was financing these rebates on the basis of the maintenance of its higher prices in the rest of Ireland, and was thereby preventing the development of free competition across Ireland. However, the Court emphasised that Irish Sugar had more than 88 per cent of the relevant market and that its ruling was made as regards 'an undertaking in a dominant position with the characteristics of that of the applicant at the time in question'.[248] Accordingly, it appears that conduct of this nature may not be an abuse in the absence of such 'super-dominance'.

Price discrimination: competitive disadvantage under Article 82(c).   Where a **10.083** dominant firm charges its customers different prices for the same product, this may place the customers paying the higher prices at a real competitive disadvantage. In the absence of economic justification, such a practice may therefore constitute an abuse within Article 82(c). That will be the case where the customers are direct competitors in the downstream market, or where the practice has an indirect effect as between the two categories of customer. In *Aéroports de Paris*, the Court of First Instance upheld the Commission's finding of infringement of Article 82(c) through the different charges imposed by the operator of the Paris airports for a licence to provide groundhandling services to aircraft, as between

---

The Commission subsequently adopted a further decision reimposing the fines: *Compagnie Maritime Belge*, OJ 2005 L 171/28, on appeal Case T-276/04, not yet decided.

[246] For the block exemption for liner conferences, see paras 12.021 *et seq*, below.

[247] Case T-228/97 *Irish Sugar v Commission* [1999] ECR II-2969, [1999] 5 CMLR 1300, [2000] All ER (EC) 198, paras 173 *et seq*; appeal on other grounds dismissed, Case C-497/99P *Irish Sugar v Commission* [2001] ECR I-5333, [2001] 5 CMLR 1082.

[248] ibid, paras 187–189. See also the application of the EC case law by the UK Competition Appeal Tribunal (applying the UK equivalent of Art 82) in *NAPP v Director General of Fair Trading* [2002] CAT 1, [2002] CompAR 13, paras 337–339: Napp had over 90 per cent market share and its conduct was directed at its only significant competitor.

those who provided such services to third parties and those airlines that provided the services themselves (self-handling).[249] The Court of First Instance rejected the argument that the different charges did not distort competition, finding on the evidence that the groundhandlers subject to the higher charges indeed suffered a competitive disadvantage: for example, the lower rate of fee could encourage some airlines to take up self-handling instead of using a third party provider. On further appeal, the Court of Justice upheld this approach.[250] In some cases, the dominant supplier is itself a competitor of its customer in a downstream market, and the resulting disadvantage to that customer therefore arises in competing with the dominant firm itself.[251]

10.084 **Price discrimination: differential tariffs.** Although the condition of 'competitive disadvantage' is not to be ignored, in other cases involving differential tariffs that are not justified by cost and effectively cover the same service, the Community Courts and Commission have given 'competitive disadvantage' an expansive reading, in particular where the discrimination effectively favours the domestic

---

[249] Case T-128/98 *Aéroports de Paris v Commission* [2000] ECR II-3929, [2001] 4 CMLR 1376, para 215.

[250] Case C-82/01 *Aéroports de Paris* [2002] ECR I-9297, [2003] 4 CMLR 609, para 116. See also AG Mischo, Opinion at paras 210–212. For other cases of price discrimination under Art 82(c), see, eg Case T-229/94 *Deutsche Bahn v Commission* [1997] ECR II-1689, [1998] 4 CMLR 220, appeal dismissed, Case C-436/97P, [1999] ECR I-2387, [1999] 5 CMLR 776 (charges for transporting containers higher on some routes than others); *Irish Sugar* (n 247, above) paras 125, 137 *et seq* (export rebates on sale of industrial sugar to customers exporting part of their production); *Deutsche Post AG—Interception of cross-border mail*, OJ 2001 L331/40, [2002] 4 CMLR 599, paras 121–132 (surcharge on 'remail' originating from senders in Germany). See also *P&I Clubs, IGA*, OJ 1999 L125/12, [1999] 5 CMLR 646, paras 134–136 (terms for access to reinsurance market discriminatory prior to amendment). Note also national court judgments: the Swedish Market Court in *Föreningen Svenska Tonsättares Internationella Musikbyrå (STIM) u.p.a. v TV3 Broadcasting Group Ltd*, 16 April 1998, held that the remuneration model for reimbursement for performance rights to copyright protected music on television discriminated against certain TV channels and also constituted a barrier to entry; similarly, in *SABAM*, 3 November 2005, [2006] ECC 195, the Brussels Court of Appeal found that the practice of SABAM, the Belgian copyright collection society for authors, composers and editors, in applying a different tariff according to the length and intensity of the commercial relations between SABAM and the undertaking in question could not be justified and accordingly infringed Art 82(c). In *Luftfartsverket (LFV) v Scandinavian Airline Systems*, 27 April 2001, the Göta Court of Appeal upheld a decision that LFV had abused its dominant position on the market for granting access to Arlanda Airport to airlines by requiring SAS, in addition to paying fees according to a tariff applicable to all airlines based on the characteristics of the airplanes and number of passengers, to pay additional costs for the provision of a terminal in accordance with agreements negotiated with SAS individually. The Court of Appeal found this to be discriminatory behaviour, for which there was no objective justification, violating Art 82 and its Swedish domestic counterpart. See further Pettersson and Alwall, 'Discriminatory pricing: comments on a Swedish case' (2003) ECLR 295.

[251] eg *Irish Sugar* (n 247, above) paras 150 *et seq*: abuse on the market for industrial sugar by charging sugar packers who competed with Irish Sugar in the downstream retail market a higher price for bulk sugar than those packers who did not compete; Case C-242/95 *GT Link v DSB* [1997] ECR I-4449, [1997] 5 CMLR 601: port did not levy duty on its own ferry service (and those of its trading partners) that were charged on independent ferry companies.

market or internal operators.[252] The analysis is sometimes sparse, but it appears that although the customers charged the higher and lower rates are not competing directly as regards their use of the goods or services supplied to them by the dominant firm, it is sufficient if they operate in the same market more broadly defined. In *Corsica Ferries*, the Court of Justice, on a reference from the Italian court, considered the different tariffs charged by the port of Genoa for piloting services: if a vessel held a cabotage licence for the Italian coast (a licence restricted to Italian flag vessels), it received piloting at substantially lower rates.[253] The Court clearly regarded this as an abuse, but the statement to that effect in the judgment makes no reference to the condition in Article 82(c) of a resulting competitive disadvantage.[254] The point was significant since the Italian government had argued that the domestic shipping activity of cabotage was not in competition with intra-Community shipping which was subject to the higher rate of charge. However, the earlier part of the judgment shows that the Court regarded the differential tariffs as placing Corsica Ferries at a competitive disadvantage in the provision of maritime transport services.[255] Similarly, there have been a series of decisions finding that Article 82 is infringed by differential bases of charging landing fees at airports. In *Portuguese Airports*, the Court of Justice upheld the Commission's decision that, *inter alia*, the 50 per cent reduction in fee for domestic flights as opposed to international flights infringed Article 82(c), irrespective of whether that had the effect of discriminating on the grounds of the nationality of the airlines.[256] The fact that international flights would almost certainly operate in a different product market or markets from the domestic flights[257] was not seen as an impediment to the finding of competitive disadvantage to the airlines subject to the higher charge. The affected airlines were competing with each other generally and the Court noted that 'a measure of this type . . . confers an advantage on carriers who operate more than others on domestic rather than international routes and so leads to dissimilar treatment being applied to equivalent transactions,

---

[252] See Whish (n 1, above), p 721, suggesting that this element of Art 82(c) may be applied in a particularly liberal manner when the discrimination is practised on national lines.

[253] Case C-18/93 *Corsica Ferries* [1994] ECR I-1783.

[254] *ibid*, para 43. See also the Opinion of AG van Gerven, para 32, suggesting that it is not necessary for the trading partners of the dominant undertaking to suffer a competitive disadvantage either against it or against each other.

[255] *Corsica Ferries*, above, para 21. See also the Commission's subsequent decn, *Port of Genoa*, OJ 1997 L301/27, [1998] 4 CMLR 91.

[256] Case C-163/99 *Portugal v Commission ('Portuguese Airports')* [2001] ECR I-2613, [2002] 4 CMLR 1319: infringement of Art 86 in conjunction with Art 82. See also *Ilmailulaitos/ Luftfartsverket ('Finnish Airports')*, OJ 1999 L69/24, [1999] 5 CMLR 90; *AENA ('Spanish Airports')*, OJ 2000 L208/36, [2000] 5 CMLR 967. cf *Brussels airport*, OJ 1996 L216/8, [1996] 4 CMLR 232 (direct competitive disadvantage to British Midland in competing with Sabena on Brussels–London route).

[257] See para 4.097, above, for market definition in the air transport sector.

thereby affecting free competition'.[258] However, the Commission appears to have gone further than this, holding that Article 82(c) is infringed when the customer discriminated against suffers a commercial handicap in competing in any market, on the basis that price discrimination may sometimes constitute exploitative rather than specifically exclusionary abuse.[259]

10.085 **Commercial price discrimination.** Appellate courts in the Member States have recognised that a dominant firm is not required to reach the same pricing arrangement with all its customers, but can negotiate arrangements that take account of its customers' different commercial situation. The issue arose before the German Federal Supreme Court and the English Court of Appeal, curiously in both cases in a dispute over the charges levied in connection with the televised broadcasting of horse racing to betting shops. In *Horserace transmission ('Galopprennübertragung')*,[260] the horse racing clubs which held the exclusive right to commercialise the television of German horse racing charged a licence fee for transmission to bookmakers who took their own bets that was substantially higher than the fee charged to betting shops which offered only totalisator bets. Although the Court found that the transactions were equivalent, it held that the discriminatory pricing was not abusive since the companies being charged the lower fees were new market entrants whom the defendants wished to aid: the defendants were legitimately seeking to promote the totalisator business which was ultimately of benefit for them. In *Attheraces v British Horseracing Board*,[261] the defendant ('BHB') arranged the supply of the precise details of the horses and riders in each race ('pre-race data') for use in conjunction with the broadcast of British races. BHB charged one company which held the broadcast rights to the majority of racecourses for transmission to overseas betting shops a higher rate of royalty than a new entrant which had equivalent rights to a smaller number of courses. The Court of Appeal held that such price discrimination was not an abuse, and observed: 'The mere fact that BHB has negotiated different deals with two

---

[258] *Portuguese Airports* (n 256, above) para 66.

[259] See COMP/38.745 *BdKEP – restrictions on mail preparation*, 20 October 2004, [2006] 4 CMLR 981, paras 92–96: infringement of Art 86 in conjunction with Art 82 by German postal law barring commercial mail preparation firms from earning discounts for handing over pre-sorted letters at Deutsche Post ('DP') sorting centres, the relevant provisions inducing DP to discriminate between bulk mailers, who have access to sorting centres and related discounts, and commercial providers of such services, who do not have such discounts. DP argued that bulk mailers and commercial senders acting for third parties were not competing. However, it seems that competitive disadvantage could have been found on the same basis as in *Aéroports de Paris*: see para 10.083, above. The decn is on appeal, Case T-490/04 *Germany v Commission*, not yet decided, and it may be that the CFI will clarify this point.

[260] Cases KZR 14/02 & 13/02, BGH judgment of 10 February 2004, WuW/E DE-R 1251 (annulling the judgment of the Düsseldorf Higher Regional Court).

[261] [2007] EWCA Civ 38, [2007] UKCLR 309 (reversing the judgment of the High Court).

customers, each in the absence of the other, cannot by itself render the difference objectionable'.[262]

Price discrimination on grounds of nationality. Price discrimination based on **10.086** the national location of the buyer is likely to infringe Article 82, as shown by *United Brands*.[263] United Brands unloaded at Rotterdam and Bremerhaven bananas of similar quality with virtually identical unloading costs and then sold the bananas to customers from various Member States at widely varying prices. Delivery was taken by the customers at the port of unloading in Europe; they then paid all import duties and the costs of carriage to their own ripening rooms in their respective countries. United Brands argued that its pricing merely reflected current retail prices in the relevant Member States, prices which themselves reflected different and often rapidly changing patterns of demand in the different countries. The Court of Justice held that United Brands was not entitled to discriminate. In principle, the quayside price should be the same for all customers, whatever the ultimate destination of the bananas; discriminating according to local conditions was an obstacle to the free movement of goods, the effect of which was intensified by a clause forbidding the resale of bananas while still green and by reducing the deliveries of the quantities ordered. A rigid partitioning of national markets was thus created at price levels which were artificially different, placing certain distributor/ripeners at a competitive disadvantage; competition had thereby been distorted. Thus a dominant firm is at serious risk under Article 82 if it pursues price discrimination designed to maintain national boundaries.[264] However, the Court of First Instance has recently interpreted *United Brands* as permitting a dominant undertaking to set different prices as between various Member States where those are already distinct geographical markets and the differences relate to the variations in the conditions of marketing and competition.[265]

---

[262] ibid, para 271. The Court stressed that on the facts there was no question of discrimination seeking to partition the market, distinguishing *United Brands*, nor was the price exploitative.

[263] Case 27/76 *United Brands v Commission* [1978] ECR 207, [1978] 1 CMLR 429. See Zanon di Valgiurata, 'Price Discrimination under Article 86 of the EEC Treaty, The United Brands Case' (1982) 32 ICLQ 36; and Bishop, 'Price Discrimination under Article 86: Political Economy in the European Court' (1981) 44 MLR 282, for a trenchant criticism of this aspect of *United Brands* as leading to a redistribution of income from poorer to richer countries.

[264] eg Case 226/84 *British Leyland v Commission* [1986] ECR 3263, [1987] 1 CMLR 184 (prices based on whether LHD or RHD certificates of conformity were required were designed to deter parallel importation). See also *Tetra Pak II* (n 217, above). *Corsica Ferries* (para 10.084, above) can also be explained on this basis; and cf Case C-266/96 *Corsica Ferries France v Gruppo Antichi Ormeggiatori del Porto di Genoa* [1998] ECR I-3949, [1998] 5 CMLR 402 (ports could charge different tariffs, which applied to any vessel irrespective of its nationality, based on the particular characteristics of each port).

[265] Case T-168/01 *GlaxoSmithKline v Commission* [2006] ECR II-2969, [2006] 5 CMLR 1589, para 177; on appeal, Cases 515/06P, etc, *GlaxoSmithKline Services v Commission*, not yet decided. The case concerned Art 81 so the observation was, strictly, *obiter*.

See also the decisions based on non-price discrimination on grounds of national-ity, referred to at paragraph 10.097, below.

10.087 **Other forms of price discrimination.** Predatory pricing, discussed above, and fidelity rebates and similar practices, discussed below, can often also be regarded as a form of price discrimination placing customers at a competitive disadvantage. For example, in *AKZO*,[266] AKZO's policy of offering lower prices to those cus-tomers who bought from its smaller competitor, ECS, but not to its other custom-ers, had adverse consequences not only for ECS but also for those customers of AKZO who continued to pay higher prices while their own competitors enjoyed the selectively reduced price. Similarly in the case of fidelity rebates, customers paying the lower price may have an unjustified advantage over other customers not receiving such a rebate. The introduction of competition in the utilities gives rise to extensive issues concerning discrimination, particularly in relation to access to network infrastructure.[267]

10.088 **Price discrimination which damages consumers.** Although price discrimina-tion which does not place one party at a competitive disadvantage cannot fall within Article 82(c), the Commission has held that practices by a dominant company that discriminate between ultimate consumers who are in a like position can, in itself, constitute an abuse. That is the case for non-price discrimination,[268] and in *Deutsche Post — Interception of cross-border mail*, both non-price and price discrimination were at issue in the treatment by the German postal monopoly of cross-border mail from the United Kingdom.[269] In an attempt to counter the practice of German senders of bulk mail of routing their mailings via the United Kingdom to take advantage of lower tariffs, Deutsche Post ('DP') intercepted incoming mailings from the United Kingdom; when such 're-mail' (that is, mail originating from a sender in Germany) was found, DP imposed a surcharge corresponding to its domestic tariff. The delay caused by the interception gave rise to non-price discrimination. The Commission held that the senders of the disputed mailings were consumers of postal services who were adversely affected both by reason of the delay and by having to pay higher prices than other senders.[270]

---

[266] *AKZO*, discussed at paras 10.072 *et seq*, above.

[267] See, eg the Commission's Guidelines on the Application of EEC Competition Rules in the Telecommunications Sector, OJ 1991 C233/02: Vol II, App E.23, paras 95–98.

[268] See cases in n 313, below.

[269] *Deutsche Post AG — Interception of cross-border mail* (n 250, above). This was an alternative ground of the decn to the finding of anti-competitive abuse within Art 82(a) and (b) and as a con-structive refusal to supply. See also Cases C-147 & 148/97 *Deutsche Post* [2000] ECR I-825, [2000] 4 CMLR 838, paras 56–61.

[270] ibid, para 133. The German addressees were similarly regarded as consumers affected by the non-price discrimination.

Identifying equivalent transactions. In order to establish that a dominant **10.089** undertaking has engaged in discriminatory pricing, it is necessary to identify equivalent transactions which have been treated differently by the dominant firm. In *Scandlines*,[271] the complainants sought to compare the prices which the port authority charged for services provided to passenger ferry operators with the services provided to cargo vessels. The Commission found that the services provided were not comparable since the ferry operators use ramps and gangways for embarking and disembarking vehicles and passengers whereas the cargo vessels use cranes and other equipment for loading and unloading cargo. The complainant argued that in determining whether transactions were equivalent, the Commission should examine whether the costs of providing the two different services were the same since only differences which affected the costs incurred by the dominant undertaking were relevant. The Commission rejected this approach. According to its analysis, differences in prices could be justified although the costs incurred in the provision of the respective transactions were equivalent. If equivalent transactions cannot be found, there was no need to examine the costs of those transactions.

Objective justification for differential pricing. The factors on which a domi- **10.090** nant firm may rely as objective justification for differentiation in price have not been fully identified. In particular, it is not clear whether, and if so in what circumstances, a dominant firm may justify offering a lower price to one customer than to another on the grounds that the lower price was needed in response to an offer to the same customer made by a competitor.[272] In *United Brands*, the Court of Justice stated:

> 'Although it is true . . . that the fact that an undertaking is in a dominant position cannot disentitle it from protecting its own commercial interests if they are attacked, and that such an undertaking must be conceded the right to take such reasonable steps as it deems appropriate to protect its said interests, such behaviour cannot be countenanced if its actual purpose is to strengthen this dominant position and abuse it. Even if the possibility of a counter-attack is acceptable that attack must still be

---

271 COMP/36.568 and 36.570 *Scandlines v Port of Helsingborg; Sundbusserne v Port of Helsingborg*, 23 July 2004, [2006] 4 CMLR 1224 and 1298, paras 249 *et seq*.

272 cf the 'meeting competition' defence under s 2(b) of the US Robinson-Patman Act (15 USC para 13(b)). In *Tetra Pak II*, OJ 1992 L72/1, [1992] 4 CMLR 551, the measures ordered by the Commission did not allow for meeting competition but required that 'Tetra Pak . . . shall not grant to any customer any form of discount on its products or more favourable payment terms not justified by an objective consideration. Thus discounts on cartons should be granted solely according to the quantity of each order and orders for different types of cartons may not be aggregated for that purpose'. cf *ECS/AKZO*, OJ 1983 L252/13, [1983] 3 CMLR 694, where the Commission, in ordering interim measures to stop predatory pricing, provided for an exception to enable AKZO to match (but not price below) a lower offer made to its customer by a competitor. Although that was not reproduced in the final order (OJ 1985 L374/1, [1986] 3 CMLR 273), note the observations of the ECJ in the appeal: *AKZO v Commission* (n 209, above) paras 153–156.

proportionate to the threat, taking into account the economic strength of the under-takings confronting each other.'[273]

In both *Compagnie Maritime Belge*[274] and *Irish Sugar*,[275] discussed above,[276] a meeting competition argument was rejected in circumstances where the price reduction was made by a 'super-dominant' company in order to exclude competitors altogether. However, the Community Courts stressed the particular features of those cases, involving virtually complete foreclosure of competition, and they should not be seen as laying down a general rule.[277] As in relation to rebates and discounts, it is well established that discrimination is permissible on the basis of differences in the costs of production or delivery, including savings resulting from economies of scale, but much less clear how far a dominant undertaking is entitled to confer differential advantages on wider strategic grounds.

(iii) Fidelity rebates and similar practices

10.091 **Fidelity rebates and similar practices.** Special financial rebates or discounts granted by dominant firms in return for securing all or an increased proportion of the business of customers may well infringe Article 82 in the absence of some objective justification. This principle was first established in *Suiker Unie*, where the Court of Justice held that Article 82 was infringed when a dominant undertaking operated a system of pricing which:

'... is not to be treated as a quantity rebate exclusively linked with the volume of purchases from the producer concerned but has rightly been classified by the Commission as a "loyalty" rebate designed, through the grant of a financial advantage, to prevent customers obtaining their supplies from competing producers.'[278]

The principle has since been affirmed and extended. In *Hoffmann-La Roche*[279] the Court of Justice stated that where a dominant undertaking ties purchasers by an obligation or promise on their part to obtain from it all or most of their

---

[273] *United Brands* (n 263, above) paras 189–190.

[274] Cases C-395 & 396/96P *Compagnie Maritime Belge Transports v Commission* [2000] ECR I-1365, [2000] 4 CMLR 1076, [2000] All ER (EC) 385.

[275] Case T-228/97 *Irish Sugar v Commission* [1999] ECR II-2969, [1999] 5 CMLR 1300, [2000] All ER (EC) 198, paras 173 *et seq*; appeal on other grounds dismissed, Case C-497/99P *Irish Sugar v Commission* [2001] ECR I-5333, [2001] 5 CMLR 1082.

[276] See paras above.

[277] In the Discussion Paper (para 10.005, above) para 5.5.2, DG Comp suggests that a 'meeting competition' defence may be made out provided that the price is above average avoidable cost and that the reduction is a proportionate response. In Cases IV/35.471, etc, *Digital Equipment Corp*, 9 October 1997, (1998) ECLR 112, the Commission accepted undertakings to end proceedings under Art 82 that allowed non-standard price reductions where justified as a proportionate response to a competitor.

[278] Cases 40/73, etc, *Suiker Unie v Commission* [1975] ECR 1663, [1976] 1 CMLR 295, para 518.

[279] Case 85/76 *Hoffmann-La Roche v Commission* [1979] ECR 461, [1979] 3 CMLR 211.

requirements, that undertaking abuses its dominant position within the meaning of Article 82; the same applies if, without the purchasers being tied by a formal obligation, the dominant supplier adopts, either under the terms of agreements concluded with the purchasers or unilaterally, a system of fidelity rebates.[280] It is irrelevant that the obligation is willingly accepted, and the fact that the term did not result from pressure being brought to bear on the other contracting party does not detract from the abusive nature of the term since the abuse consists of the further weakening of the structure of competition in a market where the firm is already dominant.[281] In *Almelo*,[282] the Court of Justice confirmed that it was abusive for a dominant undertaking to include loyalty obligations in its contracts even at the buyer's request. In *BPB Industries/British Gypsum*, the Court of First Instance stated that where such arrangements were made in respect of a substantial proportion of purchases they constituted an unacceptable obstacle to entry; the fact that the promotional payments represented a response to requests and to the growing buying power of customers did not justify the inclusion of exclusivity clauses.[283] British Gypsum later sought negative clearance for its revised rebate schemes and the Commission's Notices[284] in respect of those applications give some indication of the kind of rebate schemes that the Commission regards as acceptable: the notified schemes were essentially volume related, subject to a qualifying level of purchases and without a loyalty element.

Turnover related discounts: annual sales targets. The principles set out in **10.092** *Hoffmann-La Roche* were applied in *Michelin*[285] to turnover related discounts, which are capable of operating with the same effects as fidelity rebates.[286] In that case,

---

[280] ibid, para 89.

[281] ibid, para 120, reiterated in *Almelo* (n 282, below) paras 44–51. See also Cases T-24/93, etc, *Compagnie Maritime Belge Transports v Commission* [1996] ECR II-1201, [1997] 4 CMLR 273, paras 84–86 (insistence on exclusivity provision in an agreement that expressly enabled derogations to be accepted); *UCB/Almirall*, *XXIVth Report on Competition Policy* (1994), p 362 (free 'samples' as a fidelity discount); *Digital*, *XXVIIth Report on Competition Policy* (1997), point 69 and pp 152–153 (fidelity rebates on condition no supplies obtained from competitors); *Deutsche Post AG – mail order parcel services* (n 215, above) (discounts linked to exclusivity). See also the decision of the French NCA (Conseil de la Concurrence) relating to practices by the *Société des Caves et des Producteurs réunis de Roquefort*, Decn 04-D-13, 8 April 2004, BOCCRF 31 March 2005 (granting retrospective price reductions to major distributors and supermarkets in return for agreement to purchase all or almost all of their requirements of Roquefort cheese condemned under French equivalent of Art 82).

[282] Case C-393/92 *Almelo* [1994] ECR I-1477.

[283] See Case T-65/89 *BPB Industries and British Gypsum v Commission* [1993] ECR II-389, [1993] 5 CMLR 32, para 68 (upheld on appeal, Case 310/93P [1995] ECR I-865, [1995] 5 CMLR 14).

[284] *British Gypsum (Rebate Schemes)*, OJ 1992 C321/9, 10, 11, 12, [1993] 4 CMLR 143, 145, 147, 149.

[285] *Michelin*, OJ 1981 L353/33, [1982] 1 CMLR 643.

[286] See also *Coca-Cola*, *XIXth Report on Competition Policy* (1989), point 50; COMP/38.113 *Prokent/Tomra*, decn of 29 March 2006, [2006] 4 CMLR 1417 (fidelity rebates and individualised

Michelin NV offered its dealers an annual variable discount determined according to the dealer's turnover in Michelin heavy vehicle, van and car tyres in the previous year. The dealer received its discount, or the full rate thereof, only if it achieved an annual sales target fixed by Michelin NV. Neither the discount system as a whole nor the scale of discounts was published by Michelin NV. The Commission concluded that Article 82 was infringed, since under the discount system Michelin NV (i) bound tyre dealers in the Netherlands to itself; and (ii) applied to them dissimilar conditions in respect of equivalent transactions, the latter finding being reached on the basis that the discounts varied as between Michelin's dealers without objective justification. On appeal, the Court of Justice asked itself whether, in giving an advantage not justified by the provision of any economic service, the discount tended to remove or restrict the buyers' freedom to choose their sources of supply, to bar competitors from access to the market, to apply dissimilar conditions to equivalent transactions with other trading parties or to strengthen the dominant position by distorting competition.[287] On the issue of the binding of dealers to Michelin NV, the Court found that the system was calculated to prevent dealers from being able to select freely, at any time in the light of the market situation, the most favourable of the offers made by the various companies and to change supplier without suffering any appreciable economic disadvantage.[288] The Court emphasised the length of the period by reference to which the discount was calculated, the pressure on dealers to stay with Michelin NV throughout the period to achieve the sales target, the fact that the discount applied to the total purchases, the difficulty faced by competitors in matching the Michelin discounts and the lack of transparency of the system.[289] The Court of Justice returned to the issue in *Portuguese Airports*, where one ground for the Commission's finding of abuse was the system of discounts on landing fees based on the number of landings.[290] The Court noted that the fact that larger purchasers or users receive a higher average reduction than smaller purchasers or users is inherent in a system of quantity discounts and does not in itself make the system discriminatory. However, the Court held that having a high threshold in the system

---

retroactive quantity rebates in the supply of machines for collecting used beverage containers condemned as abusive), on appeal Case T-155/06 *Tomra Systems v Commission*, not yet decided. For economic analysis of the anti-competitive effect of rebates, see Maier-Rigaud and Vaigauskaite, 'Prokent/Tomra, a textbook case? Abuse of dominance under perfect information', (2006) 2 EC Competition Policy Newsletter 19.

[287] Case 322/81 *Michelin v Commission* [1983] ECR 3461, [1985] 1 CMLR 282, para 73.

[288] ibid, para 85.

[289] ibid, paras 81–84. Note that a competitor would have had to match the accumulated discount forgone by the Michelin dealer. On the facts, the ECJ found the Commission had failed to prove that Michelin had discriminated by applying unequal criteria for sales targets (paras 87 *et seq*) or that it had abusively linked discounts paid on car tyres to sales of heavy vehicle tyres. See also Case T-228/97 *Irish Sugar* (n 275, above), paras 194–225.

[290] *Portugal v Commission* (n 256, above) paras 48 *et seq*.

which can be met by only a few particularly large customers, or the absence of a linear progression in the increase in quantity discounts, may constitute evidence of discriminatory treatment, amounting to abuse unless it is objectively justified by costs savings.[291]

Stepped discount arrangements.   In 2003, the Court of First Instance delivered **10.093** two judgments concerning discount schemes, the first of which found that Michelin had again infringed Article 82, and the second of which, concerning British Airways, was subsequently upheld by the Court of Justice. At issue in *Michelin II* were a wide variety of complex pricing schemes in respect of the supply of replacement tyres for heavy vehicles in France. The various pricing schemes being operated by Michelin included a 'progress bonus' which involved target rebates (that is, quantity rebates based on standardised volume targets), aimed at rewarding increases of purchases year-on-year. The Commission[292] objected that the target volumes were not based on estimates of each dealer's purchase requirements but rather were based on a grid with various 'steps'. When a dealer went up a step he received the extra rebate not just for the *additional* purchases but for all purchases made in the reference period; it is this element which results in the bonus having a similar effect to a more conventional loyalty rebate. The Court of First Instance,[293] upholding the decision, found that a quantity rebate system in which there is a significant variation in the discount rates between the lower and higher steps, which has a reference period of one year, and in which the discount is fixed on the basis of total turnover achieved during the reference period, is a loyalty-inducing discount system,[294] and is abusive unless based on a countervailing advantage which may be economically justified.[295] The Court also held that transparency cannot save an otherwise abusive quantity rebate system, while noting that complex pricing systems which placed dealers in positions of uncertainty and dependence contribute to their abusive nature.[296] In its subsequent decision in *British Airways*,[297] the Court of First Instance found that the performance reward schemes operated by British Airways (BA) constituted an abuse contrary

---

[291] ibid, paras 51–53. The ECJ found that this was indeed the case: only the Portuguese airlines TAP and Portugalia could qualify for the highest rate band which, moreover, involved an appreciably greater increase in discount rate than lower bands.

[292] *Michelin*, OJ 2002 L143/1, [2002] 5 CMLR 388.

[293] Case T-203/01 *Michelin v Commission ('Michelin II')* [2003] ECR II-4071, [2004] 4 CMLR 923. The CFI noted that the Commission had been incorrect in its statement, at para 216 of its decision, that the ECJ had consistently ruled against the granting of quantity rebates where the reference period exceeds three months.

[294] ibid, paras 61–66 and 95. See also *Prokent/Tomra* (n 286, above).

[295] *Michelin II* (above), para 98.

[296] ibid, para 111.

[297] Case T-219/99 *British Airways v Commission* [2003] ECR II-5917, [2004] 4 CMLR 1008, [2004] All ER (EC) 1115 (on appeal from *Virgin/British Airways*, OJ 2000 L30/1, [2000] 4 CMLR 999). See Press Release IP/99/504 (14 July 1999) setting out the principles the Commission applies

to Article 82 in that they produced discriminatory effects within the network of travel agents in the United Kingdom. On appeal,[298] the Court of Justice confirmed the lower Court's two stage approach to determining whether a rebate scheme was abusive. The first step is to ascertain whether the scheme has an exclusionary effect, that is to say, whether it is capable first of making market entry very difficult or impossible for the competitors of the dominant undertaking and, secondly, of making it more difficult or impossible for the recipients of the rebate to choose between various sources of supply or different commercial partners. The Court held that it did not have jurisdiction to substitute its own assessment for the lower Court's determination that the discount scheme in question had such exclusionary effect.[299] The second step is determining whether there is an objective economic justification for the discounts since 'an undertaking is at liberty to demonstrate that its bonus system producing an exclusionary effect is economically justified'.[300] The disadvantages for competition arising from the exclusionary effect of the scheme may be counterbalanced or outweighed by advantages in terms of efficiency which benefits consumers. If there are no such advantages, then the system is abusive. Again, the Court held that British Airways' challenge to the Court of First Instance's rejection of its arguments based on the high level of fixed costs in air transport and the importance of aircraft occupancy rates was inadmissible.

10.094 **Discounts dependent on the dominant firm's discretion.** Another element condemned in the *Michelin II* decision was a 'service bonus' scheme to which the Commission objected because Michelin enjoyed significant discretion in how it operated the scheme.[301] The Court of First Instance agreed, stating that a discount system which leaves a dominant undertaking a considerable margin of discretion as to whether the dealer may obtain the discount must be considered unfair and abusive because it has loyalty-inducing effects, creates serious uncertainty for customers and allows the dominant undertaking to behave in a discriminatory manner.[302] Similarly, membership of the 'Michelin Friends Club' was condemned as leaving too much discretion to Michelin and being at the extreme end of loyalty-inducing abuses, causing some customers to perceive that they had entered into 'lifetime' commitments. Dealers who were members of the Club

---

to such practices by airlines, namely that target discounts or any other discounts not reflecting cost savings or differences in value, are not allowed.

[298] Case C-95/04P *British Airways v Commission* [2007] 4 CMLR 982.

[299] As with the *Michelin* case, the key feature of the rebate scheme was that sales over the set threshold resulted in a greater discount for all sales so that it could be 'of decisive importance for the commission income of the travel agent as a whole whether or not he sold a few extra BA tickets after achieving a certain turnover': ibid, para 74.

[300] ibid, para 69.

[301] *Michelin II* (n 292, above).

[302] Case T-203/01 *Michelin v Commission ('Michelin II')* (n 293, above) paras 139–141.

were subject to obligations which enabled Michelin to monitor their behaviour and which tied them closer to Michelin, thereby eliminating competition from other manufacturers. The Court's judgment firmly places the burden on the dominant undertaking to demonstrate that quantity rebates are not illegal by showing that they are linked to efficiencies; and clear evidence would appear to be required in this regard. Moreover, the Court held that there is no requirement for the Commission to establish any actual effects of such conduct and that an abuse can be established by showing that the conduct in question is capable of having the effect of restricting competition.[303] In the same vein, it made clear its view that for the purposes of Article 82, anti-competitive object and potential anti-competitive effect are the same thing.[304]

Across-product rebates. In *Hoffmann-La Roche*, the fact that in certain cases the **10.095** rebates were based on all purchases of vitamins was one element condemned in the Commission's decision,[305] which was upheld by the Court of Justice.[306] Such 'across-the-board' or bundled rebates make it hard for another firm that has a narrower product range than the dominant company to compete. The undertakings given by Coca-Cola, on the basis of which the Commission discontinued proceedings for abuse of dominance in 1989, provided that such rebates would not be included in its distribution agreements.[307] In the Commission's 2005 decision[308] to accept commitments from Coca-Cola and its three main bottling companies (which were provisionally found to be jointly dominant in the supply of carbonated soft drinks), the growth and target rebates considered were set separately for colas and non-cola drinks, and thus gave rise to concern under the principles discussed above. But the Commission also objected to so-called 'assortment and range' provisions whereby payments were made to customers purchasing broad ranges of Coca-Cola's different drink products, which therefore in effect amounted to a rebate on sales. In that way, the turnover in the best selling colas was used to leverage sales of the weaker brands. The commitments accepted from Coca-Cola and the bottler companies provided, *inter alia,* that such assortment commitments would be defined separately for certain categories of brands.

Turnover related discounts: summary. When *British Airways* is considered **10.096** together with *Michelin II,* it appears that a relatively formalistic approach is

---

[303] ibid, para 239.
[304] ibid, para 241.
[305] *Hoffmann-La Roche*, OJ 1976 L223/27, [1976] 2 CMLR D25, para 60.
[306] *Hoffmann-La Roche v Commission* (n 279, above).
[307] *Coca-Cola* (n 286, above).
[308] COMP/39.116 *Coca-Cola*, decn of 22 June 2005 [2006] 4 CMLR 1680 (under Art 9(1) of Reg 1/2003). See *Report on Competition Policy 2005*, paras 147–152. See also under US antitrust law, *LePage's, Inc v 3M*, 324 F3d 141 (3d Cir, 2003) (en banc), cert denied, 542 US 953 (2004): bundled rebates by a company in a dominant position condemned as anti-competitive.

being taken. Standardised volume thresholds are unlikely, or at least less likely, to be abusive, both for aggregate and for incremental rebates. On the other hand, certain types of discounts and rebates are presumed to be exclusionary. The Court of Justice in *British Airways* clearly indicates that loyalty-inducing rebates are not necessarily abusive and may sometimes be economically justified,[309] but gives no indication of the circumstances in which advantages of such a scheme for the market and consumers might arise.[310] The Commission appears to have adopted a firm stance in proceeding against such arrangements.[311] Quantity discounts, on the other hand, may be justified by economic considerations, but it would appear that specific evidence supporting those considerations, for example of cost savings, will be required. The approach encapsulated in these two cases has attracted strong criticism from economic commentators as curbing price reductions that may benefit consumers: it has been argued that proof of likely (as opposed to merely possible) exclusionary effect should be required.[312] That criticism emphasises the risk of preventing pro-competitive price reductions, whereas the current state of the law may afford greater emphasis to avoiding the risk to competition from exclusionary discrimination.

(c) Own market abuses: exclusionary non-price conduct

10.097 **Discrimination on grounds of nationality.** Discrimination consists of not treating like cases alike (or treating unlike cases in the same way). A particularly significant aspect of discrimination under the Treaty is discrimination on grounds of nationality: a dominant firm that discriminates between customers or suppliers or persons seeking services on the ground of nationality will be acting abusively.[313]

---

309 Case C-95/04P *British Airways v Commission* (n 298, above) para 69.

310 See also Case MD 2001:4 *Konsortiet Scandinavian Airlines Systems (SAS) v Konkurrensverket*, judgment of 27 February 2001: Swedish Market Court upheld a decision of the Swedish NCA that SAS had abused its dominant position on the market for domestic scheduled air transportation passenger services by applying its frequent flyer programme, which was held to constitute a loyalty system. The Market Court held, however, that SAS should only be prohibited from applying this system in relation to traffic between destinations where SAS faced competition from new entrants or existing scheduled air passenger transport services.

311 See also the statement by Commr Van Miert at the start of the investigation of Coca-Cola's arrangements (n 308, above): 'Fidelity bonuses by dominant companies are simply not on', MEMO/99/42, 22 July 1999.

312 See, eg *Selective price cuts and fidelity rebates* (OFT804, July 2005), Economic discussion paper prepared for the OFT by RBB Economics, available at http://www.oft.gov.uk/NR/rdonlyres/DB851D94-1FBE-46EA-85A4-53E4DA0BB0F8/0/oft804.pdf.

313 See, eg Case 7/82 *GVL v Commission* [1983] ECR 483, [1983] 3 CMLR 645, paras 55–56 (discrimination by the only German music copyright collecting association against artists not resident in Germany); similarly *GEMA*, OJ 1971 L134/15, [1971] CMLR D35. cf Case 402/85 *Basset v SACEM* [1987] ECR 1747, [1987] 3 CMLR 173. See also *1998 Football World Cup*, OJ 2000 L5/55, [2000] 4 CMLR 963: ticket sales arrangements for the football World Cup in France discriminated in favour of purchasers giving an address in France. However, only a nominal fine was imposed as the arrangements were apparently similar to those for previous World Cup tournaments

Many of the findings of abusive discriminatory practices under Article 82(c) have involved protectionist fee schemes by State or State-related entities in the field of transport,[314] which were therefore condemned under Article 86 in conjunction with Article 82.

Long-term exclusive dealing.   Entry by a dominant undertaking[315] into long-term, exclusive contracts may constitute an abuse although they are readily accepted by the undertaking's customers.[316] Such contracts can make the other parties dependent on the dominant undertaking, reducing competition from its existing competitors and deterring new entrants.[317] The Commission also considers that a long-term exclusive licensing agreement between two undertakings in a dominant position on neighbouring markets is likely to be caught by Article 82

10.098

---

and the Commission, perhaps surprisingly, considered that the organisers therefore could not easily have realised that they were infringing Art 82. cf the arrangements made for the 2006 World Cup to prevent discrimination against purchasers outside the Eurozone: COMP/39.177 *2006 World Cup/Which?/DFB*, Press Release IP/05/519 (2 May 2005).

[314]   eg *Corsica Ferries* (n 253, above) (prices for port services could not discriminate between vessels trading between national ports only and those trading between Member States); *Finnish Airports, Portuguese Airports* and *Spanish Airports* (n 256, above) (airport landing charges could not vary according to the origin of flights); *Deutsche Bahn v Commission* (n 250, above) (German national railway favoured carriage by rail passing through the northern German ports). Gerard 'Price Discrimination under Article 82(c) EC: Clearing up the Ambiguities', Research Paper published by the Global Competition Law Centre of the College of Europe (n 15, above), p 130, arguing that 'protectionist abuses' should be dealt with under the free movement provisions of the Treaty rather than under Art 82 since they do not display elements of a distortion of competition.

[315]   For the position under Art 81 in respect of exclusive dealing, see paras 6.039 *et seq*, above. Given the market power of a dominant undertaking, the concerns expressed in respect of Art 81 are of course intensified.

[316]   eg *Suiker Unie v Commission* (n 278, above); *Hoffmann-La Roche* (n 279, above) para 90 (the ECJ left open the possibility of exceptional circumstances which could justify such arrangements); *IRI/Nielsen, XXVIth Report on Competition Policy* (1996), point 64 and p 144 (Nielsen undertook not to conclude agreements that restricted retailers' freedom to supply information to competitors).

[317]   See *Carlsberg/Interbrew, XXIVth Report on Competition Policy* (1994), points 209, 213 and p 351: exclusive licence by Carlsberg to Interbrew to produce or distribute certain luxury beers. The Commission acknowledged that in beer markets where there was effective competition, such exclusive licences between producers can be a highly effective way for producers in one Member State to penetrate markets in others. However, Interbrew held a dominant position on the Belgian market and the exclusivity extended the range of beers that it could offer to include a market segment which it had not penetrated with much success previously, thereby increasing barriers to entry for existing, mostly small firms and potential new entrants since they would also need to offer a full range to compete effectively with Interbrew. The exclusivity was all the more detrimental to competition because Carlsberg's beers represented around 76 per cent of the luxury Pilsener market. Note that while the agreement was alleged to infringe Art 81 (for which both parties were responsible), the allegations of abuse under Art 82 were made only against Interbrew. See also *Finnish amusement machine market, XXVIth Report on Competition Policy* (1996), p 141: exclusivity obligation removed from contracts with State-owned company that was formerly monopoly operator of amusement machines in Finland, following discussions with Commission; *IRE/Nordion, XXVIIIth Report on Competition Policy* (1998), point 74: exclusivity clauses in long-term supply agreements for molybdenum 99 removed after Commission commenced proceedings.

(as well as Article 81).[318] Even without an exclusivity clause, long-term contracts entered into by former monopolies that effectively involve the supply of most of the customer's requirements may be regarded by the Commission as capable of constituting an abuse in the context of energy markets where they can impede the process of market liberalisation.[319] Product-swapping by a dominant supplier, whereby retailers are induced to replace the products of a new entrant with those of the dominant firm's products, similarly constitutes an abuse.[320] Where a dominant undertaking entered into a five-year agreement to buy a considerable proportion of the output of one of its few competitors, the Commission's investigation resulted in the giving of commitments to bring the agreement to an end.[321] Moreover, as with fidelity rebates discussed above, an exclusivity requirement for a shorter period may constitute an abuse: either because in particular circumstances that may be sufficient to create a significant distortion of competition,[322] or when the agreement is regularly renewed and therefore has an equivalent effect to a longer-term commitment.[323]

10.099 'English clause'.   A so-called 'English clause' is a contractual provision whereby the distributor or purchaser who receives an offer at a lower price must give its supplier an option to match that offer, and only if the supplier declines to do so can the purchaser take supplies from the alternative source.[324] This is therefore

---

[318] See *Swedish Match Sverige/Skandinavisk Tobakskompagni, XXVIIth Report on Competition Policy* (1997), point 66 and p 138 (sole manufacturer and distributor of cigarettes in Sweden held an exclusive licence since 1961 for manufacture, distribution and sale of Prince brand of cigarettes belonging to dominant Danish tobacco conglomorate: agreement amended to place marketing and pricing in Sweden under control of Danish brand owner).

[319] See para 12.080, below.

[320] Case T-228/97 *Irish Sugar* (n 275, above) paras 226–235. See also *Société des Caves et des Producteurs réunis de Roquefort* (n 281, above).

[321] COMP/38.381 *De Beers*, 22 February 2006, [2006] 5 CMLR 1426 (De Beers undertook to phase out its agreement with the Russian diamond producer Alrosa for a substantial proportion of the latter's rough diamonds and to cease making any purchases after 2008. However, the decision accepting the commitments was annulled on appeal by Alrosa on the grounds that is infringed the principles of proportionality and freedom of contract: Case T-170/06 *Alrosa v Commission*, judgment of 11 July 2007.

[322] eg *FEBIAC*, Brussels Court of Appeal, 10 November 2005, holding that FEBIAC, a union with a monopoly on the market for the offering of services linked to the organisation of exhibitions of utility vehicles in Belgium, abused that dominant position by imposing on exhibitors and distributors wishing to take part in its annual transport exhibition a requirement not to participate in any similar exhibitions during a period starting six months beforehand. The Court found that there was no realistic choice as to whether to participate in FEBIAC's exhibition as it was perceived to be a necessity for all manufacturers and importing companies active on the Belgian market or wishing to enter it.

[323] See COMP/38.113 *Prokent/Tomra*, decn of 29 March 2006, [2006] 4 CMLR 1417 (exclusivity agreements over period of five years for the supply of machines for collecting used beverage containers together with fidelity and retroactive quantity rebates condemned as abusive and €24 million fine imposed: on appeal Case T-155/06 *Tomra Systems v Commission*, not yet decided).

[324] The etymology of this expression is obscure.

a qualified form of exclusive dealing which has been found to violate Article 82 nonetheless.[325] In *Hoffmann-La Roche*, the Commission held that such a clause was only a very limited relaxation of an exclusive dealing commitment.[326] Dismissing the appeal, the Court of Justice found that a clause whereby Roche's customers were obliged to inform it of more favourable offers made by competitors also placed at Roche's disposal commercially valuable information about market conditions and the actions of its competitors; and that such a clause meant that it was for Roche itself to decide (by adjusting its prices or not) whether it would permit its customers to buy from competitors.[327]

***De facto* exclusive dealing: the 'ice cream wars'.**   Even where an undertaking is   **10.100** in principle free to stock competing products, an abuse may still occur if the overall contractual position is equivalent to an exclusive dealing arrangement. In *Van den Bergh Foods*,[328] the defendant, which held 40 per cent of the market for impulse ice cream in Ireland, had a network of supply agreements with retailers whereby freezer cabinets were provided and maintained free-of-charge subject to a prohibition on the retailers using the cabinets to store products made by a third party. Acting on a complaint by Mars, the Commission found that retailers were generally unlikely to install a second freezer cabinet on their premises, and held that as well as infringing Article 81, this practice constituted an infringement of Article 82 since it had the effect of rendering those outlets '*de facto* exclusive sellers' of the defendant's ice cream. The Commission accepted that such agreements may be normal commercial practice in the ice cream market and advantageous for retailers, but held that for an undertaking in a dominant position to give such inducements to customers to prevent them from dealing with its competitors over a significant period constituted an abuse.[329] On appeal, the Court of First Instance upheld the decision of the Commission.[330] The Court found that the fact that an undertaking in a dominant position on a market ties *de facto*, even at their own request, 40 per cent of outlets in the relevant market by an exclusivity clause which in reality creates outlet exclusivity constitutes an abuse of a dominant position. These exclusivity clauses had the effect of preventing the retailers concerned from selling other brands of ice cream (or of reducing the opportunity

---

[325] For the effect of an English clause in a vertical agreement as regards Art 81, see para 6.159, above.

[326] *Hoffmann-La Roche* (n 305, above) para 65.

[327] *Hoffmann-La Roche v Commission* (n 279, above) paras 102–108. See also *Industrial Gases, XIXth Report on Competition Policy* (1989), point 62.

[328] *Van den Bergh Foods*, OJ 1998 L246/1, [1998] 5 CMLR 530.

[329] ibid, para 264.

[330] Case T-65/98 *Van den Bergh Foods v Commission* [2003] ECR II-4653, [2004] 4 CMLR 1, [2005] All ER (EC) 418. The further appeal against this part of the judgment was dismissed as partly inadmissible and partly manifestly unfounded, Case C-552/03P *Unilever Bestfoods (Ireland) v Commission* [2006] ECR I-9091, [2006] 5 CMLR 1460.

for them to do so), even though there was a demand for such brands, and of preventing competing manufacturers from gaining access to the relevant market.[331]

10.101 **Abusive enforcement of exclusivity provisions.** It may be an abuse for a dominant firm or group strictly to enforce an exclusivity provision where their agreement allows for derogations. In *Compagnie Maritime Belge*[332] the Court of Justice
upheld the finding of the Commission that it was abusive for a shipping conference, Cewal, under the terms of an agreement with Ogefrem, the Zaire maritime
trade authority, to exercise its veto on the use of other carriers. The Court noted
that it was not the exclusivity provision in itself which here constituted the abuse
but the continued pressure by Cewal on Ogefrem to refrain from giving access to
the market to the only independent shipping line with a view to excluding it from
the market. The Court of Justice dismissed this part of the appeal against the decision of the Court of First Instance, which held that:

> 'an undertaking in a dominant position which enjoys an exclusive right with an
> entitlement to agree to waive that right is under a duty to make reasonable use of
> the right of veto conferred on it by the agreement in respect of third parties' access to
> the market . . .'[333]

10.102 **Exclusionary abuse by sporting bodies.** Given the increased economic importance of sport in relation to a variety of sectors, and in particular television broadcasting, application of the competition rules to sporting bodies is an issue that

---

[331] *Van den Bergh Foods v Commission*, above; see in particular para 160. But cf *Masterfoods*,
Paris Court of Appeal, 7 May 2002, BOCCRF No. 10, 24 June 2002. Applying the second limb
of *Delimitis* and based on the particular features of the French market (contracts cancellable within
15 days; 20 per cent of freezers returned each year indicating a relatively fluid market; 27 per cent
of distributors owned their own freezers; 52.3 per cent of distributors had the option of installing
several freezers on their premises; the market did not appear to be saturated; and the co-existence
of companies of varying sizes meant that a high degree of competition could be maintained), the
Court found that there was no firm evidence that the cumulative effect of parallel contracts to
loan freezers, accompanied by brand exclusivity clauses, would have anti-competitive effects. See
also *Henkel-Ecolab*, Decn 04-D-28 of 2 July 2004, BOCCRF 8 November 2004, where the French
NCA (Conseil de la Concurrence) held, distinguishing *Van den Bergh Foods*, that the provision
of free loan of dosage equipment by a company dominant in the supply of industrial washing
powders to laundries, hospitals, etc, in return for exclusivity of supply did not constitute abuse: the
practice was common in the industry, it was not difficult for the customer to return the equipment
when seeking to switch provider and there was evidence of such switching.

[332] Cases C-395 & 396/96P *Compagnie Maritime Belge Transports v Commission* [2000] ECR
I-1365, [2000] 4 CMLR 1076, [2000] All ER (EC) 385, on appeal from Cases T-24/93, etc,
Compagnie Maritime Belge Transports v Commission [1996] ECR II-1201, [1997] 4 CMLR 273.
The ECJ, however, annulled the fines imposed on individual members of the conference on the
grounds that the Commission had not made it clear in the statement of objections that it intended
to impose fines on the shipping lines rather than just on the association. The Commission sub-
sequently adopted a further decision reimposing the fines: COMP/32.448 *Compagnie Maritime
Belge*, decn of 30 April 2004, on appeal Case T-276/04, not yet decided.

[333] Cases T-24/93, etc, *Compagnie Maritime Belge Transports* (n 332, above) paras 108–109.
See also ECJ on appeal in Cases C-395 & 396/96P (n 332, above) paras 78, 84–86.

has arisen in a variety of contexts. Although generally arising in the context of Article 81,[334] such questions potentially involve application of Article 82, in particular where a sporting body enjoys effective control over rights to participate in a major sport or to broadcast coverage of such a sport.[335] For example, a sporting organisation may infringe Article 82 by using its regulatory powers to exclude from the market, without objective justification, competing organisers or indeed market players.[336] The Commission opened formal proceedings into Formula One motor racing and the activities of the Federation Internationale de l'Automobile, to investigate the possible abuse of market power in the licensing of participants in the sport, the acquisition of television rights and the arrangements entered into with broadcasters, promoters and teams.[337] In another investigation in the sports area, the Commission found that the ticket sales arrangements implemented for the 1998 World Cup by Comité Français d'Organisation de la Coupe du Monde de Football 1998 were discriminatory and in breach of Article 82.[338]

Litigation as an exclusionary abuse.   In certain circumstances, the instigation of **10.103** legal proceedings may be capable of being characterised as an abuse of a dominant position. The balance between the undoubted right of a dominant undertaking to take legal steps to protect its legitimate interests [339] and the need to impose some limit on such a right to avoid anti-competitive and exclusionary effects raises difficult issues of proportionality and objective justification. These are similar to the issues considered below in relation to the enforcement of intellectual property rights and refusal to license such rights to competitors. In *ITT Promedia*,

---

[334]   See paras 5.156 *et seq,* above, and for the collective selling of broadcasting rights, paras 5.115 *et seq*, above.

[335]   For collective dominance on the part of sporting bodies, see para 10.052, above.

[336]   See generally Press Release IP/99/133 (24 February 1999), [1999] 4 CMLR 596, and Pons, 'Sport and European Competition Policy' in Hawk (ed), *1999 Fordham Corp. L. Inst.* (Juris, 2000). See also Commr Monti, *Competition and Sport the Rules of the Games*, Speech/01/84, 26 February 2001, in which he set out how the Commission intended to apply competition law to sporting rules.

[337]   The proceedings were eventually resolved by substantial changes made in the Formula One arrangements: *Fédération Internationale de l'Automobile - FIA* and *FIA Formula One World Championship, XXXIst Report on Competition Policy* (2001), p 203. See further para 5.165, above.

[338]   *1998 Football World Cup*, OJ 2000 L5/55, [2000] 4 CMLR 963. Although only a nominal fine was imposed on the basis that the practice was similar to those adopted for previous competitions, the Commission regards the decision as sending 'a clear signal' that future tournament organisers must fully comply with the competition rules: *XXIXth Report on Competition Policy* (1999), point 62. See subsequently the arrangements made for the 2006 World Cup to prevent discrimination against purchasers outside the Eurozone: COMP/39.177 *2006 World Cup/Which?/DFB*, Press Release IP/05/519 (2 May 2005).

[339]   The UK courts have considered this issue on a number of occasions in the context of intellectual property litigation: see para 14.138, below, and the judgment of Megarry VC in *ICI v Berk Pharmaceuticals* [1981] 2 CMLR 91. In general, they have been unsympathetic to the idea that it might be an abuse to enforce legal rights in the courts.

the Court of First Instance set out, without dissent, the view of the Commission described in the following terms:

> 'The Commission considers that "in principle the bringing of an action, which is the expression of a fundamental right of access to a judge, cannot be characterised as an abuse" unless "an undertaking in a dominant position brings an action (i) which cannot reasonably be considered as an attempt to establish its rights and can therefore only serve to harass the opposite party, and (ii) which is conceived in the framework of a plan whose goal is to eliminate competition".'[340]

Moreover, in *AstraZeneca*[341] the Commission considered whether the defence by a patent holder of an action brought for a declaration of invalidity of the patent could ever constitute an abuse. The Commission stated that the conduct of a defence cannot be equated with the institution of legal proceedings but left open the question whether, in exceptional circumstances, it might be an abuse; in that case, the conduct of the defence was regarded as a continuation of the misrepresentations which had led to the extention of the patent right and which were found to constitute an infringement of Article 82.[342]

(d) Own market abuses: exploitative pricing

10.104 **Unfairly high prices.** Article 82(a) identifies, as an example of abuse, 'directly or indirectly imposing unfair purchase or selling prices . . .'. Unfair pricing may be either unfairly low pricing, designed to eliminate a competitor, as discussed above, or unfairly high pricing designed to achieve for the dominant undertaking larger profits than it would earn in a more competitive environment. As with other forms of abuse, the boundary between the legitimate rewards of monopoly power as the fruits of successful investment, innovation or efficiency, and illegitimate use of such power, is hard to identify with any precision.[343] Nonetheless, excessive pricing is clearly established as a form of abuse by a number of cases, including

---

[340] Case T-111/96 *ITT Promedia v Commission* [1998] ECR II-2937, [1998] 5 CMLR 491, para 30. See Preece, '*ITT Promedia v Commission*: Establishing an Abuse of Predatory Litigation?' (1999) ECLR 118.

[341] COMP/37.507 *AstraZeneca*, decn of 15 June 2005 [2006] 5 CMLR 287 (on appeal, Case T-321/05 *AstraZeneca*, not yet decided).

[342] ibid, paras 736 *et seq*. See para 10.153, below.

[343] For the arguments against using competition law to control the level of prices, see Whish (n 1, above), pp 688–691. And cf the restrictive approach of the US Supreme Court: 'The mere possession of monopoly power, and the concomitant charging of monopoly prices, is not only not unlawful; it is an important element of the free-market system. The opportunity to charge monopoly prices, at least for a short period, is what attracts "business acumen" in the first place; it induces risk taking that produces innovation and economic growth. To safeguard the incentive to innovate, the possession of monopoly power will not be found unlawful unless it is accompanied by an element of anticompetitive *conduct*.' *Verizon Communications Inc v Trinko* (2004) 540 US 398 at 407, per Scalia J.

General Motors, United Brands, British Leyland[344] and *Bodson.*[345] Although there have been relatively few examples of the abuse having been found, at least in isolation from other forms of exclusionary conduct designed to preserve the dominant firm's ability to charge such prices, in recent years the Commission has become vigilant in attacking prices in the telecommunications sector that it believes do not present fair value to consumers, in particular as regards roaming and call termination charges.[346] However, decisions by the Commission and national courts demonstrate the considerable difficulties of establishing this abuse.

Jurisprudence of the Court of Justice.   In *General Motors,*[347] the Court of Justice **10.105** adopted a test of unfairness based on the relationship between the price and the 'economic value' of the goods or services provided by the dominant firm. Charging a price that is excessive in relation to the economic value of the product is *prima facie* abusive conduct. The Commission applied this test in its *Chiquita (United Brands)* decision,[348] holding that United Brands' prices in certain Member States were 'excessive in relation to the economic value of the product supplied'. The Commission relied primarily on the widely differing prices charged as between one Member State and another. Starting from the assumption that prices charged to customers in Ireland were high enough to yield a profit, and noting that prices to customers in other Member States were sometimes more than 100 per cent higher, the Commission concluded that profits were excessive. On appeal, although the Court of Justice held[349] that the Commission's findings were defective, in that there was considerable doubt whether the price in Ireland had yielded a profit, the Court confirmed that 'charging a price which is excessive because it has no reasonable relation to the economic value of the product supplied' is an abuse. The Court indicated that an objective means of determining such excess would be a comparison of selling prices with costs of production but the Commission had made no attempt to examine United Brands' costs,

---

[344]   Case 226/84 *British Leyland v Commission* [1986] ECR 3263, [1987] 1 CMLR 184.

[345]   Case 30/87 *Bodson v Pompes Funèbres* [1988] ECR 2479, [1989] 4 CMLR 984, para 31. See also, eg Case C-242/95 *GT-Link v DSB* [1997] ECR I-4449, [1997] 5 CMLR 601, paras 39–40; Case 78/70 *Deutsche Grammophon v Metro* [1971] ECR 487, [1971] CMLR 631 (at least impliedly, para 19). See also *Sterling Airways, Xth Report on Competition Policy* (1980), points 136–138; Case 247/86 *Alsatel v Novasam* [1988] ECR 5987, [1990] 4 CMLR 434, para 10 and per AG Mancini, para 6.

[346]   See Haag and Klotz 'Commission Practice Concerning Excessive Pricing in Telecommunications' (1998) 2 EC Competition Policy Newsletter 35, and para 12.162, below. See also, in the context of utility regulation, *Electricity transmission tariffs in the Netherlands, XXIXth Report on Competition Policy* (1999), p 165.

[347]   Case 26/75 *General Motors v Commission* [1975] ECR 1367, [1976] 1 CMLR 95.

[348]   *Chiquita*, OJ 1976 L95/1, [1976] 1 CMLR D28.

[349]   Case 27/76 *United Brands v Commission* [1978] ECR 207, [1978] 1 CMLR 429, para 251.

which the Court ruled should have been possible. The *United Brands* judgment continued:

> 'The questions therefore to be determined are whether the difference between costs actually incurred and the price actually charged is excessive, and, if the answer to this question is in the affirmative, whether a price has been imposed which is either unfair in itself or when compared to competing products. Other ways may be devised - and economic theorists have not failed to think of several - of selecting rules for determining whether the price of a product is unfair.'[350]

Accordingly, a high profit margin does not necessarily constitute abuse. It is necessary to consider further whether such a high profit is unfair, assessed by reference to the concept expressed somewhat cryptically as 'the economic value' of the product.[351]

10.106 **The Commission's approach: *Port of Helsingborg*.** Since *United Brands*, the Commission has been reticent about taking decisions on 'unfair prices'[352] outside the telecommunications sector or where the case involved price differentials which perpetuate market divisions.[353] In *Port of Helsingborg*[354] the Commission issued two lengthy parallel decisions rejecting complaints by ferry operators about the port fees charged by the Port. The operators argued[355] that the 'economic value' of a product or service should be calculated by adding to the costs incurred in providing it a reasonable profit which would be a percentage of the production costs. A price exceeding this amount should be found unfair. The Commission rejected this methodology as too simplistic, stating: 'It is important to note that the decisive test in *United Brands* focuses on the price charged, and its relation to the *economic value* of the product. While a comparison of prices and costs, which reveals the profit margin, of a particular company may serve as a first step in the analysis (if at all possible to calculate), this in itself cannot be conclusive as regards the existence of an abuse under Article 82'.[356] The Commission nonetheless

---

350 ibid, paras 252–253.

351 See *Attheraces Ltd v British Horseracing Board* [2007] EWCA Civ 38, [2007] UKCLR 309, where the English Court of Appeal reversed the judgment of the High Court that found an abuse on the basis of the level of profit over a notional competitive price.

352 See *XXIVth Report on Competition Policy* (1994), point 207: 'the Commission in its decision-making practice does not normally control or condemn the high level of prices as such. Rather it examines the behaviour of the dominant company designed to preserve its dominance, usually directly against competitors or new entrants . . .'. This was stated in the context of the investigation into *Microsoft* conducted in cooperation with the US Dept of Justice and closed upon Microsoft entering into an undertaking regarding its contracting practices: ibid, point 308 and pp 364–365. See also Case T-306/05 *Scippacercola and Terezakis v Commission*, not yet decided (challenge to Commission refusal to investigate alleged excessive pricing for services at Athens airport).

353 eg *British Leyland v Commission* (n 344, above).

354 COMP/36.568 and 36.570 *Scandlines v Port of Helsingborg, Sundbusserne v Port of Helsingborg*, 23 July 2004, [2006] 4 CMLR 1224 and 1298.

355 *Scandlines*, above, para 219; *Sundbusserne*, above, para 197.

356 *Scandlines*, para 102 and see also para 221; *Sundbusserne*, para 85, also para 199.

sought to establish the costs to the Port of providing the service. Having rejected the results of the Port's cost allocation exercise, the Commission attempted to arrive at some figures itself. The costs to be taken into account were, the Commission considered, not limited to those which were reflected in the company's audited accounts. It was right also to include the very high sunk costs of providing the port infrastructure; the intangible benefit of the fact that the location of the port meets the ferry operators' needs perfectly; and the opportunity cost for the City of Helsingborg of using the land for a ferry terminal rather than for some other purpose.[357] The fact that the costs allocation included some elements which were intangible and others which were based on assumptions were only some of the difficulties encountered. Moreover, the Commission was unable to establish what a 'reasonable' level of profit would be. It rejected comparisons with other ports and with the rest of Swedish industry.[358] Finally, the Commission held that the economic value of the service had to be assessed taking into account also the perspective of the buyer (the demand-side) and not only the perspective of the provider (the supply-side):

'The demand-side is relevant mainly because customers are notably willing to pay more for something specific attached to the product/service that they consider valuable. This specific feature does not necessarily imply higher production costs for the provider. However it is valuable for the customer and also for the provider, and thereby increases the economic value of the product/service.

As a consequence, even if it were to be assumed that there is a positive difference between the price and the production costs exceeding . . . . a reasonable margin (whatever that may be), the conclusion should not necessarily be drawn that the price is unfair, provided that this price has a reasonable relation to the economic value of the product/service supplied. The assessment of the reasonable relation between the price and the economic value of the product/service must also take into account the relative weight of non-cost related factors.'[359]

The Commission concluded that there was insufficient evidence to conclude that the port charges bore no reasonable relation to the economic value of the services.

Benchmark comparator. In some cases, a comparison may provide an effective benchmark. In *British Leyland*, there was a straightforward comparator since the case concerned the fee charged for the issue of certificates of conformity for left-hand drive vehicles which was considerably higher than the fee charged by the

10.107

---

[357] *Scandlines*, para 109; *Sundbusserne*, para 92.

[358] Scandlines, paras 152 *et seq; Sundbusserne*, paras 133 *et seq.*

[359] *Scandlines,* paras 227–228; *Sundbusserne,* paras 205–206. Scandlines referred the Commission to para 9-073 of the 5th edn of this work: see para 229. The Commission also rejected the allegations by Scandlines of discriminatory pricing and by both operators of cross-subsidisation (see para 10.116, below and para 10.089, above).

same company for the issue of such certificates for right-hand drive vehicles.[360] In *Bodson*, which concerned the price charged for funerals, the Court of Justice indicated that the price charged by those with an exclusive concession to operate funerals in a particular area could be compared to the prices charged in other areas that were open to competition.[361] However, in many cases an appropriate comparator is not available;[362] or if the selected comparator's price requires adjustment to account for different circumstances, that gives rise to considerable problems. In *Valium*, the German courts had to consider the findings that Roche had engaged in excessive pricing (in contravention of the German equivalent of Article 82), on the basis of a comparison with the prices charged by another supplier of equivalent tranquilizers in the Netherlands, for Valium and Librium. On appeal against the Federal Cartel Authority's order that the prices be reduced by, respectively, 40 per cent and 35 per cent, the Berlin Higher Regional Court[363] varied this order to a 28 per cent reduction after incorporating a series of substantial uplifts over the comparator price to allow for the difference in costs structures between the Netherlands and Germany, for research costs (since the Dutch company was a generic manufacturer), and for the supplementary services offered by Roche and the goodwill in the brand. But on further appeal, the Federal Supreme Court[364] annulled the judgment, in part criticising one of the uplifts but also finding that it was necessary to take account of the fact that the Dutch company was infringing patents. Altogether, the Supreme Court held that given the many uncertainties involved, only a very significant excess over such a notional competitive price could constitute an abuse.[365]

---

[360] *British Leyland v Commission* (n 344, above) paras 25–30. The abuse could equally be seen as a form of price discrimination.

[361] *Bodson v Pompes Funèbres* (n 345, above) para 31. See also Case 395/87 *Ministère Public v Tournier* [1989] ECR 2521, [1991] 4 CMLR 248, para 38; Cases 110/88, etc, *Lucazeau v SACEM* [1989] ECR 2811, [1991] 4 CMLR 248, para 25 (comparison with other Member States may indicate abuse).

[362] As in the *Port of Helsingborg* decns, para 10.106, above. See also COMP/37.761 *Euromax/IMAX*, decn of 25 March 2004, where the Commission held that the complainant Euromax had failed to produce a valid comparator against which to assess IMAX's equipment rental prices, particularly because the IMAX brand had a high value not shared by competitors' brands. The Commission also found there was no evidence that IMAX's rental charges were excessive or unfair and that it was not an abuse for IMAX to have moved from a business model where it sold projection equipment to a model where it only offered the equipment on rental terms.

[363] Case Kart 41/74 *Valium Librium*, judgment of the Kammergericht of 5 January 1976, WuW/E OLG 1645.

[364] Case KVR 2/76 *Valium I*, judgment of 16 December 1976, WuW/E BGH 1445.

[365] When the case returned to the Federal Supreme Court on appeal from the Kammergericht's revised judgment, the finding of abuse was quashed altogether since it emerged that the turnover in these drugs by the Dutch company was so very much smaller than that of Roche that it could not provide a suitable comparison at all: Case KVR 3/79 *Valium II*, judgment of 12 February 1980, WuW/E BGH 1678, [1980] ECC 220.

Benchmark price. The fact that the price charged provides a high margin over **10.108** cost is not conclusive of abuse. For example, for pharmaceutical drugs, it is generally recognised that the revenue earned from the drugs which are brought to market has to cover the manufacturer's research and development costs which embrace also other drugs that never reach production.[366] Moreover, as the English Court of Appeal emphasised in *Attheraces Ltd v British Horseracing Board*, the law on excessive pricing is about the distortion of competition and safeguarding the interests of consumers and not about controlling excessive profits. Whereas costs plus a reasonable profit margin ('cost +') may represent a baseline below which a price could not be considered excessive, a price above that figure is not necessarily abusive. While in theory it is relevant to consider the price that could be charged in a competitive market, in the absence of an effective comparator determination of that price is a speculative exercise that is difficult to carry out with sufficient certainty. As the Court of Appeal stated: 'even a hypothetically competitive market may yield a rate of profit above, as well as below, the reasonable margin represented by cost +'.[367] Furthermore, calculation of what is a 'reasonable profit' can itself be a contentious exercise.[368] The Dutch Competition Authority has adopted the approach of comparing the profit to a standard return deemed to be the minimum profit which would have to be achieved to meet the cost of capital. In determining the standard return, the Authority applies the weighted average cost of capital method ('WACC'). The WACC comprises an amount for the cost of shareholders' equity and loan capital, weighted for the relative share of the respective capital components. For example, in *UPC Nederland and NV Casema*,[369]

---

[366] See *Valium I* (n 364, above).

[367] *Attheraces Ltd v British Horseracing Board* (n 351), above, para 208, approving Laddie J in *BHB Enterprises Ltd v Victor Chandler (International) Ltd* [2005] EWHC 1074 (Ch), [2005] UKCLR 787. Note also *Telecom Corp of New Zealand v Clear Communications Ltd* [1995] 1 NZLR 385, where the Privy Council held, under the equivalent of Art 82 in New Zealand's competition law, that the test was whether the prices were higher than those that a hypothetical firm would seek in a perfectly contestable market; however, application of this principle in the light of conflicting economic evidence to determine whether charges for access to an essential facility were excessive gave rise to considerable difficulties.

[368] See, eg Case 66/86 *Ahmed Saeed Flugreisen v Zentrale zur Bekämpfung unlauteren Wettbewerbs* [1989] ECR 803, [1990] 4 CMLR 102, para 43 (according to Dir 87/601, Art 3 air tariffs 'must be reasonably related to the long-term fully allocated costs of the air carrier, while taking into account the needs of consumers, the need for a satisfactory return on capital, the competitive market situation, including the fares of the other air carriers operating on the route, and the need to prevent dumping'). Already in its *Fifth Report on Competition Policy* (1975), point 3, the Commission had observed that 'it is difficult to tell whether in any given case an abusive price has been set for there is no objective way of establishing exactly what price covers cost plus a reasonable profit margin'.

[369] Cases 3528 and 3588 *UPC Nederland and N. V. Casema*, decn of Dutch Competition Authority (the 'NMa'), 27 September 2005. See also Case 05-46 *Interpay*, NMa decn of 22 December 2005, withdrawing its earlier decn that the JV between eight banks that supplied network services for PIN payments had charged excessive tariffs, since there was insufficient proof that the tariffs were excessive (but the decn finding a violation of the prohibition on cartels by reason of the horizontal agreement between the constituent banks was confirmed).

two cable television companies were alleged to have charged excessive prices for analogue standard packages. For prices to be excessive, the Authority ruled that return rates have to be durable and significantly higher than the WACC. It also has to be likely that these rates can also be obtained in the future. On the facts of the case, the Authority found no abuse since it was unlikely that the return rates achieved were durable and significantly higher than the WACC. Furthermore, there was no guarantee that the high return rates could be realised in the near future, due to market developments in the sector. The Authority also noted that a high return, in the long run, enhances competition because it creates an incentive for new parties to enter the market.

10.109   **Economic value.**   The second limb of the test under *United Brands* involves consideration of the 'economic value' of the product. This directs attention to the nature of the product itself and the circumstances in which it is used by the purchaser. For some some products, 'economic value' needs to reflect many factors other than the seller's costs of what is being supplied, which in some cases may be minimal.[370] To charge for the supply of copyright works a royalty calculated as a percentage of the turnover or profit made by the purchaser is standard practice; whereas such a royalty could be abusive if the rate was excessive, it could not be contended that this method of charging was abusive solely on the ground that it is unrelated to the supplier's cost of production.[371] Similarly, when a sporting body or association sells the broadcasting rights to its events, what is supplied is essentially a licence to enter the stadium and film, the cost of which to the supplier is negligible. In *Attheraces Ltd v British Horseracing Board*,[372] the English courts were confronted with the allegation that the governing body of British horse racing was charging an excessive price to a television broadcaster for access to the 'pre-race data' that set out the riders and horses, with all identifying details, running in each race. The television channel was broadcast to overseas betting shops, and needed this data to complement their pictures. The Court of Appeal held it was relevant to have regard to the fact this was not a stand-alone product but a secondary product the commercialisation of which helped to fund British racing,

---

370   See, eg Case 298/83 *CICCE v Commission* [1985] ECR 1105, [1986] 1 CMLR 486: although the case concerned an allegation of unfairly *low* prices paid by French television companies for film rights, the ECJ's approach in upholding the Commission's rejection of the complaint shows that the question of fair pricing in such a case cannot be reduced to a simplistic cost + formula; see also per AG Lenz at 1114 (ECR), 497 (CMLR).

371   *Ministère Public v Tournier* and *Lucazeau v SACEM* (n 361, above). Those cases concerned discotheques: cf Case C-52/07 *Kanal 5 and TV4*, not yet decided, where the Swedish Market Court has referred the question whether a percentage of overall revenue basis for calculation of royalty is unfair as applied to television broadcasters whose use of copyright music is more limited. See also the national court decns on copyright collecting societies, para 10.134, below.

372   n 351, above.

the primary product which gave the pre-race data its value.[373] Furthermore, following the *Port of Helsingborg* cases, the revenue earned by the broadcaster in supplying the data to betting shops in a competitive downstream market was important in determining the product's 'economic value'.

The UK Competition Appeal Tribunal decision in *Napp*.   The first appeal **10.110** to come before the UK Competition Appeal Tribunal under section 18 of the Competition Act 1998 (the UK equivalent of Article 82) concerned excessive pricing and provides a rare illustration of how such abuse can be effectively established. *Napp*[374] concerned a pharmaceutical product that was supplied both in hospitals and in the community. It was found that Napp had abused its dominant position by charging abusively low and predatory prices in the hospital sector (to retain its monopoly position) and at the same time charging abusively high prices in the much larger community sector.[375] There were links between the two sectors resulting from patterns of prescribing that rendered the hospital sector the effective 'gateway' to the lucrative community sector. Thus, although both predation and excessive pricing can in general be seen as 'own market' abuses, the case provides an illustration of a linkage that can occur between the two forms of abuse, excessive prices in the community providing the rationale for predation in sales to hospitals.[376] As regards the test for excessive pricing, the Tribunal accepted as 'soundly based in the circumstances of the present case' the statement of the Director General of Fair Trading that a price was excessive:

> 'if it is above that which would exist in a competitive market and where it is clear that high profits will not stimulate successful new entry within a reasonable period. Therefore, to show that prices are excessive, it must be demonstrated that (i) prices are higher than would be expected in a competitive market, and (ii) there is no effective competitive pressure to bring them down to competitive levels, nor is there likely to be.'[377]

The Tribunal also approved the following tests that could reasonably be applied to determine whether a price was excessive:

> 'In the present case, the methods used by the Director are various comparisons of (i) Napp's prices with Napp's costs, (ii) Napp's prices with the costs of its next most

---

[373] cf the position where the primary activity is itself a profitable monopoly: *ITT/Belgacom*, *XXVIIth Report on Competition Policy* (1997), p 152: after the Commission commenced proceedings, the Belgian incumbent telephone operator reduced to a cost-oriented basis the prices on which it made available to publishers of telephone directories data regarding subscribers to its voice telephony services. See also the decision of the Brussels Commercial Court, *ITT Promedia NV v Belgacom* [1996] 3 CMLR 130.

[374] *Napp Pharmaceutical Holdings Ltd v Director General of Fair Trading* [2002] CAT 1, [2002] CompAR 13.

[375] 86–90 per cent of supply was made to the community segment of the market.

[376] The situation was thus unusual in that recoupment for the below-cost pricing was in effect immediate, through the supra-competitive prices in the community sector.

[377] *Napp*, above, paras 390–391.

profitable competitor, (iii) Napp's prices with those of its competitors and (iv) Napp's prices with prices charged by Napp in other markets. Those methods seem to us to be among the approaches that may reasonably be used to establish excessive prices, although there are, no doubt, other methods.'[378]

It was those comparisons, taken together, which led to the conclusion that Napp's prices in the community segment were well above those that would prevail in a competitive market; and the Tribunal accordingly upheld the decision. It is notable that excessive pricing was accordingly established by an accumulation of comparisons, not a single test; and that these included comparison with competitors' prices on the same market and with the dominant company's own prices for its other products.

(e) Related market abuses: exclusionary pricing

10.111 **'Leveraging' as a common form of abuse.** Many cases under Article 82 involve some form of 'leveraging' by an undertaking from a market or market sector where the dominant firm enjoys exceptional market power (often based on some form of monopoly right or superior product or service) to another market or market sector that is more readily contestable. Such cases often, but not always, involve exclusionary abuses on 'related markets'.[379] Thus, a common theme in most if not all 'related market' abuses (such as margin squeezing,[380] tying and bundling,[381] and refusal to deal[382]) is the use of market power on one market significantly to distort competition on a related market, normally to the advantage of the dominant undertaking or a related company. However, although predatory pricing,[383] exclusive dealing,[384] and fidelity rebates and selective discounting schemes[385] are naturally seen as 'own market' abuses, they can also be seen as 'leveraging' cases.[386] The underlying vice of such conduct is the use of market power (on that segment of the market where the dominant supplier has a legitimate market advantage) to prevent or restrict competition at the margins (where other smaller suppliers may

---

[378] ibid, para 392.

[379] See, eg Case C-311/84 *CBEM v CLT and IPB ('Télémarketing')* [1985] ECR 3261, [1986] 2 CMLR 558; *Napier Brown/British Sugar*, OJ 1988 L 284/41, [1990] 4 CMLR 196; Case T-30/89 *Hilti v Commission* [1991] ECR II-1439, [1992] 4 CMLR 16 (on appeal from *Hilti*, OJ 1988 L65/19, [1989] 4 CMLR 677); Case C-333/94P *Tetra Pak v Commission* [1996] ECR I-5951, [1997] 4 CMLR 662, [1997] All ER (EC) 4.

[380] Paras 10.112 *et seq*, below.

[381] Paras 10.119 *et seq*, below.

[382] Paras 10.125 *et seq*, below.

[383] Paras 10.070 *et seq*, above.

[384] Paras 10.098 *et seq*, below.

[385] Paras 10.091 *et seq*, below.

[386] See, eg *Tetra Pak v Commission (Tetra Pak II)* where Tetra Pak was found to have engaged in predatory pricing in the market for non-aseptic packaging where it was not dominant: para 10.076, above.

be able to compete more effectively). Issues of objective justification are of particular importance in such cases.[387]

(i) Margin squeezing

Price or margin squeezing.   A vertically integrated undertaking, which is dominant on an upstream market, may be able to favour its own downstream operations as against potential downstream competitors by charging the latter input prices at a level which leaves them insufficient margin to compete effectively in the downstream market. This is sometimes called 'price squeezing' or 'margin squeezing'.[388] It is of increasing significance and concern in the context of access pricing to networks, where a crucial issue is the price at which the network owner can be required to provide access and thereby to facilitate competition on the downstream market. Price squeezing can be seen as a form of price discrimination (the upstream supplier discriminates in favour of its own downstream arm against all other customers). It may also be linked to predation on the downstream market, since if a dominant undertaking lowers the prices charged by its related business on the downstream market sufficiently, competing firms may be unable to match those downstream prices at the input prices charged by the dominant undertaking on the upstream market. But if the undertaking is not dominant on the downstream market, such conduct would not constitute predatory pricing abuse, as discussed above. Price squeezing may also reflect excessive pricing on the upstream market, as the dominant undertaking uses its monopoly power to extract excess profits on that market while eliminating competition on the downstream market. However, the essence of this head of abuse is not conduct on the upstream market or on the downstream market seen in isolation, but the relation between the two. As with other pricing abuses, difficult questions of fact frequently arise in determining the appropriate margin that is required to sustain competition on the downstream market without requiring the dominant upstream supplier to allow inefficient competition to its downstream business.[389] A price squeeze may be demonstrated by showing that the dominant undertaking's own downstream operation could not trade profitably on the basis of the price charged to its competitors by its upstream arm.

10.112

---

[387] See, eg the issues of objective justification raised in the *Hilti* and *Tetra Pak II* cases in relating to tying abuses, considered at para 10.124, below. Other 'own market' abuses such as excessive (or predatory) pricing tend to involve equivalent issues of justification as an integral part of the analysis of whether the price is excessively high (or low) rather than as a distinct issue: see, eg para 10.078, above.

[388] Case T-5/97 *Industrie des Phoudres Sphériques v Commission* [2000] ECR II-3755, [2001] 4 CMLR 1020, para 178.

[389] For economic discussion arguing that only if the downstream market is uncompetitive can price squeezing constitute an abuse, see Crocini and Veljanovski, 'Price Squeezes, Foreclosure and Competition Law' (2003) 4 J Network Ind 3.

10.113 **The Commission's practice.** In *Napier Brown/British Sugar*[390] the Commission found that British Sugar contravened Article 82 by virtue of the prices it charged to packagers for the supply of bulk sugar, having regard to the prices which it was itself setting in the downstream market for packaged sugar. The margin that British Sugar allowed between its bulk and packaged prices was insufficient to cover the company's own costs in the packaged market, despite its efficiency in packaging and selling. It thus disadvantaged third party packagers and restricted competition in the packaged market. In *Deutsche Telekom*[391] the Commission found that Deutsche Telekom ('DT') had exercised a margin squeeze on its competitors. DT controlled access to the local network (or local loop) which was essential for any operator wishing to compete with DT in the downstream retail market. DT charged a price for such access which meant that its competitors downstream could not supply their retail customers at a price which covered their costs without charging much higher prices than DT. In fact, DT's wholesale prices upstream were higher than its retail prices downstream. Therefore even an equally efficient competitor was left with no possibility profitably to compete with DT's retail operation.[392]

10.114 **Domestic cases on margin squeezing: *Genzyme*.** The UK Competition Appeal Tribunal addressed the issue of margin squeeze in its judgment in *Genzyme*.[393] *Genzyme* concerned the supply of homecare services to patients being treated with the drug Cerezyme. Genzyme Homecare supplied Cerezyme to the National Health Service (the 'NHS') for the treatment of patients at home at a price of £2.975 per unit. This unit price included both the cost of the drug and the costs involved in providing homecare services, that is delivering the drug to the patient's home and administering it there. Genzyme Homecare supplied Cerezyme to other homecare service providers at the same price of £2.975 per unit. However, Genzyme Homecare, as a division of the Genzyme group, acquired Cerezyme at

---

[390] *Napier Brown/British* Sugar, OJ 1988 L284/41, [1990] 4 CMLR 196, para 66.

[391] *Deutsche Telekom*, OJ 2003 L263/9, [2004] 4 CMLR 790 (on appeal, Case T-271/03 *Deutsche Telekom v Commission*, not yet decided). See also the Commission Notice on the application of the competition rules to access agreements in the telecommunications sector, OJ 1998 C265/2: Vol II, App E.24, paras 117–119.

[392] ibid, paras 102–111 and 199. Subsequently the Commission accepted commitments to put an end to alleged margin squeeze in relation to charges for shared access to local loops: COMP/38.436 *QSC AG/Deutsche Telekom*, Press Releases IP/04/281 (1 March 2004) and IP/05/1033 (3 August 2005). See also *National Carbonising Co*, OJ 1976 L35/2, [1976] 1 CMLR D82 (an interim measures decn); COMP/38.784 *Telefónica* MEMO/07/274 (4 July 2007): the Commission fined the Spanish incumbent telecoms operator for applying a margin squeeze in the Spanish broadband Internet access markets.

[393] *Genzyme Ltd v Office of Fair Trading* [2004] CAT 4, [2004] CompAR 358. See also *Freeserve. com v Director General of Telecommunications* [2003] CAT 5, [2003] CompAR 202; *Albion Water Ltd v Water Services Regulation Authority (Dŵr Cymru/Shotton Paper)* [2006] CAT 23 and 36, [2007] CompAR 22, 328. See also CA98/20/2002 *BSkyB*, OFT decns of 17 December 2002 and 29 July 2003, [2003] UKCLR 240, 1075.

a transfer price of £2.50 per unit and could therefore earn a margin of some £0.475 per unit on its sales of Cerezyme including homecare services to the NHS. An independent homecare services provider, Healthcare at Home, having acquired Cerezyme from Genzyme Homecare at £2.975 per unit, resold Cerezyme and provided homecare services to the NHS at the same price of £2.975 per unit. Consequently, Healthcare at Home could not earn any margin on the supply of homecare services to the NHS unless it charged a higher price than was available to the NHS from Genzyme. The Tribunal found that Genzyme's pricing policy (for which there was no objective justification) of bundling together the drug and the homecare services constituted a margin squeeze, the effect of which was to force Healthcare at Home to sustain a loss in the provision of homecare services. It also found that no undertaking, regardless of how efficient it might be, could trade profitably in those circumstances in the downstream supply of homecare services.[394] Therefore the likely consequence was that Healthcare at Home would exit the market, so the effect of Genzyme's margin squeeze would be to monopolise the supply of homecare services.[395]

Genzyme: **remedies.**   As an interim remedy, Genzyme was required to supply **10.115** Healthcare at Home with Cerezyme at a fixed discount off the NHS price and ordered not to supply other third party providers on more favourable terms than those offered to Healthcare at Home.[396] In its final judgment on remedy,[397] the Tribunal described its task as having to determine what ex-manufacturer price for Cerezyme would enable a reasonably efficient homecare services provider to supply its services to patients and in so doing earn a competitive return. In dealing with that question, the Tribunal looked at information from three different sources: (i) historical information; (ii) indicative estimates by other potential providers; and (iii) detailed information about Healthcare at Home's costs. The Tribunal noted that the risks associated with a remedy that may undercompensate third party homecare services providers by setting the price too high were greater than those associated with overcompensation by setting the price too low. Overcompensation could be expected to encourage competing providers to tender for contracts to provide homecare services in future and to compete any such increased price away, over time. On the other hand, if from the start the remedy were to undercompensate third party providers, it is likely that competition would be muted immediately and possibly irremediably, since existing providers would withdraw and new providers would not enter the market.

---

[394] *Genzyme*, above, para 552.
[395] ibid, paras 553–555.
[396] *Genzyme* [2003] CAT 8, [2003] CompAR 290.
[397] *Genzyme* [2005] CAT 32, [2006] CompAR 195.

(ii) Cross-subsidisation

10.116 **Cross-subsidies.** Thus far, the Commission has dealt with the issue of cross-subsidies largely in the context of the postal services sector. Indeed, the Commission has cast doubt on whether the principles established in these decisions are of general application, outside the situation where a company operates both in an area protected by statutory monopoly and in an area open to competition. In the two *Port of Helsingborg* decisions,[398] among the complaints about the charges imposed by the Port on ferry operators was an allegation that the profits derived from the ferry operations were used to cover the losses generated by the Port's other operations. The Commission held that this could not be regarded as being an abuse in itself. Outside the context of State-supported monopoly rights as exist in the postal sector, the extension of a dominant position to another market would normally constitute an infringement only when it weakens or reduces the degree of competition in the subsidised market.[399] There was no evidence that the use of profits derived from the ferry operations to cover the losses generated by the other operations would weaken or reduce competition in the neighbouring market for the provision of port facilities and services to cargo vessels where the Port of Helsingborg was in competition with other ports.

10.117 **Cross-subsidies in the postal services sector.** *Deutsche Post*[400] was the first case in which the Commission expressly dealt with the issue of cross-subsidies (although this was implicit in the *Tetra Pak II* decision).[401] The Commission defined cross-subsidisation as follows:

> '. . . where the earnings from a given service do not suffice to cover the incremental costs of providing that service and where there is another service or bundle of services the earnings from which exceed the stand-alone costs. The service for which revenue exceeds stand-alone cost is the source of the cross subsidy and the service in which revenue does not cover the incremental costs is its destination.'[402]

Deutsche Post had a statutory monopoly in Germany over the basic letter post and had a universal service obligation in over-the-counter parcel services. It also operated in the mail order parcel market, which was open to competition. UPS, a competitor in the mail order sector, complained that Deutsche Post was using revenue from its profitable letter post monopoly to sustain a policy of below-cost selling in the mail order parcels sector, thereby cross-subsidising the activity open to competition

---

[398] *Scandlines v Port of Helsingborg, Sundbusserne v Port of Helsingborg*, para 10.106, above.

[399] *Scandlines* (n 354, above) para 271; *Sundbusserne* (ibid) para 228.

[400] *Deutsche Post AG – mail order parcel services*, OJ 2001 L125/27, [2001] 5 CMLR 99.

[401] *Tetra Pak II*, OJ 1992 L72/1, [1992] 4 CMLR 551, paras 147–159 (appeal dismissed, Case T-83/91 *Tetra Pak v Commission* [1994] ECR II-755, [1997] 4 CMLR 726; further appeal dismissed, Case C-333/94P *Tetra Pak v Commission* [1996] ECR I-5951, [1997] 4 CMLR 662, [1997] All ER (EC) 4.

[402] *Deutsche Post AG– mail order parcel services* (n 400, above) para 6.

from the activity in which it held a statutory monopoly. To evaluate this complaint, it was necessary for the Commission to identify the relevant costs for the different segments of Deutsche Post's business and in particular for the mail order parcel service. The Commission looked at the 'incremental cost' of the mail order parcel service, which it described as solely comprising 'costs incurred in providing a specific parcel service' but not including 'the fixed costs not incurred only as a result of providing a specific service (the common fixed costs)'.[403] Even using this measure of cost, the Commission found that Deutsche Post did not earn enough from its mail order service to cover costs and was operating this service at a loss. However, *Deutsche Post* does not suggest that cross-subsidisation is an abuse in itself. It was the below-cost predatory pricing of a particular service that the Commission condemned: the cross-subsidisation merely facilitated that predatory pricing. In *UPS*,[404] another case concerning Deutsche Post, the Court of First Instance upheld the rejection by the Commission of a complaint by UPS Europe that it was an abuse of Deutsche Post's dominant position to use profits which it derived from activities for which it enjoyed a legal monopoly to finance the acquisition of control in a company which was active on a non-reserved market. The Court found that in the absence of any evidence to show that the funds used by Deutsche Post for the acquisition were derived from abusive practices in the reserved letter market, the mere fact that it used those funds to acquire joint control of an undertaking active in a neighbouring market open to competition did not in itself, even if the source of those funds was the reserved market, raise any problem from the standpoint of the competition rules and could not therefore constitute an infringement of Article 82.[405]

(f) Related market abuses: exclusionary non-price practices

Tying, bundling and refusal to supply. Many of the cases under Article 82 concern the exercise of market power by a dominant undertaking that 'leverages' its legitimate success in a way that is considered illegitimate. There is now a substantial case law on the use of market power to influence conditions of competition on related markets that is not directly or essentially a matter of pricing. In that regard, the two most significant categories of recognised abuse are: **10.118**

(i) *Tying and bundling.* This is a straightforward abuse, at least in principle, in that it consists in a dominant undertaking compelling customers for one product also to acquire another product. The undertaking thereby leverages its power on the 'tying' market on which it is dominant so as to influence conditions of competition on the 'tied' market.

---

[403] ibid, para 6, fn 5.

[404] Case T-175/99 *UPS Europe v Commission* [2002] ECR II-1915, [2002] 5 CMLR 67.

[405] ibid, para 61. Similarly, see the judgment of the English High Court, *Getmapping v Ordinance Survey* [2002] EWHC 1089 (Ch), [2002] UKCLR 410.

(ii) *Refusal to supply.* This form of abuse is theoretically controversial but its essential characteristic is that an undertaking refuses access to the product market on which it is dominant and thereby prevents or restricts competition on another market, normally a market on which it also has an interest but where its market position is considerably weaker or less well protected from actual or potential competition. In the absence of such a leveraging effect, refusal to supply customers would in general simply lead to a perverse reduction in the dominant firm's business.[406]

(i) Tying and bundling

10.119 **Introduction.**[407] The abuses cited in Article 82 include, in sub-paragraph (d):

> '. . . making the conclusion of contracts subject to acceptance by the other parties of supplementary obligations which, by their nature or according to commercial usage, have no connection with the subject of such contracts'

Such an abuse involves what is often referred to as 'tying' or 'bundling'. In several important cases, the Commission has condemned the imposition of tying obligations and imposed heavy fines. A typical example of tying is where the dominant firm is prepared to supply the product in respect of which it holds a dominant position ('the tying product') only if the customer also agrees to buy another product ('the tied product'). The dominant firm may not be dominant in the supply of the tied product, the mischief being the attempt to extend its market strength into the market of the tied product, to the detriment not only of its customer but also of its competitors in the supply of the tied product. Tying and bundling arise where what is on offer comprises two distinct products rather than a combination of different components in a single product; for example, the supply of shoelaces in shoes or buttons on clothing will not be regarded as a tie-in or bundle. The issue in respect of tying and bundling is therefore essentially one of fact: to distinguish between cases where there is a sufficient connection between the two products for it to be appropriate for them to be supplied jointly, as against those cases where competition law should intervene. This may be a difficult question

---

406 The only other natural rationale for such conduct would be pressure from powerful *purchasers* to strengthen their own position on the downstream market by limiting supplies to their competitors. Such conduct can form the basis for a serious breach of Art 81 where there is collusion between competitors and their suppliers that distorts competition on the downstream market (see, eg the decn of the UK Competition Appeal Tribunal, *JJB Sports and Allsports v Office of Fair Trading* [2004] CAT 17, [2005] CompAR 29; upheld on appeal, *JJB Sports plc v Office of Fair Trading* [2006] EWCA Civ 1318, [2006] UKCLR 1135: see further para 2.049, above).
407 For a comparative study of EC and US law, considering the economic issues and arguing that there should be greater scope for objective justification for tied sales, see Carron, *Les transactions couplées en droit de la concurrence* (2004); for economic analysis, including case studies, see Nalebuff and Majerus, *Bundling, Tying, and Portfolio Effects*, UK DTI Economics Paper No. 1 (2003). The US Supreme Court considered tie-ins in *Eastman Kodak v Image Technical Services*, 504 US 451, 112 SCt 2072 (1992).

where it is alleged that the bundled or tied products should be regarded as the component parts of a single, wider system or service.[408] As Article 82(d) itself makes clear, these are questions that need to be addressed partly by reference to the characteristics of the goods or services in question ('by their nature') and partly as a matter of commercial reality ('according to commercial usage'). A helpful approach is to determine whether, from the perspective of consumer demand, there is an independent market for *each* of the products in question, that is to say including the alleged tying product in its unbundled form.[409]

'Pure' 'technical' and 'mixed' bundling.   There are no universally accepted **10.120** definitions of the various forms of tying and bundling. The two terms themselves are often used without distinction, although in the strict sense tying may be thought of as arising when an undertaking sells the tied product separately but will not sell the tying product separately, whereas bundling arises when an undertaking will not sell either product separately but only the two together as a package. Moreover, in either case similar results can be achieved indirectly by forms of pricing, and the economic effects of the different arrangements do not necessarily relate to their formal nature. In *General Electric*,[410] the Court of First Instance was concerned with a challenge to a Commission decision under the merger regime and not with abuse under Article 82, but the Court identified three kinds of bundling when considering whether the merged entity might engage in conduct that would create or strengthen a dominant position. The case involved the proposed merger of General Electric, which was found to be dominant in the supply of jet engines for large commercial aircraft, and Honeywell, which supplied avionics and non-avionic products also for incorporation into aircraft. Neither party was a supplier of the other's products prior to the merger but the Commission prohibited the merger on the ground, *inter alia*, that the combined undertaking would have the ability and incentive to force customers buying its jet engines to take its avionics and non-avionic products, and vice versa. The Court distinguished between three types of practice: pure bundling (where sales are tied by means of a purely commercial obligation to purchase two or more products together); technical bundling (where sales are tied by means of the technical integration of the

---

[408]   This issue was raised in both Case T-30/89 *Hilti v Commission* [1991] ECR II-1439, [1992] 4 CMLR 16 (not challenged in the appeal to the ECJ in Case C-53/92P [1994] ECR I-667, [1994] 4 CMLR 614, paras 45 *et seq*) and *Tetra Pak II*, OJ 1992 L72/1, [1992] 4 CMLR 551, paras 118–119. For those cases, see further para 10.121, below. Bundling of computer software is a major issue in the *Microsoft* case, para 10.122, below.

[409]   See the Irish Supreme Court in *Competition Authority v O'Regan* [2007] IESC 22, paras 116 *et seq* holding that the supply of savings protection by the Irish League of Credit Unions (ILCU) to its member unions was not a distinct product that could be distinguished from the ILCU's function in representing its members. Hence in the example given in the text, there is no demand for laced shoes without shoelaces.

[410]   Case T-210/01 *General Electric v Commission* [2005] ECR II-5575, [2006] 4 CMLR 686.

products); and mixed bundling (where a number of products are sold as a package on more favourable terms than if the products are purchased separately).[411] Mixed bundling may represent an efficiency saving, and thus not constitute an abuse at all, or it may be a form of exclusionary pricing designed to squeeze competitors in the other products out of the market.[412] An example of the latter was *La Poste/ De Post*,[413] where the Commission imposed a fine of €2.5 million on the Belgian national postal operator for offering to customers of its general letter mail service (in which it held a statutory monopoly) a preferential rate on condition that they accepted a supplementary contract with regard to a new business-to-business mail service (an area open to competition). Such pricing is equivalent to a bundled rebate, where a firm makes a rebate on the price for the product in respect of which it is dominant dependent upon the purchase also of one or more other products in which it faces competition.[414]

10.121 **Consumables tied with machinery.**   In two important cases, the Commission and the Community Courts have considered a form of tying whereby the manufacturer of a machine or machine parts ties the purchaser into buying also the associated consumables. In *Hilti*, the undertaking was dominant in the supply of power actuated nail guns and of the 'consumables' used in those guns, namely the cartridge strips and nails. However, there were a number of nail producers who were able to produce nails which were compatible with the Hilti machines but who were not able or willing to produce the cartridge strips. Hilti took steps to tie the supply of nails into the supply of cartridge strips to ensure that customers who purchased cartridge strips from Hilti also bought from Hilti the corresponding number of nails for use with those cartridges. In particular, Hilti:

(i) refused to supply customers with cartridge strips without the accompanying appropriate number of nails;

---

411 ibid, para 406.

412 In contrast, 'pure' or 'technical' bundling may not only be exclusionary but also enable the dominant firm to extract a higher effective price for the second, tied product than if it was sold separately.

413 *La Post/De Post*, OJ 2002 L61/32, [2002] 4 CMLR 1426.

414 See *Hilti*, para 10.121, below. Bundled rebates were one of the principal forms of abuse found in *LePage's, Inc v 3M*, 324 F3d 141 (3d Cir, 2003) (en banc), cert denied, 542 US 953 (2004). Note also the converse situation where a firm offers a rebate on the price of a product for which it is not dominant on condition that the purchaser also acquires the product on which it faces competition: see, eg *Telekom Austria*, Case 16 Ok 11/03, 17 November 2003, [2005] ECC 541, where the Austrian Supreme Court upheld the order of the Austrian competition authority finding abuse by the former incumbent telephone network operator through its sales offer of cordless telephones at half price on condition that the purchaser agreed to exclude call-by-call carrier pre-selection (ie the facility to select which network would carry the call); Telekom Austria was dominant in the market for fixed line call origination but not in the market for the sale of telephones.

(ii) granted special discounts for the combined purchase of nails and cartridge strips;

(iii) refused to supply the competing nail producers with cartridge strips and took steps to prevent its customers and its exclusive distributors from supplying cartridge strips to the other nail suppliers; and

(iv) refused to honour its guarantee for the tools where they had been used with consumables of other than Hilti provenance.

The Commission held that this conduct was abusive and the decision was upheld by the Court of First Instance.[415] Similarly, in *Tetra Pak II* the Commission, upheld by the Court of First Instance and the Court of Justice, condemned clauses whereby Tetra Pak tied the sale of carton packaging materials to the sale of its filling machines by requiring the purchasers of the machines to agree to purchase from Tetra Pak all their supplies of cartons.[416] Tetra Pak argued that tied sales were justified on the grounds that there was a natural link between cartons and filling machines and that tied sales of the two were normal commercial usage. The Court of Justice upheld the Court of First Instance's rejection of that argument on the facts, adding that even where tied sales of two products are in accordance with commercial usage or there is a natural link between those products, such sales may still constitute abuse within the meaning of Article 82 unless they are objectively justified.[417]

Microsoft: **technical bundling.** In *Microsoft*,[418] after an exhaustive investigation lasting more than five years, the Commission decided that Microsoft had infringed Article 82 by leveraging its near monopoly power in the market for PC operating systems onto the markets for work group server operating systems and for media players. It had done this by deliberately restricting interoperability between Windows and non-Microsoft work group servers, and by bundling its Windows Media Player (WMP), a product where it faced competition, with

10.122

---

[415] *Eurofix-Bauco v Hilti*, OJ 1988 L65/19, [1989] 4 CMLR 677; appeal dismissed, Case T-30/89 *Hilti v Commission* [1991] ECR II-1439, [1992] 4 CMLR 16 (further appeal on other grounds dismissed, Case C-53/92P, [1994] ECR I-667, [1994] 4 CMLR 617). See also *London European/SABENA*, OJ 1988 L317/47, [1989] 4 CMLR 662; *Napier Brown/British Sugar* (n 390, above); *Decca Navigator System*, OJ 1989 L43/27, [1990] 4 CMLR 627; *Novo Nordisk*, XXVIth *Report on Competition Policy* (1996), point 62 and p 142 (refusal by pharmaceutical manufacturer to honour guarantees for its 'insulin pens' when used in conjunction with other manufacturer's components).

[416] *Tetra Pak II*, OJ 1992 L72/1, [1992] 4 CMLR 551 (appeals dismissed: Case T-83/91 *Tetra Pak v Commission* [1994] ECR II-755, [1997] 4 CMLR 726; Case C-333/94P *Tetra Pak v Commission* [1996] ECR I-5951, [1997] 4 CMLR 662, [1997] All ER (EC) 4).

[417] Case C-333/94P *Tetra Pak v Commission*, above, para 37.

[418] Case COMP/37.792 *Microsoft*, 24 March 2004, [2005] 4 CMLR 965. See also *IBM settlement*, XIVth *Report on Competition Policy* (1984), points 94–95, [1984] 3 CMLR 147.

its ubiquitous Windows operating system. This enabled it to acquire a dominant position in the market for work group servers and significantly to weaken competition on the media player market. Microsoft had argued that WMP is an integral part of Windows, not a distinct product, pointing out that other software vendors integrate media playing technology into their PC operating systems. In rejecting this argument, the Commission relied strongly on the existence of a separate market in the supply of media players as demonstrating consumer demand for a distinct product.[419] The Commission levied a fine of €497.2 million in addition to imposing other remedies to improve interoperability in relation to work group servers and remove the tying effect in relation to WMP. The decision is under appeal, but Microsoft's application for interim measures suspending the decision was refused by the President of the Court of First Instance.[420]

10.123 **Tying of other ancillary services.** A tying obligation imposed in respect of services which are ancillary to the supply of the principal product may infringe Article 82. In *Tetra Pak II*[421] the Court of First Instance held that clauses requiring the customer to obtain its maintenance and repair services (including supplies of any spare parts) for the machines from Tetra Pak were abusive. The clauses were not limited to the guarantee period but applied for the whole life of the machine and were not therefore justified by the contractual responsibility which the guarantee placed on Tetra Pak. The Court further held that the restrictive terms were part of an overall strategy aimed at making the customer totally dependent on Tetra Pak for the entire life of the machine, thereby excluding competition at the level of both cartons and machines. In *Napier Brown/British Sugar*,[422] the Commission held that it was abusive to pursue a policy of delivered rather than ex-factory pricing, such that the cost of transport to the customer's site was included in the price; British Sugar thereby reserved for itself the separate but ancillary activity of delivering the sugar which could otherwise be undertaken by an independent haulage

---

[419] ibid, paras 800–825. The Commission observed that unlike other suppliers of operating systems, Microsoft's media playing technology was integrated in a manner that made it unremoveable.

[420] Case T-201/04 *Microsoft v Commission*, judgment of 17 September 2007; see Postscript below. Order of 22 December 2004, Case T-201/04R, [2004] ECR II-4463, [2005] 4 CMLR 406. In July 2006 the Commission imposed a penalty payment of €280.5 million on Microsoft for its continued non-compliance with its obligations to make interoperability information available; that order was itself subject to appeal, Case T-271/06 *Microsoft v Commission*, but Microsoft has now withdrawn the appeal; see PS.001 below, n2.

[421] Case T-83/91 *Tetra Pak v Commission* (n 416, above) para 135 (the point was not raised on the appeal to the ECJ). See also *Digital, XXVIIth Report on Competition Policy* (1997), point 69 and p 153. cf COMP/37.761 *Euromax/IMAX*, decn of 25 March 2004: IMAX's insistence that hirers of its film projection equipment use its maintenance services was held not be an abuse. The Commission distinguished *Tetra Pak*, finding that IMAX's requirements regarding maintenance were justified by the fact that the equipment remained its property so it was entitled to ensure that it was maintained in good condition. IMAX also had a right to protect its know-how.

[422] *Napier Brown/British Sugar*, OJ 1988 L284/41, [1990] 4 CMLR 196.

contractor.[423] In *Genzyme*,[424] the price of the bundled product (a medicinal drug and the ancillary homecare services to patients) was the same as the price of the primary product alone (the drug). Although this could effectively squeeze out any independent supplier of homecare services, since there was no evidence that the only customer for both products (the UK National Health Service) wished to purchase homecare services separately from the drug, the UK Competition Appeal Tribunal held that the bundled price had not been shown in itself to constitute an abuse. However, the Tribunal found that there had been a margin squeeze abuse, which the bundled price had facilitated: charging a wholesale price for the drug to a competitor in the supply of homecare services that prevented it from earning sufficient margin in itself supplying a package of both products.[425]

Objective justification of tying practices. *Hilti* and *Tetra Pak II* provide good **10.124** examples of the difficulties that face a dominant firm in seeking to defend tying practices as objectively justified. Hilti argued that its wish to prevent the use of competing nails in its guns was motivated by considerations of safety and reliability, alleging deficiencies in competitors' nails which rendered them incompatible for use in Hilti nail guns. Hilti also relied on the extent of its duty of care under the laws of the Member States concerning product liability. The Court of First Instance rejected these arguments, holding that safety was a matter for the appropriate authorities in the United Kingdom, whom Hilti had taken no steps to alert, and afforded no justification for a dominant firm to eliminate products which it thought dangerous.[426] Similarly, the Court of First Instance rejected Tetra Pak's arguments that tying eliminated the difficult question of determining whether responsibility for any defect in the system was attributable to the supplier of the machine or to the supplier of the packaging material and that it was necessary to safeguard public health because of the dangers inherent in storing milk at ambient temperatures.[427] The reality appears to be that if tying is in fact found to

---

[423] See also *FAG—Flughafen Frankfurt/Main AG*, OJ 1998 L72/30, [1998] 4 CMLR 779 (airport authority, as the exclusive provider of airport facilities, could not reserve to itself groundhandling services); and see similar resolution of groundhandling problems at Athens airport: *XXVIIth Report on Competition Policy* (1997), points 131–134. See also refusal of access to essential facilities, paras 10.135 *et seq*, below.

[424] *Genzyme Ltd v Office of Fair Trading* [2004] CAT 4, [2004] CompAR 358, paras 527–548.

[425] See further para 10.114, above. cf Case 16 Ok 11/04, judgment of the Austrian Supreme Court of 11 October 2004: withdrawal by Telekom Austria of lower tariff for connection only service, so that cheapest tariff covered both connection and calling services, contravened Austrian equivalent of Art 82 since this foreclosed competing carriers offering long-distance calling services whose customers would need to acquire connection services from Telekom Austria.

[426] Case T-30/89 *Hilti v Commission* (n 415, above) paras 118–119.

[427] Case T-83/91 *Tetra Pak v Commission* (n 416, above) paras 134–141; Case C-333/94P *Tetra Pak v Commission* (n 416, above) paras 34–38. The CFI relied on Case 85/76 *Hoffmann-La Roche* [1979] ECR 461, [1979] 3 CMLR 211, paras 89–90; Case C-62/86 *AKZO v Commission* [1991] ECR I-3359, [1993] 5 CMLR 215, para 149 and its own judgment in Case T-65/89 *BPB Industries and British Gypsum v Commission* [1993] ECR II-389, [1993] 5 CMLR 32, para 68.

be present, it will be difficult to persuade a competition authority or court that the practice can be 'objectively justified',[428] and the passage cited above from the judgment of the Court of Justice in *Tetra Pak II* indicates that this may be the case even if the practice conforms with 'commercial usage' or the 'nature' of the products concerned.[429]

(ii) Refusal to supply

10.125 **Conceptual and policy difficulties relating to refusal to supply.** In a market economy, undertakings are generally free to choose for themselves the parties with whom they wish to enter into contractual relations.[430] In the case of dominant undertakings, however, it is clear from the case law that this freedom may be curtailed and a refusal to deal may constitute an abuse of dominance. Equally, an offer to supply only on terms that the supplier knows to be unacceptable will be a constructive refusal to supply.[431] The precise boundaries of the circumstances in which a dominant undertaking's refusal to deal may constitute an abuse remain to be determined. However, it is reasonably well established that a dominant supplier may be required, in the absence of objective justification, to maintain supplies to existing customers and to grant access to 'essential facilities' on a non-discriminatory basis to new customers. In determining the circumstances in which a refusal to deal may constitute an abuse, as against a legitimate commercial choice, it is necessary to have regard to the following considerations, identified by Advocate General Jacobs in *Bronner*:[432]

(i) the need for careful justification of any incursion into the right to choose one's trading partners and freely to dispose of one's property, which are rights generally recognised in the laws of the Member States;[433]

---

[428] But see *Euromax/IMAX* (n 421, above).

[429] Mixed bundling may in certain circumstances expand output and produce welfare enhancing effects that could exceed any potential foreclosure: see, eg Bishop and Walker (n 1 above), paras 6.56 *et seq*, and the example they give at para 6.62. But this has not been recognised as a defence so far in the case law, and the CFI judgment in *General Electric* (n 410, above) shows the danger of reliance on an economic theory without firm factual foundation on the evidence in the case. See also the DG Comp Discussion Paper (para 10.005, above) sect 8.2.3, considering how the foreclosure effect of bundling and tying should be assessed.

[430] The US Supreme Court ruling in *Trinko* (n 343, above) at 408, also addresses these issues of principle and sets out a relatively restrictive approach: 'as a general matter, the Sherman Act "does not restrict the long recognized right of [a] trader or manufacturer engaged in an entirely private business, freely to exercise his own independent discretion as to parties with whom he will deal." *United States v Colgate & Co.*, 250 U. S. 300, 307 (1919)'.

[431] *TACA*, OJ 1999 L95/1, [1999] 4 CMLR 1415, para 553 (on appeal, Cases T-191/98, etc, *Atlantic Container Line v Commission* [2003] ECR II-3275, [2005] 4 CMLR 1283); Cases C-147 & 148/97 *Deutsche Post* [2000] ECR I-825, [2000] 4 CMLR 838, paras 59–60; *Deutsche Post AG - Interception of cross-border mail*, OJ 2001 L331/40, [2002] 4 CMLR 598, para 141.

[432] Case C-7/97 *Bronner v Mediaprint* [1998] ECR I-7791, [1999] 4 CMLR 112, per AG Jacobs, Opinion, paras 56–59.

[433] See in regard to the right to property generally, Case T-65/98 *Van den Bergh Foods v Commission* [2003] ECR II-4653, [2004] 4 CMLR 1, [2005] All ER (EC) 418, paras 170–172 (appeal on

(ii) the need to balance conflicting considerations when justifying interference with a dominant undertaking's freedom to contract, in particular the desirability of preserving incentives to invest in production, purchasing and distribution facilities, which may be reduced if competitors were granted access to such facilities which the undertaking has developed for the purpose of its own business; and

(iii) the fact that the primary purpose of Article 82 is to prevent distortion of competition, in the interests of consumers, rather than to protect particular competitors.[434]

Accordingly, as Advocate General Jacobs observed in a later case, the obligations under Article 82 on a dominant undertaking to supply are in various respects circumscribed, and are in particular limited by the possibility of objective justification.[435] The following discussion of refusal to supply as an abuse considers, first, the cessation of supply to an existing customer; secondly, the refusal to licence intellectual property rights; and thirdly, the refusal to grant access to essential facilities.

Discontinuing supply to an existing customer: *Commercial Solvents.* **10.126** Commercial Solvents held a dominant position within the common market in the supply of raw materials (nitropropane or aminobutanol) required for the production of ethambutol and ethambutol-based speciality drugs. Until 1970 an Italian subsidiary acted as a reseller of nitropropane and aminobutanol produced by the parent in the United States. Zoja was a customer of the Italian subsidiary, having purchased aminobutanol over a four-year period for use in the manufacture of ethambutol-based speciality drugs. In 1970, the Italian subsidiary started production of its own ethambutol-based speciality drugs and Commercial Solvents decided it would no longer supply nitropropane and aminobutanol in the European Community; instead it would supply dextro-aminobutanol, an upgraded intermediate product, which the Italian subsidiary would convert to bulk ethambutol for sale in the Community and elsewhere and for use in the manufacture of its own speciality drugs. As a result, when Zoja placed a new order for aminobutanol in 1970, Commercial Solvents replied that none was available.

---

other grounds dismissed, Case C-552/03P *Unilever Bestfoods (Ireland) Ltd v Commission* [2006] ECR I-9091, [2006] 5 CMLR 1460).

[434] Although expressed in the context of supply of essential facilities to a new customer, points (i) and (iii) appear to be of general application. The ECJ did not enter into these theoretical considerations in such detail in its judgment but made clear that the positive obligations recognised in earlier case law were to be viewed as exceptional, effectively endorsing the cautious approach articulated by AG Jacobs: *Bronner* (n 432, above) paras 37–47. For *Bronner* generally, see further para 10.137, below. Some of the earlier, more enthusiastic Commission decisions in relation to 'essential facilities' should therefore be read with caution.

[435] Case C-53/03 *Syfait v GlaxoSmithKline* [2005] ECR I-4609, [2005] 5 CMLR 7, para 67, following a discussion of the jurisprudence (the ECJ held that the reference was inadmissible).

The Commission's decision that Commercial Solvents had acted in breach of Article 82 was upheld by the Court of Justice. The Court stated that:

> '[Commercial Solvents] had decided to limit, if not completely to cease, the supply of nitropropane and aminobutanol to certain parties inorder to facilitate its own access to the market for the derivatives. However, an undertaking being in a dominant position as regards the production of raw material and therefore able to control the supply to manufacturers of derivatives, cannot just because it decides to start manufacturing these derivatives (in competition with its former customers) act in such a way as to eliminate their competition which in the case in question, would amount to eliminating one of the principal manufacturers of ethambutol in the common market'[436]

The Court held that Commercial Solvents should be required to satisfy Zoja's requirements for the raw material. The later case of *United Brands*[437] confirmed the Court's view that a dominant undertaking cannot discontinue supplies to the long-standing customer if the orders placed by that customer are in no way out of the ordinary.

10.127 **Discontinuing supply of services.** In *Télémarketing*,[438] the Court of Justice expressed the same principle somewhat differently in the context of a refusal to supply a service rather than goods. The Court held that it would be an abuse for a television station, if it held a dominant position 'on the market in a service which was indispensable for the activities of another undertaking on another market',[439] to refuse, without objective justification, to supply its services to any telemarketing undertaking other than a member of its own group:

> '. . . an abuse within the meaning of Article [82] is committed where, without any objective necessity, an undertaking holding a dominant position on a particular market reserves to itself or to an undertaking belonging to the same group an ancillary activity which might be carried on by another undertaking as part of its activities

---

[436] Cases 6 & 7/73 *Commercial Solvents v Commission* [1974] ECR 223, [1974] 1 CMLR 309, paras 23–29. See also *Napier Brown/British Sugar* (n 422, above), referred to in the context of margin squeezing at para 10.113, above.

[437] *United Brands* (n 349, above). See also *British Leyland v Commission* (n 344, above)(refusal to supply certificate of conformity for LHD vehicles required to license and use vehicles in the UK, thereby deterring imports from the other Member States); *Polaroid/SSI Europe, XIIIth Report on Competition Policy* (1983), point 157 (refusal to supply customer with a large order of instant film). See also *Liptons Cash Registers/Hugin*, OJ 1978 L22/23, [1978] 1 CMLR D19 (refusal to supply spare parts to firm which maintained and repaired Hugin cash registers held contrary to Art 82). The case was overturned on appeal because of lack of effect on trade between Member States: Case 22/78 *Hugin v Commission* [1979] ECR 1869, [1979] 3 CMLR 345. The tying cases discussed at paras 10.119 *et seq*, above, can also be regarded as refusal to supply one product without the other.

[438] Case 311/84 *CBEM v CLT and IPB* ('*Télémarketing*') [1985] ECR 3261, [1986] 2 CMLR 558. See also *Napier Brown/British Sugar* (n 422, above); Case C-18/88 *RT v GB-INNO-BM* [1991] ECR I-5941, [1992] 4 CMLR 78.

[439] *CBEM v CLT and IPB*, above, para 26.

upon a neighbouring but separate market, with the possibility of eliminating all competition from such undertaking.'[440]

The Court's reference in *Télémarketing* to the dominant undertaking 'reserv[ing] to itself' an activity reflected the facts of that case and is not a necessary condition for the refusal to supply a third party to constitute an abusive. In *JJ Burgess & Sons*,[441] the UK Competition Appeal Tribunal rejected the argument of the Office of Fair Trading ('OFT') that the elimination of one of three funeral directors from a local market did not amount to a substantial effect on competition when two viable choices remained (and there was no evidence that prices would rise). The Tribunal adopted the statement of Advocate General Jacobs in *Bronner* that it was clear from *Commercial Solvents, United Brands* and *Télémarketing* 'that a dominant undertaking commits an abuse where, without justification, it cuts off supplies to an existing customer . . .'.[442] In the *Burgess* case, the only crematorium in the area, which was under the same ownership as one of the local funeral directors, stopped accepting funerals undertaken by one of the two other local funeral directors, with the likely consequence that this funeral director would have had to close. The Tribunal referred to the purpose of the Chapter II prohibition (the UK equivalent of Article 82) as 'preserving effective competition for the ultimate benefit of consumers' and rejected as 'entirely contrary to the established case-law' the approach of the OFT which appeared to suggest that it is not abusive to eliminate a competitor (and existing customer) from the downstream market, without objective justification, so long as at least one other competitor in that market remained.[443]

The limited scope of 'objective justification' as regards an existing customer. 10.128
The commercial rationale for a policy will not constitute objective justification

---

[440] ibid, paras 25–27. See also Case T-504/93 *Tiercé Ladbroke v Commission* [1997] ECR II-923, [1997] 5 CMLR 309: Ladbroke's claim that the French racecourses were reserving to themselves or other licensees the market in French sound and pictures ancillary to the betting market, by refusing Ladbroke's a licence for the Belgian market, was rejected on the grounds that the French racecourses were not present on the Belgian market, which was the relevant market for the purposes of Art 82. This tends to confirm that the underlying principle is the 'leveraging' effect of refusal to supply rather than any free-standing obligation to supply particular competitors or customers.

[441] *JJ Burgess & Sons v Office of Fair Trading* [2005] CAT 24, [2005] CompAR 1151.

[442] *Bronner* (n 432, above) Opinion, para 43.

[443] *JJ Burgess & Sons* (n 441, above) paras 332–333. The Tribunal also observed, *obiter*, that if a competitor would be substantially weakened but not eliminated, that might be sufficient to constitute abuse (at para 312). In *Mulitplex Cinemas,* Case 16 Ok 20/04, judgment of 4 April 2005, the Austrian Supreme Court held that Constantin-Film, which was the dominant distributor of a particular category of films and also (by its subsidiaries) operated a chain of mulitplex cinemas, infringed the Austrian equivalent of Art 82 by refusing without objective justification to continue supplying film copies save on onerous terms to a competing operator of multiplex cinemas. The Court found that successful operation of multiplex cinemas required access to virtually all films released in Austria and accepted the claimant's contention that disturbance of its existing relationship with Constantin-Film would put it at a commercial disadvantage ('*Benachteiligung*').

such as would avoid a finding of abuse if that justification is in reality that the dominant supplier is seeking to reduce or eliminate competition to itself or to a related company. On the contrary, such motivation of the dominant undertaking supports the finding of abuse. For example, in *Télémarketing*[444] the dominant undertaking was in effect replacing one exclusive provider of telemarketing with another but the Court of Justice did not regard that as providing any justification for its conduct, given the linkage between the dominant undertaking and the new exclusive provider. Again, if a manufacturer takes over the distribution and servicing of its own products it may be better able to compete with other brands, but that will not necessarily justify stopping supplies to existing distributors and thereby weakening competition on the downstream market.[445] If a dominant undertaking refuses to supply in response to a competitive challenge, its response must be fair and proportional to the threat: it cannot normally, for example, withdraw all supplies immediately from a long-standing customer only because that customer has become associated with a competitor.[446] On the other hand, a dominant firm may be justified in refusing to supply further goods to a customer from whom payment is overdue,[447] and the Court in *United Brands* indicates that the dominant supplier will not be required to meet orders from a customer that does not abide by 'regular commercial practice' or whose orders are 'out of the ordinary'.[448] Moreover, in *Syfait*, Advocate General Jacobs considered that it was possible for a dominant undertaking to justify a refusal to supply aimed at restricting parallel imports in the particular circumstances of the market for pharmaceutical products where prices are largely determined by State regulation.[449] Although the Court of Justice held that the reference in that case was inadmissible[450] and so did not decide the point, at the time of writing the issue is before the Court of Justice again in pending references from the Athens Court of Appeal in private actions arising out of the same facts.[451] Such cases raise issues similar to those involving refusal to supply new customers, considered below. It has been held by the Irish High Court that since the onus rests on the plaintiff to prove abuse, it must prove not only the conduct alleged to constitute the abuse, such as

---

[444] *CBEM v CLT and IPB* (n 438, above).

[445] *Hugin v Commission* (n 437, above). Where the market is narrowly defined, as in *Hugin* (limited to the supply of parts for Hugin's own products), the manufacturer's inability to adopt its preferred means of distribution and servicing may impede its ability to compete effectively in the wider market with other, possibly more powerful, suppliers of competing products.

[446] *BBI/Boosey & Hawkes*, OJ 1987 L286/36, [1988] 4 CMLR 67 (an interim measures decision). For application in the English court, see *Norbain SD Ltd v Dedicated Micros Ltd* [1999] Eu LR 266 (QB).

[447] See, eg *Leyland DAF v Automotive Products* [1994] 1 BCLC 245 (English Court of Appeal).

[448] *United Brands* (n 349, above).

[449] *Syfait v GlaxoSmithKline* (n 435, above).

[450] Because the reference had been made by the Greek competition authority which was held not to be a 'court' within Art 234.

[451] Cases C-468/06, etc, *Sot Lélos kai Sia v GlaxoSmithKline*, not yet decided.

refusal to supply, but also that there was no objective justification for the practice.[452] However, the Court of First Instance has made clear that it is for the dominant undertaking to put forward any ground of objective justification relied on, supported by evidence, which the party alleging abuse then has to rebut.[452a]

Refusal to license intellectual property rights. A system of intellectual property **10.129** rights which confers legal monopolies poses particular problems for the application of Article 82. Many of the issues which arise are discussed in Chapter 9, above, which considers the application of the principles of free movement of goods and of Articles 81 and 82 to the exercise of patents, trade marks and other similar rights. The mere existence of a patent, trade mark or copyright is not sufficient to establish a dominant position, nor is the exercise of an intellectual property right by a dominant undertaking in itself abusive. However, an abuse has been found in the registration of trade marks to divide markets;[453] in enforcing trade mark rights in markets opening up to competition;[454] in the insistence on unfair terms in licence agreements;[455] in the bringing of infringement suits to compel the defendants to enter into restrictive licences;[456] in the acquisition by a dominant undertaking of an exclusive patent right;[457] and in a pattern of misleading representations to patent authorities and national courts aimed at acquiring an extension of patent protection.[458] The charging of an excessive price for a product protected by intellectual property rights may also be an abuse.[459] Particular

---

[452] *Meridian Communication Limited and Cellular Three Limited v Eircell* [2002] IR 17.

[452a] Case T-201/04 *Microsoft v Commission*, judgment of 17 September 2007, para 688; see Postscript below.

[453] See, eg *Bayer/Tanabe, VIIIth Report on Competition Policy* (1978), point 125; *Airam/Osram XIth Report on Competition Policy* (1981), point 97, [1982] 3 CMLR 614.

[454] *France Télécom v Cegetel*, French Court of Appeal, 29 April 2003, BOCCRF No. 8, 11 July 2003 (clauses in contracts offered by France Télécom to new entrant Cegetel restricting use of trade marks 'special numbers' (information numbers, toll-free numbers, shared-cost numbers and flat-rate numbers) constituted abuse under French equivalent of Art 82).

[455] *Eurofima* [1973] CMLR D217; Case T-30/89 *Hilti v Commission* (n 415, above) (charging greatly in excess of the accepted patent licence fee held abusive); Case T-151/01 *Der Grüne Punkt – Duales System Deutschland v Commission* [2007] 5 CMLR 300 (requiring payment of user fees irrespective of whether service used was that of licensor or a competitor) (on appeal, Case C-385/07P, not yet decided). See further para 10.150, below.

[456] *Zip Fasteners (patent aspects)*, Press Release IP/78/111 (9 June 1978), [1978] 3 CMLR 44. See also *Intel v VIA Technologies* [2002] EWCA Civ 1905, [2003] FSR 33, [2003] EuLR 85, per Morritt VC at para 87: 'If the willingness to grant licences but only on terms which involve breaches of Article 81 is part of the abusive conduct of which complaint is made then I see no reason why those facts may not be relied on both for the purposes of the defence under Article 82 and as a free-standing defence under Article 81'. See also paras 9.066 *et seq*, above.

[457] Case T-51/89 *Tetra Pak Rausing v Commission* [1990] ECR II-309, [1991] 4 CMLR 334, paras 23–24.

[458] COMP/37.507 *AstraZeneca*, 15 June 2005, [2006] 5 CMLR 287 (on appeal Case T-321/05 *AstraZeneca v Commission* not yet decided).

[459] Case 24/67 *Parke, Davis & Co v Probel* [1968] ECR 55, [1968] CMLR 47; Case 78/70 *Deutsche Grammophon v Metro* [1971] ECR 487, [1971] CMLR 631; *Volvo v Veng* (n 461, below); Case 53/87 *CICRA v Renault* [1988] ECR 6039, [1990] 4 CMLR 265.

difficulties arise in the context of refusal to grant licences to intellectual property, where any obligation to licence may encroach upon the substance of the right. This is discussed in the following paragraphs.[460]

10.130

The essential subject-matter of the right. For many years discussion of this issue revolved around attempts to reconcile the judgments of the Court of Justice in *Volvo v Veng* and *Magill*. In *Volvo v Veng*,[461] the Court of Justice considered whether a car manufacturer, which owned the registered industrial design of the body panels for its cars, had *prima facie* acted abusively by refusing to grant a licence to a third party to supply body panels which were imitations of the protected design. The Court held that the right of the proprietor of a protected design to prevent third parties manufacturing, selling or importing, without its consent, products incorporating the design constituted the very subject-matter of the exclusive rights. A refusal to grant a licence could not therefore, of itself, constitute an abuse. By contrast in *Magill*,[462] the Court of Justice, upholding the Court of First Instance, concluded that the refusal by broadcasting organisations in Ireland and the United Kingdom to grant licences to third parties to reproduce their copyright television programme schedules was an abuse. The Court of Justice recognised, following *Volvo v Veng*, that refusal to grant a licence in intellectual property cannot *in itself* constitute an abuse of a dominant position. However, as was also clear from *Volvo v Veng*, the exercise of an exclusive right by the proprietor may in exceptional circumstances involve abusive conduct. The Court found that there were exceptional circumstances justifying a finding of abuse. In that connection, the Court of Justice relied upon three circumstances taken into account by the Court of First Instance:[463] first, that there was consumer demand for a composite weekly television guide covering all the channels and this demand could not be met without the input from all the broadcasters; secondly, there was no objective

---

460 See generally Temple Lang, 'Anticompetitive Abuses under Article 82 involving Intellectual Property Rights', in Ehlermann & Atanasiu (n 1, above), 589; 'Mandating Access: The Principles and the Problems in Intellectual Property and Competition Policy' (2004) EBLR 1087. For the position under US antitrust law, see Hovenkamp, Janis and Lemley, 'Unilateral Refusals to License in the US' in Lévêque and Shelanski (eds), *Antitrust, Patents and Copyright* (2005), Chap 2.

461 Case 238/87 *Volvo v Veng* [1988] ECR 6211, [1989] 4 CMLR 122. See also Case 53/87 *CICRA v Renault* (n 459, above). For the application of these principles in the English courts, see paras 14.140 *et seq*, below.

462 Cases C-241 & 242/91/P *RTE and ITP v Commission* [1995] ECR I-743, [1995] 4 CMLR 718, [1995] All ER (EC) 416, upholding Case T-69/89 *RTE v Commission* [1991] ECR II-485, [1991] 4 CMLR 586, Case T-70/89 *BBC v Commission* [1991] ECR II-535, [1991] 4 CMLR 669 and Case T-76/89 *ITC v Commission* [1991] ECR II-575 [1991] 4 CMLR 745 (all on appeal from the Commission's decn in *Magill TV Guide*, OJ 1989 L78/43, [1989] 4 CMLR 749). See also *Tiercé Ladbroke* (n, above) (refusal by French racecourses grant licences to transmit sound and pictures of French races for use in its betting shops in Belgium held not abusive because the racecourses were not active on the Belgian market and the licences were not essential to the creation of a new product for which there was consumer demand).

463 *RTE and ITP v Commission* (above) paras 52–56. See also *Bronner* (n 432, above) paras 40–41.

justification for the refusal; and thirdly, by their conduct the appellants reserved to themselves the secondary market of weekly television guides by excluding all competition on that market since they denied access to the indispensable raw material for the compilation of such a guide. The Court of Justice also upheld the legality of the remedies ordered by the Commission,[464] which required the appellants to supply third parties on request and on a non-discriminatory basis with their advance weekly listings. The decision provided that if the appellants chose to provide the listings by means of a licence, any royalty requested should be reasonable.[465]

10.131

IMS Health: **refusal of access to a copyright protected database.** The question of when a refusal to licence intellectual property is abusive was again considered in *IMS Health*. That case concerned a computer programme for representing regional pharmaceutical sales data in Germany, known as the '1860 brick structure', over which IMS claimed copyright. IMS's competitors attempted to develop similar brick structures but IMS obtained interim injunctions in the German courts to restrain their use as an infringement of copyright. IMS's competitors complained to the Commission that IMS's refusal to license the 1860 brick structure meant that it was not possible for them to provide pharmaceutical data services as they could not present data in a way which was acceptable to customers without infringing IMS's copyright. On an application for interim measures, the Commission concluded that IMS's brick structure had become a *de facto* industry standard which the pharmaceutical companies had become locked into and that a refusal of access to the 1860 brick structure was likely to eliminate all competition. There were no actual or potential substitutes for the structure and no objective justification for IMS's refusal to license. 'Exceptional circumstances' in the *Magill* sense were therefore established. The Commission therefore made an interim decision ordering IMS to grant a licence for the 1860 brick structure.[466]

10.132

IMS Health: **the Court of Justice's judgment.** Meanwhile, the German Court had made a preliminary reference to the Court of Justice asking questions about the interpretation of Article 82 in the context of IMS's refusal to license. The

---

[464] *Magill TV Guide* (n 462, above).

[465] The appellants were also entitled to include in any such licences to third parties such terms as were considered necessary to ensure comprehensive, high quality coverage of all their programmes including those of a minority or regional appeal.

[466] *NDC Health/IMS: Interim Measures*, OJ 2002 L59/18, [2002] 4 CMLR 111. IMS appealed and the President of the CFI suspended the decision pending the appeal: Case T-184/01 RI *IMS Health v Commission* [2001] ECR II-2349, [2002] 4 CMLR 46 (interim suspension); Case T-184/01 RII *IMS Health v Commission* [2001] ECR II-3193, [2002] 4 CMLR 58 (interim suspension confirmed); appeal against the suspension, dismissed: Case C-481/01 P(R) *IMS Health v Commission* [2002] ECR I-3401, [2002] 5 CMLR 44.

Court of Justice,[467] which to a large extent followed the Opinion of Advocate General Tizzano, set out the conditions in which a refusal to supply a copyright is an abuse. It confirmed that the exercise of an intellectual property owner's rights (including refusal to grant a licence) cannot in itself constitute abuse of a dominant position.[468] The Court stated that:

'. . . in order for a refusal by an undertaking which owns a copyright to give access to a product or service indispensable for carrying on a particular business to be treated as abusive, it is sufficient that three cumulative conditions be satisfied, namely that that refusal is preventing the emergence of a new product for which there is a potential consumer demand, that it is unjustified and such as to exclude any competition on a secondary market'.[469]

For the purposes of the application of the earlier case law, it is sufficient that a potential market or even hypothetical market can be identified. Such is the case where the products or services are indispensable in order to carry on a particular business and where there is an actual demand for them on the part of undertakings which seek to carry on that business. Accordingly, it is necessary that two different stages of production may be identified and that they are interconnected, inasmuch as the upstream product is indispensable for the supply of the downstream product.[470]

10.133   *Microsoft*: 'exceptional circumstances'.   Following the judgment in *IMS Health*, it remains unclear whether the three conditions there set out by the Court of Justice as *sufficient* to give rise to an obligation to licence are also *necessary* to constitute the exceptional circumstances which establish that obligation. In the *Microsoft* case,[471] decided a month before the Court's judgment in *IMS Health*, the Commission held that the refusal by Microsoft to supply full interoperability (interface) information for its Windows work group servers to producers of work group operating systems constituted an abuse. The Commission stated that it was

---

467 Case C-418/01 *IMS Health* [2004] ECR I-5039, [2004] 4 CMLR 1543, [2004] All ER (EC) 813. As a result, the Commission decided not to proceed to a final decision. The interim measures had by that time been withdrawn: *NDC Health v IMS Health:Interim Measures*, OJ 2003 L268/69, [2003] 5 CMLR 820.

468 Case C-418/01 *IMS Health* (above) para 34.

469 ibid, para 38.

470 ibid, paras 44–45. Although there was no suggestion that IMS had ever contemplated selling or licensing the scheme to others, the ECJ nonetheless found that there could be a 'market' for the scheme.

471 Case COMP/37.792 *Microsoft*, 24 March 2004, [2005] 4 CMLR 965. See also *Digitechnic v Microsoft*, Paris Court of Appeal, 24 May 2005, BOCCRF 20 September 2005, holding that Art 82 applied to a refusal by Microsoft to licence computer assemblers in France with an original equipment manufacturer licence unless they paid the retail price for the software. Note also see *IBM settlement, XIVth Report on Competition Policy* (1984), points 94–95, [1984] 3 CMLR 147 (proceedings alleging abuse by IBM settled, upon an extensive undertaking by IBM to modify its business practices).

no answer to the complaint that the information was sought by an undertaking which was hardly present in the market when that undertaking had an interest in entering the market.[472] Because of Microsoft's very large market share, the information at issue was found to be a key factor in enabling entry into the work group server operating system market, and the refusal to supply therefore risked eliminating competition. However, the Commission rejected the argument that there was an exhaustive 'checklist of exceptional circumstances' which had to be satisfied before finding an abusive refusal to supply but held that the issue is to be looked at on a case-by-case basis.[473] In that regard, the Commission did not find that the competing producers requesting supply were prevented from producing a specific, new product but that they were hindered in the development of 'innovative work group server operating system features'. Since so many consumers were locked into Windows, unless other systems were interoperable with Windows consumers would not benefit from those systems and there was accordingly little prospect for rival producers to market them successfully, which in turn discouraged those producers from developing such products.[474] If the Court of Justice's ruling in *IMS Health* indeed requires drawing a line between a 'new product' and an enhanced feature of an existing product, that distinction is particularly difficult to apply in the context of computer systems and software. In this regard, the Commission based its ruling on Article 82(b) which refers to 'limiting . . . technical development to the prejudice of consumers'. Microsoft also argued that refusal to supply to its competitors intellectual property which was secret and valuable was objectively justified as protecting its incentives to develop and innovate, and therefore entirely different from the situation in *Magill*. However, the Commission concluded that 'on balance, the possible negative impact of an order to supply on Microsoft's incentives to innovate is outweighed by its positive impact on the level of innovation of the whole industry (including Microsoft)'.[475] These issues may be clarified in Microsoft's appeal, which is currently pending before the Court of First Instance.[476]

Copyright associations.   In several cases, the Commission and the Community **10.134** Courts have been concerned with the activities of associations exploiting the copyright rights of their members. The general rules are that, where such an undertaking occupies a dominant position, it should not impose on its members obligations

---

[472] *Microsoft*, above, para 562.

[473] ibid, para 555.

[474] ibid, paras 693–701.

[475] ibid, para 783.

[476] Case T-201/04 *Microsoft v Commission*, judgment of 17 September 2007; see Postscript below. In his judgment refusing interim relief, the President of the CFI noted that the questions of whether the *IMS Health* conditions are necessary or merely sufficient, and whether secret information should be treated differently, were matters to be determined in the substantive case: Case T-201/04R, order of 22 December 2004, [2004] ECR II-4463, [2005] 4 CMLR 406, paras 206–207.

which are not absolutely necessary for the attainment of its objects and which thus encroach unfairly upon a member's freedom to exercise his copyright.[477] Moreover, since many such undertakings have *de facto* monopolies, they must not unreasonably refuse to supply services to persons dependent upon them,[478] or conduct their activities so that their effect is to partition the common market and thereby restrict the freedom to supply services, which constitutes one of the objectives of the Treaty.[479] Such societies must also ensure that their tariff structures do not discriminate against certain users in favour of others. The Swedish Market Court has held[480] that a royalty tariff discriminated against broadcasters with a lower coverage compared with those with higher coverage, since the former had to pay a disproportionately higher cost, and thus constituted a barrier to entry. The Brussels Court of Appeal found[481] that SABAM's system of discounts from the set tariffs was not transparent and kept rights users in a state of legal uncertainty. It also held that the level of discount given to major users of the rights was disproportionate giving rise to discrimination between new and established users. The tariffs were therefore an abuse under Article 82.

10.135

Refusal of access to 'essential facilities'. The concept of access to 'essential facilities' is a relatively late addition to EC competition law but was developed by the Commission in a series of cases concerning access to transport facilities.[482] The doctrine had not been considered by the Court of Justice, as a form of abuse independent of the two categories of refusal to supply considered above, until the *Bronner* case discussed below. In its earlier decisions, the Commission had defined an essential facility as 'a facility or infrastructure, without access to which competitors cannot provide services to their customers'.[483] From the perspective of the principles underlying competition law, there is no magic in the words 'essential' or 'facilities'. The principles may refer as much to the monopoly supplier of a raw material as to the controller of a network or the holder of an exclusive right under

---

[477] Case 127/73 *BRT v SABAM* [1974] ECR 313, [1974] 2 CMLR 238, para 15.

[478] Case 7/82 *GVL v Commission* [1983] ECR 483, [1983] 3 CMLR 645.

[479] Case 22/79 *Greenwich Film Production v SACEM* [1979] ECR 3275, [1980] 1 CMLR 629.

[480] Case MD 1998:5 *Föreningen Svenska Tonsättares Internationella Musikbyrå (STIM) v TV3 Broadcasting Group Ltd*, judgment of Swedish Market Court, 16 April 1998.

[481] *M v SA Productions & Marketing*, Brussels Court of Appeal, 11 November 2005.

[482] The doctrine originates from a US Supreme Court decision, *United States v Terminal Railroad Association*, 224 US 383 (1912). See Pitofsky, Patterson and Hooks, 'The Essential Facilities Doctrine under US Antitrust Law' (2002) 70 Antitrust LJ 443. However, the US Supreme Court appears to have reined back the doctrine, which had attracted much criticism, in *Verizon Communications Inc v Trinko* (2004) 540 US 398 at 407. For discussion under EC law, see Temple Lang, 'The Principle of Essential Facilities in European Community Competition Law - the Position since Bronner' (2000) 1 Journal of Network Industries 375; Bavasso, 'Essential Facilities in EC Law: The Rise of an "Epithet" and the Consolidation of a Doctrine in the Communications Sector' in Eckhout and Tridimas (eds), *Yearbook of European Law*, Vol 21, 2001–2002 (2003).

[483] *B&I Line/Sealink Harbours*, 11 June 1992, [1992] 4 CMLR 255, para 41; *Sea Containers/ Stena Sealink*, OJ 1994 L15/8, [1995] 4 CMLR 84, para 66. Both are interim measures decisions.

statute or public law. What constitute 'essential facilities' will depend upon the presence of 'technical, legal or even economic obstacles' preventing the would-be user of the facilities from competing on the relevant market.[484] Such impediments may arise, for example, through the exercise of intellectual property rights, through an exclusive licence to operate a facility, exceptional investment costs or through some natural advantage which cannot be replicated, such as the location of a port. As Advocate General Jacobs explained in *Bronner*:

> 'An essential facility can be a product such as a raw material or a service, including provision of access to a place such as a harbour or airport or to a distribution system such as a telecommunications network. In may cases the relationship is vertical in the sense that the dominant undertaking reserves the product or service to, or discriminates in favour of, its own downstream operation at the expense of competitors on the downstream market. It may however be horizontal in the sense of tying sales of related but distinct products or services.'[485]

However, (i) the degree of control over the 'essential' facility or input, and (ii) the degree of necessity for competitors in obtaining access to the facility or input, are both highly material in determining whether a refusal to allow access is unlawful. It follows that these obligations are most stringent in respect of a monopoly controller of a 'network' that forms the basis for competition on a clearly identifiable and significant downstream market, as is the case in many privatised utilities.[486]

10.136

The principle of access to essential facilities.   The Commission first stated what is sometimes referred to as the 'essential facilities doctrine' in the following terms:

> 'An undertaking which occupies a dominant position in the provision of an essential facility and itself uses that facility . . ., and which refuses other companies access to that facility without objective justification or grants access to competitors only on terms less favourable than those which it gives its own services, infringes Article [82] if the other conditions of that Article are met.'[487]

This reasoning stems from the approach of the Court of Justice in *Hoffmann-La Roche*, categorising as abusive conduct which 'has the effect of hindering the maintenance of the degree of competition still existing in the market or the growth of that competition',[488] and follows the underlying rationale of cases such as

---

[484]   *Bronner v Mediaprint* (n 432, above) para 44.

[485]   Case C-7/97 *Bronner v Mediaprint* [1998] ECR I-7791, [1999] 4 CMLR 112, Opinion at para 50. Tying is treated separately in this work but the last sentence of the passage quoted illustrates the overlaps that arise in identifying the various forms of abuse. Tying can be analysed as refusal to supply the 'tying' product except on the unreasonable condition of accepting the 'tied' product.

[486]   Such obligations may have specific statutory underpinning: see, eg paras 12.106 *et seq*, below for the telecommunications sector.

[487]   *Sea Containers/Stena Sealink* (n 483, above) para 66.

[488]   Case 85/76 *Hoffmann-La Roche* [1979] ECR 461, [1979] 3 CMLR 211, para 91; applied in, eg *Sea Containers/Stena Sealink* (n 483, above) para 67.

Commercial Solvents, Télémarketing and *Magill*, discussed above.[489] However, the conditions for application of this doctrine are likely to be strictly applied, as the Court of Justice has recognised the force of the public policy considerations already discussed.

10.137 **The approach of the Court of Justice:** *Bronner.* The cautious view of the Court of Justice is illustrated by its decision in *Bronner*,[490] on an Article 234 reference concerning refusal of access in relation to a new customer. The issue was whether it was an abuse for a newspaper publisher to refuse a competitor access to its home delivery service which was the only nationwide service available. The case was the first occasion on which the Court of Justice considered the 'essential facilities' doctrine developed by the Commission.[491] The Court of Justice applied (i) *Commercial Solvents*,[492] on the basis that the refusal was likely to eliminate all competition on the part of the firm seeking supplies of the goods and services which were indispensable to its business; and (ii) *Magill*,[493] on the basis that, to the extent applicable to the exercise of property rights generally, it would apply in a situation such as *Bronner* only if refusal of access to the home delivery service was likely to eliminate all competition on the part of the would-be customer and was incapable of objective justification, and also only if the service was itself indispensable to the customer's business in that there was no actual or potential substitute for the home delivery service.[494] Thus, although it was clear that refusal of access to its delivery service conferred a competitive advantage on the incumbent publisher on the newspaper market, this was not considered by the Court of Justice to be sufficient justification for a finding of abuse. The principles derived from *Commercial Solvents* and *Magill* were narrowly construed, and the essence of the abuse was analysed to be the refusal, without objective justification, of access to goods or services for which there is no alternative and without which the would-be customer would be unable to compete at all on the downstream market.

10.138 **The criterion of 'necessity': application.** In *Tiercé Ladbroke*,[495] the applicant (Ladbroke) operated betting shops in Belgium taking bets on horse races

---

489 See paras 10.126 *et seq*, above.
490 Case C-7/97 *Bronner v Mediaprint* [1998] ECR I-7791, [1999] 4 CMLR 112.
491 eg *Port of Rødby*, discussed at para 10.139, below. However, only the AG, not the ECJ, referred to any of the prior Commission decisions on 'essential facilities'.
492 Cases 6 & 7/73 *Commercial Solvents v Commission* [1974] ECR 223, [1974] 1 CMLR 309 discussed at para 10.126, above.
493 The cases cited at n 462, above and discussed at paras 10.129 *et seq*, above.
494 *Bronner v Mediaprint* (n 490, above) paras 38–41.
495 T-504/93 *Tiercé Ladbroke v Commission* [1997] ECR II-923, [1997] 5 CMLR 309, paras 124–132. The CFI also held that the *Commercial Solvents* jurisprudence did not assist Ladbroke since the French societies were not themselves operating on the relevant downstream market.

run abroad but the French racecourse societies refused its request for supply of televised broadcasts of French horse racing. The Court of First Instance dismissed Ladbroke's appeal against the Commission's rejection of its complaint of an infringement of Article 82, holding that since the French societies had not granted any such broadcasting licences for Belgium, there was no question of discrimination; and further that the the the fact that such broadcasts would assist Ladbroke's Belgian operation did not suffice to make the supply essential. In *Bronner*,[496] the Court of Justice concluded that the newspaper publisher was not acting abusively by withholding access to its home delivery service since that service was not indispensable for the would-be customer's business. There were no legal, technical or economic obstacles that made it impossible, or even unreasonably difficult, for the competitor to establish its own competing home delivery service. The substitutes also included other forms of delivery, such as by post or sale in shops and kiosks, although they might be less advantageous. As for the creation of an alternative home delivery system, the Court held that, to demonstrate the indispensability of the existing system, it was not enough to argue that it would not be economically viable by reason of the small quantities delivered; it would be necessary at the very least to show that it was not economically viable to create a second system for the distribution of newspapers with a circulation comparable to that of the papers delivered by the existing system.[497]

The Commission's early decisions: narrow market definitions.   Prior to the   **10.139** ruling of the Court of Justice in *Bronner*, the Commission had developed the

---

See also Cases T-374/94, etc, *ENS v Commission ('European Night Services')* [1998] ECR II-3141, [1998] 5 CMLR 718, paras 207–219, a case under Art 81 where, in annulling the Commission's decn that certain railway services should be supplied to third parties, the CFI held that it had not been established that access those services was essential.

[496] *Bronner v Mediaprint* (n 490, above).

[497] ibid, para 46. See also Case 04-12.388 *Messageries Lyonnaises de Presse (MLP) v Nouvelles Messageries de Presse Parisienne (NMPP)*, judgment of 12 July 2005, BOCCRF No. 11, 16 December 2005, where the Cour de Cassation annulled the judgment of the Paris Court of Appeal which had upheld a decision of the Conseil de la Concurrence giving interim measures directing NMPP to allow MLP access to its 'Presse 2000' software package which MLP had claimed was an essential facility. Applying the French counterpart to Art 82, the Cour de Cassation emphasised that access to an essential facility must be subject to strict conditions in order not to discourage investment. One of these conditions is that the facility cannot be duplicated by competitors under reasonable economic conditions. If, as in the present case, a competitor has developed or is able to develop an alternative solution, even under less advantageous conditions, the authorities should not enjoin the dominant company to give access to its facility. On *renvoi*, the Court of Appeal, judgment of 31 January 2006, quashed the Conseil's decision accordingly. Note also the assessment by the UK Monopolies and Mergers Commission that Solicitors' Property Centres did not provide 'essential facilities' for the marketing of residential property: *Solicitors' Estate Agency Services in Scotland* (Cm. 3699, 1997).

doctrine of 'essential facilities' in a series of cases relating to the ports and airports of the Community.[498] In many of these early decisions, the outcome of the case has depended on the issue of market definition, in that the Commission defined the downstream market so narrowly that access to the facilities in question was necessarily indispensable if the would-be customer were to compete on the relevant market as defined. Thus in the cases involving denial of access to port facilities, with the relevant downstream market defined by reference to services into and out of the port in question, access to the facilities is inevitably indispensable for the applicant to compete on that narrowly defined market, leaving only the question of whether there is any objective justification for refusal of access (for example, capacity limitations). Similarly, in *Flughafen Frankfurt*,[499] with the relevant market defined as the provision of ramp handling services at Frankfurt Airport, it inevitably followed that access to the ramp at Frankfurt was indispensable for any would-be competitor in that market and denial of access would eliminate all competition from such competitor, again leaving only the question of objective justification.[500] In *European Night Services*,[501] the Court of First Instance held that the Commission's order that the joint venture partners should give third parties access to their railway infrastructure, products and services was not sustainable. Although this arose in the context of the conditions of exemption under Article 81(3), the Court addressed the issue on the basis of the *Magill* and *Tiercé Ladbroke* judgments, finding that such access could be regarded as essential only if the relevant market could be defined on a much narrower basis than in fact applied.

10.140 **Dominant undertaking's presence in downstream market.** In its decisions before *Bronner*, the Commission had on occasion asserted a broader doctrine, whereby denial of access to an essential facility would constitute an abuse even if

---

[498] See, eg *Port of Rødby*, OJ 1994 L55/52, [1994] 5 CMLR 457; *Sealink/B&I Line* [1992] 5 CMLR 255; *Sea Containers/Stena Sealink* (n 483, above); *Brussels Airport*, OJ 1995 L216/8, [1996] 4 CMLR 232; and see Maltby, 'Restrictions on Port Operators' (1993) ECLR 223. cf the Northern Irish decision, *Application by the Anley Maritime Agencies Ltd for JR* (1995) [1999] Eu LR 97 (QB, N Ir): Warrenpoint harbour not the relevant market as Belfast was an alternative. Note that although in *Sea Containers/Stena Sealink* the Commission found (at paras 63–64) that Holyhead was the only port capable of serving the 'central corridor' route between the UK and Ireland and that Liverpool was not a realistic substitute, Sea Containers did not in fact take up the opportunity to operate from Holyhead but eventually started a competing service out of Liverpool: Bishop and Ridyard, 'Oscar Bronner: Legitimate Refusals to Supply', in Grayson (ed), *European Economics and Law* (1999), 24–25.

[499] *FAG - Flughafen Frankfurt/Main*, OJ 1998 L72/30, [1998] 4 CMLR 779. See Armani, 'One step beyond in the application of the essential facility theory' (1999) 3 EC Competition Policy Newsletter 15.

[500] Such justification may include the fact that a facility owner who has invested in the introduction of a new product may need to have sufficient opportunity to use the facility to place that product on the market: see the Opinion of AG Jacobs in *Bronner v Mediaprint* (n 490, above) para 57.

[501] Cases T-374/94, etc, *ENS v Commission* (n 495, above) paras 207–219.

the operator of the facility, either directly or through an associated undertaking, was not itself making use of the facility and so competing with the third party seeking access.[502] It is doubtful that such an extended proposition is correct in the light of the judgment in *Bronner*.[503] In its more recent decisions on access to essential infrastructure, the Commission has expressed the principle in narrower terms, referring to the dominant undertaking itself using the facilities to which it denies access by its competitors.[504] However, it is difficult to set out a categorical statement since 'essential facilities' should not be regarded as a discrete doctrine but rather a concept within the broader framework a refusal to supply, which always has to be considered within its specific economic context to determine whether it constitutes an infringement of Article 82. Hence, if the dominant undertaking is not itself operating in the downstream market but its refusal to supply prevents the emergence of a new product downstream, that may be abusive as discussed above.[505]

Essential facilities and cross-border discrimination. In *Clearstream*, the **10.141** Commission found that Clearstream Banking AG and its parent company had infringed Article 82 by refusing to supply cross-border securities clearing and settlement services and by applying discriminatory prices.[506] Clearstream had refused to supply to Euroclear Bank clearing and settlement services for registered

---

[502] See the interim measures decision regarding the Port of Roscoff, *Irish Continental Group v CCI Morlaix* [1995] 5 CMLR 77, para 59: although the defendant port authority held a minority interest in Brittany Ferries, that was expressly not regarded as a condition of the decision. See also *SWIFT, XXVIIth Report on Competition Policy* (1997), point 68 and p 143: Commission alleged that because the SWIFT cooperative (owned by 2000 banks) was the only operator on the international networks for transferring payment messages and the only network to supply connections for worldwide banking establishments, it provides an essential facility: refusal of access amounts to exclusion from the international transfers market. Reservation of access to shareholder members, and specifically the refusal of access to La Poste, that operates in the French retail banking market, was therefore alleged to be an abuse; but this view does not appear to depend upon the nature of SWIFT's ownership. The proceedings were settled by formal undertakings to make access available to any entity that meets the EMI criterion for domestic payment systems: *La Poste/SWIFT & GUF*, OJ 1997 C335/3.

[503] *Bronner v Mediaprint* (n 490, above). In the United States where the doctrine of essential facilities originated, a claim to access requires that the owner of the essential facility is competing in the downstream market: *Intergraph Corp v Intel* Corp, 195 F 3d 1356 (Fed Cir, 1999).

[504] See, eg *Georg/Ferrovie*, OJ 2004 L111/17, [2004] 4 CMLR 1446 (Italian national railway carrier abused its dominant position by refusing to grant access to the Italian railway network to a small German competitor). Note that under German competition law, the equivalent provision to Art 82 includes in effect an 'essential facilities' doctrine that is expressly limited to the situation where the party refused access is thereby prevented from operating as a competitor of the dominant undertaking on the upstream or downstream market: GWB, s 19(4).4.

[505] See the discussion of *Magill, IMS Health* and *Microsoft* in paras 10.130–10.133, above. Although in each of those cases the supplier could be regarded as active itself in the relevant market, the statements of principle could have wider application. See also per AG Jacobs in *Syfait* (n 435, above) Opinion, para 66.

[506] COMP/38.096 *Clearstream*, 2 June 2004, [2005] 5 CMLR 1302, Press Release IP/04/705 (2 June 2004). The Commission decided to impose no fine because the infringements had ceased

shares issued under German law. The Commission found that the refusal to supply breached Article 82 because (i) Clearstream was the only final custodian of German securities kept in collective safe custody and was an unavoidable trading partner; (ii) new entry into this activity was unrealistic in the foreseeable future; (iii) Euroclear could not duplicate the services that it was requesting; and (iv) Clearstream's behaviour had the effect of impairing Euoclear's ability to provide efficient cross-border clearing and settlement services to clients in the single market. The Commission found that Clearstream had discriminated contrary to Article 82 because it had charged a higher transaction price to Euroclear Bank than to other securities depositaries outside Germany for equivalent clearing and settlement services, with no quality of service cost justification. The Commission stressed that the application of Article 82 in this case was for the protection of consumers and not of competitors and that it was important to facilitate smooth cross-border trade.

10.142 **Essential facilities in the telecommunications sector.** Deregulation has made the issue of third party access particularly important in the telecommunications sector.[507] The concept of access to essential facilities is considered in the Commission's Telecoms Access Agreements Notice,[508] setting out the circumstances and conditions on which access will or must be granted in that field and the factors that the Commission will take into consideration.

10.143 **Essential facilities in the energy sector.** The transmission and distribution of electricity and gas are the subject of extensive regulation at the Community level. This regulation is designed in part to ensure that the national monopolies which had traditionally both transported and sold energy make their facilities available to enable third parties to compete with them in the sale of energy. Thus the Electricity Transit Regulation[509] introduced a common framework in relation to tariffs for cross-border transactions for electricity and the allocation of available interconnection capacity so as to tackle congestion. The Gas Directive[510] obliged Member States to put in place a system of third party access to the gas transmission, distribution system, and to storage facilities, based on published tariffs and applicable to all eligible customers. The proposals for a new European energy

---

and there was no EC jurisprudence dealing with the competition analysis of clearing and settlement. On appeal, Case T-301/04, *Clearstream v Commission*, not yet decided.

[507] See generally Chap 12, below.

[508] Commission Notice on the application of the competition rules to access agreements in the telecommunications sector, OJ 1998 C265/2: Vol II, App E.24, paras 87–91; see paras 12.153 *et seq*, below.

[509] Reg 1228/2003, OJ 2003 L176/1. See para 12.064, below.

[510] Dir 2003/55, OJ 2003 L176/57: Vol II, App E.15. See paras 12.075–12.076, below.

policy, announced by the Commission in January 2007, included further provisions to facilitate access to networks by new entrants.[511]

Refusal to supply in relation to other forms of abuse. Altogether, refusal to **10.144** supply should be seen within the spectrum of abuse under Article 82, in the context of the fundamental purpose of that provision. On appropriate facts, refusal to supply may be an abusive limitation of output within Article 82(b) or a form of discriminatory conduct within Article 82(c). Moreover, tying constitutes one possible manifestation of a constructive refusal to supply, where the 'tying' product is supplied only on condition that the 'tied' product is also supplied, an abuse within the scope of Article 82(d). Thus, in the case of the supply of airline interlining facilities (enabling one airline to issue tickets covering travel partly carried on the services of another airline), the Commission suggested in *British Midland v Aer Lingus* that both the withdrawal of existing facilities and the refusal to grant new facilities may be abusive.[512] The Commission decided that Aer Lingus acted abusively in refusing to supply interline services to British Midland in respect of the latter's new Heathrow–Dublin route, although interlining was not indispensable to British Midland's ability to compete. This was the case although British Midland had not previously been a customer of Aer Lingus for the services in question[513] and the refusal had not prevented British Midland from obtaining a significant market share.[514] The Commission based its decision on the definition of abuse in *Hoffmann-La Roche*,[515] finding that the conduct of Aer Lingus constituted recourse to methods different from those governing normal competition and had the effect of hindering the level of competition existing on the market. It may be that, in the light of *Bronner*, the decision in *British Midland v Aer Lingus* should be seen not so much as a matter of refusal to supply but rather as discriminatory treatment in breach of Article 82(c).[516]

---

[511] Communication from the Commission to the Council and the European Parliament, 'Prospects for the internal gas and electricity market', COM(2006) 841 final; see further para 12.056, below.

[512] *British Midland v Aer Lingus*, OJ 1992 L96/34, [1993] 4 CMLR 596, para 26.

[513] The mechanics of the refusal by Aer Lingus involved withdrawal of its concurrence to British Midland's participation in the IATA Multilateral Interline Traffic Agreement, but it does not appear that British Midland had been an existing customer of Aer Lingus for interline services (and certainly not for such services on the Heathrow–Dublin route).

[514] ibid, para 29.

[515] Para 10.060, above.

[516] Interlining was not only common practice in the airline industry but Aer Lingus had been interlining with British Airways. Moreover, Aer Lingus' action was clearly taken with the aim of protecting its dominant position: it withdrew consent to British Midland's participation only when BM started to compete on the London–Dublin route. See also *London European/Sabena*, OJ 1988 L317/47, [1989] 4 CMLR 662, paras 29–31: on one view Sabena was refusing London European access to the airline booking system of which Sabena were the Belgian operators but the Commission

(g) Other forms of abuse

10.145 **Generally.** As in relation to Article 81(1), the specific instances of abusive conduct set out in Article 82 are merely illustrative of its scope and do not limit its application:

> 'It must, moreover, be stressed that the list of abusive practices set out in the second paragraph of Article [82] of the Treaty is not exhaustive.'[517]

Therefore, conduct by an undertaking which is made possible only by its dominant position and which can objectively be considered different from 'normal' competition may be considered an abuse.[518]

10.146 **Unfair trading conditions.** Article 82(a) identifies the imposition of 'unfair trading conditions' as a form of abuse. There are many such respects in addition to those categorised above in which a dominant firm may abuse its position by imposing anti-competitive conditions on customers, many of which may also infringe Article 81(1). Such anti-competitive conditions include attempts to restrict exports,[519] restrictions relating to the resale of goods,[520] restrictions on the freedom to innovate,[521] and restrictions on the provision of guarantees.[522] The terms of a licence of intellectual property rights can also infringe Article 82.[523]

---

approached the question of abuse as the limiting of markets in breach of Art 82(b) and/or unlawful tying in breach of Art 82(d).

[517] Case C-333/94P *Tetra Pak v Commission* [1996] ECR I-5951, [1997] 4 CMLR 662, [1997] All ER (EC) 4), para 37.

[518] See, eg *BT's use of customer billing information*, OFTEL Comp Bull. 10 (Oct 1998), p. 12: when British Telecommunications (BT) used its telephone calling records to identify customers that were using the internet and then targeted those customers with promotion of its own, competing, internet service, the UK telecommunications regulator (OFTEL) alleged that this constituted abuse of its dominant position, contrary to the 'fair trading' condition in its licence; the investigation was discontinued on BT's undertaking that its internet telesales staff would no longer have access to such data.

[519] Cases 40/73, etc, *Suiker Unie v Commission* [1975] ECR 1663, [1976] 1 CMLR 295, paras 396 *et seq.* See also *Hachette, VIIIth Report on Competition Policy* (1978), points 114–115. But the exercise of a trade mark right by a dominant firm to restrain importation is not itself an abuse provided the exercise of the right is lawful under Arts 28–30 and is not intended to partition markets or distort normal conditions of competition: Case 102/77 *Hoffmann-La Roche v Centrafarm* [1978] ECR 1139, [1978] 3 CMLR 217. For the exercise of trade mark rights, see generally Chap 9, above.

[520] Case 27/76 *United Brands v Commission* [1978] ECR 207, [1978] 1 CMLR 429 (the green banana clause).

[521] An agreement between Microsoft and AT&T required any relevant developments by AT&T to be compatible with Microsoft's original software: *XXVIIth Report on Competition Policy* (1997), point 79. The Commission regarded as anti-competitive Sega and Nintendo's reservation of the right to vet games developed by independent producers for their consoles: *XXVIIth Report on Competition Policy* (1997), point 80.

[522] *Novo Nordisk, XXVIth Report on Competition Policy* (1996), point 62 and p 142 (refusal to honour guarantees for its 'insulin pens' when used in conjunction with other manufacturers' components).

[523] Para 10.150, below.

Unfair trading conditions: *Tetra Pak II*. In *Tetra Pak II*, the Commission and **10.147** the Court of First Instance condemned a wide variety of clauses which they found were intended to bind the customer to the group to the maximum extent possible and eliminate competition.[524] Those clauses included:[525]

(i) restrictions preventing the customer from adding accessories to or modifying the machine without Tetra Pak's consent;[526]

(ii) an obligation to advise Tetra Pak of any technical improvements or modifications made to the machines or cartons and to grant Tetra Pak ownership of the intellectual property rights to such improvements or modifications;

(iii) a requirement that Tetra Pak's consent be obtained for the resale or transfer of use of the equipment and a right on the part of Tetra Pak to repurchase the equipment;[527]

(iv) a stipulation that honouring of the guarantee was subject to compliance with all the terms of the contract, not limited to those terms which affected the operation of the equipment;

(v) the duration of lease agreements.[528]

Unfair trading conditions: *TACA*. In *TACA*,[529] the members of the **10.148** Transatlantic Conference Agreement were held to occupy a collective dominant position and to have abused that position in various ways. As regards the terms

---

[524] *Tetra Pak II*, OJ 1992 L72/1, [1992] 4 CMLR 551, para 106; on appeal, Case T-83/91 *Tetra Pak v Commission* [1994] ECR II-755, [1997] 4 CMLR 726, paras 210–214 (further appeal dismissed, Case C-333/94P *Tetra Pak v Commission* [1996] ECR I-5951, [1997] 4 CMLR 662, [1997] All ER (EC) 4). The Commission did not examine the extent to which these clauses were invoked or enforced by Tetra Pak in practice. See also the terms imposed by Michelin on its dealers through the 'Michelin Friends Club', condemned in *Michelin II*: para 10.094, above.

[525] The Commission in addition condemned a number of clauses allowing Tetra Pak to inspect the customers' premises or audit the customers' company documents or impose penalties for breach of any of the terms at its discretion since these were aimed at ensuring compliance with the other abusive conditions.

[526] The Commission held that these clauses were clearly abusive in cases where Tetra Pak sold the machine to the customer. With regard to leases of the machines, the Commission stated (at para 131) that 'clauses intended to ensure respect for the machine's integrity form part of the attributes of ownership and do not therefore in themselves constitute abuses ... when they are imposed on a leaseholder by an undertaking in a dominant position'. However, because the payment terms imposed by Tetra Pak for rental of machines made leasing 'equivalent in economic terms to sale' these conditions were abusive even in the rental contracts.

[527] The clause unduly limited the right of the purchaser of the machine to dispose of his asset as he wished and also prevented a market in second-hand machines from developing, thus supporting the compartmentalisation of national markets.

[528] The Commission held that a lease term which equals or exceeds the technological, if not physical, life of the machines was abusive; even a lease of three years unduly bound the customer to Tetra Pak in a market where there was rapid technological development.

[529] *TACA*, OJ 1999 L95/1, [1999] 4 CMLR 1415, paras 553–557.

of the contracts which were set by the members, the Commission held that the following were abusive:

(i) the outright prohibition between 1994 and 1995 on members entering into individual service contracts with shippers,[530] thereby forcing shippers to enter into service contracts with the conference members taken together;

(ii) once that prohibition had been lifted, the application in any individual service contract of certain terms and conditions collectively agreed by the conference;

(iii) the application in the conference service contract of certain terms and conditions.

The collectively agreed terms in the individual or conference service contracts which the Commission condemned were the prohibition of contingency clauses,[531] the minimum duration for the contract, the ban on multiple contracts and the level of the penalties imposed on shippers who breached the service contract.

10.149 *TACA*: **standard practice in the industry.** The Court of First Instance upheld the Commission's findings in relation to these clauses.[532] It rejected the conference members' arguments that the clauses were necessary to support the conference rate agreement which benefited from the block exemption in Regulation 4056/86.[533] The Court also rejected the argument that the clauses were justified by commercial usage because they were standard practice in the industry:

> '... conduct cannot cease to be abusive merely because it is the standard practice in a particular sector; to hold otherwise would deprive Article [82] of the Treaty of any effect.... Even if the practices on services contracts in question represent the standard practice of maritime carriers, therefore, Article [82] of the Treaty prevented the TACA parties, given their special responsibility as a collective dominant unit on the transatlantic trade, from adopting such practices, notwithstanding the fact that they were adopted by most, if not all, of their competitors.'[534]

Finally, the Court found, as a matter of fact, that provisions of US law did not provide any objective justification for the inclusion of the offending clauses.

---

[530] A service contract involves a commitment by the shipper to provide a minimum quantity of cargo over a particular period and by the carrier to a specified rate (usually lower than the normal rate because of the shipper's volume commitment) and defined level of service.

[531] A contingency clause is where the service contract provides that if the tariff rate (for ad hoc shipments) drops below the shipper's service contract rate, or if the conference enters into another service contract with a smaller volume commitment and a lower rate, the shipper which signed the first contract is automatically entitled to the lower rate.

[532] Cases T-191/98, etc, *Atlantic Container Line v Commission* [2003] ECR II-3275, [2005] 4 CMLR 1283, paras 1105–1191. Other findings of abuse were annulled by the CFI.

[533] See para 12.021, below for discussion of this block exemption.

[534] Cases T-191/98, etc, *Atlantic Container Line* (n 532, above) paras 1124–1125.

Unfair trading conditions: IP licences. The Commission settled a series of **10.150** complaints by manufacturers of pre-recorded compact discs against Philips and Sony which operated a joint licensing programme.[535] The complaints alleged that Philips and Sony had breached Articles 81 and 82 by setting up a patent pool which included non-essential and expired intellectual property and fixed royalties at an unfair level. Philips and Sony had jointly developed the specifications for CDs and CD-ROMs which had become the highly successful industry standard. By 2002 all CD Audio patents had expired in the majority of countries where they had been granted. The Commission, having arrived at the preliminary conclusion that Philips and Sony were jointly dominant in the market for the licensing of CD technology, identified a number of 'doubtful practices' in the joint licensing programme. The standard licensing agreement on offer did not make clear in which countries the patents were still extant; expired or useless patents were not systematically deleted from the list of patents being licensed; many patents which were not essential for the manufacture of CD Audio were included; and licensees were not informed of changes introduced into later versions of the agreement. The result was that the administration of the programme lacked transparency and created confusion amoung licensees, many of which were very small independent firms, in ways which could amount to the imposition of unfair trading conditions contract to Article 82(a). Following the Commission's intervention, Philips and Sony notified revised versions of their standard licensing agreements. Only essential patents were licensed and licensees could opt to take the joint licence or individual licences from Philips or Sony.

Limiting production, markets or technical development. As a category of **10.151** abuse, Article 82(b) specifically identifies 'limiting production, markets or technical development to the prejudice of consumers'. Conduct falling within that category could include limitation by a dominant undertaking of its own output (for example, with a view to raising prices by ensuring that demand exceeds supply); or action on the part of a dominant undertaking that limits the ability of third parties to increase production or enter new markets or develop new techniques.

---

[535] *Ingman Disc VDC v Philips and Sony, etc, XXXIIIrd Report on Competition Policy* (2002), p 197, and see Peña Castellot, 'Commission settles allegations of abuse and clears patent pools in the CD market' (2003) 3 EC Competition Policy Newsletter 56. Case T-151/01 *Der Grüne Punkt – Duales System Deutschland v Commission*, [2007] 5 CMLR 300, on appeal, Case C-385/07P, not yet deicded (standard agreement used by dominant operator of waste packaging recycling scheme that licensed use of well-known 'Green Dot' trade mark and also provided for collection of waste packaging: method of determination of licence fee was unfair and disproportionate in that it depended on the amount of packaging to which the mark was applied, irrespective of whether the licensee used the collection service); Press Release IP/02/1651 (12 November 2002) (clearance granted to agreements for patent pool of competing technologies for 3G mobile services after modification of the arrangements to ensure that competing technologies were not bundled together); Brenning, 'Commission closes probe into IBM's licensing terms for speech recognition engines' (2002) 3 EC Competition Policy Newsletter 57 (termination for challenge clause and 'must add value' clause amended after Commission's intervention).

For example, in *Suiker Unie*[536] the Court of Justice found that the sugar compa-nies had infringed Article 82(b) by compelling dealers to channel their exports to specific destinations and to impose restrictions on their own customers, thereby restricting the outlets of dealers and indirectly of their purchasers. In *British Telecommunications*,[537] the Commission held that by prohibiting message-forwarding agencies in the United Kingdom from retransmitting telex messages originating in and destined for locations abroad, British Telecommunications was infringing Article 82(b) by limiting the development of a new market and also the use of new technology, to the prejudice of relay operators and their customers. In the same way, in *Magill*[538] the Court of Justice held that the appellants' refusal to provide programme scheduling information to third parties prevented the appear-ance of a new product, namely a comprehensive weekly television guide, and thus constituted an abuse under Article 82(b).

10.152 **Abusive alteration of the structure of the market.** In *Atlantic Container Line (TACA)*,[539] the Court of First Instance also considered a challenge to a finding by the Commission that the liner conference members had infringed Article 82 'by altering the competitive structure of the market so as to reinforce the domi-nant position of the Transatlantic Conference Agreement'. The Court found that the Commission had not established the factual basis for this allegation, namely that the conference members had induced market entrants to join the liner conference rather than operate on the route as independent carriers. The Court noted that where a liner conference adopts measures in order to restrict the ability of potential competitors to enter the market as independent carriers, this might constitute an abusive alteration of the competitive structure of the market. In such a case, the mere fact that potential competitors enter the market in any event does not necessarily mean that the conference's conduct is not abusive since without such measures the entry to the market might have occurred under different condi-tions. However, the neutralisation of potential competition condemned by the Commission resulted not from measures intended to restrict the ability of poten-tial competitors to enter the market but, conversely, from measures described as inducements to enter the market as TACA parties. Accordingly, the fact that this result was not achieved sufficed to show that the measure in question was not a sufficient inducement to join the conference and, therefore, that there was no abuse of a dominant position in that regard.[540]

---

536 Cases 40/73, etc, *Suiker Unie v Commission* [1975] ECR 1663, [1976] 1 CMLR 295.
537 *British Telecommunications*, OJ 1982 L360/36, [1983] 1 CMLR 457; upheld in Case 41/83 *Italy v Commission* [1985] ECR 873, [1985] 2 CMLR 368.
538 *Magill*, discussed at para 10.130, above.
539 Cases T-191/98, etc, *Atlantic ContainerLine* (n 532, above).
540 ibid, paras 1338 and 1339.

Misconduct in acquisition of property rights: *AstraZeneca*.   The Commission's   **10.153**
decision in *AstraZeneca*[541] concerned AstraZeneca's strategy for marketing its anti-
ulcer medicine, Losec. The active ingredient in Losec was omeprazole which
existed in a neutral 'free base' form or in the form of a magnesiun salt. AstraZeneca
held a number of patents protecting the different formulations of the active substance and initially marketed Losec in capsules incorporating omeprazole in its
neutral form. The first abuse concerned the company's applications for
Supplementary Protection Certificates ('SPCs')[542] which extended the life of the
patent protection for the active ingredient. The Commission found that there was
a pattern of misleading representations made by the company to patent agents,
patent offices and national courts in order to acquire (or preserve) SPCs for omeprazole. Through these misrepresentations, the Commission found, AstraZeneca
aimed to keep generic manufacturers away from the market. The Commission
emphasised that AstraZeneca's conduct 'did not constitute normal business behaviour' and that the patent offices exercised a limited degree of discretion when
assessing the information submitted by the SPC applicants. The Commission
rejected the argument that it was interfering with the principle that it is for the
national legislature to determine the conditions and rules regarding the protection conferred by intellectual property rights. The Commission held that the laws
of the Member States are not affected by treating as abusive, misleading representations made in the context of applications for intellectual property rights, in the
absence of which the right or rights in question would not normally have been
granted. Referring to *Tetra Pak I* the Commission stated that since the acquisition
of a right may amount to an abuse:

> '. . . there is therefore no reason why the conduct in the procedure relating to the
> acquisition of the right cannot be considered as an abuse. The use of public proce-
> dures and regulations, including administrative and judicial processes, may, in spe-
> cific circumstances, constitute an abuse, as the concept of abuse contrary to AZ's
> arguments, is not limited to behaviour in the market only.'[543]

The Commission also held that the fact that the legislation governing the grant of
SPCs contained separate sanctions for the provision of false information did
not preclude the application of Article 82 since abuse is not limited to conduct
which does not infringe any other laws. Moreover, it was necessary to establish
that the misleading representations were relied upon by patent agents, patent
offices and courts. Whether or not the national patent offices or courts relied on

---

[541] COMP/37.507 *AstraZeneca*, 15 June 2005, [2006] 5 CMLR 287 (on appeal Case T-321/05 *AstraZeneca v Commission*, not yet decided).

[542] Pursuant to Reg 1768/92, OJ 1992 L182/1: SPCs are designed to compensate the patent holder for the research and development period between the grant of the original patent and the date when marketing of the drug can begin.

[543] ibid, paras 742–743.

the representations simply reflected AstraZeneca's degree of success in the strategy which it implemented.[544]

10.154 **Impeding parallel imports and launch of competing products:** *AstraZeneca.* The second abuse concerned AstraZeneca's alleged strategy to make the parallel import of Losec capsules more difficult and to minimise the effect of the intro- duction of generic versions of omeprazole once patent protection had expired in three Member States. Generics manufacturers can take advantage of a simplified authorisation procedure [545] if they can establish that their product is the same as the formerly patented product which is authorised[546] for sale on the market under a market authorisation. By withdrawing its Losec capsules from the market and seeking to deregister its authorisation, AstraZeneca sought to deprive the generic manufacturers of an authorised product with which they could compare their generic version. The legal framework governing the licensing of parallel imported products also relied on the parallel importer being able to point to an identical authorised drug being marketed in the country of import.[547] The deregistration of the Losec capsule and its replacement with a different version of the product in three Member States was therefore intended to frustrate parallel imports by removing the reference product. The Commission found that AstraZeneca adopted a strategy involving a number of actions in order to delay generic market entry through various technical and legal hurdles and prevent parallel trade of Losec capsules. The abuse found was one aspect of that strategy, namely the sel- ective requests for deregistration of Losec capsules in Denmark, Norway and Sweden combined with the switch to a differently formulated Losec tablet in

---

[544] ibid, para 764. See also Case T-30/89 *Hilti v Commission* [1991] ECR II-1439, [1992] 4 CMLR 16, para 99: abuse for dominant company to demand fee for patent licences of right approximately six times higher than the figure ultimately granted by the UK Comptroller of Patents, thereby needlessly protracting the proceedings.

[545] See the description of the legal regime in paras 258 *et seq* of the decn. For other decisions where the abuse involved the hindrance of parallel trading, see *Amministrazione Autonoma dei Monopoli di Stato*, OJ 1998 L252/47, [1998] 5 CMLR 786, upheld on appeal Case T-139/98 *Amministrazione Autonoma dei Monopoli di Stato v Commission ('AAMS')* [2001] ECR II-3413, [2002] 4 CMLR 302 (Italian State distributor used various means to restrict the import of cigarettes from other Member States). See also Cases 40/73, etc, *Suiker Unie v Commission* [1975] ECR 1663, [1976] 1 CMLR 295, in which pressure not to export from Belgium to other member states was held to be an abuse; Case 226/84 *British Leyland v Commission* [1986] ECR 3263, [1987] 1 CMLR 185 where British Leyland's pricing policy was condemned because it had the effect of reducing imports of British Leyland cars into the UK; *Eurofix-Bauco v Hilti*, OJ 1988 L65/19, [1989] 4 CMLR 677, where one of Hilti's abuses was to impose pressure on its distributors in the Netherlands not to supply certain products to the UK (appeal on other grounds dismissed, *Hilti v Commission* (n 544, above)).

[546] The ECJ held that it was sufficient if the comparable authorisation was in place at the time the application for the generic licence was made even it had been withdrawn by the time the applica- tion was being considered: see Case C-223/01 *AstraZeneca* [2003] ECR I-11809.

[547] Subsequently, the ECJ held in a different case that the deregistration of the marketing author- isation of the reference product did not necessarily mean that the licence for the parallel import should be revoked: see cases cited in *AstraZeneca* (n 541, above) para 264.

those markets. The Commission emphasised the limits of its decision: it stated that no objective justifications for AstraZeneca's use of public procedures and regulations could be found in the alleged uncertain nature of the law or legal disputes or in the relevant pharmaceutical legislation and that AstraZeneca's strategy did not, at least at the relevant time, constitute standard industry practice. Single acts involving the launch, withdrawal or requests for deregistration of a pharmaceutical product would not normally be regarded as an abuse and the launch of a new formulation of Losec and/or the withdrawal of Losec capsules would not as such constitute an abuse. The decision is on appeal to the Court of First Instance.[548] Moreover, in *Syfait*,[549] Advocate General Jacobs did not regard the refusal by a pharmaceutical manufacturer to supply sufficient product to its customers to enable them to engage in parallel trade as a *per se* abuse. In the particular circumstances of the highly regulated pharmaceutical sector, which led to different prices in different Member States, such a refusal could be justified, albeit in limited circumstances.

Failure to satisfy demand. The above examples of abuses within Article 82(b) **10.155** may be regarded as exclusionary, in that they involved keeping out new market entrants or limiting their growth. In other circumstances, abuses within Article 82(b) may be exploitative in nature, with dominant companies limiting the extent to which they satisfy demand. Thus, in *P&I Clubs IGA*[550] the Commission considered that, prior to their amendment, the arrangements between the International Group of P&I Clubs gave rise to an abuse within the meaning of Article 82(b) since they offered a single insurance product which left a very substantial share of demand unsatisfied. The Commission said that it could only intervene in the matter if there was 'clear and uncontroversial evidence that a very substantial share of demand is being deprived of a service that it manifestly needs'.

Inefficiency as an abuse. Inefficiency, idleness, mismanagement or wilful **10.156** neglect may be an abuse of a dominant position, contrary to Article 82(b), which prohibits 'limiting production, markets, or technical development to the prejudice of consumers'. Thus in *Port of Genoa*,[551] where an undertaking in Italy had been granted the exclusive right to organise dock work at Genoa's port, the Court of Justice held that the undertaking's conduct was abusive in that it refused to

---

[548] Case T-321/05 *AstraZeneca v Commission*, not yet decided. Note also Case T-198/98 *Micro Leader v Commission* [1999] ECR II-3989, [2000] 4 CMLR 886, [2000] All ER (EC) 361: potential abuse by Microsoft through enforcement of copyright to prevent parallel importation of French-language software from Canada.

[549] Case C-53/03 *Syfait v GlaxoSmithKline* [2005] ECR I-4609, [2005] 5 CMLR 7, Opinion, paras 73 *et seq* (the ECJ held that the reference was inadmissible).

[550] *P&I Clubs, IGA*, OJ 1999 L125/12, [1999] 5 CMLR 646, paras 128–133.

[551] Case C-179/90 *Merci Convenzionalli Porto di Genova* [1991] ECR I-5889, [1994] 4 CMLR 422.

use modern technology, resulting in an increase in costs and prolonged delays in performance.[552] Similarly, in *Höfner and Elser*,[553] the Court of Justice was considering the conduct of an employment services agency which was granted under German law the exclusive right to provide employment agency services to the Federal Labour Office. The agency failed to ensure that it was able adequately to meet the demand for its services and the Court of Justice held that this was an abuse within the meaning of Article 82(b).[554] In a somewhat different application of Article 82(b), in *London European/Sabena* indirect pressure imposed by a dominant company on a competitor to encourage the latter to be less price competitive or to abandon its plan to provide a competing service was construed by the Commission as an abuse.[555]

---

[552] ibid, para 19.

[553] Case C-41/90 *Höfner and Elser* [1991] ECR I-1979, [1993] 4 CMLR 306.

[554] See also Case C-55/96 *Job Centre* [1997] ECR I-7119, [1998] 4 CMLR 167; and AG Tesauro's Opinion in Case C-250/92 *Gøttrup-Klim v Dansk Landbrugs Grovvareselskab AmbA* [1994] ECR I-5641, [1996] 4 CMLR 191, para 24.

[555] *London European/Sabena*, OJ 1988 L317/47, [1989] 4 CMLR 662. See also Cases 110/88, etc, *Lucazeau v SACEM* [1989] ECR 2811, [1991] 4 CMLR 248, para 29 (high costs resulting from lack of competition not necessarily a defence to abuse).

11

THE COMPETITION RULES AND THE
ACTS OF MEMBER STATES

1. Introduction

Competition law and the activities of Member States. Where a State or state- **11.001**
owned body engages in economic activity, it may be regarded as an undertaking
and thus be subject to the direct application of the competition rules. The principles for determining where this is the case are discussed in Chapter 2. This Chapter
is concerned with how the competition rules affect the sovereign activities of the
State when it is not acting as an undertaking for the purposes of Articles 81 and 82.
The Member States' sovereign activities may be affected by the application of
competition law in various ways:

(i) A Member State may legislate in a way which compels an undertaking to
engage in conduct which would be regarded as a breach of Article 81 or 82 if
the undertaking had done the same thing on its own initiative.

(ii) National measures promulgated by the Member State may themselves be
contrary to the competition rules and associated Treaty provisions. Under
Article 86(1), measures adopted by the Member States in relation to public
undertakings and undertakings enjoying special or exclusive rights are
expressly made subject to Articles 81 and 82. The Court of Justice has held
that Member States have a duty under Article 10 of the Treaty to abstain

from enacting or enforcing laws that could jeopardise the effectiveness of the competition rules. Article 31 constrains the manner in which Member States may confer State monopolies of a commercial character.

(iii) Special derogations are available to undertakings and/or Member States in certain highly regulated sectors: Article 86(2) allows Member States and the undertakings to which they entrust the operation of services of general economic interest to derogate from the competition rules to the extent necessary for the fulfilment of the relevant public service tasks; and Article 296 allows a Member State to take the measures necessary to protect its essential security interests connected with the production of or trade in military equipment.

However, some activities carried on by private undertakings at the behest of the State do not qualify as economic in character, and those engaged in them are therefore not regarded as 'undertakings' and are not subject to competition law at all. This aspect of the meaning of the term 'undertaking' is also considered in Chapter 2.

11.002 **The Commission's policy.** In a series of pronouncements since the mid-1990s, the Commission has stressed the importance of the provision of services which public authorities class as being of general interest to the 'European model of society'.[1] In its First Communication on Services of General Interest,[2] the Commission recognised that although the operation of market forces generally produces better quality services at lower prices, these mechanisms sometimes have their limits because the potential benefits may not extend to the entire population and the objective of promoting social and territorial cohesion may not be attained. One of the principles underlying the Commission's policy in this area is therefore that Member States should be able to make the fundamental choices concerning their society, whereas the job of the Community is to ensure that the means which they employ are compatible with their European commitments.[3]

---

[1] Communication, 'Services of General Interest in Europe' OJ 1996 C281/3, ('the First Communication on Services of General Interest'); Communication, 'Services of General Interest in Europe' OJ 2001 C17/4; Communication, 'Green Paper on Services of General Interest', COM (2003) 270 final; Communication, 'White Paper on Services of General Interest', COM(2004) 374 final.

[2] Above. See also *XXVIth Report on Competition Policy* (1996), points 113 *et seq*, and point 22 where the Commission states that 'the need to ensure that balance is maintained means that the Commission must adopt a prudent, gradual and balanced approach in applying Article [86] of the Treaty'.

[3] See First Communication on Services of General Interest (n 1, above) para 17; White Paper on Services of General Interest (n 1, above) p 7 ('general interest . . . missions are protected rather than the way they are fulfilled'). See also generally: Blum and Logue, *State Monopolies under EC Law* (1998); Buendia Sierra, *Exclusive Rights and State Monopolies under EC Law* (1999).

Article 16. The importance of general interest services is also underlined by **11.003**
Article 16, introduced into the EC Treaty by the Treaty of Amsterdam,[4] which
provides:

> 'Without prejudice to Articles 73, 86 and 87 and given the place occupied by services
> of general economic interest in the shared values of the Union as well as their role in
> promoting social and territorial cohesion, the Community and the Member States,
> each within their respective powers and within the scope of application of this Treaty,
> shall take care that such services operate on the basis of principles and conditions
> which enable them to fulfil their missions.'

2. State Compulsion

Compliance with State measures. An undertaking may contend that its con- **11.004**
duct is based on a national measure, whether in the form of legislation or ministerial order, and so should not attract the operation of Article 81 or 82. In assessing
this contention, it is necessary to distinguish between national legislation that in
itself restricts competition, in which case the undertaking will not be in violation
of the competition rules; and legislation that facilitates or purports to legitimise
anti-competitive conduct by enterprises, in which case such conduct may contravene the competition rules notwithstanding the legislation. An agreement or
conduct which is not *required* by law may be caught by the competition rules[5]
even if it is done following consultation with the national authorities,[6] or with
their encouragement or approval,[7] and even if it is later expressly ratified by

---

[4] Art 16 was numbered Art 7d prior to the re-numbering pursuant to the Treaty of Amsterdam.
The Declaration on Article 7d adopted by the Amsterdam Conference states that the new article
'shall be implemented with full respect for the jurisprudence of the Court of Justice, inter alia as
regards the principles of equality of treatment, quality and continuity of such services'. See the
Commission's comments on this in *XXVIIth Report on Competition Policy* (1997), point 5 and points
96 *et seq*. See also the Protocol on the System of Public Broadcasting in the Member States, annexed
to the EC Treaty by the Treaty of Amsterdam, OJ 1997 C340/109, *Encyclopedia of European Union
Law (Constitutional Texts)*, Vol 1, para 12.3292.

[5] *SSI*, OJ 1982 L232/1, 24, [1982] 3 CMLR 702, on appeal Cases 240/82, etc, *SSI v Commission*
[1985] ECR 3831, [1987] 3 CMLR 661 (private agreements not required by Community and
Netherlands legislation affecting tobacco taxation); *Aluminium imports from Eastern Europe*, OJ
1985 L92/1, [1987] 3 CMLR 813 (governments neither participated themselves nor obliged the
undertakings to enter into the cartel so as to give rise to 'an act of State'); Cases 89/85, etc, *Åhlström
v Commission ('Wood Pulp I')* [1988] ECR 5193, [1988] 4 CMLR 901 (US legislation relied on did
not require the parties to enter into the cartel but merely exempted the conclusion of export cartels
from the application of US antitrust laws); *IJsselcentrale*, OJ 1991 L28/32, [1992] 5 CMLR 154,
paras 33–38.

[6] *SSI*, above.

[7] Cases 43 & 63/82 *VBVB & VBBB v Commission* [1984] ECR 19, [1985] 1 CMLR 27, para
40; *Zinc Producer Group*, OJ 1984 L220/27, [1985] 2 CMLR 108; *Aluminium imports from Eastern
Europe* (n 5, above) (encouragement by national authorities); *Fire Insurance (D)*, OJ 1985 L35/20,
25, [1985] 3 CMLR 246, on appeal Case 45/85 *Verband der Sachversicherer v Commission* [1987]

national law.[8] The critical question is whether or not the individual undertakings enjoyed commercial autonomy. In *Commission and France v Ladbroke Racing*, the Court of Justice stated:

> 'Articles [81 and 82] apply only to anti-competitive conduct engaged in by undertakings on their own initiative . . . If anti-competitive conduct is required of undertakings by national legislation or if the latter creates a legal framework which itself eliminates the possibility of competitive activity on their part, Articles [81 and 82] do not apply. In such a situation, the restriction of competition is not attributable, as those provisions implicitly require, to the autonomous conduct of the undertakings. . . .
>
> Articles [81 and 82] may apply, however, if it is found that the national legislation does not preclude undertakings from engaging in autonomous conduct which prevents, restricts or distorts competition.'[9]

Although the question of whether mandatory measures by a non-Member State may shield an agreement or conduct from the application of competition law has not been conclusively decided, it seems that the same principle should be applied in such a case.[10]

11.005 *Asia Motor France.* The proceedings in *Asia Motor France*[11] illustrate the application of the distinction discussed above. Parallel importers of Japanese cars into mainland France and Martinique complained of an agreement between the

---

ECR 405, [1988] 4 CMLR 264 (Art 81 cannot be subordinated to national rules in the insurance sector); *ENI/Montedison*, OJ 1987 L5/13, [1989] 4 CMLR 444 (fact that the agreement was in accordance with directives under the Italian government's Chemical Plan did not preclude application of Art 81(1)); *COAPI*, OJ 1995 L122/37, [1995] 5 CMLR 468, paras 44–47 (although Spanish legislation expressly enabled the professional association of industrial property agents to fix their scale of charges, the association was not obliged to do so); Case C-198/01 *CIF* [2003] ECR I-8055, [2003] 5 CMLR 829, para 56; Cases T-191/98, etc, *Atlantic Container Line v Commission (TACA)* [2003] ECR II-3275, [2005] 4 CMLR 1283, paras 1130–1131; Cases T-217 & 245/03 *FNCBV and FNSEA v Commission ('French Beef')*, judgment of 13 December 2006, para 92 (on appeal, Cases C-101/07P, etc, *Coopération De France Bétail et Viande v Commission*, not yet decided). See also *Sarabex, Eighth Report on Competition Policy* (1978), points 35–37, [1979] 1 CMLR 262 (terms of admission to London foreign exchange market reached under auspices of Bank of England).

   [8] *AROW/BNIC*, OJ 1982 L379/1, [1983] 2 CMLR 240, paras 53–57 (antecedent industry agreement on minimum prices given statutory effect under French law); Case 123/83 *BNIC v Clair* [1985] ECR 391, [1985] 2 CMLR 430, para 23.

   [9] Cases C-359 & 379/95P *Commission and France v Ladbroke Racing* [1997] ECR I–6265, [1998] 4 CMLR 27, paras 33–34.

   [10] Although the argument has been raised, it has always failed on the facts: eg *Aluminium imports from Eastern Europe* (n 5, above); *Franco-Japanese ballbearings*, OJ 1974 L343/19, [1975] 1 CMLR D8; *French-West African Shipowners' Committees*, OJ 1992 L134/1, [1993] 5 CMLR 446. See also Cases C-395 & 396/96P *Compagnie Maritime Belge Transports v Commission* [2000] ECR I–1365, [2000] 4 CMLR 1076, [2000] All ER (EC) 385, para 78; *Atlantic Container Line v Commission* (n 7, above) para 1131.

   [11] Case T-387/94 *Asia Motor France v Commission (No. 3)* [1996] ECR II–961, [1996] 5 CMLR 537. The Commission's previous decision rejecting the complaints had been annulled on the same grounds: Case T-7/92 *Asia Motor France v Commission (No. 2)* [1993] ECR II–669, [1994] 4 CMLR 30. Remarkably, the Commission adopted the decision again without any further evidence other than as regards Martinique, thereby giving rise to the further proceedings.

authorised distributors of Japanese cars who had undertaken to the French authorities not to import more than a specified quota, which they shared out amongst
themselves, with consequent restrictions on other (parallel) Japanese car imports.
The Commission rejected their complaints on the basis of a statement by the
French government that the conduct in question was connected to a regulatory
system laid down by the public authorities that left the distributors no freedom of
independent action. However, the Court of First Instance found that no legally
binding restrictions had been imposed and, as regards metropolitan France, there
was no evidence that the importers had been placed under 'irresistible pressures'
by the national authorities to engage in such conduct.[12] The mere risk that such
pressures might be imposed in furtherance of the French government policy to
reduce imports of Japanese cars was insufficient and that part of the decision was
accordingly annulled. By contrast, there was evidence establishing that operation
of the import scheme in Martinique was imposed on the authorised dealers unilaterally by the public authorities; the Commission's dismissal of the complaint in
that regard was therefore upheld.[13]

Scope for residual competition. The statement by the Court of Justice in **11.006**
Ladbroke[14] envisages the possibility that the competition rules will not apply if
national measures preclude the possibility of independent competition. However,
arguments to that effect made by parties subject to investigation seldom succeed
and the Commission is concerned to protect such residual competition as may
be possible. In *Sugar*,[15] several of the defendants argued that the Community's
common organisation of the sugar market, with a determination of minimum

---

[12] The CFI cited as an example the threat to adopt State measures likely to cause them to sustain substantial losses: *Asia Motor France (No. 3)*, above, para 65. In the subsequent appeal, Case
C-401/96P *Somaco v Commission* [1998] ECR I-2587, [1999] 4 CMLR 35, AG Tesauro observed
that this reference 'seems to suggest unlawful conduct by a public authority': Opinion at para 22, n 20.
[13] *Asia Motor France (No. 3)*, above, paras 73–100. The appeal by the Martinique complainant
was dismissed, *Somaco v Commission,* above.
[14] See para 11.004, above.
[15] Cases 40/73 *Suiker Unie v Commission* [1975] ECR 1663, [1976] 1 CMLR 295. See also *Re
Sugar Beet*, OJ 1990 L31/32, [1991] 4 CMLR 629 (Community sugar regime leaves residual field
for competition); Cases 209/78, etc, *Van Landewyck v Commission* [1980] ECR 3125, [1981] 3
CMLR 134, paras 123–136; Cases 240/82, etc, *SSI v Commission* (n 5, above); *UK Agricultural
Tractor Registration Exchange*, OJ 1992 L68/19, [1993] 4 CMLR 358, para 49 (availability of
information also from Government sources did not detract from unlawfulness of information exchange agreement), appeals on other grounds dismissed: Case T-34/92 *Fiatagri and Ford
New Holland v Commission* [1994] ECR II–905; Case C-8/95P *New Holland Ford v Commission*
[1998] ECR I–3175, [1998] 5 CMLR 362; Case T-35/92 *John Deere v Commission* [1994] ECR
II–957 (on appeal Case C-7/95P *Deere v Commission* [1998] ECR I–3111, [1998] 5 CMLR
311); Case T-65/99 *Strintzis Lines Shipping v Commission* [2003] ECR II-5433, [2005] 5 CMLR
1901, paras 119–124 (appeal dismissed by order, Case C-110/04P [2006] ECR I-44); Case T-
66/99 *Minoan Lines v Commission* [2003] ECR II-5515, [2005] 5 CMLR 1957, paras 176–178
(appeal dismissed, Case C-121/04P, order of 17 November 2005); Case T-168/01 *GlaxoSmithKline
Services v Commission* [2006] ECR II-2969, [2006] 5 CMLR 1589, paras 66 *et seq* (on appeal, Cases
C-501/06P, etc, *GlaxoSmithKline Services v Commission*, not yet decided).

and intervention prices and also national quotas, eliminated any effective competition. While recognising that certain aspects of this system reduced the scope for competition, the Court of Justice held that 'if it leaves in practice a residual field of competition, that field comes within the provisions of the rules of competition.'[16] That was the case with the general Community regime. But in the particular case of Italy, that regime was supplemented by Italian domestic regulations which organised the Italian national market by matching supply with demand and largely removed the freedom of buyers and suppliers to choose their trading partners. Accordingly, the Court found that the concerted practice which the Commission had found as regards the Italian market could not appreciably impede competition and the decision was annulled in that respect.[17]

11.007 **Concurrent liability of Member States and undertakings.** As discussed at paragraphs 11.029 *et seq*, below, State measures that restrict competition may be contrary to Articles 81 or 82 applied in conjunction with Articles 10 and 3(1)(g) or Article 86(1). In the *Ladbroke case*,[18] the Court of Justice held that the question of whether the national measures involve a breach by the Member State of Article 10 is irrelevant to the analysis of the position of private undertakings under Article 81(1). It follows that in certain circumstances an agreement or conduct may infringe Article 81 or 82; and a national measure endorsing or giving binding force to that agreement or decision may also be in breach of Community law. For example, the governing body of the Italian customs agents (CNSD), who are classed as an independent profession, was empowered by law to set the rates to be charged by the agents for customs clearance procedures; those rates then became binding on all agents. In infringement proceedings brought by the Commission under Article 226, the Court of Justice held that Italy was in breach of the Treaty by adopting legislation that delegated to private operators the fixing of rates by

---

[16] *Suiker Unie v Commission,* above, para 24. In *ÁB-Aegon/Allianz Hungária/Generali-Providencia/ OTP Garancia/Uniqua* Vj-149/2003 the Hungarian Competition Office held that an agreement creating a consortium of insurance companies for the purpose of bidding jointly to provide state accident insurance fell within the equivalent of Art 81. The domestic legislation on public procurement, although it facilitated undertakings in submitting joint bids did not make joint bids mandatory and therefore did not eliminate the autonomy of undertakings in deciding whether to bid independently or join the consortium.

[17] ibid, paras 29–73. In *Verbindung von Telefonnetzen*, 10 February 2004, WuW/E DE-R 1254, the German Federal Supreme Court held that the charging of prices approved by a regulatory authority can nevertheless constitute an abuse of a dominant position. In that case, the regulator's approval procedure was triggered by an application by the defendant and although the procedure was intended to ensure that prices were not abusive, approval did not conflict with a finding of abuse.

[18] *Commission and France v Ladbroke Racing* (n 9, above) paras 30–33. For discussion of the case law and criticism of the Courts' approach, see Martinez Lage and Brokelmann, 'The Application of Articles 85 and 86 to the Conduct of Undertakings that are Complying with National Legislation', in Dony and De Walsche (eds), *Mélanges Michel Waelbroek*, Vol II, p 1247 (1999).

agreement and prohibited any customs agents from departing from those rates.[19] In separate proceedings, the Commission found CNSD itself to be in breach of Article 81(1) by reason of its rate-fixing decision.[20] On appeal, the Court of First Instance dismissed CNSD's argument that its conduct was effectively prescribed by the Italian legislation, holding that the legislation allowed a margin of discretion to CNSD and therefore left scope for competition, which CNSD was obliged not to hinder.[21] The decision to impose minimum rates and prohibit lump sum charges was not required under the legislation and had the effect of impeding competition; it therefore violated Article 81(1).

Liability of undertakings when State compulsion is lifted. A national **11.008** court must disapply national measures contrary to Articles 81, 3(1)(g) and 10 or Articles 86(1) and 82.[22] Where measures which compelled an undertaking to act in a way which would otherwise be contrary to the competition rules are disapplied, can the undertaking be penalised for its conduct during the period when it believed it was obliged to comply? In *CIF*,[23] the Italian court referred to the Court of Justice two questions arising out of the Italian Competition Authority's investigation into a domestic match producers consortium. The Court of Justice held that a national competition authority which is competent to apply Article 81 EC must similarly disapply national measures contrary to Articles 81, 3(1)(g) and 10. The Court then discussed the effect of such a disapplication on the liability of the undertakings who may have been obliged to act in a manner which contravened the competition rules. The Court held that, if the general Community law principle of legal certainty is not to be violated, the disapplication of the law cannot expose the undertakings concerned to any penalties in respect of their past conduct in compliance with the law; the law constitutes 'a justification which shields the undertakings concerned' from the consequences of the infringement *vis-à-vis* both the public authorities and other economic operators.[24] However, once the decision to set aside the legislation 'becomes definitive' and binding upon them, they can be penalised for any subsequent infringing conduct.

---

[19] Case C-35/96 *Commission v Italy* [1998] ECR I–3851, [1998] 5 CMLR 889.

[20] *CNSD*, OJ 1993 L203/27, [1995] 5 CMLR 495. See also *COAPI* (n 7, above).

[21] Case T-513/93 *CNSD v Commission* [2000] ECR II–1807, [2000] 5 CMLR 614. See also Case T-35/92 *John Deere v Commission* (n 15, above) para 58.

[22] See paras 11.034–11.035, below.

[23] Case C-198/01 *CIF* [2003] ECR I-8055, [2003] 5 CMLR 829, paras 49–50.

[24] *CIF*, above, para 54. The ECJ held that it was for the national court to determine whether the Italian legislation did, in fact, require the undertakings to commit the infringements.

3. The Application and Enforcement of the Prohibition in Article 86(1)

11.009 **In general.**   Article 86(1) provides that:

> 'In the case of public undertakings and undertakings to which Member States grant special or exclusive rights, Member States shall neither enact nor maintain in force any measure contrary to the rules contained in this Treaty, in particular to those rules provided for in Article 12 and Articles 81 to 89.'

Article 86(1) is addressed not to undertakings but to Member States. In *INNO v ATAB*,[25] the Court of Justice stated that Article 86 was only a particular application of certain general principles which bind the Member States. The Court was referring in particular to the obligation imposed on Member States, by virtue of Article 10, not to jeopardise the attainment of the objectives of the Treaty.[26] Article 86(1) has direct effect, in that it can be invoked by an individual against the Member State in a national court,[27] but it seems that a breach of some other article of the Treaty having direct effect must be shown.[28]

11.010 **Public undertakings.**   The use of the word 'public' indicates that a public undertaking is to be distinguished from a private one. Just as there is no definition in the Treaty of an undertaking, so there is no definition in the Treaty of a public undertaking. In its Notice regarding the postal sector,[29] the Commission states that the term includes every undertaking over which the public authorities may exercise, directly or indirectly, a dominant influence by virtue of ownership of it, or their financial participation in it or the rules which govern it. A dominant influence on the part of the public authorities may be presumed where they hold a majority of the capital or of the voting rights in the undertaking.[30] For this purpose it does not

---

[25] Case 13/77 *INNO v ATAB* [1977] ECR 2115, [1978] 1 CMLR 283, para 42. See also generally Cases 188/80, etc, *France, Italy and the United Kingdom v Commission* [1982] ECR 2545, [1982] 3 CMLR 144.

[26] *INNO v ATAB* (n 25, above) paras 30–38.

[27] Case 155/73 *Sacchi* [1974] ECR 409, [1974] 2 CMLR 177, para 18.

[28] See, eg Case C-179/90 *Merci Convenzionale Porto di Genova* [1991] ECR I-5889, [1994] 4 CMLR 422 (Art 86 in conjunction with Arts 28, 39 and 82). Art 86(1) could not be invoked in the case of a breach of a provision not having direct effect, such as Art 87.

[29] Notice on the application of the competition rules to the postal sector and on the assessment of certain State measures relating to postal services, OJ 1998 C39/2, [1998] 5 CMLR 108. See also the definition in similar terms in the Transparency Directive (Dir 2006/111, OJ 2006 L318/17: Vol II, App F.2), but note that the ECJ has stated that the definition of public undertaking in the earlier version of the Directive was not a definition of the concept as it appears in Art 86 of the Treaty: *France, Italy and the United Kingdom* (n 25, above) paras 22–26.

[30] Notice, ibid, para 4.1. See also, eg COMP 38.745 *BdKEP – restrictions on mail preparation*, 20 October 2004, [2006] 4 CMLR 981 (63 per cent of Deutsche Post owned directly or indirectly by German government, hence it is a public undertaking) (on appeal, Case T-490/04 *Germany v Commission*, not yet decided).

matter whether the State carries out the economic activities by way of a distinct body over which it can exercise a dominant influence or whether it carries out the activities directly through a body forming part of the State administration. The fact that a body has or does not have legal personality under national law separate from that of the State is irrelevant in deciding whether it is a public undertaking within the meaning of Community law.[31]

Undertakings granted special or exclusive rights. These undertakings are included within the ambit of Article 86(1) because a Member State that accords undertakings special or exclusive rights might be disposed to adopt measures that would favour these undertakings and thus distort competition.[32] Thus, for example, the granting of exclusive rights to an undertaking to engage in radio and television transmissions was held by the Court of Justice to fall within the ambit of Article 86(1).[33] On the other hand an authors' rights society that benefited from legislation requiring authors to exercise their rights only through such a society did not fall within the scope of Article 86(1) since it was open to any other authors' rights society to benefit from that legislative provision.[34] Where the measure confers the exclusive rights to carry out a particular kind of work on a class of people who are then employed by a number of different undertakings, Article 86 does not apply because the workers are not undertakings for the purposes of that Article.[35]

11.011

Special and exclusive rights. In the *Leased Lines* case,[36] the Court of Justice considered in what circumstances an undertaking has 'special or exclusive' rights in the context of the United Kingdom's implementation of the Leased Lines Directive.[37] The Court held that a licence under such a system could not be

11.012

---

[31] Case 118/85 *Commission v Italy* [1987] ECR 2599, [1988] 3 CMLR 255; Case C-69/91 *Decoster* [1993] ECR I-5335.

[32] *Commission v Italy*, above; *Decoster*, above.

[33] *Sacchi* (n 27, above) and see Case C-260/89 *ERT* [1991] ECR I-2925, [1994] 4 CMLR 540. See also Case 90/76 *Van Ameyde v UCI* [1977] ECR 1091, [1977] 2 CMLR 478 (grant of sole responsibility for the settlement of foreign accident insurance claims apparently regarded as within Art 86(1)); Case 83/78 *Pigs Marketing Board v Redmond* [1978] ECR 2347, [1979] 1 CMLR 177, paras 41 *et seq*, where the ECJ appeared to accept that the Pigs Marketing Board (Northern Ireland), a body that administered the marketing of pigs in Northern Ireland pursuant to the Agricultural Marketing Act (Northern Ireland) 1964, was an undertaking granted special or exclusive rights within the meaning of Art 86(1); Case 66/86 *Ahmed Saeed Flugreisen v Zentrale zur Bekämpfung unlauteren Wettbewerbs* [1989] ECR 803, [1990] 4 CMLR 102 (the right to operate on an air route alone or with one or two other undertakings is a special or exclusive right).

[34] *GEMA*, JO 1971 L134/15, [1971] CMLR D35.

[35] Case C-22/98 *Becu* [1999] ECR I-5665, [2001] 4 CMLR 968.

[36] Case C-302/94 *The Queen v Secretary of State for Trade and Industry, ex p British Telecommunications* [1996] ECR I-6417, [1997] 1 CMLR 424. See also the definitions of 'exclusive rights' and 'special rights' in Art 2(f) of the Transparency Directive, Dir 206/111 (n 29, above).

[37] Dir 92/44, OJ 1992 L165/27. The UK had imposed an obligation on BT to make leased lines available on the basis that BT was a 'telecommunications organisation', a term defined for the

described as the grant of exclusive or special rights because the licences were granted according to objective, proportionate and non-discriminatory criteria which did not have the effect of limiting the number of undertakings which can operate as PTOs.[38] But the Court went on to hold that because British Telecommunications ('BT') and Mercury alone were licensed to operate international lines and because that licence was granted according to criteria which were not objective nor proportionate nor free from discrimination, BT was a undertaking with special and exclusive rights. In *Ambulanz Glöckner*,[39] the Court adopted a somewhat different approach. Advocate General Jacobs suggested that there were three essential elements: (i) the right is granted by the authorities of a Member State; (ii) it is granted to one undertaking or to a limited number of undertakings; and (iii) it substantially affects the ability of other undertakings to exercise the economic activity in question in the same geographical area under substantially equivalent conditions.[40] The fourth criterion as to whether the rights were granted according to objective, proportionate and non-discriminatory criteria was relevant in the Leased Lines Directive but not, according to the Advocate General, in the application of Article 86(1). The Court of Justice seems to have followed this approach, stating that special and exclusive rights may be found to exist where 'protection is conferred by a legislative measure on a limited number of undertakings which may substantially affect the ability of other undertakings to exercise the economic activity in question in the same geographical area under substantially equivalent conditions'.[41]

11.013 **Measures of the Member State.** It seems that the measures referred to in Article 86(1) are acts directed towards the categories of undertakings set out in Article 86(1).[42] The term 'measures' would seem to include legislative acts affecting the undertakings in question, administrative directions, the exercise of

---

purposes of the Directive as being an undertaking which had been granted 'exclusive or special rights for the provision of public telecommunications networks'. Note that in Dir 94/46, OJ 1994 L268/15, [1996] 4 CMLR 87, which amends the Telecommunications Terminal Equipment and Services Directives, the Commission has now incorporated a more precise definition of special rights.

[38] The ECJ also held that privileges granted to PTOs to acquire land compulsorily and to place network equipment under the highway was not enough since they were conferred equally on all PTOs, did not give their holders a substantial advantage over their potential competitors.

[39] Case C-475/99 *Ambulanz Glöckner* [2001] ECR I-8089, [2002] 4 CMLR 726, para 89.

[40] ibid, Opinion, para 87.

[41] *Ambulanz Glöckner*, above, para 24 of the judgment. See also AG Colomer in Case C-451/03 *Servizi Ausiliari Dottori Commercialisti v Giuseppe Calafiori*, Opinion of 28 June 2005, at fn 12 The ECJ did not refer to this point, [2006] ECR I-2941, [2006] 2 CMLR 1135.

[42] Cases 46/90 & C-93/91 *Procureur du Roi v Lagauche* [1993] ECR I-5267 where the ECJ held that a power of authorisation conferred on a minister within the normal framework of his powers was not a measure within Art 86(1) because it was not adopted in regard to a favoured undertaking.

shareholders' rights and even non-binding recommendations.[43] Article 86(1) covers State measures so that conduct hindering competition which is simply adopted by the undertakings on their own initiative rather than having been required or induced by the State may be challenged only under Articles 81 and 82.[44] Conversely, where the public undertaking in practice operates in a less restrictive manner than required by the measure, this does not absolve the Member State of its responsibility for the infringing measure.[45]

The grant of special or exclusive rights can itself be a measure. In the *Telecommunications Terminal Equipment* case,[46] the Court of Justice held that the grant of such rights could themselves be regarded as measures contrary to Article 86. The case arose out of proceedings brought by France to annul Commission Directive 88/301 on competition in the telecommunications terminal equipment market. The Directive was adopted on the basis of Article 86(3), and Article 2 of the Directive provided that Member States which had granted special or exclusive rights to undertakings, *inter alia*, to import, market, connect and maintain terminal equipment must ensure that those rights were withdrawn. France[47] contended that by requiring the withdrawal of special or exclusive rights, the Commission had exceeded its powers under Article 86; Article 86(1) presupposes the grant of such rights so that those rights themselves

11.014

---

[43] See also the wide definition given to the word 'measure' as used in Art 28 which has been held to cover non-binding recommendations: eg Case 249/81 *Commission v Ireland ('Buy Irish')* [1982] ECR 4005, [1983] 2 CMLR 104; *Greek Insurance*, OJ 1985 L152/25 (non-binding recommendation held to be a measure).

[44] Case C-202/88 *France v Commission ('Telecommunications Terminal Equipment')* [1991] ECR I-1223, [1992] 5 CMLR 552, paras 55–56; Case C-323/93 *Centre d'Insémination de la Crespelle v Coopérative de la Mayenne* [1994] ECR I-5077. In Case E-4/05 *HOB-vín v The Icelandic State and Áfengis- og tóbaksverslun ríkisins (The State Alcohol and Tobacco Company of Iceland)* [2006] 2 CMLR 1098, it appears that approval by the Icelandic Minister of Finance of the rules adopted by the monopoly undertaking's Board was regarded as sufficient to make those rules 'measures' for the purposes of Art 59 EEA (the equivalent of Art 86 EC).

[45] COMP 38.745 *BdKEP – restrictions on mail preparation*, 20 October 2004, [2006] 4 CMLR 981, para 78 (on appeal Case T-490/04 *Germany v Commission*, not yet decided). See note on this case in (2005) 3 EC Competition Policy Newsletter, 31. See also *Guaranteed day- or time-certain delivery in Italy*, OJ 2001 L63/59, [2001] 5 CMLR 595 (Italian legislation reserving new postal service to public undertaking infringed Art 86 in conjunction with Art 82 although the undertaking was not in fact providing the new service).

[46] *Telecommunications Terminal Equipment* case (n 44, above). See also the later similar judgment in Cases C-271/90, etc, *Spain v Commission* [1992] ECR I-5833, [1993] 4 CMLR 110, concerning the Telecommunications Services Directive 90/388.

[47] France was supported by Italy, Belgium, Germany and Greece. See also *Towercast v TDF*, decn 03-MC-03 of 1 December 2003, BOCCRF 13 February 2004, where the Conseil de la Concurrence held that the grant of exclusive right to TDF to broadcast all Radio France programming on FM frequencies was an abusive extension of TDF's rights because Dir 2002/77, which would outlaw such exclusivity, was due shortly to come into force. This decn was upheld by the Court of Appeal of Paris in *Towercast v TDF*, decn of 8 January 2004, BOCCRF 4 May 2004.

cannot constitute a measure within its terms. The Court rejected this argument stating:

> '. . . even though that article presupposes the existence of undertakings which have certain special or exclusive rights, it does not follow that all the special or exclusive rights are necessarily compatible with the Treaty. That depends on different rules, to which Article [86(1)] refers.'[48]

The Court of Justice went on to hold that the existence of exclusive rights to import and market terminal equipment deprives market operators of the opportunity to have their products bought by consumers. Further, given the wide range of products available on the market and the pace of technological change, one could not be sure that the State monopoly would be able to offer the full range of models existing on the market. The grant of exclusive rights contravened the free movement provision in Article 28 and thus the Commission had power under Article 86(3) to require such rights to be withdrawn.

11.015 **Application in conjunction with Treaty provisions.** Article 86(1) is infringed only in conjunction with another provision of the Treaty. Frequently, it is applied together with provisions that are themselves addressed to Member States such as Article 28 (free movement of goods),[49] Article 49 (free movement of services)[50] and Article 43 (right of establishment).[51] In such cases, Article 86(1) simply confirms that those other provisions apply to national measures adopted in relation to public undertakings and undertakings having special and exclusive rights. As Article 86(1) specifically states, it also applies in conjunction with Articles 81 and 82,[52] although those provisions are addressed to undertakings, not Member States.

11.016 **Link between the measure and the breach by the undertaking.** In some of its judgments, the Court of Justice has suggested that a State measure will only breach Articles 86(1) and 82 EC if it leads *inevitably* to an abuse of a dominant position in that the public or privileged undertaking concerned 'cannot avoid infringing' Article 82. In *Centre d'Insémination de la Crespelle*,[53] the Court of Justice considered whether a statutory framework which permitted insemination centres holding a local exclusive right to set their own charges was consistent with Articles 86(1) and 82. The Court held that a Member State contravenes the prohibitions contained in those two provisions only if, in merely exercising the

---

[48] *Telecommunications Terminal Equipment* case (n 44, above) para 22.

[49] See, eg *Telecommunications Terminal Equipment* case (n 44, above); Case C-18/88 *GB-Inno-BM* [1991] ECR I-5941.

[50] See, eg *Spain v Commission* (n 46, above); Case C-18/93 *Corsica Ferries* [1994] ECR I-1783.

[51] See, eg *Greek Insurance*, OJ 1985 L152/25, upheld on appeal, Case 226/87 *Commission v Greece* [1988] ECR 3611, [1989] 3 CMLR 569.

[52] See, eg *Porto di Genova* (n 28, above).

[53] Case C-323/93 *Centre d'Insémination de la Crespelle v Coopérative de la Mayenne* [1994] ECR I-5077. See also the *Telecommunications Terminal Equipment* case (n 44, above) at para 56.

exclusive right, the undertaking in question must necessarily abuse its dominant position. In more recent cases, however, the Court of Justice appears to be adopting a less exacting standard in order for a breach of Articles 86(1) and 82 to be established. Thus, in *Deutsche Post*, the Court was prepared to find such a breach where a State measure 'creates a situation where [the undertaking involved] may be led . . . to abuse its dominant position . . .'[54] In its recent case law, the Court has on several occasions stated that a Member State would infringe the Treaty if 'the undertaking in question, merely by exercising the exclusive rights granted to it, is led to abuse its dominant position or when such rights are liable to create a situation in which that undertaking is led to commit such abuses'.[55]

Inability to satisfy demand. In a number of cases, a State measure has been **11.017** challenged on the grounds that the undertaking which has been granted the exclusive right to provide a particular service is unable to satisfy the demand for that service in the Member State concerned and is thus placed in breach of Article 82 of the Treaty. In *Höfner and Elser*[56] the Court of Justice considered the grant by Germany of exclusive rights to an employment recruiting agency. It was apparent on the facts that the agency did not have the resources to meet all the demand for those services which arose in the market but German law rendered any agreement between private individuals for the provision of such services unenforceable. The Court held that the grant of exclusive rights in those circumstances contravened Article 86(1) in conjunction with Article 82, because the agency was forced, since it was manifestly incapable of meeting the demand for its services, to limit the provision of those services on the market.[57]

Extension of dominance into neighbouring markets. Measures which assist the **11.018** undertaking which has exclusive rights to extend its market power into a neighbouring market will be contrary to Article 86 in conjunction with Article 82. In *GB-INNO-BM*[58] the Court of Justice considered whether it is lawful for a

---

[54] Cases C-147 & 148/97 *Deutsche Post* [2000] ECR 825, [2000] 4 CMLR 838, para 48.

[55] Case C-163/96 *Raso* [1998] ECR I-533, [1998] 4 CMLR 737, para 27; Case C-209/98 *Sydhavnen* [2000] ECR 3743, [2001] 2 CMLR 936, para 66; Cases C-180 & 184/98 *Pavlov* [2000] ECR I-6451, [2001] 4 CMLR 30, para 127; *Ambulanz Glöckner* (n 39, above) para 39; *Servizi Ausiliari Dottori Commercialisti* (n 41, above) para 23. See also *HOB-vín v The Icelandic State and Áfengis- og tóbaksverslun ríkisins (The State Alcohol and Tobacco Company of Iceland)* (n 44, above) where the ESA in its submissions used the more stringent test (judgment, para 43) but the EFTA Court adopted the more recent formulation (para 50).

[56] Case C-41/90 *Höfner and Elser* [1991] ECR I-1979, [1993] 4 CMLR 306, para 31. See also *Pavlov*, above, paras 127–129.

[57] See similarly Case C-55/96 *Job Centre* [1997] ECR I-7119, [1998] 4 CMLR 708; Case C-258/98 *Carra* [2000] ECR I-4217, [2006] 2 CMLR 285. See also *Ground handling services at Athens Airport*, XXVIIth Report on Competition Policy (1997), point 131.

[58] Case C-18/88 *GB-INNO-BM* [1991] ECR I-5941. See also cases concerning the extension of the national postal monopoly to added value courier services: *Dutch Courier Services*, OJ 1990 L10/47, [1990] 4 CMLR 947, annulled on appeal on procedural grounds in Cases C-48 & 66/90

Member State to confer on the public telephone network operator the power to lay down specifications for telephone apparatus and to grant approval to other suppliers of apparatus when the network operator itself competed in the market as a supplier of apparatus. The Court of Justice held that it is contrary to Article 82 for a dominant undertaking to reserve for itself, without any objective justification,[59] an ancillary activity which could be carried out by a third party on a neighbouring market, with the aim of eliminating competition on that market. If the extension of the dominant undertaking's power to that neighbouring market is the result of a State measure, that measure contravenes Article 86(1) in conjunction with Article 82.[60] In two decisions concerning the market for mobile telephone services using the GSM standard, the Commission condemned measures placing financial burdens on new entrants to a market where they had to compete with an incumbent that had not been similarly burdened.[61] The public telephone network operator in Italy, Telecom Italia, had exclusive rights to provide services in the neighbouring markets for fixed wire telephony and mobile analogue radiotelephony. Telecom Italia was also granted a licence to operate in the new digital radiotelephony market. The government licensed a second operator to compete in the new market but imposed on the second operator a very substantial financial payment for the concession which was not required from Telecom Italia. The Commission held that Telecom Italia had been granted a special right in the new market because the licences were not designated according to objective and non-discriminatory criteria. Because of its dominance in the neighbouring markets, it would be an abuse for Telecom Italia to try to extend its

---

Netherlands PTT v Commission [1992] ECR I-565, [1993] 5 CMLR 316; and *Re Spanish Courier Services*, OJ 1990 L233/19, [1991] 4 CMLR 560; Case C-320/91 *Corbeau* [1993] ECR I-2533, [1995] 4 CMLR 621; to mail preparation and consolidation services: *BdKEP – restrictions on mail preparation* (n 45, above) paras 59–63; and to the day- or time-certain delivery phase of hybrid electronic mail service: *Guaranteed day- or time-certain delivery in Italy*, OJ 2001 L63/59, [2001] 5 CMLR 595.

[59] The ECJ held in this case that there were less restrictive ways in which the integrity of the public network could be protected.

[60] In Case T-175/99 *UPS Europe v Commission* [2002] ECR II-1915, [2002] 5 CMLR 67, para 61, the CFI upheld the Commission's decn that Deutsche Post had not infringed Art 82 when it acquired DHS using income obtained on a market exclusively reserved to it. Cross-subsidisation from the reserved market was not in itself to be regarded as abusive.

[61] *Decision concerning the conditions imposed on the second operator of GSM radiotelephony services in Italy*, OJ 1995 L280/49, [1996] 4 CMLR 700; *Re GSM Telephony services in Spain*, OJ 1997 L76/19. Note that in the first case the Commission ordered Italy to impose the same charge on Telecom Italia and in the second it ordered Spain to reimburse the fee to the second operator. For the follow up to these cases, see *XXVIIth Report on Competition Policy* (1997), points 107–108. See also Case C-462/99 *Connect Austria v Telekom Control Kommission* [2003] ECR I-5197, [2005] 5 CMLR 302 (grant of frequencies to incumbent without charge not contrary to Art 86 if the fee imposed on the dominant public undertaking for its GSM 900 licence, including subsequent allocation of additional frequencies in the DCS 1800 band without additional payment, is equivalent in economic terms to the fee imposed on the competitor which was granted the DCS 1800 licence).

dominance into the new market, for example by increasing the costs of its new rival. By imposing the additional financial burden on the second operator, the government put Telecom Italia in the position of having to choose one of two commercial strategies, either of which would be in breach of Article 82. The measure imposing the charge was therefore contrary to Article 86.

Creation of conflict of interest.   Measures which place the privileged undertak-   **11.019** ing in a position where it can control aspects of its competitors' business have been condemned by the Court of Justice and the Commission. In *Raso*,[62] the Court of Justice held that the Italian legislation which reserved to the port authority the exclusive right to supply temporary dock work labour in the port of La Spezia was contrary to Article 86 in conjunction with Article 82 where that port authority also had a licence to compete in the market for dock services with those companies who had to acquire their temporary labour from it. The Court stressed that it was immaterial that the national court did not identify any particular case of abuse: the legal framework created by the Italian measure was in itself contrary to the Treaty.[63] By contrast in the *Dutch Sectoral Pension Funds* cases,[64] the Court distinguished the situation where a pension fund, to which affiliation (and therefore the payment of contributions) was generally compulsory, had the power to grant exemptions to firms that were otherwise bound to use it. The Court held that since complex evaluation was needed to determine whether exemption was appropriate and the grant of exemptions involved risks for the financial equilibrium of the fund which had the obligation to accept any firm in the sector, a Member State was not obliged to confer the power of exemption on a separate entity.

Fee tariffs.   If the State measure does not stipulate the charges to be imposed by   **11.020** the favoured undertaking, the fact that the undertaking may charge excessive

---

[62]   Case C-163/96 *Raso* [1998] ECR I-533, [1998] 5 CMLR 737. See also *GB-INNO-BM* (n 58, above) and *France v Commission* (n 44, above) where the ECJ held that to entrust to an undertaking which markets terminal equipment the task of approving its competitors' equipment gave it a clear advantage over its competitors which was contrary to the Treaty. This is the case even where the operation of the network and the approval of terminal equipment are carried out by different departments within central government: *Decoster* (n 31, above). See also *La Poste*, OJ 2002 L120/19 (La Poste's ability to determine the financial and technical conditions offered to mail preparation service providers created a conflict contrary to Art 86 in conjunction with Art 82).

[63]   See also *La Poste*, above, where the Commission found that the French ministry responsible for supervising La Poste's conduct was 'insufficiently independent and neutral in relation to La Poste' and the legislation therefore infringed Art 86.

[64]   Case C-67/96 *Albany* [1999] ECR I-5751, [2000] 4 CMLR 446; Cases C-115–117/97 *Brentjens* [1999] ECR I-6025, [2000] 4 CMLR 566; Case C-219/97 *Drijvende Bokken* [1999] ECR I-6121, [2000] 4 CMLR 599 (collectively, 'the *Dutch Sectoral Pension Funds* cases'). The ECJ also held that the criteria for exemption were such that it was unlikely that their application could be abused by the pension fund, but that the decision to refuse exemption should be subject to review before the national court to verify that the power was not used in an arbitrary or discriminatory manner.

prices does not place the Member State in breach of Article 86.[65] But where the State measure does set or confirm the tariff to be charged by the undertaking, this can result in a breach of Article 86. In *GT-Link v DSB*,[66] port duties charged by the port authority were set out in regulations for each port drawn up in accordance with regulations prepared by the competent minister. The Court of Justice held that a Member State infringes Article 86(1) in conjunction with Article 82 if, by adopting rules governing the port duties to be paid for the use of the port belonging to a public undertaking, it induces that undertaking to abuse its dominant position. The fact that the public undertaking was able to waive the application of the duties for its own ferry services also amounted to an abuse.[67] Similarly in *Portuguese Airports*[68] the Court of Justice upheld the Commission's findings that a tariff system for landing charges established in Portuguese legislation which offered substantial discounts for high volume users and for domestic flights unfairly favoured the national carriers over carriers from other Member States and thus was a breach of Article 86 in conjunction with Article 82.

11.021 **Effect of Article 86(1) on undertakings.** Article 86(1) does not affect the position under the rules of competition of public undertakings and undertakings to which Member States grant special or exclusive rights. Those undertakings, as is

---

[65] See *Centre d'Insémination de la Crespelle* (n 53, above). In Cases C-147 & 148/97 *Deutsche Post/GZS (Remail)* [2000] ECR I-825, [2000] 4 CMLR 838, the ECJ held that it was not a breach of Art 86(1) in conjunction with Art 82 that Deutsche Post had been given the right to charge internal postage for the delivery of mail in large quantities in Germany for which the sender was resident in Germany but which had been posted in another Member State, provided that the charge imposed took into account the terminal dues paid to Deutsche Post by the foreign postal service for those mail items. This case is discussed at para 12.192, below.

[66] Case C-242/95 *GT-Link v DSB* [1997] ECR I-4449, [1997] 5 CMLR 601. See also *BdKEP – restrictions on mail preparation* (n 45, above) (inability of commercial mail preparation service providers to earn the same discounts as public undertaking's own mail preparation customers was discriminatory and a breach of Art 86 in conjunction with Art 82).

[67] See also *Re tariffs for piloting in the Port of Genoa*, OJ 1997 L301/27, [1998] 4 CMLR 91; *Brussels Airport*, OJ 1995 L216/8, [1996] 4 CMLR 232; *Port of Elsinore*, Press Release IP/96/205 (6 March 1996), [1996] 4 CMLR 728 (access to port facilities for competing ferry operator). The Port of Genoa has made a substantial contribution to the case law in this area: in *Porto di Genova* (n 28, above), the ECJ held that the exclusive right to supply labour was contrary to Art 86; and the Commission subsequently held that the legislation as revised in order to comply with that ruling was still contrary to the Treaty: see *Re provisions of Italian ports legislation relating to employment*, OJ 1997 L301/17, [1998] 4 CMLR 73. In Case C-18/93 *Corsica Ferries* (n 50, above), the ECJ condemned the tariffs set for pilotage services in Genoa and again the Commission has held that the subsequently amended tariff still infringed Art 86: *Re tariffs for piloting in the Port of Genoa*, above. cf Case C-266/96 *Corsica Ferries France v Gruppo Antichi Ormeggiatori del Porto di Genova* [1998] ECR I-3949, [1998] 5 CMLR 402, where it was held that the mere grant of exclusive rights for the supply of mooring services did not in itself breach Art 86(1) and that the tariffs required to be charged fell within the derogation under Art 86(2).

[68] Case C-163/99 *Portugal v Commission* [2001] ECR I-2613, [2002] 4 CMLR 1319, dismissing the appeal against *Portuguese Airports*, OJ 1999 L69/31, [1999] 5 CMLR 103. See also *AENA*, OJ 2000 L208/36, [2000] 5 CMLR 967 (systems of discounts for aircraft landing fees unduly favoured national carrier).

emphasised by Article 86(1) itself, are subject to all the provisions of the Treaty including, in particular, the rules on competition.[69] Articles 81 and 82 continue therefore to have direct effect as regards undertakings of the type described in Article 86(1) and to give rise to individual rights which national courts must safeguard.[70] In *GT-Link v DSB*,[71] the Court of Justice held that persons or undertakings, on whom duties incompatible with Article 86(1) in conjunction with Article 82 have been imposed by a public undertaking which is responsible to a national ministry and whose budget is governed by the budget law of the State, are in principle entitled to repayment of the duties.

Enforcement: Article 86(3). Article 86(3) provides that:　　　　　　　　　　　**11.022**

> 'The Commission shall ensure the application of the provisions of this Article and shall, where necessary, address appropriate directives or decisions to Member States.'

Whenever any undertaking, including one within the meaning of Article 86(1), is suspected of violating Article 81 or Article 82, the Commission may institute proceedings against such an undertaking under Regulation 1/2003. In addition, or independently, if the relevant Member State is in breach of Article 86(1), the Commission may take action against that State. The Commission may proceed against a Member State either under Article 226 or under Article 86(3).[72] Article 86(3) provides the Commission with two distinct instruments with which to enforce Article 86(1), namely directives and decisions. The Commission has increasingly used its powers to legislate under Article 86(3) as a means of bringing about the liberalisation of industry sectors that have traditionally been reserved for a monopoly public undertaking.[73]

Commission's discretion as to enforcement. The Court of Justice has held that **11.023** the wording of Article 86(3) and the scheme of Article 86 as a whole confers on the Commission a wide discretion in relation to the decision whether to investigate an

---

[69] This was confirmed, in relation to Art 82, in *Sacchi* (n 27, above) at paras 14 *et seq*, and generally in *France, Italy and the United Kingdom* (n 25, above) and *Porto di Genova* (n 28, above). Note, however, Art 86(2) which provides for certain derogations for special types of undertakings: see paras 11.046 *et seq*, below.

[70] *Sacchi* (n 27, above); *Van Ameyde v UCI* (n 33, above) paras 23–25; *Porto di Genova* (n 28, above). Subject, however, to Art 86(2) if applicable: paras 11.046 *et seq*, below.

[71] Case C-242/95 *GT-Link v DSB* [1997] ECR I-4449, [1997] 5 CMLR 601.

[72] Art 226 is a general provision covering a Member State that has failed to fulfil any obligation under the Treaty: the Commission must first allow the State the opportunity to submit observations, then deliver a reasoned opinion on the matter, and if the State does not comply with that opinion the Commission may then bring the matter before the ECJ. In the *Sixth Report on Competition Policy* (1976), point 274, the Commission stated that whether Art 86(3) or Art 226 would be used would depend on the nature of the State measure involved.

[73] See, eg Ungerer 'Use of EC Competition Rules in the Liberalisation of the European Union's Telecommunications Sector: Assessment of Past Experience and some Conclusions' which refers to the Commission's extensive use of Art 86 powers as a 'major innovation and a unique feature of the EU telecommunications liberalisation drive': (2001) 2 EC Competition Policy Newsletter 16.

alleged breach by a Member State and in the choice of the means of enforcement. A Member State cannot complain that the Commission chose to adopt a decision directed against it rather than a generally applicable directive, even when there are other Member States engaging in the conduct condemned in the decision.[74] There may be circumstances in which an individual does have standing to challenge a decision taken by the Commission against a Member State.[75] Where the complaint is about inaction rather than action on the part of the Commission, the position in less clear. In *Bundesverband der Bilanzbuchhalter*, the Court of Justice did not rule out that there may be exceptional circumstances in which an individual or, possibly, an association constituted for the defence of the collective interests of a class of individuals, would have standing to bring proceedings against a refusal by the Commission to adopt a decision under Article 86(3).[76] But more recently, the Court appears to have hardened its approach, holding that the Court of First Instance was entitled to reject such appeals against the Commission's failure as inadmissible.[77]

11.024 **Decisions.** The Commission adopted its first individual decision under Article 86(3) in 1985 in *Greek Insurance*.[78] A decision is different from a directive in that it relates to a particular situation existing in one or more Member States and determines the legal consequences of that Member State's conduct. In adopting such a decision the Commission must respect the rights of the defence, in particular the right of the Member State to a precise statement setting out the different elements alleged to constitute the infringement and the Member State must be afforded a right to be heard.[79] Once adopted, a decision under Article 86(3) is binding in its entirety on the Member State to which it is addressed.[80]

---

[74] Case C-163/99 *Portugal v Commission* (n 68, above) para 22.

[75] Case C-107/95P *Bundesverband der Bilanzbuchhalter v Commission* [1997] ECR I-947, [1997] 5 CMLR 432.

[76] *Bundesverband der Bilanzbuchhalter*, above. The ECJ held also that an individual may not, by means of an action against the Commission's failure to adopt a decision under Art 86(3), indirectly compel it to adopt legislation of general application. In Case T-52/00 *Coe Clerici Logistics v Commission* [2003] ECR II-2123, [2003] 5 CMLR 539, the CFI, following *Bundesverband der Bilanzbuchhalter*, examined the Commission's rejection of a complaint and held that there were no exceptional circumstances justifying the challenge.

[77] Case C-141/02P *Commission v T-Mobile Austria* [2005] ECR I-1283, [2005] 4 CMLR 735, paras 69–74 (on appeal from Case T-54/99 *max.mobil v Commission* [2002] ECR II-313, [2002] 4 CMLR 1356). See Hocepied, 'The Maxmobil judgment: the Court of Justice clarifies the role of complainants in Article 86 procedures' (2005) 2 EC Competition Policy Newsletter 51.

[78] *Greek Insurance*, OJ 1985 L152/25. See also *XVth Report on Competition Policy* (1985), points 258–259.

[79] Cases C-48 & 66/90 *Netherlands PTT v Commission* (n 58, above), annulling the Commission's decision for failure to respect these rights. As to rights of the defence, see paras 13.028 *et seq*, below.

[80] *Commission v Greece* (n 51, above) which also held that the validity of a decision under Art 86(3) cannot be challenged in the course of proceedings by the Commission under Art 226 to enforce it.

The power to legislate under Article 86(3). In contrast to the other Articles **11.025**
of the Treaty that enable the Council to enact implementing legislation,[81]
Article 86(3) states that it is the Commission, not the Council, which may address
appropriate directives or decisions to Member States. In *France, Italy and United
Kingdom v Commission*,[82] the Court of Justice upheld the right of the Commission
to issue general legislative provisions under Article 86(3). Accordingly, the
Commission's powers under Article 86(3) include the adoption of preventive
legislative measures to ensure that Member States comply with the Treaty.[83]

The Transparency Directive. The principal purpose of Directive 80/723, **11.026**
on the transparency of financial relations between Member States and public
undertakings, was to verify that public undertakings do not receive hidden
aids from public authorities.[84] It required that Member States ensure that
financial relations between public authorities and public undertakings are
transparent so that the amount of public funds made available, directly or
indirectly, to public undertakings, and the use to which these funds are put,
emerge clearly. The Directive was amended several times following its adoption
in 1980 and was recently replaced by Directive 2006/111 which consolidates
the changes made.[85] Directive 80/723 originally did not apply to public undertakings carrying on activities in the sectors of water and energy, post and telecommunications, transport and public credit institutions, but its scope was extended to
cover those undertakings from 1 January 1986.[86] The next extension of the
obligations was in 1993 when Member States were required to provide certain
financial information in relation to public undertakings operating in the

---

[81] eg Arts 83 and 89. For a comparison of the powers under Art 86(3) with those of the Council
under Arts 87 and 95, see *Telecommunications Terminal Equipment* case (n 44, above).

[82] Cases 188/80, etc, *France, Italy and the United Kingdom v Commission* [1982] ECR 2545,
[1982] 3 CMLR 144; see also The *Telecommunications Terminal Equipment* case (n 44, above).

[83] See also *Sixth Report on Competition Policy* (1976), points 274 *et seq*. The two examples
there mentioned were a Directive on transparency in the accounts of public undertakings and a
Directive on the award of contracts by public undertakings. The first of those was subsequently
adopted as Dir 80/723.

[84] Dir 80/723, OJ 1980 L195/35. The Commission re-issued its Communication on the
application of Art 5 of the Transparency Directive with appropriate amendments, after the original
version was annulled by the ECJ as being *ultra vires*: Case C-325/91 *France v Commission* [1993]
ECR I-3283: 1993 C307/3 Vol II, App F.3.

[85] Dir 2006/111, OJ 2006 L318/17: Vol II, App F.2. This repealed all the amending Directives
as well as Dir 80/723 but without prejudice to the obligations of the Member States to transpose
those Directives into their national law: Art 10. Annex II to the Directive sets out a useful correlation
table between the provisions of the old and new Directives.

[86] See Dir 85/413, OJ 1985 L229/20, now Art 5 of Dir 2006/111. See *XVth Report on Competition
Policy* (1985), point 257. However central banks and the Institut Monetaire Luxembourgeois are
still excluded as well as public credit institutions as regards deposits of public funds placed with them
by public authorities on normal commercial terms.

manufacturing sector.[87] In 2000 Member States were required[88] to ensure that any undertaking which falls within Article 86(1) or (2) and which receives a State aid in any form draws up its accounts in a way which distinguishes the cost and revenues associated with the activities in respect of which it has been granted special or exclusive rights, or which constitute services of a general economic interest, from those associated with its other business activities. The undertaking must also give full details of the methods by which its costs and revenues are allocated to its different activities. Most recently, in 2005, accounting obligations were imposed not only on public undertakings but also on companies which operate services of general economic interest and which receive compensation in the form of payments or special or exclusive rights where the same company also carries on commercial operations.[89] Directive 2006/111 thus enables the Commission to investigate possible overcompensation of public service costs and cross-subsidisation of commercial activities.[90]

11.027 **The Telecommunications Directives.** The Commission has adopted a series of directives pursuant to Article 86(3) concerning the process of liberalisation of the markets for fixed and mobile telecommunications. These are discussed, along with the Commission's notices and guidelines on the application of competition law to the telecommunications sector, in Chapter 12.

11.028 **Postal services.** Many Member States have traditionally reserved to themselves, or have granted on an exclusive basis, the right to provide a universal postal service within their territories. In a number of cases, the Court of Justice and the Commission have considered the permissible scope of such rights under Article 86.[91] The relevant case law is discussed further in Chapter 12.

---

[87] Introduced by Dir 93/84, OJ 1993 L254/16, now see Art 8 of Dir 2006/111.

[88] This requirement applied with effect from 1 January 2001; see Dir 2000/52, OJ 2000 L193/75, now see Art 2(d) of Dir 2006/111.

[89] By Dir 2005/81, OJ 2005 L312/47, now see Art 2(d). But some of the obligations under the Dir are disapplied for certain small undertakings where the compensation received by the undertaking for carrying the services was fixed 'following an open, transparent and non-discriminating procedure': see Art 5(2)(b) and (c) of Dir 2006/111.

[90] See Arts 6 and 8 of Dir 2006/111. Following the ECJ's judgment in Case C-280/00 *Altmark* [2003] ECR I-7747, [2003] 3 CMLR 339, [2005] All ER (EC) 610, payments in compensation for the performance of a public service will not qualify as State aid provided that they meet the criteria laid down by the Court. See paras 11.048 and 15.025, below.

[91] See the *Telecommunications Terminal Equipment* case (n 44, above); *GB-INNO-BM* (n 58, above); *Dutch Courier Services*, OJ 1990 L10/47, [1990] 4 CMLR 947, annulled on appeal on procedural grounds in Cases C-48 & 66-90 *Netherlands PTT v Commission* [1992] ECR I-1565, [1993] 5 CMLR 316; and *Re Spanish Courier Services*, OJ 1990 L233/19, [1991] 4 CMLR 560; *Corbeau* (n 58, above); Case C-340/99 *TNT Traco* [2001] ECR I-4109, [2002] 4 CMLR 454.

4. Unenforceability of National Measures: Article 10

The *INNO* principle.   Although the rules on competition apply only to under-   **11.029**
takings, Member States have a duty under Article 10 of the Treaty to abstain from
enacting or enforcing national laws which could jeopardise the effectiveness of the
rules on competition contained in Articles 81 to 89. That duty was first expressed
by the Court of Justice in *INNO*,[92] a case in which it was argued that Belgian fiscal
legislation compelling manufacturers and importers of tobacco products to fix
minimum retail prices had the effect of encouraging an abuse of a dominant
position by the undertakings concerned, contrary to Article 82. The Court of
Justice said:

> 'The second paragraph of Article [10] of the Treaty provides that Member States shall
> abstain from any measure which could jeopardize the attainment of the objectives of
> the Treaty.
>
> Accordingly, while it is true that Article [82] is directed at undertakings, nonetheless
> it is also true that the Treaty imposes a duty on Member States not to adopt or main-
> tain in force any measure which could deprive that provision of its effectiveness.'[93]

Although the Court in *INNO* specifically referred to Article 82, Article 10 has
most frequently been applied in combination with Article 81 in holding that a
national law is unenforceable insofar as it gives rise to agreements that would
infringe the EC competition rules.

Development of the *INNO* principle: *Van Eycke v ASPA*.   In a number of cases[94]   **11.030**
following *INNO*, the Court of Justice applied this principle, stating many times

---

[92] Case 13/77 *INNO v ATAB* [1977] ECR 2115, [1978] 1 CMLR 283. The principle has generated much debate: see, eg Pescatore, 'Public and Private aspects of Community Competition Law'
in Hawk (ed), *1986 Fordham Corp. L. Inst* 381; Joliet, 'National Anticompetitive Legislation and
Community Law' in Hawk (ed), 1988 *Fordham Corp. L. Inst* 16–1; Gyselen, 'State Action and
the Effectiveness of the EEC Treaty's Competition Provisions' (1989) 26 CML Rev 33; Bacon,
'State Regulation of the Market and EC Competition Rules: Articles 85 and 86 compared' (1997)
ECLR 283; Thunström and Lindeborg, 'State Liability under the EC Treaty arising from Anti-
Competitive State Measures' (2002) 25 (4) *World Competition* 515. For strong criticism of the ECJ's
approach, see Buendia Sierra (n 3, above) paras 7.24 *et seq.*
[93] *INNO v ATAB*, above, paras 30–31.
[94] For a summary of the relevant case law up to 1993, see Opinion of AG Tesauro in Case C-2/91
Meng [1993] ECR I-5751, paras 8–17. The principal cases are: Cases 177 & 178/82 *Van de Haar*
[1984] ECR 1797, [1985] 2 CMLR 566; Case 229/83 *Leclerc v Au Blé Vert* [1985] ECR 1, [1985]
2 CMLR 286 (French legislative requirement that publisher fix a minimum resale price for books
held not to contravene the Treaty on the grounds that competition rules on national resale price
maintenance were not yet sufficiently well defined: judgment, paras 10–20); Case 231/83 *Cullet v
Leclerc* [1985] ECR 305, [1985] 2 CMLR 524; Case 123/83 *BNIC v Clair* [1985] ECR 391, [1985]
2 CMLR 430; Cases 209/84, etc, *Ministère Public v Asjes* [1986] ECR 1425, [1986] 3 CMLR 173;
Case 188/86 *Ministère Public v Lefevre* [1987] ECR 2963, [1989] 1 CMLR 2; Case 136/86 *BNIC
v Aubert* [1987] ECR 4789, [1988] 4 CMLR 331; Case 311/85 *VVR v Sociale Dienst* [1987] ECR
3801, [1989] 4 CMLR 213.

that although national legislation or government measures cannot contravene Article 81(1), their compatibility with the rules of competition law can be examined on the basis of Article 10 in conjunction with Articles 3(1)(g) and 81. Subsequently, in *Van Eycke v ASPA*,[95] a case concerning national legislation providing tax exemption for income from savings deposits, the Court of Justice refined the *INNO* principle in the following terms:

> '... Articles [81 and 82] of the Treaty, read in conjunction with Article [10], require the Member States not to introduce or maintain in force measures, even of a legislative nature, which may render ineffective the competition rules applicable to undertakings. Such would be the case, the Court has held, if a Member State were to require or favour the adoption of agreements decisions or concerted practices contrary to Article [81] or to reinforce their effects or to deprive its own legislation of its official character by delegating to private traders responsibility for taking decisions affecting the economic sphere.'[96]

National measures will therefore infringe Article 10, in conjunction with Article 81, in two broad categories of case: (i) where the measure requires or favours the adoption of an agreement prohibited by Article 81 or where it reinforces the effects of such an agreement;[97] and (ii) where it delegates to private undertakings power to take collective decisions concerning intervention in economic matters.[98]

---

[95] Case 267/86 *Van Eycke v ASPA* [1988] ECR 476, [1990] 4 CMLR 330. See also *Ahmed Saeed* (n 33, above).

[96] *Van Eycke,* above, para 16. The ECJ has applied this elaboration of the *INNO* principle in numerous cases: Case C-2/91 *Meng* [1993] ECR I-5751, para 14; Case C-185/91 *Reiff* [1993] ECR I-5801, [1995] 5 CMLR 145, para 14; Case C-245/91 *Ohra Schadeverzekeringen* [1993] ECR I-5851, para 10; Case C-153/93 *Delta Schiffahrts und Speditiongesellschaft* [1994] ECR I-2517, [1996] 4 CMLR 21, para 14; Case C-96/94 *Centro Servizi Spediporto v Spedizioni Marittima del Golfo* [1995] ECR I-2883, [1996] 4 CMLR 613, paras 21–22; Cases C-140/94, etc, *DIP v Comune di Bassano del Grappa and Commune di Chioggia* [1995] ECR I-3257, [1996] 4 CMLR 157, paras 14–15; Case C-70/95 *Sodemare v Regione Lombardia* [1997] ECR I-3395, [1997] 3 CMLR 591, paras 41–42; Case C-35/96 *Commission v Italy* [1998] ECR I-3851, [1998] 5 CMLR 889, paras 53–54; Case C-266/96 *Corsica Ferries France* (n 67, above) para 49; Case C-38/97 *Librandi v Cuttica* [1998] ECR I-5955, [1998] 5 CMLR 967, para 26; *CIF* (n 23, above) para 46; Case C-35/99 *Arduino* [2002] ECR I-1529, [2002] 4 CMLR 866, paras 34–35. For consideration as to whether Art 10 may be infringed in cases falling outside the two categories enumerated in *Van Eycke,* see AG Tesauro in *Meng,* paras 23–33 and AG Fennelly in *DIP,* para 43.

[97] As to agreements existing prior to the legislation, if the legislation incorporates wholly or in part the terms of agreements concluded between traders and requires or encourages those traders to comply with it, the legislation will be regarded as reinforcing the effect of the pre-existing agreements and will contravene the Treaty: see, eg *VVR v Sociale Dienst* (n 94, above) where the ECJ considered a Belgian law requiring travel agents to observe prices set by tour operators and held that, by transforming an originally contractual prohibition falling within Art 81(1) into a legislative provision, the government gave the rule a permanent character in that it could no longer be rescinded by the parties. The legislative provision also imposed sanctions for breach of the rule. In these circumstances the measures contravened Art 10. See also explanation of *VVR* by AG Tesauro in *Meng* (n 96, above) para 14.

[98] *Arduino* (n 96, above) para 35. (AG Léger there divided the first category into two: Opinion, para 37).

Requiring or favouring the adoption of an anti-competitive agreement or rein- **11.031**
forcing its effects. As to the first category of case, the Court of Justice has subsequently held, in *Meng*,[99] that there must be a link between the State measure and
conduct on the part of undertakings of the kind falling within Article 81. Thus the
mere fact that national legislation has an anti-competitive effect equivalent to that
of an agreement prohibited by Article 81 does not bring that legislation within
Article 10.[100]

Delegating collective decisions concerning interaction in economic matters. As **11.032**
to the second category of case identified in *Van Eycke v ASPA*,[101] in a number of
cases[102] concerning the fixing of tariffs, the Court of Justice found that the Member
State had not delegated its powers even where rates were set by committees which
included representatives appointed by undertakings or trade associations, in circumstances where the legislation required that the public interest[103] be taken into
account in the setting of rates and where the public authority retained the power
to substitute its own decision on rates for that of the committee.[104] In *Arduino*,[105]
the Court of Justice was asked to consider Italian legislation empowering the

---

[99] Case C-2/91 *Meng* [1993] ECR I-5751, para 22 and AG Tesauro, paras 24, 32–33. See also
the Opinion of AG Darmon in *Reiff* (n 96, above), particularly at paras 58–77; Case C-35/96
Commission v Italy (n 96, above). But cf Cases C-359 & 379/95P *Commission and France v Ladbroke
Racing* [1997] ECR I-6265, [1998] 4 CMLR 27; and see comment by Jowell, (1998) ECLR 302.

[100] See further on this point, AG Fennelly in *DIP v Comune di Bassano del Grappa* (n 96, above)
paras 34–39.

[101] See para 11.030, above.

[102] See *Reiff* (n 96, above); Case C-153/93 *Delta Schiffahrts* (n 96, above); Case C-96/94 *Centro
Servizi Spediporto* (n 96, above); and Case C-38/97 *Librandi v Cuttica* (n 96, above). The principles
applicable to the transport tariff cases have been extended to other areas: see *DIP v Comune di Bassano
del Grappa* (n 96, above) (shop licensing); *Sodemare v Regione Lombardia* (n 96, above) (provision
of social welfare health care services); Case C-266/96 *Corsica Ferries France* (n 67, above) (tariffs
for mooring services). In Case C-35/96 *Commission v Italy* (n 96, above), the ECJ held that Italian
legislation which supported a compulsory tariff set by the national council of customs agents and to
be charged by all customs agents was contrary to Arts 10 and 81. Note also the further proceedings
brought by the Commission against the council of customs agents itself under Art 81(1): Case T-
513/93 *CNSD v Commission* [2000] ECR II-1807, [2000] 5 CMLR 614: see para 11.007, above.

[103] As to the scope and determination of the public interest, see *Librandi* (n 96, above) paras 35–
48. The ECJ also held that even if the majority of the rate-fixing commission was made up of trade
appointees this did not bring the legislation within Art 10. cf *Commission v Italy* (n 96, above).

[104] Such cases are distinguishable from earlier cases such as *BNIC v Clair* (n 94, above); *BNIC
v Aubert* (n 94, above); and *Ministère Public v Asjes* (n 94, above), where the legislation merely
confirms an agreement reached between representatives of private undertakings based solely on the
interests of those undertakings: see *Reiff* (n 96, above) paras 16–19 and AG Darmon paras 43, 44,
125–128; *Delta Schiffahrts* (n 96, above) per AG Darmon at paras 25–29; and *DIP v Comune di
Bassano del Grappa* (n 96, above) per AG Fennelly at para 59. Similarly in *Commission v Italy* (n 96,
above), the ECJ distinguished these tariff cases because in that case all representatives on the national
council were appointed by members of the trade and, in setting rates, the council was not required
to take account of the public interest or indeed any interest other than that of the customs agents.

[105] *Arduino* (n 96, above) paras 38–39. Similarly, Cases C-94 & 202/04 *Cipolla*, [2006]
ECR I-11421, [2007] 4 CMLR 286, [2007] All ER (EC) 699.

Minister for Justice to fix minimum and maximum lawyers' fees on the basis of a proposal prepared by a committee of lawyers. The Court was not persuaded that the lawyers comprising the committee were to be regarded as experts, given that they were elected by their fellow lawyers and that there was no public-interest criteria in the legislation for them to take into account when formulating their proposal. However, the Court nonetheless concluded that no impermissible delegation had taken place: the committee's proposal was not binding on the Minister; and Italian national courts were free to deviate from the fee scales in exceptional cases when determining what fees were appropriate.[106]

11.033 **Narrow application of Articles 81, 3(1)(g) and 10.**   Although the *INNO* principle as subsequently refined is now firmly established, in practice the Court of Justice has only rarely found national measures to be illegal on this basis.[107] It seems clear that Articles 81 and 82 do not affect the powers of Member States to maintain national price controls,[108] impose taxes,[109] or collect levies.[110] Such matters are affected, if at all, by other provisions of the Treaty.[111]

11.034 **Direct applicability of Article 10.**   Article 10 of the Treaty has direct effect. It follows that where a Member State enacts or maintains in force legislation in breach of Article 10, that breach can be relied on by private parties in the national courts to render the legislation *pro tanto* unenforceable. Many of the cases in the Court of Justice on Article 10 in conjunction with the competition rules have

---

[106] *Arduino*, above, paras 41–43; *Cipolla*, above, paras 50–53.

[107] eg *BNIC v Clair, BNIC v Aubert* and *Asjes* (n 94, above); *Ahmed Saeed* (n 33, above); *VVR v Sociale Dienst* (n 94, above); and *Commission v Italy* (n 96, above). The principle has also been relied upon before English Courts: see *R. v Dearlove* [1988] Cr App R 279 (CA), where a prosecution under the Theft Act 1968 succeeded although the relevant deception was intended to evade the application of a policy of price discrimination contrary to Art 81(1); *R. v MAFF, ex p DTF* [1998] Eu LR 253, where there was an arguable case that the Minister was in breach of Art 10 by approving a new milk marketing scheme which itself constituted an abuse within Art 82 and by failing to remedy that abuse; *MTV Europe v BMG Records (UK) Ltd* [1998] EWCA Civ 430, where it was accepted that Art 10 meant that the court must consider whether it was appropriate to make an order for discovery which might detract from the effectiveness of Arts 81 and 82.

[108] eg Case 5/79 *Buys* [1979] ECR 3203, 3231, [1980] 2 CMLR 493, 520; Cases 177 & 178/2 *Van de Haar* [1984] ECR 1797, [1985] 2 CMLR 566; *Cullet v Leclerc* (n 94, above) paras 12–18; *Leclerc v Au Blé Vert* (n 94, above); Cases 11/84, etc, *Gratiot* [1985] ECR 2907; Case 355/85 *Cognet* [1986] ECR 3231, [1987] 3 CMLR 942; *Ministère Public v Lefevre* (n 94, above).

[109] Case 811/79 *Amministrazione Delle Finanze Dello Stato v Ariete* [1980] ECR 2545, [1981] 1 CMLR 316, para 15. See also the Opinion of AG Poiares Maduro in Case C-72/03 *Carbonati Apuani* [2004] ECR I-8027, [2004] 3 CMLR 1282, para 20 (the ECJ did not refer to this point).

[110] Case 2/73 *Geddo v Ente Nazionale Risi* [1973] ECR 865, [1974] 1 CMLR 13, para 18.

[111] See, eg Art 28. In this regard, see AG Tesauro in *Meng* (n 94, above) paras 8, 10, 30–32 and AG Darmon in *Reiff* (n 96, above) paras 31–38, 75. In *Cipolla* (n 105, above), the ECJ followed *Arduino* (n 96, above) in dismissing a challenge to the Italian legislation on lawyers' fees under the competition rules, but held that the law constituted a restriction on the freedom to provide services under Art 49.

been references from national courts in the course of domestic proceedings. The issue may arise when an undertaking that faces the imposition of a sanction or penalty by a public authority for violation of a national measure argues in its defence that the measure involves a breach of Article 10. For example, the case of *Meng*[112] concerned an insurance broker who was fined for passing commission to clients contrary to a provision of the German insurance supervision law. His contention that that provision was contrary to Article 10 in conjunction with Article 81(1) was rejected by the Court of Justice on the grounds that the regulatory law set out a self-contained prohibition that was not linked to any unlawful agreement by undertakings that infringed Article 81(1). By contrast, if the German legislation had authorised an association of insurance brokers to adopt rules to prevent the passing of commission to clients and had provided for the imposition of criminal sanctions for breach of such rules, a broker who was prosecuted for breach of the rule would have been able to rely on the fact that this provision of national law infringed Article 10, read in conjunction with Article 81(1), and that its application was therefore precluded by Community law. The issue can also arise in a private action based on national legislation which the defendant similarly contends is unenforceable. The *INNO* case[113] itself involved a claim for unfair competition brought by the Belgian association of tobacco retailers against a supermarket chain for selling cigarettes at below the price on the tax label, contrary to Belgian law. If, as alleged, the Belgian legislation gave rise to a breach by Belgium of Articles 10 and 82, the proceedings for unfair competition could not succeed.[114]

Duty of national competition authorities to apply Articles 81, 3(1)(g) and 10.   **11.035** In *CIF*, the Court of Justice held that a national competition authority, one of whose responsibilities is to apply Article 81, has a duty to disapply a national measure, including legislation, that is contrary to Articles 81, 3(1)(g) and 10.[115] Since the coming into effect of the Modernisation package revising the procedure for the enforcement of the competition rules, all national competition authorities in the Community are competent to apply Article 81 by virtue of Article 5 of

---

[112] C-2/91 *Meng* [1993] ECR I-5751. See also *Ohra Schadeverzekeringen* (n 96, above) (Dutch insurance company breaching supervision law by dealing directly with the public); Case C-250/03 *Mauri* [2005] ECR I-1267, [2005] 4 CMLR 723 (candidate in Bar exams seeking annulment of decision that he failed on basis that legislation constituting exam committee contravened Art 10 in conjunction with Arts 81 and 82).

[113] *INNO v ATAB* (n 92, above). See also *BNIC v Aubert* (n 94, above); *Ahmed Saeed* (n 33, above).

[114] The ECJ did not decide this question, holding that the national court must determine whether the measure as such was capable of affecting trade between Member States, having regard to the barriers to inter-State trade that resulted from fiscal arrangements.

[115] Case C-198/01 *CIF* [2003] ECR I-8055, [2003] 5 CMLR 829, [2004] All ER (EC) 380, paras 49–50, 58. See, eg the application of this principle by the UK Competition Appeal Tribunal in *Floe Telecommunications v Office of Communications* [2006] CAT 17. On the consequences of such disapplication for the liability of undertakings that were compelled by the national measure in question to act contrary to Art 81, see para 11.008, above.

Regulation 1/2003[116] and are therefore all subject to the duty established by the Court in *CIF*.

5. State Monopolies of a Commercial Character: Article 31

11.036   **Article 31(1).**   Article 31(1), as amended by the Treaty of Amsterdam, provides as follows:

> 'Member States shall adjust any State monopolies of a commercial character so as to ensure that no discrimination regarding the conditions under which goods are procured and marketed exists between nationals of Member States. The provisions of this Article shall apply to any body through which a Member State, in law or in fact, either directly or indirectly supervises, determines or appreciably influences imports or exports between Member States. These provisions shall likewise apply to monopolies delegated by the State to others.'

11.037   **Article 31 and the free movement of goods.**[117]   The purpose of Article 31 is to reconcile the desire of the Member States to maintain certain monopolies of a commercial character as instruments for the pursuit of public interest aims with the requirements of the establishment and functioning of the common market. It aims at the elimination of obstacles to the free movement of goods save for the restrictions on trade which are inherent in the existence of the monopolies in question.[118] Article 31 comes in the Title of the EC Treaty that concerns free movement of goods,[119] and is part of Chapter 2 of that Title, which relates to the elimination of quantitative restrictions between Member States. Thus Article 31 applies only to goods[120] that are capable of being traded between Member States[121] and not to trade with third countries.[122]

---

116 See paras 1.058, above and 14.010, below.

117 See generally Oliver and Jarvis, *Free Movement of Goods in the European Community* (4th ed, 2003), Chap XI.

118 Case C-189/95 *Franzén* [1997] ECR I-5909, [1998] 1 CMLR 1231; Case C-438/02 *Hanner* [2005] ECR I-4551.

119 Title I of Part Three of the Treaty, Vol II, App A.4.

120 It does not apply to services: Case 155/73 *Sacchi* [1974] ECR 409, [1974] 2 CMLR 177 (television); Case 271/81 *Amélioration de l'Élevage v Mialocq* [1983] ECR 2057, paras 8–13 (insemination centres); Case C-6/01 *Anomar* [2003] ECR I-8621, [2004] 1 CMLR 1357, paras 59–60 (gambling). In Cases 46/90 & C-93/91 *Procureur du Roi v Lagauche* [1993] ECR I-5267, the ECJ held that Art 31 relates to monopolies over the provision of services only insofar as such monopoly discriminates against imported products to the disadvantage of products of domestic origin; see also Case 30/87 *Bodson v Pompes Funèbres des Régions Libérés* [1988] ECR 2479, [1989] 4 CMLR 984, para 10. But the supply of electricity and gas constitutes the supply of goods: see eg Case 6/64 *Costa v ENEL* [1964] ECR 585, [1964] CMLR 425; Case 158/94 *Commission v Italy* [1997] ECR I-5789, [1998] 2 CMLR 463, paras 14–19. See also Case C-379/98 *PreussenElektra* [2001] ECR I-2099, [2001] 2 CMLR 833, [2001] All ER (EC) 330, paras 68–81 and Opinion of AG Jacobs, para 197.

121 *Costa v ENEL* (above), at 598 (ECR), 459–460 (CMLR).

122 Case 91/78 *Hansen v Hauptzollamt Flensburg* [1979] ECR 935, [1980] 1 CMLR 162.

Relationship between Article 31 and Article 28.   When examining regulations   **11.038**
adopted by a Member State it is necessary to determine whether they fall to be
examined under Article 28 (the general prohibition on discrimination against
goods from other Member States) or under Article 31: the two prohibitions are
mutually exclusive. Article 31 applies where the rules relate to the existence and
operation of the monopoly and are specifically applicable to the exercise by a
domestic commercial monopoly of its exclusive rights. Domestic legislation
setting rules which are separable from the operation of the monopoly, although
they have a bearing upon it, fall to be examined under Article 28.[123] In *HOB-vín
v The Icelandic State and the State Alcohol and Tobacco Company of Iceland*,[124]
for example, the EFTA Court held that the crucial factor was that the statutory
requirements concerning warehouse deliveries applied only to the State monopoly
undertaking ('ÁTVR') and not to other undertakings operating warehouses.
Since they exclusively regulated ÁTVR's contractual relationships, the requirements at issue were inseparable from the operation of the monopoly and hence fell
to be considered under Article 16 EEA, the equivalent of Article 31 EC.

State monopoly of a commercial character.   This is defined in the second para-   **11.039**
graph of Article 31(1) as 'any body through which a Member State, in law or in
fact, either directly or indirectly supervises, determines or appreciably influences
imports or exports between Member States' and also includes 'monopolies delegated by the State to others'. In order to fall within Article 31, the State must be in
a position to control, direct or influence appreciably trade between Member States
through a body established for the purpose or through a delegated monopoly.[125]
Bodies which have been held to fall within the ambit of this provision include, for
example, State alcohol monopolies,[126] tobacco monopolies,[127] monopolies for the
retail sale of medicinal products,[128] and various monopolies in respect of the
import and sale of natural gas and electricity.[129] An example of a monopoly delegated by the State to another body was the grant by Belgium of the exclusive right

---

[123] Case 91/75 *Hauptzollamt Göttingen v Miritz* [1976] ECR 217, [1976] 2 CMLR 235; *Franzén*
(n 118, above).
[124] Case E-4/05 *HOB-vín v The Icelandic State and Áfengis- og tóbaksverslun ríkisins (The State
Alcohol and Tobacco Company of Iceland)* [2006] 2 CMLR 1098 (on a reference from the Reykjavík
District Court).
[125] *Bodson v Pompes Funèbres* (n 120, above); Case C-393/92 *Almelo* [1994] ECR I-1477.
[126] See, eg *Fifteenth Report on Competition Policy* (1985), point 262 (France); *Seventeenth Report*
(1987), point 295 (Germany); *Eighteenth Report* (1988), point 313 (Portugal); *XXVIIth Report*
(1997), point 140 (Norway); *Franzén* (n 118, above), (Sweden); *HOB-vín v The Icelandic State and
Áfengis- og tóbaksverslun ríkisins (The State Alcohol and Tobacco Company of Iceland)* (n 124, above).
[127] See, eg *Seventeenth Report* (1987), points 292, 293 (Spain and France); *XXVIIth Report*
(1997), point 144 (Austria).
[128] See *Hanner* (n 118, above).
[129] Case C-157/94 *Commission v Netherlands*, Case C-158/94 *Commission v Italy*, Case
C-159/94 *Commission v France* [1997] ECR I-5699, 5789, 5815, [1998] 2 CMLR 373.

to import and market natural gas to Distrigaz.[130] But the Court of Justice has held that Article 31 does not apply to national provisions which do not concern the exercise by a public monopoly of its exclusive rights but which apply in general to the production and marketing of the product in question. Thus, an Italian body which had a monopoly on the distribution of tobacco products made in Italy did not fall within Article 31 because the State could not use it to intervene in the procurement choices of retailers or to ensure an outlet for the monopoly's products or to discourage imports or encourage exports.[131] Similarly, where French legislation empowered local authorities to delegate the provision of funeral services within their area to private undertakings, the fact that several local authorities had appointed companies within the same group, thereby putting those companies in a position to influence imports, did not make the companies a national monopoly within the meaning of Article 31. The national and local authorities were not using the companies as a means of exerting influence on the movement of goods.[132] It appears that Article 31 covers monopolies limited to part of the territory of a Member State.[133]

11.040 **Monopolies for import and export.** The Court of Justice has held that Article 31 precludes the establishment of bodies with exclusive rights to import or export a particular product,[134] because such rights automatically give rise to discrimination against importers established in other Member States. For Article 31 to apply it is not necessary for the exclusive right to import to relate to all the imports; it is sufficient that those rights relate to a proportion such that they enable the monopoly to have an appreciable influence on imports.[135]

11.041 **Extent of prohibition under Article 31(1) for other monopolies.** Where the monopoly relates to the distribution of the product within a Member State rather

---

[130] See *Thirteenth Report on Competition Policy* (1983), point 291.

[131] Case C-387/93 *Banchero* [1995] ECR I-4666, [1996] 1 CMLR 829.

[132] *Bodson v Pompes Funèbres* (n 120, above).

[133] *Bodson v Pompes Funèbres* (n 120, above) para 13 and per AG Cruz Vilaça at paras 41–43. See also AG Roemer in Case 82/71 *Pubblico Ministero Italiano v SAIL* [1972] ECR 119, 143, [1972] CMLR 723, 728–729. cf AG Reischl in Case 83/78 *Pigs Marketing Board v Redmond* [1978] ECR 2347, [1979] 1 CMLR 177.

[134] Case 59/75 *Pubblico Ministero v Manghera* [1976] ECR 91, [1976] 1 CMLR 557; Case 347/88 *Commission v Greece* [1990] ECR I-4747. See also Case E-1/94 *Restamark* [1994–1995] EFTA Court Report 15; Case E-4/01 *Karlsson v Iceland* [2002] EFTA Court Rep 240 (failure to abolish monopoly on imports of alcohol after coming into force of the EEA infringed Art 16 EEA; compliance of wholesale distribution monopoly was a matter for the national court to determine on the facts. The Court went on to hold that Iceland would be liable to compensate the claimant who had suffered loss because of the unlawful prolongation of the monopoly). The Commission has opened an infringement procedure against Malta for maintaining its import monopoly on petroleum products: Press Release IP/06/1391 (13 October 2006).

[135] Thus the fact that end users are allowed to import for their own needs does not preclude the application of Art 31: *Commission v Netherlands* (n 129, above).

than to the import or export of the product, Article 31(1) does not require the total abolition of national monopolies having a commercial character. Rather it requires that they should be adjusted in such a way as to ensure that no discrimination regarding the conditions under which goods are procured and marketed exists between nationals of Member States.[136] This means that the organisation and operation of monopolies must be arranged so as to exclude any discrimination between nationals of Member States as regards the conditions of supply and the provision of outlets so that goods from other Member States are not put at a disadvantage in law or in fact in relation to domestic goods and that competition between the Member States is not distorted. In *Franzén*,[137] the Court of Justice considered the Swedish monopoly on the retail sale of alcohol, challenged by a Swedish shopkeeper prosecuted for selling spirits at his premises on 1 January 1995, the date of Sweden's accession to the European Union. The Court examined the criteria on which the Swedish monopoly selected the goods which it would stock at its outlets and concluded that there was no discrimination against imported goods. It also considered that the number of outlets was not so limited as to compromise the ability of consumers to obtain supplies of imported products and the advertising and promotion of alcohol by the monopoly did not disadvantage imported products. The monopoly therefore was not contrary to Article 31.

Application of Article 31 post *Franzén*.   By contrast, in *Hanner*,[138] the Court   **11.042**
concluded that the Swedish monopoly on the retail sale of medicinal products did infringe Article 31(1). It applied similar criteria to those employed in *Franzén*, but this time concluded that the manner in which the monopoly in question was organised and operated was liable to place trade in medicinal preparations from other Member States at a disadvantage as compared with trade in Swedish medicinal preparations. In particular, as regards the system for selecting products sold by the monopoly, the governing rules made no provision for a purchasing plan or for a system of 'call for tenders' within the framework of which producers whose products were not selected would be entitled to be apprised of the reasons for the selection decision. Nor did the rules provide any opportunity to contest such decisions before an independent supervisory authority. More recently, the EFTA Court has held that a requirement imposed by ÁTVR, the Icelandic alcohol distribution monopoly, requiring suppliers to deliver their products on pallets and to include the price of the pallet in the price of their products did not infringe

---

[136] *Manghera* (n 134, above); *Hansen v Hauptzollamt Flensburg* (n 122, above); Case 78/82 *Commission v Italy* [1983] ECR 1955, 1967; *Hanner* (n 118, above) para 34.

[137] Case C-189/95 *Franzén* [1997] ECR I-5909, [1998] 1 CMLR 1231. See also Case E-1/97 *Gundersen v Oslo kommune* [1997] Rep. EFTA Court 110, concerning the Norwegian alcohol monopoly and Case E-6/96 *Wilhelmsen v Oslo kommune* [1997] EFTA Court Report 53.

[138] Case C-438/02 *Hanner* [2005] ECR I-4551, paras 42–43.

Article 16 EEA (the equivalent to Article 31 EC).[139] The plaintiff in that case referred to an incident where a domestic supplier had in fact been allowed to retrieve his pallets from ÁTVR. The Court, while confirming that discrimination can arise 'not only in obvious ways, but also in day-to-day decisions in areas such as pricing, advertising and deliveries' held that one incident of minor importance, even if it had discriminatory effect, was not enough to establish an infringement of Article 16 EEA on the part of the State monopoly. To be relevant, such incidents would have to be part of the policy of the monopoly or of its outlets or a consequence of failure to enforce the monopoly's rules.[140]

11.043 **Standstill provision: Article 31(2).**   Article 31(2) provides as follows:

> 'Member States shall refrain from introducing any new measure which is contrary to the principles laid down in paragraph 1 or which restricts the scope of the Articles dealing with the prohibition of customs duties and quantitative restrictions between Member States.'

In *Cordless Telephones in Germany*,[141] the Commission took the view that the planned extension of the monopoly of the Bundespost (the federal post and telecommunications organisation) to include exclusive marketing rights for cordless telephones was in breach of not only Article 31(1) but also Article 31(2). After intervention by the Commission, the German government abandoned the planned extension of the Bundespost's marketing rights.

11.044 **Agricultural products: Article 31(3).**   Article 31(3) provides as follows:

> 'If a State monopoly of a commercial character has rules which are designed to make it easier to dispose of agricultural products or obtain for them the best return, steps should be taken in applying the rules contained in this Article to ensure equivalent safeguards for the employment and standard of living of the producers concerned.'

In *Miritz*,[142] the Court of Justice held that Article 31(3) did not constitute an exception to the specific and unconditional obligations laid down by Article 31(1) and (2), but that its purpose was to enable national authorities, if necessary in cooperation with the Community institutions, to promulgate various measures designed to compensate for the effects which the abolition of the discrimination may have on the employment and standard of living of the producers concerned.

---

139 Case E-4/05 *HOB-vín v The Icelandic State and Áfengis- og tóbaksverslun ríkisins (The State Alcohol and Tobacco Company of Iceland)* [2006] 2 CMLR 1098. See also Case E-9/00 *EFTA Surveillance Authority v Norway* [2002] EFTA Court Rep 72 (Norwegian retail alcohol monopoly's distinction between beer (mainly produced domestically) which could be sold outside its own stores and other beverages of the same alcohol content (mainly imported) which could only be sold through its stores infringed Art 16 EEA); *Karlsson v Iceland* (n 134, above).

140 *HOB-vín*, above, para 37.

141 *Cordless Telephones in Germany*, Press Release IP/85/92 (26 March 1985), [1985] 2 CMLR 397.

142 Case 91/75 *Hauptzollamt Göttingen v Miritz* [1976] ECR 217, [1976] 2 CMLR 235.

Article 31(3) is likely to be relevant only in respect of those agricultural products for which no common organisation of the market has yet been established.[143]

Remedies. Article 31(1) and Article 31(2) have direct effect and so can be relied **11.045** upon by parties before national courts.[144] The Commission may enforce the obligation as against a Member State by bringing proceedings under Article 226 of the Treaty.[145]

6. Derogations under Articles 86(2) and 296

(a) Article 86(2): services of general interest

In general. Article 86(2) provides that: **11.046**

'Undertakings entrusted with the operation of services of general economic interest or having the character of a revenue-producing monopoly shall be subject to the rules contained in this Treaty, in particular to the rules on competition, in so far as the application of such rules does not obstruct the performance, in law or in fact, of the particular tasks assigned to them. The development of trade must not be affected to such an extent as would be contrary to the interests of the Community.'

In contrast to Article 86(1), Article 86(2) is addressed to undertakings, albeit of a particular kind. Article 86(2) confirms that those undertakings are, in general, subject to the Treaty rules although, in appropriate circumstances, it provides them with a limited derogation. Moreover, Article 86(2) may be relied on in combination with Article 86(1) by a Member State to justify the grant to an undertaking entrusted with the operation of services of general economic interest of exclusive rights that would otherwise involve the breach of another provision of the Treaty.[146] As the Court of Justice has stated:

'that provision seeks to reconcile the Member States' interests in using certain undertakings, in particular in the public sector, as an instrument of economic or fiscal

---

[143] The provisions of a common organisation of the market prevail over Art 31: see *Pigs Marketing Board v Redmond* (n 133, above).

[144] *Manghera* (n 134, above) (Art 31(1)); *Costa v ENEL* (n 121, above) (Art 31(2)).

[145] See, eg the cases concerning the electricity and gas monopolies cited at n 129, above; see also the Commission notice to Malta regarding the ending of its import monopoly for petroleum products, Press Release IP/06/1391 (13 October 2006).

[146] See the infringement proceedings concerning energy monopolies: Case C-157/94 *Commission v Netherlands*, Case C-158/94 *Commission v Italy* and Case C-159/94 *Commission v France* (n 129, above). The ECJ stopped short in each case of holding that justification under Art 86(2) had been made out: rather it held that the Commission (which relied on its legal arguments that Art 86(2) was not available) had not established the breach of Art 226 to the necessary standard because it had failed to meet the points put forward by the respondent Member States. See also Case C-209/98 *Sydhavnen* [2000] ECR 3743, [2001] 2 CMLR 936 (exclusive right to treat industrial waste granted to only three undertakings held to be justified).

policy with the Community's interest in ensuring compliance with the rules on competition and the preservation of the unity of the Common Market.'[147]

11.047 **The relevant Treaty rules.** The Treaty rules from which the derogation in Article 86(2) is sought most frequently are Articles 81 and 82.[148] But the Court of Justice has held that Article 86(2) may also be relied upon as a defence to an infringement of Article 31 of the Treaty[149] and to justify the grant of a State aid contrary to Article 87.

11.048 **Article 86(2) and State aids.** In *FFSA*[150] the Court of First Instance reviewed a decision by the Commission rejecting a challenge to the grant of tax concessions to the French Post Office on the ground that the concession did no more than offset the burden of public service constraints to which the Post Office was subject.[151] The Court held that provided that the sole purpose of the aid was to offset the additional costs incurred in performing the particular task assigned to the undertaking and that the grant of the aid was necessary in order for that undertaking to be able to perform its public service obligations 'under conditions of economic equilibrium', the State aid could be justified under Article 86(2). The Court of Justice in the *Altmark* judgment later developed this principle, holding that where a State measure constitutes compensation for the services provided by the recipient undertaking in order to discharge public service obligations, those undertakings do not enjoy a real financial advantage putting them in a more favourable position than their competitors.[152] This means that one of the key criteria for defining when a payment constitutes a State aid is not met so that the measure is not caught by Article 87. Reliance on Article 86(2) would not, in those circumstances, be necessary.

11.049 **The task entrusted.** For an undertaking to have been 'entrusted' with the operation of services of general economic interest, there must have been an act of public authority.[153] Thus the express legal approval by Member States of the

---

[147] *France v Commission* (n 129, above) para 12; repeated in subsequent judgments, eg *Albany* and *Brentjens* (n 64, above) para 103; *Drijvende Bokken* (n 64, above) para 93.

[148] See generally cases cited in this Section.

[149] *Commission v Netherlands, Commission v Italy, Commission v France* (n 129, above); *Hanner* (n 138, above).

[150] Case T-106/95 *FFSA v Commission* [1997] ECR II-229, [1997] 2 CMLR 78 (appeal dismissed, Case 174/97P *FFSA v Commission* [1998] ECR I-1303). See also Case C-387/92 *Banco Exterior de España* [1994] ECR I-877, [1994] 3 CMLR 473.

[151] In particular, the obligation to ensure that there were post offices distributed throughout the country.

[152] Case C-280/00 *Altmark* [2003] ECR I-7747, [2003] 3 CMLR 339, [2005] All ER (EC) 610. See also Case C-451/03 *Servizi Ausiliari Dottori Commercialisti v Giuseppe Calafiori* [2006] ECR I-2941, paras 54 *et seq*. The *Altmark* judgment is discussed at paras 15.025 *et seq*, below.

[153] See Case 123/73 *BRT v SABAM* [1974] ECR 313, [1974] 2 CMLR 238; Case 66/86 *Ahmed Saeed Flugreisen v Zentrale zur Bekämpfung unlauteren Wettbewerbs* [1989] ECR 803, [1990] 4 CMLR 102, para 55.

Eurocheque clearing system did not bring the banks operating it within Article 86(2).[154] The legal method of entrustment may take the form of a specific national law[155] or other act of public authority.[156] Identifying the scope of the 'particular tasks' assigned to the undertaking is important in order to establish which restrictions are necessary for the performance of those tasks. In *Commission v France*,[157] the Court of Justice considered the links needed between the public act conferring the exclusive rights and the application of the derogation. France had argued that the monopoly importers of gas and electricity were not only entrusted with supplying power subject to important public service obligations[158] but also with contributing to environmental and regional policies. The Court rejected those additional grounds, holding that for obligations imposed on an undertaking to be regarded as falling within the task entrusted, they must be linked with the subject-matter of the service and designed to make a direct contribution to satisfying the general economic interest relied upon. Further, the 'task entrusted' must be distinguished from other services carried on by the undertaking which are dissociable from that task. Restrictions on competition in relation to the dissociable services cannot be justified unless the absence of those restrictions would compromise the 'economic equilibrium' of the service of general economic interest.[159]

Services of general economic interest.   The Commission has defined this term   **11.050** as referring to services of an economic nature which Member States or the Community subject to specific public service obligations by virtue of a general interest criterion.[160] This may cover, for example, transport networks, energy and communications. Article 86(2) does not, however, apply to non-economic services.[161] A service of general economic interest does not include one that is

---

154 *Uniform Eurocheques*, OJ 1985 L35/43, [1985] 3 CMLR 434.

155 See, eg *British Telecommunications*, OJ 1982 L360/36, [1983] 1 CMLR 457 (a UK Act of Parliament), upheld in Case 41/83 *Commission v Italy* [1985] ECR 873, [1985] 2 CMLR 368.

156 *Commission v France*, below (legislative measure or regulation is not required); *Almelo* (n 125, above) para 47 (concession granted by public law). The public authority need not be part of central government: see *NAVEWA-ANSEAU*, OJ 1982 L167/39, [1982] 2 CMLR 193.

157 Case C-159/94 *Commission v France* [1997] ECR I-5815, [1998] 2 CMLR 373.

158 Namely, the obligation to ensure continuity of supply, offer competitive tariffs and equal treatment of customers.

159 Case C-320/91 *Corbeau* [1993] ECR I-2533, [1995] 4 CMLR 621; *Flughafen Frankfurt/ Main*, OJ 1998 L72/30, [1998] 4 CMLR 779, para 102. See also *BUPA Ireland Ltd v Health Insurance Authority*, judgment of 23 November 2006: Irish High Court held that dominant State-owned medical expenses insurer came within Art 86(2) since it was compelled to apply 'community rating' in setting insurance premiums (ie charge same premium for all who take out the same policy); on appeal to the Supreme Court, not yet decided.

160 See White Paper on Services of General Interest, COM(2004) 374 final, Annex 1.

161 On the distinction between economic and non-economic activities, see paras 2.005 *et seq*, above. In its First Communication on Services of General Interest, 'Services of General Interest in Europe' OJ 1996 C281/3, para 18, the Commission suggested as examples of non-economic

available only to certain undertakings,[162] or one that is concerned only with managing private interests.[163] The Court of Justice has held that the tasks of ensuring the navigability of a State's most important waterway falls within Article 86(2),[164] as do the operation of a universal and continuous mooring service at ports,[165] operation of the public telephone network,[166] the broadcast of television services,[167] the operation of the national public electricity supply,[168] the basic postal service,[169] the provision of a supplementary pension scheme,[170] the

---

activities compulsory education, social security and matters of vital national interest which are the prerogative of the State, such as security, justice, diplomacy or the registry of births, deaths and marriages. In the more recent Communication, 'Services of General Interest in Europe' OJ 2001 C17/4, Vol II, App F.5, the Commission refers to 'many activities conducted by organisations performing largely social functions, which are not profit oriented and which are not meant to engage in industrial or commercial activity' such as trade unions, political parties, churches and religious societies, consumer associations, learned societies, charities as well as relief and aid organisations (para 30). See also the White Paper on Services of General Interest (n 160, above) pp 16–17, re choices Member States may make for delivery and financing of social and health systems.

[162] Case 10/71 *Ministère Public of Luxembourg v Muller* [1971] ECR 723, per AG Dutheillet de Lamothe at 739. See also Case C-108/98 *RI.SAN* [1999] ECR I-5219, [2000] 4 CMLR 657, per AG Alber at para 43: the undertaking must itself be active in offering services to the public; therefore a state-owned financing company that participates in companies together with public authorities should not fall within Art 86(2) (the ECJ did not address the issue for lack of sufficient factual information).

[163] *BRT v SABAM* (n 153, above) para 23 (Belgian copyright collecting society).

[164] *Muller* (n 162, above) p 730.

[165] Case C-266/96 *Corsica Ferries France v Gruppo Antichi Ormeggiatori del Porto di Genova* [1998] ECR I-3949, [1998] 5 CMLR 402.

[166] See *British Telecommunications* (n 155, above); Case C-18/88 *GB-INNO-BM* [1991] ECR I-5941; and see Chap 12, below, cf *Deutsche Telekom AG*, OJ 2003 L263/9, [2004] 4 CMLR 790: Commission doubtful whether DT was entrusted but found in any event that the margin squeeze was not necessary to fulfil its role (on appeal on other grounds, case T-271/03, *Deutsche Telekom v Commission*, not yet decided).

[167] *Sacchi* (n 120, above) paras 15–17; Case C-260/89 *ERT* [1991] ECR I-2925, [1994] 4 CMLR 540; Case T-69/89 *Radio Telefis Eireann v Commission* [1991] ECR II-485, [1991] 4 CMLR 586, para 82. But see *Exclusive right to broadcast television advertising in Flanders*, OJ 1997 L244/18, [1997] 5 CMLR 718, para 14 (upheld on appeal Case T-266/97 *Vlaamse Televisie Maatschappij v Commission* [1999] ECR II-2329, [2000] 4 CMLR 1171): right to broadcast advertisements not within Art 86(2). The BBC was considered by the Commission to fall within Art 86(2) in *BBC/Valley Printing, Sixth Report on Competition Policy* (1976), point 163, but the issue is not raised in *BBC/Grenfell/Holt, Fourteenth Report* (1984), point 86. See also Communication from the Commission on the application of State aid rules to public service broadcasting, OJ 2001 C320/5.

[168] *Almelo* (n 125, above); Case C-157/94 *Commission v Netherlands*, Case C-158/94 *Commission v Italy*, and Case C-159/94 *Commission v France* (all at n 129, above). Similarly for water authorities, see the Commission's decision in *NAVEWA-ANSEAU* (n 156, above).

[169] *Corbeau* (n 159, above); *FFSA v Commission* (n 150, above); Cases C-147 & 148/97 *Deutsche Post* [2000] ECR 825, [2000] 4 CMLR 838; Cases C-83/01P, etc, *Chronopost v Commission* [2003] ECR I-6993, [2003] 3 CMLR 303; COMP 38.745 *BdKEP–restrictions on mail preparation*, 20 October 2004, [2006] 4 CMLR 981, para 105 (on appeal Case T-490/04 *Germany v Commission*, not yet decided and see note on this case in (2005) 3 EC Competition Policy Newsletter 31).

[170] Case C-67/96 *Albany* [1999] ECR I-5751, [2000] 4 CMLR 446; Cases C-115–117/97 *Brentjens* [1999] ECR I-6025, [2000] 4 CMLR 566; Case C-219/97 *Drijvende Bokken* [1999] ECR I-6121, [2000] 4 CMLR 599 (collectively, *the Dutch Sectoral Pension Funds* cases). See also

environmental management of waste,[171] the wholesale distribution of pharmaceutical products when subject to an obligation to maintain adequate and accessible stocks within a given territory,[172] and the operation of an air route which is not commercially viable, but which it is necessary to operate for reasons of the general interest.[173] Conversely, the services of authors' rights societies,[174] and banks,[175] and the provision of port services do not fall within Article 86(2).[176] It would not seem necessary that the services of general economic interest performed by the entrusted undertaking should benefit the whole of the national economy, but merely a certain group of the population.[177]

Undertakings having the character of a revenue-producing monopoly. Undertakings that enjoy a fiscal monopoly by exploiting their exclusive rights in order to raise money for the State often benefit from a commercial monopoly as well and are therefore also subject to Article 31 of the Treaty which concerns the adjustment of 'State monopolies of a commercial character'.[178]   **11.051**

Obstructing the performance of the tasks. Undertakings within the meaning of Article 86(2) are subject to all the rules of the Treaty unless it is shown that the application of those rules would be incompatible with the performance of their tasks.[179] The derogation, which is granted directly by the Treaty without the need   **11.052**

Cases C-264/01, etc, *AOK-Bundesverband* [2004] ECR I-2493, [2004] 4 CMLR 1261, where AG Jacobs stated (Opinion, para 87) that the parties had correctly accepted that the provision of a solidarity-based system of statutory health insurance was a service of general economic interest (the ECJ did not address this issue).

[171] *Sydhavnen* (n 146, above) para 75.

[172] Case C-53/00 *Ferring* [2001] ECR I-9067.

[173] *Ahmed Saeed* (n 153, above); Case T-260/94 *Air Inter v Commission* [1997] ECR II-997, [1997] 5 CMLR 851.

[174] See *GEMA*, JO 1971 L134/15, [1971] CMLR D35; *BRT v SABAM* (n 153, above); Case 7/82 *GVL v Commission* [1983] ECR 483, [1983] 3 CMLR 645.

[175] Case 172/80 *Zuchner v Bayerische Vereinsbank* [1981] ECR 2021, [1982] 1 CMLR 313, para 7; *Uniform Eurocheques* (n 154, above); *Lombard Club*, OJ 2004 L56/1, [2004] 5 CMLR 399, para 398 (on appeal Cases T-259/02, etc, *Raiffeisen Zentralbank Österreich v Commission*, judgment of 14 December 2006). The position of central banks is not, however, necessarily the same. Note that in Case C-309/99 *Wouters v Algemene Raad van de Nederlandse Orde Van Advocaten* [2002] ECR I-1577, [2002] 4 CMLR 913, [2002] All ER (EC) 193, AG Léger (Opinion, paras 170–176) considered that lawyers, by reason of their role in the administration of justice and in enabling a system governed by the rule of law to operate effectively, perform services that are 'of general economic interest' within Art 86(2); *sed quaere* (and the ECJ did not address this issue).

[176] Case C-179/90 *Merci Convenzionale Porto di Genova* [1991] ECR I-5889, [1994] 4 CMLR 422, above, and the other port cases cited in n 67, above.

[177] AG Roemer in Case 82/71 *Pubblico Ministero Italiano v SAIL* [1972] ECR 119, 144, [1972] CMLR 723, 730–731. But cf the submissions of the Commission in Case 90/76 *Van Ameyde v UCI* [1977] ECR 1091, [1977] 2 CMLR 478.

[178] See paras 11.036 *et seq*, above.

[179] *Sacchi* (n 120, above) para 14; Case 311/84 *CBEM v CLT and IPB* ('*Télémarketing*') [1985] ECR 3261, [1986] 2 CMLR 558; *Ahmed Saeed* (n 153, above); Case C-41/90 *Höfner and Elser*

for notification to the Commission, is available not to particular undertakings as such but rather in respect of particular tasks assigned to those particular undertakings.[180] In a series of cases concerning monopolies on the import and export of electricity and natural gas, the Court of Justice reformulated the test to be applied in assessing whether the derogation applies. The Commission brought actions for breach of Article 31[181] of the Treaty against the Netherlands, Italy and France.[182] It argued that the States had not discharged the burden of proving that the continued existence of the national bodies would be threatened by the application of Article 31 or that there was no alternative way to achieve the performance of the task entrusted to them. The Court held that to satisfy Article 86(2) it is sufficient that the Treaty rules obstruct the performance in law or in fact of the special obligations entrusted to the undertaking. It is not necessary that the survival of the undertaking itself would be threatened in the absence of the derogation. Although the burden of showing that Article 86(2) is fulfilled rests on the Member State, it is enough to show that the special or exclusive rights are necessary to enable the holder to perform the task assigned to it 'under economically acceptable conditions'.[183] Further, the burden of proof on the Member State was 'not such as to require member States to prove positively that no other conceivable measure, which by definition would be hypothetical, could enable those tasks to be performed under the same conditions'.[184]

[1991] ECR I-1979, [1993] 4 CMLR 306; *Radio Telefís Eireann* (n 167, above). For other unsuccessful attempts to rely on Art 86(2), see *IJsselcentrale*, OJ 1991 L28/32, [1992] 5 CMLR 154, and the postal services cases cited in n 58, above. In *Albany* (n 170, above) para 122, the ECJ referred, when considering the application of Art 86(2) to the 'margin of appreciation enjoyed, according to settled case-law, by the Member States in organising their social security systems.' It may therefore be that the rigour of the test under Article 86(2) varies to some degree from sector to sector. See AG Jacobs in *AOK-Bundesverband* (n 170, above) Opinion at para 95 (the ECJ did not address this issue).

[180] See Case 258/78 *Nungesser v Commission* [1982] ECR 2015, [1983] 1 CMLR 278, paras 8–9; *NAVEWA-ANSEAU* (n 156, above); *British Telecommunications* (n 155, above).

[181] For Art 31, see paras 11.036 *et seq*, above.

[182] Case C-157/94 *Commission v Netherlands*, Case C-158/94 *Commission v Italy*, Case C-159/94 *Commission v France* [1997] ECR I-5699, 5789, 5815, [1998] 2 CMLR 373. A similar infringement action against Spain was dismissed on the grounds that the Commission had not established that the legislation challenged in fact conferred an exclusive right to import or export at all: Case C-160/94 *Commission v Spain* [1997] ECR I-5851, [1998] 2 CMLR 373.

[183] See also *Almelo* (n 125, above): 'it is necessary to take into consideration the economic conditions in which the undertaking operates, in particular the costs it has to bear and the legislation, particularly concerning the environment, to which it is subject' (para 49). In *BdKEP – restrictions on mail preparation* (n 169, above) the Commission held that the test was not satisfied on the facts, para 114.

[184] *Commission v Netherlands* (n 182, above) para 58; *Commission v Italy* (ibid) para 54; *Commission v France* (ibid) para 101. The ECJ dismissed the proceedings on the grounds that the Commission had not adduced sufficient evidence for it to decide whether the exclusive rights went further than was necessary for the undertakings to perform under acceptable conditions the tasks of general economic interest entrusted to them.

The *Dutch Sectoral Pension Funds* cases.   The Court of Justice applied the **11.053** reformulated test in three decisions[185] concerning the position under Dutch law whereby, pursuant to a collective labour agreement, a designated pension fund was granted the exclusive right to manage a supplementary pension scheme in a particular industrial or economic sector. Firms in the relevant sector were obliged to affiliate to the relevant fund for the purpose of securing a supplementary pension for their employees unless the fund granted them a specific exception. In each case, firms that were bound by the legislation to affiliate to the designated sectoral fund argued that they could obtain the same or better levels of benefits for their employees by making arrangements for comprehensive pension cover with an insurance company, yet they had been refused exceptions and were being sued for contributions to the sectoral fund. The Court found that each sectoral pension fund had been granted an exclusive right and held that it occupied a dominant position within the meaning of Article 82. Further, the fact that undertakings that wanted to supplement the basic state pension were unable to make arrangements for a supplementary pension scheme with the insurer of their choice resulted in a restriction of competition which derived directly from the grant of an exclusive right. It was therefore necessary to consider the application of the derogation in Article 86(2). The Court found that if the exclusive right were removed, undertakings with young employees in good health engaged in non-dangerous activities would seek more advantageous terms from private insurers leaving the fund with the 'bad risks' so that it would no longer be able to offer pensions at an acceptable cost. The removal of the exclusive right might therefore make it impossible for the fund to perform the task of general economic interest entrusted to it under economically acceptable conditions and threaten its financial equilibrium. The restriction on competition therefore fell within the derogation and Article 82 did not apply.[186]

---

[185] Case C-67/96 *Albany* [1999] ECR I-5751, [2000] 4 CMLR 446; Cases C-115–117/97 *Brentjens* [1999] ECR I-6025, [2000] 4 CMLR 566; Case C-219/97 *Drijvende Bokken* [1999] ECR I-6121, [2000] 4 CMLR 599 (collectively, 'the *Dutch Sectoral Pension Funds* cases'). The ECJ dismissed a separate argument under Art 81 on the grounds that the collective agreement between employers' and labour organisations to seek designation of a compulsory pension fund fell outside the scope of Art 81 altogether: see para 2.034, above. See also Case C-266/96 *Corsica Ferries France* (n 165, above) where the ECJ held that the inclusion in the price of mooring services of a component designed to cover the cost of maintaining a universal service was necessary for the provision of that service of general economic interest and so benefited from Art 86(2).

[186] See also *BUPA Ireland Ltd v Health Insurance Authority* (n 159, above): Irish High Court held that imposition of a 'risk equalisation scheme', whereby a competing insurer (BUPA) had to make substantial payments to the dominant medical expenses insurer which was obliged to carry a higher risk profile, satisfied Art 86(2). Since the level of payments exceeded its profits, BUPA has in consequence withdrawn from the Irish healthcare insurance market altogether. The decn is on appeal to the Supreme Court of Ireland, not yet decided.

11.054 **The 'tailpiece': adverse development of trade.** Even if an undertaking is able to show that the normal application of the Treaty obstructs the performance of its entrusted task, the 'tailpiece' to Article 86(2) provides that it is entitled to benefit from the derogation only if the development of trade is not 'affected to such an extent as would be contrary to the interests of the Community'. This wording is narrower than the concept of effect on trade between Member States in Articles 81 and 82, for if any effect on trade between Member States were sufficient to prevent the application of the derogation there would be little ground covered by Article 86(2). It appears that the application of the tailpiece involves an appraisal of the particular task entrusted to the undertaking concerned and the protection of the interests of the Community in relation to the development of trade.[187]

11.055 **Article 86(2) in national courts.** It is now clear that Article 86(2) is directly effective and that once a national court holds that an undertaking comes within the scope of that provision it should determine whether the conditions of the derogation are satisfied.[188] If an undertaking invokes the provisions of Article 86(2) as a defence in proceedings relating to a provision of Community law having direct effect, such as Articles 81 or 82, before a national court, that court is under a duty to investigate whether the undertaking has in fact been entrusted by a Member State with the operation of a service of a general economic interest.[189] If the national court rules that the undertaking is not an entrusted undertaking within the meaning of Article 86(2), it should apply the normal rules of the Treaty, including Articles 81 and 82.[190]

11.056 **Article 86(3).** The Commission may specify the meaning and extent of the exception under Article 86(2) and may set out rules intended to enable effective monitoring of the fulfilment of the criteria set out in Article 86(2) by adopting decisions and directives pursuant to Article 86(3).[191] For example, following the

---

187 In *Commission v Netherlands* (n 182, above), the ECJ held that since the Netherlands had stated that all the available capacity for cross-border trade in electricity was taken up under the monopoly regime, it was incumbent on the Commission to define the Community interest in relation to which the development of trade must be assessed and to show how development of direct trade between producers and consumers or between the major networks would have been possible given the existing capacity and arrangements for transmission and distribution in the country (para 71).

188 *Almelo* (n 125, above); *Corbeau* (n 159, above). It appears, however, that a national court may not apply Art 86(2) to an aid that has not been notified to the Commission under Art 88 of the Treaty. See Case C-387/92 *Banco Exterior de España* [1994] ECR I-877, [1994] 3 CMLR 473, para 17; AG Léger in *Altmark* (n 152, above) para 56 of the Opinion. But cf AG Tizzanno in *Ferring* (n 172, above) paras 78–80 of the Opinion.

189 *BRT v SABAM* (n 153, above) para 22; *Ahmed Saeed* (n 153, above).

190 *Sacchi* (n 120, above) paras 15–18.

191 See generally paras 11.022 *et seq*, above.

Court's judgment in *Altmark*,[192] the Commission adopted a decision on the application of Article 86(2) of the Treaty to State aid in the form of public service compensation granted to certain public service undertakings entrusted with the operation of services of general economic interest.[193]

(b) Article 296: military equipment

Article 296.   Article 296(1)(b) provides that: **11.057**

'Any Member State may take such measures as it considers necessary for the protection of the essential interests of its security which are connected with the production of or trade in arms, ammunitions and war material; such measures shall not adversely affect the conditions of competition in the common market regarding products which are not intended for specifically military purposes.'

Article 296(2) provides that: **11.058**

'The Council may, acting unanimously on a proposal from the Commission, make changes to the list, which it drew up on 15 April 1958, of the products to which the provisions of paragraph 1(b) apply.'

The Article is not, of itself, a derogation from any Treaty obligation. Rather it permits the Member States when enacting domestic legislation, for example, to implement a Directive, to derogate in respect of the essential interests covered by Article 296 (1)(b).

Application of Article 296.   The list of products covered by Article 296(1)(b)   **11.059**
has never been amended since it was drawn up.[194] The Commission has held[195] that Article 296(1)(b) is inapplicable to a clause restricting the right of a licensee to grant sub-licences in respect of applications of a patented invention to military equipment. The Commission considered that this restriction did not come within Article 296 since the engines to which the patents related were not intended for specifically military purposes but on the contrary were intended primarily for non-military use. The Commission's view is that Article 296 can be invoked only by Member States and not by undertakings[196] and it has been invoked to prevent

---

[192] *Altmark* (n 152, above).

[193] Commission Decision 2005/842/EC of 28 November 2005 on the application of Article 86(2) of the Treaty to State aid in the form of public service compensation granted to certain public service undertakings entrusted with the operation of services of general economic interest, OJ 2005 L312/67. See further para 15.068, below.

[194] The list has not been published but is at Vol II, App A.7.

[195] *French State/Suralmo, Ninth Report on Competition Policy* (1979), points 114–115. Art 296 does not seem to have been raised in *WANO Schwarzpulver*, OJ 1978 L322/26, [1979] 1 CMLR 403.

[196] In the Commission's view, Art 296(1)(b) can only be invoked by Member States and not by undertakings; and the government measures can only preclude application of the competition rules where they required or encouraged undertakings to take particular action within the terms of Art 296(1)(b): Parliamentary answer to a written question, OJ 1991 C130/2. See also the Commission's Green Paper on Defence Procurement, September 2004 (COM(2004) 608).

parties to a concentration concerning the defence sector from submitting information to the Commission under the Merger Regulation.[197] If a Member State or the Commission considers that improper use is being made of the powers under Article 296, it may bring the matter directly before the Court of Justice.[198]

---

[197] See para 8.105, above.
[198] Art 298 EC. This is in derogation of the normal procedures under Arts 226 and 227 and the ECJ must give its ruling *in camera*.

12

SECTORAL REGIMES

1. Introduction

12.001   **Accommodating different social goals.**   The economies of the Member States are based on the assumption that free and open markets and vigorous competition are the best way to ensure the efficient allocation of resources. However, since the early implementation of the Community competition rules, there has been a recognition that in some sectors of the economy, the application of those rules must be tempered to accommodate other potentially conflicting policy goals. The need to modify the application of competition rules varies as between different sectors. In the agricultural sector, for example, the objectives expressed in Article 33 of the EC Treaty of stabilising markets, ensuring a fair standard of living for the agricultural community and maintaining availability of supplies might not be achieved if unrestrained competition were allowed to take place. Similarly, the need to ensure universal provision of utilities or services which are fundamental to society means that a provider of such services subject to a universal service obligation requires a degree of protection from competition and must be allowed to cross-subsidise certain groups of consumers.

12.002   **Liberalisation of former national monopolies.**   In other sectors, the need to temper the application of competition rules is pragmatic, arising from the fact that traditionally certain services were provided by a single, State-owned undertaking which owned and operated the infrastructure needed to provide the service. Here the introduction of effective competition can only be achieved in conjunction with liberalising measures restricting the ability of the Member State to reserve to itself the provision of those services. In these areas, notably telecommunications and energy, the Community institutions rely on a combination of liberalising directives and competition law enforcement gradually to open up markets to competing undertakings and break down national barriers. There is also an international aspect in that some constraints on the application of competition law result from the Member States' adherence to international treaties and conventions. For example, creating contestible markets in air transport between the Community and third countries involves modification of long-standing treaties governing international carriage, and the rules governing the activities of liner conferences derive from a UN Convention.

12.003   **Plan of this Chapter.**   This Chapter considers the sectors of the economy which are subject to special competition regimes which either supplement or replace the general application of Articles 81 and 82. Section 2 considers the application of the competition rules in relation to different modes of transport and the changes made, particularly in relation to procedure, by Regulation 1/2003. Section 3 considers the different energy markets where the Commission has sought to encourage competition by adopting liberalising measures as well as applying competition rules to areas traditionally reserved to State control. Section 4 concerns electronic communications where the Commission has been particularly concerned to ensure that the bringing to market of rapidly developing technologies is not hindered by the market power enjoyed by former national monopolies. The last three Sections deal with insurance, postal services and agriculture, where it has been recognised that wider social policy requires an adaptation of competition law. Reference should also be made to Chapter 11, above, which covers the application of Article 86 of the EC Treaty and the control of public undertakings and undertakings to which the State has granted special or exclusive rights.

2. Transport

(a) Introduction

Scope of this Section.   This Section deals with the application of the competition rules in the field of transport. Despite increasing liberalisation, special rules remain for the application of Articles 81 and 82 to all three main transport sectors: rail, roads and inland waterways; maritime transport; and air transport.   **12.004**

Generally.   Article 3(1)(f) of the EC Treaty provides that the activities of the Community shall include the adoption of a common policy in the sphere of transport. The special provisions of the Treaty relating to transport, namely Articles 70 to 80, are to be found under Title V in Part Three of the Treaty concerned with 'Community Policies'. Article 80(1) provides that the provisions of Title V apply to transport by rail, road and inland waterway. Article 80(2) provides that the Council may, acting by a qualified majority, decide whether, to what extent and by what procedure, to adopt appropriate measures in the context of sea and air transport. In a series of judgments the Court of Justice ruled that the general rules of the Treaty[1] (in the absence of a specific derogation[2]), the provisions on State aids,[3] and the rules on competition,[4] are applicable to all modes of transport.   **12.005**

Implementation of Articles 81 and 82 in the transport sector.   When Regulation 17 was adopted to provide an enforcement regime for Articles 81 and 82 for most sectors of the economy, Council Regulation 141/62[5] excluded the transport sector from the potential exercise of those powers. Subsequently, the Council   **12.006**

---

[1] Case 167/73 *Commission v France* [1974] ECR 359, [1974] 2 CMLR 216.
[2] Such as Art 51(1) EC: see Case C-49/89 *Corsica Ferries France v Direction Générale des Douanes* [1989] ECR 4441, [1991] 2 CMLR 227.
[3] Case 156/77 *Commission v Belgium* [1978] ECR 1881.
[4] Cases 209/84, etc, *Ministère Public v Asjes ('Nouvelles Frontières')* [1986] ECR 1425, [1986] 3 CMLR 173. See also Case C-185/91 *Reiff* [1993] ECR I–5801, [1995] 5 CMLR 145.
[5] Reg 141/62, OJ 1962 2751, OJ 1959–62, 291, Art 1 as amended by Reg 1002/67.

adopted three sectoral regulations: Regulation 1017/68 applying the rules on competition to transport by rail, road and inland waterways; Regulation 4056/86 applying them to international maritime transport; and Regulation 3975/87 applying them to international and domestic[6] air transport. Each of these Regulations had substantive provisions, in particular incorporating block exemptions for certain categories of agreement, and also procedural provisions empowering the Commission to enforce the Regulations.

12.007 **Transport and the Modernisation of enforcement procedure.** As part of the Modernisation package replacing Regulation 17 with a new regime for the enforcement of the Community competition rules, it was decided to incorporate transport into the general enforcement regime. Regulation 1/2003[7] therefore applied on its introduction to most transport sectors: it repealed Regulation 141/62 and amended Regulations 1017/68, 4056/86 and 3975/87 by deleting the procedural provisions which they contained.[8] The remaining provisions of Regulation 3975/87 were repealed by Regulation 411/2004, save for some transitional provisions, with the result that all air transport is now covered by Regulation 1/2003.[9] This left only two sectors outside the new Regulation 1/2003 regime: international tramp vessel services as defined in Article 1(3)(a) of Regulation 4056/86; and 'cabotage' services, that is maritime transport services that take place exclusively between ports within the same Member State as foreseen in Article 1(2) of Regulation 4056/86. These two sectors were finally brought within the ambit of Regulation 1/2003 by Regulation 1419/2006.[10] That Regulation also repealed the liner conference block exemption, discussed below. Article 82, by contrast, has since the adoption of Regulation 17 been fully effective and can be invoked by individuals without any prior decision of the Commission or national authorities.[11]

12.008 **EEA Agreement.** The Regulations applying the competition rules to the various transport sectors have been adopted so as to apply to the EEA.[12]

---

6 Domestic air transport was included by virtue of Reg 2410/92, OJ 1992 L240/18.

7 Reg 1/2003, OJ 2003 L1/1: Vol II, App B.3.

8 Arts 36–38 of Reg 1/2003. Reg 1/2003 is incorporated into the EEA Agreement by EEA Joint Committee Decn 130/2004, OJ 2005 L64/57. For the detailed procedural rules governing the enforcement of Arts 81 and 82, see Chap 13, below.

9 Reg 411/2004, OJ 2004 L68/1. The transitional provisions relate to the continuation in force of the individual exemptions granted under the Reg.

10 Reg 1419/2006 repealing Art 32 of Reg 1/2003, OJ 2006 L269/1. The repeal came into effect on 18 October 2006, 20 days after the publication of the Reg in the Official Journal.

11 Case 66/86 *Ahmed Saeed Flugreisen v Zentrale zur Bekämpfung unlauteren Wettbewerbs* [1989] ECR 803, [1990] 4 CMLR 102.

12 EEA Agreement, Annex XIV, points 10–11c and Protocol 21, Arts 1 and 3(1)(6)–(14). See para 3.093, above, for a table showing the Annex XIV provisions implementing the various transport block exemptions. See also Clarification of the Commission Recommendations on the application of the competition rules to new transport infrastructure projects OJ 1997 C298/5: Vol II, App E.13.

(b) Rail, road and inland waterway transport

(i) Application of Community competition rules

Introduction.[13]   Previously, both the procedural and substantive rules on com-   **12.009**
petition which applied in this sector were contained in Regulation 1017/68.[14]
The relevant procedural rules are now contained in Regulation 1/2003 which
made substantial amendments to Regulation 1017/68. The only substantive
provisions of Regulation 1017/68 which remain in force are Articles 1, 3 and 4.
Article 1 governs the scope of the Regulation, Article 3 provides for the negative
clearance of certain agreements, and Article 4 provides for block exemption of
certain agreements between small- and medium-sized undertakings. The
Commission has accordingly prepared a draft codifying Regulation to replace
Regulation 1017/68 and, at the time of writing, this proposal is pending before
the Council and the Parliament.[15]

Scope of Regulation 1017/68.   By Article 1, Regulation 1017/68 applies to   **12.010**
agreements, decisions or concerted practices concerning transport by road, rail or
inland waterway (and also to the operations of providers of services ancillary to
transport) which have as their object or effect the fixing of transport rates and
conditions; the limitation or control of the supply of transport; the sharing of
transport markets; the application of technical improvements or technical coordination; or in certain circumstances, the joint financing or acquisition of transport
equipment or supplies where such operations are directly related to the provision
of transport services and are necessary for the joint operation of services by a
grouping of road or inland[16] waterway transport undertakings.[17] In the *UIC*
case,[18] the Court of Justice held that the application of Regulation 1017/68
depends upon the nature of the agreements in question, as regards their objects
and effect, and does not require identification of the relevant market. There was
substantial jurisprudence developed by the Community Courts prior to the
changes made by Regulation 1/2003, delineating the boundary between
Regulation 1017/68 and Regulation 17 and defining the 'ancillary services'
referred to in the second sentence of Article 1.[19] This is now largely of historical

---

[13] See generally Faull & Nikpay (eds), *The EC Law of Competition* (2nd ed, 2007), paras 14.149
et seq.
  [14] Reg 1017/68, OJ 1968 L175/1 (as amended by Reg 1/2003): Vol II, App E.1.
  [15] COM(2006) 722 final of 27 November 2006, Vol II, App E.4.
  [16] This is defined in Art 4 of Reg 1017/68.
  [17] Thus the provision of rail equipment such as rolling stock would appear to be governed by the
general Treaty provisions and Reg 17 (now superseded by Reg 1/2003) rather than Reg 1017/68: see
Eurofima, *IIIrd Report on Competition Policy* (1973), point 68, [1973] CMLR D217.
  [18] Case C-264/95P *Commission v UIC* [1997] ECR I-1287, [1997] 5 CMLR 49, para 42.
  [19] See, eg *French inland waterway traffic: EATE Levy*, OJ 1985 L219/35, appeal dismissed
Case 272/85 *ANTIB v Commission* [1987] ECR 2201; *Eurotunnel III*, OJ 1994 L354/66, [1995]
4 CMLR 801 (annulled on other grounds in Cases T-79 & 80/95 *SNCF and British Railways v*

interest since the provisions of Regulation 1017/68 which remain in force do not appear to depend upon the ambit of Article 1 for their scope.

12.011 **Exception for technical agreements.** Article 3 of Regulation 1017/68 (as amended) excepts from the prohibition in Article 81(1) certain agreements the sole object and effect of which is to apply technical improvements or to achieve technical cooperation.[20] Agreements which may be construed as having a commercial purpose, as well as a technical one, are therefore outside the exception.[21] The excepted categories include the standardisation of equipment, transport supplies, vehicles or fixed installations, the coordination of transport timetables for connecting routes, the grouping of single consignments and the establishment of uniform rules as to the structure of tariffs and their conditions of application, provided such rules do not lay down transport rates and conditions.[22]

12.012 *Exemption for groups of small- and medium-sized undertakings.* Article 4 of Regulation 1017/68 (as amended) exempts from the prohibition in Article 81(1) agreements the purpose of which is the constitution and operation of groupings of road or inland waterway transport and undertakings or the joint financing or acquisition of equipment or supplies where this is directly related to providing transport services and necessary for the grouping's joint operations. The exemption only applies where the individual undertakings and the grouping are within certain carrying capacity thresholds.[23] Where the implementation of such an agreement has effects which are incompatible with the general exemption rules, the Commission can require the undertakings to make such effects cease.

Commission [1996] ECR II-1491, [1997] 4 CMLR 334); Case T-14/93 *Union Internationale des Chemins de Fer v Commission* [1995] ECR II-1503, [1996] 5 CMLR 40, paras 55–56 (the ECJ did not address this issue on the appeal in *UIC* (n 18, above) paras 47–51). The boundary between Reg 1017/68 and Reg 4056/86 dealing with maritime transport was also important: see para 12.019, below, for Reg 4056/86 (now repealed).

20 See *HOV SVZ/MCN*, OJ 1994 L104/34, para 91 (on appeal, Case T-229/94 *Deutsche Bahn v Commission* [1997] ECR II-1689, [1998] 4 CMLR 220, further appeal dismissed Case C-436/97P [1999] ECR I-2387, [1999] 5 CMLR 776). The word 'sole' is omitted before 'object and effect' in Art 3 only in the English version but appears in the original (1968) language versions. See also the Eighth Recital of Reg 1017/68, and Ortiz Blanco and Van Houtte *EC Competition Law in the Transport Sector* (1996), 71.

21 See *Tariff structures in the combined transport of goods*, OJ 1993 L73/38, corr OJ 1993 L145/31, para 41; *ACI*, OJ 1994 L224/28; and *Night Services*, OJ 1994 L259/2, [1995] 5 CMLR 76 (locomotives), annulled in part on appeal, Cases T-374/94, etc, *ENS v Commission* [1998] ECR II-3141, [1998] 5 CMLR 718 (the exclusion in the latter decn was not considered by the CFI in the appeal). In *Deutsche Bahn* (n 20, above), the CFI held (para 37) that an agreement whose purpose is the joint fixing of prices could not come within the Art 3 exception.

22 See *Tariff structures in the combined transport of goods* (n 21, above).

23 1,000 tonnes individually and 10,000 tonnes in aggregate for road transport undertakings; 50,000 tonnes individually and 500,000 tonnes in aggregate for inland waterway transport undertakings.

Individual application of Article 81(3).   Consortia agreements that do not **12.013** come within the terms of Regulation 1017/68 may nonetheless benefit from the application of Article 81(3) if they fulfil the criteria set out there.[24] Prior to the repeal of the procedural provisions of Regulation 1017/68, the Commission granted individual exemption to a number of agreements under Article 5 of Regulation 1017/68 which set criteria very similar to those in Article 81(3). In *EATE*,[25] the Commission refused an exemption under Article 5 on the grounds that the restrictions were disproportionate to any benefits likely to accrue and that the levy as applied neither contributed to any of the necessary improvements nor benefited users. A number of cooperation arrangements between public railway undertakings in relation to the Channel Tunnel have been granted exemption on the basis of conditions designed to facilitate access by other operators.[26] The Commission has noted the importance of developing such high quality rail services which provide increased competition with traditional sea and air transport.[27]

Article 82.   In addition to the liberalisation measures, described below, the **12.014** Commission has sought to address concerns over access by the use of Article 82. In October 2001, the Commission warned Deutsche Bahn about discriminating against a private operator.[28] In *GVG/FS*,[29] the Commission found that Ferrovie dello Stato's ('FS') repeated and long-standing refusal to give access to GVG, a small German railway operator, amounted to an abuse of a dominant position: first, FS discriminated in its charges for traction; secondly, it subsequently declined to provide traction altogether; and thirdly, it imposed a requirement that GVG must hire FS staff.

(ii) Liberalisation measures in the railway sector

Separation of railway services provision from rail infrastructure.   The process **12.015** of opening up railway services to competition has focused on the need to remove the Member States' railway infrastructure from the absolute control of the former monopoly provider of railway services. The process of liberalisation began with

---

[24] For Art 81(3), see generally Chap 3, above.

[25] *EATE levy* (n 19, above).

[26] See *ACI*, OJ 1994 L224/28; *Night Services*, OJ 1994 L259/2, [1995] 5 CMLR 76 (on appeal, the requirement imposed by the Commission to make specialised rolling stock for Channel Tunnel services available to new extrants as a condition for exemption was set aside: *ENS v Commission* (n 21, above)).

[27] *XXIVth Report on Competition Policy* (1994), point 190. See also *CIA*, OJ 1994 C130/3, *XXIVth Report on Competition Policy* (1994), point 191: cooperation agreement between 13 European rail companies regarding the international carriage of new motor vehicles exempted under the objections procedure for three years. On its expiry, and in response to a fresh notification, the Commission expressed concern about the basis of the tariff set out in the agreement; the tariff was withdrawn and the Commission issued a 'negative clearance' comfort letter in December 1999.

[28] Press Release IP/01/1415 (5 October 2001).

[29] *GVG/FS*, OJ 2004 L11/17, [2004] 4 CMLR 1446.

the introduction of Directive 91/440 on the development of the Community's railways.[30] Directive 91/440 introduced a requirement to distinguish between 'railway undertakings' which provide rail transport services and 'infrastructure managers' which are responsible for establishing and maintaining railway infrastructure.[31] It also provided that 'international groupings', defined as an association of at least two railway undertakings established in different Member States, had to be granted rights of access and transit in the Member States where they are established, as well as transit rights in other Member States for international services between the Member States where the undertakings constituting the grouping are established. Agreements for the allocation of railway infrastructure capacity were then covered by Directive 95/19 which also covered the charging of infrastructure fees,[32] where access is made available pursuant to Directive 91/440.[33]

12.016 **The 2001 railway package of measures.** In February 2001, the Council and the European Parliament adopted three directives comprising the first railway package.[34] These measures extend rights of access to all types of international rail freight operating over a specified trans-European rail freight network until 2008, and over the whole EU network thereafter.[35] The three directives are as follows:

- Directive 2001/12 on the development of the Community's railways, sets out the general framework for European railways. It includes separation of certain essential functions such as licensing, charging for track access, capacity allocation,

---

30 Dir 91/440, OJ 1991 L237/25. Dir 95/18, OJ 1995 L143/70, made provision for an EU-wide licence for railway undertakings providing the services referred to in Art 10 of Dir 91/449.

31 Dir 91/440, Art 3.

32 Dir 95/19, OJ 1995 L143/75 (no longer in force).

33 See Clarification of the Commission's recommendations on the application of the competition rules to new transport infrastructure projects, OJ 1997 C298/5; Vol II, App E.13, concerning the balance between the interests of promoters of costly and high-risk infrastructure projects who wish to reserve capacity for transport companies that contribute to the financial viability or equilibrium of the project on the one hand and the need on the other hand to allow freedom of access to infrastructure. See also the position adopted by the Commission in relation to the reservation of train paths on the Channel Tunnel Rail Link for the Eurostar by the parties financing its construction: OJ 1999 C6/7.

34 The first railway package Directives were all published in OJ 2001 L75. For consolidated texts of Dir 91/440 and Dir 95/18 incorporating the changes from the first package (but not the second package), see the website of the UK Office of Rail Regulation (www.rail-reg.gov.uk) under International Regulation/EU Developments. Dir 2001/14/EC was amended by Commission Decn 2002/844, OJ 2002 L289/30. The second package of railway measures (para 12.017, below) also amends these Directives; eg Dir 2004/49 replaces the provisions in Dir 2001/14 concerning safety certification.

35 The deadline for transposition of the first railway package expired on 5 March 2003. The requirements of the Directives have been transposed in the UK through two sets of Regs: the Railway (Licensing of Railway Undertakings) Regs 2005, SI 2005/3050, which transposed Dir 95/18 as amended by 2001/13 and 2004/49, and the Railways Infrastructure (Access and Management) Regs 2005, SI 2005/3049 which transposed Dir 91/440, as amended by Dirs 2001/12 and 2004/51, and Dir 2001/14 as amended by Dir 2004/49. These Regs repeal the Railways Regs 1998, SI 1998/340, as amended by SI 1998/1519.

safety certification, rolling stock certification and the setting of safety standards and rules, from the undertakings involved in operating rail transport services. It also provides for open access for international freight services on the Trans-European Rail Freight Network (TERFN), which comprises the major railways routes in each Member State. Open access to the entire European rail network for all international freight is meant to be achieved within seven years of the adoption of the Directive.

- Directive 2001/13 covers the licensing of railway undertakings (train operators). It establishes a common licence for train operators across the European Union and the European Economic Area. It applies to most domestic train operators and gives Member States a discretion to include domestic regulatory provisions in licences (for example, for consumer benefit) provided that they are not discriminatory.

- Directive 2001/14 replaced Directive 95/19 and covers capacity allocation and charging. It requires each Member State to establish a regulatory body and sets out the key principles for, and requires transparency in, allocating and charging for track access.

The second railway package. The Commission's White Paper *European Transport Policy for 2010: Time to decide*[36] resulted in the adoption of the second railway package,[37] comprising a Directive to liberalise market access by opening up domestic and cabotage freight services,[38] a Directive on rail safety,[39] a Directive amending Directive 96/48 on the interoperability of the trans-European high speed rail system and Directive 2001/16 on the interoperability of the trans-European conventional rail system,[40] and a Regulation creating a European Railway Agency to provide technical support for interoperability and safety work.[41] The period within which the Member States had to implement the second railway package expired on 30 April 2006.[42] **12.017**

---

[36] COM(2001) 370 final, 12 September 2001.

[37] Adopted on 29 April 2004.

[38] Dir 2004/51 on the development of the Community's railways, OJ 2004 L164/164 (corr, OJ 2004 L220/58).

[39] Dir 2004/49 on safety on the Community's railways and amending Dir 95/18 and Dir 2001/14, OJ 2004 L164/44 (corr, OJ 2004 L220/16). The period within which the Member States had to implement this Directive expired on 30 April 2006.

[40] Dir 2004/50, OJ 2004 L164/144.

[41] Reg 881/2004, OJ 2004 L164/1 (corr, OJ 2004 L220/1). This instrument was included in Annex XIII of the EEA Agreement as of 11 June 2005: 2005 OJ L268/13. The Agency now has a website at www.era.eu.int.

[42] The Commission has announced that it is commencing infringement proceedings against 10 Member States that had failed to communicate national implementing measures to transpose Dirs 2004/49 and 2004/50: Press Release IP/07/368 (21 March 2007).

12.018 **Further proposals.** The Commission announced on 3 March 2004 a proposed third railway package containing measures to revitalise the European railways.[43] This package consists of four proposals: a further opening of the market for international passenger transport by rail;[44] a regulation on the rights and obligations of international rail passengers;[45] a regulation on rail freight quality;[46] and a Directive for train driver licences.[47] On 24 July 2006, the Council adopted its common position on the third package which, at the time of writing, is at second reading stage.

(c) Maritime transport

(i) Scope of application of the competition rules

12.019 **Repeal of Regulation 4056/86.** Regulation 4056/86 used to provide a bespoke procedural and enforcement regime for applying the competition rules to maritime transport. These procedural provisions were repealed by Regulation 1/2003[48] leaving only the substantive provisions of Regulation 4056/86 governing the application of Articles 81 and 82 to maritime transport services.[49] After the Commission and Council concluded that the criteria for the application of Article 81(3) were no longer satisfied by liner conference agreements, the remaining provisions of Regulation 4056/86 were repealed by Regulation 1419/2006[50] but with effect only from October 2008. Acknowledging the fact that liner conferences are permitted in other jurisdictions, the Commission has described the consequence of the ending of the block exemption in the following terms:

> 'The decision to end the exemption from the competition rules means that as of October 2008 all EU and non-EU carriers which currently take part in conferences operating on trades to and from the EU will have to end their conference activities, that is price fixing and capacity regulation, on those trades. Nothing would prevent them from taking part in price fixing conferences on non-EU trade routes. To give a concrete example, an EU carrier like Maersk Line, member of the Trans-Atlantic Conference Agreement (TACA), can no longer be involved in price fixing and capacity regulation

---

[43] Further integration of the European rail system: third railway package, Communication COM(2004) 140 final, 3 March 2004.

[44] Proposal for a Directive of the European Parliament and of the Council, amending Council Directive 91/440/EEC on the development of the Community's railways, COM(2004) 139 final.

[45] Proposal for a Regulation of the European Parliament and of the Council on International Rail Passengers' Rights and Obligations, COM(2004) 143 final.

[46] Proposal for a Regulation of the European Parliament and of the Council on compensation in cases of non-compliance with contractual quality requirements for rail freight services, COM(2004) 144 final.

[47] Proposal for a Directive of the European Parliament and of the Council on the certification of train crews operating locomotives and trains on the Community's rail network, COM(2004) 142 final.

[48] Reg 1/2003, Art 38.

[49] Reg 4056/86, OJ 1986 L378/4: Vol II, App E.5. EEA Agreement, Annex XIV, point 11, adopted Reg 4056/86, subject to various amendments for the purposes of the EEA Agreement.

[50] Reg 1419/2006, OJ 2006 L269/1. See Press Release IP/06/1249 (25 September 2006) and MEMO/06/344 (25 September 2006). EEA Agreement, Annex XIV, point 11d, adopted Reg 1419/2006, subject to various amendments for the purposes of the EEA Agreement.

on the North Atlantic-EU and EU-North Atlantic trades as of October 2008, but could still do so on the US-Pacific trades. The same applies to non-EU carriers.

This is a logical consequence of the fact that different competition regimes are in force world-wide. In fact, already today there are differences in what liner shipping companies are allowed to do in different jurisdictions. For example, today US law allows carriers to fix prices jointly on inland transport, while EU law does not.'[51]

The Commission plans to issue Guidelines on the application of the competition rules to maritime transport services, with particular reference to information exchanges among liner shipping carriers and so-called 'pool agreements' among tramp shipping operators.[51A]

Agreements outside Article 81(1). Article 2 of Regulation 4056/86 provided that the prohibition in Article 81(1) of the Treaty did not apply to agreements and decisions whose 'sole object and effect' was to achieve technical improvements or cooperation by specified means.[52] The specified means were the introduction or uniform application of standards or types for means of transport, equipment, supplies or fixed installations; the exchange or pooling for operational purposes of vessels, space, slots, staff, or fixed installations, organisation and execution of successive transport operations and the establishment of inclusive rates and conditions; coordination of timetables for connecting routes; and uniform rules concerning the structure and conditions governing the application of tariffs.[53] Article 2 did not create an exemption from the operation of Article 81(1) of the Treaty. It was essentially declaratory as to the scope of application of Article 81(1) and it was strictly construed,[54] particularly as some of the operations could easily spill over into anti-competitive conduct. The preamble to Regulation 1419/2006 states that the provisions excluding these agreements from the prohibition of Article 81(1) were 'redundant' and should also be deleted.[55] Article 9 of Regulation 4056/86, which provided for the resolution of conflicts between the provisions of the Regulation and the law of third countries, was also described in the preamble as redundant.

12.020

---

[51] MEMO/06/344, above. The Commission also indicated that it will take 'all appropriate initiatives' to advance the removal of price fixing liner conferences elsewhere in the world.

[51A] See draft Guidelines, OJ 2007 C215/3.

[52] The basis for the non-applicability is that such agreements 'do not, as a general rule, restrict competition': Recital (7), Reg 4056/86.

[53] cf the list of exempted categories of agreements relating to inland transport (Art 3 of Reg 1017/68), para 12.011, above.

[54] *FETTCSA*, OJ 2000 L268/1, [2000] 5 CMLR 1011, sect 11 (agreement not to offer discounts to independent lines cannot come within Art 2), upheld on this point by the CFI, Case T-213/00 *CMA CGM v Commission* [2003] ECR II-913, [2003] 5 CMLR 268, para 100 (appeal on other grounds dismissed, Case C-236/03P *Commission v CMA CGM* [2005] 4 CMLR 557). See also the observations of the CFI on the equivalent provision in Reg 1017/68 in *Deutsche Bahn v Commission* (n 20, above). In the context of consortia, the Commission has indicated that 'there are few, if any, agreements whose sole object or effect is merely to achieve technical (ie non-commercial) improvements or co-operation': *XIXth Report on Competition Policy* (1989), point 26.

[55] Reg 1419/2006, OJ 2006 L269/1, preamble para 9.

(ii) Block exemption for liner conferences

12.021 Generally. A substantial part of Regulation 4056/86 was devoted to setting out the conditions for block exemption of liner conference agreements. This was necessitated by the notification of, or accession to, the UN Convention on a Code of Conduct for Liner Conferences by a number of Member States[56] and the subsequent need to ensure that liner conferences compatible with the Code did not infringe the Community competition rules.[57] The substance of the block exemption was in consequence strongly influenced by the Code itself.[58] The rationale for exempting what was in effect a price-fixing, market-sharing and revenue-pooling cartel was the belief that a conference brought stability to the trades which it affected because the fixing of a uniform tariff serves as a reference point for the market. Competition was not eliminated altogether because non-conference services, tramp vessels, other modes of transport and the mobility of fleets combined to provide effective competition.[59] In a series of cases concerning agreements among shipping companies, the Commission and the Community Courts emphasised the narrow boundaries of the block exemption[60] and condemned a number of price-fixing and market-sharing arrangements which were held not to fall within the block exemption. Those cases are discussed in Chapter 5, above.[61]

12.022 Transitional period of application. The Commission carried out an extensive review to determine whether liner conferences still fulfilled the four cumulative

---

[56] See Recital (3) of Reg 4056/86. See generally, Ortiz Blanco, *Shipping Conferences under EC Antitrust Law - Criticism of a Legal Paradox* (2007). The Commission has been asked by the European Parliament to review whether the ending of the block exemption means that Council Reg 954/79 concerning the conditions under which Member States may accede to the UN Convention needs to be repealed: see MEMO/06/344 (25 September 2006).

[57] See the last Recital of Reg 954/79, OJ 1979 L121/1, which called on the Commission to make proposals to ensure compatibility.

[58] Recital (3) of Reg 4056/86 states that 'as far as conferences subject to the Code of Conduct are concerned, the Regulation should supplement the Code or make it more precise'.

[59] See 8th Recital of Reg 4056/86. But where the conference members seek to extend the allocation of cargoes to the entire trade, such that competition from non-conference members becomes almost impossible, the conditions of Art 81(3) will not be met; see *French-West African Shipowners' Committee* (n 72, below).

[60] eg Reg 4056/86 does not apply to the inland leg of multimodal transport of sea containers, therefore an exemption had to be sought under Reg 1017/68 for an agreement or part of an agreement concerning the inland portion of the journey (and now that aspect needs to satisfy the criteria of Art 81(3) pursuant to Reg 1/2003): Case T-86/95 *Compagnie Générale Maritime v Commission* [2002] ECR II-1011, [2002] 4 CMLR 1115, upholding on this point *Far Eastern Freight Conference (FEFC)*, OJ 1994 L378/17. See also *Trans-Atlantic Agreement (TAA)*, OJ 1994 L376/1 (appeal dismissed on other grounds Case T-395/94 *Atlantic Container Line AB v Commission* [2002] ECR II-875, [2002] 4 CMLR 1008, [2002] All ER (EC) 684); *Transatlantic Conference Agreement (TACA)*, OJ 1999 L95/1, [1999] 4 CMLR 1415, concerning the agreement that replaced the TAA (appeal as to Art 81 largely dismissed but decn on Art 82 annulled, Cases T-191/98, etc, *Atlantic Container Line v Commission* [2003] ECR II-3275, [2005] 4 CMLR 1283). And note *Vessel Sharing Agreements*, OJ 1997 C185/4 (exemption sought under both Reg 1017/68 and Reg 4056/86).

[61] See paras 5.033–5.034, above.

conditions of Article 81(3). A White Paper was published in October 2004[62] and the Commission adopted a legislative proposal in December 2005.[63] Regulation 1419/2006 repeals Regulation 4056/86 subject to a transitional period. Article 1 of the Regulation provides that certain provisions of the block exemption continue to apply in respect of liner shipping conferences satisfying the requirements of Regulation 4056/86 until 18 October 2008.[64] The following discussion of the scope of the block exemption therefore remains relevant for liner shipping conferences before that date.[65] The Commission plans to issue appropriate guidelines on competition in the maritime sector by the end of 2007.[66]

Scope of the block exemption.   The block exemption falls into two parts.   **12.023** Article 3 of Regulation 4056/86 covers agreements, decisions and concerted practices between some or all of the members of one or more liner conferences, while Article 6 covers certain agreements between transport users and liner conferences or between transport users *inter se*. Liner conferences are defined[67] in Article 1(3)(b) as:

> '. . . a group of two or more vessel-operating carriers which provides international liner services for the carriage of cargo on a particular route or routes within specified geographical limits and which has an agreement or arrangement, whatever its nature, within the framework of which they operate under uniform or common freight rates and any other agreed conditions with respect to the provision of liner services.'

This definition makes it plain that only cargo, not passenger, carriage services are covered. As an exempting regulation, the provisions in Regulation 4056/86 that provide derogation from Article 81 are to be strictly interpreted.[68] So-called 'outsider

---

[62] See Press Release IP/04/1213 (13 October 2004).

[63] See Press Release IP/05/1586 (14 December 2005) and MEMO/04/480 (14 December 2005).

[64] These are Art 1(3)(b) and (c) which define certain terms, Arts 3–7 which contain the block exemption, Art 8(2) which empowers the Commission to withdraw the benefit of the block exemption from an individual agreement and Art 26 which empowers the Commission to adopt implementing measures.

[65] Further, although Reg 1419/2006 was incorporated into Annex XIV of the EEA Agreement by Decn 153/2006 of the EEA Joint Committee, OJ 2007 L89/25, one of the EFTA Member States has raised constitutional objections and at the time of writing it has therefore not entered into force as regards the EEA regime.

[66] See *Report on Competition Policy* (2005), point 2.1.1. See also Faull & Nikpay (n 13, above) paras 14.92 *et seq*; Power, *EC Shipping Law* (1998).

[67] The same definition as that contained in the UN Convention on a Code of Conduct for Liner Conference by a number of Member States, para 12.021, above.

[68] Cases T-24/93, etc, *Compagnie Maritime Belge Transports v Commission* [1996] ECR II-1201, [1997] 4 CMLR 273, para 48; further appeal dismissed on other grounds, Cases C-395 & 396/96P, etc, *Compagnie Maritime Belge Transports v Commission* [2000] ECR I-1365, [2000] 4 CMLR 1076, [2000] All ER (EC) 385. The ECJ, however, annulled the fines imposed on individual members of the conference on the grounds that the Commission had not made it clear in the statement of objections that it intended to impose fines on the shipping lines rather than just on the association. The Commission subsequently adopted a further decision reimposing the fines: *Compagnie Maritime Belge*, OJ 2005 L 171/28, on appeal Case T-276/04, not yet decided.

agreements', between liner conferences and one or several carriers that operate independently of the liner conference, are not within the terms of the block exemption. Multi-modal transport price-fixing is also outside the scope of the block exemption.[69] Consortia agreements, which the Commission considered fell outside the terms of Regulation 4056/86 because they pursue different objectives and are different in organisation, were made the subject of a separate block exemption.[70] The Commission has been reluctant to accept that the criteria in Article 81(3) apply to agreements not falling within Article 3. Particular examples of this reluctance can be seen in relation to multilateral cooperation agreements; discussion agreements; inland transport agreements; and capacity management programmes.[71]

12.024 **Block-exempted agreements between liner conference members.** Article 3 exempts, subject to certain conditions and obligations, agreements between liner conference members:

> 'when they have as their objective the fixing of rates[72] and conditions of carriage, and, as the case may be, one or more of the following objectives:
>
> (a) the co-ordination of shipping timetables, sailing dates or dates of calls;
> (b) the determination of the frequency of sailings or calls;

---

[69] This involves inland transport whereas Reg 4056/86 only covers 'international maritime transport services': Art 1(2). See *Far Eastern Freight Conference* (n 60, above), also *XIXth Report on Competition Policy* (1989), point 27.

[70] See paras 12.029 *et seq*, below.

[71] *Eurocorde Agreements*, OJ 1990 C162/13, [1990] 4 CMLR 803; *XXth Report on Competition Policy* (1990), point 79; which was replaced by the *Trans-Atlantic Agreement* (*TAA*), which covered also the inland leg of multi-modal transport and incorporated a capacity management programme (where carriers undertake not to use a proportion of space on their vessels for carriage of goods of a particular trade, by reference to the anticipated excess of supply over demand). The TAA was also notified and the subject of an adverse decision refusing exemption (n 60, above). Thereafter, the Revised TACA agreement was concluded and notified under Reg 4056/86, Reg 1017/68 and Reg 17. This agreement instead of setting an inland tariff included a not-below-cost clause, ie each shipping line could not price for the inland leg of multi-modal carriage below its own costs. That clause received exemption under Reg 1017/68 when the Commission decided not to raise serious doubts about it (see Art 12(2) Notice, OJ 1999 C125/6, [1999] 5 CMLR 197). The period of exemption expired without the clause having been implemented: see *Revised Trans-Atlantic Conference Agreement*, OJ 2003 L26/53, [2003] 4 CMLR 1001. Given that the exemption had expired, the CFI concluded in Case T-224/99 (Order at [2003] ECR II-2097) that there was no need to adjudicate on the action. A capacity management programme also received unfavourable consideration by the Commission in *Europe Asia Trades Agreement (EATA)*, OJ 1999 L193/23, [1999] 5 CMLR 1380. Discussion agreements were notified under Art 12 of Reg 4056/86 (now repealed) in respect of *Agreement 1237*, OJ 1990 C59/2, *Gulfway Agreement*, OJ 1990 C130/3, and see Ortiz Blanco and Van Houtte (n 20, above), 146. The Commission intervened under the opposition procedure and expressed serious doubts about the prospects for exemption.

[72] See *French-West African Shipowners' Committees*, OJ 1992 L134/1, [1993] 5 CMLR 446, and the cases referred to in para 5.034, above, holding that the block exemption does not apply to (i) allocation agreements between different liners conferences by which they refrain from operating as outsiders in each other's sphere of activity; (ii) an agreement that establishes at least two rate levels for the same service or provides for the non-utilisation of capacity; or (iii) an agreement relating to commission payable to freight forwarders or the designation of cargo brokers. For service contracts, see para 12.028, below.

(c) the co-ordination or allocation of sailings or calls among members of the conference;

(d) the regulation of the carrying capacity offered by each member;[73]

(e) the allocation of cargo or revenue among members.'

Conditions for exemption. The exemption is expressly subject to the condition in Article 4 that the agreement does not, within the common market, cause detriment to certain ports, transport users[74] or carriers by applying rates and conditions of carriage which differ according to the country of origin or destination or the port of loading or discharge to the carriage of the same goods in the area covered by the agreement, unless the differential can be economically justified. It would appear that, to breach this condition, not only must the agreement apply rates which are discriminatory on grounds of the origin or destination of the goods carried, but the discrimination must cause actual detriment[75] to ports, transport users or carriers in the Community. Breach of the condition will result in automatic invalidity of the agreement. Because the main counterweight to the exemption for liner conferences is the non-conference competition from outsider companies, the Commission takes a strict view of notice clauses in a conference agreement on the basis that a conference member must be enabled to become an outsider offering a competing service within a reasonable period. The Commission has stated that a member must be able to give notice at any time and that the maximum period of notice required for leaving a liner conference without penalty should not as a rule exceed six months, and in some cases might have to be shorter.[76] **12.025**

Obligations. Article 5 sets out a number of wide-ranging obligations attached to the exemption, the breach of which does not cause automatic invalidity but allows the Commission to take remedial steps.[77] The obligations are: **12.026**

(a) to hold consultations between transport users and conferences (at the request of either) on general issues of principle concerning rates, conditions and quality of scheduled services;

---

[73] The Commission considers that this allows only temporary or short-term adjustments, eg to meet seasonal demand fluctuations; it does not exempt wider capacity management programmes: *Trans-Atlantic Agreement* (n 60, above) paras 365–366.

[74] Art 1(3)(c) defines a transport user as (a) any association of shippers or (b) an undertaking which has, or shows it intends to have, contractual or other arrangements for the shipment of goods with a conference or shipping line.

[75] Recital (10) of Reg 4056/86 envisages the 'detriment' as being harmful 'deflections of trade' resulting from the discriminatory conditions.

[76] See *East African Conference*, where the Commission terminated proceedings after the notice period was reduced from 12 to 6 months: *XXIIIrd Report on Competition Policy* (1993), points 230–231.

[77] Under Art 38 of Reg 1/2003 the Commission has the power to take a decision against conferences which are in breach of an obligation that either prohibits conferences from carrying out, or requires Conferences to perform, certain specific acts, or that withdraws the benefit of the block exemption.

(b) in the event that the conference has a system of loyalty rebates, to abide by a number of conditions as to the rights of users to withdraw and the provision of information to users on their rights;[78]

(c) to allow transport users to choose which inland transport or quayside services they wish to use, provided that these services are not covered by the freight charge or charges agreed with the user;[79]

(d) to make available on request details (including a breakdown of the elements of the freight charge) of tariffs, related conditions, regulations and amendments to transport users;

(e) to notify the Commission forthwith of arbitral awards or accepted recommendations resolving disputes relating to discrimination under Article 4, loyalty arrangements and tying of services not covered by freight charges.

12.027 **Agreements between conferences and transports users and between users.** Article 6 of Regulation 4056/86 exempts agreements, decisions and concerted practices (a) between transport users and liner conferences and (b) between transport users *inter se* which are necessary for the former agreements, concerning the rates, conditions and quality of liners services, 'as long as they are provided for in Article 5(1) and (2)'. The exemption appears to be limited, therefore, to:

(a) consultations between conferences and transport users which comply with the conditions of Article 5(1);

(b) loyalty arrangements between conferences and transport users which comply with the conditions of Article 5(2);

(c) agreements between transport users only to the extent necessary for them to take part in the first two exempted categories.

The exemption is also subject to observance of the condition in Article 4.

12.028 **Service contracts.** A 'conference service contract' is an agreement concluded between the shipper and the liner conference whereby the shipper agrees to commit to provide a minimum cargo to the conference at rates fixed by the conference. In an 'individual service contract' the agreement on cargo and rates is between the shipper and an individual shipping company. In the *TACA* case,[80] one of the

---

[78] In *Compagnie Maritime Belge* (n 68, above), the CFI upheld the Commission's decision that a loyalty rebate scheme which imposed excessive conditions and was enforced by blacklists went beyond the exemption in Art 5(2) and constituted an abuse of a dominant position; the ECJ did not address the interpretation of Art 5(2) but upheld the finding of abuse.

[79] The implication of this obligation is that where the freight charge or agreed charge does cover inland transport and quayside services, the conference can 'tie' these additional services. However, such obligations may well be incompatible with Art 82 EC where a conference holds a dominant position. The freedom to choose between carrier haulage and merchant haulage is an important issue for shippers.

[80] See Cases T-191/98, etc, *Atlantic Container Line v Commission* [2003] ECR II-3275, [2005] 4 CMLR 1283, paras 507 *et seq*. The CFI also upheld the Commission's finding that the conference

issues was whether the mere fact that a liner conference jointly enters into a service contract was of itself a restriction of competition which fell within Article 81(1) and needed therefore to benefit from the block exemption in Regulation 4056/86 or from the individual application of Article 81(3). The Court of First Instance interpreted the Commission's decision as having condemned the conference service contract only because it was accompanied for a period of two years by a rule prohibiting the conference members from concluding individual service contracts. The Court did not therefore have to consider whether the existence of a conference service contract would have fallen within Article 81(1) had the conference members been free to enter into individual service contracts. The Court upheld the Commission's decision that the ban on members entering into individual service contracts and the later imposition of rules as to the content of such contracts after the ban was lifted fell within Article 81(1) and did not benefit either from block exemption or the individual application of Article 81(3).[81]

(iii) Block exemption for consortia

Generally.   Liner consortia involve the carrying out of activities in common by independent shipping lines in order to rationalise operations or costs. They are therefore distinguishable from liner conferences which, *inter alia*, pursue the objective of coordinating tariffs. In 1992, the Council adopted Regulation 479/92[82] as an enabling regulation that allowed the Commission to issue a block exemption for consortia agreements. This Regulation was framed in broad terms, recognising the immensely wide variety of consortia agreements and the fact that the parties and terms change frequently. In April 1995, pursuant to Regulation 479/92, the Commission finally issued a block exemption for consortia agreements.[83] This was replaced on its expiry in April 2000 by a new block exemption incorporating minor changes. This block exemption is not affected by the repeal of Regulation 4056/86.

12.029

Regulation 823/2000.   The current block exemption for consortia agreements, Regulation 823/2000,[84] came into force on 26 April 2000. Due to expire after five years, the application of the Regulation has been extended for a further

12.030

---

agreement on rates of commission payable to freight forwarders was a restriction on competition which did not fall within Art 3 of Reg 4056/86 or Art 81(3) of the Treaty: paras 560 *et seq*.

81 ibid, paras 534 *et seq*.
82 Reg 479/92, OJ 1992 L55/3: Vol II, App E.6.
83 Reg 870/95, OJ 1989 L89/7.
84 Reg 823/2000, OJ 2000 L100/24: Vol II, App E.7. Annex XIV, point 11c, to the EEA Agreement adopts Reg 823/2000 subject to amendments for the purposes of application to the EEA. For discussion of the preceding block exemption, see generally Clough, 'The Devil and the Deep Blue Sea' (1995) 7 ECLR 417. Reg 823/2000 is described in detail in (2000) 3 EC Competition Policy Newsletter 44.

five years to 25 April 2010.[85] Regulation 823/2000 was amended in 2004 and 2005[86] and has to be read in conjunction with the block exemption for liner conferences. The Regulation applies to consortia agreements defined as:

> '[A]n agreement between two or more vessel-operating carriers which provide international liner shipping services exclusively for the carriage of cargo, chiefly by container, relating to one or more trades, and the object of which is to bring about cooperation in the joint operation of a maritime transport service, and which improves the service that would be offered individually by each of its members in the absence of the consortium, in order to rationalize their operations by means of technical, operation and/or commercial arrangements, with the exception of price fixing.'[87]

Like the liner conference block exemption, the Regulation therefore does not currently apply to domestic maritime transport, tramp vessel services or passenger services. The exemption applies to consortia which have as their object the rationalisation of the members' operations through technical, operational or commercial arrangements. Article 3 sets out the activities provided for in consortia agreements which are exempt.

12.031 **Conditions for block exemption.**   The definition of 'consortium' in Regulation 823/2000 excludes an arrangement where one of the means of rationalisation is price-fixing.[88] The Regulation further provides that the exemption will not apply to arrangements concerning the non-utilisation of a certain percentage of the capacity of consortium members used within the framework of the consortium.[89] Further, for the exemption to apply, one or more of the following three conditions must be met: (i) there must be effective price competition between the members of the conference within which the consortium operates; or (ii) there must exist within that conference a sufficient degree of effective competition in terms of the services provided; or (iii) the consortium members must be subject to effective competition, actual or potential, from shipping lines outside the consortium.[90] The exemption is subject to an important market share condition: the consortium must possess on each market on which it operates a share of under 30 per cent (by volume) when it operates within a conference and 35 per cent otherwise.[91] The procedure whereby the exemption could be automatically extended to agreements notified to the Commission where a consortium exceeded those thresholds but did not exceed 50 per cent has been repealed.[92] The Regulation imposes other

---

[85] Art 4 of Reg 611/2005, OJ 2005 L101/10.
[86] Reg 463/2004, OJ 2004 L77/23 and Reg 611/2005, above.
[87] Reg 823/2000, Art 2(1).
[88] ibid, Art 2(1).
[89] ibid, Art 4 (as amended by Art 1 of Reg 611/2005).
[90] ibid, Art 5.
[91] ibid, Art 6.
[92] Art 1(1) of Reg 463/2004, repealing Art 7 of Reg 823/2000.

conditions and obligations[93] and any consortium claiming the benefit of the Regulation must be able to demonstrate, at the Commission's request, compliance with the conditions and certain obligations imposed.[94] Finally, Regulation 823/2000 sets out an exemption for agreements between transport users and consortia exempted under Article 3 insofar as they arise out of these required consultations.[95]

Recent amendments to the block exemption. Regulation 611/2005[96] introduced two minor amendments to Regulation 823/2000 as well as prolonging the life of the block exemption until 25 April 2010. The amendments allow a consortium member the right to withdraw from a consortium agreement without financial penalty after an initial period of up to 24 months, an extension of six months as compared with the previous regime. In addition, this initial period now also applies where the parties to an existing agreement have agreed to make substantial new investment in the maritime transport services offered by the consortium. Such investment must constitute at least half of the total investment made by the consortium members. Finally, one of the basic conditions for exemption, namely the existence of effective price competition within the consortium, has been amended: 'individual confidential contracts' may now also be taken into consideration to demonstrate the existence of such competition. **12.032**

Article 81(3). Consortia agreements that do not come within the terms of Regulation 823/2000 may nonetheless fulfill the criteria set out in Article 81(3) EC. Prior to the repeal of the notification system, the Commission was prepared to grant exemption to an agreement concerning regular ferry services that were not exclusively concerned with the carriage of cargo largely by container.[97] The Commission has required amendment of certain clauses in the agreement as a condition for exemption, or an undertaking that they will not be applied in the areas covered by the EC Treaty.[98] **12.033**

(iv) Abuse of a dominant position

Article 82: collective dominance of members of liner conference. The Commission has made extensive use of its powers under Article 82 in the context of the maritime shipping sector.[99] The Community Courts have consistently held **12.034**

---

93 Reg 823/2000 Arts 8–9 and Recital (22).
94 ibid, Art 9(5).
95 ibid, Art 10.
96 Reg 611/2005, OJ 2005 L101/10, see *Report on Competition Policy* (2005), points 9 *et seq*.
97 *Baltic Liner Conference Agreement*, OJ 1996 C44/2, [1996] 4 CMLR 589.
98 *Vessel Sharing Agreements* (n 60, above). On the application of Art 81(3) generally, see Chap 3, above.
99 See, eg *French West African Shipowners' Committees* (n 72, above) (request for African authorities to impose penalties on shipowners who breach the quota system was an abuse as was depriving

that the economic links between the members of the liner conference will usually justify a collective assessment of the market position of the members of that conference for the purposes of determining whether they hold a collective dominant position for the purposes of Article 82.[100] This is because the links which are inherent in them operating as a liner conference are such as to allow them to adopt together, as a single entity which presents itself as such on the market *vis-à-vis* users and competitors, the same line of conduct on that market. In the absence of evidence of significant internal competition within the conference, the conference is to be regarded as a single entity for the purpose of determining the market share of its members.[101] This does not mean that a liner conference is necessarily in a dominant position, that depends on an analysis of the competitive restraints imposed by shipping companies outside the conference.

12.035 **Article 82: acceptance of new members into the liner conference.** In *Atlantic Container (TACA)*,[102] the Court of First Instance overturned the Commission's finding that the liner conference had abused its collective dominant position by inducing new entrants to the market to join the conference rather than provide independent competition on the route. The Court emphasised that the finding of abuse was not simply that the conference had allowed new members to enter but that they had actively induced shipping companies to join.[103] The Court held that the Commission had not proved to the requisite standard that the liner conference had taken steps to induce the new members to join and left it unclear as to whether any inducement would be an abuse or only some form of improper inducement.

(d) Air transport

(i) Scope of application of the competition rules

12.036 **Legislative background.** It was not until 1987, following the Court of Justice's judgment in *Nouvelles Frontières*,[104] that the Council adopted its first package of

---

third parties of sufficient quotas to enable them to mount a viable service); *Compagnie Maritime Belge* (n 68, above) (enforcement of exclusivity with Zairian authorities, use of 'fighting ships' targeting lower rates at customers served by a competitor and loyalty rebates were abuses).

[100] See, eg Cases T-191/98, etc, *Atlantic Container Line v Commission (TACA)* [2003] ECR II-3275, [2005] 4 CMLR 1283, paras 594 *et seq.* CFI held (at para 695) that significant internal competition, if proven, could establish that in spite of the various links or factors of correlation existing between the members of a liner conference, they are not to be treated as a single entity. On the facts, however, the CFI found that internal price and non-price competition was not significant. The CFI went on to hold that the liner conference held a dominant position on the relevant market although some of the Commission's findings of abuse were annulled.

[101] ibid. The Commission is not required to prove that all competition among members of the conference has been eliminated: para 655.

[102] Cases T-191/98, etc, *Atlantic Container* (n 100, above).

[103] ibid, paras 1265 and 1272.

[104] Cases 209/84, etc, *Ministère Public v Asjes ('Nouvelles Frontières')* [1986] ECR 1425, [1986] 3 CMLR 173. Previously, the Commission invoked Art 85 EC in seeking to examine the transatlantic

measures regulating the air transport market.[105] This package laid down detailed rules for the application of Articles 81 and 82 to international air transport between Community airports[106] and empowered the Commission to adopt block exemption regulations for certain types of agreement in this sector.[107] Over the following years a number of block exemptions were adopted covering areas such as computer reservation systems and capacity allocation agreements. Further packages of liberalisation measures for the air transport sector were also adopted. The block exemptions have been allowed to expire and are therefore only of historical interest. The power to adopt block exemptions, however, has been retained and the Commission has consulted on proposals for adopting limited exemptions in this area. From a procedural standpoint, the bespoke regime for the enforcement of competition rules in the air transport sector has been repealed and agreements relating to air transport are covered by the generally applicable provisions of Regulation 1/2003.[108]

Extension to third countries: the '*Open Skies*' judgment.   A particular area of   **12.037** controversy has been the ability of the Commission to apply the principles developed in the context of the single European aviation market to air service agreements negotiated bilaterally between Member States and third countries, in particular the United States. Those bilateral agreements contained nationality clauses favouring domestic carriers. The effect of this was to deny access to those by carriers from other Member States and to act as a disincentive to restructuring in the industry since the nationality clause would prevent those routes passing to any foreign acquirer of a domestic carrier. Furthermore, such bilateral agreements also granted US operators access to intra-Community connections without offering EU operators the corresponding right to cabotage between American cities. In 2002, the Court of Justice ruled in its so-called '*Open Skies*'

'alliances' between European and US airlines. Such examination was required to be conducted 'in co-operation with the competent authorities in the Member States'. The Commission had no direct enforcement powers and was dependent upon the Member States to enforce any resulting decisions under Art 84 'in accordance with the law of their country'. In *Nouvelles Frontières*, the ECJ held that where the transitional provisions of Arts 84 and 85 applied, agreements, decisions and concerted practices would be prohibited under Art 81(1) and be automatically void under Art 81(2) only insofar as they have been held by the authorities of Member States, pursuant to Art 84, to fall under Art 81(1) and not to qualify for exemption under Art 81(3), or insofar as the Commission has recorded an infringement pursuant to Art 85(2).

[105] The first package is described in the *XVIIth Report on Competition Policy* (1987), points 43–46.

[106] Reg 3975/87, OJ 1987 L374/1: Vol II, App E.8.

[107] Reg 3976/87, OJ 1987 L374/9, since amended by Reg 411/2004, OJ 2004 L68/1: Vol II, App E.9.

[108] Art 39 of Reg 1/2003, repealing most of Reg 3975/87. Reg 1/2003 was amended to incorporate air transport between the Community and third countries by Art 3 of Reg 411/2004; see Vol II, App B.3 for the consolidated version.

judgment[109] that the Commission had exclusive competence to negotiate with third countries in those areas in which the Commission had been granted competence. This included the establishment of fares and rates on air services for intra-Community carriage and a Code of Conduct for computer reservations systems. Furthermore, the Court of Justice ruled that all Community carriers established in one Member State must be permitted to operate routes from another Member State to third countries on an equal basis to national carriers.

12.038 **Developments following the '*Open Skies*' judgment.** As a result of the Court's judgment, two Council decisions were adopted on 5 June 2003 granting the Commission a mandate to negotiate with the United States in the field of air transport and also with other third countries with regard to replacing nationality clauses in bilateral agreements with a Community agreement.[110] Regulation 847/2004[111] was adopted in April 2004 to create a legislative framework for individual negotiations between Member States and third countries. The Commission has published a Communication on developing the agenda for the Community's external aviation policy.[112]

12.039 **Exception for technical agreements.** Article 2 of Regulation 3975/87 declared that Article 81(1) does not apply to agreements, decisions or concerted practices insofar as their 'sole object and effect' is to achieve technical improvements or cooperation. A non-exhaustive list of the types of agreement falling within Article 2 was annexed to the Regulation. In view of the purely declaratory nature of Article 2 that provision has been repealed as unnecessary.[113] However, despite its repeal it probably remains a valid statement of the Commission's view that such agreements do not fall within Article 81(1) of the Treaty.

(ii) The sectoral rules applicable to the air transport sector

12.040 **Generally.**[114] The application of Article 81(1) and (3) to air transport agreements has been reflected partly in the series of block exemptions adopted under

---

[109] Cases C-466/98, etc, *Commission v United Kingdom, Denmark, Sweden, Finland, Belgium, Luxembourg, Austria and Germany* [2002] ECR I-9427, [2003] 1 CMLR 143. The action against the United Kingdom concerned the opening of the UK market to US carriers under the Bermuda II agreement. See similarly Case C-523/04 *Commission v Netherlands* [2007] 2 CMLR 1299, affirming the principle of pre-emption and in consequence the Community's exclusive competence.

[110] Press Release IP/03/806 (5 June 2003).

[111] Reg 847/2004, OJ 2004 L157/7. For the first cases considered in 2005 under this Reg see *Annual Report on Competition Policy* (2005), points 106 *et seq*.

[112] COM(2005) 79 Final. See also the Council's Conclusions: OJ 2005 C173/1.

[113] See Recital (5) and Art 1 of Reg 411/2004. With the repeal of Art 2, Reg 3975/87 is now entirely repealed save for a transitional provision, Art 6(3), which continues to apply to decisions adopted pursuant to Art 81(3) prior to the date of application of Reg 1/2003 until the date of expiry of those decisions.

[114] See generally Faull & Nikpay (eds), *The EC Law of Competition* (2nd ed, 2007), paras 14.12 *et seq*.

Council Regulation 3976/87 and partly in individual cases examined. As regards the former, policy has developed considerably since 1988 when the first block exemptions were adopted. Although all the block exemptions adopted in the sector have been allowed to expire they may offer some guidance as to the areas in which an individual agreement may satisfy the criteria set out in Article 81(3). In addition, the Commission is proposing to renew Regulation 1617/93. The competition concerns which arise from airlines coordinating their schedules and prices have to be balanced against the benefits for the consumer of 'interlining', that is where the customer can buy a single ticket covering a journey which involves flights on different airlines.

Scope of Regulation 3976/87. Regulation 3976/87[115] empowers the   **12.041**
Commission to adopt block exemption regulations in respect of joint planning and coordination of airline schedules; consultations on tariffs for the carriage of passengers and baggage and of freight on scheduled services; joint operations on new less busy scheduled air services; slot allocation at airports and airport scheduling; and common purchase, development and operation of computer reservation systems.[116] The Council in practice retains a considerable degree of control over legislation by limiting the time span for block exemptions that may be made under the Regulation.[117] All the block exemptions adopted have been subject to a large number of conditions, in part dictated by the terms of Regulation 3976/87[118] and in part reflecting the development of competition policy in the context of the liberalisation of the air transport sector. The Regulation has been amended to grant powers to the Commission to grant block exemptions to agreements in the air transport sector between the Community and third countries.[119]

Block exemptions. As originally adopted,[120] Regulation 1617/93 provided for   **12.042**
block exemption, subject to detailed conditions, for agreements with various purposes included the joint planning and coordination of the schedule of an air service between Community airports and slot allocation and airport scheduling between airports in the Community. Extensive consultations were carried out by the Commission prior to the final expiry of the Regulation at the end of June 2005. Following that exercise, the Commission concluded that a block exemption was no longer justified but that the airline industry needed a transitional period to adapt to the new situation and to assess for themselves whether their agreements and practices are compatible with Article 81.

---

115 Reg 3976/87, OJ 1987 L374/9: Vol II, App E.9.
116 The significant deletions from the list as a result of the third package of liberalisation measures are coordination of capacity, the sharing of revenue and common preparation of tariff proposals. Joint operations are a new addition.
117 Reg 3976/87, Art 3, now provides that any block exemptions must be for a specified period.
118 ibid, Art 2(2).
119 Art 2 of Reg 411/2004, OJ 2004 L68/1.
120 Reg 1617/93, OJ 1993 L155/18 and corr at OJ 1994 L15/20; notice at OJ 1993 C177/6.

12.043 **Regulation 1459/2006.** The Commission therefore adopted Regulation 1459/2006[121] granting a temporary exemption with retrospective effect to agreements which fulfilled the conditions set out in the Regulation. It applies to two different kinds of agreements: (i) the holding of consultations on slot allocation and airport scheduling insofar as they concern air services which start or finish at a point within the Community; and (ii) the holding of consultations on tariffs for carriage of passengers with their baggage on scheduled air services. In respect of both kinds of consultation, the Regulation gives the Commission and Member States the right to send observers to the consultations.[122]

12.044 **Slot allocation consultations exemption.** The conditions for the application of the block exemption to slot allocation agreements are set out in Article 2 of Regulation 1459/2006 and are as follows:

— the consultation must be open to all air carriers having expressed an interest in the slots;
— the rules of priority for the allocation of slots must not be discriminatory and must be made available on request to any interesting party;
— a specified proportion of new or unused slots are allocated to new entrants;[123]
— air carriers taking part in the consultations must have access to specified information about which carriers have which slots and what additional slots are available;
— if a request for a slot is not accepted, the air carrier must be given a statement of reasons for the rejection.

However, this exemption expired on 31 December 2006.[124]

12.045 **Passenger tariff consultation exemption.** There were three separate exemptions for passenger tariff consultations depending on whether the scheduled air services were between a point within the Community and (i) another point within the Community or in an EFTA state,[125] or (ii) a point in Australia or the United States, or (iii) a point in another third country. For consultations concerning routes in the first category, the exemption applied only until 31 December 2006; for those in the second category, it applied until 30 June 2007; and for those in the third category, it applied until 31 October 2007.[126] For all three categories, however, the

---

[121] Reg 1459/2006, OJ 2006 L272/3: Vol II, App E.12. The Reg came into force on 23 October 2006 but applies with retroactive effect: see Art 4.

[122] ibid, Arts 2(2) and 3(3).

[123] 'New entrants' are as defined in Art 2(b) of Reg 95/93 on common rules for the allocation of slots at Community airports, OJ 1993, L14/1, last amended by Reg 793/2004, OJ 2004 L138/50.

[124] Reg 1459/2006, Art 4.

[125] Recitals (20) and (21) explain that EFTA countries are treated in the same way as Member States in anticipation of the block exemption being adopted under the EEA Agreement and by virtue of bilateral arrangements with Switzerland.

[126] The Commission announced that the block exemption would not be renewed since there was little evidence that the IATA passenger tariff conferences which the exemption was designed to cover benefit consumers: Press release IP/07/973 (29 June 2007).

conditions for the application of the exemption were as set out in Article 3 of the Regulation, namely:

— the consultations must be limited to air fares and not extend to capacity on the route or agents' remuneration;

— the consultations must enable interlining, that is, to combine the service provided by one carrier with the same or a connecting service offered by another carrier, and to change a reservation from one carrier to another so far as permitted by the conditions governing the ticket;

— passenger tariffs must not discriminate between passengers on the grounds of nationality or place of residence;

— participation in the consultations must be voluntary and open to all carriers interested in operating on the route and carriers must retain the right to act independently in respect of passenger tariffs.

(iii) Particular issues

Tariff fixing. In *Ahmed Saeed*,[127] the Court of Justice acknowledged the potential difficulty in distinguishing between a price-fixing agreement and mere consultations on tariffs.[128] The former would be unlikely to benefit from exemption (except perhaps as part of a wider arrangement with certain economic benefits), whereas the latter might qualify for block exemption or the individual application of Article 81(3), provided that any consultations on fares gave rise to interlining and did not lead to price-fixing.[129] The new block exemption for passenger tariffs has been discussed above. Beyond that, agreements which involve price coordination are generally part of wider airline alliances or code-sharing agreements and will need to fulfil the criteria set out in Article 81(3). The Commission may require alliance members to enter into interlining agreements with new entrants to facilitate their entry and counteract any adverse effects on competition of the alliance.[130] The question of interlining also arises under Article 82 when interlining is refused.[131]

12.046

---

[127] Case 66/86 *Ahmed Saeed Flugreisen v Zentrale zur Bekämpfung unlauteren Wettbewerbs* [1989] ECR 803, [1990] 4 CMLR 102.

[128] For the application of Art 81 to information exchange agreements generally see paras 5.084 *et seq*, above.

[129] Reg 1617/93, Recital (5) and Art 4. That exemption was subsequently curtailed to exclude from its scope consultations on cargo tariffs, partly on the basis that these were not necessary for interlining and led to higher cargo rates: Reg 1523/96, OJ 1996 L190/11. See *XXVIth Report on Competition Policy* (1996), points 92–93.

[130] See *Lufthansa/Austrian Airlines*, OJ 2002 L242/25 [2003] 4 CMLR 252; M.3280 *Air France/KLM* (11 February 2002).

[131] See *British Midland v Aer Lingus*, OJ 1992 L96/34, [1993] 4 CMLR 596; *Lufthansa/Air Europe*, *XXth Report on Competition Policy* (1990), point 107. Note that in its *XXth Report*, point 75, the Commission stated that there is no general obligation on a dominant airline to grant interline facilities. Interline facilities need only be granted for the period necessary for the relevant airline to establish itself on the route in question, normally two years. The obligation may, however, extend to

12.047 **Airline alliances.** The Commission has adopted a number of decisions relating to cooperation agreements between airlines. Competition issues may arise from such alliances if the airlines are particularly strong on certain routes and/or where they hold a large number of slots on capacity constrained airports (such as London Heathrow). The Commission's approval[132] has usually been subject to requirements aimed at facilitating new entry into the routes affected, in particular by the surrender of a significant number of slots at the relevant airports.[133] These cases are discussed in more detail in Chapter 7, above.[134]

12.048 **Computer reservation systems.** A computerised reservation system ('CRS') is an electronic distribution platform that enables travel agents through their terminal to obtain up-to-date information on schedules, fares and availability, generally with the facility to book tickets and, sometimes, also to issue tickets directly. Although a CRS brings obvious benefits, the ownership of the major CRSs by groups of airlines also carries anti-competitive potential as most carriers need to participate in a CRS in order to compete effectively.[135] The fear has been that parent airlines may obtain more rapid access to commercially valuable information regarding discounting and capacity utilisation by their competitors, and the operation of a CRS, for example as regards display of information, may discriminate against the non-parent airlines.[136] Also, refusal by parent airlines of one CRS to

---

connecting routes and other types of fare where these are necessary for the new entrant to become established.

[132] Before 1 May 2004 (when Reg 1/2003 as amended by Reg 411/2004 came into effect), agreements relating to air transport services between Community airports could be notified under Art 5 of Reg 3975/87. Unless the Commission raised 'serious doubts' about the arrangement within 90 days of publication of the details in the Official Journal, the arrangement was treated as exempt for six years.

[133] See, eg COMP/38.284 *Air France/Alitalia*, 7 April 2004, [2005] 5 CMLR 1504; on appeal: Case T-300/04 *easyJet v Commission*, not yet decided.

[134] See paras 7.133 *et seq*, above.

[135] See, eg *London European/Sabena: refusal to grant access to a CRS*, OJ 1988 L317/47 (abuse of dominant position); *Electronic ticketing*, OJ 1999 L244/56, at rec 33. The exceptions are the low budget airlines, which do not sell through travel agents but direct to the public. See also *Global Logistics System*, OJ 1993 C76/5, [1993] 4 CMLR 632: JV between Lufthansa, Air France, Cathay Pacific and Japan Airlines to establish and market computerised cargo information logistics systems; the Commission issued an Art 19(3) Notice indicating its intention to take a favourable view on condition that the parties gave undertakings to respect the principles contained in the then block exemption for air transport CRSs, in particular as regards non-discriminatory access and freedom to participate in other systems. And note *Acriss*, OJ 1993 C149/9 (Art 19(3) Notice for code of conduct for CRS for the car rental industry).

[136] *Amadeus/Sabre, XXIst Report on Competition Policy* (1991), points 93–95. The ownership link between airlines and CRSs appears to be weakening. Galileo, Sabre and Worldspan are no longer airline-owned and Amadeus is now partly publicly owned. See The Brattle Group and Norton Rose, 'Study to Assess the Potential Impact of Proposed Amendments to Council Regulation 2299/89 with Regard to Computerised Reservation Systems', prepared for DG for Energy and Transport, October 2003, p 8.

participate in another may create a significant barrier to entry by a competing CRS. Travel agents will generally choose to subscribe to the CRS that carries the 'host' airline of their State.

CRS code of conduct.   Operation of computer reservation systems is now **12.049** regulated by the need to fulfill the criteria in Article 81(3) and by Council Regulation 2299/89 which contains the Code of Conduct for CRSs.[137] The Code, which is expressly stated to be without prejudice to the application of Articles 81 and 82,[138] targets the behaviour of parent carriers, system vendors and subscribers. It imposes mandatory requirements as regards, *inter alia*, conditions for access, non-discrimination in handling of data, and supply by parent carriers of information to competing CRSs. Infringement of the Code is sanctioned by a liability to fines of up to 10 per cent of annual turnover for the relevant activity of the undertaking concerned.[139] The first fine for infringing the CRS Code of Conduct was imposed on Lufthansa for linking incentives to travel agents with the issue of electronic tickets, thereby discriminating against Sabre since such ticketing was available only through use of Amadeus.[140]

Groundhandling services.   In 1996 the Council adopted Directive 96/67 on **12.050** access to the groundhandling market at Community airports.[141] Groundhandling services are defined as including all technical and operational services generally provided on the ground at airports (such as loading and unloading, refuelling, aircraft maintenance and servicing, passenger, mail and freight handling, and services for in-flight catering).[142] Denial of access to companies seeking to provide a competing service and refusal to permit self-handling by airlines may, in an appropriate case, amount to an abuse of a dominant position under Article 82.[143]

---

[137] Reg 2299/99 on a Code of Conduct for computer reservation systems, OJ 1989 L220/1, as amended by Reg 3089/93, OJ 1993 L278/1, corr OJ 1995 L17/18, and by Reg 323/1999, OJ 1999 L40/1: Vol II, App E.10. The Code is accompanied by an Explanatory Note, OJ 1990 C184/2: Vol II, App E.11.

[138] Recital (8).

[139] Art 16(2) of the Code.

[140] *Electronic ticketing*, OJ 1999 L244/56: fine of €10,000 for what was described as a 'relatively minor' infringement.

[141] Dir 96/97, OJ 1996 L272/36. See Goh, 'Reforming Airport Services in Europe' (1998) 9 (2) Utilities Law Rev. 44. The Dir has been implemented in the UK by the Airports (Groundhandling) Regs, SI 1997/2389, amended by SI 1998/2918. There was previously a block exemption for agreements for the supply of groundhandling services but this lapsed on 31 December 1992: Reg 82/91, OJ 1991 L10/7, [1991] 4 CMLR 715 (effectively continuing the terms of Reg 2673/88).

[142] Dir 96/97, above, Art 2(e) and the list in the Annex.

[143] See *FAG — Flughafen Frankfurt/Main*, OJ 1998 L72/30, [1998] 4 CMLR 779 (general ramp-handling services); Case T-128/98 *Aéroports de Paris v Commission* [2000] ECR II-3929, [2001] 4 CMLR 1376, appeal dismissed Case C-82/01P [2002] ECR I-9297, [2003] 4 CMLR 609 (in-flight catering services). The decision finding an infringement of Art 82 by Frankfurt airport was significantly adopted on the same day as a decision under Art 9 of Dir 96/67 approving

12.051 IATA agreements.   To date, the Commission has only adopted two formal decisions in relation to IATA resolutions.[144] These concern IATA resolutions establishing its passenger agency programme[145] and its cargo agency programme.[146] With certain important modifications the Commission was prepared to exempt both programmes for 10 years from the original notifications, without conditions but subject to close monitoring. Since June 2003, the passenger agency programme has been reviewed further pursuant to a complaint involving market partitioning, leading to the removal of geographic restrictions on the use of satellite ticket printers in Europe, and the creation of a new accreditation category that eases the process for travel agents that operate in several Member States, while providing certain required financial safeguards.[147] IATA notified its system of cargo tariff resolutions for individual exemption, following the amendment of Regulation 1617/93 that removed them from the scope of the block exemption. Although IATA argued that its tariff conferences facilitated interlining, when the Commission made clear its provisional objections that the system was not indispensable for this purpose, IATA agreed to end the joint setting of cargo rates within the EEA.[148]

3. Energy

(a) Introduction

12.052 The ECSC, Euratom and EC Treaties.   The ECSC Treaty was, and the Euratom Treaty is, concerned primarily with energy and the establishment of integrated

---

an exemption to limit the number of suppliers (*Frankfurt Airport*, OJ 1998 L173/32) and the Commission viewed the two together as ending the groundhandling monopoly at the airport: Press Release IP/98/27 (14 January 1998), [1998] 4 CMLR 398.

[144] It has, however, intervened at IATA Europe Conferences and secured amendments to existing resolutions with a view to ensuring compliance with Art 81(3). See Notice concerning the application of Art 4(1)(a) of Reg 2671/88, OJ 1989 C119/6 (application of the old block exemption on tariff consultations to consultation on inclusive tour and group inclusive tour fares). IATA rules that prevent passengers from purchasing tickets outside the country of travel origin have been modified as a result of the Commission's intervention so that they no longer apply to travel within the EC and Norway: *XXIIIrd Report on Competition Policy* (1993), point 237. See also *IATA—Cargo Surcharge*, ibid, point 238, where IATA withdrew resolutions providing for the imposition of a worldwide freight surcharge that the Commission found could not benefit from the then block exemption, Reg 1617/93, or receive individual exemption since its main purpose was to raise revenue and not to facilitate interlining.

[145] *IATA Passenger Agency Programme*, OJ 1991 L258/18, [1992] 5 CMLR 496.

[146] *IATA Cargo Agency Programme*, OJ 1991 L258/29, [1992] 5 CMLR 496.

[147] See IATA's News Brief, 9 March 2006.

[148] Press Release IP/01/1433 (19 October 2001). The Commission subsequently investigated a IATA resolution about low-density cargoes, following a complaint: *XXXIIIrd Report on Competition Policy* (2003), point 34; the case was closed in 2005 when IATA decided to cancel that resolution.

markets in coal and atomic energy.[149] The EC Treaty by contrast contains no specific provisions about these or other forms of energy. The amendments made by the Treaty on European Union, however, introduced 'measures in the sphere . . . of energy' as one of the activities of the Community listed under Article 3.[150] Title XV of the EC Treaty, introduced by the Maastricht amendments, sets out provisions aimed at the promotion of trans-European networks in the field of transport, telecommunications and energy infrastructures.[151] Article 305 states that the provisions 'shall not derogate from' those of the Euratom Treaty, but the overlapping jurisdictions of the two Treaties are not specifically addressed.

Special characteristics of energy markets.   The energy sector as a whole presents   **12.053** various problems from a competition perspective: the infrastructure required for the transmission of electricity and gas is effectively a natural monopoly and the need for security of supply tended to reinforce the justification for government regulation, subsidies and the grant of exclusive rights. These in turn have tended to isolate national markets. Significant differences exist between Member States in the scale and availability of resources and the organisation of domestic industry. The different uses of energy (raw material, fuel, power), and the substitutability of sources in some areas but not others, have compounded the problem. In addition, although products are to a certain extent interchangeable, each energy sector presents distinct problems as a consequence of differences in production, distribution/transmission and treatment of imports/exports.

Sector inquiry.   On 10 January 2007, the Commission published the final   **12.054** report of its inquiry under Article 17 of Regulation 1/2003 into the functioning of the European gas and electricity markets.[152] The report concluded that many energy markets, in particular for gas but also in some cases for electricity, are too highly concentrated, with incumbents remaining in control and limited new entry; that many markets are characterised by a high degree of vertical integration, with insufficient unbundling of network and supply activities, and also long-term

---

[149] The ECSC Treaty expired on 23 July 2002; the EC Treaty therefore in principle applies fully to the coal and steel sectors. Given that the ECSC Treaty has expired, it will not be the subject of further comment in this work. For a summary of the application of the competition and State aid rules contained in the ECSC Treaty, see Chap 17 of the 5th edn of this work. See also Communication from the Commission concerning certain aspects of the treatment of competition cases resulting from the expiry of the ECSC Treaty, OJ 2002 C152/5. It should be noted that State aid to the coal industry is now governed by Reg 1407/2002, OJ 2002 L205/8.

[150] See now Art 3(1)(u).

[151] Added as Arts 129a–d under the TEU amendments; now Arts 154–156.

[152] SEC(2006) 1724. Available in four parts at: http://ec.europa.eu/comm/competition/antitrust/others/sector_inquiries/energy/fr_part1.pdf (and similarly part 2, etc). See also See COM(2006) 851 final and Press Release IP/07/26 (10 January 2007). This inquiry should not be confused with the annual reports that the DG Energy and Transport produce, eg the 2005 Report on the functioning of the electricity and gas markets summarised in MEMO/05/427 (15 November 2005): see para 12.063, below.

contracts preventing alternative suppliers from supplying retail customers; and that there is an absence of cross-border integration or competition. A detailed consideration of the findings of the sector inquiry is beyond the scope of this work. Commenting on the report,[153] the Competition Commissioner referred to its 'disappointing conclusion . . . that more than a decade after having launched the drive for liberalisation, we are still far from having a single, competitive and well-functioning European energy market'. At the time of writing, a number of investigations by the Commission into possible violations of the competition rules are ongoing, and the Commissioner noted that if infringements are established, it is possible to impose structural remedies.[154]

12.055   **The Commission Green Paper.**   In March 2006, the Commission adopted a Green Paper, 'A European Strategy for Sustainable, Competitive and Secure Energy'.[155] The Paper highlights six priority areas where it believes action is necessary:

- Completing the internal European gas and electricity markets, in particular by focusing on creation of a single European grid, by increasing interconnection between Member States, by investing in generation capacity, by unbundling transmission and distribution activities and by boosting the competitiveness of European industry;

- Guaranteeing security of supply,[156] for example by making the state of Community oil stocks more transparent and by ensuring that the existing directives[157] on gas and electricity security of supply can deal with potential supply disruptions;

- Encouraging a more sustainable, efficient and diverse energy mix;[158]

- Adopting an integrated approach to climate change, including a review of the EU Emissions Trading Scheme and adopting an action plan for energy efficiency;

---

[153] Commr Kroes, 'Introductory remarks on the Final Report of the Energy Sector Competition Inquiry', Speech/07/4, 10 January 2007.

[154] ibid. The power is conferred by Art 7 of Reg 1/2003: see para 13.131, below.

[155] *A European Strategy for Sustainable, Competitive and Secure Energy*, COM(2006) 105 final, ch 2.3 and 2.4 (8 March 2006); and Art 174 EC. See also the accompanying Staff working document entitled 'What is at stake – Background document'; and Commr Kroes, 'Competition in the energy sctor: preliminary results of the Commission's inquiry and next steps in anti-trust enforcement', Speech at the First Annual Seminar and Conference on Energy Law and Policy, 9 March 2006 (Speech(06)159).

[156] The ruling in Case 72/83 *Campus Oil Limited v Minister for Industry and Energy* [1984] ECR 2727, [1984] 3 CMLR 544, appeared to give Member States a considerable degree of latitude in enacting measures to ensure security of oil supplies.

[157] Dir 2005/89, OJ 2006 L33/22 (electricity) and Dir 2004/67, OJ 2004 L127/92 (gas).

[158] See, eg Commission Communications 'Biomass action plan' COM(2005) 628, 7 December 2005 and 'An EU Strategy for Biofuels' COM(2006) 34, 8 February 2006.

- Encouraging innovation in new energy technologies;
- Developing a coherent external energy policy.[159]

In January 2007, the Commission issued proposals for a new European energy policy, comprising an integrated energy and climate change package.[160] The proposals include an EU objective in international negotiations of a 30 per cent reduction in greenhouse gas emissions by developed countries by 2020 compared to 1990, and call for a commitment to achieve at least a 20 per cent reduction of greenhouse gases by 2020 compared to 1990. The package also calls for commitments to further energy 'unbundling' through ownership unbundling or through a fully independent system operator;[161] to ensure effective regulation in every Member State; to establish a new Community mechanism and structure for transmission system operators; and to make further progress in realising the construction of essential new interconnectors. As part of its drive to create an effective energy policy, the Commission states that it proposes to establish an Office of the Energy Observatory within the Directorate General for Energy and Transport.[162]

Energy and the internal market. The internal market initiative has been seen as **12.056** a means for promoting competition in a single market in tandem with the enforcement of the competition rules of the EC Treaty. The first stage of the initiative involved the adoption of directives on price transparency and transit of electricity and gas.[163] The second stage included the liberalisation of electricity generation and the building of electricity and gas lines by encouraging investment; the separation of the management and accounting of production, transmission and

---

[159] On 25 October 2005, the European Union, Croatia, Bosnia and Herzegovina, Serbia, Montenegro, Albania, the Former Yugoslav Republic of Macedonia, Romania, Bulgaria and UNMIK (on behalf of Kosovo) signed the Energy Community Treaty. As a result, the *acquis communautaire* on energy, the environment and competition will be implemented in the Balkan peninsula. The Treaty is the first legally binding treaty to be signed by all of those States together. It has been consciously modelled on the ECSC Treaty. The Treaty will also create an agreed policy framework for the World Bank and the European Bank of Reconstruction and Development to support infrastructure investments and the expansion of the natural gas system to create an intermediate gas market between the Caspian Sea and the European Union: see Press Release IP/05/1346 (25 October 2005) and MEMO/05/397.

[160] Communication from the Commission to the European Council and European Parliament, *An Energy Policy for Europe*, COM(2007) 1 final (10 January 2007). This was accompanied by detailed Communication documents covering various aspects: COM(2006) 841–849 final. See at: http://ec.europa.eu/energy/energy_policy/index_en.htm.

[161] For unbundling, see para 12.056, below. The proposal for ownership unbundling is the most radical option and unlikely to prove politically acceptable: 'EU's plans for the "unbundling" of assets might prove a catalyst', *Financial Times*, 11 January 2007, p 6.

[162] *An Energy Policy for Europe* (n 160, above) point 3.10.

[163] Dir 90/377, OJ 1990 L185/16 (price transparency); Dir 90/547, OJ 1990 L313/30 (transit of electricity); Dir 91/296, OJ 1991 L147/37 (transit of gas). For discussion of these Directives, see Hancher, *EC Electricity Law* (Chancery Law Publishing, 1992).

distribution operations ('unbundling'); and the introduction of access to transmission networks. The third stage involves the full opening of the EU electricity market, legal unbundling of electricity undertakings and ex ante regulation so as to ensure non-discriminatory access to networks. The Commission has, however, acknowledged the difficulties inherent in opening up energy markets:

> 'whilst much has been done to create a competitive market, work is not yet complete. Many markets remain largely national, and dominated by a few companies. Many differences remain between Member States' approaches to market opening, preventing the development of a truly competitive European market - including powers of regulators, level of independence of network operators from competitive activities, grid rules, balancing and gas storage regimes.'[164]

The Commission has signalled its frustration with the delays in national implementation of the energy market liberalisation measures, and is pursuing defaulting Member States by infringement proceedings under Article 226 EC for failure to meet the specified deadlines.[165]

12.057 **Relevant provisions of the EC Treaty.** In promoting the policy of introducing greater competition into the energy sector, the Commission can invoke a variety of Treaty provisions in addition to Articles 81 and 82. Article 86(1) enables the Commission to scrutinise the justification for the grant of special or exclusive rights to energy companies and Article 86(2) applies the competition rules to public undertakings subject to the proviso that this 'does not obstruct the performance, in law or in fact, of the particular tasks assigned to them': see generally Chapter 11, above. Article 31 requires the adjustment by Member States of any State monopolies in order to ensure free movement of goods; and electricity and gas are treated as goods.[166] In addition, the State aid rules will in general be applied to the energy sector.[167]

---

[164] *A European Strategy for Sustainable, Competitive and Secure Energy* (n 155, above), 5–6. See also 'Energy Sector Inquiry – Issues Paper' (n 152, above); European Regulators Group for electricity and Gas (ERGEG), Assessment of the Development of the European Energy Markets, 2006 (6 December 2006), available at http://www.ergeg.org/portal/page/portal/ERGEG_HOME/ERGEG_DOCS/NATIONAL_REPORTS/2006/E06-MOR-02-03_AssessmentReport_2006-12-06.pdf.

[165] The Commission obtained judgment against Luxembourg and Spain for failure to implement Dir 2003/55 (the Gas Directive): Case C-354/05 *Commission v Luxembourg* [2006] ECR I-67, and Case C-357/05 *Commission v Spain* [2006] ECR I-118. In December 2006, the Commission sent 26 reasoned opinions to 16 Member States for breach of the 2003 Dirs concerning both electricity and gas markets: Press Release IP/06/1768 (12 December 2006).

[166] See, eg Case 6/64 *Costa v ENEL* [1964] ECR 585, [1964] CMLR 425; Case 158/94 *Commission v Italy* [1997] ECR I-5789, [1998] 2 CMLR 373, 463, paras 14–20; Case C-379/98 *PreussenElektra* [2001] ECR I-2099, [2001] All ER (EC) 330, [2001] 2 CMLR 833, paras 68–81 and Opinion of AG Jacobs, para 197. See further para 12.071, below, and for Art 31 generally, see paras 11.036 *et seq*, above.

[167] cf *PreussenElektra*, above, and see generally, Chap 15, below.

Plan of this Section.   This Section deals separately with the electricity and gas   **12.058**
sectors.[168] The rules relating to competition, together with the Commission's
single market initiatives, are considered as regards the individual sectors.

(b) Electricity

(i) Generally

Market structure: generally.   The electricity sector is characterised by the vari-   **12.059**
ety of primary energy sources which can be used to generate electricity. In particular, a large proportion of electricity generation is based on coal and nuclear power
and therefore retains a social and employment dimension (in contrast to the gas
sector). Community policy has also encouraged the use of renewable energy
sources.[169] Organisation and ownership of the electricity industry in each Member
State varies as a consequence, with electricity being generated either from indige-
nous national resources or from imports. Electricity has, therefore, traditionally
been one of the least international of energy sectors.

Market structure: objectives.   The establishment of a competitive internal elec-   **12.060**
tricity market has been a Commission objective for a long time. It has acknowledged that this must be achieved gradually in order to enable industry to adapt
and to take account of the different ways in which electricity systems in the
Member States are organised. Directive 2003/54 ('the Electricity Directive'),[170]
adopted in 2003, provided for full liberalisation of the EU electricity market by
July 2004 for all non-household customers and by July 2007 for all customers.
Regulation 1228/2003,[171] adopted at the same time, sets out conditions for access
to the network for cross-border exchanges in electricity ('the Electricity Transit
Regulation'). The Electricity Transit Regulation supplements the Electricity
Directive and is intended to facilitate the creation of an effective internal electric-
ity market.

---

[168] For further discussion, see Jones (ed), *EU Competition Law and Energy Markets* (2006);
Cameron, *Competition in Energy Markets* (2nd ed, 2007); Hardiman, 'Energy' in Korah and others
(eds), *Competition Law of the European Communities* (2nd ed, and Supp), chap 16; Van Bael & Bellis,
Competition Law of the European Community (4th ed, 2005), chap 12; Faull & Nikpay (eds), *The EC
Law of Competition* (2nd ed, 2007), Chap 12. The nuclear energy and oil sectors are not considered
in this edition of the work; for a summary, see 5th edn, paras 16-034–16-051 (nuclear energy) and
paras 16-066–16-074 (oil).

[169] See, eg Dir 2001/77 on the promotion of electricity produced from renewable energy sources
in the internal electricity market: OJ 2001 L283/33.

[170] Dir 2003/54, OJ 2003 L176/37: Vol II, App E.14, which replaced Dir 96/92, OJ 1997
L27/20. See Case C-17/03 *Vereniging voor Energie, Milieu en Water v Directeur van de Dienst uitvoer-
ing en toezicht energie* [2005] ECR I-4983, [2005] 5 CMLR 361.

[171] Reg 1228/2003, OJ 2003 L176/1.

(ii) Liberalisation

12.061 **The Electricity Directive.** The Electricity Directive[172] is intended to create a fully-competitive single market for electricity in the Community. It sets out common rules for the generation, transmission, distribution and supply of electricity. It lays down *ex ante* rules to ensure legal unbundling of transmission system operators ('TSOs')[173] and distribution system operators ('DSOs');[174] non-discriminatory access to networks;[175] and market opening. The Electricity Directive also imposes obligations on Member States to ensure that all household customers[176] enjoy universal service[177] and to take appropriate measures to protect final customers,[178] in particular vulnerable customers, including measures to help avoid disconnection.[179]

12.062 **National regulatory authorities.** The Electricity Directive obliges Member States to designate one or more independent authorities ('NRAs') to be responsible for ensuring non-discrimination, effective competition and the efficient functioning of the market (Article 23(1)).[180] NRAs are also responsible for fixing

---

[172] Dir 2003/54 (n 170, above). However, most Member States did not respect the deadline for implementation of the Electricity Directive (nor that for the implementation of the Gas Directive) into national law: see *XXIVth Report on Competition Policy* (2004), point 294. At the time of writing, certain Member States had still not implemented the Electricity Directive and the Commission has sent reasoned opinions to those States as a prelude to infringement proceedings under Art 226 EC: see n 165, above.

[173] As to the tasks of TSOs, see Dir 2003/54 (n 170, above) Art 9.

[174] As to the tasks of DSOs, see Dir 2003/54 (ibid) Art 14.

[175] An operator may only refuse access where it lacks the necessary capacity (Article 20(2)). Substantiated reasons must be given. However, certain new direct current interconnectors may be exempted from the provisions relating to access: see Reg 1228/2003 (n 171, above) Art 7. A similar exemption is provided in relation to gas interconnectors, LNG and storage facilities: see Dir 2003/55, OJ 2003 L176/57, Art 22. The Commission has noted that this possibility of exemption from the third party access regimes is one of the most controversial points of the Electricity Transit Reg, the exemption provisions seeking 'to strike a balance between creating incentives for new infrastructure and the creation of a common market': *XXXIIIrd Report on Competition Policy* (2003), point 90.

[176] For the definition of 'household customers', see Art 2(10).

[177] 'Universal service' is defined as the right to be supplied with electricity of a specified quality within the territory at reasonable, easily and clearly comparable and transparent prices: see Art 3(3).

[178] For the definition of 'final customers' see Art 2(9).

[179] Member States must also ensure a high level of consumer protection, in particular in relation to transparency of contractual terms and conditions, general information and dispute settlement mechanisms. They shall also ensure that the eligible customer (as to which see Art 2(12)) is able to switch to a new supplier: see Art 3(5) and Annex A.

[180] Art 23(1) provides a non-exhaustive list of particular monitoring tasks that NRAs must perform. In December 2003 the Commission founded the European Regulators Group for Electricity and Gas ('ERGEG') in order to encourage cooperation and coordination between NRAs: Decn 2003/796, OJ 2003 L296/34 and see n 163, above. See also Dir 2003/54 (n 169, above) Recital (16). In 2004 the Commission also established an Energy Subgroup of the European Competition Network. Its aim is to provide a forum to discuss key issues and develop a common approach to the application and monitoring of EC competition law in the energy sector: see *XXXIVth Report on Competition Policy* (2004), point 117. The process of liberalisation of the European energy markets is also discussed, on an annual or biennial basis, by the Commission, national authorities and industry representatives at the so-called Florence and Madrid Forums.

or approving the methodologies used to calculate or establish the terms and conditions for connection and access to national networks, including transmission and distribution tariffs (Article 23(2)).

Reporting. The Commission must produce annual progress reports to the **12.063** European Parliament and the Council of Ministers covering *inter alia* experience gained and progress made in creating a fully operational internal market, unbundling, system capacity, security of supply and progress achieved with regard to bilateral relations with third countries (Article 28).

The Electricity Transit Regulation. Regulation 1228/2003,[181] which applies **12.064** from 1 July 2004,[182] introduces a common framework in relation to tariffs for cross-border transactions and the allocation of available interconnection capacity so as to tackle congestion. Its aim is to set fair rules for cross-border exchanges in electricity, thus enhancing competition within the internal electricity market.[183]

Other recent developments. Security of supply is one of the principal concerns **12.065** of both Member States and the Commission.[184] In January 2006, the Council and the European Parliament adopted a Directive concerning measures to safeguard security of electricity supply and infrastructure investment.[185]

(iii) Long-term arrangements and exclusivity

Length of exclusivity. In *Pego*,[186] the Commission refused to approve a 28-year **12.066** exclusive supply arrangement which would have prevented the consortium generator of a coal-fuelled station in Portugal from delivering electricity to consumers other than Electricidade de Portugal (EDP), from whom the consortium was purchasing the project. The agreements were then modified and the Commission issued a comfort letter on the basis that Article 81(3) was satisfied by provisions limiting capacity and output exclusively to EDP for the first 15 years with an option during the subsequent period for the generator to supply outside the franchise system if there was surplus capacity not required by the grid.[187]

---

181 Reg 1228/2003 (n 171, above).
182 Art 15.
183 Art 1.
184 See, eg Dir 2003/54 (n 170, above) Arts 3(2) (public service obligations) and 4 (monitoring of security of supply); *A European Strategy for Sustainable, Competitive and Secure Energy* (n 155, above) Ch 2.2.
185 Dir 2005/89, OJ 2006 L33/22.
186 Electricidade de Portugal/Pego project, XXIIIrd Report on Competition Policy (1993), point 222.
187 The same time limit was considered acceptable in *REN/Turbogás*, where the Commission sent a comfort letter in respect of a 15-year agreement for supply from the largest power station in Portugal, once this had been amended to delete a clause giving the purchaser a first option to obtain power from the generator after the 15 years: *XXVIth Report on Competition Policy* (1996), point 134. See also *Transgás/Turbogás*, ibid, 135; *Gas Natural/Endesa*, Press Release IP/00/297 (27 March 2000).

12.067 **Exclusivity and Article 82.** In *Almelo*,[188] a case concerning the Dutch electricity sector, the Court of Justice considered the exclusive purchasing obligation imposed on local distributors through the regional distributors' general conditions for the supply of electricity, which prohibited local distributors from obtaining supplies from other suppliers including those in other Member States. The Court held that the use of such an exclusive purchasing obligation by a regional electricity distributor that was part of a group of undertakings occupying a collective dominant position in a substantial part of the Community would breach Article 82. It was for the national court to decide if the links between the regional electricity distributors were sufficient to constitute such collective dominance.[189]

12.068 **Electricity pricing mechanisms.** Pricing mechanisms in national electricity industries which reinforce monopolies through price-fixing or excessive or unfair pricing have been considered by the Commission under the competition rules.[190] The Commission has stated that transmission charges will not be considered an abuse under Article 82 provided that they are linked to the actual cost and there is no double payment where electricity is traded across national borders.[191]

12.069 **National or European markets.** The Commission's position on the identification of an effect on trade between Member States in electricity markets depends on the particular circumstances.[192] Those include the different stages of development in the national markets, which should change following liberalisation, and the electricity sector involved.[193] This approach has not prevented the Commission

---

[188] Case C-393/92 *Almelo* [1994] ECR I-1477, paras 43–44.

[189] On exclusivity and foreclosure, see *Electrabel*, *XXVIIth Report on Competition Policy* (1997), point 94; See also *Jahrhundertvertrag*, OJ 1993 L50/14: para 12.070, below.

[190] See, eg *National Association of Licensed Opencast Operators v British Coal Corporation*, 23 May 1991, [1993] 4 CMLR 615 (discrimination in purchase prices offered by electricity generators to British Coal). The Commission's decn was taken under both Arts 82 EC and Art 63(1) ECSC, and on a reference from the English court in the damages claim by the small mine owners, the ECJ held that such coal supply contracts were exclusively covered by the ECSC Treaty: Case C-18/94 *Hopkins v National Power and PowerGen* [1996] ECR I-2281, [1996] 4 CMLR 795. See also *IJsselcentrale*, OJ 1991 L28/32, [1992] 5 CMLR 154, considering the cost equalisation mechanism imposed by Dutch regional electricity distributors on their customers to eliminate differences in its costs of distribution (supplying rural regions) and the costs of municipal and regional distributors (supplying mainly city areas).

[191] *Electricity transmission tariffs in the Netherlands*, *XXIXth Report on Competition Policy* (1999), p 165.

[192] See, eg the Commission's analysis of UK privatisation (5th edn of this work, para 16-023). See also, in relation to national markets and import/export bans, *IJsselcentrale* (n 189, above) paras 25 and 32; *Jahrhundertvertrag* (n 188, above) para 25. For an application of Case C-234/89 *Delimitis* [1991] ECR I-935, [1992] 5 CMLR 210, see *Almelo* (n 187, above) (exclusive purchasing clause contained in general conditions of supply that applied in the network of contractual arrangements between regional distributors and local distributors in the Netherlands had the cumulative effect of compartmentalising the national market: they prohibited local distributors from obtaining supplies of electricity from distributors or producers in other Member States).

[193] The Commission has divided the activities of the electricity industry into four different types of operation: generation, transmission, distribution, and supply to the final consumer: each of these

from accepting that national policy considerations may justify provisions which breach Article 81(1): see Section (iv), below.

(iv) National policy considerations

Jahrhundertvertrag: Article 81(3). In *Jahrhundertvertrag*,[194] the Commission **12.070** considered a series of agreements whereby the German public and private electricity producers were required for the period 1981–1995 to purchase stipulated amounts of coal from German coal mines for the purpose of electricity generation. The Commission stated that the supplementary agreements to *Jahrhundertvertrag* qualified for exemption under Article 81(3) EC and for authorisation under Article 65(2) ECSC. The agreements contributed to improving electricity generation and coal production in a market where production and demand had to be in constant equilibrium since electricity cannot be produced for storage.[195] Electricity supply and distribution is therefore a branch of the energy sector in which it is of particular importance to safeguard the procurement of primary energy sources. The agreement made such an energy source available in the form of coal and this promoted security of supply in Germany, which represented a benefit for both industrial and private consumers. However, the Commission approved the purchasing commitments only insofar as they related to actual requirements; the carrying forward of purchasing commitments from one period to the next did not contribute to security of supply and was an unjustifiable tying of customers. Exemption and authorisation were given on condition that the amount of coal covered by the purchasing commitment did not exceed a stated amount.

(v) Imports and exports

National monopolies investigated under Article 31. The Commission has **12.071** used both Article 81 and Article 31 as the basis for challenging national import and export monopolies. Infringement proceedings were brought under Article 226 against several Member States each of which granted a particular undertaking exclusive import and export rights for electricity.[196] Although the Court dismissed all the actions on the basis that the Commission had failed to meet the defence raised under Article 86(2), its willingness to find a contravention of Article 31

---

constitutes, in the Commission's view, a separate product market, which may be purely national. See, eg Case M.3440 *ENI/EDP/GdP* (9 December 2004), paras 31 *et seq* (product markets), 78 *et seq* (geographic market); appeal on other grounds dismissed, Case T-87/05 *EDP v Commission* [2005] ECR II-3745, [2005] 5 CMLR 1436.

[194] *Jahrhundertvertrag*, OJ 1993 L50/14.

[195] ibid, para 31.

[196] Cases C-157/94 *Commission v Netherlands*, C-158/94 *Commission v Italy*, C-159/94 *Commission v France*, C-160/94 *Commission v Spain* [1997] ECR I-5699, 5789, 5815, 5851, [1998] 2 CMLR 373. The monopoly granted by the Netherlands related only to electricity imports; France had also granted a similar monopoly in respect of gas.

may have helped to secure a consensus among the Member States for the adoption of the liberalisation directives. In *Almelo*,[197] the Court of Justice held that Article 31 did not apply because the regional distributor had not been granted an exclusive concession giving it a monopoly in supply within the territory of its concession. Furthermore, the contracts at issue were concluded with local distributors, not with public authorities, and did not transfer to those distributors the concession granted to the regional undertaking. The conditions for the application of Article 31, that national authorities are in a position to control or appreciably influence trade between Member States through a body established for that purpose or a delegated monopoly, were not present.

12.072 **Cumulative effect to establish import/export ban.** In the *IJsselcentrale* case,[198] the Commission concluded that the company (SEP) established by the four Dutch electricity generators was able to exercise total control of imports and exports and that this monopoly was sustained in several ways which led to a breach of Article 81(1). The Cooperation Agreement between SEP and the generating companies prohibited the import and export of electricity by undertakings other than SEP both horizontally, by prohibiting the generators from exporting or importing, and vertically, by requiring them to impose the same ban on distributors in their supply agreements. First, the succession of exclusive purchasing obligations as between distributors and customers formed 'a coherent system' with the Cooperation Agreement. Secondly, SEP's operation and ownership of all international interconnectors and the impracticality of privately owned lines meant that private importers were dependent on the cooperation of SEP. The Commission also considered that SEP's refusal to make power lines available to others was a concerted practice between the generators that could constitute a separate infringement of Article 81.

(c) **Gas**

(i) *Generally*

12.073 **Market structure.** Similarities between the gas and electricity sectors in industry organisation, regulation and Commission approach arise from the fact that both are grid-based industries. The main difference from electricity lies in the fact that natural gas is a primary fuel and reserves are located only in certain Member States. This means that transportation (pipelines), security of supply and dependence on imports are significant.[199] The priorities in the industry have tended to reinforce national monopolies with public distribution and transmission

---

[197] *Almelo* (n 187, above) paras 29–32. See Hancher, (1995) 32 CML Rev 305.
[198] *IJsselcentrale*, OJ 1991 L28/32, [1992] 5 CMLR 154.
[199] The 'vast majority' of the EU's gas supply comes via pipeline from Russia and Norway: 'Energy Sector Inquiry – Issues Paper', 15 November 2005, para 9 available, with other information from this Inquiry, at http://ec.europa.eu/comm/competition/antitrust/other/sector_inquiries/energy/.

undertakings granted exclusive operating rights and imports/exports and foreign investment subject to control. This is reflected by diversity in the Member States' market structures, ranging from deregulation to dominance by a single company.[200]

Market structure: objectives. The establishment of a competitive natural gas market has been an important element in the Commission's objective of the completion of the internal energy market.[201] The adoption by the Council and the European Parliament of Directive 2003/55 concerning common rules for the internal market in natural gas on 26 June 2003 (the same date on which the Electricity Directive was adopted) marked the most recent stage in the process of achieving this objective.[202] Directive 2003/55 ('the Gas Directive') was to be implemented and applied by July 2004.[203] **12.074**

(ii) Liberalisation

The Gas Directive. Directive 2003/55[204] established common rules for the transmission, distribution, supply and storage of natural gas, including liquefied natural gas ('LNG'). It laid down rules relating to the organisation and functioning of the natural gas sector including access to the market and the criteria and procedures applicable to the granting of authorisations. The Gas Directive broadly followed the principles of the Electricity Directive. Authorisations for construction or operation of natural gas facilities may, for example, be granted according to a system provided that the criteria are objective and non-discriminatory (Article 4). All provisions relating to transmission, storage, distribution and supply emphasise the need for non-discrimination between users (Articles 7, 10).[205] As with the Electricity Directive,[206] provisions are established to ensure the legal unbundling **12.075**

---

[200] eg, deregulation in the UK but dominance by a single supplier in France and Spain. France imports about 90 per cent of its natural gas consumption; Belgium has depleted most of its natural gas reserves and now relies on imports. See also *A European Strategy for Sustainable, Competitive and Secure Energy* (n 155, above), Annex (Staff working document).

[201] The first phase involved measures to improve transparency, expansion of the European gas pipeline network and the use of common carriage to decompartmentalise national gas markets: see the Council Directives on the transit of natural gas through grids, Dir 91/296, OJ 1991 L147/37, am by Dir 95/49, OJ 1995 L233/86; and a Community procedure to improve the transparency of gas and electricity prices charged to industrial end-users, Dir 90/377, OJ 1990 L185/61. See also Dir 98/30, OJ 1998 L204/1, corr L245/43 (the 'First Gas Directive'), which established common rules for the transmission, distribution, supply and storage of natural gas. For a detailed overview of the First Gas Directive, see the fifth edition of this work, paras 16-054–16-057.

[202] Dir 2003/55, OJ 2003 L176/57: see Vol II, App E.15.

[203] ibid, Art 33. However, many Member States failed to do so: see n 165, above. Note that Member States may postpone the implementation of the unbundling obligation on DSOs until 1 July 2007: Art 33.

[204] Dir 2003/55, OJ 2003 L176/57: see Vol II, App E.15.

[205] See also *Irish interconnector, XXIXth Report on Competition Policy* (1999), p 165.

[206] Dir 2003/54, OJ 2003 L176/ 37, discussed at para 12.061, above.

of TSOs and DSOs (Articles 9 and 13 respectively)[207] and the unbundling of accounts of all natural gas undertakings (Article 17).[208]

12.076 **Access to transmission and distribution system.** The Gas Directive obliged Member States to put in place a system of third party access to the gas transmission and distribution system,[209] and to LNG facilities, based on published tariffs and applicable to all eligible customers. It also required measures to be put in place to ensure that natural gas undertakings and eligible customers[210] were able to obtain access to upstream pipeline networks, including facilities supplying technical services incidental to such access. Guidelines for Good Practice were adopted by the European Gas Regulatory Forum in 2002 and 2003, and in 2005 a further instrument, Regulation 1775/2005, was adopted by the Council and the European Parliament aiming 'to tackle remaining barriers to the completion of the internal market in particular regarding the trade of gas'.[211] The Annex to the new Regulation sets out guidance on third party access services, the principles underlying the capacity allocation mechanisms, congestion management procedures and the technical information necessary for network users to gain effective access to the system. This guidance can be amended by the Commission in accordance with a procedure set out in the Regulation.

12.077 **Security of Supply Directive.** In April 2004 the Council adopted a Directive concerning measures to safeguard security of natural gas supply,[212] under which Member States are obliged to define the roles and responsibilities of the different gas market operators in achieving national policies aimed at ensuring adequate levels of security of supply and to specify adequate minimum security of supply standards that must be complied with.[213] Household customers' supplies must also be protected to an appropriate extent.[214]

---

[207] Market experience of full ownership unbundling suggests that it significantly changes the behaviour of the transport undertaking – a fully unbundled TSO will focus on optimising the use of its network: 'Energy Sector Inquiry – Issues Paper' (n 199, above) point 28.

[208] Member States, or any competent authority designated for the purpose, shall, in addition, have a right of access to the accounts of natural gas undertakings. This right of access is subject to a general duty to respect confidentiality, albeit Member States may provide for disclosure where necessary for the competent authorities to carry out their functions: Dir 2003/55 (n 202, above) Art 16.

[209] Art 19 of the Gas Directive also deals with access to storage facilities and the Directive provides for the possibility of limited derogations.

[210] For 'eligible customers', see Art 23.

[211] Reg 1775/2005, OJ 2005 L289/1, Recital (1).

[212] Dir 2004/67, OJ 2004 L127/92.

[213] ibid, Art 3.

[214] ibid, Art 4. The Directive also imposes reporting and monitoring mechanisms (Arts 5 and 6 respectively) and establishes a Gas Coordination Group, comprising representatives of the Member States and representative bodies of industry and of relevant consumers, to facilitate the coordination of security of supply measures: Art 7.

(iii) Application of competition rules

Articles 81–82 and liberalisation. Since liberalisation commenced, the **12.078** Commission has on a number of occasions invoked the competition and merger control rules in an attempt to ensure that the liberalisation process is not thwarted.[215] The Commission has stated that '[t]he adoption of legislation aimed at liberalising European energy markets must be accompanied by the strict application of European competition law. The contribution of European competition law to the liberalisation process is likely to increase over the next few years'.[216] This Section sets out certain such cases.

Territorial restrictions. In *GDF-ENEL, GDF-ENI*,[217] the Commission adopted **12.079** two decisions concerning the arrangements for the supply of natural gas by Gaz de France to, respectively, the Italian electricity company and the Italian gas company, which contained clauses requiring the gas to be used outside France. The Commission confirmed that territorial restriction clauses of this kind traditionally included in gas supply and transportation contracts infringe Article 81. They prevent customers from obtaining supplies from operators in other Member States and constitute a sizeable obstacle to the creation of a truly competitive and integrated EU gas market.[218] In 2005, the Commission closed its investigation into gas supply contracts between the Russian gas producer, Gazprom, and the Austrian incumbent gas wholesaler, OMV. OMV will no longer be prevented from reselling, outside Austria, the gas which it buys from Gazprom, and Gazprom will be free to sell to other customers in Austria without having first to offer the gas to OMV (so-called 'right of first refusal'). OMV also agreed to contribute to increasing capacity on the TAG pipeline which transports Russian gas through Austria to Italy.[219]

---

[215] eg, *Marathon, XXXIVth Report on Competition Policy* (2004), point 296: Commission accepted commitments from Gaz de France and Ruhrgas improving TPA to their networks following an investigation into alleged refusals to grant a Norwegian subsidiary of Marathon, a US energy company, such access (the Commission having previously settled similar cases).

[216] *XXXIInd Report on Competition Policy* (2002), point 81.

[217] Case COMP 38.662 *GDF-ENI, GDF/ENEL*, decn of 26 October 2004, *XXXIVth Report on Competition Policy* (2004), Vol 1, points 81–83. Since these were the first decisions concerning such clauses in the gas sector in the process of liberalisation, no fines were imposed. And see Note on the decns by Cultrera in (2005) 1 EC Competition Policy Newsletter 45.

[218] See also *ENI/Gazprom, XXXIIIrd Report on Competition Policy* (2003), point 98: Commission investigated territorial sales restrictions contained in gas supply contracts between gas producers and European gas wholesalers/importers. A settlement was reached after the companies deleted the relevant clauses from their existing supply contracts. Additionally, ENI agreed to adopt a number of further measures, including the offer to sell significant volumes of gas outside Italy.

[219] *Annual Report on Competition Policy* (2005), point 48. A similar result was achieved as regards the contract between Gazprom and the biggest German wholesale company, E.on Ruhrgas (removal of territorial restrictions and Gazprom will no longer be bound by a 'most favoured customer' provision which obliged Gazprom to offer Ruhrgas similar conditions to those it offered to Ruhrgas' competitors on the wholesale market in Germany), ibid, point 49.

12.080 **Long-term contracts and developing markets.** The Commission has identified the existence of long-term supply contracts for the supply of gas as a particular problem impeding the erosion of traditional national monopolies. Such contracts prevent customers from taking advantage of the development of competition in the market and foreclose opportunities for market entrants.[220] In *Transgás/ Turbogás*,[221] the Commission considered an agreement for the supply of natural gas from Algeria to the Tapada power station in Portugal. Transgás concluded a long-term agreement with the Algerian supplier for gas to be transported along a new pipeline. Transgás and Turbogás entered into a 25-year supply and purchase agreement for the gas required by Turbogás to generate electricity required by the national grid. This would account for approximately 68 per cent of the Portuguese gas market in 1999, estimated to fall to 36 per cent by 2012. The Commission examined the project in light of the investment by the European Investment Bank to create an infrastructure in the embryonic Portuguese market. It required certain amendments to the agreement, including the deletion of an obligation on the generator to obtain Transgás' prior consent before electricity could be sold to third parties and the reduction in the duration of the clause providing that gas would be supplied only for electricity generation purposes. On that basis, a comfort letter was issued, but the Commission made clear that this does not prejudice the position which it may take with respect to other long-term agreements.[222] In *Gas Natural/Endesa*, the Commission closed its investigation under Article 82 into the long-term gas supply agreement for electricity generation made between the Spanish gas company, Gas Natural, and the Spanish electricity generator, Endesa, following amendment of the terms of the agreement.[223] The Commission had identified the long-term supply obligation and the own-use requirement on Endesa as potential restrictions of competition. It noted that the market position of Gas Natural was strong, with a high market share and with control of the gas infrastructure. The Commission was concerned that the agreement should not impede entry into the Spanish gas market at the start of domestic liberalisation and in the initial stages of liberalisation of the European market. The parties undertook to amend the agreement to reduce the volumes to be supplied and the

---

[220] See Annual Report on Competition Policy (2005), points 44–46.

[221] *XXVIth Report on Competition Policy* (1996) p 135; see also para 12.066, above.

[222] *XXVIth Report on Competition Policy* (1996), point 103. In its *XXXIInd Report on Competition Policy* (2002), point 80, the Commission stressed that it was important 'to underline that long-term gas supply contracts are not *ipso facto* incompatible with EU competition law but the Commission will monitor whether such an incompatibility arises in individual cases. To the extent that restrictions in gas supply contracts are necessary to underpin significant investments, e.g. in a new gas field, the Commission will take this into account.'

[223] See Fernández Salas, 'Long-term supply agreements in the context of gas market liberalisation: Commission closes investigation of Gas Natural' (2000) 2 EC Competition Policy Newsletter 55; see also Press Release IP/00/297 (27 March 2000).

duration of the contract, and to remove the own-use requirement so that Endesa could resell the gas.[224]

Third party access.   Certain TPA regimes have been improved as a result of **12.081** Commission investigations. An entry/exit regime was introduced in Germany following commitments offered by the German gas company, BEB.[225] In *Dong/ DUC*, the Commission clarified that so-called 'use restrictions', clauses restricting the use to which gas may be put by the buyer, and 'reduction clauses', allowing the buyer to reduce the volumes bought from the seller if the latter starts selling into the supply area of the buyer, were incompatible with Community law.[226]

Article 86 and domestic legislation.   The introduction of new French domestic **12.082** legislation led to the Commission dropping the proceedings which it had brought following a complaint against France and Gaz de France for breach of Articles 82 and 86. The new law allows operators to distribute gas in France in areas at present not connected to the public network, provided that they are approved by the Minister for Energy. The trade association for non-nationalised gas companies had complained that the law then in force prevented them from extending their services to certain areas in spite of the fact that Gaz de France was refusing to install distribution networks there because of the requirement that it must make a profit. The Commission had adopted a decision on 9 July 1997 finding against France but postponed its implementation in order to give the French authorities time to adopt remedial legislation.[227]

Mergers and joint ventures.   In *Energais de Portugal/Gás de Portugal*,[228] the **12.083** Commission blocked the acquisition of joint control over GDP, the incumbent gas company in Portugal, by EDP, the incumbent electricity company in Portugal, and ENI. The Commission found that the operation would have strengthened EDP's dominant position in both the electricity wholesale retail markets and the gas markets in Portugal. In particular it would have removed potential competition from GDP in the electricity markets as well as EDP's most likely entry in the gas markets. It would also have made those electricity producers which use gas as a fuel reliant on their main competitor for their gas supplies. Finally, the acquisition would have foreclosed a significant part of gas demand, at the time

---

[224] Various other clauses which could have had the effect of discriminating in favour of Endesa compared with other customers were modified: ibid. See also the proposed commitments from the Belgian supplier, *Distrigaz*, OJ 2007 C77/48.

[225] *BEB, XXXIIIrd Report on Competition Policy* (2003), point 99; see also Press Release IP/03/1129 (29 July 2003).

[226] *XXXIIIrd Report on Competition Policy* (2003), point 99.

[227] Press Release IP/99/291 (3 May 1999), [1999] 4 CMLR 1171. The new French Law No. 98-546 of 2 July 1998 is implemented by Decree No. 99-278 of 12 April 1999, JO 14 April 1999, 5483.

[228] Case M.3440 *ENI/EDP/GDP*, decn of 9 December 2004. See also *XXXIVth Report on Competition Policy* (2004), point 298.

controlled by EDP. In the Commission's view, it would have discouraged cross-border competition and pre-empted the effectiveness of the liberalisation of the electricity and gas markets in Portugal. EDP's appeal to the Court of First Instance was dismissed.[229] The issues arising when potential competitors enter into joint ventures to build and exploit natural resources infrastructure are further considered in Chapter 7, above.[230]

(d) Energy and the environment

12.084 **Generally.** Article 3(1)(l) of the EC Treaty identifies a policy in the sphere of environment as one of the activities of the Community,[231] and Article 174 elaborates what this involves, including pursuit of the objective of environmental protection and prudent utilisation of natural resources and adoption of the 'polluter pays' principle. The Commission has proposed common policies for a greener Europe, including the need to promote a sustained and increased use of renewable resources (for example, wave power, biomass, solar, geothermal and wind energy).[232]

12.085 **State aids.** The Commission has acknowledged that State aid may be permissible to support the cost of developing renewable energy sources or assist in reducing gas emissions and energy consumption.[233]

12.086 **Competition rules.** In *CECED*,[234] a decision primarily based on the environmental benefits, the Commission granted exemption under Article 81(3) to an agreement between virtually all the European importers and manufacturers of

---

[229] Case T-87/05 *EDP v Commission* [2005] ECR II-3745, [2005] 5 CMLR 1436. See also *GVS* (clearance of the acquisition of a regional gas wholesaler by EnBW, a German electricity company, and ENI, an Italian gas and petroleum company, after the parties undertook to grant early termination rights to all local gas distributors which had entered into long-term supply contracts with GVS or other subsidiaries controlled by EnBW), *XXXIInd Report on Competition Policy* (2002), point 85; and *Verbund/EnergieAllianz* (clearance of a merger between the Austrian power producer and several regional supply companies; merging parties agreed to assist in the creation of a stronger competitor and offered to make certain amounts of energy available for sale by auction to smaller competitors), *XXXIIIrd Report on Competition Policy* (2003), point 100.

[230] See paras 7.111 *et seq*, above.

[231] Added by the Maastricht Treaty (as Art 3(k)).

[232] See *A European Strategy for Sustainable, Competitive and Secure Energy* (n 155, above) 9–13. See also Dir 2001/77 on the promotion of electricity produced from renewable energy sources in the internal electricity market, OJ 2001 L283/33, under which Member States are obliged to set national objectives for the future consumption of electricity produced from renewable sources of energy, introduce a certification system for green electricity and put measures in place to promote renewable sources in the internal market.

[233] See para 15.060, below.

[234] *CECED*, OJ 2000 L187/47, [2000] 5 CMLR 635. See also *EACEM*, *XXVIIIth Report on Competition Policy* (1998), p 152; *CEMEP*, Press Release IP/00/508 (23 May 2000) and Martínez-López, 'Horizontal agreements on energy efficiency of appliances: a comparison between CECED and CEMEP', (2000) 2 EC Competition Policy Newsletter 24; *CECED: dishwashers and water heaters*, Press Release IP/01/1659 (26 November 2001).

domestic washing machines to stop importing or producing the least energy-efficient machines, thereby reducing the polluting emissions from power generation. The environmental benefits for society were stated to meet the criteria for exemption although there may be no benefits for individual purchasers. This distinction is reflected in the Commission's Horizontal Cooperation Guidelines, adopted in December 2000.[235] The Guidelines include a specific section on 'environmental agreements', defined as agreements whereby the parties undertake to achieve pollution abatement or environmental objectives, in particular those set out in Article 174 of the EC Treaty.[236]

4. Electronic Communications

(a) Regulatory framework

A 'dynamic' regulatory regime.   The communications sector within the Community underwent a radical transformation towards the end of the 1990s. The combined effects of ever increasing liberalisation, legislative harmonisation and, to a large degree, technological change have brought about a much more dynamic and competitive environment for communications. At the same time, the sector has been increasing in its economic importance to the Member States and the Community as a whole. These developments were noted by the Commission in its 1999 review of the communications sector,[237] where it recognised, in particular, the need to encourage competition by increasing harmonisation and reducing administrative burdens, the need to protect consumers, the pace of technological change and the effects of the convergence of telecommunications, media and information technology sectors. The Commission's findings led to the adoption of revised regulatory framework in 2002, intended to meet the challenges posed by the industry and designed to provide flexibility and adaptability in order to promote competition, while enabling sufficient oversight by regulators and competition authorities alike.

12.087

Council of Ministers statement.   A useful introduction to the policy underpinning the regulatory framework is provided by the following statement of reasons made by the Council of Ministers, which accompanied the common position on the 2002 regulatory framework:

12.088

> 'The purpose of the regulatory package proposed is to bring current Community legislation on telecommunications into line with the far reaching changes which have taken place in the telecommunications, media and information technology sectors. The convergence of these sectors underlies the approach of the Commission's

---

[235] OJ 2001 C3/2: Vol II, App C.12. For the Guidelines, see further para 7.027, above.
[236] ibid, Section 7, paras 179 *et seq.*
[237] '*Towards a new framework for Electronic Communications infrastructure and associated services. The 1999 Communications Review*' COM(1999) 539.

proposals which seek to bring all transmission networks and associated services together under a single regulatory framework. The proposed new regulatory framework has been designed as an intermediate phase between the current framework and an anticipated future situation where the telecommunications market will be sufficiently mature to allow it to be governed solely by general competition law.'[238]

12.089 **Overview of regulatory framework.** The Community's vision for telecommunications regulation is now embodied in a series of five directives which, together with a Commission decision on radio spectrum policy,[239] make up the 2002 regulatory framework.[240] These in turn envisage the adoption of further decisions, guidelines and recommendations to bring about the objectives of the framework. The architecture of the 2002 regulatory framework is set out in the aptly named 'Framework Directive'[241] which prescribes the fundamental rules and objectives of the regulatory framework found in each of its constituent directives. The Framework Directive refers[242] to the 'Specific Directives', which are as follows: (1) the 'Access Directive';[243] (2) the 'Authorisation Directive';[244] (3) the 'Universal Service Directive';[245] and (4) the 'Directive on privacy and electronic communications'.[246] In conjunction with the Framework Directive, these Directives seek to bring about both greater harmonisation and liberalisation of the communications sector. The 'Directive on Competition in the Markets for Electronic Communications Services'[247] is also relevant to the subject-matter of the regulatory

---

[238] Council's statement of reasons of 20 July 2001, OJ 2001 C337/15.

[239] This reform has brought about a desirable simplification by reducing the number of applicable directives from 20 to 6: see the 1999 Review (n 237, above) p 17, for a helpful diagram illustrating how the past regime has been transformed into the current regime.

[240] Since the entry into force of the 2002 regulatory framework, the Commission had opened proceedings under Art 226 EC against the Member States in some 90 cases due to failures to implement correctly the requirements of the framework. The alleged failures cover a wide range of provisions within the regulatory framework, eg the powers that national regulatory authorities are to be given, the independence of NRAs, the provision of transitional measures to ensure that there is no legal vacuum during the transition period, the provision of number portability systems and directory enquiry services: see Commission MEMOs (05) 478 of 14 December 2005 and (06) 487 of 13 December 2006.

[241] Dir 2002/21 on a common regulatory framework for electronic communications networks and services (Framework Directive), OJ 2002 L108/33: Vol II, App E.17.

[242] See Recital (5).

[243] Dir 2002/19 on access to, and interconnection of, electronic communications networks and associated facilities (Access Directive), OJ 2002 L108/7: Vol II, App E.18.

[244] Dir 2002/20 on the authorisation of electronic communications networks and services (Authorisation Directive), OJ 2002 L108/21: Vol II, App E.19.

[245] Dir 2002/22 on universal service and users' rights relating to electronic communications networks and services (Universal Service Directive), OJ 2002 L108/51: Vol II, App E.20.

[246] Dir 2002/58 concerning the processing of personal data and the protection of privacy in the electronic communications sector (Directive on privacy and electronic communications), OJ 2002 L201/37. This Directive replaces Dir 97/66/EC on the processing of personal data and protection of privacy, OJ 1998 L24/1.

[247] Dir 2002/77 on competition in the markets for electronic communications networks and services, OJ 2002 L249/21: See Vol II, App E.21. The following directives are consequently

framework. This Directive consolidates and recasts pre-existing liberalisation directives adopted under Article 86 of the Treaty[248] so as to take account of the Framework Directive, the Specific Directives, technological developments and experience gained through the implementation of the Telecommunications Services Directive.[249]

Scope of the regulatory framework. The 2002 framework replaces or repeals **12.090** much of the pre-existing telecommunications legislation at the Community level. It does not, however, cover Community legislation concerned with telecommunications terminal equipment,[250] which establishes a framework for the sale, use and free movement of radio equipment and telecommunications terminal equipment.[251] It excludes obligations imposed by national law, in accordance with Community law, or other obligations imposed by Community law in respect of services provided using electronic communications networks or services.[252] National measures pursuing general interest objectives, in particular relating to content regulation or audio-visual policy, are also excluded.[253]

The plan of this Section. This Section addresses the key provisions in each **12.091** of the directives within the regulatory framework, except for the Directive on privacy and electronic communications that does not concern issues of competition law. Reference is also made to the important aspects of the Radio Spectrum Decision and to initiatives for reform. A more comprehensive treatment of the communications regulatory framework is provided in specialist works on communications policy and regulation.[254]

(i) The Framework Directive

Harmonisation. The Framework Directive[255] is designed to create a harmonised **12.092** framework for communications regulation across the Community and is aimed at

---

repealed: (1) Dir 90/388 (Telecommunications Services Directive); (2) Arts 2 and 3 of Dir 94/46 (Satellite); (3) Dir 95/51 (Cable); (4) Dir 96/2 (Mobile); (5) Dir 96/19 (Full Competition); (6) Dir 1999/64 (Cable Ownership).

[248] Dir 90/388, OJ 1990 L192/10.

[249] Dir on Competition in the Markets for Electronic Communications Services (n 245, above) Recital (6).

[250] Dir 1999/5 on radio equipment and telecommunications terminal equipment and the mutual recognition of their conformity, OJ 1999 L91/10.

[251] Framework Directive (n 241, above) Art 1(4).

[252] Framework Directive, Art 1(2).

[253] Framework Directive, Art 1(3). See para 12.095, below.

[254] Nihoul and Rodford, *EU Electronic Communications Law* (2004); Garzaniti, *Telecommunications, Broadcasting and the Internet – EU Competition Law & Regulation* (2nd edn, 2003); Koenig, Bartosch and Braun (ed), *EC Competition and Telecommunications Law* (2002). See also Faull & Nikpay (eds), *The EC Law of Competition* (2nd ed, 2007), Chap 13; Larouche, *Competition Law and Regulation in European Telecommunications* (2000).

[255] Dir 2002/21 on a common regulatory framework for electronic communications networks and services (Framework Directive), OJ 2002 L108/33: Vol II, App E.17.

fostering effective competition, contributing to the development of the internal market and promoting the interests of consumers.[256] In order to bring about these objectives, the Framework Directive sets out the obligations on regulatory authorities ('NRAs'), indicates the powers and resources that they should have, and sets out a cooperation mechanism between NRAs and the Commission.[257]

12.093 **Obligations on NRAs.** Article 8 of the Framework Directive sets out the key regulatory principles and policy objectives that NRAs must observe when carrying out their tasks under the framework. Notably, the promotion of competition features prominently in these duties,[258] thus emphasising the increased relevance of competition law principles and case law to the communications sector. There are, however, further obligations interspersed throughout the Framework Directive. These include the obligations (i) to act impartially and transparently;[259] (ii) to consult with interested parties where the regulatory measures intended have a significant impact on the relevant market;[260] (iii) to act according to objective, transparent, non-discriminatory and proportionate criteria in the management of radio frequency and numbering resources;[261] (iv) to ensure the confidentiality of information collected from undertakings;[262] and (v) to resolve disputes.[263] The Framework Directive also requires effective rights of appeal for undertakings affected by a decision of a NRA to a body which has the appropriate level of expertise and which is able to take into account the merits of the case.[264]

12.094 **Technology neutrality.** One of the central aims of the regulatory framework is to promote technology neutrality in the approach to regulation so that a single framework governs the transmission of communications across the increasingly converging telecommunications, media and information technology sectors.[265] Consequently, whereas the different technologies were each previously governed

---

[256] Framework Directive (n 255, above) Art 8, which sets out these policy objectives and regulatory principles in greater detail.

[257] See, for example, the Framework Directive: Recitals (11) and (16); Art 3 (National Regulatory Authorities); Art 4 (Rights of Appeal); Art 5 (Provision of Information); Art 7 (Consolidating the internal market for electronic communications); Art 8 (Policy objectives and regulatory principles); Art 9 (Management of radio frequencies for electronic communications services); Art 10 (Numbering, naming and addressing); Art 11 (Rights of way); Art 17 (Standardisation); Art 18 (Interoperability of digital interactive television services) and Art 19 (Harmonisation procedures).

[258] Framework Directive (n 255, above) Arts 8(2) and 8(3)(c).

[259] ibid, Art 3(3).

[260] ibid, Art 6.

[261] ibid, Arts 9(1) and 10(1).

[262] ibid, Arts 5(3) and 20(4).

[263] ibid, Art 20.

[264] ibid, Art 4.

[265] Framework Directive (n 255, above) Recitals (5) and (18) and Art 8. However, the Framework Directive distinguishes between the regulation of transmission and the regulation of content: see Framework Directive (Recital (5)) and para 12.095, below.

by separate measures, the Framework Directive (and consequently the framework) applies to all electronic communications networks ('ECNs') and electronic communications services ('ECSs'), which are accordingly defined in broad terms.[266] This requirement does not, however, preclude a NRA from taking proportionate steps to promote a specific service where justified, such as digital television.[267]

Exclusion of content. Despite its broad scope, the regulatory framework does **12.095** not extend to national measures relating to content regulation and audiovisual policy. It does not therefore cover television content delivered over ECNs or using ECSs. This recognises the fact that content regulation will take into account distinct policy objectives such as cultural and linguistic diversity and media pluralism.[268] Accordingly, the Television without Frontiers Directive[269] remains in place. At the end of 2005, the Commission announced proposals for the reform of the Television Without Frontiers Directive so that the modernised replacement directive would govern TV and TV-like services in order to take account of technological developments.[270]

---

[266] These terms are defined in Art 2 of the Framework Directive, which refers to 'the conveyance of signals by wire, by radio, by optical or by other electromagnetic means, including satellite networks, fixed (circuit- and packet switched, including Internet) and mobile terrestrial networks, electricity cable systems, to the extent that they are used for the purpose of transmitting signals, networks used for radio and television broadcasting, and cable television networks, irrespective of the type of information conveyed.'

[267] Framework Directive (n 255, above) Recital (18).

[268] The Framework Directive does not provide a specific definition of 'content'. Recital (5) indicates that broadcasting services (audiovisual content), financial services and 'information society services' do not fall within the regulatory framework. The term 'information society service' is defined in Dir 98/34 (as amended by Dir 98/48) to encapsulate a wide range of services that are or will be delivered over the internet. These services (as defined in these directives) are specifically excluded from the definition of an ECS increased convergence may make it difficult in the future to distinguish between those internet services that are covered by the framework and those that are not. Recital (10) of the Framework Directive, however, indicates that most online services are not intended to be covered by the framework and emphasises that only those services which consist 'wholly or mainly' of the conveyance of signals on electronic communications networks are intended to be covered. It also recognises that the same undertaking, eg an internet service provider, may provide services that are covered by the framework, such as access to the internet, and other services which are not covered, such as the provision of web-based content. Voice telephony and email are explicitly indicated to constitute ECSs. Voice over Internet Protocol (VoIP) is also covered by the Framework Directive. See the Commission Staff Working Document, 'The treatment of Voice over, Internet Protocol (VoIP) under the EU Regulatory Framework – An Information and Consultation Document', 14 June 2004.

[269] See Dir 89/552 on the coordination of certain provisions laid down by Law, Regulation or Administrative Action in Member States concerning the pursuit of television broadcasting activities (as subsequently amended), OJ 1989 L298/23.

[270] See the Commission's 'Proposal for a Directive of the European Parliament and of the Council Amending Council Directive 89/552/EEC on the coordination of certain provisions laid down by law, regulation or administrative action in Member States concerning the pursuit of television broadcasting services', COM(2005)646 final and Press Release IP/05/1573 (13 December 2005). The proposal distinguishes between 'linear' services (eg scheduled broadcasting via traditional TV,

12.096 **Derogations.**   The Framework Directive and the Specific Directives are without prejudice to further measures that Member States adopt to ensure the protection of essential security interests, to safeguard public policy and public security and to permit the investigation, detection and prosecution of criminal offences.[271]

12.097 **Imposition of regulatory obligations on undertakings.**   The Authorisation Directive[272] introduces a harmonised and 'self executing' framework for the authorisation of undertakings to provide ECNs and ECSs (the 'general authorisation regime'). As a result, they may commence operations without the need for a licence or other form of specific authorisation by a NRA,[273] so long as they comply with a set of pre-set conditions. However, the Framework Directive[274] enables the imposition of further *ex ante* obligations on undertakings that are found to be in a position of significant market power ('SMP').[275] There are also specific provisions within the Directive (i) allowing NRAs to impose non-SMP related conditions on undertakings in order to encourage co-location and facility sharing;[276] and (ii) requiring NRAs to impose accounting separation and financial reporting obligations on undertakings that provide public ECNs or public ECSs and enjoy special or exclusive rights (in other sectors) in the same or another Member State.[277]

12.098 ***Ex ante* conditions on operators with SMP.**   The Framework Directive requires NRAs to analyse relevant markets within the communications sector by carrying out market reviews in order to determine whether or not those markets are 'effectively competitive'.[278] Where a NRA determines that a market is not effectively competitive, it is required to identify undertakings with SMP on that market and impose on them appropriate specific regulatory obligations, or maintain or amend such obligations where they already exist. These regulatory obligations

---

the internet, or mobile phones, which 'pushes' content to viewers), and 'non-linear' ones, such as on-demand films or news, which the viewer 'pulls' from a network. It is proposed that today's TV broadcasting rules would apply to linear services in a modernised, more flexible form, whereas non-linear ones would be subject only to a basic set of minimum principles, eg to protect minors, prevent incitement to racial hatred and outlaw surreptitious advertising. It is hoped that harmonising these rules across the Community will ensure that the regulatory burden on audiovisual media service suppliers is reduced so that they will need only to comply with the rules of the Member State in which they are established, and not with the disparate rules of all the Member States receiving their services. See also the Commission's MEMO(05)475 of 13 December 2005: 'The Commission Proposal for a Modernisation of the Television without Frontiers Directive: Frequently Asked Questions.'

271 Framework Directive (n 255, above) Recital (7) and Art 1.
272 Authorisation Directive (n 244, above).
273 Paras 12.111–12.112, below, and Authorisation Directive, Recital (8). Regulatory obligations may also be imposed pursuant to other provisions of the Specific Directives, Recital (8).
274 Framework Directive (n 255, above).
275 See para 12.098, below.
276 Framework Directive (n 255, above) Art 12.
277 ibid, Art 13.
278 ibid, Art 16.

are mandated in the Access Directive (Articles 9–13)[279] and the Universal Service Directive (Articles 16–19).[280] Where a NRA finds that a relevant market is 'effectively competitive', the NRA is required to withdraw any pre-existing sector specific obligations imposed on undertakings operating in that market.[281] The aim of this mechanism is to reduce *ex ante* sector-specific obligations as competition within markets develops.

The link between 'effectively competitive' and SMP.   Although the Framework   **12.099**
Directive does not define the concept of 'effectively competitive',[282] Recital (27) of the Directive indicates that a market will not be effectively competitive where there are one or more undertakings with SMP and where national and Community competition law remedies are not sufficient to remedy the problem. The notion of effective competition therefore turns upon the existence of undertakings with SMP in a relevant market. SMP itself is defined in Article 14(2) of the Framework Directive as a 'position equivalent to dominance' under Article 82, as defined by the Community Courts,[283] and includes the concept of 'joint dominance'.[284]

SMP requires a 'prospective' analysis.   In most respects, the exercise of deter-   **12.100**
mining SMP is similar to that of determining dominance.[285] It begins with the process of market definition and applies competition law methodology[286] to the review of the conditions of competition on that market. However, unlike the retrospective analysis of dominance under Article 82, the concepts of 'effective

---

[279] See paras 12.105 *et seq*, below, on the Access Directive (n 243, above): Art 9 (transparency); Art 10 (non-discrimination); Art 11 (accounting separation); Art 12 (access to and use of specific network facilities)); and Art 13 (price control and cost accounting obligations).

[280] See paras 12.113 *et seq*, below on the Universal Service Directive (n 245, above): Art 16 (review of existing obligations); Art 17 (regulatory controls on retails services); Art 18 (regulatory controls on the minimum set of leased lines)); and Art 19 (carrier selection and carrier pre-selection).

[281] Framework Directive (n 255, above) Art 16(3).

[282] See also Koenig, Bartosch and Braun (n 254, above) for discussion of the concept of 'effective competition' in EC law.

[283] Framework Directive (n 255, above) Recital (25). The notion of SMP also existed under the 1998 regulatory framework. However, it was defined more rigidly whereby undertakings with more than 25 per cent market share in a specified market (such as fixed telephony, mobile telephony and leased lines) were presumed to have SMP. See, eg Dir 97/51 (ONP Framework Directive), OJ 1997 L295/23; Dir 98/10 (Voice Telephony Directive), OJ 1998 L101/224 and Dir 98/61 (Interconnection Directive), OJ 1998 L268/37.

[284] See, eg Case IE/2004/0121: notification under the Art 7 procedure (para 12.102, below) by the Irish NRA of its finding that Vodafone and O2 were jointly dominant on the wholsesale market for mobile access and call origination; the Commission did not object but noted that the analysis had focused on competitive effects at retail level and recommended that the NRA should monitor the performance of competitors at wholesale level. The UK NRA, Ofcom, also notified a provisional finding of SMP based on collective dominance in the market for broadcasting transmission services, but this was withdrawn after the Commission expressed doubts: see on both these cases, Bernaerts and Kramer, 'First collective dominance cases under the European consultation mechanism in electronic communications' (2005) 3 EC Competition Newsletter 47.

[285] See Chap 10, above on Art 82 generally and Chap 4, above on market definition.

[286] Access Directive (n 243, above) Recital (13).

competition' and SMP under the Framework Directive require a prospective analysis in order to ascertain whether the market is prospectively competitive and thus whether any lack of effective competition is durable.[287] In this regard, it may be said that the analysis required under the Framework Directive draws upon the analytical techniques developed under the EC Merger Control Regulation. A NRA's assessment of the prospective state of competition on a relevant market, in other words whether an undertaking's position of SMP is durable, therefore determines whether an undertaking has SMP.[288] The outcome of this assessment plays an important role in the setting of further specific regulatory obligations on the undertaking(s) concerned.[289]

12.101 **The Recommendation on Relevant Markets.** In order to assist NRAs, the Commission has adopted a 'Recommendation' on relevant product and services markets within the communications sector.[290] The Recommendation provides a list of relevant markets that it regards as potentially susceptible to *ex ante* regulation, determined in accordance with competition law principles and differentiating between markets at wholesale and retail level.[291] Although the Recommendation is not binding on the NRAs, they are nevertheless required to take 'utmost account' of it.[292] Where, for example, a NRA wishes to define a relevant

---

287 Framework Directive (n 255, above) Recital (27). The SMP Guidelines (para 12.102, below) note (at para 28) the similarity between merger control analysis and SMP analysis but also note the distinction in that SMP analysis is intended to be carried out periodically, unlike merger control analysis. For EC merger control more generally, see Chap 8, above.

288 The Framework Directive (n 255, above) leaves to the Member States to determine (under national legislation) the temporal scope of their respective NRAs' market reviews. The SMP Guidelines state that the actual period used should reflect the specific characteristics of the market (para 20).

289 Para 12.098, above. See, eg *Hutchison 3G Ltd v Office of Communications* [2005] CAT 39, judgment of 29 November 2005, where the UK Competition Appeal Tribunal held that Ofcom had erred in its assessment of market power in the mobile voice telephony market by failing to consider the extent of countervailing buyer power; *Hutchison 3G Ireland Ltd v Commission for Communications,* Decn 02/05 of 26 September 2005, where the Irish Electronic Communications Appeals Panel annulled a similar determination of SMP by the Irish NRA; *Kroniklijke KPN NV v Independent Post and Telecommunications Authority,* Cases AWB 05/903, etc, judgment of 29 August 2006, where the Netherlands Trade and Industry Appeals Tribunal annulled a decn by the Dutch NRA that each of the mobile operators had SMP in the markets for mobile call termination and the resulting imposition of price controls.

290 Commission Recommendation on relevant product and service markets within the electronic communications sector susceptible to *ex ante* regulation in accordance with Dir 2002/21/EC of the European Parliament and of the Council on a common regulatory framework for electronic communication networks and services, OJ 2003 L114/45: Vol II, App E.22. This recommendation is accompanied by an Explanatory Memorandum, available at http://europa.eu.int/information_society/policy/ecomm/doc/info_centre/recomm_guidelines/relevant_markets/en1_2003_497.pdf.

291 For market definition generally, see Chap 4, above. For further discussion of the Recommendation, see Hocepied, 'The approach to market definiation in the Commission's Guidelines and Recommendation' in Buigues and Rey (eds), *The Economics of Antitrust and Regulation in Telecommunications* (2004), Chap 5.

292 Framework Directive (n 255, above) Art 16, which indicates that analysis shall be carried out in collaboration with the national competition authorities where appropriate.

market which differs from those defined in the Recommendation and would affect trade between Member States, it is required to notify the Commission in advance.[293] If the Commission has serious doubts as to the compatibility of the NRA's proposal with the single market, Community law and, in particular, the objectives of the regulatory framework, the Commission is entitled to require the NRA concerned to withdraw the measure.[294] In June 2006, the Commission published for consultation a draft revised Recommendation as part of its proposals for reform of the regulatory framework.[295] The draft revised Recommendation reduces from 18 to 12 the number of relevant markets suitable for *ex ante* regulation. Following the consultation, the Commission expects to adopt a new Recommendation in the first part of 2007, to take immediate effect.[296]

The SMP Guidelines. The Commission has also adopted guidelines for market **12.102** analysis and the assessment of SMP (the 'SMP Guidelines').[297] These provide a very useful analytical framework for both NRAs and undertakings, in particular, by providing guidance in relation to the prospective nature of a market review. In this regard, the SMP Guidelines clarify that the NRAs are required to conduct a 'forward looking, structural evaluation of the market, based on existing market conditions';[298] that NRAs should take into account 'expected or foreseeable market developments over the course of a reasonable period' and that 'NRAs enjoy discretionary powers which reflect the complexity of all the relevant factors that must be assessed (economic, factual and legal) when identifying the relevant market and determining the existence of undertakings with SMP'.[299] The Commission has therefore acknowledged that a market defined for the purpose of the regulatory framework, in the context of *ex ante* regulation, may differ from that adopted for the purpose of application of the competition rules to a situation occurring in the past.[300] The SMP Guidelines also set out the relevant criteria for assessing SMP. These draw from the criteria developed by the Community Courts and the Commission itself in relation to both Article 82 and cases under the EC Merger

---

[293] ibid, Art 15(3).

[294] ibid, Art 7(4).

[295] SEC(2006)837, available at http://ec.europa.eu/information_society/policy/ecomm/doc/info_centre/public_consult/review/recommendation_final.pdf. For the reform proposals, see para 12.120, below.

[296] See Bernaerts, 'Time to deregulate – Commission consultation on a new EU framework for electronic communications' (2006) 3 EC Competition Policy Newsletter 7.

[297] Commission guidelines on market analysis and the assessment of significant market power under the Community regulatory framework for electronic communications networks and services (the 'SMP Guidelines'), OJ 2002 C165/6: Vol II, App E.25. NRAs are required to take utmost account of these guidelines in their market reviews: Framework Directive (n 255, above) Art 15(3)).

[298] SMP Guidelines (above) para 20. The SMP Guidelines also note that, 'NRAs' market analyses should not ignore, where relevant, past evidence when assessing future prospects of the relevant market' (para 27).

[299] SMP Guidelines (above) para 22.

[300] ibid, para 37.

Regulation, such as market shares, barriers to entry, countervailing buyer power and levels of competition on the market.[301]

12.103 **SMP Conditions.**   SMP conditions may be imposed under the Framework Directive, in conjunction with either the Universal Service Directive or the Access Directive. Once an undertaking is determined to have SMP, the imposition of appropriate conditions on that undertaking becomes mandatory.[302] The conditions deriving from the Universal Service Directive[303] relate mainly to the protection of end-users, some of whom may be entirely dependent on the undertaking in question for their communication services.[304] These conditions include the provision of retail services,[305] leased lines[306] and carrier selection/carrier pre-selection.[307] The conditions deriving from the Access Directive[308] relate mainly to ensuring adequate access, interconnection and interoperability between communications operators in the interests of end-users.[309] These conditions include the obligations of transparency,[310] non-discrimination,[311] accounting separation,[312] access to, and use of, specific network facilities[313] and price control and cost accounting obligations.[314] In imposing each of these conditions on undertakings, NRAs must have regard to the principles of objectivity, proportionality, transparency and non-discrimination.[315] Provisions for the enforcement of these specific conditions and for the provision of information under them is set out in the Authorisation Directive.[316]

---

[301] ibid, paras 72–106. Dominance for the purpose of Art 82 is discussed in Chap 10, above.

[302] Universal Service Directive (n 245, above) Arts 17–19; Access Directive, Art 8(2).

[303] Universal Service Directive (n 245, above).

[304] ibid, Recital (26).

[305] ibid, Art 17.

[306] ibid, Art 18.

[307] ibid, Art 19.

[308] Access Directive (n 243, above).

[309] Access Directive, Recital (6).

[310] ibid, Art 9.

[311] ibid, Art 10.

[312] ibid, Art 11.

[313] ibid, Art 12.

[314] ibid, Art 13. Such obligations are justified where the NRA's market analysis indicates that a lack of effective competition means that the operator concerned might be able to sustain excessive prices or apply a price squeeze to the detriment of end-users. However, in setting these obligations, NRAs are required to (1) take into account the investment made by the operator and (2) the risks involved and allow him a reasonable rate of return on adequate capital employed. The controls employed by the NRA must promote efficiency, sustainable competition and maximum consumer benefits. In the UK, and several other Member States, a 'LRIC' (long run incremental cost) model is used as the basis for deriving applicable cost controls. The Commission has implicitly authorised the use of LRIC-based measures by several NRAs pursuant to the Article 7(4) notification procedure. The burden of proving that an operator has complied with the cost obligations, lies with the operator concerned.

[315] Universal Service Directive (n 245, above) Arts 3(2), 9(5) and 17(2); and Access Directive, Arts 5(3) and 8(4).

[316] Authorisation Directive (n 244, above) Arts 10 and 11.

The Commission's review of SMP designations. Prior to designating an **12.104**
undertaking with SMP, NRAs are required to consult with the Commission and
other NRAs in accordance with the requirements of Article 7 of the Framework
Directive.[317] The Framework Directive provides for this consultation to be conducted in parallel with the NRA's consultation with interested parties.[318] Where
the Commission expresses serious doubts as to the proposed designation, either
because it involves the adoption of a market definition that differs from the
Commission's Recommendation[319] or as regards the decision concerning SMP,
then the NRA is required not to adopt the proposed measure for a further two
months.[320] During this time, the Commission may take a decision requiring the
NRA to withdraw the proposed measure (a 'veto decision') and provide detailed
and objective reasons to the NRA in question. In practice, thus far, the Commission
has expressed serious doubts in relatively few cases and issued veto decisions only
in rare cases.[321] On those occasions where the Commission has indicated serious
doubts or required withdrawal of a draft measure, the Commission's review of the
proposed designation/measure has indicated a careful evaluation of the evidence
collected by the NRA in question and a thorough review of the NRA's analysis.[322]

---

[317] Framework Directive (n 255, above) Arts 6 and 7(3). See also the Commission
Recommendation on notifications, time limits and consultations provided for in Article 7 of
Directive 2002/21 of the European Parliament and of the Council on a common regulatory framework for electronic communications networks and services, OJ 2003 L190/13. The Commission
published a review of the working of the consultation mechanism in the Framework Directive:
Communication on Market Reviews under the EU Regulatory Framework, COM(2006) 28 final,
6 February 2006.

[318] Recognising the administrative burden that this process would entail, the Commission
has set up two internal 'Task forces' to manage the consultation process; one task force is in DG
Competition and the other is in DG Information Society. It is understood that the two task forces
cooperate closely. See, Krüger and Di Mauro, 'The Article 7 consultation mechanism: managing
the consolidation of the internal market for electronic communications' (2003) 3 EC Competition
Policy Newsletter 33.

[319] See para 12.101, above.

[320] Framework Directive (n 255, above) Art 7(4).

[321] MEMO (06) 59 (7 February 2006), 'Electronic communications: the Article 7 Procedure
and the role of the Commission – frequently asked questions'. The Commission comments on
measures proposed by NRAs are available on DG Information Society's website.

[322] See, eg Case DE/2005/0144, letter of 11 March 2005, German NRA's review of the market
for call termination on individual public telephone networks provided at a fixed location; Cases
FI/2003/0024 and FI/2003/0027, Decn of 20 February 2004 requiring withdrawal of the notified draft measure by Finnish NRA in relation to the market for publicly available international
telephone services provided at a fixed location for residential and non-residential customers; Case
FI/2004/0082, Decn of 5 October 2004 requiring withdrawal of the notified draft measure by
Finnish NRA in relation to market for access and call origination on public mobile telephone networks in Finland; Case AT/2004/0090, Decn of 20 October 2004 requiring withdrawal of the
notified draft measure by the Austrian NRA in relation to the market for transit services in the fixed
public telephone network in Austria. These decns are available on DG Information Society's website
and summarised in *Report on Competition Policy* (2004), Vol 1, points 301–304. For discussion, see
Di Mauro and Inotai, (2004) 2 EC Competition Policy Newsletter 52; Grewe, Inotai and Kramer,
(2005) 1 EC Competition Policy Newsletter 49.

Once the Commission announces its serious doubts in relation to a notified designation/measure, third parties are invited to submit observations prior to the Commission adopting its final decision and NRAs are at liberty to withdraw their notification.[323]

(ii) The Access Directive

12.105 **Access and interconnection.** 'Access'[324] and 'interconnection'[325] are crucial to the operation of a communications network and to deliver benefits to end-users. Without access and/or interconnection agreements between operators, users subscribing to one network would not be able to communicate with (or make calls to) users subscribing to other networks; in other words, there would be no 'end-to-end connectivity'.[326] Agreements on access and interconnection also lead to the interoperability of services between operators, by conforming technical standards, interfaces and/or network functions. Greater interoperability of services benefits end-users by improving freedom of choice.[327]

12.106 **Aims of the Access Directive.** The Access Directive[328] is designed to harmonise the way in which Member States regulate 'access' to and 'interconnection'[329] of ECNs and associated facilities between undertakings in order to achieve sustainable competition, interoperability and consumer benefits.[330] The Directive also establishes rights and obligations for undertakings seeking interconnection and sets out NRAs' regulatory objectives and the procedures that NRAs are required to follow to ensure that any obligation imposed remains appropriate.[331] There are also provisions for the distribution of digital television services.[332]

---

323 Framework Directive (n 255, above) para 16.

324 'Access' is defined in Art 2(a) of the Access Directive. It means the making available of facilities and/or services, to another, under defined conditions, on either an exclusive or non-exclusive basis for the purposes of providing ECNs. This definition is non-exhaustive and the Access Directive gives examples of what access can include, such as, access to the local loop and to facilities and services necessary to provide services over the local loop.

325 'Interconnection' is a specific type of access implemented between public network operators. It is defined in Art 2(b) of the Access Directive as 'the physical and logical linking of public communications networks used by the same or a different undertaking in order to allow the users of one undertaking to communicate with users of the same or another undertaking, or to access services provided by another undertaking'.

326 Access Directive, Recital (8).

327 ibid.

328 Dir 2002/19 on access to, and interconnection of, electronic communications networks and associated facilities ('Access Directive'), OJ 2002 L108/7: Vol II, App E.18.

329 Although 'interconnection' is specifically defined to be a subset of 'access' (n 325, above), the Access Directive continues to use both terms throughout. The text here follows the terms of the Directive in this regard.

330 Access Directive, Art 1.

331 ibid.

332 See, eg Access Directive (n 328, above) Art 4(2). For these purposes, the Directive also provides a definition of 'wide-screen television services': Art 2(d).

Framework for access and interconnection. Member States are required to **12.107** create a framework for interconnection and access.[333] They must ensure that there are no restrictions preventing undertakings from the same Member State or from different Member States negotiating between themselves on technical or commercial arrangements for access and/or interconnection.[334] Member States must also ensure[335] that there are no legal or administrative measures which oblige operators[336] to grant access or interconnection on different terms for equivalent services and/or impose conditions that are not related to the actual access or interconnection services provided.[337]

Rights and obligations for undertakings. Operators of public communications **12.108** networks[338] have a right, and an obligation when requested by other undertakings so authorised, to negotiate interconnection[339] with the requesting undertaking in order to secure the provision.[340] Operators are also obliged to offer access and interconnection on terms which are consistent with the obligations imposed on them by their NRAs.[341] There are also confidentiality obligations in respect of information obtained through interconnection negotiations.[342]

Powers and responsibilities of NRAs. Article 5 of the Access Directive sets out **12.109** a range of powers for NRAs to impose obligations on undertakings in order to

---

[333] Access Directive (n 328, above). Recital (6) of the Access Directive notes the importance of creating a framework to ensure that the market functions effectively because in some markets there will be significant disparities in bargaining power between undertakings or certain undertakings may rely on others for the delivery of services. The Directive states that NRAs should have the power to secure, where commercial negotiation fails, adequate access and interconnection and interoperability of services in the interest of end-users. In particular, NRAs may ensure end-to-end connectivity by imposing proportionate obligations on undertakings that control access to end-users. See para 12.109, below.

[334] ibid, Art 3. Where undertakings from different Member States are concerned, the Directive states that the undertaking requesting access or interconnection does not need to be authorised in the Member State where the request is made so long as it is not operating an ECN or providing an ECS in that State.

[335] These obligations are without prejudice to obligations imposed under the Universal Service Directive (n 245, above) (see paras 12.113 *et seq*, below) and the Authorisation Directive (see paras 12.110 *et seq*, below)

[336] The Access Directive (n 328, above) also provides a specific definition for 'operator' (at Art 2(c)), although it also continues to use the term 'undertaking' (as defined in competition law). 'Operator' means an undertaking 'providing or authorised to provide a public communications network or an associated facility'.

[337] These obligations are designed to prevent market distortion: see Access Directive, Recital (7).

[338] Note that these rights and obligations apply to a limited class of operator; providers of associated facilities are excluded.

[339] Note also that these rights and obligations are limited to 'interconnection' and have not been extended to 'access'.

[340] Access Directive (n 328, above) Art 4(1).

[341] ibid, Art 4(1).

[342] ibid, Art 4(3).

ensure access and interconnection.[343] These obligations are distinct from the obligations to provide access and interconnection imposed on undertakings in a position of SMP[344] and can also be imposed on undertakings regardless of whether they have SMP. The obligations that NRAs may impose under Article 5 include (1) the obligation to interconnect where necessary to ensure end-to-end connectivity; and (2) the obligation to provide access on fair, reasonable and non-discriminatory terms to other facilities (as set out in Annex I, Part II of the Directive) where these are necessary to ensure accessibility for end-users to digital radio and television broadcasting services.[345] NRAs may lay down technical or operational conditions on providers or beneficiaries of such access where necessary to ensure the normal operation of the network.[346] NRAs must also be authorised to intervene on their own initiative (where justified) or at the request of one of the parties in order to secure the policy objectives of the regulatory framework.[347] Chapter III of the Access Directive contains obligations on NRAs to review existing obligations on operators to provide access and interconnection,[348] obligations to review markets[349] and further powers on NRAs to impose conditions on operators, such as obligations relating to conditional access systems and other facilities[350] and conditions on operators with SMP.[351] Chapter IV of the Access Directive contains procedural provisions.

(iii) The Authorisation Directive

12.110   **The general authorisation regime.**   The aim of the Authorisation Directive[352] is to implement an internal market in ECNs and ECSs through the harmonisation[353] and simplification of authorisation rules and conditions throughout the Community.[354] In order to achieve this, the Directive requires Member States to

---

[343] The conditions or obligations imposed must be objective, transparent, proportionate and non-discriminatory and must be implemented in accordance with the provisions of Arts 6 and 7 of the Access Directive.

[344] The SMP obligations are set out in Arts 8–13 of the Access Directive.

[345] Access Directive (n 326, above) Art 5(1).

[346] ibid, Art 5(2).

[347] ibid, Art 5(4). The policy objectives of the framework are set out in the Framework Directive (n 253, above) Art 8.

[348] Access Directive (n 328, above) Art 7.

[349] See para 12.098, above.

[350] Access Directive, Art 6. These obligations relate *inter alia* to conditional access to digital television and radio services.

[351] Specifically in relation to conditions on operators with SMP, see para 12.098, above.

[352] Dir 2002/20 on the authorisation of electronic communications networks and services (Authorisation Directive), OJ 2002 L108/21: Vol II, App E.19.

[353] Authorisation Directive, Recital (9) notes the importance of ensuring a level playing field throughout the Community and the importance of facilitating cross-border negotiation of interconnection between public communications networks.

[354] ibid, Art 1. The scope of the Authorisation Directive is, however, limited in respect of rights to use radio frequencies and conditional access systems: Authorisation Directive, Recitals (5) and (6).

ensure the freedom of undertakings to provide ECNs and ECSs. This freedom is subject to certain conditions stipulated in the Directive itself (the conditions of 'general authorisation'[355]) and can be curtailed where Member States consider it necessary to prevent such activities for the reasons set out in Article 46(1) of the EC Treaty, in particular, measures regarding public policy, public security and public health.[356] Consequently, undertakings are no longer required to apply for a licence, or any another form of *a priori* authorisation, in order to provide ECNs or ECSs;[357] so long as they comply with the relevant conditions of general authorisation (as transposed into national law), they can automatically start to provide ECNs and ECSs.[358] At most, undertakings may be required to a submit notification of their intention to provide ECNs and ECSs.[359] These conditions are distinct from the specific obligations imposed on undertakings with SMP[360] and should be considered to create rights and obligations which are legally separate from those created under the specific obligations.[361] In addition to the introduction of the general authorisation regime, the Authorisation Directive also contains provisions relating to the installation of facilities[362] and administrative charges.[363]

The conditions of general authorisation.   The general authorisation of undertakings for the provision of ECNs and ECSs may be subject only to the conditions listed in the Annex to the Directive.[364] The specific subject-matter of each of these conditions varies considerably and includes matters such as interoperability of services and interconnection of networks,[365] consumer protection rules,[366]

12.111

---

[355]   See para 12.111, below.

[356]   Authorisation Directive (n 352, above) Art 2.

[357]   The definition of ECNs and ECSs adopted in Dir 2002/21 on a common regulatory framework for electronic communications networks and services (Framework Directive), OJ 2002 L108/33 continues to apply for the purposes of the Authorisation Directive; the Authorisation Directive therefore also adopts a technology neutral approach. The recitals to the Authorisation Directive note the exclusion of content from its scope and recognise that where an undertaking provides an ECS together with broadcasting content services, additional obligations may be imposed on it in respect of activities as a content provider: see Recital (20).

[358]   The minimum rights conferred by general authorisation are set out at Art 4 of the Authorisation Directive. The Directive also lays down guidelines for enforcement of the conditions of general authorisation and for the provision of information under the general authorisation: see Arts 10 and 11 of the Authorisation Directive.

[359]   The Licensing Directive (Dir 97/13, OJ 1997 L117/15) is repealed by the Authorisation Directive. Telecommunications licences under which ECN or ECS providers in the Community previously operated have been repealed with the implementation of the Authorisation Directive into national law.

[360]   See para 12.098, above.

[361]   Authorisation Directive (n 352, above) Art 6(2).

[362]   ibid, Arts 9 and 13.

[363]   ibid, Art 12.

[364]   The Annex covers conditions which may be attached to (1) general authorisation; (2) rights of use for radio frequencies; and (3) rights of use of numbers.

[365]   ibid, Annex (Part A), condition 3.

[366]   ibid, Annex (Part A), condition 8.

enabling of legal interception by competent national authorities,[367] and 'must carry' obligations.[368] These conditions overlap with the conditions that may be imposed by NRAs under the remaining Specific Directives[369] and consequently refer back to these Directives. When implemented into national law, the Authorisation Directive also requires that the general authorisation conditions must be objectively justified in relation to the network or the service concerned, non-discriminatory, proportionate and transparent.[370]

12.112 **Special provisions for radio frequencies and numbers.** The provisions of the Authorisation Directive also apply to rights of use of radio frequencies and numbers and, accordingly, it introduces conditions of general authorisation for both these resources.[371] Parts B and C of the Annex to the Directive list the conditions of general authorisation applicable to both radio frequencies and numbers respectively. However, the Directive does not preclude Member States from authorising the use of radio frequencies or numbers under a separate grant of specific right (under, for example, licences)[372] in order *inter alia* to promote their efficient use, prevent interference or where a separate grant is unavoidable in view of the scarcity of resources.[373] Where specific rights are to be granted, the Authorisation Directive sets out general rules for the procedure and principles to be employed in making the grant.[374]

(iv) The Universal Service Directive

12.113 **Overview.** The Universal Service Directive (the 'USD') defines the minimum set of services (of a specified quality and at an affordable price) that all end-users, irrespective of their geographical location, are entitled to receive from designated undertakings providing publicly available electronic communications.[375] The USD's aim is to ensure the provision of such services through effective

---

367 ibid, Annex (Part A), condition 11.

368 ibid, Annex (Part A), condition 6.

369 Para 12.089, above.

370 Authorisation Directive (n 352, above) Recital (7) indicates that the least onerous authorisation system possible should be used in order to stimulate the development of new ECNs and ECSs, pan-European communications networks and services and to allow service providers and consumers to benefit from the economies of scale of the single market. Where ECNs and ECSs are not to be provided to the public, fewer and lighter conditions may be justified: Authorisation Directive, Recital (16).

371 ibid, Art 6(1). However, the general authorisation regime for radio frequencies is limited to situations where their use is for the provision of ECNs or ECNs for remuneration: Authorisation Directive, Recital (5).

372 Authorisation Directive (n 352, above) Recitals (11) to (14).

373 ibid, Recital (11) and Art 5.

374 ibid, Arts 5, 7 and 8.

375 Dir 2002/22 on universal service and users' rights relating to electronic communications networks and services ('Universal Service Directive'), OJ 2002 L108/51: Vol II, App E.20, Arts 1(2) and 2. The meaning of ECNs and ECSs is the same as in the Framework Directive (n 357, above), ie electronic communications network and electronic communications service.

competition and choice.[376] However, the USD recognises that regard must be had to specific national conditions, which may mean that ensuring universal service requires the provision of some services to some end-users at prices that depart from those resulting from normal market conditions.[377] It is left to Member States to determine the most efficient and appropriate means for ensuring the implementation of universal service, subject to observing the principles of objectivity, transparency, non-discrimination and proportionality.[378] Where the provision of these services requires a departure from normal market conditions, Member States are required to ensure a minimisation of market distortions whilst safeguarding the public interest.[379]

Structure of the USD.   Chapter II[380] of the USD sets out *inter alia* the services   **12.114** that are to be made available to end-users,[381] the designation of undertakings as universal service providers, quality of services, and the financing for universal service provision. Chapter III[382] of the USD deals with the imposition of obligations on undertakings with SMP.[383] Chapter IV[384] of the USD prescribes end-users' rights and interests. Chapter V[385] of the USD includes the 'general' and 'final' provisions, such as permitting Member States to include additional services within the universal service obligation, provisions for consultation with interested parties and an out-of-court dispute resolution system for disputes involving consumers in respect of issues covered by the USD. Further details in respect of the individual obligations are set out in Annexes to the USD.

Designation and financing of undertakings.   Member States may designate one   **12.115** or more undertakings to guarantee the provision of universal service.[386] Different undertakings (or sets of undertakings) may be designated to provide different elements of the universal service or to cover different parts of the national territory.[387]

---

[376] ibid, Art 1(1).
[377] ibid, Recital (4) and Art 1(2).
[378] ibid, Art 3.
[379] ibid, Art 3(2).
[380] ibid, Articles 3–15.
[381] These include the provision of access at a fixed location (Art 4); directory enquiry services (Art 7); public pay telephones (Art 6); special measures for disabled users (Art 7); affordability of tariffs for end-users (Art 9); measures which allow end-users to control their expenditure and avoid paying for services that have not been requested (Art 10); the setting of quality and service standards (Art 11).
[382] ibid, Arts 16–19.
[383] See also para 12.098, above, in relation to the imposition of *ex ante* conditions on operators with SMP.
[384] Universal Service Directive (n 375, above) Arts 20–31.
[385] ibid, Arts 32–40.
[386] ibid, Art 8(1).
[387] ibid, Art 8(1). eg, in the UK, both BT and Kingston Telecommunications have been designated as universal service providers. Kingston's designation covers only the Kingston upon Hull area whereas BT's designation covers the remainder of the territory.

However, the provision of universal services at affordable prices can lead to significant financial costs for designated undertakings. Where NRAs find that universal service obligations are leading to an unfair financial burden, they may introduce a mechanism to compensate that undertaking for their determined 'net costs'[388] from public funds and/or share the net cost of the universal service obligations between providers of ECNs and ECSs[389] within the Member State.

(v) The Directive on competition in the market for ECNs and ECSs

12.116 **Abolition of special and exclusive rights.** Article 86 of the Treaty requires the Commission to ensure that, in the case of public undertakings and undertakings enjoying special or exclusive rights,[390] Member States comply with their obligations under Community law. The Directive on competition in the market for ECNs and ECSs ('Directive on Competition')[391] consolidates and recasts the provision of several pre-existing directives, in particular Directive 90/388,[392] which required Member States to abolish special and exclusive rights for the provision of telecommunications services.[393] It also updates these provisions and the definitions employed so that they are in line with the 2002 regulatory framework. The obligations in this Directive relate not only to the special or exclusive rights of public undertakings, including vertically integrated undertakings, but also rights to use frequencies, directory services, universal service obligations, satellites and cable television networks.[394] In *Towercast v TDF*,[395] Towercast objected to a contract by which TDF was given a monopoly for broadcasting all Radio France programmes on FM frequencies until 31 December 2007, alleging that it contravened the Directive on Competition. The Conseil de la Concurrence referred to jurisprudence of the Court of Justice holding that the national authorities of Members States must refrain from applying national law if it does not comply with the stated aims of a directive that has not been transposed in time or which has been incorrectly transposed. Consequently, the Conseil found that the fact

---

[388] For the method for calculating the net cost, see Universal Service Directive, Art 12.

[389] ibid (n 375, above) Art 13.

[390] For Art 86 generally, see Chap 11, above.

[391] Dir 2002/77 on competition in the market for electronic communications networks and services ('Directive on Competition'), OJ 2002 L249/21: Vol II, App E.21. See COMP/39.157 *Teracom*, Press Release IP/05/343 (21 March 2005) (Commission calls on Sweden to abolish the monopoly of State-owned company, Teracom AB, as regards analogue terrestrial broadcasting and transmission services in order to comply with the Directive).

[392] Dir 90/388 on competition in the markets for telecommunications services, OJ 1990 L192/10.

[393] Directive on Competition, Recitals (1)–(6). For some recent instances of the Commission taking action to remove exclusivity obligations, see *Annual Report on Competition Policy* (2005), points 31 *et seq*.

[394] ibid, Arts 3–8.

[395] Conseil de la Concurrence, decn 03-MC-03 of 1 December 2003, BOCCRF 13 February 2004.

that the Directive on Competition had not been adopted by France at the time of the signature of the extended contract did not rule out the possibility that the extension of TDF's exclusive rights was abusive. This decision was confirmed by the Court of Appeal of Paris.[396] The Court of Appeal noted that it was very likely that TDF, at the time of the signature of the contract with Radio France in July 2000, was aware that its monopoly might be removed as a result of a forthcoming European directive.

(vi) Overview of the current position on radio spectrum policy

Radio spectrum policy. Spectrum policy is an important part of the regulatory framework and is one of the specific areas within the framework where the legislature has created a system of cooperation between the Member States in order to foster greater harmonisation and the development of an internal market.[397] In this regard, the Framework Directive requires Member States to ensure the effective management of radio frequencies.[398] NRAs are specifically required to encourage efficient use, and ensure the effective management, of radio frequencies.[399] In addition to these general objectives, the Framework Directive also requires Member States to promote the harmonisation of use of radio frequencies across the Community,[400] in accordance with the Radio Spectrum Decision, and enables Member States to make provision for undertakings to transfer rights to use radio frequencies under national rules.[401] The Authorisation Directive contains provisions for the licensing and use of radio spectrum. **12.117**

Radio Spectrum Decision. This is the principal legislative instrument relating to spectrum policy in the 2002 regulatory framework.[402] The Decision echoes the Framework Directive and emphasises the desirability of further harmonisation of Community policy on radio spectrum, in particular for services and applications with Community and European coverage, and in order to ensure the implementation of certain decisions of the CEPT.[403] In order to achieve its objectives, the **12.118**

---

[396] *Towercast v TDF*, judgment of 8 January 2004, BOCCRF 4 May 2004.

[397] The Commission has also emphasised the importance of a successful spectrum policy in achieving economic success: see Commission MEMO (05) 345 and Press Release IP/05/1199 (29 September 2005).

[398] Framework Directive (n 253, above) Art 9.

[399] ibid, Art 8(2)(d).

[400] ibid, Art 9(2).

[401] ibid, Art 9(3). In 2006, the Commission consulted with the Member States with regard to the introduction of both spectrum trading and spectrum liberalisation.

[402] Decn 676/2002 of the European Parliament and of the Council on a regulatory framework for radio spectrum policy in the European Community ('Radio Spectrum Decision'), OJ 2002 L108/1. Art 2 defines 'radio spectrum' to mean radio waves in frequencies between 9kHz and 3,000 GHz. 'Radio waves' means electromagnetic waves propagated in space without artificial guide.

[403] The European Conference of Postal and Telecommunications Administrations. For further clarification, see Radio Spectrum Decision, Recital (13). See also para 12.133, below.

Decision establishes procedures to facilitate policymaking with the aims of (i) optimising the use of radio spectrum and avoiding harmful interference; (ii) ensuring the effective implementation of radio spectrum policy, in particular, establishing a general methodology to ensure harmonised conditions for the availability and efficient use of radio spectrum; (iii) ensuring the coordinated and timely provision of information concerning the allocation, use and availability of radio spectrum in the Community; and (iv) ensuring the effective coordination of Community interests in international negotiations.[404] In order to assist the Commission, the Radio Spectrum Decision mandates the creation of a Radio Spectrum Committee[405] and outlines its functions and the framework for cooperation with the Commission.[406] Measures adopted pursuant to the Radio Spectrum Decision are, however, without prejudice to measures taken at a Community or national level to pursue general interest objectives, in particular, relating to content regulation and audio-visual policy, or measures taken by Member States' for public security or defence purposes.[407]

12.119 **Radio Spectrum Policy Group.** In conjunction with the Radio Spectrum Committee, a Radio Spectrum Policy Group was also established[408] as a high level consultative group[409] to advise and assist the Commission on radio spectrum policy, including methods for granting rights to use spectrum, spectrum 'refarming'[410] and spectrum valuation.[411] The recitals to the Decision establishing the Group make explicit that the work of the Group should not interfere with the work of the Radio Spectrum Committee.[412]

(vii) Forthcoming changes

12.120 **Reform.** The Framework Directive and Specific Directives[413] require the Commission periodically to review their functioning, in any event no later than three years after the date of their application.[414] Accordingly, in June 2006 the

---

[404] Radio Spectrum Decision (n 402, above) Art 1.

[405] ibid, Art 3.

[406] ibid, Art 4.

[407] ibid, Art 1(4).

[408] Commission Decn of 26 July 2002 establishing a Radio Spectrum Policy Group, OJ 2002 L198/49 ('Radio Spectrum Policy Group Decision').

[409] This group includes high-level governmental experts from the Member States and high-level representatives of the Commission. Other persons may also be invited to attend meetings as appropriate, including national regulators, national competition authorities, market participants and user or consumer groups: Radio Spectrum Policy Group Decn, Recital (5).

[410] This is sometimes referred to as spectrum liberalisation, which involves the change in use of pre-allocated spectrum.

[411] Radio Spectrum Policy Group Decn (n 406, above) Recitals (2)–(5).

[412] ibid, Recital (7). The operational arrangements for the Group are set out in Art 4.

[413] See para 12.089, above.

[414] This date is 25 July 2003, except in the case of the Directive on Privacy and Electronic Communications, which applied only from 31 October 2003.

Commission launched a public consultation on options for updating the regulatory framework, including a new draft Recommendation on relevant markets.[415] The consultation period concluded at the end of October 2006 and the Commission expects to put forward new legislative measures to the Council and Parliament in the first half of 2007, with a view to full incorporation of the new rules by the Member States by 2009–2010. Proposals for common rules for radio spectrum are included within the scope of this review.[416]

'i2010' initiative. The Commission's longer term objectives for this sector are outlined in its 'i2010 – European Information Society 2010' initiative.[417] This was proposed in the Community's 2005 Lisbon agenda, where the Commission recognised the importance of information and communications technologies ('ICT') as key to future growth and employment. It calculated that a quarter of EU GDP, and 40 per cent of productivity and growth, were attributable to ICT. The three broad areas to be covered by this initiative include (i) the completion of a 'Single European Information Space' to promote an open and competitive internal market for information society and media; (ii) the strengthening of innovation and investment; and (iii) the achievement of an inclusive European information society.[418] These goals were reiterated by the Commission at the launch of its 2006 review of the existing regulatory framework, and it was indicated that greater harmonisation in the application of the framework, in particular the regulation of spectrum, would be one of the Commission's objectives.[419] **12.121**

(b) Application of competition law

(i) Generally

Position of communications providers. The competition law rules of the Treaty and the implementing provisions (in particular Regulation 1/2003[420]) **12.122**

---

[415] See Press Release IP/06/874 (29 June 2006) and MEMO/06/257. For the draft revised Recommendation, see para 12.101, above. In relation to the Universal Service Directive, see also the Commission's *Report regarding the outcome of the Review of the Scope of Universal Service in accordance with Article 15(2) of Directive 2002/22/EC*, COM(2006) 163 Final.

[416] See Bernaerts, loc cit n 294, above; and Commr Reding, 'From Service Competition to Infrastructure Competition: the Policy Options Now on the Table', speech to ECTA Conference, 16 November 2006 (Speech/06/697). For progress of the reform proposals, see the DG Information Society website at: http://europa.eu.int/information_society/policy/ecomm/tomorrow/index_en.htm.

[417] See the 'Communication from the Commission to the Council, the European Parliament, the European Economic and Social Committee and the Committee of the Regions' COM(2005) 229 Final, 1 June 2005. See also Press Release IP/05/643 (1 June 2005) and the speech by Commr Reding to the i2010 Conference, 6 September 2005 (Speech/05/486).

[418] The Commission provides in the Communication (ibid) a detailed work programme for the achievement of these goals.

[419] See the speech by Commr Reding to the annual meeting of BITKOM, 27 June 2006 (Speech/06/422).

[420] For Reg 1/2003, see generally Chap 13, below.

apply in full to the electronic communications sector. There are no sector-specific implementing regulations. It is clear that communications providers are undertakings within the meaning of Articles 81 and 82 to the extent that they carry on an economic activity for the manufacturing or sale of electronic communications equipment or the provision of electronic communications services. Articles 81 and 82 apply regardless of any other facts, for example, whether the nature of the communications provider is commercial or whether it is a legally distinct entity or forms part of the State organisation.[421] In particular, an undertaking cannot avoid the competition rules merely because compliance with those rules would make it more difficult for it to discharge a task of general economic interest: it would have to show that it was actually prevented from discharging the task.[422]

12.123 **Exception for services of general economic interest.** It has always been recognised that the exception from competition rules, pursuant to Article 86(2), is to be applied very narrowly. The extent of the exception arose for the first time in relation to the communications sector in *British Telecom*,[423] where the Commission found that BT had abused its dominant position in seeking to prevent third parties from providing a telex forwarding service.[424] Accordingly, it found that Article 82 should in this case be applicable to BT. The Court of Justice upheld this decision.[425]

12.124 **Consistency between the regulatory framework and competition rules.** Neither Member States nor the Commission or Council may introduce rules which conflict with the provisions of Articles 81 or 82.[426] NRAs also have an overriding duty not to approve any practice or agreement contrary to Community competition law. Consequently, the regulatory framework and other Community acts adopted in the electronic communications sector must be interpreted in such a way as to ensure consistency with the competition rules; the regulatory framework itself often combines the goals of ensuring effective competition and achieving consumer welfare.

---

[421] See Competition Guidelines, OJ 1991 C233/02: Vol II, App E.23, point 20.

[422] See generally Chap 11, above, on Art 86.

[423] *British Telecommunications*, OJ 1982 L360/36, [1983] 1 CMLR 457.

[424] BT claimed that Art 82 should not be applied to it on the basis that application of the competition rules would obstruct it in the performance of tasks of general economic importance. The Commission accepted that BT was entrusted with such tasks (the provision of telecommunications systems in the UK), but held that BT was not prevented from discharging these tasks by allowing third parties to provide telex forwarding services, particularly as business attracted by the third parties would increase traffic on BT's network.

[425] Case 41/83 *Italy v Commission* [1985] ECR 873, [1985] 2 CMLR 368. Allowing third parties to use new technology to speed up the transmission of messages was in the public interest and the applicants had failed to demonstrate that the result of third party activity would be unfavourable to BT or would jeopardise the performance of the tasks entrusted to BT.

[426] See Arts 3(1)(g) and 10 EC.

(ii) Relationship of competition rules and sector-specific regulation

The role of competition rules in a regulated sector. Competition policy and   **12.125**
the principles of the Treaty's competition rules are at the heart of the 2002 regulatory framework.[427] The policy and regulatory principles of the framework (set out
in Article 8 of the Framework Directive) make explicit that NRAs are required to
introduce competition into the sector. The Specific Directives also recognise that
greater competition within the sector will bring about greater consumer welfare.[428]
The designation of undertakings as possessing SMP under Articles 14–16 of the
Framework Directive is also based on competition law principles, in particular the
concept of dominance under Article 82. However, the regulatory framework also
pursues other public interest objectives, which may not be best delivered through
the application of competition rules alone; these include cultural diversity and
media pluralism,[429] consumer welfare for specific social groups,[430] ensuring 'end-
to-end connectivity'[431] and the provision of 'universal service' to end-users.[432]
This duality of objectives and the potential for the full application of competition
rules where sector-specific regulation already exists means that it is necessary to
understand the interaction between these rules.

Parallel application of sectoral regulation and competition laws. Key features   **12.126**
of the 2002 regulatory framework draw heavily upon competition law principles
and methodologies to set the conditions for regulation. But, as the Commission
clarifies in its SMP Guidelines,[433] this does not mean that the analysis carried out
pursuant to the regulatory framework will always lead to the same results as
that carried out under Articles 81, 82 or the EC Merger Regulation.[434] In respect of
market definition, for example, the Commission distinguishes between markets

---

[427] See para 12.088, above.

[428] See, eg Universal Service Directive (n 373, above) Recital (26). See also Commr Reding,
speech to the 1st Meeting of the Centre for European Policy Studies Taskforce on Electronic
Communications, 15 September 2005 (Speech/05/515). See para 12.089, above, for 'Specific
Directives'.

[429] Dir 2002/19 on access to, and interconnection of, electronic communications networks and
associated facilities ('Access Directive'), OJ 2002 L108/7: Vol II, App E.18, Recital (10).

[430] Framework Directive (n 255, above) Art 8(4)(e).

[431] Access Directive (n 429, above) Art 5(4)(a), which mandates NRAs to impose interconnection obligations on networks without prejudice to the measures that may be taken regarding
undertakings with SMP.

[432] Universal Service Directive (n 375, above) Recital (4). 'Universal service' means a defined
minimum set of services to all end users at an affordable price. The Universal Service Directive recognises that this may involve the provision of some services to some end-users at prices that depart
from those resulting from normal market conditions.

[433] Commission guidelines on market analysis and the assessment of significant market power
under the Community regulatory framework for electronic communications networks and services,
OJ 2002 C165/6: Vol II, App E.25. See para 12.102, above.

[434] SMP Guidelines, above, at paras 24–28.

defined on an *ex ante* basis, under the regulatory framework,[435] and markets defined on an *ex post* basis, per Articles 81 and 82.[436] Therefore, the Commission concludes that markets defined for the purposes of the regulatory framework may not always coincide with those defined for the purposes of competition enforcement. The Commission also states that a SMP designation under the framework does not mean that the undertaking in question is necessarily dominant for the purposes of Article 82.[437] Moreover, it states that a SMP designation has no bearing on whether the undertaking in question is guilty of an 'abuse' under Article 82 or national competition laws. According to the Commission, the SMP designation is confined to its regulatory purposes.[438] However, although the Commission acknowledges that the possibility of parallel procedures under *ex ante* regulation and competition laws cannot be excluded, it intends that instances of dual investigation should be limited by close cooperation between NRAs and national competition authorities.

12.127   **Sector-specific guidance on the application of competition rules.**   The adoption of the regulatory framework has not been accompanied by updated guidance in relation to the application of competition rules. Some recent guidance is available from the SMP Guidelines[439] and the Commission's annual reports, though these do not purport to set out the Commission's position on the future enforcement of Articles 81 and 82. Consequently, the Commission's 'Competition

---

[435] Framework Directive (n 255, above) Art 15(1), itself provides that markets defined for the purposes of the regulatory framework are without prejudice to those defined for the application of competition laws. This includes the market definition procedure under Art 15 of the Framework Directive and those markets listed in the Commission's recommendation on regulatory markets.

[436] Commission guidelines on market analysis and the assessment of significant market power under the Community regulatory framework for electronic communications networks and services (the 'SMP Guidelines'), OJ 2002 C165/6: Vol II, App E.25, para 26: the Commission distinguishes between the starting points for market definition for competition enforcement and regulatory purposes.

[437] SMP Guidelines, para 30.

[438] The Commission invests much effort during the Art 7 consultation process to ensure that there is consistency between *ex ante* regulatory decisions and *ex post* antitrust enforcement decisions: Van Ginderachter (then Head of Unit C-1, DG Comp), 'Electronic communications markets: current activities / objectives of DG Competition and review of recent cases', paper to 9th Annual Conference, Communications and Competition Law, Brussels, 14 October 2004. He indicated that the Commission would use its 'veto powers' (see para 12.104, above) against draft regulatory measures by NRAs that conflict with existing jurisprudence or the Commission's own decisional practice.

[439] The SMP Guidelines (n 436, above) state, at para 24, that they are based on (i) the existing case law of the CFI and the ECJ concerning market definition and the notion of dominance under Art 82 and Art 2 of the EC Merger Reg; (ii) the Guidelines on the Application of Competition Rules in the Telecommunications Sector, (n 438, below); (iii) the notice on the definition of relevant markets for the purposes of Community competition law, OJ 1997 C372/5 (see generally Chap 4, above); (iv) the Notice on the application of competition rules to access agreements in the telecommunications sector (n 442, below). It is likely that these guidelines will also be revised in conjunction with the Commission's 2006 review of the the regulatory framework (see para 12.120, above).

Guidelines',[440] developed in 1991, continue to be relevant although some of the concepts and examples in those Guidelines may no longer apply as a result of developments in technology and changes in legislation.[441] In 1998, the Commission published a Notice on the Application of the Competition Rules to Access Agreements in the Telecommunications Sector ('the Telecoms Access Agreements Notice').[442] This provides some helpful guidance in relation to one of the most prevalent types of agreement in the sector, namely, interconnection agreements.

Sector inquiry into 3G mobile communication. In September 2005, the **12.128** Commission and EFTA Surveillance Authority concluded a sector inquiry into the competitive situation in the market for new systems of mobile communication that are able to transmit audiovisual content (3G). The inquiry was initiated with a view to ensuring that sports content, which is critical for the take-up of new mobile services, is not held back by anti-competitive conduct. The report[443] highlighted a number of potentially anti-competitive business practices which may limit the availability of innovative mobile sport services to consumers. The report focuses on four main areas of competition concerns:

- Bundling: situations where powerful media operators have bought all audiovisual rights to premium sports in a bundle in order to secure exclusivity over all platforms with no view to exploiting or sublicensing 3G rights.

- Embargoes: situations where overly restrictive conditions (serious time embargoes or unnecessary limitations of clip length) are imposed upon mobile rights that limit the practical availability of 3G content.

- Joint selling: situations where 3G rights remain unexploited, because collective selling organisations do not manage to sell the 3G rights of individual sports clubs.

- Exclusivity: exclusive attribution of 3G rights in situations leading to the monopolisation of premium content by powerful operators.

The report invited market players to redress the possible anti-competitive effects resulting from their business practices and announced that the Commission will,

---

[440] Guidelines on the Application of EEC Competition Rules in the Telecommunications Sector, OJ 1991 C233/02: Vol II, App E.23. The EFTA Surveillance Authority issued equivalent Guidelines on the application of the EEA competition rules: OJ 1994 L153/35.

[441] eg the Competition Guidelines pre-date the directive that introduced full competition to the telecommunications sector by opening up the last reserved services to competition. As a result, the distinction made in the Guidelines between agreements between communications providers in relation to reserved services and other horizontal agreements between communications providers is now largely obsolete.

[442] Telecoms Access Agreements Notice, OJ 1998 C265/02: Vol II, App E.24.

[443] Report on the sector inquiry into the provision of sports content over third generation mobile networks, 21 September 2005, available at http://ec.europa.eu/comm./competition/antitrust/others/sector_inquiries/new_media/3g/final_report.pdf.

together with the national competition authorities concerned, review potentially harmful case situations with a national dimension identified during the sector inquiry.

(iii) Application of Article 81

12.129 **Prevalence of agreements.** Whilst the regulatory framework emphasises the harm that may be caused to competition by the presence of undertakings with SMP, or dominance, on a particular market, the provisions of Article 81 are equally relevant to the communications sector. The industry depends on agreements (both horizontal and vertical) between different communications providers in order, *inter alia* (i) to ensure that communications between consumers using different networks can be completed ('end-to-end connectivity'); (ii) to ensure technical interoperability; and (iii) to further 'convergence'.[444] Competing communications companies must, for example, enter into interconnection agreements with one another to secure end-to-end connectivity. Similarly, some operators will need to enter into vertical agreements for the supply of wholesale services, such as 'wholesale line rental' or content for their pay-TV services, so that they can supply their own services over the communications infrastructure of another undertaking.

12.130 **The Commission's objectives.** In applying Article 81 to agreements within the communications sector, the Commission has regard to the need for communications providers to cooperate in order to ensure network and services interconnectivity, one-stop shopping and one-stop billing and, in particular, to cooperate in such a way as to enable the provision of Europe-wide services and optimum service to users. On the other hand, the Commission is conscious of the overriding objective to develop market conditions which allow users greater variety of communications services, better access to content, better quality and lower cost; and of the need therefore to safeguard a strong competitive market structure.[445]

12.131 **Restrictive effect of certain agreements.** The Competition Guidelines[446] point out that an agreement between network providers could limit the extent to which those providers compete against each other to attract and retain large telecommunications users for their telecommunications centres, so-called 'hub competition',[447] or could limit the number of services (in particular 'packages of services' or 'managed data network services') that communications providers

---

[444] eg the supply of television content transmission through telephone networks.
[445] Ungerer, 'EU Competition Law in the Telecommunications, Media and Information Technology Sectors' in Hawk (ed) *1996 Fordham Corp. L. Inst.* (1996), Chap 11.
[446] Competition Guidelines (n 440, above).
[447] ibid, points 41–42.

would offer.[448] Equally important, such agreements could restrict competition by third parties if the communications providers were to refuse to provide facilities to those third parties, to agree to impose discriminatory or inequitable trading conditions on such users, or to favour their own offerings over those of third parties.[449] The Commission will rarely, if ever, be prepared to accept restrictions in agreements between communications providers which seek to deny access to third parties or which lead to an appreciable strengthening of a dominant position.[450] The following Section deals with the Commission's approach to some common restrictions in agreements.

Price agreements.   Agreements between communications providers as to prices, discounting or collection charges for international services are apt to restrict competition to an appreciable extent.[451] Similarly, an agreement between a network provider and another operator (such as a communications service provider) on prices, discounts or charges for domestic services could restrict the ability of a third party to compete. Coordination on or prohibition of discounting could cause particularly serious restrictions of competition. The Commission has always taken the view that price agreements between competitors should be tolerated only under exceptional circumstances. Article 81(3) might apply to a price agreement entered into for the sole purpose of introducing or maintaining a common tariff structure. Even then, it would probably need to be shown that the tariff arrangements were transparent and provided a substantial competitive benefit, for example stimulating a trend towards cost-oriented tariffs.[452]

12.132

***CEPT*.**   The stance the Commission is likely to adopt on price agreements was seen in *CEPT*[453] (Conférence européenne des administrations des postes et des télécommunications), where the Commission found that a recommendation that telecommunications operators impose a 30 per cent surcharge on an access charge where third party traffic was carried on an international telecommunications leased circuit (or if such a circuit was interconnected to the public

12.133

---

[448] ibid, points 57–58.

[449] ibid, points 42 and 59.

[450] ibid, point 62. Thus, in considering an arrangement for a Europe-wide managed data network service (MDNS) promoted by 22 communications providers, the Commission made it clear that it could grant approval only if the parties gave guarantees to prevent discrimination against third party service providers and not to cross-subsidise the MDNS service: Press Release IP/89/948 (14 December 1989). The arrangement was abandoned for commercial reasons.

[451] Competition Guidelines (n 438, above) points 44–46. On 'most favoured nation' clauses where one party promises the other that it will enjoy the most favourable terms on offer see by analogy the Commission's approach to Hollywood movie studios: Case COMP/38.427 *Pay Television Film Output Agreements*, Press Release IP/04/1304 (26 October 2004) and *XXXIVth Report on Competition Policy* (2004), p 47.

[452] ibid, points 45 and 46.

[453] *CEPT*, Press Release IP/90/188 (6 March 1990).

telecommunications network) was restrictive of competition. Following the Commission's intervention, CEPT agreed to abandon its recommended policy of applying surcharges to third parties.[454]

12.134 **Agreements on conditions other than price.** Network providers may limit competition between themselves and inhibit competition by third parties by reaching agreement on terms other than price. To the extent that such terms restrict competition, they are likely to fall within Article 81(1). In *CEPT*,[455] the Commission objected under Article 81(1) to recommendations making the supply of leased circuits subject to a restriction as to the use for those circuits; a ban on subleasing; authorisation of private networks only for customers tied to each other by economic links and carrying on the same commercial activity; and prior consultation between the network providers before approving any private network. In *GEN*,[456] the Commission objected to an agreement between network providers which sought to exclude third parties from access to an optical fibre telecommunications network.

12.135 **Agreement on technical and quality standards.** The Commission acknowledges that standardisation brings substantial benefits which can often be relevant to the application of Article 81(3). Adoption of common standards may be vital if Europe-wide markets are to be developed; and common standards may be beneficial in permitting economies of scale (and, as a result, cheaper products or services). Having a single set of standards may also facilitate new entry. However, standard-setting can also be restrictive if it is used to hinder innovation or block network access. The Commission has indicated that assessment of whether standard-setting (other than European standards developed pursuant to Community law[457]) is pro-competitive or anti-competitive is complex and inevitably needs to be made on a case-by-case basis.[458]

12.136 **Agreements on standards and Article 81(3).** Agreements setting standards are more likely to benefit from the application of Article 81(3) where users are directly involved in the standardisation process in order to contribute to deciding what products or services will meet their need. Similarly, if service operators other than network providers or manufacturers (who will be in control of the

---

[454] See also *GEN (Global European Network)*, *XXVIIth Report on Competition Policy* (1997), point 73: the Commission objected to pricing provisions in an agreement between large network providers designed to set up a high quality, heavy-capacity optical fibre telecommunications network to enhance trans-European services. Although the Commission welcomed the objectives of the agreement and ultimately allowed the creation of the network, it required as a condition of its approval that provisions on the setting of prices were deleted.

[455] n 453, above.

[456] *GEN*, n 452, above.

[457] eg pursuant to the regulatory framework discussed in paras 12.092 *et seq*, above.

[458] Competition Guidelines (n 438, above) point 49.

communications hardware used in the network) are involved, the process is more likely to be seen to be for industry benefit, rather than as creating a restriction which inhibits service operators other than network providers from competing. Licensing other manufacturers may be deemed necessary in order to ensure that the standardisation agreement satisfies the Article 81(3) criteria (so as to avoid foreclosure of the market to those other manufacturers). The difficulties in designing agreements to promote competition by the setting of standards were apparent when ETSI (the European Telecommunications Standards Institute) notified an arrangement designed to ensure that standards which were subject to intellectual property rights were not wasted, but were made generally available. The Commission, assessing the agreement under the pre-Modernisation procedure, challenged the proposed arrangements according to which members would agree in advance to let their intellectual property rights be included in a given ETSI standard, unless the rights owner specifically withheld the rights (so-called 'licensing by default'), as a compulsory licensing system in breach of Articles 81 and 82. ETSI's general assembly withdrew the arrangement and substituted one whereby its members were obliged to use 'reasonable efforts' to inform ETSI in a timely manner of rights which they learn of in a given standard.[459] The Commission did not object to this revised arrangement.[460]

Interplay between agreements on standards and intellectual property rights. More recently, the Commission also identified the risk of 'patent ambushes' in the context of agreements on technical standards. A 'patent ambush' arises where, during the development of a standard, a company intentionally conceals that it has essential IPR for that standard and only declares and identifies these after the standard has been agreed. Concerns about 'patent ambushes' were raised by the Commission in relation to ETSI's rules where it considered that this potentially raised an unjustified barrier to entry or prevent the consideration of alternative technologies, thereby distorting the competitive process. After ETSI approved changes to its rules put forward by the Commission, the investigation was closed.[461] **12.137**

Agreements on information exchange. While the Commission recognises that a general exchange of information could assist the functioning of international communications services and could help in enabling interconnectivity and one-stop shopping, it is nonetheless concerned about the exchange of competitively **12.138**

---

[459] If the member will not grant the rights, ETSI will seek an alternative technology and, if no such technology is found, work on the standard will cease. Once ETSI becomes aware of any rights in a particular standard, it shall ask the owner if it will grant an irrevocable non-exclusive licence on fair, reasonable and non-discriminatory terms and conditions. Refusal can lead to the non-recognition of the standard.

[460] *ETSI Interim IPR Policy, XXVth Report on Competition Policy* (1995), p 131.

[461] See Press Release IP/05/1565 (12 December 2005).

sensitive information such as tariff information, customer details and commercial strategy (including new products).[462] Such exchanges may limit the autonomy of the communications providers affected and would not be necessary to ensure the benefits of interconnectivity and one-stop shopping. Where major network providers have formed global alliances,[463] the Commission has sought undertakings to ensure that there will be no disclosure of commercial information that would confer a substantial competitive advantage. The Commission raised similar concerns in relation to the GSM Association Infocentre, which collected price information from competing operators in relation to their international roaming tariffs.[464]

12.139 **Agreements on infrastructure sharing.**   Following the acquisition of 3G licences around Europe, certain mobile network operators applied to share one another's infrastructure as a means of achieving their network roll-out obligations under their 3G licences and reducing their financial burden. In 2002, T-Mobile and O$_2$ notified their intention to share each other's networks in the UK and Germany. The Commission's decision[465] in relation to the notified agreements found that site sharing would not restrict competition in this case because the cooperation only extended to basic network elements and each of the parties retained control of their own core networks. It also noted that site sharing may be beneficial for environmental and health reasons. In relation to the national roaming aspects of the notified arrangements, however, the Commission was concerned that this could restrict competition at the wholesale level with harmful effects in downstream retail markets[466] although it granted an exemption for five years subject to conditions. The Court of First Instance annulled[467] those parts of the Commission decision in the *O$_2$ Germany* case that related to the finding that the national roaming agreement fell within Article 81(1). The Court found that the Commission had simply assumed that because O$_2$ Germany was present in

---

[462] Competition Guidelines (n 440, above) point 53. See, eg *Mobile telephony*, Paris Court of Appeal, judgment of 12 December 2006, dismissing the appeal by the three major mobile operators in France from the decn of the Conseil de la Concurrence condemning arrangements for regular exchange of information about the numbers of new and terminating subscribers (ie 'churn'): this was commercially sensitive information that enabled each operator to know precisely the market position and success of the strategy of its competitors.

[463] See, eg *Unisource*, OJ 1997 L328/1, [1998] 4 CMLR 105; *Uniworld*, OJ 1997 L3218/24, [1998] 4 CMLR 145; *Atlas*, OJ 1996 L239/23, [1997] 4 CMLR 89.

[464] See the Commission's 'Working Document on the Initial Findings of the Sector Enquiry into Mobile Roaming Charges' adopted on 13 December 2000.

[465] *T-Mobile Deutschland/O$_2$ Germany – Network Sharing Rahmenvertrag*, OJ 2004 L75/32, and *O$_2$ UK Limited/T-Mobile UK Limited- UK network sharing agreement*, OJ 2003 L200/59, [2004] 4 CMLR 1401. For more detailed discussion, see paras 7.125 *et seq*, above.

[466] This was because roaming undermines infrastructure-based competition as it limits competition on coverage, quality and transmission speeds. It may also limit competition on price: *XXXIIIrd Report on Competition Policy* (2003), p 195.

[467] Case T-328/03 *O$_2$ Germany v Commission* [2006] ECR II-1231, [2006] 5 CMLR 258, para 77.

the mobile telecommunications market in Germany, it would inevitably have entered the 3G market even in the absence of the roaming agreement. Given that there had not been objective examination of the competitive situation in the absence of the agreement, the Commission had not properly assessed the extent to which the agreement was necessary for O$_2$ Germany to penetrate the new 3G market. The Court rejected the Commission's argument that roaming agreements necessarily restricted competition by making an operator dependent on the network of its competitor, and held that factors which the Commission had considered relevant only to Article 81(3) might take the agreement outside Article 81(1) altogether.

Discriminatory treatment.   Agreements discriminating in favour of certain undertakings, such as manufacturers, may also be found to infringe Article 81 especially where one of the parties is dominant in the relevant network or services market. In past cases, the Commission has identified foreclosure risks to third parties.[468]   **12.140**

Risks of foreclosure.   The increasing convergence of communications markets has resulted in greater demand for premium content over different and competing transmission platforms, such as sports content over cable, the internet or 3G mobile phones.[469] These changes have brought both existing and new arrangements for the licensing and distribution of content under closer scrutiny.[470] The Commission approach to date has primarily indicated concerns of foreclosure whereby competitors and consumers are prevented from accessing content as a result of long contract durations,[471] exclusivity provisions and/or joint selling.[472] Exemptions under Article 81(3) have been granted, or commitments under Article 9 of Regulation 1/2003 have been accepted, where the parties have modified their agreements to take account of the Commission's concerns.[473]   **12.141**

Research and development agreements.   The telecommunications industry has been characterised by a large number of joint ventures, where competitors have collaborated with a view to keeping pace with technological progress and ensuring   **12.142**

---

[468] See, eg *STET, Italtel, AT&T and AT&T-NSI*, OJ 1992 C333/03, where the Commission required STET's subsidiary, Telecom Italia, not to discriminate in favour of Italtel.

[469] See the Commission's concluding report on the 'Sector Inquiry into the provision of sports content over third generation mobile networks', para 12.128, above.

[470] See also para 12.146, below in relation to mergers. The Commission has noted the risks posed to media plurality and cultural diversity as a result of greater market concentration.

[471] See COMP 38.287 *Telenor/Canal+/Canal Digital*, decn of 29 December 2003, Press release IP/04/2 (5 January 2004). See also *XXXIIIrd Report on Competition Policy* (2003), p 196, and see further paras 7.118 *et seq*, above.

[472] See *Telenor/Canal+/Canal Digital*, above, and *UEFA Champions League*, OJ 2003 L291/25, [2004] 4 CMLR 549. See also *Bundesliga*, OJ 2005 L134/46, [2005] 5 CMLR 1715. See further paras 5.115–5.118, above.

[473] eg *UEFA Champions League* (individual exemption); *Bundesliga* (commitments).

they provide innovative and competitive services. The Commission recognises[474] that, within the telecommunications industry, joint research and development may often be vital to achieving these objectives, particularly as research and development in this area often involves greater important financial, technical and human resources than many undertakings (even very large undertakings) can generate individually. Some telecommunications joint ventures will fall within the block exemption, Regulation 2659/2000,[475] which exempts joint research and development agreements, provided that all parties have access to the results (and, if the agreement does not provide for joint exploitation, that each party has the right to exploit the results independently) and that the agreement does not contain any of the expressly prohibited restrictions.[476]

12.143 **Joint distribution.** According to Regulation 2659/2000, where the agreement provides also for joint exploitation, that must relate to results which are protected by intellectual property rights or constitute know-how, which substantially contribute to technical or economic progress, and which are decisive for the manufacture of the products or application of the processes in question.[477] Accordingly, joint distribution linked to joint research that does not fulfil this condition would not appear to play a crucial role in the exploitation of the results; Article 81(3) is therefore unlikely to apply to joint distribution arrangements that fall outside the block exemption for this reason.[478]

(iv) Joint ventures and mergers

12.144 **Background.** Technological advances and the rapid uptake of communications services towards the end of the 1990s led to rapid consolidation within the communications sectors which has continued into this decade. The benefits of liberalisation also meant that many cooperation alliances between market participants had an effect on inter-State trade and therefore came to be analysed under either Article 81 or Article 82 or both.[479] Clearly, liberalisation would serve little purpose if new concentrations led to the creation of undertakings with significant market power.[480] On the other hand, the Commission has supported the necessity

---

474 Competition Guidelines (n 440, above) point 73.

475 Reg 2659/2000, OJ 2000 L304/7: Vol II, App C.5. See paras 7.078 *et seq*, above.

476 Where the participants are competitors, the exemption applies only if their combined market share does not exceed 25 per cent of the relevant market. If none of the participants are competitors, this market share condition does not apply and the exemption will pertain for the duration of the R&D stage and, if the results are jointly exploited, for seven years from the time the products are first put on the market.

477 Art 3(4) of Reg 2659/2000.

478 See Competition Guidelines (n 440, above) point 77.

479 For more detailed treatment, see the works cited in n 254, above.

480 See Lowe, 'Media Concentration & Convergence: Competition in Communications,' speech to Oxford Media Convention, 13 January 2004.

of cooperation, particularly in order to promote the development of trans-European services and strengthen the competitivity of the European industry throughout the Community and in the world markets.[481]

Joint venture decisions under Article 81.   The Commission has taken the view that a number of telecommunications and broadcasting joint ventures ('JVs') do not fall within Article 81(1) on the basis that the objectives pursued by the parties cannot realistically be achieved by the companies acting independently,[482] although particular restrictions in the governing agreement may fall within Article 81(1) if they are not ancillary and therefore require assessment under Article 81(3).[483] Most JVs or 'strategic alliances', however, have been found to fall within Article 81(1), on the basis that the parties might have been expected to be active independently in the products or services concerned in the absence of the JV.[484] But the Commission has recognised that a JV may benefit from the application of Article 81(3) on the basis that: (i) it provides parties with no prior presence in a particular market with the ability (through association with another such company or with a network provider or other telecommunications company) to enter the market;[485] (ii) it allows the parties to keep up with the pace of technological progress or to innovate and provide services which they could not do independently as quickly;[486] (iii) it provides the parties (whether network providers or other telecommunications companies) with the structure and resources necessary to enable them to move into global markets.[487] In many cases, the Commission demanded amendments to the notified arrangements or that the parties give

12.145

---

[481] See, eg Competition Guidelines (n 440, above) point 36.

[482] See, eg *International Private Satellite Partners*, OJ 1994 L354/75; *Konsortium ECR 900*, OJ 1990 L228/31, [1992] 4 CMLR 54; *Iridium*, OJ 1997 L16/87, [1997] 4 CMLR 1065.

[483] *Cégétel+4*, OJ 1999 L218/14 (corr L237/10), [2002] 4 CMLR 106: see further paras 7.121–7.124, above; *TPS*, OJ 1999 L90/6, [1999] 5 CMLR 168, appeal dismissed, Case T-112/99 *Métropole Télévision-M6 v Commission* [2001] ECR II-2459, [2001] 5 CMLR 33 [2002] All ER (EC) 1: see further paras 7.115–7.117, above.

[484] In the past, the Commission seems to have taken an expansive view of when telecommunications companies might have been expected to compete in a particular telecommunications product or service. See, eg Competition Guidelines (n 440, above) point 66, which concludes that a communications provider should be regarded as a potential competitor where it 'may have the required financial capacity, technical and commercial skills to enter the market … and could reasonably bear the technical and financial risk of doing it'. See also *Astra*, OJ 1993 L20/23 where the Commission concluded BT must be regarded as a potential competitor to its JV partner SES in leasing of transponders on satellites because of its technical and financial capabilities.

[485] eg *Eirpage*, OJ 1991 L306/22, [1993] 4 CMLR 64 (before the JV, Motorola had provided telecommunications equipment but not paging services).

[486] eg *BT/MCI*, OJ 1994 L223/36, [1995] 5 CMLR 285 (global, value-added services and enhanced applications for large commercial customers); and *British Interactive Broadcasting/Open* ('*BIB*'), OJ 1999 L312/1, [2000] 4 CMLR 901 (digital interactive TV services).

[487] eg *BT/MCI* (above); *Atlas* OJ 1996 L239/23, [1997] 4 CMLR 89; *Phoenix/GlobalOne*, OJ 1996 L239/57, [1997] 4 CMLR 147; *Unisource*, OJ 1997 L381/1, [1998] 4 CMLR 105; *Uniworld*, OJ 1997 L381/24, [1998] 4 CMLR 145.

undertakings (primarily to ensure access to third parties on non-discriminatory terms), but in only very few cases has the Commission blocked a communications JV.[488] The Commission's earlier decisions now have to be considered in the light of the more economics-based approach to JVs developed in recent years, and adumbrated in the Hoorizontal Cooperation Guidelines issued in 2000.[489] The position is discussed in more detail in Chapter 7, above.

12.146 **Mergers and full-function joint ventures.** Almost all of the concentrations in the communications sector have been cleared by the Commission. The strength of competitors has meant that the Commission has only very rarely found there to be a risk of creating or strengthening a dominant position.[490] In fact, of the four instances involving a major telecommunications company where the Commission has, to date, blocked a concentration, three related to JVs engaged in the supply of pay-TV services, where (broadly) the dominant positions of the television companies and of the telecommunications/cable companies could, through the ventures, be mutually reinforcing.[491] Only in *MCI WorldCom/Sprint*[492] has the Commission blocked a 'pure' telecommunications merger, in that case because of the effect in the market for internet connectivity.

(v) Application of Article 82

12.147 **Article 82: significance in the communications sector.** In most countries in the Community, network providers hold individually or collectively a dominant position for the creation and the exploitation of their own network.[493] Until the mid-1980s, the provision of telecommunications services and equipment was reserved to state-owned, national network providers. These special and exclusive rights reserved to network providers were gradually abolished over a period of 10 years, and since 1 January 1998 most communications providers in the Community have been exposed to 'full competition'. However, many communications providers retain large market shares and a significant degree of market power, in particular by virtue of the range of services which they offer and the

---

[488] See, eg *Astra* (n 484, above); *GEN, XXVIIth Annual Report on Competition Policy* (1997), point 73.

[489] Guidelines on Horizontal Cooperation Agreements, OJ 2001 C3/2: Vol II, App C.12.

[490] For some recent decisions, see eg M.3916 *T-Mobile Austria/Tele.ring* (26 April 2006); M.2876 *NewsCorp/Telepiu*, OJ 2004 L110/73, [2004] 5 CMLR 1619; Case M.2803 *Telia/Sonera* (10 July 2002); Case M.1845 *AOL/Time Warner*, OJ 2001 L268/28, [2002] 4 CMLR 454.

[491] Case M.469 *MSG Media Service*, OJ 1994 L364/1; Case M.490 *Nordic Satellite Distribution*, OJ 1996 L53/20; Case M.993 *Bertelsmann/Kirch/Premiere*, OJ 1999 L53/1, [1999] 4 CMLR 700.

[492] Case M.1741 *MCI WorldCom/Sprint*, OJ 2003 L300/1 (annulled on appeal since the parties had informed the Commission that they had abandoned the merger: Case T-310/00 *MCI v Commission* [2004] ECR II-3253, [2004] 5 CMLR 1274).

[493] See, eg the Telecoms Access Agreements Notice (n 442, above) point 63; Competition Guidelines (n 440, above) point 79.

breadth of their distribution networks.[494] Although their *de jure* monopoly has been ended, many national network providers retain *de facto* dominance in a number of markets. Article 82 therefore assumes particular importance in the communications sector.[495]

The Commission's guidance. The alignment of the regulatory framework with **12.148** competition law and, moreover, the equivalence of the concept of SMP under the framework with the concept of dominance under Article 82 means that the Commission's SMP Guidelines provide very helpful guidance as to how Article 82 will be applied in the sector.[496] As regards market definition, the Commission's Relevant Markets Recommendation is similarly of considerable assistance.[497] Supplementary guidance may also be found in the Commission's Competition Guidelines[498] and its Telecoms Access Agreements Notice.[499]

Dominance in the telecommunications sector. The Commission's SMP **12.149** Guidelines[500] indicate that the relevant factors for an assessment of whether a communications provider is dominant include the following:

(i) *Market share.* The Commission believes that a market share of over 50 per cent is usually in itself evidence of dominance (although it will obviously have regard to other factors including the existence of other network providers and satisfactory alternative infrastructures). The SMP Guidelines note that in the Commission's decision-making practice dominance arises where undertakings have market shares over 40 per cent, although in some cases dominance may arise with smaller market shares, but that the existence of a dominant position cannot be established solely on the basis of large market shares.[501]

(ii) *Dominance on neighbouring markets (leverage of market power).* In assessing dominance on a particular communications market, the Commission is likely to consider whether the company concerned is dominant on any neighbouring horizontal or vertical market. The Commission envisages a number of situations where there will be closely related markets where an

---

[494] See Competition Guidelines (n 440, above) points 80–81.

[495] For Art 82 generally, see Chap 10, above. See also, in addition to the works cited at n 252, above, the UK Office of Telecommunications (OFTEL) Guideline to the Competition Act 1998 (which enacts a domestic equivalent of Art 82), *The Application in the Telecommunications Sector* (OFT 417, March 2000).

[496] See para 12.102, above.

[497] See para 12.101, above; for market definition generally, see Chap 4, above.

[498] Competition Guidelines, OJ 1991 C233/02: Vol II, App E.23. The EFTA Surveillance Authority issued equivalent Guidelines on the application of the EEA competition rules: OJ 1994 L153/35.

[499] Telecoms Access Agreements Notice, OJ 1998 C265/02.

[500] SMP Guidelines (n 436, above).

[501] ibid, paras 75, 78.

operator will have a very high degree of market power in at least one of those markets.[502]

(iii) *Essential facilities.* The expression 'essential facility' is used to describe a facility or infrastructure which is essential for reaching customers or enabling competitors to carry on their business, and which cannot be replicated by reasonable means.[503] In the communications sector, ownership of an essential facility may well be the factor which leads the Commission to conclude that a company occupies a dominant position.

(iv) *Other relevant factors.* There is no exhaustive list of factors which the Commission will take into account in assessing dominance. But other matters to which it is likely to have regard in the telecommunications sector include: high barriers to entry; whether an operator has easy or privileged access to capital; economies of scale and scope; absence of or low countervailing buyer power; and absence of potential competition.[504]

12.150 **Collective dominance.** Although at the time of writing there has been no finding of collective or joint dominance in the communications sector pursuant to Article 82,[505] the Commission refers in the SMP Guidelines to the jurisprudence of the Community Courts as a guide to the criteria that should apply.[506] It cites also its own decisions in the field of communications mergers where it has considered whether any of the notified transactions could give rise to a finding of collective dominance.[507]

12.151 **Types of abuse.** There are many ways in which a dominant communications company can seek to exploit its market power in a manner that constitutes anti-competitive abuse. Broadly speaking, these can be divided into four categories: (i) action which may restrict the activities of competitors; (ii) action which may extend the dominance of the operator into areas where it is not already dominant; (iii) action imposing prices on customers which they would not accept under conditions of effective competition; and (iv) action forcing terms on suppliers which they would not grant other than to dominant purchasers. The following paragraphs consider briefly under these heads which particular types of conduct

---

502 ibid, paras 83–85.

503 For essential facilities generally, see paras 10.135 *et seq*, above.

504 See the SMP Guidelines (n 436, above) paras 78 *et seq*.

505 But cf para 12.099 at n 282, above, as regards the finding of collective dominance under the regulatory framework.

506 SMP Guidelines (n 436, above) paras 86–101. In *Westel900/PANNON GSM*, Case Vj-22/2002, 28 July 2003, the Hungarian Competition Office held that the three Hungarian mobile phone service providers were not collectively dominant in the retail market: although the market was highly concentrated and transparent, both in respect of contracts and prices, it was a dynamic market with rapidly developing technology (other aspects of the decn concerning the wholesale market are under appeal).

507 SMP Guidelines, paras 102–106.

are most likely to arise in the communications sector. For full analysis of these issues, see Chapter 10, above.

Restricting activities of competitors. A dominant communications company **12.152** can restrict the activities of competitors by refusing to supply essential services to a competitor, by supplying such a service only on discriminatory or excessive terms or by imposing restrictions as to how a competitor may make use of a facility which is supplied.[508] Alternatively, a dominant company may make the supply but then restrict the opportunities available to that competitor by offering to supply the competitor's customers in the downstream market at prices which are predatory or give rise to a 'margin squeeze.'

Refusal to supply. A refusal to supply communications services will infringe **12.153** Article 82 only if it has exploitative or anti-competitive effects.[509] This may be the case as regards a company dominant through its control of facilities if (i) the dominant company is already supplying one or more customers in the same downstream market (discriminatory refusal); or (ii) if the service requested is an essential facility; or (iii) if the refusal involves withdrawal of a service which the competitor had been receiving.[510] But refusal to supply will not constitute an abuse if it is objectively justified, for example on the grounds that the company requesting supply is a credit risk, or that the dominant company lacks capacity to make further supply or that there is a technical incompatibility. However reliance on such grounds will be subject to careful scrutiny and the action of the dominant operator must be proportionate. Undue or inexplicable delays in responding to requests for access may themselves constitute an abuse.

Examples of refusal to supply. Thus, in *Télémarketing*,[511] the Court of Justice **12.154** held that a refusal by RTL (then the only channel offering television advertising in Belgium) to supply advertising 'spots' to third parties soliciting telephone call responses unless those spots specified a telephone number belonging to Information Publicité was an abuse of a dominant position. The refusal by *SWIFT* (Society for Worldwide International Financial Telecommunications), a cooperative owned by 2000 banks, to grant access to its network on the basis of admission criteria which were clearly discriminatory led the Commission to commence proceedings

---

[508] The Commission investigated under Art 82 the practices of registry operators of domain names who were alleged to be abusing their dominant positions, eg by requiring registrants to have their domicile or a legal establishment in the country to which the domain name was allocated, by limiting the number of domain names available per registrant, or by restricting the choice of name to the business activity of the user. In four cases, the registration rules were relaxed by the operators resulting in the closure of the proceedings. See the *XXXIIIrd Annual Report on Competition Policy* (2003), para 121.

[509] Telecoms Access Agreements Notice (n 499, above) point 83.

[510] ibid, paras 83–100.

[511] Case 311/84 *CBEM v CLT and IPB* [1985] ECR 3261, [1986] 2 CMLR 558.

for breach of Article 82. SWIFT then gave undertakings to grant access to any entity that met objective criteria laid down by the European Monetary Institute and the proceedings were suspended.[512] By contrast, in a number of cases,[513] German courts have held that a mobile operator's refusal to allow SIM-cards to be used in GSM gateways (in effect enabling the user to take advantage of the lower charges for calls within the same GSM network thereby avoiding the higher rates which mobile operators charge for the switching of calls) does not constitute an abuse of a dominant position.

12.155 **Supplying on discriminatory or excessive terms.** A dominant company's duty is to provide access in such a way that the goods and services offered to downstream companies are available on terms no less favourable than those given to other parties, including the supplier's own downstream operations. Discrimination may take the form of restrictions or delays in connection to the public switched network or leased circuits, in installation, maintenance and repair, in effecting interconnection of systems or in providing information concerning network planning, signalling protocols or technical standards.[514] In the *Télémarketing*[515] case, the Court of Justice commented that even if RTL's offer to supply via Information Publicité was not to be treated as a refusal to supply to third parties, it should be treated as an offer to supply on discriminatory terms. As a seller of television time, it had sought to impose on all other undertakings wishing to carry out telemarketing operations a condition that they must not advertise their own telephone number whereas it did not impose this condition for its own operations.

12.156 **Imposing restrictions on customers.** A dominant supplier could also damage the ability of other operators to compete by agreeing to supply only on condition that the operator accept restrictions. The most common conditions imposed by dominant telecommunications service suppliers are a prohibition on third parties connecting private leased lines to the public switched network or using private leased lines for providing services; and conditions imposing extra charges (such as

---

[512] *La Poste/SWIFT, XXVIIth Report* on Competition Policy (1997), point 68; OJ 1997 C335/3.

[513] *GSM-Gateway*, judgment of the Kammergericht Berlin of 15 January 2004, WuW/E DE-R 1274; *GSM-Wandler*, judgment of the Munich Court of Appeal of 22 April 2004, WUW/E DE-R 1270; Case VI-U (Kart) 35/03, judgment of the Düsseldorf Court of Appeal of 24 March 2004, MMR 2004 p 618; Case 88 O (Kart) 60/04, judgment of the Cologne District Court of 16 December 2004. The cases were decided under both Art 82 and German domestic competition law and the reasoning of the judgments differs: some held that a dominant company is not obliged to foster the business of its competitors to its own direct detriment, whereas the Düsseldorf court found that granting access would have overloaded the cells of the mobile network. The courts distinguished the *British Telecommunications* case (n 517, below).

[514] Telecoms Access Agreements Notice (n 499, above) point 98. For supply at excessive prices more generally, see paras 10.104 *et seq*, above.

[515] Case 311/84 *CBEM v CLT and IPB* [1985] ECR 3261, [1986] 2 CMLR 558.

access charges to leased circuits).[516] In *British Telecommunications*,[517] the Commission found against the restrictions imposed by BT which limited the ability of message forwarding agencies to provide a service transmitting international messages on behalf of third parties. This term, and a condition which allowed international telex forwarding only if the prices charged did not undercut the cost of a direct telex message bypassing the United Kingdom, were found to offend against Article 82, and BT was required to cease applying such conditions. Similarly, following a complaint from a private supplier of value added telecommunications services, the Commission required the Belgian Régie des Télégraphes et Téléphones (RTT) to abandon conditions under which telecommunications circuits were to be leased.[518] In *France Télécom v Cegetel*[519] the telephone company Cegetel complained to the Competition Council about the practices of France Télécom with respect to *numéros d'accueil*, that is special call-centre or information numbers, a segment that includes toll-free numbers (known as *numéros verts*), shared-cost numbers (known as *numéros azur*) and *numéros indigos* (billed at a flat nationwide rate). France Télécom's contracts by which it allocated a special number to a customer included a licence to that customer of the trade mark for the use of the relevant *numéros* term. These terms were strongly associated in the public's mind with that kind of special number. The licence terminated immediately if the user moved to another telecoms provider even if they took the actual number with them. The surrender of the right to describe the number as a *numéro vert* therefore limited the portability of the telephone number itself. The Paris Court of Appeal held that France Télécom was dominant since, despite the opening of the market to competition, it still held more than 85 per cent of the toll-free numbers and 80 per cent of the shared-cost numbers at the relevant time. Further, the clauses challenged by Cegetel risked forcing France Télécom's customers to abandon number portability, since they would either lose a key element for identifying their service or would be forced to make costly revisions to their advertising and supporting documentation to remove the references to the marks to which they no longer had a licence. This created an obstacle to market entry by other operators.

---

[516] Telecoms Access Agreements Notice (n 499, above) points 89–97.

[517] *British Telecommunications*, OJ 1982 L360/36, [1983] 1 CMLR 457; upheld by Case 41/83 *Italian Republic v Commission* [1985] ECR 873, [1985] 2 CMLR 368.

[518] *XXth Report on Competition Policy* (1990), point 55; Press Release IP/90/67 (29 January 1990).

[519] Paris Court of Appeal, 29 April 2003, BOCCRF No. 8, 11 July 2003. The Court granted interim relief but held that the relief ordered by the Conseil de Concurrence went too far in requiring the holder of a trade mark to license its use unwillingly to third parties. The Court therefore limited the interim measures to enabling clients who cancelled their 'special number' contracts to continue to use those trade marks in publicity materials, of whatever nature, that already existed at the time of the Conseil's decision.

12.157 **Predatory behaviour.**   A dominant company can hamper the efforts of other operators to compete in its markets by engaging in predatory conduct. The most common form of predatory behaviour is predatory pricing, which according to *AKZO*[520] involves selling below the dominant company's average variable cost or, if its pricing strategy forms part of an anti-competitive plan, selling below average total cost. Both tests were applied by the Commission in *Wanadoo Interactive*,[521] pursuant to which the Commission found that Wanadoo had engaged in predatory pricing on the market for high-speed internet access for residential customers, and imposed a fine of €10.35 million.[522] However, in the telecommunications sector, average variable cost may be negligible, making it an inappropriate cost base for assessment of predatory conduct. The Commission considers that the analysis should have regard to the need to recover also the cost of capital investment, and may therefore resort to long run average incremental cost in analysing whether a company's services are operated at a loss.[523]

12.158 **Conduct on dominated market having effects on other markets.**   An attempt by a communications provider to exploit a dominant position on one market (usually monopoly control of the public network) so as to compete more effectively on a market subject to competition will constitute a breach of that provider's dominant position. Certain practices, however, will infringe Article 82 specifically on the basis that they are likely to extend the dominant position held by the operator to a neighbouring competitive market. Such practices include: a dominant undertaking reserving to itself an ancillary activity in a neighbouring market; bundling; and using information obtained by virtue of an operator's dominant

---

[520] Case C-62/86 *AKZO v Commission* [1991] ECR I-3359, [1993] 5 CMLR 215; see further paras 10.070 *et seq*, above on predatory pricing generally.

[521] Case COMP/38.233 *Wanadoo Interactive*, 16 July 2003, [2005] 5 CMLR 120 (upheld on appeal Case T-340/03 *France Télécom v Commission* [2007] 4 CMLR 919, further appeal pending, Case C-202/07P *France Télécom v Commission*).

[522] The *Wanadoo* case raised two important questions for competition law: (1) whether it is appropriate for companies to engage in selling services below cost for the purposes of developing a market and reaching profitability in the medium term; and (2) whether it is appropriate for the Commission to intervene in nascent markets. In relation to (1), the Commission did not accept Wanadoo's arguments, in particular its economic evidence and financial calculations which took account of investment decision-making and showed that the losses would be recouped in five years. The Commission considered that the recoupment of losses after the initial period is the very objective of predatory behaviour. In relation to (2), the Commission acknowledged that the market for high-speed internet connection in France had not reached a phase of maturity but considered that to defer the application of competition rules until the market had matured would deprive competition authorities of the power to act in time and before the effects of the abuse are consolidated and irreversible. It also noted that the intervention of the Commission was justified as first mover advantages are considerable in the internet sector. See *XXXIIIrd Report on Competition Policy* (2003), p189.

[523] Telecoms Access Agreements Notice (n 499, above) points 113–115. See also the DG Competition discussion paper on the application of Art 82 to exclusionary abuses, December 2005, para 126.

activities to the operator's advantage in competitive markets. In some instances, the Commission has introduced legislation to limit the ability of companies to extend a dominant position on one telecommunications market to another market.[524]

Reservation by a dominant undertaking of an ancillary activity.   A dominant   **12.159** company will infringe Article 82 when it seeks to reserve to itself an activity on a market where competition is possible. In *RTT v GB-INNO*,[525] RTT (which then had a legal monopoly) sought to prevent third parties from selling telephones to users on the basis that those telephones did not have type-approval (RTT being the body responsible for deciding which telephones should have type-approval). In its judgment, the Court of Justice confirmed that an abuse is committed where an operator in a dominant position on a particular market reserves to itself an ancillary activity (in that case importation, marketing, connection, commissioning and maintenance of equipment) which might be carried out by another undertaking. The effect of such reservation would otherwise be to permit a company dominant in one telecommunications market to achieve or maintain dominance in the neighbouring market. The *Télémarketing* case was decided on a similar basis.[526]

Bundling.   Bundling, or tying, involves a dominant operator obliging its cus-   **12.160** tomers, without adequate justification, to purchase not just the service in which the operator is dominant but other services which the customers may not wish to buy. The Commission has indicated its firm intention to intervene should it find there to be cases of unjustified bundling.[527]

Other methods of extending dominance into neighbouring markets.   A domi-   **12.161** nant company would be found to abuse its position if it were to tie the provision of services in which it was dominant to the agreement of a user to enter into cooperation with the dominant company as to the competitive services to be carried on the network. It might also be found to abuse its position if it were to use information acquired as a result of the activities in which it was dominant in order to compete more effectively in areas where it was not dominant.[528]

---

[524] See, eg Dir 1999/64, OJ 1999 L175/39, requiring cable and telecommunications activities carried on by a company dominant in one or other market to be run by separate legal entities. See also the *XXIXth Report on Competition Policy* (1999), points 65–67.

[525] Case C-18/88 *GB-Inno-BM* [1991] ECR I-5941, [1992] 4 CMLR 78.

[526] See n 511, above.

[527] See Competition Guidelines (n 498, above) point 98; Telecoms Access Agreements Notice (n 499, above) point 103. Also note that in *Astra* (n 484, above), the Commission objected to the JV between BT and SES partly on the basis that the bundling of SES's transponders and BT's uplink forced customers to acquire services which they may not have wanted.

[528] Competition Guidelines (n 498, above) point 98.

12.162 **Imposing excessive prices.** A dominant company abuses its position if it charges a price which is excessive in relation to the value of the service provided.[529] In practice, it is always difficult to apply this principle since it is not easy to calculate the proper value of the service provided. But in the past, it was particularly problematic in the telecommunications sector where many of the dominant suppliers were until recently state monopolies providing the whole range of telecommunications services: no internal cost allocation was necessary, and it is now difficult or impossible to make a fair allocation. Nonetheless, the Commission has recently been vigilant in attacking prices which it believes have not represented fair value.[530]

12.163 *ITT Promedia.* The Belgian subsidiary of the US telephone directory publisher, ITT, brought a complaint in 1995 accusing Belgacom, the Belgian TO, of applying discriminatory and excessive prices for access to the data on its subscribers for voice telephony services. The Commission found that, since directory publishers were dependent on telecommunications operators, access to the data should be allowed on non-discriminatory prices, calculated on the basis of the operator's own costs. Belgacom, by demanding a fee from ITT Promedia related to the turnover of that company derived from its directory publishing activities in Belgium, had clearly abused its dominant position. The Commission halted proceedings when Belgacom agreed to adopt a method of calculation based on the ratio of total annual costs to the number of publishers.[531]

12.164 *Deutsche Telekom.* A number of providers of corporate network services in Germany lodged a complaint with the Commission after encountering problems in gaining access to Deutsche Telekom's network. The Commission objected to the tariffs charged by Deutsche Telekom and invited the company to conclude more favourable agreements on access to the public telephone network with competitors. The company put forward an agreement which included prices which its competitors found unacceptable. The Commission arranged a comparative market study, based on the premise that, unless there were clear reasons for the

---

[529] See paras 10.104 *et seq*, above. See also *Verbindung von Telefonnetzen*, judgment of 10 February 2004, WuW/E DE-R 1254: German Federal Supreme Court held that the charging of prices approved by the regulatory watchdog can nevertheless constitute an abuse of a dominant position.

[530] See Haag and Klotz 'Commission Practice Concerning Excessive Pricing in Telecommunications' (1998) 2 EC Competition Policy Newsletter 35, and para 12.165, below.

[531] *XXVIIth Report on Competition Policy* (1997), point 67. The Commission rejected ITT Promedia's further grounds of complaint, a decision upheld by the CFI in Case T-111/96 *ITT Promedia v Commission* [1998] ECR II-2937, [1998] 5 CMLR 491. Note also the judgment of the Brussels Commercial Court ordering Belgacom to supply the subscriber data to ITT Promedia at a 'fair, reasonable and non-discriminatory price': Decn of 11 June 1996, [1996] 3 CMLR 130. The Court followed the conclusion of the designated expert and made its order in advance of the Commission's determination on the basis that it would be automatically amended to conform to the Commission's eventual decision.

divergence, a price was likely to be abusive if it exceeded by more than 100 per cent prices found on comparable competitive markets. Following the study, Deutsche Telekom agreed substantial tariff reductions.[532] In a subsequent case, the Commission investigated Deutsche Telekom's pricing strategy for local access to the fixed telephony network. The Commission found that Deutsche Telekom was engaging in a 'margin squeeze'[533] by charging competitors higher fees for wholesale access to broadband services in the upstream market than its own subscribers in the downstream market had to pay for retail lines.[534] The Commission found that Deutsche Telekom had abused its position although it was subject to price controls under national regulatory measures, because those controls left Deutsche Telekom sufficient scope to modify its pricing practices so as to avoid such abuse.[535] The methodology developed in the *Deutsche Telekom* decision has been used by the Commission to assess a potential margin squeeze in subsequent cases.[536] Generally, the position of vertically integrated dominant providers and the degree of intermediary services offered in the telecommunications sector makes this an area particularly susceptible to margin squeeze.[537]

International roaming charges.   In 1998, the Commission expressed its concern   **12.165** at the continuing high cost of mobile communications in Europe, in particular of calls from fixed lines to mobile phones, and the level of 'accounting rates' charged for transferring international telephone calls. In 2004, it issued statements of objection to O_2 and Vodafone in the United Kingdom[538] and in 2005 similarly

---

[532] *Deutsche Telekom*, Press Release IP/96/975 (31 October 1996).

[533] A margin squeeze may be created where a vertically integrated operator charges prices for wholesale services so high that even an equally efficient competitor in the downstream retail market is forced to charge end users prices that are higher than those charged by the vertically integrated operator to its own end users for similar services: ie the vertically integrated operator is either supplying wholesale services to its competitors at excessive prices or is supplying the same services at a 'loss' to its retail business. In the case of *Deutsche Telekom*, the Commission held that the latter was the case.

[534] *Deutsche Telekom*, OJ 2003 L263/9, [2004] 4 CMLR 790 (on appeal, Case T-271/03 *Deutsche Telekom v Commission*, not yet decided).

[535] See also the *XXXIIIrd Annual Report on Competition Policy* (2003), p 188 and Annual Report on Competition Policy (2005) para 31–32.

[536] eg Case COMP/38.436 *QSC, Report on Competition Policy* (2005), point 77: Commission (working closely with the German NRA) accepted commitments from Deutsche Telekom to put an end to alleged margin squeeze in relation to charges for shared access to local loops. See Note by Grewe (2005) 3 EC Competition Newsletter 57. See also COMP/38.374 *Telefónica* MEMO/07/274 (4 July 2007): the Commission fined the incumbent telecoms operator for applying a margin squeeze in Spanish broadband Internet access markets.

[537] See, eg in France, *ETNA v France Télécom and SFR*, Cour de Cassation, 10 May 2006, annulling the judgment of the Paris Court of Appeal and thereby restoring the finding of the Conseil de la Concurrence of 14 October 2004 that France Télécom and SFR had applied a margin squeeze through the call termination charges imposed by their mobile networks for fixed- to-mobile calls, thereby infringing both Art 82 and the equivalent provision of French competition law.

[538] *UK Roaming*, Press Release IP/04/994 (26 July 2004).

to T-Mobile and Vodafone in Germany,[539] alleging excessively high rates for international roaming at wholesale level (so-called 'inter-operator tariffs') which are keeping retail roaming charges unduly high.[540] In June 2007 the Eu Roaming Regulation was adopted obliging mobile phone operators to offer a 'Eurotariff' to all thier customers by the end of September 2007. The Regulation also sets wholesale caps on the prices that operators can charge each other for roaming.[541]

12.166 **Abuses of a dominant purchasing position.**   Dominant telecommunications operators may abuse their position (and indeed attempt to strengthen it) by seeking excessively favourable prices or trading conditions from their suppliers; by seeking exclusivity from their suppliers; or by excluding or giving unfavourable terms to suppliers. Thus, in *Télémarketing*,[542] the Commission condemned an arrangement where a broadcaster with a dominant position required advertisers placing telemarketing spots to deal exclusively with its associated telecommunications company.

12.167 **Purchasing from domestic suppliers.**   When in public ownership, many telecommunications operators tended to purchase in whole or in part on the basis of nationality, buying locally. Public procurement rules[543] in part eliminate this problem, requiring telecommunications companies covered by the rules to award contracts on the basis that the tender is either economically the most advantageous (taking into account such factors as delivery date, period for completion, running costs, cost-effectiveness, quality, aesthetic and functional characteristics, technical merit, after-sales service and technical assistance, commitments with regard to spare parts, security of supplies and price) or simply lowest price. Dominant telecommunications operators awarding contracts which, in any particular case, are not covered by the procurement rules may nonetheless abuse their position if they discriminate in the award of the contract.[544]

(vi) Application of Article 86

12.168 **Discriminatory licensing by Member States.**   The Commission has been active in proceeding under Article 86 against Member States that favour the incumbent telecommunications operator in granting licences for new services.[545] The issue has arisen in a number of Member States as regards the conditions for granting

---

[539] *Report on Competition Policy* (2005), point 77.

[540] See also the Commission's MEMO (05) 247 (11 July 2005), 'International Roaming Charges: Frequently Asked Questions'.

[541] Reg 717/2007, OJ 2007 L171/32.

[542] Case 311/84 *CBEM v CLT and IPB* [1985] ECR 3261, [1986] 2 CMLR 558.

[543] ie under Dir 2004/18/EC, OJ 2004 L134/114.

[544] Competition Guidelines (n 496, above) points 116–120.

[545] For Art 86 generally, and for other telecommunications cases thereunder, see paras 11.009 *et seq*, above.

GSM mobile licences.[546] The Commission adopted a decision under Article 86(3) in conjunction with Article 82 addressed to Italy in respect of the requirement of a licence entry fee from one licensee without a similar payment having been requested from the first GSM operator, Telecom Italia Mobile, which would therefore be left with a commercial strategy that abused its dominance.[547] In response, Italy took a package of remedial measures to correct the situation.[548] A similar decision was adopted as regards Spain, leading to a package of corrective measures approved by the Commission.[549]

5. Insurance

Generally. There was initially some uncertainty as to whether insurance   **12.169** and other financial services fell within the ambit of Articles 81 and 82. The Commission expressed the view as early as 1972 that in principle the competition rules applied to the insurance sector.[550] However, activity by the Commission in the sector was limited until 1984 when it adopted two formal decisions, *Nuovo CEGAM*[551] and *Fire Insurance (D)*.[552] The latter decision was appealed to the Court of Justice in *Verband der Sachversicherer*.[553] The insurance companies argued that Articles 81 and 82 could not be given effect in relation to insurance without implementing legislation. They pointed out that certain characteristics of the industry required collaboration between undertakings which was reflected in the regulation of the insurance sector by national law. Those characteristics

---

[546] *XXVth Report on Competition Policy* (1995), points 108–110.

[547] OJ 1995 L280/49, [1996] 4 CMLR 700. See further para 11.018, above.

[548] *XXVIIth Report on Competition Policy* (1997), point 108.

[549] *Spanish GSM*, OJ 1997 L76/19, and *XXVIIth Report on Competition Policy* (1997), point 107.

[550] *Second Report on Competition Policy* (1972), point 60. There is increasing convergency between banks and insurance companies and the Commission has given negative clearance to cooperation agreeements: see, eg comfort letter for joint venture between AMB and Commerzbank for distribution of banking and insurance products on the basis that the market overlaps were minimal and the parties would face strong competition from other groups: *XXXIst Report on Competition Policy* (2001), points 204–206. For banking, see paras 5.041 *et seq*, above.

[551] *Nuovo CEGAM*, OJ 1984 L 99/29, [1984] 2 CMLR 484. See also *Insurance Intermediaries*, OJ 1987 C120/5; *Dutch Banks*, OJ 1989 L253/1, [1990] 4 CMLR 768 (uniform commission and exchange rates, etc); *TEKO*, OJ 1990 L13/34, [1990] CMLR 957 (common premiums specified by reinsurer); *Concordato Incendio*, OJ 1990 L15/24, [1991] 4 CMLR 199; *Assurpol*, OJ 1992 L37/16, [1993] 4 CMLR 338 (common basic premiums specified by reinsurer in relation to environmental damage); *Re the Institute of London Underwriters and Lloyd's Underwriters' Association*, OJ 1993 L4/26 (negative clearance granted after restrictions deleted). See also the analysis of the English courts in the Lloyd's litigation, in particular *Higgins v Marchant & Eliot Underwriting* [1996] 2 Lloyd's Rep 31, [1996] 3 CMLR 349 (Court of Appeal); *Society of Lloyd's v Clementson (No. 2)* [1996] CLC 1590, [1996] ECC 193 (QBD, Comm Ct).

[552] *Fire Insurance (D)*, OJ 1985 L35/20, [1985] 3 CMLR 246.

[553] Case 45/85 *Verband der Sachversicherer v Commission* [1987] ECR 405, [1988] 4 CMLR 264.

included the fact that individual insurance companies are not in a position accurately to calculate premiums based on their own experience and it is necessary for them to share information with other undertakings in order accurately to calculate the reserves to be held in case an insured risk materialises. The Court confirmed the Commission's view that the insurance sector was indeed covered by Articles 81 and 82 but said that this did not preclude the possibility of exemption in appropriate cases.[554]

12.170 **Insurance block exemption.** The first block exemption Regulation adopted by the Commission under the Council enabling Regulation 1534/91[555] expired on 31 March 2003[556] and was replaced by Regulation 358/2003.[557] Although Council Regulation 1534/91 also empowers the Commission to grant block exemptions in respect of agreements concerning the settlement of claims and registers of, and information on, aggravated risks, it has not done so because it considers that it lacks sufficient experience in handling individual cases to make use of the power in these areas.[558] Such agreements may nevertheless fulfill the criteria for the application of Article 81(3).

12.171 **Categories of agreements covered.** Article 1 of Regulation 358/2003 defines six types of agreements to which Article 81(1) is disapplied pursuant to Article 81(3). The subsequent Articles of the Regulation set out various conditions which must be satisfied before an agreement falling within one of the listed categories can benefit from exemption. The categories listed are:

— the joint establishment and distribution of calculations of the average cost of covering a specified risk in the past, and, in connection with insurance involving an element of capitalisation, mortality tables, and tables showing the frequency of illness, accident and invalidity;[559]

---

[554] ibid, para 15.

[555] Reg 1534/91, OJ 1991 L143/1: Vol II, App E.26.

[556] Reg 3932/92. See also the Report from the Commission to the Council and the European Parliament on the operation of the Commission Regulation 3932/92, COM(1999) 192 final, 12 May 1999.

[557] Reg 358/2003, OJ 2003 L53/8: Vol II, App E.27. It expires on 31 March 2010. Reg 358/2003 is incorporated into the EEA Agreement by EEA Joint Committee Decn No. 82/2003, OJ 2003 L25/37.

[558] Recital (3), Reg 358/2003; *XXVIth Report on Competition Policy* (1996), pp 131–132.

[559] See also Commission comfort letter to Inreon, a business-to-business online exchange enabling insurers and insurance brokers to obtain bids from reinsurers on certain risks (property and catastrophic risks) and conclude reinsurance contracts. This followed assurances from Swiss Re and Munich Re that there were safeguards in place to prevent the exchange of sensitive commercial information and that the exchange would not enable joint selling: *XXXIInd Report on Competition Policy* (2002), p 188. In Press Release IP/05/361 (23 March 2005) the Commission announced that (i) aviation insurers have given undertakings to promote consistency and transparency with standard wording in aviation insurance policies to be drawn up by insurers in consultation with customers; and (ii) that terms of reference of the liaison between the International Underwriting

— the joint conduct of studies regarding the impact of external circumstances on the frequency of future claims and profitability;

— the joint establishment and distribution of non-binding standard policy conditions for direct insurance;[560]

— the joint establishment and distribution of non-binding models illustrating profits to be realised from certain policies;

— the operation of co-insurance or co-reinsurance groups (so-called 'pools') to cover certain types of risks;[561] and

— the establishment, recognition and distribution of technical specification of security devices, considered further below.

Joint calculations, tables and studies of risks.   In a number of decisions, the   **12.172** Commission concluded that collaboration by insurers in relation to certain information restricts competition under Article 81(1) but that there are counter-vailing benefits which satisfy the criteria set out in Article 81(3).[562] Collaboration between insurers in relation to information is now covered by Articles 1, 3 and 4 of Regulation 358/2003. Two separate types of cooperation are covered:

— the joint establishment and distribution of calculations of the average cost of covering a certain risk in the past ('calculations') and, in cases of life insurance involving an element of capitalisation, mortality tables and tables showing the frequency of illness, accident and invalidity ('tables'); and

— the joint carrying out of studies on the probable impact of extraneous circum-stances on either the frequency or scale of future claims for a given risk or risk category or on the profitability of different types of investment ('studies'), and the distribution of the results of such studies.[563]

The Recitals to Regulation 358/2003 state that cooperation in relation to this type of information leads to an improvement of the knowledge of risks and the rating of risks for individual insurers thereby facilitating new entry.[564] The greater scale on which such information can be gathered, the greater its reliability.

Association of London and the Lloyd's Market Association have been redefined to avoid unneces-sary coordination.

[560] Direct insurance is insurance that is sold directly by insurance companies rather than through an independent agent.

[561] Co-insurance groups are defined as groups of insurance companies that agree to underwrite a specific risk on behalf of all members of the group or that entrust the underwriting of that risk to another undertaking, broker, or common body on their behalf. Co-reinsurance groups are defined as groups of insurance companies set up to reinsure mutually their liabilities with respect to a certain risk and/or to accept the reinsurance of that risk on behalf of all members of the group: Reg 358/2003, Arts 2(5) and 2(6).

[562] *Concordato Incendio*, OJ 1990 L15/25, [1991] 4 CMLR 199; *TEKO*, OJ 1990 L13/34, [1990] 4 CMLR 957; *Assurpol*, OJ 1992 L37/16, [1993] 4 CMLR 338.

[563] Reg 358/2003, Art 1(a) and (b).

[564] Recitals (10)–(13).

Accordingly, the participation of insurers with high market shares in such arrangements is desirable. The exemption provided for in relation to calculations or tables will only apply if the conditions set out in Article 3 of the Regulation are satisfied. The exemption will not apply where participating undertakings enter into an undertaking or commitment among themselves, or oblige other undertakings not to use calculations or tables that differ from those established or not to depart from the results of the studies carried out pursuant to the arrangements.[565]

12.173 **Standard policy conditions and models.** Also exempted are arrangements for the joint establishment and distribution of standard policy conditions for direct insurance and standard models illustrating the profits to be realised from an insurance policy involving an element of capitalisation.[566] Such standard policy conditions or standard models can produce benefits in terms of efficiencies for insurers, facilitating market entry by small or inexperienced insurers and helping insurers to meet legal obligations. They can also be used by consumer organisations as a benchmark to compare insurance policies offered by different insurers.[567] Again, Articles 5 and 6 of the Regulation set out the parameters of the exemption, for example that standard policy conditions and models must not lead either to the standardisation of products or to the creation of a significant imbalance between the rights and obligations arising from the contract. Furthermore the exemption for standard policy conditions does not apply to certain prohibited clauses.

12.174 **Common coverage of certain types of risk: insurance pools.** Regulation 358/2003 exempts the setting up and operation of groups of insurers or of reinsurers for the common coverage of a specific category of risks in the form of co-insurance or co-reinsurance.[568] Co-insurance or co-reinsurance groups (often called 'pools') can allow insurers and reinsurers to provide insurance or reinsurance for large or undeterminable risks for which they might not otherwise be able to provide cover.[569] They can also help insurers and reinsurers to acquire experience of risks with which they are unfamiliar.[570] However, such groups can involve restrictions of competition, such as the standardisation of policy conditions, amounts of cover and premiums.

---

[565] Art 4.

[566] Art 1(c) and (d).

[567] See Recital (14).

[568] Art 1(e).

[569] For earlier cases where the Commission examined the system of mutual maritime insurance through P&I Clubs, see *P&I Clubs*, OJ 1985 L376/2, [1989] 4 CMLR 178; *P&I Clubs IGA and P&I Clubs Pooling Agreement*, OJ 1999 L125/12, [1999] 5 CMLR 646; and *XXVIIIth Annual Report on Competition Policy* (1998), points 111–119.

[570] See *Assurpol*, OJ 1992 L37/16, [1993] 4 CMLR 338.

Exemption for pools covering new risks. For genuinely new risks, it is not **12.175** possible to know in advance what subscription capacity is necessary to cover the risk, nor whether two or more such groups could co-exist for the purposes of providing this type of insurance. Pooling arrangements which are for the exclusive co-insurance or co-reinsurance of such new risks (not of a mixture of new risks and existing risks) are exempted for a period of three years,[571] which the Commission considers should provide sufficient historical information on claims to assess the necessity or otherwise of a single pool. No market share limits apply to the exemption for new risks. The definition of 'new risks' clarifies that only risks which did not exist before are covered, thus excluding, for example, risks which hitherto existed but were not insured.[572] Moreover, a risk whose nature changes significantly (for example, a considerable increase in terrorist activity) falls outside the definition, as the risk itself is not new. A 'new risk' requires an entirely new insurance product, and cannot be covered by additions or modifications to an existing insurance product.

Exemption for pools covering risks that are not new. For risks which are not **12.176** new, Regulation 358/2003 grants an exemption to co-insurance or co-reinsurance groups which have existed for more than three years, or which have not been created in order to cover a new risk, subject to certain market share thresholds not being exceeded.[573] Such co-insurance and co-reinsurance groups which involve a restriction of competition can also, in certain limited circumstances, involve benefits which justify an exemption under Article 81(3), even if they could be replaced by two or more competing insurance entities. They may, for example, allow their members to gain the necessary experience of the sector of insurance involved, or allow cost savings, or reduction of premiums through joint reinsurance on advantageous terms. However, exemption for such groups is not justified if the group in question benefits from a significant level of market power, since in those circumstances the restriction of competition deriving from the existence of the pool would normally outweigh any possible benefits. The threshold for co-insurance groups is lower because the co-insurance pools may involve uniform policy conditions and commercial premiums. These exemptions, however, only apply if the group in question meets the further conditions laid out in the Regulation, which are intended to keep to a minimum the restrictions of competition between the members of the group.[574]

---

[571] Reg 358/2003, Art 7(1).
[572] Art 2(7).
[573] Art 7(2). There is a tolerance in respect of agreements where the market share exceeds the limit for a short period.
[574] Art 8.

12.177 **Individual application of Article 81(3) to insurance pools.** Pools falling outside the scope of the Regulation may fulfil the criteria in Article 81(3), depending on the details of the pool itself and the specific conditions of the market in question. An individual analysis would be necessary in such cases in order to determine whether or not the conditions of Article 81(3) are met.[575]

12.178 **Security devices.** Regulation 358/2003 exempts the establishment, recognition and distribution of technical specifications, rules or codes of practice for certain security devices for which there is no harmonised Community-level technical specification. This covers also technical specifications for the installation and maintenance of security devices, and procedures for assessing and approving the compliance of undertakings which install or maintain security devices with such specifications, rules or codes of practice.[576] Such agreements can be beneficial in providing a benchmark to insurers and reinsurers when assessing the extent of the risk they are asked to cover in a specific case, which depends on the quality of security equipment and of its installation and maintenance. However, where there are Community-level harmonised standards, any agreements among insurers on the same subject will not be covered by the Regulation, since the objective of such harmonisation at European level is to lay down exhaustive and adequate levels of security for security devices which apply uniformly across the Community.[577] Any agreement among insurers on different requirements for safety devices could undermine the achievement of that objective.[578]

---

[575] The Commission issued a negative clearance-type comfort letter to the Swedish, Italian and Spanish nuclear insurance and reinsurance pools *Svenska Atomforsakringspoolen, Pool Italiano Rischi Atomici* and *Aseguradores Riesgos Nucleares* (*XXXIst Report on Competition Policy* (2001), point 204) covering the markets for nuclear property insurance, nuclear reinsurance and UK nuclear liability insurance. See also *Pool Reinsurance Co Ltd* [2004] UKCLR 893: Office of Fair Trading granted individual exemption under the UK equivalent of Art 81(3) to a pool set up to provide reinsurance against terrorism risk for commercial property in Great Britain, after insurance against such risk had become unavailable following 1992 IRA bombing in London. Although the arrangements restricted competition because they required members to offer terrorism cover only in conjunction with general cover for commercial property; to reinsure all their terrorism insurance for commercial property with Pool Re and stipulated that policyholders who buy terrorism insurance for commercial property must buy such cover for their entire portfolio of commercial properties with Pool Re, an exemption was granted because of the benefits of ensuring that all commercial properties have access to terrorism cover.

[576] Reg 358/2003, Art 1(f).

[577] See Council Resolution of 7 May 1985 on a new approach to technical harmonisation and standardisation, OJ 1985 C136/1; Council Resolution of 21 December 1989 on a global approach to conformity assessment, OJ 1990 C10/1.

[578] In *Association of Norwegian Insurance Companies*, EFTA Surveillance Authority (ESA) Annual Reports 1998, point 5.1.2.2.4, 2002, point 6.2.6, the rules of the Norwegian insurers' association (considered under Art 53 EEA) were found to come outside the scope of the equivalent provision in the earlier block exemption, apparently as common standards and common approval of firms were imposed; after amendments to make the approval process fairer, the ESA found the criteria for individual exemption were satisfied and closed the cases by comfort letters.

Insurance intermediaries.   Vertical agreements in the insurance sector, including   **12.179**
agreements involving intermediaries, fall to be assessed under the block exemption for vertical agreements. Where an agreement is a genuine agency agreement
it will not fall within the scope of Article 81(1).[579] However, an agreement among
insurers as to which intermediaries they will use may infringe Article 81(1).
In *Institute of Independent Insurance Brokers and Association of British Travel
Agents*,[580] the United Kingdom Competition Appeal Tribunal found that the
rules of GISC, which prevented its insurer members from dealing with insurance
intermediaries unless they were themselves members of GISC, fell within the
Chapter I prohibition (the domestic equivalent to Article 81(1)).

6. Postal Services

(a) Generally

The EC Treaty and characteristics of the sector.   The application of the EC   **12.180**
competition rules to postal services involves consideration not only of Articles 81
and 82 but also of Article 86 of the Treaty. Moreover, postal services constitute
'services' within the meaning of Article 49 EC. The market for postal services is
characterised by the need, widely recognised in the Member States, to ensure a
certain degree of universal service. Those living and conducting business in remote
parts of a Member State should have access to postal services since they remain an
important method of communication notwithstanding advances in electronic
communications. Furthermore, this access should be on terms no less favourable
than those in well connected urban conurbations. Determining the extent to
which parts of the postal services sector should be 'reserved' to legal monopolies
in the general interest is, however, a complex policy question.

Development of Community policy.   Community policy in the field of postal   **12.181**
services has come about relatively recently.[581] It has to a large extent been inspired
by, and based around, the judgment of the Court of Justice in *Corbeau*,[582] which
set out the limits of permissible postal monopolies. In 1992 the Commission
published a Green Paper proposing that all postal services excluding ordinary

---

[579] Commission Notice (Guidelines on Vertical Restraints), OJ 2000 C291/1, paras 12–20
(Agency Agreements). See further paras 6.028 *et seq*, above.
[580] *Institute of Independent Insurance Brokers and Association of British Travel Agents v Director
General of Fair Trading* [2001] CAT 4, [2001] CompAR 62.
[581] The DG Internal Market and Services has a useful webpage dealing with EU Postal
legislation: http://ec.europa.eu/internal_market/post/legislation_en.htm. See also Van Bael &
Bellis, *Competition Law of the European Community* (4th ed, 2005), paras 12.13–12.15.
[582] Case C-320/91 *Corbeau* [1993] ECR I-2533, [1995] 4 CMLR 621.

internal letter deliveries be liberalised.[583] The Green Paper led in turn to legislation designed to liberalise access to the majority of postal services within the Community.[584] In recent years, this legislation has been amended with a view to completing the internal market by 2009.[585]

12.182 *Corbeau.*   In *Corbeau*,[586] the Court of Justice dealt with the central question of the extent to which Member States could rely on Article 86(2) EC in reserving parts of the postal services market to legal monopolies.[587] The Court held that the exclusion of competition was justified as regards services properly linked to the service of general interest. It accepted that in the absence of a monopoly, undertakings could 'concentrate on the economically profitable operations' to the detriment of the loss making aspects of a service.[588] However, there are limits to the permissible reservation of the market:

> 'the exclusion of competition is not justified as regards specific services dissociable from the service of general interest which meet special needs of economic operators and which call for certain additional services not offered by the traditional postal service, such as collection from the senders' address, greater speed or reliability of distribution or the possibility of changing the destination in the course of transit, in so far as such specific services, by their nature and the conditions in which they are offered, such as the geographical area in which they are provided, do not compromise the economic equilibrium of the service of general economic interest performed by the holder of the exclusive right.'[589]

(b) Liberalisation

12.183 **The Postal Directive.**   Directive 97/67 ('the Postal Directive'),[590] which entered into force in February 1998, established common rules concerning the provision of a universal postal service within the Community; the criteria defining the services which may be reserved for universal service providers[591] and the conditions governing non-reserved services; tariff principles and transparency of accounts for

---

[583] *The Development of the Single Market for Postal Services*, COM(91) 476 final.
[584] viz the Postal Directive, discussed below.
[585] Directive 2002/39, OJ 2002 L176/21. See further para 12.186, below.
[586] Case C-320/91 *Corbeau* [1993] ECR I-2533, [1995] 4 CMLR 621.
[587] For Art 86(2), see generally Chap 11, above.
[588] *Corbeau* (n 586, above) para 18.
[589] ibid, para 19.
[590] Dir 97/67, OJ 1998 L15/14, am by Dir 2002/39, OJ 2002 L176/21: Vol II, App E.28. Dirs 97/67 and 2002/39 are incorporated into the EEA Agreement by EEA Joint Committee Decns 91/98 and 168/2002, OJ 1999 L189/64, OJ 2003 L38/30. For various points on the interpretation of the Dir see COMP 38.745 *BdKEP – restrictions on mail preparation*, 20 October 2004, [2006] 4 CMLR 981 (on appeal Case T-490/04 *Germany v Commission*, not yet decided) and *La Poste*, OJ 2002 L120/19. See note on *BdKEP* decn in (2005) 1 EC Competition Policy Newsletter 31.
[591] 'Universal service provider' is defined as the public or private entity providing a universal postal service or parts thereof within a Member State whose identity has been notified to the Commission: Dir 97/67, Art 2(13).

universal service provision; the setting and monitoring of quality standards for universal service provision; the harmonisation of technical standards; and the creation of independent national regulatory authorities.[592] The Postal Directive was amended by Directive 2002/39[593] which defined further steps in the process of gradual and controlled opening up of the postal market. It also further limited the service sectors that can be reserved by the Member States to the universal service provider.

Reservation of services.   To the extent necessary to ensure the maintenance of **12.184** universal service, Member States may reserve services limited to the clearance, sorting, transport and delivery of items of domestic correspondence and incoming cross-border correspondence weighing not more than 50 grams and costing less than two and a half times the basic tariff.[594] Outgoing cross-border mail may also continue to be reserved subject to specified limits.[595]

Universal service.   The Postal Directive lays down a right to a universal service **12.185** involving the permanent provision of a postal service of specified quality at all points in their territory at affordable prices for all users. Universal service providers must guarantee as a minimum one clearance and one delivery to the home or premises of every legal or natural person every working day and not less than five days a week, save in exceptional circumstances.[596] Furthermore, universal service must include the clearance, sorting, transport and distribution of postal items weighing up to two kilograms and of postal packages weighing up to ten kilograms.[597] The Postal Directive sets out a number of further requirements with respect to universal service provision[598] and obliges Member States to establish one or more independent national regulatory authorities for the postal sector.[599]

---

[592]   ibid, Art 1.

[593]   Dir 2002/39 (n 585, above).

[594]   Dir 97/67 (n 590, above) Art 7(1) (as amended). From 1 January 2003 to 1 January 2006 Member States could reserve such services relating to correspondence with a weight limit of 100g: ibid. On the interpretation of Art 7 in relation to 'self-provision' (ie the provision of postal services by the natural or legal person who is the originator of the mail or collection or routing of these items by a third party acting solely on behalf of that person), see Case C-240/02 *Asempre* [2004] ECR I-2461.

[595]   ibid. As of 14 October 2003, six Member States had decided not to liberalise this market: *XXXIIIrd Report on Competition Policy* (2003), point 103.

[596]   Dir 97/67 (n 590, above) Art 3. Deliveries may, by way of derogation, be made to 'appropriate installations' subject to conditions imposed at the discretion of the national regulatory authority: ibid, Art 3(3).

[597]   ibid, Art 3(4). Member States must ensure that packages received from other Member States weighing up to 20 kilograms are delivered: ibid, Art 3(5).

[598]   ibid, Arts 5–6 (service to users); Arts 12–14 (as amended) (tariff principles and transparency of accounts); Arts 16–19 (quality of services).

[599]   ibid, Art 22.

12.186 **Commission reports and proposed full liberalisation.** The amendments to the Postal Directive introduced by Directive 2002/39 included an obligation on the Commission to report every two years to the European Parliament and the Council on the application of the Postal Directive.[600] Further, the Postal Directive set a target date of 2009 for the full opening of postal markets to competition (the Directive itself expires on 31 December 2008).[601] In October 2006, the Commission proposed that the target date should be confirmed and accordingly published a proposal for a new Directive that would remove the concept of 'reservable areas' while maintaining the provisions of the existing Directive, including the universal service obligation.[602] The proposal was accompanied by a study on the impact on universal service of the full accomplishment of the postal internal market in 2009.[603] If the proposal is adopted, this is likely to lead to more operators carrying business mail, but the impact on private consumers in the short-term is likely to be more limited.

12.187 **Commission Notice on the postal sector.** In 1998, the Commission published guidance on the application of the EC competition rules to the postal sector.[604] The Notice set out, for the benefit in particular of postal operators and Member States, the Commission's interpretation of the relevant Treaty provisions and the guiding principles according to which it intended to apply the competition rules to the postal sector in individual cases. The Notice considers, *inter alia*, issues surrounding market definition; dominance; potential forms of abuse, in particular cross-subsidisation; freedom to provide services; measures adopted by Member States; State aid; and the concept of services of general economic interest.

(c) Application of competition rules

12.188 **Jurisprudence of the Community Courts and the Commission.** The area of postal services has been the subject of several judgments of the Community Courts and decisions of the Commission, notably in relation to the application of Articles 81 and 82 but also concerning Article 86[605] and the question of the proper

---

[600] Art 23 of Dir 97/67 as amended (n 588, above). See first report, 2002 (COM/2002/632); second report, March 2005 (COM/2005/102); third report, 2006 (COM/2006/595).

[601] ibid, Arts 7(3) and 27 (as amended).

[602] COMP/2006/594 final.

[603] COMP/2006/596 final.

[604] Notice from the Commission on the application of the competition rules to the postal sector and on the assessment of certain State measures relating to postal services, OJ 1998 C39/2: Vol II, App E.29.

[605] See *Corbeau* (n 586, above); *Spanish International Courier Services*, OJ 1990 L233/19, [1991] 4 CMLR 560 (infringements of Arts 82 and 86 by Spanish laws reserving to incumbent PPO the ancillary activity of international express courier services); *New Postal Services with a Guaranteed Day- or Time-certain Delivery in Italy*, OJ 2001 L63/59, [2001] 5 CMLR 595 (infringement of Arts 82 and 86 by an Italian law excluding competitors of the incumbent PPO from providing 'hybrid mail' services such as guaranteed delivery of electronically-created items at a pre-determined

interpretation of the Postal Directive.[606] The following paragraphs concentrate on the application of Articles 81 and 82.[607]

Article 81(1): *REIMS II.*   In *REIMS II,*[608] the Commission granted an exemp-   **12.189**
tion to the Remuneration and Exchange of International Mails II Agreement ('REIMS II'), which set fees ('terminal dues') for the delivery of cross-border mail among most EC and EEA public postal operators ('PPOs'). Historically, deliveries had been made without charge by the operator in the State of destination with the sender making a payment only to the postal authority in the state where the item is posted. But that cooperative approach, based on the assumption that international mail would move in equivalent volumes among countries and so balance out the cost, became unrealistic. Under REIMS II, terminal dues were linked to domestic mail tariffs in the country of destination and to the quality of service provided by the postal operator which delivered the mail. Terminal dues were not to exceed a certain percentage of the applicable domestic tariff.[609] The Commission considered that the agreement was caught by Article 81(1) in that it amounted to a price-fixing agreement, albeit one with 'unusual characteristics'.[610] However, the Commission held that Article 81(3) applied, setting stringent conditions to enable it to monitor the agreement and ensure that the final level of terminal dues reflected actual costs.

REIMS II: **2001 exemption.**   The Commission renewed the exemption in respect   **12.190**
of a revised version of REIMS II[611] which took into account the transparent

---

date and time; competition in these markets, which were distinct from the basic postal service, would likewise not jeopardise the PPO's economic position); Case C-340/99 *TNT Traco v Poste Italiane* [2001] ECR I-4109, [2002] 4 CMLR 454 (compatibility with Arts 86 and 82 of Italian law requiring independent providers of express mail services to pay the universal service provider ('USP') postal dues for the provision of this service equivalent to the postage charge normally payable to the USP by its customers); *France/La Poste* (the 'SNELPT case'), OJ 2002 L120/19 (infringement of Art 86 in conjunction with Art 82 by French law not ensuring supervision by an independent regulatory authority of the relationship between the incumbent PPO and private mail preparation firms); *BdKEP–Restrictions on mail preparation* (n 590, above) (infringement of Art 86 by German postal law barring commercial mail preparation firms from earning discounts for handing over pre-sorted letters at Deutsche Post's ('DP') sorting centres, the relevant provisions (i) prompting DP to extend its market power from the reserved market for basic postal services into the liberalised market for mail preparation services, and (ii) inducing DP to discriminate between bulk mailers (which have access to sorting centres and related discounts) and commercial providers of such services (which do not have such discounts), hence inducing DP to abuse its dominant position).

[606] See, eg Case C-240/02 *Asempre and Asociación Nacional de Empresas de Externalización y Gestión de Envíos* [2004] ECR I-2461.

[607] For a detailed account of jurisprudence of the Community Courts in this area up to June 2001, see Flynn and Rizza, 'Postal Services and Competition Law. A Review and Analysis of the EC Case-Law' (2001) 24 (4) World Competition 475–511.

[608] *REIMS II,* OJ 1999 L275/17, [2000] 4 CMLR 704.

[609] ibid, para 17.

[610] ibid, paras 63–65.

[611] *REIMS II, renewal of exemption,* OJ 2004 L56/76, [2004] 5 CMLR 123. The exemption was valid for five years and expired on 31 December 2006. See the Note on this case in (2004) 1 EC

cost-accounting system required by both the Commission's *REIMS II* decision and the Postal Directive. The accounting data submitted by the PPOs indicated that maximum terminal dues of 80 per cent, which the parties had provided for in the revised version of the agreement submitted to the Commission, did not reflect actual costs and were therefore not indispensable to the attainment of the agreement's benefits. The Commission therefore insisted on the fees not exceeding a given proportion of the domestic tariffs. The revised agreement also obliges the parties to deliver incoming cross-border mail on behalf of private third party postal service providers on the same terms and conditions as those applied to other parties to the agreement.

12.191 **Article 82 and cross-subsidy issues.** In *Deutsche Post*,[612] the Commission found that Deutsche Post ('DP') had infringed Article 82 in relation to its activities on the business parcel services market. DP was found to have unlawfully cross-subsidised its mail order parcel services business from profits made in the reserved area of the basic postal service in the period 1990–1995.[613] The Commission considered whether the earnings from DP's mail order parcel services business covered the incremental costs of providing the services. In doing so, it only took account of the additional costs incurred solely as a result of providing those services rather than of common fixed costs.[614] By contrast, in *UPS Europe v Commission*[615] the Court of First Instance upheld a decision of the Commission rejecting a complaint against the acquisition by DP of a holding in parcels operator DHL. The fact that DP used profits made in the reserved area to fund the acquisition of joint control of an undertaking in a neighbouring market did not, in itself, raise a competition problem.[616]

Competition Policy Newsletter. Under the post-Modernisation regime, no new individual exemptions are granted and Art 81(3) is directly applicable if its conditions are satisfied.

[612] *Deutsche Post*, OJ 2001 L125/27, [2001] 5 CMLR 99.

[613] The Commission also characterised this abuse as predatory pricing: ibid, paras 35–36. Note that no penalty was imposed in respect of this head of abuse because, (i) the relevant measure of cost that a multi-service postal operator benefiting from a reserved area had to meet in activities open to competition had not previously been clarified, and (ii) DP undertook structurally to separate its business parcel services from reserved services: para 47.

[614] ibid, in particular Recital (7). The Commission took into account that DP, as a 'carrier of last resort', was under an obligation to remain ready to offer a standard parcel delivery service at a uniform tariff as part of its universal service obligations (maintenance of 'network reserve capacity'). That obligation increased the proportion of common fixed costs that a carrier of last resort bears in comparison with companies not under such an obligation: paras 9–10.

[615] Case T-175/99 *UPS Europe v Commission* [2002] ECR II-1915, [2002] 5 CMLR 67.

[616] ibid, para 61. The CFI pointed out that (i) there was no evidence that DP had been able to fund the acquisition as a result of abusive practices on the reserved market (para 59); and (ii) DP had undertaken to the Commission not to engage in cross-subsidisation of DHL's business in the parcels market (para 64).

Article 82: charging for remail. The *REIMS II* case concerned the payment of **12.192** terminal dues by the sender's postal authority to the postal authority in the territory of the addressee. The Universal Postal Convention makes separate provision for 'remail' cases where the sender is in fact resident in the same State as the addressee but posts letters (or causes letters to be posted) in a different State, either in large quantities or in order to take advantage of lower postal tariffs in that other State. Remail can be either physical (where the letters are actually transported to the other State to be posted there) or non-physical (where the text of the letter is transmitted electronically to the other State to be printed out, put in envelopes and posted there). The Universal Postal Convention allows the postal service in a Contracting State to refuse to deliver remail items or to deliver them subject to the imposition of a charge to be paid by the sender on each item of mail. In *Deutsche Post/GZS (Remail)*,[617] two companies resident in Germany challenged DP's right under German legislation implementing the Convention to charge them for remail items. On a reference from the German Court, the Court of Justice held that if DP were obliged to forward and deliver to addressees resident in Germany mail posted in large quantities by senders resident in Germany using postal services of other Member States, without being able to charge for providing that service, the performance of its task of providing a universal letter service would be jeopardised. The Court noted that the terminal dues paid to DP by the sending postal authority did not cover the actual costs of processing and delivering the letters. That being the case, DP was entitled to impose a charge on the sender to compensate it for the costs incurred in handling the item. On the other hand, insofar as part of the forwarding and delivery costs had been offset by receipt of terminal dues, it was not necessary for DP to charge the full internal rate on remail items in order to recoup its costs. Since DP had a statutory monopoly over internal letter mail and hence held a dominant position, it would be an abuse by DP (and hence a breach by Germany of Article 86) if DP were to charge the full internal postage tariff for the letter when it had already recovered part of its costs from the terminal dues paid by the State of posting.

---

[617] Cases C-147 & 148/97 *Deutsche Post/GZS (Remail)* [2000] ECR I-825, [2000] 4 CMLR 838. This case was referred to in Case VI-U (Kart) 32/99, judgment of the Düsseldorf Court of Appeal of 3 March 2004. The Düsseldorf Court held that DP was entitled to seek information from several defendants active in the mail order trade about the number of non-physical remail items they had sent, in order to charge them with internal postage as provided under the Universal Postal Convention and the corresponding German law. The Court referred to the ECJ's judgment in *Deutsche Post/GZS (Remail)* and held that since, on the facts, the charges imposed by DP did not, when added to the terminal dues received, exceed its costs, there was no abuse. See also *Deutsche Post – Interception of cross-border mail*, OJ 2001 L331/40, [2002] 4 CMLR 598 (finding of abuse by DP consisting in the interception, surcharging and delaying of incoming cross-border mail erroneously classified as circumvented domestic mail (known as 'A-B-A remail')).

12.193 **Article 82 and customer loyalty issues.** Once elements of the postal service which used to be reserved to the national monopolist have been opened up to competition, it becomes important to ensure that fledgling suppliers and potential market entrants are not forced out of the market or deterred from entering by abusive behaviour on the part of the former monopolist.[618] In *La Poste/De Post*,[619] the Commission found that the Belgian PPO had abused its dominant position by offering to customers of its general letter mail service (the reserved area) a preferential rate on condition that those customers accepted a supplementary contract with regard to a new business-to-business mail service (an area open to competition). This amounted to a form of tying contrary Article 82(d).[620] In the *Deutsche Post* case,[621] the Commission found that DP had unlawfully granted fidelity rebates over a period of 16 years to mail order parcel customers: DP granted a discount in return for an undertaking to send all or a significant part of the customer's parcels or catalogues via DP.[622] The Swedish Market Court has held that a new pricing tariff whereby Posten Sverige[623] charged substantially lower prices for customers in major cities where Posten Sverige was encountering competition constituted an abuse. The Court held that the announcement of the proposed new tariff was itself abusive because it was introduced just as Posten Sverige's new competitor was planning to expand its business. Since the tariff was drawn up at a time when Posten Sverige had not fully analysed its cost structures, the Court found that the tariff could not have been based on cost savings.

7. Agriculture

(a) The objectives of Article 33 of the EC Treaty

12.194 **The EC Treaty.** Among the activities of the Community set out in Article 3 of the EC Treaty are the establishment of a common agricultural policy[624] and of a system to ensure undistorted competition.[625] The authors of the Treaty recognised

---

[618] The Commission has emphasised the need for vigilance by the competition authorities (both EC and national) to ensure that the benefits of the liberalisation process are not cancelled out by anti-competitive behaviour by the dominant operator, in particular by leveraging its position from the market of monopoly services to adjacent markets open to competition: *Report on Competition Policy 2005*, point 95.

[619] *La Poste/De Post*, OJ 2002 L61/32, [2002] 4 CMLR 1426.

[620] ibid, paras 53–62.

[621] *Deutsche Post*, OJ 2001 L125/27, [2001] 5 CMLR 99.

[622] ibid, in particular paras 23 and 34.

[623] Case MD 1998:15 *The Competition Authority v Posten Sverige*, judgment of the Swedish Market Court, 11 November 1998. The Court held that a revised two zone tariff was not abusive because it did reflect cost savings.

[624] Art 3(1)(e).

[625] Art 3(1)(g).

that these two objectives might prove difficult to reconcile.[626] Accordingly, Article 36 of the Treaty provides that the rules on competition in Articles 81–89 shall apply to production of and trade in agricultural products only to the extent determined by the Council acting within the framework of Article 37(2) and (3)[627] and taking into account the objectives of Article 33. Those objectives are:

(a) 'to increase agricultural productivity by promoting technical progress and by ensuring the rational development of agricultural production and the optimum utilisation of factors of production, in particular labour;

(b) thus to ensure a fair standard of living for the agricultural community, in particular by increasing the individual earnings of persons engaged in agriculture;

(c) to stabilise markets;

(d) to ensure the availability of supplies;

(e) to ensure that supplies reach consumers at reasonable prices.'

Relationship between Article 36 and competition law objectives. Article 36 **12.195** simultaneously recognises the precedence that the specific rules on agriculture have over the competition rules of the Treaty and the wide discretion given to the Council in deciding how far the rules on competition should apply to the agricultural sector.[628] In *Milk Marque*,[629] the Court of Justice had to consider whether the Member States are in principle competent to take steps under their national competition law in an agricultural sector governed by a common organisation of the market. The Court described the relationship betweeen Article 36 and the Community competition rules in the following terms:

'It must first of all be observed that the maintenance of effective competition on the market for agricultural products is one of the objectives of the common agricultural policy and the common organisation of the relevant markets. Whilst Article 36 EC has conferred on the Council responsibility for determining the extent to which the Community competition rules are applicable to the production of and trade in agricultural products . . . that provision nevertheless establishes the principle that the Community competition rules are applicable in the agricultural sector . . . .

As the common organisations of the markets in agricultural products are therefore not a competition-free zone, . . . Community competition law and national competition law apply in parallel, since they consider restrictive practices from different points

---

[626] For discussion of the issues, see speech by the then Competition Commr Monti, 'The relationship between the CAP and competition policy: does EU competition law apply to agriculture?', 13 November 2003 (SPEECH/03/537).

[627] These provisions now require a Commission proposal, consultation of the European Parliament and qualified majority vote for the Council to make regulations, issue directives or take decisions.

[628] Case 139/79 *Maizena v Council* [1980] ECR 3393, para 23; see also, per AG Capotorti in Case 114/76 *Bela-Mühle v Grows-Farm* [1977] ECR 1211, 1236, [1979] 2 CMLR 83, 114.

[629] Case C-137/00 *Milk Marque and National Farmers' Union* [2003] ECR I-7975, [2004] 4 CMLR 293. The ECJ went on to hold that the recommendations by the Competition Commission did not undermine the common organisation of the milk market.

of view. Whereas Articles 81 and 82 EC regard them in the light of the obstacles which may result from trade between Member States, national law proceeds on the basis of the considerations peculiar to it and considers restrictive practices only in that context.'[630]

12.196 **The agricultural sector.** As the Treaty provides for limited application of the competition rules in the agricultural sector, it is important to identify what that sector comprises. Article 32(1) defines 'agricultural products' as 'the products of the soil, of stockfarming and of fisheries and products of first-stage processing directly related to those products'. Article 32(3) provides that the products 'subject to Articles 33 to 38' (the Agriculture Title) are listed in Annex I to the Treaty. It is settled that the classification of a product as within or outside the agricultural sector for the purposes of application of competition rules depends on whether it is within Annex I rather than within the Article 32(1) definition,[631] and that Annex I falls to be interpreted, insofar as it adopts Common Customs Tariff headings, in accordance with interpretation of the Tariff itself.[632]

12.197 **Council measures.** Under Article 37(2) and (3), the Council may choose whether the common agricultural policy is to be achieved, in relation to any given commodity, by instituting a common organisation of the market in that commodity. The Council has exercised that choice, in applying competition rules to trade in agricultural products, in two ways. First, in 1962 it adopted Regulation 26 applying certain rules of competition to the production of and trade in agricultural products.[633] Secondly, it has varied and extended the application of those rules in the specific regulations implementing the various common organisations. Regulation 26 was replaced by Regulation 1184/2006 which came into force on 24 August 2006.[634] The new Regulation does not change the substantive law but was adopted 'in the interests of clarity and rationality'[635] to codify the amendments to the earlier Regulation.

12.198 **Analysis of agricultural product agreements.** Accordingly, in analysing the application of the competition rules to production of or trade in any product commonly regarded as agricultural, it is necessary to ask two questions: (i) whether the product appears in Annex I EC: if so, Regulation 1184/2006 applies to it; and (ii) whether the product is subject to a common organisation of the market: if so,

---

[630] ibid, paras 58–61.
[631] Case 61/80 *Coöperatieve Stremsel-en Kleurselfabriek v Commission* [1981] ECR 851, [1982] 1 CMLR 240. The definition of agricultural products contained in Art 32(1) EC is only indicative; the binding definition is that contained in Art 32(3) which refers to Annex I: per AG Warner at 877 (ECR), 250 (CMLR).
[632] Case 77/83 *CILFIT v Ministero della Sanità* [1984] ECR 1257.
[633] Reg 26, JO 1962, 993, OJ 1959–1962,129.
[634] Reg 1184/2006, OJ 2006 L214/7: Vol II, App E.30.
[635] ibid, Recital (1).

the specific rules of the common organisation also require examination to identify whether they vary or supplement the competition rules that apply to the product by Regulation 1184/2006.[636]

EEA Agreement.   Although the European Economic Area aims to eliminate **12.199** trade barriers between the Community and the participating EFTA States, it was recognised that the task of assimilating agricultural support measures for that purpose was unmanageable at commencement and would need to be deferred.[637] Article 8(3) of the EEA Agreement provides that, unless otherwise specified, the Agreement applies only to the products identified in that Article.[638] Agricultural products are not included under Article 8(3) nor are they specified in Part IV of the Agreement (competition and other common rules). Accordingly, the competition rules of the EEA Agreement do not apply to agricultural products.

(b) Application of competition rules

Operation of Regulation 1184/2006.   Article 1 of Regulation 1184/2006 **12.200** provides that Articles 81–86 of the Treaty and any implementing provisions shall apply to all agreements, decisions and practices referred to in Articles 81(1) and 82 which relate to production of, or trade in, the agricultural products listed in Annex I to Treaty, subject to Article 2 of that Regulation. Article 2(1) provides that:

> 'Article 81(1) of the Treaty shall not apply to such of the agreements, decisions and practices referred to in the preceding article as form an integral part of a national market organisation or are necessary for attainment of the objectives set out in Article 33 of the Treaty.

> In particular, it shall not apply to agreements, decisions and practices of farmers, farmers' associations, or associations of such associations belonging to a single Member State which concern the production or sale of agricultural products or the use of joint facilities for the storage, treatment or processing of agricultural products, and under which there is no obligation to charge identical prices, unless the Commission finds that competition is thereby excluded or that the objectives of Article 33 of the Treaty are jeopardised.'

---

[636] eg wool is a product commonly regarded as agricultural which does not appear in Annex I: see *CILFIT* (n 632, above); potatoes are Annex I products of which there is still no common organisation of the market. In *Milk Marque and National Farmers' Union* (n 629, above), it was held that national authorities in principle retain jurisdiction to apply national competition law in relation to the common organisation of the market in milk and milk products in the UK.

[637] See Arts 17–20 EEA.

[638] Art 8(3) applies the EEA Agreement to products falling within Chapters 25–97 of the Harmonised Commodity Description and Coding System, excluding the products in Protocol 2; this system was set up by International Convention, signed in Brussels on 14 June 1983. Agricultural Products fall within Chapters 1–24.

Article 2 relates only to Article 81 EC and as a derogation from the general rule on competition is to be interpreted strictly.[639] It follows from Article 1 that Article 82 EC applies in full to agricultural products.

12.201 **Annex I products.** There is an advantage, for an undertaking whose practices might otherwise infringe Article 81(1), in establishing that the product in which it deals falls within Article 2(1) of Regulation 1184/2006 since this means that Article 81(1) applies only subject to the exceptions applicable to the agricultural sector. However, for Article 2(1) to apply, the agreement, decision or practice in question must relate to a product listed in Annex I to the Treaty. Accordingly an undertaking cannot invoke the exceptions contained in Regulation 1184/2006 in respect of an agricultural product that does not fall within Annex I, even if it is a substance ancillary to the production of a commodity within Annex I.[640]

12.202 **The first Article 2(1) exception: national market organisations.** The first kind of agreements, decisions and practices to which Article 81(1) EC does not apply by virtue of Article 2(1) of Regulation 1184/2006 (formerly Article 2(1) of Regulation 26) are those that 'form an integral part of a national market organisation'. Most national market organisations have now been replaced by common organisations of the market set up under Council regulations, and those that remain must be compatible with Community law.[641] Consequently this provision is significant only in residual areas, for example potatoes, where an Annex I product is not yet subject to a common organisation of the market, or in areas where the common organisation itself authorises the continued existence of a national market organisation.[642]

---

[639] Cases T-70 & 71/92 *Florimex and VGB v Commission* [1997] ECR II–693, [1997] 5 CMLR 769, [1997] All ER (EC) 798, para 152; upheld on appeal, Case C-265/97P *VBA v Florimex* [2000] ECR I–2061, [2001] 5 CMLR 1343, para 94 (decided under the analogous Reg 26).

[640] See, eg *Coöperatieve Stremsel* (n 631, above) where it was held that rennet could not benefit from Reg 26; similarly, cognac: Case 123/83 *BNIC v Clair* [1985] ECR 391, [1985] 2 CMLR 430; fur farming: Case T-61/89 *Dansk Pelsdyravlerforening* [1992] ECR II–1931; and fertilisers and pesticides: Case C-250/92 *Gøttrup-Klim v Dansk Landbrugs Grovvareselskab AmbA* [1994] ECR I–5641, [1996] 4 CMLR 191.

[641] See *New Potatoes*, OJ 1987 C159/2 and *French New Potato Marketing Regulations*, OJ 1988 L59/25, [1998] 4 CMLR 790. See also *Bloemenveilingen Aalsmeer*, OJ 1988 L26/27, [1989] 4 CMLR 500, where the Commission rejected the argument that exclusive purchasing agreements could form part of a national organisation of the market. Any national market organisation must, after the expiry of the original transitional period under the Treaty on 1 January 1970, and, as far as the new Member States are concerned, after the expiry of the transitional periods provided under the relevant Accession arrangements, comply with the general rules on the free movement of goods: see Case 288/83 *Commission v Ireland* [1985] ECR 1761, [1985] 3 CMLR 152 (import licensing system for third century potatoes could not extend to such potatoes once in free circulation elsewhere in the Community); Cases T-217 & 245/03 *Fédération National de la Coopération Bétail et Viande v Commission ('French Beef')*, judgment of 13 December 2006, para 199 (on appeal, Cases C-101/07P, etc, *Coopération De France Bétail et Viande v Commission*, not yet decided).

[642] See, eg Reg 1421/78, OJ 1978 L171/12, Reg 1422/78, OJ 1978 L171/14, and Reg 1565/79, OJ 1979 L188/29, which between them provided for the UK Government to be authorised, subject

The second Article 2(1) exception: necessary under Article 33. The second **12.203**
category of agreements, etc, to which Article 81(1) does not apply are those which
are 'necessary for the attainment of the objectives set out in Article 33 of the
Treaty'. All the objectives of Article 33 must be attained before this exception can
apply. In *Frubo*, the Court of Justice held that, even if the agreement met some of
those objectives, the agreement had not been necessary to meet the remaining
requirements of Article 33, namely 'to increase agricultural productivity' or 'to
ensure a fair standard of living for the agricultural community'; consequently it
had been reasonable for the Commission to conclude that this exception did not
apply to the agreement in question.[643] In *French Beef*, although the measures
adopted to help French cattle breeders at the time of crisis caused by BSE
('mad cow' disease) satisfied the objective of 'ensur[ing] a fair standard of living for
the agricultural community', the Court of First Instance found that it was not
designed to stabilise the market, nor was it necessary for that objective, since it did
not seek to reduce supply but simply to keep prices artificially high.[644] Normally,
the means for attaining the objectives of Article 33 are defined in the Council
regulation setting up the common organisation of the market for the products
concerned.[645] In such a case it is only where the application of Article 81(1) would
jeopardise the attainment of the objectives of Article 33 as given effect by the
relevant regulation that it is possible to invoke the second exception contained in

to conditions, to maintain the milk marketing schemes in the UK, which survived until brought
to an end pursuant to the Agriculture Act 1993 and the Agriculture (Northern Ireland) Order,
SI 1993/2665 (N.I. 10). cf *Scottish Salmon Board*, OJ 1992 L246/37, [1993] 5 CMLR 602, where,
in the absence of such an authorisation, the Commission held that a salmon price-fixing arrangement clearly could not be justified as an integral part of a national market organisation, since such
an organisation was precluded by the establishment of the relevant common organisation.

[643] Case 71/74 *Frubo v Commission* [1975] ECR 563, [1975] 2 CMLR 123, paras 22–27 and
AG Warner at 594 (ECR), 138 (CMLR). The Court expressed the justification as entirely a matter of
reasonableness on the part of the Commission, whereas the AG expressed it primarily as a matter
of legal analysis. The latter is more consistent with the text of Art 2(1), taken alone (but cf discussion of Art 2(2), below) and has been confirmed in the *Florimex* case (n 636, above) where the
Commission's statement of reasons for deciding that the second exception applied was annulled as
deficient. The CFI stated (para 153): 'In the event of a conflict between those sometimes divergent
objectives, the Commission's statement of reasons must, at the very least, show how it was able to
reconcile them so as to enable the first sentence of Article 2(1) of Regulation 26 to be applied'. The
ECJ stated (para 99): '... the Commission was required to state reasons for its decision by showing
how the agreements concluded within the VBA were necessary for attainment of each of the objectives set out in Article 33 of the Treaty or, in any event, how those objectives could be reconciled.'

[644] Cases T-217 & 245/03 *FNCBV and FNSEA v Commission*, judgment of 13 December 2006,
paras 201–204 (decided under the analogous Reg 26) (on appeal, Cases C-101/07P, etc, *Coopération
De France Bétail et Viande v Commission*, not yet decided).

[645] See, eg *MELDOC*, OJ 1986 L348/50, [1989] 4 CMLR 853, a case involving milk where the
means to be employed in the dairy sector to fulfil the objectives of Art 33 were held to be set out in
Reg 804/68 on the common organisation of the market in milk and milk products. See also *Frubo*
(n 643, above); *Cauliflowers*, OJ 1978 L21/23, [1978] 1 CMLR D66; *Bloemenveilmegen Aalsmeer*
(n 641, above); and Case 212/87 *Unilec* [1988] ECR 5075, [1990] 1 CMLR 592.

Article 2(1) of Regulation 1184/2006.[646] Thus in *Cauliflowers*,[647] an agreement between cauliflower producers' associations and dealers limiting the right of dealers to obtain supplies from other sources could not benefit from the exception; the common organisation of the market in fruit and vegetables under Regulation 1035/72[648] was focused on producers alone in attaining Article 33 objectives, and consequently the attainment of those objectives could not be adversely affected by the application of Article 81(1) to arrangements involving dealers. In practice, therefore, it would appear to be difficult to establish that an agreement is necessary for Article 33 objectives in any case where there is a common organisation of the relevant market unless the rules of the common organisation expressly or impliedly contemplate such an agreement.[649]

12.204   **The third Article 2(1) exception: farmers' associations.**   The second paragraph of Article 2(1) of Regulation 1184/2006 provides that:

> 'In particular, [Article 81(1)] shall not apply to agreements, decisions and practices of farmers, farmers' associations, or associations of such associations belonging to a single Member State which concern the production or sale of agricultural products or the use of joint facilities for the storage, treatment or processing of agricultural products, and under which there is no obligation to charge identical prices, unless the Commission finds that competition is thereby excluded or that the objectives of Article 33 are jeopardised.'

This sentence reproduces the second sentence of Article 2(1) of Regulation 26 and is ambiguously drafted. Although there was at one time doubt as to whether this formed no more than an illustrative example within the ambit of the previous sentence or constituted a free-standing exception of its own,[650] the matter was settled by the Court of Justice which held that the second sentence constituted an independent exception. It was material that, as a matter of legislative history, the sentence was added to Regulation 26 at the behest of the European Parliament

---

[646]   See *Milchförderungsfonds*, OJ 1985 L35/35, [1985] 3 CMLR 101; *MELDOC*, above.

[647]   See *Cauliflowers* (n 642, above). See also *Breeders Rights–Maize Seed*, OJ 1978 1286/23, [1978] 3 CMLR 434, on appeal Case 258/78 *Nungesser v Commission* [1982] ECR 2015, [1983] 1 CMLR 278; *Milchförderungsfonds* (n 643, above); *Preserved Mushrooms*, OJ 1975 L29/26, [1975] 1 CMLR D83.

[648]   Since replaced by Reg 2200/96, OJ 1996 L297/1.

[649]   See *Re Sugar Beet*, OJ 1990 L31/32, [1991] 4 CMLR 629; *Scottish Salmon Board* (n 639, above); *Sicasov*, OJ 1999 L4/27, [1999] 4 CMLR 192, para 68. However, in the *Florimex* case (n 639, above) where the Commission dismissed a complaint on the basis that the agreements in question concerning cut flowers fell within this exception, the products were subject to a common organisation by Reg 234/68; although this decision was annulled, the effect of a common organisation formed no part of the reasoning of the CFI or ECJ.

[650]   See, eg *Milchförderungsfonds* (n 643, above) in which the Commission stated that an agreement falling within the scope of the second sentence of Art 2(1) could not benefit from the derogation granted by Art 2 if it failed to satisfy either of the two conditions laid down in the first sentence of Art 2(1), but went on to justify why the agreement in question was objectionable by reference to the second sentence even if it were independent.

and did not appear in the Commission's original legislative proposal; and that, had the sentence no independent meaning, 'the Commission could scarcely find that an agreement jeopardised the objectives of Article 33 of the Treaty if, by virtue of the derogation set out in the first sentence, it had already been established that that agreement . . . was necessary for the attainment of those objectives'.[651] The same interpretation clearly applies to the identical Article 2(1) of Regulation 1184/2006.

Scope of the third exception. This exception applies only where the agree- **12.205** ment involves farmers and/or their associations exclusively; an agreement involving farmers and dealers cannot benefit from it,[652] whereas obligations arising between a farmer and a farming cooperative to which he belongs will be capable of doing so.[653] The condition requiring there to be no obligation in the agreement to charge identical prices is probably intended to prevent price-fixing cartels of the ordinary kind, for example an agreement between farmers not to sell their cattle to slaughterhouses below a minimum price; it should not apply to an arrangement whereby producers selling through a cooperative receive proportionally the same realised price for their produce.[654] Finally, this exception does not apply if the Commission finds that competition is excluded or that the objectives of Article 33 are jeopardised. Hence the combination of clauses in the statutes of an agricultural cooperative requiring exclusive supply by its members to the association and excessive fees for withdrawal, thereby tying the members to the association, could have the effect of restricting competition and be incompatible with the objective of the common agricultural policy of increasing farmers' earnings.[655]

Varying or supplementing operation of the regime. Regulations governing **12.206** groups of producers of certain specified commodities may contain derogations

---

[651] Cases C-319/93, etc, *Dijkstra v Friesland (Frico Domo) Coöperatie* [1995] ECR I–4471, [1996] 5 CMLR 178, para 20.

[652] See *Cauliflowers* (n 644, above).

[653] Case C-399/93 *Oude Luttikhuis v Coberco* [1995] ECR I–4515, [1996] 5 CMLR 178.

[654] If it were otherwise, it would be virtually impossible for any agricultural cooperative marketing arrangement to benefit from Art 2(1); however, the whole purpose of the second sentence of Art 2(1) is to enable standard agricultural cooperative arrangements to avoid being caught as a matter of routine by Art 81(1) EC.

[655] *Oude Luttikhuis* (n 653, above). See also *Campina*, *XXIst Annual Report on Competition Policy* (1991), points 83–84, where the Commission regarded a widening of opportunity to leave the cooperative (three times a year rather than once) and a reduction of the leaving fee (from 10 per cent to 4 per cent of the average annual milk price paid by the cooperative to the member, or nothing if two years' notice were given) as covered by the exemption in Reg 26; *Milk Marketing Board*, *XXIInd Annual Report on Competition Policy* (1992), points 161–167, where, given the potentially dominant position of the England and Wales Board's prospective successor cooperative, the Commission's decision not to take action under Arts 81 and 82 was assured in effect only for the purpose of monitoring over an initial two year period.

from the regime established by Regulation 26 and continued by Regulation 1184/ 2006.[656] Although in general common organisations of markets in particular agricultural commodities do not add to or vary the regime in its application of Articles 81 and 82, those which give special status to producer groups may do so.[657]

12.207 **Procedure.** Article 2(2)–(3) of Regulation 1184/2006 provides that subject to consulting the Member States and hearing the undertakings concerned and any other natural or legal person that it considers appropriate, the Commission has the sole power to determine which agreements, decisions and practices fulfil the conditions specified in Article 2(1). In a number of cases the equivalent criteria in Regulation 26 were found by the Commission to have been fulfilled.[658]

12.208 **Role of national courts.** Where there has been no decision by the Commission under Article 2(2) of either Regulation 26 or 1184/2006, the course to be followed by a national court faced with a challenge to an agreement will be closely analogous to that governing the position of national courts regarding Article 81(3) in general.[659]

12.209 **Article 81(3).** If the conditions in Article 2(1) of Regulation 1184/2006 are not satisfied, the consequence is that Article 81 applies in full to the agreement, decision or practice in question. Therefore, an agreement concerning agricultural products, like any other products, may fall within a general block exemption or fulfil the criteria for individual exemption. Hence in *Sicasov*,[660] the standard form agreements of the French plant breeders' cooperative for the production and sale of breeders' seeds (an Annex I product) were granted individual exemption under Article 81(3) for 10 years although the Commission found that they were not necessary for the Article 33 objectives and so did not come within the exception in Article 2(1) of Regulation 26.

---

[656] See, eg Council Reg 1360/78, OJ 1978 L166/1 (repealed) which contained a specific derogation for groups of producers of certain specified commodities in Belgium, Italy and part of France.

[657] See, eg Reg 2200/96 on the common organisation of the market in fruit and vegetables (n 648, above) Art 20.

[658] See Cases 40/73, etc, *Suiker Unie v Commission* [1975] ECR 1663, [1976] 1 CMLR 295; *Preserved Mushrooms*, OJ 1975 L29/26, [1975] 1 CMLR D83; *Nungesser v Commission (maize seed)* (n 647, above).

[659] This was the approach taken in *Dijkstra* (n 648, above), which applied the principles applicable prior to the introduction of Reg 1/2003.

[660] *Sicasov*, 1999 OJ L4/27, [1999] 4 CMLR 192.

13

ENFORCEMENT AND PROCEDURE

1. Introduction

13.001 **Plan of this Chapter.**   This Chapter deals with the enforcement of Articles 81 and 82 by the Commission.[1] The enforcement of Article 81 and 82 by national competition authorities (NCAs) is dealt with in Chapter 14, and procedural issues concerning mergers and State aids are dealt with, respectively, in Chapters 8 and 15. Section 2 of this Chapter briefly describes the former enforcement regime under Regulation 17. The transitional provisions moving from that regime to the post-Modernisation regime under Regulation 1/2003 that came into force on 1 May 2004 were very limited. In consequence, infringements occurring prior to 1 May 2004 that are dealt with subsequently are handled under the new regime. However, knowledge of the Regulation 17 regime is important for an understanding of the case law, most of which is of course prior to May 2004. Section 3 describes the process of allocation of cases as between the Commission and NCAs and also covers the Commission's power to make declarations of inapplicability or to issue guidance letters. Section 4 deals with the Commission's powers of investigation. Section 5 covers the duties of the Commission with respect to the handling of complaints. The formal procedure followed in cases leading to substantive adverse decisions is discussed in Section 6. The Commission's new power to accept binding commitments is discussed in Section 7, and the ancillary power of the Commission to order interim measures is discussed in Section 8. The Commission's powers to order termination of infringements are discussed in Section 9 and the Commission's powers to impose fines for infringement of the substantive rules and its policy in that regard in Section 10. Review of Commission decisions by the Court of First Instance and the Court of Justice is discussed in Sections 11 and 12.

13.002 **The Commission's role in enforcing Article 81 and 82.**   Since 1962, the Commission has had the task of enforcing the competition rules under the EEC (and then the EC) Treaty. This task encompasses the duty to pursue a general policy designed to apply, in competition matters, the principles laid down by the Treaty and to guide the conduct of undertakings in the light of those principles.[2] Under Regulation 1/2003,[3] this system has been transformed so that the

---

[1] For works offering a detailed treatment of the subject-matter of this Chapter, see Kerse and Khan, *EC Antitrust Procedure* (5th edn, 2006); Ortiz Blanco, *EC Competition Procedure* (2nd edn, 2006). See also Tosato and Bellodi (eds), *EU Competition Law, Vol I: Procedure* (2006); Siragusa and Rizza (eds), *EU Competition Law, Vol III: Cartel Law* (2007), Chaps 2–5.

[2] Cases 100/80, etc, *Musique Diffusion Française v Commission* [1983] ECR 1825, [1983] 3 CMLR 221, para 105; Case C-344/98 *Masterfoods v HB Ice Cream* [2000] ECR I-11369, [2001] 4 CMLR 449, [2001] All ER (EC) 130, paras 45 *et seq*.

[3] Reg 1/2003, OJ 2003 L1/1, Vol II, App B.3.

Commission now shares the task of enforcing Articles 81 and 82 with the NCAs of the Member States. However, although the Regulation imposes duties and confers powers (including with regard to the application of Article 81(3)) on the NCAs, the Commission retains what may be said to be a 'leading role', or *primus inter pares*,[4] in the enforcement of the EC competition rules, a role which is further enhanced by the fact that as a matter of Community law decisions of the Commission have a special status as far as national courts are concerned.[5]

The Commission's role in enforcing Articles 53 and 54 of the EEA **13.003**
Agreement. Where conduct being investigated by the Commission affects trade between the EC Member States and trade between the contracting EFTA States of the EEA, the Commission has jurisdiction to apply the competition provisions of the EEA Agreement. The powers it uses in such an investigation are the same as the powers it uses when investigating purely EC conduct. This aspect of the Commission's procedure is discussed in Chapter 1, above.[6]

2. The Former Enforcement Regime under Regulation 17

Regulation 17. Under the previous regime implementing Articles 81 and 82, **13.004**
set out in Regulation 17,[7] the Commission was, broadly speaking, the sole body charged with the task of enforcing Articles 81 and 82 as a matter of Community law. Save in limited sectors of the economy to which Regulation 17 and other implementing regulations did not apply, NCAs were not as a matter of Community law obliged to enforce Article 81 or 82 themselves. Moreover, the Commission was the only body able to apply Article 81(3). Regulation 17 established a procedure whereby parties could notify agreements or conduct to the Commission seeking a formal decision on whether the agreement or conduct was caught by Articles 81 and 82 and if so, whether an agreement could benefit from the application of Article 81(3). This Section describes that procedure with a view to explaining the terms used since they appear in the case law of the Commission and Community Courts.

Application for negative clearance. Under Article 2 of Regulation 17, the **13.005**
Commission was able to certify that, on the basis of the facts known to it, there were no grounds for action on its part under Article 81(1) or Article 82 in respect

---

[4] See Lowe, 'The Role of the Commission in the Modernisation of EC Competition Law', p 6 (speech to UKAEL Conference, 23 January 2004, available on DG Comp website).
[5] See paras 14.075 *et seq*, below.
[6] See paras 1.090 *et seq*, above.
[7] Council Reg 17, OJ 1962 13/204, in force from 1962 until the coming into force of Reg 1/2003 on 1 May 2004: Vol II, App B.1. For a fuller description of the notification process see the 5th edn of this work, Chap 11.

of an agreement, decision, practice or other conduct. The purpose of applying for negative clearance was therefore to establish whether or not the agreement or conduct fell within Article 81(1) or Article 82. Unlike a notification, discussed below, an application for negative clearance did not give interim protection from fines. Since an application for negative clearance and a notification for exemption under Article 81(3) could be made on the same form, it was common practice for undertakings to make a combined application seeking either negative clearance or, if that was refused, exemption.

13.006 **Notification to obtain individual exemption.** Under Regulation 17, agreements had to be notified to the Commission in order to obtain a declaration that, pursuant to Article 81(3), the prohibition in Article 81(1) was inapplicable to a particular agreement, decision or concerted practice. A decision making such a declaration was commonly referred to as the grant of an 'individual exemption'[8] although this term is not found in Article 81(3) itself. Failure to notify an agreement did not in itself attract any penalties and was not a breach of any duty but it generally ruled out the possibility of the grant of individual exemption.[9] The effect of notification was, first, that the parties were protected from the imposition of fines in respect of their conduct pending the Commission's consideration of the agreement.[10] Secondly, if the Commission decided to grant an individual exemption, the parties to a notified agreement could benefit from the power of the Commission to declare that the exemption applied with retroactive effect back to the date of notification.[11] However, notification did not of itself render a new agreement enforceable in the period pending the Commission's consideration.[12] Moreover, an exemption decision had to be for a specified period;[13] upon its expiry the parties had to apply again for a further exemption decision.

13.007 **Notifiable and non-notifiable agreements.** Article 4(2) of Regulation 17 provided that some agreements did not need to be notified to the Commission in order to obtain exemption under Article 81(3). Such agreements could be notified if the parties so wished but if, as a result of a complaint, or in the course of an investigation undertaken on the Commission's own initiative, the Commission came to consider an agreement to which Article 4(2) applied, it could grant

---

8 The reference to 'individual' being in contrast with the 'block' exemption conferred on categories of agreement by Commission regulation: see generally Chap 3, above.

9 See Case T-67/01 *JCB Service v Commission* [2004] ECR II-49, [2004] 4 CMLR 1346 (sending replacement agreements under cover of a letter instead of under the prescribed form did not constitute notifying them): appeal dismissed, Case C-167/04P, [2006] ECR I-8935, [2006] 5 CMLR 1303.

10 Reg 17 (n 7, above) Art 15(5). This immunity was subject to the application of Art 15(6) discussed in para 13.010, below.

11 Reg 17, Art 6.

12 Case 48/72 *Brasserie de Haecht v Wilkin (No. 2)* [1973] ECR 77, [1973] CMLR 287.

13 Reg 17, Art 8(1).

an individual exemption under Article 81(3) even if the agreement had not been notified. The exemption could be backdated to the date of the conclusion of the agreement. The categories of agreement which fell within Article 4(2) were:

(i)   domestic agreements, that is agreements between undertakings from one Member State which do not relate either to imports or to exports between Member States;

(ii) vertical agreements;[14]

(iii) agreements made between two undertakings imposing only unilateral restrictions on the exercise of the rights of the assignee or user of industrial property rights;

(iv) certain agreements which have as their sole object either the development or uniform application of certain standards or types, or joint research and development or specialisation in manufacture.

In addition, agreements which fell within the terms of a block exemption did not need to be notified.

Article 19(3) notices.   Where the Commission was minded to issue a formal decision giving negative clearance or individual exemption under Article 81(3), a summary of the notification or application was published in the *Official Journal* pursuant to Article 19(3) of Regulation 17 in order to give third parties an opportunity to comment. The publication of a so-called 'Article 19(3) Notice' was not always followed by a formal decision but could result in the Commission closing its file with the issue of a comfort letter.[15] The publication of such a notice did not create a legitimate expectation that no infringement decision would be issued.[16]

13.008

Carlsberg Notices.   A Carlsberg Notice was a notice published in the *Official Journal* whereby the Commission informed third parties of a notification and invited them to submit information or comments concerning the notified case. The notice contained a short summary of the case and was published with the consent of the parties directly involved in the matter. This way of obtaining case-related information takes its name from the case in which it was first used by the Commission in 1992.[17] In contrast to an Article 19(3) Notice, a Carlsberg Notice

13.009

---

[14] This category was added by Reg 1216/1999, OJ 1999 L148/5, as part of the reform of the treatment of vertical restraints so that those vertical agreements which did not benefit from block exemption under Reg 2790/1999 did not need to be notified as a pre-condition for individual exemption.

[15] For comfort letters see para 13.011, below.

[16] Case T-65/98 *Van den Bergh Foods v Commission* [2003] ECR II-4653, [2004] 4 CMLR 14, [2005] All ER (EC) 418 (on appeal from *Van den Bergh Foods*, OJ 1998 L246/1, [1998] 5 CMLR 530); appeal to the ECJ dismissed, Case C-552/03P *Unilever Bestfoods (Ireland) v Commission* [2006] ECR I-9091, [2006] 5 CMLR 1460.

[17] *Carlsberg-Tetley*, OJ 1992 C97/21.

was neutral and gave no indication of any provisional view formed by the Commission about the case.

13.010 **Article 15(6) decisions.** Article 15(6) of Regulation 17 provided that the Commission could inform the parties that after a preliminary examination of an agreement which had been notified to it, it had formed the view that the application of Article 81(3) was not justified. Such a decision could only be taken in the case of a manifestly serious infringement of Article 81(1). Such a communication put an end to the parties' protection from fines so that a fine could be imposed for the continued operation of the agreement in the period following the notification of the decision to the parties concerned.

13.011 **Comfort and discomfort letters.** The Commission took relatively few formal decisions on notified agreements. Most notifications were settled informally, usually by the sending of a comfort letter. A comfort letter was usually signed by a senior official of the Directorate-General of Competition and indicated that the Commission was closing its file and intended to take no further action. It would normally state whether the notified agreement was considered to fall outside Article 81(1) ('a negative clearance-type comfort letter') or to fall within Article 81(1) but to benefit from the application of Article 81(3) ('an exemption-type comfort letter'). Although the informal outcome meant that there was no published decision, the Commission could publicise the case, for example mention in a press release or in a subsequent annual Report on Competition Policy or Competition Newsletter.[18] Further, comfort letters could be 'formal' (usually following the publication of an Article 19(3) Notice) or informal. The effect of a comfort letter in civil proceedings in which the validity of the agreement was challenged in a national court was less certain than the effect of a formal decision.[19] The Notice on cooperation between the national courts and the Commission stated that whilst not binding a comfort letter 'constitutes a factor which the national courts may take into account in examining whether the agreements or conduct in question are in accordance with the provisions of Article [81]'.[20] Another possible outcome of notification, albeit rarer, was a 'discomfort' letter indicating that the agreement fell within Article 81(1) and was unlikely to benefit from Article 81(3) but that it was not sufficiently important to justify the Commission taking action to terminate the infringement.

13.012 **Effect of grant or refusal of individual exemption.** If a notified agreement obtained an individual exemption under Article 81(3), it was rendered fully valid

---

[18] The protection from fines continued in respect of acts falling within the notification even if the Commission decided to close the file or issue a comfort letter without taking a formal decision.

[19] See discussion in the 5th edn of this work, paras 11-016 and 11-017.

[20] Notice on cooperation between national courts and the Commission, OJ 1993 C39/6, the precursor to the current Notice issued post-Modernisation.

and enforceable in the national courts for the period specified by the Commission in its decision. If, on the other hand, the exemption under Article 81(3) was refused, then those provisions of the agreement falling within Article 81(1) were void *ab initio* notwithstanding the notification.

Conditions and obligations attached to individual exemption. Under **13.013** Article 8(1) of Regulation 17, the Commission was empowered to attach conditions and obligations to a decision granting individual exemption. If a condition was not satisfied by the parties, the exemption would automatically not apply and the agreement would be subject to Article 81(1). In contrast, if an obligation was breached, the Commission had power to impose a fine for breach of the obligation but there was no immediate effect on the enforceability of the agreement. Conditions typically required amendment to the notified agreement to remove certain objectionable clauses. Typical obligations required regular reporting by the parties about their compliance with conditions or the provision of financial information to the Commission for the duration of the exemption.

Opposition procedure. Several block exemptions provided for an opposition **13.014** procedure.[21] Under such a procedure, if an agreement fell within the general ambit of the block exemption but contained restrictions which went beyond those strictly permitted, it could be notified to the Commission. If it was not opposed by the Commission within six or four months (depending on the regulation) the agreement would be deemed to be exempted pursuant to the block exemption.

Notification in the transport sector. Regulation 17 did not apply in the trans- **13.015** port sector. Rules for the application of Articles 81 and 82 were contained in separate regulations.[22] A significant difference from Regulation 17 was that notification was not necessary in order to obtain exemption under the transport regulations. Exemption under those regulations was therefore possible from a date earlier than notification. However, notified agreements benefited from protection from fines only under the regulations covering internal maritime transport and air transport.

Objections procedure in the transport sector. The three regulations imple- **13.016** menting the competition rules in the transport sector provided for exemptions to be made by way of an 'objections' procedure. The Commission would publish

---

[21] eg in the block exemption for liner shipping consortium agreements (Art 7 of Reg 823/2000, OJ 2000 L100/24) and the old block exemptions for technology transfer agreements (Art 4 of Reg 240/96, OJ 1996 L31/2), franchise agreements (Art 6 of Reg 4087/88, OJ 1988 L359/46), specialisation agreements (Art 4 of Reg 417/85, OJ 1985 L53/1) and R&D agreements (Art 7 of Reg 418/85, OJ 1985 L53/5).

[22] Reg 1017/68 (transport by rail, road and inland waterway), Reg 4056/86 (international maritime transport) and Reg 3975/87 (air transport). See Chap 12, above, for a discussion of the provisions of these Regs post-Modernisation.

a summary of a request for exemption in the *Official Journal* and invite comments from interested third parties. Unless the Commission notified the parties to the agreement within 90 days of the date of such publication that there were serious doubts about the agreement, the agreement would be deemed to be exempt for the number of years which was specified in the relevant Regulation. These procedures were repealed by Regulation 1/2003 which brought the transport sectors within the general enforcement regime.

3. The European Competition Network and the Allocation of Cases

13.017 **Case allocation under Regulation 1/2003.** Regulation 1/2003 provides that NCAs and the Commission are to apply the competition rules 'in close cooperation'.[23] The only provision in the Regulation dealing with how cases are to be allocated for investigation and enforcement action is Article 11(6). This provides, first, that the initiation of proceedings by the Commission relieves NCAs of their competence to apply Articles 81 and 82 and, secondly, that the Commission must, if it intends to initiate proceedings, consult with any NCA which has already initiated proceedings. Apart from that, the Regulation is silent as to how cases are to be allocated as between the Commission and NCAs, or as to when the Article 11(6) power is to be exercised, or how disputes are to be resolved where NCAs and the Commission disagree as to who should handle a case. The Commission has stated that it 'cannot and will not act as a clearing house between independent national authorities, but will leave it to the authorities to agree on the appropriate case allocation'.[24]

13.018 **The European Competition Network.** The 15th recital to Regulation 1/2003 states that 'the Commission and [the NCAs] should form together a network of public authorities applying the [EC] competition rules in close cooperation'. That intention was confirmed on the adoption of Regulation 1/2003 when the Council and the Commission issued a Joint Statement stating that a network of close liaison between NCAs and the Commission would be established and setting out the general principles that would govern that network.[25] Those principles

---

[23] Reg 1/2003, OJ 2003 L1/1, Vol II, App B.3, Art 11(1). See, in relation to the matters dealt with in this section, Bremmer, 'Case Allocation under Regulation 1/2003' (2005) 42 CML Rev 1383; Gerber and Cassinis, 'The Modernisation of EC Competition Law' (2006) ECLR 10 and 51.

[24] Speech by Lowe (n 4, above) page 6.

[25] Joint Statement of the Council and the Commission, Council doc no. 15435/02 ADD1 of 10 December 2002: Vol II, App B.7. The Joint Statement cannot be relied on as establishing any rights or obligations: Case T-339/04 *France Télécom v Commission*, judgment of 8 March 2007, para 85.

have subsequently been fleshed out by a Notice issued by the Commission (the Network Notice).[26] The composition of the Network (known as the 'European Competition Network' or 'ECN') and the provisions of the Joint Statement and the Network Notice are discussed in Chapter 14, below.[27] The general principle is that the authority which receives a complaint or starts an *ex officio* procedure will remain in charge of the case provided that it is well-placed to deal with the matter.[28] Under Regulation 1/2003, an NCA must inform the Commission in writing before, or without delay after, commencing the first formal investigative measure,[29] and may make that information available to other NCAs.[30]

Meaning of 'well-placed'. A case will be reallocated from the initiating **13.019** authority only if that authority considers it is not well-placed to act or where other authorities consider themselves well-placed.[31] An NCA is well-placed if (a) the putative infringement has substantial direct effects on competition in its territory or originates within its territory; (b) it is able to bring the infringement to an end and sanction the infringement adequately; and (c) it can gather the evidence required to prove the infringement (including with the cooperation of other NCAs).[32] In cases where an infringement by undertakings in State A has effects mainly in State A, the NCA of A will be well-placed to deal with it.[33] In cases affecting two States, one NCA will be well-placed if both the undertakings concerned are on its territory;[34] but if they are each in a different State, the NCAs will be well-placed to deal with it in parallel,[35] perhaps designating one of them as the lead authority.[36] The Commission will be regarded as particularly well-placed if (a) the infringement affects more than three States;[37] or (b) the case is closely linked to other Community provisions applied by the Commission; or (c) if the Community interest requires a Commission decision to develop EC competition policy, to resolve a new enforcement issue or to ensure effective enforcement.[38]

---

[26] Network Notice, OJ 2004 L1/1, Vol II, App B.8.

[27] See paras 14.011 *et seq*, below.

[28] Network Notice (n 26, above) paras 6 and 19; Joint Statement (n 25, above), para 12.

[29] Reg 1/2003 (n 23, above) Art 11(3).

[30] ibid and see para 14.018, below.

[31] Network Notice (n 26, above) para 6.

[32] ibid, para 8.

[33] ibid, para 10.

[34] ibid, para 11.

[35] ibid, para 12.

[36] ibid, para 13.

[37] ibid, para 14. For cases referred from NCAs to the Commission on that basis, see, eg OFT press release 3 December 2004 'OFT refers iTunes complaint to the Commission'; and the Flat Glass cartel referred to by Commissioner Kroes in 'Taking Competition Seriously - Anti-Trust Reform in Europe', SPEECH/05/157 of 10 March 2005 to the International Bar Association/EC Commission conference. In a case involving Deutsche Post, the Commission and the German Bundeskartellamt each looked at a different aspect of the complaint: ibid.

[38] Network Notice (n 26, above) para 15.

13.020 **Reallocation period.** Reallocation issues should be resolved swiftly, usually within two months from the date of notification to the ECN.[39] The authorities will endeavour to agree reallocation or a procedure for joint handling,[40] but there is no mechanism for resolving a dispute in default of agreement. Although it is stated that the Advisory Committee could serve as the forum for the discussion of case allocation,[41] it has no power to resolve a dispute beyond issuing an 'informal statement'.[42] Once the reallocation period is over, the authority or authorities charged with the case should continue to deal with it until the completion of proceedings, unless the facts known about the case change materially in the course of proceedings.[43] If a case is reallocated, the undertakings concerned and the complainant (if there is one) should be informed as soon as possbile.[44] Where an NCA has already informed the ECN that it is looking at the matter and the reallocation period has expired, the Network Notice provides that the Commission will in principle trigger the application of Article 11(6) of Regulation 1/2003 to take over the handling of the case only if (i) NCAs envisage conflicting decisions in the same case; (ii) NCAs envisage a decision in obvious conflict with the case law (including decisions and regulations of the Commission) or which significantly diverges from previous factual assessments by the Commission; (iii) NCAs are unduly prolonging proceedings; (iv) there is a need to develop a Community policy on an issue, in particular where the same issue arises in a number of Member States or to ensure effective enforcement; or (v) where the NCAs do not object.[45]

13.021 **Challenging decisions as to case allocation.** The Network Notice states that the provisions concerning the allocation of cases do not create any rights for the undertakings involved to have their case dealt with by a particular authority.[46] The Network Notice observes that all competition authorities apply EC competition law and that there are mechanisms to ensure consistent application of those rules. However, given the lack of procedural harmonisation between NCAs the decision that a matter will be dealt with by one authority rather than another may have significant consequences for the parties. The Court of First Instance, rejecting the Commission's argument, has held that a challenge to a decision to carry out an inspection as contrary to the principle of cooperation between the Commission and NCAs was admissible, albeit that in the case in question the Court found

---

[39] ibid, para 18.
[40] ibid.
[41] ibid, para 62. For the Advisory Committee, see para 13.107, below.
[42] Network Notice (n 26, above) para 62.
[43] ibid, para 19.
[44] ibid, para 34.
[45] ibid, para 54. See also the Joint Statement (n 25, above). For Art 11(6), see para 13.017, above.
[46] Network Notice (n 26, above) para 31. See also Joint Statement (n 25, above) para 3.

that there was no violation of the Commission's powers under Regulation 1/2003, and that the Network Notice was indicative and not mandatory in its guidance on case allocation, preserving a broad discretion for the Commission to initiate proceedings.[47]

Declarations of inapplicability.   Article 10 of Regulation 1/2003 provides that   **13.022**
the Commission may, where the Community public interest so requires, decide that Article 81 does not apply to an agreement (either because the agreement does not fall within Article 81(1) or because it fulfils the criteria in Article 81(3)). The Commission may also decide that Article 82 does not apply to particular conduct. Before the Commission takes a decision under Article 10, it must publish a concise summary of the case and set a date (not less than one month) for third parties to comment on the proposed course of action.[48] Such declarations are envisaged only in exceptional cases, in particular as regards new types of agreements or practices not settled by the existing case law.[49] At the time of writing, no decisions have as yet been taken under this provision.

Informal guidance.   Recital 38 to Regulation 1/2003 refers to the Commission's   **13.023**
power to issue letters giving informal guidance in cases where genuine uncertainty arises because of novel or unresolved questions under the competition rules. The Commission has issued a Notice setting out when it will issue such guidance (the Informal Guidance Notice).[50] Such letters will be issued only if (a) there is no relevant case law or decisions or existing guidance; (b) guidance is useful, having regard to the economic importance of the goods or services affected, the extent to which the agreement or practice in question is widespread, and whether a substantial level of investment depends on the agreement or practice; and (c) the Commission can issue guidance on the basis of the application without further fact-finding.[51] The Commission will not issue guidance letters where the matter is before national or Community courts, or the Commission or an NCA.[52] Nor will it issue guidance on hypothetical situations, although it will be prepared to issue guidance on plans which have reached a sufficiently advanced stage.[53] An application for informal guidance should be made by submission of a detailed

---

[47] Case T-339/04 *France Télécom v Commission* (n 25, above) paras 77–84. The challenge there was to the Commission's carrying out of an inspection in a matter that was already under consideration by the French NCA, not to the allocation of a case as between NCAs. For possible human rights aspects, see Wils, *Principles of European Antitrust Enforcement* (2005), Chap 2.
[48] Reg 1/2003 (n 23, above) Art 27(4).
[49] ibid, 14th recital.
[50] Informal Guidance Notice, OJ 2004 C101/78: Vol II, App B.11.
[51] Informal Guidance Notice, above para 8.
[52] ibid, para 9.
[53] ibid, para 10.

memorandum giving comprehensive information about all relevant facts and matters and attaching relevant documentation. The memorandum must explain how the conditions in (a) to (c) above are met.[54] The Commission will evaluate the request on the basis of the information provided and any public material; it can share the material provided with NCAs. If a request for guidance is withdrawn, the Commission can use the information provided to it in proceedings under Regulation 1/2003.[55] An informal guidance letter will set out its conclusion and reasoning and will be published on the Commission's website.[56] A guidance letter does not preclude the Commission looking at the matter under Regulation 1/2003, although it will take the informal guidance into account. It also does not bind the Community courts and although NCAs and national courts may take account of guidance letters, they are not bound by them.[57] At the time of writing, no applications for informal guidance have been made.

13.024 **The Commission's priorities.** The Commission has long been faced with many more potential cases than it has the resources to investigate. Even before the coming into force of Regulation 1/2003, the Community Courts had confirmed that the Commission is entitled to set priorities among the potential cases before it.[58] In particular, it can reject otherwise well-founded complaints on the basis of a lack of sufficient Community interest, leaving the matter to be dealt with by national courts or authorities.[59] Even where a case does have a sufficient Community interest, the Commission may concentrate its resources on one case, leaving complainants in other cases to pursue remedies before NCAs or national courts.[60] In the new framework created by Regulation 1/2003, the Commission has stated that its enforcement resources will be focused towards cases in which it is well-placed to act,[61] concentrating on the most serious infringements, and cases in which the Commission can define Community policy or further the coherent application of the competition rules.[62]

---

[54] ibid, section III.
[55] ibid, section IV.
[56] ibid, section V.
[57] ibid, section VI.
[58] Case T-24/90 *Automec v Commission ('Automec II')* [1992] ECR II-2223, [1992] 5 CMLR 431, para 77; see also para 13.072, below.
[59] See para 13.072, below.
[60] See Case T-219/99 *British Airways v Commission* [2003] ECR II-5917, [2004] 4 CMLR 1008, [2004] All ER (EC) 1115, para 70 (appeal on other grounds dismissed, Case C-95/04P [2007] 5 CMLR 982). See also Cases T-189/95, etc, *SGA v Commission* [1999] ECR II-3587, [2001] 4 CMLR 215, para 59; Cases T-9 & 211/96 *Européene automobile v Commission* [1999] ECR II-3639, [2001] 4 CMLR 245, para 49.
[61] See para 13.019, above.
[62] Complaints Notice, OJ 2004 C101/65: Vol II, App B.10, para 11.

4. The Commission's Powers of Investigation

Generally. The Commission has wide powers to require information from **13.025**
Member States and from individual undertakings under Articles 18 and 19 of
Regulation 1/2003. It also has power to conduct inspections under Articles 20
and 21 of Regulation 1/2003 (so-called 'dawn raids') in order to carry out its functions. This Section discusses those powers of fact-finding and investigation, considering first the legal principles which form the background to the Commission's
exercise of its powers.

(a) Fundamental rights and the Commission's powers of investigation

General principles of EC law. The relevance of the norms laid down in the **13.026**
European Convention on Human Rights to the procedures for the enforcement
of the competition rules has developed considerably since Regulation 17 was
adopted. Although the jurisprudence of the European Court of Human Rights
under the Convention is not binding on the Community Courts,[63] fundamental
rights form an integral part of the general principles of Community law whose
observance the Community Courts ensure.[64] In formulating those general principles, the Community Courts draw inspiration 'from the constitutional traditions
common to the Member States and from the guidelines supplied by international
treaties for the protection of human rights on which the Member States have
collaborated or of which they are signatories'.[65] The Human Rights Convention
has 'special significance'[66] in this regard. Article 6(2) of the Treaty on European
Union declares that the Union shall respect the fundamental rights protected
by the Convention, as they result from the constitutional traditions common to
the Member States.[67] In practice, the Community Courts frequently have regard
to the jurisprudence of the European Court of Human Rights in assessing whether
the acts of the Community institutions have been consistent with those general
principles. Recital (37) to Regulation 1/2003 provides that it must be interpreted
and applied with respect to the rights and principles contained in the Charter
of Fundamental Rights adopted by the Member States in December 2000.[68]

---

[63] Case T-112/98 *Mannesmannröhren-Werke v Commission* [2001] ECR II-729, [2001] 5 CMLR
54, para 59; Case T-347/94 *Mayr-Melnhof v Commission* [1998] ECR II-1751, para 311.

[64] Opinion 2/94 on Accession by the Community to the ECHR [1996] ECR I-1759, [1996]
2 CMLR 265, para 33.

[65] Opinion 2/94, ibid.

[66] Opinion 2/94, ibid.

[67] See paras 1.016 *et seq*, above. Art 46 TEU renders Art 6(2) justiciable and gives the ECJ jurisdiction to review the acts of EC institutions to determine their compliance with these principles.

[68] For the significance of the Charter of Fundamental Rights, see paras 1.010 and 1.012, above. In
Case C-105/04P *Nederlandse Federatieve Vereniging voor de Groothandel op Elektrotechnisch*

13.027 **Significance of case law of the Court of Human Rights.** The European Court of Human Rights has ruled that a State which is a signatory to the Convention remains responsible for all its acts and omissions, even where the act or omission in question was the consequence of the need to comply with international legal obligations, such as those which flow from Community law.[69] Although there are some instances in which there has been a marked divergence between the approach of the Community Courts and that of the Court in Strasbourg, in general the Community Courts seek to apply the case law of the Court of Human Rights. In *Roquette Frères*,[70] the Court of Justice considered a question referred by the French Cour de Cassation as to the possible effect on the principles established by the Court in *Hoechst*[71] of certain developments which had taken place in the Strasbourg jurisprudence since delivery of the judgment of the Court of Justice in *Hoechst*. Given that the national court was applying EC legal principles rather than enforcing Convention rights, should it nonetheless have regard to case law of the Strasbourg Court decided after the relevant case law of the Court of Justice? The Court of Justice held that it should. In *Hoechst*, the Court had recognised that the need for protection against arbitrary or disproportionate intervention by public authorities in the sphere of the private activities of any person, whether natural or legal, constitutes a general principle of Community law. For the purposes of determining the scope of that general principle in relation to the protection of business premises, regard must be had to the case law of the European Court of Human Rights subsequent to the judgment in *Hoechst*.

13.028 **Relevant rights.** The general principles of EC law to which the Community Courts have regard include both procedural and substantive rights.[72] In addition to the right to a fair and independent legal process, involving the protection of a wide range of procedural rights encompassed in 'the rights of the defence', the

---

Gebied v Commission [2006] ECR I-8725, [2006] 4 CMLR 1223, Opinion, fn 59, AG Kokott referred to Recital (37) and observed that the Charter 'must be taken into account in cartel proceedings'; however, the ECJ in its judgment did not address the Charter. See also Case C-540/03 *European Parliament v EU Council* [2006] ECR I-5769, [2006] 3 CMLR 779, [2007] All ER (EC) 193, paras 38 and 59 (reliance by the ECJ on the Charter along with other human rights instruments in determining challenge to validity of a Directive on the right to family reunification).

[69] Application no. 45036/98 *Bosphorus Hava Yollart Turizm ve Ticaret Anonim Şirketi (Bosphorus Airways) v Ireland*, judgment of 30 June 2005, (2006) 42 EHRR 1, para 152. See also para 1.017, above.

[70] Case C-94/00 *Roquette Frères* [2002] ECR I-9011, [2003] 4 CMLR 46, [2003] All ER (EC) 920, paras 22 *et seq*. See also Cases C-238/99P, etc, *Limburgse Vinyl Maatschappij ('LVM') v Commission ('PVC II')* [2002] ECR I-8375, [2003] 4 CMLR 397, para 274 (ECtHR case law on self-incrimination post *Orkem* taken into account).

[71] Cases 46/87 & 227/88 *Hoechst v Commission* [1989] ECR 2859, [1991] 4 CMLR 410, see para 13.046, below.

[72] See Cases C-204/00P, etc, *Aalborg Portland v Commission* [2004] ECR I-123, [2005] 4 CMLR 251, paras 64–67.

rights and principles recognised by the Community Courts as protected by the Community law include the following:[73]

(a) a right of privacy, in terms of guarantees against unreasonable or dispropor-tionate searches of premises for documents;[74]

(b) the privilege against self-incrimination;[75]

(c) attorney/client privilege, in terms of the protection of the confidentiality of communications with independent lawyers;[76]

(d) *non bis in idem*, that is the principle that an undertaking should not be punished twice for the same conduct;[77]

(e) that legislation, particularly that which imposes penalties, should not be imposed with retroactive effect;[78]

(f) that legitimate expectations should be respected;[79]

(g) the principle of equal treatment;[80]

(h) the principle of proportionality;[81]

(i) the principle of sound administration;[82] and

(j) the right to have a decision taken, and judicial proceedings resolved, within a reasonable time.[83]

Right to a fair trial.   Articles 6 and 8 of the European Convention on Human   **13.029**
Rights are the most relevant to the Commission's powers of investigation.[84]
Article 6(1) of the Convention provides that 'in the determination of his civil rights and obligations or of any criminal charge against him, everyone is entitled to a fair and public hearing within a reasonable time by an independent and

---

[73] See Tridimas, *The General Principles of EU Law* (2nd edn, 2006); Schermers and Waelbroeck, *Judicial Protection in the European Union* (6th edn, 2001), Chap 1(B); Roth, 'Ensuring that Effectiveness of Enforcement Does Not Prejudice Legal Protection: Rights of Defence. Fundamental Rights Concerns' in Ehlermann and Atanasiu (eds), *European Competition Law Annual 2006: Enforcement of Prohibition of Cartels* (2007), 627; Hartley, *The Foundations of European Community Law* (5th edn, 2003), Chap 5; Toth, *The Oxford Encyclopaedia of European Community Law*, Vol 1: Institutional Law (1990).

[74] See paras 13.031 and 13.046, below.

[75] See paras 13.057 *et seq*, below.

[76] See paras 13.055–13.056, below.

[77] See para 13.207, below.

[78] See, eg para 13.147, below.

[79] See para 13.228 and also para 13.200, below (as regards the provisions for leniency) and para 15.106 below (in the context of State aid).

[80] In competition cases, this principle is usually invoked in relation to fines: see, eg para 13.203, below.

[81] In addition to the works cited in n 73 above, see Craig, *EU Administrative Law* (2006), Chaps 17–18. In competition cases, this is similarly most relevant in the context of fines.

[82] This is expressed in Art 41 of the Charter of Fundamental Rights. For application, see, eg para 13.067, below.

[83] See para 13.078, below. As regards Commission decisions, this can be seen as part of the right to good administration, above.

[84] Art 8 of the Convention is considered at para 13.031, below.

impartial tribunal established by law'. Legal as well as natural persons are entitled to the protection of this provision.[85] The Court of Justice has held that the entitlement to a fair legal process, inspired by those fundamental rights, is a general principle of Community law.[86] The right to a fair trial has been frequently invoked before the Community Courts in support of the contention that the Commission has breached the rights of the defence.[87] The Convention has played a role in the reasoning of the Community Courts in answering such pleas, particularly in respect of challenges based upon the privilege against self-incrimination, delay, the burden of proof and access to the file. A particular aspect of the right to a fair trial is the right to be heard, which has been elaborated in the context of Commission proceedings[88] and encompasses at least the following aspects:

(a) the guarantee of notice of the allegations of infringement and the evidence relied on in support of them, prior to any adverse decision being taken, so as to have an opportunity to respond: this is achieved by the issue of a statement of objections;[89]

(b) the right of access to the Commission's file;[90]

(c) the right of the undertaking, during the administrative procedure, to make known its views on the truth and relevance of the facts and circumstances alleged and on the documents relied on by the Commission;[91]

(d) the right to an oral hearing.[92]

13.030 'Criminal charge'. The Court of Human Rights has ruled that Contracting States have a greater latitude for the purpose of Article 6 when dealing with cases concerning civil rights and obligations than when dealing with criminal cases.[93] Moreover, there are guarantees afforded by Article 6(2) and 6(3) which generally apply only to the determination of a criminal charge. In *Société Stenuit v France*,[94] the Commission of Human Rights held that the decision of the French Minister of the Economy and Finance to levy a fine against the applicant company for

---

[85] eg *Dombo Beheer v Netherlands* A/274 (1994) 18 EHRR 213. cf the position in the USA, where corporate bodies are not entitled to rely on the Fifth Amendment to the US Constitution: *Hale v Henkel* 201 US 43, 26 SCt 370 (1906) (re the antitrust laws); *Braswell v US* 487 US 99, 108 SCt 2284 (1988) (corporate officer). See also Emberland, *The Human Rights of Companies: Exploring the Structure of ECHR Protection* (2006).

[86] Case C-185/95P *Baustahlgewebe v Commission* [1998] ECR I-8417, [1999] 4 CMLR 1203, para 21.

[87] For rights of the defence generally, see paras 13.075 *et seq*, below.

[88] See para 13.080, below.

[89] See paras 13.083 *et seq*, below.

[90] See paras 13.088 *et seq*, below.

[91] See para 13.086, below.

[92] See paras 13.101 *et seq*, below.

[93] *Dombo Beheer* (n 85, above) para 32.

[94] *Société Stenuit v France* (1992) 14 EHRR 509. The case was settled by agreement between the parties before the Court ruled on the application.

breaches of French competition law amounted to the determination of a criminal charge for the purposes of the Convention, notwithstanding the non-criminal nature of the penalty under French law. In reaching that view, the Commission of Human Rights emphasised the nature of the penalty at issue (it was intended to be a deterrent) and its severity, amounting as it did to up to 5 per cent of the turn-over of the company.[95] Both these features are, of course, characteristics of the EC competition rules (indeed fines in Community cases may amount to as much as 10 per cent of worldwide turnover). The Community Courts have held that given the nature of the infringements in question and the nature and degree of severity of the ensuing penalties, the principle of the presumption of innocence resulting from Article 6(2) of the Convention applies to procedures that may result in the imposition of fines or periodic penalty payments.[96] It therefore appears that for the purposes of Article 6 of the Convention, proceedings by the Community for infringement of the competition rules should be regarded as the determination of a criminal charge, notwithstanding the fact that Article 23(4) of Regulation 1/2003 declares that such decisions 'shall not be of a criminal law nature'.[97]

Article 8 of the Convention: respect for private and family life. Article 8 of **13.031** the Convention confers the right to respect for private and family life, home and correspondence. In a number of cases, the Court of Justice had held that 'dawn raids' of business premises (that is to say, unannounced inspections, considered in detail below[98]) raised no issue under Article 8 of the Convention on the basis that Article 8 did not cover such premises.[99] That case law was, however,

---

[95] The Commission also pointed out that the alternative to fining the company was to refer the case to the prosecuting authorities. For decisions of the ECtHR holding that national proceedings involve the determination of a criminal charge although they were not so regarded in national law, see *Öztürk v Germany* A/73 (1983) 6 EHRR 409; *Janosevic v Sweden* No. 34619/97 (2004) 38 EHRR 22. The national classification of proceedings as non-criminal is relevant but not decisive: *Dombo Beheer* (n 85, above).

[96] Case C-199/92P *Hüls v Commission* [1999] ECR I-4287, paras 149 and 150, [1999] 5 CMLR 1016; Case C-235/92P *Montecatini v Commission* [1999] ECR I-4539, [2001] 4 CMLR 691, paras 175 and 176; Case T-38/02 *Group Danone v Commission* [2005] ECR II-4407, [2006] 4 CMLR 1428, para 216. See also Opinion of Judge Vesterdorf in Cases T-1/89, etc, *Rhône-Poulenc v Commission* [1991] ECR II-869, 885, [1992] 4 CMLR 84, 101 and Opinion of AG Léger in *Baustahlgewebe* (n 86, above) para 31. See also the UK Competition Appeal Tribunal in *Napp Pharmaceutical Holdings Ltd v Director General of Fair Trading* [2002] CAT 1, [2002] Comp AR 13, para 98.

[97] Similarly, beforehand, Art 15(2) of Reg 17. The admissibility decision of the ECtHR in *OOO Neste St Petersburg v Russia*, 3 June 2004, does not affect this conclusion since it turned largely on the particular nature of the Russian legislation in question which did not involve penal or deterrent sanctions.

[98] See Art 20 of Reg 1/2003 (n 23, above), paras 13.041 *et seq*, below.

[99] Case 136/79 *National Panasonic v Commission* [1980] ECR 2033, [1980] CMLR 169, para 20; Case 5/85 *AKZO v Commission (AKZO No. 2)* [1986] ECR 2585, [1987] 3 CMLR 716, paras 24–26; Cases 46/87 & 227/88 *Hoechst v Commission* [1989] ECR 2859, [1991] 4 CMLR 410, para 18; Cases T-305/94, etc, *LVM v Commission ('PVC No. 2')* [1999] ECR II-931,

considered by the Court of Human Rights in *Colas Est v France*.[100] The application concerned a challenge to a raid carried out by the French competition authorities upon the applicant's premises. The Court of Human Rights ruled that 'the time has come to hold that in certain circumstances the rights guaranteed by Article 8 of the Convention may be construed as including the right to respect for a company's registered office, branches or other business premises'. In *Roquette Frères*,[101] the Court of Justice expressly followed the judgment in *Colas* in this regard, departing from its previous case law. In the case of natural persons, the Court of Human Rights has developed a generous interpretation of the concept of 'private life' so as to encompass 'any information relating to an identified or identifiable individual',[102] including information relating to a business of a seemingly anodyne nature.[103] However, interference with the right set out in Article 8(1) can be justified under Article 8(2) where the interference 'is in accordance with the law and is necessary in a democratic society in the interests of' materially, 'the economic well-being of the country' or 'the prevention of . . . crime'.[104] In *Colas Est*, the Court of Human Rights was prepared to assume (without deciding) that the entitlement to interfere with Article 8(1) rights may be more far-reaching where the business premises of a legal person are concerned than where the rights of a natural person are involved.[105]

(b) Power to obtain information

13.032 **Information from undertakings.**   Under Article 18 of Regulation 1/2003, the Commission has wide powers to obtain from undertakings and associations of undertakings 'all necessary information' either by 'simple request' or by decision.[106] The power to request information includes the power to seek documents

---

[1999] 5 CMLR 303, paras 419, 420. See also the English High Court in *X v OFT* [2003] EWHC 1042, [2003] 2 All ER (Comm) 183, [2004] ICR 105.

    100 *Société Colas Est v France*, No. 3791/97, [2004] 39 EHRR 17, para 41. Art 8 also extends to the business premises of private individuals: *Niemietz v Germany* A/251-B (1992), [1993] 16 EHRR 97, para 31; *Amann v Switzerland* [2000] 30 EHRR 843, para 65. For a recent survey of the Strasbourg and UK case law on the scope of Art 8 see *R (Countryside Alliance) v Attorney General* [2006] EWCA Civ 817, [2006] 3 WLR 1017.

    101 *Roquette Frères* (n 70, above) para 29. See further paras 13.046–13.047, below.

    102 *Rotaru v Romania* (2000) 8 BHRC 449, para 43; *Amann* (n 100, above) para 65. The Courts expressly drew upon the Council of Europe's Convention of 28 January 1981 for the Protection of Individuals with regard to Automatic Processing of Personal Data.

    103 See *Amann* (n 100, above) para 66.

    104 This aspect of Art 8 is discussed in para 13.046, below.

    105 *Colas Est* (n 100, above) para 49; *Niemietz* (n 100, above) para 31; *Roquette Frères* (n 70, above) para 28; Case C-301/04P *Commission v SGL Carbon* [2006] ECR I-5915, [2006] 5 CMLR 877, Opinion of AG Geelhoed, para 64 (point not addressed by ECJ).

    106 Art 18(1) of Reg 1/2003 (n 23, above). There is no requirement that the Commission should make a simple request before taking a decision seeking information, in contrast to the former position under Art 11(5) of Reg 17, OJ 1962 13/204: Vol II, App B.1.

containing that information.[107] A simple request must state the legal basis and purpose of the request, specify what information is required and fix the time within which the information must be provided. The request must therefore make clear the subject-matter of the inquiry and the presumed facts which the Commission intends to investigate.[108] There is no obligation to comply with a request but there are penalties for supplying incorrect or misleading information, and this sanction must be indicated in the request.[109] By contrast, compliance with a decision requiring information is mandatory. The decision must state the legal basis and the purpose of the request, specify what information is required and fix the time within which it must be provided.[110] It must indicate the potential penalties for failing to supply information or supplying incorrect or misleading information, or impose penalties for failing to supply information pursuant to an earlier decision.[111] It must further indicate the right to have the decision reviewed by the Court of Justice.[112] There is no obligation to publish such decisions.[113] The owners of the undertakings or their representatives are under an obligation to furnish the information requested.[114] Lawyers duly authorised to act may supply the information on behalf of their clients, although if they do, the clients remain fully responsible if the information supplied is incomplete, incorrect or misleading.[115] If the undertaking defaults in the supply of information, the Commission may adopt a further decision imposing a fine.[116] The Commission must without delay forward a copy of the simple request or decision to the competition authority of the Member State in whose territory the seat of

---

[107] The ECJ has held that the fact that an inspection under Art 14 of Reg 17 (broadly equivalent to Art 20 of Reg 1/2003; see para 13.041, below) had taken place did not deprive the Commission of its powers to request information under Art 11 and the Commission is entitled to include in its request for information a request for the disclosure of documents: see Case 374/87 *Orkem v Commission* [1989] ECR 3283, [1991] 4 CMLR 502, para 14; Case 27/88 *Solvay v Commission* [1989] ECR 3355, [1991] 4 CMLR 502.

[108] Case C-36/92P *SEP v Commission* [1994] ECR I-1911, para 21, upholding AG Jacobs at para 34; Case T-34/93 *Société Générale v Commission* [1995] ECR II-545, [1996] 4 CMLR 665, para 40. The purpose must be indicated with enough precision to be able to judge that the request is necessary: *SEP*, ibid.

[109] Art 18(2) of Reg 1/2003 (n 23, above). For penalties for supplying incorrect or misleading information, see para 13.035, below.

[110] Art 18(3) of Reg 1/2003 (n 23, above).

[111] ibid.

[112] ibid. The Court of Justice has unlimited jurisdiction to review Commission decisions which fix a fine or periodic penalty payment under Reg 1/2003 and may cancel, reduce or increase the fine or penalty payment imposed: ibid, Art 31. The 'Court of Justice' is a single institution: Art 7 EC. In fact, such cases are heard by the CFI pursuant to its jurisdiction under Art 225 EC.

[113] Art 30 of Reg 1/2003 (n 23, above).

[114] ibid, Art 18(4).

[115] ibid. There was previously no express provision for lawyers to supply information under the equivalent provision, Art 11(4) of Reg 17.

[116] See para 13.035, below.

the undertaking or association of undertakings is situated and the competition authority of the Member State whose territory is affected.[117]

13.033 **Addressees of requests for information.** Frequently the addressees of the request will be those undertakings whose conduct is under investigation. But the Commission may also seek information from undertakings which are not themselves suspected of infringement.[118] It is unclear whether the Commission has the right to obtain information from undertakings situated outside the Community, although in practice it does, on occasion, seek to do so.[119]

13.034 **'Necessity' for information requested.** It is for the Commission to decide whether particular information is necessary. Even if it already has evidence, or indeed proof, of the existence of an infringement, the Commission may legitimately take the view that it is necessary to request further information to enable it better to define the scope of the infringement, to determine its duration or to identify the undertakings concerned.[120] Such information will typically include background information and market data, as well as details of alleged infringements and copies of documents.[121] The connection between the document or information requested and the infringement under investigation must be such that the Commission could reasonably suppose that the document or information would help it to determine whether the alleged infringement had taken place.[122] The Commission will not permit an undertaking to refuse information on the ground the information is not 'necessary',[123] but the undertaking may

---

[117] Art 18(5) of Reg 1/2003 (n 23, above).

[118] See the wording of Art 18(1).

[119] Information which is sought from undertakings in the EC may also relate to undertakings outside the EC: *CSV*, OJ 1976 L192/27. See also Cases 97/87, etc, *Dow Chemical Iberica v Commission* [1989] ECR 3165, [1991] 4 CMLR 410, for the use of powers to obtain information in a new Member State relating to a period prior to Accession. In *UKWAL*, OJ 1992 L121/45, [1993] 5 CMLR 632, a 'dawn raid' under Art 18 of Reg 4056/86 took place at the premises of a liner conference some of whose members were based outside the EC. However, the 8th recital to Reg 17 referred to the Commission as empowered 'throughout the common market' to require information to be supplied.

[120] *Orkem* (n 107, above) para 1; Case 27/88 *Solvay v Commission* (n 107, above); *National Panasonic* (n 99, above); Case T-39/90R *SEP v Commission* [1990] ECR II-649, [1992] 5 CMLR 27, on appeal Case C-36/92P (n 108, above); Case T-39/90 *SEP v Commission* [1991] ECR II-1497, [1992] 5 CMLR 33, para 30.

[121] Copy documents were requested in, eg *Comptoir Commercial d'Importation*, OJ 1982 L27/31, [1982] 1 CMLR 440.

[122] Case C-36/92P *SEP* (n 108, above) para 21, following the Opinion of AG Jacobs, para 21; and see *Société Générale* (n 108, above) para 40.

[123] See, eg *RAI/Unitel*, OJ 1978 L157/39, [1978] 3 CMLR 306 (refusal on number of grounds alleging inapplicability of Art 81(1)); see also *Fire Insurance (D)*, OJ 1982 L80/36, [1982] 2 CMLR 159 (refusal on grounds that agreement not caught by Art 81); *Olympic Airways*, OJ 1985 L46/51, [1985] 1 CMLR 730 (refusal on grounds that Arts 81 and 82 did not apply to airport handling services); *CSM—Sugar*, OJ 1992 L305/16 (refusal on grounds of relevance); Case C-36/92P *SEP* (n 108, above) (refusal on grounds of risk of disclosure to State controlled competitor).

challenge the Commission's decision before the Court on the grounds that the request for information is excessive.[124] The obligation to furnish information should not represent a burden for the enterprise which is disproportionate to the needs of the investigation.[125]

Penalties in respect of information.   The sanctions which apply to undertak-   **13.035**
ings from whom the Commission seeks to obtain information vary depending upon whether the information was sought by a 'simple request' under Article 18(2) or on the basis of a decision under Article 18(3). Article 23(1)(a) of Regulation 1/2003[126] provides for the Commission to adopt a decision imposing fines where undertakings or associations of undertakings intentionally or negligently supply incorrect or misleading information in answer to a simple request for information by the Commission. The fine must not exceed 1 per cent of the undertaking's total turnover in the preceding business year. There is no sanction for failure to supply information pursuant to a simple request.[127] The Commission has held in relation to the equivalent provision in Regulation 17 that:

> 'Any statement is incorrect which gives a distorted picture of the true facts asked for, and which departs significantly from reality on major points. Where a statement is thus false or so incomplete that the reply taken in its entirety is likely to mislead the Commission about the true facts, it constitutes incorrect information within the meaning of Article 15(1)(b) [of Regulation 17].'[128]

The Commission may also impose such a fine where, in response to a request made by decision, incorrect, incomplete or misleading information is supplied, or information is not supplied within the required time limit.[129] Where a decision requiring information is disobeyed, the Commission also has power to impose periodic penalty payments in order to compel the undertaking or association of

---

[124] See, eg Case 5/62 *San Michele v High Authority* [1962] ECR 449, [1963] CMLR 13 (Art 47 ECSC); *National Panasonic* (n 99, above). An undertaking may challenge the legality of a request although it has been complied with: Case T-46/92 *Scottish Football Association v Commission* [1994] ECR II-1039.

[125] *SEP* (n 108, above) and, at first instance, Case T-39/90 *SEP v Commission* (n 120, above) para 51.

[126] Reg 1/2003, OJ 2003 L1/1: Vol II, App B.3.

[127] Art 23(1)(a) and Art 23(1)(b) of Reg 1/2003 (n 126, above). The Commission's remedy if the undertaking fails to respond to a simple request is to adopt a decision requesting the same information.

[128] *Telos*, OJ 1982 L58/19, [1982] 1 CMLR 267. See also *Comptoir Commercial d'Importation* (n 121, above); *National Panasonic (France)*, OJ 1982 L211/32, [1982] 3 CMLR 623; *National Panasonic (Belgium)*, OJ 1982 L113/18, [1982] 2 CMLR 410; *Peugeot*, OJ 1986 L295/19, [1989] 4 CMLR 371; *Secrétama*, OJ 1991 L35/23, [1992] 5 CMLR 76 (request under Reg 4056/86). In *Anheuser-Busch/S&N*, OJ 2000 L49/37, [2000] 5 CMLR 75, fines of €3000 were imposed on each of two parties to an agreement for failing to supply information requested; the fact that it was the parties themselves who later supplied the information meant that the infringement was not major.

[129] Reg 1/2003, Art 23(1)(b).

undertakings to provide complete and correct information.[130] Periodic penalty payments may not exceed 5 per cent of the average daily turnover in the preceding business year per day, calculated from the date appointed by the decision.[131] The undertaking has a right to be heard before the Commission takes any decision to impose a fine, or when it fixes the definitive amount of the periodic penalty payment once the undertaking has complied with the obligation.[132] The Advisory Committee on Restrictive Practices and Dominant Positions must also be consulted.[133] The power to impose penalties in respect of requests for information is subject to a limitation period of three years.[134] The power to enforce such a penalty is subject to a limitation period of five years.[135]

13.036 Information from Member States.   Article 18(6) of Regulation 1/2003 provides that at the request of the Commission the governments and competition authorities of the Member States must provide the Commission with all necessary information to carry out the duties assigned to it by Regulation 1/2003.

13.037 Statements.   The Commission has the power to interview any natural or legal person who consents to be interviewed for the purpose of collecting information relating to the subject-matter of an investigation.[136] Since the interview is voluntary, the proposed interviewee can refuse to consent unless his lawyer is present. When the Commission conducts such an interview on the premises of an undertaking, it must inform the Member State in whose territory the interview takes place.[137] At the beginning of the interview, the Commission must state the legal basis and purpose of the interview, and 'recall its voluntary nature'.[138] It must also inform the person interviewed of its intention to make a record of the interview.[139] The interview may be conducted by telephone or electronic

---

[130] Reg 1/2003, Art 24(1)(d).

[131] ibid and Cases 46/87 & 227/88 *Hoechst v Commission* [1989] ECR 2859, [1991] 4 CMLR 410, paras 59–65. Where the obligation which the period penalty payment was intended to enforce has been satisfied, the Commission may fix the definitive amount of the penalty at a figure lower than that which would arise under the original decision: Art 24(2) of Reg 1/2003.

[132] Reg 1/2003 (n 126, above) Art 27(1).

[133] ibid, Art 14(1).

[134] ibid, Art 25(1). Any action taken by the Commission or by the competition authority of a Member State for the purpose of the investigation or proceedings in respect of an infringement will interrupt the limitation period with effect from the date on which the action is notified to at least one undertaking which participated in the infringement: ibid.

[135] Reg 1/2003 (n 126, above) Art 26(1). The notification of a decision varying the original amount of the penalty or refusing an application for variation, or any action of the Commission or a Member State designed to enforce payment of the penalty, will interrupt the limitation period and start time running afresh: Arts 26(3), (4) of Reg 1/2003.

[136] ibid, Art 19(1).

[137] ibid, Art 19(2). The officials of the competition authority of that Member State may assist the Commission in conducting the interview if they so request: ibid.

[138] Art 3(1) of Reg 773/2004, OJ 2004 L123/18: Vol II, App B.4.

[139] ibid.

means[140] (presumably, email). The Commission may record the statements made by the persons interviewed in any form, but must make a copy of any recording available to the person interviewed for approval.[141] There is no sanction for the supply of incorrect or misleading information in such an interview, in line with the approach of Regulation 1/2003 of not providing for penalties on individuals (except if they are undertakings).

Privilege.   The power to obtain information is subject to the protection given by the privilege against self-incrimination and for communications between lawyers and their clients. The scope of these privileges is discussed below.[142]   **13.038**

Investigations into sectors of the economy and types of agreements.   Under Article 17 of Regulation 1/2003, the Commission has power to conduct a general inquiry into any economic sector or type of agreement across various sectors. This power arises where the trend of trade between Member States, the rigidity of prices or other circumstances suggest that competition is being restricted or distorted within the common market. In the course of such an inquiry, undertakings concerned may be required to communicate to the Commission all agreements, decisions and concerted practices.[143] Where the Commission conducts such an inquiry, it may publish a report and invite comments from interested parties.[144] The Commission's powers to obtain information or to take statements and to carry out inspections apply in respect of such inquiries.[145] In January 2007, the Commission published its final reports in two sectoral inquiries, into retail banking[146] and energy markets,[147] and at the time of writing there is an ongoing inquiry into business insurance.[148]   **13.039**

Exchange of information.   As the Network Notice observes, a key element of the functioning of the ECN[149] is the ability of all the competition authorities to exchange and use information (including documents, statements and digital information) collected by them for the purpose of applying Article 81 or Article 82 of the Treaty.[150] The Commission considers this power to be a precondition for   **13.040**

---

[140] Art 3(2) of Reg 773/2004 (n 138, above).
[141] Reg 773/2004 (n 138, above) Art 3(3). Where necessary, the Commission may set a time limit within which the person interviewed may make any correction to the statement: ibid.
[142] See, below, paras 13.057 *et seq* (self-incrimination) and 13.055 *et seq* (lawyer/client privilege).
[143] Reg 1/2003 (n 126, above) Art 17(1).
[144] ibid.
[145] Reg 1/2003 (n 126, above) Art 17(2) provides that Arts 14, 18, 19, 20, 22, 23 and 24 apply *mutatis mutandis* in respect of an investigation under Art 17.
[146] See para 5.047, above.
[147] See para 12.054, above.
[148] The final report in this inquiry is expected in the autumn of 2007.
[149] See paras 13.017 *et seq*, above, for the the Network Notice and the ECN generally.
[150] Network Notice, OJ 2004 L1/1: Vol II, App B.8, para 26.

efficient and effective handling of cases.[151] Article 12 of Regulation 1/2003 contains the rules governing such exchange of information and is discussed in Chapter 14, below.[152]

(c) Powers of inspection

13.041 **Powers of inspection.** Article 20 of Regulation 1/2003[153] empowers the Commission to conduct all necessary inspections of undertakings and associations of undertakings in order to perform its duties. Inspections may be carried out by Commission officials either under an authorisation from the Commission[154] or under a formal decision[155] and either with or without prior notice to the undertakings involved. Inspections under decision without prior notice are often informally referred to as 'dawn raids'.[156] There is no need for a two-stage procedure with an attempted inspection under authorisation preceding an inspection under a decision.[157] The Commission's choice of method of inspection depends 'on the need for an appropriate enquiry, having regard to the special features of the case.'[158] Article 21 of Regulation 1/2003 introduced a new power for the Commission to order an inspection at 'any other premises, land and means of transport, including the homes of directors, managers and other members of staff' of the relevant undertakings or associations of undertakings. This was in recognition of the fact that sensitive documents, particularly in the case of illegal cartels, are sometimes kept at private homes in the hope of evading discovery.[159] However, because of the heightened concerns about invasion of privacy in the case of a 'dawn raid' on a domestic residence, inspection of such 'other premises' requires a formal Commission decision and can be executed only with the authority of a court in the Member State concerned.[160] An inspection does not constitute the opening of proceedings and the fact that the same matter is being considered by a NCA

---

[151] ibid.

[152] See paras 14.022 *et seq*, below.

[153] Reg 1/2003, OJ 2003 L1/1: Vol II, App B.3. For discussion of powers of inspection under Reg 1/2003, see Wils, 'Powers of Investigation and Procedural Rights and Guarantees in EU Antitrust Enforcement' (2006) 29 World Competition 3.

[154] Reg 1/2003, above, Art 20(3).

[155] ibid, Art 20(4).

[156] Simultaneous 'dawn raids' may take place in a number of different Member States, if the Commission is investigating several undertakings in the same industry.

[157] *National Panasonic v Commission* (n 99, above). Thus there is no right to be heard before such a decision is taken: ibid, para 21. See also *AKZO No. 2* (n 99, above).

[158] *National Panasonic* (n 99, above) para 29. The Commission has a broad discretion to determine the need for an inspection: see, eg Case T-340/04 *France Télécom v Commission*, judgment of 8 March 2007; Case T-266/03 *Groupement des cartes bancaires (CB) v Commission*, judgment of 12 July 2007, paras 63 *et seq*.

[159] Recital (26) to Reg 1/2003 (n 153, above).

[160] See para 13.044, below.

in the relevant Member State does not affect the Commission's discretion as to whether to carry out an inspection.[161]

Inspection of undertakings under authorisation.   In the case of an inspection **13.042** under authorisation, the officials of the Commission are required to produce to the undertaking the form of authorisation. This must indicate the subject-matter and purpose of the inspection, and the penalties which may be imposed for failure to cooperate fully.[162] Occasionally, the Commission will give notice of their visit by telephone. An authorisation is not equivalent to a 'search warrant' and the undertaking is entitled to refuse to submit voluntarily to inspection.[163] However, if it does submit, the undertaking is bound to accept all the ensuing obligations and to produce the required books and other business records in complete form, upon pain of penalties. The Commission must give notice of the inspection to the competition authority of the Member State in whose territory it is to be conducted in good time before the inspection is carried out.[164] Where the premises identified in the authorisation are in fact owned by an agent of the suspected undertaking rather than by the undertaking itself, the Commission is still entitled to carry out the inspection provided that the agent was aware of the reasons for the inspection.[165]

Inspection of undertakings pursuant to decision.   Before taking a decision to **13.043** carry out an inspection, the Commission must consult the competent authority of the Member State in whose territory the inspection is to be carried out.[166]

---

[161] Case T-339/04 *France Télécom v Commission*, judgment of 8 March 2007.

[162] Art 20(3) of Reg 1/2003 (n 153, above). For penalties, see para 13.050, below.

[163] In such a case, however, the Commission is likely to take a formal decision to inspect: see *VdF*, OJ 1978 L10/32, [1978] 1 CMLR D63; *Fides*, OJ 1979 L57/33, [1979] 1 CMLR 650; *AM&S Europe*, OJ 1979 L199/31, [1979] 3 CMLR 376, on appeal Case 155/79 *AM&S v Commission* [1982] ECR 1575, [1982] 2 CMLR 264; *AKZO No. 2* (n 99, above).

[164] Art 20(3) of Reg 1/2003 (n 153, above).

[165] Case T-59/99 *Ventouris Group Enterprises v Commission* [2003] ECR II-5257, [2005] 5 CMLR 1781, paras 145–147; Case T-66/99 *Minoan Lines v Commission* [2003] ECR II-5515, [2005] 5 CMLR 1957, paras 75–77, (appeal dismissed Case C-121/04P, Order of 17 November 2005); Case T-65/99 *Strintzis Lines Shipping v Commission* [2003] ECR II-5433, [2005] 5 CMLR 1901, paras 65–67 (appeal dismissed Case C-110/04P, [2006] ECR I-44). The Commission was entitled to carry out an inspection at the premises of a separate legal entity to that under investigation where the entity was legally separate to but 'merged with' that of its principal, and it had all the information necessary to judge whether it was obliged to consent to the Commission's investigation: *Ventouris*, paras 145–147. The undertaking under investigation had the right to challenge the decision to investigate that separate entity: *Strintzis*, paras 27–30.

[166] Art 20(4) of Reg 1/2003 (n 153, above). The consultation may be informal, and the Commission is not obliged to share the information on which it bases its decision with the Member State concerned: *AKZO No. 2* (n 99, above) para 24. See also generally *Hoechst* (n 99, above); Case 85/87 *Dow Benelux v Commission* [1989] ECR 3137, [1991] 4 CMLR 410 and *Dow Chemical Iberica v Commission* (n 119, above). But the Commission's practice is to visit the national authority, produce a draft decision and provide any explanation requested: Answer to Parliamentary Question 677/79, OJ 1979 C310/30. The decision can be taken by the Competition Commissioner under

The decision must state the subject-matter and purpose of the inspection, the date it is to begin, the penalties for non-compliance and the fact that the decision may be appealed.[167] The Commission need not inform the undertaking of the information it already has in its possession or set out any precise legal analysis of the suspected infringement, but it must clearly indicate the presumed facts which it intends to investigate.[168] Failure to submit to the decision renders the undertaking liable to a subsequent decision imposing a fine and periodic penalty payments.[169] There is no obligation on the Commission to inform an undertaking of its intention to adopt a decision to search premises.[170] Nor is there any obligation upon the Commission to publish such decisions.[171] The fact that such inspections have taken place does, however, sometimes receive press coverage. An undertaking against which the Commission has ordered an inspection by decision may bring an action against the Commission under Article 230 EC.[172]

13.044 **Inspection of other premises.** Inspection of premises other than that of an undertaking may only be carried out pursuant to a decision. Article 21(1) of Regulation 1/2003[173] provides that if a reasonable suspicion exists that books or other records which relate to the business and to the subject-matter of the inspection and which may be relevant to prove a serious violation of Articles 81 or 82 are being kept in any premises, land and means of transport, the Commission may by decision order an inspection to be conducted on those premises, land or

---

delegated powers: *AKZO No. 2* (n 99, above) paras 30–40. (An application to suspend a decision to investigate under Art 14(3) of Reg 17 enforced by a decision to impose periodic penalty payments under Art 16(1)(d) of Reg 17 was refused in Case 46/87R *Hoechst v Commission* [1987] ECR 1549, [1988] 4 CMLR 430).

167 Art 20(4) of Reg 1/2003 (n 153, above); and see *National Panasonic* (n 99, above) and *Hoechst* (n 99, above). There is no further requirement for detailed reasoning: *AKZO No. 2* (n 99, above) para 20; *Dow Benelux* (n 166, above) para 10; *Roquette Frères* (n 70, above) para 82.

168 *Hoechst* (n 99, above) para 41; *Groupement des cartes bancaires* (n 158, above).

169 Arts 23(1)(c) and 24(1)(e) of Reg 1/2003 (n 153, above); see *Hoechst* (n 99, above) paras 49–64; suspension refused in Case 46/87R *Hoechst* (n 166, above). The undertaking is in breach even if the refusal is only temporary: *CSM–Sugar* (n 123, above); *MEWAC*, OJ 1993 L20/6, [1994] 5 CMLR 275.

170 *AKZO No. 2* (n 99, above) para 20.

171 Art 30 of Reg 1/2003 (n 153, above).

172 Art 20(4) of Reg 1/2003 (n 153, above). Where such a decision is annulled, the Commission is prevented from using, for the purposes of proceeding in respect of an infringement of the Community competition rules, any documents or evidence which it might have obtained in the course of that investigation, as otherwise the decision on the infringement might, insofar as it was based on such evidence, be annulled: Case C-94/00 *Roquette Frères* [2002] ECR I-9011, [2003] 4 CMLR 46, [2003] All ER (EC) 920, para 49; Case 46/87R *Hoechst v Commission* (n 166, above) para 34; Case 85/87R *Dow Chemical Nederland v Commission* [1987] ECR 4367, para 17. cf the European Convention on Human Rights which does not preclude the admissibility of unlawfully obtained evidence: *Khan v United Kingdom* [2001] 31 EHRR 45. For the dismissal of challenges to an inspection decn, see Case T-339/04 and Case T-340/04 *France Télécom v Commission*, judgments of 8 March 2004. For actions pursuant to Art 230 generally, see paras 13.217 *et seq*, below.

173 Reg 1/2003 (n 153, above).

means of transport.[174] Inspections may thus be carried out at the homes of directors, managers and other members of staff of the undertakings and associations of undertakings concerned. As is the case for an inspection of undertakings, the decision must state the subject-matter and purpose of the inspection, the date it is to begin, and the right to have the decision reviewed by the Court of Justice.[175] The decision must in particular state the reasons which have led the Commission to conclude that a reasonable suspicion exists in the sense of paragraph 21(1) of Regulation 1/2003.[176] The Commission may only take such a decision after consulting the competition authority of the Member State in whose territory the inspection is to be conducted.[177] Significantly, the Commission may not carry out such an inspection without prior authorisation from the judicial authority of the Member State concerned.[178] There is no provision in Regulation 1/2003 for penalties on those who refuse to comply with the decision, but since the inspection will be carried out pursuant to authority from a national court, penalties may apply under national law.

Assistance by Member States. Articles 20(5) and 21(4) of Regulation 1/2003 **13.045** provide that officials of the Member State in whose territory the inspection is to be conducted as well as those authorised or appointed by the competition authority of that Member State must, at the request of that authority or of the Commission, actively assist the officials and other accompanying persons authorised by the Commission.[179] Further, Article 20(6) of Regulation 1/2003 provides that where an undertaking refuses to submit to an inspection under a decision, Member States are required to afford the Commission officials the necessary assistance for the carrying out of their duties, requesting where appropriate the assistance of the police or of an equivalent enforcement authority, so as to enable the Commission to conduct the inspection.[180] This provision also applies, *mutatis mutandis*, to an inspection of other premises.[181] Where such assistance in the case of an inspection of an undertaking requires authorisation from a judicial authority according to national rules, such authorisation must be

---

[174] See further *XXXIVth Annual Report on Competition Policy* (2004), p 37.
[175] Reg 1/2003 (n 153, above) Art 21(2). For the 'Court of Justice' see n 112, above.
[176] ibid.
[177] ibid. For the scope of such consultation see n 166, above.
[178] Reg 1/2003, Art 21(3). See further para 13.047, below.
[179] Art 20(5) of Reg 1/2003 (n 153, above), applicable also to inspection of other premises by Art 21(4). Such persons enjoy the powers specified in Art 20(2) of Reg 1/2003 (see para 13.048, below). In the UK, officials of the Commission are generally accompanied by a small team of officials of the OFT. These officials are present to facilitate the investigation and not as guardians of the undertaking's interests: Answer to Parliamentary Question of 8 November, 1979, *Hansard*, HL, Col 1084.
[180] Art 20(6) of Reg 1/2003 (n 153, above).
[181] ibid, Art 21(4). This appears to suggest that compliance with an inspection of other premises is compulsory although Reg 1/2003 does not prescribe any sanctions for non-compliance.

applied for.[182] In the case of an inspection of 'other premises', such as a private residence, judicial authority must be applied for in any event.[183] Under Article 22(2) of Regulation 1/2003, the Commission may call upon the competent authorities of a Member State to undertake the inspections of undertakings which the Commission might otherwise undertake under Article 20.[184] If so requested by the Commission or by the competition authority of the Member State in whose territory the inspection is to be conducted, officials and other accompanying persons authorised by the Commission may assist the officials of the authority concerned.[185]

13.046 **Inspections and the right to privacy.** An inspection may interfere with the right conferred by Article 8 of the European Convention on Human Rights.[186] Such interference may nonetheless be permissible where it falls within Article 8(2) as it 'is in accordance with the law and is necessary in a democratic society in the interests of', materially, 'the economic well-being of the country' or 'the prevention of . . . crime'. In *Colas Est v France*,[187] the Court of Human Rights accepted that raids carried out by the French competition authorities were 'manifestly in the interests of both "the economic wellbeing of the country" and "the prevention of crime" '.[188] However, such interference can only be justified under Article 8(2) if it is proportionate to the aim pursued. In *Funke*,[189] the Court of Human Rights

---

182 ibid, Art 20(7). Such assistance may be applied for as a precautionary measure: ibid. See also Cases 46/87 & 227/88 *Hoechst* (n 99, above) para 32. eg in the UK, sect 62 of the Competition Act 1998 provides for the issue of a warrant by the High Court in England and Wales or the Court of Session in Scotland where the Commission has ordered an inspection under Art 20 of Reg 1/2003. Such a warrant permits the use of reasonable force to secure entry, and to search for books and records on the premises, to take copies of those books and records and to seal the premises or books or records. The proportionality of measures ordered by the national judge at the request of the Commission cannot be challenged before the CFI: *Groupement des cartes bancaires* (n 158, above) para 74.

183 Art 21(3) of Reg 1/2003 (n 153, above). eg in the UK, see sect 62A of the Competition Act 1998.

184 Surprisingly, this provision does not apply to inspections of 'other premises'. Under Art 22(1) of Reg 1/2003 (n 153, above) the competition authority of a Member State may in its own territory carry out any inspection or other fact-finding measure on behalf and for the account of the competition authority of another Member State in order to establish whether has been an infringement of Arts 81 or 82. See para 14.021, below.

185 Reg 1/2003 (n 153, above) Art 22(2). In the United Kingdom, sect 62B of the Competition Act 1998 provides that for the purposes of Art 22(2) of Reg 1/2003, an authorised officer of the OFT has the powers specified in Art 20(2) of Reg 1/2003, as to which see para 13.048, below. Sect 63 of the Competition Act 1998 provides for the issue of a warrant where the Commission has requested the OFT to conduct an Art 22(2) inspection and the inspection is being, or is likely to be, obstructed and the measures that would be authorised by the warrant are neither arbitrary nor excessive having regard to the subject matter of the Art 22(2) inspection.

186 See para 13.031, above, as to when business premises fall within the remit of Art 8.

187 *Société Colas Est v France*, No. 3791/97 (2004) 39 EHRR 17, para 44.

188 ibid, para 44.

189 *Funke v France* A/256-A (1993) 16 EHRR 297, [1993] 1 CMLR 897; see also *Miailhe v France*, A/256-C (1993) 16 EHRR 332; and *Crémieux v France*, A/256-B (1993) 16 EHRR 357.

held that in order for a State to rely on Article 8(2), there must be safeguards against abuse of the power in question. On the facts of that case, the Court found that the absence of a judicial warrant and the exclusive competence of the relevant authorities to determine the nature and scale of the investigation meant that the safeguards were inadequate. Similarly, in *Colas Est*, the Court of Human Rights found a breach of Article 8 since there was an absence of adequate and effective safeguards where the investigating officers had exclusive competence to determine the expedience, number, length and scale of inspections, and the inspections took place without any prior warrant being issued by a judge and without the presence of a senior police officer.[190] In *Hoechst*,[191] the Court of Justice held that it was for national courts to determine whether or not the exercise by the Commission of its powers under Article 14 of Regulation 17 was arbitrary or excessive. In *Roquette Frères*,[192] the Court of Justice affirmed this approach but went on to explain the proper scope of such a review, having regard to the Article 8 issues which arise and the more recent jurisprudence under the Convention.[193]

Authorisation of an inspection by the courts of a Member State. *Roquette* **13.047**
Frères was a reference under Article 234 from the French Cour de Cassation on the interpretation of the power to inspect the premises of an undertaking under Article 14 of Regulation 17, the precursor of Article 20 of Regulation 1/2003. The Court of Justice explained that where a national court is called upon to authorise entry and seizures, it must satisfy itself that there are reasonable grounds for suspecting an infringement of the competition rules by the undertaking concerned. It may not, however, substitute its own assessment of the need for the inspections for that of the Commission. The national court must also verify the proportionality of the measures. Therefore, it is open to the national court to refuse to grant the measures applied for where the suspected impairment of competition is so minimal, the extent of the likely involvement of the undertaking concerned so limited, or the evidence sought so peripheral, that the intervention appears manifestly disproportionate. The Court of Justice discussed in detail the nature of the material which the Commission should produce to the national court and the limits on what the court may require. The terms of the judgment are reflected in Articles 20(8) and 21(3) of Regulation 1/2003 concerning, respectively, inspection at the premises of an undertaking (or association of

---

[190] *Colas Est* (n 187, above) para 49.
[191] Cases 46/87 & 227/88 *Hoechst v Commission* [1989] ECR 2859, [1991] 4 CMLR 410.
[192] Case C-94/00 *Roquette Frères* [2002] ECR I-9011, [2003] 4 CMLR 46, [2003] All ER (EC) 920. See also *Groupement des cartes bancaires* (n 158, above) paras 70 *et seq*.
[193] In *X v OFT* [2003] EWHC 1042, [2004] ICR 105, [2003] 2 All ER (Comm) 183, para 13, the English High Court held that the interference with Art 8 arising out of the grant to the OFT of search warrants under the Competition Act 1998 was justified.

undertakings), and at 'other premises', in particular the private homes of directors or employees. These Articles provide that:

(i) to control the proportionality of the coercive measures applied for, the national court may ask the Commission, either directly or through the national competition authority, for explanations of the grounds on which the Commission suspects an infringement, the seriousness of the infringement, and the nature of the involvement of the undertaking concerned; and in the case of inspection at 'other premises', of the reasonable likelihood of the books and records being kept at those premises and the importance of that evidence;

(ii) however, the national court may not call into question the necessity for the inspection or demand that it be provided with the information in the Commission's file;

(iii) the lawfulness of the Commission's decision to make an inspection may be reviewed only by the Community Courts.

The control that may be exercised by the national court is therefore circumscribed. Neither *Colas Est* nor *Roquette Frères* concerned inspection at a private residence, for which the concerns under Article 8 are inevitably greater. Subsequently, the Court of Human Rights has considered the compatibility with Article 8 of search and seizure measures at a private home. Acknowledging that it may well be considered necessary to provide for such inspections to obtain evidence in a sphere where it is otherwise impossible to detect the guilty, the Court held that: 'having regard to the severity of the interference with the right to respect for his home of a person affected by such measures, it must be clearly established that the proportionality principle has been adhered to.'[194] It appears that the Commission may need to produce particularly full information to the national court in such a case to satisfy the court that the proportionality standard is complied with.

13.048 **Powers that can be exercised during an inspection.** The general purpose of the power to carry out an inspection is to enable the Commission to check 'the actual existence and scope of a given factual and legal situation'[195] and to enable the Commission to obtain evidence directly through its own officials.[196] Article 20(2)

---

[194] *Buck v Germany*, Appl no. 41604/98, [2006] 42 EHRR 21, para 51.
[195] Case 136/79 *National Panasonic v Commission* [1980] ECR 2033, [1980] CMLR 169, para 21. The Commission is not obliged to identify in advance which documents or files it wishes to inspect: *Hoechst* (n 191, above); *Dow Benelux* (n 166, above); and *Dow Chemical Iberica* (n 166, above). In *Société Générale* (n 108, above) para 40, it was said that the Commission is entitled to require disclosure only of information or documents which may enable it to investigate putative infringements of the competition rules that justify the enquiry and are set out in the request.
[196] *National Panasonic* (n 195, above) at 2066 (ECR), 177 (CMLR), per AG Warner.

specifies that during an inspection, Commission officials, and other authorised accompanying persons, are empowered:

'(a) to enter any premises, land and means of transport of undertakings and associations of undertakings;

(b) to examine the books and other business records related to the business, irrespective of the medium on which they are stored;

(c) to take or obtain in any form copies of or extracts from such books or records;

(d) to seal any business premises and books or records for the period and to the extent necessary for the inspection;[197]

(e) to ask any representative or member of staff of the undertaking or association of undertakings for explanations on [*sic*] facts or documents relating to the subject-matter and purpose of the inspection and to record the answers.'

The powers in (a) to (c) above, but notably not (d) and (e), apply to an inspection under Article 21 at 'other premises'.[198]

Scope of the inspection.   The subject-matter of the inspection will be described **13.049** in the authorisation or decision but it is for the Commission officials to determine what documents are relevant to be examined.[199] The Commission has the power to search premises[200] in the sense that its officials have the power to require the production of documents and of the contents of furniture.[201] The Commission has no express power to demand oral explanations from particular individuals;[202] or to conduct inspections outside the Community.[203] It is not clear whether an undertaking may be required to produce at its premises within the Community documents which it keeps outside the Community.[204] Where oral explanations are sought, the explanations given may be recorded in any form.[205] A copy of any

---

[197] There was no equivalent power to seal premises, books or records under Art 14 of Reg 17.

[198] Art 21(4).

[199] *AM&S v Commission* (n 163, above). See also *Fabbrica Pisana* and *Fabbrica Sciarra*, OJ 1980 L75/30 and 35, [1980] 2 CMLR 354 and 362; *FNICF*, OJ 1982 L319/12, [1983] 1 CMLR 575. Note that the Commission has stated that if after the investigation it finds that it has taken copies of irrelevant documents, those documents will be returned to the firm as rapidly as possible and will therefore not appear on the file to which access may be granted at a later stage to other undertakings: Access to the File Notice, OJ 2005 C325/7: Vol II, App B.12, para 9.

[200] *Hoechst* (n 191, above) para 27.

[201] ibid, para 31. If the exercise of these powers is obstructed, the relevant Member State must assist: para 13.045, above.

[202] See Cases T-25/95, etc, *Cimenteries CBR v Commission* ('*Cement*') [2000] ECR II-491, [2000] 5 CMLR 204 [summary], para 735. cf *Fabbrica Pisana* (n 199, above) where the Commission stated that it is the undertaking's responsibility to designate competent representatives to reply to requests from Commission inspectors.

[203] But see paras 1.096 *et seq*, above for international cooperation.

[204] cf *Stahlwerke Röchling—Burbach GmbH*, OJ 1977 L243/20, [1977] 2 CMLR D25 (a decision under Art 47 of the ECSC Treaty) where the company had removed relevant files from its head office in Germany. See also *Dow Chemical Iberica* (n 166, above) for the use of powers of investigation under Reg 17 to obtain documents relating to a period prior to Accession.

[205] Reg 773/2004, OJ 2004 L123/18: Vol II, App B.4, Art 4(1).

such recording must be made available to the undertaking concerned after the inspection.[206] Where a member of staff who lacks the necessary authority has been asked questions in the course of an inspection, the Commission must set a time limit within which the undertaking concerned can communicate any rectification, amendment or supplement to the explanations given, to be added to the record made of the explanations given.[207] Although it appears that an inspection may be properly conducted even in the absence of a lawyer to advise the undertaking,[208] the Commission's policy is to allow the undertaking to consult a lawyer and to have a lawyer in attendance if one is available on the premises or to wait a short time for the undertaking's lawyer to arrive, on condition that the business records are not disturbed in the meantime and that the Commission officials are given access to the relevant offices.[209] The same protection should clearly apply to an inspection at a private home. At the conclusion of the inspection, the Commission officials will normally record what occurred during the inspection, including any oral explanations relating to facts or documents, in a protocol in which the representatives of the undertaking may record their own comments and which they will be asked to sign.[210]

13.050 **Penalties in respect of inspections.** The Commission may by decision impose a fine not exceeding 1 per cent of the total turnover in the preceding business year where, intentionally or negligently: (i) an undertaking refuses to submit to inspections ordered by a decision or produces the required books or other records related to the business in an incomplete form during inspections under Article 20;[211] (ii) in response to a question asked in the course of an inspection, the undertaking gives an incorrect or misleading answer, fails to rectify an incorrect, incomplete or misleading answer given by a member of staff within a time limit set by the Commission, or fails or refuses to provide a complete answer;[212] or (iii) seals affixed by the Commission in the course of an inspection have been broken.[213] If an undertaking refuses to submit to an inspection ordered by formal decision of the Commission under Article 20(4) the Commission may, by a further decision, impose periodic penalty payments not exceeding 5 per cent of the average daily

---

206 ibid, Art 4(2).

207 ibid, Art 4(3).

208 *National Panasonic* (n 195, above) at 2069 (ECR), 181 (CMLR), per AG Warner.

209 See Faull & Nikpay, *The EC Law of* Competition (2nd edn, 2007), para 8.383. The Commission will only wait for the lawyer if the delay is reasonable: *MEWAC* (n 169, above) (the premises were sealed until the following day). The Commission will not wait for external advice to be obtained if there are in-house advisers available.

210 Faull & Nikpay, above, para 8.386. Such a report does not constitute an 'act' susceptible to challenge under Art 230: Case T-9/97 *Elf Atochem v Commission* [1997] ECR II-909, [1997] 5 CMLR 844.

211 Reg 1/2003 (n 153, above) Art 23(1)(c).

212 ibid, Art 23(1)(d).

213 ibid, Art 23(1)(e).

turnover in the preceding business year per day, calculated from the date appointed by the decision.[214] The undertaking has a right to be heard before the Commission takes any decision to impose a fine, or when the Commission fixes the definitive amount of the periodic penalty payment once the undertaking has complied with the obligation.[215] The Advisory Committee on Restrictive Practices and Dominant Positions must also be consulted.[216] The power to impose penalties in respect of the conduct of inspections is subject to a limitation period of three years.[217] The power to enforce such a penalty is subject to a limitation period of five years.[218] There is no provision for the imposition of penalties as regards an order for inspection at other premises, such as private homes. Altogether, Regulation 1/2003 does not enable the imposition of fines on individuals, except where the individual is himself an undertaking. However, as an inspection at other premises may be carried out only under the authority of the national court, penalties for non-compliance may well apply under national law.

Limits on the Commission's use of information acquired.   The Commission   **13.051**
is subject to two principal obligations in relation to the information it acquires during its investigation.[219] First, Article 28(1) of Regulation 1/2003 provides that information obtained by the Commission under Articles 17 to 22 of Regulation 1/2003 may be used only for the purpose for which it was acquired.[220]

---

[214] ibid, Art 24(1). Where the obligation which the period penalty payment was intended to enforce has been satisfied, the Commission may fix the definitive amount of the penalty at a figure lower than that which would arise under the original decision: Art 24(2) of Reg 1/2003. See *AKZO Chemicals*, OJ 1994 L294/31; *UKWAL* (n 119, above) (maximum fine imposed); see also *CSM—Sugar* (n 123, above) and *MEWAC* (n 169, above) (fines imposed although refusals to allow inspection were only temporary).

[215] Reg 1/2003 (n 153, above) Art 27(1).

[216] ibid, Art 14(1) and see para 13.107, below.

[217] ibid, Art 25(1). Any action taken by the Commission or by the competition authority of a Member State for the purpose of the investigation or proceedings in respect of an infringement will interrupt the limitation period with effect from the date on which the action is notified to at least one undertaking which participated in the infringement: ibid.

[218] Reg 1/2003 (n 153, above) Art 26(1). The notification of a decision varying the original amount of the penalty or refusing an application for variation, or any action of the Commission or a Member State designed to enforce payment of the penalty will interrupt the limitation period and start time running afresh: Art 26(3)–(4) of Reg 1/2003.

[219] The provisions on disclosure in the EC-USA and EC-Canada Cooperation Agreements (paras 1.100–1.102, above) are subject to the EC rules on confidentiality: see the interpretative letters at OJ 1995 L95/51 and OJ 1999 L175/59. The Commission has set out the steps it takes to make sure that its officials do not breach these rules in discussions with their opposite numbers in the US: *XXVIth Report on Competition Policy* (1996), p 306, para 5. The Commission has also stated that effective cooperation between the EC and US authorities can be inhibited in the absence of a waiver on confidentiality by the undertaking concerned; ibid, pp 308–309 and 316. In *IRI/Nielsen*, ibid, pp 314–316, the waiver of confidentiality by AC Nielsen enabled close cooperation between the EC and US authorities and facilitated the closure of the case by the Commission once undertakings were obtained from that company; the US authorities then felt able to close their files avoiding the expense of parallel investigations and the risk of inconsistent remedies.

[220] Art 28(1) of Reg 1/2003, OJ 2003 L1/1: Vol II, App B.3.

This obligation is, however, without prejudice to the exchange and use of information foreseen by the provisions regarding cooperation with national competition authorities and national courts.[221] If the Commission wants to use such documents in a further investigation it can issue a request under Article 18 to the undertakings for fresh copies.[222] Secondly, Article 28(2) of Regulation 1/2003 provides that the Commission and the competition authorities of the Member States, their officials, servants and other persons working under the supervision of those authorities must not disclose information acquired or exchanged by them pursuant to Regulation 1/2003 if that information is of the kind covered by the obligation of professional secrecy. This is also without prejudice to the exchange and use of information foreseen by the provisions of Regulation 1/2003 concerned with cooperation.[223] These provisions are to be read with Article 287 of the Treaty, which places an obligation on the Community institutions not to disclose such information, referring specifically to 'information about undertakings, their business relations or their cost components'. The concept of 'professional secrecy' covers both business secrets and other types of confidential information. 'Business secrets' are 'information of which not only disclosure to the public but also mere transmission to a person other than the one that provided the information may seriously harm the latter's interests'.[224] Other 'confidential information' covered by the obligation of professional secrecy is information (i) that is known to only a limited number of people, (ii) the disclosure of which is liable to cause serious harm to the person who provided it or to third parties, and (iii) where the interests that would be harmed are worthy of protection.[225] The protection of confidential information is considered further in the context of access to the file.[226]

13.052 **Cooperation between the Commission and national courts.** The Commission's obligations in respect of confidentiality do not apply in relation to its cooperation with national courts under Article 15 of Regulation 1/2003.[227]

---

[221] Arts 12 and 15 of Reg 1/2003, above. See paras 14.022 *et seq*, below.

[222] Cases T-305/94, etc, *LVM ('PVC No. 2') v Commission* [1999] ECR II-931, paras 476–477.

[223] Arts 11, 12, 14, 15 and 27 of Reg 1/2003 (n 220, above).

[224] Case T-353/94 *Postbank v Commission* [1996] ECR II-921, [1997] 4 CMLR 33, [1996] All ER (EC) 817, paras 86–87; Case 145/83 *Adams v Commission* [1985] ECR 3539, para 34. See also Case T-9/99 *HFB v Commission* [2002] ECR II-1487, para 367. Access to the File Notice, OJ 2005 C325/7: Vol II, App B.12, para 18, lists as examples of business secrets: 'technical and/or financial information relating to an undertaking's know-how, methods of assessing costs, production secrets and processes, supply sources, quantities produced and sold, market shares, customer and distributor lists, marketing plans, cost and price structure and sales strategy'.

[225] Case T-198/03 *Bank Austria v Commission* [2006] ECR II-1429, [2006] 5 CMLR 639, paras 70–71.

[226] See paras 13.088 *et seq*, below.

[227] Art 28 of Reg 1/2003 (n 220, above); in *Postbank* (n 224, above) para 66, it was held that the Commission's obligation to assist courts in applying Arts 81 and 82 in private law proceedings lay outside the scope of what was then Reg 17 and took effect pursuant to the duty of cooperation in Art 10 EC.

Therefore the Commission may in general disclose information, including business secrets, obtained in the course of its investigation to national courts. Moreover, undertakings seeking to rely on Articles 81 or 82 may use in proceedings before national courts information disclosed to them by the Commission in the course of an administrative procedure. Regulation 1/2003 does not apply to such use and the Commission is not required to impose on undertakings to which it discloses information for the purposes of the administrative procedure an obligation not to use that information in private law proceedings.[228] It is for the national court, pursuant to Article 10 of the Treaty, to guarantee the protection of the confidential information or business secrets and the Commission should take the necessary precautions to ensure that this is achieved.[229] The Commission should not decline to transmit the information to a national court unless that is the only way to ensure that professional secrecy is respected.[230] The Commission will therefore, before transmitting the information to the national court, remind it of the court's obligation to uphold the rights conferred by Article 287 EC and ask the court whether it can and will guarantee protection of confidential information and business secrets. Unless such guarantees are offered, the Commission will not transmit the information. If they are, then the Commission will transmit the information, indicating those parts which are covered by professional secrecy and cannot be disclosed.[231]

Confidential information passed to NCAs.   Both of the Commission's obliga- **13.053** tions under Article 28 of Regulation 1/2003[232] are expressed to be without prejudice to Article 12 which permits the Commission and NCAs to exchange information with each other. However, in relation to professional secrecy, the Commission must nonetheless respect the obligations in Article 287 of the Treaty. Moreover, Article 12(2) of Regulation 1/2003 restricts the use of exchanged information in evidence to (i) the application of Article 81 or Article 82 'in respect of the same subject-matter for which it was collected by the transmitting authority'; or (ii) to the application of national competition law in the same case and in parallel to Community competition law where it does not lead to a different outcome. Article 12(3) imposes restrictions on the use in evidence of exchanged information as regards the imposition of sanctions on individuals,

---

228 *Postbank* (n 224, above) paras 66–68. Note that as a matter of English law the converse is true: the courts will not impose an obligation on parties not to pass material obtained on discovery to the Commission: *Apple Corps v Apple Computer* [1992] 1 CMLR 969 (ChD).

229 This may include telling the national court what information should be regarded as confidential or a business secret: *Postbank* (n 224, above) para 69.

230 *Postbank* (n 224, above) paras 89–93.

231 Commission Notice on Cooperation with National Courts, 2004 OJ C101/54: Vol II, App B.9, para 25.

232 See para 13.051, above.

with an absolute prohibition on its use to impose custodial sanctions. This provision is discussed in Chapter 14, below.[233]

13.054 **Consequences of breach.** Community officials and servants who breach confidentiality provisions risk disciplinary procedure.[234] The Commission may also be liable in damages to the party affected under Article 288 of the Treaty if wrongful disclosure is made.[235]

(d) Privilege

13.055 **Lawyer/client privilege.** In *AM&S v Commission*,[236] the Court of Justice recognised that the protection of the confidentiality of certain communications between lawyer and client is an essential corollary to the rights of the defence and serves the important requirement that everyone should be able without restraint to consult a lawyer to obtain independent legal advice. The communications protected are, however, limited to those between a client and an independent lawyer entitled to practise his profession in one of the Member States.[237] Internal documents of an undertaking summarising advice obtained from independent lawyers are also protected.[238] The protection extends to documents emanating from the undertaking to the lawyer, not merely those passing from the lawyer to the undertaking. The communications in question are those made 'for the purposes and in the interests of the client's rights of defence', that is to say which come into existence after the initiation of the proceedings or which, although made earlier, 'have a relationship to the subject-matter of that procedure'.[239] Moreover, a preparatory document which was drawn up *exclusively* for the purpose of seeking legal advice, for example summarising information gathered within the undertaking as to particular practices, is also within the scope of the privilege, even if it was not intended actually to send that document to the lawyer.[240]

---

[233] See para 14.027, below.

[234] *XVth Report on Competition Policy* (1985), points 50 to 51.

[235] Cases 145/83, etc, *Adams v Commission* [1985] ECR 3539, [1986] 1 CMLR 506.

[236] Case 155/79 *AM&S v Commission* [1982] ECR 1575, [1982] 2 CMLR 264, paras 18 and 23. See also Cases T-125 & 253/03 *Akzo Nobel Chemicals v Commission*, judgment of 17 September 2007, para 86.

[237] Annex VII to the EEA Agreement adds to the scope of Dir 77/249 lawyers qualified in the relevant EFTA states.

[238] Case T-30/89 *Hilti v Commission* [1990] ECR II-163, [1992] 4 CMLR 16, upheld on appeal Case C-53/92P *Hilti v Commission* [1994] ECR I-667, [1994] 4 CMLR 614. cf the broader definition of privileged communications in sect 65A of the Competition Act 1998.

[239] *AM&S v Commission* (n 236, above) para 23. The *AM&S* decn suggests that this requirement is likely to be broadly interpreted; in that case the privilege was held to extend to communications arising six years previously.

[240] *Akzo Nobel Chemicals v commission* (n 236, above) para 123. However, this requirement is interpreted restrictively: in that case the CFI held that the privilege did not apply to a memorandum

Lawyer/client privilege: *Akzo*.   In *AM&S*, it was held that the privilege does not   **13.056**
apply to communications with in-house lawyers.[241] In the *Akzo* case, decided 25 years
later, the Court of First Instance declined to extend the scope of the ruling in
AM&S, either to cover communications with employed lawyers who are members
of a professional Bar or more generally.[242] The Court noted that although there had
been some changes in this regard under the laws of Member States since *AM&S*, it
was impossible to identify a practice which had clear majority support across the various Member States. In many Member States communications with the undertaking's
employed lawyer were not protected, even if the lawyer was a member of a Bar or
Law Society, and in some Member States an employed lawyer is indeed precluded
from being a member of the relevant professional body.[243] The Court recognised that
the self-assessment required by reason of modernisation may give rise to a greater
need for legal advice, but found that this was not a reason for applying the privilege
to communications with in-house counsel since such exercises could always be conducted by an outside lawyer in cooperation with the staff of the undertaking, including its in-house lawyer.[244] Although a further appeal to the Court of Justice is pending,
so far *Akzo* has brought no change to the substance of the privilege. However, the
Court of First Instance gave important guidance which strengthened the procedures
to be followed when a claim to privilege was raised. It is for the undertaking contending that a document is protected by the privilege to provide the Commission officials
with material showing the basis on which the claim rests, for example by identifying
the author and purpose of the document or the context in which it was prepared.[245]
But the Court held that the Commission is not entitled to take a cursory look at
the document when the undertaking explains that even such a brief look may reveal

---

summarising certain practices and seeking agreement from a senior manager for recommendations
in that regard, although the document was discussed with the company's external lawyer.

[241] *AM&S v Commission* (n 236, above) para 27. See also *London European/Sabena*, OJ 1988
L317/47, [1989] 4 CMLR 662 (opinion of a member of Sabena's legal department quoted
in Commission decision). In *VW-Audi*, OJ 1998 L124/60, [1998] 5 CMLR 33, para 199, the
Commission rejected a claim of privilege in respect of advice from the undertaking's separate legal
division: since the lawyers in question were all employees of the undertaking, their administrative
separation from the parts of the undertaking involved in the infringement was irrelevant.

[242] Cases T-125 & 253/03 *Akzo Nobel Chemicals v Commission* (n 236, above). However, the
CFI's judgment is under appeal to the ECJ: Case C-550/07P, not yet decided. For a full discussion
of the issues, arguing in favour of retention of the *AM&S* limitation, see Grippini-Fournier, 'Legal
Professional Privilege in Competition Proceedings Before the European Commission: Beyond the
Cursory Glance' in Hawk (ed), *2004 Fordham Corp Law Inst* (2005), 587. See also Vesterdorf, 'Legal
Professional Privilege and the Privilege Against Self-Incrimination in EC Law: Recent Developments
and Current Issues', ibid, 702. (Both articles are also in (2005) 28 Fordham Int Law J 967, 1179).

[243] *Akzo Nobel Chemicals v Commission* (n 236, above) paras 170–171; see also paras 154–155.
In that case Akzo's in-house lawyer was a member of the Netherlands Bar.

[244] Ibid, para 173. This of course disregards the economic considerations for having an in-house
lawyer in the first place.

[245] Ibid, paras 79–80. In some cases, the undertaking may be able to show that the document
bears the heading of the Chambers or law firm from which it emanates, or the document's title may
demonstrate that it concerns legal advice, without revealing the contents of the document.

its contents.[245A] If the Commission officials are not satisfied by the material presented that the document is privileged, they must place it in a sealed envelope and may remove it for safe-keeping; and the Commission should then take a decision which enables the undertaking to refer the matter to the Court, with a request for interim relief where appropriate. The Commission argued that no harm was done by permitting a cursory look at the document to ascertain if the privilege applied, since if the document was privileged it could not be relied on in a subsequent decision. The Court rejected this, holding that if a document is privileged, that means not only that it cannot be relied on as evidence but that the Commission must not read it at all, otherwise it might be used indirectly to seek other information or evidence.[245B]

13.057   **Privilege against self-incrimination:** *Orkem.*   In the 1989 case of *Orkem,*[246] the Court of Justice held that the privilege against self-incrimination – which it found was not consistently recognised in the legal systems of Member States save in the purely criminal context – extends only to answering questions put by the Commission to an undertaking where the answer might lead it to an admission of an infringement of the competition rules. The undertaking is not, however, otherwise entitled[247] under Community law to refuse to supply information or documents that could be used to prove the existence of an infringement of the competition rules.[248] In *Orkem*, the Court held that the Commission is entitled 'to compel an undertaking to provide all necessary information concerning such facts as may be known to it and to disclose to it, if necessary such documents relating thereto as are in its possession, even if the latter may be used to establish against it or another undertaking the existence of an anti-competitive practice'.

[245A] Ibid, paras 81–85.

[245B] Accordingly, the CFI found that the Commission had infringed the proper procedure by taking a cursory look at some of the documents for which Akzo claimed privilege before placing them in a sealed envelope and by reading the other documents for which the Commission rejected the claim to privilege and placing them in the file before Akzo had the opportunity to challenge this decision: ibid, paras 95–101.

[246] Case 374/87 *Orkem v Commission* [1989] ECR 3283, [1991] 4 CMLR 502. See also Case T-34/93 *Société Générale v Commission* [1995] ECR II-545, [1996] 4 CMLR 665, paras 72–74 (no such privilege lay in order to justify a refusal to comply with investigative measures that would require the production of evidence of an infringement).

[247] The Commission is entitled to question the undertaking under investigation about the conduct of all the other undertakings under investigation: Cases C-204/00P, etc, *Aalborg Portland v Commission* [2004] ECR I-123, [2005] 4 CMLR 251, para 207; Case T-67/00 *JFE Engineering v Commission* [2004] ECR II-2501, [2005] 4 CMLR 27, para 192 (appeal dismissed, Cases C-403 & 405/04P *Sumitomo Metal Industries Ltd v Commission* [2007] 4 CMLR 650). The privilege against self-incrimination does not permit a trade association to refuse to answer questions about the conduct of its members: *Aalborg Portland*, above, para 208

[248] cf the position in English law, where an undertaking is entitled to assert privilege in respect of information or documents that could be used to prove a breach of EC competition rules: *Rio Tinto Zinc v Westinghouse* [1978] AC 547 (HL). In practice, however, this may be an unattractive point for a defendant to raise.

In short, the *Orkem* principle does not restrict the matters on which questions can be asked but merely the type of questions that may be asked.[249]

Self-incrimination: developments in human rights jurisprudence. The scope **13.058** of the privilege against self-incrimination has been the subject of developing human rights jurisprudence. In *Funke*,[250] it was held that Mr Funke's rights under Article 6(1) of the European Convention on Human Rights were violated when he was required to produce bank statements and financial information by customs authorities investigating charges against him of infringement of exchange control legislation, and then convicted for refusing to supply those documents. The scope of the ruling in *Funke* was, however, cast into doubt by the subsequent judgment of the Court of Human Rights in *Saunders*.[251] There the Court held that the use in criminal proceedings against Mr Saunders of answers obtained under compulsion from him during an investigation by inspectors under the (English) Companies Act 1985 was a violation of his rights under Article 6. But the Court went on to observe that 'the right not to incriminate oneself . . . does not extend to the use in criminal proceedings of material which may be obtained from the accused through the use of compulsory powers but which has an existence independent of the will of the suspect such as, *inter alia*, documents acquired pursuant to a warrant. . . '.[252] There is an apparent tension between this decision and that of *Funke*, in which a requirement to produce pre-existing documents was held to give rise to a violation of Article 6.[253] The Court of Human Rights has,

---

[249] See, per AG Gulmann in Case C-60/92 *Otto v Postbank* [1993] ECR I-5683, para 10; at para 9 the AG observed that the *Orkem* rule can be seen as preventing questions where the answer would require the undertaking to perform a subjective appraisal of whether or not it has breached the competition rules. In that case, the ECJ held that national courts are not required, as a matter of EC law, to apply the *Orkem* principle in ordinary civil proceedings which do not lead to the imposition of a penalty. But it followed that the Commission was not entitled to use information obtained in the course of such proceedings, which may come to its attention, in order to establish an infringement or as evidence justifying the initiation of an investigation: para 20.

[250] Case A/256-A *Funke v France* [1993] 16 EHRR 297, [1993] 1 CMLR 897.

[251] App No. 19187/91 *Saunders v United Kingdom* [1997] 23 EHRR 313. See Riley, '*Saunders* and the power to obtain information in Community and United Kingdom competition law' (2000) 25 EL Rev 264.

[252] *Saunders*, para 69.

[253] See the dissenting opinion of Judge Martens, ibid, paras 11–12. It has been suggested that it is unclear on what basis Mr Funke could be said to have been deprived of a fair trial since the information and documents were never used in any trial: see *R v Hertfordshire CC ex p Green Environmental Industries* [2000] 2 AC 412, [2000] 1 All ER 773, per Lord Hoffmann at 381–382, declining to follow *Funke* on the basis that Art 6(1) ECHR is concerned with the fairness of the trial and not with extra-judicial inquiries. The ECtHR has however since reaffirmed that there is no requirement that allegedly incriminating evidence obtained by coercion should actually be used in criminal proceedings before the privilege against self-incrimination applies: *Heaney and McGuinness v Ireland* (2001) 33 EHRR 12, paras 43–46; *Weh v Austria* (2005) 40 EHRR 37 paras 39–45; and *Shannon v United Kingdom* No. 6563/03, (2006) 42 EHRR 31 paras 32–35, in which the ruling of the House of Lords in *Green Environmental Industries* to contrary effect was considered and, effectively, disapproved. As the Court explained in *Weh*, there are two types of cases in which a violation of the

however, subsequently affirmed the approach taken in *Funke* in a case concerning the use in criminal proceedings of information obtained under compulsion. *In JB v Switzerland*[254] the Swiss tax authorities had instituted tax avoidance proceedings against the applicant. He was required to produce documents and information about his income and the Court of Human Rights found there had been a breach of the privilege against self-incrimination. It ruled that unlike *Saunders*, the case did not involve material which 'has an existence independent of the will of the accused, and is not, therefore obtained by means of coercion and in defiance of the will of that person'.[255] It is difficult to understand this reasoning: plainly, the documents that the Swiss authorities sought had an existence independent of the will of the accused, even if actions of the accused were required in order to produce those documents to the authorities.[256]

13.059 **Subsequent case law of the Community Courts.**   Although the case law of the Court of Human Rights has thus developed considerably since the Court of Justice's judgment in *Orkem*, the principles governing the Commission's requests for information have subsequently been confirmed by the Community Courts.[257] *Mannesmannröhren-Werke*[258] concerned the Commission's investigation into cartels in the seamless steel tubes market. The Commission sent a series of questions to the undertakings identifying different kinds of meeting at which cartel discussions allegedly took place asking for: the dates, places and names of the firms participating in each meeting; the names of the persons who represented the undertaking at the meetings together with their travel documents; and copies of all the invitations, agendas, minutes, internal memoranda, records and any other document in the possession of the undertaking or employees concerning the meetings.

---

privilege against self-incrimination may arise: cases relating to the use of compulsion for the purpose of obtaining information which might incriminate the person concerned in pending or anticipated criminal proceedings (eg *Funke* and *JB*), and cases concerning the use of incriminating information compulsorily obtained outside the context of criminal proceedings in a subsequent criminal prosecution (eg *Saunders*): *Weh*, paras 42–43.

[254] No. 31827/96 *JB v Switzerland*, judgment of 3 May 2001.

[255] *JB*, above, para 68.

[256] See Ward and Gardner, The Privilege Against Self-incrimination: In Search of Legal Certainty (2003) Comp Law 200, (2004) EHRLR 388. In *X v OFT* [2003] EWHC 1042, [2004] ICR 105, [2003] 2 All ER (Comm) 183, paras 7–11, the English High Court held that where a search warrant was issued under the Competition Act 1998, the right of the investigating officers to take documentary material was compatible with Art 6.

[257] For discussion prior to the *SGL Carbon* judgment, see Wils, 'Self-incrimination in EC antitrust enforcement: A legal and economic analysis' (2003) 26 World Competition 567.

[258] Case T-112/98 *Mannesmannröhren-Werke* [2001] ECR II-729, [2001] 5 CMLR 54, paras 66, 67; Cases T-305/94, etc, *LVM ('PVC No. 2') v Commission* [1999] ECR II-931, para 448 (the ECJ did not rule on the point on appeal: Cases C-238/99P, etc, *Limburgse Vinyl Maatschappij NV ('LVM') v Commission ('PVC II')* [2002] ECR I-8375, [2003] 4 CMLR 397, para 279). In *Trioplast Nyborg A/S v Competition Authority*, 28 March 2003, U 2003.1328 H, the Danish Supreme Court applied the ECJ and CFI case law, holding that requiring answers to questions relating only to facts does not infringe the privilege against governing self-incrimination unless the answer would imply a confession.

The Commission's final request, in relation to meetings for which the undertaking was unable to find relevant documents, was that the undertaking should 'describe the purpose of the meeting, the decisions adopted and the type of documents received before and after the meeting'. The Court of First Instance held that an undertaking was obliged to produce the 'purely factual' information requested and documents already in existence. However, the last request was such that it might compel the applicant to admit its participation in an unlawful agreement and thus was a breach of the rights of the defence. The Court of First Instance went on to hold that whether the undertaking had a right not to incriminate itself under German law was irrelevant since in the field of competition law such a right was not generally accepted among Member States.[259] In *Commission v SGL Carbon*,[260] the Advocate General expressly applied the *Saunders* distinction as regards existing documents[261] and the Court of Justice followed his Opinion, reversing the Court of First Instance to hold that an undertaking is obliged to produce contemporaneous documents although they evidenced the meetings and discussions of a cartel.[262] In that case, the Commission had also asked SGL Carbon to inform it of which cartel members it had tipped off about the Commission's planned inspection visit. The Court found that although SGL Carbon had not been obliged to answer this question, it had purported to do so but the information which it gave was misleading and incomplete.

Foreign law prohibitions. In 1976, the Commission held in *CSV*[263] that an **13.060** undertaking established within the Community could not refuse to disclose information on the grounds that to do so would amount to unlawful disclosure, rendering the officers of the undertaking liable to fines or imprisonment under the laws of Switzerland.[264] However, in the light of subsequent developments in

---

259 *Mannesmannröhren-Werk*, above, para 84.

260 Case C-301/04P *Commission v SGL Carbon* [2006] ECR I-5915, [2006] 5 CMLR 877 (on appeal from Cases T-236/01, etc, *Tokai Carbon v Commission (Graphite Electrodes)* [2004] ECR II-1181, [2004] 5 CMLR 1465). The Commission appealed against the reduction in the level of fine which the CFI had granted because SGL Carbon had cooperated with the Commission's investigation by voluntarily providing information which it claimed was covered by privilege. The ECJ agreed with the Commission that no such reduction was justified: the material was not in fact privileged and SGL Carbon had therefore done no more than comply with its legal duty to respond to the Commission's requests.

261 *SGL Carbon*, above, Opinion of AG Geelhoed, paras 65–66.

262 See also Cases T-259/02, etc, *Raiffeisen Zentralbank Österreich v Commission*, judgment of 14 December 2006, para 543 (on appeal on other grounds, Cases C-125/07P, C-133/07P, C-135/07P and C-137/07P, not yet decided).

263 *CSV*, OJ 1976 L192/27.

264 See *Adams v Staatsanwaltschaft des Kantons Basel-Stadt* [1978] 3 CMLR 480 (Swiss Supreme Court upheld conviction under Swiss law for having unlawfully communicated information to Commission). It is submitted that a different view should be taken in a case where the undertaking in question was itself situated in the third country. A number of third countries have legislation which may prohibit such disclosure: see, eg Jacobs, 'Problems arising from Extraterritorial Application of Competition Laws' (1980) ECLR 199; and cf *Restatement (Third) of the Foreign Relations Law of the United States* (1987), para 442(2).

the case law on human rights, this decision should not now be followed. But information cannot be withheld on grounds that its disclosure would involve the undertaking in breach of a fiduciary duty.[265]

5. Complaints

13.061 **Generally.** This Section describes the procedure whereby an interested person can complain to the Commission about an alleged infringement of Article 81 or Article 82, the obligations on the Commission to examine such complaints and, when an investigation is ordered, the complainant's right to take part in any infringement proceedings.[266] The Commission has issued a Notice on the handling of complaints under Article 81 and 82 ('the Complaints Notice').[267] The Complaints Notice records the fact that information supplied by undertakings and consumers benefits the enforcement of the competition rules and that the Commission wishes to encourage citizens and undertakings to inform the Commission and NCAs about suspected infringements.[268] Part of the Complaints Notice is therefore devoted to assisting a complainant who is deciding whether to complain to the Commission or bring an action before the national court. Part III of the Notice explains the procedure for the handling of complaints under Regulation 1/2003.

13.062 **Complaints and provision of information.** Under Article 7(2) of Regulation 1/2003, Member States or natural or legal persons who can show 'a legitimate interest' may lodge with the Commission a complaint that there has been an infringement of Article 81 or Article 82. Under Article 5 of the Implementing Regulation, Commission Regulation 773/2004, such complaints must contain the information set out in Form C (annexed to the Regulation).[269] However, a person who cannot show a legitimate interest or who does not want to provide the information required by Form C may nonetheless draw the matter to the attention of the Commission. Such information can be a starting point for a Commission investigation,[270] but the informant will not be regarded as a complainant for the purposes of the rules relating to the Commission's treatment of complaints. The Commission's only promise to such an informant is to deal with correspondence from it in accordance with its principles of good

---

[265] *Fides*, OJ 1979 L57/33, [1979] 1 CMLR 650.

[266] For a thorough analysis by the UK Competition Appeal Tribunal of the rules governing the handling of complaints before the Commission as they stood immediately before the coming into force of Reg 1/2003, see *Pernod-Ricard v OFT* [2004] CAT 10, [2004] CompAR 707.

[267] Complaints Notice, OJ 2004 C101/65: Vol II, App B.10.

[268] Complaints Notice, paras 2–3.

[269] Reg 773/2004, OJ 2004 L123/18: Vol II, App B.4.

[270] Complaints Notice, para 4.

administrative practice.[271] A person can acquire the rights that attach to being a complainant within Article 7(2) even if his complaint was not the trigger for the subsequent Commission investigation.[272]

Legitimate interest: generally. A complainant under Article 7(2) must be able **13.063** to show a 'legitimate interest', the onus being on him to do so.[273] The use of the word 'legitimate' suggests that the complainant's interest should be significant and reasonably direct. Member States are deemed always to have a legitimate interest,[274] but the Commission considers that sub-national public authorities have a legitimate interest only if they themselves are buyers or users of the relevant goods or services and do not have such an interest insofar as they pursue a complaint for the general benefit of their residents.[275]

Legitimate interest of consumers of products and services. The question **13.064** whether a person who is simply a consumer of the goods or services affected by the alleged cartel can establish a legitimate interest was considered by the Court of First Instance in *Österreichische Postsparkasse*.[276] The applicants objected to the disclosure of a non-confidential version of the statement of objections alleging a banking cartel to a political party, the FPÖ, whose only interest was as a consumer of retail banking services. The Court held that 'there is nothing to prevent a final customer who purchases goods or services from being able to satisfy the notion of legitimate interest'. The Court rejected the argument that this would effectively render the notion of legitimate interest meaningless or 'pave the way for an alleged "*actio popularis*"'. Acknowledging that a consumer who can show that his economic interests have been harmed as a result of a cartel complained of by him may have a legitimate interest is not the same, the Court held, as considering that any natural or legal person has such an interest. The FPÖ could therefore validly rely

---

[271] ibid, para 4, fn 4. Such informants will, however, benefit from the general rules regarding the handling of confidential information and the Commission's duties to safeguard confidentiality; see, eg Case 145/83 *Adams v Commission* [1985] ECR 3539, [1986] 1 CMLR 506.

[272] Cases T-213 & 214/01 *Österreichische Postsparkasse v Commission* [2006] ECR II-1601, [2007] 4 CMLR 506.

[273] Complaints Notice (n 267, above) para 40.

[274] Complaints Notice, para 33.

[275] ibid.

[276] *Österreichische Postsparkasse* (n 272, above). See also the Commission decisions following complaints from individual consumers in *Greek Ferries*, OJ 1999 L109/24, [1999] 5 CMLR 47, para 1 (on appeal: Case T-65/99 *Strintzis Lines Shipping v Commission* [2003] ECR II-5433, [2005] 5 CMLR 1901, Case T-66/99 *Minoan Lines v Commission* [2003] ECR II-5515, [2005] 5 CMLR 1957; further appeals dismissed: Cases C-110/04P *Strintzis Lines*, [2006] ECR I-44; C-121/04P *Minonan Lines* [2006] 4 CMLR 1405 and Case T-59/99 *Ventouris Group v Commission* [2003] ECR II-5257, [2005] 5 CMLR 1781); and *Volkswagen*, OJ 2001 L262/14, [2001] 5 CMLR 1309 (appeal allowed, Case T-208/01 *Volkswagen v Commission* [2003] ECR II-5141, [2004] 4 CMLR 727, [2004] All ER (EC) 674; Commission's appeal dismissed, Case C-74/04P *Commission v Volkswagen* [2006] ECR I-6585).

on its capacity as a customer of banking services in Austria and the fact that its economic interests were harmed by anti-competitive practices in order to show a legitimate interest in lodging a complaint. The Commission's Complaints Notice states in general terms that 'Consumer associations can . . . lodge complaints with the Commission'[277] but that individuals or organisations acting *pro bono publico* would not have a legitimate interest.[278]

13.065 Legitimate interest: the practice. Persons whose 'legitimate interest' has been accepted by the Community Courts and the Commission[279] include a competitor,[280] a person excluded from a distribution system,[281] a distributor bound by an export ban,[282] a trader unable to make parallel imports by reason of an export ban,[283] a member of a trade association punished for breach of the association's rules,[284] a licensee subject to restrictive provisions in a licence agreement,[285] a trader unable

---

[277] Complaints Notice (n 267, above) para 37.

[278] Complaints Notice (n 267, above) para 38. See also Case 246/81 *Lord Bethell v Commission* [1982] ECR 2277, [1982] 3 CMLR 300, para 16. In Case T-114/92 *BEMIM v Commission* [1995] ECR II-147, [1996] 4 CMLR 305, the Commission did not contest the *locus* of a consumers' organisation to make a complaint. However, in *Distribution system of Ford Werke AG (Interim Measures)*, OJ 1982 L256/20, [1982] 3 CMLR 267, BEUC (a consumers' organisation) was a complainant, but recitals to the Commission's decision do not suggest that proceedings were initiated on the complaint itself. However BEUC was allowed to intervene in the subsequent ECJ proceedings: [1984] ECR 1129, [1984] 1 CMLR 649. In *BP/TGWU*, XVIth Annual Report on Commission Policy (1986) a trade union was held to have a legitimate interest to make a complaint about the closure of a refinery where its members were employed but not to complain about other agreements that had no bearing on the closure. And cf Case T-2/03 *Verein für Konsumenteninformation* [2005] ECR II-1121, [2005] 4 CMLR 1627, [2005] All ER (EC) 813, concerning the right under Reg 1049/2001, OJ 2001 L145/43, of a consumers' association to have access to documents in the Commission's file *after* the issue of a cartel decision for the purpose of bringing a damages claim: see para 13.100, below.

[279] The test applied by the Courts is whether the application is of direct and individual concern to the applicant. This is not necessarily the same as the question of whether the complainant has a legitimate interest under Art 7(2) of Reg 1/2003. Nonetheless, the Commission's practice under Art 7 (formerly Art 3 of Reg 17) of following the Courts' approach under Art 230 EC avoids a situation a person is treated as a complainant under Art 7 but cannot apply under Art 230 for review of decisions taken upon that complaint.

[280] See, eg Cases 142 & 156/84 *BAT v Commission* [1987] ECR 4487, [1988] 4 CMLR 24; *ECS/AKZO (No. 2)*, OJ 1985 L374/1, [1986] 3 CMLR 273, on appeal Case C-62/86 *AKZO v Commission* [1991] ECR I-3359, [1993] 5 CMLR 215.

[281] Case 26/76 *Metro v Commission (No. 1)* [1977] ECR 1875, [1978] 2 CMLR 1; Case 210/81 *Demo-Studio Schmidt v Commission* [1983] ECR 3045, [1984] 1 CMLR 63; Case 75/84 *Metro v Commission (No. 2)* [1986] ECR 3021, [1987] 1 CMLR 118; Case T-19/92 *Leclerc v Commission* [1996] ECR II-1851, [1997] 4 CMLR 995.

[282] *The Distillers Company Ltd*, OJ 1978 L50/16, [1978] 1 CMLR 400; *Nintendo*, OJ 2003 L255/33, [2004] 4 CMLR 421, para 85, on appeal Cases T-12/03 *Itochu Corporation v Commission*, T-13/03 *Nintendo v Commission*, T-18/03 *CD Contact Data v Commission*, not yet decided.

[283] Case 792/79R *Camera Care v Commission* [1980] ECR 119, [1980] 1 CMLR 334; *Johnson & Johnson*, OJ 1980 L377/16, [1981] 2 CMLR 287. For the position of a consumer unable to purchase because of an export ban, see *Kawasaki*, OJ 1979 L16/9, [1979] 1 CMLR 448.

[284] *CBR*, OJ 1978 L20/18, [1978] 2 CMLR 194.

[285] *AOIP/Beyrard*, OJ 1976 L6/8, [1976] 1 CMLR D14; *Breeders' rights: roses*, OJ 1985 L369/9, [1988] 4 CMLR 193.

to penetrate a market because customers were tied to other suppliers,[286] persons subject to refusal of supply by a dominant company,[287] a supplier being paid low prices by monopoly purchasers,[288] a dealer subject to an allegedly abusive discount structure,[289] an undertaking injured by predatory pricing,[290] the 'target' of a takeover,[291] a trade union representing workers made redundant following the closure of a refinery allegedly as a result of a concerted practice,[292] and an association of undertakings entitled to represent the interests of those adversely affected.[293] However, an undertaking does not have a legitimate interest by virtue of the involvement of a trade association of which its parent company is a member in the Commission's administrative procedure,[294] or because the lawfulness of the Commission's actions are relevant to a dispute involving the undertaking before national courts.[295] In *IECC v Commission*,[296] the Court of First Instance upheld the Commission's rejection of part of a complaint by a trade association whose members were not involved in that aspect of the matters complained of.

Requirements of Form C. In addition to showing a legitimate interest, Form C requires[297] the complainant to provide the following information, unless the

13.066

---

[286] *Vaessen/Moris*, OJ 1979 L19/32, [1979] 1 CMLR 511; see also Cases T-528/93, etc, *Métropole Télévision v Commission* [1996] ECR II-649, [1996] 5 CMLR 386 (actual or potential competitors denied access to the market).

[287] *Zoja-CSC/ICI*, OJ 1972 L299/51, [1973] CMLR D50, on appeal Cases 6 & 7/73 *Commercial Solvents v Commission* [1974] ECR 223, [1974] 1 CMLR 309.

[288] Case 298/83 *CICCE v Commission* [1985] ECR 1105, [1986] 1 CMLR 486.

[289] *Nederlandsche Michelin*, OJ 1981 L353/33, [1982] 1 CMLR 643, on appeal Case 322/81 *Michelin v Commission* [1983] ECR 3461, [1985] 1 CMLR 282.

[290] *ECS/AKZO (No. 2)* (n 280, above).

[291] *British Sugar/Berisford*, *XIIth Report on Competition Policy* (1982), points 104–106; see also *Philip Morris/Rembrandt/Rothmans*, *XIVth Report on Competition Policy* (1984), points 98–100, on appeal Cases 142 & 156/84 *BAT v Commission* (n 280, above).

[292] *BP/TGWU* (n 278, above). But the Commission held in the same case that the complainant trade union had a legitimate interest to complain about processing contracts only to the extent that these had a bearing on the closure of the refinery.

[293] *BEMIM* (n 278, above) (association of discotheque operators affected by practices relating to performance rights; the association will need to establish its authority to act on its membership's behalf). See the Complaints Notice (n 267, above) para 35. Note that in Case T-37/92 *BEUC and NCC v Commission* [1994] ECR II-285, [1995] 4 CMLR 167, neither the CFI nor the Commission challenged the legitimate interest of the applicant consumers associations.

[294] Case T-87/92 *Kruidvat v Commission* [1996] ECR II-1961, [1997] 4 CMLR 1046; appeal dismissed, Case C-70/97P, [1998] ECR I-7183, [1999] 4 CMLR 68.

[295] ibid, para 32 (ECJ).

[296] Cases T-133 & 204/95 *IECC v Commission* [1998] ECR II-3645, [1998] 5 CMLR 992 at para 68 (upheld on appeal Case C-450/98P, [2001] ECR I-3947, [2001] 5 CMLR 291).

[297] For Form C, see para 13.062, above. If these requirements are not complied with, the Commission will not regard the correspondence as amounting to an Art 7(2) complaint, although it may use it as the basis of an *ex officio* inquiry: Complaints Notice (n 267, above) para 32.

Commission dispenses with part of this obligation:[298]

(a) details of the complainant including corporate structure and contact information;

(b) details of the subject of the complaint including corporate structure and contact information;

(c) facts showing an infringement, including details of the nature of products concerned, the agreements or practices in question, and market shares;

(d) relevant documents;[299] details of witnesses and market statistics;

(e) geographical scope of the infringement and effect on trade between Member States;

(f) the remedy sought; and

(g) details of any approach to an NCA or legal proceedings brought in a national court in relation to the subject of the complaint or related matters.

Three paper copies and (if possible) an electronic version[300] should be submitted to the Commission, along with a non-confidential version. The complaint must be made in one of the Community's official languages.[301]

13.067 **Extent of the Commission's duty to consider a complaint.** The Commission is under no obligation to initiate procedures to establish possible infringements of Community law.[302] Since it is not obliged to come to a decision as to whether or not there has been an infringment in a particular case, it is also not obliged to carry out an investigation because such an investigation could have no purpose other than to seek evidence of the existence or non-existence of an infringement which it is not required to establish. This does not mean, however, that the Commission has an unlimited discretion as to how it handles a complaint. On receipt of a complaint, the Commission is under a duty to consider the factual and legal elements of it so as to decide whether, if established, the facts would constitute an infringement and whether there is a Community interest in pursuing the matter.[303]

---

[298] Reg 773/2004 (n 205, above) Art 5(1). The Commission considers that the possibility of dispensation may in particular play a role in facilitating complaints by consumers or consumers' associations: Complaints Notice (n 267, above) para 31.

[299] The Commission expects the provision of copies of material 'reasonably available' to the complainant; where information or documents are unavailable, the complainant should to the extent possible provide the Commission with indications as to where they might be found; Complaints Notice; ibid.

[300] Complaints Notice (n 267, above) para 30. The link referred to in the Notice is no longer effective: an electronic version of Form C is currently available at http://ec.europa.eu/comm/competition/antitrust/others/anticompetitive/formc.html.

[301] Reg 773/2004 (n 205, above) Art 5(2) and (3). For the Community languages, see para 1.039, above.

[302] See, eg Case T-204/03 *Haladjian Frères v Commission* [2006] ECR II-3779, [2007] 4 CMLR 1106, paras 26 *et seq.*

[303] See generally Case T-24/90 *Automec v Commission ('Automex II')* [1992] ECR II-2223, [1992] 5 CMLR 431; and Case C-119/97P *Ufex v Commission* [1999] ECR I-1341, [2000]

The principle of sound administration means that in doing so, it must undertake a diligent and impartial examination of the complaint.[304] However, the Commission is not obliged, before rejecting a complaint, to examine facts which have not been brought to its notice by the complainant and which the Commission could only have discovered by investigation.[305] The Commission is also entitled to treat different complaints on the same subject-matter differently if some of them reveal an infringement and a Community interest and others do not.[306] Even if similar complaints are made against a number of undertakings between whom there is no relevant distinction the Commission is entitled to take one case and leave the other complainants to pursue their remedies in national courts.[307] In deciding which case to take, it will be relevant how long ago each complaint was made.[308] The Commission is obliged, if it decides not to proceed with a complaint, to take a decision on it that can be challenged before the Community courts, and to do so within a reasonable time.[309] It is not under a duty to consider every aspect of the complainants' arguments as long as its sets out its reasoning and conclusions on the main arguments.[310]

Procedure: first stage. In *Automec I*,[311] the Court of First Instance identified **13.068** three successive stages to the procedure for the investigation of a complaint. Following the adoption of Regulation 1/2003, these three stages[312] are now incorporated into the relevant provisions governing handling of complaints in Article 7(2) of Regulation 1/2003 and Article 7 of Regulation 773/2004.[313]

---

4 CMLR 268. See also *Demo-Studio Schmidt* (n 281, above) para 19; *CICCE* (n 288, above); Case 114/83 *Sté d'Initiatives et de Co-operation Agricoles v Commission* [1984] ECR 2589, [1985] 2 CMLR 767; Case T-575/93 *Koelman v Commission* [1996] ECR II-1, [1996] 4 CMLR 636 (on appeal: Case C-59/96P, [1997] ECR I-4809); *Haladjian Frères*, above.

304 Case T-54/99 *max.mobil v Commission* [2002] ECR II-313, [2002] 4 CMLR 1356, referring also to Art 41(1) of the Charter of Fundamental Rights.

305 Case T-319/99 *FENIN v Commission* [2003] ECR II-357, [2003] 5 CMLR 34, [2004] All ER (EC) 300, para 43 (appeal dismissed Case C-205/03P *FENIN v Commission* [2006] ECR I-6295, [2006] 5 CMLR 559). But where there are several complaints on the same subject, the Commission must take account of all the information in them and not merely assess them separately: Case T-26/99 *Trabisco v Commission* [2001] ECR II-633, para 35.

306 *Trabisco*, above, para 36.

307 Case T-219/99 *British Airways v Commission* [2003] ECR II-5917, [2004] 4 CMLR 1008, para 70 (appeal on other grounds dismissed, Case C-95/04P, [2007] 4 CMLR 982).

308 ibid, para 69.

309 Case C-282/95P *Guérin Automobiles v Commission* [1997] ECR I-1503, [1997] 5 CMLR 447.

310 eg Case T-62/99 *Société de distribution de mécaniques et d'automobiles (Sodima) v Commission* [2001] ECR II-665, [2001] 5 CMLR 1309, para 44.

311 Case T-64/89 *Automec Srl v Commission (Automec I)* [1990] ECR II-367, [1991] 4 CMLR 177.

312 This procedure does not apply when the rejection is on the basis that an NCA is dealing with the matter; such rejections are governed by Art 13 of Reg 1/2003. In such a case, the Commission must tell the complainant which NCA is dealing with the matter: Art 9 of Reg 773/2004, OJ 2004 L123/18: Vol II, App B.4.

313 Formerly Art 6 of Reg 2842/98, OJ 1998 L354/18. For a comparison of the *Automec* procedure with the procedure set out in Reg 773/2004, see Case T-411/05 *Annemans v Commission*, judgment of 12 July 2007.

In the first stage, which follows the receipt of the complaint, the Commission obtains the information that will enable it to decide whether to take action on the complaint.[314] This stage may comprise an informal exchange of opinions and information between the Commission and the complainant with a view to specifying the factual and legal matters which are the subject of the complaint and giving the complainant an opportunity to substantiate his allegations, if necessary, in the light of an initial reaction by the Commission staff.[315] The Commission has set an indicative period of four months for this stage.[316] However, the Commission may not need to investigate the matter; it can proceed to the second stage once it has examined the matters of fact and law set out in the complaint.[317]

13.069 **Procedure: second stage.** In the second stage, the Commission, if it is minded to reject the complaint, informs the complainant of the reasons why it considers that there are insufficient grounds for acting on the complaint and gives him a time limit of not less than four weeks[318] in which to submit any further comments in writing.[319] This communication is often referred to as an 'Article 7(1) letter'. The complainant may request access to the documents on which the Commission has based its provisional assessment, apart from business secrets and confidential information,[320] although normally the Commission will annex the relevant documents to the Article 7(1) letter.[321] The complainant is not entitled to access to the file.[322] The Commission is not obliged to take account of written submissions received after the expiry of that time limit, and the complaint is deemed to have been withdrawn if the complainant fails to respond within the time set.[323] If the

---

[314] The Commission must, where there are several complaints on the same matter, aggregate the evidence in those complaints: *Sodima* (n 310, above) para 35.

[315] See para 55 of the Complaints Notice. The Commission often sends a copy of the complaint (with business secrets deleted) to the undertaking against whom the complaint is made, inviting comments.

[316] Complaints Notice, OJ 2004 C101/65: Vol II, App B.10, para 61.

[317] Case C-19/93P *Rendo v Commission* [1995] ECR I-3319, [1997] 4 CMLR 392, para 27.

[318] Article 7(1) of Reg 773/2004 (n 312, above) and Complaints Notice (n 316, above) para 70.

[319] Complaints Notice, para 56. In Case T-77/94 *VGB v Commission* [1997] ECR II-759, [1997] 5 CMLR 812, [1997] All ER (EC) 812, the Commission wrote a reasoned letter to the complainant saying that unless it heard from the complainant with further comments it would close the case in four weeks' time. This was held to be a letter under what is now Art 7(1), particularly as the Commission had already given an initial reaction to the complaint.

[320] Reg 773/2004, OJ 2004 L123/18: Vol II, App B.4, Art 8, which also provides that the complainant may use the documents only for the purposes of administrative or judicial proceedings under Arts 81 or 82.

[321] Complaints Notice (n 316, above) para 69.

[322] Case T-17/93 *Matra-Hachette v Commission* [1994] ECR II-595, 608–10; Case T-65/96 *Kish Glass v Commission* [2000] ECR II-1885, [2000] 5 CMLR 229, para 34 (appeal dismissed, Case C-241/00P [2001] ECR I-7759, [2002] 4 CMLR 586).

[323] Reg 773/2004 (n 320, above) Art 7(1) and (3); Complaints Notice (n 316, above) para 57. But see *VGB* (n 319, above); in that case, the Art 7(1) communication was sent at the beginning of

Commission does not issue an Article 7(1) letter within a reasonable time, a complainant may challenge its failure to act under Article 232 of the Treaty, but the issue of the Article 7(1) letter prevents such a challenge.[324] The Article 7(1) letter does not itself amount to a decision capable of review by the Courts; it is a purely procedural step designed to safeguard the rights of the complainant to submit its observations on the grounds on which the Commission intends to rely.[325]

Procedure: third stage.   In the third stage of the procedure outlined in *Automec I*,   **13.070** the Commission takes note of the complainant's comments. The complainant is entitled to insist upon the Commission adopting a formal decision, capable of being challenged under Article 230, in respect of the complaint. If the Commission fails to do so within a reasonable time,[326] the complainant may bring proceedings for failure to act pursuant to Article 232 of the Treaty.[327] Once a formal decision rejecting a complaint has been taken, the complainant may not seek to re-open

---

August; the CFI held that the Commission should have realised that given the timing of the letter in the holiday season and the undertaking's previous persistence in its complaint, the Commission could not draw the conclusion that silence within the four weeks allotted for reply indicated consent. When the undertaking did respond after the expiry of the four weeks it was entitled to a decision. The complainant may also request extra time, which the Commission may grant depending on the circumstances; Complaints Notice (n 316, above) para 71.

[324] Case T-38/96 *Guérin Automobiles v Commission* [1997] ECR II-1223, [1997] 5 CMLR 352.

[325] *Automec I* (n 311, above); *Annemans* (n 313, above); Case C-282/95P *Guérin Automobiles v Commission* [1997] ECR I-1503, [1997] 5 CMLR 447 (paras 34–35). In the *Guérin* case, AG Tesauro pointed out that a complainant dissatisfied with progress on his complaint would be obliged first to initiate an action under Art 232, which would become devoid of purpose once the communication was issued. The complainant would then be obliged to respond to that communication in order to generate a final decision capable of being challenged under Art 230 or, if no such decision is adopted within a reasonable time, to commence a fresh action under Art 232.

[326] Case C-282/95P *Guérin*, above, para 37; in AG Tesauro's opinion, three to six months was a reasonable time (para 34). In Cases T-213/95 & T-18/96 *SCK and FNK v Commission* [1997] ECR II-1739, [1998] 4 CMLR 259, para 55, the CFI stated that the amount of time that was reasonable for the Commission to take before issuing a decision would depend on the context, the conduct of the parties and the complexity of the case; see Cumming, 'Stichting & Federatie' (1997) ECLR 397. In Case T-95/96 *Gestevisión Telecinco v Commission* [1998] ECR II-3407, the CFI found that the Commission had failed to resolve allegedly complex proceedings within a reasonable time. In Case T-127/98 *UPS Europe v Commission* [1999] ECR II-2633, [2000] 4 CMLR 94, [1999] All ER (EC) 794, the CFI held that in deciding whether a delay at the third stage was reasonable, it was necessary to bear in mind the years already spent on the investigation of the complaint; a four-month delay in that case was not reasonable. The fact that a decision was taken only after the lapse of an unreasonably long time is not a ground for annulment: *Trabisco* (n 305, above) paras 51–53; and *Sodima* (n 310, above) paras 93–95.

[327] *Automec II* (n 303, above). In these further proceedings the Commission conceded that a complainant was entitled to a decision capable of review (para 27). The issue as to the stage at which the failure of the Commission to act crystallises sufficiently to become the subject of proceedings under Art 232 is a difficult one and each case depends on its own circumstances: ibid, para 33. If, after the commencement of the Art 232 action, the Commission takes a decision rejecting the complaint, the applicant cannot convert the action into one for annulment of the decision under Art 230: Case T-28/90 *Asia Motor France v Commission* [1992] ECR II-2285, [1992] 5 CMLR 484, para 44.

the matter without significant new evidence and the Commission will not regard further correspondence as a new complaint.[328]

13.071 **Decision upon a complaint.**   In practice, it has often been difficult to discern from the communication sent by the Commission whether it constitutes a definitive decision. This has given rise to disputes about the admissibility of actions to annul such communications.[329] It appears that a decision rejecting the complaint is characterised by the fact that it terminates the investigation; it contains an assessment of the agreements or conduct in question[330] and it prevents the complainant from asking for the investigation to be re-opened unless new information comes to light.[331] A letter closing the file will normally be the final step in a procedure and therefore constitutes a 'decision'.[332] Conversely, a letter which states that its conclusions are provisional only and are subject to any further comment the complainant might make will not be regarded as a reviewable act.[333] A final decision may be appealed to the Court of First Instance under Article 230 of the Treaty by the complainant who has a legitimate interest within the meaning of Article 7 of Regulation 1/2003.[334] If the reason given by the Commission for rejecting the

---

[328] Complaints Notice (n 316, above) para 78. In Case C-172/01P *International Power and Commission v NALOO* [2003] ECR I-11421, [2005] 5 CMLR 987, AG Alber said at para 99 that a Commission letter refusing to re-consider a rejected complaint in response to a letter from the complainant raising no fresh facts was not a decision that could be challenged but simply confirmation of its earlier rejection.

[329] See, eg *Automec I* (n 311, above) and the position of Asia Motor France in the further proceedings; see also Case T-131/89R *Cosimex v Commission* [1990] ECR II-1, [1992] 4 CMLR 395; Case C-282/95P *Guérin* (n 325, above); *BEUC and NCC* (n 293, above); and Case C-39/93P *SFEI v Commission* [1994] ECR I-2681.

[330] Case T-241/97 *Stork Amsterdam v Commission* [2000] ECR II-309, [2000] 5 CMLR 31. The reasoning in the decision can be stated shortly, particularly where it cross-refers to earlier correspondence: Case T-504/93 *Tiercé Ladbroke v Commission* [1997] ECR II-923, [1997] 5 CMLR 309, para 27.

[331] In *Guérin* (n 325, above) AG Tesauro complained of the high volume of litigation in this area caused by the ambiguity of the Commission's letters: para 14. In *Rendo* (n 317, above), para 28, the ECJ held that the applicants were entitled to challenge under Art 230 that part of the Commission's decision that refused to rule on part of their complaint.

[332] In *SFEI* (n 329, above) the ECJ stated that a letter closing the file on the complaint could be analysed as a preliminary or preparatory statement of position (rather than as a decision capable of challenge under Art 230) only if the Commission has clearly indicated that its conclusion is valid only subject to the submission by the parties of further observations. Further, it is not relevant that the letter is signed by a Commission official and not by a member of the Commission: *Stork Amsterdam v Commission* (n 330, above).

[333] Case T-95/99 *Satellimages TV 5 v Commission* [2002] ECR II-1425, [2002] 4 CMLR 1416.

[334] *Demo-Studio Schmidt* (n 281, above); *CICCE* (n 288, above); *BAT* (n 280, above) (complaint rejected because agreement amended in accordance with Commission's request). For a letter containing a decision rejecting a complaint, see, eg the letter sent to Plessey in *Plessey v General Electric and Commission*, 7 September 1989, [1992] 4 CMLR 471. But cf *Cosimex* (n 329, above) where the CFI declined to decide whether the terms of the letter sent by the Commission amounted to a reviewable act because it was not prepared in any event to require the Commission to reconsider the application for interim measures.

complaint is inconsistent with its earlier treatment of the conduct complained of, the decision rejecting the complaint may be challenged on the grounds of lack of reasoning.[335] The Commission may be entitled to reject a complaint under Articles 81 and 82 before completing an investigation into the complaint under Article 86.[336]

Lack of Community interest. Even where the complaint does appear to dis- **13.072** close a breach or potential breach, the Commission may[337] still reject it on the basis of lack of Community interest,[338] unless the complaint involves a matter which is within the Commission's sole jurisdiction (such as a request for the withdrawal of the benefit of a block exemption in a case where the 'distinct geographic market' provision does not apply).[339] In such a case the complainant is entitled to a reasoned decision on the merits.[340] When assessing whether a complaint has a Community interest, the Commission has a wide discretion, but this discretion is not unlimited.[341] It must assess in each case the seriousness and duration of the interferences with competition and the persistence of their consequences,[342] for example it must take into account the existence of other similar complaints.[343] Where the Commission rejects a complaint on the grounds that there was no infringement of Article 81(1), it cannot avoid the Court of First Instance's scrutiny of its reasoning by asserting on appeal that there was no Community interest in pursuing the complaint.[344] The Complaints Notice sets out[345] a number of criteria which have been employed in the assessment

---

[335] Case T-206/99 *Métropole Télévision v Commission* [2001] ECR II-1057, [2001] 4 CMLR 39 (Commission initially granted agreement individual exemption under Art 81(3) and, after this was annulled by CFI, rejected further complaint on the grounds that agreement fell outside Art 81(1). CFI held that since the earlier decision presupposed that Art 81(1) applied, the Commission should have explained why it had changed its position).

[336] Cases C-359 & 379/95P *Ladbroke Racing v Commission* [1997] ECR I-6265, [1998] 4 CMLR 27 (reversing the CFI on the point, Case T-32/93, [1994] ECR II-1015).

[337] But is not obliged to: Case T-77/92 *Parker Pen v Commission* [1994] ECR II-549, [1995] 5 CMLR 435, para 64.

[338] *Automec II* (n 303, above) para 83; *BEMIM* (n 278, above); Case C-91/95P *Tremblay v Commission* [1996] ECR I-5547, [1997] 4 CMLR 211, and see at first instance Case T-5/93 [1995] ECR II-185, [1996] 4 CMLR 305; Case T-458/04 *Au Lys de France v Commission*, judgment of 3 July 2007; Case T-229/05 *AEPI v Commission*, judgment of 12 July 2007.

[339] Reg 1/2003, OJ 2003 L1/1: Vol II, App B.3, Art 29.

[340] *Automec II* (n 303, above) para 75. However, the fact that the Commission has the sole competence to withdraw a block exemption does not mean that a complainant is entitled to decision as to the scope of a block exemption; *Sodima v Commission* (n 310, above) para 38.

[341] Case T-193/02 *Piau v Commission* [2005] ECR II-209, [2005] 5 CMLR 42 (appeal dismissed, Case C-171/05P *Piau v Commission* [2006] ECR I-37).

[342] *Ufex* (n 303, above) paras 88–95; *Piau* (n 341, above) para 80.

[343] *Sodima* (n 310, above) para 34.

[344] Cases T-197 & 198/97 *Weyl Beef Products v Commission* [2001] ECR II-303, [2001] 2 CMLR 459, para 74.

[345] Complaints Notice, OJ 2004 C101/65: Vol II App B.10, para 44.

of Community interest, making the point that the list of such criteria is not closed:[346]

(a) that the complainant can bring an action before the national courts[347] – the Commission must examine whether the complainant's rights can be adequately safeguarded in those proceedings and whether the national court is in a position to gather the facts necessary to determine the issue;[348]

(b) the duration and extent of the alleged infringements and their effects on competition in the Community – the Commission may not regard certain situations as excluded in principle from its purview;[349]

(c) the balance between the probability of establishing an infringement and the scope of the investigation required as against the significance of the alleged infringement;[350]

(d) the stage of the investigation;[351]

(e) the fact that the practices in question have ceased – if they have, the Commission must still assess whether the anti-competitive effects persist and whether the seriousness of the complaint or the persistence of effects gives the complaint a Community interest;[352]

(f) the fact that the undertakings involved have given appropriate assurances to change their conduct.[353]

13.073 **Complainant's rights after initiation of procedure.** Once the Commission decides to proceed with an investigation initiated by a complaint, it must conduct the investigation with the requisite care, seriousness and diligence so as to be able

---

[346] Complaints Notice, above, para 43. See also *Piau* (n 341, above) para 80.

[347] *Tremblay* (n 338, above).

[348] *BEMIM* (n 278, above) paras 86–88. In Case T-95/94 *Sytravel v Commission* [1995] ECR II-2651, para 77, the CFI regarded it as relevant to point out (in a State aid case) that it may be more difficult for a private party to obtain information about the alleged infringement than it would be for the Commission. That will be the case in particular where the necessary information is to be found in a number of Member States. In *Koelman* (n 303, above), the CFI dismissed a complainant's challenge to the Commission's decision to reject his complaint based on the difficulty he would face in bringing national proceedings; the CFI remarked that the complainant had not shown that it was impossible for him to do so (para 79). See also *AEPI* (n 338, above) para 44; *Au Lys de France* (n 338, above).

[349] *Ufex* (n 303, above) paras 92–93; *Sodima* (n 310, above) para 47. The Commission is entitled to take into account whether the agreement complained about would benefit from the application of Art 81(3): *Piau* (n 341, above) paras 100 *et seq*.

[350] *Automec II* (n 303, above) paras 86–87; *Sodima* (n 310, above) para 46.

[351] Case C-449/98P *IECC v Commission* [2001] ECR I-3875, [2001] 5 CMLR 238, para 37.

[352] *Ufex* (n 303, above) para 95; *Sodima* (n 310, above) para 52; Cases T-185/96, etc, *Riviera Auto Service v Commission* [1999] ECR II-93, [1999] 5 CMLR 31, para 83; Case T-115/99 *Système Européen Promotion SARL ('SEP') v Commission* [2001] ECR II-691, [2001] 5 CMLR 579, para 33.

[353] Cases T-133 & 204/95 *IECC v Commission* [1998] ECR II-3645, [1998] 5 CMLR 992, para 147 (appeal dismissed Case C-450/98, [2001] ECR I-3947, [2001] 5 CMLR 291, para 70); *Piau* (n 341, above) paras 83 *et seq*. See paras 13.113 *et seq*, below.

to assess with full knowledge of the case the factual and legal particulars submitted for its appraisal by the complainants.[354] If the Commission issues a statement of objections, it must provide the complainant with a copy of the non-confidential version of the Statement and set a time limit within which the complainant may make known its views in writing.[355] If the complainant wishes to express its views at the oral hearing, the Commission may afford it such an opportunity where appropriate.[356] However, the complainant does not have a right of access to the Commission's file under Article 15 of Regulation 773/2004.[357] In relation to persons other than complainants under Article 7 who have a sufficient interest, the Commission shall, if they apply to be heard, inform them of the subject-matter and nature of the proceedings and set a time limit within which they may make known their views in writing. The Commission may also permit them where appropriate to develop their arguments at the oral hearing.[358]

6. Formal Procedure Prior to an Adverse Decision

(a) The nature of Commission proceedings

Generally. This Section is concerned with the procedure that the Commission **13.074** must follow before taking a substantive adverse decision under Regulation 1/2003. Although this Section focuses on the formal procedure, there is often considerable scope for informal settlement with the Commission.[359] The procedure for dealing with complaints and third party rights of intervention is dealt with separately in Section 5, above.

An 'administrative' procedure. Proceedings before the Commission are admin- **13.075** istrative rather than judicial in nature.[360] There is no formal separation between

---

[354] See Case T-7/92 *Asia Motor France v Commission* [1993] ECR II-669, [1994] 4 CMLR 30, para 36; Case T-206/99 *Métropole Télévision v Commission* (n 335, above) para 59; *Haladjian Frères* (n 302, above) para 29.

[355] Reg 773/2004 (n 320, above) Art 6(1); Complaints Notice (n 345, above) para 64.

[356] Reg 773/2004 (n 320, above) Art 6(2); Complaints Notice (n 345, above) para 65. The complainant has no right to an oral hearing before the rejection of his complaint: Case T-57/91 *NALOO v Commission* [1996] ECR II-1019, [1996] 5 CMLR 672.

[357] For access to the file and Reg 773/2004, see paras 13.088 *et seq*, below. And see para 13.100, below, for the possibility of a request to the Commission under Reg 1049/2001.

[358] Reg 773/04 (n 320, above) Art 13. The Commission may also invite any other person to express their views in writing or at the oral hearing; ibid; the Commission enjoys a reasonable margin of discretion in that regard: Case T-86/95 *Far Eastern Freight Conference* [2002] ECR II-1011, [2002] 4 CMLR 1115, para 468.

[359] Paras 13.113 *et seq*, below.

[360] Case 45/69 *Boehringer Mannheim v Commission* [1970] ECR 769, 798, [1972] CMLR D121; Case T-11/89 *Shell v Commission* [1992] ECR II-757, para 39; Case T-348/94 *Enso Española v Commission* [1998] ECR II-1875, paras 55–65. And see generally *Hasselblad Ltd v Orbinson* [1985] QB 475 (English Court of Appeal). As to whether the proceedings are 'criminal' for the

the investigation, prosecution and decision-making functions.[361] Although the final decision is the decision of the Commission as a whole,[362] the procedure is conducted by the Directorate-General for Competition, the organisation of which has already been set out.[363] Although the Commission's procedures are administrative, Article 27(2) of Regulation 1/2003 declares that 'the rights of the defence shall be fully respected' in proceedings under that Regulation. This echoes the case law of the Court of Justice which has stressed that 'the necessity to have regard to the rights of the defence is a fundamental principle of Community law which the Commission must observe in administrative procedures which may lead to the imposition of penalties under the rules of competition laid down in the Treaty'.[364] Thus the Commission must conduct its procedure fairly and not with a closed mind.[365]

13.076 **Presumption of innocence and burden of proof.** There is a presumption of innocence in favour of the party accused of an infringement.[366] Article 2 of Regulation 1/2003 provides that it is for the party or authority alleging an

---

purposes of Art 6 ECHR, see para 13.030, above. For the status of investigations by the UK Office of Fair Trading, see Competition Appeal Tribunal in *Napp Pharmaceutical Holdings Ltd v Director General of Fair Trading* [2001] CAT 3, [2001] CompAR 33, paras 70 *et seq*.

361 The establishment of the post of independent Hearing Officer, para 13.102, below, was intended to answer criticisms of the Commission's procedure: see, eg Report of House of Lords Select Committee on the European Communities, *Competition Practice*, Session 1981–82, 8th Report (HL 91). The same team of officials normally takes a case from the original investigation stage through to the drafting of the decision; see discussion in *Shell* (n 360, above) paras 31 *et seq*, where the CFI held that the fact that certain Commission officials acted both as investigators and as *rapporteurs* did not render the decision unlawful. Note that this organisation is different from that relied on by the Commission in its submissions in Case 155/79 *AM&S v Commission* [1982] ECR 1575, [1982] 2 CMLR 264 on appeal from OJ 1979 L199/31, [1979] 3 CMLR 376 and before the House of Lords Select Committee: see *XVth Report on Competition Policy* (1985), point 45.

362 For the Commission's procedure in drawing up and adopting decisions, see para 13.108, below.

363 Paras 1.052 *et seq*, above.

364 Case 322/81 *Michelin v Commission* [1983] ECR 3461, [1985] 1 CMLR 282, para 7; in the context of lawyer/client privilege in *AM&S v Commission* (n 361, above) para 20; *Enso Española* (n 360, above) para 80; Cases C-238/99P, etc, *Limburgse Vinyl Maatschappij NV ('LVM') v Commission ('PVC II')* [2002] ECR I-8375, [2003] 4 CMLR 397, para 85; Cases T-125 & 253/03 *Akzo Nobel Chemicals v Commission*, not yet decided, para 86; Cases C-204/00P, etc, *Aalborg Portland v Commission* [2004] ECR I-123, [2005] 4 CMLR 251, para 63.

365 See, eg Case 86/82 *Hasselblad v Commission* [1984] ECR 883, 914, [1984] 1 CMLR 559, 567, *per* AG Slynn.

366 Case T-30/91 *Solvay v Commission* [1995] ECR II-1775, [1996] 5 CMLR 57, para 73; Case C-199/92P *Hüls v Commission* [1999] ECR I-4287, [1999] 5 CMLR 1016, paras 149–150; and Case C-235/9 *Montecatini v Commission* [1999] ECR I-4539, [2001] 4 CMLR 691, paras 175–176; Case T-38/02 *Group Danone v Commission* [2005] ECR II-4407, [2006] 4 CMLR 1428, para 216 (appeal dismissed, Case C-3/06P [2007] 4 CMLR 701). In this regard the Community Courts invoke Art 6(2) ECHR: eg *Montecatini*, ibid; Case T-67/00 *JFE Engineering v Commission* [2004] ECR II-2501, [2005] 4 CMLR 27, para 178 (appeal dismissed, Cases C-403 & 405/04P [2007] 4 CMLR 650), and see more generally 13.030, above. See also the UK Competition Appeal Tribunal in *Napp Pharmaceuticals Holdings Ltd v Director General of Fair Trading* [2002] CAT 1, [2002] CompAR 13, para 99.

infringement of the competition rules to prove its existence and for the undertaking invoking the benefit of a defence against such a finding to demonstrate that the conditions for applying such a defence are satisfied.[367] The Commission must therefore establish to the requisite standard each element of the infringement, including its duration.[368] An undertaking which has been shown to have attended meetings at which cartel discussions took place bears the burden of proving that it expressly distanced itself from the conduct at the meeting if it wishes to argue that it did not intend to participate in the implementation of an agreement established at that meeting.[369]

Evidence of infringement. Where the Commission alleges a breach of the **13.077** competition rules, it is accordingly necessary for it to produce sufficiently precise and consistent evidence to support the firm conviction that the alleged infringement took place.[370] It is not, however, necessary for every item of evidence produced by the Commission to satisfy those criteria in relation to every aspect of the infringement; it is sufficient if the body of evidence relied on by the institution, viewed as a whole, meets that requirement.[371]

---

[367] For the compatibility of such a presumption with Art 6(2) ECHR, see *Salabiaku v France* [1991] 13 EHRR 379, and the more recent European and UK authorities discussed by the House of Lords in *Sheldrake v DPP* [2004] UKHL 43, [2005] 1 AC 264, [2005] 1 All ER 237. The factual evidence on which a party relies may be of such a kind as to require the other party to provide an explanation or justification, failing which it is permissible to conclude that the burden of proof has been discharged: *Aalborg Portland* (n 364, above) para 79.

[368] Case T-120/04 *Peróxidos Orgánicos v Commission* [2007] 4 CMLR 153, paras 50 *et seq*. Thus where the Commission had lost relevant documents and failed to adduce any evidence as to the date of termination of an anti-competitive agreement, an assumption adverse to the Commission's case will be drawn: Case T-44/00 *Mannesmannröhren-Werke v Commission* [2004] ECR II-2223, para 263 (appeal dismissed, Case C-411/04P [2007] 4 CMLR 682); *JFE Engineering* (n 366, above) para 343.

[369] See, eg *Hüls v Commission* (n 366, above) para 155; Case T-303/02 *Westfalen Gassen Nederland v Commission* [2007] 4 CMLR 334, paras 74 *et seq*, and the case law discussed at para 2.054, above.

[370] Cases 29/83 and 30/83 *CRAM and Rheinzink v Commission* [1984] ECR 1679, para 20; Cases C-89/85, etc, *Åhlström Osakeytiö v Commission* ('Wood Pulp II') [1993] ECR I-1307, [1993] 4 CMLR 407, para 127; Cases T-68/89, etc, T-78/89 *SIV v Commission* [1992] ECR II-1403, [1992] 5 CMLR 302, paras 193–195, 198–202, 205–210, 220–232, 249–250 and 322–328; T-62/98 *Volkswagen v Commission* [2000] ECR II-2707, [2000] 5 CMLR 853, paras 43 and 72 (appeal dismissed Case C-338/00P, [2003] ECR I-9189, [2004] 4 CMLR 351); Case T-44/00 *Mannesmannröhren-Werke* (n 368, above) para 260; *JFE Engineering* (n 366, above) para 179; *Group Danone* (n 366, above) para 217. Evidence of an anti-competitive agreement may be 'fragmentary and sparse', requiring inferences to be drawn as to the existence of an anti-competitive agreement or practice: *Aalborg Portland* (n 364, above) paras 56–57: See also *Claymore Dairies Ltd and Express Dairies Plc v Office of Fair Trading (Stay of Proceedings)* [2003] CAT 18, [2004] CompAR 177, paras 3 and 10; *Napp Pharmaceuticals Holdings Ltd* (n 366, above) paras 110–111.

[371] Cases T-305/94, etc, *LVM ('PVC No. 2') v Commission* [1999] ECR II-931, paras 768–778; Cases C-238/99P, etc, *Limburgse Vinyl Maatschappij NV ('LVM') v Commission* ('PVC II') [2002] ECR I-8375, [2003] 4 CMLR 397, paras 513–523; *Group Danone* (n 366, above) para 218; *JFE Engineering* (n 366, above) para 180.

13.078 **Delay.** There is a general principle of Community law that the procedure leading to the adoption of the contested decision must be completed within a reasonable time.[372] In *SCK and FNK*,[373] the Court of First Instance stated that it had had
regard to the case law on delay under Article 6 of the European Convention on
Human Rights in considering whether or not the Commission had taken a more
than reasonable time to reach its decision.[374] The Court held that a lapse of 11
months between notification and the issue of a statement of objections (preparatory to lifting the undertakings' immunity from fines under Article 15(6) of
Regulation 17) was 'relatively short' in the light of all the documents in the case.
Nor could a further lapse of 16 months between that statement of objections and
the Article 15(6) decision be criticised. A further lapse of six months before a final
statement of objections with a view to refusing exemption and ordering termination of the infringement was 'not unreasonable'; nor was a lapse of 11 months
between the undertakings' reply to that statement of objections and the final decision, particularly having regard to translation difficulties. The Court stated that
the Commission was entitled to proceed more slowly on cases having a lower
priority. In *FEG and TU*,[375] the Commission itself reduced the fine imposed on
each party by €100,000 to reflect the 'considerable' duration of the proceedings
(eight years) for which it accepted some of the responsibility. In *Baustahlgewebe*,[376]
the Court of Justice found that delays by the Court of First Instance of 32 months
between the end of the written procedure and the decision to open the oral procedure and of 22 months between the end of the oral procedure and judgment failed
to satisfy the requirements of EC law concerning completion within a reasonable

---

[372] Case T-67/01 *JCB Service v Commission* [2004] ECR II-49, [2004] 4 CMLR 1346, paras 36
et seq. The CFI held therefore that it was not necessary to rule on whether Art 6(1) ECHR imposed
an obligation on the Commission to act without undue delay (appeal dismissed, Case C-167/04P
[2006] ECR I-8935, [2006] 5 CMLR 1303). See also *SCK and FNK v Commission*, below, para 56.

[373] Cases T-213/95 & T-18/96 *SCK and FNK v Commission* [1997] ECR II-1739, [1998]
4 CMLR 259, para 56.

[374] See para 13.029, above and, eg *Eckle v Germany* A No 51 (1983) 5 EHRR 1, para 73; *Buchholz
v Germany* A No 42 (1983) 3 EHRR 597, para 51 (existence of a backlog of cases is no answer to a
complaint of delay).

[375] *FEG and TU*, OJ 2000 L39/1, [2000] 4 CMLR 1208 (on appeal Cases T-5 & 6/00 *Nederlandse
Federative Vereniging voor de Groothandel op Elektrotechnisch Gebied v Commission* [2003] ECR
II-5761, [2004] 5 CMLR 969; further appeal partly dismissed C-105/04P *Nederlandse Federatieve
Vereniging voor de Groothandel op Elektrotechnisch Gebied ('FEG') v Commission* [2006] ECR I-8725,
[2006] 5 CMLR 1223).

[376] Case C-185/95P *Baustahlgewebe v Commission* [1998] ECR I-8417, [1999] 4 CMLR 1203.
The fine was reduced by €50,000 (a reduction of less than 2 per cent). For criticism of the ECJ's
reasoning, see Toner, (1999) CML Rev 1345. cf Cases C-403 & 405/04P *Sumitomo Metal Industries
v Commission ('Seamless Steel Tubes')* [2007] 4 CMLR 650, paras 115–122: four-and-a-quarter years
before CFI was not unreasonable where virtually all facts disputed and seven undertakings appealed.
In Case T-228/97 *Irish Sugar v Commission* [1999] ECR II-2969, [1999] 5 CMLR 1300, [2000]
All ER (EC) 198, para 285, the CFI stated that *Baustahlgewebe* is not authority for the view that the
Commission is obliged to reduce the fine for delays in the *administrative* proceedings (appeal on
other grounds dismissed, Case C-497/99P [2001] ECR I-5333, [2001] 5 CMLR 1082).

time; the appropriate remedy in such a case was a (modest) reduction in the fine, since no influence of the delay on the outcome of the case could be shown.[377]

Effect of unreasonable delay.   Where it has not been established that the undue **13.079** delay has adversely affected the ability of the undertakings concerned to defend themselves effectively, failure to comply with the principle that the Commission must act within a reasonable time cannot affect the validity of the administrative procedure.[378] In other circumstances, the consequences will merely be to found a cause of action for damages based on Articles 235 and 288 of the Treaty.[379] However, it is important to consider whether the rights of the defence have been adversely affected by delay during the Commission's investigation stage prior to the issue of the statement of objections as well as delay between the issue of the statement of objections and the adoption of the ultimate decision.[380]

The right to be heard.   The most fundamental aspect of the rights of the defence **13.080** is the right to be heard. The Court of Justice has held that observance of the right to be heard requires:

'... that the undertaking concerned must have been afforded the opportunity, during the administrative procedure, to make known its views on the truth and relevance of the facts and circumstances alleged and on the documents used by the Commission to support its claim that there has been an infringement of the Treaty.'[381]

Article 27(1) of Regulation 1/2003 provides there is a right to be heard before the Commission adopts a decision requiring that an infringement of Article 81 or 82 be brought to an end,[382] ordering interim measures[383] or imposing certain fines or periodic penalty payments.[384] The implementing provisions of Regulation 773/2004 give substance to that right.[385] In outline, the formal procedure

---

[377] cf *per* AG Léger in *Baustahlgewebe*, above, who considered that the appropriate remedy was an action for damages against the CFI brought before the ECJ.

[378] *JCB Service* (n 372, above) para 40; Cases T-305/94, etc, *LVM v Commission* (n 371, above) para 122; Case C-104/04P *FEG* (n 375, above), Opinion of AG Kokott, para 123.

[379] Cases T-305/94, etc, *LVM v Commission* (n 371, above) para 122.

[380] See *per* AG Kokott in Case C-104/04P *FEG* (n 375, above) paras 126 *et seq* (CFI had erred in law by failing to consider whether excessive delay at the investigation stage had adversely affected the appellant).

[381] Cases 100/80, etc, *Musique Diffusion Française v Commission ('Pioneer')* [1983] ECR 1825, [1983] 3 CMLR 221, para 10. See also Case 85/76 *Hoffmann-La Roche v Commission* [1979] ECR 461, [1979] 3 CMLR 211, para 11; Case 322/81 *Michelin v Commission* [1983] ECR 3461, [1985] 1 CMLR 282, para 11; Case 17/74 *Transocean Marine Paint v Commission* [1974] ECR 1063, [1974] 2 CMLR 459; *Aalborg Portland* (n 364, above) para 66.

[382] Reg 1/2003, OJ 2003 L1/1: Vol II, App B.3, Art 7.

[383] Reg 1/2003, above, Art 8.

[384] ibid, Arts 23 and 24(2).

[385] Reg 773/2004, OJ 2004 L123/18: Vol II, App B.4, came into force on 1 May 2004. It repealed Reg 2842/98, OJ 1998 L354/18, which governed the hearing of parties. Procedural steps taken under Reg 2842/98 continue to have effect for the purpose of Reg 773/2004: Art 19 of Reg 773/2004.

established by Regulation 773/2004 is that, first, the Commission must inform the undertakings in writing of the objections raised against them. It does this by sending a statement of objections.[386] Article 11(1) of Regulation 773/2004 provides that the Commission must give the parties to whom it has addressed a statement of objections the opportunity to be heard before consulting the Advisory Committee[387] and, accordingly, before taking any decision. Secondly, the undertakings have the opportunity to respond in writing within a stated period, setting out all matters considered by them to be relevant and submitting any documentary evidence.[388] The undertakings may also request an oral hearing.[389] Thirdly, the Commission must in its decision deal only with those objections in respect of which the undertakings have been given the opportunity to make known their views.[390] These and related matters are discussed below in more detail.

13.081 **Hearing by 'an independent and impartial tribunal'.** The position of the Commission as prosecutor and judge in competition cases has attracted widespread criticism,[391] despite the establishment of a Hearing Officer with some administrative independence from the Competition Directorate-General.[392] In *Enso Española v Commission*,[393] the Court of First Instance confirmed the earlier case law[394] to the effect that the Commission was not a tribunal for the purposes of Article 6 ECHR, but observed that the judicial control which the Court exercised itself over the Commission and its power under Article 230 of the Treaty to examine whether the Commission's conclusions were soundly based in fact and law satisfied the requirements of Article 6.[395] Moreover, pursuant to Article 229

---

[386] Reg 773/2004, above, Art 10(1). See para 13.083, below.

[387] The Advisory Committee on Restrictive Practices and Dominant Positions, which the Commission is required to consult before taking any decision finding an infringement of Article 81 or 82 EC: Art 14 of Reg 1/2003 and see para 13.107, below.

[388] Reg 773/2004 (n 385, above) Art 10(3). See para 13.086, below.

[389] ibid, Art 12. See paras 13.101 *et seq*, below.

[390] ibid, Art 11(2).

[391] See, eg Brent 'The Binding of Leviathan?—The Changing Role of the European Commission in Competition Cases' (1995) 44 ICLQ 255; Montag, 'The Case for a Radical Reform of the Infringement Procedure' (1996) ECLR 28. cf Wils, *Principles of European Antitrust Enforcement* (2005), Chap 6.

[392] See para 13.102, below.

[393] Case T-348/94 *Enso Española v Commission* [1998] ECR II-1875, paras 55–65. The point was not pursued on appeal: Case C-282/98P *Enso Española v Commission* [2000] ECR I-9817. See also Case T-156/94 *Aristrain v Commission* [1999] ECR II-645, paras 27–30 (under the ECSC Treaty); Cases T-25/95, etc, *Cimenteries CBR v Commission* [2000] ECR II-491, [2000] 5 CMLR 204 [summary], para 718.

[394] Cases 209/78, etc, *Van Landewyck v Commission* [1980] ECR 3125, [1981] 3 CMLR 134; *Musique Diffusion Française ('Pioneer')* (n 381, above). See also Case T-11/89 *Shell v Commission* [1992] ECR II-757, para 39.

[395] For discussion of the Strasbourg case law, see Simor, *Human Rights Practice* (2006), paras 6.106–6.111.

the Court of First Instance has unlimited jurisdiction over decisions imposing a fine.[396]

(b) Initiation of procedure and the statement of objections

Initiation of proceedings.   The first stage of the Commission's investigation **13.082** normally involves the fact-finding measures discussed in Section 4, above. If the Commission wishes to move to the decision-making stage the first formal step to be taken is 'the initiation of proceedings'. The Commission may decide to initiate proceedings at any point in time, but no later than the date on which it issues a preliminary assessment in respect of an infringement of Article 81 or 82,[397] or a statement of objections,[398] or the date on which it publishes a notice of its intention to adopt a decision rendering commitments offered by undertakings binding,[399] or publishes a notice in respect of a decision that Article 81 or 82 is inapplicable,[400] whichever is the earlier.[401] The Commission may exercise its powers of investigation, or reject a complaint, without the initiation of proceedings.[402] The initiation of proceedings by the Commissioner for Competition under delegated authority from the full Commission is a preparatory step and is therefore not a 'decision' subject to review under Article 230 of the Treaty.[403] The Commission is not obliged to publish a notice of a decision to initiate proceedings, but may make the step public 'in any appropriate way'.[404] Before it does so, it must inform the parties concerned.[405] The main legal significance of the initiation of proceedings is that it precludes action under Articles 81 or 82 by the competent authorities of the Member States.[406] A delay in notifying the parties of the initiation of a procedure does not infringe their essential rights.[407]

---

[396] See paras 13.214 *et seq*, below, as to the grounds on which the CFI may annul or vary decisions of the Commission. In Case T-352/94 *Mo och Domsjö v Commission* [1998] ECR II-1989, paras 423–427, the applicant argued that Art 6 ECHR required that the CFI should make a full examination of the facts and all the legal aspects of the case. The CFI dismissed the argument on the grounds that the allegations were 'so unspecific that the Court is not able to evaluate them'.

[397] Reg 1/2003 (n 382, above) Art 9(1).

[398] Reg 773/2004 (n 385, above) Art 10(1).

[399] Reg 1/2003 (n 382, above) Art 9(1). For commitments generally see paras 13.113 *et seq*, below.

[400] ibid, Art 10.

[401] Reg 773/2004 (n 385, above) Art 2(1).

[402] ibid, Art 2(3), (4).

[403] See generally para 13.220, below and Case 60/81 *IBM v Commission* [1981] ECR 2639, [1981] 3 CMLR 635.

[404] Reg 773/2004 (n 385, above) Art 2(2).

[405] ibid.

[406] Art 11(6) of Reg 1/2003 (n 382, above). If a competition authority of a Member State is already acting on a case, the Commission may only initiate proceedings after consultation with it: ibid and para 14.015, below. Initiation of proceedings also serves to stop time running for the purposes of Art 25(3)(c) of Reg 1/2003, which provides for limitation periods in respect of penalties; see para 13.208, below.

[407] Cases 48/69, etc, *ICI v Commission* [1972] ECR 619, [1972] CMLR 557.

13.083 **The statement of objections: its purpose and status.** Respect for the rights of the defence requires that an undertaking should be afforded the opportunity, during the administrative procedure, to make known its views on the truth and relevance of the facts and circumstances alleged and on the documents used by the Commission to support its claim that there has been an infringement of the Treaty.[408] To that end, the Commission is required to inform the parties in writing of the objections raised against them.[409] The communication by the Commission of these objections is by means of a document known as the 'statement of objections'. Its purpose has been described as being to enable the undertaking concerned to submit its observations and to ensure that the Commission is provided with the fullest information possible before it adopts a decision affecting the undertaking's interests.[410] Although of considerable legal and practical importance, the issue of the statement of objections is not a 'decision' subject to review under Article 230 of the Treaty.[411] The statement of objections must be notified to each of the parties concerned[412] and may be sent to an address outside the Community.[413]

13.084 **Contents of the statement of objections.** The statement of objections serves to crystallise the Commission's objections at the start of the procedure.[414] The Commission may, in its decision, deal only with objections in respect of which the parties have been able to comment.[415] Thus in *Archer Daniels Midland*[416] the

---

[408] Cases C-204/00P, etc, *Aalborg Portland v Commission* [2004] ECR I-123, [2005] 4 CMLR 251, para 67.

[409] Art 10(1) of Reg 773/2004 (n 385, above). The function of the statement of objections does not vary accordingly to the specific situation of the undertaking to which it is addressed. Thus, however much that undertaking cooperates with the Commission, that function is still to give undertakings and associations of undertakings all the information necessary to enable them to defend themselves properly, before the Commission adopts a final decision (*Wood Pulp II* (n 370, above) para 42, and *Mo och Domsjö* (n 396, above), para 63; Case T-15/02 *BASF v Commission* [2006] ECR II-497, [2006] 5 CMLR 27, para 58).

[410] *IBM* (n 403, above) para 14. See also Case T-351/03 *Schneider Electric v Commission*, judgment of 11 July 2007, paras 145 *et seq*.

[411] ibid, para 19. But the possibility of challenging a statement of objections lacking 'even the appearance of legality' was left open at para 23. See also Cases T-10/92R, etc, *Cimenteries CBR v Commission* [1992] ECR II-2667, [1993] 4 CMLR 243, paras 34 and 49.

[412] Art 10(1) of Reg 773/2004 (n 385, above).

[413] *ICI v Commission* (n 407, above).

[414] *IBM* (n 403, above) para 18.

[415] Art 11(2) of Reg 773/2004 (n 385, above); Cases C-238/99P, etc, *LVM* (n 371, above) para 86. A supplementary statement of objections may be required where the Commission seeks to rely upon new information; see para 13.106, below. The Commission is not required to communicate to the parties a decision to abandon an allegation: *Cimenteries CBR* (n 411, above) paras 439–440, confirmed on appeal: *Aalborg Portland* (n 408, above) para 193.

[416] Case T-59/02 *Archer Daniels Midland v Commission* [2006] ECR II-3627, [2006] 5 CMLR 1494, para 424 (on appeal, Case 511/06P, not yet decided). The CFI did not reduce the fine despite annulling part of the decision. See also *Schneider Electric v Commission* (n 410, above) where the CFI held that the defects in the statement of objections which had earlier led the Court to annul the prohibition of a merger were so egregious that they engaged the Commission's non-contractual liability to pay damages.

Court of First Instance annulled the decision insofar as it alleged that the parties had restricted and closed down citric acid production capacity because the statement of objections had alleged only that they had allocated market share quotas. In practice, the statement will contain a description of the facts regarded as relevant, together (if appropriate) with supporting evidence and a statement of the legal conclusions to be drawn from them. It is not necessary for the Commission to set out in great detail or at great length all the matters on which it proposes to rely: it is sufficient if the statement of objections sets out succinctly all the essential facts.[417] The 'essential facts' are those on which the Commission relies in its final decision.[418] The objections raised must be sufficiently clear to enable the parties concerned to understand what conduct is complained of by the Commission and to give them all the information they need to defend themselves properly.[419] However, the assessment of the facts and their legal classification in the statement of objections is only provisional, and a subsequent Commission decision cannot be annulled on the ground that the definitive conclusions do not correspond precisely with that intermediate assessment: indeed, respect for the rights of the defence requires the Commission to take account of any observations made in response to the objections by amending its analysis accordingly.[420] A single statement of objections may be addressed to more than one party, without specifying which objections apply to any particular party, so long as the parties are in fact placed in a position to comment on the relevant objections.[421] Where fines are proposed, a section on considerations relevant to the imposition of fines will also be included.[422] It is not necessary for the Commission to give an indication of the

---

[417] Case 45/69 *Boehringer Mannheim v Commission* [1970] ECR 769, [1972] CMLR D121, paras 9–10, a formulation repeated in subsequent cases; eg more recently: *Aalborg Portland* (n 408, above) para 67; Cases T-71/03 *Tokai Carbon v Commission (speciality graphite)* [2005] ECR II-10, [2005] 5 CMLR 489, para 138, on appeal Case C-328/05 *SGL Carbon v Commission* [2007] 5 CMLR 16. For the approach of the UK Tribunal, see *Apex Asphalt & Paving v OFT* [2005] CAT 4, [2005] Comp AR 507, para 100.

[418] See, eg Case 107/82 *AEG v Commission* [1983] ECR 3151, [1984] 3 CMLR 325 (failure to state in SO individual cases relied on in decision); *Pioneer* (n 381, above) paras 12–23 (duration of infringement stated in decision longer than alleged in SO); Case T-48/00 *Corus UK v Commission* [2004] ECR II-2325, [2005] 4 CMLR 182, para 144.

[419] *Wood Pulp II* (n 370, above); *Mo och Domsjö* (n 396, above) paras 63–74; Cases T-25/95, etc, *Cimenteries CBR v Commission ('Cement')* [2000] ECR II-491, [2000] 5 CMLR 204 [summary], paras 852–860; *Mannesmannröhren-Werke* (n 368, above) para 99; Cases T-236/01, etc, *Tokai Carbon v Commission (Graphite Electrodes)* [2004] ECR II-1181, [2004] 5 CMLR 1465, para 47 (Commission's further appeal allowed, Case C-301/04P *Commission v SGL Carbon* [2006] ECR I-5915, [2006] 5 CMLR 877; other appeals dismissed, Cases C-289/04P *Showa Denko v Commission* and C-308/04P *SGL Carbon v Commission* [2006] ECR I-5859, 5977, [2006] 5 CMLR 840, 922; *BASF* (n 409, above) para 46).

[420] *Mannesmannröhren-Werke* (n 368, above) para 100; *Aalborg Portland* (n 408, above) paras 66–67. See further para 13.110, below.

[421] Cases 40/73, etc, *Suiker Unie v Commission* [1975] ECR 1663, [1976] 1 CMLR 295.

[422] For fines see paras 13.135 *et seq*, below.

probable amount of any fine, or the criteria upon which the Commission proposes to calculate the fine, for to do so would prejudge the outcome of the procedure.[423] However, the Commission must make clear in the statement of objections which undertakings are susceptible to a fine: if that is stated only as regards an association of undertakings, no fines may be imposed on the individual members;[424] and if the statement is addressed only to a subsidiary, no fine may be imposed on the parent company.[425] The statement must provide a brief provisional assessment as to the duration of the alleged infringement, its gravity and the question whether the infringement was committed intentionally or negligently.[426] A statement of objections vitiated by a defect will not be annulled by the Community Courts if the defect has no repercussions for the defence of the undertakings concerned.[427]

13.085 **Obligation to supply relevant documents.** Where the Commission relies on particular documents as evidence of infringement, copies of those documents must be supplied so as to enable the defendant undertakings to comment on their probative value.[428] If that is not done, the Commission may not rely on the documents.[429] However, if a document providing additional evidence for an

---

[423] *Pioneer* (n 381, above) para 21; Case 322/81 *Michelin v Commission* (n 381, above) para 19; Case T-16/99 *Lögstör Rör v Commission* [2002] ECR II-1633, para 200 (case upheld on appeal in Cases C-189/02P, etc, *Dansk Rørindustri v Commission* [2005] ECR I-5425, [2005] 5 CMLR 796; *Tokai Carbon (Speciality Graphite)* (n 417, above) paras 138–145; *BASF* (n 409, above) para 62. There is no breach of the rights of the defence against an undertaking A alleged to be one of two leaders of the cartel in the statement of objections where the Commission ceases to allege that undertaking B is a leader, and accordingly increases the fine upon undertaking A: *Tokai Carbon*, paras 148–150. The Commission is not required to mention in the statement of objections the possibility of a change in its policy as regards the general level of fines: *Pioneer* (n 381, above) para 22; *Lögstör Rör v Commission*, above, para 203; *BASF* (n 409, above) para 59.

[424] Cases C-395 & 396/96P *Compagnie Maritime Belge Transports v Commission* [2000] ECR I-1365, [2000] 4 CMLR 1076, [2000] All ER (EC) 385, paras 142–147. And vice versa: Cases T-25/95, etc, *Cement* (n 419, above) paras 480–485.

[425] Case C-176/99P *Arbed v Commission* [2003] ECR I-10687, [2005] 4 CMLR 530.

[426] *Pioneer* (n 381, above) para 21; *Lögstör Rör* (n 423, above) para 193, upheld on appeal in *Dansk Rørindustri* (ibid) para 428; *Corus* (n 418, above) para 146. BASF (n 409, above) para 48. The adequacy of that provisional assessment must be evaluated in relation not only to the wording of the measure in question but also to its context and the entirety of the legal rules governing the matter concerned: *Corus*, para 146, applying by analogy Cases T-371/94, etc, *British Airways v Commission* [1998] ECR II-2405, [1998] 3 CMLR 429, paras 89 *et seq*.

[427] *Corus* (n 418, above) para 155; followed by the UK Competition Appeal Tribunal in *Apex Asphalt & Paving Co* (n 417, above) para 100.

[428] eg Case T-4/89 *BASF v Commission* [1991] ECR II-1523, para 36. In Case C-310/93P *BPB v Commission* [1995] ECR I-865, [1997] 4 CMLR 238, the ECJ stated that this obligation was essential in order that the defendants could express their views effectively.

[429] See, eg Cases T-30/91 *Solvay v Commission* [1995] ECR II-1775, [1996] 5 CMLR 57 and T-36/91 *ICI v Commission* [1995] ECR II-1775 and 1847, [1996] 5 CMLR 57, [1995] All ER (EC) 600; the failure by the Commission to disclose inculpatory documents meant only that those documents were inadmissible to support the Commission's allegations; since the allegations could be supported by other evidence, the decision could not be annulled on that ground. A defendant

allegation included in the statement of objections is supplied after the statement of objections, or even after the hearing, but in good time for the defendant to comment on the document before the Commission takes its decision, the Commission is entitled to rely on the document.[430] The Commission must supply such documents even where the documents in question emanate from the defendant, who therefore has knowledge of them, because the defendant is entitled to be made aware of the importance attached to them by the Commission.[431] Similarly, the fact that documents are included in the Commission's file to which the undertaking is given access does not entitle the Commission to rely on the document in its decision.[432] If a document is annexed to the statement of objections but not referred to in the body of the statement, it can only be relied on by the Commission if the undertaking could reasonably deduce from the statement what use the Commission intended to make of the document.[433] In *Shell v Commission*[434] the applicant complained that the Commission had referred to a particular document in the statement of objections in support of one allegation but had relied on it in the decision in support of a different allegation, in respect of which Shell had not had the opportunity to make representations. Shell also complained it had put forward a document in exculpation of one aspect of the case whereas the Commission had used the document in the decision as support for a different allegation, without giving Shell the opportunity to comment on the supposedly incriminating parts of that document. The Court of First Instance rejected both complaints holding that in respect of the first document, Shell had been able reasonably to deduce the conclusions which the Commission intended to draw from the document and in the second that Shell 'ran the risk' that the Commission might use documents put forward in exculpation as material to incriminate the applicant. Where the Commission wishes to rely on a document, it cannot 'pick and choose' the parts it makes available to the defendant undertakings for comment.[435] The statement of objections normally annexes a list of the

---

against whom a document is not relied on by the Commission is not entitled to disclosure of that document on the ground that it is used as evidence against another defendant (unless the document is disclosable under the Access to the File Notice: para 13.088, below): *Cement* (n 419, above) paras 284, 318.

[430] Case T-334/94 *Sarrió v Commission* [1998] ECR II-1439, [1998] 5 CMLR 195, paras 40–41; Case T-23/99 *LR AF 1998 v Commission* [2002] ECR II-1705, [2002] 5 CMLR 571, para 190.

[431] Case 107/82 *AEG v Commission* [1983] ECR 3151, [1984] 3 CMLR 325, para 27, followed by the UK Competition Appeal Tribunal in *Aberdeen Journals Ltd v Director General of Fair Trading* [2002] CAT 4, [2002] CompAR 167, paras 162–178.

[432] Case T-4/89 *BASF* (n 428, above) paras 31 *et seq*; Case T-8/89 *DSM v Commission* [1991] ECR II-1833, para 37; *ICI* (n 407, above) para 34–35.

[433] Case T-4/89 *BASF* (n 428, above) para 37.

[434] Case T-11/89 *Shell v Commission* [1992] ECR II-757, paras 48–68.

[435] ibid, para 24; Cases T-68/89, etc, *Società Italiano Vetro v Commission* [1992] ECR II-1403, [1992] 5 CMLR 302. Note also Case 30/78 *Distillers v Commission* [1980] ECR 2229, 2295–2298, [1980] 3 CMLR 121, 159–162, per AG Warner.

relevant documents; however, as is described in the following paragraph, the defendant now has a general right of access to documents in the Commission's possession.

13.086 **Reply to the statement of objections.** The Commission must fix a date within which the parties may inform it in writing of their views.[436] To permit the proper exercise of the right to comment, the Commission must allow the parties a reasonable period of time.[437] Between two and three months appears to be the norm, although in complex cases periods of six months, or even longer, have been allowed.[438] In *Volkswagen v Commission*,[439] the Court of First Instance held that a period of two months (and two weeks to take account of the Christmas period) was a reasonable time within which to expect an undertaking to respond to a statement of objections even in a case with a large number of documents which the Commission had taken a year to analyse. An undertaking is under no duty to reply to the statement of objections and is free to raise new arguments on appeal against a decision, even if these could have been raised in answer to the statement of objections.[440] Where a party chooses to respond, it may make written submissions [441] setting out all the facts known to it which are relevant to its refutation of the objections raised by the Commission, attaching any relevant documents. The reply may also propose that the Commission should hear persons who are able to corroborate the facts set out in those submissions.[442]

---

[436] Art 10(2) of Reg 773/2004 (n 385, above). The Commission is not obliged to take into account written submissions received after this date: ibid.

[437] Cases 6 & 7/73 *Commercial Solvents v Commission* [1974] ECR 223, 274, [1974] 1 CMLR 309, 334, per AG Warner (15 days 'patently unreasonable' and 'oppressive'); cf Case 27/76 *United Brands v Commission* [1978] ECR 207, [1978] 1 CMLR 429, para 273 (two months 'normal' and 'cannot be criticised on the grounds that it was rushed'). See also Cases 40/73, etc, *Suiker Unie v Commission* [1975] ECR 1663, [1976] 1 CMLR 295, para 98.

[438] See, eg Case 6/72 *Continental Can v Commission* [1973] ECR 215, [1973] CMLR 199 (five months); *IBM v Commission* (n 403, above) (eight months, after extensions); Case T-44/00 *Mannesmannröhren-Werke* (n 368, above) paras 62–75 (two and a half months sufficient). See also *XXIIIrd Report on Competition Policy* (1993), point 207.

[439] Case T-62/98 *Volkswagen v Commission* (n 370, above) paras 311–318. The CFI observed that the Commission had power to speed up cases which in its view involved a serious violation of the competition rules; the law at issue was clear and since the documents came from the undertaking itself and its subsidiaries, it would need less time to analyse them than did the Commission.

[440] Case T-30/89 *Hilti v Commission* [1991] ECR II-1439, [1992] 4 CMLR 16, para 38; upheld on appeal Case C-53/92P, [1994] ECR I-667, [1994] 4 CMLR 614. The CFI left open the question whether an undertaking can retract admissions made during the course of the administrative proceedings. For the approach of the UK Competition Appeal Tribunal, see *Argos v OFT (Case Management: Witness Statements)* [2003] CAT 16, [2004] Comp AR 80, para 66.

[441] A paper and electronic copy of the submission must be provided: Art 10(3) of Reg 773/2004 (n 385, above). Where no electronic copy is provided, the party must provide 28 paper copies of their submission and the documents attached to it: ibid.

[442] Art 10(3) of Reg 773/2004.

Submissions from third parties. The Commission may accept written com- **13.087** ments from a third party without admitting that it has a 'sufficient interest'.[443] Where the Commission intends to adopt a decision that Article 81 or 82 is inapplicable to an undertaking,[444] it must publish a concise summary of the case and the main content of the proposed course of action. Interested third parties may submit their observations within a time limit fixed by the Commission of not less than one month. In publishing such a summary, the Commission must have regard to the legitimate interest of undertakings in protecting their business secrets.[445]

(c) Access to the file

Access to the file. Access to the Commission file[446] is one of the procedural **13.088** guarantees intended to apply the principle of equality of arms[447] and to protect the rights of the defence.[448] Until 1991 it appeared that, as a matter of law, the defendant had no right to have the full file made available to him.[449] However, in 1991 the Court of First Instance observed that although there was no mandatory rule of Community law requiring it to do so, the Commission had undertaken to permit undertakings involved in the procedure to inspect the file in the case.[450] The Court of First Instance held that the Commission could not depart from rules which it has thus imposed on itself.[451] The right has now been recognised by the Court

---

[443] Case 8/71 *Komponistenverband v Commission* [1971] ECR 705, [1973] CMLR 902.

[444] ie: a decision pursuant to Art 10 of Reg 1/2003.

[445] Art 27(4) of Reg 1/2003 (n 455, below); this provision also applies where the Commission proposes to accept commitments; see para 13.115, below.

[446] See further Ortiz Blanco, *EC Competition Procedure* (2nd edn, 2006), paras 10.28–10.46; Kerse and Khan, *EC Antitrust Procedure* (5th end, 2005), paras 4.028 *et seq*.

[447] The ECtHR has held that the principle of equality of arms requires that each party should have the opportunity to 'comment effectively' on evidence adduced by the other side: *Mantovanelli v France* (1997) 24 EHRR 370, para 36. See Cases T-305/94, etc, *LVM v Commission* [1999] ECR II-931, [1999] 5 CMLR 303, para 1012 (on further appeal: Cases C-238/99P, etc, *Limburgse Vinyl Maatschappij NV ('LVM') v Commission ('PVC II')* [2002] ECR I-8375, [2003] 4 CMLR 397); *Solvay* (n 429, above) para 83; Case T-36/91 *ICI* (n 429, above) para 93.

[448] *Group Danone* (n 366, above) para 33; Cases T-191/98, etc, *Atlantic Container Line v Commission* [2003] ECR II-3275, [2005] 4 CMLR 1283, para 334; *Aalborg Portland* (n 408, above) para 68.

[449] See, eg Cases 56 & 58/64 *Consten and Grundig v Commission* [1966] ECR 299, [1966] CMLR 418; Cases 43 & 63/82 *VBVB and VBBB v Commission* [1984] ECR 19, [1985] 1 CMLR 27, paras 23–25; Case C-62/86 *AKZO v Commission* [1991] ECR I-3359, para 16.

[450] Case T-7/89 *Hercules v Commission* [1991] ECR II-1711, [1992] 4 CMLR 84, paras 52–53, referring to *XIIth Report on Competition Policy* (1982), points 34 and 35; appeal dismissed, Case C-51/92P *Hercules Chemicals v Commission* [1999] ECR I-4235, [1999] 5 CMLR 976.

[451] Cases T-7/89 *Hercules*, above, paras 53–54 and several other *Polypropylene* appeals, eg Case T-9/89 *Commission v Hüls* [1992] ECR II-499, para 48; if a party wishes to challenge the adequacy of access to the file and the Commission claims to have given full access, it is up to the party to adduce evidence to show that the Commission has been selective in the documents disclosed: see *Hercules*.

of Justice[452] and incorporated into the procedural rules. The Community Courts have indicated that the right of access to the file is a procedural safeguard intended to ensure that the right to be heard can be exercised effectively.[453] Thus, in the *Soda Ash* cases,[454] the Court referred to the right of access to the file in the context of 'the general principle of equality of arms' and held that it was irrelevant that the Commission had considered the documents to see whether they were exculpatory. The Commission should have given the undertakings the opportunity to examine the documents and make their own appraisal.

13.089 **The Commission's Notice.** The right of access to the file is now guaranteed by Article 27(2) of Regulation 1/2003[455] and Article 15(1) of Regulation 773/2004.[456] The Commission's Access to the File Notice, first published in 1997[457] and replaced by a revised notice in 2005,[458] sets out who is entitled to access to the file, what documents must be made available, how confidential information is treated and the procedure for implementing access.

13.090 **Effect of lack of access on validity of decision.** In the landmark *Cement* judgment,[459] the Court of First Instance stressed that access to the file 'is not an end in itself, but is intended to protect the rights of the defence'. Therefore failure to give proper access does not necessarily lead to annulment of the decision. The Court proceeded to set out an analytical framework for considering an action for annulment based on non-disclosure by the Commission of documents in the file.[460] The Court should require production of the documents in question and examine them. That examination will first consider whether there is an objective link between those documents and an objection adopted in the Commission's decision against the applicant concerned. If there is not, the challenge to the decision fails. If, on the other hand, there is such a link, the Court will examine the evidence adduced by the Commission in support of that objection to assess whether, in the light of that evidence, the documents not disclosed might have been signficant.

---

[452] *Aalborg Portland* (n 408, above) para 68; Case C-199/99P *Corus UK v Commission* [2003] ECR I-11177, para 126.

[453] Cases T-10/92, etc, *Cimenteries CBR v Commission* [1992] ECR II-2667, [1993] 4 CMLR 259, para 38; see also Case T-65/89 *BPB v Commission* [1993] ECR II-389, [1993] 5 CMLR 32, para 30 (upheld by ECJ (n 428, above) but without dealing with this point).

[454] *Solvay* and *ICI* (n 429, above).

[455] Reg 1/2003, OJ 2003 L1/1: Vol II, App B.3.

[456] Reg 773/2004, OJ 2004 L123/18: Vol II, App B.4. See also and Art 18(1) and (3) of Reg 139/2004, OJ 2004 L24/1: Vol II, App D.1 for access to the file in merger cases.

[457] Commission notice on the internal rules of procedure for processing requests for access to the file in cases under Articles 85 and 86 of the EC Treaty, Articles 65 and 66 of the ECSC Treaty and Council Regulation (EEC) No 4064/89, OJ 1997 C 23/3: App 52 to the 5th edn of this work.

[458] Access to the File Notice, OJ 2005 C325/7: Vol II, App B.12.

[459] Cases T-25/95, etc, *Cimenteries CBR v Commission* ('*Cement*') [2000] ECR II-491, [2000] 5 CMLR 204 [summary], para 156.

[460] ibid, paras 241–248.

The rights of the defence will be infringed if there was 'even a small' chance that the Commission's decision might have been different if the applicant could have relied on the document before the Commission. However, if an exculpatory document was available to the applicant or in its possession during the procedure before the Commission, it cannot rely on non-disclosure as a ground of annulment.

Exculpatory and incriminating documents.   In the appeal against the *Cement* **13.091** judgment, the Court of Justice upheld the approach of the Court of First Instance and explained that the significance of a failure to communicate a document depends on whether the document is incriminating or exculpatory.[461] As regards an incriminating document, the failure to make the document available constitutes a breach of the rights of the defence only if the undertaking concerned shows, first, that the Commission relied on that document to support its objection concerning the existence of the infringement,[462] and secondly, that the objection could be proved only by reference to that document.[463] Thus, where an undertaking challenges the failure to provide such a document, it must show that the result that the Commission arrived at in its decision would have been different if the document in question was held to be inadmissible.[464] Where, however, an exculpatory document[465] has not been communicated, the undertaking concerned need only establish that the non-disclosure of that document was able to influence, to its disadvantage, the course of the proceedings, and the content of the Commission's decision.[466] The possibility that a document which was not

---

[461] Cases C-204/00P, etc, *Aalborg Portland v Commission* [2004] ECR I-123, [2005] 4 CMLR 251, paras 71–77.

[462] *Aalborg Portland*, above, para 71; Case 322/81 *Michelin v Commission* [1983] ECR 3461, [1985] 1 CMLR 282, paras 7 and 9.

[463] *Aalborg Portland* (above) para 71; *AEG* (n 431, above) paras 24–30; *Solvay* (n 429, above) para 58. If there was other documentary evidence of which the parties were aware during the administrative procedure that specifically supported the Commission's findings, the fact that an incriminating document not communicated to the person was inadmissible as evidence would not affect the validity of the objections upheld in the contested decision: *Aalborg Portland*, para 72; *Pioneer* (n 381, above) para 30; *Solvay* (n 429, above) para 58.

[464] *Aalborg Portland* (n 461, above) para 72. Moreover, if an undertaking is unable to draw any exonerating evidence from documents disclosed to it during the procedure before the CFI, it cannot argue that non-disclosure of those documents during the earlier administrative procedure before the Commission should lead to annulment of the decision: *Hercules Chemicals v Commission* (n 450, above) para 80.

[465] The question whether a document is potentially exculpatory is a question of law amenable to review by the ECJ: *Aalborg Portland* (n 461, above) para 125.

[466] *Aalborg Portland* (n 461, above) para 72 and see also para 131; *Solvay* (n 429, above) para 68. It is sufficient for the undertaking to show that had it been able to rely on the documents during the administrative procedure, it would have been able to put forward evidence which did not agree with the findings of the Commission and thereby influence the Commission's assessment, at least as regards the gravity and duration of the conduct, and accordingly, the level of the fine: *Aalborg Portland*, para 75; *Solvay*, para 98.

disclosed might have influenced the course of the proceedings and the content of the Commission's decision can be established only if a provisional examination shows that the documents might have been significant.[467] For that purpose, the Court of First Instance may arrange full access to the file to determine whether the Commission's refusal to disclose or communicate a document may have been detrimental to the defence, although access at a later stage may not suffice to remedy a breach of the rights of the defence.[468] The Commission need not make available previously published documents.[469] Refusal to grant access to the file after the final decision has been adopted cannot affect the validity of that decision.[470]

13.092   **When the right to access to the file arises.**   Access must be granted before the Commission takes an infringement decision, orders interim measures or imposes certain penalties.[471] Prior to notification of the statement of objections, the parties have no right of access to the file.[472] After notification of the statement of objections, the Commission, if so requested, must grant access to the file to the parties[473] to whom the statement of objections is addressed.[474] Such access on request is normally granted on a single occasion.[475] Since access to the file is regarded as part of the rights of defence, access is generally not granted to other parties' replies to the Commission's objections, save where those replies contain new evidence which is incriminating or exculpatory.[476]

13.093   **The documents to which access is granted.**   The 'Commission file' in a competition investigation consists of all documents[477] which have been obtained, produced or assembled by DG Competition during an investigation.[478] The purpose

---

[467] *Aalborg Portland* (n 461, above) para 76; *Solvay* (n 429, above) para 68.

[468] *Aalborg Portland* (n 461, above) paras 100–106.

[469] *BPB* (n 453, above) para 25.

[470] Case T-229/94 *Deutsche Bahn v Commission* [1997] ECR II-1689, [1998] 4 CMLR 220, para 102.

[471] Access must be granted before taking decisions on the basis of Arts 7, 8 23 and 24(2) of Reg 1/2003.

[472] Access to the File Notice (n 458, above) para 26.

[473] For the position of complainants, see para 13.100, below.

[474] Art 15(1) of Reg 773/2004 (n 456, above); Access to the File Notice (n 458, above) para 7.

[475] ibid, para 27.

[476] Access to the File Notice (n 458, above) para 27. There is no general principle that the parties are entitled to attend the interviews carried out or receive copies of all the documents taken into account in the case of other persons: *Aalborg Portland* (n 461, above) para 70. The Commission has occasionally allowed parties to see a non-confidential version of each other's responses and to comment on them at an oral hearing, and in Cases T-236/01, etc, *Tokai Carbon* (n 419, above) paras 45–48 the CFI held that in those circumstances the undertakings concerned could not complain of an infringement of the right to be heard in relation to other parties' responses.

[477] Irrespective of storage medium, and including electronically stored data: Access to the File Notice (n 458, above) para 8 fn 6.

[478] Access to the File Notice (n 458, above) para 8. Documents returned because irrelevant to the investigation no longer form part of the file: ibid para 9. The Commission is entitled to exclude irrelevant material from the administrative procedure: *Aalborg Portland* (n 461, above), para 126.

of access is to enable the parties to acquaint themselves with the information in the Commission's file, so that they can effectively express their views on the preliminary conclusions reached by the Commission in its statement of objections.[479] A party who requests access to the file will obtain all documents[480] except business secrets, other confidential information and internal documents of the Commission or the competition authorities of the Member States. The right of access does not extend to correspondence between the Commission and the competition authorities of the Member States, or between those authorities.[481] However, the Commission is not precluded from disclosing and using information necessary to prove an infringement.[482] Thus, if the Commission intends to rely on documents to which there would not otherwise be a right of access, it must nonetheless disclose them.[483] Where documents are obtained through access to the file, they must only be used for the purposes of judicial or administrative proceedings for the application of Articles 81 or 82.[484] The Commission's Access to the File Notice[485] explains the nature of these exclusions and sets out the Commission's internal procedures for regulating access to the file. Where the Commission accidentally discloses a document when giving access to the file, it is entitled to remove it from the file and the applicant may not rely upon it.[486]

Internal Commission documents. Access will not be granted to internal **13.094** Commission documents, such as drafts, opinions, memoranda or notes[487] from the Commission departments or other public authorities, and documents prepared for the Advisory Committee.[488] The Commission considers that such

---

[479] Access to the File Notice (n 458, above), para 10.

[480] It is not for the Commission to decide which documents may be useful for the purposes of the defence: See Case T-305/94 *LVM* (n 447, above) para 1012; *Solvay* (n 429, above) paras 81–86; Case T-36/91 *ICI v Commission* (n 429, above) paras 91–96.

[481] Art 27(2) of Reg 1/2003 (n 455, above); Arts 15(2) and 16(1) of Reg 773/2004 (n 456, above); Case T-7/89 *Hercules* (n 450, above) para 54.

[482] Art 27(2) of Reg 1/2003 (n 455, above) and Art 15(2) of Reg 773/2004 (n 456, above).

[483] See para 13.097, below.

[484] Art 15(2) of Reg 773/2004. On the face of it, that would permit a party to use documents disclosed through access to the file in private enforcement proceedings.

[485] Access to the File Notice, OJ 2005 C325/7: Vol II, App B.12.

[486] Case T-62/99 *Société de distribution de mécaniques et d'automobiles (Sodima) v Commission* [2001] ECR II-665, paras 24–26.

[487] In the case of a study commissioned in connection with proceedings, correspondence between the Commission and its contractor containing evaluation of the contractor's work or relating to financial aspects of the study, are considered internal documents: Access to the File Notice (n 485, above) para 14.

[488] Access to the File Notice, ibid, para 12, Art 27(2) of Reg 1/2003 (n 455, above). See *Mannesmannröhren-Werke* (n 368, above) para 56; Cases T-236/01, etc, *Tokai Carbon* (n 419, above) para 40; COMP/37.370 *Sorbates*, 1 October 2003, [2005] 5 CMLR 2054, paras 25, 26. For the Advisory Committee, see para 13.107, below. There is no obligation on the Commission departments to draft any minutes of meetings with any person or undertaking: Cases T-191/98, etc, *Atlantic Container Line* (n 448, above) paras 349, 359. Agreed minutes will, however, be made

documents can be neither incriminating nor exculpatory.[489] Further, correspondence between the Commission and other public authorities and the internal documents received from such authorities (whether from Member States or non-Member countries) are considered to be internal documents.[490] This includes correspondence between the Commission and the competition authorities of the Member States,[491] or between the latter;[492] correspondence between the Commission and other public authorities of the Member States;[493] correspondence between the Commission, the EFTA Surveillance Authority and public authorities of EFTA States;[494] and correspondence between the Commission and public authorities of non-Member countries, including their competition authorities, in particular where a Community and a third country have concluded an agreement governing the confidentiality of the information exchanged.[495] Access is granted in exceptional circumstances to documents originating from Member States, the EFTA Surveillance Authority or EFTA States, after deletion of any business secrets or other confidential information where such documents contain allegations against the parties or form part of the evidence in the investigation,[496] or, in respect of documents originating from Member States or the EFTA Surveillance Authority, insofar as they are relevant to the parties' defence with regard to the exercise of competence by the Commission.[497] The Commission will consult the entity submitting the document to identify business secrets or other confidential information prior to granting access.[498]

---

accessible after deletion of any business secrets or other confidential information: Access to the File Notice (n 485, above) para 13. Results of a study commissioned in connection with proceedings are accessible together with the terms of reference and methodology of the study, although the Access to the File Notice notes that '[P]recautions may however be necessary in order to protect intellectual property rights': para 11.

[489] Access to the File Notice (n 485, above) para 12.

[490] Access to the File Notice, ibid, para 15.

[491] eg documents drawn up for the purposes of Art 11 of Reg 1/2003: Art 27(2) of Reg 1/2003 (n 455, above).

[492] ibid. See also Art 15(2) of Reg 773/2004 (n 456, above).

[493] Order of the CFI in Cases T-134/94, etc, *NMH Stahlwerke v Commission* [1997] ECR II-2293, para 36; Case T-65/89 *BPB* (n 453, above) para 33.

[494] Access to the File Notice (n 485, above) para 15.

[495] ibid. The Commission refers in particular to Art VIII.2 of the EC-USA Cooperation Agreement, which obliges the Commission to protect the confidentiality of information supplied by the US competition authorities 'to the fullest extent possible', and notes that this creates an international-law obligation binding on the Commission.

[496] These considerations apply in particular to documents and information exchanged pursuant to Art 12 of Reg 1/2003 (n 455, above) and information provided to the Commission pursuant to Art 18(6) of Reg No 1/2003 and complaints lodged by a Member State under Art 7(2) of Reg 1/2003. See further para 13.036, above.

[497] Access to the File Notice (n 485, above) para 16.

[498] ibid.

Business secrets and other confidential information. There are two further **13.095**
categories of information to which access to the file may be partially or totally
restricted, namely 'business secrets' and 'other confidential information'.[499]
Business secrets must not be disclosed even to undertakings which have a right to
be heard[500] since this covers 'information of which not only disclosure to the public but also mere transmission to a person other than the one that provided the
information may seriously harm the latter's interests'.[501] Examples of information
that may qualify as business secrets include: technical and/or financial information relating to an undertaking's know-how, methods of assessing costs, production secrets or processes, supply sources, quantities produced and sold, market
shares, customer and distributor lists, marketing plans, cost and price structure
and sales strategy.[502]

Other confidential documents. The precise scope of the 'confidential informa- **13.096**
tion' referred to in Article 16 of Regulation 773/2004 remains indeterminate.[503]
This category includes information other than business secrets which may be
considered as confidential, insofar as its disclosure would significantly harm a person
or undertaking.[504] The Commission's Access to the File Notice explains that this
category may include information provided by third parties about undertakings
which are able to place very considerable economic or commercial pressure on
their competitors or on their trading partners, customers or suppliers, including
information that would enable the parties to identify complainants or other third
parties which have a justified wish to remain anonymous, and military secrets.[505]

---

[499] Reg 773/2004, Art 16(1); Access to the File Notice, para 17. See also para 13.051, above.
See, in addition to the more recent works cited in n 446, above: Lavoie, 'The Investigative Powers
of the Commission with respect to business secrets under Community Competition Rules' (1992)
17 ELRev 20; Joshua, 'Balancing the Public Interests: Confidentiality, Trade Secret and Disclosure
of Evidence in EC Competition Procedures' (1994) ECLR 69; Ehlermann and Drijber, 'Legal protection of enterprises: Administrative proceedings, in particular access to the file and confidentiality'
(1996) ECLR 375.

[500] Access to the File Notice (n 485, above) para 18; and see Case T-353/94 *Postbank v Commission*
[1996] ECR II-921, [1997] 4 CMLR 33, [1996] All ER (EC) 817, para 87. See also Case 53/85
AKZO v Commission [1986] ECR 1965, [1987] 1 CMLR 231, para 28; Cases 142 & 156/84 *BAT
v Commission* [1987] ECR 4487, [1988] 4 CMLR 24, para 21.

[501] *Postbank v Commission* (n 500, above) paras 86–87; Case 145/83 *Adams v Commission* [1985]
ECR 3539, para 34. See also Case T-9/99 *HBF Holding v Commission* [2002] ECR II-1487, [1986]
1 CMLR 506, para 367.

[502] Access to the File Notice: (n 485, above) para 18.

[503] In *Cartonboard*, OJ 1994 L243/1, [1994] 5 CMLR 547, para 124, the Commission said that
the obligation of professional secrecy extended to all information obtained from the undertaking
'except that which is so trivial that it is not worthy of consideration'.

[504] Access to the File Notice (n 485, above) para 19.

[505] ibid; Case T-65/89 *BPB* (n 453, above) para 33; Case C-310/93P *BPB Industries* (n 428,
above) para 26; Case T-221/95 *Endemol v Commission* [1999] ECR II-1299, [1999] 5 CMLR 611,
[1999] All ER (EC) 385, para 69; and Case T-5/02 *Tetra Laval v Commission* [2002] ECR II-4381,
[2002] 5 CMLR 1182, [2003] All ER (EC) 762, para 98; Case T-203/01 *Michelin v Commission*

In *Bank Austria*,[506] the Court of First Instance considered the different levels of protection afforded to business secrets as compared with information covered by 'professional secrecy'. Information which is covered by professional secrecy must not be disclosed to the general public and so will be redacted for example, from the text of the published decision. But such information can be disclosed to parties who have a right to be heard under Article 27 of Regulation 1/2003. By contrast, information which constitutes business secrets is not made accessible even to parties with a right to be heard.[507]

13.097 **Disclosure of non-accessible documents.** Non-accessible documents may be disclosed by the Commission where necessary to prove an infringement of Article 81 or 82.[508] The Access to the File Notice explains that confidentiality is not a bar to disclosure if such information is either incriminating or potentially exculpatory.[509] The assessment as to whether disclosure is justified is carried out by the Commission, with regard to the relevance of the information, whether it is indispensable, the degree of sensitivity involved and its preliminary view of the seriousness of the alleged infringement.[510] Where the Commission intends to disclose non-accessible information, the person or undertaking in question will be granted the opportunity to provide a non-confidential version of the documents which contain that information with the same evidential value as the original documents.[511]

13.098 **Obligation to identify confidential information when submitted.** A person who submits information or comments to the Commission in the course of competition proceedings must clearly identify information which it considers to be confidential, giving reasons.[512] It must also provide a separate non-confidential version by the date set by the Commission for making its views known.[513] Information will be classified as confidential only where an undertaking makes a claim to that effect which is accepted by the Commission.[514] In addition to that

---

[2003] ECR II-4071, [2004] 4 CMLR 923, para 124. The ECtHR has ruled that on a criminal charge, anonymous evidence may be relied on only if the witnesses have an genuine interest worthy of protection and if the rights of the defence can be respected: see, eg *Van Mechelen v Netherlands* (1997) 25 EHRR 647.

[506] Case T-198/03 *Bank Austria Creditanstalt v Commission* [2006] ECR II-1429, [2006] 5 CMLR 639, paras 28 *et seq.*

[507] See *Postbank* and *AKZO* (n 500, above).

[508] Art 27(2) of Reg 1/2003 (n 455, above); Art 15(2) of Reg 773/2004 (n 456, above).

[509] Access to the File Notice (n 485, above) para 24.

[510] ibid.

[511] Access to the File Notice (n 485, above) para 25.

[512] ibid, para 35; Art 16(2) of Reg 773/2004.

[513] Art 16(2) of Reg 773/2004; Access to the File Notice, para 22.

[514] ibid, paras 21 and 22. Confidentiality claims can be made only by the person or undertaking which is the source of the document: para 22. As a general rule, information about turnover, sales,

obligation placed on undertakings providing information, the Commission also has power to require such undertakings to identify the documents or parts of documents which they consider to contain business secrets or other confidential information belonging to them, and to identify the undertakings with regard to which such documents are considered to be confidential.[515] If an undertaking fails to comply with the obligation to identify confidential material, the Commission may assume that the documents do not contain confidential information and that the undertaking has no objection to the disclosure of the documents or the statements they contain in their entirety.[516] Where the undertaking does assert that documents are confidential, the Commission will either provisionally accept the claims which seem justified or inform the person or undertaking in question that it does not agree with the confidentiality claim in whole or in part.[517] The Commission may reverse its provisional acceptance of the confidentiality claim in whole or in part at a later stage.[518] Where there is a risk that an undertaking which is able to place very considerable economic or commercial pressure on its competitors or on its trading partners, customers or suppliers will adopt retaliatory measures as a consequence of their collaboration in the investigation carried out by the Commission, the Commission will protect the anonymity of the authors by providing access to a non-confidential version or summary of the responses in question.[519] Where a confidentiality claim is rejected, or the provisional acceptance of confidentiality is reversed so that the Commission intends to disclose information, it will inform the person or undertaking in writing, give its reasons and set a time limit within which that person or undertaking may express its views. If a disagreement on the confidentiality claim persists, the matter will be referred to the Hearing Officer.[520]

Procedure for granting access to the file. The Commission may grant access to the file on CD-ROM, by paper copies or by inviting the parties to inspect the file on the Commission's premises.[521] The Commission will provide the parties or

13.099

---

market-share data and similar information which is more than five years old is no longer regarded as confidential: ibid, para 23.

[515] ibid, para 36 and Art 16(3) of Reg 773/2004 (n 456, above). The Commission may set a time limit within which undertakings may substantiate their claim to confidentiality, provide a non-confidential version of any document and provide a description of each piece of deleted information: Access to the File Notice (n 485, above) para 27 and Art 16(3) of Reg 773/2004.

[516] Art 16(4) of Reg 773/2004 (n 456, above); Access to the File Notice (n 485, above) para 39.

[517] Access to the File Notice, para 40.

[518] ibid, para 41.

[519] ibid, para 43; Case T-5/02 *Tetra Laval* (n 505, above) paras 98, 104 and 105. Requests for anonymity in such circumstances, as well as requests for anonymity on the part of complainants (see para 13.096) are dealt with in accordance with the procedure set out in that paragraph: Access to the File Notice (n 485, above) para 43.

[520] ibid, para 42. For the Hearing Officer, see para 13.102, below.

[521] Access to the File Notice (n 485, above) para 44.

complainant with a list setting out the contents of the file[522] but is under no obligation to provide translations of documents.[523] The non-confidential versions and the descriptions of the deleted information must be established in a manner that enables any party with access to the file to determine whether the information deleted is likely to be relevant for its defence and therefore whether there are sufficient grounds to request the Commission to grant access to the information claimed to be confidential.[524] If a party considers that, having obtained access to the file, it needs to see specific non-accessible information for its defence, it may submit a reasoned request to the Commission. Any dispute will be resolved by the Hearing Officer.[525]

13.100   **Provision of documents from the file to third parties.**   Complainants do not have the same rights and guarantees as the parties under investigation and cannot claim a right of access to the file.[526] A complainant who, pursuant to Article 7(1) of the Implementing Regulation,[527] has been informed of the Commission's intention to reject its complaint may request access to the documents on which the Commission has based its provisional assessment.[528] The complainant will be given access to such documents on a single occasion, following the issuance of the Article 7(1) letter.[529] Complainants do not have a right of access to business secrets or other confidential information which the Commission has obtained in the course of its investigation. An alternative avenue by which any third party may gain access to the file appears to be by the exercise of rights under Regulation 1049/2001 which governs public access to the documents of the Community institutions.[530] In *VIK*[531] the Court of First Instance considered the application of this Regulation to the Commission's file relating to the finding of a cartel infringement in *Austrian Banks: Lombard Club*. VIK was an Austrian consumer organisation pursuing compensation claims in the national court against banks involved in that cartel. It requested access under the Regulation to the Commission's file as being indispensable to its ability to prove its claim. The Commission rejected the request, on the grounds that the documents fell within various categories which were exempt from disclosure under the Regulation and that, since the file

---

[522] ibid, para 45.

[523] ibid, para 46; Cases T-25/95, etc, *Cimenteries* (n 459, above) para 635.

[524] Access to the File Notice (n 485, above) para 38.

[525] ibid, para 47.

[526] See Case T-17/93 *Matra-Hachette v Commission* [1994] ECR II-595, para 34 (ruling in relation to Art 19 of Reg 17 now replaced by Art 27 of Reg 1/2003).

[527] Reg 773/2004, OJ 2004 L123/18: Vol II, App B.4.

[528] See Access to the File Notice, paras 29–32.

[529] For Art 7(1) letters, see para 13.069, above.

[530] Reg 1049/2001, OJ 2001 L145/43. The Reg came into effect in December 2001.

[531] Case T-2/03 *Verein für Konsumenteninformation v Commission* [2005] ECR II-1121, [2005] 4 CMLR 1627, [2005] All ER (EC) 813.

comprised about 47,000 pages of documents it would be disproportionate for the Commission to have to examine and justify the non-disclosure of each individual document. The Court held that the Commission had erred in law in failing to examine the individual documents to determine how the Regulation applied to them. The Court acknowledged that the Commission could, in a case where 'concrete, individual examination of the documents' would entail an unreasonable amount of administrative work, balance the interest in public access to the documents against the burden of work so caused. But it was only justified declining to carry out such an individual examination in exceptional circumstances and after having considered all possible alternative ways of meeting the request. The Court therefore annulled the Commission's rejection of the request without considering how the exemptions set out in the Regulation would apply in this context.

(d) The hearing and subsequently

Hearings. Any undertaking to which the Commission has addressed a statement **13.101**
of objections must be given the opportunity to develop its arguments at an oral hearing, if it so requests.[532] As discussed above, complainants and other interested parties may also attend and speak at the oral hearing.[533] Hearings are conducted by a Hearing Officer who is fully independent of the Commission[534] and charged with ensuring the proper conduct of the hearing.[535] The hearing date, duration and venue of hearing are fixed by the Hearing Officer.[536] The Commission may also invite NCAs or representatives of other authorities of the Member States to take part.[537] Those invited to attend may appear in person or be represented by legal representatives, properly authorised representatives or authorised permanent members of staff. They may be assisted by legal advisers or other qualified persons admitted by the Hearing Officer.[538]

---

[532] Art 12 of Reg 773/2004 (n 527, above).

[533] See para 13.073, above with regard to complainants.

[534] Art 14(1) of Reg 773/2004.

[535] Art 5 of the Decision on the Hearing Officer, decn 2001/462, OJ 2001 L162/21: Vol II, App B.2.

[536] Art 12(1) of the Decision on the Hearing Officer (n 535, above).

[537] Reg 773/2004 (n 527, above) Art 14(3). In 1997, officials from the US Department of Justice attended hearings in the *British Airways/American Airlines* case: *XXVIIth Report on Competition Policy* (1997), point 327.

[538] Reg 773/2004 (n 527, above) Art 14(4) and (5). Parties may choose not to put forward officers of the company who were involved at the time of the infringement; but as to the inferences which the Commission may draw from this, see Case T-12/89 *Solvay v Commission* [1992] ECR II-907, para 48. The Hearing Officer may decide what persons are heard on behalf of a party: Decision on the Hearing Officer, Art 12(3). In a case where there were 14 separate undertakings, the Commission could not be expected to take into account the needs of each undertaking, and the fact that one of the parties' lawyers could not attend one of the hearings did not infringe its rights of

13.102 **Hearing Officer.** To help counter criticism of the administrative nature of the decision-making process, the Commission established the post of Hearing Officer in 1982.[539] The current 'terms of reference' of the Hearing Officer are contained in Commission Decision 2001/462 of 23 May 2001 (the Decision on the Hearing Officer).[540] The Hearing Officer is attached for administrative purposes to the member of the Commission responsible for competition matters, and is not part of the Competition Directorate-General.[541] In addition to his function of overseeing the proper conduct of the oral hearing, he is also charged with ensuring the objectivity of the Commission's decision, including, in particular, ensuring that due account is taken of all facts favourable and unfavourable to the undertakings concerned, including facts relating to the gravity of the infringement.[542] The Hearing Officer must be kept informed of the procedure up to the stage of the draft decision to be submitted to the Competition Commissioner and may at any time present to the Commissioner his observations on any matter arising out of the proceedings.[543] Additionally, the Hearing Officer submits his own report to the Competition Commissioner on the hearing and other matters concerning the right to be heard, such as disclosure of documents and access to the file. That report may also make observations on the further progress of proceedings, including as to further information required, the withdrawal of certain objections, or the formulation of further objections.[544] Once a draft decision is ready to be submitted to the Advisory Committee, the Hearing Officer prepares a final report in respect of the right to be heard, considering whether the draft decision deals only with objections in respect of which the parties have had the opportunity of making known their views. That final report is submitted to the Competition Commissioner, the Director-General for Competition, the director responsible

defence: Case T-86/95 *Far Eastern Freight Conference* [2002] ECR II-1011, [2002] 4 CMLR 1115, para 466.

[539] See, eg *XIIIth Annual Report on Competition Policy* (1983), points 75–76; *XVIIIth Report* (1988), point 44.

[540] Decision on Hearing officers decn 2001/462, OJ 2001 L162/21: Vol II, App B.2. This replaced the earlier decn 94/810, OJ 1994 L330/67. On the role of the Hearing Officer see Durande and Williams, 'The practical impact of the exercise of the right to be heard: A special focus on the effect of Oral Hearings and the role of the Hearing Officers' (2005) 2 EC Competition Policy Newsletter 22.

[541] Decision on the Hearing Officer, above, Art 1(2); until 2001 the Hearing Officer was part of DG Comp. Art 2(1) provides that his appointment may be interrupted or terminated, or he may be transferred, only by a reasoned decision of the Commission.

[542] Decision on the Hearing Officer, Art 5.

[543] Art 3(3).

[544] Art 13. The Hearing Officer is not obliged to include reference to complaints by the parties that are irrelevant and unfounded: Cases T-236/01, etc, *Tokai Carbon v Commission* [2004] ECR II-1181, [2004] 5 CLMR 1465, para 53 (Commission's further appeal allowed, Case C-301/04P *Commission v SGL Carbon* [2006] ECR I-5915, [2006] 5 CMLR 877; other appeals dismissed, Cases C-289/04P *Showa Denko v Commission* and C-308/04P *SGL Carbon v Commission* [2006] ECR I-5859, 5977, [2006] 5 CMLR 840, 922).

for the case, the NCAs and the EFTA Surveillance Authority.[545] That final report is also attached to the draft report submitted to the full Commission. It is also provided to the parties with the final decision and is published with the decision in the *Official Journal*.[546]

Conduct of the hearing.   Hearings are held in private.[547] Parties and complain-   **13.103** ants may be heard separately or in the presence of the other persons summoned to attend, in which case consideration must be given to the protection of business secrets.[548] Although the Commission does not accept that it has a duty to hear all interested persons together,[549] its preferred practice appears to be to hear all co-defendants as well as other interested parties (including complainants) at the same time, clearing the room when business secrets are under discussion. The statements made are recorded on tape and made available on request.[550] Usually the official of the Commission in charge of the case (the *rapporteur*) will open the proceedings briefly then the parties make their presentation. If the Hearing Officer so allows, the parties, complainants, other invited persons, the Commission and the representatives from the Member States may ask questions.[551] Such questions are not necessarily confined to matters arising out of the parties' presentation. The Hearing Officer is also responsible for deciding whether fresh documents should be admitted at the hearing[552] and may permit the submission of further written comments after the hearing.[553] The oral hearing is ancillary to the written procedure,[554] but the Commission has stated that the direction taken by a number of cases as presented in the statement of objections has been changed following the oral hearing.[555] The Commission is not required to afford the undertaking concerned the opportunity to cross-examine the author of an incriminating document.[556]

---

[545] Decn on the Hearing Officer, Art 15.

[546] ibid, Art 16.

[547] Reg 773/2004 (n 527, above) Art 14(6).

[548] ibid. The decision is taken by the Hearing Officer: Art 12(3) of the Decision on the Hearing Officer.

[549] See Cases 40/73, etc, *Suiker Unie v Commission* [1975] ECR 1663, [1976] 1 CMLR 295, paras 423–426 (where the Commission's refusal to supply to one party the written comments of other parties was upheld), and note *FEDETAB* (n 559, below) (complainants excluded at request of defendants).

[550] Reg 773/2004 (n 527, above) Art 14(8).

[551] ibid, Art 14(7).

[552] Decision on the Hearing Officer (n 535, above) Art 12(3).

[553] ibid, Art 12(4).

[554] *FEDETAB* (n 559, below) paras 16–25.

[555] *XXIIIrd Report on Competition Policy*, para 23.

[556] Cases C-204/00P, etc, *Aalborg Portland v Commission* [2004] ECR I-123, [2005] 4 CMLR 251. The ECJ has held that parties have no absolute right under Art 6 ECHR to call witnesses as part of the Court's proceedings: Cases C-189/02P, etc, *Dansk Rørindustri v Commission* [2005] ECR I-5425, [2005] 5 CMLR 796, para 70.

13.104 **Third party participation in the hearing.** Even where a third party is not the original complainant[557] it has the right to be heard before the Commission takes an infringement decision, orders interim measures or imposes a fine,[558] if it has a 'sufficient interest'.[559] The competition authorities of the Member States may also ask the Commission to hear other natural or legal persons.[560] If a third party applies to be heard and shows a sufficient interest, the Commission must inform it in writing of the nature and subject-matter of the procedure and set a time limit within which it may make known its views in writing.[561] The third party may, if it so requests in its written comments, be invited to attend the defendants' oral hearing.[562] The Commission may invite any other person to express its views in writing and to attend the oral hearing.[563]

13.105 **Issues concerning admissibility of evidence.** Provided that evidence has been obtained lawfully by the Commission, the principle that prevails in Community law is that of the unfettered evaluation of evidence: it is only the reliability of the evidence that is decisive when it comes to its evaluation.[564] The Commission frequently relies on the evidence of one member of a cartel to incriminate others[565] and evidence from an informant is admissible even if his identity is not disclosed.[566]

---

557 As to the position of such complainants, see para 13.073, above.

558 ie: a decision pursuant to Arts 7, 8, 23 or 24(2) of Reg 1/2003: Art 27(1),(3) of Reg 1/2003, OJ 2003 L1/1, Vol II, App B.3.

559 Reg 1/2003 (n 558, above) Art 27(3). For 'sufficient interest' see, eg Cases 228 & 229/82 *Ford v Commission (No. 1)* [1984] ECR 1129 esp *per* AG Slynn at 1174–1175, [1984] 1 CMLR 649, 666–669. See also Cases 209/78, etc, *Van Landewyck v Commission ('FEDETAB')* [1980] ECR 3125, [1981] 3 CMLR 134, paras 16–18; and Cases 43 & 63/82 *VBVB and VBBB v Commission* [1984] ECR 19, [1985] 1 CMLR 27, paras 15–20 (refusal to admit on grounds of insufficient interest accepted by the ECJ). Recital 11 to Reg 1/2003 expressly recognises that consumer associations should generally be regarded as having sufficient interest.

560 Art 27(3) of Reg 1/2003 (n 558, above).

561 Art 13(1) of Reg 773/2004 (n 527, above).

562 ibid, Art 13(2).

563 ibid, Art 13(3).

564 C-411/04P *Salzgitter Mannesmann v Commission* [2007] 4 CMLR 682, para 45 upholding the judgment of the CFI in Case T-44/00 *Mannesmannröhren-Werke v Commission* [2004] ECR II-2223.

565 Cases C-204/00P, etc, *Aalborg Portland v Commission* [2004] ECR I-123, [2005] 4 CMLR 251, para 207; Cases T-67/00, etc, *JFE Engineering v Commission* [2004] ECR II-2501, [2005] 4 CMLR 27, para 192, appeal dismissed Cases C-403 & 405/04P *Sumitomo Metal Industries v Commission* [2007] 4 CMLR 650.

566 *Salzgitter Mannesmann* (n 564, above) para 44 where the ECJ, rejecting the analogy with ECtHR jurisprudence relating to criminal trials, held that evidence could be used to incriminate a party even though that party was not allowed to know its source but that anonymous evidence cannot in itself establish the infringement. In Case T-224/00 *Archer Daniels Midland v Commission* [2003] ECR II-2597, [2003] 5 CMLR 583, the CFI declined to rule on whether statements from co-conspirators and recordings of private conversations provided to the Commission by the FBI in the United States were admissible since it held that the Commission did not need to rely on them

Developments during the course of the procedure.   New facts or documents   **13.106**
may emerge during the course of the procedure. Where the Commission wishes
to rely upon these to the detriment of the undertakings, it may do so, provided
that those new matters are brought to the attention of the undertakings to enable
them to exercise effectively their right to comment.[567] There is no provision
which prevents the Commission from sending to the parties after the statement of
objections fresh documents which it considers support its argument, subject to
giving the undertakings the necessary time to submit their views on the subject.[568]
Therefore, it is not necessary to restart the entire procedure,[569] although in certain
cases (for example, where substantial changes are made to the agreements or
practices the subject of the statement of objections), a second or supplementary
statement of objections may be issued.[570] Where information about the draft
decision is leaked to the media before the decision is adopted, this will not result
in the annulment of the decision unless it can be shown that the leak affected the
Advisory Committee or the College of Commissioners.[571]

Advisory Committee.   Before taking any decision under Article 81 or 82   **13.107**
finding an infringement or non-applicability, imposing interim measures, accepting commitments, imposing fines or periodic penalty payments, or withdrawing
the benefit of a block exemption, the Commission must consult the Advisory

to prove the infringement: para 348 (further appeal dismissed, Case C-397/03P *Archer Daniels
Midland v Commission* [2006] ECR I-4429, [2006] 5 CMLR 230).

[567] Cases 100/80, etc, *Musique Diffusion Française v Commission ('Pioneer')* [1983] ECR 1825,
[1983] 3 CMLR 221 (evidence to support a longer period of infringement); *FEDETAB* (n 559,
above) paras 67–74 (further specific complaints covering the same conduct as gave rise to the
original SO). In *Far Eastern Freight Conference* (n 538, above) para 447, the CFI held that a party
could not complain of a breach of its rights of defence when the Commission relied on the party's
own argument in response to the statement of objections: a party had to expect that the Commission
would take into account the arguments put to it. In a case where the number of extra documents put
to the parties was small, one month was enough time for comments: Case T-9/99 *HFB v Commission*
[2002] ECR II-1487, paras 345–346.
[568] Case T-334/94 *Sarrió v Commission* [1998] ECR II-1439, [1998] 5 CMLR 195, paras 40–41;
Case T-23/99 *LR AF 1998 v Commission* [2002] ECR II-1705, [2002] 5 CMLR 571, para 190.
[569] See, eg *FEDETAB* (n 559, above) (further SO covering new complaints unnecessary); *Pioneer*
(n 567, above) paras 28–29 (sufficient if opportunity to comment during the oral hearing); Case
107/82 *AEG v Commission* [1983] ECR 3151, [1984] 3 CMLR 325, para 29 (able in fact to comment on document).
[570] *FEDETAB* (n 559, above); Case 71/74 *Frubo v Commission* [1975] ECR 563, [1975] 2
CMLR 123 (second SO on amended agreements unnecessary on the facts). See also Case T-328/03
O2 (Germany) v Commission [2006] ECR II-1231, [2006] 5 CMLR 258, para 98: Commission's
failure to adapt its analysis of the effect of the agreement to take account of amendments to the
agreement made during the course of the investigation vitiated its assessment, resulting in the
annulment of the decision.
[571] Case C-338/00P *Volkswagen v Commission* [2003] ECR I-9189, [2004] 4 CMLR 351,
paras 163–165.

Committee on Restrictive Practices and Dominant Positions,[572] which is composed of representatives of NCAs.[573] The Advisory Committee delivers a written opinion,[574] of which the Commission must take the utmost account.[575] The Advisory Committee's opinion is annexed to the draft decision, and, if the Committee recommends publication, the Commission must publish it.[576]

13.108 **Adoption and authentication of the decision.** The Court of Justice has emphasised that proper adoption and authentication of a decision is so fundamental a procedural requirement for the purpose of legal certainty that lack of authentication must lead to annulment of a decision whether or not the defendant has thereby been prejudiced.[577] There is, however, a general presumption that measures are valid and that notified and published measures are in conformity with the original authentic measure.[578] In *Re the PVC Cartel*[579] the Community Courts considered in detail the procedures whereby decisions are drawn up, adopted and authenticated by the Commission. The Court of First Instance found that the Commission had failed to comply with its Rules of Procedure[580] in several respects and that the failures were so serious that the decision was in fact 'non-existent'. On appeal, however, the Court of Justice held that there was a decision; a finding of non-existence should be reserved for 'quite extreme situations' and that it was plain that the College of Commissioners had decided to adopt the operative part

---

[572] Art 14(1) of Reg 1/2003, OJ 2003 L1/1: Vol II, App B.3. The Committee must meet not less than 14 days after despatch of a notice convening it unless a shorter notice period is given and no Member State objects: Art 14(3). The Committee is provided with a summary of the case, an indication of the most important documents, and a preliminary draft decision: Art 14(1).

[573] Reg 1/2003 (n 572, above) Art 14(2). If the meeting is not discussing individual cases, a Member State may appoint a representative, competent in competition matters, of a domestic authority which is not a member of the ECN.

[574] ibid. The Commission can also consult by a purely written procedure, but if any Member State objects, a meeting must be convened: Art 14(4).

[575] ibid, Art 14(5).

[576] ibid, Art 14(6).

[577] Case C-286/99P *Commission v ICI*, Cases C-287 & 288/95P *Commission v Solvay* [2000] ECR I-2341, 2391, [2000] 5 CMLR 413, 454, [2001] All ER (EC) 439 (dismissing appeals by the Commission). See also Cases T-80/89, etc, *BASF v Commission* [1995] ECR II-729.

[578] This point emerged from the appeals from the *Polypropylene* decision where the applicants sought to reopen the oral proceedings following the judgment in *PVC*. See, eg Case T-11/89 *Shell v Commission* [1992] ECR II-757, para 374: 'a measure which has been notified and published must be presumed to be valid. It is thus for a person who seeks to allege the lack of formal validity or the inexistence of a measure to provide the Court with grounds enabling it to look behind the apparent validity of the measure which has been formally notified and published'. See also Case T-34/92 *Fiatagri and New Holland Ford v Commission* [1994] ECR II-905, where the CFI refused to initiate an investigation into the procedure of adoption unless the applicant produced evidence to rebut the presumption of validity (appeals on other grounds dismissed, Case C-8/95P *New Holland Ford v Commission* [1998] ECR I-3175, [1998] 5 CMLR 311).

[579] Cases T-79/89, etc, *BASF v Commission* [1992] ECR II-315, [1992] 4 CMLR 357; on appeal Case C-137/92P *Commission v BASF* [1994] ECR I-2555.

[580] JO 1963 17/181 (as then applicable).

of the decision.[581] However, the Court of Justice annulled the decision[582] for breach of essential procedural requirements. The essential procedural requirements that had been infringed were that:

(a) once an act has been adopted by the College of Commissioners it may not be altered, save for spelling and grammar, except by the College. In this respect there was no distinction to be drawn between the operative part of the decision and the statement of reasons;[583]

(b) where the Commission intends to adopt a single measure which is binding on a number of legal persons for whom different languages must be used, the decision must be adopted in each of the languages in which it is binding. It must also be authenticated in each such language by the President and Executive Secretary as required by the (then applicable) Rules of Procedure. The adoption of an infringement decision in a language in which it was binding could not be delegated to a single member of the Commission.

Rules of Procedure on adoption of decisions. The procedure by which the **13.109** Commission adopts its decisions is set out in the new Rules of Procedure which came into effect on 1 January 2006.[584] Decisions as to management or administrative measures, such as the decision to initiate an investigation under Article 20 of Regulation 1/2003, may be made by a single Commissioner under delegated authority from the full Commission,[585] or, by sub-delegation,[586] by the Director-General of DG Competition.[587] However, decisions under Articles 7–10 of

---

[581] *Commission v BASF* (n 579, above) paras 50–52.

[582] The Commission subsequently adopted another decision to the same effect; *PVC II*, OJ 1994 L239/14, appeal dismissed, Cases T-305/94, etc, *LVM v Commission* [1999] ECR II-931, [1999] 5 CMLR 303, further appeal dismissed, Cases C-238/99P, etc, *Limburgse Vinyl Maatschappij ('LVM') v Commission ('PVC II')* [2002] ECR I-8375, [2003] 4 CMLR 397.

[583] *Commission v BASF* (n 579, above) paras 67–68, following Case 131/86 *United Kingdom v Council ('battery hens')* [1988] ECR 905, [1988] 2 CMLR 364. But cf Case T-29/92 *SPO v Commission* [1995] ECR II-289, where the CFI found that apparently serious evidence of changes to the texts after adoption by the Commission was in fact the result of technical defects in the Commission's email system; there were no grounds for annulment.

[584] Commission decn of 15 November 2005 amending its Rules of Procedure, OJ 2005 L347/83. The decn amended the earlier Rules (OJ 2000 L308/26) by replacing all the earlier articles though not the Annex to those earlier Rules. The Annex sets out the Code for good administrative behaviour for the staff of the Commission in their dealings with the public.

[585] Case 5/85 *AKZO Chemie v Commission* [1986] ECR 2585, [1987] 3 CMLR 716, para 38, and *Commission v BASF* (n 579, above), para 71, and see now Art 13 of the present Rules of Procedure, above. This is sometimes referred to as the habilitation procedure.

[586] Commission Rules of Procedure (n 584, above) Art 13(3) and Art 14.

[587] The Commissioner for Competition may delegate to the Director-General her duty to notify parties of her decision; thus statements of objection, though approved by the Commissioner, are usually signed by the Director-General.

Regulation 1/2003[588] must be taken by the full Commission.[589] Under the present Rules, the Commission may adopt a decision either (a) at a meeting of the Commissioners or (b) by means of a 'written procedure' set out in Article 12. It should be noted that the present Rules of Procedure differ from those applicable at the time that the *PVC* decision was taken.[590]

13.110   **Relationship between the decision and the statement of objections.**   A decision must not contain any allegation which was not contained in the statement of objections or subsequently properly notified to the parties, nor must it contain any new evidence.[591] But it is not necessary for the decision to be an exact copy of the statement of objections. The Commission is entitled to take into account factors arising in the course of the administrative procedure and may either abandon objections which have proved groundless or supplement the arguments in support of objections it maintains.[592] Moreover, the rights of the defence are not breached by the existence of a discrepancy between the statement of objections and the final decision unless a criticism appearing in the latter is not adequately set out in the former in such a way as to enable the addressees to defend themselves; and unless the addressees' defence is adversely affected by the discrepancy, there is no ground for an annulment of the decision.[593] The decision must specify the evidence on which the case hangs; it is not necessary for it to enumerate exhaustively all the evidence, but may refer to it in general terms.[594]

13.111   **Legal status of the decision.**   A single decision in a major cartel case is to be treated as a bundle of individual decisions against each cartel member. If one addressee does not appeal, the annulment of the decision on appeal by another

---

[588] ie decisions finding infringement, ordering interim measures, accepting commitments or finding inapplicability of Arts 81 or 82.

[589] In such a case, the Commissioner for Competition will circulate a draft decision and summary to her colleagues.

[590] See also Case T-219/99 *British Airways v Commission* [2003] ECR II-5917, [2004] 4 CMLR 1008, paras 46–57 (resignation of the Santer Commission did not invalidate decn since it continued exercising its full powers until the appointment of the replacement Prodi Commission in September 1999); appeal on other grounds dismissed, Case C-95/04P *British Airways v Commission* [2007] 4 CMLR 982.

[591] Case T-2/89 *Petrofina v Commission* [1991] ECR II-1087, para 39; Cases C-89/85, etc, *Åhlström Osakeytiö v Commission ('Wood Pulp II')* [1993] ECR I-1307, [1993] 4 CMLR 407.

[592] *FEDETAB* (n 559, above) para 68; Case T-9/89 *Hüls v Commission* [1992] ECR II-499, para 59 (appeal on other grounds dismissed; Case C-199/92P, [1999] ECR I-4287, [1999] 5 CMLR 1016); Cases T-24/93, etc, *Compagnie Maritime Belge Transports v Commission* [1996] ECR II-1201, [1997] 4 CMLR 273, para 113 (appeal on other grounds partially allowed: Cases C-395 & 396/96P, [2000] ECR I-1365, [2000] 4 CMLR 1076, [2000] All ER (EC) 385); Case T-325/01 *DaimlerChrysler v Commission* [2005] ECR II-3319, [2007] 4 CMLR 559, paras 188–195; *Aalborg Portland* (n 565, above) para 192.

[593] Case T-48/00 *Corus v Commission* [2004] ECR II-2325, [2005] 4 CMLR 182, paras 100–104.

[594] Case T-43/92 *Dunlop Slazenger v Commission* [1994] ECR II-441.

party does not affect the addressee which did not appeal.[595] It is the operative part of the decision (that is the concluding paragraphs setting out the finding of infringement) rather than the statement of reasons preceding it that sets out definitively the scope of the Commission's conclusions.[596] Thus, where the operative part of the decision sets out two distinct cartel agreements, the Commission cannot rely on statements in the body of the decision to argue that in fact both agreements were part of a single infringement.[597] An undertaking cannot argue that it is not the correct addressee of a decision if it has not contested responsibility for its subsidiaries during the administrative procedure.[598]

Publication of decisions. Subject to the obligation to respect business secrets, **13.112** the Commission is obliged to publish the names of the parties and the main content of decisions taken by it finding an infringement of Articles 81 or 82, the non-applicability of Articles 81 or 82, imposing interim measures, accepting commitments, or imposing fines or periodic penalty payments.[599] Occasionally, the Commission makes press statements about alleged infringements before the parties have been heard; this practice has been described as 'regrettable' by the Court of Justice.[600] The practice of the Commission is to communicate the '*dispositif*' of the decision immediately after the decision has been taken, supplying the full text later. Issue of the press release accompanying a decision may in practice antedate receipt of the full text by the defendant undertakings.[601] Although decisions used to be published in full in the *Official Journal* (subject to

---

[595] Case C-310/97P *Commission v AssiDomän* [1999] ECR I-5363 (addressees of the *Wood Pulp* decn who had paid fines without appealing not entitled to refund when decn later annulled); Case C-238/99P *LVM ('PVC II')* (n 582, above).

[596] Case T-59/99 *Ventouris v Commission* [2003] ECR II-5257, [2005] 5 CMLR 1781, paras 31 *et seq.*

[597] ibid.

[598] Case T-354/94 *Stora Kopparbergs Bergslags v Commission* [1998] ECR II-2111.

[599] Art 30 of Reg 1/2003 (n 572, above). For the principles governing the redaction of information from the published decision see Case T-198/03 *Bank Austria Creditanstalt v Commission* [2006] ECR II-1429, [2006] 5 CMLR 639.

[600] Case 27/76 *United Brands v Commission* [1978] ECR 207, [1978] 1 CMLR 429, para 286; and see Cases 40/73, etc, *Suiker Unie v Commission* [1975] ECR 1663, [1976] 1 CMLR 295, paras 89–93; cf AG Mayras at pp 2065–2066 (ECR), pp 328–329 (CMLR). Note also Cases 96/82, etc, *IAZ v Commission* [1983] ECR 3369, [1984] 3 CMLR 276, para 16 (regrettable that decision published before being made available to addressees). In Case T-308/94 *Cascades v Commission* [1998] ECR II-925 the CFI held that the leak of a decision before it was published did not affect its validity: para 58; similarly, Case T-62/98 *Volkswagen v Commission* [2000] ECR II-2707, [2000] 5 CMLR 853, paras 279–284, where the CFI stated that the fact and amount of a fine were covered by professional secrecy during the Commission's procedure so that leaks to the Press contravened principles of good administration (appeal dismissed Case C-338/00P, [2003] ECR I-9189, [2004] 4 CMLR 351). See also Press Release IP/99/564 (26 July 1999) (apology for statements made concerning the investigation into Formula One motor racing as part of the settlement of proceedings under Art 288 EC: Case T-85/98 *FIA v Commission*, unpublished order of 6 December 1999).

[601] See *IAZ v Commission* (n 600, above). This practice can create problems where the press release refers to matters not covered in the decision; see, eg Case T-30/89 *Hilti v Commission* [1991]

any redaction for business secrets), in recent years only a summary of cartel decisions has been published while the full text is available on the DG Competition website.

7. Commitments and Settlement

13.113 **Informal settlement pre-Modernisation.** Regulation 17, the predecessor to Regulation 1/2003, did not contain any provision for the settlement of cases without an infringement decision. However, in practice many cases were resolved informally by negotiation between the Commission and the undertakings concerned.[602] Indeed, it was established that in accordance with the principles of good administration the Commission should give due consideration to any proposals by the parties to amend their agreements since one of the purposes of the procedure is to provide 'the undertakings concerned with an opportunity to bring the practices complained of into line with the rules of the Treaty'.[603] Cases settled in this way might be publicised by the Commission by the issue of a press release or a reference in the following annual Report on Competition Policy, in order to provide information and guidance. The promises made by the undertaking concerned are not, however, legally enforceable and the Commission's only recourse in case of breach of such promises is to institute an investigation for infringement of Article 81 or 82. Notwithstanding the new procedures resulting in formal commitment decisions, the Commission continues to resolve cases by way of informal settlement.[604]

ECR II-1439, [1992] 4 CMLR 16, para 136; and Case T-14/89 *Montedipe v Commission* [1992] ECR II-1155, paras 52–54.

[602] It is estimated that more than 90 per cent of all competition cases were settled by the Commission without taking a formal decision: Van Bael & Bellis, *Competition Law of the European Community* (4th edn, 2005), 1136. Examples of cases resolved without formal proceedings can be found in the annual Reports on Competition Policy, passim. Sometimes settlement was achieved by a 'suspension' of the proceedings: see, eg *IBM* [1984] 3 CMLR 147, and *XIVth Report on Competition Policy* (1984), points 94 and 95; *XVIth Report* (1986), point 75; *Electrabel*, *XXVIIth Report on Competition Policy* (1997), point 94; *Euro bank charges XXXIst Report on Competition Policy* (2001), page 205. Sometimes, the terms of the settlement were published in the *Official Journal*, eg *Swift*, OJ 1997 C335/3. See also the provisions in the EC-USA Agreement on positive comity, para 1.100, above, for suspension of enforcement activity by the Commission where the US authorities are in a position to take effective action. In the first *Microsoft* case, the Commission's investigation was settled by undertakings given after joint negotiations between Microsoft and the EC and US authorities: *XXIVth Report on Competition Policy* (1994), page 364.

[603] Cases 96/82, etc, *IAZ v Commission* [1983] ECR 3369, [1984] 3 CMLR 276, para 15; Cases 43 & 63/82 *VBVB and VBBB* [1984] ECR 19, [1985] 1 CMLR 27, para 52. cf Case 226/84 *British Leyland v Commission* [1986] ECR 3263, [1987] 1 CMLR 185.

[604] See, eg *OMV/Gazprom* and *E.on Ruhrgas/Gazprom, 2005 Report on Competition Policy*, points 48–49; *Philips CD-Recordable Disc Patent Licensing*, IP/06/139 (9 February 2006).

Article 9 of Regulation 1/2003. The 13th recital to Regulation 1/2003[605] states **13.114** that where, in the course of proceedings which might lead to the prohibition of an agreement or practice, undertakings offer commitments to the Commission such as to meet its concerns, the Commission should be able to adopt decisions which make those commitments binding. The relevant provisions are found in Article 9 of Regulation 1/2003.[606] Under Article 9, the power to adopt such a decision exists when the Commission intends to adopt a decision requiring that an agreement or practice be brought to an end and where the undertakings involved offer commitments to meet the concerns expressed to them by the Commission in its preliminary assessment. The decision may be adopted for a specified period[607] and should state the Commission's conclusion that there are no longer grounds for action by the Commission, without concluding whether or not there has been an infringement. The Commission has stated that the conditions for the use of the new procedure are flexible and it can consider accepting commitments where (a) the companies under investigation are willing to offer commitments which remove the Commission's initial competition concerns as expressed in a preliminary assessment; (b) the case is not one where a fine would be appropriate; and (c) efficiency reasons justify the Commission limiting itself to making the commitments binding without issuing a formal prohibition decision.[608] However, the Commission must only exercise its power under Article 9 to make commitments bindings insofar as they are necessary and proportionate to the concerns which it has identified.[609] Although the Commission cannot substitute itself for the parties so as to amend the commitments offered, it is not obliged to consider proposed commitments on a 'take it or leave it basis': it should make the proposed commitments binding only in part or to a particular extent if that is necessary to

---

[605] Reg 1/2003, OJ 2003 L1/1: Vol II, App B.3.

[606] See Temple Lang, 'Commitments under Reg 1/2003: Legal Aspects of a New Kind of Community Instrument' (2003) ECLR 347; Heim, 'Settling EU Anti-Trust Proceedings' (2004) Comp Law 258; Sousa Ferro, 'Committing to Commitments: Unanswered Questions on Article 9 Decisions' (2005) ECLR 451; Whish, 'Commitment Decisions under Article 9 of the EC Modernisation Regulation: Some Unanswered Questions' in Johansson, Wahl and Bernitz (eds), *Liber Amicorum in Honour of Sven Norberg - A European for All Seasons* (2006); Cook, 'Commitment Decisions: The Law and Practice under Article 9', (2006) 29 World Competition 209; Wils, 'Settlements of EU Antitrust Investigations: Commitment Decisions under Article 9 of Regulation No 1/2003' (2006) 29 World Competition 345.

[607] All the decisions taken to date have been for a specified period. However, the CFI has confirmed that commitments can be binding indefinitely: Case T-170/06 *Alrosa v Commission*, judgment of 11 July 2007, para 91.

[608] See MEMO/04/217 (17 September 2004) setting out some frequently asked questions regarding commitment decisions (available on DG Competition website under 'Legislation - Regulations').

[609] *Alrosa* (n 607, above) paras 88, 100, 105: 'The fact that an undertaking considers, for reasons of its own, that it is appropriate at a particular time to offer certain commitments does not of itself mean that those commitments are necessary'.

ensure that the principle of proportionality is respected.[610] At the time of writing, the Commission has accepted commitments in six cases.[611]

13.115 **Procedure.** The fact that Article 9 of Regulation 1/2003 refers to the Commission having conducted a preliminary assessment could suggest that commitments would be considered only after the issue of a statement of objections.[612] However, it appears from Article 2(1) of Regulation 773/2004 that a preliminary assessment for the purpose of Article 9[613] is not the same as a statement of objections and the Commission has accepted commitments before issuing a statement of objections,[614] as well as after.[615] In cases where commitments have been accepted before the issue of a statement of objections, the Commission has set out its concerns in a letter. The Commission must, before adopting a decision to accept commitments, publish a concise summary of the case and the main content of the commitments. Although plainly the Commission is not required to establish the existence of an infringement, it must nonetheless establish that the competition concerns which justify the adoption of a commitments decision are real. This presupposes an analysis of the market and an identification of the infringement envisaged that is sufficient to allow a review of the appropriateness of the commitments.[616] A period of at least one month must be fixed for interested parties to submit their observations,[617] and the Commission must also consult the Advisory Committee.[618] A final commitments decision must be published.[619]

13.116 **Effects of a commitment decision.** Although commitment decisions can be made only when the Commission intends to adopt a decision requiring an agreement or practice to be brought to an end, they are without prejudice to the ability

---

[610] ibid, para 139.

[611] *German Bundesliga*, OJ 2005 L134/46, [2005] 5 CMLR 1715; Case COMP/38.173 *Premier League*, 22 March 2006, [2006] 5 CMLR 1396; Case COMP/38.381 *De Beers*, 22 February 2006, [2006] 5 CMLR 1426 (decision annulled, Case T-170/06 *Alrosa v Commission* (n 607, above)); COMP/39.116 *Coca Cola*, 22 June 2005, [2006] 4 CMLR 1680; COMP/38.348 *Repsol*, Press Release IP/06/495 (12 April 2006); COMP/38.772 *Cannes Extension Agreement*, Press Release IP/06/1311 (4 October 2006).

[612] Temple Lang (n 606, above).

[613] In *Coca Cola* (n 611, above), the Commission published a notice of the initiatation of proceedings (2004 OJ C289/04) and then an Art 27(4) Notice.

[614] eg *German Bundesliga* (n 611, above); in that case (originally notified to the Commission for exemption under Reg 17) the Commission had indicated it was minded to grant an individual exemption before deciding (after the coming into force of Reg 1/2003) to accept commitments. See Wilbert, 'Joint selling of Bundesliga media rights' (2005) 2 EC Competition Policy Newsletter 44. See also *De Beers* and *Coca Cola* (n 611, above).

[615] eg *Premier League* (n 611, above).

[616] *Alrosa* (n 607, above) para 100.

[617] Reg 1/2003 (n 605, above) Art 27(4). In *Alrosa* (n 607, above) the CFI held that Alrosa's right to be heard had been infringed: paras 196 *et seq*.

[618] ibid, Art 14(1); see para 13.107, above.

[619] ibid, Art 30(1).

of NCAs or national courts to make findings of infringement.[620] Commitments decisions may adversely affect third parties. If the third party was a complainant and contends that the commitments accepted do not go far enough to resolve the infringement complained of, the third party should be able to challenge the decision before the Community Courts.[621] If, on the contrary, the third party was involved in arrangements which are adjusted to its detriment as a result of the commitments, it may also be able to bring a legal challenge. In the *De Beers* case,[622] the Commission accepted a commitment from De Beers that it would phase out and then cease entirely as from 1 January 2009 all direct and indirect purchases of rough diamonds from Alrosa. In determining a challenge by Alrosa to the Commission's decision, the Court of First Instance annulled the decision on the grounds, amongst others, that the commitment accepted infringed the principles of proportionality and freedom of contract.[623] The Court stressed that although a decision under Article 9 of Regulation 1/2003 was predicated on the offer of commitments by the undertaking concerned, it was the decision and not that offer that produced legal effects. The Commission is therefore the 'sole author' of the commitments and assumes responsibility for them. Part of that responsibility is to ensure that the commitments are necessary and proportionate having regard to the competition concerns identified. The Court rejected the Commission's argument that the application of the principle of proportionality is different when assessing commitments from when assessing orders terminating an infringement under Article 7 of Regulation 1/2003. The Court held that it would be contrary to the scheme of the Regulation for it to be possible to take a decision under Article 9 which would have been condemned as disproportionate under Article 7 if the infringement had been established. The Court held that by obliging Alrosa, which was not subject to the procedure initiated under Article 82 EC, to make significant changes to its structure and activity in order to compete with De Beers, the Commission had exceeded its powers under Article 82.

Enforcement and withdrawal. A failure to comply with a commitment deci- **13.117** sion exposes the undertaking to liability to a fine of up to 10 per cent of its business

---

[620] ibid, Recital (13). However, if by a commitment decision the Commission has at least implicitly reached the view that conduct consistent with the commitments does not infringe the competition rules, *quaere* whether NCAs would be excluded by Art 10 EC from taking action in respect of conduct consistent with commitments: see Sousa Ferro (n 606, above). The Commission's view is that a decision to accept commitments cannot be taken as such a determination: see, eg *Premier League* (n 611, above).

[621] Since by the commitments decision, the Commission cannot take further action on the complaint save in the circumstances specified in Art 9(2). See Faull & Nikpay (n 209, above) para 2.136.

[622] *De Beers* (n 611, above).

[623] Case T-170/06 *Alrosa v Commission*, judgment of 11 July 2007. The CFI also held that Alrosa's right to be heard had been infringed.

turnover in the preceding business year.[624] The Commission may also by decision impose on an undertaking a daily penalty payment of up to 5 per cent of its average daily turnover in the previous year in order to compel it to comply with a commitment decision.[625] The Commission may also reopen the original infringement proceedings where there has been a material change in the facts upon which the decision was based; where the undertakings concerned breach their commitments; or where the decision was based on incomplete, incorrect or misleading information provided by the parties.[626] No express provision is made for NCAs or national courts to enforce commitment decisions by the Commission and it is unclear whether breach of such decisions creates a right to damages by third parties.[627]

8. Interim Measures

13.118 **Background.** Regulation 17, which governed the procedure for enforcing the competition rules prior to 1 May 2004, made no express provision for interim measures. However, the Court of Justice held in *Camera Care*[628] that Article 3(1) of that Regulation conferred on the Commission the power to take interim measures which were 'indispensable for the effective exercise of its functions and, in particular, for ensuring the effectiveness of any decisions requiring undertakings to bring to an end infringements which it has found to exist'. Article 8 of Regulation 1/2003[629] expressly gives the Commission the power, on the basis of a *prima facie* finding of infringement, to impose interim measures in cases of urgency where there is a risk of serious and irreparable damage to competition. A decision ordering interim measures must specify the period of time for which the measures apply, but may be renewed so far as this is necessary and appropriate. Although Article 8 refers to the Commission taking such a decision on its own initiative, there is no reason why the Commission cannot act in response to a complaint; but

---

[624] Reg 1/2003 (n 605, above) Art, 23(2)(c).

[625] ibid, Art 24(1)(c).

[626] ibid, Art 9(2).

[627] Sousa Ferro (n 606, above) argues that NCAs may derive a duty and right to do so from Art 10 EC; Wils (ibid) points out that if national competition law provides for equivalent settlement decisions that can be enforced by the NCA or give rise to private damages claims, the principle of equivalence should require the same consequences to apply in national law to Commission decisions. The Commission apparently considers that national courts are under a duty to enforce commitment decisions by any means provided for by national law, including the adoption of interim measures: MEMO/04/217 (n 608, above).

[628] Case 792/79R *Camera Care v Commission* [1980] ECR 119, [1980] 1 CMLR 334, para 18. See also Case 109/75R *National Carbonising Company v Commission* [1975] ECR 1193, [1975] 2 CMLR 457; *NCB/National Smokeless Fuels/NCC*, OJ 1976 L35/6, [1976] 1 CMLR D82.

[629] Reg 1/2003, OJ 2003 L1/1: Vol II, App B.3.

the Commission has stated that interim measures cannot be applied for and has suggested that those seeking interim relief should apply to national courts or (where they possess equivalent powers) NCAs.[630] Indeed, the wording of Article 8 (as compared with Article 7) suggests that it is not intended to confer any procedural rights on those who may seek to persuade the Commission to impose interim measures.

Criteria for the grant of interim measures.   The criteria in Article 8 of Regulation   **13.119**
1/2003 are based on those established by the Court of First Instance in *La Cinq v Commission*.[631] In that case, the Court made it clear that the requirement of a *prima facie* breach is entirely different from a requirement of certainty; the Commission is not, for example, required to show a clear or flagrant breach of the competition rules.[632] As to the requirement of urgency, the Court held in *La Cinq* that damage is considered irreparable if it cannot be remedied by the decision which the Commission takes on the termination of the administrative procedure. Irreparability could be established although the undertakings adversely affected by the conduct could have a remedy in damages in the national court.[633] Under Article 8, the damage must be damage to competition (rather than, for example, to particular competitors). Financial loss is not regarded as irreparable unless the survival of the undertaking concerned is threatened.[634] Damage will be regarded as irreparable if it leads to market developments that will be very difficult to reverse.[635]

Commission procedure.   When considering whether to impose interim measures   **13.120**
the Commission must respect the right to be heard of the prospective addressee of the decision.[636] Article 27 of Regulation 1/2003 applies to interim measures decisions, so that the addressee enjoys a right to be heard, and therefore be informed of and comment on the Commission's objections, to have access to the

---

[630]   Complaints Notice, OJ 2004 C101/65: Vol II App B.10, para 80.

[631]   Case T-44/90 *La Cinq v Commission* [1992] ECR II-1, [1992] 4 CMLR 449. In fact, La Cinq was granted interim relief by the Paris Court of Appeal, *La Cinq v Fédération française de football*, judgment of 10 February 1992, BOCCRF, 21 February 1992, p 69, noted in (1992) 3 ECLR R-71 (appeal to the Cour de Cassation dismissed, no. 91–16.751, 1 March 1994, JCP éd G 1994, IV, p 1199). Interim measures were granted in Cases T-24 & 28/92R *Langnese Iglo v Commission* [1992] ECR II-1839; and in *Port of Roscoff* [1995] 5 CMLR 177, to allow the applicant access to port facilities.

[632]   *La Cinq*, above, paras 61–62.

[633]   ibid, para 79. Note, however, that under Art 8 the focus is on damage to competition rather than to a particular complainant.

[634]   Case T-184/01R *IMS Health v Commission* [2001] ECR II-3193, [2002] 4 CMLR 58, para 121; upheld on appeal Case C-481/01P(R) *NDC Health v IMS Health and Commission* [2002] ECR I-3401, [2002] 5 CMLR 44.

[635]   Case T-184/01R *IMS Health*, above, paras 128–129.

[636]   *Camera Care* (n 628, above) para 18; see generally Cases 228 & 229/82 *Ford v Commission (No. 1)* [1984] ECR 1129 1172–1176 (ECR), 664–669 (CMLR) (AG Slynn).

file, and to have an oral hearing.[637] The Advisory Committee must be consulted.[638] The decision must be reasoned, if only concisely.[639] None of the provisions relating to rights of complainants under Article 7 of Regulation 1/2003 applies in respect of interim measures decisions under Article 8, and it is unclear to what extent, in the light of that absence and the fact that Article 8 refers only to actions on the Commission's own initiative, the Community Courts will now require the Commission to consider complaints or consult complainants in relation to failures by the Commission to take Article 8 decisions.

13.121 **Likely timescale.** The need to issue a statement of objections, provide access to the file and allow time for an oral hearing inevitably means that interim measures cannot be imposed in a shorter time period than a few weeks. The Commission is assisted by the reduction in interim measures cases of the minimum period to be allowed for a response to a statement of objections from the usual four weeks to one week.[640]

13.122 **Types of order that may be made.** The power extends to ordering positive measures to be taken, as well as to the issue of prohibitory orders.[641] Thus the Commission has been prepared to order the resumption of supplies,[642] the cessation of predatory conduct,[643] or issue of an instruction to dealers,[644] or the grant of an intellectual property licence,[645] and has considered granting measures to prevent the imposition of a tying clause,[646] or an exclusivity clause.[647] The interim measures must be measures of a kind that the Commission could include in a final order.[648] The measures ordered must be temporary and conservatory and must

---

[637] See paras 13.080 *et seq*, above.

[638] Art 14(1) of Reg 1/2003 (n 629, above).

[639] *Camera Care* (n 628, above) para 18.

[640] Reg 773/2004, OJ 2004 L123/18: Vol II, App B.4, Art 17(2).

[641] *Distribution system of Ford Werke AG (Interim Measures)*, OJ 1982 L256/20, [1982] 3 CMLR 267; *B & I Line v Sealink Harbours* [1992] 5 CMLR 255; *Irish Continental Group v CCI Morlaix* [1995] 5 CMLR 177; *IMS Health: Interim measures*, OJ 2002 L59/18 (suspended on other grounds on appeal, see n 634, above); *Boosey & Hawkes*, OJ 1987 L286/36, [1988] 4 CMLR 67.

[642] *Boosey & Hawkes*, above.

[643] *ECS/AKZO (No. 1)*, OJ 1983 L252/13, [1983] 3 CMLR 694. See also *British Sugar/Napier Brown*, Press Release IP/86/398 (21 August 1986), [1986] 3 CMLR 594.

[644] *Ecosystem/Peugeot*, OJ 1992 L66/1, [1993] 4 CMLR 42; appeal dismissed, Case T-23/90 *Peugeot v Commission* [1991] ECR II-653, [1990] 4 CMLR 674.

[645] *IMS Health: interim measures* (n 641, above); *IGR Stereo Television*, XIth Report on Competition Policy (1981), point 94; *Ford (body panels)*, XVth Report on Competition Policy (1985), point 49.

[646] *Hilti*, OJ 1988 L65/19, [1989] 4 CMLR 677 (tying the supply of nails to the supply of nailguns).

[647] *Langnese—Iglo/Mars*, OJ 1993 L183/19, [1994] 4 CMLR 83.

[648] *Ford v Commission (No. 1)* [1984] ECR 1129, [1984] 1 CMLR 649, annulling the *Ford Werke* decision (n 641, above) on the ground that the Commission could not, in relation to an allegation of an allegedly anti-competitive distribution agreement, order the manufacturer to grant supply.

not exceed what is necessary in a given situation.[649] Infringement of an interim order may be penalised by fines or periodic penalty payments.[650]

Review by the Community Courts.   The grant of interim measures may be   **13.123**
reviewed by the Court of First Instance.[651] An application for interim suspension of the measures may be granted by the President of the Court of First Instance pending the full hearing of the application to suspend the measures.[652] Given the absence of reference to complainants in the current rules, it is not clear to what extent the Community Courts now can or will review a decision not to grant interim measures sought by a complainant. Where the measures are withdrawn during the period of suspension, the Court may still determine their legality if they had a legal effect on the addressee of the decision.[653]

9. Declarations of Infringement and Orders to Terminate

Declaratory decisions.   The Commission may decide simply to declare that   **13.124**
an infringement is or has been committed without imposing any remedies.[654] Article 7(1) of Regulation 1/2003 provides that the Commission may find that an infringement has been committed in the past but only if it has a legitimate interest in doing so, and in *GVL*[655] the Court of Justice held that the Commission would have such a legitimate interest if there is a real risk of resumption of previous infringing practices. The Commission has taken decisions of this kind.[656]

---

[649] Cases 228 & 229/82R *Ford Werke v Commission* [1982] ECR 3091, [1982] 3 CMLR 673 (order that Ford meet all orders for RHD vehicles in Germany suspended and replaced by a requirement to meet such orders only up to the limits set by the ECJ, which broadly corresponded to the level of deliveries prior to Ford's original suspension of supplies); *Ecosystem/Peugeot* (n 644, above); *B & I Line v Sealink Harbours* (n 641, above) (order to Sealink to return to its earlier published ship schedules in respect of certain crossings).

[650] Reg 1/2003 (n 629, above), Arts 23(2)(b) and 24(1)(b); see paras 13.135 *et seq*, below for a discussion of fines and periodic penalty payments.

[651] *Camera Care* (n 628, above) and see paras 13.211 *et seq*, below.

[652] See, eg *IMS Health: interim measures* (n 641, above): interim measures suspended by the President of the CFI pending an appeal by IMS Health: Case T-184/01R, [2001] ECR II-3193, [2002] 4 CMLR 58 (confirmed on appeal to the ECJ: Case C-481/01 P(R) *NDC Health v IMS Health and Commission* [2002] ECR I-3401, [2002] 5 CMLR 44). The order was then withdrawn when the Commission investigation was superseded by the judgment of the ECJ in an Art 234 reference concerning the same subject-matter: see Case T-184/01, [2005] ECR II-817.

[653] Case T-184/01 *IMS Health v Commission* [2005] ECR II-817.

[654] The finding of an infringement does not of itself require the Commission to adopt a termination decision, at least where national courts share competence with the Commission: Case T-16/91 *Rendo v Commission* [1992] ECR II-2417, paras 98–99 (appeal on other grounds allowed: Case C-19/93P, [1995] ECR I-3319, [1997] 4 CMLR 392).

[655] Case 7/82 *GVL v Commission* [1983] ECR 483, [1983] 3 CMLR 645.

[656] See, eg COMP/38.337 *Thread*, 14 September 2005, paras 407–417 (limitation period prevented imposition of a fine; risk of repetition demonstrated by subsequent cartels involving the undertakings concerned and possible abortive attempts to restart it, on appeal Cases T-446/05

However, a legitimate interest must be demonstrated by reasoning in the decision and cannot simply be asserted.[657] The fact that the limitation period for the imposition of fines has expired does not preclude the adoption of a declaratory decision.[658]

13.125 Power to terminate infringements. Under Article 7(1) of Regulation 1/2003 the Commission may, by decision, require an undertaking or association of undertakings to bring to an end the infringements that have been found. Such a decision is binding in its entirety upon those to whom it is addressed.[659] Decisions of the Commission ordering termination of an infringement must be published.[660] The Commission is not entitled to order parties to behave in a way that would contravene the national law of a Member State without an assessment of whether that national law is contrary to the Treaty.[661]

13.126 Orders to terminate. Decisions ordering termination of infringements normally take effect forthwith,[662] although in appropriate cases the parties will be given a short period in which to comply.[663] The Commission is not required to specify

---

Amann & Söhne and Cousin v Commission, Case T-448/05 *Oxley Threads v Commission*, T-452/05 *Belgian Sewing Thread v Commission*, T-456/05 *Gütermann v Commission*, T-457/05 *Zwicky v Commission*, not yet decided).

[657] Cases T-22 & 23/02 *Sumitomo v Commission* ('*Vitamins*') [2005] ECR II-4065, [2006] 4 CMLR 42, paras 129–140; the Commission asserted before the CFI (although such reasoning was absent from the decision) that possible legitimate interests could include the need to prevent repetition, the seriousness of the infringements, the need to promote exemplary behaviour by the undertakings, and the interest in enabling injured parties to bring the matter before national courts. However, the CFI found that these grounds were simply hypothetical; there was no evidence of recidivism or that legal actions were being taken or were even capable of being envisaged by injured parties. The decision was therefore annulled.

[658] ibid, paras 34–64; at paras 76–112 the CFI rejected submissions that fundamental principles of Community law precluded the adoption of a declaratory decision.

[659] Art 249 of the Treaty.

[660] Reg 1/2003, OJ 2003 L1/1: Vol II, App B.3, Art 30(1).

[661] *Rendo* (n 654, above) para 106 (CFI).

[662] See, eg *ECS/AKZO (No. 2)*, OJ 1985 L374/1, [1986] 3 CMLR 273, on appeal Case C-62/86 *AKZO v Commission* [1991] ECR I-3359, [1993] 5 CMLR 215, and more recently COMP/38.281 *Raw Tobacco (Italy)*, 20 October 2005, OJ 2006 L353/45, [2006] 4 CMLR 1766 (cartel agreement); COMP/36.623 *SEP/Peugeot*, 17 December 2005, [2006] 5 CMLR 714 (agreement impeding parallel trading). Such decisions usually include an order that the undertakings shall refrain from repeating or continuing any of the measures constituting the infringement and from adopting any measures having equivalent object or effect: see para 13.127, below.

[663] See, eg *British Telecommunications*, OJ 1982 L360/36, [1983] 1 CMLR 457 (two months allowed); *IJsselcentrale*, OJ 1991 L28/32, [1992] 5 CMLR 154 (three months for parties to make proposals to bring infringements to an end); *Magill TV Guide*, OJ 1989 L78/43, [1989] 4 CMLR 757 (two months to submit proposals to the Commission of terms on which the parties would permit third parties to publish programme listings; for appeals see n 679, below); *Soda-Ash—Solvay*, OJ 1991 L152/21, [1994] 4 CMLR 645 (three months in which to notify new discount and rebate systems and to renegotiate supply contracts); *Alpha Flight Services/Aeroports de Paris*, OJ 1998 L230/10, [1998] 5 CMLR 611 (two months to apply a non-discriminatory system of fees to suppliers of groundhandling services); *Frankfurt Airport*, OJ 1998 L72/30, [1998] 4 CMLR 779

its requirements in detail, provided the infringement to be terminated is reasonably clear from the decision as a whole.[664] The Commission may additionally order the parties to refrain in future from similar conduct.[665] The Commission may order parties to refrain from certain conduct even if they have ceased that conduct or if the Commission cannot be certain that they have ceased,[666] and it is irrelevant that the parties may have intended to cease the infringement regardless of what the Commission did.[667] However, in *Automec II*,[668] the Court of First Instance held that in relation to the exercise of its powers to terminate an infringement of Article 81(1), the Commission must respect the principle of freedom of contract and cannot order a party to enter into a contractual relationship where there are other suitable means at its disposal for compelling an enterprise to terminate the infringement. In that case, a complainant alleged that the selective distribution network operated by BMW infringed Article 81(1) and sought an order that it be admitted to the network. The Court held that the infringement could be terminated in a number of ways, such as giving up or altering the distribution system,

---

(three months to produce a plan for the reorganisation of groundhandling services at the airport); *Ilmailulaitos/Luftfartsverket ('Finnish airports')*, OJ 1999 L69/24, [1999] 5 CMLR 90 (infringement to be brought to an end within two months and Commission to be informed of measures taken). In COMP/37.792 *Microsoft*, 24 March 2004, [2005] 4 CMLR 965, the Commission ordered Microsoft to bring its infringements to an end setting out the detailed steps by which Microsoft had to make available information to competitors in accordance with the timetable set out in the decn. Microsoft was also ordered to submit proposals for a mechanism whereby the Commission could monitor its compliance with the order (on appeal Case T-201/04 *Microsoft v Commission*, judgment of 17 September 2007; see Postscript below).

[664] Cases 25 & 26/84 *Ford v Commission (No. 2)* [1985] ECR 2725, [1985] 3 CMLR 528; Case T-128/98 *Aeroports de Paris v Commission* [2000] ECR II-3929, [2001] 4 CMLR 1376, paras 82–83 (requirement to end non-discriminatory charging scheme clear in context of decision as a whole).

[665] See, eg *Hasselblad*, OJ 1982 L161/18, [1982] 2 CMLR 233; *Toltecs/Dorcet*, OJ 1982 L379/19, [1983] 1 CMLR 412; *Polypropylene*, OJ 1986 L230/1, [1989] 4 CMLR 347. In *Hilti*, OJ 1988 L65/19, [1989] 4 CMLR 677, Hilti was required to refrain from measures 'having an equivalent effect' to those found to have been abusive; upheld on appeal Case T-30/89, [1991] ECR II-1439, [1992] 4 CMLR 16. In Cases T-305/94, etc, *Polypropylene II ('LVM')* [1999] ECR II-931, [1999] 5 CMLR 303, the CFI upheld a requirement that the undertakings not exchange information that indirectly allowed an identical or similar result to the exchanges covered by the decision (para 1254).

[666] eg *Citric Acid*, OJ 2002 L239/18, [2002] 5 CMLR 24, paras 196–197; *Austrian Banks, (Lombard Agreement)*, OJ 2004 L56/1, [2004] 5 CMLR 399, para 492 (appeals largely dismissed Cases T-259/02, etc, *Raiffeisen Zentralbank Österreich*, judgment of 14 December 2006; on further appeal on other grounds, Case C-125/07P, C-133/07P, C-135/07P and C-137/07P, not yet decided).

[667] Case T-354/94 *Stora Kopparbergs Bergslags v Commission* [1998] ECR II-2111, para 99 (appeal on other grounds largely dismissed, Case C-286/98P, [2000] ECR I-9925, [2001] 4 CMLR 370).

[668] Case T-24/90 *Automec Srl v Commission* [1992] ECR II-2223, [1992] 5 CMLR 431. See similarly Case T-170/06 *Alrosa v Commission*, judgment of 11 July 2007, where the CFI annulled a commitments decn holding that to force a market operator which was not the subject of proceedings under Art 82 to work towards a change in the structure of the market for the production and supply of rough diamonds exceeded the power of the Commission under Art 82: para 149.

and it was not for the Commission to impose upon the parties its own choice among the different potential courses of action which would all conform with the Treaty.

13.127 **'Like effect' orders.** The Commission may order undertakings not to enter into further agreements or conduct to the like effect as the infringing agreement or conduct. In *Fiatagri*,[669] it was held that such orders are no more than declaratory since the competition rules would in any event prohibit the putative future agreement or conduct; however, they fall within the Commission's powers,[670] and are used.[671] In *Langnese-Iglo* and *Schöller*,[672] the Court of First Instance annulled the contested decisions insofar as they withdrew the benefit of the exclusive purchasing block exemption in force at the time (Regulation 1984/83) for future agreements falling within the exemption and prohibited the applicants from concluding such agreements. The Court held that such agreements could only be prohibited insofar as they significantly contributed to the partitioning of the market and that Regulation 1984/83 did not provide a legal basis for a decision withholding its application from future agreements. The Court pointed out that the effect of such a decision would be to distort competition as the suppliers' competitors would remain free under the block exemption to conclude equivalent agreements.

13.128 **Power to order positive action.** The Commission's powers under Article 7 of Regulation 1/2003 to require the termination of infringements include the power to impose any 'behavioural or structural remedies which are proportionate to the infringement committed and which are necessary to bring the infringement effectively to an end'. The Commission can therefore order undertakings to take positive action. Indeed, even under Regulation 17, which did not contain those words, the Court of Justice had reached the conclusion that the Commission could order positive action to be taken.[673] The action ordered may amount to no more than an obligation to inform interested third parties that the infringement has been brought to an end,[674] or to make information available periodically to

---

[669] Case T-34/92 *Fiatagri v Commission* [1994] ECR II-905, para 39 (on appeal Case C-8/95P, [1998] ECR I-3175, [1998] 5 CMLR 311).

[670] Case T-305/94 *Polypropylene II ('LVM') v Commission* [1999] ECR II-931, [1999] 5 CMLR 303, para 1253.

[671] eg *Methionine*, OJ 2003 L255/1, [2004] 4 CMLR 1062 (fine reduced on appeal Case T-279/02 *Degussa v Commission* [2006] ECR II-897).

[672] Case T-7/93 *Langnese-Iglo v Commission* [1995] ECR II-1533, [1995] 5 CMLR 602, [1995] All ER (EC) 908, paras 205–211; cross-appeal dismissed, Case C-279/95P, [1998] ECR I-5609, [1998] 5 CMLR 933, [1999] All ER (EC) 616; Case T-9/93 *Schöller v Commission* [1995] ECR II-1611, [1995] 5 CMLR 659.

[673] Cases 6 & 7/73 *Commercial Solvents v Commission* [1974] ECR 223, [1974] 1 CMLR 309, para 45.

[674] See, eg *Johnson & Johnson*, OJ 1980 L377/16, [1981] 2 CMLR 287; *Hasselblad* (n 665, above); *VW-Audi*, OJ 1998 L124/60, [1998] 5 CMLR 33 (notification to dealers).

the Commission,[675] but in other cases there may be a need for further action. Thus, in *Commercial Solvents*,[676] where a dominant undertaking refused supplies in breach of Article 82, the Commission required the undertaking to resume supplies within 30 days and to make proposals for subsequent supply arrangements within two months of the Commission's decision. In *Magill TV Guide*,[677] the Commission ordered the television companies to supply to each other and to third parties on request and on a non-discriminatory basis their weekly programme listings.[678] The order further provided that if the companies chose to do this by way of licence, the royalty charged had to be reasonable. The order expressly allowed the companies to include in any such licences granted to third parties such terms as they considered necessary to ensure comprehensive high quality coverage of all their programmes, including those of minority and regional appeal. The orders were upheld on appeal as the appropriate and necessary means to bring the infringement to an end, and a challenge on the grounds of proportionality was accordingly rejected.[679] In *Microsoft*,[680] the Commission ordered the disclosure of interoperability information to enable the development of group server operating systems able to interface with Windows domain architecture. The Commission cannot, however, order positive action to remedy conduct which is not in itself contrary to Articles 81 or 82.[681] Further, in *Atlantic Container Line*[682] the Court of First Instance cast doubt on whether the Commission was entitled in a cartel

---

675 See, eg *United Brands*, OJ 1976 L95/1, [1976] 1 CMLR D28; *ECS/AZKO* (n 662, above).

676 *Commercial Solvents*, OJ 1972 L299/51, [1973] CMLR D50, on appeal *Commercial Solvents v Commission* (n 673, above); see also *Hugin/Liptons*, OJ 1978 L22/23, [1978] 1 CMLR D19, appeal allowed on other grounds, Case 22/78 *Hugin v Commission* [1979] ECR 1867, [1979] 3 CMLR 345.

677 *Magill TV Guide*, OJ 1989 L78/43, [1989] 4 CMLR 757.

678 See also *Der Grüne Punkt - Duales System Deutschland*, OJ 2001 L166/1, [2001] 5 CMLR 609: order to refrain from imposing charges under trade mark agreement in cases where the licensee did not participate in the licensor's exemption system under the German Packaging Ordinance; appeal dismissed, Case T-151/01 *Duales System Deutschland v Commission* [2007] 5 CMLR 300.

679 Case T-69/89 *Radio Telefis Eireann v Commission* [1991] ECR II-485, [1991] 4 CMLR 586; Case T-70/89 *BBC v Commission* [1991] ECR II-535, [1991] 4 CMLR 669; Case T-76/89 *ITP v Commission* [1991] ECR II-575, [1991] 4 CMLR 745; and on further appeal Cases 241 & 242/91P *RTE and ITP v Commission* [1995] ECR I-793, [1995] 4 CMLR 718, [1995] All ER (EC) 416.

680 *Microsoft* (n 663, above) paras 995 *et seq.*

681 Cases 228 & 229/82 *Ford v Commission (No. 1)* [1984] ECR 1129, [1984] 1 CMLR 649. In that case the ECJ held that an order to resume supplies of right hand drive cars in Germany was not permissible where the refusal to supply was not of itself contrary to Art 81 or Art 82, although it might preclude exemption under Art 81(3) of the relevant dealer agreement. For subsequent proceedings, see Cases 25 & 26/84 *Ford v Commission (No. 2)* (n 664, above).

682 Case T-395/94 *Atlantic Container Line v Commission* [2002] ECR II-875, [2002] 4 CMLR 1008, [2002] All ER(EC) 684. The CFI held that the Commission had not given sufficient reasons why it was necessary to impose a similar remedy in that case. cf *Astra*, OJ 1993 L20/23, [1994] 5 CMLR 226, where Astra was required to notify customers of their ability to renegotiate their contract terms or terminate on reasonable notice.

case to make a direction that the participants should renegotiate contracts with third parties the terms of which were affected by the cartel agreement.[683]

13.129 **Power to control prices.** The power of the Commission to impose prices on an undertaking has not been finally determined by the Court of Justice. In *United Brands*,[684] the Commission held that United Brands had abused its dominant position by charging discriminatory and excessive prices and, without actually imposing prices, subsequently monitored the company's pricing policy. On appeal, the Advocate General indicated[685] that the Commission was empowered to impose prices. The Commission imposed minimum prices in its interim measures decision in *ECS/AKZO (No. 1)* which concerned an allegation of predatory pricing.[686] In practice, there are formidable difficulties in imposing prices, since the Commission is not in a good position to judge the costs incurred by the undertaking concerned; moreover, the effect of such an order may be to freeze prices at a level above that which the market might produce or (if the imposed price is less than the market price) inhibit entry by other undertakings. However, in *Tetra Pak II*, the Commission made orders requiring the defendant to ensure that any differences in prices charged for its products as between the Member States 'result solely from market conditions', and that it would not grant to any customer a discount or more favourable payment terms 'not justified by an objective consideration' but solely on the basis of the quantity of products ordered.[687] This remedy was upheld by the Court of First Instance.[688]

13.130 **Appointment of experts and monitoring trustees.** Where the Commission's order terminating the infringement requires a series of complex steps on the part of the addressee, the Commission may rely on experts or monitoring trustees to assist it in ensuring compliance. For example, in *IMS Health*,[689] the Commission ordered IMS Health to to grant a copyright licence 'without delay' to all

[683] *Atlantic Container Line*, above, paras 410–420. The CFI found that the direction was in any event vitiated by lack of reasoning, and insufficient notice had been given in the statement of objections that such an order could be made. But it also observed that the civil law consequences of an infringement of Art 81 were in principle determined by national law, that the remedy in question was highly unusual, and that the third party contracts in question were in any event only for one year.

[684] *United Brands*, OJ 1976 L95/1, [1976] 1 CMLR D28.

[685] AG Mayras in Case 27/76 *United Brands v Commission* [1978] ECR 207, 342, [1978] 1 CMLR 429, 475–476.

[686] *ECS/AKZO (No. 1)*, OJ 1983 L252/13, [1983] 3 CMLR 694. There was no appeal against this decision.

[687] *Tetra Pak II*, OJ 1992 L72/1, [1992] 4 CMLR 551.

[688] Case T-83/91 *Tetra Pak v Commission* [1994] ECR II-755, [1995] 1 CMLR 34, paras 220–223; further appeal on other grounds dismissed, Case C-333/94P, [1996] ECR I-5951, [1997] 4 CMLR 662.

[689] *IMS Health: Interim measures*, OJ 2001 L59/18; and see n 652, above for the procedural history of this case.

undertakings present on the relevant market, on request and on a non-discriminatory basis. The order also provided that the royalties should be determined by agreement between IMS and the undertaking requesting the licence but that if an agreement was not reached within two weeks of the date of the request for a licence, appropriate royalties would be determined by an independent expert. If the parties could not agree on the appointment of an expert, the Commission would make the choice. The expert was enjoined to make a determination on the basis of transparent and objective criteria, within two weeks of being chosen to carry out this task. In *Microsoft*, the initial decision in March 2004 finding an infringement required Microsoft to submit proposals for a suitable mechanism to assist the Commission in monitoring Microsoft's compliance with the decision and stipulated that that mechanism must include an independent monitoring trustee.[690] In July 2005, the Commission adopted a decision pursuant to Article 7 of the initial decision and to Article 7(1) of Regulation 1/2003, setting out in detail the terms under which a trustee would be appointed and describing the role that the trustee would fulfil.[691] In October 2005, the Commission appointed a computer scientist to act as monitoring trustee. Although the Commission retained exclusive responsibility for ensuring compliance with the decision, the trustee provided impartial expert advice to the Commission on compliance issues, for example in assessing whether Microsoft's disclosures of interface documentation were complete and accurate and whether the terms under which Microsoft makes the protocol specifications available are reasonable and non-discriminatory.[692] Thereafter, the Commission approved a trustee mandate and the appointment of two advisors to the trustee. The trustee's reports led the Commission to conclude that Microsoft had failed to comply with the decision and a substantial periodic penalty was imposed.[693]

Power to order divestiture. In *Continental Can*,[694] the Commission required a **13.131** dominant undertaking to divest itself of a company which it had acquired in breach of Article 82. Since the Commission's decision was quashed on its merits by the Court of Justice,[695] the order never took effect. Article 7(1) of Regulation 1/2003

[690] COMP/37.792 *Microsoft*, 24 March 2004, [2005] 4 CMLR 965, paras 1043 *et seq.* (on appeal Case T-201/04 *Microsoft v Commission*, judgement of 17 September 2007; see Postscript below.) Microsoft's application for interim suspension of the decn pending its appeal was rejected by the President of the CFI: Case T-201/04R *Microsoft v Commission* [2004] ECR II–4463, [2006] 4 CMLR 311.

[691] COMP/37.792 *Microsoft*, decn of 28 July 2005. The decn makes clear that the costs incurred are to be borne by Microsoft: para 31. Microsoft also lodged an appeal against a decision in a letter of 1 June 2005 in which the Commission indicated the scope of the disclosure required: Case T-313/05, now withdrawn; see para PS.001 below, n1.

[692] See Press Release IP/05/1215 (5 October 2005) and MEMO/06/119 (10 March 2006).

[693] See *Microsoft*, decn of 12 July 2006, Press Release IP/06/979 (12 July 2006); on appeal, Case T-271/06, now withdrawn: discussed further para 13.202, below.

[694] *Continental Can*, OJ 1972 L7/25, [1972] CMLR D11.

[695] Case 6/72 *Continental Can v Commission* [1973] ECR 215, [1973] CMLR 199.

makes express reference to 'structural' remedies; however, structural remedies may be imposed only where either there is no available behavioural remedy or where any behavioural remedy would be more burdensome for the undertaking concerned than would a structural remedy. The remedy would also be subject to the principle of proportionality. At the time of writing, it has not yet been used.

13.132 **Lapse of time or delay.** In *Commercial Solvents*,[696] the Court of Justice upheld the Commission's order although it was not made until two years after the supplies had first been refused. It is not clear how far Commission decisions requiring positive action may be impugned on the ground of lapse of time or delay on the part of the Commission.

13.133 **Recommendation.** Regulation 1/2003 does not refer to the possibility that the Commission might simply issue a recommendation that an agreement or conduct be brought to an end. The previous power to issue recommendations in Article 3(3) of Regulation 17 was hardly ever used.[697]

13.134 **Consequences of non-compliance with directions.** A refusal to comply with directions may of itself amount to an infringement of Article 81 or 82 and give rise to liability to pay a penalty. But in addition, Article 24(1)(a) of Regulation 1/2003 provides that the Commission may impose periodic penalty payments on undertakings that fail to put an end to an infringement in accordance with an Article 7 final direction; those payments may not exceed, per day, 5 per cent of the average daily turnover of the undertaking concerned in the previous business year. In *Microsoft*, the Commission issued a decision[698] under that Article imposing a penalty of €2 million a day from a date five weeks after the date of the decision in respect of certain contraventions of directions given in the original Article 7 decision. Article 24(2) provides that when the undertaking has satisfied the obligation in question, the Commission may fix the definitive amount of the penalty at an amount lower than that which would arise under the original decision.

---

696 *Commercial Solvents* (n 673, above).

697 There were no formal recommendations after the Commission's first case under Reg 17, *Convention Faience* (1964): see *First Report on Competition Policy* (1971), point 20.

698 COMP/37.792 *Microsoft*, decn of 10 November 2005. The Commission subsequently quantified at €280.5 million the amount due for failure to comply for the period to 20 June 2006 and raised the amount of daily penalty to which Microsoft would be liable for continued failure to comply after 31 July 2006 to €3 million: decn of 12 July 2006, Press Release IP/06/979 (12 July 2006); on appeal, Case T-271/06, now withdrawn; see Postscript, para PS.001 below, n1.

10. Fines for Substantive Infringements

(a) Generally

The jurisdiction to fine.   The Commission is entitled to impose fines where   **13.135**
undertakings or associations of undertakings 'intentionally or negligently' infringe
Article 81(1) or Article 82 of the Treaty.[699] The fines imposed may not exceed
10 per cent of turnover of the undertaking concerned in the preceding business
year.[700] In fixing the amount of the fine the Commission must have regard to the
gravity and to the duration of the infringement.[701] The Commission has power to
impose fines even if the conduct in question has ceased[702] and is not precluded by
the fact that no fine was imposed in other cases.[703] There is no power to fine individual directors or employees of undertakings. In 1998 the Commission issued
Guidelines on the Method of Setting Fines, and those Guidelines have now in
turn been superseded by further Guidelines issued in June 2006.[704] Before the
1998 Guidelines, the Commission's reasoning on the level of fines was generally
opaque[705] and it was not always easy to tell why, in any particular case, the parties
escaped a fine.

The nature and purpose of fines.   Decisions imposing fines are expressed to be   **13.136**
not of a criminal law nature.[706] In the *Pioneer* case, in which the Court of Justice
approved a substantial increase in the level of fines, the Court stated that the

---

699   Reg 1/2003, OJ 2003 L1/1: Vol II, App B.3, Art 23(2)(a).

700   In Case T-33/02 *Britannia Alloys v Commission* [2005] ECR II-4973, [2006] 4 CMLR 1046,
the applicant had sold the business in question some five years before the decision and had ceased to
trade. Its turnover in the business year preceding the decision was therefore zero. The CFI held, however, that, having regard to the need to ensure the effectiveness of the Regulation, the Commission
was entitled, notwithstanding the actual words of (what was then) Reg 17, in exceptional circumstances, such as those where the person concerned had ceased trading, to take the last year of normal
trading by the undertaking concerned as the relevant year for the purposes of applying the 10 per
cent maximum (appeal dismissed, Case C-76/06P [2007] 5 CMLR 251).

701   Reg 1/2003, Art 23(3).

702   Cases 41/69, etc, *ACF Chemiefarma v Commission* [1970] ECR 661, para 175. For limitation
periods, see para 13.208, below.

703   Cases 32/78, etc, *BMW v Commission* [1979] ECR 2435, [1980] 1 CMLR 370, para 52.

704   Guidelines on the method of setting fines imposed pursuant to Article 23(2)(a) of Regulation
1/2003, OJ 2006 C210/2: Vol II, App B.13.

705   See the criticism made by the CFI in Case T-148/89 *Tréfilunion v Commission* [1995] ECR
II-1063, para 142.

706   Reg 1/2003, Art 23(5) (a provision originally inserted into Reg 17 to meet constitutional
objections raised by some of the original Member States). Fines imposed for infringement of
Art 81(1) have been held in England to be 'penalties' for the purposes of sect 14 of the Civil Evidence
Act 1968 and sect 3 of the Evidence (Proceedings in Other Jurisdiction) Act 1975: *Re Westinghouse
Uranium Contract Litigation* [1978] AC 547 (HL), [1978] 1 All ER 434, [1978] 1 CMLR 100.
Art 23(5) is not determinative of whether proceedings for infringement of Arts 81 or 82 constitute
a 'criminal charge' for the purpose of Art 6 ECHR: see para 13.030, above.

general purpose of fines is to secure the implementation of Community competition policy.[707] Thus, while their immediate object is to 'suppress illegal activities and to prevent any recurrence',[708] the Commission may also use fines as a general deterrent to other undertakings.[709]

(b) Intentional or negligent infringement

13.137 **Generally.** Article 23(2)(a) of Regulation 1/2003 provides that a fine may be imposed only where the infringement is committed 'intentionally' or 'negligently'. There is no clear analysis of the difference between 'intention' and 'negligence' and the Commission's practice is not consistent.[710] In very broad terms the distinction is probably between whether the parties acted deliberately, plainly intending to restrict competition, and whether the parties at least ought to have known that anti-competitive effects would result.[711] However, the characterisation of an infringement as intentional or negligent does not affect the amount of the fine; a fine can therefore be determined without having to decide whether the infringement was intentional or whether it was negligent.[712] In a number of cases there has been an express finding of intentional infringement.[713] On other occasions, the Commission has not sought expressly to characterise the nature of the infringement, relying instead on formulations such as 'intentionally, or at least negligently'.[714] This practice appears to have the support of

---

[707] Cases 100/80, etc, *Musique Diffusion Française v Commission ('Pioneer')* [1983] ECR 1825, [1983] 3 CMLR 221, paras 101–110. A fine cannot be challenged on the basis that fines in similar cases may have been lower: Case T-338/94 *Finnboard v Commission* [1998] ECR II-1617, para 340.

[708] Case 45/69 *Boehringer Mannheim v Commission* [1970] ECR 769, para 53; and AG Mayras in Cases 40/73, etc, *Suiker Unie v Commission* [1975] ECR 1663, 2120, [1976] 1 CMLR 295, 396–397.

[709] *Pioneer* (n 707, above). See also Case T-13/89 *ICI v Commission* [1992] ECR II-1021, para 385.

[710] eg in *Nederlandsche Michelin*, OJ 1981 L353/33, [1982] 1 CMLR 643, it is not clear why the Commission characterised one infringement relating to a dealer bonus as 'at least negligent' and a similar infringement relating to an extra dealer bonus as 'intentional, or at least negligent'. Similarly in *Windsurfing International*, OJ 1983 L229/1, [1984] 1 CMLR 1, without explanation some infringements were characterised as 'negligent', others as 'grossly negligent' and others as 'intentional'.

[711] *Pioneer* (n 707, above); Cases 96/82, etc, *IAZ v Commission* [1983] ECR 3369, [1984] 3 CMLR 276, paras 43–45; Case 322/81 *Michelin v Commission* [1983] ECR 3461, [1985] 1 CMLR 282, para 106; Cases 240/82, etc, *SSI v Commission* [1985] ECR 3831, [1987] 3 CMLR 661.

[712] Case C-137/95P *SPO v Commission* [1996] ECR I-1611, paras 53–57.

[713] See, eg *Woodpulp*, OJ 1985 L85/1, [1985] 3 CMLR 474; *Opel*, OJ 2001 L59/1, [2001] 4 CMLR 1441, para 174 (appeal on other grounds largely dismissed, Case T-368/00 *General Motors Nederland and Opel Nederland v Commission* [2003] ECR II-4491, [2004] 4 CMLR 1302; further appeal dismissed, Case C-551/03P [2006] ECR I-3173, [2006] 5 CMLR 9).

[714] See, eg *Cast iron and steel rolls*, OJ 1983 L317/1, [1984] 1 CMLR 694 ('intentionally, or perhaps in the case of one or two firms in the early stages, at least negligently'); *Irish Sugar*, OJ 1997 L258/1, [1997] 5 CMLR 666; *FEG and TU*, OJ 2000 L39/1, [2000] 4 CMLR 1208.

the Community Courts.[715] Sometimes, the Commission has not formally characterised the nature of the infringement at all.[716]

'Intentionally'. It appears that an intentional infringement requires at least **13.138** the deliberate commission of an act which is designed to achieve anti-competitive ends, or which is committed in the knowledge that plainly anti-competitive effects would ensue.[717] Thus an infringement is not intentional simply because the act complained of was deliberate rather than inadvertent or accidental.[718] For the purpose of establishing intentional infringement an undertaking is liable for the acts of its responsible employees,[719] but it is not necessary to identify any particular individual who acted improperly or who was responsible for the default.[720]

Knowledge of Treaty not prerequisite to intention. While in many cases the **13.139** Commission has established that the parties knew that they were acting contrary to the Treaty,[721] or were apparently reckless as to whether or not their action infringed the Treaty,[722] actual knowledge of the Treaty provisions is not necessary to a finding of intentional infringement. In *Miller*, the Court of Justice said:

'... the clauses in question were adopted or accepted by the applicant and the latter could not have been unaware that they had as their object the restriction of competition between its customers. Consequently, it is of little relevance to establish

---

[715] Cases 40/73, etc, *Suiker Unie v Commission* (n 708, above), paras 606–617, implicitly rejecting the applicants' arguments at pp 1874–1875 (ECR); and see *SPO* (n 712, above).

[716] eg *SSI*, OJ 1982 L232/1, [1982] 3 CMLR 702. On appeal the Commission contended that the infringement had been at least negligent: Cases 240/82, etc, *SSI v Commission* (n 711, above). In cases of price-fixing cartels, the Commission appears to consider such characterisation superfluous: eg COMP/38.337 *Thread*, 14 September 2005 (on appeal Cases T-446/05, etc, *Amann & Söhne and Cousin v Commission*, not yet decided); COMP/38.281 *Raw Tobacco (Italy)*, 20 October 2005, [2006] 4 CMLR 1766 (on appeal, Cases T-11/06, etc, *Romana Tabacchi v Commission*, not yet decided).

[717] *Pioneer* (n 707, above); Cases 96/82, etc, *IAZ v Commission* [1983] ECR 3369, [1984] 3 CMLR 276. In more recent cases, the Commission sometimes uses the phrase 'deliberate and manifest' rather than 'intentional': eg COMP/38/443 *Rubber Chemicals*, 21 December 2005, [2007] 4 CMLR 723, para 334 (on appeal, Cases T-85/06, etc, *General Quimica v Commission*, not yet decided).

[718] Thus the 'intention' found by the Commission in *General Motors*, OJ 1975 L29/14, [1975] 1 CMLR D20, was probably insufficient for a finding of deliberate infringement: see AG Mayras in Case 26/75 *General Motors v Commission* [1975] ECR 1367, 1389, [1976] 1 CMLR 95, 106.

[719] *Pioneer* (n 707, above) para 97. See also Case T-77/92 *Parker Pen v Commission* [1994] ECR II-549, [1995] 5 CMLR 435, paras 77–82, where the undertaking was held to have acted intentionally although the agreement was entered into by one senior employee, who failed, contrary to company policy, to seek legal advice on the contract at issue.

[720] Case C-338/00P *Volkswagen v Commission* [2003] ECR I-9181, [2004] 4 CMLR 351, paras 95–98.

[721] eg because they had been heavily fined before: *Soda-Ash—Solvay, ICI* (n 663, above). See also para 13.160, below.

[722] See, eg *Woodpulp* (n 713, above).

whether the applicant knew that it was infringing the prohibition contained in Article [81].'[723]

Thus ignorance or mistake of law is no bar to the finding of intentional infringement, at least where an anti-competitive intention is plain and obvious.[724] The Commission may regard the existence of a competition law compliance programme as evidence that an undertaking knew that its actions contravened the competition rules.[725] An undertaking's intention may be confirmed by internal documents,[726] but may also be inferred from the fact that anti-competitive consequences will, or will foreseeably, follow from the conduct at issue.[727] A high degree of awareness of antitrust rules is expected of major undertakings.[728]

---

[723] Case 19/77 *Miller v Commission* [1978] ECR 131, [1978] 2 CMLR 334, para 18; see also *IAZ v Commission* (n 717, above) paras 43–45; *BMW v Commission* (n 703, above) paras 40–47; Case T-62/98 *Volkswagen v Commission* [2000] ECR II-2707, [2000] 5 CMLR 853, para 334 (appeal dismissed Case C-338/00P, [2003] ECR I-9189, [2004] 4 CMLR 351); Cases T-202/98, etc, *Tate & Lyle v Commission* [2001] ECR II-2035, [2001] 5 CMLR 859, [2001] All ER (EC) 839, para 127; Cases T-259/02, etc, *Raiffeisen Zentralbank Österreich v Commission*, judgment of 14 December 2006, para 205 (on appeal on other grounds, Cases C-125/07P, C-133/07P, C-135/07P and C-137/07P, not yet decided); see also Case T-65/89 *BPB v Commission* [1993] ECR II-389, [1993] 5 CMLR 32, para 165.

[724] *Kawasaki*, OJ 1979 L16/9, [1979] 1 CMLR 448; *Miller* and *BMW* (n 723, above); *Pioneer* (n 707, above) at 1952 (ECR), 310–311 (CMLR) *per* AG Slynn; *Roofing Felt*, OJ 1986 L232/15, [1991] 4 CMLR 130; Case C-279/87 *Tipp-Ex v Commission* [1990] ECR I-261; *Viho/Toshiba*, OJ 1991 L287/39, [1992] 5 CMLR 180. Parties entering an agreement with the object of price-fixing, or of placing wholesalers outside the exclusive dealing agreement at a competitive disadvantage, will be regarded as intentionally infringing Art 81: Case T-5/00 *FEG & TU v Commission* [2003] ECR II-5761, [2004] 5 CMLR 969, para 396. Similarly an agreement with the object of market-sharing and impeding imports (even if the parties – who were small – may not have recognised it as being anti-competitive): Cases T-49/02, etc, *Brasserie Nationale v Commission* [2005] ECR II-3033, [2006] 4 CMLR 266, paras 155 *et seq*. The fact that the infringement involves professional services is irrelevant, since such services are plainly subject to the competition rules in the Treaty: COMP/38.549 *Belgian Architects*, 24 June 2004, [2005] 4 CMLR 677, para 125.

[725] *British Sugar/Tate & Lyle/Napier Brown*, OJ 1999 L76/1, [1999] 4 CMLR 1316, para 192 (appeals largely dismissed Cases T-202/98, etc, *Tate & Lyle v Commission* [2001] ECR II-2035, [2001] 5 CMLR 859, [2001] All ER (EC) 839 and Cases C-359/01P *British Sugar v Commission* [2004] ECR I-4933, [2004] 5 CMLR 329).

[726] *VW-Audi*, OJ 1998 L72/60, [1998] 5 CMLR 33, para 214 (internal minutes demonstrated VW's knowledge that its conduct was contrary to the competition rules); *FEG & TU* (n 724, above) para 398 (internal note to the effect that Dutch competition law would prohibit the practices in question); COMP/38.233 *Wanadoo Interactive*, 16 July 2003, [2005] 5 CMLR 120, para 397 (internal documents showed company not unaware of risks of below-cost selling) (appeal on other grounds dismissed, Case T-340/03 *France Télécom v Commission* [2007] 4 CMLR 919. COMP/37.507 *AstraZeneca*, 15 June 2005, [2006] 5 CMLR 287, para 907 (internal document referred to free movement and competition provisions of the Treaty) (on appeal Case T-321/05 *AstraZeneca v Commission*, not yet decided). See also the UK Competition Appeal Tribunal in *Napp Pharmaceuticals Holdings Ltd v Director General of Fair Trading* [2002] CAT 1, [2002] CompAR 13, para 456.

[727] See *Napp*, above.

[728] *AstraZeneca*, above; *Belgian Beer Cartel Interbrew and Alken-Maes*, OJ 2003 L200/1, [2004] 4 CMLR 80, para 343 (basic amount of the fine multiplied by a factor of five for Interbrew and by a factor of two for Alken-Maes to take account of the fact that Interbrew, as a large international

'Negligently'. An infringement is probably committed negligently when the **13.140** undertaking concerned could reasonably foresee that its conduct would have anti-competitive effects of the kind prohibited by Article 81(1) or Article 82.[729] A negligent infringement may also occur when the conduct complained of is inadvertent, for example, where an export ban is maintained in error.[730] The fact that particular conduct has not previously been found to be in breach of the Treaty does not necessarily absolve an undertaking from negligence, at least where the anti-competitive effects of the conduct are foreseeable.[731] Although in the 1970s the Commission had sometimes found that the absence of any previous decision may rebut negligence and therefore remove the jurisdiction to impose a fine,[732] the Commission's subsequent practice has been to regard the novelty of a decision finding an infringement as a matter of mitigation that may lead to no penalty, or only a nominal fine, being imposed.[733]

Awareness to be expected from the parties. Advocate General Warner has sug- **13.141** gested that all undertakings should be taken to be aware of the law as laid down by

---

undertaking and Alken-Maes as a member of an international group 'have easier access to legal and economic knowledge and infrastructures which enable them more easily to recognise that their coduct constitutes an infringement and be aware of the consequences stemming from it under competition law' (on appeal small reduction in fine: Case T-38/02 *Groupe Danone v Commission* [2005] ECR II-4407, [2006] 4 CMLR 1428; further appeal dismissed C-3/06P [2007] 4 CMLR 701).

[729] See AG Mayras in Case 26/75 *General Motors v Commission* (n 718, above). Note in particular *BMW Belgium*, OJ 1978 L46/33, 42, [1978] 2 CMLR 126, 143, where the Commission considered that the BMW dealers other than those represented by the Belgium BMW Dealers Advisory Committee had acted negligently because on 'reasonable reflection, they should have realised without difficulty that in signing the circular letter they agreed to a general export prohibition which went beyond the needs of a selective distribution system and thereby infringed the competition rules of the EEC Treaty'; upheld on appeal in *BMW v Commission* (n 703, above). See also *SSI v Commission* (n 711, above) (participants could not overlook fact that their conduct restricted competition in a way likely to affect trade between Member States); *Windsurfing International*, OJ 1983 L229/1, [1984] 1 CMLR 1 (licensor 'negligent' in maintaining certain restrictions in patent licence after scope of patent had been decided under national law: negligence upheld on appeal in Case 193/83 *Windsurfing v Commission* [1986] ECR 611, [1986] 3 CMLR 489); Case C-277/87 *Sandoz v Commission* [1990] ECR I-45.

[730] *Deutsche Philips*, OJ 1973 L293/40, [1973] CMLR D241. Similarly an undertaking could still be guilty of negligent infringement if employees acted in disregard of standing instructions designed to ensure compliance with the competition rules, although the existence of such instructions may lead to a reduction in the fine. On the other hand, the existence of such instructions may go to show that the undertaking knew that what it was doing was contrary to the competition rules: *Irish Sugar* (n 714, above).

[731] See, eg *Zoja/CSC—ICI*, OJ 1972 L299/51, [1973] CMLR D50, on appeal Cases 6 & 7/73 *Commercial Solvents v Commission* (n 673, above).

[732] eg *Fourth Report on Competition Policy* (1974), point 64, discussing *IFTRA Glass Containers*, OJ 1974 L160/1, [1974] 2 CMLR D50; *Franco-Japanese Ballbearings*, OJ 1974 L343/19, [1975] 1 CMLR D8; *Preserved Mushrooms*, OJ 1975 L29/26, [1975] 1 CMLR D83 (as to Taiwanese parties); *Vegetable Parchment*, OJ 1978 L70/54, [1978] 1 CMLR 534, 551.

[733] See para 13.170, below. But see also *DSD*, OJ 2001 L166/1, [2001] 5 CMLR 609 (upheld on appeal, Cases T-151 & 289/01 *Duales System Deutschland v Commission* [2007] 5 CMLR 300, 356, where no fine was imposed in an Art 82 case without any explanation of the reason.

the Treaties, by implementing Regulations and perhaps by decisions of the Courts,[734] and the Commission is prepared to fix undertakings with knowledge of its own previous decisions[735] as well as those of the Courts. The Commission considers that an undertaking's management has the responsibility to establish effective internal rules for compliance with EC competition law. The nature and extent of such rules will vary from enterprise to enterprise and also from one part of the enterprise to another.[736] Even small undertakings are expected to know the basic Treaty rules, for example on export bans,[737] as are non-EC undertakings.[738] A high degree of antitrust awareness is expected from major undertakings, especially those which enjoy a dominant position.[739] Conversely, in some early cases a lower degree of awareness of general competition law was imputed to individuals or small undertakings,[740] although it is unlikely that even a small company could now hope to persuade the Commission that it was not aware of, for example, the law relating to price-fixing cartels.

13.142   Rebutting intention or negligence.   An undertaking is not guilty of intentional or negligent infringement if it relies reasonably on a public communication made by the Commission.[741] The same would appear true as regards reasonable reliance

---

[734] *Miller* (n 723, above) 160 (ECR), 345 (CMLR).

[735] See, eg *AEG—Telefunken*, OJ 1982 L117/15, 27, [1982] 2 CMLR 386; *AROW/BNIC*, OJ 1982 L379/1, 13, [1983] 2 CMLR 240; *Toltecs/Dorcet*, OJ 1982 L379/19, 28, [1983] 1 CMLR 412; *Windsurfing International*, OJ 1983 L229/1, [1984] 1 CMLR 1.

[736] *Viho/Toshiba* (n 724, above).

[737] eg note the fines for export bans imposed on the distributors in *BMW Belgium* (n 729, above); in *Hasselblad*, OJ 1982 L161/18, [1982] 2 CMLR 233; and in *Windsurfing International* (n 735, above).

[738] Among many examples, see *Woodpulp* (n 713, above) where all the participants were outside the Community. In *Austrian Banks* (n 666, above) paras 494 *et seq*, the Commission held that undertakings in new Member States cannot invoke their lack of knowledge of Community law to avoid liability to fines.

[739] See, eg *Nederlandsche Banden Industrie Michelin*, OJ 1981 L353/33, [1982] 1 CMLR 643, para 56: NBIM as part of the Michelin group was expected to 'follow developments in European law attentively and gear its policy to them'. In *Michelin*, OJ 2002 L143/1, [2002] 5 CMLR 388, para 352, the Commission referred to Michelin's previous infringements and the existence of an in-house legal department as support for categorising the infringement as intentional. Note also Case 27/76 *United Brands v Commission* [1978] ECR 207, [1978] 1 CMLR 429, para 299 ('UBC . . . [being] engaged for a very long time in international and national trade, has special knowledge of anti-trust laws and has already experienced their severity'); Case 85/76 *Hoffmann-La Roche v Commission* [1979] ECR 461, [1979] 3 CMLR 211, paras 128 *et seq*; cf AG Reischl ibid at 595 (ECR), 257 (CMLR) *et seq*. See also *Methylglutamine*, OJ 2004 L38/18, [2004] 4 CMLR 1591, para 239.

[740] See, eg *Toltecs/Dorcet* (n 735, above) (in relation to Segers); *Roofing Felt* (n 724, above) (even by 1978 the members, particularly the smaller ones, may have been unaware that a 'national' cartel was prohibited by Art 81(1)).

[741] Cases 40/73, etc, *Suiker Unie v Commission* (n 708, above) paras 555–557; Case 19/77 *Miller v Commission* (n 723, above) *per* AG Warner (on the facts no reliance on public communication); *Ford Agricultural*, OJ 1993 L20/1, [1995] 5 CMLR 89 (Commission's action contributed to allowing Ford to believe its conduct was legitimate). It is not clear how far the parties would be

on views communicated to the undertaking by the Commission.[742] Similarly, a fine might not be imposed if the undertaking reasonably but incorrectly believed itself to be covered by a block exemption.[743] But much will turn on the Commission's assessment of the reasonableness of the reliance.[744] Further, ignorance or mistake of law is no defence.[745]

Involuntary infringement. It is irrelevant to the question of intent or negli- **13.143** gence that the undertaking may have been forced into participation in the infringement by its competitors or because of its market position.[746] But, depending on the circumstances, the Commission may reduce the fine or impose no fine.[747]

(c) The calculation of the fine

Generally. Having established that the infringement was intentional or negli- **13.144** gent, the Commission is required under Article 23(3) of Regulation 1/2003 to take into account both the gravity and the duration of the infringement in setting the amount of the fine.[748] The Court of Justice has indicated that the gravity of an infringement:

'has to be determined by reference to numerous factors such as, in particular, the particular circumstances of the case, its context, and the dissuasive effect of fines; moreover, no binding or exhaustive list of criteria which must be applied has been drawn up.'[749]

---

immune from the imposition of fines in cases where, eg a Commission Notice has been overtaken by subsequent case law. If a Notice is formally withdrawn (such as the Patent Notice withdrawn with effect from 1 January 1985, OJ 1984 C220/14) it presumably cannot be relied on for the future.

[742] See, eg *Hasselblad* (n 737, above) at para 72 of the Decision (reliance not reasonable in circumstances); *Soda-Ash—Solvay*, OJ 1991 L152/21, [1994] 4 CMLR 454, para 71 (possibility that Solvay was led to believe that exclusive purchasing contracts limited to 85 per cent of requirements would not be abusive). See also the UK OFT decision in *Lladró Comercial* [2003] UKCLR 652, para 124 (no penalty imposed under parallel provisions in the UK Competition Act as Lladró reasonably (albeit, according to the OFT and the Commission, incorrectly) interpreted a Commission letter to it as including a favourable competition assessment of its agreement).

[743] This appears on the facts to have been the case in *BP Kemi—DDSF*, OJ 1979 L286/32, [1979] 3 CMLR 684.

[744] eg *Hasselblad* (n 737, above).

[745] Case 125/78 *GEMA v Commission* [1979] ECR 3173, [1980] 2 CMLR 177. But if the law is unclear a fine may not be imposed until it has been clarified: see para 13.169, below.

[746] Case T-50/00 *Dalmine v Commission* [2004] ECR II-2395, para 333 (appeal dismissed Case C-407/04P *Dalmine v Commission* judgment of 25 January 2007); Cases T-25/95, etc, *Cimenteries CBR v Commission* [2000] ECR II-491, [2000] 5 CMLR 204, para 2557.

[747] See para 13.170, below.

[748] The same criteria applied under Art 15(2) of Reg 17. For a table of fines imposed in the period 1996–June 2005, see Ortiz Blanco (ed), *EC Competition Procedure* (2006), Appdx 14.

[749] Case C-137/95P *SPO v Commission* (n 712, above) para 54; Case C-219/95P *Ferrière Nord v Commission* [1997] ECR I-2411, [1997] 5 CMLR 575, para 33; Case T-334/94 *Sarrió v Commission* [1998] ECR I-1439, [1998] 5 CMLR 195, para 328.

However, the Court of Justice has indicated that these criteria include:

' . . . the nature of the restrictions on competition, the number and size of the undertakings concerned, the respective proportions of the market controlled by them within the Community and the situation of the market when the infringement was committed.'[750]

The Court of Justice has also said:

' . . . regard must be had to a large number of factors, the nature and importance of which vary according to the type of infringement in question and the particular circumstances of the case. Those factors may, depending on the circumstances, include the volume and value of the goods in respect of which the infringement was committed and the size and economic power of the undertaking and, consequently, the influence which the undertaking was able to exert on the market.'[751]

In addition:

' . . . regard must be had to the duration of the infringements established and to all the factors capable of affecting the gravity of the infringements, such as the conduct of each of the undertakings, the role played by each of them in the establishment of the concerted practices, the profit which they were able to derive from those practices, their size, the value of the goods concerned and the threat that infringements of that type pose to the objectives of the Community.'[752]

13.145　**Discretion of the Commission.**　Since the fines are an instrument of its competition policy, the Commission is allowed a margin of discretion when fixing their amount in order that it may best direct undertakings towards compliance with the competition rules.[753] The role of the Court of First Instance in review under Article 229 of the Treaty is to verify that the amount of the fine is proportionate to the duration of the infringement and to the various factors capable of affecting the assessment of its gravity.[754] The Commission's practice in previous cases does not serve as a legal framework for fines in competition matters,[755] and it is free to change the weight that it gives to particular factors in its assessment of gravity.[756]

---

[750] *Boehringer Mannheim* (n 708, above) para 53.

[751] *Pioneer* (n 707, above) para 120; to the same effect Case 322/81 *Michelin v Commission* (n 711, above) para 111; *IAZ v Commission* (n 717, above) para 52.

[752] *Pioneer* (n 707, above) para 129.

[753] Case T-150/89 *Martinelli v Commission* [1995] ECR II-1165, para 59; Case T-49/95 *Van Megen Sports v Commission* [1996] ECR 1799, [1997] 4 CMLR 843, para 53; Case T-229/94 *Deutsche Bahn v Commission* [1997] ECR II-1689, [1998] 4 CMLR 220, para 127.

[754] ibid; *Pioneer* (n 707, above) paras 120 and 129. The CFI has observed that it is desirable that the decision's reasoning should enable the undertakings to determine in detail the method of calculation of the fines imposed on them: Case T-148/89 *Tréfilunion v Commission* [1995] ECR II-1063, para 142. In Case T-141/94 *Thyssen Stahl v Commission* [1999] ECR II-347, [1999] 4 CMLR 810, the Commission's decision was upheld after examining in detail additional figures produced during the proceedings before the CFI (paras 610–611).

[755] Case T-52/02 *SNCZ v Commission* [2005] ECR II-5005, [2006] 4 CMLR 1069, para 77.

[756] Case T-347/94 *Meyr-Melnhof v Commission* [1998] ECR II-1751, para 368; Case T-241/01 *SAS v Commission* [2005] ECR II-2917, [2005] 5 CMLR 922, para 132 (fact that Commission may have taken a less serious view in the past of the type of infringement at issue irrelevant).

The Commission cannot be criticised for failing to mark infringements of comparable gravity in different cases with fines that represent the same proportion of turnover.[757] Moreover, the Commission is entitled to increase the general level of fines if, for example, it believes that such an increase is necessary to achieve a deterrent effect in the light of the frequency of contraventions of the competition rules.[758] However, any significant change of approach by the Commission requires detailed explanation.[759] The Commission must set out in its decision the factors which it took into account to determine the gravity and duration of the infringement but it need not set out the detailed quantification of the fine.[760]

The Commission's Guidelines on Fines. The Commission published its first **13.146** Guidelines on the level of fines in January 1998.[761] In June 2006 it issued revised Guidelines[762] which differ from the 1998 Guidelines in a number of important respects. The 2006 Guidelines on Fines apply in all cases where a statement of objections is notified after 1 September 2006.[763] The following parts of this Section set out the structure of the 2006 Guidelines on Fines and then discuss the various factors mentioned in them in the light of the case law.

Retroactive application of revised Guidelines. The marked increase in fines **13.147** brought about by the 1998 Guidelines, and the similar increase expected to result from the application of the 2006 Guidelines on Fines, has given rise to the question whether their immediate application to all subsequent fining decisions (including decisions relating to conduct during periods before the Guidelines were promulgated) violates the principle of non-retroactivity or (by giving rise to differences in treatment of identical infringements depending on when the decision was taken) the principle of equal treatment. Those questions were settled in the Commission's favour by the Court of Justice's judgments concerning the *Pre-Insulated Pipes* cartel[764] and in *Archer Daniels Midland (amino acids)*.[765] The Court held that it was reasonably foreseeable that the Commission might alter its fining policy at any time and that no legitimate expectation could arise

---

[757] *SNCZ v Commission* (n 755, above) para 79.

[758] *Pioneer* (n 707, above) paras 105–108; *Sarrió* (n 749, above) para 331.

[759] Case 73/74 *Papiers Peints* [1975] ECR 1491, [1976] 1 CMLR 589, para 31.

[760] *Sarrió* (n 749, above) para 73; but providing information as to the actual calculation is nonetheless desirable in the interests of transparency: ibid, paras 76–77 (and to the same effect the ECJ judgments delivered on the same day in the other *Cartonboard* appeals).

[761] Guidelines on the method of setting fines, OJ 1998 C9/3: Vol II, App B.5.

[762] Guidelines on the method of setting fines, OJ 2006 C210/2: Vol II, App B.13. See Wils, 'The European Commission's 2006 Guidelines on Antitrust Fines: A Legal and Economic Analysis' (2007) 30 World Competition 197.

[763] Being the date the Guidelines were published in the *Official Journal*: see 2006 Guidelines on Fines, para 38.

[764] Cases C-189/02P, etc, *Dansk Rørindustri* [2005] ECR I-5425, [2005] 5 CMLR 796, paras 222–229.

[765] Case C-397/03P *Archer Daniels Midland v Commission* [2006] ECR I-4429, [2006] 5 CMLR 230, paras 15 *et seq.*

that fining would not be based on a new policy. Moreover, the fact that the Commission was free to increase the level of fines at any time meant that the plea of breach of the principle of equal treatment could not succeed.

(d) Basic amount

13.148 **The basic amount: the 2006 Guidelines on Fines.** Under the 2006 Guidelines on Fines, the Commission starts by setting a 'basic amount'.[766] The 2006 Guidelines on Fines mark a return to the Commission's practice[767] before the issue of the 1998 Guidelines of determining the amount of the fine (except in cases where nominal fines were imposed) by reference to a turnover figure; that is to say, the amount of the fine would be determined by multiplying the turnover figure by a percentage determined by reference to the gravity of the violation. The turnover figure chosen for this purpose before 1998 was usually[768] the undertaking's turnover in the relevant product and geographical market.[769] One difficulty with that method was that, since the relevant turnover figure was usually considered to be a business secret,[770] it could not be mentioned in the published version of the decision (nor notified to other addressees of the decision in cases with more than one defendant undertaking). This made it difficult to know what proportion of turnover the fine represented in any particular case. One policy objection to an approach based on turnover is that there is no obvious reason in principle why the level of a fine should be directly related to a turnover figure; it is not clear that turnover is a good proxy for the harm caused by a violation although it may be related to the gain which the undertaking expected to make from the infringement.[771] In *Pioneer*, the Court of Justice stated that, while it was permissible for the

---

[766] 2006 Guidelines on Fines (n 762, above) para 10.

[767] See, eg *Cartonboard*, OJ 1994 L243/1, [1994] 5 CMLR 353; and *Cement Cartel*, OJ 1994 L343/1, [1995] 4 CMLR 327 (on appeal Cases T-25/95, etc, n 746, above).

[768] But not invariably: see *Benelux Flat Glass*, OJ 1984 L212/13, [1985] 2 CMLR 350 (fines on BSN and Saint-Gobain assessed on flat glass turnover in other countries as well as Benelux; fines on other parties assessed on Benelux turnover only); *ECS/AKZO (No. 2)*, OJ 1985 L374/1, [1986] 3 CMLR 273 (fine of 10 million ECUs represented just under 10 per cent of AKZO's total turnover in the UK but appears to have been very high in relation to AKZO's UK turnover in the products affected by the infringement; reduced on appeal to 7.5 million ECUs, Case C-62/86, [1991] ECR I-3359, [1993] 5 CMLR 215); Case T-30/89 *Hilti v Commission* [1991] ECR II-1439, [1992] 4 CMLR 16 (Hilti sought a reduction of fine on the grounds that it was well over 10 per cent of Hilti's EC turnover in the relevant product market but the CFI rejected this argument in the light of the gravity of the infringement).

[769] In cases where the Commission bases the level of the fine upon a turnover figure, it must take into account the fact that the figure is abnormally high in the relevant year for a particular undertaking and reduce the fine accordingly: Case T-142/89 *Boël v Commission* [1995] ECR II-867. cf Case T-319/94 *Fiskeby Board v Commission* [1998] ECR II-1331; the Commission is entitled to take into account intra-group sales by the undertaking: Case T-304/94 *Europa Carton v Commission* [1998] ECR II-869, paras 120–131.

[770] As to which, see para 13.095, above.

[771] See Wils (n 762, above).

Commission to have regard to the total turnover of the undertaking and to the percentage of that turnover accounted for by the products in respect of which the infringement was committed, it was important not to accord disproportionate importance to either figure: the fixing of a fine should not be derived from a simple calculation based on turnover.[772] Nonetheless, the Commission is permitted to have regard both to total turnover and to turnover in the relevant market in setting the fine.[773]

Value of sales. According to the 2006 Guidelines on Fines, the basic amount **13.149** will constitute a proportion of the 'value of sales', adjusted for duration. The value of sales is defined as the undertaking's sales of goods or services to which the infringement directly or indirectly relates in the relevant geographic area within the EEA. The Commission will normally take the sales made by the undertaking during the last full business year of its participation in the infringement.[774] The Commission does not refer to the value of sales in the 'relevant market' in this context; in particular it makes it clear[775] that in a horizontal cartel case sales of goods or services whose prices are based on the price of the cartelised product will be included in the 'value of sales'. In any event, the Commission is not obliged precisely to define the relevant market in relation to agreements with an anti-competitive object.[776] It has also been held that it was not obliged to reach a precise market definition for the purposes of setting a fine under the 1998 Guidelines.[777]

Appropriate proportion of the value of sales. As a general rule, the proportion **13.150** of sales taken into account will be set at a level of up to 30 per cent.[778] The proportion set will depend on the gravity of the infringement.[779] The 2006 Guidelines on Fines give a (non-exhaustive) list of factors to which the Commission will have regard: the nature of the infringement; the combined market share of all the undertakings concerned; the geographic scope of the infringement; and whether or not the infringement has been implemented.[780]

---

772 *Musique Diffusion Française ('Pioneer')* (n 707, above) para 121. See also *Dansk Rørindustri* (n 764, above) para 260. Now that the 2006 Guidelines on Fines have reverted to an approach essentially based on relevant turnover, care will have to be taken by the Commission to avoid a mechanical approach.

773 *Parker Pen* (n 719, above) para 94.

774 2006 Guidelines on Fines, para 13.

775 See fn to the word 'indirectly', ibid.

776 See paras 2.097 and 4.006, above.

777 *SAS v Commission* (n 756, above) para 99; Case T-48/02 *Brouwerij Haacht v Commission* [2005] ECR II-5259, [2006] 4 CMLR 621, para 59.

778 2006 Guidelines on Fines, para 21. The Commission does not explain in what circumstances the proportion might be set at more than 30 per cent, but an example might be where the undertaking's turnover in the last year of the infringement was abnormally low.

779 2006 Guidelines on Fines, para 19.

780 ibid, para 22.

13.151 **Approximation.** The 2006 Guidelines on Fines provide that the Commission may set an identical basic amount for undertakings participating in the same infringement where their value of sales is similar but not identical. Further, the Commission states that it will use rounded figures.[781]

13.152 **Basic amount: the 1998 and 2006 Guidelines on Fines compared.** The main difference made by the 2006 Guidelines on Fines is that the basic amount of the fine will now be determined as a proportion of 'value of sales'. Under the 1998 Guidelines, a particular range of basic amounts, in euros, was set for each category of seriousness (minor, serious and very serious). This system had the effect of bearing disproportionately on smaller undertakings.[782] However, the Commission's decision to move to a value of sales basis is a policy decision on its part: Article 23 of Regulation 1/2003 does not oblige the Commission to set fines by reference to turnover (whether total turnover or relevant market turnover) although it imposes a cap by reference to total turnover.[783] The difference between the 1998 and 2006 Guidelines on Fines in this respect should not be exaggerated. First, in cases where the market was relatively small, the Commission would set a fine at a level that reflected that fact.[784] Secondly, the 1998 Guidelines themselves provided that the basic amount would be set so as to 'take account of the effective capacity of offenders to cause significant damage to other operators, in particular consumers'.[785] Where a number of undertakings were fined for the same infringement (as in cartel cases), the 1998 Guidelines contemplated that it might be necessary in some cases to apply weightings to the amounts determined for gravity in order to take account of the real impact on competition of the offending conduct of each undertaking. This was particularly so where there was considerable disparity between the sizes[786] of the undertakings committing infringements of the

---

[781] ibid, para 26.

[782] See Speech by Commissioner Kroes, 7 April 2005 'The First Hundred Days', SPEECH/05/205: 'what does puzzle me is the rigidity of the present [1998] guidelines. The current system of fixed minima according to the gravity of the infringement appears to hit small and medium sized enterprises harder than larger businesses. If an ongoing analysis of the evidence proves this perception, I will not hesitate to look at ways to improve the current guidelines in this respect'.

[783] *Dansk Rørindustri* (n 764, above) para 312.

[784] eg COMP/38.337 *Thread*, decn of 14 September 2005 (on appeal Cases T-446/05 *Amann & Söhne and Cousin v Commission*, Case T-448/05 *Oxley Threads v Commission*, T-452/05 *Belgian Sewing Thread v Commission*, T-456/05 *Gütermann v Commission*, T-457/05 *Zwicky v Commission*, not yet decided); *Seamless steel tubes*, OJ 2003 L140/1.

[785] 1998 Guidelines on Fines (n 761, above) para 1A.

[786] In assessing 'size' under the 1998 Guidelines, the Commission was entitled to take account of total turnover or relevant turnover. See Case T-224/00 *Archer Daniels Midland v Commission* ('*Amino acids*') [2003] ECR II-2597, [2003] 5 CMLR 583, para 187: 'It is appropriate to observe that the [1998] Guidelines do not provide that fines are to be calculated according to the overall turnover of undertakings or their turnover in the relevant market. However, nor do they preclude the Commission from taking either figure into account in determining the amount of the fine in order to ensure compliance with the general principles of Community law and where circumstances

same type.[787] Thirdly, the 1998 Guidelines referred to the need for a fine to be set at a level which had a sufficiently deterrent effect.[788] This would in some cases lead the Commission to multiply the fine[789] imposed on undertakings with a larger overall turnover than others with a similar turnover in the relevant market.

Hard-core cartels. The 2006 Guidelines on Fines state that horizontal price-fixing, market-sharing and output-restriction agreements, which are usually secret, are, by their very nature, among the most harmful restrictions of competition. As a matter of policy, they will be heavily fined. Therefore, the proportion of the value of sales taken into account for such infringements will generally be set at the higher end of the scale, that is at or near 30 per cent.[790] This reflects the approach in the 1998 Guidelines, regarding such agreements as 'very serious' infringements, although in practice that principle was not always applied.[791]   **13.153**

Basic amount: seriousness of infringements. One difference between the 2006   **13.154**
and 1998 Guidelines is that the 1998 Guidelines required an infringement to be categorised as 'very serious', 'serious' or 'minor'. The 1998 Guidelines contain the following indicative list of which types of infringement would fall into which category:

> '*Minor infringements:* These might be trade restrictions, usually of a vertical nature, but with a limited market impact and affecting only a substantial but relatively limited part of the Community market.'

> '*Serious infringements:* These will more often than not be horizontal or vertical restrictions of the same type as above but more rigorously applied, with a wider market impact, and with effects in extensive areas of the common market. However, these might also be abuse of a dominant position (refusals to supply, discrimination,

---

demand it' (appeal dismissed, Case C-397/03P *Archer Daniels Midland Co v Commission*, [2006] ECR I-4429, [2006] 5 CMLR 230). This statement was approved by the ECJ in *Dansk Rørindustri* (n 764, above) para 258. In *SAS v Commission* (n 756, above) para 166, the CFI said that 'the Commission is free to take into account the turnover figure of its choice, provided it does not appear unreasonable by reference to the circumstances of the case'.

[787] Case T-224/00 *Archer Daniels Midland*, above, para 186.
[788] 1998 Guidelines on Fines (n 761, above) para 1A.
[789] *Brouwerij Haacht* (n 777, above) paras 61–67.
[790] 2006 Guidelines on Fines (n 762, above) para 23.
[791] See, eg *Luxembourg Brewing Industry*, OJ 2002 L253/21, [2002] 5 CMLR 1279 (agreement confined to Luxembourg only 'serious'), appeals dismissed Cases T-49/02, etc, *Brasserie Nationale v Commission* [2005] ECR II-3033, [2006] 4 CMLR 266; see also COMP/37.750 *French Beer*, 22 December 2004, OJ 2005 L184/57, [2006] 4 CMLR 577. cf *Austrian Banks (Lombard Agreement)*, OJ 2004 L56/1, [2004] 5 CMLR 399 ('very serious' infringement despite limitation to Austria). The facts that a cartel relates only to 'reference' rather than actual prices, and is informal and without an effective enforcement mechanism, do not make it less serious: Case T-64/02 *Heubach v Commission* [2005] ECR II-5137, [2006] 4 CMLR 1157.

exclusion, loyalty discounts made by dominant firms in order to shut competitors out of the market, etc).[792]

'*Very serious infringements:* These will generally be horizontal restrictions such as price cartels and market-sharing quotas, or other practices which jeopardize the proper functioning of the single market, such as the partitioning of national markets[793] and clear-cut abuse of a dominant position by undertakings holding a virtual monopoly.'

Although the 2006 Guidelines on Fines are not based on this three-fold classification, it is nonetheless likely that the Commission will adopt a similar approach when it comes to determining the appropriate point in the range from 0–30 per cent of value of sales at which the basic amount should be set.[794] The Court of First Instance has held that the seriousness of an infringement does not depend on the proportion of EEA sales affected by the infringement.[795] It is not necessary for the Commission to demonstrate the actual effects of an agreement with an anti-competitive purpose, and it is entitled to estimate the probability of its having had substantial adverse effects.[796]

13.155   **Duration of infringement.**   The 2006 Guidelines on Fines provide that the basic amount will be multiplied by the number of years in which the undertaking was involved in the infringement, with periods of less than six months being counted as six months, and periods of over six months but less than a year being counted as a year.[797] This represents a marked difference from the approach adopted by the 1998 Guidelines,[798] which was that (a) in the case of infringements of medium duration (that is to say of between one and five years), the amount determined for gravity would be increased by up to 50 per cent; and (b) in the case of infringements of long duration (more than five years) the amount determined for gravity would be increased by up to 10 per cent per year.

---

[792] See COMP/38.113 *Tomra*, 29 March 2006, [2006] 4 CMLR 1417 (loyalty rebates and foreclosure agreements a serious abuse). As regards predatory pricing, see COMP/38.233 *Wanadoo Interactive*, 16 July 2003, [2005] 5 CMLR 120 (appeal dismissed, Case T-340/03 *France Télécom v Commission* [2007] 4 CMLR 919).

[793] eg COMP/36.623 *Peugeot*, 7 December 2005, [2005] 5 CMLR 120, [2006] 5 CMLR 714 (restrictions on dealers selling cars to non-Dutch purchasers, on appeal Case T-450/05, not yet decided); *Raiffeisen Zentralbank Österreich* (n 723, above) paras 249–265.

[794] See para 13.153, above. In addition to cartels, distribution agreements that partition the Community will also be regarded as serious infringements (eg COMP/37.980 *Souris – Topps*, 26 May 2004, OJ 2006 L353/5, [2006] 4 CMLR 1713 (concerning the distribution of Pokémon collectibles) as will resale price maintenance: COMP/37.975 *Yamaha*, decn of 16 July 2003, see Press Release IP/03/1028.

[795] Case T-38/02 *Groupe Danone v Commission* [2005] ECR II-4407, [2006] 4 CMLR 1428, para 191; see also Case T-241/00 *SAS v Commission* (n 756, above) (market-sharing agreement very serious even though only certain routes to and from Denmark affected).

[796] *SAS v Commission* (n 756, above) para 122.

[797] 2006 Guidelines on Fines, para 24.

[798] 1998 Guidelines on Fines, para 1B.

Legal considerations affecting duration. Under Article 23(3) of Regulation **13.156** 1/2003, duration and gravity are separate matters which must both be taken into account. The Commission is therefore entitled to impose a substantial increase for duration even where the infringement is categorised as very serious and is conceived as a long-term infringement.[799] Since Article 23(3) specifically refers to the duration of an infringement, the Commission must clearly indicate to the parties the period in respect of which it proposes to make a finding of infringement.[800] Further, the Commission's finding must be limited to the period for which it has evidence of infringement.[801] However, the duration of a cartel agreement is to be determined by reference to the existence of the agreement (which is the fact that constitutes the infringement) and not by the period in which it was implemented.[802] Even where the infringement varies in seriousness over time, the Commission is entitled not to take that into account in assessing the increase based on duration.[803] Fines may be mitigated if an infringement is prolonged as a

[799] Cases T-236/01, etc, *Tokai Carbon v Commission (Graphite Electrodes)* [2004] ECR II-1181, [2004] 5 CMLR 1465, para 259 (Commission's further appeal allowed on other grounds, Case C-301/04P *Commission v SGL Carbon* [2006] ECR I-5915, [2006] 5 CMLR 877; other appeals dismissed, Cases C-289/04P *Showa Denko v Commission* and C-308/04P *SGL Carbon v Commission* [2006] ECR I-5859, 5977, [2006] 5 CMLR 840, 922); Case T-64/02 *Heubach v Commission* [2006] ECR II-5127, [2006] 4 CMLR 1157, para 45. It is not necessary that the duration of the arrangement of itself caused harm to the Community interest: Cases T-202/98, etc, *Tate & Lyle v Commission* (n 725, above) para 106 (appeal on other grounds dismissed, Cases C-359/01P, ibid).

[800] *Pioneer* (n 707, above) paras 15–16. cf Case 226/84 *British Leyland v Commission* [1986] ECR 3263, [1987] 1 CMLR 184, where the ECJ held that the Commission had sufficiently indicated the duration despite some ambiguity that had arisen during the administrative proceedings. The burden of proving the end date of the infringement lies with the Commission: Case T-120/04 *Peróxidos Orgánicos v Commission* [2007] 4 CMLR 153; and if the Commission fails to adduce evidence, an inference adverse to its case may be drawn: Case T-44/00 *Mannesmannröhren-Werke v Commission* [2004] ECR II-2223, para 263.

[801] Case 85/76 *Hoffmann-La Roche v Commission* [1979] ECR 461, [1979] 3 CMLR 211; see also Cases T-24/93, etc, *Compagnie Maritime Belge Transports v Commission* [1996] ECR II-1201, [1997] 4 CMLR 273, para 241 (appeal on other grounds partially allowed: Cases C-395 & 396/96P, [2000] ECR I-1365, [2000] 4 CMLR 1076, [2000] All ER (EC) 385). But it is easy to infer continuation of a cartel agreement in circumstances where no positive action is taken to bring it to an end: see, eg Cases C-65 & 73/02P *ThyssenKrupp Stainless v Commission* [2005] ECR I-6773, [2005] 5 CMLR 773, paras 31–39. The fact that cartel meetings have ceased does not prove that the agreement has come to an end: *SAS v Commission* (n 756, above) para 193. It is also possible for the Commission to find that there was a continuous agreement between two separate contacts between the parties if those contacts are sufficiently close in time; Case T-61/99 *Adriatica v Commission* [2003] ECR II-5349, [2005] 5 CMLR 1843, para 125 (appeal dismissed Case C-111/04P, [2006] ECR I-22).

[802] Case T-213/00 *CMA CGM v Commission ('FETTCSA')* [2003] ECR II-913, [2003] 5 CMLR 268, para 280; *SAS v Commission* (n 756, above) para 186; *Brasserie Nationale v Commission* (n 724, above) para 185.

[803] Case T-203/01 *Michelin v Commission* [2003] ECR II-4071, [2004] 4 CMLR 923, para 278 (although this case concerns the rather smaller uplifts for duration under the 1998 Guidelines). Note that the Commission must take account of a period when the cartel failed to reach agreement on prices and prices fell drastically as part of its assessment of seriousness: Case T-279/02 *Degussa v Commission* [2006] ECR II-897.

result of the failure of the Commission to act reasonably promptly.[804] In respect of an infringement before 1 May 2004, the Commission cannot take into account any period when the activity in question was covered by a notification under Regulation 17, except in relation to a period covered by a decision under Article 15(6) of that Regulation lifting immunity from fines.[805]

13.157 **The 'entry fee'.** The 2006 Guidelines on Fines further provide that irrespective of the duration of the infringement, in the case of horizontal price-fixing, market-sharing, and output-limitation agreements, an additional amount of between 15 and 25 per cent of the value of sales will be included in the basic amount in order to deter undertakings from entering into such agreements at all. In the case of other infringements, a similar additional amount may be imposed.[806]

(e) Aggravating and mitigating circumstances and deterrence

13.158 **Generally.** The basic amount, as determined by the approach set out in the preceding part of this Section, will be increased or decreased to reflect any aggravating and mitigating circumstances, examples of which are set out in the 2006 Guidelines on Fines. The increases and decreases will be applied simultaneously to the basic amount. The Commission is not entitled to apply the percentage increases or decreases to an amount that has already been increased or decreased to reflect aggravating or mitigating factors.[807]

13.159 **Aggravating circumstances.** The 2006 Guidelines on Fines list a number of circumstances that may lead to an increase in the basic amount:[808]

(a) repeat infringements;

(b) refusal to cooperate with the Commission's investigation;

(c) being the leader or instigator in the infringement.

13.160 **Repeat infringements.** The 2006 Guidelines on Fines state that where an undertaking continues or repeats the same or a similar infringement after the Commission or a national competition authority has made a finding that

---

[804] Cases 6 & 7/73 *Commercial Solvents v Commission* [1974] ECR 223, [1974] 1 CMLR 309; cf Cases 32/78, etc, *BMW v Commission* [1979] ECR 2435, [1980] 1 CMLR 370; see also Case 322/81 *Michelin v Commission* [1983] ECR 3461, [1985] 1 CMLR 282.

[805] See para 13.010, above. In *SCK and FNK*, OJ 1995 L312/79, [1996] 4 CMLR 565, the Commission imposed a fine after lifting immunity under Art 15(6) of Reg 17. The fine was reduced on appeal: Cases T-213/95 & T-18/96 *SCK and FNK v Commission* [1997] ECR II-1739, [1998] 4 CMLR 259. Where an agreement had been communicated to the Commission, albeit without completing the formalities of a notification, the Commission could not take that period into account in assessing the fine: Case C-338/00P *Volkswagen v Commission* [2003] ECR I-9181, [2004] 4 CMLR 351, paras 175–180 (dismissing the Commission's cross-appeal).

[806] 2006 Guidelines on Fines, para 25.

[807] Case T-224/00 *Archer Daniels Midland* (n 786, above) para 378.

[808] 2006 Guidelines on Fines, para 28.

the undertaking[809] infringed Article 81 or 82, the basic amount will be increased by up to 100 per cent for each such infringement established. This differs from the position under the 1998 Guidelines in two ways. First, in line with the modernisation of the competition rules, reference is made to previous findings by an NCA as well as by the Commission itself. Secondly, the 2006 Guidelines on Fines make it clear that there will be a very large uplift of up to 100 per cent for repeat infringements; this is a substantial increase on the 50 per cent increase normally applied by the Commission for recidivism.[810] However, an uplift for recidivism is a matter in which the Commission has a margin of discretion and is not bound by previous practice. It has long regarded the fact that undertakings have persisted in conduct in breach of previous orders of national authorities or of the Commission as an aggravating factor.[811] Moreover, the Commission is obliged to ensure that a fine has a sufficient deterrent effect.[812] The Commission is entitled to increase a fine for recidivism even when the previous infringement occurred before the start of the limitation period in what is now Article 25 of Regulation 1/2003.[813] It may also increase the fine if the previous infringements were in a different market, provided that the infringement is of a similar nature.[814] However, the Commission is not entitled to increase a fine for recidivism when the infringement being punished took place before the decision penalising the earlier infringement.[815]

---

[809] In Case T-203/01 *Michelin v Commission* (n 803, above) the applicant argued that it should not be treated as a recidivist because it was not the same legal person as the undertaking fined on the previous occasion; the CFI rejected that argument (para 290), noting that the applicant and the previously-fined company both belonged to the same economic unit.

[810] COMP/37.533 *Choline Chloride*, 9 December 2004, OJ 2005 L190/22, [2006] 4 CMLR 159, para 15; COMP/37.857 *Organic Peroxides*, 10 December 2003, OJ 2005 L110/44, [2005] 5 CMLR 578, para 23 (appeal dismissed, Case T-120/04 *Peróxidos Orgánicos v Commission* [2007] 4 CMLR 153).

[811] *ECS/AKZO (No. 2)*, OJ 1985 L374/1, [1986] 3 CMLR 273; *Benelux Flat Glass*, OJ 1984 L212/13, [1985] 3 CMLR 250; COMP/38.638 *Butadiene Rubber*, decn of 29 November 2006, Press Release IP/06/1647.

[812] In Case T-203/01 *Michelin v Commission* (n 803, above) paras 292–293, an uplift of 50 per cent – larger than in previous cases – was justified.

[813] Case C-3/06P *Groupe Danone v Commission* [2007] 4 CMLR 701, para 39: 'repeated infringement is an important factor which the Commission must appraise, since the purpose of taking repeated infringement into account is to induce undertakings which have demonstrated a tendency towards infringing the competition rules to change their conduct. The Commission may therefore, in each individual case, take into consideration the indicia which confirm such a tendency, including, for example, the time that has elapsed between the infringe ments in question'. There, the previous infringement was 20 years earlier. For limitation periods see para 3.208, below.

[814] *Belgian Beer Cartel Interbrew and Alken-Maes* (n 728, above) para 314, where the Commission also regarded it as relevant that the same person occupied the post of chairman and chief executive at the time both infringements took place and at least two directors who had been responsible for the sector covered by the earlier infringement were now responsible for the sector covered by the instant cartel.

[815] Case T-141/94 *Thyssen Stahl v Commission* [1999] ECR II-347, [1999] 4 CMLR 810, para 618; see also COMP/37.667 *Speciality Graphite*, 17 December 2002, OJ 2006 L180/20,

An undertaking is not entitled to a reduction in the fine for not having infringed the competition rules before.[816]

13.161 **Refusal to cooperate with Commission investigation.** A refusal to cooperate or an attempt to obstruct the Commission in carrying out its investigations will lead to an increase in the fine.[817] An identical provision was contained in the 1998 Guidelines. The Commission is entitled to regard 'tipping off' other undertakings about a Commission investigation as an aggravating factor, and indeed as an even more serious aggravating factor than destruction of an undertaking's own documents.[818]

13.162 **'Ring leaders' of infringements and retaliatory measures.** The undertaking which plays the role of leader in, or is the instigator of, the infringement will be fined more heavily. The Commission will also pay particular attention to any steps taken to coerce other undertakings to participate in the infringement and/or any retaliatory measures taken against other undertakings with a view to enforcing the practices constituting the infringement. The Court of First Instance has agreed that acting as an instigator or ringleader is an aggravating factor.[819]

---

where the Commission accepted that no increase on the basis of recidivism should be imposed on undertakings who were at the same time party to the graphite electrodes cartel (also subject to a fining decision); on appeal, fines were reduced Cases T-71/03, etc, *Tokai Carbon v Commission* [2005] ECR II-10, [2005] 5 CMLR 489 (appeal dismissed, Case C-328/05P *SGL Carbon v Commission* [2007] 5 CMLR 16).

[816] Cases T-305/94, etc, *Re PVC (No. 2)* [1999] ECR II-931, [1999] 5 CMLR 303, para 1163.

[817] Conversely, cooperation is an attenuating factor; see para 13.167, below. In *Greek Ferries*, OJ 1999 L109/24, [1999] 5 CMLR 47, the proposal by Minoan to restructure the cartel, after the Commission had begun to investigate, so as to make it harder to detect, was regarded as an aggravating factor justifying an increase of 10 per cent in the basic amount; this was upheld by the CFI (Case T-66/99 *Minoan Lines v Commission* [2003] ECR II-5515, [2005] 5 CMLR 1956, paras 335–338; further appeal dismissed Case C-121/04P, [2006] 4 CMLR 1405). In *Pre-Insulated Pipe Cartel*, OJ 1999 L24/1, [1999] 4 CMLR 402, an aggravating factor in the case of De Henss/Isoplus was that it attempted to mislead the Commission about its corporate structure; if it had succeeded, the Commission might have inappropriately imposed a lower fine or found recovery more difficult; this uplift was again upheld by the CFI, which dismissed arguments based on rights of the defence and fiduciary duties of confidence owed by the undertakings to third parties in relation to the information: Case T-9/99 *HFB v Commission* [2002] ECR II-1487, paras 555–564.

[818] *Tokai Carbon v Commission (Graphite Electrodes)* (n 799, above) paras 312–315, where the Commission did not impose an uplift for destruction of documents. On appeal, the ECJ set aside a reduction by the CFI in SGL Carbon's fine for having answered a Commission request for the names of the undertakings it had warned, on the grounds that SGL Carbon's answer had been incomplete and misleading: Cases C-301/04P, etc, *SGL Carbon* (n 799, above) para 69. In *Nintendo*, OJ 2003 L255/33, [2004] 4 CMLR 421, paras 413–419, an uplift of 10 per cent was imposed for inaccurate answers to Commission questions (on appeal Cases T-12/03 *Itochu Corporation v Commission*, T-13/03 *Nintendo v Commission*, T-18/03 *CD Contact Data v Commission*, not yet decided). See also *Eurocheque: Helsinki Agreement*, OJ 1992 L95/50, [1993] 5 CMLR 323.

[819] *Tokai Carbon v Commission (Graphite Electrodes)* (n 799, above) para 301 (uplift of 50 per cent upheld: para 310); see also Case T-15/02 *BASF v Commission* [2006] ECR II-497, [2006] 5 CMLR 27, paras 280–282. A 50 per cent uplift was also imposed on the ringleader in COMP/38.238 *Raw Tobacco (Spain)*, 20 October 2004, [2006] 4 CMLR 866, para 438 (on appeal, Cases T-24/05 *Standard Commercial*; T-29/05 *Deltafina*; T-33/05 *Cetarsa*; T-37/05 *World Wide Tobacco Espana*;

In finding that an undertaking is an instigator, the Commission must show that the undertaking persuaded or encouraged others to join; being a founding member of a cartel is not enough. The Commission must also distinguish between instigation of a new cartel and taking a leading role in a cartel, and justify its finding by evidence going beyond the undertaking's market position or motivation.[820] As to retaliatory measures, the Commission has regarded such measures (or threats to take such measures) as deserving a substantial uplift.[821]

Mitigating circumstances.   The 2006 Guidelines on Fines identify as mitigating circumstances:[822]   **13.163**

(a) immediate termination of the infringement following the Commission's intervention;

(b) where the infringement has been committed as a result of negligence;

(c) limited involvement and failure to implement the anti-competitive agreement;

(d) cooperation with the Commission beyond the undertakings' legal obligations to do so;

(e) encouragement or authorisation to engage in the infringing conduct by a public authority.

Prompt termination of infringement.   The 2006 Guidelines on Fines provide   **13.164** that where the undertaking concerned provides evidence that it terminated the infringement as soon as the Commission intervened, this is a mitigating factor. This reflects the Commission's long-standing practice that prompt and effective remedial action may result in substantial mitigation of the fine.[823]

T-38/05 *Agroexpansion*; T-41/05 *Dimon*, not yet decided) and in COMP/36.756 *Sodium Gluconate*, re-issued 29 September 2004 (on appeal, Case T-492/04 *Jungbunzlauer v Commission*, not yet decided). In Case T-15/02 *BASF* (above) the CFI found that BASF was not an instigator, but considered that an uplift of 35 per cent was justified on the basis that it took a leading role.

[820] Case T-15/02 *BASF* (n 819, above) paras 296 and 321 (paras 304–464 contain a detailed analysis of the evidence relied on to prove BASF's role as an instigator).

[821] eg *Volkswagen*, OJ 2001 L262/14, [2001] 5 CMLR 1309, para 121: 20 per cent for threats to terminate dealer contracts (annulled on appeal on other grounds, Case T-208/01 *Volkswagen v Commission* [2003] ECR II-5141, [2004] 4 CMLR 727, [2004] All ER (EC) 674; Commission's appeal dismissed Case C-74/04P *Commission v Volkswagen*, [2006] ECR I-6585); *JCB*, OJ 2002 L69/1, [2002] 4 CMLR 1458, para 255: basic amount increased by twice the amount of the sanction imposed on a dealer by JCB for non-compliance. In *Interbrew and Alken Maes ('Belgian beer')*, OJ 2003 L200/1, [2004] 4 CMLR 80, the Commission increased the fine on Danone by 50 per cent on this ground but the CFI reduced it to 40 per cent because the threat had no effect on Interbrew's decision to participate: *Group Danone* (n 795, above).

[822] 2006 Guidelines on Fines (n 762, above) para 29.

[823] See, eg *General Motors*, OJ 1975 L29/14, [1975] 1 CMLR D20 (immediate steps to remedy infringement by reducing scale of charges and refunding excess amounts collected); *United Brands*, OJ 1976 L95/1, [1976] 1 CMLR D28 (steps taken to terminate one infringement 'voluntarily' prior to Commission decision); Case 85/76 *Hoffmann-La Roche v Commission* [1979] ECR 461, [1979] 3 CMLR 211, para 140 (cooperative attitude by company in offering to amend agreements); *Floral*,

In *National Panasonic*, initiation of proceedings in respect of a Treaty infringement by a United Kingdom subsidiary led the Japanese parent company to establish, in consultation with the Commission, an antitrust compliance programme covering the activities of all European subsidiaries. This action led to the fine imposed on the United Kingdom subsidiary being substantially mitigated.[824] Effective implementation and monitoring are essential to achieve a stated compliance objective.[825] In *Woodpulp*, the fines were substantially reduced in return for an undertaking as to the parties' future behaviour designed to increase competition in the relevant market.[826] The Commission is however entitled not to give any discount for the introduction of a compliance system after the event and in recent cases has tended not to do so, with the approval of the Community Courts.[827] In *Michelin II*,[828] the Court agreed that the Commission was entitled to give a 20 per cent reduction to reflect the fact that Michelin abandoned the conduct in question before the statement of objections. But the Commission is not *obliged* to take into account the fact that an infringement was terminated upon initiation of its investigation,[829] so that it appears that the Commission is entitled, as the 2006 Guidelines on Fines make clear, not to accept this point as mitigation in the case of secret infringements.[830] Conversely, the Commission may increase the basic amount where the infringement was continued even after the Commission has begun its enquiries.[831]

OJ 1980 L39/51, [1980] 2 CMLR 285 (dissolution of joint selling company prior to Commission decision); *Gosme/Martell-DMP*, OJ 1991 L185/23, [1992] 5 CMLR 586 (export ban removed from invoices following Commission's intervention); *Viho/Toshiba*, OJ 1991 L287/39, [1992] 5 CMLR 180; *Far East Trade Tariff Charges and Surcharges Agreement (FETTCSA)*, OJ 2000 L268/1, [2000] 5 CMLR 1011, para 188 (20 per cent reduction for termination of infringement on receipt of Commission's warning letter). See also *Zinc Producer Group*, OJ 1984 L220/27, [1985] 2 CMLR 108; *British Leyland*, OJ 1984 L207/11, [1984] 3 CMLR 92, on appeal Case 226/84 *British Leyland v Commission* [1986] ECR 3263, [1987] 1 CMLR 184 (fine upheld); *Polistil/Arbois*, OJ 1984 L136/9, [1984] 2 CMLR 594; *Sperry New Holland*, OJ 1985 L376/21, [1988] 4 CMLR 306; *Souris - Topps* (n 794, above); *Yamaha* (n 794, above).

[824] *National Panasonic*, OJ 1982 L354/28, [1983] 1 CMLR 497; *Viho/Toshiba* (above) ('very constructive' action towards compliance taken by Toshiba).

[825] *Viho/Toshiba* (n 823, above).

[826] *Woodpulp*, OJ 1985 L85/1, [1985] 3 CMLR 474; decision largely annulled on other grounds: Cases C-89/85, etc, *Åhlström Osakeytiö v Commission* ('*Wood Pulp II*') [1993] ECR I-1307, [1993] 4 CMLR 407.

[827] Case T-15/02 *BASF* (n 819, above) para 266; *Dansk Rørindustri* (n 764, above) para 373.

[828] Case T-203/01 *Michelin v Commission* [2003] ECR II-4071, [2004] 4 CMLR 923, paras 298–299.

[829] *Fiskeby Board* (n 769, above) para 82; Case T-352/94 *Moch och Domsjö v Commission* [1998] ECR II-1989, para 418. In *Lysine*, OJ 2001 L152/7, a 10 per cent discount was however granted to reflect the cessation of the infringement at the outset of the investigation.

[830] See, eg *Choline Chloride* (n 810, above): no discount given to reflect the fact that the secret cartel had ended before the Commission began its investigation; the Commission commented that the ending of the infringement was reflected in the calculation of duration.

[831] *Pre-insulated Pipe Cartel* (n 817, above); *French Beef*, OJ 2003 L209/12, [2003] 5 CMLR 891, para 174 (on appeal, fine reduced further to reflect extraordinary market circumstances: Cases

Negligent commission of infringement. The 2006 Guidelines on Fines state **13.165**
that where the undertaking provides evidence that the infringement has been
committed as a result of negligence, this will be regarded as a mitigating factor.[832]
The existence of a compliance system has been held to be a potential mitigating
factor,[833] but the Commission may refuse to take its existence into account if it is
ineffective[834] or flouted by the most senior management level.[835] In *British Sugar*,
the Commission said that the conduct of British Sugar was aggravated by the
fact that the conduct contravened its own compliance programme, as that
programme had been taken into account in a previous case as a mitigating factor.
The infringement showed that the promise in its compliance system to take every
step to avoid an infringement had not been fulfilled.[836]

Limited involvement and non-implementation. Where the undertaking shows **13.166**
that its involvement in the infringement was 'substantially limited' and that it
engaged in competitive conduct in the market despite being a party to the offending agreement, that will be a mitigating factor. This provision reflects the way
in which the apparently less restrictive provision in the 1998 Guidelines ('Non-
implementation in practice of the offending agreements or practices') was actually
interpreted. First, the drafting of the 2006 Guidelines on Fines in this respect
emphasises that 'cheating' or periods where the cartel failed to operate very successfully will not provide mitigation. The practice of the Commission, approved
by the Court of First Instance,[837] has been to refuse to reduce fines to reflect the
fact that the undertaking concerned has 'cheated' by not honouring agreements
reached at cartel meetings. In such cases the undertaking is held to have been
exploiting the cartel for its own benefit. The Commission has also refused to
reduce the fine to reflect periods where the cartel was less successful.[838] Secondly,
it is clear that to benefit from this ground of mitigation the undertaking must have
behaved competitively, which probably involves showing that its prices differed

T-217 & 245/03 *Fédération nationale de la coopération bétail and viande (FNCBV) v Commission*,
judgment of 13 December 2006).

[832] For negligence, see para 13.140, above. In Case C-137/95P *SPO v Commission* [1996] ECR
I-1611, para 55, the ECJ held that 'as the Commission emphasises, infringements committed negligently are not, from the point of view of competition, less serious than those committed intentionally'. However, it seems that the Commission had in fact submitted that negligent infringements
were *not necessarily* less serious than intentional ones; see Wils (n 771, above) 260, n 29.

[833] Case T-77/92 *Parker Pen v Commission* [1994] ECR II-549, [1995] 5 CMLR 435, para 93.

[834] Case T-327/94 *SCA Holdings v Commission* [1998] ECR II-1373, [1998] 5 CMLR 195,
para 118.

[835] *Pre-Insulated Pipe Cartel* (n 817, above) para 172.

[836] *British Sugar/Tate & Lyle/Napier Brown*, OJ 1999 L76/1, [1999] 4 CMLR 1316, para 208
(appeals largely dismissed Cases T-202/98, etc, *Tate & Lyle v Commission* [2001] ECR II-2035,
[2001] 5 CMLR 859, [2001] All ER (EC) 839 and Cases C-359/01P *British Sugar v Commission*
[2004] ECR I-4933, [2004] 5 CMLR 329).

[837] *SCA Holdings v Commission* (n 834, above).

[838] eg *Austrian Banks* (n 791, above) paras 530 and 540.

significantly from those of other parties. This reflects the interpretation of the non-implementation factor in the 1998 Guidelines by the Court of First Instance in *Archer Daniels Midland ('Amino Acids')*.[839] The removal of the provision in the 1998 Guidelines relating to 'an exclusively passive or "follow-my-leader" role in the infringement' and its replacement by 'substantially limited' involvement emphasises that the undertaking should have behaved in a way that distanced itself from the cartel, for example by attending cartel meetings infrequently,[840] rather than that it simply followed other participants.[841] The expression does not mean involvement limited in time since this will be dealt with by the provisions relating to duration. Finally, the onus of proof of limited involvement and competitive conduct is clearly placed on the undertaking.[842]

13.167 **Cooperation with Commission investigation.** The 2006 Guidelines on Fines provide that where the undertaking concerned has effectively cooperated with the Commission outside the scope of the Leniency Notice and beyond its legal obligation to do so, this is a mitigating factor. The Leniency Notice is discussed below,[843] but for present purposes it should be noted that its application is confined to covert cartel cases. Therefore it does not apply in, for example, cases

---

[839] Case T-224/00 *Archer Daniels Midland v Commission* [2003] ECR II-2597, [2003] 5 CMLR 583, para 268 (not raised on appeal to the ECJ, Case C-397/03P, [2006] ECR I-4429, [2006] 5 CMLR 230); see also Case T-62/02 *Union Pigments v Commission* [2005] ECR II-5057, [2006] 4 CMLR 1105, paras 127–130 (on appeal from *Zinc Phosphate Cartel*, OJ 2003 L153/1, [2003] 5 CMLR 731).

[840] Infrequent attendance is not however a mitigating factor when the undertaking is represented at meetings by another undertaking and is also involved in other meetings: Case 236/01 *Tokai Carbon (graphite electrodes)* (n 799, above) para 335.

[841] See *Austrian Banks* (n 791, above) paras 538–540 (division of roles between undertakings who played a greater part and other who played a lesser part not relevant to fine); *Citric Acid*, OJ 2002 L239/18, [2002] 5 CMLR 24, para 283 (no discount for minor player: it could have reported the matter to the Commission), appeals as to fine dismissed: Cases T-59/02 *Archer Daniels Midland* [2006] 5 CMLR 1494 and T-43/02 *Jungbunzlauer*, judgment of 27 September 2006. cf other cases under the 1998 Guidelines where the Commission granted reductions for a purely 'passive' role, eg *Industrial and Medical Gases*, OJ 2003 L84/1, [2003] 5 CMLR 144, paras 351 and 442 (15 per cent discount). See also *Cheil Jedang*, discussed below.

[842] In Case T-220/00 *Cheil Jedang v Commission* [2003] ECR II-2473, paras 165 *et seq* (on appeal from *Amino Acids*, OJ 2001 L 152/24, [2001] 5 CMLR 322) the CFI said that a passive role could be proved by sporadic attendance at cartel meetings, late entry (but this factor is expressly disallowed under the 2006 Guidelines on Fines) and declarations by other undertakings that it was not regarded as an active participant (but the absence of declarations to the contrary was not probative). In Case T-48/02 *Brouwerij Haacht v Commission* [2005] ECR II-5259, [2006] 4 CMLR 621, paras 74 *et seq*, the CFI held that the applicant's systematic participation in the anti-competitive meetings throughout the entire duration of the infringement and the absence of factors showing reluctance on its part to pursue the objectives of the cartel ruled out any discount on the grounds of passive involvement; it was irrelevant that others had been found to play a leading role in the cartel. See also *Union Pigments* (n 839, above) para 126: applicant failed to show that it had a 'low profile' by reference to those criteria.

[843] See paras 13.182 *et seq*, below. Briefly, it provides for immunity or a reduction in fines for 'whistle-blowers' who disclose the existence of a cartel to the Commission.

under Article 82 or involving vertical agreements. It should not necessarily be assumed that the very substantial reductions available under the Leniency Notice (of up to 100 per cent) will be applied in cases outside its scope, given that the Notice deals with cases which are intrinsically very difficult to detect so that there is a policy reason supporting substantial discounts.[844] The reference to 'effective' cooperation emphasises that the cooperation must produce 'value added', so that it provides facts and explanations that lead to a better understanding of the case by the Commission.[845] Where an undertaking's cooperation reveals matters that increase the severity of the fine (for example, that the infringement lasted longer than initially supposed), the Commission may well calculate the amount of the reduction so as to cancel out the increase in its fine that would otherwise have resulted.[846] Conversely, only a limited discount can be given for cooperation that does not relate to matters that could give rise to an increase in fine on the undertaking concerned.[847] If an undertaking does not expressly acknowledge the correctness of the Commission's case during the administrative procedure but simply fails to comment on it, that cannot be regarded as cooperation since the Commission still has to prove its case.[848] Nor is an undertaking to be regarded as cooperating if it admits that certain facts would in law constitute an infringement but continues to deny those facts.[849] Submitting responses which purport to clarify facts but which in fact amount to contesting the Commission's account of them cannot be regarded as cooperation.[850] Further, as the reference to 'beyond its legal obligation' suggests, simply complying with legal requirements to disclose information and documents to the Commission cannot be regarded as cooperation.[851] On the other hand, admitting facts of which the Commission already has ample evidence can give rise to a (modest) reduction since the

---

[844] But cf *Nathan-Bricolux*, OJ 2001 L54/1, [2001] 4 CMLR 1122 (fines reduced due to active cooperation in a case concerning vertical agreements); *Raw Tobacco (Spain)* (n 819, above) (reductions of 20–40 per cent).

[845] *Austrian Banks* (n 791, above) paras 548–550.

[846] *Choline Chloride* (n 810, above).

[847] Case T-224/00 *Archer Daniels Midland* (n 839, above) paras 295–298; however, in Case T-236/01 *Tokai Carbon (Graphite Electrodes)* (n 799, above) paras 434–440, the CFI stated that providing the Commission with information concerning a disloyal Commission official who had leaked information was cooperation that should have been taken into account.

[848] Case C-297/98P *SCA Holding v Commission* [2000] ECR I-10101, [2001] 4 CMLR 413, paras 34–37.

[849] Case T-213/00 *CMA CGM v Commission ('FETTCSA')* (n 802, above) para 306.

[850] *Group Danone* (n 795, above) para 515.

[851] *CMA CMG* (n 802, above) para 303. See also Case C-301/04P *Commission v SGL Carbon* [2006] ECR I-5915, [2006] 5 CMLR 877 (on appeal from *Tokai Carbon (Graphite Electrodes)* (n 799, above)) where the ECJ held that the respondent was not entitled to a reduction in fine for cooperation because the documents provided in answer to one request were not covered by the privilege against self-incrimination and the response to another request was incomplete and misleading and therefore did not reflect the 'spirit of cooperation' required to justify a reduction.

admission spares the Commission work and shortens proceedings.[852] Cooperation can be of value to the Commission and can lead to a discount even though it is oral rather than written and even if the undertaking declines to permit the information in question to be used as evidence (since the information may enable the Commission to make enquiries of its own).[853]

13.168 **Encouragement by public authorities.** Where the anti-competitive conduct of the undertaking has been authorised or encouraged by public authorities or by legislation, this will lead to a reduction in fine. In *Greek Ferries*,[854] the Commission granted a reduction of 15 per cent in the basic amount to reflect possible doubt caused by the fact that domestic prices were subject to a process of consultation involving the Greek Ministry of the Merchant Marine. Reductions of 40 per cent were granted for similar reasons in *Spanish Raw Tobacco* in order to reflect the fact that a legal framework for public negotiations between producers and processors contributed to circumstances in which processors reached secret agreements between themselves.[855] In *French Beef*, a reduction was granted because of the 'forceful intervention' of the French Minister of Agriculture in support of the agreement, although that mitigation did not apply to those parties who had demonstrated in favour of the agreement and put pressure on the Minister to intervene.[856] The fact that national legislation may have created an ambiguity about the compatibility of concertation with the rules of the Treaty may also be a mitigating factor.[857]

13.169 **Uncertainty as to the law.** The Court of Justice has stated that uncertainty as to the law should lead to a reduction in the fine,[858] and fines have been set at a lower level in cases which are the first of their kind where fines have been imposed.[859]

---

852 *Austrian Banks* (n 791, above) para 559. If the undertaking then contests the facts on appeal, the Commission may ask the CFI to increase the fine to cancel out the reduction: see para 13.215, below.

853 Case T-236/01 *Tokai Carbon (Graphite Electrodes)* (n 799, above) para 431.

854 *Greek Ferries*, OJ 1999 L109/24, [1999] 5 CMLR 47. On appeal: Case T-65/99 *Strintzis Lines Shipping v Commission* [2003] ECR II-5433, [2005] 5 CMLR 1901, Case T-66/99 *Minoan Lines v Commission* [2003] ECR II-5515, [2005] 5 CMLR 1957 (further appeals dismissed: Cases C-110/04P *Strintzis Lines* [2006] ECR I-44; C-121/04P *Minoan Lines* [2006] 4 CMLR 1405) and Case T-59/99 *Ventouris Group v Commission* [2003] ECR II-5257, [2005] 5 CMLR 1781.

855 COMP/38.238 *Raw Tobacco (Spain)*, 20 October 2004, OJ 2007 L102/14, [2006] 4 CMLR 866, para 438 (on appeal see n 819, above) the producers' fines were reduced to a nominal €1,000 to reflect this factor – they were involved only in the public discussions, which took place according to Spanish law, were on occasion hosted by the Spanish Ministry of Agriculture, and the prices agreed were published in the Spanish Official Gazette (paras 427–429).

856 *French Beef*, OJ 2003 L209/12, [2003] 5 CMLR 891, para 176. The reduction was increased further by the CFI on appeal Cases T-217 & 245/03 *FNCBV* (n 831, above).

857 *Building and Construction industry in the Netherlands*, OJ 1992 L92/1, [1993] 5 CMLR 135.

858 Case 62/86 *AKZO v Commission* [1991] ECR I-3359, [1993] 5 CMLR 215, para 163.

859 See, eg *Toltecs/Dorcet*, OJ 1982 L379/19, [1983] 1 CMLR 412, on appeal Case 35/83 *BAT v Commission* [1985] ECR 363, [1985] 2 CMLR 470 (non-use of trade mark agreement;

The 1998 Guidelines referred as an attenuating circumstance to the 'existence of reasonable doubt on the part of the undertaking as to whether the restrictive conduct does indeed constitute an infringement'. Although this is not similarly identified in the 2006 Guidelines, it appears to be covered by the more general statement that 'in certain cases' the Commission may impose a symbolic fine.[860] However, the practice in this regard is not altogether consistent. Thus, in *Tetra Pak*, the Court of First Instance upheld the Commission's refusal to reduce the fine to reflect the unprecedented nature of certain legal assessments made in that case.[861] The Commission has also been held to be justified in refusing to reduce a fine to reflect the fact that it is the first to be imposed under a particular Regulation implementing Articles 81 and 82[862] or the first in a particular sector,[863] although in some cases it has been prepared to reduce fines where a sector has been investigated for the first time.[864] However, in other cases the novelty of a decision finding an infringement has led to no financial penalty, or only a nominal penalty, being imposed[865] and in *Transatlantic Conference Agreement (TACA)*, where the Court of First Instance annulled the fine, an element in the reasoning was that the issue of service contracts by a shipping conference raised complex legal issues and did

---

fine quashed); *Windsurfing International*, OJ 1983 L229/1, [1984] 1 CMLR 1, on appeal Case 193/83 *Windsurfing International v Commission* [1986] ECR 611, [1986] 3 CMLR 489 (restrictive patent licence; fine reduced); *Woodpulp* (n 826, above) para 146 (re members of the KEA, a US association registered under the Webb-Pomerene Act and thereby exempt from the US antitrust laws).

860 2006 Guidelines on Fines, para 36.

861 Case T-83/91 *Tetra Pak v Commission* [1994] ECR II-755, [1997] 4 CMLR 726, paras 228, 234, upheld on further appeal in Case C-333/94P, [1996] ECR I-5951, [1997] 4 CMLR 662, [1997] All ER (EC) 4, paras 48–49; the legal assessments in question related to the link between the market in which the abuse took place and the market in which the undertaking was dominant: see para 10.004, above).

862 Cases T-24/93, etc, *Compagnie Maritime Belge Transports* (n 801, above) para 248 (the first fines under Reg 4056/86 but the abuse found was in no way novel); the Commission had stated in the decision under appeal (*CEWAL*, OJ 1993 L20/1, [1995] 5 CMLR 89) that although it was customary to moderate the fines in the cases of the first application of legislation, no such moderation was appropriate where the parties were fully informed of the effect of the competition rules (the fines were annulled by the ECJ on other grounds). But cf *Far Eastern Freight Conference*, OJ 1994 L378/17 (symbolic fines in first case of the application of Reg 1017/68 to a liner conference).

863 Case T-229/95 *Deutsche Bahn v Commission* [1997] ECR II-1689, [1998] 4 CMLR 528, para 130. In COMP/38.549 *Belgian Architects*, 24 June 2004, OJ 2005 L4/10, [2005] 4 CMLR 677 the Commission refused to accept as a mitigating factor doubt as to the application of the competition rules to the professional services in question, although it imposed a modest fine of €100,000 to reflect a 'gradual approach' to fining professional associations for anti-competitive practices.

864 *Eurocheque: Helsinki Agreement*, OJ 1992 L95/50, [1993] 5 CMLR 323, para 91 (banking); *Building and construction in the Netherlands*, OJ 1992 L92/1, [1993] 5 CMLR 135, para 41 (construction); *Distribution of package tours during 1990 World Cup*, OJ 1992 L326/31, [1994] 5 CMLR 253 (tickets for sporting event).

865 See para 13.170, below.

not constitute a 'classic abuse'.[866] The existence of uncertainty has also been taken into account in assessing the seriousness of the infringement.[867] Conversely, the Commission will take into account the fact that an undertaking has been warned, for example by its own lawyers[868] or third parties,[869] that its conduct contravenes the competition rules.

13.170 **No penalty or nominal fine.**   In cases where an important aspect of the decision is novel, the Commission may impose no financial penalty or set only a symbolic fine. In *Italian Flat Glass*,[870] no fine was imposed for the abuse of a collective dominant position because the concept was used for the first time in that case. Similarly, in *Clearstream*[871] the Commission imposed no fine, taking into account the facts that the infringements had been brought to an end, that there was no EC case law dealing with the competition analysis of clearing and settlement, and that the decision came at a time when cross-border trade in securities was assuming greater significance within the EU. In other cases, the Commission has imposed only a symbolic fine, and the 2006 Guidelines on Fines provide that in such cases the Commission will set out its reasoning in its decision.[872] For example,

---

[866] Cases T-191/98, etc, *Atlantic Container Line v Commission* [2003] ECR II-3275, [2005] 4 CMLR 1283, paras 1615–1633; the CFI also noted that the agreement had been notified for exemption under Art 81(3) and the Commission had never before fined under Art 82 conduct in respect of which there was a notification.

[867] *Deutsche Telekom*, OJ 2003 L263/9, [2004] 4 CMLR 790, para 206 (on appeal, Case T-271/03, not yet decided). See also *FNCBV* (n 831, above) paras 356–361, where the CFI allowed a further reduction in the fine (which had already been reduced by the Commission by 60 per cent for exceptional circumstances) in part because this had been the first time the Commission had fined conduct of this kind. But cf *AstraZeneca*, OJ 2006 L332/24, [2006] 5 CMLR 287, para 922, where the Commission states that the novel features of the infringements were taken into account in the assessment of gravity, but for abuses described as not 'clear-cut' (para 908) total fines of €60 million were nonetheless imposed (on appeal, Case T-321/05 *AstraZeneca v Commission*, not yet decided).

[868] See, eg *Quinine*, OJ 1969 L192/5, [1969] CMLR D41; *Meldoc*, OJ 1986 L348/50, [1989] 4 CMLR 853; and note AG Warner in Cases 36–82/78, etc, *BMW v Commission* [1979] ECR 2435, 2495, [1980] 1 CMLR 370, paras 391–392; *London European/Sabena*, OJ 1988 L317/47, [1989] 4 CMLR 662 (undertaking advised by its in-house lawyer that its behaviour could be contrary to Art 82). As to lawyer/client privilege, see paras 13.055 and 13.056, above.

[869] eg *Toltecs/Dorcet* (n 859, above).

[870] *Italian Flat Glass*, OJ 1989 L33/44, [1990] 4 CMLR 535, para 84(a). However, fines were imposed for infringement of Art 81. (On appeal, the decn was partly annulled, Cases T-68/88, etc, *SIV v Commission* [1992] ECR-1403, [1992] 5 CMLR 302.)

[871] COMP/38.096 *Clearstream*, 2 June 2004, [2005] 5 CMLR 1302 (on appeal, Case T-301/04 *Clearstream v Commission*, not yet decided). See also *GVG/FS*, OJ 2004 L11/17, [2004] 4 CMLR 1446: no fine on the Italian state railway monopoly for refusal to supply access to its track on the basis that the infringement found was novel; COMP/38.662 *Gaz de France*, decn of 26 October 2004, Press Release IP/04/1310: no fine in relation to market partitioning restrictions since liberalisation of the energy sector had required substantial changes in commercial practices. In *DSD*, OJ 2001 L166/1, [2001] 5 CMLR 609, no fine was imposed, without explanation (appeal against infringement dismissed, Cases T-151 & 289/01 *Duales System Deutschland v Commission* [2007] 5 CMLR 300, 356. But cf *AstraZeneca* (n 867, above).

[872] 2006 Guidelines on Fines, para 36.

in *Organic Peroxide*[873] the Commission imposed a fine of €1000 on AC Treuhand, a company that did not itself operate in the relevant market but which acted as an organiser and facilitator of the cartel; the nominal fine was based on the fact that the Commission's finding of infringement against it in that case was 'to a certain extent a novelty'.[874]

Other aggravating and mitigating circumstances.   The lists of aggravating   **13.171**
and attenuating circumstances in the 2006 Guidelines on Fines are not exhaustive; indeed, the Commission is obliged to take all relevant circumstances into account.[875] There are a number of other factors which have in the past been regarded by the Commission as aggravating or mitigating circumstances, in particular duress, the payment of compensation to third parties damaged by the anticompetitive conduct, and dismissal of the staff responsible for the infringement.

Pressure from others.   In some cases, the Commission has refrained from impos-   **13.172**
ing a fine at all where the undertaking was effectively forced by other undertakings to take part in the infringement. That has in particular been the case for vertical agreements involving a significant disparity in bargaining power. Thus, in *VW-Audi*, VW dealers in Italy were put under strong commercial pressure by VW to agree not to supply VW cars for the German and Austrian markets; no fines were imposed on those dealers.[876] In other cases, fines have been reduced where

---

[873] COMP/37.857 *Organic Peroxide*, 10 December 2003, OJ 2005 L110/44, [2005] 5 CMLR 579, para 454 (on appeal, Cases T-99/04 *AC Treuhand v Commission*, not yet decided).

[874] See also *Deutsche Post - interception of cross border mail*, OJ 2001 L331/40, [2002] 4 CMLR 598, para 193: €1,000 fine because of uncertainty as to the legal position; *Raw Tobacco (Spain)* (n 855, above) and COMP/38.281 *Raw Tobacco (Italy)*, 20 October 2005, [2006] 4 CMLR 1766: €1,000 fines on producer representatives on the basis that their conduct had never been challenged under either national or EC law although their agreements had been communicated to the authorities (substantial fines were imposed on the producers, whose appeals are not yet decided). In *1998 Football World Cup*, OJ 2000 L5/55, [2000] 4 CMLR 963, the Commission imposed a fine of €1,000 on the French organisers of the tournament for infringing Art 82 by discriminating in favour of consumers in France in the ticketing arrangements. Although such discrimination was 'a breach of fundamental Community principles' (para 122), the Commission felt that a symbolic fine was appropriate since arrangements for previous World Cup tournaments had been similar, the application of the EC competition rules was unclear, the Commission had been told of the arrangements and they had subsequently been amended at the Commission's request. For criticism, see Weatherill, 'Fining the Organisers of the 1998 Football World Cup' (2000) ECLR 275.

[875] See para 13.144, above.

[876] *VW-Audi*, OJ 1998 L252/47, [1998] 5 CMLR 47 (appeal dismissed Case T-62/98 *Volkswagen v Commission* [2000] ECR II-2707, [2000] 5 CMLR 853). Similarly, *BMW Belgium*, OJ 1978 L46/33, [1978] 2 CMLR 126 (lower fines imposed on some participating dealers); *Opel*, OJ 2001 L59/1, [2001] 4 CMLR 1441 (no fines on Opel dealers); *Kawasaki*, OJ 1979 L16/9, [1979] 1 CMLR 448 (no fines on dealers); *Johnson & Johnson*, OJ 1980 L377/16, [1981] 2 CMLR 287 (no fines on chemists); *Hasselblad*, OJ 1982 L161/18, [1982] 2 CMLR 233 (lower fine imposed on dealers participating under pressure); *NAVEWA/ANSEAU*, OJ 1982 L167/39, [1982] 2 CMLR 193 (no fine on some undertakings 'practically obliged to participate'); *Windsurfing International* (n 859, above) (fines not imposed on patent licensees 'who had to submit' in order to obtain a licence; small fines imposed on distributors maintaining export bans); *John Deere*, OJ 1985 L35/58,

undertakings took action as a result of pressure from public authorities.[877] In *French Beef*, there was a substantial reduction in the fines on the two slaughterers' federations who had concluded the offending agreement only after forceful intervention by the Minister of Agriculture placing pressure on them to do so and following illegal action blockading the plants of their members and in some cases physical violence.[878] But in other cases, particularly horizontal cartels, the view has been taken that this ground of mitigation should not be accepted since the undertaking in question could have protected itself by informing the Commission.[879]

13.173 **Compensation paid to third parties.**   In *Pre-insulated pipes*,[880] the Commission accepted as a ground of mitigation the payment of substantial damages to a third party competitor whose elimination was an object of the cartel. Similarly, in *Nintendo*[881] the Commission reduced the fine by €300,000 to take account of substantial financial compensation paid to third parties after Nintendo had decided to cooperate with the investigation but before the statement of objections was issued. However, the Commission has refused to grant such reductions in other cases and the Court of First Instance has held that undertakings have no right to obtain such reductions.[882] Moreover, it is irrelevant that the undertaking has had to pay substantial damages, for example in the United States, in respect of damage outside the EEA.[883]

13.174 **Dismissal of staff responsible for the infringement.**   The fact that disciplinary sanctions are imposed by the undertaking on staff responsible for the infringement is of particularly little weight if they are imposed selectively with senior staff

---

[1985] 2 CMLR 554 (no fines on dealers); *Sperry New Holland*, OJ 1985 L376/21, [1988] 4 CMLR 306 (no fines on dealers who were held to be 'acting under duress and against their own interests'); *Roofing Felt*, OJ 1986 L232/15, [1991] 4 CMLR 130 (no fines on non-members); *Tipp-Ex*, OJ 1987 L222/1, [1989] 4 CMLR 425; *Gosme/Martell-DMP*, OJ 1991 L185/23, [1992] 5 CMLR 586 (fine not imposed on wholesaler who accepted restrictions contrary to its own interests).

[877] eg *British Telecommunications*, OJ 1982 L360/36, [1983] 1 CMLR 457 (no fine imposed in part because conduct was in response to pressure from some national telecommunications authorities).

[878] *French Beef* (n 856, above) paras 176–177.

[879] *Citric Acid* (n 841, above); Cases T-109/02, etc, *Bolloré v Commission* [2007] 5 CMLR 66, paras 638–639; *Group Danone* (n 795, above) para 423.

[880] *Pre-insulated Pipe Cartel* (n 817, above) para 172.

[881] *Nintendo*, OJ 2003 L255/33, [2004] CMLR 421 (on appeal, Cases T-12/03 *Itochu Corporation v Commission*, T-13/03 *Nintendo v Commission*, T-18/03 *CD Contact Data v Commission*, not yet decided).

[882] Case T-59/02 *Archer Daniels Midland v Commission* [2006] 5 CMLR 1494, paras 349–355 (on appeal on other grounds, C-511/06P, not yet decided).

[883] Case T-236/01 *Tokai Carbon (Graphite Electrodes)* (n 799, above) para 348. For the avoidance of double jeopardy where an undertaking has already been fined by another competition authority see para 13.207, below.

responsible escaping entirely.[884] But the Commission is entitled to take no account even of dismissal of all responsible staff before the decision.[885]

Conduct pending appeal of decision.   The Court of First Instance has unlim-   **13.175**
ited jurisdiction to review the level of a fine.[886] That gives rise to the question of the extent to which the Court can take account of conduct by the undertaking after the decision. The Court's position is that:

> 'the case-law does not show that a fine may be reduced in consideration of conduct adopted subsequently to the issuing of the decision imposing a fine. Such a reduction, even if it were possible, could in any event be operated by the Community judicature only with great care and in altogether exceptional circumstances, particularly because such a practice could be perceived as an incentive to commit infringements while speculating on a possible reduction in the fine by reason of alteration of the undertaking's conduct after the decision'.[887]

Other factors.   The fact that a pricing agreement is designed as a response to an   **13.176**
unexpected currency fluctuation is not an attenuating circumstance.[888] A shortage of supplies is not mitigation in respect of an export ban.[889] The fact that an agreement has been operated covertly is an aggravating factor;[890] conversely, the fact that an agreement has been operated openly may be an attenuating factor.[891] It is not a mitigating circumstance that there has been a change of ownership and management since the infringement.[892] There is no general rule to the effect that fines are less severe on undertakings in the agricultural sector.[893] Physical violence and threats of violence are an aggravating factor.[894] In a market-sharing agreement, it is not a mitigating factor that the parties were making losses in the parts of the market from which they agreed to withdraw.[895]

---

[884] *Pre-Insulated Pipe Cartel* (n 817, above) para 172. It was also irrelevant that the most senior official responsible had recently left, since his departure was not a disciplinary measure resulting from his behaviour.

[885] Case T-15/02 *BASF* (n 819, above) para 266.

[886] See paras 13.214 *et seq*, below.

[887] Case T-241/01 *SAS v Commission* [2005] ECR II-2917, [2005] 5 CMLR 922, para 228 (resignation of the board of SAS and dismissal of the senior vice-president after the decision not sufficiently exceptional).

[888] *Ferry Operators*, OJ 1997 L26/23, [1997] 4 CMLR 798.

[889] *Moët et Chandon*, OJ 1982 L94/7, [1982] 2 CMLR 166 (chronic shortage of supplies held not to justify export bans supporting national quota allocations imposed by supplier).

[890] eg *Polypropylene*, OJ 1986 L230/1, [1998] 4 CMLR 347, para 107; *SAS/Maersk*, OJ 2001 L265/15, [2001] 5 CMLR 1119.

[891] *Building and Construction industry in the Netherlands* (n 857, above).

[892] In *British Sugar/Tate & Lyle* (n 836, above) para 211, the Commission explained that a new owner purchases an undertaking with all its liabilities including those under the competition rules.

[893] Case T-228/97 *Irish Sugar v Commission* [1999] ECR II-2969, [1999] 5 CMLR 1300, [2000] All ER (EC) 198, para 254 (appeal dismissed, Case C-497/99P, [2001] ECR I-5333).

[894] *French Beef* (n 856, above) para 173.

[895] *SAS v Commission* (n 887, above). Generally speaking, the poor state of the industry is no excuse for the formation of a cartel: see para 13.179, below.

13.177 **Specific increase for deterrence.**   The 2006 Guidelines on Fines provide that:[896]

'The Commission will pay particular attention to the need to ensure that fines have a sufficiently deterrent effect; to that end, it may increase the fine to be imposed on undertakings which have a particularly large turnover beyond the sales of goods or services to which the infringement relates'.

The 1998 Guidelines referred to the need 'to set the fine at a level which ensures that it has a sufficiently deterrent effect'.[897] Under those Guidelines, the Commission would seek to ensure a deterrent effect by imposing multipliers (of between 1.5 and 3 times) on the basic amount.[898] The Court of First Instance expressly approved multipliers of that order, based on the need to deter, in cases where an undertaking was large. It referred to 'the rule that an infringement committed by an undertaking with vast financial resources may, in principle, be sanctioned by a fine proportionately higher than that imposed in respect of the same infringement committed by an undertaking without such resources'.[899] It was also able to take account of the fact that an undertaking had a large turnover beyond the sales of goods or services to which the infringement related when it came to group the undertakings according to size for the purpose of setting the basic amount[900] (although it was not required to do so, at least where the disparity in overall size was not so great as to require a difference between them[901]). The fact that an undertaking has a large turnover outside the relevant market is of obvious relevance to deterrence; as Advocate General Geelhoed has put it:

'it is common sense that a large undertaking with diversified resources will be in a different position from a small undertaking which relies for its existence on a single product. For a large, diversified undertaking any fine which related only to the affected market would be smaller by reference to its overall resources than would a fine for an undertaking whose products are all concerned by the cartel agreement.

---

[896] Guidelines on the method of setting fines, OJ 2006 C210/2: Vol II, App B.13, para 30. For discussion of fines and deterrence, see Wils, 'Optimal Antitrust Fines: Theory and Practice' (2006) 29 World Competition 183.

[897] 1998 Guidelines, para 1A.

[898] eg *Choline Chloride*, OJ 2005 L190/22, [2006] 4 CMLR 159, paras 203–204; *Nintendo* (n 881, above), paras 392–396.

[899] Cases T-236/01, etc, *Tokai Carbon v Commission (Graphite Electrodes)* [2004] ECR II-1181, [2004] 5 CMLR 1465, paras 238–245 (although the CFI reduced the multiplier in that case to reflect unequal treatment in that respect between the applicant and a comparator) (Commission's further appeal allowed, Case C-301/04P, *Commission v SGL Carbon* [2006] ECR I-5915, [2006] 5 CMLR 877; other appeals dismissed, Cases C-289/04P *Showa Denko v Commission* and C-308/04P *SGL Carbon v Commission* [2006] ECR I-5859, 5977, [2006] 5 CMLR 840, 922); see also Case T-15/02 *BASF* (n 819, above) paras 217–262.

[900] Case C-397/03P *Archer Daniels Midland v Commission* [2006] ECR I-4429, [2006] 5 CMLR 230, paras 33–35.

[901] *Union Pigments v Commission* (n 839, above) para 157; Case T-230/00 *Daesang and Sewon Europe v Commission* [2003] ECR II-2733, paras 69–77.

Thus, a like fine for the same infringement does not have the same deterrent effect'.[902]

In determining the fine in *Microsoft*, the Commission doubled the basic amount of the fine in order to ensure a sufficient deterrent effect, given Microsoft's 'significant economic capacity'.[903] It remains to be seen how the Commission will approach the interrelated questions of total size and deterrent effect under the 2006 Guidelines on Fines, where the basic amount is calculated on the 'value of sales' basis.

Benefit from the infringement. The 2006 Guidelines on Fines further provide **13.178** that:

'The Commission will also take into account the need to increase the fine in order to exceed the amount of gains improperly made as a result of the infringement where it is possible to estimate that amount.'[904]

This provision is in the same terms as the equivalent in the 1998 Guidelines. Even before the 1998 Guidelines, the Commission used to take into account how far the parties benefited from their infringement.[905] In *Eurocheque: Helsinki Agreement*,[906] the Commission calculated that the French banks had derived an illegal income of approximately five million ECUs from the operation of the agreement and imposed a fine of that sum upon them.[907] In 1991, the Commission stated that the financial benefit which companies derived from their infringements would become an increasingly important consideration and might even be the starting-point in the calculation of the fine.[908] However, the difficulty with this approach is that, given the possibility of non-detection, infringements can effectively be deterred only if fines substantially exceed the expected benefit contemplated by the undertaking.[909] Nonetheless, the equivalent provision in the

---

[902] Case C-289/04P *Showa Denko v Commission* [2006] ECR I-5859, [2006] 5 CMLR 840, Opinion, para 37.

[903] COMP/37.792 *Microsoft*, 24 March 2004, [2005] 4 CMLR 965; on appeal Case T-201/04, judgment of 17 September 2007; see Postscript below.

[904] 2006 Guidelines on Fines, para 31.

[905] eg Cases 100/80, etc, *Musique Diffusion Française v Commission* ('*Pioneer*') [1983] ECR 1825, [1983] 3 CMLR 221, paras 104 and 129; *Gosme/Martell-DMP*, OJ 1991 L185/23, [1992] 5 CMLR 586 (distinction drawn between an undertaking that did benefit from market partitioning and one that did not).

[906] *Eurocheque: Helsinki Agreement*, OJ 1992 L95/50, [1993] 5 CMLR 323.

[907] The fines were reduced or annulled by the CFI on other grounds: Cases T-39 & 40/92 *CB and Europay v Commission* [1994] ECR II-49. For another example, see *BASF Lacke + Farben/ Accinauto*, OJ 1995 L272/16, [1996] 4 CMLR 811, para 103.

[908] *XXIst report on Competition Policy (1991)*, point 139.

[909] See Wils (n 771, above).

1998 Guidelines was held to be lawful by the Court of Justice.[910] The absence of any gain from an infringement is not a mitigating factor.[911]

13.179 **Ability to pay and performance of the sector.** The 2006 Guidelines on Fines state that account may, on request, be taken of an undertaking's 'inability to pay in a specific social and economic context'.[912] In general, an undertaking's ability to pay is relevant to the amount of the fine,[913] but the Court of Justice has held that the Commission should not take account of the adverse financial situation of the infringer, since this would be tantamount to conferring an unjustified competitive advantage on the undertaking least well adapted to the conditions of the market.[914] The 2006 Guidelines on Fines reflect that principle by expressly providing that no reduction will be granted simply on the basis that the undertaking is in an adverse or loss-making situation. Rather, a reduction could be granted 'solely on the basis of objective evidence that imposition of the fine . . . would irretrievably jeopardise the economic viability of the undertaking concerned and cause its assets to lose all their value'.[915] If, therefore, the undertaking's business could be sold to a new owner, a plea that the present owners could not afford the fine is unlikely to be successful. However, where an undertaking's financial circumstances had caused it to exit the market in question, so that it was no longer carrying on the business to which the infringement related, that can justify the non-imposition of a fine.[916] A non-profit making body may be fined.[917] In fixing the level of fines the Commission does not take into consideration whether or not a fine may be deducted for tax purposes.[918] The Court of First Instance has stated

---

[910] Cases C-189/02P, etc, *Dansk Rørindustri v Commission* [2005] ECR I-5425, [2005] 5 CMLR 796, paras 290–296.

[911] *SAS v Commission* (n 895, above) para 146; Case T-64/02 *Hans Heubach v Commission* [2005] ECR II-5137, [2006] 4 CMLR 1157.

[912] 2006 Guidelines on Fines, para 35.

[913] per AG Slynn in *Musique Diffusion Française* (n 905, above) paras 310–311.

[914] Cases 96/82, etc, *IAZ v Commission* [1983] ECR 3369, [1984] 3 CMLR 276, para 55; applied in *Thyssen Stahl* (n 815, above) para 630; and Case T-175/95 *BASF Coatings v Commission* [1999] ECR II-1581, [2000] 4 CMLR 33, para 158. See also, eg *Choline Chloride* (n 898, above) paras 215–216.

[915] 2006 Guidelines on Fines, OJ 2006 C10/2, para 35.

[916] Cases T-24/93, etc, *Compagnie Maritime Belge* [1996] ECR II-1201, [1997] 4 CMLR 273, para 237 (appeal on other grounds partially allowed: Cases C-395 & 396/96P, [2000] ECR I-1365, [2000] 4 CMLR 1076, [2000] All ER (EC) 385).

[917] *IAZ v Commission* (n 914, above) paras 56–59. A farmer's cooperative may also be fined: *Meldoc* (n 868, above).

[918] Case 44/69 *Buchler v Commission* [1970] ECR 733, 761. In the UK, HM Revenue & Customs take the view that financial penalties imposed under the UK Competition Act (and, it is assumed, Art 81 and 82) will not be deductible in computing trading profits for tax purposes. This is because civil or criminal penalties imposed by or under the authority of an Act of Parliament are not deductible: they are 'losses not connected with or arising out of the trade' and so not deductible by virtue of sect 74(1)(e) of the Income and Corporation Taxes Act 1988. See the Office of Fair Trading competition law guideline, *Enforcement* (OFT 407, December 2004), para 5.15.

that the Commission is not required to take any account of poor financial performance of the sector concerned; it accepted the Commission's observation that, since cartels tend to arise in poorly-performing sectors, treating this as a ground of mitigation would lead to a reduction in virtually all cases.[919] However, in some case the Commission has accepted that the fact that the market generally is in a poor state is a mitigating factor.[920]

Reduction of fine for delay.   Delay in the conduct of the proceedings by the   **13.180**
Commission cannot be characterised as a 'mitigating' factor but exceptional delay may lead the Commission to reduce the fine. Exceptional delay can constitute an infringement of the fundamental rights of the defendant, as discussed above.[921] But without adopting any such conclusion, the Commission in *FETTSCA* reduced the fines by €100,000 because of the considerable duration of the administrative proceedings.[922] On appeal,[923] the Court of First Instance robustly dismissed the argument that the reduction should have been greater, holding that the statutory provisions (now Article 25 of Regulation 1/2003)[924] provide a complete code governing the imposition of fines so that a penalty imposed within the limitation period cannot be impugned on the ground of delay. The Court stated that the fact that the Commission had itself allowed a reduction in the fine for delay did not undermine that conclusion since the Commission was entitled to make such a reduction in its discretion although it was under no obligation to do so. Somewhat surprisingly, the Court considered that unreasonable delay which infringes the rights of defence may justify the annulment of a decision altogether, but will not warrant a reduction in the fine. This appears to create an inconsistency between the approach to delay on the part of the Commission and to delay on the part of the Court itself, since for the latter a reduction in the fine was ordered by the Court of Justice in *Baustahlgewebe*.[925] Perhaps reflecting its uncertainty over this distinction, the Commission has subsequently again reduced a

---

[919] *Tokai Carbon (Graphite Electrodes)* (n 899, above) para 345; *Hans Heubach v Commission* (n 911, above).

[920] See, eg *White Lead*, OJ 1979 L21/16, [1979] 1 CMLR 464 (no fines imposed in 'exceptional circumstances' of a case involving a market in terminal decline). In *Alloy Surcharge*, OJ 1998 L100/55, [1998] 4 CMLR 973, the fact that economic situation in the sector at the commencement of the agreement was 'particularly critical' helped to justify a 10 per cent reduction in the basic amount. For an example of extreme market conditions justifying a substantial reduction in fine, see *FNCBV* (n 831, above) (cartel in French beef sector in response to crisis arising from mad cow disease).

[921] See paras 13.078–13.079, above.

[922] *FETTSCA*, OJ 2000 L268/1, [2000] 5 CMLR 1011. This amounted to a reduction of between 10 and 40 per cent in the individual fines.

[923] Case T-213/00 *CMA CGM v Commission ('FETTCSA')* [2003] ECR II-913, [2003] 5 CMLR 268, paras 317–326.

[924] At that time, Reg 2988/74.

[925] Case C-185/95P *Baustahlgewebe v Commission* [1998] ECR I-8417, [1999] 4 CMLR 1203: see para 13.078, above.

cartel fine by €100,000 on account of the 'unduly long' duration of a procedure.[926]

13.181 **Maximum fine and consequential adjustment.** Article 23(2) of Regulation 1/2003 provides that fines must not exceed 10 per cent of the undertaking's turnover in the preceding business year. This provision therefore sets an absolute limit on the amount of the fine that may be imposed and if the result of the application of the Guidelines is to produce a result above that level then the fine will be reduced accordingly. It does not, however, necessarily follow that the Commission is obliged to determine the amount of a fine below that limit by reference to a turnover figure, nor is it possible to criticise the Commission for discrimination or unequal treatment resulting from the fact that the application of the 10 per cent limit may mean that a reduction has to be made in the fine of one undertaking but not of another, otherwise materially identical, undertaking.[927] Where an undertaking had not achieved any turnover in the business year preceding the decision, the fine can be determined and the maximum applied by reference to the undertaking's last full year of normal economic activity.[928]

(f) The Leniency Notice: cartel cases

13.182 **The Leniency Notice 2006.** The Commission published its first Notice on the non-imposition or reduction of fines in July 1996.[929] The 1996 Notice set out the circumstances in which undertakings that assist the Commission by providing information concerning their participation in a secret cartel can expect to be exempted from a fine, or to have their fine reduced. The 1996 Notice was replaced by a revised version of the Notice in 2002.[930] That Notice eased the conditions which undertakings must satisfy in order to obtain full immunity whilst making it more difficult for applicants to benefit from reductions in fines. The 2002

---

[926] COMP/37.766 *Netherlands Beer Cartel*, IP/07/509, 18 April 2007: procedure exceeded seven years.

[927] *Dansk Rørindustri* (n 910, above) para 323; Case T-304/02 *Hoek Loos v Commission* [2006] ECR II-1887, [2006] 5 CMLR 590, para 112.

[928] Case C-76/06P *Britannia Alloys v Commission* [2007] CMLR 251, applying a purposive construction to the equivalent provision in Reg 17. The ECJ dismissed the argument that this involved unequal treatment compared with other participants in a cartel (for whom the business year preceding the decision was applied), since they are not in a comparable situation.

[929] Commission Notice on the non-imposition or reduction of fines in cartel cases, 1996 OJ C207/4 ('the 1996 Notice'). The 1996 Notice was inspired by the US Dept of Justice's corporate leniency policy (introduced in 1993) of granting automatic amnesty for whistle-blowers in cartel cases. For the US and EC leniency programmes and the policy issues involved, see Wils, 'Leniency in Antitrust Enforcement: Theory and Practice' (2007) 30 World Competition 25; and the papers by Klawiter and Bloom in Ehlermann and Atanasiu (eds), *European Competition Law Annual 2006: Enforcement of Prohibition of Cartels* (2007).

[930] Commission Notice on immunity from fines and reduction of fines in cartel cases, OJ 2002 C45/03, Vol II, App B.6 ('the 2002 Notice').

Notice led to a substantial increase in applications for leniency.[931] In December 2006, the Commission issued a further revised version of the Leniency Notice.[932] This clarifies the information that an applicant needs to provide to the Commission in order to benefit from immunity and introduces the 'marker' system whereby applicants can establish their status as the first 'whistleblower' on the cartel whilst providing the necessary detailed information at a later date. The 2006 Leniency Notice also clarifies the protection given to corporate statements made by companies in their application for leniency from being made available to claimants in civil damages proceedings. The 2006 Leniency Notice applies as from 8 December 2006 in all cases in which no undertaking has contacted the Commission under the earlier Notice.[933] But the provisions in the 2006 Notice relating to the protection of corporate statements from disclosure apply both to new applications and those pending under the earlier Notice.[934]

Immunity from fines under the Leniency Notice. In contrast to the 1996 Notice which only guaranteed a 75 per cent reduction in fine for the first-reporting company, the 2002 Notice introduced full immunity from fines for qualifying leniency applicants who are 'first through the door'.[935] This is carried forward in the 2006 Leniency Notice which offers full immunity from fines for the first undertaking to submit information and evidence which, in the Commission's view, will enable it either to carry out a targeted inspection in connection with the alleged cartel ('paragraph 8(a) immunity') or to find an infringement of Article 81 ('paragraph 8(b) immunity').[936] **13.183**

Paragraph 8(a) immunity. The evidence which must be provided by the applicant in order to qualify for paragraph 8(a) immunity is specified in paragraph 9 of the Leniency Notice. It comprises, first, the 'corporate statement' which must set out the full extent of the applicant's knowledge regarding the aims, activities and **13.184**

---

[931] See Van Barlingen and Barennes, 'The European Commission's 2002 Leniency Notice in practice' (2005) 3 EC Competition Policy Newsletter 6, 7. For a table setting out all leniency decisions under the 1996 and 2002 Notices to September 2006, see Siragusa and Rizza (eds), *EU Competition Law, Vol III: Cartel Law* (2007), Annex 3.1, pp 396–425.

[932] Commission Notice on immunity from fines and reduction of fines in cartel cases, 2006 OJ C298/17: Vol II, App B.14 ('Leniency Notice'). See also the Leniency Application form at Vol II, App B.15.

[933] ie the date of its publication in the *Official Journal*: Leniency Notice, para 37.

[934] ibid.

[935] For commentary on the 2002 Notice, see Swaak and Arp 'A tempting offer: immunity from fines for cartel conduct under the European Commission's New Leniency Notice' (2003) ECLR 24(1) 9; Van Barlingen 'The European Commission's 2002 Leniency Notice after one year of operation' (2003) 2 Competition Policy Newsletter 16; Reynolds and Anderson 'Immunity and Leniency in EU Cartel Cases: Current Issues' (2006) 27 ECLR 82.

[936] For commentary on the 2006 Notice, see Suurnäkki and Tierno Centella, 'Commission adopts revised Leniency Notice to reward companies that report hard-core cartels' (2007) 1 EC Competition Policy Newsletter 7.

functioning of the cartel giving specific dates, locations and content of meetings and the names and addresses of individuals who have been involved both on the applicant's behalf and on behalf of the other cartel members. The corporate statement must also state whether other competition authorities either inside or outside the European Union have been approached or are intended to be approached in relation to the alleged cartel. Secondly, the applicant must submit any other evidence in its possession including in particular any contemporaneous evidence of the infringement. Paragraph 8(a) immunity will not be granted if, at the time of the submission, the Commission already has sufficient evidence to adopt a decision to carry out an inspection or if it has in fact already carried out an inspection.

13.185 **Paragraph 8(b) immunity.** In order to qualify for immunity under paragraph 8(b) the applicant must be the first to provide contemporaneous, incriminating evidence of the alleged cartel. A corporate statement must be provided covering the same material as is required for paragraph 8(a) immunity. In addition, this form of immunity will only be available where the Commission did not have sufficient evidence, at the time of the leniency submission, to find an infringement in respect of the alleged cartel and no other undertaking has been granted conditional paragraph 8(a) immunity.

13.186 **Additional conditions.** In order to qualify for definitive immunity at the end of the procedure, the applicant must also have satisfied a number of further cumulative conditions. It is required to cooperate genuinely, on a continuous basis and expeditiously throughout the administrative procedure, and to provide the Commission promptly with all the evidence that comes into its possession or is available to it relating to the suspected infringement.[937] The duty of cooperation requires the applicant to remain at the Commission's disposal to answer swiftly any request that may contribute to the establishment of the facts concerned[938] and not to reveal the existence of the immunity application to third parties before the Commission has issued a statement of objections, unless otherwise agreed.[939] The applicant must also have ended its involvement in the alleged cartel immediately following its application for leniency,[940] must not have taken steps to coerce

---

[937] Leniency Notice, para 12(a). See Case C-301/04P *Commission v SGL Carbon* [2006] ECR I-5915, [2006] 5 CMLR 877, para 68, in which the ECJ held, in relation to the 1996 Leniency Notice, that a reduction can only be justified where the information provided and, more generally, the conduct of the undertaking concerned, might be considered to demonstrate a genuine spirit of cooperation on its part.

[938] Leniency Notice, para 12(a). This includes making current and if possible former employees and directors available for interviews with the Commission.

[939] ibid. Nor must the undertaking have disclosed to others that it was contemplating an application: para 12(C).

[940] ibid, para 12(b). But since such action may alert the other cartel members, there is an important caveat that such involvement may continue if, in the Commission's view, it is necessary to preserve the integrity of inspections.

other undertakings to participate in the infringement,[941] and must not have destroyed, falsified or concealed evidence of the alleged cartel when contemplating making its application to the Commission.

Procedure for applications for immunity.　An undertaking wishing to apply for **13.187** immunity from fines should contact the Commission's Directorate-General for Competition.[942] The undertaking may initially apply either for a marker or may make a formal application for immunity straight away. If the undertaking decides to make a formal application for immunity, it may either provide all the information and evidence required with its application or it may present the information in hypothetical terms. If it becomes apparent that immunity is not available or that the undertaking has failed to meet the conditions in paragraph 8, the Commission will inform the undertaking in writing. In that case the undertaking may either withdraw the evidence it has disclosed or may convert its application into one for a reduction in fine. However, the Commission is not prevented from using its normal powers of investigation to obtain the information.[943]

Securing a marker for immunity.　Since only the first whistleblower can benefit **13.188** from full immunity from fines under the Leniency Notice, each of several cartel members may be anxious to establish itself as the first to approach the Commission once a cartel has begun to break up. An innovation introduced by the 2006 Notice is that an undertaking can secure its place in the queue by applying initially for a marker which allows it further time to gather the information and evidence that it needs to submit in order to qualify for immunity.[944] To be eligible to secure a marker, the applicant must provide the Commission with limited information about the cartel as well as informing the Commission whether it has made or intends to make immunity applications to any other competition authorities. It must also justify its request for the marker. If the Commission grants the marker, it will set a date by which the undertaking must 'perfect the marker' by providing the full information required to meet the relevant threshold for either paragraph 8(a) or paragraph 8(b) immunity. If the undertaking does so, then the full application will be deemed to have been submitted on the date when the marker was granted. If the undertaking does not perfect the marker within the set time limit and an extension is not granted, it may still present a formal application

---

[941] ibid, para 12(c). This is weaker than the requirement in the 1996 Leniency Notice that the applicant had not acted as an instigator of or played a determining role in the cartel.

[942] ibid, para 14.

[943] ibid, para 20. It would also be unrealistic to expect the Commission to adopt 'acute amnesia' in respect of evidence which it has seen: cf Case C-67/91 *Direccion General de Defensa de la Competencia v Asociacion Espanola de Banca Privada ('Spanish Banks')* [1992] ECR I-4785; and Kerse and Khan *EC Antitrust Procedure* (5th edn, 2005), para 7–064.

[944] Leniency Notice, para 15.

for immunity at any time but its place in the queue is no longer protected and its application will not date back to the provision of the marker.[945]

13.189 **Formal application and grant of conditional immunity.** Once an undertaking is ready to make a formal application for leniency, it must provide the Commission with all the information and evidence relating to the alleged cartel as required by paragraphs 8 and 9 of the Leniency Notice. A criticism of the 1996 Notice was that a decision as to the grant of immunity was taken at the end of the procedure with the adoption of the substantive decision imposing the fine. Under the 2002 and 2006 Leniency Notices, conditional immunity is granted at an earlier stage. The undertaking will be informed if immunity is not available.[946] If immunity is available and the Commission has verified that the information and evidence submitted meets the criteria, the Commission grants conditional immunity in writing.[947] The Commission will not consider other applications for immunity from fines before it has taken a position on an existing application in relation to the same suspected infringement, irrespective of whether the immunity application is presented formally or by requesting a marker.[948]

13.190 **Hypothetical applications.** The making of an application in hypothetical terms enables applicants to obtain a conditional decision from the Commission that they will be entitled to full immunity before the evidence has been submitted.[949] A hypothetical application must include a detailed descriptive list of the evidence which the applicant proposes to disclose at a later agreed date.[950] Although the applicant need not reveal its own identity, it must at least identify the relevant product or service sector (for example, the transport sector or the chemical sector), the geographic scope of the alleged cartel and the estimated duration. The descriptive list should be sufficiently detailed to enable the Commission to assess whether the conditions for immunity (under either limb of the test) are fulfilled. Copies of documents from which sensitive sections have been redacted may be used to illustrate the nature of the evidence.[951]

13.191 **Joint applications and applications by parents and subsidiaries.** The Commission recommends that where the infringing undertaking is a subsidiary, the leniency application be made by the parent company as the Commission will assume, in that case, that all subsidiaries under the control of the parent are

---

[945] Suurnäkki and Tierno Centella (n 936, above) p 10.

[946] Leniency Notice, para 20.

[947] Leniency Notice, para 18.

[948] ibid, para 21.

[949] The hypothetical procedure cannot be used by an undertaking which is seeking to perfect a marker which has been granted: para 15.

[950] Leniency Notice, para 16(b).

[951] ibid.

covered by the leniency application. The Commission will not interpret an application by the parent company as an admission of liability on the part of the parent.[952] Different considerations may, however, apply in respect of joint ventures.[953] The Court of First Instance has held, in the context of the 1996 Notice, that where several undertakings ask to meet the Commission with a view to cooperating for the purposes of a leniency application, the Commission should ensure that this does not itself have an impact on the conditions for the grant of leniency.[954]

'Partial immunity'.   Undertakings that do not meet the conditions for complete   **13.192**
immunity may nevertheless be eligible for a reduction in their fine.[955] To qualify for so-called 'partial immunity', undertakings must provide the Commission with evidence which represents 'significant added value' compared to the evidence in the Commission's possession at the time of the submission.[956] Whether significant added value has been provided depends on whether the evidence, by its nature and level of detail, enhances the Commission's ability to prove the infringement.[957] The Commission will generally consider written evidence originating from the period of time to which the facts pertain to have a greater value than evidence subsequently established.[958] Applications for reductions can, nonetheless, be made orally. Greater value will also be attached to evidence of direct rather than indirect relevance,[959] and evidence which does not require corroboration in order to be relied upon against other undertakings is preferred over evidence such as statements which does require corroboration if contested.[960] Although the 2006 Leniency Notice, like the 2002 Notice, is silent on the possibility of hypothetical applications for reductions, the Commission does in practice accept such hypothetical applications.[961] The Commission will determine, in its final decision, whether the undertaking provided significant added value and, if so, the level of reduction to be given to the undertaking.[962]

Level of reduction.   Reductions are calculated by reference to the timing of the   **13.193**
submission, with the first undertaking to provide evidence of significant added

---

[952] See Van Barlingen and Barennes (n 931 above) p 8.
[953] ibid, for discussion of issues facing JVs.
[954] Case T-15/02 *BASF v Commission* [2006] ECR II-497, [2006] 5 CMLR 27, paras 504 and 505.
[955] Leniency Notice (n 930, above) para 23.
[956] ibid, para 24.
[957] ibid, para 25. See Van Barlingen and Barennes (n 931, above) at p 13 which notes that corroboration of existing evidence may in certain circumstances provide significant added value.
[958] Leniency Notice, para 25.
[959] ibid.
[960] ibid.
[961] See Ortiz Blanco, *EC Competition Procedure* (2nd edn, 2006), para 6.18.
[962] Leniency Notice, para 26.

value being eligible for a 30–50 per cent reduction, the second undertaking being eligible for a 20–30 per cent reduction, and subsequent undertakings being eligible for a reduction of up to 20 per cent.[963] In determining the level of reduction, the Commission will also take into account both the time at which the evidence was submitted and the extent to which it represents added value.[964] The Leniency Notice therefore seeks to reward early cooperation and undertakings may find themselves in a race to submit their applications.[965] If an undertaking provides evidence relating to facts previously unknown to the Commission which have a direct bearing on the gravity or duration of the suspected cartel, the Commission will not rely on those facts to the detriment of that undertaking when setting the fine to be imposed upon it.[966]

13.194 **Procedure for the grant of a reduction.** An undertaking which has applied for a reduction can request written acknowledgement of receipt, recording the date and time of each submission of evidence supporting the application for a reduction.[967] The Commission will not take a position on any application for a reduction before it has taken a position on any existing application for conditional immunity from fines in relation to the same suspected infringement.[968] As with decisions on immunity, the Commission will inform the undertaking in writing, no later than the date on which the statement of objections is notified, of its preliminary conclusion on the application, identifying the applicable band of reduction.[969] The Commission will take a final decision in respect of any reduction in fine in the infringement decision.[970]

13.195 **Leniency and the European Competition Network ('ECN').** Regulation 1/2003 includes a number of provisions which facilitate the sharing of information between national competition authorities. These include Article 11(2) which obliges the Commission to transmit to the national competition authorities

---

[963] ibid. See, eg COMP/38.645 *Methacrylates (acrylic glass)*, decn of 31 May 2006, paras 401–422; on appeal as regards *inter alia* the refusal of leniency to ICI, Case T-214/06 *ICI v Commission*, and on other grounds, Cases T-206/06 *Total and Elf Aquitaine v Commission*, T-217/06 *Arkema France v Commission*, T-216/06 *Lucite International v Commission*, not yet decided. The Commission may not allow reductions to be based on purely random factors such as the order in which companies are questioned by, or answer to, the Commission: see Case T-48/98 *Acerinox v Commission* [2001] ECR II-3859, para 140.

[964] Leniency Notice, para 26.

[965] The Commission may disregard any application submitted after the statement of objections has been issued: ibid, para 29.

[966] ibid.

[967] Leniency Notice (n 930, above) para 28.

[968] ibid. There is, however, no requirement for the Commission to take a position on a first application for a reduction in fine before it can start to examine a second application for a reduction in fine.

[969] ibid, para 29.

[970] ibid, para 30.

'copies of the most important documents it has collected'.[971] The sharing of information in this way creates a potential disincentive for an undertaking wishing to apply for leniency, given the risk that it could trigger a domestic competition investigation. The Commission has sought to address this concern in its Notice on cooperation within the network of competition authorities ('the Network Notice').[972] These provisions are considered at paragraphs 14.028 *et seq*, below.

Multiple leniency applications in different Member States.   There is no 'one-stop shop' for applying for leniency in the Community: an application to the Commission for lenient treatment does not operate as a leniency application in any other jurisdiction.[973] Therefore, an undertaking applying to the Commission for leniency should consider the need for further leniency applications where there is a risk that the infringement could be investigated by one or more national competition authority.[974] The Commission has taken the view that it is typically best placed to handle matters where effects are felt in three or more Member States.[975] Where the Commission initiates proceedings, Regulation 1/2003 provides that national competition authorities ('NCAs') are relieved of their competence to apply Articles 81 and 82.[976] Accordingly, cases which concern effects in only one or two Member States may be more appropriately dealt with by one or two NCAs.[977] It follows that an undertaking which applied to the Commission for leniency may be denied lenient treatment if the case is subsequently allocated to a NCA to which another undertaking had been the first to apply for leniency.[978] The applicant may therefore wish to make leniency applications to all potentially interested NCAs at the same time as its makes its submission to the Commission, and the differences between leniency regimes may require the applications to be tailored accordingly. To reduce the burden of such multiple applications, in

13.196

---

[971] Arts 11(2) of Reg 1/2003, OJ 2003 L1/1: Vol II, App B.3. See also Art 12, ibid, which supercedes the ECJ judgment in *Spanish banks* (n 943, above) on the constraints on the use by Member States of information which was obtained by the Commission under Reg 17.

[972] Notice on Cooperation within the network of competition authorities ('the Network Notice') OJ 2004 C101/43: Vol II, App B.8 and Leniency Notice, para 35. See Blake and Schnichels, 'Leniency following Modernisation: safeguarding Europe's leniency programmes' (2004) 2 EC Competition Policy Newsletter, 7.

[973] For commentary, see Reynolds and Anderson (n 935, above), 8.

[974] See para 38 of the Network Notice (n 972, above), which advises applicants to consider filing simultaneous leniency applications with the relevant authorities.

[975] Network Notice (n 972, above) para 14; and see para 13.019, above.

[976] Art 11(6) of Reg 1/2003 (n 971, above). The effect of Art 3 of Reg 1/2003 is also to preclude the application of domestic competition law in these circumstances. See further para 14.060, below.

[977] See section 2.1 of the Network Notice on principles of case allocation.

[978] Thus, if single applications for immunity are made by different parties to different authorities, the decision on case allocation may determine who enjoys immunity from fines: see Kerse and Khan (n 943, above), para 7–071.

September 2006 the ECN issued a Model Leniency Programme.[979] The Model seeks to harmonise Member States' leniency programmes and introduces the concept of summary applications. If an undertaking applies for leniency with the Commission, it can file summary applications, containing only very limited information, to those NCAs which have accepted this process. The NCAs then grant an indefinite marker to the applicant that protects the applicant's position until they decide to take up the case, whereupon the summary application will have to be completed within a certain time frame. A list of Member States which accept such summary applications is available on the DG Competition website.[980]

13.197 **Oral applications for leniency.** In response to concerns about the risk of discovery of corporate statements in civil damages proceedings, the Commission accepts corporate statements in the form of oral evidence.[981] The applicant will be asked to attend a meeting with the Commission for the purposes of recording its statement on tape. The tape forms part of the Commission's investigation file. The undertaking has the opportunity to check the technical accuracy of the recording and once the recording has been approved, must check the accuracy of the transcript within a given time limit. Failure to check the transcript may lead to the loss of any beneficial treatment.[982] As an internal Commission document, it may be less susceptible to disclosure in civil litigation.[983] However, the Court of First Instance has noted that oral evidence must be regarded, in principle, as a less advantageous means of cooperation as it requires cooperation on the part of the Commission and is therefore subject to the availability of the Commission's resources.[984]

---

[979] See Vol II, App B.16 and also http//ec.europa.eu/comm/competition/ecn/model_leniency_en.pdf.

[980] http://ec.europa.eu/comm/competition/ecn/accepting_nca.pdf. At the time of writing, 15 NCAs accept such applications.

[981] Leniency Notice, para 32. As to the admissibility of oral evidence, see *Tokai Carbon (Graphite Electrodes)* (n 899, above) para 431, in which the CFI recognised the admissibility of oral evidence under the 1996 Notice; also Case T-15/02 *BASF* (n 954, above) para 506. In *Citric Acid*, OJ 2001 L239/18, [2002] 5 CMLR 24, the Commission for the first time granted a reduction of 90 per cent of the fine imposed on Cerestar Bioproducts on the basis of its oral evidence (appeals dismissed: Case T-59/02 *Archer Daniels Midland* [2006] 5 CMLR 1494 and T-43/02 *Jungbunzlauer*, judgment of 27 September 2006; on further appeal, Case C-511/06P *Archer Daniels Midland*, not yet decided). See Van Barlingen and Barennes (n 931 above), 10 and Reynolds and Anderson (n 935, above) on procedure for oral applications. In particular, note that the act of scheduling a meeting with the Commission does not have the effect of laying down a marker, so that the applicant will not have reserved its place in the queue in the event that evidence is received prior to the meeting.

[982] Leniency Notice, para 32.

[983] However, commentators have pointed out that this is not necessarily the case: see Kerse and Khan (n 943, above), para 7–064 and note 26; and Ortiz Blanco (n 961, above), para 6.19 note 64.

[984] Case T-15/02 *BASF* (n 954, above) para 503.

Protection of corporate statements from disclosure. The 2006 Leniency   **13.198**
Notice includes specific provision for the protection from disclosure of corporate
statements made to the Commission. The Notice includes a clear policy statement that participation in the leniency programme should not be discouraged by
discovery orders issued in civil litigation.[985] Access to corporate statements on the
Commission's file is granted only to the addressees of the statement of objections
and not to third parties such as complainants. Undertakings granted access, and
their legal advisers, must commit not to take copies of the statement and must
ensure that the information in the statement will be used solely for judicial or
administrative proceedings for the application of the Community competition
rules at issue in the related administrative proceedings.[986] The Commission has
also stated that it considers that public disclosure of documents and written or
recorded statements received in the context of the Notice would undermine public or private interests within the meaning of Article 4 of Regulation 1049/2001[987]
which concerns public access to documents held by the Community institutions.
This protection applies irrespective of whether the applicant finally obtains full or
partial immunity;[988] but it will be lost if the applicant itself discloses its corporate
statement to third parties.[989]

Review by the Community Courts. The European Court of Justice has   **13.199**
endorsed the principles underlying the Leniency Notice in the following terms:

> 'while the Commission may not compel an undertaking to admit its participation in
> an infringement, it is not thereby prevented from taking account, when fixing the
> amount of the fine, of the assistance given by that undertaking, of its own volition,
> in order to establish the existence of the infringement.

> In that connection, it is clear from the judgment in Case C-298/98P *Finnboard v
> Commission* . . . that the Commission may, for the purpose of fixing the amount of a
> fine, take account of the assistance given to it by the undertaking concerned to estab-
> lish the existence of the infringement with less difficulty and, in particular, of the fact
> that an undertaking admitted its participation in the infringement. It may grant an
> undertaking which has assisted it in that way a significant reduction of the amount
> of its fine and grant a substantially lesser reduction to another undertaking which did
> no more than fail to deny the main factual allegation on which the Commission
> based its objections.'[990]

---

[985] Leniency Notice, para 6.
[986] Leniency Notice (n 930, above) para 33. Para 34 of the Leniency Notice lists the sanctions
available to the Commission if the undertaking or legal advisor reneges on these commitments.
[987] Reg 1049/2001, OJ 2001 L145/43: see Leniency Notice, para 40.
[988] Suurnäkki and Tierno Centella (n 936, above), 14.
[989] Leniency Notice, para 33.
[990] Cases C-65 & 73/02P *ThyssenKrupp Stainless v Commission* [2005] ECR I-6773, [2005]
5 CMLR 773, paras 50–51; Case C-57/02P *Acerinox v Commission* [2005] ECR I-6689, [2005]
5 CMLR 712, paras 87–88. The ECJ was there concerned with the 1996 Notice.

13.200 **Status of the Leniency Notice.** The Court of First Instance has held, in relation to the 1996 Notice, that it creates legitimate expectations on which undertakings may rely when disclosing the existence of a cartel to the Commission.[991] This is expressly recognised in the 2006 Notice[992] and the Commission is therefore obliged to adhere to the Notice for the purposes of determining the fine. The Court of First Instance has also confirmed that a reduction in fine for cooperation is justified only if the conduct of the undertaking enabled the Commission to establish the infringement more easily, and, where relevant, to bring it to an end.[993] The Commission is not entitled to disregard the principle of equal treatment so that a difference in treatment of undertakings which participated in the infringement must be attributable to degrees of cooperation which are not comparable 'in so far as they consisted in supplying different information or in supplying that information at different stages of the administrative procedure, or in circumstances that were not similar'.[994] An express admission of infringement may therefore give rise to a reduction in fine which is greater than that given to an undertaking which cooperated but did not make any such express admission.[995] The Court of Justice also ruled, in relation to the 1996 Notice, that the Commission is entitled to take account of cooperation at a later stage in the proceedings, even after notification of the statement of objections to the undertaking concerned.[996] Any reduction in fine must not, however, take account of purely random factors, such as the order in which the undertakings are questioned by the Commission.[997] The provision of information in respect of facts for which the undertaking could not be fined, for example, because it concerned the conduct of another undertaking, does not amount to cooperation within the scope of the Leniency Notice,[998]

---

[991] Case T-15/02 *BASF AG* (n 954, above) para 488; and Case T-26/02 *Daiichi Pharmaceutical v Commission* [2006] ECR II-713, [2006] 5 CMLR 169, para 181.

[992] Leniency Notice, para 38.

[993] Case T-48/02 *Brouwerij Haacht v Commission* [2005] ECR II-5259, [2006] 4 CMLR 621, para 104; Case T-327/94 *SCA Holding v Commission* [1998] ECR II-1373, [1998] 5 CMLR 195, para 156; Cases T-67/00, etc, *JFE Engineering v Commission* [2004] ECR II-2501, [2005] 4 CMLR 27, para 499 (appeals dismissed, Cases C-403 & 405/04P *Sumitomo Metal Industries v Commission* [2007] 4 CMLR 650).

[994] *Brouwerij Haacht*, above, paras 108–109; Cases T-45 & 47/98 *Krupp Thyssen Stainless and Acciai Speciali Terni v Commission* [2001] ECR II-3757, [2002] 4 CMLR 521 appealed to the ECJ: Cases C-65 & 73/02P *ThyssenKrupp Stainless* (n 990, above) paras 245 and 246; *JFE Engineering*, above, para 501.

[995] Cases C-65 & 73/02P *ThyssenKrupp Stainless* (n 990, above) para 60.

[996] ibid, para 59.

[997] Case T-48/98 *Acerinox* (n 963, above) paras 139–140; not a point taken on appeal to ECJ: Case C-57/02P *Acerinox* (n 990, above).

[998] Case T-224/00 *Archer Daniels Midland v Commission* [2003] ECR II-2597, [2003] 5 CMLR 583, paras 295–298 in respect of the 1996 Notice (further appeal dismissed, Case C-397/03P, [2006] ECR I-4429, [2006] 5 CMLR 230). The CFI held that it could however amount to cooperation which is a mitigating circumstance under the Guidelines on Fines.

but the Commission may take such cooperation into account more generally as a mitigating factor in setting the fine.[999]

(g) Periodic penalty payments

Periodic penalty payments. Under Article 24 of Regulation 1/2003, the **13.201** Commission may by decision impose on undertakings default fines, called periodic penalty payments, in order to enforce a requirement to put an end to an infringement of Article 81 or Article 82 of the Treaty.[1000] The default fine may not exceed 5 per cent of the average daily turnover in the preceding business year per day.[1001] A decision to impose such penalties in respect of a substantive infringement can only be taken if there is also a decision under Article 7 of Regulation 1/2003 requiring the termination of the infringement.[1002] The Commission may also impose penalty payments to ensure compliance with an order for interim measures or with a commitment made binding under Article 9.[1003] The rules set out in Article 23(4) regarding the payment of fines by members of an insolvent association of undertakings apply to periodic penalties as they apply to fines imposed under Article 23. The fixing of periodic penalty payments under Article 24 involves two stages. In its first decision, the Commission imposes a periodic payment expressed in euros calculated from a specified date. Since that decision does not determine the total amount of the periodic penalty payment, it cannot be enforced.[1004] The amount can be definitively fixed only in another decision. If the parties comply with the Commission's requirements, the Commission may reduce the amount of the penalties when fixing the definitive sum due.[1005] The obligation to hear the undertaking concerned and to consult the Advisory Committee is fulfilled if the hearing and consultation take place before the fixing of the definitive amount of the payment so that all parties are

---

[999] See para 13.167, above.

[1000] For periodic penalty payments in support of the Commission's powers of investigation, see paras 13.035 and 13.050, above.

[1001] Reg 1/2003 (n 971, above) Art 24(1). Note that Art 16(1)(b) of Reg 17 empowered the Commission to impose periodic penalty payments to enforce an order under Art 8(3) to prohibit acts by the parties to an agreement which had been granted individual exemption under Art 81(3) EC. Art 43 of Reg 1/2003 maintains Art 8(3) of Reg 17 in force until the expiration of the individual exemption decisions but does not expressly retain this Art 16(1)(b) power of enforcement.

[1002] Art 24(1) of Reg 1/2003.

[1003] Art 24(1)(b) and (c) of Reg 1/2003.

[1004] Cases 46/87 & 227/88 *Hoechst v Commission* [1989] ECR 2859, [1991] 4 CMLR 410, para 55.

[1005] Art 24(2) of Reg 1/2003. See, eg *Baccarat*, OJ 1991 L79/16, [1992] 5 CMLR 189 (decision fixing the amount of the fine after an earlier decision imposing a periodic penalty; the Commission reduced the total amount of the fine because Baccarat believed that the withdrawal of the complaint which had led to the request for information released it from the obligation to supply the information).

in a position to express their views on the basis on which the Commission has imposed the penalty.[1006]

13.202 **Periodic penalty payments: *Microsoft*.** The procedure involved in imposing a periodic penalty is illustrated by the *Microsoft* case, where the Commission has sought to enforce its decision adopted in March 2004.[1007] In addition to fining Microsoft €497 million for its infringements of Article 82, the Commission ordered Microsoft to disclose to competitors, within 120 days, the interoperability information required for their products to be able to 'talk' with the Windows operating software. Further, Microsoft was required to allow the use of the information on reasonable and non-discriminatory terms.[1008] In November 2005, the Commission adopted a decision under Article 24(1)(a) of Regulation 1/2003 concluding that Microsoft had failed to comply with both these obligations.[1009] In setting the amount of the periodic penalty the Commission took into account (i) the extent to which Microsoft's failure to meet its obligations under the original decision has reduced the effectiveness of the remedy imposed by the Commission; and (ii) the necessity of imposing periodic penalty payments sufficient to ensure Microsoft's compliance.[1010] The Commission considered that Microsoft's failures 'have frustrated the effectiveness of the remedy and left in place the unlawful barriers hindering companies from competing in the work group server operating system market'.[1011] It was also necessary, having regard to Microsoft's size and financial resources to set periodic penalty payments 'which show that it is not possible to avoid or delay complying with a requirement in a Decision imposed to bring an infringement to an end but instead to continue to receive the benefits of failing to comply with such a requirement'. The Commission therefore allowed Microsoft a further month, until 15 December 2005, in which to comply, failing which a penalty of €2 million per day would be payable, calculated from that date. On 22 December 2005[1012] the Commission issued a statement of objections alleging that Microsoft was still failing to comply with the obligation to make the information available and on 12 July 2006, the Commission adopted a decision under Article 24(2) setting the definitive amount of the periodic penalty for the

---

[1006] *Hoechst* (n 1004, above) para 56.

[1007] COMP/37.792 *Microsoft*, 24 March 2004, [2005] 4 CMLR 965 (on appeal Case T-201/04 *Microsoft v Commission*, judgment of 17 September 2007; see Postscript below.).

[1008] Microsoft's application to suspend the operation of the decn pending its appeal was rejected by the President of the CFI: Case T-201/04R *Microsoft v Commission* [2004] ECR II-4463, [2006] 4 CMLR 406. For the appointment of the monitoring trustee in this case, see para 13.130, above. Microsoft also lodged an appeal against a decision in a letter of 1 June 2005 in which the Commission indicated the scope of the disclosure required: Case T-313/05, now withdrawn; see para PS.001 below.

[1009] COMP/37.792 *Microsoft*, decn of 10 November 2005.

[1010] ibid, para 198.

[1011] ibid, para 201.

[1012] See Press Release IP/05/1695 (22 December 2005).

period 16 December 2005 to 20 June 2006 for that failure.[1013] The Commission stated that it would be fully entitled to impose the full €2 million per day amount but that, since it wanted to leave open the possibility of imposing a periodic penalty in respect of the failure over the same period to offer information on reasonable terms, it would calculate the penalty at the level of €1.5 million per day.[1014] The Commission therefore imposed a fine of €280.5 million. In the same decision, the Commission increased the daily level of the periodic penalty payable in the event of continued non-compliance after 31 July 2006.[1015]

(h) Ancillary matters of law and practice

Allocation of fines between infringing parties.   Where more than one party is   **13.203** to be fined, the liability of each party is to be determined separately in the light of a 'consideration of the situation and of the individual conduct of each undertaking and of the importance of the role which it played in the agreement'.[1016] The Commission is not permitted to depart without explanation in a particular case from the general criteria which it has set out in that case for assessing fines.[1017] In appropriate cases, fines may be imposed on some parties, while other parties may escape the imposition of fines altogether,[1018] especially if they were in a subordinate position.[1019] But undertakings having the same responsibility may be

---

[1013] Press Release IP/06/979 and MEMO/06/277 (both 12 July 2006). The decn fixing the amount of the periodic penalty was appealed: Case T-271/06 *Microsoft v Commission*, now withdrawn, see Postscript below, para PS.001, n1.

[1014] The Commission calculated that the 5 per cent maximum set under Art 24(1) would amount to €4.82 million per day.

[1015] The operative part of this decision adds an additional sentence to the operative part of the 10 November 2005 decision to achieve this.

[1016] Case 45/69 *Boehringer Mannheim v Commission* [1970] ECR 769, 806; Cases 100/80, etc, *Musique Diffusion Française v Commission ('Pioneer')* [1983] ECR 1825, [1983] 3 CMLR 221, paras 129 and 135 *et seq*. The Commission is, however, entitled to impose a number of small flat-rate fines on a number of undertaking without seeking to distinguish between them: Case T-49/95 *Van Megen Sports v Commission* [1996] ECR II-1799, [1997] 4 CMLR 843, para 54.

[1017] Case T-309/94 *Koninklijke KNP v Commission* [1998] ECR II-1007, para 108.

[1018] See, eg *NAVEWA/ANSEAU*, OJ 1982 L167/39, [1982] 2 CMLR 193 (parties other than initial signatories); *Benelux Flat Glass*, OJ 1984 L212/13, [1985] 2 CMLR 350 (participants other than BSN and St. Gobain); *Roofing Felt*, OJ 1986 L232/15, [1991] 4 CMLR 130 (non-members of Belasco); per AG Vesterdorf, *Re Polypropylene Cartel* [1991] ECR II-869, [1992] 4 CMLR 84; *French-West African Shipowners' Committees*, OJ 1992 L134/1, [1993] 5 CMLR 446 (four companies who drew attention of the Commission to the infringements were exempted from fines); Case T-49/95 *Van Megen Sports v Commission* [1996] ECR 1799, [1997] 4 CMLR 843, para 56; *FEG and TU*, OJ 2000 L39/1, [2000] 4 CMLR 1208 (fines imposed on trade association and on its biggest and most powerful member).

[1019] cf cases under Art 81(1) such as *VW-Audi*, OJ 1998 L72/60, [1998] 5 CMLR 33 where dealers are in effect forced by their supplier to participate in an agreement containing an export ban; in such cases, the dealers are not usually fined, see para 13.172, above. See also *Floral*, OJ 1980 L39/51, [1980] 2 CMLR 285 (Firma Schiffer a minor instrument); *Toltecs/Dorcet*, OJ 1982 L379/19, [1983] 1 CMLR 412 (Mr Segers inexperienced and owner of small firm); reasoning approved by AG Slynn in Case 35/83 *BAT v Commission* [1985] ECR 363, [1985] 2 CMLR 470.

fined identical amounts.[1020] The imposition of a penalty does not infringe the principle of equal treatment merely because other undertakings in a similar position, whose infringements are not before the Court, have not been fined.[1021] So far as possible, the Commission should work on comparable data.[1022] Since the Commission is allowed to change the level of fines over time[1023] and to alter its view of the gravity of particular matters in different cases, challenges to the fine based on contravention of the principle of equal treatment tend to be based on comparisons with other undertakings fined in the same case.[1024] In relation to such challenges based on differences in total turnover or turnover in the relevant market, the Court of First Instance has stated:

> '[the Commission] is not required to ensure, where fines are imposed on a number of undertakings involved in the same infringement, that the final amounts of the fines resulting from its calculations for the undertakings concerned reflect any distinction[1025] between them in terms of their overall turnover or their turnover in the relevant product market'[1026]

1020 *Siemens/Fanuc*, OJ 1985 L376/29, [1988] 4 CMLR 945; see also *Alloy Surcharge*, OJ 1998 L100/55, [1998] 4 CMLR 973, in which the Commission applied its 1998 Guidelines on Fines to a case under the ECSC and refused to distinguish between the undertakings on the ground of the gravity of their infringements.

1021 Case T-77/92 *Parker Pen v Commission* [1994] ECR II-549, [1995] 5 CMLR 435, para 83–86; Cases C-89/85, etc, *Åhlström Osakeytiö v Commission ('Wood Pulp II')* [1993] ECR I-1307, [1993] 4 CMLR 407, para 146; Case T-219/99 *British Airways v Commission* [2004] All ER (EC) 1115, [2004] 4 CMLR 1008, para 66 (appeal on other grounds dismissed, Case C-95/04P, [2007] 4 CMLR 982); Case T-303/02 *Westfalen Gassen Nederland v Commission* [2007] 4 CMLR 334, para 141.

1022 *Musique Diffusion Française* (n 1016, above) para 122. See also Case T-142/89 *Boël v Commission* [1995] ECR II-867, where the Commission was held to have erred in not taking into account the fact that the undertaking's turnover in the relevant year was abnormally high compared to the turnover of the other undertakings involved.

1023 See para 13.147, above.

1024 eg Case T-220/00 *Cheil Jedang v Commission* [2003] ECR II-2473 (CFI reduced increase for duration on the basis that it inexplicably contradicted the approach taken in respect of the other parties to the cartel); Cases T-236/01, etc, *Tokai Carbon v Commission (Graphite Electrodes)* [2004] ECR II-1181, [2004] 5 CMLR 1465 (Commission's further appeal allowed, Case C-301/04P *Commission v SGL Carbon* [2006] ECR I-5915, [2006] 5 CMLR 877; other appeals dismissed, Cases C-289/04P *Showa Denko v Commission* and C-308/04P *SGL Carbon v Commission* [2006] ECR I-5859, 5977, [2006] 5 CMLR 840, 922) (applicants wrongly placed in same group as larger undertaking).

1025 However this phrase in the English version of the judgment – which suggests that the Commission is entitled to take no account of any distinction in turnover – is not reflected in the other language versions. eg the French language version (*'toute différentiation'*) makes it clear that the Commission is entitled not to take account of 'every' such difference in turnover; ie the Commission is not required to reflect every single difference in turnover, however minor.

1026 Case T-21/99 *Dansk Rørindustri v Commission* [2002] ECR II-1681, para 202, upheld by the ECJ Cases C-189/02P, etc, *Dansk Rørindustri* [2005] ECR I-5425, [2005] 5 CMLR 796, para 312; see also Case T-62/02 *Union Pigments v Commission* [2005] ECR II-5057, [2006] 4 CMLR 1105, para 159.

The test is whether the Commission has exercised its discretion in a coherent and objectively justified manner.[1027] As far as turnover beyond the relevant market is concerned, the Commission is entitled to take total turnover, or global turnover in the affected product,[1028] into account. The Court of First Instance has upheld the imposition of a similar basic amount on undertakings whose total turnovers differed by a factor of 10.[1029] However, the appropriate remedy for a successful plea of unequal treatment may be to increase the fine on the favoured party, although that could only happen if (a) the favoured party has also appealed and (b) has had sufficient notice of that possibility to respond to it.[1030]

Trade associations. A non-profit making trade association may be indepen- **13.204** dently fined in proportion to its participation.[1031] However, if the statement of objections is addressed only to an association, the Commission may not impose fines on its members; for an undertaking to be fined, it must be notified individually that it is susceptible to the imposition of a penalty.[1032] If a fine is imposed on a trade association taking account of its members' turnover, and the association is not solvent, the association is required to call on its members to contribute up to 10 per cent of their turnover in the preceding business year so as to cover the fine. If they do not do so, the Commission may require payment of the fine by those members whose representatives were members of the decision-making bodies of the association, unless those undertakings show that they have not implemented the infringing decision and either were unaware of it or distanced themselves from it before the Commission's investigation.[1033]

[1027] Case T-15/02 *BASF v Commission* [2006] ECR II-497, [2006] 5 CMLR 27, at, eg para 170.

[1028] *Tokai Carbon (graphite electrodes)* (n 1024, above).

[1029] Case T-230/00 *Daesang v Commission* [2003] ECR II-2733; *Union Pigments* (n 1026, above) para 157 (similar disparity 'not so great as to make it necessary to place [the applicant] in a different group [from the comparator]'). In COMP/38.337 *Thread*, decn of 14 September 2005, the Commission imposed the same basic amount on a company whose total turnover was 71 times smaller than the comparator (on appeal Cases T-446/05 *Amann & Söhne and Cousin v Commission*, Case T-448/05 *Oxley Threads v Commission*, T-452/05 *Belgian Sewing Thread v Commission*, T-456/05 *Gütermann v Commission*, T-457/05 *Zwicky v Commission*, not yet decided).

[1030] Cases T-67/00, etc, *JFE Engineering v Commission* [2004] ECR II-2501, [2005] 4 CMLR 27 at paras 575 *et seq* (on appeal Cases C-403 & 405/04P *Sumitomo Metal Industries v Commission* [2007] 4 CMLR 650) but see also para 13.216, below.

[1031] Cases 96/82, etc, *IAZ v Commission* [1983] ECR 3369, [1984] 3 CMLR 276 (ANSEAU); *Woodpulp*, OJ 1985 L85/1, [1985] 3 CMLR 474 (KEA and others); *Roofing Felt*, OJ 1986 L232/15, [1991] 4 CMLR 130 (Belasco); cf *Building and construction industry in the Netherlands*, OJ 1992 L92/1, [1993] 5 CMLR 135 (no fine for association which performed purely administrative function).

[1032] Cases C-395 & 396/96P *Compagnie Maritime Belge Transports v Commission* [2000] ECR I-1365, [2000] 4 CMLR 1076, [2000] All ER (EC) 385, paras 142–147 (fines on members of a liner conference annulled).

[1033] Reg 1/2003 (n 971, above) Art 23(4).

13.205 **Fines on parents and subsidiaries.** The respective responsibilities of parent companies and their subsidiaries for infringements and their consequent liability to fines will depend on the facts of the case.[1034] The evidence may show that parent and subsidiary acted together in the commission of the infringement, or that the parent exercised control over the subsidiary.[1035] The Commission is entitled[1036] to impose a fine on the parent where more than one subsidiary is involved or where the subsidiary has no real independence, assets or staff.[1037] The Commission cannot merely find that an undertaking was able to exert such a decisive influence over the other undertaking, without checking whether that influence actually was exerted. Rather, the Commission must demonstrate such decisive influence on the basis of factual evidence, including, in particular, any management power one of the undertakings may have over the other.[1038] However, when a parent company holds 100 per cent of the shares in a subsidiary which has been found guilty of unlawful conduct, this is a strong indication that the parent company actually exerted a decisive influence over its subsidiary's conduct. In that situation, only some further factors indicating likely influence rather than evidence of actual influence needs to be shown so as to establish a presumption of decisive influence; and it is then for the parent to reverse that presumption by adducing evidence to

---

[1034] For the Commission's analysis of the questions discussed in this and the succeeding paragraph, see *Cartonboard*, OJ 1994 L243/1, [1994] 5 CMLR 547, paras 140 *et seq*; and *Pre-Insulated Pipe Cartel*, OJ 1999 L24/1, [1999] 5 CMLR 47, paras 154 *et seq*. See generally Montesa and Givaja, 'When Parents Pay for their Children's Wrongs: Attribution of Liability for EC Antitrust Infringements in Parent-Subsidiary Scenarios', (2006) 29 World Competition 555; Wils, 'The undertaking as subject of EC competition law and the imputation of infringements to natural or legal persons' (2000) 25 EL Rev 99, 108–116. The principle that a parent may be responsible for its subsidiary also applies to the responsibility of a principal for its agent in a case where the agent would not be regarded as a separate undertaking; Case T-66/99 *Minoan Lines v Commission* [2003] ECR II-5515, [2005] 5 CMLR 1957, paras 121 *et seq* (further appeal dismissed C-121/04P *Minoan Lines* [2006] 4 CMLR 1405) and see paras 2.020 and 6.028, above.

[1035] See, eg Cases 48/69, etc, *ICI v Commission* [1972] ECR 619, [1972] CMLR 557; Cases 6 & 7/73 *Commercial Solvents v Commission* [1974] ECR 223, [1974] 1 CMLR 309; *United Brands*, OJ 1976 L95/1, [1976] 1 CMLR D28; *Hugin/Liptons*, OJ 1978 L22/23, [1978] 1 CMLR D19; *Johnson & Johnson*, OJ 1980 L377/16, [1981] 2 CMLR 287; *AEG—Telefunken*, OJ 1982 L117/15, [1982] 2 CMLR 386, upheld on appeal Case 107/82 *AEG v Commission* [1983] ECR 3151, [1984] 3 CMLR 325, paras 47–53; *Moët et Chandon*, OJ 1982 L94/7, [1982] 2 CMLR 166; *Benelux Flat Glass*, OJ 1984 212/13, [1985] 2 CMLR 350; *John Deere*, OJ 1985 C L35/58, [1985] 2 CMLR 554; *Sandoz*, OJ 1987 L222/28, [1989] 4 CMLR 628; Case C-294/98P *Metsä-Serla Oyj v Commission* [2000] ECR I-10065, [2001] 4 CMLR 322, para 34; Case C-286/98P *Stora Koppabergs Bergslags v Commission* [2000] ECR I-9925, [2000] 4 CMLR 370, para 26–29; Cases C-65 & 73/02P *ThyssenKrupp Stainless v Commission* [2005] ECR I-6773, [2005] 5 CMLR 773, paras 66–69. For the application of these principles in the case of a joint venture, see Case T-314/01 *Avebe v Commission* [2006] ECR II-3085, [2007] 4 CMLR 9.

[1036] But not bound; the Commission may choose to address its decision to the subsidiary in such a case: *Tokai Carbon (Graphite Electrodes)* (n 1024, above) paras 279–285.

[1037] Case T-352/94 *Mo och Domsjö v Commission* [1998] ECR II-1998, paras 94–95; appeal dismissed, Case C-283/98P, [2000] ECR I-9855, [2001] 4 CMLR 322.

[1038] Case T-314/01 *Avebe v Commission* [2006] ECR II-3085, [2007] 4 CMLR 9, para 136.

establish that its subsidiary was independent.[1039] The fact that the subsidiary has its own infrastructure or constitutes an insignificant proportion of group turnover does not rebut the presumption.[1040] Undertakings may be treated as members of the same economic unit, so that a fine may be imposed on one in respect of the conduct of the other, by virtue of the fact that they are each owned by the same individual, provided that it is established on the evidence that the individual actually controls both undertakings.[1041] In *BPB Industries*,[1042] the Commission imposed a fine on a wholly-owned subsidiary company, British Gypsum, in respect of its activities in the British market, but imposed a fine on the parent, BPB, in respect of British Gypsum's activities in the Northern Irish market where British Gypsum sold products supplied by the Irish subsidiary of BPB. The Court of First Instance noted that BPB and British Gypsum constituted a single economic entity and that it was apparent that the executive committee of BPB had kept itself regularly informed of the practices of British Gypsum and the Irish subsidiary on the Northern Ireland market, whereas it had displayed no such interest in British Gypsum's activities on the mainland. The Court held that although the Commission could have fined BPB for all British Gypsum's activities, the Commission was entitled instead to attribute only some of the abuses to the parent. If one undertaking later becomes the parent of another undertaking which is party to the same cartel agreement, it may be held to be liable for the conduct of that undertaking thereafter.[1043] Where fines are imposed on both parent and subsidiary, they may be imposed jointly and severally.[1044]

[1039] Case C-286/98P *Stora Koppabergs v Commission* (n 1035, above) paras 21–30, and Opinion of AG Mischo, paras 17–62. In Cases T-109/02 *Bolloré v Commission* [2007] 5 CMLR 66, the CFI held that such additional indicia of influence could be an overlap in the board of directors or at management level. See also Case T-325/01 *DaimlerChrysler v Commission* [2005] ECR II-3319, [2007] 4 CMLR 559, paras 218–221; *Avebe*, above, where it was held by analogy that the parents of a joint venture were presumed to control the activity of their subsidiary in which they held 50 per cent shares and so could be held liable for its infringement. cf the Commission's rejection of any rebuttal of the presumption in COMP/38.443 *Rubber Chemicals*, 21 December 2005, [2007] 4 CMLR 723, para 258 *et seq*; on appeal, Cases T-85/06, etc, *General Química v Commission*, not yet decided. The principle that an undertaking can be fined for the behaviour of another undertaking over which it has control has been extended to the case where a trade association infringes the competition rules on the instructions of, and on behalf of, its members; in such a case the members may be held jointly and severally liable for the fine imposed on the association: *Metsä-Serla Oyj v Commission* (n 1035, above).

[1040] *Bolloré v Commission*, above, paras 142–144.

[1041] *Dansk Rørindustri* (n 1026, above) para 118–130.

[1042] Case T-65/89 *BPB Industries v Commission* [1993] ECR II-389, [1993] 5 CMLR 32. See also *Distribution of package tours during 1990 World Cup*, OJ 1992 L320/31, [1994] 5 CMLR 253.

[1043] *Stora* (n 1035, above) para 82.

[1044] See, eg *Zoja/CSC—ICI* [1972] JO L299/51, [1973] CMLR D50 (upheld on appeal, Cases 6 & 7/73 *Commercial Solvents* [1974] ECR 223, [1974] 1 CMLR 309, para 41); *Johnson & Johnson* (n 1035, above); *Pre-Insulated Pipe Cartel* (n 1034, above) (De Henss/Isoplus group).

13.206 **Liability of successor undertaking.** By the time the Commission seeks to impose fines, the undertaking sought to be fined may be a different legal entity from the undertaking which committed the infringement. Thus in *Sugar*, the Court of Justice upheld a fine on Suiker Unie, a company, in respect of activities carried on before its incorporation by an association of four cooperatives, all of which had been dissolved by the time of the Commission's decision. Since Suiker Unie had assumed the rights and liabilities of the cooperatives (which had also traded under the name 'Suiker Unie') and was run by the same persons from the same address, the Court held that Suiker Unie was the 'economic successor' of the dissolved undertakings.[1045] When the legal person in control at the time of the infringement has ceased to exist by the time the fine comes to be imposed, it is necessary to identify the collection of material and human resources responsible at the date of the infringement and then identify the owner of those resources at the time of the decision. This will ensure that the disappearance of the legal person does not mean that the undertaking escapes liability.[1046] That principle also applies where the person in control at the time of the infringement still exists, but is structurally linked to the new owner.[1047] In *Cartonboard*,[1048] the Commission held that the question to be asked was whether there was a 'functional and economic continuity' between the infringing undertaking and its putative successor. Where a parent was properly considered to be party to the infringement, its responsibility for the period prior to the transfer would not pass to the acquirer of

---

[1045] *Sugar*, OJ 1973 L140/17, [1973] CMLR D65, on appeal Cases 40/73, etc, *Suiker Unie v Commission* [1975] ECR 1663, [1976] 1 CMLR 295, paras 74–88. See also Cases 29 & 30/83 *CRAM and Rheinzink v Commission* [1984] ECR 1679, [1985] 1 CMLR 688, para 9; *Floral*, OJ 1980 L39/51, [1980] 2 CMLR 285, para 59; *Zinc Producer Group*, OJ 1984 L220/27, [1985] 2 CMLR 108, para 91; *Aluminium Imports from Eastern Europe*, OJ 1985 L92/1, [1987] 3 CMLR 813, para 19; *Welded Steel Mesh*, OJ 1989 L260/1, [1991] 4 CMLR 13, para 194; *Cartonboard* (n 1034, above).

[1046] Case T-6/89 *Enichem Anic v Commission* [1991] ECR II-1623, para 237–239, comparing the position of Enichem where the legal person responsible for the control of the undertaking at the time of the breach was still in existence at the time of the decn and so was liable to a fine, with the position of SAGA Petrokjemi where the legal person had ceased to exist on fusion with Statoil; upholding in this regard *Polypropylene*, OJ 1986 L230/1, [1988] 4 CMLR 347, paras 96–101; further appeal on this ground dismissed, Case C-49/92P *Commission v Anic Partecipazioni* [1999] ECR I-4125, [2001] 4 CMLR 602, paras 139–147. See also Case C-297/98P *SCA Holding v Commission* [2000] ECR I-10101, [2001] 4 CMLR 413, paras 24–28; Cases T-259/02, etc, *Raiffeisen Zentralbank Österreich v Commission*, judgment of 14 December 2006, paras 325 *et seq*, also dealing with some instances where the infringing entity ceased to exist on being absorbed into its acquiring undertaking and some where the legal entity remained in existence so that the original owner could be held liable (on appeal on this ground, Case C-125/07P *Erste Bank der österreichischen Sparkassen v Commission*, not yet decided); *NAVEWA/ANSEAU (No. 2)*, OJ 1982 L325/20, [1983] 1 CMLR 470, where, on special facts, subsequent acquisition of part of the assets of an undertaking was held not to render the acquirer liable to fines imposed on parties responsible for the original infringement.

[1047] Cases C-204/00P, etc, *Aalborg Portland* [2004] ECR I-123, [2005] 4 CMLR 251, para 359.

[1048] *Cartonboard* (n 1034, above) para 145.

its subsidiary; on the other hand, where the decision would have been addressed to a subsidiary which had subsequently been transferred, the former parent had no responsibility for the infringement and responsibility passed with the subsidiary. Liability as between the new parent and the subsidiary in respect of the period after the transfer would depend on the factors discussed in the previous paragraph. The new parent is not liable for the conduct of the subsidiary prior to its acquisition, even if the new parent could not have been unaware of its involvement in the cartel.[1049] It is possible for an undertaking to accept liability for the conduct of another undertaking, but such an acceptance of responsibility must be strictly construed.[1050]

Double jeopardy. Conduct constituting an infringement of Article 81 or Article 82 may also infringe the competition law of a Member State or a third country. Where fines are imposed under the law of a Member State in respect of conduct which is also an infringement of Treaty, the principle of *non bis in idem* applies, so that the Commission is obliged to take account of the fines already imposed by the Member State.[1051] However, the position is different when fines are imposed by a non-Member State. Arguments that the Commission when penalising participants in an international cartel should take account of the fines imposed in the United States have been decisively rejected by the Court of Justice. A fine under the EC regime is concerned with safeguarding competition within the Community whereas the exercise of powers by authorities of non-Member States is concerned with the requirements of those States regarding competition within their own territorial jurisdiction.[1052]

13.207

Limitation period for imposition of fines. Under Article 25(1)(b) of Regulation 1/2003 the Commission's power to impose fines for substantive infringements

13.208

[1049] Cases C-65 & 73/02P *ThyssenKrupp Stainless* (n 1035, above) para 69. In that regard it is irrelevant if the new parent had at that time itself been a participant in the cartel on its own account: Case C-279/98P *Cascades v Commission* [2000] ECR I-9693, paras 73–82; *Stora Koppabergs Bergslags v Commission* (n 1035, above) paras 35–39. But cf Cases T-259/02, etc, *Raiffeisen Zentralbank Österreich* (n 1046, above) paras 333–334.

[1050] Cases C-65 & 73/02P *ThyssenKrupp Stainless* (n 1035, above) paras 81–88.

[1051] Case 14/68 *Wilhelm v Bundeskartellamt* [1969] ECR 1, [1969] CMLR 100; Case 7/72 *Boehringer v Commission* [1972] ECR 1281, [1973] CMLR 864; *Cast iron and steel rolls*, OJ 1983 L317/1, [1984] 1 CMLR 694; Case T-149/89 *Sotralentz v Commission* [1995] ECR II-1127, para 29. cf the converse position under the UK Competition Act 1998, sect 38(9). For discussion of the principle, see Wils, *Principles of European Antitrust Enforcement* (2006), Chap 3. Note that while the *non bis in idem* principle traditionally applies only within the same national jurisdiction, the EU Charter on Fundamental Rights, Art 50, expresses the protection against double jeopardy as regards any criminal proceedings within the EU.

[1052] Cases C-289/04P *Showa Denko v Commission* and C-308/04P *SGL Carbon v Commission* ('*Graphite Electrodes*') (n 1024, above); Case C-328/05P *SGL Carbon v Commission* ('*Specialty Graphites*'), judgment of 10 May 2007. See also Case C-397/03P *Archer Daniels Midland v Commission* ('*Amino Acids*') [2006] ECR I-4429, [2006] 5 CMLR 230, paras 46–76.

of the rules on competition cannot be exercised more than five years after the cessation of the infringment.[1053] Time begins to run on the day upon which the infringement is committed, but in the case of a 'continuing or repeated' infringement, time begins to run on the day on which the infringement ceases.[1054] When the infringement ceases may be a difficult question of fact[1055] and the burden of proving the end date rests on the Commission even where the date is relevant to a limitation period defence, because duration is an essential element of an infringement.[1056] The running of time for limitation purposes is 'interrupted' by 'any action' taken by the Commission, or by a Member State at the Commission's request, for the purpose of the preliminary investigation or proceedings in respect of the infringement. Such 'action' includes, amongst other things, requests for information, authorisations issued by the Commission to its officials, the commencement of proceedings by the Commission, or the service of the statement of objections.[1057] However, such actions must be 'necessary' if they are to interrupt the limitation period.[1058] Action against any one party 'interrupts' the running of time as regards all the undertakings participating in the infringement.[1059] Each interruption starts the full limitation period running afresh, subject to an overall limit of twice the limitation period, although that maximum is extended by the period of any appeals.[1060]

[1053] Reg 1/2003, OJ 2003 L1/1: Vol II, App B.3. For infringements of provisions covering requests for information and carrying out of inspections the period is three years: Art 25(1)(a). There appears to be no express limitation period in respect of behavioural or structural remedies under Art 7 of Reg 1/2003, a matter which could create difficulties, eg in respect of divestiture orders: see para 13.131, above. In *Ford Agricultural*, OJ 1993 L20/1, [1995] 5 CMLR 89, the Commission regarded the age of the infringements (six years) as relevant although the limitation rules did not apply. Note that the fact that the limitation period for the imposition of a fine has expired does not preclude an investigation and finding of infringement by the Commission if it has a legitimate interest to pursue the case: see para 13.124, above.

[1054] Art 25(2) of Reg 1/2003. See, eg Case T-7/89 *Hercules v Commission* [1991] ECR II-1711, [1992] 4 CMLR 84, para 307–311, appeal on other grounds dismissed, Case C-51/92P, [1999] ECR I-4235, [1999] 5 CMLR 976.

[1055] See generally *Zinc Producer Group* (n 1045, above).

[1056] Case T-120/04 *Peróxidos Orgánicos v Commission* [2007] 4 CMLR 153, paras 50 *et seq*. The CFI also held in that case that the fact that the Commission may have applied the limitation period principles incorrectly in relation to one cartel member did not entitle another to a reduction in its fine.

[1057] Art 25(3) of Reg 1/2003 (n 1053, above). The limitation period is interrupted as from the date on which the action is notified to at least one undertaking, or association of undertakings, participating in the infringement, ibid.

[1058] Case T-213/00 *CMA CGM v Commission* ('*FETTCSA*') [2003] ECR II-913, [2003] 5 CMLR 268, paras 480–517 (Commission completed its investigation in 1995; subsequent requests for updated turnover figures were insufficient to interrupt the running of the limitation period).

[1059] Art 25(4) of Reg 1/2003.

[1060] Art 25(5) and (6) of Reg 1/2003. It is irrelevant that the eventual decision of the Commission is later annulled. Moreover, appeals for annulment of a decision suspend the running of time, whether or not they succeed. See Cases T-305/94, etc, *Re PVC (No. 2)* [1999] ECR II-931, [1999] 5 CMLR 303, paras 1089–1104.

Payment of the fine. The Commission is entitled to specify the amount of the **13.209** fine in euros,[1061] and that is now its practice.[1062] The Commission is also entitled to indicate the period within which, and the bank account to which, payment must be made. Normally the fine is payable within three months, after which the Commission is entitled to charge default interest.[1063] The rate of such interest is now usually specified in the decision.[1064] In cases of hardship, it seems that the Commission may accept payment by instalments against provision of a bank guarantee.[1065] The Commission is entitled to attribute part payments as payments of interest rather than of the principal, and interest remains payable even if the fine is reduced on appeal.[1066] If the decision is appealed, payment may be suspended pending the appeal against provision of a bank guarantee in which case default interest is applied (which must also be covered by the guarantee) at a rate lower than that applicable for non-payment.[1067]

Enforcement of penalties. Decisions of the Commission which impose **13.210** pecuniary obligations are enforceable under Article 256 of the Treaty. Enforcement is governed by the rules of civil procedure in the Member State where enforcement is carried out. In the United Kingdom, the Commission may cause a decision to be registered with the High Court (or Court of Session in Scotland) whereupon it is to have the same force and effect as if it were a judgment or order given or

---

[1061] Case T-334/94 *Sarrió v Commission* [1998] ECR II-1439, [1998] 5 CMLR 195, para 328, paras 393–397; in that case (where the Commission had followed its then practice of fixing fines by reference to a turnover figure) the CFI also held that the Commission was entitled to convert the relevant turnover figure into ECUs on the basis of the average rates for the last complete year of the infringement and not on the date of the decn; it was irrelevant that exchange rates had subsequently altered. See also Case T-348/94 *Enso Española v Commission* [1998] ECR II-1875. Since 1 January 1999, fines have been fixed in euros.

[1062] If the decn states that payment may be either in euros or in the currency of the Member State where the bank nominated for payment is situated, the relevant rate of exchange is that prevailing on the day preceding payment; see, eg *British Midland v Aer Lingus*, OJ 1992 L96/34, [1993] 4 CMLR 596 (re ECUs).

[1063] Case 107/82 *AEG v Commission* (n 1035, above) paras 139–143; Case T-275/94 *CB v Commission* [1995] ECR II-2169, [1995] 5 CMLR 410, [1995] All ER (EC) 717.

[1064] Generally the rate applied by the European Central Bank to its main refinancing operations on the first day of the month in which the decision is adopted, plus 3.5 percentage points. A challenge to this rate as unreasonable was dismissed in Case T-23/99 *LR AF 1998 v Commission* [2002] ECR II-1705, [2002] 5 CMLR 571, paras 395–399.

[1065] The Commission is thought to have done so in *Amino acids*, OJ 2001 L152/24, [2001] 5 CMLR 322. See also *CEWAL*, OJ 1993 L34/20, [1995] 5 CMLR 89, Press release IP/92/1110 (23 December 1992); Case T-18/96R *SCK and FNK* [1996] ECR II-407, [1996] 5 CMLR 307, para 31. A facility to pay by instalments has to be negotiated with DG Budget.

[1066] *CB v Commission* (n 1063, above).

[1067] Generally the European Central Bank rate (n 1064, above) plus 1.5 percentage points. The Commission is entitled to insist on a bank guarantee and need not accept other forms of security: Cases T-236/01, etc, *Tokai Carbon v Commission (Graphite Electrodes)* (n 1024, above) paras 478–479. See further para 13.248, below.

made by that Court on the date of registration.[1068] No such decision may be registered unless an order for enforcement has been appended by the Secretary of State, but such order must be appended by the Secretary of State without any formality other than verification of the authenticity of the decision.[1069] Enforcement proceedings cannot be taken more than five years after the date of the Commission's decision, excluding periods during which the Commission allowed time to pay or the decision was suspended by the Court of First Instance.[1070] The period is interrupted, so that time starts running afresh, by any action of the Commission (or a Member State at the Commission's request) to enforce the fine or by notification of a variation in the amount of the fine or of the rejection of a request to vary the fine.[1071]

11. Review by the Court of First Instance

13.211 **Generally.** Although a full description of the role of the Community Courts lies outside the scope of this work,[1072] the following paragraphs briefly discuss the jurisdiction of the Court of First Instance and the principal heads under which it may review decisions of the Commission in the sphere of Articles 81 and 82.

13.212 **The Court of First Instance.** The Court of First Instance was originally established by a Council Decision of 24 October 1988,[1073] and is now directly constituted by Article 220 of the EC Treaty, as amended by the Treaty of Nice.[1074] Pursuant to Article 225, the Court of First Instance has jurisdiction to hear virtually all direct actions against Community institutions under the Treaty brought by private persons as well as, broadly speaking, direct actions by Member States challenging executive action by the Community institutions, primarily

---

[1068] The European Communities (Enforcement of Community Judgments) Order 1972 (SI 1972 No. 1590) and CPR 50.1 and Sch 1, RSC, Ord 71, Part II.

[1069] See Art 256 EC.

[1070] Case T-153/04 *Ferriere Nord v Commission* [2006] ECR II-3889, [2006] 5 CMLR 1382: recovery may be time barred although part of the fine has been paid and a banker's guarantee given pending appeal is still in place (an appeal, Case C-516/06P, not yet decided).

[1071] Art 26 of Reg 1; as to suspension by, now, the CFI see paras 13.248 *et seq*, below.

[1072] For specialist works on the Community Courts, see generally: Arnull, *The European Union and its Court of Justice* (2nd edn, 2006); Lenaerts, Arts and Maselis, Bray (ed), *Procedural Law of the European Union* (2nd edn, 2006); Schermers and Waelbroeck, *Judicial Protection in the European Communities* (6th edn, 2001); Anderson and Demetriou, *References to the European Court* (2nd edn, 2002). With particular regard to procedure, see Lasok and Millet, *Judicial Control in the EU* (2004); Kerse and Khan, *EC Antitrust Procedure* (5th edn, 2005); Ortiz Blanco, *EC Competition Procedure* (2nd edn, 2006); Siragusa and Rizza (eds), *EU Competition Law, Vol III: Cartels* (2007), Chap 5(4).

[1073] Dec 88/591, OJ 1988 L319/1, adopted pursuant to the then version of the former Art 168a EC.

[1074] See Vol II, App A.6.

the Commission. The Court of First Instance also has jurisdiction under the EC Treaty to deliver preliminary rulings in specific areas laid down by the Protocol on the Statute of the Court of Justice but no such areas have as yet been specified.[1075] An appeal lies on a point of law from a decision of the Court of First Instance in a direct action to the Court of Justice.[1076] However, if the Court of First Instance should be given jurisdiction in Article 234 proceedings,[1077] an appeal will lie only exceptionally, in a case where there is a serious risk of the unity or consistency of Community law being affected.[1078]

The jurisdiction for review. The Court of First Instance has jurisdiction to review the actions of the Commission under the following heads: **13.213**

(a) unlimited jurisdiction pursuant to Article 229 to review decisions of the Commission imposing a fine or penalty payment;

(b) jurisdiction under the second paragraph of Article 230 to review the legality of all decisions taken by the Commission;

(c) jurisdiction under the third paragraph of Article 232 to declare that the Commission has failed to act; and

(d) jurisdiction to grant interim relief under Articles 242 and 243.

(a) Review under Articles 229 and 230

(i) The scope of review

Article 229: unlimited jurisdiction regarding fines. The Court of First Instance   **13.214**
has unlimited jurisdiction, as regards matters of fact and law, to review decisions whereby the Commission has imposed fines or periodic penalty payments. This jurisdiction is conferred pursuant to Article 229 of the Treaty by Article 31 of Regulation 1/2003 (and previously by Article 17 of Regulation 17). It is regarded as an enlargement of the jurisdiction under Article 230 of the Treaty to review the legality of Commission decisions and is accordingly subject to the same time limit.[1079] The Court may cancel, reduce or increase the fine or penalty

---

[1075] Art 225(3) EC.

[1076] Arts 56–58 of the Protocol on the Statute of the Court of Justice, published at OJ 2001 C80/53 and as amended most recently by Council Decn of 3 October 2005, 2005 OJ L266/60. A consolidated version of the Statute is on the ECJ website, also in *Encyclopedia of European Law (Constitutional Texts)*, Vol 3, para 60.0214. See also Art 225(1) EC and see paras 13.252 *et seq*, below.

[1077] Art 225(3) EC: this requires areas for such jurisdiction to be specified by the Statute of the Court of Justice and, at the time of writing, no such amendment to the Statute has been made.

[1078] The First AG of the ECJ may propose that the decision be reviewed by the ECJ on that ground: Art 62 of the Protocol on the Statute of the Court of Justice.

[1079] ie within two months of either publication of the decision or its notification to the applicant or, in the absence thereof, of the date when it came to the knowledge of the applicant: Art 230 EC, fifth paragraph. See Case T-252/03 *FNICGV (French beef-limitation)* [2004] ECR II-3795, [2005] 4 CMLR 785, where the CFI stated that an action invoking the unlimited jurisdiction as regards the

payment imposed. It has often reduced or quashed fines imposed by the Commission.[1080] Although the Court of First Instance is not bound by the Commission's Guidelines on the imposition of fines when exercising its jurisdiction under Article 229, it has tended to follow the approach of the Commission as set out in those Guidelines in calculating reductions in fines.[1081] However, an applicant who has been partially successful cannot be certain that the reduction in fine awarded by the Court will be at the level which the Guidelines might suggest. Thus, where the Court finds that the duration of an infringement was less than that determined by the Commission, it will not necessarily make a proportional reduction in the fine.[1082] The Court of Justice has confirmed that the Court of First Instance is not necessarily bound by the same considerations as those which the Commission takes into account in determining the fine.[1083] However, the Court does not have power to replace an addressee of the decision with a different legal entity.[1084]

13.215 **Increase in fines.** The Court of First Instance is generally reluctant to increase fines but has done so where, for instance, an undertaking challenged facts before the Court of First Instance which it had not disputed during the administrative procedure for which it received a reduction in fine.[1085] The Court of Justice may increase the fine where it overturns the legal basis for the grant of a reduction by the Commission or the Court of First Instance.[1086]

13.216 **Adjustment of fines in cases of unequal treatment.** Where an appellant establishes that the Commission erred by imposing too low a fine on another addressee of the decision, the question arises whether the Court will reduce the appellant's fine in circumstances where it cannot increase the fine on the favoured undertaking. In *Hoek Loos*, the Court held that the alleged misapplication by the

---

fine 'necessarily comprises or includes a request for annulment, in whole or in part, of that decision' (para 25).

[1080] See also Art 16 of the Merger Reg, Reg 2004/139, and Art 31 of Reg 1/2003.

[1081] See paras 13.146 *et seq*, above for the Guidelines on Fines.

[1082] Case T-62/98 *Volkswagen v Commission* [2000] ECR II-2707, [2000] 5 CMLR 853, para 347; upheld by the ECJ on appeal Case C-338/00P *Volkswagen v Commission* [2003] ECR I-9189, [2004] 4 CMLR 351.

[1083] Case C-388/00P *Volkswagen v Commission*, above.

[1084] Cases T-259/02, etc, *Raiffeisen Zentralbank Österreich v Commission*, judgment of 14 December 2006, para 72.

[1085] *Tokai Carbon (Graphite Electrodes)* (n 1024, above), para 112. See also Case T-322/01 *Roquette Frères v Commission* [2006] ECR II-3137, paras 301–315: CFI imposed slight increase in calculation of the fine due to erroneous reply given by Roquette to Commission's questions during investigation. cf *Raiffeisen Zentralbank Österreich*, above, para 572 (increase not appropriate); Case T-241/01 *SAS v Commission* [2005] ECR II-2917, [2005] 5 CMLR 922, paras 234–242 in which the CFI rejected the Commission's application to have the fine increased on the basis that the undertaking did not contest the infringement but only the level of the fine.

[1086] eg Case C-301/04P *Commission v SGL Carbon* [2006] ECR I-5915, [2006] 5 CMLR 877.

Commission of the upper limit on penalties which favoured another undertaking did not give rise to a ground of appeal because 'compliance with the principle of equal treatment must be reconciled with the principle of legality, according to which a person may not rely in support of his claim, on an unlawful act committed in favour of a third party'.[1087] However, in the earlier case of *JFE Engineering* where the Commission had wrongly failed to take account of the fact that some addressees had committed two infringements and others only one, the Court reduced the fines of those falling in the latter category because it was unable to increase the fines on the former.[1088]

Review under Article 230: generally.   Under Article 230 of the Treaty, appeals   **13.217** may be lodged against decisions of the Commission. The grounds of appeal are expressed to be 'lack of competence, infringement of an essential procedural requirement, infringement of the Treaty or of any rule relating to its application, or misuse of powers'. The role of the Court in an application for annulment of an infringement decision is to assess whether the evidence and other information relied on by the Commission in its decision is sufficient to establish the existence of the alleged infringement.[1089]

Nature of a decision reviewable under Article 230.   Regulation 1/2003 requires   **13.218** that the Commission act by way of formal decision in a number of circumstances. However, there will also be situations in which the Commission, although not acting by virtue of a formal decision, adopts measures which may affect the legal position of the party to whom it is addressed. In those circumstances, it will be necessary to ascertain whether the Commission's act comprises a reviewable decision. The problem was considered in detail in *IBM v Commission*[1090] where the Court of Justice held that the category of acts reviewable under Article 230 should not be defined restrictively and depended on the substance rather than the form. As to the substance, a measure of the Commission is reviewable so long as it:

(a) produces legal effects binding on the applicant;
(b) is capable of affecting the interests of the applicant by bringing about a distinct change in its legal position; and
(c) represents the culmination of a distinct administrative procedure.[1091]

1087 Case T-304/02 *Hoek Loos v Commission* [2006] ECR II-1887, [2006] 5 CMLR 590, para 113; *Peróxidos Orgánicos*.

1088 *JFE Engineering* (n 1030, above) para 579. See also the English Court of Appeal in *Argos & Littlewoods v Office of Fair Trading* [2006] EWCA Civ 1318, [2006] UKCLR 1135, para 280.

1089 *JFE Engineering* (n 1030, above) para 175.

1090 Case 60/81 *IBM v Commission* [1981] ECR 2639, [1981] 3 CMLR 635; see also Case 5/85 *AKZO v Commission* [1986] ECR 2585, [1987] 3 CMLR 7169.

1091 *IBM v Commission* (n 1090, above); Case T-113/89 *Nefarma v Commission* [1990] ECR II-797; Cases T-10/92, etc, *Cimenteries CBR v Commission* [1992] ECR II-2667, [1993] 4 CMLR 259;

Challenges to an act which is non-existent, for example, because of procedural irregularities in its adoption, are inadmissible.[1092]

13.219 **Examples of reviewable acts.** By abolishing the notification system, Regulation 1/2003 has introduced a measure of certainty in this area given that questions concerning the legal status of acts such as comfort letters will no longer arise. However, different uncertainties may arise under the new system, for example, in respect of decisions concerning the allocation of cases. A decision may be capable of challenge even if it has already been acted upon by the Commission if it prevents a repetition of the act complained of or has consequences for the subsequent stages of the Commission's investigation.[1093] Although it is not possible to attempt a definitive list, reviewable acts of the Commission include:

(a) a decision under Article 7 of Regulation 1/2003 that an infringement be brought to an end;

(b) the adoption of interim measures under Article 8;[1094]

(c) the acceptance of commitments under Article 9;[1095]

(d) a finding of inapplicability under Article 10;[1096]

(e) a decision to impose a fine under Article 23 (failure to comply with request for information) or to fix a periodic penalty payment under Article 24;[1097]

Cases T-213 & 214/01 *Österreichische Postsparkasse v Commission* [2006] ECR II-1601, [2007] 4 CMLR 506, paras 64–73 (challenge to decn of Hearing Officer to recognise the legitimate interest of a third party for the purposes of Art 3(2) of Reg 17 and to send that third party a copy of the non-confidential version of the statement of objections was admissible). For an example of a Commission decision which was deemed a preparatory statement of position, see Case T-95/99 *Satellimages TV 5 v Commission* [2002] ECR II-1425, [2002] 4 CMLR 1416.

[1092] Cases 1 & 14/57 *Soc des Usines à Tubes de la Sarre v High Authority* [1957–8] ECR 105. See, eg Cases T-79/89, etc, *Re the PVC Cartel* [1992] ECR II-315, [1992] 4 CMLR 357, where the CFI declared the decision to be non-existent, accordingly dismissed the applications for annulment, but ordered the Commission to pay the costs. (The ECJ on appeal held that the decision did exist but should be anulled, Case C-137/92P, [1994] ECR I-2555). Time limits do not apply to challenges in such circumstances because the non-existence of a measure is a matter of public interest: Case 15/85 *Consorzio Co-operative D'Abruzzo v Commission* [1987] ECR 1005, [1988] 1 CMLR 841; and *PVC*, above.

[1093] *Österreichische Postsparkasse* (n 1091, above) para 55 (challenge to handing over of the statement of objections admissible although it had in fact been handed over).

[1094] It is not yet clear whether a refusal by the Commission to adopt interim measures may be characterised as a decision susceptible to review.

[1095] See the annulment of the commitments accepted from De Beers in Case T-170/06 *Alrosa v Commission*, judgment of 11 July 2007. Note the CFI contrasted its role in reviewing the acceptance of commitments under the Merger Regulation with its role in relation to commitments decisions under Art 9 of Reg 1/2003: para 109.

[1096] Note that in Case T-112/99 *Métropole télévision (M6) v Commission* [2001] ECR II-2459, [2001] 5 CMLR 1236 (on appeal from *TPS*, OJ 1999 L90/6) the CFI held that the parties were entitled to challenge a decn by the Commission to grant an exemption under Art 81(3) for three years rather than for the 10 years the parties had requested.

[1097] Case T-596/97 *Dalmine v Commission* [1998] ECR II-2383, paras 30–32 (decision to impose a periodic penalty payment is only a preliminary step so that it is the decision which definitively fixes the amount of the periodic penalty payment which is reviewable).

(f) the rejection of a complaint under Article 7 of Regulation 773/2004;[1098]

(g) the refusal to accept the confidential nature of information supplied to the Commission.[1099]

The above list is by no means exhaustive and new issues will undoubtedly arise under the new regime.

Non-reviewable 'acts' of the Commission.   It is not finally decided whether **13.220** reviewable acts under Article 230 include certain matters that need to be decided in the course of administrative proceedings, such as whether third parties have a 'sufficient interest' to be heard, and if so whether orally or in writing.[1100] Letters from the Commission asking complainants for submissions are not reviewable acts.[1101] A decision that merely confirms an earlier decision without consideration of any further material facts is not reviewable.[1102] An applicant may seek review only of a decision that produces legal effects as regards his own interests; therefore a party to a cartel which is the subject of a decision imposing fines cannot challenge the Commission's decision to drop allegations against other parties.[1103] Other acts of the Commission which have been held not to be capable of challenge under Article 230 are:

(a) the initiation of a procedure and issue of a statement of objections;[1104]

(b) a finding of dominance without a finding of abuse;[1105]

[1098] See cases cited in paras 13.071 *et seq*, above.

[1099] eg Case T-198/03 *Bank Austria Creditanstalt v Commission* [2006] ECR II-1429, [2006] 5 CMLR 639, paras 27 *et seq* (decn of Hearing Officer under Art 9 of Decn 2001/462 as to what material should be redacted from the published version of the substantive decision was amenable to challenge).

[1100] See para 13.100, above. In *Österreichische Postsparkasse* (n 1091, above) the CFI reviewed the Hearing Officer's decn to treat the FPÖ as having a legitimate interest since this was a necessary step in his decn to release the statement of objections to it. It is not clear whether the status of the FPÖ would have been reviewable by itself. Note that even if a decision is reviewable, it may nonetheless not be susceptible to challenge until a final decision is taken at the conclusion of the Commission's administrative procedure; that is the position as regards decisions on access to the file: Cases T-10/92, etc, *Cimenteries CBR v Commission* [1992] ECR II-2667, [1993] 4 CMLR 259.

[1101] See also Case C-282/95P *Guérin Automobiles v Commission* [1997] ECR I-1503, [1997] 5 CMLR 447; Case T-411/05 *Annemans v Commission*, judgment of 12 July 2007.

[1102] Case C-480/93P *Zunis Holding v Commission* [1993] ECR II-1169, [1994] 5 CMLR 154.

[1103] Case T-25/95, etc, *Cimenteries CBR v Commission* ('*Cement*') [2000] ECR II-491, [2000] 5 CMLR 204 [summary], paras 80–82.

[1104] Case 60/81 *IBM v Commission* (n 1090, above); *Cement*, above.

[1105] Cases T-125 & 127/97 *The Coca-Cola Company and Coca-Cola Enterprises v Commission* [2000] ECR II-1733, [2000] 5 CMLR 467, [2000] All ER (EC) 460; followed by the Brussels Court of Appeal in *Beroepsinstituut van Vastgoedmakelaars* judgment of 7 June 2004 (Case ref 2002/MR/2).

(c) the rejection of a complaint from an undertaking requesting the Commission to take action against a Member State under Article 86(3) of the Treaty (otherwise than in exceptional circumstances);[1106]

(d) the publication of a non-confidential version of a decision on the Commission's website prior to its publication in the *Official Journal.*[1107]

13.221 **Standing to bring appeal.** Proceedings may be brought by any natural or legal person to whom the decision is addressed;[1108] they may also be brought by any natural or legal person against a decision which, although addressed to another person, is of direct and individual concern to the applicant (for example, a complainant with a legitimate interest).[1109] A Member State may lodge such an appeal as of right.[1110] Although Member States frequently intervene in competition cases brought by private parties, it is rare for a Member State to exercise this independent right of appeal.

(ii) The grounds of annulment

13.222 **Grounds of annulment generally.** In large measure the grounds of annulment referred to in Article 230 overlap. However, infringement of an essential procedural requirement must be raised by the Court of its own motion, whereas infringement of a rule relating to the application of the Treaty (such as a manifest error of assessment) provides a ground for annulment of a decision only if it is

---

[1106] Case T-84/94 *Bundesverband der Bilanzbuchhalter v Commission* [1995] ECR II-101 (upheld on appeal Case C-107/95P, [1997] ECR I-947, [1997] 5 CMLR 432); Case T-52/00 *Coe Clerici Logistics v Commission* [2002] ECR II-2553, [2003] 5 CMLR 531.

[1107] *Bank Austria Creditanstalt* (n 1099, above).

[1108] This is so even if no pecuniary sanctions have been imposed: Case 77/77 *BP v Commission* [1978] ECR 1513, [1978] 3 CMLR 174. But when the Commission found that Art 81 did not apply due to lack of effect on trade (a negative clearance decision in pre-Modernisation language), the addressee could not challenge the decision in order to overturn the finding of anti-competitive effect: Case T-138/89 *Nederlandse Bankiersvereniging and Nederlandse Vereniging van Banken v Commission* [1992] ECR II-2181, [1993] 5 CMLR 436.

[1109] A party which is entitled to bring a complaint under Art 7(2) of Reg 1/2003 and Art 5 of Reg 773/2004 will also also be entitled to bring proceedings under Art 230: see paras 13.063 *et seq*, above. In addition to the examples mentioned there, a parent company will normally have locus standi to challenge a decision addressed to its subsidiary: Cases 228 & 229/82 *Ford v Commission (No. 1)* [1984] ECR 1129, [1984] 1 CMLR 649, para 13. Shareholders in the affected undertakings do not have locus to challenge a Commission decision: Case T-83/92 *Zunis Holding v Commission* [1993] ECR II-1169, [1994] 5 CMLR 154; appeal dismissed on other grounds, Case C-480/93P, [1996] ECR I-1, [1996] 5 CMLR 219, but see the Opinion of AG Lenz at paras 36 *et seq*. Where a commitment made binding by the Commission in a decn under Art 9 of Reg 1/2003 required the undertaking concerned to terminate its long standing contract with a third party, that third party had locus to challenge the decn: Case T-170/06 *Alrosa v Commission*, judgment of 11 July 2007. See also Case T-231/99 *Joynson v Commission* [2002] ECR II-2085, [2002] 5 CMLR 123, paras 24–25: brewery tenant still had locus to challenge the Commission's decision to exempt a beer tie agreement even if he was no longer party to the beer tie, in particular given that he had brought proceedings in the national courts.

[1110] Case 41/83 *Italy v Commission* [1985] ECR 873, [1985] 2 CMLR 368.

pleaded by the applicant.[1111] In any event, applicants tend these days to frame their cases in general terms, namely, that the Commission has not proved the infringement rather than relying on the formal grounds of Article 230. The following paragraphs briefly discuss those types of argument most frequently relied upon in appeals against Commission decisions in competition matters, and the general approach of the Court of First Instance in considering them.[1112]

Procedural irregularities.　Many appeals in competition matters have relied on alleged defects in the Commission's procedure. To succeed on this ground under Article 230, it is necessary to establish breach of an 'essential procedural requirement' or infringement of 'any rule of law relating to the application of the Treaty'. Where a particular procedural requirement is expressly imposed by law, such as the obligation properly to consult other bodies, failure to comply will normally result in the decision being quashed.[1113] Similarly, a decision will be annulled if the proceedings were taken under the wrong legislation, but only if this deprives the defendant of certain safeguards.[1114] In other cases, however, a procedural irregularity may lead to the decision being quashed 'only if it were shown that in the absence of such irregularity the contested decision might have been different'.[1115] Examples of procedural irregularities which have been held not to vitiate the Commission's decision include delay in communicating the minutes of the oral hearing;[1116] notification of a statement of objections to a trade association and not to its individual members;[1117] communication of documents in languages other

13.223

[1111]　Case C-367/95P *Commission v Sytraval* [1998] ECR I-1719, para 67.

[1112]　In relation to competition matters, see also Kerse and Khan, *EC Antitrust Procedure* (5th edn, 2005), Chap 8. The CFI considers that its powers to review Commission decisions in competition cases are sufficiently broad for it to constitute the independent tribunal required by Art 6 of the ECHR: see para 13.081, above.

[1113]　See generally, eg Case 138/79 *Roquette Frères v Council* [1980] ECR 3333. As to failure to consult the Advisory Committee under Art 14 of Reg 1/2003, see as regards the previous Art 10 of Reg 17, Case 30/78 *Distillers Company v Commission* [1980] ECR 2229, 2290, [1980] 3 CMLR 121, 154, *et seq, per* AG Warner; Cases 228 & 229/82 *Ford v Commission (No. 1)* [1984] ECR 1129, 1173, [1984] 1 CMLR 649, 666, *per* AG Slynn.

[1114]　See Case T-14/93 *Union Internationale des Chemin de Fer v Commission* [1995] ECR II-1503, [1996] 5 CMLR 40, upheld on appeal Case C-264/95P *Commission v UIC* [1997] ECR I-1287, [1997] 5 CMLR 49: decn annulled because the Commission's proceedings should have been governed by Reg 1017/68 and not Reg 17; cf Case T-213/00 *CMA CGM v Commission* ('*FETTCSA*') [2003] ECR II-913, [2003] 5 CMLR 268: CFI upheld decn in which Commission had failed clearly to state what reg it was applying but where it had complied with all potentially applicable procedural safeguards for the parties.

[1115]　Cases 209/78, etc, *Van Landewyck v Commission* ('*FEDETAB*') [1980] ECR 3125, [1981] 3 CMLR 134, paras 46–47, and 3299–3300 (ECR), 174 (CMLR), *per* AG Reischl. See also *Distillers* (n 1113, above) para 26 and *per* AG Warner at 2290 *et seq*; and AG Slynn in *Pioneer* (n 1016, above), 1927 (ECR), 285 (CMLR).

[1116]　Cases 48/69, etc, *ICI v Commission* [1972] ECR 619, [1972] CMLR 557, paras 27–33.

[1117]　Case 71/74 *Frubo v Commission* [1975] ECR 563, [1975] 2 CMLR 123. But individual members may not be fined if they are not addressees of the statement of objections: Cases C-395 & 396/96P *Compagnie Maritime Belge Transports v Commission* [2000] ECR I-1365, [2000]

than the Community language of the addressee;[1118] failure of all the Commission officials involved to attend throughout the oral hearing;[1119] unauthorised disclosure of confidential information to third parties;[1120] premature publicity of the proceedings or of the decision;[1121] failure to follow up initiatives aimed at settling proceedings;[1122] and the notification of a decision to a subsidiary within the Community on behalf of its non-EC parent.[1123] In contrast, the Court of First Instance held that the fact that an addressee of a cartel decision had not been given the opportunity to comment on the statement of objections amounted to a procedural irregularity which resulted in the decision being quashed in part.[1124]

13.224 **Failure to respect the rights of the defence.** The observance of the rights of the defence is a fundamental requirement of Community law.[1125] One of its most important aspects is the right to be heard: defendant undertakings must be given a full opportunity to comment on the facts alleged against them and on the documents relied on by the Commission. On occasion, decisions have been quashed in whole or part for failure to respect the right to be heard,[1126] but the Court will not quash the decision if in substance the undertakings did have the opportunity to be heard.[1127] Moreover, if the breach of the right to be heard relates to matters of secondary importance, the decision as a whole will not be vitiated.[1128] A failure to respect the right to be heard will not lead to annulment if the allegation in question can be substantiated on the basis of other evidence in the decision on which the undertaking was given the opportunity to comment,[1129] or in certain

---

4 CMLR 1076, [2000] All ER (EC) 385. Similarly, Case C-176/99P *Arbed v Commission* [2003] ECR I-10687, [2005] 4 CMLR 530: notification only to a subsidiary; decn against parent annulled.

[1118] Case 41/69 *ACF Chemiefarma v Commission* [1970] ECR 661.

[1119] Cases 43 & 63/82 *VBVB and VBBB v Commission* [1984] ECR 19, [1985] 1 CMLR 27.

[1120] *FEDETAB* (n 1115, above) paras 41–47.

[1121] See para 13.112, above.

[1122] Cases 96/82, etc, *IAZ v Commission* [1983] ECR 3369, [1984] 3 CMLR 276, paras 12–16.

[1123] *ICI* (n 1116, above) paras 34–39.

[1124] Cases T-45 & 47/98 *Krupp Thyssen Stainless and Acciai Speciali Terni v Commission* [2001] ECR II-3757, [2002] 4 CMLR 521, paras 55–67.

[1125] See generally para 13.028, above. The importance of the rights of the defence was reaffirmed by the ECJ in Case C-204/00P *Aalborg Portland v Commission ('Cement')* [2004] ECR I-123, [2005] 4 CMLR 251, paras 64–67 *et seq*.

[1126] See, eg the *Soda Ash* cases discussed at para 13.088, above; and *Krupp Thyssen Stainless* (n 1124, above).

[1127] See, eg Cases 40/73, etc, *Suiker Unie v Commission* [1975] ECR 1663, [1976] 1 CMLR 295, paras 434–438; *FEDETAB* (n 1115, above) para 69–74; Cases 100/80, etc, *Musique Diffusion Française v Commission ('Pioneer')* [1983] ECR 1825, [1983] 3 CMLR 221, paras 18–19; *Ford v Commission (No. 1)* (n 1113, above) 1172 (ECR), 665 (CMLR) *per* AG Slynn.

[1128] Case 107/82 *AEG v Commission* [1983] ECR 3151, [1984] 3 CMLR 325, paras 21–30 and 136–138; *Musique Diffusion Française* (n 1127, above) paras 29–30.

[1129] Cases T-191/98, etc *Atlantic Container Line v Commission ('TACA')* [2003] ECR II-3275, [2005] 4 CMLR 1283, para 196; T-109/02, etc, *Bolloré v Commission* [2007] 5 CMLR 66, para 80.

circumstances if the irregularity has been put right without prejudice to the undertaking in proceedings before the Court.[1130] Nor is it possible to establish a breach of the right to be heard simply by comparing the Commission's decision with the statement of objections: the Commission's decision is not required to be a replica of the statement of objections.[1131] The rights of defence are not breached by the existence of a discrepancy between the statement of objections and the final decision unless a criticism, which appears in the decision, is not adequately set out in the statement of objections in a way which enables the addressees to defend themselves.[1132] Where the Commission has dropped certain objections which were contained in the statement of objections, respect for the rights of the defence does not require that the appellant be allowed to submit observations on the dropping of those objectons where it did not in any way change the legal and factual context of the objections raised against the appellant.[1133] Access to the file is complementary to the right to be heard, not only because it enables a defendant to comment on the documents relied on by the Commission but because it encompasses the right to see exculpatory documents that may assist the defence in making its case on an equal footing with the Commission's case against it.[1134] Failure to give proper access therefore infringes the rights of the defence and is a ground for annulment of the Commission's decision.[1135]

Inadequacy of reasoning. The requirement under Article 253 of the Treaty that **13.225** a decision be reasoned is intended (a) to enable the Community Courts to review the legality of the decision and (b) to provide the person concerned with sufficient details to allow him to ascertain whether the decision is well founded or is vitiated by a defect which will allow its validity to be contested.[1136] In cases where a decision has been inadequately reasoned, the Court must raise the point whether or not the applicant does so.[1137] The Court of Justice has criticised the Court of First Instance for characterising errors of fact or law by the Commission as

---

[1130] Case 85/76 *Hoffmann-La Roche v Commission* [1979] ECR 461, [1979] CMLR 211, paras 15–17; *per contra* AG Warner in *Distillers* (n 1113, above) 2297–2298 (ECR), 161–162 (CMLR).

[1131] *FEDETAB* (n 1115, above) paras 68–70; *Pioneer* (n 1127, above) paras 19–20; *IAZ v Commission* (n 1122, above) paras 4–7.

[1132] T-48/00 *Corus UK v Commission* [2004] ECR II-2325, [2005] 4 CMLR 182, paras 100–106.

[1133] See *Aalborg Portland* (n 1125, above) paras 192–193.

[1134] See paras 13.090 *et seq*, above, and *Aalborg Portland* (n 1125, above) para 68.

[1135] See the *Soda Ash* cases discussed at para 13.088, above.

[1136] See, eg *VBVB* (n 1119, above) para 22, following a long line of cases on Art 190, starting with Case 24/62 *Germany v Commission* [1963] ECR 63, 69. Note especially *Suiker Unie* (n 1127, above) para 118; Cases T-24/93, etc, *Compagnie Maritime Belge Transports v Commission* [1996] ECR II-1201, [1997] 4 CMLR 273, para 61.

[1137] Case C-166/95P *Commission v Daffix* [1997] ECR I-983, para 24; Case T-44/00 *Mannesmannröhren-Werke v Commission* [2004] ECR II-2223, para 126 (appeal dismissed, Case C-411/04P *Salzgitter Mannesmann v Commission* [2007] 4 CMLR 682).

infringements of Article 253.[1138] The fact that the Commission's reasoning may be incorrect in law or contain a wrong assessment of the evidence is not of itself a breach of the requirement to state reasons.[1139] Whether a statement of reasons is adequate must be assessed in all the circumstances of the case, including in particular the context of the decision and the interest of the addressee in obtaining an explanation.[1140] It is generally sufficient if the decision mentions the principal issues of law and fact in such a way that the Commission's essential reasoning may be understood.[1141] It is not necessary for the decision to consider all the points of law and fact put forward by the parties,[1142] and the Commission is not obliged to adopt a position on all the arguments that were relied on. It need only set out those facts and legal considerations which are of decisive importance in the context of the decision.[1143] A decision which breaks new legal ground may, however, require to be more fully reasoned than those in other cases.[1144] If an applicant challenges its liability before the Commission, the decision must contain a detailed account of the grounds for holding it liable.[1145] Subject to fulfilling the requirement that its essential reasoning may be understood, a single decision may cover a number of distinct infringements, not all of which are alleged against particular parties.[1146] But where the decision relates to several addressees and raises a problem as to which is liable for the infringement, the decision must contain an adequate statement

---

[1138] *Commission v Sytraval* (n 1111, above) paras 68–72.

[1139] See the Opinion of Judge Vesterdorf (acting as AG) in Cases T-1/89, etc, *Polypropylene* [1991] ECR II-869 at 908, [1992] 4 CMLR 84 at 125. cf the distinct ground of annulment for lack of adequate proof or manifest error of assessment: paras 13.226 *et seq*, below.

[1140] *Commission v Sytraval* (n 1111, above) para 63; applied in Case C-265/97P *VBA v Florimex and Commission* [2000] ECR I-2061, [2001] 5 CMLR 37, para 93.

[1141] *ACF Chemiefarma v Commission* (n 1118, above) para 78 (re a decision imposing a fine), a test repeated in subsequent cases. Note also Cases 8/66, etc, *Cimenteries CBR v Commission* (n 1103, above); Case 86/82 *Hasselblad v Commission* [1984] ECR 883, 915, [1984] 1 CMLR 559, 567–568, *per* AG Slynn. In Case T-16/91 *RV Rendo v Commission* [1996] ECR II-1827, [1997] 4 CMLR 453, the CFI stated that a person concerned by a decision can be expected to interpret the reasons if the text is not immediately clear; if any ambiguities can thereby be resolved, Art 253 EC is not infringed (para 46).

[1142] See, eg *FEDETAB* (n 1115, above) para 66; *VBVB* (n 1119, above) para 22; Case 246/86 *Belasco v Commission* [1989] ECR 2117, [1991] 4 CMLR 130; Case T-155/04 *SELEX Sistemi Integrati v Commission* [2007] 4 CMLR 372, paras 117 *et seq* (appeal on other grounds, Case C-113/07P, not yet decided).

[1143] Case 6/72 *Europemballage and Continental Can v Commission* [1973] ECR 215, [1973] CMLR 199, paras 4–7; Case T-206/99 *Métropole Télévision v Commission* [2001] ECR II-1057, [2001] 4 CMLR 39 at para 44. See also T-464/04 *Impala v Commission* [2006] ECR II-2289, [2006] 5 CMLR 1049, paras 278–281, in which the CFI held that although the Commission is not under any specific obligation to give reasons where it has changed its position from that which it adopted in the statement of objections, such a reversal in the Commission's position was, in that case, a relevant factor in assessing the adequacy of the statement of reasons.

[1144] Case T-38/92 *AWS Benelux v Commission* [1994] ECR II-211, [1995] 4 CMLR 43.

[1145] *Suiker Unie* (n 1127, above) para 111; *FEDETAB* (n 1115, above) para 77.

[1146] Case T-38/92 *AWS Benelux v Commission* [1994] ECR II-211, [1995] 4 CMLR 43.

of reasons with respect to each of them.[1147] In the *Publishers' Association* case, the Commission decision was annulled for failure adequately to explain the Commission's rejection of the applicants' submissions based on the judgment of a national court and for citing as a precedent a case which on analysis was on quite different facts.[1148] In relation to fines, in 1995 the Court of First Instance criticised the thin reasoning that had generally been employed by the Commission in relation to the amount of the fine.[1149] Failure to include adequate reasoning will result in the decision being quashed.[1150] It is possible that an *implied* decision to reject a complaint could be regarded as properly reasoned.[1151] But only in exceptional circumstances will the Court take into account *ex post facto* explanations of the Commission's reasoning.[1152] However, arguments dressed up as lack of reasoning frequently turn on the Commission's evaluation (or lack of evaluation) of the substance of the case, in which event the Court will deal with the matter in its review of the merits.[1153]

Lack of adequate proof. Article 2 of Regulation 1/2003 enshrines the rule **13.226** established in the case law that the burden of proving the infringement lies on the Commission.[1154] Where there is doubt, the benefit of that doubt must be given to the undertakings accused of the infringement.[1155] The Commission must produce 'sufficiently precise and coherent proof'[1156] to support its allegations and

---

[1147] Case 73/74 *Papiers Peints v Commission* [1975] ECR 1491, [1976] 1 CMLR 589, para 31.

[1148] Case C-360/92P *Publishers' Association v Commission* [1995] ECR I-23, [1995] 5 CMLR 33.

[1149] Case T-148/89 *Tréfilunion v Commission* [1995] ECR II-1063, para 142. However, the decision was not annulled and the CFI has subsequently refused to annul fining decisions taken before the *Tréfilunion* judgment where (on the basis of that judgment) the reasoning was inadequate, when the Commission was able to explain its reasoning to the court: see Case T-319/94 *Fiskeby Board v Commission* [1998] ECR II-1331, paras 130–132.

[1150] See, eg Cases 8/66, etc, *Cimenteries CBR v Commission* (n 1103, above); *Papiers Peints* (n 1147, above); Cases 19 & 20/74 *Kali und Salz and Kali-Chemie v Commission* [1975] ECR 499, [1975] 2 CMLR 154.

[1151] *Rendo* (n 1141, above) para 57–60.

[1152] Case T-61/89 *Dansk Pelsdyravleforening v Commission* [1992] ECR II-1931, para 131; Case T-30/89 *Hilti v Commission* [1991] ECR II-1439, [1992] 4 CMLR 16, para 136; *Rendo v Commission* (n 1141, above) para 55. See also Case E-2/94 *Scottish Salmon Growers Association v EFTA Surveillance Authority* [1994–5] Rep EFTA Ct 59, [1995] 1 CMLR 851 (provision of reasons over the telephone cannot satisfy requirement for proper statement of reasons).

[1153] See, eg Cases 40/73, etc, *Suiker Unie* (n 1127, above); Case 7/82 *GVL v Commission* [1983] ECR 483, [1983] 3 CMLR 645.

[1154] See generally Cases 100/80, etc, *Musique Diffusion Française v Commission ('Pioneer')* [1983] ECR 1825, [1983] 3 CMLR 221, *per* AG Slynn.

[1155] Case T-67/00 *JFE Engineering v Commission* [2004] ECR II-2501, [2005] 4 CMLR 27, para 177. The CFI went on to rule that the presumption of innocence under Art 6(1) ECHR applies in that context (appeal dismissed, Case C-403&405/04P *Sumitomo Metal Industries v Commission* [2007] 4 CMLR 650).

[1156] Cases 29 & 30/83 *CRAM & Rheinzink v Commission* [1984] ECR 1679, [1985] 1 CMLR 688, paras 16–20; See also, eg Case 27/76 *United Brands v Commission* [1978] ECR 207, [1978] 1 CMLR 429, 267 (failure by Commission to adduce 'adequate legal proof'); Case 86/82 *Hasselblad v Commission* (n 1141, above) (allegations on servicing not proved); Cases T-68/89, etc, *Società Italiano Vetro v Commission ('Italian Flat Glass')* [1992] ECR II-1403, [1992] 5 CMLR 302.

must sufficiently show 'the facts and assessments' on which its decision is based.[1157] Where the Commission relies on documentary evidence to support its finding of infringement, it is not enough for the applicant to put forward a plausible alternative to the Commission's view but it must also show that the evidence relied on by the Commission is insufficient.[1158] An admission by one undertaking accused of having participated in a cartel, the accuracy of which is contested by other alleged participants, cannot be regarded as constituting adequate proof in the absence of corroboration.[1159] However, a lesser degree of corroboration may be required where the statement in question is particularly credible.[1160] The Commission may rely on hearsay evidence,[1161] and may prove a course of conduct by sufficiently clear and numerous examples.[1162] Evidence provided by an anonymous informant is admissible although its provenance could affect the probative value of such evidence.[1163] For discussion of the evidence that will be sufficient to establish participation in a cartel or the existence of a concerted practice, and the presumptions that apply, see Chapter 2, above.[1164] The Commission must prove not only the primary facts but must also adduce sufficient evidence to establish its economic analysis, for example as regards the relevant market.[1165] Instances where the evidence is equivocal will be resolved in favour of the undertaking.[1166] Failure to fulfil these requirements will result in total or partial annulment of the decision or a reduction in the fine.[1167]

13.227 **Scope of review by the Court of First Instance.** The extent to which the Court of First Instance will carry out a detailed review of the facts on which the Commission's decision was based depends on the nature of the proceedings.[1168] On an appeal by an addressee of a decision, the Court of First Instance will review

---

[1157] Case 6/72 *Europemballage and Continental Can v Commission* (n 1143, above) para 37; see also Case 85/76 *Hoffmann-La Roche v Commission* (n 1130, above) para 28 ('insufficient evidence'); Cases T-44/02, etc, *Dresdner Bank v Commission* ('German Banks - Eurozone currency exchange') [2006] ECR II-3567, [2007] 4 CMLR 467, para 167 (existence of agreement not established to requisite standard).

[1158] *JFE Engineering* (n 1155, above) para 187. For the shifting to the Commission, in unusual circumstances, of an evidential burden that would otherwise rest on the applicants, see Case T-44/00 *Mannesmannröhren-Werke* (n 1137, above) paras 259–263.

[1159] Case T-337/94 *Enso-Gutzeit v Commission* [1998] ECR II-1571, para 91.

[1160] *JFE Engineering* (n 1155, above) paras 219–220. The CFI also held in that case that there is no bar to the Commission relying, as against an undertaking on statements made by other incriminated undertakings, para 192.

[1161] *Suiker Unie* (n 1127, above) para 164.

[1162] Case 107/82 *AEG v Commission* [1983] ECR 3151, [1984] 3 CMLR 325.

[1163] See *Mannesmannröhren-Werke* (n 1137, above) paras 84–85.

[1164] See paras 2.045–2.046 and 2.050–2.056, above.

[1165] See, eg *Continental Can* (n 1143, above); *Italian Flat Glass* (n 1156, above) para 159.

[1166] See, eg *CRAM and Rheinzink* (n 1156, above); *Suiker Unie* (n 1127, above) para 210, 304, 354, 363, 420 and 497.

[1167] But failure to prove some matters will not necessarily result in annulment or reduction of the fine: *AEG* (n 1162, above).

[1168] See Bailey, 'The Scope of Judicial Review under Article 81 EC' (2004) 41 CML Rev 1327.

all the facts and circumstances in considerable detail.[1169] In a recent judgment, the Court of First Instance described its role as follows:

' . . . the Court hearing an application for annulment of a decision applying Article 81(1) EC must undertake a comprehensive review of the examination carried out by the Commission . . . unless that examination entails a complex economic assessment, in which case review by the Court is confined to ascertaining that there has been no misuse of powers, that the rules on procedure and on the statement of reasons have been complied with, that the facts have been accurately stated and that there has been no manifest error of assessment of those facts. . . . Furthermore, that review is carried out solely by reference to the elements of fact and of law existing on the date of adoption of the contested decision . . . without prejudice to the possibility afforded to the parties, in the exercise of their rights of defence, of supplementing them by evidence established after that date, but for the specific purpose of contesting or defending that decision.'[1170]

Decisions which the Court of First Instance considers involve the complex economic analysis which calls for more limited review are primarily those where the Commission has applied Article 81(3)[1171] and those where the Commission has rejected a complaint.[1172] In such cases, the Court considers that the Commission has a 'margin of appreciation' and will limit judicial review of the Commission's evaluation to an examination of the relevance of the facts and of the legal consequences which the Commission draws from them.[1173] But where a manifest error

---

1169 See, eg *Italian Flat Glass* (n 1156, above) and cases such as *Cement* (n 1103, above) (which runs to 5,134 paragraphs, the bulk of which deal with factual issues). See also para 13.081, above: CFI's view that its powers to review are sufficiently broad for the appeal to the CFI to constitute the fair hearing before an independent and impartial tribunal required by Art 6 ECHR.

1170 Case T-168/01 *GlaxoSmithKline Services v Commission* [2006] ECR II-2969, [2006] 5 CMLR 1589, paras 57–58 (on appeal, Cases C-501/06P, etc, *GlaxoSmithKline Services v Commission*, not yet decided).

1171 This principle has been stated many times: see, eg Cases 56 & 58/64 *Consten and Grundig v Commission* [1966] ECR 299, 347, [1966] CMLR 418, 477; Case T-18/96R *SCK and FNK* [1996] ECR II-407, [1996] 5 CMLR 307, para 190; Case T-112/99 *Métropole Télévision (M6) v Commission* [2001] ECR II-2459, [2001] 5 CMLR 1236, para 156; Case T-131/99 *Shaw v Commission* [2002] ECR II-2023, [2002] 5 CMLR 81, para 38. Note, however, that the test for whether a decision refusing the grant of an exemption should be suspended by interim measures is the same as the test for suspending any other Commission decn: Case T-184/01R *IMS Health v Commission* [2001] ECR II-3193, [2002] 4 CMLR 58, para 56 (confirmed on appeal to the ECJ: Case C-481/01P (R) *NDC Health v IMS Health and Commission* [2002] ECR I-3401, [2002] 5 CMLR 44).

1172 See, eg Case T-115/99 *Système Européen Promotion SARL ('SEP') v Commission* [2001] ECR II-691, [2001] 5 CMLR 579, para 34; Case T-204/03 *Haladjian Frères v Commission* [2006] ECR II-3779, [2007] 4 CMLR 1106, para 30.

1173 Case 71/74 *Frubo v Commission* (n 1117, above) para 43 and *per* AG Warner at 597 (ECR), 142 (CMLR); Case 26/76 *Metro v Commission (No. 1)* [1977] ECR 1875, [1978] 2 CMLR 1, para 50 and *per* AG Reischl at 1924 (appeal by third party against decision granting exemption); Case 75/84 *Metro v Commission (No. 2)* [1989] ECR 3021, [1987] 1 CMLR 118; *GlaxoSmithKline Services v Commission* (n 1170, above) paras 241–245. In Case T-528/93, etc, *Métropole Télévision v Commission* [1996] ECR II-649, [1996] 5 CMLR 386, the CFI annulled a decision under Art 81(3) on the basis that the Commission had not adequately explained the relevance of certain facts. See also Case T-170/06 *Alrosa v Commission*, judgment of 11 July 2007, where the

of fact by the Commission influences its analysis of the economic effects of a practice or agreement, the Court will annul the decision on that basis.[1174] Although an error of fact does not necessarily entail an absence of reasoning,[1175] there is inevitably a grey area within which it is unclear whether a particular error of fact should be characterised as an absence of reasons (for example, a failure to deal with a particular argument or issue) or an error of appreciation. Moreover, the Court has also allowed the Commission a 'margin of appreciation' in some cases under Articles 81(1) and 82, and the boundary between those issues which are said to involve complex economic assessment leading to less intensive judicial review and those subject to full appellate scrutiny is not altogether clear.[1176]

13.228 **Error of substantive law.** The Community Courts have on occasion annulled decisions of the Commission on the ground that the Commission's analysis of the substantive law was incorrect.[1177] More frequently, the Court has annulled decisions of the Commission on the ground that the facts as established did not support the application of a particular rule of substantive law.[1178] The general principles of Community law apply in competition cases as in other cases.[1179] Thus breach of the principles of proportionality,[1180] equal treatment or

---

CFI rejected the Commission's argument that review of a decision accepting commitments under Art 9 of Reg 1/2003 should be limited, on the grounds that the Commission had not, in fact, undertaken a complex economic analysis in that case and that, on any basis, the decision was vitiated by a manifest error of assessment: paras 122 *et seq*.

[1174] See, eg Cases T-79 and 80/95 *SNCF and BRB v Commission* [1996] ECR II-1491, [1996] 5 CMLR 26. Judge Bellamy (speaking extra-judicially) expressed the parameters through which the CFI works as follows: 'are the facts established; is the economic appreciation supported by the evidence; have the important arguments been answered in a credible way', in Hawk (ed) *1998 Fordham Corp. L. Inst.* (1999), 392.

[1175] See para 13.225, above; and see Legal, 'Standards of Proof and Standards of Judicial Review in EU Competition Law' in Hawk (ed), *2005 Fordham Corp. L. Inst.* (2006), Chap 5.

[1176] See, eg Case 42/84 *Remia v Commission* [1985] ECR 2545, [1987] 1 CMLR 1, para 34 (permissible duration of vendor's non-compete covenant); applied in Cases 142 & 156/84 *BAT and Reynolds v Commission* [1987] ECR 4487, [1988] 4 CMLR 24, para 62 (effect on competition of acquisition of shareholding in a competitor); Case T-65/98 *Van den Bergh Foods v Commission* [2003] ECR II-4653, [2004] 4 CMLR 14, [2005] All ER (EC) 418, para 80 (foreclosure of market resulting from exclusivity clauses), appeal dismissed Case C-552/03P *Unilever Bestfoods v Commission* [2006] ECR I-9091, [2006] 5 CMLR 1494 (although the CFI there appeared to carry out a careful analysis). See Bailey, n 1168, above. cf the similar issues on appeals from merger decisions, paras 8.244 *et seq*, above; and see Case T-201/04 *Microsoft v Commission*, judgment of 17 September 2007, discussed in the Postscript on *Microsoft*, at the end of this volume.

[1177] See, eg Case 258/78 *Nungesser v Commission* [1982] ECR 2015, [1983] 1 CMLR 278 (application of Art 81(1) to exclusive patent licence); Cases 40/73, etc, *Suiker Unie* (n 1127, above) para 473–498 (application of Art 81 to agency agreements). Case T-41/96 *Bayer v Commission* *('ADALAT')* [2000] ECR II-3383, [2001] 4 CMLR 126, [2001] All ER (EC) 1, appeal dismissed. Cases C-2 & 3/01P *BAI and Commission v Bayer* [2004] ECR I-23, [2004] 4 CMLR 653.

[1178] See para 13.227 and cases there cited.

[1179] See para 13.026, above.

[1180] Proportionality is usually relevant to the amount of the fine, but see also Case 226/84 *British Leyland v Commission* [1986] ECR 3263, [1987] 1 CMLR 184; *Alrosa* (n 1173, above).

non-discrimination,[1181] legitimate expectation,[1182] or infringement of fundamental rights,[1183] may be pleaded in an action under Article 230.

Lack of competence.   Lack of competence relates to the absence of powers on   **13.229**
the part of the Commission in respect of actions taken by it. For example, if
interim measures ordered by the Commission exceed the measures that could be
ordered,[1184] or if a decision was not regularly adopted,[1185] the decision will be
quashed for lack of competence. Lack of competence has been invoked unsuccessfully in cases where the jurisdiction of the Commission to take decisions against
non-EC undertakings has been contested.[1186]

Misuse of powers.   Misuse of powers relates to the exercise of powers for   **13.230**
improper purposes and has not hitherto been successfully invoked in any competition case.[1187] The Court of First Instance has said that for a decision to be annulled
on this ground, it would have to be apparent on the basis of objective, relevant and
consistent factors that the sole or main purpose of the contested decision was
other than that stated.[1188]

(iii) Procedural aspects

The Court's procedure.   The procedure before the Court of First Instance is   **13.231**
set out in the Rules of Procedure.[1189] The procedure depends largely on written
submissions[1190] with fact-finding procedures different from those found in
common law jurisdictions. After the written procedure there is a relatively brief

---

1181 See, eg *British Leyland*, above.

1182 See, eg *Suiker Unie* (n 1127, above) at paras 555–557.

1183 See paras 13.026 *et seq*, above.

1184 Cases 228 & 229/82 *Ford v Commission (No. 1)* (n 1109, above). See also *Metro (No. 2)* (n 1173, above) (whether Commission had jurisdiction to renew exemption in absence of new notification).

1185 Cases T-79/89, etc, *Re the PVC Cartel* (n 1092, above).

1186 See, eg Case 6/72 *Europemballage and Continental Can v Commission* [1973] ECR 215, [1973] CMLR 199; as to extraterritorial jurisdiction, see generally paras 1.105 *et seq*, above, and Cases 89/85, etc, *WoodPulp I* [1988] ECR 5193, [1988] 4 CMLR 901.

1187 cf *Metro (No. 1)* (n 1173, above); Case 22/84 *British Leyland v Commission* [1986] ECR 3263; Case 5/85 *AKZO v Commission* [1986] ECR 2585, [1987] 3 CMLR 716; *Metro (No. 2)* (n 1173, above); Case T-57/91 *NALOO v Commission* [1996] ECR II-1019, [1996] 5 CMLR 672.

1188 Case T-143/89 *Ferriere Nord v Commission* [1995] ECR II-917, para 68.

1189 CFI Rules of Procedure, OJ 1991 L136/1, corr OJ 1991 L317/34; as amended by OJ 1994 L249/17, OJ 1995 L44/64, OJ 1995 L172/3, OJ 1997 L103/6 (corr OJ 1997 L351/72), OJ 1999 L135/92, OJ 2000 L322/4, OJ 2003 L147/22, OJ 2004 L132/3, OJ 2004 L127/108, OJ 2005 L298/1, OJ 2006 L386/45. An up-to-date version is available on the CFI website; also in *Encyclopedia of European Union Law (Constitutional Texts)*, Vol. 3, paras 61.0260 *et seq*.

1190 The procedure consists of a written application, followed by defence, reply and rejoinder. Third parties may intervene. See CFI Practice Directions, OJ 2002 L 87/48.

oral hearing,[1191] followed in due course by the judgment.[1192] Five issues of procedure are considered below:

(a) time limits for bringing actions;

(b) how far new material may be adduced before the Court;

(c) measures of organisation and measures of inquiry;

(d) interveners; and

(e) the order of the Court, including the question of costs.

13.232   **Time limits for bringing actions.**   Under Article 230 of the Treaty, proceedings must be instituted within two months of publication of the decision in the *Official Journal*, or of its notification to the applicant, as the case may be; probably that means whichever of the two events is the earlier.[1193] In practice, the addressee of a decision is likely to receive notification (that is, the full text) of the decision prior to its publication. Time starts to run from the day following receipt.[1194] The same time limit applies to appeals pursuant to Article 229 of the Treaty in respect of the level of the fine.[1195] Where persons who are not recipients of the decision wish to institute proceedings, time runs from the fifteenth day following publication in the *Official Journal*.[1196] The above time limits are extended to take account of

---

[1191] Arts 55–63 Rules of Procedure of the CFI (n 1189, above). The oral hearing seldom lasts more than one day, often less. Counsel should be prepared to summarise the principal arguments in half an hour at most. See the CFI's Guidance Notes to Counsel for the oral procedure, [1999] All ER (EC) 643, also in *Encyclopedia of European Union Law (Constitutional Texts)*, Vol. 3, paras 61.1220 *et seq*. (See also the Guidance Notes for the ECJ published May 2006 available on the ECJ's website.) Exceptionally, one of the Judges of the CFI may be designated by the CFI to perform the function of an Advocate General when the CFI sits in plenary session (eg Case T-51/89 *Tetra Pak v Commission* [1990] ECR II-309, [1991] 4 CMLR 334) or if it is considered that the legal difficulty or the factual complexity of the case so requires (eg the *Polypropylene* cases, where AG Vesterdorf gave an opinion on all the appeals together but the CFI delivered a separate judgment in each case: see Arts 2(2) and 17–19 of the Rules of Procedure).

[1192] Arts 81–86 of the Rules of Procedure.

[1193] Art 230 EC, 5th para. For the meaning of 'notification' and the scope for 'excusable error' see Case T-12/90 *Bayer v Commission* [1991] ECR II-219, [1993] 4 CMLR 30; upheld on appeal Case C-195/91P, [1994] ECR I-5619, [1996] 4 CMLR 32.

[1194] Rules of Procedure of the CFI, Art 102(1) (n 1189, above). The period expires at the end of the day which, in the month determined by the period, bears the same number as the day which caused the period to run, namely the day of notification: Case 152/85 *Misset v Council* [1987] ECR 223. If the period would otherwise expire on a Saturday, Sunday or official holiday, the period is extended to the next working day: Art 102(1). Notification of the *dispositif* without the reasoning is almost certainly not 'notification' for the purposes of Art 230. But the time limit does not apply to challenges to non-existent measures: Case 15/85 *Consorzio Co-operative D'Abruzzo v Commission* [1987] ECR 1005, [1988] 1 CMLR 841. The burden of proof that an application was lodged out of time lies on the party that alleges that it was out of time: Cases T-70 & 71/92 *Florimex and VGB v Commission* [1997] ECR II-693, [1997] 5 CMLR 769, [1997] All ER (EC) 798.

[1195] Case T-252/03 *FNICGV (French beef - limitation)* [2004] ECR II-3795, [2005] 4 CMLR 785.

[1196] Art 102(1) of the Rules of Procedure of CFI (n 1189, above). In the case of unpublished decisions, time begins to run from the date on which the decision came to the knowledge of the applicant: Art 230 EC. However, this is of mainly theoretical significance given that the

distance from Luxembourg and public holidays.[1197] The Court of First Instance takes a strict approach to compliance with time limits as illustrated by a recent case in which the the Court of First Instance gave judgment by default as the Commission had failed to lodge its defence in time.[1198]

Fast-track procedure.   By amendment to the Rules of Procedure that took effect on 1 February 2001, the Court may, on the application of either party, institute an expedited procedure in a case of particular urgency.[1199] Cases which have been fast tracked are generally dealt with in under a year.[1200] This procedure has been predominantly (although not exclusively) used in appeals against Commission merger decisions where time is of the essence.[1201] Access to the fast track is not granted as of right: the party seeking expedition must file a request which is then heard and decided by the President of the Court of First Instance.[1202]   **13.233**

Whether decisions can be supported by new material.   An appeal to the Court under Article 230 is by way of review of the Commission's decision, and not by way of re-hearing.[1203] On occasion, the Commission has successfully sought to justify its decision by reference to arguments other than those relied on in the decision.[1204] But only rarely will this be possible without infringing the right to be   **13.234**

Commission is now required by Art 30 of Reg 1/2003 to publish at least a summary of decisions which it takes pursuant to Art 7–10, 23 and 24. Where the third party is not an addressee but has full notice of the decision prior to publication, it is unclear whether time starts to run as from that time.

[1197] See Annexes I and II to the Rules of Procedure (n 1189, above). The extension for the UK is 10 days. Note that the appeal must be physically lodged at the CFI within the permitted period: Art 43(3) of the Rules of Procedure of the CFI. There is a limited *force majeure* provision under Art 42 of the Statute of the Court.

[1198] Case T-44/02 *Dresdner Bank v Commission*, judgment of 14 October 2004 (unpublished). See also Case T-125/89 *Filtrona Española v Commission* [1990] ECR II-393, [1990] 4 CMLR 832 (application lodged two days late rejected by CFI).

[1199] Rules of Procedure of the CFI, Art 76a. This 'fast track' procedure dispenses with written pleadings after the application and defence and instead involves a more extensive oral hearing. See Barbier de la Serre, 'Accelerated and expedited procedures before the EC courts: a review of the practice' (2006) 43 CML Rev 783.

[1200] See, eg Case T-310/01 *Schneider Electric v Commission* [2002] ECR II-4071, [2003] 4 CMLR 768, [2004] All ER (EC) 314; Case T-5/02 *Tetra Laval v Commission* [2002] ECR II-4381, [2002] 5 CMLR 1182; Case T-87/05 *EDP v Commission* [2005] ECR II-3745, [2005] 5 CMLR 1436.

[1201] In the first six years to the end of 2006, applications for expedited procedure were granted in 28 cases, of which 17 were merger cases: see House of Lords EU Committee, 15th Report 2006–07, *An EU Competition Court* (HL 75), para 55. For the merger cases, see further para 8.236, above.

[1202] Art 76 of the Rules of Procedure of the CFI (n 1189, above).

[1203] *per* AG Warner in Cases 19 & 20/74 *Kali und Salz and Kali-Chemie v Commission* [1975] ECR 499, [1975] 2 CMLR 154, 165–166. But the CFI has a wider jurisdiction as regards fines under Art 229 and even under Art 230 the CFI's review is, in practice, detailed: see para 13.227, above.

[1204] See, eg *ICI v Commission* [1972] ECR 619, [1972] CMLR 557, paras 143–145.

heard and the requirement that the decision be adequately reasoned,[1205] and the Commission is not permitted to rely on evidence that is not contained in the decision.[1206] However, in some cases defects in the Commission's administrative procedure may be rectified in the course of proceedings before the Court.[1207] By contrast, the applicant is entitled to raise substantive arguments in the appeal which it did not raise during the administrative proceedings.[1208] But any new evidence introduced by the applicant, or obtained by the Court of its own initiative,[1209] is relevant only to whether the facts stated in the decision may be substantiated in the light of the circumstances at the time the decision was taken.[1210] Where a party becomes aware of a document in the context of measures of organisation of procedure granting access to the Commission's file, it may rely on that document although it had not pleaded breach of its right of access to the file in its appeal.[1211] It follows from the limited nature of the Court's jurisdiction that if the decision is vitiated by manifest errors of appreciation or significant procedural breaches, it must be annulled: the Court is not able to retake the decision on the merits in the light of fresh external evidence.[1212]

[1205] See, eg Cases 8/66, etc, *Cimenteries CBR v Commission* [1967] ECR 75, [1967] CMLR 77; *Papiers Peints v Commission* [1975] ECR 1491, [1976] 1 CMLR 589; Cases 19 & 20/74 *Kali und Salz* (n 1203, above).

[1206] Case T-67/00 *JFE Engineering* (n 1155, above) para 176. However, the CFI went on to hold that the Commission is entitled to refer to documents not before the court on which the undertakings challenging the decision seek to rely. In *Metro v Commission (No. 2)* [1986] ECR 3021, [1987] 1 CMLR 118, paras 75–78, the Commission was entitled to refer to the Macintosh report prepared after the decision was taken to show that the factual basis set out in the decision was adequate.

[1207] Case 85/76 *Hoffmann-La Roche v Commission* [1979] ECR 461, [1979] 3 CMLR 211, para 15–17.

[1208] Case T-30/89 *Hilti v Commission* [1991] ECR II-1439, [1992] 4 CMLR 16. The CFI held that since an undertaking is under no obligation to reply to the statement of objections at all, it cannot be prevented from raising arguments that were not raised in any such reply. In Case T-354/94 *Stora Koppabergs Bergslags v Commission* [1998] ECR II-2111, [2002] 4 CMLR 1397, para 50, the CFI held that an applicant may dispute before the CFI factual or legal matters conceded before the Commission; however the earlier concession would be taken into account by the Court 'as evidence' in determining the dispute. The CFI has jurisdiction to increase the level of the fine where an undertaking which has benefited from a reduction in fine for not contesting facts in the statement of objections proceeds to contest those facts before the CFI: see Case T-241/01 *SAS v Commission* [2005] ECR II-2917, [2005] 5 CMLR 922, paras 231–242, and see para 13.215, above.

[1209] See AG Slynn in *Pioneer* (n 1154, above) 1931 (ECR) and 289 (CMLR).

[1210] Case T-168/01 *GlaxoSmithKline* (n 1170, above) paras 58 *et seq*. See also *per* AG Warner in *Kali und Salz* (n 1203, above) at 526 (ECR). Note *Metro v Commission (No. 2)* [1989] ECR 3021, [1987] 1 CMLR 118 (Commission entitled to refer to Macintosh report prepared after the decision was taken).

[1211] Case C-238/99P *Limburgse Vinyl Maatschappij('LVM') v Commission ('PVC II')* [2002] ECR I-8375, [2003] 4 CMLR 397, paras 369–375.

[1212] See para 13.240, below, and Vesterdorf, 'Judicial Review in EC Competition Law: Reflections on the Role of the Community Courts in the EC System of Competition Law Enforcement (2005) 1 Competition Policy Int'l, No 2, at 20–22.

Measures of organisation and inquiry.   Articles 64–76 of the Rules of Procedure   **13.235**
of the Court of First Instance provide for the taking of measures of organisation of
procedure, measures of inquiry and the summoning and examination of witnesses
and experts. Measures of organisation of procedure are intended to ensure that
cases are prepared for hearing, procedures carried out and disputes resolved 'under
the best possible conditions'. They are prescribed by the Court and can be proposed by the parties.[1213] The measures may include putting questions to the parties, asking the parties or third parties for information or particulars, asking for
documents and summoning the parties to meetings.[1214] Measures of inquiry may
include the taking of oral testimony, the commissioning of an expert's report and
'an inspection of a place or thing in question'.[1215] The Court of First Instance may,
of its own motion or on the application of a party, order that certain facts be
proved by witnesses. It can summon a witness who may be questioned by the
members of the Court and, subject to the control of the President of the Court, by
the representatives of the parties.[1216]

Interveners.   Member States, Community institutions and 'any other person   **13.236**
establishing an interest in the result of any case submitted to the Court' (except in
cases between Member States, between Community institutions or between
Member States and Community institutions) may intervene before the Court of
First Instance.[1217] The application to intervene should be limited to supporting
the form of the order sought by one of the parties[1218] and the intervener must

---

[1213] Rules of Procedure of the CFI (n 1189, above) Art 64.

[1214] ibid, Art 64(3). See, eg Cases T-68/89, etc, *Società Italiano Vetro v Commission ('Italian Flat
Glass')* [1992] ECR II-1403, [1992] 5 CMLR 302 (measures taken by Judge Rapporteur to produce
agreed summary of positions, single common file of documents, agreed statistical evidence); Cases
T-79/89, etc, *Re the PVC Cartel* [1992] ECR II-315, [1992] 4 CMLR 357 (measures taken to request
production of documents by the Commission). See also appointment of experts by ECJ in Cases
C-89/85, etc, *Åhlström Osakeyhtiö v Commission ('WoodPulp II')* [1993] ECR I-1307, [1993]
4 CMLR 407. If a party requests the production of an apparently material document on which
it relies for its allegations, the CFI cannot refuse to order production of the document while also
dismissing those allegations on the grounds that the existence of the document was unconfirmed
and its contents unsubstantiated: Case C-119/97P *Ufex v Commission* [1999] ECR I-1341, [2000]
4 CMLR 268, annulling the decision of the CFI (the document was a letter from the Competition
Commissioner to the President of the Commission). Where non-disclosure of documents is a
ground of appeal, the CFI will require those documents to be produced: para 13.090, above.

[1215] Rules of Procedure of the CFI (n 1189, above) Art 65.

[1216] ibid, Arts 68–76. See, eg T-141/94 *Thyssen Stahl v Commission* [1999] ECR II-347, [1999]
4 CMLR 810, paras 68 and 482.

[1217] Art 40 of the Protocol on the Statute of the Court of Justice, published at OJ 2001 C80/53
and as amended most recently by Council Decn of 3 October 2005, 2005 OJ L266/60. A consolidated version of the Statute is on the ECJ website, also in *Encyclopedia of European Law (Constitutional
Texts)*, Vol 3, para 60.0214. See also Case T-193/02 *Piau v Commission* [2005] ECR II-209, [2005]
5 CMLR 42, paras 35–36 (appeal dismissed, Case C-171/05P, [2006] ECR I-37).

[1218] Art 40 of the Statute of the Court of Justice, above.

'accept the case as he finds it'.[1219] In deciding whether to grant leave to intervene, the Court of First Instance will distinguish between parties which have a direct interest in the ruling on the specific act whose annulment is sought and those which can establish only an indirect interest in the result of the case by reason of similarities between their situation and that of one of the parties.[1220] Accordingly, the intervener's interest must be in the actual form of the order sought rather than merely in abstract legal arguments.[1221] The Court of First Instance has held that where the Commission has taken a decision following a complaint, the undertaking which has lodged the complaint has the necessary interest to intervene, in particular when it has participated in the procedure before the Commission.[1222] Undertakings which compete on the affected market with the undertaking found by the Commission to have infringed Article 81 or 82 have a direct and existing interest in the appeal proceedings.[1223] The right to intervene is given a broader interpretation in the case of associations of undertakings which will be deemed to have the necessary interest where their object is to protect their members in cases raising questions of principle that are liable to affect those members.[1224] The Court of First Instance has held more specifically that an association may be granted leave to intervene if it represents an appreciable number of undertakings active in the sector concerned, its objects include that of protecting its members' interests, the case may raise questions of principle affecting the functioning of the sector concerned and the interests of its members may therefore be affected to an appreciable extent by the forthcoming judgment.[1225]

13.237 **Interveners – procedure.** An application to intervene must be made within either six weeks of the publication of the notice in the *Official Journal* or before the decision to open the oral procedure has been taken.[1226] In the latter case, the

---

[1219] Rules of Procedure of the CFI, Art 116(3) and see Case T-2/03 *Verein für Konsumenteninformation v Commission* [2005] ECR II-1121, [2005] 4 CMLR 1627, [2005] All ER (EC) 813, para 52: 'Although those provisions do not preclude an intervener from using arguments different from those used by the party it is supporting, that is nevertheless on the condition that they do not alter the framework of the dispute and that the intervention is still intended to support the form of order sought by that party'.

[1220] Cases C-151/97P(I) and C-157/97P *National Power and Powergen v Commission* [1997] ECR I-3491, [1998] 4 CMLR 502, para 53.

[1221] ibid.

[1222] See Case T-367/94 *British Coal v Commission* [1997] ECR II-469, para 31.

[1223] Case T-201/04R *Microsoft Corp v Commission* [2004] ECR II-4463, [2005] 4 CMLR 949, para 67.

[1224] See, eg Case T-201/04R *Microsoft Corp v Commission* [2004] ECR II-2977, [2004] 5 CMLR 1073, paras 37–38.

[1225] Case T-253/03 *Akzo Nobel Chemicals v Commission* [2004] ECR II-1617, para 18. In that case, the CFI rejected the application to intervene by the Section of Business Law of the International Bar Association on the basis that it is not a representative association whose object is to protect the interests of in-house lawyers: paras 20–23.

[1226] Rules of Procedure of the CFI (n 1189, above) Art 115.

intervener forfeits the right to submit written pleadings but may make oral submissions on the basis of the Report for the Hearing.[1227] Where an application to intervene has been made within the six-week period, the interveners will receive copies of every document subject to applications by either of the parties to omit secret or confidential documents.[1228]

Powers of partial annulment. The Court of First Instance has power to limit   **13.238**
its annulment to only part of a Commission decision. However, in *Italian Flat Glass*,[1229] the Court of First Instance held that the finding in the Commission decision of a close, institutionalised cartel in the market had not been proved to the requisite legal standard but that there were some documents on the file which were proof of a more episodic concertation among two or three producers. The Court held that although it could partially annul a Commission decision, it did not have jurisdiction to remake the contested decision. Such a jurisdiction would disturb the institutional balance established by the Treaty and would risk prejudicing the rights of the defence. In such circumstances, therefore, the Court held that it should not carry out a comprehensive reassessment of the evidence before it or draw new conclusions from that evidence. The Court had only to consider whether the conditions for partial annulment of the decision had been fulfilled or whether the whole decision had to fall. The test for partial annulment was whether the scope of the operative part of the decision, read in the light of the grounds for the decision, could be limited *ratione materiae*, *ratione personae* or *ratione temporis* in such a way that its effects were restricted but its substance remained unaltered; and whether the undertakings had been given an opportunity of replying effectively to the objections so revised.

Consequences of successful appeal by some addressees of the decision. A Com-   **13.239**
mission decision resulting from a single administrative procedure may, based on similar findings of law and fact, impose fines on a number of undertakings. If only some of the defendants apply to the Court of First Instance for annulment and the decision against them is annulled by the Court, the Commission has no duty under Article 233 of the Treaty to re-examine whether fines paid by the remaining addressees of the decision should be repaid.[1230] A infringement decision addressed to a number of undertakings is in reality a 'series of individual decisions' applying to each of the addressees. The annulment of one of those decisions at the instance of one applicant does not have an effect *erga omnes*; that

---

[1227] ibid, Art 116.
[1228] ibid.
[1229] *Italian Flat Glass* (n 1214, above).
[1230] *Re PVC (No. 2)* [1999] ECR II-931, [1999] 5 CMLR 303, paras 169 *et seq*.

is to say, it has no effect on the validity of the decision *vis-à-vis* addressees who have not challenged the decision.[1231]

13.240 **Consequences of total annulment.** Although the Court of First Instance has unlimited jurisdiction to review fines, the mere bringing of an action does not entail the definitive transfer to the Court of the power to impose penalties. Where a Commission decision has been annulled in its entirety on the basis of a procedural defect in the manner in which the decision was adopted, the Commission may take a fresh decision on the basis of the same facts but avoiding the procedural defects that vitiated its first decision.[1232] The Commission is entitled to restart the administrative proceedings at the point at which the original procedural error occurred, since the validity of earlier procedural steps is not affected by an annulment based on later procedural errors. But if the Court has found that allegations made by the Commission in its decision are unproven, the Commission is not permitted to take a further decision in respect of the same conduct.[1233] Where the Court of First Instance annuls a decision, the Commission is required, under Article 233 of the Treaty, to take the measures necessary to comply with the Court's judgment.[1234] In doing so, the Commission must observe not only the operative part of the judgment but also the grounds which constitute the 'essential basis' of the judgment.[1235] The Court has held that when it annuls a decision concerning the grant or refusal of individual exemption under Article 81(3) that had been sought under the former regime of Regulation 17, the Commission must still take a decision on the application of Article 81(3).[1236] However, this approach seems questionable since the procedure for exemption under Regulation 17 has been abolished by the Modernisation Regulation without any transitional provision, and at the time of writing the issue is pending on appeal before the Court of Justice.[1237]

[1231] Cases C-238/99P, etc, *Limburgse Vinyl Maatschappij* (n 1211, above) para 100; Case C-310/97P *Commission v AssiDomän Kraft Products* [1999] ECR I-5363, [1999] 5 CMLR 1253, [1999] All ER (EC) 737. See comment by Moloney, (2000) CML Rev 971.

[1232] Cases C-238/99P, etc, *Limburgse Vinyl Maatschappij v Commission* (n 1211, above) para 693. Thus the Commission re-adopted decisions against certain participants in the *Alloy Surcharge* case: Press Release IP/06/1851 (20 December 2006) and in the *Steel Beams* cartel case: Press Release IP/06/1527 (8 November 2006).

[1233] *Re PVC (No. 2)* (n 1214, above) paras 71–99, 183–193.

[1234] Case T-206/99 *Métropole Télévision v Commission* [2001] ECR II-1057, [2001] 4 CMLR, para 35.

[1235] ibid.

[1236] Case T-328/03 *O2 (Germany) v Commission* [2006] ECR II-1231, [2006] 5 CMLR 258, paras 47–48; Case T-168/01 *GlaxoSmithKline Services v Commission* [2006] ECR II-2969, [2006] 5 CMLR 1589, paras 318–320.

[1237] Cases C-513 & 515/06P *GlaxoSmithKline Services v Commission*, not yet decided. In *O2 (Germany)*, above, the statement was *obiter*.

Powers of the Court of First Instance following annulment of decision. In an **13.241** action for annulment under Article 230 of the Treaty, the jurisdiction of the Court of First Instance is limited to reviewing the legality of the contested act. If the action is well-founded, the Court declares the decision to be void and it is then incumbent on the Commission to take the necessary measures to comply with the judgment. The Court cannot grant relief directing the Commission to take particular steps.[1238] The Court of First Instance does, however, have power under Article 235 to award damages for 'non-contractual liability' which a Community institution is liable to pay under Article 288 of the Treaty. In *Schneider Electric*, the Court of First Instance stressed that it was only in the case of grave and manifest illegality that the Commission's non-contractual liability to pay damages for loss caused by a competition law enforcement decision would arise.[1239] In that case, however, the Court held that the Commission's breaches of the rights of the defence which had previously led to the annulment of a prohibition of a merger could not be justified or explained by the pressures under which the Commission operated and an award of damages was therefore appropriate.

Costs and other orders. If the applicant is unsuccessful, the Court will dismiss **13.242** the application and order the applicant to pay the costs of the Commission[1240] and often those of intervening parties[1241] if costs have been requested.[1242] If the applicant is wholly successful, the decision will be annulled, and the Commission ordered to pay the costs,[1243] including those of successful interveners.[1244] The costs recoverable include disbursements and the fees of outside lawyers and,

---

[1238] Case T-102/92 *Viho v Commission* [1995] ECR II-17, [1997] 4 CMLR 469, [1995] All ER (EC) 371, paras 28–29 (appeal on other grounds dismissed, Case C-73/95P, [1996] ECR I-5457, [1997] 4 CMLR 419, [1997] All ER (EC) 163); Case T-114/92 *BEMIM v Commission* [1995] ECR II-147, [1996] 4 CMLR 305, paras 33–34; Case T-266/03 *Groupement des cartes bancaires (CB) v Commission*, judgment of 12 July 2007, para 78.

[1239] Case T-351/03 *Schneider Electric v Commission*, judgment of 11 July 2007. See also Case T-212/03 *MyTravel v Commission*, not yet decided.

[1240] The Commission's costs are often trivial, comprising in effect only their travelling expenses to Luxembourg for the oral hearing. The Commission cannot recover costs in respect of its in-house lawyers: Case 126/76 *Dietz v Commission* [1977] ECR 2431, [1978] 2 CMLR 608.

[1241] See, eg Cases T-5/00 and 6/00 *Nederlandse Federatieve Vereniging voor de Groothandel op Elektrotechnisch Gebied and Technische Unie v Commission* [2003] ECR II-5761, [2005] 5 CMLR 962 (appeals partially dismissed Cases C-105/04 and C-113/04P, [2006] ECR I-8725, 8831, [2006] 5 CMLR 1223); Case 226/84 *British Leyland v Commission* [1986] ECR 3263, [1987] 1 CMLR 185; but cf., eg Cases 25 & 26/84 *Ford v Commission (No. 2)* [1985] ECR 2725, [1985] 3 CMLR 528 (BEUC to bear its own costs). Intervening Member and EFTA States and Community or EEA institutions must bear their own costs (Art 87(4) of the Rules of Procedure of the CFI (n 1189, above)).

[1242] Art 87(2) of the Rules of Procedure of the CFI.

[1243] See, eg Case 53/85 *AKZO v Commission* [1986] ECR 1965, [1987] 1 CMLR 231.

[1244] See, eg Cases 228 & 229/82 *Ford v Commission (No. 1)* [1984] ECR 1129, [1984] 1 CMLR 649 (Commission to pay costs of intervening dealers, but not costs of BEUC).

where appropriate, experts such as economists.[1245] If the level of costs is not agreed between the Commission and the applicant, the Court will make an order as to the amount of costs recoverable.[1246] In determining the level of costs, the Court is not obliged to take account of any national scale of lawyers' fees or any agreement between the party and its lawyers but determines the necessity of the work involved and makes an equitable assessment of the amount of fees.[1247] Where a fine has been annulled or reduced, the Commission must repay not only the principal amount of the fine overpaid but also default interest on that amount.[1248] A more usual result is that the parties succeed on some heads but not others, in which event the parties and interveners are normally ordered to bear their own costs.[1249] Where the applications lodged are so voluminous as to amount to an abuse, the parties may be ordered to bear their own costs in spite of the fact that some heads of the application were upheld.[1250] If a decision is annulled in part, the Court will ensure that its order is couched in such a way as to preserve for the partly successful applicant the fruits of its success.[1251] In the exercise of its unlimited jurisdiction

---

[1245] The costs recoverable are defined by Art 91 of the CFI Rules of Procedure. See generally Mail-Fouilleul, *Les dépens dans le contentieux communautaire* (2005); and specifically as regards competition cases, Siragusa and Rizza (eds), *EU Competition Law, Vol III: Cartel Law* (2007), paras 5.244 *et seq*; Kerse and Khan, *EC Antitrust Procedure* (5th edn, 2005), paras 8.018–8.019.

[1246] Art 92 of the CFI Rules of Procedure. The Court has no power to tax the costs as between the applicant and its own lawyers.

[1247] The equitable assessment will be based on the subject-matter and nature of the dispute and its significance from the point of view of EC law, the difficulties presented by the case, the amount of work caused for the lawyers, and the financial interest of the parties in the proceedings: Case T-120/89 (92) *Stahlwerke Peine-Salzgitter v Commission* [1996] ECR II-1547, para 28. There is usually a shortfall between the costs determined by the Court and the amount actually incurred by private parties in competition cases. See, eg Case T-342/99 DEP *Airtours v Commission* [2004] ECR II-1787: despite the complexity of the case and its significant financial interest for the applicant, CFI substantially reduced the fees claimed for lawyers and economic experts, holding that there was unnecessary duplication in the work and that some of the fees appeared excessive.

[1248] Case T-171/99 *Corus UK v Commission* [2001] ECR II-2967, [2001] 5 CMLR 1275. See also Case C-123/03P *Commission v Greencore Group* [2004] ECR I-11647, [2005] 4 CMLR 11 on the Commission's obligation to reimburse unpaid interest.

[1249] See, eg Case 155/79 *AM & S v Commission* [1982] ECR 1575, [1992] 2 CMLR 264; Case 86/82 *Hasselblad v Commission* [1984] ECR 883, [1984] 1 CMLR 559; Cases 29 & 30/83 *CRAM and Rheinzink v Commission* [1984] ECR 1679, [1985] 1 CMLR 688 (Commission to pay costs in Case 29/83, parties to bear own costs in Case 30/83). cf Case T-168/01 *GlaxoSmithKline Services* (n 1236, above) where the appellant failed to overturn the Commission's finding that the agreement fell within Art 81(1) but the Commission's decn that Art 81(3) did not apply was annulled. Both parties were ordered to bear half of their own costs and half of the costs of the other party and of the interveners.

[1250] Cases T-191/98, etc, *Atlantic Container Line v Commission* [2003] ECR II-3275, [2005] 4 CMLR 1283, paras 1646–1647; see also Case T-464/04 *Impala v Commission* [2006] ECR II-2289, [2006] 5 CMLR 1049, paras 544–554, where the CFI ordered that the successful applicant should bear a quarter of its own costs given that it had 'insisted' that the case be dealt with under the expedited procedure but then failed to conduct itself accordingly, in particular, in respect of the volume of the application and the number of pleas in law and arguments submitted.

[1251] Case 17/74 *Transocean Marine Paint v Commission* [1974] ECR 1063, [1974] 2 CMLR 459; see also *AM&S v Commission* (n 1249, above) and note Case 264/82 *Timex v Commission* [1985] ECR 849, [1985] 3 CMLR 550.

under Article 229, the Court may substitute its own order regarding fines whilst entirely dismissing the application for annulment of the Commission's decision on the substance.[1252]

(b) Action under Article 232 in respect of failure to act

Generally. An action may be brought for a declaration that the Commission **13.243** has failed to act under Article 232 of the Treaty. The action is admissible only if the Commission has first been specifically called upon to act and if, within a further period of two months, it has not defined its position. Proceedings under Article 232 may be brought by any natural or legal person, but only if that person's complaint is that the Commission has failed to address to him an act other than a recommendation or opinion.[1253]

Conditions for successful application. Although the precise ambit of **13.244** Article 232 is unclear, a number of cumulative conditions must be met before an individual may bring a successful action under Article 232.[1254] Although Article 232 states that a natural or legal person may bring proceedings for a failure 'to address [an act] to that person', the Courts have interpreted this as not imposing a standing requirement for such proceedings. An action under Article 232 for failure to act is regarded as the converse of an action under Article 230 for annulment of an act; and accordingly there is standing if the act is one which, if taken, would be of direct and individual concern to the applicant within the fourth paragraph of Article 230.[1255] However, there are a number of further cumulative conditions that must be satisfied:

(a) the failure by the Commission to act involves an infringement of the Treaty; if the Commission has no duty to take the particular act requested, no action lies under Article 232;[1256]

[1252] See, eg Cases 6 & 7/73 *Commercial Solvents v Commission* [1974] ECR 223, [1974] 1 CMLR 309.

[1253] Art 232 EC, 2nd and 3rd paras. See Case 246/81 *Lord Bethell v Commission* [1982] ECR 2277, [1982] 3 CMLR 300, paras 16–17, and *per* AG Slynn at 2295–2299 (ECR), 305–306 (CMLR); AG Capotorti in Case 125/78 *GEMA v Commission* [1979] ECR 3173, 3199–3200, [1980] 2 CMLR 177, 189–190.

[1254] See also para 13.071, above, on the position of complainants seeking judicial review of the handling of their case by the Commission.

[1255] Case C-68/95 *T. Port v Bundesanstalt für Landwirtschaft und Ernährung* [1996] ECR I-6065, [1997] 1 CMLR 1, para 59; Case T-17/96 *TFI v Commission* [1999] ECR II-1757, [2000] 4 CMLR 678, paras 27–28 (appeal dismissed on other grounds, Case C-302/99P, [2001] ECR I-5603). For standing under Art 230, see para 13.221, above.

[1256] *GEMA* (n 1253, above) para 18; *Lord Bethell* (n 1253, above) at 2296 (ECR), 306 (CMLR); Case T-32/93 *Ladbroke v Commission*, paras 37–38.

(b) the Commission has failed to address to an individual 'any act other than a recommendation or an opinion';[1257]

(c) the individual has clearly called upon the Commission to act for the purposes of Article 232, specifying the nature of the act required;[1258] and

(d) the Commission failed to define its position within the two month period.[1259]

Where the definition of position consists of a refusal to adopt the act requested, this nonetheless operates as a bar to action under Article 232.[1260] The remedy of the applicant is then to appeal the decision of refusal under Article 230 of the Treaty.[1261] In practice, the applicant may be well advised to bring simultaneous actions under both Articles.[1262] But circumstances may arise where a definition of position is not reviewable under Article 230;[1263] or where an applicant has to bring successive proceedings for failure to act in order to obtain a final decision that is susceptible to review.[1264]

[1257] Art 232, 3rd para. It seems clear that the concept of 'act' is wider than that of 'decision' under Art 249: see AG Roemer in Case 8/71 *Komponistenverband v Commission* [1971] ECR 705, 715, [1973] CMLR 902, 907–908 (procedural matters such as the grant of a right to be heard) and AG Capotorti in *GEMA* (n 1253, above) at 3198 (ECR), 191 (CMLR) (sending an Art 6 letter under Reg 2842/98: now Art 7 of Reg 773/2004). See also Case 15/70 *Chevally v Commission* [1970] ECR 975, para 6 (concept of 'measure' identical under Arts 230 and 232).

[1258] AG Roemer in *Komponistenverband*, above.

[1259] Art 232, 2nd para. In Case T-186/94 *Guérin Automobiles v Commission* [1995] ECR II-1753, [1996] 5 CMLR 685, the Commission defined its position outside the two-month period and only after the action had been commenced; the CFI held that it therefore did not need to rule on the Art 232 complaint but ordered the Commission to bear all the costs: paras 45–46; appeal dismissed, Case C-282/95P, [1997] ECR I-1503, [1997] 5 CMLR 447.

[1260] *GEMA* (n 1253, above) at paras 19–22. If an Art 232 action has already been brought, it cannot be converted into an Art 230 action for the annulment of a decision subsequently taken by the Commission: Case T-28/90 *Asia Motor France v Commission* [1992] ECR II-2285, [1992] 5 CMLR 431, para 44.

[1261] *GEMA* (n 1253, above) at 3200 (ECR), 190 (CMLR) *per* AG Capotorti. See also Case 792/79R *Camera Care v Commission* [1980] ECR 119, [1980] 1 CMLR 334, *per* AG Warner.

[1262] See *Camera Care*, above; cf Cases 109 & 114/75 *National Carbonising Company v Commission* [1977] ECR 381 (ECSC).

[1263] Thus if a complainant brings Art 232 proceedings for failure by the Commission to respond to his complaint, an 'Article 7 letter' from the Commission under Reg 773/2004 will frustrate those proceedings but since it is only a provisional decision that notification cannot be reviewed under Art 230; once the complainant has submitted his observations in response, if the Commission then does not proceed within a reasonable time either to initiate proceedings against the subject of the complaint or to adopt a definitive (and therefore reviewable) decision rejecting the complaint, the complainant's remedy is to commence a fresh Art 232 action: see Case C-282/95P *Guérin Automobiles v Commission* (n 1259, above). Assessed in the context of the totality of the procedure, the Commission may be expected to act within the two months period set out under Art 232: Case T-127/98 *UPS Europe v Commission* [1999] ECR II-2633, [2000] 4 CMLR 94, [1999] All ER (EC) 794.

[1264] Thus a refusal by the Commission to take action under the Treaty that it is under no duty to take will not ordinarily be a 'decision' for the purposes of Art 230: Case 247/87 *Star Fruit v Commission* [1989] ECR 291, [1990] 1 CMLR 733, paras 10–14 (refusal at the instance of an individual to take Art 226 proceedings against a Member State not a reviewable decision under

Time limits for action. If the Commission fails to define its position within two **13.245** months of being called upon to act, proceedings must be brought within a further two-month period.[1265] This period is extended in accordance with the Rules of Procedure of the Court to take account of distance and public holidays.[1266]

(c) Interim relief from the Court

Generally. Article 242 of the Treaty provides that the institution of proceedings **13.246** before the Court of First Instance does not have automatic suspensive effect but that the Court may suspend the operation of the contested decision. Under Article 243 of the Treaty the Court additionally has power in any cases before it to prescribe 'any necessary interim measures'.[1267] An application for interim relief can thus be made only if a substantive action (eg under Article 230) is already pending before the Court.[1268] The application should be made by separate document, setting out the grounds relied on,[1269] and will normally be decided by the President of the Court sitting alone.[1270] Interim relief may be, but is not normally, granted on an *ex parte* basis, and third party interventions may be accepted.[1271] Any interim relief ordered may be varied on further application.[1272] If the admissibility of the application for annulment is contested, it is for the

---

Art 230); see also Case T-83/97 *Sateba v Commission* [1997] ECR II-1523, [1998] 4 CMLR 528 (public procurement). cf the position with regard to Art 86(3): Case T-84/94 *Bundesverband der Bilanzbuchhalter v Commission* [1995] ECR II-101 (upheld on appeal Case C-107/95P, [1997] ECR I-947, [1997] 5 CMLR 432); Case T-52/00 *Coe Clerici Logistics v Commission* [2002] ECR II-2553, [2003] 5 CMLR 531.

    1265 Art 232, 2nd para.
    1266 Rules of Procedure of the CFI, Art 102(2) and Annexes I and II to the Rules of Procedure of the ECJ.
    1267 In Case T-322/94R *Union Carbide v Commission* [1994] ECR II-1159, the CFI stated that it had no power to grant measures addressed to the parties to a joint venture which the Commission had decided was compatible with the common market (the decision which the applicant was seeking to have annulled); the application for suspension of the Commission's decision itself was rejected.
    1268 Rules of Procedure of the CFI (n 1189, above) Art 104(1). Application for the suspension of the operation of a decision may be made by a person challenging a decision addressed to a third party: Case 26/76R *Metro v Commission* [1976] ECR 1353. Interim measures may be sought in proceedings brought under Art 232 for the Commission's failure to act: see *Camera Care* (n 1261, above).
    1269 Rules of Procedure, Arts 104(3).
    1270 Statute of the Court, Art 39 and Rules of Procedure, Art 106. Exceptionally, the President may refer the application to the Chamber or plenary of the CFI to which the main case has been assigned.
    1271 Rules of Procedure of the CFI (n 1189, above) Art 105(2) and eg Case T-184/01 R *IMS Health v Commission* [2001] ECR II-3913, [2002] 4 CMLR 46. See also Cases 228 & 229/82 *Ford v Commission (No. 1)* [1984] ECR 1129, [1984] 1 CMLR 649. But note however Leaver, 'The Ford Case: The Right of Intervention' (1982) LS Gaz. 1551; and Case T-23/90R *Peugeot v Commission* [1990] ECR II-195, [1990] 4 CMLR 674 (complainant and consumer organisation allowed to intervene).
    1272 Rules of Procedure of the CFI, Art 108.

Court hearing the application for interim measures to establish that the application reveals *prima facie* grounds for concluding that there is a certain probability that it is admissible.[1273] No application can be made to suspend a Commission decision until the decision has actually been taken.[1274]

13.247 **Interim relief in competition cases.** In the present context the question of interim relief under Articles 242 or 243 of the Treaty usually arises:

(a) where the Commission has imposed fines and the parties wish to postpone payment until after the appeal has been heard;

(b) where the Commission has issued an order that action be taken, or not taken, and the parties wish to suspend operation of the order pending the hearing of the appeal;

(c) where the Commission has refused to act on a complaint and the complainant wishes to obtain interim measures pending the hearing of his appeal;

(d) where the Commission has decided to take a certain step in its proceedings and the parties wish to prevent it from taking that step pending their challenge to the decision.

Those circumstances are briefly considered in turn.

13.248 **Interim relief to suspend fine.** Although a fine is normally payable within three months of a decision, it is usually not necessary to seek a formal suspension of the obligation to pay the fine since the Commission will agree to defer seeking enforcement on condition that the undertaking agrees to pay default interest if the appeal fails and provides a bank guarantee as to eventual payment.[1275] Bank guarantee charges are not, however, recoverable in the event that the Commission's decision is annulled and the fine revoked.[1276] Normally, imposition of these two requirements is a prerequisite to deferring payment.[1277] However, the Court of Justice has held that a decision imposing a fine would be suspended without the requirement of a bank guarantee if the undertaking would have difficulty in obtaining such a guarantee or if the cost of obtaining it would cause serious and irreparable damage.[1278] In subsequent cases, the Court of First Instance has

---

1273 Case C-117/91R *Bosman v Commission* [1991] ECR I-3353, [1991] 3 CMLR 938; Cases T-10/92R, etc, *Cimenteries CBR v Commission* [1992] ECR II-2267, [1993] 4 CMLR 243.

1274 Case T-395/94R(II) *Atlantic Container Line v Commission* [1995] ECR II-2895, [1997] 5 CMLR 195.

1275 See para 13.209, above.

1276 Case T-28/03 *Holcim (Deutschland) v Commission* [2005] ECR II-1357, [2005] 5 CMLR 75 (appeal dismissed, Case C-282/05P, judgment of 15 March 2007).

1277 Case 107/82R *AEG v Commission* [1982] ECR 1549; Case 86/82R *Hasselblad v Commission* [1982] ECR 1555, [1982] 2 CMLR 233. The ECJ confirmed that default interest is payable in Case 107/82 *AEG v Commission* [1983] ECR 3151, [1984] 3 CMLR 325, paras 139–143.

1278 Case 234/82R *Ferriere di Roè Volciano v Commission* [1983] ECR 725 (under the ECSC Treaty); see also Case 213/86R *Montedipe v Commission* [1986] ECR 2623 (no serious or irreparable harm shown on the facts).

repeated that the grant of such a suspension is exceptional and that evidence that the undertaking is unable to provide a guarantee must be adduced.[1279] An application was made to the European Court of Human Rights challenging the requirement for a bank guarantee.[1280] However, no ruling was made as the Court of First Instance annulled the fines at issue[1281] and the case was accordingly withdrawn.[1282]

Suspension of Commission order. If the Commission's decision orders the **13.249** undertaking to take or refrain from taking certain action, it appears that the Court will suspend the order pending the hearing of the appeal if:

(a) the applicant raises a serious question as to the correctness of the Commission's decision;
(b) there is urgency in the sense that the upholding of the decision pending final judgment will probably cause serious and irreparable damage to the applicant;[1283] and
(c) the grant of the measures requested will not prejudice the final outcome.[1284]

[1279] See Case T-301/94R *Laakmann Karton v Commission* [1994] ECR II-1279; Case T-295/94R *Buchmann v Commission* [1994] ECR II-1265; Case T-104/95R *Tsimenta Chakidos v Commission* [1995] ECR II-2235; Case T-18/96R *SCK and FNK* [1996] ECR II-407, [1996] 5 CMLR 307; and Case T-9/99R *HFB Holding v Commission* [1999] ECR II-2429, [2001] 4 CMLR 1066. The effect of the adverse conclusions which business associates or creditors might draw from the lodging of security on the appeal cannot in any circumstances amount to serious and irreparable damage: Case 263/82R *Klöckner—Werke v Commission* [1982] ECR 3995. See also Case T-308/94R *Cascades v Commission* [1995] ECR II-265, where the obligation to provide a guarantee for part of the fine was suspended for six months on condition that the parent company of the appellant undertaking undertook to procure the provision of the balance of the guarantee in that period. For more recent case law, see, eg Case C-364/99P(R) *DSR-Senator Lines v Commission* [1999] ECR I-8733, [2000] 4 CMLR 600, para 48; Case C-361/00P(R) *Cho Yang Shipping Co v Commission* [2000] ECR I-11657, [2001] 4 CMLR 1102, para 88.

[1280] Application 56672/00 *DSR Senator Lines v Fifteen Member States of the EU*.

[1281] Cases T-191/98, etc, *Atlantic Container Line v Commission* [2003] ECR II-3275, [2005] 4 CMLR 1283.

[1282] The question thus remains open whether the requirement of a bank guarantee for a stay of the fine, and the conditions on which this requirement is dispensed with, are consistent with Art 6 ECHR: Kerse and Khan (n 1245, above), para 8–068, consider that the CFI's position is open to objection, relying on *Västberga Taxi and Vulic v Sweden*, Appl no 36985/97, ECtHR judgment of 23 July 2002, para 120.

[1283] See, eg Case T-201/04R *Microsoft v Commission* [2004] ECR II-4463, [2006] 4 CMLR 311, para 240. For commentary see Madero and others 'The Court of First Instance rejects Microsoft's request for interim measures concerning the Commission's decision of 24 March 2004' (2005) 1 EC Competition Policy Newsletter 53.

[1284] See, eg Cases 60 & 190/81R *IBM v Commission* [1981] ECR 1857, [1981] 3 CMLR 93, para 9; Cases 76/89R, etc, *Radio Telefis Eireann v Commission* [1989] ECR 1141, [1989] 4 CMLR 749; Case 56/89R *Publishers' Association v Commission* [1989] ECR 1693, [1989] 4 CMLR 816; Case T-29/92R *SPO v Commission* [1992] ECR II-2161; Cases T-24 & 28/92R *Langnese-Iglo* [1992] ECR II-1713; Case T-88/94R *Sté Commerciale des Potasses et de l'Azote v Commission* [1994] ECR II-401 (condition of clearance in a Merger Reg case was that a party dispose of its shares in another company; this likely to cause dissolution of other company and serious and irreparable

In a number of cases the Court has accepted that the dismantling of an agreement prior to the hearing of the appeal could cause serious and irreparable damage.[1285] Similarly an order which would require the addressee to change how it conducts its business in a way which would be difficult to reverse may be suspended.[1286] Purely financial loss may not be considered to be serious damage, in particular where the applicant has substantial financial power.[1287] Where a national court had reached a different view from the Commission regarding infringement of the EC competition rules, that will be a relevant factor.[1288] But the Court will take into account the interests of third parties and competing undertakings[1289] and the balance of convenience[1290] and will refuse suspension if a proper case is

---

harm to its other shareholders); Case T-41/96R *Bayer v Commission* [1996] ECR II-381, [1996] 5 CMLR 290.

[1285] See, eg Case 20/74R *Kali-Chemie v Commission* [1974] ECR 337, 339. Case 71/74R *Frubo v Commission* [1974] ECR 1031, [1975] 1 CMLR 646; Case 209/78R *Van Landewyck v Commission* [1978] ECR 2111; Cases 43 & 63/82R *VBVB and VBBB v Commission* [1982] ECR 1241; *Publishers' Association* (above); *SPO* (above). In some cases, the Court has emphasised that it did not thereby confer validity on the agreements and also ordered that no penalties should be imposed under the agreements pending the hearing of the appeal. In Case T-395/94R *Atlantic Container Line v Commission* (n 1274, above) the CFI suspended that part of the Commission's decision that prevented the shipping companies from jointly exercising rate-making authority in respect of the inland portions of intermodal transport on the ground that the resulting changes to the framework of operations would be difficult to reverse if the decision were eventually annulled (upheld Case C-149/95(P)R, [1995] ECR I-2165, [1997] 5 CMLR 167, [1995] All ER (EC) 853). See also Case 27/76R *United Brands v Commission* [1976] ECR 425, [1976] 2 CMLR 147.

[1286] See Case T-184/01R *IMS Health v Commission* [2001] ECR II-3913, [2002] 4 CMLR 46 (considering the test of serious and irreparable damage in the context of an appeal against interim measures imposed by the Commission). cf Case T-201/04R *Microsoft* (n 1283, above) para 298: the fact that Microsoft was already subject to similar orders under its settlement with the US antitrust authorities meant that compliance with the Commission's order would not require a fundamental change in business policy. The CFI also made clear that the mere fact that an order to grant intellectual property licences would breach the exclusive prerogatives of the rights holder is not of itself enough to constitute serious and irrepable damage: para 250.

[1287] See, eg *Microsoft* (n 1283, above) para 257.

[1288] Case T-65/98R *Van den Bergh Foods v Commission* [1998] ECR II-2641, [1998] 5 CMLR 475 (where the judgment of the Irish High Court was under appeal). But see now Case C-344/98 *Masterfoods v HB Ice Cream* [2000] ECR I-11369, [2001] 4 CMLR 449, [2001] All ER (EC) 130.

[1289] See, eg Case C-481/01P(R) *NDC Health Corporation v IMS Health* [2002] ECR I-3401, [2002] 5 CMLR 44, para 84 in which the CFI was criticised for excluding the interests of competing undertakings from the assessment.

[1290] Thus, in *Union Carbide Corporation* (n 1267, above) the CFI rejected an application to suspend the operation of a decision clearing a concentration on the ground, *inter alia*, that there was a strong public interest in implementing decisions taken under the Merger Reg which was adopted primarily in order to ensure that there was effective control of concentrations and to provide legal certainty to the parties to the concentration. See, eg Cases 6 & 7/73R *Commercial Solvents v Commission* [1973] ECR 357; Case 3/75R *Johnson and Firth Brown v Commission* [1975] ECR 1, [1975] 1 CMLR 638; and Cases 160 & 161/73R *Miles Druce v Commission* [1973] ECR 1049, [1974] 1 CMLR 224 and [1974] ECR 281, [1974] 2 CMLR D17 (contested takeovers); see also Case 26/76 *Metro v Commission (No. 1)* [1977] ECR 1875, [1978] 2 CMLR 1.

not made out.[1291] If the Commission's decision is itself an interim measures decision, the Court will intervene if the measures ordered by the Commission exceed what is necessary.[1292]

Interim measures at complainant's behest. If the Commission has failed to take action sought by a complainant and the complainant has brought a properly constituted appeal before the Court, the Court has jurisdiction to order interim measures under Article 243 of the Treaty. However, in such circumstances it may be more appropriate for the Court to order the Commission to take any necessary interim measures.[1293] If the complainant has not requested the Commission to order interim measures, it is impossible for the Court of First Instance to adopt such measures in the Commission's stead.[1294] If the complainant is appealing against a decision of the Commission in favour of a third party, the Court has jurisdiction to suspend the operation of that decision so as to avoid irreparable damage to the complainant[1295] but may be reluctant to do so.[1296] **13.250**

Interim measures to suspend step in Commission investigation. Where an undertaking challenges a Commission decision taken in the course of an investigation under Regulation 1/2003, any attempt to suspend the operation of the decision in the interim risks causing considerable disruption to the progress of the Commission's procedure. In *AKZO and Akros*,[1297] the appellants challenged the decision of the Commission to conduct an inspection at their premises and also sought the suspension of the operation of that decision.[1298] While those **13.251**

1291 Suspension was refused, eg in *Metro v Commission* (n 1290, above) (interests of third parties); *IBM v Commission* (n 1284, above) (no *prima facie* case); Case 62/86R *AKZO v Commission* [1986] ECR 1503, [1987] 1 CMLR 225 (no suspension of obligation not to discriminate). See also Case T-543/93R *Gestevisión Telecinco v Commission* [1993] ECR II-1409; Cases T-79 & 80/95R *SNCF and British Rail v Commission* [1995] ECR II-1433, [1996] 5 CMLR 26; and Case C-174/94R *France v Commission* [1994] ECR I-5229.

1292 Cases 228 & 229/82R *Ford v Commission* (n 1271, above) para 13.

1293 Case 109/75R *National Carbonising v Commission* [1975] ECR 1193, [1975] 2 CMLR 457, acted on in *NCB/National Smokeless Fuels/NCC*, OJ 1976 L35/6, [1976] 1 CMLR D82; Case 792/79R *Camera Care v Commission* (n 1261, above).

1294 Case T-235/95R *Goldstein v Commission*, Order of 27 February 1996 (unrep but see in ECJ judgment dismissing the appeal, Case C-148/96P(R), [1996] ECR I-3883, [1997] 5 CMLR 27, para 7).

1295 *Johnson & Firth Brown* (n 1290, above); *Miles Druce*, ibid (ECSC cases suspending the Commission's authorisation of a takeover under Art 66 ECSC).

1296 *Metro v Commission* (n 1290, above) (no suspension of decision of exemption under Art 81(3) at instance of a complainant).

1297 Cases T-125 & 253/03R *AKZO and Akcros v Commission* [2003] ECR II-4771, [2004] 4 CMLR 744.

1298 Case T-125/03 sought the annulment of the decn 'in as far as it has been interpreted by the Commission as legitimating and/or constituting the basis of the Commission's action (which is not severable from the decision), of seizing and/or reviewing and/or reading documents covered by [legal professional privilege]'. For the proceedings seeking the interim suspension of the decision, see Case T-125/03R. The CFI held that this application was inadmissible because complaints about

challenges were pending before the Court of First Instance, the Commission further decided that certain documents found during the inspection were not covered by legal professional privilege. The appellants then brought further proceedings to annul that decision and also to suspend its operation in the interim.[1299] Ultimately, the President of the Court of Justice overturned the grant of the interim suspension in the latter case since the Commission accepted that, if the challenge was successful, it would have to remove the documents from its file and would not be able to rely on them as evidence, and accordingly there was no risk of serious damage to the appellants simply from the Commission reading the documents in the interim.[1300] Although the order of the President of the Court of First Instance was overturned, the reasoning in his decision contains a valuable discussion of the need to balance observance of the rights of the defence with the Commission's claims that the uncertainty over the proper handling of the documents was causing major problems in allocating its resources and determining its priorities.[1301]

12. Appeals to the Court of Justice

13.252 **Appeal from judgments of the Court of First Instance.** An appeal lies from a judgment of the Court of First Instance to the Court of Justice on a point of law only[1302] and is limited to the following grounds:[1303]

(a) lack of competence of the Court of First Instance;

(b) a breach of procedure before the Court of First Instance which adversely affects the interests of the appellant;

(c) infringement of Community law.

An appeal must be brought within two months of the notification of the decision appealed against.[1304] As an exception, an appeal against a judgment of the Court

---

the way in which the inspection had been carried out did not form grounds for impugning the decn to carry out the inspection: para 69.

[1299] Case T-253/03 is the substantive challenge to this decision and Case T-253/03R is the application for its interim suspension.

[1300] Case C-7/04P(R) *Commission v AKZO and Akcros* [2004] ECR I-8739, [2004] 5 CMLR 1200. The ECJ noted that the Commission had given an undertaking that it would not make the contentious documents available to any third parties given access to the Commission's file pending the determination of the appeal.

[1301] Cases T-125 & 253/03R *AKZO and Akcros* (n 1297, above) paras 179 *et seq.*

[1302] Art 225 EC; Art 58 of the Protocol on the Statute of the Court of Justice published at OJ 2001 C80/53 and as amended most recently by Council Decn of 3 October 2005, 2005 OJ L266/60. Consolidated versions of the Statute of the Court and of its Rules of Procedure as at 1 January 2007 are available on the Court's website.

[1303] For detailed discussion, see further the works cited under para 13.211, above.

[1304] Art 56 of the Statute of the Court of Justice.

dismissing an application to intervene must be brought within two weeks of the notification of the decision.[1305] The procedure for appeals from the Court of First Instance is set out in the Rules of Procedure of the Court of Justice.[1306] The Rules of Procedure allow the President of the Court to decide that a case of particular urgency shall be determined according to an expedited procedure.[1307]

Restricted review by the Court of Justice. In *John Deere v Commission*,[1308] the **13.253** Court of Justice stated that:

> 'an appeal [from the Court of First Instance] may be based only on grounds relating to the infringement of rules of law, to the exclusion of any appraisal of the facts. The Court of First Instance has exclusive jurisdiction, first, to establish the facts except where the substantive inaccuracy of its findings is apparent from the documents submitted to it and, second, to assess those facts. When the Court of First Instance has established or assessed the facts, the Court of Justice has jurisdiction under Article [225] of the Treaty to review the legal characterisation of those facts by the Court of First Instance and the legal conclusions it has drawn from them . . . . The Court of Justice thus has no jurisdiction to establish the facts or, in principle, to examine the evidence which the Court of First Instance accepted in support of those facts. Provided that the evidence has been properly obtained and the general principles of law and the rules of procedure in relation to the burden of proof and the taking of evidence have been observed, it is for the Court of First Instance alone to assess the value which should be attached to the evidence produced to it . . . The appraisal by the Court of First Instance of the evidence put before it does not constitute, save where the evidence has been fundamentally misconstrued, a point of law which is subject, as such, to review by the Court of Justice.'

The Court of Justice also observed that it is not enough for an appellant merely to repeat arguments before that Court which the Court of First Instance has rejected. The appellant must specifically contest the judgment appealed against.[1309] The appellant is not, however, entitled to rely on legal arguments that he did not advance before the Court of First Instance.[1310] Appraisal of the evidence by the

---

[1305]   ibid, Art 57.

[1306]   For a codified text of the Rules of Procedure of the ECJ, see OJ 2001 C34/1 and the ECJ's website.

[1307]   Art 62a of the Rules, which took effect on 1 February 2001.

[1308]   Case C-7/95P *John Deere v Commission* [1998] ECR I-3113, [1998] 5 CMLR 311, [1998] All ER (EC) 481, para 21; see also Case C-19/95 *San Marco v Commission* [1996] ECR I-4435.

[1309]   *John Deere*, above, para 20. See also Case C-338/00P *Volkswagen v Commission* [2003] ECR I-9189, [2004] 4 CMLR 351, para 47: 'where an appeal merely repeats or reproduces verbatim the pleas in law and arguments previously submitted to the Court of First Instance, without even including an argument specifically identifying the error of law allegedly vitiating the judgment under appeal, it fails to satisfy the requirements under Article 58 of the Statute of the Court of Justice and Article 112(1)(c) of its Rules of Procedure. In reality, such an appeal amounts to no more than a request for re-examination of the application submitted to the Court of First Instance, which, under Article 56 of that Statute, falls outside the jurisdiction of the Court of Justice'.

[1310]   ibid, paras 61–62, repeating observations to that effect in Case C-136/92P *Commission v Brazelli Lualdi* [1994] ECR I-1981, para 59.

Court of First Instance does not constitute, for the purposes of an appeal, a point of law except where 'the clear sense of the evidence has been distorted'.[1311] The duty on the Court of First Instance to state reasons for its decisions does not require it to provide an account that follows exhaustively all of the arguments. The reasoning may therefore be implicit provided that it enables the persons concerned to know why the measures in question were taken and provides the Court of Justice with sufficient material for it to exercise its power of judicial review.[1312] On interim measures applications,[1313] the appeal is also limited to points of law and may not call into question the Court of First Instance's assessment of the facts in deciding whether or not to grant such measures.[1314]

13.254 **Exercise of the jurisdiction.** The Court of Justice has, however, been prepared to set aside judgments of the Court of First Instance. Thus, in the *Publishers' Association* case,[1315] the Court of Justice set aside a judgment of the Court of First Instance on the basis that it had taken insufficient account of a relevant decision of a national court. Moreover, the Court of Justice has also considered allegations of breach of procedures before the Court of First Instance.[1316] In the case of challenges to fining decisions under Article 229 of the Treaty, the Court of Justice has stated that it is not for it, even on grounds of fairness, to substitute its assessment of a fine for that of the Court of First Instance exercising its unlimited jurisdiction under that Article.[1317] However, the Court of Justice will examine whether the court below has responded to all the applicant's arguments on the question of the fine to a sufficient legal standard.[1318] The Court of Justice, on the basis of the principle of equal treatment, will also reduce a fine when the Court

---

[1311] *NDC Health Corporation* (n 1289, above) para 88. See also Cases C-65 & 73/02P *ThyssenKrupp Stainless v Commission* [2005] ECR I-6773, [2005] 5 CMLR 773, paras 80–87; Case C-204/00P *Aalborg Portland v Commission ('Cement')* [2004] ECR I-123, [2005] 4 CMLR 251, paras 48–49.

[1312] Case C-397/03P *Archer Daniels Midland* [2006] ECR I-4429, [2006] 5 CMLR 230, para 60.

[1313] Under Art 39 of the Statute of the Court of Justice (n 1302, above).

[1314] Case C-149/95P(R) *Atlantic Container Line v Commission* (n 1285, above); Case C-148/96P(R) *Goldstein v Commission* (n 1294, above).

[1315] Case C-360/92P *Publishers' Association v Commission* [1995] ECR I-23, [1995] 5 CMLR 33.

[1316] Case C-185/95P *Baustahlgewebe v Commission* [1998] ECR I-8417, [1997] 4 CMLR 1203 (allegation of delay before the CFI). In such a case, an appellant will have to advance arguments he did not put to the CFI. In the event, the ECJ accepted the allegation of delay and reduced the fine imposed. See also Case C-119/97P *Ufex v Commission* (n 1214, above). Art 51 of the Statute of the Court of Justice refers to appeals to the ECJ on the basis of the CFI's lack of competence and a breach of procedure adversely affecting the interests of the appellant.

[1317] Case C-310/93P *BPB and British Gypsum v Commission* [1995] ECR I-865, [1997] 4 CMLR 238, para 34; Case C-359/01P *British Sugar v Commission* [2004] ECR I-4933, [2004] 5 CMLR 329, para 48; Case C-397/03P *Archer Daniels Midland v Commission* (n 1312, above) para 105.

[1318] Case C-219/95P *Ferrière Nord v Commission* [1997] ECR I-2411, [1997] 5 CMLR 575, para 31.

of First Instance has (without good reason) applied a harsher approach to one undertaking than to others involved in the same infringement.[1319]

No suspensory effect.   An appeal to the Court of Justice does not lead to the **13.255** automatic suspension of the effects of the judgment of the Court of First Instance.[1320] However, by virtue of Articles 242 and 243 of the Treaty, the Court of Justice may order the suspension of the Court of First Instance's decision and prescribe any necessary interim measures. Furthermore, decisions of the Court of First Instance declaring a Regulation void do not take effect until the time period allowed for lodging an appeal against the decision has expired or, if an appeal has been brought within that period, until that appeal has been dismissed.[1321]

Effect of an appeal.   If an appeal to the Court of Justice is successful and the **13.256** decision of the Court of First Instance is quashed, the Court of Justice may either proceed to give final judgment in the matter[1322] or refer the case back to the Court of First Instance for final judgment. In the latter case, the Court of First Instance is of course bound by the judgment of the Court of Justice on points of law.[1323]

[1319] Case C-280/98P *Moritz J. Weig v Commission* [2000] ECR I-9757, paras 67–68.
[1320] Art 60 of the Statute of the Court of Justice (n 1302, above).
[1321] ibid.
[1322] eg Case C-519/04P *Meca-Medina and Majcen v Commission* [2006] ECR I-6991, [2006] 5 CMLR 1023, [2006] All ER (EC) 1057.
[1323] Art 61 of the Statute of the Court of Justice (n 1302, above). See, eg Case T-354/94 *Stora Kopparbergs Bergslags v Commission* [2002] ECR II-843, [2002] 4 CMLR 1397, where the ECJ had remitted the calculation of the fine to the CFI having found that the CFI had wrongly imposed liability for the cartel activity of a subsidiary prior to its acquisition.

14

THE ENFORCEMENT OF THE COMPETITION RULES IN THE MEMBER STATES

1. Introduction

14.001 **Direct effect and the supremacy of Community law.** The EC Treaty establishes an independent legal order which is capable of creating obligations and rights affecting not only the governments of the Member States but also individuals within those States. Community law provisions which have 'direct effect' confer rights on individuals which the national courts must safeguard, and obligations which the national courts must enforce.[1] Within the sphere of application of Community law, such provisions take precedence over the domestic law of a Member State. All organs of the Member State (including its administrative authorities and courts) have a duty to ensure that those rights are protected and can be exercised effectively.[2]

14.002 **Acceptance of supremacy.** Provisions in the EC Treaties and Regulations are 'directly applicable' in the sense that they do not require specific implementation measures to take effect as an integral part of the Member State's national legal system. Some Member States follow this 'monist approach'; others require a specific domestic legislative provision recognising the limitation of national sovereignty. By virtue of sections 2(1) and 3(1) of the European Communities Act 1972, Articles 81 and 82 have been imported into the law of the United Kingdom since 1 January 1973.

Section 2(1) of the Act provides:

> 'All such rights, powers, liabilities, obligations and restrictions from time to time created or arising by or under the Treaties,[3] and all such remedies and procedures

---

[1] Art 10 EC as interpreted by the ECJ in Case 26/62 *Van Gend en Loos* [1963] ECR 1, [1963] CMLR 105. The doctrine of 'direct effect' has generated a vast literature, much of which discusses the application of this doctrine to directives. For its application to Treaty provisions, see Hartley, *The Foundations of European Community Law* (5th edn, 2003) Chap 7; Craig and de Búrca, *EU Law – Text, Cases and Materials* (3rd edn, 2002) Chap 5. For recent statements regarding the direct effect of Arts 81 and 82, see Cases C-295/04 etc, *Manfredi v Lloyd Adriatico Assicurazioni* [2006] ECR I-6619, [2006] 5 CMLR 980, para 39; Case C-453/99 *Courage v Crehan* [2001] ECR I-6297, [2001] 5 CMLR 1058, [2001] All ER (EC) 886, para 23.

[2] See, eg Case 106/77 *Amministrazione delle Finanze dello Stato v Simmenthal* [1978] ECR 629, [1978] 3 CMLR 263; Case C-198/01 *Consorzio Industrie Fiammiferi ('CIF')* [2003] ECR I-8055, [2003] 5 CMLR 829, [2004] All ER (EC) 380, para 48; Case 213/89 *Factortame* [1990] ECR I-2433, [1990] 3 CMLR 1, para 19. See also in the UK the comments on the supremacy of EC law in the speech of Lord Bridge in *R v Secretary of State for Transport, ex p Factortame (No. 2)* [1991] 1 AC 603 at 658–659, [1991] 1 All ER 70 at 107–108; discussed further by Laws LJ in *Thoburn v Sunderland City Council* [2002] EWHC 195 (Admin), [2003] QB 151, [2002] 4 All ER 156, paras 60–70.

[3] 'The Treaties' now include the EC and Euratom Treaties (the ESCS Treaty expired on 23 July 2002), the Accession Treaties, the Single European Act, the EEA Agreement of 1992 (together with the adjustment Protocol of 1993), Titles II, III and IV of the Treaty of European Union 1992 and the Protocols adopted at Maastricht annexed to the EC Treaty (with the exception of the Protocol on Social Policy), certain provisions of the Treaty of Amsterdam 1997, certain provisions of the

from time to time provided for by or under the Treaties, as in accordance with the Treaties are without further enactment to be given legal effect or used in the United Kingdom shall be recognised and available in law, and be enforced, allowed and followed accordingly. . .'[4]

Section 3(1) (as amended by the European Communities (Amendment) Act 1986) further provides:

'For the purposes of all legal proceedings any question as to the meaning or effect of any of the Treaties, or as to the validity, meaning or effect of any Community instrument, shall be treated as a question of law (and, if not referred to the European Court, be for determination as such in accordance with the principles laid down by and any relevant decision of the European Court or any court attached thereto).'

By section 3(2) of the 1972 Act (also amended by the 1986 Act), judicial notice is to be taken of the Treaties, the *Official Journal* and decisions of the European Court of Justice and the Court of First Instance.

Modernisation. The enforcement of the competition rules throughout the Community has changed significantly as a result of the Modernisation regime, introduced by Regulation 1/2003, of which the implementation coincided with the enlargement of the Union to 25 Member States on 1 May 2004.[5] In a move away from the previously centralised administration by the Commission under Regulation 17, national competition authorities ('NCAs') and national courts have been given the power to apply Articles 81 and 82 in their entirety, and they are obliged to do so when applying their national competition law to an agreement or conduct that falls within the scope of Article 81 or 82. The Commission, although not relieved of its general responsibility for competition enforcement, will concentrate its resources on prosecuting the most serious infringements and those that involve several Member States.[6]   **14.003**

Treaty of Nice 2001 and Treaties with third countries entered into by the Communities, and other ancillary treaties: see in the UK s 1(2) of the European Communities Act 1972, as amended by (*inter alia*) Acts dealing with Accession States in 1979, 1985, 1994, 2003 and 2006, by the European Economic Area Act 1993, and by European Communities (Amendment) Acts of 1986, 1993, 1998 and 2002.

[4] With regard to the power in s 2(2) to make secondary legislation to implement a Community obligation see the amendments proposed in Part 3 of the Legislative and Regulatory Reform Bill (HL Bill 146) which empower Ministers to make orders, rules or schemes rather than regulations and enable ambulatory references to Community instruments to be included in subordinate legislation.

[5] Reg 1/2003, OJ 2003 L1/1: Vol II, App B.3. For details of the Modernisation regime, see Chaps 1 and 13, above.

[6] For details of the division of powers between the Commission and the NCAs, see Chap 13, above.

14.004 **Direct effect of Articles 81 and 82.** Articles 81(1) and 82 have direct effect and create individual rights which the NCAs and national courts must safeguard.[7] Broadly speaking, if an agreement falls within Article 81(1) and does not fulfil the criteria in Article 81(3), two separate civil consequences follow. First, pursuant to Article 81(2) the agreement is 'automatically void' in respect of the offending provisions without a prior decision to that effect being necessary.[8] Secondly, any party injured by the infringement (including a counterparty to the agreement in question[9]) may be able to pursue a civil claim for damages, restitution or an injunction.[10] In general, the same principles apply to Article 82, in that the infringement may render a contract unenforceable or give rise to an action in damages or restitution.

14.005 **Direct effect of Article 81(3).** Following Modernisation, Article 81(3) now has direct effect[11] in the same way as Articles 81(1) and 82. The new regime is based on a 'directly applicable exception system',[12] whereby NCAs and national courts may prohibit agreements or practices or declare that the conditions for the application of Article 81(3) are satisfied without any prior decision by the Commission to that effect being necessary. Regulation 1/2003 has abolished the procedure whereby agreements were notified to the Commission for its assessment. Rather than obtaining competition clearance *ex ante*, a party to an agreement has to rely on Article 81(3) *ex post*, in the event of a challenge, directly before an NCA or a national court.

14.006 **National courts.** National courts may be called upon to apply Articles 81 and 82 in civil, administrative or criminal proceedings. They play a specific role in the private enforcement of Community competition law which is different from that carried out by NCAs acting in the public interest.[13] National courts will be responsible for determining claims between individuals and for awarding remedies

---

[7] Case 127/73 *BRT v SABAM* [1974] ECR 51, [1974] 2 CMLR 238, para 16; Case C-234/89 *Delimitis* [1991] ECR I-935, [1992] 5 CMLR 210, para 45; Case C-282/95P *Guérin automobiles v Commission* [1997] ECR I-1503, [1997] 5 CMLR 447, para 39; Case C-453/99 *Courage v Crehan* (n 1, above) para 23. For the position as to State aids under Arts 87–89, see paras 15.108 *et seq*, below.

[8] See para 14.098, below.

[9] Case C-453/99 *Courage v Crehan* (n 1, above) para 24; see further paras 14.114–14.115, below.

[10] See paras 14.108 *et seq*, below.

[11] Art 81(3) has direct effect by virtue of Arts 1(2), 5 and 6 of Reg 1/2003 (n 5, above). But note that Reg 1/2003 does not apply to mergers even if they lack a Community dimension and are therefore not subject to control under the EC merger regime: Art 21(1) of Reg 139/2004: Vol II, App D.1. See further para 14.043, below.

[12] Recital (4) of Reg 1/2003.

[13] Case T-24/90 *Automec* [1992] ECR II-2223, [1992] 5 CMLR 431, para 85; and see Commission Notice on cooperation with the courts of the Member States ('Cooperation Notice'), OJ 2004 C101/54: Vol II, App B.9, para 4.

such as injunctive relief, declarations of invalidity and damages.[14] Their assessment will be carried out according to domestic rules of procedure and evidence and within the national framework of applicable causes of action and remedies.[15] In contrast to the position of competition authorities, national courts are able to refer questions for preliminary rulings by the Court of Justice under Article 234 of the Treaty.[16]

Relationship between Community and domestic competition law. Regulation 1/2003 is directly applicable and, from 1 May 2004, must be fully and uniformly applied in all Member States. The devolution of Community competition law enforcement has affected the scope of national competition law and vice versa. Many Member States have amended their domestic competition legislation and procedures so as to replicate the European model to ensure that there is no conflict between the two systems.[17] There is a developing body of case law from the Member States, which it is intended should be circulated within the European Competition Network ('ECN') of NCAs and posted on the DG Competition website.[18]   **14.007**

Convergence and consistency. Since 1 May 2004, NCAs and national courts apply Articles 81 and 82 in conjunction with their domestic competition law. Regulation 1/2003 contains provisions to ensure convergence between the parallel regimes. Where an agreement or practice is capable of affecting inter-State trade, NCAs and national courts must apply the Community competition rules[19] and ensure that the rights conferred on individuals are respected in their own territories. NCAs and national courts must ensure that the application of their national competition law does not prohibit agreements or concerted practices that would otherwise remain valid under Article 81 or permit unilateral conduct   **14.008**

---

[14] For a comparative analysis of the national rules and procedures applicable to damages claims, see the Ashurst Comparative Report prepared for the European Commission, *Study on the conditions of claims for damages in case of infringement of EC competition rules*, 31 August 2004 ('the Ashurst Report'), available on the DG Comp website. However, there have been developments in several Member States since the Report was compiled.

[15] Reg 1/2003 does not seek to harmonise the standards of proof or evidential requirements applicable in the domestic legal system (Recital (5)). National courts retain their procedural autonomy subject to the principles of equivalence and effectiveness: see further, Cooperation Notice (n 13, above) paras 9–10 and paras 14.095 *et seq*, below.

[16] Case C-53/03 *Syfait v GlaxoSmithKline* [2005] ECR I-4609, [2005] 5 CMLR 7, para 34: see further para 14.090, below.

[17] In the UK, by virtue of s 209 of the Enterprise Act 2002, the Secretary of State is empowered to enact regulations to amend the Competition Act 1998 to eliminate or reduce any inconsistency with Community competition law, including notably Reg 1/2003.

[18] See at http://ec.europa.eu/comm/competition/antitrust/national_courts/index_en.html. However, the listing is very incomplete and judgments are posted in the original language. Note also that cases concerning only national competition law are not included, although the issues involved may be identical to those which arise under Arts 81 and 82.

[19] Art 3(1) of Reg 1/2003; see para 14.056, below.

that would otherwise be prohibited under Article 82.[20] Moreover, Article 16 of Regulation 1/2003 requires national courts and NCAs to avoid adopting a ruling in a particular case that would conflict with a decision contemplated by the Commission in any pending investigation or that would run counter to a prior Commission decision.

14.009 **Plan of this Chapter.** This Chapter is divided into seven sections. After this Introduction, Section 2 deals with the jurisdiction and powers of NCAs when enforcing Articles 81 and 82 and their duties of cooperation with the Commission and NCAs in other Member States. It includes a description of the role of the United Kingdom NCAs, the Office of Fair Trading and the sectoral regulators post-Modernisation. Section 3 explains the relationship between Community competition law and national competition law and describes the mechanisms in place to ensure convergence and consistency between the two parallel regimes. This Section also explains the role of national courts in competition law enforcement and their relationship to the European Commission. Section 4 deals with various factors affecting the jurisdiction of national courts when dealing with competition law claims in civil proceedings. It also explains potential overlaps in jurisdiction with other NCAs, national courts and the Commission and the duties of consistency and cooperation that are incumbent on national courts under the Modernisation regime. Section 5 covers remedies, including declaratory and injunctive relief and damages. Section 6 considers issues of practice and procedure in the English courts. Finally, Section 7 discusses the application of competition rules in the context of arbitration proceedings.

2. Enforcement by National Competition Authorities

(a) The National Competition Authorities

14.010 **Role prior to Modernisation.** The role of the NCAs in the enforcement of Articles 81 and 82 has been greatly enhanced by the Modernisation package.[21] Prior to the coming into effect of Regulation 1/2003, Community legislation governing the implementation of Articles 81 and 82[22] envisaged a limited role for NCAs in enforcement. In particular, there was no requirement in Community law that national authorities should enforce the EC competition rules at all; whether they had the jurisdiction to do so was therefore dependent upon national

---

[20] Art 3(2) of Reg 1/2003; see para 14.060, below.

[21] For the background to the Modernisation package, see paras 1.058 *et seq* and Chap 13, above.

[22] Primarily Reg 17, adopted under Art 83 of the Treaty: Vol II, App B.1.

rules or legislation.[23] Moreover, even where the NCAs could apply the EC competition rules, they could not declare Article 81(1) to be inapplicable by applying Article 81(3). Only in the limited areas of the economy where there had been no Community implementing regulation for the competition rules,[24] were the NCAs subject to the obligation under Article 84 to apply Articles 81 and 82, including the power to apply Article 81(3).

Regulation 1/2003 and the Joint Statement.   The new arrangements are set out   **14.011**
primarily in Regulation 1/2003.[25] Article 35(1) of Regulation 1/2003 requires Member States to designate the competition authority or authorities responsible for the application of Articles 81 and 82 'in such a way that the provisions of this regulation are effectively complied with'.[26] When Regulation 1/2003 was adopted, a Joint Statement[27] of the Council and the Commission on the functioning of the network of NCAs was entered in the Council Minutes. The Joint Statement sets out the common political understanding shared by the Member States and the Commission on the principles of the functioning of the network. The Statement describes the Commission as 'the guardian of the Treaty' with the 'ultimate but not the sole responsibility for developing policy and safeguarding efficiency and consistency'. It also sets out the guiding principles on case allocation, outlining the factors which determine whether an NCA is 'well placed' to deal with a particular case. The Regulation and Statement make clear that the NCAs are to be regarded as partners of the Commission in the enforcement of Community competition rules rather than as having merely a subsidiary or residual jurisdiction. Although, as before, the initiation of proceedings by the Commission deprives the NCA of their power to apply Articles 81 and 82,[28] the allocation of tasks is now based on the parallel competences of the Commission and the NCAs 'on the basis of equality, respect and solidarity'.[29]

Commission's Notice on Cooperation with the NCAs.   The Commission's   **14.012**
Notice on Cooperation within the Network of Competition Authorities ('the

---

[23] Save that if an NCA had such jurisdiction, it could no longer act if the Commission opened a procedure: Art 9(3) of Reg 17.

[24] These were air transport between the Community and third countries, international maritime tramp vessel services, domestic maritime transport services (cabotage) and international maritime transport services wholly outside the Community. All of these are now within the scope of Reg 1/2003: the first by amendment made by Reg 411/2004, OJ 2004 L68/1; and tramp vessel services and cabotage with effect from 26 October 2006 by amendment made by Reg 1419/2006, OJ 2006 L269/1: Vol II, App B.3.

[25] Reg 1/2003 (n 5, above).

[26] See para 14.013, below, for the members of the ECN.

[27] Joint Statement of 10 December 2002, Doc no. 15435/02 ADD 1: Vol II, App B.7. The Joint Statement cannot be relied on as establishing any rights or obligations: Case T-339/04 *France Télécom v Commission*, judgment of 8 March 2007, para 85.

[28] Art 11(6) of Reg 1/2003. See further para 14.015, below.

[29] Joint Statement (n 27, above) para 7.

Network Notice')[30] elaborated on the principles to be applied in case allocation as between the Commission and the network and as among the NCAs themselves. It also provides guidance on some of the key provisions of Regulation 1/2003 dealing with exchange of information within the network and the role and functioning of the Advisory Committee[31] under the new system.[32] Annexed to the Notice was a statement for NCAs to sign indicating their agreement to adhere to the principles set out in the Notice.[33]

14.013 **Members of the European Competition Network.** Member States retain procedural autonomy for allocating the relevant investigation, prosecution and enforcement responsibilities among their administrative and judicial bodies. Article 35(1) of Regulation 1/2003 requires the Member States to designate the competition authority or authorities responsible for the application of Articles 81 and 82 EC, and Recital (15) to the Regulation refers to those authorities together forming a network of authorities applying the competition rules in close cooperation. In some Member States, national courts have been designated under Article 35(1) and they will be bound in their dual capacity as an NCA and as a national court.[34] For the designated NCAs of each of the Member States, see the Table at pages 1486 *et seq*.[35] Where a public authority has not been designated as an NCA, such as the Competition Commission in the UK, it will lack the power to apply Articles 81 and 82 and cannot participate in the European Competition Network ('ECN').

(b) Avoidance of multiple proceedings

14.014 **Case allocation.** The detailed rules which determine whether a particular case is dealt with by the Commission or an NCA and, if the latter, by which NCA are discussed in Chapter 13, above.[36] In summary, section 2 of the Network Notice emphasises that each member of the Network retains full discretion in deciding whether or not to investigate a case. The authority which receives a complaint or which starts an ex-officio procedure will generally remain in charge. Where reallocation is necessary, it should be a quick and efficient process and not hold up the investigation.[37] The principle behind reallocation is the assessment of which NCA

---

[30] Network Notice, OJ 2004 C101/43: Vol II, App B.8. There is a separate Notice regarding cooperation between the Commission and the national courts (n 13, above).

[31] For the Advisory Committee, see para 13.107, above.

[32] See further paras 14.020 *et seq*, below.

[33] Para 14.031, below.

[34] Cooperation Notice (n 13, above) para 2. See further para 14.075, below.

[35] For a general overview of the applicable administrative procedures in each Member State, see FIDE 21st Congress, National Reports in Cahill (ed), *The Modernisation of EU Competition Law Enforcement in the EU* (2004).

[36] See paras 13.017 *et seq*, above.

[37] In the overview in its *Report on Competition Policy 2004*, point 106, the Commission states: 'As expected, re-allocation of cases notified to the network was extremely rare (less than 1 per cent

is 'well-placed' to deal with the matter, based on three criteria: (i) whether the agreement or practice has substantial effects within its territory, is implemented within or originates from its territory; (ii) whether the NCA is able effectively to bring an end to the infringement and impose appropriate sanctions; and (iii) whether the NCA can gather, possibly with the assistance of other NCAs, the evidence required to prove the infringement. The Commission will always be regarded as well-placed to deal with a case, but particularly so if the agreement or practice has effects on competition in more than three Member States; if the case is closely linked to other Community provisions which may be exclusively or more effectively applied by the Commission; or if the Community interest requires the adoption of a Commission decision to develop Community competition policy when a new issue arises. The rules on case allocation do not create any rights for parties to insist that their case is dealt with by any particular authority.[38]

Effect of initiation of Commission proceedings on jurisdiction of NCAs. Article 11(6) of Regulation 1/2003 provides that the initiation by the Commission of proceedings[39] for the adoption of a decision 'shall relieve the competition authorities of the Member States of their competence to apply Articles 81 and 82 of the Treaty'. If an NCA is already acting on a case, the Commission will only initiate its own proceedings after consulting that NCA. Article 11(6) refers only to the NCA's jurisdiction to apply Articles 81 and 82. It is not clear whether the effect of this, in conjunction with Article 3 of the Regulation, is also to deprive the NCA of the power to apply its national competition law since in those circumstances the NCA cannot apply EC competition law together with its national law as Article 3 requires.[40] Moreover, insofar as most national competition laws of the Member States are now modelled on Articles 81 and 82, once proceedings against an undertaking by the Commission under EC

14.015

---

of all cases). Cases normally remain with the authority which started to investigate them'. See also *Report on Competition Policy 2005*, points 211–214, noting that work-sharing takes place when several NCAs report indications of the same price-fixing cartel, or receive complaints concerning the same matter.

38 Network Notice (n 30, above) para 31.

39 Para 52 of the Network Notice explains that the initiation of proceedings is a formal act by which the Commission indicates its intention to adopt a decision under Reg 1/2003, that can occur at any time during a Commission investigation.

40 There are indications that the Commission thinks that it does: see Blake and Schnichels, 'Leniency following Modernisation: safeguarding Europe's leniency programmes' (2004) 2 EC Competition Policy Newsletter 7. See also Wils, *Principles of European Antitrust Enforcement* (2005) para 147. Note that in *Mastercard Europe/International, XXXIIIrd Report on Competition Policy* (2003), points 182–184, the Commission issued a statement of objections starting proceedings regarding MasterCard's cross-border multilateral interchange fee ('MIF') in September 2003, but several NCAs are also continuing proceedings under their national competition laws concerning the domestic MIF (which in some cases mirrors the cross-border MIF) applied by MasterCard in their respective States.

competition law have concluded, for an NCA then to pursue the undertaking in respect of the same matter under domestic competition law would appear to offend against the principle of *ne bis in idem*, as set out in Article 50 of the EU Charter of Fundamental Rights.[41] However, Article 11(6) should not apply to proceedings for the imposition of criminal penalties on individuals under domestic law because such proceedings do not involve the *application* of Article 81 or 82: the Community provisions apply only to undertakings.[42]

14.016 **Effect of initiation of Commission proceedings on national courts which are also NCAs.** In some Member States, the NCA is a court which is therefore bound by the principle of direct effect to apply Articles 81 and 82. Article 35(3) of the Regulation provides that the effects of Article 11(6) apply to courts which have been designated as NCAs insofar as they exercise functions regarding *the preparation and the adoption* of the types of decisions referred to in Article 5 of the Regulation, that is to say decisions of an NCA applying Articles 81 or 82 EC. Article 11(6) does not extend to courts 'insofar as they act as review courts' in respect of those kinds of decisions. Further, where the procedure in the Member State provides for the NCA to bring an action before a judicial authority which is separate from the prosecuting authority, the effect of Article 11(6) is that the authority prosecuting the case must withdraw its claim before the judicial authority, thereby bringing the national proceedings to an end.[43]

14.017 **Effect of initiation of proceedings by one NCA on the jurisdiction of other NCAs.** In contrast to the prohibition on NCAs applying Articles 81 and 82 once the Commission has initiated proceedings, Regulation 1/2003 empowers rather than obliges NCAs to halt their proceedings in favour of another NCA. Article 13 provides that the fact that one authority is dealing with a case shall be sufficient grounds for any other NCA to suspend or terminate any proceedings which it has commenced or to reject a complaint received in relation to the same conduct. Similarly, where an NCA or the Commission receives a complaint about conduct which has already been dealt with by another competition authority, it

---

[41] See the expansive scope to what can be considered to be the same offence under Art 4 of Protocol 7 to the ECHR applied by the ECtHR in *Fischer v Austria*, No. 37950/97, judgment of 29 May 2001. Although Art 4 applies to double jeopardy in criminal proceedings 'under the jurisdiction of the same State', as the ECHR is regarded as setting out fundamental principles of EC law, it should be regarded in the Community context as applicable to the jurisdictions of the Member States, a position reflected in Art 50 of the Charter. See Wils (above), paras 422–435. For the Charter generally, see para 1.010, above. See also *per* AG Colomer in Cases C-213/00P *Italcementi v Commission* and C-217/00P *Buzzi Unichem v Commission*, Opinions at [2004] ECR I-230, paras 81–104, and [2004] ECR I-267, paras 170–184 (the ECJ in its composite judgment in the *Cement* case, did not address the issue).

[42] See also Recital (8) to Reg 1/2003; but for critical discussion of that recital, see Wils (n 40, above) paras 153–157.

[43] Art 35(4) of Reg 1/2003 and see Recital (35).

may reject it.[44] The Network Notice[45] stresses the importance of leaving scope for 'appreciation of the peculiarities of each individual case'. If a case was rejected by an NCA following an investigation of the substance of the case, another NCA may not want to re-examine it. On the other hand, if a complaint was rejected for other reasons, for example because the authority was unable to collect the necessary evidence, another NCA may wish to carry out its own investigation. Article 13 can be applied to part of a complaint or part of the proceedings in a case.[46] The Commission also has power to reject a complaint on the ground that an NCA is dealing with the case.[47] The initiation of proceedings by an NCA and any step taken in those proceedings is important with regard to the limitation period for the imposition of penalties by the Commission under Regulation 1/2003.[48]

Notification of proceedings.   In order to facilitate both the resolution of any **14.018** case allocation issues and the operation of Articles 11(6) and 13, Regulation 1/2003 provides for the Commission and the NCAs to notify each other about the initiation and progress of investigations into infringements of Articles 81 or 82 EC. Article 11(3) imposes an obligation on NCAs to inform the Commission either before, or as soon as possible after, the first formal investigative measure is taken.[49] All this information may also be made available to the other NCAs. Network members may inform each other of pending cases by means of a standard form containing limited details of the case.[50] The Commission is also obliged to provide to the NCAs copies of the most important documents that it has collected with a view to exercising its enforcement functions under the Regulation.[51] Statistics as to the cases notified by NCAs are published in the ECN section of the DG Competition website.[52]

---

[44] Reg 1/2003, Art 13(2).

[45] Network Notice (n 30, above) paras 20 *et seq.*

[46] ibid, para 24.

[47] Reg 1/2003, Art 13(1).

[48] See Art 25(3) of Reg 1/2003. cf Art 2 of the original Reg 2988/74, OJ 1974 L319/1, under which only steps taken by the NCA acting at the request of the Commission interrupted the limitation period in proceedings, whereas under Reg 1/2003 procedural steps taken independently by the NCA also interrupt a limitation period: see Recital (31) and Art 37 of Reg 1/2003.

[49] Para 17 of the Network Notice (n 30, above) describes the rationale for this obligation as 'to allow the network to detect multiple procedures and address possible case re-allocation issues as soon as an authority starts investigating a case'.

[50] ibid. The form sets out basic details of the case, such as the product, territory and parties concerned and the nature and duration of the suspected infringements; in practice, that form is placed onto an intranet between members of the ECN.

[51] Reg 1/2003, Art 11(2).

[52] http://ec.europa.eu/comm/competition/ecn/statistics.html. As of 31 March 2007, 708 investigations had been notified through the ECN. The five leading authorities in terms of numbers of cases notified were (in order) the Commission, France, Germany, the Netherlands and Hungary (see n 55, below, for statistics for NCAs' notification of intended decisions). It appears that about half the cases notified raised Art 81 alone, with around one third raising Art 82 alone.

14.019 **Subsequent liaison in a case being dealt with by an NCA.** NCAs may consult the Commission on any case involving the application of Community law.[53] A dedicated unit within DG Competition acts as a contact point for NCAs and has the task of assisting consistent application of competition law across the ECN.[54] Article 11(4) of the Regulation 1/2003 requires NCAs to give at least 30 days' notice to the Commission before adopting a decision applying Articles 81 or 82 and requiring an infringement to be brought to an end, accepting commitments, or withdrawing the benefit of a block exemption regulation. They must provide the Commission with a summary of the case and the proposed decision (or other document indicating the proposed course of action). This information may be shared with the ECN.[55] NCAs can also inform the Commission and ECN about other types of proposed decision, such as rejection of complaints or orders of interim measures,[56] and should inform the ECN of the closure of proceedings which had been previously notified.[57]

(c) Cooperation within the Network

14.020 **Generally.** Article 11(1) of Regulation 1/2003 provides that the Commission and the competition authorities of the Member States shall apply the Community competition rules 'in close cooperation'. The NCAs play an important role in the proceedings of the Commission, for example by their participation in the Advisory Committee on Restrictive Practices and Dominant Positions[58] and their attendance at oral hearings during Commission investigations. Those aspects of the NCAs' involvement are discussed in Chapter 13, above.

14.021 **Investigations on behalf of another NCA: Article 22(1).** Regulation 1/2003 also envisages that NCAs will help each other in carrying out cross-border investigations into anti-competitive conduct. Article 22(1) provides that an NCA may, in its own territory, carry out any inspection or other fact-finding measure under its national law[59] on behalf of and for the account of the NCA of another

---

53 Reg 1/2003, Art 11(5).

54 See Lowe, 'The Role of the Commission in the Modernisation of EC Competition Law', Speech to UKAEL Conference, 23 January 2004 (accessible on the DG Comp website). For the power of national courts to make similar inquiries, see paras 14.065 *et seq*, below.

55 Network Notice (n 30, above) para 45. As of 31 March 2007, 192 anticipated NCA decisions had been notified to the ECN; for these the leading NCAs in number were (in order) France, the Netherlands, Germany, Denmark and Italy. The United Kingdom was joint ninth (with Greece, behind Sweden, Spain and Hungary, and just ahead of Finland). See ECN statistics (n 52, above).

56 ibid, para 48.

57 ibid, para 49.

58 Reg 1/2003, Art 14. See para 13.107, above.

59 It is not clear whether this reference to the NCA's 'national law' means that Art 22 does not, of itself, confer a power to carry out an investigation and that the NCA must be empowered under its domestic legislation or whether it means only that the inspection or other measure must be carried out in accordance with any procedural requirements set down in the NCA's domestic legislation.

Member State in order to establish whether there has been an infringement of Articles 81 or 82.

(i) Exchange of information

Powers and safeguards. Article 12(1) of Regulation 1/2003 confers a wide power **14.022** on the Commission and the NCAs to provide one another with, and use in evidence, any matter of fact or of law, including confidential information. Article 12 should take precedence over any contrary law of a Member State.[60] There are various safeguards incorporated into the Regulation and into the Network Notice which constrain the *use* which can be made of information exchanged under Article 12. These constraints cover information gathered by the Commission using its power to request information (Article 18) or to take statements and inspect premises (Articles 19, 20 and 21) and information gathered by an NCA carrying out inspections in its territory on behalf of the Commission or another NCA (Article 22). It is not clear, however, whether the power to disclose information extends to information obtained by an NCA as a result of a criminal investigation, whether conducted by the NCA or another authority with prosecutorial powers, that may be subject to special protection under the national rules of criminal procedure.[61]

Obligation not to disclose: 'professional secrecy'. According to Article 28(2) of **14.023** Regulation 1/2003, the Commission, the NCAs and their officials and employees as well as officials and civil servants of other authorities of the Member State must not disclose information acquired by them 'of the kind covered by the obligation of professional secrecy'.[62] That obligation covers all information collected or exchanged 'pursuant to the Regulation' generally and therefore extends to information gathered under national law powers for the purposes of an Article 81 or 82 investigation.[63] The scope of information covered by obligations of professional

---

[60] See Recital (16) of Reg 1/2003 and Network Notice (n 30, above) para 27, which also states that the question whether information was gathered in a legal manner by the transmitting authority is governed by the law applicable to that authority.

[61] Recital (8) to the Regulation states that it does not apply to national laws which impose criminal sanctions on individuals except to the extent that such sanctions are the means whereby the competition rules applying to undertakings are enforced: for comment on that Recital, see Wils (n 40, above) paras 153–157. Note also the Statement by the German delegation annexed to Joint Statement of the Council and the Commission (n 27, above), recording Germany's view that national criminal procedural law provisions cannot be amended on the basis of Art 83 EC, which is the legal basis of Reg 1/2003: available at http://register.consilium.europa.eu/pdf/en/02/st15/15435-a1en2.pdf. However, that view seems doubtful following Case C-176/03 *Commission v Council* [2005] ECR I-7879, [2006] All ER (EC) 1.

[62] According to the Network Notice, para 28(a), the term 'professional secrecy' is a Community law concept and includes in particular business secrets and other confidential information. This will create a common minimum level of protection throughout the Community.

[63] The obligation does not apply to the power to disclose within the ECN under Art 12(1) since Art 28(2) is expressly without prejudice to the former provision.

secrecy, and the protection which it should be given, were considered by the Court of First Instance in the *Bank Austria* case.[64] The Court stated that to be covered by an obligation of professional secrecy, (i) the information must be known only to a limited number of persons; (ii) it must be information whose disclosure would cause serious harm to the person who provided it or to third parties; and (iii) the interests liable to be harmed by disclosure must be worthy of protection.[65] The Court also set out, in effect, a hierarchy of confidentiality, whereby 'business secrets' are a category within the broader concept of documents subject to 'professional secrecy' and are entitled to 'very special protection'. The Court stated that the obligation on officials and other servants of the institutions not to disclose information in their possession covered by the obligation of professional secrecy was mitigated in regard to persons who had a right to be heard in the Commission's proceedings. The Commission may communicate to such persons certain information covered by the obligation of professional secrecy insofar as it is necessary to do so for the proper conduct of the investigation. But information covered by the obligation of professional secrecy cannot be disclosed to the general public. The term 'business secrets' concerns information of which not only disclosure to the public but also mere transmission to a person other than the one who provided the information may seriously harm the latter's interests.[66]

14.024 **Restrictions as to use.** Articles 12(2) and (3) and 28(1) of Regulation 1/2003 impose important constraints on the use which can be made of information collected and/or exchanged within the ECN. Article 28(1) of Regulation 1/2003 sets out the general principle that information collected pursuant to Articles 17 to 22 of the Regulation is to be used only for the purpose for which it was acquired. That restriction applies to Commission investigations and to 'cross-border' situations where NCAs use their national law investigatory measures on behalf of the competition authority of another Member State or the Commission, but it is not clear whether it extends to purely domestic investigations into potential infringements of Community competition law. Article 12(2) imposes a similar restriction on information that is exchanged within the ECN: such information can only be used as evidence for the purpose of applying Articles 81 or 82 and in respect of the same subject-matter for which it was collected by the transmitting NCA. It may also be used for the application of national competition law, subject to certain conditions discussed below.[67]

---

[64] Case T-198/03 *Bank Austria Creditanstalt v Commission* [2006] ECR II-1429, [2006] 5 CMLR 639.
[65] ibid, para 71.
[66] ibid, paras 29–30.
[67] See para 14.027, below.

'Subject-matter' and 'use in evidence'. There is no definition of 'subject-   **14.025**
matter' in Article 12 but the procedure for obtaining evidence by inspection of
premises in Articles 20 and 21 of the Regulation requires the Commission to
specify 'the subject-matter' of the inspection, and the meaning given to this
expression in Article 12 should be the same. The Court of Justice held, as regards
the equivalent provision concerning inspection under Regulation 17, that specification of the 'subject-matter', although not covering all the information at the
Commission's disposal, referred to the presumed facts which the Commission
intended to investigate.[68] Accordingly, if the information is obtained concerning
a suspected cartel in product A and exchanged through the ECN, it seems that
Article 12 prevents this information being used in evidence for proceedings
concerning an agreement covering product B. Whether it could be so used in proceedings concerning an abuse of a dominant position in the market for product A
is perhaps less clear, but the same limitation should probably apply. However, the
constraint in Article 12 is confined to 'use in evidence'. The Commission or NCA
that receives the information is not required to disregard it altogether: it can be
taken into account for the purpose of deciding whether to launch a new investigation,[69] and indeed those documents can then be specifically requested again for
the purpose of the second investigation.[70] Accordingly, whether the original
documents can form the basis of a new investigation by an NCA would appear
to depend on whether the necessary steps for an initial investigation require that
information to be given 'in evidence' in any formal sense under the relevant
national procedure.

Use against undertakings. There is no further restriction on the ability to use   **14.026**
the information in evidence based on the degree of protection afforded to undertakings under the law of the Member State where the information was obtained
('the transmitting State'). Therefore if the transmitting State provides only limited
protection from disclosure of confidential information than the law of the
Member State whose NCA receives the documents through the ECN ('the receiving State'), for example as regards legal professional privilege, Article 12(1)
permits the latter NCA to use those documents in evidence although they
would not otherwise be admissible under the law of the receiving State. This is
subject only to any overriding protection on human rights grounds.[71] Moreover,

---

[68] Cases 46/87 & 227/88, *Hoechst v Commission* [1989] ECR 2859, [1991] 4 CMLR 410,
para 41.
[69] See Case 85/87 *Dow Benelux v Commission* [1989] ECR 3137, [1991] 4 CMLR 410, 474,
para 19; Case 67/91 *Asóciacion Española de Banca Privada ('Spanish Banks')* [1992] ECR I-4785,
para 36.
[70] Cases C-238/99P, etc, *Limburgse Vinyl Maatschappij v Commission ('PVC II')* [2003] ECR
I-8375, [2003] 4 CMLR 397, paras 298–308. See also the Opinion of AG Mischo, paras 178–197.
[71] Since protection of human rights is a fundamental principle of EC law; and see the express
reference to the EU Charter of Fundamental Rights in Recital (37) of Reg 1/2003.

Article 12(2) provides that the information can also be used for proceedings under national competition law where that is applied (i) in the same case; (ii) in parallel with Community competition law; and (iii) does not lead to a different outcome. The meaning of the third condition is unclear. It seems that if the NCA concludes that, for example, Article 81 does not apply because there is no effect on trade between Member States, the NCA is then precluded from using the information in evidence in proceedings under national competition law; indeed, if that were evident at the outset, Article 81 would not be applied in the same case at all. It appears that the third condition may have been designed to cover the situation where national competition law condemns unilateral conduct as abusive on a stricter basis than Article 82:[72] in those circumstances, information exchanged cannot be used by the receiving NCA to secure condemnation under national law of conduct that escapes censure under Article 82. However, this condition may present problems in practice if it becomes clear only in the course of proceedings that Community competition law is inapplicable or would produce a different result.

14.027 **Use against individuals.** Regulation 1/2003 does not impose any further limits on the use that one NCA can make of information transmitted to it under Article 12 in its proceedings against undertakings, on the basis that the sanctions imposed on undertakings in all the Member States are 'of the same type' and the rights of defence granted to undertakings in the various systems are therefore 'sufficiently equivalent'.[73] As indicated above, the differences which remain may nonetheless have significant implications.[74] However, as regards natural persons, there is a substantial difference as regards the type of sanctions which can be imposed for violations of competition law, ranging from imprisonment in some Member States to an absence of any personal penalty at all in others (except where the individual is an undertaking in his own right). Consequently, the rights of defence determining what material can be received in evidence in such proceedings differs as between Member States. Regulation 1/2003 recognises that it is therefore important that information transmitted to an NCA under Article 12 should only be used to impose sanctions on individuals if the information has been collected in the transmitting State in a way that meets the same level of protection of the rights of defence as the law of the receiving State.[75] Article 12(3) provides that information

---

[72] As is permissible by Art 3(2) of Reg 1/2003. See para 14.061, below.
[73] Recital (16) of Reg 1/2003.
[74] Moreover, the financial penalty imposed on undertakings constitutes a criminal penalty in some Member States but an administrative fine in others: see the Table at p 1486 *et seq*, below.
[75] Recital (16) of Reg 1/2003.

exchanged can only be used in evidence to impose sanctions on individuals where one of two conditions is satisfied:

(i) the law of the transmitting State[76] 'forsees sanctions of a similar kind' in relation to an infringement of Articles 81 or 82;

(ii) where that condition is not satisfied, where it is possible to demonstrate that the information has been collected in a way which respects the same level of protection of the rights of defence of individuals as is guaranteed by the law of the receiving State.

However, this second condition cannot be relied on by the receiving authority to impose a custodial sanction on an individual. This means that information exchanged can only be used to impose a prison sentence on an individual if the law of the transmitting State also provides for imposition of such a sanction. In that situation, it is assumed that the rights of defence in both systems offer equivalent protection. But this is not necessarily the case since a difference in the means of protection can have substantial consequences in the context of an exchange of information.[77]

(ii) Exchange of information and leniency programmes

Exchange of information and leniency programmes.   The potential for the wide-   **14.028**
spread disclosure of information between the Commission and NCAs, and among the NCAs, to undermine the Commission's leniency programme has caused the Commission considerable concern.[78] Under the Leniency Notice,[79] the Commission encourages members of cartels to disclose details of the cartel to the Commission in return for total or partial immunity from fines. Many, but not all, Member States also operate their own leniency programmes, conferring immunity from fines on 'whistleblowers'.[80] The concerns expressed focus on three aspects of the operation of Regulation 1/2003: the notification of the commencement of proceedings

---

[76] Art 12(3) in fact refers to the law 'of the transmitting authority' but clearly means the law of the State governing the transmitting authority's conduct.

[77] eg where both transmitting and receiving States provide for criminal penalties on individuals who, as managers or directors, were knowingly involved in an infringement by their company, but the protection against self-incrimination in the transmitting State is that the information collected from an individual can be used only against the company, whereas the protection in the receiving State is that an individual liable to prosecution does not have to provide any information at all. For the privilege against self-incrimination in human rights law, see paras 13.057 *et seq*, above.

[78] Blake and Schnichels 'Leniency following Modernisation: safeguarding Europe's leniency programmes' (2004) 2 EC Competition Policy Newsletter 7.

[79] Commission Notice on immunity from fines and reduction of fines in cartel cases, OJ 2006 C298/17: Vol II, App B.14. The Notice is discussed at paras 13.182 *et seq*, above.

[80] See the Table at p 1486 *et seq*, below. For an updated list of the NCAs that offer leniency programmes, see the DG Comp website at http://ec.europa.eu/comm/competition/ecn/leniency_programme_nca.pdf.

under Article 11; the exchange of information under Article 12; and the obligation of the Commission to provide information to national courts under Article 15.

14.029   **Notifications under Article 11.**   Where an undertaking's leniency application triggers an investigation by one authority, the notification of this around the ECN pursuant to Article 11 might trigger an investigation by another authority to which the applicant has not also applied for leniency. Paragraph 39 of the Network Notice seeks to meet this by providing that information submitted to the Network in a case which has been initiated as a result of a leniency application will not be used by other members of the network as the basis for starting an investigation on their own behalf either under the Community competition rules or under national competition or other national laws. This is without prejudice to the power of an authority to open an investigation on the basis of information received from other sources.

14.030   **Information exchange under Article 12.**   The Network Notice also places limits on the use that can be made of information acquired by the Commission or an NCA as a result of a leniency application and then transmitted to other members of the Network pursuant to Article 12 of Regulation 1/2003. These limits apply not only to the material actually provided to the transmitting authority by the applicant itself but also to any information obtained as a result of inspections or other fact finding measures which would not have been carried out except as a result of the leniency application. Generally, paragraph 40 of the Network Notice stipulates that this information may only be transmitted where the leniency applicant consents to the transmission. Once consent is given, it cannot be withdrawn. Paragraph 41 of the Notice provides that, if no consent is forthcoming from the leniency applicant, transmission under Article 12 is only permitted in three circumstances:

(i)   where the receiving authority has also received a leniency application relating to the same infringement from the same applicant, provided that at the time the information is transmitted, it is not open to the applicant to withdraw the information which it has submitted to the receiving authority. This is because by choosing to submit applications to two or more authorities, the applicant is taken to have accepted that those authorities will be able to exchange information about their investigations without the need for further consent.

(ii)   where the receiving authority gives a written commitment[81] that it will not use the information to impose sanctions on the leniency applicant, on any other person who would be protected under the transmitting authority's

---

[81]   A copy of this commitment must be given to the leniency applicant: para 41(2) of the Network Notice.

programme (such as subsidiaries of the applicant) or on any employee or former employee of a protected entity. The commitment given covers not only the information transmitted between the authorities but also any information the receiving authority acquires subsequently and binds not only the receiving authority but also any other authority to which the information is later transmitted by that receiving authority.

(iii) where the leniency application was made to the receiving authority and the information is collected by the transmitting authority on behalf of the receiving authority pursuant to Article 22(1) of Regulation 1/2003.[82]

The legal effect of the Network Notice limitations. These restrictions in the **14.031**
Notice should be sufficient to protect leniency applicants as regards the future conduct of the Commission,[83] but a Commission Notice cannot bind the NCAs. Paragraph 42 of the Network Notice provides that information relating to cases initiated as a result of a leniency application[84] will only be transmitted by the Commission pursuant to Article 11(3) to those NCAs who have signed the statement of principles referred to in paragraph 72, and that statement is annexed to the Notice.[85] The statement commits the NCA to acknowledge the principles set out in the Network Notice and declare that it will abide by those principles, in particular relating to the protection of applicants claiming the benefit of a leniency programme.[86] As regards the position of information exchanged under Article 12, rather than Article 11 of Regulation 1/2003, such exchange can take place with an NCA even if it has not signed the statement, provided that the conditions set out in paragraphs 40 and 41 of the Notice are met; and in its Leniency Notice, the Commission states that it will not transmit a corporate leniency statement to NCAs unless the conditions of the Network Notice are met and the NCA provides an equivalent measure of protection against disclosure to that conferred by the Commission.[87]

Disclosure of leniency programme information to national courts. Article 15 **14.032**
of Regulation 1/2003 provides that courts of the Member States may ask the

---

[82] However, it is unclear whether in those circumstances any restriction on use applies to the transmitting authority.

[83] The Commission must act in accordance with the principles which it lays down in its guidance notices: see Cases C-189/02P, etc, *Dansk Rørindustri v Commission* [2005] ECR I-5425, [2005] 5 CMLR 796, para 219.

[84] This applies to any transmission by the Commission, whether it relates to a Commission investigation triggered by a leniency application to the Commission or the onward transmission by the Commission of information notified to it under Art 11(3) by an NCA which has initiated an investigation as a result of a leniency application under its jurisdiction.

[85] A list of those NCAs who have signed is published on the DG Comp website.

[86] The legal effect of the NCA's adherence to this statement of principles probably depends on its domestic law.

[87] Leniency Notice (n 79, above) para 35.

Commission to transmit to them information in its possession concerning the application of the Community competition rules. A cartel participant contemplating making a leniency application to the Commission might be discouraged by the possibility that information which it voluntarily submitted to the Commission as part of the leniency application might subsequently be disclosed to a national court in the context of a claim for damages against it as a cartel participant. The Commission's Notice on cooperation between the Commission and the courts of the Member States provides that the Commission will not transmit to a national court information submitted by a leniency applicant without the consent of that applicant.[88] However, the business community expressed concerns that companies might be deterred from applying for leniency, thereby revealing the existence of cartels, by the risk that their leniency application would then be subject to disclosure in third party damages claims, in particular in the United States. The Commission's revised Leniency Notice therefore incorporates new provisions whereby a corporate applicant is able to request that its leniency statement is made orally, and the recording and transcription of the statement are then checked by the applicant at the Commission's premises. In that way, no copy of the statement need come into the possession of the applicant. For the same reason, addressees of a statement of objections with a right of access to the file are permitted to see the statements only on condition that they undertake not to make any copies of it; and complainants are not given access to the statements at all. Moreover, addressees of the statement of objections may make use of the information thereby obtained only for the purpose of administrative or judicial proceedings concerning the application of the Community competition rules at issue in the Commission's administrative proceedings.[89] This protection applies even if the applicant is not ultimately granted leniency; but it is lost if applicant itself discloses the content of its leniency statements to third parties.

(d) Enforcement of Community competition rules in the United Kingdom

14.033 **Generally.**   The Office of Fair Trading ('OFT') is the body which has primary responsibility for the enforcement of Community competition law within the United Kingdom. Most of this responsibility derives from the provisions of Regulation 1/2003 and has been implemented by amendments to the Competition

---

[88] Cooperation Notice, OJ 2004 C101/54: Vol II, App B.9, para 27.

[89] Leniency Notice (n 79, above) paras 32–34. The distinction appears to be as regards use in the application of, eg US antitrust law. Note the steps the Commission threatens to take if this condition is violated, including requesting the Community Courts to increase any fine and reporting the relevant legal advisers to their professional body: ibid, para 34. For the background to these provisions, see Suurnäkki and Tierno Centella, 'Commission adopts revised Leniency Notice to reward companies that report hard-core cartels' (2007) 1 EC Competition Policy Newsletter 7 at 14–15.

Act 1998. In addition to the OFT, the sectoral regulators in the United Kingdom are designated as competition authorities pursuant to Article 35 of Regulation 1/2003 and exercise jurisdiction concurrent with the OFT. Each of these aspects of the United Kingdom's implementation of its obligation to enforce Community competition law is briefly considered below.[90]

(i) The OFT's powers and obligations under Regulation 1/2003

The Competition Act 1998 before Modernisation.   Before the implementa-   **14.034**
tion of Regulation 1/2003, the Competition Act 1998 ('the 1998 Act') conferred powers on the OFT to investigate and impose fines in respect of anti-competitive agreements which might affect trade within the United Kingdom and abuses of a dominant position. The operation of these provisions is considered further in Section 6, below. Although Regulation 17 contemplated that NCAs could apply Articles 81 and 82 themselves in cases where the Commission had not initiated proceedings,[91] there was no provision in the United Kingdom empowering the OFT or any other body to do so.

The designation of the competition authorities.   In preparation for the   **14.035**
coming into effect of Regulation 1/2003, the Competition Act 1998 and Other Enactments (Amendment) Regulations 2004[92] ('the 2004 Regulations') made substantial changes to the 1998 Act, conferring powers and imposing obligations on the OFT to enable it to fulfil its role as one of the United Kingdom's competition authorities. Regulation 3 of the 2004 Regulations designated the OFT and the sectoral regulators to be the United Kingdom's NCAs. The OFT and the other sectoral regulators have signed the statement annexed to Regulation 1/2003 indicating their commitment to adhere to the principles set out in the Regulation, in particular regarding the handling of information gathered as a result of an application under a leniency programme.[93]

Implementation of Regulation 1/2003.   Schedule 1 to the 2004 Regulations   **14.036**
made extensive amendment to the 1998 Act with effect from 1 May 2004 to coincide with the coming into force of Regulation 1/2003. As a result:

- section 25 empowers the OFT to conduct an investigation not only where there are reasonable grounds for suspecting that the prohibitions in Chapters I and II

---

[90] For more detailed discussion, see O'Neill and Sanders, *UK Competition Procedure* (2007).
[91] See para 14.010, above.
[92] The 2004 Regulations, SI 2004/1261. The Regulations were made partly under s 2(2) of the European Communities Act 1972 and partly under s 209 of the Enterprise Act 2002. S 209 confers a power on the Secretary of State to modify the 1998 Act for the purpose of eliminating or reducing any differences between the domestic provisions of the 1998 Act and Community competition law (defined as any Act or subordinate legislation which gives effect to a regulation or directive made under Art 83 EC).
[93] See para 14.031, above.

of the 1998 Act have been infringed but also where there are reasonable grounds for suspecting that infringements of Article 81 or 82 have taken place. Further, section 31 empowers the OFT to adopt decisions that the prohibitions in Article 81 or 82 has been infringed.[94] This enables the OFT to comply with the obligations under Article 3(1) of Regulation 1/2003 and to exercise its powers under Article 5 of that Regulation;[95]

- the provisions which empower the OFT to enter and inspect premises either with[96] or without[97] a warrant apply only to business premises[98] but can be used for investigations into infringements of Articles 81 and 82 and include the power to take steps to preserve evidence found on the premises;[99]

- the OFT may apply to the court for a warrant to enter and inspect domestic premises;[100]

- the OFT may accept commitments from undertakings instead of adopting a decision following an investigation;[101]

- the previous powers in Part II of the 1998 Act for a judge of the High Court to issue a warrant, on the application of the OFT, to enter and search premises in order to assist a Commission investigation were amended so as to implement the United Kingdom's obligations to assist the Commission in its investigations under Articles 20, 21 and 22(2) of Regulation 1/2003;[102]

- the OFT may conduct an investigation in the United Kingdom on behalf and for the account of an NCA pursuant to Article 22(1) of Regulation 1/2003;[103]

---

[94] The powers in ss 32–34 to give and enforce directions to bring infringements to an end and the power to impose a fine in s 36 were also amended to cover infringements of Arts 81 and 82.

[95] It also has the effect that the powers in s 26 Act to request documents and information now apply to investigations of 1998 Act infringements and also to infringements of Arts 81 or 82.

[96] s 27 of the 1998 Act, which applies to the business premises of an undertaking suspected of engaging in the infringement or to the business premises of another undertaking. In the latter case, two days notice of the intended entry should be given where possible: s 27(2) and (3).

[97] s 28 of the 1998 Act, which allows entry using reasonable force to any business premises where there is a reasonable suspicion that if the documents were required to be produced they would be concealed, removed tampered with or destroyed.

[98] cf the earlier definition of 'premises' for the purposes of these powers: see s 59(1) of the 1998 Act.

[99] s 27(5)(f) of the 1998 Act reflects Art 20(2)(d) of Reg 1/2003. Such a power was already included in s 28 (2)(c) and (d).

[100] s 28A of the 1998 Act.

[101] ss 31A–31E (which mirror the Commission's powers under Art 9 of Reg 1/2003) and Sch 6A to the 1998 Act. Pursuant to the obligation in s 31D, the OFT has published guidance on when it considers it appropriate to accept commitments.

[102] ss 61–65B of the 1998 Act.

[103] ss 65C–65N of the 1998 Act.

- decisions by the OFT finding that Article 81 or 82 has been infringed, or imposing any penalties in consequence, may be appealed to the Competition Appeal Tribunal.[104]

OFT Guidance. The OFT updated and expanded its guidance to take account of the changes brought about by the 2004 Regulations and the coming into force of Regulation 1/2003. It has published[105] guidance on Modernisation, guidance as to the appropriate amount of a penalty (which incorporates the OFT's leniency programme for immunity from fines for cartel members who inform the OFT of the existence of a cartel), guidance on vertical agreements and restraints, market definition and the assessment of market power, enforcement and powers of investigation, abuse of a dominant position and agreements and concerted practices. **14.037**

(ii) Jurisdiction of sectoral regulators to apply Articles 81 and 82

Concurrent powers of sectoral regulators. Pursuant to Article 35 of Regulation 1/2003, the United Kingdom has designated a number of sectoral regulators as competition authorities having concurrent jurisdiction with the OFT in their respective industry sectors. However, the OFT is the only authority designated in relation to the provisions in Chapter V of Regulation 1/2003, which cover the obligations of the NCAs to assist the Commission and other NCAs in carrying out their investigations.[106] The concurrent powers to apply Articles 81 and 82 are conferred by the legislation establishing and governing the functions of the particular regulator that were amended to reflect their post-Modernisation functions by Schedule 2 to the 2004 Regulations.[107] The provisions are drafted in similar terms, providing that the regulator shall be entitled to exercise, concurrently with the OFT, the functions[108] of the OFT under the provisions of Part 1 of the 1998 Act so far as relating to agreements, decisions or concerted practices of the kind mentioned in Article 81(1), or conduct which amounts to abuse of **14.038**

---

[104] s 46 of the 1998 Act.
[105] The guidance is available on the OFT's website.
[106] Reg 3 of the 2004 Regulations (n 92, above).
[107] 2004 Regulations (n 92, above).
[108] Other than publishing guidance about commitments (under s 31D of the 1998 Act) or penalties (under s 38) or making procedural rules (under s 51).

the kind mentioned in Article 82. The designated sectoral regulators[109] and their respective empowering legislative provisions are as follows:

Regulatory body	Industry sector	Empowering provision
Office of Communications (Ofcom)	Activities connected with communications matters	The Communications Act 2003, section 371(2)
Gas and Electricity Markets Authority (Ofgem)	The shipping, conveyance or supply of gas	The Gas Act 1986, section 36A
	The generation, transmission or supply of electricity	The Electricity Act 1989, section 43(3)
Northern Ireland Authority for Energy Regulation	The conveyance, storage or supply of gas in Northern Ireland	The Gas (Northern Ireland) Order 1996, Article 23(3)
	The generation, transmission or supply of electricity in Northern Ireland	The Electricity (Northern Ireland) Order 1992, Article 46(3)
Director General of Water Services (Ofwat)	The supply of water, securing a supply of water or provision or securing of sewerage services	The Water Industry Act 1991, section 31(3)
Office of Rail Regulation (ORR)	Services relating to railways	The Railways Act 1993, section 67(3)
Civil Aviation Authority (CAA)	Supply of air traffic services	The Transport Act 2000, section 86(3)

14.039 Concurrency Regulations. The Competition Act 1998 (Concurrency) Regulations 2004[110] ('the Concurrency Regulations') contain provisions for the coordination of the performance of concurrent functions under the 1998 Act by the OFT and the regulators. In particular, the Concurrency Regulations require the OFT and the regulators (a) to agree who shall exercise the relevant functions in relation to a particular case; (b) to refer a case to the Secretary of State for determination where agreement cannot be reached; and (c) to agree when they wish to transfer a case between each other. The OFT has issued guidance on the operation of concurrent jurisdiction.[111]

14.040 Case allocation in the United Kingdom. Regulation 6 of the Concurrency Regulations stipulates that neither the OFT nor the regulators may exercise functions in relation to a case where it appears that they may have concurrent jurisdiction until the question of which of them is to deal with the case has been determined under Regulations 4 or 5 of the Concurrency Regulations. Once the

---

[109] Listed in s 54(1) of the 1998 Act.
[110] Concurrency Regulations, SI 2004/1077, made pursuant to s 54(4) of the 1998 Act.
[111] *Concurrent application in regulated industries* (OFT 405, December 2004).

matter has been so determined, Regulation 6 prohibits any other United Kingdom authority from exercising functions in relation to that case unless it is formally transferred to that authority under the procedures laid down in Regulation 7. Even where Regulation 6 does not apply (because a determination has not been made under Regulations 4 or 5 and it is not yet proposed to exercise the relevant functions), it is the policy of the OFT and the regulators that, once it has been decided which United Kingdom authority should deal with a case, only that authority will handle the investigation, decision-making and enforcement, unless the case is subsequently transferred from that authority to another. The general principle is that a case will be dealt with by whichever of the OFT or the relevant regulators is better or best placed to do so. In determining this, the relevant factors include the sectoral knowledge of a regulator, whether the case affects more than one regulatory sector, any previous contacts between the parties or complainants and a regulator or the OFT, and any recent experience in dealing with any of the undertakings or similar issues which may be involved in the proceedings. In many cases, the undertakings whose agreement or conduct is relevant will be licensees, franchisees or similar rights holders under one of the statutes conferring concurrent powers. However, it is the subject-matter to which the agreement or conduct relates rather than the identity of the undertakings involved which will determine whether there is concurrent jurisdiction.

Scope of concurrent powers.   A regulator seised with the case may consider **14.041** complaints about possible infringements of Article 81 or 82,[112] may impose interim measures to prevent serious and irreparable damage and may carry out investigations both on its own initiative or in response to complaints. The regulators have the same powers as the OFT to require the production of documents and information and to search premises. They may also impose financial penalties, having regard to the guidance on penalties issued by the OFT; give and enforce directions to bring an infringement to an end; accept commitments that are binding on an undertaking; offer information and confidential informal advice on how the Community competition rules apply in their sector; and publish an Opinion where a case raises novel or unresolved questions and the regulator considers that there is an interest in issuing clarification for the benefit of a wider audience. Only the OFT, however, has powers to issue guidance on penalties, to issue guidance on commitments and to make and amend procedural rules. The regulators' approach to the exercise of their concurrent powers is explained in their sector-specific guidelines on the application of competition law to their particular sectors.[113]

---

[112] As well as considering the application of the Chapter I or Chapter II prohibitions under Part 1 of the 1998 Act.

[113] *The Application in the Telecommunications Sector* (OFT 417, 2000); *Application in the energy sector* (OFT 428, 2005); *Application to the Northern Ireland energy sectors* (OFT 437, 2001); *The*

3. Enforcement by National Courts: Jurisdiction

14.042 Jurisdiction of national courts. As stated above,[114] Articles 81 and 82 of the Treaty have direct effect and therefore in principle create rights and obligations that can be enforced directly in the national courts. It therefore appears at first sight curious that Regulation 1/2003 should expressly provide in Article 6 that national courts have the power to apply Articles 81 and 82 of the Treaty.[115] However, the application of Article 81(3) is dependent on an implementing regulation pursuant to Article 83. Under the former implementing regime of Regulation 17, only the Commission had power to apply Article 81(3) by individual or block exemption. It is pursuant to Regulation 1/2003 that Article 81(3) has become directly applicable and the Regulation therefore makes clear that national courts can accordingly apply Article 81 in full.[116] This raises the question whether the substantive jurisdiction of national courts is restricted in the now very limited areas to which Regulation 1/2003 does not apply. Mergers and certain kinds of joint ventures are the subject of a special jurisdictional regime and there is an express exclusion in the field of agriculture. In addition, the courts may be subject to limits on their personal jurisdiction over defendants by virtue of Council Regulation 44/2001 on jurisdiction in civil and commercial matters (the 'Brussels I' Regulation).[117]

(i) Limitations on jurisdiction in relation to certain subject-matter

14.043 Limited jurisdiction over mergers and joint ventures. For mergers and certain kinds of joint ventures, the position is somewhat complicated and it is necessary to differentiate (a) between the application of Article 81 and of Article 82; and (b) between concentrations that have and that do not have a 'Community dimension'. Mergers and full-function joint ventures[118] constitute 'concentrations' under the terms of Regulation 139/2004 ('the Merger Regulation').[119] If such a concentration has a 'Community dimension', defined in terms of turnover thresholds, it is subject to mandatory notification and assessment by the Commission under the regime set out in the Merger Regulation, discussed in

---

Application in the Water and Sewerage Sectors (OFT 422, 2000); *Applications to services relating to railways* (OFT 430, 2005). The CAA has not issued general guidance, but see *Air Traffic Services and Competition Law* (CAA Policy Document, April 2006).

114 See para 14.004, above.
115 See Kerse and Khan, *EC Antitrust Procedure* (5th edn, 2005), para 1-066, who describe this provision as exhibiting 'a conceptual muddle'.
116 See Recital (7) to Reg 1/2003. The reference in Art 6 of Reg 1/2003 to Art 82 EC is otiose but was no doubt included since omission of a mention of Art 82 could have led to confusion.
117 See paras 14.045 *et seq*, below.
118 For the meaning of 'full-function joint venture', see paras 8.052 *et seq*, above.
119 Reg 139/2004, OJ 2004 L 24/1: Vol II, App D.1.

Chapter 8, above. Article 21(1) of the Merger Regulation provides for the extent to which Regulation 1/2003 can be applied to concentrations which do not fall to be assessed under the Merger Regulation. This states that Regulation 1/2003 shall not apply to a concentration except in relation to joint ventures that do not have a Community dimension and which have as their object or effect the coordination of the competitive behaviour of undertakings that remain independent. The current position with regard to the application of Article 81 can thus be summarised as follows:

(i) it is generally accepted that Article 81 does not apply to true merger agreements at all;[120]

(ii) by reason of the proviso to Article 21(1) of the Merger Regulation, any full-function joint venture *without* a Community dimension that falls within Article 81(1) is subject to the regime of Regulation 1/2003 and a national court accordingly has jurisdiction to apply Article 81 in such a case;

(iii) as regards a full-function joint venture *with* a Community dimension, since such joint ventures are not covered by Regulation 1/2003 whereas a national court's power to apply Article 81(3) derives from Regulation 1/2003, there is no implementing provision that enables the application of Article 81(3) in such a case. On the basis of the ruling of the Court of Justice concerning the analogous situation that previously prevailed as regards international air transport,[121] a national court should not have jurisdiction to apply Article 81 to such a joint venture. This result supports the objective of the Merger Regulation of achieving a single jurisdiction for the assessment of the coordinative aspects of concentrations with a Community dimension.

(iv) joint ventures which are not full-function fall outside the Merger Regulation altogether and national courts therefore have jurisdiction to apply the EC competition rules to those agreements in full.

As regards Article 82, a national court retains jurisdiction to apply Article 82 because that provision has direct effect: the court's jurisdiction in that regard accordingly comes directly from the Treaty and is not dependent on Regulation 1/2003.[122] However, as regards a concentration *with* a Community dimension, that jurisdiction is more theoretical than real, since a national court would be bound by the duty of loyal cooperation with the Commission[123] not to act inconsistently with the Commission's evaluation of such a concentration under the

---

[120] See para 8.257, above.
[121] Cases 209-213/84 *Ministère Public v Asjes ('Nouvelles Frontières')* [1986] ECR 1425, [1986] 3 CMLR 173, paras 60–68.
[122] Case 66/86 *Ahmed Saeed Flugreisen v Zentrale zur Bekämpfung unlauteren Wettbewerbs* [1989] ECR 803, [1990] 4 CMLR 102, paras 32–33. For application of Art 82 to mergers, see para 8.259, above.
[123] See para 14.054, below.

Merger Regulation. It is only as regards a concentration *without* a Community dimension that this jurisdiction to apply Article 82 could have practical significance.[124]

14.044 **Agricultural agreements.** Article 2(1) of Regulation 1184/2006 provides that Article 81 shall not apply to agreements, decisions or concerted practices that form an integral part of a national market organisation, such as an agricultural farmers' association, or which relate to the production, sale or joint use of storage, treatment or processing facilities for agricultural products.[125] Accordingly, national courts have no power to apply Article 81 to such agreements but they retain jurisdiction to apply Article 82 in full.

(ii) Limitations on personal jurisdiction over defendants

14.045 **Foreign jurisdiction.** Private actions involving the application of Community competition law will frequently involve claimants and defendants established in different Member States or even different continents. Such proceedings may follow on from a finding of infringement by the Commission or an NCA or may be self-standing claims for relief. To determine jurisdiction over a defendant, the courts of the Member States are bound in all 'civil and commercial matters' to follow the harmonised rules of Regulation 44/2001 ('the Brussels I Regulation') where the defendant is domiciled in one of the other Member States, or the similar Lugano Convention where the defendant is domiciled in an EFTA State.[126] Although designed to provide harmonised rules of jurisdiction and produce certainty, there remains the possibility of forum-shopping in competition actions, particularly in claims arising from cartels that encompassed several States.

14.046 **The Brussels I Regulation and the Lugano Convention.** Regulation 44/2001 was adopted at the end of 2000[127] and has now fully replaced the earlier Brussels Convention of 1968. The Lugano Convention was concluded between the

---

[124] There could of course be issues as to the interaction of such proceedings in a national court with any administrative control of the concentration under a Member State's domestic merger regime.

[125] Reg 1184/2006 applying certain rules of competition to production of, and trade in, agricultural products, OJ 2006 L214/7: Vol II, App E.30 and see Chap 12, above.

[126] For full discussion of the Brussels I Reg and the Lugano Convention, see Collins (ed), *Dicey, Morris and Collins on The Conflict of Laws* (14th edn, 2006); Briggs and Rees (eds) *Civil Jurisdiction and Judgements* (4th edn, 2005). See also on the particular issues concerning competition law, Withers, 'Jurisdiction and Applicable Law in Antitrust Tort Claims' (2002) JBL 250–271.

[127] Reg 44/2001 on jurisdiction and the recognition and enforcement of judgments in civil and commercial matters, OJ 2001 L12/1 (corr OJ 2001 L307/28). Denmark became subject to Reg 44/2001 only on 1 July 2007 on the coming into force of its additional agreement with the EC of 19 October 2005, OJ 2005 L299/62. The Reg has been amended on several occasions to take account of the accession of additional Member States. A consolidated version of the Reg taking account of accessions prior to Bulgaria and Romania is available at http://eur-lex.europa.eu/LexUriServ/site/en/consleg/2001/R/02001R0070101-en.pdf.

EU Member States and the EFTA States (excluding Liechtenstein) in 1988 and remains in force.[128] The relevant provisions of the Lugano Convention are largely identical to those of the Brussels I Regulation, and save where relevant differences are referred to, the discussion below is by reference to the Regulation. A revision of the Lugano Convention that will bring the Convention fully into line with the Brussels I Regulation was agreed between the European Community and the Contracting EFTA States on 28 March 2007.[129] However, it is unlikely to come into force before 2009.

Scope of application. The Brussels I Regulation now applies to all of the EC **14.047** Member States. The Brussels I Regulation governs jurisdiction only in civil and commercial matters and excludes areas such as administrative matters[130] and arbitration.[131] Civil proceedings between private individuals or undertakings under Articles 81 and 82 constitute civil and commercial matters within the scope of the Regulation.[132]

General and special jurisdictions. The general jurisdictional rule laid down by **14.048** Article 2(1) of the Brussels I Regulation is that a defendant should be sued in the national court of the Member State where he is domiciled. However, as exceptions to the general rule, the Regulation also provides for a series of special jurisdictions which provide an alternative venue in the limited circumstances set out. There are also additional rules concerning jurisdiction clauses ('prorogation of jurisdiction')

---

[128] The Lugano Convention also applies where the defendant is domiciled in Norway, Iceland or Switzerland. However, of the 12 Member States that joined the EU in 2004 and 2007, at the time of writing only Poland has ratified the Lugano Convention. For consolidated versions of the original Brussels Convention and the Lugano Convention see the Schedules to the UK Civil Jurisdiction and Judgments Act 1982 as amended.

[129] The European Community rather than the individual Member States will be parties to the new Lugano Convention pursuant to Opinion 1/2003 [2006] ECR I-1145, where the ECJ held that the EC has exclusive competence to conclude the Convention.

[130] Actions between a public authority (such as an NCA) and a person governed by private law are 'administrative matters' that fall outside the scope of the Brussels Regulation where the authority is acting in the exercise of public powers, see Art 1(1) of the Brussels I Regulation; Case C-167/00 *Verein für Konsumenteninformation v Henkel* [2002] ECR I-8111, [2003] All ER (EC) 311, para 26. For the same reason, jurisdiction over damages claims brought by consumer associations may depend on their constitution as a statutory or private law entity.

[131] Disputes concerning arbitration clauses are excluded from the scope of the Brussels I Reg by Art 1(2)(d). For the extent of the exclusion of arbitration (under the equivalent provision of the Brussels Convention), see Case C-190/89 *Rich v Società Italiana Impianti (The Atlantic Emperor)* [1991] ECR I-3855, [1992] 1 Lloyd's Rep 342; Case C-391/95 *Van Uden Maritime v Deco-Line* [1998] ECR I-7091, [1999] QB 1225, [1999] All ER (EC) 258. The English Court of Appeal has held that the exclusion does not prevent the grant of an anti-suit injunction in support of arbitration proceedings: *Through Transport Mutual Insurance Assn Ltd v New India Assurance Assn Ltd* [2004] EWCA Civ 1598, [2005] 1 Lloyd's Rep 510, [2005] 1 All ER (Comm) 715.

[132] See, eg in Germany, the Dortmund Regional District Court in the *Vitamins Cartel* case, judgment of 1 April 2004, WuW/E DE-R 1349; and in England, the High Court in *Provimi Ltd v Aventis* [2003] EWHC 961 (Comm), [2003] UKCLR 493, [2003] 2 All ER (Comm) 683, [2003] EuLR 517, para 9.

and *lis alibi pendens* that restrict the taking of jurisdiction. The principal special jurisdictions that affect competition claims are the following:

- in matters relating to a contract: under Article 5(1), subject to any agreement between the parties as to jurisdiction, a defendant may be sued in the place of performance of the obligation in question;
- in matters relating to tort, delict or quasi-delict: under Article 5(3), a defendant may be sued in the courts for the place where the harmful event occurred or may occur;[133]
- as regards a dispute arising out of the operation of a branch, agency or other establishment: under Article 5(5), a defendant may be sued in the courts for the place in which the branch, agency or establishment is situated;
- in matters concerning a contract with a consumer: under Article 15, the consumer may bring proceedings against the other party in the State in which the consumer is domiciled;[134]
- where the defendant is one of a number of defendants: under Article 6(1), he may be sued in the courts for the place where any one of those defendants is domiciled, provided that the claims are so closely connected that it is expedient to hear and determine them together to avoid the risk of irreconcilable judgments resulting from separate proceedings.[135]

14.049 **Matters relating to a contract or tort.** Matters relating to a contract or to a tort are autonomous concepts of Community law that are not defined by reference to national law.[136] In matters relating to a contract, the relevant obligation, identified by the proper law of the contract,[137] for the purpose of Article 5(1), is the contractual obligation which forms the basis of the dispute.[138] In matters relating to a

---

[133] The extension to a place where the event 'may occur' is not included in Art 5(3) of the Lugano Convention; however, the ECJ interpreted the equivalent provision of the Brussels Convention as covering an action to prevent the occurrence of damage: Case C-167/00 *Henkel* [2002] ECR I-8111, [2003] All ER (EC) 311.

[134] These provisions cannot be circumvented by a jurisdiction clause save in limited circumstances: see Art 17 of Reg 44/2001.

[135] Note that this proviso, which could be significant in some cases, does not appear in Art 6(1) of the Lugano Convention.

[136] Case C-26/91 *Handte v Traitements Mécano-Chimiques des Surfaces* [1992] ECR I-3967, para 10; Case C-265/02 *Frahuil* [2004] ECR I-1543, [2004] All ER (EC) 373, para 22.

[137] Determined pursuant to the provisions of the Rome Convention on the law applicable to contractual obligations 1980 (consolidated version at OJ 1998 C 27/34). On 14 January 2003, the Commission issued a Green Paper (COM (2002) 654 final) proposing the modernisation of the Convention and its conversion to a Community legal instrument. On 15 December 2005, the Commission presented a draft regulation ('Rome I') COM (2005) 650 final, 2005/0261 (COD).

[138] Case 14/76 *De Bloos v Bouyer* [1976] ECR 1497. For the difficulties in applying this concept to Community-wide negative restraints such as non-compete clauses and exclusivity obligations, see Case C-256/00 *Besix* [2002] ECR I-1699, [2004] All ER (EC) 229, where the ECJ refused to apply Art 5(1) on the ground that it could not identify a single place of performance or link the

tort, delict or quasi-delict (such as restitution), 'the harmful event occurred' under Article 5(3) has been interpreted by the Court of Justice as meaning that the claimant may commence proceedings either in the courts of the place where the damage occurred or of the place of the event giving rise to that damage.[139] However, if the latter basis is relied upon, jurisdiction is confined to claiming damages for loss suffered within the State of the court.[140] Given the relative paucity of private enforcement claims, there is no authority as at the time of writing identifying which precise competition issues should be characterised as falling within Article 5(1) and which within Article 5(3). A division between Article 81 restrictive agreements and Article 82 abusive practices would be an over-simplification. Article 5(1) covers disputes between contractual parties or other situations where the parties 'freely assume' binding obligations towards one another.[141] It will therefore cover situations such as the relationship between an association and its members,[142] enforceability of vertical restraints, declarations of invalidity and, possibly, exploitative contractual abuse practised by a dominant company. Article 5(3) is a subsidiary jurisdiction in that it covers all claims which seek to establish the liability of a defendant which 'are not matters relating to a contract within the meaning of Article 5(1)'.[143] It will therefore cover situations where no contract has been formed (including unreasonable refusal to supply or refusal to give access to essential facilities) or situations where the parties are not in a contractual relationship, such as allegations of exclusionary conduct against a competitor or damages claims by an indirect purchaser against participants in a cartel.[144]

Co-defendants. Article 6(1) of the Brussels I Regulation enables a plaintiff **14.050** suing one defendant under the general jurisdictional rule in the place where the defendant is domiciled thereby to establish jurisdiction over any number of co-defendants to the same or a closely connected claim. This provision gives significant scope for forum-shopping in competition law damages claims arising out of an international cartel where an 'anchor' defendant is likely to be available in several

---

contractual obligation to one particular court that would be particularly suited to hear and determine the dispute. Instead, the ECJ reverted to the place of the defendant's domicile under Art 2.

[139] Case C-21/76 *Bier v Mines de Potasse d'Alsace* [1976] ECR 1735, [1977] 1 CMLR 284.

[140] Case C-68/93 *Shevill v Press Alliance* [1995] ECR I-415, [1995] 2 AC 18, [1995] All ER (EC) 289. See the application of this principle in a competition case by the English High Court, *Sandisk Corp v Koninklijke Philips Electronics NV* [2007] EWHC 332 (Ch), [2007] FSR 22, where Pumfrey J succinctly observed at para 25: 'the jurisdiction based upon the place of the harmful event will be international, while the jurisdiction based on the relevant harm will be restricted to England and Wales'.

[141] *Handte* (n 136, above) para 15.

[142] Case 34/82 *Peters* [1983] ECR 987, [1984] 2 CMLR 605, para 13.

[143] Case 189/87 *Kalfelis* [1988] ECR 5565. The applicable law in the case of such a non-contractual claim is governed by Art 6(3) of the Rome II Reg: see para 14.096, below.

[144] See, eg judgment of the Dortmund Regional District Court (n 132, above).

jurisdictions.[145] The proviso in Article 6(1) of Regulation 44/2001 about the risk of irreconcilable judgments should not be difficult to satisfy.[146] In *Provimi*, the English High Court ruled that a close connection will be established when private law damages claims are brought against several defendants involved in the same alleged infringement of Article 81. It also held that as the law on the scope of private damages claims across the Community was 'very undeveloped', national courts were likely to adopt different approaches to some of the issues, leading to irreconcilable judgments.[147]

14.051 **Declining jurisdiction.** The Brussels I Regulation also contains provisions designed to avoid multiple proceedings leading to irreconcilable judgments. If there is an agreement governing the dispute between the parties conferring jurisdiction on the courts of a Member State, Article 23 provides that this jurisdiction is exclusive and the courts of other Member States may not entertain the dispute unless the parties otherwise agree.[148] Where proceedings involving the *same cause of action* between the *same parties*[149] are brought before the courts of

---

[145] Art 6 may be relied on to assert jurisdiction over a foreign co-defendant even when the action against the 'anchor' defendant is inadmissibile under a provision of national law, so long as the latter claim is not made for the sole purpose of removing one of the co-defendants from the jurisdiction of the courts of the Member State where it is domiciled: Case C-103/05 *Reisch Montage* [2006] ECR I-6827. If, as the English High Court held was arguable in *Provimi Ltd v Aventis* (n 132, above), a purchaser in one Member State from a subsidiary of a cartel participant is entitled to recover damages from a subsidiary in another Member State on the basis that it implemented the cartel agreement, the choice of forum is wider still. However the judgment was only on an application summarily to dismiss the case, which subsequently settled: see para 14.117, below. Once the criteria of Art 6(1) are fulfilled, the scheme of Reg 44/2001 suggests that the court has no discretion to decline jurisdiction: Briggs and Rees (n 126, above) para 2.176.

[146] On the assumption that this is interpreted in the broader terms applied to the same wording in Art 28(3): see *The Tatry* (n 149, below) and the discussion in Briggs and Rees (n 126, above) para 2.175.

[147] *Provimi* (n 132, above) paras 46–49. See also in the UK Competition Appeal Tribunal, *Emerson Electric Co v Morgan Crucible Co plc*, not yet decided.

[148] Note that the formal and material validity of a jurisdiction clause will be assessed exclusively by reference to the conditions in Art 23 without reference to principles of national law: Case C-269/95 *Benincasa v Dentalkit* [1997] ECR I-3767, [1998] All ER (EC) 135; C-159/97 *Castelletti v Trumpy* [1999] ECR I-1597. However, the national court will have to decide (i) whether the dispute arose out of the legal relationship governed by the contract; and (ii) whether the scope of the jurisdiction clause covers the dispute before the court: see *Provimi* (n 132, above) paras 76–88, where the court held that the intention of the parties did not extend to agreeing jurisdiction in respect of a claim arising from a secret price-fixing cartel. If pursuant to a jurisdiction clause the jurisdiction is in a court other than that of the defendant's domicile, the claimant cannot rely on Art 6(1) to join co-defendants to the proceedings.

[149] Identity of cause of action means that the two actions must have the same 'object' and be based on the same facts and legal principles: Case C-406/92 *The Tatry* [1994] ECR I-5439, [1995] All ER (EC) 229. An action for damages for breach of contract will share identity with one for a declaration of invalidity. In some circumstances, there may be identity between an Art 81 claim and an Art 82 claim arising from the same contractual relationship.

two or more Member States, Article 27 provides that all national courts other than the court first seised[150] must stay their proceedings of their own motion until the jurisdiction of the court first seised has been established; and once the jurisdiction of the first court has been established, they must dismiss the claim. The rule applies even where the first court has wrongly assumed jurisdiction.[151] Where *related proceedings* between different parties are pending in courts of more than one Member State, Article 28 provides that a court other than the one first seised has a discretion. It may assume jurisdiction and proceed with the claim, or stay its proceedings to await the outcome of the proceedings before the court first seised, or on the application of one of the parties, decline jurisdiction if the claim can be consolidated with the proceedings before the court first seised. The approach will depend on the extent to which the two sets of proceedings are closely connected and the expediency of hearing them together. This test is the same as that which applies for the purpose of the proviso to Article 6(1).[152] These rules on *lis alibi pendens* and related actions do not, however, apply to applications for interim relief.[153]

(iii) Jurisdiction in disputes involving third countries

Disputes involving parties from non-contracting countries. Where the 14.052 defendant is domiciled outside the Community altogether, jurisdiction will be determined by the *lex fori* (the rules of the court determining the dispute) save where the parties have conferred jurisdiction on the court or courts of a Member State by agreement or where one of the heads of exclusive jurisdiction in Article 22 applies.[154] Pursuant to Chapter III of the Brussels I Regulation and Title III of the Lugano Convention, a judgment of the national court of a Member State or Contracting EFTA State against a defendant over whom jurisdiction was established on this basis, will be recognised and enforceable throughout the Community and the Contracting EFTA States.

Articles 81 and 82 in the courts of third countries. An agreement operating 14.053 in the Community may become the subject of dispute in the courts of a third country. If the proper law of the agreement is that of one of the Member States, it is clear that Articles 81 and 82 may legitimately be raised, if pertinent to the proceedings. If, however, the proper law of the agreement is that of a country outside the Community, whether Articles 81 and 82 are applicable will depend on the rules of private international law applied by the foreign court hearing the case.

---

150 The point at which a national court is seised is defined in Art 30 of the Reg.
151 Case C-351/89 *Overseas Union Insurance* [1991] ECR I-3317.
152 See para 14.050, above.
153 Brussels I Reg, Art 31.
154 ibid, Art 4. The heads of exclusive jurisdiction in Art 22 are unlikely to apply in competition law claims.

Many jurisdictions will refuse to enforce an agreement which is unlawful under the law of the place of performance (*lex loci solutionis*) although the agreement is lawful under its proper law. In such circumstances, Articles 81 and 82 may be pleaded in the foreign proceedings in question.[155]

4. Convergence, Cooperation and Consistency in the Application of the Competition Rules

(a) Parallel application of Community and national competition law

14.054 **Generally.** Article 83(2)(e) of the Treaty provides that the Council may, in giving effect to Articles 81 and 82, determine the relationship between national laws and the Community competition rules. Articles 3 and 16 of Regulation 1/2003 therefore stipulate how the NCAs and the national courts in the Member States are to reconcile their obligations under Community law with their role in applying domestic competition legislation. Article 16 concerns the position where the Commission has already adopted a decision in relation to the agreement or conduct in question. Broadly, the national authority or court must not take a decision which runs counter to the decision taken by the Commission. The application of Article 3 is not dependent on the Commission having already examined the agreement or conduct. It provides that NCAs and national courts must apply Articles 81 and 82 when they are applying their national competition law to a matter falling within the Community rules and, subject to some qualifications, must not arrive at a different result under national law from the result achieved under the Community rules. The pre-Modernisation duty of sincere cooperation under Article 10 of the Treaty[156] has thus been cemented into a legal rule applying to both NCAs and national courts.

14.055 **General duties owed under the Treaty.** Issues concerning the effect of Community proceedings on national courts arose from the application of the doctrine of direct effect and the supremacy of Community law long before the adoption of Regulation 1/2003. The Community Courts have interpreted Article 10 of the Treaty as imposing a duty of consistent interpretation on national courts as well as a mutual duty of loyal cooperation with the Commission. The same obligations are incumbent on NCAs as organs of the State.[157] Consistency

---

[155] eg in the US Federal Court: *Verson Wilkins v Allied Products Corp*, judgment of 16 July 1987 (ND Ill), where the defendant unsuccessfully pleaded Art 81 to resist a claim for an interlocutory injunction under an agreement governed by the law of Illinois. Both sides filed expert evidence on EC law: see 723 F Supp 1 (1989) at 5.

[156] See paras 14.055 *et seq*, below.

[157] Case C-198/01 *Consorzio Industrie Fiammiferi ('CIF')* [2003] ECR I-8055, [2003] 5 CMLR 829, [2004] All ER (EC) 380, paras 49–50.

and cooperation are distinct but convergent obligations. National courts and NCAs are obliged under Articles 10 and 3(1)(g) of the Treaty to ensure that competition in the internal market is not distorted and to abstain from any measure that could jeopardise the attainment of that objective. That duty extends to setting aside national rules which make the exercise of rights under Articles 81 or 82 virtually impossible or excessively difficult or otherwise prevent Community competition law from taking full effect.[158] Due to the primacy of Community law, national courts and NCAs will be required to disapply a conflicting national law provision, even if it was adopted before the Community rule.[159] That obligation is known as the duty of 'consistent interpretation'.

Duties to apply Articles 81 and 82.   Article 3(1) of Regulation 1/2003 provides   **14.056** that where NCAs or national courts are applying their national competition law to conduct which constitutes an agreement, a decision of an association of undertakings or a concerted practice within the meaning of Article 81(1) which may affect trade between Member States, they must also apply Article 81 of the Treaty. Similarly, where they are applying national competition law to conduct which would constitute an abuse prohibited by Article 82, they must apply Article 82 in parallel with their national law. It is clear from this that, whether or not the legal concepts established in the national legal provisions reflect the Community concepts of undertakings, agreements, concerted practices or abuses, it is the Community concepts which the NCA or national court must overlay upon its national law.[160] Moreover, the power of NCAs to apply Articles 81 and 82 derives directly from Article 5 of Regulation 1/2003. This is a change from the position pre-Modernisation when it was dependent upon national law, with the result that in some Member States the NCAs did not have this jurisdiction.[161]

Differences between the national court and NCA in applying Articles 81   **14.057** **and 82.**   In the context of litigation between private parties, the national court has not only the jurisdiction but the duty to protect directly effective Community rights.[162] The position of the national court, which must uphold the individual rights of private persons in their relations *inter se*, therefore differs from that of the Commission and NCAs which may reject complaints for lack of Community

---

[158] Cases 33/76 *Rewe v Landwirtschaftskammer Saarland* [1976] ECR 1989, [1977] 1 CMLR 533, para 5; and Notice on cooperation between the Commission and the courts of the EU Member States ('Cooperation Notice'), OJ 2004 C101/54: Vol II, App B.9, para 10.
[159] Case 106/77 *Simmenthal* [1978] ECR 629, [1978] 3 CMLR 263, para 21; and *CIF* (n 157, above) para 49.
[160] See Recital (8) of Reg 1/2003.
[161] eg in the United Kingdom.
[162] See Recital (7) of Reg 1/2003; and Case C-213/89 *Factortame* [1990] ECR I-2433, [1990] 3 CMLR 1, para 19.

interest or as a matter of administrative priority.[163] Moreover, the range of remedies that the NCAs may impose under Articles 81 and 82 are derived from Community law. Article 5 of Regulation 1/2003 sets out the various decisions that NCAs 'may take' when applying Articles 81 and 82: requiring the infringement to be brought to an end, ordering interim measures, accepting commitments and imposing fines. They may also decide that there are no grounds for action on their part. By contrast, in cases before the national court, the remedies are a matter of domestic law, subject to the principles of effectiveness and equivalence.

14.058 **Raising competition law of the court's own motion.** An important distinction between the different national legal systems of the Community is the extent to which courts may raise issues of their own motion. In civil law systems, the court is deemed to know the law ('*curia novit legem*') and will conduct research independently from the parties' submissions. In the common law adversarial system, the court is traditionally more passive and dependent upon the submissions advanced by counsel for the parties. The Court of Justice has confirmed that, since Articles 81 and 82 are directly applicable within the national legal order, national courts may raise issues of Community competition law of their own motion even if the issue is not pleaded by the parties. In *Van Schijndel*,[164] the Court of Justice held that where national procedural law permits a court to raise an issue of its own motion, the national court is required to raise an issue of Community competition law. However, the obligation does not apply where the national court would not be allowed to raise a point of domestic law of its own motion or is prevented by national procedural rules from straying beyond the ambit of the dispute defined by the parties.[165] Notwithstanding Member States' procedural autonomy, the national procedural rule will remain subject to the fundamental principles of effectiveness and equivalence.[166] In *Peterbroeck*,[167] the Court of Justice held that,

---

[163] See Case 91/95P *Tremblay* [1996] ECR I-5547, [1997] 4 CMLR 211, per AG Jacobs at para 22.

[164] Cases C-430 & 431/93 *Van Schijndel and van Veen v SPF* [1995] ECR I-4705, [1996] 1 CMLR 801, paras 13–15; Cooperation Notice (n 158, above) para 3: Arts 81 and 82 'are a matter of public policy and are essential to the accomplishment of the tasks entrusted to the Community'. cf the position in an arbitration: paras 14.167 *et seq*, below.

[165] In *Van Schijndel* (above), Opinion at paras 33–38 and 49–50, AG Jacobs suggested that where an agreement was 'manifestly illegal' under Art 81 (eg a price-fixing agreement), the national court could and should raise the point of its own motion as a matter of public policy, since no court would enforce a transaction which was manifestly illegal as a matter of national law. However, no such duty would arise in cases of less obvious infringements.

[166] *Rewe* (n 158, above) para 5; Cases C-6 & 9/90 *Francovich v Italian Republic* [1991] ECR I-5357, [1993] 2 CMLR 66, para 43. For the significance of these principles generally in competition law, see Oliver, 'Le Règlement 1/2003 et les Principes d'Efficacité et d'Équivalence' (2005) 3–4 CDE 351.

[167] Case C-312/93 *Peterbroeck v Belgian State* [1995] ECR I-4599, [1996] 1 CMLR 793. See also similar reasoning in Case C-126/97 *Eco Swiss v Benetton International* [1999] ECR I-3055, [2000] 5 CMLR 816.

where the effect of the national procedural rule would be to preclude any national court from considering an issue of Community law and thereby deny effective relief, the national court must disapply the national rule and consider the matter of its own motion.

Contractual exclusion of Community competition law.   The court's duty to apply Article 81 or 82 cannot be circumvented by contractual provisions to the contrary. There is authority for the proposition that private parties cannot by agreement exclude or waive rights and obligations arising from Community law.[168] To do so would undermine the supremacy, uniformity and effectiveness of Articles 81 and 82 as fundamental principles of Community law.[169] Since the protection of Community law rights is a matter of public policy (*'ordre publique'*), and therefore independent of the will of the parties to the contract, Articles 81 and 82 are likely to be considered to be mandatory in nature, so that it is not possible to derogate from them even with consent.[170] Even if the proper law of the contract in question is that of a State outside the Community, it appears that it would nonetheless be the duty of the court to apply the provisions of Articles 81 or 82 to an agreement or conduct which has a close connection with a Member State, either as a matter of public policy or as a 'mandatory rule' under the Rome Convention.[171]

14.059

(b) The convergence rule

Duty to arrive at a consistent result under national law.   Where an agreement may affect trade between Member States, Article 3(2) of Regulation 1/2003 provides that the application by a national authority, whether an NCA or national court, of national competition law must not operate to prohibit the agreement (i) if it does not restrict competition within the meaning of Article 81(1) of the Treaty;

14.060

---

[168] Case 246/80 *Broekmeulen v Huisarts Registratie Commissie* [1981] ECR 2311, [1981] 1 CMLR 91; Case 102/81 *Nordsee v Reederei Mond* [1982] ECR 1095, [1982] CMLR 154; *Alabaster v Woolwich Plc* [2000] ICR 1037 (EAT) para 55. But see *Milk Marketing Board v Tom Parker Farms and Dairies Ltd* [1998] 2 CMLR 721, [1999] EuLR 154, where the English High Court., whilst recognising the principle, held that it did not apply to a compromise of litigation under which a party settled its claim based on a breach of the Community principle of legitimate expectation. For English law principles of contracting out of statutory rights and obligations, see Beale (ed), *Chitty on Contracts* (29th ed, 2004 and Supp, 2006) Vol. 1, paras 16-016 and 16-030.

[169] The ECJ has emphasised the importance of Art 81 as a matter of public policy in *Eco Swiss v Benetton* (n 167, above) paras 36–40; see further para 14.167, below.

[170] See by analogy in relation to the transfer of undertakings: Case 324/86 *Tellerup v Daddy's Dance Hall* [1988] ECR 739, [1989] 2 CMLR 517, paras 14–15.

[171] Rome Convention on the Law Applicable to Contractual Obligations, Arts 3(3), 7(2) and Art 16. For more detailed discussion of the Rome Convention, see *Dicey, Morris & Collins on the Conflict of Laws* (n 126, above) 1537 *et seq*. cf the analogous position in the field of commercial agents: Case C-381/98 *Ingmar v Eaton* [2000] ECR I-9305, [2001] 1 CMLR 215, [2001] All ER (EC) 57.

(ii) if it fulfils the conditions of Article 81(3) of the Treaty; or (iii) if it is covered by a block exemption. This is referred to in the Network Notice as the 'convergence rule'.[172] Where, however, the agreement falls outside Article 81(1) because it has no effect on trade between Member States, the convergence rule is not engaged and there is no restriction on the application of national competition law.[173]

14.061 **The convergence rule and Article 82.** The relationship between Article 82 and national competition rules dealing with unilateral conduct is different from that between Article 81 and national rules relating to anti-competitive agreements. Article 3(2) of Regulation 1/2003 provides that although national authorities are required to apply Article 82 when they are applying their national competition law, they are not precluded 'from adopting and applying in their own territory stricter national laws which prohibit or sanction unilateral conduct engaged in by undertakings'. Accordingly, whereas conduct which is prohibited by Article 82 cannot escape sanction, conduct which affects trade between Member States but is not caught by Article 82 may be condemned under national competition law relating to unilateral conduct. The Preamble to the Regulation gives as an example of the kind of stricter national law that is envisaged, provisions which may prohibit or impose sanctions on abusive behaviour towards economically dependent undertakings.[174]

14.062 **Application of national laws serving a different purpose.** Article 3(3) of Regulation 1/2003 makes clear that the convergence rule does not apply when the national authorities apply national merger control law or provisions of national law that 'predominantly pursue an objective different from that pursued by Articles 81 and 82 of the Treaty'. With regard to merger control, the Merger Regulation contains its own rules regarding division of jurisdiction between the Commission and national authorities.[175] With regard to national laws serving a different purpose, Recital (9) of the Regulation gives as an example legislation which prohibits unfair

---

[172] Network Notice, OJ 2004 C101/43: Vol II, App B.8, para 43. Recital (8) of Reg 1/2003 describes this as necessary 'to create a level playing field for agreements' within the internal market. This rule applies where the Community institutions have not taken a position on the conduct in question: as to the duty to abide by a Commission decision, see paras 14.076 *et seq*, below.

[173] For application of the convergence rule, see, eg *Koninklijke Gilde van Vlaamse Antiquairs v NV MSA, Belgian State*, judgment of the Brussels Court of Appeal, 29 September 2004 (Case No. 2002/MR/3-2003/MR/8), setting aside an order by the Belgian NCA concerning a rule of an antique dealers' guild on the basis that the rule had an appreciable effect on inter-State trade and so could not be condemned under Belgian competition law since it did not infringe Art 81(1). However, since the court found that the effect on cross-border competition was *de minimis*, the holding that it had an appreciable effect on inter-State trade appears questionable.

[174] Reg 1/2003, Recital (8). eg there are provisions restricting refusal to supply in several Member States that are not dependant on a finding of dominance. In the United Kingdom, the unilateral conduct of undertakings may be examined under the market investigation provisions of the Enterprise Act 2002.

[175] These are discussed in Chap 8, above.

trading practices, whether unilateral or contractual, for example legislation controlling unfair or disproportionate contract terms or conditions. Thus, although an agreement which may affect trade between Member States cannot be condemned under national competition law if, for example, it falls within an EC block exemption, it may still be struck down by other national legislation controlling unfair contract terms. Further, Article 3 should not restrict the application of national laws which impose criminal sanctions on natural persons since Articles 81 and 82 can apply only to undertakings.[176]

Convergence and the English doctrine of restraint of trade. In *Days Medical Aids v Pihsiang Machinery*[177] the English High Court held that an agreement for the distribution of motor scooters did not infringe Article 81(1) because it did not have an appreciable effect on competition. However, the agreement would, on one possible interpretation, offend against the doctrine of restraint of trade thus making it void. Although Article 3 of Regulation 1/2003 was not yet in force, the judge accepted that the convergence principle had its origin in the Opinion of Advocate General Tesauro in the *Volkswagen* case[178] and held that because the agreement did not infringe Article 81(1) it could not be condemned under the domestic restraint of trade doctrine.[179] The judge considered that that doctrine could not be said to pursue an objective different from Articles 81 and 82 but rather that the two had a 'close relationship'.   **14.063**

(c) Cooperation between the Commission and the national authorities

Generally. The Court of Justice has interpreted Article 10 of the Treaty as imposing *reciprocal* duties of loyal cooperation on the Commission and the Member States with a view to attaining the competition law objectives in Article 3(1)(g). Therefore, as a matter of Community law, the Commission has a 'duty of sincere co-operation' with the national court.[180] Equally, the national court may be   **14.064**

---

176 See Reg 1/2003, Recital (8) which sets out the proviso 'except to the extent that such sanctions are the means whereby competition rules applying to undertakings are enforced'. However, the Preamble cannot change the substantive text of the Reg; see further Wils, *Principles of European Antitrust Enforcement* (2005) paras 153–157. The UK Office of Fair Trading considers that the cartel offence under s 188 of the Enterprise Act 2002 is not a means whereby competition rules applying to *undertakings* are enforced, so that the investigation or prosecution of an individual under the cartel offence would not require the OFT to apply Art 81 as well: see *Modernisation* (OFT 442, December 2004) para 4.21.

177 *Days Medical Aids Ltd v Pihsiang Machinery Co Ltd* [2004] EWHC 44 (Comm), [2004] 1 All ER (Comm) 991, [2004] UKCLR 384, paras 254 *et seq*. See also *WWF v World Wrestling Federation* [2002] EWCA (Civ) 196, [2002] UKCLR 388, para 64.

178 Case C-266/93 *Bundeskartellamt v Volkswagen and VAG Leasing* [1995] ECR I-3477, [1996] 4 CMLR 505, esp paras 58–59 of the Opinion.

179 *Days Medical Aids* (n 177, above) para 265.

180 Case C-2/88 *Zwartveld* [1990] ECR I-3365, [1990] 3 CMLR 457, paras 17–18 and 22–26; Case C-275/00 *First and Franex* [2002] ECR I-10943, [2005] 2 CMLR 257, para 49; and see Cooperation Notice (n 158, above) para 15.

obliged to assist the Commission in the fulfilment of its tasks[181] and to avoid adopting measures that could jeopardise the Commission's function. The Commission has adopted two Notices providing guidance to national authorities on what it expects from them and also what assistance it can provide to them. The Network Notice relating to cooperation and exchange of information between the Commission and the NCAs has been discussed in the previous Section of this Chapter. The Notice on cooperation between the Commission and the national courts (the 'Cooperation Notice')[182] is discussed in this Section.

(i) Mutual assistance

14.065 **Cooperation between national courts and the Commission.** Regulation 1/2003 does not contain any precise procedural rules governing such cooperation mechanisms: their implementation is left to national law, subject to the principles of equivalence and effectiveness.[183] The reciprocal duty of sincere cooperation takes different forms at different stages of the proceedings. For instance, the national court may be called upon to assist the Commission at the preliminary stages of an investigation by granting judicial authorisation for inspections at business or other premises.[184]

14.066 **The Cooperation Notice.** Section III of the Cooperation Notice describes the steps that the national court can take to seek the assistance of the Commission in the application of Community competition rules. Three kinds of assistance may be available: the transmission of information, the provision of an opinion on questions of competition law and the Commission's submission of observations to the national courts. In all cases where it intervenes, the Commission's role is that of a neutral *amicus curiae*, acting in the public interest and in order to ensure the coherence of Community competition law.[185] It will not hear representations from the parties to a particular dispute before it makes its submissions. In addition to transmitting any relevant documents to the Commission, the national court should also ensure that a copy of its eventual judgment is forwarded to the Commission.[186]

14.067 **Transmission of information by the Commission.** Under Article 15(1) of Regulation 1/2003, the Commission may, on request, assist a national court in proceedings for the application of Articles 81 or 82 by providing information in the form of documents in its possession or an update as to the status of any

---

[181] Case C-94/00 *Roquette Frères* [2002] ECR I-9011, [2003] 4 CMLR 46, [2003] All ER (EC) 920, para 31.
[182] The Cooperation Notice, OJ 2004 C101/52: Vol II, App B.9.
[183] ibid, para 17. See also Oliver (n 166, above).
[184] Reg 1/2003, Art 20(7) and (8), and see para 13.045, above.
[185] Cooperation Notice (n 182, above) paras 19 and 32.
[186] Reg 1/2003, Art 15(2).

Commission investigation into the same agreement or conduct.[187] The extent to which the parties can make use of Article 15(1) as a indirect means of discovery is unclear.[188] The Commission has indicated that it will endeavour to provide such information within one month of receiving the request.[189]

Exceptions to the obligation to transmit information. In *First and Franex*,[190] **14.068** the Court of Justice held that the duty of loyal cooperation in Article 10 of the Treaty requires the Commission to provide information requested by a national court as soon as possible, unless refusal to do so is justified by overriding reasons relating to the need to avoid interference with the functioning and independence of the Community or to safeguard its interests. As an example of this, a national court cannot require the Commission to produce an expert report to determine the role of that institution in events which allegedly caused damage and loss. Similarly, the Commission cannot be obliged to disclose information of a privileged or confidential nature.[191] In *Postbank v Commission*, the Commission disclosed a copy of the statement of objections to a complainant and then sanctioned the disclosure of that document by the complainant in the course of national proceedings in the Netherlands. The Court of First Instance annulled the decision to transmit due to the Commission's failure to protect confidentiality.[192] The Court held that, although in principle the Commission is not required to prohibit disclosure to national courts of documents containing confidential information and business secrets, it must take steps to seek to protect such information, for example by informing the national court of the parts of the documents which are confidential.[193] In exceptional circumstances where it is not possible adequately to protect the confidential information, the duties of confidentiality will prevail and the Commission will be justified in refusing disclosure to the national court.[194]

The Commission's opinion on questions concerning the application of **14.069** **competition rules.** The national court may ask the Commission for its opinion

---

187 In 2005, the first full year of implementation of the modernisation reforms, the Commission provided information in reply to three requests from national judges: *Report on Competition Policy 2005*, point 219.

188 The CFI has held that the restriction on purpose does not override the Commission's duty of sincere cooperation under Article 10 EC to transmit documents relating to an administrative investigation for use in civil proceedings before the national courts: Case T-353/94 *Postbank v Commission* [1996] ECR II-921, [1997] 4 CMLR 33, paras 64–67.

189 Cooperation Notice, para 22.

190 Case C-275/00 *First and Franex* [2002] ECR I-10943, [2005] 2 CMLR 257, para 49.

191 Case C-234/89 *Delimitis* [1991] ECR I-935, [1992] 5 CMLR 210, para 53.

192 *Postbank* (n 188, above) paras 74–76. See also para 14.032, above.

193 ibid, paras 89–93.

194 See *Zwartveld* (n 180, above) paras 10–11; also Cooperation Notice, paras 23–26.

on economic, factual and legal matters.[195] As soon as the national court makes a request, the Commission and the NCA of that Member State will inform each other. The Commission will endeavour to respond within four months of receiving the request. To date, the opinions have tended to set out the analytical framework under Articles 81 or 82, provide conceptual guidance (for example, explaining how to define the relevant market or to determine foreclosure) and draw the national court's attention to relevant case law and Commission Guidelines and Notices.[196] The Commission will not consider the merits of the case and its opinion is not binding on the national court.

14.070   **Submission of observations to the national court.**   Article 15(3) of Regulation 1/2003 provides that both the NCA of the Member State concerned and the Commission may submit written observations on their own initiative to the national court.[197] Oral observations may only be submitted with the permission of the national court. The Commission may only intervene in this way '[w]here the coherent application of Article 81 or Article 82 of the Treaty so requires'. This power is likely to be used sparingly, and as at the end of 2006 the Commission had exercised it only once, to make written and oral submissions to the Paris Court of Appeal in a case concerning the application of the motor vehicle block exemption.[198] The NCA and the Commission are entitled to ask the court for copies of the documents which they need in order to assess the case and prepare their observations.[199]

14.071   **Assistance to the Commission from the national court.**   Article 15(2) of Regulation 1/2003 requires Member States to send to the Commission a copy of any written judgment applying Articles 81 or 82.[200] National courts may also wish to relay pleadings or evidence disclosed during the course of civil proceedings to

---

[195] Reg 1/2003, Art 15(1); and Cooperation Notice, paras 21–30.

[196] In 2005, the Commission issued six opinions in response to requests from courts in Belgium, Lithuania and Spain: *Report on Competition Policy 2005*, points 225–236. In 2006, the Commission issued one opinion to a court in the Netherlands and another to a Belgian judge while a request from a Swedish court was pending at the end of the year: *Report on Competition Policy 2006*, point 70.

[197] Although Art 15(3) presupposes that the Commission will ask to intervene on its own initiative, the UK Competition Appeal Tribunal in Cases 1054-56/1/1/05 *MasterCard Members Forum v OFT* informed the Commission of the proceedings and invited it to participate, an invitation which the Commission declined.

[198] *Report on Competition Policy 2006*, point 72; and see *Garage Gremeau v Daimler Chrysler France*, no. 188/07, judgment of the Paris Court of Appeal of 7 June 2007: para 6.117.

[199] Art 15(3), 2nd para. See also Cooperation Notice, paras 31–35.

[200] In 2005, 54 judgments were notified from various Member States, with the greatest number being submitted (in descending order) by Germany, France, Spain and the United Kingdom: *Report on Competition Policy 2005*, point 222. With the exception of Lithuania, the new Member States have not notified any judgments to date. The majority of the judgments (43 out of 54) resulted from private enforcement actions rather than appeals from NCA decisions. In 2006, only some 30 judgments were notified to the Commission: *Report on Competition Policy 2006*, point 71. The non-confidential version of the judgment in the original language of the case is posted on the DG

NCAs or the European Commission for use in parallel administrative proceedings.[201] The procedural framework for such transmission will be determined by national law or by the court itself.[202] However, although such information may be brought to the authorities' attention, the Commission or the NCAs will not be allowed to use it as evidence or by way of justification for initiating proceedings if such evidence has been obtained in breach of the rights of defence.[203] National court also have certain obligations to assist the Commission in the conduct of its investigations, particularly regarding the inspection of business or other premises. These obligations are discussed in Chapter 13, above.

(ii) Effect of national authority's action on the Commission

Effect of national decision on the Commission. Before Modernisation, the **14.072** Commission took the view that its assessment of an agreement or practice was not affected by a prior decision of an NCA or national court applying its national competition law to that same conduct. This approach was upheld by the Community Courts. In *JCB Service*,[204] the Court of First Instance stated that '[i]t is settled case law that any similarity there may be between the legislation of a Member State in the field of competition and the rules laid down in Articles 81 EC and 82 EC certainly cannot serve to restrict the Commission's freedom of action in applying those Articles so as to compel it to adopt the same assessment as the authorities responsible for implementing the national legislation'. Further, even where a national court was applying Articles 81 and 82 rather than its equivalent national legislation, the Court of Justice has held that the Commission cannot be bound by the national court's decision. The Commission is therefore entitled to adopt at any time its own decisions, even where an agreement or practice has already been the subject of a decision by a national court and the decision contemplated by the Commission conflicts with that national court's decision.[205] The Commission has, however, stated that it will normally not adopt a decision

---

Comp website, unless the transmitting authority classes the judgment as confidential. However, it seems clear that not all national court judgments are being duly notified.

[201] In *Apple Corps Ltd v Apple Computer Inc* [1992] 1 CMLR 969 (ChD), the English High Court allowed the claimant to forward to the Commission documents disclosed by the defendant on discovery in the course of proceedings alleging that an agreement infringed Art 81(1) because the Commission was in the course of investigating the same agreement.

[202] In *MasterCard* (n 197, above), the OFT was criticised for providing copies of the parties pleadings to another NCA without notifying the parties or seeking the Tribunal's permission in advance.

[203] Case C-60/92 *Otto v Postbank* [1993] ECR-I 5683, para 20.

[204] Case T-67/01 *JCB Service v Commission* [2004] ECR II-49, [2004] 4 CMLR 1346, para 93. The CFI cited Case 298/83 *CICCE v Commission* [1985] ECR 1105, [1986] 1 CMLR 486, para 27.

[205] Case C-344/98 *Masterfoods and HB* [2000] ECR I-11369, [2001] 4 CMLR 449, [2001] All ER (EC) 130, para 48.

which is in conflict with a decision of an NCA provided that it has been properly informed of the investigation and decision by the NCA under Article 11(3) and (4) of Regulation 1/2003 and has not chosen to act under Article 11(6) so as to relieve the NCA of its jurisdiction at the time.[206] Moreover, under the principle of *ne bis in idem*, if a fine has been imposed by an NCA in respect of the same conduct under either Community law or the equivalent provisions of national law, no further fine should be imposed by the Commission.[207]

(iii) Effect of commencement of Commission investigation

14.073 **Effect on investigation by an NCA.**   Article 11(6) of Regulation 1/2003 provides that the initiation by the Commission of proceedings[208] for the adoption of a decision 'shall relieve the competition authorities of the Member States of their competence to apply Articles 81 and 82 to the Treaty'. The application of Article 11(6) is considered in paragraphs 14.015 *et seq*, above.

14.074 **Effect on proceedings in national courts.**   Unlike NCAs, national courts (save where they act as public enforcers) will not be automatically relieved of their competence if the Commission commences its own investigation.[209] However, they are required by Article 16(1) of Regulation 1/2003 to avoid giving a decision which would conflict with a decision contemplated by the Commission in proceedings which it has initiated. According to the Cooperation Notice,[210] the national court should ascertain from the Commission's website[211] or through the Article 15 cooperation procedure,[212] whether the Commission has initiated a procedure, the progress of any investigation and the likelihood of the Commission taking a final decision. In practice, this information may in many cases be supplied by the parties. If the Commission is investigating the relevant agreement or

---

[206] See Network Notice (n 172, above) para 57; and Joint Statement (n 27, above) para 23. For the Art 11 obligations, see para 14.018, above.

[207] See the Opinions of AG Colomer in the *Cement* cases (n 41, above); see further para 13.207, above.

[208] Para 52 of the Network Notice explains that the initiation of proceedings by the Commission is a formal act by which the Commission indicates its intention to adopt a decision under Reg 1/2003, which can occur at any time during a Commission investigation.

[209] See Case 127/73 *BRT v SABAM* [1974] ECR 51, [1974] 2 CMLR 238; for 'initiation of a procedure', see paras 13.082, above. In some Member States (eg Ireland), national courts have been designated as NCAs under Art 35 of Reg 1/2003. Where the national court performs an investigative or prosecuting role with a view to adopting enforcement decisions under Art 5 of Reg 1/2003, it will not be allowed to apply Arts 81 and 82 in parallel with the Commission: see Art 11(6) read in conjunction with Art 35(3) and 35(4) and Cooperation Notice (n 182, above) para 11.

[210] Cooperation Notice (n 182, above) paras 21–26.

[211] The Commission will adopt a public decision when it decides to initiate proceedings: see Art 2(2) of Reg 773/2004. The initiation of proceedings is an authoritative administrative act which evidences the Commission's intention to take a decision: Case 48/72 *Brasserie de Haecht* [1973] ECR 77, [1973] CMLR 287, para 16.

[212] See para 14.067, above.

conduct, the national court should consider whether to stay its proceedings until the Commission has taken its decision and, if necessary, grant interim relief.[213] The Commission has stated that it will endeavour to give priority to cases which are the subject of stayed national proceedings. Where, however, it is clear how the Commission will deal with the matter or where it is possible to take a non-conflicting decision, the national court may take its own decision without waiting for the conclusion of the Commission's proceedings.[214] Where the pending investigation is conducted not by the Commission but by an NCA, the national court is under no obligation as a matter of Community law to stay parallel proceedings: whether or not to order a stay will accordingly be decided according to national rules.[215]

(d) Duty to ensure consistency with decisions of European Commission

The importance of consistent decision-making. The Court of Justice has stressed the importance of consistency within concurrent enforcement proceedings for the uniformity and practical effectiveness of the Community competition law regime.[216] Consistency is important not just to secure fairness in the particular case pending before the Commission and the national court but also to secure equal treatment of parties in similar or related circumstances. That wider perspective is necessary to underpin the principle of legal certainty, which is one of the general principles of Community law, and to create a level playing field for agreements, concerted practices and conduct within the internal market.[217] **14.075**

---

[213] Art 16(1) of Reg 1/2003. See also Cooperation Notice, para 12. See eg the approach of the English court, upheld by the Court of Appeal, in *MTV Europe v BMG Records (UK) Ltd* [1995] 1 CMLR 437 (ChD), [1997] 1 CMLR 8676, [1997] 1 CMLR 867, [1997] EuLR 100 (CA) (English proceedings could continue up to setting down for trial, at which point a stay until after the Commission's decision).

[214] *Delimitis* (n 191,above) para 47; and Case C-344/98 *Masterfoods and HB* (n 205, above) paras 51 and 58. Art 16(1) of Reg 1/2003 follows the principle established by these cases.

[215] eg in England the High Court stayed private civil proceedings involving Arts 81 and 82 when the same matter was being actively considered by the Office of Fair Trading: *Synstar Computer Services (UK) Ltd v ICL (Sorbus) Ltd* [2001] ICR 112, [2001] UKCLR 585. The approach of the national court may differ according to whether the investigation is being conducted by an NCA of its own State or of another Member State. Under Art 15(3) of Reg 1/2003, the NCA has the right to intervene in proceedings before a court of its own State on issues relating to the application of Arts 81 and 82 and could no doubt draw attention to the pending investigation that either it or a foreign NCA is carrying out. In practice, however, an application for a stay is likely to be made by one of the parties. As regards pending proceedings before other national courts, see Arts 27–28 of the Brussels I Reg, discussed at para 14.051, above.

[216] Case 14/68 *Walt Wilhelm v Bundeskartellamt* [1969] ECR 1, [1969] CMLR 100, para 6. Cases 253/78, etc, *Procureur de la République v Giry and Guerlain* [1980] ECR 2327, [1981] 2 CMLR 99.

[217] Recital (8) of Reg 1/2003. As regards legal certainty in this context, see the observations of the President of the CFI granting interim measures in Case T-65/98R *Van den Bergh Foods v Commission* [1998] ECR II-2641, [1998] 5 CMLR 475, para 72.

14.076 **Effect of prior Commission decisions: generally.** Article 16 of Regulation 1/2003 sets out, under the heading 'uniform application of Community competition law', the general rule that when a national court or NCA rules on agreements, decisions or practices under Articles 81 or 82 that are already the subject of a Commission decision, they cannot take decisions that would 'run counter' to the decision adopted by the Commission.[218] This provision is intended to reflect the case law of the Community Courts as to the effect of Commission decisions on the courts and competition authorities of the Member States.[219] However, the application of this apparently simple principle depends on the nature of the decision taken by the Commission and whether the parties to the proceedings in the national courts are the same as the parties involved in the Commission proceedings.

14.077 **Prior infringement decisions.** A finding of infringement by the Commission will be binding on the addressee of the decision under Article 249 EC. Already before the adoption of Regulation 1/2003, it was held that it would be an abuse of process for the addressee of the decision to seek to contest the Commission's findings in proceedings before the national courts.[220] The proper course is for the addressee to challenge the Commission's findings of fact and law by bringing an action for annulment before the Court of First Instance under Article 230 EC. Similarly, interested third parties that have participated in the Commission's investigation (such as a complainant) or a third party that is directly and individually concerned (for example, a co-contractor) cannot seek an inconsistent decision from a national court.[221] Such third parties should make use of their rights of appeal under Article 230 to contest any adverse findings rather than challenging them in domestic proceedings. If the national court doubts the legality of the Commission's decision, it must either stay proceedings pending the judicial review

---

[218] As to the effect of a contemplated Commission decision on proceedings in the national court, see para 14.074, above.

[219] Reg 1/2000, Recital (22). See in particular Case C-344/98 *MasterFoods and HB* [2000] ECR I-11369, [2001] 4 CMLR 449, [2001] All ER (EC) 130.

[220] Case C-128/92 *Banks* [1994] ECR I-1209, [1994] 5 CMLR 30, Opinion of AG Van Gerven, para 60. See in the English High Court, *Iberian (UK) Ltd v BPB Industries plc* [1996] 2 CMLR 601, [1997] EuLR 1 (ChD); and in the field of State aid, *Betws Anthracite Ltd v DSK Anthrazit Ibbenburen* [2003] EWHC 2403 (Comm), [2004] 1 CMLR 381, [2004] 1 All ER (Comm) 289. See also s 47A of the UK Competition Act 1998 which provides that Commission infringement decisions are binding on the Competition Appeal Tribunal in any follow-on claims for damages.

[221] *Banks*, ibid, *per* AG van Gerven, para 60. See also, *Inntrepreneur Pub Company v Crehan* [2006] UKHL 38, [2007] 1 AC 333, [2006] 4 All ER 465, para 61, *per* Lord Hoffmann. Hence in *Eddy Lodiso v La SPRLU MONDE* (2002/MR/6), judgment of 28 September 2004, the Brussels Court of Appeal applied Art 16(1) of Reg 1/2003 in holding that the Commission's decision in *Belgian Architects*, OJ 2005 L4/10, [2005] 4 CMLR 677, meant that it was not open to the national court to determine the compatibility of the Belgian Architects' Association's recommended minimum fee scale with Arts 81–82, and that the practice accordingly could not be enforced against third parties.

of the decision by the Community Courts or make an Article 234 reference to the Court of Justice.[222] However, it should be noted that the obligation under Article 16(1) of Regulation 1/2003 is carefully expressed so as to prevent the national court reaching a decision that is *inconsistent* with that of the Commission; the court is not required to reach an identical decision.

Subsequent infringment decisions.   Where the Commission initiates proceed-   **14.078**
ings only after the national court has delivered its judgment on the same matter, and then comes to a decision which is inconsistent with that of the national court, the effect on the national court's judgment is unclear. That this situation is not fanciful is illustrated by the *Masterfoods* cases, where the Irish court held that there was no infringement of the competition rules by a practice which the Commission subsequently condemned. As part of its distribution arrangements, the largest supplier of ice cream in Ireland, HB Ice Cream (subsequently Van den Bergh Foods), provided retailers of 'impulse' ice cream with freezer cabinets free-of-charge on condition that the cabinets would be used exclusively for its own products. This form of exclusivity was challenged by Masterfoods, a later entrant to the Irish ice cream market, as contrary to Articles 81 and 82, both in proceedings commenced in the Irish courts and, subsequently, by a complaint to the Commission. The High Court in Ireland first granted HB Ice Cream an interim injunction restraining Masterfoods from inducing retailers to breach the exclusivity,[223] and two years later, after trial, concluded that there was no infringement of EC competition law, issued a final injunction and dismissed Masterfoods' action.[224] At that point the Commission had still not instituted proceedings, and it was only several years later that the Commission finally issued its decision whereby it reached the opposite conclusion and prohibited continuation of the freezer exclusivity.[225] This gave rise not only to inconsistent decisions but to inconsistent mandatory orders. Van den Bergh Foods challenged the Commission's decision before the Court of First Instance and while that case was pending,[226] the Irish Supreme Court, on appeal from the lower court's judgment, made a reference to the Court of Justice seeking guidance. Emphasising the primacy of the

---

222 Cooperation Notice (n 182, above) para 13; and Case 314/85 *FotoFrost* [1987] ECR 4199, [1988] 3 CMLR 57, paras 12–20. The possibility of an Art 234 reference is expressly referred to in Art 16 (1) of Reg 1/2003.

223 *H.B. Ice Cream Ltd v Masterfoods Ltd* [1990] 2 IR 4637.

224 *Masterfoods Ltd v H.B. Ice Cream Ltd* [1992] 3 CMLR 830, [1993] ILRM 145.

225 *Van den Bergh's Foods Limited*, OJ 1998 L246/1, [1998] 5 CMLR 530.

226 The President of the CFI granted interim measures suspending the Commission decision pending the appeal to avoid concurrent incosistent judgments in view of the earlier Irish High Court decision: Case T-65/98R *Van den Bergh Foods v Commission* (n 217, above). Thereafter the CFI stayed its proceedings pending the outcome of the reference before the ECJ.

Commission's role in ensuring the proper application of the EC competition rules, the Court of Justice held that:

'The Commission is therefore entitled to adopt at any time individual decisions under Articles [81 and 82], even where an agreement or practice has already been the subject of a decision by a national court and the decision contemplated by the Commission conflicts with that national court's decision.'[227]

Accordingly, the national court should stay its proceedings pending a final judgment in the annulment action before the Community Courts, notwithstanding the decision of the national court of first instance.[228] In *Masterfoods*, the position could therefore be resolved because an appeal in the national proceedings was still pending at the time when the Commission started its proceedings, and the ruling of the Court of Justice has been effectively enacted in Article 16(2) of Regulation 1/2003. But this solution is not available if the national proceedings had finally concluded by the time the Commission reached its decision. It is open to question whether in those circumstances Community law requires that the judgment of the national court be set aside.[229]

14.079 **Which aspects of the Commission decision are binding.** A Commission decision, even if not one of infringement, may contain useful findings of fact or economic appraisal (including, for example, conclusions on market definition, effect on trade, dominance or appreciable effect) that litigants may seek to rely on in subsequent proceedings before national courts. There has been some debate as to whether the national court is bound not just by the outcome of the decision or the Commission's findings of law but also by its findings of fact and economic appraisal.[230] In *Banks*,[231] Advocate General van Gerven concluded that if the national court considers that issues of fact or law decided by the Commission are incorrect or has serious doubts in that regard, then as regards findings which carried no weight in the final decision and do not underlie the reasoning of the Commission, the national court is free to adopt a different interpretation. Where the findings did have an influence on the Commission's decision, the national court should either seek information from the Commission or make a reference to the Court of Justice.[232]

---

[227] Case C-344/98 *MasterFoods and HB* [2000] ECR I-11369, [2001] 4 CMLR 449, [2001] All ER (EC) 130, para 48.

[228] ibid, para 59. The ECJ accordingly applied the guidelines in *Delimitis* (n 191, above) and held that as an alternative the national court could make a reference as to the validity of the Commission's decision. For the final resolution of the substantive issue, see para 6.158, above.

[229] eg that the national courts should permit the judgment to be appealed out of time.

[230] By analogy, ss 58 and 58A of the Competition Act 1998 make findings of fact by the OFT and the Competition Appeal Tribunal binding on the court in certain circumstances.

[231] Case C-128/92 *Banks v British Coal* [1994] ECR I-1209, [1994] 5 CMLR 30, para 61.

[232] However, it seems doubtful that the ECJ would have jurisdiction on an Art 234 reference to revisit a Commission finding of fact, as distinct from a question of law.

Commission decisions in similar or related cases. Litigants may seek to rely **14.080** on Commission findings in decisions involving other parties but relating to the same market or involving a similar type of agreement. Regulation 1/2003 gives no guidance as to whether the obligation in Article 16 not to 'run counter' to the Commission decision has any application in this situation. However, this issue arose directly in the *Crehan* litigation before the English courts. The claimant contended that the tied public house agreement with his landlord foreclosed competition to such an extent as to infringe Article 81, and sought to rely on the Commission's findings in various other decisions concerning similar beer tie agreements offered by different brewing companies. In *Inntrepreneur v Crehan*,[233] the House of Lords held that Commission findings are not binding where a national court is considering an issue arising between different parties in respect of different subject-matter.[234] Lord Hoffmann confined the duty of consistency to a situation where there was 'an inconsistency between the legal effects of the two decisions' in the sense that the binding authority of the national court's decision conflicts with the grounds and operative part of the Commission's decision.[235] A situation of conflict could not arise where the legal and factual context of the case before the Commission is not completely identical to that before the national court, for example because it involved different parties operating in the same market.[236] In such a situation, the Commission decision is not binding on the national court but can be taken into account by the judge as part of the evidence, albeit that it may be regarded as highly persuasive.[237] In the case itself, the judge had therefore been fully entitled, on assessment of all the evidence, to reach a different view from that of the Commission.[238]

---

[233] *Inntrepreneur Pub Company v Crehan* [2006] UKHL 38, [2007] 1 AC 333, [2006] 4 All ER 465.

[234] The judgments took account of the fact that a national court could not make a reference to the ECJ in respect of a question of fact and that the matter properly remained within the jurisdiction of the national court.

[235] *Inntrepreneur v Crehan* (above) paras 44–52, relying on the opinion of AG Cosmas in *Masterfoods and HB* (n 227, above) para 16.

[236] ibid, paras 49–51, 56 and 64.

[237] See also the Cooperation Notice (n 182, above) para 8, where the Commission states that national courts may find guidance in decisions 'which present elements of analogy with the case they are dealing with'.

[238] *Crehan* concerned the effect on the national court of the Commission's prior decision. The same approach should apply as regards the effect on an NCA, but the affected geographic market considered by the NCA may be narrower than that considered in the Commission's decision. This issue arose in the United Kingdom in *Mastercard Members Forum v Office of Fair Trading*, where Visa contended that the OFT could not reach an infringement decision against Mastercard's domestic interchange arrangements that was inconsistent with a prior exemption decision issued by the Commission in favour of Visa. However, as the OFT withdrew its decision on 19 June 2006, the issue was not determined. See also the Network Notice (n 172, above) para 54(b), which states that the standards defined in previous Commission decisions and regulations should 'serve as a yardstick' for subsequent cases.

14.081 **Non-applicability decisions.** The Commission may under Article 10 of Regulation 1/2003 issue a decision finding that Article 81 is not applicable to an agreement either because it does not fall within Article 81(1) or because the conditions in Article 81(3) have been satisfied. The Commission may make a similar finding of inapplicability in relation to Article 82. Where the national proceedings concern the same agreement or conduct, the duty of consistency in Article 16 will apply and the national court will not be able to issue a judgment under EC competition law that 'runs counter' to the decision. As regards the application of national competition law, the power of the national court is discussed in paragraphs 14.060 *et seq*, above.

14.082 **Rejection of a complaint or a refusal to award interim measures.** The fact that a complainant has initiated proceedings before the Commission will not deprive it of its rights to seek redress from the national courts.[239] However, once the Commission refuses to initiate proceedings or award interim relief, the accused undertaking may seek to rely on such refusal in its defence to a claim of infringement. A challengeable decision by the Commission rejecting a complaint does not prevent a national court from ruling upon the application of Article 81(1) or 82. However, the effect of any such decision depends on the Commission's reasons for its refusal. If the decision does not rule on whether or not there has been an infringement of Articles 81 or 82, it has no binding legal status.[240] Likewise, if the decision is based predominantly on the Commission's assessment of its administrative priorities, then the decision is of little relevance as to the substance of the infringement.[241]

---

[239] See, by analogy, in the State aid field, Case C-390/98 *Banks* [2001] ECR I-6117, [2001] 3 CMLR 1285, paras 117–119. The ECJ refused to limit the obligation upon the national courts to apply the EC law provisions simply because a complaint, raising similar questions, had been referred to the Commission. It stressed that, although the Commission and the national courts have concurrent jurisdiction, they do not necessarily have the same powers. An individual complainant cannot be required to pursue his action with the Commission in all circumstances, where appropriate by bringing proceedings for failure to act, until the Commission adopts a position on his complaint. The complainant should be allowed to keep both options open so that in the event that the Commission shows no intention of dealing with the complaint, the complainant can pursue its interest by giving priority to a private enforcement action before the national courts.

[240] Case T-575/93 *Koelman v Commission* [1996] ECR II-1, [1996] 4 CMLR 636, paras 42–43; *BEMIM v Commission* [1995] ECR II-147, [1996] 4 CMLR 305, para 65.

[241] See, eg the English cases *Aero Zipp Fasteners v YKK* [1973] CMLR 819 (ChD), [1978] 2 CMLR 88 (Court of Appeal) where it was held that the fact that the Commission has decided to institute proceedings may show that there is a *prima facie* case of infringement but the fact that the Commission has declined to start proceedings does not necessarily indicate that no infringement has been committed; *Holleran v Thwaites* [1989] 2 CMLR 917 (ChD) (when considering the grant of an interlocutory injunction court held 'it is notorious that the Commission is overburdened with work and the fact that it refused to take an interim decision is no more than a factor to be taken into account').

Commitment decisions. Decisions accepting commitments under Article 9 of Regulation 1/2003 are binding on the undertakings concerned. Commitment decisions are, however, silent on whether there was or still is an underlying breach of the EC competition rules. Accordingly, they do not affect the power of national courts to apply Articles 81 and 82 in third party private damages actions,[242] but the claimant will need to establish the illegality of the undertaking's behaviour.[243]   **14.083**

Informal guidance. The Commission may give informal guidance in cases of genuine uncertainty that present novel or unresolved questions regarding the application of Articles 81 or 82.[244] Guidance letters are not Commission decisions and do not bind national courts as such. However, it remains open to the national court to take account of the Commission's guidance as to the application of Community competition law as it sees fit in the context of a particular case.[245]   **14.084**

Decisions under the old notification regime. The notification and negative clearance procedures[246] are now obsolete under Regulation 1/2003 and, according to Article 34 of the Regulation, any such applications to the Commission lapsed with effect from 1 May 2004.[247] Article 34 is silent as to the effect of any decisions made by the Commission under the old regime. However, the obligation on national courts in Article 16 not to take decisions running counter to a decision adopted by the Commission is not limited to decisions adopted under the new regime, and it would therefore appear that the obligation applies equally to decisions, whether finding infringement or granting exemption, adopted under Regulation 17.[248] Indeed, the Commission's power to withdraw an individual exemption granted under the former regime is expressly saved on a transitional basis under Regulation 1/2003 until the expiration of the decision,[249] indicating   **14.085**

---

242 Recitals (13) and (22) of Reg 1/2003.

243 Whether the breach of a commitment decision in itself gives rise to a private right of action is of course a distinct question: see para 13.117, above.

244 Commission Notice on informal guidance relating to novel questions concerning Articles 81 and 82 ('Informal Guidance Notice'), OJ 2004 C101/78: Vol II, App B.11, para 35; and Recital (38) of Reg 1/2003. The Commission will not issue a guidance letter in relation to an agreement or practice which is subject to proceedings pending before an NCA: Informal Guidance Notice, para 9.

245 Informal Guidance Notice, above, para 25. In the UK, the informal guidance will amount to a 'statement' for the purposes of s 60(3) of the Competition Act 1998.

246 See paras 13.004 *et seq*, above for a brief description of the former regime.

247 Similar applications made under the sectoral transport regimes also lapsed: Art 34(1) of Reg 1/2003.

248 See Case T-289/01 *Der Grüne Punkt – Duales system Deutschland v Commission* [2007] 5 CMLR 356, para 197 (applying the principle under *MasterFoods and HB* (n 227, above) rather than Reg 1/2003).

249 Art 43(1) of Reg 1/2003 preserving Art 8(3) of Reg 17; and see similar provisions for exemptions granted under the transport sector regimes: Art 36(4) of Reg 1/2003 in relation to Reg 1017/68 and Art 38(4) of Reg 1/2003 in relation to Reg 4056/86.

that the Commission regards itself as bound by them. Accordingly, it seems that the Commission retains exclusive jurisdiction to determine whether there has been such a change in circumstances that an individual exemption should be disapplied.

14.086 **Negative clearance under Regulation 17 and comfort letters.**   A Commission decision under Regulation 17 giving negative clearance was considered not to bind national courts.[250] Unlike the grant of individual exemption, such a 'decision' was formally only a statement that 'on the basis of the facts in its possession, there are no grounds under Article 81(1) or Article 82 of the Treaty for action' on the part of the Commission.[251] There is no reason to suggest that Article 16 of Regulation 1/2003 has changed the status of such a negative clearance under the former regime so as to render it binding on national courts. Negative clearance under Regulation 17 is accordingly different from a finding of inapplicability under Article 10 of Regulation 1/2003, which is a formal decision within the scope of Article 16.[252] Prior to Modernisation, the Commission frequently dealt with notifications and applications for exemption by way of comfort letter. The Court of Justice held that a comfort letter did not prevent a national court from reaching a different finding as regards the agreement concerned on the basis of the information available to it. However, the Commission's stated opinion constitutes a factor that the court may take into account in examining whether the agreement is compatible with Article 81.[253] Given that a comfort letter always reserves the right for the Commission to re-open the procedure in the light of additional information of which it was unaware when the letter was issued,[254] there should be no bar to the claimant adducing new evidence showing a material change in

---

[250] See Case 37/79 *Marty v Lauder* [1980] ECR 2481, [1981] 2 CMLR 143, *per* AG Reischl at 2507 (ECR), 152 (CMLR) (the ECJ did not address the point); and Case C-128/92 *Banks* [1994] ECR I-1209, [1994] 5 CMLR 30, Opinion of AG van Gerven, para 60. cf *MTV Europe v BMG Records Ltd* [1995] 1 CMLR 437, paras 32–33, where the English High Court took the view that whether a formal decision of negative clearance was conclusive in national proceedings depended upon the terms and reasoning used by the Commission in their decision (although the cited Opinion of AG van Gerven is not authority for this view); on appeal on other grounds, [1997] 1 CMLR 867, [1997] EuLR 100.

[251] Art 2 of Reg 17: Vol II, App B.1.

[252] cf the finding by the Commission in a commitment decision under Art 9 of Reg 1/2003: para 14.083, above.

[253] Cases 253/78, etc, *Procureur de la République v Giry and Guérlain* [1980] ECR 2327, para 13; *Marty v Lauder* (n 250, above) para 10; Case 99/79 *Lancôme v Etos* [1980] ECR 2511, [1981] 2 CMLR 164, para 11; and Case 31/80 *L'Oréal* [1980] ECR 3775, [1981] 2 CMLR 235, para 11.

[254] This happened in the German ice cream cases, *Schöller Lebensmittel*, OJ 1993 L183/1, [1994] 4 CMLR 51; and *Langnese-Iglo*, OJ 1993 L183/19, [1994] 4 CMLR 83. The defendants' contention that the Commission could not 'go behind' its comfort letters were dismissed on appeal: Case T-7/93 *Langnese-Iglo v Commission* [1995] ECR II-1533, [1995] 5 CMLR 602, [1995] All ER (EC) 902, paras 37–42, upheld in Case C-279/95P *Langnese-Iglo v Commission* [1998] ECR II-5609, [1998] 5 CMLR 933, para 30; Case T-9/39 *Schöller v Commission* [1995] ECR II-1611, [1995] 5 CMLR 659, paras 111–116.

circumstances to undermine the weight that might be attributed to the existence and conclusions of the comfort letter.

Decisions of NCAs. The effect on the national court of a decision of an NCA applying Article 81 or 82 is a matter of national law. The national rules in question may differ according to the nature of the decision and, more fundamentally, distinguish between a decision by the NCA of the court's own State and by an NCA of another Member State. For example, in the United Kingdom, a decision by the Office of Fair Trading that the prohibition in Article 81(1) or Article 82 has been infringed is binding in a private action for damages once any appeal against that decision has been determined, but a decision rejecting a complaint does not have the same conclusive effect,[255] and there is no statutory provision concerning decisions by foreign NCAs. In Germany, a decision by the NCA of any Member State finding an infringement of Articles 81 or 82 is binding in a private civil action.[256] In almost all Member States, decisions of an NCA of another Member State at least constitutes evidence that the national court is likely to take into account. The position is summarised in the comparative Table at pages 1486 *et seq*. The effect on the national courts of a decision of the NCA applying *national* competition law is beyond the scope of this work.[257] **14.087**

Transitional application of Article 81(3). Although national courts are given power by Regulation 1/2003 to apply Article 81(3), that Regulation only takes effect as from 1 May 2004.[258] Since the Regulation contains no general transitional provisions, the question arises whether a national court is able to apply Article 81(3) to an agreement in respect of the period up to 30 April 2004. A national court could well be faced with this issue when having to rule on the validity of an agreement, for example in a damages claim, in respect of a period starting earlier than 1 May 2004. Three different potential situations can be distinguished: **14.088**

(i) where the parties had applied to the Commission under Regulation 17 for an exemption under Article 81(3) but the Commission had not taken a decision on that application;

---

[255] Competition Act 1998, s 58A and see also s 47A(9) as regards claims brought before the Competition Appeal Tribunal. However, the court is also bound by a finding of fact made by the OFT in the course of an investigation, whether the final decision is of infringement or non-infringement, 'unless the court directs' otherwise: s 58.

[256] GWB Art 33(4), pursuant to the 7th Amendment that took effect on 1 July 2005. The same applies to the decision of a court on an appeal from the NCA decision.

[257] But if a decision of the NCA applying national competition law is binding on the national court, under the EC law principle of equivalence, so also must its decisions applying EC competition law: for the principle of equivalence, see para 14.095, below.

[258] Art 45 of Reg 1/2003.

(ii) where no application for an exemption had been made but the agreement satisfies the conditions of Article 4(2) of Regulation 17, whereby the Commission could issue an exemption decision retroactively;[259]

(iii) where no application for an exemption had been made and the Commission had no power under Regulation 17 to grant an exemption prior to the date of an application.

In cases (i) and (ii), it would appear that the national court should have power to apply Article 81(3) for the period before Regulation 1/2003 took effect. Any other conclusion would cause substantial injustice to the parties to the agreement. But in case (iii), the position is problematic. Whereas the national court should be able to apply Article 81(3) to the agreement for the period after 1 May 2004, if the court could also apply it in respect of the earlier period that would appear to change retrospectively the rights which the parties otherwise would have had.[260]

(e) Relationship between national courts and the Community courts

14.089 **Generally.** The Community Courts are not bound by a previous inconsistent finding by a national court regarding the application of Community law.[261] The supremacy of Community law means that the judgments of the Community Courts are binding on issues of law and national courts are required by Article 10 of the Treaty to follow them.[262] This is to be contrasted with the position as regards findings of fact. In competition matters, the Community Courts do not have jurisdiction to determine primary facts, but on an appeal against a Commission

---

[259] The most common examples were agreements between undertakings from the same Member State that did not relate either to imports or exports, and vertical agreements. See Art 4(2) of Reg 17: Vol II, App B.1 and for full discussion, the 5th edn of this work, paras 11-019 *et seq*.

[260] See Lever, 'Article 81(3) EC, Modernisation and the Lack of Transitional Arrangements' (2006) Comp Law 165, referring to this as 'an interesting conundrum' which only the ECJ could resolve. See *Citroën*, judgment of the German Federal Supreme Court of 13 July 2004, WuW/E DE-R 1335, where on a claim by car dealers that certain clauses in the Citroën car dealership agreement infringed Art 81, the court applied as regards the time before 1 May 2004 only the relevant block exemption, but as regards the time after 1 May 2004, the block exemption and also Art 81(3). In that case the proceedings had been commenced before Reg 1/2003 came into effect: see para 6.115, above. See also *Marketing Displays International v VR*, judgment of 24 March 2005, NJF 2005/239, where the Hague Court of Appeal held that Art 81(3) could not be applied by the national court (or arbitrators) to an agreement in respect of a period prior to 1 May 2004.

[261] *Masterfoods and HB*, para 14.078, above. See also, on the substantive appeal against the Commission's decn, Case C-552/03P *Unilever Bestfoods (Ireland) v Commission* [2006] ECR I-9091, [2006] 5 CMLR 1460, para 128.

[262] See, eg Case 61/79 *Amministrazione Delle Finanze Dello Stato v Denkavit Italiana* [1980] ECR 1205, [1981] 3 CMLR 694, para 16, and the general principle of the primacy of Community law: paras 14.001 *et seq*, above. For the UK, see the European Communities Act 1972 as amended, s 3(1) and 3(2) which require that judicial notice be taken of any judgment of the ECJ or CFI on any question of law (see para 14.002, above) and as regards national competitive law, s 60(2) of the Competition Act 1998.

decision, they may adjudicate upon the factual findings of the Commission. For example, if the addressee of a Commission decision condemning undertakings for price-fixing contrary to Article 81(1) challenged the Commission's evaluation of the facts under Article 230 EC on appeal to the Court of First Instance, the Court could determine that the Commission had failed sufficiently to prove that prices were fixed over as long a period as set out in the decision and that only a shorter infringement was established (and the Court would probably then reduce the fine accordingly). If that undertaking were then sued for damages in the national court, it could not seek to argue that the infringement was even shorter or did not occur at all: that would now result from Article 16(1) of Regulation 1/2003, since the effect of the Court of First Instance's judgment would be to vary the Commission's decision.[263] However, as a matter of Community law, the claimant seeking damages would not be precluded from arguing before the national court that prices were in fact fixed for as long as the Commission had found, although it would need to produce additional evidence beyond that which was in the Commission decision. Such a finding by the national court, based on new evidence, would not be inconsistent with the judgment of the Court of First Instance just as it would not 'run counter' to the Commission's decision as varied.[264] Similarly, if the Community Courts annulled the Commission's finding of infringement in its entirety for lack of sufficient proof, a national court could nonetheless find on new evidence in a subsequent private action that price-fixing had indeed occurred. The supremacy of Community law, as interpreted by the Community Courts, only precludes the national courts from reaching a different interpretation of the legal consequences of substantially the same facts. Similarly, if in a reference under Article 234 the Court of Justice ruled that a restriction of competition was not appreciable, the Court would be basing its ruling on the facts set out in the reference from the national court.

Article 234 references.   If the allegation of infringement made in the course   **14.090**
of proceedings in the national court gives rise to an issue as to the interpretation of either the Treaty or secondary EC legislation, the national court may stay the domestic proceedings and seek a preliminary ruling on that question from the Court of Justice under Article 234 EC.[265] Only a 'court or tribunal' within the meaning of Article 234 may make a reference. The definition of 'court or tribunal'

---

[263] Prior to Reg 1/2003, the English High Court found that for an addressee of a Commission cartel decision against which it had unsuccessfully appealed to the CFI and the ECJ to seek to contest it in national proceedings consituted an abuse of process: *Iberian (UK) Ltd v BPB Industries plc* [1996] 2 CMLR 601, [1997] EuLR 1, paras 36–50.

[264] See para 14.077, above.

[265] A detailed discussion of Art 234 is beyond the scope of this work. See generally Lasok and Millett, *Judicial Control in the EU* (2004); Anderson and Demetriou, *References to the European Court* (2nd edn, 2002).

is governed by Community law alone.[266] Moreover, there must be a case pending before the national court where it is called upon to give judgment in proceedings intended to lead to a decision of a judicial nature.[267] An NCA will not constitute a court or tribunal for the purposes of Article 234 where, amongst other things, it may be relieved of its competence by the European Commission under Article 11(6) of Regulation 1/2003.[268] An arbitration tribunal is not a court or tribunal for the purposes of Article 234.[269] The jurisdiction of the Court of Justice on a preliminary reference is limited to interpreting Community provisions: it will not apply Articles 81 and 82 to the facts of the particular case nor will it construe or apply domestic law provisions.[270] However, if the principles or concepts of the equivalent Community law are binding in the application of national law, a reference to the Court of Justice of questions of interpretation of Community law may be made in proceedings that concern only national law.[271] Accordingly, the Court of Justice held that it had jurisdiction to determine a reference from the Austrian court of questions under Article 82 in a case where the national court was applying Austrian competition law;[272] and similarly from the Spanish court of questions under Article 81 where the court was applying Spanish competition law.[273]

14.091 **Admissibility.** The Article 234 procedure is based on a clear separation of judicial functions between the Court of Justice and the national court.[274] The Court of Justice has reaffirmed that it is solely for the national court, before which the dispute has been brought and which must assume responsibility for the subsequent judicial decision, to determine in the light of the particular circumstances of the case both the need for a preliminary ruling in order to enable it to deliver judgment and the relevance of the questions which it submits

---

[266] The ECJ takes account of a number of factors, such as whether the body is established by law, whether it is permanent, whether its jurisdiction is compulsory, whether its procedure is *inter partes*, whether it applies rules of law and whether it is independent. See, in particular, Case C-54/96 *Dorsch Consult* [1997] ECR I-4961, [1998] 2 CMLR 237, [1998] All ER (EC) 262, para 23; Case C-516/99 *Schmid* [2002] ECR I-4573, [2004] 3 CMLR 249, para 34.

[267] Case C-134/97 *Victoria Film* [1998] ECR I-7023, [1999] 1 CMLR 279, para 14.

[268] Case C-53/03 *Syfait v GlaxoSmithKline* [2005] ECR I-4609, [2005] 5 CMLR 7. The ECJ did not follow the Opinion of AG Jacobs.

[269] Case 102/81 *Nordsee v Reederei Mond* [1982] ECR 1095, [1982] CMLR 154: see further para 14.166, below.

[270] Case C-346/93 *Kleinwort-Benson* [1995] ECR I-615, [1995] All ER (EC) 514, para 18.

[271] The national provisions need not implement the Community provisions so long as they apply similar concepts within a domestic context: Case C-306/99 *BIAO* [2003] ECR I-1, paras 88–94, distinguishing the *Kleinwort-Benson* case.

[272] Case C-7/97 *Bronner v Mediaprint* [1998] ECR I-7791, [1999] 4 CMLR 112, paras 12–20. The ECJ there rejected the argument of the Commission that the reference was inadmissible.

[273] Case C-217/05 *Confederación Española v CEPSA* [2006] ECR I-11987, [2007] 4 CMLR 181, paras 14–24. Therefore, it is irrelevant that the agreement may have no appreciable effect on trade between Member States.

[274] Case 36/79 *Denkavit* [1979] ECR 3439, para 12.

to the Court.[275] Only in exceptional circumstances will the Court refuse to rule, for example where it is obvious that the interpretation of Community law that is sought bears no relation to the facts of the main action or its purpose, where the problem is hypothetical, or where the Court does not have before it the factual or legal material necessary to give a useful answer to the questions submitted to it. [276]

Factual issues for the national court. The Court of Justice will leave the **14.092** determination of all preliminary factual issues involved in establishing a breach of Article 81 or 82 to the national court. For example, in *Télémarketing*, a reference from a Belgian court, the Court of Justice stated that the nature and geographical extent of the markets in issue, the position in law and in fact of the defendants on those markets, the existence of any effect on trade between Member States and any possible justification for the alleged abusive conduct, were matters for the national court alone to assess.[277] However, especially in competition law, it is not always easy to disentangle issues of Community law from issues of fact which cannot be referred. In *Manfredi*, where the question referred was, in essence, whether the disputed agreement was capable of affecting trade between Member States, the Court stated that although it was for the national court to determine whether such an effect had been proved, the Court was able to 'provide clarification designed to give the national court guidance in its interpretation'.[278] Determination of purely economic issues, which are prevalent in the application of Article 81(3), are in principle inadmissible under Article 234.[279] However, given the novelty of the jurisdiction of national courts to determine issues under Article 81(3) and the aspiration to achieve a consistent approach across the Community, it remains to be seen to what extent the Court of Justice may be willing to provide assistance to national courts on the evaluation of the factors arising under Article 81(3) if such questions were referred.

Exercise of the discretion to refer. Unless the national court is a court of final **14.093** resort,[280] it has discretion to make a reference where it considers that a ruling is

---

275 Cases C-295/04, etc, *Manfredi v Lloyd Adriatico Assicurazioni* [2006] ECR I-6619, [2006] 5 CMLR 980, [2007] All ER (EC) 27, paras 26–27.

276 Case C-415/93 *Bosman* [1995] ECR I-4921, [1996] 1 CMLR 645, [1996] All ER (EC) 97, para 59; Case C-340/99 *TNT Traco* [2001] ECR I-4109, [2003] 4 CMLR 13, para 31.

277 Case 311/84 *Telemarketing CBM v CLT and IPB* [1985] ECR 3261, [1986] 2 CMLR 558.

278 *Manfredi* (n 275, above) para 48.

279 In Case C-134/03 *Viacom Outdoor v Giotto* ('*Viacom II*') [2005] ECR I-1167, [2006] 1 CMLR 1255, paras 25–28, the ECJ treated economic issues such as the determination of the relevant product and geographic market and the calculation of the undertakings' market shares as part of the factual context that the referring national court should determine.

280 Art 234(3) EC imposes an obligation upon a final court to make a reference. A final court is not just a supreme court but any court or tribunal from which there is no further right of appeal or judicial review under national law: Case 6/64 *Costa v ENEL* [1964] ECR 585, [1964] CMLR 425.

necessary for it to give judgment in the case pending before it.[281] In *R v Stock Exchange, ex p Else Ltd*,[282] the English Court of Appeal summarised its understanding of the correct approach that a national court (other than a final court) should take in deciding whether to make an Article 234 reference in the following terms:

> '... if the facts have been found and the Community law issue is critical to the court's final decision, the appropriate course is ordinarily to refer the issue to the Court of Justice unless the national court can with complete confidence resolve the issue itself. In considering whether it can with complete confidence resolve the issue itself the national court must be fully mindful of the differences between national and Community legislation, of the pitfalls which face a national court venturing into what may be an unfamiliar field, of the need for uniform interpretation throughout the Community and of the great advantages enjoyed by the Court of Justice in construing Community instruments. If the national court has any real doubt, it should ordinarily refer.'

14.094 **The approach of English courts to making a reference.** The Court of Justice has issued guidance to national courts on the reference procedure, including as regards the framing of the reference.[283] The Court has also emphasised the need for precision in setting out the factual and legislative context in competition law cases, which are characterised by complex factual and legal situations.[284] English courts have held that, in general[285] it is premature to refer issues to the Court of Justice before pleadings have been exchanged[286] or before the facts have been determined by the national court.[287] However, in certain cases an early reference may be convenient to limit the scope of the facts which the national court is

---

A court may be a final court where it refuses permission to appeal: Case C-99/00 *Lyckesog* [2002] ECR I-4839, [2004] 3 CMLR 593, para 16.

[281] Art 234(2) EC.

[282] *R. v Stock Exchange, ex p Else Ltd* [1993] QB 534, [1993] 2 CMLR 677, [1993] 1 All ER 420, *per* Sir Thomas Bingham MR at 545C-G (QB), 426 (All ER). In *Trent Taverns Ltd v Sykes* [1999] EuLR 492, the Court of Appeal cited *Else* but declined to make a reference on the grounds that the same point might be referred by the House of Lords in another pending case.

[283] Information Note on references from national courts for a preliminary ruling, OJ 2005 C143/1.

[284] Case C-134/03 *Viacom II* (n 279, above) para 23; and the Opinion of AG Stix-Hackl in Case C-231/03 *Consorzio Aziende Metano (Coname) v Comune di Cingia de' Botti* [2005] ECR I-7287, [2006] 1 CMLR 17, paras 15–17. She recommended that the ECJ impose 'particularly stringent criteria' in the context of competition law and that the order for reference should contain, in particular, information on the undertakings concerned or on the practices which, in the view of the referring court, fall within the scope of Art 81.

[285] See generally Civil Procedure Rules 1998 ('CPR') Part 68 and the Practice Direction (References to the European Court), 68PD, annexing the ECJ's Information Note (n 283, above).

[286] *DDSA Pharmaceuticals v Farbwerke Hoechst* [1975] 2 CMLR 50 (ChD).

[287] *Bulmer v Bollinger (No. 2)* [1974] FSR 263; *Church of Scientology of California v Commissioners of Customs & Excise* [1981] 1 All ER 1035 (CA); *Bethell v SABENA* [1983] 3 CMLR 1 (QBD).

required to determine; for example, a trial of preliminary issues may be ordered even if those issues might involve an Article 234 reference.[288]

5. Enforcement by National Courts: Remedies

Introduction. National courts are under a duty under Article 10 of the Treaty to ensure the effectiveness of the prohibitions in Articles 81 and 82 and to provide adequate protection for those that have suffered loss.[289] Regulation 1/2003 is not intended to be a harmonising enforcement measure. It is not intended to modify national rules on the standard of proof nor the obligations of competition authorities and courts of the Member States to ascertain the relevant facts of a case.[290] In the absence of any harmonising Community rules governing procedural matters, it is for the domestic legal system of each Member State to designate the courts and tribunals having jurisdiction in competition law matters and to lay down the detailed procedural rules. The only constraints on such national procedural rules is that they must not be not less favourable than those governing similar domestic actions (the principle of equivalence) and that they must not render practically impossible or excessively difficult the exercise of rights conferred by Community law (the principle of effectiveness).[291]

14.095

Cause of action. As a matter of Community law, an action for damages for breach of Articles 81 or 82 may be tortious or contractual in nature, depending on the facts of the individual case. The Rome II Regulation on the law applicable to non-contractual obligations[292] provides that for a non-contractual obligation

14.096

---

288 *PSA Wholesale Ltd v Fordham Engineering Co Ltd* [1997] ECC 587 (CA) *per* Beldam LJ. In *R. v Sec of State for Transport, ex p Factortame Ltd* [1997] EuLR 475, [1998] 1 CMLR 1353, the Divisional Court made a reference of the fundamental question of whether damages were available as a matter of EC law, in advance of discovery or a substantive hearing. See also *Courage Ltd v Crehan (No. 1)* [1999] EuLR 834, [1999] UKCLR 110, where the Court of Appeal made a reference on points of 'the greatest importance' on an application for summary judgment and prior to any findings of fact on the application of Art 81(1), and despite the fact that there was a prior Court of Appeal decision on the same issue: see para 14.114 and n 359, below.

289 Case C-312/93 *Peterbroeck v Belgian State* [1995] ECR I-4599, [1996] 1 CMLR 793; and Cases 430 & 431/93 *Van Schijndel and van Veen v SPF* [1995] ECR I-4705, [1996] 1 CMLR 801. Note also Art 47 of the EU Charter of Fundamental Rights, OJ 2000 C364/1, which provides that everyone whose rights guaranteed by EC law are violated is entitled to an effective remedy before an independent tribunal.

290 Recital (5) of Reg 1/2003.

291 Case C-261/95 *Palmisani* [1997] ECR I-4025, [1997] 3 CMLR 1356, para 27; Case C-453/99 *Courage v Crehan* [2001] ECR I-6297, [2001] 5 CMLR 1058, [2001] All ER (EC) 886, para 29; *Manfredi* (n 275, above) para 61. See Oliver, 'Le Règlement 1/2003 et les Principes d'Efficacité de d'Équivalence' (2005) 3–4 CDE 351; and more generally, Tridimas, *The General Principles of EU Law* (2nd edn, 2006), Chap 9.

292 Reg 864/2007 on the law applicable to non-contractual obligations ('Rome II'), OJ 2007 L199/40.

arising out of a restriction of competition, the applicable law will be the law of the country where the market is, or is likely to be, affected; save that where that market is in more than one country, a claimant seeking compensation in the court of the domicile of the defendant may instead base his claim on the law of that court provided that the market in that Member State is among those directly and substantially affected.[293] Obligations arising in the context of a contractual relationship will be determined, subject to the application of mandatory rules, by the parties' choice of law, or failing that, the presumptions applied by the Rome Convention to establish the country with which the contract is most closely connected.[294] In due course, the Convention will be superceded by the Rome I Regulation which, in the draft current at the time of writing, replaces the presumptions under the Convention with a series of firm rules according to the type of contract involved.[295] Although matters of evidence and procedure are excluded from the conflict of laws regulations, the applicable law will determine not just the interpretation of the agreement but also procedural issues such as the burden of proof,[296] evidential presumptions and rules of prescription and limitation.[297] It will also determine the consequences of the total or partial breach of obligations, including the nature and assessment of damages, and the consequences of nullity of the contract.[298] Accordingly, characterisation of the cause of action will have a bearing not just on the applicable procedural rules of law (such as causation and remoteness) but also on the measure and type of damages available.

---

[293] Art 6(3). This covers both claims under EC law and under national competition law: see Recital (23).

[294] Art 4 of the Convention on the Law Applicable to Contractual Obligations ('the Rome Convention'). For a consolidated text, see OJ 1998 C27/34, subsequently amended after the accession of further Member States, OJ 2005 C169/01. The main presumption is that the contract is most closely connected with the country of the habitual residence, or in the case of a body corporate or incorporate the central administration, of the party who is to effect the performance which is characteristic of the contract. For detailed discussion, see Collins (ed), *Dicey, Morris & Collins on The Conflict of Laws* (14th ed, 2006), Chap 32.

[295] See Art 4 of the proposal for a Regulation of the European Parliament and the Council on the law applicable to contractual obligations ('Rome I') COM (2005) 650 final, 2005/0261 (COD). eg a distribution agreement will be governed by the law of the country of the habitual residence of the distributor; a contract for sale by the law of the seller's habitual residence; and a contract relating to intellectual or industrial property rights by the law of the IPR-holder's habitual residence. Other contracts which are not listed in Art 4(1) are to be governed by the law of the country where the party who is required to perform the service characterising the contract has its habitual residence at the time of the conclusion of the contract or, failing identification of such law, the law of the country with which the agreement is most closely connected. 'Habitual residence' for companies and incorporated or unincorporated entities is defined in Art 18 as the principal establishment unless the the contract is concluded or performed by a subsidiary, a branch or other establishment, in which case the place of this establishment is the habitual residence.

[296] Art 17 of Rome I and Art 22 of Rome II.

[297] Art 11(d) of Rome I and Art 15(h) of Rome II.

[298] Art 11 of Rome I and Art 15 of Rome II.

Type of remedy available. There may be a range of remedies available within   **14.097**
the domestic legal system, such as declarations of invalidity, damages and injunctive relief. Similarly, invalidity resulting from infringement of the competition
rules may be raised as a defence to the enforcement of a contract or an intellectual
property right. This Section considers the general principles applicable to main
types of remedy. Specific issues of practice and procedure in the English courts are
discussed in Section 6, below, although the present Section also makes extensive
reference to the English case law.

(a) Declarations of invalidity

Generally. An agreement which contravenes either Article 81(1)[299] or Article 82[300]   **14.098**
is void and unenforceable as between the parties. Article 81(2) provides a remedy
in and of itself by stating that agreements or decisions prohibited by Article 81(2)
are automatically void. National courts can use a declaration of nullity as a
sanction for infringement of Articles 81 or 82 in any civil proceedings. Thus
Articles 81 and 82 may in principle be pleaded, for example, to defeat a contractual obligation to pay royalties,[301] or an obligation to pay rent under a lease,[302]
to avoid a contract of sale,[303] to avoid an agreement not to market certain goods
in the United Kingdom,[304] to set aside an arbitration award[305] or as a defence to a

---

[299] Case 22/71 *Béguelin Import v G L Import Export* [1971] ECR 949, [1972] CMLR 81, paras 25
et seq. There is no duty to amend an agreement to comply with a block exemption but if the agree-
ment does not comply with the block exemption Art 81(1) may be applicable: Case 10/86 *VAG v
Magne* [1986] ECR 4071, [1988] 4 CMLR 98; Case C-234/89 *Delimitis v Henninger Brau* [1991]
ECR I-935, [1992] 5 CMLR 210; Case C-230/96 *Cabour and Nord Distribution Automobile v
Arnor* [1998] ECR I-2055, [1998] 5 CMLR 679, paras 46–52.

[300] Although there is no equivalent to Art 81(2) under Art 82, agreements infringing Art 82
are unenforceable by virtue of the direct effect of that provision: Case 127/73 *BRT v SABAM*
[1974] ECR 51, [1974] 2 CMLR 238, para 16; Case 66/86 *Ahmed Saeed Flugreisen v Zentrale
zur Bekämpfung unlauteren Wettbewerbs* [1989] ECR 803, [1990] 4 CMLR 102, para 45. See, eg
in Sweden: *Luftfartsverket v Scandinavian Airlines System*, case no. T 33-00, judgment of the Göta
Court of Appeal of 27 April 2001: para 14.123, below; in England: *English Welsh & Scottish Railway
Ltd v E.ON UK plc* [2007] EWHC 599 (Comm), High Court judgment of 23 March 2007 (on
appeal to the Court of Appeal, not yet decided).

[301] eg in the English courts, *Dymond v G B Britton & Sons (Holdings) Ltd* [1976] 1 CMLR 133
(ChD); *Chemidus Wavin v TERI* [1978] 3 CMLR 514, [1977] FSR 181 (Court of Appeal).

[302] eg *Heathrow Airport Ltd v Forte (UK) Ltd* [1998] ECC 357, [1998] EuLR 98, 109 (English
High Court, ChD). The defence under Art 82 failed, but the judge considered the extent to which,
if established on the facts, the alleged abuse of charging an excessive rent could constitute a defence
to the claim for the rent.

[303] eg *Felixstowe Dock & Railway Co v British Transport Docks Board* [1976] 2 CMLR 655
(English Court of Appeal CA) (Art 82).

[304] *Sirdar v Les Fils de Louis Mulliez* [1975] 1 CMLR 378 (English High Court, ChD).

[305] See Case 174/84 *Bulk Oil v Sun International* [1986] ECR 559, [1986] 2 CMLR 732, a
defence under Art 81 apparently being raised for the first time in the course of an Art 234 reference.
See also Case C-126/97 *Eco Swiss v Benetton International* [1999] ECR I-3055, [2000] 5 CMLR
816, and para 14.167, below.

statutory debt.[306] In *Ciments et Betons*,[307] the Court of Justice confirmed the effect of previous case law holding that Article 81(2) applies only to those individual elements of the agreement which fall within the prohibition of Article 81(1). Any contractual provisions which are not affected by the prohibition fall outside Community law and are enforceable provided that those elements are severable from the agreement as a whole. The consequences of the nullity of the relevant contractual provisions are determined by national law, including its principles of severance.[308] A defence based on Article 81(3) must be established not only on the law but on the evidence, and may raise difficult factual issues. In several cases before the English courts, the party relying upon Article 81 or 82 has failed to satisfy the court, on the evidence adduced, of the requisite facts.[309]

14.099 **Effect of nullity in general.** Two particular issues arise from the nullity provided for in Article 81(1); first, its temporal application and secondly, the extent to which the whole or part of a contract is affected by the nullity.

(i) The temporal effect of nullity

14.100 **Temporal effect of nullity.** The question arises as to whether the nullity provided for in Article 81(2) renders an agreement or a provision in an agreement void and unenforceable for all time or whether it applies only for so long as the

---

[306] eg in the English courts, *Potato Marketing Board v Robertsons* [1983] 1 CMLR 93 (County Court); *Potato Marketing Board v Drysdale* [1986] 3 CMLR 331 (Court of Appeal); *Potato Marketing Board v Hampden-Smith* [1997] EuLR 435 (CA); *Yorkshire Water Services Ltd v Jarmain & Sons* [1997] EuLR 577 (QBD) (Art 82).

[307] Case 319/82 *Soc de Vente de Ciments et Betons v Kerpen & Kerpen* [1983] ECR 4173, [1985] 1 CMLR 511, paras 11, 12. The ECJ referred to the earlier case Case 56/65 *Société Technique Minière* [1966] ECR 235, 250, [1966] CMLR 357, 376; see also Cases 56 & 58/64 *Consten and Grundig v Commission* [1966] ECR 299, [1966] CMLR 418.

[308] *Ciments et Betons v Kerpen & Kerpen* (n 307, above) paras 11, 12.

[309] See, eg *Potato Marketing Board v Robertsons* (n 306, above) (the court rejected the evidence of a professor of economics on the existence of a dominant position); *Potato Marketing Board v Hampden-Smith* (n 306, above) (no effect on trade between Member States); *Panayiotou v Sony Music Entertainment (UK) Ltd* [1994] EMLR 229, [1994] ECC 395 (ChD); *Heathrow Airport Ltd v Forte (UK) Ltd* (n 302, above) (no arguable case on abuse or effect on trade). Particularly difficult issues arise if the national court is required to consider the cumulative effect of a network of agreements under Art 81: see *Delimitis* (n 299, above), in which the ECJ clearly contemplates the possibility of nullity in such circumstances, and subsequent English cases relating to brewery ties, eg *Cutsforth v Mansfield Inns* [1986] 1 CMLR 1, [1986] 1 All ER 577 (QBD); *Harrison v Matthew Brown plc* [1998] EuLR 493; *Gibbs Mew plc v Gemmell* [1998] EuLR 588; *Inntrepreneur Pub Co (CPC) Ltd v Price* [1998] All ER (D) 598 (where Neuberger J cited *Delimitis* and emphasised the need to produce evidence of anti-competitive effect). However in *Byrne v Inntrepreneur Beer Supply Co Ltd* [1999] EuLR 834, [1999] UKCLR 110, the CA held (paras 134–142) that whether a clause constituted an additional restriction of competition within Art 7(1) of the then block exemption, Reg 1984/83, was in the first place a question of construction of the clause and did not depend upon evidence of its actual effect. See also *Masterfoods Ltd v H B Ice Cream Limited* [1992] 3 CMLR 830, [1993] ILRM 145, where the Irish High Court, after hearing six expert witnesses on economic issues in a trial lasting over three weeks, rejected the claims based on Arts 81 and 82.

agreement itself is prohibited under Article 81(1). The issue of temporal effect was addressed by the English Court of Appeal in *Passmore v Morland*.[310] The claimant, a pub tenant, had entered into a 20-year tied house lease of a public house with Inntrepreneur, which subsequently transferred its interest as landlord to the defendant, a small regional brewer. The foreclosure effect of the exclusive purchasing obligation (the beer tie) depended on the size of the landlord's tied estate. The defendant contended that the assignment removed the anti-competitive effect so that the nullity under Article 81(2) only applied to the lease between the claimant and Inntrepreneur. Chadwick LJ referred to *Brasserie de Haecht (No. 1)*[311] and *Delimitis*,[312] and held that Article 81(1) only prohibits agreements which have a particular offensive economic objective or effect and that in order to determine whether an agreement was prohibited it is necessary to assess all the relevant economic facts 'at the time or times in respect of which the question fell to be decided'. He concluded:

> 'It follows that an agreement which is not within Article [81(1)] at the time when it is entered into—because in the circumstances prevailing in the relevant market at that time, it does not have the effect of preventing, restricting or distorting competition—may, subsequently, and as the result of a change in those circumstances, come within Article [81(1)]—because, in the changed circumstances, it does have that effect. . . .
>
> It must follow, also, by parity of reasoning, that an agreement which is within the prohibition in Article [81(1)] at the time when it is entered into—because, in the circumstances prevailing in the relevant market at that time, it does have the effect of preventing, restricting or distorting competition—may, subsequently and as the result of a change in those circumstances, fall outside the prohibition contained in that Article—because, in the changed circumstances, it no longer has that effect.'

Chadwick LJ concluded, referring to *Société Technique Minière* and *Ciment et Betons*[313] that as the prohibition in Article 81(1) is transient rather than absolute, the agreement could not be void for all time.[314] The consequence of this ruling is that the enforceability of an agreement (or a particular provision) may vary according to changes in external market circumstances which may be beyond the control or even knowledge of a party. The approach in *Passmore v Morland* applies equally to the question whether an agreement satisfies the conditions of Article 81(3). It is notable, for example, that Regulation 2790/99,[315] the block exemption for

---

[310] *Passmore v Morland plc* [1999] 3 All ER 1005, [1999] 1 CMLR 1129, [1999] EuLR 501 (at first instance, [1998] 4 All ER 468).

[311] Case 23/67 *Brasserie de Haecht v Wilkin* [1967] ECR 407, [1968] CMLR 26.

[312] *Delimitis* (n 299, above).

[313] *Ciments et Bétons* (n 307, above) paras 10–12.

[314] See, eg the application of this principle to another 'pub tie' agreement by the English High Court in *Barrett v Inntrepreneur Pub Co Ltd* [2000] ECC 106.

[315] Reg 2790/99, OJ 1999 L336/21: Vol II, App C.3, Arts 3 and 9. Similar provisions apply in other block exemption regulations.

vertical agreements, provides that if the 30 per cent market share ceiling in the block exemption comes to be exceeded during the lifetime of an agreement, the agreement will continue to benefit from the block exemption for only a limited transitional period. Conversely, it seems clear that an agreement could gain the benefit of the block exemption only at the point when the relevant party's market share falls below the ceiling some years after the agreement took effect. More generally, the Commission's Article 81(3) Notice[316] states that the assessment of restrictive agreements under Article 81(3) must be made within the actual context in which they occur and on the basis of the facts existing at any given point in time. Accordingly, it appears that, as a matter of Community law, the assessment of the prohibition is sensitive to material changes in fact. However, the temporal extent of the nullity of an agreement whose very *object* is to restrict competition may be different.[317]

(ii) Severance

14.101   **Extent of nullity in English law.**   A doctrine of severance exists in English law,[318] the general rule being that:

> 'where you cannot sever the illegal from the legal part of the contract the contract is altogether void; but where you can sever them, whether the illegality be created by statute or by the common law, you may reject the bad part and retain the good.'[319]

Severance in domestic law concerns the ability not only to salvage the rest of an agreement by excising the illegal restrictive covenant but also to salvage a legal restrictive covenant by excising the words which extend the ambit of the restraint too far. The latter process has been described as the 'blue pencil' rule: if one is left with a reasonable covenant after striking through the offending words with a blue

---

[316] Commission Notice Guidelines on the application of Art 81(3) of the Treaty, OJ 2004 C101/8: Vol II, App C.18, para 44.

[317] See per Laddie J in *Passmore v Morland* at first instance (n 310, above) at 473. *Delimitis* (n 299, above) paras 13–14, upon which the analysis of Laddie J and Chadwick LJ was based, was concerned only with agreements whose *effect* (rather than object) was restrictive of competition.

[318] See, eg Beale (ed), *Chitty on Contracts* (29th edn, 2004), Vol. 1, paras 16-188 *et seq*; Peel (ed), *Treitel on the Law of Contract* (12th edn, 2007) paras 11-151 *et seq*, making the distinction, not always clear in decided cases, between enforcement of a valid promise where part of the consideration for that promise is illegal (severance of consideration) and enforcement of a valid promise where the promisor has made other promises which are illegal (severance of promises).

[319] *Pickering v Ilfracombe Ry* (1868) LR 3 CP 235, 250. On severance generally, see also *Amoco Australia v Rocca Bros* [1975] AC 561 (PC) (whether what was unenforceable was part of the main purpose and substance, or whether the deletion altered entirely the scope and intention of the agreement or, on the contrary, left the rest of the agreement a reasonable arrangement between the parties); *Alec Lobb Ltd v Total Oil* [1985] 1 All ER 303 (CA); *Marshall v NM Financial Management Ltd* [1995] 1 WLR 1461, [1997] 1 WLR 1527, [1997] ICR 1065 (CA) (whether the agreement was in substance an agreement for an invalid restraint). See the discussion of the various tests for severance in *Crehan v Courage Ltd, Byrne v Inntrepreneur Beer Supply Co Ltd* [1999] UKCLR 110, [1999] EuLR 834 (CA), paras 157–159.

pencil, severance is possible.[320] However, the 'blue pencil' test is a necessary, but not sufficient, condition for severance. The courts will not make a new contract for the parties, and will not sever if to do so would 'alter entirely the scope and intention of the agreement'[321] or if the invalid promise was 'the whole or substantially the whole consideration for the promise' sought to be enforced[322] or if severance would be contrary to public policy.[323]

Chemidus Wavin v TERI.   The first important English case on the effect of a   **14.102** breach of Article 81(1) is *Chemidus Wavin v TERI*[324] in which a licensor claimed sums due under a minimum royalties provision contained in a patent licence agreement between a British licensor and a French licensee. Both Walton J at first instance and the Court of Appeal treated the clause sued upon as valid, although many other provisions of the agreement were arguably contrary to Article 81(1). In upholding Walton J in the Court of Appeal, Buckley LJ said:

> 'Whether it is right to regard the matter as one of severance of the contract or not, I do not think it is necessary for us to consider now. I doubt whether it is really a question of severance in the sense in which we in these courts are accustomed to use that term in considering whether covenants contained in contracts of employment and so forth are void as being in restraint of trade, and, if they are to any extent void, whether those covenants can be severed so as to save part of the covenant, although another part may be bad. It seems to me that, in applying Article [81] to an English contract, one may well have to consider whether, after the excisions required by the Article of the Treaty have been made from the contract, the contract could be said to fail for lack of consideration or on any other ground, or whether the contract would be so changed in its character as not to be the sort of contract that the parties intended to enter into at all.'[325]

Changing the nature of the contract.   In a number of subsequent cases the   **14.103** English courts have applied the test laid down in *Chemidus Wavin*. In some cases, where the party relying upon Article 81(1) has sought to escape other obligations in the agreement, the courts have been ready to find that the covenant which is prohibited under Article 81(1) can be severed, leaving the remaining covenants of

---

321 *Attwood v Lamont* [1920] 3 KB 571, 580 (CA); see also *Days Medical Aids Ltd v Phisiang* [2004] EWHC 44 (QBD), [2004] 1 All ER (Comm) 991, para 228.
322 *Bennett v Bennett* [1952] 1 KB 249 (CA). It is not clear whether this is an additional or an alternative requirement for severance: see *Marshall* (n 319, above), where although stated as an additional requirement, it appears to have been the principal test applied.
323 See *Chitty* (n 318, above) para 16-196; and *Marshall* (n 319, above).
324 *Chemidus Wavin v TERI* [1978] 3 CMLR 614 (CA), on appeal from [1976] 2 CMLR 387, [1977] FSR 19 (ChD). The decision was followed as stating a general test for severance in English law in *Alec Lobb Ltd v Total Oil* (n 319, above), and in *Marshall*, ibid, at first instance. See also AG Warner in Case 22/79 *Greenwich Film Production v SACEM* [1979] ECR 3275, 3296, [1980] 1 CMLR 629, 640.
325 *Chemidus Wavin*, above, paras 519–520 (CMLR), 186–187 (FSR). See also per Goff LJ [1978] 3 CMLR at 523, [1977] FSR at 189.

the same party valid and enforceable. For example, in the brewery tied house cases, the courts have held that the invalidity of the tie is not sufficient to render the lease a sufficiently different transaction, with the result that the landlord remains entitled to enforce the tenant's obligation to pay rent.[326] In other cases, where the party relying upon Article 81(1) has sought to contend that the remaining obligations in the agreement are valid, the courts have found that the deletion of the clauses which fall within Article 81(1) would be such as fundamentally to change the nature of the contract. Such a case was *Richard Cound Ltd v BMW (GB) Ltd*,[327] where the plaintiff motor dealer contended that BMW's standard distribution agreement infringed Article 81(1) and was not covered by the then motor vehicle block exemption, Regulation 123/85, but went on to argue that the remaining parts of the agreement remained valid and enforceable. Balcombe LJ approved the following statement in the judgment at first instance:

> 'the effect of the excision of so many clauses in the agreement is to make the agreement of a completely different character. Instead of being a dealership agreement under which [BMW GB] supplied BMW cars and BMW spare parts to [Cound], and [Cound] undertook to resell those cars and those spare parts to the public within a public area and to provide servicing facilities for BMW cars for anyone owning such a car, whether or not bought from [Cound], the agreement would become an agreement, the essence of which would be that [BMW GB] would be obliged to sell BMW cars and parts to [Cound] and [Cound] would be obliged to pay for them. That is an agreement so different that, in my judgment, it is apt to regard the effect of severance as 'altering entirely the scope and intention of the agreement' or as removing the heart and soul of the agreement.'[328]

---

[326] *Inntrepreneur Estates Ltd v Mason* [1993] 2 CMLR 293 (QBD); *Inntrepreneur Estates (GL) Ltd v Boyes* (1994) 68 P & CR 77, [1993] 2 EGLR 112 (CA); *Star Rider Ltd v Inntrepreneur Pub Co* [1998] 1 EGLR 53 (ChD). But every case depends on the particular contract and terms at issue: see the Court of Appeal in *Byrne v Inntrepreneur Beer Supply* (n 326, above) paras 161–168, applying the test of substantial consideration in the context of Art 81 by considering whether compliance with the invalid exclusive purchasing obligation agreement 'constituted the "substance" or "substantially" the whole, of the consideration' for the grant of the option to renew a lease. Whilst recognising that the tenant provided other consideration for the option, the Court concluded that due performance of the purchasing obligations 'must be viewed as at least one integral aspect of the substance of the consideration, without which [the option] would amount to something quite different'. It was therefore held that if the exclusive purchasing obligation was invalid then so was the option to renew the lease.

[327] *Richard Cound Ltd v BMW (GB) Ltd* [1997] EuLR 277 (QBD and CA). See also, eg *Clover Leaf Cars Ltd v BMW (GB) Ltd* [1997] EuLR 535 (ChD and CA); *First County Garages Ltd v Fiat Auto (UK) Ltd* [1997] EuLR 712 (ChD); *Parkes v Esso Petroleum Co Ltd* [1999] 1 CMLR 455, [1998] EuLR 550 (ChD); and *Frazer (Willow Lane) Limited v Nissan* [2003] EWHC 3157, [2004] EuLR 445, paras 51–52; *English Welsh & Scottish Railway Ltd v E.ON Ltd* (n 300, above).

[328] *Richard Cound*, above, at 309G–310B. A similar approach was followed in *Intel Corp v VIA Technologies Inc* [2002] EWHC 1159 (Ch D), [2003] FSR 12, [2002] EuLR 502, [2002] UKCLR 576, paras 147–149, where the High Court refused to sever an allegedly illegal limitation as to use contained in a patent license agreement as the effect of its removal would be that Via obtained an unlimited licence to use the patents for all Intel microprocessors, including the new Pentium 4. Lawrence Collins J held that removal of the restriction would make the contract one into which

Express contractual severance clauses.   Where a contract contains an express **14.104**
severance clause, the question whether this is effective to save the remaining provisions of an agreement depends upon construction of the clause and the contract
as a whole. However, unless very clear words are used, such a clause will not
displace common law principles of severance and will not be effective where the
effect of deleting the void provisions is to alter entirely the scope and intention
of the agreement.[329] Difficult questions also arise as to extent to which the prohibition in Article 81(1) applies to other particular clauses related to the principal
prohibited clause and how far the invalidity of the latter affects the validity of
the former.[330]

Non-compliance with conditions for block exemption.   An agreement may **14.105**
contain a number of restrictions within Article 81(1), some of which are allowed
under the terms of a block exemption regulation but others of which are expressly
not permitted. The block exemption may itself make clear whether the effect of
the inclusion of a clause which is not permitted is to deprive the whole agreement
of the benefit of the block exemption or simply to require individual assessment
of those clauses but allowing the rest of the agreement still to fall within the exemption. For example Regulation 772/2004 on technology transfer agreements[331]
contains a list of 'hard-core restrictions' which, if included in a licence will take
the whole agreement outside the scope of the Regulation but contains a different
list of 'excluded restrictions' the inclusion of which does not affect the validity of
the rest of the agreement. Generally, however, it is not possible to sever restrictions
not expressly covered by the block exemption so as to allow the remainder of
the agreement to benefit from block exemption. Insofar as other obligations fall
within Article 81(1) they, together with the restriction going beyond what is
allowed by the block exemption, will be void under Article 81(2), unless the block
exemption regulation contains express provision to the contrary. In *Delimitis*,[332]

---

the parties had not intended to enter, and that its deletion would alter entirely its scope and intention, and disappoint one of its main purposes; (appeal on other grounds allowed, [2002] EWCA
(Civ)1905, [2003] FSR 33, [2003] UKCLR 106, [2003] EuLR 85).

[329] *Richard Cound* (n 327, above), *per* Balcombe LJ at 310; *English Welsh & Scottish Railway Ltd*
(n 300, above) para 29. cf *Inntrepreneur v Boyes* (n 326, above).

[330] See, eg differing conclusions reached on the same provisions in *Inntrepreneur v Mason* (n 324,
above) and *Inntrepreneur v Price* (n 309, above) (supported by *Inntrepreneur v Boyes*, n 326, above).
An individual sale contract, entered into pursuant to an exclusive purchasing agreement falling
within Art 81(1), is not itself void or illegal: *Courage Ltd v Crehan (No. 1)* [1999] EuLR 834 (CA),
[1999] UKCLR 110, paras 60, 64. See also *Trent Taverns v Sykes* [1998] EuLR 571 (QBD); and
Matthew Brown plc v Campbell [1998] EuLR 530, 538A–B (QBD).

[331] See Arts 4 and 5 of Reg 772/2004, OJ 2004 L123/11: Vol II, App C.7 discussed in Chap 9,
above; and to the same effect Arts 4 and 5 of the vertical restraints block exemption Reg 2790/1999,
OJ 1999 L336/21, Vol II, App C.3.

[332] See C-234/89 *Delimitis v Henninger Brau* [1991] ECR I-935, [1992] 5 CMLR 210,
paras 38–42. See also *Cabour and Nord Distribution Automobiles v Arnor* (n 299, above) paras 47–48
and per AG Tesauro, para 42. cf Case C-39/92 *Petrogal* [1993] ECR I-5659.

the Court of Justice held that if certain conditions specified in a block exemption are not met, the block exemption 'ceases to be applicable in its entirety'. It added, however, that the fact that the agreement did not satisfy the conditions for block exemption does not necessarily mean that the whole of the contract is void under Article 81(2) but that only those aspects of the agreement which are prohibited by Article 81(1) are void. Whether the remainder of the agreement is void is a question of severability. In answer to a further question, the Court also held[333] that 'the national courts may not extend the scope of [a block exemption regulation] to . . . agreements which do not explicitly meet the conditions for exemption laid down in that regulation'. In *Byrne v Inntrepreneur*, the Court of Appeal applied this approach in considering a pub tie, holding that the presence of clauses not covered by the block exemption simply means that the conditions for the block exemption are not satisfied and that there is no basis for examining first any clauses which took the agreement out of the block exemption with a view to severing such clauses and then going back to reconsider the block exemption:

> 'European authority . . . demonstrates clearly that compliance with the block exemption is a matter which must be assessed looking at the particular agreement as a whole, and that (unless, perhaps, there is specific contractual provision for severance in such circumstances), once an agreement is found to contain any restriction beyond those provided, the block exemption ceases to apply and the focus reverts to Article [81(1)].'[334]

14.106 **Severance under English law: a summary.** As a result of *Chemidus Wavin* and subsequent cases, where a particular clause falls within the prohibition of Article 81(1), the English courts will be prepared to enforce other provisions in an agreement so long as the provisions that are void did not constitute the substantial consideration for those that are sought to be enforced or the effect of deletion of the offending clause or clauses is not to alter entirely the scope and intention of the agreement. Therefore, each case will turn on its own facts and requires assessment of the point at which a 'severed' agreement becomes so different from the original agreement that the court will decline to enforce it.[335]

---

[333] *Delimitis*, above, paras 46, 55.

[334] *Crehan v Courage Ltd, Byrne v Inntrepreneur Beer Supply Co Ltd* [1999] EuLR 834, [1999] UKCLR 110, para 154. Other cases before the English courts have been argued and decided on the assumption that the loss of the protection of the block exemption renders void the restrictions which would otherwise fall within the block exemption: *Richard Cound* (n 327, above); *Clover Leaf Cars Ltd v BMW (GB) Ltd* (n 327, above) at 546–547; *First County Garages v Fiat Auto (UK) Ltd*, ibid, at 716–717, 719.

[335] eg if a dealer-supply agreement prohibits the dealer from reselling the goods 'inside or outside the EC' the blue pencil rule would presumably enable one to salvage the restriction on exporting outside the EC to be salvaged by deleting the words 'inside or'. A restriction on exporting outside the Community does not usually fall within Art 81(1). Conversely, if the covenant merely prohibited 'exports to other dealers', possibly the blue pencil rule could not apply and the whole clause would be void, irrespective of whether the breach consisted of exporting inside or outside the Community.

Severance: other Member States. In Germany, the Court of Appeal of **14.107** Düsseldorf held that the possible invalidity of a minimum purchase obligation in a contract for reprocessed glass did not affect the validity of the contract as a whole. The glass processor was therefore entitled to recover payment for services provided since the payment obligation could be severed from the purchase obligation.[336] By contrast, a judgment of the Court of Appeal of Celle[337] held that the whole of an agreement under which two producers of construction vehicles agreed to limit their product range to complementary products which would be distributed under the same trade mark was unenforceable. The provisions in the agreement regarding the use of the trade mark were void because their sole purpose was to distribute the complementary products under the same brand: the parties' single-brand-strategy only made sense as long as competition was eliminated between them. In Sweden, in a case where the payment obligations on an airline for use of an airport were found to be discriminatory and abusive, the court struck down only the offending terms and upheld the remainder of the contract.[338] Indeed, Swedish law, like that of other Scandinavian countries, permits the court to adjust the remaining provisions of a contract if one of the terms is unenforceable.[339]

(b) Action for damages

Private enforcement: developments at Community level. The Commission **14.108** is actively seeking to encourage private enforcement of Articles 81 and 82 by damages claims in the national courts, including collective claims and consumer claims. Although public and private enforcement serve the same aims, namely deterring anti-competitive behaviour and protecting consumers and competitors from harm, private damages actions provide a direct and immediate remedy for those whose interests have been adversely affected in the past. Furthermore, the Commission has noted that direct engagment contributes to the observance of the competition rules because this 'first hand experience increases the relevance of the competition rules for firms and consumers'.[340]

The Ashurst Report and the Green Paper. Despite the benefits which can be **14.109** obtained by private enforcement, there have been few judgments on claims for damages for the infringement of EC and national competition law in the majority

---

For doubts as to the appropriateness of applying the 'blue pencil' test to Art 81, see *Chemidus Wavin* (n 324, above), *per* Walton J, [1976] 2 CMLR 389, 391, [1977] FSR 19, 21.

[336] Case VI-U(Kart)39/03, Oberlandesgericht Düsseldorf, judgment of 16 March 2005 (published at: www.justiz.nrw.de/RB/nrwe/index.html).
[337] Case 13 U 227/02, Oberlandesgericht Celle, judgment of 6 June 2003.
[338] *Luftfartsverket v Scandinavian Airlines System* (n 300, above).
[339] Swedish Contracts Act 1915:218, s 36.
[340] *Report on Annual Competition Policy 2005*, point 31.

of Member States. In 2004, the Commission published the Ashurst Study[341] which provides a comparative analysis of the procedural rules and case law in each of the then 25 Member States. The Study concluded that the prospect of private enforcement in the enlarged Union was subject to 'astonishing diversity and total underdevelopment'.[342] At the time of writing, the Commission is reviewing the conditions under which private parties can bring actions for damages before the national courts of the Member States with a view to facilitating more effective remedies. To this end, in December 2005 the Commission published a Green Paper[343] with an annexed Staff Working Paper on damages actions. The Study and the Green Paper highlight various factors which could account for the lack of progress. For example, claimants bear the burden of proof and face a high evidential standard in some Member States in circumstances where they have limited access to documents and restricted opportunities to demand disclosure from the defendant. In many Member States, claimants have to establish fault in addition to establishing proof of the infringement. The quantification of damages is a 'key difficulty' which deters claimants from bringing actions and the lack of any generalised model for quantifying loss, uncertainty as to possible defences together with restrictions as to the amount that can be recovered all act as disincentives. The combination of these elements with the likelihood that the high costs incurred will not be recoverable led the Commission staff to conclude that '[t]he risk/reward balance in antitrust litigation is skewed against bringing actions'.[344] Inevitably, the conditions governing private enforcement vary widely as between Member States, but the Commission is likely to produce a White Paper in early 2008 with proposals to remove some of the disincentives to the bringing of damages claims.

14.110 **Cause of action as a matter of Community law.** The Court of Justice has consistently stated that the consequences of the nullity of the contract, or certain terms in it, are governed by national law and not Community law. However, national courts are under a duty under Article 10 of the Treaty to ensure the

---

[341] *Study on the conditions of claims for damages in case of infringement of the EC Competition rules* (31 August 2004) ('the Ashurst Study') available on the DG Comp website.

[342] The Ashurst Study reported that as at December 2004, there had been a total of 60 adjudicated claims for damages and 28 successful awards in the whole of the Union: see Introduction. However, since many claims result in settlements and never reach the stage of a judgment, the Ashurst Study significantly understates the extent of private enforcement activity.

[343] Damages actions for breach of the EC antitrust rules, 19 December 2005, COM (2005) 672 final. Over 140 responses were submitted during the following consultation process.

[344] Commission Staff Working Paper SEC(2005) 1732, para 45. The Commission contrasts, at paras 46–47, the situation in Europe with the US system which offers strong financial incentives to claimants, including the availability of treble damages, adapted rules on costs and class action procedural rules. However the Commission is keen not to promote vexatious litigation and to achieve some form of moderation in the enforcement system by removing legal uncertainty and introducing Community measures to improve conditions for bringing claims.

effectiveness of the prohibitions in Articles 81(1) and 82 and to provide adequate protection for those that have suffered loss.[345] In *Courage v Crehan*,[346] the Court of Justice clarified that Member States were required, as a matter of Community law, to allow claims for compensation for breaches of Articles 81(1) and 82 as well as enforcing the illegality of the infringing conduct. In that case the Court was asked whether a party to a contract which was held to infringe Article 81 could be barred by a rule of domestic law from seeking damages arising out of that unlawful agreement. The Court recalled that the national courts whose task it is to apply the provisions of Community law in areas within their jurisdiction must ensure that those rules take full effect and must protect the rights which they confer on individuals. The Court went on to say:

> 'The full effectiveness of Article [81] of the Treaty and, in particular, the practical effect of the prohibition laid down in Article [81(1)] would be put at risk if it were not open to any individual to claim damages for loss caused to him by a contract or by conduct liable to restrict or distort competition. Indeed, the existence of such a right strengthens the working of the Community competition rules and discourages agreements or practices, which are frequently covert, which are liable to restrict or distort competition. From that point of view, actions for damages before the national courts can make a significant contribution to the maintenance of effective competition in the Community. There should not therefore be any absolute bar to such an action being brought by a party to a contract which would be held to violate the competition rules.'

Accordingly, a right to claim for damages for breach of Article 81(1) is available as a matter of Community law and the Court considers that such claims serve a Community interest. The same reasoning applies to Article 82.[347]

Who can sue?   There is a wide range of persons who may suffer damages from an infringement of Article 81 or 82. Whether there is a limit to the class of persons who can recover and, if so, where the line is to be drawn, raise difficult questions.[348] In particular, it is not clear whether the question of who can recover is to be determined by Community law or by national law.[349] The Court of Justice has

14.111

---

[345] See para 14.095 and nn 289, 291, above

[346] Case 453/99 *Courage v Crehan* [2001] ECR I-6297, [2001] 5 CMLR 1058, [2001] All ER (EC) 886, paras 26–31.

[347] See in the UK, the judgment of the House of Lords in *Garden Cottage Foods v Milk Marketing Board* [1984] AC 130, [1983] 3 CMLR 43, [1983] 2 All ER 770, holding that a breach of Art 82 inevitably gave rise to a right to claim damages for loss caused by the contravention. The cause of action as a matter of English law was categorised as a breach of statutory duty. See comments at (1993) 8 ELRev 353, (1984) 100 LQR 189.

[348] See in particular C Jones, *Private Enforcement of Antitrust Law* (1999), Chap 16; Whish, 'The Enforcement of EC Competition Law in the Domestic Courts of Member States' (1994) ECLR 60.

[349] The class of persons who may sue can be characterised as one of the 'conditions' for liability: see Cases C-46 & 48/93 *Brasserie du Pêcheur and Factortame ('Factortame III')* [1996] ECR 1029, [1996] 1 CMLR 889, [1996] All ER (EC) 301, paras 37–74; and Case C-128/92 *Banks* [1994]

confimed in *Manfredi* that the principle of invalidity can be relied on by *anyone*, without having to show a relevant legal interest in relying on the invalidity of an agreement or practice.[350] In that case, private individuals sought repayment of the increased car insurance premiums that they had paid under their compulsory civil liability contracts, which reflected an unlawful information exchange between the insurance companies concerned. The Court of Justice based their entitlement to damages not just on the direct effect of Article 81(1) but also on the absolute nature of the invalidity, as follows:

> 'Since the invalidity referred to in Article 81(2) EC is absolute, an agreement which is null and void by virtue of this provision has no effect as between the contracting parties and cannot be invoked against third parties . . . Moreover it is capable of having a bearing on all the effects, either past or future, of the agreement or decision concerned . . .'

In various cases, subject to rules on remoteness, claimants could, in theory, include actual and potential purchasers, whether direct or indirect, actual or potential suppliers, competitors, shareholders and the undertakings who are party to the unlawful agreements themselves. However, questions such as who can sue, who can be sued, and issues of remoteness can causation, are all interrelated. Although the rulings of the Court of Justice in *Courage v Crehan* and *Manfredi* evidently preclude the application of at least some conditions previously imposed in some jurisdictions as qualifying the right to bring a damages claim, the extent to which Community law overrides rules of national law in this field has still to be determined as private enforcement develops.

14.112 **Qualifying interest.** In the *Crehan* litigation that followed the Court of Justice's ruling, the English Court of Appeal considered the requirements for a claim for damages for breach of Article 81.[351] Although the cause of action was classified as the tort of breach of statutory duty under English law, the court held that some of the constraints usually applicable for such a claim (including notably that the duty

---

ECR I-1209, [1994] 5 CMLR 30, *per* AG van Gerven at paras 49–54. But it could also be characterised as a rule relating to the extent of damage recoverable and thus governed by national law: *Brasserie du Pêcheur*, paras 81–90. As a matter of English law, the relevant rules may depend upon the characterisation of the cause of action, eg breach of statutory duty, economic tort or *sui generis*: see now *R. v Secretary of State, ex p Factortame (No. 6)* [2001] 1 CMLR 1191 (QBD). However such characterisation will not be permitted to undermine the paramount principle of effectiveness: see para 14.095, above.

350 Cases C-295/04, etc, *Manfredi v Lloyd Adriatico Assicurazioni* [2006] ECR I-6619, [2006] 5 CMLR 980, [2007] All ER (EC) 27, paras 56–59. This would appear to preclude conditions imposed in some jurisdictions, such as a 'personal, existing real and legitimate interest' (France) and an 'acquired, personal, direct, legal and immediate interest' (Belgium).

351 *Crehan v Inntrepreneur Pub Co CMC* [2004] EWCA Civ 637, [2004] UKCLR 1500, [2004] EuLR 693, paras 162–167. The decision was reversed on other grounds by the House of Lords (n 233 above).

owed to the claimant was in respect of the kind of loss he has suffered[352]) do not apply to competition law claims since they would render it impossible to succeed in any claim. Accordingly, the defendant could not rely on the fact that the loss suffered was at the retail level when the distortion of competition arose at the distribution level of the supply chain so as to defeat the claim on the basis that the kind of damage suffered did not fall within the scope of the duty. In Italy, the Corte di Cassazione held that an insurance company that participated in an upstream cartel, which the NCA had found fixed premiums for motor insurance, could be sued for damages by a consumer whose individual insurance charged him a higher premium as a result in implementation of the cartel agreement.[353] The Court thereby departed from its earlier ruling that competition law was for the direct benefit of competitors and that as consumers were only the indirect beneficiaries they could not bring a claim for damages founded directly on competition law. In Germany, the 7th Amendment to the Act against Restraints of Competition has removed the requirement that only those whom the provision 'serves to protect' are entitled to claim damages, which had been interpreted restrictively by some courts. Moreover, a German court has held admissible a follow-on claim for damages resulting from a cement cartel brought by Cartel Damages Claims NV, a Belgian company that took assignments of the causes of action from 29 commercial customers who had purchased cement.[354]

Indirect purchasers.   The question of indirect purchaser standing is inherently   **14.113** linked to the passing-on defence.[355] The Court of Justice's ruling in *Manfredi*[356] would suggest that, in line with the effectiveness of Community law, both direct and indirect purchasers have the right to bring a claim.[357] However, the Court went on to state that in the absence of Community rules governing the matter, it is for the domestic legal system of each Member State to prescribe the detailed rules governing the exercise of that right, provided that the Community right was not dealt with less favourably than the equivalent domestic law right.[358] This appears to preserve domestic rules as to remoteness of damage.

---

[352] See *South Australia Asset Management Corporation v York Montague Ltd* [1997] AC 191 at 211, [1996] 3 All ER 365, *per* Lord Hoffmann.

[353] *Compagnia Assicuratrice Unipol spa v Ricciarelli*, Cass. civ. Sez. Unite (united sections), 4 February 2005, no. 2207.

[354] *Cement Cartel*, 34 O (Kart) 147/05, interim judgment of 21 February 2007 of the Regional Court of Düsseldorf. The case was decided on the basis of the old version of the Act Against Restraints of Competition (GWB).

[355] See para 14.124, below.

[356] *Manfredi* (n 350, above).

[357] Indirect purchaser claims are permitted in Germany (following the 7th Amendment) and Sweden.

[358] *Manfredi* (n 350, above) para 64.

14.114 **Co-contractor's right to claim damages.** The Court of Justice has confirmed in *Courage v Crehan*[359] that, in order to ensure the practical effect of the prohibitions, national procedural rules must make it possible for one party to an unlawful contract to claim damages for loss caused by the anti-competitive conduct. However, the Court of Justice stated that provided that the principles of equivalence and effectiveness are respected,[360] Community law does not preclude national law from denying a party who is found to bear 'significant responsibility' for the distortion of competition the right to obtain damages from the other contracting party. Where a party is partly responsible for the conduct or benefits from it, the extent of any damages may be apportioned to reflect their contribution or the need to prevent unjust enrichment.

14.115 **'Significant responsibility'.** The principle that a litigant should not profit from his own unlawful conduct was one which is recognised in most of the legal systems of the Member States. The matters to be taken into account include the economic and legal context in which the parties find themselves and the respective bargaining power and conduct of the two parties to the contract. As the Court of Justice observed in *Crehan*, the national court must ascertain whether the claimant 'found himself in a markedly weaker position than the other party, such as seriously to compromise or even eliminate his freedom to negotiate the terms of the contract and his capacity to avoid the loss or reduce its extent, in particular by availing himself in good time of all the legal remedies available to him'. For example, where a contract falls within Article 81(1) only because it is part of a network of similar contracts which have a cumulative effect on competition, the party contracting with the person controlling the network cannot bear significant responsibility for the breach of Article 81, particularly where in practice the terms of the contract were imposed on him by the party controlling the network. Before the High Court and the Court of Appeal, the defendant, Inntrepreneur, sought to argue that Mr Crehan shared responsibility for the infringement as he had entered into the leases voluntarily. The Court of Appeal dismissed the argument holding that there was no equality of bargaining power in any real sense as Mr Crehan was dealing with the single largest tied house landlord in the UK and the tying terms in their standard form agreement were not negotiable. Mr Crehan was in a markedly weaker position than Inntrepreneur: if he wanted to lease the pubs he had to agree to the tie.[361]

---

[359] *Courage v Crehan* (n 346, above) paras 26–31. Accordingly, the English High Court was required to disapply the common law rule precluding recovery by a party of money paid or goods transferred under an illegal contract: cf previous case law cited in *Gibbs Mew plc v Gemmell* [1998] EuLR 588 (Court of Appeal).

[360] Para 14.095, above.

[361] *Crehan v Inntrepreneur Pub Co CPC* (n 351, above) para 153.

Derivative claims.   In *O'Neill v Ryan*,[362] the Supreme Court of Ireland struck **14.116** out a claim by a shareholder contending that the value of his shareholding in Ryan Air had been reduced by alleged infringements of Articles 81 and 82 on the part of several defendants. The court held that since the damage was caused to the company, it was Ryan Air and not the plaintiff who could bring such a claim as a matter of Irish law; and Community law did not require the national court to create a new remedy which lay beyond those already provided under national law. A similar issue arose before the English court in *Intergraph Corpn v Solid Systems*[363] where shareholders and directors brought a counterclaim for loss of their investment in, and dividend income from, a company alleged to have been damaged by its competitor's infringements of Articles 81 and 82. There the judge, although strongly inclined to follow the Irish Supreme Court, refused to strike out the counterclaim as unarguable since he considered that the issue might ultimately be one of Community law to be resolved by the Court of Justice.[364] However, even where a shareholder or other person with a 'derivative' claim[365] falls within the class of permissible claimants, he should not be allowed to duplicate any recovery by the principal victim of the infringement of the competition rules.

Who can be sued: the *Provimi* case.   An international cartel will frequently be **14.117** concluded at the level of parent or group companies whereas the actual sales of the product involved are made in different countries by local subsidiaries. The resulting questions of liability confronted the English court in *Provimi*,[366] which concerned damages claims arising out of the Commission's decision condemning the global cartel in *Vitamins*.[367] The Swiss company, Hoffmann-La Roche AG ('HLR') and the French company, Aventis SA ('Aventis') were among the addressees of the decision fined by the Commission. A German company, Trouw Nutricia,

---

[362]   *O'Neill v Ryan* [1993] ILRM 557.

[363]   *Intergraph Corpn v Solid Systems CAD Ltd* [1998] EuLR 223 (ChD).

[364]   The argument for the exclusion of such claims is based on the principle of English tort law in *Prudential Assurance v Newman Industries Ltd (No. 2)* [1982] Ch 204 (ChD), [1982] 1 All ER 354, and whether the claim is to be characterised as only reflective of the company's loss: see *Johnson v Gore Wood & Co* [2002] 2 AC 1, [2001] 1 All ER 481; also *Giles v Rhind* [2002] EWCA Civ 1428, [2003] Ch 618, [2002] 4 All ER 977 (exceptionally shareholder may cliam where company unable to do so).

[365]   Similar considerations are likely to apply to others sustaining 'derivative' loss flowing from the direct loss sustained by a company, eg employees, directors, creditors, third party suppliers of goods and services. Note that in the *Factortame* litigation, those claiming damages include not only the owners of the vessels excluded from registration as British fishing boats, but also shareholders and directors of the owning companies and companies managing the vessels: see *Factortame III* (n 349, above) para 14. But save for the requirement of direct causal link between the breach and the damage sustained, the ECJ did not address recovery of losses sustained by these persons and the litigation was subsequently settled without the matter being decided.

[366]   *Provimi Ltd v Aventis Animal Nutrition SA* [2003] EWHC 961 QBD (Comm Ct), [2003] UKCLR 493, [2003] EuLR 517, [2003] 2 All ER (Comm) 683.

[367]   *Vitamins*, OJ 2003 L6/1, [2003] 4 CMLR 1030.

brought claims against HLR's English subsidiary ('Roche UK'), along with HLR's German subsidiary ('Roche Germany') and HLR itself. It brought a parallel action against Aventis' English subsidiary ('Rhodia') along with Aventis and another French subsidiary of Aventis that was a direct party to the cartel discussions. However, all the defendants in both actions sought to strike out Trouw Nutricia's claims on the basis that it had not bought vitamins from, respectively, Roche UK or Rhodia. If Trouw Nutricia's claims were bound to fail against those UK defendants, it could no longer assert jurisdiction in the English courts over the non-UK defendants since that jurisdiction was based on the co-defendants provision of Article 6(1) of the Lugano Convention and the Brussels I Regulation.[368] There was no suggestion that either of the English subsidiaries had knowledge of the cartel agreement entered into by their respective parents. However, applying the concept of an undertaking in Community law, the judge held that it was arguable that:

> 'where two corporate entities are part of an "undertaking" (call it "*Undertaking A*") and one of those entities has entered into an infringing agreement with other, independent, "undertakings", then if another corporate entity which is part of *Undertaking A* then implements that infringing agreement, it is also infringing Article 81.'[369]

For the purpose of Article 81, the legal entities that are part of one undertaking have no independence of will and are to be regarded all as one. This therefore led to the conclusion that where one legal entity in a group had infringed Article 81 by agreeing to fix prixes and another entity had implemented that agreement, the latter was also an infringer. But the court also had to consider whether Trouw Nutricia could claim that Roche UK and Rhodia caused its loss, since it had not bought vitamins from either company. As to that question, the judge held that it was arguable that since each infringing entity upheld the cartel prices by implementing the cartel, the English subsidiaries contributed to the situation whereby Trouw Nutricia could not buy at a lower price and their actions thus had sufficient causal link to the loss.[370] The attribution of liability in the first part of the judge's reasoning seems inherent in the scheme of Article 81, whereby both an offending agreement and its implementation are prohibited but fines can be imposed and damages awarded only against a legal entity. However, as regards the application of similar reasoning to causation, it should be emphasised that the court decided only that the point was *arguable*, and since the cases then settled the issue was never finally determined or tested on appeal.[371]

---

[368] For Art 6, see para 14.050, above.

[369] *Provimi* (n 366, above) para 31.

[370] ibid, paras 39–41. The judge also found that it was arguable that in the absence of the cartel Trouw Nutricia might have been able to buy vitamins at a lower price in the UK.

[371] Although the case is always referred to as *Provimi*, that was in fact a parallel set of claims by a different claimant against the same defendants that did not raise this issue but was covered in the same judgment.

Fault. In many Member States, damages claims, as tortious actions, require **14.118** proof of fault[372] whereas in others, fault is presumed from the illegality of the infringement[373] or there is a no-fault or strict liability regime.[374]

Causation. In *Manfredi*,[375] the Court of Justice held that any individual can **14.119** claim compensation for harm suffered provided there is a causal relationship between that harm and an agreement or practice prohibited under Article 81. However, it held that, subject to the principles of equivalence and effectiveness, the detailed rules governing the concept of 'causal relationship', were to be determined by national law. In *Crehan*, the English Court of Appeal held that the judge is entitled to make prudent assumptions when determining causation in a competition case on the balance of probabilities.[376] In the earlier case of *Arkin v Borchard Lines*, a damages claim alleging breaches of both Articles 81 and 82 by the members of a shipping conference, the High Court emphasised that the burden of proof of causation rests on the claimant and that he must establish that the defendant's conduct was the 'predominant cause' of the claimant's loss.[377] The chain of causation will only be broken if, applying a 'common-sense approach', the claimant's own conduct displaces that of the defendant. The court found that the predominant cause of the losses was the claimant's failure to withdraw from the market and its decision to cut its rates to unsustainably low levels. In Germany, the Federal Supreme Court dismissed an independent distributor's claim for refusal to supply by the members of a car manufacturer's selective distribution network because the claimant could not establish that it was the unlawful aspect of the manufacturer's arrangement which caused the refusal.[378] Although the manufacturer's arrangement for 'pricing discipline' by its German distributors was a prohibited practice under Regulation 1495/95, the then motor vehicle block exemption, the Court held that the system was deprived of the benefit of the block exemption only for the geographical market in which the practice distorted competition; and since the claimant had not solicited supplies in Germany but only in the Netherlands and Denmark where the selective system therefore continued to benefit from the block exemption, the claim was unfounded.

---

[372] As at 2004, such countries inlcuded Denmark, Greece, Spain, Poland, Portugal, Finland and Sweden: Ashurst Report (n 341, above).

[373] eg Belgium, Germany, France, Italy, the Netherlands, Hungary, Estonia and Austria: ibid.

[374] eg the United Kingdom, Ireland, Cyprus, the Czech Republic and the Slovak Republic: ibid.

[375] *Manfredi* (n 350, above) paras 61–64.

[376] *Crehan v Inntrepreneur Pub Co CMC* (n 351, above) paras 169–171.

[377] *Arkin v Borchard Lines Ltd* [2003] EWHC 687 (Comm), [2003] 2 Lloyd's Rep 225, para 536.

[378] *Wegfall der Freistellung*, judgment of the Bundesgerichtshof of 30 March 2004, WuW/E DE-R 1263: see para 6.124, above.

14.120 **Extent of damages recoverable.** In *Manfredi*,[379] the Court of Justice also addressed the measure of damages. After confirming the principle of procedural autonomy, the Court considered whether the extent of the damages recoverable was confined to actual loss or extended to consequential loss. The Court ruled:

> '. . . it follows from the principle of effectiveness and the right of any individual to seek compensation for loss caused by a contract or by conduct liable to restrict or distort competition that injured persons must be able to seek compensation not only for actual loss (*damnum emergens*) but also for loss of profit (*lucrum cessans*) plus interest.[380]

> Total exclusion of loss of profit as a head of damage for which compensation may be awarded cannot be accepted in the case of a breach of Community law since, especially in the context of economic or commercial litigation, such a total exclusion of loss of profit would be such as to make reparation of damage practically impossible . . .'

14.121 **Damages cases.** The problem of proof and quantification of damage resulting from infringements has proved a significant disincentive to the bringing of damages claims. The position inevitably varies as between Member States according to the rules of domestic law and procedure, but subject to the fundamental principles of Community law discussed above. In England, the Court of Appeal in *Crehan*[381] applied the standard tortious measure of damages, namely 'the sum of money which will put the party who has been injured, or has suffered, in the same position as he would have been in if he had not sustained the wrong'.[382] Reversing the trial judge, the Court held that the damages are to be assessed at the time of the loss, not at the time of the judgment. That equated to the dates on which Mr Crehan had to give up the business of the two pubs that were subject to the exclusive purchasing beer tie, and the damages were accordingly quantified as the value of the unexpired terms of the two leases had they been free of the tie (plus the lost profits to the dates the businesses ceased).[383] However, since the judgment on liability was reversed on further appeal to the House of Lords, Mr Crehan in the end recovered nothing.[384] *Crehan* was a 'stand-alone' action. Most of the successful damages claims to date have been in 'follow-on' cases after an infringement decision by the Commission or an NCA. In Spain, there have been a few

---

379 *Manfredi* (n 350, above) paras 95–100.

380 The Court referred to its previous ruling in Case C-271/91 *Marshall II* [1993] ECR I-4367, [1993] 3 CMLR 293, [1993] 4 All ER 586, para 31, as support for its conclusion than the payment of interest constitutes an essential component of compensation.

381 *Crehan v Inntrepreneur Pub Co CMC* (n 351, above) paras 179 *et seq*.

382 *Livingstone v Rawyards Coal Co* (1880) 5 App Cas, p 39 *per* Lord Blackburn.

383 The result was a substantial reduction to £131,336 from the damages quantified at first instance (£1,311,500).

384 For the same reason, Mr Crehan's cross-appeal against the quantification of damages was not determined.

judgments awarding damages for breach of Article 82 and/or the equivalent provision in Spanish competition law. For example, an abusive refusal of supply of an input product resulted in an award of damages including lost profits based on the number of clients and potential clients that the claimant proved it had lost.[385] In Germany, in a claim brought by a sweets and confectionery manufacturer arising from the vitamins cartel, the Dortmund District Court applied the principles of German procedural law that enable the judge to a certain degree to estimate the damage and held that the claimant's loss was to be measured by the difference between the prices during and after the ending of the cartel.[386] If courts generally adopted such assumptions, or at least presumptions that shift the burden to the defendant, as to what prices would have been at the relevant time in the absence of the infringement, this would undoubtedly simplify and facilitate a damages claim.

Exemplary damages. The majority of legal systems in the Community regard damages as compensatory in nature rather than punitive. However, in many competition law claims, the amount of loss suffered by the claimant will be considerably less than the economic advantage gained by the infringing party to the prohibited agreement or concerted practice. Punitive or exemplary damages augment the compensable amount and therefore increase deterrence. The question whether a national court should, of its own motion, award exemplary damages arose in *Manfredi*.[387] The Court of Justice reaffirmed the principle of procedural autonomy, stating that the availability of exemplary damages was a matter for the domestic legal system of each Member State provided that they did not result in the unjust enrichment of the claimant. However, where exemplary damages are available for similar actions founded on domestic law, the principle of equivalence will require that it is possible for such relief to be awarded in claims founded on the Community competition rules. As a matter of English law, a claimant may recover exemplary damages where the defendant has calculated that wrongful conduct will result in a profit that may well exceed the compensation

14.122

---

[385] Case 811/07 *lasist v 3M*, judgment of First Instance Judge no. 71 of Madrid of 1 June 2007. See also *Conduit Europe SA v Telefónica de España*, judgment of Commercial Court no. 5 of Madrid, 11 November 2005.

[386] *Vitaminpreise Dortmund*, Dortmund District Court judgment of 1 April 2004, WuW/E DE-R 1352. The defendant appealed but the case was then settled. Note that in a case involving administrative fines (ie not private enforcement) that were calculated by reference to the unlawful gain, the Federal Supreme Court reversed the ruling of the Düsseldorf Higher Regional Court that it was insufficient to assume that the gain equated to the difference between the cartel price and the subsequent lower prices: Bundesgerichtshof, judgment of 28 June 2005, WuW/E DE-R 1567. See further Böge and Ost, 'Up and Running, or is it? Private enforcement - the situation in Germany and Policy Perspectives' (2006) ECLR 197.

[387] *Manfredi* (n 350, above) paras 89–94.

payable to a claimant.[388] In Ireland, the Competition Act 2002 expressly provides that exemplary damages may be granted in claims for breach of the Act's prohibitions.[389]

14.123 **Restitution and prevention of unjust enrichment.**   Restitution may overlap with compensation in that it seeks to place the victim of anti-competitive behaviour in the same position as if the infringement had not occurred. However, rather than focusing solely on the loss or harm that has been suffered by the victim, it aims to prevent the unjust enrichment of the undertaking that has committed the wrongful infringement. The claimant may decide to frame his action in terms of recovering the illegal gain that has been enjoyed by the infringer, which may in certain cases be more advantageous than pure compensation or easier to prove.[390] In the *Luftfartsverket* case,[391] concerning the charges imposed on the Scandinavian Airlines System (SAS) for use of Arlanda airport in Sweden, the Göta Court of Appeal upheld the finding that the Swedish Airport and Navigation Services Board had abused its dominant position by discriminatory pricing contrary to Article 82 and the equivalent provision of Swedish competition law by requiring SAS to pay part of the costs of the Terminal 2 building at the airport in addition to standard landing fees. Relying on the judgment of the Court of Justice in *GT-Link v DSB*[392] concerning an infringement by a State body of Article 86(1) in conjunction with Article 82, the Swedish Court held that the defendant should repay to SAS approximately €55 million, corresponding to the monies paid under the provisions of the agreement that were invalid.

14.124 **'Passing-on' defence.**   The passing-on defence concerns the legal treatment of the fact that an undertaking which purchases from a supplier that has engaged in anti-competitive conduct may be able to mitigate his loss by 'passing-on' the excess charge to its own customers. The defendant may raise this pass-on as a defence so that only the final consumer can succeed in bringing a claim. There is no detailed

---

388 *Rookes v Barnard* [1964] AC 1129, [1964] 1 All ER 367. See generally McGregor, *McGregor on Damages* (17th edn, 2003 and 3rd Supp, 2006), paras 11-021 *et seq.* But cf *Devenish Nutrition Ltd v Sanofi-Avensis SA* [2007] EWHC 2394 (ch), where in a claim arising out of the vitamins cartel, the court held that exemplary damages would not be awarded against defendants who had been fined for the same infringement.

389 Competition Act 2002, s 14(5)(b).

390 In German law, the amount of the gain made by the infringement may be the basis for the administrative fine: see, eg judgment of the Federal Supreme Court of 28 June 2005 (n 386, above). In *Consumers' Association v JJB Sports plc*, not yet decided, the claimant acting on behalf of 130 consumers in a follow-on action before the UK Competition Appeal Tribunal claims restitutionary damages as well as compensatory damages.

391 *Luftfartsverket v Scandinavian Airlines System*, case no. T 33-00, judgment of 27 April 2001. The Swedish Supreme Court refused both permission to appeal and to make a reference to the ECJ. See further Bernitz, 'The Arlanda Terminal 2 Case: Substantial Damages for Breach of Article 82' (2003) Comp Law Journal 195.

392 Case C-242/95 *GT-Link v DSB* [1997] ECR I-4449, [1997] 5 CMLR 601.

analysis of the passing-on defence in competition law proceedings before the Community Courts but parallels can be drawn from analogous fields, such as the non-contractual liability of the Community under Article 288(2) EC[393] and the right of recovery of illegal taxes from Member States.[394] Moreover, in *GT-Link v DSB*, the Court of Justice ruled that while the Danish national railway company was obliged as a matter of Community law to repay discriminatory port charges levied in abuse of its dominant position, this would not apply where it was established that the traders had actually passed them on to others.[395] The Court of Justice has recognised in *Courage*[396] and *Manfredi*[397] that national courts are free to ensure that the exercise of Community rights does not result in the unjust enrichment of claimants in competition law claims. However a statement that Community law does not *preclude* the defence of passing-on is not the same as establishing a positive general principle.[398] The Court of Justice has, at the very least, insisted the mere existence of a passing-on defence cannot operate as an automatic or absolute presumption, without any detailed assessment of the extent of pass-on or the level of unjust enrichment that would entail in the particular circumstances of the case under review.[399] For instance, even if a claimant passes on the overcharge through increased retail prices, he may suffer reduced sales as a result.

Examples of passing-on in the Member States. In the United Kingdom, the **14.125** passing-on defence has been raised in claims for repayment of unlawful taxes[400] and for restitution of sums paid under an unlawful contract.[401] In a damages claim arising from the vitamins cartel, *BCL v Aventis*,[402] the defendants asserted the

---

[393] Case 238/78 *Ireks-Arkady v Council and Commission* [1979] ECR 2955, para 14.

[394] See Cases C-441 & 442/98 *Kapniki Michailidis* [2000] ECR I-7145, [2001] 1 CMLR 350. In Cases 199/82 *Amministrazione delle Finanze dello Stato v SpA San Giorgio* [1983] ECR 3595, [1985] 2 CMLR 658, and Case 68/79 *Just v Danish Ministry for Fiscal Affairs* [1980] ECR 501, [1981] 2 CMLR 714, the ECJ recognised that national rules permitting the passing-on defence do not infringe the principles of equivalence and effectiveness.

[395] *GT-Link v DSB* (n 392, above) paras 58–59. The ECJ proceeded to emphasise that even if the charges were passed on, the traders could still claim compensation for any losses suffered (para 60).

[396] *Courage v Crehan* (n 346, above) para 30.

[397] *Manfredi* (n 350, above) para 94. For a stronger pronouncement, see Opinion of AG van Gerven in Case C-128/92 *Banks v British Coal* [1994] ECR I-1209, [1994] 5 CMLR 30 paras 48–51.

[398] See AG Slynn in Case 331/85 *Bianco* [1988] ECR 1099, 1989] 3 CMLR 36.

[399] Case C-147/01 *Weber's Wine World v Abgabenberufungskommission Wien* [2003] ECR I-11365, [2004] 1 CMLR 147, [2005] All ER (EC) 224, paras 110–117

[400] *Marks and Spencer v Commssioners for Customs and Excise* [1999] STC 205; *CCE v National Westminster Bank* [2003] EWHC 1822, [2003] STC 1072.

[401] *Kleinwort Benson v Birmingham City Council* [1997] QB 380, [1996] 4 All ER 733 (the Court of Appeal rejected the availability of the defence on the basis that the bank had hedged its losses under the unlawful swap deal).

[402] *BCL Old Co Ltd v Aventis SA* [2005] CAT 2, [2005] Comp AR 485, [2005] ECC 39, paras 33–39.

'passing-on defence', namely that the claimants had suffered no loss, either because any higher prices were absorbed by the first purchasers in line, who then sold on at normal prices to the claimants, or because the claimants themselves passed-on to their customers any higher prices which they might have paid. The Competition Appeal Tribunal commented that questions such as whether the defendants were entitled to raise the defence, what the effect of the defence was and who bore the burden of proof, were 'novel and important issues' both for the United Kingdom and the rest of the Community.[403] The Tribunal remarked that whether or not the passing on defence is available to defendants will be an important consideration to potential claimants in future when considering whether or not to issue proceedings. In view of the uncertainty of the defence at that preliminary stage of the proceedings, the Tribunal refused to award security for the defendants' costs since it did not consider that the financial risk on the issue should be borne by the claimants. The case settled before any decision was given on this issue. In Germany, a passing-on defence is permitted but the effect of the 7th Amendment of the Act Against Restraints of Competition, that took effect on 1 July 2005, is to place upon the defendant the burden of establishing that the prices were passed on.[404] In Denmark, after trial in the *GT-Link v DSB* case,[405] the Danish Supreme Court held on appeal that an undertaking which has infringed competition law has the burden of proving a contention that the claimant has passed on to his customers the losses claimed: since the defendant had failed to substantiate that argument, the claimant recovered in full.[406] In France and Italy, courts have held that a passing-on defence is available without applying any particular presumptions.[407]

14.126 **United States experience.** Under US antitrust law, there is a substantial jurisprudence on the question of standing to sue for damages.[408] In addition to establishing causation, a plaintiff claiming damages must also establish that he falls within other established limitations placed upon the class of persons who

---

[403] ibid, para 33.

[404] GWB, Art 33(3) as amended.

[405] See para 14.124, above.

[406] *GT-Linien v DSB*, judgment of 20 April 2005, U.2005.2171 H.

[407] France: *Arkopharma v Roche and Hoffmann-La Roche*, judgment no. RG 2004F02643 of Nanterre Commercial Court of 11 May 2006 (the comprehensive nature of the vitamins cartel meant that direct purchasers were able to pass-on the increased prices to their customers); Italy: *Indaba Incentive Co v Juventus FC*, judgment of Turin Court of Appeal of 6 July 2000 (damages not recoverable by provider of ticket distribution service as court found that he had passed on extra costs to its consumers).

[408] The right to recover damages is expressly conferred by s 4 of the Clayton Act 1914 as amended, 15 USC, para 15. See in general Areeda and Hovenkamp, *Antitrust Law* (2nd edn, 2002), Vol II, paras 330 *et seq*; Jones, (n 348, above) Chaps 13–15.

can sue. These include rules on proximity,[409] 'antitrust injury',[410] passing-on and indirect purchasers.[411]

Limitation. In *Manfredi*,[412] the Court of Justice ruled that the issue of limita- **14.127** tion was a matter of national procedural autonomy, subject to the principles of equivalence and effectiveness. Accordingly, the start date and length of the limitation period must not make it practically impossible or excessibly difficult for claimants to exercise their right to seek compensation. The Court gave the following examples where the remedy would be ineffective: where the limitation period starts to run from the day on which the agreement or concerted practice was adopted; where the national rule imposes a short limitation period which is not capable of being suspended and/or where there are continuous or repeated infringements so that the limitation period expires before the infringement is brought to an end. The Commission is concerned that some Member States impose too stringent limitation periods which lead to a denial of justice for the victim of anti-competitive behaviour. This is particularly so where limitation periods do not take account of the length of the administrative procedure so any claim is effectively time-barred before the decision establishing liability is issued.[413] It is also concerned that short limitation periods prevent claimants from assembling evidence in time. The Commission is consulting as to whether all limitation periods for damages actions should be suspended pending any administrative

---

[409] See *Blue Shield of Virginia v McCready* 457 US 465, 102 SCt 2540 (1982); *Associated General Contractors of California v California State Council of Carpenters* 459 US 519, 103 SCt 897 (1983). Under this principle, 'derivative' claims by persons such as shareholders, suppliers, employees, creditors, and lessors of the company primarily injured by the antitrust violation are likely to be excluded. See also *Loeb v Eastman Kodak Co*, 183 F 704 (3rd Cir., 1910).

[410] ie injury of the type which the antitrust laws were intended to prevent and which flows from that which makes the defendants' conduct unlawful. The rationale for this limitation is that antitrust laws are enacted for the protection of competition and not competitors. Thus damages which result from increased competition (or from the loss of opportunity to participate in an uncompetitive market) are not recoverable: see *Brunswick Corp v Pueblo Bowl-O-Mat Inc*, 429 US 477, 97 SCt 690 (1977).

[411] Under Federal antitrust law, where an excessive price, charged by a monopolist or as a result of a cartel, is passed on by the first purchaser to his customers, the first purchaser can recover (*Hanover Shoe Inc. v United Shoe Machinery Corp*, 392 US 481, 88 SCt 2224 (1968) but the customers, as indirect purchasers, cannot recover (*Illinois Brick Co v Illinois*, 431 US 720, 97 SCt 2061 (1977); ie there is no defence of 'passing-on', but 'passing-on' cannot be used offensively. However, the position is complicated because recovery by indirect purchasers under State antitrust law has been upheld by the US Supreme Court: *California v ARC America Corp* 490 US 93, 109 SCt 1661 (1989). The resulting position has attracted much criticism in the United States. See, eg Baker, 'Revisiting History — What Have We Learned About Private Antitrust Enforcement That We Would Recommend To Others' (2004) 16 Loyola Consumer Law Rev 379; and generally, Hovenkamp, *Federal Antitrust Policy* (3rd edn, 2005), para 16.6.

[412] *Manfredi* (n 350, above) paras 77–82.

[413] Commission Staff Working Paper SEC (2005) 1732, pp 74–75.

proceedings before an NCA or the Commission or only start to run once the court of last instance has determined the issue of infringement.[414]

(c) Injunctive relief

14.128 **Injunctive relief.** Due to the principle of procedural autonomy, the Community Courts have had little cause to assess the conditions for injunctions. However, following the development of effective private enforcement in *Courage v Crehan*, injunctive relief should as a matter of Community law be available to anyone suffering loss as a consequence of anti-competitive conduct.[415] Such relief may be more relevant and effective on an interim basis than on a final determination.

14.129 **Test for interim injunction is a matter for national law.** In *Pharma Lab v Glaxosmithkline*,[416] the French Cour de Cassation considered the question whether, in a claim for interim measures, the test to be applied was the test which the Commission applies in deciding whether to grant interim measures or whether French case law applied. The Commission's test requires the claimant to establish a *prima facie* case, whereas French law requires only evidence that the alleged practice seriously and immediately threatens the general economy, the relevant sector, the interest of consumers or the complainant and that there is a causal link between the alleged practice and the alleged infringement. The Cour de Cassation, overturning the decision of the Court of Appeal, held that the procedural rules of national and Community authorities remain independent and the national authorities should apply their own national procedural rules unless that would make it impossible or more difficult to implement Community competition law.

14.130 **Development of English case law.** In England, injunctions are available on an interim or final basis to prevent the continuation of a breach of Articles 81(1) or 82. They may be mandatory or prohibitory in nature. In *Cutsforth v Mansfield Inns*,[417] for example, suppliers of amusement machines obtained an injunction on the basis of Article 81(1) restraining a brewery company from excluding them from the brewery's tied houses. In *Endtotal v S.P. Radio*,[418] an interim injunction was granted requiring continuance of supplies by a manufacturer to one of its

---

[414] Green Paper on Damages Actions for Breach of the EC Antitrust Rules, COM (2005) 672 final, p 11.

[415] See the Opinion of AG Jacobs in Cases C-264/01, etc, *AOK Bundesverband* [2004] ECR I-2493, [2004] 4 CMLR 1261, para 105.

[416] *Pharma Lab SA v Glaxosmithkline GSK*, Cour de Cassation, 14 December 2004, Bull. Civ. IV, no. 225, p 254.

[417] *Cutsforth v Mansfield Inns* [1986] 1 CMLR 1, [1986] 1 All ER 577. See also *Holleran v Thwaites* [1989] 2 CMLR 917. In both these cases damages were not an adequate remedy as the plaintiffs were threatened with a complete loss of their business.

[418] *Endtotal Ltd v S.P. Radio*, judgment of 7 August 1996 (QBD). The terms of the order carefully circumscribed the circumstances and extent of the obligation to supply. At trial, the plaintiff's claim failed on the facts (judgment of 30 April 1997).

long-standing distributors, on the basis, *inter alia*, of a claim that in terminating the distribution agreement the manufacturer was seeking to operate a selective distribution system in breach of Article 81(1), where there was a risk of the plaintiff going out of business before the action could be tried. In *Adidas*,[419] an interim injunction was granted to restrain the introduction by the the organisers of the Wimbledon and US Open tennis tournaments of a revised dress code that would have prevented players wearing clothing with the long-established adidas '3-Stripes' design and which was the result of an agreement alleged to be contrary to Article 81 and an abuse of collective dominance under Article 82. The following paragraphs discuss some of the issues arising in the English courts as regards interim injunctions in competition cases.

Conditions for relief. In principle, the normal rules governing injunctions **14.131** apply in competition cases. Hence, to grant an interim injunction, the court must usually be satisfied (i) that there is a serious issue to be tried; and (ii) that the balance of convenience is in favour of the grant of interim relief; or (iii) if the balance of convenience does not point either in favour or against the grant of relief, that an injunction will best preserve the status quo.[420] These principles apply equally where an injunction is sought to prevent an infringement of competition law and where the claimant seeks an interim injunction to enforce his contractual rights and the defendant alleges that the agreement is prohibited by Article 81(1).[421]

The balance of convenience. As expressed by Hoffmann J in *Films Rover* **14.132** *International*,[422] the court should take the course that involves the lower risk of injustice should the interim decision be found at trial to have been 'wrong'. In *Garden Cottage Foods*, the House of Lords held, on the facts, that damages would be an adequate remedy and refused an injunction, referring also to the difficulty of drafting an injunction in sufficiently precise terms.[423] In *Macarthy*

---

[419] *Adidas-Salomon AG v Lawn Tennis Association* [2006] EWHC 1318 (Ch), [2006] UKCLR 823, [2006] ECC 29.

[420] *American Cyanamid Co v Ethicon Ltd* [1975] AC 396 (HL), [1975] 1 All ER 504.

[421] For the latter, see, eg the cases concerning 'pub ties' where the claimant brewer sought to enforce contractual rights under the tie which the defendant alleged was unenforceable as it contravened Art 81(1): *Inntrepreneur Estates (CPC) Ltd v Bayliss* [1998] EuLR 483 (ChD) (injunction refused to party seeking to enforce agreement pending Commission decision on notification); *Greenalls Management Ltd v Canavan* [1998] EuLR 507 (Court of Appeal made final determination of Art 81 points of law); *Greenalls Management Ltd v Philbin* [1998] EuLR 540 (QBD, Mercantile Ct).

[422] *Films Rover International Ltd v Cannon Film Sales Ltd* [1987] 1 WLR 670, [1986] 3 All ER 772. These dicta have been followed on numerous occasions and were approved by Lord Jauncey in *R v Transport Sec, ex p Factortame Ltd (No. 2)* [1991] 1 AC 603 at 683, [1991] 1 All ER 70 at 128.

[423] *Garden Cottage Foods Ltd v Milk Marketing Board* (n 347, above) at 142E–143F, 145H–146D: *sed contra* Lord Wilberforce at 152D–155E. See also in Scotland, *Argyll Group v Distillers* [1986] 1 CMLR 764 (interdict refused by the Outer House for lack of a *prima facie* case and on balance of

v UniChem,[424] a competitor sought to restrain a share allocation and discount scheme introduced by a pharmaceutical wholesaler, alleging that it infringed Article 81. Relief was refused, in part on the grounds that an interim injunction would hinder the ability of the court to determine damages. If an injunction was not granted, but at trial the claimant established a right to damages, its loss could be calculated on the basis of its trading history in the intervening period until trial; whereas if an injunction was granted but the defendant then succeeded at trial, there would be no trading history upon which the court could assess the defendant's loss and thus the plaintiff's liability under its cross-undertaking in damages.[425] However, in other cases the difficulty of determining the claimant's loss has weighed heavily in favour of the grant of interim relief, sometimes coupled with an order for a speedy trial so that the effects on the market participants of the interim remedy last no longer than necessary. In *Adidas,*[426] the court had regard to the fact that if the injunction were refused, the tennis players sponsored by adidas would be unable to wear the '3 Stripes' clothing at the forthcoming Wimbledon and US Open tournaments, with a knock-on effect for sales of the claimant's fall/winter range. The court was not satisfied that forensic accountancy would be able to estimate the loss to a sufficient degree of accuracy given the uncertainties in sales from one year to the next.[427] Similarly, in *Attheraces,*[428] the court found that if an interim injunction were refused, the supply of pre-race data, which was essential to the claimant's business, would be stopped: although similar data could be obtained from newspapers, it was not as up-to-date or accurate. The court held that the loss of business to the claimant could not be readily calculated and interim relief was granted.

---

convenience); in Ireland, *RTE v Magill TV Guide* [1990] ILRM 534, 541–542, [1990] ECC 273, 282 (injunction refused by the High Court despite complaint to Commission). Other examples in the English courts include *Budgett v British Sugar*, noted (1979) 4 ELRev 417; *Chelmkarm Motors v Esso Petroleum* [1979] 1 CMLR 73 (ChD) (injunction to restrain breach of Arts 81 and 82 refused, mainly on grounds of balance of convenience); *ECS/AKZO*, referred to in OJ 1985 L374/1, [1986] 3 CMLR 273 (interlocutory injunction to restrain predatory pricing contrary to Art 82); *Plessey v GEC and Siemens* [1990] ECC 384 (injunction preventing a takeover bid discharged as it would prevent compliance with the City Panel rules and probably be equivalent to final judgment); *EasyJet Airline Co Ltd v British Airways plc* [1998] EuLR 350 (QBD Comm. Ct) (despite serious issue that cross-subsidisation infringed Art 82, injunction refused on grounds of balance of convenience).

[424] *Macarthy PLC v UniChem Ltd* [1991] ECC 41.

[425] See also *Norbain SD Ltd v Dedicated Micros Ltd* [1998] EuLR 266, [1998] ECC 379 (QBD) at 277D-E where Toulson J considered *obiter* that a mandatory injunction to continue supplies would complicate the question of damages because the existence of the proceedings themselves would lead to an artificial situation with regard to trading.

[426] *Adidas-Salomon AG v Lawn Tennis Association* (n 419, above).

[427] The court also found that the 'loss of face' that an injunction would cause to the regulatory bodies of the tournaments, although exaggerated, could not be compensated financially and therefore granted an injunction to preserve the status quo: ibid, paras 69 et seq.

[428] *Attheraces Ltd v The British Horseracing Board Ltd* [2005] EWHC 1553 (Ch), [2006] ECC 12, [2006] EuLR 76, para 65.

Mandatory relief. Mandatory, interim injunctions carry a higher risk of **14.133** injustice in that they require the respondent to take a positive step rather than simply preserve the status quo. Accordingly, before granting such an injunction, the court should consider whether it 'feel[s] a high degree of assurance that the plaintiff will be able to establish this right at a trial'. But even without that degree of assurance, there will be circumstances in which a mandatory interim injunction is appropriate 'where the risk of injustice if the injunction is refused sufficiently outweighs the risk if it is granted'.[429] The issue arises acutely in cases where the alleged infringement of Article 82 is a refusal to supply. In *Norbain v Dedicated Micros*,[430] Toulson J considered that the grant of an injunction which involved the requisitioning of goods from an unwilling seller under the duress of a court order, should be approached with considerable caution. Since the likely period for any permanent relief would have expired before even a speedy trial could take place (so that the grant of an interim injunction would be tantamount to granting a final injunction), and as the plaintiff's claim on dominance was unlikely to succeed, an interim injunction was refused. In *Sockel v The Body Shop International*,[431] an injunction was refused on the grounds that there was no serious issue to be tried, but Rimer J considered that if the claimant had shown an arguable case for continued supplies and the likely consequence of being deprived of them was that it went out of business, he would probably have granted an injunction. Referring to the difficulties in drafting and enforcing such a mandatory order, the judge stated:

> 'I do not consider that there is or can be any general principle to the effect that an injunction cannot be granted in cases such as these. If there were, it would seem to me to represent a deficiency in the law.'[432]

---

[429] The quotations are from the judgment of Chadwick J in *Nottingham Building Society v Eurodynamic Systems* [1993] FSR 468 at 474, cited with approval by Phillips LJ in *Zockoll Group Ltd v Mercury Communications Ltd* [1998] FSR 354 at 366 as 'being all the citation that in future should be necessary'.

[430] *Norbain SD Ltd v Dedicated Micros Ltd* (n 425, above).

[431] *Sockel GmbH v The Body Shop International plc* [2000] EuLR 276, [2000] UKCLR 262 (ChD).

[432] ibid, at 291 (EuLR), 227 (UKCLR). See also *Jobserve Ltd v Network Multimedia Television Ltd* [2001] EWCA (Civ) 2021, [2002] UKCLR 184 (Court of Appeal upheld injunction restraining operator of internet website from refusing to deal with customers who used competitor); *Endtotal v S.P. Radio* (n 418, above); *A&N Pharmacy Ltd v United Drug Ltd* [1996] 2 ILRM 42 (Irish High Court): interim injunction granted under provision of Irish Competition Act equivalent to Art 82, requiring collectively dominant wholesaler to supply claimant on cash-on-delivery terms. cf *Getmapping Plc v Ordnance Survey* [2002] EWHC 1089 (Ch); *Suretrack Rail Services Limited v Infraco JNP Limited* [2002] EWHC 1316 (Ch), [2002] UKCLR 410, [2003] ICR 1, para 15, where Laddie J held in a case of abuse of dominant position the claimant seeking an injunction had to demonstrate that there was a real prospect of showing that the decision taken by the defendant was 'incapable of objective justification'.

14.134   **The status quo.**   In *Garden Cottage Foods*,[433] the House of Lords identified the status quo as the state of affairs existing during the period immediately preceding the issue of the claim form or, in the event of delay, before the application for the injunction. In *Adidas*,[434] the parties had spent several months trying to reach a settlement before the commencement of proceedings. The court refused to take such delay into account when identifying the status quo; Sir Andrew Morritt VC held that the *status quo ante bellum* referred to the situation prevailing before the dispute arose rather than that brought about by the changes to the dress code. That meant that the status quo related to the time when adidas-sponsored players were permitted to wear clothing with a larger '3 Stripes' design.

14.135   **Cross-undertaking in damages.**   Normally, as a condition of obtaining interim relief, the claimant must offer a cross-undertaking to pay such damage as the defendant may sustain by reason of the making of the order if it is discharged at trial and which the court considers that the claimant should pay. However, this is an undertaking not an order of the court, so it is given voluntarily to the court and cannot be compelled or imposed restrospectively.[435] In some cases, interim relief may have a direct effect also on third parties, and the court has jurisdiction to require as the condition for the grant of an injunction that the claimant should give a cross-undertaking also for the benefit of such affected third parties.[436]

(d) Reliance on Articles 81 and 82 as a defence

14.136   **Introduction.**   Article 81 can be relied upon by a defendant as a defence to claims for payments due or performance of an agreement, on the basis that the court will not enforce an unlawful agreement. Relying on the nullity provided in Article 81(2), the defendant will seek to strike out the claim and/or seek a declaration of invalidity or counterclaim in damages.[437] Although Article 82 does not expressly provide for nullity in the same way as Article 81, the courts will not sanction conduct or enforce a contractual term that violates the prohibition of abuse of a dominant position.[438]

14.137   **Articles 81(1) and 82 as a defence for third parties.**   In certain circumstances both Articles 81(1) and 82 can be pleaded as a defence by a defendant who is not

---

[433] *Garden Cottage Foods* (n 347, above) *per* Lord Diplock at 140
[434] *Adidas-Salomon AG v Lawn Tennis Association* (n 419, above) para 75.
[435] *Smithkline Beecham plc v Apotex Europe Ltd* [2005] EWHC 1655 (Ch), [2006] 2 All ER 53, paras 38–41.
[436] *Smithkline Beecham plc v Apotex Europe Ltd* [2006] EWCA Civ 658, [2007] Ch 71, [2006] 4 All ER 1078, [2007] FSR 6, para 31. In *Adidas* (n 419, above), such a broader cross-undertaking was given.
[437] For a recent (unsuccessful) example, see *P & S Amusements Ltd v Valley House Leisure Ltd* [2006] EWHC 1510 (Ch), [2006] UKCLR 876.
[438] See para 14.098, above.

a party to any relevant agreement. The principal context in which this has arisen has been in national proceedings for infringement of intellectual property rights. In such cases it may be relevant to consider the free movement rules in Articles 28 and 30 EC in addition to Articles 81 and 82.[439]

Articles 81 and 82 as a defence to infringement of intellectual property rights. The basic principle is that Article 81(1) or 82 may give rise to a defence but there must be some credible nexus[440] between the relief sought in the action and the alleged breach of competition law. The English case law in this area mainly concerns actions brought by the owner of the right rather than by a licensee. In *ICI v Berk Pharmaceuticals*,[441] in defence to a claim for passing-off, it was alleged that the plaintiffs were abusing their dominant position by excessive pricing and that by copying the 'get-up' of their product to enter the market the defendant was therefore restoring competition. Granting an application to strike out this defence on the grounds that there was no nexus between the alleged infringement of Article 82 and the enforcement of the right to prevent passing off, Sir Robert Megarry VC stated:

14.138

'Article [82] prohibits any abuse which falls within the ambit of the Article. Many other acts by the plaintiffs are also prohibited, whether by statute, common law or equity, or under the Treaty. I do not think that it could be said that a person in breach of some statutory or other prohibition thereupon becomes an outlaw, unable to enforce any of his rights against anyone. If the plaintiffs are imposing unfair selling prices in that they charge too much for their product, I cannot see why this breach of the prohibitions of Article [82] means that the defendants are thereby set free from

---

[439] For Engish cases on Arts 28 and 30 as defence to infringement proceedings, see, eg *British Leyland v Armstrong* [1984] 3 CMLR 102 (CA) (Arts 28 to 30 held not to apply); *Allen & Hanburys v Generics (UK) Ltd* [1986] 1 CMLR 101 (CA), in which an Art 234 reference was later made by the House of Lords (Case 434/85, [1988] ECR 1245, [1988] 1 CMLR 701) on the issue whether Art 30 provides a defence to an infringement action where there is no 'licence of right' under s 46 of the Patents Act 1977; Case 35/87 *Thetford Corporation v Fiamma* [1988] ECR 3585, [1988] 3 CMLR 549 (Art 28 as defence to infringement action, Art 234 reference by CA); *Sandvik v Pfiffner* [1999] EuLR 755 (Arts 28–30 giving rise to arguable defence through consent to marketing in non-patent protected Member States); Jarvis, *The Application of EC Law in National Courts: The Free Movement of Goods* (1998). In *Sportswear SpA v Stonestyle Ltd* [2006] EWCA Civ 380 (CA), [2006] UKCLR 893, [2006] ECC 27, the Court of Appeal reversed the decision of the first instance judge striking out those parts of a defence to a trade mark infringement claim relying on Art 81 on the basis that Art 28 could be used instead; the Court held that a breach of Art 81 might well strengthen the defence.

[440] In the context of Art 81, the ECJ has used the formulation that the infringement action is brought as the 'object, means or consequence' or 'subject, means or result' of the prohibited agreement or practice: see Case 56/64 *Consten & Grundig v Commission* [1966] ECR 299, [1966] CMLR 418; Case 40/70 *Sirena v Eda* [1971] ECR 69, [1971] CMLR 260, para 9; Case 15/74 *Centrafarm v Sterling Drug* [1974] ECR 1147, [1974] 2 CMLR 480, para 40; and in the English courts, *Glaxo Group Ltd v Dowelhurst Ltd* [2000] FSR 371, [2000] ECC 193, [2000] EuLR 493; and *Sportswear SpA v Stonestyle Ltd* (above).

[441] [1981] 2 CMLR 91 (ChD).

any liability to the plaintiffs if they, the defendants, commit the tort of passing off (or, indeed, any other tort) against them.'

This was adopted and applied by the Court of Appeal in *British Leyland v Armstrong*,[442] where the defendant to an action for infringement brought by a copyright owner sought to rely on Article 81(1) on the grounds that the plaintiff was party to agreements with third parties (its licensees) which contravened Article 81(1). However, in *British Leyland v T.I. Silencers*,[443] a defence based on Articles 81(1) and 82 was allowed to stand when the allegation was that the owner of the right was using the threat of infringement proceedings to force the defendant to enter into a copyright licence which arguably infringed Articles 81(1) and 82.[444] And in *British Leyland v Armstrong*, where the defendant also raised a defence under Article 82, Oliver LJ accepted that unlike the allegation under Article 81, the contention under Article 82 could in principle give rise to a defence since:

'... the allegation here is that the relief is claimed by the plaintiffs in order to compel the defendants to enter into an agreement which would, if entered into, constitute an abuse under Article [82], so that the relief claimed is thus itself an abuse.'[445]

---

[442] *British Leyland v Armstrong* [1984] 3 CMLR 102, [1984] FSR 591; reversed on other grounds, [1986] AC 577, [1986] 1 All ER 850. The House of Lords did not consider the EC law issues and the Court of Appeal judgment remains a good illustration of how a national court can approach the difficulties raised by 'Euro-defences'; see also *Sportswear SpA v Stonestyle Ltd* (n 439, above).

[443] [1981] 2 CMLR 75 (CA). Similarly in *Lansing Bagnall v Buccaneer Lift Parts* [1984] 1 CMLR 102 (CA) there was a clear nexus between the defence under Art 82 and the relief sought in the action, since it was alleged that the plaintiff was using its dominant position in the supply of its own spare parts to sue for infringement and thus put into effect a policy of charging high prices and preventing competition. Both Templeman and Lawton LJJ distinguished *ICI v Berk Pharmaceuticals* (n 441, above), on the ground that it was a passing off action not a copyright action, but, it is suggested, the real issue is the presence or absence of nexus. See also *IBM v Phoenix International (Computers) Ltd* [1994] RPC 251 at 271–273 (ChD).

[444] The broader principle in the *British Leyland* case has been applied in cases unrelated to intellectual property rights. In *Holleran v Thwaites* (n 417, above), two public house tenants obtained an injunction against their brewery landlord to restrain the enforcement of the landlord's contractual right to serve a notice to quit, on the grounds that the reason for giving notice was their refusal to enter into a new tied house agreement which they alleged contravened Art 81(1). The court can prevent the exercise of a *contractual* right when a nexus is perceived between the exercise of that right and an arguable illegality. See also *Marchant & Eliot Underwriting Ltd v Higgins* [1996] 3 CMLR 313 (on appeal, [1996] 2 Lloyd's Rep 31, [1996] 3 CMLR 349), rejecting such an argument: in that case the contractual rights were not being exercised for the purpose of implementing an unlawful arrangement.

[445] n 442, above, at 128 (CMLR). Similarly in *Hoover v George Hulme (STO) Ltd* [1982] 3 CMLR 186 (ChD), a defence under Art 82 was rejected on the facts. See also *Ransburg-Gema AG v Electrostatic Plant Systems Ltd* [1989] 2 CMLR 712, [1990] FSR 287 (ChD); and *Pitney Bowes v Francotyp-Postalia* [1990] 3 CMLR 466, [1991] FSR 72 (ChD). In both these cases, the defendants alleged, *inter alia*, that the threat of proceedings for infringement of intellectual property rights was in itself abusive. These allegations were rejected on the basis that the mere threat of legal proceedings had no credible connection to abuse of a dominant position; but cf now Case T-111/96 *ITT Promedia v Commission*, para 14.140, below.

However, on analysis of the facts, the Court found that the royalty terms of the licence agreement were not abusive.

Other cases. In *Philips v Ingman*,[446] the defendant alleged, *inter alia*, that the **14.139** patent infringement proceedings had been brought to force acceptance of the terms of the plaintiff's standard patent licence that infringed Article 81(1). Laddie J distinguished two types of case: in *British Leyland v T.I. Silencers* the owner of the intellectual property right was bringing the proceedings to force the defendant or others to enter into an agreement which would infringe Article 81; whereas in *Armstrong*, the alleged infringing agreements had already been entered into with third parties and were unrelated to the infringement. Laddie J held that the defendant's allegation fell within the *T.I. Silencers* category and was therefore maintainable. The defendant also pleaded that the infringement proceedings had been brought as part of the implementation of a prior patent pooling agreement between the plaintiff and a third party which also infringed Article 81(1). This was held to be sustainable as a matter of law. In *Intel v VIA Technologies*,[447] an Article 81 defence was re-instated by the Court of Appeal, which found the proposed asymmetric licence was, on its face, restrictive and sufficiently pleaded as such. Although the then Technology Transfer block exemption, Regulation 240/96, applied to reciprocal cross-licences, the benefit of the block exemption was withdrawn where the cross-licence imposed non-reciprocal conditions on competitors. The Vice-Chancellor therefore held that it was arguable with a real prospect of success that any anti-competitive restriction could not be cured by the block exemption.

The nexus between infringement and abuse under Article 82: the Community **14.140** **Courts' approach.** In *Volvo v Veng*,[448] the plaintiff brought proceedings for infringement of registered designs of Volvo car body panels. The defendant pleaded a defence under Article 82, but the only abuse upon which it relied was Volvo's refusal to grant it a licence. The Court of Justice held that a refusal to grant such a licence 'cannot in itself constitute an abuse of a dominant position'. But the Court added:

> 'It must however be noted that the exercise of an exclusive right by the proprietor of a registered design in respect of car body panels may be prohibited by Article [82] if it involves, on the part of an undertaking holding a dominant position, certain

---

[446] *Philips Electronics NV v Ingman Ltd* [1998] 2 CMLR 839 at 868–874, [1998] EuLR 666. Laddie J's reasoning was followed in *Sandvik v Pfiffner* (n 439, above), where Neuberger J held that, even if territorial and field of use restrictions in a patent licence arguably fell within Art 81(1), that did not provide, of itself, a defence to a patent infringement action. The limitations arose not out of the agreement but out of the patentee's right to grant only a limited licence.

[447] *Intel Corporation v VIA Technologies Inc* [2002] EWCA Civ 1905, [2003] FSR 33, [2003] ECC 16, [2003] EuLR 85.

[448] Case 238/87 *Volvo v Veng* [1988] ECR 6211, [1989] 4 CMLR 122, para 9.

abusive conduct such as the arbitrary refusal to supply spare parts to independent repairers, the fixing of prices for spare parts at an unfair level or a decision no longer to produce spare parts for a particular model even though many cars of that model are still in circulation, provided that such conduct is liable to affect trade between Member States.'

In the *Magill* case,[449] the Court of Justice, applying *Volvo v Veng*, held that, although the mere refusal to grant a licence by the owner of an intellectual property right with a dominant position cannot of itself constitute an abuse of a dominant position, the exercise of an exclusive right may, in exceptional circumstances, involve abusive conduct. On the facts of that case there were such exceptional circumstances and the Commission was entitled to order the grant of licences on payment of a reasonable royalty. Moreover, in *ITT Promedia*[450] the Court of First Instance has indicated that the mere bringing of proceedings may itself constitute an abuse of a dominant position, where the proceedings cannot reasonably be considered to be an attempt to assert the rights of the dominant undertaking and can therefore only serve to harass the defendant. And in *AstraZeneca*,[451] the Commission found that procuring supplementary protection certificates ('SPCs') for patented pharmaceutical products by misleading representations to patent offices and then persisting in these representations to courts in defence of those SPCs, constituted an abuse.

14.141   **Article 82 as a defence to an infringement action: the English courts' approach.**   In *Pitney Bowes*[452] (decided before *Magill*), Hoffmann J considered that the passage from the judgment in *Volvo v Veng* was:

> '. . . a fairly clear affirmation of the view that the abuses need not be a direct or even an indirect consequence of the relief claimed in the particular action. It is sufficient that the existence of the intellectual property right creates or buttresses the dominant position which the plaintiff is abusing. The remedy contemplated by the Court is that the plaintiff may have to be deprived of the means of maintaining his dominant position.'

---

[449] Cases C-241 & 242/91P *RTE and ITP v Commission ('Magill')* [1995] ECR I-743, [1995] 4 CMLR 718, [1995] All ER (EC) 416 (on appeal from Case T-69/89 *RTE v Commission* and Case T-76/89 *ITP v Commission* [1991] ECR II-485, 575, [1991] 4 CMLR 586, 745). See also Case T-504/93 *Tiercé Ladbroke v Commission* [1997] ECR II-923, [1997] 5 CMLR 309; Case T-198/98 *Micro Leader v Commission* [1999] ECR II-3989, [2000] 4 CMLR 886, [2000] All ER (EC) 361, para 56. For discussion of these cases and refusal to licence intellectual property rights under Art 82, see further paras 10.129 *et seq*, above.

[450] Case T-111/96 *ITT Promedia v Commission* [1998] ECR 2937, [1998] 5 CMLR 491, paras 55–58 and 72–73. See further para 10.103, above.

[451] *AstraZeneca* [2006] 5 CMLR 287, paras 737–739; on appeal, Case T-321/05 *AstraZeneca v Commission*, not yet decided. Since the defences were a continuation of prior conduct, the Commission observed that it was unnecessary to decide whether, in exceptional circumstances, a defence based on misleading representations might on its own constitute an abuse.

[452] *Pitney Bowes v Francotyp-Postalia* (n 445, above) 471 (CMLR), 77 (FSR).

Although this analysis has been adopted in subsequent cases,[453] the decision of the Court of Appeal in *Chiron Corp v Murex Diagnostics (No. 2)*[454] raises questions as to its scope, particularly in relation to the appropriate remedy where the owner of the right is abusing a dominant position. In *Chiron*, the defendant's defence to a patent infringement action was that the plaintiff was abusing its dominant position by pursuing a policy of excessive prices for, *inter alia*, sales of its own products and that the infringement action 'had been brought as a result of and in pursuance of' the abuses; accordingly the plaintiff was entitled to no relief or only to payment of a reasonable royalty. The court at first instance, applying the reasoning of *Pitney Bowes*, refused to strike out that part of the defendant's defence relating to this aspect of abuse (although the defence was struck out for an inadequate plea of effect on trade between Member States). The Court of Appeal dismissed the defendant's appeal. The majority upheld the judge's view that there was an arguable case of abuse, but not an effect on trade. In relation to the question of abuse and nexus, Balcombe LJ (expressing the majority view) said:

> '. . . [the plaintiffs] submit that, if there has been a breach of Article [82], Murex's proper remedies are an action for damages under Article [82], a complaint to the European Commission or, in due course, an application for a compulsory licence. To suggest that there is a sufficient nexus between the abuse and the relief sought is to make the plaintiffs outlaws, unable to enforce their rights against anyone and to leave Murex free to continue infringement of Chiron's patent. I find this an attractive submission which undoubtedly has some support in the English authorities [*ICI v Berk, British Leyland v Armstrong*]. Nevertheless I am . . . unable to say that the judge was plainly wrong in his conclusion that there was a nexus sufficient at any rate to allow the pleading to stand.'[455]

Staughton LJ, although agreeing that the appeal should be dismissed, decided to 'grasp the nettle' on the issue of nexus, in the following terms:

> 'Even if it be shown that Chiron (i) have a dominant position in a relevant market and (ii) are abusing that position, (iii) so as to affect trade between Member States, in my opinion that does not in the present case lead to the conclusion that a national court should refuse to enforce Chiron's patent.'[456]

---

[453] See *Chiron Corp v Murex* (reported *sub. nom. Chiron v Organon Teknika Ltd)* [1992] 3 CMLR 813, 824–825) (ChD); and in *Sandvik v Pfiffner* (n 439, above).

[454] *Chiron Corp v Murex Diagnostics Ltd (No. 2)* [1994] 1 CMLR 410, [1994] FSR 187.

[455] ibid, para 419. See *Intergraph Corp v Solid Systems CAD Ltd* [1998] EuLR 223, 241 (ChD) where Ferris J considered that this majority view did not involve a rejection of the approach in *Pitney Bowes*.

[456] ibid, paras 421–423.

After referring to the opinion of Advocate General Roemer in *Parke Davis & Co v Probel*,[457] *ICI v Berk* (as approved in *British Leyland v Armstrong*[458]) and *Pitney Bowes*, Staughton LJ continued:

'In the ordinary way I consider that the remedy for abuses such as are alleged in this case is not to refuse relief to the holder of the patent as against the infringer. That could be altogether lacking in proportionality. It might also, as Megarry V-C points out, give rise to a fluctuating situation whereby a patent was sometimes enforceable and sometimes not. There are other remedies available, as the Advocate General indicated in *Parke Davis*, such as action taken under Article 3 of Regulation 17 . . . There may be extraordinary cases, where the holder of a patent should be refused relief against an infringer on the ground that he is in breach of Article [82]. But I can see nothing to indicate that this case is in that class.'

In *Philips v Ingman*, Laddie J examined the relationship between *Volvo v Veng* and *Magill*, concluding, first, that 'it is not an abuse for the owner of an intellectual property right to refuse a reasonable royalty'[459] and then stating:

'If a party is to rely upon *Magill* to resist enforcement of an intellectual property right it is incumbent on him to plead explicitly what are the exceptional circumstances which take the case outside *Volvo v Veng*. Mere assertion will not do. Bearing in mind the cost and time implications of raising this type of plea in an action, it is reasonable to require the pleader to set out the essential facts on the basis of which he will invite the court to decide that an exceptional case exists.'[460]

14.142 **Developing jurisprudence: *Intel v VIA Technologies*.** The interaction between intellectual property rights and competition law is a contentious area, so that on some issues it is impossible to set out a settled legal position. That is of particular significance to the assessment of whether there is an arguable case, for the purpose of interim relief or summary judgment. In *Intel v VIA Technologies*,[461] Article 82 was the basis of the primary competition law defence raised to patent infringment claims: it was alleged that where the patents represented an industry standard, by refusing to grant licences save on terms that it was contended infringed Article 81 and then by bringing proceedings for patent infringement, Intel was abusing its dominant position. At first instance, Intel obtained summary judgment on the basis that the defendant had not shown either that the proposed licence terms infringed Article 81 or that a refusal to licence would eliminate all competition in

---

[457] Case 24/67 *Parke Davis v Probel* [1968] ECR 55, 80, [1968] CMLR 47, 57.
[458] See n 442, above.
[459] *Philips Electronics NV v Ingman Ltd* (n 446, above) para 856.
[460] *Philips v Ingman*, above, at 864. See also *Sandvik v Pfiffner* (n 439, above) where, however, Neuberger J declined to strike out a defence under Art 82 in respect of wider allegations of abuse on the market. Relying upon *Magill* (para 14.140, above) and *Pitney Bowes* (para 14.141, above) he concluded that it was conceivable that an effective grant of a compulsory licence under the patent would be the appropriate relief.
[461] *Intel Corporation v VIA Technologies Inc* (n 447, above).

the market or exclude an entirely new product from the market since Intel would still face competition from its licensees who would develop new components. The Court of Appeal reversed this decision, finding that it was arguable that the concept of 'exceptional circumstances' for the purpose of an abusive refusal to licence was not limited to the two criteria set out by the Court of Justice in its case law to date, and that in any event the criterion of the exclusion of competition did not mean all competition for all sources.[462] Whilst it was important to ensure that a defence was not unmeritorious, the Court of Appeal noted that the jurisprudence of the Court of Justice in this particular field was in the course of development. The Court of Appeal therefore cautioned against assuming that existing case law will not be extended or modified by the Court of Justice so as to encompass the defence advanced in those proceedings. Final determination of the case might require a reference under Article 234, but the national court should not summarily dismiss the arguments raised as bound to fail.[463]

6. Practice and Procedure in the UK

Community or national law?   The Community Courts have often stressed that, **14.143** in the absence of Community rules governing the matter, it is for the national courts to determine the procedures by which the directly effective rights under Articles 81 and 82 are enforced. However, this devolution of responsibility is subject to two important qualifications, namely that the national methods and procedures must be no less favourable than those applying to like remedies for the protection of rights founded on domestic provisions (the principle of equivalence or non-discrimination) and that they must not be such as to render practically impossible or excessively difficult the exercise of the rights which the courts are obliged to protect (the principle of effectiveness).[464] In a number of cases, therefore, the Court of Justice has directed national courts to set aside national procedural rules which unduly impede the enforcement of Community law rights.[465]

---

[462] ibid, *per* Morritt V-C at paras 48–51.

[463] ibid, paras 32, 95. See also *Intergraph Corp v Solid Systems CAD Ltd* (n 455, above), where Ferris J remarked upon the difference in approach between that of Hoffmann J in *Pitney Bowes* and that of the minority view of Staughton LJ in *Chiron* and was not prepared, on a strike out application, to reject the approach in *Pitney Bowes*.

[464] See para 14.095, above.

[465] See Case 453/99 *Courage v Crehan* [2001] ECR I-6297, [2001] 5 CMLR 1058, [2001] All ER (EC) 886; and Cases C-295/04 etc, *Manfredi v Lloyd Adriatico Assicurazioni* [2006] ECR I-6619, [2006] 5 CMLR 980.

14.144 **Specialist jurisdiction.** In the United Kingdom, cases raising competition issues under either Community or domestic law are assigned to particular courts.[466] The Competition Appeal Tribunal[467] has a special jurisdiction to hear follow-on damages claims which rely upon the findings of infringement in a decision of the European Commission or the Office of Fair Trading. However, the Tribunal's jurisdiction in private actions is limited to monetary claims; it cannot hear actions between private parties for interim, injunctive or other declaratory relief. All claims in England and Wales relating to the application of Article 81 or 82 that are not commenced before the Tribunal are assigned to the Chancery Division of the High Court, except for 'commercial actions' which may be commenced in, or may be assigned to, the Commercial Court.[468] Any such proceedings commenced in a County Court, district registry or the Queens Bench Division must be transferred to the Chancery Division or the Commercial Court.[469] The Enterprise Act 2002 enables the making of regulations to permit courts to transfer to the Competition Appeal Tribunal the determination of the question whether or not there has been an infringement of competition law which may arise in any case, but no such regulations have as yet been made.[470]

14.145 **Follow-on damages claims.** Sections 47A and 47B of the Competition Act 1998 enable monetary claims following a finding of infringement by either the Commission or the Office of Fair Trading to be brought before the Competition Appeal Tribunal. Section 47B makes special provision for 'consumer claims', whereby a specified body approved by an order of the Secretary of State, may bring such proceedings on behalf of at least two named individuals who have consented to such representation.[471] The advantage of this statutory procedure is that the

---

[466] For more detailed discussion of competition claims in the United Kingdom, see Ward and Smith (eds), *Competition Litigation in the United Kingdom* (2005).

[467] The Competition Appeal Tribunal was created by s 12 of and Sch 2 to the Enterprise Act 2002. In France, Decree no. 2005-1756 of 30 December 2005 allocated the jurisdiction to hear cases under French and EC competition law to a designated list of Tribunals of first instance. Other Member States also accord first instance jurisdiction over damages claims to higher courts, eg Czech Republic, Italy, Ireland and Slovakia: *Study on the conditions of claims for damages in case of infringement of the EC Competition rules* (31 August 2004) ('the Ashurst Study'), p 31; available on the DG Comp website.

[468] Practice Direction - Competition Law - Claims relating to the Application of Articles 81 and 82 of the EC Treaty, para 2.1, *Civil Procedures 2007*, paras B12-001 *et seq*. 'Commercial action' is defined in CPR, rule 58.1(2).

[469] ibid, para 2.3. In Scotland, there is no provision for transfer, but in practice a pursuer would be more likely to raise a competition action in the Court of Session (sitting as a court of first instance) than in the Sheriff Court.

[470] Enterprise Act 2002, s 16(1).

[471] See also CAT Rules, rule 33. Pursuant to this provision, the Consumers' Association has been approved as a specified body: see Case No. 1078/7/9/07 *Consumers' Association v JJB Sports plc*, not yet decided: damages claim on behalf of some 130 consumers who purchased football replica shirts, arising out of the OFT decn no. CA 98/06/2003 *Football replica kit*, finding an infringement of the Chap 1 prohibition under the Competition Act 1998. The claim was

Tribunal is bound by the findings of infringement in the relevant decision[472] and the proceedings will accordingly focus on remedy, causation and quantum. The relevant procedure is set out in the Tribunal's Rules.[473] However, this special procedure, which is available only after the time for any appeals has expired, does not preclude the bringing of a follow-on damages claim in the High Court or Court of Session.[474] Accordingly, in some cases, the claimant may choose whether to bring his claim before the specialist tribunal or the ordinary court or a combination of the two. Although at the time of writing the experience is limited, determining factors might include matters such as timing, cost, complexity and, given the limited jurisdiction of the Tribunal, type of relief. At the request of the parties or on its own initiative, the Competition Appeal Tribunal may transfer a claim under section 47A to the High Court or Court of Session, and conversely the latter may transfer to the Tribunal so much of the proceedings before them as relate to a claim to which section 47A applies.[475]

Other private actions: binding OFT determination. The Competition Act **14.146** 1998 also contains provisions that give effect to findings by the Office of Fair Trading ('OFT') in claims other than follow-on damages claims before the Tribunal. Under section 58, a finding of fact made by the OFT in the course of an investigation is binding on the court in proceedings alleging an infringement of Article 81(1) or 82, unless the court otherwise directs. Under section 58A, in damages claims the court is bound by a decision of the OFT that Article 81(1) or 82 has been infringed. Determinative effect is similarly given to OFT findings or decisions concerning the analogous provisions of UK competition law, the Chapter I and Chapter II prohibitions. But, in any case, this effect applies only once any appeal in respect of that finding or decision has been resolved or the time for such an appeal has expired. These provisions of the domestic legislation give effectively the same status in private proceedings to decisions of the OFT as are given to decisions of the European Commission pursuant to Article 16(1) of Regulation 1/2003.[476] Moreover, aside from these statutory provisions, it may be an abuse of process for the addressee of a Commission or NCA decision to seek to contest the findings in that decision in a subsequent private action.[477]

---

commenced following the final dismissal of JJB's appeal by the Court of Appeal, *Argos & Littlewoods and JJB Sports v Office of Fair Trading* [2006] EWCA Civ 1318, [2006] UKCLR 1135.

[472] Competition Act 1998, ss 47A(9), 47B(5).
[473] Competition Appeal Tribunal Rules 2003 ('CAT Rules'), SI 2003/1372, rules 30–47.
[474] Competition Act 1998, s 47A(10).
[475] Enterprise Act 2002, s 16(4)–(5); CAT Rules, rules 48–49. A claim under s 47B may not be transferred.
[476] For Art 16(1) of Reg 1/2003, see para 14.076, above.
[477] *Iberian (UK) Ltd v BPB Industries plc* [1996] 2 CMLR 601, [1997] EuLR 1 (ChD). See also in the field of State aid, *Betws Anthracite Ltd v DSK Anthrazit Ibbenburen* [2003] EWHC 2403 (Comm), [2004] 1 CMLR 381, [2004] 1 All ER (Comm) 289.

14.147 **Parallel competence.** In addition to ordinary rules of service, any statement of case that raises an Article 81 or 82 issue must be served on the Office of Fair Trading.[478] The Chancery Division has indicated that where a party has made an approach to the competition authority in connection with competition law issues that are raised in parallel proceedings before the High Court, there should be a duty on that party and on its legal advisers, to disclose to the court the fact of the approach and, if the competition authority has indicated a willingness to proceed with an investigation, to disclose that fact as well.[479] Such disclosure will enable the court to consider whether to stay its proceedings in whole or part pending any investigation and to avoid any conflict between the findings of the court and any decision of the authority and/or the outcome of any appeal before the Competition Appeal Tribunal.

14.148 **Standing and security for costs.** Claims may be brought in the United Kingdom by any natural or legal person of full capacity who has suffered loss or damage as a result of an infringement.[480] Where, in particular, the claimant is an individual or company that is resident outside the United Kingdom and is not someone against whom a claim can be enforced under the Brussels I Regulation or Lugano Convention,[481] or there is some reason to believe that he will be unable to pay the defendant's costs, the court may make an order for security for costs.[482]

14.149 **Limitation period.** Since an infringement of the competition rules is regarded in English law as analogous to a breach of statutory duty, a cause of action arises when the claimant suffers damage by reason of the breach.[483] The limitation period is six years and when an isolated event causes a chain of damage that period begins to run on the date when the first damage is suffered. However, in *Arkin v Borchard Lines*,[484] the court held that the implementation of an agreement contrary to Article 81 or of a decision to carry out conduct contrary to Article 82 represents a continuing breach or series of breaches of the duty derived from the competition rules. Therefore, if such implementation continued and caused damage within six years before the start of proceedings, the claim will not be

---

[478] Practice Direction (n 468, above) para 3.

[479] *Ineos Vinyls Ltd v Huntsman Petrochemicals (UK) Ltd* [2006] EWHC 1241 (Ch), paras 264–265.

[480] ie there is not additional requirement such a direct personal concern nor is the right of action restricted to undertakings: cf the Ashurst Study (n 467, above) p 38.

[481] See paras 14.046 *et seq*, above, for the Brussels I Reg and the Lugano Convention.

[482] CPR rules 25.12–25.13; CAT Rules, rule 45.

[483] See *R. v Secretary of State for Transport, ex p Factortame Ltd* [1997] EuLR 475, [1998] 1 CMLR 1353, where it was held that an action against a *Member State* for breach of Community law is an action for breach of statutory duty and thus an action founded upon a tort within s 2 of the Limitation Act 1980.

[484] *Arkin v Borchard Lines* [2000] EuLR 232, [2000] UKCLR 495 (QBD Comm. Ct).

time-barred in respect of that damage. For follow-on damages claims,[485] there is a time limit of two years from the date on which the cause of action accrued, the date of the expiry of any right of appeal from the relevant decision or the date of the determination of any such appeal, whichever is the later.[486] However, this special time limit can give rise to practical problems when an appeal is brought by only some of the addressees of a Commission decision whom the follow-on claimant wishes to sue and the duration of their appeal is likely to exceed two years, by which time the limitation period will have expired for bringing a follow-on action against the other addressees of the decision who did not appeal.[487]

Requirement of fault.   Unlike many other Member States, there is no require-   **14.150** ment under the law in the United Kingdom that the claimant must establish fault (in the form of intention or negligence).[488]

Pleading.   As a matter of pleading, a party raising an issue under Article 81 or 82   **14.151** must expressly state that fact in his statement of case and adequately set out full and proper particulars of his case on that issue, including the essential facts.[489] Particular care will be expected of a party pleading competition law infringements as they are notoriously burdensome allegations, leading to extensive evidence and lengthy trials. Mere assertion in a pleading will not do.[490] In *P & S Amusements*,[491] the High Court highlighted that the general requirement for the party to plead the facts on which he relies applies to claims or defences under competition law as to any others. The judge stated:

> 'Thus, as with claims or defences under Articles 81 or 82 EC Treaty, so with claims or defences under ss. 2 or 18 of the Competition Act 1998 the party relying on the same must plead the primary facts on which he relies for the relevant conclusion, ... For example it is insufficient merely to aver that a given concerted practice has as its

---

[485] See para 14.145, above.

[486] CAT Rules, rule 31; Competition Act 1998, ss 47A(7) and (8), 47B(5).

[487] See *Emerson Electric Co v Morgan Crucible Co plc*, not yet decided, a claim pursuant to s 47A of the Competition Act 1998 where this issue is raised.

[488] See the Ashurst Study (n 467, above), although the position has changed in some Member States as a result of subsequent legislation.

[489] See CPR, Pt 16 and Practice Direction (n 468, above) para 2.2. In particular, a statement of case must specifically plead the fact of any illegality and all pleadings (statements of case) must be verified by a statement of truth by the party or his legal representative. See *Sandvik v Pfiffner* [1999] EuLR 755 (ChD); *Intergraph Corp v Solid Systems CAD Services Ltd* [1998] EuLR 223 (ChD); see also *per* Neuberger J in *Esso Petroleum v Gardner* (8 July 1998 unreported), approved by the Court of Appeal in *Parks v Esso Petroleum Co Ltd* [1999] EWCA Civ, [2000] EuLR 25.

[490] *BHB Enterprises Plc v Victor Chandler (International) Ltd* [2005] EWHC 1074 (Ch), [2005] EuLR 924, [2005] ECC 40, paras 42–43.

[491] *P & S Amusements Ltd v Valley House Leisure Ltd* (n 437, above) para 15. cf *Intel Corporation v VIA Technologies* (n 447, above) para 32: as the defence simple alleged a future hypothetical state of affairs, namely that a breach of Art 81 would be committed if VIA were forced to take a licence, it would be unreasonable to expect specific pleadings of fact to the same degree as where there had been an existing breach.

effect the distortion of competition within the United Kingdom. This is a mere reci-
tation of the statutory condition or conclusion imposed or required by s.2(1)(b)
without alleging any primary facts from which it might be inferred or found. In any
event such claims or defences require careful scrutiny so as to prevent cases lacking in
sufficient merit going to long and expensive trials'.

14.152 **Strike out.** Unparticularised allegations may be struck out.[492] However, the
degree of particularity will depend upon the nature of the allegation. For example,
in *Solid Systems*,[493] Ferris J held that it was not necessary to particularise in further
detail the facts relied upon to support the pleaded definition of the relevant
market and that, in respect of an allegation of anti-competitive effect, it was sufficient to set out how the effect flows from the agreement or concerted practice as
a whole. In *Sandvik v Pfiffner*,[494] Neuberger J held that it was necessary to plead
in some detail the facts relied upon to support allegations of dominant position,
abuse and the effect on trade between Member States. He referred to the relevant
balance as follows:

> 'On the one hand the Court should not make it too easy for a defendant to raise what
> turns out to be a baseless allegation of Article [82] infringement against a plaintiff,
> with a view to frightening off the plaintiff, or at least increasing the cost and delay to
> the plaintiff in establishing his right. On the other hand, it would be wrong to make
> it too difficult for a defendant with a valid case of Article [82] infringement to put his
> case before the Court.'

14.153 **Burden of proof.** The burden of proving that conduct constitutes a breach of
the Treaty lies on the party who asserts the infringement.[495] The burden of proving
the fulfilment of the conditions of Article 81(3) rests on the party claiming the
benefit of that provision.[496] An *evidential* burden will lie on the defendant generally in relation to any positive assertion it may make in rebuttal of the allegations
made by the claimant.[497]

---

[492] *Ransburg-Gema AG v Electrostatic Plant Systems Ltd* (n 445, above), where all five defences
were struck out. Striking out a claim or defence as disclosing no reasonable grounds or an abuse of
process is governed by CPR Pt 3.4. In practice, where the question of adequate particularisation is
raised, the Court will hear at the same time an application to strike out by one party and an application to amend by the other: eg *Sandvik v Pfiffner* (n 439, above); *Chiron Corp v Organon Teknika Ltd*
[1992] 3 CMLR 813, 816–817.

[493] *Intergraph Corpn v Solid Systems CAD Ltd* [1998] EuLR 223, 241 (ChD).

[494] ibid. See also *Huggins & Co Ltd v Capital Radio Restaurants Ltd*, 4 May 1999 (QBD), citing
Sandvik, in relation to a failure adequately to plead a case establishing infringement of Art 81(1) of
a beer supply agreement. For the need for particularity in pleading abuse under Art 82, see *HMSO
and Ordnance Survey v The Automobile Association Ltd* [2001] EuLR 80, [2001] ECC 34 (ChD).

[495] Art 2 of Reg 1/2003.

[496] ibid. See also Case C-552/03P *Unilever Bestfoods (formerly Van Den Bergh Foods) v Commission*
[2006] ECR I-9091, [2006] 5 CMLR 1460, paras 102–105.

[497] Case T-128/98 *Aéroports de Paris v Commission* [2000] ECR II-3929, [2001] 4 CMLR 1376,
para 202, applied in *The Racecourse Association and British Horse Racing Board v Office of Fair Trading*
[2005] CAT 29, [2006] Comp AR 99, paras 130–134 and *Attheraces Ltd v British Horse Racing*

Standard of proof. Regulation 1/2003 does not regulate the standard of proof, **14.154** which remains a matter for national law.⁴⁹⁸ Nor does it remove the requirement for national courts to ascertain the relevant facts. In *Napp*,⁴⁹⁹ the Competition Appeal Tribunal stated that although proceedings concerning a penalty for infringement of competition law are 'criminal' for the purpose of Article 6 of the European Convention on Human Rights, the Convention has not laid down a particular standard of proof and did not oblige the Tribunal to apply the criminal standard of 'proof beyond all reasonable doubt'. The Tribunal considered that the civil standard of 'the preponderance on the balance of probabilities' was more appropriate for determining factual issues requiring complex assessment of economic data which might involve conflicting expert evidence. In *Replica Kits*,⁵⁰⁰ the Tribunal reconsidered its ruling in *Napp* in the light of the introduction of the criminal cartel offence and confirmed that the applicable standard of proof was the civil standard on the balance of probabilities. This standard is also applied in competition law claims in the High Court.⁵⁰¹

Quality of evidence. The standard of proof is distinct from the quality and the **14.155** weight of the evidence required to discharge it. In *Napp*,⁵⁰² the Tribunal observed that, as the potential fines for an infringement were severe and were intended to have a deterrent effect, the more serious the allegation, the more cogent the evidence would have to be. The degree of probability will therefore be commensurate with the seriousness of the infringement alleged. In the Tribunal's view, 'strong and compelling evidence' would be required before an infringement can be found to be proved, even to the civil standard. In *Replica Kits*,⁵⁰³ the Tribunal resisted the attempt by the appellants to interpret 'strong and compelling' as introducing the criminal standard by the back door. It emphasised that such comments were directed towards the nature of the evidence: in all cases the Tribunal

---

Board Ltd [2005] EWHC 3015 (Ch), [2006] FSR 20, [2006] ECC 12, [2006] EuLR 76, para 127 (appeal on other grounds allowed, [2007] EWCA Civ 38, [2007] UKCLR 309, [2007] ECC 7).

⁴⁹⁸ Recital (5) of Reg 1/2003. The ECJ has previously held that questions of proof are a matter for national law subject to the principles of equivalence and effectiveness: Case C-242/95 *GT-Link v DSB* [1997] ECR I-4449, [1997] CMLR 601, paras 24–27. In its case law, the ECJ often does not distinguish between burden and standard and refers obliquely to the 'requisite standard of proof': see, eg Cases C-204/00P, etc, *Aalborg Portland v Commission* [2004] ECR I-123, [2005] 4 CMLR 251, para 81.

⁴⁹⁹ *Napp v Director General of Fair Trading* [2002] CAT 1, [2002] CompAR 13, paras 98 – 109.

⁵⁰⁰ *Allsports and JJB v Office of Fair Trading ('Replica Kits')* [2004] CAT 17, Comp AR 29, paras 187–208.

⁵⁰¹ *Attheraces Ltd v British Horse Racing Board Ltd* (n 497, above) para 126; *Ineos Vinyls Limited v Huntsman Petrochemicals (UK) Limited* [2006] EWHC 1241 (Ch), paras 210–211.

⁵⁰² *Napp* (n 499, above) paras 107–109, citing *Re H* [1996] AC 563 at 586, *per* Lord Nicholls.

⁵⁰³ *Allsports and JJB* (n 500, above) paras 187–208.

should be satisfied that the quality and weight of the evidence was sufficient to overcome the presumption of innocence.[504]

14.156 **Hierarchy of evidence.**   The legal systems of all Member States observe the principle of the free evaluation of evidence, ie that the judge is free to decide the value of each piece of evidence presented to him.[505] In *Replica Kits*,[506] the Tribunal emphasised that it would make its findings of fact on the basis of the totality of the evidence before it. In so doing, it established an informal hierarchy stating that it would attribute most weight to contemporaneous documents unless there was good reason not to do so. Next, the Tribunal takes account of the background evidence dealing with the economic and market context in determining whether it was likely that the infringements occurred. As to oral evidence from cross-examination, the Tribunal was sensitive to the complication that particular witness evidence might be coloured, at least subconsciously, by different motivations or that their recollection of events might deteriorate after some time. The Tribunal would assess the witnesses' credibility by testing their evidence and look for corroboration from the wider context or documentary evidence.[507] Overall, the Tribunal stressed that the question whether the evidence is sufficiently convincing to prove the infringement will depend on the circumstances. The Tribunal, relying on the *Cement* appeals,[508] took account of the fact that some anti-competitive practices, such as cartels, take place in a clandestine fashion where the production of documentary evidence may be suppressed. As in such cases evidence is sparse and fragmentary, the Tribunal may have to reconstitute the factual details by inferring the existence of an agreement or practice from a number of coincidences where there is no other plausible explanation for the behaviour. The Tribunal concluded that, in some cases, even a single item of evidence, or wholly circumstantial evidence may, depending on the particular context and the particular circumstances of the case, be sufficient to meet the required standard.[509]

---

[504] This appears to be in common with most Member States, although it seems that some countries, eg the Slovak Republic, Greece, Lithuania and Slovenia, impose higher standards based on absence of doubt: see *Study on the conditions of claims for damages in case of infringement of the EC Competition rules* (31 August 2004) ('the Ashurst Study') available on the DG Comp website, p 55.

[505] Ashurst Study (above) p 55.

[506] *Allsports and JJB* (n 500, above) paras 285–294.

[507] Note that in *Mastercard Members Forum v Office of Fair Trading*, the Tribunal objected to using expert reports as a means of presenting issues of primary fact: transcript of the CMC dated 31 March 2006.

[508] *Aalborg Portland v Commission* (n 498, above) paras 55–57.

[509] *Allsports and JJB* (n 503, above) para 206.

Admissible evidence. Expert economic evidence is admissible on such issues **14.157** as market dominance or restriction of competition.[510] Since the introduction of the Civil Evidence Act 1995, hearsay evidence is in principle admissible, although it is a matter for the Court to assess the weight to be given to such evidence.[511] Further, as a matter of Community law, the principle of effectiveness may place a limitation upon the application of domestic rules of evidence.[512]

Disclosure of documents as between parties. The Commission regards access **14.158** to evidence as 'key' to making damages claims effective, especially in stand-alone actions.[513] In England, the court will order pre-trial discovery if it is satisfied that disclosure is necessary to dispose of the proceedings fairly or prevent the need for proceedings at all or to save costs.[514] Otherwise disclosure is governed by the provisions for 'standard disclosure' under the Civil Procedure Rules, which require a party to disclose to the other party the documents on which he relies and the documents which adversely affect his own case or support or adversely affect another party's case.[515] The duty of disclosure continues throughout the proceedings. Disclosure is made by the party's solicitors who will serve a list of documents and a disclosure statement setting out any limitations to disclosure and the extent of the search that has been conducted.[516] The other party is permitted to inspect and take copies of the documents on the list. In addition, a party has the right to

---

[510] See, eg *Crehan v Inntrepreneur Pub Co (CPC)* [2003] EuLR 663, where the Court heard evidence from eight experts, including economists, surveyors and an analyst who had made a particular study of the brewing industry, and partly on the basis of that evidence concluded that the Commission's findings about the degree of foreclosure in the UK brewing industry were not correct; *Attheraces v British Horse Racing Board* (n 497, above), where three economists gave evidence on the issues of market definition and externalities relevant to the allegation of excessive pricing; *Chester City Council v Arriva Plc* [2007] EWHC 1373 (Ch), judgment of 15 June 2007, where the court accepted that evidence as to market definition could be given by an industry expert who was not an economist, albeit that it found that he had not established the definition that he put forward.

[511] cf *Macarthy v UniChem* [1991] ECC 41 (ChD), a case prior to the Civil Evidence Act 1995 where it was held that a report of the Monopolies and Mergers Commission following an investigation of an anti-competitive practice under the Competition Act 1980 was not admissible as evidence at the trial of an action based upon Art 81.

[512] AG van Gerven in Case C-128/92 *Banks* [1994] ECR I-1209, [1994] 5 CMLR 30, Opinion, para 48, citing Case 199/82 *San Giorgio* [1983] ECR 3595, [1985] 2 CMLR 658.

[513] Green Paper (n 414, above) para 2.1.

[514] CPR, rule 31.16. 'England' is used as shorthand in the text for England and Wales, the jurisdiction to which the CPR applies. For detailed discussion, see Matthews and Malek, *Disclosure* (3rd edn, 2007).

[515] CPR, rule 31.6. The Competition Appeal Tribunal follows similar principles and has broad powers to order the production of documents under rule 19(k) of the CAT Rules as it sees fit to secure the just, expeditious and economical conduct of proceedings.

[516] In giving standard disclosure, the party concerned is required to make a reasonable search for such documents; reasonableness will depend on a number of factors, including the nature and complexity of the proceedings, the number of documents involved, their significance and the ease and expense of their retrieval: see CPR, rule 31.7.

inspect any document that has not been disclosed but which is referred to in the other side's statement of case, witness statements or affidavits.[517] Moreover, a party can apply for disclosure of documents from third parties, who are not parties to the litigation, where the court is satisfied that such disclosure is likely to support the case of the applicant or adversely affect the case of one of the other parties to the proceedings and is necessary in order to dispose fairly of the claim or to save costs.[518]

14.159 **Limitations on disclosure.** A party may have a right to withhold certain documents from disclosure or inspection and should indicate those documents in the list or disclosure statement.[519] Among the most important examples are 'without prejudice' communications between the parties and documents protected by legal professional privilege. Documents prepared for the purpose of responding to an investigation by the competition authorities, even if that investigation did not envisage proceedings that could lead to the imposition of a penalty, should be protected by legal professional privilege.[520] It is not clear whether a party may claim a right to withhold documents on the ground of freedom from self-incrimination on the basis that disclosure of the document might incriminate him and lay him open to the imposition of a fine for breach of Article 81 or 82.[521] In certain cases, the court may dispense with or impose limits on standard disclosure[522] or order specific disclosure of documents or classes of documents

---

[517] CPR, rule 31.14.

[518] CPR, rule 31.17.

[519] CPR, rule 31.19.

[520] eg in connection with a market study by the Office of Fair Trading or a market investigation by the Competition Commission: see *Three Rivers District Council v Governor and Company of the Bank of England (No. 6)* [2004] UKHL 48, [2005] 1 AC 610, [2005] 4 All ER 948, holding that privilege applied to the documents prepared by the Bank of England to respond to the investigation into the collapse of BCCI. In the United Kingdom, legal professional privilege is wider than that observed in some other Member States as it protects communications with internal legal advisers: see Case 155/79 *AM & S Europe v Commission* [1982] ECR 1575, [1982] 2 CMLR 264, [1983] 1 All ER 705.

[521] In *Westinghouse Uranium Contract Litigation* [1978] AC 547, [1978] 1 CMLR 100, [1978] 1 All ER 434 (followed in *British Leyland v Wyatt Interpart* [1979] 3 CMLR 79 (ChD)), the House of Lords held that such a privilege could be claimed. However, the *Westinghouse* case concerned third party discovery in aid of US proceedings and the English law of privilege against self-incrimination in civil proceedings has subsequently been refined: see *Istel v Tully* [1993] AC 45 (HL), [1992] 3 All ER 523. Further, the ECJ has held that the Commission cannot use directly incriminating information obtained in the course of civil proceedings before a national court as evidence of a breach of competition rules: Case C-60/92 *Otto v Postbank* [1993] ECR I-5683, para 20. Were it otherwise, the privilege could frustrate the principle of EC law that national courts must provide effective remedies for infringement of the Community competition rules: see para above. See further on privilege against self-incrimination, Cumming, 'Otto v Postbank and the Privilege against self-incrimination in Enforcement Proceedings of Articles 85 and 86 before the English Courts' (1995) ECLR 400; and Temple Lang, 'The Devices of National Courts under Community Constitutional Law' (1997) 22 ELRev 3.

[522] CPR, rule 31.5 and CAT Rules, rule 22.

following a request.[523] However, applications for disclosure amounting to 'fishing expeditions' will not be ordered.[524] Disclosure in cases involving Article 81 or 82 potentially involves a very wide range of documents. In *MTV Europe v BMG Records*[525] the Court of Appeal upheld a decision that a very extensive request for discovery by the defendants was unduly burdensome and that the plaintiff should be permitted to serve schedules of figures, rather than the underlying documents which evidenced those figures. The court accepted that in ordering inspection of confidential documents, it was required to consider its duty under Article 10 of the Treaty to ensure the effectiveness of the EC competition rules, but that this had to be balanced against the public interest in a defendant's right to defend himself against allegations of infringement of Articles 81 and 82. On this basis, the court rejected the plaintiff's argument that disclosure of highly sensitive information to an undertaking operating in the same market would itself breach Article 81. However, although there is no rule protecting business secrets from disclosure, the commercial confidentiality of the information may influence the court in exercising its discretion as to the scope of disclosure to be ordered.[526] If disclosure is ordered, the court may restrict inspection of the documents to a 'confidentiality ring' of external legal advisers, experts and, where necessary, named individuals in the parties.[527]

Alleviating the claimant's burden. In the Green Paper, the Commission **14.160** highlighted the information asymmetry that exists when the claimant bears the burden of proving an infringement of competition law yet the defendant tends to have greater control or access to the underlying evidence.[528] The Commission put forward various proposals to improve access to evidence, including a procedure for mandatory disclosure of classes of documents by court order, orders to preserve evidence and/or sanctions for the destruction of evidence, procedures for access by the claimant to documents submitted by the other party to an NCA or the Commission during administrative proceedings or access by the national court to documents held in the Commission's possession. The Green Paper also considers the option of alleviating the evidential burden on the claimant by making all NCA infringement decisions binding on national courts, or reversing or lowering the *evidential* burden of proof to take account of any information asymmetry or unreasonable refusal to disclose documents.[529] It is expected that

---

[523] CPR, rule 31.12.
[524] *British Leyland v Wyatt Interpart* (n 521, above).
[525] *MTV Europe v BMG Records (UK) Ltd (No. 2)*, judgment of 10 March 1998.
[526] See Matthews and Malek (n 514, above) para 8.25.
[527] See, eg *Claymore v Director General of Fair Trading (Confidentiality)* [2003] CAT 12, [2004] Comp AR 63 (Competition Appeal Tribunal on an infringement appeal).
[528] Commission Staff Working Paper SEC (2005) 1732, paras 81 *et seq*.
[529] Working Paper (above) paras 29–30.

the Commission will publish a White Paper in early 2008 making concrete proposals for legislative development at Community level.

14.161 **Summary judgment.** The Civil Procedure Rules provide for summary judgment procedures, which are designed for the swift disposal of straightforward cases without trial. These are only available where the applicant demonstrates that the defence (or the claim, as the case may be) has no 'real' prospect of success and if there is no other compelling reason why the case or issue should be disposed of at a trial.[530] The court will be prepared to determine questions arising from a plea of Article 81(1) or 82 on a summary basis.[531] However, the Court of Appeal has, on several occasions, expressed caution about the efficacy of using the summary judgment procedure in cases involving conflicts of fact, developing areas of the law or a potential preliminary reference to the Court of Justice.[532] The court must heed the warning, when exercising its summary jurisdiction, against conducting a mini-trial.[533]

14.162 **Defence to summary judgment.** A plea based on Article 81(1) or 82 may result in the dismissal of an application for summary judgment.[534] However, a party relying upon Article 81(1) or 82 to resist summary determination will be required

---

[530] CPR, rule 24.2.

[531] See, eg *Unipart Group Ltd v O2 (UK) Ltd (formerly BT Cellnet Ltd)* [2004] EWCA Civ 1034 (CA) (Civ Div) [2004] UKCLR 1453, [2005] ECC 9, [2004] EuLR 969, upholding the summary judgment at first instance on the basis that Cellnet's alleged policy of adopting a margin squeeze was unilateral rather than an agreement between undertakings. Note that under CPR Part 24, a person resisting summary judgment must now show a real prospect of success (or 'some other reason' for a trial). See *Huggins & Co Ltd v Capital Radio Restaurants Ltd* (n 494, above) injunction and damages granted under CPR Pt 24 as the defendant has 'no real prospect of success' in its Art 81(1) defence; *The British Horseracing Board v William Hill Organisation Ltd* and *HMSO v The Automobile Association Ltd* (n 494, above) (pleas under Art 82 struck out as having no real prospect of success).

[532] *Intel Corpn v VIA Technologies Inc* (n 447, above), Court of Appeal, where Sir Andrew Morritt VC, sounded a cautionary note regarding the level of scrutiny to be given to 'Euro defences' when determining an application for summary judgment and warned against the dangers of assuming that the ECJ jurisprudence would not be extended to encompass the defence being advanced. He also warned that a Euro defence that could form the subject of an Art 234 reference is likely to be one that should be disposed of at trial not on a summary application. See also *Adidas-Salomon AG v Lawn Tennis Association* [2006] EWHC 1318 (Ch), [2006] UKCLR 823, [2006] ECC 29; *Doncaster Pharmaceuticals Group Ltd v The Bolton Pharmaceutical Co 100 Ltd* [2006] EWCA Civ 661, [2007] FSR 3, paras 17–18.

[533] See *Swain v Hillman* [2001] 1 All ER 91; *Three Rivers Council v Bank of England (No. 3)* [2001] UKHL 16, [2003] 2 AC 1, 260, [2001] 2 All ER 513, per Lord Hope at paras 94–95; *P & S Amusements Ltd v Valley House Leisure Ltd* [2006] EWHC 1510 (Ch), [2006] UKCLR 876, para 14.

[534] For cases of leave to defend being granted under former RSC Ord 14, see *Dymond v G B Britton & Sons (Holdings) Ltd* [1976] 1 CMLR 133 (ChD); *Yorkshire Water Services Ltd v Jarmain & Sons Ltd* [1997] EuLR 577 (QBD, Comm Ct) (conditional leave to defend where Art 82 defence 'shadowy'). See also *Sandvik v Pfiffner (UK) Ltd* (n 439, above) (some of the Art 81 defences could not be determined under Ord 14A where the point of EC law was difficult). *The Society of Lloyd's v Clementson* [1995] 1 CMLR 693, [1995] CLC 117 (CA) (application of Art 81 to Lloyd's bye-laws could not be determined as a preliminary point of law).

to demonstrate by credible evidence that he has a real prospect of establishing his case.[535] If the defence is based on a counterclaim arising out of Article 81 or 82, the defendant will have to establish, as a matter of English law, that the counterclaim gives rise to a set-off.[536] If the same or a similar issue has already been litigated in a court of competent jurisdiction the defendant must adduce good reasons to resist summary judgment even if the matter is not strictly governed by issue estoppel.[537] However, a court may take account of the defence even if an estoppel would otherwise operate since Articles 81 and 82 raise issues of public interest of which the Court should take cognisance. The Commercial Court has held that, where there is a strong *prima facie* case under Article 81, the Court cannot simply ignore the matter once it has been brought to its attention and there remains the possibility of dealing with it on the basis of full argument and evidence.[538]

7. Arbitration Proceedings

In general.   It is well established that issues of competition law are arbitrable and   **14.163**
that arbitrators therefore have power to apply Articles 81 and 82.[539] International joint venture agreements frequently incorporate an arbitration clause and provisions for arbitration are also common in distribution and licence agreements. Disputes heard by arbitrators under such agreements, in particular, may therefore involve arguments of competition law and there have been many arbitral awards

---

535 Note that under CPR Part 24, a person resisting summary judgment must show a real prospect of success (or 'some other reason' for a trial). See *Huggins & Co Ltd v Capital Radio Restaurants Ltd* (n 494, above) (summary judgment for an injunction and damages granted as the defendant has 'no real prospect of success' in its Art 81(1) defence); *The British Horseracing Board v William Hill Organisation Ltd* and *HMSO v The Automobile Association Ltd* (n 494, above) (pleas under Art 82 struck out as having no real prospect of success).

536 See *Courage Ltd v Crehan* [1999] EuLR 834, [1999] UKCLR 110, paras 57–78.

537 *Potato Marketing Board v Drysdale* [1986] 3 CMLR 331 (CA). (Subsequently in *Potato Marketing Board v Hampden Smith* [1997] EuLR 435, the defendant did adduce good reasons to resist summary judgment, but failed at trial to establish a defence under Art 82). For the position as regards judgments of the CFI and ECJ, see para 14.089, above. cf the special legislative provisions that apply to decisions under Art 81 or 82 by the Commission (paras 14.076 *et seq*, above) and the Office of Fair Trading (para 14.146, above).

538 *Bim Kemi AB v Blackburn Chemicals Ltd* [2004] EWHC 166 (Comm), [2004] EuLR 575, para 59.

539 See further Nazzini, *Concurrent Proceedings in Competition Law: Procedure, Evidence and Remedies* (2004) Chaps 10–11; Ward and Smith (eds), *Competition Litigation in the UK* (2005) Chap 11 (by Bowsher); Ehlermann and Atanasiu (eds) *European Competition Law Annual 2001: Effective Private Enforcement of EC Antitrust Law* (2003), Panel 3; and in general works on arbitration, Redfern and Hunter, *Law and Practice of International Commercial Arbitration* (4th edn, 2004) paras 3-16–3-18; Mustill and Boyd, *Commercial Arbitration* (2nd edn) *2001 Companion*, 79–82. For a detailed study, see Landolt, *Modernised EC Competition Law in International Arbitration* (2006).

determining competition law issues.[540] It is a question of the construction of the arbitration clause in any particular case as to whether it embraces disputes concerning competition law.[541] Since Modernisation, arbitrators should have the power to apply Article 81(3) in the same way as courts.

14.164   **Separability of the arbitration agreement.**   When a contract offends against competition law, since only those provisions which give rise to the violation are automatically void, the clause or term providing for arbitration should, as a matter of national law, be severable and survive.[542] The principle of the separability (or autonomy) of the arbitration agreement from the agreement of which it forms a part is widely accepted in international arbitration, and in England it is embodied in section 7 of the Arbitration Act 1996.[543] Arbitrators may therefore determine matters concerning the validity of the remainder of the agreement under Article 81 or 82. Nonetheless, in some cases the matters relevant to the impeachment of the substantive contract could also affect the validity of the arbitration agreement.[544] But those circumstances are exceptional, having regard to the reasons for the illegality and the policy favouring arbitration. In *Fiona Trust Corporation v Privalov*,[545] the English Court of Appeal upheld an arbitration agreement in a contract which it was alleged had been induced by bribery and could therefore be rescinded. The court held that an arbitration agreement would not be impeached only because the whole contract of which it was part was to be impeached, but only if there is some special reason for saying that the bribery impeached the arbitration clause in particular. Thus, although it is theoretically possible, for example, that a provision for arbitration in a bid-rigging agreement would be held invalid by the court of a Member State, in practice the objection on competition law grounds can be raised before the arbitrator, and any award which gave effect to such an agreement would probably not be enforceable in any Member State.[546]

---

[540] See the examples referred to by Baudenbacher, 'Enforcement of EC and EEA Competition Rules by Arbitration Tribunals Inside and Outside the EU', in Ehlermann & Atanasiu (eds) *European Competition Law Annual 2001* (above), pp 351–352.

[541] See, eg *ET Plus SA v Welter* [2005] EWHC 2115 (Comm), [2006] 1 Lloyd's Rep 251, para 51.

[542] See para 14.098 and, for discussion of severance under national law, paras 14.101 *et seq*, above.

[543] Authoritatively stated to be 'as close to a universal precept as any proposition of arbitration law can be': Mustill & Boyd (n 539, above), 79.

[544] See the discussion in the judgment of the English Court of Appeal, holding that jurisdiction of the arbitrator in that case was valid: *Harbour Assurance Co (UK) Ltd v Kansa General International Insurance Co Ltd* [1993] QB 701, [1993] 3 All ER 897, [1993] 1 Lloyd's Rep 455. See also Joseph, *Jurisdiction and Arbitration Agreements and their Enforcement* (2005) para 4.37.

[545] *Fiona Trust & Holding Corp v Privalov* [2007] EWCA Civ 20, [2007] 1 All ER (Comm) 891.

[546] See para 14.169, below.

Arbitrators' duty to apply EC competition rules. In *Nordsee*,[547] the Court of **14.165** Justice stated that Community law must be observed in its entirety throughout the territory of all the Member States and that parties to a contract are not free to create exceptions to it. The parties cannot seek to evade the application of the EC competition rules by the selection of the law of a non-Member State as their contractual choice of law. Moreover, when a party raises a competition law argument before the arbitral tribunal, the arbitrators are obliged to rule upon it: their failure to do so will be a ground for annulment of the award.[548] It is less clear whether the arbitrators are under a duty as a matter of Community law to apply EC competition law of their own motion if it is not raised by one of the parties. In the *Eco Swiss* case, discussed below,[549] Advocate General Saggio considered that they had no such duty but the Court of Justice did not rule on this point.[550] In practice, however, it seems that arbitrators may well themselves raise a competition law issue if the case concerns one or more States of the Community or the EEA.[551] If a relevant issue of competition law is not addressed in the arbitration, there is a risk that any resulting award may be susceptible to challenge on public policy grounds and many widely used arbitration rules, such as those of the International Chamber of Commerce (ICC), impose an obligation on the arbitral tribunal to seek to ensure that its award is legally enforceable.[552]

References to the Court of Justice. The Court of Justice held in *Nordsee*[553] that **14.166** arbitrators do not have power to refer questions of Community law to the Court of Justice under Article 234, since an arbitral tribunal which owes its jurisdiction to a consensual decision of the parties is not a 'court or tribunal' within the meaning of Article 234(2). The position may be otherwise in the case of mandatory arbitration imposed by national law.[554] However a national court within a Member

---

[547] Case 102/81 *Nordsee v Reederei Mond* [1982] ECR 1095, [1982] CMLR 154, para 14.

[548] See, eg judgment of the Swiss Federal Tribunal of 28 April 1992, ATF 118 II 193, annulling an award on those grounds. The governing law of the contract is irrelevant for this purpose: judgment of the Swiss Federal Tribunal of 13 November 1998, (1999) ASA Bulletin 529 (where the contract was governed by Swiss law).

[549] See para 14.167, below.

[550] Case C-126/97 *Eco Swiss v Benetton International* [1999] ECR I-3055, [2000] 5 CMLR 816, Opinion paras 21–26. See also Prechal and Shelkoplyas, 'National Procedures, Public Policy and EC Law. From Van Schijndel to Eco Swiss' (2004) ERPL 589 at 608; Van Houtte, 'Arbitration and Arts. 81 and 82 EC Treaty A State of Affairs' (2005) 23 ASA Bulletin 431, 438–441; Ward and Smith (n 539, above) para 11-056.

[551] See the examples cited by Derain, 'Specific Issues arising in the Enforcement of EC Antitrust Rules by Arbitration Courts', in Ehlermann & Atanasiu (eds) *European Competition Law Annual 2001* (n 539, above), 333–335.

[552] ICC Rules of Arbitration, rule 35: '... the Arbitral Tribunal ... shall make every effort to make sure that the Award is enforceable at law'. Similarly, London Court of International Arbitration, Arbitration Rules, art 32.2.

[553] *Nordsee* (n 547, above).

[554] ibid, paras 9–13.

State that is considering an appeal from an arbitration award or the enforcement of an award does have power to make a reference to the Court of Justice, even where the national court is required to determine the appeal on general principles of fairness and not in accordance with any particular system of law.[555] Moreover, it remains an open question whether the EFTA Court, which is not bound to follow the Court of Justice in this regard, might accept the jurisdiction of an arbitrator to make a reference to it under Article 34 of the EFTA Surveillance and Court Agreement.[556]

14.167 *Eco Swiss v Benetton.* In *Eco Swiss v Benetton*,[557] a Dutch company brought proceedings in the Dutch courts to set aside awards given by an arbitral tribunal in the Netherlands under which it had been ordered to pay substantial damages to a Hong Kong company for wrongful termination of a long-term licensing agreement. Although Benetton had not raised the issue before the arbitral tribunal, it contended before the Dutch courts that the licence agreement infringed Article 81 and that the awards were thus contrary to public policy. As a matter of Dutch law, there was no obligation upon the arbitrators to raise of their own motion EC competition law issues, and the fact that the award did not deal with such issues did not render enforcement of the award contrary to public policy. Moreover, an application for annulment on grounds of public policy had to be made within three months of registration of the awards and under Dutch procedural law the application was therefore out of time. However, the Dutch Supreme Court was concerned whether the principle in *Van Schijndel*,[558] which requires a court in certain circumstances to raise Community competition law issues of its own motion, should also apply to arbitrators and, further, whether a national court itself was obliged to set aside an award which was incompatible with Article 81(1). Accordingly the Supreme Court referred a number of questions to the Court of Justice under Article 234. In its judgment, the Court of Justice held that a national court must grant an application for annulment of an arbitration award if it considers that the award is in fact contrary to Article 81 where its domestic rules of procedure require it to grant such an application on failure to observe national rules of public policy ('*ordre public*'). The Court referred to the inability of arbitrators to make an Article 234 reference[559] and, although remarking that review by the courts of arbitration awards should be limited,

---

[555] Case C-393/92 *Almelo* [1994] ECR I-1477.

[556] OJ 1994 L344/3; for the Agreement, see para 1.087, above. See Baudenbacher (n 540, above), 355–356, 360–361 (Judge Baudenbacher is the President of the EFTA Court).

[557] Case C-126/97 *Eco Swiss v Benetton International* [1999] ECR I-3055, [2000] 5 CMLR 816.

[558] Cases C-430 & 431/93 *Van Schijndel and van Veen v SPF* [1995] ECR I-4705, [1996] 1 CMLR 793. See para 14.058, above.

[559] See para 14.166, above.

emphasised that by virtue of Article 3(1)(g) of the Treaty, Article 81 is a fundamental provision essential for the accomplishment of the tasks entrusted to the Community. Accordingly, where national procedural rules provide for annulment on grounds of national public policy, a national court must apply such rules where the application to annul is based on infringment of Article 81(1). The Court went on to hold that the provisions of Article 81(1) are to be regarded as a matter of public policy within Article V.2(b) of the New York Convention.[560] Moreover, Community law requires that questions concerning the interpretation of Article 81(1) should be open to examination by national courts when asked to determine the validity of an arbitration award and that it should thereby be possible for those questions to be referred to the Court of Justice under Article 234. However, Community law did not require the Dutch courts to refrain from applying their limitation period under domestic law for an application to annul the award. The period of three months did not deny a party an effective remedy, and since the application to annul was out of time it could be dismissed.[561]

Public policy and challenges to awards. Following the ruling by the Court of **14.168** Justice that the rules of EC competition law constitute rules of public policy within the Community, there has been much discussion as to the extent to which arbitration awards are therefore open to challenge on this basis.[562] The issue can arise on an application to annul an award or when the party in whose favour the award was made seeks to enforce it through the courts. In either case, there is a tension between the desire to ensure that the rules of competiton law, as a matter of public policy, are properly applied and concern that extensive review of awards by the courts on competition law grounds would undermine a fundamental attribute and attraction of arbitration, the finality of a decision given by the parties' chosen tribunal. *Eco Swiss* notably acknowledged the procedural autonomy of the Member States and did not require national courts to depart from their rules governing the manner or circumstances in which public policy can be raised as a challenge to an arbitral award, provided that some scope for review remained.[563] In consequence, there appears to be divergence in the degree of scrutiny given to

---

[560] The New York Convention on the Recognition and Enforcement of Foreign Arbitral Awards 1958.

[561] For the principle of effectiveness, see para 14.095 above.

[562] In addition to the works cited in n 539, above, see the articles in the special issue of Concurrences 2006, No. 3: 'Ordre public, concurrence et arbitrage' and the further articles cited therein.

[563] See the analysis of the judgment by Nazzini (n 539, above) paras 10.20–10.21. See also Case C-168/05 *Mostaza Claro* [2006] ECR I-10421, [2007] 1 CMLR 661 (national court should allow annulment of award on public policy grounds where contract violated Dir 93/13 conferring consumer protection).

awards on competition grounds.[564] In *Thalès v Euromissile*,[565] no argument of competition law had been raised before the arbitral tribunal and it was only on an application in the French courts to annul the award of substantial damages that the unsuccessful party first alleged that the agreement was anti-competitive and unenforceable. The Paris Court of Appeal found that the award was still susceptible to review,[566] but that only if the violation of the public policy rules was flagrant, effective and specific (*flagrante, effective et concrète*) would an award be set aside on that ground. In particular, the court would not embark upon a detailed examination of the complex issues involved in a competition case that had not been advanced before the arbitrators. Subsequently, in *SNF v Cytec Industries*,[567] the Paris Court of Appeal dismissed on the same grounds a challenge to the enforcement of another ICC arbitration award where the issues of competition law had been fully argued before, and dismissed by, the arbitrators. The court referred to the threat to the arbitral process posed by the depth of review of an arbitral award sought by the appellant. By contrast, in *Marketing Displays International*,[568] the Dutch courts were faced with an application under the New York Convention to enforce awards made by US arbitrators concerning an exclusive licence for the Benelux countries. An EC competition law defence had not been argued before the arbitrators but the unsuccessful defendant sought to resist enforcement before the Dutch courts on this ground. Applying Article 81 as fundamental public policy on the basis of *Eco Swiss*, the Hague Court of Appeal reviewed the agreement, found that several of its key provisions violated Article 81 and were not covered by the relevant block exemptions, and concluded that the whole agreement was void; enforcement of the awards was accordingly denied.

14.169 **Public policy challenges: England and Wales.** In *Bulk Oil v Sun International*,[569] the unsuccessful party in an English arbitration sought to appeal specifically so

---

[564] See Idot, 'Ordre Public, Concurrence et Arbitrage: État de la Rencontre' in *Concurrences* (n 562, above) pp 12–15.

[565] *Thalès Air Défence v GIE Euromissile*, judgment RG no. 2002/19606 of 18 November 2004, JCP E no. 18-19 of 5 May 2005, p 759, [2006] ECC 52. The award was in an ICC arbitration.

[566] ie the award had not become *res judicata*.

[567] *SNF-SAS v Cytec Industries BV*, judgment RG no. 04/19673 of 23 March 2006, Gazette du Palais 21-22 April 2006, p 48. See also in Sweden, Case T 6730-3 *Republic of Latvia v JSC Latvijas Gaze*, judgment of the Svea Court of Appeal of 4 May 2003, rejecting a challenge to an award on the basis of the EC State aid rules and suggesting (apparently *obiter*) that only in obvious cases of non-compliance with EC competition law would an arbitration award violate public policy.

[568] *Marketing Displays International v VR*, judgment of 24 March 2005, NJF 2005/239. For trenchant criticism of this approach, see Mourre and Radicati di Brozolo, 'Towards Finality of Arbitral Awards: Two Steps Forward and One Step Back' (2006) 23(2) Journal of Int'l Arbitration 171.

[569] *Bulk Oil Ltd v Sun International Ltd* [1984] 1 WLR 147, [1984] 1 All ER 386, [1983] 2 Lloyd's Rep 587. In due course the question was referred to the ECJ: see [1984] 2 CMLR 91 (QBD) and Case 174/84 *Bulk Oil v Sun International* [1986] ECR 559, [1986] 2 CMLR 732.

that a reference could be made by the English court to the Court of Justice. The Court of Appeal upheld the decision to grant leave to appeal against the award where the point of Community law was complex and 'capable of serious argument', noting the duty of national courts to ensure the observance of Community law and that only the courts, and not an arbitrator, can make a reference to the Court of Justice.[570] *Bulk Oil* was decided under the Arbitration Act 1979 whereas the subsequent Arbitration Act 1996 has narrowed the circumstances in which an award can be challenged before the English courts. Although the court may still give leave to appeal a domestic award[571] on a point of law, it may not do so if the question was not raised before the arbitrators.[572] Similarly, although the 1979 Act provides that a domestic award may be challenged on the grounds of 'serious irregularity' where the award is contrary to public policy, this applies only where in consequence 'substantial injustice' is caused to the applicant, and it appears that the right to make such an application is lost if the ground of objection was not taken before the arbitral tribunal.[573] It is unclear whether the condition that the competition issue had been raised before the arbitrator is to be regarded as a domestic procedural rule, which is applicable equally to national rules of public policy, such that the requirement prescribed by the Court of Justice in *Eco Swiss* is satisfied.[574] For a foreign arbitral award to which the New York Convention applies, the English court may refuse recognition or enforcement where that would be contrary to public policy and there is no equivalent condition that the ground of objection was taken in the arbitration.[575] At the time of writing, the issue has not yet arisen so as to establish the intensity of review that the English courts would be prepared to conduct in order to comply with *Eco Swiss* and assess whether an arbitration award violates EC competition law.

Public policy challenges: third countries.   The ruling in *Eco Swiss* of course   **14.170** binds only the courts of Member States. The approach of the courts in other

---

[570] In *Bulk Oil*, the desire to seek a reference to the ECJ was already made clear before the arbitrator.

[571] ie an award where the seat of the arbitration is in England and Wales or Northern Ireland.

[572] Arbitration Act 1996, s 69(3).

[573] ibid, ss 68(2)(g), 73. In *Lesotho Highlands Development Authority v Impregilo SpA* [2005] UKHL 43, [2006] 1 AC 221, [2005] 3 All ER 789, the House of Lords held that, save in exceptional cases, the finality of arbitration should not be undermined in a s 68 application by a review of the merits of the arbitrators' decision by the national courts. Presumably, therefore the grounds for setting aside an award on competition related policy grounds would have to fall within this category of exceptional cases.

[574] See para 14.167, above. In *Eco Swiss*, AG Saggio considered that a party cannot be precluded from raising an EC law objection in the court by reason of his failure to raise it in the arbitration: Opinion, paras 41–45; however the ECJ did not address this question.

[575] Arbitration Act 1996, s 103(3). This effectively reproduces Art V(2)(b) of the New York Convention.

countries to a challenge to an award on public policy grounds for failure to comply with EC competition law may well be different from that of the courts of Member States. Switzerland plays an important role in international arbitration, and a judgment of 8 March 2006 of the Swiss Federal Tribunal,[576] on an application to set aside the award in an ICC arbitration on competition law grounds, has therefore attracted considerable attention. The dispute concerned a cooperative arrangement between two Italian companies to tender for the supply of cables for the construction of bridges for the high-speed Milan–Naples railway line. The award of the arbitrators, whose seat was in Switzerland, considered in detail but rejected the respondent's contention that the agreement was void under both EC and Italian competition law. An application to annul the award was brought under the relevant Swiss law on the basis that the award was contrary to public policy. The Swiss Federal Tribunal conducted an extensive consideration of the relationship between competition law and public policy. Acknowledging that the concept of public policy was difficult to define, the Tribunal determined that for the purpose of the applicable Swiss statute, an award is inconsistent with public policy 'if it disregards those essential and widely recognised values which, according to the prevailing values in Switzerland, should constitute the foundation of any legal order'.[577] On that basis, the Tribunal held that the differences between the various laws on competition are too marked to enable a finding that competition law expressed a transnational or international rule of public policy. The Tribunal distinguished the judgment in *Eco Swiss* as based upon the fundamental role of competition law in achieving the objectives of the European Union. The Tribunal concluded that the provisions of competition laws, whatever they may be, do not belong to the essential and broadly recognised values which, according to Swiss concepts, would have to be found in any legal order.[578] However, the question of enforcement of that award then came before the Italian courts, where competition law was of course to be regarded, following *Eco Swiss*, as part of public policy. Nonetheless, the Milan Court of Appeal rejected the defendant's challenge to the award.[579] The Court considered the reasoning of the award, on the basis that this was to be distinguished from the arbitrators' evaluation of the facts and the evidence, and found that it showed that the principles of

---

[576] *X SpA v Y Srl*, ATF 132 III 389, ASA Bulletin 3/2006, p 521. An unofficial English translation is at ASA Bulletin 3/2006, p 550. The Federal Tribunal is Switzerland's highest court.

[577] ibid, para 2.2.3 (amended translation).

[578] However, the Tribunal made clear that its decision was taken on the basis of the narrow interpretation given to public policy on an application to set aside an award before a court, whereas an arbitrator can apply EC competition law as a foreign mandatory law in any case affecting trade between Member States: ibid, para 3.3.

[579] *Terra Armata Srl v Tensacciai SpA*, judgment no. 1897/06 of 5 July 2006.

competition law had been applied correctly. Accordingly, there was neither a need for a reference to the Court of Justice nor any conflict with public policy. This approach, involving scrutiny by the court that is far removed from a substantive appeal, appears to be a way of meeting the concern that the requirements of Community law should not be allowed to develop into a full appeal on the merits.[580]

8. Table of National Enforcement Regimes

See over for Table of National Enforcement Regimes.   **14.171**

---

[580] cf the approach laid down by the US Supreme Court when holding that claims for violation of antitrust law could go to arbitration, with the public policy enshrined in the antitrust laws protected by the exception to enforcement of a resulting award: 'While the efficacy of the arbitral process requires that substantive review at the award-enforcement stage remain minimal, it would not require intrusive inquiry to ascertain that the tribunal took cognizance of the antitrust claims and actually decided them'. *Mitsubishi Motors Corp v Soler Chrysler-Plymouth*, 473 US 614, 638, 105 SCt 3346 (1985), per Blackmun J giving the majority judgment. See also *Baxter International, Inc v Abbott Laboratories*, 315 F 3d 829 (7th Cir, 2003) (rehearing den'd, 325 F 3d 954; cert den'd, 540 US 963, 124 S Ct 387 (2003)), rejecting a challenge on antitrust grounds to enforcement of an arbitral award as an 'attempt to litigate the antitrust issues anew'. However, *Eco Swiss* clearly requires the national court to allow a challenge if scrutiny of the award reveals serious doubt as to the application of EC competition law such that the award may be contrary to Art 81 or 82 or a reference should be made to the ECJ.

	National authority(ies)	Maximum financial penalty	Criminal sanctions	Leniency policy	Appeal from national competition authority (NCA)	Status of the NCA decision in subsequent private action	Status of another MS's NCA decision in subsequent private action
Austria	Prosecuting authorities: – Bundeswettbewerbsbehörde (Federal Competition Authority) – Budeskartellanwalt (Federal Cartel Prosecutor) Judicial authority: Kartellgericht (Cartel Court)	10% of annual worldwide turnover	No (except for bid-rigging in public procurement proceedings: up to 3 years' imprisonment)	Yes, but not for criminal sanctions	Appeal against Kartellgericht decisions to the Kartellobergericht (Supreme Court)	Kartellgericht decisions binding in subsequent court proceedings (*res judicata*)	Not binding
Belgium	Investigating authorities: Dienst voor de Mededinging/Service de la concurrence (Competition Service)[1] Auditoraat/Auditorat[2] Administrative adjudicating authority: Raad voor de Mededinging / Conseil de la concurrence (Competition Council)	10% of annual turnover on the national market and by way of exports from Belgium	No	Yes	First Instance: Court of Appeal of Brussels Second instance: Supreme Court (on points of law only)	Take into account as evidence	Taken into account as evidence

[1] Part of the Federal Public Service Economy, SMEs, Self-employed and Energy.

[2] Guides and organises the investigation, and monitors the implementation of the decisions of the Competition Council of which it is formally a part.

Bulgaria	Комисия За защита на конкуренцията (Commission on Protection of Competition)	300 000 BGN (500 000 BGN for repeat offenders)[3]	No	Yes	Supreme Administrative Court	Taken into account as evidence	As yet undetermined
Cyprus	Επιτροπή Προστασίας του Ανταγωνισμού (Commission for the Protection of Competition (CPC))	10% of annual turnover[4]	No (except for continuing to give effect to an agreement or engage in abusive conduct in contravention of a decision by the CPC)	Yes	Cyprus Supreme Court	Binding	No special provision in that regard
Czech Republic	Úřad pro ochranu hospodářské soutěže (Office for the Protection of Competition)	10% of annual net worldwide turnover	No (except for bid-rigging in public procurement)	Yes	Regional Court Brno	Binding	Taken into account as evidence
Denmark	Konkurrencerådet (Competition Council) decides on major cases and test cases on the basis of submissions from the Konkurrencestyrelsen (Competition Council) Konkurrencestyrelsen is responsible for day-to-day management on behalf of the Council	No legal maximum. (annual worldwide turnover taken into account; highest fine to date: 30 million DKK)	Yes (all sanctions are criminal: fines imposed by Criminal Courts both on undertakings and individuals—no imprisonment)	Yes	First instance: Competition Appeal Tribunal Second instance: Ordinary courts	Binding	Taken into account as evidence

[3] However, new law in draft at time of writing is expected substantially to increase penalties.

[4] The legislation does not specify whether this is national or worldwide turnover.

	National authority(ies)	Maximum financial penalty	Criminal sanctions	Leniency policy	Appeal from national competition authority (NCA)	Status of the NCA decision in subsequent private action	Status of another MS's NCA decision in subsequent private action
Estonia	Konkurentsiamet (Competition Board)	Maximum varies according to nature of violation: lesser violations attract civil penalties imposed by Competition Board; more serious violations are criminal. Figures below are for serious violations, ie: infringement of Art 81 (or equivalent); or repeated abuse of dominant position, violation by undertaking with special or exclusive rights or in control of essential facilities, in respect of the same act. For a legal person: 250 million EEK For an individual: 500 'daily rates' (calculated on the basis of the individual's average daily income).	Yes – serious violations are crimes under the Penal Code, for which penalties are imposed by the criminal courts: see previous column. Up to 3 years' imprisonment for individuals	Yes – under the general rules of criminal procedure	Ordinary courts	Taken into account as evidence	Taken into account as evidence

Finland	Kilpailuvirasto (Competition Authority): takes decisions on infringement and acts as prosecuting authority for penalties Market Court: judicial authority for penalties	10% of worldwide turnover in the preceding year	No	Yes	a) Market Court – from decisions of the Kilpailuvirasto b) Supreme Administrative Court – from decisions of the Market Court	Taken into account as evidence	Taken into account as evidence
France	Conseil de la Concurrence (Competition Council) and Ministre de l'Economie – Direction Generale de la Concurrence, Consommation et Repression des Fraudes (Minister of Economy – DGCCRF)	10% of highest worldwide turnover (net of tax) in any financial year in which the infringement was carried out, preceding the year in which it was terminated — save that where the undertaking is not a company, maxiumum penalty of €3 million.	Yes (up to 3 years imprisonment and criminal fines for individuals)	Yes, but not for criminal sanctions	Paris Court of Appeal	CC decision taken into account as evidence	Taken into account as evidence
Germany	Bundeskartellamt (Federal Cartel Office) and Landeskartellbehörden (State Cartel Offices)	10% of annual worldwide turnover + disgorgement of illicit profits if they exceed the fine; penalties on individuals up to €1 million.	No (except for bid-rigging in public tenders: criminal fines on individuals and up to 5 years imprisonment)	Yes, but not for criminal sanctions	First instance: Court of Appeal Düsseldorf (or the respective Federal Court of Appeal) Second instance: Federal Supreme Court	Binding	Binding

	National authority(ies)	Maximum financial penalty	Criminal sanctions	Leniency policy	Appeal from national competition authority (NCA)	Status of the NCA decision in subsequent private action	Status of another MS's NCA decision in subsequent private action
Greece	Επιτροπή Ανταγωνισμού (Hellenic Competition Commission)	15% of annual worldwide turnover	Yes, where the individual is the undertaking (whether as sole owner or partner) or a representative of the undertaking that committed the infringement (criminal fines up to €30,000; doubled for repeat offence).	Yes	Ordinary administrative courts	Binding	Taken into account as evidence
Hungary	Gazdasági Versenyhivatal (GVH) (Competition Authority)	10% of annual worldwide turnover	No (except for bid-rigging in public procurement and concession proceedings – up to 5 years' imprisonment for individuals and criminal sanctions on undertakings)	Yes – both for admini-strative and criminal sanctions	First instance: Metropolitan Court, Budapest Second instance: Metropolitan Court of Appeal, Budapest	Binding	Taken into account as evidence

					Ordinary courts	Taken into account as evidence	Taken into account as evidence
Ireland	Prosecuting authorities: – Competition Authority (summary offence) – Director of Public Prosecutions (prosecution on indictment) Judicial authority: every Court in Ireland	€4 million or 10% of annual turnover, whichever is the higher[4a]	Yes: all sanctions are criminal. For an individual, up to 5 years imprisonment.	Yes	Ordinary courts	Taken into account as evidence	Taken into account as evidence
Italy	Autorità Garante della Concorrenza e del Mercato (Italian Competition Authority)	10% of annual worldwide turnover	No	Yes	First instance: Latium Regional Administrative Tribunal Second instance: Consiglio di Stato (Council of State)	Taken into account as evidence	Taken into account as evidence
Latvia	Konkurences padome (Competition Council of Latvia)	10% of annual net worldwide turnover	No	Yes	Administrative Courts	Taken into account as evidence	Taken into account as evidence
Lithuania	Lietuvos Respublikos konkurencijos taryba (Competition Council of the Republic of Lithuania)	10% of gross annual worldwide income (ie before tax)	No	Yes	Vilnius Regional Administrative Court	Taken into account as evidence	Taken into account as evidence
Luxembourg	Prosecuting authority: Inspection de la concurrence (Competition Inspectorate) Administrative adjudicating authority: Conseil de la concurrence (Competition Council)	10% of annual net worldwide turnover	No	Yes	First instance: Administrative Court Second instance: Administrative Court of Appeal	Taken into account as evidence	Taken into account as evidence

[4a] Probably refers to the turnover of the legal person before the court and not the group of which it is part, but as yet unclear.

	National authority(ies)	Maximum financial penalty	Criminal sanctions	Leniency policy	Appeal from national competition authority (NCA)	Status of the NCA decision in subsequent private action	Status of another MS's NCA decision in subsequent private action
Malta	Prosecuting authority: 1-Ufficċju tal-Kompetizzjoni Ġusta (Office for Fair Competition) Administrative adjudicating authority: il-Kummissjoni għall-Kummerċ Ġust (Commission for Fair Trading)	10% of annual turnover on the market affected by the infringement	Yes (all fines are of criminal nature and are imposed by criminal courts)	No	Judicial review under administrative law	Taken into account as evidence	Taken into account as evidence
Netherlands	Nederlandse Mededingingsautoriteit (NMa) (Netherlands Competition Authority)	€450,000 or 10% of annual worldwide turnover, whichever is the higher	Yes: fines up to €450,000 for the executives of the undertaking which committed the infringement	Yes	Initially an internal administrative review by the NMa and thereafter (or directly with the NMa's consent) appeal to: First instance: Rotterdam District Court Second instance: Trade and Industry Appeals Tribunal	Taken into account as evidence	Taken into account as evidence

Norway	Konkurransetilsynet (Competition Authority) – responsible for enforcement and able to impose administrative fines. Fornyings- og administrasjonsdepartementet (Minister of Government Administration and Reform) – responsible for determining competition policy and priorities for the Competition Authority	10% of annual net worldwide turnover	Yes, but not for abuse of dominance. Criminal fines and imprisonment of up to 3 years (or 6 years in 'severely aggravating circumstances')	Yes — both for administrative and criminal sanctions	Ordinary courts, save that a decision ordering the termination of an infringement (but not the imposition of an administrative fine) may be appealed to the Ministry of Renewal and Government Administration	Taken ito account as evidence	Taken ito account as evidence
Poland	Prezes Urzedu Ochrony Konkurencji i Konsumentow (President of the Office for Competition and Consumer Protection)	10% of annual worldwide turnover	No	Yes	First instance: Court for Competition and Consumer Protection – a division of the Warsaw District Court. Second instance: Court of Appeal in Warsaw.	Binding	Probably taken into account as evidence
Portugal	Autoridade da Concorrência (Competition Authority)	10% of annual turnover[4b]	No special criminal offence, except for bid-rigging	Yes, but not for criminal sanctions	Lisbon Court of Commerce	Creates a rebuttable presumption	Taken into account as evidence

[4b] It is unclear whether this applies to national or worldwide turnover, but to date it has been applied in respect of national turnover.

	National authority(ies)	Maximum financial penalty	Criminal sanctions	Leniency policy	Appeal from national competition authority (NCA)	Status of the NCA decision in subsequent private action	Status of another MS's NCA decision in subsequent private action
Romania	Consiliul Concurentei (Competition Council)	10% of annual worldwide turnover	Yes (criminal fines and up to 4 years' imprisonment)	Yes, but not for criminal sanctions	Court of Appeal Bucharest, Administrative Section	Taken into account as evidence	Taken into account as evidence
Slovak Republic	Protimonopolný úrad Slovenskej republiky (Antimonopoly Office of the Slovak Republic AMO)	10% of annual worldwide turnover	Yes (criminal fines and up to 6 years' imprisonment)	Yes, but not for criminal sanctions	First instance: Council of the AMO Second instance: Judicial review in Regional court in Bratislava (administrative section)	Binding	Probably binding
Slovenia	Urad RS za varstvo konkurence (Competition Protection Office)	Legal persons: - €375,000 Individuals:- €12,500	No – except for art 321 of the Criminal Code (creation of monopoly) that is currently under review	No	Administrative Court for administrative decisions Ordinary courts for misdemeanour decisions	Probably binding	Taken into account as evidence

						Taken into account as evidence
Spain	Comisión Nacional de la Competencia (CNC) (National Competition Commission) (Investigations are carried out by the Investigation Division of the CNC and decisions are taken by the Council of the CNC)	Legal persons: – for 'serious' infringements: up to 5% of annual worldwide turnover of the undertaking, or if turnover cannot be determined, from €501,000 to €10 million; – for 'very serious' infringements:[5] up to 10% of annual worldwide turnover of the undertaking, or if turnover cannot be determined, at least €10 million. Individuals: €60.000	No	Yes[6]	First instance, Audiencia Nacional, Sala de le Contencioso-Administrativo (National Audience, Contentious-Administrative Chamber) Cassation: Supreme Court	Taken into account as evidence / Taken into account as evidence
Sweden	Konkurrensverket (Competition Authority): takes decisions on infringement and acts as prosecuting authority for penalties. Judicial authority for penalties: Stockholm District Court	10% of annual worldwide turnover of the undertaking	No	Yes	First instance: Stockholm District Court Second instance: Market Court	Taken into account as evidence / Taken into account as evidence

5 eg, infringement of Art 81 by actual or potential competitors or of Art 82 by company in a recently liberalised market or having a near monopoly market share.

6 At time of writing, an implementing regulation has still to be adopted.

	National authority(ies)	Maximum financial penalty	Criminal sanctions	Leniency policy	Appeal from national competition authority (NCA)	Status of the NCA decision in subsequent private action	Status of another MS's NCA decision in subsequent private action
United Kingdom	Office of Fair Trading and sectoral Regulators	10% of annual worldwide turnover of the undertaking	Yes – for individuals as regards 'hardcore' horizontal agreements Up to 5 years' imprisonment	Yes	First instance: Competition Appeal Tribunal Second instance: – Court of Appeal (England and Wales) – Court of Session (Scotland) – Court of Appeal in Northern Ireland (Northern Ireland)	Findings of fact and of infringement are binding	Probably can be taken into account as evidence

15

STATE AIDS

1. Introduction

Generally. The establishment of a true single market and a system of undistorted **15.001**
competition requires that Member States are prohibited from granting to
undertakings aids that distort, or threaten to distort, competition and trade
between Member States. It is therefore not surprising that the EC Treaty includes
provisions[1] regulating the granting of aids by Member States. As the Commission
has stated:

> 'State aid control comes from the need to maintain a level playing field for all
> undertakings active in the Single European Market, no matter in which Member

---

[1] Arts 87–89: Vol II, App A.2. Similar provisions are included in the EEA Agreement, see
para 15.004, below. The ECSC Treaty, which expired on 24 July 2002, also made provision with

State they are established. There is a particular need to be concerned with those State aid measures which provide unwarranted selective advantages to some firms, preventing or delaying market forces from rewarding the most competitive firms, thereby decreasing overall European competitiveness. [Such measures] may also lead to a build-up of market power in the hands of some firms .... As a result of such distortions of competition, customers may be faced with higher prices, lower quality goods and less innovation.'[2]

However, the rules on State aid have considerable flexibility. While Article 87(1) of the EC Treaty prohibits State aids, Articles 87(2) and (3) allow the Community to approve particular types of State aids that are generally beneficial.[3] Therefore, although the main aim of the Commission, which has the principal responsibility for administering the State aid rules, is to avoid distortions of competition and to strengthen the unity of the common market, the Commission also recognises that:

'State aid measures can sometimes be effective tools for achieving objectives of common interest. They can correct market failures, thereby improving the functioning of markets and enhancing European competitiveness. They can also help promote, [for example], social and regional cohesion, sustainable development and cultural diversity, irrespective of the correction of market failures.

However, State aid should only be used when it is an appropriate instrument for meeting a well defined objective, when it creates the right incentives, is proportionate and when it distorts competition to the least possible extent. For that reason, appreciating the compatibility of State aid is fundamentally about balancing the negative effects of aid on competition with its positive effects in terms of common interest.'[4]

The growing importance of the rules on State aid can be seen from the fact that, in 2006, the number of State aid cases registered with the Commission reached 921, a 36 per cent increase on the previous year.[5] In 2006 the Commission issued

---

regard to State aids in Arts 4(c) and 67. With regard to the law and policy of EC State aid regulation, see generally Hancher, Ottervanger and Slot, *EC State Aids* (3rd edn, 2006); Dony (ed), *Contrôle des aides d'Etat* (2007); Quigley and Collins, *EC State Aid Law and Policy* (2003); Sanchez-Rydelski, *State Aid Regime – Distortive Effects of State Aid on Competition and Trade* (2006); Nicolaides, Kekelekis and Buyskes, *State Aid Policy in the European Community – A Guide for Practitioners* (2005); Biondi, Eeckhout and Flynn (eds) *The Law of State Aid in the European Union* (2004); Feltkamp, 'Some reflections on the structure of the state aid rules in the Treaty of Rome' (2003) 1 EC Competition Policy Newsletter 29. For procedural issues, see Ortiz Blanco (ed), *EC Competition Procedure* (2nd edn, 2006), Chaps 21-27 (by Keppenne). See also the Commission's Vademecum Community Rules on State Aid (February 2007) containing summaries of some of the guidelines and regulations, available at: http://ec.europa.eu/comm/competition/state_aid/studies_reports/vademecum_on_rules_2007_en.pdf.

[2] *State Aid Action Plan – Less and better targeted State aid: a roadmap for State aid reform 2005-2009*, COM(2005) 107 final–SEC(2005) 795, 7 June 2005, para 7. The Plan is available in the State aid section of DG Comp's website and at (2005) 2 EC Competition Policy Newsletter 3.

[3] See paras 15.039 *et seq*, below.

[4] *State Aid Action Plan 2005* (n 2, above), paras 10–11.

[5] *Annual Report on Competition Policy* (2006), point 24. These figures are based on a corrected methodology that avoids double counting, and therefore differ from the figures in the 2005 Report.

710 decisions in the State aid field, a 12 per cent increase on 2005. In the great majority of cases, the Commission approved the examined measure, concludng either that it was compatible with the State aid rules or that it did not constitute State aid.[6]

State aid reform. The Community rules on State aid are currently undergoing a process of modernisation and reform pursuant to the Commission's State Aid Action Plan.[7] The Action Plan is directed at achieving the goal of 'less, and better targeted, State aid' which forms part of the 'Lisbon Strategy'[8] for improving the competitiveness and dynamism of the European economy.[9] One of the key aims of the Action Plan is to simplify the State aid rules by reference to a coherent set of fundamental principles which can be consistently applied in different settings. As the Commission has noted: **15.002**

> ' . . . the increasing complexity and number of documents progressively adopted by the Commission over time have created a need to streamline State aid policy, focus attention on the most distortive types of aid and make State aid control more predictable and user-friendly, thereby minimising legal uncertainty and the administrative burden both for the Commission and for Member States.'[10]

The Commission has stated that in general the positive impact of an aid depends on: (i) how accurately the accepted objective of common interest (whether social, regional, economic or cultural) has been identified; (ii) whether State aid is an appropriate instrument for dealing with the problem as opposed to other policy instruments; and (iii) whether the aid creates the needed incentives and is proportionate. On the other hand, the level of distortion created by an aid generally depends on: (i) the procedure for selecting beneficiaries and the conditions attached to the aid; (ii) characteristics of the market and of the beneficiary; and (iii) the amount and type of aid. For example, restructuring aid or investment aid

---

[6] ibid.

[7] See *State Aid Action Plan 2005* (n 2, above); also http://ec.europa.eu/comm/ competition/ state_aid/overview/sar.html.

[8] Agreed at the European Council meeting in Lisbon in March 2000: see European Council, Lisbon, 23–24 March 2000, Presidency Conclusions, in particular points 16–17. The declared aim of the Lisbon Strategy is to make the EU the most competitive and dynamic knowledge-based economy in the world by 2010.

[9] In March 2005 the European Council relaunched the Lisbon Strategy, calling on Member States 'to continue working towards a reduction in the general level of State aid, while making allowance for any market failures. The movement must be accompanied by a redeployment of aid in favour of support for certain horizontal objectives such as research and innovation, and the optimisation of human capital. The reform of regional aid should also foster a high level of investment and ensure a reduction in disparities in accordance with the Lisbon objectives', European Council, Brussels, 22–23 March 2005, Presidency Conclusions, Doc 05/1, point 23.

[10] *State Aid Action Plan 2005* (n 2, above) para 17.

to large companies should be carefully monitored to address clearly an objective of common interest, since the impact of such measures on competition and trade will normally be significant.[11]

15.003 **Recent legislative developments.** The Commission has stated that it is seeking to refocus and modernise State aid controls.[12] One of the first steps in implementation of the Action Plan was the adoption, in November 2005, of a Community Framework on services of general economic interest, as well as a block exemption for certain forms of public service compensation.[13] The Commission has also adopted revised guidelines on both regional aid[14] and risk capital[15] that came into force on 1 January 2007. In addition, the Commission issued a new Communication on State aid and innovation and adopted a new Community framework for research and development, in order to promote cross-border research cooperation and focus aid on addressing market failures that inhibit innovation.[16] A further significant change will be the adoption of a general block exemption. At the time of writing, the Commission is reviewing responses to a consulation on a draft Regulation which will replace the the existing block exemptions for training, SMEs, employment and regional aids,[17] with one block exemption which consolidates and simplifies the existing block exemptions, and further provides for the first time block exemption for environment aid,[18] aid in the form of risk capital and research and development aid in favour of large enterprises. The general block exemption is likely to be adopted by the end of 2007 with retrospective effect.[19]

---

[11] *State Aid Action Plan 2005* (n 2, above) para 20. See further Kleiner, 'Reforming state aid policy to best contribute to the Lisbon Strategy for growth and jobs' (2005) 2 EC Competition Policy Newsletter 29.

[12] With respect to the criticism that the current State aid regime is poorly focused and over-inclusive in its application, see, eg Lever, 'The EC State Aid Regime: The Need for Reform', in Biondi, Eeckhout and Flynn (eds), *The Law of State Aid in the European Union* (2004), Chap 16.

[13] See para 15.068, below.

[14] See para 15.046, below.

[15] Community guidelines on State aid to promote risk capital investments in small and medium-sized enterprises, OJ 2006 C194/2: Vol II, App G.21. See Schwarz, 'New Guidelines on State aid promoting risk capital invetsments in SMEs' (2006) 3 EC Competition Policy Newsletter 19.

[16] Communication on State Aid for Innovation COM(2005) 436 Final (21 September 2005); Press Release IP/05/1169 (21 September 2005). The new Community Framework for State Aid for Research and Development and Innovation was adopted on 22 November 2006: OJ 2006 C323/1 and see Press Release IP/06/1600 and MEMO/06/441 (both 22 November 2006).

[17] For the current block exemptions, see paras 15.052 and 15.067, below.

[18] The current Guidelines on State aids for environmental protection measures, OJ 2001 C37/3: Vol II, App G.18, lapse at the end of 2007.

[19] See the draft Regulation for a general block exemption, published on 24 April 2007: Vol II, App G.16. DG Competition has published a full explanatory memorandum on the draft: Vol II, App G.17.

European Economic Area.   Article 61 of the EEA Agreement[20] contains provi-   **15.004**
sions on State aids largely equivalent to Article 87 of the EC Treaty. Jurisdiction to
apply Article 61 is divided between the Commission and the EFTA Surveillance
Authority. As regards the three EFTA States within the European Economic Area,
the provision is applied by the EFTA Surveillance Authority[21] according to a procedural and enforcement framework[22] which closely correspond to the EC rules.
As regards the EC Member States, the provision is applied by the Commission
and in effect the existing EC procedural and enforcement rules are extended to
cover the EFTA States that are parties to the EEA Agreement.[23] Most of the EC
regulations, directives and guidelines as regards State aids have been adopted, with
necessary modifications, to apply under the EEA Agreement to the European
Economic Area.[24] As with the application of the other competition rules, the
Commission and the EFTA Surveillance Authority cooperate closely in the field
of State aid.[25]

Other international agreements.   The decision of 22 December 1995 of the   **15.005**
EC–Turkey Association Council implementing the final phase of the customs
union under the Association Agreement with Turkey ('the Ankara Agreement')
contains rules on State aid similar to those in the EC Treaty.[26] The Community
is party to the WTO Agreements,[27] one of which, the Agreement on Subsidies
and Countervailing Measures, imposes an obligation to report subsidies during
the previous calendar year and to notify prior to implementation certain types

---

[20] Art 61(3) EEA has not been amended to incorporate the sub-paragraph concerning aid to
promote culture and heritage conservation that was added to the EC Treaty at Maastricht, now
Art 87(3)(d) EC: see para 15.064, below. However, the ESA seeks to authorise such aid under other
heads of Art 61(3). There is also no equivalent provision in Art 61(2) EEA to Art 87(2)(c) EC: see
para 15.040, below. See *Encyclopedia of European Union Law* (*Constitutional Texts*) (Sweet & Maxwell),
Vol 2, paras 30.0042 *et seq*. See also Joint Declarations [10]–[12] annexed to the Agreement: ibid,
paras 30.2418–30.2430.

[21] Art 62(1)(b) and Protocol 26 to the EEA Agreement. The three EFTA States within the EEA
are Norway, Iceland and Liechtenstein. For the application by the EFTA Surveillance Authority of
the State aid rules, see its annual Reports.

[22] The primary procedural rules corresponding to Art 88 EC are in Art 1 to Protocol 3 of the
EFTA Surveillance and Court Agreement.

[23] Art 62(1)(a) EEA.

[24] Pursuant to Art 63 and Annex XV to the EEA Agreement. The EC Guidelines were adopted
by the EFTA Surveillance Authority on 19 January 1994 as one document, the Guidelines on the
application and interpretation of Arts 61 and 62 of the EEA Agreement and Art 1 of Protocol 3 to
the Surveillance and Court Agreement (published in OJ 1994 L231, EEA Supp No 32), which is
updated by amendment. For a consolidated, up-to-date text, see the Authority's website at http://
www.eftasurv.int/fieldsofwork/fieldstateaid/guidelines/.

[25] See Art 62(2) and Protocol 27 EEA.

[26] Arts 34–35 of Decn 1/95, OJ 1996 L35/1. For agreements between the Community and third
countries generally concerning cooperation in competition matters see paras 1.096 *et seq*, above.

[27] See para 1.103, above.

of aid.[28] Account needs also to be taken of the OECD Arrangement on Guidelines for Officially Supported Export Credits, to which the Community is a party.[29] More information about arrangements for cooperation on competition matters with countries outside the EEA are included in the international section of DG Competition's website.

15.006 **Plan of this Chapter.**   This Chapter deals first with the substantive question as to what constitutes State aid under Article 87(1) and then considers, in Sections 3 and 4, the compatibility of certain aid with the common market under Article 87(2) and (3). Section 5 discusses the procedural rules relating to review and notification of State aid. Section 6 considers briefly Article 89, which grants the Council certain legislative powers. The consequences of, and remedies for, unlawful aid and misuse of aid are examined in Section 7. Section 8 considers the judicial remedies in respect of Articles 87 and 88. Finally there is discussion in Section 9 of the relationship between Articles 87–89 and other provisions of the EC Treaty.

2. The Concept of an Aid

(a) Generally

15.007 **The aim of Article 87.**   Article 87(1) of the Treaty provides:

> 'Save as otherwise provided in this Treaty, any aid granted by a Member State or through State resources in any form whatsoever which distorts or threatens to distort competition by favouring certain undertakings or the production of certain goods shall, in so far as it affects trade between Member States, be incompatible with the common market.'

The Court of Justice has stated that the aim of Article 87 is to prevent trade between Member States from being affected by benefits granted by public authorities which, in various forms, distort or threaten to distort competition by favouring certain undertakings or the production of certain products.[30]

---

[28] Agreement on Subsidies and Countervailing Measures, OJ 1994 L336/156. See also the Commission letter to the Member States of 2 August 1995, D/20506. The WTO Agreement permits the adoption of anti-subsidy measures. See Eighteenth Annual Report from the Commission to the European Parliament on the Community's anti-dumping and anti-subsidy activities (1999), COM (2000) 440 final.

[29] See OJ 1993 L44/1. The Community was instrumental in preparing an OECD Agreement respecting normal competitive conditions in the commercial shipbuilding and repair industry, OJ 1995 C355/1, but this never entered into force.

[30] Case C-387/92 *Banco Exterior de España v Ayuntamiento de Valencia* [1994] ECR I-877, [1994] 3 CMLR 473, para 12; and Case 173/73 *Italy v Commission (Aids to the Textile Industry)* [1974] ECR 709, [1974] 2 CMLR 593, para 13.

Wide concept of an aid.　The concept of 'aid' is wide, going beyond mere sub- **15.008**
sidy, and comprises any form of intervention or assistance which has the same or
similar effects to a subsidy. In *Steenkolenmijnen*,[31] a case under the ECSC Treaty,[32]
the Court of Justice held:

> 'A subsidy is normally defined as a payment in cash or in kind made in support of an
> undertaking other than the payment by the purchaser or consumer for the goods or
> services which it produces. An aid is a very similar concept, which, however, places
> emphasis on its purpose and seems especially devised for a particular objective which
> cannot normally be achieved without outside help. The concept of an aid is never-
> theless wider than that of a subsidy because it embraces not only positive benefits,
> such as subsidies themselves, but also interventions which, in various forms, mitigate
> the charges which are normally included in the budget of an undertaking and which,
> without, therefore, being subsidies in the strict meaning of the word, are similar in
> character and have the same effect.'[33]

An aid is therefore defined by reference to its effects[34] although a consideration
of the objects of the measure may also be necessary to see whether it falls outside Article 87(1).[35] Unlike the assessment of the compatibility of aid under

---

[31] Case 30/59 *Steenkolenmijnen v High Authority* [1961] ECR 1. See also *Italy v Commission,*
above, para 15; Case 61/79 *Amministrazione delle Finanze v Denkavit Italiana* [1980] ECR 1205,
[1981] 3 CMLR 694, para 31; *Banco Exterior de España* (n 30, above) para 13; Case C-39/94 *SFEI*
[1996] ECR I-3547, [1996] 3 CMLR 369, [1996] All ER (EC) 685, para 58; Case C-200/97
Ecotrade v AFS [1998] ECR I-7907, [1999] 2 CMLR 804, para 35; Case C-256/97 *DMT* [1999]
ECR I-3913, [1999] 3 CMLR 1, [1999] All ER (EC) 601, para 19.
[32] See Arts 4(c) and 67 of the ECSC Treaty.
[33] *Steenkolenmijnen*, para 19. To the same effect see also AG Warner in Case 74/76 *Iannelli v
Meroni* [1977] ECR 557, 584, [1977] 2 CMLR 688, 702. *Steenkolenmijnen* has been approved on
several occasions by the ECJ: see, eg *Banco Exterior de España* (n 30, above) para 13; *Ecotrade v AFS*
(n 31, above) para 34; Case C-75/97 *Belgium v Commission (Maribel I)* [1999] ECR I-3671, [2000]
1 CMLR 791, para 23; Case C-156/98 *Germany v Commission (new Länder)* [2000] ECR I-6857,
para 25; Case C-53/00 *Ferring v ACOSS* [2001] ECR I-9067, [2003] 1 CMLR 1001, para 15; Case
C-501/00 *Spain v Commission* [2004] ECR I-6717, para 90.
[34] *Italy v Commission* (n 30, above) para 13; see also *R v Attorney General, ex p ICI* [1987]
1 CMLR 72, 103–104 (English Court of Appeal) (*per* Lord Oliver); Case 310/85 *Deufil v
Commission* [1987] ECR 901, [1988] 1 CMLR 553; Case T-67/94 *Ladbroke Racing v Commission*
[1998] ECR II-1, para 52, in which the CFI stated that the relevance of the causes or aims of
State measures fall to be considered only in the context of Art 87(3) (not raised on appeal in Case
C-83/98P *France v Ladbroke Racing and Commission* [2000] ECR I-3271, [2000] 3 CMLR 555);
Case T-14/96 *Bretagne Angleterre Irlande (BAI) v Commission* [1999] ECR II-139, [1999] 3 CMLR
245, para 81; Case C-480/98 *Spain v Commission (Magefesa)* [2000] ECR I-8717. There is no
such thing as a measure of equivalent effect to a State aid: see AG Mancini in Case 290/83
Commission v France (Caisse nationale de crédit agricole) [1985] ECR 439, 440–442, [1986] 2 CMLR
546, 547–550, whose view was endorsed by the ECJ at para 18.
[35] Thus Art 87(1) is inapplicable where, eg a payment of money is for the supply of goods or
services; a measure is justified by reference to the market investor principle (see para 15.013, below),
or is otherwise commercially justified (see, eg Cases 67/85, etc, *Van Der Kooy v Commission* [1988]
ECR 219, [1989] 2 CMLR 804); or where the measure is an inherent feature of the protection of
insolvent companies against their creditors (*Ecotrade v AFS* (n 31, above) para 36) or of employment legislation (Cases C-72 & 73/91 *Sloman Neptun v Bodo Ziesemer* [1993] ECR I-887, [1995]
2 CMLR 97, para 21; AG Jacobs in Cases C-52/97, etc, *Viscido v Ente Poste Italiane* [1998] ECR

Article 87(3), the Commission does not enjoy a broad discretion in its definition of a measure as aid, save in particular circumstances owing to the complex nature of the State intervention in question. This flows necessarily from the fact that the characterisation of a measure as State aid is the responsibility of both the Commission and the national courts.[36]

15.009 Elements of a State aid. The elements that make up a State aid are: (i) an advantage; (ii) granted by a Member State or through State resources; (iii) favouring certain undertakings or the production of certain goods; (iv) distorting competition; and (v) affecting inter-State trade. Those elements are discussed in turn, although the cases indicate that there is some degree of overlap between them. There are a number of conceptual difficulties with the first three elements which are reflected in the evolution of the case law. As a result of recent cases, caution needs to be exercised when considering the analysis and result in some of the older cases.[37] Many illustrations of aids are to be found in the Commission's Annual Reports on Competition Policy; some examples are listed in paragraph 15.030, below.

15.010 An advantage. In *Denkavit*, the Court of Justice held that Article 87(1):

'. . . refers to the decisions of Member States by which the latter, in pursuit of their own economic and social objectives, give, by unilateral and autonomous decisions, undertakings or other persons resources or procure for them advantages intended to encourage the attainment of the economic and social objectives sought.'[38]

It is necessary to distinguish between advantages designed to attain particular economic and social objectives of a Member State and measures which are commercially justifiable in the sense that a private undertaking or investor in a similar position would adopt an equivalent measure.[39] The latter are generally not

---

I-2629, [1998] All ER (EC) 857, paras 11–16); or where a differential rate of taxation is justified to prevent tax avoidance (Case C-308/01 *GIL Insurance* [2004] ECR I-4777, [2004] 2 CMLR 22, [2004] All ER (EC) 954). See also Art 86(2), discussed at para 15.068, below; and Case T-106/95 *FFSA v Commission* [1997] ECR II-229, [1997] 2 CMLR 78, upheld on appeal Case C-174/97P, [1998] ECR I-1303.

[36] See *Ladbroke Racing v Commission* (n 34, above) at para 52, upheld on appeal, Case C-83/98P *France v Ladbroke Racing and Commission* (ibid). For the relationship between the national courts and the Commission in determining the existence of State aid, see paras 15.108 *et seq*, below.

[37] In particular, see the judgments in Case C-280/00 *Altmark Trans and Regierungspräsidium Magdeburg* [2003] ECR I-7747, [2003] 3 CMLR 339, [2005] All ER (EC) 610 (on compensation for public service obligations, see further paras 15.011 *et seq*, below); Case C-379/98 *PreussenElektra* [2001] ECR I-2099, [2001] 2 CMLR 833, [2001] All ER (EC) 330 (on the need for State resources, see further paras 15.017–15.020, below), and Case C-482/99 *France v Commission (Stardust Marine)* [2002] ECR I-4397, [2002] 2 CMLR 1069, [2003] All ER (EC) 330 (on the need for imputability to the State, see para 15.021, below).

[38] *Amministrazione delle Finanze v Denkavit Italiana* (n 31, above) para 31.

[39] See AG Jacobs in Cases C-278/92, etc, *Spain v Commission (Hytasa No. 1)* [1994] ECR I-4103, para 28 where he states that 'state aid is granted whenever a Member State makes available to an

State aids. Thus in *Van Der Kooy*,[40] in order to decide whether a preferential natural gas tariff for horticulturists was aid, the Court of Justice had to determine whether that tariff was commercially justified by the wish to prevent a switch by such users from gas to coal. On the facts, the Court found that the tariff was lower than necessary to prevent a switch by the users to coal and was therefore an aid. Likewise in *BAI*,[41] the Court of First Instance held that the advance payment by a local authority to a ferry company for a block of transport vouchers to be used on a route operated by that ferry company was an aid since the surrounding circumstances indicated that the transaction did not have the character of a normal commercial transaction. The question in each case is whether the recipient of the advantage is receiving a benefit which it would not have received under normal market conditions and which improves its financial position or reduces the costs which it would have otherwise borne.[42] In *GEMO*,[43] for example, the State funding of a service for the disposal of animal carcasses and slaughterhouse waste constituted State aid because it relieved farmers and slaughterhouse operators of a financial burden which they would otherwise have had to bear as an inherent cost

---

undertaking funds which in the normal course of events would not be provided by a private investor applying ordinary commercial criteria and disregarding other considerations of a social, political or philanthropic nature'. For an example, see Case T-98/00 *Linde v Commission* [2002] ECR II-3961, [2003] 2 CMLR 234.

[40] Cases 67/85, etc, *Van Der Kooy v Commission* [1998] ECR 219, [1989] 2 CMLR 804, paras 39–55. See also Case C-169/84 *CdF Chimie AZF v Commission* [1990] ECR I-3083, [1992] 1 CMLR 177: price difference between a subsequent preferential gas tariff and the general tariff constituted a State aid to the extent that the difference was not justified by cost savings to the supplier. See also para 15.023, below.

[41] T-14/96 *Bretagne Angleterre Irlande (BAI) v Commission* [1999] ECR II-139, [1999] 3 CMLR 245. See also Cases C-442 & 471/03P *P&O European Ferries v Commission* [2006] ECR I-4845.

[42] *SFEI* (n 31, above) para 60; Case C-241/94 *France v Commission* [1996] ECR I-4551, [1997] 1 CMLR 983, paras 34–40; C-353/95P *Tiercé Ladbroke v Commission* (n 35, above) para 25; Case T-67/94 *Ladbroke Racing v Commission* (n 34, above) para 52. See also AG Slynn in Case 84/82 *Germany v Commission (Textiles)* [1984] ECR 1451, 1500–1501, [1985] 1 CMLR 153, 168; *R v Attorney General, ex p ICI* (n 34, above) at 104–105 (CA); *Hytasa (No. 1)* (n 39, above) para 28, per AG Jacobs; *DMT* (n 31, above) para 22; Case C-342/96 *Spain v Commission (Tubacex)* [1999] ECR I-2459, [2000] 2 CMLR 415, paras 41–42; Case C-237/04 *Enirisorse v Sotacarbo* [2006] ECR I-2843, where the ECJ held that a measure which prevented a company's budget being burdened with a charge which in a normal situation would not have existed was not an advantage. The Commission has held that the reduction of concession fees payable by a public broadcaster was not aid because it simply reduced the advantage enjoyed by its private competitors who paid even lower fees: *XXIXth Annual Report on Competition Policy* (1999), point 229. See also N264/02 *London Underground*, decn of 2 December 2002, in which the Commission decided that compensation paid to infrastructure companies to renovate parts of the London Underground did not constitute aid since the amount of compensation was the result of a competitive procurement process which eliminated any possible advantage. With regard to the provision of advantages to undertakings through a failure to adhere to public procurement processes, see Arrowsmith, *The Law of Public and Utilities Procurement* (2nd edn, 2005), paras 4.36–4.50.

[43] Case C-126/01 *Ministre de l'Economie v GEMO* [2003] ECR I-13769, [2004] 1 CMLR 259, paras 28–33.

of the economic activities in which they were engaged. It therefore distorted competition in their favour. It does not matter whether the advantage is permanent or of limited duration.[44] A measure can still be an advantage where the beneficiary has contributed wholly or partially to its financing as a result of a State levy,[45] or if the recipient undertaking has to do something in return (for example, if an undertaking receives money on condition that it rationalises or expands its production capacity).[46]

15.011 **Compensation for public service obligations.** The provision to an undertaking, whether by way of a subsidy paid directly out of State funds or some other means (such as the right to collect a levy from certain other undertakings), of compensation for the carrying out of public service obligations imposed on, or undertaken by, that undertaking does not, in principle, constitute the conferral of 'an advantage'.[47] In order to avoid the possibility of Member States providing State aid to undertakings in the form of excessive compensation for the discharge of public service obligations, a tight fit must be shown between the costs of discharging the public service obligations and the level of 'compensation' provided.

15.012 **The *Altmark* criteria.** In the leading case of *Altmark*[48] the Court of Justice held that four criteria must be satisfied for public service compensation to escape classification as State aid:

(a) the recipient undertaking must actually have public service obligations to discharge and those obligations must have been clearly defined;

---

[44] Case T-67/94 *Ladbroke Racing* (n 34, above) para 56.

[45] Case 78/76 *Steinike und Weinlig v Germany* [1977] ECR 595, [1977] 2 CMLR 688, para 22; *Caisse nationale de crédit agricole* (n 34, above) para 14; Cases T-197 & 198/97 *Weyl Beef Products v Commission* [2001] ECR II-303, [2001] 2 CMLR 459, para 81. See also Case 47/69 *France v Commission* [1970] ECR 487, [1970] CMLR 351; AG Warner in Case 177/78 *Pigs and Bacon Commission v McCarren* [1979] ECR 2161, 2201–2202, [1979] 3 CMLR 389, 401–403; AG Rozes in Case 222/82 *Apple and Pear Development Council v Lewis* [1983] ECR 4083, 4133, [1984] 3 CMLR 733, 747–748; Cases C-78/90, etc, *Compagnie Commerciale de l'Ouest v Receveur principal des douanes de la Pallice-Port* [1992] ECR I-1847, para 35; Cases C-149 & 150/91 *Sanders Adour v Directeur des Services Fiscaux des Pyrénées-Atlantiques* [1992] ECR I-3899; AG Tesauro in Cases C-17/91, etc, *Lornoy en Zonen v Belgium* [1992] ECR I-6523, 6536–6539. cf *Regeling Bijzondere Financiering*, XXVIIth *Report on Competition Policy* (1997), point 219, in which the Commission took the view that a State guarantee scheme financed by premiums paid by beneficiaries did not constitute State aid.

[46] Case 323/82 *Intermills v Commission* [1984] ECR 3809, [1986] 1 CMLR 614. See also Case C-251/97 *France v Commission (collective agreements)* [1999] ECR I-6639, paras 39–47.

[47] *Ferring v ACOSS* (n 33, above) paras 23–29; *Altmark* (discussed below) paras 83–87; Cases C-34/01, etc, *Enirisorse v Ministero delle Finanze* [2003] ECR I-14243, [2004] 1 CMLR 296, para 31; Case C-451/03 *Servizi Ausiliari Dottori Commercialisti v Calafiori* [2006] ECR I-2941, [2006] 2 CMLR 1135, paras 51–71, para 60.

[48] Case C-280/00 *Altmark Trans and Regierungspräsidium Magdeburg* [2003] ECR I-7747, [2003] 3 CMLR 339, [2005] All ER (EC) 610, paras 88–93. See Santamato and Pesaresi, 'Compensation for services of general economic interest: some thoughts on the Altmark ruling' (2004) 1 EC Competition Policy Newsletter 17.

(b) the parameters on the basis of which the compensation is calculated must have been established in advance in an objective and transparent manner so as to avoid the conferral of an economic advantage which might favour the recipient undertaking over competing undertakings;

(c) the compensation must not exceed what is necessary to cover all or part of the costs incurred in the discharge of the public service obligations, taking into account any relevant receipts and allowing for a reasonable profit; and

(d) where the selected undertaking was not chosen pursuant to a public procurement procedure which would allow for the selection of the tenderer capable of providing those services at the lowest cost to the community, the level of compensation needed must have been determined on the basis of an analysis of the costs which a typical efficient undertaking with the means to meet the public service requirements would have incurred in discharging the public service obligations, taking into account any relevant receipts and allowing for a reasonable profit.

If the *Altmark* criteria are fully satisfied, the compensation paid will not fall within Article 87(1) at all.[49] It will frequently be difficult for public service compensation to satisfy these exacting criteria, however, particularly in circumstances where the undertaking chosen to discharge the obligations has not been selected following a tendering procedure designed to identify the undertaking capable of providing the service for the lowest level of subsidy. Where the criteria are not satisfied, the compensation will constitute 'an advantage' and may therefore fall within Article 87(1) but may nevertheless be compatible with Community law pursuant to Article 86(2).[50]

The 'market economy investor' principle. In order to decide whether the provision of public funds, whether by way of loan, capital injection or purchase of shares, to an undertaking constitutes an aid, it is necessary to examine whether the terms on which the funds are provided go beyond those that a private investor, operating under normal market economy conditions and having regard to the information available and foreseeable developments at that time, would find acceptable when providing funds to a comparable private undertaking.[51] This 'market economy investor' **15.013**

---

49 An early example of the application of these criteria by the ECJ was provided in *Enirisorse* (n 47, above) paras 32–40.

50 See para 15.068, below.

51 See Case 234/84 *Belgium v Commission (Meura)* [1986] ECR 2263, [1988] 2 CMLR 331, paras 14–15; Case 40/85 *Belgium v Commission (Boch No. 2)* [1986] ECR 2321, [1988] 2 CMLR 301, para 13; Case C-301/87 *France v Commission (Boussac)* [1990] ECR I-307, para 39; Case C-303/88 *Italy v Commission (ENI–Lanerossi)* [1991] ECR I-1433, paras 21–24; Case C-305/89 *Italy v Commission (Alfa Romeo No. 1)* [1991] ECR I-1603, paras 19–23; Case C-261/89 *Italy v Commission (Aluminium undertakings)* [1991] ECR I-4437, paras 8–14; Case C-42/93 *Spain v Commission (Merco)* [1994] ECR I-4125, [1996] 2 CMLR 702, paras 13–19; Case T-358/94 *Air France v Commission (CDC–P)* [1996] ECR II-2109, [1997] 1 CMLR 492, para 134 (subscription

principle applies to all public enterprises whether profitable or loss-making.[52] The application of the principle requires an examination of whether there will be an acceptable return on the provision of funds within a reasonable period of time.[53] In comparing the position of the State with that of a private investor, the comparator need not be the ordinary investor placing his capital with a short-term view of its profitability; it is appropriate to look at 'the conduct of a private holding company or a private group of undertakings pursuing a structural policy—whether general or sectorial—and guided by prospects of profitability longer term'.[54] Where a capital injection forms part of a restructuring and modernisation plan, it will constitute an aid if it fails to fulfil the market economy investor principle.[55]

---

by the State to virtually all the securities issued by an undertaking in a grave financial situation for a restructuring that was clearly incapable of improving the heavily indebted undertaking's situation constituted aid); Case T-16/96 *Cityflyer Express v Commission* [1998] ECR II-757, [1998] 2 CMLR 537, paras 51–53, 88–90 (since a regional airline would have been able to receive a loan at a market rate of interest, the interest-free element of the loan constituted aid); *DMT* (n 31, above) paras 22–30; Case T-98/00 *Linde v Commission* [2002] ECR II-3961, [2003] 2 CMLR 234 (subsidy to an undertaking not an aid where State had assigned the performance of a loss-making contract to that undertaking and the value of the subsidy did not exceed the price that would have been agreed between economic operators as consideration for the recipient's discharge of its contractual obligations). See generally, Slocock, 'The Market Economy Investor Principle' (2002) 2 EC Competition Policy Newsletter 23. See also Commission Communication on the application of Arts [87] and [88] of the Treaty and of Art 5 of Commission Directive 80/723 to public undertakings in the manufacturing sector, OJ 1993 C307/3: Vol II, App F.3 and para 15.015, below. For the application of the principle to financial services, see *Crédit Lyonnais*, OJ 1998 L221/28; *GAN*, OJ 1998 L78/1; also Case T-228/99 *Westdeutsche Landesbank Girozentrale and Land Nordrhein-Westfalen v Commission* [2003] ECR II-435, [2004] 1 CMLR 529.

52 *Westdeutsche Landesbank*, above. For investment in public undertakings, the Commission adopts a refined test: see Friederiszick and Tröge, (Chief Economist Team), 'Applying the Market Economy Investor Principle to State Owned Companies - Lessons Learned from the German Landesbanken Cases' (2006) 1 EC Competition Policy Newsletter 105.

53 *Boussac* (n 51, above). See also Case T-296/97 *Alitalia v Commission* [2000] ECR II-3871, [2001] All ER (EC) 193, paras 84, 96–99. A high profile example of the Commission finding that a package of measures constituted State aid because the 'private investor test' had not been met was *Ryanair/Charleroi*, OJ 2004 L137/1; on appeal, Case T-196/04 *Ryanair v Commission*, not yet decided.

54 *Alfa Romeo No. 1* (n 51, above) para 20; *SFEI* (n 31, above), per AG Jacobs at para 60; *Merco* (n 51, above) para 14. See also Cases T-124/95, etc, *Neue Maxhütte Stahlwerker and Lech-Stahlwerke v Commission* [1999] ECR II-17, recognising that in the private sector, a parent company may for a limited period take over the losses of its subsidiaries if there is a prospect of the subsidiary returning to profitability; *Alitalia* (n 53, above) para 96.

55 Case C-142/87 *Belgium v Commission (Tubemeuse)* [1990] ECR I-959, [1991] 3 CMLR 213: Tubemeuse's prospects of profitability were not such as to induce private investors operating under normal market economy conditions to enter into such financial transactions and it was unlikely that Tubemeuse could have raised the amounts necessary for its survival on the capital markets. On capital injections, see also AG Slynn in *Textiles* (n 42, above) 1499–1501 (ECR), 166–169 (CMLR); Cases 296 & 318/82 *Netherlands and Leeuwarder Papierwarenfabriek v Commission* [1985] ECR 809, [1985] 3 CMLR 380; Case 52/84 *Commission v Belgium (Boch No. 1)* [1986] ECR 89, [1987] 1 CMLR 710; *Boussac* (n 51, above); *Alitalia* (n 53, above) paras 76–94; Case C-328/99 *Italy v Commission (Seleco)* [2003] ECR I-4035, [2005] 2 CMLR 1169.

In *Leeuwarder Papierwarenfabriek*[56] the Court of Justice upheld the Commission's decision that the provision of capital was an aid because, on the facts, it was very unlikely that Leeuwarder could have raised the necessary capital from private investors. Where a State body is not acting as a public investor but as a public creditor, its conduct must be compared to that of a private creditor in a similar position and not to a private investor.[57]

Absence of private investor comparator. Where the public undertaking giving the alleged aid is in a unique position on the market it may be inappropriate to compare its situation with that of a private undertaking acting under normal market conditions. In *Chronopost v UFEX*[58] a competitor alleged that the assistance offered by the French postal service, La Poste, to Chronopost, the private company entrusted with the management of La Poste's express delivery service, constituted a State aid. The assistance was in part logistical (in particular La Poste made available to Chronopost the use of the postal infrastructure for the collection, sorting, transport and delivery of its dispatches) and in part commercial (Chronopost's access to La Poste's customers and enjoyment of its goodwill). The question arose of how the market investor principle applied given that La Poste operated a monopoly in the supply of ordinary postal services and was subject to a universal service obligation whereas Chronopost operated in the competitive market for express delivery services. The Court of Justice, overturning the judgment of the Court of First Instance, noted that the national infrastructure created by La Poste in order to satisfy its universal service obligation would never have been created by a private company. Accordingly, it was not possible to compare the situation of La Poste with that of a private group of undertakings not operating in a reserved sector. To determine whether the charges made to Chronopost constituted an aid, it was necessary to look at objective and verifiable elements, in the present case, the costs borne by La Poste in respect of the provision of the logistical and commercial assistance. On that basis, the Court held, there would be no question of State aid to Chronopost if, first, it was established that the price charged properly covered all the additional, variable costs incurred in providing the logistical and commercial assistance, an appropriate contribution to the fixed costs arising from use of the postal network and an adequate return on the capital investment insofar as it is used for Chronopost's competitive activity; and if,

15.014

---

[56] *Netherlands and Leeuwarder Papierwarenfabriek v Commission,* above. The relevant facts for the Commission were (i) the financial structure of the company; (ii) its urgent need for new machinery; and (iii) the overcapacity in the paperboard processing industry.

[57] *Tubacex* (n 42, above) paras 46–48; *DMT* (n 31, above) paras 24–25.

[58] Cases C-83/01P, etc, *Chronopost v UFEX* [2003] ECR I-6993, [2003] 3 CMLR 303 (on appeal from Case T-613/97 *UFEX v Commission* [2000] ECR II-4055). The ECJ remitted the matter to the CFI which then annulled the Commission's original rejection of the complaint: Case T-613/97, judgment of 7 June 2006, [2006] ECR II-1531.

secondly, there was nothing to suggest that those elements had been underestimated or fixed in an arbitrary fashion.

15.015 **The application of the market economy investor principle to public undertakings.** The Commission has issued a Communication[59] which is intended, *inter alia*, to clarify the application of the market economy investor principle to State funds made available to public undertakings in the manufacturing sector. It is not the aim of the Commission to replace the investor's judgment. Any request by an undertaking for funds calls for an analysis on the part of public or private bodies of the risk and the likely outcome of the project.[60] The analysis involves considering the overall position of the recipient undertaking, including earlier capital injections that constituted aid and whether it is possible to sever consideration of one capital injection from another.[61] In *Alfa Romeo*[62] the Court of Justice upheld the Commission's decision that the capital injection made by public holding companies into Alfa Romeo constituted aid in view of Alfa Romeo's persistent losses, excess production capacity and excessive production costs and the failure of an earlier investment plan to redress Alfa Romeo's financial situation. The Commission recognises a wide margin of judgement on the part of the investor: the Commission will only conclude that there is a State aid when it considers that there are no objective or bona fide grounds, at the time of the investment or financing decision, to expect an adequate rate of return that would be acceptable to a private investor in a comparable private undertaking.[63] Where the public authority has full control of the undertaking, it is reasonable for the authority to be less motivated by purely short-term profit considerations than would be the case if it had a minority or non-controlling holding.[64] The Commission has made it clear that the market economy investor principle applies to any cross-subsidisation by a profitable part of a public group of undertakings of an unprofitable part, save where there are good hopes of a long-term gain or there is a net benefit

---

[59] Commission Communication on the application of Arts [87] and [88] EC and Art 5 of Dir 80/723 to public undertakings in the manufacturing sector, OJ 1993 C307/3: Vol II, App F.3. The original 1991 Communication was annulled by the ECJ in Case C-325/91 *France v Commission* [1993] ECR I-3283 as being *ultra vires* Dir 80/723 (the Transparency Directive). The 1993 Communication was adopted on the basis of an amended version of the Transparency Directive: see para 15.016, below.

[60] Commission Communication, above, para 27.

[61] Case T-11/95 *BP Chemicals v Commission (No. 1)* [1998] ECR II-3235, [1998] 3 CMLR 693, paras 170–180. cf Cases C-329/93, etc, *Germany v Commission (Bremer Vulkan)* [1996] ECR I-5151, [1998] 1 CMLR 591: Commission's application of the market economy investor principle in that case was annulled as too formalistic.

[62] Case C-305/89 *Italy v Commission (Alfa Romeo No. 1)* [1991] ECR I-1603, paras 21–22. See also *BP Chemicals*, above.

[63] Commission Communication (n 59, above) para 28. The need for an adequate rate of return casts doubt on the much earlier statement of the Commission that the acquisition of shares for non-profit motives falls outside Art 87, see *Second Report on Competition Policy* (1972), point 124.

[64] Commission Communication, para 30.

to the group as a whole.[65] In a case where one of the activities of a public group is being run down because it has no medium or long-term viability, it is legitimate to have regard to the impact on the overall credibility and structure of the group, because this is a factor which would influence a private group.[66] In *Spain v Commission (Hytasa)*[67] the Spanish government sought to justify a capital injection made to three loss-making companies it owned on the grounds that the cost of rescuing the companies was preferable to the high costs of liquidation which would entail the payment of redundancy and employment benefits and the restructuring of the industrial infrastructure. The Commission considered that the payments involved State aid according to the market economy investor principle because the capital contributions exceeded the State's debt liabilities in these limited companies. The Court of Justice agreed, ruling that a distinction must be drawn between the obligations which the State must assume as the owner of the share capital of a company and its obligation as a public authority. As the owner of the three companies, the State's liability was limited to the liquidation value of their assets. The other costs arising from the liquidation such as redundancy payments and unemployment benefit were liabilities of the State as public authority not as shareholder and so could not be taken into consideration as costs which would be borne by a comparable market economy investor.[68]

The Transparency Directive. In order to scrutinise the transactions between a **15.016** Member State and its public undertakings, the Commission adopted Directive 80/723 on the transparency of financial relations between Member States and public undertakings.[69] The Directive was amended several times and at the end of 2006 the Commission adopted as a consolidated version, Directive 2006/111.[70] Article 5 of Directive 80/723 enabled the Commission to request information concerning financial relations between public authorities and public undertakings. Following the annulment of the original Communication of October 1991 as being *ultra vires* the Directive,[71] Directive 80/723, was amended by Directive 93/84.[72] This inserted a new provision, now Article 8 of Directive 2006/111,

---

65 ibid, para 29.
66 ibid, para 30.
67 Cases C-278/92, etc, *Spain v Commission (Hytasa No. 1)* [1994] ECR I-4103.
68 See also *Merco* (n 51, above); *XXIVth Report on Competition Policy* (1994), point 344; *XXVth Report on Competition Policy* (1995), point 159; and AG Jacobs in *SFEI* (n 31, above) paras 61–62.
69 Dir 80/723 on the transparency of financial relations between Member States and public undertakings, OJ 1980 L195/35, as amended by Dirs 85/413 (OJ 1985 L229/20), 93/84 (OJ 1993 L254/16), 2000/52 (OJ 2000 L193/75) and 2005/81 (OJ 2005 L312/47). See also Commission Communication (n 59, above).
70 OJ 2006 L318/17: Vol II, App F.2.
71 Case C-325/91 *France v Commission* [1993] ECR I-3283.
72 Dir 93/84, OJ 1993 L254/16.

which requires Member States to supply financial information for public undertakings in the manufacturing sector. Pursuant to this provision, the 1993 Commission Communication[73] requires Member States to provide, on an annual basis, details of particular forms of State intervention in all public undertakings whose principal activity is manufacturing and whose annual turnover is over 250 million euros. Following a growing number of complaints about undertakings which have special or exclusive rights and/or receive compensation payments for rendering services of general economic interest engaging in cross-subsidy of their competitive activities, the Commission adopted Directive 2000/52[74] which further amended Directive 80/723 so as to require public undertakings to maintain separate accounts for separate activities to ensure financial transparency within the accounts of such undertakings.[75] The aim of such accounting is to identify any such cross-subsidisation.

15.017 **'By a Member State or through State resources'.** It is now clear that for advantages to be capable of being categorised as aid, they must, first, be granted directly or indirectly through State resources and, secondly, they must be imputable to the State. The first requirement was unequivocally confirmed by the Court of Justice in *PreussenElektra*[76] in which it was held that a requirement imposed by the State on private electricity companies to purchase electricity from renewable sources at prices higher than the real economic value of that type of electricity did not constitute State aid. That was because the obligation did not involve the transfer of State resources to companies producing renewable energy. The Court stated:

> '. . . the case-law of the Court of Justice shows that only advantages granted directly or indirectly through State resources are to be considered aid within the meaning of Article [87(1)]. The distinction made in that provision between aid granted "by a Member State" and aid granted "through State resources" does not signify that all advantages granted by a State, whether financed through State resources or not, constitute aid but is intended merely to bring within that definition both advantages which are granted directly by the State and those granted by a public or private body designated or established by the State . . . .'[77]

---

[73] Commission Communication (n 59, above). Art 8 of Dir 2006/111 (n 70, above) was previously Art 5A of the amended Dir 80/723.

[74] Dir 2000/52, OJ 2000 L193/75.

[75] See now Arts 1 and 3 of Dir 2006/111. There a number of limited exceptions: the rule does not apply to sectors for which another Community instrument already requires separation of accounts (eg postal, telecommunications, or electricity sectors), to cases where the contract to provide the service of general economic interest has been awarded and/or the special or exclusive right has been granted by means of an open and transparent procedure, to undertakings whose supply of services is not liable to affect trade between Member States to an appreciable extent or to undertakings with a total net turnover of less than €40 million.

[76] Case C-379/98 *PreussenElektra* (n 37, above). See discussion of this case in Colin-Goguel, 'Le caractère public d'un avantage en droit communautaire: après les arrêts PreussenElektra et Stardust' (2003) 3 EC Competition Policy Newsletter 26.

[77] ibid, para 58.

The expression 'through State resources' 'serves only to preclude circumvention of the State aid rules through decentralised or "privatised" distribution of aid'.[78] Accordingly, the inclusion of that expression in Article 87(1) does not mean that there can be 'aid granted by a Member State' even where no State resources are being used or forgone.[79] For example the non-applicability of general employment legislation to certain undertakings is not an aid because it does not involve any direct or indirect transfer of State resources to that undertaking.[80]

Bodies caught. The reference in Article 87 to a Member State and State resources includes the resources of regional or local authorities,[81] as well as public bodies set up by the State[82] (including public undertakings within the meaning of the Transparency Directive[83]). The Court of First Instance has held that a public body does not fall outside the scope of Article 87 although, as a matter of domestic law, it is a constitutionally independent institution, provided that its conduct is

15.018

---

[78] Case C-482/99 *France v Commission (Stardust Marine)* [2002] ECR I-4397, [2002] 2 CMLR 1069, Opinion of AG Jacobs, para 54.

[79] See, eg Case T-95/03 *AEESCAM v Commission*, judgment of 12 December 2006, paras 95 and 104, rejecting the submission that a benefit provided to certain undertakings by the State could constitute aid if it distorted competition, without any active or passive disbursement by the State needing to be shown. Although the national measures at issue plainly conferred certain advantages, with regard to planning controls, on one class of undertakings (hypermarkets) within the retail market for petroleum, the CFI found on the facts that State resources were not being forgone and so upheld the Commission's decision that there was no State aid. See also Case C-345/02 *Pearle* [2004] ECR I-7139, [2004] 3 CMLR 182, para 35; and AG Fennelly in *Ecotrade v AFS* (n 31, above) at para 23, drawing a distinction between the situation where the State acts as intermediary between those who finance a measure and those who benefit from it (which involves State resources) and the situation where the State does not so act (no State resources). In *Commission v France (Caisse Nationale de crédit agricole)* (n 34, above), the ECJ stated that aid did not need necessarily to be financed from State resources; but that statement now needs to be seen in the context of the particular facts of that case, which involved the disbursement of private funds by a public body under State control.

[80] *Viscido* (n 35, above) (the non-application of legislation covering fixed-term employment conditions). See also *Sloman Neptun* (n 35, above) (working conditions and rates of pay for third country nationals that are not subject to the legislation of the Member State until the vessel is registered); Case C-189/91 *Kirsammer-Hack v Sidal* [1993] ECR I-6185 (exclusion of small businesses from unfair dismissal legislation); *Ecotrade v AFS* (n 31, above) paras 35–44, and Case C-295/97 *Piaggio v Ifitalia* [1999] ECR I-3735, paras 34–43 (a system of special administration for insolvent undertakings).

[81] See Case 323/82 *Intermills v Commission* [1984] ECR 3809, [1986] 1 CMLR 614; *Leeuwarder Papierwarenfabriek* (n 56, above); Case C-5/89 *Commission v Germany (BUG-Alutechnik)* [1990] ECR I-3437, [1992] 1 CMLR 117, where the aid in question was granted by regional bodies in Belgium, the Netherlands and Germany respectively.

[82] *Stardust Marine* (n 78, above) paras 34–38. For public bodies, see the granting of an export bonus by the Pigs and Bacon Commission in Case 177/78 *Pigs and Bacon Commission v McCarren* [1979] ECR 2161, [1979] 3 CMLR 389; the payments made by the Caisse nationale de crédit agricole, in *Commission v France* (n 34, above); the funds provided by ENI in *ENI-Lanerossi* (n 51, above); the funds provided by IRI in *Alfa Romeo No. 1* (n 51, above).

[83] See para 15.016, above.

imputable to the State.[84] Likewise in *Caisse Nationale de crédit agricole*,[85] the Court of Justice held that Article 87(1) covered a payment made by the Caisse, a public body, to farmers. Although the money came from accumulated surpluses generated by the management of private funds and not from the State as such, the decision to pay the money was instigated by the State and had to be approved by the State, thus demonstrating that the funds were under State control. Payments made by private bodies also fall within Article 87(1) if those bodies are established or appointed by the State to administer the aid.[86] Where, however, private bodies administer aid that does not come from State resources and without the intervention of the State or a public body, Article 87 does not apply.[87]

15.019 **State resources.**   Although in the light of *PreussenElecktra* it is clear that the presence of State resources is an essential prerequisite of an aid, the case law on what constitutes State resources is not easy to follow. After *PreussenElecktra*, the question was considered in *Stardust Marine*.[88] In that case, France challenged a Commission decision which found that loans, guarantees and recapitalisation granted by public undertakings in favour of Stardust involved State resources. France argued that the use by a public undertaking of its own resources could not constitute State resources. That argument was rejected by both the Advocate General and the Court of Justice. The Advocate General's view was that resources were State resources where the State had direct or indirect control over them and that resources used by a public undertaking falling within the Transparency Directive were therefore State resources.[89] State resources can, of course, come directly from the State budget, for example, revenue from taxation. However, as is clear from *Stardust Marine*, resources can be State resources even if they do not come from the State budget, provided that the State has control over them. Indeed, the resources over which the State has control need not even be permanent assets of the public sector. In *France v Ladbroke Racing and Commission*,[90] for example,

---

[84] *Air France v Commission (CDC-P)* (n 51, above) paras 55–62.

[85] *Caisse nationale de crédit agricole* (n 34, above) paras 14–15. The ECJ appears to have been influenced by the fact that the French government had notified this measure under Art 87(3) as part of a body of measures in favour of farmers. See also, in this context, the Commission's pleading in *Apple and Pear Development Council v Lewis* (n 45, above) at 4108 (ECR), where it argued that the financing of a promotion campaign by use of the growers' own contributions was a State aid because the contributions were levied under public law and the decision as to how to use the money was made by a public body set up by the Ministry of Agriculture, Fisheries and Food whose members were appointed by the Minister. This view was upheld by AG Rozes at 4133 (ECR), 747–748 (CMLR).

[86] *Steinike und Weinlig v Germany* (n 45, above) para 21.

[87] *Pearle* (n 79, above) para 35.

[88] *Stardust Marine* (n 78, above).

[89] ibid, paras 37–41.

[90] Case C-83/98P *France v Ladbroke Racing and Commission* [2000] ECR I-3271, [2000] 3 CMLR 555, paras 45–50, approving *Air France (CDC-P)* (n 51, above) where the CFI held that funds deposited by private individuals with the Caisse des Dépôts et Consignations, a public body

the Court of Justice held that the funds derived from unclaimed winnings held by the PMU, a body controlled by the French State, were State resources owing to the fact that use of the funds was governed by statutory conditions, the non-compliance with which led to the reversion of the funds to the Treasury. State resources can also be derived from a compulsory State levy on private undertakings or individuals which is then redistributed under the State's direction.[91] In *Pearle*, however, monies spent by the Netherlands Central Industry Board for Skilled Trades (a trade association established by law and having the power to promulgate byelaws) on funding an advertising campaign to benefit the opticians' profession was held not to constitute State resources. This was because the funds spent by the association were offset in full by the compulsory levies which it exacted from opticians, who were the intended beneficiaries of the advertising campaign, for that specific purpose. The funds did not therefore tend to create an advantage which constituted an additional burden either for the State or for the association.[92]

No transfer of resources required.   In reaching their conclusions in *Stardust*   **15.020**
Marine, both the Advocate General and the Court held that the presence of State resources does not require the *transfer* of resources to an undertaking.[93] The Advocate General held, for example, that a waiver of tax revenue will involve State resources even though there is no transfer of resources.[94] In cases decided before *PreussenElecktra,* it had been held that a tax exemption granted to certain undertakings would constitute aid, since the effect would be to mitigate the charges normally included in the budgets of the recipient taxpayer.[95] Those cases are probably still good law although they did not focus on the need to identify State resources, because a tax exemption can be regarded as a waiver of revenue and hence involving the waiver of State resources. A special insolvency regime may

---

established by statute, constituted State resources even though the sums deposited could be withdrawn by the individual depositors: the Caisse was able to use and invest the available balance at its own risk in the same way as if that investment had been financed from taxation or compulsory contributions.

[91] Case 173/73 *Italy v Commission* (n 30, above) para 16; *Steinike und Weinlig v Germany* (n 45, above). See also *Kinderkanal and Phoenix,* and *BBC News 24 (TV licence fees), XXIXth Report on Competition Policy* (1999), point 226 and p 103.

[92] *Pearle* (n 79, above) para 36.

[93] *Stardust Marine* (n 78, above), the ECJ at para 36, AG at para 40.

[94] ibid. The Commission has stated that a loss of tax revenue is equivalent to consumption of State resources in the form of fiscal expenditure: see the Commission Notice on the application of the State aid rules to measures relating to direct business taxation, OJ 1998 C384/3: Vol II, App G.25 at para 10 (see further para 15.031, below), cited with approval by the English Court of Appeal: *R v Commissioners of Customs and Excise, ex p Lunn Poly* [1999] 1 CMLR 1357 (*per* Clarke LJ).

[95] *Banco Exterior de España* (n 30, above) para 14; Case T-106/95 *FFSA v Commission* (n 35, above) para 167, upheld on appeal, Case C-174/97P, ibid; Case C-6/97 *Italy v Commission* [1999] ECR I-2981, [2000] 2 CMLR 919, paras 16–17; Case C-156/98 *Germany v Commission (new Länder)* [2000] ECR I-6857, paras 23–28.

also involve the mitigation of liabilities through a loss of State resources, although whether the mitigation constitutes an aid in any particular case will depend on the overall nature and purpose of the regime.[96]

15.021 **Imputability of the measure to the State.** The other main issue raised in *Stardust Marine* was in what circumstances measures adopted by public undertakings could be imputed to the State. The Commission had simply assumed that the measures granted by those public undertakings in favour of Stardust were imputable to the State because the undertakings were in the public sector. The Court of Justice rejected this approach. It stated that even if the State is in a position to exercise control over the body which grants the alleged aid, such control cannot be assumed in a particular case. The Court recognised that it might be difficult to prove an actual instruction from the State to the public undertaking in question. The test it laid down provides for the drawing of inferences from the circumstances of the case and the context in which the measure was taken, for example, the fact that the company had to take account of directions from a public authority, rather than being permitted to exercise autonomy in its commercial decision-making.[97] The Court of Justice referred to its earlier judgment in *Van Der Kooy*,[98] where it held that the grant of a preferential tariff for natural gas to horticulturists by Gasunie, a company in which the Dutch State held 50 per cent of the shares, was an aid granted by a Member State. This was because Gasunie did not enjoy autonomy in fixing gas tariffs but acted under the control and on the instructions of the public authorities. A measure cannot be imputed to the State, however, where the State is merely implementing Community legislation, even if State resources are involved. Thus, in *Deutsche Bahn*,[99] the Court of First Instance held that Germany's exemption of aviation fuel, but not fuels used by competing forms of transportation, from the tax on mineral oil could not constitute State aid because the exemption arose from an act of the Community legislature and could not, therefore, be imputed to the State.

---

[96] *Ecotrade v AFS* (n 31, above); *Piaggio* (n 80, above).

[97] Case C-482/99 *France v Commission (Stardust Marine)* [2002] ECR I-4397, [2002] 2 CMLR 1069, [2003] All ER (EC) 330, paras 50–58. For comment on the judgment, see Lübbig and von Merveldt, (2003) ECLR 629. See also the range of circumstances taken into account by the Commission in the *Ryanair/Charleroi* decision (n 53, above) in deciding that the resources of the Charleroi Airport management company were State resources and that the measures adopted by that company in support of Ryanair's use of the airport were imputable to the regional authority of Walloonia.

[98] Cases 67/85, etc, *Van Der Kooy v Commission* [1998] ECR 219, [1989] 2 CMLR 804, paras 32–38. See also *ENI-Lanerossi* (n 51, above) paras 10–15, where the ECJ considered that aid granted by ENI fell within Art 87 since ENI was a body under the control of the Italian State. A further example is Case C-328/99 *Italy v Commission (Seleco)* [2003] ECR I-4035, [2005] 2 CMLR 1169.

[99] Case T-351/02 *Deutsche Bahn v Commission* [2006] ECR II-1047, [2006] 2 CMLR 1343.

Community resources.   In *BALM*,[100] the Court of Justice held that the phrase **15.022**
'through State resources' presupposes that the resources from which the aid is
granted come from the Member State. In that case, the mistaken grant of a favourable Community quota by a Member State fell outside Article 87 since the levy
that was waived was part of Community resources and not those of the Member
State.[101]

Favouring certain undertakings.   Article 87 refers to an aid which distorts **15.023**
or threatens to distort competition by favouring certain undertakings[102] or the
production of certain goods. It is therefore necessary to distinguish between
an advantage granted to undertakings generally and one that is granted only to
certain undertakings.[103] It is only the latter that falls within Article 87, for example where the advantage is granted only to one or more specified undertakings
or only to undertakings in a particular region[104] or industry, or of a particular age
or size. However, the fact that an aid granted to a particular economic operator
may indirectly benefit a number of others whose business depends on that
operator's principal activities does not render the aid in question a general measure falling outside the ambit of Article 87(1).[105] In the case of social or economic
measures, it is not always easy to determine whether or not a measure favours

---

[100] Cases 213/81, etc, *Norddeutsches Vieh-und Fleischkontor v BALM* [1982] ECR 3583,
3602. See also *R v Ministry of Agriculture, Fisheries and Food, ex p BPISG* [2000] EuLR 724
(QBD).

[101] cf AG Verloren Van Themaat in *BALM*, above at 3617, and AG Lenz in Cases 133/85, etc,
Rau v BALM [1987] ECR 2289, 2307 who stated, *obiter*, that the Community was also bound by
Art 87, although the provision was directed at Member States. Aids granted to EUREKA projects
were subject to the normal notification procedure and the Commission used the same criteria as
it applied to national measures, while paying particular attention to the transnational character of
these activities: *XVIIth Report on Competition Policy* (1987), point 176. See also the Commission's
De Minimis Notice: para 15.028, below, which included within the 100,000 ECUs ceiling both aid
financed by public bodies in the Member States and by the Community from Structural Funds and
in particular the European Regional Development Fund (ERDF).

[102] As to undertaking, see Case C-237/04 *Enirisorse v Sotacarbo* [2006] ECR I-2843,
paras 28–36, and generally paras 2.003, *et seq*, above.

[103] See the analysis by AG Darmon in *Sloman Neptun* (n 35, above) at paras 58–78 of his
Opinion. See also Case T-55/99 *CETM v Commission* [2000] ECR II-3207, paras 39–55.

[104] Where a Member State confers an advantage only on undertakings within a particular region
of its territory, rather than across its territory as a whole, this will normally be sufficient to amount
to the 'favouring of certain undertakings'. An exception appears, however, to be recognised in circumstances where the advantage arises from measures adopted by a regional government in exercise
of its autonomy over the territory for which it is responsible. In those circumstances, it appears
that it is that territory, and not the entire territory of the Member State, which constitutes the
relevant context for the assessment of whether the measures concerned favour certain undertakings
in comparison with others in a comparable legal and factual situation: see Case C-88/03 *Portugal v
Commission (Azores)* [2006] ECR I-7115, [2006] 3 CMLR 1233, para 58, discussed further at para
15.034, below.

[105] *Ladbroke Racing v Commission* (n 34, above) para 79; not raised on appeal in Case C-83/98P
France v Commission (n 90, above).

particular undertakings.[106] A reduction in employers' contributions to a sickness insurance scheme which was greater in the case of women than men was an aid, because it favoured certain industries employing large numbers of female employees, such as in the textile, clothing, footwear and leather-goods sectors.[107] The situation would have been different if the reduction of employers' contributions had applied equally to all sectors of the economy.[108] In *France v Commission (Kimberly Clark)*,[109] the Court of Justice held that the financial participation by the State in an undertaking's social plan was an aid because, although the State's participation in such plans was not limited by sector or territorially or by reference to a restricted category of undertakings, there was an element of discretion in the selection of beneficiaries, the amount of assistance and the conditions under which it was provided. The Court of Justice has also held that an insolvency regime favoured particular undertakings because it was intended to apply selectively to large industrial undertakings in difficulties that owed debts to mainly public creditors and its application was in part motivated by a concern to maintain the undertaking's economic activity in the light of national industrial policy conditions.[110] The granting of a preferential discount rate for exporters has been held to be an aid because it was a measure which did not apply to the undertakings

---

[106] In Case 249/81 *Commission v Ireland (Buy Irish)* [1982] ECR 4005, [1983] 2 CMLR 104, the Commission took the view that State action favouring all domestic products as against imports, such as subsidising a public body to carry out promotion for domestic products, was not caught by Art 87 since the measure was too general to favour certain, but not all, undertakings within that Member State. AG Capotorti at 4031–4032 (ECR), 117–119 (CMLR), took a different view, considering that Art 87 embodied a general principle of the prohibition of public aids to domestic products. However such action could contravene Art 28. See para 15.130, below.

[107] Case 203/82 *Commission v Italy* [1983] ECR 2525, [1985] 1 CMLR 653. With regard to the principle that aid may be selective even where it concerns a whole economic sector, see also Case 173/73 *Italy v Commission* (n 30, above); Case 52/83 *Commission v France (clothing)* [1983] ECR 3707; Case C-75/97 *Belgium v Commission (Maribel I)* [1999] ECR I-3671, [2000] 1 CMLR 791, para 33; Case C-251/97 *France v Commission (collective agreements)* [1999] ECR I-6639; Case C-148/04 *Unicredito Italiano v Agenzia delle Entrate* [2005] ECR I-11137, paras 45–49; Cases C-393/04 & 41/05 *Air Liquide Industries Belgium v Ville de Seraing* [2006] ECR I-5293, [2006] 3 CMLR 667.

[108] Case 203/82 *Commission v Italy*, above, at 2533 (ECR), 655 (CMLR), per AG Rozes. See also recital 6 of Reg 2204/2002, OJ 2002 L337/3, corrigendum OJ 2002 L349/126: Vol II, App G.12, which seeks to clarify the distinction between aid and general measures in the labour market. In *Maribel I,* above, the ECJ held that the reduction of social security charges under the Maribel bis/ter schemes was a selective measure since it excluded certain sectors of the manufacturing industry, the tertiary and the building sectors. The diversity of the eligible sectors and the large number of undertakings covered was not sufficient to render this measure one of general application.

[109] Case C-241/94 *France v Commission (Kimberly Clark)* [1996] ECR I-4551, paras 16–24. Following its earlier case law the ECJ held that the social character of the assistance did not exclude it from Art 87.

[110] Case C-200/97 *Ecotrade v AFS* [1998] ECR I-7907, [1999] 2 CMLR 804, paras 37–42; *Piaggio* (n 80, above) paras 36–39. See also *DMT* (n 31, above) paras 26–28; *Magefesa* (n 34, above) paras 17–21 (failure to enforce tax and social security obligations in the case of specific undertakings).

in that Member State that manufactured only for the domestic market.[111] In *CdF Chimie AZF v Commission*,[112] the Court of Justice treated as an aid a revised gas tariff that continued to favour ammonia producers although one non-ammonia producer was also able to benefit from the tariff.[113] Similarly, in *GEMO*,[114] the Court held that a free collection and disposal service for animal carcasses and slaughterhouse waste favoured farmers and slaughterhouse operators, although the provision of the service was not restricted to those categories of undertaking and could therefore be taken advantage of by other persons (such as zoos and owners of domestic animals). In *Ramondín*,[115] the Court of First Instance stated that the fact that measures benefited only newly-founded undertakings was sufficient to render them selective.

Difference in treatment not always favouring certain undertakings. A difference in treatment between economic activities or undertakings will not constitute an advantage favouring those activities or undertakings if the difference can be objectively justified by reference, for example, to the different regulatory conditions applicable to those activities or undertakings.[116] An exemption for particular undertakings from the normal application of a levy may therefore fall outside Article 87(1) if it is justified 'on the basis of the nature or general scheme

15.024

---

[111] See Opinion of AG Roemer in Cases 6 & 11/69 *Commission v France* [1969] ECR 523, 552, [1970] CMLR 43, 57, and paras 20–21 of the judgment.

[112] Case C-169/84 *CdF Chimie AZF v Commission* [1990] ECR I-3083, [1992] 1 CMLR 177.

[113] cf Case C-56/93 *Belgium v Commission* [1996] ECR I-723: revised version of the gas tariff which had been condemned as a State aid in *CdF Chimie* was justified for commercial reasons and did not favour Dutch ammonia producers.

[114] Case C-126/01 *Ministre de l'Economie v GEMO* [2003] ECR I-13769, [2004] 1 CMLR 259. The ECJ rejected the Member State's argument that the free service did not selectively favour certain undertakings but was a health and safety measure which benefited society generally. In that regard the Court noted, at para 34, that Art 87(1) did not distinguish between measures by reference to their aims, but defined them in relation to their effects.

[115] Case T-92/00 & 103/00 *Diputación Foral de Álava v Commission (Ramondín)* [2002] ECR II-1385, paras 49–50 (appeal on other grounds dismissed: C-186/02P *Ramondín v Commission* [2004] ECR I-10653, [2005] 1 CMLR 787); and see Kelinheisterkamp, (2002) 2 EC Competition Policy Newsletter 61. See also Case C-351/98 *Spain v Commission (Plan Renove Industrial)* [2002] ECR I-8031, paras 40–43 (fiscal measures granted only to SMEs to aid the replacement of vehicles); Case T-127/99 *Daewoo Electronics Manufacturing (DEMESA) v Commission* [2002] ECR II-1275, para 157 (measure capable of benefiting only large-scale undertakings due to the size of the required investment) (the ECJ dismissed an appeal in which DEMESA put forward different arguments from those advanced before the CFI: Case C-183/02P, [2004] ECR I-10609). See also *Kiener Deponie Bachmanning*, OJ 1999 L109/51: part-financing by the State of the clean-up of a contaminated landfill site did not constitute aid for the polluter, since it was no longer exercising any business activity, but in favour of the current owner of the site, since it would be spared the costs.

[116] Case C-353/95P *Tiercé Ladbroke v Commission* [1997] ECR I-7007, paras 33–36, discussed at para 15.033, below. See also Case C-237/04 *Enirisorse v Sotocarbo* (n 102, above) paras 40–51; Case T-475/04 *Bouygues v Commission* (judgment of 4 July 2007); and in the English Court, *Great North Eastern Railway v Office of Rail Regulation* [2006] EWHC 1942.

of the system'.[117] Thus, the application of a levy to one class of undertakings, and not to another class with whom the former class is in competition, will not amount to conferring a selective advantage on the latter class if the difference in treatment is directed at preventing a distortion of competition caused by costly public service obligations imposed only on the latter undertakings in circumstances where the levy does not exceed the level necessary to place the two classes of undertakings on an equal competitive footing.[118] Furthermore, in *R (BT3G Ltd) v Secretary of State for Trade and Industry*,[119] the English Court of Appeal held that a Member State does not confer a selective advantage on an undertaking when it treats one undertaking differently from a competitor undertaking in circumstances where the difference in treatment can be objectively justified.

15.025 **The effect on competition.** The test is whether the measure is liable to distort competition and not whether competition has actually been distorted.[120] When deciding that an aid is within Article 87, the Commission must set out the circumstances which show that the aid is capable of distorting or threatening to distort competition.[121] In *Philip Morris*,[122] the Court of Justice held that where financial aid granted by a State strengthens the position of an undertaking compared with other undertakings competing in intra-Community trade, competition must be regarded as distorted. In that case, the Commission had prohibited an aid designed to help enlarge Philip Morris's production capacity in the Netherlands.

---

[117] Case 173/73 *Italy v Commission* (n 30, above); paras 23–27 of the Commission's Notice on the application of the State aid rules to measures relating to direct business taxation (n 94, above); Case C-308/01 *GIL Insurance* [2004] ECR I-4777, [2004] 2 CMLR 22, [2004] All ER (EC) 954.

[118] *Ferring v ACOSS* (n 33, above) paras 20–29.

[119] *R (BT3G Ltd) v Secretary of State for Trade and Industry* [2001] EWCA Civ 1448, [2001] 3 CMLR 1588. The Secretary of State had delayed granting 'third generation' mobile phone licences to two of the successful bidders for such licences until they complied with rules which in effect required them to divest themselves of association with one another, since no entity could hold more than one licence: it was held that this delay, which advantaged the two bidders concerned by delaying the time when payment for the licences had to be made, did not constitute State aid because it was objectively justified by the Secretary of State's paramount objective of ensuring compliance with a rule that was itself non-discriminatory (since all successful bidders were required to comply with it).

[120] *Air Liquide v Ville de Seraing* (n 107, above) para 34.

[121] Cases 296 & 318/82 *Netherlands and Leeuwarder Papierwarenfabriek v Commission* [1985] ECR 809, [1985] 3 CMLR 380, para 24: decision annulled which contained no information on the relevant market, the place of the aided undertaking on that market, the pattern of trade between Member States in the relevant products or the undertaking's export. See also Cases C-329/93, etc, *Germany v Commission* [1996] ECR I-5151, [1998] 1 CMLR 591, paras 49–55; Cases C-15/98 & 105/99 *Italy and Sardegna Lines v Commission* [2000] ECR I-8855, [2001] 1 CMLR 237, para 67.

[122] Case 730/79 *Philip Morris v Commission* [1980] ECR 2671, [1981] 2 CMLR 321; cf the more rigorous approach of the ECJ subsequently in *Netherlands and Leeuwarder Papierwarenfabriek* (n 121, above). See also Case 248/84 *Germany v Commission (Regional Aid Programme)* [1987] ECR 4013, [1989] 1 CMLR 591; Case T-214/95 *Vlaamse Gewest v Commission* [1998] ECR II-717; *Germany v Commission (new Länder)* (n 95, above) paras 29–31; *CETM* (n 103, above) para 86. On the need for reasoning, see further para 15.120, below.

This would then amount to nearly 50 per cent of cigarette production in that country, of which 80 per cent was destined for export to other Member States. Philip Morris criticised the Commission for not identifying the relevant market, the territory and the pattern of the market in question. But the Court found that the Commission's conclusion that the proposed aid would threaten to distort competition between undertakings and affect trade between Member States was justified on the facts set out in the decision.[123] Where an undertaking competes in a market which experiences economic difficulties, any aid granted to an undertaking runs the risk of seriously distorting competition.[124] Similarly, where an aid is granted to an undertaking operating in a sector which is characterised by intense competition, there is a distortion, or a risk of a distortion, of competition.[125]

The effect on trade between Member States.   Unlike Articles 81 and 82 which   **15.026**
refer to practices *which may affect* trade between Member States, Article 87 simply refers to aids *which affect* trade between Member States. There is no indication, however, that the omission of the word 'may' in Article 87 is material. On the contrary, in *France v Commission (FIM)*,[126] the Court of Justice held that an aid

---

[123] The Commission is not obliged to provide exact details in its decision as to the competitive advantage which the recipient undertaking would receive in comparison with their competitors in other Member States who had not been aided by those States: see, eg Case C-113/00 *Spain v Commission ('Aid for horticultural products')* [2002] ECR I-7601, [2003] 1 CMLR 549, paras 49–54. Thus, where the Community Courts have found that a measure was likely directly or indirectly to favour certain undertakings or to constitute an advantage which the recipient undertaking would not have obtained under normal market conditions, those Courts will generally have little difficulty in inferring that there must at least be a risk of competition being distorted: see, eg Case C-451/03 *Servizi Ausiliari Dottori Commercialisti v Calafiori* [2006] ECR I-2941, [2006] 2 CMLR 1135, paras 51–71 (ECJ appears to have been willing to hold that remuneration provided by the Italian State to undertakings which assisted in the collection of taxes constituted State aid, unless the *Altmark* criteria for public service compensation were satisfied, without any discussion of whether there was any effect on competition, even though the market on which the service was provided appears to have been essentially national in character and the State was willing to provide remuneration, on equivalent terms, to undertakings from other Member States who provided the service in question). See also Cases E-5/04, etc, *Fesil and Finnfjord* [2005] EFTA Ct Rep 117, [2005] 3 CMLR 470, paras 93–94.

[124] Case C-42/93 *Spain v Commission (Merco)* [1994] ECR I-4125, [1996] 2 CMLR 702, para 41.

[125] *Vlaamse Gewest* (n 122, above) para 46. The aid in that case was characterised as operating aid which was held in principle to distort competition: see para 43. See also *Germany v Commission (new Länder)* (n 95, above) para 30; Case C-288/96 *Germany v Commission (Jadekost)* [2000] ECR I-8237, para 77.

[126] Case 102/87 *France v Commission (FIM)* [1988] ECR 4067, [1989] 3 CMLR 713, where the ECJ held that a subsidised loan to a French brewer was capable of affecting trade between Member States and distorting competition where that undertaking's products competed with products coming from other Member States even if the aided undertaking did not itself export its products. See also *Vlaamse Gewest* (n 122, above); *Maribel I* (n 107, above) paras 45–51; and the Commission decisions discussed in Könings, 'State aid and the effect on trade criterion. The Netherlands: measures in favour of non-profit harbours for recreational crafts' (2004) 1 EC Competition Policy Newsletter 86.

fell within Article 87 if it was capable of affecting trade between Member States. In *Associazione Italiana Tecnico Economica del Cemento (AITEC) v Commission*,[127] the Court of First Instance annulled a Commission decision approving aid granted to a Greek cement producer when the Commission had failed to examine the effect that the aid was likely to have on inter-State trade. It was not sufficient to confine the examination to the time when the aid was granted and there was no inter-State trade in the relevant product.[128] Where there is inter-State trade in the products affected by the aid, however, the Commission may conclude that there is an effect on that trade without having to describe the market or set out a detailed explanation of the trade flows between Member States for the product concerned.[129] That will be so even if the aid recipient is not himself engaged in inter-State trade.[130] Subject to the question of whether a *de minimis* rule applies to State aids,[131] there are parallels to be drawn between the phrases used in Articles 81 and 82, on the one hand, and Article 87 on the other hand.[132] Thus, if trade in a specified product is affected at a purely local or national level Article 87 will not apply,[133] although even matters which appear to be confined to a single State may have effects on trade between Member States.[134] This is a question of fact. Aids directed to exports or direct investment outside the Community will still fall within Article 87 if the necessary effect on inter-State trade is shown.[135]

---

[127] Cases T-447/93, etc, *AITEC v Commission* [1995] ECR II-1971, paras 138–139.

[128] See also AG Jacobs in Cases C-278/92, etc, *Spain v Commission (Hytasa No. 1)* [1994] ECR I-4103, paras 33–35. cf *Italy and Sardegna Lines* (n 121, above) paras 68–73.

[129] Cases C-346 & 529/03 *Atzeni v Regione autonoma della Sardegna* [2006] ECR I-1875, para 75.

[130] In *Air Liquide v Ville de Seraing* (n 107, above) at para 35, for example, the ECJ stated: 'where aid granted by a Member State strengthens the position of an undertaking compared with other undertakings competing in intra-Community trade, the latter must be regarded as affected by that aid. . . . [I]t is not necessary that the recipient undertaking itself be involved in the said trade'. See also Case C-66/02 *Italy v Commission* [2005] ECR I-10901, para 77; *Unicredito Italiano v Agenzia delle Entrate* (n 107, above) paras 56–58.

[131] See paras 15.027 and 15.028, below.

[132] See AG Capotorti in *Philip Morris v Commission* (n 122, above) at 2697 (ECR), 329 (CMLR). In Case C-142/87 *Tubemeuse* [1990] ECR I-959, [1991] 3 CMLR 213, paras 42–43, the ECJ rejected the view that if there was a market share of less than five per cent Community trade was not affected.

[133] See also the discussion of aid for deprived areas in Pieké and Ghoreishi, 'State aid control and regeneration: rubber straitjacket or passepartout?' (2003) 3 EC Competition Policy Newsletter 17. In February 2004, the Commission issued two draft communications which, if adopted, would have provided for a simplified investigation process for aid measures which could be presumed to have only a small distortive effect on trade between Member States, whether by reason of the small amount of aid involved, or because the economic sector concerned was characterised by low volumes of inter-State trade. The Commission ultimately decided not to adopt these proposals: see Hancher, Slot and Ottervanger *EC State Aids* (3rd edn, 2006) para 3–062.

[134] *Philip Morris* (n 122, above); *Altmark Trans* (n 48, above) paras 77–81.

[135] *Tubemeuse* (n 132, above). See also *XXVIIIth Report on Competition Policy* (1998), points 228–229. In *R v Secretary of State for National Heritage, ex p J Paul Getty Trust* [1997] EuLR 407 a grant to assist a British museum purchasing a work of art when otherwise it would go to

De minimis: **the case law.** The Community Courts have not recognised a **15.027**
de minimis rule similar to that applied under Article 81(1) of the Treaty.[136] Instead,
they have rejected arguments to the effect that a particular aid was *de minimis* in
its effect on competition and trade between Member States on the basis that the aid
in question distorted or threatened to distort competition and was liable to affect
trade between Member States.[137] Thus in *France v Commission*[138] the Court of
Justice held that even aid of a relatively small amount is liable to affect trade between
Member States where there is strong competition in the sector in question.[139]
In *Italy v Commission (ENI-Lanerossi)*[140] the Court of Justice held that the grant of
aid to undertakings which accounted for 2.5 per cent of Italian production of men's
clothing and 0.33 per cent of Italian exports in that sector was capable of affecting
competition by reason of the significant inter-State trade in such products.[141]

---

the USA was held by the English Court of Appeal not to be capable of affecting trade between
Member States. See also Cases T-304 & 316/04 *Italy v Commission (WAM)* [2006] ECR II-64,
where the CFI annulled a Commission decision for lack of reasoning on how aid granted to an
undertaking for use in the Far East was liable to affect trade between Member States (on appeal,
Case C-494/06P *Commission v Italy*, not yet decided). See also Commission Communication pursuant to Art [88(1)] applying Arts [87] and [88] of the Treaty to short-term export credit insurance,
OJ 1997 C281/4: Vol II, App G.24, which sought to bring to an end certain aspects of export credit
insurance systems operated by Member States; *XXVIth Report on Competition Policy* (1996), point
224; *XXVIIth Report on Competition Policy* (1997), point 230; Heinisch, 'EU - rules on State aid do
not allow for export aid' (2003) 2 EC Competition Policy Newsletter 81. The Communication has
been subsequently amended and extended to 2010, see para 15.060 below.

[136] For the applicability of the *de minimis* rule to Art 81, see paras 2.121 *et seq*, above. But see
Germany v Commission (new Länder) (n 95, above) para 40.

[137] See, eg Case 259/85 *France v Commission (Textiles and clothing)* [1987] ECR 4393, [1989]
2 CMLR 30; Case T-67/94 *Ladbroke Racing v Commission* [1998] ECR II-1, para 59 (not raised on
appeal in Case C-83/98P *France v Ladbroke Racing and Commission* [2000] ECR I-3271, [2000]
3 CMLR 555); *Vlaamse Gewest* (n 122, above) paras 78–79; Case T-14/96 *Bretagne Angleterre
Irlande (BAI) v Commission* [1999] ECR II-139, [1999] 3 CMLR 245, para 77; *CETM* (n 103,
above) para 92; *Germany v Commission (new Länder)* (n 95, above) paras 37–42; *Altmark Trans*
(n 48, above) paras 77–81; Case C-382/99 *Netherlands v Commission ('Dutch petrol stations')* [2002]
ECR I-5163, paras 66–68. In *GEMO* (n 114, above), however, AG Jacobs suggested (Opinion,
para 145) a number of indicators that trade between Member States would not be affected by an
aid measure: (i) the level of competition of the market is low; (ii) the amount of aid is low; (iii) the
companies concerned are small; and (iv) the markets have a local dimension. The AG's remarks
do not appear to fit well with the ECJ's reasoning in *Altmark* but may at least suggest that the case
law in this area is still developing. See also the discussion of the *Dutch petrol stations* case: Brenning,
(2002) 3 EC Competition Policy Newsletter 69.

[138] Case 259/85 *France v Commission (Textiles and Clothing)* [1987] ECR 4393, [1989] 2 CMLR
30, para 24.

[139] See also Cases C-329/93, etc, *Germany v Commission* [1996] ECR I-5151, [1998] 1 CMLR
591, para 52 where the ECJ stated that it is settled law that the fact that the level of aid is relatively
low does not *a priori* exclude the possibility of aid; *Ladbroke Racing* (n 137, above); *Vlaamse Gewest*
(n 122, above); *BAI* (n 137, above); Case C-113/00 *Aid for Horticultural Products* (n 123, above).

[140] Case C-308/88 *Italy v Commission (ENI-Lanerossi)* [1991] ECR I-1433, paras 26–29.

[141] See also *Van Der Kooy* (n 98, above) where a price reduction of 5.5 per cent off the standard
tariff for gas supplies was, in view of the amount of gas used by Dutch horticulturists, sufficient
to distort competition within the common market. In C-234/84 *Belgium v Commission (Meura)*

Similarly, in *Heiser*[142] the ECJ rejected a submission that a tax advantage granted to medical practitioners was not capable of affecting trade between Member States, stating that it was 'not inconceivable ... that medical practitioners special-ising in dentistry, such as Mr Heiser, might be in competition with their colleagues established in another Member State'. In *Enirisorse* the Court of Justice stated that 'there is no threshold or percentage below which it may be considered that trade between Member States is not affected'.[143]

15.028 *De minimis:* **The Commission's approach and the adoption of block exemptions.**   The Commission's position has changed over time. Originally it took the view that there was no *de minimis* rule.[144] From 1992 it applied a *de minimis* rule, similar to that applied under Article 81, but only in relation to small- and medium-sized undertakings (SMEs).[145] In 1996, the Commission issued a Notice setting out a new general *de minimis* rule[146] which indicated that the Commission would presume that aid below a certain threshold granted to under-takings of any size fell outside Article 87(1). The ceiling for aid covered by the *de minimis* rule was 100,000 ECUs granted over a three-year period. The Notice did not, however, apply to export aid, nor to aid to the transport, agriculture, fisheries and ECSC sectors. Article 2 of Council Regulation 994/98[147] gives the Commission the power to adopt a Regulation laying down a *de minimis* rule for aids which are exempted from notification under Article 88(3). This was intended to remove doubts over the Commission's power to define the scope of Articles 87(1) and 88(3) of the Treaty. In January 2001, the Commission adopted Regulation 69/2001,[148] which set the *de minimis* threshold at €100,000 over a three-year period. A new block exemption was adopted in December 2006, Regulation 1998/2006.[149] Certain sectors continue to be excluded from the *de minimis* exemption but, unlike Regulation 69/2001, the new Regulation applies to the transport sector and to the processing and marketing of agricultural products. The general threshold was raised to €200,000, except for undertakings in the

---

[1986] ECR 2263, [1988] 2 CMLR 331 at 2274 (ECR) and in *FIM* (n 126, above) 4078–4079 (ECR), 718–719 (CMLR), AG Lenz stated that there should be no *de minimis* rule under Art 87.

[142] Case C-172/03 *Heiser v Finanzamt Innsbruck* [2005] ECR I-1627, [2005] 2 CMLR 402, paras 31–35.

[143] Cases C-34/01, etc, *Enirisorse v Ministero delle Finanze* [2003] ECR I-14243, [2004] 1 CMLR 296, para 28.

[144] See, eg its submissions in *Meura* (n 141, above) recorded at 2272 (ECR).

[145] See para 18–013 of the 4th edn of this work and the 1st Supplement thereto. For a current definition of an SME, see Commission Recommendation of 6 May 2003 concerning the definition of micro-, small- and medium-sized enterprises, OJ 2003 L124/36: Vol II, App C.15.

[146] Commission Notice on the *de minimis* rule for State aid, OJ 1996 C68/9. As to the legal effects of Reg 69/2001, see *Dutch petrol stations* (137, above) paras 22–28.

[147] Reg 994/98, OJ 1998 L142/1: Vol II, App G.9; see also para 15.067, below.

[148] Reg 69/2001, OJ 2001 L10/30.

[149] Reg 1998/2006, OJ 2006 L379/5: Vol II, App G.14.

transport sector where the threshold remains at €100,000.[150] Before the adoption of the new Regulation, the Commission showed signs of taking a less severe approach than the Court, in cases where the threshold is exceeded, to the question of whether advantages provided to undertakings offering services of a purely local character should be regarding as capable of affecting trade between Member States.[151]

Calculating the amount of the advantage. Some aid measures involve staggered payments over time, for example, the grant of soft loans. The Commission has laid down the rules[152] to measure the grant equivalent of the aid so disbursed and to calculate the aid element in soft loans. It determines a reference rate for each Member State. The rates are intended to reflect the average level of interest rate charged in the various Member States on medium- and long-term loans, backed by normal security. These reference rates are used in the calculation of aid for the purposes of the *de minimis* rule and of ordering the repayment of illegally granted aid.[153]   **15.029**

(b) Particular applications

Examples of State aids. Examples of State aids include[154] investment grants,[155] subsidies to cover operating losses,[156] loans at reduced rates of interest,[157]   **15.030**

---

[150] See Press Release IP/06/283 (9 March 2006); and *Revised Commission proposal for an amended de minimis rule*, 20 September 2006 (available in the overview section of DG Comp's State aid pages). The Commission is also proposing to adopt a new Reg on *de minimis* aid specifically for fisheries: see Commission Press Release IP/06/825 (22 June 2006).

[151] See, eg *Irish Hospitals* N543/2001 (27 February 2002); *Dorsten swimming pool*, Press Release IP/00/1509 (21 December 2000); *Danish newspapers*, IP/04/761 (16 June 2004). See also *Brighton West Pier* N560/01 & NN17/02 (9 April 2002), explained in the Commission's 'Non-paper' on *Services of General Economic Interest and State Aid*, 12 November 2002 (available in the State aid section of DG Comp's website) at para 51, as being justified on the basis that aid to restore the West Pier would not impact on inter-State trade since piers were a peculiarly English attraction that would not attract tourists from other Member States. A rival pier operator lodged an appeal with the CFI (Case T-252/02, OJ 2002 C261/18), but subsequently withdrew it after its subject-matter became irrelevant: the West Pier fell into the sea before it could be restored.

[152] Commission Notice on the method for setting the reference and discount rates, OJ 1997 C273/3: Vol II, App G.27.

[153] See para 15.028, above and para 15.098, below. For current and recent reference rates, see Vol II, Apps G.29–31.

[154] For more illustrations, see the State aids section of the annual Reports on Competition Policy.

[155] *Philip Morris* (n 122, above); Cases 62 & 72/87 *Executif Regional Wallon v Commission (Glaverbel)* [1988] ECR 1573, [1989] 2 CMLR 771; *German Joint Regional Aid Programme*, OJ 1987 L12/17; *City of Hamburg*, OJ 1991 L215/11. See also *English Partnerships*, Press Release IP/99/1040 (22 December 1999).

[156] eg aids to the coal industry under Decn 3632/93/ECSC, OJ 1993 L329/12, and aids to the shipbuilding industry under Reg 1540/98, OJ 1998 L202/1. See also Case 94/87 *Commission v Germany (Alcan No. 1)* [1989] ECR 175, [1989] 2 CMLR 425; Case C-305/89 *Italy v Commission (Alfa Romeo No. 1)* [1991] ECR I-1603.

[157] Case 323/82 *Intermills v Commission* [1984] ECR 3809, [1986] 1 CMLR 614; Case 84/82 *Germany v Commission (Textiles)* [1984] ECR 1451, 1500–1501, [1985] 1 CMLR 153, 167–168, *per* AG Slynn; and *Vlaamse Gewest* (n 122, above).

loan guarantees,[158] preferential fiscal treatment,[159] selective reduction of public charges such as employers' social security payments,[160] preferential energy tariffs that are not commercially justified,[161] non-subjection to industrial levies that are imposed on competitors,[162] the provision without charges of services which the recipient undertakings would normally have had to pay themselves,[163] the provision of logistical and commercial assistance by a public undertaking to its subsidiaries on terms that differ from those that an undertaking acting under normal market conditions would offer,[164] cross-subsidy by a public undertaking,[165] debt write-offs,[166] payment of bonuses needed to attract workers to a particular industry,[167] discretionary State financing of an employer's social plan,[168] and funding of television channels by licence fees.[169] Aid for exports to other Member States are classic examples of aids caught by Article 87.[170] Aid to exports outside the Community and aid for direct investment abroad can also fall within Article 87 where they have an effect on competition within the Community.[171]

---

[158] See Commission Notice on the application of Arts 87 and 88 EC to State aid in the form of guarantees, OJ 2000 C71/14: Vol II, App G.26; *EFIM*, OJ 1993 C267/11, and *Jadekost* (n 125, above).

[159] Case C-387/92 *Banco Exterior de España v Ayuntamiento de Valencia* [1994] ECR I-877, [1994] 3 CMLR 473; *Germany v Commission (new Länder)* (n 95, above); *R v Commissioners of Customs and Excise, ex p Lunn Poly* [1999] 1 CMLR 1357 (CA), and see para 15.031, below.

[160] See the cases referred to in para 15.023, above.

[161] *Van Der Kooy* (n 98, above); *CdF Chimie AZF* (n 112, above); *EdF/Pechiney, XIXth Report on Competition Policy* (1989), point 168.

[162] Case C-53/00 *Ferring* [2001] ECR I-9067, [2003] 1 CMLR 1001.

[163] *GEMO* (n 114, above): the State funding of a service for the disposal of anima carcasses and slaughterhouse waste constituted State aid because it relieved farmers and slaughterhouses of a financial burden which they would otherwise have had to bear as an inherent cost of the economic activities in which they were engaged, and was therefore liable to distort competition.

[164] Case C-39/94 *SFEI* [1996] ECR I-3547, [1996] 3 CMLR 369, [1996] All ER (EC) 685. See also the Transparency Directive: para 15.016, above.

[165] Case T-106/95 *FFSA v Commission* [1997] ECR II-229, [1997] 2 CMLR 78, appeal dismissed Case C-174/97P, [1998] ECR I-1303; and sections 3 and 7 of the Commission Notice on the application of the competition rules to the postal sector and on the assessment of certain State measures relating to postal services, OJ 1998 C39/1: Vol II, App E.29.

[166] See, eg *Rover Group*, OJ 1989 L25/92; and see Case C-294/90 *British Aerospace and Rover v Commission* [1992] ECR I-493, [1992] 1 CMLR 853.

[167] See Case 30/59 *Steenkolenmijnen v High Authority* [1961] ECR 1: German government's payment of a miners' shift bonus held to be a subsidy because such bonus was necessary in order to attract men into the industry.

[168] *Kimberly Clark* (n 109, above).

[169] *Kinderkanal and Phoenix*, and *BBC News 24 (TV Licence fees)*, *XXIXth Report on Competition Policy* (1999), para 226 and p 105. See also N37/03 *BBC Digital Curriculum* (1 October 2003).

[170] See, eg Cases 6 & 11/69 *Commission v France* [1969] ECR 523, 552, [1970] CMLR 43, 57 (preferential discount rates in respect of credits for export transactions); see also *Greek export aids*, OJ 1986 L136/61 (*XVth Report on Competition Policy* (1985), point 227), upheld in Case 57/86 *Greece v Commission* [1988] ECR 2855, [1990] 1 CMLR 65.

[171] See *Tubemeuse* (n 132, above) paras 31–34.

Other examples of State aids include the use of a levy for collective research and the renewal of industrial and commercial structures[172] and for the advertising and promotion of the products of a particular industry.[173] The provision of capital can also be a State aid.[174]

Tax measures. The concept of an 'aid' embraces not only positive benefits, such **15.031** as payments of subsidies, but also measures which mitigate the charges which would normally be included in the budget of an undertaking and are similar in character to, and have the same effect as, subsidies. Accordingly, tax measures which favour certain undertakings or the production of certain goods by relieving them of tax liabilities which they would otherwise 'normally' have to bear are likely to constitute State aid.[175] Such measures may, for example, include tax exemptions,[176] special deductions, reliefs and credits,[177] lower rate social security contributions,[178] special or accelerated depreciation arrangements,[179] and deferment,[180] cancellation or even special rescheduling of tax debt. For a tax measure to be an aid, it must be selective as opposed to general, a general measure being one that is open to all economic agents.[181] Thus measures pursuing general

---

[172] Case 47/69 *France v Commission* [1970] ECR 487, [1970] CMLR 351. However, aids granted to bodies engaged in research on a non-profit-making basis are not caught by Art 87(1); *Second Report on Competition Policy* (1972), point 121; see also the new Community Framework for State Aids for Research and Development, OJ 2006 C323/1: Vol II, App G.22. See also Art 163 EC, discussed at para 15.136, below

[173] See Case 78/76 *Steinike and Weinlig v Germany* [1977] ECR 595, [1977] 2 CMLR 688; Case 222/82 *Apple and Pear Development Council v Lewis* [1983] ECR 4083, 4133, [1984] 3 CMLR 733, 747, per AG Rozes.

[174] See, eg *Alfa Romeo (No. 1)* (n 156, above). See also the Commission decn, *Viridian growth fund (Northern Ireland)*, Press Release IP/01/197 (13 February 2001) (contribution by UK authorities as well as the EIB in a venture capital fund).

[175] *Banco Exterior de España* (n 159, above) paras 13–14; Commission Notice on the application of the State aid rules to measures relating to direct business taxation, OJ 1998 C384/3: Vol II, App G.25, para 9.

[176] See, eg, Case 173/73 *Italy v Commission (Aids to the Textile Industry)* [1974] ECR 709; *Banco Exterior de España* (n 159, above); *Air Liquide v Ville de Seraing* (n 107, above). See *Fesil and Finnfjord* (n 123, above) for the application of this principle in the EEA. For the Commission's approach to several cases conerning eco-taxes, see Lannering and Renner-Loquenz, 'State aid and eco-taxes: bundling of eco-taxes for State aid Assessment' (2003) 3 EC Competition Policy Newsletter 75 (tax exemptions as aids).

[177] See, eg Case C-6/97 *Italy v Commission (Fuel tax credits)* [1999] ECR I-2981, [2000] 2 CMLR 919; *Germany v Commission (new Länder)* (n 95, above); Case T-269/99 *Diputación Foral de Guipúzcoa v Commission* [2002] ECR II-4217, [2003] 1 CMLR 298.

[178] See, eg *Maribel I* (n 107, above).

[179] See, eg Decn 96/369, OJ 1996 L146/42, on fiscal aid given German airlines in the form of a depreciation facility; appeal dismissed as inadmissible, Case T-86/96 *Arbeitsgemeinschaft Deutscher Luftfahrt-Unternehmen and Hapag-Lloyd v Commission* [1999] ECR II-179.

[180] *Ladbroke Racing* (n 137, above) paras 118–122, not disturbed on appeal, Case C-83/98P ibid; *Germany v Commission (new Länder)* (n 95, above); Case C-256/97 *DMT* [1999] ECR I-3913, [1999] 3 CMLR 1, [1999] All ER (EC) 601.

[181] Notice on direct business taxation (n 175, above) paras 13–14.

economic policy objectives through a reduction of the tax burden related to certain costs, eg R & D, environment or training costs, do not constitute State aid provided they apply without distinction to all firms and to the production of all goods. According to the Commission the fact that some firms or some sectors benefit more than others is not decisive.[182] In considering whether the advantage has been granted through State resources, a loss of tax revenue is treated as equivalent to consumption of State resources in the form of fiscal expenditure.[183] The need to show such a loss may mean, however, that the measure must be properly characterised as involving the *relieving* of a tax liability from the advantaged undertakings (thus demonstrating that the advantage is being 'funded' by the State), rather than as the imposition of an exceptional tax burden on the disadvantaged undertakings to the State's financial benefit. In *GIL Insurance*,[184] for example, Advocate General Geelhoed argued that the imposition of a higher rate of Insurance Premium Tax (IPT) on domestic appliance insurance arranged through the suppliers of the appliances was properly characterised as an 'exceptional burden' placed on such suppliers, rather than a State-resourced benefit conferred on other insurance suppliers who paid IPT at the standard rate. It was thus was not capable of constituting State aid.[185] The Court of Justice did not decide whether the Advocate General's distinction between the conferral of an advantage and the imposition of an exceptional burden was valid, instead holding that, even if the higher rate of IPT was an advantage for operators subject to the standard rate, the imposition of the higher rate was objectively justified.

15.032 **Tax measures: incidental differential result.** A conceptual problem in the application of these principles is that, although it is desirable to capture 'hidden aids' provided by way of reliefs from tax liabilities which the 'recipient' undertakings would 'normally' have to bear, any tax regime is bound to include rules which will have unintended results in terms of advantaging some undertakings

---

[182] ibid. Tax concessions which are only open to certain classes of undertaking will amount to the conferral of a selective advantage on those undertakings, however, where the difference in treatment is not objectively justified by the environmental or other policy objectives pursued: see, eg Case C-143/99 *Adria-Wien Pipeline and Wietersdorfer & Peggauer Zementwerke* [2001] ECR I-8365, [2002] 1 CMLR 1103, [2002] All ER (EC) 306 (the payment of energy tax rebates to producers of goods but not to providers of services was not justified since the effect of energy consumption on the environment was the same whether that consumption was in connection with the production of goods or the provision of services). Following this judgment, the Commission reviewed similar measures in force in the three Scandinavian Member States: see Infeldt, 'Eco-tax reliefs for companies in Denmark, Finland and Sweden after the Court ruling in Adria-Wien Pipeline GmbH case' (2003) 1 EC Competition Policy Newsletter 103. See also, under the EEA regime, *Fesil and Finnfjord* (n 123, above).

[183] Notice on direct business taxation (n 175, above) para 2; *Germany v Commission (new Länder)* (n 95, above) paras 26–28.

[184] Case C-308/01 *GIL Insurance* [2004] ECR I-4777, [2004] 2 CMLR 22, [2004] All ER (EC) 954.

[185] ibid, Opinion paras 68–89. *GIL* is discussed further in para 15.033, below.

vis-à-vis their competitors. The case law suggests two principles by which the Court of Justice seeks to keep the application of Article 87 to differences in tax treatment within reasonable bounds. The first is that a measure will not be found to be an aid if the reduced tax liability of certain undertakings is merely an incidental result of non-tax measures. In *Sloman Neptun*, for example, the Court of Justice held that provisions of German maritime law which subjected contracts for the employment of sailors who were EC nationals to German law did not constitute State aid although they had the effect of requiring shipowners who employed EC nationals to pay social security contributions which their competitors who employed non-EC nationals did not have to pay. Such effects were inherent in the social security system and did not constitute a means of affording the undertakings concerned a specific advantage.[186]

Tax measures: objective justification.   The second principle is that a measure   **15.033** will not be found to be an aid if it can be objectively justified 'on the basis of the nature or general scheme of [the tax] system'[187] or, in the words of the Commission Notice, if it is necessary to the functioning and effectiveness of the tax system.[188] In *Tiercé Ladbroke*,[189] for example, the Court of Justice held that the different fiscal treatment of totalisator bets placed in France on Belgian and French races was justified by the different regulatory and economic conditions in those countries, including the different fiscal treatment of bets, and by the logic of the totalisator betting system whereby the share of the stakes paid out to the winners could not vary according to the State in which the bets were placed. Accordingly, the difference in fiscal treatment fell outside Article 87(1). In *British Aggregates*, the Court of First Instance held that a levy imposed on virgin aggregates which was intended to encourage use of recycled aggregates was justified by the pursuit of environmental objectives and so did not constitute State aid in favour of those types of aggregates that were exempt from the levy.[190] Tax measures introduced in order to remedy distortions in competition[191] or reduce the scope for tax

---

[186] Cases C-72 & 73/91 *Sloman Neptun v Bodo Ziesemer* [1993] ECR I-887, [1995] 2 CMLR 97, para 21. See also *Ecotrade v AFS* (n 110, above) para 36.

[187] *Italy v Commission (Aids to the Textile Industry)* (n 176, above) para 15; Case C-88/03 *Portugal v Commission (Azores)*, [2006] ECR I-7115, [2006] 3 CMLR 1233, para 52; Notice on direct business taxation (n 175, above) paras 23–27; *Application of the tax on non-domestic property to telecommunications infrastructure in the UK*, OJ 2006 L383/70, pts 174–176.

[188] Notice on direct business taxation (n 175, above) para 23.

[189] Case C-353/95P *Tiercé Ladbroke v Commission* [1997] ECR I-7007, paras 33–36.

[190] Case T-210/02 *British Aggregates Association v Commission* [2006] ECR II-2789; on appeal, Case C-487/06P, not yet decided.

[191] See, eg *Ferring* (n 162, above) (a levy imposed on pharmaceutical manufacturers as a means of redressing the competitive disadvantage imposed on wholesale distributors by their subjection to legal obligations to hold certain stocks of medicines did not constitute a genuine selective advantage to the wholesalers unless the benefit conferred on them exceeded the costs they had to bear in discharging their public service obligations).

avoidance come within the same principle. Thus, in *GIL Insurance*,[192] the Court of Justice held that the United Kingdom was entitled to apply a higher rate of Insurance Premium Tax (IPT), equal to the prevailing rate of VAT, specifically to domestic appliance insurance arranged through the supplier of the appliance. The purpose of the application of the higher rate to such insurance was to remove the incentive for suppliers of domestic appliances to shift the value of those appliances from the prices charged for the appliances themselves to the prices charged for insuring those appliances, thereby profiting from the fact that the standard rate of IPT was substantially lower than the standard rate of VAT. The application of the higher rate to the transactions to which it was applied was therefore justified by the nature and general scheme of the United Kingdom tax system.[193] In contrast, in *Belgium v Commission ('Maribel I')*,[194] the Court of Justice held that an increase in the reduction in employers' social security contributions which had been targeted at economic sectors most exposed to international competition, and which had not been linked to the performance of any social obligations, lacked objective justification and constituted unlawful aid.[195]

15.034 **Selectivity of regional taxation measures.**   In *Portugal v Commission (Azores)*,[196] the Court of Justice considered an appeal brought by Portugal against the

---

[192] Case C-308/01 *GIL Insurance* [2004] ECR I-4777, [2004] 2 CMLR 22, [2004] All ER (EC) 954.

[193] The English Court of Appeal had previously reached a different conclusion, albeit in a different setting, as to whether the application of a higher rate of IPT to certain insurance transactions was objectively justified: see *Lunn Poly* (n 159, above) where it was held that the application of higher rate IPT to travel insurance sold through travel agents could not be justified as an anti-avoidance measure but, rather, involved the provision of a selective advantage to those undertakings whose supplies of travel insurance were subject to IPT at the lower rate. That advantage was directly or indirectly provided from State resources since the provision of that advantage involved a loss of revenue by the State: see in particular Clarke LJ at paras 49, 58–59. For another example of the English courts' application of these principles, see *Professional Contractors' Group v Commissioners of Inland Revenue* [2001] EWCA Civ 1945, [2002] 1 CMLR 1332: Court of Appeal held that any apparent discrimination caused by a taxation rule which had been introduced to stop a popular form of tax avoidance was objectively justified and did not, therefore, constitute the provision of a selective advantage to undertakings that were unaffected by the rule.

[194] Case C-75/97 *Belgium v Commission (Maribel I)* [1999] ECR I-3671, [2000] 1 CMLR 791.

[195] For another example of a tax measure which the ECJ found not to have been objectively justified, see *Adria-Wien* (n 182, above).

[196] Case C-88/03 *Portugal v Commission (Azores)* [2006] ECR I-7115, [2006] 3 CMLR 1233, paras 52–85. AG Geelhoed contrasted the Azores' measure with (1) a scenario where the central government unilaterally decides that the national tax rate should be reduced within a defined geographic area. Such a measure is clearly selective, as taken by a single body applying only to part of the geographical territory within its competence; (2) a scenario where all local authorities at a particular level (regions, districts, etc) have the autonomous power to set the tax rate for their geographical jurisdiction, whether with or without reference to a 'national' tax rate. In such a case it makes no sense to take the whole Member State territory as a framework for comparison for selectivity purposes because in reality, the tax rate would likely differ between each region: 'the essence of selectivity in the direct tax field is that the tax measure should form an exception or derogation to the general tax system', Opinion, paras 51–53.

Commission's finding that a tax measure adopted by the legislative body of the Azores region constituted a State aid because it imposed a lower tax rate on undertakings in the Azores than was applicable to undertakings in the rest of Portugal. The measure was adopted pursuant to powers conferred by central government on the Azores, enabling them to adapt the national tax system to the region's specific characteristics. The Commission contended that the measure was 'selective' because it applied to Azores undertakings and not to other Portuguese undertakings. Portugal, supported by the United Kingdom, argued that when considering a measure adopted by a regional body, the issue of selectivity had to be determined within the framework of the region within that body's remit, not the whole Member State. Since the measure applied equally to all undertakings in the Azores, therefore, it was not selective. The Court confirmed that measures conferring an advantage in only one part of the national territory are not selective on that ground alone for the purposes of Article 87(1).[197] The Court went on to state:

> 'It is possible that an infra-State body enjoys a legal and factual status which makes it sufficiently autonomous in relation to the central government of a Member State, with the result that, by the measures it adopts, it is that body and not the central government which plays a fundamental role in the definition of the political and economic environment in which undertakings operate. In such a case it is the area in which the infra-State body responsible for the measure exercises its powers, and not the country as a whole, that constitutes the relevant context for the assessment of whether a measure adopted by such a body favours certain undertakings in comparison with others in a comparable legal and factual situation, having regard to the objective pursued by the measure or the legal system concerned.'[198]

In order for a regional entity to be regarded as 'sufficiently autonomous' for this purpose, the Court proceeded to hold that the decision to adopt the measure must, first of all, have been taken by a regional or local authority which has, from a constitutional point of view, a political and administrative status separate from that of the central government. Next, it must have been adopted without the central government being able to directly intervene as regards its content. Finally, the financial consequences of a reduction of the national tax rate for undertakings in the region must not be offset by aid or subsidies from other regions or central government. Thus, in order for political and fiscal independence to be sufficient, the intra-State body must not only have powers in the territory within its competence to adopt measures reducing the tax rate, regardless of any considerations related to the conduct of the central State, but it must also assume the political and financial consequences of such a measure. The Court held, on the facts, that the Azores regional authority was not sufficiently autonomous and that the

---

[197] ibid, para 57.
[198] ibid, para 58.

Commission had been right to characterise the measure as conferring an aid on Azores undertakings.

15.035 **Privatisation and the sale of public assets.**   The principles that the Commission applies to privatisations have been set out in its *XXIIIrd Report on Competition Policy* (1993).[199] When privatisation is effected by the sale of shares on the stock exchange, the presumption is that the sale is on market conditions and no aid is involved. Debt may be written off or reduced before flotation without giving rise to a presumption of aid if the proceeds of the sale exceed the reduction in debt. If the public company is privatised via a trade sale, there is no aid where (i) a competitive tender is held that is open to all comers, transparent and not conditional on the performance of other acts;[200] (ii) the company is sold to the highest bidder;[201] and (iii) bidders are given enough time and information to carry out a proper valuation of the assets as the basis for their bid.

15.036 **Sales of land and buildings.**   The Commission has issued a Communication on State aid elements in sales of land and buildings by public authorities.[202] Where there is a sale to the highest or only bidder in a sufficiently well-publicised, open and unconditional bidding procedure comparable to an auction,[203] the sale will be treated as having taken place under normal market conditions and so not involve any aid.[204] Other forms of sales will not be considered to constitute aid where an independent market valuation has been undertaken and the land has been sold at or above that value.[205] Funding to cover the gap between the

---

[199] *XXIIIrd Report on Competition Policy* (1993), points 402–403. See also *XXVIth Report on Competition Policy* (1996), points 169–170; *British Aerospace and Rover v Commission* (n 166, above).

[200] In *Hytasa (No. 1)* (n 128, above) paras 27–29: the imposition of certain conditions on prospective buyers limiting temporarily the disposal of the shareholding acquired and their right to request permission to carry out temporary lay-offs meant that there was aid although the business was sold to the highest bidder.

[201] Thus the sale of British Coal Enterprises (BCE) by British Coal Corporation at a price below the nominal value of its debts to the seller did not involve aid since the sale had been the outcome of a transparent and non-discriminatory bidding process and in view of the nature of BCE's business, which included taking a number of social measures to promote employment, the seller could not expect reimbursement of the sums owed to it within a reasonable foreseeable period: *XXVIth Report on Competition Policy* (1996), point 170.

[202] Communication on State aid elements in sales of land and buildings by public authorities, OJ 1997 C209/3: Vol II, App G.23.

[203] See Section II of the Notice on land and buildings for definitions of 'sufficiently well publicised,' 'open' and 'unconditional.'

[204] Section II(2) of the Notice on land and buildings.

[205] State valuation offices and public officers or employees are regarded as independent provided that there is no undue influence on their findings. In *Derbyshire County Council/Toyota*, OJ 1992 L6/36, the Commission found that the difference of £4.2m between the District Valuer's valuation of the land and the price paid by Toyota constituted aid. For other examples of the sale of public land at an undervalue, see *Land Berlin/Daimler-Benz*, OJ 1992 L263/15, *XXVth Report on Competition Policy* (1995), points 157–158; *Mainz/Siemens*, OJ 1996 L283/43, on appeal Case

estimated development cost of a project and its estimated capital final value constitutes aid.[206]

The provision of infrastructure. The Commission stated long ago that the pro- **15.037** vision by public authorities of infrastructure that is traditionally paid for out of public funds does not normally constitute an aid, but may do so if the works are carried out specifically in the interests of one or more undertakings or of a certain type of product.[207] In *Matra v Commission*,[208] the Court of Justice upheld the Commission's decision that the provision of infrastructure in the context of the establishment of a new vehicle factory by VW and Ford did not constitute aid since it would not benefit exclusively VW and Ford. The Commission has held that public support for managers of infrastructure does not constitute aid, if the infrastructure manager is selected through a non-discriminatory, competitive tender procedure open to all bidders. Such a procedure is the best means of ensuring that the public support corresponds to the minimum needed to carry out the project thereby reflecting the market price for its execution.[209]

State guarantees. A State guarantee in respect of a loan or other financial **15.038** obligation entered into by an undertaking is likely to constitute an aid unless a private investor in the situation of the State would have been prepared to provide that guarantee.[210] In 2000, the Commission reviewed its policy in respect of State aid in the form of guarantees and issued a Notice on the subject[211] providing more

---

T-155/96R *City of Mainz v Commission* [1996] ECR II-1655 (application for interim relief dismissed, appeal withdrawn). The State aid issues arising from land purchase schemes in the former German Democratic Republic have been dealt with in the Commission's decision, *German Indemnification and Compensation Act*, OJ 1999 L107/21. See also Case T-366/00 *Scott v Commission*, judgment of 29 March 2007, where the CFI annulled the Commission's decision on calculating the market value of land said to have been sold at an under-value (on appeal, Case C-290/07P *Commission v Scott*, not yet decided).

206 *English Partnerships* (n 155, above). See further, D'Sa, 'When is aid not state aid? The implication of the English Partnerships decision for European Competition law and policy' (2000) 25 EL Rev 139.

207 Commission Answer to Written Question, JO 1967 2311. In *Daimler-Benz AG, XVIIth Report on Competition Policy* (1987), point 220, the Commission considered that the use of State funds to prepare a site for industrial use would be a State aid but that the cost of site clearance and connection to utilities did not amount to a State aid.

208 Case C-225/91 *Matra v Commission (No. 1)* [1993] ECR I-3203, para 29. For an example of infrastructure measures that have been held to constitute aid, see *Kimberly Clark, XXVth Report on Competition Policy* (1995), point 158.

209 See, eg N264/02 *London Underground*, decn of 2 December 2002. See also *XXIXth Report on Competition Policy* (1999), para 235; Community guidelines on financing of airports and start-up aid to airlines departing from regional airports, OJ 2005 C312/01, paras 55–67.

210 See, eg Cases T-204/97 & 270/97 *EPAC v Commission* [2000] ECR II-2267.

211 Notice on State guarantees, OJ 2000 C71/14: Vol II, App G.26. The Notice replaced the Commission Letters to Member States, SG(89) D/4328 of 5 April 1989 and SG(89) D/12772 of 12 October 1989 and para 38 of the 1993 Commission Communication on the application of Arts [87] and [88] EC and Art 5 of Dir 80/723 to public undertakings in the manufacturing

detailed guidance as to its approach. The Notice states that the aid beneficiary of a State guarantee is usually the borrower, who is able to obtain better financial terms for a loan or other financial obligation than those normally available on the financial markets. The Notice states further that in certain circumstances, however, the lender will also benefit from State aid, for example if a State guarantee is given *ex post* in respect of a loan or other financial obligation already entered into without the terms of the loan or financial obligation being adjusted.[212] The Notice gives detailed guidance as to how the aid element of such guarantees should be calculated and as to the conditions under which it will consider that State guarantees or guarantee schemes will not constitute aid. These are that:

(i) the borrower is not in financial difficulty;

(ii) the borrower could in principle obtain a loan on market conditions from the financial markets;

(iii) the guarantee is linked to a specific transaction, is for a fixed maximum amount, does not cover more than 80 per cent of the outstanding loan and is not open-ended; and

(iv) the market price is paid for the guarantee.

Further conditions apply to State guarantee schemes and include the requirement that the premium paid by recipient firms should be calculated in such a way as to render the scheme self-financing. However, failure to comply with the above conditions does not automatically render the relevant guarantee or guarantee scheme an aid. The Notice explains the consequences of the failure to provide prior notification of an aid but does not provide guidance as to the compatibility of aid in the form of State guarantees with the common market; this must be examined on a case-by-case basis. The Notice specifies that the question whether the illegality of aid affects the legal relationships between the State and third parties (that is, the lender) is a matter for national law but advises lenders to verify as a standard precaution that the Community rules on State aid have been observed. At time of writing, the Commission is consulting on a revised Notice.

---

sector: see para 15.016, above. See also *Jadekost* (n 125, above) paras 29–33, upholding the Commission's decision that State security for a loan, in a case where the borrower could not have obtained the loan without the security, was an aid; the value of the aid was the entire amount of the secured loan. For a discussion of guarantees in the banking sector, see Bufton, 'Where state guarantees supporting commercial banking activities distort competition, they must be abolished: the case of CDC IXIS' (2003) 2 EC Competition Policy Newsletter 26.

212 For a detailed discussion of when State guarantees constitute aid to the lender, and whether and when EC law renders State guarantees unenforceable by the lender against the State, see Lever, 'State guarantees as State aid: The effects of European Community law', Butterworths Journal of International Banking and Financial Law, Special Supp, February 2002.

3. Aids that are Compatible with the Common Market

Article 87(2).   Article 87(2) provides that an aid will be compatible with the **15.039** common market if it falls within any of the three categories identified in the Article. Each of these categories is to be interpreted narrowly.[213] Although the position is not entirely beyond doubt, it appears that aid which falls within one of these three categories, and which is therefore automatically compatible with the common market, must nevertheless be notified to the Commission prior to being put into effect, even though the Commission has no discretion to declare incompatible with the common market any aid which falls within Article 87(2).[214] The first category is described in Article 87(2)(a):

> 'aid having a social character, granted to individual consumers, provided that such aid is granted without discrimination related to the origin of the products concerned'.[215]

The Commission considers that discrimination under this provision refers to the geographical origin of the supplier of the product concerned and not to measures distinguishing between that product and competing products.[216] The second type of aid is set out in Article 87(2)(b):

> 'aid to make good the damage caused by natural disasters or exceptional occurrences.'

---

[213] See, eg Case C-156/98 *Germany v Commission (new Länder)* [1999] ECR I-6857, para 49; Cases T-132 & 143/96 *Freistaat Sachsen v Commission* [1999] ECR II-3663, [2000] 3 CMLR 485, para 132, appeals dismissed Cases C-57 & 61/00P [2003] ECR I-9975.

[214] See Case 730/79 *Philip Morris v Commission* [1980] ECR 2671, [1981] 2 CMLR 321, para 17, where an obligation to notify such aid appears to have been assumed. It has been suggested that aids falling within Art 87(2)(a) may constitute an exception to the obligation for prior notification, on the grounds that aids to individual consumers, as opposed to aids to undertakings, do not fall within Art 87(1) and are not, therefore, aid measures which are *prima facie* incompatible with the common market pursuant to that provision: see Hancher, Slot and Ottervanger, *EC State Aids* (3rd edn, 2006), para 4-003. The better view is that aids falling within Art 87(2)(a) are, in fact, subject to a requirement of prior notification, and that 'aids' to individual consumers which do not also constitute advantages to one or more undertakings are not aids at all and are entirely outside the scope of Art 87.

[215] In Case 52/76 *Benedetti v Munari* [1977] ECR 163, AG Reischl considered that the buying of wheat at the intervention price and its resale at a lower price by a State agency with the object of making bread cheaper might be an aid having a social character granted to individual consumers within the meaning of Art 87(2)(a). However the aid in question cannot be linked to the amount of the product disposed of: see Commission Answer to Written Question, OJ 1970 C123/2. Even where a measure consists of a subsidy granted directly to consumers and without discrimination related to the origin of the product concerned, it may not necessarily follow that the measure, insofar as it advantages certain undertakings, is compatible with the common market. See, eg *Digital terrestrial television in Berlin-Brandenburg*, OJ 2006 L200/14, para 133(a) (Commission stated that Member States could consider granting subsidies to consumers for the purchase of digital decoders, so as to promote take-up of digital television, but only if those subsidies did not entail an unnecessary distortion between different technologies or companies).

[216] See *XXIVth Report on Competition Policy* (1994), point 354, where the Commission states that unless the measure distinguishes between products it is not an aid at all.

The phrase 'exceptional occurrences', which must be interpreted narrowly,[217] has included internal disturbances or strikes, and with certain reservations and depending on their extent, major nuclear or industrial accidents and fires which result in widespread loss.[218]

15.040 German reunification. Article 87(2)(c) declares a third type of aid compatible with the common market:

> 'aid granted to the economy of certain areas of the Federal Republic of Germany affected by the division of Germany, in so far as such aid is required in order to compensate for the economic disadvantages caused by that division.'

That provision,[219] which refers to the division of Germany into two zones in 1948, relates only to economic disadvantages caused by that division and cannot be used to compensate the economic backwardness of the new German Länder following German reunification.[220] Following German reunification, aids to the areas specified in Article 87(2)(c) are now generally considered by the Commission under Article 87(3)(a) and 87(3)(c).[221]

4. Aids that may be Compatible with the Common Market

(a) Generally

15.041 Authorisation of aids by Commission or Council. Article 87(3)(a)–(d) specifies four types of aid which may be compatible with the common market:

(a) aid to promote the economic development of areas where the standard of living is abnormally low or where there is serious underemployment;

(b) aid to promote the execution of an important project of common European interest or to remedy a serious disturbance in the economy of a Member State;

---

[217] There must be a direct link between the aid provided and the damage caused by a specific exceptional occurrence. It is insufficient for a Member State to point to a crisis in the market concerned, high interest rates or other expressions of the market forces which must be faced by any business. See Cases C-346 & 529/03 *Atzeni v Regione autonoma della Sardegna* [2006] ECR I-1875, paras 79–82.

[218] See Community Guidelines for State aid in the agriculture sector, OJ 2000 C28/2, section 11.

[219] There is no equivalent provision in Art 61(2) of the EEA Agreement.

[220] Cases T-132 & 143/96 *Freistaat Sachsen* (n 213, above) paras 134–148, upheld on appeal in Cases C-57 & 61/00P, ibid, paras 22–26; *Germany v Commission (new Länder)* (n 213, above) paras 51–55. The Commission's established policy has been that Art 87(2)(c) can only apply to the areas of former West Germany and the former GDR close to the border between the two States. The derogation does not extend to the entire territory of the former GDR: see *German Indemnification and Compensation Act*, OJ 1999 L107/21.

[221] See *Freistaat Sachsen* (n 213, above), and *XXth Report on Competition Policy* (1990), point 178; *XXIst Report on Competition Policy* (1991), point 181. See also *Berlin/Daimler Benz*, OJ 1992 L263/15.

(c) aid to facilitate the development of certain economic activities or of certain economic areas, where such aid does not adversely affect trading conditions to an extent contrary to the common interest;[222]

(d) aid to promote culture and heritage conservation where such aid does not affect trading conditions and competition in the Community to an extent contrary to the common interest.'[223]

Article 87(3)(e) empowers the Council, acting by qualified majority on a proposal from the Commission to specify additional categories.[224] As derogations, these provisions are to be interpreted strictly.[225] Except where an aid measure falls within a block exemption adopted by the Commission,[226] all such measures must be notified in advance to the Commission and individually approved by it. In addition, pursuant to the third paragraph of Article 88(2), the Council also has power to declare an aid compatible with the common market 'if such a decision is justified by exceptional circumstances'.[227] It is also necessary to consider the application of Article 86(2) in the case of aid granted to undertakings falling within the scope of that Article.[228]

The exercise of the Commission's discretion.   Article 87(3) confers a broad dis-   **15.042**
cretion[229] on the Commission to authorise aid on the basis of examination and appraisal of economic facts and circumstances which are often complex and liable to change rapidly.[230] The derogations in Article 87(3)(a) and (c) are based on the aim of Community solidarity and require the Commission to reconcile

---

[222] The Treaty of Amsterdam deleted the last sentence of former Art 92(3)(c): 'However, the aids granted to shipbuilding as at 1 January 1957 shall, insofar as they serve only to compensate for the absence of customs protection, be progressively reduced under the same conditions as apply to the elimination of customs duties, subject to the provision of this Treaty concerning common commercial policy towards third countries'.

[223] Inserted by Art G(18) of the Treaty on European Union. The TEU also inserted a new provision in the EC Treaty dealing solely with culture, now Art 151. Although no corresponding amendment was made to the EEA Agreement, the EFTA Surveillance Authority adopts an equivalent approach to the assessment of aid schemes: see *Aid for audio-visual productions*, ESA Annual Report 1995, point 4.7.4.2.

[224] See para 15.065, below.

[225] See AG Capotorti in Case 730/79 *Philip Morris v Commission* [1980] ECR 2671 at 2701, [1981] 2 CMLR 321 at 334.

[226] See para 15.067, below.

[227] For an example, see Case C-122/94 *Commission v Council* [1995] ECR I-881. As to Art 89, see para 15.090, below.

[228] See paras 15.068 and 15.134, below.

[229] AG Slynn in Case 84/82 *Germany v Commission (Textiles)* [1984] ECR 1451, 1499–1500, [1985] 1 CMLR 153, 166–169. See also Case 310/85 *Deufil v Commission* [1987] ECR 901, [1988] 1 CMLR 553; Cases T-371 & 394/94 *British Airways v Commission* [1998] ECR II-2405, para 79; *Germany v Commission (new Länder)* (n 213, above), para 67; Case T-55/99 *CETM v Commission* [2000] ECR II-3207, para 109. For the review by the CFI and ECJ of the exercise of the Commission's discretion, see para 15.122, below.

[230] Case C-301/87 *France v Commission (Boussac)* [1990] ECR I-307, para 15; *SFEI* (n 164, above) para 36; Case C-169/95 *Spain v Commission (PYRSA)* [1997] ECR I-135, para 18;

the aims of free competition and Community solidarity while complying with the principle of proportionality.[231] The Commission has stated that in examining whether to authorise State aid proposals it takes into account the following three factors:[232]

(a) that the aid should promote a development which is in the interest of the Community as a whole; the promotion of a national interest is not enough to justify the Commission exercising its discretionary powers under Article 87(3);

(b) that the aid is necessary to bring about that development, ie the recipient would not attain that objective in normal market conditions; and

(c) that the modalities of the aid, ie its intensity,[233] duration, the dangers it creates of transferring difficulties from one Member State to another, the degree of distortion of competition, etc, are commensurate with the importance of the objective of the aid.

These guidelines were set out in the light of *Philip Morris*,[234] in which the Court of Justice endorsed the Commission's exercise of its discretion under Article 87(3). In particular, the Court upheld the Commission's argument that an aid could contribute to fulfilling one of the objectives laid down in Article 87(3) only if it could be shown that in normal market conditions the recipient firms would not attain those objectives themselves.[235] Moreover, in exercising its discretion the Commission has to make economic and social assessments in the context of the Community and not just one Member State.[236] In balancing regional objectives against the impact of a proposed aid on a particular sector, the Commission has a broader discretion under Article 87(3)(a) than 87(3)(c).[237] It is for the Commission to consider each proposal for aid individually within the framework

---

Case T-67/94 *Ladbroke Racing* (n 137, above) para 147, upheld on appeal Case C-83/98P *France v Commission*, ibid.

[231] See Case T-380/94 *AIUFFASS and AKT v Commission* [1996] ECR II-2169, [1997] 3 CMLR 542, para 54.

[232] *Twelfth Report on Competition Policy* (1982), point 160.

[233] The 'intensity' of an aid refers to the proportion of the costs which would otherwise be incurred by the recipient undertaking which would be met instead by the aid granted. Determining the intensity of an aid may involve discounting the value of aid intended to be paid in instalments over a number of years to arrive at a present value and carrying out a similar calculation in respect of the costs to which the aid relates.

[234] Case 730/79 *Philip Morris v Commission* [1980] ECR 2671, [1981] 2 CMLR 321.

[235] ibid, para 16.

[236] ibid, para 24 and *Boussac* (n 230, above) para 49; Case C-278/95P *Siemens v Commission* [1997] ECR I-2507, para 35. However this does not mean that an aid with positive effects on the development of a sector in only one Member State cannot benefit from a derogation under Art 87(3)(c) where it is in the Community interest for a particular economic sector to have an efficient organisation and infrastructure in one Member State, Case T-67/94 *Ladbroke Racing* (n 137, above) para 158. See also *AIUFFASS* (n 231, above) para 54.

[237] *AIUFFASS* (n 231, above) para 55. On the other hand the derogation in Art 87(3)(c) is wider in scope than that under Art 87(3)(a): see para 15.055, below.

of its discretion in the light of first the specific circumstances surrounding the aid, and secondly, of Community law and its own guidelines.[238] In exercising its discretion the Commission can impose conditions on the approval of aid.[239]

Operating aid.   Operating aid is aid which is intended to relieve an undertaking **15.043** of the expenses which it would normally have to bear in its day-to-day management or its usual activities.[240] Operating aid is considered by the Commission to be generally incompatible with the common market and can be authorised under Article 87(3) only in exceptional circumstances.[241]

Commission guidelines, frameworks and disciplines.   The Commission has **15.044** adopted a large number of guidelines, frameworks and disciplines[242] specifying the criteria and principles which it applies when assessing the compatibility of various types of aid with Article 87(3).[243] The Court of Justice has stated that the

---

[238] See Case T-214/95 *Vlaamse Gewest v Commission* [1998] ECR II-717, para 92.

[239] See Cases T-244 & 486/93 *TWD Textilwerke Deggendorf v Commission* [1995] ECR II-2265. Aids have been approved on condition that previous unlawfully granted aid had been recovered; *Air France*, OJ 1994 L254/73 and *British Airways* (n 229, above) paras 290–291; *Crédit Lyonnais*, OJ 1998 L221/28: aid approved subject to a number of conditions, including sale of various of assets and a commitment by France to privatise Crédit Lyonnais within a fixed period.

[240] Case T-459/93 *Siemens v Commission* [1995] ECR II-1675, paras 48 and 77, upheld on appeal in Case C-278/95P [1997] ECR I-2507, paras 39–56, where aid to marketing activities was treated as operating aid; *Vlaamse Gewest* (n 238, above) para 43; Cases T-298/97, etc, *Alzetta v Commission* [2000] ECR II-2319, para 133; *Germany v Commission (new Länder)* (n 220, above) para 30; *CETM* (n 229, above) para 83.

[241] See *XXVIIth Report on Competition Policy* (1997), point 232, which sets out the exceptional circumstances in which operating aid may be authorised (though certain of the Commission documents referred to have since been replaced). See also the Guidelines on State aids for environmental protection measures, OJ 2001 C37/3: Vol II, App G.18. cf Aid in the broadcasting sector (n 303 below and Art 86(2) discussed at para 15.068, below. The CFI and ECJ have endorsed the Commission's reluctance to approve operative aids: see eg *Siemens v Commission* (above) and Case C-288/96 *Germany v Commission (Jadekost)* [2000] ECR I-1827, paras 77–79, 88–91.

[242] A discipline is a communiction addressed by the Commission to the Member States which sets out the course of conduct which the Commission intends to follow once the Member States' have given their assent. See, eg Case C-313/90 *CIRFS v Commission* [1993] ECR I-1125, paras 32–37, which concerned, *inter alia*, the legal effects of a Commission communication which stated that Member States should desist from granting aid which would lead to increases in production capacity in the synthetic fibres industry. In that case, the rules set out in the discipline and accepted by the Member States had the effect of withdrawing certain aid falling within its scope from an authorisation which had previously been granted, and hence of classifying it as new aid which was subject to the obligation of prior notification. It followed that the discipline was of binding effect and that the ECJ was entitled, at the instance of a third party, to consider the correctness of the interpretation which the Commission had given to that discipline.

[243] The guidelines are set out on DG Comp's website at http://ec.europa.eu/comm/competition/index_en.html. See also the section on State aids in the Commission's annual Reports on Competition Policy. Further, the EFTA Surveillance Authority has issued comprehensive State Aid Guidelines, which are based on those issued by the EC Commission, on the application and interpretation of the State Aid provisions of the EEA Agreement: see para 15.004, above. See further Hancher, Ottervanger and Slot, *EC State Aids* (3rd edn, 2006), Chaps 8–24. In exercising its discretion as to whether to declare an unlawfully granted aid compatible with the common market,

Commission may publish guidelines on the approach it will follow when exercising its discretionary powers in applying the State aid rules, provided that those guidelines do not derogate from the provisions of Articles 87 and 88.[244] It is outside the scope of this work to examine in detail the guidelines, frameworks and disciplines laid down by the Commission and what follows is an examination of the Treaty provisions together with a brief mention of Commission publications where particularly relevant.

(b) Article 87(3)(a)

15.045   **Article 87(3)(a): aid to promote economic development.**   Article 87(3)(a) provides that 'aid to promote the economic development of areas where the standard of living is abnormally low or where there is serious under-employment' may be compatible with the common market. In *Philip Morris*,[245] the Court of Justice held that the question whether there is an abnormally low standard of living or serious underemployment has to be judged on a Community not a national standard. Thus the mere fact that a particular region of a Member State is suffering serious underemployment as compared with other regions in that Member State is not sufficient to bring it within Article 87(3)(a). The application of Article 87(3)(a) requires the Commission to take into consideration not only the regional implications of the aid but also its impact on trade between Member States and thus the sectoral repercussions to which it might give rise at Community level.[246]

15.046   **Guidelines on national regional aid: Article 87(3)(a) and (c).**   The Commission assesses regional aids in accordance with its guidelines on national regional aid. The Guidelines published in 1998[247] expired at the end of 2006. Since the publication of those Guidelines, important political and economic developments have

---

the Commission will apply the substantive criteria set out in any relevant frameworks, guidelines, communications and notices which were in force at the time when the aid was granted: see Notice on the determination of the applicable rules for the assessment of unlawful State aid, OJ 2004 L140/1: Vol 1, App G.4. See further n 402, below.

[244] *Deufil v Commission* (n 229, above) para 22; *CIRFS* (n 242, above) paras 34 and 36; *AIUFFASS* (n 231, above) para 57; T-149/95 *Ducros v Commission* [1997] ECR II-2031, para 61; *Vlaamse Gewest* (n 238, above) para 79; Case T-16/96 *Cityflyer Express v Commission* [1998] ECR II-757, [1998] 2 CMLR 537, para 57; Case T-296/97 *Alitalia v Commission* [2000] EC II-3871, [2001] All ER (EC) 193, para 99.

[245] *Philip Morris* (n 234, above). See also Case 248/84 *Germany v Commission (Regional aid programme)* [1987] ECR 4013, [1989] 1 CMLR 591, para 19; *Spain v Commission (PYRSA)* (n 230, above) para 15.

[246] *PYRSA* (n 230, above) paras 17–25, where the ECJ rejected the argument that under Art 87(3)(a) the Commission should take no account of Community interest because of the absence of the words 'where such aid does not adversely affect trading conditions to an extent contrary to the common interest' in Art 87(3)(a), unlike in Art 87(3)(c).

[247] Guidelines on National Regional Aid, OJ 1998 C74/9, modified in OJ 1999 C288/2 and OJ 2000 C258/5.

occurred; most notably, the enlargement of the European Union from 15 to 25 Member States on 1 May 2004, and the accession of Bulgaria and Romania on 1 January 2007. New Guidelines[248] published in 2006 (the '2006 Guidelines') came into effect on 1 January 2007[249] following a comprehensive review of the national regional aid regime.[250] It is important to bear in mind that national regional aid can be authorised under Article 87(3)(c) as well as Article 87(3)(a) and the Guidelines cover national regional aids justified under both limbs. A greater distortion of competition can be accepted in the case of the most disadvantaged regions,[251] which fall within Article 87(3)(a).[252] As a general rule, regional aid should be granted only under a multi-sectoral aid scheme which forms an integral part of a regional development strategy with clearly defined objectives.[253]

The nature and purposes of national regional aid. The 2006 Guidelines contain **15.047** the following exposition of the nature and purposes of national regional aid:

'National regional aid consists of aid for investment granted to large companies, or in certain limited circumstances, operating aid, which in both cases are targeted on specific regions in order to address regional disparities. Increased levels of investment aid granted to small and medium-sized enterprises located within the disadvantaged regions over and above what is allowed in other areas are also considered as regional aid.

By addressing the handicaps of the disadvantaged regions, national regional aid promotes the economic, social and territorial cohesion of Member States and the European Union as a whole. This geographical specificity distinguishes regional aid from other forms of horizontal aid, such as aid for research, development and innovation, employment, training or the environment, which pursue other objectives of common interest in accordance with Article 87(3) of the Treaty, albeit sometimes with higher rates of aid in the disadvantaged areas in recognition of the specific difficulties which they face.

National regional investment aid is designed to assist the development of the most disadvantaged regions by supporting investment and job creation. It promotes the expansion and diversification of the economic activities of enterprises located in the less favoured regions, in particular by encouraging firms to set up new establishments there'.[254]

---

[248] Guidelines on National Regional Aid for 2007–2013, OJ 2006 C54/13: Vol II, App G.20; discussed in Papantoniou, 'New Guidelines on national regional aid for 2007 - 2013' (2006) 1 EC Competition Policy Newsletter 18.

[249] The Commission applies the 2006 Guidelines on National Regional Aid to all regional aid granted after 31 December 2006. Only regional aid awarded before 2007 is assessed under the 1998 guidelines: see the 2006 Guidelines, para 105.

[250] See the 2006 Guidelines, para 4.

[251] A 'region' is defined as a 'NUTS level II geographical unit' under Reg 1059/2003 on the establishment of a common classification of territorial units for statistics (NUTS), OJ 2003 L154/1: see the 2006 Guidelines, para 16.

[252] 2006 Guidelines, para 5.

[253] ibid, para 10.

[254] ibid, paras 1–3.

15.048 **Areas eligible for regional aid.**   Under the 2006 Guidelines, the proportion of the EU population living in areas eligible for regional aid is fixed at 42 per cent, a figure similar to that fixed in 1998 notwithstanding the accession of 10 new Member States in the interim. A safety net is provided, however, in the form of provisions which ensure that no Member State loses more than 50 per cent of its entitlement under the 1998 Guidelines.[255]

15.049 **Disadvantaged regions.**   Regions with less than 75 per cent of the EU average per capita GDP fall within the Article 87(3)(a) derogation and qualify for the highest rates of investment aid, as well as for operating aid (see further below).[256] These regions, in which 27.7 per cent of the EU's population live, are divided into three subcategories:

(i) regions with a per capita GDP which is between 60 and 74 per cent of the EU average (in which aid for large companies is capped at 30 per cent intensity[257]);

(ii) regions with a per capita GDP of 45–59 per cent of the EU average (40 per cent cap on intensity); and

(iii) regions whose per capita GDP is less than 45 per cent of the EU average (50 per cent cap on intensity).[258]

---

[255] Although the 1998 Guidelines set the eligible population ceiling at 42.7 per cent, by 2005 the proportion of the EU's population actually living in eligible regions had grown to 52.2 per cent, largely as a consequence of EU enlargement (see Press Release IP/05/1653 (21 December 2005)). That percentage was made up of the 34.2 per cent of the population who were living in regions considered to be 'disadvantaged' and which were therefore eligible for the highest rates of aid (40–50 per cent); the other 18 per cent were living in regions which were relatively less disadvantaged and therefore eligible only for lower aid rates of aid of 10–20 per cent. The 'safety net' arrangement under the new guidelines is expected to lead to regional aid in fact covering 43.1 per cent of the total EU population (or 46.6 per cent following the accession of Romania and Bulgaria) (see paras 13–14 of the 2006 Guidelines), but this will still represent a very considerable cut in the entitlements of many of the original 15 Member States, though the full effect of that cut will not be felt until the transitional arrangements provided for in the new guidelines expire.

[256] Because of their specific handicaps, the 'outermost regions' (as identified by Art 299(2) of the EC Treaty) automatically qualify as 'disadvantaged' under Art 87(3)(a) irrespective of their relative GDP.

[257] Aid intensity percentages are calculated in terms of gross grant equivalents (GGE), ie the discounted value of the aid expressed as a percentage of the discounted value of the eligible costs: see point 41 of the new guidelines. fn 44 of the 2006 Guidelines states that the Commission is discontinuing its former practice of converting regional aid notified by Member States into net grant equivalents in order to take account of the judgment of the Court of First Instance of 15 June 2000 in *Alzetta* (n 240, above). There the CFI ruled that the Commission is not empowered to take into consideration the incidence of tax on the amount of financial aid allocated when it assesses whether it is compatible with the Treaty. Furthermore, the Commission considers that the use of GGEs, which are also used to calculate the intensities of other types of State aid, will contribute to increasing the simplicity and transparency of the State aid control system, and also takes account of the increased proportion of State aid which is awarded in the form of tax exemptions: see *Alzetta*, para 89.

[258] See the 2006 Guidelines, para 44. Outermost regions with a per capita GDP of less than 75 per cent of the EU average are eligible for a further 20 per cent permitted GGE; and even

To mitigate the impact on regions which would otherwise lose their status as a result of the enlargement of the EU from 15 to 25 Member States, the 2006 Guidelines also make provision for so-called 'statistical effect regions', that is, regions which have less than 75 per cent of average EU-15 GDP but more than 75 per cent of average EU-25 GDP. These regions will continue to benefit from 'disadvantaged' status and qualify for the lowest (30 per cent) rate of investment aid under Article 87(3)(a) until 31 December 2010 when the situation of every such region will be reviewed.[259] In order to implement the new Guidelines, the Commission approves a regional map for each Member State for the period 2007–2013 which identifies the areas eligible for aid and the maximum intensities allowed.[260]

Areas entitled to aid at lower rates under Article 87(3)(c). As regards regions **15.050** with more than 75 per cent of the EU average per capita GDP, the 2006 Guidelines allow Member States to allocate regional aid at lower rates (between 10 and 15 per cent) under Article 87(3)(c) to areas which they can define themselves in line with a national regional development policy.[261] This is discussed further in paragraph 15.055, below.

Other aspects of entitlement to regional aid. The 2006 Guidelines also **15.051** simplify the rules for granting operating aid in the outermost regions,[262] and include provisions designed to target regional aid at SMEs and business start-ups: aid rates can be increased in all assisted areas by 20 per cent where aid is given to small enterprises and 10 per cent where it is given to medium-sized enterprises;[263] a new form of aid will be allowed to encourage business start-ups in assisted areas, which will apply to the establishment and expansion phases of small enterprises during the first five years;[264] and a new form of operating aid will also be allowed to counter depopulation in the least populated areas.[265] In addition, the

---

outermost regions with a per capita GDP of above 75 per cent will receive a 10 per cent bonus on top of the 30 per cent GGE to which they are in any event entitled by virtue of their assumed disadvantaged status: para 45.

[259] See paras 18–20 of the 2006 Guidelines. If the situation of any such a region has declined during the transitional period, that region will be permitted to continue to be eligible for national regional aid under Art 87(3)(a). Otherwise, as from 1 January 2011, it will instead become eligible for such aid only under Art 87(3)(c) at a maximum rate of 20 per cent: see point 46.

[260] For Estonia, Greece, Hungary, Latvia, Poland Slovenia and Slovakia, see Press Release IP/06/1176 (13 September 2006); for Luxembourg and Malta, see IP/06/1393 (13 October 2006); for Lithuania, Ireland and the Czech Republic, see IP/06/1451 (24 October 2006), and for Germany, see IP/06/1528 (8 November 2006).

[261] 2006 Guidelines, paras 21–32 and 47.

[262] ibid, paras 80–83. On operating aid under the 1998 Guidelines, see Case C-88/03 *Portugal v Commission (Azores)* (n 196, above) paras 99-107.

[263] 2006 Guidelines, para 49.

[264] ibid, paras 84–91.

[265] ibid, paras 76, 80 and 81.

Guidelines incorporate the rules on aid for very large investment projects (costing more than €50 million)[266] which had formerly been set out in separate multi-sectoral frameworks on regional aid for large investment projects, published in 1998 and 2002.[267]

15.052 **Block exemption for regional aid.** The application of the Guidelines on national regional aid did not obviate the need for regional aids falling within the limits to be individually notified to the Commission. However, in 2006 the Commission adopted a block exemption which frees Member States of the obligation to notify regional investment aid schemes which fulfil the conditions laid down in that block exemption, including conditions in respect of transparency and monitoring.[268] Regulation 1628/2006 exempts from notification transparent forms of regional investment aid, that is schemes where it is possible to calculate precisely the aid intensity as a percentage of the investment costs from the start, without the need for a risk assessment. Regional aid schemes involving public shareholdings, risk capital and state guarantees are presumed not to fulfil this criterion and so must still be notified. All aid for very large investment projects must continue to be individually notified to the Commission. By the end of 2007, provisions granting block exemption for regional aid are likely to be incorporated in a general block exemption regulation and Regulation 1628/2006 will be repealed.[269]

(c) Article 87(3)(b)

15.053 **Article 87(3)(b): aid for important projects or to remedy a serious disturbance.** Article 87(3)(b) enables the Commission to authorise 'aid to

---

[266] ibid, paras 60–70.

[267] Communication from the Commission: Multisectoral framework on regional aid for large investment projects, OJ 2002 C70/8. The Framework was intended to reduce excessive amounts of regional aid to very large mobile capital-intensive investments which seriously distorted competition and jeopardised jobs elsewhere in the EU. Under the Framework, a stricter regime was imposed in respect of regional aids granted for large investment projects that were likely to have a highly distortive effect on competition. The Commission applied an aid ceiling by reference to the characteristics of the project, the degree of competition in the relevant market, the impact on regional development, and the maximum ceiling of intensity authorised in the region concerned. Since regional aid for large investment projects are included in the 2006 Guidelines, the 2002 Multisectoral Framework does not apply to any aids granted after 31 December 2006.

[268] Reg 1628/2006 on the Application of Articles 87 and 88 of the Treaty to national regional investment aid, OJ 2006 L302/29: Vol II, App G.15. See Press Release IP/06/1453 (24 October 2006). On the same day the Commission adopted Reg 1627/2006, OJ 2006 L302/10, which modified the prescribed forms on which aids not covered by the block exemption must be notified to the Commission.

[269] See the draft Regulation for a general block exemption, published on 24 April 2007: Vol II, App G.16.

promote the execution of an important project of common European interest[270] or to remedy a serious disturbance in the economy of a Member State'.[271] In *Exécutif Régional Wallon v Commission (Glaverbel)*,[272] the Court of Justice endorsed the Commission's view that a project is not of common European interest unless it forms part of a transnational European programme supported jointly by a number of Member States or arises from concerted action by a number of Member States to combat a common threat such as environmental pollution. An aid will not fall within the provision if it leads to the transfer of an investment which could have taken place in another Member State which is in a less favourable situation.[273]

(d) Article 87(3)(c)

Article 87(3)(c): aid for development of certain economic activities or **15.054**
areas. Under Article 87(3)(c) the Commission can authorise 'aid to facilitate the development of certain economic activities or of certain economic areas, where such aid does not adversely affect trading conditions to an extent contrary to the common interest'. Article 87(3)(c) thus enables the Commission to authorise a much wider range of aids than under either Article 87(3)(a) or (b) and is the most frequently used discretionary exception.[274] The compatibility of the aid under Article 87(3)(c) must also be determined in the context of the Community and

---

270 It is important to draw a distinction between measures which mostly benefit economic operators in one Member State and those which genuinely benefit the Community as a whole: see Case C-148/04 *Unicredito Italiano v Agenzia delle Entrate* [2005] ECR I-11137, paras 72–77. Important projects of common European interest have included the manufacture of aircraft and aircraft parts, *Second Report on Competition Policy* (1972), point 100; and *XIXth Report on Competition Policy* (1990), point 172, where the Commission approved aid to a new subsidiary of the German Airbus consortium; energy saving schemes, *Seventh Report on Competition Policy* (1977), point 250; improvements to the environment, *Tenth Report on Competition Policy* (1980), point 222; and R&D projects which are quantitatively and qualitatively important, transnational in character and related to the definition of industrial standards that can allow Community industry to benefit from all the advantages of the single market (eg aid granted to the high-definition TV project), *XXIst Report on Competition Policy* (1991), point 180.

271 Art 87(3)(b) was used by the Commission to approve aids involving financial reorganisation of companies in the Greek public sector as it considered that the crisis in the Greek economy went beyond any one sector of the economy. The severity of the situation was reflected by the safeguard measures Greece had been allowed to take under the EEC Treaty: *XVIIth Report on Competition Policy* (1987), points 185–187. See also Cases T-447/93, etc, *AITEC v Commission* [1995] ECR II-1971, paras 113–132. Following annulment by the CFI in *AITEC* of the Commission decision to authorise aid to Heracles, a Greek cement manufacturer, the Commission adopted a new decision declaring some of the aid to be compatible with the common market under Art 82(3)(b), *Heracles*, OJ 2000 L66/1. See also *Freistaat Sachsen* (n 220, above) paras 166–172.

272 Cases 62 & 72/87 *Exécutif Régional Wallon v Commission (Glaverbel)* [1988] ECR 1573, [1989] 2 CMLR 771, paras 20–26.

273 *Philip Morris* (n 234, above) para 25.

274 See para 15.056, below.

not of a single Member State.[275] An aid can only 'facilitate' development if in normal market conditions the development would not have occurred without the aid.[276] The Commission generally takes an unfavourable view of general investment aid schemes (that is, schemes offering aid for investment regardless of sectoral or regional considerations).[277]

15.055 **Regional aid: development of certain economic areas.** Article 87(3)(c) is wider in scope than Article 87(3)(a) since it permits the Commission to authorise aids for the development of regions that do not meet the test laid down by Article 87(3)(a) but are disadvantaged in relation to the national average within a Member State.[278] The Commission's Guidelines on National Regional Aid set out principles for applying Article 87(3)(c) in relation to such areas;[279] first, the method and procedure by which the Commission calculates the Article 87(3)(c) regional aid population eligibility ceiling in respect of each Member State; and secondly, the method and procedure by which each Member State may identify the regions which are to be eligible for such aid. The maximum aid intensity for aid to large companies under the Article 87(3)(c) derogation is capped at 15 per cent (or 10 per cent in the case of regions which enjoy both a higher per capita GDP, and a lower unemployment rate, than the EU average).[280] However, certain low population density regions, regions adjoining a region with Article 87(3)(a) status, and regions sharing a land border with a State which is a member of neither the EEA nor EFTA are always eligible for an aid intensity of 15 per cent.[281] The Court of Justice has upheld the Commission's refusal to authorise an aid under Article 87(3)(c) as contributing to the development of a region where the aided undertaking is not in a position to ensure its own viability.[282]

15.056 **Sectoral aid: development of certain economic activities.** This limb of Article 87(3)(c) permits aid to be granted to develop a sector of the economy. It is necessary for the aid to have the effect of facilitating the development rather than merely intending to do so.[283] The aid must ensure that there is an improvement

---

[275] *Philip Morris* (n 234, above) para 26.

[276] ibid.

[277] See Hancher, Ottervanger and Slot, *EC State Aids* (3rd edn, 2006) at paras 4-042 *et seq.*

[278] Case 248/84 *Germany v Commission (Regional aid programme)* [1987] ECR 4013, [1989] 1 CMLR 591. See section 5 of the 2006 Guidelines on National Regional Aid, OJ 2006 C54/13: Vol II, App G.20; and para 15.046, above. On the application of Art 87(3)(c) to the new German Länder, see also *XXth Report on Competition Policy* (1990), points 173–179, *XXIst Report* (1991), point 181, and *Freistaat Sachsen and VW* (n 220, above).

[279] 2006 Guidelines (n 248, above) paras 21–32.

[280] ibid, para 47. Aid intensity percentages refer to Gross Grant Equivalents: see (n 257, above).

[281] ibid, para 48.

[282] Case C-142/87 *Belgium v Commission (Tubemeuse)* [1990] ECR I-959, [1991] 3 CMLR 213, para 54; Case C-42/93 *Spain v Commission (Merco)* [1994] ECR I-4125, [1996] 2 CMLR 702, paras 25–30.

[283] See AG Slynn in *Germany v Commission (Textiles)* (n 229, above) 1501–1502 (ECR) 169–170 (CMLR).

in the way in which the economic activity is carried out, such as rationalisation or reorganisation.[284] The overall position in a particular sector has to be considered, rather than the position of just a few undertakings operating in the sector.[285] An aid can only facilitate development within the meaning of Article 87(3)(c) if the beneficiaries are at least potentially competitive.[286] Operating aid does not promote the development of any economic sector.[287] Replacement investment, even if it incorporates new technology, has been considered not to be an economic development within the meaning of Article 87(3)(c)[288] but the position may depend on the facts of the particular case.[289] The Commission's guidelines for judging the compatibility of particular sectoral and other types of aids are listed below.[290]

The tailpiece to Article 87(3)(c): not contrary to the common interest. To fall **15.057** within Article 87(3)(c) an aid 'must not affect trading conditions to an extent contrary to the common interest'. This requires the Commission to balance the beneficial effects of the aid in the development of certain economic activities or regions against its adverse effects on trading conditions and the maintenance of undistorted competition.[291] In assessing this balance, the Commission must

---

284 ibid. See also Case C-75/97 *Belgium v Commission (Maribel I)* [1999] ECR I-3671, [2000] 1 CMLR 791, para 57, upholding the Commission's negative decision under Art 87(3)(c) because the selective reductions in social security contributions were granted without any direct social or economic compensating contribution on the part of the recipient undertaking.

285 ibid. But where the restructuring is of one of the largest undertakings in the sector, that will facilitate the economic development of the sector as a whole: see *British Airways* (n 229, above) para 235.

286 AG Slynn in *Germany v Commission (Textiles)* (n 229, above) 1505 (ECR), 172–173 (CMLR). See also *Boussac* (n 230, above) upholding the Commission's conclusion that aid which lowered the costs of the beneficiary and weakened the competitive position of other undertakings which had to reorganise their activities without the benefit of State aid fell outside Art 87(3)(c); *Tubemeuse* (n 282, above) para 54; Cases C-278/92, etc, *Spain v Commission (Hytasa No. 1)* [1994] ECR I-4103, para 67.

287 *Siemens v Commission* (n 240, above) para 77; appeal on other grounds dismissed, Case C-278/95P [1997] ECR I-2507.

288 *Deufil v Commission* (n 229, above) paras 16–19; *Exécutif Régional Wallon v Commission (Glaverbel)* (n 272, above) paras 27–34; *Boussac* (n 230, above) para 54; *Alzetta* (n 240, above) para 133; cf AG Slynn in *Textiles* (n 229, above), who considered that modernisation would constitute economic development.

289 See *British Airways* (n 229, above) where the CFI annulled, for lack of reasoning, the Commission's decision approving aid granted to enable Air France to modernise its fleet in the context of its restructuring plan. The Commission had failed to explain how its approval was consistent with *Deufil* and *Glaverbel* and its own decision-making practice. The Commission then adopted a new decision (OJ 1999 L63/66) in which it distinguished the position from that in the earlier cases, principally on the basis that the acquisition of new aircraft formed part of Air France's restructuring plan and a failure to renew the fleet might jeopardise the viability of the plan.

290 See para 15.059, below.

291 *XIVth Report on Competition Policy* (1984), point 202, expressly endorsed by the CFI in *British Airways* (n 229, above) at para 283. See also Case 47/69 *France v Commission* [1970] ECR 487, [1970] CMLR 351, para 7; AG Slynn in *Textiles* (n 229, above) at 1506–1508 (ECR),

take into consideration all those factors which characterise the measure in question including its intensity, nearness to market activity[292] and the method of financing the aid,[293] as well as information as to the situation on the markets in question, in particular the positions of the beneficiary of the aid and of competing undertakings.[294] In a sector where there is overcapacity an aid will normally be contrary to the common interest because the aid will affect the position of other undertakings in that sector.[295] Similarly, the fact that a particular aid improves the competitiveness of its beneficiaries in a sector which is already characterised by intensive competition between undertakings in different Member States implies that the measure is not aimed at developing the sector in general, but rather affects trading conditions to an extent which is contrary to the common interest.[296]

15.058 **The Commission's general policy on sectoral aids.** In 1978 the Commission set out the main criteria used in examining sectoral aid proposals:

'(i) sectoral aid should be limited to cases where it is justified by circumstances in the industry concerned;

(ii) aid should lead to a restoration of long-term viability by resolving problems rather than preserve the status quo and put off decisions and changes which are inevitable;

(iii) nevertheless, since adjustment takes time, a limited use of resources to reduce the social and economic costs of change is admissible in certain circumstances and subject to strict conditions;

173–175 (CMLR); Case 259/85 *France v Commission (Textiles and clothing)* [1987] ECR 4393, [1989] 2 CMLR 30, para 24, where the ECJ held that the Commission had not exceeded the limits of its discretion in deciding that even aid on a small scale could, in a sector where profit margins are small, affect trade to an extent contrary to the common interest. For the Commission's balancing of the beneficial and adverse effects of a proposed aid, see, eg N307/2004 *Broadband in Scotland*, decn of 16 November 2004, paras 44–48. See also Hencsey, Raymond, Riedl, Santamato and Westerhof, 'State aid rules and public funding of broadband' (2005) 1 EC Competition Policy Newsletter 8; Papadias, Riedl and Westerhof, 'Public funding for broadband networks — recent developments' (2006) 3 EC Competition Policy Newsletter 13.

[292] In the Guidelines on State aid for Small and Medium-sized Enterprises ('SMEs'), OJ 1996 C213/4, the Commission stated that aid for activities that are relatively distant from the market place, such as consultancy to improve general management, affect trade only indirectly and to a comparatively small degree. Aid for near-market activities, such as investment, arguably affects trade less when it is granted to SMEs than when the beneficiaries are large firms. The Commission stated that, provided certain acceptable intensities of aid are not exceeded, the effect of aid to SMEs on trading conditions would generally not be so great as to be against the interests of the Community. The Guidelines have been replaced by the block exemption on aid to SMEs, Reg 70/2001 (see para 15.067, below), but the principle is still relevant.

[293] Case 47/69 *France v Commission* (n 291, above) paras 17–23. In that case the Commission considered that the aid itself (promotion of research in the textiles sector) was compatible with Art 87(3)(c) but that its method of financing, namely a levy on the sale of both domestic and imported textile products, was contrary to the common interest since importers contributed to the levy without receiving any benefit in return.

[294] *British Airways* (n 229, above) para 273.

[295] *Glaverbel* (n 272, above) paras 27–34.

[296] See *Unicredito Italiano v Agenzia delle Entrate* (n 270, above) paras 79–82.

(iv) unless granted over relatively short periods, aids should be progressively reduced and clearly linked to the restructuring of the sector concerned;

(v) the intensity of aid should be proportionate to the problem it is designed to resolve so that distortions of competition are kept to a minimum; and

(vi) industrial problems and unemployment should not be transferred from one Member State to another.'[297]

Although the Commission has stated that it takes a generally negative attitude to sectoral aid,[298] it has authorised large numbers of sectoral aids. Since its statement in 1978, the Commission has issued a number of codes or frameworks relating to particular sectors or industries.[299] It would appear that sectoral rules take precedence over regional rules. In *AIUFFASS and AKT v Commission*, the Court of First Instance stated that in considering a planned regional aid, even under Article 87(3)(a), the Commission was under a duty to evaluate the sectoral effect of the planned aid in order to avoid a situation in which, as a result of the aid measure, a sectoral problem was created at the Community level which was more serious than the initial regional problem.[300] Where the Commission authorises regional aid to be granted without prior notification under Article 88(3) subject to the aid not falling within any binding discipline for a particular sector, the Commission cannot, by a subsequent individual decision, unilaterally alter the scope of any such discipline.[301]

Guidelines and rules on sectoral aid. There are rules or codes laid down in the **15.059** following sectors:

— audiovisual production;[302]
— broadcasting;[303]

---

[297] *Eighth Report on Competition Policy* (1978), point 176. According to D'Sa, *European Community Law on State Aids* (1998), para 5–01, although these criteria have rarely been discussed in the Commission's annual Reports, they are routinely applied in Commission decisions involving sectoral aid.

[298] *XXIVth Report on Competition Policy* (1994), point 363.

[299] See para 15.059, below. As already indicated, the various codes, frameworks and guidelines constitute guidance setting out the course of conduct which the Commission intends to follow and with which it asks Member States to comply but they do not derogate from the provisions of Arts 87 and 88 of the Treaty, see para 15.044, above.

[300] See *AIUFFASS and AKT* (n 231, above) para 54 (aid for a textile plant in Northern Ireland). See also D'Sa (n 297, above) para 5–02.

[301] *CIRFS* (n 242, above) paras 32–49.

[302] Communication from the Commission to the Council, the European Parliament, the Economic and Social Committee and the Committee of the Regions on certain legal aspects relating to cinematographic and other audiovisual works, OJ 2002 C43/6; Communication from the Commission to the Council, the European Parliament, the Economic and Social Committee and the Committee of the Regions on the follow-up to the Commission communication on certain legal aspects relating to cinematographic and other audiovisual works (Cinema communication), OJ 2004 C123/1.

[303] Communication from the Commission on the application of State aid rules to public service broadcasting, OJ 2001 C320/5. For application of the Communication, see, eg N54/2005

— coal;[304]

— electricity (stranded costs);[305]

— postal services;[306]

— shipbuilding;[307]

— steel;[308]

— agriculture;[309]

Chaîne française d'information internationale (7 June 2005), *Report on Competition Policy 2005*, points 496–497. In addition, the Commission Communication on the transition from analogue to digital broadcasting, COM (2003) 541 final, notes the potential for public financial support to be used to promote 'digital switchover'. See further Hobbelen, Harris and Dominguez, 'The Increasing Importance of EC State Aid Rules in the Communications and Media Sectors' (2007) ECLR 101. See also the Protocol (No 32) to the EC Treaty on the system of public broadcasting in the Member States (1997): 'The provisions of the Treaty establishing the European Community shall be without prejudice to the competence of Member States to provide for the funding of public service broadcasting insofar as such funding is granted to broadcasting organisations for the fulfilment of the public service remit as conferred, defined and organised by each Member State, and insofar as such funding does not affect trading conditions and competition in the Community to an extent which would be contrary to the common interest, while the realisation of the remit of that public service shall be taken into account'.

[304] Communication from the Commission concerning certain aspects of the treatment of competition cases resulting from the expiry of the ECSC Treaty, OJ 2002 C152/5; Council Reg 1407/2002 on State aid to the coal industry, OJ 2002 L205/1.

[305] Commission Communication relating to the methodology for analysing State aid linked to stranded costs, Commission letter SG (2001) D/290869 of 6 August 2001. See discussion by Allibert, (2001) 3 EC Competition Policy Newsletter 25.

[306] Notice on the application of the competition rules to the postal sector and on the assessment of certain State measures relating to postal services, OJ 1998 C39/2: Vol II, App E.29. This deals mainly with the applicability of Art 86 to the postal sector, see further paras 15.068 and 15.134, below.

[307] Commission Communication on the submission of individual notifications on the application of regional investment aid schemes in the shipbuilding sector and on the proposal for appropriate measures pursuant to Art 88(1) of the EC Treaty, OJ 2003 C263/2; Framework on State aid to shipbuilding, OJ 2003 C317/11. The Framework provided for new rules for the assessment of State aid to shipbuilding that came into force following the expiry, on 31 December 2003, of Reg 1540/98, which had been an act of the Council under Art 87(3)(e). The Framework simplified the State aid rules applicable to the shipbuilding sector and also completed the 'normalisation' process initiated by the 1998 Regulation, which provided for the phasing out of operating aid. The Framework was due to expire at the end of 2006 but has been extended until the end of 2008: see Commission Communication, OJ 2006 C260/7.

[308] Communication from the Commission: Rescue and restructuring aid and closure aid for the steel sector, OJ 2002 C70/21; Communication from the Commission concerning certain aspects of the treatment of competition cases resulting from the expiry of the ECSC Treaty, OJ 2002 C152/5.

[309] See, eg Community guidelines for State aid in the agriculture and forestry sector 2007 to 2013, OJ 2006 C319/1; Commission Reg 1857/2006 on the application of Articles 87 and 88 of the EC Treaty to State aid to small- and medium-sized enterprises active in the production, processing and marketing of agricultural products, OJ 2006 L358/3; Commission Reg 1860/2004 on the application of Arts 87 and 88 of the EC treaty to 'de minimis' aid in the agricultural and fisheries sectors, OJ 2004 L325/4. There are convenient links to these texts on the DG Agriculture website at: http://ec.europa.eu/agriculture/stateaid/leg/index_en.htm.

—fisheries;[310]

—transport.[311]

Some of these codes or frameworks have been adopted as 'appropriate measures' under Article 88(1) of the Treaty.[312] Where no special rules exist in relation to a particular sector, the Commission may indicate its approach towards specific industries in its annual Reports.

Guidelines on horizontal aid. The Commission has also issued the following   **15.060**
guidelines relating to non-sector-specific or 'horizontal' aid:[313]

—aid for research and development;[314]
—aid for environmental protection;[315]
—regional aid;[316]
—rescue and restructuring aid;[317]
—risk capital.[318]

---

[310] Guidelines for the examination of State aid to fisheries and aquaculture, OJ 2004 C229/5; Commission Reg 1595/2004 on the application of Arts 87 and 88 of the EC Treaty to State aid to small- and medium-sized enterprises active in the production, processing and marketing of fisheries products, OJ 2004 L291/3; Commission Reg 1860/2004, above. There are links to these texts on the DG Fisheries website at: http://ec.europa.eu/fisheries/legislation/state_aid_en.htm.

[311] See, eg Council Reg 1107/70 on the granting of aids for transport by rail, road and inland waterway, OJ 1970 L130/1; Application of Articles 92 and 93 of the EC Treaty and Article 61 of the EEA agreement to State aids in the aviation sector, OJ 1994 C350/07; Commission Communication – Community guidelines on financing of airports and start-up aid to airlines departing from regional airports, OJ 2005 C312/1; Commission Communication C(2004) 43-Community guidelines on State aid to maritime transport, OJ 2004 C13/3. See also http://ec.europa.eu/dgs/energy_transport/state_aid/transport_en.htm.

[312] See further para 15.071, below.

[313] A list of currently applicable guidelines can be found at: http://ec.europa.eu/comm/competition/state_aid/legislation/aid3.html.

[314] Community Framework for State Aid for Research and Development, OJ 2006 C323/1: Vol II, App G.22 (replacing an earlier framework adopted in 1996).

[315] Guidelines on State aids for environmental protection, OJ 2001 C37/3: Vol II, App G.18. The Guidelines adopt a favourable approach to aid for renewable energy sources and permit, *inter alia*, certain types of operating aid and tax reductions for a limited period. For application of the Guidelines, see, eg Case T-176/01 *Ferriere Nord v Commission* [2004] ECR II-3931, [2005] All ER (EC) 851; Könings, 'The rehabilitation of polluted industrial sites in the Netherlands' (2002) 2 EC Competition Policy Newsletter 65; *Kiener Deponie Bachmanning*, OJ 1999 L109/51. See also Van Calster, 'Greening the EC's States Aid and Tax Regimes' (2000) ECLR 294. Information about EC competition policy and the environment can be found at: http://ec.europa.eu/comm/competition/environment/. The current Guidelines will lapse at the end of 2007 and the Commission will be issuing new Guidelines in the course of 2007, in accordance with its State Aid Action Plan: see para 15.002, above.

[316] See para 15.046, above.

[317] See para 15.061, below.

[318] Community guidelines on State aid to promote risk capital investments in small- and medium-sized enterprises, OJ 2006 C194/2: Vol II, App G.21. See Tranholm Schwarz, 'New Guidelines on State aid promoting risk capital investments in SMEs' (2006) 3 EC Competition Policy Newsletter 19.

The Commission has also issued notices on State guarantees[319] and fiscal aid,[320] and communications on land sales by public authorities[321] and short-term export-credit insurance.[322]

15.061 **Aid for rescuing and restructuring firms in difficulty.** The Commission assesses rescue and restructuring aids in accordance with its Guidelines on rescuing and restructuring firms in difficulty, the most recent version of which was published in 2004 (the 'Rescue Guidelines').[323] As the Rescue Guidelines state:

> 'The exit of inefficient firms is a normal part of the operation of the market. It cannot be the norm that a company which gets into difficulties is rescued by the State. Aid for rescue and restructuring operations has given rise to some of the most controversial State aid cases in the past and is among the most distortive types of State aid. Hence, the general principle of the prohibition of State aid . . . should remain the rule and derogation from that rule should be limited.'[324]

The Commission regards a firm as being 'in difficulty' where it is unable, whether through its own resources or with the funds it is able to obtain from its owner/shareholders or creditors, to stem losses which, without State intervention, will almost certainly condemn it to going out of business in the short or medium term.[325] Rescue and restructuring aids must normally be individually notified to, and approved by, the Commission. However, the Guidelines provide that such aids do not need to be notified if the beneficiary is a small- or medium-sized enterprise and the proposed aid satisfies certain criteria.[326]

15.062 **Distinction between rescue and restructuring aid.** The Rescue Guidelines draw a distinction between 'rescue' and 'restructuring' aid. The term 'rescue aid'

---

[319] Commission Notice on the application of Articles 87 and 88 of the EC Treaty to State aid in the form of guarantees, OJ 2000 C71/14: Vol II, App G.26. See para 15.038, above. At time of writing, the Commission is consulting on a revised Notice.

[320] Commission Notice on the application of the State aid rules to measures relating to direct business taxation, OJ 1998 C384/3: Vol II, App G.25. See para 15.031, above.

[321] Commission Communication on State aid elements in sales of land and buildings by public authorities, OJ 1997 C209/3. See para 15.036, above.

[322] Communication of the Commission to the Member States pursuant to Art [88(1)] of the EC Treaty applying Arts [87] and [88] of the Treaty to short-term export-credit insurance, OJ 1997 C281/4, amended OJ 2001 C217/2, OJ 2005 C325/22: Vol II, App G.24. It applies until 31 December 2010.

[323] Communication from the Commission, Community guidelines on State aid for rescuing and restructuring firms in difficulty, OJ 2004 C244/2: Vol II, App G.19. The Rescue Guidelines, which came into force in respect of all aids notified from 10 October 2004 onwards, apply to firms in all sectors except coal and steel, and are without prejudice to any sector-specific rules relating to firms in difficulty: see para 18. See the discussion by Valle and Van de Casteele in (2004) 3 EC Competition Policy Newsletter 58. Sector-specific rules exist for the aviation sector: OJ 2004 C350/5.

[324] Rescue Guidelines, para 4.

[325] ibid, para 9.

[326] ibid, Chap 4, esp para 79.

refers to temporary support provided to a firm which has experienced a marked deterioration in its financial position reflected by an acute liquidity crisis or technical insolvency. The purpose of such aid, which can be approved only so as to avoid serious social difficulties,[327] is to keep the ailing firm afloat long enough to allow a restructuring or liquidation plan to be devised. Accordingly, such aid must be granted for no more than six months, and must be provided by way of reversible liquidity support in the form of loan guarantees or loans with an interest rate at least comparable to those typically applied to loans to healthy firms and the reference rates adopted by the Commission.[328] The Commission endeavours to decide within one month whether to approve a notified rescue aid.[329] 'Restructuring aid', on the other hand, is intended to address the causes of the firm's difficulties, and must be based on a feasible, coherent and far-reaching plan to restore the firm's long-term viability.[330] The Rescue Guidelines take a more pragmatic approach to the distinction between 'rescue' and 'restructuring' aid than was taken by the previous guidelines,[331] under which, in principle, restructuring measures financed by State aid could not be undertaken during the 'rescue aid' phase (ie before a full restructuring plan had been devised). Under the Rescue Guidelines, rescue aid can now be used for the taking of steps, including structural measures such as withdrawal from a loss-making activity, if these are needed immediately to stem losses.[332] Restructuring aid can only be compatible with the common market if it is clear that any resulting distortion of competition will be offset by the benefits flowing from the firm's survival, for example, where the net effect of redundancies resulting from the firm's going out of business would be to exacerbate employment problems or, exceptionally, where the firm's disappearance would result in a monopoly or tight oligopolistic situation.[333]

Other conditions for rescue and restructuring aid.   The Rescue Guidelines take   **15.063**
a stricter approach than their predecessor to the requirement that the beneficiary firm must make a substantial contribution to the cost of its own restructuring. They set out the minimum contributions normally expected from different sizes of firm: 25 per cent for small enterprises; 40 per cent for medium-sized enterprises; and 50 per cent for large enterprises.[334] In addition, the amount of restructuring aid provided must be strictly limited to the minimum necessary to restore the firm to viability in accordance with the restructuring plan.

---

[327] ibid, para 25(b).
[328] ibid, para 15.
[329] Rescue Guidelines, section 3.1.2 (para 30). The one month period only applies where the amount of the rescue aid does not exceed €10 million and certain other criteria are also satisfied.
[330] Rescue Guidelines, para 16.
[331] The 1999 guidelines: OJ 1999 C288/2.
[332] Rescue Guidelines, para 16.
[333] ibid, Section 3.2.1 (para 31).
[334] ibid, paras 43–44.

Any receipts generated by the restructuring, for example, from the sale of surplus assets, must therefore be taken into account when assessing the amount of aid that may be paid.[335] Furthermore, unless the beneficiary is a small enterprise, restructuring aid will normally be approved only if the adverse effects of such aid on competition are minimised by compensatory measures, such as a requirement that the beneficiary divest itself of certain assets or reduce capacity.[336] The Commission also applies a 'one time, last time' rule under which, save in exceptional circumstances, rescue and restructuring aids will not be permitted to be paid to firms which have received any such aid in the past 10 years.[337] This reflects the intention that the rescue and restructuring of a firm by means of State aid should be a 'one-off operation' that enables the firm to return to being viable without State assistance, rather than a means by which inefficient firms or economically unviable industries can be repeatedly 'rescued'. In addition, since rescue and restructuring aid is designed to assist established firms who need short-term assistance to enable them to return to viability, rather than to promote the establishment of new firms, such aid cannot be granted to an undertaking which is less than three years old.[338] The Guidelines apply to rescue and restructuring aid granted to firms in assisted areas,[339] as well as unassisted ones. However, the conditions for authorising restructuring aid for firms in assisted areas may be less stringent as regards the implementation of compensatory measures and the size of the beneficiary's contribution.[340]

(e) Article 87(3)(d)

15.064 **Aid to promote culture and heritage conservation.** It is unclear whether this derogation has widened the scope of Article 87(3) since aids which can be authorised under Article 87(3)(d) (which was added in 1993) were previously authorised under what is now Article 87(3)(c). Thus, prior to the entry into force of the Treaty on European Union on 1 November 1993, the Commission was prepared to authorise under Article 87(3)(c) aids with a cultural objective.[341] Since the entry into force of Article 87(3)(d) the Commission has authorised aid to a

---

[335] See Case T-349/03 *Corsica Ferries France v Commission* [2005] ECR II-2197. See also, eg N370/2004 *Imprimerie Nationale* (20 July 2005), *Report on Competition Policy 2005*, points 447–449; *British Energy plc*, OJ 2005 L142/26.

[336] Rescue Guidelines, para 38–39.

[337] ibid, Section 3.3 (paras 72–73).

[338] ibid, para 12.

[339] See para 15.046, above.

[340] Rescue Guidelines, Section 3.2.4 (paras 55–56).

[341] See, eg its approval of an aid scheme for the export of French language books in view, *inter alia*, of the cultural aim of the scheme. The decision was annulled on essentially procedural grounds in Case T-49/93 *SIDE v Commission* [1995] ECR II-2501. See also Case C-332/98 *France v Commission (CELF)* [2000] ECR I-4833.

national film industry as within that provision whereas previously aid to the film industry was capable of being authorised under Article 87(3)(c).[342]

(f) Aid authorised by the Council

Authorisation by the Council: Article 87(3)(e).   Article 87(3)(e) provides that **15.065** the Council, acting by qualified majority on a proposal from the Commission, may specify 'other categories of aid' which may be compatible with the common market. This provision does not appear to enable the Council to authorise aids on an individual basis. Rather, it enables the Council to specify categories of aid, in addition to those already specified in Article 87(3)(a)–(d), in respect of which the Commission has a discretion. The Council has used its power under Article 87(3)(e) to specify a number of such 'other categories of aid', most notably in respect of aids to the shipbuilding and coal industries.[343]

Authorisation by the Council: Article 88(2).   In addition to the power under **15.066** Article 87(3)(e), the Council also has power to authorise specific aids, but only where certain strict conditions are satisfied. This power arises under the third sub-paragraph of Article 88(2), which provides:

> 'On application by a Member State, the Council, may, acting unanimously, decide that aid which the State is granting or intends to grant shall be considered to be compatible with the common market, in derogation from the provisions of Article 87 or from the regulations provided for in Article 89, if such a decision is justified by exceptional circumstances. If, as regards the aid in question, the Commission has already initiated the procedure provided for in the first sub-paragraph of this paragraph,[344] the fact that the State has made its application to the Council shall have the effect of suspending that procedure until the Council has made its attitude known. If however the Council has not made its attitude known within three months of the said application being made, the Commission shall give its decision on the case.'

The difficulties of obtaining such an authorisation are apparent from the fact that there must be a unanimous decision of the Council in a situation where the Commission is likely to take the view that the aid is incompatible with Article 87.[345]

---

[342] See *XXVIIth Report on Competition Policy* (1997), point 283; *XXVIIIth Report* (1998), points 272–273. On the Commission's policy in the audio-visual sector, see n 302, above. For examples of earlier aids to the film industry authorised under Art 87(3)(c), see *XXIInd Report on Competition Policy* (1992), point 442.

[343] See, eg Council Reg 1540/98 establishing new rules on aid to shipbuilding, OJ 1998 L202/1 (which expired on 31 December 2003); Council Reg 1407/2002 on State aid to the coal industry, OJ 2002 L205/1.

[344] See paras 15.081 *et seq*, below.

[345] But such authorisations have been given increasingly frequently to agricultural aids, see, eg *XVIIth Report on Competition Policy* (1987), point 274 and *XIXth Report* (1989), point 221 and the figures produced by the Commission in its pleading in Case C-122/94 *Commission v Council* [1996] ECR I-881, 897. See also Council Decn of 19 December 1960, JO 1960, 1972.

In order to invoke this provision, an application must be made to the Council before the Commission has taken its decision.[346] Once the Commission has declared aid to be unlawful, with the result that the Member State is under an obligation to seek repayment of that aid, the Council cannot then frustrate the effectiveness of that obligation by adopting a decision under Article 88(2) authorising a new aid aimed at reimbursing the recipients of the original aid for the costs of repaying that aid.[347] In *Commission v Council (wine)*,[348] the Court of Justice upheld two Council decisions adopted under the third sub-paragraph of Article 88(2) granting special aid for the distillation of certain wines in Italy and France. The Court of Justice held that the Council, in deciding what constitutes exceptional circumstances, is called upon to carry out an assessment of a complex economic situation and that on the facts the Council had not committed a manifest error of assessment.[349]

15.067 **Block exemptions pursuant to Regulation 994/98: SMEs, training and employment aids.** The Commission has adopted block exemptions for State aid to SMEs and for training and employment aids. All three block exemptions set out a category of aids that are deemed to be compatible with the common market under Article 87(3). They are therefore exempt from notification requirement in Article 88(3). The SME block exemption,[350] which is without prejudice to special legislative rules in specific sectors,[351] exempts investment aid (including aid to job creation), and aid for outside consultants and for trade fair participation, and has now been amended[352] also to exempt certain research and development ('R&D') aid. When the investment takes place in areas which qualify for regional aid, the block exemption permits an increase in the intensity of the aid above the regional aid ceilings.[353] The training block exemption[354] exempts, at different levels of aid intensity, both specific training, that is to say training involving tuition directly

---

[346] Case C-110/02 *Commission v Council (Pig Farmers)* [2004] ECR I-6333, [2004] 2 CMLR 1330, [2005] All ER (EC) 397, paras 30–34. See also Case C-399/03 *Commission v Council (Belgian co-ordination centres)* [2006] ECR I-5629.

[347] Case C-110/02 *Commission v Council (Pig Farmers)*, above, paras 38–51.

[348] Case C-122/94 *Commission v Council (wine)* [1996] ECR I-881.

[349] ibid, paras 17–25.

[350] Reg 70/2001, OJ 2001 L10/33, as amended by Reg 364/2004, OJ 2004 L63/22 and Reg 1857/2006, OJ 2006 L358/3: Vol II, App G.11. See also Commission Recommendation of 6 May 2003 concerning the definition of micro, small- and medium-sized enterprises, OJ 2003 L124/36: Vol II, App C.15.

[351] See, eg Reg 1857/2006 on the application of the State aid rules to SMEs active in the production of agricultural products, OJ 2006 L358/3.

[352] By Reg 364/2004, above.

[353] Reg 70/2001, Art 4(3). For regional aid ceilings, see paras 15.046 *et seq*, above.

[354] Reg 68/2001, OJ 2001 L10/20: as amended by Reg 363/2004, OJ 2004 L63/20: Vol II, App G.10.

and principally applicable to the employee's position in the assisted firm, and general training which involves tuition which is applicable not only, or principally, to the employee's position in the firm but provides qualifications that are transferable to other firms or fields of work.[355] The employment block exemption[356] exempts certain aids for the creation of employment, the recruitment of disadvantaged and disabled workers, or to cover the additional costs of employing disabled workers.[357] The coal and shipbuilding sectors are excluded from the scope of the block exemption, as are aids for the creation of employment in the transport sector.[358] As part of the implementation of the Commission's State Aid Action Plan, the existing block exemptions for training, SME and employment aids, along with the 2006 block exemption for regional aid,[359] are to be replaced by a new general block exemption which consolidates and simplifies these existing block exemptions, and further introduces block exemption for three new types of aid: environmental aid, aid in the form of risk capital and R&D aid also in favour of large enterprises.[360] The new general block exemption is likely to be introduced by the end of 2007 when the SME, training and employment aids block exemptions expire.[361]

(g) Article 86(2)

Individual exemptions for service of general economic interest: Article 86(2). Article 86 of the Treaty prohibits Member States from adopting or maintaining in force measures which contravene Articles 81–89 of the Treaty in relation to undertakings to which they have granted special or exclusive rights. Article 86 is considered more generally in Chapter 11, above. Article 86(2)   **15.068**

---

[355] Art 4. The basic rule is a maximum of 25 per cent of the project's eligible costs in the case of specific training (35 per cent for SMEs) and 50 per cent in the case of general training (70 per cent for SMEs).

[356] Reg 2204/2002, OJ 2002 L337/3, corrigendum OJ 2002 L349/126: Vol II, App G.12. The application of this Reg has been extended until 30 June 2008: Reg 1976/2006, OJ 2006 L368/85. The Reg enables Member States to grant aid for the creation of new jobs and the recruitment of disadvantaged or diabled workers. In the case of the long-term unemployed and other disadvantaged workers, Member States may meet up to 50 per cent of one year's wage costs plus compulsory social security contributions. In the case of disabled workers, up to 60 per cent of one year's wage costs can be met by the State. See Slocock, 'Commission adopts Regulation exempting State aid for employment from notification under Article 88(1)' (2003) 1 EC Competition Policy Newsletter 21.

[357] The employment block exemption is the only State aid block exemption the legality of which has been challenged before the ECJ: Case C-110/03 *Belgium v Commission* [2005] ECR I-2801, [2006] 2 CMLR 5 (the challenge was dismissed).

[358] Reg 2204/2002, Art 1(2).

[359] See para 15.052, above.

[360] The draft Regulation for a general block exemption was publishsed on 24 April 2007 and is available on the DG Comp website: see Vol II, App G.16. DG Comp has also published a very full explanatory memorandum on the draft Regulation: Vol II, App G.17.

[361] They have been extended until 31 December 2007 by Reg 1040/2006, OJ 2006 L187/8.

provides a derogation from the application of the competition rules in respect of such undertakings if an undertaking has been entrusted with the operation of services of general economic interest[362] in a case where the application of such rules obstructs its performance, in law or in fact, of the tasks assigned to it. The grant of aid to an undertaking entrusted with the operation of a service of general economic interest will therefore escape the prohibition in Article 87 provided that the sole purpose of the aid is to offset the additional costs incurred in performing the particular task assigned to the undertaking entrusted with that service and that the grant of aid is necessary in order for that undertaking to be able to perform its public service obligation under conditions of economic equilibrium.[363] Reliance on Article 86(2) will only be necessary if the undertaking concerned is actually receiving State aid. In *Altmark*[364] the Court of Justice held that compensation provided to an undertaking for its performance of a public service obligation does not, as a matter of principle, confer a true 'advantage' on that undertaking falling within Article 87(1) provided that there is a sufficiently precise and demonstrable correspondence between the amount of compensation provided and the costs of discharging the obligation.[365] However since reliance on Article 86(2) is only possible where there is a similarly close correspondence between the level of aid provided and the costs of providing the service,[366] it is conceptually difficult to envisage situations where compensation would fall within Article 87(1) but could then escape the prohibition on State aid in reliance on Article 86(2).[367] Following the *Altmark* judgment, the Commission adopted a Community Framework[368] setting out the approach it will take to providing individual

---

[362] Although Member States have a broad margin of appreciation in identifying a service as one of 'general economic interest', it is necessary that the service in question carry a general interest that goes beyond the general interest in promoting economic activity: Case C-179/90 *Merci Convenzionali Porto di Genova* [1991] ECR I-5889, [1994] 4 CMLR 422, para 27.

[363] Case T-106/95 *FFSA v Commission* [1997] ECR 11–229, [1997] 2 CMLR 78, upheld on appeal in Case C-174/97P, [1998] ECR I-1303. See, eg the three conditions that need to be fulfilled as set out in the Commission's Communication on Broadcasting (n 303, above) para 29.

[364] Case C-280/00 *Altmark Trans and Regierungspräsidium Magdeburg* [2003] ECR I-7747, [2003] 3 CMLR 339, [2005] All ER (EC) 610.

[365] See para 15.012, above.

[366] See, eg Case C-53/00 *Ferring v ACOSS* [2001] ECR I-9067, [2003] 1 CMLR 1001, paras 31–32. It is not always necessary, however, for payments to undertakings in respect of their performance of services of general economic interest to have been awarded following a tender procedure in order for such payments to be compatible with the common market under Art 86(2): see, eg Case T-17/02 *Fred Olsen v Commission* [2005] ECR II-2031, para 239.

[367] This was one of the concerns expressed by AG Léger in *Altmark*, whose Opinion the ECJ declined to follow: (n 364, above) AG Opinion, paras 79–82.

[368] Community Framework for State aid in the form of public service compensation, OJ 2005 C297/4. See Svane, 'Public service compensation in practice: Commission package on State aid for Services of General Economic Interest' (2005) 3 EC Competition Policy Newsletter 34.

exemptions under Article 86(2), as well as a Decision[369] providing block exemption for public service compensation payments that meet certain conditions.[370] The approach of the Commission and the conditions for the application of the block exemption are in some respects more generous, and provide greater certainty, than the exacting criteria set out in the *Altmark* judgment that must be satisfied if public service compensation is to fall outside Article 87(1). In particular, whereas the *Altmark* criteria require that the amount of compensation is set either through a competitive tendering process or by another method directed at identifying the costs of an efficient provider in providing the services in question, the Framework and Decision do not specify this requirement. It may therefore be possible for public service compensation to come within the framework and/or the block exemption where the amount of compensation has been set by reference to the costs of the undertaking entrusted with the performance of the services in question, although those costs exceed those which would have been incurred by a more efficient undertaking. Article 86(2) therefore seems likely to have continued relevance in the State aid context by protecting provisions of public service compensation that do not satisfy the *Altmark* criteria but may nevertheless fall within the block exemption or qualify for individual exemption by the Commission.[371]

---

[369] Commission Decn 2005/842 on the application of Article 86(2) of the Treaty to State aid in the form of public service compensation granted to certain public service undertakings entrusted with the operation of services of general economic interest, OJ 2005 L312/67. The Decn essentially provides that public service compensation provided to an undertaking which provides public services in accordance with a clearly defined public service mandate will be compatible with Art 86(2) provided that over-compensation is avoided. Such compensation does not have to be notified to the Commission in advance where the amount of compensation provided is less than €30 million per year and the beneficiary of that compensation has an annual turnover of less than €100 million. Compensation provided to hospitals and social housing undertakings for the carrying out of services of general economic interest does not need to be notified irrespective of whether those limits are exceeded, and special provision is also made for ports, airports, and air and maritime links to certain islands.

[370] At the same time as the Commission adopted the Framework and the block exemption Decision, the Commission also amended the Transparency Directive (Dir 80/723) to clarify that undertakings receiving public service compensation and operating on both public service and other markets must maintain separate accounts for their different activities in order that compliance with the prohibition of over-compensation can be verified. As to the Transparency Directive generally, see para 15.016, above.

[371] See, eg *State aid awarded by Italy to the Adriatica, Caremar, Siremar, Saremar and Toremar maritime transport companies ('Tirrenia Group')*, OJ 2005 L53/29, declaring compatible certain of the payments made by Italy to the Tirrenia Group on the basis that they constituted compensation for providing public services and fell within Art 86(2). (Italy's appeal against the imposition of a suspension by the Commission was largely dismissed: Case C-400/99 *Italy v Commission (Tirrenia Group)* [2005] ECR I-3657, [2005] 3 CMLR 611; the shipping companies' appeal on the substance of the decn was dismissed: Case T-246/99 *Tirrenia di Navigazione v Commission*, judgment of 20 June 2007). See also *Ad hoc measures implemented by Portugal for RTP*, OJ 2005 L142/1, and *Chaîne française d'information internationale* (n 303, above), in which the Commission noted that the

5. Supervision under Article 88

15.069 **Procedures under Article 88 and Regulation 659/1999.** Article 88 of the Treaty does not lay down any detailed procedural rules for the application of the State aid provisions. The procedural rules applicable to the notification, approval and recovery of State aid have therefore developed from the case law of the Community Courts and the administrative practice of the Commission. In order to introduce greater certainty and transparency into the field of State aid, the Council adopted Regulation 659/1999[372] ('the Procedural Regulation') laying down detailed rules for the application of Article 88 of the Treaty. The aim of this Regulation was to codify and, in some areas, extend the existing procedural rules.[373]

(a) Review of existing aids

15.070 **Concept of an existing aid.** It is important to distinguish between existing aids, which are subject to review under Article 88(1) but not to pre-notification, and new aids and alteration to existing aids, which require pre-notification. 'Existing aids'[374] comprise:

(i) aids in operation when the Treaty came into force or when new Member States acceded to the Treaty;[375]

---

proposed measures did not satisfy the *Altmark* criteria, but nevertheless went on to find them compatible with the common market under Art 86(2).

[372] Procedural Reg, Reg 659/1999, OJ 1999 L83/1, as amended by Act of accession of the Czech Republic, Estonia, Cyprus, Latvia, Lithuania, Hungary, Malta, Poland, Slovenia and Slovakia, OJ 2003 L236/345: Vol II, App G.1. Reg 659/1999 has been supplemented by Commission Reg 794/2004 laying down detailed rules for the application of Art 93 of the EC Treaty, OJ 2004 L140/1: Vol II, App G.2. See further n 402, below.

[373] Since Reg 659/1999 was intended mainly as a codifying measure, the prior case law remains relevant: see Case C-400/99 *Tirrenia Group* (n 371, above) paras 23–25.

[374] See generally AG Warner in Case 173/73 *Italy v Commission (Aids to the Textile Industry)* [1974] ECR 709, 723, [1974] 2 CMLR 593, 597. See also Case 120/73 *Lorenz v Germany* [1973] ECR 1471, 1482.

[375] Procedural Reg, Art 1(b)(i). Measures taken after the entry into force of the Treaty to grant or alter aid must, however, be regarded as new aids, whether the alterations relate to existing aid or to plans previously notified to the Commission: Case C-295/97 *Piaggio v Ifitalia* [1999] ECR I-3735, para 48; Cases C-346 & 529/03 *Atzeni v Regione autonoma della Sardegna* [2006] ECR I-1875, paras 51–52. For an example of a pre-Accession aid being an existing aid, see Case C-387/92 *Banco Exterior de España v Ayuntamiento de Valencia* [1994] ECR I-877, [1994] 3 CMLR 473. With regard to the 10 Member States who acceded to the EU on 1 May 2004, the Accession Treaty (signed on 16 April 2003) provides that the following aid measures are to be regarded as existing aid from the date of accession: (a) aid measures put into effect before 10 December 1994; (b) aid measures listed in an appendix to the Accession Treaty (the 'Treaty list'); and (c) aid measures which, prior to the date of accession, were assessed by the State aid authority of the new Member State and found to be compatible with the *acquis*, and to which the Commission did not raise any objection

(ii)   authorised aid, namely, individual aids[376] and aid schemes[377] which have
       been authorised by the Commission or Council[378] (including individual
       aids granted under such aid schemes[379]);

(iii) aid which is deemed to have been authorised as a result of a failure on the
       part of the Commission to take a decision as to the compatibility or other-
       wise of a notified aid;[380]

(iv)   aid which is deemed to have been authorised as a result of no action having
       been taken by the Commission to recover that aid within ten years of its
       award;[381] and

(v)   aid which is deemed to be existing aid because it can be established that at
       the time it was put into effect it did not constitute an aid, and subsequently
       became an aid due to the evolution of the common market and without
       having been altered by the Member State.[382]

---

on the ground of serious doubts as to the compatibility of the measure with the common market
(the 'interim procedure'). See the following discussions of existing aid in the context of the 2004
enlargement: Roebling, 'Existing aid and enlargement' (2003) 1 EC Competition Policy Newsletter 33; Dias, 'Existing State aid in the acceding countries' (2004) 2 EC Competition Policy
Newsletter 17; Čierna, 'Determining Commission's competence: past aid and new aid-application
on restructuring aid to Polish shipbuilding' (2005) 3 EC Competition Policy Newsletter 100.

376   Procedural Reg, Art 1(e) defines an individual aid as 'an aid that is not awarded on the basis
of an aid scheme and notifiable awards of aid on the basis of an aid scheme'.

377   ibid, Art 1(d) defines an aid scheme as 'any act on the basis of which, without further implementation measures being required, individual aid awards may be made to undertakings defined
within the act in a general and abstract manner and any act on the basis of which aid which is not
linked to a specific project may be awarded to one or several undertakings for an indefinite period
of time and/or for an indefinite amount'.

378   ibid, Art 1(b)(ii). See also Case C-313/90 *CIRFS v Commission* [1993] ECR I-1125,
para 25.

379   Individual aids which are granted in accordance with an existing aid scheme will themselves be classified as existing aids: see Case C-321/99P *ARAP v Commission* [2002] ECR I-4287,
[2002] 2 CMLR 949, para 60. Where the Commission receives complaints about such an aid, the
Commission will assess whether that aid falls within the terms of the existing aid scheme and, if
it does, will not have to further consider the compatibility of the aid with the EC Treaty: *ARAP*,
paras 76 and 83. Where the aid does not fall within the terms of the existing aid scheme, however,
the aid will be a new aid and liable to be assessed as such: see Case C-36/00 *Spain v Commission
(State-owned shipyards)* [2002] ECR I-3243, paras 20–38.

380   Procedural Reg, Art 1(b)(iii). See *Lorenz v Germany* (n 374, above) para 6; cf *Piaggio* (n 375,
above) paras 44–49.

381   ibid, Arts 1(b)(iv) and 15.

382   ibid, Art 1(b)(v). In Cases T-298/97, etc, *Alzetta v Commission* [2000] ECR II-2319,
paras 141–150, the CFI annulled that part of the Commission's decision which found that measures
which became aid subject to the Treaty after liberalisation of part of the transport sector were new
aids; they were to be classified as existing aids. Importantly, however, that case related to a liberalisation which had occurred prior to the coming into force of the Procedural Reg, the last sentence
of Art 1(b)(v) of which provides that, where certain measures become aid following liberalisation
of an activity by Community law, such measures shall not be considered as existing aid after the
date fixed for liberalisation. In Cases T-346/99, etc, *Diputación Foral de Álava v Commission* [2002]
ECR II-4259, para 84, the CFI held that Art 1(b)(v) did not include aids that the Commission
had only considered to be aids as a result of a change in its position which was independent of any

In *Namur-les Assurances*[383] the Court of Justice held that the question of whether aid is existing, new aid or an alteration of existing aid is to be determined by reference to the legislative or other provisions providing for it and not by its scale or amount.

15.071 **Review of existing aids.** Article 87(1) requires the Commission to keep existing aids under constant review and to propose to the relevant Member State 'any appropriate measures required by the progressive development or by the functioning of the common market'. For the review of existing aid schemes,[384] the Commission must obtain all the necessary information from the Member State concerned.[385] Since 1989, the Commission has been in the process of conducting a wide-ranging review of existing aid schemes and provisions, many of which were approved when economic circumstances were different and which may no longer be compatible with the common market.[386] The review has been of both individual Member State schemes and general schemes concerning particular sectors or particular aid types across the Community and began by considering schemes most likely to distort competition and trade within the Community, in particular general investment aid schemes.[387] The Commission also undertakes general reviews of policy in relation to aids for particular purposes and publishes new or codified rules which it intends to apply to new and amended schemes and to its review of individual existing aid schemes.[388]

15.072 **Implementation of existing aid.** Existing aid or measures adopted under an existing aid scheme may be implemented as long as the Commission has not found such aid to be incompatible with the common market. In *Italy v Commission (Italgrani)*,[389] the Court of Justice stated that where the Commission has before it a specific grant of an aid alleged to be made in pursuance of a previously authorised scheme, it must first examine whether the aid is covered by the general scheme and satisfies the conditions laid down in the decision approving the scheme. If the Commission has doubts as to the conformity of an individual aid

---

evolution of the common market: 'whether a State measure is existing or new aid cannot depend on a subjective assessment by the Commission and must be determined independently of any previous administrative practice it may have had'.

[383] Case C-44/93 *Namur-les Assurances du Crédit v OND* [1994] ECR I-3829. See also *Alzetta*, above.

[384] For definition of aid scheme, see n 377, above.

[385] Procedural Reg, Art 17(1). See also Case C-135/93 *Spain v Commission (Motor vehicle framework No. 1)* [1995] ECR I-1651, para 24.

[386] See *XIXth Report on Competition Policy* (1989), points 120–121; *XXth Report* (1990), point 171; and *XXIst Report* (1991), point 13 and points 240 *et seq.*

[387] ibid.

[388] eg Community Framework for State Aid for Research and Development (n 314, above); Guidelines on State aid for environmental protection (n 315, above). See para 15.060, above.

[389] Case C-47/91 *Italy v Commission (Italgrani)* [1994] ECR I-4635, para 24. See also Case C-278/95P *Siemens v Commission* [1997] ECR I-2507, para 31.

with the general aid scheme, it can require the Member State concerned to provide the necessary information.[390] If the Member State fails to provide the relevant information, the Commission can take an interim decision suspending the aid and directly assess the compatibility of the aid with the Treaty as if it were a new aid.[391]

Existing aids no longer compatible with the common market. If the **15.073** Commission considers that an existing aid is not or is no longer compatible with the Treaty, it must first inform the Member State concerned and provide it with the opportunity to submit its comments within a period of one month.[392] Where the Commission, in the light of the information provided by the Member State, concludes that the existing aid scheme is not or is no longer compatible with the common market, it must issue a recommendation proposing appropriate measures to remedy the situation by substantive or procedural amendment, or abolition of the scheme.[393] Such a proposal is not legally binding[394] but has important legal consequences since if the Member State accepts the proposed measures, the Commission's recommendation becomes binding.[395] If, however, the Member State concerned does not accept the Commission's recommendation, the Commission is then able to proceed to the formal investigation procedure under Article 88(2),[396] discussed below.[397]

---

[390] Procedural Reg, Art 10; *Italgrani*, above, para 35.

[391] Procedural Reg, Art 11; *Italgrani* (n 389, above). For an individual aid under an approved general aid scheme that required notification, see, eg Cases T-447/93, etc, *AITEC v Commission* [1995] ECR II-1971, paras 124–132. See also *ASPEC* (n 396, below) para 105.

[392] Procedural Reg, Art 17(2).

[393] ibid, Art 18.

[394] Art 249 EC; and see Cases T-132 & 143/96 *Freistaat Sachsen and VW v Commission* [1999] ECR II-3663, [2000] 3 CMLR 485, para 209.

[395] Procedural Reg, Art 19(1). Case C-288/96 *Germany v Commission (Jadekost)* [2000] ECR I-8237, paras 64–65.

[396] ibid, Art 19(2). In Case T-435/93 *ASPEC v Commission* [1995] ECR II-1281 and in Case T-442/93 *AAC v Commission* [1995] ECR II-1329, the CFI applied to State aid decisions the principles laid down in Case C-137/92P *Commission v BASF* [1994] ECR I-2555 on the rules concerning the Commission procedure for adopting competition decisions. Where the Commission is required to take a decision which involves a thorough examination of complex factual and legal questions, that cannot be regarded as a measure of management or administration which can be taken under the habilitation procedure. The CFI concluded on the facts that an examination of whether a particular measure fell within a previously approved general aid scheme could not be regarded as a measure of management or administration. The Commission's decision was annulled since it violated the principle of collegiality: there were significant differences between the draft letter considered by the Commission and the letter signed by the Commissioner for Agriculture and Rural Questions.

[397] See para 15.081, below. This procedure was initiated against Spain and Germany when they refused to accept the Community framework for State aid to the motor vehicle industry (see para 15.123, below). In the case of Spain, the procedure was closed after the Spanish authorities decided to apply the framework from 1 January 1990. In the case of Germany, the Commission adopted a negative decision which required Germany to notify in advance all aid covered by the framework; aid granted subsequently without prior notification would be illegal and could be subject to recovery: OJ 1990 L188/55.

(b) Notification of new aids

15.074 **Pre-notification of new aids.** Article 88(3) concerns aid other than existing aid which is dealt with by Article 88(1), that is to say new aid. It provides:

'The Commission shall be informed, in sufficient time to enable it to submit its comments, of any plans to grant or alter aid. If it considers that any such plan is not compatible with the common market having regard to Article 87, it shall without delay initiate the procedure provided for in paragraph 2. The Member State concerned shall not put its proposed measures into effect until this procedure has resulted in a final decision.'

Article 2 of the Procedural Regulation (Regulation 659/1999) requires notification of any plans to grant 'new aid'.[398] The Procedural Regulation defines new aid as aid schemes and individual aid, which is not existing aid, including alterations to existing aid.[399] Such notifiable aid awards include those where the Commission has set certain thresholds for the notification of individual aids once the Commission has accepted the general scheme under which the aids are granted or where the Commission has imposed individual notification requirements amongst the terms and conditions of its authorisations. Further, certain of the Commission's Codes and Frameworks in relation to particular industries or particular types of aid require notification of all individual aids exceeding a certain amount granted pursuant to an authorised scheme.[400] There is no obligation to notify any other interested party.[401] Notifications of new aid must be made using the prescribed standard form.[402]

---

[398] Procedural Reg, Reg 659/1999, OJ 1999 L83/1, amended OJ 2003 L236/345: Vol II, App G.1. 'Aid' is defined in Art 1(a) of the Procedural Reg as any measure fulfilling all the criteria laid down in Art 87(1) EC.

[399] Procedural Reg, above, Art 1(c). See Cases T-195 & 207/01 *Government of Gibraltar v Commission* [2002] ECR II-2309, [2002] 2 CMLR 826, [2002] All ER (EC) 838, paras 111–114, where the CFI held that alterations to an existing aid scheme are themselves to be regarded as new aids, but that the existing aid scheme is not itself normally to be so regarded. It is only when the alteration affects the substance of the original scheme that the latter is transformed into a new aid scheme. There is no substantial alteration where the new element is clearly severable from the original scheme.

[400] See, eg Multisectoral framework on regional aid for large investment projects, OJ 2002 C70/8.

[401] Cases 91 & 127/83 *Heineken v Inspecteur de Vennootschapbelasting* [1984] ECR 3435, [1985] 1 CMLR 389, paras 12–15.

[402] Reg 794/2004 (Vol II, App G.2). As a result of the coming into force of Reg 794/2004, a number of documents which the Commission had previously published regarding procedural issues in the State aid field were rendered obsolete: see Commission communication concerning the obsolescence of certain State aid policy documents, OJ 2004 C115/1: Vol II, App G.7. The forms set out in the Annexes to Reg 794/2004 were recently amended by Reg 1627/2006, OJ 2006 L302/10. See also Communication on professional secrecy in State aid decisions, OJ 2003 C297/6: Vol II, App G.6; details of arrangement for the electronic transmission of State aid notifications, OJ 2005 C237/3: Vol II, App G.8. Notification under the EEA regime is governed by EFTA Surveillance Authority Decn 195/04/COL, OJ 2006 L139/27 supplemented by a Notice on electronic transmission, OJ 2006 C286/9.

Complete notification. The notification requirement extends to all necessary **15.075** information in order to enable the Commission to undertake an assessment of the aid in question.[403] Thus the entire aid scheme must be notified. Where the method of financing an aid measure is an integral part of that measure (for example, where a Member State wishes to impose a specific levy on a certain category of undertakings in order to fund aid provided to other undertakings, rather than funding that aid out of general tax revenues), the notification of the proposed aid measure will not be complete unless the Member State includes in its notification details of the method by which the proposed aid measure will be financed.[404] Any modifications to the proposed scheme subsequent to the initial notification must also be notified, since an unnotified alteration to a proposed scheme will prevent the Member State from putting the whole scheme into effect unless the alteration is a separate aid measure which should be assessed separately.[405] However, it would seem that there is no need to notify minor adjustments made only in order to take account of inflation.[406] Similarly, there is no need to notify increases in the authorised budget of an existing aid scheme provided that such increase represents not more than 20 per cent of the budget originally notified.[407] Where the Commission considers that information provided by the Member State concerned with regard to a notified measure is incomplete, it must request all necessary additional information to be provided within a specified period. If such information is not provided, or if incomplete information is provided, the notification is deemed to be withdrawn and the aid thus becomes unnotified notifiable aid.[408] In the case of public undertakings, there are reporting requirements additional to the notification requirement in Article 88(3).[409]

---

[403] Procedural Reg (n 398, above) Art 2(2).

[404] Cases C-261 & 262/01 *Belgium v Van Calster* [2003] ECR I-12249, [2004] 1 CMLR 607, paras 50–52. See also para 15.107, below.

[405] *Heineken* (n 401, above) para 21.

[406] AG Warner in Case 177/78 *Pigs and Bacon Commission v McCarren* [1979] ECR 2161, 2204, [1979] 3 CMLR 389, 404; AG Rozes in Case 222/82 *Apple and Pear Development Council v Lewis* [1983] ECR 4083, 4134, [1984] 3 CMLR 733, 748; AG Darmon in Cases 166 & 220/86 *Irish Cement Ltd v Commission* [1988] ECR 6473, [1989] 2 CMLR 57, para 34. But an extension of the validity of an aid beyond the term originally notified is considered an alteration: see Case 70/72 *Commission v Germany* [1973] ECR 813, [1973] CMLR 741, paras 15–20 and Case 171/83R *Commission v France* [1983] ECR 2621, 2625.

[407] See the Letter from the Commission to the Member States on standardised notification and annual reports, SG(94) D/2484 of 22 February 1994, *XXIIIrd Report on Competition Policy* (1993), Annex IIB and point 385. But this is to be read in the light of *Namur-les Assurances* (n 383, above) para 28, that the emergence of new aid or the alteration of existing aid cannot be assessed according to the scale of the aid if the aid is provided under earlier statutory provisions which remain unaltered. Similarly, enlargement of the field of activity of the undertaking in receipt of the aid does not constitute an alteration of aid subject to notification (ibid).

[408] Procedural Reg (n 398, above) Art 5.

[409] See the Transparency Directive, Dir 80/723, discussed at para 15.016, above.

15.076 **Aids covered by a block exemption.** Council Regulation 994/98[410] enables the Commission to adopt block exemption regulations in relation to certain categories of aid. It empowers the Commission to declare, by regulation, aid in favour of SMEs, research and development, environmental protection, employment and training and certain regional aid as compatible with the common market and, as such, exempt from the notification requirements of Article 88(3).[411] In January 2001, the Commission adopted block exemptions in respect of aids for training and to SMEs.[412] These have now been joined by a block exemption for employment aids[413] and a block exemption for *de minimis* aids.[414] As required by Regulation 994/98,[415] the block exemption Regulations specify conditions subject to which the exemption applies, including the purpose of the aid, the category of beneficiaries, the threshold below which the exemption will apply and the sectors which are excluded. Aids which fall within a block exemption do not have to be notified to the Commission.

15.077 **Suspension on putting into effect new aid.** Aid measures notifiable pursuant to Article 88(3) EC and Article 2(1) of the Procedural Regulation must not be put into effect before the Commission has authorised, or is deemed to have authorised such aid.[416] This suspension applies equally to new aid that may benefit from the derogation in Article 86(2).[417] The Commission takes the view that an aid is put into effect when the legislative measures that enable the aid to be granted without

---

[410] Council Reg 994/98, OJ 1998 L142/1: Vol II, App G.9.

[411] ibid, Art 1(1).

[412] Vol II, Apps G.10 and G.11; see also para 15.067, above.

[413] Reg 2204/2002, OJ 2002 L337/3, corrigendum OJ 2002 L349/126: Vol II, App G.12. The application of this Reg has been extended until 30 June 2008: Reg 1976/2006, OJ 2006 L368/85. See also para 15.067, above.

[414] Reg 1998/2006, OJ L379/5: Vol II, App G.14 (replacing Reg 69/2001, OJ 2001 L10/30). See para 15.028, above.

[415] Art 1(2) and (3) of Reg 994/98.

[416] Art 88(3) EC, third sentence, and Procedural Reg (n 398, above) Art 3. The prohibition in Art 88(3) extends to aids schemes that are implemented without notification to the Commission, *Lorenz v Germany* (n 374, above) para 8, and see, in the English court, *R v Attorney General, ex p ICI* [1987] 1 CMLR 72 (CA). The need to obtain the Commission's authorisation before putting new aid into effect can prove highly inconvenient in situations where aid may need to be provided very quickly if it is to come in time to serve its purpose: see, eg NN101/2002 *Rescue aid to British energy* (decn of 27 November 2002), in which the Commission expressed regret that the UK had implemented a rescue aid scheme for a nuclear electricity generating company without first obtaining authorisation, but nevertheless found the scheme to be compatible with the common market. The degree of inconvenience has been ameliorated, though not removed, in relation to rescue aid, by the Commission's commitment to endeavour to decide whether to authorise such aid within one month of notification, at least where the amount of the notified aid is less than €10 million and certain other conditions are also satisfied: see Communication from the Commission – Community guidelines on State aid for rescuing and restructuring firms in difficulty, OJ 2004 C244/2: Vol II, App G.19, section 3.1.2, para 30; also para 15.061, above.

[417] *CELF* (n 341, above) paras 31–32 and *Van Calster* (n 404, above) para 61. Note, however, the block exemption for public service compensation: see para 15.068, above.

further formality have been adopted.[418] Breach of the suspension obligation enables the Commission to issue interim orders.[419]

Time limit for review of new aid.   The Treaty does not lay down any time limit   **15.078** for the Commission to rule on the notification. It was held in *Lorenz*[420] that a period of two months is sufficient time for the Commission to form a view on the compatibility of the notified aid with the Treaty. That time limit has been adopted in the Procedural Regulation.[421] Time starts to run only from the receipt of a complete notification.[422] By the end of that period, the Commission must adopt, after a preliminary examination, one of the decisions set out in Article 4(2)–(4) of the Procedural Regulation.[423] Where new aid has been put into effect in breach of Article 88(3), however, the Commission is not bound by the two month period.[424] A Member State cannot terminate that period unilaterally.[425]

Deemed authorisation.   If the Commission has not defined its position   **15.079** within the two-month period, the aid is deemed to have been authorised by the Commission and the Member State may implement the plan after giving prior notice to the Commission, unless the Commission takes a decision within 15 days of such prior notice.[426]

Preliminary examination of a notification.   Following a preliminary examina-   **15.080** tion of the notification, the Commission must adopt one of three types of decision. The first is that the notified measure does not constitute aid.[427] The second type of decision is where it has no doubts as to the compatibility with the common market of the notified measure, insofar as it falls within Article 87(1) of the Treaty. In that case it must then decide that the measure is compatible with

---

[418] Commission letter to Member States SG(89) D/5521 of 27 April 1989.

[419] See Case 301/87 *France v Commission (Boussac)* [1990] ECR I-307, paras 18–20; and see Procedural Reg Arts 10(3), 11(1) and (2); and para 15.095, below.

[420] Case 120/73 *Lorenz v Germany* [1973] ECR 1471, paras 4–6; Case 84/82 *Germany v Commission (Textiles)* [1984] ECR 1451, [1985] 1 CMLR 153, paras 11–12; Case C-213/90 *Spain v Commission* [1992] ECR I-4117; Case C-39/94 *SFEI* [1996] ECR I-3547, [1996] 3 CMLR 369, [1996] All ER (EC) 685, para 38; Case C-367/95P *Commission v Sytraval and Brink's France* [1998] ECR I-1719, para 37; Case T-187/99 *Agrana Zucker und Starke v Commission* [2001] ECR II-1587, para 37.

[421] Procedural Reg (n 419, above) Art 4(5).

[422] ibid. See also Case C-99/98 *Austria v Commission (Siemens)* [2001] ECR I-1101, which related to a notification made before the Procedural Reg had come into being.

[423] ibid, Art 4(1).

[424] ibid, Art 13(2) See *Boussac* (n 419, above) paras 25–28; a period of three months between the provision of full particulars and the initiation of the Art 88(2) procedure was acceptable. See also, *per* AG Slynn in Case 223/85 *RSV v Commission* [1987] ECR 4617, 4646–4647, [1989] 2 CMLR 259, 268.

[425] See *Lorenz v Germany* (n 420, above) para 4; Cases C-278/92, etc, *Spain v Commission (Hytasa No. 1)* [1994] ECR I-4103, paras 14–15.

[426] Procedural Reg (n 398, above) Art 4(6).

[427] ibid, Art 4(2).

the common market, stating which exception under the Treaty has been applied.[428] The third type of decision is where it entertains doubts as to the compatibility of the notified measure with the common market. It is then obliged to initiate proceedings under Article 88(2) of the Treaty.[429] In general, therefore, if the Commission is unable to reach the view that the aid is compatible with Article 87 within a two-month period it should initiate the formal procedure under Article 88(2). In making its preliminary examination of the compatibility of the aid with the Treaty, the Commission is under no obligation to consult anybody other than the Member State that notified the aid.[430] In *Sytraval*,[431] the Court of Justice held that the Commission is not obliged to give complainants an opportunity to state their views at the stage of preliminary examination.

(c) The formal investigation procedure under Article 88(2)

15.081   **The formal investigation procedure: existing aid.**   The formal investigation procedure under Article 88(2) starts with a Commission decision to initiate proceedings. This decision summarises the relevant issues of fact and law and contains the Commission's preliminary assessment of the measure concerned, including its doubts as to its compatibility with the common market.[432] That decision calls upon the Member State concerned and other interested parties to submit their comments within a prescribed period.[433] Other Member States and private parties are informed of the initiation of the procedure by a notice in the *Official Journal*.[434] The aim of this notice is 'to obtain from persons concerned all

---

[428]   ibid, Art 4(3). See also Case T-49/93 *SIDE v Commission* [1995] ECR II-2501, para 58.

[429]   ibid, Art 4(4). See *Germany v Commission (Textiles)* (n 420, above) paras 12–17. In that case the Commission entered into lengthy negotiations with the Belgian government (the notifying Member State), which went on for 14 months longer than the two-month period within which the Commission should generally form its preliminary view, without opening the Art 88(2) procedure. The ECJ concluded from that and other factors that the Commission encountered serious difficulties in considering whether the aid scheme was compatible with the common market and should therefore have initiated the Art 88(2) procedure. See also Case C-198/91 *William Cook v Commission* [1993] ECR I-2487, [1993] 3 CMLR 206, para 29; Case C-225/91 *Matra v Commission (No. 1)* [1993] ECR I-3203, para 33; Case T-11/95 *BP Chemicals v Commission (No. 1)* [1998] ECR II-3235, [1998] 3 CMLR 693, para 164; *Sytraval* (n 420, above) para 39; Case T-73/98 *Prayon-Rupel v Commission* [2001] ECR II-867, paras 35 & 42–44 (in which the CFI rejected the Commission's plea that it did not need to open the formal procedure where it considered it inappropriate to do so on the basis of 'principles of sound administration and economy of procedure').

[430]   See *Textiles*, above, para 13; *Matra (No. 1)*, above, para 16.

[431]   *Commission v Sytraval and Brink's France* (n 420, above) paras 58–59. The complainant's remedy is to bring proceedings against the implicit refusal to initiate proceedings under Art 88(2): ibid, paras 47–48.

[432]   Procedural Reg (n 398, above) Art 6(1).

[433]   ibid, Art 1(h) defines interested party as any Member State and any person whose interests might be affected by the granting of aid, in particular the beneficiary of the aid, competing undertakings and trade associations.

[434]   This is sufficient notice for the purposes of Art 88(2): Case 323/82 *Intermills v Commission* [1984] ECR 3809, [1986] 1 CMLR 614.

the information required for the guidance of the Commission with regard to its future action'.[435] In the case of existing aids, the initiation of the formal procedure under Article 88(2) does not prevent the continued payment of the aid.[436]

The initiation of the formal investigation procedure: new aid. The formal investigation procedure is initiated in the same way as in the case of existing aid, the difference being that the Commission will remind the parties of the terms of Article 88(3) of the Treaty and require that the proposed measures are not put into effect until the termination of the Article 88(2) procedure. The Commission also refers the parties to its Notice of 24 November 1983 to the effect that the illegal grant of aid carries with it the risk of repayment of the aid if it is found to be incompatible with the common market.[437] **15.082**

The operation of the formal investigation procedure. The Commission hears the views of all interested parties. If an interested party wishes to participate in the formal investigation procedure on an anonymous basis, it may request the Commission to refrain from disclosing its identity to the Member State concerned.[438] The Member State concerned may respond to comments received.[439] The Commission cannot rely on information against a party on which that party has not been afforded an opportunity to comment[440] unless the communication of that information to the party would not have led to a different outcome of the formal investigation procedure.[441] The Court of Justice stated in *Sytraval* that although the Commission was not obliged to examine of its own motion objections which could and would have been raised by the complainant if it had had access to all of the information before the Commission, 'in the interests of sound administration of the fundamental rules of the Treaty relating to State aid', the Commission must conduct a diligent and impartial examination of the complaint, which may require it to examine matters not expressly raised by **15.083**

---

[435] Case 70/72 *Commission v Germany* [1973] ECR 813, [1973] CMLR 741, para 19.

[436] See para 15.072, above.

[437] Notice on repayment of illegal aid, OJ 1983 C318/3, [1984] 1 CMLR 214; and see paras 15.096 *et seq*, below.

[438] Procedural Reg (n 398, above) Art 6(2).

[439] ibid.

[440] Case 234/84 *Belgium v Commission (Meura)* [1986] ECR 2263, [1988] 2 CMLR 331, paras 27–29; Case 40/85 *Belgium v Commission (Boch No. 2)* [1986] ECR 2321, [1988] 2 CMLR 301, paras 28–30; Case 259/85 *France v Commission (Textiles and clothing)* [1987] ECR 4393, [1989] 2 CMLR 30, para 12. The rights of the recipient of an aid are less than those of a Member State but if the Commission ignores the submissions of the recipient it risks the annulment of its decision to recover aid: Case T-366/00 *Scott v Commission*, judgment of 29 March 2007, paras 52–63 (on appeal, Case C-290/07P *Commission v Scott*, not yet decided). See also para 15.119, below.

[441] *Boussac* (n 419, above) para 31; Case C-142/87 *Belgium v Commission (Tubemeuse)* [1990] ECR I-959, [1991] 3 CMLR 213, paras 45–48; *Jadekost* (n 395, above) paras 92–106.

the complainant.[442] In the case of an aid scheme, the Commission may confine itself to examining the general characteristics of the scheme in question without being required to examine each particular case in which it applies.[443] Where there is a complaint, the Commission is obliged to terminate the Article 88(2) procedure by way of a decision[444] which must be taken as soon as any doubts as to the compatibility with the common market of the measure in question have been resolved.[445] The Procedural Regulation now provides that the Commission shall, as far as possible, endeavour to adopt a decision within a period of 18 months from the opening of the procedure.[446] That time limit may be extended by agreement between the Commission and the Member State concerned.[447] If the Commission has not taken a decision within 18 months, the Member State concerned may request the Commission to take a decision within a further two months on the basis of the information available to it. Where, however, the Commission considers that the information provided is not sufficient to establish compatibility of the aid with the common market, the Commission is obliged to take a negative decision.[448]

15.084 **Application to the Council.** After the initiation of the Article 88(2) procedure, if a Member State makes an application to the Council for a decision that the aid is compatible with the common market, the application has the effect of suspending that procedure until the Council has made its attitude known.[449] If the Council grants the application, its decision can be challenged by any party who has *locus standi* under Article 230 of the Treaty.[450] If, however, the Council rejects the application, the procedure under Article 88(2) is reactivated. If the

---

[442] Case C-367/95P *Commission v Sytraval and Brink's France* [1998] ECR I-1719, para 62.

[443] Cases C-15/98 & 105/99 *Italy and Sardegna Lines v Commission* [2000] ECR I-8855, [2001] 1 CMLR 237, para 51.

[444] Procedural Reg (n 398, above) Art 7(1); *Lorenz v Germany* (n 420, above) para 5.

[445] ibid, Art 7(6).

[446] ibid.

[447] Prior to the adoption of the Procedural Reg, the ECJ stated that the Commission has a reasonable period of time within which to conclude the Art 88(2) procedure; Case 59/79 *Fédération nationale des producteurs de vin de table et vins du pays v Commission* [1979] ECR 2425. In *RSV v Commission* (n 424, above), the ECJ annulled a Commission decision which required repayment of an aid but which was taken 26 months after the Art 88(2) procedure was initiated in circumstances where the aided company had reasonable grounds for believing that the aid would encounter no objection. In considering what constituted a reasonable period of time for the Commission to conduct its investigation, regard was also had to the promptness of notification by the Member State. See *Boussac* (n 419, above) paras 22–28, where a large part of the delay in the Commission's procedure arose from the failure of the French government to provide the Commission with full particulars (32 months between initiation and termination of procedure but only two months between receipt of all relevant information by the Commission and the final decision).

[448] Procedural Reg (n 398, above) Art 7(7); Case T-171/02 *Regione autonoma della Sardegna v Commission* [2005] ECR II-2123, para 149.

[449] Art 88(2) EC, third sub-paragraph.

[450] See generally paras 15.112 *et seq*, below.

Council has not made its attitude known within the three months following the application, the Commission must give its decision on the case.[451]

Final decision under Article 88(2). The Commission must close the formal **15.085** investigation procedure by adopting one of the following decisions:

(i) that, where appropriate following modification by the Member State concerned, the notified measure does not constitute aid;[452]

(ii) that, where appropriate following modification, and where doubts as to the compatibility of the notified measure have been removed, the notified measure is compatible with the common market: 'a positive decision';[453]

(iii) that, where the Commission finds that the aid is not compatible with the common market, the aid concerned shall not be put into effect: 'a negative decision'.[454]

Any decision must be properly reasoned.[455]

Conditional positive decisions. The Commission may attach to a positive deci- **15.086** sion conditions subject to which an aid may be considered compatible with the common market and obligations to enable the Commission to monitor compliance with the decision.[456] In *TWD Textilwerke Deggendorf (No. 2)*, the Commission approved grants and loans by the German government but required suspension of payment of the aid until recovery of the aid previously paid to the same company that had been held unlawful.[457] The Commission's approach was upheld.[458] In a case where the Commission has approved aid subject to certain conditions and one or more of those conditions is not met, there is a presumption that implementation (or further implementation) of the aid is incompatible with the common market and such aid cannot be awarded without a further Commission decision granting a formal derogation from the condition(s) in question.[459] Such a derogation can be granted only following an initial consideration of whether the derogation would lead to the aid becoming incompatible

---

[451] Art 88(2) EC, fourth sub-paragraph.

[452] Procedural Reg (n 398, above) Art 7(2).

[453] ibid, Art 7(3). See also Art 7(4) and para 15.086, below.

[454] ibid, Art 7(5).

[455] Art 253 EC. See para 15.120, below.

[456] Procedural Reg, Art 7(4).

[457] *TWD Textilwerke Deggendorf (No. 2)*, OJ 1991 L215/16, OJ 1992 L183/36 and OJ 1986 L300/34. See also *MobilCom AG*, OJ 2005 L116/55: structural aid conditional upon a behavioural measure; and the note on this case by Crome and Sölter, (2004) 3 EC Competition Policy Newsletter 55.

[458] Cases T-244 & 486/93 *Textilwerke Deggendorf v Commission (No. 2)* [1995] ECR II-2265, [1998] 1 CMLR 332; upheld on appeal, Case C-355/95P [1997] ECR I-2549, [1998] 1 CMLR 234.

[459] Case T-140/95 *Ryanair v Commission* [1998] ECR II-3322, [1998] 3 CMLR 1022, paras 86–88.

with the common market.[460] If upon such consideration, the Commission is of the view that the aid has become incompatible, or is unable to overcome the difficulties involved in determining whether the aid remains compatible with the common market, it is obliged to initiate or re-open the formal investigation procedure under Article 88(2) in order to carry out the requisite consultation.[461] Payment of the aid at issue must be suspended until the Commission adopts a final decision. The Commission is relieved of the obligation to initiate or re-open the formal investigation procedure only in the event of minor deviations from the original conditions which raise no doubt as to whether the aid remains compatible with the common market.[462] Non-compliance with a conditional decision may also constitute misuse of aid[463] by the beneficiary and may trigger the formal investigation procedure pursuant to Article 16 of the Procedural Regulation.

15.087 Variation of conditions.   In cases where aid has been granted subject to conditions and where such aid is to be implemented over a relatively long period of time, the Commission may, in order properly to manage and monitor such implementation, vary the conditions governing the implementation in response to a subsequent change in external circumstances. The Commission may do so without re-opening the formal investigation procedure provided that any variation proposed does not give rise to doubts as to compatibility.[464]

15.088 Failure to comply with a negative or conditional decision taken pursuant to Article 88(2).   If the Commission's decision is not complied with by the prescribed date, the Commission or any other interested Member State may, in derogation from the provisions of Articles 226 and 227 of the Treaty, refer the matter directly to the Court of Justice for a declaration that the defendant Member State has failed to comply.[465] Alternatively, the Commission may bring proceedings under Article 226 but it cannot thereby circumvent the procedural guarantees laid down in Article 88(2) which, *inter alia*, enable a Member State to apply for a special derogation from the Council.[466] If the defendant Member State fails to challenge a negative decision within the two-month time limit laid down by Article 230 of the Treaty, it cannot later challenge the validity of the decision in

---

460 ibid.
461 ibid.
462 ibid.
463 ibid. See now Procedural Reg (n 398, above) Art 1(g).
464 ibid, para 89.
465 Art 88(2) EC, second sub-paragraph. See Case 156/77 *Commission v Belgium* [1978] ECR 1881; Case 52/84 *Boch (No. 1)* [1986] ECR 89, [1987] 1 CMLR 710. If a Member State is required to repeal legislation it is not sufficient for it to cease paying the aid in question: Case 130/83 *Commission v Italy* [1984] ECR 2849, [1985] 1 CMLR 753.
466 Case 290/83 *Commission v France (Caisse nationale de crédit agricole)* [1985] ECR 439, [1986] 2 CMLR 546.

enforcement proceedings brought by the Commission.[467] Similarly, in *TWD Textilwerke Deggendorf (No. 1)*[468] the Court of Justice held, on a reference for a preliminary ruling, that a national court is bound by a decision under Article 88(2) where the recipient of the aid had failed to bring an action for annulment within the time limit laid down by Article 230 of the Treaty.

Monitoring. The Procedural Regulation[469] contains provisions which are **15.089** designed to enable the Commission to supervise and enforce the State aid rules in a manner which was not possible prior to its enactment. Member States are now subject to an obligation to allow Commission officials, together with independent experts, to undertake on-site monitoring visits when the Commission has serious doubts that a decision concerning State aid is being complied with.[470] Such visits may include an inspection of the undertaking in receipt of the aid. Commission officials must be allowed to enter any premises or land of the undertaking concerned; to ask for oral explanations on the spot; and to examine books and other business records and take, or demand, copies. The Commission must inform the Member State concerned in good time of the intended visit and the identity of the authorised officials and experts.[471] There is no requirement in the Procedural Regulation for the Commission or the Member State to notify the undertaking concerned in advance and the Commission's decision to undertake a visit need not be published in the *Official Journal*.[472] Article 22(6) imposes a duty on Member States to assist the Commission in cases where the undertaking objects to a monitoring visit. It remains unclear whether the Commission is obliged to undertake such a visit whenever it entertains a serious doubt concerning compliance with its decisions, with the consequence that a failure to do so may amount to a procedural irregularity leading to a decision being annulled.[473] In addition to these

---

[467] Case 156/77 *Belgium* (n 465, above); Case 52/83 *Commission v France (clothing)* [1983] ECR 3707, [1985] 3 CMLR 278; Case 93/84 *Commission v France (Fishing)* [1985] ECR 829. See also *Lener Ignace SA v Beauvois* [1994] 2 CMLR 419: French Cour de Cassation held that a lawyer could not be liable in damages for failing to make a timely application, on behalf of his client, to the French State for aid which was later declared by the Commission to be incompatible with Art 87.

[468] Case C-188/92 *TWD Texilwerke Deggendorf* [1994] ECR I-833, [1995] 2 CMLR 145. See also Case C-232/05 *Commission v France (Scott Paper SA/Kimberly Clark)* [2006] ECR I-10071, [2007] 3 CMLR 69.

[469] Procedural Reg, Reg 659/1999, OJ 1999 L83/1, amended OJ 2003 L236/345: Vol II, App G.1.

[470] ibid, Art 22(1). The Member State must be given an opportunity to submit comments before the visit takes place.

[471] ibid, Art 22(3). The Member State may object on justified grounds to the Commission's choice of experts in which case experts are to be appointed by agreement with the Member State concerned.

[472] There is no reference to such decisions in Art 26 which deals with publication of decisions.

[473] This question was raised in Case T-111/01 *Saxonia Edelmetalle v Commission* [2005] ECR II-1579, but was not decided because the CFI accepted the Commission's submission that 'serious doubts' had not arisen in that case.

powers of on-site investigation, the Procedural Regulation also requires Member States to report annually to the Commission on all existing aid schemes to which no specific reporting obligation has been attached.[474]

6. The Council's Legislative Powers

15.090 **Article 89.** Article 89 of the Treaty provides that:

> 'The Council, acting by a qualified majority on a proposal from the Commission and after consulting the European Parliament, may make any appropriate regulations for the application of Articles 87 and 88 and may in particular determine the conditions in which Article 88(3) shall apply and the categories of aid exempted from this procedure'.[475]

Pursuant, *inter alia*, to Article 89 the Council has adopted Regulation 1107/70 on the granting of aids for transport by rail, road and inland waterway,[476] Regulation 994/98[477] and the Procedural Regulation.[478] The power of the Council to adopt Regulations on the application of Articles 87 and 88 does not prevent the Commission legislating on the transparency of financial relations between Member States and public undertakings pursuant to Article 86(3).[479]

7. Unlawful Aid and Misuse of Aid

15.091 **In general.** This Section discusses the grant of unlawful aid. Unlawful aid is defined in the Procedural Regulation as new aid put into effect in breach of Article 88(3).[480] Article 10(1) of the Procedural Regulation provides that where the Commission has in its possession information from whatever source regarding alleged unlawful aid, it must examine that information without delay. Further, according to Article 20(2), an interested party may inform the Commission of alleged unlawful aid and alleged misuse of aid.[480A] Misuse of aid is defined as aid used by the beneficiary in contravention of a decision by the Commission pursuant to Article 4(3) of the Procedural Regulation (a decision not to raise

---

[474] Procedural Reg (n 469, above) Art 21.

[475] As amended by the TEU.

[476] Reg 1107/70, JO 1970 L130/1, amended by Reg 1472/75, OJ 1975 L152/1, Reg 1658/82, OJ 1982 L184/1, Reg 1100/89, OJ 1989 L116/24, and Reg 543/97, OJ 1997 L84/6.

[477] See para 15.076, above.

[478] See para 15.069, above.

[479] Cases 188/80, etc, *France, Italy, United Kingdom v Commission* [1982] ECR 2545, [1982] 3 CMLR 144.

[480] Procedural Reg (n 469, above) Art 1(f). See further Hancher, Ottervanger and Slot, *EC State Aids* (3rd edn, 2006), paras 26–003–26–004.

[480A] Any individual or company may submit a complaint to the Commission using the Form for the submission of complaints concerning alleged unlawful State aid, OJ 2003 C116/3: Vol II, App G.5.

objections following a preliminary examination of the aid) or in contravention of a positive or conditional decision following a formal investigation procedure under Article 7 of the Procedural Regulation.[481]

Unnotified aid not automatically incompatible with the common market. Article 88(3) provides: **15.092**

'The Commission shall be informed, in sufficient time to enable it to submit its comments, of any plans to grant or alter aid. If it considers that any such plan is not compatible with the common market having regard to Article 87, it shall without delay initiate the procedure provided for in paragraph 2. The Member State concerned shall not put its proposed measures into effect until this procedure has resulted in a final decision.'

In *Boussac*,[482] the Court of Justice rejected the Commission's submission that a failure to comply with the notification requirement of Article 88(3) automatically rendered an aid incompatible with the common market. The Court considered that the Treaty requires that any finding that an aid is incompatible with the common market should be the outcome of a formal investigation procedure by the Commission under Article 88(2). Thus, even where the Commission finds that an aid was unlawful by reason of the Member State's failure to notify, the Commission will go on to consider whether that aid was compatible with the common market and, if it was, the Commission will not order the aid to be recovered from its recipients.[483]

Aid granted in breach of a Commission decision. In *British Aerospace v Commission*,[484] the Court of Justice annulled a Commission decision requiring the United Kingdom to recover £44.4 million. In an earlier Commission decision **15.093**

---

[481] Procedural Reg, Art 1(g).

[482] Case 301/87 *France v Commission (Boussac)* [1990] ECR I-307, paras 11–24. See also *Tubemeuse* (n 441, above) paras 14–20; *SIDE v Commission* (n 428, above) para 84; Case T-149/95 *J Richard Ducros v Commission* [1997] ECR II-2031, para 49.

[483] See para 15.098, below. A Commission decision finding that unlawful aid was 'compatible with the common market' does not have the effect, however, of regularising *ex post facto* implementing measures that were invalid because they were taken in disregard of the prohibition laid down in the last sentence of Art 88(3). The practical consequences of this are, in principle, to be determined by the national courts, whose duty it is to protect the rights of individuals in circumstances were the obligation of prior notification has not been complied with: see Case C-368/04 *Transalpine Ölleitung in Österreich v Finanzlandesdirektion für Tirol* [2006] ECR I-9957, [2007] 1 CMLR 588, paras 40–59. See also para 15.109, below. In Case C-199/06 *CELF v SIDE*, AG Mazàk stated that a national court remains under a duty to order recovery of aid which was granted in contravention of the notification and standstill obligations in Art 88(3), even if that aid was subsequently declared compatible with the common market by the Commission: Opinion of 24 May 2007, paras 31–33. The judgment of the Court in this case is awaited. In exercising its discretion as to whether to declare an unlawfully granted aid compatible with the common market, the Commission will apply the substantive criteria set out in any relevant frameworks, guidelines, communications and notices which were in force at the time when the aid was granted: see Notice on the determination of the applicable rules for the assessment of unlawful State aid, OJ 2002 C119/22: Vol I, App G.4.

[484] See Case C-294/90 *British Aerospace and Rover v Commission* [1992] ECR I-493, [1992] 1 CMLR 853.

taken in 1989,[485] the Commission had authorised aid consisting of a capital contribution from the United Kingdom government intended to absorb certain debts of the Rover Group in connection with its acquisition by British Aerospace. The aid was authorised subject to a condition, *inter alia*, that the United Kingdom would refrain from granting any further aid to Rover. The Commission later discovered that the United Kingdom had granted British Aerospace a number of financial concessions which were not covered by the 1989 Decision. The Commission took the view that the additional concessions constituted aid and that they were incompatible with the common market since they had been granted in breach of the 1989 Decision. The Commission therefore adopted the contested measure in which it decided that the aid was illegal and should be repaid. The Court of Justice rejected this approach, holding that if the Commission had considered the aid to be in breach of the earlier decision it should have brought the matter to the Court of Justice under the second sub-paragraph of Article 88(2).[486] If, on the other hand, the new aid fell outside the scope of the earlier decision, the Commission had to open the Article 88(2) procedure. What the Commission could not do was to declare the new aid incompatible with the common market without opening the Article 88(2) procedure. In cases of misuse of aid, the Commission may institute or re-institute the formal investigation procedure.[487]

15.094 Request for information and information injunction. When the Commission has information about an alleged unlawful aid or misuse of aid[488] it is entitled to request information from the Member State concerned.[489] The Member State is obliged to provide all necessary information to enable the Commission to take a decision under the preliminary examination or formal investigation procedure.[490] If the Commission's request for information is not complied with, or is only partially complied with, the Commission must issue a formal decision (known as an 'information injunction') requiring the information to be provided within the specified period of time.[491] If the Member State, in breach of the information injunction, fails to provide the requested information the Commission can terminate the procedure and take its decision on the basis of the information available to it.[492]

---

[485] *United Kingdom aid to the Rover Group*, OJ 1989 L25/92.

[486] See also *Ryanair* (n 459, above).

[487] Procedural Reg (n 469, above) Art 16.

[488] ibid, Art 16.

[489] ibid, Art 10(2). Indeed, the Commission may be obliged to invite comments from the Member State: see para 15.119, below.

[490] ibid, Arts 2(2), 5(1) and (2), which, by virtue of Art 10(2), apply to information requested pursuant to that provision.

[491] ibid, Art 10(3).

[492] ibid, Art 13. However, that will not absolve the Commission of the obligation to adopt a properly reasoned decision: see *Saxonia Edelmetalle* (n 473, above) para 145. See also *Scott v Commission* (n 440, above) paras 143–155: a general request to produce information is not sufficiently precise to constitute an information injunction and consequently the Commission was not entitled to base its decision on Art 13.

Suspension injunction. The Commission is entitled, after giving the   **15.095**
Member State an opportunity to comment, to take an interim decision requiring
suspension of unlawful aid or aid that is being misused[493] pending the outcome of
the examination of the aid.[494] If the Commission has doubts as to whether an
individual aid falls within a previously authorised general aid scheme and is thus
uncertain as to the classification of such aid as new or existing aid, it cannot order
suspension but must first order the Member State to supply all information necessary to examine the compatibility of the aid with the previous authorisation.[495]
If the Member State fails to supply the requested information, the Commission
can then seek suspension.

Recovery injunction.   Prior to the adoption of the Procedural Regulation, the   **15.096**
Commission, in the face of continuing breaches of Article 88(3), issued a
Communication[496] to Member States giving notice of its intention to take, in
appropriate cases, a provisional decision (prior to the conclusion of any assessment
of compatibility) ordering a Member State to recover any aid granted in breach of
Article 88(3). The Commission considered that in some cases an interim decision
merely requiring suspension of aid would not go far enough to counteract the
infringement which may have been committed, particularly where all or part of the
aid has already been awarded.[497] However, the Court of First Instance[498] stated that
the only interim measure the Commission may take in relation to non-notified aid
is to direct suspension of the aid and to require provision of all necessary information.
Any legal uncertainty as to the jurisdiction of the Commission to order interim
recovery of unlawful aid was subsequently resolved by Article 11(2) of the Procedural
Regulation which provides that the Commission is entitled, after giving the
Member State an opportunity to submit its comments, to take an interim decision
requiring provisional recovery of the aid pending the outcome of the examination
of the aid. Recovery is effected in the same manner and in accordance with the same
provisions as relate to recovery following a negative decision.[499]

Interrelationship between Article 88(3) and national courts.   A national court   **15.097**
has jurisdiction to declare a new aid put into effect in breach of Article 88(3)
unlawful even if the Commission later decides that the aid is compatible with the

---

493 ibid, Art 16.

494 ibid, Art 11(1). See also *Boussac* (n 482, above); Cases C-342/90 *Germany and Pleuger Worthington v Commission* [1994] ECR I-1173, [1994] 3 CMLR 521, paras 25–26; *SIDE v Commission* (n 428, above) paras 78–87; Case T-107/96 *Pantochim v Commission* [1998] ECR II-311, para 51; *J Richard Ducros* (n 482, above) para 51.

495 Case C-47/91 *Italy v Commission (Italgrani)* [1994] ECR I-4635, paras 34–35.

496 OJ 1995 C156/5. See also its earlier communication on aids granted illegally, OJ 1983 C318/3, [1984] 1 CMLR 214.

497 *XXVth Report on Competition Policy* (1995), point 154.

498 *Pantochim* (n 494, above) para 51.

499 Procedural Reg (n 469, above) Art 11(2).

common market.[500] Such a decision cannot *a posteriori* validate unlawfully granted aid. There is no need for the Member State to make a fresh notification to the Commission after a national court has found the aid to be unlawful because it was not notified in accordance with Article 88(3).[501]

15.098 **Recovery decision.** When the Commission decides[502] that an aid is incompatible with the common market, it issues a decision requiring the Member State concerned to take all necessary measures to recover the aid from the beneficiary (a recovery decision).[503] The Commission cannot, however, require the recovery of aid if this would be contrary to a general principle of Community law.[504] Since recovery of unlawful State aid is the logical consequence of a finding that it is unlawful and the aim of recovery is to restore the previous situation, such recovery is not, in principle, to be regarded as disproportionate to the objectives of the Treaty provisions on State aid. The Commission will, save in exceptional circumstances, not exceed the bounds of its discretion in seeking recovery.[505] The nature of the recovery decision in determining the measures to be taken in order to remove any distortions in competition and to restore the situation prevailing prior to the payment of aid will depend on the nature of the aid measure. For example, in *Cityflyer Express*[506] the Court of First Instance held that the method of recovering two separate aids, one a capital injection and one a repayable loan, could differ.

---

[500] Case 120/73 *Lorenz v Germany* [1973] ECR 1471, para 8. Case C-354/90 *FNCEPA v France* [1991] ECR I-5505, confirmed that the judgments in *Boussac* (n 482, above) and *Tubemeuse* (n 441, above) did not by implication overrule the earlier judgment in *Lorenz*. The ECJ's decision in *FNCEPA* is based on the distinction between the role of national courts, which is that of protecting rights of individuals under Art 88(3), and the role of the Commission which has the exclusive jurisdiction and obligation to examine whether aids are compatible with the common market. See also Cases C-261 & 262/01 *Belgium v Van Calster* [2003] ECR I-12249; [2004] 1 CMLR 607, paras 62–65. See further paras 15.108 *et seq*, below, on the jurisdiction of national courts.

[501] AG Jacobs in *FNCEPA*, above, para 33. It is not the plan to grant aid that is unlawful but the decision to give effect to the aid prematurely.

[502] See Procedural Reg, Reg 659/1999, OJ 1999 L83/1, amended OJ 2003 L236/345: Vol II, App G.1, Art 1(f) and paras 15.091 *et seq*, above.

[503] ibid, Art 14(1). The Commission will lift the corporate veil and seek recovery not just from the original recipient but also from other undertakings controlled by the same persons to which the beneficiary's assets have been transferred: *XXIXth Report on Competition Policy* (1999), point 314. Art 14 does not deal with the situation where the Commission's authorisation of an aid as being compatible with the common market is subsequently annulled by the Community Courts. In Case T-354/99 *Kuwait Petroleum (Nederland) v Commission* [2006] ECR –II-1475, paras 67–68, the CFI held that in the case of an aid scheme, the Commission is not obliged to identify exactly the amount of aid received by individual recipients; the specific circumstances of one of the recipients can be assessed only at the stage of recovery.

[504] Procedural Reg (n 502, above) Art 14(1).

[505] See, eg *Tubemeuse* (n 441, above) para 66; Case C-350/93 *Commission v Italy* [1995] ECR I-1699, para 21; Case C-75/97 *Belgium v Commission (Maribel I)* [1999] ECR 3671, [2000] 1 CMLR 791, paras 64–66; Cases T-298/97, etc, *Alzetta v Commission* [2000] ECR II-2319, para 69; Case C-148/04 *Unicredito Italiano v Agenzia delle Entrate* [2005] ECR I-11137, para 113.

[506] Case T-16/96 *Cityflyer Express v Commission* [1998] ECR II-757, [1998] 2 CMLR 537, paras 54–56.

The Commission could, in the case of a capital injection, decide that the abolition of the competitive advantage granted requires the repayment of the capital; with regard to a loan, however, if the competitive advantage lies in the preferential interest rate rather than the value of the funds made available, the Commission could require the interest rate which would have been charged by a private investor under normal market conditions to be applied and may require the recovery of the difference between that interest rate and the interest actually paid. The Commission, when taking a decision ordering the recovery of unlawful aid, will specify a period of time within which the Member State must inform the Commission of the measures which have been taken in order to comply.[507] The Commission is not required, however, to identify the exact amount of aid which is to be recovered. Rather, it is sufficient for the Commission's decision to include information which will enable the amount of aid to be calculated by the Member State concerned without too much difficulty.[508]

Recovery where recipient's assets have been sold.   Where the recipient of an aid **15.099** has sold the business which benefited from the aid between the time the aid was granted and the time that recovery is sought, it is important to determine whether the proceeds of sale reflected the value of the business including the aid. In *Italy v Commission (Seleco)*,[509] the Court of Justice acknowledged the concern expressed in the Commission's decision that the State aid rules can be frustrated if, once the Commission has begun an investigation into an alleged aid, the assets and liabilities of the firm as an ongoing concern are transferred to another firm controlled by the same persons at below-market prices or by way of procedures that lack transparency. Such transactions cannot be allowed to place the assets out of reach of the Commission decision and continue the economic activity in question indefinitely. In that case, Seleco had sold its shares in its subsidiary, Multimedia.

---

[507] Art 88(2) EC. Strict adherence to the deadline specified by the Commission is required. Dates subsequently specified by the Commission for responding to its reminder or warning letters are without prejudice to the deadline for compliance set in the recovery decision and cannot be regarded as extending it unless they do so expressly: see Cases C-485/03, etc, *Commission v Spain*, [2006] ECR I-11887, paras 53–60.

[508] Case C-480/98 *Spain v Commission (Magefesa)* [2000] ECR I-8717, para 25; *Saxonia Edelmetalle* (n 473, above) para 124; Case C-355/95P *Textilwerke Deggendorf v Commission (No. 2)* [1997] ECR I-2549, [1998] 1 CMLR 234, para 21; Case C-415/03 *Commission v Greece (Aid to Olympic Airways)* [2005] ECR I-3875, [2005] 3 CMLR 207, paras 39–41. See also Case C-382/99 *Netherlands v Commission (Dutch petrol stations)* [2002] ECR I-5163, where the ECJ stated, at para 91, that 'the obligation on a Member State to calculate the exact amount of aid to be recovered ... forms part of the more general reciprocal obligation to co-operate in good faith in the implementation of Treaty rules concerning State aids'. For the Commission's methods for calculating the amount of the unlawful advantage, see para 15.029, above.

[509] Case C-328/99 *Italy v Commission (Seleco)* [2003] ECR I-4035, [2005] 2 CMLR 1169, paras 68–86. See also *Saxonia Edelmetalle* (n 473, above) paras 114–115: since the purpose of recovery of unlawful or misused aid was to remove the competitive advantage and restore the pre-existing situation, recovery had to be effected from the undertaking that actually benefited from the aid.

The Commission had not put forward any evidence to suggest that the valuation of those shares had been reduced because the purchaser accepted a risk that the assets of the subsidiary might be depleted if the aid had to be repaid. The Court therefore held that the Commission was wrong to order recovery against a former subsidiary without having regard to the fact that shares in that company had subsequently been sold to a third party at a public sale pursuant to a court order (and thus apparently at market price). Since the proceeds of sale increased the assets of the parent company which had received the aid, it was possible that the benefit of the aid had remained entirely with the parent rather than being carried by the subsidiary to its new owner.

15.100 **Interest and tax.** In its recovery decision, the Commission must order the payment of interest at a rate determined by it, calculated from the date on which the unlawful aid was at the disposal of the beneficiary until the date of its recovery.[510] The Commission applies compound interest at the commercial rate.[511] In *Siemens*, the Court of First Instance stated that the Commission is not obliged when ordering recovery of the State aid to determine the incidence of tax on the amount of aid to be recovered since that calculation falls to be made under national law.[512] The Court held that this does not preclude the national authorities from deducting certain sums where appropriate from the gross sum to be recovered (such as tax paid) pursuant to internal rules provided that the application of such rules does not render recovery impossible in practice or discriminate in relation to similar cases governed by national law.

15.101 **Limitation period.** The Commission is not entitled to order recovery of aid after a limitation period of 10 years from the day on which the unlawful aid was awarded to the beneficiary either as an individual aid or as aid under an aid scheme.[513] Any action taken by the Commission or by a Member State, acting at the request of the Commission, with regard to the unlawful aid interrupts the limitation period, which then starts to run afresh. Accordingly, the limitation period is interrupted if the Commission writes to the Member State seeking

---

[510] Procedural Reg (n 502, above) Art 14(2).

[511] See Chap V of Commission Reg 794/2004 implementing Council Reg 659/1999 laying down detailed rules for the application of Article 93 of the EC Treaty, OJ 2004 L140/1: Vol II, App G.2. This was in line with the prior Commission communication on the interest rates to be applied when aid granted unlawfully is being recovered, OJ 2003 C110/21. For the rates themselves, see the current edition of the annual Commission notice on State aid recovery interest rates and reference/discount rates, available at http://ec.europa.eu/comm/competition/state_aid/others/reference_rates.html. (For the 2007 rates, see OJ 2006 C317/2.) Similarly, under the EEA regime, see the EFTA Surveillance Authority Decn 195/04/COL, OJ 2006 L139/37, Art 11.

[512] Case T-459/93 *Siemens v Commission* [1995] ECR II-1675, para 83; see also Case T-67/94 *Ladbroke Racing v Commission* [1998] ECR II-1, para 188 (on appeal in Case C-83/98P *France v Ladbroke Racing and Commission* [2000] ECR I-3271, [2000] 3 CMLR 555).

[513] Procedural Reg (n 502, above) Art 15.

information on the suspected aid scheme, even if the aid recipient is not notified of the Commission's concerns at that stage.[514]

The duty of a Member State to seek repayment. The Court of Justice has stated **15.102** that the purpose of the obligation upon Member States to recover aid regarded as incompatible with the common market is to re-establish the previously existing situation.[515] Once a recovery decision is made, the Member State must seek recovery without delay in accordance with national law, acting with the diligence of a private creditor and taking all necessary steps which are available in the domestic legal system, without prejudice to Community law.[516] The recovery of illegally granted aid must take place in accordance with the relevant procedural provisions of national law, subject to the proviso that those provisions are to be applied in such a way that the recovery required by Community law is not rendered practically impossible.[517] Where the recipient is unable to repay the aid the Member State must institute winding-up proceedings and pursue repayment of the aid as an unsecured creditor in the bankruptcy procedure.[518] In certain

---

[514] Case T-366/00 *Scott v Commission* [2003] ECR II-1763, [2004] 1 CMLR 133, [2004] All ER (EC) 473; appeal dismissed, Case C-276/03P *Scott v Commission* [2005] ECI I-8437.

[515] See, eg *Hytasa No. 1* (n 425, above) para 75; Case C-24/95 *Land Rheinland-Pfalz v Alcan Deutschland (Alcan No. 2)* [1997] ECR I-1591, [1997] 2 CMLR 1061, [1997] All ER (EC) 427, para 23. Thus recovery cannot in principle be regarded as disproportionate: see, eg *Tubemeuse* (n 441, above) para 66. See also *Magefesa* (n 508, above) para 33.

[516] Procedural Reg (n 502, above) Art 14(3). See also *Seleco* (n 509, above) paras 65–69. For an analysis of Member States' performance in enforcing recovery, see Mariñas, 'Enforcement of State aid recovery decisions' (2005) 2 EC Competition Policy Newsletter 17; and see generally *Study on Enforcement of State Aid at National Level, Part 2: Recovery of unlawful State aid: enforcement of negative Commission decisions by the Member States* (March 2006), prepared for the EC Commission, available at http://ec.europa.eu/comm/competition/state_aid/studies_reports/study_part_2.pdf.

[517] Case 94/87 *Commission v Germany (Alcan No. 1)* [1989] ECR 175, [1989] 2 CMLR 425, para 12; *Tubemeuse* (n 441, above) para 61; Case C-5/89 *Commission v Germany (BUG-Alutechnik)* [1990] ECR I-3437, [1992] 1 CMLR 117, paras 18–19; and *Alcan (No. 2)* (n 515, above) para 50. In Case C-119/05 *Ministero dell'Industria v Lucchini*, judgment of 18 July 2007, the ECJ ruled that Community law precluded the application of the principle of *res judicata* in Italian law insofar as it would prevent the recovery of aid which an Italian court had determined the aid recipient to be entitled to, but which had been declared by the Commission to have been incompatible with the common market. In the UK, see *Dept of Trade and Industry v British Aerospace* [1991] 1 CMLR 165 (QBD) in which proceedings brought by the DTI pursuant to a Commission decision to recover £44.4m from British Aerospace and Rover were stayed pending the outcome of the appeal of British Aerospace and Rover against that decision, Case C-294/90 *British Aerospace and Rover v Commission* [1992] ECR I-493, [1992] 1 CMLR 853.

[518] *Boch (No. 1)* (n 465, above) para 14; Case C-349/93 *Commission v Italy* [1995] ECR I-343. See also *Tubemeuse* (n 441, above) paras 58–68: the Belgian State had lodged an appeal in the national court against a decision at first instance rejecting its application to be registered as one of the unsecured creditors of the recipient of the aid that was subject to a scheme of composition (ie a form of collective liquidation). The Commission considered that this was sufficient compliance with the State's duty to seek recovery. See also *Magefesa* (n 508, above): a national law which provided that interest could not be claimed on debts of an insolvent undertaking after it had been declared insolvent pursued a general interest objective and did not, therefore, render the recovery of aid required by EC law virtually impossible.

circumstances, such as where the assets of a recipient of an unlawful aid have been transferred to another firm during the formal inquiry phase, the Commission may require recovery to be extended to the latter firm provided that that firm is continuing the economic activity of the aid recipient and certain elements of the transfer point to economic continuity between the two firms.[519] As part of its State Aid Action Plan, the Commission has signalled an intention to be more active in pursuing actions under Articles 88(2), 226 and 228 of the Treaty against Member States who fail to effect recovery of aids 'in an immediate and effective manner'.[520] Repayment of an unlawful aid may take the form of repayment to a public body responsible for managing State funds, the principal objective of repayment being that the recipient forfeits its advantage, provided that the grant of funds to the public body by the State has not been found to be aid incompatible with the common market.[521]

15.103 **Defences open to the Member State: absolute impossibility.** The only defence that a Member State can raise is that it is absolutely impossible for it to implement the Commission decision requiring it to recover the illegal aid from the recipient.[522] A Member State cannot plead absolute impossibility if it has failed to take any step to recover the aid as required by the Commission decision.[523] Nor can a Member State rely on administrative difficulties[524] or provisions, practices or circumstances existing in its internal legal order to justify a failure to

---

[519] *Seleco* (n 509, above) paras 76–78; *Saxonia Edelmetalle v Commission* (n 473, above). See also *Aid to Olympic Airways* (n 508, above) paras 33–36, in which the ECJ held that Greece had failed to fulfil its obligation to recover unlawful aid which had been paid to Olympic Airways. Although the Greek authorities had adopted a decision to proceed with recovery against Olympic Airways of €41 million of unlawful aid, that company had been permitted to transfer all of its assets to a new company, Olympic Airlines, free of all debts, and that transfer had been effected in such a way as to make it impossible under national law for the debts of Olympic Airways to be recovered from the new company. For a case where the proviso referred to in the text did not apply, see Case T-324/00 *CDA Datenträger Albrechts v Commission* [2005] ECR –II-4309, paras 76–117.

[520] *State Aid Action Plan – Less and better targeted State aid: a roadmap for State aid reform 2005-2009*, COM(2005) 107 final–SEC(2005) 795, 7 June 2005, para 53, first indent. With respect to the Action Plan more generally, see para 15.002, above.

[521] Case C-348/93 *Commission v Italy (Alfa Romeo No. 2)* [1995] ECR I-673, paras 24–29.

[522] *Boch (No. 1)* (n 465, above) paras 14–16; *Alcan (No. 1)* (n 517, above) para 8; Case C-349/93 *Commission v Italy* (n 518, above) para 12; Case C-404/97 *Commission v Portugal (EPAC)* [2000] ECR I-4897, para 39. In *Maribel I* (n 505, above) para 86, the ECJ held that absolute impossibility of recovery cannot invalidate the decision where it emerges only at the stage of implementation. See also Case C-378/98 *Commission v Belgium (Maribel II)* [2001] ECR I-5107, paras 30–32, 40–53; Case C-310/99 *Italy v Commission* [2002] ECR I-2289, paras 98–106; *Dutch petrol stations* (n 508, above) paras 91–94; *Aid to Olympic Airways* (n 508, above) para 35.

[523] *Alcan (No. 1)* (n 517, above) paras 10–11; Case C-280/95 *Commission v Italy* [1998] ECR I-259, para 16: mere apprehension of insuperable difficulties could not justify a failure to apply Community law; Case C-6/97 *Italy v Commission (tax credits)* [1999] ECR I-2981, [2000] 2 CMLR 919, para 34; *EPAC* (n 522, above) para 52.

[524] Case C-280/95 *Commission v Italy*, above; *Maribel I* (n 505, above) para 90. See also Case E-2/05 *ESA v Iceland* [2005] EFTA Ct Rep 205, for similar principles applied in the EEA.

comply with its obligations under Community law.[525] The absence of a cause of action under national law for recovery of the sums required by the Commission decision does not absolve a Member State from the obligation to seek recovery of the aid.[526] In *BUG-Alutechnik*,[527] the Court of Justice stated that it is not a defence for a Member State that it has failed to comply with a national time limit for the revocation of an administrative act. In this respect, the Court of Justice has made clear that Community interests must prevail over the national time limits where the Commission decision orders recovery of aid found to be incompatible with the common market.[528] If a Member State encounters, in giving effect to a decision requiring it to obtain repayment, unforeseen and unforeseeable difficulties or perceives consequences overlooked by the Commission it must inform the Commission and propose suitable amendments to the decision.[529] In such a case the Commission and the Member State must respect the principle of sincere cooperation under Article 10 of the Treaty[530] and must work together in good faith with a view to overcoming difficulties whilst fully observing the Treaty provisions, in particular the provisions on aid.[531]

The position of the recipient of the aid.   The recipient of an unlawfully   **15.104** granted State aid is unlikely to be able to avoid repayment and therefore assumes significant risks in accepting aid without consideration of Community State aid rules. Confirming its earlier decisions, the Court of Justice stated in *Alcan (No. 2)*:

> 'Although the Community legal order cannot preclude national [law] which provides that the principles of the protection of legitimate expectations and legal certainty are

---

[525] *BUG-Alutechnik* (n 517, above) paras 18–19; Case C-374/89 *Commission v Belgium* [1991] ECR I-367 (failure to comply with judgment in Case 5/86 *Commission v Belgium* [1987] ECR 1773, [1988] 2 CMLR 258); and *Hytasa (No. 1)* (n 425, above) para 80. cf *Magefesa* (n 508, above) paras 36–39. See also Cases C-485/03, etc, *Commission v Spain* (n 507, above) paras 72–76: a Member State which needs to overcome difficulties in its domestic legal order so as to be able to recover unlawful aid will nevertheless be in breach of its Treaty obligations unless it has, before the implementation deadline specified in the Commission's recovery decision, informed the Commission both of the difficulties and the Member State's proposed means of overcoming them.

[526] Case C-303/88 *Italy v Commission (ENI-Lanerossi)* [1991] ECR I-1433, para 60. The ECJ rejected Italy's argument that because Italian law did not enable recovery from a purchaser of sums that were not taken into account in the conditions of sale it was impossible to comply with the obligation to recover the aids found to be incompatible with the common market. It would therefore seem that a Member State which cannot recover the aid by judicial means may be obliged to enact the necessary legislation in order to achieve recovery.

[527] Case C-5/89 *Commission v Germany (BUG-Alutechnik)* [1990] ECR I-3437, [1992] 1 CMLR 117, para 19. See also *Alcan (No. 2)* (n 515, above) para 37.

[528] *Alcan (No. 2)* (n 515, above) paras 34–38.

[529] *Boch (No. 1)* (n 465, above) para 16. *Alfa Romeo (No. 2)* (n 521, above) para 13; *Maribel I* (n 505, above) para 88; *EPAC* (n 522, above) para 40.

[530] See para 1.030 above.

[531] *Alcan (No. 1)* (n 517, above) para 9; *EPAC* (n 522, above); *Aid to Olympic Airways* (n 508 above) para 42.

to be observed with regard to recovery, it must be noted that, in view of the mandatory nature of the supervision of State aid by the Commission under Article [88] of
the Treaty, undertakings to which aid has been granted may not, in principle, entertain a legitimate expectation that the aid is lawful unless it has been granted in compliance with the procedure laid down in that article. A diligent businessman should
normally be able to determine whether that procedure has been followed.'[532]

15.105 **Legitimate expectation as a defence.** A Member State whose authorities
have granted aid contrary to the rules laid down in Article 88 cannot rely on any
legitimate expectations on the part of the beneficiaries of the aid in order to justify
a failure to seek repayment of the aid; to do so would enable national authorities
to rely on their unlawful conduct in order to deprive Commission decisions of
their effectiveness.[533] The Court of Justice has also rejected arguments that the
State could not recover the aid because this would be a breach of good faith towards
the recipient or because national legislation precluded the recovery of an aid which
had been spent by the recipient and therefore no longer existed. Those arguments
could not succeed because the recipient did not have a legitimate expectation that
the aid was lawful.[534] It is for the recipient undertaking, in the context of proceedings before the public authorities or before the national court, to invoke the existence of exceptional circumstances on the basis of which it entertained legitimate
expectations.[535] However, an aid recipient can rely on the principle of legitimate
expectation to preclude recovery of an unlawfully granted aid only 'in exceptional
circumstances'.[536] Little guidance has been given on what is capable of constituting

---

[532] Case C-24/95 *Land Rheinland-Pfalz v Alcan Deutschland (Alcan No. 2)* [1997] ECR I-1591,
[1997] 2 CMLR 1061, [1997] All ER (EC) 427, para 25. See also *BUG-Alutechnik* (n 527, above)
paras 13–16; *PYRSA* (n 533, below) para 51. See also *Alzetta* (n 505, above) para 121, where the CFI
stated that the recognition of a legitimate expectation presupposes in principle that the aid is granted
in accordance with the procedure in Art 88. Accordingly, an aid recipient cannot rely even on the
conduct of the Commission as creating a legitimate expectation that aid is lawful if the aid has not
been notified to the Commission under Art 88(3): see Cases C-183 & 187/02P *Daewoo Electronics
Manufacturing (DEMESA) v Commission* [2004] ECR I-10609, [2005] 1 CMLR 761, para 45;
Unicredito Italiano (n 505, above) para 104. Nor can an aid recipient rely on the Commission's
delay in taking a decision as founding a legitimate expectation where the aid scheme had been put
into operation before being notified: see Cases C-346 & 529/03 *Atzeni v Regione autonoma della
Sardegna* [2006] ECR I-1875, paras 64–66.

[533] *BUG-Alutechnik* (n 527, above) para 17; Case C-169/95 *Spain v Commission (PYRSA)* [1997]
ECR I-135, para 48 (although the ECJ appeared nonetheless to entertain Spain's argument that the
recovery decision itself was invalid because it breached the recipient's legitimate expectation); Case
T-67/94 *Ladbroke Racing* (n 512, above) para 181. The ECJ rejected France's appeal on this point
on other grounds in Case C-83/98P *France v Ladbroke Racing*,(ibid), para 59.

[534] See *Alcan (No. 2)* (n 515, above) paras 39–54.

[535] *BUG-Alutechnik* (n 527, above) para 16; *Ladbroke Racing* (n 512, above) paras 180–183. It is
not clear whether a beneficiary can rely on exceptional circumstances before the Community Courts
or can only raise this as a defence to recovery proceedings in the national court: see Case T-55/99
CETM v Commission [2000] ECR II-3207, paras 115–123.

[536] *BUG-Alutechnik* (n 527, above) para 16. In *Siemens v Commission* (n 512, above) para
104, the CFI held that Community law does not prevent national law from having regard to the
protection of legitimate expectation in connection with the recovery of State aid, provided that the

'exceptional circumstances'.[537] The Court has referred to the possibility of a national court making a preliminary ruling under Article 234 of the Treaty.[538] The Court of First Instance has not distinguished between the position of beneficiaries of an aid and creditors where the aid is in the form of a State guarantee.[539] The absence of a product from an aid code does not give rise to a legitimate expectation on the part of an aid recipient;[540] nor does the fact that the Commission initially decided to raise no objections to an aid, when its decision was challenged in due time by a third party (and was subsequently annulled).[541] The position may be different when the aid is duly notified and authorised by the Commission and the Commission's authorisation is subsequently annulled by the Community Courts.[542] By contrast, once a decision to open the formal procedure in relation

conditions laid down are the same as those for the recovery of purely national financial benefits and the interests of the Community are fully taken into account; appeal dismissed, Case C-278/95P [1997] ECR I-2507.

[537] In *BUG-Alutechnik* (n 527, above) AG Darmon referred to doubts which some undertakings may have in respect of 'atypical' forms of aid and the requirement of notification: Opinion, para 26. In Case C-39/94 *SFEI* [1996] ECR I-3547, [1996] 3 CMLR 369, [1996] All ER (EC) 685, AG Jacobs, in considering the concept of exceptional circumstances, noted that the provision of logistical and commercial assistance by the French Post Office to a subsidiary did not 'self-evidently constitute aid' and also referred to the fact that the Commission initially decided not to open proceedings: Opinion at paras 73–77. In Case 223/85 *RSV v Commission* [1987] ECR 4617, [1989] 2 CMLR 259, the ECJ annulled a Commission decision ordering repayment of an unlawfully granted aid because of the undue length of the Art 88(2) procedure (26 months). Note, however, that the facts of that case arose prior to the Notice of 24 November 1983 on the risk of repayment of unlawfully granted aid, OJ 1983 C318/3, [1984] 1 CMLR 214. In Case T-171/02 *Regione autonoma della Sardegna v Commission* (n 448, above) paras 64–70, the CFI rejected a submission that a legitimate expectation had arisen on the basis of the exceptional duration of the Art 88(2) procedure, including a seven-month period of silence from the Commission following the Member State's response to the Commission's last information request, since the Commission had remained under an obligation to close the formal investigation procedure by taking a decision. See also *CETM*, above, paras 119–154; Case T-6/99 *ESF Elbe-Stahlwerke Feralpi v Germany* [2001] ECR II-1523, para 190.

[538] *BUG-Alutechnik* (n 527, above) para 16.

[539] *EPAC* (n 522, above) para 144. See also, *per* AG Cosmas, Opinion at para 102, in Cases C-329/93, etc, *Germany v Commission (Bremer Vulkan)* [1996] ECR I-5151, [1998] 1 CMLR 591, and paras 6.4–6.5 of the Commission Notice on the application of Arts 87 and 88 of the Treaty to State aid in the form of guarantees, OJ 2000 C71/14 and para 15.038, above. See also Lever, 'State guarantees as State aid: The effects of European Community law', *Butterworths Journal of International Banking and Financial Law*, Special Supp, February 2002.

[540] Case 310/85 *Deufil v Commission* [1987] ECR 901, [1988] 1 CMLR 553, paras 20–25. The ECJ held that the market situation did not justify polypropylene yarn being treated differently from other synthetic yarns although at the relevant time, it was excluded from the aid code on synthetic fibres. In any event the omission of polypropylene yarn from the aid code at the relevant time was simply because it was a new product; it was subsequently included in the revised aid code in 1985.

[541] *PYRSA* (n 533, above) para 53. The successful challenge was in Case C-198/91 *William Cook v Commission* [1993] ECR I-2487, [1993] 3 CMLR 206.

[542] In Case C-199/06 *CELF v SIDE*, however, AG Mazàk stated that the principle of legitimate expectation should not normally prevent recovery of aid the grant of which was authorised by a Commission decision which was subsequently annulled, since a diligent businessman should be aware that Commission decisions took effect subject to the possibility of their being declared invalid

to a particular measure has been published, potential beneficiaries of that measure are put on notice of the uncertainty concerning its legality and cannot, therefore, have a legitimate expectation that the measure is lawful.[543] Since repayment of the aid together with interest is the logical consequence of a decision that an aid is incompatible with the common market and is intended to re-establish the previous existing situation, such a result is unlikely to be in breach of the principle of proportionality.[544]

15.106 **Legitimate expectation: existing aids.** The Commission accepts that where it decides that an existing aid is no longer compatible with the common market, recipients of that aid are entitled to a transitional period in which to adjust their businesses to the removal of the aid. The Court of Justice considered the extent of this entitlement in *Belgian Coordination Centres*.[545] The Commission had examined the tax regime for authorised 'coordination centres' when it was adopted in 1982 and had issued decisions in 1987 finding that it did not contain any aid element. However, following a comprehensive review of tax arrangements, the Commission took a decision finding that the regime was an existing aid which was incompatible with the common market. The Commission decision recognised the legitimate expectation of the authorised coordination centres that their exempt tax status would last until December 2010. However, under the decision, centres whose authorisation expired before 2010 would not be able to renew it even temporarily. The Court of Justice stated that it was common ground that the Commission's initial decision in 1987 had created an expectation that the regime did not contain an aid element. Further, the facts established that coordination centres would ordinarily expect their authorisation to be renewed without any difficulty. In the light of this, the Court held that the centres had a legitimate expectation that a Commission decision reversing its previous approach would give them the time necessary to address that change in approach. Those coordination centres with an application for renewal of their authorisation pending on the date on which the contested decision was notified, or with an authorisation which expired at the same time as or shortly after that decision was notified, had a legitimate expectation that a reasonable transitional period would be granted in order for them to adjust to the consequences of that decision. In that regard, the

---

by the Community Courts: Opinion of 24 May 2007, paras 42–46. The judgment of the Court is awaited in this case.

[543] Cases E-5/04, etc, *Fesil v EFTA Surveillance Authority* [2005] 3 CMLR 470, para 172. See also Case C-310/99 *Italy v Commission* (n 522, above) para 102.

[544] See, eg Case C-142/87 *Belgium v Commission (Tubemeuse)* [1990] ECR I-959, [1991] 3 CMLR 213; *PYRSA* (n 533, above) para 47; *Alzetta* (n 505, above) para 169; *CETM* (n 536, above) paras 160–163.

[545] Cases C-182 & 217/03 *Belgium v Commission (Belgian Coordination Centres)* [2006] ECR I-5479, paras 161–167.

expression 'shortly after' was to be understood as referring to a date so close to that on which the contested decision was notified that the coordination centres concerned did not have the time required to adjust to the change in the regime in question. Given that there was no overriding public interest taking precedence over that expectation, the Court annulled the Commission's decision insofar as it failed to make transitional provision for centres in that category.

Right to repayment of unlawfully levied charges.   In some cases, a Member **15.107** State puts in place an unlawful aid scheme under which aid provided to some undertakings contrary to Article 88(3) is funded by a tax or fiscal charge imposed on other persons specifically for that purpose. Where the circumstances are such that the tax or charge is properly to be regarded as an integral part of the aid measure, those taxes or charges will have been levied contrary to Community law and the persons on whom they were unlawfully levied will have a right to have those charges repaid to them.[546] A tax or charge will only be regarded as an integral part of the aid measure, however, in cases where the proceeds of the tax or charge were specifically hypothecated to the provision of the unlawful aid.[547] A tax or charge will only be regarded as having been hypothecated to the provision of unlawful aid if the revenue from the tax or charge is necessarily allocated to the financing of the aid and has a direct impact on the amount of the aid.[548] The Court has held that the proceeds of a tax are not hypothecated to an exemption from the payment of that same tax.[549] In *Banks*, it was held that undertakings that have paid the tax cannot rely on the State aid rules so as obtain repayment of the tax.[550] The remedy for the unlawful aid is to require the Member State concerned to recover the value of that aid from the beneficiaries of the tax exemption. However, in *Laboratories Boirin*[551] the Court of Justice reached a different conclusion where a tax was imposed on the direct distribution of pharmaceutical products by producers

---

[546] *Belgium v Van Calster* (n 500, above) paras 52–53; Case C-174/02 *Streekgewest Westelijk Noord-Brabant v Staatssecretaris van Financiën* [2005] ECR I-85, para 16. See also Case C-526/04 *Laboratories Boiron v URSSAF* [2006] ECR I-7529, [2006] 3 CMLR 1414.

[547] *Streekgewest Westelijk Noord-Brabant*, above, paras 25–26; Case C-175/02 *F J Pape v Minister van Landbouw* [2005] ECR I-127, para 15; Cases C-266/04, etc, *Distribution Casino France (formerly Nazairdis) v Organic* [2005] ECR I-9481, paras 34–57. It does not appear to be sufficient that the funding of the aid measure was one of the express purposes of the tax or charge.

[548] See Cases C-393/04 & 41/05 *Air Liquide Industries Belgium* [2006] ECR I-5293, [2006] 3 CMLR 667, para 46.

[549] *Air Liquide*, above.

[550] Case C-390/98 *HJ Banks v Commission* [2001] ECR I-6117, [2001] 3 CMLR 1285, para 80 (a case under Art 4 of the (now expired) ECSC Treaty); *Distribution Casino France* (n 547, above) paras 42 and 44; *Air Liquide* (n 548, above) para 43; cf Opinion of AG Tizzano at paras 33–57, distinguishing the position where a tax is imposed on one sector to offset costs incurred by another sector. See also Case C-368/04 *Transalpine Ölleitung in Österreich* (n 483, above), paras 49–52.

[551] Case C-526/04 *Laboratories Boiron v URSSAF* [2006] ECR I-7529, [2006] 3 CMLR 1414. This litigation arose out of the same legislation that gave rise to the earlier case of Case C-53/00 *Ferring v ACOSS* [2001] ECR I-9067, [2003] 1 CMLR 1001.

but not on distribution by wholesalers. The purpose of the tax was to equalise the conditions of competition between the two distribution channels since wholesalers were under public interest obligations that were not imposed on producers. The Court of Justice ruled that the producers that had paid the tax were entitled to seek reimbursement as the aid measure was the tax on direct distribution rather than an exemption from a general tax.[552]

8. Judicial Remedies

(a) National courts

15.108 **Existing aids.**   In *Ianelli & Volpi*,[553] the Court of Justice held that Article 87(1) does not have direct effect since there are exceptions to its application set out in Article 87(2) and Articles 87 and 88 give the Commission a wide discretion and the Council wide powers to authorise aids in derogation from the general declaration of incompatibility in Article 87(1). The Commission has, subject to the Council's powers, exclusive jurisdiction to review aids under Article 88. Therefore, in the absence of a Commission decision, existing aids[554] cannot be prohibited by national courts. On the other hand, a national court is entitled to determine whether a measure is an aid and, if so, whether it is an existing aid rather than a new aid (including an alteration to an existing aid). This question is relevant when deciding whether that measure falls under the Treaty provisions on State aids or under other Treaty provisions,[555] and also in deciding whether there has been a violation of the last sentence of Article 88(3).[556]

---

[552] *Laboratories Boiron*, above, paras 33–48.

[553] Case 74/76 *Ianelli & Volpi v Meroni* [1977] ECR 557, [1977] 2 CMLR 688, para 11–14. See also Case 6/64 *Costa v ENEL* [1964] ECR 585, [1964] CMLR 425; Case 77/72 *Capolongo v Maya* [1973] ECR 611, [1974] 1 CMLR 230; Case 78/76 *Steinike and Weinlig v Germany* [1977] ECR 595, [1977] 2 CMLR 688; *Boussac* (n 482, above) para 15; *FNCEPA* (n 500, above) para 14.

[554] As to the meaning of an existing aid, see para 15.070, above.

[555] For a consideration of other Treaty provisions that may be relevant, see paras 15.128 *et seq*, below.

[556] See, eg the ruling by the Dutch Supreme Court that the court faced with a request for an interim injunction preventing implementation of a non-notified measure must itself reach a view on whether the measure is likely to constitute a State aid if that issue is disputed: the fact that the Commission has commenced a procedure under Art 88(2) is not sufficient: *City of Alkmaar*, judgment of 7 October 2005, NJ 2006, 131; RvdW 2005, 111 (annulling the grant of an injunction on that ground by the Amsterdam Court of Appeal regarding the financing of a new football stadium by the Alkmaar municipality). See further *UPC Nederland v City of Amsterdam*, Amsterdam Court of Appeal, judgment of 18 January 2007, 1252/06 KG, refusing an interim injunction to halt municipal funding of an optical fibre telecommunications project although the Commission had initiated a procedure under Art 88(2), on the grounds that the project was likely to satisfy the 'market economy investor' test and therefore should not constitute a State aid.

New aids (including alterations to existing aids).   In contrast to Article 87(1),   **15.109**
the prohibition, imposed by Article 88(3), on the implementation of a new aid
prior to the notification to, and the assessment by, the Commission of that aid has
direct effect.[557] In *FNCEPA*,[558] the Court of Justice stated that its judgment in
Boussac[559] did not affect the principle, established by its previous case law, that
national courts are obliged to order recovery of aid which has been granted in
contravention of the requirements of Article 88(3), and do not have jurisdiction
themselves to declare aids to be compatible with the common market. In *Boussac*,
the Court held that the Commission could not condemn a new aid or an alteration to an existing aid as being incompatible with the common market merely
because the Member State had failed to notify the aid in accordance with
Article 88(3). The Court of Justice contrasted the different roles of the Commission
and the courts of the Member States: the former has the exclusive role of deciding
whether aids are compatible with the Treaty, whereas the latter have the duty
to protect the rights of individuals in a case where there has been a breach of
Article 88(3).[560] The prohibition on implementing the aid before it is approved
is thus absolute. It is not affected by the initiation of a preliminary examination
under Article 88(3) by the Commission or indeed by any delay on the part of the
Commission in completing the preliminary examination.[561] Even if the Commission subsequently decides that the aid is compatible with the common market,
that cannot validate *a posteriori* measures taken in breach of Article 88(3). The
Commission would be acting outside its competence if it attempted to provide
express validation for such measures.[562] National courts are obliged, therefore, to
give effect to individual rights under this provision and must provide remedies,
according to national procedural rules, for a failure to notify a new aid.[563] National
courts are obliged to provide for all appropriate remedies,[564] which may include

---

[557] *Costa v ENEL* (n 553, above); *Lorenz v Germany* (n 500, above) para 8; *FNCEPA* (n 500,
above) paras 8–16; *SFEI* (n 537, above) para 39.
   [558] Case C-354/90 *FNCEPA v France* [1991] ECR I-5505. See also Case C-119/05 *Ministero
dell'Industria v Lucchini*, judgment of 18 July 2007, paras 51–52, and n 483, above.
   [559] Case 301/87 *France v Commission (Boussac)* [1990] ECR I-307, paras 11–24.
   [560] See also *SFEI* (537, above) paras 34–52.
   [561] ibid, para 44.
   [562] *FNCEPA* (n 558, above) paras 15–16; *Belgium v Van Calster* (n 500, above) paras 62–63 &
73–77; *SFEI* (n 537, above) para 67; *Transalpine Ölleitung in Österreich* (n 483, above) para 41.
   [563] See *FNCEPA* (n 558, above) para 12, and the Opinion of AG Jacobs at 5520–5522; *SFEI*
(n 537, above) paras 39–48, 67–71.
   [564] AG Jacobs in *Boussac* (n 559, above) para 37 of his Opinion. See generally the *Study on
Enforcement of State Aid at National Level, Part 1: Application of EC State aid rules by national courts*
(March 2006), prepared for the EC Commission, discussing various national court judgments,
available at http://ec.europa.eu/comm/competition/state_aid/studies_reports/study_part_1.pdf.

declarations,[565] repayment of aids illegally granted,[566] interim relief[567] and possibly also damages against the national administration arising from the illegal grant of aids.[568] As regards repayment of aid, the Court of Justice has stated that a finding by a national court that an aid had been granted in breach of the final sentence in Article 88(3) must, in principle, lead to its repayment (in accordance with domestic rules) regardless of whether any subsequent Commission decision finds the aid to be compatible with the common market.[569] In addition, where a Member State has levied a tax or fiscal charge which formed an integral part of the unlawful aid measure, any person on whom the levy was imposed will have standing before the national courts to seek repayment of that levy, regardless of whether that person is a competitor of the aid recipient.[570] In affording remedies,

---

[565] See, eg the English Court of Appeal in *R v Attorney General, ex p ICI* [1987] 1 CMLR 72. See also AG Tesauro in *Tubemeuse* (n 544, above), Opinion at para 9, referring to two judgments of the Italian Constitutional Court where laws granting aid approved by the Regional Assembly prior to the completion of the Community verification procedure were declared unconstitutional; and AG Tesauro in Cases C-17/91, etc, *Lornoy en Zonen v Belgium* [1992] ECR I-6523, 6537.

[566] AG Jacobs in *Boussac* (559, above) para 37. See Case 14 O Kart 176/04, judgment of 28 July 2006, where the Regional Court of Kiel held that a favourable tariff granted to one airline by the publicly owned operator of Lübeck airport constituted a State aid which had not been notified to the Commission and ordered the operator to give information about the tariff agreement to the plaintiff (a competing airline) so that it could pursue its claim that the rebate element be repaid.

[567] AG Tesauro in *Tubemeuse* (n 544, above) para 7 at 985 (ECR), 229 (CMLR). For guidance on how an English court would exercise its discretion in the grant of interim relief, see *R v Secretary of State for Transport, ex p Factortame Ltd (No. 2)* [1991] 1 AC 603 (HL); *R v HM Treasury, ex p British Telecommunications* [1994] 1 CMLR 621 (CA); *R v Secretary of State for Health, ex p Imperial Tobacco* [2002] QB 161. See also Case C-432/05 *Unibet* [2007] 2 CMLR 725, paras 78–83.

[568] AG Tesauro in *Tubemeuse* (n 544, above); AG Jacobs in *SFEI* (n 537, above) Opinion, para 77. For the availability of damages for breach of Community law by Member States, see Cases C-6 & 9/90 *Francovich* [1991] ECR I-5357, [1993] 2 CMLR 66; Cases C-46 & 48/93 *Brasserie du Pêcheur and Factortame* [1996] ECR I-1029, [1996] 1 CMLR 889, [1996] QB 404, [1996] All ER (EC) 301; Case C-392/93 *R v HM Treasury, ex p British Telecommunications* [1996] ECR I-1631, [1996] QB 615, [1996] All ER (EC) 411; Cases 178/94, etc, *Dillenkofer v Germany* [1996] ECR I-4845, [1996] 3 CMLR 469, [1997] QB 259, [1997] All ER (EC) 917; Case C-229/01 *Köbler* [2003] ECR I-10239, [2003] 3 CMLR 1003, [2004] QB 848, [2004] All ER (EC) 23. See also *Betws Anthracite v DSK Anthrazit Ibbenburen* [2003] EWHC 2403 (Comm), [2004] 1 CMLR 61, [2004] 1 All ER 1237, where the English High Court held that EC law did not give a person a cause of action to rely on a decision addressed to a Member State as against the recipient of unlawful State aid mentioned in that decision.

[569] *SFEI* (n 537, above) paras 67–69. See also AG Jacobs at para 70 of his Opinion. In *Transalpine Ölleitung in Österreich* (n 483, above) paras 40–59, the ECJ confirmed that the duty of the national courts to safeguard the rights of individuals against possible disregard, by the national authorities, of the prohibition on putting aid into effect before the Commission has adopted a decision authorising that aid, continues even after the Commission has declared that the aid to have been compatible with the Community. The Court stopped short, however, of holding that national courts were obliged to order repayment of such aid, instead stating that the availabilities of remedies depended on national law, subject to adherence to the principles of equivalence and effectiveness. See also n 483, above.

[570] *Streekgewest Westelijk Noord-Brabant* (n 547, above) para 19. See also para 15.107, above. In view of the Commission's application of compound interest at the commercial rate when

however, the national courts should keep in mind the objective of safeguarding the rights of individuals by neutralising the effects of the aid on competitors of the recipient undertakings. The courts should avoid ordering measures which would have the effect of extending the circle of aid recipients and thus increasing the effects of that aid rather than eliminating those effects.[571]

Enforcement of Commission decisions. Where the Commission takes a **15.110** decision pursuant to Article 88(2) holding that a particular aid is incompatible with the common market and requires repayment, the national authorities have an absolute duty to seek recovery.[572] Hence, where a Member State has failed to obtain full repayment of an unlawful aid, a third party (such as a competitor of the aid recipient) may seek a remedy from the national courts against the State to whom the Commission decision was addressed.[573] Community law does not, however, appear to require national courts to entertain a claim by such a third party directly against the aid recipient.[574] An aid recipient who did not bring an action for annulment of the Commission's decision within the time laid down by the Article 230 cannot re-open the validity of that decision before the national court and obtain an Article 234 reference to the Court of Justice, thereby circumventing the time limit.[575]

---

calculating amounts of unlawful aid that should be recovered (see para 15.100, above), thus ensuring that the full benefit of the unlawful aid is disgorged from the recipient undertaking, it may also be the case that national courts are obliged to apply compound interest when ordering the repayment of unlawfully levied charges: see *Sempra Metals Ltd (formerly Metallgesellschaft Ltd) v Inland Revenue Commissioners* [2005] EWCA Civ 389, [2006] QB 37, [2005] 2 CMLR 30 (English Court of Appeal), appeal to the House of Lords pending.

[571] See also Case C-368/04 *Transalpine Ölleitung in Österreich* (n 483, above), paras 49–52.
[572] See para 15.102, above. See also Mariñas (n 516, above).
[573] See Case T-354/99 *Kuwait Petroleum v Netherlands* (n 503, above) para 69.
[574] See *Anthracite v DSK Anthrazit Ibbenburen* (n 568, above).
[575] Case C-188/92 *TWD Textilwerke Deggendorf (No. 1)* [1994] ECR I-833, [1995] 2 CMLR 145, paras 17–18. This rule only applies, however, where the person challenging the validity of the Commission decision would have had standing to bring an action for annulment under Art 230: see *Atzeni v Regione autonoma della Sardegna* (n 532, above) paras 30–34 (although a previous action for annulment brought by Atzeni and others had been ruled inadmissible by the CFI on the ground that it had been brought out of time, the ECJ still accepted an Art 234 reference concerning the validity of the same contested decision since it was 'not self-evident' that Atzeni and the other challengers had standing to bring the previous Art 230 action). As to standing generally, see para 15.091, below. In *HJ Banks v Commission* (n 550, above) paras 111–113, the ECJ held that H J Banks' failure to bring an action for the annulment of a Commission decision authorising a series of aid measures to British Coal did not prevent H J Banks from challenging before the national courts the compatibility with the State aid prohibition in Art 4(c) of the (now expired) ECSC Treaty of its liability to pay mining licence royalties to the Coal Authority which British Coal and its successors did not have to pay; but note that the ECJ explained its conclusion on the basis that the Commission had not truly decided the compatibility of the royalty arrangements with Art 4(c), at least insofar as royalties continued to be payable after the time period in respect of which the aid measures had been authorised had expired. Thus, *HJ Banks* can be reconciled with *TWD*, at least in terms of the legal principles applied.

15.111 **Notice on cooperation between national courts and the Commission in the State aid field.** The Commission has issued a Notice on cooperation between national courts and the Commission in the State aid field[576] which is similar in nature to the Commission Notice on cooperation between national courts and the Commission in applying Articles 81 and 82 of the EC Treaty.[577] The Notice sets out the respective powers and functions of the Commission and national courts and expressly encourages national courts to contact the Commission when in difficulty. It provides a procedure for national courts to ask the Commission for information of a procedural nature in a particular case and for assistance in the application of Articles 87(1) and 88(3). The answers given by the Commission will not deal with the substance of the individual case or the compatibility of the measure with the common market. A summary of the answers given by the Commission pursuant to the Notice is published in the annual Reports on Competition Policy. The Court of Justice has held that the Commission is under a duty to respond to requests under the Notice as quickly as possible.[578]

(b) The Community Courts

(i) Reviewable acts

15.112 **Generally.** Article 230 grants the Community Courts jurisdiction to review the legality of acts of the Council and Commission.[579] All actions pursuant to Article 230 are now heard by the Court of First Instance.[580] In the field of State aids, decisions of the Commission that have been challenged by such proceedings include a decision to open the formal procedure under Article 88(2),[581]

---

[576] Notice on cooperation between national courts and the Commission in the State aid field, OJ 1995 C312/8: Vol II, App G.3.

[577] Commission Notice on the cooperation between the Commission and the courts of the EU Member States in the application of Articles 81 and 82 EC, OJ 2004 C101/54: Vol II, App B.9. See generally, paras 14.054 *et seq*, above.

[578] *SFEI* (n 537, above) para 50.

[579] As to review under Art 230, see generally paras 13.217 *et seq*, above, and the specialist works on the ECJ cited at n 1072 to para 13.211, above. On the right to seek interim relief, see paras 15.124 *et seq*, below.

[580] See para 13.000, above. There is a right of appeal from the CFI to the ECJ on points of law: Arts 56–58 of the Protocol on the Statute of the ECJ.

[581] See, eg Case C-312/90 *Spain v Commission* [1992] ECR I-4117; Case C-47/91 *Italy v Commission* [1992] ECR I-4145. A decision to initiate the formal investigation procedure in relation to a measure which is already being implemented, and to classify that measure as new aid, can itself be challenged under Art 230 since such a decision will necessarily alter the legal implications of the measure under consideration and the legal position of the recipient firms, in particular because, unless interim relief can be obtained from the Community Courts, the Member State will have to suspend its application of the measure: see Case C-400/99 *Italy v Commission (Tirrenia Group)* [2005] ECR I-3657, [2005] 3 CMLR 611; Case T-269/99 *Diputación Foral de Guipúzcoa v Commission* [2002] ECR II-4217, [2003] 1 CMLR 298; Cases T-195 & 207/01 *Government of Gibraltar v Commission* [2002] ECR II-2309, [2002] 2 CMLR 826, [2002] All ER (EC) 838,

a decision that an aid does not require notification under Article 88(3),[582] a decision not to open the formal procedure under Article 88(2),[583] a decision under Article 88(2) holding that an aid is incompatible with the common market,[584] a decision under Article 88(2) requiring repayment of an aid,[585] a decision that aid paid in breach of an earlier decision under Article 88(2) be repaid,[586] a decision terminating the procedure under Article 88(2),[587] and a decision to extend the validity of a Community framework for State aid.[588] By contrast, a refusal by the Commission to propose appropriate measures under Article 88(1) is not a decision capable of being judicially reviewed since it does not have binding legal effects.[589] A judgment given by the Court of First Instance or the Court of Justice is invested with the force of *res judicata* which prevents legal questions which it has settled from being re-examined not only by the same parties but also by third parties.[590] Actions may also lie against the Commission under

---

para 85; Cases T-346/99, etc, *Diputación Foral de Álava v Commission* [2002] ECR II-4259, paras 34–36.

[582] Case C-313/90 *CIRFS v Commission* [1993] ECR I-1125.

[583] *CIRFS*, above; *William Cook v Commission* (n 541, above); Case C-225/91 *Matra v Commission (No. 1)* [1993] ECR I-3203; Case T-11/95 *BP Chemicals v Commission (No. 1)* [1998] ECR II-3235, [1998] 3 CMLR 693; Case T-82/96 *ARAP v Commission* [1999] ECR II-1889, [1999] 2 CMLR 1411.

[584] Case 730/79 *Philip Morris v Commission* [1980] ECR 2671, [1981] 2 CMLR 321.

[585] *Boussac* (n 559, above); *Tubemeuse* (n 544, above); *ENI-Lanerossi* (n 526, above); Case C-305/89 *Commission v Italy (Alfa Romeo No. 1)* [1991] ECR I-1603.

[586] Case C-294/90 *British Aerospace and Rover v Commission* [1992] ECR I-493, [1992] 1 CMLR 853.

[587] Case 169/84 *COFAZ v Commission* [1986] ECR 391, [1986] 3 CMLR 385; Case C-169/84 *CdF Chimie AZF v Commission* [1990] ECR I-3083, [1992] 1 CMLR 177; Case T-14/96 *BAI v Commission* [1999] ECR II-139, [1999] 3 CMLR 245.

[588] Case C-135/93 *Spain v Commission (motor vehicle framework No. 1)* [1995] ECR I-1651; Case C-292/95 *Spain v Commission (motor vehicle framework No. 2)* [1997] ECR I-1931.

[589] Case T-330/94 *Salt Union v Commission* [1996] ECR II-1475. Prior to the coming into force of the Procedural Reg, the ECJ held in Case C-367/95P *Commission v Sytraval and Brink's France* [1998] ECR I-1719, that a letter informing a complainant that the Commission had decided not to initiate the procedure under Art 88(2) was not a decision subject to judicial review. Proceedings had to be brought against a decision addressed to the Member State. The reasoning of the ECJ proceeded on the basis that no provision was made in either the Treaty or State aid legislation for decisions dealing with complaints.

[590] Cases C-442 & 471/03P *P&O European Ferries and others v Commission* [2006] ECR I-4845, paras 38–52. cf Case T-354/99 *Kuwait Petroleum v Commission* (n 503, above) paras 36–39 decided on 31 May 2006, that is to say a day before the ECJ's judgment in *P&O*. The approach in *P&O* is to be contrasted with the narrower concept of *res judicata* in English law, see *Iberian UK Limited v BPB Industries* [1996] 2 CMLR 601.

Articles 232 for failure to act,[591] and for non-contractual damages under Article 288[592] of the Treaty.

(ii) Applicants before the Community Courts

15.113 **Actions by the Commission.** The Commission can enforce a negative decision under Article 88(2) by referring the matter direct to the Court of Justice under the second sub-paragraph of Article 88(2) rather than having to initiate proceedings under Article 226.[593] Where a Member State fails to comply with a suspension injunction or recovery injunction,[594] the Commission may also apply directly to the Court of Justice for a declaration.[595] In addition, the Commission can bring proceedings under Article 226. This may be appropriate if it considers that the measure is also contrary to other provisions of Community law.[596] The Commission cannot, however, unilaterally terminate the procedure under Article 88(2) and start proceedings under Article 226 to obtain a declaration that a measure is an aid that is incompatible with the common market. Such a course would deprive the Member State of the guarantees laid down under Article 88(2).[597]

---

[591] Case 59/79 *Fédération nationale des producteurs de vins v Commission* [1979] ECR 2925; Cases 166 & 220/86 *Irish Cement Ltd v Commission* [1988] ECR 6473, [1989] 2 CMLR 57; Case T-277/94 *AITEC v Commission* [1996] ECR II-351; Case T-107/96 *Pantochim v Commission* [1998] ECR II-311; Case T-95/96 *Gestevisión Telecinco v Commission* [1998] ECR II-3407, [1998] 3 CMLR 1112; Case T-17/96 *Télévision française 1 v Commission* [1999] ECR II-1757, [2000] 4 CMLR 678; and see also *Sytraval* (n 589, above) and Art 20(2) of the Procedural Reg, Reg 659/1999, OJ 1999 L83/1, amended OJ 2003 L236/345: Vol II, App G.1. Delay on the part of the Commission in responding to a complaint may provide a basis for a successful challenge under Art 232, but only where that delay is such as to amount to a failure to act: Case T-395/04 *Air One v Commission* [2006] ECR II-1343 (the failure by the Commission to take a decision within nine months as to whether to investigate the substance of a complaint or reject a request for protective measures was not, in the circumstances of the case, outside a reasonable period of time, and hence there was no failure to act). See also Case T-167/04 *Asklepios Kliniken v Commission*, judgment of 11 July 2007. The Community Courts are not competent to issue directions to other institutions in the context of an action under Art 232, but are confined to determining whether there had been a failure to act; and it is then for the institution concerned, pursuant to Art 233, to take the measures necessary to comply with the order of the Court: *Air One*, para 24.

[592] The Community Courts have jurisdiction over such actions pursuant to Art 235. See *Pantochim v Commission*, above; Case T-230/95 *BAI v Commission* [1999] ECR II-123; and also in this context Case C-55/90 *Cato v Commission* [1992] ECR I-2533, [1992] 2 CMLR 459: Art 288 action in respect of the Commission's approval of a UK scheme for decommissioning grants in the fishing industry.

[593] See also Procedural Reg (n 591, above) Art 23.

[594] See paras 15.095 and 15.096, above.

[595] Procedural Reg, Art 12.

[596] See, eg Case 73/79 *Commission v Italy* [1980] ECR 1533, [1982] 1 CMLR 1, where the Commission challenged an internal tax as being contrary to Arts 87, 88 and 90. See also Case 290/83 *Commission v France (Caisse nationale de crédit agricole)* [1985] ECR 439, [1986] 2 CMLR 546. The relationship between Arts 87–89 and other Treaty provisions is discussed at paras 15.128 *et seq*, below.

[597] *Crédit agricole*, above, paras 16–19.

Actions by Member States and regional bodies.   A Member State can seek   **15.114**
annulment under the second paragraph of Article 230 of the Treaty of any binding
act taken by one of the Community institutions.[598] A regional body can bring
annulment proceedings under the fourth paragraph of Article 230 against a decision, which, although addressed to a Member State,[599] is of direct and individual
concern to it.[600] Thus where an aid has been granted by a regional body which
has an autonomous status it has *locus standi* to bring annulment proceedings
in respect of a negative decision in respect of that aid and its interest in bringing
proceedings is not subsumed in that of the Member State.[601] An interested
Member State has the same rights as the Commission to bring proceedings before
the Court of Justice under the second sub-paragraph of Article 88(2) in order to
enforce a Commission decision.

Actions by private parties against decisions prohibiting aid.   A private party   **15.115**
will never be the addressee of a decision in the State aid field, since State aid
decisions are addressed to Member States. A private party will therefore have
locus standi to challenge a decision under Article 230 only if that decision is of
direct and individual concern to him. The main stumbling block is whether the
decision is of *individual* concern. That will be the case only 'if the decision affects
them by reason of certain attributes which are peculiar to them or by reason of
circumstances in which they are differentiated from all other persons and by
virtue of those factors distinguishes them individually just as in the case of the
person addressed'.[602] In *Philip Morris*,[603] it was not disputed that a potential
recipient of an individual aid has *locus standi* under Article 230 to challenge a

---

[598] For an action against a decision addressed to another Member State, see, eg Case 84/82
Germany v Commission (Textiles) [1984] ECR 1451, [1985] 1 CMLR 153.

[599] Commission decisions in the field of State aids are addressed to Member States and not
regional bodies.

[600] Case T-214/95 *Vlaamse Gewest v Commission* [1998] ECR II-717, para 28; Case T-238/97
Comunidad Autónoma de Cantabria v Council [1998] ECR II-2271, [1999] 3 CMLR 656, paras
42–43; Cases T-132 & 143/96 *Freistaat Sachsen and VW v Commission* [1999] ECR II-3663, [2000]
3 CMLR 485, paras 81–94 (not raised on appeal in Cases C-52 & 61/00P [2003] ECR I-9975).

[601] See, eg Cases 62 & 72/87 *Exécutif Régional Wallon and SA Glaverbel v Commission* [1988]
ECR 1573, [1989] 2 CMLR 771 (admissibility not contested by the Commission and ECJ did not
consider it necessary to raise the issue on its own initiative); *Vlaamse Gewest,* above, paras 28–30
(aid granted by the region and decision prevented it from exercising its own competence); Case
T-288/97 *Regione autonoma Friuli Venezia Giulia v Commission* [1999] ECR II-1871 (aid granted
by the region and decision prevented the region from exercising its own competence); and *Freistaat
Sachsen and VW,* above, paras 81–94 (aid granted by the region under autonomous powers and the
decision obliged the region to seek repayment of the aid). A regional body does not have *locus standi*
to seek annulment of a Regulation which is capable of generally affecting socio-economic conditions
within its territory: *Cantabria,* above, paras 49–53.

[602] Case C-78/03P *Commission v Germany and Aktionsgemeinschaft Recht und Eigentum (ARE)*
[2005] ECR I-10737, [2006] 2 CMLR 1197, para 33. See also, eg Case 25/62 *Plaumann v
Commission* [1963] ECR 95.

[603] Case 730/79 *Philip Morris v Commission* [1980] ECR 2671, [1981] 2 CMLR 321, para 5.

Commission decision addressed to a Member State prohibiting the granting of the aid. In *Van Der Kooy*,[604] however, the Court of Justice held that where an aid would potentially benefit a number of persons, a potential aid recipient could not bring an action under Article 230 against an adverse Commission decision because he was not individually concerned.[605] But the Court went on to hold as admissible an action brought on behalf of the potential aid recipients by their trade association, although only because that association had negotiated and signed the disputed gas supply tariff and had participated in the administrative procedure before the Commission.[606] A trade association will also have standing where it is acting to protect the interests of its members in circumstances where some or all of those members would themselves have standing.[607] When an undertaking is an actual recipient of aid granted under a sectoral aid scheme, it is individually concerned.[608] By contrast a quasi-governmental organisation, which

---

[604] Cases 67/85, etc, *Van Der Kooy v Commission* [1988] ECR 219, [1989] 2 CMLR 804, paras 12–16. See also Case T-86/96 *Arbeitsgemeinschaft Deutscher Luftfahrt-Unternehmen and Hapag-Lloyd Fluggesellchaft v Commission* [1999] ECR II-179.

[605] This rule was recently reaffirmed in *ARE* (n 602, above), in which the ECJ set aside a judgment of the CFI which appeared to adopt a more flexible approach in order to find that a trade association's members had *locus standi*. See also *Fesil v EFTA Surveillance Authority* (n 543, above) para 55. For a case in which a potential aid recipient was, exceptionally, able to establish individual concern in respect of a general measure, see Case T-9/98 *Mitteldeutsche Erdöl-Raffinerie v Commission* [2001] ECR II-3367, [2002] 1 CMLR 193 (a company had standing to challenge a Commission decision classifying a change to the German investment premium law as State aid, since the evidence established that the legislature had had that company specifically in mind when passing the legislation to effect that generally applicable change).

[606] The trade association's position was affected not as a recipient (it did not itself receive any aid) but as a negotiator: *Van Der Kooy* (n 604, above) paras 17–25. See also *CIRFS* (n 582, above) paras 29–30; Case T-380/94 *AIUFFASS and AKT v Commission* [1996] ECR II-2169, [1997] 3 CMLR 542, para 50. cf the position of the trade association ADL in Case T-86/96 (n 604, above), which was not a negotiator as regards the contested measure; in *ARE* (n 602, above) and that of the trade unions in Case C-106/98P *Comité d'entreprise de la Société française de production v Commission* [2000] ECR I-3659, where the ECJ upheld the CFI's judgment which had dismissed as inadmissible an application by the trade unions representing employees of an undertaking to annul a decision ordering repayment of aid granted to that undertaking. The unions did not have the same negotiating role in respect of the disputed aid measure as the trade association in *Van Der Kooy* and did not participate in the procedure under Art 88(2).

[607] See *CETM* (n 536, above) paras 23–25 (a Spanish trade association representing transporters had standing to bring an action on behalf of those of its members who were SMEs who habitually transported goods by road, to challenge a Commission decision which declared illegal, and required repayment of, aid that had been granted to such persons); and *Belgian coordination centres* (n 545, above) paras 58–64 (action brought by the trade association was admissible as it was acting for a closed class of coordination centres identifiable at the time the contested decision was taken and individually concerned). See also Case T-95/03 *AEESCAM v Commission*, judgment of 12 December 2006, para 42.

[608] Cases C-15/98 & 105/99 *Italy and Sardegna Lines v Commission* [2000] ECR I-8855, [2001] 1 CMLR 237, para 34; *CETM* (n 536, above); *Fesil v EFTA Surveillance Authority* (n 543, above) para 56. An aid recipient may even, at least in principle, have *locus standi* to challenge a decision *authorising* aid to itself, provided that the decision includes findings that have (negative) binding legal effects on its interests: see Case T-212/00 *Nuove Industrie Molisane v Commission* [2002] ECR

---

represented the interests of textile producers, did not have *locus standi* to bring proceedings under Article 230 to annul a Commission decision prohibiting aid granted to textile producers, since it was not directly and individually concerned and did not have an interest separate from that of the State.[609] In *TWD Textilwerke Deggendorf (No. 1)*,[610] the Court of Justice held that an aid recipient, who could have challenged the decision under Article 230 could not challenge the decision in the national court and seek an Article 234 reference when the time limit for challenging the decision under Article 230 had expired.[611]

Challenge by complainants to refusal to open formal procedure. The **15.116** Community Courts have adopted a more liberal approach to the standing of third parties where the Commission decision which the third party is seeking to challenge is a decision not to open the formal investigation procedure under Article 88(2),[612] compared to where the thrid party is seeking to challenge a final decision at the end of a formal procedure.[613] In *William Cook*[614] the Court of Justice held that a complainant is entitled to seek annulment of a decision refusing to open the procedure under Article 88(2) in respect of an individual aid granted to

---

II-347, [2003] 1 CMLR 257, para 38; Case T-141/03 *Sniace v Commission (No. 1)* [2005] ECR II-1197, [2006] 2 CMLR 621, para 24. That would only be so, however, where the aid recipient had, on the day the action was brought, a 'vested and present' interest in having the decision annulled, as opposed to a fear of negative consequences to itself were certain hypothetical circumstances to occur: *Sniace (No. 1)*, paras 26–27. *Locus standi* was not, on the facts, established in either case.

609 Case 282/85 *DEFI v Commission* [1986] ECR 2469, [1988] 2 CMLR 156.

610 Case C-188/92 *TWD Textilwerke Deggendorf (No. 1)* [1994] ECR I-833, paras 17 and 18.

611 See para 15.110, above.

612 For the different approaches to the two stages, see *ARE* (n 602 above) paras 33–39, and the Opinion of AG Jacobs, paras 98–120. This difference of approach has also been adopted by the EFTA Court: see Case E9/04 *The Bankers' and Securities Dealers' Association of Iceland v ESA* [2006] EFTA Court Rep 42, para 51, and the cases cited therein. For a criticism of this difference of approach, see paras 138–143 of the Opinion of AG Jacobs in *ARE* who termed the case law 'plainly unsatisfactory, being complex, apparently illogical, and inconsistent'; he recommended that the same (narrower) test be applied at both stages. The ECJ appears to have rejected that criticism by justifying the more liberal approach on admissibility to challeges intended to safeguard rights under Art 88(2) on the basis that 'persons concerned' must be able to enforce their procedural rights before the Community Courts. Where the Commission, despite having had a reasonable time to consider a complaint, has neither opened a formal investigation nor complied with a request to take a decision as to whether to open such as investigation, the Commission may be challenged under Art 230 EC for failure to act (see n 591, above).

613 Challenges by third parties to decisions taken following a formal investigation are discussed at para 15.117, below.

614 Case C-198/91 *William Cook v Commission* [1993] ECR I-2487, [1993] 3 CMLR 206. See also *CIRFS* (n 582, above); *Matra (No. 1)* (n 583, above); *BP Chemicals* (n 583, above) paras 84–93; *ARAP*, ibid, paras 39–40. In *Cook* and *Matra (No. 1)* the Commission had concluded that the aids were compatible with the common market (as was the case for some of the aids in *ARAP*); in *BP Chemicals* that there was no aid at all (as was the case also for some of the aids in *ARAP*); and in *CIRFS* (n 582, above) the aid fell within an existing aid scheme and did not require notification. See also *Sytraval* (n 589, above) paras 40–41; and Case T-266/94 *Skibsvaerftsforeningen v Commission* [1996] ECR II-1399.

a competitor where the purpose of the action is to safeguard his procedural rights as a party concerned under Article 88(2). A person who is able to show that his position might be affected by the grant of the aid, in particular a competitor, is a person concerned.[615] Where the Commission approves a general aid scheme without initiating the procedure under Article 88(2), it may be more difficult to satisfy the requirement of being a person concerned.[616] However, in *British Aggregates*[617] the Court of First Instance held that a challenge by a trade association to a tax measure imposing a levy on virgin aggregates was admissible since the competitive position of several of its members who operated quarries producing virgin aggregates was significantly affected by the levy.

15.117 **Challenge by complainants to decision following formal investigation.** By contrast, where a third party challenges the substantive merits of a decision, the Court of Justice has stated in *ARE* that the test of individual concern is stricter and it is not sufficient that the applicant is a 'person concerned'.[618] In such a case, the complainant must 'demonstrate that it has a particular status within the meaning of the *Plaumann v Commission* case-law'.[619] This was successfully demonstrated in *COFAZ*[620] where the Court of Justice held that parties who had lodged a complaint with the Commission, who took part in the formal procedure under Article 88(2), and whose position on the market would be significantly affected by the measure granting the aid were directly and individually concerned by the Commission's decision to terminate that procedure. They could thus bring proceedings under Article 230. Where a person has not lodged a complaint and its position on the market is not seriously jeopardised, it is not individually concerned.[621] If the applicant is a trade association it is necessary, unless there are special circumstances, that at least some of the members of the trade association

---

[615] Case T-188/95 *Waterleiding Maatschappij v Commission* [1998] ECR II-3713, paras 60–62; *ARE* (n 602, above) para 36.

[616] Case T-398/94 *Kahn Scheepvaart v Commission* [1996] ECR II-477, [1997] 3 CMLR 63. The CFI held that at the time of the adoption of a general aid scheme there were no identified beneficiaries and hence no identified competitors who could bring proceedings for failure to open the Art 88(2) procedure. cf the position of the applicant in *Waterleiding Maatschappij*, above, whose competitive position on the market was held to be affected by a general aid measure approved without opening the Art 88(2) procedure. See paras 110–111 of the Opinion of AG Jacobs in *ARE*.

[617] Case T-210/02 *British Aggregates Association v Commission* [2006] ECR II-2789, paras 45 *et seq.*

[618] Case C-78/03P *Commission v Germany and Aktionsgemeinschaft Recht und Eigentum (ARE)* [2005] ECR I-10737, [2006] 2 CMLR 1197.

[619] *ARE*, above, at para 37.

[620] Case 169/84 *COFAZ v Commission* [1986] ECR 391, [1986] 3 CMLR 385. Their action proved successful on the merits: Case C-169/84 *CdF Chimie AZF v Commission* [1990] ECR I-3083, [1992] 1 CMLR 177.

[621] Case T-88/01 *Sniace v Commission (No. 2)* [2005] ECR II-1165, [2005] 3 CMLR 153, paras 56, 60 and 79. Although *Sniace* is a judgment of the CFI that predates the judgment of the ECJ in *ARE* it is consistent with the latter judgment: see *ARE* (n 618, above) paras 69–73.

are substantially affected.[622] Provided that an application is brought within two months of the publication of the decision in the *Official Journal* or its notification to the applicant, the application will be in time even if the application is lodged more than two months after the applicant had knowledge of the decision.[623]

(iii) The grounds of annulment

Generally. The grounds of annulment under Article 230 are lack of compe- **15.118** tence, infringement of an essential procedural requirement, infringement of the Treaty or of any rule of law relating to its application, or misuse of powers. The following paragraphs briefly discuss the grounds of annulment most frequently relied on as regards State aids decisions.

Procedural irregularities. Commission decisions have been challenged for **15.119** the failure to initiate the formal procedure under Article 88(2);[624] the length of time taken to initiate the formal procedure under Article 88(2) in the case of new aids;[625] the length of time taken by the formal procedure itself;[626] infringement of the right to be heard;[627] and infringement of the right to comment

---

[622] *British Aggregates* (n 617, above) paras 47–48; Case T-117/04 *Werkgroep Commerciële Jachthavens Zuidelijke Randmeren v Commission* [2006] ECR II-3861.

[623] Case T-14/96 *BAI* (n 587, above) paras 32–37; Case T-110/97 *Kneissl Dachstein v Commission* [1999] ECR II-2881, paras 40–44; Case T-296/97 *Alitalia v Commission* [2000] ECR II-3871, [2001] All ER (EC) 193, paras 34–37; Case T-17/02 *Fred Olsen v Commission* [2005] ECR II-2031, paras 80–83.

[624] *Germany v Commission (Textiles)* (n 598, above) (decision annulled: 16 months between notification and favourable decision too long a time for the Commission not to have initiated the formal procedure); *British Aerospace and Rover* (n 586, above) (decision annulled: failure to initiate formal procedure in respect of alleged new aid granted in breach of an earlier Commission decision); *William Cook* (n 614, above) (decision annulled: failure to initiate formal procedure when it was unclear whether there was overcapacity in a particular economic sector); and Case T-49/93 *SIDE v Commission* [1995] ECR II-2501 (decision annulled: insufficient information on the impact on the market). The position on the opening of a formal investigation is now regulated by the Procedural Reg (n 591, above) Art 4(4) and (5): see paras 15.081 *et seq*, above.

[625] *Boussac* (n 559, above) (three months between final receipt of relevant information and initiation of procedure; decision upheld in view of late notification). Art 4(5) of the Procedural Reg lays down a time limit of two months from final receipt of information subject to an extension that must be agreed by both the Commission and the Member State concerned.

[626] Case 223/85 *RSV v Commission* [1987] ECR 4617 (26 months between initiation of procedure and unfavourable decision requiring repayment when belief that aid would be approved was held to be a breach of the aid recipient's legitimate expectation and decision annulled); *Boussac* (n 559, above) (over two years between initiation of the formal procedure and the decision requiring repayment was not too long because of serious delays in the provision of the necessary information to the Commission); see also *CETM* (n 536, above) paras 144–154; Case T-171/02 *Regione autonoma della Sardegna v Commission* [2005] ECR II-2123. Art 7(6) of the Procedural Reg requires the Commission to reach a decision, as far as possible, within 18 months from the opening of the formal procedure.

[627] Case 234/84 *Belgium v Commission (Meura)* [1986] ECR 2263, [1988] 2 CMLR 301, paras 25–30; Case 40/85 *Belgium v Commission (Boch No. 2)* [1986] ECR 2321, paras 25–31, at 2348–2349; Case 259/85 *France v Commission (Textiles and clothing)* [1987] ECR 4393, [1989] 2 CMLR 30, paras 9–13; *Boussac* (n 559, above) paras 29–31; *British Aerospace and Rover v Commission* (n 586, above) para 13; Case T-459/93 *Siemens v Commission* [1995] ECR II-1675, paras 38–41; Case T-34/02 *Le Levant 001 v Commission* [2006] ECR II-267 (failure to hear private

on documents supplied by other parties.[628] It is a fundamental principle of Community law that a person must be heard in all proceedings initiated against him which are liable to culminate in a measure adversely affecting him, even in the absence of any express procedural rules. This principle requires that a Member State must be placed in a position in which it may effectively make known its views on the observations submitted by interested third parties under Article 88(2) and on which the Commission proposes to base its decision.[629] The recipient of an aid can rely on the failure by the Commission to hear the Member State since that is a breach of an essential procedural requirement.[630] However, interested third parties within the meaning of Article 88(2) cannot enjoy the same rights to a fair hearing as Member States against whom proceedings have been instituted.[631] Indeed, the Commission is not even obliged individually to inform the beneficiaries of suspected unlawful aid of the opening of the Article 88(2) procedure, since such beneficiaries are not the addressees of Commission decisions requiring the recovery of unlawful aid. The publication in the *Official Journal* of a notice announcing the initiation of the Article 88(2) procedure is deemed to be sufficient to advise potentially interested parties of their rights to participate in that procedure.[632] Furthermore, an infringement of the right to be heard will only result in the annulment of a decision adversely affecting the person seeking its annulment if it is established that, had it not been for such an irregularity, the outcome of the procedure might have been different.[633] Where an earlier decision

---

investors who were benefiting from a tax concession which the Commission subsequently decided was incompatible State aid).

[628] *Exécutif Régional Wallon (Glaverbel)* (n 601, above) paras 36–39; *Boussac* (n 559, above).

[629] See *Glaverbel* and *Boussac*, above. Indeed, even before initiating the Art 88(2) procedure classifying the measures concerned as new aid, the Commission should first provide the Member State concerned with an opportunity to put forward the view that the measures do not constitute aid or else constitute existing aid: Case C-400/99 *Italy v Commission (Tirrenia Group)* [2005] ECR I-3657, [2005] 3 CMLR 611, paras 29–30.

[630] Cases T-228 & 233/99 *Westdeutsche Landesbank Girozentrale and Nordrhein-Westfalen v Commission* [2003] ECR II-435, [2004] 1 CMLR 529, para 142.

[631] Cases T-371 & 394/94 *British Airways v Commission* [1998] ECR II-2405, [1998] 3 CMLR 429, paras 59–64; Case T-198/01 *Technische Glaswerke Ilmenau v Commission* [2004] ECR II-2717, [2004] 3 CMLR 118, paras 191–195 (appeal on other grounds dismissed, Case C-404/04P, judgment of 11 January 2007). In the latter case, the CFI noted (at para 196) that the aid recipient had been given the opportunity to submit its comments as part of the formal investigation procedure in accordance with Art 6(1) of Reg 659/1999 (the Procedural Regulation: see further para 15.069, above). But cf Case T-366/00 *Scott v Commission*, judgment of 29 March 2007, paras 51–63 (on appeal, Case C-290/07P *Commission v Scott*, not yet decided).

[632] Case T-111/01 *Saxonia Edelmetalle v Commission* [2005] ECR II-1579, paras 47–48; Case T-354/99 *Kuwait Petroleum (Nederland) v Commission* [2006] ECR II-1475, paras 80–81. In so giving notice to interested parties, however, the Commission must 'define sufficiently the framework of its investigation so as not to render meaningless the right of interested parties to put forward their comments': *Kuwait Petroleum*, para 85. But see *Scott v Commission*, above.

[633] *Boussac* (n 559, above) para 31; Case C-288/96 *Germany v Commission (Jadekost)* [2000] ECR I-8237, paras 99–106; Case C-404/04P *Technische Glaswerke Ilmenau v Commission* (n 631, above) para 131.

of the Commission has been annulled and the Commission bases its subsequent decision exclusively on information which it had available at the time of the earlier decision, there is no need again to consult the Member State that granted the aid.[634] The Commission is required, in the interests of sound administration of the fundamental rules of the Treaty relating to State aid, to conduct a diligent and impartial examination of the complaint. This may make it necessary for it to examine matters not expressly raised in the complaint.[635] Where the Commission approves the grant of an aid under a general aid scheme, such approval is not a measure of management or administration that can be the subject of the habilitation procedure[636] where the approval involves an examination of complex factual and legal questions; such a decision must therefore be adopted by the whole Commission in conformity with the principle of collegiality.[637]

Lack of reasoning.   A number of Commission decisions have been annulled **15.120** on grounds of lack of reasoning.[638] Since the absence of reasons or inadequacy of reasoning goes to an issue of infringement of essential procedural requirements and involves a matter of public policy, the Court must examine such lack of reasoning of its own motion.[639] In *Van Der Kooy*,[640] the Court of Justice reiterated the basic requirements of Article 253 in the context of State aids:

> 'A statement of reasons required by Article [253] of the Treaty must be appropriate to the nature of the measure in question and must show clearly and unequivocally

---

634 Case C-415/96 *Spain v Commission (Hytasa No. 2)* [1998] ECR I-6993, [1999] 1 CMLR 304, where the Commission based its analysis on information available at the time of that earlier decision on which Spain had already commented.

635 *Sytraval* (n 589, above).

636 The habilitation procedure, provided for in the Commission's Rules of Procedure (Art 13 of the current Rules) enables the Commission, provided the principle of collective responsibility is fully respected, to empower one or more of its Members to take management or administrative measures on its behalf.

637 Case T-435/93 *ASPEC v Commission* [1995] ECR II-1281, and Case T-442/93 *AAC v Commission* [1995] ECR II-1329. See also *British Airways* (n 631, above) paras 116–117.

638 See, eg Cases 296 & 318/82 *Netherlands and Leeuwarder Papierwarenfabriek v Commission* [1985] ECR 809, [1985] 3 CMLR 380; *CdF Chimie AZF* (n 620, above); Cases C-278/92, etc, *Spain v Commission (Hytasa No. 1)* [1994] ECR I-4103; Cases C-329/93, etc, *Germany v Commission* [1996] ECR I-5151; *Sytraval* (n 589, above); *British Airways* (n 631, above); *Italy and Sardegna Lines v Commission* (n 608, above); *Alitalia v Commission* (n 623, above); Case T-155/98 *Société Internationale de Diffusion et d'Edition (SIDE) v Commission* [2002] ECR II-1179, [2002] 1 CMLR 1658; *Westdeutsche Landesbank Girozentrale and Nordrhein-Westfalen v Commission* (n 630, above); Cases T-304 & 316/04 *Italy v Commission (WAM)* [2006] ECR II-64 (on appeal, Case C-494/06P *Commission v Italy*, not yet decided).

639 *Sytraval* (n 589, above) para 67; Case C-351/98 *Spain v Commission (Plan Renove Industrial)* [2002] ECR I-8031, para 76; cf Case T-106/95 *Federation Française des Sociétés d'Assurances (FFSA) v Commission* [1997] ECR II-229, [1997] 2 CMLR 78, para 62, where the CFI declined of its own motion to examine a plea under Art 253 (case upheld on appeal in Case C-174/97P, [1998] ECR I-1303).

640 Cases 67/85, etc, *Van Der Kooy v Commission* [1988] ECR 219. The CFI also provided a convenient summary of the case law on the duty to give reasons in Case T-613/97 *UFEX v Commission* [2006] ECR II-1531, [2006] 3 CMLR 524, paras 63–70.

the reasoning of the institution which adopted the measure, so as to inform the persons concerned of the justification for the measure adopted and to enable the Court to exercise its powers of review.'

Article 253 does not require the Commission to go into all the relevant facts and points of law and the question whether the statement of reasons is sufficient must be assessed with regard to its wording and content, its context, and all the legal rules relevant to the matter in question.[641] In its reasoning, the Commission is not obliged to take a position on all of the arguments relied upon by the parties concerned. If it sets out the facts and legal considerations having decisive importance in the context of the decision and provides a reasoned response to each of the essential arguments put forward by the parties, that is sufficient.[642] A statement of reasons which is stated to be based on a supposedly 'clear' fact must generally be regarded as inadequate.[643] Where the decision contains a finding that the measure concerned constitutes State aid, Article 253 requires the Commission to state its reasons for its conclusion that the measure in question falls within the scope of Article 87(1).[644] As a rule, the Commission must explain how competition would be affected, by examining the relevant market, the position of the aid recipient and of competing undertakings, and the volume of inter-State trade in the relevant market.[645] In some cases, however, the circumstances in which the measure was granted may be in themselves sufficient to demonstrate a potential to distort competition and affect inter-State trade, and in such cases it is sufficient for the

---

[641] Case C-278/95P *Siemens v Commission* [1997] ECR I-2507, para 17; *Vlaamse Gewest* (n 600, above) para 63; Case T-16/96 *Cityflyer Express v Commission* [1998] ECR II-757, [1998] 2 CMLR 537, para 65; *Italy and Sardegna Lines* (n 608, above) para 65; Case C-114/00 *Spain v Commission (Aid for horticultural products)* [2002] ECR I-7657, paras 62–63; Case C-301/96 *Germany v Commission* [2003] ECR I-9919, para 87.

[642] *Vlaamse Gewest* (n 600, above); *Cityflyer Express,* above; Case T-323/99 *Industrie Navali Meccaniche Affini (INMA) v Commission* [2002] ECR II-545, [2002] 1 CMLR 1638, para 98; Case T-349/03 *Corsica Ferries France v Commission* [2005] ECR II-2197, paras 62–64. The Commission is not required to define its position on matters which are manifestly irrelevant or insignificant or plainly of secondary importance: *Sytraval* (n 589, above) para 64. Where the Commission decides that a proposed aid measure is compatible with the common market on the basis that it meets the requirements set out in Community Guidelines which the Commission has published, it is sufficient for the decision to explain why the Commission considers the proposed aid to satisfy the conditions set out in those guidelines: *Corsica Ferries France*, para 66.

[643] *Glaverbel* (n 601, above) although on the facts the ECJ accepted a statement that 'it is clear that the aid in question is not intended to promote the execution of an important project of common European interest', as constituting sufficient reasoning since the Applicants were not able to challenge that statement.

[644] *Cityflyer Express* (n 641, above) para 66; *Vlaamse Gewest* (n 600, above) para 64; *Le Levant 001*(n 627, above).

[645] *Leeuwarder Papierwarenfabriek* (n 638, above) paras 22–30; Cases C-329/93, etc, *Germany v Commission* (n 638, above) paras 51–55; *Italy and Sardegna Lines* (n 608, above) paras 66–74; *SIDE* (n 638, above) para 56; *Italy v Commission (WAM)* (n 638, above) paras 62–77.

decision to set out what those circumstances were.[646] The Commission cannot excuse a lack of reasoning by pointing to the failure of the Member State to provide adequate information if it has failed to exercise its powers to order the production of all relevant documents and information.[647]

Rejection of complaint.   Where the decision contains a finding that no State aid **15.121** as alleged by a complainant exists, the Commission must provide a sufficient explanation of the reasons for which the facts and points of law put forward by the complainant have failed to demonstrate the existence of an aid.[648] Whereas the Commission is obliged to provide reasons to a complainant for its rejection of a complaint, the Commission is not, in circumstances where it decides to open the formal investigation procedure with regard to one or more of a number of measures the subject of the complaint, obliged to provide reasons for proceeding in respect of only part of the complaint.[649] In those circumstances, the complainant's remedy is not under Article 230 but under Article 232, whereby the complainant may challenge the failure of the Commission to adopt a position on the totality of the complaint.[650] Where the Commission condemns an aid which has been granted in breach of Article 88(3), it is not necessary for the Commission to demonstrate that the aid has had an actual effect since this is not required in the case of an aid which is notified before implementation. To require the Commission to show actual effect would thus favour those Member States which grant aid in breach of Article 88(3) to the detriment of those which notify aid at the planning stage.[651] Where a decision requires repayment of unlawful aid, the Commission is not obliged to give specific reasons in order to justify the exercise of that power.[652]

---

[646] See, eg Case C-372/97 *Italy v Commission* [2004] ECR I-3679, paras 71–73; *Fesil v EFTA Surveillance Authority* (n 543, above) paras 99–100. Where there is inter-State trade in the products the producers or production of which are favoured by an aid, the Commission is able to conclude that there is an effect on inter-State trade without having to describe the market or set out a detailed explanation of the trade flows between Member States for the product concerned: see Cases C-346 & 529/03 *Atzeni v Regione autonoma della Sardegna* [2006] ECR I-1875, para 75. See also paras 15.025 and 15.026, above.

[647] Cases C-324 & 342/90 *Germany and Pleuger Worthington v Commission* [1994] ECR I-1173, [1994] 3 CMLR 521, paras 24–29; *Industrie Navali Meccaniche Affini* (n 642, above) paras 90–91; Case T-318/00 *Freistaat Thüringen v Commission (Optical Disc Service)* [2005] ECR II-4179, para 73.

[648] Case C-367/95P *Commission v Sytraval and Brink's France* [1998] ECR I-1719, paras 74–78.

[649] *Sytraval*, above, para 62.

[650] Case T-67/94 *Ladbroke Racing v Commission* [1998] ECR II-1, para 92; appeal on other grounds dismissed: Case C-83/98P *France v Commission* [2000] ECR I-3271, [2000] 3 CMLR 555.

[651] Case C-301/87 *France v Commission (Boussac)* [1990] ECR I-307, para 33; Case C-75/97 *Belgium v Commission (Maribel I)* [1999] ECR I-3671, [2000] 1 CMLR 791, para 48.

[652] *Hytasa (No. 1)* (n 638, above) para 78; *Maribel I,* above, para 82. Art 14(1) of the Procedural Reg now imposes an obligation on the Commission to require Member States to recover unlawful aid which it has found to be incompatible with the common market, subject to general principles of Community law.

15.122 **Review of the exercise of the Commission's discretion.** The Commission does not possess a broad margin of discretion in relation to the characterisation of a measure as aid under Article 87(1) save in exceptional circumstances where the nature of the State intervention is complex.[653] By contrast the Commission possesses a wide margin of discretion in deciding whether an aid may be compatible with the common market in accordance with the provisions of Article 87(3). Since the exercise of that discretion involves a complex assessment of an economic and social nature which must be made within a Community context, the Community Courts in reviewing the exercise of such a discretion confine themselves to verifying whether the Commission has complied with the rules governing the procedure, whether the statement of reasons is adequate, whether the facts on which the contested finding was based have been accurately stated, and whether there has been any manifest error of assessment or misuse of powers.[654] Thus the Community Courts can review the Commission's findings of fact, to consider whether on the material before the Commission such findings were open to the Commission, and the Commission's decision on the law.[655] The legality of a decision is to be assessed in the light of the information available to the Commission at the time when the decision was adopted.[656] Only where it appears that there is

---

[653] Case T-67/94 *Ladbroke Racing* (n 650, above) para 52; upheld on appeal, *France v Commission*, ibid, paras 24–25. See also Case C-56/93 *Belgium v Commission* [1996] ECR I-723, paras 10–11; Case T-358/94 *Air France v Commission (CDC–P)* [1996] ECR II-2109, para 71; *Alitalia* (n 623, above) para 95. The position is different where an assessment under Art 86(2) is required: see *Ladbroke Racing* at para 53, referring to Case T-106/95 *FFSA v Commission* (n 639, above). See also *CdF Chimie AZF* (n 620, above): Commission decision terminating a procedure under Art 88(2) annulled on the grounds that the Commission erred in concluding that a preferential gas tariff of Gasunie was not an aid within the meaning of Art 87 because it was justified by consequent cost savings. In view of the contradictory information submitted by the Applicants and the Commission, the ECJ obtained a report from independent experts, on which it relied in holding that the Commission had erred in assessing the cost savings.

[654] Case 730/79 *Philip Morris v Commission* [1980] ECR 2671, [1981] 2 CMLR 321 at para 24; *Boussac* (n 651, above) para 49; *Ladbroke Racing* (n 650, above) para 148; *British Airways* (n 631, above) para 209; *Jadekost* (n 633, above); *Matra (No. 1)* (n 583, above) para 25; Case C-310/99 *Italy v Commission* [2002] ECR I-2289, para 46; Case T-35/99 *Keller v Commission* [2002] ECR II-261, [2003] 1 CMLR 268, para 77; Case C-88/03 *Portugal v Commission (Azores)* [2006] ECR I-7115, [2006] 3 CMLR 1233, para 99.

[655] AG Slynn in Case 84/82 *Germany v Commission (Textiles)* [1984] ECR at 1499–1500, [1985] 1 CMLR at 166–169.

[656] *Jadekost* (n 633, above) para 34; *Alitalia* (n 623, above) para 86; *Keller* (n 654, above) para 83; Case T-17/03 *Schmitz-Gotha Fahrzeugwerke v Commission* [2006] ECR II-1139, para 54; Case C-276/02 *Spain v Commission* [2004] ECR I-8091, [2004] 3 CMLR 1038, para 3. Further, an applicant to the CFI who participated, or could have participated, in the Commission's formal investigation procedure which led to the taking of the disputed decision will not be permitted to rely on information which was unknown to the Commission at the time the decision was taken, and which the applicant did not bring to the Commission's attention during that procedure: see Case T-217/02 *Ter Lembeek International v Commission*, judgment of 23 November 2006, paras 82–92. This principle should operate even where the information was 'available' to the Commission, albeit 'unknown' by it. But the Commission's wide margin of discretion in the making

an abuse of power or manifest error can the Commission's decision be annulled.[657] The discretion of the Commission in deciding not to open the formal procedure under Article 88(2) is more limited in that any doubt at the preliminary examination stage about the compatibility of aid with Article 87 should generally be resolved in favour of opening the formal procedure.[658] Accordingly, any review by the Community Courts of the classification of a measure as State aid in a Commission decision to open the formal procedure will be limited to ascertaining whether the Commission made a manifest error of assessment in forming the view that it was unable to resolve during the initial examination all aspects of the question of whether the measure amounted to State aid.[659] Since a Commission decision not to open the formal procedure has the effect of eliminating the rights to be heard of any third party complainants, however, the Community Courts will not, in adjudicating on a challenge to such a decision, consider themselves limited to finding whether the Commission made a manifest error but will make a full assessment on the basis of all the facts which were available to the Commission at the time when the decision was made.[660]

Infringement of the Treaty or of any rule of law.   There is an overlap between   **15.123** this and the other grounds of annulment. Examples of an error of law include a failure to respect the principles of legitimate expectation and equality;[661] an individual decision of the Commission purporting to amend a measure of general scope;[662] failure to obtain the agreement of the Member States in prolonging with retroactive effect the Community framework on State aid to the motor vehicle industry;[663] and failure to categorise an aid as an existing aid.[664]

---

of economic assessments cannot excuse a failure by the Commission properly to take account of all relevant facts that are available to the Commission at the time when the decision is taken: see *Corsica Ferries France v Commission* (n 642, above) paras 266–271 and 312–313, in which the Commission's failure to take account of the proceeds of certain disposals of property by the prospective recipient of restructuring aid, although the value of those proceeds were known to the Commission, led to the annulment of the Commission's decision to approve the aid package since the total amount of authorised aid had not been strictly limited to the minimum necessary.

657 See cases cited in n 654, above.
658 See para 15.080, above.
659 *Diputación Foral de Guipúzcoa v Commission* (n 581, above) paras 44–49.
660 Case T-73/98 *Prayon-Rupel v Commission* [2001] ECR II-867, paras 47–50.
661 See, eg Case T-6/99 *ESF Elbe-Stahlwerke Feralpi v Germany* [2001] ECR II-1523, para 190. See also Cases C-182 & 217/03 *Belgium v Commission (Belgian Coordination Centres)* [2006] ECR I-5479, paras 168–173 (Commission's refusal to permit Belgium to renew, even for a transitional period, agreements to provide aid to coordination centres, despite having permitted such renewals in the past, not only infringed legitimate expectations but also infringed the principle of equal treatment since it led to some coordination centres suffering a difference in treatment in comparison with others by reference to the dates on which their aid renewals became due).
662 *CIRFS* (n 582, above).
663 Case C-292/95 *Spain v Commission (motor vehicle framework No. 2)* [1997] ECR I-1931.
664 Cases T-298/97, etc, *Alzetta v Commission* [2000] ECR II-2319.

(iv) Interim relief

15.124 Generally. For an applicant to obtain interim relief it needs to show: (i) a *prima facie* case; (ii) urgency, in the sense of serious and irreparable harm in the absence of interim relief; and (iii) that the balance of interests favours the grant of interim relief.[665]

15.125 The Commission's practice. In the case of aid granted in breach of Article 88(3), the Commission has in the past applied directly to the Court of Justice under the second sub-paragraph of Article 88(2) and/or Article 226 for an interim injunction to prevent the operation of the aid.[666] However, since the Court of Justice's judgment in *Boussac* in 1990,[667] the Commission's practice has been to adopt an interim measures decision requiring the Member State to suspend the operation of the aid scheme or payment of the aid granted in breach of Article 88(3). If the Member State fails to comply, the Commission may refer the matter directly to the Court of Justice under the second sub-paragraph of Article 88(2) and apply for interim measures if necessary. The same procedure will be followed after the adoption of a final decision under Article 88(2). The Procedural Regulation now provides an express power for the Commission to adopt an interim injunction requiring a Member State to suspend and/or provisionally recover aid and entitles the Commission to refer the matter directly to the Court of Justice if a Member State fails to comply with such an injunction.[668]

15.126 Member States. Where a Commission decision requires a Member State to recover aid, the decision will not be suspended unless the Member State can show that, in the absence of suspension, it would suffer serious and irreparable damage.[669] In principle, a Member State cannot rely on any damage that the

---

[665] See Arts 83 and 104 of the Rules of Procedure of the ECJ and CFI respectively. See also the general case law of the Community Courts on the grant of interim relief and paras 13.246 *et seq*, above.

[666] Cases 31 &53/77R *Commission v United Kingdom (Pig production subsidies)* [1977] ECR 921, [1977] 2 CMLR 359, where the ECJ considered that breach of Art 88(3) itself justified interim measures; Case 171/83R *Commission v France (Textiles and clothing)* [1983] ECR 2621, where the Commission obtained an interim order under Art 226 for breach of Art 88(3) and the ECJ explicitly held that the requirement for urgency was satisfied. See also Case 173/73 *Italy v Commission (Aids to the Textile Industry)* [1974] ECR 709, [1974] 2 CMLR 593, para 9, where the ECJ indicated that the Commission could bring proceedings directly before the ECJ pursuant to the second sub-paragraph of Art 88(2) where an aid has been introduced in breach of Art 88(3).

[667] Case C-301/87 *France v Commission (Boussac)* [1990] ECR I-307; and see *XXth Report on Competition Policy* (1990), point 172.

[668] Arts 11 and 12; see paras 15.095 and 15.096, above.

[669] Case 248/84R *Germany v Commission* [1985] ECR 1813, [1985] 3 CMLR 710; Case 57/86R *Greece v Commission* [1986] ECR 1497, [1986] 3 CMLR 596; Case 303/88R *Italy v Commission (ENI-Lanerossi)* [1989] ECR 801, [1990] 2 CMLR 818; Case 142/87R *Belgium v Commission (Tubemeuse)* [1987] ECR 2589, [1988] 2 CMLR 601; Case C-356/90R *Belgium v Commission (Boelwerf)* [1991] ECR I-2423. Indefinite future damage to the Member State is not sufficient: see *Tubemeuse* at para 25.

beneficiary of the aid might suffer.[670] Where the aid has been granted in breach of the notification requirements, an application for interim relief will be treated with great circumspection.[671]

Other applicants.   The same basic requirements apply to the grant of interim **15.127** relief by other applicants, including sufficient evidence of serious and irreparable damage to the person seeking interim relief.[672] Accordingly, an aid recipient will not obtain suspension of a Commission decision addressed to a Member State requiring the Member State to seek recovery of aid unless that person is able to show that the remedies available to him under national law are insufficient to avoid him suffering serious and irreparable damage as a result of the recovery measures taken by the Member State.[673] That does not mean, however, that an aid recipient who has brought an action for annulment in the Court of First Instance must wait until the Member State brings proceedings in its national courts to recover the aid before seeking interim relief from the Community courts.[674] As a general rule, the Community interest in ensuring that the functioning of the common market is not distorted by incompatible State aid will take precedence over the interest of the aid recipients in seeking to suspend repayments of aid which the Commission has declared incompatible.[675] It is for the person seeking

---

[670] In *Tubemeuse*, above, it appeared that enforcement of the decision was likely to cause Tubemeuse's bankruptcy, with immediate and irreparable harm not just to Tubemeuse but also to its creditors, but a stay was refused. cf *Boelwerf*, above, where there had been a notification of the aid and the President of the ECJ found that no grave and irreparable harm would be caused to the recipient by immediate enforcement of the decision.

[671] Case C-399/95R *Germany v Commission* [1996] ECR I-2441, paras 54–56 (a case under the steel aid code).

[672] Case 310/85R *Deufil v Commission* [1986] ECR 537, [1986] 3 CMLR 687, paras 22–26; Case T-239/94R *EISA v Commission* [1994] ECR II-703 (third party competitor); Case T-86/96R *Arbeitsgemeinschaft Deutscher Luftfahrt-Unternehmen and Hapag-Lloyd v Commission* [1998] ECR II-641, where an application to allow an aid to be continued pending the outcome of the annulment proceedings failed. See also Case T-155/96R *City of Mainz v Commission* [1996] ECR II-1655 (sale of land by the City at below market value); Case T-73/98R *Prayon-Rupel v Commission* [1998] ECR II-2769 (third party competitor); and Case T-198/01R *Technische Glaswerke Ilmenau v Commission* [2002] ECR II-2153, [2004] 2 CMLR 107, paras 54–58, upheld on appeal, Case C-232/02P(R) [2002] ECR I-8977.

[673] See Case 310/85R *Deufil*, above, para 22; Case 142/87R *Tubemeuse* (n 669, above) para 26. Note, in that regard, that Art 14(3) of Reg 659/99 provides that recovery of aid which is unlawful or incompatible with the common market is to be effected without delay and in accordance with the procedures under the national law of the Member State concerned, without prejudice, exclusively, to any order for interim measures made by the Community judicature: see Case T-198/01R *Technische Glaswerke Ilmenau*, above, paras 53–56.

[674] Case T-198/01R *Technische Glaswerke Ilmenau* (n 672, above) paras 54–58.

[675] ibid, paras 113–114. In that case, however, the CFI for the first time allowed an application to stay a Commission decision ordering the recovery of an aid. The President of the CFI justified the stay not only on the grounds that that the applicant had a reasonable chance of success in the main action and was likely to suffer insolvency before the case could be substantively determined if no stay was allowed, but also by reference to certain exceptional circumstances (including that the insolvency of the applicant could strengthen the dominant position of one of its

interim relief to show exceptional circumstances that justify the grant of interim relief.[676] The relief sought must be in the nature of an interim measure, must not prejudice the main action or go beyond the scope of the main proceedings[677] and must balance the interests involved.[678]

9. The Relationship between Articles 87–89 and Other Provisions of the Treaty

15.128 **Generally.** As has been seen, the Treaty provisions on State aid do not have direct effect, apart from the last sentence of Article 88(3). This raises problems when all or part of the aid in question may also be said to infringe other Treaty provisions that do have direct effect, such as Articles 28,[679] 31[680] and 90.[681] More generally, the State aid rules need to be applied in harmony with other provisions of the Treaty. Those issues are considered in this section.

15.129 **Article 28:** *Iannelli & Volpi.* In *Iannelli & Volpi v Meroni*,[682] the Court of Justice held that:

> 'the effect of an interpretation of Article [28] which is so wide as to treat an aid as such within the meaning of Article [87] as being similar to a quantitative restriction referred to in Article [28] would be to alter the scope of Articles [87] and [88] of the Treaty and to interfere with the system adopted in the Treaty for the division of powers by means of the procedure for keeping aids under constant review as described in Article [88].'

It is for the Commission to decide, pursuant to the procedure laid down in Article 88, whether an aid may be incompatible with the common market.[683] The Court, however, drew a distinction between those aspects of aid that are so indissolubly linked to the object of the aid that it is impossible to evaluate them other

---

competitors, and that the same competitor would not be seriously damaged by a delay in recovering the disputed aid).

676 Case T-198/01R *Technische Glaswerke Ilmenau* (n 672, above) paras 116–124.

677 Case C-313/90R *CIRFS v Commission* [1991] ECR I-2557; Case T-107/96R *Pantochim v Commission* [1996] ECR II-1361; Case C-89/97P(R) *Moccia Irme v Commission* [1997] ECR I-2327.

678 *EISA* (n 672, above) para 27.

679 Case 74/76 *Iannelli & Volpi v Meroni* [1977] ECR 557, [1977] 2 CMLR 688, para 13.

680 In respect of Art 31(1), see Case 59/75 *Pubblico Ministero v Manghera* [1976] ECR 91, [1976] 1 CMLR 557; in respect of Art 31(2), see Case 6/64 *Costa v ENEL* [1964] ECR 585, [1964] CMLR 425.

681 Case 28/67 *Molkerei-Zentrale Westfalen v Hauptzollamt Paderborn* [1968] ECR 143, [1968] CMLR 187.

682 *Iannelli & Volpi* (n 679, above) para 12.

683 ibid. See also Case 78/76 *Steinike und Weinlig v Germany* [1977] ECR 595, [1977] 2 CMLR 688, paras 9–10.

than under Articles 87 and 88 of the Treaty, and other aspects of aid which, although they form part of the aid system, may be regarded as not being necessary for the attainment of its object or for its proper functioning.[684] In the latter case, Articles 87 and 88 do not apply to the exclusion of other Treaty provisions that have direct effect, but any declaration of invalidity by a national court must be limited to the severable part of the aid.[685]

Article 28: subsequent cases.   In *Commission v Ireland (Buy Irish)*,[686] the Court **15.130**
of Justice held that a publicity campaign to promote the sale of domestic products was prohibited by Article 28 although a substantial part of the campaign was financed by the Irish government. The Court stated that the Irish government could not rely on Articles 87 and 88 to exclude the operation of Article 28, at least in the case where the government had not notified the measure as an aid pursuant to Article 88(3). The Court later held in *Apple and Pear Development Council v Lewis*[687] that a publicity campaign financed entirely by a charge imposed by a public body on growers to promote the sale of domestic production at the expense of imports may infringe Article 28. The Court reached this conclusion although the publicity campaign in question was almost certainly financed by an aid within the meaning of Article 87,[688] and it is difficult to see how the publicity campaign could be severed without destroying the purpose of the aid altogether. A similar approach has been adopted in subsequent cases.[689] In *Commission v Italy*,[690] the Court gave two reasons for rejecting Italy's argument that a subsidy for the purchasing of vehicles of national manufacture should be assessed under Articles 87 and 88 and not under Article 28. First, the measure had never been notified to the Commission. Secondly, the Court held that Article 28 and Articles 87 and 88

---

[684] *Iannelli & Volpi* (n 679 above) para 14.

[685] ibid, paras 16–17. See also Case C-234/99 *Nygård* [2002] ECR I-3657, discussed at para 15.135, below.

[686] Case 249/81 *Commission v Ireland* [1982] ECR 4005, [1983] 2 CMLR 104.

[687] Case 222/82 *Apple and Pear Development Council v Lewis* [1983] ECR 4083, [1984] 3 CMLR 733, paras 16–21.

[688] This was the view of the Commission and AG Rozes, at 4107–4108 and 4133 (ECR), respectively, relying on *Steinike and Weinlig* (n 683, above). However, the relationship between Art 28 and Arts 87–88 was not one of the questions put by the referring national court and the ECJ did not refer to Art 88 in its judgment.

[689] Case 18/84 *Commission v France* [1985] ECR 1339, [1986] 1 CMLR 605 (tax advantages for newspaper publishers); Case 103/84 *Commission v Italy* [1986] ECR 1759, [1987] 2 CMLR 825 (subsidies for the purchase of vehicles of national manufacture); Case C-21/88 *Du Pont de Nemours Italiana v Unità sanitaria locale No. 2 di Carrara* [1990] ECR I-889, [1991] 3 CMLR 25 (reservation of public supply contracts to local undertakings); Case C-263/85 *Commission v Italy* [1991] ECR I-2457 (aid for purchase of domestically made vehicles); Case C-351/88 *Laboratori Bruneau v Unità sanitaria locale RM24 di Monterotondo* [1991] ECR I-3641, [1994] 1 CMLR 707 (reservation of public supply contracts to local undertakings).

[690] Case 103/84 *Commission v Italy* (above) para 19. See also Case 18/84 *Commission v France*, above.

have a common purpose, namely to ensure the free movement of goods between Member States under normal conditions of competition and that the fact that a measure might constitute an aid within the meaning of Article 87 was not a sufficient reason to exempt it from the prohibition in Article 28. However, in no case has the Court had to deal with a situation where a measure challenged under Article 28 has been notified under Article 88(3). It must be doubtful whether such an aid can be considered to be contrary to Article 28, since that 'would be in effect to obliterate Articles [87] and [88], at all events as respects aids taking the form of a subsidy to domestic products'.[691]

15.131 **Article 31.** Article 31 prohibits, in respect of State monopolies of a commercial character, any discrimination between nationals of Member States regarding the conditions under which goods are procured and marketed.[692] In *Hansen v Hauptzollamt Flensburg* the Court of Justice held that Article 31 constitutes in relation to Articles 87 and 88 a *lex specialis* and therefore:

> 'State measures, inherent in the exercise by a State monopoly of a commercial character of its exclusive right must, even where they are linked to the grant of an aid to producers subject to the monopoly, be considered in the light of the requirements of Article [31]'.[693]

It follows that in most circumstances the application of the provisions on State aids will not preclude the application of Article 31 of the Treaty.

15.132 **Article 43.** An aid scheme that is incompatible with the provisions on the freedom of establishment under Article 43 of the Treaty will not be considered by the Commission to be compatible with the common market under Article 87.[694]

15.133 **Articles 81 and 82.** The Commission is under an obligation to apply Articles 87 and 88 consistently with the other provisions of the Treaty, in particular those that pursue the objective of undistorted competition.[695] In *Matra (No. 1)*[696] the Court

---

[691] *Per* AG Warner in *Ianelli & Volpi* (n 679, above) at 588 (ECR), 707 (CMLR). See also AG Warner in Case 177/78 *Pigs and Bacon Commission v McCarren* [1979] ECR 2161, 2207, [1979] 3 CMLR 389, 407; Cases C-78/90, etc, *Compagnie Commerciale de l'Ouest* [1992] ECR I-1847, paras 33–35.

[692] See paras 11.036 et seq, above and Buendia Sierra, *Exclusive Rights and State Monopolies under EC Law* (1999).

[693] Case 91/78 *Hansen v Hauptzollamt Flensburg* [1979] ECR 935, [1980] 1 CMLR 162, para 10.

[694] Case C-156/98 *Germany v Commission (new Länder)* [2000] ECR I-6857, paras 72–88. See also Commission decision on a scheme of tax concessions for investment in the Basque Country, OJ 1993 L134/25.

[695] Case C-225/91 *Matra v Commission (No. 1)* [1993] ECR I-3203, paras 42–45; Cases T-197 & 198/97 *Weyl Beef Products v Commission* [2001] ECR II-303, [2001] 2 CMLR 459, paras 75–77. See also Case T-156/98 *RJB Mining v Commission* [2001] ECR II-337, [2001] 3 CMLR 308, paras 112–115, where the CFI applied the principle laid down in *Matra* to the assessment of a merger by the Commission under Art 66 of the ECSC Treaty.

[696] Above. See also Case C-164/98P *DIR International Film v Commission* [2000] ECR I-447, [2000] 1 CMLR 619, para 29.

of Justice held that the Commission was entitled to reach a decision not to open the formal procedure under Article 88(2) in respect of a proposed aid to a factory to be operated as a joint venture by Ford and VW after the Commission had published a notice under Article 19(3) of Regulation 17 indicating its intention to exempt the joint venture under Article 81(3).[697] Where the Commission is, however, not in a position to arrive at a firm view that the recipient of the aid is not in contravention of Articles 81 and 82, a decision declaring an aid to be compatible with the common market without opening the formal procedure under Article 88(2) is liable to be annulled.[698]

Article 86. In *Banco Exterior de España*,[699] the Court of Justice held that the **15.134** power of the Commission under Article 87 to keep State aid under constant review and supervision also covers State aid granted to the undertakings referred to in Article 86(2). It followed that the distinction made in Article 88 between existing and new aid is equally applicable to aid to undertakings covered by Article 86(2). As the aid in question there was existing aid, it was unnecessary to examine whether the aid was capable of falling outside the scope of the prohibition in Article 87 by virtue of Article 86(2) of the Treaty. The Commission deduced from that judgment that the procedure under Article 88 prevails over that in Article 86(3) and that a Member State may not invoke Article 86(2) to evade the notification requirements in Article 88(3).[700] This approach has been endorsed by the Court of Justice in *France v Commission (CELF)*, where the Court held that not only the obligation to notify but also the suspension obligation in Article 88(3) applied to aids falling within the scope of Article 86(2).[701] However, if the conditions of Article 86(2) are fulfilled, an aid can be compatible with the common market.[702]

Article 90. Article 90 prohibits a Member State from imposing internal taxation **15.135** of a discriminatory nature.[703] The mere fact that the financing of an aid scheme does not infringe Article 90 does not mean the scheme is compatible with the

---

[697] In Case T-17/93 *Matra Hachette v Commission* [1994] ECR II-595, the CFI rejected the application to annul the exemption under Art 81(3).

[698] Case T-49/93 *SIDE v Commission* (n 624, above) paras 67–76.

[699] Case C-387/92 *Banco Exterior de España v Ayuntamiento de Valencia* [1994] ECR I-877, [1994] 3 CMLR 473. For Art 86 generally, see Chap 11, above.

[700] See *XXIVth Report on Competition Policy* (1994), point 492. See also Communication from the Commission on the application of State aid rules to public service broadcasting, OJ 2001 C320/5; and Commission Decn 2005/842 on the application of Art 86(2) EC to State aid in the form of public service compensation granted to certain public service undertakings entrusted with the operation of services of general economic interest, OJ 2005 L312/67: Vol II, App F.1, see further para 15.068, above.

[701] Case C-332/98 *France v Commission (CELF)* [2000] ECR I-4833. See also Cases C-261 & 262/01 *Belgium v Van Calster* [2003] ECR I-12249, [2004] 1 CMLR 607, para 61.

[702] See para 15.068, above.

[703] See also Van Calster, 'Greening the EC's State Aid and Tax Regimes' (2000) ECLR 294.

requirements laid down in Articles 87 and 88.[704] Conversely, if a taxation measure involves discriminatory taxation Article 90 is applicable, even though the
taxation in question forms part of an aid within the meaning of Article 87.
In *Commission v Italy (Sovrapprezzo)*,[705] the Court of Justice decided that although
the procedure in Articles 87 and 88 leaves a wide discretion to the Commission,
and in certain circumstances to the Council, as to whether an aid is compatible
with the common market, that procedure must never produce a result which is
contrary to the specific provisions of the Treaty concerning, for example, internal
taxation. In *Compagnie Commerciale de l'Ouest*,[706] the Court of Justice confirmed
that the use to which revenue from a parafiscal charge may be put could constitute
aid and that aid measures had to be considered pursuant to the procedure laid
down in Article 88(2), subject to the jurisdiction of the national court where there
is a breach of Article 88(3). In *Nygård*,[707] the Court of Justice applied the principle
in *Iannelli & Volpi*[708] to rule that the fact that a national levy is intended to fund
an aid scheme which had been authorised by the Commission under the State aid
rules did not preclude the national court from examining whether the levy was
compatible with Article 90. There, a scheme to support the Danish pig industry
had been authorised under Article 88, but it was held that the question whether
the levy funding the scheme infringed the prohibition on discriminatory taxation,
with regard to the use made of the revenue which the levy generated, was capable
of separate assessment in the Danish courts.

15.136 **Other Articles.** A number of other Articles of the Treaty grant the Community
competence in respect of particular policies which may be relevant to State aid
policy. Article 151 gives the Community limited powers in the field of culture
and requires action by the Community, *inter alia*, to support action by the Member
States in certain cultural areas, including the improvement of knowledge and
dissemination of European culture and history, and artistic and literary creation.
Article 157 provides that the Community and the Member States shall ensure
that the conditions necessary for the competitiveness of the Community's
industry exist. Article 158 states that, in order to promote its overall harmonious

---

[704] Case 47/69 *France v Commission* [1970] ECR 487, [1970] CMLR 351, paras 10–14 (aid
financed by taxation). See also Cases C-149 & 150/91 *Sanders Adour and Guyomarc'h Orthez v
Directeur des Services Fiscaux des Pyrénées-Atlantiques* [1992] ECR I-3899; and Cases C-17/91, etc,
Georges Lornoy en Zonen v Belgium [1992] ECR I-6523.

[705] Case 73/79 *Commission v Italy* [1980] ECR 1533, [1982] 1 CMLR 1, paras 8–11. See also
Cases 142 & 143/80 *Amministrazione delle Finanze dello Stato v Essevi and Salengo* [1981] ECR
1413, para 28; Case 17/81 *Pabst & Richarz v Hauptzollamt Oldenburg* [1982] ECR 1331, [1983]
3 CMLR 11, para 22.

[706] *Compagnie Commerciale de l'Ouest* (n 691, above) paras 33–35; *Sanders Adour and Guyomarc'h
Orthez*, (n 704, above) paras 24–26; *Lornoy v Belgium* (n 704, above) paras 28–32.

[707] Case C-234/99 *Nygård* [2002] ECR I-3657.

[708] See para 15.129, above.

development, the Community shall develop and pursue its actions leading to the strengthening of its economic and social cohesion. Article 163 lays down provisions for Community policies in the field of research and technological development. Paragraph 1 provides that:

> 'The Community shall have the objective of strengthening the scientific and technological bases of Community industry and encouraging it to become more competitive at international level, while promoting all the research activities deemed necessary by virtue of other Chapters of this Treaty.'

The Community Framework for State Aid for Research and Development has regard to that objective.[709] Article 174 of the Treaty sets out the objectives of the Community policy on the environment. Among those objectives are the 'polluter pays' principle and the need to take account of the economic and social development of the Community as a whole.[710] Environmental objectives are taken into account by the Commission in accordance with the Community guidelines on State aid for environmental protection.[711]

---

[709] Community Framework for State Aid for Research and Development, OJ 2006 C323/1, para 1.1: Vol II, App G.22.

[710] Art 174(2) and (3). See Case C-379/98 *PreussenElektra* [2001] ECR I-2099, [2001] 2 CMLR 833, [2001] All ER (EC) 330, para 76.

[711] Guidelines on State aid for environmental protection, OJ 2001 C37/3: Vol II, App G.18; see further n 315, above. See also, eg the Commission's approach to biofuels discussed in Seinen and Bernsel, 'State aid for biofuels' (2006) 2 EC Competition Policy Newsletter 65.

POSTSCRIPT ON *MICROSOFT*

Introduction. On 17 September 2007, the Court of First Instance delivered its landmark judgment in the *Microsoft* case, which attracted wide publicity.[1] It is a mark of the significance of the case that it is the first since the Court was established to be referred to a Grand Chamber, which comprised 13 judges. In a detailed judgment of 1,373 paragraphs, the Court comprehensively dismissed Microsoft's challenge both to the Commission's findings of infringement of Article 82 and to the level of the fine, only setting aside part of the remedy as regards the appointment of a monitoring trustee. Commissioner Kroes not surprisingly hailed the judgment as confirming the important precedent set by the Commission's decision for competition in high technology industries, while noting that this was in many ways an exceptional case since super-dominance of the kind enjoyed by Microsoft is rare.[2] **PS.001**

Scope of the Court's review. The Commission decision[3] found Microsoft to have committed two distinct forms of abuse: **PS.002**

(i) refusal to supply its competitors with interoperability information for its Windows work group server operating systems; and
(ii) tying or bundling Windows Media Player with its Windows client PC operating system.

Microsoft's appeal against both those conclusions raised a wide range of technical issues along with economic questions of market definition and foreclosure of

---

[1] Case T-201/04 *Microsoft v Commission*, judgment of 17 September 2007. There will not be an appeal to the ECJ: 'Microsoft Concedes Defeat in EU Battle', *Financial Times*, 23 October 2007, p 1. Microsoft subsequently withdrew its two other appeals pending before the CFI: Case T-313/05 (concerning the scope of the disclosure being demanded) and Case T-271/06 (against the imposition of periodic penalty payments for non-compliance: para 13.202, above).

[2] Kroes, 'Introductory Remarks on CFI Ruling on Microsoft's Abuse of Dominant Market Position', SPEECH/07/539, 17 September 2007.

[3] Case COMP/C-3/37.792 *Microsoft*, 24 March 2004, [2005] 4 CMLR 965. See further paras 10.122 and 10.133, above.

competition. The Court noted at the outset that review by the Community Courts of complex economic and technical appraisals made by the Commission is limited.[4] However, while recognising that the Commission has a margin of appreciation on such matters, the Court significantly stated, drawing on the decision of the Court of Justice in the *Tetra Laval* merger appeal:[5]

> 'The Community Courts must not only establish whether the evidence put forward is factually accurate, reliable and consistent but must also determine whether that evidence contains all the relevant data that must be taken into consideration in appraising a complex situation and whether it is capable of substantiating the conclusions drawn from it.'[6]

On that basis, the judgment contains an evaluation in considerable detail of the parties' arguments on technical[7] and economic questions, which indeed constitute the greater part of the judgment.

PS.003 **Refusal to supply: the criteria.** The judgment proceeded on the assumption that the information which the decision required Microsoft to disclose was protected, as Microsoft contended, by intellectual property rights ('IPRs') or equivalent trade secrets. Examining the disclosure required by the decision, the Court rejected Microsoft's arguments that this would allow its competitors to replicate Microsoft's own systems: the Court found that it would merely enable competitors to develop their own work group server products which could operate in conjunction with Windows operating systems. Surveying the case law,[8] the Court reaffirmed that only in exceptional circumstances would refusal to license IPRs constitute an abuse. The Court set out the three conditions which, if satisfied, would make the circumstances exceptional:[9]

(1) that the refusal relates to a product or service indispensable to the exercise of a particular activity on a neighbouring market;

(2) that the refusal is of such a kind as to exclude any effective competition on that neighbouring market;

(3) that the refusal prevents the appearance of a new product for which there is potential consumer demand.

---

[4] See para 13.227, above.

[5] Case C-12/03P *Commission v Tetra Laval* [2005] ECR I-987, [2005] 4 CMLR 573, [2005] All ER (EC) 1059. See paras 8.250–8.251, above.

[6] *Microsoft* (n 1, above) para 89. See also para 482.

[7] eg as to the form and degree of interoperability information that Microsoft was being required (and should be required) to disclose.

[8] See paras 10.129 *et seq*, above.

[9] *Microsoft* (n 1, above), paras 331–333. Since the CFI found all three conditions were satisfied, it did not need to consider whether the circumstances could nonetheless be exceptional, as the Commission contended, without fulfilment of all those conditions.

The Court noted that the first condition requires the identification of two distinct markets. However, the second market on which the product or service is used need only be a potential or hypothetical market, provided that the product or service was indispensible to the conduct of a particular business activity and that there was an actual demand on the part of undertakings seeking to carry on that business activity. Further, the third condition applies only where the refusal to supply concerns the licensing of an IPR.[10] When all three conditions were satisfied, the refusal to supply may nonetheless be objectively justified.

Refusal to supply: elaboration.   Applying those criteria to the facts, the Court **PS.004** found that the Commission had not made any manifest errors of assessment. In particular, the indispensibility of access was strongly affected by Microsoft's near monopoly share (over 90 per cent) of the market in client PC operating systems, which made Microsoft Windows a 'quasi-standard' for those systems.[11] As regards the second criterion, the Court upheld the finding that Microsoft was dominant on the work group server operating systems market, but noted that even if that was not the case, the abuse related to Microsoft's undoubted dominance of the distinct client PC operating systems market which it leveraged onto the former market.[12] Further, the Court made clear that the requirement of 'elimination of competition' did not mean that the Commission needed to wait for the actual, or imminent, elimination of competitors from the market. The objective of Article 82 was to safeguard the competition that still existed on the relevant market, and what had to be established was that 'the refusal at issue is liable to, or is likely to, eliminate all effective competition on the market'.[13] As regards the third criterion, the Court held that this was to be considered under Article 82(b), which prohibits abusive practices that consist of 'limiting production, markets or technical developments to the . . . prejudice of consumers'. The Court rejected Microsoft's argument that the refusal here would only prevent competitors from producing competing server operating systems that incorporated features of its own product. The Court held that the concept of 'new product' embraced technical development and was not limited to the parameters set out in *Magill*[14] and *IMS Health*.[15] Accordingly, where the refusal discouraged competitors from producing work group server operating systems differentiated by innovative features which consumers considered important, the 'new product' criterion was satisfied.[16] Having

---

[10] ibid, paras 334–335.
[11] ibid, para 387.
[12] ibid, para 559.
[13] ibid, paras 561–563.
[14] Cases C–241 & 242/91/P *RTE and ITP v Commission* [1995] ECR I–743, [1995] 4 CMLR 718, [1995] All ER (EC) 416.
[15] Case C–418/01 *IMS Health* [2004] ECR I-5039, [2004] 4 CMLR 1543, [2004] All ER (EC) 813.
[16] *Microsoft* (n 1, above) paras 647–656.

upheld the Commission's findings that the three criteria were fulfilled on the facts, the Court rejected Microsoft's arguments of objective justification, for which it bore an evidential burden although the ultimate burden of proof rested on the Commission.[17] The fact that the information was protected by IPRs that were intended to provide incentives to innovate could not in itself suffice to constitute an objective justification, otherwise refusal to license IPRs could never be an abuse.[18] Here, Microsoft failed to demonstrate that the obligation to supply would have a significant negative impact on its incentives to innovate.[19] Microsoft's arguments based on the TRIPS Agreement were also dismissed.[20]

PS.005 **Bundling/tying.** The Court held that this form of abuse need not correspond with Article 82(d) since the elaboration of abusive practices set out in Article 82 is not exhaustive; although on the facts Microsoft's conduct fell within the terms of Article 82(d).[21] The analysis of this head of abuse was based directly on the precedents of *Hilti* and *Tetra Pak II*.[22] The Court devoted much discussion to the arguments whether a client PC operating system and a streaming media player were properly to be regarded as two distinct products. The distinctiveness of a product was to be assessed by reference to customer demand, and the relevant demand was that for the *tied* product; it was not necessary to show a separate demand for the *tying* product without the tied product.[23] The two products may be complementary products, brought together from different sources, and the technical integration of one product in another does not preclude that integration from constituting the bundling of two distinct products. The existence of independent companies which specialised in the manufacture and sale of streaming media players was strong evidence that there was a separate market for that product. In its decision, the Commission had also determined, as a necessary element of the abuse, that the tying had the effect of foreclosing competition in the market. The Court upheld this approach: although in an ordinary case of tying by a dominant company such an effect could be presumed, *Microsoft* was not a classic case since users could obtain competing media players through the internet, sometimes without charge.[24] But the pre-installation of Windows Media Player in the Windows client PC operating system, without the possibility of removing it, meant that Windows Media Player benefited from the ubiquity of that operating system and

---

[17] ibid, paras 688, 697.
[18] ibid, paras 690–691.
[19] ibid, paras 696–710.
[20] ibid, paras 794–813; see further para 1.103, n 324, above.
[21] ibid, paras 860–862.
[22] Case T-30/89 *Hilti v Commission* [1991] ECR II-1439, [1992] 4 CMLR 16; Case C-333/94P *Tetra Pak v Commission ('Tetra Pak II')* [1996] ECR I-5951, [1997] 4 CMLR 662, [1997] All ER (EC) 4. See para 10.121, above.
[23] *Microsoft* (n 1, above) paras 887, 917–922.
[24] ibid, paras 1036–1037.

achieved the same level of penetration in the market without having to compete on the merits with competing media players. There was a disincentive for original equipment manufacturers ('OEMs'), who installed most of the Windows client PC operating systems into computers, to include streaming media players made by a third party. Hence the finding of anti-competitive effect derived from the nature of the impugned conduct, the conditions on the market and the essential features of the relevant products.[25] That effect was reinforced by the indirect network effects on the streaming media player market.[26] Rejecting Microsoft's arguments of objective justification, the Court emphasised that the remedy imposed was not to forbid Microsoft from supplying its Windows client PC operating system with an integrated Windows Media Player, but to require it to give purchasers the option of obtaining the operating system without Windows Media Player pre-installed.[27] Microsoft had also not shown that integration of Windows Media Player led to superior technical performance.[28]

Monitoring trustee. The Commission's decision required the appointment of a **PS.006** monitoring trustee, whose role would be to monitor compliance by Microsoft with the remedies imposed and to issue opinions on compliance on the application of third parties and, indeed, the Commission itself. Applying Regulation 17, as the governing regulation at the time of the decision, the Court held that this went beyond the Commission's powers. Although the Commission could appoint an external expert to assist it in evaluating compliance with remedies in its decisions, the role here assigned to the monitoring trustee enabled him to act on his own initiative and on direct application from third parties. This therefore delegated to an outsider a power of continuing intervention, and indeed it did so without any time limit since it was expressed to apply also to future generations of Microsoft products. Furthermore, the Commission was not entitled to require Microsoft, as the addressee of its decision, to bear the costs of implementation by the Commission of its remedies. This part of the decision was accordingly annulled.

Fine. The decision imposed a penalty on Microsoft of €497,196,304, a figure **PS.007** calculated by reference to Microsoft's overall turnover in work group operating systems and client PC operating systems in the EEA in the year 2002/03. The Commission noted that this represented only 1.62 per cent of Microsoft's

---

[25] ibid, para 1058.

[26] ibid, paras 1060–1069.

[27] The remedy imposed by the Commission did not require there to be a price differential as between the two versions of the Windows client PC operating system according to whether Windows Media Player was or was not incorporated: Decn (n 3, above), Art 6. This curious aspect of the remedy was obviously not challenged by Microsoft and is not explored in the judgment; it appears to reflect the fact that other streaming media players can be downloaded from the internet free of charge.

[28] *Microsoft* (n 1, above) paras 1148–1159.

worldwide turnover in that year[29] and the Court dismissed the appeal against the level of the fine. The abuses were not based on any new interpretation of the law, and the Commission had correctly characterised them as 'very serious'.[30] Relying on internal Microsoft communications and a public speech by Bill Gates, the Court found that both forms of abuse were part of a conscious leveraging strategy pursued by Microsoft based on its near monopoly position in the market for client PC operating systems. Moreover, the application by the Commission of a multiplier of two on grounds of deterrence was justified. This was necessary to achieve a sufficient deterrent in the light of Microsoft's economic strength, and the Court added: 'Since Microsoft is very likely to maintain its dominant position on the client PC operating systems market, at least over the coming years, it cannot be precluded that it will have other opportunities to use leveraging *vis-à-vis* other adjacent markets.'[31]

---

[29] ibid, para 1317.

[30] A 'very serious' infringement is a term used in classifying gravity under the Commission's 1998 Guidelines on Fines, OJ 1998 C9/3, which applied as at the date of the decision. See further para 13.154, above.

[31] *Microsoft* (n 1, above) para 1363.

INDEX